DICTIONARY OF AMERICAN SLANG

Dictionary
of
American Slang

Second Supplemented Edition

Compiled and Edited by

HAROLD WENTWORTH

and

STUART BERG FLEXNER

THOMAS Y. CROWELL COMPANY
New York · Established 1834

PUBLISHER'S NOTE

to the Second Supplemented Edition

THE FIRST EDITION of the *Dictionary of American Slang*, published in 1960, was in preparation for more than ten years. The late Dr. Harold Wentworth compiled a vast number of entries, chiefly regionalisms and colloquialisms, on which he had become a well-known authority with the publication of his *American Dialect Dictionary*. To this material Stuart Berg Flexner added thousands of slang definitions from the recent and contemporary worlds of the prohibition era, the underworld, jazz, the Armed Forces, business, politics, various fields of entertainment, teenagers, and the beat generation. He also included those derogatory and taboo words that form such a significant part of everyday speech, and which, although they appear with increasing frequency in current writing, seldom find their way into standard dictionaries.

Mr. Flexner prepared the Appendix and was ultimately responsible for the final redefining and editing of all the entries. He also wrote two sections of the book which have generated almost as much critical acclaim as the dictionary proper: the Preface, which contains a provocative discussion on the sociocultural factors that influence the creation of a slang vocabulary; and the Introduction to the Appendix, which analyzes the linguistic processes involved in the formation of new slang terms.

Mindful of the transient nature of much slang, and aware of the obligation to keep the *Dictionary of American Slang* a truly useful and current reference tool, the publisher in 1967 printed an edition with a 48-page supplement by Mr. Flexner. The entries in that supplement are incorporated here with an equal number compiled by Sheila Brantley and Herbert Gilbert. The supplemental material includes nearly 1,500 definitions for terms that have come into use since 1967 and for familiar terms that have taken on new meanings since that time, as well as an updated bibliography and an expanded group of word lists.

Library of Congress Cataloging in Publication Data

Wentworth, Harold, 1904–1965

    Dictionary of American slang.

    Includes bibliographies.
    1. English language in the United States—Slang—
Dictionaries.   2. Americanisms.   I. Flexner, Stuart
Berg, joint author.   II. Title.
PE2846.W4 1975   427'.09   75–8644
ISBN 0–690–00670–5

1   2   3   4   5   6   7   8   9

CONTENTS

PREFACE

by Stuart Berg Flexner

AMERICAN SLANG, as used in the title of this dictionary, is the body of words and expressions frequently used by or intelligible to a rather large portion of the general American public, but not accepted as good, formal usage by the majority. No word can be called slang simply because of its etymological history; its source, its spelling, and its meaning in a larger sense do *not* make it slang. Slang is best defined by a dictionary that points out who uses slang and what "flavor" it conveys.

I have called all slang used in the United States "American," regardless of its country of origin or use in other countries.

In this preface I shall discuss the human element in the formation of slang (what American slang is, and how and why slang is created and used). Linguistic processes are described in the appendix matter under The Mechanical Formation of New Words.

The English language has several levels of vocabulary:

Standard usage comprises those words and expressions used, understood, and accepted by a majority of our citizens under any circumstances or degree of formality. Such words are well defined and their most accepted spellings and pronunciations are given in our standard dictionaries. In standard speech one might say: *Sir, you speak English well.*

Colloquialisms are familiar words and idioms used in informal speech and writing, but not considered explicit or formal enough for polite conversation or business correspondence. Unlike slang, however, colloquialisms are used and understood by nearly everyone in the United States. The use of slang conveys the suggestion that the speaker and the listener enjoy a special "fraternity," but the use of colloquialisms emphasizes only the informality and familiarity of a general social situation. Almost all idiomatic expressions, for example, could be labeled colloquial. Colloquially, one might say: *Friend, you talk plain and hit the nail right on the head.*

Dialects are the words, idioms, pronunciations, and speech habits peculiar to specific geographical locations. A dialecticism is a regionalism or localism. In popular use "dialect" has come to mean the words, foreign accents, or speech patterns associated with any ethnic group. In Southern dialect one might say: *Cousin, y'all talk mighty fine.* In ethnic-immigrant "dialects" one might say: *Paisano, you speak good the English,* or *Landsman, your English is plenty all right already.*

Cant, jargon, and *argot* are the words and expressions peculiar to special segments of the population. *Cant* is the conversational, familiar idiom used and generally understood only by members of a specific occupation, trade, profession, sect, class, age group, interest group, or other sub-group of our culture. *Jargon* is the technical or even secret vocabulary of such a sub-group; jargon is "shop talk." *Argot* is both the cant and the jargon of any professional criminal group. In such usages one might say, respectively: *CQ-CQ-CQ . . . the tone of your transmission is good; You are free of anxieties related to interpersonal communication;* or *Duchess, let's have a bowl of chalk* (see Appendix, Rhyming Slang).

Slang[1] is generally defined above. In slang one might say: *Buster, your line is the cat's pajamas,* or *Doll, you come on with the straight jazz, real cool like.*

Each of these levels of language, save standard usage, is more common in speech than in writing, and slang as a whole is no exception. Thus, very few slang words and expressions (hence very few of the entries in this dictionary) appear in standard dictionaries.

American slang tries for a quick, easy, personal mode of speech. It comes mostly from cant, jargon, and argot words and expressions whose popularity has increased until a large number of the general public uses or understands them. Much of this slang retains a basic char-

[1] For the evolution of the word "slang," see F. Klaeber, "Concerning the Etymology of Slang," *American Speech*, April, 1926.

acteristic of its origin: it is *fully* intelligible only to initiates.

Slang may be represented pictorially as the more popular portion of the cant, jargon, and argot from many sub-groups (only a few of the sub-groups are shown below).[2] The shaded areas represent only general overlapping between groups:

Eventually, some slang passes into standard speech; other slang flourishes for a time with varying popularity and then is forgotten; finally, some slang is never fully accepted nor completely forgotten. *O.K.*, *jazz* (music), and *A-bomb* were recently considered slang, but they are now standard usages. *Bluebelly*, *Lucifer*, and *the bee's knees* have faded from popular use. *Bones* (dice) and *beat it* seem destined to remain slang forever: Chaucer used the first and Shakespeare used the second.

It is impossible for any living vocabulary to be static. Most new slang words and usages evolve quite naturally: they result from specific situations. New objects, ideas, or happenings, for example, require new words to describe them. Each generation also seems to need some new words to describe the same old things.

Railroaders (who were probably the first American sub-group to have a nationwide cant and jargon) thought *jerk water town* was ideally descriptive of a community that others called a *one-*

horse town. The changes from *one-horse town* and *don't spare the horses* to a *wide place in the road* and *step on it* were natural and necessary when the automobile replaced the horse. The automobile also produced such new words and new meanings (some of them highly specialized) as *gas buggy*, *jalopy*, *bent eight*, *Chevvie*, *convertible*, and *lube*. Like most major innovations, the automobile affected our social history and introduced or encouraged *dusters*, *hitch hikers*, *road hogs*, *joint hopping*, *necking*, *chicken* (the game), *car coats*, and *suburbia*.

The automobile is only one obvious example. Language always responds to new concepts and developments with new words.

Consider the following:

wars: *redcoats, minutemen, bluebelly, over there, doughboy, gold brick, jeep.*

mass immigrations: *Bohunk, greenhorn, shillalagh, voodoo, pizzeria.*

science and technology: *'gin, side-wheeler,*

---

[2] See Appendix, The Major Sub-Groups Contributing to American Slang.

wash-and-wear, fringe area, fallout.

turbulent eras: *Redskin, maverick, speak, Chicago pineapple, free love, fink, breadline.*

evolution in the styles of eating: *applesauce, clambake, luncheonette, hot dog, coffee and.*

dress: *Mother Hubbard, bustle, shimmy, sailor, Long Johns, zoot suit, Ivy League.*

housing: *lean-to, bundling board, chuckhouse, W.C.,¡railroad flat, split-level, sectional.*

music: *cakewalk, bandwagon, fish music, long hair, rock.*

personality: *Yankee, alligator, flapper, sheik, hepcat, B.M.O.C., beetle, beat.*

new modes of transportation: *stage, pinto, jitney, kayducer, hot shot, jet jockey.*

new modes of entertainment: *barnstormer, two-a-day, clown alley, talkies, d.j., Spectacular.*

changing attitudes toward sex: *painted woman, fast, broad, wolf, jailbait, sixty-nine.*

human motivations: *boy crazy, gold-digger, money-mad, Momism, Oedipus complex, do-gooder, sick.*

personal relationships: *bunky, kids, old lady, steady, ex, gruesome twosome, John.*

work and workers: *clod buster, scab, pencil pusher, white collar, graveyard shift, company man.*

politics: *Tory, do-nothing, mug-wump, third party, brain trust, fellow traveler, Veep.*

and even hair styles: *bun, rat, peroxide blonde, Italian cut, pony tail, D.A.*

Those social groups that first confront a new object, cope with a new situation, or work with a new concept devise and use new words long before the population at large does. The larger, more imaginative, and useful a group's vocabulary, the more likely it is to contribute slang. To generate slang, a group must either be very large and in constant contact with the dominant culture or be small, closely knit, and removed enough from the dominant culture to evolve an extensive, highly personal, and vivid vocabulary. Teen-agers are an example of a large sub-group contributing many words. Criminals, carnival workers, and hoboes are examples of the smaller groups. The smaller groups, because their vocabulary is personal and vivid, contribute to our

general slang out of proportion to their size.

Whether the United States has more slang words than any other country (in proportion to number of people, area, or the number of words in the standard vocabulary) I do not know.[3] Certainly the French and the Spanish enjoy extremely large slang vocabularies. Americans, however, do use their general slang more than any other people.

American slang reflects the kind of people who create and use it. Its diversity and popularity are in part due to the imagination, self-confidence, and optimism of our people. Its vitality is in further part due to our guarantee of free speech and to our lack of a national academy of language or of any "official" attempt to

[3] The vocabulary of the average American, most of which he knows but never uses, is usually estimated at 10,000-20,000 words. Of this quantity I estimate conservatively that 2,000 words are slang. Slang, which thus forms about 10 per cent of the words known by the average American, belongs to the part of his vocabulary most frequently *used*.

The English language is now estimated to have at least 600,000 words; this is over four times the 140,000 recorded words of the Elizabethan period. Thus over 450,000 *new words or meanings* have been added since Shakespeare's day, without counting the replacement words or those that have been forgotten between then and now. There are now approximately 10,000 slang words in American English, and about 35,000 cant, jargon, and argot words.

Despite this quantity, 25 per cent of all communication is composed of just nine words. According to McKnight's study, another 25 per cent of all speech is composed of an additional 34 words (or: 43 words comprise 50 per cent of all speech). Scholars do differ, however, on just which nine words are the most popular. Three major studies are: G. H. McKnight, *English Words and Their Background*, Appleton-Century-Crofts, Inc., 1923 (for spoken words only); Godfrey Dewey, "Relative Frequency of English Speech Sounds," *Harvard Studies in Education*, vol. IV, 1923 (for written words only); and Norman R. French, Charles W. Carter, and Walter Koenig, Jr., "Words and Sounds of Telephone Conversations," *Bell System Technical Journal*, April, 1930 (telephone speech only). Their lists of the most common nine words are:

McKnight's speech	Dewey's written	Bell Telephone conversations
	a	a
and	and	
be		
have		
	in	
		I
	is	is
it	it	it
		on
of	of	
	that	that
the	the	the
to	to	to
will		
you		you

purify our speech. Americans are restless and frequently move from region to region and from job to job. This hopeful wanderlust, from the time of the pioneers through our westward expansion to modern mobility, has helped spread regional and group terms until they have become general slang. Such restlessness has created constantly new situations which provoke new words. Except for a few Eastern industrial areas and some rural regions in the South and West, America just doesn't look or sound "lived in." We often act and speak as if we were simply visiting and observing. What should be an ordinary experience seems new, unique, or colorful to us, worthy of words and forceful speech. People do not "settle down" in their jobs, towns, or vocabularies.

Nor do we "settle down" intellectually, spiritually, or emotionally. We have few religious, regional, family, class, psychological, or philosophical roots. We don't believe in roots, we believe in teamwork. Our strong loyalties, then, are directed to those social groups—or sub-groups as they are often called—with which we are momentarily identified. This ever-changing "membership" helps to promote and spread slang.

But even within each sub-group only a few new words are generally accepted. Most cant and jargon are local and temporary. What persists are the exceptionally apt and useful cant and jargon terms. These become part of the permanent, personal vocabulary of the group members, giving prestige to the users by proving their acceptance and status in the group. Group members then spread some of this more honored cant and jargon in the dominant culture. If the word is also useful to non-group members, it is on its way to becoming slang. Once new words are introduced into the dominant culture, via television, radio, movies, or newspapers, the rapid movement of individuals and rapid communication between individuals and groups spread the new word very quickly.

For example, consider the son of an Italian immigrant living in New York City. He speaks Italian at home. Among neighborhood youths of similar background he uses many Italian expressions because he finds them always on the tip of his tongue and because they give him a sense of solidarity with his group. He may join a street gang, and after school

and during vacations work in a factory. After leaving high school, he joins the navy; then he works for a year seeing the country as a carnival worker. He returns to New York, becomes a longshoreman, marries a girl with a German background, and becomes a boxing fan. He uses Italian and German borrowings, some teen-age street-gang terms, a few factory terms, slang with a navy origin, and carnival, dockworker's, and boxing words. He spreads words from each group to all other groups he belongs to. His Italian parents will learn and use a few street-gang, factory, navy, carnival, dockworker's, and boxing terms; his German in-laws will learn some Italian words from his parents; his navy friends will begin to use some of his Italian expressions; his carnival friends a few navy words; his co-workers on the docks some carnival terms, in addition to all the rest; and his social friends, with whom he may usually talk boxing and dock work, will be interested in and learn some of his Italian and carnival terms. His speech may be considered very "slangy" and picturesque because he has belonged to unusual, colorful sub-groups.

On the other hand, a man born into a Midwestern, middle-class, Protestant family whose ancestors came to the United States in the eighteenth century might carry with him popular high-school terms. At high school he had an interest in hot rods and rock-and-roll. He may have served two years in the army, then gone to an Ivy League college where he became an adept bridge player and an enthusiast of cool music. He may then have become a sales executive and developed a liking for golf. This second man, no more usual or unusual than the first, will know cant and jargon terms of teen-age high-school use, hot-rods, rock-and-roll, Ivy League schools, cool jazz, army life, and some golf player's and bridge player's terms. He knows further a few slang expressions from his parents (members of the Jazz Age of the 1920's), from listening to television programs, seeing both American and British movies, reading popular literature, and from frequent meetings with people having completely different backgrounds. When he uses cool terms on the golf course, college expressions at home, business words at the bridge table, when he refers to whiskey or drunkenness by a few words he learned from his parents, curses his next-door neighbor in a few choice army terms —then he too is popularizing slang.

It is, then, clear that three cultural conditions especially contribute to the creation of a large slang vocabulary: (1)° hospitality to or acceptance of new objects, situations, and concepts; (2) existence of a large number of diversified sub-groups; (3) democratic mingling between these sub-groups and the dominant culture. Primitive peoples have little if any slang because their life is restricted by ritual; they develop few new concepts; and there are no sub-groups that mingle with the dominant culture. (Primitive sub-groups, such as medicine men or magic men, have their own vocabularies; but such groups do not mix with the dominant culture and their jargon can never become slang because it is secret or sacred.)

But what, after all, are the advantages that slang possesses which make it useful? Though our choice of any specific word may usually be made from habit, we sometimes consciously select a slang word because we believe that it communicates more quickly and easily, and more personally, than does a standard word. Sometimes we resort to slang because there is no one standard word to use. In the 1940's, *WAC, cold war,* and *cool* (music) could not be expressed quickly by any standard synonyms. Such words often become standard quickly, as have the first two. We also use slang because it often is more forceful, vivid, and expressive than are standard usages. Slang usually avoids the sentimentality and formality that older words often assume. Taking a girl to a *dance* may seem sentimental, may convey a degree of formal, emotional interest in the girl, and has overtones of fancy balls, fox trots, best suits, and corsages. At times it is more fun to go to a *hop.* To be *busted* or without a *hog* in one's *jeans* is not only more vivid and forceful than being penniless or without funds, it is also a more optimistic state. A *mouthpiece* (or *legal beagle*), *pencil pusher, sawbones, boneyard, bottle washer* or a course in *biochem* is more vivid and forceful than a lawyer, clerk, doctor, cemetery, laboratory assistant, or a course in biochemistry—and is much more real and less formidable than a legal counsel, junior executive, surgeon, necropolis (or memorial park), laboratory technician, or a course in biological chemistry.

Although standard English is exceedingly hospitable to polysyllabicity and even sesquipedalianism, slang is not. Slang is sometimes used not only because it is concise but just because its brevity makes it forceful. As this dictionary demonstrates, slang seems to prefer short words, especially monosyllables, and, best of all, words beginning with an explosive or an aspirate.[4]

We often use slang *fad* words as a bad habit because they are close to the tip of our tongue. Most of us apply several favorite but vague words to any of several somewhat similar situations; this saves us the time and effort of thinking and speaking precisely. At other times we purposely choose a word because it is vague, because it does not commit us too strongly to what we are saying. For example, if a friend has been praising a woman, we can reply "she's *the bee's knees*" or "she's a real *chick*," which can mean that we consider her very modern, intelligent, pert, and understanding—or can mean that we think she is one of many nondescript, somewhat confused, followers of popular fads. We can also tell our friend that a book we both have recently read is *the cat's pajamas* or *the greatest.* These expressions imply that we liked the book for exactly the same reasons that our friend did, without having to state what these reasons were and thus taking the chance of ruining our rapport.

In our language we are constantly re-creating our image in our own minds and in the minds of others. Part of this image, as mentioned above, is created by using sub-group cant and jargon in the dominant society; part of it is created by our choice of both standard and slang words. A sub-group vocabulary shows

---

[4] Many such formations are among our most frequently used slang words. As listed in this dictionary, *bug* has 30 noun meanings, *shot* 14 noun and 4 adjective meanings, *can* 11 noun and 6 verb, *bust* 9 verb and 6 noun, *hook* 8 noun and 5 verb, *fish* 14 noun, and *sack* 8 noun, 1 adjective, and 1 verb meaning. Monosyllabic words also had by far the most citations found in our source reading of popular literature. Of the 40 words for which we found the most quotations, 29 were monosyllabic. Before condensing, *fink* had citations from 70 different sources, *hot* 67, *bug* 62, *blow* and *dog* 60 each, *joint* 59, *stiff* 56, *punk* 53, *bum* and *egg* 50 each, *guy* 43, *make* 41, *bull* and *mug* 37 each, *bird* 34, *fish* and *hit* 30 each, *ham* 25, *yak* 23, *sharp* 14, and *cinch* 10. (Many of these words, of course, have several slang meanings; many of the words also appeared scores of times in the same book or article.)

that we have a group to which we "belong" and in which we are "somebody"—outsiders had better respect us. Slang is used to show others (and to remind ourselves of) our biographical, mental, and psychological background; to show our social, economic, geographical, national, racial, religious, educational, occupational, and group interests, memberships, and patriotisms. One of the easiest and quickest ways to do this is by using counter-words. These are automatic, often one-word responses of like or dislike, of acceptance or rejection. They are used to counter the remarks, or even the presence, of others. Many of our fad words and many student and quasi-intellectual slang words are counter-words. For liking: *beat, the cat's pajamas, drooly, gas, George, the greatest, keen, nice, reet, smooth, super, way out*, etc. For rejection of an outsider (implying incompetence to belong to our group): *boob, creep, dope, drip, droop, goof, jerk, kookie, sap, simp, square, weird*, etc. Such automatic counters are overused, almost meaningless, and are a substitute for thought. But they achieve one of the main purposes of speech: quickly and automatically they express our own sub-group and personal criteria. Counter-words are often fad words creating a common bond of self-defense. All the rejecting counters listed above could refer to a moron, an extreme introvert, a birdwatcher, or a genius. The counters merely say that the person is rejected—he does not belong to the group. In uttering the counter we don't care what the person is; we are pledging our own group loyalty, affirming our identity, and expressing our satisfaction at being accepted.

In like manner, at various periods in history, our slang has abounded in words reflecting the fear, distrust, and dislike of people unlike ourselves. This intolerance is shown by the many derogatory slang words for different immigrant, religious, and racial groups: *Chink, greaser, Heinie, hunkie, mick, mockie, nigger, spik*. Many counters and derogatory words try to identify our own group status, to dare others to question our group's, and therefore our own, superiority.

Sometimes slang is used to escape the dull familiarity of standard words, to suggest an escape from the established routine of everyday life. When slang is used, our life seems a little fresher and

a little more personal. Also, as at all levels of speech, slang is sometimes used for the pure joy of making sounds, or even for a need to attract attention by making noise. The sheer newness and informality of certain slang words produces a pleasure.

But more important than this expression of a more or less hidden esthetic motive on the part of the speaker is slang's reflection of the personality, the outward, clearly visible characteristics of the speaker. By and large, the man who uses slang is a forceful, pleasing, acceptable personality. Morality and intellect (too frequently not considered virtues in the modern American man) are overlooked in slang, and this has led to a type of reverse morality: many words, once standing for morally good things, are now critical. No one, for example, though these words were once considered complimentary, wants to be called a *prude* or *Puritan*. Even in standard usage they are mildly derisive.

Moreover, few of the many slang synonyms for drunk are derogatory or critical. To call a person a standard drunk may imply a superior but unsophisticated attitude toward drinking. Thus we use slang and say someone is *boozed up, gassed, high, potted, stinking, has a glow on*, etc., in a verbal attempt to convey our understanding and awareness. These slang words show that we too are human and know the effects of excessive drinking.

In the same spirit we refer to people sexually as *big ass man, fast, John, sex pot, shack job, wolf*, etc., all of which accept unsanctioned sexual intercourse as a matter of fact. These words are often used in a complimentary way and in admiration or envy. They always show acceptance of the person as a "regular guy." They are never used to express a moral judgment. Slang has few complimentary or even purely descriptive words for "virgin," "good girl," or "gentleman." Slang has *bag, bat, ex, gold digger, jerk, money mad, n.g., old lady, square*, etc.; but how many words are there for a good wife and mother, an attractive and chaste woman, an honest, hard-working man who is kind to his family, or even a respected elderly person? Slang—and it is frequently true for all language levels—always tends toward degradation rather than elevation. As slang shows, we would rather share or accept vices than be excluded from a social group. For this reason, for self-defense, and to create an aura (but not the fact) of modernity and individuality, much of our slang purposely expresses amorality, cynicism, and "toughness."

Reverse morality also affects slang in other ways. Many use slang just because it is not standard or polite. Many use slang to show their rebellion against *boobs*, *fuddy-duddies*, *marks*, and *squares*. Intellectuals and politicians often use slang to create the "common touch" and others use slang to express either their anti-intellectualism or avant-garde leanings. Thus, for teen-agers, entertainers, college students, beatniks, jazz fans, intellectuals, and other large groups, slang is often used in preference to standard words and expressions. Slang is the "official" modern language of certain vociferous groups in our population.

In my work on this dictionary, I was constantly aware that most American slang is created and used by males. Many types of slang words—including the taboo and strongly derogatory ones, those referring to sex, women, work, money, whiskey,[5] politics, transportation, sports, and the like — refer primarily to male endeavor and interest. The majority of entries in this dictionary could be labeled "primarily masculine use." Men belong to more sub-groups than do women; men create and use occupational cant and jargon; in business, men have acquaintances who belong to many different sub-groups. Women, on the other hand, still tend to be restricted to family and neighborhood friends. Women have very little of their own slang.[6] The new words applied to women's clothing, hair styles, homes, kitchen utensils and gadgets are usually created by men. Except when she accompanies her boy friend or husband to *his* recreation (baseball, hunting, etc.) a woman seldom mingles with other groups. When women do mingle outside of their own neighborhood and family circles, they do not often talk of the outside

world of business, politics, or other fields of general interest where new feminine names for objects, concepts, and viewpoints could evolve.

Men also tend to avoid words that sound feminine or weak. Thus there are sexual differences in even the standard vocabularies of men and women. A woman may ask her husband to set the table for dinner, asking him to put out the *silver*, *crystal*, and *china*—while the man will set the table with *knives*, *forks*, *spoons*, *glasses*, and *dishes*. His wife might think the *table linen* attractive, the husband might think the *tablecloth* and *napkins* pretty. A man will buy a *pocketbook* as a gift for his wife, who will receive a *bag*. The couple will live under the same roof, the wife in her *home*, the man in his *house*. Once outside of their domesticity the man will begin to use slang quicker than the woman. She'll get into the *car* while he'll get into the *jalopy* or *Chevvie*. And so they go: she will learn much of her general slang from him; for any word she associates with the home, her personal belongings, or any female concept, he will continue to use a less descriptive, less personal one.

Males also use slang to shock. The rapid tempo of life, combined with the sometimes low boiling point of males, can evoke emotions—admiration, joy, contempt, anger—stronger than our old standard vocabulary can convey. In the stress of the moment a man is not just in a standard "untenable position," he is *up the creek*. Under strong anger a man does not feel that another is a mere "incompetent"—he is a *jerk* or a *fuck-off*.

Men also seem to relish hyperbole in slang. Under many situations, men do not see or care to express fine shades of meaning: a girl is either a *knockout* or a *dog*, liquor either *good stuff* or *panther piss*, a person either has *guts* or is *chicken*, a book is either *great* or nothing but *crap*. Men also like slang and colloquial wording because they express action or even violence: we *draw pay*, *pull a boner*, *make a score*, *grab some sleep*, *feed our face*, *kill time*—in every instance we tend to use the transitive verb, making ourselves the active doer.

The relation between a sub-group's psychology and its cant and jargon is interesting, and the relation between an individual's vocabulary and psychological personality is even more so. Slang

---

[5] It would appear that the word having the most slang synonyms is *drunk*. A discussion of the reasons for this, and a list of the slang words, will be found in the Appendix, Synonyms for Drunk.

[6] Women who do work usually replace men at men's jobs, are less involved in business life than men, and have a shorter business career (often but an interim between school and marriage). The major female sub-groups contributing to American slang are: airline stewardesses, beauty-parlor operators, chorus girls, nurses, prostitutes, and waitresses.

can be one of the most revealing things about a person, because our own personal slang vocabulary contains many words used by choice, words which we use to create our own image, words which we find personally appealing and evocative—as opposed to our frequent use of standard words merely from early teaching and habit. Whether a man calls his wife *baby, doll, honey, the little woman, the Mrs.,* or *my old lady* certainly reveals much about him. What words one uses to refer to a mother *(Mom, old lady)*, friend *(buddy, bunkie, old man)*, the bathroom *(can, John, little boy's room)*, parts of the body and sex acts *(boobies, gigi, hard, laid, score)*, being tired *(all in, beat)*, being drunk *(clobbered, high, lit up like a Christmas tree, paralyzed)*, and the like, reveal much about a person and his motivations.[7]

The basic metaphors, at any rate, for all levels of language depend on the five senses. Thus *rough, smooth, touch; prune, sour puss, sweet; fishy, p.u., rotten egg; blow, loud; blue, red, square.* In slang, many metaphors refer to touch (including the sense of heat and cold) and to taste.

Food is probably our most popular slang image. Food from the farm, kitchen, or table, and its shape, color, and taste suggest many slang metaphors. This is because food can appeal to taste, smell, sight, and touch, four of our five senses; because food is a major, universal image to all people, all sub-groups; because men work to provide it and women devote much time to buying and preparing it; because food is before our eyes three times every day.

Many standard food words mean money in nonstandard use: *cabbage, kale, lettuce.* Many apply to parts of the body: *cabbage head, cauliflower ear, meat hooks, nuts, plates of meat.* Many food words refer to people: *apple, cold fish, Frog, fruitcake, honey, sweetie pie.* Others refer to general situations and attitudes: to *brew* a plot, to receive a *chewing out,* to find oneself *in a pickle* or something *not kosher,* to be unable to *swallow* another's story, to ask *what's*

cooking? Many drunk words also have food images: *boiled, fried, pickled;* and so do many words for nonsense: *applesauce, banana oil, spinach.* Many standard food words also have sexual meanings in slang. The many food words for money, parts of the body, people, and sex reveal that food means much more to us than mere nourishment. When a *good egg brings home the bacon* to his *honey,* or when a *string bean* of a *sugar daddy* takes his *piece* of *barbecue* out to get *fried* with his hard-earned *kale,* food images have gone a long way from the farm, kitchen, and table.

Sex has contributed comparatively few words to modern slang,[8] but these are among our most frequently used. The use of sex words to refer to sex in polite society and as metaphors in other fields is increasing. Sex metaphors are common for the same conscious reasons that food metaphors are. Sex appeals to, and can be used to apply to, most of the five senses. It is common to all persons in all sub-groups, and so we are aware of it continually.

Slang words for sexual attraction and for a variety of sexual acts, positions, and relationships are more common than standard words. Standard non-taboo words referring to sex are so scarce or remote and scientific that slang is often used in referring to the most romantic, the most obscene, and the most humorous sexual situations. Slang is so universally used in sexual communication that when "a man meets a maid" it is best for all concerned that they know slang.[9] Slang words for sex carry little emotional connotation; they express naked desire or mechanical acts, devises, and positions. They are often blunt, cynical and "tough."

The subconscious relating of sex and food is also apparent from reading this dictionary. Many words with primary, standard meanings of food have sexual slang meanings. The body, parts of the body, and descriptions of each, often call food terms into use: *banana, bread, cheese cake, cherry, jelly roll, meat,* etc.

---

[7] For just the last example, *clobbered* may indicate that a drinker is punishing himself, *high* that he is escaping, *lit up like a Christmas tree* that he is seeking attention and a more dominant personality, and *paralyzed* that he seeks punishment, escape or death. See Appendix list, Synonyms for Drunk.

[8] Many so-called bedroom words are not technically slang at all, but are sometimes associated with slang only because standard speech has rejected them as taboo. However, many of these taboo words do have further metaphorical meanings in slang: *fucked, jerk, screw you,* etc.

[9] On the other hand, Madame de Staël is reported to have complimented one of her favorite lovers with "speech is not his language."

Beloved, or simply sexually attractive, people are also often called by food names: *cookie, cup of tea, honey, peach, quail, tomato*, etc. This primary relation between sex and food depends on the fact that they are man's two major sensuous experiences. They are shared by all personalities and all sub-groups and they appeal to the same senses—thus there is bound to be some overlapping in words and imagery. However, there are too many standard food words having sexual meanings in slang for these conscious reasons to suffice. Sex and food seem to be related in our subconscious.

Also of special interest is the number of slang expressions relating sex and cheating. Used metaphorically, many sex words have secondary meanings of being cheated, deceived, swindled, or taken advantage of, and several words whose primary meaning is cheating or deceiving have further specific sexual meanings: *cheating, fucked, make, royal screwing, score, turn a trick*, etc. As expressed in slang, sex is a trick somehow, a deception, a way to cheat and deceive us. To curse someone we can say *fuck you* or *screw you*, which expresses a wish to deprive him of his good luck, his success, perhaps even his potency as a man.[10] Sex is also associated with confusion, exhausting tasks, and disaster: *ball buster, screwed up, snafu*, etc. It seems clear, therefore, that, in slang, success and sexual energy are related or, to put it more accurately, that thwarted sexual energy will somehow result in personal disaster.

Language is a social symbol. The rise of the middle class coincided with the period of great dictionary makers, theoretical grammarians, and the "correct

---

[10] See F. P. Wood, "The Vocabulary of Failure," *Better English*, Nov., 1938, p. 34. The vocabulary of failure is itself very revealing. Failure in one's personality, school, job, business, or an attempted love affair are all expressed by the same vocabulary. One gets the *brush off*, the *gate*, a *kiss off*, or *walking papers* in both business and personal relationships. As the previous discussion of counterwords demonstrates, slang allows no distinction or degree among individual failures. Incompetence does not apply to just one job or facet of life—either one belongs or is considered unworthy. This unworthiness applies to the entire personality, there are no alternate avenues for success or happiness. One is not merely of limited intelligence, not merely an introvert, not merely ugly, unknowing, or lacking in aggression—but one is a failure in all these things, a complete *drip, jerk*, or *square*. The basic failure is that of personality, the person is not a mere failure—he is an outcast, an untouchable; he is taboo.

usage" dogma. The new middle class gave authority to the dictionaries and grammarians in return for "correct usage" rules that helped solidify their social position. Today, newspaper ads still implore us to take mail-order courses in order to "learn to speak like a college graduate," and some misguided English instructors still give a good speaking ability as the primary reason for higher education.

The gap between "correct usage" and modern practice widens each day. Are there valid theoretical rules for speaking good English, or should "observed usage" be the main consideration? Standard words do not necessarily make for precise, forceful, or useful speech. On the other hand, "observed usage" can never promise logic and clarity. Today, we have come to depend on "observed usage," just as eighteenth- and nineteenth-century social climbers depended on "correct usage," for social acceptance.

Because it is not standard, formal, or acceptable under all conditions, slang is usually considered vulgar, impolite, or boorish. As this dictionary shows, however, the vast majority of slang words and expressions are neither taboo, vulgar, derogatory, nor offensive in meaning, sound, or image. There is no reason to avoid any useful, explicit word merely because it is labeled "slang." Our present language has not decayed from some past and perfect "King's English," Latin, Greek, or pre-Tower of Babel tongue. All languages and all words have been, are, and can only be but conventions mutually agreed upon for the sake of communicating. Slang came to America on the Mayflower. In general, it is not vulgar, new, or even peculiarly American: an obvious illustration of this is the polite, old French word *tête*, which was originally slang from a Latin word *testa*—cooking pot.

Cant and jargon in no way refer only to the peculiar words of undesirable or underworld groups. Slang does not necessarily come from the underworld, dope addicts, degenerates, hoboes, and the like. Any cultural sub-group develops its own personal cant and jargon which can later become general slang. All of us belong to several of these specific sub-groups using our own cant and jargon. Teen-agers, steel workers, soldiers, Southerners, narcotic addicts, churchgoers, truck drivers, advertising men,

jazz musicians, pickpockets, retail salesmen in every field, golf players, immigrants from every country, college professors, baseball fans—all belong to
typical sub-groups from which slang
originates. Some of these sub-groups are
colorful; most are composed of prosaic,
average people.

Many people erroneously believe that
a fundamental of slang is that it is intentionally picturesque, strained in metaphor, or jocular. Picturesque metaphor
(and metonymy, hyperbole, and irony)
does or should occur frequently in all
levels of speech. Picturesque metaphor
is a frequent characteristic of slang, but
it does not define slang or exist as an
inherent part of it. The picturesque or
metaphorical aspect of slang is often due
to its direct honesty or to its newness.
Many standard usages are just as picturesque, but we have forgotten their
original metaphor through habitual use.
Thus slang's *jerk* and *windbag* are no
more picturesque than the standard *incompetent* and *fool*. *Incompetent* is from
the Latin *competens* plus the negating
prefix *in-* and = "unable or unwilling to
compete"; *fool* is Old French, from the
Latin *follis* which actually = "bellows
or wind bag"; slang's *windbag* and the
standard *fool* actually have the same
metaphor.

As for picturesque sounds, I find very
few in slang. Onomatopoeia, reduplications, harsh sounds and pleasing sounds,
even rhyming terms, exist on all levels
of speech. Readers of this dictionary will
find no more picturesque or unusual
sounds here than in a similar length dictionary of standard words. Many slang
words are homonyms for standard words.

As has been frequently pointed out,
many slang words have the same meaning. There seems to be an unnecessary
abundance of counter-words, synonyms
for "drunk," hundreds of fad words with
almost the same meaning, etc. This is
because slang introduces word after
word year after year from many, many
sub-groups. But slang is a scatter-gun
process; many new words come at the
general public; most are ignored; a few
stick in the popular mind.

Remember that "slang" actually does
not exist as an entity except in the
minds of those of us who study the
language. People express themselves and
are seldom aware that they are using
the artificial divisions of "slang" or
"standard." First and forever, language
is language, an attempt at communication and self-expression. The fact that
some words or expressions are labeled
"slang" while others are labeled "jargon"
or said to be "from the Anglo-Saxon"
is of little value except to scholars. Thus
this dictionary is a legitimate addition to
standard dictionaries, defining many
words just as meaningful as and often
more succinct, useful, and popular than
many words in standard dictionaries.

It is clearly impossible to acknowledge specifically all the help received on
so vast a project as this dictionary. Certain people, however, contributed heavily
in particular areas. Clinton A. Sanders
and Joseph A. Blackwell, Jr., provided
indispensable glossaries from the worlds
of the circus, carnival, theater, tramps
and hoboes, the railroad, miners, jive, and
swing. Godfrey Irwin helped further
with a list of tramp and hobo terms.
During the course of the work access was
generously given to the files of Professor
Louise Pound and of the late H. L.
Mencken. Noteworthy assistance or suggestions came from Professors C. K.
Thomas, H. W. Thompson, A. H. Marckwardt, W. C. Greet, and from A. W.
Read. Jim Tully, author of *Circus Parade*, contributed much assistance and
advice on circus and hobo terms. George
Jean Nathan, J. G. Taylor Spink, E. G.
Swen, James Asa Shield, Gene Buck, as
well as many other scholars, authors,
critics, journalists, and friends, have
been most helpful. Dr. David W. Maurer
has contributed much more than the
bibliography to this book can possibly
reveal. Dr. Maurer's influence will be
found in many passages of this work,
as indeed it must in all future works on
the American language.

EXPLANATORY NOTES

A BRIEF EXPLANATION of the kind of information found in a typically full entry in the text will make this dictionary more useful. But first a note on the selection of the words themselves: In addition to including as large and representative a body of American slang as possible, some colloquialisms, cant, jargon, argot, and idioms frequently used in popular novels and movies appear because the user is likely to encounter them and want to know what they mean. Morever, in a few instances standard words are also listed because many readers still consider them slang and will expect to find them here. Naturally, priority has been given to popular and historically valuable slang words over words having but little or routine use. Entries come from every period of American history, but the emphasis is placed on modern slang. Certain categories have, by and large, been minimized: popular nicknames, abbreviations, and affectionate names for regions, states, and cities, and their inhabitants. All but the most popular neologisms and recurring nonce words have been rejected. Many words referring to the particular maneuvers and plays in sports have been excluded, but some true slang deriving from sports has been included. Many words referring to specific styles of dress, coiffeurs, food, etc., have been omitted; but the more popular, such as *black cow, crew cut, dagwood* are included. Finally, words coined and popularized for a season or two by the fashion industry or by advertising are largely excluded. Trade names are, for the most part, ignored.

The entries themselves conform to the following pattern:

Entry words. Each entry word appears in boldface type. The absolute system of alphabetization is used: multiple-word entries are listed in alphabetical order as if they were spelled as one word. Phrases and clauses which are solely and completely slang are normally entered under their first word; phrases and clauses which are slang only because a key word is used in a slang sense are listed under that slang word in almost all instances.

Since many slang words are seldom found in print, confusion exists about exact spelling and the use of hyphens. Where several variants exist, they are listed in decreasing order of popularity. When a phrase or clause may have alternate wording, the alternate words are given in parentheses, in decreasing order of popularity. When a phrase or clause includes a direct or indirect object (depending on who is being spoken to, or whether the object is animate or inanimate), the possible variant noun or pronoun uses are bracketed.

Taboo and derogatory terms. Preceding some definitions are the bracketed notations [taboo] and [derog.]. If the notation precedes only one of several definitions in the entry then only that specific use is taboo or derogatory.[1] Most taboo and derogatory terms are so obvious as to leap to the eye; in many instances where a word or expression has once been labeled derogatory or taboo in this dictionary, further uses of it in cross references, editorial comment, and the like, have not always been so qualified. Because of the loosening of taboos and moral restraints during recent years, it has not been felt necessary to place these labels next to some words and some meanings that in earlier times would have been considered offensive.

Parts of speech. Single word entries are labeled with their usual basic part of speech in italics before the definition. Many entries may be commonly used as several parts of speech and are so marked before the appropriate definition. One of the characteristics of modern slang is the blurring of parts of speech, the converting of a word historically used as one part of speech into another part of speech. Many words used historically as nouns are now used as verbs, as the standard "*to orbit* a satellite." Adding all such functional shifts would have unnecessarily lengthened this dictionary; but some of the most frequent are included.

Definitions. If a word is commonly used as more than one part of speech, definitions for other forms are given. When a word has more than one meaning for any part of speech, each is numbered in boldface type. When simple definite histories of the various meanings are known, the definitions are given in chronological order of origin. When etymologies and original usage dates are not well established or easy to follow, the various meanings are listed in decreasing order of popularity of interest. When it may not be obvious that one meaning has evolved from a previous one, an arrow (→) is placed before the dependent meaning. Quotes around

---

[1] The basic taboo words, especially those commonly called "four-letter Anglo-Saxon words," are not properly slang. They have remained outside standard speech only because of their taboo nature. When used with generalized or figurative meanings, however, they are slang, and are thus included in this dictionary.

slang words are used only to show that a word having both slang and standard meanings is used in its slang sense when this might not be obvious or to indicate that a word is referred to as a word rather than for its meaning.

Quotations and citations. Whenever possible and useful, at least one published quotation is given after each definition to support the definition and illustrate usage. Many additional quotations are included to: illustrate further meanings or connotations of the word; indicate every ten-year period when the word was in use; illustrate the extreme popularity and acceptance of the word. If illustrative quotations were not found for every ten-year period, one early and one recent quotation are usually given.

The year date is given before each quotation. The first quotation often indicates the earliest printed occurrence of the word which was found, but in no instance can it be assumed that this was its first appearance in print. Indeed, nearly all words are used orally—sometimes for years—before they appear in a published source. Before secondary citations from scholarly material, the date refers to the actual usage date of the *original* source.

Following each quotation is the citation of the publication in which it is found. When this information is abbreviated, more complete bibliographical details are given in the bibliography. (If several works by the same author are listed in the bibliography, the date of the quotation in the text will match the publication date of the specific work referred to.) When two dates for a work are given in the bibliography, the later date is that of a reprint edition from which the quotation was taken, and to which page citations refer. The year date in the text corresponds to the date of original publication.

Since most slang words are more popular orally than in writing, usage quotes occasionally are taken from speech. These oral quotes have been kept to a minimum.

Etymologies and comments. Etymologies are given only when they are valuable and of interest. Many etymologies are omitted as being obvious from glancing at the word; others are unknown; still others are so complex or so fully given in the standard etymological works[2] that they are only summarized or hinted at here. In any case, only the slang etymologies are included; if a slang word originated from a standard English or a foreign word, further etymologies of these origins are not given.

Italicized comments are added to many definitions and entries. These usually refer to possible origins, primary group users, approximate dates of origin or peak popularity, or to the spirit with which the word is uttered.

A lower case *c* before a date means *approximately*.

Some words are labeled as being colloquial (*colloq.*), obsolete (*obs.*), primarily associated with World War II (*W.W.II*), or used primarily by major sub-groups, as *railroaders' use*, *hobo use*, etc. Such comments are general: *railroaders' use* may refer to words used only by engineers, brakemen, or conductors; *hobo use* covers all uses by hoboes, tramps, and vagabonds, who actually differ greatly in their way of life and attitudes; *underworld use* covers many specific groups, most words being further restricted to pickpockets, counterfeiters, confidence men, etc.

Words marked *W.W. II use* may have originated before the war or late in the war; the label only indicates that the use is associated with or was very popular during W.W.II. *Army use* and *navy use* are comments referring to the regular army and navy, meaning that the word has seen continuing use in those branches of the armed forces, as opposed to words made popular by the large number of men in uniform during wartime.

The comments *cool use, swing use*, etc. are also general, making no distinction between East and West Coast origins or between use by actual musicians and fans. The comment *jive use* primarily refers to Harlem jive use *c*1935, though some jive terms originated outside of Harlem and before and after this approximate date of the peak of jive term popularity. The comment *Negro use* primarily refers to the slang of Negroes living in large, industrial, Northern cities; *lunch-counter use* refers to all types of small restaurants, coffee shops, etc., and most frequently to waiter and waitress uses coined *c*1935; *teen-age use* refers to those words first popularized by that group; *prison use* refers only to convict use, but prison guards eventually pick up many of these terms. Words marked *archaic* in general use may still be quite popular among certain older or regional groups.

Cross references. Words of related meaning or usage are cross referenced. When a word is a less popular slang synonym for another word an = sign tells the reader to turn to the major word where a more complete definition is given.

After many entries the reader is referred to the appendix matter for a list of words similarly formed or of similar interest. The appendix lists, however, include many words not entered in the dictionary proper.

---

[2] Interested readers would enjoy browsing in Skeat's or Weekley's etymological dictionaries, the many volumes of the *Oxford English Dictionary*, or the volumes of *A Dictionary of American English*.

Abbreviations

For abbreviations of periodicals, news services, and dictionaries, see list of abbreviations in bibliography.

abbr. abbreviation, abbreviated
ABC American Broadcasting Company
adj. adjective, attributive adjective
adv. adverb, -ial, -ially
advt. advertisement, advertising
Am., Amer. American
anon. anonymous
ant. antonym
AP Associated Press
appar. apparently
approx. approximately
art. article
attrib. attributive, -ly, attributed

bk. book
Brit. British, Briton

c. *circa*, about
C. City
cap. capitalized
CBS Columbia Broadcasting System
Cf., cf. Compare, confer
cit. citation, cited
Co. Company
col. column
colloq. colloquial, -ly, -ism
conj. conjunction

def. definition; definite
derog. derogatory, derogatory use
dial. dialect, -al
dict. dictionary

E. east, eastern
ed. edition; editor
e.g. *exempli gratia*, for example
Eng., Engl. England, English
equiv. equivalent
esp. especially
est. established
ety. etymology, etymological
euphem. euphemism, euphemistic, -ally
exclam. exclamation, exclamatory
expl. expletive

f. and the following page
fem. feminine
ff. and the following pages

fig. figurative, figuratively
fn. footnote
Fr. French
freq. frequent, -ly; frequent use

gen. generally
Ger. German

Hebr. Hebrew
hist. history

i. intransitive
indef. indefinite
inf. infinitive
interj. interjection
intr. intransitive
I.W.W. Industrial Workers of the World
Jour. Journal
1. line
lit. literal, literally
ll. lines

mag., Mag. magazine
masc. masculine
MBS Mutual Broadcasting System
ms. manuscript

n. noun; nominative
N. north, northern
naut. nautical, nautical use
NBC National Broadcasting Company
n.d. no date, no date given
newsp. newspaper
no. number
N.W. U.S. Northwest U.S.
N.Y.C. New York City

obj. object; objective
obs. obsolete
occas. occasional, -ly, occasional use
orig. original, -ly

p. page
partic. participle
perh. perhaps
pl., plur. plural
pop. popular, -ly
pp. pages
pred. predicate
prep. preposition
pret. preterit (past tense)
prob. probably
pron. pronoun
prop. proper
ptc. participle
pub. publisher; publication

ref. refer; reference
Rev. Review

S. south, southern
s. section
sing. singular
sl. slang
Sp. Spanish
specif. specifically
stand. standard; standard usage
subj. subject; subjunctive
suf. suffix
Sup. Supplement
SW southwest, southwestern
syl. syllable
syn. synonym, -ous
synd. syndicated

t., tr. transitive

univ. university
UP United Press
usu. usually

v. verb
var. variant
v.i. verb intransitive
vol. volume
v.t. verb transitive

W. west, western
W.W.I World War I
W.W.II World War II

& and
= equivalent in meaning to; means, denotes
+ and; combined with, added to (in etymologies)
→ from which is derived, whence
... in quoted material, indicates deleted material
/ in citations, separates page numbers from column numbers or separates lines of quoted verse
[ ] in entries, encloses words not in the slang expression (as direct and indirect objects); in quoted material, encloses words not in the original quotation
( ) in entries, encloses variant words which may or may not be used as part of a slang expression

A

A   *n.* Fig., a high or the best grade; success; ability.

a—   **1** Lit. and fig., a portion, share, or order of something. **2** Sometimes used as a sing. possessive pronoun = my, your, his or her. Thus "I didn't get a share of the profits" often = I didn't get my (rightful or expected) share. **3** Always used before certain sl. words or phrases, often when "the" is expected, often to give a colorful or underworld connotation. **4** Often used to mean "an order of—" when said before a specific dish, as when a lunch-counter waiter or waitress relays an order. Thus "a cup" = an order of a cup of coffee and "a bowl" = an order of a bowl of soup. *In this dictionary such expressions are listed under the second or main word of the phrase. Cf.* **the.**

AA   *n.* Antiaircraft gun; antiaircraft fire. *W.W.I and W.W.II use. See* **ack-ack.** See Appendix, Shortened Words.

ABC's   *n.* **1** The alphabet. **2** The basic facts or skills of any job or field of endeavor.

Abe's cabe   *n.* A five-dollar bill. *Orig. jive use, c1935; rock-and-roll use since c1955.*

Abie   *n.* **1** Any Jewish male. *Not common. From abbr. of proper name "Abraham." Not necessarily derog.* **2** A tailor, not necessarily a Jewish tailor. *From pop. concept of tailoring as a trade among Jews.*

Able   *n.* The first of the three squads in an Army platoon. *The other two are "Baker" and "Charlie," these names being taken from the Signal Corps convention for oral transmission of the alphabet and more readily understood than "A," "B," "C,"* etc.

A-bomb   *n.* **1** Any exceptionally fast hot rod; a car with a powerful or souped-up motor. *Hot-rod use since c1955.* **2** An atomic bomb. *Colloq. since c1945.*

abortion   *n.* **1** Any plan or act that is so unusual as to be a travesty; something that is a complete failure or does not succeed as planned or expected; any entertainment or performance that is so dull or inferior that it seems a travesty.

2 Any cheap or inferior item or object; esp. an item of poor design or quality when compared to a superior one. *Some student and young adult use since c1945.*

accidentally-on-purpose   Describing a wilful action so carried out as to appear accidental or adventitious; maliciously; slyly. *First used c1885; in vogue at frequent intervals since. Pop. student use c1940.*

ac-dc   **ac/dc**   *adj.* Bisexual. *Some jocular use since c1940.*

ace   *n.* **1** A one-dollar bill. **2** Any person of proved and outstanding skill in a given field of endeavor. **3** Any agreeable, generous, kind male person. **4** The first item in order of importance. **5** = **ace in the hole. 6** = **ace of spades.** *adj.* Excellent; diligent; proficient; skilled; experienced. **7** In baseball, a run or score. *c1850; obs.* **8** A person skilled in any specific work. *Colloq.* **9** Specif., an Air Force fighter pilot who has shot down at least five enemy planes. *Air Force use since W.W.I.* **10** = **prince.** **—s**   *adj.* Agreeable; first rate; generous; pleasing; kind; the best. 1951: " 'I just want to thank you for being such a goddam Prince, that's all.' I said it in this very sincere voice. 'You're aces. . . .' " J. D. Salinger, *Catcher in the Rye,* 47. *Usu. attrib. use. Since c1950; from ace.* *adv.* O.K., all right.

ace-deuce   *n.* Three, esp. a three or trey of playing cards. **—y - —y**   *adj.* **1** High and low; containing extremes of high and low numbers or positions; both right and wrong, or embodying contradictory elements. See **so-so.** *Orig. sports use. From card games in which the ace is the highest and the deuce the lowest card.* **2** Containing a variety of ideas or materials; general in appeal; so vague, generalized, or inclusive as to offend no one; satisfactory; O.K. *Prob. reinforced by confusion with okey-dokey. See Appendix,* **—y** *endings.* 1958: "[Jockey Eddie] Arcaro, who explained an acey-deucey rider is one with a high right stirrup, and a low left one. This gives a rider more leverage. . . ." Al Buck, N.Y. *Post,* June 22, 36.

ace-high *n.* In the card game of poker, a hand containing an ace but no pair, or a straight having an ace as the highest card. *adj.* Successful, respected. *Since c1880.*

ace in the hole **1** Any important fact, plan, argument, person, or thing held in reserve until needed, esp. until needed to turn failure into success. *From stud poker.* **2** An ace face down on the table so other players are not aware of it. *Since c1920, colloq.*

ace lane A husband or male lover; fig., one who has the right to use the "road" to a woman's ace of spades. *Orig. Negro use; some c1935 jive use.*

ace of spades **1** [derog.] A Negro, esp. a very dark Negro. *From the color of the playing card. Archaic.* **2** [taboo] The vagina; the female pudendum. *From the shape and color of the pubic hair. Not common.*

ace up [one's] sleeve A surprise; an ace in the hole. *Colloq. From the card-sharp's trick of hiding needed cards in his sleeve.*

ack-ack *n.* **1** An antiaircraft gun; antiaircraft fire. *W.W.I and W.W.II use.* **2** A machine gun. *Some W.W.II Army use.*

across, get **1** To explain successfully; to be understood, comprehended, or accepted. 1946: "He decided to devote all his energy to getting his own platform across at a series of public and labor meetings." H. Fast, *The American*, 293. *Colloq.* **2** = **get away with.** Cf. **put across.**

across, put *v.i., v.t.* **1** To perform or execute deceitfully; to swindle or cheat. **2** To present an idea or plan so that another comprehends it. *Colloq.*

across the board **1** A type of horse-racing wager in which equal amounts of money are bet on the same horse to win, place, and show. *Sporting use since c1935.* 1956: *Across the Board: Behind the Scenes of Racing Life*, title of book by T. Betts. *From the electronic totalizator board placed in the infield of racetracks, which shows the odds on each horse, the total amount bet on each horse to win, place, and show, and the value of winning tickets on the first three horses to pass the finish line.* **2** Inclusive; pertaining in the same ratio to all members of a group. Thus an "across the board" raise to the employees of a factory is a raise given to each employee at the same time and in the same percentage of increase. *Mainly labor union and political use; since c1940.*

action *n.* **1** Gambling activity, esp. fast play for high stakes. Cf. **play.** **2** Activity; excitement. **3** Any motivational inducement to individual or group enthusiasm. *Not common.* **4** A plan, proposition, proposal, esp. for a business or social project.

Adam and Eve on a raft Bacon and eggs. *Lunch-counter use in relaying an order; never common.*

ad lib **ad-lib** *v.t., v.i., n., adj.* To speak extemporaneously, to deviate from a written script; to improvise in music. 1950: "They did a lot of ad-libbing in ragtime style with different solos or group in succession, not in a regular routine, but just as one guy would get tired and let another musician have the lead." A. Lomax, *Mr. Jelly Roll*, 56. *Orig. radio use.* **2** To make a spontaneous, short, witty remark. *Colloq.* **3** To contribute new elements to a discussion or other undertaking, whether or not they are desirable. **4** A remark or passage that a performer interpolates in an established script or musical score.

adobe dollar A Mexican peso. *S.W. dial. use.*

A for effort A phrase applied, sometimes disparagingly, to those who have blundered or failed in spite of great earnestness.

African dominoes Dice. *Usu. jocular. Commonly used in ref. to craps, thus implying the game's popularity among Negroes. Game of "coups" was first introduced from France in New Orleans, where large Negro and Creole population quickly accepted it. Since c1920.*

African golf = **African dominoes.**

agony-pipe *n.* A clarinet. *Jive use, but prob. synthetic. Never common.*

air *v.i., v.t.* **1** To jilt. "[He] has aired the femme that got him the job." O'Hara, *Pal Joey*, 6. **2** To broadcast by radio or television. *Colloq.*

air, get the To be jilted; to be fired from one's job; to be dismissed, as by a lover or friend. Cf. **air.**

air, give [someone] the To dismiss an employee, lover, or friend; to reject or jilt; to throw out; to snub someone. 1924: "How about my studies?" "I suppose you want me to give them the air." Marks, *Plastic Age*, 202. *First common c1920; still in wide use.* Cf. **air.**

air, go up in the **1** To miss a cue or forget one's lines; said of an actor. *Theater use.* **2** To lose self control through vexation; to become angry, confused, or excited. 1914: "You will rouse his anger, and he may 'go up in the air.' " D. S. Martin, *Living Age*, Aug., 374. Cf. **blow [one's] top, hit the ceiling.**

air, grab a handful of   To apply the brakes quickly to a bus or truck. *From the fact that such vehicles usu. employ air brakes. c1953. Bus and truck driver use.*

air, take the   To go away.   *imp.* Go away! 1942: "Take the air. Scram. Push off." Chandler, *High Window*, 59.

air [one's] belly   To vomit. *Dial.*

air-breather   *n.* **1** A jet airplane whose fuel is burned by being mixed with air taken into the engine during flight. *Air Force and pilot use.* **2** A guided missile whose fuel is burned by being mixed with air taken into its engine during flight. *Air Force and rocketry use.*

airedale   airdale   *n.* **1** An ugly, ill-mannered, uncouth, or boring man or youth; an unattractive youth. *Some c1920 use.* **2** Any member of the Naval Air Force, esp. a member of an aircraft carrier crew, as a mechanic or flight-deck worker. *Some W.W.II USN use.*

airing, take [someone] out for an = take for a ride.   1932: "When Dave the Dude takes a guy out for an airing the guy very often does not come back." Runyon.

air-log   *n.* An altimeter. *Some aviation use.*

air out   **1** To stroll; to saunter. *Orig. Negro use.* **2** To leave; to flee. *Not common.*

airplane   aeroplane   *n.* An interlinear translation of a foreign text. *Some c1920 college use. An attempt to update "pony"; obs.*

airs, put on   **1** To assume manners, refinement, or prestige which one does not have. **2** To act or be snobbish or aloof.

air strip   A single concrete, asphalt, or hard-packed earth strip used as an airplane runway in takeoffs and landings.

aisles, in the   Fig., so humorous or entertaining that the audience falls out of their seats for freer expression of their exuberance. Said of an audience wowed by a superlative stage show. Often in **knock [or lay] them in the aisles.** 1951: "I was splendid [as a public speaker] and laid them in the aisles. . . ." W. Pegler, *synd. newsp. col.*, Oct. 8.

A.K.   a.k. [taboo]   **1 = alter kocker. 2 = ass kisser.** *This use is now the more common. Orig. prob. reinforced by first meaning.* See Appendix, Shortened Words.

akey-okey   *interj.* & *adj.* O.K.; all right; satisfactory. See Appendix, Reduplications.

A1   *n.* The shoe width A. *Retail shoe salesman use. Much more common than the full "Alfred."*

Alabama   *n.* The South, those states which were part of the Southern Confederacy during the Civil War; Dixie. *Not now common; associated with Negro use.*

alarm clock   A chaperon. *Some c1920 student use.*

albatross   *n.* Roasted, boiled, or stewed chicken served at a meal. *Some W.W.II Army use.*

Albert   *n.* A watch chain, esp. a gold one. *Underworld and hockshop use; archaic.*

alfalfa   *n.* **1** Smoking tobacco. *Underworld use. Obs.* Cf. **hay. 2** Whiskers; a beard. *Dial.* **3** Money; esp. a small, insignificant sum of money. Cf. **cabbage, lettuce. 4 = boloney.** *Not common.*

Alfred   *n.* **= A1.**

Alibi Ike   One who habitually makes excuses or offers alibis for his actions.

alkali   *n.* **1** Coffee. *Some archaic hobo use.* **2** Whisky of any kind; esp. inferior or bootleg whisky. *Not common.* See **alky.**

alkied   alkeid   alkeyed   *adj.* Drunk.

alky   alki   alchy   *n.* **1** Alcohol; specif. liquor. 1846: "Alchy." *DAE.* "*Alky*" *is now the only common form.* **2** Whisky, esp. inferior or bootleg whisky. *Most common c1920.* **3** Methanol as used for engine fuel. **4** Commercial alcohol. **5** A drunkard, esp. a jobless, homeless alcoholic.

all   *n.* Everything or everyone; anything or anyone. *Often added to a stand. or sl. v.t. after "it," esp. in utterances of exasperation, anger, or desperation; e.g., "Damn it all," "fuck it all," etc.*   *adv.* Completely, thoroughly. *Often used before sl. verbs and phrases for emphasis, thus: "All balled up," "all burned up," "all fucked up," "all dolled up," etc.*

—alley   See Appendix, Suffixes and Suffix Words.

alley apple   alley-apple   **1** A piece of horse manure. **2** A rock or stone. 1946: "A fellow's blonde usually stepped in . . . and slugged the other gee with an alley apple or a ground biscuit, meaning a rock done up in a stocking. . . ." D. Runyon, *synd. newsp. col.*, Sept. 14.

all-fired   *adj.* & *adv.* Extreme(ly); "damn(ed)." 1835: *DAE.* 1941: "There's a mighty all-fired mystery about the gentleman. . . ." A. R. Hilliard, *Justice*

Be Damned, 130. *As Bartlett and Gree-nough & Kittredge pointed out, this is a euphem. for "hell-fired."*

all get out To an extreme degree; usu. preceded by "as" or "like" to make a metaphor. 1884: *DAE.* 1950: "Prepared to work like all get out. . . ." Billy Rose, *synd. newsp. col.,* Aug. 30. *Somewhat archaic; mainly rural use.*

all get up = all get out. 1952: "I'm prouder than all get up to get such letters." Nick Kenny in N. Y. *Daily Mirror,* July 8, 18/5.

alligator *n.* **1** A Mississippi River keelboat sailor. *c1800–1860. The mouth of the Mississippi River is in swamp territory; many old tales relate exaggerated heroic battles between "alligators" and the early river boatmen. As the grizzly bear in the West or the ox in timber country, the "alligator" became the symbol of tough, strong, mean manliness along the lower Mississippi; and to best an "alligator" in combat was to prove one's strength and manliness, as well as to create a legend about oneself. Obs.* **2** Any tough, self-reliant frontier hunter or Indian fighter; any man known for his strength, fighting ability, capacity for drinking large quantities of whisky, success with women, or any other combination of manly traits. *Obs.* **3** A dude, a sport, a well-dressed, hep, swaggering male. *Mainly Negro use. Once it no longer was necessary or even possible to prove one's manliness by fighting "alligators" or Indians, one could demonstrate manliness only in swaggering, drinking, wenching, and gambling.* **4** Specif., a jive or swing music enthusiast; a hep person. *Mainly swing use. Usu. shortened to "gator" or "gate." Common in the rhyming "See you later, alligator" = Good-by, which saw wide swing use and still has some general use.* **5** A white jazz musician. *A mildly disparaging term used by Negro jazzmen in New Orleans, c1915 and later.* **6** A jitterbug. *c1935.* **7** An amphibian tank. *Some W.W.II USN use.*

alligator, make like an = drag ass. *Because an alligator's tail drags on the ground. Some teenage use since c1955.*

alligator bait **1** [derog.] A Negro, esp. one from Florida or Louisiana. *Dial.* **2** Fried or boiled liver served at a meal. *Some archaic hobo use.*

all in **1** Exhausted; tired. *Colloq. since c1910.* **2** All-out; inclusive, total. *Not common. Mainly British use.*

all of a doodah Completely or suddenly confused or disorganized. *Archaic.*

all-out *adj.* Complete, thorough, exhaustive. *E.g.,* "*He made an all-out effort.*" *Colloq.*

all quiet on the Potomac Lit., a period of no fighting in a war; a peaceful period. *Used jocularly and ironically. From the phrase as freq. issued by Sec. of War Cameron or Gen. McClellan during the Civil War. Obs. by c1910.*

all quiet on the Western front **1 = all quiet on the Potomac.** *From the stand. official phrase as issued daily by the War Dept. during relatively calm or peaceful periods during the stagnant trench warfare of W.W.I.* **2** Fig., peaceful; without fighting, quarreling, bickering, or nagging. *Some use since W.W.I.*

all reet all reat all root *interj.* All right. 1943: " 'All reat' . . . is the rug-cutters' way of saying 'all right.' " *New Yorker,* June 19, 15/1. *Orig. jive use c1935; pop. student use c1940; archaic.*

all-right *adj.* Dependable, trustworthy, friendly; also hep. *Usu. attrib. use.* 1941: "These are . . . all-right guys trying to make a living. . . ." · Cain, *Mildred Pierce,* 22. 1951: "Decker was an all-right guy." Spillane, *Big Kill,* 25.

all right already "That's enough, my patience is at an end; stop talking, teasing, criticizing, or nagging." *The most common "already" phrase.*

all rightie all righty all rightey all rightee *interj.* All right. 1929: "All righty, I'm coming." A. Kober in *New Yorker,* Feb. 2, 44/3. 1939: "She: All rightie." Elizabeth Moyers, "All Rightee," *Better Eng.,* Nov., 8. *Dial. use since c1890. Fairly common c1935–c1940; now considered affected or cute.*

all root = all reet.

all shook all shook up Excited, stimulated, disturbed, upset. 1958: *All Shook Up,* pop. rock and roll song, orig. recorded by Elvis Presley. *Orig. rock and roll use, c1955; at present the only major rock and roll contribution to general sl.*

all six, hit on To do well; to do all that one is capable of doing. 1920: "He's sure hittin' on all six." Gillilan, *Literary Digest. Orig. in ref. to the smooth-running automobile engines when all six cylinders were working well.*

all that kind of crap [taboo] And so forth; et cetera. 1951: "The first thing you'll probably want to know is where I was born, and what my lousy childhood was like, and how my parents were occupied before they had me, and all that kind of crap. . . ." J. D. Salinger, *Catcher in the Rye*, 1.

all the way   **1** Completely; for all time; without reservation. Usu. used to indicate agreement or support for a person or venture. **2** Chiefly in phrase "to go all the way" = sexual intercourse, or complete sexual satisfaction as opposed to necking or a feel. *Mainly student use.*

all to the mustard   O.K.; all right. 1905: "Petroskinski is a discovery of mine, and he's all to the mustard." McHugh, *Search Me*, 17. *Archaic since c1935.*

all wasted   **1** Wrong, inappropriate; not adequate. *Cool, far out, and beat use since c1955.* **2** Not hip. *Mainly beat use.*

all wet   Mistaken, misguided, wrong; esp. convinced of, portraying, or loudly arguing a mistaken idea or belief. *Colloq. since c1930.*

almost, the   Describing something or someone not quite the most. *Cool use since c1955, not common.*

along, get   To make a living; to exist; to continue living one's life regardless of adversity or disappointment.

along with, go   To agree with a suggestion, idea, or person; to accept another's idea, plan or deduction.

already   *adv.* Sometimes used at the end of a phrase or sentence to indicate emphasis, immediacy, impatience, or exasperation. Thus "Let's go already," or "Shut up already." Sometimes jocular use, implying Yiddish speech patterns. See **all right already.**

also-ran   *n.* One who fails to achieve a specific goal; in general, a person whose talent or luck is only moderate. *From the horse-racing term = a horse that has finished no better than fourth in a race.*

alter kocker   alter cocker   1 [taboo] An elderly man who pursues young women; a lecherous old man. *Lit. an old cock; from the Ger. and Yiddish.* **2** An elderly but active man, usu. one who is stubborn or shrewd. *This use is now more common than the first.*

altogether, in the   Naked. *Colloq.* Cf. **birthday suit.**

alum   alumn   *n.* An alumnus or alumna. See Appendix, Shortened Words.

alvin   Alvin   *n.* A rustic; an unsophisticated or inexperienced person; one who can be hoaxed easily. *Some carnival, circus, and underworld use.*

alyo   *n.* **1** Any routine task; a state of calm or safety; a person who is not easily excited or confused. *Mainly underworld and sports use.* **2** An agreement between

criminals and police, leading to protection and safety for the criminals; the fix.

am   *n.* An amateur performer or actor; a ham. 1936: "Major Bowes' [the conductor of a radio program for amateur performers] amateurs gave rise to [the word] ams. . . . " A. Green in *Esquire*, Sept., 160/3. See Appendix, Shortened Words.

—ama   See Appendix, Suffixes and Suffix Words.

amateur night   **1** Fig., any time or place in which professional workers or athletes perform ineffectively. **2** Any occasion in which many children or youths participate. **3** Any occasion of sexual intercourse between a male and a chance acquaintance who is not a professional prostitute.

ambish   *n.* Ambition; aggressiveness. *Theater use.* See Appendix, Shortened Words.

ambulance chaser   Lit., a lawyer who follows an ambulance to the scene of an automobile accident or other disaster to offer his professional services to the injured; an unethical or overly aggressive lawyer. *Since c1920.* Fig., a shyster. 1897: *DAE.* 1930: "Some [cops] collect revenue . . . from ambulance chasers." Lavine, *Third Degree*, 166.

Ameche   *n.* A telephone. *From Don Ameche, an actor who played the film role of Alexander Graham Bell, founder of the Bell Telephone Company.* 1942: "You can get me on the Ameche." S. Billingsley in *Harper's Bazaar*, July. *Usu. jocular use.*

Americano   *n.* An American; specif. a person from the United States. 1945: "Some ingenious Americano. . . ." Mencken, Sup. I, 202. *From Sp.* See Appendix, —o endings.

ammo   *n.* **1** Ammunition of all kinds. 1945: "The fat ammo barge rocked up and down stubbornly against the tide. . . ." F. R. Sammis in *This Week*, May 26, 19/2. *Since c1930; common W.W.II use by Armed Forces.* **2** Any information or other material that can be used as evidence in an exposé, argument, defense, or the like. 1947: "Some woman is going . . . to delve . . . into the matter of artificial fishing lures. [She] can acquire enough 'live ammo' to squelch . . . any remarks about hats, styles, or similar female foibles." J. Pancoast in Phila. *Bulletin*, Nov. 12, 24/1. **3** Money. See Appendix, Shortened Words.

ammonia   *n.* Carbonated water. *From its resemblance to ammonia water, possibly* reinforced by spirits of ammonia, also added to nonalcoholic drinks during Prohibition era. 1934: "I went downstairs to fix myself a coke. I hadn't any more than squirted the ammonia in it than she was at the door." Cain, *Postman*, 110f.

amp   *n.* An ampere. *Colloq.* See Appendix, Shortened Words.

amscray   *v.i.* To scram; to beat it. 1941: "Amscray on the porchola." Radio, *Lum & Abner*, Oct. 28. 1951: "This [phone call] is personal! Amscray!" Dick Brooks, *synd. newsp. col.*, Oct. 15. *The most common word carried over from Pig Latin to sl.* See Appendix, Little Languages.

Amy-John   *n.* A female homosexual, esp. one who plays the dominant male role. *Not common. From a mispronunciation of "Amazon," plus the pun from combining a female and a male name.*

anchor   *n.* **1** A pickax. 1956: "Metal miners . . . call a pick an *anchor*. . . ." *Labor's Special Language from Many Sources.* Hobo, railroad, and labor use since c1915. **2** An emergency brake. *Railroad and truck-driver use since c1925.*

anchor man   **1** The student having the lowest academic standing in his class. *c1920 college use; archaic.* **2** In sports, the player who defends his team's goal or goal line. *Both uses from the tug-of-war term.*

—— **and**   *conj.* → *n.* Conventional lunch-counter usage to signify the second of two items that always go together; e.g., "coffee and" = coffee and doughnuts, "ham and" = ham and eggs, "pork and" = pork and beans, etc.

And how! = You said it!—an emphatic affirmative. 1930: " 'Were you on duty?' 'And how!' . . ." Weeks, *Racket*, 90. 1951: "He had [responded] to the first and second [remarks], respectively, with 'And how!' and 'Check!' " P. De Vries in *New Yorker*, Nov. 24, 39/1. *Colloq. since c1920.*

and such   "And similar items." 1956: "A French purse with two change compartments (one for lipstick and such. . .)." "Mark Cross" purse advt. in *New Yorker*, Dec. 8, 10.

angel   *n.* **1** One who donates money to a politician's campaign fund. *Since c1920.* **2** One who finances any undertaking, esp. a stage show or play. *Theater use since c1925.* **3** A thief's or confidence man's victim. *Underworld use since c1935.* **4** A homosexual, esp. one who plays the male role and supports or

frequently buys gifts for his partner. *Since c1935.* **5** One who treats another to food or drink. *Some W.W.II Army use.* *v.t.* To finance an enterprise, esp. a stage play or show. 1948: ". . . a revue angeled by gangster dough. . . ." Lait–Mortimer, *New York Confidential*, 160. *Theater use since c1935.*

angel-factory   *n.* A theological seminary. *Some c1930 student use; never common.*

angel food   Mission-house preaching. *Hobo use c1925.*

angel teat   **1** Any mellow whisky with a rich bouquet. 1956: "Distillery workers smack their lips over *angel teat*—a mellowed whiskey of good bouquet. . . ." *Labor's Special Language from Many Sources.* **2** Any pleasant or easy task.

angle   *n.* **1** One's selfish motive; any unethical way of profiting or benefiting. **2** That part of a plan, action, or scheme from which a person hopes to profit or benefit. **3** The profit or benefit a person expects to gain from a seemingly altruistic or profitless plan, action, or scheme.

animal   *n.* **1** = **pony**: a literal translation of a foreign text used unfairly. *Some student use since c1920.* **2** Any ugly, vulgar, or sexually aggressive person. *Student and Army use c1940–c1950.* Cf. **beast.**

ankle   *v.i.* To walk; to amble. *Orig. c1935.* *n.* An attractive girl or young woman. 1946: "She strikes me as an ankle who doesn't yell easy." Evans, *Halo in Blood*, 67. *Not common.*

Annie   *n.* = **Annie Oakley.**

Annie Oakley   **1** A meal ticket, esp. one issued to circus performers, workers, hoboes, etc., that is valid for a specific number of meals at a specific eating place, a hole being punched in the ticket each time it is used. *Orig. circus, theater, hobo, and laborer use. From Annie Oakley, the famous trick shot artist of the Buffalo Bill Wild West Show who could throw a playing card into the air and shoot so many holes in it before it fell that it resembled a punched meal ticket. Obs.* **2** A free ticket or pass to a prize fight, theatrical performance, circus, etc. *Wide circus and prize fight use until c1910; now mostly obs.*

—Anonymous   See Appendix, Suffixes and Suffix Words.

answers, [one who] knows all the   **1** A wise guy; a person who has a brash or audacious answer to everything. **2** A cynic; one who claims to have seen and done everything and cannot feel enthusiasm.

ante　　*v.t., v.i.* **1** In poker, to contribute one's share to the pot before a hand is played. **2** To put up money for any wager. **3** To contribute to any undertaking.　　*n.* In poker, each player's initial wager, or his share of the pool or pot established before a hand is dealt.

ante up　　*v.t., v.i.* = **ante**. 1934: " 'To ante up' might pass as a proper expression when one sits in a poker game, but it is slang when one is asked for a contribution to the church collection." J. W. Redway in *N.Y. Times*, Nov. 1, 2/2.

anti　　*n.* One who is not in favor of, or who is against, any specific plan or action. *From the stand. prefix.*

ants　　*n.pl.* Anxiety; concern; eagerness; lust; anger. 1946: "The papers play up [the killing of a prominent person] and the mayor starts getting ants about the third day...." Evans, *Halo in Blood*, 73. *From* **ants in [one's] pants.**

ant's eyebrows, the = **cat's meow, the** *Since c1920; never common.*

ants in [one's] pants, to have　　Fig., to fidget with anxiety, anger, lust, or eagerness. 1943: "She dilates her nostrils a lot, the way Valentino used to do it in the silent movies to indicate that he had ants in his pants." H. A. Smith, *Putty Knife*, 136.

A-number-1　A-number-one = **A-1.** *A more emphatic form. Colloq. since c1835. From the way in which ships were once classified, Class A, Number 1 being the newest, fastest type of ship.*

anxious　　*adj.* Wonderful; attractive. *Jive use. Obs.*

any, get　　To have sexual intercourse; lit. to "get" sex. *Often in the male greeting, "Getting any?" = "How is your sex life?"*

anyhoo　　*adv.* Anyhow. 1953: "She bids him, 'Anyhoo, sit ye doon.' " Ogden Nash, "Visit," *Time*, Apr. 13, 112/3. *A jocular mispronunciation considered sophisticated c1945–c1950.*

any old　　Any; typical, a typical example of; unspecified; e.g., "any old house," "any old woman," etc. *Since c1910.* '

A-1　A-one　　*n.* Any excellent or first-rate person or thing; the best; the most agreeable. *Often used attrib.; colloq.* *adj.* Superior; likable.

ape　　*n.* **1** [derog.] A Negro. **2** The apex; the climax; the ultimate. *Far out, beat, and rock and roll use c1958.* **3** A hoodlum or strong-arm man; a gorilla.

adv. & adj. Good, well; the best; completely; thoroughly exciting or satisfying. 1958: " 'Maybe we could dig each other the ape,' he says." Sam Boal, *Cool Swinging in N.Y.*, 26. *Far out, beat, and rock and roll use.*　　**—d**　　*adj.* Drunk. *c1915. Never common; obs.* See Appendix, Drunk.

apple　　*n.* **1** A saddle horn. *Old Western use. Obs.* **2** A fellow, a guy. *Usu. preceded by an adj., e.g., "smooth apple," one who is or thinks he is suave or charming; "wise apple," an impertinent youth. Colloq.* **3** The earth; the globe. **4** Any large town or city. **5** A street or district in which activity or excitement may be found. **6** A ball, esp. a baseball. *Since c1925.* Cf. **onion, potato. 7** A bomb or hand grenade; a "pineapple." 1939: "... To have any airplane come along and drop a few hot apples on them." D. Runyon, 79. **8** = **alley apple. 9** = **square.**　　*adj.* O.K. *Not common.*

applebutter　　*n.* Smooth talk; idle conversation. *Dial.*

apple-head　　*n.* A stupid person. 1951: " 'You, sir,' thundered the Old Arbitrator, 'are an apple-head.' " A. Daley, *N.Y. Times*, Sept. 24, 34/3. *Not common.*

apple knocker　appleknocker　　*n.* **1** Any fruit picker; itinerant workers who harvest fruit crops. *c1915; from the mistaken urban belief that fruit is harvested by being knocked from the trees with long sticks.* **2** A farmer; a rustic; an inexperienced or unsophisticated person. 1949: "Even in good clothes, Floyd looked like an apple knocker." A. Hynd, *Public Enemies*, 81.

apple-pie　　*adj.* Neat; perfect; orderly; easy. *Usu. attrib. or pred. adj. use. Colloq.*

apple-polish　apple polish　　*v.i. & v.t.* To curry favor; to bestow flattery in order to gain personal advantage. 1951: "Are you trying to apple-polish me?" Movie, *Skirts A-hoy. Not as old as apple-polisher.*　　**—er**　　*n.* One who curries favor with a superior, specif. a student who truckles to his teacher. 1939: "We do not know ... who was the first *Joe College*, or *apple-polisher.*" Hixson, *Word Ways*, 154. *Student use since c1925. Common since c1935. From the traditional figure of the student who gives his teacher an apple as a gift.*

apple sauce　applesauce　　*n.* Nonsense; flattery; boloney; bunk. 1927: " 'I hear you dislike to be interviewed by newspaper women.' Dempsey retorted, '... That's applesauce!' " *Word Study,*

Dec., 3. 1937: "Karl Marx . . . called these loose-floating ideas *ideologies*, . . . which freely translated into American means 'applesauce.' " Max Eastman, *Harper's. Now mostly obs.*

apple-shiner apple shiner *n.* = **apple-polisher.** 1935: "Dean J. R. Schultz of Allegheny College states that in his section of Pennsylvania *apple shiner*, not *apple polisher*, is the term invariably used. . . ." *Word Study*, Sept., 2/1. *Dial.*

appropriate *v.t.* **1** To steal or take something, usu. an item of small value. **2** To obtain something by pilferage. *W.W. II Army use.* Cf. **liberate.**

apron *n.* A bartender. 1946: "The nearer of the two aprons unfolded his arms and drifted over. . . ." Evans, *Halo in Blood*, 34. *From the white apron bartenders wear.*

aqua *n.* Water. *Some student and jocular use since c1915; from the Latin.*

aquarium *n.* A Roman Catholic rectory, priest's house, or chaplain's quarters. *Some student and Army use. Because the fish live there.*

Arab arab *n.* **1** Any wild-looking person; an excitable or passionate person. *Since c1850.* **2** Any dark-complexioned person, esp. if belonging to a group traditionally considered to be somewhat excitable or primitive in emotional matters; specif. a Jew or a Turk. **3** A huckster or street vendor, esp. those who possess a Central European or Middle Eastern cast of countenance. 1935: "These [watermelons] are mighty good when we get them in our markets or from the Arabs that peddle them around." Baltimore *Sun*, July 15, 4/5. *v.t.* To sell or peddle, as a huckster. *Not common.*

Archie *n.* An antiaircraft gun; an antiaircraft battery. *Fairly common W.W.I use, though more among British than U.S. soldiers. Some archaic W.W.II use.*

—arino See Appendix, Suffixes and Suffix Words.

Arizona *n.* Buttermilk. *Some lunch-counter use; mainly in the West.*

Arkansas lizard *n.* A louse. *Some Army and hobo use; archaic.*

Arkansas toothpick Any hunting knife when used for fighting, esp. a Bowie knife; a bayonet. *Since c1840; now dial.*

Arky Arkie *n.* **1** A migratory worker from Arkansas. **2** Any poor Southern farmer, esp. a sharecropper.

3 A farmer who fled the dust-storm region of the West, specif. Oklahoma, during the 1930's. *From confusion of "Arkie" and "Okie."*

arm *n.* A policeman. *Not common. From traditional phrase "arm of the law."*

arm, on the 1 On credit; credit; often implying that no payment will be made. 1950: "We . . . took a taxi down to the Paradise. We could put it on the arm there." Toots Shor, quoted by John Bainbridge, *New Yorker*, Nov. 11, 74. 1951: "They'll wind up putting drinks on the arm." *I, Mobster*, 107. *Based on "on the cuff."* **2** Free of charge. 1951: "Commissioner Murphy said he had got in touch with 'twelve to fifteen . . . lawyers to represent a cop when he is in trouble and to do it on the arm.' " N.Y. *Her. Trib.*, Mar. 12, 1/5.

armchair — See Appendix, Prefixes and Prefix Words.

armchair general Fig., one who freely gives his opinions on technical matters with which he is not personally concerned and on which he may be ill informed; a kibitzer, a Monday morning quarterback. *Orig. W.W.II use.*

arm on [someone], put the 1 To detain or restrain by physical force, specif. to arrest. 1943: "No hick cop is going to put the arm on me." Chandler, *Lady in Lake*, 233. 1950: "It was a signal for the waiter to hustle over and put the arm on the customer who was trying to stiff him." M. Zolotow, *SEP*, July 15, 124/3. **2** To hit with the fist; to beat up. **3** To ask for, demand, or borrow money from. 1939: "I had a lot of fun out of it, writing a letter to my friend Ted without putting the arm on him for a couple of bucks." O'Hara, *Pal Joey*, 64.

armored cow *n.* Canned milk; powdered milk. *Ex. of term supposedly common in the Armed Forces but actually synthetic.*

armored heifer = **armored cow.** *Synthetic.*

Armstrong armstrong *n.* **1** A locomotive fired by hand, as opposed to one fired mechanically. *Railroad use, in allusion to the strong arm required. Usu. cap.* **2** A high note or series of notes played on a trumpet, esp. in jazz. *From Louis Armstrong, jazz musician who first exploited the instrument's upper register. adj.* Operated by hand; requiring muscle power; said of tools and machinery. E.g., Armstrong mower = a scythe; Armstrong starter = a crank handle for starting an engine.

Armstrong heater(s) The arm(s) of one's sweetheart. *Some c1920 student use; prob. synthetic.*

arm-waver *n.* One whose enthusiasm, self-righteousness, patriotism, etc., leads to wild arguments or inopportune speeches. See **flag-waver.**

army banjo = **banjo.**

army chicken Beans and frankfurters. *Supposedly some W.W. II Army use; prob. synthetic.*

army strawberries Prunes. *Some W.W.II Army use.*

—aroo See Appendix, —eroo, Suffixes and Suffix Words.

—around See Appendix, Suffixes and Suffix Words.

—arounder See Appendix, Suffixes and Suffix Words.

around the bend   around-the-bend Having completed the longest, most difficult, or crucial part of a task.

around the world [taboo] To kiss or lick the entire body of one's lover, often in preparation for fellatio or cunnilingus.

arrive *v.i.* 1 To attain success; to become accepted in a profession or social group. *Colloq.* 2 To become or be hip. *Orig. jive use c1935.*

arrowhead *n.* A wallflower; an unpopular girl. *Some student use c1935.*

art *n.* 1 Photographs of wanted criminals. 1949: "Information began to appear under art of Karpis on post office bulletin boards." A. Hynd, *Public Enemies,* 110. 2 Newspaper photographs of celebrities. 3 = **pin-up.**   **—y** *adj.* Pretentiously artistic; ostentatiously bohemian in speech or manner. *Since c1900, colloq. since c1930.*

Arthur Duffy (Dan O'Leary, Jesse Owens), take it on the To run away fast; to flee; to take it on the lam. 1935: "I am figuring on taking it on the Dan O'Leary away from there before somebody gets to thinking we do Cecil some great wrong." Runyon, 273. 1939: "It may be a good idea for you to take it on the Jesse Owens until the beef is chilled." Runyon, 92. 1948: "He would take it on the Arthur Duffy up the avenue before the cops got there." Runyon, *synd. newsp. col.,* Sept. 14. *Except for ". . . Jesse Owens," underworld use. "Jesse Owens" is used, of course, because of his fame as a track star. No use common.*

article *n.* 1 A person. Usu. modified by an adjective of quality; e.g., a "smart article," a "slick article," etc. 1948: "Hundreds of smart New York articles

. . . thrive because they . . . know the right people. . . ." Lait-Mortimer, *N.Y. Confidential,* 219. 2 A Negro slave, considered as an "article" of merchandise. *c1830–1865; obs.* 3 A fellow, a guy; esp. a person considered shrewd or quick to advance his own interests.

artillery *n.* 1 A revolver, pistol, shotgun, knife, or other hand weapon. *Since c1920; associated with underworld use. Cf.* **heat, heater.** 2 A hypodermic needle. *Drug addict use since c1935.*

—artist See Appendix, Suffixes and Suffix Words.

ash can   ashcan *n.* A high-explosive depth charge used by surface ships to destroy submarines. *USN use since W.W.I. From their appearance.* 2 A large German artillery shell. *Some W.W. I Army use; obs.*

ash-cat *n.* A locomotive fireman. *Railroad use.*

ashes hauled, get [one's] To have sexual intercourse, to be sexually satisfied; usu. with a prostitute, chance acquaintance, or a stranger. 1939: "Well, you see that spider climbin' up that wall,/Goin' up there to get her ashes hauled." Jelly Roll Morton, "Winin' Boy Blues," song written before 1910. 1951: "We'll get a box at the Comique, then go get our ashes hauled. Never had an Indian girl myself." S. Longstreet, *The Pedlocks,* 102. *Used only by men; not now common and prob. unknown to many younger men.*

Asiatic *adj.* Crazy; wild; eccentric. *W.W.II USN use.*

ask for it Lit. and fig., to ask for trouble; to act in a way that invites trouble. *Since c1900.*

asleep at the switch Off one's guard; unaware or unwary; derelict in one's duty. 1939: "[He] wasn't asleep at the switch." Gardner, *D. A. Draws,* 205. *From railroad use.*

ass *n.* 1 A fool; a stupid or foolish person. *Colloq.* 2 [taboo] The rectum. *Colloq.* → 3 [taboo] The buttocks. *Colloq.* 4 [taboo] The vagina; generally, the female sexual function. *Colloq. Cf.* **piece, piece of ass.**   **—y** *adj.* 1 Mean; malicious; stubborn; impolite; debased. 2 Shiny, said of the seat of a pair of trousers or a skirt.

ass, on [one's] [taboo] In straitened circumstances of any kind; down and out; broke; despairing of success. *Fig., hit so hard by circumstances as to have been knocked into a sitting position.*

ass backwards [taboo]   Lit., in reverse order; fig., wrong(ly), confused(ly), without order or system.

ass in a sling, to have one's [taboo] To be or to appear to be sad, rejected, tired, or defeated.

ass-kisser [taboo]   *n.* = **apple-polisher,** but more emphatic; suggests subject will submit to any degree of humiliation in order to obtain favor. *Though very common and often heard in semipolite, mixed society, the orig. being ignored or forgotten.*

ass man [taboo]   A youth or man who devotes much time to coitus, pursues a variety of women for coitus, and often talks about coitus; a youth or man whose obsession or hobby is sex. Often in "big ass man." *Often used with envy or admiration, esp. by students; seldom used as a moral reprimand.*

—ateria   See Appendix, —eteria, Suffixes and Suffix Words.

at liberty   Unemployed.

—atorium   See Appendix, Suffixes and Suffix Words.

attaboy!   *exclam.* = **That's the boy!** An expression of approval for deserving behavior or a successful performance. Also "attagirl!" *Since c1910.*

— atter   See Appendix, Suffixes and Suffix Words.

attic   *n.* The head. *Jocular or disparaging; archaic.*

auger in   1 To crash; to crash-land an airplane. *Some W.W.II Air Force use.* 2 To become unconscious from drinking too much liquor. *Not common.*

aunt   Aunt   *n.* 1 A brothel madam; an old prostitute. 2 An elderly male homosexual.   **—ie**   *n.* 1 = **aunt.** 2 Any elderly Negress, esp. a nursemaid or one who takes care of children. *Since c1830; not now common.* See Appendix,—ie ending. 3 An antimissile missile. *Air Force use.*

Aussie   *n.*   An Australian. 1951: "Seems the Aussies go in for fish contests, too. How do you like the gall of those Aussies?" Stan Smith in N.Y. *Daily News,* Aug., 30, c14/4. *Since W.W.I. adj.* Australian. 1945: "Returning Aussie brides . . . will have a hard time. . . . Hundreds of Aussie girls. . . . Aussie men and women. . . ." H. Boyle, AP, Oct. 27. *These uses not at all derog.*

Aussie steak   *n.* Mutton. *Some W.W. II Army use reported, but prob. synthetic.*

author   *v.t.* To write or compose, as a book, play, or the like. 1952: "The name of him who authored what/I used to

know but have forgot." H. P. Boynton, *Atlantic Monthly,* Jan., 99/1. 1952: "Murray Rose, who authors the column, 'Sports Roundup,' . . ." AP, July 18.

auto   *n.* An automobile. 1899: *DAE.* 1901: Greenough & Kittredge, 61. 1913: "Why don't he use his auto?" *SEP,* Mar. 1, 10. 1930: "Frowned upon by the elegant . . . are auto, gent, ad, rep, exam, memo. . . ." *Word Study, Dec.,* 4/1. 1934: *colloq. Web.* See Appendix, Shortened Words.   **—mobile**   *n.* A fast worker; a fast-moving, fast-talking, or fast-thinking person. 1956: "Garment workers . . . are . . . distrustful of *automobiles*—fast operators. . . ." *Labor's Special Lang. From Many Sources. Orig. Amer. Yiddish sl.*

Auzzie   *n.* = **Aussie.**

avoirdupois   *n.* Body weight, personal fat. *Since c1850; euphem.; colloq.*

aw   *interj.* A speech sound signifying disapproval, disappointment, disbelief, etc.; often followed by an additional sl. word or phrase, as "Aw, gee!" "Aw, heck!" "Aw, nuts!" etc. *Colloq. Exceedingly common in speech but seldom adopted in literature, even in vernacular writing.*

away   *adv.* 1 In prison. *Underworld use.* 2 In baseball, out; used only in phrase "There is one away," "There are two away," etc., meaning there is one out, two are out, etc.

away, put   1 To commit to an asylum or jail. *Colloq.* 2 To knock unconscious, usu. by a blow from a blunt instrument. 3 To kill. 4 To eat or drink. 1946: "That man can put away more whiskey than any other two men I know." *Word Study,* Dec., 6/1. 5 To classify; to categorize. 1934: "It is this innocent expression that causes many guys to put Ambrose away as slightly dumb." Runyon, 370.

away, put it   To eat large quantities of food; to eat voraciously.

— awayer   See Appendix, Suffixes and Suffix Words.

away with [something], get   1 To win or capture; to succeed. 1926: "He will 'get away' well enough with what he undertakes." J. W. Beach. 2 To do something that is illegal or forbidden without getting caught or punished. Often in the phrase "get away with it." 1934: "You think you can get away with lies now? . . ." Cain, *Postman,* 61. *Since c1920, the most common use.* 3 To steal or take something; to make a getaway with something. **4** To finish eating or drinking something. Cf. **put away.**

awful   *adj.* Very unpleasant; very sad; exceedingly disagreeable, ugly, unskillful or otherwise objectionable. 1809: *DAE*. 1909: "In present use . . . 'an awful job,' 'awful weather,' 'an awful bore,' . . .'' Krapp, *Mod. Eng.*, 202. *Colloq.*   **—ly** *adv.* **1** Very; very much; a general intensive. 1839: *DAE*. 1893: " 'Awfully' was British first, and is now American also.'' *Colloq.* **2** Very badly. 1816: *DAE*. *Colloq.*

A.W.O.L.   a.w.o.l.   awol Absent without leave. *Armed Forces use since W.W.I. Used to designate a soldier who does not answer rollcall but has not been away long enough to be classified as a deserter. During W.W.I and for some years after, the initials only were used in both speech and writing. Since c1935 the letters have been pronounced and written as one word. Also occasionally used in nonmilitary establishments, e.g., schools.*

ax   axe   *n.* A musical instrument, esp. in a modern jazz context. 1957:

"Axe—any musical instrument, even a piano." E. Horne, *For Cool Cats and Far-Out Chicks. Far out and beat use; not common.*

ax, get the   To be fired or dismissed; lit., to be severed from one's employment or school, or from a relationship. See **get it in the neck.**

ax, give [someone] the   To fire or dismiss someone; to fire an employee; to dismiss a student from school; to dismiss one's boy friend or girl friend. 1951: "They give guys the ax quite frequently at Pencey [a prep school]. It has a very good academic rating." J. D. Salinger, *Catcher in the Rye*, 9.

ax, the   *n.* **1** Fig., a sudden separation from one's job; a firing or discharge. → **2** A dismissal from school. → **3** Rejection by one's fiancé, lover, etc. *All uses colloq.*

axle grease   Butter.

ax to grind   **1** A grievance, esp. one that the complainant wishes to discuss. *Colloq.* **2** An idea, cause, argument, etc., to which one continually reverts; an obsession.

B

B   *n* Benzedrine. *Orig. narcotic addict use; some student use since c1950.*

b.a. [taboo]   *adj.* = **bare-assed.** See Appendix, Shortened Words.

Babbitt   *n.* A smug, self-satisfied conformist; specif., a middle-class, successful, small-town businessman who does not question society or the prevailing ethics, politics, homey virtues, religion, etc.; one who is satisfied with society as he finds it; one who has no interest in thinking about, contemplating, or enjoying art, philosophy, religion, politics, ethics, etc. 1958: "It is not just the Babbitts who think there's something odd about people who read poetry." K. Rexroth in *Esquire*, May, 20. *From the chief character in the novel Babbitt, by S. Lewis.*

babbling brook   A talkative woman; a chronic talker, esp., a gossip.

babe   *n.* A girl, a woman of any age; specif., a sexually attractive girl or young woman. 1943: "I remembered the babe who threw the drink in his face." Chandler, *Lady in Lake*, 117. 1950: " 'Babe,' used in the United States for a pretty girl or almost any female. . . .'' M. Berger in N.Y. *Times Bk. Rev.*, July, 23,

7/1f. 1950: "The bird, which had the habit of greeting women with a low, expressive whistle and a 'hiya, babe.' '' AP, Sept. 1. *Implies familiarity, or that the girl or young woman is spirited. c1925–c1940, often in direct address. From "baby."* See Appendix, Shortened Words.   **Babe**   *n.* A large, fat man; esp., a large, fat baseball player;— used as a nickname. *As irony, and because many fat men have baby faces. Reinforced by Babe Ruth, the baseball star of the 1920s who was a heavy-set man.* **—s**   *n. sing.* = **babe.**

Babe-Ruth   *n.* In baseball, a home run. *From Babe Ruth, the famous home-run hitter.*

baby   *n.* **1** = **babe,** esp. one's sweetheart or a babe who is the object of one's special attention. 1924: "Gloria Nielsen [a movie actress] is there, and she's a pash baby." Marks, *Plastic Age*, 24. 1950: "I'm sure happy my baby wore her war paint." UP, Jan. 27. *Since at least c1900. "Babe" is more common = a girl; but "baby" alone may have the connotation of "sweetheart." 2* A man, a fellow, a guy; esp., a mean or intimidating man, a tough guy. 1939: "I did not want them babies to think they had me under contract." J. O'Hara, *Pal Joey*, 33. 1921: "That baby packed a nasty wallop." Witwer, *Leather*, 10. 1950: "Those boys I used to sing with were really tough babies . . . nobody fooled with *them*." A. Lomax, *Mr. Jelly Roll*, 15. **3** Anything which, like a baby or a "baby," is the object of one's special attention, interest, or masculine admiration or affection; anything that gives a man pride or a feeling of power to possess, create, or build; that with which familiarity or association gives a man a feeling of masculine pride or power. 1929: "That baby [a painting] set me back 150 berries." Burnett, *Little Caesar*, 131. 1942: "Must take a good man to run them fast babies [elevators]." Chandler, *High Window*, 82. 1943: "This baby [a ship] can turn on a dime." H. Wren in *Word Study*, May, 4/1. 1945: "The crime had been one of my babies." L. F. McHugh, *Chicago Murders*, 185. 1949: "He sniffed [at the gun]. 'Oh yeah, this baby's been working.' " Chandler, *Little Sister*, 215. 1951: "It was a tough season. Even the oaters [cowboy movies], my babies, were off." W. Fuller in *Collier's*, Feb. 10, 22/1. 1951: "Mr. Carter picked the Bible up and bore it to Scribner's. 'It's my baby to sell,' said Mr. Randall." *New Yorker*, Feb. 17, 22/3. *adj.* Nice. *Applied to anything. Mainly teenage girl use; obs.*

baby doll A pretty girl.

baby kisser A politician, esp. one campaigning for public office. *Because the traditional politician is supposed to shake the hands of adults and kiss babies in an attempt to seem friendly and win votes.*

baby-lifter *n.* A brakeman on a passenger train. *Railroad use.*

baby-sit **baby sit** *v.i.* To stay with a child or with children while the parents are away; to be responsible for a child or children in the absence of the parents. *The person who baby sits may be either a professional, as a nurse or a teenager who works for a fee, or a friend or relative who assumes the responsibility as a favor.* 1951: "It was her idea for Hoke to babysit!" D. Brooks, *synd. comic strip*, "*The Jackson Twins*," Oct. 15. *Since c1945; the changes in living conditions and attitudes during and since W.W.II have made baby-sitting a common practice; the war saw people marry and have children at a younger age; these young families moved to new neighborhoods or* suburban areas away from older family members who could have taken care of their children when the young couple wished an evening away from home; consequently the idea of paid workers to watch over children in the absence of parents became popular.
—ter *n.* One who baby-sits. *Orig. teenage use c1945; now very common among all age groups.*

baby-skull *n.* An apple dumpling. *Archaic and dial.*

bach **batch** *n.* A bachelor; an unmarried man. *Since c1850.* See Appendix, Shortened Words. *v.i.* To live alone; to live as a bachelor. *Since c1870; often used in "to bach it."*

bachelor girl An unmarried, self-sufficient young woman who lives alone or with another woman. *A euphem., the term often implies that the woman is unmarried by choice, usu. because of her devotion to a career.*

back *v.t.* To give one's support to a person, project, or plan; lit., to wager one's money on the success of someone or something. 1958: "UAW [United Auto Workers union] Plans $50 Million Fund to Back Contract Demands." Headline in N.Y. *Post*, Jan. 24, 4.

back, get off [someone's] To stop harassing, teasing, criticizing, or otherwise molesting someone; usu. a command or entreaty. *Lit.* = "stop riding me." See **on [someone's] back.** *Very common during and since W.W.II.*

back, on [someone's] **1** A phrase used with the verb "to be" to signify the action of criticism, teasing, or harassment. **2** A phrase used with the verb "to be" to signify a moral, emotional, financial, or physical dependency. 1956: ". . . Tamkin for thirty or forty years had gotten through many a tight place, . . . he would get through this crisis too and bring him, Wilhelm, to safety also. And Wilhelm realized that he was on Tamkin's back. It had made him feel that he had virtually left the ground and was riding upon the other man. He was in the air. It was for Tamkin to take the steps." Saul Bellow, *Seize the Day*, 96. **3** Teasing, criticizing, nagging, or annoying a person acutely or constantly. See **ride.**

back alley **1** Any alley, street, or part of a cheap, disreputable section of a city or town; a slum area; a section of a city or town where vice abounds. 1952: "Saturday night in Reno. Back-alley Reno. Colored Reno by the railroad tracks. . . ." L. Hughes, *Laughing to Keep from Crying*, 65. **2** A slow, sensuous type of jazz, played in a rhythm as if accompanying a strip-tease dance or even coitus and often with the instruments imitating human sounds.

backasswards [taboo]   *adv.* = **ass backwards.** 1951: "You always do everything backasswards. No wonder you're flunking out of here. You don't do one damn thing the way you're supposed to." J. D. Salinger, *Catcher in the Rye*, 35.

Back Bay   **1** A fashionable, wealthy, upper-class residential district of Boston, Mass., situated on the end of the inner harbor. *Obs.* → **2** Any fashionable residential area in any city or town. *Not common.*   *adj.* Fashionable, wealthy.

backbone   *n.* Courage; perseverance; honesty.

back-cap   *v.t.* To disparage. *Some use since c1890.*

—backer   See Appendix, Suffixes and Suffix Words.

back-gate (-door) parole   The death of a prisoner, from a natural cause. *Underworld and prison use.*

back number   A thing that or, esp., a person who is old-fashioned, out of date, or behind the times; a has-been. 1882: *DAE.* 1891: "For a back number, George Hanley seems to be holding up." N.Y. *Sporting Times*, June 13, 15/2. 1905: "Mr. Stale is a back number." McHugh, *Search Me*, 53. *Still in use. From the term as applied to old magazines no longer on current sale at magazine stands.*

back off   **1** To stop teasing, annoying, or riding someone. *Usu. an imperative or an entreaty.* → **2** To slow down; to speak slower or explain in more detail; to ease one's foot off the gas pedal of a car in order to slow its speed. *Teenage use since c1950.*

backroom   *adj.* Of, by, for, or from political expediency; associated with the people or opinions concerned with current politics.

backroom, boys in the   Those politically wise; politicians, their staffs and friends.

back talk   Impudent talk; an impertinent retort. *Colloq.*

back to the salt mines   See **salt mines.**

back up   *v.t.* To support, verify, testify in favor of, or back a person, statement, or plan.   *v.i.* To talk slower, to explain more fully, to restate or repeat.

back up, to have one's   To be angry, to be in an angry or critical mood.

back yard   Collectively, the performers in a circus, as opposed to the administrative staff. *Circus use.* Cf. **front door.**

bacon   *n.* **1** Chicken served at a meal. *Some W.W.I Army use.* Cf. **turkey. 2** Plunder. *A little underworld use.* **3** See **bring home the bacon.**

bad   *adj.* Eminently appropriate or suitable; excellent, wonderful; orig., adroitly played or arranged. *Cool and far out use. In order to be cool and to demonstrate a lack of emotion, cool and far out sl. and jargon sometimes relies on understatement. Saying that something one likes or considers good is "bad" is, of course, the ultimate understatement.*

—die   *n.* **1** The villain in a movie, play, or other entertainment; an actor who plays the role of a villain, a heavy; specif., a movie bad man. 1951: "If you booed today's stage baddie...." J. Chapman in N.Y. *Sunday News*, Sept. 30, 19C/1. **2** A criminal, hoodlum, or tough guy; a mischievous person. **3** An unsuccessful attempt.

bad actor   **1** A mean, vicious, or poorly trained animal. **2** A mean, malicious, or deceitful person. **3** A confirmed criminal.

bad egg   See **egg.**

badge   *n.* A policeman. *Some c1920 underworld use.*

badge bandit   **1** A motorcycle policeman. *Hot rod use. It is motorcycle policemen that try to stop unofficial drag races on public roads.* → **2** A policeman. *Some general teenage use since c1955.* Cf. **badge, bandit.**

badger   **badger game, the**   *n.* **1** A method of blackmailing a man whereby a female accomplice of the blackmailer entices the victim into a compromising sexual situation, at which point the blackmailer enters and threatens exposure of the man unless money is paid. *Since c1920.* → **2** Fig., any blackmail, extortion, or intimidation; any deception for personal or political gain.

bad hat   *n.* A bad egg; a bad actor; a rascal. 1940: "As for Amthor, he's a bad hat." Chandler, *Farewell*, 242. *Never common in U.S., fairly common in Brit. use before W.W.II.*

bad man   Orig., in the cowboy days of the old West, a villainous robber and psychopathic murderer; now, in movies about the old West, a robber or gunman; the villain. 1936: "The actual 'bad man' was 'short on conversation.' He spoke infrequently, and when he opened his mouth what he said was to the point. He usually talked in quiet tones, for his nerves were always well in hand. His nerves had to be thus in order for him to do the jobs which he essayed. All actual 'bad men' were wholly untrustworthy, were natural killers, were moral and mental degenerates, inhuman brutes who would slay for personal gain or merely to gratify a whim. All of them were among the horse thieves and train robbers, the 'hold-up men' and 'road agents'. . . ." P. A. Rollins, *The Cowboy*, 55.

bad news A bill for money owed, esp., as given personally to the customer by a waiter in a nightclub.

bad shit [taboo] **1** A dangerous or deceptive person, task, or situation; malicious actions or deeds. *The most common use.* **2** Ill fortune, bad luck.

bad time 1 = **hard time**. **2** A situation that is dangerous, frightening, or uncomfortable. **3** Time that has been spent in the guardhouse and is not credited toward one's required period of military service. *Some Army use during and since W.W.II.*

Baedeker *n.* A guide book. *From Karl Baedeker, of Leipzig, Ger., publisher who issued a series of travel guide books so widely used that his name has become a common synonym for guide book.*

baffle-gab *n.* The ambiguous, verbose, and sometimes incomprehensible talk or writing often done by bureaucrats; officialese. 1952: "The word [baffle-gab], gaining steadily in use, was dreamed up only last May by a young lawyer named Milton A. Smith of the U.S. Chamber of Commerce." W. A. Garrett, GNS, Oct. 28.

bag *n.* **1** A discharge from one's job, the sack. *Some use since c1915; never common.* **2** [taboo] A woman's douche bag. *Once assoc. with prostitutes or promiscuous women, the article and the word are respectable and common now.* → **3** [taboo] A prostitute; a promiscuous woman; a woman considered solely as a sexual object. 1924: "I don't chase around with filthy bags." Marks, *Plastic Age*, 202. 1939: "The highest paid bag in Chi. . . ." J. O'Hara, *Pal Joey*, 60. 1951: "Some old bag said she had to take on thirty, forty customers a day." I, *Mobster*, 132. *The word is now somewhat archaic, and most often applied to old women.* → **4** An unattractive or ugly girl or young woman; an old woman, esp. a gossipy old shrew. 1949: "The old bag

told you." J. Evans, *Halo*, 166. *Since c1925. Now much more common than "bag" = prostitute. Orig. and still derisive, but now freq. used as a term of jocular familiarity or even affection, as by a man in talking or referring to his wife or sweetheart, or by a woman talking in a jocular mood about a friend or herself; the "old" connotation thus may become "old friend," or a humorous ref. to one the same age as the speaker. A man may call a woman "bag" after she is 20 years old, a woman may call another "bag" after both are 30.* **5** [taboo] The scrotum. *Not common.* **6** [taboo] A thin rubber sheath worn over the penis during coitus, as a contraceptive or prophylactic; a rubber. **7** [taboo] A woman's rubber diaphragm or pessary. **8** In baseball, a base. 1951: "Thomson didn't realize that Lockman had stepped on second and headed for that bag only to find Lockman occupying it." J. Hand, AP, Oct., 3. *Since before 1930.* **9** See **have a bag on**. **10** A uniform. 1958: "Bag— Uniform." G. Y. Wells, *Station House Slang. Not common.* **11** A dress or style of dress which hangs loosely from the shoulders, is not fitted at the waist, and is gathered or tapered near the hem line. *A style pop. during 1958. Not as common as "sack."* —*v.t.* **1** To dismiss an employee from his job. See **sack**. **2** To arrest a person. 1947: "The police at once bagged her as a 'vag.' " J. Bruce in *San. Fran. Murders*, 206. *From the now stand. to bag = to seize.* **3** To be unnecessarily absent from school; to skip school. 1948: "Threatening him with castor oil, when he seemed set to bag school, never did any good." T. Daly in Phila. *Bulletin*, Jan. 15, 14. 1950: "[After my mother's death] I took to baggin' school in [Philadelphia]." Toots Shor, quoted by J. Bainbridge in *New Yorker*, Nov. 11, 60. *May be regional use.*

—**gage** *n.* **1** See **blind baggage**. **2** A girl or woman, esp. one's wife, sweetheart, or date. Cf. **bag**. *Perh. influenced by stand. baggage = prostitute.* **3** See **excess baggage**. ——**ger** *n.* In baseball, a hit that enables the batter to reach the specified base. *Thus two bagger = a double; three bagger = a triple; four bagger = a home run.* 1881: "Two-bagger." *DAE.* 1910: "A sizzling three-bagger." Johnson, *Varmint*, 123. 1953: "Slammed a two-bagger." L. Thomas, CBS radio, Mar. 9. ——**ging** *n.* = **bag-play**. —**man** *n.* One who is assigned to collect bribe, extortion, or kidnaping

money. 1952: "The defendant was described by the court as 'bagman' or collector for 'higher-ups' in the [police] department." N .Y. *Times*, Sept. 3, 1/1.
—s   *n.pl.* **1** Trousers. *Some jitterbug and jive use in U.S., not as common as in Eng.* **2** [taboo] The testicles. *Not common.*
bag, in the   **1** Certain; sure; safe; secure; cinched. 1949: "Losing this race after we appeared to have it in the bag. . . ." AP, Oct. 3. **2** Rigged or fixed in advance, as a crooked sporting event. 1933: ". . . The sinister implication of 'in the bag' may or may not be included when the phrase is used even now." Kieran, *Sat. Rev. Lit.* **3** Completed successfully. 1954: "It's in the bag. The fix is in." W. R. & F. K. Simpson, *Hockshop*, 188. *Colloq.*
baggage smasher   **1** One whose work is handling baggage. *Since c1850; still used, mainly railroad, airplane, and trucker use.* **2** A rough, brutal person. 1851: "Gamblers, emigrant-robbers, baggage-smashers, and all the worst classes of the city." N.Y. *Trib.*, Nov. 23. *Obs.*
bag of wind   = **windbag.**
bag on, have (get, tie) a   To go on a drinking spree; to be on a drunken spree; to be drunk. 1951: "He had half a bag on and looked it." Spillane, *Big Kill*, 37. 1952: "You still tie a bag on now and again." W. Pegler, *synd. newsp. col.*, July 31. See Appendix, Drunk.
bag-play   *n.* Currying favor; an act or instance of attempting to curry favor; an attempt to impress a superior with one's ability or importance.
bag-puncher   *n.* A boxer.
bags of   Much or many. *Fig., possessing bags full of something.*
bail   *v.t.* To shovel coal into a firebox. *Railroad use; archaic.*
bail out   **1** To help another who has met with failure; to relieve someone of debt, embarrassment, or the like; to come to another's aid. *From "bail."* **2** To abandon a project, task, or relationship that is unsuccessful before losing further time and/or money; specif., to rid oneself of a girl friend or fiancé. *From the term = to parachute from an airplane.* **3** To make a parachute jump from a crippled airplane. *Colloq.* **4** To avoid work; to goof off. 1943: "Later on, when he [an air-force recruit] has been a soldier a little longer, he will goof off with finesse, but by then he will say he has bailed out, another term taken over from actual flying." R. A. Herzberg,

Word Study, Apr., 5/1. *W.W.II Air Force and some Army use.*
bait   *n.* **1** A man who is pretty or seems effeminate, or a woman who is handsome and seems masculine, and thus is attractive to or receives the unwanted attentions of homosexuals. **2** A person, esp. a youth, living in a neighborhood or having psychological problems which, or assoc. with friends who, may lead him to become a drug addict; a potential drug addict. *Not common.*
—bait   See Appendix, Suffixes and Suffix words.
baked wind   = **hot air.**
bake-head   *n.* **1** A locomotive engineer. *Railroad use. Obs.* **2** A locomotive fireman. *Railroad use. Archaic.*
Baker   *n.* Used instead of any intended word beginning with the letter "b," esp. as a euphem. for "bitch" in "son of a bitch" or for "bastard." *From the Army use as the second letter in the spoken alphabet. Some use during and since W.W.II.* See **Able.**
baker, the   *n.* The electric chair. *Not common.*
Baker flying   **1** Danger; keep off; keep out. *From USN use; a red Quartermaster B or Baker flag is flown to indicate danger, as when a ship is loading ammunition or fuel.* **2** = **have the rag on.**
baker's dozen   Thirteen of anything. *From the bakers' traditional custom of giving 13 when a dozen is asked for, to ensure full measure and as a bonus to the customer.*
bald   *adj.* **1** Not wrapped; usu. said of a handout lunch. *Hobo use. Usu. in "bald lump."* **2** Fig., bald-faced.
bald face   Unaged or inferior whisky; homemade or bootlegged whisky. *Since c1850; not common.*   **—(d)**   *adj.* Obvious; bare; fig., unmasked; usu. in "bald-faced lie."
bald-headed row   Orig. and mainly, the front row of seats in a burlesque theater where wealthy, elderly men sit to have the best view; fig., men or a group of men, esp. if old, who stare at women; fig., the front row or rows of seats in any theater where wealthy, elderly men and their companions sit.
baldy   baldie   *n.* **1** A bald man. 1953: "Baldies are more romantic. . . ." F. Bayle, AP, Jan. 20. See Appendix, —ie, —y endings. → **2** An old but not necessarily bald man. *Orig. underworld and hobo use c1925. Not common.* **3** An Army haircut. *Because the hair is cut very short. Some W.W.II Army use.*

ball *n.* **1** A dollar; orig., a silver dollar. *Some use from before 1895 until c1925. Mainly underworld use.* → **2** A prisoner's allowance, from which he buys tobacco, candy, and the like. *Underworld and prison use c1910–c1935.* → **3** Lit., a party, esp. a wild, unrestrained, uninhibited, boisterous, or noisy party. Fig., any good time or way of life; any place in which or period during which one enjoys oneself thoroughly, and any thing or person that adds to one's pleasure or is pleasing or enjoyable; specif., that which or one who contributes to complete, unrestricted, exciting, or thrilling good times or enjoyment. *Some early c1935 Negro jive use. Orig. pop. by bop and cool use, and assoc. with jazz and avant-garde groups. Now common student and teenage use, with less emphasis on being unrestricted and exciting, and some general use. Of multiple orig.: from ball = dollar and prison allowance; of course, from ball = formal dance or masquerade; and at least reinforced by obs. ball off = to treat or be generous, goof ball = narcotic pill, and balls = testicles. Cf.* **have a ball.** → **4** Specif., a pill or portion of a narcotic drug, orig. marijuana. *Addict use.* See **goof ball. 5** Specif., a passionate, uninhibited session of necking or petting; an evening or period of sexual abandonment, a sex orgy. **6** A single scoop of ice cream. *Some lunch-counter use in relaying an order.* *v.i.* To have a good time, esp. an exciting one; to play cool or far out music pleasingly; to enjoy oneself or have a good time within the cool, far out, or beat milieu; to have an uninhibited, personally satisfying, unique, cool, or beat good time. 1958: "A good-time town where everybody comes to ball." E. Klein, N.Y. *Daily News,* Feb. 20, 36. 1958: "A pretty little department store model approaches a man at a party, takes off her sweater, then her bra, and says, 'Let's ball, dig,'—by which she [in this instance] means, Let's try a new far-out sound on the hi-fi." H. Gold, *The Beat Mystique,* 20. **—ing** *n.* Having fun, esp. uninhibited, wild, or exciting fun; orig. having fun by dancing; specif., having fun by dancing, drinking, necking, in coitus, or at an exciting, wild party. *Jive and some Negro use since c1935.*

ball, get on the To become alert, adroit, knowledgeable, or hep. *Usu. said as a command or as an urgent request.* See **on the ball.**

ball, have [oneself] a To enjoy oneself thoroughly and without reservations, restrictions, or inhibitions; to have a good time. *Orig., c1945, bop talk; by c1955 common with teenagers, college students, and others. From "ball" = formal dance party and "ball" = marijuana.*

ball, keep [one's] eye on the To be alert.

ball, on the **1** To be alert and have vitality and ability; to be in the know, to be hep. 1949: "That *Inquirer* [newspaper] is on the ball." Advt., in the Phila. *Inquirer,* Sept. 4. *First pop. assoc. with bop and cool use; some student use since c1935; common since c1940; very popular during W.W.II.* **2** Alert; active; diligent, efficient; prompt; clear-thinking. 1949: "FBI Agents were very much on the ball in the Bremer snatch...." A. Hynd, 124. **3** In baseball, to pitch effective curves, or to have a wide variety of effective pitches, said of a pitcher. *There is no indication that this baseball use is older than the general sl. use.*

ball and chain **ball-and-chain** **1** One's wife. 1948: "What a lovely ball-and-chain!" Movie, *Look for the Silver Lining. Always jocular.* → **2** One's mistress or steady girl friend. *Not common.*

ballast *n.* Money. *Some c1920 use.*

ball-breaker [taboo] *n.* = **ball-buster.**

ball-buster [taboo] *n.* **1** A job, task, activity, or goal that is extremely difficult to accomplish. *From balls = testicles. Fig., that which strains one.* → **2** The person who assigns, demands, or supervises such arduous tasks. *Both uses attained some pop. use during the Korean war, though known much earlier.*

balled up **balled-up** Confused; disorganized; perplexed; abounding with mistakes or blunders. 1920: "He's got me all balled up. I've misjudged him." F. S. Fitzgerald, *This Side of Paradise,* 133. 1922: "They get so sloppy and uncultured in their speech, so balled-up in their thinking!" S. Lewis, *Babbitt,* reprinted in *The American Twenties,* 231. *Colloq. Orig. ref. to the accumulation of snow in the curve of a horse's hoof or shoe in winter. This could cause a horse to slip or fall and had to be removed. Cf.* **fouled up; fucked up.**

ball off To treat, to be generous to. *Obs. since c1895.*

ball of fire A brilliant, energetic person; an energetic person who strives hard for rapid success; a go-getter or dazzling performer of any kind. 1949: "He was sometimes enviously referred to

as a go-getter, a hot shot, a ball of fire."
"Maybe he was a ball of fire in the
business world, but he was just a nice
fellow to go out with." *Fact Detec.
Mysteries*, 21; 27. 1952: "Governor
Adlai Stevenson [Democratic candidate
for President] hasn't actually been a ball
of fire himself, up to this time." J.
Marlow, AP, Aug. 28. *Since before 1900.*
2 A fast or express train. *Railroad use.*

ball one   An order to prepare or
serve one hamburger or meat ball. *Some
lunch-counter use c1940 in relaying a
customer's order. From the ball-like form
of the meat patty, plus a jocular allusion
to the baseball expression.*

balloon   *n.* **1** A bed-roll or roll of
blankets carried on the back; a bindle.
Some hobo use c1920. **2** A frankfurter.
Not common.   *v.i., v.t.* To forget one's
lines entirely during a theatrical performance; to go up in one's lines. *Some
theater use.*

balloon-head   *n.* A stupid person.
—ed   *adj.* Stupid. 1937: "Listen, you
balloon-headed fool." Weidman, *Wholesale,* 34.

balloon juice   **1** Empty, noisy talk;
lit., hot air. *Some use since c1900.* **2** Gas
as used in a balloon, specif. helium.
Some use during and since W.W.I.

balloon room   A room where marijuana is smoked; a marijuana pad. *Some
addict use.*

balloon soup   An attempt to deceive;
false or deceptive talk; balloon juice.
Not common.

balls [taboo]   *n.pl.* The testicles. *Colloq.
interj.* An expression of incredulity, disappointment, disgust, or the like.

balls, have [someone] by the [taboo]
To have power over someone; to be in a
position to rule, boss, hurt, or impugn
the reputation of, expose, act maliciously toward, or cause trouble to
someone. *Fig. to have a person helpless
and in one's power, specif. to be needed or
necessary to a disliked person, who thus
must bear one's abuse or malicious deeds
or words; to have someone dead to rights.
Known to most men since W.W.II.*

balls on [something], put   To make
more emphatic, colorful, attractive, or
the like. 1958: "That copy is too weak.
Rewrite it and put balls on it!" *Oral,*
from a N.Y.C. advertising agency
manager.

ball the jack   **1** To go, move, or work
very rapidly or fast. *Orig. logger use,
from highballing.* → **2** To gamble or risk
everything on one attempt or effort.

ball up   **1** To fail at recitation or on
an examination. 1856: Hall, *College
Words. Regional student use.* → **2** To
confuse, mix up; to ruin or spoil by
confusion or blundering. 1887: *DAE.*
1930: "Eppingham can't ball me up."
Weeks, *Racket,* 201. *Colloq. From balled
up.*   **ball-up**   *n.* Confusion; a mess.
1952: "The ball-up abroad has been
supervised by Harry's [Truman's] advisers." R. C. Ruark, *synd. newsp. col.,*
Oct. 6. *Some use since c1900.*

bally   *v.i.* To attract a crowd to a
side-show by describing the show loudly
and sensationally, usu. on a platform in
front of it, as by a barker; to advertise
vocally a side-show and urge people to
come and see it. *Carnival and circus use.
From* "*ballyhoo.*"   *v.t.* To urge one's
wares on a crowd which one has attracted
by a spiel. *Pitchmen's use.*   *n.* **1** =
bally stand. *Carnival and circus use.*
2 = **ballyhoo**; publicity. 1948: "Looks
like some advance bally." *Variety,* Aug.,
25, 55/3. See Appendix, Shortened Words.
—hoo   bally-hoo   *n.* **1** A short,
free exhibition or sample of a side-show,
accompanied by a barker's spiel, given
on a platform or bally stand in front of
the side-show tent in order to attract
spectators and lure them inside as paying
customers. *Carnival and circus use since
at least c1910.* → **2** Lit. and fig., advertising, favorable publicity; esp., loud,
colorful advertising; lit. and fig., boisterous, happy noise created to give an
impression that one's customers are
satisfied, or an impression that a good or
attractive performance, entertainment,
product, or plan is available. 1949:
"Working without benefit of ballyhoo
to date, tiny Haiti has outdone itself in
building a world's fair." King Features
Synd., Oct. 18. *Since c1925.* → **3** Exaggerated talk; boloney. *Since c1930; not
common.*

bally show   A carnival side-show;
esp., one having continuous or regularly
scheduled performances. *Carnival and
circus use.*

bally stand   The platform in front of
a side-show tent on which the barker
stands, and on which a free exhibition
or a sample of the show may be performed
in order to lure spectators inside. *Carnival and circus use; also used by pitchmen.* See **ballyhoo.**

balmy   *adj.* **1** Drunk. 1850: *DAE.
Still some use.* See Appendix, Drunk.
2 Daffy; loony, nuts. *Never as common in*

U.S. as in Eng. **3** Nervous; afraid. *Some W.W.I Army use.*

baloney   *n.* = **boloney.**

Baltimore steak (beefsteak)   Cow's or calf's liver served at a meal. *Orig. USN and hobo use; not common.*

bam   *v.t.* To strike or hit. 1918: "Heads may be biffed or bammed or bumped." M. Doolittle in *Outlook*, Nov., 433. *Of imitative orig.*

bambino   *n.* **1** A baby; a young child. *From the Italian.* **2** A man, esp. a strong or tough man; a fellow, a guy. *Since c1920;* see **bimbo.**

bamboo   *adj.* = **jerkwater.** *Never common.*

bamboo juice   Wine. *Some W.W.II Air Force use from Flying Tigers' use = rice wine, sold in a section of bamboo.*

bamboozle   *v.t.* To hoax; to deceive, trick, or swindle. 1703: Farmer & Henley. 1923: "Bamboozling the public." N.Y. *World*, Mar. 28. 1955: "He has been bamboozled by Miss Pat Ward." E. Trujillo, *I Love You, I Hate You*, 139. *Colloq.* —**d**   *adj.* Drunk. 1851: "In use at one time or another." Hall, *College Words*, 302. *Obs.* See Appendix, Drunk.

bamboula   *n.* **1** A primitive African drum, as used by New Orleans Creoles *c1830–c1900.* 1956: "Bamboula was the name of a drum covered with cowhide, a drum made of a length of bamboo." S. Longstreet, *The Real Jazz Old and New*, 5. *Archaic.* → **2** A primitive, often erotic dance as performed by New Orleans Creoles since c1900. → **3** A drum. *Some early jazz use.* → **4** Any wild, exciting dance. *Obs.*

banana   *n.* **1** A comedian, specif. in a burlesque show. *The most important, best, or senior comedian `is the "top banana," the next is "second banana," and so on.* 1953: " 'So they made me into a comedian,' [Red Buttons] says, 'third banana.' " G. Millstein in N.Y. *Times Mag.*, Feb. 22, 24/3f. *At least reinforced by the soft, water- or air-filled banana-shaped bladder club carried as a stand. item by such comedians and usu. used to hit other comedians over the head. Similar to the phallic symbols carried by the comedians on the ancient Greek stage. Orig. theatrical use, but fairly well known generally.* **2** A sexually attractive mulatto or light-skinned Negro woman; a trim high-yellow girl. *Some Negro use.* **3** The nose; esp., a large or long hooked nose. **4** [taboo] The penis. *Not common.* → **5** [taboo] Fig., coitus; the act or an instance

of ejaculation. *Usu. in "have one's banana peeled." Not common.* See Appendix, Sex and Food. **6** An automobile bumper guard. *Some automobile factory use.*

banana-head   *n.* A stupid person.

banana oil   **1** = **bananas! 2** Nonsense; insincere talk, exaggeration; bunk, apple sauce.

banana peeled, have [one's] [taboo], **have [one's] nuts cracked** [taboo] = **get one's ashes hauled.**

bananas!   *interj.* Nonsense! *An expression of refutation or incredulity, usu. addressed to someone who has told a small exaggeration or lie.*

banana stick   A baseball bat made of inferior wood. *Some baseball use.*

band   *n.* A woman. *Some Negro use. Prob. from "bantam."*

bandbox   *n.* A small or rural workhouse or jail; a county jail, esp. one from which it seems easy to escape. *Some convict use. Reinforced by "bandhouse."*

bandhouse   *n.* A prison. *Underworld use, obs. by c1925.*

bandit   *n.* An enemy aircraft. *W.W.II Air Force and Army use, orig. in combat communications.* Cf. **one-armed bandit.**

bandwagon   *n.* **1** A railroad pay car. *Some railroad use.* **2** Extreme nationwide popularity of a politician, entertainer, plan, or endeavor which pays that person or persons associated with him or it well in money or prestige. See **hop on the bandwagon.**

bandwagon, hop (get, jump, climb, leap) on the   To join the majority or most popular faction after withholding one's opinion or vote until the majority or relative popularity is known; to like, praise, accept, or show enthusiasm for a person, idea, or product only after popularity and general acceptance are assured; specif., to vote for or campaign for a political party or candidate after one is assured of the party's or candidate's popularity and relatively sure chances of winning an election, so as to be sure of being with the winning party or candidate.

bang   *n.* **1** An interjection of a narcotic drug. 1951: "He'd given himself a bang before he showed up." *I, Mobster*, 142. *Addict use.* → **2** A thrill; excitement or pleasure. *Almost always in "to get a bang out of."* 1951: "I started imitating one of those guys in the movies. I hate the movies like poison, but I get a bang imitating them." J. D. Salinger, *Catcher in the Rye*, 27. See **get a bang out of.**

3 A criminal charge or arrest. 1951: " 'What they got you locked up for?' 'Ah, Sergeant Dooley got me. It's a bum bang.' " J. B. Martin in *SEP*, Mar. 24, 78/4. *Underworld use, not common.* See **rap**.   *v.t.* **1** To have coitus (with); to fornicate. **2** To take narcotic drugs, esp. heroin, intravenously. *Common addict use.* *adv.* Exactly; smack. 1949: ". . . Not to nail people until they have them bang to rights. . . ." A. Hynd, *Public Enemies*, 115. 1952: "She arrived there bang on time." CBS radio, May 3. *v.t.* To knock oneself against an object in passing, as a door or chair; to bump or bruise oneself. *Colloq.*

bang-bang   *n.* **1** A gun. *Not in common, serious use.* → **2** A Western movie; a horse opera. *From the high incidence of gunshots in such films.* See Appendix, Reduplications.

banger   *n.* A club or stick; a stout cane. 1849: DAE. 1897: "Twenty years ago the college man had a most picturesque vocabulary. What color there was in such words as 'banger'. . . ." *Bookman*, Aug., 448/2. *Obs. since c1915.* See Appendix, —er endings.

bang out of, get a   To enjoy; to be pleasantly excited by; to get a thrill or a kick from. 1932: "Dave seems to be getting quite a bang out of the situation." Runyon. 1949: "The younger set is not 'getting a bang' out of things any more." N.Y. *Times Mag.*, Mar. 6, 33/1. See **bang**.

bangtail   *n.* A racehorse. 1947: "Tom used to wager as much as $50,000 a day on the bangtails." *Life*, May 26, 10. 1950: "The bangtail [Man o' War] was retired to stud." Billy Rose, *synd. newsp. col.*, Apr. 7. *Still common horse-racing use; is becoming archaic.*

bang to rights   In the act of committing a crime; dead to rights.

bang-up   *adj.* **1** Excellent, first-rate; excitingly proficient; modern, stylish; elegant;—said of both people and things. 1830: *DAE.* 1901: "Genuine slang." Greenough & Kittredge, 313. 1944: "I have some bang-up gin." Fowler, *Good Night*, 5. 1947: "The reporters had done a bang-up job of coverage." J. H. Jackson in *San Fran. Murders*, 158. 1953: "A bang-up novel." "We have a bang-up novelist in our midst." H. Breit in N.Y. *Times*, Apr. 5, 8/3. **2** Having no money; broke. 1854: *DAE. Never common; obs.*

banjo   Irish (Army) banjo   *n.* A shovel, esp. a short-handled shovel, as used to dig potatoes or dig a fox hole. 1956: "To coal miners, a *banjo* is a

shovel." *Labor's Special Language from Many Sources. Hobo and railroad use since c1920; railroad and Army use since c1940.*

banjo hit   In baseball, a hit between the infield and outfield. *Some baseball use.*

bank   *n.* A rest room; a toilet. *Not common.*

bank on   To depend or rely on. 1947: "When Ike [General Dwight Eisenhower] tells you anything about this country you can bank on it being true." Ernie Pyle, *Home Country*, 73.

bankroll   *v.t.* To finance, esp. to finance a theatrical production or nightclub. 1947: "Most of the joints were bankrolled by gents who wore .38s on their key rings." Billy Rose, *synd. newsp. col.*, Nov. 4.

bantam   *n.* = **chick**. *Primarily Negro use.*

baquero   *n.* See **bucker**.

barb   *n.* **1** A college student who is not a member of a fraternity. *Wide student use c1900; still a little use, but nearly obs. From "barbarian."* See Appendix, Shortened Words. **2** A barbecued meat sandwich. *Some lunch-counter use in relaying an order.* See Appendix, Shortened Words.

barbecue   *n.* **1** A sexually attractive girl or young woman. c1925: "Struttin' with Some Barbecue." Pop. song title. *Negro use.* See Appendix, Sex and Food. **2** A gathering, esp. an informal social or business gathering. 1957: "The Hick Cops Bust Up Joe's Nice Barbecue [a meeting of alleged criminals at Joseph Barbaro's home in Apalachin, N.Y.]." Headline, *Life*, Dec. 9, 57.

barbed-wire captain (major, colonel, general)   An officer allegedly promoted after being captured by the enemy, because he is a hero. *Some W.W.II Army and Air Force use.*

barber   *n.* **1** A talkative baseball player. *Some baseball use since c1925. Because barbers traditionally are talkative, esp. while shaving a customer who cannot talk back. Reinforced by baseball announcer "Red" Barber, whose job is talking.* **2** A baseball pitcher who is willing and able to force batters away from the plate by pitching fast balls close to their heads. *From close shave, reinforced by the famous pitcher Sal Maglie, who was nicknamed "the Barber" and was known for this type of pitch.* *v.i.* To talk; to chat or gossip. 1940: "I shouldn't ought to barber with you." Chandler, *Farewell*, 24. *Not common.*

barber bait *n.* A recruit or recruits. *Some W.W.II, mainly USN, use. In ref. to extremely short haircuts given to all new Armed Forces personnel.*

barber-shop *n.* Close-harmony singing, esp. of songs pop. *c1875–c1910. From the traditional style of barber-shop (employees') quartets.*

barbwire *n.* Whisky; esp., raw whisky. *Never common.*

bare-ass(ed)   bare ass(ed) *adj.* Naked. *Fairly common. Not taboo in ref. to men, as it is assumed "ass" = rump; considered vulgar in ref. to women, and considered taboo in ref. to women when "ass" = vagina.*

bareback   bare-back [taboo] *adj. & adv.* Without a contraceptive; said of the male only, in ref. to the act of coitus.

bareback rider [taboo]   A male who enters into sexual intercourse without using a contraceptive or prophylactic device. *Often used jocularly to imply that the encounter was unexpected and hurried.*

bareface(d)   bare-face(d) *adj.* **1** Undisguised; bold; impertinent; obvious; said of a speech or act. *Usu. in "a barefaced lie."* → **2** Impertinent, bold, obvious; specif., flaunting lies, exaggerations, or unsuitable, unbecoming, unacceptable words or acts; said of a person.

barefoot *adj.* Having no brakes; said of a railroad car or engine. *Railroad use.*

barf *v.i., v.t.* To vomit. *Some student use.*

bar-fly *n.* **1** A person of either sex who often and protractedly drinks at a bar; a heavy drinker of whisky; a souse, a tippler. 1928: "Andy Jackson, Kit Carson and General Grant—all good American bar-flies in their day." B. de Casseres in *Amer. Mercury,* Aug., 133/4. → **2** Specif., an alcoholic who frequents bars in order to beg or mooch free drinks from others.

bargain *n.* (Seldom if ever used as a sl. term in the affirmative.) See **no bargain.**

barge *v.i.* To move, to walk; to come, to go. 1929: "Bugs was reached after eleven-thirty and commanded to barge right over." K. Brush, *Young Man,* 44. *Not common.* See **barge in.**

barge in   1 To walk into or enter a place without hesitation or ceremony; to intrude. 1934: "The secretary barged in with a gun." Chandler, *Finger Man,* 59. 1942: "We can't have a lot of people barging in." W. B. Johnson, *Widening Stain,* 61. → **2** To interrupt, esp. to interrupt a conversation in order to add one's own opinion or advice; to offer or give one's advice or aid when not requested to do so; to butt in.

bar-girl = **B-girl.**

bark *n.* **1** Money. **2** Human skin. **3** Fur pelts, as used in fur coats. *v.i., v.t.* To give orders, criticize, or talk in a loud, curt, angry voice. *Colloq.* **—er** *n.* **1** One who draws a crowd of potential customers to a sideshow tent by describing the show and introducing the performers in sensational terms; a sideshow spieler or ballyhoo man. 1897: *DAE.* 1923: "The cries of the barkers [at an amusement park]." C. MacArthur, *Rope.* 1945: "He has been employed as a talker—the side-show term for barker —on the box at the gate at Hubert's." Mitchell, *McSorley's,* 96. *General use. Carnival and circus people prefer "spieler" or "talker."* **2** A pistol; an artillery cannon. *Some continued Army and underworld use.* **3** A funny joke or saying. **4** A first-base coach in baseball.

bar-keep *n.* A barkeeper or bartender. 1846: *DAE. Colloq.* See Appendix, Shortened Words.

barking dogs   Tired or sore feet. Cf. **dogs.**

barks *n.pl.* Shoes. *Not common.*

barn-burner *n.* Anything remarkable or sensational. *Dial.*

barn door *interj.* "Bon jour"; good day. *Some W.W.I Army use.* *n.* Any large object. *Usu. used in the colloq. phrase "big as a barn door."* **—s** Prominent front teeth, esp. the two upper center incisors.

barney *n.* **1** A bad recitation. 1810 [1851]: "Harvard College use about 1810." Hall, *College Words.* **2** Any bad performance. *Not common in U.S. use; from Brit. sl.* **3** Something done dishonestly, as a fixed prizefight or race. 1938: "[The fight] looked like a barney— as if there were some collusion." Liebling, *Back Where,* 136. 1946: "Not too much [drug could be given to the dogs], for fear the contest might look like the barney it was." P. Jones in Phila. *Bulletin,* Jan. 7, 10.

barn-storm *v.i.* To travel as an entertainer, making short or one-night stands in rural towns. **—er   1** One who barn-storms; orig. an actor, now often a traveling carnival act or stunt man. → **2** Specif., an inferior actor.

barnyard golf   The game of pitching horseshoes. *Jocular.*

barracks 13   An Army guardhouse. *Some W.W.II Army use.*

barracks lawyer   A soldier who is free with unwanted advice, is argumentative, habitually complains, or pretends to a knowledge of military rules and regulations. *W.W.II Army use.*

barrel   *v.i.* To speed, to go fast; specif., to drive a car rapidly. *Since c1930, mainly student use; now general use and common hot rod use, where technically barrel = an engine cylinder.* n. A fat person. *Not common.*

barrel, in the   Without money; broke. 1942: "A red hot pimp like you ain't got no business in the barrel." Z. Hurston, 86. *Negro use. Fig., having no clothing and wearing a barrel.*

barrel, over a   1 Fig., to be helpless; specif., to be helpless before one's creditors; to be in dire need of money, to be broke and in debt, to owe a debt which one cannot pay, esp., to have too little money to continue operating a business; fig., to be in another's power, so that one has to accept business, personal, or social conditions set by another, or bear his insults and malicious words or deeds. *In allusion to the state of a person put over a barrel to clear his lungs of water after a water mishap.* 1939: "Then you'd be over a barrel." Chandler, *Big Sleep*, 190.

barrel ass   [taboo]   To drive a car rapidly; to speed. *From "barrel." Lit., to move oneself forward rapidly, as when driving a car.*

barreled up   Drunk. *Obs.* See **barrelhouse.** See Appendix, Drunk.

barrel-house   barrelhouse   *n.* 1 A cheap saloon. 1883: *DAE.* 1913: "Barrelhouse kings, with feet unstable. . . ." V. Lindsay, "The Congo," 1, 2. *Archaic.* → 2 A brothel; orig. a combination cheap saloon, brothel, and rooming house. 1950: "Storyville opened in 1897 and offered regular, well-paid jobs to any musician who wasn't too proud to earn a dollar in a barrelhouse." A. Lomax, *Mr. Jelly Roll*, 72. → 3 A tail-gate form or style of jazz; a rough and ready manner of performing, usu. associated with ensemble improvisations and a driving rhythm. *The term is a hark-back to the early days of the century in New Orleans, but whether or not it was actually used then, or only later, is uncertain.*

barrel-house bum   An urban, wine-drinking beggar. *Some c1920 hobo use.*

base, get to first   To achieve the first step toward one's objective, often intimacy with the opposite sex. *Almost invariably in the negative, "He won't get to first base with her." From the baseball term.*

base, off   1 A place or situation in which one is an intruder. 2 Descriptive of an unfounded statement or a person who utters such a statement; intrusive; interfering. *From the baseball use.*

base, off [one's]   1 Mistaken; wrong. 1882: *DAE.* 1909: "A person . . . may be said 'to be off his base,' a metaphor apparently taken from base-ball." Krapp, *Mod. English*, 205. 1913: "Professor McClintock is quite off his base in knocking the use of slang." Washington *Post* quoted in *Lit. Digest*, Sept. 6, 379/1. *Obs.* → 2 Crazy. *Some use c1890–c1910.*

bash   *n.* 1 Any exciting, memorable party; an exciting, or violently exciting, good time; a "ball." 2 = **jam session.** 1950: "Some of these bashes were impromptu at 4 in the morning by trumpet players." L. Sobol, *Home Mag.*, Apr. 2, 8. 3 A banquet; a meal consisting of several days' rations stored up. *Some W.W.II Army use.*   *v.t.* To hit; to strike. *Colloq.*   *v.i.* To act as a prostitute. *Not common in U.S.*

basket   *n.* 1 The pit of the stomach; the solar plexus. 1929: "[A blow] flush to the basket." J. Auslander, *Hell in Harness*, 39. *From "bread-basket."* 2 [taboo] The scrotum. *Not common.*

bassackwards = **ass backwards.**

bastard [derog.]   *n.* A despicable man; an untrustworthy, selfish, unethical man; a thoroughly disliked person of either sex; a son of a bitch. 1951: "Big Eddie Stover was legally born a bastard; the other two [men] made the grade on their own." T. Capote, *Grass Harp*, 67. *The stand. but taboo meaning of "illegitimate" is present only as a fig. implication reinforcing "despicable." One of the most common derog. sl. terms. As many other such derog. words, this may be used between friends as a familiar, jocular, even affectionate term of address. The word is so common that virtually all children learn the sl. meaning long before they know the stand. meaning.*

basted   *adj.* Drunk. *Obs.* See Appendix, Drunk.

bastile   bastille   *n.* A jail. 1884: *DAE.* Still some use. *Common in rural journalism and facetious speech.*

bat   *n.* 1 A prostitute, orig. one who walks the streets; a promiscuous woman. 1612: Farmer & Henley. 1951: "The [good-conduct] code [drawn up by television broadcasters] specifically bans a number of words and phrases, among them: *bat* (applied to a woman). . . ." *Time*, Oct. 29, 50. *Used mainly by youths and students.* Cf. **bag.** → **2** A girl or young woman; esp., an unattractive or ugly girl. *Mainly used by youths and students. Since c1910. Not necessarily uncomplimentary.* Cf. **bag.** → **3** A gossipy or mean old woman; a shrew or termagant. *Colloq.* **4** A spree; specif., a drinking spree, a binge. 1848: *DAE.* 1908: "[Motor cars] carry our daughters on their shopping bouts and their calling 'bats.' " H. Copley Greene in *Atlantic Monthly*, Aug., 190/2. 1914: "Your bat's over, ain't it?" S. Lewis, *Our Mr. Wrenn*, 147. 1929: "Don't go on a bat with that two-bits." Burnett, *Little Caesar*, 26. → **5** A souse; an habitual tippler; one given to carousing. *Some c1915 use.* **6** A dollar. *Some c1900 use. From bat hides.* **7** A jockey's whip. 1935: "Belting away at him [a race horse] with his bat. . . ." Runyon, 239. *Common horse-racing use.* **8** A watchman. *Never common.*   *v.i.* To go on a spree or binge to carouse.

bat, go to   To be sentenced to prison.

bat, on a   On a drunken spree. See **bat.**

bat against [someone], go to   To testify against someone. 1927: "None of her victims would go to bat against her. . . ." Hammett, *Blood Money*, 10.

bat around   To loaf or idle; to move, seek entertainment, or live aimlessly. 1928: "I want [the kids] home, instead o' battin' around the streets," E. Rice, *Street Scene*, I.

bat carrier   A police informer. *Some c1925 underworld use.*

batch   *v.* = **bach.**

batch out   To start and accelerate a hot rod from a standing start. *Hot rod use since c1955.*

bateau   *n.* A boat. *From the Fr. Dial. and some jocular use since c1700.*

bat for [someone], go to   To come to the aid of someone; to stand up for; to stick up for; to defend someone. *Common.*

bat [one's] gums   To converse; to talk idly but volubly; to chat. *Some W.W.II Army use.*

bath, take a   To go into bankruptcy.

bat hides   *n.pl.* Paper money.

bathtub   bath-tub   *n.* **1** A motorcycle sidecar. *The most common use.* **2** A very large car, as a limousine or an old touring car. **3** A small ship.

baton   *n.* A club, esp. a policeman's club or nightstick. 1958: "Baton—Nightstick." G. Y. Wells, *Station House Slang.*

bat [something] out   To create or make something quickly; specif., to create and write something, as an article, quickly on a typewriter. 1941: "I had to bat out my [newspaper] column." "He kept batting out scenes [for a play]." Schulberg, *Sammy*, 5; 118.

bats   *adj.* Crazy; nuts. 1944: "I must be going bats." Ford, *Phila. Murder*, 72. *From bats in [one's] belfry.*

bats in [one's] belfry, have   To be crazy, very eccentric, or odd. 1907: "Bats in his belfry." A. Bierce in *Cosmopolitan*, July, 335/2. 1951: "The creature [professor] is absurdly harmless, with bats in his belfry and harpsichords in his study." College Eng. Assoc. *Critic*, Apr., 6/4.

batter   *v.t.* To solicit a person for a gift, as of money, food, or the like; to beg of passers-by in the street; to knock on a door with intent to beg. 1893: "Standing in front of shops and 'battering' the ladies as they passed in and out." J. Flynt. 1907: "The hungry hoboes 'battered' the back doors of the homes of the citizens." J. London, *My Life*. *Hobo use.*   *v.i.* To beg food, money, or the like; to beg. 1893: "How well [the tramps] are fed . . . they have 'battered' in this community [Newark, N.J.] for years." "A tramp in Milwaukee can 'batter' for breakfast successfully from 6 until 11." J. Flynt. 1907: "Not until eight o'clock could I begin to batter for my breakfast." J. London, "My Life."
—ed   *adj.* Drunk. 1851: Hall, *College Words*, 302. *Obs.* See Appendix, Drunk.

battery acid   Coffee. *W.W.II Army use.*

bat the breeze   To gossip; to talk, esp. to talk idly. *W.W.II Army use.*

battle   *n.* An ugly or dull girl. *Not common. From "battle-ax."*

battle-ax   *n.* **1** A strong man who is disliked or considered mean. *Never common. Obs. by c1920.* **2** A stout, sharp-tempered, mean, and/or belligerent woman, usu. an old woman. 1936: "That's the old battle-ax." Movie, *My Man Godfrey.*

battleship   *n.* The heaviest type of railroad locomotive; a large, heavy passenger car. *Railroad use.*   **—s** *n.pl.* **1** The feet. *Not common.* **2** Overshoes. *Not common.*

battlewagon   *n.* **1** A battleship. 1938: "Three new 35,000-ton battlewagons." *Newsweek*, Nov. 14, 11. *Orig. USN use; now generally known.* **2** An iron railroad coal-car. *Some c1925 railroad and hobo* *use.* **3** A police patrol wagon. *Some c1925 underworld use.*

batty *adj.* Crazy; nuts. 1921: "The crowd goes batty again." Witwer, *Leather*, 35. *Colloq. From "bats in [one's] belfry."* Cf. **bats.**

baum *v.t.* To fawn upon; to flatter; to curry favor. 1851: Hall, *College Words*, 16. *Never common; obs.* *n.* A failure; usu. in "to make a baum of it." *Dial. Obs.*

bawl *v.i., v.t.* To weep. 1929: "I could bawl." K. Brush, *Young Man*, 111. *Common use.*

bawlbaby *n.* = **crybaby.** 1939: "I'm an awful b-b-bawl baby." Gardner, *D. A. Draws*, 212. *Not common.*

bawling out A loud angry reprimand. 1917: "Claudio gave Hero an awful bawling out." Utter in *Harper's*, June, 67/1. 1951: "President Truman on Tuesday dealt the new Czechoslovak Ambassador a first-class bawling out." N.Y. *Daily News*, Aug. 30, 11C/1. *Since before c1915.*

bawl out **ball out** To scold someone angrily and usu. loudly; to reprimand. 1922: "I was bawlin' him out." O'Neill, *Hairy Ape*, 4. 1930: "Lebovitz went wild and bawled her out." Weeks, *Racket*, 125. *Colloq. Since before c1910.*

bawl-out *n.* = **bawling-out.** 1951: "The general bawl-out." A. Green, *Show Biz*, xix. *Not common.*

bay, over the Drunk. *Dial. c1830–c1930. Obs.*

bayou blue Inferior or bootleg whisky. *Dial. and archaic.*

bay window A person's, esp. a man's, protuberant stomach or abdomen. 1879: "Since his bay window began to form." Cimarron (N.M.) *News*, Nov. 27, 3. 1923: "You don't see no bay window here." C. MacArthur, *Rope. Colloq.*

bazoo *n.* A person's mouth, esp. regarded as an organ of speech. 1952: "If you would close that big bazoo and let me—" W. Kelly, *synd. comic strip*, "Pogo," May 22. 1956: "I said will you kindly shut your loud bazoo?" W. Pegler, *synd. newsp. col.*, Apr. 30. *Since c1860. From the Dutch "bazuin"* = *trumpet.*

bazooka *n.* A small, antitank rocket launcher. *W.W.II Army use. From the musical instrument of comedian Bob Burns, which resembled a length of 2-inch pipe.*

B-boy *n.* A mess sergeant. *Some W.W.II Army use reported. From "busboy," based on "B-girl."*

beach, on the Out of work; unemployed. 1941: "I was . . . strictly on the

beach." D. McFerran, 578. *Radio employee use; from nautical use.*

beagle *n.* **1** A sausage. *From "dog."* **2** A lawyer; a judge. *Underworld use, archaic.* Cf. **beak.**

beak *n.* **1** A mayor, magistrate, or trial judge. 1848: J. S. Farmer. *Still some archaic underworld use. From the Celtic "beachd"* = *a judgment or a judge.* **2** A person's mouth. *Not now common.* → **3** A lawyer. *From uses 1 and 2. Some archaic underworld use.* **4** A person's nose. 1953: "The beak-buster in the opening round was the first punch [prizefighter Archie] Moore had thrown." AP, Jan. 28. *Prob. now the most common use.*

beak-hunting *n.* Poultry-stealing. *Some hobo use before c1920; obs.*

bealer *n.* The head. *Never common. Obs.*

beam, off the Incorrect, wrong, mistaken; not pertinent or applicable; functioning poorly. 1942: "I was 'way off the beam. . . ." Advt., *Life*, Aug. 31, 34. *Popular c1940–c1945.*

beam, on the Correct, right; fig., on the right track or course; functioning well; on the ball; said of people. 1941: "We're on the beam." *Daring Detec.*, Nov., 7. *Since c1940; from aviation use. Popular during W.W.II.*

bean *n.* **1** A five-dollar gold piece. 1859: Matsell. *Underworld use, obs. In Brit. sl. bean still* = *one pound sterling.* → **2** A dollar. 1941: "Without a coat on his back or a bean in his pocket." J. Lilienthal, *Horse Crazy*, 11. 1944: "There wasn't a bean of Laurel's money left." Ford, *Phila. Murder*, 108. *Not common.* → **3** In the card game of poker, a poker chip. *Since c1900; not common.* **4** The head; specif., the human head. 1910: "Why, bean is baseball language for head." F. L. Chance, *The Bride and the Pennant*, 69. 1924: "You certainly used the old bean." Marks, *Plastic Age*, 10. *By far the most common use. If not orig., at least pop. by baseball players and announcers.* **5** The sun. *Some c1935 jive use.* **6** A commissary or mess sergeant; a cook or cook's helper; usu. as a nickname. *Some Army use since W.W.I.* *v.t.* To hit a person on the head with a stone, club, or other weapon; specif., to hit a baseball batter on the head with a pitched ball. 1949: "A truant officer who beaned me with a milk bottle." Roeburt, *Tough Cop*, 87. 1950: "The slugging rookie was struck just above the left ear by a pitched ball. The 'beaning' occurred in the fifth inning." AP, Aug. 16.

—s *n.pl.* **1** money. **2** Ammunition. *Some W.W.I Army use.* **—er** *n.* An excellent person or thing. *Some c1910 use.* **—ery** *n.* **1** A restaurant, specif. a cheap one. 1905: "A swell joint is the St. Regis, but hereafter me for the beanery with the high stool and the low prices." McHugh, *Search Me*, 20. 1950: "A beanery in Hell's Kitchen." J. McCarten in *New Yorker*, Dec. 2, 116. *Still used. From "bean wagon."* See Appendix, —ery endings. **2** A jail. *Some dial. use. Because beans are a traditional staple of the prison diet.* **—ie** *n.* Specif., a skull cap which covers only the crown of the head; any cap or beret. *Since c1945, mainly children and student use. Specif., student use = the skull cap worn by college freshmen to distinguish them as such; the cap is usu. in the school colors. During the late 1940s a children's fad was wearing elaborately ornamented beanies. From "bean" = head.* See Appendix, —ie endings.

bean ball A pitched baseball that intentionally or unintentionally comes near or hits the batter's head. 1906: "While pitching Mr. Bender places much reliance on the bean ball." C. Dryden, *The Athletics of 1905*, 16. 1951: "The bean ball—a pitch around the batter's head—is designed to make the batter apprehensive and keep him from getting set to make his best swing at a later pitch." AP, July 31.

bean-eater *n.* **1** A resident of Boston, Mass. *Because Boston baked beans are the traditional favorite of Bostonians.* → **2** A native of New England. *Not common.* **3** A Mexican, esp. a poor Mexican. *Dial.*

bean gun A mobile kitchen. *Some W.W.II Army use reported.*

bean-head *n.* A stupid person. *From the small size of a bean. Not common.*

bean pole   bean-pole   beanpole *n.* Any tall, skinny person. 1837: *DAE.* 1939: "She was tall but no bean-pole." Chandler, *Big Sleep*, 177. 1951: "The beanpoles went gaily on their way." Syracuse (N.Y.) *Post-Standard*, Apr. 15, 5/2. *Fig., one as tall and slim as a bean pole.*

bean rag A red pennant flown from a ship to indicate that only a minimum crew is on duty because it is mealtime; a red pennant raised at mealtime. *USN use.*

beans *n.* Nothing. *interj.* An expression of disbelief.

beans, know [one's] To know the facts of or be skilled in one's chosen field of endeavor.

bean shave (cut) A very short haircut; a crew cut. *Not common.*

bean-shooter *n.* **1** = **bean,** *n.sing.* **2** A small-caliber pistol.

bean wagon Any small restaurant, often having only a lunch counter and stools, with no tables and chairs, that serves inexpensive meals and snacks quickly and with a minimum of ceremony.

bear *n.* **1** A remarkable, first-rate person or thing; a humdinger. c1915: "Everybody's doin' it. Doin' what? Turkey Trot. Ah, my honey, honey, I declare! It's a bear! It's a bear! It's a bear!" Pop. song. *A student fad word c1910–c1915.* **2** = **beast,** an ugly girl. *Some teenage use since c1955;* cf. **bearcat.** *adj.* Tending to favor low or stable values and prices of corporate stocks; favorable to the holding of, or long-term investment dealing in, corporate stocks. *Stock market use, common.* **—ish** *adj.* Cf. **bear,** adj.

bearcat *n.* **1** A powerful, aggressive person; an excellent or fervent fighter. **2** A beautiful, spirited, or passionate girl or young woman. 1929: "Ain't she a bearcat!" Burnett, *Little Caesar*, 83. *Archaic.*

beard *n.* An intellectual person; an egghead; a cool, far out, or beat person; a member of the avant-garde. 1957: "Beard—An avant-garde type; also a hipster." E. Horne, *For Cool Cats and Far-Out Chicks. Bop musicians introduced beards, usu. goatees, into fashionable hip society. Since the early 1950s beards have become somewhat common, as a mask of nonconformity, with various avant-garde, cool, far out, beat, and intellectual groups.*

beast *n.* **1** A literal translation used unfairly; a pony. *Some c1900 student use.* **2** A new cadet. *c1940 West Point use.* **3** A cheap prostitute or B-girl; fig., one who preys on men. *Orig. pop. by W.W.II USN use.* Cf. **sea gull.** → **4** An ugly girl; a disliked girl. *Student and teenage use since c1945.* → **5** Any girl, whether ugly and stupid or beautiful and passionate, but esp. the latter. 1956: "A girl is a beast." S. Longstreet, *The Real Jazz Old and New*, 150. *Modern jazz use.* Cf. antym. **bearcat.** **6** A fast, experimental airplane; a fast airplane that is difficult or dangerous to handle. *W.W.II Air Force Use.* **7** A high-powered car, esp. a hot rod that has been souped up with great success. *Hot rod use since c1950.*

→ **8** A rocket or guided missile. *Some Armed Forces use since c1950.* **—ly** *adj. & adv.* Awful; unpleasant; awfully; very. 1909: "The crude 'beastly' and the unmeaning 'bally'—those two overworked adjectives of our English cousins." *Scribner's,* Aug., 250/1. *Universally known.*

beat *n.* **1** A remarkable or unexcelled person or thing. *c1825–c1900; never common. Obs. Fig., that which or one who "beats" anything or anyone else in being remarkable.* **2** A loafer; a moocher. *Since c1860. From "deadbeat."* **3** Lit. and fig., a neighborhood, area, or field of endeavor in which an employee is assigned to work. *Orig. the area assigned to a foot policeman, and which he walked and guarded; specif., the area or field of endeavor from which a reporter gathers news. Colloq.* **4** News published first in a given newspaper; the reporting and publishing of a news item by a newspaper before its competitors; a scoop; the news item so reported. *Newspaper use since c1870.* **5** The rhythm of a piece of music; specif., the basic rhythm of a jazz performance as accented by the drums, bass viol, and other rhythm instruments. 1956: "Swinging jazz with an audible beat." Advt. for a phonograph record, *Metronome,* Apr., 34. *Mainly jazz use; has been adopted more and more by classical musicians.* **6** = **hipster;** the world and time of the hipster; fig., the generation of the hipster; any attitude, belief, fashion, fad, or manner characteristic of hipster life. 1958: "The 'BEAT GENERATION' is really a private vision. The 'originals' —Jack Kerouac (*On the Road* [a novel]), John Clellon Holmes (*Go!* [a novel]), and Allen Ginsberg (*Howl* [a long poem]) —dreamed of a 'generation of crazy illuminated hipsters suddenly rising and roaming America, serious, curious, bumming and hitchhiking everywhere, ragged, beatific, beautiful in an ugly, graceful new way.' "San Francisco is the home of the 'beats.' Of this there is no doubt. Partly this is because of the natural beauty, the bridge-arched foggy eeriness of the place, the salt air and the freedom of a port town. Partly it is because of the lack of racial prejudice, the existence of a floating Bohemia around North Beach." E. Burdick, "The Innocent Nihilists Adrift in Squaresville," *The Reporter,* Apr. 3, 30; 31. *Common since c1955.* *adj.* **1** Astonished, surprised; shocked. *Since c1840; not now common.* **2** Physically exhausted, tired,

completely weary. *Since c1930; wide student and teenage use since c1945.* → **3** Emotionally exhausted; exhausted by emotional or nervous strain or concentration; discouraged. *A logical growth from the previous meaning; pop. by bop use c1946.* → **4** = **beat up;** dilapidated or disheveled; ugly. 1942: "Didn't I see you last night with dat beat chick, scoffing a hot dog? Dat chick you had was beat to de heels. You was with a beat broad." Z. Hurston. *Negro jive use since c1935.* **5** Intensely believing in and protecting one's own true nonemotional, nonintellectual, nonsocial, amoral identity, to the exclusion of any commercial, material, and social interests or desires; cool; in rapport with, believing in, or appreciative of hipsters and their attitudes, beliefs, fashions, and fads; of, by, for, or pertaining to the hipster or hipsters' attitudes, beliefs, fashions, or fads. 1958: "The 'Beat' Generation in the Village [N.Y.C.'s Greenwich Village]," title of an article by E. Klein in *N.Y. Daily News,* Feb. 20, 36. 1958: "Writer Jack Kerouac prepares for his interview on TV. 'We're beat, man,' he says. 'Beat means beatific, it means you got the beat, it means something. I invented it.' " H. Gold, *The Beat Mystique,* 84. 1958: " 'Beat,' meaning down and out but full of intense conviction. The 'beat' man was in a muted, low-pitched, inarticulate revolution, but disenchanted enough to know that political action was not the way out. The trick was to stay free, dig friends, but man, really dig them deep and true; with strangers use the implacable cruel language of the hipster and you're safe; and, above all, keep 'them' away from you, keep that big safe, fat, cold world away from you." E. Burdick, *The Reporter,* Apr. 3, 30. *v.t.* **1** Orig., to ride free of charge, or, specif., to avoid paying one's fare on a train; to avoid paying, as a bill owed to a merchant; to see an entertainment without buying a ticket of admission. 1931: "A hobo is a man who can travel by train without paying his fare: 'beating the trains,' that is." C. Ashleigh in *Everyman,* May 21, 520/1. *Orig. hobo use. Now general use. From "deadbeat."* → **2** To escape or avoid punishment or a reprimand. 1949: " . . . Confident of beating any drunken-driving charge with which the Traffic Bureau might confront him." N. Algren, *Man with the Golden Arm,* 94.

beat around   To wander aimlessly,

as a pastime or in search of fun; to loaf or idle.

beat around the bush To talk around a subject, to avoid being frank and direct in talking, esp. in telling someone bad news or expressing one's opinion or conclusion.

beat [one's] brains out To work hard in an attempt to solve a problem; to attempt to solve a tedious, difficult, or complex problem. 1951: "Let somebody else have the privilege of beating his brains out on these tough defense production problems." P. Edson, NEA, Aug. 9.

beaten down to the ankles Completely exhausted or beat.

beaten-up *adj.* = **beat-up.** 1951: "They were the most beaten-up group of people I've ever seen. . . ." UP, Dec. 31.

beater See **egg-beater, world-beater.**

beat [one's] gums (chops) To talk, esp. to talk volubly but without point. "Quit beating your gums." Mitchell, *McSorley's,* 175. 1956: *"To beat your chops* is to talk." S. Longstreet, *The Real Jazz Old and New,* 148. *Assoc. with hip use, but pop. by W.W.II Armed Forces use. Often in the negative as "now you're not just beating your gums" = now you are talking sensibly.*

beating, a *n.* **1** A defeat or loss that one has suffered. **2** A massage; a facial.

beat it To go or go away; to leave or depart; to scram; —often as an imperative, as to children or inferiors. c1600 [1952]: "Ben Jonson used 'beat it' for go." I. Brown in N.Y. *Times Mag.,* May 4, 2/4. 1914: "I've got to beat it." S. Lewis, *Our Mr. Wrenn,* 14. 1924: "He beats it for the tall timber." Marks, *Plastic Age,* 101f. *Common since c1905, when it replaced "skedaddle."*

beatnik *n.* A beat person; one who lives a beat life; specif. any atypical member of the beat generation. *Orig. synthetic newsp. use, now becoming common.*

beat-out *adj.* Exhausted, fatigued. *Since c1750; never common; now dial.* See **beat.** Cf. **beat-up.**

beat out [something] **1** To play a piece of jazz emphasizing the rhythm or tempo. See **beat. 2** In baseball, to reach first base safely on a bunt or a weakly hit ball by running fast enough to arrive at the base before the ball thrown by the fielding player. **3** To compose on a typewriter or to typewrite

rapidly. Cf. **bat out. 4** To talk about or discuss something. *c1935 jive use.*

beat pad A marijuana joint, esp. one which sells inferior reefers. Cf. **beat, pad.**

beat the band, to To do anything excessively, intently, or remarkably. *Since c1900.*

beat the drum **1** To talk too much. → **2** To brag, advertise, or seek attention or appreciation.

beat the dummy [taboo] To masturbate; —said of a male.

beat the gong To smoke opium. *Addict use; now archaic.*

beat the rap To be acquitted of a legal charge in court; to escape punishment. 1930: "Through political connections and similar ties or by intimidation and bribery of complainants and witnesses, gangsters almost invariably 'beat the rap.'" Lavine, *Third Degree,* 5. 1949: "She will most likely beat the Texas rap by turning state's evidence. . . ." *Life,* Oct. 25, 26. See **rap.**

beat [someone's] time To court or pay too much attention to another's girl or boy friend; to become a competitor for a girl someone else is courting; esp. to win the girl someone else has been courting; to win out over a rival. *Student use since c1930.*

beat to the ground Completely beat or exhausted. 1949: "Frankie Machine, looking beat to the ground, brushed past the pair of them without a word or a nod to either." N. Algren, *Man with the Golden Arm,* 67.

beat-up *n.* Fig., a person battered by time, life, and fortune; hence, one who is more or less a bum. *Not common. adj.* **1** Dilapidated, worn out, shabby, damaged; said of things. 1951: ". . . A beat-up car. . . ." *I, Mobster,* 110. **2** Tired out; exhausted. 1951: "Finally beat up as we were, we . . . decided to return to camp." UP, Dec. 31. *Not common.* Cf. **beat; beat-out. 3** Ugly, disheveled; said of people.

beat up [one's] gums (chops) = **beat [one's] gums (chops).**

beat [one's] way To travel without paying; to travel in the cheapest possible manner.

beau *n.* **1** A male lover or steady boy friend. *Archaic.* **2** A female sweetheart; a girl friend. *Never common.*

beaujeeful   beaugeeful *adj.* Ugly; garish; in bad taste, loud, corny. *From the Jewish immigrant mispronunciation of "beautiful." To turn a word into its* *antonym by mispronouncing it is common, but such corruptions are usually nonce words.*

beaut   *n.* An unusually beautiful or remarkable person, thing, or situation; specif., a beautiful woman. *Often used ironically when applied to things or situations.* 1910: [Said about an advt. sign] "It's a beaut." Johnson, *Varmint,* 16. 1946: "It's [an odd name] a beaut, all right." Evans, *Halo in Blood,* 7. 1950: "While the president doesn't go off on these tangents often, when he does, they are beauts." Drew Pearson, *synd. newsp. col.,* Sept. 11. *Since c1850. From "beauty."*   *adj.* Good; well done; also used ironically to mean odd. *Not common.*

beaver   *n.* **1** A full beard. **2** A person wearing a beard. **3** One who works diligently; a hard-working, diligent, active man. *Since c1850; colloq.* Cf. **eager beaver.**

bebop   be-bop   *n.* **1** = **bop.** *An earlier form; archaic.* **2** An intricate form of jazz music characterized by fast tempo, curt phrasing, dissonance, close harmonies over a wide tonal range, etc.; also the attitudes, fashions, etc., of those following the bop craze. 1956: "The true meaning of *be-bop,* also called *re-bop* and *ripbop,* is a fast, frenzied, and mechanical jazz." S. Longstreet, *The Real Jazz Old and New,* 148. *The term was quickly replaced by "bop" as serious listeners began to appreciate the merits of the work done by Charlie Parker, Dizzy Gillespie, and other early exponents of advanced jazz. Obs. by c1948.*

bed   See **get up on the wrong side of bed, go to bed, put to bed with a shovel.**

bed, go to   To go to press; to be printed. 1945: "Whose angle on any story . . . I can predict before the paper goes to bed. . . ." W. Pegler, *synd. newsp. col.,* Dec. 13. *Newsp. use.*

bedbug   *n.* A Pullman porter, traditionally Negro. *Railroad and Negro use.*

beddie-weddie   *n.* A bed. 1945: "Sweet, sweet chick! Enjoy your beddie-weddie all day long!" S. Lewis, *Cass Timberlane,* 259. *One of the more common baby-talk terms used by adults in talking to young children.* See Appendix, Reduplications.

bed house   **1** A brothel. *Some Negro use.* **2** The caboose of a railroad train. *Railroad use.*

bedpan commando   A medical attendant. *Some jocular W.W.II Army use.*

bedpost = **devil's bedposts.**

bedrock   *n.* The basic facts; the underlying facts.   *adj.* Basic.

bedstead = **flying bedstead.**

bed with [someone], go to   To have sexual intercourse with someone.

bee   *n.* An obsession; any unusual or unfounded idea or belief which another cherishes. *From "bee in one's bonnet."*

bee-bee   *n.* A machine-gun bullet. *Some W.W.II Armed Forces use. From "BB," a size of small shot often used in air rifles.*

beef   *n.* **1** A complaint, esp. a complaint to the police; the cause of a complaint; an argument, a quarrel. 1928: " . . . They wouldn't have no beef against him." E. Booth, *Amer. Mercury,* May, 81. 1950: " 'What's the beef?' . . . 'Murder.' " *Gangbusters,* network radio program, Jan. 28. 1950: " . . . Her mother called up to register a beef." Billy Rose, *synd. newsp. col.,* Feb. 17. 1951: "I walked in on a beef they were havin'." *Las Vegas Story,* movie. *Since c1900; from the older "cut a beef." →* **2** A mistake. *Some c1900 student use.* **3** A fat or husky person. **4** A customer's bill or check. *Some hotel, night club, and restaurant use.*   *v.i.* **1** To complain, find fault, protest or object; specif., to complain to the police; to inform; to argue or quarrel. 1930–37: "Three others came back to beef. . . ." J. T. Farrell, 113. 1949: "The hospital beefed when the city announced plans. . . ." *Phila. Bulletin,* Sept. 2, 4/1. *Since c1900.* **2** To make an error. *Student use c1900.* **3** To loaf, to waste time. *Some use c1900–c1935.* *v.t.* = **beef up.**   **—er** *n.* **1** One who complains; esp. an habitual complainer. 1952: "The Yanks . . . were an irreverent bunch and steady beefers about their lot." *New Yorker,* Apr. 12, 138. *Since c1915.* **2** An informer. *Underworld use c1930.* **3** A football player. *See Appendix,* —er words.   **—ing** *n.* Complaining; arguing; quarreling. 1938: "Pegler [newspaperman Westbrook] . . . doesn't like the [Newspaper] Guild . . . and he has done a lot of beefing. . . ." Heywood Broun, *New Republic,* Aug. 17, 45/2.

beefcake   *n.* A photograph or photographs of a man or men wearing little clothing. 1950: "The actor has no objections to male cheesecake, or beefcake as it is called in Hollywood." Bob Thomas, AP, Sept. 29. *Not common. Based on "cheesecake."*

beefeater *n.* **1** An Englishman. **2** A strong, muscular person.

beef-squad *n.* A gang of tough men or hoodlums organized or employed for any specif. violent purpose. 1956: "*Beef-squad*—A gang of toughs, used either by a company to break up a picket line or by a union to enforce one." *Labor's Special Lang. from Many Sources.*

beefsteak *v.t.* To saddle or ride a horse so poorly that his back becomes raw, as a beefsteak. *Some cowboy use.*

Beefsteak and Onions The Balti-more and Ohio railroad. *Hobo use, with some jocular use by those otherwise acquainted with the term.*

beef trust *n.* Any group of stout or fat people; specif., a chorus of large, stout, or fat girls or women, or a baseball or football team composed of exceptionally large, stout, or fat players. Cf. **meat, meat-show.**

beef up **1** To slaughter a cow for beef. *Lit. = to store up on beef by slaughtering a cow. Rural use.* → **2** To add strength, impact, meaning, or meat to a play, book, entertainment, or plan; to add vigor. *Since c1860.* 1953: "Thousands of Chinese infantrymen swarmed recklessly southward as the Communists boldly beefed up [their own] troops." George McArthur, AP, Seoul, Korea, July 18. *Not common.* **3** To kill deliberately, as troops in battle.

bee in [one's] bonnet, a An idea, exp. an eccentric or obsessive idea or an unfounded conviction. *Colloq.*

beekie *n.* **1** Any nosy person. *From "beak."* **2** A company spy. 1949: "If there is ever going to be peace on the transit lines, there'll have to be some changes. . . . The 'beekies' . . . must go." M. Quill [labor leader] quoted in N.Y. *Times,* Sept. 18.

been = **has-been.**

been had   been taken   been took To have been taken advantage of, deceived, cheated, or tricked; overcharged, sold misrepresented merchandise; swindled.

bee on [someone], put the **1** To knock out an opponent. *Prize fight use. Archaic.* **2** To ask a person for a loan or gift of money. 1941: "He came in to put the bee on me." Schulberg, *Sammy,* 134. 1951: "He asked if I would lend him 15 dollars to get back to New York. It was an accolade to have a man of the world put the bee on me." F. Sullivan in *New Yorker,* Aug. 4, 20/3. 1953: "I

have been subjected to scores of communications from New Haven . . . , mostly putting the bee on me for cash contributions." G. T. Hellman in *New Yorker,* Jan. 10, 22/1. *The more common use, equally as common as "put the bite on [someone]."* **3** To make a request of a person. 1948: "Sullivan continues putting the bee on other Government agencies." *Variety,* Aug. 25, 9/2. **4** To harass; to annoy. *All uses since c1920.*

beep *n.* A small reconnaissance car, a jeep. *Some W.W.II use, but never common.* Cf. **peep.**

beer See **cat beer, drink [one's] beer.**

beer belly **1** A greatly protruding abdomen; lit. and fig., assumed to be caused by excessive beer drinking. *Since c1920.* → **2** Any man with a protruding abdomen.

beer-jerker *n.* One whose work is drawing beer from a bar tap into glasses or growlers; a waiter or waitress who serves beer. 1936 [c1865]: " . . . Served at little tables by waiter girls, popularly known as 'beer-jerkers.' . . . " Herbert Asbury, *The French Quarter,* 232f.

beer-joint = **joint.**

beer-shell = **shell.**

beer-slinger *n.* A bartender. 1875: *DAE. Still some use.*

beer up To drink a lot of beer. 1952: "The mechanics, beering up with the guys and driving off to Detroit. . . . " Clellon Holmes, N.Y. *Times Mag.,* Nov. 16, 10.

bees and honey Money. See Appendix, Rhyming Slang.

bee's knees, the = **cat's meow, the.** Obs.

beeswax *n.* Business. *Usu.* in "Mind your own beeswax" = "Mind your own business" and "none of your beeswax" = "none of your business." *Common in child speech since c1920; also some adult euphem. use.*

beetle *n.* **1** A girl. 1933: "If we went to a hop we could find plenty of nice beetles to rub ourselves against." J. T. Farrell, 70. → **2** Specif., an independent, ultramodern, somewhat tomboyish girl, typically one with a short hair style, a preference for wearing slacks, a good education, and an interest in jazz, bullfighting, and motorcycles. *Though not as common, the beetle is to the post-W.W.II period what the flapper was to the post-W.W.I period. Intellectually, she is close to the "lost generation" and has contributed much to the "beat generation."* **3** A race horse. 1934: "Customers are clamoring for a chance to lay their money on some beetle whose neck will feel the caress of a floral horseshoe." H. McLemore in Fort Worth *Press*, Feb. 2. Cf. **roach.** **4** A Volkswagen automobile, made in Germany. *From its appearance.*

beeveedees   *n.* = **B.V.D.**'s.

beewy   *n.* Money, esp. coins or small change. *USN use, from pronouncing "B.W.I.", the abbr. for British West Indies. All traders in the Caribbean area understand the question, "How much beewy?"*

beezer   *n.* **1** A person's nose. 1932: "This Izzy . . . has a large beezer. . . . " Runyon. 1951: "Shield the Beezer," article title, *New Yorker*, Feb. 10, 38. *Orig. hobo and prize fight use.* **2** The face; the head. *Various ety. have been suggested, including the "-beza" from Sp. "cabeza" = head and the Peking dial. "pi-tyu" = nose.*

be for it   See **for it.**

beggar's velvet   Light rolls of woolly dust such as collect under furniture in a seldom swept room; house moss. *Archaic.*

Be good   *interj.* Good-by; so long. *Fairly common valediction since c1930.*

behind   *n.* The buttocks, rump. 1956: "Ulanova . . . her broad, plain, Slavic face, absence of waistline, and enormously broad behind detract not one flicker from the impression she gives of a willful gentle, magnetically young Juliet." *Vogue*, May 15. *Colloq.*

behind the cork   Drunk. *Never common.*

behind the eight ball   In a troublesome, unfortunate, or losing position. 1939: " . . . By putting me behind the eight ball." Gardner, *D. A. Draws*, 208. 1951: "The Dodgers [baseball team] got behind the eight ball quickly at Philadelphia." AP, Oct. 1. *From the term in the game of pool.*

beholden   *n.* A euphem. for "bejesus." 1944: " . . . Beating the beholden out of the gang . . . in the next street. . . . " Walter Davenport, *Collier's*, Sept. 23, 12/4.

beige   *n.* A light-complexioned Negro. *Negro use.*

be into [someone] for [a certain amount of money]   To owe a person a certain amount of money. 1954: "He was into me for 20 grand." CBS radio, *People Against O'Hara*, Mar. 9.

bejesus, the   **be-Jesus, the** Fig., the stuffing or insides of a person. *Always in such expressions as "knock [hit, kick, beat] the bejesus out of him."* 1941:

"He would . . . get the bejesus kicked out of him." Schulberg, *Sammy*, 222. Cf. **Jesus.**

belch   *n.* A complaint; a beef. 1946: "What's the belch, friend? Am I supposed to have bent a law?" Evans, *Halo in Blood*, 9. *Circus, hobo, and underworld use.   v.i., v.t.* To complain; to 'beef'; to inform; to squeal. 1951: "I feel good that I didn't belch on a pal. . . . " Morris Lipsius, quoted in *New Yorker*, Dec. 1, 106. *Circus, hobo, and underworld use.*

belfry   *n.* The head. *Not common in U.S. except in "bats in [one's] belfry."*

bell   See **be there with bells on, dumbbell, Hell's bells, ring the bell.**

bell, hit the = **ring the bell.**

bell, [that, it] rings a (the)   To recall something to one's mind, to be remembered or recognized; to bring forth a response of recognition.

bellhop   **bell-hop**   *n.* **1** In a hotel, any employee, usu. a youth who carries suitcases to one's room and does other such errands; a bellboy. 1924: "Stealing from the bell-hop. . . . " *Lit. Digest*, Nov. 1, 30/1. *Because he comes hopping in response to a bell signal. "Bellboy" is now standard, but "bellhop" has not yet been so listed by major dictionaries. →* **2** A Marine. *In allusion to the fancy uniform. Some W.W.II use.* See **seagoing bellhop.   *v.i.* To work as a bellboy. 1951: "Summers he bell-hopped at Lake Tahoe. . . . " Davis H. Beetle, GNS, Sept. 19.

bell-ringer   *n.* **1** A door-to-door salesman or canvasser. → **2** A local politician. **3** A fact or bit of information that enables one to remember or comprehend something. **4** A tobacco chewer. *From the joke, common in vaudeville, of causing a bell to ring at the instant a chewer scores a bull's-eye on a cuspidor.* **5** A locomotive fireman. *Railroad use.*

bells   *n.pl.* **1** In non-nautical use, equivalent to "o'clock" in phrases telling the time of day. 1929: " . . . Three bells it is." Dunning & Abbott, *Broadway*, III. 1932: "One morning along about four bells. . . . " Runyon. *This sense is derived from but is very different from the nautical sense.* **2** A vibraphone, specif. when used as a jazz instrument. 1956: "Bells—Vibraphones." E. Horne, *For Cool Cats and Far-Out Chicks. Some cool and far-out use.*

bells (knobs, tits) on, be there with ["Tits" variant, taboo] **1** To be, fig., dressed in one's best, present in a given place; always used in the future tense, indicating enthusiasm or a definite promise to be present. Cf. **with knobs on. 2** Emphatically; definitely. *Often used after a criticism or oath. E.g.,* "*He is a jughead with bells on.*"

belly   *n.* **1** Courage; guts. *Not common.* Cf. **stomach. 2** = **bellylaugh.** 1952: " . . . We get a real belly from the opening gag. . . . " L. Stander, *Esquire,* June, 132/3. *Mainly theatrical use.* See **beer belly, melon-belly, possum belly, sow-belly, yellow-bellied.** —**ache**   *v.i.* To complain, esp. to complain either loudly or for a long time. 1939: " . . . Always bellyaching about me." J. T. Farrell, 188. 1951: "Bernard M. Baruch . . . said that the best advice for Americans in the present emergency is: 'Don't bellyache.'" AP, N.Y., Aug. 20. *Common since c1915.* *n.* A complaint; a session of nagging. 1930: "Now start your bellyache." Burnett, *Iron Man,* 10. —**r**   *n.* One who complains frequently.

belly brass   *n.* Fraternity, fraternal, honorary, or civic insignia, keys, seals, decorative emblems, usu. gold, worn as charms dangling from a watchchain across the belly or chest of a vest, esp. by college youths. *c1920; the Eng. syn. is gastric jewelry, attrib. to H. G. Wells.*

belly-burglar   *n.* = **belly-robber.**

belly-buster   *n.* = **belly-whopper.**

belly button   The navel. *Colloq.*

belly fiddle   A guitar. *Some synthetic jazz use.*

belly-flopper   *n.* = **belly-whopper.**

bellyful   *n.* Fig., as much as or more than one can stand of something unpleasant; a surfeit.

belly gun   A pistol; a short-barreled revolver of any caliber, inaccurate at a distance, but effective at very close range, as at the belly of a person being held up. 1942: "A revolver, not an automatic . . . a small revolver, about .32 caliber, a belly gun, with practically no barrel." Chandler, *High Window,* 165. 1950: " . . . a .38 belly gun. . . . " Starnes, *Another Mug,* 66.

belly laugh   A deep, loud, long, uninhibited laugh, esp. a convulsion powered chiefly by action of abdominal muscles. *Colloq.*

belly-robber   *n.* Any person whose work is to buy and/or prepare food, esp. a USN commissary steward, an Army mess sergeant, or a logging camp cook. *Orig. USN and Army use c1915.*

belly-rub   *n.* A dance or dancing party, esp. a student dance or dancing

at a dance hall or meeting place where one may dance with strangers.

belly-smacker   *n.* = **belly-whopper.**

belly stove   An old-fashioned coal or wood-burning stove. 1935: "They like to sit in rickety armchairs around the big belly stove which heats the saloon." Mitchell, *McSorley's,* 2. *Archaic.*

belly to belly   **1** [taboo] In the act of sexual intercourse. **2** Dancing. c1955: "Belly to Belly and Back to Back," title of a pop. calypso song.

belly up to   To approach something straight on, to move straight ahead; fig., to push one's belly toward or up to something. 1953: " . . . For a fellow to belly up to a bar and buy a round of drinks. . . . " Hal Boyle, AP, Feb. 27.

belly-wash   *n.* Almost any commercially prepared beverage or other drinkable liquid; whisky, beer, coffee, tea, soft drinks, or soup.

belly-whopper   belly-buster   belly-smacker   belly-flopper   *n.* In diving, the act of striking the water stomach first; in sledding, the act of striking one's stomach against the sled; in riding, to fall on one's stomach; such a dive, sled ride, or fall. *Mainly children's use. Dial. variations include belly-bump, belly-bumper, belly-bust, belly-whop, belly-flop, etc.*

belt   *n.* **1** A blow with the fist. **2** In baseball, a hit. **3** A thrill or kick. 1934: "He always seems to be getting a great belt out of life. . . . " Runyon, 106. *Not common.* **4** A marijuana cigarette; the effect of smoking a marijuana cigarette. **5** A swallow or swig of a drink, specif. of whisky. 1943: "He . . . handed me the bottle and I took a belt at it. Then he took one. . . . " H. A. Smith, *Putty Knife,* 124. 1950:"I wanted to take a vigorous belt at a jug of bourbon. . . . " Starnes, *And When She Was Bad,* 12.   *v.t.* **1** To hit a blow with the fist. *Colloq.* **2** To swallow; fig., to put a swallow of something under one's belt. 1846: *DAE.* **3** To drink any specif. beverage, usu. a variety of whisky, habitually; to drink a lot, esp. of whisky; to drink greedily or quickly. 1932: "Jack takes to belting. the old grape right freely. . . . " Runyon, 23.

belt around   To travel; to go junketing. 1953: "As for the propriety of Godfrey's belting around in Air Force planes, I see nothing wrong in it." John Crosby, N.Y. *Her. Trib.,* Mar. 11, 25. *Not common.*

belted earl   One who assumes or pretends to noble birth. 1936: "In certain sections of Texas, during the final seventies and early eighties, to people unfamiliar with both London and America's West, it might well have seemed that all the most intimate male friends of the late King Edward VIII had received his reluctant consent to their absence from court, and for a monthly wage of twenty-five dollars, were herding sheep in Texas. The more insistent men of this type were sometimes referred to as 'belted earls.' " P. A. Rollins, *The Cowboy*, 25. *Western use. Obs.*

belt in, pull [someone's]   **1** To confine a soldier to the stockade or to his barracks. *Some W.W.I use; obs. Because when a soldier was so confined, his belt and side arms were taken from him.* **2** To prepare for hard times, a difficult job, or the like. *Colloq.*

belt the grape   To drink heavily.

bench warmer   An athlete who is not good enough to play as a regular performer with his team and hence spends most of his time sitting on the players' bench; a substitute or idle athlete. *Since c1925.*

bend   *v.t.* **1** To slur a note in playing jazz. 1956: " . . . When they are playing jazz and alter pitch between notes, they call it *bending*." S. Longstreet, *The Real Jazz Old and New*, 149. Cf. **scooping pitch. 2** To steal. *Underworld use.* See **bent. 3** To "break" a law; to violate common ethics or principles of behavior, but not break any existing law. 1946: "What's the belch, friend? Am I supposed to have bent a law?" Evans, *Halo in Blood*, 9.   *v.i.* To fight; to have a fight. *Some teenage street gang use.*   *n.* **1** A spree. 1887: *DAE. Never common. Obs. A short form of "bender."* **2** Lit. and fig., a bow made, usu. by a performer, in acknowledgment of applause. 1936: "Then only do the stars . . . producers and technical crew rate any bends for their efforts. . . . " A. Green, *Esquire*, Sept., 64/2. *Theater use.* See **corner (bend), go around the   —er** *n.* **1** A spree of whisky-drinking; often in on a bender. 1820: [U.S. use] *OED Suppl. Colloq.* 1928: "He was on a bender last night." W. Gibbs, *New Yorker*, Nov. 17, 27/1. 1934: "If you lads . . . provide the bottle, I'm all set for a bender tonight." J. T. Farrell, 131. 1950: "He [a Maine farmer] is going on a [alcoholic] vanilla-extract bender." J. Alexander, *SEP*, Apr. 1, 17/1. → **2** A spree involving something other than drinking. 1857: *DAE.* 1938: "He goes on a regular

rocking [in a rocking chair] bender." Liebling, *Back Where*, 209. 1951: "You can see . . . Shelton running around the Beverly Hills streets when he's on a reducing bender. . . . " Bob Thomas, AP, Nov. 7. **3** A stolen car. 1948: "It may be a bender." Evans, *Halo for Satan*, 101. See **bend, bent.**

bend [someone's] ear   **1** To talk to an interested listener; to talk on an important, secret, or interesting subject. 1952: "MacArthur is supposed to have bent . . . [President] Eisenhower's ear with a new plan . . . [concerning] Korea." Hal Boyle, AP, Dec. 19. → **2** To talk too much, to bore another with talk; to gossip or tell all of one's personal plans.

bend (crook, tip)[one's][the] elbow   To drink or tipple; to have a drink. 1830: *DAE.* 1938: "He tips the elbow." R. Connell, *Parade.*   **—s** To drink whisky with a person, as at a bar; esp. to drink to excess.

bender, on a   On a drunken spree. *Colloq.* See **bender.**

benders   *n.pl.* The human legs. 1849: *DAE.* 1923 [1905]: "American and especially Boston ladies . . . are reported to be [prudish], speaking of their own benders instead of legs. . . . " Jespersen, *Growth & Structure*, 248. *Euphem; obs.*

bends, the   *n.* The acute pains caused by too rapid depressurization, as when a deep-sea diver returns too quickly to the surface. *Colloq.*

bend the throttle   **1** To fly a plane faster than its regular cruising speed. *Some W.W.II Air Force use.* → **2** To drive very rapidly. *Some teenage use since c1945.*

Benjamin   An overcoat. *Orig. Eng. use.*

benny   bennie   Benny   Bennie *n.* **1** = **Benjamin.** *Usu.* "*Benny.*" See Appendix, **—ie, y** ending. **2** The shoe width B. *Retail shoe-salesman use.* **3** Any amphetamine pill, esp. Benzedrine. 1956: "Of course, you can take bennies (Benzedrine) . . . but they make me too nervous." S. Longstreet, *The Real Jazz Old and New*, 146. See Appendix, Shortened Words. *Addict and student use since c1945.* **4** A break in a military formation, as caused by an inexperienced soldier. *W.W.II Army use.* **5** A man's overcoat. *From Brit. underworld sl., archaic underworld use.* **6** A man's bowler or derby hat. *Archaic.*

bent   *adj.* **1** Drunk. *Fairly common; most pop. c1925.* **2** Having very little money; nearly broke. **3** Stolen, said esp. of a stolen car. 1930: "For having sold a stolen or *bent* car to a complainant." Lavine, *Third Degree*, 39. *Underworld use.*

bent eight A car with an eight-cylinder engine; an eight-cylinder engine. *Orig. and mainly hot-rod use.*

Bermudas *n. sing. & pl.* **1** A species of large, sweet onion; onions. **2** A species of lawn grass; grasses. **3.** Knee-length shorts; walking shorts. *Pop. since c1953. The most common use of this word. All three of the above items supposedly orig. on the island of Bermuda.*

Bernice *n.* Cocaine crystals as inhaled by addicts. *Narcotic addict use. Archaic.*

berries, the *n.* Any remarkable, attractive, or satisfying person or thing. 1925: "She is the berries." *English Jour.,* Nov., 704. 1949: "It's the berries—jujube candy." *Advt. sign. Common c1920–c1930 student use = an attractive, popular student of the opposite sex. Archaic.* Cf. **berry.**

berry *n.* **1** Any easy task or assignment. *Common c1900. Obs.* → **2** Any agreeable, attractive, or remarkable person or thing. *Some c1900 student use.* See. **berries, the. 3** A dollar. 1924: "I'm nearly a hundred berries to the good." Marks, *Plastic Age*, 231. *Most common c1920–c1930. Still in use.* **4** An egg. *From "cackle-berry." Not common. adj.* Good looking; handsome. *A little c1900 student use.* See **berries, the.**

best fellow A girl's sweetheart; one's beau. *Colloq.*

best girl A boy's sweetheart. *Colloq.*

Betsy Betsey *n.* **1** A gun, whether a pistol, revolver, rifle, or shotgun. 1935: "A slug from a Betsey." Runyon, 302. 1953: "I [holding shotgun] got a lot of votes in ol' Betsey here. That's law." Walt Kelly, *synd. comic strip*, "Pogo," May 15. **2** The sun. *Some farmer and dial. use.*

better half **1** One's wife. 1887: *Lantern*, New Orleans. *Usu. jocular use. The most common use.* **2** One's husband. *Not common.*

betwixt and between Undecided; uncertain.

bewitched *adj.* Drunk. *Dial.*

B-girl *n.* **1** Lit., a nonprofessional prostitute who sits in bars in order to meet prospective clients, esp. soldiers. *W.W.II use. An abbr. for "bar girl," reinforced by the connotation of "grade B."* → **2** A girl employed by a bar or cheap

nightclub, either as an entertainer or as a shill, i.e., as a customer who allows male patrons to buy her drinks. *The girl may receive a commission on each such drink sold, and often the drinks given to her are only tea or colored water instead of the whisky that the male patron has paid for. Sometimes the girls receive no compensation but the permission of the owner to use the premises for soliciting.* → **3** Any promiscuous girl or woman. 1941: "I seem to meet nothing but B-girls here." Schulberg, *Sammy*, 132. Cf. **V-girl.** *Since c1938. Orig. "bar-girl," which form was almost immediately made archaic by this abbr. use.* See Appendix, Shortened Words.

bialystok *n.* A semihard, round onion roll with a hole in the center. 1958: "The shop specializes in an onion roll that resembles a bagel but is softer. It [the bakery shop] is called a Bialystoker. . . ." "Hunt a Motive in Blast that Razed Bakery." N.Y. *Daily News*, Feb. 20, 9. *From the town of orig., Bialystok, Russia.*

bib *n.* A napkin; usu. a paper napkin. *Some lunch-counter use.* **—ful** *n.* A lot of talk, esp. by one person, and specif. gossip or talk about personal subjects.

bibble-babble *n.* Babble. 1901: Greenough & Kittredge, 332. See Appendix, Shortened Words.

bible *n.* **1** Any authoritative book, listing, reference, guide, catalog, compilation of data, or set of rules; specif. the Sears Roebuck mail order catalog [rural use], the program of a circus, stage show, or movie [circus and theater use], the various Armed Forces regulations and the articles of war [W.W.II Armed Forces use], salesman's catalog and price list, or an employee's bills or receipts which must tally with the money in the cash register. *All uses since c1930.* **2** At a circus, the hinged platform of planks that the reserved seats stand on. *So called because it opens like a book and closes with a slap.* **3** The truth.

bicker *n.* The period during which prospective members of eating clubs are rushed. 1950: "As the annual 'bicker' period drew near last month. . . . As the bicker began, sophomores . . . waited." *Time*, Mar. 20, 78. *Mainly Princeton Univ. use.*

bicycle *n.* A student's literal translation or list of answers unethically used during an examination or recitation. *Some student use, c1900, in an attempt to update "pony."*

bicycle, on [one's]   Retreating from an opposing fighter, fighting a defensive fight, dodging and stepping back from blows. *Prize fight use since c1920.*

bid   *n.* **1** An invitation, esp. to a major student social affair, as a prom, or to join a college fraternity or sorority. 1887: *DAE.* 1924: "He wouldn't accept a bid from any fraternity." Marks, *Plastic Age*, 114. 1934: "The chatter of my Junior home-room girls with their 'bids' to 'hops'...." *English Journal*, Nov., 740. *Common student use since c1900; colloq.* → **2** A ticket of admission to a prom. *Student use. Not common.*   *v.t.* To invite a person to become a member of a fraternity or sorority. 1924: "Perhaps no fraternity would bid him...." Marks, *Plastic Age*, 81. *Some student use since c1915; not common.*

biddies on a raft   Eggs on toast. *Lunch-counter use in relaying an order; some use since c1915. Not common. From "biddy" = hen.* Cf. **Adam and Eve on a raft.**

biddle = **bindle.**

biddy   *n.* **1** An Irish servant girl, esp. one whose passage to the U.S. has been paid by an employer in return for future work. 1858: *DAE. Obs. by c1935; from "Biddy," diminutive of the name "Bridget."* → **2** An Irishwoman. *Never common. Obs.* **3** Any maid or housekeeper. 1924: "If I leave this liquor around here, the biddy'll get hold of it...." Marks, *Plastic Age*, 18. *Archaic by c1935.* **4** A woman, esp. an old, gossipy woman; a termagant or shrew. 1951: "Charley had met an old biddy named Zoe Winthrop...." William Fuller, *Collier's*, Feb. 19, 22/1. **5** = **chick.** *From "biddy" = hen, prob. reinforced by earlier meanings of "biddy."* See **hen.**

biff   *n.* **1** A blow with the fist; a slap or punch. 1890: *DAE.* 1929: "Biff on the kisser." J. Auslander, *Hell in Harness*, 39. *Not common.* **2** An unsuccessfully played high note on a brass instrument. *Musician use.* **3** = **biffer.** *Some Negro use.*   *v.t.* **1** To strike, as with the fist. 1892: *DAE.* 1918: "Heads may be ... biffed or bammed or...." M. Doolittle, *Outlook*, Nov., 433. *Fairly common since c1900.* **2** To take or win a card or trick in a card game, or a checker or chess piece. *Not common.* **—er**   *n.* A homely girl who compensates for her lack of attractiveness by being promiscuous; a homely but promiscuous girl. *Some Negro use.*

biff-guy   *n.* A hoodlum or thug. *Underworld use; never common.*

biffy   *n.* A bathroom; a toilet. *Not common in the U.S.*

big   *n.* = **Mister Big.** *Underworld and teenage street gang use since c1950.*   *adj.* **1** Important, the most important. *Colloq.* → **2** Successful; celebrated; influential; famous; popularly accepted, esp. said of entertainers or entertainment. 1953: "If I do say it, we were very big." Bing Crosby, *SEP*, Feb. 14. 1956: "Joe might ask a groom, 'How's the big horse?' referring to the stable's star." T. Betts, *Across the Board*, 196.   *adv.* Successfully.   **—gie**   *n.* A big shot; a prominent person. 1937: "Bob Burns is the easiest of the biggies to sign for a benefit." *Hollywood* (mag.), Jan., 10. 1948: "Sullivan continues putting the bee on other Government biggies." *Variety*, Aug. 25, 9/2.

big, go over   To become a popular success, esp. as an entertainer or entertainment; said of an entertainer, song, book, or the like.

big, make   To succeed, esp. in one's chosen career.

Big Apple, the   big apple, the   1 Any large city; specif., New York City. 1956: "New York is the Big Apple...." S. Longstreet, *The Real Jazz Old and New*, 148. → **2** The main business and entertainment section or street of a city. **3** = **big time, the. 4** A dance briefly pop. among jitterbugs c1936.

big-band   *adj.* Pert. to swing or jazz music played by a large band, usu. composed of 14 to 20 men, as opposed to smaller or pick-up groups. 1950: "In 1930, Jelly tried half-heartedly to enlarge his band; he tried to play big-band swing, but he couldn't bring it off." A. Lomax, *Mr. Jelly Roll*, 206.

big band   *n.* A large jazz band; specif., a swing band. 1956: "Kirk, Cootie Williams, Diz, and Bill were members of the big band...." "Charlie Parker, 1920–1955," *The Metronome Year Book*, 40.

Big Bertha   big Bertha   1 A type of very large, long-distance cannon used by the German forces in W.W.I; any large cannon. 1957: "The cannon is forever bogging down, and the peasants resort to some heroic but implausible methods in their efforts to give Big Bertha a semblance of rolling along." *New Yorker*, July 13, 48. → **2** A fat woman.

big boy 1 Any tall youth or man, usu. in direct address. 2 An important person, a big shot. 1934: "He tried to shake down one of the big boys." Chandler, *Finger Man*, 110. 3 Any recognizably large or important item, specif. a hundred-dollar bill [underworld use] or a hamburger sandwich with two hamburgers on it [lunch-counter use].

big brother Specif., a police or welfare state; any society or any aspect of any society, national organization, or accepted political belief that originates, enforces, or encourages group welfare and group values over individual freedom, thought, or emotion. From the term as used in George Orwell's 1949 novel, *1984*.

big browneyes The female breasts.

big bug An important person; a big shot. 1827: *DAE*. 1928: "Even among the big bugs of his own Cabinet." R. Lynd, *New Statesman*, Feb. 4. *Archaic.*

big butter-and-egg man See **butter-and-egg man.**

big cage A state or federal reformatory or penitentiary. 1949: "He . . . had . . . friends in the big cage." A. Hynd, *Public Enemies*, 19. *Underworld use. Not common.* Cf. **big house, the.**

big cheese 1 An important person, a big shot. 2 A stupid or rude male; a lout. *Both uses since c1925.*

Big D Dallas, Texas.

Big Daddy **big daddy** 1 One's father. 2 = **daddy.** 3 An affectionate nickname, usu. used in direct address, for any male, esp. a large, active, extroverted male. *Exclusive female use. Far-out and beat use.*

big deal 1 Anything important, exciting, satisfying, interesting, lavish, or highly publicized, be it a business deal or a social or athletic function. 1949: "My brother pulled off a big deal today. I think we're going into business together." A. Miller, *Death of a Salesman*, 99f. 1955: "She tried to make everything sound like a big deal." E. Trujillo, *I Love You, I Hate You*, 40. → 2 An important, influential, interesting, or well-known person. *Wide student use since c1940.* → 3 Sarcastically, anything or anyone believed to be unimportant, uninteresting, or unimpressive. 1951: "The game with Saxon Hall was supposed to be a very big deal around Pencey. It was the last game of the year, and you were supposed to commit suicide or something if old Pencey didn't win." J. D. Salinger, *Catcher in the Rye*, 8. *Wide*

student use since c1940. Often used as a belittling exclamation to deflate another's enthusiasm, as in reply to a suggestion or an eager proposal. This use is fast supplanting the earlier uses. Said in a flat tone of voice and with an overemphasis on "big." Popularized by comedian Arnold Stang on the Henry Morgan network radio program, c1946, and on the Milton Berle network program, c1950.

Big Dick In crap-shooting, the point 10.

Big Ditch, the 1 The Erie Canal. *c1825–c1875; obs.* 2 The Atlantic Ocean. *Since c1900.* 3 The Panama Canal.

big drink 1 The Mississippi River. 1846: *DAE. Obs.* → 2 The Atlantic Ocean. *Since c1915.* → 3 Either the Atlantic or the Pacific Ocean. *Since c1940. The last two uses pop. by W.W.I and W.W.II Armed Forces, respectively. The three meanings clearly indicate the growth of global awareness in the U.S.*

big drink of water A youth or man, esp. if tall, who is uninteresting, dull, or boring.

big drive, the A large or comparatively pure injection of narcotics. 1949: "Man, their *eyes* when that big drive hits 'n goes tinglin' down to their toes. They retch, they sweat, they itch—then the big drive hits 'n here they come out of it cryin' like a baby or laughin' like a loon." N. Algren, *Man with the Golden Arm*, 76. *Addict use; not common.*

big eights Long woolen winter underwear. *Some Negro use.*

big George A quarter; the sum of 25¢. *From the face of George Washington which appears on the U.S. 25¢ piece.*

big gun An important or influential person; a high official. *Since c1840.*

biggy *adj.* Drunk. *Some colonial use until c1750; obs.* See Appendix, Drunk.

big head **big-head** *n.* 1 A hangover; any or all of the physical, mental, and psychological reactions to having consumed too much whisky on the previous night. 2 Conceit. 1805: *Thornton.* 1850: *DAE. Colloq.* → 3 A conceited person. *Colloq.* **—ed** *adj.* Conceited. *Colloq.*

big hole The low gear of a truck or an automobile. *Truckdriver use.*

big house, the **Big House, the** Any state or federal penitentiary. 1850: Farmer & Henley. 1930: "20 years in the 'Big House' . . . doing 'a stretch in the Big House.'" Lavine, *Third Degree*, 38, 194. 1942: "To go to the big house for the rest of his life." W. Bolingbroke

Johnson, *Widening Stain*, 75. *Underworld use; universally known.*

big idea   *n.* An unwelcome suggestion, proposal, or action.

big Joe = **big John.**

big John   An Army recruit. *Some W.W.II Army use. Not common.*

big joint = **big house, the.** *Underworld use since c1920. Not common.*

big-league   *adj.* Professional; on a large scale.

big lie, the   A major political misrepresentation or complex of misrepresentations freq. repeated by political leaders in the hope that it will eventually be believed. *A cold war term, since 1948.*

big man   1 An important or influential man; one who is in authority. *Since c1885; colloq.* 2 = **big man on campus.** 1920: "The prep school 'big man.'" Fitzgerald, *This Side of Paradise*, 39.

big man on campus   Lit., a popular, important student, usu. a leader in social, athletic, and extracurricular activities. *Traditionally the big man on campus is much sought after by female students.*

big moment   One's sweetheart or lover. *Some student use since c1935.*

big mouth   A person who talks often and/or loudly; a person who always has an opinion to state; one who talks about the personal life of others or says things better left unsaid.

big name   A prominent, famous, or celebrated person, usu. in the field of entertainment. **big-name**   *adj.* Famous; celebrated. 1949: "A big-name trumpeter." Billy Rose, *synd. newsp. col.*, July 25. See **name.**

big noise   1 An important, sensational, or highly publicized statement or deed. 1956: "Big Noise from Moscow, Mumbled Words from Washington." Title of an editorial, N.Y. *Post*, Nov. 16, 43. 2 An influential person. 1929: "The warden is the big noise...." Givens, *SEP*, 50/3.

big number = **big man.**

big O   1 A train conductor. *Railroad use.* 2 Opium used for smoking. *Narcotic addict use; not common.*

big one   1 A thousand-dollar bill; a thousand dollars. 1958: "... [He] lost, picking up 42 Big Ones ($42,000 that is) in consolation money." Paul Sann, "It Happened All Over," N.Y. *Post*, Jan. 12. 2 A bowel movement. *Part of the euphem. bathroom vocabulary taught to young children.*

big one, the   An important entertainment. 1956: "The Big One Is No More! [headline:] Word that John Ringling North had closed down the Ringling Bros. Barnum & Bailey Circus...." N.Y. *Post*, July 17, 3.

big ox   A train conductor; a "big O." *Railroad use.*

big picture, the = **picture, the.** *Some use since c1955. From the large movie screens accommodating exceptionally wide pictures; several trade-name processes such as "Vista-Vision," "Cinerama," and "Cinemascope" were widely advertised by film makers and distributors as giving "the big picture," c1955.*

big pipe   A baritone saxophone. 1957: "Big Pipe or baritone saxophone...." E. Horne, *For Cool Cats and Far-Out Chicks. Some cool and far-out use.*

big pond, the   The Atlantic Ocean. 1840: *DAE. Fairly common.*

big pot = **big shot.** 1950: "The chamber occupied by the big pot." Starnes, *Another Mug*, 14.

big rag = **big top.** The main tent of a circus. *Circus use.*

big red apple = **Big Apple, the.**

big school   A state or federal penitentiary. *Hobo and underworld use since c1920.*

big shit [taboo] = **big deal.**

big shot   bigshot   *n.* A very important person, usu. one who is highly successful and famous in a specif. field, or one who is an executive or person in authority; esp. a very influential person in politics, crime, business, society, or the like. 1930: "The Chief, the Boss, or the Big Shot." Weeks, *Racket*, 51. 1944: "I'd like to show them that I'm a big shot now." Moss Hart, quoted in *Amer. Mercury*, Aug., 176/1. 1946: "Here [in the Appendix to the *Congressional Record*, 1945], among 33 names [prefixed by the title 'Hon.'], are those of eight big shots of famous farmers', manufacturers', or veterans' organizations." H. L. Mencken in *Amer. Speech*, Apr., 83. 1951: "Wives who suddenly find their husbands have become bigshots who need a well-dressed wife for background and business entertainment purposes...." H. Boyle, AP, Sept. 10. *The one-word form is not common; c1930. The term often implies dislike or distrust, and that the person has gained his importance through unethical or aggressive practices, motivated by a love of power.* **big-shot**   *adj.* 1 Very important, influential, successful, or wealthy. 1939: "Those big-shot criminal lawyers." Gardner, *D.A. Draws*, 152. → **2** Ostentatious, garish, expensive; suitable for a big shot. 1943: "He was a big shot in a big shot car." Wolfert, *Underworld*, 49.

big stick An aerial ladder. *Firefighter use.*

big sticks A forest, a large wooded region, usu. remote from a town. *Logger use.*

big stiff See **stiff**, *n.*, 3.

big stink **1** A loud, sustained complaint, harangue, or angry commotion. 1951: "The way I met her, this Doberman pinscher she had used to come over and relieve himself on our lawn, and my mother got very irritated about it. She called up Jane's mother and made a big stink about it. My mother can make a very big stink about that kind of stuff." J. D. Salinger, *Catcher in the Rye*, 60–1. **2** A scandal.

big-talk big talk *n.* Boastful or exaggerated talk. *v.t.* To talk boastfully to another, to talk to another as if one is superior in authority. 1951: "Don't try and big talk the other deckhands." R. Bissell, *Stretch on River*, 14.

big ticket A sale of an expensive item; a big sale to one customer. *Because a large amount of money is registered on the salesman's ticket. Salesman use.*

big time, the **1** A theater or theatrical circuit in which high-salaried vaudeville acts are staged only twice a day; the two-a-day. *Theater use. Archaic.* → **2** Any endeavor from which large salaries or profits are obtained; the higher strata of business, crime, entertainment, sports, or the like. 1934: "The grafters on the big time." Chandler, *Finger Man*, 7. **big-time** *adj.* **1** Of, part of, or pert. to the big time. → **2** Highly remunerative, highly remunerated; famous. → **3** Important; major. 1950: "Korea begins the big-time use of jet planes in battle." Lowell Thomas, radio, July 7.

big-time operator **1** = **big shot**. *Not common now; some c1940 use.* → **2** One who figures in many exchanges of favors; one who plays petty politics to achieve minor goals. *W.W.II Army use.* → **3** A student who is prominent in school and social activities; a student who is a leader in extracurricular activities and is quick to accept current fads of student dress, speech, and belief; a male student who is adroit in establish-ing relationships with female students. *Very common student use c1940–c1945, and has retained some popularity.*

big-timer *n.* **1** = **big shot**. → **2** Esp., a professional gambler.

big top **1** Specif., the main tent of a circus; generally, the circus, circuses, or circus life. 1949: "Hypnotized by life under the big top...." H. Basso in *New Yorker*, Nov. 5, 58. *Orig. circus use; colloq. since c1890.* **2** A bank. *Underworld use; archaic.*

big trouble, the The depression of the 1930's. *Hobo use.*

big wheel **1** An important, influential person; a person in authority; a big shot. 1950: "All the big wheels from the Capitol...." Starnes, *Another Mug*, 109. 1951: "Up to that juncture I was boss man of the family and big wheel...." S. J. Perelman in *New Yorker*, June 30, 20/3. *Common since W.W.II. A logical metaphor from mechanics' "to roll a big wheel" = to be important or influential, was in use before 1850. Influenced by "wheel horse."* → **2** One who has a little authority; a loyal, diligent subordinate. *Not as common as the first meaning; some W.W.II Army use.* → **3** A student important in school and social activities; a big-time operator.

bike *n.* **1** A bicycle. *Colloq. since c1880.* → **2** A motorcycle. *Common since c1945.* → **3** A motorcycle policeman. 1958: "Bike—Motorcycle cop." G. Y. Wells, *Station House Slang.* See Appendix, Shortened Words.

bikini *n.* **1** An abbreviated women's two-piece bathing suit consisting of just enough material to cover the crotch and breasts. *Introduced c1950, this revealing style orig. in Europe; it has become somewhat modified and is now less daring than it was.* → **2** Any short, revealing bathing suit, men's swimming trunks, shorts, or other sports clothes.

bilge *n.* Worthless talk or writing; tripe; blah. *From the seafaring term. Orig. maritime use; universally known by c1920.* *v.i.* To fail in one's course of study or a class. *Annapolis use since c1925.* *v.t.* To fail a student; to expel a student. Cf. **bilge out**.

bilge out = **bilge** 1951: "We ought to have you bilged out of the [Coast Guard] Academy." Movie, *Fighting Coast Guard*.

bilk *n.* A swindler, a crooked gambler, a cheat. 1869: *DAE. Now stand. but not common.*

bill *n.* **1** The human nose. 1952: "There is a shortage of fighters. The GI Bill of Rights allowed a lot of impoverished [ex-soldiers] to get educated instead of getting their bills busted." R. C. Ruark, *synd. newsp. col.*, June 27. *Colloq.* **2** Any knife, esp. a small one that can be carried and concealed easily, used as a weapon. *Some Negro use until c1935. Obs.* **3** A $100 bill; the sum of $100. 1950: "I went five bills for that [Chinese vase]." H. Sobol, quoted in *New Yorker*, Nov. 18, 60.

Bill Daley A long lead in a race, esp. a long lead early in the race. 1941: "She [a race horse] beat a flock of platers here last year. She might go out on the Bill Daley and hang on." J. Lilienthal, *Horse Crazy*, 29. *After "Father" Bill Daley, the famous jockey instructor, who always advised his pupils to take the lead and keep it.*

Bill Daley, on the See **Bill Daley.**

billiard drinker One who drinks whisky quickly and to excess; a habitual drunkard. *Never common.*

Bill-Jim **Billjim** *n.* An Australian soldier. *Some W.W.I Army use.*

Bill Shears A farmer; a rustic. *c1920 hobo use: from "scissorbill" by metathesis and substituting "shears" for "scissors."*

billy *n.* **1** A policeman's club. *Since at least 1850. Colloq.* **2** A bucket or large can used for heating wash water or for cooking. *Some hobo use. From Australian use.*

billy can = billy, 2.

billy-goat *n.* Mutton served at a meal. *Some W.W.II USN use reported. Prob. synthetic.*

bim *n.* Any girl or woman, esp. one's girl friend. 1925: "John took his bim to a dance." R. W. Cowden in *Eng. Jour.*, Nov., 700. 1943: "Usually the bim tries to give her boy friend a bit more alibi than that." Chandler, *Lady in Lake*, 208. *Some c1920 use; a jocular term of disrespect. Archaic. From "bimbo."* **—bo** *n.* **1** A kind of blow or punch with the fist. 1837: *DAE. Obs.* **2** A man, esp. a strong or tough man; a fellow, a guy. 1921: "One of them bimbos which hurls a mean hammer...." Witwer, *Leather*, 8. 1927: "These bimbos once helped pluck a bank...." Hammett, *Blood Money*, 6. *Although this meaning of "bimbo" is usu. said to be derived from "bambino," it seems to have derived from the earlier meaning of a kind of punch or blow.* **3** A baby. *Some c1920 use; prob*

confused ety. from "bambino." **4** Any girl or woman. 1947: "What kind of a bimbo did he think I am?" Quoted by H. Boyle, AP, May 19. *Most common c1925; common student use c1925. Although this meaning is usu. said to be derived from "bimbo" = baby as a term of endearment, it was used in jocular disrespect and then and now implies a certain moral cynicism on the part of the speaker.* → **5** A prostitute; a girl or woman who is promiscuous. *Since c1930 the most common use.* **6** An Army recruit. *Some W.W.II Army use. This is a specif. meaning for the second definition given above.* **7** An insignificant, unimportant person. *Since c1840.*

bind *n.* A predicament, as caused by conflicting obligations, an overfull work schedule, or the like; a tight spot; a jam. 1951: "He was in too much of a bind to think of that." P. Hogan, *Collier's*, Nov. 24. 1952: "The bind I'm in." Movie, *Kansas City Confidential.*

bindle *n.* **1** A blanket rolled up so that it may be carried easily across one's back, often with one's clothes and other possessions rolled up inside it; a bedroll. *Hobo use since before c1880.* → **2** Any package or bundle. 1947: "A little 'bindle' of ground coffee (a cloth bag like a five-pound salt sack, which could be rolled up as the dry coffee was consumed) was the sort of package usually carried by itinerants." L. G. Offord in *San Fran. Murders*, 233. *Hobo use since c1900.* → **3** Specif., a packet of narcotics, esp. when folded inside as an envelope. *Underworld use since c1920.*

bindle man = bindle stiff.

bindle stiff **bindlestiff** *n.* **1** A migratory harvest worker; esp. a hobo who carries a bundle of blankets or a bedroll, usu. containing all his possessions. 1907: "... A world of 'strong arms' and 'bindle-stiffs.' " J. London, *The Road*, 159. 1936: "They were the familiar 'bindle stiffs' or men who carried bundles in a wandering world." Tully, *Bruiser*, 88f. 1953: "I was a bindlestiff. That's the class that will do some work once in a while. The grifters are the desperate characters, the 'boes are the philosophers." J. R. Kennedy in N.Y. *Times Bk. Rev.*, Mar. 15, 16/5. *Since c1890. See* **bindle; stiff.** **2** Any poor, homeless, jobless, unskilled tramp, beggar, or wanderer. *Since c1900.*

bing *n.* **1** A packet of narcotics. *Underworld use c1920; archaic. Reinforced by and superseded by "bindle."* **2** A prison cell used for solitary confinement of prisoners; the hole. *Prison use.*

bing-bang *n.* Zest; energy; pep. 1953: "He is full of confidence and bing-bang all day long." J. McNulty in *New Yorker*, Apr. 11, 25/1. *Not common.*

binge *n.* **1** A drunken spree. 1934: "The good old-fashioned he-man binge." DeJournette in *Esquire*, Apr., 36. 1954: "He would sally out to enjoy a hell-raising binge." W. R. & F. K. Simpson, *Hockshop*, 96. 1958: "Drinking drivers, great bangs [collisions] from little binges grow. . . ." Burma Shave shaving cream roadside verse, near Toledo, Ohio. → **2** A spree of any kind; a period of self-indulgence. 1948: "With the [movie] studios on an economy binge for the past year. . . ." *Variety*, Aug. 25, 9/1. 1949: ". . . So she could go on one last banana binge." Earl Selby in Phila. *Bulletin*, Aug. 31, 4/1. 1951: "If the nation's baseball fans have cooled out from their emotional binge of the past ten days. . . ." G. Talbot, AP, Oct. 12. **—d** *adj.* Vaccinated. *c1918 Army use.* **—r** *n.* A rejection; a squelch. *Some c1915 student use; obs.*

bingle *n.* **1** In baseball, a hit, usu. a single. 1902: "He loses bingle after bingle near second base." *Sporting Life*, Sept. 6. *Still common baseball use.* **2** A poker or gambling chip, usu. worth 10¢ or 25¢. *Not common.* **3** A large supply or cache of narcotics. *Addict use.*

bingo! *exclam.* An exclamation denoting sudden action, success, or comprehension. *From the game of bingo, in which the winner shouts "Bingo!" to signify that he has won. The usage very much resembles the classical "Eureka!" = "I have found it!"*

bingo-boy *n.* A drunkard. 1946: Boy gang use, N.Y.C., reported in *Life*, Apr. 8, 89/1.

bing spot A vaccination scar. *Some W.W.I Army use. Obs.* See **binged.**

binnacle list A list of sailors too sick to report for duty; a sick list. *Some USN use.*

binny *n.* **1** = **benny**, an overcoat. → **2** An extra large or concealed pocket in a shoplifter's overcoat where stolen items are secreted. *Underworld use.*

bird *n.* **1** An excellent, extraordinary, or unusual person, animal, or thing. 1909: "Slang has taken *bird* and has used [it] in all manner of commendatory senses; anything admirable or excellent may be spoken of as a *bird.*" Krapp, *Mod. Eng.*, 205. *Often used ironically. Since c1845; not common in this general sense since c1910.* **2** Any youth. 1851:

Hall, *College Words*, 266. *Obs.* → **3** Any man; a fellow, a guy. 1920: "I'm a literary bird myself." Fitzgerald, *This Side of Paradise*, 51. 1924: "College isn't anything like what these old birds say it is." Marks, *Plastic Age*, 17. 1943: "The third man was a tall bird in a gray suit, an anxious-looking bird." "Lavery was a fascinating bird—to women." Chandler, *Lady in Lake*, 3; 111. *The most common use.* **4** A girl or woman. 1940: "She was a tall old bird with a chin like a rabbit." Chandler, *Farewell*, 90. *Some use since c1900; in the U.S. the word has never meant "prostitute," as it does in Brit. sl.* **5** An odd or unusual person; a weird person, as a neurotic or psychopath; a homosexual. 1920: "If only that St. Paul's crowd at the next table would not mistake *him* for a bird, too." Fitzgerald, *This Side of Paradise*, 56. *This meaning prob. stems from freq. ironical use of the first meaning given above. Although it is now becoming pop. with students, this meaning has not been common since c1880.* **6** = **Bronx cheer; raspberry.** 1922: "Give him the boid—the raspberry!" O'Neill, *Hairy Ape.* 1929: "Roy makes derisive sound known as 'the bird.'" Dunning & Abbott, *Broadway*, I. *Universally known.* **7** The eagle used as an insigne of rank (U.S. Army colonel, U.S. Navy captain). *Armed Forces use since W.W.I.* **8** A rocket; a guided missile. *Military use since c1947.* **9** A gold coin with an eagle stamped on it. *Obs.* **10** = **yardbird.** See Appendix, Shortened Words. **—ie** **—y** *n.* **1** A bird;—a child's word also used by adults. **2** = **bird.** See Appendix, —ie ending. *adj.* Unusual, eccentric, weird. *Said of a disliked person. Common student use since c1955.* **—ies** *n.pl.* = **bird legs.** **—man** *n.* An aviator; any airman. *Common in early years of aviation; considered affected at end of W.W.I. Some continued use through W.W.II.* **—seed** *n.* Any dry, packaged breakfast cereal. **—seye** *n.* A small packet or portion of a narcotic drug. *Addict use.* **—wood** *n.* Marijuana cigarettes. *Addict use.*

—bird See Appendix, Suffixes and Suffix Words.

bird-brain *n.* A person of slight intelligence; a stupid or foolish person. 1952: "One is racked with sobs in sympathy to whatever bird-brain is rendering one of the ditties of the day." R. C. Ruark, *synd. newsp. col.*, Mar. 26. *Since c1940; wide student, children, and* *teenage use c1945, esp. in semijocular direct address or as epithet.*   **—ed** *adj.* Stupid.

birdcage   *n.* **1** A prison cell. *Underworld use.* **2** A sleeping area in a flophouse. 1949: " 'Bird cages' are six feet by four feet and contain a bed and a locker." W. J. Slocum in *Collier's,* Aug. 27, 60. *Often the beds are separated by chicken wire to reduce the incidence of robbery.* **3** A brothel. *Not common.* **4** A lady's bustle. *Universally known c1870.* **5** A small furnished room, as rented by the day. *Maritime use.* **6** A lantern used in signaling by railway brakemen and switchmen. *Railroad use.* **7** A student's dormitory. *Student use, never common.*

bird colonel = **chicken colonel.**

bird dog   **1** Anyone whose job is to hunt or find objects or people; specif., an antique dealer or art dealer commissioned to find a specif. object, a detective who specializes in finding missing persons, a business agent who hunts for prospective customers, a talent scout who looks for promising young entertainers, or a baseball, football, or basketball scout who searches for promising athletes. *Since c1930; because bird dogs are raised for hunting.* **2** A chaperon at a school dance. *Some prep-school and college use since c1935.* **3** An Air Force fighter or intercepter plane. *Some W.W.II Air Force use.*

bird-dog   *v.i.* **1** To -dance with or become overly friendly with a superior's girl or wife. *Mainly Army use; since W.W.II.* **2** To attempt to or to steal another's girl; to beat [someone's] time. *Student use since c1945.*   *exclam.* Used as a warning that an officer is approaching. *Some W.W.II Army and USN use.*

birdie   *adj.* = **nuts.** *A fairly new teenage use.*

bird legs   Skinny legs.

birds and the bees, the   The basic facts of sex, conception, and birth, esp. as explained to children. *Colloq.*

bird's-eye maple   *n.* A light mulatto girl, esp. if sexually attractive. *Since c1925.*

birthday suit   *n.* One's completely bare skin; a state of nakedness; usu. in "one's birthday suit." *Because the bare skin is fig. the "suit" which one was given when one was born. Colloq.*

biscuit   *n.* **1** The face or head. *Mainly prize fight use; since c1920.* **2** Any coin; any banknote of comparatively low denomination. **3** A woman, esp. a worldly or cruel woman. 1952: ". . .

Favors to certain ladies in residence. . . . Some of these biscuits were married to men less broad-minded than they." Advt. for *True,* N.Y. *Her. Trib.,* Jan. 24, 12/2. *A biscuit is harder and less sweet than a cookie.* Cf. **cold biscuit.** See Appendix, Sex and Food. **4** A pillow. *Some c1935 jive use.* **5** A payroll timekeeper. *From his former additional work of buying food for the workmen. Some railroad labor crew and telephone lineman use, often as a nickname.*

biscuit hooks   The hands.

biscuit-roller   *n.* A cook. *Some ranch use since c1870.*

biscuit-shooter   *n.* **1** A waitress. 1898: *DAE. Obs.* **2** A cook, esp. on a ranch. 1920: *DAE. Reinforced by "biscuit-roller."*

bishop   *n.* The bustle of a woman's dress. *c1775–c1875; obs.*

bistro   *n.* A restaurant; a café. 1947: "The big Broadway bistros. . . ." Billy Rose, *synd. newsp. col.,* Nov. 4.

bit   *n.* **1** A prison sentence, not necessarily a short one. 1917: "Ferrati, whose 'bit' was three to seven years. . . ." P. L. Quinlan in *New Repub.,* Jan. 13, 294/1. 1951: "The only question was how much of a bit Lucky would get, for it was clear they were fixing to throw the book at him." *I, Mobster,* 35. **2** A small part in a play or entertainment. *Theatrical use since c1920. Now colloq.* → **3** Any expected or well-defined action, plan, series of events, or attitudes, usu., but not necessarily, of short duration; one's attitude, personality, or way of life; fig., the role which one assumes in a specif. situation or in life. *Orig. bop and cool use.*

bitch   *n.* **1** A woman, usu., but not necessarily, a mean, selfish, malicious, deceiving, cruel, or promiscuous woman. 1941: "A cold-hearted bitch." Schulberg, *Sammy,* 139. *Very old. Since past studies usu. have omitted such "vulgar" words, the history of this one is hard to trace.* → **2** [taboo] A prostitute. *Very old.* **3** In playing cards, a queen of any suit. *Fairly common by c1900.* **4** Any difficult or unpleasant task; anything unpleasant. 1949: "That wind's sure a bitch." J. Evans, *Halo,* 77. *Common by c1900. Very common.* **5** = **bitch lamp. 6** A complaint; a gripe. *Since c1910. Wide use during and since W.W.II.*   *v.t.* **1** To bungle or spoil something. 1888: *OED. Some W.W.I use. Superseded by "bitch [something] up."* **2** To cheat someone. 1941: "You never tried to bitch me out of anything." Schulberg, *Sammy,* 279.   *v.i.*

To complain, to gripe; to criticize; to nag. 1941: "What have you got to bitch about?" Schulberg, *Sammy*, 120. *Common since W.W.II.* *adj.* Substitute; makeshift; home-made; not of usual quality or value. Cf. **bitch lamp.** *As many such "vulgar" words "bitch" has a definite taboo connotation; during W.W.I this connotation became acceptable in the speech of rough or socially unacceptable people, and during and since W.W.II many such formerly taboo words have become common in the speech of many, esp. of young adults.* **—y —ey** *adj.* **1** Having the attributes of a bitch. **2** Striking in appearance; classy. 1930: "A pearl-gray Stutz, a bitchey roadster all right." J. T. Farrell, 137. *Some c1930 use.* **3** Sexually provocative; having sex appeal. 1941: "Two bitchy strip [tease] queens." *Time*, Oct. 13, 36/1.

bitch box A public-address loudspeaker. *W.W.II Army and USN use.*

bitch kitty 1 An obstinate, disagreeable, or bad-tempered girl or woman. → **2** A difficult or disagreeable task. *Both uses since c1930.*

bitch lamp A makeshift lamp, usu. a container of grease or oil with a rag for a wick; an oil lantern. 1956: "The light from the bitch lamp kept him awake. The lamp had been made by fixing a rag wick to a stone and setting it in a vessel half-filled with whatever was left in the frying pan after the morning bacon was finished." N. Algren, *A Walk on the Wild Side*, 34. *Orig. hobo use, c1920.*

bitch session 1 = **bull session.** **2** A meeting for the presentation of grievances, as when union representatives present employees' complaints to their employer.

bitch up [something] **bitch [something] up** To ruin or spoil something. 1928: "You've just bitched up my whole life!" Hecht & MacArthur, *Front Page*, III. 1948: "She bitched up no lines in the next act." Lait-Mortimer, *N.Y. Confidential*, 22.

bite *v.i.* To be gullible; to believe a deception; to allow oneself to be tricked. *v.t.* To borrow money from a person; to ask a person for money. 1949: "Remember that last five bucks you bit me for?" *Synd. cartoon*, "Major Hoople," Dec. 3. Cf. **put the bite on.**

bite, the *n.* **1** A request for money; the act or instance of borrowing money. 1935: "Nobody can remember when the bite is as painful as it is in Miami this season." Runyon, 233. See **put the bite on.** → **2** Expense; cost. 1951: "I could have had one of these fancy places without even feeling the bite." *I, Mobster*, 79. **3** One's proportion or share of the cost; the price, the money one has to pay; specif., money demanded of one, as for a bribe or extortion.

bite on [someone], put the **1** To ask for a loan or gift of money; to put the bee on [someone]. 1943: "He put the bite on me for two dollars." H. A. Smith, *Putty Knife*, 93. 1952: "He put the bite on me for a nickel to buy a glass of vichy." A. J. Liebling, *New Yorker*, Sept. 27, 58. *The most common use.* **2** To blackmail; to extort money from; to shake down. 1942: "Or did he just happen to see what happened and put the bite on you and you paid him a little now and then to avoid scandal?" Chandler, *High Window*, 183. 1951: "He was blackmailing some people.... There's a chance he was putting the bite on you." R. S. Prather, *Bodies in Bedlam*, 94. → **3** To request, borrow, or try to obtain an item from someone known to possess it. *All uses since c1935.*

bite the dust **1** To die. *Since c1870.* → **2** To meet with disaster; to fail.

biz *n.* Business. Now specif. theatrical or show business. *Mainly theater use.* 1862: *DAE.* 1894: "It's our biz to do anybody out o' our class." J. Flynt. 1910: "A newspaper that would put the *Lawrence* out of biz." Johnson, *Varmint*, 128. 1948: "Jack Pulaski [died] July 18. He helped coin much of *Variety's* lingo, such as 'show biz.' ..." N.Y. *Times*, July 18, 2E/7. See Appendix, Shortened Words.

blabbermouth *n.* One who talks too much or reveals secrets. *Colloq.*

blab off **1** To reveal a secret; to say what is better left unsaid. **2** To talk too much.

black *n.* **1** A Negro. *Not necessarily derog.* **2** Chocolate ice cream; chocolate sauce. *Not common.* *adj.* **1** Shameful; discouraging. *Colloq.* **2** Without cream; said of a cup of coffee.

black, in the **1** To run a business at a profit; operating at a profit. **2** To be solvent. *From the black ink commonly used on the credit side of business ledgers, as opposed to red ink.* See **in the red.**

black and tan **1** The name of the faction of the Republican party favoring proportional representation of Negroes and whites in the party after the Civil War. *Those vehemently in favor were called "blacks," those mildly in favor* *"tans"; the faction was thus black and tan.* *Obs.* **2** A mulatto; mulatto. *Since c1880.* **3** Catering to an audience of both Negroes and white persons. 1950: "The Commissioner looked at me—'You heard what the Captain said, boy. We'll close you down if you allow dancing.' I guess what worried them was my place was black and tan—for colored and white alike." A. Lomax, *Mr. Jelly Roll*, 157.

black and white An ice-cream soda made with vanilla ice cream and chocolate sauce. *Mainly Eastern use.*

blackbaiter *n.* **1** Any person in favor of Negro slavery. 1946: ". . . A furious argument between an Abolitionist and a blackbaiter." H. Fast, *The American*, 20. *c1840–c1865; obs.* See **black.** → **2** A person with an intolerant attitude toward Negroes. *Dial.* See Appendix, —er endings.

Black Betsy A baseball bat. *Baseball use. Orig. the name of Babe Ruth's bat.*

blackbirder *n.* A Negro slave merchant; one who financed or sailed ships operating in the Negro slave trade. 1956: "The stinking ships of the blackbirders crossed the bars below the delta and came up-river." S. Longstreet, *The Real Jazz Old and New*, 3. *Pre-Civil War use. Obs.*

black-coat *n.* **1** An undertaker. **2** A clergyman.

black cow **1** Root beer; an order of root beer. *Some lunch-counter use c1930.* → **2** A soda made with root beer and vanilla ice cream. *The most common Eastern use.* **3** Chocolate milk. *Some use since c1940.* **4** = **black and white.** *The most common Western use.*

black diamonds Coal. *Orig. railroad use.*

black eye Fig., a lowered status or reputation; something that will injure one's prestige. *Since c1900.*

black gang The engine-room workers on a ship. *From the days when Negroes were usu. employed as stokers on coal and wood-burning vessels.*

Black Maria **1** A police wagon or truck used to take arrested persons to jail. 1847: *DAE.* 1954: "New Orleans had fine big horses to pull the patrol wagons and the Black Maria." L. Armstrong, *Satchmo, My Life in New Orleans*, 12. **2** A hearse. → **3** A large, high-explosive shell used in W.W.I. *W.W.I Army use.*

black market **black-market** *n.* Fig., the market where contraband is sold or bought; illegal or unethical sales, usu. of contraband or stolen or government-rationed items. *Orig. W.W.II sl., applied to the obtaining, often by theft, selling, and buying of scarce or rationed items that were in scant civilian supply owing to their military use. Now stand.* *adj.* Illegal, unethical; pert. to contraband or stolen merchandise. 1956: "Conviction of seven U.S. marines for black-market operations in Japan, involving theft and sale of military supplies, was disclosed by the Navy today." AP, Nov. 16.

Black Mike A meat and vegetable stew. *Hobo and logger use.*

black out **1** To faint, to lose consciousness. *Colloq.* **2** To lose one's memory of a specif. happening. *Colloq.*

blackout *n.* Coffee. *Some W.W.II Army use.* Cf. **black-strap.**

black snake A train made up exclusively of coal-carrying cars. *Railroad use.*

blackstick *n.* A clarinet. *Never common; some c1935 jive use.*

black-strap *n.* Coffee. *Implying that it is as thick as black-strap molasses. Logger use and some Armed Forces use.* Cf. **blackout.**

black stuff Opium. *Narcotic addict use.* Cf. **white stuff.**

black widow An unpopular girl. *Some c1940 student use. In allusion to the poisonous black widow spider.*

bladder *n.* **1** A toy balloon. *Circus use, archaic since c1935.* **2** A newspaper. *Orig. underworld use. From the Ger. "blatt" = newspaper.* Cf. **blat.**

blade *n.* A young man, esp. one who believes himself socially adroit, sophisticated, and witty. 1949: "I retired to a cloakroom with several other blades." S. J. Perelman, *Listen to the Mocking Bird*, 79. *Almost always used in a jocular sense.*

blah *n.* Senseless or exaggerated talk; useless talk; bunk, boloney. 1928: "A lot of romantic blah." W. Gibbs in *New Yorker*, Nov. 3, 79. 1950: "The case of the People v. Inescapable Blah. . . ." *New Yorker*, Feb. 4, 22/3. *adj.* **1** Nonsensical; worthless. **2** Bland; unexciting, unappetizing, or unappealing. 1958: "ACCENT ends blah meals for good!" Headline for an advt. for a commercially packaged, trademarked, pure monosodium glutamate, a pop. cooking additive that intensifies natural food flavors. N.Y. *Sunday News*, "Coloroto Magazine," Apr. 20, 19.

blah-blah   blah blah   blahblah
n. = **blah**. 1921: "A long debate with
himself which was mostly blah blah."
Witwer, *Leather*, 140. See Appendix,
Reduplications.
blame(d)   *adj.* = **darn(ed), blast(ed)**.
Since c1825.
blanket   *n.* **1** A pancake; a hotcake.
2 A cigarette paper.   **—s**   *n.pl.* Pancakes; a stack of pancakes.
blanket drill   *n.* Sleep. *Army use since
before c1930.*
blankety-blank   *n. & adj.* A euphem.
for any taboo word or expression. 1953:
"Say—who the blankety-blank are you?"
"Well, you're just the blankety-blank
I've been looking for." Quoted by Bob
Thomas, AP, Feb. 24.
blanko water   Coffee. *Some W.W.II
Army use reported.*
blast   *n.* **1** A blow, as with the fist.
Colloq. Cf. **put the blast on.** → **2** In
baseball, a powerful hit, esp. a home run.
1952: "Gionfriddo's catch of Joe DiMag-
gio's 'home run' blast into the bullpen. . . ." A. Daley in N.Y. *Times Mag.*,
Sept. 28, 28/1. 1952: "Mize's third home
run in as many days—a three-run blast
into the right-field stands." W. Grimsley,
AP, Oct. 8. → **3** Fig., any attack, as a
verbal assault or speech. 1950: "Senator
Chance had begun his blast." Starnes,
Another Mug, 4. → **4** Fig., any violence,
as a robbery. 1928: "He came out of
K.C. hot from that P.O. blast." E. Booth
in *Amer. Mercury*, May, 80. **5** A thrill;
a feeling of great satisfaction; a kick, a
charge. 1952: "You get a blast takin'
care of me, givin' me presents." Radio
play, *Broadway Is My Beat*, Dec. 20. →
6 That which gives a thrill, esp. a drink
or narcotics. 1953: "Maybe it's a little
early in the day for that first blast. . . ."
Dean Harris, radio, Apr. 21. → **7** A
party, esp. a wild or abandoned one; a
period of excitement. **8** = **gasser. 9** A
complete or conspicuous failure. From
"bomb."   *v.t.* **1** In baseball, to hit.
1951: "Torgeson walloped his 19th home
run, blasting Tom Poholsky's pitch into
the right pavilion." AP, Aug. 27 **2** In
sports, to defeat a team or opponent, esp.
by a decisive score. **3** To shoot someone.
1939: "I wasn't told to blast anybody."
Chandler, *Big Sleep*, 107. **4** To attack
another verbally.   *v.i.* **1** To criticize
publically; to complain; to broadcast;
to advertise; to proclaim the merits of
a product extravagantly. 1956: "Touts
were allowed to advertise winners they
did not have. This was called 'blasting.' "

T. Betts, *Across the Board*, 240. **2** To
take injections of narcotic drugs, as an
addict; to smoke a marijuana cigarette.
1957: " 'You all right, honey? You ain't
just had a jolt of junk? I don't play with
hopheads.' 'I'm fine,' I said, 'No, I don't
blast.' " S. Longstreet, *The Promoters*, 14.
blasted   *adj.* **1** Without funds, completely broke. **2** Exceeding; damned.
1682: "Adv." *OED*. 1854: *DAE*. Cf.
dad-blasted.
blaster   *n.* **1** A gunman. *Underworld
use.* → **2** A gun.
blast off   To leave a place or gathering, esp. quickly, without ceremony, or at
the request of another; often used as a
request or command; to beat it.
**blast on [someone], put (lay) the
1** To criticize a person severely, either in
speech or in print; to take someone to
task. 1949: "He . . . went back to his
paper and put the blast on the Federals."
A. Hynd, 33. **2** To hit with the fist.
1935: "I turn around figuring to put a
large blast on the guy who slaps me."
Runyon, 3.
blast party   *n.* A party of narcotic
addicts, esp. marijuana smokers. 1958:
"Blast party—Get-together of marijuana
smokers." G. Y. Wells, *Station House
Slang.*
blat   *n.* A newspaper. See **bladder.**
bleed   *v.t.* To obtain money from a
person, esp. to obtain an exorbitant
amount or to obtain it by extortion.
Colloq.   v.i. To complain; to nag.
Some c1940 use.   **—er**   *n.* In baseball, a one-base hit, a lucky hit, or a
weakly hit ball.
bleenie   *n.* A frankfurter or weenie.
Dial.
blimp   *n.* **1** An obese person. **2** A
promiscuous girl, fig., one who "floats"
from one man to another. *Some c1930 use.*
3 An old or dilapidated car. *Not common.
Orig. taxi-driver use.*
blind   *adj.* Drunk. 1933: "I was blind
last night." J. T. Farrell, 62. 1942: "She
loses count of her drinks and is liable to
get a little blind." P. Wylie, *Generation
of Vipers*, 202. See Appendix, Drunk.
n. **1** = **blind baggage.** 1907: "Then
[the tramp] must jump onto the blind
again." J. London, *My Life.* **2** =
blind date. 3 A fine, as imposed by
a court. 1933: "With a good defense
counsel he'll get three [months] and
a blind." H. T. Webster. **4** A letter
bearing an illegible or incomplete address; a nixie. *Post office use.   v.i. &
adj.* To know or do something perfectly;

fig., to know or be able to do something so well that one need not use one's eyes; to answer all questions asked by an examiner. *Since c1900; mainly student use.* See **cold.** **—ed** *adj.* Drunk. 1955: "We used to drink until Pat was blinded." E. Trujillo, *I Love You, I Hate You,* 37. See Appendix, Drunk.

blind baggage A railroad baggage or mail car with no door or a locked door at the front end; the space between such cars where hobos may hide and ride. 1907: "One [act] was to catch the blind baggage on the west-bound overland." J. London, *My Life. Hobo use.*

blind Charley A lamp-post; a protective light. *Underworld use. Archaic.*

blind date A social engagement at which one's partner is a previously unknown person of the opposite sex, usu. the friend of a friend; also, such a partner. *Student use since c1920. Colloq.*

blind drag = blind date.

blindfold a pair An order to fry two eggs on both sides. *Lunch-counter use in relaying a customer's order. Dial.*

blind pig A speakeasy; an unlicensed saloon. 1887: *DAE.* 1948: "Of the 50-odd blind pigs only two remained." Lait-Mortimer, *N.Y. Confidential,* 43.

blind-pigger *n.* The proprietor of a blind pig. 1894: *DAE. Obs. since c1925.* See Appendix, —er endings.

blind robin A smoked herring. 1889: *DAE. Archaic.*

blind tiger **1** = blind pig. 1883: *DAE. Obs. since c1935.* **2** Cheap or inferior whisky.

Blind Tom A baseball umpire. *In allusion to the traditional allegation that umpires cannot see the pitches, etc., that they judge. Baseball use.*

blinger *n.* An extreme instance or example of anything. 1949: "241 [persons] caught one or more colds, some of them 5 or 6. 179 of them developed real blingers going through to the phase of secondary infections." P. de Kruif in *Reader's Digest,* Dec., 18/1.

blink, on the **1** Not in working order; not functioning or not functioning properly; not in good condition, in disrepair; said of tools, machines, and the like. 1951: "Did you call about a television set on the blink?" Robert Day, *New Yorker,* Feb. 17, 22. 1958: ". . . I'm looking for a [sympathy] card for someone whose television set is on the blink." Cartoon caption by Modell, *New Yorker,* Mar. 29, 76. *Since c1920.* → **2** Not feeling well; without vigor; said of people. → **3**

Dead; said of people. 1944: "1926 it had pretty nearly put me on the blink. . . ." John Barrymore, quoted by G. Fowler, *Good Night,* 234. **4** Drunk. *Not common.*

blinkers *n.pl.* The eyes. 1952: "Cast your limpid blinkers on this!" M. Blosser, *synd. comic strip,* "Freckles," Sept. 20.

blinkie *n.* A beggar who feigns blindness. *Orig. hobo use.* See Appendix, —ie endings.

blip *n.* A nickel; the sum of 5¢. 1956: "A *blip* is five cents." S. Longstreet, *The Real Jazz Old and New,* 148. *adj.* **1** Excellent; very good. *Jive use since c1935.* → **2** = **hip.** *Cool use since c1950.*

blip jockey A human monitor of electronic equipment, especially warning or detecting equipment, giving off visual responses. Cf. **ping jockey.**

blip off To kill; to murder, esp. by shooting. 1927: "If he blipped Beno off, he knows me." Hammett, *Blood Money,* 30.

blister *n.* **1** An annoying person; one whose presence detracts from the peace or gaiety of a gathering. 1854: *DAE. Still some use.* **2** A promiscuous girl or woman; a prostitute. *Dial.* → **3** Any sexually attractive girl or woman. *Some W.W.II Army and USN use.* **4** A woman hobo. **5** A semispherical glass or transparent plastic covering, as for an airplane cockpit or gun turret.

blisterfoot *n.* **1** An army infantryman. *Fairly common W.W.I use; archaic.* **2** A uniformed policeman who walks a regular beat. *Not common.*

blitz *v.i.* To absent oneself from a class or an examination; to cut a class. *Some c1900 student use.* *v.t.* To polish the buttons and buckles of one's uniform; to polish and clean a barracks in preparation for inspection. *W.W.II Army use. After the commercial "Blitz Cloth," a polishing cloth.* *n.* **1** = **blitzkrieg.** **2** An important conference; a major flap. *W.W.II use.*

blitzkrieg **Blitzkrieg** *n.* A quick line used to gain sympathy from an attractive girl or someone who has money that can be borrowed; the rush act. *W.W.II Army use.*

blizzard head In telecasting, a very blonde actress for whom the lighting must be subdued. 1948: "The television boys have already worn out *blizzard head.*" H. L. Mencken in *New Yorker.*

bloated *adj.* Drunk. *Some c1920 use, not now common.* See Appendix, Drunk.

blob *n.* A mistake. *Some c1900 student use.* *v.i.* To make a mistake.

block *n.* **1** The head. *Common since before 1900. Not now generally used absolutely, but common in such colloq. expressions as "knock [one's] block off."* **2** A watch; *orig.*, a man's pocket watch. *Underworld use, archaic.* **3** = **blockhead**. *v.t.* To look at, inspect, or watch someone or something. *Not common.*

block and tackle One's wife, boss, or superior; anyone who can or does restrain one's actions. *Colloq.*

blockhead *n.* A stupid person. *1594: OED. Still in freq. use, this is the oldest of the many "—head" words.*

bloke *n.* **1** A stupid person. *1887: New Orleans Lantern. Not now common. From the Celtic "ploc" = a large, bull-headed person, reinforced by "plocach" = a strong, coarse person. Common in Eng. since c1850, this word has been little used in the U.S. Since c1900 it has been considered affected and pseudo-English when used.* → **2** A man, a fellow, a guy. *1900:* "Look at the bloke ridin'." *Dreiser, Carrie, 342. 1949:* ". . . Handing [cash] to some bloke who needs a pair of shoes." *Billy Rose, synd. newsp. col.,* Sept., 5. **3** A drunkard. *Some c1915 use.*

blonde and sweet Coffee with sugar and cream in it. *Some W.W.II USN use reported.*

blood *n.* **1** A perfect recitation. *Student use c1850–c1910.* → **2** A socially active male college student, a leader of student activities, a big man on campus. *1939:* "Her hair is cut crew cut like the college blood." *O'Hara, Pal Joey, 57.* **3** Ketchup. *Since c1910.* **—y** *adj & adv.* Very; blooming, blasted, goddamn(ed). *Although now considered only a Briticism, this word was in some use in the U.S. c1845–c1890.*

blood disease Syphilis. *A very old euphem.*

bloody murder **1** A decisive defeat; complete ruin or failure; an exhausting task. **2** Loud or emotional anger. *Almost always in "to yell (scream, etc.) bloody murder."*

blooey, go   **blooie, go**   **flooey, go**
flooie, go To cease operating properly; to collapse or fall apart; to fail suddenly. *Lit. = to explode. 1931:* "Right there some of the good will went blooie." *J. Sayre, Hex, 416. 1944:* "Careful you don't get that dynamite too warm holding it. A little overheating and she'll go blooie, just like that." *Shulman, Feather Merchants, 117.*

bloom *n.* In television, a televised glare from some white object, as a shirt front, within range of the camera lens; a womp.

bloomer *n.* **1** An empty or nearly empty safe. *Underworld use, archaic.* **2** A location where, or a day when, business is bad; a poorly attended show or place of business; a business failure. *Orig. circus use.* **3** A blunder; a mistake; a boner. *1935:* "I made a gorgeous bloomer in my list of one hundred Best Books." *W. L. Phelps in Scribner's, Dec., 378/2. 1949:* "A 'bloomer' by [President Harry S.] Truman and [General George C.] Marshall about a grave that was not there. . . ." *UP, Aug. 13.*

bloomer boy *n.* A paratrooper. *Some W.W.II use. From the cut of his jump-uniform trousers.*

bloomer girl *n.* A popular, attractive, somewhat daring girl or young woman. *In tribute to those c1910 beauties who first wore bloomers at the beach and while bicycle riding or playing tennis. Archaic.*

bloomers *n.pl.* Gun covers. *Some W.W.II USN use.*

blooming *adj. & adv.* A euphem. for a taboo word; blasted, bloody, darned, etc. *Although now considered a Briticism, this word was in some U.S. use c1900–c1920.*

bloop *n.* **1** The grating sound of a voice unsuitable for recording. *Early movie use. Of imitative orig.* → **2** An extraneous dull sound in a record, caused by improper splicing of two sections of a tape recording. *Since c1945.* **3** A fluke; a blunder. *v.i.* To make a howling sound; said of a radio receiver. *Radio amateur use since c1925.* *v.t.* To hit someone, esp. to hit someone with a long, slow punch. *1952:* "[Prizefighter Gil] Turner blooped a bolo to the heart. Turner walked in and stabbed four lefts to the nose." *J. Jennings in N.Y. Daily Mirror, July 8, 24/1.* **—er** *n.* **1** A blow with the fist, esp. a long, slow punch. *1939:* "So I could hang a blooper on your kisser." *O'Hara, Pal Joey, 64.* **2** In baseball, a slow, high-arching pitch; a weakly hit, high-arching ball, a fluke hit, a Texas leaguer. *The baseball pitch was first used successfully by pitcher "Rip" Sewell during the 1945 baseball season.* **3** = **bloomer**, a blunder. *1951:* "But on one subject—'security'— [Eisenhower] may have felt he pulled a political blooper." *J. Marlow, AP, Nov. 8.*

blot out To kill. *Underworld use.*

blotter *n.* **1** The ledger of arrests and arrested persons kept at a police station.

1958: "Blotter—The official log of a station house in the handwriting of the desk officer in charge—a lieutenant or captain." G. Y. Wells, *Station House Slang*. **2** A drunkard.

blotto   *adj.* **1** Drunk; esp. unconscious from drink. 1928: "Newark gin that knocks you blotto. . . ." P. Cummings in *New Yorker*, Dec. 8, 46. 1950: "The surgeon was quite blotto." *SEP*, Apr. 1, 78/3. *Of Brit. orig. Usu. a pred. adj., but used attrib.* **2** Confused, baffled. *Not common.*

blouse   *v.i.* To leave, to depart, esp. hurriedly. *Some c1920 use. A fad word. considered cute. Based on "blow."*

blow   *n.* **1** A storm. *Orig. maritime use. Colloq.* → **2** Any loud or angry confusion. → **3** A drinking spree. 1827: *DAE. Archaic since c1890.* → **4** One who goes on a drinking spree; an irresponsible person; one who spends much money on entertainment and nonessential items. *Some c1850 use.* **5** A gun. *Some underworld use.* **6** A greeting or other sign of recognition; a tumble. 1939: ". . . A couple of old characters among them give Blooch a blow, and he stops to talk with them." Runyon. *v.t.* **1** To inform against someone; to squeal on someone; to betray someone. 1848: *DAE. Underworld use.* → **2** To expose a scandal to the public; to unearth and broadcast illegal or unethical dealings. **3** To treat someone to something, as to a drink, meal, or entertainment. 1896: *DAE.* 1912: "I blew myself to a few glad rags." Johnson, *Stover at Yale*, 162. 1930: "The ambulance surgeon is supposed to blow the staff to a spread." Lavine, *Third Degree*, 67. **4** To play a musical instrument, esp. in jazz style, whether a wind instrument or not. *Musician use before c1920. Some c1935 jive use; jazz use; very common cool and way out use.* → **5** To perform any act, esp. to perform any act well. 1957: "Blow— To perform an act: 'He blows great conversation,' 'She blows scrambled eggs from endville,' etc." E. Horne, *For Cool Cats and Far-Out Chicks.* **6** [taboo] To perform cunnilingus or fellatio on someone. *Although taboo, this is the most common word for oral intercourse and is in wide use.* **7** To lose something, as a prize, in defeat; to lose one's chance of success or of winning; to fail to use one's opportunity to advance or succeed, esp. by one's own blunder or apathy. 1949: "We should have won the [baseball pennant] last week, but we blew it." AP, Oct. 3. 1952: "Between the [Navy's

spoiled] meat and the oyster forks you'd think the old senior service had already blown World War 3." R. C. Ruark, *synd. newsp. col.*, Mar. 11. *Common since c1920.* **8** To spend or lose money, usu; quickly or on unnecessary items. 1949: "The state blew my money buying votes for Roosevelt. . . ." W. Pegler, *synd. newsp. col.*, Oct. 26. **9** To eliminate or cancel part of an agreement or business. **10** To forget or blunder one's lines in a stage show. *Theater use.* **11** To throw a baseball fast and hard. 1952: "Joe Black, Brooklyn's rookie, blowing his fast one past Yankee bats for a 4–2 win. . . ." W. Grimsley, AP, Oct. 8.   *v.i.* **1** To brag; to exaggerate. *Since c1850.* → **2** To recite in school. *Some c1930 use.* **3** To become angry, to lose one's temper. **4** To take a narcotic by inhalation. *Addict use.* → **5** To smoke tobacco. *Some prison use. v.i. & v.t.* To go away, to depart; to leave a place, esp. rapidly or secretly; to escape, as from prison; to desert an enterprise. 1921: "The female shakes the Kid's hand and blows." Witwer, *Leather*, 85. 1929: "I'm blowing. I got a job in Detroit." D. Parker, "Big Blonde," reprinted in *The American Twenties*, 148. 1949: "Alive, you're ready to blow town." Radio play, *Sam Spade*, Aug. 28. *The most common use.   interj.* A command or entreaty, usu. in anger, to leave, to scram.

blow a fuse   To lose one's temper, to become violently angry, to blow one's top. 1949: "Relax . . . or you'll blow a fuse." S. J. Perelman, *Listen to the Mocking Bird*, 120. *Colloq.*

blow a gasket = **blow a fuse**. 1953: "The higher-ups blew a gasket when they heard. . . ." B. Crosby in *SEP*, Feb. 14.

blow away   To depart; to blow.

blow-boy   *n.* A bugler. *Some Army use.*

blow [one's] cap = **blow [one's] top**. 1956: ". . . Blowing your cap . . . is to go mad." S. Longstreet, *The Real Jazz Old and New*, 148.

blow [one's] cork = **blow [one's] top**.

blowed-in-the-glass   Genuine; first-rate; refined; of the highest order. *Hobo use. From liquor bottles with the brand name blown in the glass.*

blowen   *n.* Any woman, but esp. a prostitute or promiscuous woman. *Underworld use since c1850.*

blower   *n.* A handkerchief.

blow for canines   To play in the very highest register of a trumpet. 1957:

"Blows for canines—Plays long successions of high notes; screeches." E. Horne, *For Cool Cats and Far-Out Chicks. Cool and far-out use; prob. synthetic. In allusion to the ability of dogs to hear notes at a pitch above the range of the human ear.*

blowhard *n.* **1** A braggart. *Since c1860.* **2** A loud, freq. emotionally upset or fault-finding talker.

blow in **1** To spend money, usu. foolishly and quickly. 1886: New Orleans *Lantern.* 1929: "And blow it in on smokes." J. Auslander, *Hell in Harness,* 2. **2** To arrive at or enter a place, esp. suddenly, unexpectedly, and from a distant place. Usu. in past tense. 1895: *DAE.* 1934: "I blew in there in a hurry." Cain, *Postman,* 1. **blow-in** *n.* **1** A spree. *Logger use.* **2** A new arrival at a place or gathering. *Hobo use.*

blowing *n.* Playing jazz music; the act or an instance of playing jazz music. 1956: "This music is the culmination of all my [Duke Ellington's] writing and blowing." Advt. for the "Ellington Showcase" record in *Metronome,* April, 34. *adj.* Drunk. *c1850; obs.* See Appendix, Drunk.

blowing cat A jazz musician. 1956: "There are lots of blowing cats (musicians). . . . " S. Longstreet, *The Real Jazz Old and New,* 147.

blow job **1** [taboo] The act of or an instance of cunnilingus or fellatio. See **blow.** **2** A jet-propelled airplane. *Some Air Force use since c1950.* **3** = **snow job.**

Blow Joe An enlisted man. *Some Army use since c1940. An inversion of "Joe Blow."*

blown *adj.* Drunk. *c1850; obs.* See Appendix, Drunk.

blown up Drunk. *Dial.* See Appendix, Drunk.

blow-off **blowoff** *n.* **1** A climax; the end, the conclusion; esp. the final or climactic insult or indignity which precipitates a fight. 1951: "[We] went to the Spreckles' house for dinner. That was the blow-off." L. Rogow in *Collier's,* Nov. 17, 10/3. → **2** A quarrel; the cause of a quarrel. 1943: "It was funny a five-dollar bet should come to be the blowoff." Wolfert, *Underworld,* 27. 1952: "She and Hobart have had a big blow-off on the night in question, mostly over her getting too cozy with Bob Dumas." J. Kelly in New York *Times Bk. Rev.,* Aug. 17. **3** A pitchman's first customer, who often is given a free item in order to induce further sales. *Carnival use.* *v.t.* To defeat an

opponent or opposing team, esp. with ease. *Not common.*

blow off [one's] mouth (trap, yap) To talk too much; to reveal a secret. *Archaic by c1910.*

blow off steam = **let off steam.**

blow one An order to draw a glass of beer. *Used in relaying orders to a bartender. In allusion to the foam on top of a glass of beer, which can be blown off.*

blow one up To light a cigarette; to begin smoking a fresh cigarette. *Some prison use.*

blow-out **blowout** *n.* **1** An outbreak of disagreement, disorder, or loud noise. 1825: *DAE. Archaic.* → **2** A celebration or spree, esp. a festive, noisy, or extravagant one. 1834: *DAE.* → **3** A public oration. *Some use c1910.* **4** A large outdoor crowd. *Pitchman use.* **5** An unsuccessful robbery attempt. *Underworld use.* **blow out** **1** To spend money, usu. quickly and foolishly. Cf. **blow in.** **2** To leave; to depart. *Some c1920 use.* See **blow.**

blowpipe *n.* A rifle.

blow smoke To boast, to brag, to exaggerate. *Implying that the speaker is having a pleasant dream, as induced by smoking opium.*

blow [one's] stack = **blow [one's] top.**

blow the gaff To inform. *Underworld use; archaic.*

blow the lid off To expose a scandal to the public; to expose illegal or unethical practices.

blow the whistle **1** To inform, to sing. 1948: "She had a faint idea who had done it. But she hadn't been Dutch Schultz's wife for four years not to know the penalty for blowing the whistle." Lait-Mortimer, *N.Y. Confidential,* 19. *Underworld use.* **2** To expose a scandal; to threaten to expose a scandal.

blow [one's] top (stack, wig, topper, cork, noggin, roof, lump, etc.) **1** To become insane. 1932: "They think I will blow my topper." Runyon. *Not now common.* **2** To commit suicide. *Some underworld use.* **3** Fig., to become insane with excitement or enthusiasm. *Orig. jive use, now cool use.* **4** To lose one's temper; to become violently angry; lit. and fig., to have a tantrum as a result of uncontrollable rage. 1946: "We usually consider any statement in its context before blowing our tops. . . . " A. E. Gower in *Sat. Rev. Lit.,* Apr. 6, 11/2. 1949: "I'd blow my roof." A. Granley in Phila. *Inquirer,* "Everybody's Weekly," Sept.

4, 7/2. 1952: "When Andrew [Carnegie] received the minutes and read them he blew his stack a mile high." R. Bissell, *The Monongahela*, 189. *The most common use.* "*Blow [one's] top*" *is the orig. and most freq. term.* Cf. **flip [one's] lid.** 5 To talk too much. *Underworld use.* 6 To do something exceedingly well, esp. to play a musical passage with skill and enthusiasm. *Cool use.* 7 To become insane or sick from narcotics, esp. marijuana. *Addict use.*

blowtop   *n.* A person who angers easily; one who often blows his top.

blowtorch   *n.* A jet fighter plane. *Air Force use since c1950.*

blow-up   **blowup**   *n.* **1** A fit of anger. 1837: *DAE.* 1944: "A mere journalistic blow-up." Fowler, *Good Night*, 101. → **2** Fig., an explosion; an uproar; a quarrel; a fight. 1950: "[She] was worried about Liz and Nick getting out of Europe in case of an international blow-up." Bob Thomas, AP, July 18. **3** An enlarged photograph.   *v.t.* To enlarge a photograph. *v.i.* **1** = **blow [one's] top.** 1939: "He blew up. He cussed and raved around a while." Gardner, *D. A. Draws*, 184. **2** = **blow,** to forget or blunder one's lines in a stage performance. 1944: "[John] Barrymore 'blew up' in his lines." Fowler, *Good Night*, 309.

blow up a storm   To play jazz with spirit and skill. 1954: "I first heard Buddy Bolden play. . . . He was blowing up a storm." L. Armstrong, *Satchmo, My Life in New Orleans*, 23. *Jazz use.*

b. l. t.   An order of a bacon, lettuce, and tomato sandwich. *Common lunch-counter use in relaying an order.*

blub   *n.* Empty talk; false promises. *Some c1900 student use.*

blubber   *v.i.* To cry.

blubberhead   *n.* A stupid person; a fathead. 1952: "Listen, blubberhead!" Movie, *We're Not Married.*

blue   *adj.* **1** Lewd, lascivious, obscene, erotic. *Colloq. by c1900; perhaps because the color of blue is associated with burning brimstone.* **2** Drunk. 1838: *DAE.* 1929: "When you were blue you got the howling horrors." D. Parker, "Big Blonde," reprinted in *The American Twenties*, 146. See Appendix, Drunk. **3** Risqué; vulgar; suggesting the obscene. 1930: " . . . Blue gags = jokes in questionable taste." *Variety*. 1953: "In burlesque [comedian Red] Buttons had a reputation for being, if not lily white, at least no bluer than. . . . " G. Millstein

in N.Y. *Times Mag.*, Feb. 22, 74/2. **4** Melancholy; sad; depressed. *Colloq.*   *n.* **1** A conscientious, law-abiding student. 1842: *DAE.* **2** [derog.] A very dark complexioned Negro. **3** The sky. → **4** Heaven. *Jive use.*   *v.t.* To perform music in blues manner. See **blues.**

blue balls [taboo]   A case of venereal disease, esp. gonorrhea. 1947: "They were talking about syphilitic spots when Wintermine interrupted to describe the blue balls." C. Willingham, *End As A Man*, 244.

bluebelly [derog.]   *n.* **1** A Union soldier during the Civil War. 1954: "This time aided only by Cole [Younger] and brother Frank, he [Jesse James] ambushed a company of eighty Federals. The murderous crossfire 'left twenty bluebellies laying in the dirt.' " W. Henry, *Death of a Legend*, 26. *Confederate use. From the color of the Union uniforms.* **2** Any person in, state of, or sympathizer with the Union during the Civil War. *Obs.*

blue-book   **Blue Book**   **bluebook**   *n.* **1** A test or examination. 1951: " . . . Students [at the University of Michigan] fearful of flunking a bluebook. . . . " Cornell (Univ.) *Daily Sun*, Nov. 10, 3. *Student and college use since c1890. From the thin, blue-covered notebook of blank pages commonly provided by colleges for students to use in writing answers to examination questions.* **2** Any list or directory. 1950: "*The Blue Book*, a directory of the [New Orleans] tenderloin, printed for the convenience of tourists and on sale at Storyville bars for twenty-five cents, carried ads from every madam of reputation." A. Lomax, *Mr. Jelly Roll*, 98.

blue-eyed   *adj.* **1** Drunk. *c1850; obs.* See Appendix, Drunk. **2** Innocent, gullible; idealistic; unworldly.

blue-eyed boy = **fair-haired boy.**

blue fizzle   A very bad recitation. 1851: "He made a blue fizzle." Hall, *College Words*, 130. *Obs.*

blue funk   A state of emotional depression, esp. when caused by romantic disillusionment, losing a lover, or confusion. A state of loneliness, aimlessness, or confusion.

blue-gum [derog.]   *n.* A Negro. *Civil War use.*

bluejeans   **blue jeans**   *n.* Blue denim pants, worn by teenagers and adults of both sexes. *Originally "jeans" or "Levis," now rarely called "slacks." Accent first syllable.* See **jeans, Levis.**

blue loco   1 Loco weed. → **2** = **loco.**
blue man   A uniformed policeman.
blue murder = **bloody murder.**
blue nose   *n.* A person with strongly puritanical moral convictions; one who believes that having a good time is immoral; an ultraconservative. 1956: "It was 1917 and America was at war and the moral bluenoses were sniffing around the army camps and keeping our boys pure, so they could make the world safe for democracy." S. Longstreet, *The Real Jazz Old and New*, 61. *Orig. in Colonial times = an aristocrat.*
blue note   A flatted note characteristic of the blues. 1956: "*Blue notes* are the flattened thirds and sevenths in the blue scale." S. Longstreet, *The Real Jazz Old and New*, 149. See **the blues.**
blue ruin   1 Inferior liquor, esp. gin. 1827: *DAE. Archaic and dial. since c1920.* 2 A catastrophe; complete ruin, failure, or disgrace.
blues, the   *n. sing.* 1 Despondency; a sad, melancholy, depressed mood. See **blue.** 2 Specif., a fundamental part, specific form, and mood of jazz music. One of the main origins of jazz was the sad or melancholy Negro work, prison, and funeral songs of slavery and oppression. The mood of these songs, combined with the melancholy theme and mood of lost or rejected love expressed in diminished 13ths, 5ths, and 3ds, usu. played in a slow tempo, have given us the mood, themes, and form of jazz known as "the blues." In general use = any slowly played jazz or popular musical piece with sad lyrics of lost or rejected love. 1905: "The Jelly Roll Blues," composed by Jelly Roll Morton, copyright 1915 by Will Rossiter, Chicago, widely recognized as the first published jazz composition. According to the list in Alan Lomax's *Mr. Jelly Roll*, Jelly Roll Morton wrote at least 24 songs with "blues" in their copyrighted title. 1956: ". . . Around 1870 . . . in the farmlands, the cotton and tobacco fields . . . they were already calling it the blues. 'It was mostly voice, because beyond the banjo and a little drumming there just were not the tools to make it instrumental.' " S. Longstreet, *The Real Jazz Old and New*, 17.
blue-skin   [derog.]   *n.* A Negro, esp. a very dark complexioned one. *Used by James Fenimore Cooper in "The Spy"; obs. by c1865.*
blue-stocking   *n.* A woman student, esp. a studious, unfeminine one. *c1900*

student use. *In Colonial times orig.* = aristocrat.
blue ticket   A discharge without honor from the Army, not as desirable as a discharge with honor, but more desirable than a dishonorable discharge. *Some c1930 Army use. Because such discharges were printed on blue paper.*
blunt   *n.* Money. *c1850 underworld use. Obs.* —**ed**   *adj.* Having much money; wealthy, esp. temporarily wealthy. *Archaic underworld use.*
blurb   *n.* 1 A short laudatory essay or review of a new book, printed on its jacket to entice prospective readers to buy it. *Since c1915.* → 2 Any laudatory article, advertisement, short sales talk, or the like, whether given freely or as part of a paid advertising campaign, which increases the sales appeal of an item, performance, or entertainment; the mention of a commercial product, firm, or performer of entertainment in a published source. *The word was coined by Gelett Burgess and first used in his "Burgess Unabridged" (1914).*
blushing bunny   Welsh rabbit with tomato soup as one of the ingredients.
BMOC   **B.M.O.C.** = **big man on campus.** *A very common student abbr. since c1940.* See Appendix, Shortened Words.
BO   **B.O.**   1 Abbr. for "body odor," esp. underarm perspiration odor. *Popularized c1940 by heavy Lifebuoy Soap advertising campaign. Among other manifestations of the term was "B. O. Plenty," a character introduced c1945 in the synd. comic strip "Dick Tracy."* 2 Theatrical business conditions; specif., the "box office" receipts for the sale of tickets to a play or other entertainment. *Theater use.* → 3 The appeal or ability of an entertainer that attracts audiences to buy tickets to his performances. *Theater use.* See Appendix, Shortened Words.
bo   '**bo**   *n.* 1 A hobo. 1907: "From some bo on the drag I managed to learn what time a certain freight pulled out." J. London, *My Life.* 1937: "Rank and file 'bos find the problem amusing." *Lit. Digest*, Apr. 10, 11. 1956: "As soon as his thirst was quenched, the 'bo was washing his one shirt." N. Algren, *A Walk on the Wild Side*, 18. See Appendix, Shortened Words. 2 A boy or youth; orig. a catamite. *Prison use.* 3 A man; used only in direct address, usu. to a stranger. *Prob. from the Sp. "vos" = you.*
board   *n.* 1 A restaurant check. *Not*

common. **2** A ticket to an entertainment. **—s** *n.pl.* Playing cards; a deck of playing cards.

boat *n.* An automobile. 1949: "The little boat (automobile, in the argot of '22). . . ." S. J. Perelman, *Listen to the Mocking Bird,* 82. *Since c1920.*

boater *n.* A man's stiff straw hat, with a flat crown. *Archaic.*

boat race A dishonest race; specif., a horse race in which one entry is allowed to win by the others. 1956: "BOAT RACE—A fixed race." T. Betts, *Across the Board,* 312.

bob *n.* **1** Money. *From the Brit. "bob" = a shilling, reinforced by the nickname "Bob" suggested by the synonym "Jack".* → **2** A dollar; the sum of $1. 1932: "Twenty-five bobs per week." "I like to turn a few honest bobs." Runyon. **3** A shoplifter. *Obs. underworld use.*

bobble *n.* A mistake; an error. *Since c1900. Colloq.* *v.i.* & *v.t.* To make a mistake; esp., in sports, to fumble.

bobby-socker **bobby-soxer** *n.* **1** An adolescent girl. *From the bobby socks which most such girls wore as part of the fashionable high school costume during the early 1940's.* → **2** A young teenager of either sex, esp. one whose interests dress, and personality conform to adolescent fashions.

bobby socks **bobby sox** *n.* Long white cotton socks worn to a length just below the knee or as anklets with thick cuffs. *Orig. pop. with teenage girls c1940.*

bob tail **bobtail** *n.* A dishonorable discharge from military service. *Armed Forces use since W.W.I. From the former custom of cutting out the phrase ". . . service honorable and faithful" from the bottom of the discharge certificate.*

Boche [derog.] *n.* A German; esp. a German soldier. *Wide W.W.I use; not common in W.W.II.* *adj.* German.

bodega *n.* **1** A liquor store, a store that sells whisky by the bottle. *Some S.W. dial. use since c1850. From the Sp. In Spanish-speaking countries a "bodega" is a grocery store, which also sells liquor.* **2** A grocery store. *Some N.Y. City dial. use, through Puerto Rican immigrant use.*

bodgie *n.* A male jitterbug. 1952: "A bodgie is a jitterbug-crazy boy 'who wears his hair curled and long and a sport coat too big for him.' " H. Boyle, AP, Sept. 10. *Archaic.*

bodo *n.* A friend. *Some c1920 use.*

body *n.* A sexually attractive girl or young woman with a good figure. *Starting in the middle 1940's, a succession of actresses, singers, and movie stars were nicknamed "The Body," and referred to as such by columnists, newsmen, and the public. Marie McDonald was probably the first to be so dubbed, and later any physically attractive girl, whether a celebrity or not, was likely to be so nicknamed.*

body and breeches Entirely; completely. 1878: *DAE. Obs. by 1900.*

body and soul A lover; a member of the opposite sex with whom one is sexually, emotionally, and mentally compatible. *An example of sl. derived from aptness of expression, as it actually implies that the other person is one's own metaphoric body and soul. Probably orig. with the pop. song "Body and Soul."*

body-snatcher *n.* **1** An undertaker. **2** A kidnaper. **3** A stretcher-bearer. *Some W.W.II use.*

boff *v.t.* & *v.i.* To hit; to cuff, to slap; to treat roughly. 1932: ". . . Trying to boff Big Jule with his blackjack. . . ." Runyon, 130. 1950: "LaGuardia bade his cops to muss them up and boff them around on sight. . . ." W. Pegler, *synd. newsp. col.,* Apr. 10. *v.i.* **1** [taboo] To have sexual intercourse. 1937: ". . . You wouldn't even let me take time out to get boffed. . . ." Weidman, *Wholesale,* 5. Cf. **lay.** **2** To vomit. 1952: oral: "He needs to boff"—said by a bartender of a sick customer. *n.* **1** A blow, with the fist or open hand. **2** A laugh elicited from an audience, or the joke causing the laugh. 1945: "[The movie script writers are] always trying for a boff . . . a laugh. . . ." Vera Vague, quoted by Robbin Coon, AP, Jan. 22. 1952: ". . . Getting the boff, handing a laugh." The N.Y. *Times Bk. Rev.,* Oct. 5, p. 8/1. *Although probably used by show-business people much earlier, the word begins to appear in mass media c1945.* **3** Any television, radio, movie, or stage show, or any book, piece of music, or other entertainment, that pleases the audience. *Most often used to refer to a popular play or muscial comedy.*

boffo *n.* **1** A dollar. 1931: ". . . Not if you got a jernt that's worth a million boffos." J. Sayre, *Hex,* 416. 1948: "If the L[ong] I[sland] Railroad] needs money why not make the phone company split some of its extra revenue from commuters calling up to say they'll be late? Must amount to quite a few boffoes." C. B. Palmer, The N.Y. *Times Mag.,* Jan. 18, 38/4. *Note plural is either*

"—*s*" *or* "—*es*." **2** A year; esp. a one-year prison sentence. *Some underworld use since c1930.* **3** A loud laugh or a joke; a boff. **4** A very successful or popular movie, stage show, story, or other entertainment. 1950: "Betty [Grable] was signed by 20th-Fox and started her string of box-office boffos." Bob Thomas, AP, July 17. See Appendix, —o ending.   *adj.* **1** Loud; said of a laugh. 1947: "... The zany Brewsters [in the play *Arsenic and Old Lace*] and their basement cemetery still get laughs—boffo laughs." Phila. *Evening Bulletin*, May 19, 22/4. **2** Very favorable; enthusiastic; said of a critical comment or review. 1945: "... A 'boffo' *Variety* review means money in the bank." Helen Colton, *Pageant* [mag.], Apr., 71/1. *Theater use.* **3** Highly successful and popular;—said of a performer or an entertainment. 1949: "... Red-blooded boffo entertainment for both sexes." S. J. Perelman, *Listen to the Mocking Bird*, 61. **4** Slapstickish, funny, uproarious.

boffola   buffola   *n.* **1** A laugh, esp. a deep, loud laugh; a belly laugh. 1949: "This ability [to think of gags] brought out the old boffolas from coast to coast." Booton Herndon, *SEP*, May, 28, 35/1–2. *Since c1945.* **2** A joke that should or does elicit loud laughter. 1947: "All I [comedian Fred Allen] need is a funny hat and a buffola." Network radio, April 20. 1949: "The dialogue progresses inevitably toward the gag line, the old buffola." John Crosby, "Radio in Review," col. in Phila. *Eve. Bull.*, Aug. 9. *One of the most common of the "—ola" words.* See Appendix, —ola ending.

boff out   To lose one's money; to be without funds. 1956: "New money moved up to the tables as soon as a player was boffed out." J. Cannon, *Who Struck John?* 75. Cf. **tap out.**

bog-hopper   *n.* An Irishman; a person of Irish descent.

bogie   bogy   *n.* **1** A policeman. *Some underworld use; not as common in U.S. as in Eng.* **2** An enemy airplane, specif. an attacking fighter plane. *W.W.II Air Force use; more commonly = a Japanese fighter plane than a German one.* **3** In golf, a score of one point over par.

bog-pocket   *n.* A stingy or thrifty person.

bog-trotter   *n.* = **bog-hopper.**

bogue   *adj.* Bogus; false; fake. *Far-out use.*

bohn   Bohn   *n.* A translation; a pony. 1855: *DAE. Common student use c1850. From "Bohn's Classical Library," a series of translations. Obs.* Cf. **bone.**

bohunk   Bohunk   *n.* **1** [derog.] An immigrant from central Europe, usu. a Czech, Slav, Hungarian, Pole, or Austrian. *Most common c1900–c1930.* → **2** A clumsy or stupid person. **3** [derog.] Any uneducated, unskilled immigrant from central Europe. See **Hunkie.** *From "Bohemian" plus "Hungarian" reinforced by "Hunk."*

boiled   *adj.* Drunk. *With "stewed" and "fried," one of the common cooking terms = drunk.* See Appendix, Drunk.

boiled leaves   A cup of tea. *Some lunch-counter use. Never common.*

boiled rag = **boiled shirt.** 1886: *DAE.*

boiled shirt   **1** A dress shirt, usu. one with a heavily starched bosom. 1861: *DAE.* 1912: "He had arrayed himself in boiled shirt, high collar, and derby." Johnson, *Stover at Yale*, 2. *Archaic.* Cf. **fried shirt. 2** Any person or activity which is formal or lacking in human warmth. 1928: "Conversation is speech freed from the conventions and yet not arrayed in the 'boiled shirt' of formality." R. Lynd in *New Statesman*, Feb. 4. Cf. **stuffed shirt.**

boiler   *n.* **1** One who cooks as by boiling; hence an inexperienced, uninspired, or inferior cook. *Logger use.* **2** An automobile, esp. an old or dilapidated one. *c1930.* **3** A steam locomotive. 1952: "Casey [Jones] and me'd sneak a boiler out of the roundhouse an' take our girl friends fer a ride." M. Blosser, *synd. comic strip*, "Freckles," Dec. 17. *Railroad use.* **4** A tobacco pipe. *Some c1930 college use.* **5** A still. *Dial.*

boiler-maker   boilermaker   *n.* **1** A virile, sexually attractive man; a ladies' man. *Some c1910–c1925 use.* **2** A drink consisting of a jigger of whisky in a glass of beer. *The most common meaning. Colloq.* → **3** Any strong alcoholic drink. See **boilermaker's delight.**

boilermaker's delight   Fig., an alcoholic drink only suitable for the strongest of men; moonshine; inferior whisky. *Since c1910.*

boil out   To leave quickly. *Obs.*

boil up   To wash clothes. *Hobo use c1920.*

boing   boing-boing   *exclam.* An expression of appreciation or acknowledgment of and toward a sexually attractive girl or young woman. 1956: "When she [Marilyn Monroe] came in, everybody stopped doing what they were doing and their eyes went 'Boing, boing.' " Pete Martin, "The New Marilyn Monroe," *SEP*, May 5, 151. *Orig. and mainly wide W.W.II Armed Forces use, some W.W.II student use, and universally known. A W.W.II fad word, now almost obs. Can be almost lewd or complimentary, depending on the mood. The sound is almost certainly imitative of the sound a spring makes when it suddenly expands upon being relieved of any weight or pressure, and thus orig. suggested that the penis was becoming erect. In general use the suggestion is that a male's eyes are popping or springing out of his head in an approving, almost incredulous stare.* See **wolf whistle**.

boke   *n.* The nose. *Underworld use.* Cf. **beak**.

boko   *n.* = **boke**. *Never as common in U.S. as in Eng. and Australia*.

bolexed up = **bollixed up**.

Bolivar   *n.* A pistol or revolver. *Some underworld use since c1935*.

bollixed   bolaxed   *adj.* = **bollixed up**.

bollixed up   bolaxed up   bolexed up   Confused; mixed up; balled up. 1937: "Watch your script. You're getting your cues all bollixed up." Weidman, *Wholesale*, 36. *Usu. as a euphem. for "fucked up," though it implies somewhat less confusion than the latter term.*

boll weevil   boll-weevil   *n.* **1** A nonunion worker; a scab. 1950: "Bunk Johnson ran into Jelly at this time ... round in 1903 and 1904.... The longshoremen had two parades—one for the union men and one for the boll weevils, the scabs." A. Lomax, *Mr. Jelly Roll*, 105. → **2** Any unwanted fellow worker; a worker who threatens the job security of an older employee; a new worker. 1956: "To coal miners a *boll-weevil* is a new miner." *Labor's Special Lang. from Many Sources.*

bolo   *n.* **1** An unskilled rifleman. *Army use since c1930. Implying that, like a "bolo," a bullet fired by an unskilled rifleman may return to harm the shooter or those near him.* **2** In boxing, a slow, high overhand or sidearm punch, as opposed to a short, fast direct jab. 1952: "[Fighter Gil] Turner blooped a bolo to the heart of [his opponent] Jim Jennings." N.Y. *Daily Mirror*, July 8, 24/1.

boloney   baloney   bologny   *n.* **1** An inferior prize fighter. 1921: "... To bounce some boloney at this fight club." Witwer, *Leather*, 28. *Never common.* See **sausage**. **2** An uninformed, stupid, or useless person. 1937: "... You dumb baloney." Weidman, *Wholesale*, 9. *Fairly common until c1940; archaic.* **3** Nonsense; false information or talk, even if believed by the speaker; worthless or pretentious talk; tripe, bunk, hokum, hot air, blah. 1929: "... One of the young men ... dismissed the whole speech as 'a bunch of tripe.' The other ... concluded, 'Oh, of course there was a certain amount of bologny in what he said....' " Philip Curtiss, *Harper's*, Aug., 385/1. 1930: "Medical journals are largely filled with boloney." H. L. Mencken, *Amer. Mercury*, Nov., 285/2. *Also used as a one-word comment or interj. From the colloq. pronunciation of "bologna," the sausage.* **4** An automobile or truck tire. *Never common.* **5** Insulated electric cable. *Electronic and construction use.   adj.* Spurious; phoney.

bolus   *n.* A physician. *Underworld use since c1850. From "bolus" = a large pill, usu. for a horse.* Cf. **pill-pusher**.

bomb   *n.* **1** A inflammatory or startling statement. → **2** An unbelievable or unreal object or action. → **3** A conspicuous failure, esp. a performance or entertainment which receives bad reviews and public disapproval. Fig., a dud. **4** A car. *Hot-rod use since c1950.*

bomber   *n.* A marijuana cigarette; a stick. *Addict use, esp. among young and teenage addicts. Since c1945.*

bombosity   *n.* The buttocks. *Never common; some jocular c1930 use. From "bombous" = convex, reinforced by "bum."*

bomb-shell   bombshell   *n.* **1** A stunningly attractive, energetic, or sexy girl or woman [or person] whose appearance or actions attract immediate attention or enthusiasm. 1949: "Bonnie Parker was a rootin', tootin', whiskey-drinking blonde bombshell." A. Hynd, *Public Enemies*, 41. *Orig. the term implied wildness, audacity, and lust for life; but soon it was used by columnists, press agents, and the like to refer to any physically attractive female. At one time, c1935–c1940, the word was very pop. in phrase "blonde bombshell" and was applied to virtually every fair-haired actress or singer in the world of professional entertainment.* → **2** A young woman, esp. a showgirl, with a reputation for being promiscuous.

bone *n.* **1** A dollar. 1905: ". . . To see me cough up those two bones." McHugh, *Search Me*, 38. 1922: "This is the real stuff. . . . Twelve bones—if you want it." S. Lewis, *Babbitt*, reprinted in *The American Twenties*, 232. → **2** Specif., a silver dollar. *Dial. only.* **3** A diligent student. *c1860–c1910. From the Bohn publishing company, publisher of "Bohn's Classical Library."* See **bohn.** **4** A trombone. *Some jazz use, esp. c1915.* See Appendix, Shortened Words. **5** [taboo] The penis, esp. the erect penis. **6** An argument or disagreement; a task that is not carried out according to instructions and thus brings on criticism and ill feeling. *From the colloq. phrase, "I have a bone to pick with you."* *v.i.* **1** To work hard. 1841: *DAE.* → **2** To study diligently, esp. to concentrate on studying during a brief period prior to an examination. *Since c1850.* 1910: "The student 'bones' or 'crams' for the coming examination." *Rev. of Revs.,* July, 116/1. 1949: "You will simply have to bone up on your lessons." W. Pegler, *synd. newsp. col.,* Sept. 29. *The most common use.* *v.t.* **1** To desire or strive for something. *Not common.* **2** To annoy, bother, or nag a person; to dun a person for payment of a debt. 1858: *DAE.* 1950: "You boned me in front of a stranger! . . . Don't bone me!" Movie, *Asphalt Jungle.* **3** To beg or solicit from a person; to offer a person an illegal or unethical business proposition. *Underworld use.*

bone-bender *n.* A physician.

bone-breaker *n.* **1** A physician. **2** A task, job, or goal that is extremely difficult. Cf. **ball-buster.** **3** A wrestler.

bone-cracker *n.* **1** A wrestler; a bone-breaker. **2** A chiropractor or osteopath. *Not common.*

bone-crusher *n.* A wrestler.

bone-eater *n.* A dog.

bone-factory *n.* **1** A hospital. **2** A cemetery. *Primarily Eastern use.*

bone-head **bonehead** *n.* **1** A stupid person. 1920: "Four sons, all bone-heads." F. S. Fitzgerald, *This Side of Paradise*, 37. *Colloq.* → **2** A stubborn person. → **3** An error committed through stupidity. **—ed** *adj.* Stupid. *Since c1860.*

bonehead play In sports, an error caused by bad judgment.

bone orchard A cemetery. *Primarily Western use.*

bone out To study a subject or text. 1912: "Boning out the Greek?" Johnson,

Stover at Yale, 148. *Never common.* See **bohn, bone.**

bone-polisher A vicious dog. *Hobo use c1920.*

boner *n.* **1** A mistake; an error or blunder. *Has seldom, if ever, been used in U.S. with the Eng. sl. meaning, i.e., a blow with the fist on the lowest vertebra. c1830. Colloq.* Cf. **bone-head.** **2** A diligent student. *Some c1900 student use. From "bone."*

boner, pull a To make an error or blunder. 1917: *DAE.* 1929–1930: "Chris pulled a boner?" K. Brush, *Young Man*, 116. 1951: ". . . Pull a boner." *Word Study*, Feb., 3/1. See **boner.**

bones *n.pl.* **1** Dice. 1887: "To shake the bones." *New Orleans Lantern.* 1920: "They bent over the bones." F. S. Fitzgerald, *This Side of Paradise*, 91. *According to Farmer & Henley, this word was used by Chaucer in 1386. In allusion to the fact that dice were orig. made of bone.* **2** Any thin person. **3** Traditionally, the end man in a minstrel show; a nickname for any blackface comedian. *From the fact that such an entertainer often played the bones.* **4** Two short rods, such as two rib bones, used to keep a clacking rhythm as an accompaniment to music or dancing. *The bones are held loosely between adjacent fingers of one hand and clacked together by rapidly agitating the hand.* **5** Money. *From "bone" = a dollar.*

bone-shaker *n.* Any unstable or dilapidated vehicle, specif. an early model bicycle, an early model Ford automobile.

bone-top *n.* A stupid person.

bone up **1** To study. See **bone, bohn.** **2** To pay a debt. 1910: "You said you were going to clean off the whole slate with Al, sure as Turkey boned up." Johnson, *Varmint*, 58. See **bone.**

bone up on To study or review a specific subject intensively during a short period. See **bone.**

bone-yard **boneyard** *n.* A cemetery. *Since c1870.* 1957: ". . . In nice weather you [a boy and a girl] lie on a blanket out on the boneyard. . . ." Tennessee Williams, *Orpheus Descending,* I.

bonfire *n.* A cigarette, esp. a stub of a cigarette smoked by another.

bong *adj.* Excellent. *In allusion to the colloq. "to ring the bell."*

bonzer *adj.* Good; excellent; admirable. *n.* An object or action that is so well constructed or accomplished as to fit its use perfectly. *Orig. Australian sl., intro. into U.S. during W.W.II.*

boo   *n.* = **bo.**   *adj.* Excellent; remarkable; satisfying. 1952: "A teen-ager has to keep up on his slang. At the moment something that used to be known as the cat's whiskers is now called 'sly,' 'really neat,' 'the real George,' or 'deadly boo.' " H. Boyle, AP, June 30. *Cf.* **tickety-boo.**

boob   *n.* **1** A stupid person; a simpleton, a sap, one easily victimized. *Since c1900.* 1922: "There are still boobs, alack, who'd like the old-time gin-mill back." S. Lewis, *Babbitt*, reprinted in *The American Twenties,* 227. *Since c1910.* → **2** A person who is extremely innocent or too trusting for his own good. → **3** Specif., a person who is innocent politically and culturally. 1916: "You poor boob!" M. Eastman. *Pop. by H. L. Mencken c1925–c1935.* **4** A jail. *Some underworld use. From "booby hatch." In the U.S. never used in the sense of the Eng. sl. verb = to make a mistake.* **5** = **Babbitt.**

boobie   bubie   *n.* A term of endearment or affection. *Pop. by comedian Jerry Lewis c1950–1955. Seems to be, but is not, a Yiddish word. The "—ie" is the usu. affectionate diminutive ending.* See Appendix, Synthetic Words.

boobies   *n.pl.* = **boobs.**

boo-boo   *n.* **1** A dollar. 1905: "I have a hundred thousand booboos in the kick." McHugh, *Search Me,* 116. *Never common.* **2** A minor flesh wound; an accident causing such a wound. *Limited to children's use in ref. to a scratch, etc. Prominent among Jewish children in N.Y.C. Seems to be, but is not, a child's word.* → **3** A faux pas; an embarrassing mistake; in sports, a blunder or error. 1957: "The original boo-boo that started all this public confusion. . . ." H. R. King, *Harper's,* Aug., 52. *Popularized by comedian Jerry Lewis. c1950.* See Appendix, Synthetic Words.

booboos   *n.pl.* The testicles. 1951: "Catherine said, 'In the booboos. Collin, kick his old booboos.' So I did. Big Eddie's face curdled. . . ." T. Capote, *Grass Harp,* 67.

boobs   *n.pl.* The breasts. *Usu. to refer to the prominent breasts of a well-developed young woman (appreciatively) or to the sagging breasts of an elderly woman (depreciatively). The word is almost always used by a male in talking about a woman to another male, but is not taboo.*

boob trap   A nightclub. *From "boob" plus "trap," reinforced by "booby trap."* *Cf.* **boob, booby trap.**

booby hatch   *n.* **1** A police wagon used to transport arrested persons to jail. [Orig. "booby hutch," 1766: *DAE.*] *Archaic, but some underworld use as late as c1925.* → **2** A prison. → **3** An insane asylum. 1938: "If any of my friends heard you, they'd say you belonged in the booby hatch." J. T. Farrell, 167. 1956: "All that time, King [Buddy] Bolden cut hair in the booby-hatch [East Louisiana State Hospital]. . . ." S. Longstreet, *The Real Jazz Old and New,* 11. *The only meaning in use now. Universally known.*

booby trap   **1** A hidden explosive device triggered to a common object, in order to kill or injure a person who is expected to touch or handle the object. *Wide use during W.W.II.* → **2** Any plot, plan, or situation that may lead to death, injury, distress, embarrassment, or financial disaster.

boodle   *n.* **1** An entire lot; a large number or amount of anything. See **kit and boodle; caboodle.** **2** Counterfeit money. 1858: *DAE. Archaic underworld use.* → **3** Bribe money; money stolen from public funds; esp. graft. 1893: "Such terms as 'boodle' . . . belong to the more recent unsavory imbecilities of politics." Anon. in *Atlan. Mon.,* Mar., 425/2. → **4** A petty, grafting jail official; a corrupt politician. *Cf.* **boodler.** → **5** Money. 1884: *DAE.* **6** Cake, candy, ice cream, or similar food. *Usu. delicacies sent to prisoners, students, or soldiers by friends or relatives.* *v.i. & v.t.* To neck. *Some c1940 student use.* **—r** *n.* **1** A corrupt politician. 1887: *DAE. Archaic by c1925.* **2** A hobo who lives at the public expense by spending the winter in jail. *Hobo use.*

boog   *v.i., v.t.* To dance. 1941: ". . . To go booging." *Life,* Jan. 27, 78. *Not common; from "boogie-woogie."*

boogerboo   *v.i., v.t.* To pretend; to fake. *n.* An insincere person, a phoney. *Some Negro use.*

boogie   *n.* **1** [taboo] Syphilis, esp. secondary syphilis. **2** [derog.] A Negro. **3** = **boogie-woogie.** **4** An enemy aircraft, esp. a fighter plane. *Wide W.W.II use, esp. in reference to Japanese fighter planes.* *adj.* [derog.] Negro.

boogie-woogie   *n.* **1** Secondary syphilis. *Archaic. Southern Negro use; quite old.* See **boogie.** **2** In jazz, a fast blues with an iterative bass figure played in double time, i.e., eight beats to the measure, associated with the Kansas City mode of jazz. 1928: "Pine Top's Boogie Woogie." Title of a jazz song composed by "Pine Top" Smith, one of the earliest boogie-woogie pianists. 1956: "Jimmy Yancey as much as anyone created the boogie-woogie blues, and his followers—Meade Lux Lewis, Pine Top Smith, Albert Ammons and others—carried on the job." S. Longstreet, *The Real Jazz Old and New*, 37. **3** Loosely, any jazz, jive, swing. *Since c1935.* *v.i.* To enjoy oneself thoroughly. *Some Negro use.*

boogily-woogily *adv.* Confused; disorderly. 1956: "*Boogily-woogily* is not to be confused with *boogie-woogie*, but means pell-mell." S. Longstreet, *The Real Jazz Old and New*, 148. *Not common.*

book *n.* **1** A one-year prison sentence. *Most freq. underworld use until c1930. Usu. "a book."* **2** A life sentence in prison. *Most freq. underworld use since c1930. Usu. "the book."* → **3** Any maximum or extreme punishment, penalty, or criticism. See **throw the book at [someone]**. **4** = **bookie**; a bookie's establishment.

bookie *n.* A horse-racing bookmaker. 1909: "Did the bookies get you?" G. Chester, *Bobby Burnit*, 9. 1949: "The super had been in office fourteen years without having a single bookie door nailed shut in his territory without his personal consent. No man can manage that without the help of heaven and the city's finest precinct captains." N. Algren, *Man with the Golden Arm*, 8f.

book keeper *n.* A flagman. *Railroad use.*

books, hit the To study, esp. to study hard. *A colloq. among students.*

boom-boom *n.* **1** A bowel movement. *Part of young children's euphem. bathroom vocabulary.* **2** A pistol or small-caliber rifle. *Some W.W.II Army use.*

boomer *n.* **1** A migratory, itinerant, or transient worker. → **2** A railroad worker, logger, construction crew member, or other worker who changes jobs often; a worker who works steadily for one employer but on projects far removed from his own home. **3** A ladies' man; a youth preoccupied with pursuing women. *Usu. used as a nickname; most common c1930.*

booms *n.pl.* A set of drums, specif. as used to play jazz. *Some cool and far-out use, not common.*

boom stick *n.* **1** An itinerant railroad worker, a railroad worker who often

moves from job to job or from one region to another. *Hobo use.* **2** A gun. **—s** *n.pl.* A pair of drumsticks, esp. as used by a jazz or rock-and-roll musician. *Some synthetic jazz use; some teenage rock-and-roll use since c1955.*

boondock *v.i.* To neck. *Never common. From the inference that necking, usu. in a parked car, is done in isolated places.* See **boondocks**. *adj.* Used or suitable for rough outdoor use, such as hiking. 1950: "Today Marines use boondock clothes and boondock shoes for hikes and maneuvers." Harvey L. Miller, *Word Study*, Oct., 7/1. **—er** *n.* One who likes to live in, or who is stationed in, a jungle or tropical swamp. *W.W.II USN and U.S. Marine use.* See Appendix, —er ending. **—ers** *n.pl.* Shoes suitable for rough outdoor use, specif. heavy-duty G.I. shoes. *W.W.II Marine use.* **—s** *n.pl.* An isolated forest, swamp, mountain, or jungle region; uncivilized country; wild terrain. *W.W.II Armed Forces use. From the Tagalog "bundok" = mountain.*

boondoggle *n.* A gadget, a whatchamacallit, a thingamajig. *Not common.* *v.i.* To do unnecessary or trivial work at public expense. *Fairly common c1930.*

Boone Boon *n.* A talent scout. *Theater use. Not common.* See **pull a Daniel Boone**.

booshwah *n.* = **bushwa**.

boost *v.i. & v.t.* **1** To steal, esp. by shoplifting; to pilfer. 1958: "Jeez, when I slept on park benches and boosted from the A & P, I did it because I had to." H. Gold, *The Beat Mystique*, 84. *Since c1915.* **2** To make a false bid over a real one, as is sometimes done by an auctioneer's accomplice to raise the bidding on an auctioned item. **3** To compliment, praise, recommend, endorse. or encourage someone or something. *Colloq.* **—er** *n.* **1** A shoplifter or thief, often female. 1925: "The lowest type of thief is the booster. . . ." McLennan, *Collier's*, Aug. 8. 1943: "Got a booster for you. The chunky girl in blue at the lace counter." D. Hammett, *Assistant Murderer*, 124. **2** A pitchman's assistant who pretends to buy in order to start real buying; a shill. **3** An enthusiast; one who admires and habitually praises a person, place, or thing. See Appendix, —er endings.

boot *v.t.* **1** To kick someone or something. *Colloq.* **2** To discharge; to fire; to sack. 1907: " 'To fire out,' which latterly has become . . . 'to fire,' is . . . more vivid than 'to sack,' or 'to boot.' " *Living*

Age, July, 117/1. **3** To criticize or give a person a bad recommendation. **4** To make a specific error or blunder; to ruin something. 1951: "As one who 'boots' [misspells] a word now and then, I'm glad to report that . . . youngsters are . . . boning up on their spelling. . . ." Cedric Adams, *New Yorker*, Dec. 1, 191. **5** To lose an opportunity. *From the image of kicking away one's chances of success, reinforced by the specif. baseball use = to kick a baseball while attempting to pick it up.* **6** To introduce one person to another. → **7** To introduce a person to the facts concerning a specif. situation; to explain something.   *n.* **1** A USN or Marine recruit; a newly enlisted sailor. *Colloq. Orig. USN use. In ref. to the leggings once worn during training; the word has remained pop. through W.W.I and W.W.II.* See **boot it. 2** In baseball, an error. 1951: "[Shortstop Alvin] Dark atoned for his boot by making a good play on Kiner's slow roller through the box. . . ." Jim McCulley, N.Y. *Daily News*, Aug. 30, C201. **3** A social or business error or blunder. *Not common.* **4** A thrill, a pleasing or exciting sensation; a kick. 1943: "You don't get much of a boot out of that, do you?" Chandler, *Lady in Lake*, 183. 1951: "You schoolteachers must get a big boot out of doing different things every vacation to earn extra money!" Eldon Dedini, *Esquire*, Dec., 114. *Not as common as "kick." Becoming archaic.* Cf. **bang. 5** A handsome, socially prominent male student, one who gives the coeds a boot. *Not common.* **6** A discharge or dismissal. 1939–40: "I would give the boot to that rum-pot you have now. . . ." O'Hara, *Pal Joey*, 23. **7** An introduction.   *adj.* Newly recruited, new on a job; inexperienced.

boot, get the   To be fired from one's job. *Fig. = to be kicked out.* Cf. **boot.**

boot, the   *n.* An act or instance of dismissal, either by an employer or a friend; the termination of a relationship. 1955: "He had given Judy the boot, because that was his way—no sense in higgling around. . . . No girl liked the idea of being given the boot. They liked to *give* the boot, not to *receive* it. If Judy, for example, had happened to give *him* the boot. . . ." C. Willingham, *To Eat a Peach*, 79; 81.

boot camp   The first training center to which naval recruits go for their initial training. *Colloq.* See **boot, boot it.**

booter   *n.* **1** = **bootlegger.** 1928: "There must be 5,000 booters on Manhattan Island alone. . . ." Mencken, *Amer. Mercury*, July, 295/1. *Never common.* **2** A soccer player. *Not common.*

bootie   *n.* = **bootlegger.** 1929: "That new bootie . . . carries a powerful line of hooch!" *SEP*, Apr. 13, 76. *Some c1920 use.*

boot it   **1** To walk or march. *Since c1900.* **2** To make a mistake or blunder. See **boot.**

bootleg   *n.* **1** Coffee, esp. inferior coffee. *Since c1915. A little Armed Forces and prison use.* **2** Bootleg liquor. *Since c1920. Not common.*   *v.t.* To carry the ball deceptively, as in football and other sports. **—ger**   *n.* A dealer in or seller of illicit liquors. *Colloq.* See Appendix, —er endings.

bootlick   *v.t.* To curry favor, as with a superior or teacher. *Most common c1900; mainly student use.*   *n.* One who bootlicks. **—er**   *n.* = **bootlick.**

boot one   To make a mistake or blunder, esp. in baseball. 1952: "Berry [an umpire] . . . has never made a wrong decision, or as the trade says, 'booted one.' " Gilbert Millstein, The N.Y. *Times Mag.*, Sept. 14, 19/1. See **boot.**

boots laced, have [one's]   To be aware. *Not common.*

booze   *n.* **1** Any type of liquor. c1303: "Bouse." Farmer & Henley. 1890: *DAE*. 1914: ". . . On the booze." "Hit the booze." S. Lewis, *Our Mr. Wrenn*, 18, 145. *Colloq. Said to have been popularized in U.S. by Philadelphia distiller, E. G. Booze, c1840.* **2** A liquor-drinking spree. 1894 [1891]: ". . . Gay cats who've been on a booze." J. Flynt. *Never common.*   *v.i.* To drink liquor or to go on a drinking spree; esp., to spend a relaxing afternoon or evening slowly drinking whisky or beer and conversing with one's fellow drinkers. *Not common.* **—d**   *adj.* Drunk. 1887: "By getting boozed." *Lantern*, New Orleans. *Not common.* **—ry**   *n.* A saloon; esp. a speakeasy. *Main use c1915–c1930.*

boozed up   *adj.* Drunk. *Common 19th cent. sl. expression; still used.* See **boozed.**

booze-fighter   *n.* **1** One who habitually drinks large quantities of whisky; a drunkard. 1930: ". . . Among American governors the booze-fighters are plainly the best." Mencken, *Amer. Mercury*, Sept., 127/1. *Since c1910. The most common of the "-fighter" words, for a list of which see Appendix.* **2** A narcotic addict. *Not common.*

booze hound = **booze-fighter.**

booze up To drink liquor; to fill up on liquor.

boozy *adj.* Drunk. 1737: *Pa. Gazette. Obs. by c1900.*

bop *v.t.* **1** To strike, esp. with the fist. 1932: "Dave ... reaches across the table and bops One-eyed Solly right in the mouth...." Runyon, 65 (2). 1953: "Nina reached out and bopped her on the head." Hal Boyle, AP, Feb. 3. *Common since c1930.* **2** To kill. *c1935 underworld use.* *n.* **1** A blow; a hit. *Since c1930.* **2** A form and style of jazz music characterized by triadal chords with the first and third notes played an octave below the second and a little after it. The last two notes of a phrase thus often resemble the vocal sound "re-bop" or "be-bop," from which the word "bop" is commonly thought to have evolved. *Prob. from the Sp. "arriba" = up, which Afro-Cuban musicians shout to each other while playing, by way of encouragement. Often shortened to "riba," its use is directly equivalent to the U.S. "go" and "go man go." Thus Sp. "arriba" → Sp. "riba" → U.S. sl. "rebop" → "bop."* The music is also characterized by syncopation in which the beat precedes the melody, wind and wood instruments playing in a flat tone, the use of short double and triple notes replacing longer notes, sudden changes in the octave or register, and sudden changes in key and rhythm, sometimes accompanied by scat lyrics. Bop was the most modern and popular jazz style c1946–c1953; it was then superseded by "cool." It was the first of the cool jazz forms consistently based on chord progressions and having an intellectual appeal. *The second quotation below gives a brief history of the orig. of bop music.* 1950: "Bop is 'cool' jazz in contrast to the 'hot' variety of the swing or Dixieland schools." *Am. Sp.,* 25, 215. 1956: "Bop ... grew from the main body of jazz and a lot of people had to do with it, Billy Eckstine for one. Not just as a singer but as a bandman too. His band was once a part of Earl Hines' group when he reorganized it in 1934. Dizzy Gillespie joined the band, too, and Dizzy did as much as anyone to make it bop.... He and Dizzy made some records for Bluebird [record company label]—*Woodyn You, Disorder at the Border, Rainbow Mist*—that settled bop as a pattern. Billy Eckstine's band was pure bop. Dizzy [with Charlie Parker] led a band of his own playing bop in 1945.... A man named Tadd Dameron, often called The Disciple, expanded bop.... He wrote the music the bop players used, arranging new and old stuff his way." S. Longstreet, *The Real Jazz Old and New,* 174. **3** A fight between members of rival teenage street gangs, a rumble. *adj.* Of, by, for, or pertaining to devotees of bop, their attitudes, modes, fashions, and fads. 1956: "... Dizzy Gillespie and his followers got into bop uniform. It called for real home-grown goatees on the chin ["bop" beards], horn-rimmed glasses ["bop" glasses], and berets." S. Longstreet, *The Real Jazz Old and New,* 175. *v.i. & v.t.* To fight, esp. to fight as a member of a teenage street gang, against a rival gang; to fight a rival teenage street gang. 1958: "You gotta go on bopping (gang fighting) and hanging around street corners all your life?" "A Gang Leader's Redemption," *Life,* April 28, 78. *Teenage street gang use.*

bop glasses *n.* Horn-rimmed spectacles. 1958: "The horn rims of the intellectual came to be known as bop glasses." H. Gold, *The Beat Mystique,* 84. *The dress of the bop musician often included heavy horn-rimmed glasses, esp. glasses with tinted lenses. Pop. by Dizzy Gillespie, an early bop musician, c1946. Heavy horn rims for spectacles have regained some general popularity owing to the bop fad.*

boppo *n.* A one-year prison sentence; one year of a longer prison sentence. *Underworld use, c1935. Cf.* **boffo.**

borax *n.* **1** Cheap or inferior material or merchandise. *Orig. used by Jewish immigrants.* → **2** Lies; exaggeration; misrepresentation; horse shit. **3** Any gaudy object, colorful knickknack, souvenir, or small cheap item. *adj.* **1** Cheaply made; of inferior quality. **2** Gaudy; showing bad taste. *exclam.* An expression of incredulity at an exaggeration, lie, triviality, or unbelievably cheap or gaudy item or action. *Not common.*

border, the *n.* The U.S.–Mexican border. c1940: "South of the Border." Title of pop. song. 1952: "BORDER is a proper noun to many Texans, and it does not refer to the border of the tablecloth or the garden. Naturally, it is the Texas-Mexican border. The Rio Grande country." J. Randolph, *Texas Brags,* 55.

borscht circuit, the Summer vacation hotels in the Catskill Mountains.

Theater use. Many of these hotels have a predominantly Jewish clientele, and borscht (beet and potato soup) is associated with their European ancestry. The hotels constitute a circuit in which many well-known entertainers perform. Since c1935.

bosh   *v.t.* To annoy, disturb; to ruin; to put the kibosh on [something]. *Never common in U.S.*   *n.* Nonsense; blah. *Colloq.*

boss   *n.* See **crumb boss, straw boss.**

bossy   Bossy   *n.* **1** A cow. *From the affectionate name traditionally given cows by farmers.* → **2** Beef. *Since c1930. Mainly lunch-counter use. "A slice of bossy" = an order of roast beef; "Bossy in bowl" = beef stew.*   *adj.* Dominating; autocratic. *Colloq.*

Boston coffee   **1** Tea. *In allusion to the "Boston tea party" of 1773.* **2** A mild drink that is half coffee and half cream or milk; café au lait. *Because Boston is assoc. in the popular mind with an effete way of life. Neither usage is common.*

Boston strawberries   Beans. 1884: "'One plate of Boston strawberries,' yelled that functionary [a waitress]." N.Y. *Weekly,* June 23. *Lunch-counter use. Not common. Because Boston is traditionally famous for its beans.*

bot   *n.* A bottle. 1910: "How many bots did you bring?" Johnson, *Varmint,* 295. *Never used in U.S. in Australian sense of "a habitual borrower."* See Appendix, Shortened Words.

botch = **potch.**

both hands   **1** A prison sentence of ten years. *Underworld use, c1935. From the number of fingers on both hands.* → **2** Ten.

bottle   *n.* **1** A glass insulator. *c1900. Railroad lineman use; later telephone lineman use.* **2** An electronic vacuum tube. *c1925. Early radio and radio amateur use. Obs.* **3** A bottle of whisky. 1953: "Let's take a bottle to the bash...." *Oral,* student at Ohio State University. *The most common use. In the U.S. the word is never used in the Eng. sl. sense = a lecture or reprimand.* See **giggle bottle, hit the bottle.**   **—d**   *adj.* Drunk. *Not as common in the U.S. as in Eng.* See Appendix, Drunk.

bottle, hit the   sauce, hit the   booze, hit the   redeye, hit the   hit the [etc.]   To drink alcoholic beverages frequently or habitually, usu. to excess; to take one or more large drinks; to drink from or of whisky or wine; to become drunk. 1921: "That was the

first ... time the Kid hit the redeye. ..." Witwer, *Leather,* 116. 1939–40: "... He almost began hitting the sauce...." O'Hara, *Pal Joey,* 37. 1943: "... With all the booze he hits." Wolfert, *Underworld,* 138. 1944: "He gave me the bottle, and I drank eagerly.... I hit the bottle again, hard." Shulman, *Feather Merchants,* 128. 1949: "... A dame who hits the bottle on the sneak." Billy Rose, *synd. newsp. col.,* Aug. 19. *"Hit the bottle" is very common.*

bottle baby   **1** An infant fed from a bottle rather than suckled. *Colloq.* **2** An alcoholic. 1958: "Bottle baby—A derelict, a Bowery bum." G. Y. Wells, *Station House Slang.*

bottle club   A private drinking club; specif., an association of people, often unknown to one another, for the sole purpose of providing themselves with liquor and a place to drink it after the legal closing hours of public bars or in a city or county where the public sale of alcoholic beverages is prohibited. 1956: "District Attorney Hogan's special task force raided the Gold Key, one of the better-known after hours bottle clubs [in N.Y.C.]." N.Y. *Post,* Feb. 10, 5. See **bottle.**

bottle-man   *n.* A drunkard or habitual drinker. 1944: "A profound bottle-man." Fowler, *Good Night,* 87.

bottom   *n.* The buttocks. 1949: "..The murmuring rumdums were being let out of their cells to wash, spit, and scratch their hairy bottoms." N. Algren, *Man with the Golden Arm,* 20. *Since c1790.*

bottom man   The person with the least seniority, skill, experience, authority, or importance in a specif. group. 1956: "Joseph (Joe Peelo) Carlino voiced compassion yesterday for the late Abe Telvi, whom Carlino, as bottom man on a totem pole of intermediaries, enlisted for the acid attack on labor columnist Victor Riesel." N. Abrams & N. Patterson, N.Y. *Daily News,* Nov. 16, 5. *Almost always as part of the phrase "bottom man on the totem pole."*

bottom's up [taboo] = **dog fashion.** *A facetious play on the common drinking expression "bottoms up."*

boudoir   *n.* An Army squad tent. *Some jocular W.W.II Army use.*

bounce   *v.i.* To fail of payment by a bank;—said of a check. 1954: "The pay checks had bounced." W. R. & F. K. Simpson, *Hockshop,* 269. *Generally speaking, a check bounces because there are not enough funds in the payer's account to*

cover it. Cf. **rubber check.**   *v.t.,v.i.*
1 Lit. and fig., to throw or kick out of a
place; to expel, as from college or a
classroom; to eject or expel forcibly, or
to be ejected or expelled. 1876: Thornton.
1877: *DAE.* 1887: "Tommy got bounced
out of a picnic...." *Lantern,* New
Orleans. 1929–30: "I was bounced out
of college...." K. Brush, *Young Man,*
18. 1939–40: "...Threaten to get me
bounced out of town...." O'Hara, *Pal
Joey,* 14. 1948: "...You may be
bounced out [of a night club]." Lait-
Mortimer, *N.Y. Confidential,* 221. *A
prime example of a sl. word derived from
the standard image of an inanimate
object and applied to a person, in this
case the image of a ball that bounces when
thrown.* **2** To discharge; to fire from
a job; to be so discharged or fired. 1876:
DAE. Still fairly common. **3** To try to
influence [a person] by flattery. *Univ.
use c1925; obs.* **4** To pay [a bill]. 1951:
"Knowin' you gals have to bounce for
this [soft drink] sure improves the
flavor!" Merrill Blosser, "Freckles,"
synd. newsp. comic strip, Oct. 18.   *n.*
1 Pep; energy; vitality. 1958: "Occasionally a ringer for Mark Twain's Colonel
Mulberry Sellers, he is also himself, a
man of curious learning and unfailing
bounce." W. Havighurst in *N.Y. Her.
Trib.,* bk. rev. section, Apr. 6, 1. **2** In
jazz, a lively tempo; a tune customarily
played in such a tempo. 1956: "*Bounce*
is a buoyant beat.*" S. Longstreet,
The Real Jazz Old and New, 149.   **—r**
n. **1** A tough, burly man employed to
throw unwelcome people out of a public
place, as a theater, hotel, saloon, or
dance hall; occasionally the one who is
thrown out. 1886: *Lantern,* New Orleans.
1888: *DAE.* 1940: "He had bouncer
written all over him." Chandler, *Farewell,* 4. *From the standard image of
"bounce," perhaps reinforced by the Eng.
sl. "bounce" = a remarkable specimen.*
2 A check written against a bank
account that does not contain enough
funds to pay the amount. 1930: "...He
slips me a bouncer...." *Amer. Mercury,*
Dec., 454. **3** A forged check. *Underworld
use.* **4** A railroad train caboose. *Railroad
use.*
bounce, the   *n.* **1** An act or instance
of dismissal, esp. from a public place;
any forcible ejection of a person from a
public place. Cf. **bum's rush, the
heave-ho. 2** Expulsion; a discharge.
1877: *DAE.* 1926: "They gave me the
grand bounce." Schwesinger, *Jour. of*

Applied Psych., 258. Cf. **Hollywood
kiss off, kiss off.**
bouncy-bouncy   *n.* [taboo] The act
or an instance of coitus. *Some jocular use.*
See Appendix, Reduplications.
bovine extract   Milk. *Prob. synthetic.*
bowl   *n.* **1** An outdoor stadium or
arena, esp. a football stadium. *From the
shape, often like a bowl. Colloq.* **2** An
order of a bowl of soup. *Very common
lunch-counter use.* **3** The world; the
globe. *Maritime use.* "Around the bowl"
= *around the world.* See **fish-bowl.**
bowlegs   *n. & n.pl.* A cavalryman;
the cavalry. *Army use, archaic.*
bow-wow   bowwow   *n.* **1** A dog.
1950: "The country is going to the bow-
wows." Billy Rose, *synd. newsp. col.,*
Aug. 23. *Baby talk; very old.* **2** A sausage,
a frankfurter, a "dog." *Since c1900. Jocular use.* **3** A person in authority; a boss or
superior. *Since c1925. Archaic. Because
such a person can bark at underlings.*
4 A gun. *From the common use in sensational fiction of the word "bark" to describe
a gun's report.*   **—s**   *n.pl.* The
feet; the dogs.   *adj.* Beautiful; perfect; remarkable. 1932: "He saw an
athletically built blonde who was just
bow-wows, the kind to look at and
weep." J. T. Farrell, 122. *Analogous to
"the cat's meow," but see* **whistle bait.**
bowzed   *adj.* Drunk. 1737: "Bowz'd."
Pa. Gazette. Obs. See Appendix, Drunk.
bowzered   *adj.* Drunk. *Archaic.* See
Appendix, Drunk.
box   *n.* **1** A coffin. 1954: "Personally,
I'll believe he's [Jesse James] dead when
the box is shut and covered up." W.
Henry, *Death of a Legend,* 66. *Colloq.*
2 A safe; a vault. *Common underworld
use.* **3** [taboo] The vagina. 1954: "I didn't
realize that the experience [masturba-
tion] was akin to intercourse without
the 'box.' " H. K. Fink, *Long Journey,*
14. **4** Any stringed instrument, specif. a
guitar, c1930, or a piano, c1955; an
accordion. 1957: "Box—Piano." E.
Horne, *For Cool Cats and Far-Out
Chicks. Jive and cool use.* **5** The mouth;
the mouth and larynx; the voice "box."
1951: "First crack outa Don's box is
'What is with you, Sonny?' " A. Kober
in *New Yorker,* May, 12, 32/2. **6** A
camera; specif. a simple camera in the
shape of a box with a preset lens opening
and exposure time. 1954: "Photographers
kept running in yelling, 'Quick, gimme
my box!' " W. R. & F. K. Simpson,
Hockshop, 43. **7** An ice box; a refrigerator.
Colloq. See Appendix, Shortened Words.

8 A phonograph. **9** The trailer of a truck. *Truck driver use.* **10** = **pad.** *Some cool and far-out use.* **11** A police telephone operator. 1958: "Boxes—Policemen assigned to the switchboard for call boxes." G. Y. Wells, *Station House Slang. Police use.* —**er** *n.* A railroad freight or box car. *Hobo use c1920.*

box, go home in a To die or be killed.

box, in a In difficulty or trouble; in a dilemma. 1864: *DAE.* 1934: "Suppose I walk out on you, and you get in a box?" Chandler, *Finger Man,* 6. 1953: "Now we are in an awful box." H. Breit, N.Y. *Times Bk. Rev.,* Aug. 9, 8/3.

box, in the [taboo] Having sexual intercourse; said of a man. See **box.**

—**box** See Appendix, Suffixes and Suffix Words.

boxcar box-car *n.* **1** A large freight-carrying plane; a large four-engine bomber. *Some W.W.II Air Force use.* **2** Whisky. *Some c1920 use.* *adj.* Long, high, as in "long odds," "high odds." *Mainly racetrack use; from the high numbers freq. seen on the sides of railroad freight cars.* —**s** *n.pl.* **1** In craps, a throw of double-6, i.e., a throw in which each dice turns up a 6; the highest number in craps, a 12. **2** Shoes, esp. large shoes.

boxcars, grab an armful of To jump on a moving freight train in order to get free transportation. *c1915. Hobo use.*

box man 1 A specialist in opening locked safes; a safe-cracker. 1930: "A notorious safe, or 'box' man. . . ." Lavine, *Third Degree,* 224. **2** A professional dealer in the game of blackjack or 21. *Because orig. the cards were drawn from a box.* → **3** A gambling-house employee, as a cashier or croupier, directly involved with a gambling game. 1956: "The box men, who are the cashiers of the tables. . . ." J. Cannon, *Who Struck John?* 72.

box of dominoes The mouth. *Not common.*

box of teeth An accordion. 1956: "Words that jazzmen don't use much, but which most people think are real jazz words . . . *box of teeth* for an accordion." S. Longstreet, *The Real Jazz Old and New,* 150.

boy *n.* **1** [derog.] A male Negro of any age. 1952: "'Don't call me *boy,*' said the Negro. 'I'm as old as you, if not older.'" L. Hughes, *Laughing to Keep from Crying,* 12. → **2** Any menial servant, regardless of age, working in a public

place; a porter, elevator operator, or the like. **3** A male who plays the female role in a homosexual relationship; a catamite; any effeminate man. Cf. **peg boy.**

— **boy** See Appendix, Suffixes and Suffix Words.

boy friend A girl's or young woman's sweetheart. 1922: ". . . Having left her 'boy friend' at or near the door." Phila. *Eve. Bulletin,* Mar. 8. *Colloq.*

boyo *n.* A fellow, a youth or adult male. *Almost always in direct address to a friend, but not a close friend, and usu. in "me boyo."* 1951: "And we can't afford to wait much longer, me boyo." S. Longstreet, *The Pedlocks,* 75.

boys, the *n.pl.* **1** Men, esp. the drinking and poker companions of the speaker and the like. **2** A gang of hoodlums or organized criminals.

boys uptown, the 1 The organized political bosses of a city or district. *From Tammany Hall, the N.Y.C. Democratic organization, which has its headquarters in uptown Manhattan.* → **2** Any group of influential or notorious criminals; influential criminals. 1956: "The 22-year-old Telvi, according to Carlino, was 'tricked, lied to, and swindled' into blinding Riesel. The tricksters, said Carlino, were 'the boys uptown,' not yet identified in the conspiracy prosecution testimony, who sponsored the attack." N. Abrams & N. Patterson, N.Y. *Daily News,* Nov. 16, 5.

bozo *n.* **1** A man; fellow; guy; esp. a large, rough man or one with more brawn than brains. 1934: "Drive the heap, bozo!" Chandler, *Finger Man,* 95. 1951: "The Battlin' Bozos of Company B." Advt. for movie, *Breakthrough. From Sp. dial. "boso" (from "vosotros") = you (pl.), which resembles a direct address.* **2** An army recruit. *Some W.W.II Army use.*

boz-woz *n.* Bragging; excessive talk. *Carnival use. Obs. Prob. of imitative orig., allied to "buzz."* See Appendix, Reduplications.

bra *n.* A brassière. *Since c1920. Colloq.* See Appendix, Shortened Words.

brace *v.t.* **1** To accost a person and beg or solicit money from him; to ask for or borrow money from a person. 1939: "This pan handler came up to me and braced me and said I look as if I had a warm heart and I gave him a two-bit piece." J. O'Hara, *Pal Joey,* 39. 1951: "The money I'd figured I would be making from Black Tony. . . . I'd even had it in mind to brace him for enough

to start me off on my own." *I, Mobster,*
43. → 2 To accost or meet a person in
order to accuse him of a misdeed, to
challenge him, or to arrest him; to find
and confront someone. 1951: "When I
braced the guy he proved that Decker
had paid him back." Spillane, *Big Kill,*
62. 1952: "Two patrolmen had spotted
Willie. When braced, Willie had naturally denied his identity." *Time,* Mar. 3,
22/1.   *n.* An extremely exaggerated
posture of standing to attention. *Some
Armed Forces and military academy use.*
—r   *n.* A drink of liquor. 1920: "And
later she made use of [this trouble]—
especially after several astounding bra-
cers." F. S. Fitzgerald, *This Side of
Paradise,* 4.

brace, take a   To improve; usu. said
of an athlete or gambler.

bracelets   *n. pl.* A pair of handcuffs.
1929: "You can't put no bracelets on
me." Burnett, *Little Caesar,* 143. 1950:
"Iron bracelets." Starnes, *And When
She Was Bad,* 183. *Since before 1900.*

brad   *n.* A small saw, such as a
prisoner might use in an attempt to cut
his handcuffs. *Perh. back slang from
"darb(ies)"* = *manacles. Archaic.* See Appendix, Back Slang.

brag-rags   *n.pl.* Ribbons representing military decorations and campaign
medals. See Appendix, Rhyming Slang.

brain   *n.* **1** A good student; an
intelligent or intellectual person; a
thinker or scholar. 1941: "The names of
brains and grinds are flaunted before the
bored student body." *Dict. of Exeter
Lang.,* 9. 1952: "The publicity of being
a brain did not further her movie
career as a glamor girl." Bob Thomas,
AP, Jan. 14. **2** An electronic computer;
any complex navigational unit, usu. containing an electronic computer. **3** A
detective. *Some underworld use.*   *v.t.*
To hit someone on the top of the head, as
with a club.   **—ery**   *n.* A university. 1895: W. A. Merril in APA
[*Journal*], July, lxix. *Obs.* See Appendix,
—ery ending.   **—s**   *n. sing.* **1** A
train conductor. *Some railroad use.* **2** A
ship's officer. *Some maritime use.* **3** Anyone in authority, a boss; an official.
—y   *adj.* Intelligent; intellectual. 1874:
DAE. Colloq.

brain-box   *n.* **1** The head. **2** The
caboose of a freight train. *Some railroad
use.* **3** The pilot house on a river towboat.
Bissell, *The Monongahela,* 217.

brain child   **1** Any product of one's
intellect or imagination, as a plan,

invention, work of art, or the like.
Colloq. **2** A good student; a brain. *Not
common.*

brain picker   One who develops,
exploits, or profits from the ideas or
artistic concepts of others. 1950: "Whatever he [Jelly Roll Morton] played,
however, it had to be good and it had
to be Morton. He had nothing but
scorn for brain pickers and imitators."
A. Lomax, *Mr. Jelly Roll,* 100. *Colloq.*

brain storm   A sudden idea, usu. one
that leads to action or the solution of a
problem; a brilliant and spontaneous
insight; a good idea.

brain tablet   A cigarette. *Some Western use.*

brainwash   brain wash   *v.t.* **1** To
induce an attitudinal change in a person,
usu. a captive, by means of psycho-
educational methods, sometimes supplemented by drugs and physical coercion.
1953: "This Red label makes us feel like
criminals. We are all completely innocent. I never even heard the term
'brainwash' before I got back home."
A U.S. prisoner of war in Korea after his
release, quoted by AP, May 4. *This form
of psycho-educative conditioning developed
in the USSR, based upon the original
work of Pavlov with conditioned reflexes
of dogs.* → **2** To change another's opinion;
to convince someone of something.   *n.*
A conversion from one belief to another;
persuasion.

brain wave   = **brain storm.**   1934:
"Lou had a brain wave. He offered the
boy a C note to let him drive the cab into
San Angelo." Chandler, *Finger Man,* 23.
1951: "I get a brain wave." *I, Mobster,*
14.

brakie   brakey   *n.* A railroad
brakeman, esp. on a freight train. *Hobo
use since c1885; railroad use since c1910.
Not now as common as "shack."*

bran   *n.* A bran muffin; an order of a
bran muffin. *Lunch-counter use in relaying an order.*

brannigan   branigan   *n.* **1** A spree.
1928: "He may seek escape by going on
prolonged crossword puzzle brannigans."
B. de Casseres in *Amer. Mercury,* May,
100/1. 1943: "This party was a stag
dinner and brannigan." H. A. Smith,
Putty Knife, 146. → **2** A loud quarrel,
row, or fracas; a fight; noisy and violent
confusion. 1949: ". . . A violent brannigan
they'd had because he kidded her." Burnett, *Jungle,* 120. 1951: ". . . Wave after
wave of ugly vituperation [in Con-
gress]. . . . Republicans and Democrats

alike are guilty of this branigan." P. Edson, AP, Aug. 30.

brass *n.* **1** Impudence; effrontery. *Since Elizabethan times. Colloq.* **2** Money. *c1750–c1875. Obs.* **3** Cheap, imitation, or fake jewelry. *Hobo, circus, pitchman, and underworld use.* **4** Military officers, esp. high-ranking military officers; a military officer. *Often preceded by a sl. adj. = high-ranking, such as "heavy," "top," "big," etc.* 1949: "Top Navy Brass Hits at [Naval budget] Slashes." Headline, Syracuse (N.Y.) *Post-Standard*, Oct. 13/1. 1949: "Hamlet, like the G.I., hated the guts of the high brass." "Many a G.I. hated the brass and the enemy [equally]." J. B. Douds in *CEA Critic*, Nov., 3/2. *Common during and since W.W.II. From the officers' brass insignia, but see* **brass collar, brass hat.** → **5** Military authority. → **6** High-ranking civilian police officials. 1949: "The top police brass spreads out a hot carpet for the local cops." Phila. *Bulletin*, Sept. 14, 4/1. → **7** An official; officials; influential people; persons in authority; executives.

brass collar A railway official. *Some railroad use c1930.*

brassed-off **brassed off** *adj.* Fed up; bored. *Some W.W.II Air Force use, from the common Royal Air Force sl.*

brass hat **1** A military officer, esp. a staff officer. *Some W.W.I use, from Brit. Army sl. Some W.W.II use, but superseded by "brass."* → **2** An official; any important or influential person; one in authority, a boss. 1935: "The brass hats of the press call this the fascination of the game." *Amer. Mercury*, May, 102/1.

brass louie **brass Louie** A second lieutenant in the U.S. Army. *More common W.W.I than W.W.II use.* See **brass, louie.**

brass pounder A telegrapher; an amateur radio operator. *Newspaper, railroad, Army, and radio amateur use since c1925; archaic.*

brass tacks The essential facts; the practical realities. 1914: ". . . Highbrow sermons that don't come down to brass tacks." S. Lewis, *Our Mr. Wrenn*, 42. *Colloq.*

brat *v.i.* To baby-sit. *Never common.*

brawl *n.* **1** A dancing or social party that develops into a rough, drunken, or wild party. 1924: "The Prom had been an 'awful brawl.'" Marks, *Plastic Age*, 274. **2** A fight.

Brazil-water *n.* Coffee. 1949: ". . . Over the third cup of Brazil-water."

Billy Rose, *synd. newsp. col.*, Nov. 28. *Synthetic sl. occasionally used by newspaper columnists.*

bread *n.* **1** [taboo] The vagina. *Never common.* **2** Money. 1957: "Bread—Money." E. Horne, *For Cool Cats and Far-Out Chicks. Orig. c1935 jive use. Now associated with cool and hip use.* **3** One's employer, manager, or boss. *From the worker's dependency on him for wages with which to buy the necessities. Often introduced into conversation to warn other employees that the boss is watching or listening.*

breadbasket *n.* The stomach. 1753: Farmer & Henley. *Mainly child, prize fight, and sports announcer use.*

break *v.t.* **1** To subdue or, fig., "break" the spirit of a wild horse so that he may be trained and ridden; to train a horse to be ridden. *c1847.* [1956] "Having no other resources I stayed with him until the next summer doing general farm work and breaking wild colts to the saddle." Samuel Chamberlain, "My Confession," *Life*, July 23. *Orig. Western use. Universally known.* **2** To separate, as two boxers. **3** To take a short rest period from work, as for refreshment. **4** To escape from prison. **5** To bankrupt someone. 1956: "You could throw New York away if they ruin the bookmakers. It'll break the town." J. Cannon, *Who Struck John?* 164. → **6** To ruin another's chance for success; to impugn someone's reputation. *n.* **1** = **lick.** In jazz, an improvised interpolation between two passages of music, usu. played by a solo instrument while the other instruments of the ensemble, including the rhythm instruments, rest; the improvisation itself. 1950: "Without breaks . . . you can't play jazz. It's always necessary to arrange some kind of a spot to make a break. A break, itself, is like a musical surprise which didn't come in until I [Jelly Roll Morton] originated the idea of jazz." Quoted in A. Lomax, *Mr. Jelly Roll*, 58. *Morton's claim for himself is wildly exaggerated.* **2** An escape from prison or from any confining or disagreeable situation. **3** A social error or blunder; a faux pas. 1884: *DAE.* 1914: ". . . He had, even at this moment of social triumph, 'made a break.'" S. Lewis, *Our Mr. Wrenn*, 193. **4** Luck; opportunity; a stroke of fate, either good or bad. 1944: "It was just that I got all the breaks that time." Ford, *Phila. Murder*, 14. *Since c1925; colloq.* **5** Specif., a reduction in a prison sentence by a parole board. *Underworld use.* **6** A short rest period from work, usu. 10 or 15 minutes, often used for refreshments, esp. coffee. *Colloq. since c1945.*

break a hamstring To do one's best. *c1930 logger use.* Cf. **bust a gut.**

break-away *adj.* Pertaining to an object made to collapse easily at the pull of a string, press of a concealed button, or the like. *Thus a break-away dress is made to fall off the wearer, a strip-tease dancer, at the pull of a string; a break-away knife has a blade which recoils into the hilt at the push of a button, etc.*

breaker-upper *n.* One who or that which breaks up. c1940: "And from breakfast time till supper/Who's the leading breaker-upper?/It's the kid in the three-cornered pants." Pop. song. 1948: "Don't come near me! You godfather breaker-upper, you!" Phil Harris, NBC radio, Feb. 15. *A fairly common "—er- —er" word;* see Appendix.

break in **1** To gain entry, specif. to enter a prison by any means other than violence; to surrender voluntarily for imprisonment. **2** To tame or train, as a horse; to attune, adapt, or adjust a new article of merchandise by using it, as a new pair of shoes or a new automobile.

break-in *n.* A burglary. 1950: "100 or so break-ins." CBS radio play, *Gangbusters,* Jan. 14.

break it up **1** To stop fighting or quarreling;—usu. a command. *Colloq.* **2** To win a lot of money, fig., to win so much money in a gambling game that the game must end because the other players are broke.

break-off *n.* A joke at another's expense. *Some c1900 student use.*

break over To make an exception to one's usu. rule or practice. 1929: "Don't be mean. Let Toby break over, just this once." K. Brush, *Young Man,* 45. *Dial.*

break the ice **1** To accomplish a specific deed for the first time. → **2** To become initiated; to begin an apprenticeship. → **3** To become friendly or intimate with another or others; to overcome strangeness, shyness, aloofness, or formality with another person, persons, or esp. with an entire group of people, as at a social gathering. *Most common use.*

break the news To beat up someone. 1930: ". . . 'Breaking the news' . . . and numerous other phrases are employed by the police as euphemisms." Lavine, *Third Degree,* 3.

breakthrough *n.* An important or critical advance toward completion or

the success of a project or endeavor. *From the freq. W.W.II military aim of breaking through the enemy's defenses.*

break up To cause lovers, friends, or relatives to separate or become angry with one another. *Colloq.* **break-up** *n.* A separation, as between lovers.

break wind To eruct. 1949: "The murmuring rumdums were being let out of their cells to wash, break wind. . . ." N. Algren, *Man with the Golden Arm,* 20.

breath *n.* An order for a slice of onion, as in a sandwich. *Some lunchcounter use in relaying an order, since c1930.*

breathe easy To be relieved of worry; to be assured of success; to escape from danger. *Colloq.*

bree *n.* See **breigh.**

breech loader Any early breech-loading, long-range rifle. 1887: Used in "The Extermination of the American Bison," Report of the National Museum. *Such rifles were introduced in the American West during the 1870's, and the term was common there for some decades. Now archaic.*

breeze *n.* **1** Compressed air used in air brakes. *Railroad use.* **2** The escape of a prisoner or prisoners. 1948: "We had a breeze today." Wyer in N.Y. *Sun,* 30/2. *Not common.* **3** An easy task; a cinch. 1950: "Time-telling is just a breeze for this wrist piece [watch]." NEA photo caption, Sept. 14. 1951: "Flying is a breeze compared to highway travel, pilot Cassidy's experience indicates." AP, Aug. 11. *v.i.* **1** To depart; to leave; to go away, esp. quickly. 1937: "I did get a quick look at her before she breezed out of here." Weidman, *Wholesale,* 85. 1949: "Take the dough and breeze." Chandler, *Little Sister,* 62. **2** To travel or move, either rapidly or easily. **3** Specif., to flee, to escape from jail. 1958: "If I didn't get out [of the reformatory] legally . . . I would breeze [run away]." "A Gang Leader's Redemption," *Life,* April 28, 70.

breeze in To arrive or enter as though with or on a breeze; to saunter in; hence to win a race without great effort. 1949: "[He] breezed in." J. Evans, *Halo,* 195.

breeze off **1** To be quiet; to shut up. **2** To leave; to depart.

breezer *n.* An open touring car; a convertible car. *c1925 use; obs.*

breezy *adj.* **1** Drunk. *c1850; obs.* See Appendix, Drunk. **2** Affable; nonchalant; supercilious.

breigh   bree   *n.* A girl or young
woman. *Some c1930 student use; some
c1935 jive use.*
briar   *n.* A file or hacksaw.*Underworld use since c1830.*
briar-hopper   *n.* A farmer. *Dial.*
brick   *n.* **1** A happy, carefree person.
1851: Hall, *College Words*, 25. *From the
Celtic "brigh" = energy, spirit, and the
superlative "brigheil" = high spirits.* →
2 A pleasant, thoughtful, trustworthy,
generous person; an admirable person.
1939: "Aunt Laura is a brick." A.
Christie, *Sad Cypress*, 14. *Since c1910;
colloq.* **3** A homely girl. *Annapolis use,
c1930.*   **—yard**   *n.* See **Hogan's
brickyard.**
bricks, hit the   **1** To go on the street
on foot; to start walking on a sidewalk
or pavement. → **2** To leave a public
place; to withdraw to the street. → **3**
To be released from prison. *Underworld
use.* → **4** To go on strike; to stage a
walkout. 1949: "It is obvious that any
union always hitting the bricks and
calling showdowns cannot get what it
asks for at the end of the year." Phila.
Bulletin, Sept. 3, 6/1. 1956: "*Hit the
bricks*—To go out on strike, to walk out."
*Labor's Special Language from Many
Sources.* **5** Specif., to walk the streets all
night because one does not have a place
to sleep; to beg on the streets; to walk a
beat; to march on a picket line. *Hobo,
police, and union use; some general use.*
bricks, the   *n. sing.* **1** The pavement
or sidewalk; the street. → **2** The world
outside prison walls. *Prison use.*
beat; *Hobo, police, and union use; some
general use.*
bricks and mortar   School notes and
books. *From the notion of a school as
nothing but a brick and mortar building;
reinforced by "mortarboard." Rock and
roll use, c1955.*
bricktop   *n.* A red-haired person;—
often used as a nickname; a head of red
hair. *Since at least 1850.*
bride and groom on a raft = **Adam
and Eve on a raft.**
bridgey   *adj.* Drunk. 1737: *Pa. Gazette.
Obs.* See Appendix, Drunk.
briefs   *n. sing.* A pair of men's cotton
undershorts with an elastic waist. *They
are usu. white and are legless, as opposed
to the skivvy, which has short legs. Colloq.*
brig   *n.* A naval prison or cell; a
guardhouse; any prison. 1852: *DAE.*
bright   *n.* Day; the daytime. *Orig.
c1935 jive use; bop and cool use since
c1946.*

brig rat   A prisoner. *Some Armed
Forces use.*
bringdown   *n.* **1** A disappointing,
unsatisfactory, or depressing performance or job. **2** A habitually sad,
gloomy person. 1956: "A *bringdown* is a
depressing character." S. Longstreet,
The Real Jazz Old and New, 149.   *adj.*
1 Unsatisfying; incompetent; inexperienced. **2** Depressing; gloomy. *All uses
cool and far-out; since c1953.*
bring down the house   To elicit a
big ovation from an audience, as in a
theater. 1949: "Old Man Dillinger strode
onto the stage and brought down the
house." A. Hynd, *Public Enemies*, 42f.
bring home the bacon = **bring home
the groceries.**
bring home the groceries   **1** Fig.,
to earn money with which to buy the
necessities of life. → **2** To succeed in a
job or task; to produce tangible results;
to accomplish what one has set out to do.
briny, the   *n.* The ocean. *Since c1900.*
Brit   *adj.* British. 1951: "Brit flick =
British film." A. Green, *Show Biz*, 567.
Not common; synthetic. See Appendix,
Abbreviations.
broad   *n.* **1** A young woman or girl;
a woman. 1932: "He refers to Miss Perry
as a broad, meaning no harm whatever,
for this is the way many of the boys speak
of the dolls." Runyon, 89. 1958: "Mrs.
Elsie Bambridge, daughter of Rudyard
Kipling, refused to approve a new Frank
Sinatra recording of 'On the Road to
Mandalay.' You see, Frankie substituted
the word 'broad' for girl." P. Sann, N.Y.
Post, Apr. 13, M6. **2** A promiscuous
woman; a prostitute; a woman whom
the speaker does not respect. 1926:
"*Broad* is usually applied by New
Yorkers to women who, it is hoped or
believed, are of uncertain morals. It is
derived from *bawd*." L. B. N. Gnae-
dinger in *Amer. Mercury*, Mar., 369f.
1934: " 'I saw plenty wrong with your
broad's manners.' 'She's not a broad.' "
Chandler, *Finger Man*, 13. 1943: "I *read*
that book. Only had one dame in it and
she was a broad." H. A. Smith, *Putty
Knife*, 96. *It is virtually impossible to say
which of the above meanings is most
common. The connotation of promiscuous, however, is disappearing from
the second use given, and the modern
speaker is usu. showing his dislike of the
woman in question without questioning
her sexual morality.* **3** The shoulders of a
man or a man's coat. *Some c1935 jive use.*
Broadway boy   A loud, garishly

dressed, small-time gambler or ladies' man.

brodie **Brodie** *n.* A failure, mistake, or blunder; a mixup. *After Steve Brodie who claimed to have jumped from the Brooklyn Bridge on July 23, 1886. Although he was found in the water under the bridge, his feat was never proved, and thus if he didn't jump he received much mistaken acclaim; if he did jump he made the mistake of having no accredited witnesses to attest the validity of his claim and thus jumped in vain.* *v.i.* **1** To fail; to make a mistake. 1936: "An act brodied." A. Green in *Esquire*, Sept., 162/3. **2** To commit suicide, esp. by jumping off a bridge or building.

broke *adj.* Without money; penniless. 1894: "I've been broke myself." J. Flynt. 1900: "I'm 'broke' now." Dreiser, *Carrie*, 308. 1914: "Are you broke?" S. Lewis, *Our Mr. Wrenn*, 148. 1956: "It was Phoce [E. Phocian Howard] who gave [Damon] Runyon that melody, orchestrated with so many lively orchestrations, 'All horse players must die broke.' " T. Betts, *Across the Board*, 166. *Usu. pred. adj., occasionally attrib. adj.*

broken arm Food that has been uneaten or only partially eaten after being served at a meal; a plate of such food; leftovers; table scraps. c1915 [1954]: "He brought 'broken arms'... the leftovers from the tables he served." L. Armstrong, *Satchmo, My Life in New Orleans*, 29.

broken-striper *n.* A warrant officer. *USN use.*

bromide *n.* **1** An old joke or saying. **2** A trite saying; a trite homily; a dull person. 1906: *Are You a Bromide? A book by Gelett Burgess who coined the sl. meaning of this term from the medical usage = a sedative; perhaps influenced by the Sp. "broma" = a joke.*

bronc **bronk** *n.* **1** = bronco. **2** A bad-tempered horse. *Dial.* **3** A catamite. *Some c1925 hobo use.*

bronco *n.* A wild, untrained horse; a horse not yet broken for riding. *Orig. western use = a bad-tempered wild horse.* 1936: " 'Bronco' (from Spanish 'broncho,' meaning rough, rude) often was contracted into 'bronc' or 'bronk.' Texans, when speaking technically, restricted 'mustang' to the unmixed wild horse, and limited 'bronco' to such of these as were particularly 'mean' in nature." P. A. Rollins, *The Cowboy*, 28.

bronco buster A cowboy; lit., one who breaks or tames broncos. 1936:

"The cowboy was not always called 'cowboy.' To various legitimate titles, conscious slang added 'bronco buster,' 'bronco peeler,' 'bronco snapper,' 'bronco twister.'..." P. A. Rollins, *The Cowboy*, 39f. *Colloq.*

bronco peeler = bronco buster.

bronco snapper = bronco buster. 1936: "A man's competence to ride the most violent of bucking animals did not, of itself, make him an efficient cowboy. As a 'bronco snapper' he might be thoroughly proficient and yet...." P. A. Rollins, *The Cowboy*, 25.

bronco twister = bronco buster.

bronk *n.* = bronco.

Bronx cheer *n.* **1** Any loud, derisive noise, such as a hiss, a boo, or a raspberry. 1933: "...Got nothing but the Bronx cheer." AP, Oct. 25. 1946: "[Baseball fans] make a lot of noise, they let off steam via the Bronx cheer and the boo." J. K. Hutchens in N.Y. *Times Mag.*, July 14, 18. 1951: "What policemen think of cops-and-robbers films is perhaps best expressed by a Bronx cheer." AP, Mar. 13. *The Bronx cheer is the direct opposite of applause. Although it is said to have orig. in the National Theater in The Bronx, N.Y.C., the term may have come from the Spanish "brazo" or Span. sl. and dial. "branca," orig. = an affectionate hug, but later = the "Olé!" shout of approval voiced by bullfight fans, and now = any mass audience noise, whether of approval or disapproval. Cf.* **raspberry.** → **2** An adverse criticism or remark; any written or spoken statement of ridicule or derision.

brook *n.* See **babbling brook.** **—ie** *n.* A brook trout. 1952: "Good looking trout... brookies, grays and rainbows." L. R. Blanchard, GNS, July 12. See Appendix, **—ie** endings.

broom *n.* A cigar. *Jocular use, obs.* *v.i.* To run or walk away, esp. to flee. *Negro use.* **—stick** *n.* **1** One's wife. *In allusion to "witch," the traditional rider of broomsticks. Dial.* **2** Any thin person.

broom in (up) [one's] tail (ass), get (have) a [taboo] To have or show enthusiasm over a job or task; to work hard; to become or be a diligent honest worker. 1949: "Why don't I get a broom in my tail and go to work on the legit." N. Algren, *Man with the Golden Arm*, 33. *From a pop. joke about an employee whose hands are busy but whose boss gives him the additional task of sweeping the floor; hence he must*

hold the broom in this unorthodox manner.
broom tail   *n.* A mare. 1936: " . . .
'Broom tails' (range mares). . . ." P. A.
Rollins, *The Cowboy,* 28. *Ranch use.*
brother   *n.* **1** A man, fellow, guy.
*Some use in direct address to strangers, as
in the street beggar's traditional, "Brother,
can you spare a dime?" From the freq.
religious use of the word.* **2** In direct
address, a man who has aroused the
speaker's resentment, often leading to
quarrelsome or threatening talk or blows.
1948: "The word 'brother,' as a means of
address, is never used unless the speaker
is willing to clout the person addressed."
J. McNulty, *PM,* June 10, 13.
brow   *adj.* Of low intelligence. *From
"lowbrow." Some use since c1920. Not now
common.*
brown   *n.* **1** A penny. *Some Negro and
jive use. Never as common in U.S. as in
Eng.* **2** Butterscotch sauce. *Some student
use.*
brown Abe   *n.* A penny. *Orig. c1935
jive use; cool use, some rock and roll use.*
See **brown.**
brown bucks   Buckwheat cakes; an
order of buckwheat cakes. *Lunch-counter
use, used in relaying an order, c1880; obs.*
browned off, *adj.* **1** Bored; restless as a
result of waiting or inactivity. *Orig.
W.W.II Air Force use from Brit. Royal
Air Force sl. Never common. Obs.* → **2**
Angry, esp. angry with disappointment,
as at another's mistake, slight, or
tardiness. 1940: ". . . Has almost completely displaced the colloquial 'to be
fed up.' " H. L. Mencken in *Reader's
Digest,* May, 39. *The most common use.*
3 Finished, completed. *Not common.*
Brownie   *n.* **1** A demerit. 1942: "I
got a pair of Brownies for that one."
D. McFerran. *Railroad use. From the
surname of the originator of the disciplinary system.* **2** An apple polisher. *Some
W.W.II use.* See **brown noser. 3** A
penny. See **brown, brown Abe.** See
Appendix, —ie ending.
brown-nose [taboo]   *v.t.* To curry favor
with a superior.   *n.* **1** One who curries
favor with a teacher or superior. **2** A
teacher's pet. *c1940, student use, prob.
carried into W.W.II Armed Forces by
students. Term replaced "apple polisher"
and is derived directly from image of the ass
kisser.* Cf. **apple polisher.   —r**   *n.*
One who brown-noses. *Colloq.* See Appendix, —er ending.
brown off   To make a mistake or
blunder; to ruin or spoil something.
1956: "Musically . . . to break time out

of tempo is to *brown off.*" S. Longstreet,
The Real Jazz Old and New, 148.
Brown Top   The main tent at a
chautauqua; a chautauqua big top.
brud   *n.* A brother. 1945: "Where's
your brud?" E. Kasser, 131. *From dial.
"brudder."* See Appendix, Shortened
Words.
bruised   *adj.* Drunk. *c1850; not common.* See Appendix, Drunk.
bruiser   *n.* A big, strong male, esp.
one with a rough appearance or manner.
Usu. in "big bruiser." Colloq.
brunch   *n.* A late morning meal eaten
in lieu of both breakfast and luncheon,
a combined breakfast and luncheon.
*Since c1900. From telescoping "breakfast'
and "lunch."* 1938: "[Batista] likes to
sleep until 11 A.M., then brunches, sees
visitors. . . ." *Time,* Nov. 21,12.
brush   *n.* **1**   =   **brush-off.** Usu. in
give [someone] the (*or* **a**) **brush.**
1939–40: "She . . . was glad to see me
instead of giving me the brush which was
what I was afraid of. . . ." O'Hara, *Pal
Joey,* 50. 1951: "I'd hate to give you the
brush on that story." Network radio
program, *Can You Top This?* Apr. 10.
2 A beard; whiskers. **3** An encounter, esp.
one involving a fight, quarrel, or un-
pleasantness; a skirmish.   *v.i., v.t.* To
fight; to defeat by fighting; to beat up.
adj. **1** Bearded; bewhiskered. *Not common, but used in such combinations as
"brush-face," "brush-peddler"* (an actor
who gets a part because he has natural
whiskers, *Hollywood use c1925),* etc. **2**
Rural, rustic. *In such combinations as
"brush-show"* = *a rural nonprofessional
show; "brush-canary"* = *female singer of
hillbilly songs; "brush-whisky"* = *illegal
whisky, as made in rural or mountain
districts, and the like.*
brush, give [someone] the   To ignore
or snub someone; to dismiss someone
curtly and without much concern. Cf.
brush.
brush, the   *n.* **1** The jungle; forested
country; uncivilized regions of any kind.
Colloq. **2**   =   **brush-off.**
brush ape   *n.* A hillbilly; a rustic. *Not
common.*
brush cut   A mode of hair cut in
which all the hair (front top, and sides)
is cut to the same short length, usu. less
than an inch. *c1910. A male haircut,
forerunner of the crew cut. c1950, a
fashionable women's hair style. Orig.
because the short, straight hair resembles
the bristles·of a brush.*

brush-down *n.* The act of brushing clothes.

brushes *n. pl.* A pair of thin drumsticks with flat soft brushes of wires or plastic on the ends. They are used to give the drums a soft, smooth, muted sound. *Orig.* jazz use; now the most common word for these items in all forms of jazz and popular music.

brush off **brush-off** **1** To ignore, snub, or get rid of a person or thing; fig., to brush aside. 1941: "He'd only brush me off." Schulberg, *Sammy*, 124. **2** To go away, to leave. *Usu. as an entreaty or command.* **brush-off** *n.* The act of brushing off a person or thing, esp. the act of jilting a suitor; an instance of ignoring a friendship or a friend's request; a rejection. 1951: "... An overwhelming 'yea' from 38 critics with five giving it the brush-off." D. Dempsey in N.Y. *Times Bk. Rev.*, Sept. 2.

brush up **1** To brush clothes or the like. → **2** To clean up; to dress up; to spruce up. **3** To review, relearn, or acquire additional information about a specific subject. *Colloq.*

bruss *n.* An extremely exaggerated position of attention. *From* **brace.** *Army use.*

BS **B.S.** **b.s.** **1** A Bachelor of Science degree; one who holds such a degree. *Stand.* **2** [taboo] = **bullshit; bullshitter.** *Like other such abbrs. of taboo terms, this is somewhat euphem.* See Appendix, Shortened Words.

BTO **B.T.O.** **b.t.o.** = **big-time operator.** *This abbr. is at least as common as the full expression.* See Appendix, Shortened Words.

bub *n.* **1** A boy or youth. *Used in direct address. Colloq.* → **2** *A derog. or humorous form of direct address to an adult male, implying that the person is insignificant. Very common since c1940.*

bubbies [taboo] *n. pl.* The female breasts. *Often = bubs, but as a true diminutive is also applied to smaller shapely breasts.*

bubble-chaser *n.* A U.S. Air Force bombardier. *Some W.W.II use.*

bubble dance To wash dishes. *Army kitchen duty. Some W.W.II Army use.* —**r** **bubble-dancer** *n.* A person who washes dishes. *Lunch-counter use and W.W.II Army use. Common and one of the more successful sl. terms based on a humorous image.*

bubble-head **bubblehead** *n.* A stupid person. *Often used as a term of address or as a nickname.* 1952: "Bubble-

head [Henry] Wallace...." W. Pegler, *synd. newsp. col.*, Mar. 11.

bubble queen A girl worker in a laundry.

bubbly *n.* Champagne. *Orig. Eng. use, introduced into U.S. sl. during W.W.I. Common with newsp. columnists and writers, some facetious general use.*

bubie = **boobie.**

bubs [taboo] *n.pl.* The female breasts, esp. if large or ponderous. 1941: "... Those bubs of hers." Schulberg, *Sammy*, 260. *Very common since c1900.*

buck *n.* **1** A dollar; the sum of $1. 1923: "A hundred bucks." C. MacArthur, *Rope*, 183. 1939: "Skins were classified [c1800] as 'bucks' and 'does,' the former being larger, and more valuable. Americans still refer to dollars as 'bucks'... echoing the business terminology of their ancestors." John Bakeless, *Master of the Wilderness*, 38. *In wide colloq. use since at least c1850. The true origin is not definitely known.* See **fast buck, half-buck, pass the buck, sawbuck.** **2** An Army private. *From "buck private." Fairly common use between W.W.I and W.W.II.* See Appendix, Shortened Words. **3** A Roman Catholic priest. *It is said that frontiersmen orig. called priests "bucks" and nuns "does"; hobo use c1925; because a hobo could depend on receiving a dollar from a priest if he begged from him.* **4** A young male Indian → **5** Any young male, esp. a muscular or spirited one. *Colloq.* **6** Specif., a young male Negro. **7** A tooth, not necessarily a buck tooth. *Not common.* —*v.t.* To resist, to defeat. *Usu. in the negative, as in such phrases as "you can't buck the system"; "it's fate, don't buck it," etc. Colloq.* —*v.i.* **1** To strive in any way for personal advancement, as by dressing neatly, studying hard, or competing for favors or promotion. 1952: "He is bucking for the job." R. C. Ruark, *synd. newsp. col.*, Sept. 12. *Wide W.W.II use; perh. from "buck private," the lowest Army rank and hence the one in which one must work most for promotion.* → **2** To side with or seek favor from those in authority. —*adj.* Good, excellent, pleasant, agreeable. *Some c1850 college use. Obs.* —**ed** *adj.* Proud; pleased. *Some W.W.I use.* —**er** *n.* **1** One who curries favor with his superiors; an aspirant to promotion. 1946: "To be called a bucker is a condemnation." F. Elkin. **2** A cowboy. 1936: "The cowboy was frequently called 'baquero,' 'buckeroo,' 'buckhara,' or 'buckayro,' each a perversion of either the Spanish 'vaquero,' or the Spanish 'boyero,' and each subject to be contracted into 'bucker.' " P. A. Rollins, *The Cowboy*, 39. **—o** *n.* **1** A fellow; guy. *Since c1900. Used by old sailors and cowboys. Connotation of an independent, outdoor person.* **2** A bully. *Orig. seaman use. adj.* **1** Brutal; mean; sadistic; usu. applied to a ship's officer. *Seaman use. Obs.* **2** Strong, rough, tough, self-reliant. 1950: "A bucko mate who sailed the horn in the barbarian days of seafaring. . . ." W. Pegler, *synd. newsp. col.*, Aug. 25. See Appendix, —o ending. **—ra** *n.* A white man, esp. a poor or mean white man. *Lorenzo D. Turner's "Africanisms in the Gullah Dialect" indicates that this word is of African origin. It spread from the slaves to Southern whites, who used it derogatorily. Archaic.*

buck, pass the   To pass on to someone else a problem, responsibility, or a person having a problem requiring attention. *Since c1910; colloq.*

buckayro *n.* = **bucker.**

buckeroo *n.* = **bucker.**

bucket *n.* **1** An automobile, esp. a large, old automobile. 1939: "I got out the old bucket and we drove down to Clinton Street." Runyon. **2** A ship, esp. an old or slow ship; in the Navy, esp. a destroyer. 1953: "You're going on that French bucket." Nathaniel Benchley, *New Yorker*, Feb. 7, 82/2. *Often used as a term of familiarity or affection rather than derision.* See **can, rust bucket.** **3** Any ugly or unpleasant girl or woman. *In the U.S. the word is never used as a v. = to travel fast, as it is in Eng. sl., but see* **barrel.** See **gutbucket, kick the bucket, messy bucket, murky bucket, tar bucket.** **4** The rump, the buttocks. **5** A disliked, objectionable, dull person. *Some student use since c1945.* **6** A toilet.

bucket-head [derog.]   *n.* **1** A German soldier. *Some W.W.I and W.W.II use. Orig. in allusion to the shape of the German field helmet, which resembled a "bucket" = toilet or chamber pot.* → **2** A German. *Not common.* Cf. **Jerry.** **3** A stupid person.

bucket of bolts   A car, esp. an old, dilapidated car that rattles when in motion.

bucket-shop   bucket shop *n.* **1** A saloon. *c1880.* **2** An office where illegal, worthless, or highly speculative stocks are sold, often by telephone and with unethical sales talks; posing as a legitimate stockbroker's office, but using aggressive means and misrepresentation bordering

on swindling. 1957: "Boiler Room or Bucket Shop—Can You Tell the Difference?" Sam Dawson, financial writer, N.Y. *Post*, March 26, 18.

buck general   A brigadier general in the U.S. Army.

buckhara *n.* = **bucker.**

buckle down   To replace frivolity or apathy with a serious attitude and hard work, in order to succeed.

buck naked   Completely naked. 1955: " 'Don't you dare turn around,' said Madeleine. 'What are you, buck naked?' asked Jimmy, idly." C. Willingham, *To Eat a Peach*, 180.

buck out   To prepare, as a lesson. *c1900; college use.*

buck private   An Army private, esp. a new recruit.

bucks, in the   In funds; having money. 1948: ". . . Everybody was in the bucks." F. Brown, *Dead Ringer*, 1.

buckshee *adj.* **1** Spare; extra; loose. **2** Free. *Some maritime use since W.W.I, from Brit. sailor sl.* **3** Faked; surreptitious. *Some W.W.I use, from Brit. Army sl. Prob. of Arabic orig., from "buckshes" = tip.*

buck slip   Any written paper which passes a given problem on to another person or office. See **pass the buck.**

buck up   To cheer up. 1924: "Come on, old man; buck up." Marks, *Plastic Age*, 44. *Since c1840.*

bud *n.* Friend; fellow. *Always used in direct address, often to a stranger, usu. in the vocative at the end of a sentence, and always to a male. Since c1850. Colloq. From "brother."* **—dy** *n.* **1** = **bud.** 1930: "Sure, buddy. . . ." Lavine, *Third Degree*, 77. *Equally as common as "bud" and used in exactly the same way. Also since c1850.* **2** A partner. **3** A man's male friend; a chum; a comrade, esp. a close friend whom one will aid or protect. *Colloq. v.i.* = **buddy up.** To be a close friend to someone; to move about with another; to share living quarters. *Often in the phrase, "They buddy together."* See Appendix, —y ending. **—dyroo** *n.* = **buddy,** 3. 1951: "You should've seen the way they said hello. You'd have thought they'd taken baths in the same bathtub or something when they were little kids. Old buddyroos. It was nauseating." J. D. Salinger, *Catcher in the Rye*, 97. See Appendix, —eroo ending.

buddy-buddy *n.* **1** A close friend. *W.W.II Army and USN use.* → **2** One who is not a friend; an enemy; a disliked person. *This sarcastic use is by far the most common since c1945. The reduplication has been used to strengthen the word "buddy" and also to reverse its meaning.*→ **3** An overly friendly person; one who tries too hard to make friends, join a group, or be hep. *v.i.* To be overly friendly; to curry favor. *adj.* Too friendly; insincere; presuming. See Appendix, Reduplications.

buddy gee A young man. *Some jive use c1930.*

Buddy poppy **1** A paper replica of a Flanders poppy sold by W.W.I veterans on Memorial Day. → **2** To use sentimentality and assumed intimacy in order to convince or persuade; to buddy up. *Not common.*

buddy seat **1** A motorcycle sidecar. Cf. **bathtub.** *c1940. Because the two riders are close together.* **2** A position of authority; *c1950. Because others must now try to be friendly or curry favor.*

buddy up **1** To share living quarters; to combine resources. *Male student use.* **2** To seek out, court, or ingratiate oneself with another for personal advancement or gain; to form a friendship for ulterior motives; to apple-polish. 1958: ". . . He's hanging out with Walson now and buddying up to him. . . ." Earl Wilson, *synd. newsp. col.,* Feb. 16.

buddy [someone] up **buddy up to [someone]** To curry favor with someone, usu. someone in authority. 1950: "The wisdom of buddying up to Franco of Spain. . . ." Billy Rose, *synd. newsp. col.,* Jan. 13. *From "butter up" with the mispronunciation reinforced by "buddy."*

buff *v.i.* To give evidence; to swear. *Underworld use. Obs.* *n.* **1** A devotee, a fan, a bug; one whose hobby or passion is collecting specific items, going to specific events, or associating with a specific occupational group. 1930: "There are several varieties of police buffs. . . ." Lavine, *Third Degree,* 67. **2** A girl or young woman. *c1910. Not common.* **3** A buffoon. *Archaic.* See Appendix, Shortened Words.

buffalo *v.t.* **1** To confuse another purposely. *Since c1870.* → **2** To cheat or take advantage of another, usu. by confusing him. → **3** To intimidate, frighten, or bluff someone; to cow someone. *Since c1900.* → **4** To control a situation. *n.* **1** [derog.] A Negro. *Not common.* **2** A girl or woman, esp. if she is extremely fat. Cf. **cow.**

buffaloed *adj.* Deceived; tricked; cheated.

buffalo head A nickel.

buffer *n.* **1** A dog, esp. a watchdog. *Underworld use. Obs.* **2** A chief boatswain's mate. *U.S.N. use.*

bug *n.* **1** An enthusiast; one who is obsessed by an idea or pursuit. 1841: *DAE.* 1921: ". . . A coupla thousand bugs fought to get in." Witwer, *Leather,* 54. *Colloq.* → **2** An obsession; an idea or belief with which one is obsessed. 1932: "He has a bug that he is a wonderful judge of guys' characters." Runyon, 78. 1957: "Stanley Kramer has succumbed to the Cecil B. deMille bug. Mr. Kramer, newcomer though he is [as a movie producer] in the spare-no-expense and crowd-the-screen line, is a man to be reckoned with if you happen to have an unemployed army around." *New Yorker,* July 13, 48. → **3** An insane person. 1922: "Only a bug is strong enough for that." O'Neill, *Hairy Ape. Not common.* See **bugs.** → **4** An irrational mood; a grouch or bad mood. *Since c1930. Mainly prison use.* Cf. **bug up [one's] ass (nose).** → **5** An angry mood. *Usu. in "to have a bug on."* → **6** A psychologist. *Some prison use.* **7** A trick or hoax. 1848: *DAE. Obs.* **8** Any defect or cause of trouble in a machine, equipment, or plan; specif. a defect in a new machine that becomes apparent only when the machine is put into operation. *Colloq.* **9** Any impurity or unwanted particle found in food served for eating, as a fishbone, nutshell, dirt, etc. *Some c1930 Army use.* **10** A prostitute. *Some underworld use c1920. Obs.* **11** An asterisk. *Printing and publishing use.* → **12** Specif., an asterisk appearing next to the weight a horse is carrying in a horse race, as on a program, to indicate that a 5-pound weight decrease has been granted because the horse is being ridden by an apprentice jockey. *Racetrack use.* → **13** In horse-racing, the 5-pound allowance in weight given to a horse being ridden by an apprentice jockey. 1941: "Apprentices [jockeys] get a five-pound allowance in weights—the 'bug' it's called." J. Lilienthal, *Horse Crazy,* 20. → **14** An apprentice jockey who has ridden his first race within the present year or who has not won his 40th race. → **15** A race horse that has never won a race. *Also from the asterisk that used to be placed next to the name of such a horse, as on a program.* Cf. **maiden.** → **16** [taboo] The hymen; virginity. *Jocular use, from horse-racing use. Not*

common. **17** A small, usu. printed, label
or trademark; specif., the union label
printed on publications to show they
have been printed in a union workshop.
1956: "*Bug*—Name for the Union label
on printing." *Labor's Special Language
from Many Sources. From the shape.* **18**
An automobile, esp. a small one. *Some
c1920 use. Because early car enthusiasts
and drivers were bugs = enthusiasts.* →
19 A truck, specif. an Army supply
truck. *Some W.W.II Army use.* → **20**
Specif., a hot-rod; the driver of a hot-rod.
Hot-rod use since c1950. → **21** Specif., a
Volkswagen, the small German car; any
small, inexpensive foreign car. *From
their appearance.* **22** A semiautomatic
telegraph key, operating from side to
side instead of up and down, which sends
"dashes" automatically, speeding message sending. 1943: "The dots and
dashes on the bug. . . ." "He began
practicing on the bug with his left
hand." Wolfert, *Underworld*, 88. *Telegrapher, radio amateur, railroad, and USN
use since c1920.* → **23** A confidential
message or signal; confidential information. *Underworld use c1925.* → **24** A
burglar alarm. *Underworld use. Here
"bug" may be a shortened form of "burglar alarm," and a possible orig. of meanings 22 through 25.* → **25** A dictaphone or other such recording device
concealed to record conversations without the speakers' knowledge; any device
allowing a third person to overhear
a conversation, esp. a telephone conversation, without the speakers' knowledge; any wire-tapping device. 1950:
"We-can't-talk-because-the-phone-has-
a-bug-on-it." Starnes, *Another Mug*,
24. **26** A bacterium; a germ or microbe
or virus; any micro-organism. *Colloq.* →
27 Any virus disease or infection; a cold;
dysentery. *Common during and since
W.W.II.* **28** A lantern; a flashlight. *Not
common. Orig. railroad use, then underworld use. Since such lights are used in
signaling, this use has contributed to and
reinforced "bug" = burglar alarm, telegraph key, recording device, etc.* **29**
Any small, cheap item of merchandise,
as sold by a novelty vendor or pitchman.
Circus use since c1800. **30** A large
industrial ladle, as used in pouring
molten steel, baker's dough, or the
like. *v.t.* **1** To examine a person
psychiatrically or psychologically; to
pronounce a person mentally irresponsible for his actions; to pronounce a
person insane. *Mainly prison use, since*

c1930. **2** To install a burglar alarm
in a specif. location. *Underworld use.*
3 To conceal a microphone-recording
device in a room or other location in
order to record conversation surreptitiously; to listen to a recorded telephone conversation without the speakers'
knowledge.   *v.i., v.t.* To be angry or
irritated (at someone); to bother, irritate, or anger someone; to confuse or
bewilder someone. 1954: "I   suspected something was bugging her from
the way she used to give me hell every
time I came home only a half hour late."
L. Armstrong, *Satchmo, My Life in New
Orleans*, 164. 1956: "Mother is bugged
(angry) at me." S. Longstreet, *The Real
Jazz Old and New*, 147.
—bug   See Appendix, Suffixes and
Suffix Words.
bugaboo   *n.* A nemesis; a real or
imagined obstacle that cannot be overcome; something that always causes
failure or bad luck; ungrounded or
unnecessary fear or dislike of a real or
imagined thing, as a child's fear of the
dark. *Colloq.*
bug doctor   A psychiatrist or psychologist, as one employed by a penal
institution. *Since c1930.*
bug-eyed   *adj.* **1** Having protruding
eyeballs. **2** Astonished, surprised; struck
with wonder or amazement. 1951:
"Joseph laughed. 'I kill best with a
Bowie knife.' The child went bug-eyed."
S. Longstreet, *The Pedlocks*, 39f.
bugger   *n.* **1** A fellow; a chap; a
thing. *Esp. applied to small or cute persons
or things, as a small boy.* **2** [taboo] A
male who practices active rectal intercourse; a sodomite.   *v.t.* [taboo] **1** To
have rectal intercourse. **2** [taboo] To
have intercourse with animals.
buggy   *n.* **1** A caboose of a train, esp.
of a freight train. *Railroad use since
c1895.* Cf. **crummy.** **2** A wheelbarrow.
c1915; not common. **3** An automobile;
esp. an old dilapidated automobile.
*Since c1925; has been very common, esp.
in jocular use.* **4** Any vehicle. See **gas
buggy, hell buggy, Irish buggy,
struggle-buggy.** **5** [derog.] A Negro.
*Not common. Orig. prison use, implying
that Negroes are all crazy, reinforced by
"boogie."* **6** = **bus.**   *adj.* **1** Foolish;
silly. *Some use since c1920.* → **2** Crazy.
1952: "Ross Bagdasarian . . . is the guy
who was responsible for [the song] 'Come
Ona My House,' which was driving the
nation buggy a year ago." AP, Aug. 29.
Very common since c1930. See **bugs.**

—buggy See Appendix, Suffixes and Suffix Words.

buggy bitchers **1** Field artillerymen. *Some Army use. Archaic.* → **2** U.S. cavalrymen assigned to motorized equipment. *Some Army use. c1930; archaic.*

bughouse *n.* **1** An insane asylum. 1947: "Who cares whether you're free or locked in a bughouse? You're crazy." C. Willingham, *End As A Man*, 228. 1958: "Ezra Pound: 'When I was in the bughouse, I used to think there were 160,000,000 worse cases outside.' " Paul Sann in N.Y. *Post*, May 4, M6. **2** A wartime trench dugout. *Some W.W.I Army use, taken from Brit. Army sl. adj.* Insane, crazy; eccentric; nuts. 1894 [1891]: "A fellow had said that 'tramps were bughouse.' . . ." Josiah Flynt, *Contemporary Review*, 255. 1924: "You're just plain bug-house. . . ." Marks, *Plastic Age*, 52. 1944: "I drew those bug-house cartoons. . . ." Fowler, *Good Night*, 96. *Still in use by older people.*

bug-hunter *n.* An entomologist; a naturalist. *Since c1890.*

bug in [one's] ear **1** = **bug up [one's] ass.** *A euphem.* **2** An obsession; a cherished concept, idea, or plan. **3** A rumor, gossip, or secret or private information which one believes to be true.

bug in [one's] ear, put a To warn someone by implanting an idea in his mind, to forewarn; to insinuate, imply, or suggest something to a person, esp. so that he may reach his own conclusion or not remember from whom he received an impression or idea. See **bug.**

bug-juice *n.* **1** Liquor, esp. inferior whisky. *Since c1875.* **2** Any beverage, esp. a synthetic or artificially colored beverage; any soft drink. **3** Gasoline. **4** The residue of tobacco in the bowl of a frequently used pipe. *All uses orig. from the tobacco-colored secretion of grasshoppers.*

bugle *n.* **1** The nose. 1930: "It ain't no skin off of Hymie's bugle." Joel Sayre, *Amer. Mercury*, Dec., 420. 1951: "My pappy, Jasper Hoople, had the same bugle on him, same size, same color!" "Major Hoople," *synd. newsp. cartoon*, Aug. 27. *Not common.* **2** The head. *c1920. Not common.*

bugle-warmer *n.* A hat. *c1920. Not common.*

bug man *n.* A circus concessionaire who sells chameleons and turtles. Cf. **bug.**

bugologist *n.* A entomologist. *Since c1875.*

bugology *n.* **1** Entomology. *Since c1850.* → **2** Biology. *Some student use since c1900.*

bug on [to have a] See **bug.**

bug out **1** To protrude. *Since c1870. Now usu. in ref. to naturally protruding, staring eyes.* **2** To withdraw, retreat, lose one's enthusiasm, or compromise, owing to exhaustion, cowardice, or fear; to turn chicken. → **3** To leave or drive away rapidly. *Hot-rod and teenager use since c1950.* *n.* **1** One who habitually withdraws or compromises; one who cannot be depended upon. → **2** A military retreat. *Korean War Army use.* 1951: "Commanding officers hated the word because of the psychological overtones of defeatism. Men talked of 'bug-out gas' and 'bug-out jeeps' and 'bug-out routes.' They anticipated retreat and they prepared for it." M. R. Johnson in N.Y. *Her. Trib.*

bugs *n.* Biology. *Student use.* *adj.* **1** Insane; crazy; eccentric; obsessed. 1922: "Yuh're bugs." O'Neill, *Hairy Ape*, I. *Very common.* **2** A student or teacher of biology. *Some c1900 student use.*

—bugs See Appendix, Suffixes and Suffix Words.

bug-sharp *n.* An entomologist. *c1875. Student use. Obs.*

bug test **1** An intelligence test. *c1930.* **2** A psychological test. *c1945.*

bug torch A lantern. *Railroad use.*

bug up To become or be excited; to become or be confused or bewildered. See **bug.**

bug up [someone's] ass (nose), to have [taboo] To have an obsession; to have an idea or plan from which one refuses to be deterred.

build *v.t.* **1** To prepare a person for victimizing; to build up. 1930: "We build the sap for the score." *Amer. Mercury*, Dec., 454. *Orig. underworld use.* **2** To exaggerate, project, or predict something. *v.i.* To increase, to grow in complexity, quantity, or intensity; may be said of a jazz performance. 1949: "I am afraid, and it builds all the time." Movie, *Scene of the Crime.* 1956: "When he [Dave Brubeck] plays twelve choruses of a number, as he does in 'Balcony Rock,' the number 'builds' constantly." A. Shaw, *West Coast Jazz*, 127. 1957: "The song 'Love Is a Many Splendored Thing' builds to a climax of strings, voices, brass, and woodwinds." Hedda Hopper, *synd. newsp. col.*, Mar. 17. *n.* **1** The work of preparing a person for victimizing; a build-up. *c1930. Orig. underworld use.* **2** A show whose earnings continue to increase. *Theater use.* **3** A person's physique, shape, or figure, specif., of an attractive young woman. *Colloq.* **—er** = **stew-builder.**

builder-upper *n.* One who or that which builds up, esp. one who or that which increases physical stamina or morale in a person. 1936: "You Mr. Sports Fan—it is you who plays the role of 'builder-upper' [of athletes' morale]. . . ." J. F. Hennessey in *Esquire*, Sept., 59/3. 1940: "Counselors make a point of encouraging such builder-uppers as a new hair-do for an awkward girl." C. Mackenzie in N.Y. *Times Mag.*, Apr. 4, 21. 1949: "V-8's the builder-upper." Advt. for a vegetable juice concoction, CBS radio, Sept. 2. See Appendix, —er - —er endings.

build-up **buildup** *n.* **1** Preparations, esp. advance publicity, to make a person, product, or plan of action acceptable, well known, or desirable; the art of creating a demand, usu. for an entertainer or a product. 1936: "A build-up for the championship. . . ." Tully, *Bruiser*, 108. 1952: "Jean Peters [actress] actually turned down a buildup as a sexy dish." Hollywood, Sept. 30. *Usu. in "to give [someone or something] the build-up."* **2** Anything said or done to win the confidence of a prospective victim of a confidence man; anything said or done to win the confidence of a customer. *Orig. underworld use.* **build up** *v.t.* To create self-confidence or determination in another by compliments or flattery; lit., to build up another's ego.

bulge *n.* **1** An advantage; a lead. 1951: "Brooklyn [the Brooklyn Dodgers, baseball team] retained its 5½-game bulge over the N.Y. Giants in the National League race. . . ." Joe Reichler, AP, Sept. 8. **2** Any part of the body that easily shows signs of obesity; esp. the buttocks, stomach, or breasts. *After W.W.II the name of the last major German offensive, "The Battle of the Bulge," was humorously applied to woman's constant fight for a trim figure.* **3** Any unusually big or important thing. *c1835. Obs.*

bull *v.t., v.i.* **1** To talk, discuss, or converse; esp. to talk at great length; to pass the time by talking. 1924: "He passed an open door. . . . 'Hi, Hugh. Come in and bull a while.' . . ." Marks, *Plastic Age*, 42. 1951: "Loafing, 'bulling'

with my colleagues, hunting and fishing. . . ." R. P. Basler, *Amer. Assoc. of Univ. Professors Bulletin*, Autumn, 587. **2** To talk insincerely; to exaggerate; to talk with more intensity or at a greater length than one's knowledge warrants. *Since c1850.* **3** To recite poorly. *Obs.* **4** To bluff; to accomplish a task crudely or without knowledge owing to one's aggressiveness, energy, or enthusiasm. 1939: "You can't bull me into spilling anything." Gardner, *D. A. Draws*, 167. *Since c1850. Colloq.* **5** To fail in a subject or school course. *c1930. Student use. Not common.* *n.* **1** A locomotive. *Railroad use since c1885.* **2** A policeman; a law enforcement officer of any kind, as a uniformed policeman, detective, plain-clothes man, F.B.I. agent, prison guard, railroad policeman, or the like. 1893: "I have seldom met a hobo who was very angry with a New York City 'bull.'" J. Flynt. 1929: *Used 36 times in* Burnett, *Little Caesar.* 1936: "Railroad bulls . . . eat three squares a day. . . ." John Dos Passos, *New Republic*, July 22, 322/1. *Prob. earlier than c1800; see* **bull pen.** *Orig. hobo and underworld use; since c1920 very common with all ranks of the underworld. Prob. of gypsy orig. from Sp. sl. "bul"* = *policeman, reinforced by the image of a bull as big and aggressive. Often used in combinations to designate the type of law enforcement officer.* Cf. **cinder bull, fly bull, harness bull, yard bull.** **3** Stupidity; insincerity; idle talk; exaggeration; lies; cant; esp. stupid, insincere, exaggerated, or untruthful talk, attitudes, or deeds; nonsense, hokum, boloney; conceit; bluff. 1924: "You're full of bull . . . she's more interesting than all your bull." Marks, *Plastic Age*, 48. 1937: "Don't give me any of that bull . . . sending flowers . . . is the bull." Weidman, *Wholesale*, 4. 1953: "It must be bull. . . ." J. R. Williams, *synd. cartoon*, "Out Our Way," Apr. 6. *Often used as a one-word reply or opinion. Orig. c1915, student use. Some W.W.I USN use. c1925 the usage started to gain popularity and has now been in universal sl. use for many years. Possibly same origin as gypsy "bul"* = *policeman. There is little to substantiate this, particularly as the present usage was neither orig. hobo nor Sp. Prob. euphem. for "bullshit."* Cf. **bulldoze** *for a further possible orig.* Cf. **bull session, shoot the bull, throw the bull.** **4** An ox. *Logger use.* **5** An elephant of either sex. *Circus use since c1920.* **6** Beefsteak. *Some logger and prison use since c1925.* **7** The boss of

a labor crew, esp. a ranch foreman. *c1930.*
8 An ace playing card. *From "bullet."*
bull   Bull   *n.*   **1** Bull Durham
tobacco. *A very popular brand before the
days of machine-made cigarettes.* **2** Any
smoking tobacco. 1920: "He wandered
about the gardens and along the shore
in a state of superloneliness, finding a
lethargic content in smoking 'Bull' at the
garage with one of the chauffeurs."
F. S. Fitzgerald, *This Side of Paradise,* 23.
adj. **1** Causing or favoring high prices, esp.
in the stock market. *Stock market use.*
2 Large; largest; strong; most powerful.

bull bitch [taboo]   Any woman having
a masculine appearance, gestures, or
traits. *Wide rural use.*

bull cook   **1** A male cook in a
logging or mining camp or ranch. *Logger
miner, rancher, and hobo use. Archaic.* →
2 One who does menial tasks around a
ranch, lumber camp, or the like; a camp
flunky, kitchen helper, or errand boy.
*Since c1920. Hobo, logger, and rancher
use. Because such flunkies usu. are
responsible to the chief cook.*

bulldog   *n.* The earliest daily edition
of a newspaper. *Newspaperman use.   v.t.*
1 To exaggerate or lie for personal gain
about one's past or success; to attempt to
increase demand for a product or service
by exaggeration of merit. **2** To wrestle
a steer or calf to the ground by its horns,
head, or neck. 1952: "When a Texas
cattleman hears 'BULLDOG,' his mental
impression is not canine. He thinks of
the cowboy sport of grabbing a steer by
the horns and rasslin' him to the ground."
J. Randolph, *Texas Brags,* 55.   **—dog-
ging**   *n.* **1** The act of wrestling a steer
or calf to the ground, so that it may be
branded. 1956: "Beside the bronc riding
and calf roping, of course, the [cow-]boys
were trying to stay on wild Brahma bulls
and wrestle with steers, a pastime which
used to be known as bulldogging." L.
Silvers in N.Y. *Daily News,* Sept. 27, 74.
Colloq. **2** Exaggerating or lying about
one's success for personal gain; trying to
increase the demand for a product or
service by blatantly exaggerating its
merits. 1956: "Touts were allowed to
advertise winners they did not have.
This was called 'bulldogging.' " T. Betts,
Across the Board, 240. **3** A short or snub-
nosed revolver. *Mainly police and underworld use.*

bulldoze   *v.t.* To cow; to coerce. 1876:
DAE. 1930: "If an Assistant District
Attorney attempts to bulldoze a wit-

ness. . . ." Lavine, *Third Degree, 197f.*
—r   *n.* **1** One who bulldozes. 1876:
DAE. Archaic. **2** A revolver. *c1880; obs.*

bulldyke   bulldike [taboo]   A
large-boned, muscular female homosexual who has many masculine traits;
a female homosexual who plays the
aggressive male role. *Orig. West Coast
use; not as common as the shorter "dyke."
Even among homosexuals, often used as
a term of derogation.*

bullet   *n.* **1** A doughnut; a biscuit or
cracker; any small item of bread or
pastry that can be heavy, hard, or stale.
c1880. Obs. **2** Dollars; silver money;
money. *Western and underworld use
since c1900. Archaic.* **3** In card-playing,
an ace. *Usu. used in poker in the plural,*
e.g., *"two bullets beat a pair of kings."
Since c1930. Because, like bullets, no
player can argue with aces.* **4** A rivet.
Airplane factory use during W.W.II.
—s   *n. pl.* **1** Any beans other than
green or string beans. *Since c1900, orig.
prison and USN use. Because such beans
traditionally cause explosive stomach rumb-
lings and eructations.* → **2** Peas, esp. the
hard varieties such as chickpeas or
cowpeas. *Since c1920, orig. USN use.*

bullet bait   Soldiers, sailors, or
marines. esp. when young or untrained,
who are likely to be exposed to enemy
fire; esp. marines. *See* **cannon fodder.**
Some use during and after W.W.II.

bull-fest   *n.* = **bull session.** 1924:
"Nothing but 'bull fests.' . . ." Marks,
Plastic Age, 286. *Not common. Some
student use c1920–30.*

bull fiddle   The double-bass viol.
Colloq.

bull-fighter   An empty railroad
freight car. *Railroad and hobo use.*

bullfrog's head, the = **cat's meow.**
Never common.

bullgine   *n.* A steam locomotive. *Some
railroad use since c1900. From "bull"
+ "engine."*

bullhead   bull-head   *n.* **1** A
stupid or stubborn person. *Since
c1850.* **2** A nickel; five cents. 1945:
"Then slip me a bullhead. I need a java."
Chas. Carson. *Archaic. From the figure
of a buffalo on the nickel.*

bullheaded   *adj.* Stubborn. *Colloq.*

bullish   *adj.* Tending to favor high
values and prices of corporate stocks;
favorable to the selling of or short-term
dealings in corporate stocks. *Stock-market
use.*

bull of the woods, the   **1** A
logging-camp foreman or boss. *Logger*

use since c1920. → **2** A trucking company foreman or district manager. *Trucker use. c1935.* → **3** Any important person; one who acts with or assumes authority. *Since c1940.*

bullpen   bull pen   *n.* **1** A small prison room used to confine convicts awaiting transfer, interrogation, or punishment. 1809: *DAE.* 1930: "The officer ... ordered them thrown into the bull pen." Lavine, *Third Degree*, 240. *Orig. prison use.* **2** A prison; any enclosure serving as a temporary cell or prison for those awaiting official judgment. 1943: "Waiting for arraignment with the others in the bullpen adjoining the courtroom...." Wolfert, *Underworld*, 103. *Orig. prison and underworld use, c1900.* → **3** An [enclosed] area near a baseball diamond where pitchers practice throwing and limber up as they wait to be called upon to enter the game. 1951: "Jim Hearn is my pitcher. Everybody else ... will be in the bullpen." Leo Durocher [baseball manager], *quoted by AP*, Oct. 1. *Baseball use since c1920.* **4** A prize fight ring. 1921: "Whilst waitin' for the gladiators to enter the bull pen...." Witwer, *Leather*, 161. *Not common.* **5** A bunkhouse. *Logger use since c1930.* → **6** Company-maintained dressing or sleeping rooms used by railroad workers and train crews between shifts. *Railroad use since c1935.* → **7** A men's college dormitory. *Some student use.* **8** A living room or other room of a house or sorority house where a male student waits for his date while he is judged by the girl's family or sorority sisters. *Student use, c1940*

bull session   *n.* **1** An informal and often lengthy conversation or series of discussions, freq. idle or boastful, on a variety of topical or personal subjects, esp. among a group of male students. 1924: "Religion and sex, the favorite topics for 'bull sessions.' ...." Marks, *Plastic Age*, 77. *Universally used by male students since c1920. Also common W.W. II Army use.* → **2** Any discussion, short or long, either serious or for the purpose of passing idle time. *Since c1940.* 1956: "When I [Wes Santee, track star] was still at Kansas University ... at a bull session among [Fred] Wilt, Bob [Richards], Mal [Whitfield] and myself. ...." Wes Santee, "Names, Places, and Pay-Offs," *Life*, Nov. 19, 99.

bullseye, hit the   **1** To succeed. **2** To satisfy a specific taste or desire.

bullshit   bull-shit [taboo]   *n.* **1** Anything that is distasteful, useless, or unnecessary. **2** Insincerity, lies, exaggeration. *The most common use.* **3** Menial tasks or jobs. *Not as common as the euphem. "bull."* Cf. **chicken shit.**   *v.i.* & *v.t.* To speak or write insincerely or with exaggeration; to brag; to speak idly, without thought; to pass the time by talking; to gossip.   *expl.* An expletive showing incredulity and contempt.   **—ter** [taboo]   *n.* **1** One who habitually talks too much or talks in an exaggerated or nonsensical way; one who speaks bull. **2** A voluble male egotist; a conceited man. See Appendix, —er ending.

bullshit artist [taboo]   *n.* = **bull-shitter.** *One of the most common sl. terms using "artist."*

bullshooter   *n.* One who exaggerates, brags, or talks nonsense. *Prob. a euphem. for "bullshitter."*

bullshot = **bullshit.**

bullskate   *v.i.* **1** = **bullshit.** **2** To brag. *Primarily Negro use.*

bullstaller   *n.* One whose inefficiency impedes the progress of a specific task. 1956: "A *bullstaller*—a poor carpenter." *Labor's Special Lang. from Many Sources.*

bull's wool   *n.* Stolen clothes. See **bull.**

bull work   *n.* Hard work. *Logger, miner, rancher, and maritime use. Not common.*

bully   *adj.* Fine, excellent, first-rate. 1910: "Say, that's a bully idea," Johnson, *Varmint*, 67. *Used 12 other times in the book. Associated with students c1850–1920. No longer common; now considered affected or pseudo-Brit.*   *n.* A railroad track workman; a gandy dancer. *Railroad use, c1900–35.*

bum   *n.* **1** A spree. 1871: *DAE. c1900 common use, esp. with students. Archaic.* **2** Generally, a beggar, tramp, hobo, vagrant, or loafer; also, any jobless man or youth having little or no income; a poor, poorly dressed, and unkempt frequenter of saloons; a down-and-outer; sometimes, a hoodlum. 1893: "The 'C. B. & Q.' [railroad] ... was called 'the bums' line. ...." J. Flynt. 1900: "It's a well-dressed class of customers. No bums. ...." "... A chronic type of bum and beggar." Dreiser, *Carrie*, 223, 334. 1936: "I consider the word 'bum' a term of reproach to men who are unemployed and unfortunate." H. F. Kane, *New Republic*, July 15, 289/2. 1952: "A hobo will work, a tramp won't, a bum can't." CBS, *radio network*, Aug.

25. *Common since c1880, the word has degenerated. Orig.* = *a vagabond or wandering hobo, by 1900 had taken on the connotation of beggar, one who has not the romantic wanderlust or pride of some early vagabonds. Later* = *a moneyless, prideless, filthy, hopeless derelict and habitual drunkard. During the Depression the word took on a little more status owing to the vast number of unemployed and tramps. During times of prosperity, however, the connotation of drunken derelict is the main one. No self-respecting vagabond or hobo would allow anyone to call him a bum today. From the German "Bummler," a good natured vagabond, an idler, a stroller* + *the British word "bum"* = *the buttocks. Hence, "bum" has the connotation of an irresponsible vagabond and of one whom life, fate, or bad habits have fig. knocked to a sitting position.* → **3** A drifter; a grifter. **4** Any male without a professional occupation, goal in life, or social prestige; any disreputable or disliked youth. *Since c1920.* → **5** A prize fighter, esp. one who is not a successful or good fighter. *Prize fight use since c1920.* → **6** Any well-known athlete of country-club sports, such as tennis or golf, who lives on the hospitality of socially prominent sports fans. *Since c1920.* → **7** Any sports enthusiast, usu. of skiing, tennis, or golf, who changes his job location frequently in order to be near ski slopes, golf courses, or the like; any sports fan who follows a sport, athlete, or team to various cities or locales, to the complete disruption of jobs and home life. *Since c1920.* → **8** Any unskilled worker or athlete. *Since c1925.* → **9** A promiscuous woman, esp. if uneducated and unsophisticated; a cheap prostitute. 1930: "Picking up bums in public dance halls. . . ." J. T. Farrell, 161. *Very common since c1940.* → **10** An orphaned animal; an animal deserted by its mother. *Western ranch and farm use since c1930.* → **11** An inferior farm animal or breed of livestock. *Farm and market use since c1930.* → **12** An inferior racehorse; a slow-running racehorse. **13** A fellow, a guy. *Used jocularly or affectionately since c1945.* **14** Fig., anything considered as useless or unsatisfactory or as having the traits of a bum. 1951: "Money is a bum, a no-good." Hal Boyle, AP, May 1. See **crumb-bum, on the bum, stew-bum, stumblebum.** **15** Any person less successful than others think he

should be; any person with but little money or status; a person without energy or ambition. 1957: "In a recent movie Humphrey Bogart's screen wife asked him why he was so eager for big money. Bogart intoned the national ethos: 'All I know is, if you haven't got it, they call you a bum.' " F. Morton, *The Art of Courtship,* 156. **16** The human posterior. *Colloq.* *v.i.* **1** To live as a tramp or bum. 1894 [1891]: "What a foolish business 'bumming' was. . . ." J. Flynt. *Since c1870.* → **2** To beg; to go begging. *Since c1880.* → **3** To loaf. *c1900, student use. Obs. in favor of "bum around."* **4** To hitch-hike; to travel to a place by asking free rides with passing motorists. *Usu.* in "I bummed to ――." *Short form of "bum* [= *beg*] *a ride." Common student use c1920. Archaic.* *v.t.* **1** To beg food, drink, money, a smoke, a ride, or the like. 1925: "He was probably bumming his way home." F. Scott Fitzgerald, *The Great Gatsby,* 137. 1939: "He thought of bumming the price of a pack of cigarets off someone. . . ." J. T. Farrell, 211. 1948: "I had started out to bum a feed." Cain, *Moth,* 77. *Since c1865; in common use by c1900.* → **2** To beg from a person. → **3** To borrow something, esp. to borrow an item so insignificant that its return or replacement is not expected, such as a cigarette, match, or pencil. *Since c1940; very common. Colloq.* *adj.* **1** Of inferior quality; inferior; unsatisfactory; not serving an intended purpose. 1888: *DAE.* 1910: "It's a bum hat." Johnson, *Varmint,* 154. 1920: "He's a bum dancer." Fitzgerald, *This Side of Paradise,* 157. → **2** False, untrue; inaccurate; unreliable. 1934: "I told a bum story first." Cain, *Postman,* 52. 1952: "But the rap that sends Frankie away was a bum one." R. C. Ruark, *synd. newsp. col.,* Aug. 19. **3** Sickly; without energy. **4** Spoiled; overripe. *Said of food.* **―mer** *n.* **1** A lamb deserted by its mother. *Farm use since c1860.* **2** A worthless youth or man, esp. one given to habitual borrowing." 1952: "An old bummer named Rumson." A. J. Lerner, *Paint Your Wagon,* I. See **bum.** See Appendix, **―er** ending. **―my** *adj.* **1** Slightly ill. **2** Spoiled or overripe. *Said of food.*

bum, on the **1** Living as a beggar or hobo; living and wandering as a tramp; begging. 1907: "A poor hobo on the bum." Jack London, *My Life. Colloq. since c1900.* → **2** Living any disreputable, disorderly life. **3** In bad condition. *Said* *of a sick or indisposed person or a non-functioning or improperly functioning thing. Since c1900.*

bum around **1** To loaf; to wander idly; to do nothing. *Since c1860.* → **2** To associate with as a friend; to pass the time loafing, idling, or wandering with another. 1950: "Fellows with whom I've bummed around. . . ." Billy Rose, *synd. newsp. col.*, Jan. 6.

bumblepuppy *n.* **1** In the card game of bridge, a game played without a plan or thought. → **2** A card player who plays without much thought or interest. *Both uses since c1935. From the fictional and satirical game of "bumblepuppy," a highly organized, rule-ridden game described in Aldous Huxley's "Brave New World." Also a 19th-century children's tennis game in which the ball was hit so as to arc as high as possible over the net.*

bum-out *n.* An assignment to easy work. *Some prison and Army use. c1950.*

bump *v.t.* **1** To dismiss an employee; to fine a person. *Since c1915.* → **2** To reassign work from an employee of lesser seniority to one of great seniority in order to retain the older employee and dismiss the younger. *Railroad and general union worker use since 1860.* → **3** In U.S. federal government agencies, to replace another employee who is less retainable. 1953: "Riffing sets up a chain reaction through . . . 'bumping.' . . . A person is bumped by someone with a larger number of retention points. In turn, if the person bumped has civil service status, he bumps someone else. . . . Right now bumping is affecting thousands of government employees. . ." Jane Eads, *synd. newsp. article*, Aug. 25. *Since cW.W.II.* **4** To defeat an opponent or opposing team. *Fig., to bump a person or team off a list of victors.* **5** To kill; to murder. 1934: "You bumped Low Harger." Chandler, *Finger Man*, 34. *Underworld use since c1920. Not as common as "bump off."* **6** To cause something to happen; to give; to make a contact with another; to meet, write, or telephone another; to "hit." *Since c1930. Not common.* **7** To make pregnant; to knock up. 1935: "She had to blame somebody for bumping her. . . ." Len Yinberg, *Amer. Mercury*, May 84/2. **8** To give an employee an increase in salary or responsibility; to promote someone. 1957: "After . . . six months, they bumped me to $100 a week." AP, Aug. 20. *Since c1935.* **9** In the card game of poker, to raise or increase the amount

each player must bet to stay in the game. *Since c1935. Note the opposite meanings of 1, 2, 3, and 9.* *v.i.* **1** To die. *Some use since c1940.* **2** In dancing or during a striptease, to thrust the pelvis forward suddenly. *n.* **1** A murder. 1934: "Maybe he needed the bump—but you gave it to him. . . ." Chandler, *Finger Man*, 34. **2** A promotion; an increase in salary. 1949: "I see old Pipkin has got a bump to full professor. . . ." Morris Bishop, *New Yorker*, Dec. 3, 123/1. *Since c1940.*
—er *n.* **1** In the card game of bridge, a two-game rubber. *c1934. Archaic.* **2** A striptease performer or erotic dancer; one who does bumps. 1957: "A show full of . . . grinders, peelers, and bumpers. . . ." L. Sobel, *synd. newsp. col.*, Apr. 2.

bump [one's] gums To talk; esp. to talk often, at length, idly, or futilely. 1943: "You may as well stop bumping your gums." *Time*, July 26, 56. *Orig. jive talk. Never as common as "beat [one's] gums."*

bumpman **1** A professional, hired killer. *c1925.* **2** A pickpocket. 1939–40: "A bump man I use to see out at the track . . . it will be a fine thing for the joint in case he happens to bump into one of the socialites and the socialites lose a handsome wallet stuffed with a liberal supply of folding." O'Hara, *Pal Joey*, 52. *Not common.*

bump off **bump-off** **bumpoff** *v.t.* To kill; to murder. 1921: "Guys has been bumped off for no more cause than a . . . grin." Witwer, *Leather*, 71. 1930: "If I'm going to bump off the enemy I'll need some practice. . . ." *All Quiet on the Western Front*, movie. *Underworld use since c1915. Freq. W.W.I Army use.* *v.i.* To die. *Since c1920. Orig. hobo use.*
bump-off **bumpoff** *n.* A murder. 1949: "It's . . . a gangland bump-off. . . ." *Fact Detec. Mysteries*, 178. *Since c1920.*

bum-rush *v.t.* To give someone the bum's rush. 1944: "I bum-rushed him the hell out of there. . . ." Shulman, *Feather Merchants*, 123.

bum's rush, the **1** The ejection of a person from a room or public place by physical force. 1922: "Dey gimme de bum's rush." O'Neill, *Hairy Ape*, 5. → **2** Fig., any discourteous treatment used in getting rid of a person. 1949: "Those not in sympathy with the strike got the bum's rush." W. Pegler, *synd. newsp. col.*, Dec. 28.

bum steer A false clue; advice or information that proves to be wrong. 1937: "Would I give you a bum steer?.." Weidman, *Wholesale*, 211. 1942: "A bad tip or bum steer...." Henry McLemore, *Look*. *Common since c1925.*

bun *n.* **1** A state of drunkenness; a jag. 1938: "A bun is a light jag." R. Connell, *Parade. Perhaps from "bungey."* *Since c1920.* See **have a bun on. 2** The human posterior. **—ned** *adj.* Drunk. *A little use since c1920.* Cf. **have a bun on.** See Appendix, Drunk.

bunch *v.i.* **1** To leave, depart, or withdraw. **2** To quit a job. *Hobo use; c1925.* *n.* **1** = **mob.** *Underworld use.* **2** Money, esp. a large sum of money; a bankroll.

bunch of calico A girl or woman. *c1900; logger and ranch use. Obs.*

bunch of fives A fist; lit., the five fingers bunched into a fist. *Since c1850. Now archaic.*

bunch of rags = **bunch of calico**; a girl or young woman.

bunco **bunko** *v.t.* To swindle; to cheat; to fake; to bluff. 1901: "He was buncoed out of his seat in the House of Representatives." Greenough & Kittredge, 351. *c1875–c1910; obs.*

bunco artist **bunko artist** A professional swindler; a confidence man. 1945: "The other fellow is, in most instances, a bunko artist who is looking for a chance to prove how good he is." *Time*, June 11, 22/2. *Newsp. and police use. Synthetic underworld use.* Cf. **bunco.**

bunco-steerer *n.* A shill; esp. an accomplice in a confidence game. 1900: "A stranger ... in the city ... became entangled with a bunco-steerer." Dreiser, *Carrie*, 143. *Since c1875. Newsp. and police use. Synthetic underworld use. Archaic.*

bundle *n.* **1** An amount of money; esp. a large amount of money. 1905: "Did they sting you for the whole bundle?" McHugh, *Search Me*, 15. *Since c1900. Common since c1920 with the connotation of money illegally or unethically obtained; since c1935 such a connotation is not necessarily implied.* **2** A sexually desirable girl or young woman, esp. if small and cute. *Since c1930.*

bun-duster *n.* A meek male who frequents teas and other mild entertainments, making no effort to repay his social obligations; a cake-eater. *Some c1920 use.* Cf. **bun-struggle.**

bungalow sailor A Coast Guardman, esp. when on shore duty. *Said to be some W.W.II USN use, but sounds synthetic.*

bungey *adj.* Drunk. *c1730; obs.*

bunhead *n.* A stupid person. *Some use c1915.* Cf. **bum.**

bunion-breeder *n.* An infantry soldier. *Prob. synthetic.*

bunk *n.* Boloney; exaggeration; lies; cant. 1927: "Among the words now in good usage which within recent memory were but slang, I recall ... 'bunk.'" J. A. Work in *Educational Rev.*, Apr., 224. *Colloq.* *v.t.* To cheat. 1926: "He bunked me out of my pile." Court testimony.

bunk fatigue *n.* **1** Sickness requiring the patient to remain in bed. *W.W.I Army use. Obs. →* **2** A period of sleep or rest in bed; sleep. *Wide W.W.II Armed Forces use. This meaning orig. C.C.C. and Army use c1935.*

bunk flying Talking about flying; exaggerated recounting of stories of flying. *W.W.II Air Force use.*

bunk habit = **bunk fatigue.**

bunkie *n.* A roommate or bunkmate; a buddy. *More common than "buddy" during W.W.I Army use. Mainly student use since W.W.I. Colloq.* See Appendix, —ie ending.

bunk lizard A chronic sleeper; one who is able to hide away from work; a gold brick. *W.W.I use, orig. USN use.*

bunkum **buncombe** *n.* Nonsense; bunk. *Archaic.*

bunny *n.* **1** Welsh rabbit. 1910: "Dish out the bunny." Johnson, *Varmint*, 289. *c1900; student use.* See **blushing bunny. 2** A person; a guy or girl; a bewildered, confused, or habitually perplexed person. *Usu. in a phrase such as "tough bunny," "cuddle bunny," or "dumb bunny."* 1951: "And she is always criticizing some poor bunny." S. Lewis, *World So Wide*, 4. *Usu. preceded by an adj. such as "poor," "helpless," or "lost," the term implies affection or sympathy more often than criticism. It seems to be applied to those whose appearance or predicament brings out the maternal or paternal instinct in the speaker. Since c1925.* **3** [taboo] A female prostitute to lesbians. **4** A male prostitute to male homosexuals.

bun on, have a **1** To be drunk. *Fairly common since c1925. →* **2** To be under the influence of a narcotic. See Appendix, Drunk.

bun pup A frankfurter on a roll; a hot dog. *Not common.*

bun-struggle *n.* A formal tea. *Some*

c1920 use. Not as common as the orig. Brit. sl. term.

Bunyan camp   A logging or construction camp that does not furnish bedding for workers. *From Paul Bunyan, who lived primitively.*

burg   *n.* A town; a city. 1928: "Two weeks . . . in a burg he hated." J. T. Farrell, 73. *Since c1850. From "burgh." The word is assuming a connotation of a city or town that is disliked, because it is either too small and quiet or too big and noisy.*

—burger   See Appendix, Suffixes and Suffix Words.

burglar   *n.* Anyone who swindles, cheats, or takes advantage of another; any unethical businessman. See **gut-burglar.**

burgle   *v.t.* To burglarize. *Since c1850. Now considered jocular.* See Appendix, Back Formations.

buried   *adj.* **1** Drunk. *Some 1920 use. Now archaic.* **2** Serving a life or a very long prison sentence. *Underworld and prison use.*   *v.i., v.t.* To be in prison; to be put in prison, esp. if held incommunicado or in solitary confinement. *Since c1930; underworld use.*

burlap, the   *n.* = **the sack.** 1951: "There's no reason why he should be fired . . . or given the gate, the burlap, the sack, or the mitt." C. Stinnett, *SEP*, Dec. 8, 44/1. *Jocular.*

burleycue   burlecue   burlicue   *n.* A burlesque show. 1948: "Pony in a burlecue. . . ." F. Brown, *Dead Ringer*, 48.

burly   *n.* Burlesque. 1953: "Even when [comedian Red] Buttons was in burly." Eli Basse quoted by G. Millstein, N.Y. *Times Mag.*, Feb. 22, 14/2.

burn   *v.t. & v.i.* **1** To cheat a partner out of his business profits or criminal loot. 1928: ". . . To burn a partner." E. Booth, *Amer. Mercury*, May, 80. 1950: "He will not burn . . . his partners." DeBaun, 72. *Since 1800.* → **2** To rob, swindle, cheat, or take advantage of another. *Since c1800.* → **3** To be disappointed bitterly in business or love; to lose confidence or faith in others owing to past disappointments. *Since c1940.* **4** To electrocute a person, as legal punishment, in the electric chair. 1929: "They burned him in the chair." J. Auslander, *Hell in Harness*, 1. → **5** To kill; esp. by shooting. 1949: "Burn them." Ellson, *Duke*, 7. *Since c1935.* **6** To anger a person; to burn up. 1939–40: "I was plenty burned. . . ." O'Hara, *Pal Joey*, 12. 1949: "That's

what burns me, Chief." *Mr. District Attorney*, network radio play, Oct. 26. **7** To fight or assault a rival gang or member of a rival gang, esp. with clubs or knives. *Teenage street gang use since c1955.* **8** To apply pressure, mistreatment, or "heat" to a person to induce his resignation or to break down his morale. 1943: "I'll burn you right off the [police] force." Wolfert, *Underworld*, 235. **9** [taboo] To become infected with, or to infect another with, a venereal disease.   *v.i.* **1** To die by penal electrocution. 1930: "No one wants to burn for just having a guy knocked off. . . ." Lavine, *Third Degree*, 32. **2** To become angry; to show one's anger; to burn up. 1939–40: "He began making cracks . . . I burned but went on singing. . . ." O'Hara, *Pal Joey*, 4. *Since c1930.* **3** To move with great speed. *Colloq.*   *n.* See **slow burn.**   **—er**   *n.* **1** A swindler; a thief. *Archaic.* Cf. **burn. 2** The electric chair. *Not as common as "hot seat" or "the chair."* See **grease-burner, hash-burner, slum-burner;** also **cook on the front burner, hay-burner.**

burn down   **1** To shoot a person. Cf. **burn. 2** To refuse or reject another, or to deflate another's ego, or another's optimism, work, or plan, by severe criticism, sarcasm, or angry remarks.

burned-out   *adj.* **1** Tired, exhausted; specif., exhausted and depressed after the effects of a drug have worn off. *Drug addict use.* **2** Bored.

burnese   *n.* = **Bernice.**

burnie   *n.* A partially smoked marijuana cigarette; a marijuana cigarette shared between two or more addicts. *Drug addict use.* See Appendix, **—ie** ending.

burn off = **burn up.** *Some use since late W.W.II; later popularized by freq. use in Walt Kelly's synd. newsp. comic, "Pogo." Reinforced by "browned off."*

burn one   **1** A glass of beer. *Since c1930. Used by bartenders in relaying an order.* **2** A malted milk. *Some lunch-counter use since c1935. Used by waitresses in relaying an order.*

burn one over   In baseball, to pitch a fast ball.

burn the breeze   To run at full speed; to drive a car at full speed. *Mainly Southwestern use, since c1930.*

burn the road   To drive a car fast. *Since c1930.*

burn [someone] up   **1** To make [a person] angry; to enrage; to irritate. 1929–30: "And that burns me up!"

K. Brush, *Young Man*, 91. 1940: "I'll bet the Army boys are burned up now!" *Life*, Nov. 18, 2. *Very common. Cf.* **burn.** **2** To electrocute a criminal in the electric chair. **3** To cheat, swindle, exploit, or take advantage of; esp. to do so in such a manner or so thoroughly as to prevent future cheating, swindling, or exploiting in the same place or of the same person. *c1930. Circus use.* **4** To do one's job or to perform sensationally; to better previous records. *Common in sports since c1940.* **5** To search a place thoroughly. **6** To do anything intensely, rapidly, or thoroughly. *Colloq.*

burn with a low blue flame   To be in the most extreme stage of intoxication.

burp   *v.i., v.t.* To belch.   *n.* A belch. *Of echoic origin. "Burp" has largely replaced "belch" in popular U.S. speech. Colloq.*

burp gun   **1** A small automatic gun used by the German Army during W.W.II. *Wide Army use during W.W.II. So called from its sound in firing.* → **2** Any machine gun.

burr   *n.* = **cold shoulder.**

burr cut = **crew cut.**

burr-head [derog.]   *n.* A Negro.

burrole   *n.* **1** The human ear. → **2** An eavesdropper; one who seeks information; a stool pigeon. *Some underworld use since c1930. From Eng. underworld use.* **3** Begging. See **on the burrole.**

burrole (burrola), on the   To live the wandering life of a criminal, person wanted by the police, confidence man, or even of a hobo or beggar; to live the life of a drifter.

bury   *v.t.* To betray a friend or co-worker. See **buried.**

bury yourself!   *interj.* = **drop dead!**

bus   *n.* **1** A car, esp. one's own. 1934: "That your bus outside?" Chandler, *Finger Man*, 17. *Since c1915; often implies that car is old; always said affectionately.* → **2** A military tank or armored vehicle. *Some W.W.I use. Not used during W.W.II.* → **3** An airplane. *Some W.W.I and W.W.II use. Some commercial aviation use.* *v.t.* To clear used dishes and silver from tables, esp. in a restaurant or cafeteria, and take them to the dishwasher. 1950: "Right now I'm bussin' dishes at the automat." *Eddie Cantor's radio network show*, Apr. 9. *Common since c1925. Prob. from the four-wheeled cart used in many public eating places. Colloq.* **—boy bus-boy bus boy**   *n.* One who busses dishes. 1932: ". . . Talking very tough

to a bus boy. . . ." Runyon. 1939–40: "This busboy . . . use to fix me up a sandwich once in a while. . . ." O'Hara, *Pal Joey*, 54. *Common since c1925.*

buscar   *n.* **1** Borrowed money. *Some W.W.II Army and USN use.* → **2** Unexpected or forbidden pleasure; boodle; that which provides unexpected pleasure. *Thus "buscar" can be a woman or provided by a woman, the unexpected arrival of money, or a box of sweets, etc. Some W.W.II use.* → **3** A close friend, esp. one from whom one can borrow money or with whom one shares a pleasurable experience. *A new slang word, still gaining popularity.*

bush   *n.* **1** = **bush league.** *Fairly common since c1930. Cf.* **the bushes. 2** A list of students whose scholastic standing or conduct is unsatisfactory. *Since c1925, student use.* See **tree. 3** A beard. 1952: " 'So I grew a beard . . . the director . . . told me to keep the beard.' Gene [Evans] has had the bush ever since. . . ." Bob Thomas, AP, Hollywood, Dec. 12. **4** [taboo] The vagina; the female crotch. *In reference to pubic hair. Cf.* **bush patrol.** → **5** A girl or young woman, esp. if attractive. *A new usage; the word is usu. not derog. Since c1950, mainly student use.* *adj.* Pertaining to or reminiscent of small towns or rural areas; unsophisticated, non-professional, amateurish. *Cf.* **bush league.** *v.t.* To tire a person out; said of a task or action; to exhaust someone physically, mentally, or emotionally; to sap someone's energy. *From "bushed."* **—ed**   *adj.* **1** Lost in the forest or bushes; confused and walking in circles in the forest; lost. *c1870. Obs.* **2** Tired, fatigued, exhausted, as if from being lost or walking in circles. *Since c1870.* 1947: "I'm bushed!" H. Boyle, AP, May 19. 1951: "On the one hand, she was curious to know what was up there. On the other hand, she was bushed." *New Yorker*, July 28, 15/1. *Common since W.W.II.* **—er**   *n.* **1** A baseball player in or from a minor league. *See* **bush league.** → **2** An inept, inexperienced, unsophisticated person; esp. an athlete. → **3** A hick; one with hick concepts or manners.

bush, on the   Close to failure, esp. in a course of study. *Not common; mainly Annapolis use. Since c1925.* See **bush.**

bushes, the   Small towns or rural communities; the sticks. 1949: "When I was . . . working 12-hour tricks as a newspaper cub in the bushes." W. Pegler, *synd. newsp. col.,* Oct. 26. Cf. **bush league.**

bush league   bush-league   *n.* In baseball, a minor league of professional or semiprofessional teams, usu. composed of players lacking the experience or ability, or players who are too old, to be able to compete in the major leagues. *Common since c1925; colloq.   adj.* Fig., small-time; second-rate; amateurish, nonprofessional, unsophisticated. 1949: "He was . . . a bushleague Chicago gambler. . . ." A. Hynd, *Public Enemies,* 108.

bush parole   An escape from prison; one who has escaped from prison. *Prison and underworld use since c1920.*

bush patrol   1 = **necking.** *Usu. jocular use, implying that one is going to take one's date into the seclusion of a clump of bushes or a park.* → **2** Sexual intercourse. Cf. **bush.**

bush-tail   *n.* A horse. *Archaic.*

bushwa(h)   booshwa(h)   boushwa(h) Bunk; boloney; blah. 1938: "There has been a lot of bushwa tossed around about how moving pictures aren't worthy of their audience." Otis Ferguson, *New Republic,* Aug. 31, 104/2. 1939: "The usual boushwah of the Reds." J. T. Farrell, 204. *Often used as a one-word comment and as an exclam. Common since c1920; not now heard from young people who prefer the more vulgar "bull," "bullshit," and "horseshit."*

business   *n.* A bowel movement; feces, usu. said of a household pet. *Euphem.*

business, give [someone] the   See **the business.**

business, know [one's] = **know [one's] onions.**

business, the   *n.* **1** Rough treatment; murder; a beating; a bawling out; planned rudeness. 1942: "He gives him the business with his own gun." Chandler, *High Window,* 140. 1949: "[We]'ve been getting the business [a reprimand] down at Headquarters." Burnett, *Jungle,* 17. **2** The equipment necessary for giving oneself an injection of a narcotic drug—hypodermic needle, cotton, etc.— or the substitutes often used, i.e., a pin, an eye-dropper, a bent spoon, etc. *Drug addict use.* **3** [taboo] The penis; the vagina; sexual intercourse.

business end of [something]   The dangerous, critical, or most important part of something; the front section or end of a piece of machinery. Thus, "the business end of a gun" = a gun's muzzle;

"the business end of a truck" = a truck's engine.

businessman's bounce   Dance music or a popular song played in fast tempo, satisfying to those with little knowledge of dancing or of jazz. 1956: ". . . The *businessman's bounce,* a two-beat played fast." S. Longstreet, *The Real Jazz Old and New,* 149. *Derisive use by musicians.*

bus ride! = **subway!**

buss = **bus.**

bust   *n.* **1** A failure of any kind; one who cannot complete a specif. task successfully or who has failed to attain a specif. goal; an inferior or worthless thing, an item which does not serve its intended purpose. 1842: *DAE.* 1958: "I'm a bust as a father, and my son's a bust at making money." Movie, *Hot Spell.* → **2** A notice of failure, as a note dismissing a student from a school or an order demoting a soldier in rank. *Since c1890.* **3** A drinking spree; a spree; a wild party. 1844: *DAE.* 1957: "What did I do? I went on a real bust." Movie, *The Young Don't Cry. Most common use c1900.* → **4** A drunkard; a bum or hobo. *Dial.* Cf. **busthead. 5** A punch with the fist. 1929: "You think I'm gonna let a guy take a bust at me?" Burnett, *Little Caesar,* 167. *Since c1915.* **6** A raid by the police. 1938: "One whiff [of marijuana] and we get a bust." Berger in *New Yorker,* 48/2.   *v.t.* **1** To break something. *Colloq.* **2** To fail an examination, recitation, or course of study; to fail a student. *Common student use by c1900.* → **3** To demote a military man in rank; specif., to demote a noncommissioned officer to the rank of private. *Common Army use since W.W.I.* **4** To tame a wild horse, fig. to break the spirit of a wild horse. 1936: "[The cowboy], by reason of his inability to handle cattle, might be useless save for the single task of 'busting' horses which the average puncher could not sit on." P. A. Rollins, *The Cowboy,* 25. Cf. **bronco buster. 5** To hit, as a person. *Since c1920.* **6** To break open or crack a safe or strong box; to enter or break into a place in order to rob it. *Underworld use.* **7** To ruin something; to make a mistake. **8** To catch another in the act of doing something illegal or unethical. *Rock-and-roll and some general teenage use since c1955.* **9** To disperse a gang or group; to force a gang or group to leave a specific public place, street corner, or the like. *Teenage gang use since c1955.   adj.* Broke; penniless. *Fairly common.*

—ed　　*adj.* **1** Reduced in rank. *Army use since cW.W.I.* **2** Without money; broke. 1956: "You're not wealthy but you're not busted, either." J. Cannon, *Who Struck John?* 51. **3** Arrested. 1958: "Although I had been busted (arrested) less than two weeks ago. . . ." "A Gang Leader's Redemption," *Life*, April 28, 70.　　**—er**　　*n.* **1** A spree. 1848: *DAE. Obs. From "bust."* See Appendix, —er ending. **2** An unusually large person. 1943: "The young un come. He was a buster. He was nigh as big as his Mammy. He come afore his time and all of a sudden but he was a buster." R. P. Warren, *Sewanee Rev.*, Spring. *Since c1850. Dial.* **3** A fellow, a guy, esp. a wise guy. *Almost always in direct address to a stranger, usu. one who has aroused the speaker's anger.* **4** A square, a Babbitt. *Some far-out use since c1955.*

bust a gut　　To use all one's strength in attempting to accomplish a specif. task, either a manual or other task, successfully; to try to the best of one's ability; fig., to try so hard that one ruptures oneself. *Since c1945.*

bust [one's] conk　　To work hard; to apply oneself diligently. Cf. **bust a gut.**

busthead　　bust-head　　*n.* **1** Inferior or cheap whisky, liquor, or wine; fig., whisky so raw that one's head will burst from drinking it. 1863: *DAE.* → **2** A drunkard, esp. a hobo or derelict who is a drunkard.

bust out　　*v.i.* To be dismissed from a college or university because of failing grades. See **bust.**　　**bust-out**　　*n.* The conclusion of a swindle, when the victim surrenders his money; the trick or swindle that causes a victim to lose money. 1958: "Bust-out—High point of a confidence game, when the swindle occurs." G. Y. Wells, *Station House Slang. Police use; synthetic underworld use.*　　*v.i., v.t.* To lose all one's money gambling, specif. at dice; to win all of someone's money at gambling, specif. at dice, and specif. by crooked means.　　**—s**　　Crooked or loaded dice.

bust-out joint　　A notoriously crooked gambling house. 1953: "Percentage dice . . . common in bust-out joints all over the country." W. S. Fairfield in *Reporter*, June 9, 16/1. 1956: "BUST-OUT JOINT —A crooked gambling house. Horse players in a losing streak sometimes apply the term to a race track." T. Betts, *Across the Board*, 313. See **joint.**

bus up = **bus.**

busy　　*n.* A detective. *Never common.*

but　　*conj.* And.　　*adv.* Very; definitely. 1939: "He noticed it and began making cracks but loud." O'Hara, *Pal Joey*, 4. 1953: "So I let him have it—but good." Radio, *Phone Call from a Stranger*, Jan. 5. 1958: "Nobody but nobody undersells Gimbels." Advt. for N.Y.C. dept. store. *Often used only to emphasize the word following; sometimes used to signal a coming repetition of the preceding word. Typically, it joins a monosyllabic, flat adverb (such as "good," "loud," "quick," "soon," "bad," etc.) to a preceding predicate or other verbal construction. Occasionally it precedes an adj.*

Butch　　butch　　*n.* **1** The youngest male child of a family. *Dial. and archaic.* **2** A tough or rough youth or man; a tough or rough-looking man. **3** A type of men's haircut. 1949 "His hair disfigured by a butch haircut." Burnett, *Jungle*, 24. 1957: "A more radical version of the Crew is the 'Butch.' Prof. L. Sherman Trusty, manager of the American Barber College, says the genuine Butch has the top, side and back hair cut short, following the natural shape of the head." H. Mitgang, *About—Men's Haircuts.* Cf. **crew cut.** **4** A medical officer. *Some W.W.II Army use. From "butcher."* See Appendix, Shortened Words. **5** A vendor, a butcher. See Appendix, Shortened Words. 1947: ". . . News butcher. . . . The butch sometimes helped the conductor to pick up the ticket markers." S. H. Holbrook in *Amer. Mercury*, Apr., 435/2. **6** A mistake. **7** A female homosexual who plays the male role.　　*v.t.* To spoil or ruin something.　　**—er**　　*n.* **1** A vendor of small items, as newspapers or candy, as in a train or at a circus. 1947: "Drink and peanut butchers." *Fortune*, July, 110/2. *Colloq.* **2** An inferior surgeon. **3** An inferior barber. **4** Any person who is particularly clumsy at work requiring manual dexterity.

—butcher　　See Appendix, Suffixes and Suffix Words.

butcher shop　　A hospital.

butcher wagon　　An ambulance.

butt　　*n.* **1** The rump. 1859: *DAE.* 1943: "So drunk he couldn't find his butt with both hands." H. A. Smith, *Putty Knife*, 129. *Colloq.* **2** The remainder, esp. the last year or few months of a military enlistment or prison sentence. *Since c1915.* → **3** A short time; a short enlistment or prison sentence. **4** A whole cigarette, an unsmoked cigarette. 1924: "Anybody got a butt?" Marks, *Plastic Age*, 161. 1951: "He gave me a pack of butts." *I*, *Mobster*, 31. *From stand.* *"butt"* = *the stub of a partially smoked cigarette or cigar.* *v.i.* To smoke. *Not common.*

butter *n.* **1** Dynamite. *Never common.* **2** Flattery. *Colloq.* **3** Soldering paste. *Some radio amateur use c1930.* *v.t.* = **butter up.**

butter-and-egg man A wealthy, unsophisticated, small-town businessman who tries to become a playboy, esp. one when visiting a large city; a wealthy Western farmer or businessman visiting in a big Eastern city. 1930: "The visiting Butter and Egg Men [had] their Whoopee in New York." C. Bragdon in *Outlook*, Oct., 301/1. *Common since c1920. Popularized by nightclub entertainer Texas Guinan.*

butter-ball *n.* Any plump person, esp. a young woman.

butter-box [derog.] *n.* A Dutchman. *Never common.*

butter brown An order of buttered toast. *Some lunch-counter use in relaying orders. Not as common as "an order of down."*

buttercup *n.* A girl, esp. an attractive, innocent girl.

butterfingers *n. sing.* A clumsy person, esp. a person who habitually drops things; specif., a baseball player who drops the ball when attempting to catch it. *Since c1900; colloq.*

butterflies **butterflys** *n. pl.* Fluttery sensations in one's stomach, caused by anxiety or nervous tension. 1951: "I've got butterflies, and I don't want to be alone." Movie, *Night into Morning.* *n. sing.* Nervousness; apprehension. *From the expression "to have butterflies in one's stomach," descriptive of nervous tension.*

butterfly ball **butterfly pitch** In baseball, a slow, floating pitch; a knuckleball. 1951: "Maybe all this exertion took the butter off his butterfly pitches in the next disastrous inning." D. Young in N.Y. *Daily News*, Aug. 30, C20.

butterfly kiss A caress given by winking one eye so that the lashes brush against the face of the receiver. 1940: "She worked her eyelashes and made butterfly kisses on my cheeks." Chandler, *Farewell*, 112. *Since c1920.*

butterfly pitch = **butterfly ball.**

butterfly's boots, the = **cat's meow, the.**

Butternut **butternut** *n.* A Confederate soldier; a Confederate or Confederate sympathizer during the Civil War. *Confederate homespun was traditionally dyed with butternut extract, but the use may have orig. been a Northern one, used derog. to indicate the poverty of the South. Civil War use. Obs.*

butter up To flatter someone; to flatter or court someone so that person will be receptive to a request for aid or a favor. 1950: "He began buttering me up." Starnes, *Another Mug*, 107.

butt in (on) To interfere; to intrude; to give one's advice or opinion when one has not been asked to do so; orig., to interrupt a person who is speaking, in order to talk or give one's own opinion. 1914: "If a bobby butts in. . . ." S. Lewis, *Our Mr. Wrenn*, 58. 1949: "The Wagner Act forbade any employer to butt in on such matters." W. Pegler, *synd. newsp. col.*, Sept. 29. Cf. **barge in.** **butt-in** *n.* An unwelcome intruder; one who butts in.

buttinsky **buttinski** *n.* One who habitually interrupts a speaker, interferes, or tries to give advice or opinions to others; lit., one who butts in. *One of the few U.S. words with a "—sky" suffix denoting "one who," rather than the usual "—er" suffix. Based on the Central European "—sky," "—ski" suffix.*

button *n.* **1** The chin, the point of the jaw. 1921: ". . . A right cross to the button." Witwer, *Leather*, 48. *Prize fight use. Colloq.* **2** A baby. *Dial.* **3** [taboo] The clitoris. **—s** *n. sing.* Any uniformed worker whose uniform trationally has a double row of buttons on the jacket; specif., a bellboy, occasionally a policeman. 1946: " 'Matter of fact, she called the buttons herself.' 'Buttons?' 'Police.' " Evans, *Halo in Blood*, 66. *Since c1900; archaic.* *n. pl.* Premiums or bonuses paid to a salesman for selling outmoded or hard-to-sell merchandise. *Retail salesman use, esp. furniture salesman use.* Cf. **spiff.**

button, on the **1** On the point of the chin, said of a perfectly aimed blow. See **button.** → **2** Exactly; completely right or correct; comprehending basic issues, revealing; satisfying. 1949: "Right on the Button," title of an article giving the review of a book, The N.Y. *Times Book Rev.* Sept. 25, 14. **3** Exactly on time, on the dot. 1952: "I . . . then strolled . . . over to Ricky's, at five o'clock on the button." St. Clair McKelway, *New Yorker*, May 18, 30/3.

button chopper A laundry; a laundryman or proprietor of a laundry. *Some W.W.II Army use.*

Button down

button down **button-down** *v.t.*
1 To classify, recognize, or peg someone. 1953: "I got you buttoned down
a long time ago." Radio, *Phone Call
from a Stranger*, Jan. 5. **2** To finish
or complete a task, to be confident that
one will complete or finish a task successfully. *Not as common as "button up."*
3 To lock up or make secure a room or
building; to clean or straighten up a room
or building. *n., adj.* A men's style
of shirt collar, in which the points of the
collar button to the shirt front. *Colloq.*
buttons, have all [one's] To be of
normal mentality or behavior. 1949:
"... Whether you have all your buttons. ..." The *N.Y. Times Book Rev.*,
Sept. 25, 14.
button(s) missing, have a (few) To
be crazy; to be eccentric. *Colloq. Also
common in Eng.*
button up **1** = **button up [one's] lip**
2 To accomplish a task successfully.
During and since W.W.II. **3** To lock up,
close up, or make secure an item, room,
or building. 1957: "I told John Sanderson to button up the generators in a
nearby concrete bunker and to secure
the control building." J. C. Clark in
SEP, July 20, 64.
button up [one's] lip To stop
talking; to shut up; to keep a secret.
1747: Farmer & Henley. 1930: "Button
up yer lip." Lavine, *Third Degree*, 239.
1952: "If the general will kindly button
his lip. ..." S. Pett, AP, Oct. 17.
butt out To stop interrupting; to stop
giving unwanted advice or opinion. *Usu.
a command.* 1951: "We're busy. Butt
out!" Movie, *Up Front. Antonym of "butt
in."*
butt-room *n.* A smoking room. 1941:
"In smoke-filled butt-rooms. ..." *Dict.
of Exeter Lang.*, 4. *Never common.*
buy *v.t.* **1** To agree to something or
with someone; to believe; to acquiesce;
to accept as true; to approve. 1948:
"'I'm just a friend of his.' 'She wouldn't
buy that.'" F. Brown, *Dead Ringer*, 69.
1951: "Before U.S. taxpayers buy the
proposition that the appointment of
collectors [of internal revenue] be put
under civil service, they should take a
closer look at what they might get."
D. Larsen, NEA, Nov. 30. **2** To accomplish or effect. 1949: "She pointed [a gun]
at me. I said, 'What're you trying to buy
with that?'" J. Evans, *Halo*, 146. **3** To
hire; to engage the services of. 1949:
"If you give me any rough stuff, I'll buy
me a lawyer." Burnett, *Jungle*, 18.

buzz *n.* **1** A telephone call; a ring, usu.
in "give [someone] a buzz." 1929: "I
think I'll give the Guilded Child a buzz."
K. Brush, *Young Man*, 79. 1941: "I gave
Sammy a buzz." Schulberg, *Sammy*, 42.
Colloq. **2** Whispering, talking secretly;
the act or an instance of giving information in confidence. *Some c1930 use.*
3 A thrill, a kick, a charge, a feeling of
excitement, pleasure, satisfaction, or the
like. *Since c1935.* **4** A police squad car.
*Rock-and-roll and some general teenage use
since c1955. From the siren's sound, but
see* **buzzer** *and* **buzz,** *v.t.,* 7. **5** A kiss,
esp. a quick compassionate kiss, as on the
cheek. *v.t.* **1** To flatter; to court. *c1900,
dial.* **2** To telephone a person. 1933: "Why
not buzz Eddie for the brawl?" H. T.
Webster, 367/2. **3** To give information to
someone in confidence, to whisper to
someone. 1951: "You'll buzz me later?"
Spillane, *Big Kill*, 28. **4** To announce
one's arrival to another, as by ringing a
doorbell; to call for someone by ringing
a buzzer. **5** To beg from someone or at a
place. *Hobo use since c1920.* → **6** To
pilfer from a place; to rob a person.
Underworld use since c1925. **7** To question
or investigate someone, as by the police.
c1930 use. **8** While flying, to swoop low
and fast over a place with a great noise
of engines; said of an airplane or pilot.
→ **9** To go on a spree in a specif. town or
bar. *W.W.II Air Force and Army use.*
10 To intoxicate. 1950: "Deane, comfortably buzzed by his cocktails, mono-
polized what conversation there was."
Starnes, *And When She Was Bad*, 33.
*From "buzz" = a thrill, reinforced by pre-
vious meaning of "to go on a spree."*
—ey **—y** *adj.* Drunk. 1737: *Pa.
Gazette. Obs.* See Appendix, Drunk.
buzz along To leave, to depart, esp.
from a social visit. *Since c1935.* Cf. **buzz
off.**
buzzard *n.* **1** A contemptible man;
specif., an old, unkempt man. *Since
c1800.* **2** Chicken served at a meal;
turkey served at a meal. *Army,
prison, and student use.* **3** An eagle
insigne, as worn by an Army or USN
officer. *Since c1920; Armed Forces use.*
buzzard colonel A full colonel in the
U.S. Army, as opposed to a lieutenant
colonel. *Some W.W.II use.* See **buzzard.**
Cf. **chicken colonel.**
buzz around the barrel To get
something to eat; to eat, esp. a snack.
Rock-and-roll use since c1955.
buzz bomb **buzzbomb** *n.* A flying bomb, specif. the German V1 or V2

ram-jet and rocket missile used to bomb London toward the end of W.W.II. 1953: "The British called those devastating German rockets 'buzz bombs.'" K. Vidor, *A Tree Is a Tree*, 234. *Obs. Although the W.W.II "bombs" were the first successful modern self-propelled missiles, the word was replaced by the stand. "missile" as this element of military technology became more familiar to the public through its development in the postwar period.*

buzz-buggy   *n.* An automobile; an early model automobile, whether gas, steam, or electric powered. *Some c1915 use.*

buzz-buzz   *n.* Buzz; noise; specif. the noise of a crowd, as at an athletic contest. 1908: "All the buzz-buzz from without may be said to go in one ear and out the other." *Atlan. Monthly*, July, 143/1. See Appendix, Reduplications.

buzzer   *n.* A policeman's badge; a badge worn or carried by any officer of the law. 1948: "I brought out the 1928 deputy sheriff's star I carried to show people who wanted to see a buzzer." Evans, *Halo for Satan*, 25.

buzz off   **1** To go away; to leave; specif., to beat it. *Usu. a command.* 1942: "Buzz off!" Chandler, *High Window*, 63. **2** To stop making noise; to be quiet. *Not common.*

buzz-saw, monkey with the   To touch, handle, or interfere with something dangerous or important. 1901: "Don't monkey with the buzz-saw." Greenough & Kittredge. *Archaic.*

buzz-wagon   *n.* = **buzz-buggy.**

B.V.D.'s   *sing.* A suit of men's underwear. *From the trade-mark "B.V.D.," a well-known brand.*

by   For phrases beginning with "by," see under principal word of phrase.

by   *prep.* **1** With. 1930: "Five skins is jake by me." *Amer. Mercury*, Dec., 456. **2** From; at. 1949: "I'll buy you a drink by Antek." N. Algren, *Man with the Golden Arm*, 34. *This use resembles the Fr. "chez," but derives from Yiddish usage.*

bylow   *n.* A Barlow knife; usu. a single-bladed folding knife with a bone handle; any knife with a large, flat blade. c1915 [1954]: "Mary Jack whipped out a bylow, a big knife with a large blade." L. Armstrong, *Satchmo, My Life in New Orleans*, 74. *A corruption of "Barlow."*

byway   *n.* A sidewalk; a road; an aisle.

by with [something], get   **1** = **get away with [something]. 2** To be mildly successful; to be adequate, but not ambitious enough to be truly successful. **3** To be almost caught or punished, but to escape.

C

C   *n.* **1** A hundred dollars; orig. a hundred-dollar bill. 1845: *DAE.* 1954: "We gotta have 500 bucks. If we can just lay our hands on 5 C's." W. R. & F. K. Simpson, *Hockshop*, 220. *From "century" or the Roman numeral "C" which at one time was printed on all $100 bills.* See Appendix, Shortened Words. **2** Cocaine; sometimes, heroin. *Drug addict use.* See Appendix, Shortened Words. **3** A bookmaker's commission. *Racing use.*

cab   *n.* **1** The cockpit of an airplane. → **2** An airplane. *Some W.W.II Air Force use.*

cabbage   *n.* **1** Money; banknotes; paper money. *Colloq.* Cf. **lettuce, spinach. 2** Tobacco. *Dial.* **3** [taboo] The female genitalia. *Negro use.* See Appendix, Sex and Food. → **4** A young girl. 1947: "The little cabbage spoke up for her generation." Billy Rose, *synd. newsp.*

col., May 8.   *v.t.* To steal. 1846: *DAE. Obs.*

cabbage-head   *n.* **1** A person's head; —used disparagingly. 1845: *DAE.* 1907: "My poor old cabbage head wobbled about." R. H. Bainton, *G. L. Burr*, 100. → **2** A stupid person. 1865: *DAE. Colloq.*

cabbage leaves   Paper currency. See **cabbage.**

cabbie   cabby   *n.* A cab-driver; now specif. a taxi-driver. 1900: "Cabby." Dreiser, *Carrie*, 165. 1946: "Racing Stork Just Normal to Cabbie." Headline, AP, Mar. 7. *Colloq.*

cabin girl   A chambermaid, esp. a girl or woman whose job it is to make the beds and straighten up the rooms each day on a ship, at a motel, or the like.

caboodle   *n.* An entity, group, or lot; the entire lot of people or things. 1848: *DAE.* 1910. "The best thing in the whole caboodle." Johnson, *Varmint*, 71. See **boodle, kit and boodle.**

caboose *n.* A jail. *Prob. shortened from or suggested by syn. "calaboose." Not common.*

cack-broad *n.* = **cackle-broad.** 1942: "I knocks de pad with them cack-broads up on Sugar Hill." Z. Hurston, 89. Cf. **kack.**

cackle *n.* An egg. *From "cackleberry." Not common.* See Appendix, Shortened Words.

cackleberries and grunts Bacon and eggs. See **cackleberry; grunts.**

cackleberry *n.* An egg. *Obs.*

cackle-broad cack-broad *n.* A fashionable, wealthy, or society woman; lit., a woman who talks a lot in a hifalutin manner.

cackle-jelly *n.* = **cackleberry.** *Not common.*

cackler *n.* An office worker; a pencil-pusher. *Hobo use c1920.*

cad *n.* **1** A hobo. 1894: "Every cad you meet up the road is bound South." J. Flynt. *Some hobo use, never common. Obs.* **2** An academy or preparatory-school student. *Common use c1870–c1910; obs. From "cadet."* See Appendix, Shortened Words. **3** = **Caddy.** 1953: "So I join him in his leather-lined Cad." B. Thomas, AP, Mar. 19.

Caddy Caddie *n.* A Cadillac automobile. *Some use since c1925. Most common since c1945.* See Appendix, Shortened Words.

cadet *n.* A pimp; a procurer. *Obs.*

cadge *v.t. & v.i.* To borrow or beg; to sponge. *Some W.W.I use.*

Cadillac *n.* An ounce of heroin; heroin; sometimes, cocaine. *Addict use. From "C"; as is true with much argot, once "C" becomes known to those outside the addict groups, and can be classified as sl., the addicts need a new word and build it on "C." Once "Cadillac" is somewhat familiar to those outside the group, it will be replaced by another word. Reinforced by the fact that an ounce of heroin, or any drug, seems just as expensive and desirable to an addict as a Cadillac automobile might be to someone else.*

cady caddy cadi kady katy *n.* A man's hat or cap. *Underworld use since c1850; now somewhat archaic.*

Caesar *n.* A type of men's haircut. 1957: "Another hair style coming up fast is the 'Caesar,' a swirl job worn by young and old attempting to cover bare patches. If worn short, it's brushed forward instead of back, is unparted, and has a straight-line cut across the temple." H. Mitgang, *About—Men's Haircuts. Because it resembles the hair style seen on typical busts of Julius Caesar and was first popularized by actor Marlon Brando, who wore such a hair style while playing Mark Antony in the movie "Julius Caesar."*

cage *n.* **1** A prison. 1636: *DAE. Until c1920; archaic.* **2** A train caboose. *Railroad use.* **3** The human body; the human skeleton. *v.t.* To imprison. 1949: "The bars clanged shut. Behind his easy boasting the punk concealed a genuine terror of being caged." N. Algren, *Man with the Golden Arm*, 7.

caged *adj.* Drunk. *Never common.* See Appendix, Drunk.

cager *n.* **1** A basketball player. *Some use since c1925.* **2** A drunkard. *Dial.* See **caged.**

cagey cagy *adj.* Crafty; cunning; wary; sly. 1927: "He who is arraigned as 'cagey' knows his pigeon-hole forthwith." J. A. Work in *Educational Rev.*, Apr., 223. 1944: "I couldn't tell whether he was being honest or cagey." Ford, *Phila. Murder*, 61. *Colloq.*

cahoole *v.i. & v.t.* To cajole, wheedle, deceive; to procure. 1851: Hall, *College Words*, 40. *Never common.*

cake *n.* **1** [taboo] The female genitalia. *Negro use.* See Appendix, Food and Sex. → **2** A sexually attractive or personable girl or young woman. **3** = **cake-eater.** 1932: "His brown hat, fixed square-shaped the way the cakes were wearing them...." J. T. Farrell, 121. *Never common.* See Appendix, Shortened Words.

cake, take the **1** To merit or win the highest place, fig. to win a cake as a prize. *c1840; now archaic.* **2** Of an action, person, thing, or concept, to be so unusual as to be unbelievable; to be extremely audacious; to have unusual behavior or characteristics; fig. to win a cake as being the most unusual freak ever encountered. *Orig. to win the prize in a cakewalk (dancing) contest. Usu. in "You take" (or "that takes") the cake."* 1900: "Pack up and pull out, eh? You take the cake." Theodore Dreiser, *Sister Carrie*, 155. *Colloq. and very popular since c1890.*

cake-cutter *n.* One who short-changes the public. *Circus use.*

cake-eater *n.* A ladies' man, a dude; a male flirt; a playboy. 1922: "A hard-boiled cake-eater." Phila. *Eve. Bulletin*, Mar. 8. 1932: "All the cake-eaters were wearing [powder-blue suits]." J. T.

Farrell, 121. 1951: "A generation ago the devils of their day were the daring flapper and her long-haired baggy-pants boy friend, the cake-eater." H. Boyle, *AP*, June 11. *Lit., prob. a young man who often attends ladies' tea parties, where cake may be served; but may orig. have been in taboo ref. to "cake."* Cf. **lounge-lizard, bun-duster, heavy-cake.**

calabash   *n.* The human head. 1723: *DAE. Obs.*

calaboodle   *n.* = **caboodle.**

calaboose   *n.* A prison or prison cell; a jail. 1792: "Chiefly Southern, elsewhere jocular." *DAE.* c1847 [1956]: "[In Mexico] I was thrust into the 'Calaboose,' a room about 20 feet square. . . ." Samuel E. Chamberlain, "My Confession," *Life*, July 23, 78. 1956: "The garb some [women] wear now would have landed them in the calaboose in my day." Quote from a 77-year-old woman, *AP*, Oct. 8. *From the Sp. "calabozo."*

calf love   *n.* = **puppy love.**

calf-slobber   *n.* Meringue, as on pies.

calic   *n.* A girl or woman. *Some c1890 use. From "calico."* See Appendix, Shortened Words.

calico   *n.* 1 A girl or woman. 1861: *DAE. In use until c1920. From the material most closely assoc. with women's clothes in 19C; term = modern "skirt."* Cf. **dry-goods.** 2 A flirtation; a love affair. *Some c1890 student use. v.i. & v.t.* To court the ladies; to flirt. 1887: *DAE. Obs. by c1900. adj.* Of, pertaining to, suitable for, or popular with women students. *Some c1895 student use.*

California   *n.* A type of men's haircut, similar to the Detroit.

California bible = **California prayer book.**

California blanket   *n.* Newspaper used as bedding. 1929: "The old-timer who spends his nights on a park bench under California blankets. . . ." *World's Work*, Nov., 40. *Hobo use.*

California kiss (-off) = **kiss-off.** *East Coast use.*

California prayer book   **California bible**   *n.* A deck of playing cards. *Some c1855 use.*

California widow   A woman deserted by her husband. *Some c1875 use. Orig. meaning that the husband had deserted to join the California gold rush.*

calk   *n.* A failure in reciting. 1851: "Used in some Southern U.S. colleges." Hall, *College Words*, 85.

calk off = **caulk off.**

call   *n.* 1 Stew, esp. one consisting mainly of onions or potatoes. *Hobo use, archaic by c1925.* 2 The act of or an instance of one's name being called, as over a public address system. 3 A telephone call, specif. for the purpose of waking a person. 4 A meeting; an interview; a period or session during which a director or producer of a play or movie interviews and tries out prospective actors, dancers, singers, etc., for jobs; a rehearsal. *Theater use.* 5 A desire to urinate or, usu., to have a bowel movement. *Because one must answer "Nature's call."*

call-back   *n.* 1 A request to return; an instance of being called back, in person, on the phone, etc. 2 A person who is requested to or who returns; specif., a person who returns to a store to buy an item previously seen. *Retail salesmen's use.*

call down   *v.t.* To rebuke, scold, bawl out, etc. 1897: *DAE.* 1914: "Mr. Wrenn had been 'called down' by the office manager." S. Lewis, *Our Mr. Wrenn*, 1. *Colloq. n.* A reprimand. *Not common.*

call girl   1 A prostitute; lit., a prostitute who works in a call house. → 2 By confusion and popular misconception = a prostitute who visits a known or recommended customer at his hotel room or apartment when called on the telephone to do so, as opposed to a prostitute who solicits customers in a public place or works in a brothel; a prostitute whose known or recommended clients visit her apartment after making an appointment by telephone. 1958: "A high-priced call girl who nets over $250 a week. . . ." E. Klein, "The 'Beat' Generation in the Village," N.Y. *Daily News*, Feb. 20, 36. *Use of the telephone makes the call girl less conspicuous, and less apt to arrest, than the average prostitute. The arrangement usu. insures her of a wealthy, socially prominent clientele. Call girls have been in business since c1935, and their existence known to the general public since c1950.*

call house   1 A brothel; lit., a brothel in which the clients may call upon the prostitutes to do anything at any time. → 2 By confusion and popular misconception = a house, apartment, or room where telephone messages are received and relayed to call girls; a place where call girls live; a brothel where appointments are made by telephone.

calliope   *n.* A railway locomotive, esp. a steam locomotive having a multitoned whistle. *Railroad use, c1920; archaic.*

call it quits To give up one's attempt to do something; specif., to become divorced, separate, break one's engagement, or the like. 1950: "Any sensible assassin would have called it quits." Billy Rose, *synd. newsp. col.,* Jan. 18.

call joint = **call house.** 1937: "This charge account you go with [to] that . . . call joint." Weidman, *Wholesale,* 129. See **call girl, joint.**

call-up *n.* The act of mustering or calling up a group of men for military duty. 1950: "A Marine Corps spokesman who disclosed this said a statement on the call-up for extended duty may be issued later today." AP, July 20. *Not common.*

cally *n.* A local jail; a police station. *Hobo use c1920; from "calaboose."*

camel *n.* A railway locomotive having the engineer's cab in the center. *Railroad use.*

camel flags Camouflage. *Some W.W. I Army use. A corruption.*

campus *v.t.* **1** To discipline or punish a student by confining him to the campus. 1950: "They therefore campused him during house party weekend." Cornell (Univ.) *Daily Sun,* May 18, 8. *Some student use since c1920.* **2** To discipline a student by withdrawing a privilege, not necessarily the privilege of leaving campus.

campus butcher In college, a ladies' man; one who slays the girls.

can *n.* **1** A dollar. *Some c1850 use. Obs.* **2** A toilet; a rest room. 1943: "The gents' room at the Radio City Music Hall [N.Y.C. theater] is the biggest and most magnificent can on earth." H. A. Smith, *Putty Knife,* 122. 1951: "Places like Jacques', where they don't put any signs on the Men's Room or the Ladies' Room . . . so that [only] the habituées know how to find the can." R. S. Prather, *Bodies in Bedlam,* 53. *Since c1900. Though still considered vulgar, became common during W.W.II.* **3** The human rump; usu. used of men only to indicate that part of the body which bears the brunt of a fall, or in "fat can," indicating obesity or that the man sits too much and is lazy; usu. used of women only to indicate the rump as contributing to or detracting from sexual appearance. 1932: "Wanting to see him tossed out on his can. . . ." J. T. Farrell, 126. 1937: "A dame with a can like an elephant."

Weidman, *Wholesale,* 4. 1952: "This kid's old man threw our police reporter out of the house on his can." J. Thurber in *New Yorker,* Jan. 5, 21/2. **4** A jail, a prison; a police station. 1927: "Throwing her in the can. . . ." Hammett, *Blood Money,* 144. 1956: "The book [*Somebody Likes Me Up There*] is about the Army and my life in the can. I [Rocky Graziano] spent about nine years in prison." J. Cannon, *Who Struck John?* 208. **5** A safe or strongbox. *Underworld use since at least c1910.* **6** The human head. *Some use since c1915.* **7** A boat, specif., a destroyer. *USN use during and since W.W.I, wide W.W.II USN use.* See **tin can. 8** Any vehicle, including an airplane, but usu. an automobile. 1938: "Tooling along with the kiddies and the little woman in his costly can." W. Pegler, quoted in *Better Eng.,* Jan., 59/2. *Since c1920, orig. a lightweight early-model car, implying "tin can." Not now common.* → **9** Specif., a hot rod, a car redesigned by the, usu. teenage, owner to give it greater speed or acceleration. 1951: "Guy your age gets ahold of one of these cans . . . he's a hot-rod." J. A. Maxwell, *New Yorker,* Sept. 8, 81. *Hot-rod use since c1950.* **10** A railroad tank car for carrying fluids. *Railroad use since 1935.* **11** A storage battery. *Orig. W.W.II USN use.* *v.t.* **1** To expel a student from school. 1904: *DAE. Student use.* → **2** To discharge or fire an employee. 1912: *DAE.* 1938: "He is not the first commentator to be canned by an editor." H. Broun in *New Repub.,* Sept. 28, 211/1. 1951: "He tactfully wrote canning me. . . ." S. Lewis, *World So Wide,* 206. *Colloq.* → **3** To eject a person from a place; to forbid a person entrance to a place, almost always a public place, as a bar, restaurant, night club, or the like. **4** To stop, cease, or put an end to something, usu. to cease talking, or talking about a specif. subject or with a specif. attitude, at least temporarily. 1913: "Can the high-brow stuff." *Nation,* Aug. 21, 161/2. 1928: "Aw, can all that talk!" E. Rice, *Street Scene,* II. **5** To complete successfully; to clean thoroughly. 1938: "Why only this morning Dominick had canned [swept with a broom] this block beautiful." Liebling, *Back Where,* 188. **6** To imprison.

can, (put) in the **1** To approve the final sequence or shots of a movie; lit., to put a reel of finished film in a metal container, or can, ready for distribution to movie houses. *Movie use.* → **2** To finish a project or task; to put a project into effect. *Not common.*

canal boats   Feet, esp. large feet; shoes, esp. large shoes. *Not common.* Cf. **tugboats.**

canary   *n.* **1** A girl or young woman. 1886: New Orleans *Lantern.* 1956: "*Canary* . . . for woman is just used in smart fiction about jazz." S. Longstreet, *The Real Jazz Old and New,* 150. Cf. **chick, pigeon, quail.** → **2** Specif., a woman singer, a professional female vocalist, almost always one who sings popular songs or jazz music with a band. *Orig. radio and jazz use.* **3** An informer; lit., one who "sings." 1951: "They've got plenty of trained canaries to sing any way they tell them." *I, Mobster,* 132. **4** A gas mask. *Some W.W.II Army use, from Brit. sl.* **5** A compliment; praise; critical acclaim. *From the Yiddish "kein nahurra" (Yiddish sl. "canurra") = no evil eye or no bad luck.*   *v.i.* To sing, usu. professionally. 1944: "She had to go back to canarying." C. Macon in *Collier's,* Sept. 23, 69/1.

candy   *n.* Cocaine. *Drug addict use.* Cf. **needle candy, nose candy.**   *adj.* Stylish or garish—said of dress; frivolous; facetious. 1951: "I don't like razzin' from any of you candy comics!" J. R. Williams, *synd. cartoon,* "Out Our Way," Sept. 21. Cf. **candy kid.**

candy kid   **1** A fine, showy, or stylish person; one who is flashily dressed; a dude. *Wide use c1910; obs. by c1920.* → **2** A ladies' man. *Obs. by c1925.* → **3** A protégé; a person favored by another; a star pupil. 1941: "She's been Mr. Hannen's candy kid. . . ." Cain, *M. Pierce,* 189. *Some use c1900–c1925; replaced by "fair-haired boy."*

cane corn   Lit., corn whisky, as made from corn and cane sugar; moonshine; home-made or bootleg whisky.

can-house   canhouse   can house   *n.* A brothel. 1930: "He was too lousy for a decent girl like her, him playing the races and going to can houses." J. T. Farrell, 161. 1956: ". . . the whole Storyville era when jazz grew up in the canhouses of New Orleans. . . ." S. Longstreet, *The Real Jazz Old and New,* xi.

canned   *adj.* **1** Drunk. 1928: "They was already pretty canned, 'cause they both of them had a pint of corn on their hip." J. M. Cain in *Amer. Mercury.* See Appendix, Drunk. **2** Recorded, as on a phonograph recording; said of music or talk. *Since c1925.* → **3** Photographed on movie film; filmed.

Movie use. **4** To be a prisoner. 1958: "Canned—Imprisoned." G. Y. Wells, *Station House Slang.*

canned cow   Condensed milk. *Orig. logger, ranch, and maritime use, c1925. Some W.W.II Army use.*

canned goods   *sing.* A virgin; a male or female without sexual experience.

canned up   Drunk. 1928: "So the old man give them a drink of some hard cider, and they got canned up a little more." J. M. Cain, *Amer. Mercury.* See **canned.** See Appendix, Drunk.

cannery   *n.* A jail. *From "can."*

cannister   *n.* A revolver. *Some c1925 underworld use.*

cannon   *n.* **1** A pistol; a revolver; any gun. 1901: *DAE.* 1934: "He holstered his own cannon." Chandler, *Finger Man,* 128. **2** A professional thief or robber. *Contrary to pop. belief, this use did not evolve because a thief carries a cannon = gun. This use grew out of the Yiddish "gonif" = a thief, shortened to Amer. sl. "gon" or gun. Thus "gun" = thief, and "cannon" = a big or important thief. Orig. underworld use. Since c1910.* → **3** Specif., a pickpocket; in a team or gang of pickpockets, the one who actually removes the wallet from the victim's pocket. 1928: "Mob of cannons." E. Booth in *Amer. Mercury,* 78. 1956: "He taught me the difference between a horse's cannon and hock. To a city bred kid who saw nothing but wagon horses, a cannon was a pickpocket and hock was always a verb." T. Betts, *Across the Board,* 270. *Since c1920. Orig. underworld use.*   *v.t.* To rob a person or a place, esp. by picking pockets. 1947: "You're too small to cannon the street-cars." N. Algren, "The Face."

cannon ball   **1** A fast express train; orig., a fast freight train. *Since c1915. Orig. hobo use. From its speed.* **2** A message sent from one prisoner to another, as via a trusty or known guard; a message surreptitiously sent from prison by a prisoner, as to his underworld friends. **3** A grapefruit. *Some reported W.W.II Army use; prob. synthetic.*

cannon fodder   Infantry troops, esp. young, inexperienced troops, who are likely to suffer many casualties; troops, sent to attack the enemy, who have little chance to win the battle, owing to bad planning, inexperience, poor equipment, or the like. *Wide W.W.I use, some W.W.II use.*

canoe   *v.i.* To have sexual intercourse; to kiss and caress, esp. intimately;

to neck. 1954: "Her old man had been hearing about me and Daisy canoeing from the first night we'd got together." L. Armstrong, *Satchmo, My Life in New Orleans*, 154. *Obs. Because, before the automobile became popular, canoes were assoc. with romantic endeavors.* Cf. **canoodle.** **—s** *n. pl.* = **canal boats.** Cf. **tug-boats.**

can of corn **1** In baseball, a high, slow fly ball. *Baseball use.* **2** A man, a fellow, or a guy, esp. one who has done something audacious. 1949: "Where would a hot can of corn like Dillinger hide out?" A. Hynd, *Public Enemies*, 13.

can of worms A very complex, unsolved problem. *Not common.*

can on, get a To be or become drunk. 1929: "A gal used to throw herself out the window every time she got a can on." D. Parker, "Big Blonde," reprinted in *The American Twenties*, 153. Cf. **growler.** See Appendix, Drunk.

canoodle *v.i., v.t.* **1** To kiss and caress; to neck. 1859: *DAE. Obs. For a possible orig. see* **canoe.** → **2** To cajole or coax, as by a display of affection. 1867: *DAE. Obs.*

can-opener *n.* Any tool used to open a safe in order to rob it. *Underworld use.* See **can.**

cans *n. pl.* Radio earphones; any radio or telephone earphones worn on the head. *Orig. radio amateur use.*

cantaloupe *n.* A baseball.

canto *n.* A regular division of any sports contest; a round of a prize fight; an inning of baseball; a quarter of a football game; etc.

Canuck **Canuk** [derog.] *n., adj.* A Canadian, esp. a French-Canadian. *Since c1855; the ref. is often to a strong, rough woodsman or logger.*

cap *n.* **1** A captain. 1759 [1895]: S. Merriman's diary quoted in Sheldon, *Hist. of Deerfield*, I. *Colloq.* See Appendix, Shortened Words. → **2** A man, esp. in direct address to a stranger who commands respect. *Used by beggars, porters, and servants who wish to practice concealed flattery upon their clients.* See **captain. 3** A capsule, esp. of a narcotic, such as heroin. 1952: "I didn't have the money to buy a cap with." D. Hulburd, *H is for Heroin*, quoted in N.Y. *Times Bk. Rev.*, Nov. 30, 34. *v.t.* To do better than another; to overbid another person, tell a better joke, or the like.

cap, go-to-hell *n.* = **overseas cap,** Army or Marine. *Esp. when worn at a*

rakish angle. *W.W.II Army and Marine use.*

Cape Cod turkey Codfish. *Some jocular use.*

caper *n.* **1** A whisky-drinking spree. *Some use since c1875.* → **2** Any spree; a period or instance of fun, excitement, or exhilaration. *Common student use since c1945.* → **3** A prank. → **4** Specif., an instance of a crime, esp. a robbery; a job. *Since c1925, orig. underworld use.*

caper-juice *n.* Whisky; a drink of whisky. 1888: *DAE. Obs. by c1910.* See **caper.**

capon *n.* An effeminate man, usu. a homosexual. *From "capon."*

capper *n.* **1** A cardsharp's confederate. 1870: *DAE. Obs. by c1920.* **2** A pitchman's assistant who makes false purchases so that real buying will start; a shill. *Pitchman use; archaic.*

captain *n.* **1** A generous person; a free spender. *Hobo use.* **2** A train conductor. *Some railroad use since c1930.*

captain of the head **1** Lit., one in charge of the latrine aboard ship; fig., a novice or stupid person, a useless or blundering person, who cannot be assigned to important work. *W.W.II Armed Forces jocular use, orig. USN use.* → **2** A new or inexperienced worker. *Not common.*

car catcher A railroad brakeman. *Some railroad use since c1925.*

card *n.* **1** A remarkable person, usu. a prankster; a joker; a wit; a character. 1840: *DAE.* 1942: "That old Witch-Hammer was really quite a card." W. B. Johnson, *Widening Stain*, 39. *Becoming archaic. Colloq.* **2** A portion of a drug used by an addict. See **deck.** **—er** *n.* A professional gambler, esp. a card player. *Some use since c1850.*

cards, in the Expected; impending. *Often negative, as "It's not in the cards."* 1949: ". . . Coffee has gone up at wholesale . . . with another 10-cent boost in the cards." AP, N.Y., Nov. 17.

card shark (sharp) See **shark, sharp.** *Colloq.*

car-hop **carhop** *n.* A waiter or, usu., a waitress who serves food to patrons in parked cars. 1949: "Out of a Texas car hop . . . [Hollywood] will make a courtesan." Chandler, *Little Sister*, 161. *Based on "bell-hop." v.i.* To work as a car-hop.

carny **carney** **carnie** *n.* **1** A carnival. 1948: "Carney" in this sense occurs at least 95 times between pp. 1 and 212 in F. Brown, *Dead Ringer.* →

2 A carnival worker. 1939: "60,000 outdoor show people, the 'carnies,' who travel from town to town with carnivals. . . ." Liebling in *New Yorker.* 1948: "Carney" in this sense occurs at least 25 times between pp. 1 and 212 in F. Brown, *Dead Ringer.* → **3** The special idiom or argot spoken by carnival workers. 1948: "I thought you talked carney by now." F. Brown, *Dead Ringer*, 161. *adj.* Of or characteristic of a carnival. 1948: "A Carney kid." "The carney lights." "Carney girls." "Carney" as an adj. occurs at least 18 times between pp. 1 and 212 in F. Brown, *Dead Ringer.* See Appendix, —y and —ie endings.

carpet, on the   **1** Summoned to appear before one's employer, administrative superior, or the like, as in his office, for a reprimand. *Since c1900; colloq. Freq., the one summoned walks in onto a carpeted floor from his uncarpeted workroom, and stands on the carpet while being adversely criticized.* → **2** Reprimanded, scolded, severely criticized, by anyone. *Always used with the past tense.*

carpetbag   *v.i.* To try to make a favorable impression on a superior; to bagplay. *Some c1935 student use.*

carps   *n. sing.* A stage carpenter; often a⁻ a nickname. *Theater use.*

carrot-top   *n.* A red-haired person; often as a nickname.

carry   *n.* A sick, wounded, or injured person who must be taken to a hospital by stretcher or ambulance. 1958: "Carry—Any stretcher case." G. Y. Wells, *Station House Slang.*

carry a (heavy) load   **1** To be drunk. *Has been gaining in pop. since c1940.* See Appendix, Drunk. **2** To be tired, depressed, or worried. *Some W.W.II Army use.*

carry a lot of weight   To be very influential.

carrying weight   The blues. 1956: "*Carrying weight* is a load of the blues." S. Longstreet, *The Real Jazz Old and New*, 148.

carry the banner   To walk the streets all night for want of a place to sleep. 1907: "I have 'carried the banner' in infernal metropolises, bedded in pools of water." J. London, *The Road*, 149. 1949: "The bum who says he is 'carrying the banner.' . . ." W. J. Slocum, *Collier's*, Aug. 27, 60.

carry the difference   To go, or be, armed; to carry a gun. 1941: "If you're going to fool around with that guy,

don't you think you ought to carry the difference?" Movie, *Johnny Eager.*

carry the load   To be depended upon by others to do most of the work; to have much work to do; to be responsible for the successful accomplishment of a specif. task.

carry the mail   To be depended upon to do the most work; to accomplish a task successfully, esp. a task that is necessary to others.

carry the stick   To be a hobo because one is homeless; to be a vagrant; to loaf or loiter. *Not common.*

carry the torch (for [someone])   To suffer or be sad, melancholy, or self-pitying from unrequited love. 1949: "[He] fell in love with a beautiful girl, only to discover that she was carrying the torch for W. C. Fields." E. Johnson in Phila. *Bulletin*, Sept. 6, 45/4. 1951: "After Miss Jones divorced him, Walker was said to 'carry the tallest torch in town.' " UP, Aug. 30.

car toad   A railroad terminal worker who inspects or services railroad cars. *Railroad use since c1925.*

cart-wheel   **cartwheel**   *n.* **1** A silver dollar. 1952: "He returned with two paper sacks straining with silver dollars. He said he picked up the 'cartwheels' on trips into Wyoming." AP, Dec. 3. *Since c1850. Archaic.* → **2** A dollar; the sum of one dollar. 1953: "Exactly 32 cart wheels and some stray change!" M. Blosser, *synd. comic strip*, "Freckles," May 12. *Some use since c1900. Never common.*

carve   *v.t.* To give one a thrill; to send. 1943: "Next to T. D. [Tommy Dorsey] I like him [Benny Goodman] best. He carves me. Does he carve you?" M. Shulman, *Barefoot Boy with Cheek*, 88. *Swing use c1935–c1945.*

casaba   *n.* A ball, as a basketball or baseball. *Some use since c1925; mainly West Coast use. Because a ball resembles a casaba melon.*

Casanova   **casanova**   *n.* A man who is charming to, courts, and is sexually successful and adroit with a variety of women. *Colloq; from the name of the famous lover.*

case   *n.* **1** An odd, unusual, or eccentric person; a precocious child. 1840: *DAE. Colloq.* **2** A dollar. 1859: *DAE.* 1878: "Half case" = a half-dollar. *DAE. Archaic.* Cf. **case note**. **3** The act or an instance of being romantically attached to one of the opposite sex; an obsession for one of the opposite sex; a crush. *Colloq.* 4 The act of inspecting a place to be robbed in order to gain useful information; an inspection. *Orig. underworld use.* 5 A brothel. *Not common in U.S.* → 6 The last of any item; mainly card-playing use. Thus in the game of poker the case ace is the last or fourth ace in the deck. See **case ace**. *v.t.* 1 To look something over carefully with the view of dealing with it later, esp. the scene, as a bank, of a prospective robbery. 1928: "Has it been cased?" E. Booth in *Amer. Mercury*, May., 81. 1941: "Another man was casing the joint." G. Homes, *40 Whacks*, 43. 1950: "Casing [a heist] is important. This word is from the argot of faro [and] means gathering information from observation." DeBaun, 73. *Orig. underworld use.* 2 To scrutinize a person; orig. to scrutinize a prospective victim to ascertain how much money he is carrying. 1939: "So I feigned an interest in the dog kingdom and cased the mouse and got a look at her kisser." O'Hara, *Pal Joey*, 17.

case-ace   *n.* In card games, esp. poker, the fourth ace after three aces have already been dealt. *From the game of faro.*

case-dough   *n.* A small amount of money, specif., as saved for use in emergencies.

case note   A dollar; a one-dollar bill. Cf. **two-case note**. See **case**.

case out   To follow or befriend another so as to help earn and share in profits, earnings, winnings, or loot; to bet with or on another. 1949: " 'Can't I case out wit' you, Frankie? Where you goin'?' He hadn't been left out of any fast hustle of Frankie's since they'd been together. 'Maybe I could help like before.' " N. Algren, *Man with the Golden Arm*, 72.

cash in [one's] chips   1 To terminate a business transaction, sell one's share of, or stock in, a business, or the like, in order to realize one's cash profits. *From the gambling term.* → 2 To die. *The most common use.*

cash in on [something]   To obtain a profit or an advantage, esp. due to one's having superior or confidential knowledge; to take full advantage of any opportunity; to realize the maximum profit, publicity, promotion, or advantage of a specific situation.

caspar   *n.* A stupid or cowardly person. *Some c1930 student use.* See **milquetoast**.

cast a kitten = **have kittens**. To express one's anger, anxiety, fear, excitement, amusement, or the like, esp. violently; to have a fit. 1920: "Kerry . . . rolled on the floor in . . . laughter. '. . .Oh, my Lord, I'm going to cast a kitten!' " Fitzgerald, *This Side of Paradise*, 56.

casting   *n.* A coin. *Some c1850 use. Obs.*

castle   *n.* Any dwelling. *Jocular use.*

cat   *adj.* Drunk. 1737: "He's cat." *Pa. Gazette. Obs.* See Appendix, Drunk. *n.* 1 A hobo, tramp, or migratory worker. *Since before c1900; archaic.* Because they often move from place to place like a cat, esp. a stalking cat. 2 A prostitute. *Very old; not now common.* 3 A spiteful woman; a malicious gossip. *Colloq.* See **catty**. 4 A lion, tiger, leopard, or any other animal of the cat family. *Circus use.* 5 A man who dresses in the latest style and pursues women; a dude, a sport; one who tomcats; one who is worldly, wise, or hep. c1920 [1954]: "I had on a brand new Stetson . . . my fine black suit and new patent leather shoes . . . I was a sharp cat." Louis Armstrong, *Satchmo, My Life in New Orleans*, 164. 1945: "The cool chick down on Calumet/ Has got herself a brand new cat,/ With pretty patent-leather hair./And he is man enough for her./" Gwendolyn Brooks, *A Street in Bronzeville*, 11. *Prob. from "alligator"* → *"gator"* → *"gate" and then corrupted to "cat," reinforced by "tomcat." Mainly Negro use.* 6 A jazz musician. 1924 [1956]: " 'Their [jazz] playing was going to lead to Chicago style and they 'vo-do-de-o-doed' maybe a bit too much, but in 1924 it was all right to the early cats." S. Longstreet, *The Real Jazz Old and New*, 102. 1957: ". . . Musicians are cats. . . ." Leonard Feather, "Jazz Millionaire [Norman Granz]." *Esquire*, May. 1957: "Our Cats the Greatest [headline]" '. . . They are the best,' exclaimed [symphony conductor] Igor Markevitch." Douglas Watt, N.Y. *Daily News*, July 16, 41. *Because orig. jazz personalities were cats in the sense of definition 5, reinforced by the fact that jazz musicians often moved from place to place to play, definition 1; and perhaps reinforced by a cat's howling. Associated with and pop. by swing use, but has much older and more general jazz meaning. Wide bop use, but cool and far-out musicians are not referred to as cats by their devotees. Fairly well known general use since c1940.* 7 A devotee of jive or swing, a hepcat. *Jive and swing use c1935–c1942.* 8 A devotee of, or a member of, a group that is, or anyone that understands or appreciates, bop, cool, far-out, or beat; anyone who is a member of the avant garde of music, art, or literature; any nonconformist; specif., a hipster. *Used by members of these groups since c1950; fairly common general use since c1955, mainly owing to the sensational newspaper articles about hipsters and the beat generation.* **9** A man, a fellow, a guy; since c1950, any human being. 1947: "In jive talk, 'cat' = fellow, guy." *Time*, Feb. 10, 12. 1953: " 'The old cat's all right, man. He's humble. . . . But that other cat, man, he's been dragging me all night . . . there's nothing worse than a self-confident square.' " D. Wallop, *Night Light*, 157f. *Some c1938 jive and swing use. Wide bop, cool, far-out, and beat use since c1950.* **10** A tractor, orig. and specif. a caterpillar tractor (with treads instead of wheels). *Logger, construction crew, and some farm use since c1935. From "caterpillar." See Appendix, Abbreviations.*   *v.i.* **1** To court or seek women for sexual reasons; to consort with prostitutes or promiscuous women. *Some use, mainly Negro, since c1900. From* **tomcat. 2** To gossip. to make disparaging remarks. See **catty. 3** To loaf or idle; to spend one's time idling on street corners. *Some teenage street gang use since c1950.*   **—ty** *adj.* Spiteful; prone to malicious gossip. *Colloq.; in ref. to a cat's sharp claws, reinforced by a cat's spitting.*

catamaran   *n.* A quarrelsome person. *Some use c1830–c1910. Obs.*

cat beer   Milk. *Some W.W.II Army use reported; prob. synthetic.*

catch   *v.t.* **1** In "to catch a smoke" = to smoke a cigarette. *Since c1925.* **2** To attend, see, or hear any entertainment, performance, or performer. 1939: "I am on just before the local station hooks up with NBC, but I don't think you can catch me in New York." O'Hara, *Pal Joey*, 5. **3** To receive a complaint, strong criticism, a bawling out, punishment, or the like. *Usu. in* "to catch it" *or* "to catch hell." *Colloq.*   *n.* A person highly desirable for a specif. job or relationship; esp. a worthwhile, attractive, popular, or wealthy person of the opposite sex who will make a highly desirable husband or wife. *Colloq.*   *v.i.* To receive a complaint or bawling out. 1958: "Assignment of a detective to the complaint-receiving desk. One so assigned says: 'I'm catching today.' " G. Y. Wells, *Station House Slang*.

catch, the   *n.* The flaw, the part of an otherwise good plan or easy task that may cause difficulty or be difficult; a trick.

catch flies   **1** To distract an audience's attention from another performer on the stage by making an unnecessary motion or motions. *Theater use.* **2** To yawn, esp. in boredom.

caterpillar's kimono, the   *n.* = **the cat's meow.**

catfit   *n.* A fit of anger; any emotional outburst due to extreme anger, disappointment, or the like.

catgut   *n.* = **rotgut.** 1924: "That stuff [in a flask] was catgut and that you wouldn't drink." Marks, *Plastic Age*, 18. *Never common.*

cat-haul   cat haul   cathaul   *v.t.* To subject a person to prolonged, severe questioning. 1950: "Brafferton's cat-hauling by the Harford Committee commanded a banner headline [in a newspaper]." Starnes, *And When She Was Bad*, 104. *From the earlier lit. sense (1840: DAE) of dragging a clawing cat down the bare back of a person tied prone.*

catholic   *n.* A pickpocket.

cat house   cathouse   cat-house   *n.* **1** A cheap lodging house; a flophouse. *Some c1915 hobo use.* **2** A brothel, esp. a cheap brothel. 1954: "I had sex with a number of girls—off the street, out of bars, or in cat houses." H. K. Fink, *Long Journey*, 21. 1956: "It was maybe the oldest profession . . . but New Orleans was proud *and* ashamed of its cathouses." S. Longstreet, *The Real Jazz Old and New*, 54. **3** = **barrelhouse,** style of jazz music.

cat lick   A Catholic. *A jocular and derog. corruption.*

cat out of the bag, let the   To disclose a secret, often, though not always, inadvertently. *Colloq.*

cat plant   An oil or gasoline refinery. 1956: "Oil workers use the term *cat plant*—a plant where crude oil is split by catalysis." *Labor's Special Lang. from Many Sources. From "catalysis." See Appendix, Shortened Words.*

cat's, the   *n.* = **the cat's meow.** *Some c1920 use. Obs.*

cats and dogs   **1** Low-priced stocks, as those yielding no revenue or being of dubious value. *Financial use since c1900.* **2** Odds and ends, bits and pieces. **3** See **rain pitchforks.**

cat's eye   A type of boy's playing marble, of any color, having a crescent-shaped area of a second color in the center. *Young boy use.* **—s** *n. sing.* Tapioca pudding.

cat's meow, the *n.* Any person, thing, plan, etc., that is remarkable, noteworthy, excellent, or the like. 1926: "Substitute for *meow, whiskers, eyebrow, ankle, tonsils, adenoids, galoshes, pajamas, cufflinks, roller skates,* and the result is the same." "The ant, gnat, bee, and elephant are also called in such [expressions]." R. P. Bond, *AS,* II, 58; 60. *One of the most pop. fad expressions of the 1920's; archaic.*

cat's pajamas, the *n.* = **the cat's meow.** 1924: "It's a good poem. It's the cat's pajamas." Marks, *Plastic Age,* 102.

cat's-paw *n.* A pawn; a dupe. 1958: "You know the kid hasn't the slightest notion he was our cats-paw." "Dondi," *synd. newsp. comic strip,* Feb. 9.

cat's whiskers, the *n.* = **the cat's meow.** 1952: "A teen-ager has to keep up on his slang. At the moment something that used to be known as the cat's whiskers is now called 'sly, really neat, the real George,' or 'deadly boo.' " H. Boyle, AP, June 30.

cattle train A Cadillac automobile. *Negro use.*

caulk off **1** To sleep; to go to sleep. *USN use since c1925.* → **2** To rest from one's work; to take a break. *Some W.W. II USN use.*

cavalier *n.* In prize fighting, a skilled boxer, as opposed to a strong slugger. *Some use since c1920.* Cf. **caveman.**

cave *n.* **1** A room; a pad. *Some use since c1935. Orig. jive use, now far-out use.* → **2** A small or windowless office. **—man** *n.* **1** A strong, virile, rough, or rude man; esp. one who is sexually attractive. **2** In prize fighting, a strong slugger, as opposed to a skillful boxer. *Some use since c1920.* Cf. **cavalier.**

cayuse *n.* A horse, esp. a small, hardy animal descended from the wild horses of the Northwest. 1936: ". . . From Oregon came the horse's name, 'cayuse.' That state was the home of the Cayuse tribe of Indians, an equestrian people." P. A. Rollins, *The Cowboy,* 63. *Western colloq. use.*

c c pills Laxative pills of any kind. *From the laxative pills dispensed by the Armed Forces Medical Corps. W.W.II use.*

Cecil *n.* Cocaine. *Addict use.* See **Cadillac.**

Cee *n.* = **C.**

ceiling, hit the **1** To fail in an examination or recitation, esp. when due to

nervousness; to blow up. *c1900; college use. Obs.* → **2** To become greatly excited or violently angry; to go up in the air; blow one's top. 1914: "He will . . . 'get warm round the collar,' and may even 'hit the ceiling.' " D. S. Martin, *Living Age,* Aug., 374. 1952: "I have to be in by 11 or . . . Father hits the ceiling!" Merrill Blosser, "*Freckles,*" *synd. comic strip,* Oct. 27.

celeb *n.* A celebrity. 1952: "Each a certified celeb from the realms of cafe, style or theatrical society. . . ." B. Gross in N.Y. *Daily News,* Aug. 11, 27C/5. *Since c1910; orig. theatrical and newsp. columnist use.* See Appendix, Shortened Words.

cellar *n.* The lowest standing in a baseball league.

cement-mixer *n.* **1** Any act, as dancing, that includes a vertical rotation of the pelvis; a person who performs such movements, but usu. a strip-tease dancer or prostitute. 1956: "A dance is a cement-mixer." S. Longstreet, *The Real Jazz Old and New,* 150. *From the rotary motion of a cement-mixing machine.* Cf. **grind. 2** A truck or other vehicle having a noisy motor, a broken muffler, or the like. 1952: "Some jerk pulls alongside and guns his cement mixer!" Fagaly & Shorten, *synd. comic strip,* "There Oughta Be a Law!" Sept. 16. *Orig. truckdriver use, since c1935.*

century *n.* **1** A hundred dollars; a $100 bill. 1859: Matsell. 1930: "There is only a century in the deal." Lavine, *Third Degree,* 32. 1949: "New bills . . . I riffled them. Ten centuries, an even thousand dollars." Chandler, *Little Sister,* 239. Cf. **C.** → **2** One dollar. 1859: Matsell. *Still some use.*

chain See **ball and chain.**

chain-gang **chaingang** *n.* A gang of prison laborers, usu. Negroes, chained together or wearing shackles and working at hard manual labor, as roadbuilding. 1956: "The work-songs are still sung in the chain-gangs, the farm jails of Texas, Louisiana and Mississippi." S. Longstreet, *The Real Jazz Old and New,* 25. *Colloq. Chain-gangs are still common in the South.*

chain lightning Inferior liquor. 1843: *DAE. Dial.*

chain-locker *n.* A cheap, dirty, dockside bar. *Maritime use; from the nautical term.*

chain-man *n.* A watch thief. *Obs. underworld use.*

chain-smoke *v.i., v.t.* To smoke

cigarettes continuously, lighting the second from the first, the third from the second, and so on. 1946: "He chain-smoked American cigarets." *PM*, Jan. 20, M5. **—r** *n.* One who chain-smokes.

chair, the *n.* **1** A chairman or mediator of a meeting or organization. *Stand. parliamentary use.* **2** The electric chair; death in the electric chair.

chair-warmer *n.* An idle person.

chalk *n.* **1** A horse favored to win a race; a betting favorite. **2** A cigarette. *Not common.* **3** Milk; esp. powdered milk. *Prison use; W.W. II Armed Forces use.* *adj.* Favored to win;—said of a race horse; playing favored race horses or short odds;—said of a bettor. 1956: "CHALK PLAYERS—Also chalk eaters: favorite bettors. The term goes back to the days when bookmakers, marking the odds with chalk on slates, frequently erased and reduced the odds on heavily played horses." T. Betts, *Across the Board*, 313.

chalk-eater **chalk eater** *n.* One who bets only on favorites. 1939: "A chalk-eater [at a racetrack] being a character who always plays the short-priced favorites." Runyon, 18. *Common horse-racing use.*

chambermaid *n.* A machinist in a roundhouse. *Railroader use.*

Chamber of Commerce A toilet. *From "chamber pot."*

champ *n.* **1** A sports champion, esp. in boxing. 1957: "Who will be the new champ...?" AP, Mar. 23. *Colloq.* **2** A bum; an unsuccessful person. *Owing to the popular image of prize fighters as men of more brawn than brain, and to various scandals in modern ring history, the word is as often used sarcastically or condescendingly as to convey honor or respect.*

change *n.* Money. 1953: "$350 weekly may seem like a sizable chunk of change to you and me." Bob Thomas, AP, July 22. Cf. **piece of change.**

change breath To have a drink of liquor. *Obs.*

change [one's] luck To have sexual intercourse, esp., in the South, with a Negress; used only by white males.

change the channel To change the topic of conversation. *Teenage use since c1955. From the television use.*

change-up **changeup** *n., v.t., adj.* In baseball, a pitch delivered with an impressive windup but little speed, used to confuse the batter and destroy his timing. *Since c1940.*

chank **chanck** **shank** *n.* A chancroid or chancre; a case of venereal disease, esp. syphilis.

channel *n.* A vein, usually in the crook of the elbow or the instep, into which narcotics addicts inject drugs. 1954: D. W. Maurer & V. H. Vogel, *Narcotics and Addiction*, 267. See **main line.**

chant *n.* **1** A person's name. *Underworld use c1850.* ↦ **2** A man, a fellow, a guy. *Obs; never common in U.S.*

chaplain *n.* See **see the chaplain.**

chappie *n.* A fellow, a chap. 1939: "... Which may amuse the chappies around Lebuses." O'Hara, *Pal Joey*, 42. See Appendix, —ie ending.

chaps *n.pl.* Leather or fur leggings worn by cowboys to protect their legs from cactus and brush while riding. 1948: "He donned chaps ... with traveling Wild West shows." *Time*, Jan. 26, 20/2. *Since c1820. Orig. Sp. "chaparajos," used by Sp. cowboys [Mexico and S. A.] as a protection against the chaparral bush.*

chapter *n.* **1** An inning of baseball. Cf. **canto.** **2** Any complete action or episode, such as a particular sequence of experiences in the life of a person.

chapter and verse **1** Rules; a list of rules, taboos, commands, etc. 1956: "He knows the chapter and verse of General Electric policy. He's a good employee." *Oral*, at the General Electric Company's "Electronic Park," Syracuse, N.Y. **2** Exact knowledge; remembered data; detailed or itemized intelligence of any kind. 1957: "He can quote you chapter and verse, anything about baseball." *Oral. Orig. ref. to ability to quote exact chapters and verses from the Bible.* 1957: "The Giants will play in San Francisco next season. That became clearly evident yesterday when prexy Horace Stoneham received chapter and verse of the city's offer from Mayor George Christopher and described it as 'a very fair and firm offer.'" N.Y. *Daily News*, Aug. 9, 38.

chaqueta *n.* A leather or thick cloth jacket worn by cowboys for protection against the chaparral bush. *Obs.* See **chaps.**

character *n.* **1** A vagabond. *c1920.* **2** An eccentric; a person whose mental or behavioral processes are unusual. *Common since c1940.* 1948: "The character who always has an ax to grind...." J. B. Roulier, "Service Lore: Army Vocab.," N.Y. *Folk Quart.*, Spring. *The term is used to show either deprecation of a person's eccentricity or affection for a* *person's individuality.* **3** A person; a man; esp. one who is not personally known to or respected by the speaker. 1939: "The idea is so humorous that many characters laugh right out loud." Runyon, 14. 1949: "Ever hear of a character called Freud?" Burnett, *Jungle,* 4.

charcoal *n.* **1** An Abolitionist. *Civil War use.* → **2** A white person who champions the Negro cause. *Obs.*

charcoal nigger [derog.] A very dark-skinned Negro. *c1840 southern use; obs.*

charge *n.* **1** An injection of a narcotic. *Underworld and addict use since before c1925.* → **2** Marijuana. *Addict use.* → **3** A thrill; a feeling of excitement or satisfaction; a kick. 1951: "What kind of an old creep'd get a charge out of this stuff?" S. J. Perelman in *New Yorker,* Mar. 3, 28/3. *Orig. jive use; some c1945 bop use; general jazz use since c1935. Now considered archaic.* **4** An extreme sensual or psychological response. 1956: "Kids get a charge out of the circus." *Oral,* Madison Sq. Garden, N.Y.C. See **kick.** **5** Sexual excitement, esp. from merely visual contact with the opposite sex. 1956: "I get a charge from [movie actress] Marilyn Monroe." *Oral,* in lobby of movie theater. **6** [taboo] An erection. *Orig. from the popular image of activation through an electric charge and/or the sensation of electric shock.* *v.t.* To rob. 1948: "A little bank just itchin' to be charged." Movie, *They Live by Night. May derive from psy. excitement thieves experience in their work.*

chariot *n.* Any vehicle; esp. an automobile or a train caboose. 1953: "Step into my chariot." Movie, *Jalopy.*

charity girl A sexually promiscuous young woman. *Applied only to young, unmarried, seemingly respectable females.* Cf. **for free.** *Became somewhat common during W.W.II.*

Charley *n.* **1** Any minor stiffness or pain of the joints or muscles. *Orig. Charley horse.* **2** The shoe width size C. *Retail shoe salesman use.* **3** A stupid or blundering soldier. *c1945, Army use.* See **Able.** Cf. **fuck off, sad sack.** **charley** *n.* A watchman. 1805: *DAE. Underworld use; obs.*

Charley Coke A cocaine addict. 1953: *Obs.* D. W. Maurer & V. H. Vogel, *Narcotics & Addiction,* 267. **Charley coke** *n.* Cocaine. *Addict use.* See **C.**

Charley horse A soreness and stiffness in arm or leg muscles induced by strain or excessive exercise. 1903: "We

are indebted to the turf when an attack of rheumatism is denominated a 'dose of the Charley-horse.'" H. Spencer, 659/2. *Colloq.*

Charley Noble **Charlie Noble** A ship's funnel; also a ship's galley smoke-stack or exhaust pipe. *Maritime use.*

Charlie *n.* = **Charley coke.** See **C.**

Charlie Brown! *exclam.* An exclamation indicating surprise. *From the character in the synd. comic strip "Peanuts," whose behavior freq. elicits from other characters the expression, "Good grief, Charlie Brown!"*

charm *v.t.* To court, flatter, or attempt to impress a person, usu. one of the opposite sex or a superior, esp. with a line.

chart *n.* **1** Specif., published information showing the past performances of race horses so that bettors may compare the merits of horses in a race. **2** A musical score or written arrangement. 1957: "Charts—Musical Arrangements." E. Horne, *For Cool Cats and Far-Out Chicks. Some cool and far-out use since c1950.*

chase *v.t.* **1** To serve or pass food at table. *c1925, logging camp use; c1955, lunch counter use.* **2** To court a girl; to seek sexual contact with a particular woman. **3** To pursue a business opportunity. **4** To look for a job, a rare item, etc. See **go chase yourself.** *n.* Any rapid, confusing activity. 1957: "I'm glad that chase [task] is over." *Oral.* See **rat race.** **—r** *n.* **1** An order, glass, or drink of water, soda, beer, or other mild liquid, taken immediately after a drink of neat liquor. *Colloq.* **2** A glass of water. *c1935, lunch-counter use.* **3** A woman chaser. 1941: "Mark always was a lady-killer, a chaser." A. R. Hilliard, *Justice Be Damned,* 81. 1949: "Your old man was a souse and a chaser." Movie, *Mr. Soft Touch.* **4** An employee whose assignment is to hurry other manual workers in their work. *c1956: oral,* truck-driver ref. to foreman of loading platform. **5** See **ambulance chaser, dog-chaser, fly-chaser, monkey-chaser.** **6** An exit march; music played as an audience leaves a theater; the finale in an entertainment. *Circus and theater use.*

chase [oneself], (go) Lit., to depart; to beat it; fig., to stop annoying or bothering. 1900: "He expected to hear the common, 'Aw! Go chase yourself!'" Dreiser, *Carrie,* 42. *Often used absolutely.*

—chaser See Appendix, Suffixes and Suffix Words.

chassis *n.* The human body, esp. the female torso. 1930: "These dames whose mugs and chassis were in the paper . . ." J. T. Farrell, *Short Stories*, 106. See also **classy chassis.**

Chattanooga *n.* A railroad train. 1942: Sherman Billingsley, *Harper's Bazaar*, July. *An example of literary sl., used only in fiction and newsp. Derived from pop. song of 1940's, "Chattanooga Choo-Choo."*

chatterbox *n.* 1 A machine gun. *c1925.* 2 An anti-aircraft machine gun. *W.W. II.* 3 A radio, esp. an automobile radio. *c1940. Auto factory and garage use.* 4 An announcing or intercommunication system. *W.W. II.* See **squawk box.**

Chautauqua salute The waving of handkerchiefs to show appreciation and approval. *c1900; obs.*

chaw *n.* 1 A bite or portion of chewing tobacco. *Colloq.* 2 A trick; a deception. *Some c1850 use; obs.* **—ed** *adj.* Angry. 1956: "The American Southernism, 'chawed,' meaning 'mad.' " *Vogue,* Oct. 15, 73. *Since c1830; dial.*

cheap *adj.* 1 Stingy. *Colloq.* 2 Unrefined; open to accusations of being promiscuous (said of a girl or woman). 3 Having a bad reputation, as of one who gives and withdraws affection, loyalty, or sexual favors easily. **—ie** *n.* 1 Any cheaply made, dilapidated, or secondhand item. 1950: "A couple of real cheapies . . . 1929 Essex sedan . . . $39; 1930 Chevrolet Tudor . . . $59." Advt., Ithaca (N.Y.) *Journal*, July 25, 12/9. 1952: "Low-cost pictures [movies] . . . known in the trade as 'cheapies.' " *Time,* May 12, 103.

Cheap John *adj.* Inferior; unknown; unimportant; said of people and places. 1951: " 'I'm an old man now,' he used to say, 'pottering around with rancid children in some riverfront slum, running a Cheap John clinic, and begging the rich for a few dollars for healing salve for bedbug-bitten bodies.' " S. Longstreet, *The Pedlocks*, 88. *n.* A flophouse, cheap brothel, or esp. a dirty, dilapidated saloon.

cheapskate *n.* A stingy, niggardly person; a person who seeks cheap goods or pleasures; a person who attempts to avoid his share of expenses. *Now stand.*

cheat *v.i., v.t.* To be sexually unfaithful to one's spouse or permanent sexual partner. **—er** *n.* 1 An unfaithful person. 2 A rear-view mirror on an automobile. *c1940; auto factory and garage use.* **—ers** *n.pl.* 1 Spec-

tacles. 1932: "A little guy who wears horn [rimmed] cheaters." Damon Runyon, *Guys and Dolls.* 2 Marked cards. **—ing** *n.* The act or an instance of being sexually unfaithful to one's spouse. See Appendix, Sex and Deceit.

cheat stick 1 A slide rule or other such calculating device that can be used instead of manual calculation. 2 A scaler's rule by which a lumberman's pay is determined. *Logger use.* → 3 A wage-rate scale by which any employee's pay is determined.

check *interj.* O.K.; definitely; "I understand"; "I'll do it"; and the like. *Usu. a one-word reply.* *n.* 1 A dollar. 2 A certain quantity, a small package, esp. of contraband or narcotics. 3 See **hand in [one's] checks, pass in [one's] checks, rubber check.**

check bouncer One who writes checks against nonexistent bank accounts or against accounts containing insufficient funds to cover the check.

check crew (gang, mob, team, etc.) Working groups composed of both Negro and white members.

checker, the *n.* The very thing; the exact thing called for or needed. *c1850; obs.* See **ticket.**

checkerboard *n.* A town, neighborhood, public gathering place, factory, etc., which contains both Negro and white elements.

checkeroo *n.* 1 A check or bill for food, drink, etc., ordered in a restaurant, night club, hotel, etc. 1940: cited from *Variety* [n.d.] in *AS. Not common.* 2 A name applied to any item, such as a shirt, dress, etc., made of checked cloth. 1947: "Checker-oo . . . checked gingham in brown or black and white checks, $8.95." Advt. for "McCreery's Dept. Store," N.Y. *Times,* June 15, 12.

checks, cash in [one's] = **cash in [one's] chips.**

checks (chips), hand in [one's] To die. *c1865 colloq.; still in use but not common.* See **pass in [one's] checks.**

checks (chips), pass in [one's] To die. *Since c1870.* Cf. **cash in [one's] chips.**

cheechako *n.* A newcomer; a tenderfoot or inexperienced person. 1897, 1945: M. M. Mathews, *Americanisms,* 1951, I, 302/2. *Alaska and fur trader use. Orig. Chinook jargon.*

cheek *n.* Impudence; audacity; nerve. 1887: "Have got the cheek to flirt with every girl. . . ." New Orleans *Lantern.* 1901: "He had the cheek to tell me."

Greenough & Kittredge, *Words & Their Ways*, 69. *Colloq.* **—y** *adj.* **1** Impudent. 1941: "I could tell by the cheeky look on your face." James M. Cain, *Mildred Pierce*, 55. *Colloq.* but more common in *Eng.* than in *U.S.* **2** Audacious; having a lot of nerve; rude. 1956: "The hustler from Western Canada, where they spawn the cheekiest hustlers in the world, was telling the United States how to run racing." T. Betts, *Across the Board*, 160.

cheek it To bluff; to deceive, esp. a teacher or employer, by pretending to have knowledge or ability not actually possessed. *c1900, college use.*

cheerio cheero cheery *interj.* **1** Good-by. *Colloq. An Eng. sl. term; in the U.S. it is almost invariably a humorous colloq., often implying that the meeting has been cheerless or dull. Also, further corrupted to mean* → **2** Hello.

cheers *interj.* **1** A common informal toast, meaning "To your health," "To our health," etc. **2** A one-word compliment signifying approval; = "Well done!" → **3** A one-word comment to signify disapproval or defeat; used sarcastically.

cheese *n.* **1** Any important person or object, usu. in such phrases as the big piece of cheese, the big cheese, the real cheese, etc. 1924: "She's the real cheese." A. Lewis, *Lit. Dig. Prob. from Per.* "*chiz.*" 1929: " 'He's the whole cheese' was originally Anglo-Indian slang ... from Hindustani and, before that, from ... Persian ... 'chiz,' meaning 'the thing' and was ... current in London ... generations ago." P. E. Curtiss, "The Psy. of Tripe," *Harper's*, Aug., 388. **2** An insignificant person, esp. an unworthy person in a position of authority. 1934: "So the big cheese give me the job." R. Chandler, *Finger Man*, 108. See also **big cheese.** **3** A lie, nonsense, cant, exaggeration. 1951: "What a line of cheese!" Richard Bissell, *Stretch on the River*, 10. *A good example of sl. degeneration.* **4** Money. 1956: "I didn't have any cheese." *Oral, N.Y.C.* **5** See **rat cheese.** *v.t.* To stop; to leave off. See **cheese it.** **—cake** *adj.* Sensual; provocative; said of pictures or photographs of girls. 1953: " ... The scantily clad girls in the cheesecake magazines." D. Wallop, *Night Light*, 148. *n.* **1** Published photographs of young women in clothes and poses that emphasize their sex appeal; also, one such photograph. 1939: ship news photographer use. *Better Eng.*, Oct.,

22. *Much popularized during W.W.II.* 1943: "Cheesecake hasn't been rationed." *Life*, May 3, 104. See **pin-up.** *Such photographs, produced in large quantities in Hollywood, were favorite wall decorations for servicemen in W.W.II. Term orig. from photographers' asking subjects to say "cheese" in order to simulate a smile. One of many sl. terms relating food and sex.* → **2** A sexually attractive young woman. See **sweater girl. 3** The revealing garments—shorts, bathing suits, tight sweaters, etc.—or the poses used in provocative photographs. **4** Photographs of virile men. *W.W.II,* Women's Army Corps use. 1944: K. Noble, *Word Study*, Apr. *Not common.* **—cloth** *n.* An obvious person; one who is "seen through" easily. *Not common.*

cheese bun An informer. 1944: longshoreman use, N.Y.C. J. A. Knoetgen, *Encore*, 336. See **cheese eater.**

cheesed off *adj.* Bored; disgusted; angry. 1943: Eng. Royal Air Force use, adopted by U.S. Air Force during W.W. II. *Time,* Mar. 22, 51. Cf. **browned off, pissed off, T'd off.**

cheese eater One who cheats, doublecrosses, or informs. *Euphem. for rat, which orig. meant an informer or stool pigeon.*

cheesehead *n.* A stupid person. 1939: "You let this cheesehead ... insult me ... ?" R. Chandler, *Big Sleep*, 75.

cheese it cheeze it *exclam.* **1** A warning or command to cease an improper activity in order to avoid detection. **2** To run away or disperse. *c1810 to present. Orig. "cheese it, the cops."* Cf. **chickie, jiggers.**

cheesy *adj.* **1** Lacking in style; worthless; of cheap or inferior material, design, or workmanship; unsatisfactory for any reason. 1954: "She looked around the room, mentally rearranging furniture, throwing out table lamps, removing artificial flowers. In her opinion it was an altogether hideous room—expensive but cheesy." J. D. Salinger, "Just Before the War with the Eskimos," reprinted in *Manhattan*, 24. 1948: "For a man with 25,000,000 bucks, Wirtz certainly lives in a cheesy neighborhood." J. E. Evans, *Halo for Satan*, 15. **2** Stylish. 1934: Smart, sl. *Web.*

chef *n.* One who prepares opium for smoking. *Addict use.*

cherry *n.* **1** Other than sexually, one who has not been initiated. 1956: "He's ridden a couple of [horse] races and'll make a good jockey some day; but he's still got his cherry." *Oral*, said of a young jockey who hadn't yet won a race, Churchill Downs, Louisville, Ky., May. **2** Lack of experience, savoir faire, or confidence. **3** [taboo] Virginity; lit., the hymen. 1956: "One bet I'll make you— not a girl in this place still has her cherry." Comedian "Pinky" Lee, N.Y.C. nightclub, "Club Savannah," Oct. 6. *Another of the sl. words relating food and sex*. Cf. **box**, **bug**, **virgin coke**. See Appendix, Sex and Food.   *adj*. Virginal; new; in good condition; specif. as good as new; said of merchandise, esp. used or secondhand merchandise. *From "cherry" = virgin*.

cherry picker   1 A man who desires young girls. See **cherry**. **2** A railroad switchman. *Railroad use, orig. from the red lights on switch stands*.

cherry pie   1 Something easily attainable, easy or pleasant to accomplish. **2** Money readily obtained; money acquired unexpectedly or from work other than one's usual occupation. *Circus use*.

chest hardware   Military medals. *W.W.II Armed Forces use*.

chestnut   *n*. An old, often repeated joke, story, musical composition, etc. *Colloq. since c1885*.

chev   *n*. See **shiv**.   **—y**   See **chivey**.

chevy chase   The face. *Rhyming sl.; much more common in Eng. than in U.S.* See Appendix, Rhyming Terms.

chew   *v.i., v.t.* **1** To eat; to be able to obtain food. 1891: "Now there's Schenectady. You can chew all right there . . . I had heard Buffalo was a good chewing town." J. Flynt, "The American Tramp," *Contemporary Rev.*, Aug. **2** To talk, converse, gossip. 1948: "The stoop-sitters . . . are chewing about it." Lait-Mortimer, *N.Y. Confidential*, 42.   *n*. An overbearing, disliked person. 1927: "I was tempted to paste the big chew. . . ." D. Hammett, *Blood Money*, 76. *Orig. "a big chew of tobacco."*   **—ed**   *adj*. Angry, tired, defeated. 1942: Harlem use: "I know you feel chewed." Z. Hurston, "Story in Harlem Sl.," *Amer. Mercury*, July. See **chew out**.   **—ings**   *n.pl.* Food. 1907: "We went down the river 'on our own,' hustling our 'chewings.' . . ." J. London, "My Life in the Underworld," *Cosmopolitan*, May–Oct.

chewallop   chewalloper   *n*. A fall or a dive that makes a big splash or flopping noise. *Onomatopoeia*.

chew a lone [something]   To do something by oneself that is usu. done with others; e.g., "to chew a lone drink," "to chew a lone song," "to chew a lone summer." *Used by young people, students, etc., in moods of self-pity*.

chew [one's] cabbage   See **chew [one's] tobacco**.

chew [someone's] ear off   To deliver a long monologue; to talk tediously. 1953: "Our society considers it the privilege of the frail sex to chew a gentleman's ear off if she chooses." R. Fontaine, *SEP*, July 4, 34/1.

chewed fine   *adj*. Composed of small particles; e.g., sawdust, ground beef, etc. *c1935: lunch-counter use: "chewed fine on a toasted bun" = a hamburger. Not common*.

chewed up   *adj.* **1** = **chawed**. " 'Chewed Up,' a wash drawing by Paul Klee with its look of thorough and proper rage, was done in 1933, when Klee abandoned Nazi Germany." *Vogue*, Oct. 15, 73. **2** Thoroughly beaten or defeated. → **3** Depressed.

chewing gum   Double talk; cant; utterance garbled as if the speaker were chewing gum; information that is incomplete or mixed up. 1927: "That's probably a lot of chewing gum. . . ." D. Hammett, *Blood Money*, 26.

chew out   *v.t.* To reprimand a person severely; to bawl out. *W.W.II.* 1943: "I got chewed out." J. B. Roulier, "Service Lore: Army Vocab.," *N.Y. Folk Quart.*, Spring. 1951: "The way he chewed out the bos'n. . . ." Movie, *You're in the Navy Now*. 1951: "Everything must be . . . so finalized that the chief won't . . . entertain the idea of chewing out anybody." P. Hogan, "Pentagonese," *Collier's*, Nov. 24. *Very common during W.W.II; still in frequent use among civilians as well as servicemen. Orig. to chew or bite someone's ear, nose, finger, etc., in a frontier fight; hence, angry enough "to chew him up" = demolish, vanquish*.

chew over   To discuss, talk over. 1939: "Drop up, and chew it over." R. Chandler, *Big Sleep*, 149.

chew the fat   1 To talk; to gossip; to chat at length, esp. about trivial matters. **2** A visit, esp. for the purpose of discussing "old times." *Orig. British Army sl., W.W.I*.

chew the rag   1 See **chew the fat**. **2** To argue. 1909: "How better is conversational impotence characterized than by 'chewing the rag'?" *Scribner's*, Aug., 250/2. Cf. **rag chewing**.

chew [one's] tobacco To make a statement; esp. to deliver a homily or a rustically philosophical opinion. Usu. in the cliché: "I don't chew my tobacco but once." *Archaic and dial.*

chib *n.* = **shiv.** 1954: "The big knife called the chib." L. Armstrong, *Satchmo, My Life in New Orleans*, 76.

Chicago *adj.* Resembling a gangster; giving a tough appearance, hinting of illegality or brutality. Often used in phrase, "that Chicago look," to signify the dark, closely tailored clothing popularly associated with gangsters. *n.* 1 A pineapple sundae, sometimes a pineapple soda. *In allusion to gangsters' bombs or pineapples. c1935, lunch-counter use.* 2 In sports, a contest in which one side does not score. *Obs.*

Chicago flats = **St. Louis flats.**

Chicago overcoat A coffin. 1929: "A Chicago overcoat is what blasting would get you...." R. Chandler, *Big Sleep*, 161. *Not common.* See **Chicago**.

Chicago pineapple A small bomb or grenade. *Because such items were associated with Chicago hoodlums during the Prohibition era.* See **pineapple**.

chi-chi **chichi** *n.* Something or someone stylish or fancy; fanciness; stylishness. 1951: "Is that what you want in a girl—chi-chi, frou-frou, fancy clothes, permanent waves?" M. Shulman, *Dobie Gillis*, 73. 1951: "Another bit of chichi that has come to our notice lately is Eleanor Roosevelt's letterhead." *New Yorker*, Dec. 1, 39/1. *adj.* Smart, stylish; pretentious, affected; fancy. 1951: "This rather chichi experiment [i.e., allergy skin tests for nail polish, nylon, chrome, and chrysanthemums] has increased her allure." *New Yorker*, Dec. 1, 39/1.

chick *n.* 1 Prison food. *Underworld use.* 2 A girl or young woman, esp. if attractive, pert, and lively; a hip girl or woman. *c1935, jive use, esp. in Harlem.* 1938: jitterbug use [hip chick = snooty girl], *Variety.* 1951: "Any guy could keep his chick contented with a hundred-grand annuity." *SEP*, Apr. 21, 12. *Orig. "chicken"; ref. to a live, perky chicken with secondary connotation of food, another ex. of relation between food and sex. Also ex. of sl. word used only by males.* 1954: "Luckily she was a woman, and a good-looking chick at that." L. Armstrong, *Satchmo, My Life in New Orleans*, 179. 1957: *For Cool Cats and Far-Out Chicks*,

title of a modern jazz lexicon by E. Horne. 1958: "He runs after all the chicks . . . all of them . . . young and old. . . ." Saul Bellow, "Leaving The Yellow House," *Esquire*, Jan., 116. *Associated with jazz, now common.* Cf. **chicken, hen, hipchick, pigeon, quail, slick chick.** —**en** *n.* 1 An attractive young woman. 1956: "George Jessel is dating a bevy of young girls—some barely out of their teens. His colleagues at the Friars Club in Hollywood saw him with some of the young ladies. And when George next visited the club, he saw a sign: 'Why does a chicken cross the road? Because George Jessel is on the other side of it?'" L. Lyons, N.Y. *Post*, Feb. 21, 48. *Since c1900.* See **spring chicken.** 2 A coward; a sissy. *c1935.* 3 A young and puny or innocent Army or USN inductee. 4 A victim of a robbery, kidnaping, confidence game, etc. 5 Insignia of a U.S. Army colonel or a USN captain, used disparagingly. *W.W.II.* 1953: "But when a man is placed in a position of authority primarily because he has chickens or even stars [U.S. Army general's insignia] on his shoulders. . . ." C. B. Seib, GNS, June 2. *Often used in term "chicken colonel" to distinguish a full colonel from a lieutenant colonel and also to imply "chicken shit" colonel.* 6 An excessive show of authority; unnecessary discipline or regimentation, in either military or civilian life. *Orig. in colonel's insignia, reinforced by "chicken shit."* 7 Cant; boloney, bunk; testiness in discourse or behavior. 8 Small tasks or duties that are boring or perhaps unnecessary. 1952: "Cut the chicken [unnecessary amenities] and let's get through with it." Movie, *My Six Convicts. Short and more acceptable form of "chicken shit."* *adj.* 1 Afraid; cowardly; yellow. 1941: "Gets chicken. . . ." *Life*, Dec. 15, 89. 1956: "He's chicken, that's what's the trouble." John & Ward Hawkins, "The Cowardice of Sam Abbott," *SEP*, Oct. 20, 112/2. 2 Underhanded; sneaky; thoughtless or inconsiderate. 3 Strictly conventional in conduct; following (esp. Army) rules too closely; misusing authority; petty, mean. *v.i.* To grin foolishly, mockingly, or apologetically. *c1935, Negro use.*

chicken colonel *n.* A U.S. Army colonel.

chicken coop See **rain pitchforks.**

chicken feed Small change; any small amount of money, esp. compared to what one expects to have in the future. 1836: "I stood looking on, seeing him pick up the chicken feed from the green horns." *Col. [Davy] Crockett's Exploits*, 49. 1952: "Charley was . . . ahead $38, . . . he knew that was only the merest chicken feed to the others. . . ." R. M. Coates, *New Yorker*, Oct. 4, 32/1. 1956: "Chickenfeed Campaign Cash [headline:] The $2,500 offered by an oil lobbyist for the campaign of Sen. Case was only small change—that is, as money for political purposes is rated among some big oil moguls." T. L. Stokes in N.Y. *Post*, Feb. 21, 48. Cf. **scratch.**

chicken guts   Gold trimming on military uniforms, as epaulets. c1865 [1951]: "It showed a proud young man in Rebel gray, with the gold trimming the soldiers called 'chicken guts' on the cuffs." S. Longstreet, *The Pedlocks*, 18. *Archaic.* See **scrambled eggs.**

chicken-head   *n.* A stupid person.

chickenheart   *n.* A coward.   **—ed** *adj.* Cowardly; lacking persistence. Cf. **yellow.** 1956: "He sized me up. Here's a potbellied, chickenhearted slob—this is what he thinks—here's a slob with no backbone, no guts. He won't fight. He's afraid to fight." John & Ward Hawkins, "The Cowardice of Sam Abbott," *SEP*, Oct. 20, 110/4.

chicken-livered   *adj.* Cowardly.

chicken money   See **chicken feed.** *Colloq. since c1850.*

chicken out   To withdraw from a plan, task, or endeavor because of fear; to quit. See **chicken.** Cf. **pig it.** 1950: "The Harvard Student Council . . . just plain chickened out. . . . [They] considered the proposal . . . and sent the resolution back to committee on a technicality." *Cornell (Univ.) Daily Sun*, Mar. 24, 4.

chicken shit [taboo]   **1** Practically any order, system, state of affairs, or the like that is disagreeable for any reason; esp., a close adherence to rules of discipline. 1947: " 'That's putting it straight,' said Munro. 'Now and then I like a freshman who comes out and says something, instead of this eternal dreary chicken shit.' " C. Willingham, *End as a Man*, 96. **2** Pettiness; mean and unliked assignments. **3** Something that is worthless or of small size or value. **4** Unnecessary rules of conduct; an excessive show of authority. **5** A lie; cant; an attempt to deceive. *adj. & adv.* **1** Petty; worthless; boring. **2** Degrading; menial. **3** Small. *v.i.* **1** To lie; to

attempt to deceive. **2** To stall; to waste time or effort purposely. **—s** Diarrhea. Cf. **bullshit, horse shit, GI shits.** See **chicken.**

chicken tracks   *pl.* = **hen tracks.** Illegible handwriting. 1953: "The teacher had us all try to write the first letters of the alphabet . . . when she saw mine she said . . . 'I'd better put you in the chicken tracks row.' " Hal Boyle, AP, Sept. 12.

chickie   *imp.* A warning or command to cease an improper activity in order to avoid detection; an imperative warning to run or disperse. *Very pop. among N.Y.C. adolescents and juvenile delinquents since c1945.* 1956: "We use 'chickie' more than 'cheese it.' " *Oral*, by a Bronx adolescent girl.

chickie the cops!   *imp.* See **chickie.**

Chic Sale   An outdoor toilet; an outhouse. *From humorist Chic Sales, who wrote a widely circulated catalogue of outhouses, a satirical booklet; archaic.*

chief   *n.* **1** One's boss or superior. **2** A fellow or guy; usu. used in direct address to strangers.

chief itch and rub   The most important person; the head of any group, e.g., school principal, Army officer, office overseer, etc.

chief of staff   An officer's wife. *Army argot.* 1951: P. Hogan, "Pentagonese," *Collier's*, Nov. 24. *Picturesque, but not common.*

child   *n.* See **brain child.**

chili-bowl   *n.* A haircut that leaves the hair too short and untapered, as if the barber had placed a bowl over the head and shaved around it.

chill   *v.t.* **1** To effect a permanent solution, esp. in an emotionless and hypereffective manner. **2** To resolve a complaint or awkward situation; to square a complaint. 1932: "There is plenty of trouble . . . in chilling the blonde doll's beef over Lillian snagging her Peke. . . ." D. Runyon, *Guys & Dolls*, 57. **3** To render (someone) unconscious, either in the boxing ring or elsewhere. *Underworld use.* **4** To kill. 1949: "Remember the night Stein got chilled out front?" R. Chandler, *Little Sister*, 247. **5** To cause another to become angry; to elicit anger. 1944: Longshoreman use. J. A. Knoetgen, "Longshoreman's Lingo," *Encore*, Sept.–Oct.   *v.i.* **1** To submit willingly to another's domination, to let oneself be taken advantage of. → **2** To submit to arrest without resisting. **3** To become suspicious or cold toward a plan or person. **4** To become discouraged, to lose enthusiasm (also *v.t.*). *adj.* & *adv.* Perfect(ly), exact(ly); having perfect mastery of a scheme, topic, situation, etc.; having "it [a body of data or a procedure] down cold." *1900, student use.* See **cold, put the chill on.** **—off** *v.i.*, *v.t.* = **chill.**

chill, put on the To act coldly toward a person; to snub.

chiller *n.* **1** A melodrama; a horror story or thriller. 1952: "The documentary chiller is based on a famed . . . court case." *Syracuse (N.Y.) Post Standard*, Sept. 22, 18/7. **2** A gun.

chiller-diller *n.* A book, movie, or play, esp. a movie, which fascinates its audience by suspense, mystery, or scenes of fear and horror. *Based on "chiller" plus "dilly."* See Appendix, Rhyming Slang.

chill on [someone], put the **1** To ignore, reject, or treat someone coldly; to withdraw one's affection or friendship. 1956: "John F. Curry, leader of Tammany Hall, could not understand why [Mayor Jimmy] Walker greeted him so coldly when they met at the funeral of Judge Rosalsky. 'Why does he put the chill on me?' Curry asked." T. Betts, *Across the Board*, 185. *Not common.* **2** To kill someone. 1949: "Moyer had the chill put on Sunny Moe Stein. . . ." Chandler, *Little Sister*, 57.

chime *n.* An hour. 1948: Harlem use. Lait-Mortimer, *N.Y. Confidential*, 235. *Not common.*

chime in To interrupt and intrude in a conversation or discussion; to give unasked-for advice or an opinion; to butt in.

chimney *n.* The human head. *Negro use.*

chin *v.i.*, *v.t.* To talk; converse. 1883: *DAE.* 1934: "The cop was . . . chinning a nurse." J. M. Cain, *Postman*, 55. *n.* A chat, talk, conversation. 1912: "Coming up for a chin?" O. Johnson, *Stover at Yale*, 270. 1952: "We'd like to have a little chin with you right now." S. J. Perelman, *New Yorker*, Jan. 12, 24/1. *Replaced the older "chin music."*

chin, take it on the **1** = **take it.** *No longer common in this sense, has been replaced by "take it."* **2** To suffer a severe failure; to undergo complete defeat or frustration. *Now common.*

china *n.* **1** The teeth. 1950: "Smile and show that china." Movie, *Riding High*. **2** Money. 1956: "Money is *china*."

S. Longstreet, *The Real Jazz Old and New*, 150. *Never common.*

china chin = **glass jaw.** 1950: "What is known in the prizefight game as a china chin. . . ." J. Lardner in *New Yorker*, Sept. 30, 52.

china-clipper *n.* A person whose job is washing dishes. *Pop. among servicemen, W.W.II.*

China cracker A firecracker. *Obs.*

Chinaman *n.* A sailor who works in a ship's laundry.

Chinaman's chance An extremely poor chance. Only used in phrase "hasn't got a Chinaman's chance" = no chance at all. *Orig. from Calif. gold rush, 1849, when Chinese worked old claims, streams, and even wash abandoned by white prospectors, in hope of finding gold; reinforced by poor lot of Chinese in a segregated society.*

chinch *n.* A bedbug. 1956: "A *chinch* is a bedbug." S. Longstreet, *The Real Jazz Old and New*, 148. *Some hobo, ranch, logger, and Army use.* **—pad** *n.* A cheap hotel or rooming house. Cf. **pad.**

Chinee *n.* **1** A Chinese. *Since c1870.* **2** A complimentary ticket of admission to an entertainment, esp. a sporting event. 1935: "Bill Corum . . . gives me a Chinee for a fight at Madison Square Garden, a Chinee being a ducket with holes punched in it like old-fashioned Chink money, to show that it is a free ducket. . . ." D. Runyon, *Money from Home*, 211.

Chinee ducket *n.* See **Chinee.**

Chinese See **knock for a loop.**

Chinese ace A pilot who lands a plane with one wing low. *From the pun "one wing low"* = *Wun Wing Lo.*

Chinese landing A plane landing made by a (q.v.) **Chinese ace.** *Orig. aviator use; common in Army Air Force, W.W.II.*

Chinese three-point landing An airplane crash, esp. an airplane crash caused by a pilot's error while attempting a landing. *W.W.II Air Force use.* Cf. **Chinese ace.**

Chinese tobacco Opium. 1950: "If you think I've been lacing my coffee with Chinese tobacco and want to check on [this story], go ahead." Billy Rose, "Pitching Horseshoes," *synd. newsp. col.*, Jan.

chin fest A session of idle talk and gossip; a discussion; a bull session.

chinjaw *n.* Talk; esp. small talk. *Logger use.*

Chink   **chink**   *n.* **1** [derog.] A Chinese. *Since c1900.* 1951: "Lee, the Chinese cook, born in San Francisco, did not speak like a Bret Harte Chink." S. Longstreet, *The Pedlocks,* 63. **2** Coins, metal money; money in general. 1573: Sl., *OED.* 1934: Sl., *Web. Obs. adj.* [derog.] Chinese. 1938: "A Chink joint." A. J. Liebling, *Back Where I Come From,* 102. 1951: "We were out in the Chink lines . . . ; the red chinks hit us hard." Letter from U.S. soldier during Korean War. **—s** *n.pl.* Chinese food as served in a Chinese restaurant in the U.S.

chin music   **1** Talk; esp. unnecessary conversation, small talk, gossip. 1952: "After endless chin music calculated to allay her trepidation. . . ." S. J. Perelman in *New Yorker,* Sept. 20, 35/1. *Since c1835.* **2** Impertinent retorts; protestations. *Obs.*

chinny   *adj.* Talkative. 1883, colloq.: *DAE. Obs.*

chino   *n.* **1** [derog.] A Chinese. 1936: Addict use. D. W. Maurer, "Argot of Narcotic Addicts," *AS,* 119. **2** A variety of cotton twill cloth. *Orig. the cheap cotton worn by Chinese coolies, applied by U.S. soldiers stationed in China (pre-W.W.II) to their own cotton summer uniforms, transferred to civilian use by post-W.W.II Army surplus clothing stores, and now applied to* → **3** A style of trousers having tapered legs, a belt in the back, and made of a cotton twill cloth. *Such garments have now become associated with the Ivy League style of dress; an outstanding example of word upgrading.*

Chinook wind   Warm spring winds; the beginning of spring. *Alaskan and northwest U.S. use.*

chintzy   *adj.* Unfashionable; unsophisticated; unenlightened; corny or cheap. 1951: "How chintzy can you get?" Movie, *The Guy Who Came Back.* 1953: "In New York City, the all-white costume is considered 'CHINTZY' (that's the newest word for unfashionable). . . . White shoes with a dark dress is [sic] considered very definitely . . . 'chintzy.'" Helen Humphrey, woman's page, *Syracuse (N.Y.) Post-Standard,* May 28, 19/4.

chip   *n.* **1** A news item. *Since c1890.* **2** A dollar. *c1920.* **3** A cash register. *c1935.* **4** A tip (gratuity). 1956: "I used to get $15 a week plus maybe another $15 in chips; since Roosevelt was president I get $50 a week and up to maybe $35–40 in tips." *Oral,* a N.Y.C. waiter. *Although it is used by some older people, all four*

uses of this word are virtually obs. It is preserved in the standard gambling "chip" as used in poker, etc. See **in the chips, chip in, pass in [one's] checks (chips).** *v.t.* To steal. **—ie** See **chippie.** **—s** *n.* **1** Money. *Since c1860.* See **chips are down, in the chips. 2** A ship's carpenter; the common nickname for a ship's carpenter. 1948: R. de Kerchove, *International Maritime Dict.* **3** French fried potatoes. *Eng. sl., used by U.S. troops during W.W.II.*

chip in   **1** To pay one's share of an expense; to contribute money toward a group undertaking. *Colloq. From the game of poker. Since c1860.* 1949: "The crew chipped in and bought him a . . . chair." *Syracuse (N.Y.) Post-Standard,* Sept. 29, 9. → **2** To contribute to a discussion. 1953: "State Assembly Speaker Oswald D. Heck chipped in with: 'The state's budget reflects . . . integrity. . . .'" AP, Jan. 29.

chippie   **chippy**   *n.* **1** A promiscuous woman or delinquent girl; orig. a prostitute, dance-hall girl, female bartender, or the like. c1915 [1954]: "Around the honky-tonks on Liberty and Perdido life was the same as in Storyville except that the chippies were cheaper." L. Armstrong, *Satchmo, My Life in New Orleans,* 95. 1934: "Men are really much nicer to chippies than to ladies." P. Wylie, *Finnley Wren,* 112. *Now usu. jocular, as sounding archaic. Although this word prob. does not come from "chip," it once was used in the same sense as "piece."* → **2** A simple, straight-cut dress that buttons down the front, as worn in place of a robe. 1950: "A chippie is a dress that women wore, knee length and very easy to disrobe." A. Lomax, *Mr. Jelly Roll,* 21. *Obs. adj.* Amateurish; small.

chippie joint   A brothel.

chips, cash in [one's]   To die. *Since c1875; from the gambling usage.*

chips (checks), hand in [one's]   To die. *From gambling use, where one actually hands one's chips or checks to a cashier or the dealer on leaving the game.*

chips, in the   Affluent; having money. In reference to poker chips. 1944: "I am now in the chips." Fowler, *Good Night,* 3.

chips are down, the   Signifying a situation of urgency or ultimacy, sometimes portending failure or disaster; signifying a situation in which the consequences of any action will be irrevocable. 1949: "When the chips are down a man shows what he really is." Radio program, *Martin Kane, Private Eye*, N.Y.C. station WOR, Sept. 4.

chip the ivories To talk. 1945: "A skivvy-waver and a bellhop were chipping the ivories." Riordan in *Calif. Folk Quart.*, Oct. *Some W.W.II USN use.*

chirp *v.i., v.t.* **1** To sing; said of a female singer, usu. professional. *c1930*. 1950: "She chirps with the orchestra." AP, Mar. 29. **2** To inform, to give information to the police; to "sing." R. Chandler, *Big Sleep*, 152. 1949: "If I'd chirped. . . ." Movie, *Johnny Stool Pigeon*. *n.* = **twerp.** *By euphem. rhyming.* **—er** *n.* **1** A female singer. 1950: "An ork [orchestra] chirper is a gal who sits . . . before a dance band. . . . Every 10 minutes . . . she . . . chirps with the orchestra." Bob Thomas, AP, Mar. 29. **2** An informer. 1939: "I am by no means a chirper." D. Runyon, *Take It Easy*, 70. *Orig., British use., "chirp" = mouth.*

chisel *v.i., v.t.* To cheat (someone); to take advantage of (someone); to obtain (something) by unfair or niggling means. *Since c1830.* **2** To borrow with little expectation of repaying, esp. something of insignificant value. *Ex.: one chisels a cigarette or a few cents but borrows $50 or a cup of replaceable sugar.* **—er** *n.* A petty crook; a schemer associated with trivial enterprises. 1932: "In use about a hundred years ago . . . and then for many years discarded. It [chiseler] has now returned to general use." J. L. Kuethe, "John Hopkins Jargon," *AS*, June. 1951: "There is no place for the phony economics of the chiseler." Charles E. Wilson, Sec. of Defense, in an official radio address, Feb. 23. **—ing —ling** *adv.* 1949: "A chisellin' heel of a louse." A. Kober in *New Yorker*, Nov. 5, 82.

chit *n.* **1** An insignificant person; a rude, vulgar, audacious, or obnoxious person;—always a young person. 1956: "In the late twenties every dance left at least a half-dozen of the chits—high school girls, debutantes, and convent-bred misses—dead drunk in the corners." S. Longstreet, *The Real Jazz Old and New*, 96. **2** A paper, card, or ticket entitling the bearer to merchandise, usu. food or service; private "script" issued by a business firm. 1956: ". . . Martin had been signing his meal chits, but not touching his food." Al Stump, "He's Never Out of Trouble," *SEP*, Aug. 18, 44.

chitchat *n.* Chat; amiable or idle conversation. 1943: ". . . Enough of this

pecuniary chitchat." M. Shulman, *Barefoot Boy with Cheek*, 55.

Chiv *n.* A Southerner. *c1860: Obs. Orig. a Western term for "Southerner." Abbr. of "chivalry."*

chiv *n.* = **shiv.** **—ey chivvy** *v.i., v.t.* To badger (someone); to nag (someone). 1934: chiv(v)y, chevy. *Web.* 1949: "So Mr. Dubinsky's union not only chivvies the subjects to get the vote out but warns them to register. . . ." W. Pegler, *synd. newsp. col.*, Sept. 29.

chocolate *adj.* Negro; pertaining to Negroes. 1952: "Valerio was handsome with olive-yellow skin and Spanish-black hair, more foreign than Negro. His sleek-haired yellow star rose in a chocolate sky." L. Hughes, *Laughing To Keep from Crying*, 38.

chocolate drop [derog.] A Negro.

choke **choke in** **choke up** *imp.* An order or command to stop talking. *v.i.* **1** To stop talking; to stop doing whatever one is doing. **2** To slow down; to take it easy. **3** To be on the verge of tears; to be unable to speak as the result of emotional stress. **—r**

chocker *n.* **1** Anything worn closely around the throat, esp. a tie, stiff collar, or necklace. 1922: "Brew's going stepping. Sinners and claw-hammers and stiff chocker [collar], and bear grease in his hair." A. L. Bass, "Univ. Tongue," *Harper's*, Mar. 1934: Chiefly sl. *Web.* 1949: "I was sent up because they caught me with a couple of chockers [necklaces] that the guy from the jewelry store said was his." *Oral*, from a petty thief. 1956: "If you double it in back, like this, you can wear it [a long necklace] as a chocker." *Oral*, sales clerk in R. H. Macy's store, N.Y.C. *As a necklace, a definite and popular fashion, no longer sl.* **2** A cheese, large pie, or any other big, solid article of food. **3** See **grub-choker.** **4** A man's tie, esp. a bow tie. *Archaic.*

choke-dog *n.* Strong, raw-tasting liquor, usu. home-made. *c1821.*

chokey **chokee** **choky** *n.* A prison. *Anglo-Indian; more common in Eng. than U.S.* See **pokey.**

chop *n.* **1** Quality. 1950: "Imported champagne of the very first chop." R. Starnes, *Another Mug*, 110. *Orig. Hind. "chāp" = a seal or stamp, such as would indicate official clearance or approval.* **2** The mouth or jaws. See **beat [one's] gums (chops), flap [one's] chops, lick [one's] chops. 3** A very critical or insulting remark, a dig; lit., a cutting remark. *Some use since c1950.* **—s** *n.sing.* **1** The mouth; the lips. **2** The legs, esp. the thighs; the hips. *Negro use.* *n.pl.* **1** The teeth, natural or false. 1949: "He made with the choppers [bared his teeth]." A. Kober in *New Yorker*, Nov. 5, 86. 1951: "One of Randy Turpin's [Irish prize fighter] first experiences in this country was to sink his choppers into the exalted hot dog. . . ." NEA photo caption, Aug. 27. **2** The chin, mouth, jaws, or cheeks.

chop-chop *imp. & adv.* Hurry up; to do [something] promptly, correctly, and in a satisfactory manner. *W.W.II. A pidgin Eng. term used by Chinese and Armed Forces; used humorously by U.S. civilians.* 1946: "'Chop-chop' is Army slang for make it snappy." W. Winchell, *synd. newsp. col.*, June 4. *Orig. may be reduplication of Hind. "chāp" = a seal or stamp, hence in India or China official approval or a mark of high quality.* *n.* Food, eating, or anything related to either. *Used by U.S. soldiers in Korean War. Orig. may be reduplication of stand. Eng. "chop" or from the Hind.; note most common use by U.S. Armed Forces via Korea.*

chopped top A convertible car. *Teenage use, c1955; not common. Orig. hot-rod use = a car with the top section of its windshield removed, and/or with its roof and sometimes its windows removed also, so that only the bare frame is left above the door level.* See Appendix, Rhyming Slang.

chopper *n.* **1** A ticket taker or conductor; one who tears a ticket into two parts to show that it has been used. **2** A machine gun (usu. the Thompson submachine gun); a machine gunner. 1929: "Johnny Head . . . had met the 'chopper' [machine-gunner]. . . ." John Gunther, *Harper's*, Oct., 532/2. 1931: A machine gunner for a mob. D. W. Maurer, "Argot of Underworld," *AS*, Dec., 105. 1934: "The chopper raked the room. . . . The man with the chopper. . . ." R. Chandler, *Finger Man*, 124–5. 1950: "Izzatto gave Sam a chopper. . . ." J. B. Martin, *SEP*, May 27, 67/2. *Mainly mobster use; seldom adopted in armed forces.* **3** A helicopter. 1951: Used by U.S. soldiers in Korean War. M. R. Johnson, "New Lexicon for War," N.Y. *Her. Trib.*, Dec. 16. Cf. **egg beater.** **4** See **button-chopper.**

chop [one's] teeth To talk idly; to interject unnecessary remarks into a conversation. Often in phrase "now you're just chopping your teeth" = you're saying something worthless. Cf. **beat [one's] gums.**

chow *n.* **1** Food; mealtime. 1856: "Ah, Chow . . . [=] Mr. Chow, something good to eat." *Sacramento (Calif.) Spirit of Age*, Nov. 27, 2/2, in M. M. Mathews, *Americanisms*, 1956, I, 321/1. 1905: *U.S. sl.* "A shortening of Pidgin chow-chow, mixed pickles." E. Partridge, *Sl.*, 429. 1921: "Let's get some chow." Witwer, *Leather Pushers*, 57. W.W.I: Stallings & Anderson, *What Price Glory*, Act I, III, 1926. 1918: *Armed Forces use.* "Attributed to the Chinese chow dog, which has a reputation for insatiable hunger." E. S. McCartney, "Trench Talk," *Texas Rev.*, Oct., 284/2. 1943–5: "In the Army one never eats a meal but always 'chow.'" J. B. Roulier, "Service Lore; Army Vocab.," *N.Y. Folk Quart.*, Spring, 1948. *Very common during and after W.W.II. Var. attributed to "chow-chow," Pidgin Eng., and to Chinese chow dogs. E. Partridge traces to 19C Eng. nautical argot; first U.S. uses recorded near Sacramento, Calif., Pacific Coast. Said to have been used by Chinese railroad workers in West, which may indicate orig. directly from Chinese "chow" = food.* **2** A Chinese. *More common in Australia than in U.S.* *v.i.* To eat. *W.W.I and W.W.II.*

chowderhead *n.* A stupid person; one who uses poor judgment. **—ed** *adj.* Stupid. *Since c1835.*

chow down To eat a meal. 1945: "Let's knock off . . . and chow down." J. L. Riordan, "Amer. Naval Sl. in the Pacific," *Calif. Folk Quart.*, Oct. 19. *n.* A meal. *W.W.II.*

chow fight A dinner. 1933: "After we pull that chow fight for the Johnsons." H. T. Webster, "They Don't Speak Our Lang.," *Forum*, Dec., 367/1. *Synthetic.*

chow hall An eating place; esp. an Army mess hall, school dining room, etc., where members of a group are required to eat and where mass-produced, usu. bland, food is served. *adj.* Unimaginatively prepared food; sloppy serving. 1943: "A chow-hall breakfast." R. A. Herzberg, "Army Sl.," *Word Study*, Apr., 5/2.

chow hound A hearty eater; a glutton; one whose table manners leave something to be desired. *W.W.II use by all branches of the Armed Forces.* 1943: "He is not necessarily a prodigious eater;

his unpopularity is usually caused by his roughshod methods in getting first to the best of the food." J. B. Roulier, "Service Lore: Army Vocab.," *N.Y. Folk Quart.*, Spring. *Orig. one who, like a hound dog, scents food before the signal is given to begin feeding, and hence is able to obtain bigger helpings and the best food by being first in the chow line. Now frequently used in civilian speech.*

chow line **1** A line, as of soldiers, students, etc., waiting to be admitted to an eating place or waiting to be served (cafeteria-style) inside. 1940: "I was standing in the chow line." *Life*, Nov. 18, 6. 1949: "So you will stand in chow line. . . ." W. Pegler, *synd. newsp. col.*, Oct. 13. *Very common W.W.I and W.W.II use.* **2** Any clique of soldiers found usu. together, as in a chow line. **3** The row of counters from which food is dispensed in a cafeteria; also the employees who tend the counters and steam tables.

chow time Mealtime.

Christer *n.* **1** A pious, sanctimonious college student; a prude. **2** A person who shuns drinking, dancing, or other group activities; a wet blanket. 1930: "A regular Christer, that sap." B. Brown, "The Great Amer. Sl.," *Outlook*, Nov. 12, 417. 1951: "Non-drinkers are called all sorts of names—one in popular usage is 'Christer.'" *Cornell (Univ.) Daily Sun*, Oct. 23, 4/2.

Christmas *n.* **1** Any ostentatious display, as of clothing, jewelry, etc. **2** A garish article of clothing or jewelry, or one that sparkles. **3** A shower of metallic foil dropped by an airplane or artillery shell to jam enemy radar or communications systems. *W.W.II use. Orig. "all lighted up like a Christmas tree."*

Christmas tree *n.* The piping constituting and controlling an oil or gas well; the derrick of an oil or gas well. 1952: "Texans do not cut CHRISTMAS TREES. Nor do they throw them away come New Year's Day. They build them of steel and use them the year 'round. A Christmas tree is a maze of pipes, joints, valves and gauges on an oil well, used to control it." J. Randolph, *Texas Brags*, 55. *Dial.*

chromo *n.* **1** Any person or object that is ugly or offensive. 1939: "His sister . . . is the chromo sitting behind him. . . . She is older than he is, and has a big nose and a mustache." D. Runyon, *Take It Easy*, 161. **2** A difficult customer or client, one who buys only after much

hesitation and then is rarely satisfied. *c1930: salesman use. Although term is commonly derived from ugliness of chromo-lithographs, see* **chromosome***. Or it may orig. in rapid pronunciation of "crumb-o." In any case, obs.*

chromo, take the To vie with; to "take the cake." *c1880. Obs.*

chromosome *n.* An insignificant or small person. *c1945: student use.*

chronicker *n.* **1** A back-door beggar; a panhandler. *c1920.* **2** A watch or clock. **3** A newspaper.

chub *n.* A Texan. *c1870. Colloq.*

chuck *n.* **1** Food; a meal. 1891: "You can batter for clothes, chuck, and booze. . . ." J. Flynt, "The Tramp at Home," *Cent. Mag.*, Feb., 1894. **2** Money. *v.t.* **1** To have done with. 1951: "Is it possible that she has chucked her aloofness . . . ?" S. Lewis, *World So Wide*, **2** To eat. *v.i.* **1** To pitch for a baseball team; to throw a ball. *Colloq.* **2** To be quiet; to "shut up." **3** To vomit. *c1940; student use.* See **up-chuck**. **—er** *n.* **1** A baseball pitcher. 1934: M. H. Weseen, *Dict. Amer. Sl.* 1956: "The pitching size-up will have to wait until the chuckers can throw a few innings." AP, Apr. 16. **2** A baseball inning. *Orig. a polo term.* **—s** See **chuck habit**.

chuck a dummy To feign a fainting fit in order to win sympathy. *Hobo use.*

chuck-a-lug = **chug-a-lug**.

chucker-out *n.* One whose job is to expel undesirable customers; a bouncer. 1929: "Other chuckers-out such as Handsome Harry at the Chatham [bar]. . . ." J. K. Winkler, "That Was N.Y.: Some Bounce Easy," *New Yorker*, Feb. 9, 38/2. *Orig. British; "bouncer" much more common in U.S.*

chuck habit **chuck horrors** **1** The craving for food experienced by a dope addict whose supply of narcotic is suddenly discontinued. **2** A fear of not having enough to eat; therefore the compulsion to eat as much as possible whenever food is available. *Hobo use.* **3** A fear of, obsession for, or horror of food, esp. one kind of food, as a reformed drug addict for sweets. 1949: "Back on the street at last, he'd gotten the chuck horrors: for two full days he'd eaten candy bars, sweet rolls and strawberry malteds. It had seemed that there would be no end to the hunger for sweets." N. Algren, *Man with the Golden Arm*, 78. **4** A psychotic fear or obsession with prison; insanity resulting from confinement in prison.

chuck it   *imp.* A command to "shut up" or cease whatever one is doing. 1957: "If you've got the crazy idea that you're going to take my place, just chuck it." *Oral*, an experienced employee to a younger one, N.Y.C. See **chuck**, *v.t.*

chucklehead   *n.* A stupid person. 1913: "Slang . . . knows how . . . to work the poppycock racket on any daffy squirt or dotty chucklehead or dippy mushhead, or any crazy kioodle or concatenated chump." F. K. Sechrist, "The Psy. of Unconventional Lang.," *Pedagogical Seminary*, Dec. **—ed** *adj.* Stupid. 1950: "The chuckleheaded infants who think it's a good idea to stage raids on other campuses. . . ." *Cornel (Univ.) Daily Sun*, Oct. 7, 4.

chuck wagon   **1** A wagon carrying food and a cookstove, used to feed cowboys and other outdoor workers on the job. 1890: Western use, *DAE*. **2** Any small roadside or neighborhood lunch counter. *c1940.* **3** A buffet meal of unlimited servings for a nominal, pre-fixed price. *c1950.* 1954: "In [Las] Vegas you scoff either downtown at the Golden Nugget [famous gambling saloon] or else you eat chuck wagon on the strip." *Oral*, Las Vegas shill.

chug-a-lug   *v.i., v.t.* To drink a glassful of a beverage, or the amount of a beverage remaining in a glass, in one gulp or in a series of uninterrupted swallows without pausing for breath. *Common student use c1940–c1950. The beverage was usu. beer and was chug-a-lugged in haste, on a dare, or to demonstrate one's capacity for alcoholic drink.* 1956: "If you chug-a-lug that [bottle of beer] I'll pay for the next one." *Oral*, St. Louis bar. *Onomatopoetic from sounds of swallowing and imbibing.*

chug wagon   A car. *c1910. Obs; never common.*

chum   *n.* **1** A roommate. 1851: "Now very generally used in U.S. and English colleges and universities, replacing 'chamber-mate.' " B. H. Hall, *College Words*, 41. 1901: " 'Chum' was defined in 1650 as 'chamber-fellow' and is usually regarded as a corruption of this term, but evidence is lacking. It has been [British] university slang since the latter part of the 17th century. . . ." Greenough & Kittredge, *Words & Their Ways*, 67. *Obs.* → **2** A close personal friend. Still used by preteenagers, but elsewhere almost invariably replaced by "buddy." **3** Now used sarcastically for "chump." *v.i.* **1** To occupy a room with another. **2** To curry favor with someone, esp. a teacher. See **new chum**. Cf. **apple polish, brown-nose**. **—my** *n.* A chum. *c1850.* *adj.* Friendly.

chum-buddy   *n.* A particularly close friend; more than a chum. 1952: "Yesterday's villains are tomorrow's chum-buddies." R. Ruark, *synd. newsp. col.*, Mar. 20.

chump   *n.* **1** A dupe, one who is easily deluded; a stupid person. **2** A paying customer, esp. a patron of a carnival, circus, burlesque show, etc. See **off [one's] chump**.

chump, off [one's]   Insane. 1922: "You'll go off your chump. . . ." O'Neill, *Hairy Ape*, I. 1952: "You're off your chump." *New Yorker*, Feb. 16, 24/1.

cider barrel   An ocean-going tug.

cig   *n.* A cigarette. See Appendix, Shortened Words.

cigar   *n.* **1** A compliment. *From the carnival barker's "give the man a big cigar," a prize for winning at a game.* **2** A reprimand from one's employer. *From associating authority with those who smoke cigars; not common.*

cigaroot   *n.* A cigarette. *Used facetiously. Orig. cigarette + cheroot.* Cf. **root**.

cinch   *n.* **1** A certainty; someone assured of success or something easily accomplished. 1893: "From the Southwest came 'cinch,' from the tightening of the girths of the pack-mules, and so by extension indicating a grasp of anything so firm that it cannot get away." B. Matthews, "The Funct. of Sl.," *Harper's*, July, 307/2. 1905: "We can't lose if we handle this cinch right. . . ." H. McHugh, *Search Me*, 23. 1910: "The windows are a cinch [to open]." Johnson, *Varmint*, 174. 1941: "He was a cinch to defeat the mayor." G. Homes, *40 Whacks*, 14. 1957: "It's a cinch to get a husband. The trick is getting the right one." S. McNeil, *High-Pressure Girl*, 49. *Colloq. Since before 1875. From the cinch of a saddle, which secures it.* → **2** An advantage. *Some c1900 student use.* See also **lead pipe cinch.**   *v.t.* **1** To make sure of anything. 1909: "Now slang use. Originally used of buckling a saddle to a horse's back. . . ." G. P. Krapp, *Mod. Eng.*, 205. **2** To bring someone else into difficulty; to spoil another's schemes.

cinchers   *n.pl.* The brakes on a truck or car. *c1935; garage and bus and truck driver use.*

Cincinnati cracklings   Cincinnati oysters   Cincinnati quail   Pork scraps; pork products. 1845: cracklings = pork scraps. M. M. Mathews, *Americanisms*, 1951, I, 329/1. 1877: oysters = pigs' feet. *DAE*. 1884: quail = fat pork. *Waiter use. Orig. from Cincinnati's location as a terminal on the Ohio river for livestock shipments and the production in its stockyards of large quantities of pork products.*

cinder — Of or pertaining to the railroad. Thus "cinder bo" = a hobo long experienced with hopping freight trains; "cinder-shark" = a cardshark or gambler who fleeces railroad travelers; and the like.

cinder bull A private policeman or detective employed by a railroad. 1926: "The cinder bull double-crossed me." Court testimony, quoted in *AS*, 1944. *Hobo use.*

cinder crusher A railroad switch tender. *Railroad use.*

cinder dick A railroad detective. See **dick.** Cf. **cinder bull.**

circuit blow (clout) (wallop) A home run in baseball.

circuit slugger A baseball player who hits frequent home runs. 1951: "Gil Hodges . . . became the greatest circuit slugger ever to wear Dodger flannels." Dick Young, N.Y. *Daily News*, Aug. 20, 20C.

circular file A waste basket. *Fairly common in business offices.*

circus *n.* **1** An obscene show; a naked dance or naked dancing. 1950: "Small-time houses where the price was from fifty cents to a dollar and they put on naked dances, circuses." "Those years [c1905] I worked for all the houses, even Emma Johnson's Circus House. They did a lot of uncultured things there that probably couldn't be mentioned, and the irony part of it, they always picked the youngest and most beautiful girls to do them . . . right before the eyes of everybody. People are cruel, aren't they?" A. Lomax, *Mr. Jelly Roll*, 47, 118. **2** Any large, colorful spectacle. **3** Excitement. **4** A feigned fainting spell. *Hobo use.*

circus — See Appendix, Prefixes and Prefix Words.

cit *n.* A citizen. 1901: "[Has] passed into the accepted vocabulary." Greenough & Kittredge, *Words & Their Ways*, 61. *Obs. adj.* Civilian clothes, as opposed to a uniform. 1915: West Point use. "When will he get used to these cit clothes?" *The Howitzer* (West Point senior annual). **—s** *n.pl.* Civilian

clothing. 1899: *DAE. Obs. Replaced by civvies.*

city cow Canned milk. *W.W.II. Serviceman use.* 1944: A. Ostrow, "Service Men's Sl.," *Amer. Mercury*, Nov. *Like much servicemen's sl. for food, such as battery acid, etc., this is synthetic, more picturesque than common.*

city slicker A city dweller, specif. a shrewd, worldly, stylishly dressed one, regarded by rural people as a swindler; almost always disparaging use by rural people. 1948: "The average 'city slicker' wouldn't use such a homespun term [as 'folks']." A. Hynd, *Pinkerton*, 137. 1949: ". . . Distinctions between hick and city slicker." D. L. Cohn in N.Y. *Times Bk. Rev.*, Nov. 6, 5/2. See **slicker.**

civvies *n.pl.* **1** Civilian clothes; mufti. 1943: "When a man changes from civvies to a uniform. . . ." A. Ostrow, "Service Men's Sl.," *Amer. Mercury*, Nov. 1951: "General MacArthur was fitted for 'Civvies' for the first time in 11 years." *Ithaca* (*N.Y.*) *Journal*, May 10, 1/3. *Used during W.W.I. but very common during and after W.W.II.* **2** Clothes other than work clothes; whatever one wears off the job. *Primarily referring to clothes other than Armed Forces uniforms but also used by any uniformed workers; used by convicts to mean clothes other than prison uniforms.* **3** Civilians. 1919: "A prewar [W.W.I] word in England." E. Verney, "Sl. in War-Time," *Athenaeum*, Aug. 1, 695/1. 1945: *USN use.* E. F. Stuckey, "How the Navy Talks," *Author & Journalist*, Oct. Cf. **cits.**

clacker *n.* A dollar. 1951: Movie, *My Favorite Spy*, used twice.

claim agent A bettor who "claims" to have placed a winning bet, though there is no proof of this, in hopes of collecting winnings. 1956: "CLAIM AGENTS— Bettors who claim that the bookmaker, or the clerk, made a mistake in recording a losing transaction, that the bet intended was on a winner." T. Betts, *Across the Board*, 313.

clam *n.* **1** The mouth. *c1825.* **2** A stupid or unknowing person; one who can be tricked. *c1890.* **3** An uncommunicative person; one who will not divulge desired information; one who can keep a secret. 1931: "I'm the original clam." E. Queen, *Dutch Shoe Mystery*, 106. 1949: "Stu is a clam." J. Evans, *Halo in Blood*, 100. **4** A dollar. 1939: "I hit a crap game for about 80 clams. . . ." J. O'Hara, *Pal Joey*, 20. 1953: "Schwartz is now pulling down 1,750 clams a week. . . ."

AP, Aug. 20. **5** A mistake; a boner. 1952: "Radio men speak no worse English than the general average of American professional men, and . . . on the average there are not really so horribly many out-and-out clams coming over the air." Letter in *N.Y. Her. Trib.*, Apr. 3, 24/5.   *v.i.* See **clam up.**

clambake   *n.* **1** A party or gathering, usu. for the purpose of entertainment; a loud or raucous party or gathering. **2** A session of swing music; a jam session. 1956: "A *clambake* is a jam session." S. Longstreet, *The Real Jazz Old and New,* 149. **3** Any discordant or lively gathering, such as a political convention, business meeting, or the like. 1951: "Nowhere can one have as stimulating an intellectual clambake, or gam, as this [Melville conference] promises to be." Form letter invitation from the Melville Society of America, Aug. **4** An insufficient radio rehearsal; hence an unsuccessful radio program. → **5** A showy failure. **6** A private gathering for official or business purposes, the public disclosure of which might harm the participants; a confused or fruitless official meeting. 1952: "A recent act to prevent the broadcast, televising, or filming of any clambake where the witnesses get hauled in under subpoena. . . ." R. Ruark, *synd. newsp. col.,* Apr. 18. See **kettle of fish.**

clamp down   **1** To become stricter, as in the enforcement of regulations; to strengthen authority; to increase supervision. 1957: "If you [employees] don't start coming in on time I'm going to clamp down. I can always get a time clock, you know." *Oral,* N.Y.C. office. **2** To clean up a room, house, office, ship, etc. *Orig. USN use.*

clamps on, put the   **1** To marry. 1910: "Sis is going to put the clamps on that." Johnson, *Varmint,* 391. *Not common.* **2** To steal.

clam shells   **1** The jaws. *c1835.* **2** The mouth. *c1880; obs.*

clam shovel   A shovel, esp. a short-handled shovel, used to dig trenches, truck gardens, etc.

clam trap   The mouth. *c1800.* Cf. **trap.**

clam up   To refrain from talking or to stop talking; to refuse to disclose information, esp. to the police or a judge. 1942: "Even if I had the legal right to stay clammed up. . . ." R. Chandler, *High Window,* 124. 1950: "Frank Erickson [accused racketeer before U.S. Senate crime investigating committee] clammed

up today and refused to answer Senators' questions. . . ." AP, Apr. 28.

clanker   *n.* A dollar. *Circus and hobo use. Obs.*

clanks, the   *n.* Delirium tremens; the shakes. 1947: "He told me he had the clanks from [drinking] Purple Passions." H. Boyle, *synd. newsp. col.,* May 19.

clap   **clapp** [taboo]   *n.* A case of venereal disease, esp. syphilis. 1951: "Very good girls, no loose tramps like you pick 'em up in the saloons and get a the clap." Stephen Longstreet, *The Pedlocks,* 241.

claptrap   *n.* Nonsense; lies; exaggerated talk; bull. See Appendix, Rhyming Slang.

claret   *n.* Blood. 1908: "He 'drew the claret' from his 'mug.' . . ." J. H. Morse, *Independent,* Oct. 1, 766/2. 1957: "Basilio [a prize fighter] is not known to give up his claret very easily." N.Y.C. radio broadcast. *Since c1860; prize fighter use.*

class   *n.* High quality; elan; tone; stylishness; savoir faire; dignity. 1947: "Besides, he had class." Billy Rose, *synd. newsp. col.,* Nov. 5. 1950: "A class mob. . . ." E. DeBaun, "The Heist," *Harper's,* 75. 1956: "Class, class, class. If I like a guy I say he has class. If I don't like a guy I say he's got no class. If I don't know about a guy I say I got no figure on his class." T. Betts, *Across the Board,* 295. *Since c1890; now colloq.* **—y**   *adj.* Highly fashionable; stylish. 1914: "I had a classy hangover. . . ." S. Lewis, *Our Mr. Wrenn,* 148. 1916: "'Classic' . . . is a Latin equivalent of the slang word, 'classy.'" M. Eastman, "Poetic Education & Sl.," *New Republic,* Dec. 16, 183/2. 1941: "[The British actor, Sir John] Gielgud, seen as a very classy Hamlet ten years ago. . . ." *Newsweek,* Mar. 17.

classis chassis   **classy chassis**   *n.* A sexually attractive or healthy-looking physique, specif. of a girl or young woman. *Assoc. with swing use.* See Appendix, Rhyming Slang.

claw   *n.* A policeman.   *v.t.* To arrest. See **put the claw on.**

clawhammer   *n.* A dress coat. *c1850; obs.*

claw on [someone], put the   **1** To arrest, detain, or esp. to identify another for arrest or detention. *Underworld use.* **2** To ask another for a loan of money. See **claw.** Cf. **put the bite on.**

clay eater   **1** A native of the South Carolina or Georgia low country. *Orig. from clay-eating habit common among*

Negroes and poor whites. → **2** Any Southern farmer or local rustic.

clay pigeon **1** A vulnerable person or thing; a person easy to victimize, cheat, or take advantage of; a job that is a cinch. *From the "clay pigeon" targets used in trapshooting.* See **sitting ducks.** **2** An airplane catapulted from a ship. **3** An easy task.

clean *adj.* **1** Innocent of carrying illegal goods, usu. arms, contraband, or narcotics; esp. used in ref. to those searched by police. *Underworld use.* 1934: "This one's clean [no gun]." R. Chandler, *Finger Man,* 94. 1950: "He's clean [no gun, after searching for one]." Movie, *Where the Sidewalk Ends.* 1952: "I'm clean." Comedian Ronnie Graham, pulling out a pack of standard brand cigarettes to convince police he is not carrying marijuana cigarettes, Broadway review, *New Faces of 1952,* Act I. → **2** Innocent in general; not guilty of a supposed crime. **3** Free of dangerous radioactive contamination. 1958: "The U.S. is testing a 'clean' bomb in its current series in the Pacific, according to Lewis L. Strauss, chairman of the Atomic Energy Commission. The AEC chairman said that scientists had been able to produce weapons 95 to 96 per cent clean of all radioactive by-products." N.Y. *Post,* May 26, 8. *Since c1955.* Cf. **dirty.** **4** Without money; broke. 1939: "He is cleaner than a jaybird." D. Runyon, *Take It Easy,* 6. **5** Inoffensive; not obscene or lewd; not dirty; free of sexual or sinful connotations. *Colloq.* 1956: "It was a very clean party; I even heard two funny clean jokes." *Oral,* N.Y.C. **6** Technically proficient, without mistakes; free of distracting or inharmonious elements, esp. as applied to art or design. 1957: "The clean lines of this year's Pontiac [automobile] make it the most desirable of...." Radio advt., Mar. 22. 1956: "I [Charlie Parker] was crazy about Lester [Young, the "Pres."]. He played so clean and beautiful." Charlie Parker, 1920–1955, *The Metronome Year Book,* 39 f. 1957: "Lester Young [a jazz musician] plays clean on this record." *Oral,* N.Y.C. **—er** **—ers** *n. & n.pl.* Used in phrase "taken to the cleaners" to signify having lost one's money or possessions through gambling, theft, natural disaster, etc. 1950: "They [dice players] took me to the cleaners. Six hundred bucks gone. I ain't been so broke since my ex-wife lit out and took the bank-

book." *Oral,* N.Y.C., after a crap game.

cleaners, go to the To have all one's money taken away through gambling or being robbed or cheated. *Fig. to have one's pockets "cleaned" of money.* 1934: "I'm in a jam. But I'm not going to the cleaners.... Half of this money is mine...." Chandler, *Finger Man,* 25.

clean out *v.t.* To win all someone's money. "I'm cleaned out, lost my wad on the 5th [race]." *Oral,* Jamaica race track, N.Y., May 12, 1957.

clean up To make a large profit quickly; to win a large bet. "That show must be cleaning up." Budd Schulberg, *What Makes Sammy Run?,* 110. **clean-up** **cleanup** *n.* **1** A big profit. *c1910.* **2** Police or vice squad activity to eradicate crime and immorality in a particular area.

clean up the kitchen *imp.* Order for a hamburger or a serving of hash, stew, etc. *c1935; lunch-counter use.*

clear *n.* A member of the I.W.W. (International Workers of the World). *Obs.*

clear sailing Easy to accomplish successfully; easy; without worry or strain; enjoyable.

cleek *n.* A sad or melancholy person. 1956: "A sad type is a *cleek.*" S. Longstreet, *The Real Jazz Old and New,* 150. *Not common.*

clef *v.t.* To compose a song. 1948: "Two new songs cleffed for the film ... are good...." *Variety,* Aug. 25, 8/2. **—fer** *n.* A songwriter. *Synthetic.*

Clem **clem** *n.* **1** A small-town resident; a rustic; one who can be hoaxed easily; esp., to circus people, the members of the local community in which the circus is playing temporarily. → **2** A fight between carnival or circus employees and local townspeople. 1948: "I wouldn't tangle in a crowd of rubes.... It'd start a clem, with me in the middle." F. Brown, *Dead Ringer,* 15. → **3** A rallying call for help from circus people when a fight with townspeople seems imminent. *1931: circus use.* *v.t.* To disperse rioting townspeople at a circus.

clemo *n.* **1** Executive clemency; a parole or commutation of a prison sentence. → **2** An escape from prison.

click *v.i.* **1** To be a success; to be received favorably by an audience. 1933: "It's going to click!" J. T. Farrell, *Short Stories,* 64. 1952: "Teen-age fashion shows have clicked for a number of stores around the country." AP. Aug.

29. 2 To fall into recognizable or apprehendable patterns of thought or feeling; to be classified or remembered; to fit together exactly, to match in color, size, shape, or value.   *n.* 1 A commercial success in the entertainment field. 2 A clique.

cliffdweller   *n.* A resident of a large apartment house.

cliffhanger   **cliff hanger**   *n.* A melodramatic story, play, book, or movie. *From early movie serials when each installment ended in suspense, as with the heroine hanging precariously over a cliff.* 1948: "Before Pearl White was making cliff hangers. . . ." J. Evans, *Halo for Satan*, 31.

climb   *v.t.*   To reprimand, scold, or criticize (someone) severely. *W.W.II Army use.*

clinch   *n.* An embrace. 1929: " 'Darling!' and they go into a clinch." W. Root, "Effect of Movies on Eng. Lang.," *Bookman*, Feb., 68.   *v.t., v.i.* 1 To embrace. 2 To determine conclusively; to complete.   **—er**   *n.* A deciding factor; the crux of an argument.   **—es** *n.pl.* Automobile brakes. *c1935, factory and garage use.*

clink   *n.* 1 A jail, prison, prison cell, or guardhouse. 16C: Eng. sl. E. Partridge, *Slang*, 363. 1949: "Joe Cool's in the clink." "To stay out of the clink." "Saved him from the clink." "A night in the clink." W. R. Burnett, *Asphalt Jungle*, 8, 13, 78, 149. 1950: "If I ain't in the clink and there's something to drink, you can tell 'em I'll be there." Pop. song, "In the Cool Cool Cool of the Evening." *Orig. the proper name of a famous prison in Southwark, London. Reinforced onomatopoetically from sound of jail door closing.* 2 A Negro. *Negro use.*   **—er** *n.* 1 A biscuit. *c1900.* 2 A jail. 1935: "In the clinker." J. Hargan, "Psy. of Prison Lingo," *Journal A. & S. Psychol.*, Oct., 362. See **clink.** 3 An unwanted noise heard on a long distance telephonic transmission line. 4 A squeak or unwanted reed sound produced by a clarinet or saxophone player. Hence, any mistake, error, or boner, esp. a sour note in music or an error in baseball. 1953: "If one of the singers hits a clinker. . . ." J. Crosby, N.Y. *Her. Trib.*, Mar. 11, 25. 1956: "A clinker is a bum note." S. Longstreet, *The Real Jazz Old and New*, 150. 5 Anything of inferior quality, esp. a movie, play, or other work of mass entertainment. 1950: "Almost all the 24 films . . . have been real clinkers. . . ." M. Zolotow, "The Great Schnozzola," *SEP*, July 15, 126/4. 1951: "Gee, that joke was a clinker." Comedian Robert Q. Lewis, radio, Aug. 8. *Orig. from the clinker, or unburnable cinder, in a coal fire.*

clinker boy   A railroad fireman. *Railroader use.*

clinks   *n.pl.* 1 Money. 2 Ice cubes; small pieces of ice. *Orig. onomatopoeic.*

clip   *n.* 1 A sharp blow. 1950: "You hit him a good clip. . . ." P. Starnes, *Another Mug for the Bier*, 54. Since *c1830.* 2 A thief or robber. *Underworld use.* 3 A Jew. *Orig. "clipped dick," i.e., one who has been circumcised.* 4 A clever person; a trickster.   *v.t.* 1 To hit a person sharply, usu. with the fist or a heavy object. *Colloq.* 1934: "She was to . . . clip him from behind with a blackjack. . . ." J. M. Cain, *Postman*, 15. 1943: "If he don't stop [whimpering] . . . I'll clip him." I. Wolfert, *Underworld*, 101. *Since c1860.* 2 To cheat, swindle, or rob someone. 1949: "He'd just been clipped for $1300." Burnett, *Jungle*, 34. 3 To kill, usu. by shooting. 4 To steal. 1951: "Dough that he was supposed to have clipped during a robbery. . . ." M. Spillane, *The Big Kill*, 25. See **put the clip on.** 5 To arrest.   **—per**   *n.* 1 An attractive girl. *c1835.* 2 A killer; a thug.   **—ping**   *n.* A sharp blow; esp. a foul blow, or an illegal block in football. 1956: "The Rams [Los Angeles football team] were penalized for clipping." *Radio*, Dec.

clip-artist   *n.* A professional swindler, cheater, or robber. 1956: "A gentle clip-artist, Abadaba robbed bookmakers as well as bettors." T. Betts, *Across the Board*, 268. See **clip.** See Appendix, Artist.

clip-joint   **clip joint**   *n.* A place of public entertainment where one is likely to be overcharged, swindled, cheated, or robbed. 1939: "They [taxidrivers] steer fares to clip joints for a standard 40% of the sucker's bill. . . ." *Fortune*, July, 160. 1949: "A lot of people think of Broadway as one big clip joint. . . ." Billy Rose, *synd. newsp. col.*, Dec. 28.

clip on [someone], put the   To overcharge; to clip. *Not common.*

clipped dick [taboo]   A Jew. *In ref. to circumcision.*

cloak-and-suiter [derog.]   *n.* A Jew. *From the concept that many Jews are tailors or are employed in the garment industry.*

clobber   *n.* Clothing. *Mainly British*

use. *v.t.* **1** To defeat decisively, thoroughly; to beat up; to attack aggressively and with concentrated power. *Colloq.* 1949: "In their first start of the year the Wolverines [football team] clobbered their opponents 42 to 3." *Radio.* 1950: "They [U.S. troops in W.W.II] clobbered 'em [the enemy troops] good." Movie, *Breakthrough.* 1951: " 'Poor loser!' They kept yelling as they clobbered me." M. Shulman, *Dobie Gillis,* 206. → **2** To berate; to criticize or reprimand severely. 1951: "In the Pentagon an individual can be clobbered by his superior." P. Hogan, "Pentagonese," *Collier's,* Nov. 24, 67/2. **—ed** *adj.* Drunk. 1951: "The game is also tough on . . . those who are, to use a word presently popular with the younger drinking set, clobbered." J. Thurber in *New Yorker,* Sept. 29, 27/2–3. See Appendix, Drunk.

clock   *n.* The face. *W.W.I.* *Not common.* *v.t.* **1** To hit. 1950: "[The one] who clocked me when I wasn't looking." R. Starnes, *Another Mug for the Bier,* 77. Cf. **cluck.** See **alarm clock, doubleclock. 2** To time, to keep time.   **—er** *n.* One who times the workouts of race horses in order to rate their performances.

clock watcher   **1** A person who takes little interest in his work; lit., one who watches the office or factory clock in expectation of quitting time. 1943: "A hard worker, no clock watcher." I. Wolfert, *Underworld,* 483. → **2** One who will not do a favor; an ungenerous person. 1956: "Sure he'd have to give me the car if I asked him; but do you think he'd offer it? That clock watcher!" *Oral,* Chicago.

clodhopper   *n.* **1** A sturdy or cumbersome shoe; esp. a man's work shoe. 1934: standard. *Web.* → **2** An awkward, unsophisticated person; esp. a farmer. 1934: standard. *Web.* **3** An old, dilapidated car, bus, train, or plane that is only useful for short trips; transportation used in local areas.

clog dancer   The clog orig. a cross between a soft-shoe dance and an Irish jig; therefore one who performed such a dance. Later, a soft-shoe dancer. *Obs. since c1930.*

clonk   *v.t.* To hit or strike. See **clunk.**

close   *adj.* **1** Warm and humid; said of the weather. *Colloq.* **2** Stingy. *Colloq.* **3** In complete control, in complete mastery, as of one's life, creativity, musical instrument, or the like. 1957:

"He's close, man!—The musician has done just about everything attainable." E. Horne, *For Cool Cats and Far-Out Chicks. Far-out use since c1955. Prob. from the gambling phrase "to play close to one's vest"* = *to keep one's cards out of the sight of others and thus to play skillfully or to take no unnecessary risks.*

closed   closed down   closed up *adj.* Out of business, usu. owing to official prohibition; said esp. of a town or region in which gambling houses, brothels, etc., have been closed by police action. 1955: "Since the election we're closed down tight; I take a few bets from friends, but the wire service [communication system for receiving information from race tracks] isn't so good—if you want to make a big bet you got to go out in the county. We're closed up in town, but the county's wide open." *Oral,* Louisville, Ky., bookie.

close shave   Lit. and fig., avoidance of or rescue from imminent danger, destruction, or failure; a narrow escape.

close up   To stop talking. See **closed.**

close-up   *n.* **1** A near view. *Orig. the picture made by a camera set close to the object; popularized by pioneer movie producer D. W. Griffith, c1920.* → **2** A close scrutiny. → **3** A biography. 1932: "It is becoming a commonplace for the literary critic to describe a biography as a 'close-up.' " E. Weekley, "Eng. As She Will Be Spoke," *Atlantic Mon.,* May, 559.

clothes   *n.pl.* See **monkey clothes.**

clotheshorse   clothes horse   *n.* An extremely well-dressed or fashionable person; usu. implies that sartorial elegance is the subject's only merit. 1930: "Along Broadway O. O. McIntyre and Mayor Jimmy Walker are the most striking clothes horses." H. Salpeter, "O! O! McIntyre," *Outlook,* Sept. 3, 6/3.

clothesline   *n.* **1** Personal problems; family disagreements. 1951: "Do you have to let everybody in the neighborhood see our clothesline?" *Oral,* N.Y.C. See **dirty wash. 2** In baseball, a line drive, i.e., a ball hit so sharply that its flight appears virtually level.

cloud, on a   **1** Extremely happy; fig., so elated as to be unaware of mundane obligations or occurrences. **2** Under the influence of narcotics; in a dream state induced by drugs. *Some narcotic addict use.*

cloud buster   **1** In baseball, a high fly ball. **2** A skyscraper. **3** A fast, new airplane.

cloud seven, on   **1** Completely happy,

perfectly satisfied; in a euphoric state. **2** = **on a cloud.**

clout   *v.t.* **1** To hit or strike a person or object with force. *Colloq.* 1955: "If I'd acted that way when I was his age, my old man would have clouted the hell out of me." C. Willingham, *To Eat a Peach*, 201. **2** To steal; esp. to shoplift or to steal an automobile or from an automobile. **3** In baseball, to hit a pitched ball with great force. 1952: "Steve Bilko clouted a homer in the eighth." AP, Sept. 26.   *n.* **1** A hit or blow. **2** In baseball, a hit.   **—er**   *n.* **1** An automobile-stealing gang, esp. the member who actually does the stealing. **2** One who looks over an establishment to see how it may best be robbed. **3** In baseball, a heavy hitter.

clover, in   clover, in the   Wealthy; successful; in a position in which one can enjoy wealth or the results of success. 1919: "The firm was on 'easy street' again, as the expression went, 'in clover.'" T. Dreiser, reprinted in *The American Twenties*, 432.

clover-kicker   *n.* A farmer; a country boy. Cf. **Clem, Rube.**

clown   *n.* **1** An ebullient, ineffectual, boastful, or purposeless person whose words or actions cannot be taken seriously; hence an incompetent or unreliable person. 1924: "What do you know about this other clown?" "Can you imagine that clown . . . takin' up that man's time talking about a fifty-thousand-dollar policy; and him in debt to his eyes. . . ." "I don't want Frank Hyland goin' around payin' out thousand-dollar bills on account of this clown." G. Kelly, *The Show Off*, Acts I, II, III. 1957: "Cut out the clowning." *Oral; common.* **2** Any rustic. **3** A rural police officer, esp. a sheriff, constable, or deputy. **4** = **square.** *Cool and far-out use since c1955.*   *v.i.* **1** To tease; to scuffle; to refuse to act or talk seriously. **2** To fake a prize fight; to take a dive. *c1920.*

Clown Alley   Lit., the aisle of tents or wagons where circus clowns live and prepare for their performances; fig., circus life in general. 1956: "Tears Flow in Clown Alley [headline:] . . . 'The tented circus is a thing of the past,' [said] John Ringling North." N.Y. *Post*, July 17, 3.

clown around = **clown**, *v.i.* **1.**

clown-wagon   *n.* A freight train's caboose.

club   *n.* See **deuce of clubs, war club.**

clubhouse lawyer   A member of a sports team, social group, etc., who freely offers his personal opinions to fellow members. *Baseball use.*

club-winder   *n.* A railroad brakeman.

cluck   kluck   *n.* **1** A stupid, dull, or incompetent person; a dunce; a dope. 1930: "The champion cluck of all time." J. Sayre, "Bong Soir," *Amer. Mercury*, Dec., 415/1. 1931: "I must be the world's prize cluck." Queen, *Dutch Shoe*, 199. 1949: "No booster I of books by clucks." F. P. Adams in N.Y. *Times Bk. Rev.*, Dec. 18, 7/4. 1951: "It's his cluck of a wife that really gets me down." S. Lewis, *World So Wide*, 3. 1951: "It's obscure clucks like you who've nourished our banking system." S. J. Perelman in *New Yorker*, Jan. 27, 30/2. **2** [derog.] A very dark Negro. *Negro use.* **3** An egg. *Western use; not common.*   *v.t.* To do well; esp. to make a high grade in an examination.   *adj.* Stupid.

cluck and grunt   Eggs and ham.

cluckhead   *n.* See **cluck.**

clue   *v.t.* To inform someone of a fact or opinion; to reveal a fact or opinion; to reveal a confidence or a secret. *Pop. c1945–c1955.*   *n.* A piece of news; a pertinent fact; a personal opinion.

clunk   *v.t.* **1** To hit or strike, esp. on the head. 1934: "Barnaby clunked you." Movie, *Babes in Toyland.* 1943: "Sit down or I'll clunk your other ear." I. Wolfert, *Underworld*, 265. **2** To throw down; to plunk down, esp. money; to pay cash. 1957: "Before I ask the listeners to clunk down their hard-earned dollar or two dollars or even more. . . ." Radio program, *Big Joe's Happiness Exchange*, N.Y.C. station WMGM, Apr. 17.   *n.* **1** A stupid person, a cluck. 1934: "Because you'll be listed among the clunks." W. Winchell, foreword to D. Runyon's *Blue Plate Special.* 1952: "Love-addled youths allow themselves to be coaxed down the aisle by scheming maids who have been working on the poor clunks all spring." Robert Ruark, *synd. newsp. col.*, Sept. 19. **2** An old or worn-out piece of machinery; an old bus or car. *c1935.* **3** A hit; a blow. 1943: "One clunk on the knuckle." R. Stinson, "Said the Marine to the Jap," *SEP*, Mar. 20. **4** Any cumbersome object; esp. a heavy shoe. **5** A person's foot.   **—er**   *n.* **1** Something that is inferior or worthless. 1948: "You might be buying a clunker." F. W. Brown, *Dead Ringer*, 190. **2** A dilapidated, worn out car, bus, or other machine. 1950: "Before you sell a clunker [an old car] to the junkman . . . smash the transmission. . . ." AP, Feb.

18. 1951: "Teague [a racing car driver] plans to meet two touring clunkers, a 1911 Stoddard-Dayton and a 1913 Stanley Steamer, at the Geneva [N.Y.] city line and race them. . . ." AP, Sept. 13. **3** An awkward person; esp. an inferior golfer, tennis player, etc.; a duffer. 1951: "Tell one of those clunkers [golfers] what a great stroke he has, and he'd vote for you." G. Edson, "The Gumps," *comic strip*, Aug. 13.

clunkhead *n.* A stupid person. 1952: "Some clunkhead sent me three live quail!" Arthur Godfrey, radio, Jan. 1. *Increased in pop. after frequent use by Arthur Godfrey on radio and television.*

clutch *n.* **1** An embrace. See **clinch. 2** An emergency, predicament, or exigency; in sports, a decisive or critical play in a close contest; the decisive moment in any sequence of events or operations. 1951: "We need 3 or 4 men who could step in and hit for us in the clutch." Al Lopez, baseball team manager, quoted by AP, Oct. 12. 1951: "Groza and . . . Graham [pro football players] . . . came through in the clutch again today." AP, Nov. 12. *adj.* Dependable in a crisis, said esp. of athletes. 1951: "Jackie Robinson, Brooklyn's great clutch player. . . ." AP, Oct. 3. 1951: "The Boston Celtics are proving to be the 'clutch' team of the National Basketball Association. Their ability to win the close ones is making them the surprise of the professional circuit." AP, Dec. 17. *Very common sportswriter use.* *v.t.* To smoke a cigarette. *c1925.* See **slip the clutch.** **—ed** *adj.* Angry. 1956: "Be careful, the boss is clutched today." *Oral,* N.Y.C. office.

clutch the gummy To fail; to be left to take the blame; to be cheated. *Orig. on model of "hold the bag" = to clutch the gunny bag or sack; reinforced by "gummy" = sticky.*

C-note *n.* = **C,** specif. a $100 bill. 1939: "A couple of C notes." Chandler, *Big Sleep,* 151. *More recent than C-speck.*

coach See **slow coach.**

coal *v.t., v.i.* See **deal in coal, pour on the coal.**

coal box A type of artillery shell which emitted dense black smoke upon exploding; hence any heavy, low-velocity shell. *W.W.I only.*

coalhole *n.* A prison, prison cell, or guardhouse. *c1850; obs.*

coal-pot *n.* A stove; a tobacco pipe. 1942: "Wait till I get my coal-pot." Z.

Hurston, "Story in Harlem Sl.," *Amer. Mercury,* July, 84.

coast *n.* **1** To inhabitants of the Atlantic seaboard, the Pacific coast; to inhabitants of the Pacific seaboard, the Atlantic coast. **2** A sensation of utter relaxation, buoyancy, or satisfaction, esp. as the result of drugs or listening to jazz. *v.i.* **1** To do or obtain something without great effort; to rely on one's reputation or past achievements in order to succeed or gain fame without making further effort. *Colloq.* **2** To pass a school examination or course easily. *Student use.* **3** To experience a sensation of utter relaxation, buoyancy, or satisfaction, esp. as the result of drugs or listening to jazz music. *Drug addict and jazz musician use.* 1949: "That first fix had only cost him a dollar, and sent him coasting one whole week end." N. Algren, *Man with the Golden Arm,* 77.

coattail, on [someone's] **1** Dependent upon someone for success, usu. said of an unknown or unpopular candidate in a political election who wins on the strength of the popularity of another candidate on the same ticket. → **2** Dependent upon someone, usu. a friend or relative, for success in business, sports, or any enterprise.

cob *n.* A farmer or small-town local. See **off the cob, on the cob.**

cob, off the = **corn, corny.** 1943: "Your vocabulary . . . is off the cob." *Time,* July, 26, 56. 1948: "The music was strictly off the cob. . . ." F. Brown, *Dead Ringer,* 38. *Orig. teenage use, c1940.*

cob, on the See **corny.** Cf. **off the cob.**

cobber *n.* A good friend or comrade. *Much more common in Australia than in U.S. Orig. probably in Australia, but perhaps from Hebrew "chaver" = "pal," common among Jews in the U.S.*

cob-roller *n.* Any small or very young farm animal, esp. a small pig. *Implies that the animal is too small to eat properly and merely pushes the corn cobs with its nose when trying to take a normal bite.*

cock *n.* **1** [taboo] The penis, esp. considered only as a sexual organ; specif., the erect penis. 1599: "And Pistol's cock is up. . . ." Shakespeare, *Henry V,* II, 1. *One of the most common sl. words = penis.* → **2** A swaggering boastful male. → **3** The leader of a group or organization. **—ed** *adj.* Drunk. 1737: *Pa. Gazette.* 1865: *DAE.* Archaic. See Appendix, Drunk.

cock-and-bull　**cock-and-bull story**

An exaggerated account; a story re-counted with embellishment or lies. *Colloq.*

cock-eye   cockeye   *n.* In baseball, a left-handed pitcher. *Not common.* **—d**   *adj.* **1** Cross-eyed, wall-eyed. *Archaic.* **2** Eccentric; confused or chaotic; crazy, screwball. 1929: "Who in this cockeyed world. . . ." *Nation*, Sept. 4, 240. 1934: "I'll say stuff that's cock-eyed." J. M. Cain, *Postman*, 46. 1938: "Anybody who thinks I'm kidding is cock-eyed." H. Broun, "Shoot the Works," *New Republic*, Aug. 17, 45/2. 1948: "This plan appears to be com-pletely 'cockeyed.' " A. H. Marckwardt & F. G. Cassidy, *Scribner Hndbk. of Eng.*, 310. 1950: "As cockeyed as the recent dispatch from Moscow. . . ." Billy Rose, *synd. newsp. col.*, Jan. 18. **3** Drunk. 1737: "He's Cock Ey'd." *Pa. Gazette.* 1934: slightly inebriated, sl., *Web.* 1934: "Getting cockeyed under the stars. . . ." J. DeJournette & L. V. Berrey, "Popping the Corks," *Esquire*, Apr., 36. 1938: "A more advanced stage [of drunkenness] is denoted by *cock-eyed* which means that you see [double]." R. Connell in *Parade*, quoted in *Better Eng.*, July–Aug., 17/2. 1941: "We were absolutely cockeyed." B. Schulberg, *What Makes Sammy Run?*, 160. 1952: "When you get cockeyed. . . ." T. Robinson, "How to Disappear," *Harper's*, Mar., 91/1. See Appendix, Drunk. → **4** Unconscious. 1932: "Izzy knocks him cock-eyed." Runyon, 12. *Colloq.* → **5** Crazy; insane. *Colloq.* → **6** Wrong; mistaken; misstated. 1950: "It's all cockeyed that a man who makes his living with a pen would rather wallow in a greasy boat bilge." F. Tripp, AP, July 31. *Colloq.* **7** Askew; crooked. 1936: "Her hat was on cock-eyed." J. Weidman in *Amer. Mercury*, May, 90/1. *Colloq.* **8** Mean; contemptible. *Never common.*   *adv.* Very.

cockroach   *n.* **1** A person interested in small schemes, esp. a small businessman. 1931: "I.W.W. use." C. Ashleigh in *Everyman*, May 21, 520/3. **2** A person who is exceptionally busy, esp. with many small projects.

cock sucker [taboo and derog.]   **1** A fellatrice; the one who plays the female role in a male homosexual relationship. **2** One who attempts to curry favor with a superior; a sycophant. Cf. **ass kisser**. **3** A degrading name applied to any male who is disliked, esp. a sneak.

cock teaser [taboo] A girl or young woman who displays affection and sexual interest in a male, assumes sexually inviting postures, speaks inti-mately, allows petting or necking, and perhaps indulges in sexual foreplay, but does not allow coitus or satisfy the male. *Universally known by male students.*

coco   *n.* The head. 1909: "Wear pads in your derby . . . the hammer's going to drop on your coco." G. Chester, *Bobby Burnit*, 170. *From coconut.* See Appendix, Shortened Words.   **—nut** *n.* **1** The head. 1834: *DAE. Still in use.* **2** A dollar. 1930: "The whole hundred thousand coconuts." J. Sayre, *Amer. Mercury*, Dec., 420.

codd   *v.t.* To fool or bluff a person. *Some c1909 N. Eng. dial. use. Obs.*

coddler   *n.* A louse. *Some W.W.I Army use.*

co-ed   coed   *n.* A girl or woman student at a coeducational college or university. 1893: *DAE. A prime example of a word once sl. and now universally accepted as stand.; since c1900.*   *adj.* **1** Coeducational; appropriate to both sexes. *Colloq. since c1900.* **2** Dove-tailed; fitting together perfectly, as a joint.

coffee and   **1** Coffee and cake; coffee served with doughnuts, rolls, or the like. *Lunch-counter use in relaying an order.* → **2** The cheapest meal obtainable. 1949: "A saloon on Stanton Street hands out 'coffee and' each morning." W. J. Slocum, *Collier's*, Aug. 27, 27. → **3** The necessities of life. 1958: "If I'm lucky I make my week's 'coffee and' by Tuesday, and don't work the rest of the week." *Oral*, N.Y.C. street vendor, June 24. *Used by gamblers, small-time con men, vagabonds, etc.* **4** Coffee with cream and sugar. *Since c1935; lunch-counter use in relaying an order.*

coffee and cake(s)   A small salary, a small amount of money; lit., just enough money for the necessities of life; chicken-feed. 1950: "1938 found him playing for coffee and cakes in an obscure Washington nightspot." A. Lo-max, *Mr. Jelly Roll*, x.

coffee-and-cake-job   (—joint   —lay-out   —place   —spot, etc.)   A job or place of business that is very limited in scope and financial remunera-tion.

coffee-and-cake-time   **1** The point at which one's funds are exhausted and it is necessary to earn more money. → **2** A time or place that seems well suited to the obtaining of money; esp. by a robber, con man, etc.

coffee bag   Any pocket. *Never common.*

coffee break   See **break.**

coffee cooler   One who seeks easy work; a shirker.

coffee grinder   **1** A strip teaser or other female performer who makes suggestive grinding motions with her hips and abdomen. Cf. **cement mixer.** **2** A prostitute. **3** A professional movie-studio cameraman. **4** An aircraft engine. *Air Force use since c1940. All four meanings allude to the grinding movement of a coffee grinder; the first two meanings also imply that one needs to perform such movements to earn one's coffee and.*

coffee-pot   coffee pot   *n.* **1** A lunch counter or small restaurant. 1951: "The Marx brothers ate in coffee pots and greasy spoons." J. Sayre in *Time*, Dec. 31, 29/2. **2** A small railroad steam locomotive. *Railroad use.*

coffin   *n.* **1** A large shoe. 1851: *DAE. Still in some use. From the size and shape of a coffin, and from the shoe width "C."* **2** A safe for valuables. **3** Any car, bus, plane, etc., considered to be unsafe. **4** An armored car or tank. *Some W.W.II use.* See **flying coffin.**

coffin corner   **1** In football, any of the four corners of the playing field. *So called because a ball-carrier trapped in these corners may be easily tackled.* **2** In baseball, third base. *Not common.*

coffin nail   **1** A cigarette. 1951: "Dutch took the cigarette from between his thick lips and extended it toward me. 'Have a coffin nail,' he chuckled." R. S. Prather, *Bodies in Bedlam*, 118. *Since c1890. From the saying that each cigarette one smokes drives one more nail into one's coffin.* → **2** One who smokes a lot. → **3** Anything regarded as likely to shorten one's life.

coffin tack = **coffin nail.**

coffin varnish   Inferior whisky; esp. bootleg or home-made whisky. *c1920.*

coil   *n.* **1** Life. *Some jocular use, from the literary "mortal coil."* **2** Any electrical device or gadget, esp. a condenser or generator.

coin   *n.* Money. *Extremely pop. c1900–c1935. Later use usu. restricted to small amounts of money.* See **loot.** *v.t.* To earn something, as money or praise.

coke   *n.* **1** Cocaine. 1913: "A coke user." *SEP*, Feb. 15, 6. 1942: "Out of the apartment houses came cookies and coke peddlers." R. Chandler, *High Window*, 54. 1956: "This Sherlock Holmes.... People get put in jail by a coke fiend. How could you trust this bum?" J. Cannon, *Who Struck John?*, 202.

Orig. addict use. **2** Coke, a popular shortened form of Coca-Cola, a carbonated beverage. *The makers of Coca-Cola have registered as trademarks both the full and shortened name and insist that they be printed with initial capitals.* **3** Cement. *Shipyard use.* **—d**   *adj.* Under the influence of a narcotic, orig. of cocaine. 1930: "Many of the newer generation of 'coked' or 'hopped up' gunmen will kill a merchant." Lavine, *Third Degree*, 227.

coked up = **coked.**

coke frame   A shapely girl or young woman, lit., one whose figure resembles the shape of a Coca-Cola bottle. *Some c1935 jive use.*

coke head   **1** A cocaine addict. **2** Any stupid, dull, slow-reacting person.

cokie   cokey   *n.* **1** A narcotic addict; esp. a cocaine addict. 1949: "Some cokie client." W. Burnett, *Jungle*, 131. **2** A boy; anyone who lacks experience. *adj.* Sleepy-looking; relaxed; inattentive. *c1930; Negro use.*

cold   *adj.* **1** Basic; ungarnished; without frills. **2** Disinterested; lacking in ambition, skill, energy, or luck. 1941: "He was certainly in the money. He'd made it gambling. 'Playing ... cold horses when they were hot.'" J. Lilienthal, *Horse Crazy*, 11. **3** Dead. → **4** Unconscious; completely unconscious. 1924: "A man 'passed out cold.'" Marks, *Plastic Age*, 254. **5** Sexually frigid. **6** Without, or without showing, emotion or interest, esp. love or sexual passion. *The above meanings ref. to a lack of motion or life, as if one were actually frozen. The following meanings ref. to something frozen while at the peak of perfection.* **7** Without error; excellent. 1942: "He was cold on that trumpet." Z. Hurston. Cf. **cool.** 1953: "I passed the final [examination] easily; I knew it cold." *Oral*, Ohio State Univ. **8** Well performed, esp. without practice or forewarning. *adv.* Certainly, really.

cold biscuit   **1** An unattractive or dull girl. 1933: "He couldn't rate a blind date with a cold biscuit." H. T. Webster. → **2** A person of either sex who lacks sex appeal.

coldcock   cold-cock   *v.t.* **1** To knock someone unconscious, with the fist, a club, etc. **2** A specif. way of hitting someone over the head with a blackjack or strangling someone with a piece of wire, always without warning, in order to render the person completely incapable of action.

cold deck   cold-deck   *n.* A stacked or marked deck of playing cards. *adj.* Unfair; with planned or prearranged results in another's favor. *v.t.* To take advantage of; to make unable to succeed owing to some previous and unalterable condition; to plan or prejudice against some result or person.

cold feet, to have   To lose courage; to be afraid.

cold fish   A person of reserved temperament; one who is unfriendly, reserved, withdrawn, dull, unemotional, or lacking in vivacity or sex appeal; dispassionate, one who displays no love, passion, or affection.

cold haul   *v.t.* **1** To take advantage of; to victimize. **2** To accomplish a task or obtain a goal easily and without effort. → **3** To accomplish a task or attain a goal in a slipshod manner, without enthusiasm or the necessary effort that would have made the accomplishing or attaining worthwhile; to fail to take full advantage of an opportunity. *v.i.* **1** To expend no more effort than necessary. **2** To depart rapidly; to flee.

cold in hand   Without money; broke. *Negro use.*

cold meat   A dead person; a cadaver. 1819: *OED Sup. Still in use. May have orig. meant a person killed or knocked unconscious in the boxing ring.*

cold-meat box   A coffin. *Some use since c1890.*

cold-meat cart   A hearse. *Since c1820.*

cold-meat party   A wake; a funeral. 1946: "You were at that cold-meat party, I spotted you coming out of the cemetery." Evans, *Halo in Blood,* 9.

cold pack   **1** A knockout or knockout blow. *Prize fight use.* **2** A certainty or sure thing; a cinch. *Some c1925 use.*

cold shoulder   A coldness of manner; the obvious and conscious ignoring of a person or plan. *v.t.* To obviously and consciously ignore (someone). 1949: "Some admirals have tried to cold-shoulder Denfield." D. Pearson, *synd. newsp. col.,* Oct.

cold storage   **1** A grave; a cemetery. **2** The imaginary place where an idea or project is stored until one is ready to act upon it. 1954: "It's a good idea; put it in cold storage until we're ready to use it." *Oral,* N.Y.C. publisher's office.

cold turkey   cold-turkey   1 The act of being suddenly and completely deprived of the use of narcotics, usually during a medical cure of narcotics addiction. *Addict use.* **2** At an auction, to stop the bidding and sell an item at a previously set price. **3** On the spur of the moment; without preparation or forewarning. 1950: "Anyone . . . can simply walk in cold turkey and talk things over. . . ." D. H. Beetle, *GNS,* Aug. 29. **4** To know a subject or to be able to perform so well that no practice or research is necessary. **5** Objective; frank; blunt; unemotional. 1952: "Stalin didn't like certain cold-turkey facts Kennan reported about Russia. . . ." N.Y. *Daily News,* Oct. 4, 9C/1.

coll   *n.* A stew or hash made from any available items; esp. a very tasty or very welcome stew, to one who is very hungry. *c1920; hobo use.*

collar   *n.* **1** A policeman. → **2** An arrest. 1930: "The bull makes a collar on me." *Amer. Mercury,* Dec., 455. 1952: "'The best collar in recent years,' said the [police] commissioner." *Time,* Mar. 3, 22/1. *v.t.* **1** To arrest. → **2** To comprehend; to understand thoroughly. Cf. **latch on.**

collar a nod   To sleep. 1942: "You can't collar nods all day." Z. Hurston.

collar the jive   To understand and feel rapport with what is being said; to be in the know; to be hip. *c1935 jive term.*

collateral   *n.* Money.

college   *n.* A jail; a reform school; any penal institution. *Some archaic underworld use.*

collision mat   **1** A waffle. *Some USN use since c1920.* → **2** A pancake; a hotcake. *Some W.W.II USN use. Although used occasionally in the Marine Corps and Army, this is mainly USN use.*

colly   *v.t.* To understand, to comprehend. *Primarily Negro use, used in the rural areas of the South as much as in Harlem and in jive circles; it seems to predate "collar."*

color blind   Unable to tell the difference between one's own money and someone else's; in other words, not averse to stealing or cheating. *Jocular use.*

combo   *n.* **1** A combination of things; esp. of foods in a sandwich or salad or of beverages in a mixed drink. 1934: "Orange juice and gin combo." DeJournette in *Esquire,* Apr., 86. **2** A combination of people; esp. a professional dancing team, a dance orchestra, and, since c1940, specif. a small jazz band, usu. of three or four members. 1946: "Guitar or

Bass man needed for small combo."
Advt. in *TV News*, Dec. 9, 3/1. 1948:
". . . He had formed a bop combo—a
small band. . . ." Harry Henderson and
Sam Shaw, "And Now We Go Bebop!"
Collier's, 88, March 20. *Pop. by bop and
cool use. Progressive music is usu. played
by such small bands, as opposed to large
swing bands.* 3 The combination of a
lock on a safe or vault. 1948: "My
fingers kept working the combo." J. M.
Cain, *Moth*, 95. *All meanings from
"combination."* See Appendix, Shortened
Words.

come   cum   *n.* [taboo] 1 Semen;
the viscid whitish fluid sometimes produced in the female reproductive tract
at sexual climax. 2 Any viscous liquid
resembling semen, esp. cream gravy,
mayonnaise, or the like. *Derisive use.*
v.i. 1 [taboo] To ejaculate; to reach a
sexual climax; to experience an orgasm.
→ 2 To feel extreme excitement; to reach
a high peak of enthusiasm; to experience
a thrill or kick, as while watching a
sports contest or listening to music, etc.
1956: "When Dizzy [Gillespie, jazz
musician] plays 'Night in Tunisia,' man,
I come." *Oral*, bop music fan at "Birdland," N.Y.C. nightclub. → 3 To display
a sudden surge of power, as by an
athlete, entertainer, or the like. 1956:
"I thought my [race] horse could run real
fast/ but now I know he'll finish last./
I'm standing by the [race-track] rail,/
waiting for my horse to come. . . ."
Parody song by comedian Joe E. Lewis
at N.Y.C. nightclub "Copacabana,"
Oct. 6. 4 To start; esp. a race or series
of gambling plays. 5 To show promise of
being successful.   —r   *n.* One who
or that which shows great promise of
being a success; one who is making a
rapid advance in a specif. field of
endeavor. 1879: *DAE.* 1949: "He said
the club [the New York Yankees] is a
comer." D. Cresap in Phila. *Eve.
Bulletin*, Sept. 9, 41/2.

come a cropper   1 To fall, esp. on
one's posterior. 2 Fig., to fall; to fail; to
make a mistake. *More common in Eng.
than in U.S.*

come across   1 To pay money owed;
to produce what is expected of one.
1917: "If you can't go across with guns,
'come across' with funds!" *Pop. W.W.I
slogan for War Bonds.* 2 To pay a bribe;
to bribe. 1938: "You could get almost
anything if you stood in with 'the
boys' and were willing to come across."
Atlan. Mon., Aug., 219. 3 To surrender

information or allegiance to another.
4 [taboo] To surrender sexually; to
grant sexual favors when expected or
asked to; said only of the female.

come again   To repeat what one has
just said, because the listener has not
heard or because the matter in question
needs further clarification. 1952: "Would
you come again, please?" Radio, *Town
Meeting of the Air*, Apr. 15.

come-along   *n.* An inexperienced or
a temporary member of a work crew.
*c1900; Railroad, telephone lineman, and
construction crew use.*

come apart at the seams   To lose
one's composure; to lose one's confidence.
1957: "It was rather a long kiss. Silas
felt himself coming apart at the seams."
S. McNeil, *High-Pressure Girl.*

come around   1 To agree or acquiesce,
after initially disagreeing or refusing;
to be persuaded or convinced. *Common
use.* 2 [taboo] To menstruate later than
expected, relieving one of the fear of an
unwanted pregnancy.

comeback   *n.* 1 A recovery of health,
prosperity, success, public acceptance,
or the like. 1908: *DAE.* 1920: "You
could still stage a comeback." F. S.
Fitzgerald, *This Side of Paradise*, 108.
Colloq. 2 A retort; a riposte. *Colloq.* 3 A
complaint or exposure of one's previous
actions; imposed retribution for an act
committed in one's past. 1930: "The
detective became nervous about a
comeback." Lavine, *Third Degree*, 63.
4 A customer who returns unsatisfactory
merchandise to a retail store; the act of
returning such merchandise; the returned
merchandise itself. *Retail salesman use.*

come clean   To tell the complete
truth; to confess, as to the police. 1930:
"We want you to come clean." Weeks,
Racket, 59.

comedown   *n.* 1 A drop in one's
social or business status. *Since c1840.
Colloq.* 2 A project giving less satisfaction,
esteem, monetary gain, etc., than expected; a disappointment. *Colloq.* 3 An
intended victim who grabs a pickpocket's hand in the act of stealing.
Underworld use.

come-in   *n.* 1 Spectators waiting in
line to buy tickets or waiting for a
performance to begin. *c1920.* 1956: "I
was clowning the come-in, you know,
entertaining the come-in until the stars
could get ready." *Oral*, circus clown,
Ringling Brothers, Barnum & Bailey
Circus, N.Y.C. → 2 The time between
the opening of the main tent and the

beginning of the grand entry at a circus. *Circus use.*

come off = **come,** *v.* **1.**

come off it To stop doing or saying what one is doing or saying; esp. because one's actions or words are meaningless or offensive; usu. a command. 1947: "Come off that crap. Keep your jaw shut." C. Willingham, *End as a Man,* 36.

come off [one's] perch To stop acting in a superior or snobbish manner.

come-on   come on   *n.* 1 Lit. and fig., an invitation. **2** That which is appealing, attractive, or enticing about any thing or person; that which attracts. **3** Specif., sex appeal. **4** Act of enticing someone to spend money, do a favor, or esp. to enter into a situation in which he will be victimized. **5** A dupe; the person who succumbs to a confidence game. 1913: "In American films the innocent dupe is spoken of as a 'sucker,' a 'come-on.' . . ." W. Faulkner in *London Daily Mail.* **6** An employee who buys the first ticket to a circus or a carnival side-show, who buys the first item a huckster offers, or who gambles, pretending to be a customer, in order to entice real customers to buy or gamble; a shill.   *adj.* Enticing; made desirable for the purpose of gaining money, esteem, etc. 1951: "Football bowls, baited with $100,000 or so of come-on money. . . ." A. Daley in N.Y. *Times,* Jan. 1, 28. *v.i.* To arrive; to enter or present oneself; to begin, as to begin talking or playing music; to participate; to perform; to do these things with a purpose or specif. attitude or skill, as if one were on a stage; always followed by an adj. telling the purpose, attitude, or skill of the one who has come on, or esp. of the initial impression made by that person on those present. 1958: "The phrase 'come on' means, roughly, present oneself. But it is not cool to come on too strong because this is aggressiveness, the very antithesis of cooldom." S. Boal, *Cool Swinging in N.Y.,* 26. *Orig. cool use, c1950. From theater and radio use; reinforced by the older "come on like gangbusters."*

come on like gangbusters To enter, arrive, begin, participate, or perform in a sensational, loud, active, or striking manner. *From the radio program "Gangbusters" which always began or came on (the airwaves) with sound effects of police sirens and machine-gun fire. Since before c1945.*

come through   1 See **come. 2** To confess; to admit one's guilt. 1930: "He won't come through." Lavine, *Third Degree,* 81. **3** To pay or give money, encouragement, or other support as expected. 1950: "I hope the folks come through with $25 for Christmas." *Oral,* Univ. of Illinois. **4** To be as successful as expected; to deliver the desired results; to excel; to please. 1957: "Jim Thorpe always came through to win and give you that good feeling." Bill Stern, WINS, June 3.

come to school To give up one's vices, unruliness, or eccentricities; to conform; to compromise.

comeuppance *n.* A deserved rebuke or punishment; esp. a rebuke that deflates the sufferer's ego or allows him to see an idea or plan in a realistic perspective. 1859: *DAE.* 1920: " 'Got his comeuppance' is a familiar phrase." *Scribner's,* Aug., 248/1. *Colloq.*

come-uppings *n.sing. & pl.* = **comeuppance.** 1896: *DAE. Replaced by comeuppance. Now only dial.*

comfortable *adj.* Drunk. *Some use since c1950.* See Appendix, Drunk.

comma-counter *n.* One who overemphasizes the importance of minor details; one who demands perfection in small things, but who lacks imagination or a comprehensive understanding of his subject or job; a pedant.

commando *n.* One who does things in a rough or obvious manner; one who is overly eager or rough, specif. in romantic or sexual matters. Cf. **bedpan commando.** *Some W.W.II Army and student use.*

commercial *n.* **1** Any laudatory statement; praise; a good reference. **2** A musical piece played by an orchestra or band at a spectator's or dancer's request. 1957: "Commercials—Request numbers. Usually played by dance bands. Some hot bands pointedly ignore requests and will play a blues, for example, if asked for 'Rosetta.' " E. Horne, *For Cool Cats and Far-Out Chicks.*

commie   Commie   Commy *n.* **1** Any plain, cheap, glass marble used in the game of marbles; esp. a cream-colored or opaque glass marble. *c1920 and c1930.* 1935: " 'The commy . . . is used to shoot marbles with.' (Commies was our word for those cheap ten-for-a-cent marbles . . .). . . ." James Thurber, *The Middle Aged Man on the Flying Trapeze,* 519. *From "common."* See

Appendix, Shortened Words. **2** A member of the Communist party or the international Communist movement; a Communist; a Communist sympathizer. *Colloq.*   *adj.* Communist; Communistic. 1945: "Chinese Commy leaders." W. Winchell, radio, Dec. 13. 1950: "The Commie problem." Speech by Francis Biddle, former Attorney General, at AAUP meeting, Mar.

commo   *n.* **1** Candy, tobacco, cigarettes, etc., obtained by a prisoner through a penal institution's inmates' commissary. *From "commissary."* **2** Commotion. 1958: "What's the commo?" *Oral*, Chicago policeman. *More common in Brit. sl. than in U.S.* See Appendix, Shortened Words.

comp   *n.* **1** A nonpaying guest or spectator, as at a hotel, restaurant, or place of entertainment. **2** A complimentary or free ticket. *The above two meanings from "complimentary."* **3** An abbr. for "composition." **4** An abbr. for "compositor."   *v.t.* An abbr. for "compose." See Appendix, Shortened Words.   **—o** *n.* **1** A cheap dress shoe that is pasted or nailed together instead of being sewn. *From "composition."* See Appendix, Shortened Words. **2** A "comprehensive examination." *Student use.* See Appendix, Shortened Words.

company man   An employee, usu. a white-collar worker, whose loyalty to his employer is greater than his loyalty to his fellow employees. 1957: "Oh, the company man, the company man,/ Look at he,/ Earning sixteen-three [\$16,300 per annum],/ What wouldn't he do,/ For seventeen-two?" From unpublished song, "The Company Man," by Irving Panken, folk song authority.

company monkey   In the Army, a company clerk. See Appendix, — monkey.

con   *n.* **1** A blow or tap on the head with the knuckles, as a teacher might give to reprimand a child. *Some c1850 student use. Obs. From Eng. schoolboy sl.; orig. from the Greek "kondylos" = a knuckle.* **2** A railroad conductor. 1893: "But soon the 'Con' appeared, and the chase began." J. Flynt. *Some c1880–c1900 hobo use. Obs. in U.S.* See Appendix, Shortened Words. **3** A convict; an ex-convict; one who is serving or has served a prison term. 1917: "You're a 'con'; you've no rights." P. L. Quinlan in *New Repub.*, Jan. 13, 294/1. *Colloq.* See Appendix, Shortened Words. → **4** A criminal; a hoodlum. **5** A confidence

game, a swindle; the world of the confidence game. 1940: *The Big Con*, a book by D. W. Maurer. See **con game.** **6** Tuberculosis. 1918: "When the con gets one of these hill billies he goes mighty fast." Irvin S. Cobb, *Escape of Mr. Trimm*, 187. *Mainly dial. From "consumption."* See Appendix, Shortened Words. → **7** A consumptive person. *Mainly prison use.* **8** A conservation officer. *Some c1910 use.* **9** The act of being, or one who is, confined to his dormitory or quarters. *Some c1930 student and Army use.*   *v.t.* **1** To swindle; to persuade, convince, or victimize another to accept or believe a deception by or as by a confidence game; to cheat. → **2** To trick; to fool; to persuade another to do something not in his best interests; to persuade. 1902: "Mansfield conned the Critics." G. Ade, *Fables in Slang*, 90. 1939: "I got delivery on this tailcoat and had to con the tailor into letting me have it for only the down payment." O'Hara, *Pal Joey*, 34. 1951: "[Prize fighter] Bucceroni revealed he injured the middle knuckle of his right hand. 'That was when I began to con [La Starza]. I yelled, "Come on, let's go." I stood up in my corner waiting for the bell, trying to con him that I felt great.'" J. Hand, AP, Dec. 22.

conchie   **conchy**   *n.* A conscientious objector to military service. 1945: "Denies That His Son Was A 'Conchie.'" Headline in Syracuse (N.Y.) *Post-Standard*, Sept. 23, 3. *W.W.I use in Eng.; W.W.II use in both Eng. and U.S. From "conscientious" with common sl. suffix of "—ie" or "—y."*

Coney Island   **1** A room in which police give the third degree. *Archaic underworld use.* **2** A lunch wagon; a quick lunch, esp. one consisting of a hot dog with lots of condiments. **3** A large hot dog, served on a roll and covered with relish, sauerkraut, etc. **4** Any large sandwich filled with hot or cold meat, vegetables, relishes, etc. 1957: "Coney Islands—your choice of two meats, two cheese, tomato; topped with sauerkraut, mustard, relish and onions." Sign in front of drive-in restaurant, Wheeling, W. Va. *The above three meanings are from the assoc. of such sandwiches with the food concessions at Coney Island amusement park in N.Y.C., esp. with "Nathan's" lunch-counter and restaurant, known for its large hot dogs, served with sauerkraut.* **5** A glass of beer that contains much foam and little beer.

Orig. "*Coney Island head.*" See **head.**
adj. Gaudy; showy; loud.
Coney Island head = **Coney Island.**
confab   *n.* A talk, conversation, or conference. 1901: Greenough & Kittredge, 62. 1945: "The infamous Munich confab." W. Winchell, *synd. newsp. col.,* Nov. 13.   *v.i.* To talk or confer. 1948: "He will confab with them again." *Variety,* Aug. 25, 5/3. *Before c1925 used as carnival sl.; now general; abbr. from "confer" and the artificial jocular word "confabulation.*" See Appendix, Shortened Words.
confetti   *n.* Bricks. 1950: "Saskatchewan Confetti [headline:] The Saskatchewan Government is building a new brick plant." N.Y. *Times,* Sept. 3, 30/5. *An example of sl. exaggeration.* See **Irish confetti.**
confisticate   *v.t.* To confiscate. 1781: *DAE. W.W.II maritime use. Maritime sl.; a prime example of group sl., known to outsiders, but after almost 200 years still used almost exclusively by the orig. group. A synthetic, humorous word formed by infixing a hard consonant to a stand. word.*
con game   1 A confidence game; a swindle. 2 Any enticement. 1902: "De girl a feller sets his heart upon/ Jes' keeps him comin wid a game of con." Coley, *Rubaiyat of the East Side,* 11. 3 Anything against the law; anything unethical. 4 Any way of earning money easily; an easy life.
Congaroo   Congeroo   Congoroo
n. A conga song, dance, dancer, or singer. 1942: "Jive-mad congaroos." Movie, *Hellzapoppin',* which also contained a song titled "Congaroo," and advertised a cast including "30 Congaroos [dancers]." *Variant spellings due to confusion of conga dance, Congo moods, and tendency to add usual —eroo sl. suffix. Never common.*
con job   = **con game.** 1955: "He was being taken in by a sharp con job." Trujillo, *I Love You, I Hate You,* 139.
conk   *n.* 1 The head. 1931: "Persistent idea has been buzzing around in my conk." E. Queen, *Dutch Shoe,* 48. → 2 The face. → 3 The nose. *From "conch."   v.t.* 1 To hit a person on the head. 1951: "He knocked over a lamp, got conked on the head, and wound up in the hospital." NEA, Dec. 13. → 2 To defeat thoroughly, esp. in sports.
conk-buster   *n.* 1 Cheap liquor. *Negro use.* See **busthead.** 2 Any difficult problem, task, or the like; fig., anything so complex that one breaks one's head

in thinking about it. *Primarily Negro use.* → 3 An intellectual Negro.
conk off   1 To stop work; to rest when one should be working. 2 To go to sleep; to sleep. 1951: "You been conking off for eight hours." M. Spillane, *I, Mobster,* 123.
conk out   1 To break down and stop running; said of an engine or machine, esp. an airplane engine. 1946: "A super[-fortress airplane] conked out. . . ." Riordan in *Calif. Folk Quart.,* Oct. 2 To tire suddenly; to stop work and rest or sleep; to become exhausted; said of a person. → 3 To die. 1939: "So she's conked out—eh?" A. Christie, *Sad Cypress,* 54.
con man   1 A confidence man; a swindler. *Colloq.* 2 Anyone who earns money easily; a person who has an easy life. 3 Any handsome, charming male; one with a beguiling smile and a persuasive way of talking.
conn   *n.* The command of a naval vessel. 1952: "The Captain thereby assumed the 'conn.'" P. Kihss in N.Y. *Times,* May 15, 23/5.
connection   *n.* A dope peddler or seller; one who can obtain narcotics. *Addict use.*
constructed   *adj.* = **stacked,** a more emphatic form; e.g. "She ain't stacked; man, she's constructed." *A very new use.*
contact   *v.t.* To call, phone, or write a person for a business or social reason; to communicate with. *Colloq.   n.* A person who can provide one with an introduction to a group or with whom one can conduct negotiations. *Colloq.*
Continental   *n.* A type of men's haircut. See **English.**
contract   *n.* A political or business favor; a bribe; the fix. 1958: "Contract— Any favor one policeman says he'll do for another." G. Y. Wells, *Station House Slang.*
convertible   *n.* A corporate security that can be converted to a security of another corporation. 1957: "A 'convertible' in Wall Street isn't an auto . . . it's a bond, debenture, or preferred stock which may be exchanged by the owner for common stock or another security. . . ." Sam Dawson, "On the Business Side," N.Y. *Post,* March 26, 18. *Common stock-market use.*
convict   *n.* 1 A zebra. *Circus use.* 2 A schemer; one who is unethical or untrustworthy.
cooch   *n.* 1 Any lascivious dance; the hootchy-kootchy. *Orig. carnival and*

circus use. **2** [taboo] The female crotch. *Not common.* **3** An unethical scheme; an unfair enticement; an obvious deceit. 1948: "Your cooch shows." F. Brown, *Dead Ringer,* 19. *One of many words relating sex and deceit.* See Appendix, Sex and Deceit.

coo-coo *adj.* **1** Unconscious. *c1915. Archaic.* **2** Insane, crazy; extremely unconventional. 1928: "I'm going nuts— bugs—coo-coo." P. Gould in *New Yorker,* Dec. 22, 53. *Colloq.* **3** Stupid; unrealistic in one's views. *n.* An insane person; one who is crazy, stupid, or unconventional. *From "cuckoo," a bird whose cry sounds somewhat demoniac to some ears.*

cook *v.t.* **1** To die by electrocution, as in the electric chair. *Fairly well known.* **2** To question or interrogate a person thoroughly; to beat up, torture, or intimidate someone, as if to extort information; to sweat information out of someone. *Underworld use; archaic.* **3** To arouse someone sexually; to tease someone sexually. *Not common.* **4** To die; fig., to die and go to hell. *Archaic.* **5** To ruin, to make a failure of. *v.i.* **1** To fail; to suffer the consequences of failure, stupidity, audacity, or the like. *Colloq.* **2** To happen, develop, evolve, take place, transpire, etc. *Used chiefly in phrases "what's cooking?" "what cooks?" Orig. from "what's cooking on the front burner?" = what's the main item of news or interest? c1940. Heavy W.W.II use, student use. Orig. jive use.* Cf. **cook up.** **3** To do or think the right or desired thing; to enter into the spirit or mood of jive, swing, or of a group of people; to agree; to be in the know, to be hep. Usu. in "Now you're cooking," said approvingly. *Orig. jive and swing use. Pop. c1940 and still some use.* **4** To be excited, stimulated, or filled with enthusiasm. *n.* **1** One who plans a course of action; a leader. See **cook up.** **2** See **bull cook.** —**book** *n.* A chemistry laboratory manual. *Student use.* —**ed** *adj.* **1** Knocked out; unconscious. → **2** Exhausted; finished without having attained one's goal. → **3** Inadequate; defeated. **4** Drunk. See Appendix, Drunk. —**er** *n.* A sexually attractive girl. *Some c1940 student use. From "cook," reinforced by "looker."* —**ie** —**ey** —**ee** *n.* **1** A cook's helper. *Maritime, logger, and ranch use. Since c1840,* See Appendix, —ie, —ey, —ee endings. → **2** A cook. *Some general but mainly maritime, logger, and ranch use.* **3** One

who cooks or prepares opium for smoking; an opium addict. *Addict use.* **4** A girl or young woman, esp. an attractive, vivacious one. 1950: "She is just the cookie." E. DeBaun, 75. **5** A man; usually a man who is self-confident, clever, or brusque; usu. in "tough cookie" or "smart cookie." 1942: "Just about the toughest cookie ever born." *Amer. Mercury,* Oct., 436/1. 1949: "You're a pretty shrewd cookie, Doctor." *Radio,* Groucho Marx, Oct. 5. **6** Any person, esp. a clever, brash, or energetic one. **7** [taboo] The female genitalia. *Negro use.* **8** A bomb. 1943: ". . . Will drop 4,000-pound cookies." INS, Dec. 3. *Not common, but a good example of sl. exaggeration.*

cookie-cutter **cooky-cutter** *n.* **1** A policeman's badge. *Circus use.* → **2** A policeman. **3** Anyone who is supposed to be tough but isn't; a weakling. *Most common use.* See **cookie-pusher.** **4** An inadequate weapon, esp. a knife.

cookie pusher **cooky pusher** **1** A man, usu. a young man, who prefers group feminine society, as tea parties, easy tasks, and nonmasculine sports; an effeminate, weak, or cowardly man; a man deeply concerned with the social graces. → **2** A man who does little hard work and tries to obtain promotion by courting his superiors; an apple polisher. **3** A government career man, esp. a State Department official. 1946: "State Department officials have long been called 'cookie pushers.'" *Word Study,* May, 2/1. *Orig. ref. to the many teas that State Department workers need to attend. During the 1952 presidential campaign, Republican politicians and editorialists used the term with double-entendre to imply that members of the Democratic administration were effeminate and that homosexuals were employed by the State Department.*

cook on the front burner = **cook with gas** **(on the front burner).**

cook-out **cookout** *n.* **1** A meal cooked out of doors, as over a back yard home grill, by camping groups, etc. → **2** A gathering, hiking trip, camping trip, or the like, during which an outdoor meal is cooked. 1950: "A cookout at the Campfire Girls' cabin. . . ." Lincoln (Nebr.) *Eve. Journal,* Sept. 9. *Used freq. by Boy and Girl Scout groups, suburbanites, etc.*

Cook's tour **Cook's Tour** A trip, a sightseeing excursion; any tour; traveling; a ride. 1958: "At the end of his 'Cook's Tour' [jockey] Ismael Valenzuela had him [the racehorse, Tim Tam] a neck in front of Ebony Pearl." *The Morning Telegraph*, Apr. 30, 1. *From Thomas Cook and Son, a prominent firm of travel agents, known for organizing European tours, esp. in the 19C.*

cook up   **1** To fabricate, as a story, alibi, or the like. 1939: "On a rap I'd cooked up myself...." E. S. Gardner, *D. A. Draws*, 204. **2** To plan or scheme; to concoct an idea or plan of action; to invent. *Colloq. May be the base for the jive and swing use of "cook."*

cook with gas (on the front burner) To do, think, or feel the right or desired action, thought, or emotion; to enter into or appreciate the spirit, modes, fashions, and fads of swing; to be in the know, to be hep. An emphatic variation of "cook" = to do the right thing. *Orig. swing use. Fairly well known c1940, still some use.*

cooky   *n.* See **cookie.**

cool   *v.t.* **1** To postpone; to wait for. *Associated with and most common as cool, far out, and beat use, but in use much earlier, as in the expression "to cool one's heels" = to wait.* **2** To kill someone. *Some use since c1920.* **3** To fail, esp. to fail an examination; to ruin a chance for success; to fail to take advantage of an opportunity. *Some student use since c1935.*   *n.* A form and style of jazz characterized by soft tones, improvisations based on advanced chord extensions, the use of harmonic and rhythmic devices adapted from "classical" music, etc. *Cool or progressive jazz was first developed by West Coast musicians and by the early 1950's had supplanted bop as the major jazz movement. The originators of cool jazz were chiefly white musicians with university training and a highly sophisticated knowledge of musical techniques, both jazz and classical. As a result the cool movement has been characterized as an "intellectual" approach to music and life in general; cool enthusiasts have looked with disdain on the eccentricities associated with former jazz movements and have fostered a conservative manner in speech, dress, etc.*   *adj.* **1** In complete control of one's emotions; hip but having a quiet, objective, aloof attitude; indifferent to those things considered nonessential to one's individual beliefs, likes, and desires; pertaining to cool or progressive jazz; similar to or sharing the taste, dress, and attitudes of cool musicians. 1957: "Willis Conover of the Voice of America explains. Cool jazz doesn't permit undue display of emotions. The cool player doesn't jump up and down, full of fire, nor does his understanding listener." N. Randolph, N.Y. *Post*, July 5, 6. *Orig. used by those who played and appreciated cool or progressive jazz; since c1948, common since c1955.* → **2** Aloof; unconcerned; disdainful; emotionless and amoral. 1958: "To express a desire or a need for anything is not cool. Coolness is relaxation, aloofness, indifference, languor. This is the governing atmosphere of the cool party ... as one chick said in describing admiringly a cat she had just met: 'Man, he's so cool he doesn't even move.' If a girl is plain she can never be cool because who really wants her, man? ... Since she isn't desirable, not desiring her would be natural and being natural is not being cool. Active lesbianism is simply not cool, just because it is active." S. Boal, *Cool Swinging in N.Y.*, 26, 50. 1958: "I stay cool, far out, alone." E. Burdick, "The Innocent Nihilists Adrift in Squaresville," *The Reporter*, Apr. 3, 31. *Beat use since c1950.* **3** Thrilling; played in an exciting, satisfying, expert way; said of any jazz music; stimulating; hot, jivy, groovy. 1951: "Bellson has been described here and there as the coolest drummer alive ('cool' being, of course, the current word for 'hot' in musical terminology)." *New Yorker*, Aug. 4, 15/2. *Some use since c1950, a logical mistake by devotees of earlier, more emotional forms of jazz and by nonlisteners.* **4** Satisfying; pleasant; in good taste; attractive. 1953: "You enjoying it? Is everything cool?" D. Wallop, *Night Light*, 205. 1956: "... Cool: tasty, pretty." S. Longstreet, *The Real Jazz Old and New*, 151. **5** Played in the style of cool music. 1958: "You feel this. You feel it in a beat, in jazz, real cool jazz...." John Clellon Holmes, "The Philosophy of the Beat Generation," *Esquire*, Feb., 35. **6** Eliciting an intellectual, psychological, and/or spiritual response; intellectually, psychologically, and/or spiritually exciting and satisfying; on a higher intellectual level than, and removed from, mere physical, sensual excitement or satisfaction; unemotional, without obvious excitement, disaffiliated. 1956: "... No blues, no swing, nothing but the cool relaxed music...." "Charlie Parker, 1920–1955," *The Metronome Year Book*, 41. 1958: "... The cats play everything cool and sex is no exception." Edward Klein, "The Beat

Generation," N.Y. *Daily News*, Feb. 19, 28. [Woman shaking hands with minister in front of church], 1956: "That was the *coolest* sermon!" Barney Tobey cartoon caption, *Look*, May 15, 115. *Orig. bop use, c1946. Now the most common bop word, with frequent far out, and beat use. Fairly well known, and fairly common student and teenage use. Some older adult use. All uses and meanings of "cool" have the basic connotation of intellectual, psychological, and/or spiritual excitement and satisfaction, negation of mere obvious, physical, sensual excitement. In this basic meaning "cool" is, of course, the direct antithesis of "hot"* (see **hot**, adj.). *Associated with this basic connotation of "cool" are various synonyms, more specialized words, and words orig. after "cool" by cool, far out, and beat groups. These words are:* **crazy** = *specif., eliciting a unique mental response;* **gone** = *specif., eliciting a pseudo-religious cultural response;* **mad** = *specif., eliciting a unique and exciting intellectual response* ("mad" *was an earlier bop and cool word than* "crazy," *and is now somewhat archaic in this sense);* **nervous** = *cool or, specif.,* **wild;** *more often used by those who write about far out and beat groups than by members of these groups, and is thus somewhat synthetic;* **wicked** = *intellectually or psychologically so satisfying that one becomes exhausted;* **weird** = *specif., eliciting a unique emotional response (early use),* **crazy; wild** = *specif., eliciting a strong psychological response. All these words are used as synonyms for "cool," but their unique and orig. bop, cool, far out, and/or beat uses are given. Note that none of these words implies a physical, sensuous excitement or response. Cf.* **far out, out.**

—er *n.* 1 Any of various cooling drinks made with liquor. 1840: *DAE. Colloq.* 2 A prison. 1884: *DAE.* 1939: "In the cooler." Chandler, *Big Sleep*, 45. *Colloq. since c1900.* → 3 A solitary confinement cell or block of cells. 1917: "One of the cells in the 'cooler' was empty." *New Repub.*, Jan. 27, 353/2. *Prison use.* 4 An attractive girl. *Common student use c1900; archaic.* 5 A sharp retort. *Some c1900 use.* 6 A certainty; a cinch.

cool cat See cat, cool. 1957: "For Cool Cats and Far-Out Chicks," title of an article by E. Horne, N.Y. *Times Mag.*, Aug. 18, 26.

cool it To relax, calm down; to work less strenuously, slow down; to stop

annoying, insulting, threatening, or being angry; to take a vacation. *Cool and far out use since c1955.* See **cool.**

cool off 1 To become calmer; to lose one's enthusiasm or anger. 2 To kill. 1934: "Somebody cools off Mr. Justin Veezee." D. Runyon.

cool out 1 To calm someone; to appease. 2 To beat up someone so that his anger or enthusiasm will be stopped. 3 To kill. 4 To investigate another's intentions; to find out if someone is angry. *Above four meanings primarily underworld and sports use.* 5 To reduce exercise slowly so that one does not become suddenly chilly; esp., to walk a horse after a race so that he will calm down slowly.

cool [something] over To think about something; to consider all the aspects of a plan, idea, or the like; to view from all angles objectively and carefully. See **cool.**

coolville Coolville *adj.* The best; wonderful; satisfying. *Associated with cool use. Not common.* See Appendix, —ville ending.

coon *n.* 1 [derog.] A Negro. 1887: *DAE.* 1944: ". . . Now one of the most familiar designations . . . originally from the name of the animal [raccoon] which Southern Negroes were supposed to enjoy hunting and eating." H. L. Mencken. 2 A stupid person; one who can be swayed easily; a strong or brutal man with little brains. *From mispronunciation of "goon."* *v.t.* To steal. 1901: *DAE. Obs. adj.* [derog.] Negro; orig. from or appealing to Negroes. 1956: ". . . The white coon songs, 'Jump Jim Crow,' 'Ole Zip Coon,' and 'Hamfoot.'" S. Longstreet, *The Real Jazz Old and New*, 7.

coop co-op *n.* 1 A co-operative store, enterprise, or society; a building in which each resident owns his own apartment; such an individually owned apartment. *From stand. abbr. for "co-operative," "co-op"; now often pronounced as one syllable and sp. without hyphen.* 2 Any small dilapidated shelter, residence, room, store, etc.; lit., a place resembling a chicken coop. 1958: "Coop—Any shelter used by a policeman to avoid the elements." G. Y. Wells, *Station House Slang.* 3 A jail. 4 A coupe. 1939: "It's a Plymouth convertible coop." J. O'Hara, *Pal Joey*, IV. *Orig. humorous; now common.*

coop-happy *adj.* Insane from confinement. See **stir crazy.**

coosie *n.* 1 A cook. *Some ranch use.*

2 [derog.] A Chinese. *Some W.W.II Armed Forces use.*

coot *n.* A fellow; esp., an old or stupid fellow. 1843: *DAE.* 1942: "She was the widow of an old coot with whiskers." R. Chandler, *High Window. Colloq.* One of many *sl. words derog. when applied to strangers or acquaintances, but a term of intimacy among friends.* —**ie** **cutie** *n.* A body louse. *From the Brit. Army sl.; W.W.I and hobo use. Some W.W.II use, but infreq., owing to improved sanitation.*

cootie garage One of a pair of hair puffs worn over a woman's ears. 1953: ". . . Unlovely puffs we used to call 'cootie garages.'" S. J. Perelman in *New Yorker*, Jan. 3, 15/1. *c1920 use.*

cop *n.* A policeman. 1859: *DAE.* 1902: "De Cops cast o'er de edifice/ Protectin' care (if you puts up de price)." Coley, *Rubaiyat of the East Side,* 49ff. 1930: "The Cop"; "It's Bad Judgment to Shoot a Cop"—chapter titles in Lavine, *Third Degree;* "cop" appears at least 114 times in the book. 1939: *Cop Killer,* title of a movie. *From the copper buttons once used on police uniforms, reinforced by the Italo-Amer. "coppo." Orig. derog., implying the speaker's superiority to law and order; now by far the most common word for "policeman." Colloq.* See **copper, fly ball, harness bull, on the cops, sparrow cop.** *v.t.* **1** To steal; to obtain; to deprive. 1949: "Don't buy it; I'll cop it for you." *Oral. From the Yiddish "chop" = to grab.* → **2** To win; to carry off a prize. 1941: "[In a race] pace in the pinches is what cops or kills." J. Lilienthal, *Horse Crazy,* 19. 1950: "'Green Pastures' copped the Pulitzer Prize. . . ." T. M. Pryar in N.Y. *Times*, Sept. 3, X3/8. **3** To understand, perceive, comprehend; to consider. **4** To give forth with or present something, as an appeal. *adj.* Very good; valuable; lit., that which is worth stealing or copping. *Not common in U.S.* —**per** *n.* **1** A policeman; esp., a tough policeman or one who is intent on enforcing the law to its fullest. 1848: Sl. *DAE.* 1900: "Look at the copper watchin'." Dreiser, *Carrie,* 431. 1925: "A 'copper' is a hard-boiled officer." McLellan in *Collier's.* 1947: "The district coppers acted immediately." D. Fairbairn in Phila. *Bulletin,* May 9, 4B/1. *From the copper buttons worn by Eng. policemen. More of an underworld term than cop, the abbr. being less derog.* **2** An informer; a stool pigeon. **3** Time subtracted from a prison sentence

because of good behavior; time off a prison sentence because the prisoner has informed on his co-criminals after the sentence was imposed. **4** A U.S. penny; one cent. *Colloq.* *v.i.* To work as a policeman. *v.t.* To bet against a person, card, roll of the dice, etc. 1864: *DAE.* 1950: "In this game you can't copper no bets." Movie, *Sugarfoot.*

copacetic **copesetic** **kopasetic** **kopesetic** **kopasetee** **kopesetee** *adj.* Fine, excellent, all right, o.k. 1926: "Kopasetee." C. Van Vechten, *Nigger Heaven,* 1934: "Copacetic." *Web.* Sl. 1948: "Kopasetic." Lait-Mortimer, *N.Y. Confidential,* 235. *From the Yiddish.*

cop a cherry **cop [her] cherry** [taboo] To deprive a female of her virginity. See **cherry, cop.**

cop a feel [taboo] To touch or manipulate a woman's sexual parts manually, specif. surreptitiously and without attempting further intimacy. 1943: "Sure you don't want to cop a feel?" M. Shulman, *Barefoot Boy with Cheek,* 77. See **cop, feel.**

cop a heel To escape from prison or a policeman; to make a getaway. *Underworld use.*

cop a mope To escape. *Underworld use.* See **cop a plea.**

cop and heel **1** An escape from prison or a policeman; a getaway. **2** A narrow escape; a close call. 1952: "Somebody saw us and everybody started running; it was cop and heel to cop a mope." *Oral,* car thief. *Underworld use.*

cop a plea To plead guilty to a criminal charge, thus saving the court time and money; esp. to plead guilty in order to receive a lighter sentence than if one pleads innocent, is tried, and found guilty. 1946: "All five men cop (make) a plea of guilty." Wyer in N.Y. *Sun.* 1957: "Most defendants 'copped a plea.' Confronted by testimony . . . nearly all . . . pleaded guilty." Ashley Halsey, Jr., "The Lady Cops of the Dope Squad," *SEP,* March 30, 101.

copeck *n.* A silver dollar. *Some c1900 use; still some jocular use.*

cop out **1** To be arrested; to be caught in the act of committing a crime. **2** To plead guilty. 1951: "I copped out." J. Lardner in *New Yorker,* Dec. 1. See **cop a plea.**

copper a tip To do just the opposite of what one is advised to do; to bet against a hunch or tip.

copper-hearted *adj.* Tending to be an informer; untrustworthy. See **copper**.

copper-on copper-off A method of gambling whereby one alternately bets for and against the dice, a card, a number, etc.; also a method of betting whereby one bets several times, then does not bet, then bets again, in a definite predetermined order. See **copper**, *v.t.*

cops, go on the See **on the cops**.

cops, on the On the police force. 1930: "Most of the men 'went on the cops' because they were square pegs who weren't succeeding. . . ." Lavine, *Third Degree*, 10. 1940: "I was on the cops once . . . being on the cops is a . . . way to make a living." Chandler, *Farewell*, 207.

copy-cat *n.* An imitator. *1896.*

cork *n.* A complete failure in reciting. *c1850.* *v.i.* To fail. *Both forms now obs.* See **pop [one's] cork.** **—ed** *adj.* Drunk. *Most common in 1920's.* See Appendix, Drunk. **—er** *n.* **1** Any thing or person that is exciting, colorful, excellent, remarkable, noteworthy, or the like. *c1835.* 1910: "Dennis is a corker!" Johnson, *Varmint*, 150f. 1952: "Honestly—you're a corker." E. Bushmiller, "Nancy," *comic strip*, Aug. 27. **2** An incredible story; a very funny joke or prank. **—ing** *adj. & adv.* Exceedingly. 1900: ". . . A corking good actress." Dreiser, *Carrie*, 118. Excellent. 1908: "'Bally,' and 'snide,' . . . and 'corking' will very naturally have but a brief day." Morse in *Independent*, Oct. 766/1.

corking mat *n.* A sleeping pad. *W.W.II USN use.*

cork off To fall asleep. 1929: "They come in tablets . . . give grains, and you cork off pretty." D. Parker, "Big Blonde," reprinted in *The American Twenties*, 155. *W.W.I Army use. Not common; now obs.*

cork opera A minstrel show, from the burnt-cork make-up used. *c1860's.*

corkscrew *n.* An auger.

corn *n.* **1** Liquor, esp. corn whisky, home-made or illegally sold. 1929: ". . . A pint of corn on their hip." J. M. Cain in *Amer. Mercury.* **2** A state of drunkenness from too much corn whisky. **3** Money. **4** Anything overly sentimental, old-fashioned, or banal; sentimentality; banality; melodrama. 1958: "Corn . . . too banal to be exciting." S. Boal, *Cool Swinging in N.Y.*, 26. **5** A corn muffin. *Lunch-counter use in relaying an order.* **—ed** *adj.* Drunk. 1823: *DAE.* 1932: "One and all are somewhat corned." Runyon, 72. *Common c1930.* Cf. **pickled.** See Appendix, Drunk. **—fed** *adj.* **1** Stout, plump; said of a girl or woman. **2** Given to or characterized by a rustic style, tastes, or ideas; unsophisticated. **3** Trained to play or appreciate classical music. *Derisive jive use, c1935.* **—y** *adj.* Sentimental; banal; obvious; old-fashioned or out of date; unsophisticated. 1935: "Corny—Derived from cornfed, meaning [music] played in country style, out of date, hill-billy, or in a style of pre-1925." *Peabody Bulletin*, Dec., 42/2. 1950: "As corny as a chorus of 'Hearts and Flowers.'" Billy Rose, *synd. newsp. col.*, Jan. 4. 1957: " . . . Gang killings are corny or old-fashioned these days." George Raft, as told to Dean Jennings, "Out of My Past," *SEP*, Sept. 21, 94. *Orig. pejorative use by musicians and theatrical folk; wide teenage use after c1940; now general use, though beginning to become archaic.*

cornball corn-ball *n.* One who likes or perpetrates sentimentality, banality, or outdated styles; a musician or other artist whose work is vapid, sentimental, or corny. 1952: "Eisenhower on no account can be called a cornball." R. C. Ruark, *synd. newsp. col.*, Mar. 17. *Based on "screwball." Mainly teenage use c1943–c1953.*

corn bill = **corn willie.**

corn cracker A good thing. *c1900; Dial. and archaic.*

corner = **hot corner.**

corner (bend), go around the To die. *Archaic and dial.*

cornfield meet *n.* A head-on collision of two trains. *c1935. Railroad use.*

corn juice Corn whisky; (inferior) whisky. *Before 1845.* 1928 [1788]: "[Corn juice has been] a nickname for 150 years." M. Meredith.

corn mule Corn whisky; specif., home-made or bootleg or inferior corn whisky.

corn-on-the-cob *n.* A harmonica. *In allusion to the manner of playing the instrument and the corny music often produced thereby. Not common.*

corn punk = **punk.**

corn shucks Tobacco. *c1940; rural and dial. use.*

corn-stealer *n.* A human hand. *c1825.*

corn willie corned willie *n.* Corned beef; also, hash made with it. *c1918; AEF use.* Corn willie also called "corn bill." *Army use; common in W.W.II.*

corpse *v.t.* To embarrass (another actor) during a stage show by forgetting one's lines, thus depriving him of his cue. *Theater use c1925.*

corral *v.t.* **1** To find; to look for. *Colloq.* **2** To catch a baseball. *c1925; baseball sl.*

cosh **kosh** *n.* A bludgeon, esp. a piece of iron pipe or a length of rubber hose filled with lead; a blackjack. 1950: "He was unconscious when he was killed. He might first have been hit on the head with a cosh." R. West in *New Yorker*, Dec. 16, 43.

cosmo *n.* A foreign student. *Student use.*

cosmolines, the *n.* The field artillery; the artillery unit or units attached to an infantry group. *W.W.II use. From the cosmoline grease used in oiling and storing guns.*

costume jewelry Women's Army Corps. officers' insignia. *Not common.*

cotton-picking **cotton-pickin'** *adj.* Common; vulgar; damned; not valuable. 1958: "Robert Stack ... is interested in politics and believes actors should assert themselves politically. ('I don't think it's anybody's cotton-pickin' business what you're doing. But don't use whatever power you have in the movie business to try to swing votes.')" S. Skolsky, N.Y. *Post*, June 1, M3. *Orig. Southern use. Somewhat jocular, because it appears to be a euphem.*

cou *n.* A girl. *From "couzie."*

couch doctor A psychoanalyst.

cough syrup Bribe money paid to keep another from informing or coughing up information. *c1925 underworld use.*

cough up **1** To pay, pay up, or pay over money. Used with or without a direct object. 1952: "... Having to cough up a thousand smackers...." Lowell Thomas, radio, Apr. 29. **2** To come forth with or present, as a confession of guilt or money owed.

countdown **count-down** *n.* The act of or an instance of counting down from a given number to zero at one-second intervals in preparation for exploding an atomic bomb or launching a missile. *The countdown is organized in such a way that each operation in a complex sequence of preparatory actions may be performed at the proper time and under the supervision of the director of the entire program; thus a failure in any preparatory operation may be the cause for interrupting the countdown and canceling the final explosion or launching.* 1957:

"We have just had the weather briefing and we agreed to continue. So go ahead with the count-down." Dr. J. C. Clark, *SEP*, July 20, 64. 1958: "For the second day, however, there were reports of delays in the count-down. Residents of nearby Cocoa Beach flocked to the beaches again on the chance the [satellite-bearing space] rocket would go up." N.Y. *Post*, Jan. 24, 4. *Orig. c1945 atomic-bomb use; now also missile-launching use.*

counter-jumper *n.* A store clerk. *c1835.*

country, go out in the To murder someone; to take for a ride. *Underworld use; c1930.*

count [one's] thumbs To kill time.

count ties To walk on a railroad trackway. *Vagabond argot.*

courage *n.* See **Dutch courage.**

course See **gut course, pipe course, snap course.**

court See **kangaroo court.**

cousin *n.* **1** In baseball, an easy pitcher; one who gives (certain) batters no trouble in making hits. 1928: G. H. Ruth, *Babe Ruth's Own Book of Baseball,* 299. **2** A dupe; an easy victim. **3** A close friend. See **kissing cousin.**

couzie **couzy** *n.* A girl.

cove *n.* A man; a fellow. 1848: J. S. Farmer. 1893: "*Pal* and *cove*, words not yet admitted to the best society...." B. Matthews in *Harper's*, July, 304/2. *Mainly c1875 underworld use; more common in Eng. than in U.S.; archaic. From the Celtic "caobh" = courteous, reinforced by the Romany "covo."*

cover *v.i.* = **cover up.** *v.t.* **1** To alibi or lie for another in order that he may escape detection or punishment. **2** To protect another.

covered wagon An aircraft carrier. *W.W.II USN use.*

cover-up *n.* An alibi, distraction, shield, or attempt to conceal. 1949: "The phoning is just a cover-up." Movie, *Johnny Allegro.* **cover up** *v.i.* To lie or take the blame for wrongdoing in order to allow another to escape undetected; to attempt to conceal or minimize a misdeed.

covess dinge [derog.] A colored woman. *Some c1850 underworld use.*

cow *n.* **1** Milk. 1903: "Drive the cow down" = pass the milk. E. Conradi. *Student, Armed Forces, hobo, ranch, and logger use since c1900.* **2** Cream. **3** Butter. **4** Beef in any form—steak, roast, hamburger, etc. **5** Any fat, ungraceful person. *Colloq.* **6** A girl of any size or shape. *Some c1935 mainly underworld use.* **7** A third-year student at West Point. *West Point use c1940.* Cf. **armored cow, black cow, canned cow, tin cow, white cow.** —**boy** *n.* **1** A "Western" sandwich. **2** A reckless, irresponsible man. 1958: "Cowboy—A motorist given to . . . jumping lights, weaving, speeding, etc." G. Y. Wells, *Station House Slang.* **3** A raucous, boisterous man. **4** A king in a deck of playing cards. **5** The leader of a criminal gang or mob. *v.t.* To murder quickly, recklessly, or in a noisy, public, or sensational manner. 1946: "He had had an assignment to kill a man and his bodyguard 'even if we had to cowboy them.' 'What does that mean?' asked Liebowitz. 'That means that we were to kill them any place we found them even if it was in the middle of Broadway.' " C. A. Wyer in N.Y. *Sun.*

cowboy coffee Black coffee without sugar. 1945: ". . . He lives on 'air, self-esteem, cigarette butts, cowboy coffee.' . . ." Mitchell, *McSorley's,* 72.

cowboy job A holdup staged by amateurs; a robbery staged recklessly.

cow-cage *n.* A railroad car that carries cattle. *Railroad use. Not common.*

cow college A small agricultural college; an agricultural college; any small, little-known college. 1958: ". . . Not 'cow colleges,' but famous institutions." M. Wallace in N.Y. *Post,* Feb. 19, 40.

cowein *n.* **1** A turtle; turtle soup; turtle-meat stew. *c1885–c1915 New Orleans Creole use.* . → **2** A party, dance, or social gathering, as where turtle soup or meat might be served. *Obs.* 1950: "*Cowein* means turtle, a dish made of turtle meat, or by extension, a social get-together." A. Lomax, *Mr. Jelly Roll,* 7.

cow-hide *n.* A baseball.

cow juice *n.* Milk. *c1845. Still used.*

cow pilot An airplane stewardess. *Aviator use.*

cowpoke *n.* Cowboy. Cf. **poke.** *c1885.*

cowpuncher *n.* A cowboy. *First use c1875. Western use.* 1936: "The cowboy was not always called 'cowboy.' He everywhere was equally well known as 'cowpuncher.' " P. A. Rollins, *The Cowboy,* 39. *Colloq.*

cow salve Butter. *c1940. Civilian Conservation Corps use.*

cow-simple *adj.* Girl-crazy; in love

with a girl. *c1935 underworld use.* See **cow.**

crab *n.* **1** A horse, usu. in "fast crab." *Obs.* **2** A strict, cross, or irritable person. **3** A native of Annapolis, Md. 1922: *U.S. Naval Academy use.* **4** An Annapolis girl. 1928: *U.S. Naval Academy midshipman use.* *v.i.* **1** To complain; to nag. 1929: "Crab, crab, crab, that was all she ever did. What a lousy sport she was!" D. Parker, "Big Blonde," reprinted in *The American Twenties,* 144. *Colloq.* **2** To borrow continually. **3** To complain. *v.t.* **1** To pilfer trifling articles. **2** To spoil (something belonging to another person). 1929: "You trying to . . . crab my party?" Dunning & Abbott, *Broadway,* II. —**s** *n.pl.* **1** Shoes. *c1850.* **2** [taboo] Crab lice; a case of infestation by crab lice. 1934: "She would have flown into a rage of protest if someone had bluntly said that her friends slobbered, ripped off girls' dresses at parties, had crabs. . . ." P. Wylie, *Finnley Wren,* 85. → **2** A type of flea. *Hobo use.*

crack *v.t.* **1** To enter or leave a building by force, as when entering a bank to rob it or when escaping from prison. *Orig. underworld use, c1850.* → **2** To open a safe by force, using either explosives or tools. → **3** To attend a social gathering uninvited; to crash the gate. → **4** Fig., to force or finally gain one's way into an occupation, social group, or the like. → **5** Fig., to solve a problem or a mystery; to reveal, explain, or comprehend. 1934: "They never cracked the [murder] case." R. Chandler, *Finger Man,* 109 f. 1949: ". . . Until science cracks the mystery of just how leprosy is transmitted." A. L. Blakeslee, AP, Oct. 4. *Colloq.* **6** To mention something; to disclose something. 1943: "When the pitchman is about to crack the price. . . ." Zolotow in *SEP.* **7** To break a banknote in making change. 1951: "Twenty bucks? Gee, I can't crack that." Movie, *Cry Danger.* *v.i.* **1** To weaken or show signs of weakening under emotional strain; to lose one's emotional control, will power, or sanity. 1939: "If Ribber thinks Carr is planning to give him a double-cross, he'll begin to crack, and if he cracks, he'll break." E. S. Gardner, *D. A. Draws,* 181. See **crack up. 2** To speak or talk. 1942: "Listen, Ben, quit cracking dumb." Cain, *Love's Lovely Counterfeit,* 6. **3** In the card game of bridge, to double. *n.* **1** [taboo] The vagina. **2** A short, often humorous, criticism; an audacious remark; a statement, esp. one that is uncomplimentary or clever; a wisecrack. *Colloq.* 1929–30: "One more crack like that, and I'm going to sock you." K. Brush, *Young Man*, 31. **3** A try at some undertaking whether large or small. 1934: ". . . To take a crack at something bigger." Cain, *Postman*, 29. **4** A remarkable person; a crackerjack. *Not common.* **—ed** *adj.* **1** Crazy; eccentric. 1909: "[This use is] derived from the metaphor of the head as a nut." Krapp, *Mod. Engl.*, 205. **2** Stupid, foolish.   **—er** See **bone-cracker,   diamond-cracker, jaw-breaker.   —erjack** *n.* An excellent or remarkable person or thing. 1897: *DAE. Archaic.* *adj.* Excellent; topnotch. *Colloq.* 1910: ". . . He's a crackerjack boxer." Johnson, *Varmint*, 43. **—ing** *adj.* Excellent. *c1925.* *adv.* Very. **—y** *interj.* Cripes! Crimus! etc. *c1850.* 1910: "Cracky, what a prize!" Johnson, *Varmint*, 70, 127, 178. *Obs.*

crack a book   Lit., to open a book; fig., to study, to cram. 1924: "I didn't crack the book till two days ago." Marks, *Plastic Age*, 100. 1951: "You haven't cracked a book since graduating from Gowdy's grammar." *Synd. newsp. cartoon*, "Major Hoople," Sept. 19.

crack a smile   To smile.

crack back   To retort.   **crackback**   *n.* A quick or clever retort.

crack down   To take admonitory or punitive action against someone; to censure. 1952: "Representative Robert W. Kean . . . warned the House at that time. It cracked down." Sid Kline in N.Y. *Daily News*, Aug. 13, 2C/2.

cracked ice = **ice.**

cracker barrel   **1** Fig., a place or locale where, or time when, men relax and talk philosophically. *From the actual cracker barrel, once found in all general stores, where town elders gathered, discussed local problems, and waxed philosophical.* **2** Resembling or pertaining to homely philosophy; unsophisticated, rustic; said of thought or philosophy. *Colloq.*

cracking, get   Start; start moving; begin working; begin to exert oneself. *Often in the phrase* **let's get cracking.** See **crack.**

crack [one's] jaw   To boast.

crack up   **1** To praise. *c1820: DAE.* 1924: ". . . Asked if a book was all that it was 'cracked up to be.'" Marks, *Plastic Age*, 228. *Colloq.* **2** To wreck an

airplane, automobile, or the like while operating it. *Colloq.*   *v.i.* To lose one's emotional control, will power, or sanity; to have a crying or laughing fit. 1934: "She cracked up." Cain, *Postman*, 23. 1955: "Jimmy felt that he was cracking up. He felt that the pressure would increase and that flesh and blood could not endure it." C. Willingham, *To Eat a Peach*, 78.   **crack-up**   *n.* **1** An accident that badly damages or destroys an automobile, airplane, or the like; a wreck. 1950: "A crack-up of his 'hot-rod' car. . . ." AP, Sept. 1. *Colloq.* **2** An emotional or mental breakdown; a loss of control.

crack wise   **1** To speak knowingly. Cf. **wisecrack.** **2** To speak jokingly; to make a wisecrack. 1942: "It's a waste of time talking to you. All you do is crack wise." Chandler, *High Window*, 23, 27, 138.

cradle   *n.* A railroad gondola car.

cradle-robber   *n.* See **cradle-snatcher.** Cf. **rob the cradle.**

cradle-snatcher   *n.* A person of either sex who marries, courts, or befriends a much younger person of the opposite sex. The British equiv. is "baby farmer."

cram   *v.i., v.t.* **1** To study hard, esp. for a school examination. **2** Fig., to pack information into one's mind, esp. in preparation for an examination. *c1850.* 1949: ". . . Heavy cramming once or twice a term. . . ." *Cornell Daily Sun*, Sept. 30, 4. *Common student use, esp. college level.*   *n.* **1** A written paper, textbook, etc. used in studying for an examination; also, a study session. **2** A course requiring hard study; esp. a lecture course for which the student must do much supplementary reading. *c1900.* **3** A student who studies hard before an examination. **4** An overly diligent student, a book worm.   *adj.* Devoted to cramming. 1952: "Many thousands more attended [Judge Medina's] bar exam cram courses." R. Halley in N.Y. *Times Bk. Rev.*, Aug. 17, 3/3.   **—mer**   *n.* **1** The stomach. *c1850.* **2** One who studies hard for an examination.

cramp [one's] style   To interfere with or hinder a person; esp. to prevent a person from expressing himself fully. 1929–30: ". . . Am I cramping your style?" K. Brush, *Young Man*, 46.

crap [taboo]   *n.* **1** Nonsense; cant; lies; exaggeration; insincerity; mendacity; bull. 1939: "I wasn't satisfied with the crap I handed her but had to put it on thicker . . . and she said, 'Pally, I never heard so much crap in such a short time in my life.' " J. O'Hara, *Pal Joey*, 59. 1949: "I'm not interested in stories about the past or any crap of that kind." A. Miller, *Death of a Salesman*, 107. *From the taboo but otherwise stand. "crap" = feces.* 2 Anything inferior, cheap, ugly, or insulting by its very presence, esp. merchandise that is of inferior material, workmanship, or over-all quality; shit. *Very common.* 3 Inferior entertainment; corn; shit; *Not as common as the more specif. "shit"; all sl. uses of "crap" synonyms for the various sl. uses of "shit."* *v.t.* To talk nonsense to a person; to deceive or lie to a person. 1930: "Don't crap me! You're still in love with her." J. T. Farrell, 162. *interj.* [taboo] An expression of disgust or disappointment; shit; an expression of incredulity. **—per** *n.* 1 A public rest room; a toilet. *Most common c1930. Still some use.* Cf. **John.** 2 A boaster; one who speaks crap or bull. **—py** *adj.* Worthless; inferior; ugly; un-pleasant. See **crap.**

crape-hanger *n.* 1 A gloomy person; a killjoy. 1921: "Don't be a crape hanger all your life." Witwer, *Leather,* 11, 193. 2 An undertaker.

crap list *n.* See **shit list.**

crap out 1 To lose; esp. to lose one's money or a bet. *From dicing and gambling use in the game of craps, in which a throw of 7 or 11 in attempting to make a point causes the player to lose his bet and his turn. Not common.* 2 To evade one's duty; to become afraid, to become cowardly; to withdraw from a scheme or activity due to cowardice. 3 To tire or become exhausted; to lose one's en-thusiasm; to withdraw from a plan or excursion; specif. to become too tired to continue enjoying, contributing to, or staying at a party or social gathering. *Wide student use since c1945 and most common use.*

crash *n.* 1 A strong romantic in-fatuation; a crush. 2 A complete flunk. 3 In baseball, a hit. *Not common.* *v.t.* 1 To break into a building; to gain admission to a place by force. 1927: "Their mob will crash the prison and turn 'em loose." Hammett, *Blood Money,* 26. 1949: "Hoover's men crashed Doc's apartment. . . ." A. Hynd, *Public Enemies,* 130. Cf. **crack.** → 2 To rob a place; to make a forced entry in order to rob a place. → 3 Fig., to gain ad-mission to, to break in; to gain admission to or acceptance in a group of field of

endeavor. 1937: "To 'crash a party.' " L. Untermeyer in *Rotarian,* Nov., 11/1. 1951: "I'm glad to see [that Buster Crabbe] crashed television successfully." Hy Gardner in N.Y. *Her. Trib.,* Dec. 12, 27/3. **—er** *n.* Anyone who goes to parties uninvited; from "gate-crasher." *c1920: flapper use.* 1950: ". . . At the Plymouth [Theater] . . . his main job after the curtain goes up is handling crashers." *New Yorker,* Dec. 9, 31/1.

crash out To break out of prison. 1949: "You going to crash out?" *White Heat,* movie. **crashout** *n.* A jail break. 1949: ". . . Prison pals who were looking . . . to a crashout. . . ." A. Hynd, *Public Enemies,* 10.

crash program See **crash project.**

crash project A project or program designed to overcome an emergency; thus, one demanding immediate and intensive exertion; a project having priority over all others; a project so vital to the life of a nation or firm that no time or effort is spared to complete it successfully. *Since c1950. Orig. applied to scientific or military programs considered vital to the national defense but now widely used in clerical departments of the government and in private business.*

crash the gate To go to a social gathering uninvited; to go to a place of entertainment without paying admission. Cf. **gate-crasher.** 1922: *flapper use.* "We crashed the gate at a swell joint." Phila. *Eve. Bulletin,* Mar. 8.

crash wagon An ambulance.

crate *n.* 1 An antiquated or dilapi-dated automobile, truck, bus, airplane, or even a ship. *c1920. Orig. California mechanic use.* 1949: "A 'crate' [auto-mobile] is a 'junker' with 'one surge left.' " N.Y. *Times,* May 1, 62. → 2 Any auto-mobile, truck, bus, or airplane, or even a ship. Cf. **egg crate.** *Very common c1938–1945.* 3 A jail. *Vagabond argot, rarely used by others.* 4 A coffin. 5 An unattractive girl. *Not common.*

crate of sand A sugar truck. *c1935, truckdriver use.*

crawfish *v.i.* To renege. *c1850.* 1914: "Had to crawfish when the miner saved him?" S. Lewis, *Our Mr. Wrenn,* 191. Fig., to back out with the devious move-ments of a crawfish.

crawk *n.* An animal imitator. *c1935, radio use.*

crawl *v.t.* 1 To have sexual inter-course with; said of a male. 1947: "Marquales saw written on the wall just by his seat the words: '*Men, I finally* *crawled Mary Jane Cummings last night. She meeowed like a kitty.'* " C. Willingham, *End as a Man*, 140. *Not common.* **2** To admonish; to bawl out. *W.W.I Army use.* 1951: " 'To crawl' meant what Second World War troops were to signify by 'chew out.' " A. J. Liebling, *New Yorker*, Mar. 10, 60.   *v.i.* To dance. *c1930, college sl.* See **pub-crawl.**   *n.* A dance.

crawl [someone's] hump   To attack a person physically; to beat a person up. *Cowboy use.*

crazy   *adj.* **1** Satisfying one's desire for the unique; new, cool, exciting, different, and personally satisfying. *Common bop use since c1945. Usu. as a one-word comment.* → **2** Wonderful; thrilling; satisfying. 1956: *"Crazy:* new, wonderful, wildly exciting." S. Longstreet, *The Real Jazz Old and New*, 151. 1956: "Dig this jive, Daddy? I think it's c-r-a-z-y." Steve Vlasich, "Before Be-bop," *Look*, May 15, 128. 1956: "Hi Fi can turn your bachelor apartment into a Harem, . . . and the crazy part is you don't have to be an engineer to operate H. H. Scott components." H. H. Scott high-fidelity phonograph component advt., *New Yorker*, Dec. 8, 159. 1957: ". . . And stopovers at crazy joints like Barcelona. . . ." Patrick Chase, "Playboy's International Datebook," *Playboy*, May, 14. 1958: "The crazy new Kraft candy with longer chocolate taste." Advt. for "Kraft" brand chocolate "Fudgies" candy, N.Y. *Daily News*, Feb. 9, comic section, 7. *Orig. bop and cool use. The order of the definitions and quotations shows how the word has become more general in meaning as its use spread from the cool groups to general usage. Common to teenagers since c1950.* See **cool.**

—crazy   See Appendix, Suffixes and Suffix Words.

crazy about [someone or something] *adj.* Crazy for; specif., in love with; having a strong liking for someone or something. 1914: "I'm crazy about her." S. Lewis, *Our Mr. Wrenn*, 212.

crazy-cat   *n.* A "crazy" person. See **cat.**

crazy for   Very eager for; in love with; attracted to; appreciative of; obsessed with. *Since c1850.*

crazy house   An insane asylum. *c1870.*

creaker   *n.* Any old person.

cream   *v.t.* **1** To obtain a selfish goal, cheat, take advantage of, rob, persuade, or gain dominance over another by glib talk, flattery, or the like. 1929: "The

college boy (in 1929) knows a smoothie who wolfed on a friend and creamed his lady." *World's Work*, Nov., 40. 1939: "I told you how I got creamed out of the hotel spot in Ohio." J. O'Hara, *Pal Joey*, 26. → **2** To accomplish a task easily and with spectacular success; specif., to pass an examination or course of study easily and with high grades. 1941: "Boy, did I cream that exam!" *Dict. of Exeter Lang.*, 12. → **3** To defeat decisively, esp. in an athletic contest.   *adj.* Easy; pleasant.

creamie   *n.* Any glass marble; esp. a clear or white marble. *Child use.*

cream puff   creampuff   *n.* **1** A weakling; a person of slight physique; a sissy. 1949: ". . . Opponents might get the idea . . . Lemonick is a cream puff." Dick Cresap, Phila. *Bulletin*, Sept. 15, 51. **2** An automobile that has been driven carefully, kept in good condition from the first, and is being offered for resale. 1949: "This car was owned by a prominent local lady and if there ever was a 'creampuff' this is it." Advt., *Cornell Daily Sun*, Oct. 25, 8.

cream-puff hitter   In baseball, a weak batter.

cream up   To carry out a task perfectly. 1952: "Now you guys [gangsters] all know what you're supposed to do and when, so let's cream this up. This is one caper I don't want any slipup on." R. Decker in *New Yorker*, Jan. 19, 27.

creep   *n.* **1** Lit., a person who gives one "the creeps"; orig. an introvert, bore, or nonsociable person whose quiet manners and gestures seem sly or surreptitious; any odd, loathsome, or objectionable person; a drip; a wet blanket; a jerk. 1938: "Quentin Reynolds: 'The man is nothing but a creep.' Heywood Broun: 'What is this thing a creep?' R.: 'Why, a creep's a creep. If you don't know when you meet up, I'm afraid I can't describe the species for you.' B.: 'But how am I to decide . . .?' R.: 'Any sensitive person can't be mistaken. The knowledge comes to you through a kind of curdling sensation in the marrow of your bones.' " *New Repub.*, Sept. 7, 129/1. 1949: "In Denver, socially boresome classmates . . . referred to as 'creeps.' " *Time*, Oct. 3, 37. 1958: "Okay . . . but I'm still not sure of that creep. . . ." "Dondi," *synd. newsp. comic strip.* Feb. 9, 6. *Wide student use c1935–c1945. Still common.* **2** Draught beer. *Not common.* **3** A clandestine meeting or mission. *Some Negro use.* **4** A slow round of golf. *Caddy use.*   **—er**   *n.* **1** In an automobile, low gear. *c1935, trucker use.* **2** A performer who comes closer and closer to a microphone during a broadcast. *Broadcasting studio use.* **3** A sneak thief. *Underworld use c1935.* **4** = **creep.** **—ers** *n.pl.* Rubbers; rubber-soled shoes; sneakers. *Orig. underworld use. c1900.* **—y** *adj.* **1** Like a creep; characteristic of a creep. **2** Cheap; inferior. 1950: "I'm just a creepy saloonkeeper." J. Bainbridge in *New Yorker*, Nov. 11, 52/1.

creep dive A cheap saloon; a saloon operated by or patronized by creeps.

Creepers! *exclam.* = **Jeepers Creepers!** *Euphemistic profanity.* See Appendix, Shortened Words.

creeping meatballism See **meatballism.** *A somewhat jocular though intrinsically serious criticism of American politics, culture, education, or the like. Since c1955, pop. by N.Y.C. disc jockey and social commentator Jean Shepherd.*

creep-joint *n.* **1** A gambling business, game, or set-up that operates in a different location every night in order to avoid police raids. *Underworld use since c1930.* **2** = **creep dive.**

creeps, the *n.sing.* **1** A physical, mental, or psychical sensation of fear, horror, disgust, or the like; revulsion; uneasiness. 1930: "She could give any man the creeps." J. T. Farrell, 89. *Colloq.* Cf. **willies. 2** Delirium tremens; the heebie-jeebies. 1952: "He was not in [Bellevue] with the creeps but with a broken leg." J. McNulty in *New Yorker*, May 10, 28/2.

crew *n.* = **crew cut.**

crew-cut crew cut *n.* A style of close haircut, usu. a man's or boy's. 1957: "Probably the most popular special hair style in the country today is the Crew Cut. It has a flat silhouette with a hair length of about an inch or less on top, closely cropped on the sides." H. Mitgang, *About—Men's Haircuts. Since c1940. From college crewmen who have favored such haircuts for many years. Orig. pop. with students, now common. adj.* In crew-cut style. 1939: "Her hair is cut crew-cut like the college blood." J. O'Hara, *Pal Joey*, 57. *adj.* Collegiate; Ivy League. 1956: "When you first hear the Brubeck Quartet, you are immediately struck by the novel blending of crew-cut and long-hair elements." A. Shaw, *West Coast Jazz*, 127.

crib *n.* **1** A set of written answers used by a student to cheat on an examination. *c1860; now colloq.* 1943: ". . . Individual

cheating is even more ingenious. . . . He made a crib out of one hundred and twenty feet of ticker tape . . . folded it into accordion pleats, and wrote an answer in each of the folds." Max Shulman, *Barefoot Boy With Cheek*, 186. **2** A student who cheats on an exam. **3** A building, office, or room of any kind. *Underworld use c1850–c1890. Obs.* **4** A brothel, esp. a cheap one; specif., a very small room, large enough to contain only a bed, in a brothel. 1950: "A crib is a room about seven feet wide." A. Lomax, *Mr. Jelly Roll*, 21. **5** A public place where thieves and hoodlums meet or congregate; a cheap saloon, esp. one patronized by drunkards and hobos. *Hobo and underworld use c1930.* **6** A nightclub; a dive. 1939: "I am singing for coffee and cakes at a crib on Cottage Grove Ave. . . ." J. O'Hara, *Pal Joey*, 15. **7** A safe or vault. *Underworld use.* **8** A caboose on a train. *Railroad use.* *v.t.* **1** To steal. **2** To cheat, esp. in an academic examination. 1951: "The exam-cribbing scandal at the U.S. Military Academy . . . he was . . . told to check the names of those who cribbed. . . . He said . . . he was asked point blank: 'Did you crib?' " AP, West Point, Aug. 9.

crimp *n.* An obstacle; a restriction, as "to put a crimp in my style." *c1880. v.t.* **1** To put a restriction on another's actions. **2** To demote. **3** To ruin a plan, idea, etc. by adding restrictions to it. **—y** *adj.* Uncomfortably cold. 1907: "I could expect 'crimpy' weather. . . ." Jack London, *My Life.*

Crimus! Euphem. for "Christ." 1944: *In def. of "cripus." Amer. Dial. Dict.*

crip *n.* **1** A crippled person. 1939: " 'Phony crips,' as the fraudulent cripples call each other. . . ." Berger, *New Yorker*, 3. **2** A crippled horse. *Farm usage.* **3** In the game of pool, a ball positioned so as to be easy to take. **4** An adversary easily beaten. **5** In college, an easy course. 1926: "Crip has about driven snap into oblivion . . . it seems . . . probably that the word came into collegiate use via the poolroom. . . ." Gilmore Spencer, *Univ. of Va. Mag.*, Oct., 16f.

Cripes! Cripus! Euphem. for "Christ." 1924: "Sweet! Cripes, that old hen made him sick. . . . Cripes! what a title!" Marks, *Plastic Age*, 6, 103.

crip-faker *n.* A professional beggar who pretends bodily injury to gain attention. *Tramp use.*

croak *v.t.* To murder. *c1850.* 1931: "He croaked a screw at Dannemora [prison]. . . ." J. Sayre, *Hex*, 415. *v.i.*

1 To die. 1932: "If Midgie Muldoon croaks. . . ." Runyon. **2** To flunk a school examination or course.   **—er** *n.* A physician; a medical doctor. 1949: "Don't say 'croaker' . . . say 'doctor.' " N. Algren, *Man with the Golden Arm*, 94. 1951: "I come to down at Bellevue [hospital] with croakers . . . standing around." *I, Mobster*, 121. *Underworld, addict, hobo, circus, etc., use.*   **—ing** *n.* A killing; a murder. 1949: "There's been a croaking in town." A. Hynd, *Public Enemies*, 79.   **—sman** *n.* A murderer. *c1850; obs.*

crock *n.* **1** A disliked youth or man, esp. one disliked for being meticulous, superior, aloof, or selfish; specif., a successful, boasting, meticulous elderly man. **2** A worthless or disliked girl or woman. 1950: "A lot of old crocks with baggy eyes and . . . corsets. . . ." Starnes, *Another Mug*, 109. **3** A bottle of liquor. **4** A drunken person; a drunkard. 1950: "The Bevins . . . lose their boozy Uncle Joe. . . . Later . . . it is discovered that the aged crock. . . ." Philip Hamburger, *New Yorker*, Sept. 2, 66/3. *From "crocked."* **5** An animal imitator. *Radio use.* **6** A bargelike freight ship made chiefly of reinforced concrete. *1945, USN use in Pacific.* **7** A guy; a geezer. 1945: "Old man Hollinan was good company. He was a funny old crock." Mitchell, *McSorley's*, 154. **8** [taboo] = **crock of shit.** *A euphem., made by shortening the term.*   **v.t.** To hit someone over the head; to bean or conk. 1940: "I crocked the orderly with a bed spring." Chandler, *Farewell*, 196.   **—ed** *adj.* **1** Drunk. 1927: "U.S., now in common use." *New Republic*, 71. 1951: "The other four laying around on a settee, sort of half crocked." S. J. Perelman in *New Yorker*, Feb. 10, 29. See Appendix, Drunk. **2** Disabled; wounded. *Some W.W.I use.*

crockery *n.* **1** The teeth. Cf. **china. 2** In baseball, a pitcher's arm that stops functioning. Cf. **crockie, glass arm.**

crockie *n.* A playing marble with a baked, glazed finish, usu. blue or brown. See Appendix, —ie ending.

crock of shit [taboo]   **1** Lies; exaggeration; mendacity. **2** A person who lies, exaggerates, or is insincere; a braggart. **3** = **pile of shit** [taboo].

crocus *n.* See **croaker.**

cronk *adj.* Drunk. *c1850.*

crook *v.i., v.t.* To steal. 1945: "He crooked my socks." E. Kasser.   **—er** See **pinky-crooker.**

crooked arm   A left-handed pitcher. *Baseball use.*

crooked stick   A dishonest person. 1848: *DAE. Dial.*

crook [one's] elbow (little finger) To drink whisky, esp. at a bar. *1836: DAE; obs.* Cf. **bend [the] elbow.**

croon *v.i., v.t.* **1** To sing popular songs with a soft, mellow style; to sing. 1947: "The Negritic word for sing, *croon.*" C. Willingham, *End as a Man*, 211. **2** = **sing.**

croot *n.* An Army recruit. *Some Army use.* See Appendix, Shortened Words.

cropper See **come a cropper.**

croppy *n.* A corpse. 1929: "That kid needs a doctor. . . . If you don't want a croppy on your hands, start firing the locomotive." G. Jones. *Railroad use.*

cross *adj.* Dishonest. *c1850.*   *n.* A double-cross. 1941: "I guess the cross is really on." *Johnny Eager*, movie.   *v.t.* **1** To cheat. **2** To deny another his rights or possessions; to do something against another's wishes.

cross-eyed See **look at [someone] cross-eyed.**

cross my heart (and hope to die)   A traditional and mild oath used to affirm the truth of a statement. *Common child use.*

cross [someone's] palms   To bribe; to pay for a noncommercial service. 1949: "Officials whose palms had been crossed by Floyd." A. Hynd, *Public Enemies*, 100.

cross-up *n.* = **double-cross.** 1953: "An' leave us have no cross-ups, hunh?" Bob Hope, *NBC radio program*, Mar. 11.

cross [someone] up   To mix one up; to confuse; to lead astray; to deceive. 1934: "That's to cross them up." Cain, *Postman*, 46.

crow *n.* **1** The eagle in various USN insignia. *W.W.I USN use, still common.* → **2** A USN chief or captain who wears such insignia. **3** Chicken. *W.W.II Armed Forces use.* **4** See **jim crow. 5** An unpopular or ugly woman or girl.

crowbait *n.* An old, useless, mean, or ugly horse. *Western use.*

crowd *n.* A gang, group, faction, or clique. 1930: "The Hip Sing and On Leong crowds." Lavine, *Third Degree*, 88.

Crow Jimism   A strong psychological attraction to Negroes; said in ref. to whites. *Usu. used to characterize a guilt attitude arising from deep-rooted Negrophobia or the operations of a politician who courts Negro votes for* *personal gain. "Jim Crowism" backwards.*

crown *v.t.* To hit a person over the head. 1928: "We'll crown him." Hecht & MacArthur, *Front Page*, III.

crown fire Fig., a severe hangover. *Logger use. From the stand. expression for a fire in the treetops.*

crow tracks Chevrons. *Army use.*

crud *n.* **1** [taboo] Dried semen, as sticks to the body or clothes after sexual intercourse. → **2** [taboo] Any venereal disease, esp. syphilis. *Orig. Army use since c1925. The above taboo meanings are now seldom used, though many adult males know them and are startled to hear the nontaboo uses by those who are unaware of the orig. meanings.* → **3** Any disease or illness, esp. those affecting the skin, such as fungus infections; any nameless and imaginary horrible or ugly disease; any mythical disease. 1951: "I gotta get him outa here—he's got the crud." Movie, *Up Front. Since c1930; common W.W.II Army use; some student use.* **4** A slovenly, unwashed fellow; a dirty, repulsive person. *Since c1935.* **5** Anything inferior, worthless, ugly, or disgusting; crap. 1956: "All music has its times when it isn't really popular crud, and yet isn't its original form any more." S. Longstreet, *The Real Jazz Old and New*, 168.

cruller *n.* **1** Specif., a yeast doughnut. *From the French; colloq.* **2** A man's head. *Not common.* **3** A failure; specif., an unsuccessful performance or entertainment. 1951: "He can have a couple of swell shows and the next week come up with a cruller." Bing Crosby, quoted by AP, Dec. 12.

crumb **crum** *n.* **1** A louse; a bedbug. *Some hobo, ranch, logger, Army, and USN use since before c1900.* → **2** A hobo's blanket roll or pack. *Some c1910 hobo use.* → **3** A dirty, slovenly, repulsive person. *Army, maritime, and hobo use. Since c1910.* **4** An untrustworthy, loathsome, or objectionable person; an insignificant, despicable person. *Since c1920; wide student use c1935–c1945.* **—s** *n.pl.* Lit., a few pieces of change or silver money; a few dollars; a small amount of money. 1957: "Crumbs—A small sum of money." E. Horne, *For Cool Cats and Far-Out Chicks. Orig. c1935 jive use; some continuing Negro and jazz use.* **—y** **—y** *adj.* **1** Infested with body lice; lousy. *Hobo, Army, maritime, ranch, and logger use c1910.* See **crumb.** → **2** Dirty, filthy; contemptible, repulsive, disgusting. 1949: "If it weren't for trouble I'd be dead of the dirty monotony

around this crummy neighborhood." N. Algren, *Man with the Golden Arm*, 18. 1957: "I wrote that crummy scene because the producers wanted it that way." R. Bissell, *Publishers' Weekly*, Apr. 22, 17. *Common use. Although "crum" for "crumb" appears so seldom as to seem illiterate, "crummy" prevails over "crumby" about 7 to 1.* *n.* **1** A train caboose. *Hobo use. From the early days when cabooses were infested with lice.* See **crumb.** **2** A railroad work-crew bunk car. *Railroad use.* See **crumb.** **3** A stingy person. *Some c1940 student use.*

crumb boss *n.* **1** A construction-camp bunkhouse janitor or porter; one who makes up beds. *Hobo and logger use.* See **crumb.** → **2** One in charge of a railroad work-crew car. *Railroad use.*

crumb-bum **crum-bum** *n.* Fig., a lice-ridden bum; a worthless person. 1951: "Boxing . . . also attracts some of the nicest [people], but they still can't outnumber the crum-bums." A. Daley in N.Y. *Times Mag.*, Mar. 4, 58. See **crumb.**

crumb house = **crumb joint.**

crumb joint A flop-house infested with lice. *Hobo use.* See **crumb.**

crumb-o **crumbo** *n.* = **crumb.** *One of the more common sl. words with —o suffix. Mainly newsp. columnist, theater, and gambler use.* See Appendix, —o ending.

crumb-roll *n.* A bed or blanket roll; a bed. *Hobo, ranch, and logger use c1915.* See **crumb.**

crumb the deal To spoil a plan or plot.

crumb up To clean clothes thoroughly, esp. by boiling, so as to rid them of lice; to clean a place. *Some W.W.I Army use; some prison use.* See **crumb.**

crump *v.i.* **1** To shell. *From the sound made by exploding shells. W.W.I use.* **2** To lose consciousness from the combination of drinking and fatigue; to pass out; to crap out. *adj.* Drunk. *Never common.* See Appendix, Drunk.

crumped out Drunk; also, fatigued, tight asleep. See **crump.** See Appendix, Drunk.

crump out = **crump.**

cruncher *n.* A road, a street; a sidewalk. *Some archaic Negro use.*

crupper *n.* A body belt. *Telephone lineman use.*

crush *n.* **1** An infatuation, esp. a one-sided one; a strong liking for a person, esp. one of the opposite sex; often in "to have (or get) a crush on someone." 1920: "You got a crush on Froggy Parker. I've got a crush, too." Fitzgerald, *This Side of Paradise*, 13. 1949: "I Have a Crush on You," title of pop. song. **2** A reception, dance, party or other large social gathering. *Some student use since c1900.* **3** A mob, a crowd; a faction, a clique. *Never common in U.S.* *v.t.* To escape from prison. Cf. **crack**, **crash.**   **—er**   *n.* A boy who is popular with girls and women; an attractive youth whom many girls have a crush on.

crush on someone, have a   To be infatuated or in love with someone. *Esp. applied to children and early teenagers. Colloq.*

crush out   To escape from prison. 1927: ". . . Who had crushed out of Leavenworth." Hammett, *Blood Money*, 42. 1944: ". . . After crushing out of stir." *Collier's*, Sept. 9, 55/2. *Underworld use.*

crush-out   *n.* An escape from prison. 1927: "Papadopoulos had arranged a crush-out for Flora." Hammett, *Blood Money*, 188.

Crusoe   = **Robinson Crusoe.**

crust   *n.* Gall, audacity, nerve. *c1900.* 1943: "You've got a hell of a crust assuming I'll go down there. . . ." Chandler, *Lady in Lake*, 173.   **—y**   *adj.* **1** Nervy; also, dirty; mean; contemptible. **2** Worthless; worn out.

crut   *n.* = **crud.**

crutch   *n.* An automobile. *Some Negro use.*

cry baby   *n.* One who cries frequently and with little provocation; fig., one who cannot bear criticism or reprimands.

crying jag   A period of uncontrolled crying. 1929: "Florence got regular crying jags and the men sought to cheer and comfort her." D. Parker, "Big Blonde," reprinted in *The American Twenties*, 152. 1954: "Mother flipped her lid, ended with a crying jag." H. K. Fink, *Long Journey*, 6.

crying towel   An imaginary towel freq. called for to be given one who complains, chronically or loudly, of minor defeats and ill fortune. Thus "Get out the crying towel [for another]" = once again [another] is talking too much about his minor defeats and ill fortune.

cry uncle = **say uncle.**

C-speck   *n.* A $100 bill. *c1850–c1900. Obs., superseded by C-note.*

c.t.   **C.T.**   [taboo] = **cock   teaser** [taboo]. See Appendix, Shortened Words.

cub   *n.* **1** A novice newspaper reporter. *Rapidly becoming obsolete.* 1929: "I was a cub . . . covering the . . . West 30th Street police station." Winkler, *New Yorker*, Feb. 9, 40. **2** A young inexperienced person.   **—by**   *n.* A room; a home, a pad. *Some Negro use.*

cube   *n.*   Lit., a three-dimensional "square"; a super "square"; one who is unbelievably innocent of current events and ideas or hopelessly ignorant of fashionable usages; an ultraconservative; a thorough bore. *Some bop and cool use since c1955, but mostly synthetic.*   **—s** *n.pl.* Dice. 1952: "He chose to . . . stake his hopes of a world championship on one throw of the cubes." Gayle Talbot, AP, Sept. 30.

cuckoo   *n.*   An insane person; an eccentric. *Since before 1600.*   *adj.* Crazy; irrational; eccentric. 1926: " . . . Even if you have gone cuckoo." Stallings & Anderson, *What Price Glory*, III. *"Coo-coo" is more common in the U.S.*   **—ed**   *adj.* Drunk. *Some c1920 use.* See **cuckoo.** See Appendix, Drunk.

cuckoo's chin, the = **the cat's meow.**

cucumber   *n.* A dollar. 1935: ". . . It may be against the law to say that a doll whose papa has all these cucumbers is dumb." Runyon.

cuddle-bunny   *n.* A promiscuous or delinquent girl. *Some teenage use c1940–c1950.*

cue   *v.t.* = **clue.**

cueball   cue-ball   *n.* **1** A man or boy who has just had a close or crew haircut. 1943: "Cueballs [are] the barber's clients." A. Ostrow. *Some W.W.II Army and student use. Because of the resemblance between a white billiard cue ball and a closely cropped head. Archaic.* **2** An eccentric or odd person; an oddball. *The "cue" stands for "q" or "queer."*

cue in   To make a specif. place for, to add to, to combine with; said of parts of radio, television, and movie scripts. 1957: "In Hollywood the writer gets a script of 'Lorna Doone' . . . to change the setting to Arizona and cue in some songs for Doris Day." R. Bissell, *Publishers' Weekly,* Apr. 22, 17.

cuff   *v.t.* **1** To borrow money from an individual, usu. without forewarning. **2** To charge (an expense) to; to put 'on the cuff.' 1953: ". . . No man . . . feels he is really forging ahead until he can cuff a few tabs on his firm." Hal Boyle, AP, Mar. 6. See **off the cuff, on the cuff, for the cuff.**   **—eroo**   *adj.* Free, gratis, or, more usu., to be paid for later; on the cuff. 1939: "A little mouse came in one nite with a party of six. It was not a spending party, strictly cufferoo." J. O'Hara, *Pal Joey*, 42. *One of the more common —eroo words; see Appendix.* **—o** *adj.* Free of charge, gratis; nonpaying; admitted free of charge. 1942: "Concerteers like a cuffo concert once in a while." *PM*, Jan. 5, 24. 1951: "Applause from the cuffo customers." A. Green, *Show Biz*, 14. *Since c1935.* See **on the cuff.** See Appendix, **—o** ending. *v.t.* To admit a person free of charge, as to a theater. 1948: "The crowds, most of which are made up of kids who are cuffoed. . . ." *Variety*, Aug. 25, 55/3. *Not common.* **—s** *n.pl.* Handcuffs; a pair of handcuffs. 1943: "Put the cuffs on." Chandler, *Lady in Lake*, 52. *Colloq.*

cuff, off the 1 Informally; extemporaneously; impromptu; unrehearsed. 1941: "A powerful "off-the-cuff orator." *Time*, Sept. 8, 4. 1951: " 'Show Biz,' the new book, talks off the cuff, splits an infinitive when it wishes and is slangy. . . ." Lewis Nichols, N.Y. *Times Book Rev.*, Nov. 11, 4/3. **2** Speaking, or giving one's opinion, advice, or confidential plan, to a person or group as a private individual rather than in one's official or business capacity.

cuff, on the 1 On credit; on a charge account; on the installment plan; not paying but promising to pay; trusted to pay later. 1930: "He puts me on the cuff for drinks." *Amer. Mercury*, Dec., 457. 1948: "He gave Harry the use of a beautiful suit and arranged for him to eat on the cuff in the cafe. . . ." Lait-Mortimer, *N.Y. Confidential*, 172. 1953: "Buying on the cuff is now at an all-time high. Billions of dollars are owed for . . . cars, television sets." Sam Dawson, AP, Mar. 16. *Because, traditionally, the amount owed was written on the creditor's cuff.* **2** Free of charge; on a basis of no monetary payment promised or expected for goods, etc., received or consumed; done without cash remuneration for one's work. 1939–40: "The press agent gets no pay but only a certan [sic] am't of drinks on the cuff. . . ." O'Hara, *Pal Joey*, 17. 1947: "When asked for a shot of liquor on the cuff the bartender . . . would pay for the drink himself." N. Algren, *The Face.* **3** Confidentially; impromptu; offhand. 1943: "But strictly on the cuff I'm willing to bet he never. . . ." Chandler, *Lady in Lake*, 79.

cuffee *n.* A Negro. *A genuine African word.*

cuff on [someone], put the To

arrest. 1950: "Why don't we have him [a detective] put the cuff on whoever it is?" Starnes, *And When She Was Bad*, 179. *Not common.*

cuke *n.* A cucumber; a cucumber prepared for eating. See Appendix, Shortened Words.

cull *n.* A cheap or inferior race horse. *Race track use; archaic.* **—s** *n.pl.* Hash. *N.W. U.S. Logger use and lunch-counter use.*

culture vulture A person interested in or a devotee of art or intellectual concerns. 1947: "Everybody can't be a culture vulture." Billy Rose, *synd. newsp. col.*, May 8. *Some teenage use since c1940.* See Appendix, Rhyming Slang.

cum [taboo] = **come.**

cunt [taboo] *n.* A girl or woman. *Depending on the tone of voice in which the word is spoken, the connotation may be of a sexually attractive girl or of a mean old woman. From the taboo but stand. "cunt" = vagina.*

cup, a *n.* An order of a cup of coffee. *Lunch-counter use in relaying an order.*

cup of tea Anything that or anybody whom a person likes. 1939–40: "I don't know what she saw in him, I'm sure he wouldn't have been my cup of tea. . . ." A. Christie, *Sad Cypress*, 77.

cupola *n.* The top of the human head; the brain. 1952: "Smoking (bad cigars) . . . finally smogged his cupola." "Our Boarding House," *synd. newsp. cartoon*, Dec. 27.

cups *n.* Sleep. *adj.* Asleep. *Some Negro use.* See **in [one's] cups.**

cups, in [one's] Drunk. *Fairly common.* See Appendix, Drunk.

curbie *n.* A waitress who serves food and drink to patrons in their automobiles parked at the curb; a carhop. 1938: "Us curbies don't get no salary for banging these trays." T. Pratt, *New Yorker.*

curbstone *n.* A cigarette or cigar butt; esp. one picked up from the street; a cigarette made from the tobacco found in the butt ends of previously smoked cigarettes.

curdle *v.t.* **1** To fail. **2** To offend; to annoy. 1941: "It curdles me. = I loathe it. *Life*, Jan. 27, 78. *Lit. to curdle one's stomach.*

cure, take the 1 Lit., to commit oneself to a hospital or sanitorium to be cured of chronic alcoholism or drug addiction. → **2** Fig., to refuse to indulge in or to refrain from participating in any pastime which one formerly enjoyed.

curl   *v.t.* To recite perfectly; to overwhelm a professor with an excellent recitation. *c1850.* 1926: "Even the indigenous ancient verb, 'to curl,' i.e., to confound a professor by a perfect recitation, is in good repute [at the Univ. of Virginia.] . . ." W. Carl Whitlock, *Univ. of Va. Mag.,* Oct., p. 5/1.

curry below the knee   To curry favor; to court a superior. *From "ass kisser."*

curtain   See **lace-curtain**.

curtains   *n.sing.* Death; disaster. 1941: "It looked like curtains for Ezra then and there. But just that moment he saw a chance of salvation." J. Lilienthal, *Horse Crazy,* 13. *From theater use when "curtain" = the lowering of the curtain in front of the stage, signifying the end of the performance.*   —**[for someone]** *n.pl.* Something ominously dire or final for a person; specif., death; the end, as of a career; a knockout; a prison sentence. 1944: ". . . Claims it would be curtains for him [if he drove a car]." Fowler, *Good Night,* 384.

cush   *n.* **1** Money; esp., profit, bribe, or spending money. 1905: "They've put up their good cush to send me on tour. . . ." McHugh, *Search Me,* 63. 1929: "Who hands out the cush?" Burnett, *Little Caesar,* 67, 74. *Common c1930. Now becoming obsolete.* **2** A wallet; esp. one found or stolen. *Both meanings from "cushy" (money easy to obtain).* **3** A form of mush or gruel. *Borrowed from the Gullah slaves by Southern whites, the word has radiated to the more prominent connotation of anything soft or pleasurable, reinforced by "cushion."* → **4** Sex or sexual gratification. See **cuzzy**. **5** Desserts; sweets.   —**ee**   —**y**   *n.* Money.   *adj.* **1** Easy; secure; pleasant; soft. Esp. an easy job, an easy way to earn money, a pleasant way to live, etc. 1951: ". . . Who . . . quit under fire his cushy $15,000 a year lifetime job. . . ." AP, Mar. 22. *Perhaps from "cushion," but maybe from the French "couchée" or "coucher." More probably from the Anglo-Indian "khushi" (pleasant) since the British used the term before it came to the U.S. c1900.* **2** Fancy. 1941: "I may not know a lot of cushy words. . . ." Schulberg, *Sammy,* 126.

cushion   *n.* **1** In baseball, the bag used to mark first, second, or third base; hence the base itself. **2** Money saved for unexpected expenses, emergencies, or one's old age.

cushions, the   *n.sing.* A passenger coach or train; first-class train travel. *Orig. hobo use, c1910; now railroad use.*

cuss   *n.* A fellow. *One of the oldest colloq. words in the U.S.; used by the colonists and still common.*

customer   *n.* A person, usu. a male; a man, guy, fellow. *Usu. preceded by an adj., e.g., "tough customer," "smooth customer."*

cut   *n.* **1** An absence from a college class; the omission of a recitation. 1851: Hall, *College Words,* 90. *Common student use.* **2** A share or percentage of profit; a commission; a share or part. 1958: "Las Vegas gambling interests have been demanding a cut of the Havana take." N.Y. *Post,* Feb. 12, 38. **3** One's turn or try; a chance or opportunity. **4** A derisive comment; a sharp, insulting, deprecatory, critical, or reprimanding remark. *Colloq.* **5** In baseball, a swing at the ball with the bat.   *adj.* **1** Diluted. 1949: "Nifty Louie was pushing a heavily cut grade of morphine." N. Algren, *Man with the Golden Arm,* 31. **2** Shortened; censored; condensed; usu. said of books, movies, plays, a piece of music, etc. **3** Drunk.   *v.t.* **1** In college, to be wilfully absent from a class or lecture. 1858: "Those who cut more than one lecture or prayer in a week received a private admonition. . . ." *Harvard Mag.,* 287. 1952: "(The course at Yale) was cut with a frequency that was ridiculous. . . ." *Atlantic Monthly,* Jan., 20/1f. **2** To refrain from greeting an acquaintance upon meeting him; to ignore an acquaintance. 1914: ". . . He wouldn't stand being cut." S. Lewis. *Our Mr. Wrenn,* 2. **3** To share the winnings or profits. 1930: "Crap games were played . . . with the keeper cutting the game." Lavine, *Third Degree,* 222. **4** To dilute a beverage, esp. whisky or another alcoholic beverage; to dilute drugs. *Colloq.* **5** To delete, shorten, or censor, as a passage of written material, esp. a book. *Universally known.* **6** To put an end to something that one is doing; to stop. 1937: "Cut the comedy, Bogen." Weidman, *Wholesale,* 186. 1952: 1952: "Cut the funnies [jokes] an' git a can-opener." Walt Kelly, "Pogo," *synd. newsp. comic strip,* Oct. 16. *Since c1930. From "cut it out," reinforced by the order a director gives to a movie cameraman, "cut" = stop filming this sequence; cut the roll of film here and use it up to this point, while discarding the rest.* **7** To ignore, evade, or reject someone. **8** To spoil or decrease someone's pleasure, enthusiasm, or happiness. *Since c1940.*

Fig., to dilute, shorten, end, or reject another's happiness. **9** To outdo another, to perform so well or be so intelligent, charming, attractive, or well dressed that one receives more attention than, or preference over, another. 1957: "All of the musicians are primed for a . . . session, i.e., each man will attempt to outdo or cut the others." E. Horne, *For Cool Cats and Far-Out Chicks. Since c1945.* **10** To annoy, bother, or irk another. *v.i.* To leave; to depart for another place. 1856 [1954]: "Let's cut. . . . We ain't no more than just time, providing we step lively." Will Henry, *Death of a Legend,* 5. Cf. **cut out.** *Fig.,* to sever oneself from a place. *v.i., v.t.* To make a phonograph recording; to record. *A groove is actually cut into a record during recording.* **—ter** *n.* **1** A six-shooter gun. 1913: *DAE. Obs.* **2** = **cutor.**

cut A (a) = **cut out.** *Some teenage use since c1955. A euphem. for "cut ass," also a syn. for "cut out."* See Appendix, Shortened Words.

cut a beef   To complain or criticize. 1905: "How often have I told you not to cut a beef about the has-happened?" McHugh, *Search Me,* 15f. *Some c1900 underworld use. Obs.* See **beef.**

cut a melon   To divide unusually large profits. *c1925.*

cut and dried   Routine; familiar; certain; characterized by agreement with known rules, schedules, or the like. 1949: "There was respect, and comradeship, and gratitude in it. Today, it's all cut and dried, and there's no chance for bringing friendship to bear—or personality." A. Miller, *Death of a Salesman,* 81. *Colloq.*

cut and run   To leave and run away; to stop what one is doing and run away; to cut out. 1856 [1954]: "We dassn't stick here and we dassn't cut and run." W. Henry, *Death of a Legend,* 10.

cut a rug   To dance; specif., to jitterbug. 1942: "Wanta cut a rug?" S. Billingsley in *Harper's Bazaar,* July. *Jive use, mostly synthetic.*

cut a rusty   To show joy; to show off. 1837: *DAE. Now dial.*

cut ass [taboo] = **cut out.** *Some teenage use since c1955.*

cut a take   **1** To record a performance; to make a phonograph recording. → **2** To explain something precisely. 1957: "Cutting a take—Explaining a point. In the recording business, literally to make a record." E. Horne, *For Cool Cats and Far-Out Chicks. Cool use.*

cutback   *n.* A reduction, specif. of work or production, as to a previously lower level. *Colloq.*

cut cake   To give short change to circus patrons. *c1930; circus use.*

cut didoes   To be frolicsome. *Colloq; obs.*

cut-dub   *n.* A best friend. *Reformatory use.*

cute   *adj.* Bow-legged. 1905: *Am. Dial. Dict.* 1945 [1943]: *Orphans' home use.*

cuter   **kyuter**   *n.* A U.S. 25-cent piece, a quarter of a dollar. *Vagabond argot, from carnival and circus use.*

cutes, the   *n.* Precocious actions or conduct. 1948: "Lina began flapping her dress to give herself air. Then she got the cutes and asked if that was allowed." Cain, *Moth,* 32.

cutie   **cut(e)y**   *n.* **1** A cute person. **2** Specif., an upstart; one who thinks himself clever. **3** A cute or good-looking person. 1939: "*Pippin* gives place to *peach, cutie,* and *smoothie.*" Hixson, *Word Ways,* 153. **4** A smart prize-fighter. 1938: "Watching a cutey spar with an ordinary dull fighter." Liebling, *Back Where,* 110 (2). **5** Anything that is cute or clever; a song, trick, etc. 1951: "The 'Scandals of '24' started this cutie on the road to fame." Song title. Martha Tilton, CBS, WHCU, Apr. 18. **6** A deception. 1951: ". . . To have you slip over a cutie. . . ." Spillane, *Big Kill,* 65. **7** A clever, charming, but selfish or unethical person.

cutie-pie   **cutie pie**   *n.* A cute person; a small, alert, energetic, winsome person. 1948: "The cutie pies got eighty cents a Sunday for [singing in the choir]." Cain, *Moth,* 12.

cut-in   *n.* A share; a "cut." 1937: "We've each got a cut-in on the profits." Weidman, *Wholesale,* 131.   **cut in** *v.i.* **1** To intercept a dancing couple; said of a male who then asks the female to dance with him. *Colloq.* **2** To interrupt; to give unasked for advice or opinion.

cut it   To stop [doing something]. *c1930.*

cut it off   To sleep. *Suggested by "saw wood"* = *to sleep.* 1930: "Boy, you sure was cutting it off. A buzz-saw ain't got nothing on you." Burnett, *Iron Man,* 7.

cut it out   An order or a plea for someone to stop what he is doing, esp. to stop annoying, bothering, teasing, or riding another. 1939: "Why don't you cut it out?" J. T. Farrell, 181. *Very common with children in 8-12-year-old age group, although common with adults.*

cut no ice   To have no effect; to make

no impression. 1896: *DAE.* 1902: "Dere preachin' cuts no ice wid me an' you." Coley, *Rubaiyat of the East Side,* 1. 20. *Colloq.*

cut off [someone's] water = **turn off [someone's] water.**

cutor *n.* **1** A prosecuting attorney; a prosecutor. 1926: "[A term] always used in the wobbly press . . . the word had its origin in crook circles." *Amer. Mercury,* Jan., 63. 1939: "She gets [the D. A.] to beg the kid off with the U.S. 'cutor." Chandler, *Big Sleep,* 45. **2** The joker in a deck of playing cards. *Never common.*

cut out ‑ **1** To leave, usu. to leave quickly, suddenly, secretly, or permanently; to depart. 1912: "Let's cut out." Johnson, *Stover at Yale,* 83. 1954: "I was not going to wait. I cut out." L. Armstrong, *Satchmo, My Life in New Orleans,* 123. 1957: "So you think you're cutting out? . . . you're not leaving until I leave with you." Tennessee Williams, *Orpheus Descending,* III. *Wide student use since c1940; some teenage and young adult use.* **2** To refrain from; to give up; to stop. 1905: "I've been speculating again after faithfully promising her to cut out all the guessing contests. So cut out the yesterday gag. . . ." McHugh, *Search Me,* 27, 28.

cut-plug *n.* An inferior horse. 1861 [1954]: "He [Jesse James] pulled the black in, easing him off to a disdainful hand-gallop. He could hold this gait all day, and gain a yard a minute on such cut-plugs as those back yonder." W. Henry, *Death of a Legend,* 48.

cut-rate cut rate *adj.* Offered at less than the usual price; cheap. *Colloq.* *n.*

A stingy person; a cheap skate. *Never common.*

cut the mouth *imp.* Shut up; keep quiet. *Reformatory use.*

cutting out [paper] dolls (dollies) Crazy. 1942: ". . . I noticed she bullied her." "It isn't just that. She has her cutting out dolls. . . ." Chandler, *High Window,* 117.

cut up **1** To meet in order to divide loot, gambling winnings, or the like. *Underworld use. From "cut up the touches."* → **2** To reminisce or gossip; to discuss. 1950: "Eddie and Pete talk the job over—'cut it up,' they say." "Heistmen with whom I have cut up this situation." DeBaun, 72, 76. **3** To joke; to play pranks; to misbehave. 1905: "Peaches thought I was only cutting up." McHugh, *Search Me,* 106. **4** To be humorous and lively. *Colloq.* **cut-up** *n.* **1** A prankster; a practical joker. *Colloq. since c1890.* 1914: "Ain't he the cut-up!" S. Lewis, *Our Mr. Wrenn,* 17. **2** An expert. *Not common.* **3** A jocular, pleasantly boisterous, entertaining person. *c1890* [1955]: "Al Burns was a great cutup. He could dance a bit, sing better than average, and had a sense of comedy that made him top the amateur minstrel shows." H. R. Hoyt, *Town Hall Tonight,* 189.

cut up [the] touches (pipes, jackpots) **1** Lit., to meet in order to divide loot. *Underworld use.* → **2** To reminisce; to gossip. *Dial.*

cuzzy [taboo] *n.* Sexual intercourse; the vagina. 1937: "What's more important than cuzzy?" Weidman, *Wholesale,* 4.

cylinder *n.* A cylindrical phonograph record. *c1915; obs.* Cf. **disc, platter.**

D

D.A. **1** Stand. abbr. for district attorney. **2** A teenage boys' hair style in which the hair is kept thick and long and combed straight back from the top and sides; strands of hair from the top and sides overlap at the back of the neck, resembling the arrangement of a duck's tailfeathers. *Common rock and roll use since c1954. From the resemblance to a duck's tailfeathers or duck's ass; an abbr. for "duck's ass."* See Appendix, Shortened Words.

dace *n.* Two cents; small change. *Obs. From the small fish called a "dace."*

dad *n.* Euphem for "God" in certain mild oaths like "dad-blamed," etc. *Colloq.*

dad-blamed *adj.* Darned. *Colloq.*
dad-blasted *adj.* Darned. *Colloq.*
dad burn Gosh darn. *Colloq.*
daddy *n.* A male lover, esp. one who supports his paramour in return for her sexual favors; one who keeps a mistress. c1912: "My little Daddy lovin' all the time." From "Daddy," pop. song. 1945: "I loved my daddy./But what did my daddy do?/Found him a brown-skin chicken/What's it gonna be/Black and

blue." G. Brooks, *A Street in Bronzeville*, 40. *Clipped form of "sugar daddy."* *Replaced "sugar daddy" c1935. A "daddy" is usu. older than a "John." c1940 a song pop. by Mary Martin, "My Heart Belongs to Daddy," includes the lines, "Good night and thank you, laddie, the evening's been perfectly swell./ But my heart belongs to daddy, because my daddy he treats me so well!" Thus, "daddy" is not young enough to be a "laddie," and he is loved only because he treats the girl "well" financially. Thus a "daddy" or "sugar daddy" is often older and wealthier than a "John," for whom the girl may have a genuinely fond attachment.* See **John, sugar daddy.**

Daddy-o **daddy-o** *n.* An affectionate term of direct address for any male who is hip, understanding, or sympathetic, whether a father or not. 1956: "Big Daddy-o's coming home." T. Williams, *Cat on a Hot Tin Roof*, I. 1958: "Daddy-o likes Nuco." Billboard advt. *Orig. bop use c1946; now one of the most common —o words.*

daffodil *n.* A homily, proverb, or aphorism. 1927: "Pope was like Ben Franklin who was always getting up little daffodils." *AS*, 2, 261.

daffy *adj.* Crazy. *Colloq.* 1915: "He tries to convince her that she is not daffy. . . ." S. J. Perelman, *New Yorker*, Oct. 20, 29/2. **—dill** *n.* An insane person. *From "daffy" plus a form of "daffodil."* 1935: "Take your pick whether Cecil is a genius or a daffydill." Runyon.

—daffy See Appendix, Suffixes and Suffix Words.

daffy about In love with; crazy about. 1932: "I do not blame . . . Jack . . . for going daffy about her." Runyon.

dag *v.t.* To jab or injure; esp. to stab. 1945 [1943]: "I'll dag you." E. Kasser. *Orphans' home use.*

dagged *adj.* Drunk.

dag-nabbed *adj.* Darned; doggoned. 1945: "It's this dag-nabbed housing shortage." NEA item, Memphis, Tenn., Dec. 18.

dago **Dago** *n.* **1** A Latin of the working class, usu. a Spaniard. 1832: *DAE. Archaic.* Cf. **spic. 2** An Italian; a person of Italian descent. 1887: *DAE.* 1901: "*Dago* is a queer misnomer. It must come from the Spanish *Diego*, yet is usually applied to Italians." Greenough & Kittredge, 66. 1908: "The Italian 'Dago' is looked down upon by the Irish." W. Z. Ripley in *Atlantic Monthly*, Dec., 753/1. 1937 [1954]: "Six floors

below, the contractor called, 'Hey, Geremio! Is your gang of dagos dead!'" P. di Donato, *Christ in Concrete*, reprinted in *Manhattan*, 135. 1948: "I can still hear . . . the kids . . . Hey, Fiorello, you're a dago." Fiorello H. La Guardia, *"The Making of an Insurgent, An Autobiography: 1882–1919*, 27. *Sometimes derog; usu. derisive.* Cf. **wop. 3** The Spanish language. 1901: [U.S. use.] *OED Sup. Archaic.* **4** The Italian language. *Since c1900.* **5** Macaroni. *Not common. Because it is the traditional food of Italians.* *adj.* [derog.] Italian.

dago bomb **Dago bomb** A white spherical firecracker. *Child use c1935.* Cf. **golf ball.**

dago red **1** Italian red wine; any cheap red wine. *Hobo sl.; became pop. during prohibition.* **2** Italian wine, specif. red Chianti. 1906: "Casks of wine (real 'Dago red') . . ." Frank W. Aitken and Edward Hilton, *A History of the Earthquake and Fire in San Francisco*, 120.

dagwood *n.* A gigantic sandwich. *From "Dagwood," a character in a synd. comic strip.* Cf. **Coney Island, Hero, poor boy, torpedo.**

daily double Success in two fields of endeavor simultaneously; winning or obtaining any two different prizes, goals, or the like. 1956: "108-pound businessman Eddie Arcaro has made a couple of million dollars traveling at high speeds on thoroughbred horses. Which explains his daily double with the New York Times sports section and financial section." N.Y. *Post*, Sept. 11, 19. *From the betting term, a combination bet on two successive races.*

daisies, the *n.pl.* In baseball the outfield. *1943 baseball use.* See **push up the daisies.**

daisy *n.* **1** Any excellent, remarkable, or admirable person or thing; a choice specimen; a honey. 1903: "That's a daisy." E. Conradi. *Colloq. Used as early as 1750 in U.S.* **2** Specif., a pretty girl. 1900: "Hello. You're a daisy." Dreiser, *Carrie*, 42. **3** A freckle. *Usu. pl.: "daisies." Beauty-parlor use.* **4** A male homosexual, usu. one who takes the female role; a male pervert. *c1940; archaic. Because flowers, as the daisy, are considered as appealing esp. to females.* See **pansy. 5** A grave; death. *From "pushing up daisies." adj.* Excellent. *c1880.* 1912: "We had a daisy bunch of boys at prep school. . . ." Johnson, *Stover at Yale*, 3. *adv.* Very. 1893: ". . . The other slang synonyms for *very* [are] *jolly . . : awfully . . .* and *daisy. . . .*" Brander Matthews, *Harper's*, July, 308/1. See **turn up one's toes to the daisies.**

daisy chain [taboo] The act or an instance of several persons having sexual intercourse with each other at the same time; a group or "chain" of persons involved in mutual, simultaneous sexual activity. 1951: "The screened, discreet box at the Comique led to an unbelievably evil circus at the Casino ('Oh, them daisy chains,' said Condon)." S. Longstreet, *The Pedlocks*, 102.

daisy-cutter *n.* **1** In baseball, a hit ball that skims the ground; a grounder. 1868: *DAE. Still in use.* **2** A tennis ball that skims the ground. 1897: *DAE. Still in use.* **3** A horse that, when trotting, does not lift its feet far off the ground. **4** An antipersonnel, shrapnel bomb, set to explode close to the ground. *Some W.W.II Army use.*

dally See **dilly-dally.**

damaged *adj.* Drunk.

dame *n.* A woman or girl, esp. a troublesome one. 1902: "De frowsy dames." Coley, *Rubaiyat of the East Side*, l. 33. 1933: "When I fallen for a little 'dame' in a jitney dance hall. . . ." G. Milburn in *Amer. Mercury*, Aug., 490/1. *Orig. "dame" implied a young woman considered attractive but not wholly respectable by the speaker. Depending on the emphasis, it can now mean a promiscuous woman (prob. the most freq. use since c1940), a sexually attractive woman, an unemotional, sexless woman worker, or even an ugly old woman.*

damn **darn** *v.t.* To condemn a person or thing as without value; to judge someone or something as worthless. *Colloq.* *adj.* Complete, hopeless. Used to intensify a derog. statement. *Colloq.* *expl.* A curse or epithet of anger, disappointment, or frustration. *Not now generally considered taboo.*

damned **darned** *adj.* = **damn, darn.** *expl.* = **damn, darn.**

damper *n.* **1** That which discourages; that which reduces the joy of success, expectation, or a good time; lit., that which "dampens" one's enthusiasm, spirit, or pleasure. *Colloq.* **2** A cash register; a drawer or compartment where money is kept, as by a store or business that has no cash register. 1939: "Chip damper = money drawer." Howsley. 1947: "You're too little to reach the damper." N. Algren, *The Face. Circus, hobo, and underworld use since c1925.* → **3** A bank. **4** Fig., a treasury.

1951: "The government racket has collected countless millions [in taxes] and the Roosevelt-Truman administrations have squandered every dime, dropping bonds into the damper which are then sold to the public." W. Pegler, *synd. newsp. col.*, Aug. 14.

damper on, put a To discourage; to dampen the enthusiasm of; to spoil another person's pleasure. Cf. **damper.**

damper pad A bankbook; a check book. *Some underworld use since c1930; not common.* See **damper.**

Dan See **fancy Dan.**

dance *v.i.* **1** To die by hanging. *Obs.* **2** To be in the power or control of another; to be forced to be subservient to another, as through threats, blackmail, or because one has a dominating boss, wife, or the like. *n.* A street fight between gangs of boys; a rumble. 1944: "With Harlem's per capita income high, the kids have plenty of time for pushing a dance." W. Davenport in *Collier's*, Sept. 23, 92/2.

dance, go into [one's] **1** To come to the point. *Theater use. Obs.* **2** To "tell a line."

dance-hall *n.* **1** A prison death-house; a room where condemned prisoners are put to death. **2** An anteroom to a prison electrocution chamber; cells where condemned prisoners spend their last hours.

dance off To die. 1939: "If you don't dance off up in Quentin. . . ." Chandler, *Big Sleep*, 84 f.

dance on air To die by hanging. 1934: "It don't cost me a thing to make you dance on air." Cain, *Postman*, 109.

dance on nothing To be hanged. *Obs.* Cf. **dance.**

dancer *n.* **1** A fickle person who changes sweethearts often. *Archaic.* **2** A coward, as a prize fighter who spends much time "dancing" away from or evading an opponent.

dance the carpet To appear before an official for an investigation of one's work or behavior, or, specif., to receive a reprimand, criticism, or punishment. See **on the carpet.**

D and D *n.* **1** Drunk and disorderly. *A common police charge in arrests of troublemakers.* **2** Deaf and dumb. → **3** Fig., deaf and dumb, i.e., afraid of telling what one knows or has heard; fear of fighting for one's rights. *N.Y.C. longshoreman and underworld use since c1950, because many who have complained* *or testified against illegal or unethical practices of the longshoremen's union have been beaten, threatened, or otherwise silenced.* See Appendix, Shortened Words.

dander up, get [one's]   To make someone become angry or concerned; to become angry or concerned.

dandy   *n.* An excellent thing or person. *Since c1785. Colloq.   adj.* Fine; excellent; first-rate. 1792: *DAE.* 1949: "A dandy present." Advt. in N.Y. *Times*, Oct. 2, 83/2. *Colloq.   adv.* Splendidly. 1952: "She and her husband get along just dandy." Bob Thomas, AP, Sept. 12.

dang   dange [taboo]   *n.* The penis. *adj.* Sexy, sexually stimulating or attractive. See **ding-dang.**

dange broad   A sexually attractive Negro girl or young woman.

dangler   *n.* A trapeze performer. *Circus use.* 1944: "He started rushing a dangler." Cliff Macon, *Collier's*, Sept. 16, 64/3.

Daniel Boone, pull a   To vomit. *Some jocular student use c1910–c1935. From the pun on the stand. and sl. meaning of the word "shoot" in the familiar sentence found in all stories about Daniel Boone, "Daniel Boone went out and shot his breakfast."*

Dan O'Leary   See **do a Dan O'Leary.**

dap   *n.* A white person. *Some Negro student use.*

darb   *n.* Any remarkable or excellent person or thing, as an apartment, a house, a vest, a story; a lulu; a honey. Also in "the darb." 1924: "We're going to have a swell joint here. Quite the darb. Three rooms, you know...." Marks, *Plastic Age*, 9. 1930: "I had . . . vests that ranged from a few modest ones . . . all the way up to a darb of flaming red with large pearl buttons. . . ." O. O. McIntyre, *Outlook*, Sept. 3, 8/3. *Obs.*

darbies   derbies   *n.* Handcuffs; orig. manacles or fetters. *c1850 maritime and underworld use. Used in 1850 ed. of Herman Melville's "White-Jacket."*

darbs, the   A person with money who can be relied upon to pay for food, entertainment, etc. 1922: Phila. *Eve. Bulletin*, March 8. *Flapper use.*

darby   *n.* Money.

darby cove   A blacksmith.

dark   *adj.* Closed; said of a theater, sports arena, or other place of entertainment, whether or not lighted by artificial lights. 1958: "Bowie [racetrack] Dark Again [headline:] Bowie racetrack closed

again today for the eighth day in the past month." N.Y. *Post*, Mar. 20. *Orig. theater use.   —y   n.* A Negro. *Colloq. c1770.*

dark, in the   Uninformed; not aware of current attitudes or happenings.

dark cloud   A Negro. *Some c1900 dial. use.*

dark horse   1 An entry in a contest, such as a horse race or other sporting match, which is unknown or seems to have little chance of winning; fig., an unknown contestant for a prize, job, honor, or the like, whose chances for success are better than generally supposed. *From horse racing use → 2* Specif., a surprise candidate for public office in an election; one nominated without advance publicity. 1884: *DAE.* 1943: "The only sharp thing to do is to run an unknown, a dark horse." M. Shulman, *Barefoot Boy with Cheek*, 161. **3** A night watchman. *Some c1930 underworld use.*

dark meat   1 [taboo] A Negro considered as an object of sexual gratification; the vagina of a Negress. See **meat.   2** In roulette, black. 1934: " 'What would you like to do?' 'Bet the wad —dark meat!' " Chandler, *Finger Man*, 11. *Not common.*

dark-setting   *n.* **1** Necking, petting, or courting a Negro girl, esp. a very dark complexioned one. *Some c1930 Negro use.* **2** Necking or petting in complete seclusion at night. *Prison use. A white man's adaptation of the Negro term.*

darning needle   See **rain pitchforks.**

darter   See **joe-darter.**

dash   *v.t.* To darn or damn. *More common in Eng. than in U.S.*

date   *n.* **1** An engagement or appointment, esp. and usu. with one of the opposite sex. See **blind date, heavy date.** 1885—1914: *Colloq. DAE.* **2** A social escort or partner of the opposite sex. 1925: "The developments of the word *date* from the meaning 'point of time' to . . . 'social engagement' and now into an agent-noun 'escort.' 'My date was late last evening.' " Louise Pound. 1949: "Just the Place To Take Your Date." Advt., Cornell Univ. *Daily Sun*, Oct. 14, 7.   *v.i., v.t.* To make or have a social engagement or engagements (with one of the opposite sex). *All uses so common as to be standard.*

date bait   An attractive, popular girl. 1957: "The love coach is an institution in our newspapers, telling Miss Anxious whether or not to tolerate a boy's hand on her waist the first evening out. And a whole library of books has been written on 'How to Be Date Bait.' " F. Morton, *The Art of Courtship*, 157. *Some teenage use since c1940. Freq. use by newsp. columnists.* See Appendix, Rhyming Slang.

date mate   A person that one goes on a date with, esp. one's steady date or sweetheart. 1950: "He soon grows weary of the chase and finds himself a date mate who'll wait to be dated." S. J. Daly, Syracuse (N.Y.) *Post-Standard*, Aug. 22, 12. *Some teenage use c1945. Never pop. Based on "date bait."* See Appendix, Rhyming Slang.

Dave   *n.* The shoe width D. *Retail shoe-salesman use.*

David   *n.* The shoe width D.

day   See **eagleday, ninety-day wonder.**

daylight (sunlight) into, let   To clarify one's thoughts or thinking on a specif. subject; to contribute facts or ideas to a specif. discussion.

daylights   *n.pl.* Consciousness; sense; life; brains or other vital organs, as "to knock the (living) daylights out of somebody."

day the eagle screams, the = **day the eagle shits, the.** *A euphem.*

day the eagle shits, the [taboo]   Pay day. *Orig. and mainly Armed Forces use; wide W.W.II Army use. The eagle represents the national symbol and thus the soldiers' employer or paymaster; reinforced by eagle symbol on U.S. currency.*

de—   See Appendix, Prefixes and Prefix Words.

deac   *n.* A deacon. 1821: *DAE.* 1913: "Look at her, deac!" *SEP*, Feb. 1, 34. See Appendix, Shortened Words.

deacon seat   The long seat along the edge of bunks in a bunkhouse. *Hobo and woodsman use.*

dead   *n.* **1** A complete failure in reciting; also, a statement that one is not prepared to recite. 1827–1851: *DAE. College slang. Obs.* 1951: Hall, *College Words*, 91. **2** A letter or package that cannot be delivered or returned to the sender, because of an incomplete or illegible address, lack of forwarding address, or the like. *Post office use.* *v.t.* To cause (a student) to fail in reciting by asking hard questions. 1851: "Have I been . . . deaded . . .?" Hall, *College Words*, 91. *Obs.* *v.i.* To be unable to recite in class. *College*

slang.   *adj.* **1** Exhausted; dead tired; said of a person. 1934: "For two days after that I was dead. . . ." Cain, *Postman*, 9. 1934: *Colloq. Web.* **2** Not working; said of a mechanism. **3** Considered and rejected; said of a plan or scheme. **4** Empty; usu. said of a beer or whisky bottle. **5** Having no chance of success; without further opportunity; said of a person. **6** Boring, dull, unexciting. **7** Completely, entirely. *In certain specific expressions, like "dead level" = completely true or honest; "dead set against it" = completely opposed to something; "dead broke" = entirely without funds; etc. Colloq.* See **drop dead!; on the dead.**   —**beat**   **dead beat** *n.* **1** A worthless person, specif. one who does not pay his debts; one who depends on the generosity of others; a moocher. **2** A hobo or tramp riding free on a train. 1891: "The Southern railways are perhaps the most hostile to these dead beats." J. Flynt. **3** Hence, any tramp or hobo. 1913: "[In American movies] 'tramp' gives way to . . . 'hobo' or 'dead beat.' " Faulkner, London *Daily Mail* [*Lit. Digest*].   *v.i.* To loaf or sponge. —**er**   *n.* **1** An exhausted person. *c1881. Used in Great Lakes region.* **2** A dead person.

dead, on the   Honestly. *Never common. From "on the (dead) level."*

dead as a dodo   Completely, irrevocably, and finally "dead," forgotten, or dismissed. See **dodo.**

dead ass [taboo]   **1** A stupid, boring, or worthless person; an insensitive person; one who is not hip; fig., one who is too stupid or insensitive to feel pain if kicked in the posterior. **2** To leave or be forced to leave; to depart speedily but with regret; to be embarrassed or feel square because one has to leave a desirable gathering or enjoyable party. *Prob. reinforced by "deadhead." Both uses orig. c1950 bop use.*

dead broke   Penniless; entirely without money. 1925: "He came to us dead broke." F. S. Fitzgerald, *The Great Gatsby*, 143. See **broke.**

dead cat   A lion, tiger, or leopard that does not perform, but is merely exhibited. 1939: *Circus use. SEP*, Mar. 25.

dead duck   Any person or thing that is doomed to failure, extinction, or the like, or that has died or failed; a goner. 1948: "The hotel grills and roofs . . . were dead ducks by now. . . ." Lait-Mortimer, *N.Y. Confidential*, 27.

deadfall *n.* A night-club or all-night restaurant; a clip joint. 1837–1911: A low saloon or gambling dive. *DAE. Colloq. or slang.* 1950: "At 16 Jimmy Durante got his first regular job in a deadfall in Coney Island known as Diamond Tony's." M. Zolotow, *SEP*, July 15, 122/4.

deadhead **dead-head** *n.* **1** A nonpaying spectator, as at the theater, a sports event, or the like. 1843: *DAE.* 1909: "The forest-covered slopes of Deadhead Hill, whose summit rim is always outlined in black by the crowding figures of the deadheads assembled to see the game." O. D. von Engeln, *At Cornell,* 319. *Archaic.* Cf. **cuffo, free-loader. 2** A nonpaying guest or customer; a passenger who rides free, as on a train, bus, or cab; one who is a guest of the management and need not pay. **3** A train, freight car, bus, cab, or truck carrying no passenger or freight, as on a return trip to a terminal. 1950: ". . . A deadhead, an empty mail car." A. Lomax, *Mr. Jelly Roll,* 109. **4** A stupid or incompetent person. *v.i.* To drive an empty taxi, as on a return trip, with no prospect of a passenger; to drive an empty truck, bus, or train; to travel empty, without passengers or freight. 1929: "He [a taxi driver] has to deadhead all the way back." G. Milburn in *Folk-Say,* 111. 1958: "We should charge a dollar extra to the motel because we have to deadhead back to town." *Oral,* taxi driver, Louisville, Ky., Aug. 25. *Orig. railroad use.*

dead heat A tie between two or more contestants. 1956: "DEAD HEAT—A tie between two or more horses." T. Betts, *Across the Board,* 314. *Colloq. Orig. horse racing use; mainly sports use.*

dead horse An issue, argument, or incident that does not affect or have any meaning to the present; an unfortunate incident or issue that cannot be rectified and is best forgotten; fig., something that one has used up but not yet paid for; an unpaid debt for something that no longer exists. *From traditional expression "to flog a dead horse." Since c1830. Colloq.*

dead hour An hour during which college classes are held but during which a given student does not have a class. *Student use since c1920.*

deadlights *n.pl.* The eyes. 1877: *Slang. DAE.* 1934: *Maritime slang. Web.*

deadly *adj.* Excellent. 1941: "An orchestra that . . . sends . . . is called deadly. . . ." *Life,* Jan. 27, 78. *Jive use.*

dead man's hand **1** In the card game of poker, a hand containing a pair of aces and a pair of eights (aces over eights). *So called because Wild Bill Hickok was reportedly holding just such a hand when Jack McCall shot him in the back at Deadwood in 1876.* → **2** Bad luck or misfortune of any kind; entering an endeavor or contest at a disadvantage.

dead marine = **dead soldier.**

dead one *n.* **1** A hobo who has retired from the road; also, a stingy person. *Hobo lingo.* **2** An inefficient, dull person.

dead pan **deadpan** *n.* **1** An expressionless face; a poker face. Cf. **pan** *n.,* **1.** 1934: "I tried some comical stuff, but all I got was a dead pan. . . ." Cain, *Postman,* 1. **2** A person who keeps his face expressionless. Said specif. of an entertainer while performing. 1935: *Peabody Bulletin,* Dec., 42/2. *adj.* Straight-faced; facially expressionless. 1938: "This is known as the deadpan system of prevarication." Liebling, *Back Where,* 34. 1951: "It's enough to make even deadpan Gromyko laugh." Letter, N.Y. *Daily News,* Sept. 12, 11C/5.

dead pigeon One who is sure to meet death, disaster, or failure; one who has no chance to succeed or escape disaster; a goner; a dead duck. 1941: "Either you plunk for Merriam around here or you're a dead pigeon." Schulberg, *Sammy,* 102. 1951: "Unless somebody would start this mob to the sugar bowl, I was a dead pigeon." M. Shulman, *Dobie Gillis,* 77.

dead president Any U.S. banknote; a piece of paper money.

dead ringer A duplicate; a person, animal, or thing that very closely resembles another person, animal, or thing; a double; a ringer. 1891: "Homan is a 'dead-ringer' for Anson." N.Y. *Sporting Times,* July 4, 10/4. 1937: "He was such a dead ringer for my ex-boss. . . ." Weidman, *Wholesale,* 38.

dead soldier (marine) *n.* **1** An empty bottle, esp. an empty beer or whisky bottle. 1929: "His aim with a dead soldier was unnerving." Winkler in *New Yorker,* Feb. 9, 40f. **2** Food or a plate of food served at a meal but only partially consumed; leftovers; table scraps. c1920 [1954]: "On the way to the kitchen with the dead soldiers, or leftovers. . . ." L. Armstrong, *Satchmo, My Life in New Orleans,* 215. *Not common.*

dead to rights   **1** Certain. *c1880*. *Colloq.* 1939: "You've got him dead to rights. . . ." Gardner, *D. A. Draws*, 185. **2** Caught in the act of or irrefutably accused of an illegal, immoral, unethical, or antisocial act.

dead to the world   **1** Drunk, esp. unconscious from drinking. *Since at least 1875.* See Appendix, Drunk. **2** Sound asleep. *Now the more common use.*

dead wagon   A vehicle, now usu. an automobile, used for carrying a corpse or corpses; a hearse. 1937 [1932]: "Calling the dead wagon for a nice ride downtown to the morgue with the stiff. . . ." H. Johanson, *Atlantic Monthly*, Dec., 775/2.

dead wood   deadwood   **1** Any useless item, esp. one that is a nuisance to carry. **2** A useless person; one who does not contribute to work or festivity. **3** Specif., an unsold theater ticket or block of tickets.

deal   *n.* An unethical transaction or agreement from which both parties benefit; an unethical agreement, the trading of favors. Specif., the securing of favored treatment by extortion or bribery. 1958: "He [a senator] had made a deal with the Republicans, these sources say, to suppress the charges against the FCC in return for their votes for the natural gas bill. Until Wednesday night the deal was on. Then . . . the deal was off." Robert G. Spivack, "The Deal That Didn't Come Off," N.Y. *Post*, Jan. 24, 4.   *v.t.* To pass food at the table. *Not common.* *v.i.* To be independently active in many varied businesses or social enterprises; to be able to make many plans and decisions; to be in command, authority, or control. 1949: "[He] didn't want to go home. Sophie [his wife] did all the dealing there." N. Algren, *Man with the Golden Arm*, 33.   **—er**   *n.* **1** Anyone who makes a living from gambling, as a casino employee, bookmaker, or card sharp, whether or not an actual dealer of cards. 1956: "A bookmaker, who is known as a dealer in refined usage. . . ." T. Betts, *Across the Board*, 317. **2** One involved in many schemes and plans; one with a varied and active social or business life. See **deal**. **3** A professional gambler, whether actually a dealer of cards or not. 1949: "He was the best dealer on Chicago's West Division Street, and he dealt the cards all night every night. . . ." A. C. Spectorsky, N.Y. *Times Bk. Rev.*, Sept. 11, 8.

deal in coal   [derog.]   **1** To associate with very dark-skinned Negroes. *Negro use.* **2** To mix with Negroes; said of whites.

deal them off the arm   To wait on table. 1934: "After she gets through dealing them off the arm all day her feet generally pain her. . . ." Runyon.

deaner   *n.* A dime [10¢]. In Eng., a shilling. See **deemer**.

deano   *n.* A month. *Thief use.*

dearie   *n.* One who is dear. *A vulgar endearment often used jocularly in direct address.* See Appendix, —ie ending.

Dear John   Orig. a letter to a soldier from his wife asking for a divorce; now a letter to a male fiancé informing him that the engagement is broken; any letter of dismissal from one's sweetheart. *Orig. W.W.II Armed Forces use.*

deb   *n.* **1** A debutante. 1924: "Society debs." A. Lewis in *Lit. Digest*, 28. See Appendix, Shortened Words. **2** A girl member of an adolescent street gang. *Orig. teenage use; since c1945.*

debunk   *v.t.* To prove a lie or an exaggeration to be false; to reduce another's stature or reputation by exposing his misdeeds. 1923: "Why, de-bunking means simply taking the bunk out of things." W. E. Woodward in *Word Study*, Dec., 5/2. See **bunk**.

decay   *n.* **1** The loss in mass of a radioactive substance during any specific time. **2** The loss in speed of a guided missile or man-made earth satellite during any specific time, owing to gravity and friction. *Rocketry use.*

deceiver   *n.* See **falsies**.

deck   *n.* **1** A pack of playing cards. 1853: *DAE. Now stand.* Cf. **cold deck**. → **2** A strong or good hand of cards. **3** The roof of a railroad car, as a passenger car. 1853: *DAE. Still hobo and railroad use.* **4** A package of narcotics wrapped in paper or an envelope; a portion of a drug. 1949: "A deck of nose candy for sale." J. Evans, *Halo*, 24. *Drug addict use since c1920.* **5** A package of cigarettes. 1952: "I got me a deck of butts." L. Stander in *Esquire*, June, 131/1.   *v.t.* To knock someone down; to floor someone with a blow of the fist. 1953: "They might wheel and deck me." Bing Crosby, *SEP*, Apr. 4, 118/4.

deck, hit the   **1** To be knocked down. *Since c1930, common boxing use. From nautical use.* **2** To get up out of bed; to rise. *Orig. maritime use. Wide W.W.II Army use.* See **deck**.

deck, on   **1** In baseball, next at bat; said of a player, esp. if he is in the area marked for batters waiting their turn at bat. *Since c1900; appar. from the nautical use.* **2** Present; on hand and ready for work, play, etc.; said of a person. *From nautical use, but strongly reinforced by the baseball term.*

deck hand   *n.* A stage hand. *Theater stage hand use.*

decks awash   Drunk.

decode   *v.t.* To explain.

decrease the volume   To speak lower. *Teenage use since c1950; usu. a command or entreaty.*

deduck   *n.* An item or an amount deducted from one's taxable income.

dee-dee = D and D.

dee-donk   *n.* A Frenchman. *Not common.*

deejay   DJ   D.J.   d.j.   = disc jockey. *Orig. radio use; common use since c1945.* 1956: "... Some 1,200 radio disc jockeys ... journeyed to Nashville ... to attend Dee-Jay (for disk jockey) convention. Officials for music and record companies also attended. *Life*, Nov. 19, 143. *From "disc jockey."* See Appendix, —jockey; Shortened Words. **2** An F.B.I. man, operating in the Dept. of Justice. *From the initials.* 1949: "The Dee-Jays." A. Hynd, *Public Enemies*, 111, 112 (2).

deek   *n.* A detective; a dick.

deemer   *n.* **1** A dime. *Vagabond argot, from carnival and circus men.* **2** Any small gratuity or tip, whether a dime or not. **3** One who gives a small tip; a cheapskate. **4** Ten.

deener   See **deaner; deemer.**

deepie   *n.* A three-dimension stereographic movie; a depthie. 1953: "The deepies released so far have been ... gimmick pictures. ..." AP, Hollywood, Aug. 24.

deep-sea chef   A dishwasher. *Hobo use.*

deep-sea turkey   Salmon. *W.W.I USN and Army use. From the serving of salmon on holidays.*

deep six   A grave. *Assoc. with jive and jazz use, esp. bop and cool use since c1946.*

defi   defy   *n.* Defiance; a notice or act of defiance. 1930: "A Hip Sing was sent to paste, on a signboard, a defi to the On Leongs." Lavine, *Third Degree*, 90. *Some common c1925 use.* See Appendix, Shortened Words.

degree   See **third degree.**

dehorn   *n.* **1** Anything in opposition to the teachings or beliefs of the International Workers of the World; anything that diverts an I.W.W. member from the class struggle, such as liquor or gambling. *c1925 I.W.W. use.* → **2** Specif., bootleg whisky or denatured alcohol. 1926: "*Dehorn* means bootleg booze." J. Lance in *Amer. Mercury*, Apr., xxx. *c1925 I.W.W. use; hobo use.* → **3** A drunkard, esp. one who drinks bootleg whisky, specif. one who drinks denatured alcohol; a drunken bum. 1951: "The Jollity Theater in Minneapolis is patronized largely by vagrants, winos, dehorns, grifters. ..." M. Shulman, *Dobie Gillis*, 215. **4** A disliked person. *Never common.*

dekko   *n.* A look. *W.W.I use, from Hindustani "deiko" to look, by way of the regular British army. Still more common in Eng. than in U.S.*

delicatessen   *n.* **1** Bullets. 1918: "As he goes over the German lines, 'Archies' ... send him delicatessen. ..." McCartney, *Texas Rev.*, 79. **2** The food commonly associated with delicatessens: cold sliced meats, smoked fish, vegetable salads, hard-crusted rye bread, dill pickles, etc.; specif., a meal consisting of these items. *Mainly N.Y.C. use.* **3** A business office. 1952: *Adman jargon. Management Rev.*, Oct., 688.

delish   *adj.* Delicious. 1951: "Gee, that was a delish dinner." M. Shulman, *Dobie Gillis*, 52. *A fairly common shortening.* See Appendix, Shortened Words.

delly   dellie   *n.* = **delicatessen.** See Appendix, Shortened Words.

demi-rep   *n.* A woman of questionable reputation. *Used in Eng. since c1750 and still more common there than in U.S. Patterned after Fr. "demimondaine" = a worldly woman of dubious or mysterious background.*

Demo   *n.* A member of the Democratic party. 1793: *DAE.* 1952: "The old-line Demos." R. C. Ruark, *synd. newsp. col.*, July 18. See Appendix, Shortened Words.

demo   *n.* **1** A member of a squad or a squad of demolition workers. *From "demolition."* See Appendix, Shortened Words. *Not common.* **2** A phonograph record made for demonstration purposes, to display the talents of a singer or musician or the merits of a new song to booking agents, bands, radio stations, and the like. *From "demonstration."* See Appendix, Shortened Words. **3** A demerit. *West Point use since c1930.* See Appendix, —o ending.   *adj.* Demolitional. *Some W.W.II Armed Forces use.* See Appendix, Shortened Words.

demon   n. A dime; the sum of 10¢. *c1935 jive use.*

den   n. A house, apartment, or room.

departee   n. One who leaves a theater at intermission. 1949: "Door checks are not issued to the departees. . . ." Richard Maney, N.Y. *Times Mag.*, June 5, 22.

depthie   n. A three-dimensional stereographic movie; a deepie. 1953: "Three-dimensional depthies . . . are luring movie-goers. . . ." AP, June 30.

derbies   See **darbies.**

Derbyville   proper n. Louisville, Kentucky. 1958: "Mayor Bruce Hoblitzell of Derbyville." *The Morning Telegraph,* Apr. 30, 3. *Because Churchill Downs, where the Kentucky Derby is run, is located there.*

derrick   n. 1 A successful thief, of expensive items. 2 A shoplifter. *Crook use.* v.t. To take a player out of a game before it is over. 1943: *Baseball use.* 1952: "The next hitter was Eddie Stanky. But Shotton derricked him in favor of Cookie Lavagetto as a pinch-hitter. . . ." Arthur Daley, N.Y. *Times Mag.,* Sept. 28, 28/1.

derrière   n. The human rump. 1938: "That little derrière would be warmed by a bed slat." Letter in *Life,* Nov. 14, 6. 1946: "To slither on what Mr. Ervine would no doubt delicately call our derrières." A. E. Gower in *Sat. Rev. Lit.,* Apr. 6, 11. *From the Fr.*

desert rat   One who likes to live in the desert; esp. an old, grizzled prospector, who lives in, prospects, and loves the desert.

designer   n. A counterfeiter. *Crook argot.*

desk jockey   An office worker; one who works at an office desk. A term modeled on "disc jockey." 1953: "Let some desk jockey in the home office envy you." Hal Boyle, AP, May 19.

desperado   n. A person who borrows or gambles larger sums than he will be able to pay; one whose standard of living is sensationally more costly than his income warrants. 1956: "Desperado— One who bets or borrows with no intention to pay; one certain to become a welcher, it being firmly established in gambling circles that a person who takes a welching chance will welch." T. Betts, *Across the Board,* 314.

destroyer   n. An extremely attractive or beautiful young woman. *Some c1940–c1945 Armed Forces and student use.*

detainer   n. A train dispatcher. *Railroad use.*

Detroit   n. A type of men's haircut in which the hair on the top of the head is cut short and the hair on the sides long. 1957: "One of the hottest haircuts is the 'Detroit' . . . cut Crew on top, normal trim on sides." H. Mitgang, *About— Men's Haircuts.*

deuce   n. 1 In playing cards, a two. *Colloq.* 2 In poker, a pair. 3 A two-dollar bill. *c1920; obs.* 4 Two dollars. 1941: "Within a week [he] was going to the races every afternoon. Sometimes he would bet a deuce." J. Lilienthal, *Horse Crazy,* 12. 5 A two-year prison sentence. 1952: "[We] did a deuce together at Joliet." Movie, *Kansas City Confidential.* 6 A quitter, a coward; a small-time crook; fig., one not worth $2 or one who is so petty in crime that he is worthy of receiving only a two-year prison sentence. *Boy street gang use since c1940.*   **—r** n. A two-dollar bill; two dollars. *From "deuce."* See Appendix, —er ending.

deuce of clubs   Both fists. *From the term in card playing. Reformatory use.*

deuce spot   1 The second act of a vaudeville show. *Stage talk.* 2 The runner-up; second place in a sports contest, dog show, etc.

devil-may-care   Irresponsible; reckless. c1847 [1956]: ". . . Scouts of our Army, and a more reckless, devil-may-care looking set it would be. . . ." Samuel E. Chamberlain, "My Confession," *Life,* July 23. *Colloq.*

devil's bedposts, the   The four of clubs. *c1930. Contract bridge use. Now obs.*

devil's dozen   Thirteen.

devil's piano   A machine gun. *Not common.*

devoon   adj. Divine, wonderful. 1947: " 'Pretty snazzy weather we're having, eh?' 'Devoon,' said Jeanie languidly." Billy Rose, *synd. newsp. col.,* May 8. *Some c1940 teenage use; some jocular use.*

dew   See **mountain dew.**

dewdrop   n. A sophomore. *Some student use. Archaic.*

dewey   n. A revolver; a gun. *Some c1930 ranch use. Dial.*

dews   n. Ten dollars.

dexie   **dexy**   n. Dexedrine; Dexedrine tablets. 1956: "Of course, you can take dexies (Dexedrine), but you can get hooked on them." S. Longstreet, *The Real Jazz Old and New,* 146. *Orig. drug addict use. Mainly student use, as dexies are taken to keep awake during all-night study sessions.*

D.I.   **DI**   n. A drill instructor; a noncommissioned officer in charge of recruits. 1956: "Marine DI Convicted of Abusing Recruits [headline:] A Marine Corps courtmartial convicted a former drill instructor today. . . ." UP, Nov. 16. *Mainly Marine Corps use.* See Appendix, Shortened Words.

diag *n.* Gold braid, as worn diagonally on the sleeve to show the wearer's class. *Annapolis use.* See Appendix, Shortened Words.

diamond-cracker *n.* A fireman on a coal-burning locomotive. *Railroad use.*

diamond-pusher *n.* A railroad fireman.

diamonds *n.* **1** Coal. Also called black diamonds. *c1920. Railroad use.* "Throwing diamonds in the firebox . . ." Song, "Casey Jones." **2** The testicles. See **the family jewels.**

diamond-thrower *n.* A railroad fireman.

dib *n.* **1** Money; esp. a share, portion, or per cent of money. 1927: "I ought to collect the kid's dib, too." Hammett, *Blood Money*, 89. *From "divvy."* → **2** A dollar. 1939: "To put down a few dibs." Runyon. 1951: "Fifty sweet dibs!" S. H. Adams in *New Yorker*, Dec. 8, 81.

dibby *adj.* Fine. *c1900. Schoolgirl use.*

dibs *n.pl.* Money; usu. a small amount of money. 1949: " 'What's your racket?' 'Racket?' 'Sure. What do you shake them for? How do you make your dibs?' " Chandler, *Little Sister*, 28.

dibs on [something] An expression used in claiming the next use of, or chance at, something. *E.g.,* "*Dibs on that magazine.*" "*Dibs on going with the team.*" *Mainly child use. From "divvy."*

dice See **no dice.**

dice house *n.* A bunkhouse. *Perhaps suggested by British "doss-house." c1920. Ranch use. Midwest U.S.*

dicer *n.* **1** A stiff hat, such as a top hat, a man's sailor straw hat, etc. 1910: *Lawrenceville School use:* "Now clap on a dicer." Johnson, *Varmint*, 323. **2** A helmet. 1918: "The man with the Gas Mask and the Tin dicer." *Stars and Stripes*, n.d. 1934: *Slang, Web.*

dick *n.* **1** A detective. 1930: "One of the more ambitious policemen would go in the Detective Bureau and become a dick. . . . The cop . . . let his dick friend get the credit for the arrest. . . ." Lavine, *Third Degree*, 13, 21. *Criminal use until c1920. Now common.* Cf. **fly-ball.** **2** A policeman. 1939: "A banker would scarcely call . . . policemen 'dicks' or 'bulls.' " Hixson and Colodny, 136. Cf. **harness-bull. 3** The dean. 1941: *Boys'*

prep-school use; *Dict. of Exeter Language*, 13. **4** [taboo] The penis. *Colloq.*

dicty   dickty   dictee *adj.* **1** Stylish, high class, wealthy. 1928: "Dickty." C. Van Vechten, *Nigger Heaven*. 1956: "*Dicty* is high-class." S. Longstreet, *The Real Jazz Old and New*, 148. → **2** Haughty, snobbish; bossy, demanding. 1942: "These dickty jigs." Z. Hurston, 91. *n.* An aristocrat; a wealthy person; a high-class person; a stylish person. 1928: "Dictees." C. McKay, "Home to Harlem." 1947: "I didn't want to be a dicty." Mezz Mezzerow, *Really the Blues*, quoted in *Time*, Feb. 10, 12. *All uses Negro use. Has been some jive use.*

diddie bag A bag for keeping valuables. A variant of standard ditty bag. *Army use.*

diddle *v.i.* **1** To make any nervous or idle gestures; to pick up an object and handle it idly; to idle away one's time wastefully. **2** [taboo] To masturbate. c1935: "There was a man from Racine/ Who invented a diddling machine;/ Both concave and convex,/ It could fit either sex. . . ." Pop. limerick. *Jocular use.* *v.t.* To cheat. 1944: "A Eurasian who diddled her out of the bulk of her substance." Shulman, *Feather Merchants*, 63.

didie *n.* A diaper. *Colloq.*

didie pins A second lieutenant's gold bars. *From "didie." Some W.W.II use.*

dido *n.* A complaint; a reprimand. 1958: "Dido—A minor complaint of a superior against a cop." G. Y. Wells, *Station House Slang.*

die *v.i.* **1** In baseball, to be left on base as a baserunner at the end of a half-inning. 1908: "Men died on bases. . . ." R. L. Hartt in *Atlan. Mon.*, Aug., 229/1. 1950: "Only one Phil reached first. He died there." AP, Oct. 4. **2** To laugh or cry uncontrollably; fig., to die of laughter. 1943: "When he puts a lampshade on his head you could die." M. Shulman, *Barefoot Boy with Check*, 95. *Colloq.* **3** To experience extreme anticipation or strong desire. 1943: "The season opens next Saturday and I'm just dying to go." M. Shulman, *Barefoot Boy with Check*, 95. *Colloq.* *n.* Death.

diesel dyke = **bull dyke.** *West Coast use.*

die standing up To fail; to flop. 1925: *Trouper talk.* "The performers have 'flopped.' They have . . . 'died standing up.' . . ."

diff   dif *n.* Difference; used almost

invariably in "What's the diff?" 1910: "What's the diff?" Johnson, *Varmint*, 58. 1914: "It wouldn't make any dif what they met." S. Lewis, *Our Mr. Wrenn*, 57. 1951: "What's the diff?" M. Blosser, *synd. comic strip*, "Freckles," Dec. 15. *"Diff"* and *"dif"* appear with equal frequency. See Appendix, Shortened Words. **—er** *n.* Difference. 1873: *DAE. Mainly dial.* See Appendix, Shortened Words. **—erence** *n.* The advantage or that which gives an advantage over an opponent, as a gun or club. 1934: "And what they let them have it with is not only their dukes, but with the good old difference in their dukes, because they all carry something in their pockets to put in their dukes in case of a fight, such as a dollar's worth of nickels rolled up tight." Runyon. 1951: "[Robert Mitchum to man who has just pulled a gun on him:] O.K., so you've got the difference." Movie, *His Kind of Woman.* **—y** *n.* A sick-bay attendant. *USN use.*

dig *n.* **1** A diligent student. 1830: *DAE. Some student use until c1910. Obs.* **2** A hiding place for contraband; a cache. *Some underworld use.* **3** A sarcastic, contemptuous, or derogatory remark. *Colloq.* *v.i.* To study hard or diligently. 1827: *DAE.* 1851: "The man who dug for sixteen hours 'per diem.' " *Harvard Register*, quoted in Hall, *College Words*, 99. *v.t.* **1** To study a subject diligently. *Some student use since c1850.* → **2** To comprehend fully, understand or appreciate something or someone; to be in rapport with someone or something. 1941: "Dig me?" *Life*, Dec. 15, 89. 1943: "Awful fine slush pump . . . you ought to dig that." M. Shulman, *Barefoot Boy with Cheek*, 90. 1954: "Before we could dig what was going on, these tough guys started shooting." L. Armstrong, *Satchmo, My Life in New Orleans*, 61. 1957: ". . . [We] think and operate the same way. That's why I dig Italy." Leonard Feather, "Jazz Millionaire, [Norman Granz]." *Esquire*, May. 1958: "Dig a bag or bar today." Advt. for "Kraft" brand chocolate "Fudgies" candy, N.Y. *Daily News*, Feb. 9, comic section, 7. *Orig. some c1935 jive use; now associated with cool use; general jazz and hip use, fairly well known to general public. May be from the Celtic "twig" = to understand.* **3** To meet or find someone or something; to dig up. 1953: "Where did you dig her, kid?" Radio, *Phone Call from a Stranger*, Jan. 5. **4** To notice, see, look at, or

identify someone. 1950: "I 'digged this baby,' when I was a frosh." L. Luce in Cornell (Univ.) *Daily Sun*, Oct. 10, 4/3. **5** To be present at, see, or listen to an entertainment, performance, or performer. Cf. **catch.**

dig [oneself] a nod   To get a night's sleep.

dig dirt   To gossip. 1924: "Everyone seems to be digging dirt about Norry's friend." Marks, *Plastic Age*, 224.

digger   **Digger** *n.* **1** An Australian soldier. *Some W.W.I use.* **2** An Australian. **3** A man; buddy; fellow countryman; pal. *From "gold-digger" in the mining sense.* **4** = **gold-digger.** 1930: "She was just a plain digger." Burnett, *Iron Man*, 32. **5** A pickpocket.

diggings *n.pl.* Lodgings; living quarters; digs. 1910: *Lawrenceville School use.* Johnson, *Varmint*, 358.

diggity   See **Hot damn.**

dig out   To leave quickly. 1912: "Supposing we dig out." Johnson, *Stover at Yale*, 23.

digs *n.pl.* A rooming house; living quarters; lodgings. *More common in Eng. than U.S.* 1951: "Come autumn, we'll probably find digs more suited to the family needs." S. Perelman, *New Yorker*, Sept. 8, p. 35/2. Cf. **diggings.**

dig [someone or something] the most   To be in complete rapport with someone or something; to arrive at complete understanding or appreciation of another. 1958: "Of her husband [Rep. Rev. Adam Clayton Powell, D., N.Y.], she [Hazel Scott Powell] said, 'Adam and I dig each other the most. We have a perfect understanding. It couldn't be better." N.Y. *Sunday News*, May 11, 2.

dig up   To find or meet someone or something, usu. something old-fashioned or unusual or someone disagreeable, ugly, or eccentric. *Usu. in "Where did you dig her [him, it] up?"*

dike   **dyke** *n.* **1** = **bulldyke.** *Fairly common since c1950.* → **2** [derog.] Any large, masculine woman, whether or not a homosexual. *Prob. from "hermaphrodite."*

dildo *n.* **1** [taboo] An artificial device resembling an erect penis, used by female homosexuals. *Not common.* → **2** A foolish, stupid person; a prick. *Common among boys between 10 and 14 who do not know the primary meaning of the term. Reinforced by "dill."*

dill   **dil** *adj.* Stupid; easy to victimize. *Never common in U.S. In Eng.*

since c1200; obs. *n.* = **dilly.** See Appendix, Shortened Words.

diller See **chiller-diller, killer-diller, thriller-diller.**

dillion *n.* An exceedingly large number; a zillion.

dilly *n.* **1** Any person or thing remarkable in size, quality, appearance, or the like, as a beautiful girl, a hard-fought football game, a striking necktie, a honey, humdinger, beaut, or lulu. *Also used ironically.* 1945: "Gosh, we had more fun. That [football] game really was a dilly." Arthur Daley, N.Y. *Times,* Oct. 23, 21. 1951: "In order to get inside you have to pass three guards at different gates. The first two aren't so tough, but the last one is a dilly if you don't have an appointment." R. S. Prather, *Bodies in Bedlam,* 48. **2** A best girl. *Prob. from first three letters of "delightful" plus "y."*

dilly-dally *v.i.* To idle; to trifle; to dally. 1948: "Folks who dilly-dally with dessert . . ." UP, July 16. *Colloq.* See Appendix, Reduplications.

dim *n.* **1** Evening. *Jive use.* **2** Night; nighttime. *Bop use.*

dimbox *n.* **1** One who smooths over disagreements. 1925: *Flapper term.* F. H. Vizetelly. **2** A taxicab.

dime, get off the To stop loafing; to stop wasting time. *Lit. = "to stop standing in one spot." Not common.*

dime a dozen, a Cheap; plentiful; almost useless, having little or no value.

dime-note *n.* A ten-dollar bill.

dime store = **five-and-ten.**

dime up In begging: to offer a merchant ten cents for food or other goods worth considerably more, with a hard-luck story to save the dime also. Cf. **nickel up.** 1927: *Vagabond argot.* "An expert . . . can generally psychologize the tradesman into not accepting the coin." C. Samolar.

dimmer *n.* **1** A dime. 1943: "Neither of us can make a thin dimmer." D. Hammett, *Asst. Murderer.* Cf. **deemer.** **2** An electric light. *Prison use.*

dimmo *n.* A dime. See Appendix, —o ending.

dim view A lack of enthusiasm; a pessimistic attitude; a critical attitude; dislike. *Usu. in "to take a dim view of [something]."*

dim-wit *n.* A stupid person.

dinah *n.* **1** Dynamite. See Appendix, Shortened Words. → **2** Nitroglycerine.

dine *n.* Dynamite. Cf. **dinah.** See Appendix, Shortened Words. **—r** *n.* The caboose of a railroad train.

dinero *n.* Money. *From Sp.*

ding *v.i.* To beg, as on a street. *v.t.* To vote against a candidate for fraternity membership; to blackball; to veto. *Student use since c1930.* *n.* A vetoing or blackballing, as of a candidate for fraternity membership. *Student use.*

ding-a-ling *n.* Fig., a person who acts queerly because of mental deficiency; an insane person, a screwball, an eccentric. *Lit., one who hears bells in his head.*

dingbat *n.* **1** Money. **2** Anything suitable as a missile, such as a stone or a piece of wood. **3** A gadget, contraption, or dingus. 1934. *Colloq.* Web. 1947: "I don't think any wire-and-glass dingbat [i.e., television set] is going to 'oontz' out cheek-to-cheek dancing." Billy Rose, *synd. newsp. col.* May 15. 1953: J. C. Swayze, NBC, Jan. 1. **4** Any of various kinds of muffins, biscuits, or buns. 1895. *Student use.* **5** A vagabond, beggar, or hobo. 1948: "Some dingbat robs a filling station." Movie, *They Live by Night.* **6** [derog.] An Italian. Cf. **ding. 7** [derog.] A Chinese. **8** A woman other than one's sister or mother.

ding-dang *v.t.* To dang; to darn; to damn. 1948: "Ding-dang it!" Song, variant lyric of "Sweet Embraceable You," Radio Station WFIL, Dec. 6.

ding-dong *n.* **1** A bell; a steel triangle struck to announce dinner; also, the signal so given. See Appendix, Reduplications. 1925. *N.W. U.S. logging camps.* "The loggers wait for the ding-dong. . . . When the breakfast ding-dong rings. . . ." **2** A gas or gas-electric coach. *Railroad use.* *adj.* Spirited; hard-fought; furious. 1952: "In a dramatic climax to a ding-dong fight with Senator Taft of Ohio, Eisenhower crashed through to the GOP accolade [i.e., nomination] on the first ballot." AP, Chicago, July 11. **—er** *n.* An aggressive go-getting vagabond. *Vagabond argot.*

dinge [derog.] *n.* A Negro. *Still in use though very old. From "dingey."* *adj.* Negro; Negroid. 1940: "You say this here is a dinge joint?" Chandler, *Farewell,* 3. *Since c1850.* **—y** *n.* **1** [derog.] A Negro. *Dial.* **2** [derog.] A Negro child. *c1900 dial use. Diminutive from "dinge."* **3** A small locomotive; a short train; a small truck. *Hobo, railroad, and trucker use.* **4** Sub-standard, unregistered, or unbranded cattle. *Farm and ranch use.* **5** Eleven; the number eleven. *Used to avoid confusion with the sound of "seven." Some USN and radio use.*

dinger   *n.* **1** Any remarkable person or thing. *Obs.* See **hum-dinger.** 1951: "President Truman used it not once, but twice, in characterizing a sermon he had heard. . . . 'That was a dinger, chaplain,' said [he], and a moment later: 'I said it was a dinger.' " Editorial: "A Dinger Indeed." *N.Y. Her. Trib*, Nov. 27, 30. 1951: [person] "I'm a real dinger." Movie, *Cry Danger.* **2** A tramp; a worthless person. **3** A person having a smattering of knowledge. 1930: *Oral use.* L. Axley. **4** A railroad yardmaster or his helper. *Railroad use.*

ding ho(w)   ding hau   ding hao *adv.* O.K.; very good; all right; swell; everything is O.K. *From the Chinese. Orig. used by Armed Forces in Burma during W.W.II; orig. prob. "Flying Tigers" air group use.*

dingle   *n.* Favor with one's superiors. *Not common.*

dingo   **1** A hobo or vagrant. *Hobo use. From "ding."* See Appendix, —o ending. **2** A small-time confidence man. 1939: "One dingo got a dollar." Berger in *New Yorker*, 43/1.

ding-swizzled   *adj.* Darned; damned.

dingus   Anything of which the correct name is unknown or forgotten; a thingamajig. *Colloq.*

dink   *n.* **1** A small and close-fitting cap worn by college freshmen; apparently from dinky = small. 1950: "Lovers of the old-fashioned dink. . . ." *Cornell Univ. Daily Sun*, May 18, 4. **2** Any hat. **3** Failure in an examination. *c1900, college use.* **4** A dude. *c1900, college use.*

dinkum   *adj.* Genuine, honest, reliable, fair; also true, real, nice, etc. See **fair dinkum.** *W.W.I and W.W.II use, via Australian soldiers. Very common in Australia, but has gained little popularity in U.S.* *n.* An Australian soldier.

dinky   *adj.* **1** Small. 1943: "A dinky trolley car. . . ." H. A. Smith, *Putty Knife*, 48. *Very common.* **2** Cute; pretty; nice. *From "dinkum." Not common.*

dinner   See **fine dinner.**

dino   *n.* **1** A Mexican or Italian laborer, usu. a Mexican, esp. a railroad section-hand, specif. one who works with dynamite. 1949: "It'd serve that pokey right if somebody slapped him silly. He's been shakin' down the greenhorns in here fourteen years. Someday he'll shake down the wrong dino." N. Algren, *Man with the Golden Arm*, 26. *From "dine."* → **2** A hobo; an old beggar. *Not common.*

dip   *n.* **1** A pickpocket. 1859: *DAE.*

1926: "The dip who slid with the ticktick." *N.Y. Times*, May 30. *Common underworld use, universally known. Lit., one who "dips" his hand into other people's pockets.* **2** A diploma. 1941: "I'm failing my dip right now." *Dict. of Exeter Lang.*, 14. *Common c1900 student use.* See Appendix, Shortened Words. **3** Diphtheria. *From the common pronunciation: "dip-theria."* See Appendix, Shortened Words. **4** A hat. *Orig., c1910–c1920, New Eng. dial. use, esp. usu. by boys. Now some Negro use. Because one "dips" or "tips" one's hat to another on meeting.* **5** An advance press agent or public relations man. *c1900 use. From "diplomat."* **6** A drunkard. *From "dipsomaniac."* See **dipso.** See Appendix, Shortened Words. **7** A stupid person. *v.t.* To rob someone by picking his pockets.   *adj.* Crazy; dippy.

dipper   *n.* **1** See **hipper-dipper.** **2** = **dipper-mouth.** *Usu. a nickname.* See Appendix, Shortened Words.   **—mouth** *n.* A person with a large mouth; lit., one with a mouth the size of a dipper. 1954: "Dipper (that was my nickname—short for Dippermouth, from the piece called 'Dippermouth Blues'). . . ." L. Armstrong, *Satchmo, My Life in New Orleans*, 27f.

dippiness   *n.* Craziness,

dippy   *adj.* Crazy; foolish; not sensible.

—dippy   See Appendix, Suffixes and Suffix Words.

dippydro   *n.* One who often changes his mind; an uncertain person.

dipsey   *n.* A workhouse sentence; a short sentence, as for vagrancy, to a local jail. *Hobo use c1925.*

dipso   *n.* A drunkard; an alcoholic; a dipsomaniac. 1943: "The reason so many [pitchmen] become dipsos. . . ." Zolotow in *SEP*, 12.

dipsy-do   dipsy-doo   *n.* **1** In baseball, a tantalizing curve. **2** One who throws a "dipsy-do" or "dipsy-doodle." 1952: "Easy Ew [*sic*] Lopat, the greatest of the dipsy-doodlers, will do nothing calculated to bring [the Brooklyn batters] to." Gayle Talbot, AP, Oct. 3. **3** A fixed prize fight.

dipsy-doodle   *n.* **1** Chicanery, deception. 1942: "I opened the front door, leaving the key in the lock. I wasn't going to work any dipsy-doodle in this place." Chandler, *High Window*, 165. **2** In baseball, a sharp curve pitch.   *v.t.* To deceive or cheat. 1951: "Now all I've got to figure out is whether we've been dipsy-doodled.'' Radio, *Meet Corliss Archer*, Mar. 4.

dip the bill (beak)   To drink. 1939: "Let's dip the bill. Got a glass?'' Chandler, *Big Sleep*, 162.

dirt   *n.* **1** Gossip; obscenity; scandal. *Colloq.* Cf. **dig dirt.** 1941: "Gibbon . . . would come up to a . . . morsel of scandal about the Romans and then, just as the reader expected him to dish the dirt, he'd go into his Latin routine. . . .'' Frank Sullivan, "A Garland of Ibids,'' *New Yorker*, Apr., 19, fn. 17. **2** Specif., a novel or other entertainment abounding in sexual reference. **3** Information; the low-down. **4** Cheating. *Prize fight use.* **5** Black pepper. *Army use. Not common.* **6** Sugar. *Convict use.* **7** Money. See **do dirt, hit the dirt, pay dirt.**   —**y**   *adj.* **1** Unethical, dishonest. *Colloq.* **2** Malevolent; spiteful; mean. 1939: "People gave him dirty looks, made dirty cracks at him.'' J. T. Farrell, 200. *Colloq.* **3** Lewd; lascivious; sexually suggestive; obscene. *Colloq.* → **4** Suggesting the lewd or obscene, as by a reedy, ragged, or slurred tone in performing jazz. 1926[1956]: "The Indiana U College newspaper voted him [Bix Beiderbecke] in 1926 the greatest 'dirty' trumpet-player in jazz circles.'' S. Longstreet, *The Real Jazz Old and New*, 106. *Jazz use.* **5** Well supplied with money; filthy rich. 1927: "Paddy was dirty with fifteen thousand or so.'' Hammett, *Blood Money*, 114. **6** Radioactive; contaminated by radioactive particles or by-products. 1958: "The U.S. is testing 'dirty' [atomic] bombs as well as 'clean' bombs in its current series in the Pacific, according to Lewis L. Strauss, chairman of the Atomic Energy Commission.'' *Since c1955.* **7** Big; impressive; remarkable. See **do the dirty on [someone].**   *adv.* Very.

dirt, hit the   **1** In baseball, to slide for a base. **2** To jump off a still moving freight train; to get off a train. *Hobo use.* **3** To fling oneself into the closest shelter or to the ground for protection from a bomb or artillery shell blast. *Wide W.W.II use.* See **dirt.**

dirt-bag   *n.* A garbage collector. *W.W.II Armed Forces use.*

dirty bird   A so-and-so. *Usu. in* "*Well, I'll be a dirty bird!*'' *indicating self-effacing surprise. A fad word pop. by comedian George Gobel c1955.*

dirty heavy   A villain. *c1925; movie talk.*

dirty linen = **dirty wash.**

dirty-neck   *n.* **1** A laborer; a farmer.

1956: "To coal miners . . . a *dirty-neck* is a miner.'' *Labor's Special Lang. from Many Sources.* → **2** A rustic; an immigrant.

dirty wash   Personal or family problems, esp. those that would cause gossip if made public; neighborhood scandal. 1957: "There's plenty of dirty wash in [the novel] *Peyton Place*. It's about this town where everybody is doing something wrong and nobody else knows it.'' *Oral, N.Y.C. Orig. in that one's neighbors see one's dirty wash being hung out on the clothesline in the view of everyone.*

dirty work   Any dishonest or unethical act.

disc   disk   *n.* A modern phonograph record, esp. of popular or jazz music. 1943: "Phonograph records are called 'discs' or 'platters.' '' M. Shulman, *Barefoot Boy with Cheek*, 149. 1957: ". . . Duke [magazine] asks a leading disc jockey for his selection of the most played records as well as the discs he feels will click in coming weeks.'' Jesse Owens, "Duke on Discs,'' *Duke*, Aug., 7. *Orig. to distinguish the disc-shaped records from the older cylindrical records. Pop. by jive use. "Disc'' now more common than "disk.''*

disc jockey   disk jockey   A radio announcer who supervises a show of recorded popular music. He selects the discs, announces them, often with some comment, reads sponsors' advertisements between recordings, and tries to increase the popularity of the show by his personality. With the advent of television, many radio stations program a majority of their time to such shows of recorded popular music. *Orig. radio use; now universally known and common teenage use; colloq. since c1950.* See **disc.**

discomboberate   discumbobulate   *v.t.* **1** To perplex. **2** To disconcert, discomfit, etc.

discouraged   *adj.* Drunk.

dise-drag   *n.* A freight car in a railroad train. *Vagabond argot.*

disguised   *adj.* Drunk.

dish   *n.* **1** A woman or a girl, usu. a beautiful, pretty, or sexually attractive one. 1939–40: "I was thinking this was going to be my favorite dish. . . .'' O'Hara, *Pal Joey*, 28. 1950: "She's a blonde dish with good gams.'' Movie, *Let's Dance. The connotation depends on the qualifying adjective. Thus, "beautiful dish,'' "hot dish,'' "dumb dish,'' "German dish,'' "old dish,'' etc. A prime example of* *a slang word relating sex and food.* See Appendix, Sex and Food. **2** A thing that is exactly suited to one's tastes or abilities, as a certain book or the music of a certain composer; a preference. 1921: "Fight scenes is my dish—I made my reputation on 'em. . . ." Witwer, *Leather*, 168. 1951: "Now, there is a book that is just my dish. . . . It's just my dish, so I buy it. . . . I still feel that it is exactly my dish. . . . It is exactly my dish. . . ." Geo. S. Kaufman, *New Yorker*, May, 26, 23. **3** In baseball, home plate. **4** An order of ice cream a la carte. *Lunch-counter use.* *v.t.* **1** To tell [something]; to disclose by talking. **2** To give or retaliate with. 1949: "He took everything [i.e., rough scrimmage] we gave and dished it right back. . . ." Dick Cresap, Phila. *Bulletin*, Sept. 15, 51. **3** To frustrate; cheat; set aside; shelve.

dish it out   To give out money, abuse, punishment, or the like; to hand out, dispense, inflict upon. 1934: [To a croupier] "You take [money] away fast enough, but you don't like to dish it out." Chandler, *Finger Man*, 10. *Lit. and fig., to attack a person violently, either physically or verbally; fig., to "dish out" or serve blows or punishment on another. Colloq.*

dish of tea   One's preference; one's environment. 1953: "Harlem is [Langston Hughes'] own habitat, . . . his forte and his dish of tea." C. Van Vechten, N.Y. *Times Book Rev.*, May 31, 5/1.

dish out   **1** To give out [talk, news, abuse, information]; to dispense or issue. 1929: "The brand of drool they dished out. . . ." J. Auslander, *Hell in Harness*, 2. 1950: "When Betty Grable dishes out advice to show business hopefuls, it pays to listen." Bob Thomas, AP, July 17. 1951: "The President . . . has been on the receiving end for more abuse than he has dished out." Peter Edson, Washington dispatch, Aug. 30. **2** To give, administer; to inflict [on]. 1951: "The beating he dished out to Tone . . . [on] Sep. 14." AP, Cloquet, Minn., Sept. 29. **3** To pay. 1950: "Janice is merely a paid performer, dishing out the sponsor's dough." Hal Boyle, AP, Oct. 8.

dish the dirt   To gossip; to gossip with malicious intent or enjoyment.

dishwasher   *n.* An engine wiper. *Railroad use.*

dishwater   *n.* **1** Soup, esp. bad-tasting soup. **2** Coffee. **3** Weak tea.

disk   See **disc.**

dissolve   *n.* A device used to make (or an instance of making) one movie or stage scene meld or blend into the next. 1951: "The reconciliation of the lovers is followed by two newsboys running back and forth across the stage shouting the headlines of the day. This device, calculated to divert and entertain the audience for the next twenty minutes, gives the stage crew time to set up the big final scene backstage. This technique of stagecraft is known as a 'dissolve' (the movies use the same trick) and allows one scene to flow into the next one." Al Hirschfeld, *Show Business Is No Business*, 48. *From the movie use where one scene dims or fades out as another comes into focus.*

ditch   *v.t.* **1** To abandon or run away from a person or thing. 1934: "We'll ditch this Greek and blow." Cain, *Postman*, 13. → **2** Specif., to bring down a crippled airplane on water in such a way that there will be time for the passengers to get out before the plane sinks.

dit-da artist (jockey, monkey)   *n.* A short-wave radio operator. *In imitation of the sounds of a dot and a dash being transmitted.*

dive   *n.* **1** A disreputable, cheap, low-class establishment or public place, esp. a bar, dance-hall, nightclub, or the like; a place of bad repute. 1929: "The girl who danced in a dive in New Orleans." K. Brush, *Young Man*, 29. 1934 [1949]: "I played in that dive for nine weeks. There were rooms upstairs and girls. I had a glass of beer on top of the piano and a half-smoke juane on the side." P. Wylie, *Finnley Wren*, 51. → **2** Specif., a place where whisky is sold illegally; a speakeasy. **3** In prizefighting, a knockdown, esp a knockdown or knockout that is feigned by prearrangement between the fighters. 1951: "[Boxing] still will come up occasionally with its 'dives.' (A dive is a phantom knockout in which a boxer 'swoons' or dives to the canvas under the impact of a light blow or, sometimes, no blow at all.)" A. Daley in N.Y. *Times Mag.*, Mar. 4, 58.

diver   See **pearl-diver.**

divot   *n.* A toupee.

divvy   *v.i., v.t.* To divide or share [something, as loot]; to divide up. *Colloq. since c1890.* 1928: "The government and the Paris crook divvy the swag." Alva Johnson, *New Yorker*, Nov. 10, 51 f.   *n.* A split; a dividend; one's part or share in the profit or spoils. 1948: "Quarterly divvy of $1.12½ per share." *Variety*, Aug. 25, 4/3.

divvy up To divide spoils or profits. 1954: "We would pass our hats and divvy up." L. Armstrong, *Satchmo, My Life in New Orleans*, 34.

Dix *n.* A ten-dollar bill. 1956: "Once, a long time ago, a New Orleans bank put out a ten-dollar bill. On each side was printed the word: Dix. Ten dollars was an impressive sum and you remembered if you got a good ole Dix, real Southern currency." S. Longstreet, *The Real Jazz Old and New*, 70. —**ie** *n.* **1** New Orleans. *From the "Dix" printed on ten-dollar bills issued from New Orleans.* See **Dix.** → **2** The South. 1956: "The word Dixie came from Dix and later Dixie was used in general as meaning the South. But at first Dixie and Dixieland meant only New Orleans." S. Longstreet, *The Real Jazz Old and New*, 70. **3** Dixieland music. *adj.* Southern. —**iecrat** *n.* A Southern Democrat, usu. an office holder or nominee, who belongs or once belonged to the Democratic party but considers local Southern loyalty, esp. to racial segregation, more important than party loyalty. *From the name of the actual "third party" that formed in 1948 but returned to the Democrats during the following Presidential· election as a somewhat unified and highly vocal faction.* —**ieland** *n.* **1** New Orleans and the surrounding bayou country. *Obs.* See **Dixie.** → **2** The South. **3** The style or form of jazz resembling the orig. jazz played by street bands in New Orleans c1910; recognized by a simple two-beat rhythm, ragged syncopation, improvised ensemble passages, etc. 1956: "Later Dixie was used in general as meaning the South. But at first Dixie and Dixieland meant only New Orleans. So when a white man named Jack Laine began to play jazz, why they called his music Dixieland. Jack Laine was born in 1873." S. Longstreet, *The Real Jazz Old and New*, 70. 1950: "The all-white Original Dixieland Jazz Band of 1917 (by chance the first band to record jazz) is generally reckoned the originator of 'Dixieland.' " A. Lomax, *Mr. Jelly Roll*, 117.

dixie *n.* An army mess tin or small pot, used for a cooking utensil or as a bowl while eating. *Army use c1920 from Brit. Army use. Archaic.*

dizzy *adj.* **1** Silly; foolish. 1937: "Some dizzy broad. . . ." Weidman, *Wholesale*, 8. **2** Given to taking chances. *c1925; aviator use.*

—**dizzy** See Appendix, Suffixes and Suffix Words.

dizzy-wizzy *n.* Any drug in pill form. 1905: "Put four of those dizzy-wizzys back in the box." McHugh, *Search Me*, 96. See Appendix, Reduplications.

DJ *n.* See **deejay.**

do *v.t.* To harm, attack, or ruin [a person]. 1894: "He is hated by all the beggars above him, and they do him every chance they get . . . 'it's our biz to do anybody who is out o' our class.' " Josiah Flynt. 1934: *Colloq. Web.* *n.* A social affair or party. 1952: "I go to the Washington's Birthday dinner dance and a few of the main do's just to put in an appearance." Budd Schulberg, *Holiday*, Jan., 42/1.

D. O. A. Dead on arrival, the official terminology of police and hospital reports and in coroners' inquests. 1958: "Don't Be a D.O.A. reads a headline over a leaflet warning against the dangers of jaywalking. 'D.O.A.'—meaning dead on arrival at a hospital—is part of a vivid police argot." G. Y. Wells, *Station House Slang.* See Appendix, Shortened Words.

do a barber To talk a lot.

do a Dan O'Leary To work diligently; specif., to work hard as a uniformed policeman. 1958: "Do a Dan O'Leary— To work every minute of a tour of duty—from the name of a very hard-working cop of yesteryear." G. Y. Wells, *Station House Slang. Not common.*

do a guy To run away.

do black To act as a Negro in a show. *Pitchman and vaudeville use.*

doby **dobee** **dobie** *v.i.* To wash clothes by hand. *Orig. Brit. maritime use; some U.S. maritime use. From Hindustani "dhobi" = a washerman or laundry boy.*

doc *n.* **1** A doctor; specif., a physician. 1854: *DAE.* 1952: "Docs find he's schizo." Photo caption, N.Y. *Daily News*, Aug. 13, C3/1. *Colloq.* See Appendix, Shortened Words. **2** An unknown fellow or guy; used in direct address.

dock *v.t.* To penalize a worker part of his pay, usu. for absence or arriving late on the job. 1956: "*Docking*—Penalizing a worker for spoilage, tardiness, absence, etc." *Labor's Special Lang. from Many Sources. Colloq.*

dock rat A bum; specif., one who hangs around docks. 1928: ". . . A gang of notorious little dock rats. . . ." Asbury, *Gangs of N.Y.*, 160.

dock-walloper *n.* One who idles

around docks, occasionally working. 1930: "I have . . . strolled among the dock-wallopers swinging a cane." O. O. McIntyre, *Outlook*, Sept. 3, 8/3.

doctor   *n*. One who drugs racehorses to affect their performance.

do-dad   doodad   *n*. **1** A useless ornament. **2** A thing.

doddy   See **hoddy-doddy.**

do [one, someone] dirt   To expose, inform on, or in some other manner cause another trouble; to cause another to lose status or the good opinion or good will of others; maliciously to damage another's good reputation.

dodo   *n*. **1** A stupid or inept person. 1951: "Just ninety-five years after its discovery it [the dodo bird] was gone, leaving behind it like an epitaph its name, which has become a synonym for stupidity and extinction." J. Williams, *Fall of the Sparrow*, 47. *From the now extinct dodo bird [Didus ineptus], a heavy, wingless fowl once found on the island of Mauritius.* **2** An old fogy; a settled, secure, dull person. 1934: "I love my wife. I have kids. A job. I'm a respectable old dodo." P. Wylie, *Finnley Wren*, 89. **3** A student pilot who has not yet made a solo flight. 1944: "[Cadet] Smith was still a dodo." C. Macon in *Collier's*, Sept. 9, 51/2. *In allusion to the dodo bird's inability to fly; orig. U.S. Air* *ᵣorce and Army use c1940.*

dodunk   *n*. A stupid or simple person. *New England use. Becoming obs.*

doe   *n*. At a dance, party, or gathering, a woman unaccompanied by a male escort. *Based on "stag."*

do-funny   *n*. A thingamajig. *Colloq.*

dog   *n*. **1** A promissory note. 1833: Mathews, *Dict. of Amer. Dial.* **2** Ostentation in dress, manner, or the like; swank; airs; often in "put on the dog." 1871: *DAE. Dial.* **3** The sandwich made of a frankfurter on a roll. **4** A frankfurter. *Both uses shortened from "hot dog."* 1948: "A lot of dogs, butter, ground meat, pop and stuff on hand." Cain, *Moth*, 32. *Colloq. since before 1900.* See **hot dog.** → **5** A lunchroom, lunch counter, or cheap restaurant; a quick lunch or snack bar. 1900 [1950]: "Half a century ago, your historian took his meals at Hank Norwood's dog." R. Berry in Cornell (Univ.) *Alumni News*, Apr. 1, 337/2. *Not now common. Prob. from "dog wagon."* **6** Something inferior; something disliked or lacking in appeal; esp. a slow-moving racehorse; merchandise that does not appeal to customers;

entertainment, a performer, or performers that does not appeal to the public; an ugly or uncouth girl; or the like. 1952: " '[The book will have] a record-breaking sale.' 'Yes, unless the book turns out to be a dog.' " D. Dempsey in N.Y. *Times Bk. Rev.*, Aug. 10, 8/3. **7** A promiscuous girl; a prostitute. **8** A college freshman; a new or inexperienced worker. **9** An automobile inspector. **10** A human foot. See **dogs.** **11** A disreputable or untrustworthy man, esp. in sexual or social matters; a cad. **12** An ugly, unrefined, or sexually disreputable girl or woman; a boring girl or young woman who does not have the compensation of beauty. *Fairly common; wide male student and teenage use.*   *adj.* Inferior; unappealing. 1956: "A dog-tune is one that isn't very good music." S. Longstreet, *The Real Jazz Old and New*, 149.   *v.t.* To pester someone; to follow another, as to collect a debt, get information, or the like; to hound. *v.i.* **1** Dog it = to shirk. 1927: "They'll all come home if they don't dog it." Hammett, *Blood Money*, 25; also 71. **2** To run away. **3** To tell a lie. **—face** *n*. **1** A soldier, specif., an infantry private. 1951: "Few [enlisting students] wanted to be dogfaces." *Time*, Jan. 1, 14/3. *Prob. orig. derisive use by USN and Marines.* **2** An ugly boy. *Some child and teenage use.* **—gie** *n*. **1** = **dog, hot dog.** See Appendix, **—ie** ending. **2** = **dogface,** soldier. **—ging** = **bull-dogging.** **—gity** See **hot-dig-gity-doggity.**

—dog   A salesman. Thus shoe-dog = a shoe salesman. *Not common.*

dog, put on the   **1** To dress in one's fanciest clothes. *Archaic and dial.* **2** = **put on airs.** See **dog.**

dog biscuit   *n*. **1** Hardtack. *Some Army use c1925–c1935.* → **2** Crackers. Some student use. **3** An unattractive girl. *Some c1940 student use.* See **dog.**

dog-chaser   *n*. A relief crew sent to bring in a train that cannot legally be moved by its own crew. 1940–43; *railroad use.*

dog-collar   *n*. A muffler clamp. *c1940; auto factory use.*

dog days   **1** Days during which one does not feel energetic or enthusiastic; dull days; the days when a woman is menstruating. **2** Hot, humid summer days that sap one's energy; specif., midsummer days. *So called because anciently reckoned from the first rising of the Dog Star.*

dog-eye *n.* A stare of reproach or supplication. *Maritime use.*

dog fashion [taboo] **1** Descriptive of sexual intercourse conducted in such a way that the male covers the female from the back. **2** Heterosexual anal intercourse. *Not common; through confusion with the main use.*

dog fight A fight between two fighter planes. *Orig. W.W.I Air Force use. Universally known. with faster planes and group flights, now archaic.*

dog food Corned-beef hash. *W.W.II USN use.*

doggo *adj.* In hiding; desiring to be left alone; meek. 1949: "Hamilton, lying doggo since killing the Chicago detective." A. Hynd, *Public Enemies*, 22. *Not common.* See Appendix, —o ending.

doggone *adj.* and *adv.* Darned.

doggy *adj.* Stylish; well dressed, esp. in a somewhat garish, conspicuous manner. 1897: "Twenty years ago the college man had a most picturesque vocabulary. What color there was in such words as 'doggy.' . . ." *Bookman*, Aug., 448/2. 1925: "A doggy scarf." Bowers in *Lit. Digest. Obs.*

doghouse *n.* **1** Any of various houselike structures more or less resembling a dog's kennel; specif., a railroad caboose, a small, temporary office shack serving a work crew, a tower on a prison wall, a bass viol, or the like. 1898: [Caboose] *DAE.* 1933: "When the bull-fiddler plucks the strings he is slapping the doghouse." H. T. Webster, 370. **2** Fig., disfavor or disgrace, esp. in "to be in the doghouse." 1950: "For the president resents opposition—as the late Bob Hannegan, who ended up in the doghouse, found out." D. Pearson, *synd. newsp. col.*, Sept. 11.

doghouse, in the See **doghouse, 2.**

dog it **1** To dress up, esp. in the latest or most gaudy style; to act haughtily or in an aloof manner; to put on the dog. **2** To make no, or but a slight, effort; to relax when one should be working hard; to fail to make one's best effort. 1941: "In Dellup's next race, Crump bet man-sized money. Also he bet a wad for the stable connections. But the horse dogged it, the same as it had done before." J. Lilienthal, *Horse Crazy*, 23. **3** To flee; esp. to retreat or withdraw from a social nuisance. **4** To travel, seek entertainment, or live very cheaply, esp. by borrowing money or letting one's friends pay various bills. **5** To avoid hard work, thought, or

creating; to evade responsibility; to produce inferior work or work meeting only the minimum standard requirements.

dog kennel = **dog house.**

dog-naper **dog-napper** *n.* A stealer of dogs. 1945: "Dog-nappers [are] a dishonest group which steal a valuable dog and sell for a high profit." George Butz, Phila. *Inquirer*, Dec. 16, S5. *From "dog" plus "kidnaper."*

do-gooder *n.* A sincere but self-righteous worker for the welfare of others. 1949: "A professional do-gooder." Billy Rose, *synd. newsp. col.*, July 25.

dog out To dress or dress up; to tog out. Cf. **dog.** 1932: ". . . He would have been feeling much better if he were dogged out in a new outfit." J. T. Farrell, 121.

dog-robber *n.* **1** An Army officer's orderly, servant, or personal attendant. *W.W.I use.* **2** A baseball umpire. *Some baseball use.*

dogs *n.pl.* The human feet; specif., a pair of human feet. *Universally known.*

dogs, the = **the cat's meow.** 1932: "Wouldn't it be the dogs to be paged like that!" J. T. Farrell, 126.

dog show Foot inspection. *W.W.II Army use.*

dog's-nose *n.* A drink containing beer or ale mixed with gin or rum. Cf. **boiler-maker.**

dog style [taboo] = **dog fashion.**

dog tag See **dog tags.**

dog tags The pair of metal identification tags worn by soldiers and sailors on chains about their necks. *The tags served as an identification of dead and wounded and provided various items of essential information.* 1952: "Hey, vets! If you still have your dog tags. . . ." Letter in N.Y. *Sunday News*, Oct. 5, C19/3. *W.W.I and W.W.II Armed Forces use. From their resemblance to dog licenses, reinforced by "dogface."*

dog tent = **pup tent.**

dog up To dress in one's best clothes. See **dog it.**

dog-wagon *n.* **1** A lunch-wagon. See **dog. 2** An antiquated truck. *Truckdriver use.*

do-hinky *n.* **1** A pimple or any minor skin eruption. **2** Any object; a thingamajig.

doily See **dome doily, scalp doily.**

do in To kill. 1939: "She did in the old woman too." A. Christie, *Sad Cypress*, 154.

do it all   To serve a life term in prison. *Underworld and prison use.*

doke   dokey   See **okey-doke, okey-dokey.**

dokus   *n.* The human posterior. 1949: "Woodrow Wilson landed on his *dokus* like the humblest of professors." H. L. Mencken in *New Yorker*, Oct. 1, 63/1. *From the Yiddish "tokus."*

doll   *n.* **1** A pretty girl or woman; esp. a pretty girl or woman whose main use in life seems to be to grace the scene rather than to make an active contribution; esp. a clear complexioned blonde, blue-eyed girl with regular features. 1920: "If a blonde girl doesn't talk we call her a 'doll.' " Fitzgerald, *This Side of Paradise*, 141. **2** Any female, esp. a pert or saucy one. 1932: *Guys and Dolls,* title of a book by Damon Runyon. *Also the title of a pop. c1950 musical play on Broadway and a successful movie c1945, all based on the writings of Runyon.* → **3** Any attractive, sweet person; a pleasant generous person of either sex. **4** An attractive, popular boy. *Common teenage-girl use since c1940.*

dollface   *n.* A boy or youth with a good-looking, pretty, or feminine face. 1951: "Hello, dollface." M. Shulman, *Dobie Gillis*, 69. *Used either as a compliment or in derision.*

doll out = **doll up.**

doll up   To dress up; to dress and groom oneself with great care or fashionably. 1922: "All dis is too . . . dolled up. . . ." O'Neill, *Hairy Ape,* 5. 1921: ". . . He . . . gives himself a swift dollin' up before the mirror. . . ." Witwer, *Leather,* 61.

dolly dancer   A soldier who receives easy duty, esp. office duty, by courting officers. *W.W.II Army use.*

—dom   See Appendix, Suffixes and Suffix words.

dome   *n.* The head; esp. of a person. See **double-dome, ivory dome.** 1922: "To get the wool sheared off my dome." H. Wentworth, *Purple Pennant.*

domecon   *n.* In colleges, a course or class of domestic economy. *Obs., now called "home economics."*

dome doily   A wig. *Never common.*

domino [derog.]   *n.* A Negro, esp. a dark-complexioned Negro whose black skin makes his teeth and eyeballs seem prominent.   *n.pl.* **1** The teeth. 1913: "To sluice the dominoes" = to drink. F.K. Sechrist. See **box of dominoes. 2** Sugar cubes pressed in the general shape of

dominoes. **3** Dice. See **galloping dominoes.**

donagher = **donnicker.**

done   *n.* A prostitute. *Some c1875 use. Obs. Prob. from Italian "donna"* = **lady.**

done in   *adj.* **1** Tired, exhausted, beat, bushed. *Colloq.* **2** See **do in.**

done up   Tired out. *Colloq.* 1951: "I was done up. . . ." S. J. Perelman, *New Yorker,* Sept. 8, 33/1.

dong [taboo]   *n.* The penis.

donk   *n.* Whisky, esp. raw, homemade corn whisky. *Dial. Because its kick is as strong as a donkey's.* See Appendix, Shortened Words.

donkey   *n.* **1** A religious student. *Obs.* **2** A section man. *Railroad use.*

donkey act   A stupid or foolish act; a blunder, mistake, or faux pas. See **ass.**

donkey puncher   One who runs a donkey engine. *Lumberjack use.*

donkey's breakfast   A straw mattress. *Maritime sl.*

donkey's years   *sing.* A very long time. 1952: "I got interested in his apprenticeship donkey's years back." R. C. Ruark, *synd. newsp. col.,* May 20. *Dial. since c1850. In allusion to the length of a donkey's ears, by elision so that the "y" of donkey makes "ears" sound like "years."*

donnicker   doniker   *n.* **1** A toilet; a rest room. *Common underworld, carnival, and circus use.* **2** A freight-train brakeman. *Railroad use.*

donnybrook   *n.* A loud, noisy argument, fight, brawl, riot, contest. *From Donnybrook Fair.* 1949: ". . . The end of the three hour and four minute donnybrook." [A scrappy baseball game.] AP, Oct. 10. 1958: "He called the cops. A donnybrook began when police arrested the operators. . . ." Robert McCarthy, "They Take Bulldozer By Horns, Get Hooked." N.Y. *Daily News,* Feb. 20, 6.

don't know from nothing, [someone]   See **know from nothing.**

doodad = **do-dad.**

doodah = **all of a doodah;** excited.

doodle   *v.t.* To deceive or cheat someone; to trick someone. *Archaic.   v.i.* To draw meaningliness patterns or figures as a nervous gesture or idle habit while doing something else.   *n.* A meaningless pattern or figure, as drawn idly.

doodle-bug   *n.* **1** A self-propelled gas, electric, or diesel railway car; a one-car train. *Railroad use.* **2** A small reconnaissance car. *Some W.W.II Army use.* **3** A tank, esp. a light tank. *Some W.W.II military use.*

doodle-e-squat *n.* Money. *Carnival use.*

dooey = **dewey.**

doohickey *n.* 1 A pimple or other skin eruption. Cf. **do-hinky, hickey.** 2 A gadget; any small object.

doojigger *n.* A gadget.

dooker *n.* One who, while appearing to be one of an audience, is employed by the management; a shill. *Carnival and circus use. Never common.*

dookie = **dukie.**

doop See **hoop-a-doop.**

dooper See **hooper-dooper, super-dooper, whooper-dooper.**

door See **barn door[s], side-door Pullman.**

doormat = **hand-painted doormat.**

doosy   doozie   doozy *n.* Anything remarkable or unusual; something enjoyable, well liked, successful; or something humorous, confusing, or exotic. 1951: "The first orchestra I ever had was really a doozie." Radio broadcast. Meredith Wilson, Feb. 18.

dooteroomus *n.* Money.

doowhistle   doowillie *n.* Anything whose name is unknown or forgotten; a gadget, a thingamajig. *Not common.*

dope *n.* 1 Any drug, esp. a narcotic such as opium or cocaine. *c1870–1920; specif.* = *opium. Drug addict use only. Since 1920, colloq.* 1927: "He had the dope habit an' he had it bad." "Willie the Weeper" [a song], Carl Sandburg, *The American Song Bag.* 2 Any substance that acts, or is thought to act, more or less like a drug; esp. alcoholic beverages. 3 The soft drink Coca-Cola. *c1920; the original formula was supposed to contain a stimulant.* See **Coke.** 1941: "A shot of dope = a coke." *Life,* Jan. 27, 79. 4 Coffee. 5 A cigarette. See **dope stick.** 6 Any thick, heavy liquid, regardless of its purpose, such as sauces, cosmetics, lubricants, etc. 1929: "All dopes [sauce put over ice cream] 5 cents extra." Sign in ice cream fountain. 7 A person who uses narcotics. *c1900.* 8 A person who acts as though drugged; hence usu. a stupid person. 1949: "So you sit and mope like a dope...." Popular song. "Don't Cry, Joe." *Colloq.* 9 Smelling salts. 10 Information; essential, true, or direct information; data. 1913: "Come across with the real dope." *Nation,* Aug. 21, 161/2. 1943: "Just got the dope on the officer election of the Audubon Club." M. Shulman, *Barefoot Boy with Cheek,* 104. 11 Gossip or news. 12 A prediction made from evaluating all the facts. *adj.* Stupid. 1939–49: "... Me calling attention to her dope boyfriend." O'Hara, *Pal Joey,* 4. *v.t.* 1 To drug. *c1880.* 2 To figure, equate, or predict from the known facts, esp. to predict a winner or result in the fields of sports or gambling. Cf. **dope out.   —ster** *n.* One who gathers data on past events in order to predict the result of future ones; esp. one who forecasts the results of sporting events. See Appendix, —ster ending.   **—y   dopy** *adj.* 1 Under the influence of a narcotic. 2 Stupid or slow, as if doped. 3 Inferior, unusual, boring, ill-planned, etc. *Said of people, objects, or actions.*

dope off 1 To sleep; to sleep very soundly, as if drugged. *c1915.* 1926: "And dope off for a little while." Stallings & Anderson, *What Price Glory,* II. 2 To act stupidly; to be inattentive or negligent. *Specif.* to be absent from one's post without authorization. *W.W.II Armed Forces use.* 1949: "I doped off for a cup of coffee." Movie, *Sands of Iwo Jima. Not as common as* **fuck off, goof off.**

dope out 1 To figure out a gambling or sports result from the available information and data. 1930: "... Doping out prospective winners at Saratoga." Lavine, *Third Degree,* 193. 2 To think or figure something out; to study available information in order to draw a conclusion, find a meaning, or plan future work. See **dope.**

dope sheet Written or printed information, as a set of written instructions; esp. printed information listing the past performances of racehorses.

dope stick *n.* A cigarette. *c1915.*

Dora = **dumb Dora.**

do-re-mi *n.* Money. *From a pun on dough* = *money, plus the second and third notes of the diatonic scale.* 1933: "Get the rubber band off the do-re-mi." Kieran, *Sat. Rev. of Lit.*

dorg *n.* A dog. *A humorous variant.* Cf. **purp.** *c1920.*

dorm *n.* A dormitory; specif., a residence hall for men or women college students. 1949–52: 'Dorm' occurs at least 278 times in the Cornell (Univ.) *Daily Sun* from Sept., 1949, to Jan. 16, 1952. 1951: "In every dorm, a little group of males/ Talks through the night of country, God, and frails." C. Welsh in *Amer. Scholar,* Autumn, 423. *Common student use since at least 1900.* See Appendix, Shortened Words. *adj.* Of, pertaining to, or provided by a dormitory. 1948–52: 'Dorm,' adj., occurs at least 165 times in the Cornell (Univ.) *Daily Sun* from Sept., 1949, to Jan. 16, 1952.

dornick   *n.* A stone. 1840: *DAE. Dial.*

dory   See **oky dory, hunky-dory.**

dose   *n.* **1** A bullet. *From "dose of lead."* 1934: "You wear a .32. . . . You caught up with him . . . slipped Harger the dose and got the money." Chandler, *Finger Man,* 34. *Not common.* **2** [taboo] A case of venereal disease, esp. syphilis or gonorrhea. See **doss house. 3** A surfeit; esp. a surfeit of being unfairly treated or deceived.

do-se-do   *n.* A dull prize fight, which consists chiefly of prancing around the ring. 1935: "The guys who are supposed to do the fighting go in there and put on the old do-se-do, and I consider this a great fraud upon the public." Runyon, 211. *From "do-si-do," a phrase recurrent in calls for square dancing.*

doss   *v.i.* To sleep.   *n.* **1** Sleep. 1894[1891]: ". . . Find good barns for a doss at night." J. Flynt. *Tramp use.* **2** A cheap, squalid lodging house; a flop house; a brothel. 1894: ". . . A queer kind of lodging house called . . . the two-cent doss." J. Flynt. **3** A bed. *All meanings more common in Eng. than in U.S.; all vagabond use.* See **dose.**
—er   *n.* A lodger or sleeper, as in a doss house.

doss house   A very cheap lodging house; a flop house; a brothel. *First two meanings more common in Eng., third meaning more common in U.S.*

do [one's] stuff   To do whatever it is one's business to do; to do as one has been doing or may be expected to do; to function in one's occupation; to work or act as one wants to. 1942: "Do your stuff—the old stufferoo." Musical comedy, *Louisiana Purchase,* Feb. 13. Cf. **strut [one's] stuff.**

dot   *n.* **1** An insignificant, worthless person. *Not common. Underworld use.* **2** The exact time; the exact amount. *Common in the colloq.* **on the dot. —s**   *n.* Money. *Obs.* **—ty**   *adj.* Senile; crazy; stupid; eccentric. *c1850.*

dot, on the   Exactly on time.

do the dirty on [someone] = do [someone] dirt.

do time   do [a specific period of time]   **1** To serve a sentence in prison. → **2** To spend or serve one's time, as by necessity or order. 1956: "Bix [Beiderbecke] did two years in the Davenport High School." S. Longstreet,

The Real Jazz Old and New, 102. 1950: ". . . Doing time in San Quentin. . . ." UP, San Francisco, July 9.

double   *n.* **1** Any alcoholic drink containing two standard portions of whisky. 1949: ". . . Something called Antek's A-Bomb Special, made simply by pouring triple shots instead of doubles into his glasses." Nelson Algren, *Man with the Golden Arm,* 89. **2** Two of anything; in sports, two victories on the same day. 1957: "[Jockey] Ted Atkinson scored a double, riding the winners of the 4th and 7th races." N.Y. *World Tel. & Sun,* July 18. **3** In horse racing, the "daily double," the first and second races bet as and considered as one. **4** One who strongly resembles another; a ringer. **5** Specif., an actor who performs dangerous feats in the place of another actor during the filming of a movie.

double, on the   **1** At "double time," a specif. number of paces per minute according to military use. *Orig. Army use.* → **2** At a run; fast; quickly. 1934: "They went with me on the double." Cain, *Postman,* 72. *Often used as a command or plea to hurry.*

double back   To reverse one's direction of travel; to return to a place one has departed from comparatively recently. 1920: "At St. Regis Amory stayed three days and took his exams with a scoffing confidence, then doubled back to New York to pay his tutelary visit." F. S. Fitzgerald, *This Side of Paradise,* 26. *Colloq.*

double-clock   *v.t.* To two-time. A fanciful variation of the colloq. **two-time.** 1933: "I told him he couldn't double-clock me." H. T. Webster.

doublecross   The betraying or cheating of one's associate[s]. *Also written* "XX" *or* "double-X." 1905: ". . . If you feel tempted to give the old gentleman the double cross. . . ." McHugh, *Search Me,* 83. 1939-40: "I know you gave me the XX. . . ." O'Hara, *Pal Joey,* 64.

double-cross   *v.t.* To betray or cheat. 1927: "Double-crossed somebody." Hemingway, *Killers.* **double-crosser** *n.* One who double-crosses. 1949: "You double-crosser!" Radio station WOR, Sept. 4. **double-crossing**   *adj.* Betraying, cheating. 1941: ". . . Doing a bit of double-crossing. . . . You double-crossing bastard!" G. Homes, *40 Whacks,* 110, 163.

double-dealing   *n., adj.* Unethical; insincere. 1957: "In music by Rodgers and Hart it [the musical play *Pal Joey*] sang of show business's double-dealing hero. . . ." *Life*, Oct. 14, 97.

double-decker   *n.* A sandwich having two layers of filling between three slices of bread or toast.

double dome   A thinker; an intellectual; a 'highbrow'; a well-educated person. 1943: "Old Double Dome Brisbane. . . ." H. A. Smith, *Putty Knife*, 141. 1956: "Princeton, N.J., where the double domes congregate." N.Y. *Post*, Aug. 2, 2. See **egghead**.   **—ed**   *adj.* Intellectual; having the high forehead commonly believed to indicate intelligence. 1950: ". . . The newspapers would have . . . called him a double-domed phony." Billy Rose, *synd. newsp. col.* Aug. 2.

double-gaited   double gaited   *adj.* Bisexual. 1939: "Duilio is not double gaited as far as I know." O'Hara, *Pal Joey*, 58. *An extension of the horse-pacing term.*

double-header   *n.* A customer who buys more than one of the same item at a time.   *adj.* Obtaining or winning two things; successful in two ways.

double in brass   **1** To play in a circus band and perform in a circus act. *Circus talk.* **2** To do any two different kinds of work; to be able to do more than one thing well.

double-o   double O   double-oo   *v.t.* To look at, or over, carefully; to examine. *From "once-over" or the resemblance of two wide-open eyes to two consecutive o's.* 1952: ". . . They got . . . a picture of me in the lobby frame. I stop for a second to double-o the frame. . . ." L. Stander, *Esquire*, June, 131/2.   *n.* **1** A close scrutiny; a once-over. *Usu. in* "the double-o." **2** A tour of inspection.

double-saw   *n.* A twenty-dollar bill or the sum of $20. *From "double sawbuck."* 1951: ". . . A terrible conspiracy which already has printed so many sheets of dollars, ten-spots and double-saws. . . ." W. Pegler, *synd. newsp. col.* Aug. 14.

double sawbuck   *n.* A twenty-dollar bill; the sum of $20. See **sawbuck**.

double scrud   *n.* = **scrud**. *Here the "double" makes the mythical disease of "scrud" even worse.*

double shuffle   **1** The act of cheating or taking advantage of a friend. Cf. **double cross**. **2** A hasty and confusing interview; a brush-off. **3** Deception, trickery, intended confusion, which one has received. *Usu. in, e.g.,* "I got the double-shuffle from him." *From the "double*

shuffle" of card mixing or dealing by which the card manipulator can cheat his opponents. **4** An instance of being ignored or given the cold shoulder.

double take   A quick second look or glance, usu. at a person; a sudden recognition that what was glanced over or thought of as common is actually remarkable. Specif., a second and admiring glance at an attractive woman. 1948: ". . . Then she turned around and . . . I did a double-take." F. Brown, *Dead Ringer*, 24. *Often in* "do a double-take." *Apparently from the photography term,* "take."   *v.i.* To do a double-take. 1952: "She was a very pretty lady . . . and that is why I double-took a little bit when she ordered a cigar with her after-dinner coffee." R. C. Ruark, *synd. newsp. col.* Apr. 28.

double-time   To double-cross; to two-time. *Not common.*

double-trouble   *n.* Extreme trouble, difficulty, or danger.   *adj.* Trouble-making. 1945. "Barbara Stanwyck/*That Double-Trouble Dame!*" *Movie advt. in newspaper.* See Appendix, Rhyming Slang.

double whammy, the   See **whammy**.

double-X = double cross.

dough   *n.* **1** Money; cash. *c1850.* 1890's: "And to get the dough we'll put our watch and chain in hock." H. S. Canby, *Harper's*, Feb., 1936, 355/2. *Orig. meant bribe money or money obtained unethically.* **2** An infantry soldier or other frontline soldier. 1933: ". . . 'A dough' that went over the hill." H. T. Webster. *From "doughboy." Army use.*

dough-ball   *n.* **1** A college student. 1851: ". . . A name given by the town's people to a student." Hall, *College Words*, 104. *Obs.* **2** Any boring, unimaginative person. **3** Fishing bait made from stale bread and cinnamon.

Doughboy   doughboy   *n.* A U.S. Army infantry soldier. *c1847* [1956]: "This bit of Army slang [Doughboys] dated to the battle of Monterey [Mexican war] . . . infantry baked a mixture of flour and rice in their campfire ashes and boasted of their first hot meal after 48 hours of fighting." Samuel E. Chamberlain, "My Confession," *Life*, July 23. *Very common during W.W.I. "G.I." more common W.W.II term. Orig. commonly supposed to be that infantrymen pound the mud of roads into dough.* **2** A baker in the U.S. Navy. *W.W.I use.*

doughfoot   *n.* An infantry soldier

1945: "Ex-doughfeet may shudder at this." NEA item, Memphis, Tenn., Dec. 18. *W.W.I and W.W.II use; not as common as "doughboy."*

dough-head   *n.* **1** A stupid person. **2** A baker. *Vagabond use.*

doughnut   *n.* An automobile tire. *Truckdriver use.*

doughnut factory   doughnut foundry doughnut house   doughnut joint **1** A very cheap eating place; a luncheonette. **2** A place where free food is dispensed. *Hobo use.*

dough-puncher   *n.* A U.S. Army or Navy baker. *Not common.*

dough-roller   *n.* A logging-camp cook. *Logger use.*

dough well done with cow to cover Having bread (or toast) and butter.

do up   To beat up. See **done up.**

do up brown   To do thoroughly; to treat severely.

dove   A term of endearment. See **turtle doves.**

dovey = **lovey-dovey.**

dow   See **row-dow, rowdy-dow, wow-dow.**

dowdy = **rowdy-dowdy.**

down   *v.t.* **1** To defeat another. *Colloq.* **2** To eat or drink, esp. to eat or drink rapidly or voraciously. *Colloq.* **3** To pass food at the table. 1943: "Down the meat." *Time,* quoting Marine Corps mag., *Chevron,* July 19, 69. *Some W.W.II Marine Corps use.*   *adj.* **1** Depressed; melancholy; pessimistic. Cf. **blue. 2** Sickly; exhausted; defeated. **3** Toasted; served on toast. *Lunch-counter use in relaying an order, usu. in "a ham sandwich down."* **4** Mean; tough; strong; skilled in fighting. *Teenage street-gang use since c1955.*   *n.* **1** In a nightclub or bar, a glass of cheap, appropriately colored liquid, as tea or a soft drink, sold to a male customer as whisky and to be drunk by a female employee of the management. **2** Toast. *Common lunch-counter use in relaying an order; usu. in, e.g., "an order of down."*

—down   See Appendix, Suffixes and Suffix Words.

down, get   Lit. and fig., to put one's money or chips down on a gambling table in making a bet; to make a bet; to make a bet on something. 1950: "That meant I had all four jacks—but they didn't know it. So I told the boys, 'All right, get down on this card.' 'Getting down' means to put some money up." A. Lomax, *Mr. Jelly Roll,* 107.

down [one's] alley = **up [one's] alley.**

down and dirty   *adj., adv.* Done to one's disadvantage; accomplished through trickery or deception. *From the card game of poker where "down and dirty" = the last card has been dealt, usu. face down on the table, and has not improved anyone's hand.* See **dirty.**

down and out   Without money; unsuccessful; straitened; destitute. 1949: "Spite is the word of your undoing. And when you're down and out, remember what did it." A. Miller, *Death of a Salesman,* 130. *Colloq.*

down-and-outer   *n.* One who is lit. or fig. a tramp, homeless and jobless, or living in poverty, and who will probably not be able to improve his way of life or become a useful member of society; a complete and helpless failure, specif. one unable to work or lead a normal life owing to having made a major mistake or to being a drunkard.

downbeat   *adj.* Of a movie, song, etc., more artistic or dramatic than entertaining; ending unhappily or without a moral; unusual. 1952: "It looks like a triumph of upbeat pictures over the downbeat." Bob Thomas, AP, Hollywood, Mar. 24. *Being replaced by "offbeat."*

downer   See in Appendix words ending in —er, of which many have downer as the second element. See **sun-downer.**

—downer   See Appendix, Suffixes and Suffix Words.

downhill   *n.* **1** The last half of a prison term. *Underworld use since c1930.* **2** The last half of an enlistment in the Armed Forces. *W.W.II use.* Cf. **over the hump.**   *adj.* **1** Decreasing; becoming less valuable, healthy, or the like; worsening. **2** Easy to accomplish; pleasurable; fig., requiring no more effort than rolling down a hill.

down in the kitchen   Low gear. *Truckdriver use.*

down on [someone], go [taboo]   To perform cunnilingus or fellatio on someone. *Fairly common. Both heterosexual and homosexual use.*

down the hatch   A pop. toast, after which a portion of whisky is drunk in one gulp.

down the line   **1** In the district of a city that contains brothels, cheap bars, or the like. **2** To go from one person to another, in decreasing order of their importance or authority, as in asking for a favor, seeking information, or the like.

Down Under   Australian; Australia and New Zealand. 1958: "Then in '51 the trek started Down Under as gold-hungry men from California set off to dig for the precious metal in Australia." A. D. Osborn, N.Y. *Her. Trib. Book Rev.*, Apr. 6, 1.

down with it To understand; to know; to dig. *Jive use. Older than "with it".*

down yonder The southern U.S.

dozen See **dime a dozen, play the dozens.**

dozer *n.* **1** A terrific blow with the fist. **2** Anything remarkable or ostentatious.

draft bait A man or men subject to immediate conscription. *W.W.II use.*

draftee *n.* A man conscripted for Army service. 1866: *DAE. Still in use.* See Appendix, —ee ending.

drag *n.* **1** A share, percentage, or portion of something. 1907: "I had a sneaking idea that [the brakeman] got a 'drag' out of the constable fees." J. London, *The Road*, 202. *Obs.* **2** Influence; pull. 1923: "We had a big drag with the waiter." E. Hemingway, "My Old Man." *Since c1890. Common c1920; archaic.* **3** A town or city street, esp. the main street. 1907: "From some bo on the drag I managed to learn what time a certain freight pulled out." J. London, *My Life.* 1948: "A block down the drag." F. Brown, *Dead Ringer*, 111. *Very common.* **4** A deep inhalation or puff of tobacco smoke, esp. of cigarette smoke; the act or an instance of taking just one or a few puffs on a cigarette; to take another's lighted cigarette, puff once or a few times, and return it to the owner. 1920: "The ponies took last drags at their cigarettes and slumped into place." Fitzgerald, *This Side of Paradise*, 61. *Common since c1915.* → **5** A marijuana cigarette. *Some c1930 addict use; obs.* → **6** A cigarette. 1956: "Sit around with a glass in your hand and a drag smoking on your lip, and just listen." S. Longstreet, *The Real Jazz Old and New*, 128. *Jazz use; orig. c1935 jive use.* **7** A homosexual gathering or party in which the participants wear clothes appropriate to the opposite sex; a gathering or party of transvestites; clothing appropriate to the sex opposite that of the wearer; transvestite clothing. 1948: "It's a law violation to appear in 'drag.'" Lait-Mortimer, N.Y. *Confidential*, 68. **8** A dancing party; a dance; a party. 1923: "Shoeshiner's Drag," title of song. *Still in wide student and teenage use.* **9** A girl or woman when escorted by a man at a social affair, esp. a dance; a man's date. 1950: "I'm his drag." Movie, *West Point Story. Orig. c1925 West Point and Annapolis use. Some student use.* **10** A dull or boring person. 1949: "A youth who used a dated expression would be strictly a 'drag.'" N.Y. *Times Mag.*, Mar. 6, 33/1. *Common since c1940.* → **11** A person, thing, event, or place that is intellectually, emotionally, or aesthetically boring, tedious, tiring, or colorless. 1954: "It's a funny thing how life can be such a drag one minute and a solid sender the next." L. Armstrong, *Satchmo, My Life in New Orleans*, 126. 1957: ". . . Her friends had come to see her [jazz singer Billy Holliday] and they weren't allowed in. She was crying and everything; it was a real drag." Leonard Feather, "Jazz Millionaire [Norman Grantz]," *Esquire*, May. *Orig. jazz use; c1946 bop use; very common with teenagers and students.* **12** A railroad train, esp. a freight train, specif. a slow or long one; a railway freight car. *Hobo and railroad use since c1920. Because the cars "draw" on the engine or "drag" freight.* **13** A short race between two or more hot-rod cars in which the car with the greatest rate of acceleration from a standing start wins. *Orig. c1950 hot-rod use; general teenage use.* See **drag race. 14** A roll of money, stock certificates, or other valuables used to entice a victim in a confidence game. 1958: "Drag—A pocketbook dropped as bait in a confidence game." G. Y. Wells, *Station House Slang. adj.* Accompanied by a partner or date of the opposite sex. *Often in "come stag or drag," used in invitations to a dance or party. Student use since c1940. v.i., v.t.* To curry favor, as with one's superior or one in authority. *Some use c1900. v.t.* **1** To understand or comprehend. *Some c1900 student use; obs.* See **dig. 2** To puff on or smoke a cigarette; to inhale deeply. **3** To take or escort a girl to a dance or party; to be escorted by a youth to a dance or party. 1924: "The other men who weren't 'dragging women' [to the Prom]. . ." Marks, *Plastic Age*, 136. **4** To bother or bore a person mentally or physically; to leave one with a nervous, unsatisfied feeling. *Usu. said of unsatisfying jazz music. Mainly bop and cool use since c1950. v.i.* **1** To attend a dance or party with a partner or date rather than alone. 1952: "The full dress uniforms [the West Point cadets] must wear to 'drag.'"

Life, Apr. 14, 147/1. *Since c1930.* **2** To be unexciting, dull, or boring; said of an entertainment. 1946: "Another problem in writing plays is action. Sometimes you have a situation where nothing is happening. People are just sitting around and talking. There is a great danger that the play will drag in such a situation, that it will become unbearably static." M. Shulman, *Zebra Derby*, 112. *Colloq.* **3** To participate in or hold an acceleration race between two or more hot-rods. *Hot-rod use since c1950.* **—ger** *n.* A patron who asks for change when giving a tip. **—ging** *n.* The act or an instance of drag racing. 1956: ". . . Dragging . . . spreads a psychological poison among the rising generation of drivers." *SEP*, Sept. 22, 10. **—gy** *adj.* **1** Unexciting, dull, boring. *Colloq.* → **2** Unsatisfying; nonintellectual; bothersome; emotionally or aesthetically colorless. *Cool use since c1950.* See **drag.**

drag [it]   To quit [a job]; to leave; to stop talking; to break off a relationship.

drag ass [taboo]   **1** To be melancholy, sad, or blue; to lack enthusiasms or energy, as from exhaustion, defeat, or apathy. **2** To leave, esp. in a hurry; to depart.

drag [one's] freight   To depart. Cf. **pull [one's] freight.**

drag in   To arrive.

drag in your rope   *imp.* Be quiet; shut up.

drag out   To tell something in a long, indirect way; to make a story, book, play, or movie longer than the action or plot demands. *Colloq.*   **drag-out** *n.* A dancing party.

drag race   A race between two or more cars, usu. hot rods, to determine which can accelerate the faster. Such formal or organized races are usu. over a quarter-mile distance on a drag strip, the competing cars starting from a complete stop. Less formal races may take place almost anywhere, including traffic-crowded streets, and begin usu. when the cars are in first or second gear and starting away from a stoplight that has turned from red to green. Such informal races are often between strangers, to show off their cars and driving ability, and from an aggressive enjoyment of being first away from a stoplight. *Hot rod use since c1945.* 1957: "Official drag race—the name apparently stems from the need to 'drag' or stay in low gears as long as possible. . . ." "The Drag Racing Rage." *Life*, April 29.

dragster   *n.* A car suitable for drag racing. *Hot rod use since c1950.*

drag strip   Any straight and flat ground, road, or strip of concrete, at least a quarter of a mile long, used for drag racing. *In formal, organized drag racing, such strips are often abandoned concrete airplane runways or small air strips.* 1957: ". . . The oldest drag strip in [the] U.S. . . ." "The Drag Racing Rage." *Life*, April 29, 132.

drag-tail   *v.t.* To move or work slowly or with difficulty, as with a burden. 1949: "Jimmy is drag-tailing it up Main St. [carrying a basket of fish]." Billy Rose, *synd. newsp. col.*, Nov. 2.

drag [one's] tail   **1** = **drag-tail. 2** To be depressed or melancholy. 1937 [1954]: "If you're givin' the men two hours off with pay, why the hell are they draggin' their tails!" P. di Donato, *Christ in Concrete*, reprinted in *Manhattan*, 138.

drap   *n.* A skirt. 1947: "A skirt is a drap. If pleated, it is a lapped drap. Buttoned, it becomes a bapped drap and if fastened with a zipper it is a zapped drap." Don Rose, Phila. *Bulletin*, Jan. 21, 13. From a school newspaper, *The Academian. Teenage usage.*

drape   *n.* **1** A suit; an ensemble of suit, shirt, tie, hat. *Jive use.* **2** A young man wearing black, narrow-cuffed slacks, a garish shirt, a loose lapel-less jacket, and no necktie; a later, more hip version of the zoot-suiter. 1950: "The true drape wore his hair seaweed-long. Drapes resent any comparison with zoot-sooters." *Time*, Jan. 30, 18/3. **3** Any article of clothing. **4** A dress. 1947: "Dresses are drapes and with belts they are shaped drapes." Don Rose, Phila. *Bulletin*, Jan. 21, 13. From a school newspaper, *The Academian. Teenage use.*

drape shape   *n.* **1** A severely draped garment, as worn by zoot-suiters. 1943: "Designing the first drape-shape coat. . . ." *New Yorker*, June 19, 14/3. *Usu. in ref. to a zoot suit.* See Appendix, Rhyming Slang. **2** A girl who has sex appeal. *Some c1940 student use; archaic.*

draw a blank   **1** To receive nothing; to obtain a negative or no result. **2** To forget; to be unable to remember a person, fact, etc. **3** To be drunk. **4** To fail to obtain another's interest or enthusiasm.

drawer   See **top-drawer, Maggie's drawers.**

draw one   To fill a glass with draft beer; usu. as an order. *Bar use in relaying an order.* **2** An order of a cup of coffee. *Common lunch-counter use in relaying an order.*

dream bait An attractive, personable, popular person of either sex; a desirable date. *Some student use since c1940.*

dreamboat *n.* **1** An exceptionally attractive person who, or thing that, fulfills one's image or "dream" of a perfect specimen; an ideal person or thing. 1957: "A dreamboat for hot-rodders is a chromed roadster like this one...." "The Drag Racing Rage," *Life,* April 29, 137. **2** Specif., an exceptionally beautiful or attractive and pleasing member of the opposite sex. 1947: "She is a dynamite dreamboat...." Popular song, "The Lady from 29 Palms." 1949: "[Ava Gardner] will star opposite James Mason, who she says is a 'dreamboat.' " AP, Hollywood, Nov. 4. **3** = **dream bait.** *All uses associated with young teenagers, but the word is considered corny by most young people.*

dreambox *n.* The head. *Jive use.*

dreamer *n.* **1** A bedsheet; a cover. → **2** A bed.

dream puss = **dream bait.** See **puss.**

dream-stick *n.* **1** An opium pill. **2** A cigarette. *Not common.*

dream up To invent; to make up; to imagine; to create. 1941: "Julian has to start dreaming up a story...." Schulberg, *Sammy,* 168. 1948: "... Conceptions of living dreamed up by such groups as the Mormons...." J. B. Roulier.

drek **dreck** *n.* **1** Any manufactured object of inferior material, design, workmanship, and over-all quality; any obviously inferior product. 1957: " '[Motion] Pictures! Drek! I am ashamed. . . . you should have seen me in such drek!' 'Drek has made you a very famous woman. A star.' " Al Morgan, "Master of the Revels," *Playboy,* May, 18. **2** Any cheap, gaudy items of merchandise; small, cheap, useless items. *From the Yiddish "dreck" = shit (feces).*

dress *v.t.* To increase the attendance at an entertainment by reducing admission prices and/or issuing free tickets. *Theater use.*

dressing down An extensive reprimand; a bawling out. 1952: "... A dressing down from the cop." R. C. Ruark, *synd. newsp. col.,* Aug. 14.

dressing out = **dressing down.**

drift *n.* **1** In automobile racing, a four-wheel skid purposely executed to turn a corner or round a curve at maximum speed; a device for maintaining full speed forward while moving sideways. 1957: "When Fangio puts his Maserati or Ferrari into a corner in a four-wheel drift (i.e., with all wheels skidding)...." *Life,* Aug. 15, 83. **2** Purport; import; meaning. 1929: "Snow again, baby, I get your drift." *Literary Digest,* Mar. 16, 23. 1934: Standard. *Web.* *v.i.* To go away; leave; depart; get out. Also "drift away." 1942: " 'Beat it,' he said. 'Drift.' " "... So speak your piece and drift away." Chandler, *High Window,* 59, 115. —**er** *n.* **1** A vagabond; a wanderer; a person without a steady job, occupation, or permanent address; a grifter. **2** A tramp. **3** An unimportant member of the underworld.

drift? get the *interrog.* An interrogatory expression meaning "Do you understand me?" Cf. **drift, 2.**

drill *v.i., v.t.* **1** To walk; to hike; to travel on foot. 1893: "I had to drill 20 miles that afternoon." J. Flynt. *Tramp use. Orig. during the Civil War.* **2** To walk idly. *Some jive use c1935.* **3** To move quickly, with force, and in a straight line; said of a bullet, baseball, car, or the like. 1957: "He noticed a car following his. As he turned into his driveway, he said, a shot from the trailing car entered the open window beside him, skimmed by his head and drilled through the closed window on the right." N.Y. *Daily News,* July 26, 12. **4** To shoot; to kill by shooting. **5** In baseball, to bat a ball. 1951: "Lockman drilled a single past Hodges into right field." Jack Hand, AP, New York, Oct. 3. *n.* See **blanket drill, sack drill.**

drink *n.* Any sizable body of water, from a small stream to an ocean; esp., however, the ocean. Often **the drink.**

drink, take a **take a fishing trip** In baseball, to strike out. *Baseball use.*

drink [one's] beer To shut up or stop talking. 1947: "Finally I had to tell him to drink his beer!" Hal Boyle, AP, May 18, 12.

drip *n.* **1** Flattery; sweet talk. 1924: "[The theme] was nothing but drip." Marks, *Plastic Age,* 297. *Some student use.* **2** Useless or idle talk, gossip. *Some c1930 hobo use.* **3** Any person, usu. a male teenager or student, who is disliked or who is objectionable, usu. because he is a bore, introverted, overly solicitous, or is not hip to the fads, fashions, and typical behavior patterns of his age group. 1948 [1954]: "Ginnie openly considered Selena the biggest drip at

Miss Basehoar's—a school ostensibly abounding with fair-sized drips." J. D. Salinger, "Just Before the War with the Eskimos," reprinted in *Manhattan*, 22. 1955: "And all these councilors and staff members [of a summer camp] are such drips. Oh, I don't mean that to sound nasty, but *you* know what I mean—they're just sort of dull." C. Willingham, *To Eat a Peach*, 48. *Teenage and student use since c1935; most pop. c1940–c1945.* *v.i.* To flatter; to sweet talk; to show greater concern than necessary. *Not common.* **—py** *adj.* Abounding in sentimentality; corny. c1940 [1952]: Shirley Temple, motion picture actress, quoted by J. Crosby, N.Y. *Her. Trib.*, Apr. 9, 29/1.

drive *n.* A stir of emotion; a thrill or kick; esp. the result of taking a portion of narcotic. 1949: "Sure I like to see it hit. Heroin['s] got the drive awright—but there's not a tingle to a ton." N. Algren, *Man with the Golden Arm*, 76. *v.i.* To play jazz or swing music with great enthusiasm and vigor. *Jazz and swing use.*

drive-in *n.* **1** A roadside restaurant equipped to serve customers food in their automobiles. *Colloq.* **2** An outdoor movie theater whose patrons watch from their automobiles. *adj.* **1** Offering customers service at their cars. Besides drive-in restaurants and movies, there are drive-in banks, cleaners, and even churches. **2** Having traveled or arrived from out of town by automobile.

driver *n.* A leg. *Railroad use.* See the Appendix for words ending in —er, many of which have "driver" as second element.

—driver See Appendix, Suffixes and Suffix Words.

drive up *imper.* Come here.

drizzle *n.* = **drip**. *Fig., a persistent or thorough drip.*

drizzle puss = **drizzle, drip.**

drone *n.* **1** A dull or boring youth. *Some teenage and student use c1940.* **2** An automatic, unmanned airplane, electronically controlled from an airbase or a manned plane. *Drones are used as moving targets for gunnery or missile practice. Air Force use since c1950.*

drool *v.i.* **1** Fig., to drool in eagerness or anticipation; to be eager or appreciative. *Usu. in jocular "stop drooling" to one who is obviously impressed by a pretty girl, stylish dress, expensive car, or the like. Common student use c1940. Still in use.* **2** To talk nonsense; to talk

vaguely or aimlessly. *c1895.* *n.* **1** Nonsense; foolish talk. 1929: "It gives me sharp and shooting pains/ To listen to such drool." Morris Bishop, *Paramount Poems*, 4. *Since c1900; very common c1940.* **2** A boy who is not approved of; a drip. **—er** *n.* A vague or aimless talker. Specif., a master of ceremonies, radio announcer, or other person with facility for impromptu speaking to fill in with talk when a program runs short of its allotted time or while waiting for a performer to arrive. **—y** *n.* An attractive and popular boy. *Very popular teenage use c1940.* See **ooly-drooly.** *adj.* **1** So good-looking as to elicit expressions of admiration from the opposite sex. 1952: ". . . Rain can turn the sharpest dressed drooly dream boat into a drizzly drip from the knees down." N.Y. *Daily News*, Aug. 26, 11c/1. **2** So attractive an object as to elicit expressions of admiration; esp. applied to articles of clothing, movies, cars, etc. **3** Excellent; wonderful; heavenly.

droop *n.* A person disliked for his languidness or stupidity. *c1940; teenage use.* **—ers** [taboo] *n.pl.* The female breasts. *Never common.*

drop *v.i.* To be arrested; to be caught in an illegal act. *v.t.* **1** To knock someone down. **2** To kill someone. **3** To catch [a thief] in possession of stolen goods. **4** To ship merchandise in small quantities to many places. **5** To supply illegal or contraband goods to a person. **6** To lose money quickly, by gambling, by making investments, or in quick business deals. *n.* **1** An ostensibly respectable place of business used as a cover for illegal business or as a hiding place for stolen goods or contraband. **2** A slum boy of unknown parentage; a homeless waif. 1944: ". . . A professional granny accepting anywhere from 25¢ to $1 a week for taking in drops, rustles, fetches or whatever you've a mind to call them." Walter Davenport, *Collier's*, Sept., 23, 13. *Harlem use.* **3** A paying passenger in a taxi. See **chocolate drop, knockout drops.** **—per** *n.* Any of various criminals who "drop" their victims; specif., a thief who knocks out or stabs the person he robs; a hired assassin. *Some underworld use c1930.*

drop a brick To blunder; to make an embarrassing mistake.

drop [one's] cookies = **shoot [one's] cookies.**

drop dead! A popular exclamation

expressing emphatic refusal, scorn, dislike, or disinterest. 1951: "Gifford announced to the loner that the loner's presence . . . was not . . . to Gifford's liking. . . . The loner shrugged his heavy shoulder. 'Drop dead,' the loner cried." Stan Smith, N.Y. *Daily News*, Aug. 9, 15C/4.

drop dead list   Fig., a list of people to be fired from a job, expelled from a school, excluded from a social activity, or given any type of refusal, punishment, or ostracism.

drop-in   *n.* A place frequented by a person or group, often to indulge in vice. 1948: ". . . Many of the furnished rooms . . . provide drop-ins for youths . . . seeking . . . marijuana revels." Lait-Mortimer, *N.Y. Confidential*, 46f.

drop joint = **drop.**

dropout   *n.* 1 A withdrawal; the act or fact of withdrawing, as from school. *Colloq.* 2 The person who withdraws.

drop quiz   A short unannounced examination; a shotgun quiz; pop quiz. *c1900; college use.*

drop the boom   1 To refuse further credit. 2 To ask a favor of someone. 3 To bawl out a person. See also **lower the boom.**

drop the lug on [a person]   To beg money from someone; to put the bite on [him]. 1945: "How's about droppin' the lug on you for thirty-five hundred?" Charles Carson.

drownder = **goose-drownder.**

drowning   *adj.* Confused; baffled; uncomprehending. 1949: ". . . It is natural . . . that . . . the pre-war slangy set should be baffled by the latest slang terms. Be 'drowning,' that is." The N.Y. *Times Mag.*, Mar. 6, 33/1.

drown [one's] troubles   To forget or try to forget one's problems and troubles by becoming drunk. *Fig. to drown one's troubles in whisky.*

drug on the market, a   1 Any item or product so plentiful as to have little value or to offer but small profit to those who sell it. → 2 Any disliked, unwanted person; a person whose presence is considered detrimental to the enjoyment of others; an average person.

drugstore cowboy   1 A western movie extra who loafs in front of drugstores between pictures. *c1928; movie talk.* 2 A man or youth who idles around public places showing off and trying to impress the opposite sex. 1949: ". . . Bell-bottom trousers so much in vogue with the drugstore cowboys of the day [1930].

A. Hynd, *Public Enemies*, 43. *The most common use. c1929; attrib. to cartoonist T. A. Dorgan.* 3 A braggart. 1952: "The Saturday night sport . . . was the forerunner of the cake-eater, the drugstore cowboy, and the modern-day corner wolf. . . . He had . . . the nonchalant air of a dead-game guy ready for any adventure." Hal Boyle, AP, Aug. 9.

drug-store race   A horse race in which one or more of the horses have been drugged or given alcohol. 1948: "What racketeers call 'a drug store race.' . . ." A. Hynd, *Pinkerton*, 80. Cf. **boat race.**

drum   *n.* 1 A saloon, nightclub, hotel, dive, joint, or the like. 1927: "Larrowy's—just one drum in a city that had a number of them. . . ." Hammett, *Blood Money*, 14. *c1900; obs.* 2 A prison cell.   *v.t.* 1 To announce; inform. 2 To try to get people enthusiastic over a product or cause; to advertise; to obtain customers or patrons. *Colloq.* 3 To sell merchandise, esp. as a traveling salesman sells to retailers. 1949: "A salesman eighty-four years old, and he'd drummed merchandise in thirty-one states." A. Miller, *Death of a Salesman*, 81. See **drummer.**   **—mer**   *n.* 1 A traveling salesman. 1900: "He was a . . . traveling canvasser . . . a class which at that time [1889] was first being dubbed by the slang of the day 'drummers.'" Dreiser, *Carrie*, 3f. 2 A railroad yard conductor. *Railroad use.*

drum-beater   *n.* A press agent.

drunk   *n.* 1 A drinking bout; a spree. *Colloq. since c1835.* 2 A state of intoxication. *Colloq. since c1840.* 3 An intoxicated person. *Colloq. since c1850.* 4 A habitual drunkard. *Colloq.* See **punch-drunk.** See Appendix, Drunk. **—ard**   *n.* A late Saturday night train. *Railroad use.*

drunk tank = **tank.**

dry   *n.* One who favors prohibiting the legal distilling or sale of liquor.   *adj.* 1 Thirsty. *Colloq.* 2 Prohibiting or in favor of prohibiting the sale of alcoholic beverages.

dry, on the   Abstaining from alcoholic beverages; on the wagon. *Never common.* See **dry.**

dryball   *n.* A boring or unsociable student; esp., a student who devotes nearly all his time to study. *College use. Not common.*

dry behind the ears   See **not dry behind the ears.** *The expression is seldom used in the affirmative.*

dry cush   Cookies.

dry-goods   *n.* **1** A girl or woman. *Since c1865.* See **calico.** **2** Clothing, esp. a suit, dress, or coat. *Negro use.*

drygulch   dry-gulch   *v.t.* **1** To murder, esp. by pushing off a cliff or from a high place. 1951: "How did your father die?" "He was drygulched." Movie, *Whirlwind. Orig. cowboy use meaning to kill sheep or cattle of rival ranches by stampeding them over a cliff or into a dry gulch.* **2** To knock unconscious; to beat up. 1940: "Then one of them got into the car and dry-gulched me." Chandler, *Farewell,* 62.

dry run   **1** Firing or shooting practice with blank or dummy ammunition. *Army use.* → **2** A rehearsal; any simulated action. **3** [taboo] Sexual intercourse during which a contraceptive is used.   *v.t.* To subject someone or something to a dry run. 1953: "The V[eterans'] A[dministration] invited Lemanowicz in a few days early so the hospital staff of 27 could 'dry run' their equipment." AP, Jan. 6.

dry up   To shut up; to stop talking. *Usu. a command or entreaty.* 1947: "Finally I just told him to dry up." Hal Boyle, Phila. *Bulletin,* May 19, 12. *Colloq. since c1850.*

D. T.'s   *sing.* Dementia tremors; delirium tremens. 1956: "When Bix [Beiderbecke] got the D.T.'s, [Paul] Whiteman treated Bix to a drunk cure." S. Longstreet, *The Real Jazz Old and New,* 106. *Universally known.* See Appendix, Shortened Words.

dualer   *n.* A double-feature movie show. *Not common.*

dub   *n.* One who does something awkwardly; a novice; a stupid person. *Colloq. since c1885.* See **flub-dub, flub the dub.**   *v.t.* To insert additional material, such as background music or commentary, into a previously recorded program, sound track, or record.

ducat   ducket   *n.* **1** A ticket of admission, as to a circus, prize fight, football game, or show. 1949: "How much d'I owe you for the [football] ducats?" Red Skelton, radio program, Oct. 30. *c1915 to present.* **2** A pass; a free ticket. **3** A union card or work permit. *Hobo use.* **4** A begging letter; a printed card asking for alms for a deaf and dumb beggar. *Hobo use.* **5** A dollar; money. 1931: ". . . Which will keep him in ducats for the rest of his life. . . ." Queen, *Dutch Shoe,* 72.

ducat-snatcher   *n.* A ticket taker.

duchess   *n.* **1** A girl; esp. a snobbish or aloof girl. **2** A girl who is in the know or who belongs to a jive or underworld group. **3** A female member of a street gang. *Teenage use.*

duck   *n.* **1** A man or boy; fellow; guy; bird. 1905: "That duck isn't a critic. . . ." McHugh, *Search Me,* 51. *Colloq. since c1870. Arch.* → **2** A simple man who is easily imposed on; a pleasant fellow; an amiable eccentric. *c1840.* → **3** A dupe, a sucker. *Underworld use.* **4** A score of zero in a game. *From "duck-egg." c1900.* **5** A bed urinal. *cW.W.I to present. Common hospital use, from its ducklike shape.* **6** A partly smoked cigarette; a butt. *Perhaps from the motion used in picking one up from the ground.* **7** Any amphibious vehicle, such as a flying boat or amphibious tank. *cW.W.II.* See **dead duck, lame duck, ruptured duck.** **8** A ticket. *From "ducket."* See Appendix, Shortened Words. **9** = **D. A.,** haircut.   *v.t.* To evade something or someone. 1950: "They always had it in their minds that a musician was a tramp, trying to duck work." A. Lomax, *Mr. Jelly Roll,* 5.

duck bumps   *n.pl.* Goose pimples; goose bumps.

duck-butt   *n.* A person of short stature. *Not common.*

duck-egg   *n.* A grade or mark of zero: a score of zero, as in a game. *c1900.* See **goose egg.**

ducket = ducat.

duck-fit   *n.* A fit of anger. 1928–29: "Clarice . . . would throw a duck-fit, if she knew." Elmer Rice, *Street Scene,* III. *Alluding to the loud squawking of an angry duck.*

duckie   ducky   *adj.* **1** Good-looking; attractive. **2** Fine; also often used ironically, e.g., "Isn't that just ducky?" 1948: "Is everything okay?" "Everything's ducky." F. Brown, *Dead Ringer,* 14. **3** Cute; dainty; corny. 1943: "Pastel phials tied with ducky satin bows." Chandler, *Lady in Lake,* 1.

ducks   *n.* **1** A pair of white flannel trousers. *A perennial summer favorite of students.* **2** A lighted cigarette stub.

duck's ass [taboo] = **D. A.,** a boy's haircut. *Common rock-and-roll use since c1954. Not as common as the abbr. "D.A."*

duck soup   **1** Any person easily overcome, convinced, or the like; one who is easy prey; a pushover. 1936: "Them big yaps are duck soup for me."

Tully, *Bruiser*, 67. **2** Anything that is easily done; a cinch.

duck tail = **D. A.**, haircut.

ducrot *n.* Anything or anyone whose name is not known. *West Point use.* See **dumbjohn, Mister Ducrot, Mister Dumbguard.**

dud *n.* **1** A shell or bomb that has been fired or thrown, but because of a faulty fuse has not exploded. *Colloq. since W.W.I. Perhaps related to "dead."* → **2** A failure; any ineffective, useless person or thing, as a worthless hand of cards, a false story, a social misfit. 1933: [Social misfit] "He was a wet smack—a social dud to you. . . ." H. T. Webster. 1947: [False story] "The story turned out to be a dud." J. H. Jackson, *San Francisco Murders*, 162. *adj.* Ineffective; useless.

duddy = **fuddy-duddy.**

dude *n.* **1** An overdressed man. *Perhaps from or related to duds = clothes.* → **2** A man from the East or a city man vacationing on a ranch. c1885. *Western use.* → **3** A well-dressed, dapper, ladies' man. → **4** A bus tourist of either sex; formerly, a stagecoach tourist. **5** A railroad conductor. *Railroad use.* **6** An Army recruit. *Some W.W.II Army use.*

dude heaver = **bouncer.**

dude up To dress like a dude; to wear one's best clothes. *Colloq. since c1890.*

dudine *n.* **1** A female dude. 1883: *DAE. Still some derisive ranch use. Dial.* **2** Any female tourist. *Dial. Not common.*

Dudley = **Uncle Dudley.**

duds *n.pl.* Clothes. *Colloq. Brought over by colonists from Eng.*

duff *n.* **1** Any sweet food, such as candy, cake, or cookies. *Not common.* **2** The posterior, butt, seat. 1952: ". . . A bunch of lazy guys sitting around on our duffs. . . ." *Time*, Aug. 25, 12/2. See **huff-duff.**

duffer *n.* **1** A dull, stupid, or unrealistic person. *Obs.* **2** Any elderly man who is somewhat senile, eccentric, or mischievous for his age. *Used either affectionately or critically; almost always in the phrase "old duffer."*

duff gen = **gen.**

dugout *n.* The refrigerator, from which it is possible to dig out food for snacks. *Teenage use.*

duke *n.* **1** A person's hand, esp. when considered as a weapon or tool. 1946: ". . . Two . . . guys started belting away with their dukes." D. Runyon, *synd. newsp. col.*, Sept. 14. *c1880.* **2** The winning decision in a prize fight. 1936: "Well,

even if I lose the duke I got forty percent of five hundred, ain't I?" Tully, *Bruiser*, 16. *From the winner's raising his hands over his head in victory.* **3** "The duke." A bull. *Farm use.* *v.t.* **1** To hand something to a person. **2** To attempt to sell some article by handing it to one person, as a child, and asking payment from his companion, as the child's parent. *Circus and pitchman use.* **3** To shortchange a person by palming a coin that is part of the change due to him. *Circus and pitchman use.* **4** To shake hands with a person. **dukie dookie** *n.* **1** A meal ticket. *Carnival use, obs. by c1935. Because it is held in the "dukes," or perh. from "ducat."* **2** A lunch wrapped up at a circus cooktent to be handed out to workmen; a box lunch. **—s** *n.pl.* **1** The hands, esp. the hands as fists. 1953: "The Cockney in his ordinary conversation calls his hands his 'dooks.' This latter comes by way of a devious route: 'dooks' from 'dukes'; 'dukes' from elliptical rhyming slang, 'Duke of Yorks' rhyming on 'forks'; 'forks' is slang for 'fingers,' and 'fingers' is used to express the hands." J. Franklyn, *The Cockney*, 291. See Appendix, Rhyming Slang. **2** The knees. *Some c1935 jive use.*

duket = **ducat.**

dukie book A book of meal tickets. *Circus use. Archaic.* See **dukie.**

dum = **rum-dum.**

dumb *adj.* **1** Stupid; foolish. *Colloq. since c1820. From Pa. Dutch, "dumm."* 1925: "You think I'm pretty dumb, don't you?" F. Scott Fitzgerald, *The Great Gatsby*, 130. **2** Damn. *Colloq. since 1780.* *adv.* Stupidly. 1934: "Don't talk so dumb." Cain, *Postman*, 31. *v.t.* To dull the mind. **—o** *n.* **1** A stupid person. 1951: "Edison was a dumbo in school." Radio station WHK, Cleveland, Jan. 27. See Appendix, **—o** ending. **2** A stupid mistake; a boner. 1952: "If you think you've seen dumbos pulled on the highways, you haven't seen anything until you [have seen careless boaters]." *SEP*, Sept. 20, 40. See Appendix, **—o** ending.

dumb-bell *n.* A stupid person. 1921: "The Crown Prince of dumb-bells." Witwer, *Leather*, 40. *Attributed to cartoonist T. A. Dorgan.*

dumb bunny A somewhat stupid person; implies a shade of endearment in or toleration of the person.

dumb cluck **dumb-cluck** *n.* A dull or stupid person; one who makes many blunders or mistakes; a careless person. 1935: "All those dumb clucks snickering at you. ..." S. Lewis in *Scribner's*, Aug., 68/2. 1949: "The dumb cluck left his key in the door." Radio network program, *Martin Kane, Private Eye*. *Colloq.* Cf. **cluck.**

dumb Dora   **1** A stupid girl. 1924: "Flappers' use, known to everyone." Vizetelly, *Literary Digest*. **2** A man's sweetheart.

dumb-head   *n.* A stupid person. 1940 [1932]: "This dumbhead . . . has just gone nuts." Queen, *Tragedy of X*, 117. *Colloq. since c1885.*

dumbjohn   *n.* **1** = **Ducrot.** *West Point use.* **2** A person easily deceived or tricked; one who is not wise or worldly; an easy mark; one who is stupid; esp. one who is not hep.

dumb otiġ   A young man from the country; an otiġ. *c1920; obs.*

dumb ox   A stupid, slow-thinking person, esp. a large, awkward one. *Colloq.*

dummy   *n.* **1** A stupid person. *Colloq.* **2** Bread. *Hobo use.* **3** A train carrying railroad employees. *Railroad use.* **4** [taboo] The penis. *Not common.*

dummy, beat the [taboo]   To masturbate; said of a male.

dummy up   To refuse to reveal information or a confidence; to refuse to talk or sing; fig., to act as if one were dumb. 1942: "You can't dummy up on a murder case." Chandler, *High Window*, 125. 1950: "When questioned, they [my children] invariably dummy up." S. J. Perelman, *New Yorker*, Apr. 22, 28/3.

dump   *n.* **1** Any unattractive, cheap, shabby, or wretched house, apartment, hotel, theater, or the like; a joint. 1930: "It's [a house] the same old dump." Lavine, *Third Degree*, 141. *The most common use.* **2** Any building, irrespective of the cost, state of repair, furnishings, or reputation, as a store, apartment, room, house, bunkhouse, nightclub, hotel, etc. 1930: "[The hotel is] a swell dump." B. Brown in *Outlook*, Nov., 417. **3** A prison. *Some underworld and prison use since c1925.* **4** A city or town. **5** A sporting contest in which one contestant or team has been bribed to lose; a fixed fight, race or game. 1951: " 'Dumps' and fixes. ..." *Time*, Mar. 4, 50/1.   *v.t.* **1** To bunt a baseball. 1927: "To dump one." F. Graham in N.Y. *Sun*, July 18. **2** To beat a person up; to assault a person. *Not common.* **3** Purposely to lose

a game or other sports contest; to play poorly in a contest because one has been bribed to do so. 1951: "Players accepting bribes to 'dump' games. ..." AP, Mar. 21. **4** To rid oneself of something; to reject or refuse a person.

dump a load [taboo]   To defecate.

dune-leaper   *n.* A Coast Guardsman on shore duty. *Not common. USN use.*

dunk   *v.t.* **1** To dip something, usu. pastry, into a liquid, usu. a beverage. 1932: "John is dunking a piece of rye bread in my coffee." Runyon, 41. 1949: "Scientific temperature readings [of a liquid] cannot be taken just by dunking a thermometer on a string." G. Hill in N.Y. *Times*, Oct. 2, 59/3. **2** To score points in a basketball game; fig., to "dump" the basketball through the basket.

dupe   *n.* A duplicate copy of something, as made from a film negative, a mimeograph or other duplicating machine, or a carbon copy of typed material. See Appendix, Shortened Words.

duper = **super-dooper.**

dust   *n.* **1** Gold dust. *c1860; California Gold Rush term; obs.* **2** Money; cash. *From gold dust. Arch.* **3** Tobacco; chewing tobacco; snuff. *Dial.* **4** The ground. **5** Powdered narcotics. See **bite the dust, sawdust, sea dust.**   *v.i.* To run away; to depart quickly. 1949: "Dillinger . . . used a Ford . . . when dusting from a job." A. Hynd, 3. *Colloq. since c1865; c1935 jive use; not common.*   *v.t.* **1** To hit or strike. 1950: "[Miners] dusted one of [the district leader's] lieutenants with an old shoe for trying to talk them back to work." *Time*, Jan. 30, 14/2. **2** To spray insecticide on crops from an airplane; to spray. *Colloq.*   **—er**   *n.* **1** In baseball, a pitch purposely thrown very close to the batter. See **dust [someone] off.** **2** A woman's smock or house-coat, worn over or instead of usual clothes. *Colloq.* **3** A chicken thief. *Obs.* See **ear-duster, feather duster.**   **—s**   *n.pl.* Brass knuckles. *From "knuckle-dusters." Underworld and street gang use.*   **—y Dusty**   *n.* = **dusty butt,** often as a nickname.

dust-dust   *n.* A newly promoted corporal, sergeant, or other noncommissioned officer. *In jocular allusion to the frequent brushing that they give their new chevrons. Some W.W.II use reported.* See Appendix, Reduplications.

dust 'em off   **1** To study. → **2** To talk

about the past; to be required to produce facts or data that have been forgotten or filed away. *From the concept of dusting off old books.* 3 To return to a job, hobby, or sport after a long absence.

dust [one's] jacket   To beat a person up.

dust [someone] off   1 To hit someone; to beat someone up. 2 In baseball, to pitch a ball close to the batter without hitting him, thus forcing him to move back from the plate and perhaps interfering with his ability to concentrate on the next pitch; the act of so pitching, or the pitch itself. → 3 To hit or try to hit a batter with a pitched ball. 1952: "This 'dusting off' of batters is a risky business. . . . it's remarkable that only one fatality has resulted from this . . . practice." Arthur Daley, N.Y. *Times*, Sept. 10, 37/1.

dust [one's] pants   dust [one's] trousers   To spank a child.

dust-raiser   *n.* 1 A farmer. 2 A locomotive fireman. *Railroad use.*

dustup   *n.* A disturbance; uproar; fuss; commotion. 1950: "There was a big dustup in the office of a vice-president . . . when a carbon of an important letter . . . couldn't be found." *New Yorker*, Sept. 2, 17/1.

dusty butt   *n.* A short person; lit., a person built so close to the ground that his butt or rump is always dusty. *Some student use.*

dutch   *v.t.* 1 Orig., to bet on each horse in a race proportionally, so that any winner will return more than the total amount bet. *The introduction of paramutuel totalizators made this kind of betting impossible.* → 2 To ruin something, as a plan; to ruin one's chance of successfully completing a task; to cause another to fail.

Dutch   *n.* A type of men's haircut, similar to the "Detroit." *v.t.* 1 To ruin or destroy a person's business, health, or social standing, and to do so with malice. 2 In gambling, to place a series of bets, in a mathematical relation or from knowledge of a prearranged outcome, so that the gambling house or owner of the game is ruined. See **Dutch act, Dutch rub, Dutch treat, go Dutch, in Dutch.**

Dutch, go   To pay for one's own refreshments or entertainment when in another's company ; to take part in a Dutch treat. 1914: "We'll go Dutch. . . ." Sinclair Lewis, *Our Mr. Wrenn*, 58.

Dutch, in   1 Having incurred the wrath or dislike of someone on whom one's success or happiness depends. 2 In trouble; in disfavor; in wrong.

Dutch act, the   Suicide; the act of committing suicide. 1935: "She only came aboard to do the Dutch act." J. O'Hara, *Butterfield 8*, 247. 1951: "The guy was ready to pull the Dutch act so I gave him back his dough. . . ." Spillane, *Big Kill*, 81.

Dutch book   A small-time handbook, specif. one that will accept horseracing bets of less than one dollar. *It is assumed that such a bookmaking establishment can be "dutched" easily, but the other "dutch" sl. words, such as "Dutch act," "Dutch treat," and "Dutch uncle," all have some basic connotation of disaster, dislike, and cheapness, indicating that there may have been a common root.*

Dutch courage   False courage or bravery inspired or supported by intoxication. *From 17th C. Brit. sl., coined during a period of belligerency between Eng. and the Dutch.* 1913: "A man in liquor . . . is full of Dutch courage." F. K. Sechrist.

Dutch rub   The act of rubbing vigorously a small area of another's head, causing minor pain. *A schoolboy's trick; term common since c1910.*

Dutch treat   An instance of each of two or more persons paying his own way or for his own refreshment and entertainment; an outing or date during which each participant pays his own way. *Colloq.*

Dutch uncle   A person, usu. a man, who talks to another severely. 1913: "A 'Dutch uncle,' whose every word is reproof." F. K. Sechrist.

duty = sack duty.

dyke   *n.* 1 A female homosexual who plays the male role, esp. a large, masculine-looking woman. → 2 One who is subservient to another. 1951: "At Virginia Military Institute [the first-year cadets] serve as 'dykes' (fags) for their seniors, run errands, polish shoes. . . ." *Time*, May 28, 50. *Some military school use. Not common.*

dynamite   *n.* 1 Part of a bet or money bet on a horse that a bookmaker bets elsewhere or transfers to another bookmaker in order to reduce possible loss. 2 Marijuana or heroin, esp. a marijuana cigarette. *Some addict use.* *v.t.* To lure customers or patrons by false or garish advertising. 1956: "Touts were allowed to advertise winners they did not have. This was called 'blasting,' 'dynamiting,' or 'bulldogging.' " T. Betts, *Across the Board*, 240. *adj.* Scandalous; shocking; certain to cause a scandal. *Attrib. use. Colloq.* **—r**   *n.* A driver who abuses a truck through unnecessary hard, fast driving. *Truckdriver use.*

E

E   *n.* **1** A flag or insigne awarded during W.W.II for proficiency in helping the war effort. *A flag with an "E" on it signified that a war plant was producing quality goods rapidly for the Armed Forces; an "E" painted on the stack of a USN ship signified the efficiency of the crew; and the like.* → **2** Any award or compliment. *Some W.W.II use.*

eager beaver   One who seems overly diligent to his coworkers or acquaintances; an extremely diligent, ambitious person; esp. one who tries to impress his superiors by his diligence and eagerness to serve. 1945: "His talk of slick chicks and eager beavers naturally bewilders the natives." L. Lee, Phila. *Bulletin*, Aug. 18, 5/2. *Wide student use since c1940. May be used as a compliment, but usu. is applied derisively to one who seems overly ambitious or aggressive in his work.*   *adj.* Ambitious; industrious; eager to please. 1951: "The eager beaver cop." Spillane, *Big Kill*, 10.

eagers, the   Anxiety; haste. *Not common.*

eagle   *n.* An adept fighter pilot; a fighter pilot who has shot down many enemy planes. *Air Force use.*

eagle-beak [derog.]   *n.* A Jew. 1939: "He works for kikes. Catch me workin' for one of them eagle-beaks." J. T. Farrell, 181.

eagle day   Payday. *W.W.II Armed Forces use. In ref. to the eagle appearing on U.S. banknotes and coins; also the eagle is popularly said to scream or shit on payday.* See **day the eagle shits.**

eagle-eye   *n.* **1** Fig., one who sees or watches as well as an eagle, which is known traditionally for its keen vision. **2** A locomotive engineer. *c1915 railroad use.* **3** A detective, esp. a detective assigned to watch for shoplifters or pickpockets.

eagle shits, the   See **day the eagle shits.**

ear   *n.* The handle of a drinking cup. 1934: "That which resembles . . . the ear. . . ." *Web., standard use.* 1953: ". . . Wrapping a finger around the ear of my coffee cup." Peter De Vries, *New Yorker*, May, 2, 27/1.   **—s**   *n.pl.* The testes. *A euphemism.* Cf. **lungs.** See **on [one's] ear, pig's ear, pin [someone's] ears back, pound [one's] ear, pull in your ears, wet behind the ears.**   **—ful**   *n.* News or gossip; a fairly large amount of talk. 1929: "I want the boys to get an earful. . . . I'll have to go over and give that bird an earful." Burnett, *Little Caesar*, 74, 83.

ear, get up on [one's] = **on [one's] ear.**

ear, on [one's]   **1** Angry or indignant, esp. to the point of being eager to argue or fight. 1879: "Why some members of this House always 'got up on their ear.' . . ." Thornton. 1926: "Don't get on your ear about it." Stallings & Anderson, *What Price Glory*, III. *Usu. in "get, get up, or be on one's ear." Obs.* **2** *Euphem. for "on one's ass."* 1939: "His hat store went kerflooie, and he's on his ear now." J. T. Farrell, 189. *Fig., to be knocked or thrown down to a sitting position.*

ear-banger   *n.* **1** One who tries to curry favor by flattery; a yes man; an apple-polisher; a handshaker. *W.W.II Armed Forces use.* **2** A braggart.

ear-bender   *n.* An overtalkative person.

ear duster   **1** In baseball, a ball pitched at or close to the batter's head. See **bean ball. 2** A gossip; one who talks at great length to another, usually revealing confidences. **3** A piece of gossip; a piece of surprising or extremely interesting personal news.

early bright   Dawn; morning; the daytime. Cf. **bright.** *Some c1935 jive use; now some bop, cool, and far out use; some teenage use since c1955.*

earn (have) [one's] wings   To prove oneself as responsible, reliable, mature, or skilled.

ears into   To eavesdrop.

easy   See **free-and-easy, speakeasy.**

easy, take it   An admonition, command, plea, or advice to another to relax, to stop worrying, to become calm and unemotional, or to enjoy life and accept it as it is. *Also often used on* *parting, in place of "good-by." Colloq.*

easy as pie   Very easy. See **pie.**

easy digging   1 Sugar. *c1900. Railroad lineman use.* 2 Anything accomplished with ease; a sure success.

easy make   1 [taboo] A girl or woman who can easily be persuaded to enter into coitus. Cf. **make.** 2 One easy to persuade or convince, esp. to victimize, deceive, or defeat; a customer who is receptive to a sales talk.

easy mark   A person who is easily convinced, victimized, or cheated. 1907: "He was . . . an 'easy mark.' " Jack London, *My Life.* See **mark.**

Easy Street   easy street   1 Financial independence. 1903: "On easy street." *DAE*, slang. 2 A way of life characterized by wealth and luxury; a pleasant and successful life; successful business dealings. *Almost always in "on easy street."* 1919: "The firm was at once as busy as a bee-hive, on 'easy street' again." T. Dreiser reprinted in *The American Twenties*, 432.

easy walkers   Rubber-soled canvas shoes. c1915 [1954]: "Black easy-walkers, or sneakers as they are now called." L. Armstrong, *Satchmo, My Life in New Orleans*, 47. *Archaic.*

eat   *v.t.* 1 To annoy or bother a person greatly; to trouble someone to distraction; usu. in "What's eating you?" 1916: "What's eating you?" *New Repub.*, Dec. 30, 244/2. 1949: "What was eating her?" Billy Rose, *synd. newsp. col.*, Dec. 30. 2 [taboo] To perform cunnilingus or fellatio on a person, esp. cunnilingus. 1951: "There must be Turkish blood in the family. I could eat you. . . ." S. Longstreet, *The Pedlocks*, 270. *Universally known. One of the major words with a stand. food meaning and a sl. sex meaning.* See Appendix, Sex and Food.   **—s**   *n.pl.* Food; meals. *Colloq. since c1910. Very popular on roadside restaurant signs, because it is the shortest word that can be put on a sign to advertise a restaurant.*

eat [someone] (up) (with a spoon)   1 To consider someone as exceptionally sweet, adorable, or cute. *Usu. said of babies or children.* 2 [taboo] = **eat.** *Considered a euphem. since in its usu. context it can be considered as having the first meaning.*

eat dirt   To take severe criticism, insults, or a reprimand meekly; to grovel in front of another. 1947: "I ate dirt and apologized to that bastard. That's how surprised I was when he

pulled that stuff about expelling me. The bastard—I'll never forget how he made me eat dirt." C. Willingham, *End as a Man*, 183.

—eater   See Appendix, Suffixes and Suffix Words.

eat [someone] out   To reprimand; bawl out; chew out. 1952: "Out came Joe McCarthy from the Boston dugout all set to eat me out." Gilbert Millstein, N.Y. *Times Mag.*, Sept. 14, 19/1.

ech!   *interj.* An expression of disgust or disinterest toward an inferior or worthless item or person. *From the Yiddish. On rare occasions used as an adj. = disgusting, ugly, inferior.*

echo   *n.* 1 An order repeated on request to clarify. *c1930; lunch-counter and Air Corps use.* 2 An underling of a politician; a close follower and popularizer of another's ideas.

Ed   *n.* A square; one who is not hip. 1943: "That G. L. [Guy Lombardo] . . . strictly a square, an Ed." M. Shulman, *Barefoot Boy with Cheek*, 90.

—ed   See Appendix, Suffixes and Suffix Words.

Eddy   *n.* The shoe width E. *Retail shoe-salesman use.* See **George Eddy.**

Edgar   *n.* The shoe width E. *Shoe-store use.*

edge   *n.* 1 A state of mild intoxication. Usu. in "have an edge [on]." 1920: ". . . We'll drink to Fred Sloane, who has a rare, distinguished edge." Fitzgerald, *This Side of Paradise*, 122. 2 A slight advantage. *Colloq.*   **—ed**   *adj.* Drunk; having an edge [on]. 1934: "When he was nicely edged he was a pretty good sort of guy. . . ." Chandler, *Finger Man*, 104.

edge on [someone], have an   To have an advantage over another person, esp. to have an advantage that will, lit. or fig., enable one to best another in a contest of strength.   **edge on, have an**   To be drunk.

—ee   See Appendix, Suffixes and Suffix Words.

eel   *n.* A clever prisoner; a smooth guy. Esp., a criminal who is too slippery for the police to catch easily or a politician or businessman who refuses to make concrete statements of opinion.

eel's hips, the   A term of strong approval equivalent to "the cat's meow"; sleek; slick. *"She's the eel's hips" was a popular c1920 term.*

eel-skin   *n.* A piece of paper money. *c1830; obs.*

egg   *n.* 1 A person, usu. male; a man,

fellow, guy, "bird," or the like. *A neutral word which takes its sense of approval or disapproval from a modifier, as "a good egg," "a bad egg," "a dumb egg," etc.* 1924: "He told him that he was a good egg." Marks, *Plastic Age*, 48. 1930: "Occasionally, a really tough egg is trained to be a killer." Lavine, *Third Degree*, 30. 1935: "He's a swell egg." "That dumb egg could sell auto paint to an Eskimo!" S. Lewis in *Scribner's*, Aug., 71/1; 72/1. 1950: "He was really a tough egg . . . terrible to get along with, always in some argument." Alan Lomax, *Mr. Jelly Roll*, 11. *Since c1850; orig. from a concern with the edibility of actual eggs; sl. use restricted to "good egg" and "bad egg" until c1885.* **2** Something egglike in shape, specif.: a zero or nought, a baseball, the human head; etc. *Various uses since c1875.* **3** A newly arrived member of the American Expeditionary Forces in France during W.W.I. *W.W.I Army use. Fig., the arrival is as new as a freshly laid egg.* → **4** A student pilot; a pilot recently graduated from flying school. *Some W.W.I and W.W.II Air Force use.* **5** Any of several kinds of explosive missiles, esp. a bomb to be dropped from an airplane, a hand grenade or small bomb to be thrown, or a naval mine. 1918: "On a bombing expedition the aviator drops the machine's 'eggs.'" McCartney in *Texas Rev.*, 79. *All these uses both W.W.I and W.W.II Armed Forces. Orig. = aerial bomb, prob. because a plane drops bombs in the manner of a hen laying an egg, rather than in ref. to the shape of the bomb.* **6** A rude boy or young man; esp. an escort who expects his date to pay for her own food and entertainment. *Some c1920 use. Used alone, without modifier. Cf.* **dutch treat.** *v.t. =* **egg on.**

egg, full as an   Very drunk. See **full.**

eggbeater   *n.* **1** An airplane propeller. *W.W.II Air Force use.* **2** A helicopter. 1952: "The 'egg-beater' took off for Inchon with its burden. . . ." AP, Korea, Aug. 21. *Colloq. From the appearance and motion of its rotor blades.* **3** A woman's hair style, shoulder length or shorter, featuring a tousled, windblown, almost disheveled effect, usu. worn with a headache band. The hair behind this band is deliberately arranged to fall over the band onto the face. *Common c1958.*

egg-crate   *n.* An automobile. 1952:

"I know the home port of that egg-crate they were driving!" Merrill Blosser, *synd. comic strip, "Freckles,"* Apr. 28. Cf. **crate.**

egghead   *n.* **1** A bald man. **2** A stupid person. *Some c1935 student use. Obs.* **3** An intellectual; one who makes decisions intellectually rather than emotionally; one who does not participate in popular fads and diversions; a person deeply interested in cultural or scientific affairs. 1957: "I have always been attracted by the egghead—the bright man with the vital, curious mind, the man with talent and imagination." F. Emerson, "Eggheads Make the Best Lovers," *Esquire*, Nov., 66. 1958: "Somebody asked Adlai Stevenson what's an egghead and the man said that an egghead is 'one who calls Marilyn Monroe Mrs. Arthur Miller.'" P. Sann, N.Y. *Post*, May 4, M6. *Pop. during presidential campaign of 1952 when the supporters of Adlai Stevenson, Democratic candidate, were called eggheads. Thus orig. the term carried the connotation of "politically minded" and "liberal"; today its application is more general. May have originated in ref. to the high forehead of Mr. Stevenson or of the pop. image of an academician.*

egg [someone] on   To persuade or goad someone into doing something, esp. to belligerent action; to encourage; to entice; to cajole.

egg orchard   A henhouse; a chicken farm; a farm. *Some archaic hobo and facetious use.*

egg-sucker   *n.* One who seeks advancement through flattery rather than work; a "weasel."

egg up   To raid the galley at night. *By analogy with coal up, water up, gas up, flick up. Not common.*

eightball   *n.* **1** A complete and thorough "square"; fig., an octagonal "square." *Some bop and cool use.* **2** [derog.] A Negro. *Because the No. 8 ball in the game of pool is colored solid black.* **3** An unsuccessful, inefficient, or maladjusted person. *Some W.W.II Army use. Not now common. From the expression "behind the eight ball" = in trouble; from a pop. pocket billiards game in which one loses if the No. 8 ball is hit into a pocket. Perhaps reinforced by "section 8."*

eight-rock [derog.]   *n.* A very black Negro. *Harlem Negro use.*

eighty   *n.* = **eighty-two.** *Not common, some c1930 lunch-counter use.*

eighty-eight   *n.* A piano. *From the number of keys in a full keyboard.* 1952: "I've been right here poundin' on the old 88." Hoagy Carmichael. Movie, *Las Vegas Story.*

eighty-four   *n.* A naval prison. *Some W.W.II USN use.*

eighty-one   *n.* = **eighty-two.** *Common c1935 lunch-counter use; succeeded by "eighty-two."*

eighty-six   **1** No, nix; nothing; there is none left; we don't have the item ordered. *Common lunch-counter use; used by the cook to inform waiters that there is no more of a specific dish.* **2** A glass of water. *Some lunch-counter use, because there is no sale, nothing rung up on the cash register.* **3** A person who is not to be served, as at a lunch counter, because he is thought to be undesirable or unable to pay; a person who is not to be served liquor, as at a bar, because he is or will become drunk and/or disorderly. 1944: "[He] was known as an 'eighty-six,' which in the patois of [liquor] dispensers means: 'Don't serve him.'" Fowler, *Good Night,* 191. *All uses because the term rhymes with "nix." Used by waiters, bartenders, etc., so that customers will not understand. See Appendix, Rhyming Slang.*

eighty-two   *n.* A glass of water; a request for a glass of water. *Lunch-counter use in relaying a customer's request. Fairly common since c1950. Perhaps from c1930 "eighty" = a glass of water, and "eighty-two" = two glasses of water.*

eke-okey = **O.K.** *Carnival slang. Obs.*

elbow   *n.* A policeman or detective. 1916: "... In the West, Central Office men are known as 'C. O. dicks,' or 'elbows,' from a habit they have of elbowing into crowds after their prey." "Star of Hope," *Lit. Digest,* Aug. 19. 1948: "Why, you lousy elbow!" Evans, *Halo for Satan,* 64. *Arch.*   *v.i.* To associate with as a friend; to bend elbows or rub elbows with.

elbow-bender   *n.* A convivial person. Cf. **bend [the] elbow.**

elbow-bending   *n.* Liquor drinking. 1934: "... The gentlemanly art of refined elbow-bending...." DeJournette, *Esquire,* Apr., 36. 1957: "... Time between ports for swimming, dancing and elbow bending...." Patrick Chase, "Playboy's International Datebook," *Playboy,* May, 14. Cf. **bend [the] elbow.**

elbow-crooking = **elbow-bending.** *c1840; obs.*

elbow grease   Hard physical work; muscular energy, expended in any manual labor.

electric   *n.* An automobile propelled by an electric motor or other electric device instead of an internal combustion engine. 1920: "Amory caught sight of his mother waiting in her electric on the gravelled station drive. It was an ancient electric, one of the early types, and painted gray." F. S. Fitzgerald, *This Side of Paradise,* 22. *Obs.*   *adj.* Played smoothly and sensuously; said of jazz. 1956: "A pretty good blues called electric doesn't hold its own with the gutty stuff of Lead Belly." S. Longstreet, *The Real Jazz Old and New,* 37. *Archaic jazz use.*

elephant ears   Apricots. *Not common.*

elephant-hunt   To go slumming. **—er**   *n.* One who goes slumming. 1880: "... A writer for the *Cincinnati Enquirer,* who went slumming, or as it was then called, elephant hunting, among the dives of New York...." Asbury, *Gangs of N.Y.,* 132. *Obs.*

elephant's eyebrows, the = **cat's meow, the.**

elevate   *v.t.* To hold up with a gun and rob; a synonym for "hold up." 1929: "Any U.S. Senator who isn't... thrilled... will have to go out and 'elevate' a bank himself." Jack Black, *New Republic,* Apr., 17, 259/2.   *v.i.* To raise one's hands on command in a hold-up. 1928: "The clerk... stubbornly refused to elevate at Slim's command." D. Purroy, *Amer. Mercury.*

elevated   *adj.* Drunk.

Elizabeth club   An informal union or society of Negro household maids, cooks, and cleaning women. *It is doubtful if there has ever existed such an organization, but Southern housewives claim Elizabeth clubs meet on the members' afternoons off from work to exchange gossip about their employers, fix salary ratzs, and the like. Because Elizabeth is considered a typical name.*

Elk   *n.* = **square, Babbitt.** 1958: "Most cats don't drink much, or at least not on a cool party. (They drink when they go out with squares in restaurants and kill themselves later with laughter over the amount of money the Elks spent.)" S. Boal, *Cool Swinging in N.Y.,* 26. *From the Elks fraternal society; beat use.*

ellybay   **elly-bay**   *n.* The belly;

the stomach. 1939: "[Hit him] in the elly-bay, Jones." Runyon, 163. *A euphem. from Pig Latin.* See Appendix, Little Languages.

Elmer *n.* **1** An overseer. **2** An inexperienced, stupid boy.

else = **or else.**

Elvis *n.* A type of men's haircut. 1957: ". . . Its prototype, of course, is atop that boy [Elvis Presley]. An Elvis is all hair and a mile high, hanging over the temples, deliberately, and with a long slashing sideburn." Herbert Mitgang, *About—Men's Haircuts. Since c1955, rock-and-roll and general teenage use.*

embalmed *adj.* Intoxicated.

embalming fluid **1** Coffee; particularly very strong coffee. **2** Whisky.

emcee *n.* A master of ceremonies. *A spelling of the letters in the abbr. "M.C."* *v.t.* To serve as master of ceremonies. 1948: "George Jessel emceed the event." *Variety,* Aug. 25, 2/1.

emery ball In baseball, a curve pitched with a roughened ball.

emote *v.i.* **1** In the theater, to act in a role which includes many emotional scenes; to act in a hyperemotional manner. 1945: "Her relatives have all been panting to see her emote in the gangster film." L. O. Parsons, *synd. newsp. col.,* July 27. *From "emotion."* See Appendix, Shortened Words. → **2** To simulate any emotion; to assume an emotion or concern which one does not feel.

emoting *n.* The act or state of displaying emotion, either by a performer in a professional capacity or by a layman who simulates an emotion that he does not feel. 1949: "During the first act he and his troupe did more ducking [vegetables] than emoting." Billy Rose, *synd. newsp. col.,* Dec. 2.

end *n.* A share, as of the spoils. 1950: "Eddie would be entitled to half an end. . . ." DeBaun, 73. *Colloq.*

end, the = **most, the;** the best. *Cool, far out, and beat use since c1955. Although new, "the end" is used exactly as was "sockdollager" in the 19C.* See **far out.**

endville **Endville** *adj.* The best; the greatest; the most. 1957: "Endville (obs.) means the best." E. Horne, *For Cool Cats and Far-Out Chicks. Some early cool use.* See Appendix, —ville.

English *n.* **1** A twisting, spinning rotation made by a tennis ball, billiard ball, or the like, as it moves forward; the untrue bounce or carom caused by this motion. 1946: "No, it [a billiard ball] was going to itch. You had a lot of English on it. It was rolling right for the pocket. I've never seen so much English. Are you sure you never played anywhere but the Y.M.C.A.?" M. Shulman, *Zebra Derby,* 43. *Colloq.* **2** An English muffin, esp. a large, comparatively flat muffin or biscuit bought precooked and needing only heating or toasting before being served; an order of such a muffin. *Lunch-counter use in relaying an order. Common since c1950.* **3** A type of men's haircut. 1957: "Another hairdo, which originated in Britain, spread to the Continent and is now widely accepted here, is the 'English.' Hair rides back from the temples, rests comfortably on top of the ears and keeps moving to the rear. Like Sir Laurence Olivier's." H. Mitgang, *About—Men's Haircuts.*

enob [taboo] *n.* The penis. *Not common. From "bone" spelled backward, reinforced by "knob." This back sl. is an attempted euphem.*

enthuse *v.i.* To show enthusiasm. *Since c1825.*

equalizer *n.* A pistol or other gun. 1932: ". . . He outs with the old equalizer and lets go at Polly. . . ." Runyon. *Although the word has seen underworld use, it is more common in fiction about the underworld.*

equestrian *n.* One who uses a translation or pony. *Some jocular c1900 student use.*

—er See Appendix, Suffixes and Suffix Words.

erase *v.t.* To kill; rub out. *More often used in fiction about than by the underworld.* **—r** *n.* A knockout. *Prize fight use.*

—er- —er See Appendix, —er, Suffixes and Suffix Words.

—eria See Appendix, —eteria, Suffixes and Suffix Words.

Erie = **on the Erie.**

Erie, on the **1** Listening; eavesdropping. 1939: "But Horsey is in there on the old Erie. . . ." Runyon, 35. *Hobo and underworld use. A pun on ear and the Erie railroad line.* → **2** Not taking chances; hiding. *Underworld use.*

—erino —erina —erini —erine See Appendix, —ino, Suffixes and Suffix Words.

—eroo See Appendix, Suffixes and Suffix Words.

—ers See Appendix, —er, Suffixes and Suffix Words.

—ery See Appendix, Suffixes and Suffix Words.

—ese See Appendix, Suffixes and Suffix Words.

Eskimo See **train to be an Eskimo.**

—ess See Appendix, Suffixes and Suffix Words.

essence peddler "A skunk." *c1845; colloq.*

estate = **real estate.**

etaoin shrdlu Confusion; mistakes. 1956: ". . . 98 per cent accurate and 2 per cent etaoin shrdlu." *N.Y. Post*, Aug. 2, 2. *Not common. These letters are formed in order by striking the two left-hand rows of keys on a linotype machine; as a line or as two words they are set by typesetters to indicate a mistake.*

—eteria See Appendix, Suffixes and Suffix Words.

Ethel *n.* **1** A coward, usu. a cautious prize fighter. *c1920.* → **2** An effeminate man.

Ethiopian paradise [derog.] The top gallery or balcony in a theater; nigger heaven.

eve *n.* A rib on an airplane wing assembly. *Airplane factory and Air Force use.* See **Adam and Eve on a raft.**

even-Steven even-steven even-Stephen even-stephen *adj. & adv.* Even, fair; evenly. 1927: "Give me the hundred and fifty and we'll call it even-steven." Hammett, *Blood Money*, 89. 1945: "And we'll do likewise for San Francisco and Odessa—or any places we want, always even-stephen." D. Fairbairn in Phila. *Bulletin*, Dec. 31, 8.

even with [someone], get To wrong another, esp. to cause another a social or business loss from spite. *Colloq.*

Eve with the lid on A piece of apple pie. *An allusion to the myth of Eve and the apple. Restaurant use.*

evil *adj.* **1** Disillusioned; disappointed; angry. *c1935 jive use. Some cool use since c1955.* **2** Wonderful; specif., thrilling, very satisfying; said of a person, act, or usu. of the playing of a piece of music, of a theatrical performance, or the like. *Pseudo cool use. Implies that, like sex, that which is really thrilling and satisfying is considered sinful by puritanical people.*

evil eye Bad luck; lit., bad luck or misfortune as caused by an enemy or demonic person casting an evil spell. 1937 [1954]: "And remember, shut-mouth to the *paesanos*! Or they will send the evil eye to our new home even before we put foot." P. di Donato, *Christ in Concrete*, reprinted in *Manhattan*, 136.

ex x *n.* **1** An examination. 1882: *DAE. Obs.* **2** An exclusive concession or right to sell a product. *Circus and pitchman use.* From the "x" that "marks the spot," reinforced by the "x" = a signature. **3** An ex-wife or an ex-husband. 1952: "Her ex." R. C. Ruark, *synd. newsp. col.*, Aug. 26 *Colloq.*

ex— See Appendix, Prefixes and Prefix Words.

exam *n.* An examination, as a formal, written test, usu. long and authoritatively administered by a school or college; a medical, physical, or civil-service examination. *Colloq. since c1870.* *adj.* Concerned with or given over to an examination or examinations, as an exam question, exam paper, exam week.

excess baggage **1** Anything or anyone not necessary, needed, or wanted; fig., that which is or could become a burden. See **baggage.** **2** Specif., immature, outmoded, undesirable, prohibiting, or limiting ideals, beliefs, or ideas that prevent one from being objective. Fig., any intangible thing that may hinder one.

excuse *v.t.* **1** To request someone to depart or leave. **2** To choose or separate one or more items from a group. *Railroad use and dial. In railroad use "to excuse three cars" is to switch three cars away from a train.*

exec *n.* **1** An executive officer. *USN use since c1925.* **2** Calisthenics; marching drill. *Some USN use, because an executive officer is in command.* *adj.* Of or by executives. For all uses, see Appendix, Shortened Words.

extension *n.* Credit; specif., the maximum credit that can be extended to a customer. 1956: " 'Unlimited extension' has come to mean a tribute to a big bettor—that he has proved himself honorable." T. Betts, *Across the Board*, 315.

extra *n.* **1** A special edition of a newspaper that is published when news of major importance occurs. *Colloq. and now obs. Since the introduction of radio and television newscasting very few newspapers consider it worthwhile to publish extras.* **2** One who plays a minor role in a movie or play; specif., one who has no speaking part in a movie but who takes part in crowd scenes. *Colloq.*

175

—curricular *adj.* Unplanned; unethical; immoral; said of one's actions, usu. sexual or flirtatious actions. *From the stand. collegiate use.*

extracurricular activity Adultery, sexual intercourse with one other than one's spouse; a girl or woman with whom one has committed adultery. 1956: "Hints His College Bride's Baby Was Extracurricular Activity [headline:] It is Leon's contention that Rae trapped him into marriage last March 23 and deserted him a month later. Leon contended that any one of a number of men could have fathered the baby who was born only last Friday." A. Albelli in N.Y. *Daily News,* Nov. 16, 4.

—ey See Appendix, —ie, —y, Suffixes and Suffix Words.

eye *n.* **1** A private detective. 1952: "I am grateful to Dale Wilmer for inventing an eye named Johnny O'John." A. Boucher in N.Y. *Times Bk. Rev.,* Sept. 14, 16/4. *From "the eye."* See **the Eye, private eye. 2** A signal light. *Railroad use.* Thus *"green eye"* = *clear; "red eye"* = *danger; "white eye"* = *clear track ahead.* **3** A television set; a television screen. *Teenage use, common since c1955.*

—s *n.pl.* [taboo] The female breasts. *Not common.* Cf. **headlights, maracas, shakers.**

eye, get the See **give [someone] the eye.**

eye (beady eye) (fish eye), give [someone] the To look or glance at a person, often admonitorily or sinisterly. 1941: "A well-fed man in tails opened the door, gave them the fish eye." G. Homes, *40 Whacks,* 129. 1942: "The maid opened the front door . . . and gave me the beady eye." Chandler, *High Window,* 2. 1951: "He was smart enough to clam up when I gave him the eye." I, *Mobster,* 122.

Eye, the   eye, the *n.* **1** The Pinkerton National Detective Agency. 1948: used at least 9 times in A. Hynd, *Pinkerton Case Book. Since soon after 1850, when the agency was founded. From the watching eye pictured on the sign posted outside places of business protected by the Pinkerton Agency.* **2** A Pinkerton detective.

eyeball *v.t.* To eye; look at; look around a place. 1942: "He would eye-ball the idol-breaker." Z. Hurston. *Harlem Negro use. Teenage and synthetic hipster use since c1950.*

eyebrow = **elephant's eyebrows.** See **cat's meow, the.**

eyed See **cock-eyed, glassy-eyed, owl-eyed, pie-eyed.**

eye on [someone], put the **1** To look at; to look over. *Not common.* **2** To flirt with, esp. to look lasciviously at one of the opposite sex. 1939: "I was having the eye put on me." Chandler, *Big Sleep,* 61. *Not common.*

eye-opener *n.* A drink of liquor, as one taken upon rising. 1865: "This patriotic beverage, this glorified cocktail, this eye-opener *in excelsis.*" G. A. Sala, *My Diary in America,* 98. *c1815; still common.*

eyes, give with the **1** = to look at; to convey a message by a glance. 1950: "She . . . gives with the big blue eyes as if to say: 'Her didn't mean to.' . . ." DeBaun, 75. **2** To start; to participate; to contribute.

eyes for [something or someone], to have To want, to desire; to admire; to work for or toward; to try to obtain. 1958: "The phrase 'to have eyes for' means 'to like,' 'to admire,' 'to want,' in either a sexual or merely material sense. But the chick who has eyes for some cat would be uncool if she told him so directly." S. Boal, *Cool Swinging in N.Y.,* 26.

eye-shut A Western variant of "shut-eye."

eyes to cool it A desire or plan to relax, withdraw from strain, work, or competition, or to take a vacation. 1957: "Eyes to cool it—The desire to relax, to get away from it all." E. Horne, *For Cool Cats and Far-Out Chicks. Some cool and far-out use since c1955. From "to have eyes for"* = *to want plus "cool it."*

eyewash *n.* Flattery; boloney. Cf. **hogwash.**

Eytie   Eyetie *n.* An Italian. *Common W.W.II Army use, though the term is much earlier in origin.*

F

face *n.* A white person. *Negro use.* See **bald face, dogface, dollface, feed [one's] face, flange-face, open [one's]**

face, paleface, pie-face, pruneface, red face.

face, open [one's] To talk; lit., to

open one's mouth. 1896: *DAE*. 1932: "Nobody as much as opens his face from the time we go in. . . ." Runyon.

factory See **gargle factory, jag factory, match factory, nut factory.**

—factory See Appendix, Suffixes and Suffix Words.

fade *n.* A low or failing grade in school. *Student use. Not common.* *v.i.* **1** To leave; go away. 1949: "He faded to Chicago." A. Hynd, *Public Enemies*, 35. **2** Fig., to fade out of sight; to disappear; to depart in haste. 1950: "Of course, nobody can go up against a knife in the hand of a man who knows how to use it, but, luckily for me, Coon Can George, one of the dealers, walked in right then, pulled out that big .45 of his and the gentleman with the knife faded." A. Lomax, *Mr. Jelly Roll*, 131. **3** To meander; wander; stroll. 1941: "Let's fade down to the Grill." *Dict. of Exeter Language*, 16. *Boy use, prep school.*

fade away To leave; disappear. *c1900.* *n.* In baseball, a pitch that arrives away from the batter. 1926: *Obvious term. Constantly used.*

faded boogie A Negro informer.

fade out To depart. 1932: "People are now apt to 'fade out' instead of departing. . . ." E. Weekley, *Atlantic Monthly*, May, 559. *c1930: from the movie term.*

fag *n.* **1** A cigarette. c1915: "Strike up a Lucifer and light your fag/ And smile, boys, that's the style. . . ." *Pop. W.W.I song*, "Pack Up Your Troubles in Your Old Kit Bag." 1952: " 'I guess I'll eat tomorrow. And smoke right now,' he said, opening the white boy's cigarette case. 'Have one,' and he passed them swell fags around. . . ." L. Hughes, *Laughing to Keep from Crying*, 29. *Some cW.W.I use, seldom heard now.* **2** A homosexual; an effeminate man; since c1940 specif., a male homosexual. 1941: "He had the body of a wrestler and the face of a fag." Schulberg, *Sammy*, 65. *Common since c1920. It has been suggested that "fag" = homosexual comes from "fag" = cigarette, since cigarettes were considered effeminate by cigar and pipe smokers when they were first introduced at the end of W.W.I. Although this may have reinforced the use of the word, "fag" = a boy servant or lackey has been common Eng. schoolboy use since before 1830, and may be the orig. of "fag" = homosexual.* *adj.* Homosexual; pertaining to homosexuals. 1939: "A

stealthy nastiness, like a fag party." Chandler, *Big Sleep*, 58. *v.t.* To smoke tobacco. *Never common.*

fag along To ride fast. *Cowboy use. Still current.*

faggart fag(g)ot *n.* A sexual pervert. *Some c1930 use. Archaic, having been replaced by the shorter "fag."* See **fag.**

fagin *n.* A teacher of crime; an old, malicious criminal. *From Fagin in Dickens' "Oliver Twist."*

faint *adj.* Drunk. *c1850. Never common.*

fair dinkum Honest; on the square; on the level. *World War I use. Taken from the Australian.* See **dinkum.**

fair-haired boy *n.* **1** A man, not necessarily a youth, who is most favored by those in power. 1947: "Joe Mooney . . . blind accordionist . . . is the latest 'fair-haired boy' of the musical world. . . ." Dave Bittan, Temple University *News*, Jan. 24, 2/3. See **blue-eyed boy, golden-haired boy, white-haired boy.** → **2** Specif. one who is expected to be elevated to the top position; the known replacement for a major political or business job or for a sports star.

fair hell A person who excels; one who is energetic and successful.

fair shake **1** An honest arrangement; a fair deal; a square deal. **2** An attempt or try under the same conditions given others. *Apparently in reference to dicing. Colloq. since c1825.*

fairy *n.* **1** A male homosexual. usu. one who assumes the feminine role. 1949: "Too bad you weren't a fairy." P. Wylie, *Finnley Wren*, 26. *After "queer," "fairy" is the most common and polite word = a homosexual.* Cf. **fag, pansy, queer.** **2** A girl; esp. a pretty girl. *c1886.*

fairy godfather A prospective sponsor, advertiser, or financial backer. *Radio, television, and stage use.*

fairy lady A lesbian who assumes the female role in a homosexual relationship. *West Coast use since c1950.*

fake *v.t.* To improvise or play compatible chords or notes on a musical instrument when one does not know or has forgotten the correct notes of the composition. *Common jazz music use.*

fake it **1** To bluff; to pretend to know or be able to do something. → **2** To improvise while playing music because one does not know the piece or the arrangement; to improvise, esp. to improvise a solo in a jazz performance.

faker See **mush-faker, poodle-faker.**

fall *n.* **1** An arrest. 1928: ". . . Another

fall meant a life sentence. . . ." D. Purroy. *Underworld use.* **2** A term in prison. *Underworld use.* **3** An unsuccessful attempt at robbery. *Underworld use.* *v.i.* **1** To be caught or arrested; drop. *Underworld use.* 1949: ". . . Best thief in the city till he fell. . . ." Burnett, *Jungle,* 12. **2** To be sentenced to a term in prison. *Underworld use.* **3** To fail in an attempted robbery. 1950: ". . . The whole mob may fall. . . ." DeBaun, 72. *Underworld use.* **4** To be or begin to be in love with a person; to fall in love with a person. See **fall for.**

fall apart **1** To be overcome with desire, enthusiasm, appreciation, excitement, nervousness, or the like. 1951: "The booming voice of the stage manager announcing 'Fifteen minutes' reacts on the novices like a sandbag dropped in a bowl of Jello. Even the seasoned troupers fall apart during these last minutes before the long walk." A. Hirschfeld, *Show Business Is No Business,* 84. *Orig. c1946 bop use.* **2** To lose one's composure; to lose one's confidence. See **come apart at the seams.** **3** Specif., to be overwhelmed by another's presence or love. *Teenage use since c1955.*

fall down   To visit or pay a call.

fall down and go boom **1** To fall down noisily; said esp. of a person. **2** To fail completely and publicly.

fall for **1** To take a strong liking for [something]. 1934: "He had fallen for [the new sign] so hard. . . ." Cain, *Postman,* 9. *Colloq. since c1905.* **2** To fall in love with a person. 1920: "He was going to fall for her." Fitzgerald, *This Side of Paradise,* 69. 1958: "But little did I dream to fall for my boss. . . ." "Smilin' Jack," *synd. newsp. comic strip,* Feb. 8. **3** To be deceived, duped, or made a sucker of by some gag or trick. 1928: "Americans would continue to 'fall for' this. . . ." R. Lynd, *New Statesman,* Feb. 4.

fall guy **1** An easy victim; a victim; a loser. → **2** Specif., a scapegoat; a person who is made to take the blame for another's crime, mistake, or failure.

fall money   Money set aside for various expenses involved in being arrested, such as for possible bribes, bail, and legal fees. 1935: "Mike [an autothief] set aside a percentage of his takings for 'fall money.' " Courtney, *SEP.*

fall off   To lose weight. *Colloq.*

fallout   *n.* Radioactive particles distributed by an aerial nuclear explosion, falling from or floating in the atmosphere.

1957: " 'Fallout'—the radioactive particles from the nuclear cloud which drop back to earth." J. C. Clark, *SEP,* July 20, 17. *Colloq.*

fall out **1** To be emotionally aroused; to be surprised; to "fall apart." *Orig. c1946 bop use; now some teenage use. Prob. reinforced by the Army command "fall out" = dismissed.* **2** To be overcome with emotion or laughter; to lose one's inhibitions in an unrestrained burst of emotion or laughter. 1956: ". . . Doing all right until I tried double tempo. . . . everybody fell out laughing. . . . I went home and cried. . . ." Charlie Parker, 1920–1955, *The Metronome Year Book,* 39. *Fig., to fall out of one's chair, as with laughter.* **3** To die; fig., to fall out of reality and consciousness.

falsie   *n.* **1** Anything that is false or artificial. 1949: "A . . . gelding . . . was disqualified . . . when its tail, a falsie, fell off." *Newsweek,* Oct. 31, 61. **2** Specif., a brassiere with built-in padding, to make a woman appear to have larger or more shapely breasts. **3** = **falsies.** **4** Any padding, as over the thighs or hips, worn by a woman to give her the appearance of having a voluptuous figure. **—s** *n.pl.* Women's breast pads worn to give the appearance of having larger or more shapely breasts. *The style and the word very common c1945 to present.* Also **gay deceivers.** Cf. **sweater girl; uplift.**

family jewels, the [taboo]   The testicles. *Jocular use. Fig., a man's most valuable possession, and the pride of his family, since the testicles provide progeny.* Cf. **balls.**

fan   *n.* **1** A devotee or enthusiastic follower, usu. of a sport or other form of entertainment. 1903: [Baseball] "The base-ball fan has a slang of his own." H. Spencer. 1917: [Movie] "A good . . . movie . . . turns up for the faithful 'fan.' . . ." Vachel Lindsay, *New Republic,* Jan. 13, 303/1. *Colloq. since before 1900.* See Appendix, Shortened Words. **2** An airplane propeller. *W.W.II Air Force use.* → **3** An airplane engine. *v.t.* **1** In baseball, to cause a batter to strike out; said of a baseball pitcher. 1952: "Maglie allowed seven . . . hits, all singles, walked only one and fanned six. . . ." AP, May 20. **2** To spank. 1931: "And don't let him out of your sight, or I'll fan your tail!" Queen, *Dutch Shoe,* 65. **3** To search a person for money or a gun; to frisk. 1935: "The gendarmes fan them to see if they have any rods on them. . . ."

Runyon. **4** To sweep one's hands over a man's clothing in lieu of searching him for a concealed weapon or contraband, or to determine the contents of his pockets. 1958: "Fan—The brush or feel a pickpocket gives a potential victim." G. Y. Wells, *Station House Slang.*   *v.i.* **1** In baseball, to strike out. **2** To chat or gossip; to converse; from "fan the breeze." 1952: "All the other chauffeurs I'd stand around fanning with at weddings and the like, they called me Moore." Harry Larkin, *New Yorker*, Jan. 19, 20/3.   **—ner**   *n.* **1** A fan dancer. **2** One who locates a wallet for a pickpocket to lift.

fancy Dan   Fancy Dan   *n.* **1** A stylishly dressed, persuasive ladies' man; a dude. 1950: "The fancy Dans, dressed fit to kill, wearing their big diamonds...." A. Lomax, *Mr. Jelly Roll*, 46. *Colloq.* **2** One who looks, talks, and acts capable but who is afraid of mussing his clothes with hard work; one who is afraid of hard work. 1949: "This is no time for 'Fancy Dans' who won't hit the line with all they have on every play." O. N. Brandley, AP, Oct. 19. **3** In prize fighting, a clever, skilled boxer, esp. one who cannot punch or hit strongly. 1952: "The 24-year-old fancy-dan has a 31-3-1 record." AP, Jan. 11. *Prize fight use.*

fancy pants   1 A sissy. *Universally known to children.* **2** An effete man; an overly fastidious man.

fandangle   *n.* **1** An ornament. **2** A mechanical gadget. *Colloq.*

faniggle = **finagle.**

fanny   *n.* The human rump. 1928: "Parking her fanny in here...." Hecht & MacArthur, *Front Page*, II. 1951: "He's still stiff and sore from Sunday's air battle. 'My back muscles are awfully sore,' he said. 'In fact, I can hardly sit down, my fanny is so sore.' " AP, May 22.

fan the breeze   To talk; usu. to talk aimlessly; to chat. See **shoot the breeze.**

fantods   *n.sing.* A mythical disease causing melancholy, nervousness, and depression; the willies. 1876 [1954]: " Cole [Younger], what the Sam Hill is eating you? I dunno. You just got the fantods that's all." W. Henry, *Death of a Legend*, 178.

fare-thee-well = **fare-you-well.**
fare-ye-well = **fare-you-well.**
fare-you-well   *n.* To a fare-you-well = to perfection; thoroughly; completely; to a finish. *Colloq. since c1885.*

far out   far-out   *adj.* **1** Descriptive of or characteristic of the most modern forms of jazz or progressive music; technically, more progressive than cool. **2** Descriptive of or characteristic of devotees of "far out" music and their behavior; intellectual. **3** Satisfying; capable of arousing enthusiasm. 1956: " 'Far-out' is the new hip term of critical approval, superseding the swing era's 'hot' and the bop era's 'cool.' " A. Shaw, *West Coast Jazz*, 79. See **way out.** **4** Extremely; "gone" or far removed from reality; intent; intense; so much in rapport with, intent on, or immersed in one's work, performance, ideas, or mode or way of life that one is as if in a trance, and unaware of or removed from all extraneous things. **5** Of, by, for, or pertaining to devotees of far-out music, their fashions, fads, and attitudes. **6** Removed from standards of criticism by being unrelated to or beyond comparison with other things; intellectually, psychologically, or spiritually so cool as to be beyond comparison. *Mainly far-out use, some cool and beat use.* Cf. **cool.**

fart, lay a [taboo]   To eruct, to fart. 1951: "All of a sudden this guy sitting in the row in front of me, Edgar Marsalla, laid this terrific fart. It was a very crude thing to do, in chapel and all, but it was also quite amusing." J. D. Salinger, *Catcher in the Rye*, 18.

fashion plate   A consistently well-dressed person of either sex, esp. one habitually dressed in the latest styles. 1930: "The present-day ... racketeer is a veritable fashion plate." Lavine, *Third Degree*, 33.

fast   *adj.* Amoral; suspected of riotous or unconventional behavior; hedonistic. 1920: "Get married and live on Long Island with the fast younger married set. You want life to be a chain of flirtation with a man for every link." F. S. Fitzgerald, *This Side of Paradise*, 175.

fast buck   Lit., a quickly or easily acquired dollar; fig., money obtained quickly or easily and often unscrupulously. 1949: "Tryin' to hustle me a fast buck." A. Kober in *New Yorker*, Nov. 5, 82.

fast one   A trick; a clever swindle; a deception; an instance of double-crossing. 1944: "I don't think you'd have the guts to pull a fast one." Ford, *Phila. Murder*, 184.

fast one, pull a   See **fast one.**
fast shuffle = **double shuffle.**

fast talk Talk meant to deceive or mislead; glib talk. **—er** *n.* One who habitually talks glibly or misleadingly; a persuasive talker; a male with more charm than sincerity.

fat *adj.* **1** Poor, slight, slim; usu. in "a fat chance" = little or no chance. *Since c1900; orig. ironical.* **2** Stupid; incompetent. *Not common.* See **fat-head**. **3** Desirable; excellent; admirable. *Orig. said of an actor's part in a play or act. Not common.* **4** Temporarily in the possession of much money; wealthy. *Some use since c1920.*

fat cat **1** The financier of a political party campaign or politician; a provider of money for political uses. → **2** One who receives or expects special privileges. *Army and student use since W.W.II.* → **3** One who has fame, wealth, and luxuries. 1949: "Hollywood celebrities, literary fat cats. . . ." B. Cerf, *Sat. Rev. of Lit.*, Apr. 16, 4. *v.* To receive or try to obtain special privileges. 1946: " 'Fat-catting' by senior officers . . . a term applied in the lower ranks to higher leaders who try to [pad] themselves with special privileges and comforts." H. Boyle, AP, Jan. 8.

fat-head   **fathead**   *n.* **1** A stupid person. 1921: "You fathead!" Witwer, *Leather*, 35. *Colloq.* **2** A stupid blunder. 1951: "[In the old days], if you pulled a fathead an' cut off too much [steel], they fired you. Nowadays if you pull a fathead th' world knows it." J. R. Williams, *synd. cartoon*, "Out Our Way," Nov. 16. **—ed** *adj.* Stupid; usu. applied to persons, sometimes to actions. 1946: "Some fatheaded motorist." Evans, *Halo in Blood*, 2. *Since c1750.*

Fats   Fat   Fatty   Fatso *masc. sing.* A nickname for a fat person. **Fatty** = *c1825*, **Fats** = *c1875*, **Fat** = *c1900*, **Fatso** = *c1925*. 1945: "The I.Q. test has shown Fats Goering [Nazi leader] to be super-intelligent. . . ." *Phila. Bulletin*, Dec. 12, 13. 1951: "The . . . piano style of the late Thomas [Fats] Waller." *New Yorker*, Aug. 18, 78. 1952: "No one will call me 'Fatso' any more." Murray Rose, AP, July 18. *Can be affectionate, jocular, or derisive.* See Appendix, **—o**, **—s**, **—y** endings.

faust *adj.* Ugly; disgusting. 1956: "*Faust* is not a poem, it means ugly." S. Longstreet, *The Real Jazz Old and New*, 148. *Cool and far out use since c1955.*

fay [derog.]   *n.* A white person. *General Negro use, less freq. than syn.* "*ofay*." See **ofay**.

featherbed *v.i.* **1** To loaf; to work halfheartedly; to seek easy tasks. *Some c1850 use.* → **2** To create extra and unnecessary work in order to earn more money; to demand work for unnecessary employees. 1956: "Feather-bedding clauses in labor agreements call for such things as the extra man in a diesel locomotive and standby musicians at a recorded program. This word goes back to the American frontier army in the 1850's. A soldier who had a soft touch was called a featherbed soldier. Hence, a job with little or no work is a featherbed job." *Labor's Special Language from Many Sources.*

feather crew A type of men's haircut, similar to the crew cut. 1957: "Casually tousled . . . [the crew cut is] a 'Feather Crew.' " H. Mitgang, *About—Men's Haircuts.*

feather cut A women's hair style with the hair shorter than shoulder length and featuring casual waves and a wind-tossed effect. *Common c1943–c1946.*

feather duster The plume or pom-pom worn vertically on the full-dress military hat. *c1936. West Point use.* H. Beukema.

feather-legs *n.sing.* An unfair, deceitful person. *Some c1940 student use. Suggested by* "*chicken*."

feather merchant *n.* **1** A civilian; specif., a slacker. 1944: *The Feather Merchants*, a novel by M. Shulman. *The author's fictitious account of the origin of the term is given on p. iv. Armed Forces use W.W.II. Suggested by* "*chicken*" *and perhaps by* "*featherbed*." → **2** A Navy Reserve officer; a person who immediately receives a commission upon entering the armed services; a sailor who has an office job. *W.W.II USN use.*

feather [one's] nest   line [one's] nest To obtain money, ethically or unethically, for oneself; to obtain money or an unfair share of money from the efforts of others; to provide for oneself with no regard to the welfare of others.

feature *v.t.* To comprehend; to understand. *Since c1930.*

fed   Fed *n.* **1** A Union soldier. *Civil War use. From* "*Federal*." See Appendix, Shortened Words. **2** A Federal prohibition enforcement officer. *c1920 use.* **3** Any Federal government officer. See Appendix, Shortened Words.

Federal case out of [something], make a To overemphasize the importance of something; esp. to exaggerate /

another's mistake or bad judgment when criticizing or reprimanding him. 1957: " 'I merely bought a new car . . . so don't try to make a Federal case out of it. Nothing is going to happen." Steve McNeil, *High-Pressure Girl.*

fed up *adj.* Bored; sated; disgusted. 1928: "When a number of people suddenly became fed up with a slang phrase like 'fed up.' . . . " Greig, *Priscian,* 16f. *Colloq. Since W.W.I, from Brit. sl. Orig. a version of the French "J'en ai soupé." In Brit. sl. since c1900. Fig., having a surfeit; no longer able or willing to bear one's job, condition, constant insults, abuse, or the like; without further patience.*

feeb *n.* A feeble-minded person; an idiot, moron, or imbecile. See Appendix, Shortened Words. **—bles** *n.pl.* A hangover; the heebie-jeebies. 1943: ". . . His several disquisitions on the jeebies, or feebles. . . ." H. A. Smith, *Putty Knife,* 58.

feed *n.* **1** A meal; anything from a light lunch to an elaborate banquet, but usu. a substantial, filling, well-cooked meal. 1927: "I was to a restaurant . . . and we had a swell feed." R. Littell, *New Republic,* Jan. 26, 277/2. *c1820 to present.* **2** Food. *c1900.* **3** Money. *c1900. Perhaps short for "chicken feed."* *v.i.* To board; to take one's meals.

feed, off [one's] Sick; indisposed; depressed or sad. *From the term used to ref. to a sick horse.*

feedbag **feed-bag** *n.* A meal, as dinner. See also **put on the feedbag.** 1929: "I'm ready for the feed-bag. . . ." Burnett, *Little Caesar,* 138.

feedbag, put on the To eat.

feedbag information = **feedbox information.**

feedbox information **feedbag information** Supposedly authentic advance information or a tip, esp. on a horse race; specif., a tip on a horse race that supposedly orig. from a horse owner or stable employee. 1941: "Neither of us had ever heard of Clam giving out feed-box information to anybody." J. Lilienthal, *Horse Crazy,* 42.

feed [one's] face To eat a meal; to eat. 1905: "Will you feed the face, Dodey?" McHugh, *Search Me,* 61. 1943: ". . . All these people began feeding their faces. . . ." H. A. Smith, *Putty Knife,* 148.

feed the kitty To contribute to a common fund. See **kitty.**

feel [taboo] *n.* The act or instance of

touching, exploring, or stimulating a girl's or woman's vagina manually. *v.t.* To touch, explore, or stimulate a girl's or woman's vagina manually. **—er** *n.* A finger, esp. the middle finger. See Appendix, —er ending.

feelers on [someone or something], put the To touch; to frisk. 1950: ". . . Creep joints where they'd put the feelers on a guy's clothes." A. Lomax, *Mr. Jelly Roll,* 47. *Not common.*

feel good To be more or less drunk. 1951: "Old Charlie was feeling good that night. He felt so good that he got his envelopes mixed. . . ." Spillane, *Big Kill,* 164.

feel no pain To be drunk. 1947: ". . . At the table with three men who were feeling no pain." C. Morley, *Ironing Board,* 116.

feel out To try to find out a person's attitude toward or opinion of a specific subject or plan, subtly or indirectly.

feel up [taboo] = **feel.**

feet See **cold feet, throw [one's] feet.**

feet first, go home To die. *See* **go home in a box.**

feeze = **pheeze.**

fellow traveler **1** Specif., a follower of Communist doctrines who does not belong to the Communist Party. *Colloq.* → **2** One who professes agreement with any idea, movement, group, or the like but does not take an active role. 1958: "Onlookers, people who secretly had jobs and 'cared' about family and money and position . . . these people are not hipsters; they are fellow travellers." E. Burdick, *The Reporter,* Apr. 3, 31.

fem **femme** *n.* A girl or woman; a female. 1939–40: "He has aired the femme that got him the job. . . ." O'Hara, *Pal Joey,* 6. *The spelling "femme" occurs four times as often as "fem"; thus orig. from Fr. "femme" = woman more important than back-clipping from "female."* Cf. **frau.** *adj.* Feminine; female. 1941· "High school femme students." W. Winchell, *synd. newsp. col.,* Jan. 16. 1951: "Mary McCarty . . : looks more like a post deb than a femme comic. . . ." Hy Gardner, N.Y. *Her. Trib.,* Dec. 12, 27/1.

fem-sem *n.* A woman's college or school. *Common c1900 student use. From "feminine seminary."* See Appendix, Rhyming Slang.

fenagle = **finagle.**

fence *n.* A person or place that deals in stolen goods. 1950: ". . . To determine if any of the loot had appeared [in

Detroit] and been handled by a fence."
AP, Feb. 9. *No longer common in
underworld as too well known to outsiders.*
v.t. To sell stolen property to or at a
fence. *1848: criminal use.* 1950 "...
The təke must be fenced, or sold."
DeBaun, 71. See **stone-fence.**

fence-hanger   *n.* **1** One whose mind
is not made up; one who has not made
a decision. **2** A gossip.

—fest   See Appendix, Suffixes and
Suffix Words.

fetching   *adj.* Pleasing; attractive.
Since c1900; colloq.

fever   *n.* A five-spot playing card.
A whimsical distortion of "fiver."

f. f.   **fr. f.**   French fried potatoes.
Used as an abbr. on lunch-counter menus.
See Appendix, Shortened Words.

F. F. V.   **1** The socially elite. *From
"First Families of Virginia."* → **2** "Fast
Footed Virginians." *Civil War Union use
in jocular reference to the retreating
Confederate armies. Obs.* → **3** A criminal
or convict. *Lit., a "first family of
Virginia," jocular reference to belief that
Virginia was first settled as a penal
colony.*

fiddle   *v.* To obtain illegally, as by
bribery or petty crime. *Not common.*
See **Swedish fiddle, second fiddle.**

fiddle-faddle   *interj. & n.* Nonsense.
1934: "She's happy about herself.
Oh ... fiddle-faddle." P. Wylie, *Finnley
Wren*, 175. 1937. "An editor crazy
enough to pay for such home-made
fiddle-faddle." A. Woollcott, *Long, Long
Ago*, 211. See Appendix, Reduplications.

fiend   **—fiend**   *n.* **1** One obsessed
with or a devotee of something, esp.
something evil or forbidden; specif.,
c1890–c1920, a cigarette smoker; c1925
a drug addict. 1944: "In the early 1890's
the users [of cigarettes were] known as
'fiends.' " Fowler, *Good Night*, 40. **2** A
devotee or addict of, or enthusiast for,
something indicated. 1889: "Free lunch
fiend." 1896: "Dope fiend." 1909:
"Botany fiend." *DAE. Colloq.* 1909:
"A vista which has been the delight of
the kodak fiend. ..." O. D. von Engeln,
At Cornell, 54. *Still in use.* See Appendix,
Suffixes and Suffix Words.

fierce   *adj.* Awful; terrible; horrible;
hard; intense. 1909: "At the time of the
present writing ... the adjective *fierce*
is much used as a general slang term of
disapproval; anything which is unpleasant is *fierce.*" Krapp, *Modern
English*, 202. 1914: "How sorry I was
for the way I spoke to you. Gee! it was

fierce of me. ..." S. Lewis, *Our Mr.
Wrenn*, 205. 1925: "That is a fierce
lesson we have today." *English Journal*,
Nov., 699, 701.   *adv.* Awful. 1914:
"He just cusses her out something
fierce. ..." S. Lewis, *Our Mr. Wrenn*,
191.

fifty-five   *n.* Root beer; an order of
root beer. *c1935 lunch-counter use in
relaying an order.*

fifty-one   *n.* Hot chocolate; an order
of a cup of hot chocolate. *Common
c1935–c1945 lunch-counter use in relaying
an order.*

fifty-six   *n.* For those who work on
Saturdays and Sundays, the time off
that takes the place of a week end.
1958: "Fifty-six—Time off between
swings of duty; a policeman's week end."
*Station House Slang. Because the time
is 56 hours.*

fifty-two   *n.pl.* An order of two cups
of hot chocolate. *c1935–c1945 lunch
counter use in relaying an order.* See
fifty-one.

fight   *n.* A party. 1950: "... The
cocktail fights frequented by the old
man." Starnes, *Another Mug*, 9.

fight a bottle   To drink from a bottle.
1950: "After fighting a bottle all
evening." Starnes, *Another Mug*, 38.
Cf. **booze-fighter.**

—fighter   See Appendix, Suffixes and
Suffix Words.

fightin' tools   Eating utensils; a table
knife, fork, and spoon. *W.W.II Armed
Forces use.*

figure   *v.i. & v.t.* To be expected or
prophesied to be; to seem reasonable;
to make sense; to stand to reason
*Sometimes the subject of "figure" appears
to be in the wrong person, but then "it"
or "that" is the subject. Often the passive
voice is meant where active is used, e.g.,
"He doesn't figure to live"* = "He is not
figured [expected] to live." 1935: "And
where is Never Despair [a race horse]
but last, where he figures." Runyon, 239.
1949: "He doesn't figure to live much
longer. You're the only person who
figured to profit by Mr. Quint's death."
"The pup figured to be in the room
when Einstein discussed the bomb with
the President." Billy Rose, *synd. newsp.
col.*, Sept. 14; Dec. 23.

filbert   *n.* An enthusiast. *A variation
on "nut."* 1951: "Francis Wallace is a
self-confessed football filbert." Arthur
Daley, N.Y. *Times Bk. Rev.*, Oct. 7, 16.

file   *n.* **1** A pickpocket. *Underworld use.*

2 A waste basket. Cf. **file seventeen, file thirteen, circular file.**

file-bone *n.* Any act by which one may gain class or academic standing. **—er** *n.* An ambitious student. *Student use.* 1944: "Everyone was surprised that a fileboner as hivey as Cunningham was D in math. . . ." Cliff Macon, *Collier's,* Sept. 23, 69/1. *West Point use.*

file seventeen A waste-basket. *W.W.II Army use.*

file thirteen A waste-basket. *W.W.II Armed Forces use.*

fill-in *n.* **1** A summary; an account that fills in gaps in the hearer's or reader's knowledge. 1951. "I no sooner got off that day coach than a friend gives me a fill-in on how Costello is running the country. . . ." Editorial, *SEP,* Apr. 21, 10/2. **2** A substitute worker. *Colloq.* *v.t.* **1** To summarize for someone. *Common since c1945.* **2** To work as a substitute.

filling station A small town. *From the concept that, to one passing through, the filling station is the most important thing.*

fillmill *n.* A bar, a saloon. *Not common.*

filly *n.* A girl or young woman. 1943: "A chorus filly." Wolfert, *Underworld,* 451.

filthy *adj.* **1** Wealthy; having much money. Often in "filthy rich." 1922: "He's filthy with dough." O'Neill, *Hairy Ape,* 6. Cf. **loaded. 2** Obscene, risque, sexy. *n.* Money. Short for "filthy lucre." 1931: "Just trying to make a bit of the filthy." Wodehouse, *If I Were You,* 21.

filthy lucre Money. *Colloq.* *From Paul's Epistle to Titus.*

fin *n.* **1** The human head. **2** The human arm. **3** A five-dollar bill; the sum of $5. 1939: "I gave my pal a fin." J. O'Hara, *Pal Joey,* 34. **—if finiff**

finiff *n.* A five-dollar bill; the sum of $5. 1932: "If I happen to have a finnif on me. . . ." Runyon, 78. 1948: "[The song] 'Listen to the Mocking Bird' sold 20 million copies up to the early 1900s, and it brought its author ['Alice Hawthorne' = Septimus Winner] $5. No wonder that finif looked big to him." P. Jones in Phila. *Bulletin,* Dec. 5, 22/6. *From the Yiddish.* See **fin.**

finagle **fenagle** **finigal** **finnagel** **faniggle** *v.t.* To contrive; to manage; to figure out a way, esp. by unethical or unusual means. 1926: "I don't want any finnagelling from you."

Stallings and Anderson, *What Price Glory,* III. **—r —er** *n.* One who contrives for others to pay or take responsibility; specif. one who stalls until someone else pays the check.

find *v.t.* **1** To discharge a cadet for deficiency or for failure in studies or conduct. 1950: ". . . Or getting found in your studies." Movie, *The West Point Story. West Point use.* Cf. **foundling.** → **2** To rate as a failure or a delinquent.

find Rover To work without enthusiasm or care; to relax on one's job; to make little or no effort. *Suggested by "dog it."*

fine *adj.* Pleasing; wonderful; exciting; cool. *Wide use since c1940; now associated with bop and cool use.*

fine dinner A pretty girl. *c1935, jitterbug and student use. Obs.*

finest, the The New York City police force; a New York City policeman. 1930: "As a motorman, he decided to become one of 'the finest.'" Lavine, *Third Degree,* 12. *Also used ironically.*

finger *v.t.* **1** To point out accusingly; to point out a victim to a gunman, or a criminal to the police. 1934: "You're the guy that fingered Manny Tinnen." Chandler, *Finger Man,* 33. Cf. **put the finger on. 2** To inform thieves as to the location, value, etc., of potential loot. 1949: "I fingered the robberies." Movie, *Scene of the Crime.* Cf. **finger man.** *n.* **1** A policeman. **2** A police informer. **3** Finger man. **4** An amount of liquor in a glass equal to the depth of the width of a finger. 1934: "Maybe I'd better have another finger of the hooch." Chandler, *Finger Man,* 24. See **butterfingers, give five fingers to, give [someone] the finger, on the finger, put the finger on. —s** *n.pl.* **1** A 10% share of loot. *In allusion to the ten fingers. Underworld use.* **2** A jazz piano player; often a nickname. *Synthetic use.*

finger, give [someone] the [taboo] To treat someone badly, unfairly, or with malice; to take advantage of; to brush off. 1941: "Let me show you how to give that guy the finger . . . she was giving me the polite finger." Budd Schulberg, *What Makes Sammy Run,* 88. *Lit.,* = **fuck you** *or* **up your ass.** *Taken from the obscene gesture of extending the middle finger to imply this.*

finger, on the On credit, on the cuff. *Never common.*

finger man A criminal who finds,

obtains detailed information on, evaluates, and/or points out prospective victims or loot to thieves, holdup men, kidnapers, or killers.

finger mob   A gang of criminals working under police protection, usu. in return for informing on other gangs.

finger on [something], put [one's]   To identify, recognize, comprehend, or the like; to remember or locate in one's memory.

finger on [someone], put the   **1** To mark or point out a victim, as for killing. *Underworld use.* → **2** To identify, inform on, or make a charge against a criminal to the police. 1957: ". . . Mrs. Maloney told police that 'the guy I shot was Frank Smith. He put the finger on my husband.' " N.Y. *Daily News*, Aug. 12, 4. *Orig. and mainly underworld use. Fig., to point out, as with the index finger.*

finger popper   Lit., one who snaps his fingers; fig., a musician or listener who is carried away by jazz music. 1957: "Finger popper—A cat (musician or hipster) who is swinging." E. Horne, *For Cool Cats and Far-Out Chicks. Some synthetic cool use. Reinforced by "joy popper."*

finger-wringer   *n.* An actor or esp. an actress given to overly emotional performances. *Movie use.* See Appendix, Rhyming Slang.

finigal = **finagle.**

finisher   *n.* A knockout blow. *Prize fight use.* See **table finisher.**

fink   *n.* **1** A worker or private policeman hired by a factory, mine, or company to help break a strike; a scab; a company spy posing as a worker in order to report union activities. 1926: ". . . [Dates] from the famous Homestead strike [1892]. It is the most derogatory term in the wobbly lingo. *Fink* was originally *Pink*, a contraction of Pinkerton." S. H. Holbrook in *Amer. Mercury*, Jan., 63. 1956: "The American frontier incubated vivid wordmaking in many fields and labor was not neglected. From this source came words like 'fink' meaning a strike replacement." *Labor's Special Language from Many Sources.* Cf. **wobbly, Pink.** → **2** A guard employed by a mine, factory, or company. *Since c1915; archaic.* → **3** A detective or policeman; a private detective or policeman. 1956: "This Sherlock Holmes. . . . Whiskey's bad enough. But this fink's on the old yockydock." J. Cannon, *Who Struck John?* 202. *Since c1920.* **4** An informer,

squealer, or stool pigeon. 1940: "Now he's looking for the fink that turned him up [*i.e.*, in] eight years ago." Chandler, *Farewell*, 27. *Since c1920. Underworld use.* **5** A contemptible person; an undesirable, unwanted, or unpleasant person. *Some use since c1925.* **6** A tramp who begs food at back doors. *Some c1930 hobo use.* **7** Any broken, defective, or small article of merchandise, as a toy balloon; a larry.   *v.i.* To inform, specif. to the police; to become cowardly or untrustworthy. 1949: "Trying to make me fink?" Burnett, *Jungle*, 18. 1957: ". . . Dutch knew I worked for his friend . . . and wouldn't fink. . . ." George Raft, as told to Dean Jennings, "Out of My Past," *SEP*, Sept. 21, 94.

Finn = **Mickey Finn.**

finnagel = **finagle.**

finnif   finniff   See **finif.**

fire   *v.t.* **1** To eject or throw someone out of a place by force. 1871: *DAE.* 1893: "We talk about 'firing' a book agent [salesman] from an office room." P. Duffield in *Dial*, Aug. 16, 86/2. *Most common c1880–c1900. Still in some use.* Cf. **bounce.** → **2** To discharge an employee from his job, esp. for reasons that reflect unfavorably upon him, as incompetence, inefficiency, tardiness, or the like. 1887: *DAE.* 1907: " 'To fire out,' which latterly has become simply 'to fire,' is more vivid than 'to sack' or 'to boot.' " *Living Age*, July, 117/1. *Colloq. since c1910.* → **3** To expel or dismiss someone from a place without using physical force; to request or require that someone leave. 1910: "They fired me [from school] for trying to kill a man." Johnson, *Varmint*, 14. 1914: "I'm going to fire that Teddem [out of the rooming house]." S. Lewis, *Our Mr. Wrenn*, 178. **4** To fling, hurl, or throw something, usu. a ball or missile, with the hand, esp. with force and speed. 1952: "[Baseball pitcher] Joe Black fires one at him in the fourth inning. . . ." N.Y. *Sunday News*, Oct. 4, C20. *Colloq. since c1910.*

fire, on the   Pending; under consideration.

fire-ball   *n.* An ambitious, efficient, and fast worker; a very active person.

fire blanks   To have sexual intercourse without impregnating the woman, when the couple wishes children; for a man to have sexual intercourse when he is physically unable to father a child.

firebug   *n.* An arsonist; a pyromaniac. 1953: "A firebug's tryin' to burn this warehouse!" L. Turner, *synd. comic strip,* "Wash Tubbs," Feb. 10. *Since c1870.*

firecracker *n.* A bomb; also, a torpedo. *W.W.II use.*

fired up **1** Drunk. *c1850. Archaic.* **2** Angry.

fire-eater *n.* **1** A firefighter. *Colloq.* **2** A brave or bold person, esp. one who is not afraid to argue with or criticize those in authority; one who loves an argument.

fireman *n.* **1** In baseball, a relief pitcher. 1949: "A four-run blast against fireman Joe [Page] in the eighth inning." AP, Sept. 27. *Because such a pitcher is called into the game to stop the opposing team in the midst of a rally, i.e. "to put out the fire."* **2** A speeding motorist. 1943: "There were two things he could paste on them firemen." Wolfert, *Underworld,* 244.

fire out = **fire.** *Obs.*

fire stick A gun. *Teenage and adolescent hoodlum use since c1950.*

fire up To start an engine. *Some W.W.II Air Force use; common hot rod use.*

fire-water *n.* Liquor. *Colloq. since c1820. A common pioneer and Western term, now used jokingly.*

fireworks *n.pl.* **1** Excitement; a spectacular display of anything fig. like fireworks. 1952: "Speeches that . . . would produce the 'fireworks' [that Eisenhower's] supporters have demanded." J. Devlin, AP, Aug. 29. **2** Shooting; esp. artillery fire. *W.W.II Armed Forces use.*

first luff A first lieutenant in the Navy. *c1850 and still used in W.W.I and W.W.II.*

first man A first sergeant. *W.W.II Army use. Not common.*

first national bank A woman's stocking. *In allusion to its use, while being worn, for carrying paper money. Usu. in the c1920 pun, "There's a run on the first national bank."*

first off First; from the very first; at first. 1949: "First off, Baby jokingly told Daddy. . . ." Earl Wilson, *synd. newsp. col.,* Sep. 30. *Colloq. since c1880.*

first-of-May *n.* A novice; a new or inexperienced employee. 1939: "A beginner at barking is known as a 'first of May.' " M. Bracker in N.Y. *Times Mag.,* June 18, 11/1. *Circus use.* *adj.* Inexperienced. 1952: "These first-of-May guys are a little off time." R. L. Taylor in *New Yorker,* Apr. 19, 40/3. *Circus use.*

first-rate *adj.* Excellent. 1914: "A first-rate stunt. . . ." S. Lewis, *Our Mr. Wrenn,* 230. *adv.* Very well. *c1845; colloq.*

first reader A conductor's trainbook. *Railroad use.*

first soldier A first sergeant. *W.W.II Army use. Not common.*

fish *n.sing.* **1** A person who is a newcomer; a novice; an inexperienced worker, a beginner. *Wide college use = "freshman" c1900; still some use. Universally known prison use = a newly arrested prisoner or one arrested for a first offense; since c1915, reinforced by "tank."* → **2** A stupid person; a dupe or sucker; one who is victimized, easy to dominate, or dominated by another. 1943: "Why should he be the fish for the big guys?" Wolfert, *Underworld,* 165. *Since c1920; not now common.* **3** A Roman Catholic. *Some derisive and jocular use since c1920, from "fish eater."* **4** A dollar. 1949: "I'm good with the cue. Used to get fifteen fish for an exhibition of six-no-count." N. Algren, *Man with the Golden Arm,* 13. **5** A person, a fellow or guy; usu. after a modifier, esp. in "poor fish" = a pitiable or unfortunate person, or "queer fish" = an odd or eccentric person. 1924: "I tried once in a play at home and made a poor fish of myself." Marks, *Plastic Age,* 53. *Since c1920.* **6** A torpedo. *W.W.II USN use.* See **tin fish.** *The above have been or are the most common meanings of "fish." The following have been or are used much less commonly.* **7** One who curries favor with his teacher. 1851: Hall, *College Words,* 129. **8** An old, worn-out worker. **9** An untrustworthy, slippery or glib person. *Some c1930 use.* **10** A prostitute. *Seemed to be gaining in pop. prior to W.W.II, but did not become pop.* **11** A corpse. *Prob. from the appearance of the eyes.* **12** A boy who is not a member of a street gang; a youth whom a street gang dislikes, considers aloof, and probably intends to beat up. *N.Y.C. adolescent gang use since c1950.* **13** A criminal; a convict. 1957: ". . . The cops catch a lot of very interesting fish. . . ." "The Hick Cops Bust Up Joe's Nice Barbecue," *Life,* Dec. 9, 57. **14** A Catholic priest. Cf. **fish eater.** *v.i.* **1** To curry favor. **2** To ask or try to get information without directly asking for it. *Colloq.* **3** To feint, esp. in boxing. *n.pl.* **1** Dollars. 1921: "A guarantee of a thousand fish." Witwer, *Leather,* 4. 1952: "The job paid only fifty fish."

L. Stander in *Esquire*, June, 84/1. **2** Torpedoes. *W.W.II USN use.* **—eater** *n.* A Roman Catholic. *Some derisive but mostly jocular use. Because most Roman Catholics eat fish on fast days.* **—er** *n.* A student who curries favor with his teacher. *Obs.* **—ery** *n.* A religious mission in a working-class neighborhood. *Hobo use.* **—skin** *n.* A dollar bill.

fish bowl A jail. *A variation of syn.* **tank.** 1942: "I'm going . . . and with a . . . hope that I won't be seeing you in the fish bowl." Chandler, *High Window*, 198.

fish eggs Tapioca pudding. *Not common.*

fish eye An expressionless glance or a questioning stare. 1941: "A well-fed man in tails opened the door, gave them the fish eye." G. Homes, *40 Whacks*, 129. **—s** Tapioca pudding. *Armed Forces, student, and prison use.*

fish-hooks *n.pl.* The fingers.

fish horn A saxophone. *Synthetic jazz use.*

fishing trip, take a = **take a drink.**

fish music = **race music.** An early, often slower and quieter form of rock and roll, which grew out of "race music."

fish or cut bait A request, demand, or comment that another act, obtain a result, or bring something to a successful conclusion soon, or else stop trying and give someone else a chance to do so. *Since c1876; archaic and dial.* Cf. **shit or get off the pot** [taboo].

fish scale A nickel, 5¢; any coin. 1952: "Without a fish scale in any purse, I gotta sit here and witness this gastronomical orgy!" Merrill Blosser, NEA *comic strip*, "Freckles," July 12. *Since c1900; not common.*

fish story An exaggerated story of one's exploits. *Colloq. since c1820.*

fishtail *n.* **1** A semaphore blade. *Railroad use.* **2** A woman's dress or dress style incorporating a tight-fitting skirt that widens out, like a fish tail, at the bottom. *Popular c1955.* **3** Automobile rear fenders that flare upward to hold the car's rear lights. *Introduced c1954 and still popular.* *v.i.* To swing or slide from side to side; said of a car or truck. 1957: ". . . Causing his rear wheels to spin or the rear end to fishtail, that is swing back and forth." "The Drag Racing Rage," *Life*, April 29, 132.

fish tale A story that sounds fishy; an improbable excuse or alibi.

fish tank = **tank.**

fish trap = **trap.**

fish-wrapper *n.* A newspaper.

fishy *adj.* **1** Suggestive of deception; dishonest, unethical, insincere, or untruthful words or deeds; improbable, unconvincing, or unbelievable; not quite right or true. 1899: ". . . The story is not at all fishy, but true in every point." Matthew P. Breen, *Thirty Years of New York Politics Up-to-Date*, 103. 1930: "Your story sounds fishy." Weeks, *Racket*, 68. *Brought to U.S. by orig. Eng. colonists.* **2** Drunk. *Archaic.*

fist *n.* **1** A telegrapher's touch or distinctive technique in operating the key, by which other telegraphers may recognize his transmitted messages. *Telegrapher and radio amateur use since c1935.* **2** A signature. *Railroad use.* **—ful** *n.* **1** A five-year prison sentence. *Underworld use.* Cf. **five fingers. 2** A large amount of money. *Shortened form of the fig.* **fistful of money.**

fistful of money A large amount of money; wealth.

fit See **cat fit, duck-fit.**

five *n.* **1** A large glass of milk; an order of a large glass of milk. *Common c1930 lunch-counter use in relaying an order. Obs.* **2** Five dollars; a five-dollar bill. *Common use.* **3** The five fingers or the hand considered as an object in shaking hands. In such jive expressions as "give me five" = shake hands, give me your hand to shake. *c1935.* **—r** ~ **1** A five-dollar bill. 1883: *DAE.* 1956: "For a fiver, cash, you could ride." N. Algren, *A Walk on the Wild Side*, 17. See Appendix, **—er** ending. **2** A five-year prison sentence. *Mainly prison use.* See Appendix, **—er** ending.

five, give [someone] To help a person; to lend him a hand. *Also, fig.* = "to give five minutes of one's time to help someone else." *Not common.*

five-and-dime *n.* A 5-and-10-cent variety store. *Colloq.*

five-and-ten-cent store *n.* A variety store or small-items department store. *Because they orig. sold only 5¢ and 10¢ items, usually "notions." Many still sell only items that cost no more than a dollar; others are actually neighborhood department stores.*

five-by-five *adj.* Fat. c1940: "Mr. Five-by-Five," title of a pop. song containing the line, "He's five feet tall and five feet wide." 1956: "Anybody fat is *five-by-five.*" S. Longstreet, *The Real Jazz Old and New*, 150.

five-case note A five-dollar bill. Cf. **case note.**

five-finger *n.* A thief.

five fingers **1** A five-year prison sentence. *Underworld use.* **2** A thief. *The movie titled "Five Fingers" about a master spy and thief was very popular c1950.*

five fingers to [someone], give To thumb one's nose at a person in derision. 1949: "Then you could give five fingers to every cop. . . ." A. Hynd, 45.

five of clubs A fist.

five-ouncers *n.pl.* The fists; a blow with the fist. *From the five-ounce minimum weight of a boxing glove. Prize fight use.*

five-per-center **five percenter** *n.* **1** One who influences or seeks to influence politicians or government agencies on behalf of clients or friends, often in return for a percentage of the profits made thereby. *Most common during President Harry S. Truman's last administration, 1948–52, when his Republican opponents coined the phrase in making accusations of scandal in the awarding of public contracts. Still used. Because the person receives a percentage, usu. 5%, of the value of the contract awarded; reinforced by "ten percenter."* See Appendix, —er ending. **2** Any lawyer, businessman, or friend of politicians who possesses undue influence in public affairs.

five-spot *n.* **1** A five-dollar bill. 1952: "Follow that cab! There's a five-spot for you if you don't lose him!" Saul Pett, AP, Oct. 17. *Since c1895.* **2** A five-year prison sentence. 1928: "Serving out a five-spot." D. Purroy. **3** A playing card or billiard ball numbered 5.

fix *v.t.* **1** To bribe a person to lose a race, contest, or the like. 1908: "A jockey or a pugilist is 'fixed.'" R. L. Hartt in *Atlantic Mon.*, Aug., 230/2. **2** To buy protection from the local police. *Underworld use since c1925.* See **the fix.** **3** To give an addict an injection of narcotics, esp. heroin; to sell an addict drugs, esp. heroin. **4** To castrate an animal, esp. a cat. *Colloq.* **5** To beat up, defeat, or cause someone to fail because of malice toward him. *Colloq.* *v.i.* To intend; to plan. *Dial.* *n.* **1** A single injection of a narcotic drug, esp. heroin. 1949: " 'Don't vomit, student,' he taunted Frankie to remind him of the first fix he'd had." N. Algren, *Man with the Golden Arm*, 75. *Addict use, generally known.* 1956: "Miss Davis escaped . . . when [Federal Narcotic] agents allowed her to search for a heroin peddler for a fix to calm her jittery nerves." San Francisco *Examiner,*

April 29, 1. *Addict use; generally known.* **2** Navigational data; the coordinates establishing a specif. location, as of a ship, airplane, or the like. **3** A stationary post, of a guard or policeman, as opposed to walking a beat. 1958: "Fix—A stationary post." G. Y. Wells, *Station House Slang.* **—ed** *adj.* **1** Having a result predetermined by bribery; unfair. 1938: "He is sure that every race is fixed." Liebling, *Back Where,* see **fix, the fix,** 83. **2** Purposely ignored or forgotten by the police or public officials owing to bribery or influence. 1953: "If we get a non-fix traffic ticket, there will be a great improvement in the morals of the people." Gov. Thomas E. Dewey in a speech, Mar. 24. **3** Castrated; said of an animal, esp. a cat. See **fix.** **—er** *n.* **1** A go-between; an adjuster. 1889: *DAE.* → **2** A dishonest lawyer; a shyster. *Underworld and circus use.* → **3** A negotiator between criminals and officials; one who arranges for "the fix." 1934: "He's a fixer you have to see if you want to open a gambling hall." Chandler, *Finger Man,* 3. **4** One who sells narcotics to addicts. 1949: "Louie was the best fixer of all because he knew what it was to need to get well. Louie had had a big habit." N. Algren, *Man with the Golden Arm,* 78. See **fix.** See Appendix, —er ending.

fix, the *n.* **1** Bribery assuring the prearranged outcome of a sporting event; an act or instance of such bribery. 1954: "It's in the bag. The fix is on." W. R. & F. K. Simpson, *Hockshop,* 188. See **fix.** **2** Bribery assuring that the police or public officials will ignore, forget, or consider lightly an illegal act or law violation; an act or instance of such bribery. 1949: "You're gettin' out in half an hour 'n' the super hisself couldn't put the fix in any faster. The case'll be dismissed by noon whether you're in court or not." N. Algren, *Man with the Golden Arm,* 29.

fix-up *n.* A single dose of a narcotic. *Addict use.*

fix [someone] up **1** To secure a date for someone. **2** To provide someone with a desired, wanted, necessary, or unique item or service. *One may be "fixed up" with a drink of whisky, a prostitute, a portion of medicine, a valuable antique, or the like, esp. a thing or service associated with illegal dealings or vice.* **3** Specif., to secure a prostitute or promiscuous woman for someone. 1951: "You come down, Mista Kozloff, and I fix you up fine. Much fine. Wine, love, a plate of *pasta*." S. Longstreet, *The Pedlocks*, 241.

fix [one's] wagon **1** To prevent another's success; to destroy another's livelihood, reputation, or expectations. → **2** To punish; to kill. 1945: "A woman who had stabbed her husband to death ... 'I sure fixed his wagon,' she said." Mitchell, *McSorley's*, 146.

fizz-fuzz   *n.* Coca-Cola; a glass of Coca-Cola. *Some student use, never common.* See Appendix, Reduplications.

fizz job   A jet airplane. *Synthetic sl.*

fizzle   *n.* Failure. 1928: "He would have been a fizzle in the cheese business." *Since c1850, colloq.*   *v.i.* To fail. *Colloq. since c1870.*

flack   flak   *n.* **1** Publicity or advertising that is widely disseminated or repeated in the hope that some percentage of it will be heeded. *Fig. respelling of "flak."* 1948: "The flack description is also worth quoting. . . ." *Variety*, Aug. 25, 55/3. → **2** A professional publicity worker or press agent. 1950: "The movie-studio flack ... my flack friend. . . ." Pete Martin, *SEP*, Apr. 1, 26/1. 1956: "And since 'flack' is Hollywood slang for publicity man. . . ." Pete Martin, "The New Marilyn Monroe," *SEP*, May 5, 149. *Mainly theater and Madison Avenue use.*

flag   *v.t.* **1** To signal a moving vehicle, such as a train, bus, or cab, to stop. *Orig. for a station master to signal, by waving a red flag, a train to stop to pick up a passenger.* **2** To refuse or to turn a person away. **3** To hail or stop someone or gain attention, as for the purpose of talking.   *n.* In baseball, the pennant awarded to the best team in each league at the end of a season; the pennant awarded to the team that wins the World Series. 1958: "The Yankees [N.Y.C. baseball team] have only six more games to win before their habitual try for the flag." AP, Sept. 9. *Baseball use.* **2** An assumed name. See **Jewish flag.**

flag-waver   *n.* Any aggressively or overly patriotic person; any song, book, play, or the like based on a patriotic theme.

flak   *n.* Fragments of artillery shells, esp. of those often used in antiaircraft and short range shells, constructed so as to explode with many destructive fragments. *W.W.II use.*

flake out   To lie down to rest or sleep. *W.W.II USN use.*

flam   *v.* **1** To be attentive to a lady or ladies; to flirt. *Some c1850 student use. Obs.* **2** To fail in an examination. *Some c1900 student use; never common. Obs.*

flamdoodle   *n.* = **flapdoodle,** nonsense. 1888: *DAE. Dial.*

flame   *n.* A sweetheart; a passionately loved person. 1920: "She's an old flame." Fitzgerald, *This Side of Paradise. Brought to U.S. by the Eng. colonists.*

flamethrower   *n.* A jet plane.

flang   *v.i.* See **fling.**

flange-face   *n.* A homely sailor. *W.W.II USN use; not common.*

flange-head   *n.* A Chinese. *W.W.II Air Force use.*

flanker   *n.* A tall person. *West Point use.*

flannel   *n.* A soft, soothing manner. *More common in Eng. than in U.S.*

flap   *n.* **1** An air raid; an air raid alert or alarm. 1940: "*Flap* originated with the airmen . . . is now in general use at the front." H. L. Mencken in *Reader's Digest*, May, 39. *W.W.II use.* **2** A fight or row; a crisis or emergency; an alarm, a scare; an urgent conference; any loud or violent confusion or tumult; excitement. 1952: "There was so much flap about the desert campaign's being fought from the terrace of Shepheard's [Hotel] that several generals moved." *New Yorker*, Feb. 9, 25/3. 1952: "Mr. Lovett expressed himself thoughtfully to a group of reporters familiar with Pentagon intrigues, 'flaps' (or crises) and negotiation." A. Stevens in N.Y. *Times*, Aug. 19. → **3** A party, esp. a noisy, rowdy party; a brawl. *Teenage use since c1955.* → **4** A fight between two rival neighborhood boys' street gangs, a rumble; an encounter with the police. *Boys' street gang use.* **5** A mistake; a social error. **6** Confusion, anxiety, disconcertion.

flap [one's] chops (jowls) (jaw) (lip)   To talk, esp. idly or indiscreetly; to argue. 1953: [talking idly] "Well, you weren't just flapping your lip that time." Peter De Vries, *New Yorker*, May 2, 27/2. 1951: [arguing] "To see Leo Durocher flapping his lip bitterly at the umpire. . . ." Dick Young, N.Y. *Daily News*, Aug. 9, c20/1.

flapdoodle   *n.* Nonsense; foolish talk; blah, boloney. 1862: "He then goes on to utter other flapdoodle for the nourishment of the mind." N.Y. *Tribune* Jan. 22. 1930: "The eloquent flapdoodle about the 'crime laboratory.' . . ." Lavine, *Third Degree*, 21. 1950: "Such educational flapdoodle." H. G. Doyle in *Pub. Mod. Lang. Assn.*, Feb., 19.

flapjaw   *n.* **1** Talk; chat. 1952: "We caught Manone and Moore for a moment's flapjaw before we left." *New Yorker*, Mar. 8, 26/2f. **2** An over-talkative person.

flapper   *n.* **1** The hand. *Since c1840.* **2** The pop. female type of the 1920's, typically a young woman characterized by a cynical attitude, a frank interest in sex, a penchant for daring fashions, including short, straight dresses, no petticoats, bobbed hair, stockings rolled below the knee, etc., together with the use of bright lipstick and eye shadow, cosmetics introduced after W.W.I. *The flapper was the often somewhat bewildered experimenter with the new freedom that came to women after W.W.I; in manner, dress, speech, and thought she assiduously practiced behavior that would seem the opposite of the "feminine" as previously conceived.* 1922: "Flapper-Filology—The New Language," headline in Phila. *Eve. Bulletin*, Mar. 8. 1927: "Poor little flapper who wants to imitate the society dames. . . ." *New Repub.*, Jan. 26, 278/2. 1927: "This jazz-attuned age of flappers. . . . Among the words now in good usage which within recent memory were but slang, I recall 'boot-leg,' 'bunk,' 'hootch,' 'flapper,' 'hokum,' 'vamp,' 'gob,' and 'jazz.' " J. A. Work in *Educational Rev.*, Apr., 223f. 1956: "John Held Jr. drew the flapper best . . . the girl with long, long legs, cropped shingled hair, a cigarette and likker flask in her hand." S. Longstreet, *The Real Jazz Old and New*, 95. *Although the article is obs., the word is still universally known and used, as often with nostalgia as with sociological objectivity.*

flaps   *n.pl.* **1** The ailerons on the wings of an airplane. *Colloq.* **2** The human ears.

flare up   To become angry or enraged. *Colloq.*   **flareup**   *n.* In jazz, to reach a climax of intensity through the playing of repeated chords, increased tempo or volume. 1956: "The *flareup* is to build a chord." S. Longstreet, *The Real Jazz Old and New*, 148.

flash   *n.* **1** Thieves' argot. 1848: J. S. Farmer. *Still in use.* **2** A look; a comprehensive glance; a peek. 1948: "We slid into the cross street to take a flash at the alley. We didn't see anything." Cain, *Moth*, 94. **3** A person who excels at something; a whiz. *Archaic.* → **4** One who has a superficial knowledge

or reputation; one who has given or occasionally gives a sensational performance but who cannot be regularly depended upon to do so. *Reinforced by the expression "flash in the pan."* **5** A display of attractive or gaudy merchandise or prizes to attract attention; valuable merchandise, ostensibly prizes, but used only for display; gaudy merchandise. 1948: "Expensive flash that the mark couldn't win." F. Brown, *Dead Ringer*, 30. *Carnival and circus use.*   *adj.* Dishonest. *Underworld use since c1850. Archaic.*   *v.t.* To set up a display of prizes at a gambling concession. 1935: "Flash the joint." *Amer. Mercury*, June, 229.   **—y**   *adj.* Gaudy; cheap and gaudy; created or designed mainly to attract attention or to give an attractive appearance.

flash-sport   *n.* An unusually gaudily or fashionably dressed, handsome, or rakish dude or sport. 1950: "I would land in a little town and walk down the street in my conservative stripe. The girls would all notice but I wouldn't so much as nod at anybody. Two hours later, I'd stroll back to my place, change into a nice tweed and stroll down the same way. The gals would begin to say, 'My, my, who's this new flash-sport drop in town?' " A. Lomax, *Mr. Jelly Roll*, 108.

flat   *n.* **1** A punctured or "flat" automobile tire. *Stand. since c1930.* **2** A simple, dull, or gullible person; one who is not mentally alert. *Some use since c1925. From "flat tire."* **3** A nickel; the sum of 5¢. *Some c1935 jive use.* **4** Canvas stretched over a wooden frame and painted to resemble scenery, a wall, or other background. *Theater use.*   *adj.* **1** Without money; broke. **2** Pertaining to or associated with any carnival gambling game, esp. one in which money, rather than merchandise, is the prize. *Carnival use.* See **flat-joint**.

—foot   **flat-foot**   *n.* **1** A sailor. *W.W.I USN use. Not common.* **2** A patrolman; any uniformed policeman or detective. 1948: "The flat-feet scratched their heads." Lait-Mortimer, *N.Y. Confidential*, 127.   **—footed**   *adj. & adv.* Unprepared; taken by surprise. *Since c1910.*   **—head**   *n.* **1** A stupid person. 1951: "Flatheads that can't even run errands straight." *I, Mobster*, 97. *Since c1885.* **2** A policeman. **3** A nontipping patron. Cf. **flat**.

—headed   *adj.* Stupid. 1929: "The speaker was a flatheaded idiot. . . ."

P. Curtiss, *Harper's*, Aug., 385/2.   **—s**
n.pl. **1** Pancakes, griddlecakes, or hotcakes. *Logger and ranch use. Obs.*
2 Horse racing in which the horse runs
and is ridden by the jockey, as opposed
to harness racing in which the horse
trots or paces and pulls a sulky containing the driver. 1956: "FLATS . . .
the running horse game, as opposed to
the harness horse game." T. Betts,
Across the Board, 315. *Common horse-
racing use. Because a running horse
appears to run flatfooted, placing his
hoofs down flatly for traction.* **3** The
human feet. **4** A type or style of woman's
shoe having no or a low heel. *Colloq.*
—tener   *n.* In prize fighting, a
knock-out blow. *Prize fight use.* See
Appendix, —er ending.   **—tie   —ty**
n. **1** A policeman. *From "flatfoot."
Some c1925 use; some boy street gang
use since c1950.* See Appendix, —ie
ending. **2 = flat-joint.** 1950: "You
should have piped the squash on that
mark when he left the flattie all tapped
out." AP, Los Angeles, Jan. 12.

flat broke   Entirely without funds;
completely and utterly broke. *Here
"flat" appears to be an adv. = entirely,
somewhat redundant when used with
"broke."* Cf. **fat.**
flat hoop   **= flat tire.** See **hoop.**
flat-joint   flat joint   *n.* **1** A carnival
gambling or game concession or booth
in which one plays for money, not
prizes. *Carnival use.* → **2** A gambling
or game concession. → **3** A crooked
gambling or game concession. *Implying
that "flat" means a wheel of chance that
is weighted or not perfectly circular.*
flat out   To obtain and/or maintain
maximum speed while flying a plane or
driving a car; flying or driving at
maximum speed. *Aviation and hot rod use.*
flat tire   An unattractive, dull, boring
person whose presence contributes
nothing to a social gathering; an unpleasant and unpopular person. 1927:
"He's a flat tire." R. Littell, *New
Republic*, Jan. 26, 277/2. *Since c1930,
mainly teenage and student use; still
heard but not as pop. as c1935. Because a
flat tire detracts from rather than adds
to a car's movement.*
flattop   *n.* A USN aircraft carrier.
*Colloq. during and since W.W.II. Because
of its wide, flat flight deck, which serves
as an airfield.*
flattop crew   A type of men's haircut,
similar to the crew cut. 1957: "A stiff
version [of the crew cut] is the Flat Top

Crew." H. Mitgang, *About—Men's Haircuts.*
flea   *n.* An insignificant, annoying
person.
flea-bag   fleabag   flea bag   *n.*
1 A bed; a mattress; specif., a sleeping
bag, sailors' hammock, or Army bunk.
*Some W.W.I use, from Brit. Army sl.;
some W.W.II USN use. Brit. sl. since
c1840.* **2** An inferior racehorse. **3** A cheap,
dilapidated hotel or rooming house;
a flop-house. *Lit. and fig., a place where
one may become a host to fleas.* 1939:
"The flea-bag where I was living did not
permit dogs." J. O'Hara, *Pal Joey*, 20.
4 Any dilapidated, dirty, or cheap
public place, as a movie theater. 1951:
"[The movie] was unveiled at an owl
show in a Forty-second Street flea bag."
S. J. Perelman in *New Yorker*, June 30,
22/1.
flea house   A cheap hotel. Cf. **flea bag.**
flea trap   A cheap hotel. Cf. **flea bag.**
1946: "The Laycroft Hotel, a flea trap
on West Madison Street. . . ." Evans,
Halo in Blood, 29.
fleece   *v.t.* To obtain money from
someone by deceptive means; to cheat
or swindle a person. 1956: "I swore to
myself that someday I'd run into
Lutzie again and get back the money
he'd fleeced me out of." J. Scarne,
The Amazing World of John Scarne, 45.
flesh, in the   In person.
flesh-peddler   *n.* **1** A pimp; a prostitute. **2** One who manages an entertainment that offers as its chief attraction the physical charms of young
women. **3** An actors' agent; a talent
salesman. 1940: "Buildings in which the
Hollywood flesh-peddlers never stop
talking money." Chandler, *Farewell*, 120.
Since c1935. **4** An employee or owner of
an employment agency.
fleshpot   *n.* Lit., a brothel or entertainment where seminude girls or women
may be seen; fig., a place catering to
the vices or weaknesses of the flesh, as
saloons, gambling houses, or the like.
1954: "He would sally out for the
fleshpots to enjoy a hell-raising binge."
W. R. & F. K. Simpson, *Hockshop*, 96.
Stand.
flick   *n.* **1** A motion picture. 1950:
"He will also play a role in the flick."
AP, June 22. Cf. **flicks.** → **2** A motion
picture theater.   **—er**   *v.i.* To faint;
to pretend to faint, as from hunger, or
to feign a fit in order to gain sympathy.
Hobo use.   *n.* **1** A beggar who pretends
to faint or have a fit. *Hobo use.* **2** A movie.

1934: "The laughs about that grand flicker [*Lady for a Day*] . . ." W. Winchell in "Foreword" to D. Runyon's *Blue Plate Special*. *Mainly used by newsp. columnists.* **—ers** *n.sing. & pl.* A movie; the movies; the motion picture industry. *Mainly newsp. columnist use.* **—s flix** *n.pl.* Motion pictures; movies. *More common in Eng. than U.S.*

flier *n.* = **flyer.**

flim *adj.* = **cool.** *Some cool use.*

flim-flam flimflam *v.t.* To trick, to deceive, to cheat or victimize. 1660: Thornton. 1934: "We've been flimflammed." Cain, *Postman*, 72. *n.* Trickery; a swindle; deception. 1910: "What's the flimflam today?" Johnson, *Varmint*, 56. 1948: "Authorities had previously lodged a detainer against him, on a flimflam charge." Phila. *Inquirer*, Aug. 11, 29/2. **—mer** *n.* A grafter or crook. 1894: *DAE*. 1957: "Thomas F. Maloney, 45, an expert flimflammer who worked up crime's ladder to the city's Most Wanted list. . . ." N.Y. *Daily News*, Aug. 12, 4. See Appendix, —er ending.

flimsy *n.* 1 A sheet of thin paper. 1950: "He consulted a sheaf of typewritten flimsies." Starnes, *Another Mug*, 69. → 2 A duplicate order, often a carbon copy, written on onion skin or tissue paper; in offices, a carbon copy of invoices; in stores and restaurants, a duplicate of the employee's bills of sale, against which the cash receipts are checked; in railroading, a train order.

fling *n.* 1 A period of irresponsible fun or enjoyment, usu. as a relief from or before one assumes responsibilities. *Usu. in "one last fling." Colloq.* 2 A try; an attempt. *Usu. in "to have a fling at."* 3 A dance; a party. *Teenage and student use.* **—er** *n.* Specif., a baseball pitcher. 1913: "Three of Henshaw's starboard flingers had gone wrong." C. E. Van Loan, *Lucky Seventh*, 164. See Appendix, —er ending.

fling woo = **pitch woo.**

flip *adj.* 1 Impudent; flippant; fresh; glib; having continuous excitement, enthusiasm, appreciation, or the like. 1903: "You're getting too flip altogether." E. Conradi, 371. 1943: "Now don't get flip with me." Chandler, *Lady in Lake*, 6. *From "flippant." See Appendix, Shortened Words.* 2 Reverse; of, on, or pertaining to the reverse or "other" side of a phonograph record; of or pertaining to the less popular song on a phonograph record

containing a popular song. 1958: "Now let's hear the flip side of [a phonograph record]." N.Y.C. radio station WMGM, June 26. *n.* 1 An airplane flight. *Some c1930 Air Force and commercial pilot use. From W.W.I Brit. Air Force sl.* 2 A favor. 1945: "Do me a flip." E. Kasser, 132. *Teenage and student use c1940.* 3 [derog.] A Filipino. *Some W.W.II Armed Forces use.* 4 A minor or less tumultuous flap. *Some c1950 Army use.* 5 Something that causes uproarious laughter. 1951: "The big flip of the year is Peter Arno's [book of cartoons]." G. Millstein in N.Y. *Times Bk. Rev.*, Dec. 2, 50/3. 6 An enthusiast; a devotee. *v.t.* 1 To catch or board a train, esp. to board a train in motion or to ride free. *Hobo and Railroad use since c1920.* 2 To score a point or points in a basketball game. *Lit., to flip the ball through the basket.* 3 To cause one to laugh uproariously. *Since c1950.* 4 To make a most favorable impression on a person; to excite or shock someone; to arouse someone's enthusiasm or sense of wonder; to overwhelm. 1951: "[This record] flipped me the first time I heard it." R. Q. Lewis, network radio, Dec. 15. *Orig. and mainly cool use.* *v.i.* 1 To burst into laughter; to laugh uproariously; to flip [one's] lid. 1951: "The funniest book of the lot is enough to make a reader 'flip' or 'flip his lid.' " G. Millstein in N.Y. *Times Bk. Rev.*, Dec. 2, 50/2. 2 To react violently; to react with enthusiasm; to have a sense of wonder and rapport with; to dig completely; to like or appreciate greatly; to be overwhelmed. 1956: "*Flip:* to react enthusiastically." S. Longstreet, *The Real Jazz Old and New*, 151. 1956: "I flip over this record." T. Brown, N.Y.C. radio station WMGM, Feb. 7. *Orig. c1950 cool use; now common to most young adults. See* **flip [one's] lid.**

flip-flop *n.* A handspring; a fluctuation; a change of direction, attitude, stature, or the like. 1944: "Heart flip-flops began to annoy me." Fowler, *Good Night*, 131. 1951: "Three key farm commodities have been doing flip-flops on the price ladder." K. Scheibel, GNS, Nov. 13. *An instance in which a reduplication conveys a fig. meaning different from that of the basic words.*

flip [one's] lid To show an extreme response; specif. to become violently angry; to lose one's sanity; to burst out laughing. 1949: [angry] "Don't go

flippin' your lid." Movie, *White Heat.*
1951: [crazy] "Present war emergencies
plus strain and stress seem to have been
too much for local governmental officials.
I fear they have flipped their lids."
Letter to the editor, Ithaca, N.Y.,
Journal, Jan. 30, 6/6. *Specif., to laugh
uproariously and without control; to go
into an uncontrolled, violent rage; to like
or approve of something without reservation. Orig. late bop and early cool use.
Fairly common since c1948.* From **blow
[one's] top.** Cf. **flip.**
flip [one's] lip   To talk; esp. to talk
idly or to talk nonsense.
flipper   *n.* **1** A human hand. *Since
cW.W.I.* Cf. **flapper. 2** The arm. **3** A
slingshot. 1951: "How any boy could
harbor the nitwit notion that pot-
shotting windows with flippers from a
speeding automobile is good clean fun
is beyond comprehension." Editorial,
Salt Lake City *Deseret News*, July 30,
2/1.
flip [one's] raspberry = **to flip [one's]
lid.**
flip side   The reverse or "other" side
of a phonograph record; specif., the
reverse or "other" side of a phonograph
record whose major side contains a
very popular song; the less popular of
the two sides of a phonograph record.
*Cool, rock and roll, and general teenage
use. Pop. by disc jockey use.*
flip [one's] wig = **flip [one's] lid.**
fliv   *n.*   An automobile; **flivver.**
v.i. To fail or flop. *Said of a performance
or performer.*   **—ver**   *n.* **1** A hoax.
→ **2** A failure. **3** A small, cheap, old,
dilapidated automobile. *Orig. an early
model Ford, c1918.* 1927: "I could buy
me a new flivver." Hal C. Evarts,
SEP, Nov. 19, 94. *The term is now used
humorously in ref. to expensive, heavy
modern cars.* → **4** A U.S. naval destroyer,
esp. an old 750-ton, four stacker.
*c1935–W.W.II, USN use. Most such
ships have now been retired from service.*
→ **5** A small, cheap, old, or dilapidated
airplane.
flix   *n.pl.* = **flickers, flicks.**
float   *v.i.* **1** To loaf on the job. *c1930.*
2 To be emotionally or spiritually
uplifted; to be extremely relaxed,
happy, optimistic, or the like; specif.
because one is in love, has been complimented or rewarded, or is under the
influence of drugs or alcohol. See
floating on air, cloud seven.   *n.* **1**
A customer who walks out on a salesman
while he is looking for merchandise.

Retail salesman use. **2** An hour or a
period in which a student has no class;
a free period.   **—er**   *n.* **1** A vagrant; an itinerant worker; a skilled or
nonskilled factory worker who changes
jobs and union locals often. 1956:
"*Floater*—A worker who continually
leaves one locality to follow his trade
in another place merely for the sake of
variety." *Labor's Special Language from
Many Sources. Colloq.* → **2** A police
order to leave town within 24 or 48
hours; a jail sentence suspended if the
offender leaves town in a short time;
often given to hobos. **3** A blunder;
a *faux pas.* 1943: "Unless the old
records have made an error, slip . . . or
floater. . . ." Sterling North, *Chicago
Daily News. More common in Eng. than
in U.S.* **4** In baseball, a slow pitched
ball that appears to float in air. **5** A loan;
money loaned or borrowed. *From the
expression "to float a loan."* **6** A theft or
fire insurance policy insuring an article
or articles anywhere, no matter where
the owner may travel.   **—ing**   *adj.*
1 Drunk. **2** Under the influence of
narcotics. **3** Sublimely happy.
floating crap game   A professional
crap game held in a different place
every day, to avoid police detection.
1954: "The floating crap game run by
an underworld gambling syndicate. . . ."
W. R. & F. K. Simpson, *Hockshop*, 7.
floating on air   Supremely happy;
fig., "high" with happiness, as from
praise, a just reward for one's efforts,
or esp. from being accepted as a lover.
floating on [the] clouds   **1** To be
sublimely happy or contented, usu.
because one is in love, but often because
one has been complimented or successful.
2 To be unrealistic; to have plans
beyond one's capabilities. *Cf.* **cloud
seven, float.**
float one   To cash a check; to make
a loan.
flock   *n.* A large number; quite a few.
1949: "A broadcaster invites a newspaperman to his program, buys him a
flock of drinks afterwards, and hopes
for the best." John Crosby, *Phila.
Bulletin*, Sep. 1, 16.
flogger   *n.* An overcoat. 1935: "Fur
coats . . . including a chinchilla flogger.
. . ." Runyon. *Underworld use; archaic.*
flooey   *adj.* Drunk. *Never common.*
See Appendix, Drunk.
flooey, go   See **go blooey.**
flookum   flookem   See **flukum.**
floor   *v.t.* **1** To knock someone down,

as to the floor; to knock someone unconscious. → **2** To shock or surprise someone, fig., so that one faints or is overcome with shock or surprise. *In this sense almost always used in the passive.* **3** To drive a car at its maximum speed; lit., to hold the gas pedal of a car all the way to its maximum position, down to the floor(boards).

floorboard *v.i.* To go fast by keeping a car's accelerator pressed all the way down to the floorboard.

floozie floosie floozy floogy flugie faloosie *n.* **1** A girl; an average girl or young woman with a good but not beautiful face, an open, honest personality, and a good spirit, but lacking in deep insight, good taste, refinement, and with no more and probably less than average intelligence. c1940: "The Flat-Foot Floogy with the Floy Floy," title of a pop. song. 1945: "The American 'floosie' is picturesque. It ... to me, at least, immediately suggests a substantial charmer with plenty of good spirits and bad scent [perfume]." I. Brown, *A Word in Your Ear*, 59. 1945: "A sugar report from a flugie." Riordan in *Calif. Folk Quart.*, Oct. *Since c1900; except for some W.W.II USN use, archaic since c1940.* **2** Specif., an undisciplined, promiscuous, flirtatious, irresponsible girl or woman, esp. a cynical, calculating one who is only concerned with having a good time or living off the generosity of men; a cheap or loose girl or woman. 1942: "He'd learn more about their psychology by taking a floozie to Atlantic City." W. B. Johnson, *Widening Stain*, 32. 1948: "It is possible to portray [on the radio] as the central figure of an adult whodunit an obviously no-good floosie." S. Helfrich in N.Y. *Times*, Feb. 22, XII/5. 1951: "He bought a red racy car and went skidding around with every floozy in town; the only nice girls you ever saw in that car were his sisters." T. Capote, *Grass Harp*, 34.

flop *v.t.* **1** To succeed by trickery or dishonesty. → **2** To fail at cheating or trickery; hence, to fail an examination. *c1900.* *v.i.* **1** To lie down to rest or sleep; to go to bed; to sleep; to stay overnight. 1907: "'Kip,' 'doss,' 'flop,' 'pound your ear,' all mean ... to sleep." Jack London, *My Life.* **2** To fail completely; specif., to fail to gain a desired reaction from others; to fail to convince or entertain. 1930: "I never flopped at an exam yet." Lavine, *Third Degree*, 11.

1951: "A performance flops. . . ." A. Green, *Show Biz*, 568. *Associated with theatrical use.* *n.* **1** Any trick used in successful cheating. **2** A place to sleep; a shelter; a bed. 1949: "Living ... in a three-dollar-a-week flop." Roeburt, *Tough Cop*, 86. → **3** A night's sleep. 1945: "Giving him enough money for a meal, a drink, or a flop. . . ." Mitchell, *McSorley's*, 35. **4** A complete failure; any person or thing that fails, as a prize fighter, an entertainer, a play, a movie, a joke, or the like. 1921: "Professional strong men are flops as a rule when they turn to the ring." Witwer, *Leather*, 149. 1934: "The worst flop of a home-coming. . . ." Cain, *Postman*, 35. 1946: "Despite a season of bad plays and flop reviews. . . ." NEA, *newsp. item*, Jan. 14. *Since c1890.*

flop, make the To beg while sitting on the sidewalk, as a crippled beggar or one who pretends to be crippled. *Hobo use. Archaic.*

flophouse *n.* A very cheap rooming house or hotel where many men sleep on cots in one room.

flopperoo floperoo *n.* = **flop**; any spectacularly unsuccessful person or thing, esp. a stage show or movie. 1937: "[Hollywood] divides the failures into three subdivisions: flop, flopperoo, and kerplunk." Quoted in *AS*, 13, 107. 1940: "The past eight years have seen more economic experiments than you could shake a lorgnette at, and most of them were spectacular flopperoos." W. Holbrook, *This Week*, June 2, 12. 1952: "The profits enable the company to absorb the losses racked up by flopperoos, of which every film company has made its full share." N.Y. *Daily News*, Aug. 25, 11C/1. *Since c1930. Pop. by "Variety,"* the theater trade paper. *One of the most common —eroo words; see Appendix.*

floss around To act the part of a floozy; to go around or play around (with someone); to socialize. *Some c1925 use. Obs.*

flossy flossie *adj.* Overfancy, over-shiny, overelegant. "A youth in 'flossy' attire." Upson in *Independent*, 2573/2. 1951: "It may be highly important to know a flossy name for the boss." F. Tripp, AP, June 25.

flour *n.* Face powder.

flower *n.* A homosexual. See **hearts and flowers, pansy, wall-flower.**

flu flue *n.* Influenza. *Since c1840. Colloq.* See Appendix, Shortened Words.

flub *n.* **1** An unattractive, stupid

person; one who makes many blunders. *Since c1910.* **2** A blunder; a mistake, esp. an embarrassing one. 1956: "The operation was a complete success with no flubs in spite of the fact that the equipment was new." E. V. Purdie, *Productionwise*, Sept., 42f. *The n. is not as common as the v.t. form.* *v.t.* **1** To make a blunder, error, or mistake, esp. an embarrassing one; to make a *faux pas.* 1924: "I have the feeling that I have flubbed this talk." Marks, *Plastic Age*, 122. *Very common.* **2** To evade one's assigned duty. Cf. **goldbrick.**

flubdub   flub-dub   *n.* 1 Awkwardness; ineptitude. 1952: "Maybe Mike Todd or [Milton] Berle should take over the management of the conventions. At any rate, they would remove much of the amateur flub-dub." N.Y. *Daily Mirror*, July 8, 11/4-5. **2** An awkward youth; one who makes many blunders. *Teenage and student use c1925–c1940. Now somewhat archaic.* **3** Nonsense; bunk. *Not common.* **—bed** *adj.* Awkward; blundering. 1952: "I made flubdubbed and increasingly abashed efforts to make myself feel good again." St. Clair McKelway in *New Yorker*, May 17, 28/2. *Never common.*

flub off   flub up = flub. See **flub the dub.** *Also euphemism for "fuck off," "fuck up."*

flub the dub   1 To evade one's duty; to loaf. **2** To think and perform inefficiently and slowly. *Both meanings common W.W.II use.* **3** To spoil or ruin by blunders or mistakes; to ruin or fail to take advantage of one's chances for success. *Mainly boy use.* See Appendix, Reduplications.

fluff   *n.* 1 A girl or young woman, usu. in "bit of fluff" or "piece of fluff." 1939: "A wan little fluff steals a dress so as to look sweet in the eyes of her boy friend." Ralph L. Woods, *Forum*, Dec., 275/1. **2** Foolish talk; vague information. *Not common.* **3** A slip of the tongue; a mispronunciation; momentarily forgetting what one is supposed to say or do, as caused by shyness or nervousness; specif., such a mistake made by an actor, announcer, or public speaker. **4** A dismissal; the brush-off. 1947: "I gave him the fluff. . . ." Hal Boyle, AP, May 19, 12. Cf. **fluff off.** **5** Any job or task that is easy to perform. *v.t., v.i.* To make a mistake in speaking, as an actor forgetting a line or missing a cue; to make a mistake in pronunciation, or the like.

**fluff, give [someone] the   To reject; to snub; to brush off a person. 1947: "I gave him the fluff. . . ." Hal Boyle, AP, May 19, 12.

fluff log   Lit. and fig., a man's small pocket notebook listing the names, addresses, and telephone numbers of accessible or available girls; a little black book. *Some W.W.II use.* See **fluff.

fluff off   1 To snub, slight, or humiliate; to dismiss someone curtly. **2** To shirk or neglect one's duties or responsibilities. *W.W.II Armed Forces use.* **3** To waste time; to idle. *W.W.II use.*   **fluff-off** *n.* A shirker; a blunderer. Cf. **fuck off.**

flug = phlug.

flugie = floozie.

fluid = embalming fluid.

fluke   *n.* 1 A failure. **2** A fortuitous accident; a freak success that could not be repeated. **→ 3** A sham; a pretension. 1921: "And call his [prizefighter's] defeat in the second [round of the fight] a fluke." Witwer, *Leather*, 79.   *v.t. & v.i.* To fail.   **—y   fluky** *adj.* Uncertain; unprepared. 1942: "He couldn't have taken [a photograph]. . . . It would have been a very fluky shot, even if he happened to have the camera in his hand. . . ." Chandler, *High Window*, 183. *Not common.*

flukum   flookum   flookem   *n.* 1 Any of various kinds of cheap, nearly worthless, but gaudy or apparently useful merchandise, as nickel-plated cigarette lighters, silverware, cleaning fluids, potato peelers, or the like, which are attractive at first sight. *Orig. c1925 pitchman use.* **2** A powder to which water and sugar are added to make a soft drink. **3** A failure; a fluke. *Never common.*

flumadiddle   flummadiddle   flummerdiddle   flummydiddle *n. & adj.* Nonsense; nonsensical. 1854: *DAE. Dial.*

flummox   *v.i.* To fail; to recite badly. 1851: Hall, *College Words*, 131. *Never common. Obs.   v.t.* To upset; to thwart. 1950: "Fu-Manchu tries to abduct a missionary who has flummoxed his plans in China." S. J. Perelman in *New Yorker*, Sept. 30, 23/3. *Not common. n.* A failure; said of a plan or action. **—ed *adj.* Perplexed; confused; in a tumult. *Never common.*

flunk   *v.t.* 1 For a teacher to give a student a failing grade. 1910: "The Roman flunked Stover on the review. . . ." Johnson, *Varmint*, 195. *Colloq. since c1845.* **→ 2** For a student to fail an examination or a course. 1924: "I'm going to flunk that exam. . . ." Marks, *Plastic Age*, 107. *Colloq. since c1910. v.i.* **1** For a student to fail in an exam or a course. → **2** To fail in a personal or business endeavor. *Not restricted to student use. n.* **1** A failure by a student in his studies, a course, a recitation, or an examination. → **2** A student who has failed to pass an examination or a course. *Not common.* → **3** A course which a student has failed; the failing grade. **—ey —ie —y —ee** *n.* **1** One who does menial work, such as a porter, errand boy, dishwasher, waiter, or the like. **2** A young worker; an apprentice; an assistant. **3** A student who fails in his studies. See Appendix, —ee ending.

flunk out To be dismissed from prep school or college because of failing work. 1920: "He'll . . . flunk out [of college]. . . ." Fitzgerald, *This Side of Paradise*, 37.

flush *adj.* In possession of sufficient money; having much money; wealthy. 1956: "It took money, and the jazzman wasn't ever too flush." S. Longstreet, *The Real Jazz Old and New*, 54. *n.* A wealthy person. 1942: ". . . A white house on Stillwood Crescent Drive. Morny took it over from a busted flush." Chandler, *High Window*, 28. *v.t.* To absent oneself from a class; to cut a class. 1951: "Oh, he got teed off because I flushed lecture on Saturdays." Cornell (Univ.) *Widow*, Apr. 17, 18. *Student use.*

flush, in a Confused, bewildered.

flute *n.* **1** A male homosexual. *From the image of fellatio, perhaps punning on "fruit." Orig. musician use. Not common.* **2** A suit. See Appendix, Rhyming Slang. **—r** *n.* A male homosexual.

fluzy = floozie.

fly *n.* **1** = **square.** *Not common.* **2** An alert, knowing person. *adj.* Knowing; nimble-minded; alert; saucy; fresh. See **bar-fly, catch flies, shoo-fly. —ing** *adj.* **1** Driving, moving, or working at great speed. *Colloq.* **2** Under the influence of a narcotic drug. → **3** Extremely happy; ecstatic; elated. *'Cool' use.* **4** On duty in a place removed from one's home city or district. 1958: "Flying—Duty in other districts, or the outer reaches of one's own." G. Y. Wells, *Station House Slang.*

fly, let **1** To begin anything, esp. a tirade or bawling out. *Fig., to let the words fly out at someone.* **2** To spit. **3** [taboo] To urinate.

fly a kite **1** To write a letter; esp. to smuggle a letter into or out of prison. *Underworld use.* **2** To send an airmail letter, often requesting money or assistance. *Modern use, mainly underworld but gaining some popularity.*

fly a kite !, Go Go jump in the lake ! Get lost !

fly-bait *n.* **1** A member of Phi Beta Kappa. *Used humorously or derogatorily; from "Phi Bate," a colloq. abbrev. of "Phi Beta Kappa."* **2** A corpse.

fly ball **1** An eccentric, unusual, undesirable person. **2** A homosexual.

fly ball fly bob fly bull fly cop fly dick fly mug A detective, a plainclothes policeman, a policeman assigned to special duty. 1907: "He was a fly-cop. . . ." Jack London, *My Life.* 1930: "An offer to make him a 'fly-cop' or detective. . . ." Lavine, *Third Degree*, 160. *"Fly cop," c1860, is the oldest and has been the most widely used term; "fly ball," "fly bob," and "fly bull" have seen wide hobo use. Note the Eng. "bob" = policeman. "Fly dick" and "fly mug" are the latest terms. All freq. with hyphen.*

fly-boy flyboy fly boy *n.* **1** An aviator, esp. a glamorous, heroic, or daring aviator. *In W.W.II usu. used ironically.* **2** A U.S. Air Force pilot; any member of the Air Force. 1948: "The generals are no full-throttle 'fly-boys.' " *Life*, Nov. 1, 87/2. *W.W.II Armed Forces use. Now derog., implying snobbishness, youth, and cautiousness.* → **3** Any airplane pilot.

fly bull = fly ball, fly bob.

fly cake Raisin cake. *Jocular use.*

fly-chaser *n.* In baseball, an outfielder.

flychick *n.* An attractive, hip girl.

fly cop = fly ball, fly bob.

fly dick = fly ball, fly bob.

flyer *n.* A chance; a gamble. *Usu. in "to take a flyer at (something)." Colloq.*

fly guy = fly-boy. See Appendix, Rhyming Slang.

flying bedstead **1** An early model Ford car. *c1920; never common. Obs.* **2** An early, lumbering, but comparatively stable and steady airplane.

flying blowtorch A jet fighter airplane. *Synthetic sl.*

flying coffin A glider or airplane. *W.W.II Air Force and paratrooper use.*

flying jinny flying-jinny *n.* **1** Any of various machines, esp. those used in the textile industry, specifically, a cotton gin.

Archaic. **2** A merry-go-round. 1940 [1951]: "The wooden horses of the flying-jinny revolved in the circle to the mechanical music." C. McCullers, *Ballad of the Sad Café*, 293. *Not common.* **3** Any early airplane; a single-engine airplane. *Archaic.*

flying time   Sleep. *W.W.II Armed Forces use, not common.*

fly light   To miss a meal; to be hungry.

fly mug = fly ball, fly bob.

fly off the handle   To lose one's temper. *Colloq.*

fly pie   Huckleberry pie. *Lunch-counter use. Not common.*

fly right   To be honest and useful; to be 'straight'; to do the ethically or socially proper thing; to live or act according to ethical standards. 1956: "He's my son. . . . I want him to fly right. . . ." John & Ward Hawkins, "The Cowardice of Sam Abbott," *SEP*, Oct. 20, 104/3.

fly the coop   To leave or depart, often secretly or guiltily. 1948: "He had flown the coop . . . via a fire-escape. . . ." A. Hynd, *Pinkerton*, 99. *Colloq. since c1910.*

fly trap   The human mouth.

f.o. [taboo] = **fuck-off**, a type of person. *Not common.* See Appendix, Shortened Words.

fofarraw   foofooraw   *n.* **1** A loud disturbance or interruption; a commotion. *Dial.* **2** Gaudy wearing apparel, particularly accessories such as bracelets, belts, etc. **3** Ostentation; show-off; bluster. *Prob. from the Sp. "fanfaron" and Fr. "frou-frou."* See L. Pound, "Another 'Fofarraw' Variant," *AS*, Vol. XXV, Oct., 167.

fog   *v.i.* **1** To move fast; to run, as a horse or a man; to hurry. *Some c1930 student use, from earlier cowboy use.* → **2** To express resentment, as of being rushed. *Some c1930 student use.* **3** To smoke cigarettes. *Dial.* See **fog up.** *v.t.* **1** To kill, usu. to kill by shooting. 1930: "I takes me heat an' fogs 'em." *Amer. Mercury*, Dec., 455. 1946: "She didn't fog him; no." Evans, *Halo in Blood*, 66. **2** To hurl, pitch, or throw something, as a baseball, with great force and speed. 1953: "Ole Diz [Dean] was in his prime then, fogging a fast ball. . . ." H. Boyle, AP, Mar. 11. *n.* Steam.   **—(g)y**   *adj.* Confused; confusing, perplexing; unrealized, not specific enough.   **—matic**   *n.* A drink of liquor. *adj.* Drunk. 1851: "In use at one time or another." Hall, *College Words*, 302.

fog, in a   Dazed; confused, baffled, perplexed. *Colloq.*

fog away   To shoot. 1929: "I fogged away with my gun." Givens in *SEP*, 54/3. *Some c1925 prison use.* See **fog.**

fog-cutter   *n.* A drink of liquor. *Fig., fancied as removing the fog from one's throat. Archaic.* Cf. **fogmatic.**

fog it in   In baseball, to pitch a fast ball; to throw hard.

fogle   *n.* A neck handkerchief. 1848: *criminal use.* J. Farmer.

fog up   *v.t.* To light or smoke a pipe, cigar, or cigarette. *Logger and ranch use until c1930.*

fogy   fogey   *n.* Money received as longevity pay on completing five years of military service in peacetime or three years in wartime. 1879: *DAE. Some W.W.II Armed Forces use.*

fold   *v.i.* To go out of business owing to lack of funds; to come to an end. 1938: "If the club folds. . . ." Liebling, *Back Where*, 80. 1950: "The show . . . folded." Billy Rose, *synd. newsp. col.*, Jan. 4.   **—ing**   *n.* Money. 1939–40: "The socialites lose a handsome wallet stuffed with a liberal supply of folding." O'Hara, *Pal Joey*, 53.

folding cabbage = **folding money.** 1951: "And since when does uncle begrudge a noble ally a bit of folding cabbage?" G. Wunder, *synd. comic strip*, "Terry," Aug. 9. See **cabbage.**

folding green   Money. 1952: "The office clerk, bookkeeper, or bank teller . . . lacks the folding green to pick up a night club tab." Hal Boyle, AP, Sept. 22.

folding lettuce = **folding money.** 1956: "Money is *folding lettuce.*" S. Longstreet, *The Real Jazz Old and New*, 150. See **lettuce.**

folding money   Paper banknotes, as opposed to coins; a comparatively large amount of money; money. 1939–40: "Any time the socialites go out they leave their folding money at home." O'Hara, *Pal Joey*, 53.

Foley Square   *n.* The Federal Bureau of Investigation. 1956: "'The FBI was involved and nobody beats Foley Square, boy,' commented Carlino." N. Abrams & N. Patterson, *N.Y. Daily News*, Nov. 16, 5. Because the main Eastern office of the FBI is located in Foley Square, lower Manhattan, N.Y.C.

folks, the   *n.pl.* A gang of yeggs. *Underworld use; archaic.*

follow through   To press one's advantage until success is gained; to follow one action with the next obvious one; to ascertain that something has been done properly. *Colloq.* **follow-through** *n.* A result; anything that happens after something else; the next logical action.

follow up = **follow through. follow-up** *n.* A consequence or expected result.

food See **angel food, dog food.**

food for the squirrels 1 A stupid or foolish person; a nut. 2 A stupid job, task, or scheme.

Fooey! *exclam.* = **Phooey!**

foo-foo *n.* 1 An outsider; a new-comer; one who does not belong or is not accepted. 1848: *DAE. Obs.* 2 A fool; a worthless person. *Dial. From "fo-farraw."* 3 Perfume. *From "fofarraw."* See Appendix, Reduplications.

foofooraw *n.* = **fofarrow.**

fool *adj.* Foolish. 1805: *DAE.* 1914: "He may make you all kinds of 'fool' promises." D. S. Martin in *Living Age,* Aug., 374. 1924: "I'll knock your fool block off." Marks, *Plastic Age,* 175. *Colloq.* *n.* An unusually able person in any field of activity, as a dancing fool, a diving fool; an enthusiast, a buff, a fan. 1937: "At the time of Lindbergh's famous flight [1927] we learned that his associates had for some time described him as a flying fool, not meaning that he flew unwisely." S. V. Byington, *AS,* 13, 159.

fool around 1 To do small, un-necessary, idle operations. 2 To tease. → 3 To handle an object idly, as if examin-ing or repairing it. → 4 To caress one of the opposite sex in a teasing way; to make a faint, idle, or jocular attempt at seduction.

foolish powder Heroin. *Underworld use, c1930.*

foot See **blisterfoot, doughfoot, flat-foot, hot foot, paddlefoot, slewfoot, tangle-foot.**

foot, give [someone] the To kick.

football = **Italian football.**

footie-footie footy-footy *n.* Lit. and fig., = **footsie.** 1945: "Town's beginning to talk. They're playing a little too much footie-footie." S. Lewis, *Cass Timberlane,* 300. 1948: "[President Harry S.] Truman is plenty burned up over the way Chiang Kai-shek and advisers played footy-footy with the Republicans and Dewey until election day." D. Pearson, *synd. newsp. col.,* Dec. 29. See Appendix, Reduplications.

foot in it, put [one's] To blunder;

to say or do the wrong thing; to be indiscreet or gauche. *Colloq.*

footsie *n.* 1 Lit., the pedal equivalent of amorous hand-holding; touching, pushing, and/or more or less clumsily caressing with one's foot, as under a table, a foot or the feet of one of the opposite sex. 1944: "I played footsie with her during Carmen." Fowler, *Good Night,* 102. → 2 Fig., any instance of friendly or intimate action, esp. as in courting business favors or to atone for past unacceptable behavior.

footsie-wootsie *n.* Lit. and fig., = **footsie.** See Appendix, Reduplications.

footsy-footsy *n.* = **footsie.** 1953: "... Trying to play footsy-footsy with the hausfrau." H. Boyle, AP, Jan. 9. See Appendix, Reduplications.

Fooy! *exclam.* = **Phooey!**

foozle *v.t.* To entangle; to blunder or bungle; to make an error. 1835: *DAE. Still in use.* *n.* 1 An old fogey; an old-fashioned, conservative person. *Since c1850. From "fossil."* → 2 An elder; a parent. *Teenage use since c1950.* 3 In sports, a bungled plan, an error. *Since c1920.*

for— See Appendix, Prefixes and Prefix Words.

for, go 1 To favor enthusiastically a person or thing; to accept. 2 To fall in love with; to love. 1939–40: "A sweeter kid never lived. I really go for her." O'Hara, *Pal Joey,* 6.

for certain Certain; sure.

For crying out loud! *exclam.* An expression signifying surprise, often surprise at another's stupidity. 1937: "Who said it's terrible? I even like it, for crying out loud." Weidman, *Whole-sale,* 166. 1948: "'For crying out loud,' a rather clumsy and Americanized 'shunt' from 'For Christ's sake.' ..." A. Hern quoted in I. Brown, *I Give You My Word,* 34.

forecastle lawyer A man who habi-tually argues, complains, or talks. *Maritime use.*

for free Free of charge; gratis; without compensation. 1949: "They gave him a sandwich absolutely for free." Arthur Daley, N.Y. *Times,* Sept. 4, 4. 1951: "At first I was glad to draw their dreamings for free, for their respect." Al Capp, *Atlantic Monthly,* May, 48/2. *From "for nothing"; usu. applied to small items or favors, often humorously.*

for it 1 In favor of something, as a proposal or plan. *Colloq.* 2 Expecting or prepared for punishment, chastisement, or a strong verbal reprimand.

fork   *v.t.* **1** To pick a person's pocket. *c1850, underworld use; archaic.* **2** To mount a horse. *Archaic and dial.*   *n.* A pickpocket. *Underworld use; archaic.* **—s**   *n.* Fingers.

fork-hander   *n.* In baseball, a left-handed pitcher.

fork out   fork over   fork up   To pay over or hand over. 1903: "Fork up the cash." E. Conradi. 1951: "There's a chance he was putting the bite on you. I imagine he used a picture of you to make you fork over the dough." R. S. Prather, *Bodies in Bedlam*, 94f. 1952: "I forked out $264 to doctors and dentists." Jay Taylor, *Harper's*, July, 62/2. *Colloq. since c1840.*

fork you   *Euphemism for* **fuck you.**

for real   **1** Real; existing; possible. *Often in* **Are you for real?** *May imply either "too good to be true" or, orig., "unbelievable." Popularized by comedian Jerry Lewis, c1950.* **2** Really.

for serious   Seriously; for a serious purpose. 1952: "All the old boys looked more natural in their positions . . . than their counterparts looked later on when the Yanks [baseball team] took the field for serious." Robert C. Ruark, *synd. newsp. col.*, Sept. 5.

fort   *n.* **1** A boarding house for students. 1851: Hall, *College Words*, 134. *Some student use until c1900. Obs.* **2** An armored car, as used to transport money. *Truck-driver use.*

for the birds   Not liked, wanted, or respected by the speaker; unacceptable to, improbable for, or corny to the speaker; fig., not for the speaker but for the birds = crazy or old people. 1952: "I won't buy it. Or any part of it. It's for the birds." J. Crosby in N.Y. *Her. Trib.*, Feb. 8, 19/1. 1958: "Robert Stack doesn't worry about things that are 'for the birds.' . . . 'Too much publicity is for the birds, I discovered.' . . . 'I enjoyed being a bachelor. But if marriage works out, and mine has, then living alone is for the birds.' . . . He sleeps in a double bed. 'A single bed is for single men, it's for the birds.' " S. Skolsky in N.Y. *Post*, June 1, M3.

for the cuff   Confidential.

for the [one's] hat = **under [one's] hat.**

forthwith   *adv.* Immediately. *Colloq. n.* An order to be carried out immediately. 1958: "Forthwith—An order to report immediately." G. Y. Wells, *Station House Slang.*

forty-eight   *n.* Week-end liberty; a 48-hour pass. *W.W.II USN use.*

forty-five   .45   *n.* **1** A 45-caliber pistol. **2** A phonograph record, usu. of popular music, made to play on a turntable that revolves at a speed of 45 revolutions per minute. See **LP.**

forty-four   *n.* **1** A cup, or an order of a cup, of coffee. *Some c1940 lunch-counter use in relaying an order.* **2** A prostitute. *From rhyming sl., "forty-four" = a whore.* See Appendix, Rhyming Slang.

forty-'leven   *n.* An indefinitely large number; a great many. 1898: "I've told more'n forty-'leven times. . . ." E. N. Westcott, *David Harum.*

forty-one   *n.* Lemonade; orangeade; a small glass of milk. *c1930 lunch-counter use in relaying an order.*

forty-rod   *n.* Cheap liquor. 1929: "Forty-rod whiskey . . . a man cannot walk more than 40 rods after taking a drink of it. . . ." V. Randolph. *Archaic.*

forty ways for (from, to) Sunday   Every which way; in all directions, in confusion. 1840: *DAE. Still in use.*

forty winks   **1** A short sleep; a nap. *Colloq.* **2** A short time.

forward   *n.* A prospective customer. *From the command "Forward!" given to salesmen in a retail store. Retail salesman use.*

fossil   *n.* **1** An old fogey; an elderly person; a conservative, old-fashioned person. 1952: "If I got to kiss old fossils to hold this job I'm underpaid." Quoted by H. Boyle, AP, Feb. 22. *From "fossil."* See **foozle.** **2** A parent; an elder. *Teenage use since c1955. From "fossil," reinforced by "foozle."*

fotog = **photog.**

foul ball   **1** An inferior prize fighter. *Prize fight use since c1920.* **2** An unsuccessful, useless person; a flat tire. 1952: "It is Scotty's boast that he hasn't sent a sponsor a foul ball yet." J. McCallum, NEA, July 3. **3** An odd person; one having unacceptable personal, religious, or political beliefs. *Since c1945.*

fouled up   fouled-up   *adj.* In a state of confusion; confused; resulting from or a product of incompetence and blundering; ruined; spoiled. 1958: "In 15 years in Washington this writer has never seen anything more fouled up than what happened yesterday at the White House after President Eisenhower conferred with eight state governors." J. Marlow, AP, Mar. 20.

foul-mouth   *n.* A person given to speaking obscenities and oaths. *Colloq.*

—ed *adj.* Given to uttering freq. obscenities. *Colloq.*

foulup   foul-up   *n.* A person who makes frequent blunders; a blunder, a mix-up. 1953: "There has been a big foulup somewhere along the line." AP, May 4. Cf. **snafu, fuck-up.   foul up** To ruin or spoil something; to make a mess of things; to demonstrate one's incompetence. *Wide use cW.W.II and after. Orig. may have been euphem. for "fuck-up."*

foundling   *n.* A dismissed cadet. *c1940, West Point use.*

foundry   *n.* A business office.

four and one   1 Friday; lit. the fifth working day of the week. → 2 Pay-day. *Negro use.*

four-bagger   *n.* In baseball, a home run. 1951: "It was Bobby's 31st four-bagger and his fourth at Ebbets Field." Joe Reichler, AP, Oct. 2.

four-ball   *n.* = **foul ball.** *Not common.*

four-bit   *adj.* Costing 50¢. 1932: "To smoke four-bit cigars. . . ." J. T. Farrell, 126.   **four bits**   *n.* Half a dollar; 50¢. *Colloq.* See **two bits.** Lit., two times two bits.

four-by-four   *n.* A four-wheel drive truck having four forward gear speeds. *Army and truck-driver use.*

four-eyes   four eyes   *n.* A person who wears glasses.

four-flush   fourflush   four flush *v.i., v.t.* To bluff, pretend; to leave one's debts unpaid; to sponge on others. 1901: *DAE.* 1905: "He's been fourflushing around for years." McHugh, *Search Me*, 56. *From the poker term. Archaic.* **—er**   *n.* One who bluffs; a pretender; esp. one who pretends to have money while living off or borrowing from others; one who does not pay his debts. 1910: *DAE.* 1916: "Jack London has made the phrase 'red blood' as nationalistic as 'four flusher.'" Anon., *New Repub.*, Nov. 11, 55. *Colloq.*   **—ing** *adj.* Living off or supported by others; borrowing from others. 1954: "Four-flushing hustlers who really knew how to gamble." L. Armstrong, *Satchmo, My Life in New Orleans*, 123.

four hundred, the   Socially prominent people (implying also refinement and wealth); the elite. c1890 [1955]: "The big number [song] was 'The Colored Four Hundred.' . . . 'We're the creme de la creme/ Of the colored population.'" H. R. Hoyt, *Town Hall Tonight*, 202. *Attrib. to Ward McAllister, New York socialite, who is said to have* drawn up a list of the four hundred people whom he considered the most prominent socially.

four letter man   A dumb or stupid man, usu. a student. *Some student use. The four letters are "d-u-m-b." See "three letter man" for the derivation.*

four-o   *adv.* Perfect; o.k. 1952: "[U.S.] Navy officers are given efficiency ratings by their superiors, and the highest grade possible is 4.0. . . . 'How are you today, Harry?' the other officers would ask, and Harry would say, 'Four-o, four-o, four-o.'" S. Wilson in *New Yorker*, Feb. 23, 76/3. *W.W.II USN use.*

four sheets in [to] the wind = **three sheets in the wind.**

four-striper   *n.* A U.S. Navy captain. *From the gold stripes worn on the sleeve. Since W.W.I.*

fourteen   *n.* A special order. *Some c1930 lunch-counter use.*

four-time   four-time loser   Fig., a desperate criminal. *In some states a person four times convicted of crime receives a mandatory sentence of life imprisonment. Because of the severity of the mandatory sentence, such a criminal may go to extreme and desperate lengths to avoid arrest.*

four wide ones   In baseball, a base on balls.

fox   *n.* A college freshman. 1847: *DAE. Obs. v.t.* 1 To follow a person stealthily in order to watch him closely; to shadow a person. 1848: J. S. Farmer. *Underworld use. Obs.* 2 To fool, outwit, or outsmart someone. 1924: "How some of the boys are going to fox 'em [the professors]. . . ." Marks, *Plastic Age*, 101. See **outfox.**

foxed   Drunk. *All forms obs.*

foxhole   *n.* A small individual trench or hole dug in the ground by a soldier as protection and concealment. *Wide W.W.II use.*

fox paw   A faux pas. 1785: Grose. *Still in use.* See Appendix, Corruptions.

fox-tail   *n.* A mustache. *W.W.I. USN use.*

fracture   *v.t.* 1 To cause uproarious laughter. 1951: "We're a riot, hey. We play all kinds of funny stuff. We fracture the people." M. Shulman, *Dobie Gillis*, 41. → 2 Used ironically, to cause someone to become sad, angry, or disgusted. *Usu. in "You fracture me."* 3 To evoke a strong reaction in someone; to cause someone to flip. *Some bop and cool use since c1946.*

fractured   Drunk. *Fairly common since c1940.*

'fraidy cat   One, esp. a boy or youth, who is timorous. *Common use by younger children; some adult use.*

frail   *n.* A girl or young woman. 1930: "In persuading frails to divulge what they know. . . ." Lavine, *Third Degree*, 152. *Common since c1930.*   *adj.* Broke, without money. *c1935 jive use.*

frail eel   A pretty girl. 1942: "I can get any frail eel I wants to." Z. Hurston. *Harlem Negro use.*

frail job   1 A woman, esp. a sexually attractive one, or one known to be promiscuous. See **frail.** 2 Sexual intercourse with a woman.

frame   *n.* 1 A human physique; a body; esp. the torso of a sexually attractive girl. 2 A pocket, pocketbook, or wallet. *Some underworld use.* 3 A heterosexual male who looks effeminate and is attractive to homosexuals. Cf. **bait.** 4 In sports, a complete unit: a round of a prize fight, an inning of baseball, a quarter of a football game, etc. 1951: "A unique play by Carl Furillo in the third inning. Mel Queen lined a single to right field to open that frame. . . ." Roscoe McGowen, N.Y. *Times*, Aug. 28, 26/4. 5 A conspiracy against an innocent person; the act of framing someone. 1934: "The dough was passed to me to make the frame tighter." Chandler, *Finger Man*, 50. 1948: "Just the victim of a frame. . . ." Evans, *Halo for Satan*, 148.   *v.t.* 1 To arrest or to cause a person's arrest by means of false evidence. 1929: "I was framed. . . ." J. Auslander, *Hell in Harness*, 16. 2 To put in running order. *Carnival use.*

frame-dame   *n.* A girl known only for her sex appeal, and who has little intelligence or personality. *Some teenage use since c1940.* See Appendix, Rhyming Slang.

frame up   To victimize an innocent person by conspiracy; esp. to arrest or to cause a person's arrest by means of faked evidence.   **frame-up**   *n.* 1 A conspiracy against an innocent person; the act of framing someone. 1930: "I'll prove to you it's a frame-up." Weeks, *Racket*, 128. 2 A display of goods for sale. *Pitchman use.*

frances   *n.* The posterior. 1952: "It gives me a pain in the frances." R. C. Ruark, *synd. newsp. col.*, Oct. 1. *Jocular euphem. for "fanny."*

frank   *n.* 1 A Dutchman. *c1848, criminal use. Obs.* 2 A frankfurter. *Colloq.*

frantic   *adj.* 1 Exciting; satisfying; wonderful; cool. *Wide bop use since c1946.*

Some cool use. → 2 Too emotional; motivated by or involved in the crass material pursuits of life; ruled by habit and a love of security; having middle-class values; worldly. 1958: "The hipster has decided to quit—resign. . . . He gives up on the issue of being human in society. He decides that the problem does not exist for him. He disaffiliates. The man who cares is now derided for being 'frantic.' " H. Gold, *The Beat Mystique. Beat use since c1955.*

frat   *n.* 1 A college fraternity. 1899: *DAE. Common student use since c1900, but officially frowned upon by most national fraternities and considered unsophisticated.* 2 A member of a fraternity. *Student use since c1900.*   *adj.* Pertaining to a fraternity or fraternity life. 1951: "Some frat men say he stole their loving cup." M. Shulman, *Dobie Gillis*, 210. *Common student use since c1900. All uses are shortened.* See Appendix, Shortened Words.   **—ernize**   *v.i.* 1 To associate closely, esp. sexually, with the women of an enemy or occupied country. *Wide W.W.II Army use.* → 2 To associate closely, esp. sexually, with any girl or woman. *Some use since c1945.*

frater   *n.* A member of a college fraternity; esp. a fellow member or fraternity brother. *From the Latin.*

frau   *n.* 1 A girl or woman; often a plump or bossy one. *Not common.* 2 One's wife. 1929: "And escort your incomparable frau to a tea dance." K. Brush, *Young Man*, 57. 1951: "His reward from the frau. . . ." H. Boyle, AP, Oct. 16. Cf. **hausfrau.**

frau-shack   *n.* A women's dormitory or sorority house in a coeducational college or university. *Some c1925 student use.*

frazzled   *adj.* Drunk.

freak   *n.* 1 A drink containing Coca-Cola and orange flavoring. *Not common.* 2 A male homosexual. 1956: "*Freak* is a homosexual." S. Longstreet, *The Real Jazz Old and New*, 150. *Mainly jazz use.*

freckles   *n.pl.* Tobacco for rolling a cigarette. *From its appearance. W.W.II USN and Marines use.*

free = for free.

free-and-easy   *n.* A saloon. Cf. **speakeasy.**

freebie   freebee   freeby   *n.* Anything that is free of charge; anything given or performed without cost to the receiver or audience. 1954: "That meal was a freebie and didn't cost me anything." L. Armstrong, *Satchmo, My*

Life in New Orleans, 92. 1956: "Going from a freebee to Carnegie Hall, the journey up for jazz is not yet over." S. Longstreet, *The Real Jazz Old and New,* 33. *adj.* Free; free of charge.

free-load   free load   freeload *v.i.* To eat, drink, be entertained, vacation, or live without charge or at another's expense. 1953: "They will successfully free load the rest of their lives." H. Boyle, AP, Apr. 9. *Common since W.W.II.*   *n.* A meal, food, whisky, or the like enjoyed at another's expense; free food or drink. 1956: "During the depression when free loads were rare. . . ." J. Cannon, *Who Struck John?* 122.   **—er** *n.* **1** One who eats or drinks without expense to himself; a nonpaying customer or guest; one who stuffs himself with free food and drink, as at a party; one who habitually eats, drinks, or vacations at the expense of another; specif., one whose host is a business firm or an employee who has a business expense account. 1951: "Congressmen are great freeloaders." L. Mortimer, quoted in N.Y. *Times Bk. Rev.,* Apr. 15, 23/3. 1956: "Very few free loaders are gourmets. They have the appetites of sea gulls." J. Cannon. *Who Struck John?* 122. *Very common since W.W.II.* **2** An open-house party; a social gathering which offers free refreshments. 1950: "Somebody was tossing a free-loader over on Park Avenue." J. Bainbridge in *New Yorker,* Nov. 25, 58.   **—ing** *n.* The act or an instance of eating or drinking without cost or at another's expense. 1956: "[The art of] free loading has diminished. Any one who can mooch a ham sandwich is considered a champion." J. Cannon, *Who Struck John?* 123.

free-rider *n.* A nonunion worker who benefits from pay scales, working conditions, privileges, or the like gained by the union workers in his factory.

free show A look or glance, usu. at a girl's or woman's thighs or breasts, or occasionally at a nude woman, most often without the female's knowledge or consent, as when a girl or woman crosses her legs, or inadvertently forgets to close a door while disrobing. *Mainly boy and young teenager use.*

freeside *adv.* Outside; specif. outside the walls of a penitentiary. *Prison use.*

free ticket = **free transportation.**

free transportation   free ticket In baseball, a base on balls.

free-wheeling *adj.* **1** Spending money liberally. 1953: "The free-wheeling out-of-towner." H. Boyle, AP, Mar. 9. **2** Unauthorized; independent; unrestricted; without concern for others.

freeze *v.i.* **1** Lit., to remain motionless or still, in hope of not being seen. **2** Fig., to remain in the place, job, location, or the like where one is; to be satisfied with what one has. 1956: "Your best bet is to freeze and wait. You can't get away." N. Algren, *A Walk on the Wild Side,* 16. *v.t.* **1** = **put the freeze on.** **2** To snub. **—r** *n.* A railroad refrigerator car. *Railroad use.*

freeze on [someone], put the **1** = **put the chill on [someone].** **2** To snub. 1953: "Women are quick to put the freeze on free loaders." H. Boyle, AP, Apr. 9.

freight See **drag [one's] freight, pull [one's] freight.**

freight, pull [one's] To leave; to go away. 1929: "This bird's gonna pull his freight." Burnett, *Little Caesar,* 156. *Used since 1885. Orig. trucker and railroad use.*

French *adj.* **1** = **AWOL.** *Some W.W.I use. From "French leave."* **2** Slender; said ₁of a girl's or woman's legs. *Not common.* **3** [taboo] Sexual satisfaction given or received orally. *Since W.W.I.* See **French way.** *n.* Spoken profanity, obscenity, or oaths; profanity. 1957: "That God damned . . . —pardon my French. . . ." Tennessee Williams, *Orpheus Descending,* I. *Almost always in "pardon my French" = excuse my profanity.*

French-inhale *n. & adj.* The act of exhaling a mouthful of smoke and then inhaling it through the nose. 1948 [1954]: "Tilting his head back, he slowly released an enormous quantity of smoke from his mouth and drew it in through his nostrils. He continued to smoke in this 'French-inhale' style." J. D. Salinger, *Just Before the War with the Eskimos,* reprinted in *Manhattan,* 28. *Considered exotic and ultrasophisticated by teenagers and students; confined to beginning smokers.*

French kiss **1** A passionate kiss in which the tongue of one person explores the tongue and mouth of the other. *Teenage use.* → **2** [taboo] An instance of cunnilingus or fellatio. *Not common. By confusion with "French way."*

French leave **1** The act or an instance of leaving or departing without proper permission, esp. to leave a USN ship or Army post without authorization;

to go or be awol. *Orig. W.W.I use.* 2 The act or an instance of departing secretly or without notifying one's host, friends, creditors, or the like.

French post card   Any pornographic photograph. *From the traditional tourists' story of Paris street vendors selling pornographic picture postcards and photographs openly.*

French walk   1 = bum's rush, the. **2** Specif., ejecting a man from a place forcibly by grabbing the seat of his pants with one hand and the back of his collar with the other and thus forcing him to walk until he reaches the door.

French way [taboo]   Sexual intercourse accomplished orally, by cunnilingus or fellatio. *Because the French are traditionally believed to prefer this form of sexual activity. The term orig. among A.E.F. soldiers in France during W.W.I.*

fresh   *n.sing.* A college freshman. 1837: *DAE. Colloq. n.pl.* College freshmen; a freshman class. *Usu. preceded by "the."* 1827: *DAE. Colloq. adj.* **1** Freshman; belonging or pertaining to college freshmen. *Above meanings are of shortened words; see Appendix.* **2** Impudent; impertinent; presumptuous; disrespectful. 1848: *DAE.* 1907: "If he got fresh two or three of us would pitch on him." J. London, *My Life. Colloq. Usu. a pred. adj., sometimes an attrib. adj.* → **3** Specif., apt to try to take sexual liberties; flirtatious. *Colloq.* **4** Drunk. *Some c1920 use. Obs.* **—ie** *n.* A college freshman. 1871: *DAE. Somewhat archaic since c1935.* See Appendix, **—ie** ending.

fresh one   1 A new prisoner. *Prison use.* **2** Another, newly made highball.

fried   Drunk. 1926: "Princeton has completed the idiom of the cuisine by adding *fried* to *boiled* and *stewed,* meaning intoxicated." G. Spencer, *Univ. of Va. Mag.,* Oct., 16/2. Cf. **boiled, stewed.**

fried egg   1 The U.S. Military Academy insigne worn on the full-dress hat. *West Point use.* **2** The flag of Japan. 1952: "Morton's Wahoo sunk about everything the Japs owned with a fried egg on its masthead." R. C. Ruark, *synd. newsp. col.,* July 4. *W.W.II use. In ref. to the red disk shown on the yellow background of the flag.*

fried shirt   1 A starched shirt. *Dial.* **2** A formal dress shirt. *Never common.* See **boiled shirt.**

frig [taboo]   *v.t.* To trick or cheat

someone. *Since c1925. Common euphem. for "fuck."*

frigging [taboo]   *adj.* Damned; fucking. *Euphem.*

frill   *n.* A girl or woman.

frip   *adj.* Very unpleasant; lousy. 1949: "Nothing, teen-agers thought, could be more 'frip' than getting down to work in the first weeks of fall. . . ." *Time,* Oct. 3, 36f. *Not common.*

Frisco   *proper n.* San Francisco, California. 1869: *DAE.* 1934: "Ever been in Frisco?" Cain, *Postman,* 57. *Colloq. A term much disapproved by San Franciscans.*

frisgig   frizgig   *n.* A silly girl or woman. *Never common.*

frisk   *v.t.* **1** To search a person for anything that he may have on him; specif., to pat or rub a dressed person in all places where a pocket is or wherever something might be carried or concealed. 1781: Farmer & Henley. 1930: "Frisk him, Bob." Weeks, *Racket,* 168. 1957: ". . . Search him, raise your hands high, frisk him." Robert Wallace, "Crime In The U.S." *Life,* Sept. 9, 53. *Underworld, police, and hobo use until c1920; now universally known. One is usu. frisked by the police, as for a concealed weapon.* → **2** To search, inspect, or look over any place, as a building, an apartment, a house, or the like, to ascertain its contents or to find contraband or evidence. 1942: "Let's go up and frisk the apartment." Chandler, *High Window,* 61. *n.* A search of a person or place.

Fritz   *n.* **1** A German soldier. *W.W.I use. More common with British soldiers than American soldiers. Very little W.W.II use.* **2** A German. *Some W.W.I use. adj.* Of German origin or manufacture.

fritz   *v.t.* To put anything out of working order. 1948: "Lightning hit some wires and fritzed the generator." F. Brown, *Dead Ringer,* 4. See **on the fritz.** **—er**   *n.* Something phoney. 1935: *underworld use.*

fritz, on the   Not functioning or not functioning properly; worthless, ruined; not in accord with the usual standards of performance or quality; in disrepair; of mechanical or electrical devices, not operating properly. 1928: "That glycerine was on the fritz. . . ." *Amer. Mercury,* Aug., 487/2. 1929: "The orchestra put that dance number on the fritz." Dunning & Abbott, *Broadway,* I. 1930: "Times Square hotel biz is on the terrific fritz." *Variety,* cited in *Bookman,* 397/2. 1943: "Putting the ritz on the fritz." Wolfert, *Underworld*, 251. *Mainly used by older people, and becoming archaic. "On the blink" is now more common.*

frivol *v.i.* To act frivolously; to amuse oneself or waste time. 1866: *DAE. Some sl. use through c1915. Now archaic and dial.* See Appendix, Shortened Words.

frog **Frog** *n.* **1** A one-dollar bill. Cf. **frogskin.** *Underworld use; not common.* **2** A Frenchman. 1947: "My dad was in France during the last war. He knows those Frogs." C. Willingham, *End as a Man*, 287. *Usu. derisive, if not derog., use. Prob. from "frog-eater." Orig. W.W.I Army use, adopted from British Army use; still common.* Cf. **tadpole.** **3** A boy whose voice is changing; an adolescent. *Not common.* → **4** A first semester freshman. *College use. Becoming archaic.* See **frosh.** Cf. **fish.** *adj.* [derog.] French. **—gie** **—gy** *n.* [derog.] A Frenchman.

frog-eater [derog.] A Frenchman. *Since c1850.*

frog-eating [derog.] *adj.* French. 1953: "That . . . frog-eating sieve. . . ." Nathaniel Benchley, *New Yorker*, Feb. 7, 87.

frogman *n.* **1** A specialist in underwater work, such as placing mines, exploring sunken ships, conducting experiments in marine biology, or the like; esp. an underwater swimmer who uses an oxygen tank strapped to his back and large rubber flippers on his feet to aid in swimming. *Since c1940.* **2** Specif., a U.S. Navy skin-diver or underwater specialist, usu. assigned to demolition. *W.W.II use.*

frogskin *n.* **1** A one-dollar bill. 1949: "I'll give you five hundred frogskins for the good will and fixtures." S. J. Perelman, *Listen to the Mocking Bird*, 120. **2** A piece of paper money; a greenback. 1949: "He not only got his quail, but a handful of frogskins as well. . . ." AP, Los Angeles, Nov. 25. *Since c1910. Archaic.* **3** Specif. a one-dollar bill. Cf. **frog, skin.**

frog-sticker *n.* **1** A long-bladed knife; esp. a pocket knife. **2** A bayonet. *W.W.II Army use.*

frog up To be confused or deceived. *Negro use. c1930; not common.*

from A to Z Completely; thoroughly.

from hell to breakfast Thoroughly; from A to Z; from one end to the other. 1928: "Police . . . clubbed the Gophers

from hell to breakfast." Asbury, *Gangs of N.Y.*, 201f.

from hunger Inferior; cheap; ugly; lowbrow; disliked; unwanted; corny; hammy. 1935: "Playing [music] from hunger: similar to 'corny,' meaning playing in a style to please the uneducated masses." *Peabody Bulletin*, Dec., 42/2. 1951: "I started giving the three witches at the next table the eye again. That is, the blonde one. The other two were strictly from hunger." J. D. Salinger, *Catcher in the Rye*, 56. *Orig. assoc. with jive, swing, and jazz use c1935.*

from Mount Shasta Addicted to drugs. 1933: *drug addict use.* Maurer. *Not common. From "high," and "snow."* See **high; snow.**

from nothing Nothing; not to know. See **know from nothing.**

frompy = **frumpy.**

front *n.* **1** A suit of clothes, esp. a new or good suit of clothes. 1931: "The real 'highgrade bum' who wears a good suit of clothes—a 'front'—under his traveling suit of overalls." C. Ashleigh, in *Everyman*, May 21, 520/1. *Orig. hobo use. Never common.* → **2** The successful or respectable appearance one conveys by one's clothing, accessories, manners, possessions, or friends; esp. an assumed or calculated appearance to impress others. 1943: "This [cigar] and his stickpin, his two diamond rings, and his shirts and the gabardine suit composed his 'front.'" Wolfert, *Underworld*, 7. *Common use.* **3** A respectable, impressive-appearing, or successful person chosen to represent a group and impart to the group an appearance of respectability or success. 1930: "[The thief's] inability to hire a professional bondsman and 'good front' results in a quick trial." Lavine, *Third Degree*, 54. **4** A prospective customer. *From the command "Front!" given to salesmen in a retail store. Retail salesmen's use, c1935. Obs.* **5** Legal or normal activities, usu. business activities, used to mask illegal activities, gambling, or the like. 1958: ". . . That radar observer routine is a great front for your real racket. . . ." *Terry and the Pirates*, synd. newsp. comic strip, Feb. 9. *v.i.* To recommend or speak favorably of a person or thing.

front and center *imp.* A command to a person to present himself immediately; a stern way of saying "Come here."

front door The administrative staff

of a circus, as distinguished from the performers, called "the back yard." *Circus use.* *adj.* Respectable, honest; said of a place of business or business venture.

front gee   See **gee.**

front names   The first name of a person; a given name; a Christian name. 1953: "What is your front name?" Groucho Marx, *radio program*, June 3.

front office   1 The administrative or main offices of a business. → 2 Administrative officers; executives. → 3 One's husband or wife; anyone who makes final decisions. *Used humorously.* → 4 A police station. *Underworld use.* *adj.* Final; authoritative; formed by executives or administrators. *Usu. in "front office decision" ". . . policy," or the like. All forms and meanings since c1940. One of the sl. terms coming from big business.*

front room   A sedan or limousine. *Not common.*

frosh   *n.sing.* A first-year student in high school, prep school, college, or university; a college freshman of either sex. 1924: "A freshman started down the aisle. . . . 'Murder the frosh!' " Marks, *Plastic Age*, 25. 1953: "One Sarah Lawrence frosh to another." *New Yorker*, Jan. 17, 20/2. *Colloq. In Germany, a student while still in the gymnasium, before entering a university, is called a "Frosch" = a frog. However, the U.S. term may merely be based on the first syllable of "freshman," with a vowel change.* *n.pl.* College freshmen of either sex or both sexes; a freshman class. 1924: " 'Never mind; we'll do the ordering next year.' 'Right you are,' said Carl, 'and won't I make the little frosh walk.' " Marks, *Plastic Age*, 22. *Colloq. adj.* Of or pertaining to freshmen. *Colloq.*

frost   *n.* 1 A failure; something, as a new book, that is coldly received. *Ascribed to F. Scott Fitzgerald.* 2 = **cold shoulder.**

frou-frou   *n.* Inordinately ornate dress or adornments, esp. women's. 1951: "Is that what you want in a girl—chi-chi, frou-frou, fancy clothes, permanent waves?" M. Shulman, *Dobie Gillis*, 73. *From Fr.*

frown   *n.* 1 A drink containing Coca-Cola and lemon flavor. 2 Lemon flavoring; lemon juice. *Not common.*

frowsy   *n.* A frowzy woman. 1929: ". . . A few frowsies in skirts." Winkler in *New Yorker*, Feb. 9, 38/3.

frozen   *adj.* Frightened.

fruit   *n.* 1 A person easily defeated, influenced, or victimized. *c1900 student use.* 2 An easy, pleasant, undemanding boss, teacher, or one in authority; a good fellow. *c1900 student use. Obs.* 3 A promiscuous person; an amoral person. *c1900 use. Obs.* 4 A shabby, unkempt, eccentric fellow; an odd person. 1912: "I'll bet we get a lot of fruits." Johnson, *Stover at Yale.* 6. *Teenage and student use c1910–c1940. Still in use.* 5 A homosexual. *Since c1930. Common teenage use since c1940. The most common meaning. Kinder than "fag," "fairy," "queer," "queen."* 6 = **jerk.** *Boy, teenage, and some student use since c1940. More common c1945 than now.* *v.i.* To be promiscuous. *Not now common.*   —**y** *adj.* 1 Pleasant; easy. *Archaic.* 2 Eccentric; odd; nutty. *Teenage use since c1935.* 3 Homosexual. See **fruit.**   —**cake** *n.* 1 An insane person. *From the popular phrase "nutty as [or "nuttier than"] a fruitcake."* 1952: "An escaped fruitcake." Movie, *Pat and Mik^.* 2 An eccentric or unusual person. 3 A homosexual. From "fruit." *Not common.*

fruit salad   Campaign ribbons, representing decorations and campaign medals, worn on the breast of the tunic by members of the Armed Forces. 1944: "Quite a fruit salad on your chest, General!" M. Caniff, *synd. comic strip*, "Male Call," Sept. 22. 1951: "You can recognize the boys from Korea by the new decoration added to the war 'fruit salad.' The [United Nations Korean War] ribbon is predominantly blue." G. Lewis in Syracuse (N.Y.) *Post-Standard*, Mar. 22, 22/1. *W.W.II use.*

fruit wagon   An ambulance. 1952: "If you squawk you leave the docks, most likely in the fruit wagon." Mary H. Vorse, *Harper's*, Apr., 29/2. *Longshoreman use.*

frump   *n.* A dowdy woman. 1941: "That floppy-looking frump he left you for." Cain, *M. Pierce*, 9. *Colloq.*   —**y** *adj.* Homely, dowdy, dilapidated.

fry   *v.i., v.t.* 1 To put to death in the electric chair; to die in the electric chair. 1946: "I built up a case against Sandmark. You could probably have fried him with it too." Evans, *Halo in Blood*, 202. *Since c1930.* 2 To chastise or be chastised; to act with malice or be the recipient of malice. 3 To remove the kinks from one's hair with a hot curling iron. *Negro use.* See **small fry.**

fu   *n.* Marijuana. 1946: *addict use.* D. W. Maurer, *Amer. Mercury*, Nov., 572/2.

fuck   [taboo]   *v.t.* To cheat, trick,

take advantage of, deceive, or treat someone unfairly. *Very common. The relationship between sex and fraud is best illustrated by this usage; see Appendix. All sl. meanings of "fuck" and all "fuck" expressions, of course, derive consciously or unconsciously from the old and stand. but taboo "fuck" = sexual intercourse or, specif., manual intercourse. All sl. meanings and expressions were widely used in W.W.II military units, became part of the sl. vocabulary of many veterans, and spread from them to students and friends. This, coupled with the lessening of moral standards and taboos, including linguistic taboos, during and after the war, has contributed to the wide, almost colloq., use of these taboo words and expressions.* n. A damn; a care; hell. *E.g., "I don't give a fuck." "What the fuck."* exclam. Hell; shit; an expression of extreme dismay, anger, disgust, or the like. *Fairly common during and since W.W.II, wide Army use.* **—ed** [taboo] adj. Cheated, tricked, deceived, defeated, done in. **—ing** [taboo] adj. **1** = damned. *Very common.* **2** Difficult to accomplish; hard to do; strenuous; harsh. **3** Inferior; unpleasant; cheap; ugly; disgusting. **4** Confusing; confused; disorganized. *Wide W.W.II use; fairly common.* **—y** [taboo] adj. = **fucking.**

fuck a duck [taboo] exclam. An expression of surprise, disbelief, dismissal, or rejection. See Appendix, Rhyming Slang.

fucked out [taboo] Exhausted.

fucked up [taboo] **1** Confused; disorganized; made unnecessarily complex; the result of a blunder: said of a plan, action, task, or the like. *Common.* Cf. **snafu. 2** In trouble; obsessed with a personal problem; confused; neurotic.

fuck it [taboo] exclam. **1** An expression of dismay or annoyance. **2** A request to change the subject, forget a plan or task, stop nagging, or the like. *Common.* **3** = **fuck,** exclam.

fuck off [taboo] **1** To masturbate. *Very common.* → **2** To spend or pass the time idly; to waste time; to loll or fool around. → **3** To tease; to refuse to work or think seriously. **4** To make a blunder or mistake. **fuck-off** n. A habitual, chronic, or stupid blunderer; anyone who cannot do anything properly; one who cannot be relied upon to do what is asked or expected of him. *Wide W.W.II Armed Forces use.*

fuck up [taboo] **1** To spend or pass

the time idly; to waste time. *Not as common as "fuck off."* **2** To tease; to refuse to work or think seriously. *Not as common as "fuck off."* **3** To ruin or spoil something, as a plan or the successful completion of a task, by blundering. *Common.* **fuck-up** n. = **fuck-off.**

fuck you! [taboo] exclam. Damn you; to hell with you; an expression of decisive rejection. *Fairly common. Complete rejection of and contempt or disgust for a person, implying that henceforth the speaker will for the person bear malice. Lit. it implies the speaker has found he has been rejected, held in contempt, insulted, doublecrossed, deceived, or cheated by the person and hopes that person will be treated the same way, and will be glad to treat him so himself. Both words are given a long pronunciation.*

fuck you Charley! [taboo] exclam. = **fuck you;** addressed to a stranger or as if to a stranger, indicating complete rejection.

fuddy adj. Untidy; disordered; inefficient; outdated. *From "fuddy-duddy."* 1944: "The year fuddy old King George III had died." Fowler, *Good Night,* 9. n. = **fuddy-duddy.**

fuddydud = **fuddy-duddy.**

fuddy-duddy n. An old-fashioned, unimaginative, conservative, and timorous person, esp. an elderly person; a senile person; a fussy, ineffectual person; an old fogy. 1947: "To this little squab, I evidently rated as a fuddy-duddy." Billy Rose, *synd. newsp. col.,* May 8. *Since c1900.* v.t. To act foolishly or ineffectively. *Archaic and dial.* adj. Ineffectual; outdated. See Appendix, Reduplications.

fudge v.i., v.t. **1** To cheat a little; to hedge; to fib; to misrepresent. 1948: "I kind of relaxed on one hip and walked with a limp, so I could fudge three or four inches on my height." Cain, *Moth,* 108. 1952: "If you're fudging on your income tax return . . . better watch out for nosey neighbors." AP, Washington, Feb. 25. **2** [taboo] To produce an orgasm in one of the opposite sex by manual manipulation of the vagina or penis. n. **1** Nonsense; bunk. **2** A polite curse word or expletive uttered when something goes wrong. *Often in* **Oh fudge.**

fuff expl. A reply to an obvious, unnecessary statement. 1934: "Oh, willy-nilly and fiddle-faddle. Fuff too." P. Wylie, *Finnley Wren,* 175.

full Drunk. *Often* **full as an egg, full as a tick.** *Archaic by c1930.* n. **1** In

205   **Futy**

football, a fullback. *Not common.* **2** =
fed up.
full-blast   full blast   *adj.* Complete; on a large scale; intense. 1839
[1948]: "[In the U.S.] full blast—something in the extreme. . . ." Captain
Frederick Marryat, *A Diary in America
with Remarks on Its Institutions,* excerpted in *America Through British Eyes,*
186.   *adv.* At or with maximum
speed, efficiency, or intensity. *Colloq.*
**full of beans   full of hops   full of
prunes   1** Actively foolish, mistaken,
exaggerating. **2** Lively, energetic, high-
spirited. *All terms have both meanings,
though first meaning much more common.
"Full of prunes" is prob. the oldest and
most popular; "full of beans" is least
popular. Note that all three foods are
cheap, easy to come by, and considered
laxatives.*
full of hot air   Mistaken, exaggerating; expounding false information.
See **hot air.**
full of piss and vinegar [taboo]   **full
of vinegar**   Lively, energetic; entertaining or interesting.
full of shit [taboo]   **full of crap** [taboo]
full of bull [taboo]   Misinformed;
possessing and offering inaccurate information and advice; malicious exaggeration. Cf. **bull, crap, shit.**
full ride   With all expenses paid.
1956: ". . . He was accused of receiving
a full ride scholarship from Michigan
as compensation for his football services." Bill Fay, "The Case For Rough
Football," *Collier's,* Nov. 23, 101.
full up   1 Completely full. **2** = **fed up.**
3 On the verge of tears; feeling strong
emotional sentiments.
fume   *v.i., v.t.* To smoke tobacco.
c1900; not common; obs.
fumigate   *v.i., v.t.* To smoke tobacco.
Some popularity c1900; obs.
fungo   *n.* **1** In baseball, a practice fly ball
(hit to a fielder) that the batter makes by
throwing the ball up a few feet and hitting
it as it falls. 1886: "Practicing fungo
batting. . . ." *Sporting Life,* Mar. 3, 2/3.
1933: " 'Fungo' . . . the term designating
the practice flies that are hit to out-
fielders with a 'fungo stick,' a bat very
much lighter than ordinary." John
Kieran, *Sat. Rev. of Lit. Fungos are used
to give fielders practice.* **2** A long, light
bat used in baseball practice. → **3** Any
baseball bat. **4** A mistake; a blooper.
5 Any unrewarding act.   *v.i.* **1** To
bat fungos. **2** To make a mistake.

fungo stick = **fungo.**
funk   *n.* A mood of idle depression.
Cf. **blue funk.**
funk hole   *n.* A dugout; any depression in the earth used as a place of
safety during a bombardment. *W.W.I
Army use.*
funnel   *n.* **1** The human mouth.
Never common. **2** A drinker or drunkard.
Not common.
funnies, the   *n.* A page or pages of
a newspaper that contain comic strips;
comic strips; a funny paper. *Colloq.*
funny   *adj.* **1** Odd; eccentric; unusual;
suspicious. *Colloq.* **2** Crazy.   *adv.* Oddly;
in an unusual manner; suspiciously.
Colloq.   *n.* A joke; a funny remark
or wisecrack. 1952: "Cut the funnies an'
git a can-opener." W. Kelly, *synd.
comic strip,* "Pogo," Oct. 16.
funny business   Deceit; trickery;
fraud; any crooked or unethical dealings.
Cf. **business, monkey business.**
funny house   1 An insane asylum.
2 A sanitorium or hospital for drug
addicts or alcoholics. 1940: "Who put
me in your private funny house?"
Chandler, *Farewell,* 151.
furniture.   *n.* A sexually attractive
girl. *Usu. in "a nice little piece of
furniture."* See **piece.**
furp   *v.i.* To go on a date; to escort a
girl to a party.   *n.* A menial servant,
lackey, assistant, or helper. *c1930
Civilian Conservation Corps use.*   **—er**
n. A ladies' man; one who devotes most
of his free time to pursuing women.
*c1930 Civilian Conservation Corps use; not
common since.*
furp up   To locate; to search for and
procure; to scare up. *c1930 Civilian
Conservation Corps use.*
fuse = **blow a fuse.**
fuss   *v.t., v.i.* **1** To visit or escort a
girl; to date a girl. **2** To neck or spoon.
Obs. See **kick up a fuss.**   **—er**   *n.*
1 A ladies' man. *c1910. Obs.* **2** A girl's
date, particularly a college girl's date.
Archaic.
fuss-budget   *n.* A fussy person; esp.
an old shrew.
future   *n.* **1** One's own fiancée or
fiancé. **2** [taboo] The scrotum. See
family jewels.
futy [taboo]   *n.* The vagina. *Although not
polite, it is not always taboo but, more
often than not, used in humorous banter
implying disinterest in the sexual connotation.*   *v.i.* **1** = **futz around. 2** To

fuss, grumble, complain. **3** [taboo] To have sexual intercourse. *A partial euphemism, from the taboo "fuck."*
futz [taboo] *n.* The vagina. *v.i.* & *v.t.* = **fuck.** *A euphem.*
futz around [taboo] **1** = **fuck off, fuck up.** *A euphem.* **2** To idle, putter, waste time. 1941: "Don't futz around with it [a play] too long." Schulberg, *Sammy,* 143. **3** Teasing; sexual playing.
futzed up [taboo] = **fucked up.** *A euphem.* 1947: "I've got her all futzed up. She does everything I tell her." C. Willingham, *End as a Man,* 301.
fuzz *n.* A policeman or detective. 1931: *policeman, East Coast use.* David W. Maurer. 1946: "I shall not discuss the findings of the fuzzes, or private detectives, in the Beverly Hills case...." Damon Runyon, *synd. newsp. col.,* Aug. 5. *Underworld, hobo, and carnival use; hot rod use since c1950.* **—y** **—ie** *n.* **1** A policeman, esp. a diligent one. **2** A range horse. c1880 [1936]: "... 'Fuzzies' (Range horses)...." P. A. Rollins, *The Cowboy,* 28. *Ranch use. Obs.* **3** A sure thing, a certainty, esp. in gambling, specif. in horse racing. 1956: "Fuzzy—A horse whose chances appear infinitely better than those of his competitors in a race; a standout, a stickout." T. Betts, *Across the Board,* 315. *adv., adj.* Partially drunk.
fuzzled Drunk.

G

G *n.* A thousand dollars. 1954: "If we can just lay our hands on five C's fast, we just can't miss grabbing off fifty G's." W. R. & F. K. Simpson, *Hockshop,* 220.
gab *n.* **1** Talk; gossip; gabble. 1905: "Skinski was a warm member with the gab...." McHugh, *Search Me,* 60. *Colloq.* Cf. **gift of gab. 2** The mouth. 1924: "Close your gabs, everybody...." "He shoots off his gab...." Marks, *Plastic Age,* 100, 197. *v.i.* To talk.
—ber *n.* A talkative person; specif., a radio commentator or critic. 1948: "A gabber is anyone who talks, but especially one who does so in a strained, hurried voice, as if his message were alarming or revolting." Mencken, *New Yorker.* See Appendix, —er ending.
—by *adj.* Talkative; overtalkative. 1931: "They have spoken of any gabby party...." Pegler, *Lit. Digest.* See Appendix, —y ending. **—fest** *n.* A talk fest; a social gathering for conversation. *Colloq. since c1895.*
gaboon = **goboon.**
Gabriel *n.* Any trumpet player. *Synthetic jive and jazz use.*
G.A.C. **G-A-C** *n.* An order of a grilled American cheese sandwich. *Common lunch-counter use in relaying an order.* See Appendix, Shortened Words.
gadget *n.* **1** A device, esp. a small mechanical device with which one is not familiar; any device whose proper name is not known. *Colloq. since c1925.* **2** Any useless item, such as trimming, added to a garment, automobile, or the like, solely to cause a change in appearance or style. **3** A girl. *Some W.W.II Armed Forces use.* **4** An Air Force cadet; also, an unimportant person. *Some Army Air Force use since c1945.*
gaff *n.* = **gimmick;** lit. and fig., a concealed device that makes something work. 1951: "People start looking for a gaff." *New Yorker,* Jan. 27, 20/3. *Carnival and pitchman use.* *v.t.* **1** To equip something with a gaff in order to trick, cheat, or deceive. 1939: "The [man-made artificial] volcano was 'gaffed' with steampipes." Liebling in *New Yorker,* 24/3. **2** To reprimand; to bawl out. *Some USN use.* **—er** *n.* **1** The manager of a circus. *Circus use.* **2** The chief electrician on a movie set. *Hollywood use.*
gag *n.* **1** Almost any kind of joke or trick, whether intended to amuse or to deceive or cheat; a ruse; a funny story, practical joke, or the like. 1823: Farmer & Henley. 1894: "But better than any of these [begging] tricks is what is called the 'faintin' gag.'" J. Flynt. 1934: "I tried some comical stuff, but all I got was a dead pan, so that gag was out." Cain, *Postman,* 1. *In both theater and general use. Colloq.* **2** A trite remark; a homily; a cliché. 1895: *DAE. Obs.* → **3** A trite or old excuse or alibi. *Hobo and underworld use.* **4** A prison sentence. *Some underworld use.*
gaga **ga-ga** *adj.* Lit. and fig., crazy; "crazy"; silly; irrational; having lost one's objectivity and perspective. 1930: "When prohibition comes up, [the wets] go ga-ga." A. Briggs in *Forum,* Nov., 277/1. 1930: "If only he

would have some rich babe go gaga over him." J. T. Farrell, 156. 1952: "The prose engineers are knocking themselves gaga to tell you that to be an American means to be an honest fellow." D. Powell in *The Nation*, May 10, 445/2. See Appendix, Reduplications.

gage *n.* 1 Cheap whisky. 2 Tobacco, cigarettes, cigars, or chewing tobacco. **Stick of gage** = a cigarette, either a standard cigarette or a marijuana cigarette. 3 Marijuana; a marijuana cigarette. *Narcotic addict use. adj.* Under the influence of marijuana. **—d** *adj.* Drunk.

gage butt   gauge butt *n.* A marijuana cigarette. *Addict use.*

gagers *n.pl.* The eyes.

gage up, get one's 1 To become angry, esp. to become so angry that one takes action against the person or thing causing the anger. 2 To become emotional. 3 To become drunk.

gagger *n.* A cigar. *Not common.*

gal *n.* A girl or woman, esp. a young, pleasant, pert woman. 1795: *vulgar or dial.* 1839 [1948]: "[Americans say:] 'She's the greatest gal in the whole Union.'" Capt. Frederick Marryat, *A Diary in America with Remarks on Its Institutions*, excerpted in *America Through British Eyes*, 185. *Colloq. and now widely accepted, "standard" speech. DAE.*

Galilee *n.* The Southern states of the U.S.; the U.S. South, specif. those states that were part of the Confederacy. c1920 [1954]: "There was no place for colored people to eat on the train in those days, especially down in Galilee (the South)." L. Armstrong, *Satchmo, My Life in New Orleans*, 229f. *Southern Negro use; archaic.*

gall *n.* Effrontery; impudence; conceit. 1951: "How do you like the gall of those Aussies disallowing a fish of that stature?..." Stan Smith, N.Y. *Daily News*, Aug. 30, C14/4. *Since c1880; now colloq.*

gallaway = **galways.**

gallery *n.* A porch; esp. a large porch with corner columns, as on a large house designed in the Federal style. c1920 [1954]: "The place we lived in had two porches... we called them 'galleries,' as the word porch was unheard of to us then." L. Armstrong, *Satchmo, My Life in New Orleans*, 160. *Southern use. Dial.*

galley-west *adv.* Thoroughly; with great force; in confusion.

galloping dominoes Dice. *Common usage, but somewhat synthetic.*

gal officer A lesbian. *Not common.*

galoot *n.* 1 A person; esp. a rustic, awkward, uneducated, or ill-mannered person. *Since c1865; somewhat archaic. Perhaps a Civil War term.* 2 A young inexperienced soldier. *1888:* Thornton. *1934: maritime sl.,* Web.

Galway *n.* A Roman Catholic priest. *From County Galway, Ireland.* 1891: "The Catholic priest is nicknamed 'The Galway.'" Josiah Flynt. *Archaic.*

galways   gallaway *n.* An ear-to-ear chin beard, as worn by a stage Irishman.

gam *v.i. & v.t.* To boast, to show off. *Negro use.   v.i.* To flirt. *Negro use, not common.   n.* 1 A discussion; a conference; a meeting or gathering which includes a discussion or much talking. Cf. **clambake.** 2 A gambler. *Obs.* 3 A social visit; a get-together. *Prob. from "gambol." Archaic and dial.* 4 A leg. *Usu. plural.* See **gams.   —s   —bs** *n.pl.* The legs of a person; usu., but not invariably, the shapely legs of an attractive girl or woman. 1941: [female legs] "Regarding her superb gams with affection...." V. Faulkner, *SEP*, Sept. 6, 35. 1951: [male legs] "Gavilan [a boxer]... has spindly gams, a thin neck and a wasp waist." Gene Ward, N.Y. *Daily News*, Aug. 30, 21/5. "Gambs" *is archaic. From the Ital. "gamba" = leg.*

gamin *n.* = **pixie.**

gander *n.* 1 A look; a glance; a visual inspection. *Usu. in* **take a gander.** 1939: "I go over and take a gander into it [a car]." Chandler, *Big Sleep*, 86. 1951: "He advised them forthwith to take a gander at page 350 of the Fourth Report on Un-American Activities." Bernard DeVoto, *Harper's*, Nov., 96/1. *Since c1930.* 2 A person who serves as a lookout for criminals. *Not common. v.i., v.t.* To look at or into something; to examine by looking. 1950: "A famous businessman who never made an important decision until she [an astrologer] had gandered at the stars for him...." Hal Boyle, AP, N.Y., Jan. 13.

gandy dancer 1 A railroad section-hand or track laborer; one who lays railroad tracks, grades roadbeds, or digs drainage ditches. *Since c1915 hobo, railroad, and lumberjack use. From the rhythmic dancelike movements made by laborers straightening rails and smoothing gravel. In the South the work was often accompanied by group chanting, the rhythm* *assuring that the laborers would simultaneously apply their crowbars to straighten the tracks.* → **2** One who works with pick and shovel; any manual laborer. *Logger use.* → **3** A seller of novelties at a carnival. *Carnival use.* **4** A weaving truck. *Truckdriver use. Not common.*

ganef   ganof = goniff.

Gangbusters   See **come on like Gangbusters.**

Gange   Kange [derog.]   *n.* A Negro. **—y   —y** *adj.* Negro; Negroid. See Appendix, —y ending.

gang shay (shag) [taboo]   A sex party in which several males take turns having sexual intercourse with one woman. *Mainly teenage use.*

gangster   *n.* One who belongs to a gang. Orig. in ref. to politicians; now mainly in ref. to criminals. 1896: "Of politicians." *DAE. Political use archaic by c1925; criminal use colloq. since c1925.*

gang up on [someone]   To unite against someone, as in a fight, argument, or the like. *Colloq.*

gap   jap   *n.* The mouth. *Not common.* *v.t.* To witness a crime without taking part in it.

gaper   *n.* A mirror, lit. that into which one gapes. *c1935 jive use.* See Appendix, —er ending.

gaposis   *n.* A mythical disease, the symptom of which is a customary gap in one's clothing, as between buttons or when one's shirt and trousers or blouse and skirt do not properly meet. *A synthetic commercialism.*

garbage   *n.* **1** Food or meals. *Hobo and logger use.* → **2** Small pieces of food, esp. fruit or greens used to add visual appeal to a main dish or drink, such as parsley on a piece of meat or a cherry in a cocktail. **3** Worthless merchandise, trinkets; worthless or insincere talk, beliefs, or ideas; exaggerations, lies; bull.

garbage can   *n.* **1** An old, dilapidated USN destroyer. See **can. 2** In television, a microwave-relay transmitter.

garbage-kisser   *n.* = **scissor-bill.** *Obs.*

garbo   Garbo   *n.* **1** An English muffin torn apart and toasted. **2** An uncommunicative person; one who prefers little or no social life. *From the actress Greta Garbo who made famous the phrase, "I want to be alone." Neither use is common.*

garden   *n.* **1** In baseball, the outfield. Called also the "outer garden." *c1925; not common.* → **2** A baseball field. *Sportswriter use.* **3** A prize-fighting arena.

From New York's Madison Square Garden. **4** A freight yard. *Railroad use.* **—er**   *n.* In baseball, an outfielder.

gargle   *v.t.* To drain and clean out the radiator of a truck. *Truck-driver use.* *n.* A drink, as of beer.

gargle-factory   *n.* A saloon. *Synthetic.*

garrison state   *n.* A country under the complete control of a dictator or a military coalition. 1951: "The Administration's military program would cost $20 or $30 billion more a year, turn the U.S. into a garrison state. . . ." *Time*, Jan., 12/3.

gas   *n.* **1** Empty talk; bragging, exaggerated talk. → **2** Talk of any kind. **3** Gasoline. *Colloq.* **4** Denatured alcohol, ether, or any such substance that can be a substitute for liquor. *Hobo and maritime use.* **5** Anything exceptional, extremely satisfying, or successful, such as a piece of music, a party, or the like. *Since c1945; orig. a Harlem Negro term; now in very common use in cool circles.* See **cook with gas, step on the gas.** *v.i.* **1** To converse, chat, or gossip. 1951: "I haven't gassed this long for a year." S. Lewis, *World So Wide*, 48. **2** To become intoxicated.   *v.t.* **1** To impress a person as remarkable, amusing, unusual, or eccentric, in either a good or a bad way but usu. good; to amuse; to attract attention; to evoke some kind of emotional response from a person. 1956: "Bird [Charlie 'Yardbird' Parker] gassed them." *The Metronome Year Book*, 39. 1957: "He plays a beautiful piano, and he played and Julie [London] sang, and she gassed me, she was that good." P. Martin, *SEP*, Aug. 17, 60. *Orig. and mainly cool and far out use. Some general use since c1955.* See **gasser. 2** To deceive or cheat a person by talking. *Since c1850.* **—bag**   *n.* A braggart; a long-winded orator; anyone who talks a lot. *Since c1870.*   **—sed**   *adj.* **1** Overcome with laughter; amazed; momentarily shocked or stunned by what one has seen or heard. See **gasser. 2** Drunk. 1953: "I begged them not to get gassed or start any fights." Bing Crosby, *SEP*, Feb. 14. *Common.*   **—ser**   *n.* **1** A loquacious or boastful person. **2** Anything exceptional, as a piece of music, etc. See **gas** → **3** Anything dull, outdated, or corny. *Freq. use in cool circles; the antithesis of "gas."* **4** Anything that is uproariously funny, as a joke or boner. *Very common.* **5** A remarkable person or thing, in either a good or a bad sense; specif. a remarkably stupid, amusing, or eccentric person; a character; a remarkably garish, complex, useless, unusual, or corny thing; or, specif., a remarkably talented, intelligent, cool person; or a remarkably well designed, simple, satisfying thing. *Orig. c1935 jive and Negro use; cool and far out use since c1950.* *adj.* **1** Uproariously funny; amusing. **2** Remarkable; amazing; noteworthy; in either a good or bad sense. **—sy** *adj.* Boastful; given to idle talk. *Since c1850.*

gas, a   *n.* = **gasser.** 1957: "When asked if the music is great (or a gas). . . ." E. Horne, *For Cool Cats and Far-Out Chicks. Synthetic cool and far out use.*

gas buggy   Orig. an automobile; now an early model automobile. *c1925; archaic.*

gash   *n.* **1** [taboo] A woman, or women, considered only in the sexual aspect; specif., a vagina; sexual intercourse; sex. 1933: "Don't you ever think of anything except gash?" J. T. Farrell, 70. 1951: "That St. Paul gash." R. Bissell, *Stretch on River*, 66. *Used only by men, and not known to many women. Not now as pop. as c1935 and earlier. →* **2** An extra issue or helping of anything, as food; an unexpected gift, pleasure, or good fortune. *Some W.W.II Army use.* **3** The mouth. *Some use since c1935.* *v.t.* To obtain something extra or unexpectedly, as a gift, or by stealing or cheating. *Not common.* See Appendix, Sex and Deceit.

gas hound   One given to drinking denatured alcohol, ether, or other substitutes for liquor. *Hobo and maritime use.*

gas house   A beer saloon; a beer garden. *W.W.II Armed Forces use. Common.*

gasoline buggy = **gas buggy.**

gasper   *n.* A cigarette, esp. a marijuana cigarette. 1957: "The prophet John P. Presmont showed up at the E. 35th St. [police] Station and handed Lt. Edward Psota a nice, fresh marijuana gasper. Had it not been for the cigarette, Psota would have shoved Presmont gently out." A. Smith, N.Y. *Daily News*, Aug. 9, 5. *Much more common in Eng. than in U.S.; now archaic in both countries.*

gas-pipe   *n.* A trombone. 1956: "Words that jazzmen don't use much, . . . gas-pipe for trombone. . . ." S. Longstreet, *The Real Jazz Old and New*, 150. *Jazz use, usu. synthetic. Not common.*

gas up   To make something more

exciting or attractive. 1957: "[Motion] picture based dimly [on a novel] . . . Warner Brothers has been around to gas things up a little." J. McCarten, *New Yorker*, Nov. 16, 108.

gat   *n.* Any hand firearm; a revolver or pistol. 1913: "That little hop fighter was poking his gat your way." *SEP*, Mar. 1, 47. 1921: "The barrels of a coupla 'gats.' . . ." Witwer, *Leather*, 11. *Orig. underworld and hobo use, c1910; now almost obs. with those groups and becoming somewhat archaic in general usage. Prob. from "Gatling gun."*

gate   *n.* **1** The amount of money collected from selling tickets to spectators at a sporting event; the "gate" receipts at a sporting event. *Since c1890.* **2** An able swing musician. *Wide swing use c1935–c1943. Prob. a shortening from "gator" or "alligator," reinforced by "swing like a gate."* **3** An engagement or appointment, esp. an engagement or a job for a jazz musician; a gig. *Thus "we've got a gate in New Jersey this week end" = our band has an engagement to play in New Jersey this week end. Jazz and swing use. Prob. from "alligator" shortened to "gate" = a swing musician or hep person; but, more possibly, from clipping of "engagement" plus "date." In any case, reinforced by "swing like a gate" = to play swing music well.* **4** Any male; esp. a hep one. *Swing use.* **5** = **cat,** *n.,* **6** & **7.** *Some jive and swing use, c1935–c1942, often in admiration of a musician or as direct address to a fellow devotee. Freq. used in jive and synthetic jive rhyming slang, for a list of which see Appendix. Pop. by comedian Jerry Colonna, on Bob Hope's radio program during W.W.II. Colonna always greeted the audience with a rhyme in synthetic jive on "gates." Thus "Greetings, gates,/ let's deliberate," "Greetings, gates,/Sorry I'm late." Thus also was the jive greeting "Greeting, gate(s)" popularized. See Appendix, Shortened Words.* **6** A railroad track switch. *Railroad use.* *v.t.* To dismiss someone; to jilt someone. See **the gate; give [someone] the gate.** **—s**   *n.sing.* A fellow swing music enthusiast. See **gate, 'gator, alligator.**

gate, give [someone] the   **1** To jilt. 1921: "Whose heiress had gave him the gate. . . ." Witwer, *Leather*, 73. → **2** To discharge a person from his job. 1951: "There's no reason why he should be fired . . . or given the gate. . . ." C. Stinnett.

gate, the   *n.* **1** Dismissal from one's

job. **2** Dismissal, rejection, or the act of being jilted by one's girl friend or boy friend. *Colloq.* **3** In baseball, a strikeout.

gate-crasher   *n.* One who, without invitation or a ticket, attends a social gathering or entertainment; an uninvited, unwelcome guest. *Colloq.*

gatemouth   *n.* One who knows and tells everyone else's business. *Orig. Negro use.*

'gator   **gator**   *n.* **1** An alligator. *Since c1840. Mainly Southern use.* See Appendix, Shortened Words. **2** = **alligator; cat.** *Some Negro use since c1925. Some jive use c1935–1942.* See **gate.** *Some swing use c1935.*

gat up   **1** Robbing at the point of a gun; a holdup. **2** To arm oneself with a gat.

gauge butt = **gage butt.**

gaunch   *n.* An unpopular girl; a female goon. *Some teenage use c1940; never common.*

gauze   *n.* Unconsciousness; a daze, as from a blow. 1929: "He's coming out of the gauze...." Wells Root. *Hollywood use.*

gay   *adj.* Homosexual (said of a person); patronized by or attractive to homosexuals (said of places or things). Cf. **queer.**

gay-cat   *n.* **1** A tramp or hobo; specif., one who is not typical or wise to the ways of hobo life, as a newcomer; a hobo willing to accept itinerant work; a hobo who is considered eccentric or unacceptable by his fellows. 1907: "Were not these other tramps mere dubs and 'gay-cats'?" J. London, *My Life. Hobo use.* **2** A criminal, esp. a young or inexperienced criminal or a youth who acts as a decoy, runner, or lookout for criminals. *Some use c1920–c1940.* **3** Variously, an active, jovial, lusty person who enjoys life; a ladies' man; a dude; one who, with or without the help of narcotics, is never worried or troubled but who takes life as it comes without being concerned or bothered. *Assoc. with jazz use, esp. cool use. The meaning is not definite, owing to the several meanings of "gay," and "cat"; for example, it is even occasionally used to mean a homosexual jazz musician.*

gay deceivers = **falsies.**

gazabo   **gazebo**   *n.* A fellow; a guy. 1930: "The gazabos they put on the jury'll know all about me...." Weeks, *Racket,* 107. *Since c1805; "gazabo" is*

about ten times more freq. than "gazebo"; archaic.

gazer   *n.* **1** A federal narcotics agent. **2** A window. *Not common.*

gazooney   **gazoony**   *n.* **1** A catamite. *c1915.* **2** A young hobo; an inexperienced or innocent youth. *Hobo use.* **3** An ignoramus. *Maritime use.*

gazoozle   *v.t.* To cheat. 1946: "Private detectives support his contention that he was gazoozled." D. Runyon, *synd. newsp. col.,* Aug. 5. *Whimsically formed from "bamboozle." Prob. a Runyonism.*

g. d.   **g.-d.**   *adj.* God-damned. 1951: "The biggest g. d. engine in the West." S. Longstreet, *The Pedlocks,* 64. *A euphem. The "g" for "God" is seldom capitalized.* See Appendix, Shortened Words.

g'dong = **gedunk.**

geared up   Drunk. *Not common.* See Appendix, Drunk.

gear-jammer   *n.* A bus driver; a truck driver. *c1935.*

gedunk   **g'dong**   *n.* Sweets, dessert; esp. ice cream or pudding. 1946: "In addition to being shown the 16-inch turrets ... the cadets were 'shown' chocolate sundaes from the 'gedunk' stand back aft." N.Y. *Times,* Aug. 11, 3/3. *W.W.II USN use.*

gee   *n.* **1** A fellow; a guy. 1930: "He was the mayor, and he was one smart gee." J. T. Farrell, 162. **Front gee** = a blind used by pickpockets; **hip gee** = a guy in the know, or who can be trusted; **mob gee** = a member of a mob; **wrong gee** = man who can't be trusted. *From the first letter of "guy," reinforced by an imitated French pronunciation.* Cf. **gee whiz.** → **2** The leader of a gang of prison or reformatory inmates; an aggressive or influential prisoner. *Underworld use.* **3** A gallon of liquor. *Hobo use.* **4** Money. **Hip gee** = smart money. See **G.**   *v.t.* To rob.   *exclam.* = **Jesus!** 1857: *DAE.* 1949: "Willy: And don't say 'Gee.' 'Gee' is a boy's word. A man walking in for fifteen thousand dollars does not say 'Gee!'" A. Miller, *Death of a Salesman,* 65. *A very common and very mild euphem., based on the first syllable of "Jesus." Used absolutely to express surprise or the like.*

Geechee   [derog.]   *n.* **1** A Southern American Negro. → **2** The dialect, habits, culture, or beliefs of the American Negro living in the South. *Used derisively. From "Gullah," the creolized dialect of Negro slaves and their descendants. Most often*

211 Gent

used in eastern Ala., Ga., and the
Carolinas.

Geechie   Cheeckee [derog.]   *n.* A
native girl; a girl native to the Pacific
islands occupied by the U.S. Armed
Forces in W.W.II. *W.W.II. Armed
Forces, esp. USN, use. Prob. from the
Japanese "Geisha" or from "Geechee" = a
Bahamas Negro.*

geed up   g'd up   *adj.* 1 Crippled;
said of a person, esp. a beggar. **2** Battered;
old; said of a coin. *Hobo use.* **3** Under
the influence of, or elated by, drugs.
Narcotic addict use.

geedus   geetis   geetus   *n.* Money.
c1935. Underworld use. 1943: "The
pitchmen must give the store a 40% cut
on the 'geedus.' . . . "Zolotow, *SEP*, 13.
Pitchman use.

gee-gee   *n.* 1 A horse, esp. a race
horse; specif., an inferior or no better
than average race horse. *Common horse-
racing use.* 1946: "I like to follow the
gee-gees. . . ." Evans, *Halo in Blood*, 7.
2 = **gigi.** See Appendix, Reduplications.

geek   *n.* 1 A carnival or circus
performer, considered a freak, who
performs sensationally disgusting acts
that a normal person would not, e.g.,
eating or swallowing live animals.
*Carnival and some circus use; fairly
widely known. The geek has a low status
in the carnival and is usu. considered
mentally deranged or perverted.* **2** A snake
charmer. *c1925; carnival and circus use.*
→ **3** A sideshow freak, usu. spurious.
Carnival and circus use. → **4** A "half
man, half animal" sideshow performer
of gory, cannibalistic feats, such as
eating live snakes, biting off the heads
of chickens, etc. *c1935 carnival use.* →
5 A degenerate; one who will do anything, however disgusting, in order to
satisfy or get money to satisfy degenerate
desires. *Often used fig., as an insult.* **6** A
drunk.

**geek it   To fail; to surrender; specif.,
to get knocked out in a prize fight. 1939:
"I put him with the punching bag, Joe
Grosher . . . and my guy geeks it in the
first good smack he gets." Runyon.
Not common.

geep   *n.* 1 = **wolf.** 1940: "Hesitating
a split second lest her suppliant turn
out to be a geep, or wolf, Miss Prim
surrenders . . . and joins the gavotte."
S. J. Perelman, *New Yorker*, Sept. 14,
19/1. *Not common.* **2** A sailor who jumps
ship in order to work for higher pay as
a longshoreman. *Longshoreman use.*

**geepo   *n.* A stool pigeon. 1951: "In

the underworld the most of them are all
geepos." Morris Lipsius, *New Yorker*,
Dec. 1, 106. See Appendix, —o ending.

geerus   *n.* A policeman. *c1890; not
common. Obs.*

geese [derog.]   *n.pl.* Jews. 1939: "I consider this disrespectful, like calling Jewish
people mockies, or Heebs, or geese."
Runyon. *Not common.*

**geets   *n.pl.* Dollars; money; purchas-
ing power; that which "gets" or buys
things. 1957: "Geets—Money." E. Horne,
*For Cool Cats and Far-Out Chicks. Some
far-out and beat use.* Cf. **gelt.**

geetus   geetis   See geedus.

gee whiz   An armed pickpocket. *Underworld use. Not common since pickpockets
seldom are armed.* Cf. **gee, whiz.   Gee
whiz   Gee whizz   *exclam.* = **gee!**
1888: *DAE.* 1922: "Awful good to get
back to civilization! Gee whiz, those
Main Street burgs are slow." S. Lewis,
Babbitt, reprinted in *The American
Twenties*, 230. *Now often used mockingly
to indicate that the surprise or its object
is insignificant.*

geezed   all geezed up   1 Drunk.
2 Under the influence of narcotics.

geezer   *n.* 1 A fellow or guy; usu. an
unknown, old, and eccentric man. 1941:
"It gave him all kinds of confidence,
just to hear the big geezer spout."
J. Lilienthal, *Horse Crazy*, 15. *Often in
the phrase,* **old geezer.** 1943: "He is a
tall geezer with chin whiskers." H. A.
Smith, *Putty Knife*, 150. *Since c1900.*
2 A drink of strong liquor. **3** An injection
or inhalation of a narcotic. *Drug addict
use.*

geezle   *n.* A man. *Not common.*

**geezo   *n.* A prisoner, a convict; esp.
an old or experienced prisoner who has
been in prison for a long time. *Prob.
from "geezer."*

geld   *n.* = **gelt.

**gelt   *n.* Money. 1859: Matsell. 1930:
"To let you guys get away with the gelt?"
Weeks, *Racket*, 29. *From the German.*

general   *n.* 1 Anyone in authority, as
a boss, school principal, head of a
household, or the like. **2** A railroad
yardmaster. *Railroad use.*

general's car   A wheelbarrow. *W.W.II
Army use. Not common.*

**geneva   *n.* Gin, a contr. of "Geneva
liquor." *Not common.*

**gent   *n.* Orig. a gentleman; now any
man. 1893: "Two clipped words there
are which have no friends—*gents* and
pants." Brander Matthews in *Harper's*,

July, 306/2. 1951: "A hefty, tough-talking gent of not quite 50 named W. Walter Watts [deputy administrator of the Defense Production Administration]." P. Edson, NEA, Aug. 9.

gentleman will take a chance, the Hash; an order of hash. *Lunch-counter use, used in relaying an order.*

gents, the *n.sing.* A public rest room for men; the john. *Because many such rest rooms have a "Gents" sign on them, to distinguish them from the "Ladies' room."*

George   george *expl., exclam.* An expression denoting the speaker's awareness or appreciation of any extraordinary, remarkable, or attractive thing or person. *Orig. pop. by comedian Jerry Lester on his network television program, "Broadway Open House," c1950.* 1900: "George, that's fine." Dreiser, *Carrie. Most common c1950, from the then pop. adj. "george." Prob. from "By George." adj.* Psychologically satisfying; perfect for a specific use or mood. *Associated with early bop talk, this use was pop. with several television and radio comedians, and later with teenagers. Basically, however, it must be considered as synthetic. n.* **1** An automatic pilot in an airplane. *Some commercial and Air Force pilot use. Prob. from the expression "Let George do it" = let someone else assume the responsibility.* **2** Anyone or anything remarkable or satisfying; anyone or anything that is "George" (adj.). 1952: "At the moment something that used to be known as the cat's whiskers is now called 'sly, really neat, George,' or 'deadly boo.'" H. Boyle, AP, June 30. *Wide fad use c1950; mainly teenage use.* **3** A theater usher. *Rock-and-roll use since c1950.   adj.* **1** Wise; mentally alert; shrewd. *Some c1920 hobo use.* **2** Fine, good, wonderful, excellent, pleasant, enjoyable; jake, swell. 1952: "That's real george of you to lend a hand like this, Sue!" M. Blosser, *synd. comic strip,* "Freckles," June 23. 1956: "When *everything is George,* everything is all right, and *George* is like saying Right." S. Longstreet, *The Real Jazz Old and New,* 150. *An example of how, by a synthetic, repeated, laugh-evoking use by a comedian, a word may become very common for a brief period, esp. a fad word of teenagers.*

George do it, let   Let someone else do it. *Said in avoiding responsibility. Common c1920 and during W.W.II when the term implied a lack of responsibility in helping the war effort.*

George Eddy   A customer who does not tip. *Lunch-counter use. Not common.*

George Washington pie   Cherry pie. *Synthetic.*

geranium *n.* **1** An attractive person; a pretty girl. **2** Anything easy or choice. *Some c1900 college use. Obs.   —s n.pl.* Cabbage served at meals. *Logger use. Not common.*

German goiter   A protruding stomach, as from being a beer drinker. *Used humorously.* Cf. **beerbelly.**

get   For phrases beginning with "get," see under principal word of phrase.

get *v.t.* **1** To annoy or bother someone. 1867: *DAE. Colloq.* **2** To understand or comprehend a person or an idea. 1907: *DAE.* 1942: "Do you get me?" Z. Hurston. 1944: "I don't get it." Ford, *Phila. Murder,* 153. **3** To return malice; to force retribution; specif., to harm, beat up, kill, or cause another trouble or failure from ill will or malice toward him. *Colloq.* 1936: "Billy the Kid, at twenty-three years of age, had committed twenty-three murders, and had made the question of his extermination a political issue in New Mexico. Incidentally, the sheriff, elected to 'get' him, loaded a weapon and 'got' him." P. A. Rollins, *The Cowboy,* 52.   *n.* **1** The progeny of a thoroughbred animal. *Dial.* **2** Profit; the "gate." *Lit., that money which has been received or gotten, reinforced by a mispronunciation of "gate."* **3** The route taken by robbers fleeing with loot. 1950: "The get, or getaway route." DeBaun, 74.

getalong *n.* One's gait; one's peculiar way of walking. *Dial.*

getaway   get-away *n.* **1** An escape, as from the police; the act of fleeing the scene of a crime. *Used lit. and fig.* 1907: "A world of 'pinches' and 'get-aways.' . . ." Jack London, *The Road,* 159. 1930: "He will make his getaway." Lavine, *Third Degree,* 38. *Orig. underworld and hobo use; now used fig. One makes a getaway from a person or task one wishes to avoid.* **2** A train, plane, or car used in a getaway. *Underworld use; obs.   adj.* Used for making a getaway. 1930: "The stolen get-away Cadillac car. . . ." Lavine, *Third Degree,* 129.

getaway day   The last day of a horse-racing track's meeting for the season. 1956: "GETAWAY DAY—The last day of a race meeting." T. Betts, *Across the Board,* 315. *Common horse-racing use.*

get lost   Lit. and fig. = "go away."

getter = **go-getter.**

get-together   *n.* A meeting or gathering, usu. social. *Colloq.*

getty-up   *n.* A racehorse. *Not common.*

get-up   *n.* **1** The night before the day, or the morning of the day a prisoner, finishes his sentence; a release from prison. *Since c1915, archaic underworld use.* **2** Clothing and face make-up, esp. if either or both are stylish or extreme; a uniform or costume. 1930: "What do you think of the get-up?" Burnett, *Iron Man,* 94. *Colloq.* **3** = **get up and go** (under **up**).   **get up**   End a jail sentence.

ghost   *n.* **1** The treasurer of a theater or theatrical company. 1934: *Web.:* "the ghost walks" = it is pay day. *Theatrical* slang. **2** One who writes a book or article for pay by another who receives credit for the writing. **3** In telecasting, a secondary image on a television screen, formed by two impulses reaching the circuitry, one the direct beam, the other a reflected beam.   *v.t.* To write something, as a book, usually for pay, for another person whose name appears as author. 1952: "I 'ghosted' my wife's cook-book." Paul Darrow in *N.Y. Times Bk. Rev.,* Mar. 9, 2.

ghost story   A plausible tale invented to deceive. *Not common.*

G. I.   GI   *adj.* **1** Of general or government issue; said of clothing and equipment issued to personnel of the Armed Forces. *Thus "G. I. shoes," "G. I. soap," "G. I. trucks," and the like. Army use since c1935; common Army use by c1940. Very wide W.W.II use.* → **2** Of, required by, assoc. with the Army or Army life. *Thus "G. I. haircut," "G. I. manners," "G. I. complaint," or the like. Abbr. for "general issue" or "government issue," but see "G. I. can" for another possible origin.* See Appendix, Shortened Words. 1957: "The Crew Cut is the big brother of what was once ridiculed as a G. I. haircut but was carried over into civilian life, with a dash of nostalgia." H. Mitgang, *About— Men's Haircuts. Common Army use since c1942. Some W.W.II use.* **3** Done according to Army regulations; in a military manner; strict in enforcing or complying with Army regulations. *Army use since c1942.* **4** Commonplace, routine; inferior; lousy. *Army use since c1942. The above four uses were widely known in the Army during W.W.II and to civilians as well.* **5** For soldiers or veterans of W.W.II; veteran of W.W.II. 1950: "25-year-old GI graduate student at the University of Wichita. . . ." AP, July 22. *Civilian use during and after W.W.II.*   *n.* **1** An enlisted man, a common soldier; esp. an infantry private; a soldier who is neither an officer nor a noncommissioned officer. *Orig. Army use, esp. by officers, at beginning of W.W.II.* → **2** A soldier; any soldier or member of the Army. 1950: "The GIs fought furiously to hold Taejon." AP, July 21. *Wide use during and since W.W.II. The most common use.* **3** A veteran, esp. an Army veteran of W.W.II. *Common.*   *v.t.* To scrub with brush and soap; to clean or polish or straighten. *Army use during and since W.W.II.*

G.I. can   *n.* **1** A large iron garbage can, or can or barrel for ashes and refuse. *Some Army use since c1920. This seems to have been the earliest use of "G.I." (adj.) and to have been abbreviated from "galvanized iron" rather than from "general issue" or "government issue." If so, "galvanized iron" may be the actual root for "G.I." or at least a reinforcement for the use of "G.I."* See Appendix, Shortened Words. **2** A large artillery shell. *Some c1930–c1940 Army use. Obs.*

giddy-apper   *n.* A Western movie. 1943: "The horse opera (known as giddy-appers). . . ." H. A. Smith, *Putty Knife,* 143. *Not common. From "giddap," the order to a horse to move or move faster.*

gidget   *n.* A gadget. *From "gadget."*

gieve   *n.* = **jive.** *Pronounced gi-eve.*

gift   *v.t.* To give; to present a gift to a person. 1951: "Actors who gifted them with more than 10% commissions. . . ." A. Green, *Show Biz,* 570.

gift of gab   **1** The ability to talk persuasively. **2** The ability to talk, or habit of talking, fluently, fast, or often.

gig   *n.* **1** A child's pacifier or any object, as a cloth square, spoon, or the like, used as a toy; any object to which a small child is attached and with which he likes to play; any object treated by a child as a fetish; a gigi or ju-ju. *Orig. Negro slave and Southern use. From "gigi," the word is very well known to about 35% of the population, unheard of by the rest.* **2** [sometimes taboo] The rectum. *From "gigi." Used euphem. by some children, as part of their bathroom vocabulary, but not common to all children. Used by some male adults [taboo] as a euphem. for "ass" in such expressions as* *"up your gig."* **3** [taboo] The vagina. From *"gigi." Not cómmon. Prob. Southern use.* **4** A party, a good time; esp. an uninhibited party; occasionally but not often, an amorous session, necking party, or even a sexual orgy between a man and a woman. c1915 [1954]: "Cornet players used to pawn their instruments when there was a lull in funerals, parades, dances, gigs and picnics." L. Armstrong, *Satchmo, My Life in New Orleans,* 100. 1958: "Life is a Many Splendored Gig," a song title. **5** A jam session; a jazz party or gathering; a party or gathering of jazz musicians or enthusiasts. *Orig. swing use.* 1920 [1954]: "Kid Ory had some of the finest gigs, especially for the rich white folk." L. Armstrong, *Satchmo, My Life in New Orleans,* 141. **6** Specif., an engagement or job for a jazz musician or musicians, esp. a one-night engagement. 1950: "If I ask you to go out on a gig, it's thirty-five or forty dollars for that night." A. Lomax, *Mr. Jelly Roll,* 204. 1954: "On a gig, or one night stand." L. Armstrong, *Satchmo, My Life in New Orleans,* 221. **7** Something, as a jazz arrangement, that is satisfying or seems perfect. *Orig. swing use.* **8** A fishing spear; a pronged fork, as used for catching fish, frogs, and the like. 1946: "The subjects' faces and the gig were in the shadows." Photo caption, showing two persons with pronged forks posed by a stream, *Free Lance Photography,* 196. **9** An unfavorable report; a demerit; a reprimand. *Army and some student use since c1940. The relations, if any, between a child's pacifier or fetish, the rectum and vagina, a party, a sex orgy, jazz music, a pronged fork, and a reprimand are most interesting, and lie in the field of psychology rather than of etymology.* See **gigi.** **10** An old car; a hot rod. *Hot rod use since c1950. From earlier "gig" = a one-horse carriage.* *v.t.* To stick, specif. with a pronged fork or gigger for catching fish, frogs, and the like. *v.i.* To play a musical instrument, specif. in a jazz band; to participate in a jam session. 1956: "Gave him a clarinet to gig on." *Metronome Year Book,* 39. 1957: "I [Dizzy Gillespie] forgot whether we're gigging in Basin St. or Buenos Aires. . . . We're just playing music for the people." John "Dizzy" Gillespie, "The Gillespie Plan," *Jazz World,* March, 5. *Jazz musicians' use.*

giggle bottle   A liquor bottle. 1952: "The St. Louis manager . . . added, 'But I never lifted the curfew or brought out a giggle bottle.'" AP, Aug. 27. *Not common.*

giggle juice   **1** Champagne. **2** = **giggle water.** *Not common.*

giggle smoke   A marijuana cigarette.

giggle water   Liquor. 1951: "[Buster Crabbe] not only crashed television . . . but has invaded the giggle water places." Hy Gardner, N.Y. *Her. Trib.,* Dec. 12, 27/3.

giggle weed   Marijuana. *Addict use, never common.*

gigi   gi-gi   gee-gee   *n.* **1** Any object, whether a toy or a common household object, cloth square, string, or the like, which a child adopts as his favorite, uses as a toy, pets, takes to bed with him, and treats as a fetish; a child's pacifier. → **2** Any object, such as a string, a pencil, or the like, with which a person habitually plays as a nervous habit. *Both meanings from the Gullah "gri-gri" = the doll-like image used in voodoo rituals, as the image of a person, in which pins are stuck to cast an evil spell. Orig. New Orleans creole U.S. use.* **3** [taboo] The vagina. **4** [taboo] The rectum. *Usu. in the term "up your gigi." This is one of several psychologically interesting words, used in ref. to both the vagina and the rectum.* See Appendix, Reduplications.

G.I. Joe   A typical or representative soldier of W.W.II; a soldier; a G.I. *Wide W.W.II use. From "G.I." plus "Joe" = fellow.*

gil   *adj.* Insincere; phony.   **—guy** *n.* A thingamajig. 1948 U.S. maritime use. De Kerchove, *Maritime Dict. Since c1925.*   **—hickey**   *n.* = **gilguy.** *Navy use.* Cf. **doohickey.**   **—hooley** *n.* **1** A country person; an insincere or phony person. **2** A thingamajig. 1947: "I forgot to press the hickeymadoodle on the gilhooley." Billy Rose, *synd. newsp. col.,* Jan. 2. **3** The skidding of a moving automobile until it faces the direction opposite from the way it has been going. *Auto racer use.*

gillion   *n.* Any very large number. Cf. **jillion, zillion.**

gills   *n.pl.* **1** The human mouth. **2** The lower part of the human face. 1944: "Abigail lay there getting weaker and paler and bluer-gilled." Ford, *Phila. Murder,* 142. Cf. **blue around the gills.**

gills, blue (green) around the   **1** Nauseated; usu. nauseated for an emotional or psychological reason such as fear or disgust at an unappetizing or

horrible sight. **2** Seasick, whether nauseated or not. **3** Showing the effects of
having consumed too much food or
alcoholic beverage, whether nauseated
or not.

gilly   *n.* **1** A small circus traveling in
cars. **2** A vehicle hired to transport
circus or theatrical equipment.

Gilroy's kite   See **higher than Gilroy's kite.**

gimmick   *n.* **1** A gadget or thingamajig; a small, ingenious device that is
useful in itself or makes a larger device
more useful. *Not common.* → **2** Any
trick, secret device, or gadget by which
a pitchman, gambler, or the like cheats
the public or stimulates business. 1947:
"A   new   gimmick—infra-red   contact
lenses which . . . enabled a card player
to read markings on the backs of cards."
Billy Rose, *synd. newsp. col.*, July 22.
Orig. circus, carnival, and gambler use.
Cf. **gaff.** → **3** Any unusual attraction,
accessory, trimming, or feature, whether
useful or useless, added to legitimate
merchandise, such as a car or garment,
to cause a change in style and attract
customers. → **4** Part of a plan or
venture that can mean success or
failure; the main selling point or a
major flaw. **5** A selfish motive; the way
in which a person hopes to benefit from
a seemingly altruistic deed or plan, or
from an obviously deceptive or unethical
plan; one's angle.

gimmies, the   *n.*   Acquisitiveness;
selfishness. 1941: "They got . . . da gimmies." "Always take, never give."
Cain, *M. Pierce*, 217. *From "give me."*

gimp   *n.* **1** A limp. **2** A lame or
deformed person; specif., one who walks
with a limp. 1929: "Jack . . . would
never hit a cripple. He'd just kick a gimp
in the good leg and leave him lay. . . ."
John K. Winkler, *New Yorker*, Feb. 9,
38/1. *Orig. hobo and underworld use.*
3 Vitality; ambition. *Now dial.*

gimper   *n.* A very competent, efficient,
dependable Air Force man. *U.S. Air
Force use.*   *v.i.* To limp. 1932: "She
. . . goes gimping away." Runyon.

gimp stick   *n.* A crutch or cane.

ginch   *n.* A girl or woman. Cf. **gaunch,
wench.** *Not common.*

ginger   *n.*   Vigor;   vitality;   spirit;
enthusiasm. 1945: "A . . . redhead . . .
imbued with an effervescent quality
that used to be called 'ginger.'"
L. F. McHugh. *Colloq; somewhat archaic.*
—bread   *n.* Money. *Introduced by
Eng. colonists; never common.*

ginhead   *n.* A drunkard. 1932: "A
busted romance that makes her become
a ginhead." Runyon, 89. Cf. **wino.**

gink   *n.* Any man or fellow; a guy;
esp. an old and eccentric or unkempt
man. 1951: "Does a gink in Minsk suffer
less from an appendectomy? . . ." Hal
Boyle, AP, May 17.

gin mill   gin-mill   ginmill   *n.*
1 Any cheap saloon, bar, or nightclub;
orig. a speakeasy. 1922: "There still are
boobs, alack, who'd like the old-time
gin-mill back." S. Lewis, *Babbitt*, reprinted in *The American Twenties*, 227.
2 Any kind of public drinking place, as a
saloon. 1928: "My gin-mill keeper
friend. . . ." D. Purroy. 1943: "In some
gin mill where they know the bartender."
Schumach, N.Y. *Times. Until c1920, the
term had a connotation of cheap, rowdy,
or dilapidated.*

ginned   Drunk. 1924: "Hold me up,
kid; I'm ginned." Marks, *Plastic Age*,
213. *Since c1890. More common c1920
than at present.*

ginned up   **1** Drunk. *Since c1900;
not common.* **2** Dressed up. *c1900. Not
common. Obs.*

ginny   Ginny   *n.* A glamorous co-
ed. *College use; not common.*

ginzo   guinzo   *n.* **1** Any foreigner
or foreign-born citizen. 1931: "He's a
Roumanian or some kinda guinzo."
J. Sayre, *Hex*, 413. **2** Specif., an Italian
or a person of Italian birth. 1939: "He
is nothing but a ginzo out of Sacramento, and his right name is Carfarelli."
Runyon. *Prob. from "Guinea."* **3** A
fellow; a guy. 1949: "Then I meet this
ginzo with her doorkey in his hand."
Chandler, *Little Sister*, 163f.

gip   *n.* = **gyp.**

G. I. party   A session of cleaning,
scrubbing, and polishing; house-cleaning.
*Some W.W.II Army use; a little civilian
use after W.W.II.* See **G.I.**

giraffe   *n.* A person who necks.
*College use; somewhat synthetic and never
common. c1930.*

girene   *n.* = **gyrene.**

girk   *v.t.* To cheat. *Not common.* Cf.
jerk.

girl   *n.* In cards, a queen of any suit.
See **B-girl, V-girl.**   **—ie**   *n.* A
girl; esp. a chorus girl. 1917: "This
girlie and her mother." S. Lewis in
SEP, Oct. 20, 67. See Appendix, —ie
ending.

girl friend   A female sweetheart; a
best girl. *Since c1930, so common as to be
standard speech.*

girlie show   Entertainment or a show whose main attraction is scantily clad girls. *Orig. applied to crude, somewhat illegal shows, tending toward the obscene; now used in ref. to any legitimate show featuring attractive females.* 1950: "Mr. Mike Todd . . . has produced a colossal spectacle and girlie show. . . ." Brooks Atkinson, N.Y. *Times*, July 9, 1/1.

G. I. shits [taboo]   Diarrhea, esp. diarrhea caused by dysentery. *Wide W.W.II Army use, some postwar civilian use.*

gismo   **gizmo**   *n.* **1** = **gadget. 2** = **gimmick.** 1956: "GISMO—A supposedly secret formula, gimmick, or angle, that assures success or at least affords an advantage in gambling; a word that insinuated itself into racing jargon in the 1950's; origin unknown to racing men." T. Betts, *Across the Board*, 315. **3** Any object; specif. a gadget or gimmick; usu. a device whose name one does not know. 1947: " 'What's this gizmo?' I asked. 'The hand brake,' she said." Billy Rose, *synd. newsp. col.*, Jan. 2. *Became common cW.W.II, may orig. have been USN use.* → **4** A person whose name one does not know; a fellow; a guy.

gitbox   *n.* A guitar. *Affected among jazz musicians.*

gits   *n.* Courage; perseverance; guts; fig., any trait that "gets" results or victories. 1958: "Having been advised that Calumet [a racing stable] has some promising two year olds, them that has gits, I went to look at them." A. Minor, *New Yorker*, July 10, 77.

git up and git   *Dial. for "get up and go."*

give   For phrases beginning with "give," see under principal word of phrase.

giveaway   *n.* **1** Anything that betrays or reveals unwittingly. *Colloq.* **2** A gift, from a business concern, given to customers or patrons to increase sales or patronage or to gain publicity.

gives   See **What gives?**

gives me a pain, [someone, something] Is disgusting, aggravating, disliked, or frustrating. *Usu. said of a person.*

gizmo = **gismo.**

g. j.   An order of a glass of grapefruit juice. *Some lunch-counter use in relaying orders.*

glad eye (glad hand), give [someone] the   To greet or look at someone in a friendly, welcoming manner. Cf. **glad eye, glad hand.**

glad eye, the   A glance, look, or expression of friendliness or welcome. *Usu. in "give [someone] the glad eye."*

glad hand, the   Lit., a warm handshake; fig., a warm welcome, esp. a warm welcome or cordial reception that is overly friendly or insincere. 1941: "He gave me that glad-hand business." Schulberg, *Sammy*, 43. **—er** One who is demonstrative in his personal contacts; one who acts more friendly or more optimistic than necessary; one, as a politician, who pretends friendliness.

glad lad   An attractive youth. *Some c1940 student use. Obs.* See Appendix, Rhyming Slang.

glad rags   **1.** One's best or fanciest clothes; one's party clothes. *Common.* 1912: "I blew myself to a few glad rags." Johnson, *Stover at Yale*, 162. *Since c1900.* **2** Formal evening wear, men's or women's.

glahm = **glom.**

glamor girl   **glamour girl**   A professional beauty, a girl or woman known to the public as glamorous; specif., a glamorous movie actress, model, starlet, chorus girl, or the like. 1956: "The glamor girl was sitting at the bar alone. It's been about 17 years since she first began to get her name in the papers as one of the stars of the younger café set. She was a beautiful thing when she started her career as a glamor girl and she still retains her basic figure and good looks." R. Sylvester, N.Y. *Daily News*, Sept. 13, 63.

glamor puss   **glamour puss**   A handsome, popular youth. 1941: "We called them superswoopers instead of glamourpusses." P. Gallico in *SEP*, June 14, 22/1. *Some c1940 student use.*

glass   *n.* **1** Sparkling imitation jewelry or gems. **2** A drunk. *Never common. Obs.* **—ie** *n.* A playing marble made of glass. *Boy use.* See Appendix, **—ie** ending.

glass —   See Appendix, Prefixes and Prefix Words.

glass arm   **1** In baseball, the stiff arm of a player, usu. a pitcher. *Now seldom used.* **2** Telegrapher's cramp; a temporary, partial paralysis of the wrist and arm caused by continuous manual operation of a telegraph or ham radio transmitting key. *Telegrapher and radio amateur use; archaic.* → **3** A poor worker; a weakling. *Longshoreman use.*

glasses on, have [one's]   To be haughty or formal. *Some Harlem Negro use.*

glass jaw   A prize fighter's jaw that cannot stand a hard punch. 1921: "The glass-jawed bimbo which can't take it and dives into a clinch when shook up. . . ." Witwer, *Leather*, 162. *Very common prize fight use.*

glassy eyed   Drunk.

glaum   *n.* A look or glance.   *v.t.* To look at; to glance at. See **glom.**

gleeps   The eyes. *Not common.*   **Gleeps** A nondenotative exclamation used in lieu of profanity. *Some teenage use.*

glim   *n.* **1** A light, as a lamp or candle; a window, considered as a source of light. "Bring the glim" = turn on the light; "douse the glim" = turn off the light. *Introduced by Eng. colonists; prob. of Irish underworld orig.* → **2** Specif., headlight of an automobile. *Taxi driver and truck driver use.* **3** An eye. *Since c1915. v.t.* To look at something or someone carefully; to examine visually; to see (something). 1933: "I glimmed him with a snuggle-puppy." H. T. Webster. **—mers** *n.pl.* **1** The eyes. **2** Headlights. See **glim.** **—s** *n.pl.* **1** The eyes. **2** Spectacles; eye-glasses. 1947: "Teen-agers' talk. 'Dark glasses, of course, are rimmed dimmed glims.' " *The Academian*, a school paper, quoted by Don Rose in Phila. *Bulletin*, Jan. 21, 13. *Since c1920; orig. hobo and underworld use.*

glim worker   One who sells plain glass eyeglasses. *Carnival and circus use.*

g'obe   *n.* A golf ball. *c1920; obs.*

globes   *n.pl.* The female breasts, considered as sexually attractive. 1954: "I'd even feel Elena's soft globes through her nighty." H. K. Fink, *Long Journey*, 15. *A favorite word of story writers and semi-pornographers. Seldom spoken.*

globule   *n.* A baseball. *Since c1905; now archaic.*

glom   glaum   glahm   *n.* A hand, considered as a tool for grabbing. *v.t.* **1** To grab; to seize; to take hold of. → **2** To steal. 1907: " 'We discovered that our hands were gloved.' 'Where'd ye glahm 'em?' I asked." Jack London, *The Road*, 131. 1951: "Under the pretense of glomming a diamond from the strongbox of a rascally broker . . ." S. J. Perelman, *New Yorker*, Mar. 3, 27/2. *The most common meaning; orig. hobo and underworld use.* *v.i.* To be arrested. *Lit.* = "*to be grabbed by the hand of the law.*" **—mer** *n.* **1** A hand, used for grabbing or stealing. *Since c1930.* → **2** One who uses his hands to grasp things, as a fruit picker. Cf. **mitt-glommer.**

glop   *n.* **1** Unappetizing food, specif. a thick semiviscous mixture. **2** Any

semiviscous liquid. **3** Sentimentality; corn. 1952: "That is very dull. I hate glop." H. Boyle, AP, June 30. *All uses mainly teenage since c1945.*

glory   *n.* A train made up of empty freight cars. *Railroad use.*

glory wagon   The caboose of a railroad train. *Railroad use.*

glow   *n.* A state of moderate intoxication. *Usu. in the phrase,* "*have a glow on.*" "When the party's getting a glow on/ and singing fills the air. . . ." *Pop. college drinking song.*

glowworm   *n.* An amateur photographer. *Synthetic.*

glue   *v.t.* To take; to steal.   *n.* **1** Liquor. *Neither use common.* **2** Money. *Because it keeps body and soul together. Not common.* **—d**   Drunk. *Not common.* **—pot** *n.* **1** A racehorse. 1952: "The Starting Price bookmakers only pay the cost the old gluepot rates when he toes the line." R. C. Ruark, *synd. newsp. col.*, May 20. *Fairly common.* **2** A postoffice. *Not common.*

G-man   *n.* A garbage man. *Jocular W.W.II Army use.*

gnat's eyebrows = **cat's meow.**

gnat's heel   A small amount. *Not common.*

gnat's whistle, the   Anything of superior quality. *Sometimes ironically used.* See **cat's meow.**

go   For phrases beginning with "go," see under principal word of phrase.

go   *n.* **1** A prize fight. 1896: *DAE.* 1930: "A ripsnorting go." Burnett, *Iron Man*, 22. *Colloq.* **2** A chance, opportunity, or try. *Always in* "to have a go at it." **3** A job; a deal; a way of life. *Thus, "I have a very good go here." Not common in U.S.* *v.i.* **1** To die. **2** To go to the bathroom; to excrete. 1949: "You couldn't keep no dog in here anyhow. What would you do when he had to go? Set him in the sink?" N. Algren, *Man with the Golden Arm*, 48. *Euphem., common.* **3** To go on; to occur; to happen or be taking place. 1949: "What goes here?" Burnett, *Jungle*, 193. *v.t.* To spend or pay money. 1950: "I went five bills for that [Chinese vase]." H. Sobol, quoted in *New Yorker*, Nov. 18, 60.   *exclam.* See **go-man-go.** **—er** *n.* Anything that is going, either good or bad. *Orig. bop use c1946; some student use since c1950.* See Appendix, **—er** ending. **—ing** *adj.* **1** Profitable; successful. *Usu. in* "*a going concern,*" *almost always said of a small business or store.* **2** Working, performing, or talking smoothly or adroitly; in full swing. 1919 [1956]: "Every person shall be spared in whose home a jazz-band is in full swing. If everyone has a jazz band going, so much the better." Letter dated March 13, 1919, sent by a jazz enthusiast and psychotic murderer, known as "The Axeman," to the editor of the New Orleans *Times-Picayune*, reprinted in *The Real Jazz Old and New*, by S. Longstreet, 65. → **3** Eliciting a response; having or conveying a mood or feeling; said of a performance, piece of music, party, gathering, or remarkable person or thing. *Orig. c1946 bop use; some student use since c1950.*

go, on the **1** Active; lit., in constant motion. 1955: "I do my best. I'm on the go night and day." C. Willingham, *To Eat a Peach*, 141. → **2** Active socially; caught up in a social whirl.

go-ahead *n.* Consent or approval to proceed. 1951: "She pleaded her case before state officials and got the go-ahead." AP, Lansing, Mich., Nov. 13.

go around together To date the same member of the opposite sex frequently; to be known as friends.

go around with [someone] To date the same member of the opposite sex frequently; to be a friend to a specific person.

goat *n.* **1** A car, esp. an old or souped-up car. *Hot rod and some general teenage use since c1950.* **2** One who takes the blame for another, or for a group's or team's failure or embarrassment; the butt of a joke. *From "scapegoat."* → **2** The junior officer in an Army outfit. *W.W.II use.* **3** A locomotive switch engine. *So called because it butts and shoves cars around. Railroad use.* **4** A racehorse, esp. an inferior racehorse. See **get [one's] goat, old goat.** **—y** *adj.* Awkward; ignorant. *Some Army use.*

goat, get [one's] To annoy a person; to cause anger or frustration. 1908: "A little detraction will 'get their goat' [baseball players']. . . ." R. L. Hartt, *Atlan. Mon.*, Aug., 223/1. 1914: 'But if you 'get his goat' you will rouse his anger. . . ." D. S. Martin, *Living Age*, Aug., 374. *Since c1908. Became common cW.W.I; now colloq.*

gob *n.* **1** A quantity, usu. a large amount. **2** The mouth. 1947: "[Gob] came to the U.S. not from Eng. but directly from Ireland . . . embodied in the phrase *shut your gob* = be silent. It is not used outside this connection,

so far as I know; and *shut your gob* is good Hiberno-English." A. E. Hutson. *Not common.* **3** A USN sailor, usu. an enlisted man. *Became common during W.W.I and has remained the most common word for USN sailor. Now colloq.*

gobble *v.t.* **1** To eat rapidly and hardily. **2** In baseball, to catch a ball.

—digook **—dygook** *n.* Talk or writing which is long, pompous, vague, involved, usually with Latinized words and much professional jargon. *So defined by the word's originator, Maury Maverick, N.Y. Times Mag., May 21, 1944, p. 11.* 1952: "When concrete nouns are replaced by abstractions, simple terms by pseudo-technical jargon, the result is gobbledygook." Watt, *Amer. Rhetoric*, 296. 1954: "Half-English, half-Yiddish gobbledegook intelligible only to experienced dealers." W. R. & F. K. Simpson, *Hockshop*, 135. **—r** [taboo] *n.* A male homosexual, or sexual degenerate or pervert of any kind. *Prison use. In ref. to "eat."*

gobble-pipe *n.* A saxophone. *Synthetic.*

gobo *n.* A black screen used to decrease the light on a movie set or television stage, or to shield a movie or television camera from bright lights and glare. *Movie use since c1925.*

goboon **gobboon** **gaboon** *n.* A spittoon. 1949: "For Antek held to the old days and the old ways. There was plenty of butchershop sawdust along the floor and an old-fashioned golden goboon for every four bar stools." N. Algren, *Man with the Golden Arm*, 57. *Archaic.* 1952: "Amazed that he didn't crown LaGuardia with a brass goboon. . . ." W. Pegler, *synd. newsp. col.*, Mar. 21. *Since c1930.*

gob-stick *n.* A clarinet. *Synthetic.*

go-by, give [someone or something] the To by-pass; to ignore; to refrain or abstain from. 1928: "People . . . become fed up with a slang phrase . . . and resolve to give it the go-by in future. . . ." Greig, *Priscian*, 16f. *Since c1905, now so common as to be standard usage.*

go-cart *n.* **1** The caboose of a railroad train. *Railroad use.* **2** A car.

god-awful *adj.* Extremely objectionable or awful. *Since c1880.*

god box **1** An organ [musical instrument]. **2** A church.

godfer *n.* A child; a kid. *Short form of rhyming sl. "god forbid" = kid.* 1949: "I took the trouble and the godfers for a whisper in the fields before Rosie." John Lardner, *Newsweek*, Oct. 31, 60/3. See Appendix, Rhyming Slang.

go-down   *n.* A basement apartment or room.

go down on [someone] [taboo]   To commit cunnilingus or fellatio with someone. Cf. **eat.**

God's medicine   Narcotic drugs; any specif. narcotic drug. 1949: "The joy-poppers had the will power, they felt, to use God's medicine once or twice a month and forget it the rest of the time." N. Algren, *Man with the Golden Arm*, 31. *Narcotic addict euphem.*

goff   *n.* = **guff.**

go-getter   *n.* **1** An energetic, ambitious person; one who tries hard to succeed. 1949: "He was sometimes enviously referred to as a go-getter, a hot shot, a ball of fire." *Fact Detec. Mysteries*, 21. *Very common.* **2** A stylish or attractive person or thing. *Not common.*

go home! = **hang up, shut up.**

goifa = **greefa.**

going, get   **1** To begin a task or project. *Colloq.* **2** = **get on the ball.**

going over   A physical beating or punishment.

go-it-all   *n.* An automobile, esp. a fast one or a sports car. *Some far out use, not common.*

goiter   See **German goiter.**

go-juice   *n.* Gasoline. *Synthetic.*

gold braid   USN officers. 1945: "It is evident that gold braid doesn't think enough of the order to...." G. W. Hibbitt.

gold brick   **1** A shirker; a loafer, esp. one who makes excuses for avoiding work. *Some W.W.I use; very common during W.W.II. Still in wide use.* **2** An Army second lieutenant appointed from civilian life. *Derog. enlisted men's term, reinforced by gold bar insigne of second lieutenant.* **3** An unattractive girl; a girl who does nothing to make herself attractive. *Some W.W.II use.* **gold-brick**   *v.i.* To avoid work by making excuses. *Some W.W.I use; common W.W.II use.*   *v.t.* To swindle; cheat; take advantage of.   **—er** = **gold brick.** *Not as common as "gold-brick."*

gold-digger   *n.* A girl or woman who befriends or becomes the lover, girl friend, or wife of a man solely for financial or material gain; a girl or woman who will associate only with wealthy men. 1950: "Lorelei Lee ... the crazy-like-a-fox gold-digger...." Billy

Rose, *synd. newsp. col.*, Jan. 9. *Very common since c1925.*

golden bantam   **Golden Bantam** = **corn.** 1950: "Miss Judy Garland is ... adroit and Mr. Gene Kelly makes his feet perform magic. This is strictly Golden Bantam—but good." Bosley Crowther, N.Y. *Times*, Sept. 3, 1/8.

goldfish   *n.* Salmon; usu. canned salmon. *Common in the Army since W.W.I; in the USN cW.W.II.*

goldfish bowl   A place without privacy.

goldilocks   *n.sing.* Any pretty blonde woman or girl. 1955: "Well, thought Jimmy, it won't be [because of] *you,* goldilocks." C. Willingham, *To Eat a Peach*, 167. *Almost always used cynically by a male to indicate rejection and imply that the woman in question is neither as innocent nor as unworldly as Goldilocks, the heroine of the famous children's story.*

gold star   A prize, compliment, victory, high rating, or the like. *From the little gold paper stars for meritorious or diligent work which teachers used to give to pupils or paste on examinations.*

golf   See **African dominoes, barnyard golf.** Cf. **African golf.**

golf ball   A small, white, spherical firecracker, resembling a golf ball, that explodes when thrown against a hard surface, usu. a wall or pavement. *Child use since c1935.*

Golfer   *n.* A Cadillac automobile. *By association with "Caddy" for "Cadillac." Not common.*

golf widow   A wife often left alone while her husband plays golf. *Based on "grass widow."*

go-long   *n.* A police truck used to take arrested persons to jail; a paddy wagon. 1942: "Joe Brown had you all in the go-long last night." Z. Hurston. *Harlem Negro use.*

go-man-go   **go man go**   *exclam.* An expression of encouragement to jazz musicians; an expression of enthusiasm to or rapport with jazz music or musicians. *Orig. a bop term, c1946, shouted by devotees to the musicians as they played particularly adroit solos or close-harmony passages. Now considered passé by jazz groups, but some general teenage use.*

goms   *n.* A policeman. *Perh. from "gumshoe." Underworld use. c1930.*

gon = **gun,** a thief. *Shortened form of Yiddish "gonif" = a thief. "Cannon" = a big or important thief.* Cf. **cannon.**

gon   **gond**   *n.* A gondola railroad car. 1948: "Then a string of gonds went past...." Cain, *Moth*, 78. *Railroad use.*

Gondola

gondola *n.* A stolen car, esp. a sedan. *Underworld use. Not common.* **—s** *n.pl.* Feet. 1932: "The old gondolas are a little extra heavy to shove around. . . ." Runyon. *Not common.*

gone *adj.* **1** Enamored; in love. 1954: "Daisy and I commenced to fall deeply in love with each other. . . . I was so gone over her." L. Armstrong, *Satchmo, My Life in New Orleans*, 152. **2** Under the influence of narcotics (usu.) or whisky (occasionally). 1956: "What they mean by gone is usually high, on reefers or booze, or both." S. Longstreet, *The Real Jazz Old and New*, 151. *Mainly addict use.* → **3** Fig., removed from reality; intent; specif., so much in rapport with, intent on, immersed in, or intense over one's work, performance, ideas, or mode or way of life that one is as if in a trance and unaware of or removed from all extraneous things. 1955: "To listen to Smith toss back his head and pray, gurgling forth a flow of words, a 'gone' expression on his face. . . ." C. Willingham, *To Eat a Peach*, 210. *Orig. and mainly cool use, and applied to cool musicians and devotees in regard to cool jazz music and a cool outlook or way of life.* → **4** Capable of arousing such intense satisfaction that one forgets all else; satisfying; cool; hep. *Cool use.* **5** Old, worn, or damaged past all use or repair. *Colloq.* **6** Orig. cool use = eliciting a pseudo-religious cultural response; cool; intellectually exciting and satisfying; pleasant. *Orig. late bop and cool use. The order of the definitions shows how the word has become more general in meaning as its use spread from cool groups to general usage, esp. to teenage use since c1950.* See **cool.** *part.* **1** Drunk. *Usu. in "about gone," "all gone." Archaic.* **2** = **real gone.** **—r** *n.* A thing or person doomed to destruction; a dying person. 1953: "You'd better pray . . . or you're a goner. . . ." San Diego *Herald*, Aug. 24, 3. 1945: "If they ever sticks their needles in your arm you is just a plain goner." Saxon, et al., *La. Writers' Project*, "Gumbo Ya-Ya, La. Folk Tales," 75.

gonef = **goniff.**

gone on In love with. *Colloq.*

gonfalon *n.* A baseball pennant. *Obs.*

gong *n.* **1** Any military medal worn on the breast of a uniform. *Some W.W.II Armed Forces use.* **2** An opium pipe. 1933: " 'Hitting the gong' . . . 'kicking the gong around.' " Maurer. Cf. **kick the gong around.**

gonger = **gong.**

goniff   gonef   gonof   gonoph   ganef   ganof *n.* A thief; a crook; one who, though not a professional thief, will take advantage of another when in a position to do so; an unethical businessman. 1927: "And who is this arch-gonnif?" Hammett, *Blood Money*, 27. 1934: "Sam the Gonoph." Runyon, 347. 1941: "A gonof-like Glick." Schulberg, *Sammy*, 113. 1951: "A lot of young goniffs (thieves)." S. Longstreet, *The Pedlocks*, 246. *From the Yiddish "goniff" = thief (n.), to steal (v.)* *v.t.* To steal; to cheat; esp. applied to petty thievery.

gonk *n. & v.t.* = **conk.**

gonof   gonoph *n.* = **goniff.**

gonsil *n.* = **gunsel.**

gonus *n.* A stupid fellow. 1842: *DAE.* 1851: Hall, *College Words*, 147. *Student use; obs.*

gonzel *n.* = **gunsel.**

goo *n.* **1** Any sticky, syrupy liquid, emulsion, or semisolid; often applied to mud, cream sauces, and oily cosmetics and hair dressings. 1951: [mud] "Cox also seemed certain of tallying on the hit, but fell in the goo rounding third base and was run down." Dick Young, N.Y. *Daily News*, Aug. 9, C20/3. *Common since c1900.* 1950: "But no goo [petroleum base cosmetic] can be trusted too far. . . . It rubs off. . . . Spreading a layer of goo [oil] on the skin. . . ." Ruth Adler, N.Y. *Times*, July 9, 21/1. **2** Insincere flattery; sweet talk. 1953: "They ladle out the old goo." Bing Crosby, *SEP*, Apr. 4, 30. *v.i.* To talk affectionately. **—by** *n.* Prison food. *Convict use.* **—ey** *n.* **1** Any crisp, browned fat on cooked meat; any sugary mixture, such as may drip from a pie or cake while baking. *Some* Appendix, **—ey** *endings.* **2** Hash. *Some W.W.I Army use.* *adj.* **1** Sticky, creamy, soft, viscous. 1950: "No one 'drinks beer or whisky and eats such sweet gooey stuff [as a banana split] at the same time.' " AP, Feb. 16. *Since c1900.* 1950: "Silly Putty, gooey, pinkish, repellent-looking commodity. . . ." *New Yorker*, Aug. 26, 19/2. 1951: "Give us honest, gooey lemon filling [in lemon pies]." GNS, Nov. 21. *Usu. said of food.* **2** Weird, unusual, odd, unnatural. *Some c1900 use.* **3** Sentimental, romantic, emotional, corny. *Since c1935.*

goober *n.* A peanut. *Prob. from the Gullah. Mainly Southern use, but also heard in other sections of the country.*

goober-grabber   *n.* **1** A native of Georgia. **2** A rustic. *Not common.*

goober grease   **1** Butter. **2** Peanut butter. See **goober.**

good, make   To succeed, esp. to succeed in business. *Colloq.*

good butt   *n.* A marijuana cigarette. *Narcotic addict use.*

goodbyee   good-by-ee   *interj. A prolonged and precious form of the interj. "good-by." Analogous to "indeedy" and "all righty." Intro. from Eng. during W.W.II.*

good deal   **1** A favorable business proposition or arrangement. *Colloq.* → **2** An easy or pleasant job or way of life; anything pleasurable. *Since c1940; W.W.II Armed Forces use; student use.   adv.* Yes; o.k.; I agree.

good egg = **egg.**

gooder   *n.* Any person or thing held in high esteem, as a girl or a joke; a good one. *May be synthetic rustic sl., more often heard on radio and television than in real life.*

good fellow   A stupid boy; a fool. *Said condescendingly. c1850 to present.*

Good God!   *exclam.* An expression of surprise or shock.

good head   An agreeable, personable person; a nice guy. *Orig. West Coast teenager usage, c1950.*

goodie   *n.* **1** A well-behaved convict. *Used in contempt. Convict use. Not common.* → **2** A prissy, self-righteous person; a sissy. **3** Sweets or small gifts. *c1950. Used by adults in a baby-talking voice to simulate the enthusiasm of childhood.* **4** An honest, brave person. *Usu. said humorously.* 1946: "It's much easier to make a gal a baddie than a goodie." *Time,* Dec. 2, 62. *Orig. used humorously to refer to the good heroes and heroines of Western cowboy movies and television shows.* See Appendix, —ie ending.   **—s**   *n.* Any adult foods, drinks, clothing, or objects of art or culture that inspire childish enthusiasm. *Used sarcastically.* 1951: "In Polynesia, the local population took to the goodies of Western culture with avidity . . . to clip bonnets, silk frocks, flintlock muskets, collars, and calendar oleographs." J. Williams, *Fall of the Sparrow,* 144. *Sophisticated use since c1948.*

good Joe   Any agreeable, pleasant, or generous man.

good-looker   *n.* **1** A good-looking person, esp. a woman or girl; a **looker.** 1943: "Is she a good looker?" S. Smith, "The Gumps," *synd. comic strip,* Jan. 29.

c1890 to present. **2** A good-looking animal or object. 1900: "The animal [a horse] was a 'good-looker,' but he hitched badly in his travel. . . ." Arthur T. Vance, *The Real David Harum,* 49.

Good night!   *exclam. A term used to express surprise, disgust, or anger; a euphem. for "Good God!"*

goods, the   *n.* **1** The necessary traits or resources for a given purpose. → **2** A person possessing the required traits or resources; a sincere person. 1924: "She's the real goods." Ada Lewis, *Lit. Digest.* → **3** The desired truth or facts. → **4** Proof of guilt. 1939: "We've got the goods on him." Gardner, *D. A. Draws,* 85. **5** Stolen merchandise; contraband.

good shit [taboo]   **1** = **good deal.** *Usu. used absolutely.* **2** Anything favorable or pleasant, esp. a pleasant task; good fortune.

good show   Any excellent accomplishment, performance, spectacle, or the like. *An expression of extreme satisfaction. Not common. Taken from the W.W.II Brit. Royal Air Force use.*

good ticket   Financially successful. *c1935. Orig. theater use.*

good time   *n.* **1** Time deducted from a prisoner's sentence because of good behavior. *c1870 to present; convict use.* **2** A period of enjoying illegal or immoral acts. *Unlike the standard "good time," both words are pronounced slowly and with the same intonation.*

goody   *n.* A woman who cares for students' rooms. 1851: ". . . Believed to be peculiar to Harvard College." Hall, *College Words,* 147. *Still used at Harvard. Prob. from "goodwife."*

goody-goody   *n.* A prissy, sissified youth or man; a sissy; an effeminate youth or man. "I'm not a mammy boy nor a goody-goody." Johnson, *Varmint,* 10. See Appendix, Reduplications.   *adj.* **1** Decorous; effeminate. *Since c1885.* **2** Excessively good. 1946: "Stewart's . . . playing of what might have been a goody-goody role is a . . . delight." *Time,* Dec., 23, 54/2.

goof   *n.* **1** A stupid, eccentric, or ineffectual man. *Unlike a sap, dope, boob, or jerk, a goof is tragically stupid on all subjects at all times, and his stupidity is not due to lack of experience or innocence and is never funny.* 1921: "Look at the big goof." Witwer, *Leather,* 171. 1951: "This goof is in the army." *Can You Top This?* national radio show, Apr. 10. *Still in freq. use, but extremely common during the 1920's when it was a popular flapper's* *term and during W.W.II.* **2** An insane person. 1941: "He couldn't have acted more like a goof. . . ." Cain, *M. Pierce*, 232. → **3** A substitute or rookie player on an athletic team. *c1925.* → **4** A cellmate; a prison buddy. *c1930; convict use.* → **5** A rookie in the Army. *Some W.W.II Army use.* → **6** Any man; a guy; a fellow. *Not common.* **7** A narcotics addict. *Addict use.* **8** A blunder, mistake, or faux pas. 1956: "We committed an almost unpardonable goof." *Metronome*, Apr., 50. *v.i.* **1** To be a narcotics addict; to be under the influence of narcotics. *Addict use; archaic.* **2** To make a mistake, blunder, or faux pas. 1956: "First be hungry. Then grab any bottle of 'Del Monte' catsup. Pour one cup into a saucepan. From here on you can't goof." Advt., *Look*, Nov. 27. 1956: "*Goof:* to blow a wrong note, or to make a mistake." S. Longstreet, *The Real Jazz Old and New*, 151. *Orig. used by hep people; W.W.II Armed Forces use; common teen-age and student use since c1950.* **3** To day-dream; to give oneself up to reverie. See **goof off.** *v.t.* To fool, josh, or kid a person. 1930–31: "I saw Clara. . . ." "That bitch!" "Don't goof your grandpa. . . ." J. T. Farrell, 162. **—ed** *adj.* Under the influence of a narcotic, specif. marijuana. *Addict use.* **—er**

goopher *n.* **1** = **goof.** 1920: "Don't be a critical goopher or you can't go!" F. S. Fitzgerald, *This Side of Paradise*, 81. See Appendix, —er ending. **2** An Air Force man one step below gimper standing. *Some W.W.I Air Force use.* → **3** A successful or daring fighter pilot. *Some W.W.II Air Force use.* **—iness** *n.* The state of being goofy. 1938: "An unparalleled tolerance for goofi-ness." Liebling, *Back Where*, 205. **—us** *n.* **1** Any small item or thingamajig. → **2** A small calliope played to attract customers to a tent show. *c1915 circus use.* → **3** A rustic; a person easily duped; an easy mark. *c1920. Orig. carnival, circus, and underworld use.* → **4** Nonartistic entertainment, gaudy styles, cheap merchandise, and the like, which is created to be sold to people with unsophisticated tastes. **—y** *adj.* **1** Silly; stupid; foolish; simple-minded. 1921: "A goofy grin." Witwer, *Leather*, 164. 1929: "You must be goofy." "I was a goofy young punk." J. T. Farrell, 150; 151. 1954: "He was the funniest-looking boy, or man—it was hard to tell which he was—she had ever seen. His hair was

bed-dishevelled. He had a couple of days' growth of sparse, blonde beard. And he looked—well, goofy." J. D. Salinger, "Just Before the War with the Eskimos," reprinted in *Manhattan*, 25. **2** Infatuated with, in love with, crazy about. 1922: "I'm goofy about Jack." Phila. *Eve. Bulletin*, Mar. 8. 1953: "He is goofy over a girl." H. Boyle, AP, Jan. 7.

goof at To look at; to be entranced by. 1952: "I'm goofing at all the things I can have." *Oral*, woman in a cafeteria line.

goof ball **1** Any barbiturate used as a narcotic drug by addicts. *Addict use.* See **goof.** **2** Marijuana; a portion of marijuana. → **3** A preparation or portion of a narcotic. 1952: "Detectives . . . found 100 goof balls in one room, 275 in another, and needle eyedroppers and cellophane bags used to package the drug. A goof ball is a narcotics prepara-tion which is burned on a spoon and inhaled." Anthony Marino, N.Y. *Daily News*, Aug. 11, C4/3. → **4** A narcotics addict. → **5** A stupid awkward person; a chronic blunderer, one who makes frequent mistakes. **6** An odd person; an eccentric. **7** A tranquilizer pill; a sleeping pill. 1956: ". . . He became a nerve-pill addict . . . took over three hundred goof balls." Al Stump, "He's Never Out of Trouble," *SEP*, Aug. 18, 44. **—y ball** *n.* Nembutal. Cf. **goof ball.**

goof-butt = **goofy-butt.**

goof off **1** To make a mistake, blunder, or faux pas; to goof. *Some c1940 use. Not now common.* → **2** To idle away one's time; to refuse to work or think seriously; to evade work; to idle or loaf. 1958: "[School] closed for the summer. My goofing off in the final period had knocked down a possible A average, but I passed." *Life*, Apr. 28, 83. *Common W.W.II Armed Forces use; some W.W.II and after civilian use, esp. among students.* **3** To complain or object. *Not common. In most of the above uses "goof off" is a milder syn. for "fuck off" or "fuck up"; it is not a euphem., however, as "goof off" has an independent existence, and always implies a milder, less vehement, less serious meaning than "fuck off" or "fuck up."* **goof-off** *n.* **1** A chronic blunderer or idler. **2** A period of rest and relaxation; a rest period. Cf. **coffee break.**

goof up *v.t.* To quash, kill, queer; to put out of working order. *v.i.* To blunder.

goofy-butt *n.* A marijuana cigarette.

goog *n.* A black eye. *Not common. In the U.S. this word never means egg, as it does in Australia.*

google *n.* The Adam's apple; the throat. *Archaic and dial.*

googlum *n.* = **goozlum.**

googly *adj.* Protruding or rolling. 1934: "A short, chubby guy, with big, round googly eyes." Runyon, 370. *n.* A bomb. *Very little W.W.II Air Force use, from the pop. Australian airmen use, who borrowed the term from the cricket field.*

googol *n.* Fig., an astronomically large number; a zillion. *Since c1950. Not common. From the specif. math. use = a "1" followed by one hundred zeros.*

goo-goo   gu gu *n.* **1** [derog.] A Filipino. *Navy use. c1925.* **2** [derog.] A native of a Pacific island occupied by U.S. Forces during W.W.II. **3** Crazy, insane; gaga. See Appendix, Reduplications.

goo-goo eyes Amorous or possessive glances. *Often in* make **goo-goo eyes at.** 1923: "Barney Google with the Goo Goo Googly Eyes." *Pop. song.*

googs *n.pl.* Eyeglasses; spectacles. *From "goggles." Pitchman use.*

gooh *n.* A prostitute. *Underworld use, archaic; boy street gang use since c1945.*

gook *n.* **1** Dirt, grime, sludge, sediment. 1956: "'Glim' gets the gook off!" Advt., N.Y. *Daily News,* Oct. 3, 49. *Very common.* **2** Any viscous, semiliquid sauce or dressing. **3** Cheap, inferior merchandise. *Not common.* **4** [derog.] Generically, a native of the Pacific islands, Africa, Japan, China, Korea, or any European country except England; usu. a brown-skinned or Oriental non-Christian. 1951: "*Gook* was used during World War II at many widely separated stations to refer to natives." *Word Study,* May, 7/1. 1951: "It just ain't so that a Russian can take it on the chin better than an American or a Zulu or a gook or a goum." H. Boyle, AP, May 17. 1951: "A soldier in Korea reported, 'Two gooks nearly shot me with burp guns,' but Army headquarters frowned on the use of *gooks,* and held that the word provided fuel for propaganda, since Asiatics were insulted by the word." *Word Study,* Feb., 4/1. *Wide W.W.II Army use; some Korean Army use. adj.* Foreign; made in any country except the U.S.A. 1953: "You'll notice it's not a gook car." *New Yorker,* Mar. 7, 23/1.

gool *n.* **1** A goal. *Since c1840. Has*

been common, humorously and dial. **2** An ill-mannered, offensive introvert. *v.t.* To elicit great applause from an audience by one's entertainment. Fig., to "knock someone for a gool."

goola *n.* A piano. *c1935 jive use.*

goola box *n.* A juke box. *Negro use. Not common.*

Go on! An exclam. of incredulity or of pleasure from a compliment. *Usu. in the phrase,* **Aw, go on!** *or* **Go on with you!**

goon *n.* **1** A hoodlum; a strong man acting or employed as a thug or to commit acts of violence or intimidation. 1956: "*Goon*—A strong-arm thug. Originally, in Chaucer. Now applied to both union and company hired muscle. Made popular by Elzie Segar's comic strip, 'Popeye the Sailor.'" [*It had a large, stupid character called "the goon," c1935–38.*] *Labor's Special Language from Many Sources.* 1957: "[It was a police] raid. He and his goons pulled out their pistols and ran." D. Jennings, *SEP,* Sept. 21, 94. **2** [derog.] A Negro. 1947: "And he commenced to choke the goon, and hollered at him some more, and after a while the nigger...." C. Willingham, *End as a Man,* 76. *Not common.* **3** A strong, stupid, unimaginative man. → **4** A boring, disliked, or silly person. *Since c1935.* 1943: "He had the face of a pure goon." H. A. Smith, *Putty Knife,* 33. → **5** An unattractive or unpopular member of the opposite sex. *Very common with teenagers and college students. Since c1935.* **6** [derog.] A German soldier or civilian. *W.W.II U.S. Air Force prisoner of war in Ger.* **7** An Army private, esp. one relegated to simple, dirty chores. *Some W.W.II Army use. In the Virgin Islands, formerly a Danish possession, native Negro workers are called "goons" or "goonies," a possible derivation.* See Appendix, Shortened Words. → **8** A man; a fellow. *Usu. disparagingly or humorously.* **9** A cargo or passenger plane, as opposed to a more exciting fighter or bomber plane. *Some W.W.II airplane factory and airfield use. adj.* **1** Stupid, goonlike. *Some teenage use c1940.* **2** Nazi German. *Used by U.S. and Eng. prisoners of war in Ger. during W.W.II.* Thus: **goon-bread, goon-soup, goon-women, goon-box** [a guard tower on a prisoner of war compound], **goon-soldier,** etc.   **—ey** *n.* A simpleton. *In N.E. dial. use c1895.*   **—ie** *n.* **1** A native Virgin

Island Negro. *The word, as well as the island, was orig. Danish.* **2** A killjoy; a married man. *A little W.W.II USN use.* **—let** *n.* A young hoodlum. 1944: "Cops handle young goonlets gently. . . ." Walter Davenport, *Collier's*, Sept., 23, 11/2. *A synthetic sl. word, never common.* **—y** *adj.* Odd; goonlike.

goonk *n.* **1** Any greasy, semiviscous liquid; esp. hair tonic, lubricants, or any unappetizing, greasy food. **2** Anything unpleasant.

goon squad **1** A group of thugs, esp. when employed in labor disputes. *c1935.* **2** The police. *Not common.*

goop *n.* **1** A goof; a mutt. 1934: "A creature invented by Gelett Burgess." *Web.* **2** Cant, nonsense, boloney. **3** = **goup.**

goopher = **goofer.**

goose *v.t.* **1** [taboo] Lit. and fig., to poke or threaten to poke a finger into someone's anus to produce shock or annoyance, either to make a joke or to start the person working or the like. 1943: "As she was bending over her work-table, a playful lab assistant goosed her." M. Shulman, *Barefoot Boy with Cheek*, 99. → **2** To outwit someone, to take advantage of another's lack of alertness. *c1930.* → **3** To start a motor or a machine; to feed spurts of gasoline or power to a motor. *c1935.* → **4** To threaten, beg, cajole, or encourage another to do something faster or better. **5** To stop a locomotive suddenly, usu. by putting it into reverse while it is moving forward. *Railroad use.* → **6** Fig., to obtain the maximum speed from an engine, machine, or esp. a vehicle. *n.* **1** The act of goosing. **2** An emergency stop of a locomotive.

goose, give [someone or something] the **1** [taboo] Lit., to goose someone. → **2** Fig., to speed up someone or something; to ask for or create action, speed, alertness, enthusiasm, or the like; specif., to accelerate a car or other motor or engine. Cf. **give [something] the gun.**

gooseberry *n.* **1** A clothesline with clothes hanging on it to dry. 1931: ". . . In the old days hoboes would rob a 'gooseberry' if they needed a new shirt." C. Ashleigh, *Everyman*, May, 21, 520/2. *c1850. Hobo use. Taking clothes from a clothesline was as easy as picking wild gooseberries.* **2** A type of barbed-wire entanglement. 1918: "In making his way through entanglements, he may trip over 'gooseberries,' wooden frames wrapped round with barbed wire." McCartney, *Texas Rev.*, 78. *W.W.I Army use.* *v.t.* To steal clothes from a clothesline. *Hobo use.*

gooseberry bush = **gooseberry.**

gooseberry lay **1** An expedition for stealing clothes hung on a clothesline. *c1850. Hobo use.* → **2** A crime that can be accomplished with little difficulty; an easy job. *Criminal use; archaic.*

goose bumps Goose pimples. *Very common.*

goose-bumpy *adj.* Frightened; having goose bumps. 1946: "He . . . goes goose-bumpy at the thought of hooking a 50-lb. sailfish. . . ." *Time*, Jan. 14.

goose-drownder *n.* A heavy rainstorm. *Dial.*

goose egg Zero, esp. in the score of a game, a grade in school, or an amount of money. *Used in schools to refer to the grade of zero; used in sports to indicate that no score has been made and a zero has been posted on the scoreboard. Since c1850. Colloq.* 1867: "The Buckeyes in this inning were treated to a goose-egg. . . ." H. Chadwick, *Scrapbooks*, Oct. 1952: "There's a scoreboard [of money spent] in City Hall where everyone is happy to see big 'goose eggs' marked up." Syracuse, N.Y., *Post-Standard*, July 1, 24/1. *v.t.* To prevent an opposing sports team from scoring; to give a student a grade of 0%; to pay no money or leave no tip for a waiter.

go out To lose consciousness. *Often in the phrase, "went out like a light."* 1934: "I went out again. . . ." Cain, *Postman*, 48. 1934: "Something swished and I went out like a light." Chandler, *Finger Man*, 15.

goozle *n.* **1** The throat. *Archaic and dial.* Cf. **wet [one's] goozle. 2** Anything more or less of the consistency of thickened gravy. *Not common.*

goozlum *n.* Syrup; molasses; gravy. *Western use, usu. logger use.*

gopher **gofer** **gofor** *n.* **1** A young thief or hoodlum. 1930: "The youths were tough West Side 'gophers' who wouldn't hesitate to use a gun. . . ." Lavine, *Third Degree*, 103. *Since c1890.* → **2** Specif., a safe-cracker. *c1930; underworld use.* → **3** A safe, considered as an object to be robbed. *Underworld use.* **4** A dupe. 1930: "Don't be a gofor all your life." *Amer. Mercury*, Dec., 456. **5** A logging camp helper; specif., one who, like a gopher, digs under logs so a rope or wire can be tied around them for moving. *Logger use.*

gopher ball   **1** In baseball, a pitched or hit ball that skims low over the ground. **2** An eccentric or dull person. *Some c1945 student use; obs.*

go places   To be successful; to have a successful career.

Gordon water   **gordon water**   Gin. *From the common brand of Gordon's gin. Pop. c1925.*

gorill   *n.* A hoodlum; a gorilla. 1939–40: "Those gorills do not care anything about law...." O'Hara, *Pal Joey*, 30. *From "gorilla."*

gorilla   *n.* **1** A person with gorilla-like strength; a person known for his strength and lack of intellect. *Since c1865.* → **2** A hoodlum or thug. 1930: "Strong-arm men, gorillas, and tough gangsters...." Lavine, *Third Degree*, 5. *Since c1930.* → **3** Specif., one hired to kill or do violence.

gorm   *v.t., v.i.* To eat voraciously. *Since c1850. Not common. From "gormandize."*

gorp   *v.t., v.i.* To eat greedily.

gosh-awful   *adj.* Terrible; very awful. *Euphem. for "god-awful."* 1945: "Boxing had had the most gosh-awful collection of ... stumblebums." Arthur Daley, N.Y. *Times*, Dec., 31, 13.   *adv.* Exceedingly. 1924: "You are getting gosh-awful high-hat lately." Marks, *Plastic Age*, 199.

gospel-pusher   *n.* A preacher.

go-to-hell cap   An overseas cap. *Armed Forces use.* See **overseas cap.**

gouge   *n.* **1** A list of correct answers, as used by students when taking an examination; a pony. *c1930. Obs.* → **2** An imposter, a cheater. *Never common.*

goulash   *n.* **1** False information. *Underworld use. c1925.* → **2** An unusual hand of playing cards; a method of dealing playing cards so that all players receive unusual hands. → **3** A small restaurant or delicatessen that is a meeting place or serves as a quasi-clubroom for neighborhood criminals or for storytellers, horse-racing bettors, and card, chess, and checker players. 1956: "He owned a goulash or card house. The goulashes served excellent Hungarian cuisine at moderate prices. Their profits came mostly from the sale of cards. Since the winner paid for the cards, losing players frequently called for fresh decks—to change their luck. In poker the goulashes' takeout was five per cent. In addition to accommodating card players, some goulashes took horse players' bets." T. Betts, *Across the Board*, 121. 1958: "Goulash—Hangout for criminal elements." G. Y. Wells, *Station House Slang.*

goulashes   **goolashes**   *n.pl.* Galoshes; overshoes. *A freq. mispronunciation.*

goulie   *n.* Any unfamiliar mixture of food. *From "goulash."* See Appendix, —ie ending.

goum [derog.]   *n.* A foreigner. 1951: "It just ain't so that a Russian can take it on the chin better than an American or a Zulu or a gook or a goum." Hal Boyle, AP, May 17. *From obs. "gome" = a man.*

goup   *n.* Any sticky or greasy liquid, such as a chocolate syrup. Cf. **goo, goop, gunk.**

go up (in [one's] lines)   Specif., to forget one's lines entirely during a theatrical performance; to confuse one's lines during a theatrical performance. *Theater use since before c1920.* See **go up in the air.**

gourd   *n.* The head. *Dial. since c1845.* See **saw gourds.**

governor   *n.* **1** A father. 1912: "An idea of the governor's...." Johnson, *Stover at Yale*, 223. **2** A superior; a manager or owner; one who governs. *Orig. carnival and circus use. c1920.*

gow   *n.* **1** Opium. 1934: "Taken directly from the Canton dialect word for 'sap' ... synonymous with opium." Buethe. *Orig. San Francisco underworld use, c1915.* → **2** Any narcotic drug. 1933: "Drug-addict use." Maurer. → **3** A marijuana cigarette. → **4** The effect obtained from taking a narcotic drug. **5** Drawings or photographs of pretty and provocatively posed females used on book and magazine covers, or on the outside packaging of products, in order to arrest the buyer's attention. 1957: "The kind of Petty [an illustrator of long-legged females] drawing that has helped sell *Esquire* [magazine] for some years now is selling Decca records. As yet, the record people haven't invented a trade word to describe this type of artwork, which in the newspaper field is called 'cheesecake' and in the paperbooks field is 'gow.'" *Publishers' Weekly*, Apr. 8, 18. See **cheesecake.**

gowed-up   **gowed up**   *adj.* Under the influence of a narcotic; hopped up. 1940: "Some gowed-up runt they took along for a gun-holder lost his head." Chandler, *Farewell*, 80. See Appendix, words taking —up.

go west 1 To die. *Orig. cowboy and Western use. Very common during W.W.I.* 2 To fail in business, said of a business concern. 1928: "Men of letters will ask you if you have heard that some firm has 'gone west.' . . ." R. Lynd, *New Statesman,* Feb. 4. *Not common.*

go with To court; to date a person of the opposite sex; to keep company with; to go around with. 1920: "Some of the boys she went with. . . ." Fitzgerald, *This Side of Paradise,* 74. *Colloq.*

go with, let 1 To fire a gun. 1930: "The gunman let go with both automatics." Lavine, *Third Degree,* 71. → 2 To release a verbal attack; to bawl out. 3 = **fly, let.**

gow job = **hot rod.**

go wrong To become involved in illegal, immoral, unethical, or socially unacceptable schemes or practices.

gowster *n.* A marijuana smoker. See Appendix, —er ending.

Goy **goy** [derog.] *n.* A non-Jew; a gentile. 1916: "My dad reads the Talmud all the time and hates Goys." S. Lewis, *The Job,* 116. 1941: "He knows no more about the Torah than a goy." Schulberg, *Sammy,* 231. *From the modern Hebrew. Orig. in ancient Hebrew, very derog. = uncivilized. From the quotes note that non-Jews have a tendency to capitalize the word to = Christian.* *adj.* Non-Jewish. 1930: "The mob's strictly goy." *Amer. Mercury,* Dec., 456.

grab For phrases beginning with "grab," see under principal word of phrase.

grab, the *n.* The main store or meeting place in a small town. *Dial. and archaic.*

grabber *n.* A passenger train conductor. *Railroad use.*

grabby *adj.* Greedy; acquisitive. 1950: "Folks are just too grabby." Movie, *Saddle Tramp.*

grab-joint *n.* 1 A booth or stand that sells hamburgers, hot dogs, cotton candy, or other food, usu. at a carnival or circus. *Orig. carnival and circus use. c1935.* 2 A booth or stand that sells souvenirs. *Carnival and circus use, since c1940.*

grad *n.* 1 A graduate of a college or university. 1924: "A college grad." Marks, *Plastic Age,* 68. *Colloq. since c1935.* 2 A graduate student; one studying for an advanced degree. *adj.* Graduate; pursuing studies leading to an advanced degree. 1920: "Grad stu-

dents." F. S. Fitzgerald, *This Side of Paradise,* 149. See Appendix, Shortened Words.

graded *adj.* Scientifically bred; thoroughbred; said of farm animals. 1936: "This breeding animals into better blood, this raising of so-called 'graded' stock was, commercially, a great advance over the prior ranching methods, which had infused no new blood into the horses and the cattle obtained from Mexico." P. A. Rollins, *The Cowboy,* 29.

graft *n.* 1 A person's calling or employment. *Archaic. Replaced by "racket."* 2 Work. *Orig. hobo use c1915. Now archaic in U.S. though still used commonly in Australia.* 3 Bribery. 1913: "There is no need for us to follow the language on the American screen and . . . describe bribery as 'graft.' . . ." Faulkner, London *Daily Mail. Since c1910 this has been the common sl. usage of the word.* **—er** *n.* A faker; a confidence man; a thief. *c1920. Hobo use. Replaced by "grifter." Has never meant a "hard worker" in U.S. sl., though this is the Australian meaning.*

gramps **Gramps** *n.sing.* A nickname for a grandfather; a nickname for any elderly man, old enough to be a grandfather whether he is or not. 1945: "Cute girl on that billboard, Gramps!" Advt., *SEP,* Oct. 20, 57. 1947: "The children do not call him [their grandfather] gramps or granddaddy." L. Lee in Phila. *Bulletin,* Feb. 19, 20.

grand *n.sing.* 1 One thousand dollars. 1939: "A banker would scarcely call one thousand dollars 'one grand.' . . ." Hixson, *Word Ways,* 136. *Orig., c1920, underworld and sporting use. By 1930 had replaced "thou" and has been common since c1935.* → 2 A thousand. *n.pl.* 1 Thousands of dollars. 1930: "Who got the ten grand?" Lavine, *Third Degree,* 40. 1952: "They got the Navy on the fire . . . for spoiling 23 grand worth of meat. . . ." Robert Ruark, *synd. newsp. col.,* March 11. [*Note the possessive pl. use.*] *Since c1930. Much more common than "grands."* → 2 Thousands. **—s** *n.pl.* Thousands of dollars. 1921: "A roll of fifteen one-thousand-buck notes or 'grands.' . . ." Witwer, *Leather,* 114. *A seldom used plur. form.*

grand bounce A dismissal or rejection; the bounce. 1956: "Didn't know what to do with her . . . could not just leave her there . . . decided that all he could do was to give her the grand bounce." J. A. Kouwenhoven, *Harper's*, July, 29. See **bounce**.

grandfather   *n*. 1 An elderly man. 2 A senior student.

grandma   *n*. 1 Any elderly woman. 2 Low gear of a motor truck.

grandmother   *n*. A short, stout howitzer. *W.W.I use*.

grand slam   1 In baseball, a home run. → 2 An instance of winning everything, defeating all competition decisively, succeeding in several fields of endeavor, or the like.   **—mer**   A home run. 1953: "A grand slammer by the Indians' Ray Boone. . . ." Joe Reichler, AP, May 11. *Baseball use*.

grandstand   *adj*. Showy; done mainly for exhibition. *Fig. = done to impress a grandstand full of spectators. Since c1890.* *v.i.* To show off; to impress spectators by performing in a needlessly spectacular way. 1927: I [a prize fighter] grandstanded." Hammett, *Blood Money*, 75.   *n*. A trick; something done to deceive. *None of the above are as common as the term "grandstand play."*   **—er** *n*. A show-off. 1951: "I know what these men want. They want a gladhander and a grandstander." Movie, *The Frogmen*.

grandstand coach = **kibitzer**. *Not common*.

grandstand play   1 In sports, a play made to look more difficult than it is, to impress the spectators. *Since c1920.* → 2 Any action, speech, or device used to gain sympathy or admiration.

grape   *n*. 1 Wine. 2 Champagne. See **belt the grape**.

grapefruit   *adj*. 1 Associated with the preseason training period of professional baseball teams. *Because such training usu. takes place in the warm citrus-fruit growing regions.* 2 Played before the baseball season officially opens. *Said of baseball games.* 1953: "The Cards dropped a 5–2 grapefruit league decision to the . . . Yankees." AP, Mar. 9.

grapes, the   *n*. Champagne.

grapevine   *n*. 1 A rumor, esp. a false rumor. 1863: *DAE. Wide Civil War use.* → 2 The means or route by which a rumor or unofficial information is conveyed; an informant whose name is not to be divulged. 1891: *DAE. Colloq.*

grappo   *n*. Wine. *Orig. bums' use*.

grass   *n*. 1 Lettuce. *Since c1935*. 2 Any green salad, esp. if chopped or shredded. *Since c1940*. 3 The straight-growing hair characteristic of Caucasians. *Some Negro use*. 4 = **grass weed**.

grass-clipper = **grass-cutter**. 1868: "Wright goes to first base on his short grass-clipper to center field. . . ." H. Chadwick, *Scrapbooks II*, 9.

grass-cutter   *n*. In baseball, a ball hit hard and low to the ground. *Since c1925*.

grasshopper   *n*. An airplane that flies low, ascending and descending as the terrain demands; a plane used to dust crops. See **knee-high to a grasshopper**.

grass weed   Marijuana. *Some addict use*.

grass widow   1 A wife whose husband is away on an extended trip. *Since c1900. Colloq.* → 2 A divorced woman; a woman legally separated from her husband. *Colloq.*

grass widower   The male counterpart of a grass widow. *Not common*.

graum   *v.i.* To worry; to fret; to complain or nag. 1956: "All a bookmaker graums about is they don't drop a atom bomb on top of New York and kill all the horse players. That's all a bookmaker worries about." J. Cannon, *Who Struck John?* 137.

gravel   See **hit the gravel, scratch gravel**.

gravel, hit the = **hit the dirt**.

gravel agitator   An infantryman. *Some W.W.I and W.W.II Army use, though never common*. See **gravel crusher**.

gravel crusher   An infantryman. *Some W.W.I use. Taken from W.W.I Brit. Army*.

gravel train   A sugar bowl. *Not common*.

graveyard   *n*. = **graveyard shift**. *adj*. Pertaining to a graveyard shift; pertaining to late-at-night or early-morning hours.

graveyard shift   *n*. 1 A working shift that begins at midnight or 2:00 A.M. *A factory working 24 hours a day usu. has three shifts of workers: the regular day shift of 8:00 A.M. to 4:00 P.M., the "swing shift" from 4:00 P.M. to midnight, and the "graveyard shift" from midnight to 8:00 A.M. Guards, ranchers, truck drivers, and others whose jobs necessitate employment 24 hours a day have used the term since c1915. It became very common during W.W.II when many factories were in 24-hr production. It refers, of course, to the ghostlike hour of employment.* 2 A method of riding a horse, often a wild horse, so that one shifts with the horse's movements to avoid being thrown off, even though no saddle or bridle is used. *c1920 Western ranch use.*

graveyard stew *n.* Milk toast. *Orig. a term popular among young children. So called because it is often served to sick people. Lunch-counter use.*

graveyard watch A period of guard or watch duty from 12 midnight to 4 A.M. or 8 A.M. *Railroad and watchman use [12 midnight to 8 A.M.]. USN use [12 midnight to 4 A.M.].*

gravy *n.* Money in excess of that expected; money in excess of that needed for necessities; money easily earned or won. 1943: "... Family endowment and so on. This is the gravy." P. Wylie, *Generation of Vipers*, 243. *Specif., money that is obtained easily and that does not have to be spent on necessities, such as money won at gambling, money earned at easy work, unexpectedly large profits, special bonuses and allowances, and the like. Since c1920.* *adj.* Easy to accomplish; soft.

gravy boat = **gravy train.** 1943: "You will have to pay me a fee for letting you ride the gravy boat...." Movie, *Crazy House.*

gravy ride Fig., a ride on or as part of a gravy train.

gravy train 1 An opportunity to receive money easily; individual prosperity; excessive pay for easy work or no work. *Often in "to ride the gravy train." Since c1920. Orig. sporting use.* 2 A person, business, or project that pays one's way or enables one to live prosperously, even though one may not actually need money of his own. → 3 An easy job; a task that can be accomplished without exertion, esp. if connected with public life, political life, shady dealings, or the like. *Colloq.*

gray [derog.] *n.* A white person. *Negro use.*

grayback *n.* A louse. *Colloq. c1865 to c1910. Still some use by soldiers in the field, and hoboes.*

gray-legs *n.pl.* West Point cadets. *Orig. derog. U.S. Naval Academy use.*

gray matter Intelligence; brains. *Colloq.*

gray mule = **white mule.**

graze *v.* To eat a meal. *Some student, Army, and prison use.*

grazing ticket A meal ticket or book of meal tickets. *Some student use.*

grease *n.* 1 Money. *c1800–c1910; archaic.* → 2 Bribe money; protection money. *c1930; underworld use.* 3 Butter.

Some use since c1930; fairly common W.W.II Army use. Cf. **axle grease, goober grease, skid grease.** 4 Nitroglycerine; dynamite. *c1925; underworld use.* 5 Influence; pull. See **elbow grease.** *v.t.* 1 To bribe. *Orig. intro by Brit. colonists.* 1951: "We can recall ... no palm we have greased or been greased by." *New Yorker*, Oct. 6, 27/1. 2 To eat, esp. rapidly. *c1940; some Negro use; some far out use since c1955.* **—d** *adj.* Drunk. *Mainly Southern hill use.* **—r** *n.* 1 [derog.] A Spanish-American or Mexican. *Since c1847. After c1925 the word usu. = Mexican.* [1956]: "He created great confusion and almost panic, cursed at everybody, ordered all the greasers [Mexican soldiers] to be shot." *Life*, July 30, 52. 2 [derog.] An Italian. *c1930; not common.* **greasy** *adj.* 1 Addicted to applepolishing. *Some student use since c1940.* See **greasy grind.** 2 Sly; unctuous; cunning. 3 Muddy, esp. muddy when the soil has absorbed all surface water and the mud has just begun to dry; slightly muddy. 1958: "It took Calumet's [racing stable] slick-striding Tim Tam just 1.39 3-5 to negotiate a 'greasy' mile before an approving audience of 15,000." *The Morning Telegraph*, Apr. 30, 1. *Horse-racing use.*

grease-ball *n.* 1 [derog.] A foreigner, esp. one from a Mediterranean country, who has thick, black, oily hair; specif., an Italian, Spaniard, Greek, or South American. 1939: "I never speak of [Italians] as wops, or guineas, or dagoes, or grease balls." Runyon, 125. 2 A dirty tramp or beggar. *Some hobo use since c1925.* 3 A cook; a kitchen worker. *Some use since c1925, never common. Some W.W.II USN use.* → 4 A hamburger stand or concession. *Circus use.* 5 An actor who uses too much make-up. *Theater use since c1930.* I 6 A disliked, sly person; specif., any young man with thick, black, oily hair, a sly or unctuous look, a sheik's mannerisms, and a cynical disregard for social acceptability. 1949: "We [police] spent the summer evenings taking knives away from greaseballs in zoot suits." Chandler, *Little Sister*, 218.

grease-burner *n.* A cook; esp. a fry cook at a lunch counter.

grease-gun *n.* 1 A rapid-firing, automatic pistol. *W.W.II Army and USN use.* 2 The M-3 submachine gun. 1953: "The Army's present standard model, the M-3 'greasegun.'" AP, Mar. 3.

grease it in To land an airplane smoothly. *W.W.II U.S. Air Force use.*

grease joint 1 The cookhouse and/or eating tent of a carnival or circus. *Since c1915.* 2 Any inexpensive place where food is cooked and served, as a lunch counter, a hamburger or hot-dog stand.

grease-monkey *n.* 1 Any of various workers who lubricate machinery, esp. a garage or gasoline-station attendant who greases cars and engines. 1952: "Good grease monkeys all, they could think better with a grease rack to lean against. . . ." Jerome Ellison, *SEP*, Sept. 20, 95/1. → 2 Anyone who works in a garage; esp. a mechanic. 3 A stoker, oiler, or wiper on a ship. *Maritime use.*

grease-pot *n.* A cook. *Some W.W.I and II use. More common in the USN than the Army.*

grease-pusher *n.* A person who makes up actors with grease paint; a make-up man. *Theater and television use.*

grease rat A deckhand on a dredge. *Navy yard use.*

grease trough A lunch counter or lunchroom. 1942: "Imagine yourself in the grease trough again." Anson, *SEP*.

greasy grind A student who studies constantly; one overzealous in his studies. *c1930. The "greasy" adds further contempt to "grind."* See **grind.**

greasy spoon An inferior or cheap, usu. small, restaurant or lunch counter. 1951: "The Marx brothers ate in coffee pots and greasy spoons. . . ." Joel Sayre, *Time*, Dec. 31, 29/2. *Very common.*

great *adj.* Excellent; fine; wonderful; splendid. 1839–1911: *Colloq., DAE. Still in wide use.* 1839 [1948]: "[In the U.S.] the word great is oddly used for fine, splendid." Capt. F. Marryat, *A Diary in America,* excerpted in *America Through British Eyes,* 185. *Colloq.* *n.* A famous person, as an actor, a baseball or football player, a musician, etc. 1945: "Weiss, a former football 'great.' . . ." Phila. *Inquirer,* Dec. 20, 16. —s *n.pl.* Famous people, often entertainers, athletes, artists, or writers. 1948: "Hollywood and Broadway greats. . . ." Lait-Mortimer, *N.Y. Confidential,* 25. 1950: "One of baseball's oldtime greats. . . ." Larry LaSoeur, CBS, *radio network.*

greatest, the *n.* Anyone or anything considered wonderful; the most exciting or satisfying; the best of one's or its kind; anything or anyone considered better than anything or anyone else; the best. 1956: "People should be proud of the President! I think he's the greatest!" A. Smith, *synd. newsp. comic strip,* "Mutt and Jeff," Nov. 7. *Orig. bop and cool use, since c1950; now wide teenage and student use.* Cf. **most, the.**

great go A final examination. *Not common in U.S.* Cf. **little go.**

great guns, go To flourish; to succeed remarkably.

great shakes *Seldom used in the affirmative.* See **no great shakes.**

greeby *adj.* Terrible. *A teenage fad word c1945. No longer common.* Cf. **grooby.**

greefa griffa goifa greeta *n.* A marijuana cigarette; a reefer. *Given in order of pop. "Griffa" may be Negro usage.*

greefo griefo gre(a)fa greapha *n.* Marijuana. *Common addict use.*

Greek *n.* 1 An Irishman. *Orig. underworld use. c1850.* 2 A Greek-letter fraternity member. *College student use.*

Greek way (fashion), the [taboo] Anal intercourse.

green *n.* Money, esp. paper money. *Since c1920. Orig. sporting and underworld use. From "long green."* Cf. **folding green.** 1957: "Green—Money." E. Horne, *For Cool Cats and Far-Out Chicks.* *An old term somewhat synthetically revived by cool and beat users.*

green-ass [taboo] *adj.* Inexperienced; young; unworldly; green. 1949: "I spent thirty-four months havin' green-ass corporals chew me up." N. Algren, *Man with the Golden Arm,* 51.

green deck, the Grass.

green folding Money in bills.

green goods Counterfeit paper money. *Since c1890.*

greenhorn green-horn *n.* 1 An immigrant, usu. unassimilated and naïve. 1917: ". . . Greenhorn . . . a contemptuous quizzical appellation for a newly arrived, inexperienced immigrant." Abraham Cahan, *The Rise of David Levinsky,* 94. 2 A naïve or unsuspecting person. 1857: "No man, boy or green-horn was ever yet victimized." Charles H. Brainard, *Tricks and Traps of New York City,* Part I, 24, Brainard's Dime Books.

green hornet Any hard, military problem that must be solved in a limited time. *W.W.II use.*

greenhouse *n.* The transparent plastic cockpit cover of an airplane.

green ice Emeralds. *Underworld use.* See **ice.**

greenie *n.* A newcomer; a greenhorn.

1948: "... If you are a greenie in Gotham. ..." Lait-Mortimer, *N.Y. Confidential*, 220.

green light Approval; permission to proceed; a go-ahead sign. *From the traffic signal.*

green money Paper money; bills of various denominations. 1949: "Shooting for green money." A. Hynd, 43.

green pea A college freshman. *College use. c1925.*

green stuff, the Money; paper money. 1952: "He really poured the green stuff to the bookies." Stanley Frank, *SEP*, Mar. 15, 148/4.

green thumb 1 An aptitude for getting plants to grow. 2 The ability to produce a success and to make money. 1948: "Cheryl Crawford . . . possessor of a green thumb when it comes to making musicals blossom on Broadway." Helen Ormsbee, *N.Y. Her. Trib.*, Aug. 8.

greeta = **greefa.**

grefa = **greefo.**

grenade = **hand grenade.**

greyhound *n.* A fast-working butcher or salesman. *Circus use.*

grid *n.* 1 A football playing field. *Since c1915. From "gridiron."* See Appendix, Shortened Words. 2 A motorcycle. *Some motorcycle use since c1925.* *adj.* Football; pertaining to football. 1950: "A member of Susquehanna University's grid squad." AP, July 7. —**iron** *n.* A football playing field. *Common since c1900. Because the playing field was originally marked off in squares or grids, including the ten-yard stripes still used, plus lengthwise stripes indicating various playing, kicking, and passing zones. Colloq.* *adj.* Of or pertaining to football.

griefo = **greefo.**

grifa **griffa** = **greefa.**

grift *n.* 1 Money made dishonestly and by one's wits, esp. by swindling. 2 In general, any dishonest or unethical way of obtaining money by one's wits, such as is done by professional swindlers, gamblers, pitchmen, confidence men, and the like. *v.i.* To swindle, gamble, or make one's living dishonestly and by one's wits. *c1925, orig. carnival and circus use; assoc. with "graft."* —**er** *n.* 1 A gambler. *Orig. a gambler who followed circuses; circus use since c1925.* → 2 A swindler, pitchman, confidence man, small-time crook, dishonest concessionaire, or the like. *Prob. older than the v.* "grift." → 3 Any vagabond or

hobo. *Since c1935, by confusion with "drifter."*

grift, on the Living, traveling, or working as a grifter.

grind *v.i.* 1 To rotate one's pelvis, in or as in sexual intercourse; said of women. *Applied to sexual intercourse or to the strip-tease and erotic dancing.* 1956: "Keep a-knockin' but you can't come in./ I hear you knockin', but you can't come in./ I got an all-night trick again;/ I'm busy grindin' so you can't come in." From "Bawdyhouse Blues," reprinted in S. Longstreet, *The Real Jazz Old and New*, 52. *A very old song.* 2 To study diligently, methodically, and for long periods of time. *Since c1850; colloq. since c1930.* 1951: "Peter and Ike and Stinky were known at Beagle as a solid trio who did not grind their studies or act longhair." S. Longstreet, *The Pedlocks*, 308. *Student use.* 3 To require too much work of students. *c1900; college use.* 4 To joke; to mimic another. *c1900, college use.* 5 To spiel at a concession; to talk to a crowd in front of a sideshow about the attractions to be seen inside. *c1925, circus talk; carnival use by c1930.* → 6 To laugh. *Not common.* *n.* 1 Any unpleasant, monotonous, annoying, or boring task, esp. such a task when it deprives one of freedom to do something more pleasant. *Since c1850; very common by 1900, esp. by students; colloq. by c1925.* → 2 A college course requiring a great deal of study and concentration. *c1880 to present.* → 3 A diligent, drudging, overstudious student, esp. one who ignores or does not care for the social aspects of school life. 1909: "... The grind with his armful of books. ..." O. D. von Engeln, *At Cornell*, 61. 1924: "No one except a few notorious grinds studied that night." Marks, *Plastic Age*, 80. 1951: "This conceited grind. ..." S. Lewis, *World So Wide*, 91. *c1890 to present; gained wide popularity by c1900. Note the word is almost always used with contempt, esp. by party-boys and wheels.* → 4 A teacher who requires too much work of his students. *c1900.* → 5 Any tiresome or boring person. *c1890.* 6 A sarcastic remark aimed at someone; a dig. 1896: *DAE. Obs.* → 7 A satire, usu. personal. *c1900; mainly student use; now archaic.* → 8 A joke of any kind. *College use, c1930; archaic.* → 9 A satirist, joker, or punster. *College use, c1930. Obs.* → 10 The loud, colorful sales talk given by a barker to entice customers into a sideshow or to a concession; a barker's or pitchman's spiel. *Circus use, c1925; carnival use by c1930.* → **11** A circus barker or sidewalk pitchman. *Circus pitchman use, c1930.* **12** The pelvic-rotation gyrations of a burlesque dancer or stripper. *Colloq.* **13** A movie. *From the grinding, winding, and unwinding of the film on its spool. c1930; obs. adj.* Running continuously, without intermission. *Said of a show or a theater.* See **grind house, grind show.** —**er** *n.* **1** A barker who talks, often continuously, in front of a sideshow about the show inside. *c1925, circus talk; carnival use by c1930.* See **spieler.** **2** A stripper; a burlesque dancer. **3** A very large overstuffed sandwich, usu. on a long roll or short loaf of bread, split lengthwise, and containing several kinds of hot or cold meat and cheese, and sometimes even vegetables. *c1945. Often used in the South and West; the East prefers "Hero."* See **coffee-grinder.** **4** A car, specif. an old or dilipidated car. 1941: "The wife had bought a brand new Chev to take the place of her old grinder." J. Lilienthal, *Horse Crazy,* 9.

grind house A theater that runs continuously, either without intermissions or for a long daily run and without closing on holidays. *Theater use. From "grind show."*

grind show A continuously running carnival show, without intermissions. *c1930; carnival use. Some grind shows featured dancers doing bumps and grinds, but the two are not necessarily related.*

grip *n.* A theater stagehand who shifts scenery; a stage carpenter or his helper. 1888: *DAE.* 1950: "Crowded with assistant directors, character actors, movie stars, grips and electricians. . . ." H. Niemeyer in N.Y. *Times,* Sept. 3, X3/4. *Wide theater and movie use.*

gripe *v.i.* To complain, object, or bitch, esp. to do so chronically and about routine matters. 1940: "He got good and sore and griped. . . ." Morris Bishop, *New Yorker,* Sept. 21, 37. *Colloq. since c1945.* *v.t.* To annoy, vex, or anger someone, esp. to do so over an extended period. 1941: "What's griping him is that he can't do anything for the kids." Cain, *M. Pierce,* 83. *Colloq. since c1945.* Cf. **gives me a pain.** *n.* **1** A complaint; a strong objection or criticism. 1949: "I want to clear my desk of various matters, mostly gripes. . . ." Bernard DeVoto, *Harper's,* Jan., 61/1. *Wide enough usage to be colloq.* **2** A cause of

annoyance or vexation; the thing or person causing a complaint; anything or anyone that is disliked or disgusting. *c1925.* → **3** A dull or boring thing or person; a stupid person. *c1930.* → **4** A chronic complainer; one who nags. *c1940.* —**r** *n.* A chronic complainer. *Since c1935.*

gripes, the *n.* **1** An instance or spell of complaining. **2** The habit of complaining.

gripe session Fault-finding conversation; a bull session in which all or most of the talk is complaint. *Common to students and servicemen. c1940.*

gripes my cookies Gripes me extremely. *Some use c1940.*

gripes my middle kidney Gripes me extremely. *Common c1945.*

gripes my soul Gripes me continually. *Common c1930.*

griping *n.* The act of, or an instance of, complaining. 1949: "A little griping now and then would have been a welcome relief." Fulton Oursler, *Modern Parables. adj.* [*attrib.*] Complaining.

grit *n.* **1** Courage; perseverance. *c1800–1935; somewhat archaic. Once popular, this term has been replaced by the modern favorite, "guts."* **2** The roadpath at the side of a railroad track. *Railroad use.* See **hit the grit.** **3** Audacity; boldness. *Not common.*

grit, hit the **1** = **hit the dirt.** 1907: ". . . The shack . . . said: 'Hit the grit, you son of a toad.' " Jack London, *The Road,* 138. **2** To run; to run away. 1908: ". . . In baseball, they chase a crook out so blamed fast his feet get hot hitting the grit!" R. L. Hartt, *Atlantic Monthly,* Aug., 230/2. *Not common.* **3** To set out on a journey; to hit the road. **4** To walk or hike. See **grit.**

grizzler *n.* **1** A gasoline-wasting car. *Garage and filling-station use.* **2** An old or peevish person. *Not common.*

groan box An accordion. *Though this term may have had some use among musicians c1930, it is considered very synthetic among present-day musicians. Mainly used by gossip columnists and teen-agers, who mistakenly consider it to be a hip expression.*

groaner *n.* A singer. *A synthetic word never used by entertainers, except in reference to "The Groaner" = singer Bing Crosby.* See **grunt-and-groaner.**

groceries *n.pl.* **1** Any meal; meals. 1942: "I got hooked for the groceries." S. Billingsley, *Harper's Bazaar,* July. **2** Any important or necessary item, mission, or result. See **bring home the groceries.**

grogged *adj.* **1** Drunk. *More common in Eng. than in U.S.* **2** Groggy. See Appendix, Drunk.

grog-hound *n.* One who likes alcoholic beverages, esp. beer. *Some student use.* For a list of terms ending in —hound, see Appendix.

grog-mill *n.* A bar, tavern, or saloon, esp. a cheap one or one that mainly sells beer. 1949: "No grog-mill cuties. . . ." J. Evans, *Halo*, 24. *Based on "gin-mill."* For a list of terms ending in —mill, see Appendix.

grollo *n.* = **growler.**

grooby *adj.* Groovy; smooth. 1943: "You, too, can get on the grooby side." *Time*, July 26, 56. *Jive use.*

groove See **groovy, in the groove.**

groove, in the **1** Playing swing music intensely, with excitement, adroitly, and in such a gratifying way as to elicit a strong response from the listeners; in rapport with or enraptured by the swing music being played. *Common swing use late 1930's and early 1940's. When a phonograph plays, its stylus or needle is in the groove of the record. Archaic.* 1938: "In the Groove," title of a pop. song. **2** Exciting; satisfying; hep; representative of or in the swing mode or fashion; of the world and time of swing. *Swing use. Archaic.* **3** Speaking sensibly; thinking correctly; in the proper mood. *Some general use c1940.* **4** In top form; running or working smoothly or .perfectly; in full swing. 1951: "The Professor of Classics was now, as he would have put it, *in canaliculo*—in the groove." M. Bishop in *New Yorker*, Jan. 13, 22/1. *Teenage and student use c1940–c1945.*

groovy *adj.* **1** In a state of mind or mood conducive to playing music, esp. swing music, well; in rapport with the piece, esp. of swing music, being played. *Orig. c1935 swing use, by musicians and devotees. Some resurrected cool and far out use since c1955. From "in the groove."* → **2** Appreciative of good swing music; hep to swing music, fads, and fashions; hep. 1944: "A boy or girl who is really 'groovy' is 'skate wacky' or a 'skate bug.' " P. Martin in *SEP*, May 13, 89/2. → **3** Excellent; satisfying; in keeping with one's desires or a situation. 1951: " 'I pitched a no-hit game,' said Georgie. 'Hey, groovy,' said Sally." M. Shulman, *Dobie Gillis*, 92. 1956: "Musically, *groovy* is real good." S. Longstreet, *The Real Jazz Old and New*, 148.

grouch-bag *n.* **1** A small money bag, usu. leather or canvas, often suspended by a string carried inside the clothing, containing enough money for an emergency, usu. enough money to move on to another town if one's schemes fail or if one quits a job. *c1930; circus use.* → **2** A purse. → **3** Money saved for an emergency. *c1930; some use among entertainers and grifters.* 1956: "Circus roustabouts took their money out of grouch-bags, pouches drawn by string, like tobacco pouches." N. Algren, *A Walk on the Wild Side*, 18.

ground apple A rock. *Some farmer and lumberjack use.*

ground biscuit A stone of a size and shape suitable for throwing. 1946: "A fellow's blonde usually stepped in . . . and slugged the other gee with an alley apple or ground biscuit, meaning a rock done up in a stocking." Damon Runyon, *synd. newsp. col.*, Sept. 14.

grounder *n.* A partly smoked cigarette, picked up from the ground to be finished; a butt. *c1930; hobo use.*

ground-gripper *n.* **1** A landlubber. **2** A nonaviator; esp. a sailor stationed at a land base, who neither flies a plane or mans a ship. *A little W.W.II USN use, but probably synthetic.*

ground-hog *n.* **1** A pilot who does not like to fly; a kiwi. *Early aviator use.* **2** A railroad brakeman. *Railroad use.* **3** A frankfurter sandwich. *Not common.*

ground rations Sexual intercourse. *Some Negro use.*

grouse *v.i.* To grumble or complain. *Orig. Brit. Army sl. imported during W.W.I.* —**r** *n.* A grumbler. *Some W.W.I soldier use, taken from Brit. sl.*

growl *n.* A set of notes used for cheating in an examination; a pony. 1947: "One of the yo-yo boys sitting next to me . . . tried to pass me his growl in a whizz quiz. . . ." Hal Boyle, Phila. *Bulletin*, May 19, 12. *v.i.* To complain; to reprimand; to express one's bad temper or ill nature verbally. *Colloq.* —**er** *n.* **1** A bucket, can, pitcher, or other suitable large container used to carry beer home from a saloon. 1893: "In New York a can brought in filled with beer at a bar-room is called a growler. . . ." Brander Matthews, *Harper's*, July, 307/2. *Very common in the 1890's. Has become archaic with the advent of bottled and canned beer. Said to have orig. in the growling noise made by the can or bucket sliding along the top of a bar.* Cf. **rush the**

growler. 2 A large pitcher or other container used to carry any liquid. 1914: "Got a growler of ice-cream soda for the ladies!" S. Lewis, *Our Mr Wrenn*, 208. 3 An electronic public-address or intercommunication system. *Orig. W.W.II USN use. In the U.S. the term has never = a hansom cab, as it does in Eng.* See **squawk box.**   **—ering** part. Selling beer by measure. *c1890.*

growler-rushing   *n.* Drinking beer or other alcoholic beverages; a drinking spree. 1914: "I hope you know growler-rushing." S. Lewis, *Our Mr. Wrenn*, 92. *adj.* Drinking; given to drinking cheap liquor. 1930: "Heslin was the contemptible, growler-rushing type of petty thief. . . ." Lavine, *Third Degree*, 72.

growley   *n.* Tomato catsup.   *v.i.* To blush. *c1935. West Point use.*

grub   *n.* 1 Food, esp. basic or filling food. *Colloq.* 1907: "Goods one can exchange at the kitchen door for grub." Jack London, *My Life. Orig. cowboy use. Now colloq. but still has a Western twang and an urgent connotation.* 2 An overly diligent student. *c1845; archaic. Replaced by "grind."* *v.i.* 1 To eat a meal. 1910: "I'd like you to come over and grub with us." Johnson, *Varmint*, 320. 2 To study hard. See also **grub out.**

grub-choker   *n.* A cook. *c1870. Ranch and cowboy use.*

grub out = **grub.**

grub-pile   *n.* A meal. *Ranch use.*

grub-slinger   *n.* A cook. *Orig. ranch use.*

grub-stake   grubstake   *n.* Money saved or borrowed to buy food and other necessities, and cover the expenses involved while prospecting, moving to a new region, looking for work, or starting a new business or venture of any kind. 1936: "A 'grub-stake,' according to the usual significance of the term, required its recipient to pay to its donor an agreed share of whatever profit might accrue from the enterprise on which the recipient was about to embark, and for the furtherance of which the grub-stake was given . . . might, on occasion, be used in a different sense to denote one's food-supply, regardless of how obtained." P. A. Rollins, *The Cowboy*, 34. 1956: "He had the reputation of never having turned down a broken guy. Nobody knows how much he gave away in grubstakes." T. Betts, *Across the Board*, 119. *Orig. Western use, from mining prospectors. Colloq.*

gruesome twosome   1 Lovers; a couple who go steady. *Orig. jive talk; c1940 wide student use.* → 2 Any two associates. 3 Army shoes. *A little W.W.II use. Except in the last usage, "twosome" is the root word; "gruesome" is only added for the rhyme and is not considered derog. Often used jocularly.* See Appendix, Rhyming Slang.

grumbler   *n.* 1 A police chief. 2 One's boss. *Not common.*

grunt   *n.* 1 An electric lineman's helper who works on the ground and does not climb poles. *c1900 to present. Telephone lineman, railroad lineman, and Army Signal Corps use.* 2 A locomotive engineer. *Railroad use.* 3 Pork or ham. *Still a little Western use. From the sounds a pig makes.* "Cluck and grunt" = *ham and eggs.* See **grunts.** 4 A bill, check, or tab for food and/or drinks. 1951: ". . . No evidence that El Twirpo ever bought a drink or picked up the grunt for a party." W. Pegler, *synd. newsp. col.,* Aug. 14. 5 Wrestling; the wrestling profession, entertainment, or sport. 6 A wrestler, esp. an inferior wrestler, or one known for grimacing, pretending to be hurt, or other emotional, crowd-pleasing devices.   **—er**   *n.* A wrestler.   **—s** *n.pl.* Bacon. *Still some Western use.* "Cackleberries and grunts" = *bacon and eggs.* See **grunt.**

grunt-and-groaner   *n.* A wrestler. *Has increased pop. with the advent of televised wrestling shows incorporating excessive facial grimaces and moans from the wrestlers.*

grunt-horn   *n.* A tuba. *Not common.* Cf. **slip-horn.**

grunt-iron   *n.* A tuba. *Synthetic use by cartoonists and newsp. columnists.*

grut   *n.* 1 A boring person; a common person. *From mispronunciation of "great." Never as common in U.S. as in Eng.* See **beaugeeful.** 2 = **crud.** *The similarity of pronunciation may have confused the two words.*

guard   See **dumbguard, home guard.**
—guard   See Appendix, Suffixes and Suffix Words.

guardhouse lawyer   *n.* 1 A soldier who, well informed or not, often quotes and discusses military law and soldiers' rights. 1943–45: "The 'guardhouse lawyer' . . . performs remarkable exploits and resolves the most formidable situations all through the medium of simple discussion." J. B. Roulier. *Orig. Army use. Since c1930.* → 2 One who likes to advise others, freely and authoritatively though not acquainted with the problem; one who knows little but talks much about a specific controversial subject.

gub = **gob.**

gubbins *n.sing.* **1** Food; an item of food obtained ashore. *A little W.W.I USN use. From Brit. Navy sl.* → **2** Left-over food; scraps of food. *Obs. Also W.W.I USN use. From Brit. Navy.* → **3** Any piece of equipment in an airplane; a gadget. *c1940. Some Air Force use.*

gubble = **ubble-gubble.**

guess-stick *n.* A slide rule. *Not common.*

guff **goff** *n.* Empty or foolish talk; chiding, exaggerated, or pompous talk, writing, or thinking; boloney. 1888: *sl. DAE.* 1921: "The newspaper guff about the kid bein' through hadn't fooled Jimmy." Witwer, *Leather,* 194. 1932: "He . . . always has a fair line of guff. . . ." Runyon. 1951: ". . . Music and story-writing and all that guff." S. Lewis, *World So Wide,* 27. 1952: "Don't take any guff from him!" *New Yorker,* June 7, 21/3. → *v.t., v.i.* To deceive, lie, or exaggerate. *Usu. in* "I'm not guffing [to] you."

Guin *n.* An Italian. *From "Guinea." Not common.*

Guinea **guinea** **Ginney** **ginney** **Ginnee** **ginee** **guinie** [derog.] *n.* **1** An Italian; a person of Italian descent. 1922: ". . .Ginee. . . ." O'Neill, *Hairy Ape,* 7. 1932: "Black Mike is a Guinea." Runyon. *Since c1885. With time, the term has become a little less derog.* **2** A native islander of New Guinea; a native of any South Pacific island; a Japanese. *Wide W.W.II use. Orig. W.W.II Army use. Very derog.* *adj.* **1** Italian. 1932: ". . . A tough Ginney bootlegger by the name of Gregorio. . . ." Runyon. **2** Japanese; related to the South Pacific islands.

guinea football A small, handmade bomb. *c1925. Associated with underworld violence, owing to the bomb throwing of Mafia gangsters.*

guinea's harp A guitar. *Not common.* See **guinea.**

guinney *n.* A racetrack stable hand. *Horse-racing use.*

guinzo = **ginzo.**

gulch = **dry-gulch.**

gull *n.* **1** Chicken or any other fowl served at a meal. *A little maritime use. From "sea gull."* **2** A prostitute, esp. one who follows a USN fleet or works near naval bases. *W.W.II USN use.*

gully-jumper *n.* A farmer. *Archaic and dial.*

gully-low *adj.* Sensuous; "dirty"; said of a style of playing jazz.

gum *v.i.* To talk, esp. to gossip or talk needlessly. 1950: "The he-gossips at the Press Club have been gumming about another romance. . . ." Starnes, *Another Mug,* 33. *v.t.* **1** = **gum up.** 1939: "Gum the works." J. Auslander, *Hell in Harness,* 40. **2** To deceive or cheat. **3** To spoil or ruin something, esp. to spoil by interfering. 1910: "Well, he's rotten. He gums the whole show." Johnson, *Varmint,* 142. *Usu. in "gum up" and "gum up the works."* See **beat [one's] gums, bump [one's] gums.**

gum-beater *n.* A talker; esp. a braggart or a loud, frequent talker; a blowhard.

gum-beating *n.* **1** A chat or conversation. *Orig. Harlem jive talk.* Cf. **beat [one's] gums.** → **2** Useless or pointless talk or discussion.

gum boot = **gumshoe.**

gum drop A pretty and sweet girl or young woman. *Usu. used cynically for a woman of doubtful reputation. Not common. Pop. by comedian W.C. Fields.* See Appendix, Sex and Food.

gum-foot *n.* A policeman, esp. a plain-clothes man.

gumheel *n.* = **gumshoe.** *v.i.* To work as a detective. 1950: "Still gum-heeling?" Starnes, *And When She Was Bad,* 70.

gummer *n.* An old, toothless man; an old decrepit man.

gummixed up **gummoxed up** Confused, mixed up. *From "gummed-up" + euphem. of "fucked up," perhaps reinforced by Eng. sl. "gummock" = fool or dolt.*

gummy *adj.* **1** Inferior; uninteresting; boring; disliked, disagreeable. *c1930.* **2** Sentimental, overly emotional. *c1940.* *n.* **1** Glue; any sticky substance. **2** A pitchman who sells miracle glue that is reputed to join any broken item or materials. *c1930. Carnival use.*

gump *n.* **1** A foolish or stupid fellow; a dolt. *c1865–1920. Obs. The term is much older than the synd. comic strip featuring Andy Gump.* **2** A chicken; esp. a live chicken that can be stolen to provide a meal. *c1915. Hobo use. Because chickens are considered among the most foolish of creatures.* **3** Gumption. *Back clipping. Not common.*

gumshoe *v.i., v.t.* To walk quietly, to sneak, esp. to walk a beat; said of a policeman. 1949: "Police now ride radio prowl cars instead of gumshoeing around the block." E. B. White, *Here Is New York*, 300. **2** To walk in, or as if wearing, rubber-soled shoes; to walk silently and stealthily. *c1910.* → **3** To work as a police detective. 1927: "He thought gumshoeing would be fun." Hammett, *Blood Money*, 29.   *n.* A detective; any policeman. *Since c1920.*   *adj.* Done quietly or stealthily.

gumshoe man = **gumshoe.**

gum-sucking   *n.* Kissing, osculation. *c1870. Not common.*

gum up   To ruin or spoil a plan or the successful completion of a task, esp. by blundering; to blunder; to confuse a person, esp. by making a mistake. 1952: "I'm awfully sorry—I gummed you up on that." Radio program, *20 Questions*, Mar. 29.

gun   *n.* **1** A professional thief or robber; esp. a pickpocket. *Since at least c1840. From the Yiddish "gonif" or "goney" = a thief and Yiddish sl. "gonif" = to steal, both of which were taken directly into Amer. sl., reinforced by "gunsel." See* Appendix, *Shortened Words. See* **cannon.** 1901: "No one knows . . . how many guns there are in New York. . . ." *McClure's*, May, 571–2. → **2** A hoodlum or thug; a gunman. 1846: "One who uses a gun." *DAE. From first meaning reinforced by "gun."* **3** The throttle or gas pedal of a car, truck, or plane. *Since c1925.* **4** An elevator. *Not common.* **5** A railroad warning torpedo placed on the tracks for signaling trains to stop or slow up. *Railroad use.* **6** A surveyor's transit. *Not common.* **7** A hypodermic needle. *Dope addict use, c1935.* **8** An important person. See **big gun.** See also **belly gun, burp gun, grease-gun, scatter-gun, shotgun, zip gun.** **9** A visual examination; a look or glance. **10** [taboo] The penis. "This is my rifle./ This is my gun./ This is for shooting./ This is for fun." Old Army poem, used to teach recruits the proper nomenclature for "rifle." *Not common.* *v.t.* **1** To look at intensely; to stare at carefully; to make a complete visual inspection. *Since c1860.* **2** To shoot a person with a gun. 1934: "Canales had no motive to gun Lou. . . ." Chandler, *Finger Man*, 54. *Since c1895.* → **3** To take a photograph; to shoot a picture. *Orig. movie maker talk. c1925.* **4** To accelerate the motor of a car, plane, or boat, specif. before releasing the

brake or starting, so that the motor is warmed up and operating at maximum speed when the vehicle begins to move. 1952: "Some jerk pulls alongside and guns his cement mixer!" Fagaly and Shorten, "There Oughta Be a Law!" *synd. cartoon,* Sept. 16. *The most common verbal usage. Almost colloq.* **5** To carry something to another; to be a waiter or errand boy to another. *c1940.*

gun, give [something] the   To accelerate a car, plane, or boat to its maximum speed; to accelerate any motor or machine; to gun an engine.

gunboat   *n.* **1** An empty one-gallon tin can. **2** An iron coal car; a railroad gondola. *Railroad use.* **—s**   *n.pl.* **1** A pair of shoes; esp. a pair of very large shoes. 1951: "He brought some of the [size 14 EE] gunboats with him from the states, but they wore out. . . ." AP, Korea, June 28. *Since c1885.* **2** A pair of overshoes, galoshes, or rubbers. **3** The feet; esp. large feet. *All uses somewhat humorous.*

guncel = **gunsel.**

guniff = **goniff.**

gunk   *n.* **1** Dirt in various forms; esp., oily grime; gook. 1949: "You can actually see the gook and gunk that drains out with your [motor] oil." Advt., NBC radio ntwk., Aug. 25. → **2** Any viscous liquid or oily fluid; gook. 1950: "After immersing parts of [a 1917 model Stanley Steamer] in a fluid known as 'gunk,' and puttering around with the rest." "Thus, out of the 'gunk' bath, Mr. Woodbury's Steamer emerged just as if it were brand new." P. Blake in N.Y. *Times Bk. Rev.*, Oct. 8, 20. **3** Make-up; any cosmetic. 1950: "I smeared additional gunk on my eye." Starnes, *Another Mug*, 107. **4** Dehydrated or powdered food. *Some USN use since W.W.II.*

gun moll   gun-moll   *n.* **1** A female thief or criminal. *From "gonif" = to steal. See* **gun.** **2** A female accomplice of a criminal. *From the mistaken belief that the expression is from "gun," a weapon, and thus a gun moll carries a gun for her underworld paramour.*

gunny   gunnie   *n.* A gunman. 1934: "Tell us the rest about the two gunnies." Chandler, *Finger Man*, 48. *Not common.*

gunpoke   *n.* A gunman; an armed robber. *A term patterned after "cowpoke."* 1939: "He . . . sends a gunpoke around to take the money. . . ." Chandler, *Big Sleep*, 140f.

**gunsel   gonzel   gonsil   guncel
guntzel**   *n.* **1** A catamite; a young
inexperienced boy, esp. a hobo, such as
a catamite would desire for a companion.
Prison and hobo use since c1915. *From
the German "gänzel" and/or the Yiddish
"gantzel" = gosling.* 1951: "Scores of
hoodlums, gunsels, informers, shyster
lawyers, and crooked shamuses. . . ."
S. J. Perelman in *New Yorker*, Mar. 3,
26/3. *Underworld use since c1925.* → **2** A
treacherous person; a sly, sneaky person;
an unethical, untrustworthy person.
3 A thief; a criminal; a member of the
underworld. 1951: "Culio, a run-of-the-
mob gunsel. . . ." Advt. for movie, *The
Mob*, Sept. 15.

gun-slinger   *n.* A gunman; a hired
killer or armed robber. 1953: "The
[Valley Stream, L.I.] gun-slinger will
spend . . . his life behind bars." AP,
Sept. 28. *Orig. an old Western term.*

gun-wadding   *n.* Bread. *Not common.*

gussied up   Dressed in one's best
clothes. 1952: [*oral*] "When I get all
gussied up, somebody says, 'Pull in
your pot!' "

gussie mollie   A girl friend. 1928:
"How's your gussie mollie?" Hecht &
MacArthur, *Front Page*, II. *Not common.*

Gusy-Gusy   *adj.* Extremely masculine or virile in gestures, speech, and
appearance, usu. said of an actor or a
theatrical character. *Not common.* See
Appendix, Reduplications.

gut   *n.* **1** The stomach. *Very common.*
2 Sausage. *In hobo lingo "punk and gut"
= bread and sausage.* **3** An easy course in
college; a pipe course. See also **gut
course.** 1952: "The Yale chaplain's
basic religion course was . . . considered
a 'gut' by at least 50% of the students
enrolled in it. . . ." W. E. Chilton III,
Atlantic Monthly, Jan. 1, 20/1. See
**guts, pinch-gut, rotgut, spill [one's]
guts, tub-of-guts.**   *v.t.* To remove all accessories, frills, or ornament
from something. *Orig. hot rod use; some
cool and beat use since c1955.*   —**s**
n.sing. Courage; perseverance; audacity.
Colloq.   *n.pl.* **1** The insides of a
person or animal. 1949: "Hamlet, like
the G.I., . . . hated the guts of the
high brass. . . ." J. B. Douds, *CEA
Critic*, Nov., 3/2. → **2** Courage; nerve.
1930: "The guy who had guts enough
to croak 'Tough Tony.' " Lavine, *Third
Degree*, 27. → **3** Solid substance; forceful
or meaty contents. → **4** The insides or
working parts of a machine.   —**sy**
adj. Having force, drive, guts. 1951:

[Pentagon Building use, Washington,
D.C.] "I think he's plenty gutsy." P.
Hogan. *Not common.*   —**ter**   *n.* In div-
ing, an attempted dive in which the diver
falls prone on the water instead of going
in head foremost; a belly-whacker. *Dial.*
—**ty**   *adj.* **1** = **back alley.** 1958:
"You feel it in a beat, in jazzy . . . or a
good gutty rock number." John Clellon
Holmes, "The Philosophy of The Beat
Generation," *Esquire*, Feb., 35. *Jazz use.*
2 Courageous. 1953: "Here Come the
Guttiest Guys of All." Advt. for movie,
The Desert Rats, June 24.

gutbucket   gut-bucket   *n.* **1** A
pail used to carry beer, food, or water.
*c1890, used by Southern chain gangs and
laborers, usu. Negro.* → **2** A bucket or
other container hung in a conspicuous
place or passed around in a crowd in
order to solicit or collect contributions of
money for beer or food. *A practice of
itinerant musicians, c1900; usu. used
in the South, esp. Mississippi river towns
such as New Orleans.* → **3** A cheap saloon
and/or gambling house where musicians
could play for patrons' contributions.
4 A cheap dive or joint. *Still in use
among Negroes.* **5** A fat, pompous
person. *Orig. such a person might
patronize a saloon or gambling house and
contribute a good sum to the musicians'
bucket, often in return for special requests
or to show off. Archaic since c1930.* **6** A
sexually suggestive, dirty style of jazz,
appropriate to a cheap saloon. *The orig.
New Orleans hot style for playing a blues.*
1956: "Louis Armstrong, World's Greatest Jazz Cornetist. He blew it good and
right, gut-bucket. . . ." S. Longstreet,
The Real Jazz Old and New, 158. *Jazz use.*

gut-burglar   *n.* A logging-camp cook.
A term based on "belly-robber."

gut course   In college, an easy course.
See also **gut.** 1951: "Eco . . . was a gut
course if I ever saw one." Cornell
Widow, Apr. 17, 18.

gut-hammer   *n.* A gong, usu. a
suspended iron triangle used as a
dinner bell for logging camps, ranches,
farms, and the like.

gutter, in the   **1** Fig., as a drunken
bum, who falls down drunk in the gutter.
Colloq. **2** Without money, respect, or
hope. **3** Preoccupied with the obscene
or lewd. *Usu. in "to have [one's] mind
in the gutter."* See **dirty.**

gutterpup   *n.* A person of the gutter;
a bum. 1924: "College men . . . talk like
a lot of gutter-pups." Marks, *Plastic Age*,
154.

guttersnipe   *n.* = **gutterpup.** *c1865.* *Archaic.*

guy   *v.t.* To ridicule; to tease or mock. 1869: *DAE. Colloq.*   *n.* **1** A boy or man; a fellow. *Orig. used without modification, often of a stranger, and implied, as it still often does, an average, pleasant fellow or "regular guy." Since c1925 sometimes takes a modifier to* = *an unpleasant fellow, as a "tough guy" or "wise guy."* 1896: "Guy." *DAE.* 1900: "Look at the guy [a stranger] in the cab." Dreiser, *Carrie*, 318. 1928: "The first time you meet a guy. . . ." S. Lewis, *The Man Who Knew Coolidge*, 106. 1932: *Guys and Dolls*, title of a book by Damon Runyon. 1950: "Just a guy keeping a chair warm until a good Republican could move in." C. F. Brannan, U.S. Secy. of Agriculture, quoted in *Time*, June 19, 23f. *Very common since c1925. Perhaps influenced by the Yiddish "goy"* = *gentile.* → **2** A person of either sex. 1944: "[Said to a man and a woman:] Where are you guys going?" Ford, *Phila. Murder*, 129. 1946: "Have Americans no other word for a human being than 'guy'?" St. J. Ervine in *Sat. Rev. Lit.*, Mar. 9, 19/1. *Some use since c1930.* **3** A friend; a chum or pal.

guyed out   Drunk. *c1930; circus use. From "guy out"* = *to tighten a rope.*

guzzle   *v.i., v.t.* **1** To drink rapidly. *Colloq.* → **2** To drink liquor. 1950: "He did some guzzling during the war. . . ." AP, Jan. 23. → **3** To drink liquor constantly or in large amounts. **4** To kill, esp. by strangling to death. 1932: ". . . If we only have a Cleopatra . . . around now guzzling guys every few minutes. . . ." Runyon. **5** To neck. 1935: "A little offhand guzzling . . . is quite permissible.. . . ." Runyon. *The last two meanings are Damon Runyon creations.*   *n.* **1** The throat. 1934: "Somebody grabs Mr. Veezee by the guzzle and cracks his neck for him. . . ." Runyon. **—d**   *adj.* **1** Arrested. **2** Drunk. **—ry guzzery** *n.* Any place where beer or whisky is sold and drunk, as a bar, nightclub, or the like. *Now common only with newspaper columnists.*

guzzle shop   A saloon. 1936: ". . . No lower guzzle-shop was ever operated in the United States." Herbert Asbury, *The French Quarter*, 231. Cf. **guzzlery.**

gym   *n.* **1** A gymnasium. 1896: *DAE. Colloq. Refers to a gymnasium as a place of athletic significance only.* See Appendix, Shortened Words. **2** Exercise taken in, games played in, or an exercise class held in, a gymnasium; specif., gymnastics.

gyp   **gip**   **jip**   *n.* **1** A gypsy. *c1890. Obs.* → **2** One who uses shrewd, unethical business methods; a swindler, a cheater. 1945: "[La Guardia's] denunciations of punks, tinhorns and gyps. . . ." W. Pegler, *synd. newsp. col.*, Dec. 13. *Colloq; orig. a carnival and circus term; c1910.* → **3** A swindle, an act of cheating; an unfair transaction or decision. 1941: "The victim of any such gyp. . . ." Cain, *M. Pierce*, 247. **4** Vim; pep. *A variation of the dial. "gimp."* **5** A female dog, esp. a racing dog. *Perhaps from the 17th c. Eng. sl. term "jip"* = *servant or trained animal.*   *v.t.* **1** To outsmart. *c1915; carnival and circus use. Obs.* → **2** To cheat or swindle. 1925: "We had over $1200 . . . but we got gypped out of it all in two days. . . ." F. Scott Fitzgerald, *The Great Gatsby*, 42. *Colloq.*   *adj.* **1** Commercial; legitimately profit-making. 1938: ". . . A gyp horseman. . . . 'Gyp,' as applied to horsemen, is . . . without opprobrium. Gyp stables try to make a profit. . . ." Liebling, *Back Where*, 232. *Obs.* **2** Dishonest. 1945: "For protection against gyp employers, I would like to have a union card. . . ." W. Pegler, *synd. newsp. col.*, Dec. 20. **—per**   *n.* A cheater, a swindler. **—po**   **jippo**   *n.* **1** Gravy. *Some W.W.I Army use, but never as common as in the Brit. Army.* **2** Part-time, temporary work; piecework. *c1920. Hobo, itinerant laborer, and logger use.* **3** A pieceworker or itinerant worker. → **4** A small factory, logging contractor, cannery, or the like that employs a pieceworker or gives a hobo a day's work. 1946: "In the Northwest they discussed gyppo logging shows." *Time*, Nov. 11, 24/1.   *v.t.* To cheat; to gyp. 1926: ". . . The contract worker is . . . being unmercifully gyppoed by the boss. . . ." *Amer. Mercury*, Jan., 63. **—ster** *n.* A swindler; a gypper. See Appendix, —ster ending.

gyp artist   **gyp-artist**   An adroit and constant swindler or cheater. See Appendix, —artist.

gyp joint   **gyp-joint**   *n.* Any public place that overcharges, cheats, or promises its customers more than it gives them. 1956: "The real gyp joints were the dance schools, the taxi-dance halls and . . ." S. Longstreet, *The Real Jazz Old and New*, 57. See Appendix, —joint. *Common since c1935.*

Gypo [derog.] *n.* An Egyptian or Arab. *W.W.II Army use. From the Brit. Army term.*

gypsy('s) leave The act or an instance of departing without warning or permission; esp., departure without settling one's debts or without official permission. *Archaic.* See **French leave.**

gypsy('s) warning No warning. *Archaic. In the U.S. this term never meant "gin," as it does in Ireland.* Cf. **gypsy('s) leave.**

gyrene *n.* A U.S. Marine. *Also spelled* "girene," "gyrine," and occas. with "j" for "g." 1940: "... The regular kicking around the sailors get from the gyrenes. ..." J. H. Jennings, *Life,* Nov. 18, 4. 1950: "U.S. Army slang from 'G.I' + 'marine.'" *Web. However, the term was used at Annapolis c1925, predating the pop. of "G.I.."* Cf. **leatherneck, seagoing bell-hop.**

gyve jive *n.* A marijuana cigaret; marijuana. 1952: "So Diane smoked jive, pod, and tea. ..." Orville Prescott, N.Y. *Times,* Apr. 29, 25. *Since c1930.*

H

H *n.* Heroin as used by addicts. *Addict use.*

haba haba *interj.* A command or request to hurry up or speed up. *W.W.II Armed Forces use, usu. USN use in the Pacific Theater.* See **hubba-hubba.** See Appendix, Reduplications.

habit *n.* Addiction to a drug. 1949: " 'Habit? Man,' he liked to remember, 'I had a great big habit. I knocked out one of my own teet' to get the gold for a fix. You call that being hooked or not?' " N. Algren, *Man with the Golden Arm,* 78.

habit, off the Cured of drug addiction; not under the influence of drugs. Cf. **on the needle.**

hack *n.* **1** A taxicab. 1912: "All into a hack." Johnson, *Stover at Yale,* 11. *Here a horse-drawn coach. Colloq. Orig. a horse-drawn hackney coach, the term was applied to automobiles used as taxicabs.* → **2** A bus; an omnibus. *Not common, except among bus drivers.* → **3** The caboose of a railroad train. *c1915. Railroad use. c1930. Some regional use. Archaic.* **4** A persistent cough, usu. caused by nervousness or throat irritation rather than a cold. **5** A prison guard, a prison official; a watchman. *Convict use.* → **6** A white person. *Prison use. Negro use. In the U.S. this term never means girl, as it does in Australia. v.i.* **1** To drive a taxicab as an occupation. 1952: "I worked in an office for years. ... Then I took to hacking." Hal Boyle, *synd. AP col.,* Sept. 22. **2** To cough repeatedly or habitually. **3** To neck, pet, or spoon. *c1940. Not common.* **—er** *n.* A cab-driver; a taxi-driver. 1949: "He enriched another hacker by an even $5,000." UP, Sept. 30. *Never as common as "hackie."* **—ie** *n.* The driver of a cab, a hack-driver. 1949: "One thousand cab drivers of [Newark, N.J.] who, like 'hackies' everywhere, have a sharp eye. ..." The N.Y. *Times,* July 24, 1/2. *Orig. the driver of a horse-drawn hackney cab, now applied to all cab drivers.*

hack-driver *n.* A chief petty officer in the U.S. Navy. 1942: USN use. E. F. Stuckey.

hack hand A truck-driver. *c1935; trucker use.*

hack-skinner *n.* A bus-driver, usu. a skillful one. *c1935; bus-driver use.*

had See **been had, have.**

had it, [one] (has, have) **1** Emotionally or physically fatigued or exhausted, so that one is unable to respond further; defeated, esp. by fatigue caused by striving to succeed; to have failed or meet with such failure, defeat, or ill fortune that one has no further spirit, enthusiasm, courage, perseverance, or desire to succeed. → **2** To have been given one's last chance to show one's worth or reliability, and to have failed; no longer liked, admired, or respected; no longer believed to be attractive, worthwhile, trustworthy or successful by the speaker. Cf. **has been.** *Both uses common since c1940.*

hag *n.* A homely young woman. **—gy** *adj.* Ugly; like a hag.

haha ha-ha *n.* A joke; a cause of merriment. 1943: "That's a ha-ha all right." Wolfert, *Underworld,* 124. See Appendix, Reduplications. See **merry haha.**

Hail Columbia **1** Euphem. for "hell," as an expression of anger or disgust. **2** Euphem. for "hell" in its sl. phrases. *Thus "to get Hail Columbia" = to get hell, to be bawled out; "to raise Hail*

Columbia" = *to raise hell. In use since c1850; from the title of the song composed in 1798.* See **hell.**

hair See **in [one's] hair, long-hair, white-haired boy.**

hair, get in [one's] To irritate, bother, or annoy a person; to get in someone's way. *Lit.* = *to annoy as would lice in one's hair.*

hair, in [one's] Annoying [a person], with the implication that the annoyer is a louse. 1880: "... You'll have one of these ... professors in your hair." Mark Twain, cited in *DAE.*

hair bag A person who remembers and speaks of or gossips about past intrigues, scandals, events, and the like. 1958: "Hair bag—A veteran policeman, especially knowledgeable about the inner workings of the Police Department." G. Y. Wells, *Station House Slang.* See **hairy.**

hairdown *n.* A most intimate conversation. From **let [one's] hair down.** *Not common.*

hair down, let [one's] To shed all of one's reserve, inhibitions, or dignity, usu. to act or talk very informally or intimately. 1937: "You can let your hair down in front of me." Weidman, *Wholesale,* 3.

hair net = **win the porcelain hair net.**

hair off the dog, take To gain experience; to grow older. *Usu. in "I've taken a little more hair off the dog." From cowboy use; lit. having branded a few more calves. Not to be confused with* **hair of the dog.**

hair of the dog A drink of liquor. *Since c1925; from "hair of the dog that bit you."*

hair of the dog that bit [you, me, him, one, etc.] *n.* The liquor or a drink of the liquor that made one drunk or sick the previous night, or caused one's present hangover. *One tradition has it that the best cure for a hangover is a drink of the liquor that caused it.*

hair pie [taboo] The vulva, esp. as considered the object of cunnilingus. See **eat.** See Appendix, Sex and Food.

hairpin *n.* **1** A man; a person of either sex. → **2** A woman, esp. a housewife. *Vagabond argot.* **3** A crackpot; fig., a person with a mind bent like a hairpin; a screwball. *v.t.* To mount a horse. *Cowboy use.*

hair-pounder *n.* A teamster. *c1925; logger use.*

hairy *adj.* **1** Old, already known, passé; usu. said of a joke or story. *Colloq.* **2**

Unpleasant, lousy, *c1950; orig. West Coast teenager use. Increasing in pop.* **3** Virile. *Not common.* *n.* A brave person. 1958: "Hairy—A chesty or boastful cop." G. Y. Wells, *Station House Slang. Usu. used jocularly to indicate a man who often tells stories of his own bravery.*

half *n.* In football, a halfback. *c1930.* See **better half, one-and-a-half-striper, two-and-a-half-striper.**

half- *A common sl. prefix used to indicate:* **1** Confusion. **2** Drunkenness. *Here the "half" ceases to be a polite prefix.* See Appendix, Prefixes and Prefix Words.

half a shake **1** Fig., half a second. *E.g., "I'll be ready in half a shake."* **2** An opportunity or chance with restrictions; an unfair chance.

half-assed [taboo] *adj.* **1** Ignorant of a specif. field of endeavor or pertinent facts; without full or proper plans, experience, knowledge, or understanding. **2** Badly planned; disorganized; the result of, or giving evidence of, many blunders; unsatisfactory; inefficient; incomplete.

half-baked *adj.* Stupid; half-witted. *Colloq. since c1915.*

half-buck *n.* A half-dollar. 1948: "The average [taxi] haul is a half-buck." Lait-Mortimer, *N.Y. Confidential. Lit.* = *half of a buck.*

half-cocked **half cocked** *adj.* **1** Drunk. *Common c1925; not now common.* See Appendix, Drunk. **2** Enthusiastic or emotional about something of which one knows little; without full or proper plans, knowledge, objectivity, experience, or understanding. 1946: "You know, we're not going into this thing half cocked. I made a thorough survey of the consumer situation before I laid my plans." M. Shulman, *Zebra Derby,* 43.

half-corned *adj.* Drunk.

half-pint *n.* **1** A person of short stature. 1929: "... The little half-pint that she was. ..." John O'Hara, *New Yorker,* Jan. 12, 64/2. *Usu. used affectionately or derog.* **2** A boy. *adj.* Short of stature; small. 1950: "Half-pint showman. ..." UP, Jan. 27.

half-portion *n.* An undersized person. *c1925; not common.*

half-screwed *adj.* Drunk. *Fairly common. c1925.*

half seas over *adj.* Drunk, usu. completely drunk. *Common from Colonial times through the 1920's; some W.W.II USN use. Orig. an Eng. sl. term, it is* *still common in Eng.* See Appendix, Drunk.

half shaved *adj.* Half drunk. *Archaic.*

half-shot **half shot** *adj.* **1** Half drunk. *Since c1835; still very common.* **2** Drunk. 1948: "Stuff for guys in college to gag about when they were half shot with beer." Cain, *Moth*, 64. See Appendix, Drunk. *Since c1925;* see **shot. 3** Dissipated; not in control of one's mind or muscles; suffering from dissipation or physical or emotional shock.

half-slewed *adj.* Drunk. *c1860; archaic.*

half-snaped *adj.* Half drunk. *c1850; never common.*

half-sprung *adj.* Drunk. *c1850; archaic. Still used in Eng.*

half-stewed *adj.* Drunk. *Common.* See **stewed.**

half the bay over = half seas over.

half under Drunk. *c1925.*

halfy *n.* A legless man.

hall *n.* Alcohol. *A respelling of the "-hol" of alcohol.* Cf. **John Hall.**

halvies *n.* Half of whatever is at hand, usu. sweets, money, or children's prizes. *Child use. To shout "Halvies!" obligates another child to give one half of his loot, purchase, or the like.*

ham *n.* **1** An amateur worker, performer, or athlete; almost always one proficient and an amateur only in that he does a thing for the fun of it, as a hobby, rather than for money; occasionally an inexperienced or inferior worker, performer, or athlete; specif., an amateur athlete (*no longer common*), actor, or radio-telegraph operator (*colloq.*). 1888: [an inferior boxer]. *DAE.* 1929: "The word 'ham' is almost exclusively identified with actors." O. Sobel, *Bookman*, Apr., 148. 1929: "[Now] no stigma is implied in its use. In the early days of radio, *ham* was a term of reproach." M. Fry, *AS*, Oct., 45 ff. *From "amateur" in its orig. meaning = one who does something for the love of it.* See Appendix, Shortened Words. → **2** Specif., an amateur or professional actor who is affected, conceited, and who strives for attention over the other actors on the stage. 1936: "*Variety* never referred to actors as 'hams' (an unpardonable, derogatory reference)...." A. Green, *Esquire*, Sept., 160/3. 1949: "The cast is filled out by a group of hams." M. James in N.Y. *Times*, Aug. 28, X3/3. → **3** A pretentious, affected person; esp. one who assumes or attempts to convey an impression of gentility not actually his; a conceited

person. 1950: "Miss Moment was no doubt the biggest ham of a teacher I've heard or seen since or before: she fooled me all the time." A. Lomax, *Mr. Jelly Roll*, 6. **4** Food; meals. *Some circus use.* *adj.* **1** Amateur. **2** Inferior. *v.i., v.t.* **1** To act a part poorly, affectedly, or obviously; to display conceit; to attempt to convey the impression that one is more important or knowledgeable than one actually is. **2** To overact; to seek attention.

ham and An order of ham and eggs. *Common lunch-counter use.*

ham-and-egger *n.* **1** An average person; a worker limited to routine tasks; one as common as ham and eggs or one who may make average wages or live an average, unexciting life. *c1900; archaic.* → **2** Specif., an average prize fighter. *Since c1920.* See Appendix, —er ending. **—y** *n.* A restaurant; esp. a small restaurant or lunch counter. See Appendix, —ery ending.

hambone *n.* **1** A trombone. *Some c1930 use. Obs.* **2** A ham (actor); a ham (nonactor). 1949: "If you are a pampered hambone living in Hollywood, come along with me; step into your chartreuse convertible." W. J. Slocum in *Collier's*, Aug. 27, 26. *Not common.* 1952: "Every hambone from the deep sticks was constrained to make a speech for the benefit of the [television] cameras." R. C. Ruark, *synd. newsp. col.*, July 9. *Not common. From "ham" plus the "Bones" or "Mr. Bones" character, usu. the comedian master-of-ceremonies or the end man of a minstrel show.*

hamburger *n.* **1** A badly scarred and often beaten prize fighter. **2** A bum or tramp; anyone who is down and out. **3** An inferior racing dog; lit., one that should be ground up for food. **4** A mixture of mud and "skin-food" used as a facial treatment in beauty parlors.

hamburger heaven Any small restaurant or lunch counter featuring hamburgers and quick meals. *Many such establishments are actually named "Hamburger Heaven," as is a chain in N.Y.C.*

hamburger out of, make To beat up; to thrash severely.

ham-fatter *n.* An inferior, obvious entertainer or entertainment; an actor or act whose subtlety is no greater than that of a Negro minstrel show. *Since c1880.* See **hambone.**

ham-hanger *n.* One who loafs on the job. *Lit. = one who sits on his "hams"* *all day doing nothing. Not common, may be restricted to U.S. postoffice worker use.*

ham joint　　1 A cheap restaurant. 2 A place where one can sit and relax, doing nothing. 1925: "[A crooks'] rendezvous is a 'ham joint,' usually a cheap all-night restaurant or pool parlor." McLellan, *Collier's.* See **ham-hanger.**

hammer　　See **gut-hammer.**

hammered　　*adj.* Drunk. *Not common.* See Appendix, Drunk.

hammerhead　　*n.* A stupid person; a hard-headed person. *1934, Obs., Web.* 1937: "The best way out is for one of the three to be a hammerhead." Weidman, *Wholesale,* 118.

hammer-man　　*n.* A person of authority. *Some Negro use.*

hammertails　　*n.sing.* A formal or dress suit; specif., a cutaway or morning coat. 1951: "Several men in cutaway coats, called 'hammertails.' " S. Longstreet, *The Pedlocks,* 71. *Archaic.*

ham up = **ham.** 1950: "The [baseball umpire] was hamming up his signals for the benefit of the television audience." *New Yorker,* May 27, 19/1.

hand　　For phrases beginning with "hand," see under principal word of phrase.

hand　　*n.* The clapping of hands in applause by a person or an audience. 1939–40: "Well she got a big hand. . . ." O'Hara, *Pal Joey,* 28. *Colloq. since c1930.* See **both hands, glad hand, forkhander, left-handed.**

handbasket, go to hell in a　　Amateurish, small-sized (handbasket-sized) dissipation of the kind indulged in, usu. by the young, as protest against a disappointment or a frustration; driving too fast, drinking too much, and the like, for a fairly short period of time.

handbasket, in a = **with knobs on.**

handbook　　*n.* 1 A place, other than a race-track, where horse-racing bets are made. 1949: "I was in a handbook near Loomis and Madison. . . ." *Fact Detec. Mysteries,* 88. 2 The owner or an employee of such a betting business.

handful　　*n.* A five-year prison sentence. *In allusion to the five fingers. Underworld use.* See **grab a handful of air.**

hand grenade　　1 A hamburger. *Supposedly W.W.II Army sl., but prob. synthetic.* 2 A baseball. *Not common.* **—r**　　*n.* A baseball pitcher. *Not common.*

handies　　*n.pl.* The act of holding

hands, as by lovers. 1953: "Beneath the counter they were playing handies." Christopher Morley, *The Ballad of N.Y., N.Y.*

hand it to someone　　To give someone credit for merit; to compliment. 1934: "I got to hand it to you. . . ." Cain, *Postman,* 10. *Colloq.*

handkerchief-head　　[derog.]　　*n.* A Negro who is subservient to or meek before whites; an Uncle Tom. 1956: "A 'handkerchief-head' is an old-fashioned Negro who doesn't know his rights." S. Longstreet, *The Real Jazz Old and New,* 147. *Not now common.*

handle　　*n.* 1 A person's name, nickname, or alias; the name of a person or the name he uses, whether or not his legal name. 1950: "He is known by that handle [Society Kid Hogan] ever since to all his pals." AP, June 22. *Since c1910.* 2 Gross profit, usu. of a sporting event, illegal activities, or short term business deal; the take. 1950: ". . . A total handle of . . . between 4 . . . and 10 billion a year in the handbooks, the numbers and the slots." W. Pegler, *synd. newsp. col.,* Apr. 17. *Since c1920.* 3 The amount of money bet on a specif. gambling or sporting event or during a specif. time with one gambling establishment; the receipts of a gambling establishment before the money returned to the customers as winnings is deducted. 1956: "HANDLE—The total amount of money in a gambling transaction, such as the amount handled on a race or in a day's racing." T. Betts, *Across the Board,* 316. 4 The nose. *Not common. In the U.S. the word has never meant a pitcher or mug from which beer is drunk, as it does in New Zealand.* See **fly off the handle, panhandle.**

hand-me-down　　*n.* 1 An item, usu. clothing, used by one person and then given to another; lit., clothes handed down from father to son or from an older child to a younger one. → 2 Secondhand clothes. 3 Ready-made clothing. *Obs.*　　*adj.* Used, secondhand.

handout　　*n.* 1 A meal or a bundle of food handed out from a house to a beggar. *Hobo use since c1880.* → 2 Old clothing handed out to a beggar. *Since c1890.* → 3 Small sums of money given to a beggar so that he may buy food or a bed for the night. → 4 Fig., any gift, donation, or loan, as from public funds or a foundation. 5 A base on balls. *Baseball use, c1930.* 6 Small brochure or other printed matter given out by people on street corners to passersby, such as advertising matter; a broadside.

handshake *v.t.* To curry favor. *Not common.* **—r** *n.* An excessive affable or obsequious person; one who curries favor, as a politician trying to impress the voters or a student toadying to a professor; a flatterer and politician, rather than a worker. *Lit. and fig.*, one who goes around shaking hands with many others, esp. the influential. Often, but not always, used scornfully. Orig. military use, c1915; by 1930 had spread to college student use; now general use. Cf. **toady.**

handsome ransom *n.* Any large sum of money. *Orig. c1935 jive and swing use; some c1940 teenage use.* See Appendix, Rhyming Slang.

hands trouble A male's propensity to touch or caress women or girls; indecorous or unwelcome familiarity in one's actions. 1949: "While slinging hash, Bonnie had encountered men with hand trouble...." A. Hynd, *Pinkerton,* 44. *Not common.*

hang *n.* 1 The balance, specif. of a pistol. 1936: "The long-barrelled, perfectly balanced Colt.... It was by the faultless 'hang' or balance of the latter weapon that the puncher's shooting reputation was made." P. A. Rollins, *The Cowboy,* 49. *Western use.* **Obs.** 2 The knack. *Colloq. Usu. in "to get the hang of it."* *v.i.* 1 To frequent a place; to associate with a person or persons. 1949: "Do they hang with anyone ... who runs the coffeepot where they hang?" Movie, *Scene of the Crime. Short for "hang out."* 2 In horseracing, to hang back, to lack reserve speed during the last stage of a race. 3 To wait; to await; to loaf or idle. 1957: "Hangin'—Waiting around; sweating out a decision." E. Horne, *For Cool Cats and Far-Out Chicks.* **—er** See **cliffhanger, crape-hanger, fence-hanger, paper-hanger.**

hang a few on **hang on a few** To drink several drinks of whisky; usu. to drink enough whisky to become at least slightly drunk. 1956: "He had only hung a few on and was, for him, slightly sober." S. Longstreet, *The Real Jazz Old and New,* 103.

hang around To loiter or linger. *Colloq.*

hang it easy = **Take it easy.** *Some teenage use since c1950.*

hang loose = **Take it easy.** *A syn. for "hang it easy."*

hang one on 1 To hit with the fist; to land a blow on someone. *Since c1900.* 1934: "... Will you hang one on my jaw?" Cain, *Postman,* 107. 2 To get completely drunk. 1950: "I'm going to hang one on." Movie, *American Guerrilla in the Philippines.*

hangout *n.* 1 Any loafing place; a recognized meeting place. *Since c1895; orig. hobo and underworld use.* 2 One's house or home. *West Coast use, c1920.*

hang out 1 To loaf or loiter in a recognized rendezvous, such as a bar, drugstore, or the like. *Very common.* 2 To reside. *West Coast use, c1920.*

hang out the laundry To drop paratroops from an airplane. *W.W.II Army Air Force use.*

hang out the wash In baseball, to hit a line drive.

hangover *n.* 1 The unpleasant physiological effects occurring after drinking too much of an alcoholic beverage. 1914: "I had a classy hangover...." Sinclair Lewis, *Our Mr. Wrenn,* 148. *Very common since c1920.* 2 Fat buttocks, which would lit. hang over a chair. *Used humorously and derog.*

hang up 1 To post a score or to score points against an opposing sports team. *c1930.* 2 A request or command for another to stop talking or teasing; shut up! cut it out! *From telephone usage.* See **hung up.**

hankie **hanky** *n.* A handkerchief. 1950: "Whenever we hear a handkerchief referred to as a hankie, we strangle the speaker." *New Yorker,* Oct. 28, 54. *Mainly women use. Colloq.* See Appendix, **—ie** ending.

hanky-pank *n.* 1 Any of several carnival games that cost 5¢ or 10¢ to play. → 2 A carnival barker's urgings to get customers to take a chance in such a game; a spiel. → 3 Anything cheap and gaudy; hanky-panky. *adj.* Costing 5¢ or 10¢; cheap and gaudy. **—y** *n.* 1 Deception; anything crooked or unethical; funny business, hocus-pocus, monkey business. *Colloq.* 2 Specif., illicit sexual activity; philandering; adultery. 1945: "... The good doctor was up to his neck in some extramarital hanky-panky...." L. F. McHugh.

Hans *n.* 1 A German soldier. *Some W.W.I Army use, taken from Brit. soldier use.* 2 A German. *Some post-W.W.I use.*

hao **hau** See **ding how, habahaba, hubba-hubba.**

happenso *n.* A happenstance. *Colloq.*

happies   *n.pl.* Arch supporters. *Shoe salesman use.*

happy   *adj.* Drunk; usu. slightly drunk. *Lit., the first stage of drunkenness, when one is in a happy mood. Very common since c1920.*

—happy   See Appendix, Suffixes and Suffix Words.

happy cabbage   Money; esp. a sizable amount of money to be spent on clothes, entertainment, or other self-satisfying things.

happy dust   **1** Cocaine. *c1925; addict use.* **2** Morphine. *c1925; addict use.*

happy-juice   *n.* Liquor. 1952: "... The increased taxes on happy-juice has cut the revenue from liquor sales...." Robert C. Ruark, *synd. newsp. col.*, May 30. *Not common. May be considered as synthetic sl.*

happy money   Money earned or saved to be spent for personal enjoyment or gratification.

hard   [taboo]   *n.* The erect penis; an erection. *Used interchangeably with "heart." "Hard" refers to the stiffening of the erect penis, "heart" to the shape of the glans. Thus they have come to mean the same thing, for different reasons, and often the final "d" of "hard" and the "t" of "heart" are slurred so that the listener cannot tell which word is actually used. The slurring also excuses the speaker in lowering his voice, which is common when pronouncing taboo words.   adj.* Excellent; fine. *Jive use.*

hard-ankle   *n.* A coal miner. *Southern hill dial.*

hard-boiled   *adj.* **1** Without sentiment; tough; mean; callous; not sentimental; cynical; unconcerned about the feelings or opinions of others. *Orig. used in W.W.I Army training camps, almost always to describe a drill officer or sergeant. May orig. have implied the stiff "boiled" collars worn by some officers as well as that one is as tough as a hard-boiled egg.* → **2** Stern, strict, exacting. 1925: "... The rather hard-boiled painting [of my great-uncle] that hangs in father's office." F. Scott Fitzgerald, *The Great Gatsby*, 11. *Colloq. since c1930.*

hard-boiled egg   **1** A stingy person. *Some student and teenage use, c1920.* **2** A hard-boiled person. 1922: "Our basic idea of a hero is really a 'hard-boiled egg.'" Philip Curtiss, *Harper's*, March, 526/1.

hardboot   *n.* Orig. a Southern cavalryman; a Southern horseman. 1956: "HARDBOOT—A bantering or derisive term for a Kentucky horseman; it stems from envy, the hardboot being shrewder than horsemen in other parts of the country." T. Betts, *Across the Board*, 316.

hard guy   See **guy.**

hard hat   **1** A derby hat. 1946: "The boys with the hard hats always ask a lot of questions about murders." Evans, *Halo in Blood*, 144. → **2** Men who wear derby hats; specif. Eastern businessmen during the 1880's and later crooks, gamblers, and detectives. *May have orig. been a cowboy term = Easterner or absentee ranch owner.*

hard-head   *n.* **1** An uncomprehending or stupid person. **2** One who will not change his mind; one who is hard to convince and is unyielding. **3** [derog.] A Negro. *White use, implying a strong skull with little brains.* **4** [derog.] A white person. *Negro use, implying an unyielding, insensitive person.* **5** A Southern hill mountaineer. *Dial.*   **—ed**   *adj.* Stubborn; strong-willed; practical.

hard John   A field agent of the FBI (Federal Bureau of Investigation). *Some underworld use. Reinforced by "John" Edgar Hoover, head of the Bureau.*

hard liquor   Whisky; esp. corn whisky drunk straight.

hard money   The currency of a nation that holds a high proportion of gold or silver in relation to its currency in circulation; money worth its full face value or more in purchasing power or international exchange; money that is hard to earn or borrow, but is worth its full face value or more. *A banking term that has become pop. since c1940.*

hard-nose   *n.* Despondency. *Not common.*   **—d**   *adj.* **1** Stubborn; prone to anger. *Orig. carnival sl.* **2** Homely; ugly.

hard on   [taboo]   An erection. 1956: "As they had the capacity and were bound to use it once in a while, people were bound to have such involuntary feelings. It was only another one of those subway things. Like having a hard-on at random." S. Bellow, *Seize the Day*, 85. *Lit., to have a "hard" on.*

hard-rocker   *n.* A prospector; a miner. 1956: "Metal miners, hard-rockers...." *Labor's Special Language from Many Sources.*

hard sell   The act or an instance of selling or advertising merchandise in an aggressive, loud, unpleasant way; an aggressive pitch. *Orig. a "Madison Avenue" term applied to television advertising.*

hard-shell *adj.* Severe; conservative. *Not as common as the ant. "soft-shell."*

hard stuff 1 Money. *Some use c1910. Orig. underworld sl.* → 2 A sizable amount of money earned in a difficult or illegal way; esp. money gained from selling contraband or illegal alcohol. *Underworld use, c1920.* → 3 Alcoholic beverages. 1951: "The troubles the hard stuff inflicts on men with no defense against it. . . ." John McCarten, *New Yorker,* Dec. 1, 155. *Not common.*

hardtack *n.* 1 Silver money, esp. dollars. *c1895; dial. and archaic.* 2 Money. *c1910; archaic.*

hardtail **hard-tail** *n.* An Army mule. *Army use. Orig. Southern hill dial. spread by hoboes, loggers, and mule skinners.*

hard time 1 Trouble; difficulty; a difficult or troublesome job or position; an act, instance, or period of trouble, difficulty, or adversity; an unpleasant experience. 1910: "I must have given you some pretty hard times?" Johnson, *Varmint,* 394. 1951: "Then a man came along who gave you a hard time and you got sour on the world." Spillane, *Big Kill,* 164. 2 Specif., difficulty or trouble caused by another's desire, wish, personality, or whim. → 3 Specif., a sexual, romantic, or personal rebuke or refusal from one of the opposite sex. Usu. in "did she give you a hard time?" *The last two uses are the more common.*
—s *sing.* A period of financial adversity, either for an individual or for a community or nation; a depression.

hard top 1 A strong-willed or hard-headed person. 2 A closed automobile with a flat roof and no upright roof supports, similar in appearance to a convertible car. *Actually a shortening for "hard-top convertible," the term signifies features introduced by the automotive industry in the post-W.W.II period.*

hard up Much in need of something or someone, usu. either money or sexual activity. 1955: "They [clients of call girls] sure must have been hard up for a dame to pay five hundred dollars. . . ." E. Trujillo, *I Love You, I Hate You,* 34.

hardware *n.* 1 Whisky; hard liquor. *Since c1850; still a little dial. use.* 2 Weapons. 1951: "More than half the bill's total is for buying military 'hardware'—tanks, planes, guns, rockets, weapons." William F. Arbogast, AP, Aug. 6. *In use since c1865; orig. implied rifles and knives, such as could be bought in hardware and general stores, and Civil War artillery; by c1920 was limited to pistols and weapons easily concealed and was used in Southern hill regions and on ranches. From then on, the movies and detective stories so used the term to mean easily concealed weapons and associated it with underworld use, which is still the most common implication. However, with W.W.II the word again obtained its meaning of any weapons, large or small, used in individual or national defense.* 3 Jewelry, esp. identification and fraternal jewelry. *Since c1935.* → 4 Military insignia or medals. *Common during W.W.II.*

hard water Whisky. *Not common.*

hard way, the 1 In crap-shooting, the instance of making or attempting to make an even-numbered point by shooting two equal numbers on the dice. *Thus, "6 the hard way" is made by two 3's, as opposed to a 5 and a 1 or a 4 and a 2.* → 2 The difficult means or method for accomplishing anything; the roundabout way.

hard-wood *n.* Theater tickets for standing room; also, those given in exchange for higher-priced tickets. *Not common.*

harlot's hello, a Something that doesn't exist; nothing; zero. 1951: "The silver ore left in our pits isn't worth a harlot's hello—beggin' your pardon, Rebecca." S. Longstreet, *The Pedlocks,* 75.

harness *n.* 1 The complete dress or uniform of a man. *Obs.* → 2 A telephone lineman's safety belt. *c1920; lineman use.* → 3 A policeman's uniform. 1930: "Wise detectives, who dread going back into 'harness' or uniform. . . ." Lavine, *Third Degree,* 11f. *Common since c1930; underworld use since c1913.* See **harness bull.** → 4 A train conductor's uniform. *c1935, railroad use.* → 5 The leather jacket, boots, gloves, and cap or goggles that make up a motorcyclist's dress. *c1945, West Coast motorcyclist use. Such a harness has become the standard dress among certain nonmotorcycling teenage groups.*

harness bull 1 A uniformed policeman; a patrolman. *Underworld, prison, and hobo use since c1915.* 2 Also used attrib. = police-like, pertaining to the police. 1949: "The harness-bull secretary. . . ." Burnett, *Jungle,* 2. *Also used 17 additional times in this book.*

harness cop = **harness bull.**

harness dick = **harness bull.**

harp Harp *n.* An Irish person, usu. an Irishman. 1924: "He's a harp. At any rate, he's a Catholic." Marks, *Plastic Age*, 169. *From the harp that is part of the Irish flag. In use since c1900; most common c1925.*

harp-polisher *n.* A clergyman, esp. a priest. 1946: "I'm curious why it should take twelve harp polishers to bury an unidentified victim." Evans, *Halo in Blood*, 71.

Hart, Schaffner, and Marx In poker, three jacks. *From the well-known firm of clothing manufacturers.*

has-been *n.* **1** A person who formerly was successful and important; esp. an aging entertainer or athlete who is no longer in the public's favor. **2** A person who has been supplanted by a rival in love, business, or the entertainment field. **3** Any person whose personality, politics, dress, personal tastes, ideas, or the like, are outmoded; one to whom past memories are more important than the present. *Since c1900; colloq. since c1930.*

hash *v.t.* **1** To discuss thoroughly; to hash over. 1920: ". . . The things . . . they had hashed and rehashed for many a frugal conversational meal." Fitzgerald, *This Side of Paradise*, 134. **2** To make a mistake, ruin a plan, confuse an idea. *v.i.* To earn one's living or to gain free board and meals by being a waiter, esp. by being a part-time waiter in a hotel or boarding house. *n.* **1** Any cooked food; all the food served at a meal; a meal. **2** News, rumors, gossip. See **sling hash.** **—er** *n.* **1** A waiter or waitress who serves food at a restaurant or lunch counter. 1930: "A man who ran a swell eating-house . . . was going to give them jobs as hashers." G. Weisberg, *American Mercury*, Nov., 345/2. *Note that a hasher may work for a better restaurant than a hash-slinger.* **2** A cook or kitchen worker. **—ery** *n.* A small restaurant or lunch counter. 1953: "We'll . . . inhale a few hamburgers at some fashionable hashery!" "Our Boarding House," *synd. newsp. cartoon*, June 17.

hash-burner *n.* A cook. *More picturesque than common; W.W.II use.*

hash driver A cook. *Orig. a combination cook and chuck-wagon driver on a ranch. c1860.*

hash foundry A cheap restaurant; a charitable institution that provides free meals to the destitute. *Hobo use.*

hash-house hashhouse *n.* A restaurant, lunchroom, boarding house, or the like, esp. a cheap one. 1897: ". . . The sort of language that one would expect to hear from a hobo in a Bowery hash-house." *Bookman*, Aug., 448/2. 1942: ". . . To get something to eat at the hashhouse around the corner." Chandler, *High Window*, 66. *Since c1875; now colloq.*

hash mark **1** A military service stripe, worn diagonally or horizontally on the lower sleeve of a uniform indicating the number of years or enlistments which a serviceman has served. *The color, width, placement, and amount of service time that each stripe indicates has varied. Recently the U.S. Army hash mark was a pale tan-yellow bar on a khaki background, sewed on the lower forearm of the uniform, while the U.S. Navy uses a short white stripe. During certain periods each such stripe indicated a two-year enlistment; at other periods each stripe indicated six months of service. Very common in both U.S. Army and U.S. Navy during W.W.II.* **2** = **hash stripe.**

hash over To discuss; esp. to discuss a subject more than once; to review a discussion or plan. 1950: ". . . Asked him in to hash over a point or two." *New Yorker*, Dec. 16, 26/1.

hash session A leisurely session of talking, arguing, and gossiping; a men's bull session or a women's gabfest. *Not as common as "bull session" or "gabfest."*

hash-slinger hashslinger hash slinger *n.* **1** A waiter or waitress in an eating place; esp. a waitress in a cheap restaurant or lunch counter whose primary job is to deliver food from kitchen to tables or the counter, without observing the niceties of good service. 1949: ". . . When movie queens were picked from the ranks of hashslingers . . ." AP, Hollywood, Sep. 7. 1953: "Hash slingers are plentiful but well-trained waitresses are scarce." AP, Salt Lake City, June 3. *Since c1865; the implication of waitress rather than waiter and of a restaurant that specializes in cheap, quickly served food rather than in quality and service became strong c1935, with an increasing number of women workers and when Americans started to eat more meals away from their own homes.* **2** A kitchen worker, a cook, cook's helper, or the like. *Since c1900.* See Appendix, Suffixes and Suffix Words.

hash stripe = hash mark.

hassel hassle *n.* A disagreement, dispute, quarrel, or argument; a struggle or fight. 1949: "A hassel between two actors touched off the ... riot...." Billy Rose, *synd. newsp. col.*, Dec. 2. 1953: "... The hassle over putting fluoride in drinking water." Nat Boynton, AP, Albany, N.Y., Mar. 5.

hassock *n.* In baseball, a base. 1931: "The Crab bingled ... with the hassocks crowded." W. Pegler, *Lit. Digest. Not common.*

hat *n.* **1** Fig., those items of clothing that are put on and those household chores done immediately before leaving a house or office. Thus "get your hat and let's go" can mean "put on your coat, gloves, hat, and overshoes, turn off the radio, close the window, and let's leave." **2** An ineffectual railroad man, often an old employee who has no specific duties. **3** Any of various helmets, such as a diver's helmet, or uniform caps. See **bad hat, brass hat, hard hat, high-hat, old hat, plug hat, red hat, straw-hat, talk through [one's] hat, tin hat, under [one's] hat.**

hat, in [one's] **1** An expression of incredulity. **2** [taboo] An expression of disrespect or strong dislike. *Fig., a euphem. request to another to "shit in your hat."*

hat, pass the **1** Lit., to pass a man's hat among the members of an audience or group as a means of collecting money. 1954: "We would pass our hats [after playing music on a street corner] and divvy up." L. Armstrong, *Satchmo, My Life in New Orleans*, 34. **2** To ask for charity; to beg.

hatch *n.* The human mouth and forethroat, esp., but not always, when considered the receptacle for alcoholic beverages. 1943: "DeCasseres would hurl the first legal drink down his hatch." H. A. Smith, *Putty Knife*, 63. See **booby hatch, down the hatch, nut hatch.**

hatchet-boy *n.* A professional murderer; a thug. *Not as common as "hatchet-man."*

hatchet-man *n.* **1** A professional gunman. *Since c1925. Successor to the oldtime "hatchet-armed killer."* **2** An aggressive, militant newspaper writer or politician's associate; one whose job is to destroy the reputation of others or to do unethical tasks for a political party, office holder, or candidate. 1957: "[Vice President] Dicky Nixon, hatchet-man for the Republican administration...." *Oral*, N.Y.C.

hatchet-thrower *n.* A Spaniard, Puerto Rican, or Cuban. *Negro use.*

hat-rack *n.* **1** Any skinny, old, or sickly farm animal; specif., an old horse or cow. → **2** Any skinny or sickly person; a bean pole.

haul [one's] ashes **1** To leave or depart; to force or request someone to leave. **2** To do physical harm to another; to beat up someone. **3** [taboo] To have sexual intercourse. See **get [one's] ashes hauled.** *Given in the order of their pop. usage, which seems to be in inverse chronological order. Note the implied relationship between sexual intercourse and violence.*

haul ass [taboo] **1** To leave; to depart. *Since c1940.* → **2** To drive a car or travel rapidly; to speed. *Since c1950. Both uses mainly student and teenage.*

haul in To arrest. *Lit. = to haul the arrested person to jail.* 1949: "... The police decided to haul them all in." *Life*, Oct. 24, 25.

haul it To run away; flee. 1942: "He cold hauled it!" Z. Hurston. *Harlem Negro use.* See **haul [one's] ashes.**

haul off on [someone] To hit someone hard with the fist. 1939: "... Counting fifty before they hauled off on a Red. ..." J. T. Farrell, 204.

haul the mail To speed up; to make up lost time by doing something faster. *Orig. railroad and trucker use.*

hausfrau *n.* A woman, esp. if unattractive, whose only or main interests are cleaning, washing, ironing, cooking, and other domestic duties. Used either as a compliment to or as a criticism of the woman. *From the German "Hausfrau."*

have For phrases beginning with "have," see under principal word of phrase.

have [taboo] *v.t.* To have sexual intercourse with a girl or woman; to have carnal knowledge of a girl or woman. *Usu. in past, past perfect, or future tenses.* 1947: "Marquales saw written on the wall just by his seat the words: '*I had Mary Jane in her own bathtub ten times. Ben Wallace, April 12, 1933.*'" C. Willingham, *End as a Man*, 140. "*Had*" and "*been had*" *again seem to relate sex and deception. See Appendix, Sex and Deceit. Cf.* **made.**

have it, let [someone] **1** To strike someone with one's fist or a weapon; to kill a person. 1934: "To feint a guy open and then let him have it, right on the chin?" Cain, *Postman*, 83. 1953: "So I let him have it—but good." Television play, *Phone Call from a Stranger*, Jan. 5. → **2** To accuse, criticize, rebuke, expose, or in any other way to harass a person or group severely and directly. 1949: ". . . Unless he 'opened up' and let the [GOP] machine have it right between the eyes." Phila. *Bulletin*, Sept. 2, 4/1.

have-not   *n.* A poor person, group, region, or nation. 1943: ". . . Being a have-not. . . ." H. A. Smith, *Putty Knife*, 19. *Colloq.*

hawk   *v.i.* To clear the throat, esp. to spit. 1949: ". . . The murmuring rumdums were being let out of their cells to wash . . . hawk, stretch. . . ." N. Algren, *Man With the Golden Arm*, 20.

hay   *n.* **1** Marijuana. *Some addict use.* **2** A small amount of money; peanuts. Usu. in "that ain't hay." 1939–40: ". . . And what they pay me in addition ain't hay." O'Hara, *Pal Joey*, 5. 1951: "That would leave him $48,000 pay, or $4,000 a month, which ain't hay." Peter Edson, NEA, Washington, D.C., Feb. 14. Cf. **alfalfa**. *Almost always in the negative "that ain't hay" = that's a substantial amount of money.* **3** Tobacco. *Not common.* **4** Sauerkraut. *Not common.* See **load of hay, make hay while the sun shines, that ain't hay**.

hay, hit the   To go to bed; to lie down to sleep. 1951: "I gotta go home now and hit the hay." E. Bushmiller, "Nancy," *synd. comic strip*, Nov. 5. *Common since c1910.* See **the hay**.

hay, make   To take full advantage of one's opportunities while one can; to profit or benefit fully from one's advantage, success, or position. *From the expression "make hay while the sun shines" = work, profit, or take full advantage when conditions are favorable, because they might not always be favorable.*

hay, the   *n.* **1** A bed. 1932: ". . . He is in his hotel in the hay. . . ." Runyon. 1950: "Dr. Peachy got Moon out of the hay. . . ." Starnes, *Another Mug*, 118. → **2** Sleep; unconsciousness. See **haymaker, hit the hay**.

haybag   *n.* **1** A woman hobo. *Orig. c1920 hobo use.* See **bag**. **2** A fat or dissipated woman, esp. an old woman. 1932: "She is nothing but an old haybag and generally ginned up." Runyon, 89. *Never common.*

hay-burner   *n.* **1** A horse; esp. a race horse and part. a slow or cheap

race horse. 1939–40: ". . . Before the hay-burners stop running at Hialeah." O'Hara, *Pal Joey*, 24 f. 1950: "Van Osten . . . preferred the company of hay-burners to that of humans. . . ." Billy Rose, *synd. newsp. col. Since c1915 very common race track term.* → **2** A cavalryman. *Some Army use.* **3** A mule. *Southern hill use. c1915.* **4** An old-fashioned, diamond-stack, wood-burning locomotive. *c1920. Railroad use. Obs.* **5** An oil lantern. *c1925; railroad use.* **6** A cheap automobile; esp. one that used much gas and oil. *c1920; obs.* **7** A tobacco pipe. See **hay**. *Not common.*

hay-eater   *n.* A white person. *Some Negro use. Not always derog.*

hayhooks   *n.pl.* The hands; the hands as fists. *Archaic.*

haymaker   *n.* **1** A heavy blow or swing with the fist; usu. a knockout punch in the boxing ring or elsewhere. 1921: ". . . Smashes the . . . kid with a wild haymaker. . . ." Witwer, *Leather*, 23. *Orig. a boxing term. Since c1910. From "make hay" + "the hay" = sleep, unconsciousness.* → **2** Fig., any crushing or final blow with any weapon. 1928: "David . . . had just hung his haymaker on Goliath. . . ." Ralph Coghlan, *Amer. Mercury*, May, 1. → **3** Fig., any crushing remark, piece of news, or event. 1949: ". . . Having her arrested . . . would be a haymaker to your father." J. Evans, *Halo*, 68. **4** Fig., any complete effort, sensational try, or last resort; often the best song, joke, or performance of an entertainer's repertory.

hay rube   A farmer; a rustic. *Not common. c1900. Patterned on "hayseed" and "hay-shaker," reinforced by a misunderstanding of "Hey, Rube!"*

hayseed   *n.* **1** A farmer or rustic; a hick or rube. *c1890.* → **2** Any inexperienced, unsophisticated, or innocent person; a greenhorn. *Common c1900–1910; now archaic.* → **3** Fig., rustic qualities. 1950: ". . . There is still a lot of hayseed in Senator . . . Chance." Starnes, *Another Mug*, 85.   *adj.* Rural, rustic; resembling, suggesting, or located in or near farms, rural areas, or small towns. 1952: "Summer is when . . . the bad actors perform in worse plays in the hayseed theaters." Robert C. Ruark, *synd. newsp. col.*, Sept. 19. *c1890.*
—er   *n.* = **hayseed**.

hay-shaker   *n.* A farmer. *Not common, some use c1920–1925.*

haywire   *adj.* **1** Broken, dilapidated; makeshift; flimsy; poorly constructed, operated, or equipped; jumbled or confused. *Since c1915. Farmer, rancher, and logger use; prob. from the use of the baling wire, used in a hay-baler, to mend farm implements, thus causing an association between "hay wire" and broken or dilapidated things.* 2 Crazy; in an unusual, confused manner; confused. 1930: "He never looked inside [an almanac] and was sure that anyone who did was haywire." S. H. Holbrook in *Amer. Mercury*, Oct., 234/1. 1939: "This radio's gone haywire." Hixson, *Word Ways*, 141. 1957: "Things will start happening, now that you have this new convertible. Just remember that I tried to talk you out of it, and don't go haywire." S. McNeil, *High-Pressure Girl.*

head *n.* 1 A headache, usu. one accompanying or constituting a hang-over. *Often in the phrase "to have a head." Common since c1920.* 2 The mouth. 1934: ". . . Keep one's head shut." *Web.* 3 Foam, usu. on the top of a glass of beer. *Colloq.* 4 One person or several, esp. considered as customers or potential customers or suckers; specif., a ticket buyer or spectator. 1941: "This was a pop concert that would attract the whole town—at twenty-five cents a head, no reserved seats." J. Lilienthal, *Horse Crazy*, 13. *From farm and ranch use, "head" = one of a herd of cattle.* 5 A young woman, esp. a sexually attainable woman. 1941: "One head that used to claim to sell stockings called . . . one day. . . ." Liebling, *New Yorker*, Apr. 26, 25/1. 6 [taboo] The glans of the penis; the erect penis. → 7 Sexual gratification. Cf. **have rocks in [one's] head, hole in [one's] head, the head, use [one's] head, white-[haired] headed boy.** 8 Fig., a person, an individual. **—ed** See **white-haired boy** = **white-headed boy. —er** *n.* 1 A head-first fall; a dive or plunge. *Colloq. since c1930.* → 2 An attempt or try; a gamble; a plunge. → 3 A failure or mistake; a fall. See **double-header.**

—head See Appendix, Suffixes and Suffix Words.

head, give [her] some [taboo] To have sexual intercourse with a girl. See **head.**

head, have a To have a hangover; to feel as if one's head is swollen and throbbing, owing to overindulgence in alcoholic beverages.

head, in above [one's] 1 = **in deep water.** → 2 Certain to fail or meet with

disaster. → 3 Unable to meet one's financial obligations.

head, off [one's] Insane, out of one's mind. 1941: "Have you gone off your head?" A. R. Hilliard, *Justice Be Damned*, 276.

head, open [one's] = **open [one's] face.**

head, the *n.* A bathroom or "men's room"; esp., a toilet or urinal. *Often in "Where's the head?" c1935. Orig. USN use, because ship's toilets are often squeezed in near a bulkhead. Wide W.W.II use in both USN and USA. In Army sl. orig. = an outdoor latrine. Still the most common word for bathroom, toilet, or urinal in the Armed Forces. Has wide verbal civilian use by men.*

headache *n.* 1 Any trouble, cause of worry or vexation. 1950: "Another headache for pro coaches is that they're now getting products of the two-platoon system. . . ." AP, Sept. 1. 1953: "No one can take on the political headaches . . . as I have this year if he has any political thoughts. . . ." Thomas E. Dewey [former Gov. of N.Y.], *newsp.*, Mar. 24. *Since c1930.* → 2 One's wife. 1930: ". . . Meet the headache." A. Green, *Esquire*, Sept.

headache band A women's hair accessory made of fabric, leather, or plastic, from one to three inches wide, and worn very tight across the line between the forehead and hair and over the ears, usu. with an eggbeater hair style. *Common c1925 and c1958.*

headbeater *n.* A policeman. 1958: "Even the headbeaters (police) . . . were not that thorough." "A Gang Leader's Redemption," *Life*, April 28, 69. *Some teenage street gang use; not common.*

headbone *n.* The skull, the head. 1952: "This boot you got stuck on yo' headbone . . . is gotta come off!" Walt Kelly, "Pogo," *synd. comic strip*, Sept. 26. *Some pop. owing to freq. use in the "Pogo" comic strip, which sometimes assumes a Southern swamp dial. Orig. from a pop. old Negro folk song.*

head hunter The owner or boss of an executive employment agency; a business executive in charge of recruiting new personnel.

headlight *n.* 1 An egg. *c1925, some hobo use; archaic.* 2 A light-skinned Negro. *Some Negro use.* 3 A large diamond; a diamond ring. 1949: "That headlight she wore on her finger is the size that poor people can't buy." *Fact Detec. Mysteries*, 61. 1951: ". . . A lurid 'headlight' in his tie." A. Green, *Show*

Biz, 11. **—s** *n.pl.* **1** The eyes. *Orig. boxing use, c1925; not very common.* **2** [taboo] Prominent, well-shaped female breasts. *Usu. in the admiring "look at those headlights." c1940. From the similarity in shape between the prominent female breasts, in uplift brassiere and tight sweater of the 1940s, and the style of automobile headlight of the same period.* **3** Large diamonds. Cf. **eyes, maracas, shakers.**

head shrinker   A psychiatrist, esp. a psychoanalyst. 1957: "You talk like one of those head shrinkers—a psychiatrist." S. McNeil, *High-Pressure Girl.*

heads up!   *imp.* A warning to get out of the way quickly, or to be careful. *Very common.*

head-up   *n.* A stupid or inattentive person.   *adj.* Confused. *Some W.W.II Air Force use.*

heap   *n.* **1** Any automobile, esp. an old or ordinary one. 1941: ". . . Get that heap of junk off the road." A. R. Hilliard, *Justice Be Damned*, 235. *From "junk heap" or "scrap heap."* → **2** A motorcycle. → **3** An airplane. *Some aviator and W.W.II Air Force use. All three meanings can be used derog. by others or affectionately by the owner or driver.* **—s**   *n.pl.* A large amount.   *adj.* Very much, much; many. *Colloq. since c1930.*

hearse   *n.* A train's caboose. *Railroad use.*

heart   *n.* **1** Courage; determination; stamina. *Most freq. used when speaking of the attributes of an athlete. Colloq.* **2** Kindness, sympathy, generosity. *The emotions that the ancients believed orig. in the heart rather than in the spleen or mind. Colloq.* Cf. **have a heart.** **3** [taboo] The glans of the penis. → **4** [taboo] The erect penis; an erection. *From the shape of the glans plus "hard."* See **hard, hard on.**

heart, have a   To be (more) generous, sympathetic, or understanding; to be less severe or exacting. *Usu. in the imperative, as a plea. Colloq.*

hear the birdies sing   To be knocked out; to be unconscious. 1944: "Mac [a knocked-out prize fighter] heard the birdies sing. . . ." Cliff Macon, *Collier's*, Sept. 16, 64/3. *Implies that one is dreaming of pleasant things and has ringing ears.*

hearthstone   *n.* In baseball, the home plate. *Not common.*

hearts and flowers   **1** Sentimentality; that which is said or done for sympathy; sob stuff. 1949: "I believed all the hearts and flowers you gave me about being in love with your husband. . . ." J. Evans, *Halo*, 210. *From the title of a mournful pop. song, c1910, which is conventionally played to indicate sadness or overt sentimentality. Sometimes the listener to a "hearts and flowers" story will mimic a violinist playing an imaginary violin to indicate his awareness of the sentimentality.* **2** A knockout. *Prize fight use.* See **hear the birdies sing.**

heart-throb   *n.* A sweetheart. *c1940. Fairly common with newsp. gossip columnists, but not common otherwise.*

heat   *n.* **1** Trouble, usu. for criminals and usu. in the form of intense police searches or other police activity. 1925: "A . . . police agitation is 'heat.' " McLellan, *Collier's*. 1950: "Types of cash mark which do not involve federal heat. . . ." DeBaun, 71. *Underworld use, c1925.* → **2** A town, county, or area in which the police are actively looking for a criminal or are very active. *c1930.* → **3** Mob violence, the resentment of a crowd or audience due to being cheated or fooled. *c1935, carnival use.* → **4** Any trouble, esp. the anger or strict orders of a boss, superior, or friend. *Since c1940.* See **the heat's on.** **5** A gun, usu. a pistol. 1946: "I was packing as much heat as you'd find in an icicle, and without a gun." Evans, *Halo in Blood*, 57. See **heater, heat-packer.** *Underworld use, c1930.* → **6** Gunfire; usu. in "give someone the heat" = to kill by shooting. *Prison use.* **7** Drunkenness; a jag. 1932: ". . . She seems to have about half a heat on from drinking gin." Runyon, 89. **8** In boxing, a round. **9** In baseball, an inning. *The above two common sports usages, since c1930, are taken from the standard racing term.* **—ed**   *adj.* Reprimanded; chastized; punished. *Rock-and-roll use since c1955.* **—er**   *n.* **1** A gun; revolver or pistol. *Since c1930 widely used in the underworld and in movies and books about the underworld.* See **heat.** **2** A cigar. 1949: ". . . He . . . begins puffin' on my four-bit heater." Arthur Kober, *New Yorker*, Nov. 5, 84. 1958: "I [Mike Todd] introduced expensive heaters. I started with cigars when I was a kid. Here I was, 18, and with striped silk shirts, and I was smoking those long Havana heaters." Quoted by E. Wilson, N.Y. *Post*, Mar. 26, 55. See **Armstrong heaters.**

heat artist   A drinker of canned heat. *Some hobo use.*

heat-can   *n.* A jet plane. *c1950, Air Force use.*

heat on [someone], put the   **1** To demand payment, work, or satisfaction from someone, esp. with a warning or threat; to harass; to take aggressive action against. → **2** To request or require intensified effort, as from an employee. See **heat.**

heat-packer   *n.* A gunman. *Lit. = one who carries trouble in the form of a gun.* See **heat.** See Appendix, Suffixes and Suffix Words.

heat's on, the   A condition of being intensely sought or pursued by the police. *The best known of expressions containing "heat," this is very popular in stories and movies of crime, though no longer common with the underworld.*

heave   *v.i., v.t.* To vomit. *c1940; very pop. student and young adult use. "Heaving" is usu. associated with modern or sophisticated dissipation, worry, or a short siege of stomach virus; it is never the result of serious illness.*   *n.* A shelter; a small room, apartment, or pad. 1958: "... Heave. Any shelter used by a policeman to avoid the elements." G. Y. Wells, *Station House Slang. Not common.* **—r**   *n.* **1** A waitress in an inexpensive restaurant or lunch counter; a hash-slinger. *c1910. Some Western use.* → **2** A woman or young lady. See **dude heaver.**

heave-ho   *n.* The act of throwing a person out of a place; any forcible ejection of a person; the bum's rush. 1949: "If you make any noise ... you get the heave-ho." W. J. Slocum, "Skid Row," *Collier's*, Aug. 27, 60. → **2** Fig., the act of rejecting or casting off a friend or intimate, dismissing a lover, denying another's friendship; the cold shoulder; the act of being fired, the bounce. *Both usages often in the phrase "the old heave-ho."*   *v.i.* To vomit. 1944: "... It became expedient to heave-ho, and quickly." Fowler, *Good Night,* 176. *Euphem. for "heave."*

heaven = nigger heaven.

heaven dust   Cocaine. *Drug addict use. Not common.* See **dust.**

heave-o = heave-ho.

heavy   *n.* **1** A hoodlum or thug; a criminal in one of the more violent phases of crime. **2** The villain in a play or movie; an actor who or a role that calls for an actor who looks or can act villainously or in a tough manner. *Theater use since c1925.* **3** A heavyweight boxer. See Appendix, Shortened Words. *adj.* **1** Plentiful. 1937: "There's jack in this, heavy jack." "I've been busy

cleaning up some heavy dough." Weidman, *Wholesale,* 5; 219. **2** Hot, esp. too hot to handle or drink. *Usu. said of liquids.* **3 = hot,** esp. meaning passionate, sexy, lascivious, lewd, or dangerous.

heavy, on the   Engaged in crime; working, living, or traveling as a criminal.

heavy artillery = artillery.

heavy-cake   *n.* A man whose main pastime is pursuing women; a ladies' man. *c1925. Based on "cake-eater."*

heavy cream   A fat girl or young woman.

heavy date   **1** An important, highly desired social engagement with one of the opposite sex; a date with one's fiancé or major love interest; usu. such dates involve heavy necking or love-making. 1929–30: "... A heavy date with a light lady." K. Brush, *Young Man,* 116. *Since c1925.* → **2** One's partner on such a date. *c1925.* **3** Any important engagement. 1930: "I got a heavy poker date for this afternoon. ..." Burnett, *Iron Man,* 158.

heavy foot   A driver who presses heavily on the gas pedal of his car; a fast driver or speeder. 1958: "Heavy foot—A speeder." G. Y. Wells, *Station House Slang.*

heavy money (sugar, dough, jack)   Much money; enough money to make one important or influential. 1956: "Why did she [Marilyn Monroe] walk out on a movie career which was paying her heavy money?" P. Martin, *SEP,* May 5, 149.

heavy necking   Extremely passionate necking; intimate caresses and kisses often including sexual foreplay but never actual coitus, carried on passionately and during a fairly extended time.

heavy-sticker   In baseball, a hard hitter.

heavy sugar   **1** Much money; a large amount of money, esp. when assembled during a brief period or from entertainment, sports, or gambling. 1929–30: "$900 in two weeks in heavy sugar...." K. Brush, *Young Man,* 176. *Since c1920.* → **2** A wealthy person. → **3** An object, such as a diamond ring or big car, that represents much money. See **heavy, sugar.**

Hebe   hebe   Heeb   heeb   *n.* [derog.] A Jew. 1939: "... The two Hebes were lucky...." J. T. Farrell, 190. 1939: "I consider this ... disrespectful, like calling the Jewish people mockies, or Heebs, or geese." Runyon. *From "Hebrew." The order of freq. is as listed.*

Mildly derog., not as objectionable as "kike."

heck *interj.* Hell. *An old well-established euphem. Considered archaic and prissy by young adults. Colloq.* **—er** *n.* A rustic. *c1900; archaic. From the traditionally rural exclam., "By heck!"* Cf. **heller.**

hectic *adj.* Confusing, busy, exciting. *Colloq.*

hedge **hedge off** *v.i., v.t.* To be indecisive or act indecisively; specif., in gambling, to bet on one team, number, or entry and then to make a smaller bet on another or the other team, number, or entry, so as to recoup part of one's loss if the larger bet loses; to transfer part of a bet one has to another, to reduce possible loss. 1956: "HEDGE OR HEDGE OFF— a bookmaker's term, primarily; to hedge is to transfer part of a large bet to another bookmaker or to the mutual machines." T. Betts, *Across the Board,* 316. Cf. **dynamite.**

hedgehopper *n.* An airplane that is flying close to the ground; esp. a pilot who flies his plane close to the ground, as does a crop duster or the pilot of a military plane whose duty it is to observe an enemy's position.

Heeb **heeb** = **Hebe.**

heebie-jeebies *n.* A feeling of nervousness, fright, or worry; the willies; occasionally, delirium tremens. 1926: "Heebie Jeebies." Title of a pop. song. 1934: "To the present Manhattan heebie-jeebies . . ." P. Wylie, *Finnley Wren,* 1.

heebies *n.sing.* = **heebie-jeebies.** Cf. **leaping heebies.**

heel *n.* **1** A sneak-thief; the lowest type of petty criminal. *c1915. Orig. underworld use.* → **2** A low-grade pitchman; a shill. *c1930; carnival use.* **3** A contemptible, despicable scoundrel of a man; a bounder, rotter, or cad; a man who lacks gentlemanly feelings and will take advantage of attractive females and double-cross his friends. 1937: *On Aug. 7, in his synd. newsp. col.,* O. O. McIntyre *commented, "I think Wilson Mizner originated this." Although most common after c1925, the word = the antithesis of a gentleman to such an old-fashioned extent that it is probably much older. Colloq.* **4** An escape from prison or the scene of a crime; a getaway. See **cop a heel, gumheel, round heel[s], rubber heel[s].** *v.t.* **1** To arm oneself; to provide arms to another.

Colloq. since c1870. **2** To provide a person with money. See **well-heeled.** **3** To seek or court; esp. to seek favor from a superior or a group; to compete for social or business status by courting the favor of special individuals or groups. 1912: ". . . Heel the right crowd. . . ." Johnson, *Stover at Yale,* 34. *v.i.* To run away; to escape or make a getaway. **—ed** *adj.* **1** Equipped. *Since c1880.* → **2** Armed; equipped with a weapon. 1936: ". . . Heeled [armed]. . . ." P. A. Rollins, *The Cowboy,* 41. 1946: "I can talk better when I know this guy isn't heeled." Evans, *Halo in Blood,* 201. *Since c1890.* → **3** Wealthy; equipped with much money. *Colloq. since c1930.* Cf. **well-heeled.** **4** Drunk. **—er** *n.* **1** One who toadies before superiors; one who curries favor with superiors or social groups in order to increase his own status. *Archaic.* See **apple polisher, ass kisser.** → **2** A contemptible person; a sneak. *c1925.* → **3** A sneak thief or heel. Cf. **ward heeler.**

heel-tap *n.* A small amount of a drink remaining in a glass. *From a leather tap for a shoe heel, reinforced by "heel" = end + "tap" = spigot.* 1930: ". . . Member . . . must drink three MARTINIS . . . absolutely no heel-taps allowed." *Amer. Mercury,* Dec., 435/2.

heesh *n.* Hashish. *Some dope addict and maritime use.*

heff *n.* A heifer. *Farm use.*

hefty **heftie** *n.* A hefty or heavy man. 1953: "While other hefties count their calories, he counts the dollars. . . ." Hal Boyle, AP, Jan. 26. *Colloq.* *adj.* Fat, heavy. *Colloq.*

heifer *n.* A woman or girl; esp. a pretty or personable young woman. *Colloq. since c1830.*

heifer dust Snuff. *Farmer use; archaic.*

he-ing and she-ing Sexual intercourse; having sexual intercourse. *Jocular and dial.*

Heinie [derog.] *n.* **1** A German soldier. ". . . Until the Heinies went back into Hunland. . . ." W.W.I Air Force ace, Eddie Rickenbacker, *Lit. Digest. Common W.W.I use in Armed Forces and fairly wide civilian use. Orig. taken from Brit. Army use. Some usage again in W.W.II, but much less common.* → **2** A German. *adj.* German; Germanic. *Most common during W.W.I.*

heist **hyst** *v.t.* **1** To steal, to take by robbing. **2** To hi-jack; esp. to hi-jack a shipment of alcoholic beverages. *c1920; some early sp.* = *"hyst."* *n.* A successful hold-up, robbery, or theft; usu. an armed robbery by professional thieves. 1950: ". . . Jewelry heisted from Aga Khan last fall. . . ." DeBaun, 71. 1958: "Heist—A holdup." G. Y. Wells, *Station House Slang. From "hoist." Usu., in underworld use, to steal an expensive item or items; children and student use, to steal an insignificant object.* **—er hister** *n.* A hold-up man; a professional robber.

— heister See Appendix, Suffixes and Suffix Words.

heist man   hist man A hold-up man; a robber. *Some early sp. = "hist man."* See **heist.**

hell   Hell *exclam. & epith.* An epithet or oath of anger, disgust, or annoyance. *adj.* Fig., unpleasant; arduous; horrible; dangerous. *Colloq. n.* **1** A bawling out; a strong verbal reprimand. *Usu. in "to catch hell" or "to get hell."* **2** A person who excels. *Some Negro and jive talker use. From "heller."* *v.i.* **1** To behave or live recklessly, immorally, or dissipatedly. *c1900.* **2** To travel fast. 1950: ". . . An ambulance, helling out the state road." Starnes, *Another Mug,* 138. *Not common.* Cf. **barrel.** See **from hell to breakfast, to hell and gone.** **—er** *n.* **1** A remarkable person. *Archaic and dial. Colloq.* **2** An aggressive or immoral person. *Archaic; colloq.*

hell, give [someone] To bawl out; to criticize severely.

hell, go to An expression of incredulity, anger, contempt, or rejection. *Taboo when said in anger or with emotion, but often jocular and not taboo when incredulity is implied.*

hell-a-mile **1** Emphatically yes. **2** Emphatically no. *Neither usage common.*

hell and gone, to **1** Irretrievably gone, spoiled, ruined, or dissipated. **2** Very far from any given place, esp. without probability of returning or being returned. 1939: "He says [Spain] is to hell and gone from here." Runyon, 72.

hell around To behave or live recklessly; to frequent unfashionable bars, chase women, and the like. *c1900.*

hell-bender *n.* A wild spree.

hell buggy A tank. *Some W.W.II Army use.*

hell cat **1** An extremely spirited, reckless young woman or girl. *Colloq.* **2** A bugler or drummer whose duty is playing reveille. *West Point and Annapolis use.*

hell-fired *adj., adv.* = **all-fired.** *c1900; archaic.*

hell-hole   hellhole *n.* Any unpleasant place; fig., any place resembling hell. 1947: "I remember when I got my first leave, when I was a freshman. I was so glad to get out of this hellhole I went out and drank a ton of beer." C. Willingham, *End as a Man,* 20.

hell of a (time, fight, thing, scare, etc.) **1** A very bad or severe time, fight, thing, scare, etc.; exceptionally or exceedingly thorough or severe. Fig., anything unpleasant, arduous, or dangerous. *Since Colonial times.* See **hell.** **2** Anything insulting, audacious, bold. **3** Anything remarkable. **4** Anything confused, disorganized, or containing many blunders.

hell of a note Anything unusual, surprising, audacious, or insulting, or the like.

hell-pup *n.* A disliked, sneaky, young man. *c1900; never common.*

hell-raiser *n.* One who causes or is liable to cause a disturbance; a spirited, outspoken, fast-acting person; esp. such a person who does not observe common propriety; one who lives recklessly. *Always very common. Now somewhat archaic.*

Hell's bells *An exclamation of surprise and/or anger; also used to make a following remark more emphatic.* See Appendix, Rhyming Slang.

hell to pay A severe punishment, penalty, or bawling out.

hell to split Fast; at a run; lickety-split. 1948: ". . . She looked back and I piled after her hell to split." Cain, *Moth,* 87.

hell-west-and-crooked **1** Much askew. **2** Violently. *Both usages obs.*

help-out *n.* An amount of work done to help a friend or neighbor. *Farm use; orig. ranch use.*

he-man *n.* A strong, healthy, virile man; a man with exceptionally strong male traits and pursuits, such as broad shoulders, a rough-hewn face, deep voice, a liking for outdoor activities, a big appetite for plain food, and the like. *Colloq. adj.* Very masculine; strong; resembling, contributing to, or the result of masculine strength. 1921: ". . . A . . . two-fisted, he-man battle!" Witwer, *Leather,* 175. 1930: ". . . A regular he-man cop. . . ." Lavine, *Third Degree,* 158. 1956: "Wheaties [a packaged breakfast food] . . . —the he-man's breakfast." *Radio advt.,* Nov. 23.

hemo-jo *n.* A shovel or spade; work

done with a shovel, such as ditch-digging; hard manual labor.

hemp   hemp, the   *n.* **1** A cigar. *From "rope," as rope is made from hemp. Not common.* Cf. **rope**. **2** A hangman's noose; death at the hands of the law. **3** Marijuana, esp. a marijuana cigarette. 1956: "The hemp—marijuana." S. Longstreet, *The Real Jazz Old and New*, 144. *Because marijuana comes from a hemp-like plant.*

hemp four-in-hand   A hangman's noose. 1952: "Father . . . said Jake would wind up . . . wearing a hemp four-in-hand." "Our Boarding House," *synd. newsp. cartoon*, Oct. 15. *Not common.*

hen   *n.* A woman; esp. a fussy old woman or a woman who likes to gossip; a termagant; a shrew. 1924: ". . . One of the old maid teachers called him sweet. Sweet! Cripes, that old hen made him sick." Marks, *Plastic Age*, 6. Cf. **biddy, chicken, quail, wet hen.**   *v.i.* To gossip; to converse. *Usu. said of women.* 1950: "Glad to see you two girls henning away." Movie, *The Furies*. *adj.* Attended by, interesting to, or composed exclusively of women.

hen-apple   *n.* An egg. *Orig. farm use.*

hencoop   *n.* A women's dormitory in a coeducational college. *c1900; college use.* Cf. **frau-shack.**

hen-fruit   *n.* Eggs. *Since c1850. Has seen wide facetious use.*

henhouse   *n.* An Army officers' club. *Some W.W.II enlisted man use. Orig. because all the "chickens" hang out there.*

hen party   A party attended by women or girls only, usu. for the purpose of talking or gossiping. 1942: "Men have stag parties; girls have hen parties." Julius G. Rothenberg, *Word Study*, Feb., 3/2. 1952: "I should've remembered—the annual hen party!" Merrill Blosser, "Freckles," *synd. comic strip*, Aug. 27.

hen-pen   *n.* A girls' school; esp. a private school for girls. *c1940; student use.* See Appendix, Rhyming Slang.

hen ranch = **hencoop.** *c1925.*

Henry   *n.* A Ford automobile. *From the maker's first name. c1920.* Cf. **lizzie.**

hen tracks = **chicken tracks.**

hep   *adj.* Aware; informed; knowing; specif.: self-aware; aware of, informed of, wise to, and with a comprehension of and appreciation for a specif. field of endeavor, modern mode, fashion, or way of life; modern. 1954: "By running with the older boys I soon began to get hep." L. Armstrong, *Satchmo, My Life in New*

Orleans, 25. 1924: "Unless some of you wake up and, as you would say, 'get hep to yourselves,' you are never going to be anything." Marks, *Plastic Age*, 195. 1951: "How little we've been personally hep to what's allegedly going on." *New Yorker*, Oct. 6, 27/1. 1951: "Publicity-hep [Victor] Mature added that such pictures aren't bad for putting an actor before the public." B. Thomas, AP, Sept. 14. *Always pred. and attrib. adj. use. Some student use since c1915. Common since c1935, when the word became assoc. with jive and swing use. Still considered a jazz term and fairly common with students and young adults. Since c1945 preceded by "hip," esp. in jazz and beat use.*   **—ster** *n.* A hep person, esp. one who completely believes, lives, and is immersed in a hep group; one who works at being hep; specif., one who really appreciates and is in rapport with jive or swing music, fashions, and fads. 1938: *Cab Calloway's Cat-alogue: A Hepster's Dictionary.* Title of a publication. 1950: "The hundred hepsters joined in the chorus." Billy Rose, *synd. newsp. col.*, Jan. 20. *Obs. Completely replaced by "hipster."*

he-pal   *n.* A girl's boy friend; a beau. *Not common; prob. synthetic.*

hep cat   hepcat   *n.* **1** A person who is hep or well informed. 1938: "A hep cat is a guy who knows what it's all about." *Cab Calloway's Cat-alogue.* 1950: "The moral of the story is that a hepcat may look at a king." Billy Rose, *synd. newsp. col.*, Aug. 7. *Archaic.* **2** Specif., a devotee of jive or swing music. *Mainly used by nondevotees who don't understand the real meaning of "hep" or "hepcat." Archaic.* **3** A dude, a sport; a young man who dresses fashionably and garishly, knows the latest news, witty sayings, and cynical opinions, and enjoys or pursues women, jazz, and a fast, tense, unrefined way of life. 1952: "During depression times . . . Valerio became what is known in Harlem as a big-timer, a young sport, a hep cat. In other words, a man-about-town." L. Hughes, *Laughing to Keep from Crying*, 38. *Orig. Harlem Negro use. The most common use by hep people. Archaic since W.W.II.*

hep to the jive   **1** Hep, esp. aware of or wise to life and its mendacity, problems, and delusions. c1915 [1954]: "As the days rolled on I commenced getting hep to the jive. I learned a good deal about life and people." L. Armstrong, *Satchmo, My Life in New Orleans,*

192. → **2** Informed of, with an appreciation and comprehension of jive and swing music. *c1935–c1942 jive and swing use; now somewhat archaic.*

herder   *n.* A prison guard. *c1930; underworld and convict use.*

Herkimer Jerkimer   A fictitious, masc., personal name applied to any rustic, fool, or screwball. 1946: "This is about a screwball named Herkimer Jerkimer." *Can You Top This?* radio program, Jan. 4.

Herman   *n.* A guy; a fellow. 1950: ". . . He figured I was a smooth Herman who'd steal the script. . . ." Starnes, *Another Mug,* 104.

Hero   *n.* **1** A very large, overstuffed sandwich on a long, hard-crusted roll or hard-crusted bread, sliced lengthwise and containing several kinds of cold meats and sometimes tomatoes and peppers. *Often called "Italian Hero sandwiches." These are usu. features of Ital. restaurants in the Eastern U.S. and often contain the peppers and spiced meats assoc. with Ital. cooking.* See **grinder, poor boy.** → **2** The hard-crusted Italian bread usu. used to make Hero sandwiches.

Heroes union, the   [derog.]   The American Legion.

herring-choker   *n.* A Scandinavian. *Not common.*

herring pond   The Atlantic ocean. *Prob. more common in Eng. than in U.S.; considered somewhat affected.*

Hershey bar   **hershey bar**   **1** A gold stripe, worn on the sleeve, denoting six months military service overseas. *W.W.II Army use. Implying that such a stripe is a prize and worth just about as much as a candy bar.* **2** A European prostitute or woman who could be sexually possessed very cheaply. *W.W.II Army use. Food was so scarce in Europe during W.W.II that the Hershey bar, which soldiers could obtain easily, was actually a medium of exchange.*

Hey!   **hey!**   *exclam.* An exclamation of surprise, wonder, or quick anger. Often used as a greeting to show pleasant surprise at meeting a friend. 1955: " 'Hey,'—saying that 'Hey' in such a nice, sweet way, with a pleasant smile— 'Hey-y,' a sort of Southern drawl, as if he was an old-old-old friend." C. Willingham, *To Eat a Peach,* 16. *Colloq.*

Hey, Rube!   **1** A call for help, or a rallying call by circus people in a fight with, or trouble with, irate townspeople. 1932: "Hey, rube. Come running quick!

Hey, rube." [*Yelled by a circus employee.*] Movie, *If I Had a Million.* 1939: "If you don't want to seem gil, don't speak of a pass as an Annie Oakley. The expression disappeared 40 years ago, along with the old rallying cry, 'Hey, Rube.' *SEP,* Mar. 25. *Circus use c1890–1930; there is some doubt if the term was ever used, certain old-time circus people claiming it is synthetic. In any case, widely used in books and movies about the circus. Definitely no circus use since c1930, perhaps because it was never used, perhaps because it was then generally understood by everyone. The term "Clem" has seen wide use for this meaning.* **2** A fight between circus workers and townspeople; a riot by townspeople against a circus, because they believe they have been cheated or because they dislike the attitudes and actions of the circus outsiders. *Like many circus terms, this one is also associated with carnivals.*

Hi!   *exclam.* Hello. 1951: ". . . The staccato cry of 'Hi!,' which we . . . judged to be the almost universal greeting. . . ." *New Yorker, "The Talk of the Town"* col., Dec. 22, 12/3. *A universal colloq. since c1920.*

hick   *n.* **1** A farmer, rustic, rube, or small-town or countrified person; an innocent; a person easily duped; a stupid, unknowing person. 1690: Farmer & Henley. 1949: "The automobile . . . largely nullified the outward distinctions between hick and city slicker." D. L. Cohn, N.Y. *Times Bk. Rev.,* Nov. 6, 5/2. *Colloq. Brought to the U.S. by the orig. colonists.* Cf. **square.** → **2** A corpse or cadaver; a stiff. *Because of the fear rustics used to have that if they came alone to the city they might be waylaid and killed so their cadavers could be used for dissection by eager medical students.* *adj.* Rural; countrified; ignorant, unsophisticated. 1921: ". . . His . . . features wasn't bad looking in a hick way." Witwer, *Leather,* 141. 1939: ". . . That hick chief of police. . . ." Gardner, *D. A. Draws,* 83.

hickboo   *n.* An enemy air raid; enemy bombardment; an enemy attack. *A little W.W.I use, taken from the Eng. sl. (Brit. folk ety. of Indian word meaning "eagle," hence air raid.) Some Eng. sl. use in W.W.II, but no U.S. sl. use.*

hick dick   A small-town policeman or detective. *Not common.* See Appendix, Rhyming Slang.

hickey   **hickie**   *n.* **1** A pimple; any skin blemish. *c1915. Very common oral* *use.* **2** Any rich dessert. *Some student use, c1940; because rich, sweet food encourages pimples.* **3** A thingamajig. *c1915.*

hickory oil   A whipping.

hick(s)ville   Hick(s)ville *adj.* **1** Corny; done by or for unsophisticated people; in an amateur way. **2** Dull; boring; in a small-town way. *Both orig. cool use; never common.* See Appendix, —ville ending.

hick town   A small, rural, and sometimes backward city, town, or village. 1938: "... Any hick town in Kansas...." *Amer. Mercury,* Sept., 45/2. *Colloq. since c1915.*

hide   *n.* **1** A pocketbook. *c1930. Some underworld use.* **2** A racehorse. 1934: "... While it is a cheap race, there are some pretty fair hides in it." Runyon. **3** A baseball. Cf. **horsehide.** **—s** *n.pl.* Drums, esp. a set of drums and traps used by a jazz musician. 1957: "Hides—Drums." E. Horne, *For Cool Cats and Far-Out Chicks. Jazz use.*

hideaway   hide-away *n.* **1** A secret refuge; a hiding place. *Colloq.* **2** A small town; a small obscure place, such as a restaurant, bar, or resort. 1929: "The vaudeville performer on the two-a-day has played to punks in the hide-aways." *World's Work,* Nov., 40. 1954: "Hernando's Hide-Away." Title of pop. song.

hide-out   hideout **1** A prisoner who hides intending to escape at night. *c1915; prison use.* **2** A hiding place, a secret meeting or living place. *c1930. Colloq.* **hide out** *v.i.* To hide, esp. from the police. *Colloq.*

hi fi   high fi   hi-fi *n.* A record player (phonograph), and its components, that will reproduce the sound impressed on a phonograph record or tape recording with a high degree of fidelity, including a wide range of high and low sounds, without introducing extraneous noises. *Since c1948.* *adj.* **1** High-fidelity, applied to the reproduction of recorded sound. **2** Of, by, or pertaining to such a record player, its components, or accessories. *The selling and buying of hi fis have reached major proportions since c1945; there are now many devotees.*

hig = high hig.

high *adj.* **1** Drunk. *Usu. pleasantly or happily drunk; not drunk to the point of unconsciousness.* 1944: "... After seeing him 'a bit high.' " Fowler, *Good Night,* 262. "High, slightly alcoholic, above the earth!" A. Miller, *Death of a Salesman,* 106. *Very common.* See Appendix,

Drunk. **2** Under the influence of a narcotic drug, esp. marijuana, and esp. when the feeling is pleasant and makes one carefree and lighthearted. 1956: "The coarse [marijuana] seeds are made into cigarettes and the user smokes them in big puffs getting high—a state in which time seems to stand still, where the top of the head is filled with all heaven, and everything seems easy to do, better, stronger, and longer." S. Longstreet, *The Real Jazz Old and New,* 144. 1957: "On that occasion, Gee assertedly supplied the drugs, spoon and needle, and then they planned to meet again at 4 P.M. He was there till about 3:30 A.M. When he wandered out, he was high, but not drunk." E. Kirkman & H. Less, N.Y. *Daily News,* Sept. 14, 4/2. *Orig. addict use, c1930; now widely known.*

high as a kite = **high,** an emphatic form.

highball   *n.* **1** A drink containing a portion of whisky mixed with soda, water, or a soft drink, and served, usu. with ice, in a tall glass. 1898: *DAE. Now stand.* **2** A railroad signal denoting a clear track; a railroad signal to start, continue moving, or increase speed. *Railroad use. Early train signals were painted metal globes hoisted to the crossarm of a tall pole beside the tracks.* **3** A train running on schedule; a fast or express train. *Railroad use since c1925.* **4** A salute. 1958: "Highball—A salute." G. Y. Wells, *Station House Slang. W.W.I and W.W.II Army use.* *v.i.* To go fast; to speed. 1947: "A train was thirty yards away, highballing down the track." C. Willingham, *End as a Man,* 172. *Railroad and hobo use since c1925. Some student use since c1940.* *v.t.* To rush something; to speed or cause something to move rapidly. 1952: "One New York distributor highballed 30 trucks [of oleomargarine] through the Holland Tunnel." AP, July 1. *adj.* Operating under an emergency speed-up program.

highball jockey   See Appendix, Suffixes and Suffix Words.

high-binder   *n.* **1** A criminal; a hoodlum. *Never common.* → **2** Influential, but dishonest or crude. 1952: "The *AFL News-Reporter* ... covered the winter meeting of the grand inner circle of high-binders at Miami Beach." Westbrook Pegler, *synd. newsp. col.,* Mar. 10. *Not common.*

high-brow   highbrow *n.* An intellectual, well-educated, or cultured person. 1926: "... One does not need

to be a 'high-brow' to read this book. . . ."
A. G. Kennedy. 1948: [1902–3] "My
husband, Will Irwin, invented both the
terms highbrow and lowbrow. He used
them in a series of articles in the N.Y.
Morning Sun, circa 1902–3. . . ." Inez
Haynes Irwin, *Word Study*, Oct., 1/2.
*A high forehead is supposed to indicate
a large and good brain. Pop. since c1910;
now colloq. The word has come increasingly
to mean a literary person or one who
appreciates the arts.* *adj.* **1** Intellectual,
cultured, educated, literary. 1914: ". . .
All them high-brow sermons . . . I hope
you won't think I'm trying to get high-
browed, Mr. Morton." S. Lewis, *Our Mr.
Wrenn*, 42. *Owing to recurring anti-
intellectualism in the U.S., the word is
sometimes used derog. or humorously.* →
2 Unreal, unrealistic. *v.t.* To impress
a person with one's learning. **High-
brow** = **Highbrowville.** **—ed**
adj. = **high-brow.**
Highbrowville *n.* Boston, Mass. *Supposedly the home of many highbrows and
a cultural center.*
high-class *adj.* In or having good
taste; refined; having good manners;
honest, trustworthy. 1956: "A high-class
man can be hurt only by a low-class
man. The low-class man can't look down
at anybody, and he has no feeling and
can't be hurt anyway." T. Betts, *Across
the Board*, 295. *Colloq.*
high cockalorum *n.* A self-important
person. *Since 1880. Not common.*
higher than a kite Extremely high
or drunk.
higher than Gilroy's kite Very drunk.
See **high.**
higher-ups *n.pl.* Superiors, those in
authority, leaders; important or influential people, esp. those who are
important socially, in business, politics,
or the underworld. 1930: ". . . A conference with the Higher-ups and Tammany Hall. . . ." Lavine, *Third Degree*,
111. 1951: "She always fought with the
movie studio higher-ups—the ones who
could fight back." AP, Hollywood,
Sept. 10.
highfalutin *adj.* Pompous; high class;
ideal. 1920: ". . . Whether to yield to
[the hired girl's] extravagant demands
or to let her depart and take one with
ideas less 'high falutin.' " *Scribner's*, Aug.,
247/1. *Since c1850.*
highgrade *v.t.* **1** To steal something.
2 To remove the best trees from a forest
by cutting them down. *Lumberman use.*
—r *n.* One who appropriates another's

property; a thief. 1950: "Highgraders
have moved in on the booming Cobalt
silver mine here. When rich ore was
struck buyers flocked in and established
contact with mine workers who steal
the ore." AP, Cobalt, Ont., Dec. 20.
high-hat *n.* **1** A snob; one who acts
superior; one who is conceited, aloof, or
exclusive. 1924: "We're a lot of low-
brows pretending to be intellectual
high-hats." Marks, *Plastic Age*, 196.
2 An expert stunt flyer. *Some early
aviator use.* *v.t.* To snub; to treat
another superiorly or patronizingly.
v.i. To act superior or patronizingly.
1937: "Jack Conway's invention, to
'high hat.' . . ." Max Eastman, *Enjoyment of Laughter.* **—ter** *n.* A
snob. 1930: "Damn dressed-up high-
hatter!" Burnett, *Iron Man*, 162. **—ty**
adj. Conceited; aloof; exclusive.
high hig *n.* A snobbish, disagreeable
girl.
High, Jack! *imp.* A command to raise
one's hands, as in surrender or before
being robbed; "stick 'em up." *Some use
until c1920; obs.* See **Jack.**
highjack = **hijack.**
high jinks **hi-jinks** *n.* An uninhibited, boisterous, irresponsible good
time; loud humorous fun, often accompanying drinking; pranks. 1953: "It is
the . . . out-of-towner, his pockets full . . .
who cuts the hi-jinks here." Hal Boyle,
AP, Mar. 9. *Since c1910.*
high lonesome A drunken spree;
drunk. 1952: *High Lonesome*, movie title.
high-muck *Very derog. and angry
form of "high-muckety-muck."*
high muck-a-muck **high-muckety-
muck** **high-muckie-muck** **high-
mucky-muck** **high-monkey-monk**
n. An important, pompous person; a
socially prominent person. *Since c1865;
used disparagingly and jocularly.* Cf.
muck-a-muck.
high on [someone or something] To
be enthusiastic about; to like exceptionally well; to have a high opinion of. 1953:
"Taylor was genuinely high on his
product. . . ." Robert M. Yoder, *SEP*,
Apr. 4, 19.
high on the hog, eat **eat high off the
hog** **eat high on the joint** **1** To
have the best of food. 1949: "You will
stand in a chow-line or eat high on the
hog, as a member of the ruling mob."
W. Pegler, *synd. newsp. col.*, Oct. 13.
1952: "They have to eat, and preferably
high on the joint. . . ." Raymond Chandler, *Atlantic Monthly*, Feb., 51/2. **2** To

prosper. 1953: "The institute [of Dr. Kinsey] will eat high off the hog." Harvey Breit in N.Y. *Times Bk. Rev.*, June 28, 8/2. 1956: "Monday, chicken. Tues., macaroni salad. Wed., baked corn beef hash. Fri., shredded lettuce. Anyway, it was high on the hog while it lasted." *New Yorker*, Sept. 29, 33. **3** To live prosperously; specif., to live much more prosperously or pleasantly than formerly. *Orig. Southern use; often jocular. Because the choice cuts of meat, the more expensive hams and bacon, are taken from high up on a hog's sides.*

high pillow   An important person; a big shot. 1940: "Some punk took the rap for the high pillow." Chandler, *Farewell*, 163.

high pitch = **pitch.**

highpockets   A tall man; also, a nickname for any tall man. 1934: "It's your money, highpockets." Chandler, *Finger Man*, 10.

high roller   **1** One who gambles large sums frequently. 1956: "HIGH ROLLER —A big gambler; the term probably reached the race track by way of the dice table." T. Betts, *Across the Board*, 316. → **2** One who spends money freely, esp. at nightclubs, entertainments, and on whisky and women; a "sport."

high shot   A big shot. 1932: "I always try to keep in with the high shots...." Runyon. *A term appar. beginning and ending with Runyon.*

high sign   Any secret gesture or signal made to another person in recognition, as a warning, or the like.

high-tail   *v.t., v.i.* **1** To make a fast getaway; to leave quickly, usu. on foot. *Orig. because certain common animals, such as mustangs and rabbits, erect their tails when startled, and then flee.* → **2** To travel fast. → **3** To drive closely behind another vehicle; to follow another closely.

high-tail it = **high-tail.**

high-tony   *adj.* High-toned; superior; tony. 1950: "Look at the high-tony bum." Toots Shor, *New Yorker*, Nov. 18, 72. *Not common.*

high-ups   *n.pl.* = **higher-ups.** 1929: "Rico got in touch with some of the high-ups...." Burnett, *Little Caesar*, 188.

high, wide, and handsome   Easily, pleasantly, and with few worries; in a carefree manner.

high-wine   *n.* A mixture of grain alcohol and Coca-Cola. *An extension of the distiller term. Hobo use.*

high yellow   A light-skinned Negro, esp. if lacking Negroid features; specif.,

a mulatto; esp. a sexually attractive mulatto girl or young woman.   *adj.* Light complexioned and sexually attractive; said of a Negro or mulatto girl. 1952: "'Hong Kong's full of yellow gals,' said the white man. 'I mean high-yellow gals,' said the Negro, 'like we have in Missouri.' 'Or in Kentucky,' said the white man, 'where half of 'em has white pappys.'" L. Hughes, *Laughing to Keep from Crying*, 12.

hijack   highjack   *v.t.* **1** To rob; specif., to rob a vehicle of its load of merchandise, as whisky. 1926: "... Hijack ... a word that has reached wide circulation since the advent of Volsteadism ... its earliest use was largely within the I.W.W. ranks. It comes from 'High, Jack!,' a command to throw up the arms." S. H. Holbrook in *Amer. Mercury*, Jan., 63. 1930: "Hijack the truck." Lavine, *Third Degree*, 165. **2** To coerce or force someone to do something, as by extortion.   *n.* = **hijacker.**

—er   highjacker   *n.* A holdup man; specif., one who robs a truck, esp. a bootlegger's truck, of its merchandise. 1951: "A highjacker who looted a truck." D. P. Wilson in *Atlantic Monthly*, Feb., 54/1. *Since c1925.* See **High, Jack!**

hike   *v.i. & v.t.* To climb or work on an electric wire or telephone pole; to work as an electrical lineman. *Lineman use since c1925.*   *v.t.* **1** To alter the figures on a check, to raise the amount of money shown. 1951: "'Did you hike those checks?' 'Yes, I raised them.'" AP, Dec. 20. *Underworld use.* **2** To save, put away, store away. *Not common.*   *n.* An increase. 1949: "... Hike in wages from 40 cents to 75." AP, Oct. 19. *Colloq.*   **—r**   *n.* **1** An electric lineman. *Lineman use.* **2** A town marshal. *c1925 hobo use.*

hill   *n.* In baseball, the pitcher's mound. See **go over the hill.**

hill, go over the   **1** To escape from prison. *Orig. by running away from a work gang.* → **2** To desert from the armed forces; to go awol. *Since c1920. Became common cW.W.II.*

hill, over the   **1** In prison; imprisoned. *Archaic underworld use.* **2** Absent without leave; deserted. *Military use.* See **awol.**

hillbilly   *n.* A poor farmer who lives in the Southern hill or Ozark regions; an uneducated, unworldly rustic. *The image is of a poor, lazy, hill farmer, or member of his family, living in an isolated region in a log cabin or shack. Such a farmer may raise a small crop of corn* *or other vegetables, own a cow and a mule, and often possesses many chickens and children. According to pop. tradition all hillbillies carry long rifles and make moonshine whisky at their own stills.* adj. Rustic; pertaining to a hillbilly. 1956: "New York's New York. This ain't no hill-billy joint. We got some class to us." J. Cannon, *Who Struck John?* 164.

hill (row) of beans, a Of little significance, importance, or benefit; insignificant, inconsequential.

hind end The rump; the rear end.

hinders *n.pl.* A person's legs, regarded as though they were the hind legs of a quadruped. 1948: "He stood up on his short little hinders and got himself a lawyer." F. Brown, *Dead Ringer*, 142.

hind hook The brakeman on a train, whose position is on the caboose or rear end. *Railroad use.*

hinge *n.* 1 A look or glance. 1939–40: "It is a good thing I only write you letters instead of getting a hinge at yr . . . kisser." O'Hara, *Pal Joey*, 64. 1950: "I . . . took a fast hinge at the sodden courtyard." Starnes, *Another Mug*, 15. *Often in "get [or take] a hinge."* 2 Fig., a look; an examination or investigation. *Not common.*

hinge, get (take) a Look at; take a look.

hinkty hincty *adj.* 1 Suspicious. 2 Pompous, overbearing. → 3 A white person. *All usage Negro.* 4 Snobbish, aloof. 1956: ". . . *Hincty* is an insult, meaning snobbish." S. Longstreet, *The Real Jazz Old and New*, 148. *Mainly Negro use.*

hip *adj.* 1 = **hep.** 1929: "Why don't you get hip to yourself?" Dunning & Abbott, *Broadway*, I. *Since before c1915. Orig. a variant of "hep," since c1945 has completely superseded "hep." Thus "hep" was assoc. with jive and swing use; "hip" is assoc. with cool, far-out, and beat use.* → 2 = **cool, gone, far-out.** 1958: "According to [Kenneth] Rexroth, to be hip is to be 'disaffiliated.' The hipster is also a pacifist, and many of them are conscientious objectors and anarchists. To be hip is also to be anti-commercial, anti-intellectual, anti-culture." E. Burdick, *The Reporter*, Apr. 3, 31. 1958: " 'I'm hip.' This phrase means: No need to talk. No more discussion. I'm with you. I got you. Cool. In. Bye-bye." H. Gold, *The Beat Mystique*, 84. 3 = **beat.** *Beat use.* See **hipster.** *v.t.* To inform a person of

something he should know; to put [someone] wise. *Not common.* —**ped** *adj.* 1 Fond of; obsessed with; steeped in. 1914: "I ain't hipped on her—sort of hypnotized by her—any more." S. Lewis, *Our Mr. Wrenn*, 233. 2 Informed; hep; knowledgeable; wise to. 1920: "Oh, just one person in fifty has any glimmer of what sex is. I'm hipped on Freud and all that, but it's rotten that every bit of *real* love in the world is ninety-nine per cent passion and one little soupçon of jealousy." F. S. Fitzgerald, *This Side of Paradise*, 241. 3 Drunk. *Not common; archaic and dial.* —**py** *n.* A person who is hip or cool. 1957: "Hippy—Generic for a character who is super-cool, over-blasé, so far out that he appears to be asleep when he's digging something the most." E. Horne, *For Cool Cats and Far-Out Chicks.* *Synthetic.* —**ster** *n.* 1 = **hepcat.** 1956: "Hipster: modern version of hepcat. . . ." S. Longstreet, *The Real Jazz Old and New*, 511. *Never common; obs. by c1950.* 2 One who is hip or hep; a hepster; specif., one who is hip to or gone on bop, cool, or far out music; a cool person, a member of the cool group; a devotee of bop, cool, or far out music. *Fairly common use c1945–c1955; still in use.* 3 A member of the beat generation; in the extreme, one who has removed himself from commercial, material, political, and all physical and intellectual reality, intensely believing in and protecting only his true, nonemotional, nonsocial, amoral identity; such a pure hipster has no formal or permanent contact with fellow human beings, and has only spontaneous relationships with those with whom he feels in rapport. There are few pure hipsters, so that a hipster may be merely an extreme cynic, amoral, disliking permanent relationships, obsessed by the futility and mendacity of modern life, having a strong psychological death urge, or be extremely cool or gone. Sociologically a typical hipster has to have a background of being born during or after the depression of the 1930's, reared during a period when his family and most middle-class U.S. families were obsessed with regaining financial and social security under the New Deal, been a teenager during or a veteran of W.W.II or the Korean war, and spent at least two sensitive years in a liberal arts college. The hipster may love speed in the form of motorcycles or cars and be cool when it comes to jazz and art, but the only things he trusts are rapport and silence. A pure hipster may actually be seeking a Nirvana-like state, and his concern with his true nonintellectual, nonemotional, nonsocial, amoral identity resembles that of a Zen Buddhist monk. 1958: "Norman Mailer . . . estimates there are only a hundred real practicing hipsters. . . ." "The surest reflex of the hipster is the refusal to discuss the rationality of what he believes. You're with it or you are not. You either dig what it is all about or you go back to Squaresville. He won't try to enroll you or convince you." E. Burdick, "The Innocent Nihilists Adrift in Squaresville," *The Reporter,* April 3, 31, 33. 1958: ". . . Into the arms of the . . . hipster society . . . ran three . . . herds: 1. Mainstreet thugs with their sideburns, their [motor] cycles, and their jeans; 2. College kids and a few literary chappies, finding in the [narcotic] addict's cool stance an expression of [their] frustration. . . . 3. Upper Bohemia . . . so ready to try anti-art, anti-sex, anti-frantic nonmovement. . . . The hipster is a spectacular instance of the flight from emotion. . . . [The hipster] is powered by . . . sex without passion; the sole passion is for the murder of feeling, the extinguishing of the jitters. . . . The word hipster came in with bop, which is a way of keeping cool musically, at the same time as narcotics addiction burgeoned—a way of keeping cool sexually. The drug-taking hipster is not a sexual anarchist; he is a sexual zero, and heroin is his mama. . . . The hipster has decided to quit—resign. . . . He gives up on the issue of being human in society. . . . He disaffiliates." Herbert Gold, *The Beat Mystique,* 84–7. 1958: "The cool hipsters of the Beat Generation . . . are likely to be the last of the bohemians. . . ." Ed. Klein, "The Beat Generation," N.Y. *Daily News,* Feb. 19, 28.

hip cat   hipcat   *n.* **1** = **hepcat.** *Obs. Never common.* **2** = **hipster.**

hip chick   An alert, sensitive girl or young woman, esp. one cognizant of modern problems, personalities, and art, esp. of modern jazz music. *Orig. jive use, now wide student and young adult use.* See **chick; hip.** See Appendix, Rhyming Slang.

hipe = **hyp.**

Hip gee   See **gee.**

hipper-dipper   *adj.* Superb, superduper. 1940: ". . . Nov. 2 . . . will see Handy Andy Kerr's Red Raiders . . . putting on a hipper-dipper display of fantastic finesse in Worcester, Mass. In short, Colgate vs. Holy Cross." John Kieran, N.Y. *Times,* Sept. 27, 29. *Note rhyming reduplication and alliteration in the newspaper quote.*   *n.* Superbly bad, usu. a fixed prize fight; a tank job. 1945: "Stories about the last fight being a 'hipper-dipper' . . . is [*sic*] entirely without foundation." H. Merrill, Phila. *Record,* June 5, 18/7. See Appendix, Reduplications.

hippings   *n.pl.* Anything used as bedding under a sleeper's hips. *Hobo use.*

hippo   *n.* **1** A hippopotamus. 1950: ". . . A hippo named Betsy 2nd. . . ." AP, N.Y., July 20. See Appendix, Shortened Words. **2** An automobile. *c1925; from the ungainly shape of early cars. Obs.*   —**ed**   *adj.* Deceived; buffaloed.

hips   *n.pl.* The unsuccessful end; "curtains." 1929: " 'They got Sam.' 'Well, that's hips for Sam.' " Burnett, *Little Caesar,* 166. See **eel's hips, snake's hips.**

his nibs   An important person; usu. a pompous or demanding person who is in authority, such as a police magistrate, school principal, ship's captain, or the like. *Always used with mockery.*

hissy   *n.* A fit of anger. *From "hiss." Dial.*

hist = **heist.**   —**er**   See **heister.**

hit   For phrases beginning with "hit," see under principal word of phrase.

hit   *n.* **1** A commercially, popularly, or critically successful play, movie, performance, theater or nightclub act, book, song, recording, author, performer, director, producer, composer, song writer; any notable or celebrated success. 1917: " 'Hit' is still recorded by conservative lexicographers as a bit of theatrical slang. . . ." Utter, *Harper's,* June, 70/2. **2** An instance of winning at gambling; a winning ticket in gambling, esp. a lottery ticket. **3** An appointment or meeting relating to illegal business or contraband; the time, place, person, or operation from which one obtains contraband, usu. narcotic drugs; a package of drugs; an instance of injecting drugs by an addict. *Underworld and narcotic addict use.*   *v.t.* **1** To arrive at or reach a town or region. 1926: "The speed at which Americans live might be inferred from the fact that a

man does not arrive; he 'hits the town.' "
Y.O., *Irish Statesman*, Aug. 21. 1949:
"I hit Wheeling, W. Va. . . ." Red Smith,
Phila. *Bulletin*, Sept. 8, 47/2. 1956:
"We'll be in Russia 20 days . . . hitting
Leningrad, Odessa, Kiev. . . ." Earl
Wilson, *synd. newsp. col.*, June 18, 15.
Since c1885. **2** Fig., to attain; to arrive.
1949: "His new book . . . hit the best-
seller list. . . ." Phila. *Bulletin*, Sept. 6,
54/2. → **3** To pass an examination or
a course with a very good mark.
Student use. → **4** To attend a meeting,
class, party, or event. **5** To beg from;
to accost with a request for money,
food, or assistance. *Orig. hobo use.*   *v.i.*
1 To beg. **2** To succeed. **3** To win at
gambling. **4** To cause a strong reaction.
1949: "It [a narcotic injection] hit all
right. It hit the heart like a runaway
locomotive, it hit like a falling wall.
Frankie's whole body lifted with that
smashing surge, the very heart seemed
to lift up-up-up—then rolled over and
he slipped into a long, warm bath with
one long orgasmic sigh of relief." N.
Algren, *Man with the Golden Arm*, 76.
adj. Celebratedly successful, publicly or
personally successful.

hit [someone]   *v.t.* **1** To borrow
money or ask for a favor; to ask for a
raise in salary; to ask for charity or beg.
2 To present a personal or business
proposition to a person. **3** To cause a
strong emotional reaction; to overwhelm or bewilder. **4** To administer a
narcotic drug to an addict.

hitch   *v.t.* **1** To marry; to be married.
1953: "Now that you two is practically
hitched. . . ." Edgar Martin, "Boots &
Her Buddies," *synd. comic strip*, Jan. 27.
Since c1875; colloq. **2** To enlist in the
Armed Forces. *Not common.* *n.* A
period of enlistment in any branch of
the Armed Forces. *Colloq. Orig. Armed
Forces use.* **—ed** *adj.* Married.
Colloq. since c1860.

hitch a ride   **1** = **hitch-hike.** See
thumb a ride. → **2** To ride in the car of
a friend, for convenience or to save
money.

hitched, get   To be married. 1954:
"We went straight down to City Hall
and got hitched." L. Armstrong, *Satchmo,
My Life in New Orleans*, 158. See
hitched.

hitch-hike   *v.i., v.t.* To travel, usu.
but not necessarily a long distance, by
standing by the roadside and asking for
rides from passing motorists. *The universally accepted method is to raise one's*

*right arm, elbow bent, with the hand
closed into a fist and the thumb extended
in the direction one wishes to travel;*
hence also **thumb a ride.**

hitch-up   *n.* A marriage. *c1890; archaic.*
v.t. **hitch up** = **hitch.**

hitchy   *adj.* Nervous; frightened;
trembling. *Prob. from "itchy."*

hitchy-koo   *n.* In baseball, a nervous
batter. *Not common.* See **hitchy.** *interj.*
A phrase endearingly and traditionally
uttered by many adults while poking or
tickling a young infant. *Also "kitchy-koo"
or "kitchy-kitchy-koo."*

hitfest   *n.* **1** A baseball game in which
many hits are made and hence many
runs are scored. 1952: ". . . The baseball
games I've seen so far this year have
largely been pathetic parodies of the old
hitfests." Robert C. Ruark, *synd. newsp.
col.*, June 27. **2** A boxing match, esp. a
lively one. *Not common.*

hit for   To start out for or toward;
to head for a place. 1948: "One time we
hit for K.C. . . ." Cain, *Moth*, 83.

Hi there = **Hi.** *Considered by the speaker
as more personal and sincere than just
plain "Hi."*

hit it off   **1** To be compatible; to like
or love one another; to get along together.
1949: ". . . The pair hit it off right from
the start." Billy Rose, *synd. newsp. col.*,
Dec. 28. **2** To be acceptable to a group
or adaptable to an occupation or
situation. **3** To succeed, to bring about
success.

hit it up   **1** To walk fast, to move fast;
to be lively or boisterous. *Obs.* → **2** To
play music.

hitter = **shoulder-hitter.**

Hit the road!   *Exclam.* = **Scram!**

hit up = **hit.**

hive   *v.t.* To understand; to discover.
c1935; West Point and some Army use.
Not common. **—y** **hivy** *adj.*
Quick to learn; sharp-witted. 1944:
"Everyone was surprised that a file-
boner as hivey as Cunningham was D
in math. . . ." Cliff Macon, *Collier's*,
Sept. 23, 69/1. *c1935; some West Point
use.*

Hi ya   **Hiya** = **Hi.** *Shortened form of
"How are you," reinforced by "Hi."
Colloq.*

hiyee   *adj.* Plenty; large; enough;
many. *Logger use, from Chinook jargon.*

hizzy = **tizzy.**

ho   See **heave-ho, right-ho.**

hoary-eyed   **orie-eyed**   **orry-eyed**
adj. Drunk. 1943: "He would be orry-
eyed before nightfall." H. A. Smith,

Putty Knife, 32. *May be from "awy-eyed," which would explain the apparent cockney-style dropping of the "h."* Cf. **oryide.**

hobby   *n.* A translation, pony, trot. *Facetiously, from "hobby horse" as related to "pony."*

hock   *v.t.* To pawn something. *1939–40:* "I finely . . . hocked my diamond ring. . . ." O'Hara, *Pal Joey*, 3. *Since c1825; more common than "pawn." Colloq.*   *n.* Pawn. *Since c1850; colloq.* See **in hock.**

hock, in   **1** In a pawnshop, pawned. *Colloq.* → **2** In debt; owing money or having many unpaid bills. **3** In prison. *Since c1850; orig. underworld use.*

hockable   *adj.* Pawnable. *1951:* ". . . The 'ice' was always hockable." A. Green, *Show Biz*, 11.

hockshop   *n.* A pawnshop. *c1875; colloq. since c1900.*

hocky   *n.* Lies; exaggeration; bull. *1947:* " 'Don't you try and hand *me* any of that hocky about being a white man!' . . . after a while the nigger agreed he was a nigger." C. Willingham, *End as a Man*, 76.

hocus-pocus   *n.* Deception; trickery; funny business; fast talk.

hod   *n.* **1** A smoking pipe. *Obs.; never common.* **2** [*derog.*] An unwanted Negro customer, client, or passenger. *Orig. c1925; taxi driver use = a Negro passenger.* Cf. **scuttle.**

hoddy-doddy   *n.* An insignificant or average person; a fool. *1934: Obs., Web.* *1951:* " 'What did he look like?' . . . 'Sam Patch? A meagre, wizened, inconsiderable little hoddy-doddy.' . . ." Samuel H. Adams, *New Yorker*, Dec. 8, 81. *Not common.* See Appendix, Reduplications.

hoedag   *n.* A hoe. *Obs.*

hoe-dig   *n.* A rural square dance; a dance. *Dial. Perh. from "hoe-down" plus "shindig."* Cf. **hoodang.**

hoedown   *n.* **1** A rural square dance; a party or dance, esp. a lively, boisterous one. *Colloq.* → **2** A lively, loud argument; an angry discussion. → **3** Any action-filled or violent event; a lively boxing match, a brawl, a riot. → **4** A gang fight between boys of rival neighborhood gangs. *1951:* "Anything can start a hoe-down." H. Lee in *Pageant*, Apr., 36/1. *It is interesting to note that the meaning of this term has become more violent as it has moved from rural to urban use.*

hog   *n.* **1** Anyone who collects or hoards specif. items, is selfish, or takes or consumes more than his share of anything. *Usu. preceded by a noun indicating what is collected, hoarded, or consumed.* **2** A railroad engine; usu. a light, console-type engine with eight drivers and four pony trucks, used on freight trains. *Hobo and railroad use since c1915. From its comparatively high consumption of coal and water.* **3** A convict; a yard bird. *From "yardpig."* See Appendix, Shortened Words. **4** A dollar; the sum of one dollar. See **hogg.**

—ger   *n.* A railroad engineer. See **hog.**

— hog   See Appendix, Suffixes and Suffix Words.

hogan = **molly-hogan.**

Hogan's brickyard   A rough, bare baseball diamond; a vacant lot used as a baseball diamond. *Baseball use.*

hog-caller   *n.* A loudspeaker; esp. a portable loudspeaker. *Some W.W.II Army use.*

hogg   *n.* A dime. *c1850; never common. Obs.* See **hogs.**

hog-head   **hogshead**   *n.* A locomotive engineer. *Since c1910; orig. Western railroad and hobo use.* See **hog.**

hog-jockey = **hog-head.** See **hog, jockey.**

hog-legg   **hog's leg**   *n.* A revolver. *1940:* "A plainclothesman with his coat off and his hog's leg looking like a fire plug against his ribs. . . ." Chandler, *Farewell*, 183. *Orig. Western use = a long-barreled, single-action six-shooter.*

hogs   *n.pl.* Dollars, usu. just a few dollars, never a large amount. *Never common, but reappears every now and then in student use. Had minor pop. with some bop groups, c1945.*

hogshead = **hog-head.**

hog's leg = **hog-legg.**

hogwash   *n.* **1** Insincere talk or writing; misleading arguments and discussions; lies, exaggerations; speech or writing aimed at convincing while purporting to give the facts; propaganda; boloney, bunk, garbage, etc. *Colloq.* → **2** Worthless or inferior objects. *Not common.* → **3** Inferior or diluted liquor. *Not common. Orig. from "hogwash" = garbage or slop fed to pigs.*

hog-wild   *adj.* Wildly excited; temporarily irrational owing to excitement, anger, or happiness.

hog-wrestle   *n.* Crude or vulgar dancing.

hoist   *v.t.* **1** To report freshman servants to the tutor for refusing to work. *1851:* "Harvard College use." Hall,

College Words, 162. → **2** To punish or reprimand anyone; to fire an employee; to relieve a person of his duties, in favor of a better worker. Fig., to "hoist" = lift a person out of his job. *Not common.* See **yank. 3** To hang a person. **4** To rob a place or a person; to steal an object. 1949: "They hoisted the place." *Mr. Soft Touch*, movie. 1949: "... Jugs he was hoisting. . . ." A. Hynd, *Public Enemies*, 4. *Common since c1935; orig. underworld use. The most common meaning for this word.* See **heist.** *v.i.* To steal or rob. 1939: "The stall . . . distracts the sales force while the hoister hoists." R. L. Woods, *Forum*, Dec., 275/2. *n.* A robbery or hold-up. 1931: "Crooks . . . speak of a job of hold-up as a 'hoist.' . . ." John Wilstach, *Sat. Rev. Lit.*, See **heist.** **—ed** *adj.* Stolen. 1952: "Among the hoisted articles recently have been various specified articles." Cedric Adams, radio network, Sept. 29.

hoity-toity *adj.* Haughty, proud, snobbish; high-hat, snooty. 1952: "In the hoity-toitiest of the Fifth Avenue shops . . . the mink coat . . . arouses . . . talk. . . ." Sam Dawson, AP, Feb. 6. *Colloq. Not as common as before c1935.* See Appendix, Reduplications.

hoke = **hokum.** 1942: "You know, the usual hoke." *Holiday Inn*, movie. *v.t.* To flatter or speak insincerely to a person; to kid a person; to refuse to consider seriously, to make light of; to do something in an affected, overly sentimental, insincere, or silly way. 1938: "It's all right to hoke the incident but not the theme." AP. 1946: "The Senator not only hokes up Allen but does the pitch. . . ." NEA, Jan. 12. 1942: "I should apologize for hokin' up your number. . . ." *Holiday Inn*, movie. *Not very common.* **—y hoky** *adj.* Containing or composed of hokum. 1945: "Equally a part of America . . . are the dull films, the tasteless, hoky confections that public taste ought to repudiate. . . ." Albert Maltz, N.Y. *Times*, Aug. 19, 3/8. *n.* An actor who deals in hokum. 1951: "I can be a hokey, I can do a straight line." Milton Berle, N.Y. *Times Mag.*, Apr. 8, 17/4.

hokey-pokey   hoky-poky *n.* **1** Cheap ice cream, candy, confections, primarily made to be attractive to children. 1949: "I was about to buy a cup of lemon ice from a hokey-pokey man. . . ." Billy Rose, *synd. newsp. col.*, July 6. 1950: "In Pittsburgh around 1900 we boys bought from the itinerant

'hokey-pokey ice-cream man' a . . . confection called a snowball." A. L. Hench. 1952: "... A minimum of six hours is spent pawing over candy bars on the hokey-pokey counter. . . ." Westbrook Pegler, *synd. newsp. col.*, Jan. 7. Cf. **Good Humor.** → **2** The seller of such items. → **3** Any cheap, gaudy, useless item. **4** = **hokum.** 1947: "I am getting . . . sick of movies lately. Too much of . . . 'Hollywood hokey-pokey.' By that, I mean they 'put it on too thick!' " Phila. *Bulletin*, July 15, 26/1. *adj.* Sentimental. 1949: "Don't be hoky-poky." *Paid in Full*, movie. See Appendix, Reduplications.

hokum *n.* **1** Flattery; insincerity; nonsense, bunk, blah. *Colloq.* → **2** Any stage device used purely to please the audience; any proved song, joke, or line that is sure to elicit laughter, tears, or applause from an audience; proved but hackneyed or trite material. *Theater use.* → **3** Cheap, sugary candy; cheap souvenirs; any cheap, useless item such as is sold at carnival booths. See **hokey-pokey.**

hokus *n.* Any narcotic drug. *c1930; common drug-addict use.*

hold *v.t.* To prepare or serve food or a specif. dish without its usu. condiment or side dish. *Thus "Lettuce and tomato salad, hold the mayonnaise" = lettuce and tomato salad without mayonnaise. Lunch-counter use in relaying an order. v.i.* To have narcotics for sale. *Narcotic addict use since c1945.*

holding *adj.* Wealthy. 1952: "... Respect . . . for people who are 'holding.' . . ." A. J. Liebling, *New Yorker*, Sept. 27, 34/2. *Fig. = "holding" much money or many possessions, reinforced by the financial term "holding." Not common.*

hold out To refuse to work, perform, or do one's duty unless one is paid more or given better treatment. 1956: "As he [a prisoner] strode into the execution room, he shouted to M. E. Elliott, a prison guard who receives $100 for pulling the switch: 'Hold out for $200.' " N.Y. *Post*, Jan. 18, 3. **hold-out** *n.* **1** An athlete, esp. a baseball player, who refuses to sign his yearly contract until he is promised a higher salary. **2** A ranch; a small piece of property that one owns. *Not common.* **3** One who withholds payment or refuses to pay, usu. one who refuses to pay graft, extortion, or bribe money. 1930: "... Raids . . . coerce reluctant hold-outs into 'kicking in' with their contribution. . . ."

Lavine, *Third Degree*, 168. **4** One who refuses to accept projected plans, sign a contract, or the like. **hold-outs** *n.* Playing cards secretly held out of a deck, thus making certain hands impossible; cards from a deck secreted on one's person, to be used as part of one's hand at the most opportune moment.

hold the bag **1** To be double-crossed; to be cheated out of one's share; lit., to be left holding an empty bag. 1906: *DAE. Still in use.* → **2** To be left with the responsibility or blame for failure. *Colloq.*

hold the sack = **hold the bag**. 1939: "... Don't you let them leave you holding the sack." Gardner, *D. A. Draws*, 118.

hold [one] up To uphold or vouch for someone; to verify another's story.

hold-up **holdup** *n.* **1** A robbery, esp. to rob a person at the point of a gun; a stick-up. 1930: "... He accidentally ran into the hold-up." Lavine, *Third Degree*, 71. 1948: "Keep quiet and give us no nonsense. This is a holdup." Phila. *Bulletin*, July 6, 1/1. *Since c1875; almost as common as the standard "robbery." Colloq.* → **2** Fig., a sale at an exorbitant price. → **3** Fig., a request for a raise in pay, usu. supported by implying an offer of a better-paying job elsewhere." 1916: "I responded to the hold-up...." E. Gilbert, *New Republic*, Nov. 4, 15/2. *v.i., v.t.* To rob, esp. at the point of a gun. 1893: "... 'Holding up' a stage-coach." Brander Matthews, *Harper's*, July, 304/2. *Now colloq.* *adj.* Of, pert. to, or working at hold-up. Usu. in "hold-up man." 1930: "The hold-up man...." "... The full-fledged hold-up business." Lavine, *Third Degree*, 71, 72.

hole *n.* **1** Any small, dirty, crowded public place. 1958: "Hole—The subway." G. Y. Wells, *Station House Slang*. See **the hole. 2** [taboo] The vagina. *Mainly young boy use.* → **3** [taboo] A woman considered solely as a sexual object; a piece. **4** [taboo] The rectum. *Never common.*

hole, in a Faced with what appears to be a disastrous difficulty, an insurmountable trouble, or an unsolvable problem.

hole, in the In debt.

hole, the *n.* **1** The solitary confinement cell. *Common convict use.* **2** A railroad spur or sidetrack. *Railroad use.* **3** A subway. *Orig. pickpocket use.* **4** One's dwelling place, house, apartment, or room. *Usu. used facetiously.* See **hole.**

hole in = **hole up**. 1948: "Long Island, where ... he might hole in for a day or two." Lait-Mortimer, *N.Y. Confidential*, 18.

hole in the (one's) head **1** The mouth. *Obs.* **2** Anything that is as completely undesirable or ridiculous as having an actual hole in the head would be. *Usu. in the expression "to need [it] like a hole in the head." A very pop. expression c1948. Pop. by comedians; contains elements of Jewish wit.* **3** A mythical symptom of stupidity. *In, e.g.,* "He's got a hole in the (*his*) head."

hole in the wall Any small residence or place of business; often implies dislike for the place.

hole in [one's] wig = **hole in the (one's) head.**

hole up **1** To hide out, as from the police; to hide or keep another person hidden. 1949: "He was holed up ... in a ... rooming house." A. Hynd, *Public Enemies*, 44. **2** To secure temporary living quarters or a place to sleep, as a hotel room. 1951: "... We've got to begin thinking about holing up for the night." S. Lewis, *World So Wide*, 135. *Cf.* **hole, hole in.**

holiday *n.* **1** A small area on a ship that has been left unpainted, owing to neglect. *Wide USN use.* → **2** A task that has been forgotten or neglected; an unfinished or unsatisfactory job. *c1935. Orig. and mainly USN use.*

holler **—holler** **holler-song** *n.* A simple, sad song with words that are spoken or shouted. 1956: "The work-holler, the river-holler, and the fisher-man-holler are all different. And the cornfield-holler called 'Arwhollie' is still heard, as 'Don't Mind de Weather.' Full of long, sliding tones, you find hollers in many of Lead Belly's recordings and songs. Huddie Ledbetter, as he was known in his more formal moments, was the last of the real holler-song singers." S. Longstreet, *The Real Jazz Old and New*, 25. *Orig. used to give work orders to slaves, and sung in unison by slave workers. Many such songs have African origins or traits and contributed to the beginning of jazz music.* *v.i.* To inform to the police or to a superior; to squeal. 1949: "You think he wouldn't holler if they turned the heat on him?" Burnett, *Jungle*, 141.

holligan A variant sp. of **hooligan.** *Archaic.* See **hooligan.**

hollow note A hundred-dollar bill,

a C note; the sum of a hundred dollars. *Never common.*

Holly   *n.* An order of food that the customer takes out or has sent elsewhere, as to his office, because he does not have time to eat it at a restaurant or lunch counter. *c1945. West Coast lunch-counter use.*

holly-golly   hully-gully   *n.* **1** Nonsense; bunk, boloney. Usu. in "That is a lot of 'holly-golly.' " **2** Hullabaloo; a disturbance; noise. Usu. in "What's all that 'holly-golly.' " *Not common.* See Appendix, Reduplications.

Hollywood   *adj.* **1** Gaudy; loud, flashy, sporty. *Said of objects, often said of clothing.* **2** Affected, insincere, mannered. *Said of people.*

Hollywood corporal   An acting corporal. *Supposedly some W.W.II Army use. Prob. synthetic.*

Hollywood kiss   kiss-off   *n.* = **kiss-off.** *East Coast, esp. N.Y.C., use.*

Holy Christ!   *exclam.* An exclam. of anger, surprise, astonishment, or consternation. *Somewhat archaic, but still common.*

Holy cow!   *An oath and an exclam. of astonishment, consternation, relief, etc. Equiv. to "Holy cats!" both being euphem. for "Holy Christ!"* 1953: "All he could manage to say upon seeing the nude blonde, was 'holy cow!' " Bem Price, AP, Korea, Mar. 11. *Although this term is considered to be very popular among teenagers, no self-respecting, red-blooded teenager would dare use such a weak oath. It is, however, the common oath and popular exclam. put into the mouth of teenagers by all script writers, and is universally heard on radio, television, and in movies. It was first popularized by the "Corliss Archer" series of short stories, television programs, and movies, which attempted to show the humorous, homey side of teenage life.*

Holy Joe   holy Joe   **1** A chaplain in the Armed Forces. *USN use since c1900; wide usage in all branches of the Armed Forces during W.W.II. Cf.* **sky pilot.** → **2** Any priest, minister, or clergyman. 1946: "No guy could have led the kind of life that needs twelve Holy Joes to get him past them Pearly Gates...." Evans, *Halo in Blood,* 6. *The wide Armed Forces use during W.W.II spread the term to civilian use, where it still retains popularity.* → **3** A devout, prissy person; a pious person, esp. one whom the speaker considers sanctimonious, sissy, or corny. 1951:

"In the East they're all holy Joes and teach in Sunday schools." S. Longstreet, *The Pedlocks,* 87.   *adj.* Pious; sanctimonious; supercilious. 1951: "I can't even stand ministers. The ones they've had at every school I've gone to, they all have these Holy Joe voices when they start their sermons. God, I hate that. I don't see why they can't talk in their natural voice. They sound so phony when they talk." J. D. Salinger, *Catcher in the Rye,* 78.

holy terror   One whose mischievous or irresponsible conduct causes worry or even terror. Usu. said of a violently mischievous child. 1903: "He's a holy terror." E. Conradi.

Homberg Heaven   Homberger Heaven   Washington, D.C.; the various federal government buildings, offices, and jobs of the Eisenhower administration. *Implies that this Republican Party administration is a haven for the wealthy and successful businessman. Based on "homberg" plus "hamburger heaven" and coined by Presidential candidate Adlai Stevenson, of the Democratic opposition.*

hombre   *n.* **1** A man of Spanish or Mexican ancestry. *Since c1840; orig. Southwestern use.* → **2** Any man. *Often in "bad hombre," "tough hombre," "wise hombre." Still retains a Western twang. Commonly used in books and movies about cowboys and ranchmen.*

home   See **go home!, nobody home.**

home cooking   Satisfying; pleasing.

home free   **1** Assured of success or winning; having such a large advantage, or lead in a contest, that one is sure to succeed or win. **2** To succeed or win easily; to reach one's goal without undue expense of effort; to be sure of winning; a race horse that is leading the rest of the horses in a race by several lengths; a baseball, basketball, or football team leading an opponent by a safe number of points; a boxer who has weakened his opponent; a businessman who has overcome the main obstacles in an important deal. *All are said to be "home free," even though the race, the game, the fight, or the deal is not yet completed.*

home guard   **1** A native or permanent resident of a place; a person with a permanent home; a retired circus worker; a street beggar, as opposed to a traveling hobo. *Orig., c1910, circus and hobo use.* → **2** One who works steadily for the same employer; a nontransient worker. *Since c1920.* → **3** A married sailor. *Since c1935.*

homer   *n.* In baseball, a home run. *Since c1890; baseball colloq.   v.i.* To hit a home run. 1951: "Bobby Thomson, who homered . . . and Monte Irwin, who also homered." AP, Oct. 2. *Baseball colloq.*

homework   *n.* Love-making, usu. necking, but sometimes coitus. 1949: "I want to do homework." "Homework," *pop. commercial song. Facetiously relating to a pop. student pastime. This is a "sly" sl. word of the kind sometimes accompanied by a wink.*

homey   *n.* **1** A new arrival from one's home town. → **2** An innocent, unworldly, non-suspicious person; a hick. **3** A new arrival (to a large Northern city) from the South. *Negro use.*

homing pigeon   The discharge emblem worn by ex-servicemen of W.W.II. *Not as common as "ruptured duck."*

homo   *n.* A homosexual of either sex. 1954: "I was curious to see what sex was like. I knew nothing about 'homos' at that time." H. K. Fink, *Long Journey,* 14. *Universally known.* Cf. **queer.**   *adj.* Of or pertaining to homosexuals or their ways. See Appendix, Shortened Words.

hon   *n.* Honey; sweetheart. *A term of endearment, usu. in direct address. Colloq.* See Appendix, Shortened Words.   **Hon** *adj.* Honorable. *When part of a title.* See Appendix, Shortened Words.   **—ey**   *n.* **1** One's sweetheart, fiancée, wife, beloved. *Used for both sexes, but most often to indicate a girl or woman. Usu. a term of direct address. Now standard.* → **2** Any person who is highly regarded in a specific field of endeavor. *Usu. in "He's a honey of a prize fighter . . . an actor." Orig. c1920, prize fight use.* → **3** Anything that is highly regarded, satisfying, or well done; a dilly. 1949: ". . . It is a honey of a taut melodrama. . . ." B. Crowther, N.Y. *Times,* Oct. 2, 1. *Fairly common.* → **4** Any sweet, attractive person; any thoughtful, kind, or gentle person. *Since c1930.* → **5** A person who is difficult to please; a difficult problem or task. *The opposite of previous meanings, indicated by accenting or emphasizing the word heavily in speech.* See **bees and honey.**   *v.t.* To choose; to desire; to hozey. *Some child use in the 6- to 10-year-old age group.*

honest   *adj.* **1** Virtuous, chaste, respectable. *Usu. said of women. Colloq. Archaic.* **2** Truthful, fair. *Colloq.*   *n.* **1** A person who can be trusted. *Colloq.* **2** Cherry syrup. *In allusion to the myth of George*

Washington's chopping down a cherry tree and, when questioned, admitting that he had done so. Some lunch-counter use. The adj. meaning = chaste and this meaning appear to have no relation; however, see **cherry.**

honey barge   A garbage scow. *Some USN use.*

honey-cooler   *n.* **1** A male who can dominate or convince his sweetheart, fiancée, wife, or any attractive girl or woman of anything, usu. by flattery or a show of affection. 1905: "That boy Bunch is a honey-cooler all right." McHugh, *Search Me,* 82. → **2** Flattery or affection, esp. as lavished on a sweetheart, fiancée, wife, or attractive girl or woman in order to make her forget anger or displeasure. *Since c1930. Both meanings lit. = that which "cools" or "cools off" a "honey." Although not common, this seems to be one of the earliest uses of "cool" in its modern sl. use. However, a v. "honey-cool" does not seem to exist.* Cf. **honeyfuggle.**

honey-fuck [taboo]   *v.i., v.t.* To have sexual intercourse in a romantic, idyllic way; to have intercourse with a very young girl.   **—ing** [taboo]   *n.* Sexual intercourse of a romantic, idyllic nature, as between two innocent children; extremely gratifying and slow intercourse; sexual intercourse with an extremely young girl.

honeyfuggle   honeyfogle   *v.i., v.t.* **1** To flatter or cajole; esp. to flatter or cajole one's sweetheart, fiancée, wife, or an attractive woman, esp. to do so to gain sexual favor or make her forget anger or displeasure. *Since c1830. Archaic.* → **2** To pursue women; to seek women for sexual satisfaction. *Archaic.*

honeyfuggling [taboo]   *n.* See **honeyfucking.** 1934: "Doris was only seven and sexual exposure might have damaged her. He was keenly aware of mysterious pains and penalties attached to 'honeyfuggling.' " P. Wylie, *Finnley Wren,* 65.

honey man   A kept man; a pimp.

honey wagon   **1** A wagon used for carrying manure. *Farm use, c1915.* → **2** A manure spreader. *Farm use. c1930.* → **3** A garbage truck. *Most common W.W.II Army use.* **4** A wagon or cart used to collect refuse and ordure in certain prison compounds. *Army use.*

honk-out   *n.* A failure; a wash-out. *Not common.*

honky-tonk   *n.* **1** A cheap saloon featuring gambling games and dancing by or with women of questionable repute. 1934: "... Rode to my honky-tonk on a bus, banged the piano for my growing clientele until midnight and slept either at my cheap hotel, or in rooms upstairs with evanescent-faced girls." P. Wylie, *Finnley Wren*, 51. 1950: "These honkey-tonks ran wide open twenty-four hours a day and it was nothing for a man to be drug out of one of them dead. Their attendance was some of the lowest caliber women in the world and their intake was from the little, pitiful gambling games they operated, waiting for a sucker to come in." A. Lomax, *Mr. Jelly Roll*, 50. **2** A cheap, small-town theater. 1925: "I was playin' the sticks ... the honky-tonks." G. Lee, "Trouper Talk," *AS.* **3** A brothel. See Appendix, Reduplications.

honorable *n.* An honorable discharge from the Armed Services. *W.W.II and after.*

hon-yock   honyock   hon-yocker *n.* A rustic; a farmer. 1943: "Speaking as a pure-bred hon-yock out of the Middle West...." H. A. Smith, *Putty Knife*, 121. *Since c1875; not common.*

hoo-boy *expl.* An expression of surprise or mock surprise, consternation or mock consternation, pleasure or mock pleasure, tiredness, relief, etc. *As many such sl. terms, can be used in many circumstances to show an emotional response, large or small, when the speaker does not wish to sound sentimental, formal, or overwhelmed. Pop. by Walt Kelly's comic strip, "Pogo," c1950.* See **hoo ha.**

hooch   hootch *n.* **1** Whisky, liquor; esp. inferior homemade or cheap whisky; orig. bootleg whisky. 1924: "... If he kept her 'well oiled with hooch.' " Marks, *Plastic Age*, 251. 1925: "We got some good hooch." S. Anderson, "The Return," reprinted in *The American Twenties*, 67. *Became common during Prohibition, when = bootlegged whisky of unknown origin; after Prohibition = any kind of whisky.* **2** The hoochy-cootch dance. *v.i.* To drink whisky. *c1920; not now common.*

hood *n.* **1** A hoodlum, thief, criminal, gangster; esp. one who applies physical violence. 1930: "... Those St. Louis hoods...." *Amer. Mercury*, 456. 1943: "Why should he ... turn hoodlum ... when ... he didn't have to turn hood?" Wolfert, *Underworld*, 165. 1951: "... The procession of hoods ... on the witness stand." Bruce Bliven, *New Republic*,

Apr. 2, 11/2. *From "hoodlum," although in "hood" the long "oo" is almost always pronounced to rhyme with "good" rather than "mood." Very common.* See Appendix, Shortened Words. **2** [derog.] A nun. *From the hoods worn by nuns, plus a pun on "hood" = hoodlum.* *adj.* Hoodlum; criminal. 1958: "Lansky, once a partner of Frank Costello, has been in the hood hierarchy for decades." *N.Y. Post*, Feb. 12, 38.

hoodang   houdang *n.* **1** Any jovial gathering, a party, a celebration; any period of merriment or noisy confusion. *Mainly dial.* **2** Specif., a rural dancing party to simple country music; a barn dance. *Dial.* See **hoe-dig.**

hoodlum *n.* A youthful ruffian; any thug, criminal, or gangster. 1872: "Colloq." *DAE.* 1891: "... The San Francisco hoodlum is different from the New York loafer." Brander Matthews, *Harper's*, July, 215. *Colloq. c1920; now in stand. use. Orig. unknown. The theory that the word derives from saying the name of a feared thug, Muldoon, backwards has little merit and no basis. From the early quotes given above, the word seems to have a West Coast, prob. San Francisco, origin.*

hooey *n.* Nonsense, cant; boloney, bunk. *Usu. in "That's a lot of hooey" and "He's full of hooey."* 1924: "... My prof's full of hooey...." Percy Marks, *Plastic Age*, 100. 1928: "... The triumphs of biology over transcendental psychopathic hooey." Benj. de Casseres, *Amer. Mercury*, May, 99/2. 1941: "... It sounds to me like a lot of hooey." Cain, *M. Pierce*, 82. *Sudden pop. c1925–1930 and common ever since.*

hoof *n.* A person's foot. *Usu. used humorously, metaphorically, or emotionally.* 1946: "Now kind of take your goddam hoof to hell off my fender." Evans, *Halo in Blood*, 11. *Since c1890; the plural is "hoofs."* *v.i.* **1** To walk. *Since c1910; cf.* **hoof it.** → **2** To do a soft-shoe dance or a step dance. *c1920, vaudeville use. Obs.* See **hoofer.** → **3** To dance on the stage or in a nightclub. *Since c1925.* → **4** To dance socially for one's enjoyment; to dance to ballroom music. **—er** *n.* **1** A professional step dancer, clog dancer, soft-shoe dancer, tap dancer, or the like; a dancer on the vaudeville stage; a nightclub dancer or member of a dance chorus. 1927: "... The hoofers and the chorines of a cabaret...." J. M. Brown, *Theatre Arts Monthly*, Nov., 83. 1954: "This young and spectacular dancer

[Paul Draper], one of the greatest popular hoofers of our time." W. R. & F. K. Simpson, *Hockshop*, 270. **2** A Negro. *Because Negroes originated the clog, step, and soft-shoe dances and first popularized them on the vaudeville stage. Vaudeville use, c1925.*

hoof it **1** To walk; to travel on foot. *Usu. implies determination to reach one's destination even though the walk is long or difficult.* 1912: "I'm going to hoof it." Johnson, *Stover at Yale*, 11. **2** To beat it; to escape on foot. *Some student use. Not now common.* → **3** To dance as an entertainer.

hoo ha *interj.* **1** A cynical and satirical expression of mock surprise, used to deflate another's unacceptable enthusiasm, innocence, or eagerness. *Pop. by comedian Arnold Stang on the "Henry Morgan" radio program, c1946, and on the "Milton Berle" television program, c1950. From a meliorative expression of genuine surprise or the state of being highly impressed. From the Yiddish sl. "hoo ha" = an exclamation indicating intense joy, excitement, surprise etc., as used by comedienne Gertrude Berg on her "Molly Goldberg" radio programs during the 1930s, 40s, and 50s.*

hook *n.* **1** An anchor; a mudhook. *Maritime and USN use.* **2** A straight razor. *Some c1915 convict and Army use. From its shape.* **3** A prostitute. *Some use before c1920. From "hooker."* See Appendix, Shortened Words. **4** A crook. *Some underworld and hobo use c1915–c1935.* See Appendix, Rhyming Slang. **5** In baseball, a curved ball pitched to a batter. **6** A hypodermic needle or bent pin used by narcotic addicts to inject a narcotic. *Addict use; not common.* → **7** A narcotic drug, esp. heroin. *By basing a word on "H," reinforced by "hook" = hypodermic needle and 'hook' (v.t.).* **8** Any means of attracting customers, as a promise of a free gift, a request to radio and television listeners to send in boxtops or their names and addresses for free gifts or discounts on merchandise, or the like. *Since c1930. The last three meanings are based on "hook" = to snare, as to make or snare an addict or customer.* *v.t.* **1** To steal; to shoplift merchandise. 1615: Farmer & Henley. 1939: "Hooking merchandise from department stores requires no training." *Forum*, Dec., 273/1. *Colloq. Lit., to snare something while no one is looking.* **2** To arrest. 1929: "My cab driver got hooked for speeding." Burnett, *Little Caesar*, 110.

Not common. Lit., to snare a lawbreaker. **3** To be cheated, tricked, victimized, or defeated in gambling, out of or for a large sum of money. 1946: "[In a card game] Mike is hooked for over seven thousand dollars]." Runyon, *synd. newsp. col.*, Aug. 5. → **4** To be forced into an unpleasant situation or difficulty, from which one cannot extract oneself gracefully. **5** To be addicted to a narcotic drug. **—ed** *adj.* Addicted to a narcotic drug, as marijuana, heroin. 1949: "Once a week wasn't being hooked. It wasn't till a man needed a quarter of a grain a day that Louie felt the fellow was safely in the vise." N. Algren, *Man with the Golden Arm*, 31f. 1952: "So Diane . . . became a junkie . . . hooked by horse. . . ." Orville Prescott, N.Y. *Times*, Apr. 29, 25. **2** Addicted to any vice, person, or cause. **3** Married.   **—er** *n., adj.* **1** A prostitute. 1941: "He . . . walked into the hooker district until he found the lowest dive in the place. . . ." Marcus Goodrich, *Delilah*, 74. 1954: "The hookers working the joints along the streets." R. & F. W. K. Simpson, *Hockshop*, 95f. *Since c1850; common until c1925.* **2** Anyone who "hooks" (snares) or hooks another, as a narcotics seller, professional gambler, etc.; one who recruits others for any purpose. 1956: "*Hooker*—A person who induces union members to act as spies for the company, then keeps them 'hooked' by threatening to expose them." *Labor's Special Language from Many Sources.* **3** A drink of liquor, usu. straight whisky. 1927: "It took a stiff hooker of whisky . . . to thaw her." Hammett, *Blood Money*, 103. **3** A warrant for arrest. *Underworld use.*

hook, get [someone] off the   To rescue a person from impending trouble, failure, or embarrassment. 1952: "He falls for Ilona, sees her in jail, and winds up by trying to get her off the hook." James Kelly, N.Y. *Times*, Aug. 17, 4/2.

hook, off the   Out of trouble; free from a specific responsibility. 1950: "Tony might get off the hook. . . ." Starnes, *And When She Was Bad*, 183.

hook, on the   **1** In difficulty; in trouble; responsible for. *Never, common.* Cf. **off the hook.** **2** To be tempted or ensnared; esp. to be too intrigued by, eager for, or involved in something, to withdraw from or ignore or refuse it. *Fig., to be hooked or on the hook in the same way a fish is immediately before being caught.*

hook arm   **1** The arm one uses most;

the right arm of a right-handed person, the left arm of a left-handed person. → **2** In baseball, a pitcher's pitching arm. *c1930.* → **3** In baseball, specif. a left-handed pitcher.

hook for [something or someone], go on the   **1** To go into debt or borrow money for something or someone. 1957: "You won't think it looks right to drive a new convertible wearing your working clothes. So you'll go on the hook for one of those eighty-dollar sports-car coats and a ten-dollar cap." S. McNeil, *High-Pressure Girl.* **2** To endanger oneself for another.

hook it   To run away, escape; to beat it; often a warning to flee. *Since c1900; not common. From "hook," perh. reinforced from the Brit. sl. term of the same meaning, from the Celtic 'thugad" = to decamp, depart.*

hook-nose [derog.]   *n.* A Jew.

hooks   *n.pl.* **1** The hands; the fingers. 1846: *DAE. Colloq.* **2** The feet. *Never common.* **3** Chevrons. *Some W.W.II Army use.*

hookshop   **hook-shop**   **hook shop** *n.* A brothel, esp. a cheap brothel. 1936: "[A dollar and a half]'ll get you into one of the cheap hookshops. . . ." R. Lull, *Amer. Mercury,* June, 208/1. 1951: "Here he was, standing in a hook shop smelling of wine and perfume and armpits and personal disinfectants. Overhead the sewing machines ground on, and he wondered vaguely if the machines helped the men and women who went to bed down there, if the vibrations drove them to madder furies and greater orgies, or to feeble, sated release." S. Longstreet, *The Pedlocks,* 240. *Somewhat archaic. From "hook" and "hooker."*

hooky   *v.t.* To steal. See **hook.** *n., adj.* To make oneself absent from school or a class for a one-day vacation. Usu., "to play hooky."

hooligan   *n.* **1** A hoodlum; a ruffian; a tough guy. 1943: "Beat me up with your hooligans." Wolfert, *Underworld,* 114. *Since c1895.* → **2** A gunman. **3** The Wild West tent in a circus. Cf. **holligan.** *Circus use.*

hooligan Navy   The Coast Guard. *USN use.*

hoop   *n.* A finger ring. 1929: "The old hoop on that finger. . . ." J. Auslander *Hell in Harness,* 2. *Orig. underworld and hobo use. Colloq. since c1930. adj.* Basketball; organized for playing basketball. 1953: "North Carolina hoop

teams. . . ." Lee Kirby, news broadcast, WBT, Feb. 17.

hoop-a-doop   **hoop-de-doop** **hoopty-do**   *n.* = **whoop-de-do.** 1940: "Cowboys and soldiers created deafening hoop-a-doop but saved us from road agents." M. Berger, N.Y. *Times,* June 7, 26/3. 1947: "His scoops were sometimes achieved through the merry use of tapped wires, convincing bluster and other journalistic hoop-de-doop." M. Berger, N.Y. *Times,* 4/2. See Appendix, Reduplications.

hooper-dooper   **hooperdoo**   **hooper-doo**   *adj.* Uproarious; very entertaining. 1941: "Folks, we got a hooperdoo quarter hour left. Radio, *Uncle Walter's Doghouse,* Feb. 25.   *n.* **1** A humdinger; anything uproarious, entertaining, or remarkable. 1941: "Next Saturday's Barn Dance is going to be another hooper-doo." Radio, *National Barn Dance,* Apr. 19. **2** An important person; a high mucky-muck. 1929: "[He] may be [a] Hooper-dooper to Ann, but he's [not] to me." K. Brush, *Young Man,* 31. See Appendix, Reduplications.

hoopla   *n.* **1** A boisterous, happy noise and confusion. **2** Advertising; ballyhoo. **3** Fanfare; a furor; hullabaloo. *Since c1875.* **4** A carnival concession. *Orig. from the exclam., reinforced from the actual hoops thrown to win a prize.*

hoop-man   *n.* A basketball player. *Sports use. Colloq.*

hoopty-do   *n.* = **whoop-de-do.** **hoosegaw**   **hoosgaw**   **hoosgow** *n.* **1** A jail. *c1920, orig. from the Sp. "husgado," first common in Army and on West Coast. Common throughout U.S. by 1935.* **2** A public rest room, outhouse, or toilet enclosure.

hoosier   *n.* **1** An incompetent or inexperienced worker; an unworldly person, a rustic, hick, or rube; a fool, a dupe. *Logger, carnival, circus, and hobo use c1925; archaic. "Hoosier" = a citizen or resident of Indiana is the only nondisparaging use of this word.* → **2** A new convict or prison guard; a prison visitor. *Prison use c1930.*

hoosier up   **1** To shirk; to malinger; to plot a slowdown of work. 1926: "When a crew of workmen purposely hoosier up on the company, it means . . . a 'conscious withdrawal of efficiency.'" S. H. Holbrook, *Amer. Mercury,* Jan., 64.

hoot = **skyhoot.**

hootch   **1** = **hooch.**   **2** = **hootchie cootchie.**

hootchie cootchie hootchie-cootchie n. 1 A mildly lascivious form of dance exhibition in which a woman sways or rotates her hips and body. *Not as sensuous as actual bumps and grinds since the hips are swayed rather than the pelvis rotated. Once common in carnival and circus shows; now somewhat archaic.* 2 A woman who dances the hootchie-cootchie.

hooted adj. Drunk. *Not common.*

hootenanny n. 1 Fig., a shout, a hoot, a damn. *Usu. in "I don't give a hootenanny" = I don't give a damn, I don't care. Dial.* 2 = **gadget; thingamajig.** *Some use since c1925. Still some maritime use and dial. use.*

Hooverville n. A group of makeshift shacks, usu. located on the outskirts of a town near the city dump, where unemployed workers live and scrounge for food. 1953: "... The early 1930's. ... Hunger-marchers and 'Hooverville' stories took up a lot of space in our press." K. Vidor, *A Tree Is a Tree*, 220. *After Herbert Hoover, President at the start of the Depression, which saw such shacks multiply with growing unemployment.*

hop For phrases beginning with "hop," see under principal word of phrase.

hop n. 1 An informal dance; a public dance; a dancing party, esp. an informal dance for students or teenagers at which only "popular" and rock-and-roll music is played. 1933: "... We went to a hop. ..." J. T. Farrell, 70. *Colloq. since c1755; very wide student and teenage use since c1950.* 2 A bellhop. 1943: "The hop was tall and thin." Chandler, *Lady in Lake*, 80. *Never common. See Appendix, Shortened Words.* 3 Opium. 1887: "So long as any smoker can obtain his hop." (New Orleans), *The Lantern*, May. 1934: "You mean that hop dream she called a confession?" Cain, *Postman*, 102. *Addict and underworld use; also used by general public = any habit-forming narcotic drug.* 4 Any narcotic drug, as morphine, opium, cocaine, or marijuana. 1898: "A Hop Fiend's Dream," title of song reprinted in L. J. Beck, *New York's Chinatown*, 165. 1930: "A little hop or dope was slipped to an anxious prisoner. ..." Lavine, *Third Degree*, 223. 1950: "A lot of them smoked hop. Those days you could buy all the dope you wanted in the drugstores. Just ask for it and you got it." A. Lomax, *Mr. Jelly Roll*, 47. *Addict use. Not now common, as*

narcotics are now widely discussed and each drug has its own specific name or names. 5 A drug addict. *Addict use.* → 6 A state of confusion. → 7 A fanciful story; nonsense; lies. 1949: "Beat it. Go peddle your hop somewhere else." Roeburt, *Tough Cop*, 90. *Orig. may be from a "pipe dream" or "full of hops."* 8 Any journey, esp. a flight by airplane. *Colloq.* v.t. To get aboard, usu. a train. 1934: "... To hop a freight east." Cain, *Postman*, 28. *Colloq.* **—per** n. 1 A partly smoked cigarette that is long enough to be smoked again. *Some hobo and young boy use.* 2 In baseball, a ball hit so that it bounces, or rolls and bounces, on the ground. **—s** n.pl. 1 Opium. c1918. 2 Beer. 3 Information; news; dope. *Not common.*

hop across the fence To associate freely with persons of another race, as Negro and white. *Not common.*

hop fiend A narcotics addict. *Still some general use.*

hop-head n. A narcotics addict. 1930: "All that is necessary is to deprive a 'hophead' of narcotics. ..." Lavine, *Third Degree*, 7. 1952: "Teen-Age Hophead Jargon." Title of an essay by De Lannoy & Masterson, *AS*, Feb., 23. *Orig. addict use, now common use by the general public. From "hop."* Cf. **weedhead.**

hop it To go away; beat it. *Much more common in Eng. than in U.S.*

hopjoint 1 A cheap saloon. *From "hops."* 2 An opium den. 1932: "They find ... speakeasies, although one is a hop joint. ..." Runyon.

hopped up hopped-up adj. 1 Under the influence of narcotics; drugged. 1930: "The newer generation of 'coked' or 'hopped up' gunmen." Lavine, *Third Degree*, 227. 1956: "These young characters who take dope ... they go around all hopped up." S. Bellow, *Seize the Day*, 101. *Orig. addict use, now some general use and almost no addict use.* → 2 Excited; enthusiastic; very alert; full of pep; nervous. 1950: "[He] is all hopped up about it." *Big Town*, radio network program, Feb. 7. 3 Emotional; emotionally upset; agitated. 4 Fig., contrived to be exciting; artificially made exciting. 1950: "[Oakley Hall's *So Many Doors* is] one of those hopped-up novels in which passion is named but not felt." W. G. Rogers, AP, July 18. 5 = **souped up.**

—hop(per) See Appendix, Suffixes and Suffix Words.

hops, full of Talking without knowledge of the facts; unrealistic, exaggerating, wrong, lying; fig., talking like a drunken man or a person under the influence of a narcotic.

hop-stick *n.* An opium pipe. *Addict use.*

hop the twig To die.

hop toad 1 An iron used for derailing railroad cars. *Railroad use.* → 2 A potent liquor, a big drink of whisky.

hop up *v.i., v.t.* 1 To take narcotic drugs, as an addict; to drug a person. *From "hop."* → 2 To give a race horse a stimulating drug so that he will run faster than he normally would. 1948: "... To hop up or slow down their own horses." A. Hynd, *Pinkerton,* 79. → 3 To increase the maximum speed, acceleration, or power of an automobile by any adjustment or added engine component or device. 1956: "How to Hop Up Chevrolet & G. M. C. Engines [title]: Another complete manual on 'souping' and speed tuning ... engines for high performance. Treats all phases, including block, con rods, pistons, fuel, carburetion ignition, supercharging." Advt. for "Floyd Clymer" Motorbooks. See **hot rod.**

horn *n.* 1 Any musical wind instrument. 2. Specif., in jazz, a trumpet. *Jazz use.* 3 The nose.

hornblowing *n.* Aggressive advertising; advertising with a hard sell. *Advertising use.*

hornet = **green hornet.**

horn in To intrude; to barge in; to butt in; to enter (anything) when one is unasked or unwanted. 1922: "Some wallie tried to horn in on our gang." Phila. *Eve. Bulletin,* Mar. 8. 1929: "To horn in on your Broadway trade...." Dunning & Abbott, *Broadway,* I. 1950: "[He] was horning into a case in which he had no client." W. Pegler, *synd. newsp. col.,* Mar. 2.

hornswoggle *v.t.* To cheat, swindle, dupe, deceive. *Since c1825.*

horny *adj.* 1 Carnal-minded, amative, lusty, sexually obsessed. *Colloq.* → 2 Virile, tough, rough, strong; said of a man. *Not common.*

—horrors See Appendix, Suffixes and Suffix Words.

horse *n.* 1 A joke, esp. a joke played on a person; a practical joke. *Some c1890 use. Obs. except in the stand. "horseplay."* 2 A literal translation or list of answers used while taking an examination; a pony. *Some c1900 student*

use. → 3 A diligent, able student; a grind. *Some c1900 student use; still some dial. use. Prob. from the expression "to work as hard as a horse" plus "pony" or "horse" (def. 2).* 4 Meat, specif. corned beef. *Sometimes modified as "young horse," "red horse," "salt horse," etc. Some student, USN, and Army use, mainly c1900–c1935.* 5 A thousand dollars; the sum of $1,000. *Some circus use. Perhaps from "G" and "gee-gee."* 6 Heroin. 1951: "Then he started on heroin, or 'horse.'" Kinkead, 16. 1952: "So Diane became a junkie, hooked by horse." O. Prescott in N.Y. *Times,* Apr. 29, 25. *Wide addict use. Fairly well known to the general public.* See **H.** 7 A stupid, rude, stubborn, or contemptible person. *Dial.* 8 A truck; a tractor. *Some farm and truck-driver use.* Cf. **iron horse.** *v.i.* 1 To joke, indulge in horseplay, or refuse to talk, think, or act seriously. 1954: "Dingus was really mad about it; he wasn't just horsing now." W. Henry, *Death of a Legend,* 32. *From "horse" (n., def. 1).* 2 [taboo] To have sexual intercourse or indulge in sexual horseplay; esp. to have sexual intercourse with a person other than one's spouse, frequently. 1956: "The [band] leader called up all the men and girl singers and piano players together. 'This is a respectable band,' he said, 'and there ain't goin' to be any immoral horsin' goin' on. Whoever you start sleepin' with this trip, that's how you end the tour!'" S. Longstreet, *The Real Jazz Old and New,* 67. *v.i., v.t.* To cheat; to hoax, cheat, or take advantage of someone. See Appendix, Sex and Deceit.

horse-and-buggy *adj.* Old-fashioned.

horse apple *n.* 1 The feces of a horse. → 2 An excl. of disbelief. *A euphem. for "horse shit."*

horse around = **horse,** *v.i.*

horseback *adj.* Quick; to be done quickly; said of a task. *Fig., done while moving, as if on horseback.*

horse collar 1 A score or mark of zero; a goose egg. *Somewhat archaic.* 2 The foam or head on a glass of beer. *interj.* An exclam. of scorn, disgust, disbelief, impatience, or the like. *Euphem. for "horse shit."*

horsefeathers   **horse-feathers** *interj.* An expression of incredulity or disgust; boloney! 1949: "Horse-feathers!" J. Evans, *Halo,* 100. 1953: "Mail comes urging that something be done to 'rescue children from guns, daggers, and soldier worship.' Horsefeathers!'' F. Tripp, AP., May 11. *Euphem. for "horse shit."* *n.* Bunk; boloney. 1928: "In present vogue on street corner and college campus. First used by Wm. De Beck, comic-strip artist. In popular song title 'Horsefeathers.' . . .'' C. E. Cason, *AS*, IV, 98.

horsehide *n.* A baseball. *Colloq.*

horse nails Money, coins. *Obs.*

horse opera **horse opry** 1 A cheaply made, stereotype movie about cowboys; a Western movie. *c1928.* 2 A circus. *Circus use.* 3 = **Western.**

horse parlor = **horse room.**

horse piano A calliope. *Circus use.*

horse room A bookmaking establishment; a bookie. 1956: "HORSE ROOM —A place on any floor of any building, including a cellar, with all the comforts of a race track, if not more, where the walls are tacked with run-down sheets displaying the names of the horses, the odds, the jockeys, descriptions of the races are relayed in soft tones by an announcer who receives information from a bureau that services bookmakers.'' T. Betts, *Across the Board*, 316.

horse's ass [taboo] One who, though not necessarily stupid, lacks subtlety or tact; one who mistakenly believes himself to be shrewd; a foolish person; one who freq. does foolish or embarrassing things; a person stubborn in his ignorance; one who clings to false ideas or beliefs. *Not much used by young people; still common among older people.* See **ass.**

horse's collar = **horse's ass.** *A euphem. From confusion with "horse collar."*

horse shit **horse-shit** **horseshit** [taboo] *interj.* An expression of scornful incredulity or disgust. *n.* 1 Mendacity; insincerity; lies; exaggeration; bunk; applesauce. 1955: "Why do you think I came up here, except to try and talk reason to you? You give me all that *horseshit* about the conditions here, you lay it on and lay it on. . . .'' C. Willingham, *To Eat a Peach*, 93. 2 Trivia; nonessential details.

horse's mouth, out of the Directly from the original or most authoritative source. 1952: "The volume . . . is directly out of the horse's mouth. . . .'' GNS, Mar. 10.

horse's neck = **horse's ass.** *A euphem.*

horse's tail = **horse's ass.** *A euphem.*

horse tail A type of women's hair style, consisting of long, straight hair drawn back toward the crown, where it is gathered and then allowed to hang free, thus resembling a horse's tail. *Orig. and still most pop. among sophisticated, artistic young women, this was the forerunner of the less severe "pony tail." Since c1950.*

hose *v.t.* 1 To flatter a person in an attempt to gain a favor. *Not common,* 2 To cheat; to try hard to win. *Not common.*

hoss = **horse.**

hot *adj.* 1 Drunk. 1851: Hall, *College Words. Obs.* 2 Moving very fast; made or modified to attain high speeds; excitingly fast or speedy. 1868 [moving very fast]: *DAE.* 1943: "Hot crate = a fast plane.'' A. Ostrow. Cf. **hot rod.** 3 Lucky; competent, skilled, talented; popularly acclaimed; specif., in the midst of a series of lucky or successful actions, prone to succeed or win; specif. favored by good fortune; so lucky as to elicit excitement. *Since c1890.* Cf. **hotshot.** 4 Angry, quick to take offense; angry and excited. *c1900–c1925; now mainly in expressions such as "hot and bothered" and "hot under the collar."* 5 Lively; vital; energetic; eliciting excitement; enthusiastic; filled with energy and activity. 1927: "This is a hot town.'' E. Hemingway, *The Killers.* 1951. "When is a magazine a HOT magazine? . . . A 'hot' magazine is one that's sizzling and bubbling with vitality. . . .'' Advt., N.Y. *Her. Trib.*, Dec. 12, 48. → 6 Passionate, sexually excited; having a strong sexual desire for a person; often in the phrase **hot for.** 1924: "This kid [a girl] was the hottest little devil I ever met.'' Marks, *Plastic Age*, 10. 1941: "What makes you so hot for me?'' B. Schulberg, *Sammy*, 167. → 7 Lascivious, lewd, sexually suggestive. → 8 Eager for; in favor of. Usu. in **hot for.** 9 Exciting; specif. said of exciting jazz music played in a fast tempo and with a heavily accented beat, eliciting an emotional or physical response. *Most uses and meanings of "hot," esp. uses 2 through 9, have a connotation of physical excitement tending toward, suggesting, or at least resembling sexual excitement. Many of the uses could be grouped under the general definition of "eliciting physical excitement." This definition is basic to "hot," and includes specific physical responses such as increased pulse beat, blood pressure, and rate of certain glandular secretions, as well as the accompanying feeling of mental and psychological excitement. This* *concept of the specific physical response is important in comparing hot jazz to cool jazz.* **10** Good, fine, admirable; competent, able; pleasing, enjoyable; charming, attractive, handsome, beautiful; popular, well liked. Often in the negative. *The negative sense always has "so" between "not" and "hot." Thus never "not hot," but always "not so hot."* 1924: "I didn't flunk out but my record isn't so hot." Marks, *Plastic Age*, 112. 1934: "Shakespeare was not so hot." *English Jour.*, Nov., 740. *Common use.* **11** Stolen recently and therefore sought actively by the police. 1925; 1934: "Stolen bonds are 'hot paper'; stolen diamonds 'hot ice.' " McLellan in *Collier's. Orig. underworld use, now fairly well known.* **12** Wanted by the police for having committed a crime; guilty and fleeing or hiding out; said of a criminal. 1932: "The Hottest Guy in the World" [title], Runyon. 1949: "Where . . . would a hot criminal like Dillinger hide out?" A. Hynd, 13. → **13** Dangerous, scandalous, leading to possible disaster, arrest, or public reprimand. 1939: "Things were getting too hot." Gardner, *D. A. Draws*, 205. 1956: "As one politician said of the slush fund: 'It's hotter than the Lindbergh ransom money.' " T. Betts, *Across the Board*, 36. → **14** Under enemy fire; dangerous. *Some W.W.II Army use.* **15** Turned on; functioning; said of a microphone. **16** Radioactive. *Some use since c1950. n.* **1** A stolen item. *Some underworld use.* **2** A meal. 1942: "You got to . . . collar yourself a hot." "He might have staked him . . . to a hot." Z. Hurston, 85, 88. *Mainly hobo use, some jive use.* From "hot meal." **3** = **hot dog.**

hot air **1** Empty talk; nonsense; flattery; exaggeration; false promises. 1905: "The Jefferson family tree will never be blown down by any hot air from me. . . ." McHugh, *Search Me*, 105. *Since c1870.* **2** Pompous speech; pompous and exaggerated speech.

hot baby A girl who is passionate and sexy; a girl who lives recklessly. *Some student use since c1900.* See **hot.**

hotbed *n.* **1** A bed or room rented to two persons, one who works during the day and sleeps in the bed at night, and one who works during the night and sleeps in the bed during the day. *Thus one gets into the bed as the other leaves, and the bed is always warm.* **2** A place, region, neighborhood, or institution that fig. produces, breeds, raises, or

houses many people of a specific type. *Thus the Southern U.S. is a Democratic hotbed; an organization controlled by followers of Communism is a hotbed of Communism. From the horticultural term.*

hotcha *interj.* An expression of delight, approval, or pleasure over seeing or hearing something or someone sexually attractive or lascivious. *Archaic.* *adj.* Attractive, esp. sexually attractive; daring, esp. sexually daring; undisciplined. 1939: "He run Sternwood's hotcha daughter, the young one, off to Yuma." Chandler, *Big Sleep*, 45. *Obs.*

hot cha A cup or an order of a cup of hot chocolate. *c1935 lunch-counter use in relaying an order.*

hot corner **1** In baseball, third base. *Because hard, fast-moving ("hot") line drives and grounders are often hit in that direction.* **2** In baseball, any base on which there is a runner. *Obs.* → **3** Any crucial place, esp. on a battlefield or politically. 1943: "The North African front . . . is a 'hot corner. . . .' " *Word Study*, May, 4/1.

hot damn! *interj.* An exclamation of delight or joyous approval; "Hot dog!"
hot-diggity-damn! *exclam.* = **hot damn!**

hot diggety dog! *interj.* = **hot dog!**
hot diggety doggity = **hot diggety dog.**
hot dog **hot-dog** *n.* **1** A frankfurter sausage; a link of wienerwurst. 1928: "Tucker went back into the plane and brought out a wienerwurst link, known as a 'hot dog.' " N.Y. *Times*, quoted in *New Yorker*, Nov. 10, 42. *Since c1900; colloq.* Said variously to be *from an earlier "dachshund sausage," and from a humorous implication that the sausage is made of ground dog meat.* → **2** A frankfurter sandwich, usu. made with a split roll and served with mustard and/or pickle relish, etc. 1910: "First bungalow is Mister Laloo's, buggies and hot dogs." Johnson, *Varmint*, 38. 1923: "The vendor of hot dogs." C. MacArthur, *Rope. Colloq.* **3** A person who has great ability and good fortune; a hot shot. *c1900 student use.* *adj.* Of, selling, or pertaining to hot dogs or hot-dog sandwiches. 1934: "A hot dog stand." "The hot dog business." Cain, *Postman*, 28; 92. **hot dog!** *exclam.* An exclamation denoting delight, enthusiasm, excitement, joyous approval, or the like. 1922: " 'Well, dear, did you have a good time?' 'Hot dog!' " Phila. *Eve. Bulletin*, Mar. 8. *Since c1900; colloq.*

hot foot   hotfoot   *v.i.* To go fast or hurriedly; to travel rapidly; to depart in haste; to hurry; to walk rapidly; to run. 1954: "The boys would hot foot back to the Home when they heard the mess call." L. Armstrong, *Satchmo, My Life in New Orleans*, 39. *Colloq. since c1895.* *n.* 1 A walk; the act of walking the streets. 1905: "He'll be doing hotfoots for the handout." McHugh, *Search Me*, 55. 2 A bail-jumper; a bond-jumper. 3 The act of sticking a paper match between the sole and upper part of a man's shoe, about where his little toe ought to be, and lighting the match. *A practical or impractical joke, the object of which is to see the victim start with pain when the match burns to his shoe.* 1945: "Drunks reel over from the Bowery, and the kids give them hot-foots with kitchen matches." Mitchell, *McSorley's*, 18. *Colloq.* *v.t.* 1 To give a hotfoot to a person. 2 Fig., to cause a person trouble.

hotfoot it   To hasten, to hurry; to run. *Since c1910, colloq.* 1941: "Tell him to hotfoot it to the sheriff's office." G. Homes, *40 Whacks*, 80.

hot for [someone or something] 1 Specif., wanting or desiring a person sexually; wanting or desiring an item or possession of an object. 1947: "Too bad she's such an old hag. She seemed hot for you." C. Willingham, *End as a Man*, 158. See **hot**. 2 Desiring a forthcoming event eagerly and openly; enthused about, ready and eager for. See **hot**.

hot grease   Trouble, esp. imminent or expected trouble.

hothead   *n.* A person easily angered or emotionally agitated; one whose anger or enthusiasm compels him to spontaneous, dangerous, or stupid actions. 1957: ". . . Having dinner with a hothead whose name was Arthur Flegenheimer." D. Jennings, *SEP*, Sept. 21, 94.

hot iron = **hot rod.**

hot mamma = **red-hot mamma.**

hot man   A jazz musician. *Obs.*

hot number 1 A passionate, sexy girl or woman. See **hot**. 2 An item of merchandise that is very attractive to customers; a good selling item of merchandise. *Salesman use.*

hot one 1 An exceptional, remarkable, striking, unusual, or good or bad person or thing. *Archaic.* 2 A very funny joke or prank. *Common use.*

hot pants   hot-pants 1 A desire for sexual intercourse; a sexual passion.

2 A male obsessed with sex; a male who is always seeking sexual intercourse.

hot patootie   A man's sweetheart; a sexually attractive, passionate girl or woman. 1935: "He calls the object of his affection a 'hot patootie.' " *Nation*, May 15, 562/2. *Fairly common c1930 use.* See **patootie.**

hot pilot   A skillful, daring fighter-plane pilot. *Some early W.W.II Air Force use.*

hot-poo   *adj.* Of or pertaining to a hot rock. *n.* 1 = **hot shit.** 2 The latest, confidential information; the latest rumor. *interj.* = **hot shit.**

hot potato   Any difficult or embarrassing practical problem. 1950: "Every one can see how the boss looks when he handles a hot potato." AP, Jan. 30. *Very common.*

hot pup   *n., exclam.* = **hot dog.** *Never common.*

hot rock 1 = **hot shot.** *Some W.W.II use.* 2 In baseball, a fast pitched ball. *Not common.*

hot rod   hot-rod   hotrod   *n.* 1 A stock car, usu. an old or dilapidated roadster, stripped of all nonessential items, with its engine adjusted, modified, rebuilt, or replaced so that the car is faster and more powerful than orig. designed. *The simplest hot rod has its engine adjusted for greater maximum speed or rate of acceleration. The true hot rod is stripped of all items not contributing to speed or accelerative power, including ornaments, rear seats, and often roof, engine cover, and all paneling. True hot rods are often combinations of various old or dilapidated cars: made up of the frame of one car, usu. a light-weight car frame reduced in height so the center of gravity and wind resistance are lower; the engine of a heavy, more powerful car; and various engine, electrical, and exhaust components which the maker-driver considers superior. Simpler hot rods are used to scare and race unsuspecting motorists on the road, and should be able to maintain a speed of between 85 and 125 miles per hour. True hot rods are built and driven by teenage boys and youths and are mainly designed to have a superior rate-of acceleration from a standing start in a drag race.* 1956: "AUTO RACES . . . modified hotrod jalopys . . . TODAY . . . SPORTS-DROME." Advt., Louisville (Ky.) *Courier-Journal*, May 6, 3. 1956: "Special Racing Sports Cars and Hot Rods [title:] A technical book, . . . explains the principles of supercharging, carburetion, suspension, shock absorbers. A complete speed manual." Advt. for "Floyd Clymer" publications. 1957: "Most of the better hot rods will break 100 mph." *Life*, Apr. 29, 132. *Since c1950. Wide teenage and student use and interest since c1945.* **2** The driver of a hot rod; a teenage devotee and enthusiast of hot rods and drag racing. 1951: "Guy your age gets a hold of one of these cans and right away he thinks he's a hot-rod." J. A. Maxwell in *New Yorker*, Sept. 8, 81. *adj.* Assoc. with or pertaining to hot rods, their teenage drivers, devotees, and enthusiasts and their dress, fashions, and fads.

hots, the **1** Love. 1947: "I'd never get the deep undying hots for that rah rah collitch [boy]. Hal Boyle, AP, May 19. **2** Sexual desire.

hot seat **1** The electric chair. 1941: "Wot was Butch's last request before dey gave him de hot seat?" *Hobo News*, Dec. 1. **2** A witness chair in a courtroom. 1950: "Deane was succeeded in the hot seat by a very small pot from the State Department...." Starnes, *And When She Was Bad*, 59.

hot shit [taboo] Wonderful; attractive, handsome; charming, dashing; daring, courageous; intelligent, shrewd, skilled; esp. ultramodern or hip; hot stuff. *Always used in the negative, usu. in "He thinks he's hot shit" = he thinks he's handsome, charming, intelligent, etc., but he's not. Thus through ironical use the term has come to = conceited. exclam. = hot damn! Never common; mainly student and young adult use.*

hot short = **short.**

hot shot **hot-shot** **hotshot** *n.* **1** An important, active, successful person; a big shot; a skillful, successful person; a person who takes risks or chances in order to succeed, and who does succeed and become important; esp. a young daring person who has become a success rapidly and is self-assured and proud of his success, possibly overly confident, daring, or ambitious. 1951: "You take somebody's mother, all they want to hear is what a hot-shot their son is." J. D. Salinger, *Catcher in the Rye*, 46. 1952: "What has been written about executives has usually dealt with the hot shots." C. W. Morton in *Atlantic Monthly*, Aug., 88/1. *Since before 1920.* See **hot.** → **2** Used ironically, one who thinks he is

or acts as if he were important, successful, and daring; a conceited man given to bragging about his success and daring; a smart aleck. 1946: "[This is your] last chance, hot-shot." "You're not pushing around some crummy client to show him what a hot-shot you are." Evans, *Halo in Blood*, 11; 72. → **3** A competent, daring fighter-plane pilot; a "hot" pilot. *Some W.W.II and earlier Air Force use; archaic.* → **4** A conceited, overconfident, overly daring, or irresponsible fighter-plane pilot. **5** The electric chair. *Some underworld use since c1925.* **6** A fast or express train. *Railroad use since c1930.* **7** News; a message; esp., a recent news bulletin or very recent piece of information; a news announcement. 1948: "When that hot-shot came in about Monahan's [death]." Movie, *Scene of the Crime.* *adj.* **1** Fast-traveling; express, nonstop. *Some railroad use since c1925; some truck-driver use since c1935.* **2** Skilled or brilliant, daring and self-confident; righteously proud of one's skill or success. 1949: "In just a year I'm claiming to be a hot-shot Columbia man myself." D. D. Eisenhower quoted in N.Y. *Times*, Oct. 9, 50/3. 1949: "He's off salary . . . working on commission. He's no hot-shot selling man." A. Miller, *Death of a Salesman*, 66. **3** Conceited. 1944: "He was a young, hot-shot second lieutenant." *Amer. Legion Mag.*, Sept., 44/2. *All uses are, of course, Rhyming Slang; see Appendix.* **4** Skilled or competent but irresponsible. 1958: ". . . As your navigator in one of those kites, Hotshot [Hotshot Charles, fighter-plane pilot]." "Terry and the Pirates," *synd. newsp. comic strip*, Feb. 9.

hot-shot Charlie = **hot shot**; an egotist. *W.W.II use, Army Air Force.*

hotsie-totsie *adj.* Satisfactory; pleasing; hunky-dory. c1926: "Everything Is Hotsie-Totsie Now," title of pop. song. See Appendix, Reduplications.

hot sketch **1** One who is remarkably lively, colorful. or the like; a card; a character. *Often used ironically.* 1921: "This Roberts is a hot sketch for a fighter, anyway!" Witwer, *Leather*, 176. **2** A pretty, sexy girl.

hot spot **1** A predicament; a troublesome situation. 1932: "Say, I am in a very hot spot." Runyon, 83. **2** The electric chair. *Some underworld use.* **3** A popular nightclub, esp. one known for a boisterous or rowdy clientele or floor show; a nightclub featuring a lascivious floor show. 1937: "Martha is doing the hot spots." Weidman, *Wholesale*, 139. 1950: "The rowdy 18 Club became [52nd] street's hot spot." L. Sobol, *synd. newsp. col.*, Apr. 2.

hot squat   The electric chair. 1949: "... You couldn't ever rise from the hot squat." A. Hynd, *Public Enemies*, 23. *Underworld use.* See Appendix, Rhyming Slang.

hot stuff   1 A person of merit or quality; a superior person, an expert; a charming, dashing, reckless person. *Almost always used ironically = an audacious, conceited person.* 1939: "I guess they think they are hot stuff." J. O'Hara, *Pal Joey*, 63. 1951: "I like you very much. I'm not gonna let you get away. Not yet. Don't you think I'm hot stuff?" R. S. Prather, *Bodies in Bedlam*, 84. *Since c1900.* 2 Sensational, exciting, violent, lascivious, or similar entertainment. 1904: *DAE.* 1924: "It [a movie] was sure hot stuff." Marks, *Plastic Age*, 28. 3 Stolen goods; loot. See **hot.** 4 Hot liquid, as coffee or soup, being carried by a person, as a waitress; used as a warning to others not to cause the carrier to spill it and not to get scalded.

hot tamale   1 A clever fellow. *c1900.* 2 A sexy girl.

hot to go (for)   Ready and eager. See **hot for [someone or something].**

hot under the collar   Angry. *Colloq.*

hot war   A war involving fighting and bloodshed, as opposed to a cold war. *Some use since c1950.*

hot water   Trouble. 1949: "American girl who has got herself into hot water by marrying a Siamese prince." *Time,* Nov. 28, 91. *Colloq.*

hot wire   News; good news.

houdang = **hoodang.**

hound   *n.* 1 A college freshman. 2 A frankfurter. *Not common.* *v.t.* To pester, bother, or annoy a person. *Colloq.*

—hound   One given to a specified practice or esp. fond of a specified act, food, drink, pastime, or the like; a devotee, addict, or habitué. See Appendix, Suffixes and Suffix Words.

hounds   *n.pl.* Feet. See **dogs.** Cf. **fiend**   *exclam.* Wonderful, remarkable, "great."   *adj.* Very satisfying, remarkable, wonderful, "great." *The last two meanings in teenage use since c1951.*

house   *n.* 1 Personal attention to and interest in another person; encouragement. *Freq. in "give a person a lot of house."* 1951: "[President] Truman told a news conference, 'Wrongdoers have no

house [*sic*] with me no matter who they are. . . .' " AP, Washington, Dec. 13. → 2 [Antonym of sense 1.] Inattention; lack of interest; discouragement. 3 A brothel, a whorehouse. See **barrelhouse, bed house, big house, bughouse, canhouse, cathouse, doghouse, doss house, flophouse, gashouse, hashhouse, joy house, lighthouse, nut house, on the house, paper house, power-house, roughhouse, roundhouse, scratch house.**

—house   See Appendix, Suffixes and Suffix Words.

house, on the   Free of charge. 1951: "Breakfasts, luncheons and dinners . . . and . . . perfect coffee. All 'on the house.' . . ." *Nation-wide newsp. advt.*, Northwest Airlines, Mar. 1.

house around   To loaf. See **horse around.**

house-cleaning   *n.* A reorganization of a business, government branch, etc., involving shifting and ousting of personnel. 1930: ". . . Honest cops, instead of welcoming a house-cleaning . . . resent it. . . ." Lavine, *Third Degree*, 17.

housefrau   *n.* = **hausfrau.**

house larry   *n.* A man who frequents a retail store without buying. 1952: ". . . The 'house larry' . . . who not only has no intention of buying but drops in two or three times a week not to buy." G. Millstein, N.Y. *Times Mag.*, Sept. 21, Part 2, 58/3. *Clothing salesman use.* Cf. **larry, cooler.**

house moss   The tufts and whorls of dust that accumulate under beds, tables, etc., in rooms seldom cleaned.

how   See **And how!, ding how, know-how.** See Appendix, Suffixes and Suffix Words.

how-come-ye-so   *adj.* Drunk. *c1850, mainly New England dial. Obs.*

how-de-do   **how-do-you-do**   *n.* A set of circumstances, a situation. *Usu. ironically in "That's a fine how-de-do."* 1952: ". . . Which is a fine how-de-do in a country that prides itself on progress." D. Dempsey in N.Y. *Times Bk. Rev.*, Aug. 17, 8/2.

howl   *n.* Something fit for ridicule; a cause for laughter; a joke. *Colloq.*

—er   *n.* A laughable mistake, esp. in something written or printed; a boner. 1949: "Howlers Recently Noted. . . . It is obvious that the writer of that howler had no idea . . . what the word nuptial means. . . ." Frank Colby, *newsp. col.*, Oct. 14, 5/6.

How's about? = How about? 1952: "How's about a drink?" B. Schulberg in *Holiday*, Jan., 41.

hozey *n.* A combination of "honey" and "floozy." *Some c1920 use, mainly by would-be wits. Obs.*

hubba-hubba *interj.* An expression of approval and delight, or calling attention to a sexually attractive girl or woman. *Saying "hubba-hubba" is akin to giving a wolf whistle. Wide W.W.II Armed Forces use. Orig. Air Force use from Chinese pilots being trained with U.S. airmen at a Florida airfield. From the Chinese "how-pu-how," a stand. familiar Chinese greeting. Universally known to civilians, and pop. by comedian Bob Hope who broadcast his weekly radio show from military bases and used much military humor and sl.; obs. at end of W.W.II. See Appendix, Reduplications. Cf.* **ding how; haba-haba.**

hubby *n.* A husband. 1798: Farmer & Henley. *Colloq.* See Appendix, —y ending.

hub cap A conceited person. *Hot rod and some general teenage use since c1955.*

huckleberry *n.* A man; specif., the exact kind of man needed for a particular purpose. 1936: "Well, I'm your huckleberry, Mr. Haney." Tully, *Bruiser*, 37. *Since c1880. Archaic.*

huddle *n.* 1 A dancing party. *c1915; obs.* 2 A conference, esp. a private conference. 3 In football, a conference held by the offensive team before each play to determine what that play will be. 4 A short period of intense thought by one person before making a decision.

huff-duff *n.* A high-frequency (radio-radar) direction finder. *W.W.II Air Force use. From the initials "H. F. D. F."* See Appendix, Reduplications.

huffy *n.* A state of anger. *adj.* Angry, petulant. 1914: "I didn't mean to get huffy...." S. Lewis, *Our Mr. Wrenn*, 58. *Since c1895, now colloq.*

hugger-mugger *adj.* Slovenly; confused; makeshift. 1947: "Her execution of the plan, if that hugger-mugger improvisation could be called a plan, was witless." J. H. Jackson in *San Fran. Murders*, 152. See Appendix, Reduplications. **—y** *n.* Deception; skullduggery. 1946: "It would be difficult to put any conviction into the acting out of all this hugger-muggery." Phila. *Bulletin*, Feb. 5, F26. See Appendix, Reduplications.

hulligan *n.* A foreign performer; a foreigner. See **hooligan, holligan.**

hully-gully = **holly-golly.**

humdinger *n.* Something or someone very remarkable or admirable. See **dinger.** *c1905; archaic and dial. now. adj.* Remarkable.

humdinging *adj.* First rate. 1943: "A real, humdinging comer." Wolfert, *Underworld*, 150. *adv.* Exceedingly. 1940: "... A humdinging good tale." J. Street, *SEP*, Jan. 6. *Archaic.*

hummer *n.* 1 = **humdinger.** 2 A false arrest or false accusation. *Underworld use.* 3 Anything given free. *adj.* 1 Free. → 2 Excellent. *Perh. from* "humdinger."

hump *v.i., v.t.* 1 To move quickly; to hurry. 1845: *DAE. Not now common.* 2 [taboo] To have coitus. 1956: "I miss the circus. I miss watching the elephant's trunk and the camels hump [laughter from the audience]." Comedian Joe E. Lewis, "Copacabana" nightclub, N.Y.C., Oct. 6. *n.* 1 See **get a hump on.** 2 A mountain; fig., an obstacle. *Mainly aviation use.* Cf. **over the hump.** 3 A camel. *Circus use.* → 4 A "Camel" brand cigarette. *Some student use.*

hump, hit the To attempt an escape from prison; to desert from the Army. See **hump, over the hill.**

hump, over the 1 Fig., successfully finished with or past the hardest or most dangerous part of a task. 2 At least halfway through a tedious task; serving the last half of one's work period, apprenticeship, term of military enlistment, or prison term. *Since c1930. Fig., to be coasting downhill.*

hump on, get a Hurry; hurry up; move or act quickly. *Since c1890.* See **hump,** *v.*

humpty-dumpty *adj.* Worthless; no good; flimsy. *Because, according to the nursery rhyme, Humpty-Dumpty couldn't be properly put together again. Not common.* See Appendix, Reduplications.

Hun [derog.] *n.* 1 A German soldier. *Some W.W.I use. Not used in W.W.II.* 2 A German. *Not now common. adj.* German; Germanic; of German origin.

hunch *n., adj.* An intuitive premonition. 1949: "This ... was too good a hunch play to let drop there." E. Selby. *v.t.* To believe on the basis of a hunch. 1950: "... As I hunch it, the answer is triple [pronged]...." Billy Rose, *synd. newsp. col.*, Aug. 30. *c1905 to present, now colloq.*

hunching *n.* A dance. *c1925; obs.*

hundred proof The best; original; genuine. *From 100-proof whisky, the highest alcohol content allowed in the U.S.*

hung *adj.* In love. *Rock-and-roll use since c1955.*

hunger = **from hunger.**

hung over hung-over *adj.* Suffering from the after effects of too much whisky; burdened with a hangover. 1943: "The guy was there on the bench. He was hung over." H. A. Smith, *Putty Knife*, 125. 1950: "Brafferton just came in, looking as hung over as you can get." Starnes, *And When She Was Bad*, 95.

hung up *adj.* **1** = **square**, *adj.;* limited by old-fashioned beliefs and attitudes; incapable of being hip. 1958: "There just ain't no word in hiptalk for 'enough,' either you're way out, pops, or you're hung up." Edward Klein, "The Beat Generation," N.Y. *Daily News*, Feb. 19, 28. **2** Delayed; detained. *Now common.* **3** Stymied by a problem; delayed in completing a task or succeeding, owing to trouble or difficulty.

hunk Hunk *adj.* All right; in good condition. 1847: *DAE.* 1856: "He now felt himself all hunk." N.Y. *Her. Trib.,* Dec. 30. *Obs.* Cf. **hunky, hunky-dory.** *n.* **1** [derog.] = **Hunkie. 2** A girl or woman considered sexually. 1946: "He came back to the hot little hunk he used to run around with." Evans, *Halo in Blood*, 217. *Lit., a hunk or piece of ass.*

hunkie hunky Hunkie Hunky [derog.] *n.* A Central European, esp. a Central European immigrant laborer; specif., a Hungarian, Slav, Pole, or Lithuanian; a bohunk. 1940: "Like a hunky immigrant catching his first sight of the Statue of Liberty." Chandler, *Farewell*, 1. *Most pop. c1925. Still common. From "hunk."* See Appendix, —ie, —y endings. *adj.* All right; hunky-dory. 1861: *DAE. Obs. From "hunk."* See Appendix, —ie, —y endings.

hunk of change = **piece of change.**

hunk of cheese A stupid, objectionable, or disliked person.

hunks *n.* A foreign laborer.

hunky-chunk A sturdy, short, muscular laborer, usu. from Central Europe. *Prob. synthetic.*

hunky-dory *adj.* Satisfactory; fine; first-rate; O.K. 1868: *DAE.* 1947: "That may be hunky-dory (if you'll pardon the antiquated phrase) with the jumping and jiving youngsters. . . ."

B. Crowther in N.Y. *Times*, July 13, X1/8. *Somewhat archaic. From the obs. "hunk" and "hunky."* See Appendix, Reduplications.

hurdy-gurdy *n.* A hand organ, such as a street organ-grinder plays. 1934: "My apartment overlooks Washington Square. Hurdy-gurdies thumb melodiously below me." P. Wylie, *Finnley Wren*, 192. *Colloq.* 1948: ". . . There had been a time when the hurdy-gurdy was the only means of bringing music to many people." Fiorello H. La Guardia, *The Making of an Insurgent, An Autobiography*, 29.

hurl *v.t.* In baseball, to pitch a game or an inning. 1951: ". . . After hurling five frames in three games. . . ." Frank Eck, AP, Sept. 22. **—er** *n.* A baseball pitcher. *Baseball use.*

hurrah *n.* A spree. 1887: ". . . On a great hurrah. . . ." *Lantern* (New Orleans). *Archaic.*

hurrah's nest Confusion; a jumble. *c1830.*

hurting *adj.* Without money. *Not common.*

hush-hush *adj.* Very secret; confidential. 1950: "Mexican secret police turned Sobell over to the FBI in a hush-hush border meeting." AP, Laredo, Texas, Aug. 19. *n.* **1** Secrecy. 1934: "But why all the hush-hush about Walden?" Chandler, *Finger Man*, 110. **2** A revolver. *Not common.* See Appendix, Reduplications.

husk *v.i., v.t.* To undress.

hustle *v.i., v.t.* **1** To beg. 1894 [1891]: "You'll hustle for an overcoat. . . ." J. Flynt. **2** To steal. *c1915.* **3** To work as a prostitute, to seek customers in order to have sexual intercourse for pay. 1954: "Whores that hustle all night." L. Armstrong, *Satchmo, My Life in New Orleans*, 58. **4** To sell something. **5** To earn or obtain money aggressively or unethically; to be active or energetic in earning money by one's wits; to seek customers or victims of a deception aggressively. **6** To hurry. *n.* **1** Any confidence game, crooked gambling game, cheating, deception, or other unethical way of earning a living or obtaining money. 1954: I must explain how our quartet used to do its hustling so as to attract an audience." L. Armstrong, *Satchmo, My Life in New Orleans*, 34. **2** Moving about energetically, pushing about. *Usu. in the phrase "get a hustle on," meaning "hurry." Colloq.* **3** A quick

examination; a search. **—r** *n.* **1**
One who earns a living by illegal or
unethical means; a petty criminal.
c1930. See **duck-hustler. 2** A prostitute.
1952: "I work on the streets and in bars.
I ain't nothing but a hustler." L.
Hughes, *Laughing to Keep from Crying*,
57. *Fairly common.*

hustle on, get a   To hurry; to work,
move, or do something faster or with
more alertness. *Usu. a command or plea.*

hut   *n.* **1** A prison cell. **2** A college
fraternity house. **3** The caboose of a
railroad train.

hyp   hype   hipe   *n.* **1** A hypodermic needle. *c1913.* → **2** A hypodermic
injection of narcotics. *c1925.* → **3** A dope
peddler, a supplier of illicit narcotics.
Addict use. 1952: ". . . Any hype that

wants to get you hooked. . . ." David
Hulburd, *H Is for Heroin.*   *v.t.* **1** To
cheat; to try to talk someone out of
what is rightfully his. See **hip. 2** To beg.
Neither use common.   *adj.* = **hip.**
Some early c1915 use.

hyped-up   *adj.* Artificial, phony, as
though produced by a hypodermic
injection of a stimulant. 1950: "No
fireworks [in this movie], no fake
suspense, no hyped-up glamour." Billy
Rose, *synd. newsp. col.*, Jan. 9. See
hopped-up.

hype-stick   *n.* A hypodermic needle.
Not common.

hypo   *n.* **1** Hypochondria. *Colloq. since*
c1900. **2** A hypodermic needle; a hypodermic injection. *Hospital use.* → **3** A
narcotics addict.

I

—ian   See Appendix, Suffixes and
Suffix Words.

I Can Catch   The Interstate Commerce Commission. ICC. *Truckdriver
use; from the initials.*

ice   *n.* **1** A diamond; collectively, diamonds. 1951: "An old pal . . . is bringin'
me a two-carat hunk of ice." "Major
Hoople," *newspaper cartoon*, March
7. Cf. **green ice.** *Very common.* **2** A gem
or jewelry set with gems. **3** Bribe money;
money paid by a criminal for police and
political protection; incidental profit
obtained illegally or unethically. 1943:
". . . One of the cashiers . . . will provide
them with all the tickets they can handle
for a slight fee—say, $100 worth of
tickets for $120. The $20 is the 'ice.'"
Maurice Zolotow, *SEP*, Nov. 20. 1950:
". . . Between a vast bookie ring and
alleged police protectors who took
'ice'—protection money." AP, N.Y.,
Sept. 16. 1951: ". . . 'Ice' . . . stems from
political funds for 'Incidental Campaign
Expenses.'" A. Green, *Show Biz*, 13f.
See **break the ice, cut no ice, on ice,
put on ice.**   *v.t.* To assure or clinch
something; to put on ice.

ice, on   **1** Sure of being won, earned,
or a success, said esp. of games, situations,
and business ventures. *Since c1890;*
see **put on ice.** Cf. **in the bag. 2** Un-
approachable, aloof, beyond reach. *Not
common.* **3** In prison; not being allowed
to communicate with others. 1941:
". . . But they could keep him on ice."
G. Homes, *40 Whacks*, 123. **4** Waiting

and ready to be called to work, perform,
or play, said of people.

ice, put on   **1** To kill.   **2** To postpone.
1937: ". . . Put it on ice for a while."
Weidman, *Wholesale*, 5. **3** To assure or
clinch something, as a victory.   See **on
ice.**

iceberg   *n.* An unemotional person.

icebox   *n.* **1** A prison cell for solitary
confinement. 1930: "When a prisoner is
sent to the 'icebox.' . . ." Lavine, *Third
Degree*, 232. **2** A prison. **3** A place where
performers or athletes await their turn
to perform or play, such as the wings
of a stage or the bull pen or dugout at
a baseball park where pitchers warm up.
See **put on ice. 4** Any place noted for its
cold weather. *Colloq.*

ice cream   Any of certain habit-
forming narcotics in crystal form. 1928
[c1910]: ". . . Lowest of all [in the scale]
were the ice cream eaters, who chewed
the crystals of cocaine, morphine, or
heroin." Asbury, *Gangs of New York*, 199.

iceman   *n.* **1** A jewel thief. **2** A
gambler, athlete, or performer who is
always objective and calmly confident,
esp. during times of excitement, confusion, or stress. 1941: "An iceman, in
race-track slang, is a gambler who never
loses his head. He isn't found among the
cheer-leaders." J. Lilienthal, *Horse Crazy*,
78.

icky   ickie   *adj.* **1** Overly sentimental; old-fashioned; neither stylish
nor striking; corny; specif., incompatible
with swing music; disliked by swing

music enthusiasts. *Orig. c1935 swing use; very common student use in late 1930s and early 1940s.* → **2** Preferring sentimentality or old-fashioned entertainment, dress, topics of conversation, or the like.   *n.* **1** One who does not appreciate swing music or the fads and fashions of swing music enthusiasts; one who is not hep. 1938: "The ickies are not hep to [jam bands]. Ickies—people who think they know what swing is all about." C. Smith in *Esquire*, 95/2. 1956: "An *icky* is a man who doesn't like swing." S. Longstreet, *The Real Jazz Old and New*, 150. *Orig. swing use c1935. Obs. by c1942.   An icky was to a swing music enthusiast as a square is to a bop or cool enthusiast (although "square" was also used somewhat in the swing era).* → **2** A dull person; one who lacks worldly knowledge and a sense of humor; specif., a student who does not follow the fads and fashions of his fellow students. 1952: "We hadn't figured on Livermore turning [our boy-friends] into overly-mannered ickies." M. Blosser, *synd. comic strip*, "Freckles," Sept. 26. *Pop. teenage use c1938–c1945.*

—ie   See Appendix, Suffixes and Suffix Words.

if bet   A bet on two or more horse races stipulating that part of the winnings from the first race will be wagered on one or more later races; if the first bet is lost, the bettor has no wager on the later races. 1956: "IF BETTING— Conditional betting with a bookmaker. The bettor 'ifs' a stipulated amount of money from the winnings of one horse onto one or more other horses." T. Betts, *Across the Board*, 316. *Horse-racing use.* Cf. **parlay.**

iffy   *adj.* Doubtful; uncertain. 1941: "His chances . . . were rather iffy." *Time*, July 14, 15.

igg   *v.t.* To ignore, to refuse to take notice of. *Orig. Negro use. Jive use c1935. From "ignore."* See Appendix, Shortened Words.

iggle   *v.t.* To persuade another to do one a favor. *Teenage use since c1955. Perhaps from "egg on," certainly reinforced by "the bald iggle," creature in Al Capp's synd. newsp. comic strip "Li'l Abner," which can look a person in the eye and make it impossible for the person to lie, exaggerate, or speak insincerely.*

ike   Ike   *n.* **1** An uncouth or stupid person. *c1895; seldom used.* See **alibi Ike.** **2** A television iconoscope.   *v.i., v.t.* [derog.] To cheat; to lower the price

by haggling; to "Jew down." See **Ikey.**

Ikey   Ikie [derog.]   *n.* A Jew.

illuminated   *adj.* Drunk. *A syn. suggested by "lit."*

immie   *n.* A kind of playing marble. 1951: "What product comes from Ferrara, Italy? The correct answer is marble aggies and immies." Jack Paar, radio broadcast, March 4.

import   *n.* An out-of-town girl brought in for a college social affair, such as a fraternity house-party or dance. *College use.*

I'm sorry   An expression of one's inability or refusal to understand, comprehend, appreciate, or agree. 1957: "I'm sorry, man—Expression of disagreement; bewilderment; failure to reach any conclusion." E. Horne, *For Cool Cats and Far-Out Chicks. As an expression of refusal: colloq. As an expression of inability to comprehend, appreciate, or dig: far-out use.*

in   For phrases beginning with "in," see under principal word of phrase.

in   *n.* **1** An advantage; esp. the advantage of knowing someone in authority. *Colloq.* **2** A friend or relative in authority or who can introduce one to or influence a person in authority. **3** An ice cream soda. *Thus "chocolate in" = chocolate ice cream in a soda, as opposed to on a plate. Some lunch-counter use in relaying orders. Since c1935.   adj.* **1** Belonging to a social clique of, or accepted by, desirable, successful, or influential people; belonging to or accepted by any specific group of people; accepted or respected by a specific person. **2** Well liked by, or able to obtain a favor from, a specific person or group.

in, get   To have sexual intercourse with a female. *Lit. "to get into the vagina."*

in-and-outer   *n.* A mediocre performer or athlete, one who is sometimes successful or even brilliant but who, just as often, is a failure or gives a dull performance; a mediocre entertainment, with some entertaining and some tedious parts. 1952: "Reynolds has 30 knockouts among his 52 victories but he has been an in-and-outer." AP, Oct. 8.

increase the volume   *imp.* Speak louder. *Teenage use since c1955. From wide teenage television listening.*

indeedy   *adv.* Indeed; certainly. 1856: *DAE.* 1914: "No, indeedy." S. Lewis, *Our Mr. Wrenn*, 160. *Occasionally becomes pop., as c1945, as a fad word. An emphatic form usu. following "yes" or* "*no.*" *Prob. influenced by stand.* "*—y*" *added to some adjs. to form advs.*

index *n.* The face. *Some c1935 jive, c1940 underworld, and since c1950 cool use.*

Indian *n.* A young staff officer. *Some Army use. Not common.*

Indian hay Marijuana. 1934 [1931]: "I . . . smoked a couple of Indian hay cigarettes." *Amer. Journal of Psychiatry,* Sept., 316.

Indian hemp Marijuana.

indie *n.* An independent movie exhibitor. *Movie use.* See Appendix, —ie ending. *adj.* Independent. *Some self-conscious movie use.*

info *n.* Information. 1913: "I can slip you the info." *SEP,* Feb. 15, 8. *A common "shortening."* See Appendix, Shortened Words.

in for [someone], have it To be angry at someone; to desire revenge on someone. *Colloq.*

in for it = **in Dutch; for it.**

inhale *v.t.* **1** To eat, esp. a light meal or between-meal snack. 1953: "We'll inhale a few hamburgers." *Synd. cartoon,* "Our Boarding House," June 17. → **2** To drink, esp. a soft drink or beer. 1957: "Let's inhale a few beers before we go." *Oral,* Univ. of Pittsburgh student, July 6. *A comparatively recent teenage and student use. Perhaps an echo of narcotic addict speech.*

ink *n.* **1** Coffee. *Hobo and soldier use; not common.* **2** Cheap wine. 1938: ". . . A cheap local 'ink.'" Berger, *New Yorker. Harlem use.* Cf. **red ink.** **3** [*Derog.*] A Negro. *v.t.* To sign a contract.

ink-slinger *n.* **1** A writer; one whose work is writing, orig. with pen and ink; specif.: an author, editor, newspaperman, or the like. 1877: *DAE. Colloq. Usu. derisive.* **2** A clerk or office worker; a timekeeper; one who keeps records. *Some derisive logger, ranch, and hobo use since c1910.*

inkstick *n.* A fountain pen. 1946: "At 15, Nellie was 'making a pitch' with inksticks. . . ." S. S. Jacobs, *Mag. Digest,* Aug., 88/1. *Pitchman use.*

inky-dink *n.* A very dark complexioned Negro. *Negro use.* See Appendix, Reduplications.

in like Flyn(n) = **in.** *adj.* See Appendix, Rhyming Slang.

—inner See Appendix, Suffixes and Suffix Words.

inning *n.* A round of boxing. *Prize fight use since c1920. From baseball.*

—ino —ini See Appendix, Suffixes and Suffix Words.

in one On the strip of the stage next to the footlights; in front of the stage curtain. 1944: ". . . He appeared . . . before a painted curtain and on a narrow strip of stage during what is known as a 'front scene in one.'" Fowler, *Good Night,* 55. *Theater use.*

insect *n.* **1** A small defect in a new automobile. Suggested by the more common "bug." *Not common.* **2** A young, inexperienced Naval ensign. *W.W.II. USN use.*

intercom *n.* An intercommunication telephone or radio system. 1950: "Marc yelled into the intercom. . . ." Billy Rose, *synd. newsp. col.,* Apr. 12. See Appendix, Shortened Words.

in the know Informed or aware of a specific situation or plan, esp. a confidential one; knowledgeable; sophisticated; cognizant of and alert to new ideas and the beliefs of others.

in there **1** Trying hard; making an effort. See **in there pitching.** **2** To be equal to a specific task; to be capable of succeeding or winning. **3** Satisfying. **4** In baseball, straight across the plate in the strike zone; said of a pitched ball.

intro *n.* **1** An introduction of two people. **2** In music, an introductory passage of any kind. *v.t.* To introduce. *All uses "shortenings."* See Appendix, Shortened Words.

invite *n.* An invitation. *Accented on the first syllable.* 1615: Farmer & Henley. 1950: "I took advantage of an invite some people give me!" "Major Hoople," *newspaper cartoon,* Jan. 19. *Colloq.*

in wrong To be in another's disfavor; to have made an unfavorable impression on another.

I.O.U. **IOU** *n.* A promissory note; a personal voucher containing only a date, the statement "I owe you" and the amount of a debt, and the signature of the debtor; a guarantee to pay, usu. between friends, esp. in ref. to a gambling debt. 1956: "At the end of the evening's play the shirt-manufacturer had won $800,000—in cash, not I.O.U.'s." J. Scarne, *The Amazing World of John Scarne,* 379. *From the words "I owe you."*

Irish banjo A shovel. 1941 [1930s *Civilian Conservation Corps* use:] "Guess we'll set you to strumming an 'Irish banjo.'" Danner, *Rotarian,* July, 48/2.

Irish (baby) buggy A wheelbarrow. *Not common.* c1915.

Irish cherry A carrot. *Not common.*

Irish confetti   Bricks, esp. when thrown in a fight. See **confetti**.

Irisher   *n.* An Irish person; a person of Irish extraction. 1807: *DAE.* 1952: "[Dennis] Day[,] probably the most exemplary Irisher in Hollywood...." J. Bacon, AP, Sept. 22. See Appendix, —er ending.

Irish fan   A shovel.

Irish grape   *n.* A potato. *Jocular use. Because Ireland is assoc. with potato-growing.*

Irish local   *n.* A wheelbarrow. 1956: "Steelworkers call a wheel barrow an *Irish local.*" *Labor's Special Language from Many Sources.* "*Local*" *because it makes many stops and moves slowly, as a local train; "Irish" because there are many Irish laborers.*

Irish nightingale   A tenor, esp. a countertenor, who sings Irish ballads with an Irish accent.

Irish pennant   A sloppy loose end, as of a sheet, rope, or blanket, that should be tucked in or straightened. *USN use.*

Irish turkey   **1** Corned beef and cabbage. *Hobo lingo.* **2** Hash. *Some Army use since c1935.*

iron   *n.* **1** A motorcycle. *Motorcyclist use. c1925.* **2** A car. **3** A gun, a shooting iron. **4** A cattle brand made with a branding iron. Weseen. **5** Silver coins. See **grunt-iron**.

iron betsy   An army service rifle.

iron-burner   *n.* A blacksmith. *Logger use.*

iron curtain   Fig., a curtain that prevents the free flow of communications and people to and from the Union of Soviet Socialist Republics and its allies in eastern Europe; the boundaries, frontier barriers, and restrictive policies (i.e., political censorship of news, etc.) of the U.S.S.R. *The term was first used by H. G. Wells in "The Food of the Gods," 1904 = an enforced break of communication with society by an individual. The present use, very common since c1946, is one of the major cold war terms. This use was orig. by Sir Vincent Troubridge, Oct. 21, 1945, in the "London Sunday Empire News," in his article "An Iron Curtain Across Europe," which described the difficulties of military government without full co-operation and exchange of information by all. Sir Vincent substantiates his claim to having orig. the present usage in AS, Feb., 1951, Vol. XXVI, No. 1, pp. 49–50.*

iron hat   A derby hat.

iron horse   A military tank. *W.W.II Army use.*

iron house   A jail.

iron man   **1** A silver dollar. **2** A dollar or the sum of $1. 1932: "Two hundred iron men snatched . . . out of his mitt!" C. MacArthur, *Rope.* **3** In sports, a tireless athlete; a team member who plays through a complete game, and in many games during a year. 1934: Weseen. **4** A calypso musician who uses an oil drum instrument. *Since c1955.*

iron men   *pl.* Dollars; orig. and usu. dollars one wagers on horse races or other gambling events and games. 1941: "The horses were at the post. Ike was already in for three hundred and fifty iron men but he went over to the windows and bet a thousand for himself, to show." J. Lilienthal, *Horse Crazy,* 82.

iron off   To pay.

iron out   **1** To kill, as with a shooting iron. 1946: ". . . They'll learn you weren't at home when he was ironed out." Evans, *Halo in Blood,* 67. **2** To solve one's problems or difficulties; to resolve one's differences with another. *Colloq.*

iron pony   A motorcycle.

iron up   To put chains on the tires of an automobile. *Truckdriver use.*

irrigate   *v.i.* To drink to excess. *c1900; student use.*

Irving   *n.* = **Melvin**.

—ish   See Appendix, Suffixes and Suffix Words.

ish kabibble   An expression meaning "I'm not worrying," or "I don't care." 1926: "We read on the sport's arm band and the flapper's pennant 'Ish Kabibbul' or 'Ishkabibble'—or 'I should worry.' Through that expression all youth declared its independence." C. T. Ryan, *AS,* II, 92. 1921 [1947]: "When he was pressed too hard, he smiled and murmured, 'Ish ka bibble.'" J. Bruce, *San Fran. Murders,* 201. *A popular c1925 rejoinder.*

island   *n.* An oasis; a growth of trees on an otherwise treeless landscape. 1952: "In West Texas, an Island is a cluster of trees growing on the bald plains or in the desert." J. Randolph, *Texas Brags,* 55.

iso   *n.* Solitary confinement cells. *From "isolation." Convict use.*

it   It   *n.* **1** A worthless, stupid fellow; a boob, dope, or sap. 1903: "You big it." E. Conradi, 371. 1925: "In slang usage, *it* means simpleton or booby." L. Pound, *AS,* I, 103/1. *Archaic by c1930.* **2** Sex appeal. 1929: "A cutie with plenty of *It*." J. Auslander, *Hell in Harness*, 40. *Pop. by the early movie actress and idol Clara Bow, billed as and known as the "It Girl" throughout most of her career, which began in c1925. Clara Bow received this title from her starring role in the then sensational E. Glyn movie "It," which also orig. and helped pop. the word. Still some use by older people.*   *adj.* Sexy; sexually attractive. 1945: "Us other guys don't think he's such/ A much./ His voice is shrill./ His muscle is pitiful./ That cool chick down on Calumet,/ Though, says he's really 'it.'/ And strokes the patent-leather hair/ That makes him man enough for her." G. Brooks, *A Street in Bronzeville*, 11. *All uses stressed or deliberately pronounced. Usu. written within quotes.*

it [for someone], have   To be in love with someone. 1939–40: "They would say that mouse has got it for Joey but bad. . . ." O'Hara, *Pal Joey*, 11.

Italian cut   A women's hair style, a modification of the poodle cut, being slightly longer and featuring ringlets of hair on the forehead, and over the cheekbones and ears. *Common c1952–c1955. Popularized by the actresses appearing in post-W.W.II realistic Italian movies.*

Italian football   A bomb. *Racketeer use.*

Italian Hero = **Hero,** sandwich.

itch   *v.i.* In pocket billiards, to fall into a pocket; said of the cue ball.   *v.t.* To cause [the cue ball] to fall into a pocket, thus incurring a penalty.   *n.* **1** In pocket billiards, an instance of or the penalty for shooting the cue ball so that it falls into a pocket. 1946: "And when the cue ball goes into the pocket, you call that an itch." M. Shulman, *Zebra Derby*, 42. **2** A Yugoslav. *From the "—ich" ending of many surnames. Not common.*

itch a mean ivory   To play the piano well. *c1920. Pacific Coast use. Obs., though "tickle the ivories" is still used.*

itchy   *adj.* Eager; fig., trembling with eagerness or impatience.

it girl   A girl with obvious sex appeal; a glamorous girl or woman. See **it.**

—itis   See Appendix, Suffixes and Suffix Words.

it off, get [taboo]   **1** To ejaculate; to bring about ejaculation by any method; to have sexual intercourse, to masturbate. **2** = **knock it off.**

it's   **1** = **it's been real. 2** "It's the truth; I'm speaking honestly."

it's been = **it's been real.**

it's been real   **1** An expression said on leavetaking, to one's host or friends, indicating the speaker's enjoyment of the time spent together or at a social function. *Orig. from "it's been real fun"; "it's been real fine (a real fine evening or party)." By omitting the last word, the implication is that the gathering, people, and conversation have been enjoyed because they were sincere, and that the evening or good time or gathering was a real experience as opposed to a mere social function.* **2** "It's been real dull, boring, stupid, insincere." *From the first use. Since the last word of the phrase is omitted, the phrase can be used to imply derision of the gathering, people, or conversation.*

it stinks   An expression of disgust toward something offensive, esp. offensive to one's sense of honesty, intelligence, aesthetic taste, or the like; specif. applied to inferior entertainment.

it to [someone], give   **1** [taboo] To have sexual intercourse with someone. 1951: "All he did was keep talking about some babe he was supposed to have had sexual intercourse with. Every time he told it, it was different. One minute he'd be giving it to her in his cousin's Buick, the next minute he'd be giving it to her under some boardwalk." J. D. Salinger, *Catcher in the Rye*, 32f. *Used by both sexes, "it" refers to either the penis, the vagina, or a good time.* **2** To beat up, chastise, or reprimand someone, usu. in anger. *Colloq.*

it with [someone], make   **1** To have sexual intercourse with someone; to establish a heterosexual or homosexual relationship with someone. 1958: "When the hipster makes it with a girl, he avoids admitting that he likes her. He keeps cool . . . while she plays bouncy-bouncy on him. When the hipster makes it with boys, it's not because he's a homosexual and cares for it—it's for money, a ride home, [to] pass the time of night. . . ." Herbert Gold, *The Beat Mystique*, 84. 1958: "They have nothing but coolness. With sex tossed in. The chicks go to bed, though they'd never dream of calling it that. 'Man,' they'd say, 'don't think you're not cool enough to make it with me.' . . . The old phrase, 'Did you make her?' has been changed, because 'making her' is personal, intimate, warm. The cool cats say, 'Man, don't think I didn't make it with her.' The insertion of the word 'it' cools it, depersonalizes it—and coolness is all."

Sam Boal, *Cool Swinging in N.Y.*, 26. *Orig. beat use, now also far-out use and the beginning of student and teenage use.* 2 To impress someone favorably; to establish rapport with someone.

ivory   *n.* 1 A billiard ball. 2 The skull. See **ivory-thumper, solid ivory.** **—ies**   *n.pl.* 1 The teeth. 1953: ". . . Beaming at each other, with as fine a display of ivories as we've seen in our time. . . ." *New Yorker*, Apr. 25, 21/3. 2 Dice. 3 Piano keys; a piano. Cf. **tickle the ivories.**

ivory dome   *n.* 1 A stupid person; a bonehead. *c1915.* 2 Any intellectual; a highly trained specialist. *c1940.*

ivory-hunter   *n.* A talent scout; esp., a baseball scout searching for talented players.

ivory-thumper   *n.* A pianist. Cf. **itch a mean ivory.** 1941: ". . . Some cheap little ivory thumper. . . ." Cain, *M. Pierce*, 131.

Ivy League   *n.* A league of football and other athletic teams representing prominent north-eastern universities (Cornell, Harvard, Yale, Princeton, Columbia, Brown, Colgate, Dartmouth, U. of Pennsylvania). **ivy-league**   *adj.*

1 Pertaining to or characteristic of the Ivy League schools and the manners and fashions cultivated by their students. *Usu. "ivy-league," adj., connotes a certain degree of wealth, sophistication, refinement, social prominence, and the like.* 2 *Esp.*, representative of the modes of dress favored by students at Ivy League schools. *Generally, the term refers to conservative but youthful men's styles, currently including narrow, striped ties, button-down shirts, narrow, unpleated trousers, blazer jackets, three-button sport jackets, and the like. The ivy-league students have presumably been dressing conservatively for generations; the specif. current style evolved after W.W.II, spreading first to "Madison Avenue" and then to the country at large when several prominent clothing manufacturers adopted the style (c1955) and advertised it heavily. Since then it has become the stylish mode for men of all ages and occupations.* 3 Conservative.

Ivy League cut = **crew cut.**

ixnay   *n.* = **nix.** 1930: "Ixnay on the kabitz." *Amer. Mercury*, Dec., 456. *From Pig Latin.* See Appendix, Little Languages.

J

jab a vein   To use heroin as an addict. 1956: "Not all jazz players smoke marijuana or opium . . . or jab a vein." S. Longstreet, *The Real Jazz Old and New*, 144. *Probably synthetic.*

jabber   *n.* A hypodermic needle. 1918. *U.S. military prison use.*

jab-off   *n.* A subcutaneous injection of a narcotic; also, the effect of such an injection.

jaboney   jiboney   *n.* 1 A newly arrived foreigner; a greenhorn. 2 A tough; specif., a gangster's muscleman or bodyguard. 1952: "He had a couple of his jiboneys with him. . . . I never saw Nicky alone." L. Stander, *Esq.*, June 84/3.

jack   *n.* 1 Money. 1921: ". . . The fans which paid their jack. . . ." Witwer, *Leather*, 79. 1937: "There's jack in this . . . heavy jack." Weidman, *Wholesale*, 5. *c1850 to present; orig. sporting term, very common c1920, and still in wide use.* 2 A small coin. *c1850; not common.* 3 A blackjack. In gambling, esp. cards, a jack-pot. 4 Anything used fig. as a jack or crutch, specif. a translation or

pony used by a student. *c1900.* 5 Simple luxuries, such as sweets and tobacco. *Convict, student, and Armed Forces use.* 6 A locomotive; a train. 7 Cavalry insignia. *W.W.II use; not common.* See **highjack, ball the jack. Jack** *n.* Any man; a fellow or guy; a term of address to a person whose name is not known. 1943: "Man, he's murder, Jack [true name, Asa]." M. Shulman, *Barefoot Boy with Cheek*, 90. *Orig. jive use.*

jack, piece of = **piece of change.**

jackass   *n.* 1 A stupid person; a dullard. *Colloq.* 2 = **ass.** *A euphem.*

jack-deuce   Askew; high on one side and low on the other. 1935: ". . . He has a brown hat sitting jack-deuce on his noggin." Runyon. See **ace-deuce.**

jackeroo   *n.* A cowboy. *Western use. Perhaps from Australian sl. "jackeroo" = young fellow, but more likely from Sp. "vaquero."*

jacker-upper   *n.* One who raises or increases something; specif. a price-raiser. 1950: "This eminent food hoarder and price jacker-upper fired a barrel . . . before a house committee." Ithaca

(N.Y.) *Journal*, Aug. 1, 6/2. *See Appendix,*
—er - —er terms.

jacket = monkey jacket; yellow jacket.

jackleg lawyer An inferior or dishonest lawyer. *c1850; colloq. Archaic.*

jack off [taboo] To masturbate. *From
"ejaculate."* *n.* An incompetent or
stupid person. *Perhaps implying feeblemindedness as a result of excessive
masturbation.*

jack out To pull a gun. 1943:
". . . A fellow who could jack his gun out
kind of fast." Chandler, *Lady in Lake,*
219.

jackpot, hit the To succeed, usu.
to a greater degree than anticipated; to
succeed in a spectacular way. *Also used
sarcastically to mean to fail dismally, to a
greater degree than anticipated. From slot-
machine gambling use.*

jackroll *v.t.* To rob; usu. to rob a
drunk man. 1949: "Father had recently
been 'jackrolled' while drunk. . . ." W. J.
Slocum, "Skid Row," *Collier's,* Sept. 3,
24. *Generally replaced by "roll."* **—er**
n. **1** A town bum who fleeces or robs
migratory workers and vagabonds. *c1915.*
2 A thief who robs money from persons
of his victims, usu. while they are drunk.
*The noun is apparently older than the
verb. Rather than orig. in "rolling a
person for jack," the origin seems to be
from "rolling"* [*lumber*] *jacks.*

Jackson *n.* A term of direct address
signifying that the addressee is hep;
usu. implies group acceptance or approval. *Orig. c1935 Harlem jive use;
wide use by jazz musicians and their
followers, W.W.II Armed Forces and
student use until c1945; now archaic.*

jack up **1** To reprimand a person.
c1895; colloq. Archaic. **2** To increase a
price.

jag *n.* **1** A spree, usu. a drinking
party. 1893: "*Jag* is a provincialism
meaning a light load. . . . The man who
has a jag on is in the earlier stages of
intoxication." B. Matthews in *Harper's,*
July, 308/2. *Colloq. and still widely used.*
2 Fig., a spree or splurge; a spell of
unrestrained activity of any kind. 1924:
"One had a 'crying jag.'" "A 'laughing
jag.'" Marks, *Plastic Age,* 213, 254. 1952:
"Everybody here is off on the annual
Christmas gift-buying jag." H. Boyle,
AP, Dec. 19. **3** A drunkard. *Never
common.* **—ged** *adj.* Drunk.
Brought to America by Eng. colonists.

—jag See Appendix, Suffixes and
Suffix Words.

jaheemy *n.* A movable drydock; a
vehicle for elevating and shifting the
position of a landing craft. Also spelled
je—, gee—, and **—bie.** 1943: **geeheebee,**
jahemy, jeramy. W. Yust, *Ten Eventful Years,* 643. *U.S. Armed Forces use.*

jail bait **1** Any person, as a minor
criminal or esp. a female, with whom
one makes an acquaintance at the risk of
getting into trouble; specif., a woman of
such compelling attractiveness that men
will take to crime in order to furnish her
wants. 1930: "She's jail bait." J. T.
Farrell, 142. **2** Specif., a sexually
attractive girl who has not reached the
legal age of consent. *Because having
"carnal knowledge" of a minor is considered a major crime in most states.*

jail-bird *n.* A convict; an ex-convict;
a prisoner or ex-prisoner. 1934: colloq.,
Web.

jake *adj.* Satisfactory; all right; O.K.;
approved of; fixed. Often used in a
context of totality, as "Everything is
jake." 1924: [all right] "She said the
whole college seemed jake to her."
Marks, *Plastic Age,* 247. 1934: [fixed]
". . . Everything was 'jake' with the
police. . . ." J. L. Kilgallen. *W.W.I
British army use, quickly spread to U.S.
troops, now in common U.S. use. Prob. a
folk ety. of "chic."* *n.* **1** A person who
is all right; one who can be trusted.
1925: "If the mob members do not
squeal, he is a 'jake.'" McLellan,
Collier's. **2** Money. *Not common.* Cf.
jack. **3** Jamaica ginger extract, used as
a cheap substitute for whisky. → **4** A
drunk person. *Not common.*

jalop *n.* **1** = **jollop.** **2** A jalopy. 1951:
"Let them search every jalopp on the
road." Radio program, *Gangbusters,*
Sept. 8.

jalopy jaloppy *n.* **1** An old and/or
battered automobile. 1949: "A jalopy is a
model one step above a 'junker' . . . it
still runs but only at great peril to life,
limb and the common weal." N.Y.
Times Mag., May 1, 62. **2** Any vehicle,
regardless of its condition or age.

jam *n.* **1** A predicament; difficulty;
trouble. 1949: colloq., *Web.* **2** Good
fortune of any kind. *W.W.I use; from
the stand. noun = a sweet fruit spread.* **3**
Something easy to do; "pie." 1931: "Yes,
pure jam for me." R. Dark, *Shakespeare,*
101. *Archaic.* **4** Small objects that are
easy to steal, such as rings and watches.
Underworld use. **5** = **jam session.** 1956:
"Later, when almost everyone had gone
home, Bix [Beiderbecke] and the boys

would blow it free and the jam was on."
S. Longstreet, *The Real Jazz Old and
New*, 104. *c1935 to present.* *v.t.* **1**
To play jazz music, esp. Dixieland or
swing, intensely and primarily for one's
own gratification; to play extemporaneously or with the enthusiasm and
intensity of an extemporaneous or
personal performance. **2** In jazz, to
improvise freely, usu. in an ensemble.
3 To auction; to act as an auctioneer.
Pitchman use. **4** To nullify a radio
broadcast by creating an interference
signal on the same frequency. *adj.*
1 Possessing the characteristics of unrestricted jazz. 1938: "Jam bands do
have styles." C. Smith in *Esquire.* **2**
Lending itself to being played or being
played in an intense, seemingly personal
and extemporaneous manner; said of
jazz music or arrangements.
jam, in a In trouble; in a difficult,
disastrous, or embarrassing position.
1949: "If you're in a jam, he'll fight for
you." Paul Jones, Phila. *Bulletin*, Sept.
1, 14. *Colloq. From the standard verb
= to be pressured into a tight place.* See
jam, n. 1.
jam auction   jam pitch A pitchman's business carried on in a store; a
store selling cheap souvenirs, imitation
jewelry, knick-knacks, and the like.
jammed *adj.* Drunk. 1922: "He got
jammed." Phila. *Eve. Bulletin*, March 2.
Flapper use.
jammed up In trouble; in a jam.
1950: "You are jammed up." Starnes,
And When She Was Bad, 141.
jammer See **gear-jammer, wind-
jammer.**
jammy *adj. & adv.* Extremely lucky;
luckily.
jamoke   Jamoke *n.* **1** Coffee; esp.
strong black coffee. *From "Java" and
"Mocha."* *Vagabond, USN, and Army
use.* **2** A fellow; a guy. 1946: "If I was
going to find out what kind of jamoke
Marlin was...." Evans, *Halo in Blood*,
32.
jams *n.pl.* See **jims, the.**
jam session Orig. an informal gathering of jazz musicians to play for their
own pleasure, usu. in free and lengthy
improvisations on well-known themes;
later a term applied commercially to
public jazz performances. 1950: "When
they were holding jam sessions in the
Onyx Club...." L. Sobel, *synd. newsp.
col.*, Apr. 2. 1957: "He [Norman Granz]
sponsored a series of jam sessions, one
night a week...." Leonard Feather,

"Jazz Millionaire [Norman Granz]"
Esquire, May.
jam-up *adj.* First-rate; bang-up.
c1840, colloq; *obs.* *n.* A jam; a
crowd, as of persons. 1941: "... To
forestall the possibility of another
jam-up." Cain, *M. Pierce*, 152.
jane *n.* **1** A girl or young woman.
c1915 [1950]: "When they would [be]
around some jane that was kind of
simple ... they'd press a button in
their pocket and light up the little-
bitty bulb in the toe of their shoes and
that jane was claimed." A. Lomax,
Mr. Jelly Roll, 16. 1922: "... A cake-
eater who lets a jane pay her own way."
Phila. *Eve. Bulletin*, Mar. 8. 1948:
"Ladies from Long Island, janes from
Jersey...." *Advt.*, N.Y. *Times*, July 18,
22/7. *Common since c1915; sometimes
capitalized.* **2** A man's sweetheart. 1922:
"His regular jane had given him the
air." Phila. *Eve. Bulletin*, Mar. 8. 1952:
"We might be able to make earrings for
our janes out of them studs." L. Hughes,
Laughing to Keep from Crying, 30. **3** A
(usu., but not necessarily, public) restroom, bathroom, or toilet as used by
women. *The women's "john."*
jang [taboo] *n.* The penis. See **jing-
jang.**
jangle = **jingle-jangle.**
janney *v.* **1** To couple. *Railroad use.*
2 To copulate. *Not common.*
Jap *n.* A professional gambler. *Obs.*
jap See **gap.**
jap (Jap), pull a To ambush someone;
to make a sneak attack or surprise
assault on someone; to deceive someone.
*Some W.W.II use. From the surprise
military attack made by the Japanese on
Pearl Harbor, Dec. 7, 1941, which was the
beginning of the U.S. participation in
W.W.II.*
Jap wise Knowing only part of a
thing; not completely informed. *Not
common.*
jar-head *n.* **1** A mule. *Southern hill
dial.* **2** [derog.] A male Negro. *Southern
and Negro use.* **3** A Marine. *W.W.II use.*
jasper   Jasper *n.* **1** A theological
student. 1926: "... A term originating
in Richmond ... from John Jasper ...
the eminent colored divine...." Gilmore
Spencer, *Univ. of Va. Mag.*, Oct., 17. → **2**
An exceptionally pious or meek person.
3 A rube. **4** A fellow; a guy. 1953: "A
Western ... needs something more than
two jaspers with a grudge...." H. Birney,
N.Y. *Times Bk. Rev.*, July 5, 13/3.

j.a.t.o.   **jato**   *n.* A jet-assisted take-off. *Applied to propeller-driven military airplanes that use jet boosters to achieve a quick take-off from a short runway.*

java   **Java**   *n.* Coffee, whether Java coffee or not. *Capitalized about 8 times in 28 occurrences.* 1907 [1892]: "I got out of them nearly a quart of heavenly 'Java.'" Jack London, *The Road,* 124. 1951: "Hail, coffee quaffers, java sippers!" J. J. Burton, *New Yorker,* March 31, 68. *Colloq. since c1850, first common with hobos, Army and USN men, and lumberjacks, now very widespread; saw increased popularity with W.W.I.*

jaw   *n.* A chat; a talk. 1930: "We ain't had a good jaw together since you left...." Burnett, *Iron Man,* 170. See **flap jaw, glass jaw.**   *v.i.* **1** To talk. *c1880 to present.* → **2** Specif., to lecture a person; to give a long reprimand. 1950: "The broker ... had kept sober for several months by jawing drunks—unsuccessfully...." J. Alexander, *SEP,* Apr. 1, 78/3. **3** To talk, esp. to argue or to wrangle inconclusively; to gossip. 1949: "... Can't stand here jawing with you all day." S. J. Perelman, *Listen to the Mocking Bird,* 122.

jawbone   *v.i.* **1** To carry on sincere, rational talk that leads to establishing financial credit or trust. → **2** To loan; to trust. → *v.t.* **1** To borrow; to buy on credit. 1952: [to borrow] "... He jawboned enough thousands of dollars to set up an office and hire his personnel...." Robert C. Ruark, *synd. newsp. col.,* Dec. 9. **2** To practice-shoot a weapon over a qualification course; to rehearse. *W.W.II Army use.*   *n.* **1** Financial credit; trust. **2** A loan. **3** One who talks too much.   *adv.* On credit.   **to buy jawbone** = to buy on credit; to buy on the installment plan. *W.W.I and W.W.II Army use, very common.*

jaw-breaker   *n.* **1** A word, esp. a long one, that is hard to pronounce. 1950: "A chemical compound with a jaw-breaker name...." AP, Apr. 12. **2** A piece of hard candy; specif. a round piece of hard candy with a piece of bubble gum in the center, sold in dispensing machines and, c1940, very popular with grade-school children.

jaw-cracker = **jaw-breaker.**

Jax   *proper n.* Jacksonville, Florida. *Widely used in Florida, rarely elsewhere.*

jay   *n.* **1** A stupid, inexperienced person, usu. with a rural or small-town background. *Since c1900.* **2** An easy victim; one who is easy to dupe. **3** A

bank. *From the "j" of syn. "jug."* *Underworld use.*   *adj.* Countrified. *c1890; archaic.*

jayhawk   *n.* An unusual or extraordinary person. *A Mid-Western term.*

Jayhawker   *n.* **1** A lawless soldier; an irregular or guerrilla fighter, usu. one whose motive for fighting is personal enrichment. *Western term much used during the Border Wars, c1855. Obs.* **2** A native of Kansas.

jaywalk   *v.i.* To walk in or across a street in violation of traffic rules, as to cross a street in the middle of a block, cross an intersection when the stop light is red, and so forth. *Colloq.*   **—er** *n.* One who jaywalks. 1949: "'Jay walkers,' who endanger themselves and others...." N.Y. *Times,* Oct. 2, 66/6.

jazz   *n.* **1** [taboo] Copulation; the vagina; sex; a woman considered solely as a sexual object. *Orig. southern Negro use, prob. since long before 1900.* → **2** Animation; enthusiasm; enthusiasm and a fast tempo or rhythm; frenzy. c1875 [1926]: "Lafcadio Hearn found the word in the creole patois of New Orleans.... It had been taken from the Negroes ... it meant 'to speed things up.'" H. O. Osgood, *AS,* I, 514. → **3** The only orig. American music, traditionally known for its emotional appeal, rhythmic emphasis, and improvisation. *This is the music first played by small Creole and Negro groups in and around New Orleans in the decades before 1900. Its rhythms were based in part on African songs, field chants used by slaves, work chants of railroad laborers and prisoners, and the Spanish and French music known to the Creoles of the region. It was first played on battered, secondhand instruments discarded by marching and military bands. The musicians were often self-taught, though some were trained in traditional methods. Jazz was orig. played for the entertainment of and to express the feelings of the musicians and their friends, at parties and dances. It soon became pop. on the streets of New Orleans, where sidewalk bands multiplied and were quickly invited to perform inside saloons, brothels, cabarets, etc., of the entertainment districts, esp. Storyville. At the same time, the music began to absorb more elements of white American music, esp. ragtime and the music traditionally associated with brass bands. Once inside the brothels of Storyville, the music became more widely known to both local men and out-of-town travelers. Thus the music grew in appeal and the* *musicians, now professional, could devote full time to playing. The brothels competed with each other for the best musicians, thus encouraging new musical talent, compositions, and improvisations. Once the appeal of the music grew and the bands and musicians had gained some fame, various musicians and bands began to travel, playing throughout the Delta region and taking jobs on the riverboats that plied northward on the Mississippi as far as Minneapolis. With the ending of legalized prostitution in New Orleans during W.W.I, more musicians were forced out of the South. Some moved to St. Louis and other Mississippi River towns, but in the 1920's Chicago became the chief attraction for New Orleans musicians. There they played in beer halls, restaurants, and eventually in nightclubs. In Chicago, too, many young white musicians heard and imitated the Negro players, and the first important school of white jazz emerged. From Chicago the interest in jazz quickly spread to other northern cities, esp. to New York. With the attraction of radio, recordings, and more cities to play in, more and bigger bands were formed. With larger audiences, many of whom had no rapport with the lives or feelings of the early jazz musicians, jazz lost some of its early earthy quality. Styles changed, the small New Orleans group (now often called, though improperly, "Dixieland") gave way to the larger group playing written arrangements, and in the 1930's the style known as "swing" became predominant. Pop. music, ballads, and dance tunes were incorporated in the jazz repertoire. Thus jazz has developed many styles and moods—the back alley or low-down dirty; the slurred gutbucket; the blaring tailgate; the smooth and mellow; the swinging. The latest developments, perh. most appealing to the modern ear, are bop and cool jazz, or progressive jazz. In general, these new styles stem from Charlie Parker, the great alto saxophonist, who introduced advanced techniques, often requiring extraordinary instrumental skill and profound musical understanding. Bop is known for its long, breathless series of notes, often in high registers, and for quick changes in key and tempo; unusual rhythms, sometimes Spanish-American in orig., are used. Cool jazz orig. on the West Coast c1950 and took much of its impetus from the work of modern classical composers. The music is known for its close, intricate harmonies, its improvisations based on chord ex-*

tensions, complex phrasing, etc. The more advanced forms of cool jazz are called "far out" or "way out." Thus in only half a century jazz has evolved in many ways. With each change or addition, the backgrounds, personalities, and interests of the musicians have changed, too. The audience has grown. But all jazz is related in its American tradition and in certain fundamental approaches to rhythm and phrasing. Since jazz music can be defined in many ways, according to one's tastes, a number of quotations are appended here from its early practitioners. It is hoped that these quotes, taken from Alan Lomax's well-documented book, "Mr. Jelly Roll," which was written while he was on the staff of the Library of Congress, will indicate the basic concepts of all jazz music: ". . . Jazz is a style that can be applied to any type of tune. I [Jelly Roll Morton] started using the word in 1902. . . . Now take *La Paloma*, which I transformed in New Orleans style. You leave the left hand just the same. The difference comes in the right hand—in the syncopation. . . . Regardless to any tempo you might set, especially if it was meant for a dance tune, you ought to end up in that same tempo. . . . About harmony, my theory is never to discard the melody. Always have a melody going some kind of way against a background of perfect harmony with plenty of riffs—meaning figures. . . . Without breaks and without clean breaks, and without beautiful ideas in breaks, you don't even need to think about doing anything else, you haven't got a jazz band and you can't play jazz. Even if a tune haven't got a break in it, it's always necessary to arrange some kind of a spot to make a break. A break, itself, is like a musical surprise. . . . Jazz music is to be played sweet, soft, plenty rhythm. When you have your plenty rhythm with your plenty swing, it becomes beautiful. To start with, you can't make crescendos and diminuendos when one is playing triple forte." "As [Alphonse] Picou saw it, jazz consisted of 'additions to the bars—doubling up notes—playing eight or sixteen for one.'" "Louis deLisle Nelson . . . went on to talk about himself. 'They claims I'm the first hot clarinet. . . . Jazz is all head music. . . . Some player he have an idea—he don't know—it kinda sound a little good to him. . . . That's how riffs come about. You must handle your tone. Happen sometime you can put some *whining* in the blowing of your instrument. There are a whole lot of different sounds you can shove in. . . . But you gotta do that with a certain measurement and not opposed to harmony. . . . Keep a lively tempo but shove in crying wherever you get a chance.' " "Johnny St. Cyr . . . went on to develop his own theory of jazz. . . . 'In New Orleans we had a system of playing, so as to get all the sweetness out of the music. We play the first theme *mezzoforte*, the second very soft, and the last time we play the second theme, everybody gets hot. No off-key playing. You had to keep within the boundaries of the melody, but our old heads had great ability to beautify a number. We would familiarize ourselves with the melody and then add what *we* wanted till we sounded like we had special orchestrations.' " Alan Lomax, *Mr. Jelly Roll*, 56–60; 62–63; 69; 80–85; 93–94. → **4** Lies; exaggeration; insincerity. 1958: ". . . All this jazz started a couple of years ago." Earl Wilson, *synd. newsp. col.* Feb. 16. **5** Nonsense; idle talk. *adj.* In the style of or similar to jazz music. *All uses have obs. spellings of "jass," "jaz," "jas," "jasy."* *v.i., v.t.* **1** [taboo] To copulate. 1929: "She's cute. I jazzed her, too." J. T. Farrell, 153. *Orig. southern Negro use, long before 1900.* → **2** To increase a tempo or rhythm with excitement; to increase the speed of something, to speed up; to generate excitement. *It is impossible to know which of the two above meanings came first, or even if the v. uses are older than the n. uses.* **3** To play jazz music or in a style similar to jazz music. 1924: "When orchestras jazz famous arias." Marks, *Plastic Age*, 271. *Since c1900.* **4** To lie, exaggerate, or attempt to generate speed for or enthusiasm about something that does not warrant it. **—ed** *adj.* Drunk. *Not common.*

jazz-bo *n.* **1** A fancily dressed, hep, sharp person; a stud. **2** [derog.] A male Negro. *Both meanings said to be older than "jazz."* **3** [derog.] A Negro soldier. *W.W.II use.*

jazz it To play jazz music, esp. to play enthusiastically. **2** To engage in sexual intercourse. *Obs.*

jazz up [something] Specif., to play any musical composition in a jazz style; fig., to enliven any activity, to make a design or presentation more colorful or appealing.

jazzy *adj.* **1** Descriptive of jazz music. c1900 [1956]: " 'Ragtime' [was] what the white folks called popular music, and what Buddy [Bolden] and his boys turned into something new, 'jazzy.' " S. Longstreet, *The Real Jazz Old and New*, 4. **2** Colorful; spirited; exciting. 1951: "He wore bow ties and . . . jazzy suits. . . ." T. Capote, *Grass Harp*, 21. *Orig. and still a little jazz use, basically in ref. to jazz music or playing; some general c1920 use in ref. to things or people.* **3** Corny, obvious, square. *The only cool use since c1950.*

jeans *n.* **1** A pair of trousers made of any material, esp. denim. 1846: *DAE*. 1907: "I had the price in my jeans." Jack London, *The Road*, 134. *Now standard. Prob. from the Fr. town Jean, famous for its denim cloth.* **2** Specif., a pair of stiff, tight-fitting, tapered denim cowboy work pants, usu. blue, with heavily reinforced seams and slash pockets. *Very pop. with teenagers of both sexes since c1945. From c1945–c1958 the cuffless bottoms of the trouser legs were worn folded up; recently the style has been to leave the trouser bottoms unfolded; a faded, well-worn appearance is favored.* **3** *In Colonial times, jeans = any garment made from a material 50% linen and 50% cotton.* See **Levis**.

jeasly **jeasely** *adj.* Measly; worthless. 1930: "Tell him . . . that here is his jeasely ol' pie and biscuit irons." Stewart H. Holbrook, *Amer. Mercury*, Oct., 236/2.

Jebby *n.* A Jesuit; the Jesuit order.

jeebies = **heebie-jeebies.** 1943: "His several disquisitions on the jeebies. . . ." H. A. Smith, *Putty Knife*, 58. 1951: "It's giving me the jeebies." Dick Turner, *synd. NEA cartoon*, Oct. 11.

jeep *n.* **1** A specific bantam, squarish, open, 1¼-ton, 4-wheel-drive Army command and reconnaissance vehicle of great versatility used in W.W.II. *Early in W.W.II, and throughout the war in the U.S. Armed Forces, the word "jeep" = a small truck and what is commonly called a "jeep" was called a "peep." From the Army term "GP" [general purpose] reinforced by the noise "jeep" made by a mythical animal who could do almost anything, in E. C. Segar's comic strip, "Popeye." c1938.* **2** Generally, any car; esp. a small car. **3** A new Army recruit; a rookie. **4** A Link trainer. *W.W.II Air Corps use.* **5** A Naval escort carrier. *W.W.II USN use.* **6** A slow, painstaking man. 1938: "But with all that practice he's still a jeep." Jerome Barry, "The Jeep," *SEP*, July 16. *Not common.*

7 A complaint. *Not common.* *v.i.* **1** To ride or to travel in a jeep. 1944: "... Jeeping ... through Maquis-held territory." A. W. Read, *Time*, Sept. 4, 27. **2** To complain; to grumble. *Not common.* *adj.* Small; of a size to be carried by a jeep. **—y** *adj.* = **screwy.** *Some W.W.II Army use.*

Jeepers = **Jeepers Creepers!** 1952: "Jeepers! I had my Christmas money in that bank." Al Vermeer, "Priscilla's Pop," *synd. comic strip*, Dec. 17. *Mainly teenage and younger use. Now mostly archaic.*

Jeepers Creepers! *exclam.* A mild expression of surprise, astonishment, wonder, or approval. c1939: "Jeepers Creepers." *Pop. song title. Euphem. for "Jesus Christ."*

jeep-jockey *n.* A truck driver. *W.W.II Army use.*

jeeter *n.* **1** A slovenly, ill-mannered person. From the character Jeeter Lester in E. Caldwell's novel, *Tobacco Road.* **2** A lieutenant. *W.W.II Army use.*

Jeez **jeez** **Jeeze** **jeeze** **Jees** **jees** *exclam.* **1** A mild exclamation of surprise or wonder. 1939: "Jeeze." Chandler, *Big Sleep*, 135. 1945: "Jeez." Mencken, *Sup. I.* 1949: "And jeez, you're going to get chewed out." Michael James, N.Y. *Times*, Aug. 28, 3/2. **2** A euphem. between the more euphem. "Gee" and the profane "Jesus." *May or may not be capitalized.*

jeezy-peezy *exclam.* An expression of surprise or disgust.

Jeff *n.* A boring person; a square. *Negro use.*

jell *v.t., v.i.* **1** To close or complete a business deal or sale. **2** To materialize; to conclude.

jelly *n.* **1** = **jelly-roll.** **2** An easy or enjoyable task. **3** Anything obtained free of charge. *v.i.* To loaf, esp. as a social occupation; to loiter for idle conversation.

jellybean **1** An inferior person; a sap. *c1915.* 1951: "... The jelly beans I went to school with. ..." R. Bissell, *Stretch on River*, 8. **2** A girl. *W.W.I use.* **3** A term of address. *Jive talk and teenage use. c1935.* **4** A new, inexperienced person, esp. an athlete. *c1945; baseball use.*

jelly-roll *n.* **1** [taboo] The vagina. → **2** A man extremely virile or obsessed with sex; a man who curries the sexual favors of women. → **3** A lover; a sweet papa or sweet mama. 1914: "... I'm most wile 'bout mah Jelly-Roll." W. C. Handy, "St. Louis Blues" [a song].

4 [taboo] Sexual activity in general; a woman considered sexually; coitus. *Very common Negro use. Most pop. with Southern Negroes c1875–c1915, associated with and made known to white people by use in early jazz groups and lyrics; perhaps esp. by the early great jazz pianist Jelly Roll Morton. Still some Negro use.*

Jenny *n.* **1** An airplane used in training. **2** Any airplane.

jeppo *v.i., v.t.* To cook, esp. to cook for a crew of workmen; to work in a kitchen in any capacity. *n.* A cook; a kitchen helper. *Both meanings northwest logger use.*

jerk *n.* **1** A short branch railway line, a small railroad. 1907 [1892]: "I had missed the main line and come over a small 'jerk' with only two locals a day on it." Jack London, *My Life. Prob. from "jerkwater," reinforced by the number of jolts and jerks trains make on such a railroad line.* **2** Any ride that costs a taxi passenger less than a dollar, as distinguished from a run. *c1925, taxi-driver use.* **3** [taboo] One who masturbates. *From "jerk off." Orig. a strongly derog. word.* **4** An ineffectual, foolish, or unknowingly dull youth or man, usu. applied contemptuously to one who is overfamiliar, unprepossessing, eccentric, stupid, unreasonable, selfish, or careless. 1938: "One might even dignify him as a jerk ... a jerk not only bores you but pats you on the shoulder as he does so." Heywood Broun, *New Republic*, Sep. 7, 129/1. 1946: " 'We'll make millions ... and to think I was wasting my time with that little jerk Ezra or Asa or whatever the hell his name was." Max Shulman, *Zebra Derby*, 94. *Very common. The orig. meaning of "masturbater" has been largely forgotten and the word becomes less and less derog. As are many other such sl. words, this can be used affectionately among friends.* **5** Any young, inexperienced worker; a rookie. **6** = **Soda jerk.** *adj.* Jerklike; jerkish; operated by jerks. 1937: "Forget about Slade and Toney Frocks and those other jerk houses." Weidman, *Wholesale*, 119. 1951: "They got a couple of jerk wops. ..." *Mobster*, 132. *v.t.* To draw a gun, as from a holster or pocket. *v.i.* =

jerk off. **—y** *adj.* Having the characteristics of a jerk. 1950: "... any jerky Joe." Billy Rose, *synd. newsp. col.*, Jan. 9.

—jerker See Appendix, Suffixes and Suffix Words.

Jerkimer = **Herkimer Jerkimer.**

Jerk McGee   A jerk; a square. 1956: "Already you become some Jerk McGee like you just got off the boat from the old country." J. Cannon, *Who Struck John?* 109.

jerk off   1 [taboo] To masturbate. 1954: "I enjoyed this new experience . . . until I heard the gang call it jerking off." H. K. Fink, *Long Journey*, 14. → 2 To waste time; to fuck off; to cause confusion; to make many mistakes.   **jerk-off**   *n.* 1 [taboo] One who masturbates. → 2 One who causes confusion, makes many mistakes, or wastes time; a dope.

jerk soda   To prepare and, usu., to serve sodas, ice cream dishes, and the like at a soda fountain; to work as a soda jerk. 1935: "They had spent their tender years jerking sodas." *Amer. Mercury*, May, 102/1.

jerk soup = jerk water.

jerk town   A small town; lit., a town known mainly as a place where trains jerk water. 1894 [1891]: "It's not in us to fool round a jerk town." Josiah Flynt. *Tramp use.* 1938: "Since coming to this jerk town. . . ." O'Hara, *New Yorker*.

jerk water   **jerk soup**   To take on water, while in motion, by scooping it from a trough between the rails; said of a railroad locomotive. *Railroad use since before c1900.*   **jerkwater**   *n.* = **jerk town**.   *adj.* 1 Like a jerk town. *Since c1900.* 2 Unimportant; insignificant.

Jerry [derog.]   *n.* 1 A German soldier. *Very common in W.W.I. U.S. soldiers adopted this British Army sl. use from the Eng. sl. "Jerry" = chamber pot, which a German helmet resembled. Also W.W.II use, but not so popular.* 1945: "'Kraut' and 'Krauthead' . . . were selected by one of the propaganda branches of the Army to replace the widely accepted 'Jerry.'" I. R. Blacker, *Sat. Rev. Lit.*, Nov. 24, 14/2. 2 A German; Germany. 3 A German Air Force fighter or bombing plane. *Most common W.W.II use.*   **jerry**   *n.* 1 A track laborer; a railroad section-hand. c1915. → 2 Any manual laborer. *Railroad and hobo use.* 3 A girl. *Underworld use.* 4 A small pistol that can be easily concealed. *Underworld use.*   *adj.* Wise, in the know. **Get jerry** = wise up, understand.

jerry gang   A railroad track-laying crew.

Jersey lightning   Applejack. *c1850; obs.*

Jerusalem Slim   Jesus Christ. *Familiar but not profane. Hobo use.*

Jesse James   Fig., anyone who cheats or misappropriates funds. 1956: "To coal miners—*Jesse James* is a company weigher." *Labor's Special Language From Many Sources.*

Jesus   *n.* The stuffing; insides. Usually in **beat** or **kick** or **knock the Jesus out of [a person].** 1944: *Maritime use.*

jet up   To work intensively, efficiently, and quickly.

Jewboy   **Jew boy** [derog.]   *n.* A male Jew, regardless of age or status. 1951: "Shut up, Jewboy [said to a man], this isn't your kosher neck of the woods." S. Longstreet, *The Pedlocks*, 319. 1958: "The Wig [a youth] is smart but not all Jew boys are. Moe Levine is a dope." H. E. F. Donohue, "Gentlemen's Game," *Harper's*, Mar., 62.

Jew down [derog.]   To bargain with a vendor or seller in an attempt to make a purchase at a price reduced from that originally asked.

jewels   *n.pl.* = **family jewels, the**

Jewish flag   **Jew flag**   [derog.] A one-dollar bill. 1929. *Vagabond use.*

jibagoo = jigaboo.

jibber-jabber   *v.i.* To jabber. 1948: "Time for Congress to quit jibber-jabbering." Phila. *Bulletin*, Mar. 23, 24/5. *n.* Jabbering.

jiboney = jaboney.

jice = new jice.

jiff = jiffy.

jiffin   **jiffing**   *n.* = **jiffy.** 1776: "In a jiffin." *DAE.*

jiffin, in a = jiffy, in a

jiffy   *n.* An indefinite but short period of time; usu. from a few seconds to a few minutes; a moment. *About 7 times out of 8, "jiffy" occurs in the phrase "in a jiffy," at the end of a sentence or clause.* 1793: "In a jiffy." T. Scott, Farmer & Henley. 1837: "In a jiffy." *DAE.* 1910: "We'll fit you out in a jiffy. . . . In a jiffy every boy was on the ground." Johnson, *Varmint*, 62, 135. 1948: "Let the clutch out slowly, and you're away in a jiffy." Advt. for Gimbel's dept. store, N.Y. *Times*, Dec. 26, 52/78. 1949: "Opens clogged drains in a jiffy!" Advt. for Draino, cleanser, *Woman's Home Companion*, Oct., 50. 1951: "For Perfect Sandwiches, Canapes in a jiffy!" Advt., *New Yorker*, Aug. 18, 78/1. 1952: "You can always drop off to sleep for a jiffy. . . ." Perelman, *New Yorker*, Sept. 21, 36/3. *Maybe from "jiffin," but orig. is unknown.*   *adv.* Quickly.

jiffy, in a   See **jiffy.**

jiffy bag   **1** A small canvas or leather bag, resembling a miniature suitcase, used for carrying small articles, usu. toilet articles, while traveling. *Common W.W.II use.* **2** Several makes of cheap, heavily insulated paper bag, produced in various sizes, used for wrapping, carrying, or mailing perishable or easily damaged items.

jig   **zig**   **jigg**   *n.* **1** [derog.] A Negro. 1939–40: "They even made this jig a lieutenant." O'Hara, *Pal Joey*, 23. 1946: "It means the jigs will throw us whites out of work." B. Chambers, *Amer. Mercury*, Apr., 481/2. *Prob. from "jigaboo," but may be related to "jig" = dance, as Negroes have been traditionally considered as exceedingly rhythmic.* → **2** [derog.] Any dark-skinned person, as a West Indian, Spaniard, or Puerto Rican. **3** A dancing party or a public dance. 1933: "How about taking in a jigg somewhere, boys?" J. T. Farrell, 69.   *adj.* [derog.] Negro, esp. a jig show = a Negro minstrel show, and jig band = a Negro orchestra. 1935: "The only other jig jocks around. . . ." Runyon, 200. 1939–40: "A jig band." O'Hara, *Pal Joey*, 23. 1948: "Tap dancer with the jig show." F. Brown, *Dead Ringer*, 6.

jigaboo   **zigaboo**   **ziggaboo** **jigabo**   **zigabo**   **jibagoo** [derog.] *n.* A Negro. 1910: "So come to your Nabob, and next Patrick's Day/Be Mistress Mumbo Jumbo Jig-ji-boo J. O'Shea." Song from the musical comedy *Yankee Girl.* 1948: "Jigaboo . . . had . . . rhythm in his feet. . . ." F. Brown, *Dead Ringer*, 7.   *adj.* Negro. 1935: "That ziggaboo jock of his. . . ." Runyon, 170.

jigamaree   *n.* Any new gadget. *From "jigger." Colloq. since 1820.*

jig-chaser   *n.* **1** A white person, esp. a white policeman. **2** A Southerner.

jigger   *n.* **1** An artificially made sore, usually on an arm or leg, used as an aid in begging. 1894: ". . . He 'sizes her up' . . . and decides whether it will pay to use his 'jigger.' " J. Flynt. **2** An ice-cream sundae. 1920: "He . . . consumed another double-chocolate jigger. . . ." Fitzgerald, *This Side of Paradise*, 42. *Most common in Eastern prep schools and colleges.* **3** A liquor glass of 1½-ounce capacity. → **4** A drink of liquor.   *v.t.* **1** To interfere with; to run. 1894 [1891]: *Tramp use.* ". . . These . . . fellows . . . jigger our [free]

riding on the railroad." J. Flynt. **2** To damn. 1951: "I'll be jiggered." Lee Rogow, *Collier's,* Nov. 17, 10/3.   **—s!**

jigger!   *interj.* Look out! Run! *A warning cry, particularly that the police or one's superiors are coming. Often in "jiggers, the cops."*

jigger-man   **jigger guy**   *n.* A lookout. See **jiggers.** *Underworld use.* 1945: "17-year-old Michael . . . who acted only as 'the two-block jiggers guy.' . . ." L. F. McHugh.

jiggery pokery   *n.* Trickery; fakery. 1946: "Why the dark hints that the editor is up to some jiggery pokery?" Paul Jones, Phila. *Bulletin,* Mar. 15, 14. 1946: "Cried another stockholder: 'Let us never forget . . . the manipulations, financial jugglery, or what some term jiggery-pokery.' " *Time,* May 6, 86/3. See Appendix, Reduplications.

jiggins   **juggins**   *n.* **1** A fool; a simple-minded person. *From "jughead."* → **2** A victim of a swindle.

Jiggs   *n.* A Negro carnival worker. *Carnival sl. Archaic.*

jig-jig [taboo]   *n.* Sexual intercourse. *One of several reduplications = coitus, which were in fairly common W.W.II Armed Forces use, usu. from folk ety. of colloq. used by native residents of occupied territories.* See Appendix, Reduplications.

jigs   *interj.* Beat it! 1945 [1943]: "Jigs, here he comes!" E. Kasser. *From "jiggers." Orphan home use.*

jig-swiggered   *adj.* Jiggered; darned. 1910: "I'll be jig-swiggered!" Johnson, *Varmint,* 113.

jillion   *n.* A great many; an indefinitely large number. Cf. **zillion.** 1950: "A jillion jackpots. . . ." *Time,* Feb. 13, 20.

Jim = **Bill-Jim.**

jim   *v.t.* To spoil; to ruin; to bungle. *Underworld use.*

Jim Crow   **1** A poor man; a common or average man. *c1850. Obs.* **2** [derog.] A Negro. 1956: "Another fake darkie [a white minstrel wearing blackface] was Thomas 'Jim Crow' Rice who, in the 1830's, invented: 'Wheel about, turn about,/ Do just so,/ And every time I wheel about/ I jump Jim Crow.' " S. Longstreet, *The Real Jazz Old and New*, 18. **3** The practice or doctrine of segregation as applied to Negroes in the U.S.; discrimination or intolerance directed toward Negroes. 1954: "My first experience with Jim Crow. . . . I had never ridden on a street car before." L.

Armstrong, *Satchmo, My Life in New Orleans, 14.* 1957: "Jim Crow killed her [Negro jazz singer Bessie Smith] ... Jim Crow and John Barleycorn. She was in an accident and bled to death while they were taking care of the white people." Tennessee Williams, *Orpheus Descending,* II. **4** A wooden railroad tie that is unfit for use or sale, usu. because it is too small. *Logger and railroad use.* *v.t.* To discriminate against Negroes; to practice or enforce rules of segregation. 1953: "I would like to ... say that the people who Jim Crow me have a WHITE heart." L. Hughes, *Simple Takes a Wife,* 13.

Jim Dandy   jim-dandy *n.* **1** An admirable person or thing. *Colloq. since c1880.* **2** A fictional hero; the one who will solve all problems; a *deus ex machina.* 1957: Popular song, "Jim Dandy to the Rescue." *adj.* Admirable; dandy. 1953: "Anacin [a pain-killer] is the jim-dandy remedy. . . ." P. Hamburger, *New Yorker,* Feb. 7, 92.

jim-jam *v.i., v.t.* To jam, to jazz up. 1956: ". . . *Jim-jam* is to jump it lively." S. Longstreet, *The Real Jazz Old and New,* 148. **—s** *n.* = **heebie-jeebies.** 1852: *DAE. Colloq.*

Jimmie *n.* A car or engine built by GMC (General Motors Corp.). *From pronouncing the initials GMC rapidly. Hot-rod use since c1955.*

Jimmie Higgins An unimportant, naïve, or new member of the Socialist Party or of a labor union. 1956: "*Jimmie Higgins*—A union member, usually with little prestige in the union, who will perform drudgery like addressing and sealing envelopes, checking name lists, etc. The name was used by the Socialist Party early in this century and Upton Sinclair used it as a novel title in 1919. It is unlikely that the name comes from any real person." *Labor's Special Lang. from Many Sources. Archaic.*

jimmies, the = **jim-jams** 1928: ". . . Him popping down the chimney—well, frankly, it gives me the jimmies." Wolcott Gibbs, *New Yorker,* Dec. 22, 18/3. *Never common.*

jimmy *v.t.* To pick [a lock]; to force open a door, window, or drawer as with a jimmy. *n.* A cork inner sole, pasted in a shoe to make it fit properly. *Retail shoe salesman use.*

jims, the *n.pl.* = **jim-jams, heebie-jeebies.** 1902: "I'll have ter shake de stuff ... / ... I ain't dead anxious ter get next de Jims. . . ." Coley, "Rubaiyat

of the East Side," last stanza. *Never common.*

jing-jang [taboo] *n.* **1** The penis. **2** The vagina. **3** Sexual intercourse. *From the Oriental symbol for this name, two teardrop shapes interlocked in a circle, symbolizing the unity of life and death, fertility and religion, male and female, etc.*

jingle *n.* A phone call; a ring. 1949: "We never hear from you, not even a jingle." Movie, *Any Number Can Play.*

jingled *adj.* Drunk. *Some W.W.I use, not now common.*

jingle-jangle *n.* Money. 1953: "I've got some jingle-jangle in my jeans." *Corliss Archer,* netwk. radio, Jan. 2. *Since c1920; never common.* See Appendix, Reduplications.

jinky board A seesaw. *Used by children; prob. from the Gullah.* Cf. **joggling board.**

jinny *n.* A speakeasy. *c1920; never common. Obs.*

jinx *n.* Bad luck; a cause of bad luck; a bad luck omen. 1926: "This town is a jinx for me." Stallings & Anderson, *What Price Glory,* III. *v.t.* To cause bad luck, to put a jinx on.

jip = **gyp.**

jippo *adj., n.* Fat. *Some W.W.I use.*

jism *n.* **1** [taboo] Semen. **2** Vigor; speed; animation; excitement; pep. 1937: "'Step on it, will you?' 'Sure. . . .' 'All right, but put a little jism into it, will you?'" Weidman, *Wholesale,* 178.

jit *n.* **1** A nickel; 5¢. *From "jitney."* **2** [derog.] A Negro. **—ney** *n.* **1** A car, usu. one owned by an individual, used to carry passengers along a standard route for a small fare; a private bus. 1924: "We found a jitney and I gave him the address. . . ." R. Lardner, "How to Write Short Stories," reprinted in *The American Twenties,* 40. **2** A nickel; 5¢. 1947: "Call that money? A jitney? A nickle?" W. Saroyan, *Jim Dandy,* 11. 1947: ". . . The pinball handler slipped Hammond five jitneys for his two bits. . . ." Don Fairbairn, Phila. *Bulletin,* Oct. 29, 4. → **3** A small 5¢ cigar. **4** = **jitney bus.** An automobile or small bus that carries passengers for a small charge, usu. 5¢. *Obs.* → **5** Any unscheduled local bus, car, or limousine used as a bus. 1945: "Camden [New Jersey] authorities cracked down today on illegal jitney service to the Garden State racetrack. . . . Last year, 32 arrests for illegal jitney operation were made." Phila. *Bulletin,* July 13,

3/1. → **6** Any automobile, esp. a small or cheap one, usu. a Ford. *c1930.* *adj.* Five-cent; cheap; improvised; inferior; miniature. 1933: [cheap] "When I fallen for a little 'dame' in a jitney dance hall. . . ." Geo. Milburn, *Amer. Mercury*, Aug., 490/1. 1920: [inferior] "Here's the old jitney waiter." Fitzgerald, *This Side of Paradise*, 120. 1935: [miniature] "The prolificity of these jitney St. Georges [the editors of American weekly newspapers] . . . has been . . . amazing." Albert S. Keshen, *Amer. Mercury*, Aug., 472/1.

jitney bag   A coin purse; a small handbag.

jitney bus = **jitney,** *n.* **4.**

jitter   *v.i.* **1** To tremble, shake, etc. 1940: "A line of . . . half-washed clothes jittered on a rusty wire in the side yard." Chandler, *Farewell*, 20. **2** To be nervous or frightened. 1943: "The next day I jittered around the house . . . unable to concentrate on anything." H. A. Smith, *Putty Knife*, 191. See **jitters, the.** **—y**   *adj.* Nervous; trembling. *Colloq.*

jitterbug   *n., adj.* **1** One who, though not a musician, enthusiastically likes or understands swing music; a swing fan. 1938: "Jitterbugs are the extreme swing addicts who get so excited by its music that they cannot stand or be still. . . . They must prance around in wild exhibitionist dances . . . or yell and scream. . . ." *Life*, Aug. 8, 56. **2** One who dances frequently to swing music. **3** A devotee of jitterbug music and dancing; one who follows the fashions and fads of the jitterbug devotee. *v.i.* To dance, esp. to jazz or swing music and usu. in an extremely vigorous and athletic manner. 1951: "Do you feel like jitterbugging a little bit, if they play a fast one? Not corny jitterbug, not jump or anything—just nice and easy." J. D. Salinger, *Catcher in the Rye*, 57–58. 1956: "*Jitterbug* [used to mean] a sexual reaction to music." S. Longstreet, *The Real Jazz Old and New*, 151.

jitters, the   *n.pl.* Nervousness; fear; cowardice. 1929: "Willie's got the jitters." Sturges, *Strictly Dishonorable*, Act II. 1934: "I had the jitters. I thought—I believed—I was losing my mind. But now—I feel all right." P. Wylie, *Finnley Wren*, 175. 1945: "[The term] is from a Spoonerism ['bin and jitters' for 'gin and bitters'] . . . and originally referred to one under the influence of gin and bitters." H. W. Fry, rev. of J. T. Shipley's *Dict. of Word*

Origins, Phila. *Bulletin*, Oct. 16, B22.

jive   *n.* **1** Ordinary, tiresome, or misleading talk or actions; exaggerations, flattery; distraction; insincere, uncouth talk or conduct; anything that should be ignored; boloney; bull. 1954 [c1920]: ". . . There was lots of just plain common shooting and cutting. But . . . that jive didn't faze me at all. I was so happy to have some place to blow my horn." Louis Armstrong, *Satchmo, My Life in New Orleans*, 150. 1941: "Don't hand me any more of that jive." *Life*, Jan. 27, 78. *Orig. Negro use, and orig. perhaps alternate sp. of "gieve."* **2** Gaudy articles, merchandise, or clothing. 1954 [c1920]: "When we collected our pay I did not know what to buy so I bought a lot of cheap jive at the five and ten cent store to give to the kids. . . ." Louis Armstrong, *Satchmo, My Life in New Orleans*, 193. **3** [taboo] Sex; sexual intercourse. **4** Fast popular music with a strongly accented two- or four-beat rhythm, as played by the pop. big swing bands c1938–c1945: fast swing music; jazz as it developed in the 1930's; swing. 1943: "G.M. [Glenn Miller]! Man, what solid jive." Max Shulman, *Barefoot Boy With Cheek*, 90. *By far the most common use.* **5** Marijuana. *Never common.* See **gyve.**   *v.t.* To mislead with words; to deceive; to kid.   *v.i.* **1** To play or dance to jive music; to jam. *Note that all the above meanings are equated with meanings of "jazz." Thus, "jive" replaced "jazz" to some extent, c1938–c1945, linguistically as well as musically.* **2** To make sense; to equate or match two items; to match with the known facts. *Very common since c1940. Prob. from "jibe."* **3** To talk idly or confusedly, in a jazzy rhythm and up-to-date slang.   *adj.* Any person, place, group, object, or idea associated with teenagers or swing music. *c1938–c1945. One could see a jive movie with Benny Goodman, then go to a jive joint for some beer ℓnd to hear some jive records on the juke box.*   **jiving**   *adj.* **1** Playing jive adroitly or in an exciting manner. *Jive use c1935.* → **2** Playing swing adroitly or in an exciting manner. *Some swing use.* **3** Attracting attention or showing off while playing cool or far-out music, as by blowing very high notes, playing very fast, or accenting close-harmony bass notes, while demonstrating little musicianship or comprehension of the piece, chord relationships, or arrangement. *This derisive cool and* *far-out use shows what these groups think of jive.*

jo   *n.* A shovel. See **hemo-jo, joe.**

J.O.   **j.o.** = **Joe,** coffee.

job   *n.* **1** Almost any item, object, procedure, machine, etc., esp. one of good quality or representing good workmanship; often an automobile or other vehicle. 1941: "The [printing] presses were special jobs." *SEP*, Jan. 18, 13. 1951: "He just got a Jaguar. One of those little English jobs that can do around two hundred miles an hour." J. D. Salinger, *Catcher in the Rye*, 1. *Common since c1925.* **2** Almost any person, but usu. a tough or cynical person. 1927: "She's a tough little job." Hammett, *Blood Money*, 128. 1934: "He was the greatest job in the way of a sucker that God ever turned out." Cain, *Postman*, 28. **3** A crime; a criminal escapade. **4** = **snow job.** See **blow job, fizz job, frail job, gow job, mental job, put-up job, shack job, tank job.**   *v.t.* To deceive; to frame or double-cross. 1928: "Crying . . . that he had been jobbed, Madden was sent to Sing Sing. . . ." Asbury, *Gangs of N.Y.*, 209. 1950: "You never know whether you are getting jobbed or not." Starnes, *Another Mug*, 24. *Mainly underworld use.*

—job   See Appendix, Suffixes and Suffix Words.

job, lay down on the   To lack alertness; to shirk; to work slowly and without enthusiasm.

job pop   To inject drugs intravenously, usu. into the arm. *Narcotic addict use.*

job shark   See **shark.**

jobster   *n.* One who is rewarded with a position under the spoils system; one who enriches himself by public office. 1897: *DAE. Obs.*

jock   *n.* **1** A jockey. 1923: word used 15 times in E. Hemingway's "My Old Man," a short story. **2** = **disc jockey.** 1952: ". . . Already the jukes and jocks are dinning our ears with Christmas songs." B. Thomas, AP, Dec. 2.

jocker   *n.* **1** A homosexual hobo who lives off the begging of his boy companion. 1893: ". . . Subject to the whims and passions of various 'jockers,' or protectors." J. Flynt. *Hobo use.* → **2** A male homosexual who is aggressive toward boys or youths. *Not common.*

jockey   *n.* **1** An athlete who taunts opposing players; one who "rides" another. **2** A cab, bus, or truck driver; an airplane pilot. 1932: [cab driver] ". . .

Jerking me into the cab and telling the jockey to go to the Penn Station." Runyon, 7. 1951: [pilot] "The jockey is in the panic rack and ready to go." AP, May 10. **3** A student who uses a pony. *College use.* See Appendix, Suffixes and Suffix Words; **desk jockey, disc jockey, highball jockey, juice jockey, plow-jockey, throttle-jockey.**

—jockey   See Appendix, Suffixes and Suffix Words.

joe   **Joe**   *n.* **1** A privy; a water closet; a bathroom; a toilet. *c1850. Replaced by "john."* **2** Coffee. *Also called "j.o." "Joe" is a useful monosyllabic synonym; it apparently derives from the "j" of "Java" or perhaps the "j" and "o" of "jamoke."* **3** A term of address; anyone whose name is unknown. → **4** A man, esp. a friendly, pleasant one; a fellow; an egg; a guy, as "a good joe," "an ordinary joe." 1947: "If he's a good Joe, he can do us a lot of good." Billy Rose, *synd. newsp. col.*, Apr. 18. 1952: "Thomas Dewey never seemed to share much of the problems of the ordinary Joe." Robert C. Ruark, *synd. newsp. col.*, Sept. 29. → **5** A soldier. *Very common during W.W.II.* → **6** Any American. *Used by natives of countries familiar with W.W.II U.S. soldiers.* See **G.I. Joe.**   *adj.* Informed; wise; hep. 1941: ". . . To get Joe to something." ". . . To put you Joe." D. W. Maurer.   *v.t.* To inform [a person]. 1941: "Let me Joe you to that racket." Maurer. See **holy Joe, Little Joe, sloppy Joe.**

Joe Blow   **1** Mealtime. *Circus slang.* **2** Any person whose name is not known. → **3** A young, male civilian. *W.W.II Armed Forces use.* → **4** An enlisted man. *W.W.II Army use.* **5** A musician. **6** An average man; any man; any man at all. See **John Doe.**

Joe-boy   *n.* The male counterpart of a flapper. 1941: *Subdeb use. Life*, Jan. 27, 78. *Prob. synthetic.*

Joe College   **1** A male college student, esp. a brash youth whose dress, manner, and speech suggest the social and sporting aspects of college life. 1939: "We do not know . . . who was the first *Joe College.* . . ." Hixson, *Word Ways*, 153. *Usu. mildly derogatory.* **2** Any callow young man whose enthusiasm for inconsequential things betrays his inexperience; a young man, not a college student, who imitates the dress and manner popularly associated with college students. 1957: "Lee Young, the drummer, was . . . a real Joe College type, with the brown-and-white shoes, the open collar, the sweater. . . ." Leonard Feather, "Jazz Millionaire [Norman Granz]," *Esquire*, May.

joed   *adj.* Tired out. *Not common.*

joe-darter   *n.* An unsurpassed person or thing. *c1850, colloq.; obs.*

Joe Doakes   Any male; a man whose name is not known; "everyman."

Joe Gish   **1** Any sailor, a typical sailor; the John Doe of the USN. *Some archaic USN use.* **2** Any midshipman. *Annapolis use.*

joepot   *n.* A coffeepot. See **joe,** *n.* 2.

Joe Sad   An unpopular person. *Negro use.*

joey   Joey   *n.* A circus clown.

Joe Yale = Joe College, but with special reference to characteristics popularly associated with the old and socially prominent eastern colleges. 1951: "On my right there was this very Joe Yale-looking guy, in a gray flannel suit and one of those flitty-looking Tattersall vests. All those Ivy League bastards look alike." J. D. Salinger, *Catcher in the Rye,* 67.

Joe Zilsch   **1** Any male college student; a typical student. *c1920, college use. Obs.* → **2** Any man; a typical common man.

joggling board   **1** A swing. *Prob. from the Gullah.* **2** A seesaw.

john   John   *n.* **1** A toilet, esp. a public toilet for males. 1735: "No Freshman shall . . . go into the Fellow[']s cus John [from 'Cousin John,' a privy]." Harvard regulation quoted in Hall, *College Words,* 1856, 216. 1946: "I made a brief visit to the john." Evans, *Halo in Blood,* 162. *Very common. Usu. not cap.* Cf. **jane.** **2** A man, esp. an average or typical man; specif. one who can be used, an easy mark. 1929: "I gotta meet a John." Dunning & Abbott, *Broadway,* Act II. 1950: "This is a highclass place. We don't want no poor johns in here!" A. Lomax, *Mr. Jelly Roll,* 118. 1952: "He's pretty smart at figgerin' out what a John'll pay—that's why he's always on the corner lookin' them over when they come along." L. Hughes, *Laughing to Keep from Crying,* 120. *Orig. Negro use.* **3** An Army recruit. 1936: "He is still a John. Why is he a John? Because many years ago models for . . . enlistment papers were . . . prepared as though for 'John Doe.' " E. Colby. 1943: "He may be called a *John,* from the 'John Doe' on the sample

recruiting forms. . . ." A. Ostrow. **4** A man who is keeping a girl, i.e., paying her rent and expenses in return for sexual favors; a male lover; a girl's steady escort or date. 1954: "Our hustlers sat on their steps and called to their 'Johns' as they passed by." L. Armstrong, *Satchmo, My Life in New Orleans,* 95. *Replaced "Daddy" c1945. "John" seems to imply more charm or sophistication than "Daddy" or "Sugar Daddy"; moreover, a "John" need not be wealthy but can be any man involved in a long illicit affair. Almost always capitalized in this use. Although such a man is "a 'John' " the word is more freq. used in the expression "her 'John.' "* → **5** A girl's steady boy friend. *The word orig. implied sexual intimacy but does not now always have a sexual connotation.* **6** A wealthy, elderly homosexual who maintains a young homosexual in a man-mistress relationship. *Not common.* **7** A policeman. 1934: Slang. *Web.* 1938: Australian use. *S.J.B.* 1946: "John or no John, I don't take that kind of stuff." Evans, *Halo in Blood,* 118. **8** A law-abiding citizen. 1940: "Negro and white prisoners' use, Woodbourne, N.Y." J. Schuyler. **9** A lieutenant. 1953 [c1945]: W.W.II use, U.S. Armed Forces in Europe. Also **first john, second john.** *Oral.* **10** Variously: An idle young dude; a Chinese; a free spender; victim of a swindle. See **Dear John, dumbjohn, long John, square John.**

John —   See Appendix, Prefixes and Prefix Words.

John B.   A hat. *From "John B. Stetson." Most common in the West.*

John B. Stetson   **1** A hat made by the John B. Stetson hat company. 1954 [c1920]: "My good old John B. Stetson. That was 'the' hat in those days. . . ." L. Armstrong, *Satchmo, My Life in New Orleans,* 165. → **2** Any man's hat, regardless of make.

John Doe   Any man at all; the mythical average man. *From the name invented anciently to stand for the fictitious lessee in court proceedings of ejectment and thereafter used wherever a fictitious person is needed.*

John dogface   Johnny dogface   An Army recruit. *Some W.W.II use.*

John Family   **1** Any person having a steady job, home, and secure life, esp. a farmer or employer. *Hobo use; obs.* **2** A professional thief or grifter.

John Farmer   A farmer.

John Hall   Alcohol. *From "-hol" respelled and personified.* Cf. **hall.** *Common vagabond use.*

John Hancock   One's signature. *Often in* **put your John Hancock on the dotted line.** *From the large signature of John Hancock, prominent on the Declaration of Independence.*

John Henry = **John Hancock.**

John Hollowlegs   A hungry man. *Hobo use.*

John Law   The police; any law enforcement officer. 1907 [1892]: "... A lot of my brother hoboes had been gathered in by John Law...." Jack London, *My Life.* *Orig. hobo and circus use.*

John L's = **Long Johns.**

Johnny = **John.**

Johnny-come-lately   *n.* A newcomer. Fig., anyone or anything that is tardy; specif., a person who joins a group after the group's success seems assured and after his support is no longer needed. 1946: "For postwar planning in these United States was no Johnny-come-lately. Our people had not waited for the last shot of the war to be fired before they began to plan for peace." M. Shulman, *Zebra Derby,* 15. *Colloq. since c1850.*

Johnny O'Brian   A boxcar. *Hobo use.*

Johnny on the spot   A person who is present and alert to his opportunities or present when needed. *Colloq. since c1895.*

John Roscoe   A gun; a roscoe. 1935: "... In each of my hands I will have a John Roscoe...." Runyon.

Johnson   *n.* A tramp; a drifter. *Underworld use.*

Johnson boys   A gang of thieves; yeggs. *Argot, now archaic. From yeggs' use of a tool resembling a locomotive's Johnson bar [reverse lever].*

Johnson rod   A mythical part of a locomotive, truck, car, or plane. *Jocular use, in referring to engine trouble the cause of which is unknown, and as a joke on those who are not in the know.*

join out   1 To join; to join up. 1935: "... All the other dogs are strays that join out with him...." Runyon. *Circus use.* 2 To get free transportation by hiring out. *Vagabond use.*

joint   *n.* 1 Almost any building, apartment, room, or sheltered area where people gather, primarily for eating, drinking, living, taking dope, lounging, conversation, dancing, listening to music, watching television, gambling, etc., but also for buying and selling. Often considered disparaging, "joint" is sometimes a neutral word for "place." A joint may mean any kind of saloon, speakeasy, nightclub, café, eating place, soda fountain, hotel, house, apartment, room, store, or any other place of business. It may be a carnival concession, a jail, a dancehall, an opium or marijuana den, a hangout, a poolroom, a garage, etc., usu. not as disreputable as a dive. Fig., any place where one person joins or may join another or others. 1883: "A place for drinking, gambling, and the like." *DAE.* 1887: "Any establishment." *DAE.* 1887: "Chinese Opium Joints ... a ... list of opium joints...." *Lantern,* New Orleans, May 14. 1894: "In Chicago ... there is a 'joint' near Madison street.... I should rather live in a barrel or box than in a 'joint.'..." Josiah Flynt. 1905: "I took Clara J. to the St. Regis to dinner.... It's a swell joint, all right...." McHugh, *Search Me,* 20. 1920: "Andrew Lang ... followed the career of one of Mr. George Ade's heroes up to his entrance into an Italian restaurant, which Ade entitled a spaghetti-joint...." B. Matthews, *Scribner's,* Nov., 622/2. 1930: "Go muscle in some beer-joint." *Amer. Mercury,* Dec., 456. 1939–40: O'Hara, *Pal Joey,* used 38 times. 1941: "A hunting lodge, a cocktail joint, a beer joint, an auto court." G. Homes, *40 Whacks,* 43, 109, 110, 118. 1949: "People sitting next to him in chili joints...." Paul Jones, Phila. *Bulletin,* Sept. 2, 14. 1949: "Beer joint." *Life,* Oct. 24, 25. 1956: "Birdland [a jazz nightclub in New York City] won its suit against a Chicago club which tried to use the same name. This is the tenth such suit won by the bop-joint. The only other Birdland the club permits to use the name is a tiny igloo-like joint in Alaska." Leonard Lyons, "The Lyons Den," N.Y. *Post,* Feb. 21, 48. 2 A thing. *Never common.* 3 A gun. *Some teenage gang use.* 4 A marijuana cigarette. 1956: "'Two or three people can get high on one joint (marijuana cigarette).'" S. Longstreet, *The Real Jazz Old and New,* 146. 5 A complete set of equipment necessary to inject narcotics. *Teenage narcotics addict use. Since c1955.*

—joint   See Appendix, Suffixes and Suffix Words.

joint hop   To go from one place of entertainment to another on a spree; to stop for a drink at several bars in succession. *Used almost exclusively in the phrase "to go joint hopping." Student use since c1945.*

joker   *n.* **1** Any single component of a multiple instrument that tends to negate or qualify the positive effect of the whole; e.g., a clause in a contract, an item on an agenda, a paragraph in a legislative bill the effect of which is to nullify or weaken the apparent purpose of the larger instrument. 1953: "A postal rate increase bill . . . had within it a 'joker' which seriously affected the nonprofit publications of organized labor in all parts of America." Rep. Harold C. Hagen, *Congressional Record*, Aug. 28, A5625. **2** That which gives one an unfair chance; that which makes a task or plan impossible or difficult to achieve. **3** A man; a fellow; a guy. 1949: "What floor does this joker live on?" Radio program, WOR, *Martin Kane*, Sept. 4. *Though not derog., it often implies that the person is ineffectual.* → **4** A wiseacre; a wise guy. *Army use, c W.W.II.*

jollop   *n.* A large portion or serving, esp. of food.

jolly   *adj.* **1** Drunk. 1737: Pa. *Gazette. Archaic.* **2** Excellent; pleasant; etc. *Colloq.   adv.* Very. *In the U.S. widely regarded as a Briticism. Some jocular use.*

jolly-o   *n.* Hell. 1941: "But the hitters wearing those baseball uniforms have been walloping the ball like jolly-o, too." John Kieran, N.Y. *Times*, May 14, 29/2. *Euphem. for "hell." Not common.*

jolly-up   *n.* An informal dancing party; a dance. *c1885–1940, student use, not common in the U.S.*

jolt   *n.* **1** The initial effects of an injection of drugs or a marijuana cigarette. → **2** An injection of a narcotic drug. **3** A prison sentence. 1928: ". . . To get a jolt in the stir." E. Booth, *Amer. Mercury*, May, 81. *Underworld use.* **4** A drink of liquor; a shot. 1920: ". . . A wee jolt of Bourbon." Fitzgerald, *This Side of Paradise*, 261. **5** A marijuana cigarette; an injection of heroin. *Addict use.   v.i.* To take injections of heroin in the arm." 1952: "We didn't want to jolt. . . ." David Hulburd, *'H' is for Heroin.*

Jonah   *n.* A hipster, a rock, a cat. *Rock and roll use since c1955.*

Joneses, keep up with the   To strive not to be outdone socially or financially by one's neighbors or others regarded as one's social equals; to spend money to keep up a front. 1926: ". . . The automocracy is everlastingly trying to

'keep up with the Joneses'. . . ." Vizetelly.

jook   *n., adj.* = **juke.**

josh   *v.i.* To joke, tease, twit, banter, or kid.   *n.* A joke. *Colloq. since c1895.*   **—er**   *n.* One who joshes. *Colloq. since c1900.*   **—ing**   *n.* Joking; teasing; kidding. 1939: ". . . From the bus top came the laughter and joshing of two young couples." J. T. Farrell, 211.

joskin   *n.* A rube; a hick.

josser   *n.* A fellow. *Not common in the U.S.*

joy house   A brothel. 1940: "I ain't been in a joy house in 20 years." Chandler, *Farewell*, 15. *Not common.*

joy-juice   *n.* Liquor.

joy knob   **1** [taboo] The penis. **2** The steering wheel of a car, esp. a hot rod, or the stick of an airplane. Cf. **joy stick.**

joy-popper   *n.* **1** A newcomer among narcotic, esp. marijuana, addicts. **2** One who claims to take narcotics only for an occasional thrill, as opposed to a true addict. 1949: "They called those using the stuff only occasionally 'joy-poppers' and wished them all great joy. For the 'joy-poppers' had no intention of becoming addicts in the true sense." Nelson Algren, *Man with the Golden Arm*, 31.

joy-powder   *n.* Morphine. *Orig. underworld use.*

joy-rider   *n.* A nonaddict who sometimes takes a narcotic drug. *Drug-addict use.*

joy smoke   *n.* Marijuana.

joy-stick   *n.* **1** The control lever of an airplane. 1918: "By manipulating the 'joy-stick' . . . the tiro ascends and descends." McCartney, *Texas Rev.* 79. **2** The steering wheel on a hot rod. **3** An opium pipe.

juane   *n.* Abbrev. for "marijuana," esp. a marijuana cigarette. 1934: "I had a glass of beer on top of the piano and a half-smoked juane on the side. They paid me a small salary." P. Wylie *Finnley Wren*, 51.

Judy   *n.* **1** A girl or woman. *Some W.W.I and W.W.II use. Never as common as "jane."* **2** Used absolutely by airfield control-tower workers and pilots in radio communication with (other) pilots = "Your plane is now close enough to be seen, I see you." → **3** Used absolutely by airfield control-tower workers and pilots in radio communication with (other) pilots = "Your plane now appears on, or is locked in, my radar screen. I have located, or see you by radar." *Both* **2** and **3** *common W.W.II Air Force use, and still in use.* → **4** "Exactly"; "I understand or agree." *Usu. used absolutely. Some use since W.W.II.* Cf. **jake.**

jug *n.* **1** A jail; a prison; usu. a local prison. *c1815; often in "in the jug."* **2** A bottle or flask of whisky. **3** A drink or shot of whisky. **4** A bank. 1958: "Jug—A bank." G. Y. Wells, *Station House Slang. Underworld use.* → **5** A safe; a strongbox. *Underworld use.* *v.t.* To imprison [a person]. 1894 [1891]: "You fellows are likely to be jugged too." J. Flynt. *Since c1835.*

jugful See **not by a jugful.**

juggins = **jiggins.**

jughead **jug-head** *n.* **1** A mule, esp. an Army mule. *Farm and Army use.* **2** A stupid person.

jug-steamed *adj.* Drunk. *c1850, now obs.*

juice *n.* **1** Liquor, esp. whisky. 1954: "When the night-lifers got full of liquor, much stronger than the present-day juice. . . ." L. Armstrong, *Satchmo, My Life in New Orleans,* 117. **2** Money used for or obtained from gambling, extortion, blackmail, or bribery, esp. a bookmaker's commission from a gambling syndicate. 1956: ". . . The juice, the C, the commission." T. Betts, *Across the Board,* 317. **3** Electricity; electric current. 1920: "The wires . . . that have to do with the promulgation of light-juice, starting-juice, ignition-juice, and juice in general." Gillilan, *Lit. Digest. c1895.* → **4** Gasoline; fuel. 1949: [airplane gasoline] "If you have a light supply of juice you climb at about 200 m.p.h." N.Y. *Times,* Sept. 25, 65/3. **5** Nitroglycerin. *Construction crew and miner use.* See **balloon juice, bug-juice, bf-juice, giggle juice, go-juice, moo juice, torpedo juice.** *v.t.* To milk a cow. 1951: "Bill takes venom from the snakes for use in research laboratories, and does it as nonchalantly as a farmer juices a gentle Jersey cow." Ben Funk, AP, Miami, Sept. 27. *adj.* Electrical; electrical engineering. *c1930, student use.* **—d** Drunk. **—r** *n.* **1** Theater stage crew or movie-studio lighting electricians. 1957: "He treated the grips and the juicers the way he had always treated them, as employees instead of like brothers. . . ." Al Morgan, "Master of the Revels," *Playboy,* May, 18. *Movie talk; c1930.* Cf. **grip.** See Appendix, **—er** ending. **2** One who chews tobacco. *Archaic.*

Juice *n.* A stage electrician. *A nickname. Theater use.*

juice-box *n.* **1** A phonograph. *W.W.I use. Obs.* **2** A car battery. **3** A junction box used for attaching electric cords. *Orig. factory and electrician use.*

juice chair The electric chair. *Not common.*

juiced up Intoxicated.

juice jockey See Appendix, Suffixes and Suffix Words.

juice-joint *n.* **1** A soft-drink tent, stand, booth, or concession. *Carnival and circus use.* **2** A speakeasy; a bar or nightclub. *Orig. 1920 use.*

juju **ju-ju** *n.* **1** A marijuana cigarette. 1940: "I knew a guy once who smoked jujus. Three highballs and three sticks of tea and it took a pipe wrench to get him off the chandelier." Chandler, *Farewell,* 60. See **juane.** See Appendix, Reduplications. **2** Any object, such as a piece of string, handkerchief, etc., with which an adult plays out of nervousness or as a habit. *Perhaps from narcotics addicts' "juju" = marijuana, implying a compulsion; perhaps an alternate form of "gee-gee."*

juke *n.* **1** = **juke house.** → **2** A roadhouse, esp. a cheap one. → **3** Music, esp. the style of music played in brothels, cheap roadhouses, and the like; an early nonprofessional form of jazz music. → **4** An automatic, coin-operated record-playing machine; a juke box. *v.i.* To tour roadside bars, usu. with one of the opposite sex; to drive to one roadside bar, drink a little and perhaps dance a little, leave and go to another, and continue in this manner for an entire evening or night. 1957: "I want you to go juking with me . . . that's riding and stopping to drink and dance, and riding some more and stopping to drink and dance again, and after awhile you just stop to drink . . . and sometimes you stop drinking and go to a tourist cabin [with your girl]." Tennessee Williams, *Orpheus Descending,* I. *Southern use.*

juke house A brothel. 1956: "Juke from juke box came from juke house—which was once a whorehouse, now called *cathouse* or *canhouse.*" S. Longstreet, *The Real Jazz Old and New,* 151.

jumbo *adj.* Large, extra large. *P. T. Barnum bought "Jumbo," the largest elephant on record, from London's Royal Zoo in 1883; in America the animal quickly caught the public imagination and became* *the first major attraction of the Barnum circus.*

jump   *v.t.* **1** To attack or assault [a person]. *Colloq. since 1890.* → **2** To rob; to hold up. **3** To pulsate or be noisy with activity, as of dancers or merrymakers. 1943: "He ... called up a couple of his friends ... and Mr. Hiller phoned two or three ... and they came, and before long the joint was jumpin'." H. A. Smith, *Putty Knife*, 60. *Orig. jive talk; c1935. Most common sl. use.* *adj.* Pulsating with excitement; fast played or playing in quick tempo, as a jump tune, a jump band. 1949: "... A couple of jump bands...." Billy Rose, *synd. newsp. col.*, July 25.   *n.* **1** = **swing music**. **2** A jive dance; any dance or other social event; a hop. *Orig. some jive and teenage street-gang use; general teenage use by c1955.* **3** = **rumble**. *Teenage street-gang use since c1955.* **—y**   *adj.* Nervous; frightened. 1957: "One of our pals in the night-club business is jumpy and he needs a bodyguard tonight." George Raft, as told to Dean Jennings, "Out of My Past," *SEP*, Sept. 21, 94. *Colloq.*

jump, get the   To take a lead in a race; to have a lead or an advantage in a contest or competition.

jump all over [someone]   To berate; to criticize severely and with anger.

jump band   A musical ensemble devoted to fast swing with a powerful, accented rhythm. 1956: "A *jump band* is a big and powerful jazz band." S. Longstreet, *The Real Jazz Old and New*, 149.

jump down [someone's] throat   To criticize severely and angrily; to berate.

jumped-up   *adj.* Hurriedly organized; improperly planned. *Colloq.*

—jumper   See Appendix, Suffixes and Suffix Words.

jump off the deep end   To act quickly and without consideration; to take drastic action; to take a bold step; to go the whole hog. 1953: "I suppose it would be a shock to June if I jumped off the deep end and married again!" Merrill Blosser, *synd. comic strip*, "Freckles," Mar. 9.

jump on   To assault verbally; to reprove; to reprimand. *Colloq. since c1885.*

jumps, the = **jitters, the**.

jump salty   To become angry; enraged; to become malicious. 1942: "If you're trying to jump salty...." Z.

Hurston. *Harlem Negro use; orig. jive and teenage street-gang use. Now some general student and teenage use.*

jump smooth   To become or go honest or straight; fig., to become calm, pleasant, or friendly. 1958: "A Gang Leader's Redemption [title] ... in a sequel [he] tells why he decided to 'jump smooth.'" *Life*, April 28, 69. *Orig. some jive use; now teenage street-gang use.*

jump the gun   To do anything prematurely. *From racing use, where a shot from a gun signals the official start of a race.*

jump the hurdle   To marry.

jump (dangle) up the line, take a   To journey; to move on to the next town. *Circus and vagabond use.*

June around   To be restless or aimless; to have spring fever.

jungle   *n.* **1** A hobo camp and rendezvous, usu. a clear space in a thicket (for fuel) near a railroad (for transportation), and ideally also near water and on the outskirts of a city. *Most jungles are surprisingly clean and well ordered; they provide a place for habitual vagrants and other unemployed men to rest, to cook and eat food, and to wash themselves and their clothes.* 1936: "... Before retiring to the 'jungle' in order to cook and eat. 'Jungles' are places ... on the outskirts of a city ... where itinerants go to cook their food. Wood, water, and seclusion are necessary to a good 'jungle.'" H. F. Kane in *New Repub.*, July 15, 288. 1948: "The real hobo always leaves the jungle like he found it...." Cain, *Moth*, 80. 1949: "Down in a hobo jungle alongside the tracks." *Life*, Oct. 24, 25. **2** A gathering place for the unemployed of a city, often near the dumping ground and usu. equipped with homemade shacks or huts for those with no other place to live. **3** Any busy, crowded living or working district in a city; the business pursued in such an area, esp. if characterized by keen competition and a lack of ethics. Thus the following book and movie titles: *The Asphalt Jungle* (about crime in a large city), *The Blackboard Jungle* (about violence in a high school), *The Garment Jungle* (about the N.Y.C. garment industry), etc., all pop. novels and movies during the 1950's.   **—s** *n.pl.* **1** Open country; woods. **2** Rural districts; the sticks.

jungle buzzard   A hobo who lives in a jungle to beg from other hobos. *Hobo use.*

jungle juice   Any alcoholic drink made from any alcohol available, as cleaning fluid, hair tonic, or lubricants, mixed with whatever fruit juice or other beverages are available. *Some W.W.II Army use. Isolated Army units, as those living in the jungle, used much ingenuity to provide alcoholic drinks.*

juniper juice   Gin. *From the flavoring.*

junk   *n.* **1** A small party during which food is served. *c1900, student use. Obs.* **2** Narcotics; a narcotic. 1934: "Canales has a noseful of junk a lot of the time." Chandler, *Finger Man*, 7. 1956: "... Sherlock Holmes. ... All he does is play a fiddle and take junk. This is a hero?" Jimmy Cannon, *Who Struck John*, 199. 1956: "The cops are still checking a report that $3,000,000 worth of drugs went down with the [ocean liner] Andrea Doria. What they're trying to discover is the identity of the person entrusted to handle the junk on board. ..." Douglas Watt, "Small World," N.Y. *Daily News*, Sept. 10, 47. *Since c1920. Orig. narcotics addict use; now fairly well known.* **3** Rubbish; trash; worthless refuse. *Colloq.* **4** Worthless talk or entertainment; cheap merchandise; dilapidated, but still useful possessions. → **5** Stuff; miscellaneous articles, often of practical and some monetary value.

1953: "Men carry more junk in their pockets than women do in their pocketbooks." AP, Mar. 30. *Colloq.* **—er** *n.* **1** One addicted to any narcotic drug. *Since c1925.* → **2** A peddler of narcotic drugs to addicts. **3** An automobile worn beyond repair. See Appendix, **—er** ending. **—ie** **—y** *n.* A drug addict. 1949: "You're not a student any more. ... You just graduated. Junkie—you're *hooked.*" N. Algren, *Man with the Golden Arm*, 32. 1952: "So Diane ... became a junkie ... hooked by horse." O. Prescott in N.Y. *Times*, Apr. 29, 25. 1957: "The man I was to find was both a junkie and a pusher. ..." Ashley Halsey, Jr., "The Lady Cops of the Dope Squad," *SEP*, March 30, 102. See **junk**. See Appendix, **—ie** ending.

junk-ball   *n.* In baseball, a pitch that is unorthodox, tricky, or anything but a straight fast ball. *adj.* Given to using such pitches; said of a pitcher. 1952: "Ed Lopat, another 'junk ball' pitcher. ..." R. Roden, AP, June 28.

junk heap   An old or dilapidated automobile; the implication is that it is ready for the junk yard.

justins   *n.pl.* Boots. 1948: "From Joseph Justin ... an early [boot] maker ... at Fort Worth." Mencken, *Sup. II. Not common.*

K

kabibble = **ish kabibble.**

kack   *n.* **1** A refined or nice person. *Negro use. Archaic.* **2** A saddle. *Ranch use.*

kadigin = **thingamajig.**

kady = **cady.**

kafooster   *n.* Unnecessary or confusing talk. 1951: "There has been a great deal of kafooster [about emasculating the price-control act]." Senator Robert Taft, quoted in *Newsweek.*

Kaiser's Geburtstag   Payday. 1956: "The brewery worker eagerly looks forward to ... *Kaiser's Geburtstag*—pay day." *Labor's Special Language From Many Sources. Archaic. In neighborhoods settled by those of Ger. descent. Because it is a time of celebrating.*

kajody   *n.* A thingamajig. *c1935; orig. West Coast use.*

kale   *n.* Money. 1936: "Among *Variety* tabus are trite slangisms, among 'em kale, dough, mazuma, etc." A. Green, *Esquire*, Sept. Cf. **cabbage, lettuce.**

kale-seed   *n.* Money. *c1900.* See **kale.**

kangaroo   *v.t.* To convict [a person] with false evidence.

kangaroo court   **1** A mock "court" held by prisoners to assess each newcomer a part of his money and tobacco. 1926: "Most jails have a court selected by the prisoners, consisting of Squire, Marshal, and Searcher. Every new prisoner faces this court and is assessed a percentage, which goes to the common fund, of any money or tobacco he has. This court often apportions the work in jail and any infringement of its rules is punished by a fine, spanking, or extra work. There is no appeal as the court often has the tacit recognition of the jail officials." *AS*, 1, 651. *Hobo lingo.* 1930: "... The toughest prisoner announced that he was president of the Kangaroo Club and would hold court...." Lavine, *Third Degree*, 241. 1947: "I'll jail her. ... I'll see her in the damn Kangaroo Court, and she can sit six weeks washing jailhouse linen!" Calder Willingham, *End As A Man*, 233. 1956: "And so The Champ [Harry "Bugsy" Segal] was summoned to appear before a Kangaroo Court, with [Al] Capone presiding as Chief Justice." T. Betts, *Across the Board*, 214. → **2** A small-town police court in which the judge levies exorbitant fines on speeding out-of-town motorists, then splits the excess money with the arresting policemen. → **3** Any local court that is harsh on vagabonds, hobos, and travelers.

kange = **gange**.

kaput *n., adj.* Out of working order, broken, useless; unsuccessful, without a chance of success; dead. 1949: ". . . Calling on the Maharajah . . . I would be 'kaput' without a folding machete. . . ." S. J. Perelman, *Listen to the Mocking Bird*, 134. *From the Ger. W.W.II Army use.*

Katy = **cady**.

katzenjammers, the = **heebie-jeebies**. *Archaic. From the synd. comic strip, "The Katzenjammer Kids," who always cause confusion, worry, and strife.*

kay *n.* A knockout. *Prize fight use. From the abbr. "K.O."*

kaydet *n.* **1** Slighting and/or humorous mispronunciation of standard "cadet." **2** Variant of sl. "cadet."

kayducer *n.* A train conductor; orig. underworld use—a train conductor who would, for a fee, allow known confidence men or gamblers to ply their trade among train passengers.

kayo = **K.O.** *A spelled pronunciation of the abbr. "K.O."*

Kazoo *n.* Kalamazoo. *Obs.*

keed *n.* Kid. *Almost always in direct address.* 1920: "Couldn't say, old keed." Fitzgerald, *This Side of Paradise*, 223. 1934: "Thanks, keed." Chandler, *Finger Man*, 7. 1941: "Glad you're gonna be with us, keed." Schulberg, *Sammy*, 43. *Considered somewhat jocular.* See Appendix, Mispronunciations.

keek *n.* **1** A peeping Tom. **2** A manufacturer's spy who reports on the newest designs, research, and business details of competitors; specif. in the garment industry.

keen *adj.* **1** Very fond of; eager or enthusiastic about. 1928: "Mr. Hardy apparently wasn't keen about having his 'life' written." R.L.L., *The New Yorker*, Dec. 29, 59. *Colloq. since c1915. Now considered a child, teenage, or affected use. Somewhat archaic.* **2** Beautiful; attractive; swell; an expression of approval. 1920: "You have keen eyes. . . .'" Fitzgerald, *This Side of Paradise*, 73. 1951: "I think she's a keen kid. . . . Tell me some more of this keen stuff. . . . That sounds keen." M. Shulman, *Dobie Gillis*, 50, 55, 91. *Since c1915. Somewhat archaic.*

keener *n.* A shrewd person. 1859: *DAE. Obs.*

keep For phrases beginning with "keep," see under principal word of phrase.

keep company To court; to go steady; to go on dates; said of a couple often, but not necessarily, planning to marry. *Colloq. since c1935.*

kee-rect *adj.* Correct; "What you said is very true; I am in complete agreement with what you have said." *Pop. by repeated use in the synd. newsp. comic strip "Abbie and Slats," though much earlier student use. A prime example of sl. emphasis by a louder or longer pronunciation of the first syllable of a stand. word.*

keester = **keister**.

kef **keef** **kief** *n.* Marijuana. *Narcotic addict use.*

keg *n.* The stomach. *c1870; obs.*

keister **keester** **keyster** **kiester** **kister** *n.* **1** The human posterior. 1951: "A swift kick in the keester." Movie, *Born Yesterday*. → **2** Either of the rear pockets in a pair of pants; a pocket. *Mainly pickpocket use.* → **3** A suitcase, valise, satchel, handbag, grip, or case, esp. a display tray that folds up into a satchel or suitcase. *Often one containing pitchman wares.* 1935: ". . . An open sample case of liberal dimensions . . . the typical 'keister' of the street hawker." Collier & Westrate, *The Reign of Soapy Smith*, 1. → **4** A safe or strongbox.

kelly *n.* **1** A hat. 1948: ". . . Checking your kellys." Lait-Mortimer, *N.Y. Confidential*, 218. **2** Esp. a derby hat or other stiff hat.

kelsey *n.* A prostitute. *Carnival use; obs.*

Kelsey's nuts See **tight as Kelsey's nuts**.

kelt **keltch** *n.* **1** A white person. *Negro use.* → **2** A Negro who is light-skinned enough to pass or who does pass as a white person.

keltch = **kelt**.

kemp *n.* A car, esp. an old car. *Some hot-rod use, c1955.*

ken *n.* A house or place of business. *Never common in U.S. underworld.*

kennebecker *n.* Any knapsack or valise. *Logger use. c1890; archaic.*

kennel *n.* **1** A house; a rented room. *Vagabond use.* **2** A freshman dining hall. *Suggested by "dog" = freshman. Not common.*

kennel rations Hash. *Appar. from the name of a brand of dog food + "s." W.W.II Army use. Not common.*

ken-ten *n.* A lamp used to prepare opium for smoking. 1951: "He had rolled the little . . . pill of opium, cooked it on the end of a pin over the little ken-ten lamp made of a sardine tin and put the sizzling, cooked pill in the pipe." S. Longstreet, *The Pedlocks*, 79.

Kentucky oyster *n.* Any of various eatable internal organs of the pig, fried in deep fat and served as a meat course. See **oysters.**

keptie *n.* A woman provided with an apartment and otherwise supported by a man in return for her sexual favors. 1948: "Park Avenue . . . is the place to hole up your 'keptie.'" Lait-Mortimer, *N.Y. Confidential*, 49.

kerflooie, go = **go blooey.**

kerflumixed *adj.* Perplexed; confused. 1950: "All of this has me a bit kerflumixed." Billy Rose, *synd. newsp. col.*, Aug. 2.

kerflummux See **flummox.**

kerseys *n.pl.* Boys' Sunday trousers. *Obs.*

ketchup, in the Operating at a deficit. From **in the red.** 1949: "Ridgway . . . has wound up in the ketchup trying to operate a gym . . . but . . . another man . . . is doing well. . . ." Dan Parker, N.Y. *Daily Mirror*, Sept. 11, 12/1.

kettle *n.* **1** A pocket watch. *Underworld use.* **2** A small railroad locomotive; a switch engine. *Called also "teakettle." Railroad use.*

kettle of fish A predicament or situation, esp. a confused or unsuccessful one. Usu. in "that's a fine kettle of fish" = that situation is a mess, it's a bad predicament.

Kewie *n.* A red-headed woman. *Recorded only by O. O. McIntyre, c1932, who claimed the word was from the "Kew Garden" residential district of New York.*

key down = **quee down.**

keyster = **keister.**

keystone *n.* In baseball, second base.

keystone hit *n.* In baseball, a two-base hit; a double. *Not common. Baseball use.*

keystone sack **keystone cushion** *n.* In baseball, second base.

key-swinger *n.* **1** A college student, graduate, or professor who wears one or more honorary society keys on his watchchain. → **2** A boaster. *Both student use.* See **belly brass.**

kibitz *v.i., v.t.* **1** To give unwanted advice or opinions; specif. to watch a card, chess, checkers, etc., game from behind a player while offering opinions and advice on the plays to be made; to offer advice or opinions to a team, coach, or manager. *Orig. a card-playing term; common since c1935. From Hebrew "kibutzi" = a member of a group.* → **2** To make jokes and humorous comments, often of a critical nature, while another is trying to work, perform, or discuss a serious matter; to joke, to make wisecracks. **—er** *n.* **1** One who kibitzes, esp. at a game, specif. a card game. **2** A joker, a jester, a wisecracker.

kibosh = **put the kibosh on.**

kibosh on [someone or something], put the To put out of action; to squelch, esp. by violent means; to beat up someone; to quash, cancel, or eliminate. 1907: "I was praying that the kid wouldn't come down out of the cab, and put the 'kibosh' on me." J. London, *The Road*, 141. *Since c1850; of Turkish orig.*

kick *v.i.* **1** To complain, protest, object, make a fuss. 1914: "She can just kick all she wants to." Sinclair Lewis, *Our Mr. Wrenn*, 148. *Colloq.* **2** To die; to "kick off." 1945: "Enoch Arden kicked [at the end of the story]." E. Kasser, 132. *Never common.* *v.t.* To jilt a male suitor. 1848: *DAE. Colloq. since c1900. Obs. since c1940.* *n.* **1** A complaint; a protest; an objection. 1893: "The kick came from those who paid over their good money. . . ." Thornton. *Colloq. since c1920.* **2** A pocket, esp. in a pair of pants. 1905: "I have a hundred thousand booboos in the kick." McHugh, *Search Me*, 116. 1939–40: "A little over 300 in my kick." O'Hara, *Pal Joey*, 14. *"Keister" = "kick" = either of the two back pockets in a pair of pants; "breech kick" = either of the two side pockets in a pair of pants; "breast kick" = an inside coat or vest pocket. Mainly pickpocket use.* See **kicks.** **3** A surge of pleasurable emotion; a thrill of enjoyment or excitement; a thrill; excitement. 1951: "It must have hurt him to stretch those raw lips into a grin, but he was having so much fun he couldn't help it. He was having a real kick." Richard S. Prather, *Bodies in Bedlam*, 115. 1953: "Sock cymbal's enough to give me my kicks, man even on the top of a cigar box with a couple of pencils is kicks when you're playing, man." D. Wallop, *Night Light*, 217. *Orig. c1930 jive use. Widely used by jive, jazz, cool, and beat groups.* → **4** Anything that gives one a thrill, excitement, or satisfaction, ranging from violence, narcotics, whisky, and sex through jazz, books, and art to food, dress, and sleep. 1934: " 'That's a kick,' he growled. 'Ridin' a guy down Wilshire in daylight.' " Chandler, *Finger Man*, 95. 1956: "Why did she smoke marijuana? Because it's kicks." S. Longstreet, *The Real Jazz Old and New*, 146. 1956: "What d'you say you and me take a swing at the hunting kick? . . . I mean ducks and geese. Maybe pheasants." John & Ward Hawkins, "The Cowardice of Sam Abbott," *SEP*, Oct. 20, 104. → **5** An intense, personal, usu. temporary, preference, habit, or passion; a fad. 1953: "The Arthur Godfrey . . . [television] show was set against the backdrop of a Paris sidewalk café. Arthur . . . is on the Paris kick." John Crosby, N.Y. *Her. Trib.*, Mar. 11, 25. *Since c1935. Most widely used by jive, jazz, cool, and beat groups.* **6** Power; strength; potency; a high alcoholic content. 1924: "One of those . . . stories with a kick." Marks, *Plastic Age*, 10. *Colloq.* **7** A sergeant. *Army use since c1925.* Cf. **top-kick.** **8** A dishonorable discharge. *Some Army use since c1930.* **—er** *n.* **1** An objector; a complainer. 1888: Thornton. See **kick. 2** A small or outboard engine used to propel a boat. *Since c1930.* **3** Something that provides a big kick or thrill. c1945: "Like the kicker in a julep or two." *Pop. song*, "You Go to My Head." 1950: "The kicker . . . was the station wagon." Starnes, *Another Mug*, 85. **4** The point of a joke; the fallacy in an argument; an item in a group that invalidates, negates, or makes worthless all the others. 1951: "The kicker to this one is simple, but the background is . . . involved. . . ." Gilbert Millstein, N.Y. *Times Mag.*, Apr. 8, 17/2. **5** A revolver. 1950: "I've still got my kicker." Movie, *Vengeance Valley. Not common.* See **joker. —s** *n.pl.* **1** Trousers. *Never common in U.S.* **2** Shoes. 1907: "I took my pick of the . . . kicks. . . ." Jack London, *My Life. Hobo and carnival use until c1935; obs.*

3 Excitement; pleasure; esp. amoral pleasure or excitement. *Wide bop use since c1940; also common cool and beat use.* See **kick.**

kick [something] around   **1** To discuss, consider, or meditate on a topic, proposal, or plan. → **2** To think over something. **3** To try a plan or idea on a small scale. **4** To take advantage of one's superior strength or status in order physically to hurt, verbally abuse or insult, or dominate another; to treat someone harshly or unfairly; to take advantage of someone. 1957: ". . . Someone is always kicking someone around. . . ." Robert Wallace, "Crime in the U.S.," *Life*, Sept. 9, 53. *Colloq.* **5** To go from place to place or from one job to another frequently; to have worldliness gained from a variety of esp. unsuccessful experiences.

kick back   **1** To return, esp. to return stolen goods or money to the owner. 1925: "Stolen goods returned to the rightful owner are 'kicked back.' " McLellan, *Collier's.* **2** To rebate; to pay part of one's wages or profits to another in return for being given a job or an opportunity to profit.   **kickback** **kick-back** *n.* **1** Money returned unethically to a firm, purchasing agent, manager, or buyer by a seller in order to increase sales or gain favors. **2** A rebate; part of one's wages or profits paid to another in return for a job or an opportunity to profit. 1950: ". . . Buying another poor devil's job for $50 or a kick-back from his pay." W. Pegler, *synd. newsp. col.*, July 3. → **3** Money paid for police and political protection. *Underworld use.* Cf. **smear.**

kick in   To contribute money; to pay with others; to pay one's share. 1917: [to contribute] ". . . A request to 'kick in' with a liberty-bond subscription. . . ." *Lit. Digest*, July 21, 29. 1937: [to pay one's share] ". . . To ask you guys to kick in your share of the expenses." Weidman, *Wholesale*, 49. **2** To die.

kick in the ass [taboo]   **1** A surprising or shocking refusal, rejection, or piece of bad news. *Fairly well known to adult males. Fig., that which shocks or hurts as much as receiving an actual, physical kick in the ass.* **2** That which causes one to hurry, become alert, feel enthusiasm or be encouraged.

kick it   **1** To rid oneself of a habit, esp. narcotic addiction. 1949: "Louie had had a big habit—he was one man who could tell you lied if you said no junkie could kick the habit once he was hooked." Nelson Algren, *Man with the Golden Arm*, 78. *Fairly common.* **2** To play jazz, jive, or swing music with enthusiasm.

kick off **1** To die. 1928: ". . . After his wife kicked off." P. G. Gumbinner, *New Yorker*, Nov. 17, 104. **2** To leave, to depart. **3** To begin anything, as a meeting or campaign. *From the football term.*

kickoff *n.* The beginning of anything, as a meeting or campaign.

kick [someone] out **1** To dismiss or expel someone. 1951: "They kicked me out. I wasn't supposed to come after Christmas vacation, on account of I was flunking four subjects and not applying myself and all." J. D. Salinger, *Catcher in the Rye*, 9. **2** To fire someone from a job. *Colloq.* **kick-out** *n.* **1** The act of dismissing. **2** A dishonorable discharge from the armed forces. *W.W.II use.*

kick over To rob; to knock over. 1930: "We kick over the spot." *Amer. Mercury*, Dec., 456. *Racketeer use.*

kicks, for See **kicks.** 1956: "*For kicks* is to get pleasure. . . ." S. Longstreet, *The Real Jazz Old and New*, 149. Cf. **kick.**

kicksie-wicksie **kinxiwinx** *n.* A woman, a wife. 1601: "'That hugges his kicksie-wicksie heare at home." Shakespeare, *All's Well That Ends Well*, II, iii. 1924: "Thus the American term 'kinxiwinx.' . . ." G. H. Bonner, *19th Century*, Dec., 836. *Neither form ever common in U.S.*

kick the bucket To die. *Since c1785. Now widely believed to refer to the last volitional act of one who, standing on an upturned bucket, fixes around his neck a noose suspended from the ceiling. Perh. also a metaphor from the more familiar dairy accident of a cow kicking over the milk pail as the farmer finishes milking her, a serious matter on a one-cow farm. Still other ety. hypotheses are given in OED, "bucket."* 1857: ". . . The gentleman . . . was in . . . a hurry . . . to see his respected uncle kick the bucket." Charles H. Brainard, *Tricks and Traps of New York City*, Part I, 27, Brainard's Dime Books.

kick the gong around **1** To smoke an opium pipe. *Narcotic addict use.* **2** To smoke marijuana. 1956: ". . . It certainly has put a lot of new chords into jazz when you're kicking the gong

around." S. Longstreet, *The Real Jazz Old and New*, 144.

kick-up *n.* **1** A dancing party. *Colloq. since c1775; now archaic and dial.* **2** A disturbance; a commotion.

kick up a fuss To make trouble; cause a disturbance; make a scene. 1930: "I don't want his lawyer to kick up a fuss about this to the commissioner." Lavine, *Third Degree*, 64.

kid *n.* **1** A child of either sex. *Colloq. since c1890.* 1950: "And I was shocked by the way the kids in high school acted." PFC Jim Pasell, quoted by Hal Boyle, AP, July 20. → **2** An offspring; a young son or daughter. 1944: ". . . One of his kids." Ford, *Phila. Murder*, 168. → **3** Any inexperienced young man or young woman. 1949: "A kid [a college freshman] from anywhere immediately feels that he belongs to a great family." Dwight Eisenhower, N.Y. *Times*, Oct. 9, 50/3. → **4** A young athlete. **5** A bomber co-pilot. *W.W.II Army Air Corps use.* **6** Humbug, kidding, a prank. 1929: "That's no kid, neither." Dunning and Abbott, *Broadway*, I. See **candy kid.** *adj.* **1** Immature; innocent. **2** Younger, as used in "kid brother," "kid sister." *v.t.* To josh a person; to deceive; to make fun of a person in his presence. 1914: [to make fun of] "Quit your kidding the little man." S. Lewis, *Our Mr. Wrenn*, 53. 1922: [to deceive] "What yuh tryin' to do, kid me . . . ?" O'Neill, *Hairy Ape*, 4. *Colloq. since c1900.* *v.i.* To speak in fun; to josh, banter, or joke. 1920: "Kerry was only kidding. . . ." Fitzgerald, *This Side of Paradise*, 82. **—der** *n.* One who kids. **—ding** *n.* Joshing; joking; bantering; facetious taunting. Often in "no kidding." Cf. **kid.** 1914: "Mr. Wrenn . . . wasn't going to stand for no kidding from nobody. . . ." S. Lewis, *Our Mr. Wrenn*, 197. **—do** **Kiddo** *n.* **1** A child or youth of either sex. 1951: "It's perfectly normal in kiddos/ For little girls to be deadlier than Black Widows." Phyllis McGinley, *The New Yorker*, Feb. 24, 32. *Since c1910.* **2** A person, usu. in direct address. 1922: "Hello, Kiddo." O'Neill, *Hairy Ape*, 5. 1951: "Just pull your head inside . . . kiddo." Walt Kelly, "Pogo," *synd. comic strip*, Oct. 20. *Familiar and jocular use.* See Appendix, —o ending. **—die** **—dy** *n.* A child. 1914: "When you're a kiddy. . . ." S. Lewis, *Our Mr. Wrenn*, 85. 1938: "The kiddies and the little woman." W. Pegler, quoted in *Better English*, Jan., 58/2. See Appendix, —ie ending.

Kid, the   *n.* The co-pilot of an airplane. *Orig. Air Force use.*

kidney-buster   *n.* 1 A horse that is hard to ride. *Obs.* 2 Any physically hard job or sport. 3 A rough road; a hard-riding truck or bus. *Truck and bus driver use.*

kid show   A circus sideshow. *Circus use.*

kid stuff   Anything childish or immature; that which presents no challenge to or interest for an intelligent adult.

kid top   The sideshow tent. *Circus use.*

kiester = **keister.**

kife   *v.t.* 1 To swindle. *Circus use.* 2 To steal.

kike   **Kike** [derog].   *n.* 1 A Jew. 1924: "You go chasing around with kikes and micks." Marks, *Plastic Age*, 201. 2 Specif. an uncouth Jewish merchant. *adj.* Jewish; unassimilated Jewish gestures and speech mannerisms.

kike-killer   *n.* A billy club; a kind of bludgeon.

kill   *v.t.* 1 To drink or eat all of any specified amount of liquor or food. 1833: "I can kill more lickur...." *Sketches of Col. David Crockett.* 1887: "The lady... killed a dozen [oysters]...." *Lantern*, New Orleans. → 2 To drink or eat the last portion. 1956: "There's just one drink left, kill it; I don't want any gin in the house." *Oral.* 3 To ruin; to ruin one's chances of success; to become disillusioned or hopeless about something; to defeat someone or something. 1941: "...[In a race] pace in the pinches is what cops or kills [a horse]." J. Lilienthal, *Horse Crazy*, 19. 4 To entertain an audience well; to make an extremely favorable impression on a person or audience. 5 To extinguish a fire, esp. a cigarette. 1942: "She killed her cigarette in Morny's copper goldfish bowl...." Chandler, *High Window*, 117. *n.* 1 A murder. 1934: "They might... indict... Tinnen for the Shannon kill. ..." Chandler, *Finger Man*, 3. 2 An enemy plane shot down; an enemy ship sunk. *Air Force and USN use, esp. submarine, use during W.W.II.*

killer   *n.* 1 A very well-dressed or charming person. → 2 A lady's man; a ladykiller. 3 A honey; a lulu. → 4 That which gives one a feeling of exhilaration. → 5 Specif. a marijuana cigarette.

killer-diller   *n.* Any remarkable, attractive, or thrilling person or thing; a humdinger. 1938: "The famed quartet of musicians which steams out 'killer-dillers.' ..." *Advt., New Yorker*, Jan. 8, 34. 1938: "He hears Benny Goodman announce his next radio number as a 'killer-diller.' ..." *Life*, Aug. 8, 56. 1956: "... A good thing is a *killer-diller*." S. Longstreet, *The Real Jazz Old and New*, 150. *Orig. jive and swing group use. Now considered outmoded.*

killjoy   *n.* A gloomy person; one whose actions or remarks deprive others of pleasure; a pessimist. *Colloq. A wet blanket may decrease the pleasure of others by being dull, timorous, or pessimistic; a killjoy may do so consciously or deliberately, for logical, official, or moral reasons.*

killout   *n.* Any thing or person that is remarkable or gives one a feeling of exhilaration; a kicker. *Negro use.*

Kilroy   A nonentity; a sad sack. *Not common. Obs. Sometimes used with no specif. meaning. From the pop. fad phrase, now obs., "Kilroy was here," scribbled on almost all lavatory walls and fences during c1940 and the early part of W.W.II. Although wide use immediately before the U.S. entered W.W.II, the phrase came to mean "the U.S. Army, or a soldier, was here"—this could be applied to an occupied town in enemy territory or to a bar in the U.S. It then came to mean an inconsequential person.*

kimona   **kimono**   *n.* A coffin. *From* **wooden kimono.** *Not common.*

kinch   **kinchen**   **kinchin**   *n.* A child. Cf. **ginch** = a girl.

kind   *n.* A large amount or quantity; used only in "that [or 'the'] kind of money." 1952: "The lack of a few billion dollars.... Uncle Sam, the only guy around with that kind of money, is still investing it in jet bombers...." Hal Boyle, AP, Dec. 12.

king   *n.* 1 The leader; the top-ranking person. Specif., the warden of a prison. *Underworld use.* 2 Specif., a yardmaster or freight conductor. *Railroad use.*

— king   See Appendix, Suffixes and Suffix Words.

King Kong   **king kong**   Strong, cheap whisky or wine. 1956: "King Kong is... cheap alcohol...." S. Longstreet, *The Real Jazz Old and New*, 148. *From the fictional ape "King Kong" of huge size and tremendous strength.*

king pin   The highest ranking person in a group; the leader. *Colloq.*

kings   *n.* A pack of king-sized cigarettes. *Colloq.*

King's English, the English as spoken and written by educated, knowledgeable people; lit. the English language as spoken by the educated upper class of Great Britain. 1954: "You could tell he was a real country boy by the way he murdered the King's English!" Louis Armstrong, *Satchmo, My Life in New Orleans*, 44.

king-size *adj.* Big; exceptionally long. *A term popularized c1940 in ads for extra-long cigarettes.* 1950: "The new king-sized rockets stopped three Red tanks." AP, Tokyo, July 21. *Pop. post-W.W.II.*

king snipe *n.* The foreman of a railroad section gang; the boss of a track-laying crew. *Hobo, logger, and railroad use.*

kinker *n.* Any circus performer. *Orig. an acrobat only. From the contortions of limbs while performing. Circus talk.*

kinky *adj.* **1** Crooked; unfair. 1954: " 'Kinky' gambling paraphernalia . . . dice and cards and roulette wheels that gave the house an unfair advantage." W. R. & F. K. Simpson, *Hockshop*, 275f. Cf. **straight. 2** Stolen. *n.* Anything stolen, usu. a stolen automobile. Suggested by "bent" = stolen.

kinky-head [derog.] *n.* A Negro.

kinneta *n.* The posterior. *Not common.*

kinxiwinx = kicksie-wicksie.

kip *n.* **1** A bed. 1939–40: ". . . In the kip. . . ." O'Hara, *Pal Joey*, 62. *Mainly underworld and vagabond use.* **2** Sleep; a sleep. *W.W.I use only, never common with any group in the U.S.* **3** A nightwatchman; a watchman. *Underworld use.* *v.i.* To sleep; to go to bed. 1907: "Then it was up to me to hunt for a place to 'kip.' 'Kip,' 'doss,' 'flop,' 'pound your ear,' all mean . . . to sleep." Jack London, *My Life. Still current hobo use.*

kip, hit the = **hit the hay.** *Obs. underworld use.* See **kip.**

kipe *v.t.* To steal, usu. something of small value.

kippy *adj.* Chic; striking; attractive; of first quality. *Archaic and dial.*

kiss = **kiss-off.** See **butterfly kiss, Hollywood kiss, New York kiss.**

kisser *n.* **1** The mouth. 1932: ". . . And wads a handkerchief into his kisser in case the guy comes to. . . ." Runyon. **2** The jaw. **3** The human face. 1941: "I do nothing but show the good side of my kisser all the time." John O'Hara, *New Yorker*, Nov. 15, 26. 1956: "You're Conn McCreary, a fat runt with a kisser like a cherub with a hangover." Jimmy Cannon, *Who Struck John?* 228. *Orig., c1850, meant mouth, by c1890 also meant the jaw or the face. Often used ambiguously so that it is impossible to distinguish if mouth, jaw, chin, cheek, or entire face is meant.*

kiss [something] goodbye To dismiss or get rid of something; to realize that something is lost or ruined. *Colloq.*

kissing cousin 1 A constant companion or friend, of the same or of the opposite sex, who is granted the same intimacy accorded blood relations. 1951: [same sex] "You guys talk like kissing cousins." Movie, *The Tanks Are Coming.* → **2** Specif., a close platonic friend of the opposite sex. → **3** Humorously, a member of the opposite sex with whom one is sexually familiar when the parties involved believe their intimacy is unknown. *Orig. the term implied blood relationship and still does when used in Southern hill dial. In the South during the Civil War, kissing cousins were relatives who had the same political views.* **4** A facsimile, someone or something closely resembling someone or something else. 1946: "A few weeks' growth [of beard], squared off to the edges of [Clifton James's] upper lip, and he had a kissing cousin of [General Montgomery's] mustache." J. Alvin Kugelmass, *This Week Mag.*, Dec. 21, 11/3. See **kissing-kin.**

kissing-kin *adj.* Matching; harmonious; made of the same fabric. **kissing kin** *n.* Those items that match; harmonious people.

kiss off 1 To dismiss or get rid of something or someone, often rudely and curtly. **2** To dodge; to evade. 1948: "The man who . . . had kissed off all raps except . . . the one . . . for income tax evasion." Evans, *Halo for Satan*, 66. **3** To kill. 1946: "He wants to know who kissed off Marlin. . . ." Evans, *Halo in Blood*, 120. **kiss-off** *n.* **1** Death. **2** A dismissal; a brush-off; the end; notice of dismissal from a job, esp. without warning. *In New York often called "the California kiss-off"; in Los Angeles often called "the New York kiss-off." Mainly advt., movie, television, and radio use.*

kiss out To be denied or cheated out of one's share of the loot or profits. 1925: "When a member of a mob is deprived of his share [of loot] he is 'kissed out.' " McLellan, *Collier's.*

kiss the canvas   kiss the resin   In prize fighting, to be knocked down or out.

kiss the dust   To die. *Colloq.*

kiss the resin = **kiss the canvas.**

kister = **keister.**

kit and boodle   *n.* The entire lot of people or things. 1931: "The whole kit and boodle of 'em wore the . . . uniform." Queen, *Dutch Shoe*, 220. *Obs. in favor of the later "kit and caboodle."*

kit and caboodle = **kit and boodle.** 1923: "I am . . . a man . . . who believes that . . . happiness . . . comes from doing one's job . . . well . . . and from letting the rest—the whole kit and caboodle— go hang." George Jean Nathan, re-printed from "The World in Falseface," in *The American Twenties*, 366. *Modern form of "kit and boodle."*

kitchen   *n.* **1** The caboose of a railroad train; the cab of a locomotive. *Railroad use.* **2** The stomach. *Hobo use. Not common.* See **clean [up] the kitchen.**

kitchen sweat   A dance; dancing party. *Logger and rural use.*

kitchy-koo   kitchy-kitchy-koo = **hitchy-koo.**

kite   *n.* **1** A note or letter, esp. a smuggled one. *Underworld use.* Cf. **fly a kite. 2** An airplane. *W.W.II Air Force use.* 1958: ". . . [He] must soon risk his . . . neck as your navigator in one of those kites." "Terry and the Pirates," *synd. newsp. comic strip*, Feb. 9.   **—d** *adj.* Intoxicated. *Not common.* See **higher than a kite.**

kittens, have   kittens, have a litter of To give violent expression to one's emotions, usu. anger, anxiety, fear, or excitement, occas. laughter or surprise; to throw a fit, blow one's top, or have pups. 1950: "I'll bet . . . Baggerly had a nice litter of kittens when he found me. . . ." Starnes, *And When She Was Bad*, 50.

kittle-cattle   *n.* An unreliable, unde-pendable person or group of people. 1949: "For women are kittle-cattle and nobody knows which way they are going to jump in any emergency." Dorothy Dix, Phila. *Bulletin*, Mar. 29, 42/5.

kitty   *n.* Fig., a pot or pool of money, made up of contributions from several people; the total amount of money so available. *Orig. used in the card game of poker = the money bet.*

kiwi   *n.* An air force man, esp. an officer who cannot, does not, or does not like to fly. *From the name of the flightless bird, the kiwi.*

ki-yi   *n.* **1** A dog. *Obs.* **2** A scrubbing brush. *A little W.W.II USN use.*

klooch   *n.* A woman. 1907: "I've sent my klooch to town." R. W. Service. *From Chinook jargon. Logger use.*

kluck   See **cluck, dumbcluck.**

klupper   *n.* A slow worker; a slow-moving, slow-talking or slow-thinking person. 1956: "Garment workers . . . are . . . distrustful of . . . kluppers—slow, inferior, inefficient workers." *Labor's Special Language from Many Sources. From Yiddish sl.: "klupper" with same meaning, from stand. Yiddish "klupper" = one who pounds a slow steady pace.*

knee-bender   *n.* A church-goer; a self-righteous person. *Underworld and hobo use.*

knee-high to a (mosquito, frog, bum-ble-bee, toad, splinter, grasshopper, hoptoad, toadfrog, duck)   Hyper-bolically, very short in stature because of youth. Usually in the context, "I knew you when you were just knee-high to a . . ." The date for each cit. below is the earliest from the *DAE*: 1824 . . . to a mos-quito; 1833 . . . to a frog; . . . to a bumbly-bee; 1840 . . . to a toad; 1841 . . . to a splinter; 1856 . . . to a grasshopper; 1880 . . . to a hoptoad; 1893 . . . to a toadfrog; 1904 . . . to a duck. *"Knee-high to a grasshopper" is now the most common.*

kneesies   *n.* Under-the-table amorous play in which one touches, rubs, or bumps with one's knees the knees of a person of the opposite sex, as a sweet-heart. 1951: "We got back to the table and played kneesies while we talked. . . ." Spillane, *Big Kill*, 77.

knob   *n.* A person's head.   **—by** = **nobby.**

knock   *n.* **1** Adverse criticism; a grudge. 1952: "Somebody writes . . . that I have always got the knock in on vegetarians." Robert C. Ruark, *synd. newsp. col.*, June 19. **2** An annoyance; a disadvantage. 1932: ". . . It is a big knock to the Clancy family to have . . . Jule hanging around." Runyon. **3** A prison sentence. *Underworld use. Not common.* **4** = **kick.** 1957: ". . . [Singers] love to sing so much that they get their knocks that way." Pete Martin, "I Call on Julie London," *SEP*, Aug. 17, 60. *Not common.*   *v.i.* **1** To find fault; to give bad publicity. **2** To talk; to discuss. *v.t.* **1** To borrow; to lend; to ask or beg. *Negro use.* **2** To give. *c1950, popular song,* "Knock Me a Kiss." **3** To find fault with; to give bad publicity to.

knock a nod   To take a nap.

knock around   To idle or loaf.

knock back   To drink a glass of whisky in one gulp. 1952: "The Colonel got his drink, and after he had knocked it back with one swift motion, he began to feel better." A. J. Liebling, *New Yorker*, Sept. 27, 61.

knock [someone's] block off   To hit someone very hard; to knock someone unconscious; to give someone a severe physical beating. *Usu. used in the boasting threat, "I'll knock your block off."*

knockdown   *n.* **1** An introduction to a person, job, fact, or concept. 1937: [to a fact] "You want a knockdown to something?" Weidman, *Wholesale*, 96. → **2** An invitation. **3** Something of the highest excellence. **4** Store money stolen from a retail sale by an employee, esp. small sums taken from the cash register; specif. small sums collected from customers but never put into the cash register; graft. 1938 [c1890]: "Most bartenders . . . considered the 'knockdown' a perfectly legitimate source of profit. . . ." E. A. Powell, *Atlantic Monthly*, Aug., 219/1.   **knock down** *v.t.* **1** To introduce. **2** To keep money received or collected for one's employer. 1949: ". . . Some . . . clerk who was knocking down on the till." J. Evans, *Halo*, 161. *Since c1865.* **3** To earn; esp. to earn a salary, a grade in school, or a compliment. 1949: [to earn a salary] ". . . Hommuch he knock down a week?" A. Kober, *New Yorker*, Nov. 5, 86. **4** For a salesman to take a customer out of turn; to take another salesman's customer. *Retail store use.* **5** To reduce the price. *Colloq.* **6** To criticize or belittle someone. **7** To drink; to kill. 1952: "I am proud of the fact that I have knocked down one quart of Scotch whisky every day for the last 24 years." Letter to editor, N.Y. *Her. Trib.*, May 31, 10/7.

knock-down-drag-out fight   knock-down, drag-out fight   *n.* A hard vicious action-filled fight. 1945: "Moe Bell Jackson's husband/Whipped her good last night./Her landlady told my ma they had/A knock-down-drag-out fight./" Gwendolyn Brooks, *A Street in Bronzeville*, 37.

knocked, have it   To have a specific situation under control; to be succeeding or winning at something. 1954: "[A jet pilot who has crashed into the sea off the Korean coast during the Korean War]: You're cold and wet . . . then you see [the helicopter coming to make a rescue] . . . and you know you've got it knocked." Movie, *The Bridges at Tokori.*

knocked out   **1** Drunk. **2** Tired, exhausted. **3** Emotionally exhausted. Cf. **knock [oneself] out, pepped out, bushed, beat.**

knocker   *n.* **1** A detractor; a fault-finder. 1898: "That pack of knockers and snapping curs that have been howling . . . at *The Billboard. . . ." The Billboard.* **2** A beautiful, handsome, or remarkable person; a knockout. *Archaic.* See **apple-knocker.**   **—s**   *n.pl.* [taboo] Female breasts; usu. the well-shaped breasts of an attractive girl. *Although an old term, very common since c1940.*

knock [someone] for a loop   Also but much less freq.: **knock [someone] for a goal (gool),   . . . for a row,   . . . for a row of ashcans,   . . . for a row of milk cans,   . . . for a row of G.I. cans,   . . . for a row of naughts,   . . . for a row of Chinese pagodas,   . . . for a row of tall red totem poles,   . . . for a row of Academy Awards . . .** for a row of practically anything that is well known and usu. upright. **1** Lit., and fig. to strike a person a terrific blow, as with the fist; to knock someone out; to make someone unconscious or drunk, said of a strong drink. 1921: "We . . . knocked the villain for a row of ash cans. . . . You knock the champ for a row of milk cans. . . ." Witwer, *Leather*, 116, 130. 1926: "I'll knock you for a row of G.I. cans." Stallings & Anderson, *What Price Glory*, III. 1929–30: "You certainly knocked him for a row of tall red totem poles." K. Brush, *Young Man*, 68. 1930: "This beer knocks you for a loop." *Amer. Mercury*, Dec., 456. 1944: "This is the type [of murder mystery] that is guaranteed to knock the keenest mind for a loop." Raymond Chandler, *Simple Art of Murder*, 145. **2** Fig., to make a strong, favorable impression on someone. 1930: "Wouldn't that knock the boys for a row or two!" J. T. Farrell, 138. 1941: "I know we're going to knock them for a row of Academy Awards." Schulberg, *Sammy*, 243. **3** To pass a test, perform, or succeed in a spectacular way. 1924: "Would he hit Math I [test] in the eye? He'd knock it for a goal." Marks, *Plastic Age*, 36.

knock in on [someone], have the   To

be eager to criticize or reprimand someone; to bear malice against someone. *Associated with underworld use; not common.*

knock it   An order or request to stop instantly. *From "knock it off."*

knock it off   An order, command, or entreaty to stop doing something immediately, esp. talking or joking; fig., an order to knock off a smile or laugh from one's face, pay attention and become serious. 1951: "Knock it off. I've got no argument with you. . . . Forget it. We apologize." Richard S. Prather, *Bodies in Bedlam*, 12. *Orig. W.W.II Army use. Based on "wipe it off."*

knock off   **1** To stop work at the end of the day or to eat lunch; to take a holiday or brief rest period from work. *Since c1850.* **2** To stop immediately whatever one is doing, esp. to stop talking, teasing, or kidding, often said as a command, order, or entreaty. 1926: "Knock off that chat." Stallings & Anderson, *What Price Glory*, I. *W.W.I and II Armed Forces use.* **3** To produce, esp. by craftsmanship, writing, painting, composing, performing, or the like. 1886: "He [a composer] knocked off a few stanzas. . . ." *Lantern*, New Orleans. 1939–40: "Well at last I am getting around to knocking off a line or two to let you know. . . ." O'Hara, *Pal Joey*, 3. 1945: "After the band had knocked off a couple of rumbas. . . ." Mitchell, *McSorley's*, 170. → **4** To finish, as food, drink, or work. 1951: "After knocking off a glass of . . . wine, he topples over. . . ." John McCarten, *The New Yorker*, Dec. 1, 155. **5** To delete, deduct, or eliminate, as in shortening or editing. *Colloq.* **6** To kill; to murder. 1923: "We're goin' t' knock off [hang] three of 'em. . . ." C. MacArthur, *Rope*, 183. 1930: "The dissenter . . . will be sent to a lonely spot and knocked off. . . . When the latter is handed a rod . . . and told to 'knock off' so-and-so. . . ." Lavine, *Third Degree*, 26, 27. → **7** To die. 1944: "There . . . waiting for me to knock off was Maloney!" John Barrymore. **8** To raid, as by police, to raid and confiscate; to arrest. 1930: "The feds knock off the scatter." *Amer. Mercury*, Dec., 456. 1950: "Local cops in New York City had free authority to knock them off." W. Pegler, *synd. newsp. col.*, Apr. 17. **9** To steal or rob; to steal or rob from. 1951: "As 'messenger boy bandits' . . . the pair knocked off several shops, a bank, and jewelry stores." AP, N.Y.,

Aug. 11. → **10** To defeat or to best another, esp. in sports. **11** To leave or depart. → **12** To hurry.

knock [oneself] out   **1** To elicit enthusiasm or an emotional response, esp. deep sympathy or laughter. 1951: "I read a lot of war books and mysteries and all, but they don't knock me out too much. What really knocks me out is a book that, when you're done reading it, you wish the author that wrote it was a terrific friend of yours and you could call him up on the phone whenever you felt like it." J. D. Salinger, *Catcher in the Rye*, 19. **2** To work excessively hard or to exhaustion. 1951: "They like 'knocking themselves out' for *Variety*." A. Green, *Show Biz*, xxi. **3** To have a good time; to exhaust oneself laughing, dancing, or the like.

knockout   **knock-out**   *n.* **1** An attractive person or thing, a handsome or beautiful person or thing. 1936–1954: "Without that smock you're always wearing, and in these clothes—saaay, you know, you're a knockout!" Jerome Weidman, *I Knew What I Was Doing*, reprinted in *Manhattan*, ed. by S. Krim, 3. **2** An attractive item of merchandise. **3** Any calamity. 1901: "A calamity may be called . . . 'a knock-out' by the amateur of pugilism." Greenough & Kittredge, iii. *Obs.*   *adj.* First-rate. 1929–30: "That was a knockout plot for a fiction story." K. Brush, *Young Man*, 29.

knock out   **1** To create; to finish a task quickly and professionally; as to write a story, type a letter, or paint a picture. 1941: "I haven't got time to knock the script out myself. . . ." Schulberg, *Sammy*, 117, 123. **2** To clean a room. *Negro use; not common.*

knockout drops   Chloral hydrate or some other drug put into a drink, usu. of whisky, to render the drinker unconscious. *Since c1900.*

knock over   **1** To rob a place, a bank, a store, or the like. 1949: "A man experienced in knocking over banks. . . ." A. Hynd, *Public Enemies*, 80. **2** To raid a place, as by the police; to arrest a person. 1951: "Assistant Chief Inspector . . . Kennedy and 11 members of his confidential squad . . . knocked over a reputed \$25,000-a-day bookmaking parlor." John Martin in N.Y. *Daily News*, Aug. 30, C4. **3** To eat or drink; to dispose of by consuming. 1921: "I step around to his oasis and knock over a powder with him. . . ." Witwer, *Leather*, 82.

knock-over   *n.* A robbery.

knock (lay) them in the aisles *Lit.* and *fig.*, to overwhelm an audience with one's talent; *specif.*, to entertain an audience with truly hilarious humor.

knock the pad = **hit the pad.**

knock together To cook; to prepare [food] by cooking. 1941: "Did you . . . mean . . . what you said about knocking something together that we could eat?" Cain, *M. Pierce*, 27. *Colloq.*

knock up **1** To prepare or to serve food. *Colloq. c1870; now archaic.* **2** To wake a person up. *Colloq.; archaic in U.S., though still used in Eng.* **3** To earn; to knock down. *Not common.* **4** [taboo] To make pregnant. *Since c1920 the most common term for "impregnate."*

knocked up **knocked-up** *adj.* Pregnant.

knothead *n.* An incompetent or stupid person. 1951: "Look at Petey—a knothead. . . ." M. Shulman, *Dobie Gillis*, 61.

knots, hit the To snore; to sleep. *Not common.*

know For phrases beginning with "know," see under principal word of phrase.

know-how *n.* Skill; practical information; knowledge of how something is done or made or operates. *Colloq.*

know-it-all *n.* A smart aleck; a person who claims sophistication and knowledge of many things.

knowledge-box *n.* **1** A schoolhouse, usu. a rural schoolhouse. *Vagabond use.* **2** A railroad yard-master's office. *Railroad use.* **3** The head. *None of the meanings is common.*

know [one's] onions **know [one's] stuff** **know [one's] business** Also less freq.: **know [one's] oil,** . . . **oats,** . . . **goulash,** . . . **bananas,** . . . **beans,** . . . **goods,** . . . **groceries,** . . . **fruit** To be competent, capable, or qualified in one's business or field of endeavor. 1922: "Mr. Roberts knows his onions, all right." A. L. Bass. 1929: "You know your goulash." Dunning & Abbott, *Broadway*, II.

know what to do with [something] **know where to put [something]** **know where to shove [something]** **know where to stick [something]** [taboo] = **stick it.** *All euphemisms.*

knuck *v.i.* To pick pockets. *Underworld use; obs.* *n.* A thief, esp. a pickpocket. *Underworld use since c1850.* **—er** *and* **—sman** *n.* A pickpocket.

knuckle *n.* **1** The head. 1943: "One clonk on the knuckle. . . ." Stinson, *SEP.* **2** Muscle; stupidity. 1950: "He's got nothin' upstairs but solid knuckle." *Asphalt Jungle*, movie.

knuckle-buster *n.* A crescent wrench.

knuckle-down *n.* In playing marbles, the standard way of shooting in which the knuckles are kept down. 1949: "Any kid who knows a heist-shot [in marbles] from a knuckle-down can tell you. . . ." Billy Rose, *synd. newsp. col.*, Aug. 1.

knuckle down To concentrate, become serious in one's attitude, and work hard.

knuckle-duster *n.* **1** One who fights well, frequently, with enthusiasm, or unfairly. 1957: ". . . He showed up with his head in a cast saying, [George] Raft's a knuckle-duster and I'm going to have him work you over." George Raft, as told to Dean Jennings, "Out of My Past," *SEP*, Sept. 21, 96. *Archaic.* **2** In baseball, a pitched ball at the height of, or pitched close to, a batter's knuckles.

knucklehead **knuckle-head** *n.* A slow-thinking or stupid person. *Cf.* **knuckle.** 1944: "You knuckle-heads . . ." *Marine Raiders*, movie. 1950: ". . . Movies are made by unappreciative knuckleheads." Pete Martin, *SEP*, Apr. 1, 100. *Common, but most popular in Marine Corps and USN.*

knuckler *n.* In baseball, a ball thrown from the knuckles rather than from the finger tips. 1951: "The Giants came up . . . hoping . . . to break through Leonard's tantalizing knucklers." Louis Effrat, N.Y. *Times*, Aug. 28, 26/1.

knucks *n.pl.* Brass knuckles. 1950: "The 'knucks' were hidden in the keel of one [hunting boot]." AP, N.Y., July 13.

K.O. *n.* In boxing, a knockout. See Appendix, Shortened Words. *v.t.* In boxing, to knock out one's opponent. *adj.* **1** Knockout, as in "It was a K.O. punch." **2** = **O.K.**

kong *n.* Whisky, esp. cheap or bootleg whisky. *Negro use.*

kook *n.* An odd, eccentric, disliked person; a "drip"; a nut. *Teenage use since 1958; rapidly becoming a pop. fad word* **—y** *adj.* Crazy, nuts; odd, eccentric; having the attributes of a "drip."

kopasetic **kopesetic** **kopasetec** **kopesetec** = **copacetic.**

kosh = **cosh.**

kosher **Kosher** *adj.* Honest; authentic; valid; ethical; fulfilling the minimum requirements of honesty or ethics. 1957: "In order for the Los Angeles authorities to make everything just Kosher by meeting the federal requiremen*s. . . ." Dick Young, "Young Ideas," N.Y. *Daily News*, Sept. 25, 59. *From "kosher" = clean and acceptable, according to Jewish dietary laws. The word has been taken from Hebrew to Yiddish to Eng.*

kraut   Kraut   n. 1 [derog.] A German; esp. a German soldier. 1945: "*The Stars and Stripes* . . . published notification of its intention to use 'Kraut' because it gave less dignity to the enemy. The word was thereafter popular in print, but was not generally used by the soldiers." I. R. Blacker in *Sat. Rev. Lit.*, Nov. 24, 14/2. 1949: "Them Krauts was scared of you, Frankie . . . you were a big man in the army." Nelson Algren, *Man with the Golden Arm*, 30. *Common in both W.W.I and W.W.II but more common in W.W.I. From the idea that Germans invented and eat a lot of sauerkraut.* **2** Any mean or grouchy person. *Not common.*

krauthead [derog.]   n.   A German soldier. *W.W.II Army use.*

Kriegie   n. An American prisoner of war in a German prisoner of war camp. 1948: "Kriegie Talk," title of article, H. Homer Aschmann, *AS*, Oct.–Dec., 217. *Used by Amer. Army and Air Force prisoners of war in W.W.II. From Ger. "krieg" = war + "-ie" ending.*

kyuter = cuter.

L

lab   n. A laboratory; a building or a room that is or contains a laboratory; a period of work done in a laboratory; also used attrib. *Very common. Orig. student use.*

labonza   n. 1 The posterior. 1943: "The day's losses—$39,374! Quite a kick in the labonza." **2** The pit of the stomach. *Now the most common use. Pop. c1955 by television comedian Jackie Gleason.*

lace [one's] boots   To put [someone] wise.

lace-curtain   adj. Well-to-do; prosperous; decent; secure. 1947: "Those [Irish] who have done rather better and become lace-curtain Irish . . . moved across the tracks and into the lace-curtain class. . . ." A. E. Hutson. 1951: "An Irish family, oh, no . . . lace-curtain Irish. Rich, well-brought-up family. Rigid Catholics, of course." S. Longstreet, *The Pedlocks*, 153.

lacy   adj. Effeminate; of or pert. to a homosexual.

la(h)-de-da(h)   la(h)-di-da   la(h) de da(h)   la(h) di dah   n. A sissy; a fancy pants. 1928: "Some lah de dah with a cane!" Hecht & MacArthur, *Front Page*, II.   adj. Sissified; affected. 1948: "Lunch place of the la-de-dah literary set." Lait-Mortimer, *N.Y. Confidential*, 168.

ladies' man   lady's man   A male of any age who is charming and courtly to, and grooms himself to please, the ladies; one who pursues women politely and with success.

lady   n. In direct address, a woman who has aroused the speaker's ill will, often expressed by sarcasm or insult. 1948: "Whenever a spoken sentence begins with 'Lady,' . . . you may be sure the rest of the sentence is sarcastic or downright insulting." John McNulty, *PM*, June 10, 13. *N.Y. City use.* See **old lady.**

lady-killer   n. A ladies' man. 1934: "Slang." *Web.* 1941: "Mark always was a lady-killer, a chaser." A. R. Hilliard, *Justice Be Damned*, 81.

lag   v.i., v.t. To hang. *c1850; obs.*   n. **1** Imprisonment. **2** A convict; an ex-convict. 1932: "Lags who escape from the country pokey." D. Runyon. **3** A criminal. *Underworld use.*   **—ger   n.** A convict; esp. an ex-convict out on parole.

lagniappe   n. Lit., something given for nothing; an extra; a dividend, a tip. 1954: "I hit her with a few real hard ones for lagniappe (or good measure), which is what we kids called the tokens of thanks the grocer gave us when we went there to pay the bill for our parents. We would get animal crackers or almost anything that did not cost very much for lagniappe, and the grocer who gave the most lagniappe would get the most trade from us kids." L. Armstrong, *Satchmo, My Life in New Orleans*, 178. *A Creole usage.*

laid out   Intoxicated. See **lay [someone] out.** 1929: *Am. Sp.*

laid, relaid, and parlayed [taboo] **1** To experience something thoroughly; to dispense with all, esp. sexual, restrictions and enjoy oneself thoroughly. *From past tense of "lay," not common.*

Cf. **screwed, blewed, and tattooed.** **2** Completely deceived, cheated or taken advantage of. *The most common use. See Appendix, Sex and Deceit, and Rhyming Slang.*

Lake, the *prop.n.* Salt Lake City, Utah. *Hobo use; never common.*

la-la *n.* **1** A male sweetheart; an attractive person. 1886: "To find their la-la's...." New Orleans *Lantern. Obs.* **2** A brash, impertinent, but sympathetic person. *Usu. in "He's some la-la."*

lallygag *v.* = **lollygag.**

lam *v.i.* **1** To come or go; usu. to depart quickly; to run away, escape. 1921: "I...lammed for Cleveland." Witwer, *Leather*, 4. 1928: "...To lam right over here." Hecht & Mac-Arthur, *Front Page*, II. **2** Specif., to elude the police. *Underworld use.* Cf. **on the lam.** **3** To leave a hotel, restaurant, night club, or the like without paying the bill. *Not common.* *v.t.* **1** To escape prison. **2** To strike or hit; to lambaste. **—baste** **lambast** *v.t.* **1** To strike; to beat up. *Colloq. since c1880. Now somewhat archaic.* **2** To attack verbally and with vehemence; to chide severely. 1952: "A woman psychologist today lambasted the idea that 'mom is to blame' for all of a child's troubles...." A. L. Blakeslee, AP, Dec. 29. **—ster** **lammister** *n.* An escaped convict; a fugitive from the law; one who is on the lam; one who has departed after posting bail. 1932: "Louie is a lammister out of Detroit." Runyon.

lam, on the **1** In flight from the police; to be a fugitive from the law. 1928: "So I went—on the lam." D. Purroy, "On the Lam," *Amer. Mercury*, 14, 475. 1949: "To offer asylum to bandits on the lam." A. Hynd, 43. *Underworld use since c1925; see* **lam.** → **2** On the move; traveling. 1937: "The girl...'took it on the lam.'" *Atlantic Monthly*, Dec., 454/2.

lamb *n.* **1** One easily fooled, tricked, or cheated; a sucker; a mark. **2** = **lambie.** **—ie** **lambie-pie** *n.* A term of endearment; a sweetheart.

lame-brain *n.* A stupid person. *Colloq.* **—ed** *adj.* Stupid. *Colloq.*

lame duck **1** A holder of public office who is finishing his term but has not been re-elected. *Since he will soon be out of office, his authority is somewhat impaired; thus he is "lame." Stand. polit. use.* → **2** One who cannot assume his share of responsibility; a weakling; an inefficient person. **3** A stock market speculator who has overbought; one who has taken options on stocks that he cannot afford to buy.

lame duck bill (amendment) (law) A bill, amendment, or law initiated by a lame duck legislator or legislature; a bill, amendment, or law that has little chance of being approved by a legislature or of being enforced if approved; a weak bill, amendment, or law.

lamp *n.* **1** An eye. *Not common.* 1924: "I'm going to have to get a beefsteak...for this lamp of mine." Marks, *Plastic Age*, 61. **2** A look. 1929: "Let's take a lamp at him." Dunning & Abbott, *Broadway*, III. *v.t.* To look at someone or something; to look over. 1913: "[to look over] Lamp the lad in blue." F. K. Sechrist. 1924: "[to look at] Carl handed him the cards. 'Lamp those,' he said...." Marks, *Plastic Age*, 127ff. **—s** *n.pl.* The eyes. 1926: "Turn your lamps on the dame." Schwesinger in *Jour. of Applied Psych.*, 260.

landsman *n.* A countryman, a compatriot. *From the Yiddish.*

lane *n.* A naïve prisoner; a fool. 1940: Negro and white prisoner use, Woodbourne, N.Y. "...A lane from Spokane." J. Schuyler. See Appendix, Rhyming Slang.

lantern *n.* An eye. **—s** The eyes. *Much less common than "lamps."*

lap *n.* **1** A round of a prize fight. *Since c1920. From the racing term.* **2** A drink or swallow, esp. of whisky.

lap organ An accordion. *Not common.*

lard-bucket *n.* A fat man. See **tub of lard.**

lard-head *n.* A stupid person.

large *adv.* Boastingly, with pride. *Usu. in "to talk large." Colloq. since c1830.* *adj.* **1** Much. *c1890. Not common.* **2** Eventful, exciting. 1945: "The good doctor has had himself a large evening." L. F. McHugh, *Chicago Murders*, 187. *Since c1895, but became very pop. c1935, esp. with jive groups, and is still common.* → **3** Well accepted; famous; popular; successful; capable of drawing large audiences; in fashion. *Usu. said of performers. Orig. theater and jazz use c1945; now common. A modern, hip variant of "big."*

large charge **1** A thrill; lit., a big charge. **2** A very important man; a big shot. *Both uses orig. jive talk; a prime example of a jive rhyming term. In vogue with students c1945–c1950.*

larrikin   n. A hoodlum. *From Austral. sl.*

larry   Larry   n. **1** Any worthless or broken small article of merchandise, as a toy balloon, doll, souvenir, or the like. *Circus use.* **2** A shopper who does not intend to buy anything. Cf. **house larry.**   *adj.* Worthless; bad; phony. *Circus use.* 1943: *Pitchman use.* "The average rad worker is pushing larry merchandise." Zolotow in *SEP.*

lash-up   n. Living quarters; a house, barracks, a tent. *W.W.II Army use. Not common.*

last   See **trade-last.**

last (long) count, take the   To die. *From prize fighting.*

latch on [to something]   **1** To obtain or take possession of a much wanted object. **2** To comprehend; to get wise to; to understand thoroughly. *More common c1940 than now; in some groups replaced by "dig."*

lately   See **Johnny-come-lately.**

lather   n. An angry or excited mood; a sweat. 1946: "This business of you being in a lather about it." Evans, *Halo in Blood,* 10.   *v.t.* To hit a baseball. **—ed**   Intoxicated. *Not common.*

latrine rumor   n. An unsubstantiated, often exaggerated story or rumor. *W.W.II Army use.*

laugh   n. A joke; a cause or object of laughter. *Colloq.*

laughing soup   Liquor. *Not common.*

laugh on the other side of [one's] face   To cry; to change one's mood from happy to sad; to become a failure or be defeated after having expected or experienced success. *Colloq.*

laundry   n. The board of faculty members that passes on flying cadets. Such a board can "wash out" cadets. *W.W.II Army use.* See **hang out the laundry.**

lavender   See **lay [someone] out in lavender.**

law   See **John Law.**

law, the   n. Any officer of the law; a policeman; the police; also, a prison guard, etc. *Orig. underworld use. Now colloq.*

lawn, the   n. The grass-covered infield of a race track. 1956: "In 1913 bookies took places on 'the lawn': in front of the grandstand. The bookmakers invented the term 'The Lawn.' They paid no license fee to the track." T. Betts, *Across the Board,* 27. *Not common.*

lawn-mower   n. **1** In baseball, a grounder. **2** A sheep. *Western use.*

lawyer   n. A friend who accompanies a customer to a store to advise him on his purchase, often resulting in the customer's not buying. *Retail salesman use.* See **forecastle lawyer, guardhouse lawyer, sea lawyer.**
— lawyer   See Appendix, Suffixes and Suffix Words.

lay   For phrases beginning with "lay," see under principal word of phrase.

lay   n. **1** An expedition of thieves for any criminal purpose; a caper, a robbery; the site of a robbery; the person or place robbed. 1848: "Gooseberry lay [= an expedition for stealing clothes hung out to dry]." "Prad lay [= a horse-stealing foray]." J. S. Farmer. *Once very common underworld use; now obs.* **2** [taboo] A female considered only sexually; coitus. 1930: "Both agreed that the two girls looked like swell lays. . . ." J. T. Farrell, 158. *Even though taboo, this use is so common as to be colloq. The ety. may be the lit. one, to "lay" a woman down for sexual purposes. However, the psychological relationship between taking or stealing and sex, as shown in several other sl. words, points to an obvious relation between the two above meanings. Thus "lay" = coitus prob. grew out of "lay" = robbery, or fig. taking or stealing sexual pleasure from a woman. Unfortunately, most dictionaries and researchers ignore such taboo words; thus it is difficult to establish a first date for this use, but it is old.* See Appendix, Sex and Deceit.   *v.t.* **1** [taboo] To have coitus with someone. 1947: "She went to a doctor and found out the truth, then rushed to General Draughton and named the man: Pete Layne. But Layne immediately produced five cadets who swore they'd all layed the girl one night on Jamaica Shore." C. Willingham, *End as a Man,* 9. *As most taboo words, this is primarily used by, but not restricted to use by, males.* **2** = **lay paper.**

lay an egg   lay a bomb   **1** To fail; esp. to flop: to sing, act, tell a story, or perform very poorly or before an unappreciative audience. *Said of any entertainer or of a play, movie, song, or story.* 1929: [to fail] "Wall Street Lays an Egg." *Variety,* headline. 1939–40: [singer] "You would just as well come wearing a shell if you ever took a job [singing] in a spot like this, that is how big an egg you would lay." O'Hara, *Pal Joey,* 38. 1940: [movie] " 'Pinocchio' is laying a financial egg." Winchell, *col.*, Apr. 15. 1952: "I ain't never laid a bomb with this [song] yet." L. Stander in *Esquire*, June 132/3. *Orig. theater use, now common.* **2** To succeed; specif., in sports, to score. *Much less common than orig. meaning.* **3** To drop a bomb on the enemy from an airplane. *W.W.II Armed Forces use.*

lay chickie To act as a lookout while others steal, rob, or commit an act of violence. 1958: "I never stole anything myself, I always lay chickie for the rest of them." *Oral,* Bronx teenage street gang member. *Since c1945, common use for teenagers and juvenile delinquents, esp. in New York.*

lay-down *n.* **1** A failure. **2** Money paid to smoke opium in a den. 1936: Addict use. D. W. Maurer.

lay for [someone] To wait for someone in order to surprise and do him physical harm, usu. to fight, hit, stab, or shoot, esp. to fight; to ambush someone. 1947: "I'd lay for him in town some night, get myself a piece of plumber's pipe, and I'd knock out his brains." C. Willingham, *End as a Man*, 106.

lay low To keep inconspicuous or hidden; said of a person. Esp., to keep hidden until another's anger has evaporated or the law has had time to forget; to curtail illegal or undesirable activities for a while. 1949: "We're layin' low a couple days . . . till I get the [gambling] tables back to the alley joint." N. Algren, *Man with the Golden Arm*, 29.

lay off **1** To dismiss from employment, esp. to dismiss from employment temporarily with the promise of rehiring once business gets better and more employees are again needed. *Colloq.* **2** To stop or ease one's criticizing or teasing; often used as a command or entreaty. 1925: "Lay off, Maud." Sherwood Anderson in *The American Twenties*, 68. **3** For a bookmaker, or gambler, to give part of a bet to another bookmaker, or gambler, to reduce his potential losses. Cf. **dynamite.** **layoff** **lay-off** **lay off** *n.* **1** A vacation. *Colloq. since 1897. Not now common.* → **2** A general dismissal of employees. **3** An unemployed actor. 1952: "A couple of layoffs . . . were walking out of the hotel. . . ." L. Stander in *Esquire*, June, 131/1. **4** A bet or part of a bet which one bookmaker gives to another, in order to reduce his own potential loss; money which a bookmaker bets at a racetrack, in order to reduce his own potential loss, and some-

times to reduce the odds on a specif. horse.

lay one on [a person] To strike or hit.

lay [someone] out **1** To knock a person down; to knock a person unconscious; to kill a person. **2** To reprimand; to scold.

lay [someone] out in lavender = **lay [someone] out.** 1952: "If that woman gets the Republican nomination . . . I will lay her out in lavender." Vivien Kellems, acc. to W. Pegler, *synd. newsp. col.*, Sept. 15.

lay paper To pass worthless checks; to pass counterfeit money.

lay them in the aisles = **knock them in the aisles.**

lead *n.* Bullets. See **get the lead out, red lead.**

lead balloon Fig., a failure; a plan, joke, action or the like that elicits no favorable response; a flop; anything that lays an egg. *Orig. in the expression,* "That [joke, performance, plan, or the like] went over like a lead balloon." *Now abbr. to* "That [joke, etc.] was a lead balloon." *From the notion of a lead balloon that could not leave the ground. Since c1950.*

lead-footed *adj.* Awkward; slow-thinking; stupid. 1957: ". . . The bungling, lead-footed fellow who is so stupid that he cannot escape. . . ." Robert Wallace, "Crime in the U.S." *Life*, Sept. 9, 59.

lead in [one's] pants, to have To move, work, act, react, or think slowly; lit., to move as if one were weighted down. *Colloq.* See **get the lead out.**

lead in [one's] pencil, have **1** [taboo] To have an erection; to be capable of and eager for sexual intercourse. **2** To be full of energy and vitality.

lead joint A shooting gallery. *Carnival and circus use.*

lead out, get the To make haste; go into action; stop loafing; be alert. 1948: ". . . Quit asking . . . questions and get the lead out." F. Brown, *Dead Ringer*, 9. *A shortened form of* "get the lead out of your pants." *Euphemism for* **get the lead out of your ass** [taboo] = *fig.,* "*get rid of the thing that is weighing you down and hurry up.*" *Became very common cW.W.II; the longer forms are now seldom used.*

lead out of [one's] pants (ass), get the [taboo] To hurry up; to become alert and active; usu. a command or entreaty.

lead-pipe cinch Something easy;

anything or anyone certain of success; a certainty. 1949: "Not early enough to move no tables, that's a lead-pipe cinch." N. Algren, *Man with the Golden Arm*, 29. See **cinch.**

lead poison   lead poisoning   Death, or a wound, caused by shooting. *Old Western term used by underworld and by W.W.II Armed Forces.*

leaf   *n.* An Air Force or Army officer holding the rank of major. *From the insigne.*

leak   *v.i., v.t.* **1** To disclose information, esp. secret information, inadvertently or with malicious intent. **2** To let news apparently "leak" in order to make it known without making a public announcement; to release or reveal official or secret information unofficially; to start a false rumor purposely. 1958: "Then the FCC report was 'leaked' to the press...." Robert G. Spivack, "The Deal That Didn't Come Off," N.Y. *Post*, Jan. 24, 4. **3** [taboo] To urinate.   *n.* **1** [taboo] The act or an instance of urinating. **2** The person who "leaks" news or secret information; the channel through which such items reach the public. *Orig. use by underworld, now most commonly refers to government officials.*

lean against   lean on   1 To raid, esp. a hideout for criminals. 1949: "A small army of cops leaned against the place...." A. Hynd, *Public Enemies*, 21. *Not common.* **2** To beat up someone; to threaten to beat up someone or a member of one's family in order to get information, to persuade someone to suppress information, or to extort money; to act or be tough with someone; to coerce.

leaping heebies, the = **heebie-jeebies.** Cf. **heebies.**

Leaping Lena   1 An automobile. *c1915; obs.* **2** In baseball, a fly ball hit beyond the infield but not far enough to be caught by an outfielder. Cf. **Texas leaguer.**

leap-tick   *n.* **1** A mattress on which clowns and acrobats leap and fall. *Circus use.* → **2** The false fat stomach of a comedian, stuffed with mattress ticking or straw. → **3** The stomach of a fat person. *Since c1920. Not common.*

leary   *adj.* = **leery.**

leather   *n.* **1** A pocketbook, wallet, or purse. *Underworld use.* **2** A football. **3** Boxing gloves. **4** Meat, esp. beef. *Some W.W.I Army use. From "as tough as shoe leather."*

leather, the   *n.* **1** A kick. 1946: "He would give his fallen foe what we called 'the leather,' meaning a few boots abaft the ears ... and spareribs. ...." Runyon, *synd. newsp. col.*, Sept. 14. **2** A hit or blow, with or without boxing gloves.

leatherhead   *n.* **1** A Pennsylvanian. *c1845; archaic and dial.* **2** A night watchman; a policeman. *c1870; obs.* **3** A stupid person. *Not common.*

leatherneck   *n.* A U.S. Marine. *From the old custom of facing the neckband of the Marine uniform with leather. Very common.*

leave a strip   To decrease one's driving speed suddenly; to brake a car; fig., to stop a car so quickly that a strip of rubber is left on the pavement from the tires. *Hot-rod use since c1950.*

leaves   *n.pl.* **1** Lettuce. **2** Dungarees, blue jeans. *Rock-and-roll and general teenage use since c1955. From "Levis."*

Leblang   *v.i., v.t.* **1** To sell theater tickets at cut rates. *From Joe Leblang, ticket promoter. Theater use since c1930.* → **2** To reduce the admission price of a show.

lech = **letch.**

leech   *n.* **1** A medical doctor, esp. a surgeon. *Obs.* **2** One who is friendly to or follows another in order to profit; one who habitually borrows; a human parasite.   *v.i., v.t.* To borrow, esp. to borrow without intending to return the money or item borrowed.

lee lurch, on the   Drunk. *Never common.*

leery   leary   *adj.* Wary; suspicious; doubtful. *"Leery" is about 3 times as common as "leary."* 1927: [wary] "He was leery of toting so much money...." Hammett, *Blood Money*, 114. 1930: [suspicious] "I was leery of him...." Weeks, *Racket*, 47. 1949: [doubtful] "He was leery of how it would work out." A. Hynd, *Public Enemies*, 28f. *Since c1850.*

left   *n.* In politics, the liberal and radical persuasion, as opposed to the "right" or conservative side. See **left wing.**

left-foot   *n.* A Protestant.   *adj.* Protestant.

left-handed   *adj.* **1** Undesirable; said of a ship. 1944: *Maritime use.* "A ship is ... 'wrong' or 'left-handed' or 'hungry.'" O. Ferguson. **2** Illicit; irregular; phony. 1946: "... Left-handed honeymoons with somebody else's husband and a pedigreed crook." Evans, *Halo in Blood*, 69.

leftie   lefty   *n.* **1** A left-handed person, esp. a baseball pitcher. 1950: "Ted Gray, a young lefty, is ready to resume pitching." AP, Sept. 11. *This use usu. spelled "lefty." Colloq.* → **2** A shoe made for the left foot; a glove made for the left hand; a tool made for left-handed users. *Colloq.* **3** A radical, socialist, or communist, or a sympathizer with liberal or radical political philosophies; since c1945, esp. a communist or communist sympathizer. 1948: "Truman's Central Error: Fear of Libero-Lefties." Title of editorial, *SEP*, Aug. 7, 120/1. See **left wing.**   *adj.* Left-handed. 1886: "Nashville presented her left-handed battery . . . to offset our 'lefty' battery." *Sporting Life*, Apr. 7, 2/4. *Colloq.*

leftist   Leftist   *n. & adj.* As or like a member or sympathizer of the left wing. 1946: ". . . Following her leftist bent, attending meetings of the Subversive Elements' League, distributing leaflets, writing letters to the editor." M. Shulman, *Zebra Derby*, 52.

left-wing   left wing   *n.* The liberal and radical elements of any group, party, state, nation, etc. *Because in the Fr. republican parliament the conservative parties sit on the right of the semicircular chamber and the liberal and radical parties sit on the left.   adj.* Pert. to liberal or radical views. 1954: "In 1950, Paul Draper's left-wing tendencies were exposed along with Larry Adler's." W. R. & F. K. Simpson, *Hockshop*, 270. *Since c1945, the term has usu. implied "communistic."*   **—er** *n.* A member of or sympathizer toward the left-wing. See Appendix, **—er** ending.

leg   *v.i., v.t.* To depart; to run away; to travel. *Often in the phrase "leg it out of here."* See **bootleg, peg leg, pull [one's] leg, red legs, shake a leg, show a leg, tangle-leg.**

leg, pull [one's]   **1** To gain favor by deception. *c1900.* → **2** To make fun of a person; to kid him. 1925: "I suspected that he was pulling my leg, but a glance at him convinced me otherwise." F. Scott Fitzgerald, *The Great Gatsby*, 73. *c1920 to present; colloq.*

legacy   *n.* A college fraternity member, pledge, or prospective pledge who is closely related by blood to a member of longer standing, as an older brother, father, or grandfather. 1950: "Legacies— freshmen whose relatives have been

closely connected with the chapter." Cornell (Univ.) *Daily Sun*, Sept. 21, 4/2. *Student use since c1920.*

legal beagle   *n.* A lawyer, esp. an aggressive or astute one. See Appendix, Rhyming Slang. See **beagle.**

legal eagle   An extremely capable, devoted, or cunning lawyer. See Appendix, Rhyming Slang.

legger   *n.* **1** = **leg man.** **2** A bootlegger.

legit   *adj.* **1** Legitimate; lawful; law-abiding; honest; authentic. 1943: "She's a legit farmer." H. A. Smith, *Putty Knife*, 126. 1950: "By legit, or honest, people." De Baun, 70. **2** Concerned with the New York commercial stage, stage plays, or serious art; classical; semi-classical; other than popular. 1936: ". . . Specialists in legit (drama) reviewing." A. Green in *Esquire*, Sept., 64/2. 1947: "The Legit Theater. . . ." Billy Rose, *synd. newsp. col.*, May 15.   *n.* The New York stage, stage plays and shows; serious or classical art, performances, performers, or composers, writers, painters, and the like. *Orig. to distinguish the professional New York theater from traveling and nonprofessional shows, now primarily to distinguish stage plays from movie and television plays.*

legit, on the   **1** Honest; legitimate; within the law. 1949: "Nothing wrong at all. . . . Strictly on the legit—just the new way of doing things. . . ." N. Algren, *Man with the Golden Arm*, 15. See **legit. 2** = **on the level.** 1950: "Ya better be on the legit, pal." Movie, *Asphalt Jungle.*

leg man   **1** A newspaper reporter who goes to the scene or a source of news to gather facts, which may be written up by someone else. → **2** Any person who earns his living by gathering news, disseminating publicity, or calling on a great many clients.

leg pull   *n.* An instance of pulling [one's] leg. 1947: "The wisecrack and the gag, the leg pull and the hotfoot. . . ." James Thurber in *New Yorker*, Dec. 6, 19/1.

Legree   See **Simon Legree.**

leg show   Any performance or show of girls dressed or undressed so as to show their legs and bodies; a performance or show whose main appeal is mild sexual excitation.

lemo   *n.* **1** Lemonade. *Since c1900.* → **2** Lemon extract, drunk as an intoxicant. *Prison and Army use.* Cf. **jungle juice.**

lemon   *n.* **1** A sharp verbal thrust, criticism, or retort. *c1900.* **2** A hand grenade. *Some W.W.I Army use. From its shape.* **3** Something unsatisfactory, inferior, or worthless. *Colloq. since c1925.* **4** A light-skinned, attractive Negress; a mulatto. *Negro use.* See **high yellow.** **5** Any disagreeable disliked person, esp. one who does not produce, buy, or assume proper responsibility. *Each of the above uses is associated with the properties of a lemon, one with its shape, one with its color, and three with its sour taste.*

lemon, hand [someone] a   To do or give something unpleasant to a person. 1939: "If they hand me a lemon. . . ." Gardner, *D. A. Draws,* 64. See **lemon.**

Lena   See **Leaping Lena.**

lens lice   Film actors who try for better positions before the camera than those assigned to them. *Early movie use.*

Leona   *n.* A female square; a woman who nags. 1957: "Leona—Generic for Buster's wife who is always giving him hell for being nowhere." E. Horne, *For Cool Cats and Far-Out Chicks. Some far-out use.*

les   *n.* A lesbian. 1956: "John and Mary, John and Mary/Mary is a les and John is a fairy." Comic song sung by Joe E. Lewis at Copacabana nightclub, N.Y.C., Oct. 6.   **—bine**   *n.* A lesbian. *West Coast jazz, beat, and cool use since c1955.* See Appendix, Mispronunciations.   **—bo**   *n.* A lesbian. 1939: "M.C. in a crib where the Lesbos even come and watch the dress rehearsals." O'Hara, *Pal Joey,* 57.

let   For phrases beginning with "let," see under principal word of phrase.

letch   lech   *n.* **1** Desire; a strong liking for; a preference; a yen. 1940: "Your letch for power." S. Lewis, *B. Merriday,* 387. 1948: "His lech for cam shafts and turbines. . . ." Cain, *Moth,* 36. **2** A lecher. 1943: "If anybody noticed what I was doing, they'd think I was an old letch." H. A. Smith, *Putty Knife,* 103. *adj.* Lecherous, seductive.

let out   To discharge from one's employment; to fire. 1938–39: "Last month he was let out. . . . Everyone in the office is afraid of being let out." J. T. Farrell, 170. *Since c1895.*   **let out   let-out**   *n.* **1** A plausible way out of a predicament; an excuse for avoiding responsibility; an out. **2** A discharge; a firing. 1948: "He checks out March 1. Other Metro executive letouts impend." *Variety,* Aug. 25, 3/4.

lettuce   *n.* Money; paper money. 1946: ". . . I should run over with my hands full of lettuce and buy it from him." Evans, *Halo in Blood,* 139.

level   *v.i.* To be honest, truthful, or serious; to speak frankly; to tell the truth. 1931: "Don't laugh, I'm levellin'. . . ." J. Sayre, *Hex,* 416. 1948: "You're going to level about that." F. Brown, *Dead Ringer,* 126.   *adj.* True; straight. See **on the level.** 1951: "There's never a place for guys like me. . . . That's level." Henry Lee in *Pageant,* April, 35/1.

level, on the (dead)   *adj.* Honest; truthful; fair; ethical; legitimate; respectable; serious; sincere. 1905: "To swear that I'm on the level. . . ." McHugh, *Search Me,* 64. 1914: "He is not 'on the level.' . . ." D. S. Martin, *Living Age,* Aug., 374.   *adv.* Honestly; legitimately; truthfully; sincerely. 1938: ". . . And would fight on the level." Liebling, *Back Where,* 121. 1941: "He hugged her, half kidding, half on the level." Schulberg, *Sammy,* 66.

level with [someone] = **level;** to treat fairly. 1921: "Are you levelin' with the kid? . . ." Witwer, *Leather,* 113. 1938: "I want you to level with me and tell me if it is true." O'Hara in *New Yorker.*

Levis   *n.* A pair of stiff, tight-fitting, tapered pants, usu. blue with heavily reinforced seams and slash pockets. *From the company name "Levi Strauss," the leading mfr. of such pants; this firm orig. produced and sold them to the 19C cowboy.* Cf. **jeans.**

lexer   *n.* A student of law. *A little student use; from Lat. "lex" = law.* See Appendix, —er ending.

lib   libe   *n.* A library.   *v.t., v.i.* To study in a library. *A little student use.*

liberate   *v.i., v.t.* **1** To loot; to take in looting, esp. from an unoccupied or partially destroyed building. *Wide W.W.II Army use, mainly in Europe. A jocular euphem., from the stand. term used by Allied propaganda in ref. to the reconquest of German and Italian occupied territories.* → **2** To steal, esp. to steal a small item. *Since W.W.II.* **3** To have sexual intercourse with, or take as a mistress, a girl native to an occupied country. *W.W.II Army use in Europe.*

liberty   *n.* A holiday; a vacation from work or school. *Some use since W.W.II. From the USN use.*

liberty cabbage = sauerkraut. *Some W.W.I superpatriotic use, to avoid using "sauerkraut," traditionally a German dish and word.*

liberty ship *n.* A cargo vessel of stand. size and design, mass-produced during W.W.II to carry military personnel and supplies to overseas bases.

lick *n.* In jazz, a break, a riff, a short phrase of improvisation introduced between phrases of the melody; sometimes a chorus of improvisation. 1938: "... With a few solid licks on the sliphorn." C. Smith in *Esquire*, 95/2. 1956: "A *lick* is a break." S. Longstreet, *The Real Jazz Old and New*, 149.

lick [one's] chops **1** To wait with anticipation. *Common use.* **2** To gloat over another's misfortune.

lickety-split *adv.* Fast; at great speed. *Since c1850.*

licorice stick A clarinet, from its resemblance to the familiar confection. *Associated with swing and jazz musicians, c1935. Now considered affected usage.* 1950: "[He] plays a full mess of licorice stick in 'Serenade.'" *Basin St.*, radio program, July 8. 1956: "It's been a long time since a real jazzman admitted his clarinet was 'some licorice stick.'" S. Longstreet, *The Real Jazz Old and New*, 147. *Some archaic jazz use; a synthetic jazz word.*

lid *n.* **1** A hat. 1931: "You may now reverently lift the lid to Col. Henry Ward Belcher." Bob Brown in *Amer. Mercury*, Dec. 403/2. → **2** A helmet. *Some W.W.I use.* **3** An unskillful telegrapher. *Telegrapher and Army Signal Corps use.* See **blow the lid off, flip [one's] lid.**

lieut *n.* = **loot.**

life, not on your *exclam.* Emphatically no. *The phrase "on your life" is never used affirmatively.*

life-boat *n.* A pardon; a commutation of a prison or death sentence; a retrial. *Underworld use.*

lifer *n.* A prisoner serving a life sentence. *Since c1800.*

lift *v.t.* **1** To steal an item. 1958: "He does know he lifted an envelope from old Frosty's desk drawer." *Dondi, synd. newsp. comic strip*, Feb. 9. *Colloq.* **2** To plagiarize. *n.* **1** A ride in a car. **2** Orig. the kick felt from taking a narcotic; generally, energy, enthusiasm, power or feeling of well-being obtained from another's encouragement, success, or a stimulant, such as whisky. 1957: "... If ... the powder [suspected of being heroin] failed to [turn a chemical solution] purple, the girl had to rush back to the pusher and complain that it didn't give her 'a lift.'" Ashley Halsey, Jr., "The Lady Cops of the Dope Squad," *SEP*, March 30, 101.

lifties *n.pl.* Men's shoes built up inside in order to increase the wearer's apparent height. 1946: "Several well-known male movie stars are said to wear 'lifties.'" AP, July 24.

light *n.* A match or cigarette lighter for lighting a cigarette; the act of lighting a cigarette. *v.i.* To depart, esp. rapidly. See **light out.** *adj.* **1** Carrying only a light weight. → **2** Hungry; not having eaten recently; underweight. *Orig. hobo use.* → **3** Lacking or missing a required or desired item or amount; lacking a sufficient amount. → **4** Lacking a specif. sum of money; owing a specif. sum of money. **5** Sympathetic to and appreciative of progressive jazz music and off-beat art; hep. 1958: "Steve [novelist and painter Stephen Longstreet] is sweet, he's light, he can dig it." Poet Kenneth Rexroth, *Night Beat*, TV DuMont network, Apr. 14. *Some far-out and beat use.*

light, out like a **1** Drunk, esp. drunk to the point of unconsciousness. *c1920–c1930; obs.* → **2** Unconscious for any reason, esp. from a hard blow on the head. 1934: "Something swished and I went out like a light." Chandler, *Finger Man*, 15. *Colloq.* → **3** Asleep, esp. sound asleep or asleep from exhaustion.

light, the *n.* Comprehension, understanding; the point or main conclusion to be drawn from a story, joke, or experience. *Usu. in "see the light."*

light colonel A lieutenant colonel. *Army use.*

light-fingered *adj.* Prone to or known to steal. *Colloq.*

lighthouse *n.* **1** One who knows and can recognize plainclothes policemen on sight; one who can inform newcomers whom to trust and where hoboes can hang out. *c1900, hobo use; now archaic.* **2** A salt or pepper shaker. *W.W.II Armed Forces use; not common.*

lightning *n.* Inferior whisky. *Colloq. since c1880.*

lightning rod A jet fighter plane. *Some Air Force use*

lightning-slinger *n.* A telegrapher. *Railroad use.*

light of, make **1** To dismiss airily, as a challenge, imputation, or obstacle. **2** To belittle, as another's achievement or person.

light out To depart for another place, esp. quickly and directly; to flee. *Mainly dial.*

light piece *n.* A silver coin; usually a

quarter; a small amount of money. 1907 [1892]: "I missed many a meal, in spite of the fact that I could 'throw my feet' with the next one when it came to 'slamming a gate' for a 'poke-out' or a 'set-down' or hitting for a 'light piece' on the street." Jack London, *My Life*.

lights out   Death. 1927: "Otherwise lights out for me." Hammett, *Blood Money*, 108.

like   1 Used at the end of a sentence in place of "as," "as if," "it will be as if," etc. 1956: "When he dies, I'll be robbed like. I'll have no more father." S. Bellow, *Seize the Day*, 92, 2 Used before nouns, adjectives, and pred. adj., without adding to or changing the meaning of the sentence. *Thus, "It's like cold" = it is cold. Used by jazz, cool, and beat groups, esp. in New York City. Prob. to avoid making a definite, forthright statement, part of the beat philosophy; reinforced by Yiddish speech patterns.*

like, make   To pretend to be; to imitate; to simulate; to caricature. 1951: "During the raid, the phone rang and a cop picked it up and made like a bookmaker and in one hour took bets totaling $650." N.Y. *Daily News*, Aug. 9, C10/5. *Colloq.*

like crazy = **like mad.** Excitedly; excessively; fig., as if crazy. 1924: "She has been . . . tearing around like crazy." Marks, *Plastic Age*, 288. 1951: "Yockin' it up like crazy. . . ." Arthur Kober in *New Yorker*, May 12, 32/3.

like hell   An expression of incredulity, negation, or refusal. Thus "Like hell I will" = I won't.

like mad = **like crazy.** *Probably now the more common of the two terms.* With abandonment; with enthusiasm; without reserve, inhibitions, or dignity; quickly; completely; thoroughly. 1938: "Then everybody laughs like mad." Liebling, *Back Where*, 71. 1955: ". . . A real nice boy though . . . flirting *like mad*. . . ." C. Willingham, *To Eat A Peach*, 16. *Orig. a jive term. Now common.*

lily   *n.* 1 An effeminate male; a male homosexual. 2 = **lulu; humdinger.** 1952: "I told my best joke . . . it's never missed, a real lily. . . ." L. Stander in *Esquire*, 132/4.

lily white   Innocent; *Usu. in a negative phrase, as "She's not so lily white."* —**s**   1 Bed sheets. Usu. in **slip between the lily whites** = go to bed. *Negro use.* 2 The hands.

limb   *n.*   A young rascal, from "limb of the devil." 1931: "For you,

young limb." Queen, *Dutch Shoe*, 186. *Obs.* Cf. **out on a limb, sprout.**

limb, out on a   Exposed; vulnerable; in danger; said of a person who has publicly championed an extreme idea, plan, procedure, etc., the failure of which may precipitate his downfall or discomfiture. 1897: *DAE.* 1944: "Don't get yourself out on a limb." Ford, *Phila. Murder*, 130.

limbs   *n.pl.* Legs; esp. shapely female legs. *Colloq.*

limburger [derog.]   *n.* A German, from the familiar cheese. *Not common.*

lime-juicer   *n.* 1 An English ship. 1907 [1892]: "He had sailed always on French merchant vessels, with the one exception of a voyage on a 'lime-juicer.' " Jack London, *My Life*. 2 A British sailor. 3 An Englishman. *Orig. W.W.I Army use.* 1935: "The 'Doctor' was a 'lime-juicer.' " Scribner's, Aug., 121. *All meanings maritime use; from the ration of limes issued by the British Navy to its sailors to prevent scurvy.*

limey   limy [derog.]   *n.* 1 = **lime juicer** in all three meanings. *The most common term for "British sailor" or an "Englishman." Became common during W.W.I.* 1938: [Englishman] ". . . Pictures in which the actors are limeys." *Amer. Mercury*, Sept., 46/1. 2 A British soldier. *W.W.I. Army use.*

limit, go the   To enter into sexual intercourse, as opposed to even the most intimate petting; said of a girl or a couple. 1957: "On the one hand the all-American girl must not, as the poetry of our love-lore has it, 'go the limit.' On the other hand, she can't be prissy. She ends up a kind of perfumed puritan." F. Morton, *The Act of Courtship*, 158.

limit, the   *n.* A person, thing, or act that exceeds the usual bounds of propriety, performance, or the like, to the annoyance, exasperation, or delight of others. 1900: "She's the limit." Upson in *Independent*, 2573/1.

limmy   *n.* A jimmy; any tool or set of tools used for house-breaking. 1848: *Criminal use.* J. S. Farmer.

limp   *adj.* Drunk.

limp sock   *n.* = **wet smack.** Cf. **wet sock.**

limp wrist   *adj.* Homosexual; said of male homosexuals; effeminate.   *n.* A homosexual or effeminate man.

line   *n.* 1 One's usual topic and mode of conversation, esp. when persuasive;

stereotyped, insincere flattery; exaggeration or attention one gives to others in order to make a good impression, ingratiate oneself, seek favor, persuade, or sell; persuasive talk; a spiel. 1920: "This incident became part of what in a later generation would have been termed her 'line.'" Fitzgerald, *This Side of Paradise*, 5. 1943: "You've got some line." Wolfert, *Underworld*, 205. *Very common.* **2** One's business, occupation, or craft. *Colloq.* **3** The cost of an item, the purchase price of an item. *Mainly Negro use.* **4** = **lick.** 1956: "[West] Coasters talk of 'lines,' not licks, breaks, or riffs." A. Shaw, *West Coast Jazz*, 127. *v.i., v.t.* To hit a baseball, esp. to hit a line drive.

line, go down the **1** To quit or be fired from one's job. *Orig. hobo use. Obs.* **2** To take a second or third choice. *Lit.* = "*to go down a list of choices.*"

line, in **1** In accord with the prevailing price, quality, standards, or code. → **2** Agreeable; causing no trouble; acting as one should according to one's age and status.

line, lay (*or* put) it on the **1** Literally, to hand over money to someone; to pay money; to pay up. 1939–40: "You fellows always put it on the line for me every pay day...." O'Hara, *Pal Joey*, 33. **2** To speak frankly; to produce evidence or information or facts; to come across with facts.

line, out of **1** Deviant; not in accord with established or accepted practices, modes, or attitudes. 1950: "You was considered out of line if your coat and pants matched. Many a time they would kid me, 'Boy, you must be from the country. Here you got trousers on the same as your coat.'" A. Lomax, *Mr. Jelly Roll*, 15. **2** Not in accord with the prevailing price, quality, standards, or code. **3** Disrespectful; troublesome, brash impertinent. See **in line.**

line, pull a See **line.**

line, the *n.* The chorus of dancing girls performing in an act or show; lit., the line of chorus girls.

lined *adj.* Drunk. *Never common.*

line-load *n.* A taxi passenger bound for a red-light district. *Taxi-driver use.*

line [one's] nest = **feather [one's] nest.**

line one In baseball, to hit a line drive. *Very common.*

ling See **ding-a-ling.**

lingo *n.* A yarn; a story. *Never common.*

lip *n.* **1** Talk, esp. insolent, impudent, or impertinent talk, usu. with a negative or other context of disapproval or warning. 1821: Farmer & Henley. 1925: "I don't want none o' yer lip." Schauffler in *Sat. Rev. Lit.* 1934: "Don't be giving me any lip." J. T. Farrell, 134. 1943: "We don't take nigger lip." Wolfert, *Underworld*, 274. **2** A lawyer; a mouthpiece. 1933: "His lip couldn't spring him." H. T. Webster. *Orig. underworld use.* See **button up [one's] lip.** *v.t.* To play a musical instrument; specif., to play jazz on a brass instrument; to blow. 1956: "That year ... 1931, Bunk [Johnson] had trouble: His trumpet was lost and his teeth fell out and he couldn't lip anything proper any more." S. Longstreet, *The Real Jazz Old and New*, 50. **—py** *adj.* **1** Insolent; impertinent. **2** Talkative.

lip fern　　lip fuzz　　lip grass　　lip hair Also **lip bush (arbor, hay, muff, spinach,** etc.) *n.* A mustache. *Jocular use only. Never common.*

lip-splitter *n.* A jazz musician who plays a wind instrument. 1956: "Words that the jazzmen don't use much, but which most people think are real jazz words. *Lip-splitter* for horn-player...." S. Longstreet, *The Real Jazz Old and New*, 150. *Prob. synthetic.*

liquidate *v.t.* To kill a person.

liquored *adj.* Drunk. *Not common.*

liquored up Drunk. *Common.*

listen *v.* To appear to be reasonable, honest, or true. 1934: "It don't listen. There's something screwy about it." Chandler, *Finger Man*, 117. **—er** *n.* An ear. *Orig. boxing use.*

listen-in *n.* The act of eavesdropping. 1946: "An occasional listen-in on the ... [telephone] line later convinced company men...." *Phila. Bulletin*, Aug. 1, 3.

lit *n.* Literature, esp. as a college course; also used attrib., as a "lit course." *Common student use since c1900. adj.* Drunk; esp. drunk in a festive mood. 1929: "He gets lit." Burnett, *Little Caesar*, 55. 1943: "[Visitors to New York City] want to get lit." H. A. Smith, *Putty Knife*, 122. *Since c1880. Very common.*

litterbug *n.* One who litters the streets or public places. *Orig. coined for use in advts. by the New York City Dept. of Sanitation, c1947. The word has gained considerable currency, esp. in jocular use. May be based on "jitterbug."*

litter of kittens See **have kittens.**

little   *adj., adv.* Slightly, somewhat, quite. *Colloq.* Cf. **pretty.**

little black book   Lit. and fig., a man's small notebook listing the name, addresses, and phone numbers of accessible or available girls; a man's address book devoted to available female companions. *Colloq.*

little go   An unimportant, unexciting, or incomplete attempt, effort, task, or performance.

little gray cells   The human brain.

Little Joe   In crap-shooting, the point 4.

little ones out of big ones, make   To break rocks in a prison work yard; hence, to serve a prison sentence.

little Percy   A 3-foot pipe wrench. *Factory and plumber use; not common.*

little school   A reformatory; a juvenile or woman's house of detention. *Underworld and hobo use.* Cf. **big school.**

little shaver   A young boy. 1947: "I was a little shaver, but I had enough sense. . . ." E. Pyle, *Home Country*, 9. *Colloq.*

little woman, the   A wife. 1938: ". . . Tooling along with the kiddies and the little woman in his costly can." W. Pegler., *synd. newsp. col. Colloq. since 1880.*

lit to the gills   Drunk. *Fairly common.*

lit to the guards   Drunk. *c1925; obs.*

lit up like a Christmas tree (Main Street, Times Square, Broadway, a store window, a church, etc.)   1 Drunk. 1905: "The house was lighted up. As soon as I opened the door I found Uncle Peter and he was also lit up." McHugh, *Search Me*, 37. 1921: "Jacques was lit up like Broadway at eight in the p.m." Witwer, *Leather*, 82. 1927: "Lit up like the sky, like the commonwealth, like a Christmas tree, like a store window, like a church." *New Repub.*, v. 50, 72. **2** Colorfully, gaudily, showily, or flashily dressed or adorned with jewelry. **3** Under the influence of narcotics; said of an addict. *Orig. addict use.*

litvak   *n.* A Lithuanian; one of Lithuanian extraction. *Usu. used jocularly rather than derog.*

live   *adj.* **1** Real or potent; ready to be detonated; usu. said of ammunition. **2** In person; staged in front of television cameras by living actors rather than filmed and then televised.

live one   *n.* A lively, exciting place or person. 1922: "I certainly been seeing some hick towns. . . . You fellows can't

hardly appreciate what it means to be here with a bunch of live ones!" S. Lewis, *Babbitt*, reprinted in *The American Twenties*, 230.

Liverpool kiss   A hit on the mouth. *Some maritime use.*

Liverpool wash   A bath from the waist up. *Maritime use.*

live wire   1 An exciting person; an active, alert, reliable person. 1924: "Jimmie's a live wire, all right." Marks, *Plastic Age*, 197. 1953: "Let him see how much fun it is to be with a real live-wire girl." H. Boyle, AP, Jan. 30. *Since c1900.* → **2** One who spends his money freely.

living room gig   An appearance on television, specif., of a jazz musician. 1957: "Living room gig—A guest shot on television." E. Horne, *For Cool Cats and Far-Out Chicks. Some general jazz use.*

Liz   See **shivering Liz.**

lizard   *n.* **1** A racehorse, esp. an inferior one. **2** A wallet or purse. → **3** A dollar.

—lizard   *n.* A hound for something, a hog; one who habitually is associated with a certain act or place. *Thus a "chow lizard" is known for eating a lot, a "couch lizard" is known for necking on a couch with his girl, etc.*

lizzie   Lizzie   *n.* **1** A cheap, dilapidated, or old automobile; orig. an early model Ford. Cf. **tin lizzie.** → **2** Any automobile. 1950: "The luxurious lizzie I've always dreamed about. . . ." Billy Rose, *synd. newsp. col.*, Aug. 7. **3** An effeminate man. 1928: "I hear the reporters in New York are all lizzies." Hecht & MacArthur, *Front Page*, I. *Never common.*

load   For phrases beginning with "load," see under principal word of phrase.

load   *n.* **1** A drink of liquor. 1887: "Whisky . . . five cents a load." New Orleans *Lantern. Obs.* **2** Enough liquor to cause intoxication. 1893: "To carry a load" [= to get drunk]. Brander Matthews in *Harper's*, July, 308/2.

—ed   *adj.* **1** Drunk; fig., carrying a load of liquor. 1886: "Men act different when they get loaded." New Orleans *Lantern.* 1936: "Right over there a man used to get good licker. I used to get load down there." Jesse Stuart in *Harper's*, May, 668/1. *The most common term for "drunk." Sometimes followed by a phrase indicating extreme intoxication, as: loaded to the muzzle, loaded to the* *plimsoll mark, loaded to the gills.* See Appendix, Drunk. **2** Containing or mixed with whisky. 1939: "We sipped our loaded coffee." Chandler, *Big Sleep*, 136. **3** Under the influence of heroin. 1952: "And then you get loaded and like it. . . ." D. Hulburd, *H Is for Heroin.* **4** Wealthy; carrying a large amount of money. *Used absolutely or in "loaded with dough" or the equiv.* 1910: "He's just loaded with the spondulix, too." Johnson, *Varmint*, 60. 1949: "He was still loaded with what the boys vulgarly referred to as moo!" Barnett, *Jungle*, 51. 1949: "The boys were loaded after the [robbery]." A. Hynd, *Public Enemies*, 20. **5** Abundantly provided with anything desirable. 1950: "If the most valuable thing in the world is a friend, then I'm really loaded." P. Silvers quoted in *New Yorker*, Nov. 18, 55/1f. **6** Lit. and fig., explosive; esp. in the sense of containing elements or materials that may become dangerous, as a 'loaded' political speech or business venture. → **7** Specif., crooked; containing or having an unfair advantage; tampered with, as dice or other gambling paraphernalia, to ensure a predetermined outcome. *From dice actually being loaded with lead or other weights to make them roll in such a way that a certain number will come up frequently.* 1956: ". . . Charges of slipping loaded dice into a game at Monte Carlo's famed Casino." N.Y. *Post.* May 21, 32. 1956: "They [a set of dice] match seven all around, and they're transparent so they can't be loaded." J. Scarne, *The Amazing World of John Scarne*, 307.

loaded for bear **1** Drunk. 1896: DAE. *Archaic and dial.* **2** Angry; prepared to expose or ruin someone's reputation; ready for a fight.

load of coal [derog.] A group of Negroes, as in a taxi or bus.

load off [one's] feet, take a To sit down; to have a seat or chair; usu., "Have a seat."

load of hay **1** A head of long hair. **2** A group of nonpaying or nontipping customers, as guests of the management at a restaurant, or people traveling, eating, or seeing shows on free passes. *Bus driver, train conductor, waiter, and theater use.*

load of post holes An empty truck. *Truck-driver use.*

load of this [that, something], get a **1** To see or look at; to evaluate; to scrutinize. *Often used in the imperative.* 1948: "Mainly it was to let him get a

load of the new suit of clothes. . . ." Cain, *Moth*, 22. **2** To listen; to listen carefully.

load of wind **1** = **wind bag.** **2** A light load of freight. *Truck-driver use.*

loaf *v.t.* To borrow, usu. without returning. 1851: Hall, *College Words*, 188; *obs.* *n.* A girl. *Not common.*

loan-out *n.* The lending of a film actor by the company which holds his contract to another company. *Hollywood use.*

lob *n.* **1** A sloppy, dull person; one easily duped. 1939: "He is generally figured as nothing but a lob as far as ever doing anything useful in this world is concerned." Runyon, 54. **2** An overzealous or overdiligent inmate or employee. **3** The act or instance of throwing an object, as a baseball, softly and gently. *v.t.* To toss lightly and easily.

lobby-gow **lobbygow** *n.* **1** One who loafs around an opium den in hopes of being offered a free pipe of opium. → **2** An opium smoker, esp. one who is also a bum. → **3** A loafer, a bum. 1956: "He flung away fortunes in grubstakes to bums, heels, and lobby-gows." T. Betts, *Across the Board*, 177. → **4** A Chinatown tourists' guide.

lobo *n.* A hoodlum. 1949: " 'You crazy lobo!' 'What's a lobo?' 'A lobo's a gun, thug, hoodlum—downstate [California].' " Movie, *Scene of the Crime. Prob. from stand. "lobo"* = *wolf.*

lobster *n.* A victim of a deception; one easily duped.

lock *n.* A certainty, a cinch. 1958: "We haven't had a 20-game winner since [pitcher Ewell] Blackwell in '47 and this guy [pitcher Bob Purkey] looks like a lock now. Not because he's won eight already, but because of the way he's pitching." A. Murray, N.Y. *Post,* June 11, 33. *From* **mortal lock.** *v.t.* To occupy a cell.

lock up **lockup** **lock-up** *n.* **1** A prison cell. **2** A jail. **3** = **lock.**

loco *adj.* Crazy; insane. 1887: DAE. *Colloq. From the narcotic loco weed of the south-west plains whose leaves, when eaten by cattle, drive them insane.* 1936: "The dangerous animals often comprised . . . horses . . . steers, and . . . cows, all seemingly deranged in brain, and all apt, without warning, savagely to attack their fellows, the ranchmen, or the latters' mounts. . . . These 'locoed' brutes were victims of feeding upon toxic plants, the so-called 'loco weeds.'

... Two species each had seed-pods that, when dried, rattled on being moved, and so gave to each of these species the colloquial and undistinctive title of 'rattleweed.' There were other popular titles ... 'stemless loco,' or, according to the blossom's color, 'blue loco,' 'purple loco,' 'white loco,' or 'pink loco.' The ranchman made their botany still more confusing by employing the grammatic singular number instead of the plural, and thus referring to the collective plants not as weeds but as weed. When whatever title employed included either the word stemless or the name of a color, the term weed usually was omitted from the title. At times the vile weeds modified their process and sent an animal upon a run amuck. These death-dealing plants injected two words into the dictionary, the words 'locoed' and 'rattled,' the first as a synonym for crazy, the second as a synonym for crazy or excitedly confused." P. A. Rollins, *The Cowboy*, 42.   *n.* A locomotive. *Railroad use.*   **—ed** = loco. *Obs.*

Locofoco   *n.* A supporter of Andrew Jackson in his campaign for the Presidency. 1950: "In 1833 left-wing Jacksonians ... 'Locofocos,' as they were called. ..." W. H. Hale, *Horace Greeley*, 37.

locomotive   *n.* A mass cheer, common at most schools, that begins slowly and increases in tempo, resembling the noise made by a steam locomotive in starting up. 1951: "The first football game of the season, he came up to school in this big goddam Cadillac, and we all had to stand up in the grandstand and give him a locomotive—that's a cheer." J. D. Salinger, *Catcher in the Rye*, 18.

locust   *n.* A policeman's club. 1930: "A detective picked out the largest and heaviest locust in the group." Lavine, *Third Degree*, 78. *Because such clubs are often made of locust wood.* c1880– c1940; obs.

lola   *n.* See **lollapalooza.**

lollapalooza   also: **lala—, lolly—, lola—, lollo—, —oozer, —oosa —ooser, —ouser.**   *n.* Any extraordinary or excellent person or thing; a humdinger. 1936: "This gal's a lolapalooza." Tully, *Bruiser*, 144. 1951: "I distinctly remembered [the book] as a lollapaloosa." S. J. Perelman in *New Yorker*, Oct. 20, 28/3. 1951: "I have a filing system for keeping track of things that is, if I do say so myself, a lolla-

palooza." Judge Harold Medina, quoted in *New Yorker*, Nov. 24, 29/3.

lollipop   *n.* A weak or cowardly man. *Not common.*

lollop   *n.* **1** A guy; a fellow. *Archaic.* **2** A strong blow or hit. **3** A large portion, usu. of soft spooned food.

lollygag   lallygag   *v.i.* **1** To idle; to enjoy oneself by doing nothing in particular. 1868: DAE. 1951: "That left most of the summer free for play, swimming, berry picking, and general lallygagging." F. Sullivan, *New Yorker*, Aug. 4, 20/1. *Archaic and dial.* **2** To kiss and fondle; to spoon; to neck. c1920. *Archaic.* **3** To copulate; to spend a period of time, as a night, in casual carousing and sexual activity. *W.W.II Armed Forces use.*   **—ger**   *n.* One who lollygags. *Some c1920 use.*

lonely pay   The increased wages or bonus union workers ask for to offset reduced working hours due to automation. *The term was first used in the Shell Oil and Esso plant at Cheshire, Eng., 1956, when workers asked for such an increase to compensate for losing the companionship of fellow workers who had been replaced by machines.*

loner   *n.* **1** One person by himself, as a single fare or customer; one who attends a social function by himself. → **2** A man who prefers to work, live, drink, etc., by himself, without taking others into his confidence. *Used both derog.* = *an eccentric or unsociable person, and compl.* = *one strong enough to get along without help; one who does not meddle in the affairs of others.* 1951: "Gifford announced to the loner that the loner's presence was not to Gifford's liking. The loner shrugged his heavy shoulders. 'Drop dead,' the loner cried." S. Smith in N.Y. *Daily News*, Aug. 9, C15/4. 1951: "Although [baseball player Joe DiMaggio] never had been a hail-fellow-well-met, he became more of a 'loner,' almost a man apart from the rest of the team." A. Daley in N.Y. *Times*, Dec. 12, 54.

lone wolf   A man who, though he may lead an active social life and have many acquaintances, does not reveal his activities, has no close friends, no confidants, and keeps himself apart from any social group. 1957: ". . . A guy that was always around . . . he was a lone wolf." Leonard Feather, "Jazz Millionaire [Norman Granz]," *Esquire*, May.

long-arm   *v.i., v.t.* To hitch-hike. *From the gesture of extending the arm* *at full length to solicit a free ride from a motorist.* **long arm** The law; a policeman.

long-arm inspection Medical inspection of the erect penis. *Usu. Army use.*

long drink of water A tall, thin man, esp., but not necessarily, if dull or boring.

long green 1 Paper money. *Since c1890. Genuine money in sl., counterfeit money in argot.* 2 Money, usu. a large amount. 1912: "I tucked away a little of the long green." Johnson, *Stover at Yale*, 224. *Since c1895.* 3 Home-grown, home-cured tobacco. *Dial.*

long-hair **longhair** *n.* 1 An intellectual; one who likes serious books, music, theater, etc.; a person with cultivated tastes. 2 Classical music. 1956: "Technically jazz is going to do a lot (if it hasn't already) to what is sometimes called Western music, sometimes European music, and sometimes just longhair." S. Longstreet, *The Real Jazz Old and New*, 16. *Jazz musicians seldom use the word; in fact, modern musicians consider their cool and far-out music as demanding just as rigorous and serious standards as any other music.* *adj.* 1 Appealing to or liked by intellectuals, usu. said of entertainment. → 2 Classical; formal; usu. said of music, or of, by, for, or pertaining to classical music or classical or conservative intellectual pursuits. 1957: "This paper will deal with the formulation of a provisional definition of jazz, with particular emphasis upon its relationship to symphonic or 'Long-hair' music." Warren James, "Jazz and its Definition," *The Metronome Year Book*, 58.

long-haired *adj.* Fig., intellectual; highbrow. 1912: "Brockhurst . . . trying for the *Lit.* Clever chap, they say, but a little long-haired." Johnson, *Stover at Yale*, 88. 1953: "American music (long-haired, not pop). . . ." *New Yorker*, Feb. 21, 116.

long-handle underwear Woolen underwear with full-length sleeves and legs. 1945: ". . . sweaters, bobby-sox, coats and long-handle underwear to fill Norway's needs." Advt., *Time*, Dec. 24, 40/1.

long-heel *n.* A Negro. *Southern white use; archaic.*

longhorn *n.* A Texan.

longies *n.pl.* 1 Long pants. *Boys' use, in the recent past when boys wore short pants and the first pair of longies was eagerly awaited. Archaic.* 2 Long under-wear. 1953: "The lace-covered pantelettes which were that day's version of today's 'longies.' " C. Lawry, AP, Jan. 22.

Long John A tall, thin, lanky man. *Often used as a nickname.*

Long Johns Long woolen underwear.

long ones Long, woolen winter underwear. 1945: "What this nation needs is a return to the practice of wearing long ones in the wintertime. A generation and more ago, men, women, boys and girls, put on long ones in October and wore long ones until spring." *Wall Street Journal.*

long rod A rifle.

long shot 1 A scene photographed from a distance; the photograph of a distant scene. 2 A race horse with little chance to win a race and hence having high odds in the betting. → 3 A person, scheme, or business venture with little chance of success but with potentially great returns if success should occur.

long time no see "It's been a long time since I've seen you." *A common student and young adult greeting c1940–c1945.*

long underwear 1 Jazz music played in a sweet, popular, or corny way. 1956: "*Long underwear* for concert stuff is still in order." S. Longstreet, *The Real Jazz Old and New*, 150. *Since c1930, orig. jive use.* → 2 A poor jazz musician, esp. one who cannot improvise; one who has a classical musical education but does not play well enough to be entrusted with a solo chorus of jazz improvisation. → 3 Written arrangements of music. → 4 Classical music. 1944: "Kay thought Howard was out of this world till she found out he was a long-underwear platterbug." Cliff Macon in *Collier's*, Sept. 16, 64/3.

—loo See Appendix, Suffixes and Suffix Words.

looey **looie** *n.* 1 A second lieutenant. *W.W.I Army use.* → 2 A lieutenant, usu. preceded by "second" or "first." 1951: "They demoted me to a second looey." S. Lewis, *World So Wide*, 157. *W.W.I and W.W.II use.*

loogan *n.* 1 = **boob**; **sap**; **dope.** 1930: "The poor loogan she is marrying will never have enough dough to buy her such a rock." D. Runyon. 2 A prize fighter. 3 A hoodlum; a thug. 1939: " 'You think he sent that loogan after you?' 'What's a loogan?' 'A guy with a gun.' " Chandler, *Big Sleep*, 136f.

look-alike *n.* A person whose appearance closely resembles that of another person. 1949: "There were enough look-alikes in the flat photography of the period to puzzle me." Roeburt, *Tough Cop*, 153. 1950: "Barratt had an interview with his noted look-alike." Bob Thomas, AP, Dec. 6.

look at [someone] cross-eyed   To commit the smallest fault; to do any trivial thing out of the ordinary, regardless of its wrongness or rightness; to get out of line in the slightest degree. 1951: "The respectable owners who would yell copper if you looked at them cross-eyed." *I, Mobster*, 89.

looker   *n.* **1** A good-looking person of either sex. 1898: *DAE. Colloq.* → **2** An exceptionally attractive or beautiful girl or woman. 1914: *DAE.* 1930: "She's a looker." Burnett, *Iron Man*, 54. 1934: She's a swell looker." Chandler, *Finger Man*, 6. Cf. **good-looker.** *Colloq.* **3** A potential customer who looks over the merchandise; one who is not able or willing to buy. 1949: "A 'looker' is to the used car lot what a browser is to a book store." N.Y. *Times*, May 1, 62.

look-see   *n.* **1** A look, esp. a visual inspection, whether cursory or protracted. 1931: "Let's have a look-see at our friend." Queen, *Dutch Shoe*, 89. 1949: "I stopped in at Jerry's for a lager and look-see." Billy Rose, *synd. newsp. col.*, Dec. 1. *Since c1925.* → **2** A medical license, as carried by a traveling medical-show doctor. *From freq. demands by authorities to be shown the license.* → **3** A license to carry a gun, a soldier's pass, or any license or pass which one may have to show to the authorities.   **look see**   To look; to have a look. 1939: "I'm dropping down to look see." Chandler, *Big Sleep*, 39.

loon   *n.* **1** A stupid person. **2** An insane person, a lunatic. *Much less common than "loony."*   **—y   —ey**   *adj.* Insane; demented; fig., silly, idiotic. 1872: Thornton. 1943: "You looney punk." Wolfert, *Underworld*, 451.   *n.* A lunatic, both lit. and fig. 1949: "The inspired looney who hated killing. . . ." Billy Rose, *synd. newsp. col.*, Nov. 18. *Ending "—y" about twice as common as "—ey." From "lunatic," perhaps reinforced by "loon," the bird with a cry that resembles insane laughter. Since c1900.*

loony bin   loony-bin   *n.* An insane asylum. 1951: "That fugitive from a loony-bin. . . ." A. Kober in *New Yorker*, May 12, 32/1.

loony Joe   A left-handed baseball pitcher. *Never common.*

loop   *n.* **1** In sports, a complete component period in a game or contest, as a "round" in boxing, an "inning" in baseball, one "hole" in golf, etc. **2** In sports, a league of member teams, such as a baseball or football league; the towns in which the member teams of a league are located. 1953: "The Class C loop [in baseball]." AP, May 21. **3** A nobody; a person unable to contribute to a cause or plan in which he is engaged; fig., a person with nothing inside. *Not common.*   *v.i.* To go on a drinking spree; to drink. *Not common.*   **—ed** *adj.* Drunk. 1951: "The sap sounded half-looped." Spillane, *Big Kill*, 33. 1953: ". . . Gents at the bar indulge in competitive hospitality, and the end result is a looped group." H. Boyle, AP, Feb. 27. *Very common since c1945, particularly among college students and young adults.*   **—er**   *n.* **1** In baseball, a high easy hit between infield and outfield; a Texas leaguer. **2** A golf caddy.   **—y** *adj.* **1** Partially intoxicated. *Not common.* **2** Stupid; slow of thought; punch-drunk. 1942. "That loopy guy whose handkerchief you cry into." Chandler, *High Window*, 77.

loop-legged   *adj.* Drunk. *Not common.*

loose   *adj.* **1** With a bad reputation, esp. of promiscuity; promiscuous; said of a girl or woman; lit. a girl or woman of loose morals. *Colloq.* **2** So skilled, adroit, charming or intelligent that one is relaxed and at ease while performing or living; cool. *Some cool, far-out, and beat use.* **3** Irresponsible, fast. **4** Eccentric; nutty. See **have a screw loose. 5** Having little money. **6** Unreliable; unethical. 1949: "We ought to get a loose crowd up there Saturday night." N. Algren, *Man with the Golden Arm*, 29. **7** Generous; free with money.

loose as a goose = **loose**, cool use. See Appendix, Rhyming Slang.

loose in the bean   loose in the upper story   Crazy, lit. and fig.

loose wig = **far out.** 1957: "Loose wig—Completely uninhibited, really way out musician." E. Horne, *For Cool Cats and Far-Out Chicks. Some far-out use. Fig., one has flipped one's wig a great distance.*

loot   *n.* Money, esp. a large sum of money. 1951: "How much loot you got? . . . Money. How much? . . . How much loot?" Max Shulman, *Dobie Gillis*, 40. 1954: ". . . Rich planters would come [to Mahogany Hall] and spend some awful large amounts of loot."

L. Armstrong, *Satchmo, My Life in New Orleans*, 147. 1957: ". . . Musicians are 'cats' and money is . . . 'loot.' " Leonard Feather, "Jazz Millionaire [Norman Granz]," *Esquire*, May. *Common since c1945, orig. jazz use. For fairly large amounts of money "loot" has replaced "coin."*

loot   lieut   lute   *n.* A lieutenant. 1942: "Don't go and tell the Loot." W. B. Johnson, *Widening Stain*, 209. *Since c1750. Some W.W.I and W.W.II use. From "lieutenant".* Cf. **looey.**

lop   *v.i., v.t.* To curry favor with one's teacher(s). *c1890; some student use; obs.*

lorelei   *n.* **1** An eclectic mixture. **2** Specif. a stew, a dish of various foods cooked together.

loser   *n.* See **two-time loser.**

lose [one's] wig = **blow [one's] top.**

lost!, get   Fig., a request or command to go away and leave the speaker alone; to stop bothering or annoying the speaker; to "drop dead."

lot   *n.* **1** A baseball diamond. **2** The grounds where carnivals and circuses are held. 1934: standard use. *Web.* *Orig. circus use.* **3** The grounds and buildings where movie studios make and process films.

lot hopper   A movie extra. *Hollywood use.*

lot-louse   *n.* A person who stands around watching a circus being set up; a person who goes to a circus just to look and does not spend money to see the various shows. 1945: "The men who never spend a dime to visit the sideshow are 'lot lice' to her." Mitchell, *McSorley's*, 98. *Circus use.*

loud   *adj.* **1** Garish; gaudy; in bad taste; said of persons or things. *Colloq.* **2** Strong-smelling. 1935: "Mindy's Limberger is very loud." Runyon, 246. *Since c1900; not common.*

loudmouth   *n.* A person who talks loud and much; one who habitually says what is better left unsaid, tells secrets, or the like. 1940: "Maybe poking Loud Mouth in the kisseroo would solve everything." D. Decker in *This Week*, June 2, 6.

loud-talk   *v.t.* **1** To cause trouble for fellow prisoners or workers by talking loudly within earshot of a guard or superior about real or supposed violations of rules. *Since c1920. Orig. prison use.* **2** To flatter; to sweet-talk.

louie   Louie   *n.* A lieutenant in the U.S. Army. *Common Army use; universally known during and since*

W.W.II. See **looey.   Louie**   *n.* A migratory worker, orig. one from Louisiana. 1948: "Now [the fruit tramps] 're called Okies and Arkies and Louies." Cain, *Moth*, 112. *Never as common as "Okie" or "Arkie."*

lounge lizard   A ladies' man, often characterized as stingy, who calls upon girls and women but does not entertain them away from their own homes. The lounge lizard's interest is in necking.

louse   *n.* Any disliked person, usu. male; esp. one lacking in kindness, generosity, and ethical standards; an unethical person. *Very common.*

louse around   To loiter, loaf, or spend one's time idly. *Not common.*

louse-cage   *n.* **1** A hat. *c1895 teenage use; c1910 logger, hobo, and ranch use. Obs.* **2** A railroad caboose; a bunkhouse. *Logger, ranch, and railroad use. Archaic.*

louse up   To spoil, ruin, botch, or mess up something. 1938: "Boy, you certanly [*sic*] loused that up." J. O'Hara in *New Yorker*. 1950: "The stage crew decided to get even by lousing up his show on opening night." Billy Rose, *synd. newsp. col.*, Jan. 13.

lousy   *adj.* **1** Bad (also freq. as a pred. adj.) 1929: "Crab was all she ever did. What a lousy sport. . . ." D. Parker, "Big Blonde," reprinted in *The American Twenties*, 144. **2** Horrible; contemptible; despicable; extremely inferior; of poorest quality; worthless; incompetent; unpleasant; unwanted; disliked; sick. 1386: *OED.* 1820: "I have incurred a quarrel with the Pope's carabiniers, who have petitioned the Cardinal against my liveries, as resembling too nearly their own lousy uniform." Lord Byron, *Letters*, Everyman ed., 259. 1849: "I wish I could never hear the word lousy again. It is 'lousy' this and 'lousy' that. The rain is lousy, the trail is lousy, the bacon is lousy." Andy Gordon's diary, July 12, quoted in W. E. Woodward, *The Way Our People Lived* (1944). 1922: "Yuh lousy boob." O'Neill, *Hairy Ape*, I. 1930: "She is the lousiest necktie-picker-out I ever saw." D. Parker, *Laments for the Living.* 1934: "It's lousy." " 'How are you?' 'Lousy.' " ". . . Steaks were lousy." Cain, *Postman*, 7; 10; 11. 1951: "[Police] Commissioner [T. F.] Murphy said [to policeman] 'you make lousy witnesses for yourself.' " N.Y. *Her. Trib.*, Mar. 12, 1/15.   *adv.* Contemptibly, etc.; in a lousy way; poorly; badly. 1948: " 'How goes it?' 'Lousy.' " F. Brown, *Dead Ringer*, 17.

lousy with [something]   Well provided with something, usu. money; loaded; having much or many of; overwhelmed with. 1850: "Lousy with gold." *DAE.* 1926: "This war's lousy with sergeants." Stallings & Anderson, *What Price Glory,* I. 1927: "Everybody will come home lousy with cash." Hammett, *Blood Money,* 25. 1941: "Problems? Hell, we're lousy with them." G. Homes, *40 Whacks,* 91. 1951: "I'm not kidding, that hotel was lousy with perverts. I was probably the only normal bastard in the whole place." J. D. Salinger, *Catcher in the Rye,* 50. *From "lousy" = covered with lice.*

love apple   The tomato. *Colloq.; archaic.*

love-bird   love bird   lovebird *n.* A lover; a person who is in love; usu. in plural = a pair of lovers. 1939: "The two lovebirds." Chandler, *Big Sleep,* 154. 1949: "Ma barged in on the love birds." A. Hynd, *Public Enemies,* 121.

lovely   *n.* A lovely woman.

lover-boy   *n.* **1** A handsome man; a masculine idol. **2** A woman-chaser; a man who brags about his sexual exploits. *Usu. jocular use.*

lovey-dovey   *adj.* **1** Affectionate; amorous. → **2** Insipid; mushy. 1886: *DAE. Not common.*   *n.* **1** Friendship; brotherly love. 1946: ". . . And bring in a reign of peace, prosperity, and lovey-dovey." H. L. Mencken quoted in *Life,* Aug. 5, 46. *Not common.* **2** A wife. 1945: ". . . To help them with their foreign lovey-doveys—and, in some cases, with a small infant besides." D. Fairbairn, Phila. *Bulletin,* Dec. 10, 14/2. *Not common.* See Appendix, Reduplications.

low   *adj.* Sad, melancholy, depressed; physically, mentally, or emotionally exhausted. 1891: "I was so . . . low and depressed that I strolled into the bar at last. . . ." Bill Nye (Edgar W. Nye), *Remarks,* 350.

lowbrow   low-brow   *n.* An uneducated or unintellectual person; a person who is uninterested in cultural or intellectual matters. 1924: "We're a lot of low-brows." Marks, *Plastic Age,* 196. 1948: "My husband, Will Irwin, invented both the terms highbrow and lowbrow. He used them in a series of articles in the N.Y. *Morning Sun circa* 1902–3." Inez Haynes Irwin in *Word Study,* Oct., 1/2.   *adj.* Pertaining to unintellectual pursuits or popular entertainment; sensational. 1914: "You ain't too lowbrow." S. Lewis, *Our Mr. Wrenn,*

56. 1924: "What are you always pulling that lowbrow stuff for?" Marks, *Plastic Age,* 100.

low-down   *adj.* **1** Unfair; unethical; degraded; vile; low. 1850: Thornton. 1869: *DAE. Colloq.* **2** In jazz, slow, intense, in the manner of the blues. **3** Low-pitched and sensuous. 1951: "A babe with a low-down voice." Spillane, *Big Kill,* 66.   **low-down   lowdown** *n.* The real truth; confidential or authentic information; relevant facts; little-known intimate facts; info; dope. 1928: "What's the low-down?" Hecht & MacArthur, *Front Page,* II. 1930: "Until a man could get the low-down on the trouble. . . ." Lavine, *Third Degree,* 92. 1938: "The speaker gave me the low-down, as we say it, on how he [became an orator]." J. F. Skelly in *Better Eng.,* Nov., 47. 1949: ". . . Eager to get the low-down on new aircraft." Phila. *Bulletin,* Sept. 2, 14. *Note that the syllables of the adj. are equally stressed; the noun is accented on first syllable.*

lower the boom   **1** To deliver a knockout punch. *Prize fight use.* → **2** To chastise or punish; to attack with criticism; to treat sternly; to demand obedience. 1951: ". . . If we lower the boom on every nonconformist in society." A. Schlesinger, CBS radio, Mar. 14. 1951: "Just as [my children] were about to pawn my studs, my patience evaporated and I lowered the boom on them." S. J. Perelman in *New Yorker,* June 30, 20f. **3** To prevent another from succeeding; to act in such a manner as to harm another's chances of success.

low fi   *n.* The opposite of hi fi. *Jocular use.*

low-life   *n.* A vile person.

LP   A "long playing" record; a phonograph record made to play at the record-player turntable speed of $33\frac{1}{3}$ revolutions per minute, permitting a longer uninterrupted playing on a smaller record than the older standard of 78 or the intermediate 45 revolutions per minute. *Almost the only term used for this modern record; with the pop. LP records, "LP" is becoming a syn. for "record." Actually this abbr. is a patented trademark of Capitol Record Corp.* See Appendix, Abbreviations. *Colloq. since c1945.*

L's, the   *n.pl.* The losers in gambling. 1956: "The L's, or the losers; the professional bettors who receive a kickback of 5 per cent from bookmakers on losing bets." T. Betts, *Across the Board,* 317. *Never common.*

L7 *n.* = **square.** 1956: "L7 . . . Hollywood's latest lingo for a square: form an L and a 7 with your fingers and that's what you get." A. Shaw, *West Coast Jazz*, 79.

lube *n.* **1** Lubrication. 1957: ". . . Experienced serviceman knows where to put his finger on each lube point." Advt. for Amoco gasoline, CBS radio, July 18. *A written and spoken abbr.* **2** Butter. *A little student use; may be synthetic. From "lubricant."*

lubricant *n.* Butter. *A little student use. May be synthetic.*

lubricated *adj.* Drunk.

Lucifer *n.* A safety match, as used to strike a fire. *Orig. called "Lucifer match," from the inventor's name, common until c1925.* c1915: "Strike up a Lucifer and light your fag/ and smile boys that's the style. . . ." from pop. W.W.I song, "Pack Up Your Troubles In Your Old Kit Bag."

luck, out of Too late to obtain whatever is desired; to have no chance or opportunity for success or gratification.

lucked out To have met with ill fortune or disaster; specif. to be killed. *Some W.W.II use; some general use.*

luck up To become lucky; to become successful. 1954: "Before I lucked up." L. Armstrong, *Satchmo, My Life in New Orleans*, 25.

lug *n.* **1** The face, chin, or jaw. *Prize fight use.* → **2** Any strong but dim-witted man, esp. a prize fighter. → **3** A fellow, a guy, esp. a stupid or dull one. 1939: "Those lugs in the band would begin to kid me about it." O'Hara, *Pal Joey*, 11. 1940: "A simple-minded lug like Moose Malloy. . . ." Chandler, *Farewell*, 26. 1951: "A few lugs that were trigger-happy. . . ." *I, Mobster*, 82. **4** A request for money; money exacted by politicians or paid for police protection. 1935: "He figures it is the lug coming up, and Meyer is not such a guy as will go for the lug from a doll." Runyon, 322. 1950: "A captain of detectives whó was collecting the lug from the gambling houses." W. Pegler, *synd. newsp. col.*, Apr. 17. *v.t.* To solicit a loan; to borrow; to extend credit. *Underworld use.*

lug-clipper *n.* A boxer. *Never common.* See **lug.**

lugger *n.* A racehorse that bears toward or away from the inner rail, usu. toward. 1938: "A rapid lugger." Liebling, *Back Where*, 236. See **lug in, lug out.**

lug in To bear toward the inner rail of a race track, said of a race horse. *Horseracing term.*

lug on [someone], put the To ask for money as a loan or gift; to put the bee on [someone]. See **lug.**

lug out To bear away from the inner rail of a race track, said of a race horse. *Horseracing term.*

lugs *n.pl.* Proud or affected manners; airs; swank. 1889: *DAE.* 1900: "They put on a lot of lugs here, don't they?" Dreiser, *Carrie*, 323. *Obs. since c1935.*

lulu *n.* **1** Anything or anyone remarkable; an outstanding example of a type; anyone or anything of extraordinary size, quality, appearance, force, absurdity, or the like; a humdinger; a honey; a corker; used often derisively as well as admiringly. 1886: "Farrell's two-baser was a lu-lu." New Orleans *Lantern.* 1889: *DAE.* 1912: "While it [lasts, my college career] will be a lulu!" Johnson, *Stover at Yale*, 6. 1939: "Anna has a shape that is a lulu." Runyon, 69. 1940: "A few more lulus heard around the studio. . . . 'Clinkers' . . . 'Weaver' . . . 'Whacky Willies.'" K. W. Strong in *Better Eng.*, Mar., 119/2. 1952: "He said the aquarium was a lulu." A. J. Liebling in *New Yorker*, Jan. 12, 29. → **2** A popular, handsome, desirable person. *Some student use c1935.* **3** Any item that may be listed in an official expense account and that is regarded as in lieu of money payment of part of a salary. 1957: "Democrats Irked as 'Lulu' Plan Fails [Headline:] Democrat resentment over the Republican decision to abandon the 'lulus' of legislators by $1,500 boiled over in the Senate today. A 'lulu' is an expense allowance that does not have to be accounted for." N.Y. *Times*, Mar. 27, 7. *From "lieu."* See Appendix, Reduplications.

lumber *n.* **1** A toothpick. *Never common.* **2** A baseball bat. *v.t.* To arrest. *Some underworld use c1935.*

lumberman *n.* A beggar with a crutch. 1949: "The 'lumberman' can beg $30 a day with ease." W. J. Slocum, *Collier's*, Aug. 27, 60.

lummox lummux *n.* A clumsy, stupid youth or man, usu. of over average size. 1854: "Lummux." *DAE.* 1919: "Lommox." *DAE. Colloq.*

lump *v.t.* **1** To accept a situation one dislikes. 1828: *DAE. Colloq.* **2** To add sugar to a beverage, either lump or granulated sugar. *Not common.* *n.* **1** A package of food handed out to a beggar. 1936: "'Lumps' or 'poke-outs'

are possible at any time during the day."
H. F. Kane in *New Repub.*, July 15,
289/1. *Common hobo use.* **2** A dull or
stupid person; a clod. 1944: "A cad's
honor! What an unspeakable lump I was
to play fast and loose with virtue, honor,
and integrity." Shulman, *Feather Merchants*, 147. **3** The face. *Not common.*

lump it　　**1** A command to be quiet.
2 To give up an idea; to accept a bad
situation in silence; to forego a plan of
action.

lumps　　*n.pl.* **1** Lit. and fig., a swelling
of any part of the body caused by violence, as a beating; often in "get [one's]
lumps." 1949: "Somebody was out to give
him his lumps." Roeburt, *Tough Cop*, 95.
1951: "Their greatest fun is to see a cop
getting his lumps." H. Lee in *Pageant*,
Apr., 34/2. **2** Death caused by physical
violence. 1950: "Hardly a nice way to
get your lumps." Starnes, *Another Mug*,
74. 1952: "Schuster died without receiving anything much but lumps for his
pains." R. C. Ruark, *synd. newsp. col.*,
Mar. 13. **3** Fig., harsh treatment other
than physical; severe criticism or
questioning; exposure; rejection. 1950:
"When such a child begins getting his
lumps from society. . . ." J. Alexander
in *SEP*, Apr. 1, 75/2. 1950: "Truman is
getting his lumps again. . . ." W. Pegler,
synd. newsp. col., Apr. 17. *The most
common use.* **4** Punishment; physical
punishment. 1956: "The boys [rodeo
cowboys] were taking their lumps trying
to stay on wild Brahma bulls and wrestle
with steers." N.Y. *Daily News*, Sept. 27,
74.

lumps, get [one's]　　To be beaten up,
defeated, bawled out, or in some other
way to meet with another's vengeance;
to be punished or rebuffed; to fail or
be caused to fail. *Often implies that the
punishment, rebuff, or failure was deserved.*
Cf. **lumps.**

lumpy　　*adj.* **1** In jazz, badly played.
See **smooth.** *Cool use.* → **2** Unsuccessful;
unsatisfactory. *Cool use.*

lunch-hooks　　*n.pl.* **1** The hands, the
fingers. *Most common c1900.* **2** The
teeth. *Some c1900 use.* **3** Fig., adverse
or critical remarks. 1952: "It is difficult
to caricature Mickey Spillane. But [Ira]
Wallach [in his *Hopalong-Freud Rides
Again*] has managed to get a set of
predatory lunch-hooks into him." G.
Millstein in N.Y. *Times Bk. Rev.*, Sept.
14, 7/1.

lung　　*n.* A draw-bar connecting two

railroad cars. *Railroad use.*　　*v.i., v.t.*
To argue. *Not common.*

lung-duster　　lung-fogger　　*n.*
A cigarette. 1944: "Sweet Caporals, a
brand of lung-foggers. . . ." Fowler, *Good
Night*, 40. *Not common.*

lunger　　*n.* A person afflicted with
tuberculosis. 1929: "Yet here is a young
man, at once a lunger and lifer, who
looks himself over. . . ." J. Black in
New Repub., Apr. 17, 259/2.

lungs　　*n.pl.* A woman's breasts. *Never
common.*

lunk　　*n.* A stupid person. *From "lunk-
head."*

lunk-head　　lunkhead　　*n.* A stupid
person. 1852: *DAE.* 1951: "He was a
bulky, duckfooted lunkhead." J. Cheever
in *New Yorker*, Mar. 24, 24/2. *Colloq.*
—ed　　*adj.* Stupid. 1884: *DAE. Colloq.*

lush　　*n.* **1** Liquor. 1848: J. S. Farmer.
Archaic since c1920. **2** Food. *Some c1900
use. Never common.* **3** Money; cash. *Not
common.* **4** A drunkard; a heavy drinker,
esp. a habitual drunkard with a job,
family, and accepted place in society.
1939: "She is still plastered, the little
lush." O'Hara, *Pal Joey*, 13. 1945: "The
father was by no means a lush, but the
son carried temperance to an extreme."
Mitchell, *McSorley's*, 6. 1949: "Evvey
time a lush gets hisself loaded." A. Kober,
New Yorker, Nov. 5, 82. 1956: "The
martini lush is the most harmless of
drunks." J. Cannon, *Who Struck John?*
176. 1956: "I was married to a lush . . . a
painful alcoholic." S. Bellow, *Seize the
Day*, 93. *The most common use; very
widespread since c1920.*　　*adj.* **1** Drunk.
1848: J. S. Farmer. *Archaic.* **2** Prosperous; flush. **3** Satisfying; exciting; modern.
Some cool and far out use since c1955.
v.i., v.t. To drink liquor. 1936: "Lushing,
stowing wine into our faces. . . ." H. S.
Canby, *Harper's*, Feb., 355/2. 1944: "A
resumption of what I liked to think of as
civilized lushing. . . ." Shulman, *Feather
Merchants*, 17.　　**—ed**　　*adj.* Drunk.
Some use since c1920. See Appendix,
—ed ending.　　**—er**　　*n.* An alcoholic;
a habitual drunkard; a frequent drinker.
1848: J. S. Farmer. 1931: "City editors
are roughnecks and urbane gentlemen,
lushers and Puritans." S. Walker in
Amer. Mercury, Sept. 26/1. *Not common.*
See Appendix, **—er ending.**

lush Betty　　*n.* A whisky bottle. 1848:
J. S. Farmer. *Obs.*

lushed up　　*adj.* **1** Drunk. **2** Under the
influence of a narcotic. *Addict use; not
common.*

lush-roller   *n.* A thief who victimizes drunks. 1938: "A lush roller rolls lushes." Liebling, *Back Where*, 222. *Underworld use.*

lush-worker   *n.* = **lush-roller.** *Underworld, mainly pickpocket, use.*

lute   *n.* = **loot.**

lynch   *v.i., v.t.* To kill by any method. 1952: "That's what they did to my Jesus/ They stoned him, they stoned him!/ Called him everything but a child of God./ Then they lynched him on the cross." L. Hughes, *Laughing to Keep from Crying*, 205. *Mainly Negro use.*

M

M   *n.* **1** Morphine. 1949: "Heroin got the drive awright—but there's not a tingle to a ton—you've got to get M to get that tingle-tingle." N. Algren, *Man with the Golden Arm*, 76. *Wide addict use.* **2** Money. 1957: "M—Money." E. Horne, *For Cool Cats and Far-Out Chicks. Some far-out and beat use.*

ma   *n.* An effeminate male; usu. followed by the name of the person. *Some Negro use.*

macaroni   *n.* Sawdust. *Logger use.*

mace   *n.* **1** A blackjack; a club. **2** A baseball bat. *Not common.*

machine oil   Syrup. *Some W.W.II Army use. Prob. synthetic.*

Mack   *n.* A masculine appellative used as a term of direct address; often used in addressing a stranger.   **mack** *n.* **1** A mackintosh raincoat. **2** A pimp.

mackerel-snapper   *n.* A Roman Catholic. *Not common.*

mad   *adj.* **1** Angry. *Colloq.* **2** Exciting; remarkable; pleasing; excellent. *Orig. bop and cool use. Since c1945. Superseded by "crazy."* **3** Fine; able; capable; talented; said of cool jazz musicians. **4** Impetuous; impromptu.   *n.* A fit of anger. 1834: *DAE.*

mad —   For phrases beginning with "mad," see under the principal word of the phrase.

—mad   See Appendix, Suffixes and Suffix Words.

mad about [someone or something] To be in love with; to admire, like, or be fond of something.

madam   *n.* The female manager or proprietor of a brothel. *Colloq. Somewhat archaic.* 1954: "Presently the door swung open to show a painted slattern in a pink silk dressing gown. This was 'Big Mary' Binistrone, a madam of the old school." W. Henry, *Death of a Legend*, 22.

madball   *n.* The glass globe used by a crystal-gazer. 1948: ". . . Made with the madball." F. Brown, *Dead Ringer*, 161. *Carnival use.*

made   *n.* Straightened hair, a head of straightened hair. *Negro use.*   *v.t.* In the passive, to have been cheated, duped, or unfairly treated. *From "to make"* = to have sexual intercourse with. See Appendix, Sex and Deceit.   *adj.* Specif., made famous, made wealthy; famous, wealthy. See **make; make good.**

made, have [something]   To be assured of success at or in something, esp. without further work or worry. See **made; make; make good.**

Madison Avenue   **1** Collectively, the communications and advertising businesses; the philosophies and social concepts implicit in the mass-media advertising businesses. *Because many such enterprises are located on Madison Avenue in N.Y.C.* **2** A type of men's haircut. *Orig. common among workers on Madison Avenue.* 1957: ". . . The 'Madison Avenue' . . . the way Perry Como wears his—an inch long, lays flat top and sides, small part on left and with a slight curl. . . ." H. Mitgang, *About—Men's Haircuts.*   *adj.* Emanating from or resembling the ideas, manners, and social concepts of the large advertising agencies in N.Y.C.

mad money   **1** Money carried by a girl or woman with which to pay her own way home if she leaves her escort, usu. because of his sexual advances. → **2** Money saved by a woman against the time when she wishes to make an impetuous or impulsive purchase.

Mae West   A vestlike life preserver. *Wide W.W.II use. From its shape, which makes the wearer appear to have a large bosom, as does the entertainer Mae West.*

mag   *n.* **1** A magazine. 1934: "I was readin' a mag. . . ." Chandler, *Finger Man*, 47. 1951: "Gals who wear the latest clothes in the fashion mags are not suitable for films. . . ." B. Thomas, AP, Sept. 20. *A written and spoken abbr.* **2** A magneto. 1939: ". . . to take the

mag out [of the car] and give it a wipe." A. Christie, *Sad Cypress*, 136. *Not common.* See Appendix, Shortened Words. *v.i.* To talk a great deal. *From abbr. of magpie, a bird that traditionally chatters excessively. Not common.*

magazine *n.* A jail sentence of 6 months. *From phrase* "to throw the book at" *someone.* Cf. **newspaper.**

Maggie **maggie** *n.* **1** An automatic revolver. *Underworld use; archaic.* Cf. **Betsy. 2** A peddler of inferior goods; a dishonest peddler. *Not common.* See Appendix, —ie ending.

Maggie's drawers *n.* A red flag used on a firing range to signal a shot that has missed the target; hence a bad shot. *Army use.*

magoo *n.* **1** A custard pie used by actors to throw at one another in comedy scenes. *Theater use.* **2** An important person; a big shot. 1946: "The book [J. Weidman's *Too Early to Tell*] brims over with thinly veiled lampoons of Washington magoos, professional bandwagon liberals, and glib slogan makers...." Wm. DuBois in N.Y. *Times Bk. Rev.*, Dec. 1, 9/5. 1949: "[Paul Douglas] has yet to meet up with Darryl Zanuck, chief magoo of the studio." T. M. Pryor, N.Y. *Times*, Apr. 24, 5/6. *Not common.* Cf. **McGoo.**

mahaha *n.* Silly talk. *Not common.* Cf. **mahoola.**

mahoola *n.* Boloney; hooey. 1941: "The local Reds are already receiving their old-time mahoola about Red Russia being actually a democracy, and some of our interventionists are falling for it." N.Y. *Daily News*, June 27. *Not common.*

maiden *n.* A racehorse, regardless of sex, that has never won a race.

maiden's delight A cherry soda; a cherry-flavored Coca-Cola. *Some lunch-counter use.* See **cherry.**

main drag A major street in a town or city, often the most important business street; often that street of which the local populace is most proud or that street which is most attractive to visitors. 1907: "We begged together on the 'main drag.' ..." J. London, *My Life.* 1948: "... Strolled along the main drag...." F. Brown, *Dead Ringer*, 21. *Very common. Orig. hobo use.* Cf. **main stem.**

main-line **main line** **1** Money. *Dial.* **2** Collectively, wealthy people, socially prominent elements in any community. 1951: "She liked to have Peter there, so young and handsome

and so popular with the Main Line...." S. Longstreet, *The Pedlocks*, 16. *From the* "*main (railroad) line*" *leading into Philadelphia, Pa., which borders a district of wealthy homes.* **3** An easily accessible blood vessel, usu. in the arm or leg, into which narcotics can be injected. *Addict use.* See **mainliner. 4** A prison mess hall. *Some prison use.* **5** A coaxial cable linking the stations on a television network. *v.t.* To inject a narcotic drug intravenously. *Addict use.*

mainliner *n.* A drug addict who takes his narcotics by intravenous injection.

main queen **1** A steady girl friend. Cf. **queen. 2** A homosexual male who takes the female role, esp. one much sought after by other homosexuals.

main squeeze The most important or highest ranking person in a specif. organization, locality, workshop, or the like; any important person, specif. one's employer or foreman, the leader of an underworld operation, the dealer in a professional poker game, etc. 1927: "Vance seems to be the main squeeze." Hammett, *Blood Money*, 24. See **squeeze.**

main stem = **main drag.** 1907: "The kids began 'battering' the 'main stem.'" J. London, *The Road*, 160. 1943: "We sifted along the main stem...." Chandler, *Lady in Lake*, 49. *Not as common as* "*main drag.*" *Often implies familiarity with or affection for the town or street.* See **stem.**

maison joie A brothel. *Corrupted from the Fr.* 1956: "The finest pianist on record hired in Storyville was for Countess Piazza's 'maison joie.'" S. Longstreet, *The Real Jazz Old and New*, 55.

make *v.t.* **1** To steal something. *Since at least c1825.* **2** To rob a person or place. *Underworld use.* **3** To recognize or identify a person; to notice, discover, or see a person. 1939: "He made me the minute he saw me, as the detectives say." O'Hara, *Pal Joey*, 38. 1949: "I tailed him. ... He made me and tried to throw me off." Evans, *Halo for Satan*, 133. *Mainly underworld use.* → **4** To understand or comprehend a person or topic. 1921: "I don't make you, kid. What did the boy do?" Witwer, *Leather*, 70. *Not common.* **5** To appoint a person to a job; to increase his rank or status; to attain success, as to be chosen by a group or to achieve a certain desirable position. *Colloq.* → **6** To attain success, fame, money, etc.; to become a success. **7** To impress favorably, esp. a member of the opposite sex; to make a good impression; to meet with acceptance in advances to one of the opposite sex. 1934: "The chatter of my Junior home-room girls with . . . their problems of 'making' some of the 'smooth' boys. . . ." E. Russell in *Eng. Jour.*, Nov., 74. *Archaic*. **8** [taboo] To seduce; to lay. *Usu. said by males in boasting of sexual liaisons, or as a promise or threat of future coitus.* See **make it with [someone]**. 1950: "The first town we hit was Yazoo, Mississippi. Immediately I started playing piano and I made the landlady of the house, so that meant plenty of food for Jack and I." A. Lomax, *Mr. Jelly Roll*, 125. See Appendix, Sex and Deceit. **9** To become a business, financial, or social success in a specif. and deliberately chosen field or group; esp. to do so by being aggressive, ruthless, or taking advantage of others; to take advantage of another, to cheat, trick, or deceive another. Fig., to **make good**. See Appendix, Sex and Deceit. **10** To go to or arrive at a specific place. **11** To defecate. *Adult use in talking to children.*   *n.* **1** An identification; the act or instance of recognizing a person, as a criminal suspect. 1950: "We got a make on his prints." Ntwk. radio prog., *Gangbusters*, Jan. 28. **2** A newly appointed cadet officer or noncommissioned officer. *Some Army use; not common.* **3** The loot taken in a robbery. **4** = **hit**.

make —   For phrases beginning with "make," see also under the principal word of the phrase.

make a pitch   To propose something that will be in one's own favor; to request money, aid, or sympathy.

make a (the) scene   To participate or become involved or interested in or concerned with a specific activity or field of endeavor. 1958: "Nobody ever 'does' anything. You 'make a scene.'" Sam Boal, *Cool Swinging in N.Y.*, 26. *The specific activity or field of endeavor always precedes "scene." Thus, "I'm going to make the political scene" could mean that the speaker is going to become a candidate for office, to vote, to read a book about or to discuss politics. Orig. c1955 beat use, some far out use. Cf.* **make**.

make for   To steal from.

make good   To succeed. *Colloq.*

make hay while the sun shines   To take full advantage of one's opportunity. *Orig. applied only to financial matters. Cf.* **that ain't hay.**

make it   **1** To succeed, either in a specif. endeavor or in general. See **make**. **2** To leave or depart hastily.

make it with [someone]   **1** To have sexual intercourse with someone. **2** To be liked, respected, or befriended by someone; to be compatible with someone. *Cool use.*

make out   **1** To fare; to get along; to succeed. *Often in "How did you make out?" = What happened?* → **2** Specif., to succeed in seducing a woman.

make-out artist   **1** A man noted for his talents in seduction. 1949: "The correct description [now] for such a fellow [a wolf] is 'make-out artist.'" N.Y. *Times Mag.*, Mar. 6, 33/1f. See **make out**. **2** One, usu. a male, who seeks to impress his superiors; a man with charm and a good line.

make something out of   To interpret as a challenge or affront. 1948: "So you heard what I said, huh? You want to make something out of it?" J. McNulty in *PM*, June 10, 13. *Usu. in the expression "Do you want to make something out of it?" = Do you want to fight over it?*

make time with [someone]   **1** To date, court, or have amorous relations with another's girl friend, fiancée, or wife. → **2** To date, court, or have amorous relations with a girl or young woman. *Fairly common student use.* → **3** To court or attempt to impress a superior favorably. *Not common.*

make with the eyes (hands, feet, mouth, etc.)   To bring the specified organ into operation. 1939: "The poor man's Bing Crosby is still making with the throat [i.e., singing] here in Chi." O'Hara, *Pal Joey*, 42. 1949: "On your way, dreamboat. Make with the feet." Chandler, *Little Sister*, 73. 1950: "I made with the shoulders [= I shrugged]." Starnes, *Another Mug*, 26. 1951: "Don't make with the hands or the feet or the eyes [don't touch me or look at me]." Movie, *Here Comes the Groom*. *N.B.: the term may also be used in connection with specific skills (make with the singing, dancing, etc.) or with specific instruments (make with the saw, typewriter, machine gun, etc.).*

makings   **makin's**   *n.pl.* The ingredients or items needed in making or doing something. 1956: ". . . Makin's being the shuckmattress, quilt coverlet, and two square pillows. . . ." N. Algren, *A Walk on the Wild Side*, 13. *Dial.*

malarkey *n.* Exaggerated talk; tedious talk; lies; boloney, bunk. 1945: "Hollywood is in the business of manufacturing malarkey as well as movies. There is more unabashed truthlessness emanating from this town. . . ." Bob Thomas, AP, July 13. 1951: "An awful lot of malarkey disappeared from journalism in the 25-year history of 'The New Yorker.' " J. Crosby in N.Y. *Her. Trib.*, Dec. 12, 29. *Colloq. since c1935. adj.* Unusual; silly. 1939: "The weather was malarkey, goofy." P. E. G. Quercus, *Sat. Rev. Lit.*, Dec. 23, 21/1. *Not common.*

mallet-head *n.* A stupid person. *Not common.*

mama *n.* Marmalade. *Some lunch-counter use. Not common.*

Mama's boy A sissy; a boy, youth, or even man, who refuses to act independently or share responsibilities commensurate with his age and sex.

mamma *n.* See **red hot mamma.**

mammy boy A mother's boy; a sissy. 1910: "I'm not a mammy boy nor a goody-goody." Johnson, *Varmint*, 310.

man *n.* **1** A dollar. 1921: "You oughta grab about 300 men. . . ." Witwer, *Leather*, 4. *From "iron man."* **2** A term of direct address, to both known men and strangers, but usu. implying that the person addressed is hip and the speaker is sincere. 1943: "Man, he's murder, Jack." M. Shulman, *Barefoot Boy with Cheek*, 90. *Perhaps from Brit. West Indies. Common since c1935, esp. among jive and cool groups.*

—man See Appendix, Suffixes and Suffix Words.

Man, the **man, the** *n.* **1** The law; a law enforcement officer; a private detective. Fig., Uncle Sam; specif., a federal law enforcement officer, as a U.S. treasury agent. 1957: "The drug trade's slang for a law enforcer was, indicatively, 'The Man.' " A. Halsey, *SEP*, Mar. 30, 101. **2** The leader of a band, esp. a jazz band or combo. 1957: "The Man—The leader of a band." E. Horne, *For Cool Cats and Far-Out Chicks. Mainly bop, cool, and far-out use; some general jazz and popular band use. To his devotees "The Man" refers to only one band leader, Stan Kenton, also composer, arranger, and pianist.*

man about town **man-about-town** A sophisticated, debonair man of any age, but usually of some wealth, who is a frequenter of the better nightclubs, restaurants, bars, and entertainments, usu. with sophisticated and lovely young women.

man-catcher *n.* An employment agency or agent. *Hobo use; archaic.*

mangy with Covered with or full of; lousy with.

man in gray A postman. *Not common.*

man-size **man-sized** *adj.* Large; great in amount or bulk. 1941: "Crump bet man-sized money. . . ." J. Lilienthal, *Horse Crazy*, 23.

map *n.* **1** The human face. 1908: *DAE.* 1921: "A funny look . . . spread over Kenney's crimson map." Witwer, *Leather*, 158. *Colloq.* **2** A check, esp. one written against a fictitious or deficient account. 1956: "MAP—A bank check; not necessarily bad, yet frequently heard in that sense." T. Betts, *Across the Board*, 317.

maps *n.* Sheet music. *Some cool musician use; many jazz musicians scorn those who need sheet music to prompt their playing.*

maracas *n.pl.* [taboo] A woman's breasts. 1939: "I forgot about Lana. . . . Yes that is how good this Melba was. Gams and a pair of maracas that will haunt me in my dreams. . . ." O'Hara, *Pal Joey*, 59. Cf. **eyes, head-lights, shakers.**

marble-dome *n.* A stupid person.

marble orchard A cemetery. 1941: "You'll get your names in this marble orchard soon enough." Cain, *M. Pierce*, 155.

march *n.* A circus parade, esp. the parade through a town to drum up customers before a performance. *Circus use; archaic.*

marfak *n.* Butter. *From the trade name of a lubricating grease. Some Army use.* See **grease, lube.**

Marge **marge** *n.* Margarine.

Mari *n.* = **Mary, 4.**

Maria *n.* See **Black Maria.**

marine *n.* An empty whisky or beer bottle; a "dead marine."

mark *n.* **1** An easy victim; a ready subject for the practices of a confidence man, thief, beggar, etc.; a sucker. 1941: "Not that he's more of a mark than a lot of other horse nuts. . . . He takes these down-and-out touts around among his friends." J. Lilienthal, *Horse Crazy*, 35. 1949: "His 'marks'—as the gullible are called by a pitchman. . . ." N.Y. *Times*, Aug. 28, 63. 1958: "Mark . . . Target or victim of a confidence game." G. Y. Wells, *Station House Slang. Mainly underworld, carnival, circus,*

and hobo use, but universally known.
2 Among carnival workers, any outsider or member of the local community. 1948: "Marks . . . aren't allowed in." F. Brown, *Dead Ringer*, 4. *Carnival use.* **3** An inexperienced or stupid person. *Not common.* **4** A place from which it is easy to obtain food or money by deception, thievery, or begging. *Underworld and hobo use.* **5** The amount of money taken in a robbery. *v.t.* To seek or find a person or place worth robbing. *Underworld use.*

marker *n.* **1** A written, signed promissory note; an I.O.U. 1932: "He is willing to take Charley's marker for a million." D. Runyon, 157. **2** A scoring point in a game.

marmalade *n.* = **malarkey.**

marquee *n.* The front entrance of the main tent of a circus. *Circus use; archaic.*

marsh grass Spinach. *Dial.*

martooni *n.* A martini cocktail. *Fairly common jocular mispronunciation.* See Appendix, Mispronunciations.

Mary *n.* **1** A male homosexual who plays the female role. *"Mary" is the female name most commonly assumed by such homosexuals.* **2** A female homosexual. **3** A woman. 1945: "And calling women Marys. . . ." G. Brooks, *A Street in Bronzeville*, 7. *Not common.* **4** Marijuana; also spelled "Mari."

Mary Ann A marijuana cigarette. *Some addict use.*

Mary Jane = **Mary Ann.**

Mary Warner Marijuana.

mash *n.* **1** Love for one of the opposite sex. c1920 [1954]: ". . . Just another mash. . . . We would use the expression, 'The lady has a mash on you. . . .' " L. Armstrong, *Satchmo, My Life in New Orleans*, 151. → **2** A love affair. → **3** A lover, of either sex. *v.t.* **1** To flirt with; to make a sexual advance toward. 1882: *DAE. Still some use.* **2** To give something to another. *Negro use.*

—er *n.* **1** A male flirt. 1882: *DAE.* 1900: ". . . A still newer term, which had sprung into general use among Americans in 1880—a 'masher.' " Dreiser, *Carrie*, 4. *Obs. by c1920.* → **2** A man who tries to force his attentions on a woman against her will. *Colloq. In the U.S. the word has never had the Eng. sl. meaning of a beau or a dandy.* See **mash.** See Appendix, —er ending.

mashed *n.* An order of mashed potatoes. *Common lunch-counter use in relaying an order.*

mash in To press in the clutch pedal

of a truck or hot rod. *Orig. W.W.II Army use. Some hot rod use since c1950.*

mash note A complimentary or flattering written message of self-introduction, used as the first step in an attempt at seduction; a short love letter or note. 1900: ". . . Letters were handed her by the doorman. . . . *Mash notes* were old affairs." Dreiser, *Carrie*, 299f. 1930: "He gets mash notes by the ton." Burnett, *Iron Man*, 52.

mask *n.* The face.

maskee *adj.* O.K. *Some W.W.II Marine Corps use.*

massage *v.t.* To beat up; to thrash. 1930: " 'Massaging' . . . and numerous other phrases are employed by the police." Lavine, *Third Degree*, 3. 1937: "The thugs have been caught and massaged with rubber hoses in the back room of some station house." H. F. Pringle, *Amer. Mercury*, Feb., 142/2.

mastermind *n.* **1** The planner, manager, or leader of any undertaking. *Now stand.* **2** A railroad trainmaster. *Railroad use.* *v.i., v.t.* To plan, direct, or command; to give orders. 1947: "The fellows who mastermind prize fights, football games, hockey, baseball. . . ." Billy Rose, *synd. newsp. col.*, May 15. 1949: "I'll do the master-mindin' around here." Movie, *Sands of Iwo Jima*.

mat *n.* **1** A woman; one's wife. *Some Negro use.* **2** The floor; the deck of a ship, esp. the deck of an aircraft carrier.

mat, hit the = **hit the deck.** See **mat.**

mat, on the = **on the carpet.** *Some student use since c1930; some W.W.II USN use.*

math *n.* Mathematics; the study of mathematics. *Still not considered stand. by some scholars, though universally used as a written and spoken abbr.*

matie *n.* **1** A shipmate; any comrade. **2** A term of direct address, usu. to a stranger. *Not common in U.S.* See Appendix, —ie endings.

maud *n.* **1** A woman. *Some underworld use.* **2** An engine, esp. a steam engine. 1956: "Oilworkers use the terms . . . *Maud*—an engine. . . ." *Labor's Special Lang. from Many Sources.*

maulie **mauly** *n.* **1** A hand; the human hand. 1848: J. S. Farmer. 1946: "Now the guys grapple with each other . . . seldom using their maulies." D. Runyon, *synd. newsp. col.*, Sept. 14. → **2** Specif. a fist. *Neither use common.* See Appendix, —ie ending.

Maw Bell The Bell Telephone Company. *Not common.*

max *adj.* Maximum. *n.* The highest possible grade in a class or course of study. 1851: *DAE. Student use until c1910.* See Appendix, Shortened Words. *v.* To achieve a maximum success. *West Point use.*

may *n.* Mayonnaise. *Some c1930 lunchcounter use. Obs. Replaced by "mayo."*

mayo *n.* Mayonnaise. *Common lunchcounter use since c1930.* Cf. **may.** See Appendix, —o ending.

mayvin *n.* A self-styled expert in men's clothing; a customer who professes to know more about tailoring, styles, etc., than a clothing salesman. 1952: "The most trying type [of customer] of all . . . is the 'mayvin.' The word is of Yiddish origin, has entered the language. . . ." G. Millstein, N.Y. *Times Mag.*, Sept. 21, 58/3. *Not common.*

mazel *n.* Luck. 1951: "Let's have another drink and toast somethin' we could both use, a little *mazel*—Jewish for luck." S. Longstreet, *The Pedlocks*, 396. *From the Yiddish "masel" = luck.*

mazoo *n.* Money. *Not common. From "mazuma."*

mazoola **mazula** *n.* Money. *From "mazuma" plus "moola." Not common.*

mazoomy *n.* = **mazuma.**

mazuma **mezuma** **mazume** *n.* Money. 1926: "As originally used by the Jewish people [*mazuma*] is '*m'zumon*' and is a Chaldean word meaning 'the ready necessary.' It is employed in the Talmud. . . ." H. Heshin, *AS*, I, 456/1. 1941: "When you die, you have to leave your mazuma behind." G. J. Nathan, *Amer. Mercury*, May., 615/1. *Common since c1915.*

McCoy *adj.* Genuine. 1937: "Like every other McCoy biz. . . ." *Variety*, Sept. 27, 63. *Since c1930.* Cf. **real McCoy. 2** Neat; tidy. *Some underworld use.* *n.* The genuine thing. *Colloq.*

McGoo *n.* Sex appeal. *Some c1930 use. Obs.*

meal *n.* A bore; a dull person; a creep or drip. 1949: "In Denver, socially boresome classmates formerly referred to as 'creeps' are now called 'meals.' " *Time*, Oct. 3, 37. *Some student use c1945–c1950. Obs.*

meal ticket **1** A prize fighter in relation to his manager or agent. 1921: "He gits in the ring with that meal ticket of yours. . . ." Witwer, *Leather*, 30. 1945: "Mike [Jacobs, a fight promoter] was . . . strolling along yesterday in company with his meal ticket, the Brown Bomber himself [fighter Joe Louis]."

A. Daley, N.Y. *Times*, Oct. 17, 24/5. → **2** Any person upon whom one depends for a livelihood, as an employer, husband, etc. → **3** Any skill, instrument, talent, part of the body, etc., which provides a living for its possessor.

mean *adj.* Orig. far out use = psychologically exciting, satisfying, and exhaustive; far out, the end, formidable, keen. 1957: "Mean—The best; the greatest." E. Horne, *For Cool Cats and Far-Out Chicks. Far out and beat use, some cool use. Usu. an attrib. modifier of the direct object in a simple clause. Since c1920.* Cf. **wicked.** See **far out.**

meany **meanie** *n.* A mean, petty, or contemptible person. 1951: "The old meanies!" S. Lewis, *World So Wide*, 206. *Now more jocular or affectionate than derog.* See Appendix, —ie ending.

meat *n.* **1** One who is easily defeated or influenced by another; a poor opponent in a sports contest, business venture, or the like. → **2** A task or enterprise that is easy and pleasing; a field of endeavor for which one possesses a natural talent. **3** [taboo] The vagina; a woman considered sexually; coitus. See Appendix, Food and Sex. Cf. **piece. 4** The gist or meaning of a story, book, play or the like; the essential factors in a given situation; principal facts, ideas, items, etc.

meat-and-potatoes *adj.* Basic; primary; major. 1949: "It's the meat-and-potatoes appeal—the old pull at the heartstrings—that'll put us over at the box office." S. J. Perelman, *Listen to the Mocking Bird*, 57.

meat bag The stomach. 1848: *DAE; obs.*

meatball **meat ball** *n.* **1** A dull, boring person; an obnoxious person; anyone regarded with disfavor, esp. one of flat or uninteresting character; a creep, a drip, a square, a wet blanket. *Fairly common W.W.II use, both by servicemen and civilians; now somewhat archaic.* **2** A tactical signal flag bearing a black dot on a yellow field; also, the Japanese national flag. *Some W.W.II USN use.* **3** A swelling of or on the face, caused by a blow in fighting. *Some prison use since c1910.* **4** In baseball, any pitched ball that can be hit readily by a given batter. *Baseball use. Not common.* Cf. **gopher ball.** *v.t.* To strike someone with the fist. *Some prison use.*

—ism *n.* **1** Anti-intellectualism; the state of willing ignorance or mediocrity. **2** A state of, or instance demonstrating, decreasing standards of integrity, ethics, intelligence, and individualism in culture, politics, education, and the like; democratic rule by an uneducated, nonthinking majority.

meat-burner *n.* A cook. *Obs. International Workers of the World use.*

meat card = **meal ticket.**

meat-fit *n.* A full meal, esp. one with plenty of meat. *Hobo use; archaic.*

meat-grinder *n.* An automobile. *Some c1940 student use.*

meathead *n.* A stupid person. 1949: "Look, meathead." Burnett, *Jungle*, 34. 1950: "The copper . . . was a big meathead." J. B. Martin in *SEP*, May 27, 20/3. **—ed** *adj.* Stupid. 1949: "Some meat-headed tart." Burnett, *Jungle*, 69.

meat-hooks *n.pl.* The hands or fists, esp. of a large, powerful man.

meat run Any fast train. *Railroad use.*

meat-show *n.* A cabaret floor-show with scantily clad or unclad dancing girls. 1951: "A divertissement known in the trade as a meat-show." W. Pegler, *synd. newsp. col.*, Dec. 27. See **meat.**

meatwagon meat-wagon meat wagon *n.* **1** An ambulance. 1939: "He must have pulled his rip cord because he woke up in the meatwagon." *Forum*, July, 42/1. *Fairly common.* **2** A hearse. 1943: "Murder-a-day Marlowe, they call him. They have the meat wagon following him around to follow up on the business he finds." Chandler, *Lady in Lake*, 103. 1956: "The band would march out behind the meat-wagon, black plumes on the hearse horses. . . ." S. Longstreet, *The Real Jazz Old and New*, 7. **3** A Black Maria; a police patrol car. *Not common.*

mechanic *n.* An expert card player, esp. one skilled in dealing and shuffling unfairly; a professional card dealer in a gambling establishment; a "shark." 1956: "In poker . . . no 'mechanics' (sharps) were tolerated." T. Betts, *Across the Board*, 121.

med *n.* **1** A medical student; medicine as a course of study. 1851: *DAE. A common written and spoken abbr.* **2** Medicine, esp. bottled patent medicine. *Not common.* *adj.* Medical. *Not common.* See Appendix, Shortened Words. **—ic** *n.* **1** A medical student. 1823: *DAE.* 1850: "And medics sing the anthem too." *Yale Banner*, Nov., quoted in Hall, *College Words*, 198. *Obs. since c1900.* **2** A physician; a member of the

Army Medical Corps. 1885: *DAE.* 1952: "Medics rushed into the tent, picked up the first stretcher and lashed it to the outside of the helicopter." AP, Aug. 21. *Most common during and since W.W.II.* **—icine** *n.* Information. *Dial.* **—ico** *n.* A physician. 1952: "'His prognosis . . . is bleak,' the VA medico had set down." N.Y. *Daily News*, Aug. 13, C3/2. *Since c1920. Never as common as "medic" now is.*

meemies *n.pl.* See **screaming meemies.** 1948: ". . . Knowing [that a chimpanzee] was on the loose gave him the meemies." F. Brown, *Dead Ringer*, 101.

meestle *n.* A dog. *Dial.*

meet *n.* **1** A point where trains are scheduled to meet. *Railroad use.* **2** An appointment; specif., an appointment to discuss or enter into illegal dealings; a hit. 1939: "I telephone Tommy and make a meet with him for dinner. . . ." Runyon, 87. 1949: "She went out to make a 'meet' to buy more bogus bills. . . ." *Fact Detec. Mysteries*, 91. **3** A sporting contest, esp. a competition in track and field sports. **4** A jam session; a gig. 1957: "Meet—A jam session." E. Horne, *For Cool Cats and Far-Out Chicks. Bop, cool, and far out use. Because bop, cool, and far out musicians do not actually jam; they just "meet" together to play.*

megger *n.* A movie director. *Some c1920–c1935 Hollywood use; archaic. From the megaphone that early movie directors used in shouting instructions to cast and crew on a large movie set.*

meller *n.* = **melo.**

mellow *adj.* **1** Mildly and pleasantly drunk. 1737: Pa. *Gazette. Still fairly common.* **2** Skillful; sincere, heart-felt; said of a jazz performance. *Orig. jive use; now some cool use.*

mellow-back *adj.* Smartly dressed. *Some Negro use.*

melo *n.* A movie melodrama. *Some Hollywood use.*

melon *n.* **1** The total profit or monetary gain from a business or enterprise, whether legal or not; the spoils. → **2** Fame, glory, or patronage obtained by a group, esp. a political party, to be distributed among the members.

melon-belly *n.* A man with a protuberant abdomen. *Not common.* See **beerbelly.**

melted *adj.* Drunk, esp. to the point of unconsciousness. *Some student use.*

melted out   1 Having lost all one's money at gambling. 2 Without funds; broke.

Melvin   *n.* A dull, uninformed, or obnoxious person; a profoundly objectionable person. *Sometimes used in direct address. Since c1950. Pop. by comedian Jerry Lewis.*

memo   *n.* A memorandum. *Colloq. A written and spoken abbr.*

men, the   *n.pl.* The police, esp. state highway patrolmen. *Truck-driver use.* See **man, the.**

mental job   One who is, or who is suspected of being, a neurotic, psychotic, paranoid, manic depressive, or otherwise psychologically abnormal.

merge   *v.t.* To marry. 1945: "He confirmed that he would merge next with [a] Mexican actress. . . ." W. Winchell, *synd. newsp. col.*, Dec. 10. *Synthetic.*

merry   *adj.* Drunk; silly or loquacious as a result of liquor. 1737: Pa. *Gazette. Still some use.*

merry-go-round   *n.* 1 A railroad turntable. *Railroad use; archaic.* 2 A race track. *Archaic.* 3 A rapid, confusing sequence of jobs, appointments, duties, or the like, usu. in the expression "to be on a merry-go-round" = to be extremely busy.

merry haha, the   Ridicule; the laugh; usu. in expression "to give someone the merry haha." See **haha.**

meshuga   *adj.* Crazy; eccentric. 1953: "You seem to be a little meshuga." Movie, *Tonight We Sing. From the Yiddish; the Yiddish feminine ending "a" is used for both sexes.*

meshugana   *n.* A crazy or eccentric person. *From the Yiddish; the Yiddish feminine ending "a" is used in referring to both sexes. Not common.* See **meshuga.**

mess   *n.* 1 A stupid person. *c1930. Still common.* 2 Pleasure; excitement; anything pleasurable or exciting; a "ball." *adj.* 1 Immoral; degenerate; ignorant. 2 Excellent; remarkable. *Some cool and beat use since c1950.* 3 An immoral person; an abnormal person. **—y** *adj. & adv.* 1 Immoral; unethical. 2 Complex or confusing; said of a situation or action. 3 Bothersome.

mess around   To waste time; to idle; to work lackadaisically.

mess around with   To insult, tease, harass; to treat with ridicule, to refuse to consider seriously. 1954: "Nobody dared to mess around with Slippers. He was a good man with a pistol. . . . He could fight

fair and he could fight dirty." L. Armstrong, *Satchmo, My Life in New Orleans,* 202.

mess up   To get into or cause trouble. *Since c1915. Fairly common during and since W.W.II.*

messy bucket = Merci beaucoup. *Some jocular W.W.II Army use.* See Appendix, Mispronunciations.

meter   *n.* A quarter; 25¢. *From the coin, which often is needed to operate a gas meter. Orig. Negro use. Never common.*

meter-reader   *n.* The copilot of an airplane. *Mildly derog. W.W.II Air Force use.* See Appendix, Rhyming Slang.

Mex   *n.* A Mexican. 1927: "I found Paddy the Mex. . . ." Hammett, *Blood Money,* 9. *adj.* Mexican. 1934: "Ensenada is all Mex." Cain, *Postman,* 97.

mex   *n.* Any foreign currency. *Some c1925 Army use, esp. at posts in Philippine Islands. Obs.*

Mexican [derog.]   *adj.* Cheap, inferior. *Not common. Some southwest dial. use.*

Mexican athlete   An unsuccessful candidate for a sports team. *Never common.*

Mexican breakfast   A breakfast the consuming of which amounts to smoking a cigarette and drinking a glass of water, usu. because one has no money, has a hangover, or is too tired to eat.

Mexican promotion   **Mexican raise** Advancement of rank or status without any accompanying increase in income.

mezonny   *n.* Money; orig. money spent for drugs. *Addict use. From Carnese.* See Appendix, Little Languages.

mezuma = **mazuma.**

mezz   *n.* A marijuana cigarette. *adj.* Sincere; excellent. *Jazz use. From the jazz clarinetist Mezz Mezzerow, a musician known for his refusal to submit to commercial standards as well as for his drug addiction.*

MG   *n.* A machine-gunner. *W.W.II use.*

mib   *n.* 1 The game of marbles. *Child use, common c1890–c1930. Still some use. Dial.* 2 A small playing marble.

Michigan roll   A bankroll with a genuine banknote, usu. of large denomination, around the outside and bills of smaller value, or newspaper or stage money, on the inside.

mick   **Mick**   *n.* [derog.] 1 An Irishman; a person of Irish descent. 1872: *DAE.* 1900: "[Shaughnessy]'s a slow, greedy 'mick!'" Dreiser, *Carrie,* 240. 1922: "Mick." O'Neill, *Hairy Ape,*

I. *From pop. Irish proper name Michael, reinforced by the surname prefix "Mc." Orig. = a poor, unskilled Irish immigrant.* 2 A Roman Catholic. 1924: ". . . you go chasing around with kikes and micks." Marks, *Plastic Age,* 201. 3 A micrometer. *Some factory use since c1920.* See Appendix, Abbreviations. *adj.* 1 Irish. 1894: *DAE.* 1922: "This Mick agitator . . . De Valera. . . ." S. Lewis, *Babbitt.* 1951: "That's what the mick bastards always say in their thick brogue." *I, Mobster,* 3. 2 Roman Catholic. 1924: "I suppose you refer to . . . my one mick friend, although he isn't Irish. . . ." Marks, *Plastic Age,* 201.   **—ey** **—y** *n.* 1 [derog.] An Irishman; a person of Irish descent. → 2 A potato, whether or not an Irish potato. 1945: "Sometimes [the children in N.Y.C.] roast mickies in the gutter fires." Mitchell, *McSorley's,* 18. 3 = **Mickey Finn.** 1938: "Mickeys act so drastically that one may kill a drunk with a weak heart." Liebling, *Back Where,* 88. 1951: "Slip her a micky." *I, Mobster,* 93.

Mickey Finn   mickey finn   1 Any strongly purgative pills, drops, or potions given to an unsuspecting person, usu. in food or drink, to force his departure or as a joke. *Since c1930. Orig. the term applied only to a laxative pill made for horses.* → 2 Any strong hypnotic or barbiturate dose administered to an unsuspecting person, usu. in an alcoholic drink, in order to render him unconscious; the drink itself.

Mickey Flynn = **Mickey Finn.** *Not common.*

mickey mouse   mickey-mouse micky mouse   micky-mouse *adj.* Sentimental, insincere, or characterized by trick effects; said of pop. dance music or the musicians who play it. 1956: "A *micky-mouse band* is a real corny outfit that pushes trombone sounds and uses out-of-tune saxes." S. Longstreet, *The Real Jazz Old and New,* 149. *Musician use.*

Mickey Mouse (movie) A documentary or short movie vividly showing the means of prevention, the causes, development, and care of venereal diseases; a documentary or short movie vividly showing methods of hand-to-hand combat. *Wide W.W.II Army use, in ref. to such movies shown as part of soldiers' training courses.*

middle-aisle it To marry or be married. *Synthetic.*

middle leg [taboo] The penis.

middy *n.* A midshipman; a U.S. Naval Academy student. *Since c1900.*

midnight *n.* A cup of black coffee. *Lunch-counter use; never common.*

midway *n.* A hall; an aisle between prison cell blocks. *Some prison use.*

miff *v.t.* To offend; to vex; to anger. **—ed** *adj.* Offended, vexed, angered. 1938: "Miffed by this raillery I asked, 'And how are you . . . so certain . . . ?' " H. Broun in *New Republic,* Sept. 14, 158/1. 1952: "Davioni . . . miffed over failure of pals to raise his bail . . . is telling what he knows." N.Y. *Daily News,* Aug. 21, 1. *Colloq. since c1935.*   **—y** *adj.* = **miffed;** also splenetic; irascible. 1951: "After a good bit of miffy correspondence between Miss Kellems and the commission, the latter issued a cease-and-desist order." A. Logan in *New Yorker,* Feb. 10, 39/3.

mig   Mig *n.* 1 A cheap playing marble, usu. made of clay or the cheapest china and often not perfectly round or smooth; the cheapest playing marble. *Boy use c1890–c1925. Usu. not cap. Such marbles have now been replaced by glass ones.* 2 A migratory worker. *Some c1935 West Coast use.* 3 Any Russian-made fighter or bomber plane. *Wide Korean War use. From the initials of the best Russian jet fighter planes used by the Communist forces. Always cap.*   **—gle** *n.* 1 A playing marble. 1895: *DAE. Dial. From "mig."* 2 A marijuana cigarette. *Addict use. Never common.* See **muggle.** **—s** *n.pl.* 1 = **mig,** a marble. 2 The game of marbles. *c1890–c1935.*

Mig Alley   Mig alley   1 A specif. area over a series of valleys in North Korea where Communist jet fighter planes began their attacks on northward-flying UN bombing missions during the Korean War. *Wide Korean War use.* See **Mig.** 2 Any street or road in the U.S. where many expensive foreign sports cars may be seen or where sports-car races are held. *From the pop. MG sports and racing car and as a pun on the first meaning. Not common.*

mighty *adv.* Very; exceedingly. *Colloq. since c1820.*

mighty mezz, the Marijuana; a marijuana cigarette. 1956: "Dreamed about a reefer five foot long/ The mighty mezz, but not too strong;/ You'll be high, but not for long/ If you're a viper." *From jazz song, "If You're a Viper."* See **mezz.**

mike *n.* 1 A microphone, esp. one used in radio or television. 1935: *Ten*

Years Before the Mike, a book by T. Husing. 1939: "I brought her up to the mike...." O'Hara, *Pal Joey*, 28. *Since c1925. A common written and spoken abbr.* See Appendix, Shortened Words. **2** A microfarad. *Electronic engineer use.* **3** A microscope. *Some student use.* **4** A Mikado engine. *Railroad use.* *v.i.* To use or speak into a microphone. *Radio use since c1925. Not common.* **—s** *n.pl.* The human ears. *Not common. From "mike."*

Mike *n.* See **Red Mike.**

Mike and Ike Salt and pepper shakers.

milkcan *v.t.* See **knock for a loop.**

milk run An easy military aerial mission, usu. a bombing mission—easy either because no opposition is encountered or because the distance covered is short. 1944: "The Fort was flying a wet beam ... and it looked like a milk run...." C. Macon in *Collier's*, Sept. 23, 69/1. *W.W.II Air Force use.*

milk toast See **milquetoast.**

milk wagon A police wagon or truck used to transport arrested persons to jail. Cf. **Black Maria, paddy wagon.**

mill *n.* **1** A prize fight. 1914: "Wonder what Wolgast will do in his mill?" S. Lewis, *Our Mr. Wrenn*, 159. 1929: "The night of the K.O. Kelly mill." J. Auslander, *Hell in Harness*, 16. *Prize fight use; somewhat archaic.* **2** A prison; a guardhouse. *Fairly common Army use since W.W.I.* **3** A railroad locomotive. *Railroad use since c1925; not common.* **4** A typewriter. *Since c1930; not common.* **5** An automobile, esp. a fast one. *Not common.* **6** A motor, esp. an airplane motor. *W.W.II Armed Forces use.* *v.i.* To fight; to be a contestant in a prize fight. *Archaic.*

— mill See Appendix, Suffixes and Suffix Words.

millionaire *n.* Any person whose wealth is great, or more than the speaker's. 1951: "In Rahway, there's a junk dealer. A millionaire, must be worth not a cent less than a hundred thousan'." S. Longstreet, *The Pedlocks*, 220.

milquetoast *n.* Any shy, timid, or extremely gentle person. *From H. T. Webster's cartoon character Caspar Milquetoast, central figure of the comic strip "The Timid Soul." First published in 1924 in the N.Y. "World"; later in many other forms and publications.*

Milwaukee goiter A large midsection if attrib. to owner's propensity for beer-drinking. *Milwaukee, settled by German immigrants, is known for the quality and quantity of beer manufactured and consumed there.*

min *n.* A policeman. *Some underworld use. From "Man, The." More common in Brit. underworld than in U.S.*

mince pies *n.pl.* The eyes. *One of the most common underworld uses of rhyming sl.* See Appendix, Rhyming Slang.

— mind See Appendix, Suffixes and Suffix Words.

mingle *n.* **1** A football game. *Student use. Not common.* **2** A dance. *Student use.*

mingy *adj.* Mean and stingy. 1946: [Attrib. to Noel Busch], *Word Study*, Apr., 2/2.

minister's face **minister's head** Pig's head cooked and served at a meal. *Hobo use.*

mink *n.* A lecher. 1949: "The ... doctor was a regular mink...." Burnett, *Jungle*, 76. *Not common.*

Minnie *proper n.* Minneapolis.

mint leaves Banknotes. *Not common.* Cf. **cabbage, kale, lettuce.**

misery pipe A bugle. *Reputedly some Army use. Prob. synthetic.*

mish-mash **mishmash** **mish-mosh** **mishmosh** *n.* A mixture composed of many ingredients, esp. a poorly integrated mixture; confusion; a hodgepodge. Usu. in reference to food, such as hash, or theatrical works. 1901: Greenough & Kittredge. 1946: "The daily blats which made a big mishmosh of [gamblers'] welching...." D. Runyon, *synd. newsp. col.*, Aug. 5. 1948: "A couple of foreign films—a mish-mosh from France called 'Passionnelle.' ... " Billy Rose, *synd. newsp. col.*, Nov. 24. 1951: "They won't fall for that kind of mish-mash." Movie, *Fixed Bayonets.* 1952: "The interior of the hotel was decorated in an engaging, if preposterous, mish-mash of ... Egyptian, Moorish, and Victorian styles." *New Yorker*, Feb. 9, 26/1. 1957: " 'The Sea Gull' broke most of the rules of the theatre of Chekhov's day and was regarded as a hopeless mishmash in St. Petersburg." Brooks Atkinson, N.Y. *Times*, Sept. 29, X. 1957: "There was Gothic melodrama with dancing girls in tights, and comedy songs, and long speeches by Stalacta, Queen of the Golden Realm; there were gnomes and demons and Zamiel the Archfiend, and Swiss peasant maids—all mishmashed together." Leonard Bernstein, "American Musical Comedy," *Vogue*, Feb. 1, 159.

miss   *v.t.* To fail to menstruate at the normal time. 1947: "A beautiful but wicked girl of a good Port George family missed one month. Then she missed another month. She went to a doctor and found out the truth, then rushed to General Draughton and named the man: Pete Layne." C. Willingham, *End as a Man*, 9.

Miss Anne   Any white woman. *Negro use. Not common.*

missionary worker   An employee hired to break a strike by nonviolent means. 1956: "*Missionary worker*—One who tries to break strikers' morale by calling at their homes, trying to convince wives of strikers that all is lost, starting rumors that the strike is over." *Labor's Special Language from Many Sources.*

mission stiff   See **stiff.**

Mississippi marbles = **African dominoes.**

Missouri River   Gravy. *Some c1915 prison use; archaic.*

miss the boat   **1** To arrive too late for any occasion. →**2** To lose an opportunity; to fail, esp. to fail to understand a command, a direction, a double entendre, etc. *The most common use.*

missus, the   missis, the   *n.* One's wife. 1930: "He wanted the missus to get some sleep." Lavine, *Third Degree*, 70. *Colloq. since c1925.*

Mister   *n.* A man, fellow, guy, used as direct address to a stranger; also, as in giving an order or reprimand to one whose name is known, to show objectivity or rejection.

Mister —   See Appendix, Prefixes and Prefix words. See also entries under **Mr.**

Mister Big   The leader, planner, director of an underworld enterprise, esp. one whose real identity is unknown. *Also used occasionally in politics.*

Mister Charlie   A white man. *Some Negro use.*

Mister Ducrot   A term of derog. direct address to any West Point plebe. 1936: " 'Mr. Ducrot,' 'Mr. Dumbguard,' and similar titles denoting the hapless plebe. . . . " H. Beukema.

Mister Dumbguard   *n.* = **Mister Ducrot.**

Mister Hawkins   A cold wind; winter; wintry weather. *Hobo use, orig. Negro use.*

Mister Right   **1** = **Mister Big.** *Because "Mister Big" is always right, by virtue of his power. A new term that may replace "Mister Big."* **2** A dream man;

the perfect man a girl hopes to marry.

Mistofer   *n.* Mr.; Mister. 1952: "Mistofer Estes Kefauver's coonskin cap. . . ." R. C. Ruark, *synd. newsp. col.,* Apr. 3. *Dial.*

mistreat two   *imp.* A command to prepare two scrambled eggs, two eggs being one order. *Some lunch-counter use in relaying a customer's order.*

mitt   mit   *n.* **1** The human hand. 1907: "The erstwhile hospitable farmers met us with the icy mit." J. London, *The Road*, 187. 1923: ". . . Snatched right out of his mitt." C. MacArthur, *Rope. Colloq.* "*Mitt*" *is considerably more common than* "*mit*." Cf. **tip [one's] mitt.** **2** A boxing glove. 1930: "Will have the big mitts on. . . ." Burnett, *Iron Man*, 123. **3** = **mitt-reader.** **4** An arrest. See **mitts.**   *v.t.* **1** To shake hands with, as in greeting. **2** To put handcuffs on someone; to make an arrest.   *v.i.* To clasp hands above the head as a signal of victory, as a boxer acknowledging a favorable decision from the ring. 1930: "Prince Pearl was sitting in his corner and mitting the crowd." Burnett, *Iron Man*, 22.

mitt, the   *n.* **1** Any charitable or religious organization that gives food or lodging to hobos. *Hobo use.* **2** An arrest. See **mitts.**

mitt camp   *n.* A fortune teller's tent. 1948: "Mitt camp." F. Brown, *Dead Ringer*, 30. *Carnival use.*

mitten   *n.* **1** In "give [someone] the mitten" = to jilt, to reject a suitor or lover; in "get the mitten" = to be jilted. 1844: "Get the mitten." *DAE.* 1847: "Give [someone] the mitten." *DAE. Archaic and dial.* **2** In "get the mitten" = to be expelled from college. *Some student use.*

mitten, get the   See **mitten.**

mitten, give the   See **mitten.**

mitt-flopper   *n.* A soldier who does favors for or shows excessive deference to his superior officers, such as saluting unnecessarily; an ass kisser. *Army use. Not common.*

mitt-glommer   *n.* A hand-shaker. See **glom, mitt.**

mitt joint = **mitt camp.** *Carnival use.*

mitt reader   A palmist; a fortune teller. 1945: "Every confounded swami-woman and mitt-reader in the nation taken to calling herself Madame So-and-So. . . ." Mitchell, *McSorley's*, 98. *Carnival and circus use since c1925.*

mitts   *n.pl.* A pair of handcuffs. *Underworld use.*

mix *n.* **1** A social meeting of many persons. *Never common.* **2** The packaged and prepared (i.e., already mixed) ingredients of a cake, pie filling, or other food, usu. in such form that only liquid need be added before cooking. *Such commercially packaged goods were introduced after W.W.II and were common by 1950. Colloq.* *v.i.* To fight. 1921: "Them last two babies mixed with each other [many] times a month...." Witwer, *Leather*, 3. *Orig. prize fight use.*

mixer *n.* Water, soda, or any soft drink used to dilute whisky. *Colloq.*

mix it = **mix it up.** 1930: "The referee told Coke to mix it." "O'Keefe ...didn't seem anxious to mix it." Burnett, *Iron Man*, 24, 189.

mix it up To fight with the fists; esp. to fight vigorously and enthusiastically. 1920: "... A prize-fight where the principals refused to mix it up." Fitzgerald, *This Side of Paradise*, 61.

mixologist *n.* A bartender. 1856: *DAE. Still some jocular use.*

mix-up *n.* A fistfight.

mo *n.* A moment. *A common spoken abbr. but seldom written. Usu. in "just a mo" or "half a mo."*

moan *v.i.* To move rapidly. *Some student use c1935.*

moan, put on the To complain.

mob *n.* **1** An underworld gang. *Colloq.* **2** A safe-cracker. *Underworld use; archaic.* **3** A group of men in one employ. *Colloq.* **4** A group, gathering, or class. 1949: "... As a member of the ruling mob." W. Pegler, *synd. newsp. col.*, Oct. 13. **—ster** *n.* A member of an underworld mob. 1939: "... A mob nickname he got from the mobsters." O'Hara, *Pal Joey*, 52. *Colloq.*

mocha *n.* Coffee. 1929: "... A couple cups of Mock-a." T. Wolfe, *Look Homeward*, 564. 1939: "I never saw you even pick up a tab for 4 mocha java coffees." O'Hara, *Pal Joey*, 64. *adj.* Negro; brown-skinned. 1943: "... Negress, tall, mocha-colored ... looks like a mocha tart...." Wolfert, *Underworld*, 251. *Since c1850; not common.*

mochalie *n.* A Chinese. *Never common.*

mockie [derog.] *n.* A Jew. 1939: "I consider this ... disrespectful, like calling Jewish people mockies, or Heebs, or geese." D. Runyon, 25. 1939: "They ... crashed their fists into a mockie." J. T. Farrell, 204. 1943: "Love thy neighbor if he's not a seventh-day adventist or a nigger or a greaser or a ginzo or a hunkie or a bohunk or a frog

or a spik or a limey or a heinie or a mick or a chink or a jap or a dutchman or a squarehead or a mockie or a slicked-up grease-ball from the Argentine...." Wolfert, *Underworld*, 484.

mocky *n.* A young mare. *Dial.*

Model-T *adj.* Cheap; primitive; run-down. 1951: "... A real Model-T speakeasy out of an early Warner Brothers movie." S. Longstreet, *The Pedlocks*, 394.

modoc *n.* **1** One who becomes an Air Force flier for publicity, social prestige, or similar reasons. *W.W.II use. Never common.* **2** One of the several small dummies set up to be knocked over by baseballs at a carnival tent; hence, a stupid person. *Carnival use.*

mogue *v.t.* To deceive. *Never common; obs.*

mohasky *n.* Marijuana. *adj.* Under the influence of marijuana. *Not common. From "mohoska."*

mohoska *n.* Muscle; energy used in work. *Some maritime use.*

mojo *n.* Any narcotic. *Addict use.*

moke *n.* **1** [derog.] A Negro, esp. a Negro minstrel. 1856: *DAE.* 1899: "Smoky Mokes," title of a pop. song. *Obs. From "mocha."* **2** [derog.] A Filipino. *Some c1930 USN use.* **3** An easy-going fellow; one who habitually asks favors; a bore. *Some c1900 use.* **4** A horse, esp. an inferior race horse; a plug. *Not common in U.S. but fairly common in Australia.* *adj.* Dark; black; Negroid. *Not common.*

mokers, the *n.* Despondency; dejection; the blues. *Some use since c1955.*

mokus *n., adj.* **1** Drunk. **2** Liquor **3** Loneliness. *Not common. All are hobo use.*

molasses *n.* A good-looking used automobile displayed to attract customers to a used-car lot. 1949: "... Casting covetous eyes toward a cream puff that was being used strictly for molasses. ..." N.Y. *Times*, May 1, 62. *From the traditional bait for catching flies.*

moldy fig **1** A prude; a pedant; one whose views or tastes are old-fashioned. **2** Specif., a person who prefers traditional jazz to the progressive forms. 1948: "... The moldy figs ... are certain that the greatest jazz ever played ... was played in New Orleans in 1915." Harry Henderson and Sam Shaw, "And Now We Go Bebop," *Collier's*, Mar. 20, 88. 1956: "A *moldy fig* is what the long-hairs of jazz call a simple admirer of Dixieland Jazz." S. Longstreet, *The Real Jazz Old and New*,

149. *c1946.* 1957:". . . Animosity that exists between moldy figs and bop-lovers. . . ." Robert Shelton, "The Professor Digs Jazz," *Jazz World,* March. *Orig. bop use c1946, now also cool use. Sometimes incorrectly used to = square, but specif. = a devotee of any prebop jazz form or style who cannot accept or appreciate bop or progressive jazz.* adj. Outmoded; old-fashioned.

moll *n.* **1** A woman or girl; a sweetheart. 1785: Farmer & Henley. 1930: ". . . To borrow one of his pal's molls." Lavine, *Third Degree,* 38. *No longer common.* **2** A prostitute. 1785: Farmer & Henley. **3** A gangster's female accomplice or sweetheart. *The most common use. Colloq. since c1930.* See **gun moll.**

moll buzzer **1** A thief who preys on women, such as a purse snatcher. *Underworld use since c1920.* **2** A tramp who begs from women. *Hobo use since c1925.*

mollie *n.* A state tax token. *Dial.*

molly-hogan *n.* Any complicated or puzzling thing. *Mainly logger use. Dial.*

Molotov cocktail A homemade bomb, specif., one consisting of a bottle filled with gasoline or an alcohol mixture, and usu. a rag wick. *Orig. used by Russian civilians in fighting against the invading Nazi army during W.W.II. Such a bomb was supposed to have been effective in destroying tanks. Molotov was the USSR foreign minister during W.W.II.*

mom **Mom** *n.* A mother; one's mother. *Colloq.* **—ism** *n.* The social phenomenon of widespread mother domination; matriarchism as an informal power structure supported by sentimentalism; popular mother worship. *Coined by Philip Wylie in his "Generation of Vipers" (1943), an attack on American social mores, the term and the idea have been much discussed.* **—my** *n.* = **mom.** **moms** **Moms** *n.sing.* = **mom.**

moment *n.* See **big moment.**

mo-mo *n.* A moron. See Appendix, Reduplications.

momzer **momser** *n.* **1** One who borrows frequently, or who expects much attention and many favors; a sponger. *From the Yiddish.* → **2** Any disliked person; a bastard.

mon *n.* Money. *Not common.* See Appendix, Shortened Words.

Monday man One who steals clothes from clotheslines. *Hobo and carnival use. Because Monday is the traditional wash-day.*

Monday-morning — See Appendix, Prefixes and Prefix Words.

Monday morning quarterback **1** Specif., a football devotee who, upon learning the results of the various plays of the football game played on the previous Saturday, as published in Monday morning papers, gives his detailed opinion as to what plays should have been attempted or initiated by the quarterback of his favorite team. **2** One who, after an event, gives advice or opinions on what should have been done.

money, in the Having money, esp. a lot of it. 1943: "I'm in the money at last. . . ." H. A. Smith, *Putty Knife,* 123.

money-bags **moneybags** *n.sing.* **1** A wealthy person. 1949: "They might annoy some aged moneybags. . . ." J. Evans, *Halo,* 173. *Colloq.* **2** A paymaster. *Some W.W.II USN use reported.*

money smash In baseball, a home run. 1951: "The most spine-chilling event of the 4½-hour game . . . was [Jackie] Robinson's money smash." H. Altschull, AP, Oct. 1.

money talks Lit., wealth is power; money buys anything. 1951: "It wasn't very crowded, but they gave me a lousy table anyway—way in the back. I should've waved a buck under the head-waiter's nose. In New York, boy, money really talks—I'm not kidding." J. D. Salinger, *Catcher in the Rye,* 55. *Now a folk saying more than a sl. term.*

mongee *n.* = **mungey.**

moni(c)ker **monniker** **monacer** **monica** *n.* A person's name, nickname, or alias; the name by which a person wishes to be known; a name. 1907: "His 'monica' was Skysail Jack. . . ." " 'Monicas' are the *nom-de-rails* that hoboes assume or accept." J. London, *The Road,* 122, 126. *Colloq. Orig. hobo use, then underworld, now common. Until c1930 usu. = an alias or nickname, as of a hobo or criminal; after c1930 usu. = one's real name.*

monk *n.* **1** A monkey. 1901: Greenough & Kittredge. 1950: "Jocko, a . . . ring-tail monkey, became . . . obnoxious. . . . A relieved Anderson took the monk on to his destination." AP, July 22. *A written and spoken abbr., universally known.* See Appendix, Shortened Words. **2** [derog.] A Chinese, specif., a Chinese living in the U.S. 1925: ". . . The Chinese—known to their Occidental neighbors, the Irish especially, as monks. . . ." Roy L. McCardell, "When the Bowery Was in Bloom," *SEP,* Dec.

19, 80. *Never common.* 3 A high-ranking judge. *Underworld use c1930.* *v.t.* To neck. *Some c1935 student use; never common.* **—ey** *n.* 1 A man. 1939: "A smart monkey." Chandler, *Big Sleep,* 190. 2 An average man; one who is not a hobo, with a carnival, or on the grift. *Hobo, carnival, and grifter use.* → 3 A dupe; a victim. *Carnival use. Not common.* 4 Any of many types of employee whose costume, uniform, movements, or actions resemble a monkey; specif., a chorus girl, porter, musician in a tuxedo, bridge worker, freight handler, etc. 1928: "One of the monkies, as they are called, sang and did [a] . . . torrid dance." J. Armstrong in *Amer. Mercury,* Aug., 399/2. See **monkey suit.** 5 A silly, frivolous, or precocious person. *Usu. used affectionately.* 6 A term of affection freq. applied to small, mischievous boys. 7 Narcotics addiction; the drug habit. 1949: "When I hear a junkie tell me he wants to kick the habit but he just can't I know he lies even if he don't know he does. He wants to carry the monkey, he's punishin' hisself 'n don't even know it." "Then I got forty grains 'n went up to the room 'n went from monkey to nothin' in twenty-eight days 'n that's nineteen years ago 'n the monkey's dead." N. Algren, *Man with the Golden Arm,* 79. *Common addict use.* See **monkey on [one's] back.** *v.i., v.t.* = **monkey around.** See **monkey with the buzz-saw.**
— monkey See Appendix, Suffixes and Suffix Words.
monkey act Any entertaining or sensational action or statement. *Not common. From the vaudeville axiom "Don't follow the monkey act," because anything after such an act will be an anticlimax.*
monkey around To occupy oneself aimlessly or without knowledge or confidence; to tinker with, often out of curiosity; to adjust, touch, poke at, interfere with, or play with; to loaf or idle. *Colloq.*
monkey business 1 Any unethical, deceitful, secret, furtive, or socially objectionable conduct or dealings, something fishy; specif., cheating in gambling or business, or attempting sexual advances with one of the opposite sex. 1883: *DAE.* 1946: ". . . A guarantee against any monkey business with the cards." D. Runyon, *synd. newsp. col.,* Aug. 5. *Colloq.* → 2 Trifling or foolish conduct; monkeyshines. 3 High-spirited,

good-natured pranks or teasing; frivolity. Cf. **monkey.**
monkey cage A prison cell. *Some prison use.*
monkey-chaser *n.* 1 [derog.] A West Indian. *Negro use since c1920.* 2 A drink composed of gin, sugar, water, and ice. 1952: "Monkey chasers are gin and ice, with a little sugar and a trace of water. That term 'monkey chaser' comes from Georgia. . . ." *New Yorker,* Aug. 30, 15/3.
monkey clothes 1 A tuxedo; formal or evening clothes. *Some c1900 use; archaic.* See **monkey suit.** 2 A full-dress uniform. *Army use.*
monkey drill Calisthenics. *W.W.II Armed Forces use, esp. USN.*
monkey-flag *n.* The flag, insigne, or standard of an Army or Navy unit; the flag or insigne of a business firm or a social or political organization.
monkey-house *n.* A caboose. *Railroad use; not common.*
monkey jacket 1 A tight coat of coarse, strong cloth. 1830: *DAE. Obs.* → 2 A full-dress blouse. *Annapolis use.* → 3 A khaki uniform coat worn in the summer. *C.C.C. use, c1935.*
monkey meat Inferior, tough beef. *Some Army use since W.W.I.*
monkey off, get the To break a drug habit. 1949: ". . . So hooked on morphine that there would be no getting the monkey off without another's help." N. Algren, *Man with the Golden Arm,* 74. *Addict use.* See **monkey on [one's] back.**
monkey on [one's] back Drug addiction, considered as a financial, physical, mental, and moral responsibility; the drug habit; lit., a strong addiction that one spends most of one's energy to support. *Common addict use, now universally known. When without drugs an addict feels weighted down and depressed, when buying drugs an addict is supporting pushers and his drug habit, thus, fig., the addict carries an extra burden; it may be a large or small monkey—some have a* $100-a-day monkey. Perhaps based on the obs. **have a turkey on one's back.**
monkey pie Coconut cream pie. *Some lunch-counter use in relaying order.*
monkey punk A bellhop or porter in uniform. *Not common.* See **monkey.**
monkeyshines *n.pl.* Tricks; pranks; trifling or foolish conduct. 1847: *DAE. Colloq.*
monkey's instep, the = **the cat's meow.** *c1920; never common.*

monkey stick   A cane; a walking stick. *Not common.*

monkey suit   Almost any uniform or uniform-like suit of clothes, trousers, blouse, jacket or coat, or often cap or hat; usu. disparaging, in allusion to the fancy outfit traditionally worn in the U.S. by an organ-grinder's monkey. Specif., formal dress or dinner clothes; an Army or Navy uniform, esp. a full-dress uniform; a porter's or bellboy's uniform; the fur-lined or electrically heated suit worn by military airmen. 1946: "Neither of my two hats went well with the monkey suit." Evans, *Halo in Blood*, 145. 1949: "The enlisted seaman's uniform, disrespectfully called a monkey suit, has changed little since 1797. Its cut and creases, its buttons and bell-bottomed trousers are all symbolic of the lore and legends of the sea." Phila. *Bulletin*, Aug. 17, 10/2. *Colloq.* See **monkey.**

monkey time   Daylight Saving Time. *Dial.*

monkey wagon   The caboose of a railroad train. *Railroad use. Not common.*

Monkey Ward   *proper n.* The business firm of Montgomery Ward, a mail-order house; a Montgomery Ward store.

monkey wire   Telegraph lines between small towns. *c1920 telegrapher term; obs.*

monniker   *n.* = **moni(c)ker.**

moo   *n.* **1** Beefsteak. 1916: " 'An order of rump steak rare,' says another [customer]. 'Slab of moo—let him chew it!' " M. Eastman, 183. *Some lunch-counter use in relaying orders.* **2** Milk; cream. *Some Army use reported; prob. synthetic.* **3** = **moola.** 1945: "What Are We Gonna Do To Get Rid of All Our Moo?" Song sung by Frank Fay in *How to Be Poor. Not common.*

moocah   *n.* Marijuana. *Addict use.*

mooch   *v.i., v.t.* **1** To beg. 1948: ". . . Asking my way to the station when I really meant to mooch." Cain, *Moth*, 77. *Since c1880.* **2** To steal. **3** To loaf, idle, or hang around. *Some use c1915.* **4** To saunter; to move slowly. *Not common.* **5** To borrow; to obtain gratis. 1956: "Free loading in the fight racket has diminished in the age of television. Anyone who can mooch a ham sandwich is considered a champion." J. Cannon, *Who Struck John?* 123. **6** To steal; to pilfer. **7** To beg food, money, or the like. 1931: "Hoboes . . . range from the lowest type who 'mooches' bread and scraps, and nothing else. . . ." C. Ash-

leigh in *Everyman*, May 21, 520/1. **8** To borrow, esp. an item of small value without intending to repay it. 1946: "These geisha girls are forever mooching chocolates. . . ." Phila. *Bulletin*, Jan. 11, 34. *Colloq.*   *n.* **1** A dupe; a gullible customer; a sucker. 1929: " 'Dynamiters,' who at the proper moment 'clip the mooch.' " *World's Work*, Nov., 40. **2** A carnival-goer; a mark. *Carnival use.* → **3** A person who watches a pitchman but does not buy. *Carnival and pitchman use.* → **4** A customer in a retail clothing store who carefully examines merchandise before buying it; used in derision. *Retail salesman use, c1940.*   **—er** *n.* **1** One who mooches, esp. a beggar. 1950: ". . . He heard a moocher deliver the following spiel to a lady. . . ." Billy Rose, *synd. newsp. col.*, Sept. 11. *Since c1890; colloq.* **2** A chronic borrower; a sponger. See Appendix, **—er** endings.

moo juice   *n.* Milk. *Some lunch-counter and Army use.*

moola   moolah   *n.* Money. 1939: ". . . No matter how much moola I had. . . ." O'Hara, *Pal Joey*, 32. 1945: "I may not have enough moola to drown my sorrows in milk-shakes." M. Blosser, *synd. comic strip,* "*Freckles and His Friends*," Aug. 18. 1951: ". . . Importunate officials [of the bank] who . . . fought to stuff moola into his pockets." S. J. Perelman in *New Yorker*, Jan. 27, 29/1. 1952: "Listeners-in at the State Capitol . . . contend also that [Governor Thomas E.] Dewey could not afford a federal job. He's reached a stage of life where he needs to make lots more moola than any federal post short of the presidency can provide." B. Davidson, AP, July 17. "*Moola*" *is prob. the most common word not in the DAE, the DOA, Merriam-Webster, the OED, Mencken, or any of their supplements. Prob. not common before c1935.*

moon   *n.* Whisky, esp. moonshine. 1950: "I would buy a couple of pints of moon. . . ." J. B. Martin, in *SEP*, May 27, 20/1. *Since c1920.*

mooner   *n.* Any pathological law breaker whose crimes are against persons rather than property and who derives more excitement than financial gain from his crimes, often committing moral offenses or offenses involving no profit; esp. rapers, transvestites, and the like. 1958: "Mooner—One of a number of people who keep policemen busy during full moons (when according to police lore many categories of crime show an increase)." G. Y. Wells, *Station House Slang. Not common.*

moon-head   *n.* A silly fellow. 1934: = a moon-struck person. *Web. Not common.*

moonlight into, let   To shoot a person. 1926: "I'll let moonlight into a captain." Stallings & Anderson, *What Price Glory*, III. *Lit., to make bullet holes in someone.*

moonshine   *n.* **1** Whisky made by unlicensed, individual distillers for their own consumption or, more commonly, for illegal sale; bootleg whisky. 1947: "The moonshine distilled in the [Tennessee] mountains when I was there was made mostly from sugar.... In Knoxville the Negroes and poor whites drank it almost exclusively." E. Pyle, *Home Country*, 101. *Because such distilling operations are traditionally conducted in rural regions by the light of the moon, to avoid detection. Orig. dial.; common since c1920.* → **2** Any inferior, unaged, cheap whisky. → **3** Any whisky or liquor. **4** Nonsense; boloney.   **—r** *n.* A rustic living in any comparatively isolated section of the Southern hill area of the U.S., whether or not he makes moonshine.

moose   *n.* A younger sister. *Some c1940 child use.*

moose-eye   *n.* A stare of reproach or supplication. *Not common.*

moose-milk   *n.* Whisky. *Dial.*

moosh   *n.* A guardroom; a prison. *Some W.W.I Army use from Brit. Army sl; obs.*

mooter   moota   mootie   mutah   mu   *n.* A marijuana cigarette. 1943: mooter, mu, *Time*, July 19, 54. 1946: mutah. D. W. Maurer, *Amer. Mercury*, Nov., 572/2. *Addict use. Not common.*

mop   *n.* **1** The Missouri Pacific Railroad. *Hobo use. Obs.* **2** The last item or act of a sequence; the final result. *Negro use.*

mope   *v.i.* **1** To escape; to beat it. *Hobo and prison use.* → **2** To move along; to keep moving; to walk.

mopery   *n.* **1** Any forbidden thing in the possession of a prisoner. *Some c1920 prison use.* **2** Any absurd, trivial, or imaginary offense against the law. 1949: "He liked to take candid camera shots. The candider the better. If he'd lived long enough you'd have had him up for mopery." Chandler, *Little Sister*, 226.

mop mop   Repetitious, loud, unimaginative jazz. 1956: "Jazz is of all kinds, and 'mop mop' jazz is the mechanical stuff full of riffs." S. Longstreet, *The Real Jazz Old and New*, 147.

mop-squeezer   *n.* In poker, the queen in a deck of cards. *Not common.*

mop-up   *n.* Extermination. 1949: "... A complete mop-up of ... a gang [by T-men]."*Fact Detec. Mysteries.*   **mop up**   *v.i.* To exterminate; to finish a military or police campaign.

mop up on   To beat up; to thrash severely.

morning chow   Breakfast. See **chow.**

morph   *n.* **1** Morphine. **2** A hermaphrodite.   **—adite**   *n.* A hermaphrodite. 1951: "You morphadite." R. Bissell, *Stretch on River*, 34. *Since c1890.*

mort   *n.* A girl or woman. *Underworld use since before 1800.*

mortal lock   A certainty; a cinch. *From the wrestling term = a deadly hold that cannot be broken. Largely replaced by the shorter "lock." Archaic.*

mose [*derog.*]   *n.* A Negro. *Negro use.*

mosey   *v.i.* To move along; to walk slowly or aimlessly. 1829: *DAE. Colloq.*

mosey along = **mosey.** *Colloq.*

mosquito's eyebrows, the = **the cat's meow.** *c1920; never common.*

moss [*derog.*]   *n.* A Negro. *From the short, kinky hair common to the descendants of certain African tribes.*

most, the   *n., adj.* The best; the most exciting; the most up to date. 1956: "DEL MONTE Catsup is 'the most.'" Testimonial by Steve Allen, advt. in *Look*, Nov. 27, inside front cover. 1957: "New Jetliner The Most, Reds Say [headline]. The Soviet government claimed today that it has put into operation 'the largest and speediest passenger aircraft in the world.'" N.Y. *Daily News*, Nov. 4, 4. *Usu. pred. adj.* See **the end.** *Far out, beat, and some cool use.*

mostest   *n., adj.* The greatest; the best; the most. 1956: "Man o' War ... the most heroic figure in the Golden Age of Sports—described for all time by his Kentucky groom, Will Harbut, as 'de mostest horse.'" T. Betts, *Across the Board*, 16. 1956: "Models with the Mostest." [Title.] Carl Bakal, *American Weekly*, Apr. 29, 18. Pop. by the song, "The Hostess with the Mostest on the Ball." c1939, orig. sung by Ethel Merman. *Associated with far out use, but in some general use since the late 1940's. Usu. pred. adj.*

mothball   *n.* A serious student; a

grind; a student who never dates a girl. *Some c1940 student use.*

mother *n.* **1** An aircraft carrier, which acts as a "mother" to the planes it carries; a fuel ship serving other ships; a command ship. *Some W.W.II USN use.* **2** A piloted plane that electronically controls an unmanned plane or "drone." *Air Force use since c1950.* **3** An effeminate male. *Some Negro use.*

Mother Hubbard **1** A railroad locomotive with the cab over the middle of the boiler. *Railroad use.* **2** A loose-fitting cotton smock or dress, usu. used to protect regular clothes while working. 1949: ". . . Taking along . . . Mother Hubbards to trade to the . . . Islanders." S. J. Perelman, *Listen to the Mocking Bird*, 134. *Colloq.*

Mother Machree **Mother McCrea** An alibi; a sad story, usu. fictitious or exaggerated, told to elicit sympathy, avoid punishment, etc.; a sob story. *From the traditional Irish song of the same name.*

mott *n.* = **mort.** 1848: J. S. Farmer.

Motzy **motzy** [derog.] *n.* = **mockie.** *Never common; obs.*

moula *n.* = **moola.**

mound *n.* In baseball, the pitcher's box. 1951: "Don Newcombe was on the mound for Brooklyn." J. Hand, AP, Oct. 3. *Colloq.*

mountain canary A burro.

mountain dew = **moonshine,** whisky.

mountain oysters Sheep or hog testicles used as food.

mouse *n.* **1** A bruise or discoloration on or near the eye, caused by a blow. 1921: "One of the Kid's eyes has a little mouse under it." Witwer, *Leather*, 38. 1948: "You'll see the beginning of a mouse on my left eye." F. Brown, *Dead Ringer*, 211. *Colloq.* **2** A mustache. *Not common.* 1939: ". . . A scared lookin' little guy wit' a mouse on his lip." *Fortune*, 115/3. Cf. **mouser.** **3** An informer; a squealer, a rat. *Underworld use. Not common.* **4** A girl or young woman, esp. an attractive or vivacious girl; usu. a term of affection. 1939: "A little mouse I got to know up in Michigan. . . ." O'Hara, *Pal Joey*, 3. → **5** A girl friend; a sweetheart; a fiancée; a wife. **6** A small rocket. *Some Air Force and Army use since c1955.* *v.t.* To neck. *Some c1940 student use; obs.* —r *n.* A mustache. 1935: "He is a little guy . . . with . . . a small mouser on his upper lip." D. Runyon, 222. —trap

n. An inferior theater or night-club. 1952: "He walked out on the stage of a mousetrap called the Blue Angel. . . ." J. Crosby, N.Y. *Her. Trib.*, Aug. 6, 17/1. *Not common.* *v.t.* **1** In sports, to feint an opponent out of position. → **2** To fool or mislead by false promises; to entice; to cajole.

mouthful *n.* An important, comprehensive, manifestly true, or otherwise impressive statement; used only in "You [he, she] said a mouthful!" an expression of vigorous affirmation or assent.

mouthpiece *n.* **1** A lawyer, esp. a criminal lawyer. 1930: "[The thief's] inability to hire a professional bondsman and 'good front,' 'mouth-piece' or lawyer, results in a quick trial." Lavine *Third Degree*, 54. 1939: ". . . The highest-priced mouthpiece in the city." E. S. Gardner, *D. A. Draws*, 66. *Underworld use since c1910; colloq. since c1930.* → **2** A spokesman. 1930: "Each tong has an official 'mouthpiece' known as a secretary." Lavine, *Third Degree*, 98. *Colloq.*

move *v.t.* **1** To steal or pilfer something. → **2** To transport or sell contraband or stolen goods. **3** To sell merchandise; to dispose of a stock of merchandise by selling it.

move back *v.t.* To cost. 1935: ". . . Fur coats, including a chinchilla flogger that moves Israel [a character in the story] back thirty G's." D. Runyon. *A variant of "set back."*

move dirt To shovel coal. *Railroad use.*

movie *n.* A motion picture. *Although some scholars still consider this word colloq. or even sl., it has been in stand. use since c1915. At first the motion-picture industry attempted to pop. "film" or "cinema," but "movie" is now the universal term in speech and is very common in writing.* —dom *n.* The motion-picture industry, considered both as an association of people and as a body of customs, attitudes, and conceptual values. 1942: "Moviedom's 'Oomph Girl.' . . ." AP, Jan. 6. 1947: "Even in its depiction of moviedom, Hollywood has seen fit to glamourize itself." E. Goodman in N.Y. *Times*, July 27, II, 4/3. *One of the most common —"dom" words, widely used by newsp. columnists and reviewers.* See Appendix, —dom ending.

movies, the *n.pl.* **1** A motion-picture theater, as in "To go to the movies." **2** Collectively, the motion-picture industry.

moxie   *n.* **1** Courage; nerve; guts. 1943: "You're young and tough and got the moxie and can hit." D. Hammett, *His Brother's Keeper,* 171. **2** Experience; skill; shrewdness. 1950: "The recruit [a baseball pitcher] from Sherwood, Ore., showed plenty of moxie as he scattered seven hits the rest of the way." AP, Apr. 19. **3** Initiative; aggressiveness. 1943: "Maybe it's because we knew you had the old moxie, the old get out and get." M. Shulman, *Barefoot Boy with Cheek,* 158.

Mr. —   Used before an item, object, or concept to personify it. *Very old Negro slave use. Still some dial. and jazz use.* See also entries under **Mister.**

Mr. Big   See **Mister Big.**

Mr. Black   Night; night time. *Jive use; obs.*

Mr. Dude   See **dude.**

Mr. Whiskers   See **whiskers.**

mu   *n.* See **mooter.**

muck   *n.* **1** = **high mucky-muck.** 1940: "DeWitt had handed him . . . a cigar. The way some of these big mucks do." Queen, *Tragedy of X,* 248. **2** Muscle. *West Point use.* **3** Antiaircraft fire. *Some W.W.II USN use.*   **—er**   *n.* **1** A young man who resides in a college town but is not a student. 1893: *DAE. Fairly common student use c1900; obs. since c1925.* **2** A coarse, rude, mean, vulgar, or untrustworthy youth or man; a common man. 1899: *DAE.* 1910: "Mucker trick! . . . I want to get at him, the great big mucker." Johnson, *Varmint,* 81. 1920: "In the U.S.A. we leave [politics] to the muckers. . . ." Fitzgerald, *This Side of Paradise,* 175. 1924: "The athletes . . . cheap muckers with fine bodies. . . ." Marks, *Plastic Age,* 168. *Mainly Eastern student use. Obs. by c1935.* **3** A laborer, esp. one who works with a shovel. See **muck stick.**

muck about   To roam idly; to occupy oneself idly. 1950: ". . . Too many bones mucking about. . . ." Starnes, *Another Mug,* 113. *Not common.*

muck-a-muck   *n.* See **high muck-a-muck.**

mucket   *n.* A toupee.

muckraker   *n.* One who searches out and broadcasts scandals, esp. in order to ruin another's reputation, usu. a politician's. *Colloq. Pop. and prob. coined by Theodore Roosevelt.*

muck stick   A shovel. *Hobo and dial. use since c1915.*

muck up   **1** To clean. *Some USN use*

since *W.W.I. Archaic.* **2** To make dirty; often used in passive. 1947: "It beats me the way these nice cadets go on. Who would think to see those pretty boys parading down that field all spick and span that they'd get themselves mucked up like this?" C. Willingham, *End as a Man,* 234. **3** = **fuck up,** a euphem.

mud   *n.* **1** Opium before it is prepared for smoking. *Addict use.* **2** Coffee prepared to drink. *Orig. hobo use. Some lunch-counter and Army use. Universally known.* **3** Any thick, dark food, as chocolate pudding. **4** Any thick, dark liquid, as molten metal, petroleum, etc. 1956: "Bricklayers . . . call for *mud*—mortar or cement. . . ." *Labor's Special Language from Many Sources.* **5** Cheap plastic figurines, souvenirs, and the like, given as prizes at a carnival concession. *Carnival use.* **6** Indistinct radio or telegraph signals. *Radio use.* **7** Vicious, derogatory talk or writing, whether true or not; "slime."

mud, in the   Of poorest quality; nearly unintelligible; said of a telegrapher's keying technique. *Radio amateur use c1925; obs.*

mud-chicken   *n.* A surveyor. *Railroad use.*

mudder   *n.* A race horse that excels when running on a muddy track. 1954: "I picked a mudder on a sunny day [and lost]." W. R. & F. K. Simpson, *Hockshop,* 109.

mud-head   *n.* **1** A Tennesseean. 1838: *DAE.* **2** A stupid person. *Not common.*

mud hook   An anchor. 1827: *DAE. Still some maritime use.* See **hook.**   **—s 1** The feet. 1850: *DAE.* 1952: "C'mon, lift them mud hooks!" M. Blosser, *synd. cartoon,* "*Freckles,*" June 25. *Not common.* **2** Heavy shoes. *Not common.*

mud hop   A railroad yard clerk or checker who lists arriving and departing trains and the identification numbers of freight cars. *Railroad use.*

mud-kicker   *n.* **1** A woman who lures a man to her room or to a secluded spot by promising sexual favors and then robs him. *Not common.* **2** A prostitute. *Not common.*

mud opera   mud show   An old-time circus that traveled in wagons. *Archaic.*

mud-slinging   *n.* **1** The act of spreading malicious, vicious, derogatory statements about another, whether such statements are true or not. *Usu. political use.* **2** Gossiping.

mud-snoot *n.* A disliked person; fig., a pig. 1873: *DAE. Never common. Obs.*

muff *n.* **1** A foolish fellow. 1856: Hall, *College Words.* **2** A duffer; a poor player. 1910: "[To one who has lost a baseball game] You're a muff, a low-down muff!" Johnson, *Varmint,* 87. **3** In sports, an error, as a fumble. 1868: *DAE.* 1952: "[Snodgrass in center field] had dropped the ball, 'the $75,000 muff,' as it was called." A. Daley, N.Y. *Times,* Sept. 28, 12/3. **4** A girl or woman. *Since c1915; never common.* **5** A beard. *Not common.* **6** A wig. 1949: "Hicks . . . wasn't wearing his muff." Chandler, *Little Sister,* 180. **7** [taboo] The vulva, esp. when covered with much pubic hair. *v.t.* **1** In sports, to make an error or mistake; to fail to take advantage of an opportunity; to bungle; to fumble. 1868: *DAE. Colloq.* 1958: "We should have muffed a couple of questions on the exam, that 100% would even make me suspicious." "Dondi," *synd. newsp. comic strip,* Feb. 9, 6. **2** Fig., to make an error as if one were clumsy because one's hands were in a muff; to fail. *Colloq.*

muffin *n.* A girl. *Not common.* See **muffins.** **—s** *n.pl.* [taboo] A woman's or esp. an adolescent girl's breasts. *Not common.* See Appendix, Food and Sex.

mug **mugg** *n.* **1** The face. 1907: "We have . . . the slang word 'mug' for face,—e.g., 'your ugly mug.' " *Living Age,* July, 116/1. 1914: "That mug of his. . . ." *SEP,* Mar. 14, 11. 1949: "As for my mugg, I don't feel it's . . . villainous. . . ." F. Neill in Phila. *Bulletin,* Aug. 31, 24/4. *From the 18C drinking mugs that were made to represent human faces. "Mugg" is becoming archaic and is used in approx. one in six instances.* **2** The mouth; the chin; the jaw. *Prize fight use since c1915.* **3** A photograph of the face, esp. a photograph used for police identification. 1940: "[The photo] was a police mug, front and profile. . . ." Chandler, *Farewell,* 29. 1958: "Mug—A police photograph; also—almost exclusively in New York—robbery by use of physical force." G. Y. Wells, *Station House Slang. Police and underworld use.* **4** A man; a fellow; a guy. 1907: ". . . A 'story' that would have melted the heart of any mug." J. London, *The Road,* 202. 1950: "The poor mug is in trouble." Bob Thomas, AP, July 7. *Common.* **5** Specif. and esp., a rough or ugly fellow. **6** A prize fighter, esp. an inferior one. *Since c1920.* **7** A criminal; a hoodlum.

Very common. **8** A policeman; a detective. *Not common.* *v.t.* **1** To photograph a person's face, esp. a prisoner's for purposes of record and identification. 1918: " 'Bertillon measurement' is as familiar a phrase to [criminals] as being 'mugged.' " *Survey,* Apr. 6, 21. 1925: "When crooks are photographed they are 'mugged.' " McLellan in *Collier's. Orig. underworld use; now universally known.* **2** To attack and then rob; to garrote, beat up, or stab a victim in order to rob him. 1948: "The police said the victims were mugged in the hallways of their homes after they had been trailed from one of the . . . subway stations. . . ." N.Y. *Times,* Aug. 15, 36. *Since c1940.* **3** To have sexual intercourse with. *Negro use.* *v.i.* **1** To neck. 1924: "I hate mugging and petting. . . ." Marks, *Plastic Age,* 271. *Some c1920 student use; obs.* **2** In acting, to use exaggerated facial expressions; to overact. 1939: ". . . One of the mice . . . is mugging even in rehearsal." O'Hara, *Pal Joey,* 57. 1946: "While Danny [Kaye] mugs through his program. . . ." *Time,* Mar. 11, 63. *Since c1925.* **3** To drink an alcoholic beverage, esp. beer. *Some c1935 student use.* **—ger** *n.* **1** An actor who grimaces to produce laughter. 1944: ". . . The theatre where this trivial mugger is performing. . . ." Fowler, *Good Night,* 10. **2** A photographer who specializes in portraits. **3** A thief who first garrotes his victims; one who mugs (*v.t.,* 2d def.). 1942: "Apparently the victim of muggers, Private Berkowitz . . . was found slain at 7:30 A.M. yesterday. . . . The police were . . . tracking down three known . . . muggers, who . . . had received suspended sentences in a mugging case." N.Y. *Times,* Oct. 3, 17/1. *The most common use. Since c1940.* **—gings** *n.pl.* Necking; a girl who necks. 1933: "She was swell muggings, too." J. T. Farrell, 63. *Not common.* See **mug.**

muggle *n.* **1** Hot chocolate or cocoa. *c1920 student use; obs.* **2** A marijuana cigarette. 1949: "Desk clerk's a muggle-smoker." Chandler, *Little Sister,* 250. *Addict use; fairly common. From "muggles."*

muggles *n.pl.* **1** Marijuana, esp. the dried but unshredded marijuana leaves. **2** A marijuana cigarette. 1956: ". . . Muggles . . . the marijuana cigarette. . . ." S. Longstreet, *The Real Jazz Old and New,* 144. *Some addict use.*

mug joint *n.* A tent, booth, or

gallery in which one's photograph is taken and printed in a short time. *Carnival and circus use.*

mug shot   A photograph of a person's face. 1950: "When police passed around a mug shot of Willie. . . ." J. Randolph, AP, Mar. 10.

mug up   1 To eat a snack. → 2 To drink coffee; to drink all the coffee one wants. *Some W.W.II USN use.*

mule   *n.* 1 A translation, a pony. *Some c1900 student use. Never common.* 2 An obstinate or stubborn person. *Colloq.* 3 Raw bootleg whisky, esp. moonshine. See **white mule.** 4 A tractor. *Dial.* 5 A railroad brakeman. *Railroad use; archaic.* 6 A plane handler on an aircraft carrier flight deck. *Some W.W.II USN use.* 7 One who acts as a delivery boy or lackey for a narcotics peddler or pusher. 1958: "Mule—One—usually a minor—who delivers or sells narcotics within his own special group." G. Y. Wells, *Station House Slang. Some addict use.*

mule-skinner   *n.* 1 A mule driver. 1870: *DAE. Colloq.* → 2 A truck driver. *Never common.*

mulled   **mulled up**   *adj.* Drunk. *Never common.*

mulligan   *n.* 1 A stew made of any available meat(s) or vegetable(s). 1907: ". . . Hundreds of hoboes, . . . with whom I . . . cooked 'mulligans.' . . ." Jack London, *The Road,* 122. 1952: "You're just in time for hot mulligan!" M. Blosser, *synd. cartoon, "Freckles,"* May 29. *Orig. hobo use, perhaps from "salmagundi." Often used facetiously about any stewlike food, however excellent.* 2 An Irishman. *Some underworld use.* → 3 A policeman.

mulligrubs, the   *n.pl.* = **the blues.** *Dial.*

mum   *n.* A chrysanthemum. *A common written and spoken abbr.* See Appendix, Shortened Words.

mumsie   **mumsy**   *n.* A mother. *Often used sarcastically.*

mung(e)y   **mongee**   *n.* Food. *Some hobo and W.W.I Army use. An approximation of French and Italian words = to eat.*

murder   *adj.* 1 Excellent; terrific; remarkable. *Used only as pred. adj.; c1935 jive use; wide jitterbug use; universally known. Archaic.* 2 Very difficult; very painful; when used in ref. to a person, very stubborn or severe. 1943: "Man, he's murder." M. Shulman. *Barefoot Boy with Cheek,* 90. *v.t.* To get the better of an opponent; to vanquish decisively.

1952: "The National Leaguers . . . eat up southpaws. They murdered them all season. . . ." G. Talbot, AP, Oct. 4.

murder, get away with   To do anything in flagrant violation of rules, laws, or decency. *A stronger form of* **get away with [something].**

murk   *n.* Coffee. *Some lunch-counter use c1915–c1935; obs.*

murky bucket   = merci beaucoup. *Some W.W.I Army use.* See Appendix, Mispronunciations.

murphy   *n.* An Irish potato. 1811: Farmer & Henley. *Still in use.*

muscle   *n.* 1 Bluff; artificiality. *Some Negro use.* 2 A strong-arm man; a thug. 1949: "Send some gowed-up muscle to search my hotel room. . . ." J. Evans, *Halo,* 98.

muscle, on the   Quarrelsome; ready or eager to fight or use force; esp. ready to commit crimes involving force or violence as opposed to skill. *Underworld use since c1925.*

muscle-head   *n.* A stupid person.

muscle in   To force one's way in; to gain by force; to encroach forcibly; to secure a share by force or threat of force. 1930: "One of the lads will . . . attempt to muscle in on some graft out of his own domain." Lavine, *Third Degree,* 38. *Orig. underworld use; now very common.*

muscle out   Lit. and fig., to force out, to eject, as a person. 1953: "If she persists, . . . she'll be muscled out of the [Free German Youth] movement." F. Sparks, NEA, Mar. 7.

mush   *n.* 1 Excessive talk; boloney. 1841: *DAE. Still in use.* → 2 The mouth. 1937: "He pulled his mush away from the plate and sighed." Weidman, *Wholesale,* 6. 1950: ". . . Who pasted Mandrel in the mush. . . ." Starnes, *Another Mug,* 19. *Since c1915.* → 3 The face. 1952: ". . . A silly grin got stuck on yo' mush." W. Kelly, *synd. comic strip, "Pogo,"* Sept. 27. 4 Sentimentality; embarrassingly sentimental talk. 5 A kiss. 6 An umbrella. From "mushroom." *Pitchman use.* Cf. **skinned mush.**   *v.i.* To earn a living by grafting or faking under cover of a legitimate occupation, such as umbrella mending. 1907: "There were two more in their [gypsy] gang, who were across the river 'mushing' in Harrisburg." J. London, *My Life.* **—er**   *n.* An itinerant faker or grafter operating in the guise of an honest worker. See **mush.** **—ing**   *n.* Love-making. See **mushy.** **—room**   *n.* An umbrella. *From its* shape. *Never common. Mainly underworld and hobo use. Not as common as the shorter "mush."* **—y** *adj.* **1** Affectionate; amorous. 1927: "The kid got mushy with the broad." Hammett, *Blood Money*, 89. *Colloq. since c1920.* **2** Sentimental; corny.

mush-faker *n.* An itinerant peddler, tinker, or esp. umbrella mender. *Hobo use.* See **mush.**

mush-head *n.* A stupid or silly person. **—ed** *adj.* Stupid. *Colloq.*

mush-mouth *n.* One who talks indistinctly.

muskrat *n.* A mustache. *Never common.*

muss *n.* **1** An uproar; a fight. 1838: *DAE. Archaic since c1920.* **2** A mess; a "mess." 1840: *DAE. Obs. by c1900.* **—y** *adj.* Rumpled; disordered. 1859: *DAE.* 1934: "Her dress . . . was . . . rumpled now, and mussy." Cain, *Postman*, 5.

musta *n.* Marijuana. *Not common.*

mustang *n.* A commissioned officer who has risen from the ranks. 1950: "A mustang who had worked his way up from the ranks in 13 years of service. . . ." *Time*, Dec. 11, 22. *USN use since c1935.*

mustard *n.* A good, alert fighter or bomber pilot. *W.W.II Army use.* See **up to snuff (the mustard).**

mutah *n.* = **mooter.**

mutt **mut** *n.* **1** A stupid person. 1910: "P. Lentz, of all the muts! . . . I

think he's a mutt." Johnson, *Varmint*, 210. 1914: "I felt like such a mutt—not being able to dance." S. Lewis, *Our Mr. Wrenn*, 205. *Archaic by c1940. From "muttonhead." The spelling "mutt" is about four times as common as "mut."* **2** A dog, esp. a mongrel. *Colloq. since c1930; usu. spelled "mut."*

muttnik *n.* The second man-made satellite launched by Russia in 1957. *Because it contained a dog for experimental purposes.* See **sputnik.**

muttonhead *n.* A stupid person. 1804: *DAE. Colloq.* **—ed** *adj.* Stupid.

mutton-top *n.* = **muttonhead.**

mux *n.* **1** A multiplex circuit. *Telerapher use, c1920. From the first two letters and the last letter of "multiplex."* **2** Teletyping. 1943: ". . . He could have learned . . . mux. . . ." Wolfert, *Underworld*, 97.

muzzle *v.t.* To kiss; to spoon.

muzzle-loader *n.* A locomotive fired by hand. *Railroad use; archaic.*

muzzler *n.* **1** A minor criminal; a punk. *Underworld use.* **2** An obnoxious person. *Maritime use.*

myrrh *n.* Rum. *A spelling phonetically equivalent to "mur" = "rum" spelled backward.* See Appendix, Back Slang.

mystery *n.* Hash. 1885: *restaurant waiter use, N.Y.C.* Walt Whitman in *North American Rev., Nov.*, 434.

N

nab *v.t.* To catch or arrest. *Colloq.* *n.* A detective or policeman. *Some teenage street gang use.* **—s** *n.sing.* A policeman. *Not common.*

nab at To snap at; to nip; to graze in an attempted bite.

Nada An oath, fig. "God be my witness;" really, truthfully. 1958: ". . . The hipster says, 'Nada, I'm beat—I'm right in there, see—I'm the most religious, the most humble—I'm swinging, man.' " Herbert Gold, *The Beat Mystique*, 86. *From the Zen-Buddhist state or place of nirvana.*

Nadaville *n.* Ecstasy. Fig., completely and successfully gone or far out. *Beat and far out use. When one leaves to get far out, his ultimate destination is Nadaville.* See Appendix, **—ville.**

nag *n.* **1** An old, small, or useless horse. 1704: *DAE.* Still in use. → **2** A race horse, esp. an inferior one. 1951:

"The gambling man who used a nursery to make dough on the nags. . . ." *N.Y. Daily News*, Aug. 9, C3/2. *Colloq.*

nail *v.t.* To capture; to arrest. *n.* A cigarette. From **coffin nail.**

naked dance **Naked Dance** A lewd dance or obscene performance. 1950: "If a Naked Dance was desired, Tony would dig up one of his fast speed tunes and one of the girls would dance on a narrow stage, completely nude. Yes, they danced absolutely stripped, but in New Orleans the Naked Dance was a real art." A. Lomax, *Mr. Jelly Roll*, 47. *Obs.*

name *n.* **1** Any famous or popular performer who attracts large audiences; a big name. **2** A famous, influential person. *adj.* Famous; of established reputation, as a name band.

Nana(w) *n.* One's grandmother. *Baby talk, prob. a childhood corruption, often carried into adult speech.*

nance *n.* **1** A male homosexual who assumes the feminine role. → **2** An effeminate man; a sissy. 1943: "... Where you need desperately a man of iron, you often get a nance." P. Wylie, *Generation of Vipers*, 248. 1941: "An esthetic nance." Schulberg, *Sammy*, 200.

Nancy *n.* A male homosexual. Cf. **Mary.**

nanny *n.* A nanny goat.

nanny, get [one's] = **get [one's] goat.** *Archaic and dial.*

nanny-goat sweat Whisky, esp. inferior whisky or moonshine.

nap [derog.] A Negro.

napoo napooh *n.* The end; death. *From Fr. "il n'y a plus" = there is no more. W.W.I Army use.*

nappy [derog.] *n.* A Negro. 1956: "To call a man *nappy* is to say his hair is kinky—a real insult." S. Longstreet, *The Real Jazz Old and New*, 150.

naps *n.pl.* Kinky hair. *Negro use.*

nark *n.* **1** A person serving as a decoy; a shill; a police informer. 1944: "... Information about known gamblers, little bookmakers, and their narks...." *Fortune*, Sept., 210. **2** A kibitzer.

narrowback [derog.] *n.* An Irishman; one of Irish descent. 1957: "When William Joseph Patrick (Pat) O'Brien, a Milwaukee-born Irishman or narrowback. ..." Gilbert Millstein, The N.Y. *Times*, Sept. 29, X3. *Never common.*

nasty *adj.* Excellent; "wicked"; "mean." 1834: *DAE. Jive use c1935.*

natch *adv.* Naturally; of course; yes. 1951: "... A comedy ... depicting the habits of the rich. In one scene all the actors will be in riding clothes (habits of the rich, natch)." J. Chapman, N.Y. *Daily News*, Aug. 9, C15/1. *Wide jive and student use c1940. Archaic.*

native, go To live in and adopt or affect the customs of a foreign country, esp. a primitive country or sea island. *Orig. USN use; W.W.II use.*

nattily *adv.* Sprucely; neatly. 1952: "The nattily dressed Finnegan sat at the counsel table. ..." AP, Mar. 15. *Colloq.*

natty *adj.* Spruce; dashing; neat; stylish. 1851: Hall, *College Words*. 1910: "A natty raincoat." Johnson, *Varmint*, 349. 1942: "A natty convertible." W. Bolingbroke Johnson, *Widening Stain*, 181. *Colloq.*

natural *n.* **1** In craps, a first throw of 7 or 11, which wins the play. → **2** Any thing, action, or person that is or will be obviously or overwhelmingly successful. 1949: "A novel which looks like a natural for Lassie." N.Y. *Times*, Aug. 28, X3/4. **3** A jail sentence of 7 years.

Nature Boy **1** A virile man. → **2** A man or youth who needs a haircut. *Jocular use. From the title of the c1949 pop. song.*

nautch [taboo] *n.* The vagina. *Archaic.*

nautch-joint *n.* A brothel. Cf. **nautch.** *Archaic.*

navigate *v.i., v.t.* To walk; often used humorously in ref. to a person who is intoxicated. 1846: *DAE.*

navy *n.* A cigar end or butt found on a sidewalk. *Perhaps from "navy" = a type of chewing tobacco. Hobo use; obs.*

navy chest A protruding belly; a bay window. *USN use.*

neat *adj.* Without being mixed with water or soda (said of whisky); straight.

neb *n.* = **nebbish.** 1941: "Poor little nebs like Julian." Schulberg, *Sammy*, 111. —**bish bisch** *n.* A drab, awkward, shy person. 1941: "The Jewish language has the best word: nebbish. A nebbish ... is not exactly an incompetent, a dope or a weakling. He is simply the one in the crowd that you always forget to introduce." Schulberg, *Sammy*, 96. 1951: "There was one poor little nebbish of a dame. ..." *Radio, "Can You Top This,"* Apr. 10. 1951: "It looks like Pa [Gross] isn't anything like the *nebbish* Ma is always making him out to be." G. Millstein, N.Y. *Times Bk. Rev.*, Oct. 7, 4/4. *From the Yiddish.*

necessary, the Money. Cf. **the needful.**

neck *v.i., v.t.* **1** To risk one's neck; to trust to luck in general. *Some c1850 use. Obs.* **2** To kiss and caress intimately; to play amatively; to pet. 1934: "But I came out here to have an experience. ... I thought ... that at least you'd want to neck me." P. Wylie, *Finnley Wren*, 109. 1937: "Once upon a time you 'spooned,' then you 'petted,' after that you 'necked' —still the most widely used term—but now you may 'smooch' or 'perch,' or, reaching the heights of college argot, you may 'pitch and fling woo.' " E. Eldridge in *SEP*, Feb. 20, 89/2. 1949: "A girl who necks with any boy." *Time*, Oct. 3, 37. *Since c1910. Student use at first but considered taboo until c1920. Wide use since c1920.* *v.t.* To neck with someone. 1939: "I was even surprised I could neck her at all. ..." O'Hara, *Pal Joey*, 20. —**ing** *n.* The act or instance of amorous play.

1926: ". . . Pupils, moving into adolescence . . . resort to necking." H. L. Mencken, reprinted in *The American Twenties*, 407. 1951: "The next thing I knew I was kissing her all over—*any*where—her eyes, her *nose*, her eyebrows and all, her *ears*—her whole face except her mouth and all. She sort of wouldn't let me get to her mouth. Anyway, it was the closest we ever got to necking." J. D. Salinger, *Catcher in the Rye*, 62.

neck, get it in the   To be refused or rebuffed; specif. to be dismissed from one's job, or by one's lover or a friend.

necker's knob   A small knob attached to a car's steering wheel for easier maneuvering; it also makes it easier for the driver to drive with one hand, as when he has his arm around a girl. *Teenage use since c1950.*

necktie   *n.* A hangman's rope. 1929: ". . . Don't get nervous with that gat . . . or they'll put a necktie on you." Burnett, *Little Caesar*, 53.

necktie party   A hanging or lynching. 1882: *DAE.* 1923: ". . . That little necktie party we're giving . . . this morning." C. MacArthur, *Rope.* 1935: "He won't stand for any necktie party." L. Zinberg, "Lynch Him!" *Amer. Mercury*, May, 84/1. *Pop by western movies; universally known.*

necktie sociable   **necktie social** = **necktie party.** 1878: necktie sociable, *DAE.*

ned   *n.* A ten-dollar gold piece. 1882: *DAE. Obs.*

needful, the   Money. *Since c1900; mainly underworld use. Never common.* Cf. **necessary, the.**

needle   *n.* **1** A hypodermic needle or syringe. *Very common among doctors, nurses, dentists, drug addicts, and the general public; colloq.* → **2** An injection from a hypodermic needle; sometimes preceded by the name of the medicine or disease involved: "penicillin needle," "polio needle," etc. *Not as common as* "*shot.*" **3** The stylus in the tone arm of a phonograph. *Colloq.* **4** A joke at another's expense; a malicious insinuation or reference made to embarrass another. *Very common during and since W.W.II, esp. among students.*   *v.t.* **1** To age an alcoholic beverage artificially by introducing an electric current into it through a special needlelike rod. → **2** To strengthen a beverage or a food with whisky, wine or spices. **3** To make fun of, tease, belittle, or otherwise embarrass by making quasi-humorous malicious

remarks; to tease or 'ride' someone. 1951: ". . . She did what she gleefully called 'needling him a little.'" S. Lewis, *World So Wide.* **5** 1951: "I have met a lot of grandparents recently, but none of them were sewing quilts. . . . The only needle she [grandma] knows is the one she gives grandpa for stopping off at a bar on his way home." Hal Boyle, AP, N.Y., Apr. 17. *Since c1940.*

needle, give [someone] the   See **needle, the needle.**

needle, on the   **1** Addicted to the use of narcotics. **2** Under the influence of narcotics. *Both uses by narcotic addicts.*

needle, the   Provoking, sarcastic talk; critical or goading remarks. *Usu. in* "*give [someone] the needle.*" *Common since c1940.* See **needle.**

needle candy   Any narcotic taken by injection. 1951: "Holmes has need of greater stimulants than needle candy. . . ." W. F. Miksch, *Collier's*, Feb. 10, 53/1. See **candy, needle.**

needled beer   Beer or near-beer, reinforced with alcohol or ether; spiked beer. *Most common c1925.*

neighbo   *adv.* No; don't; I disagree. *Negro use.*

nellie   **Nellie**   *n.* An old cow. *Farm use.* See **nice Nellie.**

neon ribbons   Excessive pride in one's military rank and decorations. *Orig. W.W.II use; still some Air Force use.*

nerf   *v.t.* To push one car with another. *Hot-rod use since c1955. From the nerfing bar that supports the bumper on most cars.*

nerts   **nertz** = **nuts.**

nerty   *adv.* See **nuts.**

nerve   *n.* **1** Audacity; impertinence. *Colloq.* → **2** Courage, guts. 1905: "I simply hadn't the nerve to tell her that I lost nearly every penny I had." McHugh, *Search Me.* 47. *Colloq. since c1930.*

nervous   *adj.* **1** Orig. cool use = eliciting a strong psychological response; wild. *Some far out, beat, and cool use, but more often used by those who assume cool talk than by actual members of the various groups.* See **cool. 2** = **jazzy.**

nervous pudding   Gelatin prepared to eat. *Because it shakes.*

nervy   *adj.* **1** Nervous. 1939–40: "He's a nice enough young fellow. Nervy, though. Looks as though he might be dyspeptic later on. Those nervy ones often are." A. Christie, *Sad Cypress*, 123. *Obs.* **2** Impudent. 1896: *DAE. Colloq.*

nest egg   Money saved; esp. money

saved over a comparatively long period for use in one's old age.

neutral   *adj.* Stupid; brainless; coo-coo. 1929: "Well, when a car is not in gear, it's in neutral. And when a man's brain is out of gear, he's neutral. He's neither coming or going." G. Milburn, *Folk-Say*, 109. *Never common.*

never-get-overs   *n.pl.* A fatal illness. 1929–30: "Cold, Toby? . . . You want to watch out you don't catch your never-get-overs." K. Brush, *Young Man*, 156f. *Dial.*

never-was   never-wuz   never wuzzer   *n.* A person who has never succeeded; one who has never had fame or fortune. *Based on "has-been."*

new   *n.* A novice, newcomer, tender-foot, or greenhorn. *Never common.* See **new chum.   —y   —ey   —ie** *n.* **1** A newly entering or freshman student. 1851: [Princeton College use] "Newy." Hall, *College Words*, 217. *Obs.* **2** An innovation; a new thing, as a joke, song, or story. 1941: ". . . A newey [teenage] fad. . . ." *Life*, Jan. 27, 79. 1948: "I heard one a joke—it's a kind of newy." NBC, Apr. 30. See Appendix, —ie, —y endings.

new chum   A novice or tenderfoot, esp. a new immigrant. *Some c1900 hobo use; more common in Austral. than in U.S.*

Newfie   *n.* A Newfoundlander. *Not common.*

new jice   A novice or newcomer, esp. a young prisoner or one serving his first sentence. *Some c1925 underworld use.*

New Look   A woman's hair style with the hair at ear-lobe length and featuring a soft "page boy," a left side part, and a deep wave or bangs over the right side of the forehead. *Common c1947–c1950. Created to be worn with the Parisian designer Christian Dior's "New Look" fashions, 1947.*

New Look, the   Any revolutionary style change of clothing or any manufactured item. *From the late Parisian designer Christian Dior's "New Look" women's clothing fashions of 1947.*

newsie   newsey   *n.* **1** A newspaper seller; a newspaper boy. 1927: "Beno, a hophead newsie. . . ." Hammett, *Blood Money*, 13. *Fairly common.* **2** A newscaster, a radio news announcer. *Not common.*

newspaper   *n.* A 30-day jail sentence. *Based on "throw the book."* Cf. **magazine.**

newt   *n.* **1** A stupid person. *Some use since c1925. Maybe from "neutral" reinforced by "nut" or may imply the simplicity of the newt.* **2** A new workman or soldier or novice. *A little W.W.II Army and factory use. By telescoping "new" + "recruit."*

New York kiss   New York kiss-off See **kiss, kiss off.**

next, get = **get next to [oneself]** 1936: "I hope he don't get next before we get out of town. She took me for a hundred before I got next." Tully, *Bruiser*, 6.

next off   Next; the next thing; then. 1928: "Next off, Hutch give a yell and. . . ." James M. Cain, "Pastorale," *Amer. Mercury. Based on "first off."*

next to [oneself], get   **1** To become wise to the fact that one is being deceived, duped, cheated, tricked, or victimized. *Not now common.* → **2** To realize how stupid, unacceptable, eccentric, dull, or disliked one is; to become realistic or wise; to become hip.

next to [someone], get   To become an intimate friend, associate, or confidant of someone; specif., to become sexually intimate with a girl or woman. 1950: "If you could shoot a good agate and had a nice highclass red undershirt with the collar turned up, I'm telling you you were liable to get next to that broad." A. Lomax, *Mr. Jelly Roll*, 16.

N.G.   n.g.   No good, worthless; untrustworthy, unethical, contemptible. *From the initials for "no good."* 1950: "Mrs.——has proven to be very rotten all the way through. She is N.G." From a letter reprinted in A. Lomax, *Mr. Jelly Roll*, 238. See Appendix, Shortened Words.

nibs = **his nibs.**

nice guy   An amiable, pleasant fellow; one who can be depended upon to be fair, understanding, and socially ethical.

nice little piece of furniture   A sexually attractive, passionate, or pert girl. See **piece.**

nice Nellie   A prude of either sex; one who prefers politeness to efficiency; prudish. 1952: "I've got to use 'heck' [for "hell"] because practically all my editors are . . . being more rabidly nice Nellie than usual." George Dixon, *N.Y. Daily Mirror*, July 8, 4/5.

nicey-nice   *adj.* Overnice, affectedly nice; when applied to males, faint-hearted, effeminate. 1930: "This little kid here with all her nicey-nice talk." Burnett, *Iron Man*, 138.

nick   *n.* A nickel. 1857: *DAE. Obs. by c1930.   v.t.* **1** To rob. 1927: ". . . The bank is gonna be nicked." Hammett, *Blood Money*, 14. → **2** To charge; to assess or tax; to demand and receive money. 1930: "... A chap in Chicago who nicks the racketeers one grand a year for horoscopes." *Variety*, cited in *Bookman*, 398/2. 1941: "I think you can nick her for one fifty [salary] if you get tough." Cain, *M. Pierce*, 40. 1951: "The individual amounts are trifling. Mrs. Smith is nicked for $2.12 for the second quarter [of assessed taxes]...." W. Pegler, *synd. newsp. col.*, Sept. 5. → **3** To withhold pay from a worker for working less than a specified time, to dock a worker. **—el** See **Don't take any wooden nickels.**

nickel note   A five-dollar bill. *Not common.*

nickel nurser   A miser; a tightwad. *Attrib. to T. A. Dorgan, cartoonist, died 1929.*

nickel up   In begging, to offer a merchant five cents for food or other goods worth considerably more. Cf. **dime up.**

nicker   *n.* A person who has been cured of drug addiction. *Never common.*

niff   *n.* A quarrel or grudge; spite; dislike. *Dial.*

niff-naw   *n.* An argument. *Dial. From Scotch-Irish dial.*

nifty   *adj.* Stylish, neat, smart, attractive; skillful; excellent. 1865: *DAE.* 1900: "One of these 'nifty' youths...." Upson, *Independent*, 2574/1. 1929: "Nifty spiel." J. Auslander, *Hell in Harness*, 40. 1938: "... They can offer a nifty tap-dance. ..." *Amer. Mercury*, Sept., 50/2. 1948: "College boys ... have developed a great many niftier and hotter words than bartenders have." H. L. Mencken, *New Yorker*, Nov. 6, 108/2. 1950: "Everything's going to be nifty in 1950." *Advt. by Dictaphone Corp.*, Jan. 1950: "Those nifty campus queens." *Universal International newsreel*, Apr. *Becoming archaic.* *n.* **1** An attractive girl. 1937: "Teddy Ast with his six blonde nifties! ..." Weidman, *Wholesale*, 94. *Somewhat archaic.* **2** Any stylish idea or object, whether useful or not. 1927: "Another nifty is the circularization of telephone subscribers...." Robert Littell, *New Republic*, Jan. 5. 196/2. **3** A funny or pertinent joke or clever remark, esp. if new or about a topical subject. 1946: "Urey's recent nifty.... Nifty eavesdropped at the Beverly-Wilshire pool. ..." W. Winchell, *synd. newsp. col.*, June 4. 1949: "[Comedian Milton] Berle ... has taken his nifties where he found

them. ..." Billy Rose, *synd. newp. col.*, Dec. 2. *All meanings common by c1930.* *v.* To wisecrack or tell a nifty. *Some c1935 use.* *adv.* Excellently. *Never common.*

nig   *n.* [derog.] Short for "nigger." 1840: *DAE. Not common.* *v.i.* **1** In playing cards, to renege. *Colloq. since c1900.* → **2** To refuse to carry out a plan or do someone a favor after promising to do so. *Some use since c1930. From "renege."* **—ger**   *n.* **1** [derog.] A Negro. 1939: "Nigger is a common expression among the ordinary Negroes and is used frequently in conversation between them. It carries no ... sting when used by themselves, but they object keenly to whites using it because it conveys the spirit of hate. ..." Lucius Harper, Chicago *Defender*, quoted in *Ken*, Mar. 9. *Traditionally most common in the South.* → **2** A black screen used for decreasing light on a stage or movie set. *Theater use.*

niggerhead   *n.* A stone or rock, esp. a dark-colored glacial boulder. 1847: *DAE. Obs. Still found in some nautical place names.*

nigger heaven   [derog.]   *n.* **1** The topmost gallery or the several highest rows of seats in a theater balcony. *Since c1850.* Cf. **peanut gallery.** *Archaic.* **2** The Harlem section of New York City; any heavily populated Negro neighborhood of a large Northern city.

niggertoe   *n.* A Brazil nut. *Colloq. From its size, shape, and color.*

niggra   [derog.]   *n.* = **nigger.** *A pronunciation used by Southerners of Southern breeding and ancestry. Conjuring up the period of Negro slavery, the pronunciation is even more derog. than "nigger."*

night   See **Good night! Saturday nights. Night**   Good night. *Affected and jocular use.* **—cap**   *n.* **1** A drink one has, as to help one relax, before retiring for the night, usu. whisky, but may be tea, warm milk, or the like; the last or farewell drink of whisky one has with friends at a bar or social gathering before leaving to go home and retire for the night. 1957: "When it's time for a nightcap, let White Horse carry you smoothly." Advt. for "White Horse" brand of scotch, *Esquire*, Jan., back cover. *Colloq.* **2** The second of two baseball games played by the same two teams on the same day, whether actually played at night or in the late afternoon. *Baseball*

use. *Colloq.*   **—ery** = **nitery.**   **—ie**
n. A nightgown, a nightdress. 1923: "Gracie ought to have a silk nightie or two. . . ." C. MacArthur, *Rope. One of the words common to children that adults use freq.*

nightingale   *n.* An informer; a squealer; one who sings; a canary. See **Irish nightingale.**

night people   1 People who work or live at night, sleeping during the day. 1957: "Night people, the professor and his wife used to retire at about 2:30 or 3 A.M." Fern Marja, "Black Coffee, Textbooks and TV." N.Y. *Post*, Sept. 29, M4. → 2 Nonconformists, *Pop.* by *N.Y. City disc jockey and social commentator Jean Shepherd, c1956.*

night soil   Human feces, esp. when used as fertilizer. *A euphem.*

night spot   A night club.

nighty-night   Good night. *Colloq. Informal and jocular use. Very much in fashion c1930 and c1950. The most freq. child word for "good night."*

—nik   See Appendix, Suffixes and Suffix Words.

nine   *v.t.* To cheat or rob. 1939: "Tomaso really is an artist in [blackmail], and can nine those old phlugs in first-class style when he is knuckling." Damon Runyon. *Never common.*

nineteenth hole, the   A drink of whisky, or period of drinking and talking about one's game, after playing golf; the bar at a golf club. *Fairly common jocular use. Because a stand. game of golf includes eighteen holes, thus, fig., the last act of the game is a drink of whisky.*

ninety-day wonder   1 A USA or USN officer commissioned after only three months of training at an Officers' Cadet School, as distinguished from an Annapolis or West Point graduate and from an officer commissioned from the ranks after years of experience. *W.W.II use. During W.W.II, esp. the early part, the USA and USN set up special three-month schools to train the required number of officers quickly. Students for these schools were required to have only a minimum of six weeks' "basic training" as a soldier or sailor prior to entry. Enlisted men and officers commissioned in the regular way often had little respect for these comparatively inexperienced and usu. youthful officers. Thus the term was used derog. or jocularly in the Armed Forces, but occasionally with pride by the officer's family.* → 2 Any youthful-looking officer, esp. an Army second lieu-

tenant or an Air Force officer. → 3 A member of the U.S. Army or USN Reserve mobilized and given a three months' refresher training course. 1951: "The movie [*You're in the Navy Now*] is the . . . story of those 90-day wonders who made it the fleet that can't be beat!" *Nationwide newsp. advt.* → 4 A resort or park employee hired for the three-month summer vacation season only, as distinguished from a permanent employee. *Not common.*

ninety-eight   *n.* The manager of a lunch counter or soda-fountain. *Common lunch-counter use since c1935. Usu. used by employees to call the manager to hear a customer's grievance.*

ninety-five   *n.* A customer at a lunch counter who walks out without paying. *Lunch-counter use since c1935.*

ninety-nine   *n.* 1 At a lunch counter or soda fountain, the chief fry cook or soda jerk. 2 Out-of-style or damaged merchandise that a salesman is paid extra for selling, esp. shoes. *Retail salesman use, esp. shoe salesman use.*

Nip   *n.* [derog.] A Japanese. 1942: "A bunch of Nips." *Time*, Feb. 9, 23. *Some W.W.II use. From "Nippon."*

nipper   *n.* A small boy: a child. *More common in Eng. than U.S.*

nippers   *n.pl.* Handcuffs. 1918: ". . . A newly appointed policeman . . . has to buy . . . a pair of nippers. . . ." *Outlook*, Sept., 126/1.

nit   *adv.* No. *Mainly dial. Some sl. use c1900.* Cf. **nix.**   *n.* Zero.   **—wit**

nit-wit   *n.* A stupid person. *Colloq.*

nitery   nightery   *n.* A nightclub. 1942: "Nightery." Maurice Zolotow, *Amer. Mercury*, Oct., 412/1. 1953: "Star of burlesque [and] niteries." Bob Thomas, AP, May 18.

nit-picker   *n.* One who looks for and finds minor errors; a pedant. Cf. **comma-counter.**

nix   *adv.* 1 No. "I disagree, refuse, or forbid." "Don't." Specif., "Don't talk about or do that now; someone is listening, watching. 1942: " 'The guy's heeled.' . . . 'Under that suit? Nix.' " Chandler, *High Window*, 38. *Colloq. From Ger. "nichts" = nothing.* 2 Not. *Not common.*   *n.* 1 Nothing. 1930–31: ". . . He probably wasn't taking her out here in the park for nix." J. T. Farrell, 163. *Not common.* 2 A refusal; a ban. 1948: "Yanks' Nix on Coupling U.S., British Pix Seen as Johnston's Trump Card. . . . If the Petrillo nix stands. . . ." *Variety*, Aug. 25, 5/1–2, 9/2. *Popularized*

by the theatrical trade paper, "Variety."
v.t. To veto; to reject; to cancel; to avoid. 1945: ". . . The blue-penciler nixed the story." W. Winchell, *synd. newsp. col.,* Nov. 13. *Popularized by the theatrical trade paper, "Variety"; that paper's traditional headline, "Stix nix hix pix," was a triumph of sl. usage. Often used imperatively.* 1905: "Nix on the hurry talk, Bunch." McHugh, *Search Me,* 17. 1922: "Nix on dat . . . stuff! Nix on de loud noise." O'Neill, *Hairy Ape,* I. 1945: "Nix on swiping anything." E. B. White, *Stuart Little,* 93. *adj.* **1** Worthless; no good. *Not common.* **2** Unfavorable. **—ie** *n.* A piece of mail so damaged or incompletely or illegibly addressed that it cannot be delivered or returned. *U.S. mail service use.* See Appendix, —ie ending.

nix out To leave; to depart.

no account ‑ **1** Worthless; untrustworthy, irresponsible. **2** A worthless or irresponsible man.

noah _**Noah** *n.* A flatboat. *Obs.*

Noah's boy Ham, as served to be eaten. *A sl. pun, prob. synthetic.*

Noah's boy with Murphy carrying a wreath Ham and potatoes with cabbage. *Some lunch-counter use has been reported.*

nob *n.* **1** A rich, influential person. **2** A person's head. **—by knobby** *adj.* Smart, stylish, natty, fashionable. 1858: "His summer hat also is as good as new, quite nobby when compared with his old cap. . . ." *Harvard Mag.,* May, 170. 1900: "Genteel business men in 'nobby' suits and clean linen." "Walking dress, with a 'nobby' hat to match." Dreiser, *Sister Carrie,* 16, 232. 1930: "Polo shirts, nobby ties." J. T. Farrell, 136. 1952: "In 1903 Larkin picked up a nobby one-cylinder Winton [automobile]. . . ." *New Yorker,* Jan. 18, 20/2. *Archaic since c1935;* "nobby" *is about five times as common as* "knobby."

no bargain A person, usu. of marriageable age, who is not particularly attractive, interesting, or convivial.

nobbler *n.* One who drugs a race horse or dog or otherwise tries to influence unethically the outcome of a sporting or gambling event. 1946: "Superior chemistry and some luck on the part of the nobblers who drugged dogs in a race." Paul Jones, Phila. *Bulletin,* Jan. 7, 10. *Not as common in U.S. as in Eng.*

no better than she should be Promis-

cuous. *One of the oldest euphem. terms in the lang.*

no-bill *n.* A worker who will not join a union. *Railroad use; obs.* See **noble.**

noble *n.* **1** A strike-breaker's guard. **2** The boss of a gang of strike-breakers; a chief fink. 1956: "*Noble*—Captain of a strike-breaking team." *Labor's Special Lang. from Many Sources. Never common.* **3** A self-righteous person; one who pretends to act from principle when actually motivated by selfish considerations.

Noble = Charlie Noble.

nobody, a *n.* A person without fame, notoriety, notable success, ambition, or distinction; a person whose life has no special value or meaning to society. Cf. **somebody, a.**

nobody home An expression applied to any person thought to be stupid, feeble-minded, inattentive, etc. *Often used jocularly, and often accompanied by the gesture of tapping the person referred to on the top of the head. Since c1915.*

no-clap medal The Good Conduct Medal. *W.W.II Army use.* See **clap.**

no count = no account.

nod, get the To be chosen or approved; to be chosen over others; to be singled out for a desired job or position. *Lit. = to get a nod of approval.* See also **nod, the.**

nod, the *n.* **1** The referee's and judge's affirmative decision. *Sports use since c1920. Usu. in* "He [a prizefighter] got the nod" = he won by the referee's or judge's decision as opposed to winning by knocking one's opponent out. → **2** One's choice; esp. an expert's choice to win a race or sports contest, or a sport team manager's choice of a player to play in a specific game. 1958: "Bold Ruler gets the nod over Gallant Man in today's renewal of the Carter Handicap." *The Morning Telegraph,* May 29, 5. **3** Sleep; a period of sleep. *Some c1935 jive use.*

noddle *n.* = **noodle.** "*Noddle*" *is prob. the older of the two, but since c1915* "noodle" *has been in much more common use.*

nod-guy *n.* = **yes-man.** 1932: "Big Nig is Dave's regular nod-guy." Damon Runyon. *Because he nods his head up and down to signify* "yes."

no dice no-dice **1** No; without success; being refused or refused permission. 1952: ". . . His lawyer got the decree in Reynosa after a Nuevo Laredo judge said no dice." Gene Spagnoli, N.Y. *Daily News,* Aug. 12, C4/3. **2** Worthless. 1952: "We have been paying a disguised subsidy to a little no-dice

paper called the Rome American."
W. Pegler, *synd. newsp. col.*, Mar. 11.
no flies on [a person]   An expression
signifying that the subject is alert, canny,
or smart. *Archaic.*
noggin   *n.* The head. 1943: "The
psychiatrist after diagnosing his noggin.
. . ." H. A. Smith, *Putty Knife*, 55.
1951: "That's using the old noggin."
M. Shulman, *Dobie Gillis*, 175. *Since
c1890; colloq. Until c1925 primarily = the
head as an object for hitting, since then also
= the head as containing the brain for
thinking.*
no-good   No-good   *n.* = **no account.**
A worthless person. 1951: "He is a
No-Good." *Hobo News*, Dec., 12. 1953:
"A high-living no-good in a derby hat."
Hal Boyle, AP, Mar. 9. *Colloq.   adj.*
Worthless; almost always said of people,
seldom of things. 1946: "His father was
a no-good drunk." *Life*, Apr. 8, 87/1.
Colloq.
no got   I [or someone] don't have the
object in question; anything not possessed by a given person. *Not common.*
no great shakes   An unimportant or
average person or group. *Usu. in "He's
no great shakes" = He's not important
or outstanding. Since c1850.*
no-hitter   *n.* A baseball game in which
a team makes no hits. 1952: "Allie
Reynolds hurled two no-hitters, on July
12 and September 28. . . ." AP, Aug. 29.
noise   *n.* **1** Unwelcome information,
unfavorable comments, bad news.
Archaic underworld use. **2** Chatter,
nonsense, blah. *Colloq.* **3** Heroin. *c1925.
Never common, even among addicts.*
4 Explosives, dynamite, nitroglycerin.
Underworld use, c1925. **5** A gun. 1946:
"Not the noise, bounce him." Wyer,
N.Y. Sun. See **big noise, red noise.**
noise tool   A pistol. 1936: "As to
practice in actual firing, the puncher
necessarily had infinitely more than had
the city dweller; but the average puncher,
after his first few years, gave himself no
undue amount, since he was wont to
consider that he had better use for his
money than the purchase of ammunition
to be fired through a 'noise tool' at a
tree or can." P. A. Rollins, *The Cowboy*,
49. *Obs.*
no kid   no kidding   A somewhat
doubting response to a statement that
seems not entirely credible.
nola   *n.* A homosexual. *Some c1925–
c1940 use; archaic.*
no more room   As cool or far out as
a person or the playing of a piece of

music can be; fig., so satisfying that there
is no room for improvement. 1957:
"There's no more room—An individual
or a group (musicians or otherwise) are
just Too Much." E. Horne, *For Cool
Cats and Far-Out Chicks. Some far-out
and beat use since c1955.*
noncom   *n.* A non-commissioned officer. *Colloq. Army use since c1930. Wide
W.W.II use.*
no never mind, makes   "It makes no
difference; it is not an influencing
factor."
noodle   noddle   *n.* **1** The human
head, esp. as considered as a thinking
organ. 1905: "I suppose the axle grease
gave him wheels in the noddle. . . ."
McHugh, *Search Me*, 86. 1929-30: "I've
been as near off my noodle as a . . . sane
man can get." K. Brush, *Young Man*,
184. 1943: "He has a foggy noodle."
H. A. Smith, *Putty Knife*, 37. 1951:
"Most of the fellows running television
today are sick in the noodle. . . ."
Philip Hamburger, *The New Yorker*,
June 30, 56. *"Noddle" was in use before
c1915, but is now obs.* **2** A stupid,
unthinking, or forgetful person. *Colloq.
v.i., v.t.* To think, to think over, to study.
1952: "Think some more. I'll noodle it
around too. Then we'll have a meeting.
. . ." Jerome Ellison, *SEP*, Sept. 20,
95/2.
noodle-head   *n.* A stupid person.
Not common.
noodle-twister   *n.* A cigar-maker who
makes cigars by hand. *Obs. Except for a
few expensive ones, cigars are now made
entirely by machine.*
noodle-work   *n.* Thinking; studying.
Not common.
nookie   nookey [taboo]   *n.* Sexual
activity; a woman considered solely as a
sexual object; the vagina; coitus; a piece.
1928: Hecht & MacArthur, *Front Page*,
I. 1941: ". . . He's a young kid tryin' to
get his first nookey!" Schulberg, *Sammy*,
227. 1948: N. Mailer, *The Naked and the
Dead*, 161. *Wide W.W.II use. Prob. from
"nook."*
noose is hanging, the   Everything is
ready; everyone is waiting, eager, and
expectant. 1957: "The noose is hanging—
All of the musicians are primed for a
real cutting session, i.e., each man will
attempt to outdo . . . the others." E.
Horne, *For Cool Cats and Far-Out
Chicks. Some far-out and beat use since
c1955.*
nope   *adv.* No. 1924: "Nope, I can't go

walking. . . ." Marks, *Plastic Age*, 28. *Colloq.*

noplaceville *adj.* Fig., a place or time suitable to squares, hence square, dull, corny. *Some cool, far-out, and beat use. Since c1955.* *n.* A dull or boring place or town; a small town, a jerkwater town. 1956: "Punkin Junction . . . why should [she] ever bury herself in a noplaceville like this?" "*Mary Worth,*" *synd. newsp. comic strip*, May 6. *Some student, teenage, and even general use.*

northpaw *n.* A right-handed baseball pitcher; any right-handed person. *Not common. Based on "southpaw."*

Norwegian steam *n.* Manpower; muscle power. *A little jocular use, esp. maritime use.*

nose *n.* A police spy; a paid informer. *Some c1930 underworld use.* See **dog's-nose, on the nose, pay through the nose, pope's nose.**

nose, by a To win a contest, best an opponent, or obtain a goal by a narrow margin. *From the horse-racing use.*

nose, on the **1** Correct, right, on the button. **2** Exactly on time, on the button.

nose-bag *n.* **1** = **feedbag. 2** Food handed out in a paper bag. *Hobo use.* → **3** A dinner pail or lunch box.

nose-bag, put on the = **put on the feed bag.**

nose candy *n.* A narcotic taken by sniffing, usu. cocaine. 1939: "A deck of nose candy for sale." J. Evans, *Halo*, 24.

nose-dive *n.* **1** The act of accepting religion at a mission revival, usu. in order to receive a free meal. *Hobo use.* **2** Lit. and fig., a sudden drop or decrease, esp. in the price of something. *Colloq.*

nose out Lit. and fig., to win by a nose; to win, succeed, or be chosen over another in a close contest or by a small margin.

nose paint Whisky; liquor. *Since c1880. Never common. Because many habitual drunks seem to have red noses.*

no shit [taboo] The truth; not shit or bullshit. Usu. in "That's no shit" = that's the truth; or in the question "No shit?" = Really, is that the truth? See **shit.**

no-show *n.* A person who fails to claim, use, or cancel his reservation, esp. on an air flight. *Since c1950. Orig. commercial airlines' use.*

no soap Nothing doing; I don't know; No. 1924: "If you don't know, just say, 'No soap.' . . ." Marks, *Plastic Age*, 99.

not all there Lacking normal intelligence or sanity; seeming to lack intelligence or sanity owing to having an obsession or eccentric attitude. 1939-40: "That poor creature who's not quite all there. . . ." A. Christie, *Sad Cypress*, 96.

not by a jugful Emphatically no. 1833: *DAE. Archaic and dial.*

notchery *n.* A brothel.

notch-house *n.* A brothel. *Not common.* Cf. **nautch-joint.**

not dry behind the ears Inexperienced or unworldly, specif., because of one's youth. *Implying that one's mother has recently washed behind one's ears or has still to remind her young child to do so.*

note See **C-note, case note, mash note.**

nothing *adj.* Insipid, colorless, dull. *As in "He's a real nothing guy," or "That's a nothing book."*

nothing, know from **don't know from nothing** To know nothing; to know nothing or little about a specific topic; esp. to know nothing, or claim to know nothing, about an embarrassing, illegal, or unethical act, to be innocent of incriminating knowledge. 1937: "If they ask you any questions, you don't know from nothing." Weidman, *Wholesale*, 194. 1941: "I know from nothing about what I'm supposed to be doing. . . ." Schulberg, *Sammy*, 84. 1945: "A dizzy blonde . . . who knows from nothing, but is got everything." ABC, *network radio play*, Nov. 18. 1951: "I don't know from nothing about a crime." *I, Mobster*, 30. *Orig. c1930 New York City use; based on Yiddish speech patterns. The insertion of the "from" points to an orig. in Yiddish speech patterns. Until c1940 the double negative form was almost always used, but the initial "don't" seems to be disappearing*

nothing doing **1** An expression meaning emphatically No; usu. said in response to a plan or idea that fails to evoke interest and agreement. **2** An attrib. expression to signify no action, excitement, or interest (in a given place or group).

no three-alarm fire A mediocre, unattractive, unexciting person or thing. *Archaic.* Cf. **no bargain.**

nougat *n.* A nut, sap, or dope. *From the fact that nuts are a principal ingredient of nougat.* 1929-30: " 'She's going to telephone you?' 'So she said.' . . . 'And then what did you say?' 'Told her not to be a nougat. I became fatherly.' " K. Brush, *Young Man*, 68f. *Never common.*

no-work   *n.* A loafer; one who can but does not work. 1946: "No-works, ashamed of their laziness, cover it up by . . . fishing. . . ." Red Smith, *N.Y. Her. Trib.*, Mar. 30. *Not common.*

nozzle   *n.* The nose. See **schnozzle.**

nub   *n.* An unattractive person, esp. an unattractive girl. *Some student use c1935–c1945.*

nudie   *n.* **1** A show or performance in which a female nude or nudes appear. **2** A nude or nearly nude female performer, esp a dancing girl, as in a cabaret floor-show. 1951: "Some of the worried little nudies." Westbrook Pegler, *synd. newsp. col.*, Dec. 27. See Appendix, —ie ending.

nudnik   *n.* An obnoxious person. *From the Yiddish "nudnik" = a pest.*

nugget   *adj.* Excellent. *Some c1925 student use.*   *n.* A baseball. *Never common.*

numb   *adj.* **1** Stupid; inattentive. Cf. **numb-headed. 2** Lit. and fig., numb with fear; afraid.   **—ie**   *n.* A stupid person. *From "numb-head," reinforced by "dummy."*

numb-brained   *adj.* Stupid. 1930: ". . . To gain . . . recruits from the numb-brained hanger-ons." Lavine, *Third Degree*, 30.

number   *n.* **1** Any person, usu. of a kind specified in a modifying word or phrase, as a "hot number," "little number," "smart number," etc.; most freq. a sexually attractive or vivacious girl. 1932: "Tonight I'm grabbing myself a keen number." J. T. Farrell, 123. 1936: "She's a sweet-tempered little number." Movie, *My Man Godfrey.* 1937: "Some dizzy broad that must have been a snappy number. . . ." Weidman, *Wholesale*, 8. 1949: "He was a . . . bored-looking number. . . ." J. Evans, *Halo*, 78. Cf. **article, job.** *Also used absolutely as in "back number" and "wrong number."* **2** A specific model, style, or article of merchandise, as an automobile or article of clothing. 1928: "Picking up a number [automobile] on the street ain't like getting your shoes shined." P.G. 1948: "I found a number [man's suit] I liked pretty well. . . ." Cain, *Moth*, 22. *Reinforced by the fact that many articles of merchandise have a specific manufacturer's style number.* See **have [someone's] number.**

number, have [someone's]   To know the hidden truth about another's character, past, behavior, or motives; to have classified or identified a person. 1934: "She knew what I meant, and she knew I had her number." Cain, *Postman*, 5.

Number One   number one   number 1   1. Oneself. *E.g., "I've got to take care of number one first."*   **2** To urinate. *Child euphem. to communicate bathroom needs.* Cf. **number two.**   **— boy   1** The one in authority, esp. the head of a business firm. → **2** A chief assistant, one's most trusted associate or employee. → **3** A yes man. **4** A movie extra who owns his own dress suit for playing in society pictures.

numbers, by the   As expected; according to the usual rules; mechanically; without enthusiasm or emotion; said of actions. *Orig. W.W.II Armed Forces use. From the army expression, which was part of an order to drilling soldiers, indicating that marching, manual of arms, or other drill would be carried out accompanied by unison counting to ensure precision.*

number two   To defecate. *Child euphem. in communicating bathroom needs.* Cf. **number one.**

numb-head   *n.* A stupid or dull person. *Some student use. Not as old as "numb-headed."*   **—ed**   *adj.* Stupid. 1847: *DAE. Colloq.*

nut   *n.* **1** The human head. *Archaic since c1930; though still used in "off [one's] nut."* **2** Any person, usu. male; a fellow, a guy. 1920: "Simple little nut." Fitzgerald, *This Side of Paradise*, 105. *Usu. jocular or derog. use. Not common.* Cf. **tough nut.** → **3** A person who is insane; a stupid, foolish, or gullible person; a person of unusual habits or beliefs; a character; an eccentric; an irresponsible or humorous person. 1914: "You poor nut [eccentric person]." S. Lewis, *Our Mr. Wrenn*, 13. 1924: "What a lot of nuts [irresponsible people] we were." Marks, *Plastic Age*, 107. 1940: "It was the laugh of a nut [insane person]." Chandler, *Farewell*, 138. 1950: "On the N.B.C. network, it is forbidden to call any character a nut [eccentric]; you have to call him a screwball." *New Yorker*, Dec. 23, 15/3. 1956: "They locked him [Buddy Bolden] up in the East Louisiana State Hospital, the place for common nuts, in 1907." S. Longstreet, *The Real Jazz Old and New*, 10. *All uses common since c1915. With the popular acceptance of psychology the word is being used less and less = an insane person. With the increasing conformity in American life the word* is being used more and more to = an eccentric, irresponsible, or humorous personality; the word is now often applied affectionately to one who performs an unusually generous, funny, or touchingly emotional act. → **4** A person fanatically enthusiastic about a particular activity, esp. about a sport; a fan. 1951: "When one football nut writes a book, another football nut should not be entrusted with the job of passing judgment on it." Arthur Daley, N.Y. *Times Bk. Rev.*, Oct. 7, 16. **5** The total expenses necessary to start or operate a business; expenses; overhead. 1939: "High pitchman . . . hopes to be off the nut [even] by the Fair's end." *Life*, July 31, 24. 1952: "Producing a daily income that barely met the nut." Liebling, *New Yorker*. **6** A jocular term of endearment. 1934: ". . . A week-end party at the home of some valuable nuts I know. . . ." P. Wylie, *Finnley Wren*, 122.   **—s** *n. sing.* A despised person. 1851: "We speak of such a person . . . as being nuts." Hall, *College Words*, 218. *Never common.* *adj.* Insane; stupid, foolish, gullible; mistaken, misinformed, confused; crazy; eccentric; irresponsible. 1930: "They decide . . . he must be going 'nuts.' " Lavine, *Third Degree*, 26. 1939–40: "He is got the cashier going nuts because he wants a report every 15 min." O'Hara, *Pal Joey*, 53. 1946: "I was going nuts trying to find a short word to fit this category." Wolfe Kaufman, *Word Study*, May 1, 7/1. 1951: "The [good conduct] code [drawn up by television broadcasters] specifically bans a number of words and phrases, among them . . . nuts except when meaning crazy. . . ." *Time*, Oct. 29, 50. 1957: "Heir Rejected 400 G; Is He Nuts?" headline, N.Y. *Daily News*, July 26, 5. Cf. **nut, nuts about.** *n.pl.* [taboo] The testicles. *Very common.*   **—tiness** *n.* Craziness. 1949: "Booth's capacity for nuttiness became . . . a legend. . . ." Billy Rose, *synd. newsp. col.*, Nov. 18.   **—ty** *adj.* = **nuts,** all meanings, like a nut. 1900: "A 'nutty' person." Upson, *Independent*, 2573/2. 1914: "I was just about nutty, I was so lonely." S. Lewis, *Our Mr. Wrenn*, 82. 1936: "They're that nutty." *My Man Godfrey*, movie.   *adv.* Crazily; idiotically. 1914: "I ain't talking too nutty, am I?" S. Lewis, *Our Mr. Wrenn*, 82. *Not common.*

—nut   See Appendix, Suffixes and Suffix Words.

nut, off [one's]   **1** Insane, crazy. 1909:

"Off his nut." Krapp, *Mod. English*, 205. 1922: "He's off his nut. . . ." O'Neill, *Hairy Ape.* 1952: "He looked at me like I was off my nut." *People Are Funny*, network radio show, Nov. 11. *The most common of the "off one's ——" = "crazy" terms.* See **nut. 2** In a tantrum; irrational. **3** Mistaken.

nut college = **nut house.** 1951: "He has been recalled by the nut college to join Napoleon . . . and Shakespeare, inventing paper dolls!" "Major Hoople," *synd. newsp. cartoon*, July 5. *Since c1900; never common.*

nut factory = **nut house.** *More common than "nut college."*

nut farm = **nut house.** *Not common.*

nut foundry = **nut house.** *Not common.*

nut hatch = **nut house.** 1949: "The Chateau Bercy . . . had a general air of having been redecorated by a parolee from a nut hatch." Chandler, *Little Sister*, 246. *Not common. Based on "booby hatch."*

nut house   *n.* An insane asylum; a prison and/or hospital for the mentally ill. 1936: ". . . And goes away to the nut house." Tully, *Bruiser*, 65. 1943: "A nuthouse wall." Wolfert, *Underworld*, 425. 1952: ". . . Working in the only nuthouse run by its inmates." Comedian Red Skelton, quoted by AP, Sept. 18.

nutpick   *n.* A psychiatrist. *Never common.*

nuts!   nerts!   nertz!   *interj.* An interjection of disgust, contempt, annoyance, or the like; a term of dislike, disbelief, scorn, or despair; an emphatic "no!" *Colloq. since c1925.*

nuts, the   nerts, the   Any excellent thing or person. 1934: "Eulogizing anything . . . as 'the nerts.' . . ." *Eng. Jour.*, Nov., 740.

nuts about   nuts over   nuts on = **crazy about;** in love with; enthusiastic about. 1939: "He's a little nut, nuts on the horse races. . . ." Gardner, *D. A. Draws*, 25. 1944: "I'm nuts about her. She's just nuts about him." Ford, *Phila. Murder*, 24. 1957: "You kissed me and that changes everything. I think I'm nuts about you." Steve McNeil, *High-Pressure Girl*.

nuts cracked, get [one's] = **get [one's] ashes hauled** [taboo].   *A later use; some fairly wide W.W.II Army use.* See **nuts.**

nutty about   nutty over = **nuts**

about. 1914: "I'd be simply nutty about the quadrangles at Oxford. . . ." S. Lewis, *Our Mr. Wrenn*, 68.

nutty as a fruitcake Extremely eccentric; very nutty. Cf. **fruitcake.**

nyet *n.* A negative decision or vote; a veto. *exclam.* No. *From the Russian, often in semihumorous mockery of the Russian government's attitude in inter-*national affairs; specif. from Russia's freq. use of the veto in the United Nations. Pop. by freq. newsp. use.

nymphokick *n.* Any erotic excitement or pleasure. 1956: ". . . An erotic excitement, also called a *nymphokick.*" S. Longstreet, *The Real Jazz Old and New*, 150. *From "nymphomaniac" plus "kick." Not common.*

O

O *n.* **1** Opium. *Narcotic addict use. Not common.* **2** = **big O.**

—o See Appendix, Suffixes and Suffix Words.

oak See **oka, sport the oak.**

Oakley = **Annie Oakley.**

oakum = **oakus.**

oakus **oakum** *n.* A pocket billfold; a wallet. *Mainly underworld use; archaic.*

oat-burner *n.* = **hay-burner.** 1952: "When the time comes . . . that even an oat-burner must sport a tax stamp on its stem or stern. . . ." *Letter*, N.Y. *Daily News*, Aug. 20, C11/4.

oater *n.* A western movie; a horse opera. 1950: "Between a third and a quarter of the Hollywood pictures are horse operas, also known as sagebrushers or oaters." Bob Thomas, AP, Hollywood, July 18. 1951: "It was a tough season. . . . Even the oaters were off." William Fuller, *Collier's*, Feb. 10, 22/1. *Movie use.*

oats opera = **horse opera.** *Movie use.*

obie *n.* A post office. *Hobo use; obs. From O.B., which is P.O. [the standard abbr. for "post office"] reversed and with P changed to B.*

obit *n.* An obituary, esp. as in a newspaper. 1953: "This is not the obit page. . . ." H. Breit, N.Y. *Times*, Aug. 9, 8/3. See Appendix, Shortened Words.

ochre **ocher** **oochre** *n.* Money. *Since c1860.*

—ocracy See Appendix, Suffixes and Suffix Words.

O. D. *n., adj.* Olive drab; hence, an olive-drab uniform, esp. the "Class A" uniform of the Army through 1959. *Orig. Army use.* *n.* Officer of the Day. *Stand. abbr. Army use.* **—'s** *n.pl.* The enlisted man's uniform, U.S. Army, through 1959, when color changed to Army green.

oday *n.* Money. *One of the more familiar Pig Latin words; from "dough."* See Appendix, Little Languages.

odd-ball **oddball** *n.* An eccentric, queer, or odd person; a screwball; an intensely introverted person; a creep; a nonconformist. *adj.* Eccentric; disorganized; prone to blunder; unreliable. *Common since c1945.*

odds-on *adj.* In gambling, having better than an even chance to win; favorite. 1941: ". . . From what I know of Ezra, it's an odds-on bet that Mrs. Vera Blackburn . . . conducted the courtship." J. Lilienthal, *Horse Crazy*, 8.

ofaginzy *n.* = **ofay.** 1956: "The white visitor is called an 'ofay' by Negroes. . . . He is also known as an 'ofaginzy,' just to make it harder." S. Longstreet, *The Real Jazz Old and New*, 147.

ofay *n.* A white person. 1931: "The plutes compromised with the blacks/ the spades inhabited Harlem and let the/ofays have Wall Street to themselves." Bob Brown, *Amer. Mercury*, Dec., 407/2. 1951: "[a Negro speaking] There's gonna be two dead ofays." Movie, *The Well*. c1920 [1954]: ". . . Ofay (white) business men and planters. . . ." "He had the features and even the voice of a white boy—an ofay." L. Armstrong, *Satchmo, My Life in New Orleans*, 147, 238. *Common Negro use since c1925. It has been suggested that this may be from "foe" as said in Pig Latin. Archaic.* Cf. **fay.** See Appendix, Little Languages.

off See **dance off, first off, get it off.** *adj.* Crazy; eccentric; loco. See **off [one's] chump, off [one's] head, off [one's] nut, off [one's] onion, off [one's] rocker, off [one's] trolley.**

off — For phrases beginning with "off," see under the principal word of the phrase.

— off See Appendix, Suffixes and Suffix Words.

off, get In swing music, an improvised solo. See **tell [someone] where to get off.**

off base Impertinent; assuming

authority or intimacy which one does not have.

off-beat *adj.* Unusual; out of the ordinary; weird; unconventional but accepted; unconventional but not unique; macabre. 1957: "The off-beat death . . . in a[n] off-Broadway hotel room. . . . In less than 12 hours . . . detectives unraveled a . . . mystery which began and ended as off-beat as the death itself." N.Y. *Daily News*, Sept. 17, 4/1. *Since c1935, but wide use only since c1950, often in reference to intellectuals and cool and beat nonconformists.*

off color   off-color *adj.* Tending to be obscene, lewd, or lascivious, but hinting at or suggesting the obscene rather than actually being obscene. *Usu. in ref. to a joke, song, or the like.* See **dirty.**

— **offer**   See Appendix, Suffixes and Suffix Words.

office *n.* **1** A place; facetiously, resembling or serving as an office; any place where one does work or spends a great deal of time. 1842: "[=] a saloon." *DAE.* 1943: "[=] the cockpit of an airplane." A. Ostrow. *Air Force use.* **2** A secret sign, a signal, or tip-off, as a wink, hand signal, clearing one's throat, or the like. 1921: "When I give you the office I want you to knock Hamilton stiff. . . ." Witwer, *Leather*, 171. 1932: "I give him the office I wish to speak to him. . . ." Runyon. *Primarily underworld use.* *v.t.* To signal a person; to give an office to someone. 1927: "Will you let her out when I office you?" Burnett, *Little Caesar*, 61. *Never common.*

offsteered *adj.* Enticed away from; sidetracked. 1949: "Too many dogs get offsteered onto water right off, they don't get no chance to make up their own minds what they really like best, beer 'r water 'r just play whiskey." N. Algren, *Man with the Golden Arm*, 71.

ogfray [derog.]   *n.* = **frog.** A Frenchman. *One of the more common Pig Latin words.* See Appendix, Little Languages.

O. Henry *n.* The climax line of a play, esp. a surprising or sentimental one. *From the pen name of W. S. Porter, Amer. author, d. 1910.* 1941: "I only had a bit part but I did have the O. Henry." D. McFerran. *Radio use; obs.*

Oh fudge   An extremely mild expression of disappointment or frustration. Sometimes a euphem. for any of the "fuck" oaths. See **fudge.**

oh yeah   An expression of challenge, incredulity, or sarcasm. *Colloq.*

Oh yes = **oh yeah.** *Not common.*

oil *n.* **1** Competence, ability, skill. *c1925, student use.* **2** Chewing tobacco. *Obs.* **3** Flattery; bunk; boloney; blah. 1937: "Aah, stop the oil, will you?" Weidman, *Wholesale*, 188. 1951: "[The movie's] virtues are almost hopelessly marinated in good old Hollywood oil." John McCarten, *New Yorker*, Dec. 1, 155. **4** Money, esp. graft. Cf. **banana oil.** See **hickory oil, olive oil.** *v.t.* **1** To hit, beat, or whip someone. **2** To pay graft or bribery money; to fix the police or other public officials.

oil-burner *n.* **1** A tobacco chewer. *Obs.* **2** Any old or dilapidated vehicle, esp. a car or ship.

oil can **1** A failure, a flop. 1929: "The vaudeville performer on the two-a-day has played to punks in the hide-aways who turned his riot into an oil can." *World's Work*, Nov., 40. *Never common.* **2** A railroad tank car. *Railroad use.* **3** A disliked, boring, or worthless person. *Some student use, c1925.*

oil changed, get [one's] = **get [one's] ashes hauled.**

oiled *adj.* Drunk. 1924: "Some . . . had got at least half 'oiled' before the dance. . . ." Marks, *Plastic Age*, 252. 1948: "He . . . got oiled. . . ." Lait-Mortimer, *N.Y. Confidential*, 161. *Common c1920. Now often replaced by "well oiled."* See Appendix, Drunk.

oiler [derog.]   *n.* A Mexican; a greaser. *Never common.*

oil [someone's] palm   To bribe; to grease. 1936: "I'll have to oil Blinky Miller's palm." Tully, *Bruiser*, 152. *Colloq.*

o. j. *n.* A glass of orange juice. *Some lunch-counter use.*

oka   oke   okey   okay   oak *adv.* O.K.; yes. *adj.* Good; satisfactory. *All from stand. O.K. Most common ety. is from presidential campaign of 1840 when term was used as abbr. of "Old Kinderhook," Martin Van Buren's nickname. For other etys. see H. L. Mencken, American Lang., Supplement IV.*

okey-doke   okie doke = **O.K.** 1938: "The modern 'O.K.' with its babyfied 'okey-doke.' " C. T. Ryan, *Better English*, Sept., 39/2. 1951: " 'Suppose I pick you up at seven.' 'Okie doke.' ". Peter De Vries, *New Yorker*, Nov. 17, 139/1. *Since c1930.* See Appendix, Reduplications.

okey-dokey   okie-dokie = **O.K.** 1946: "[The Russians liked Americans'

constant use of 'O.K.'] But they were
puzzled . . . with 'okie-dokie.' " *Word
Study*, May, 2/1. *Since c1935.*

Okie   *n.* **1** A migratory worker. *Orig.
one of the many Oklahoma and Arkansas
farmers who became migratory workers
after the dust storms of the early 1930's.*
1938: "About a fifth of [the migratory
workers in California] are Okies. . . ."
Carleton Beals, *Forum & Century*, Jan.,
12. *Since c1935.* → **2** The family of such
a migratory worker. 1940: " 'Ballads of
the Okies' [title]." N.Y. *Times Mag.*,
Nov. 17. → **3** A resident or native of
Oklahoma. **4** A native of Okinawa.
Some W.W.II Army use.

okle-dokle = **O.K.** *Fairly common jocular use.*

oky dory = **O.K.** *Never common.*

—ola   —olo   See Appendix,
Suffixes and Suffix Words.

old   *n.* A wife. *Some archaic Negro use;
never common. From "old woman."*

old —   See Appendix, Prefixes and
Prefix Words.

old army game, the   Any swindle;
any unfair or crooked gambling game
or bet. 1941: "It's nothing but the . . .
army game." Cain, *M. Pierce*, 200.

old bean   Old friend; old man; "man."
1952: "You understand, old bean, things
are done differently in America and
Britain." Hal Boyle, AP, May 1. *Considered as Brit. but occas. used in the U.S.,
usu. in direct address, to convey a jocular
or affected tone.*

old boy = **old man,** the term of direct
address. *Most common c1925–c1940.
An earlier form of "old ——" = close
friend; used only by males in addressing
males.*

old chap = **old man.** *Considered somewhat more formal, and hence affected,
than other "old ——" = close friend
forms of direct address.*

old fellow = **old man.** *Archaic.*

old file   An old soldier. *Archaic Army
use.*

old fruit = **old bean.** *Once jocular or
affected use as a recognized Briticism,
c1920, now obs. owing to homosexual
meaning of "fruit."*

old goat   Any elderly, disliked person,
most often a man but may be a woman;
esp. an elderly person disliked for being
pompous, stingy, mean, stubborn, unsympathetic to younger people, or the
like. *Colloq.*

old hat   Out of style; old-fashioned.
1949: "For that matter, tubular stuff

[furniture] is now old hat. . . ." Robert M.
Coates, *New Yorker*, Oct. 15, 61/1.

old head   An employee having seniority. *Obs.*

oldie   oldy   *n.* Any old thing or
person, usu. an old joke, story, song, or
movie, less freq. an old man. 1934: "Our
pet oldie concerns the India rubber
skin man. . . ." Walter Winchell, *network
radio*, May 23. 1939–40: "The other
song was an oldy like 'My Buddy.' . . ."
O'Hara, *Pal Joey*, 48. 1957: "[A movie]
as good as a W. C. Fields oldie. . . ."
N.Y. *Post, movie review*, Oct. 19, 23/4.

old lady   **1** A wife, esp. one's own
wife. 1871: *DAE. Colloq. Not considered
derog. Based on the earlier "old woman."*
2 A mother, esp. one's own mother.
1924: " 'Gotta write a letter.' 'Who to?'
'My old lady.' He consistently called
his mother his old lady . . . and wrote
to her every night." Marks, *Plastic Age*,
28f. 1954: "So you've been in another
man's house with his old lady?" L.
Armstrong, *Satchmo, My Life in New
Orleans*, 122. 1956: "He's just a pore
lonesome wife-left feller. . . . Losin' his
old lady is what crazied him." N. Algren,
A Walk on the Wild Side, 7. *Colloq. Not
considered derog. Based on the older "old
man." Usu. male use.* **3** A roommate,
either male or female. *Some student use.
c1935.* Cf. **old miss.**

old man   **1** A father, esp. one's own
father. 1792: *DAE.* 1924: "My old man
never went to college." Marks, *Plastic
Age*, 12. 1955: "Is that any reason for
you to be spiteful to a poor little baby?
. . . Just because your own Daddy was
mean, do you have to be? My old man
wasn't mean." C. Willingham, *To Eat a
Peach*, 201. *Colloq.; usu. male use.* **2** A
husband, esp. one's own husband. 1956:
"At a racetrack a wife will get up and
leave because she can't bear to see her
old man lose his money." J. Cannon,
Who Struck John? 46. *Colloq. since c1895.
It is interesting to note that "old man" =
"father" is older than "old lady" =
"mother," but "old lady" = "wife" is
older than "old man" = "husband." The
oldest of each of the pairs is used by men,
who coin and use more sl. than women.*
3 Old friend. *A masc. term of direct
address implying affection for the man
so addressed and his intellectual equality
with the speaker. Because of the last
connotation, the term is most often used
in serious personal conversation and
sometimes is considered as condescending.*
Cf. **old bean, old boy, old chap, old**

fellow, old fruit, old sock, old socks, old thing, old top. 4 A man who supports a woman outside marriage in return for her sexual favors; a sugar daddy or John. 1954: "I was so gone over her we never mentioned she had an 'Old Man'—the name we used to have for a common law husband." L. Armstrong, *Satchmo, My Life in New Orleans*, 152. *Archaic.* **5** The captain of a ship. *Common maritime and USN use since c1850.* **6** The commanding officer of any military unit, esp. a company commander. *Army use since W.W.I.* **7** A superintendent, foreman, or boss. 1837: "master, foreman," *DAE.*

old man with the whiskers = whiskers.

old miss A roommate, either male or female. *Some student use c1935; never as common as "old lady."*

old saw 1 A homily; a folk saying; an aphorism. 1954: "Jesse [James] had a penchant for the old saws, the pithy sayings. . . . When he was worried . . . he was wont to express that worry via the handiest aphorism." W. Henry, *Death of a Legend*, 72. **2** An old joke or story. Cf. **chestnut.**

old smoky The electric chair. *Some use since c1925; archaic.*

old sock = old socks. *A later and more common term of direct address.*

old socks = old man. 1914: "Yuh—sure, old socks." S. Lewis, *Our Mr. Wrenn*, 149. *An affectionate term used in direct address between males. Archaic.*

Old Sol The sun. 1924: ". . . They's fewer days when Old Sol don't smile down on Mother Earth. . . ." R. Lardner, "How to Write Short Stories," reprinted in *The American Twenties*, 40. *Colloq.*

old soldier 1 A cigar butt, cigarette butt, or discarded quid of tobacco. *c1850–1930; archaic.* **2 = dead soldier.**

old thing = old man. 1928: "Men of letters, who would swoon at the sight of a split infinitive, such wowsers they are in regard to pure English, will in conversation address you as 'Old thing.'" R. Lynd, *New Statesman*, Feb. 4. *Orig. one of the affectionate masculine "old——" = "close friend" terms of direct address, esp. used by educated or sophisticated males. Occas. flippant or affected use. This is the one "old ——" = "close friend" term that is also applied to and used by females.*

old top = old bean.

old woman A wife, esp. one's own wife. *Colloq.* "Old lady" *is now more popular.*

olive oil Good-bye. *A parody pronunciation of Fr. "Au revoir." Some jocular W.W.I Army use. See Appendix, Mispronunciations.*

oliver *n.* The moon. 1848: "Criminal use." J. S. Farmer. 1931: "Underworld use." D. W. Maurer.

on *adj.* **1** Aware of, wise to, or hep to something, esp. to a swindle, fake, or hoax. 1934: "I saw he was on, and quit talking. . . ." Cain, *Postman*, 2. **2** Drunk. *Never common.* **3** Willing, ready to participate or accept another's participation. *prep.* Paid for by; a treat supplied by. 1934: "This was to be on him. . . ." Cain, *Postman*, 1. *Colloq. since c1900.* **4** Betting on (someone or something). *n.* **1** A sandwich on toast. *As in "One roast beef on" = a roast beef sandwich on toast. Some lunch-counter use in relaying an order to the cook. Since c1935.* **2** A dish of ice cream or an ice cream sundae. *Thus "a chocolate on" = a dish of chocolate ice cream, lit. chocolate ice cream "on" a plate, as opposed to "chocolate in" = an ice cream soda. Some lunch-counter use in relaying an order to the soda jerk. Since c1935.*

on —— For phrases beginning with "on," see under the principal word of the phrase.

on [someone or something] An expression signifying a treat paid for by the indicated person or group. *E.g.,* "Have a drink on me" = Let me buy you a drink; "Lunch on the company" = the company is providing lunch.

once-over *n.* **1** A look or glance; a visual inspection or examination, either cursory or detailed. *Usu. in "give [someone or something] the once-over."* 1922: "Give it de once-over!" O'Neill, *Hairy Ape*, 5. 1952: "The first thing we went to buy after giving all the pavilions the once-over was tomatoes." Art Buchwald, N.Y. *Her. Trib.*, Sept. 18, 21/5. *Since c1915.* Cf. **double-o. 2** A quick, cursory cleaning or putting of things in order; doing a task quickly or temporarily. 1952: "One of his brothers gave him a . . . shirt and a razor for a hasty once-over [a shave]." Meyer Berger, N.Y. *Times*, Sept. 3, 50/2. From **once over lightly.**

once over lightly Cursorily; quickly; temporarily. *From the traditional phrase in ordering a shave from a barber.*

oncer *n.* **1** One who attends church only once a week, on Sunday. *Obs.* **2** A woman who has been, or is, emotionally and sexually faithful to only one man during her life; a one-man woman.

one *n.* **1** A specimen or instance of virtually anything, identifiable only from the context; often a blow with the fist, a pitched baseball, a tall story, an order of food, etc. 1934: "I was . . . to give her one [a signal honk] on the [automobile] horn if somebody came." Cain, *Postman*, 15. 1941: ". . . He wondered if she was going to lay one [a blow with the hand] on his jaw." G. Homes, *40 Whacks*, 61. 1941: "Sheik would run in and lay one on him." Schulberg, *Sammy*, 230. *Some common examples: "draw one" = a cup of coffee, a glass of beer; "a fast one" = a fast pitch in baseball; "a hot one" = a joke or story, often used ironically; "one with" = a hamburger with coffee or with onions; "a quick one" = a single shot of whisky.* **2** One dollar; a one-dollar bill.

one-and-a-half-striper   one-and-one-half-striper A Naval lieutenant, junior. *Wide USN use since c1925.*

one and only One's sweetheart. 1947: "I've got my own one and only." Hal Boyle, *synd. newsp. col.*, May 19.

one-arm = one-arm joint. 1939–40: "She went with me to this one-arm where I eat. . . ." O'Hara, *Pal Joey*, 19. *Archaic.*

one-armed bandit   one-arm bandit A slot machine. 1952: "The 'one-armed bandits' were banned from federal property a year and a half ago." Vern Hougland, AP, July 2. 1956: ". . . Slot machines have been referred to as one-arm bandits." J. Scarne, *The Amazing World of John Scarne*, 63. *Because the operative lever of the machine resembles an arm, and because the odds on winning are fixed against the player.*

one-arm joint Any cheap restaurant, esp. and orig. one with chairs each of which has a wide right arm that functions as a table for a patron's tray of food. 1952: "I ran around to five different one-arm joints lookin' for ya." Network radio play, *The Big Story*, Dec. 10. *Archaic.* Cf. **joint.**

one-bagger See **bagger.**

one down **1** An order of toast. *1930–1945 lunch-counter use, used in relaying an order. Since c1945 being replaced by "an order of down."* **2** The first item has been accomplished; the first obstacle has been surmounted. *From baseball use of "one down and two to go" = one man has been put out and two more outs will retire the side.*

one down and two to go See **one down.**

one foot in the graveyard An order of soup. *From its being regarded as a food for invalids. Said to be lunch-counter use, prob. synthetic.*

one for the road A last drink; lit., the last drink before leaving a bar or a party for home. 1952: "He's . . . getting one for the road." Movie, *Niagara*. 1956: "As he settled himself in the electric chair, Fairris grinned at Elliot again and said: 'Give me one for the road, big boy.'" N.Y. *Post*, Jan. 18, 3. *Perhaps in allusion to the ancient tradition of the stirrup cup.*

one from Manhattan An order of clam chowder. *From "Manhattan clam chowder." Said to be lunch-counter use, prob. synthetic.*

one-horse *adj.* Small; paltry; suitable for or typical of a small or rural community; bush-league. *Since c1850; from "one-horse town."*

one-horse town A small or rural town; a town in which nothing exciting or noteworthy takes place; fig., a town so small as to have, or need, only one horse [before the time of automobiles]. *Colloq.*

one-lunger *n.* **1** A single-cylinder engine. *c1910.* 1953: "His wheezing one-lunger car." CBS, *radio network play*, May 22. *Archaic.* → **2** An automobile with a one-cylinder engine. 1951 [1943]: "A simple old one-lunger." Bellamy Partridge, *Excuse My Dust*, 3. *Archaic.*

one of the boys An informal, popular fellow considered as a jovial companion by his male friends; a man who has similar tastes, habits, and ideas as his circle of friends. See **the boys.**

one on An order of a hamburger on a bun; an order of toast. *Some lunch-counter use since c1935; neither use common.*

one on the city An order of a glass of water. *Some c1935 lunch-counter use. "On the city" because the city is providing the water free.* See **on,** *prep.*

one on the country An order of a glass of buttermilk. *Some c1935 lunch-counter use; may be synthetic. The country is providing the buttermilk, though not free. Based on "one on the city."* See **on.**

one on the house A glass of water. *Some lunch-counter use since c1935.* See **on,** *prep.* Cf. **one on the city.**

oner   *n.* A heavy blow with the fist. See Appendix, —er ending.

one-shot   *n.* **1** In publishing, a story, article, or the like that appears once and without a sequel. *Since c1940.* **2** Any business transaction, sports event, or the like that occurs only once. 1943: "The softest affairs [plays] to knock over are the one-shots." Maurice Zolotow, *SEP*, Nov., 20. → **3** A woman who agrees to sexual intercourse once but refuses afterward. *Since c1950.   adj.* Occurring only once; performed once; not part of any regular series of programs. 1938: "He put her in a one-shot whodunit [radio mystery play]." Leitzell, *Newsweek.* 1952: "Maybe it was a one-shot shakedown. The fat man would probably never show up again." Jerome Ellison, *SEP*, Sept. 20, 9/2.

one-striper   *n.* **1** In the USN, an ensign, whose rank is shown by a single stripe. *USN use since c1920.* **2** In the Army a private first class, whose rank is indicated by a single stripe on his sleeve. *Some W.W.II Army use.*

one too many   Whisky sufficient to intoxicate a person; fig., that final drink that makes the difference between sobriety and intoxication. 1941: "It's driver had obviously had one too many." D. McFerran.

one-track mind   A mind dominated by or limited to a single idea, subject, or point of view. 1949: "The impression that you have a one-track mind." Garry Flinn, Phila. *Bulletin*, Sept. 7, 16/6.

one-two   *n.* **1** A potent combination of two punches, consisting of [one] a short left jab followed immediately with [two] a hard right cross, usu. to the jaw of one's opponent. 1936: "He was knocked to the canvas with zipping 'one-twos' to the jaw." Tully, *Bruiser*, 54. 1952: "Gavilan speared three lefts to the mouth and then sent a one-two to the jaw." Jim Jennings, *sports col.*, N.Y. *Daily Mirror*, July 8, 24/1. *Since c1920; orig. and mainly a prize fighting term. A traditional series of blows, it is often referred to as "the old one-two."* → **2** A quick fight or getaway. *Some c1930 underworld use. Fig., done as quickly and effectively as a "one-two" punch.* **3** First and second places respectively, as in a race or election.

one-two punch   **one-two blow**   **1** = **one-two.** 1929: "They were good potent one-two punches." Winkler, *New Yorker*, Feb. 9, 38/3. **2** Fig., a hard or fast blow. 1949: "The jury's verdict was a smashing one-two blow to the Communist Party in America." AP, Oct. 15.

one-two-three   **1** Anything of consequence; used with a negative to disparage a person or thing, often in ". . . not worth one-two-three." 1902: "An' wese poor mortals won't be 1-2-3." Coley, *Rubaiyat of the East Side*, 12. *Archaic.* **2** A series of three punches. 1946: "An old 'one, two, three' a certain champion . . . taught him." Janney, *Miracle of Bells*, 189. *Based on "one-two," usu. a "one-two punch" followed by a left hook.   v.t.* To explain step by step or in detail. 1950: "Let's see if I can't one-two-three it for you." Billy Rose, *synd. newsp. col.*, Mar. 16. *Not common.   adv.* Ably.

one-two-three-and-a-splash   A meal of meat, potato, bread, and gravy. *Dial.*

one up   A cup of hot chocolate; a glass of beer; a frankfurter on a roll. *Lunch-counter and bartender use. Not common.*

one-way   *n.* A nickel, esp a nickel left as a tip. *Orig. lunch-counter and food vendor use. Because a nickel was the standard one-way local bus fare in most cities. See* **subway!**

one-way guy   An honest, fair, or sincere man.

one-with   An order of a hamburger sandwich with onion. *Common lunch-counter use, in relaying a customer's order to the cook.*

onion   *n.* **1** A stupid or boring person. *Orig. Army and USN W.W.II use.* **2** A badly planned, badly executed venture or task. **3** The head. *Orig., c1920, prize fight use.* **4** The face. *Orig., c1920, prize fight use. Not common.* **5** A baseball. *Not common. Cf.* **apple.** **6** A dollar. 1951: "Any of the patients in this institution got a few onions I could take till payday?" "Major Hoople," *synd. newsp. cartoon*, Sept. 5. *Not common. See* **know [one's] onions.**

onion, off [one's]   Crazy. 1939: "Benny . . . is practically off his onion about her. . . ." Runyon, 70. *Not common. See* **onion.**

only   See **one and only.**

on the make   **1** Ambitious; usu. ruthlessly intent on, and alert to, one's own social, business, or financial advancement or profit; esp. willing or eager to do anything that will help one advance or profit; receptive toward profitable offers. 1869: *DAE. Popular since c1935.* **2**

Ready or willing to take advantage of another in order to succeed. **3** To be receptive to or to encourage sexual advances from the opposite sex, usu. said of females; to make sexual advances or desire sexual intercourse with one of the opposite sex, usu. said of males; to seek or readily enter into sexual intercourse, said of both sexes. 1939–40: "I am . . . going on the make for the tired ones dressed like girl scout masters." O'Hara, *Pal Joey*, 60. 1957: "If you ask my opinion, I think she's on the make." Cartoon, *New Yorker*, April 20, 34. See **make.**

on the rocks **1** Stranded; without funds, esp. when one is in dire need of money; fig., stranded as a ship is when it has run aground on the rocks. 1930: "Ever been on the rocks yourself?" Burnett, *Iron Man*, 151. **2** Served over ice cubes; said of a drink, esp. whisky. 1949: "Ordering a Scotch on the rocks at the bar. . . ." *Life*, Nov. 14, 63. 1949: "You pour some whiskey on some ice. This year's fashionable are saying 'whiskey on the rocks.'" B. DeVoto, *Harper's*, Dec., 69/2. 1957: "This is the only gin I've ever found that's so mellow I serve it on the rocks." Advt. for Booth's gin, *Esquire*, June, 18. *Common use.* See **rocks.** **3** Concluded unhappily or unsuccessfully, moving toward an unhappy or unsuccessful conclusion. 1958: "[Actress] Ingrid [Bergman] is expected to marry Swedish producer Lars Schmidt as soon as she's free of [Director Roberto] Rossellini, whereas the latter's headlined romance with Sonali Das Gupta is now reported on the rocks." Earl Wilson, *synd. newsp. col.*, June 1,2. *From the nautical image, fig. headed toward or having met with disaster.*

on the town Enjoying the entertainment, sights, and excitement of a city as a tourist; specif., visiting the best, most expensive, exciting, sophisticated nightclubs, shows, restaurants, and bars; spending one's money lavishly in nightclubs, esp. in the company of a chorus girl, model, actress, or the like; to go on a spree; to paint the town (red).

oo See **double-o.** *Written use only.*

—oo See Appendix, **—eroo**, Suffixes and Suffix Words.

ooch *v.i., v.t.* To move a short distance by dragging one's body; to scrouge or scooch. 1930: "He lay down on the lounge with Rose. 'Ooch over,' he said." Burnett, *Iron Man*, 112. *Not as common as "scooch."*

oochre = **ochre.**

oodles *n.pl.* A large quantity. *Since c1870; wide dial. use until c1895. Sl. since c1895, most common c1900–1920. Still common but considered effeminate and childish.*

oof *n.* **1** Money. *From "ooftish."* **2** Strength, power. *Some prize fight use.*

oofay *n.* Variant of **ofay**, a white person. *Negro use, orig. and usu. derisive. May be based on or reinforced by "oaf."*

ooftish **offtish** *n.* Money, esp. money available for gambling, entertainment, or business speculation. *Some New York and gambling use since c1900; by folk ety. from the Yiddish "auf tische" = on the table.*

oofus *n.* **1** A blundering, stupid person, an oaf. 1957: "Oofus—A dope: the kind of guy who shows up at Randalls Island with a ticket for Carnegie Hall." E. Horne, *For Cool Cats and Far-Out Chicks. Some c1935 Harlem Negro and jive use; some general jazz and hep use. Prob. orig. Negro use, based on "oofay," reinforced by "oaf."* **2** Money. *May be from "oof." Not common.*

oogle *v.i., v.t.* To ogle. *A corruption.*

oogley *adj.* Praiseworthy, excellent; attractive, esp. sexually attractive, said of a girl; lit., worthy of oogling. 1949: "It's Oogley, Also Bong." D. Willens. *May have been jive talk c1935.*

ook *n.* A jerk. 1949: "Does even an 'ook' give out with a wolf whistle?" *Time*, Oct. 3, 37. *Student use c1945. Never common.*

ookus **ooks** *n.* Money. *Some use since c1900; Prob. from the Yiddish; may be based on "oofus," from "oof" and "ooftish."*

ooly-drooly *n.* Puppy love. *Some pseudo-jive and teenage use, c1940.* See Appendix, Reduplications.

oomph *n.* **1** Sex appeal. *Also wide attrib. use.* See **oomph girl.** → **2** Excitement, enthusiasm. 1950: "The enthusiasm [or the "oomph"] which [the U.N. interpreters] put into their work." Fredus A. White, Newark, N.J., *Eve. News.* 1951: "Q—What else does [the plot of the play] lack? A—Substance, drive, authority, emotional power, and oomph." Frank Sullivan, *New Yorker*, Oct. 6, 34/1.

oomph girl A girl or young woman popularly acclaimed for her sex appeal, esp. a movie star or celebrity. 1939: "America's Oomph Girl," *article title*, *Life*, July 24, 64. 1942: "Lucie Coindreau, you know, is the oomph-girl of the Romance Language Department." W.

Bolingbroke Johnson, *Widening Stain*, 30. *Common W.W.II use; orig. popularized by movie studios and fan magazines.*

oontz *n.* The usual game played with dice; the standard dice game, craps. *Some dial. use, c1900.* *v.t.* To crowd, push, or force. 1947: "I don't think any wire-and-glass dingbat is going to oontz out cheek-to-cheek dancing." Billy Rose, *synd. newsp. col.*, May 15. *Not common.*

oops *interj.* Used in surprise and as an apology on recognizing a mistake, minor accident, or slip of the tongue. 1949: "Albert . . . had the right to blow his horn—oops, we mean cucumber—after exhibiting the 26-inch vegetable he grew. . . ." GNS, Sept. 26. 1952: "Mr. Belve—oops, I mean Webb—is ecstatic [actor Clifton Webb had acted the role of Mr. Belvedere in a movie]. . . ." Bob Thomas, AP, Jan. 11.

ooze *v.i.* 1 To move forward on one's feet slowly, esp. in a sly or sneaky way. 1931: ". . . [He] oozed forward, like a seal." Queen, *Dutch Shoe*, 105. 1950: "I did my best, oozing along Front Street furtively. . . ." Starnes, *And When She Was Bad*, 177. 2 To stroll or parade on a street, to saunter. 1950: "I'd ooze across the street and into the . . . bar." Starnes, *Another Mug*, 11.

ooze out To depart secretly; to sneak away.

op *n.* 1 A telegraph operator. *Railroad and radio amateur use; archaic.* 2 A police operative; a detective. 1927: "One of your ops." Hammett, *Blood Money*, 142. *Not common.*

O.P. o.p. *n. possessive.* Other people's. *An abbr., usu. jocular, e.g.,* "What brand of cigarettes do you smoke?" "I smoke *o.p.'s*" 1956: "O.P. Other people's money." T. Betts, *Across the Board*, 317.

ope *n.* Opium. *Never used by narcotic addicts. Prob. synthetic.*

open *adj.* Without police interference in gambling and vice; having a liberal attitude toward vice, gambling, and unethical practices. *Usu. in* "an open town." *v.t.* To rob; to hold up. 1949: " 'Why don't you open a gas station?' Buck laughed. In a way, he was opening gas stations. . . ." A. Hynd, *Public Enemies*, 45. **—er** See **can-opener, eye-opener. —ing** *n.* A robbery. 1949: "After the safety deposit opening." A. Hynd, *Public Enemies*, 20. See **open up.**

open — For phrases beginning with "open," see under the principal word of the phrase.

opener-upper *n.* That which opens or begins a program, as a piece of music that begins a radio program. 1941: "A patriotic opener-upper, 'Under the Double Eagle.' " *Network radio program*, Sept. 19. *Mainly radio use.*

open-shop pants Riding breeches. *Hobo use c1925; because they are often worn by timekeepers and foremen. Contemptuous use.* Cf. **twelve-hour leggings.**

open up 1 To begin to use all one's strength and energy in order to best an opponent, esp. in boxing; to begin a fight, to attack someone physically; to start physical violence, esp. to shoot a gun or begin firing a gun at someone. 2 To inform on another or to reveal confidential information, esp. when threatened or bribed.

opera See **cork opera, horse opera, mud opera, oats opera, soap opera.**

opera house *n.* Any building that can be used for a theater, no matter how temporarily. c1880 [1955]: "Typical of the country theater, or opera house, or town hall, or what have you. . . ." H. R. Hoyt, *Town Hall Tonight*, 13. *At one time almost every small town had an "opera house" where traveling entertainers, lecturers, etc., could perform. Archaic.*

operator *n.* 1 A thief, esp. a swindler, confidence man, or pickpocket. 1956: ". . . An operator, a swindler. . . ." S. Bellow, *Seize the Day*, 98. → 2 A charming, socially adroit young man who is popular with the girls; a bold young man with a good line. → 3 A student who is prominent in school activities, often called a "Big Time Operator" or "B.T.O." 4 A dope peddler. *Narcotic addict use.* 5 One who makes a sensational first impression, often with exaggerated talk; one who can convince anyone of anything, a fast talker. See **big-time operator.**

oral *n.* An oral examination, as opposed to a written one. *Wide student use.*

oral days *n.pl.* The "good old days" of horse racing when bettors negotiated with independent bookmakers at the track, often receiving better odds than those prevailing; horse racing before the time of the pari-mutuel totalizator machines. 1956: ". . . In 1913, the fantastic era known as the Oral Days was ushered in. . . . A player bet with a bookmaker by word of mouth or wrote the wager on a slip of paper." T. Betts, *Across the Board*, 27.

orange   *n.* A baseball. *Some baseball use, c1930.* Cf. **apple**.

orbit   *v.i., v.t.* To put a man-made object into orbit around the earth. *One of the latest examples of a noun turned into a verb.*

orc   orch = **ork.**

orchard   *n.* A baseball park or stadium. 1938: "He clouted the pellet out of the orchard." J. L. Kilgallen. *Not common.* See **bone orchard, egg orchard, marble orchard.**

— orchard   See Appendix, Suffixes and Suffix words.

orchid hunt   A furlough. *W.W.II Women's Army Corps use. Prob. synthetic.*

order of down, an   An order of toast. *Lunch-counter use.* Cf. **one down.**

or else   *Usu.* used at the end of a sentence or phrase as an implied or incompleted threat of retaliation, often by violence, if one does not do as the speaker wants.

org   *n.* **1** An organ [musical instrument]. **2** An organization. 1936: "The Joe Breen (Hays org) influence on pix. . . ." A. Green, *Esquire*, Sept.   *v.i., v.t.* To play the organ. 1926: "The humorists' . . . *org* for play the organ has its merits." Louise Pound. *Not common in any use.* See Appendix, Shortened words.

organized   *adj.* Drunk. *Fairly common jocular use, c1920; archaic.*

orie-eyed   orry-eyed   *adj.* = **hoary-eyed.** Cf. **oryide.**

—orino   See Appendix, —ino, Suffixes and Suffix words.

—orium   See Appendix, —atorium, Suffixes and Suffix words.

ork   orc   orch   *n.* An orchestra; a dance band. 1948: "Orch leader." *Variety*, Aug. 25, 8/4. 1950: "An ork chirper is a gal who sits before a dance band. . . . Every 10 minutes . . . she chirps with the orchestra." Bob Thomas, AP, Hollywood, Mar. 29. *Popularized by the trade paper, "Variety."*

ornament   *n.* A railroad station master. *Railroad use.*

oryide   *n.* A drunkard or drunk. 1907 [1894]: "The hall-men were getting drunk. 'Rover Jack' . . . was our star 'oryide.' " Jack London, *My Life.* Cf. **hoary-eyed.**

oscar   Oscar   *n.* **1** Money; cash. 1949: "He would have been glad to buy me a pail of suds if he'd had any Oscar.

. . ." John Lardner, *Newsweek*, Oct. 31, 60/2. *Little known in U.S., common in Austral. From rhyming sl. "Oscar Asche"* = *cash.* See Appendix, Rhyming Slang. **2** A gun. *Some underworld use since c1930; prob. from "Roscoe."* **3** Any of numerous gold-plated statuettes awarded annually by the Academy of Motion Picture Arts and Sciences for professional distinction. → **4** Fig., any award, medal, or plaque. *Uses 3 and 4 are always capitalized.*

ossifer   *n.* Officer. *A common derog. mispronunciation since W.W.I. Usu. refers to an Army officer, sometimes a police officer.*

ossified   *adj.* Drunk. *Some use since c1925; often jocular.* Cf. **stoned.** See Appendix, Drunk.

ostrich   *n.* One who refuses to recognize a political, economic, or personal problem or a warning of danger; one who wilfully closes his eyes to the true import of current events in any field; a know-it-all. *Some use since c1920; increasing political use since c1940. From the traditional notion that an ostrich buries his head in the sand when danger approaches.*

otie   *n.* A coyote. *Some ranch use.* See Appendix, Shortened Words.

otig   *n.* An oaf, esp. a country bumpkin; an unsophisticated youth, greenhorn, or Rube. *Obs.*

out   *adj.* Far-out; attractive and modern; in the latest sophisticated or hip style. 1957: "Out sack—An attractive dress. . . ." E. Horne, *For Cool Cats and Far-Out Chicks. Common. Far-out and beat use. From "far-out."* See **far-out, way out.**   *n.* **1** Out of doors. *Colloq.* **2** Any place away from one's home or business. *Thus one goes "out to lunch" or "out to a movie."*

out —   For phrases beginning with "out," see under the principal word of the phrase.

out —   See Appendix, Prefixes and Prefix words.

— out   See Appendix, Suffixes and Suffix words.

out!, get = **Go on!** *An exclam. of incredulity.*

— outer   See Appendix, Suffixes and Suffix words.

outer garden   See **garden.**

outer pasture = **pasture.**

outfox   *v.t.* To outwit; outsmart. *Colloq.* Cf. **fox.**

out in left field   Wrong, very wrong;

out of place, date, or order; unusual; obnoxious; off base.

outlaw strike A strike by union members despite disapproval of union officials; a wildcat strike. 1956: "... *Outlaw strike—A* walkout not approved by union officials." *Labor's Special Lang. from Many Sources.*

out-of-towner *n.* A visitor or transient from out of town. 1953: "The ... out-of-towner ... cuts the hi-jinks [in New York City]." Hal Boyle, AP., Mar. 9.

out on the town = **on the town.**

outre *adj.* = **out, far-out.** *Some far-out use. From the French.*

outside *adj.* Born out of wedlock; illegitimate. "Maybe some of us is 'outside' children, because I don't know for sure that Mama was really married to Jelly's daddy or to mine." A. Lomax, *Mr. Jelly Roll,* 33. *Not common.*

outside chance A remote possibility.

outside of, get To eat. *Lit.* = "to put *food inside*." 1938: "As he got outside of a bowl of chili." Liebling, *Back Where,* 39.

out to lunch 1 Unable to qualify socially. 2 Stupid. *Jocular imputation of brainlessness.*

oval, the *n.* A football. *Some sports use.*

over— For phrases beginning with "over," see under the principal word of the phrase.

over See **half seas over.** *prep.* When in the card game of poker one is holding two pairs, the higher pair is said to be over the lower. For example, "aces over eights" = a pair of aces and a pair of eights. *adj.* Turned, or ordered to be turned, over while being cooked; specif., fried on both sides, so that the yolk becomes hard; said of an egg. *Wide lunch-counter use in relaying an order; fairly common general use. Cf. antyn.* **sunny side up.**

over a barrel To be in a situation in which one must compromise or admit defeat; to be in another's power.

overboard *adv.* 1 Extremely enthusiastic; emotionally overwrought; wholeheartedly and perhaps irrationally in favor of. 2 Drunk. *Not common.*

overcoat *n.* A parachute. *Some W.W.II Air Force use.* See **pine overcoat, wooden overcoat.**

overland route The longest route between two places; the slow way to reach one place from another, as caused

by slow movement, frequent stops for talk, food, or drink, etc. *Usu. in a semi-jocular criticism to a late arrival, like "What's the matter? Did you take the overland route?"*

overland trout Bacon. *Not common.*

overnight *n.* 1 Any job or activity that can be planned one day and accomplished the next; a comparatively unimportant job, activity, or event; specif., a newsp. col. written one day and published the next, or a horse race for which the conditions are posted only one day in advance. 2 A short trip; lit., a journey that takes one away from home only one night. **—er** *n.* = **overnight.**

overseas cap A brimless, peakless, envelope-like cap of cotton or wool having a cuffed, sharply creased crown, worn as part of the regulation Army uniform and adopted widely for civilian uniforms of all kinds. *Orig. Army use; colloq. Cf.* **go-to-hell cap.**

overset *adj.* Drunk. *Obs.*

Over There 1 In Europe as a member of the American Expeditionary Forces during *W.W.I.* c1917: "Over There," pop. song by Irving Berlin. 2 In Europe, as a tourist or worker. *Since W.W.I.* 3 Serving in the Armed Forces anywhere outside the continental U.S.A. 1946: " 'So you were Over There too?' I said. 'Myself, I was a private in the 734th Infantry Division, late of the Pacific Theater.' " M. Shulman, *Zebra Derby,* 71. *W.W.II use; not common.*

owl *adj.* Occurring, working, performing, or open for business at night, esp. late at night. 1951: "[The movie] was unveiled at an owl show in a [42nd Street] flea bag...." S. J. Perelman, *New Yorker,* June 30, 22/1. **—ed** *adj.* = **owly-eyed.**

owl-eyed *adj.* = **owly-eyed.** *Not common.* **owly-eyed** *adj.* Drunk. *Student use c1900; decreased in popularity until it became archaic c1930. Little Prohibition use.*

owner *n.* A ship's captain; one holding a captain's rank. *Some USN use.*

ox See **big ox, dumb ox.**

oyster *n.* A person who talks little; a clam. *Not common.* See **Kentucky oyster, mountain oyster.**

oyster-berry *n.* A pearl. *Underworld use. Obs.*

ozoner *n.* Any outdoor or open air arena, specif., a drive-in movie theater. *Since c1945.*

P

pace, off the   Behind the leader, in a race or contest.

pack   *n.* A liquor made from molasses. *Dial. Orig. New Orleans use. From Gen. Packenham, an Eng. general killed at the battle of New Orleans.*   *v.i., v.t.* To carry (something). 1936: "... 'Packing' (carrying). ..." P. A. Rollins, *The Cowboy*, 41. *Colloq.*

package   *n.* **1** An attractive, usu. small and neat, girl or young woman. **2** A large sum of money. 1956: "PACKAGE—Large winnings—or losses." T. Betts, *Across the Board*, 317. Cf. **bundle.** **—ed**   *adj.* Drunk. *Not common.*

package (on), have a   To be drunk. See Appendix, Drunk.

—packer   See Appendix, Suffixes and Suffix Words.

pack heat   To carry a gun on one's person. 1949: "He started packing heat ... if you pack heat, you got to know what you're doing." Burnett, *Jungle*, 12. See **heat, heater.**

pack in   **1** To relinquish, withdraw, or close one's interest in a business, occupation, friendship, emotional entanglement, problem, or plan; fig., to pack one's interest in a suitcase and leave. 1953: "The check forger told FBI men he is 'packing in.' ..." Robert M. Yoder, *SEP*, Apr. 4, 77/3. **2** To attract a large audience. *E.g., "That rodeo really packed them in." Colloq.*

pack it in   **1** To take full advantage of a favorable position; to follow up an advantage; to earn or win as much money, fame, or power as a given situation will allow. **2** To admit defeat or failure. 1958: "... If the show isn't funny ... I'm ready to pack it in." Earl Wilson, *synd. newsp. col.*, Feb. 16.

pack mustard   To work at hod-carrying. *Hobo use; obs.*

pack-rat   *n.* **1** An itinerant prospector. *c1850 Western use; obs.* → **2** A petty thief; a stranger; one who cannot be trusted. *Still some dial. use.* **3** A porter; a bellhop.

pack the mail   To run or travel fast. See **carry the mail.**

pact   *n.* A contract. 1948: "Katz has effected a settlement of his Metro [Metro-Goldwyn-Mayer movie studio] pact, which still have five years to run." *Variety*, Aug. 25, 3/4. *Pop. by "Variety," theater trade paper, and useful to headline writers.*   *v.t.* To sign a contract with a person or organization. 1936: "MG Pacts Gable." A. Green, *Esquire*, Sept.

pad   *n.* **1** A couch, bed, or the like on which one reclines while smoking opium in an opium den. *Opium addict use. Very old.* → **2** Any room, apartment, or establishment where addicts gather to take narcotics. 1958: "... There were plenty of pads. Those were places in basements and apartments ... where kids could go and smoke reefers." N.Y. *Post*, Jan. 24, 18. *Addict use.* Cf. **beat pad, pill pad, tea pad.** → **3** A temporary bed or pallet; a bed other than one's own; a room, as a hotel room or a friend's room, in which one lives temporarily, as while traveling. *Musician's use.* → **4** One's own bed, room, apartment, or home, as opposed to temporary quarters. 1953: "Sure I knew him well. Hell, he and I used to live in the same pad for two years." D. Wallop, 212. 1958: "... Only a pad (room) but man, who has a pad these days?" Edward Klein, "The Beat Generation," N.Y. *Daily News*, Feb. 19, 28. *Musicians' use since c1935; also some W.W.II Army use.* **5** An independent prostitute's place of business; a crib. *c1915 [1954]:* "... Women walking the streets for tricks to take to their 'pads.' ..." L. Armstrong, *Satchmo, My Life in New Orleans*, 8. **6** One's conception of an ideal home or way of life, either a reasonable concept or an irrational dream, such as a narcotic addict's dream; a private world in which one would like to live. 1956: "The Pad," name of a nightclub in N.Y.C. featuring cool jazz. *Cool and far-out use since c1950.* **7** An automobile license plate. 1948: "The job [automobile] was wearing California pads. ..." Evans, *Halo for Satan*, 101.   *v.i., v.t.* To increase the length of a story, essay, book, or the like by adding material, esp. repetitious or irrelevant material. *Colloq.*

pad, hit the = **hit the hay.** See **pad.**

pad, knock the   To retire; to go to sleep. See **hit the hay.**

padding   *n.* Extra material, often irrelevant or repetitious, added to an essay, book, speech, or the like to increase its length. 1951: "There is hardly an actor alive who can restrain himself from tampering with the line given him by the playwright. This improvement is called 'padding.' " Al Hirschfeld, *Show Business Is No Business*, 64. *Colloq.*

paddle *n.* An airplane engine. *Some Air Force use.*

paddlefoot *n.* An infantry soldier. 1950: "Murray was a paddlefoot in Europe. . . ." Bill Mauldin, *Life*, Jan. 2, 98/2. *Some W.W.II Army use.*

pad down 1 To sleep. See **pad. 2** To search or frisk.

pad duty Sleeping; lying down to rest. *Some W.W.II USN use.* See **pad.** Cf. **sack duty.**

paddy Paddy *n.* An Irishman; one of Irish descent. 1852: *DAE.* 1901: Greenough & Kittredge, 66. 1908: "The Irishman used to be characterized by the Americans as a 'Mick,' or 'Paddy.' " *Atlantic Monthly*, Dec., 753/1. *Prob. from the traditional Irish name Patrick and its nickname Paddy. Archaic by c1920.*

paddy wagon *n.* **1** A police wagon used for taking arrested persons to jail. 1949: "The house was swarming with cops taking out gambling equipment. On the curb, the co-operative family was being escorted into the paddy wagon." Earl Selby, Phila. *Bulletin*, Feb. 8, 4/1. *Prob. from the association of there being many Irish policemen.* See **paddy.** Cf. **Black Maria. 2** Lit. and fig., any "wagon" or vehicle used to remove a person to a place of restriction, as to an insane asylum.

padhouse *n.* One's own bed, room, apartment, or home. 1956: ". . . A *padhouse* or bedroom." S. Longstreet, *The Real Jazz Old and New*, 148. *Not common.*

padre *n.* **1** A priest or monk. *c1840– W.W.I, some dial. use in the southwest; from the Sp.* → **2** A chaplain of any denomination. *Some W.W.I Army use; wide W.W.II Armed Forces use.*

pad room 1 A room where opium is smoked or other narcotics are used. **2** A bedroom. *Prob. synthetic.*

pads *n.pl.* The feet. *Not common.*

pad the hoof To tramp about. *Orig. hobo use.*

pageboy A women's hair style consisting of shoulder-length hair in the back, slightly shorter on the sides, forming a semi-circle at the back, with the ends curled under and worn with or without a pompadour, waves, or bangs over the forehead. *Common c1935– c1943. Said to be based on the wigs worn by page boys of the English courts.*

page-one(r) *n.* **1** A front-page newspaper article. → **2** Sensational news or gossip, worthy of being put on a newspaper's front page. → **3** An entertainer, celebrity, or other person with always newsworthy name or doings.

paid in "I am paid in" = "I have a place to sleep tonight." *Hobo use.*

pail *n.* The stomach. *Negro use.*

pain *n.* **1** Annoyance, vexation, irritation. *Often in* "He gives me a pain." *Fig., a* "pain in the neck." **2** A bothersome, tedious, or annoying person; a pain in the ass. *v.t.* To pain someone in the neck [ass].

pain in the ass [taboo] An annoying, obnoxious person; any disliked person; a disagreeable duty, job, social amenity, or obligation.

pain in the neck An annoying, obnoxious person; a disagreeable duty or obligation. 1951: "Mary Eliza is a pain in the neck." S. Lewis, *World So Wide*, 4. *Although orig. a euphem. for* "pain in the ass," "pain in the neck" *is less emphatic and has an independent use of its own.*

paint *n.* Playing cards, esp. the picture cards. *From* "paint cards." *Never common.* See **nose paint, paint the town [red], red paint, war paint.** **—ed** *adj.* Registered by appearing on a radar screen. *W.W.II Air Force use.*

paint cards *n.pl.* **1** Picture cards; jacks, queens, kings, and aces. → **2** Numerically high. 1932: "A . . . man . . . with a blood pressure away up in the paint cards must live quietly." Damon Runyon. *Not common.*

paint horse = **pinto.**

paint remover **1** = **varnish remover. 2** Inferior whisky of any kind. **3** Coffee, esp. strong or inferior coffee. *Some W.W.II Army use reported, but prob. synthetic.*

paint the town (red) To go on a wild spree in a town or city; to celebrate wildly. 1884: *DAE.* 1888: "The cowboy method of 'painting the town red.' " *Century Mag.*, 838. 1924: "Painting the Town Red," title, T. F. Crane, *Scientific Monthly*, June, 605–615. 1948: "So let's paint Milwaukee a light pink this evening. . . ." F. Brown, *Dead Ringer*, 212. 1952: "Well, sport, let's go out and paint the town a new color." Hal Boyle, AP, Aug. 9.

pair *n.* **1** [taboo] The female breasts, esp. when shapely. **2** Two orders of any food. *Common lunch-counter use in relaying two identical orders to the cook.*

pair of drawers   Two cups of coffee. *From "draw one" = a cup of coffee. Jocular lunch-counter use.*

pair-off   *n.* The act of pairing off. 1937: "In a three-cornered set-up you can't afford to have the pair-off two and one." Weidman, *Wholesale*, 118.

pair up, a   Two eggs fried on one side. *Lunch-counter use in relaying a customer's order.* See **up.**

pajamas   See **cat's pajamas, the.**

pal   *n.* A friend, usu. male but may be female, esp. one who is a close companion; a chum, buddy, side-kick. 1893: *"Pal* and *cove,* words not yet admitted to the best society." Brander Matthews, *Harper's,* July, 304/2. c1918: "Oh What A Pal Was Mary," *popular song.* 1930: "By making criminals believe that their pals have confessed . . . by telling a prisoner his pal has accused him of firing the fatal shot. . . ." Lavine, *Third Degree,* 7. 1939–40: "Pal Joey," *title,* O'Hara. 1949: "[Sir Stafford Cripps] has many devoted friends, but he is nobody's 'pal.' " *Editorial,* N.Y. *Times,* Sept. 4, 6/1. *Well over 150 years old, as shown by:* 1807: " 'Better late than never, Pal,' is a saying . . . applicable on the present occasion. . . ." Lord Byron, *letter to Eliz. B. Pigot,* June 30. *Prob. from the Romany. Considered insincere as a form of address.*   **—ly   —lie**   *adj.* Friendly; intimately familiar in manner. *Since c1900.*   *n.* A pal. 1935: "Listen, pally." Runyon. *More brash than "pal."*

palace   *n.* The caboose of a railroad train. *Railroad use.*

pal around with   To associate with as a pal. 1929: "Palling around with . . . Edwards." Dunning & Abbott, *Broadway,* II. 1943: "The people he palled around with. . . ." Wolfert, *Underworld,* 165.

pale   *n.* A white person. *Some Negro use.*

pale-face   *n.* **1** Whisky. 1846: *DAE.* **2** A circus clown.

palm   *v.t.* **1** To conceal a playing card in one's palm in order to substitute it for a card received in the deal. 1947: "Marquales felt something brush against his right knee. This time it was five cards that he palmed—three aces and a pair of queens." C. Willingham, *End as a Man,* 155. **2** To conceal anything from opponents in a sports or business competition.

palm oil   Money; fig., that which oils the palm. *Not common.*

palooka   paluka   palooker   *n.*

1 An inferior or average prize fighter. 1927: "A paluka who leads with his right." Hammett, *Blood Money,* 75. 1935: ". . . A 'hot patootie' who refused to 'middle-aisle it' with him because he is a 'palooka.' " *Nation,* May 15, 562/2. 1936: "These palookers around here. . . ." Tully, *Bruiser,* 36. *"Joe Palooka," the title and main character of a synd. newsp. comic strip, has been the world's champion for years and is still unsophisticated and a little oafish, but the name has not become associated with champions. The orig. is uncertain:* 1929: "Palooka . . . derives from a pure Gaelic word." Wm. H. Nugent, *Amer. Mercury,* Mar., 329/1. 1936: *ascribed to Jack Conway of "Variety" by A. Green in "Esquire,"* Sept. → **2** A wrestler. *Since c1940.* → **3** Any stupid or mediocre person, esp. if big or strong. → **4** An oafish hoodlum. **5** A weak or worthless hand in poker or bridge. *Not common.*

palsy-walsy   palsey-walsey   *adj.* Acting as a pal or pals; friendly, intimate. 1947: "Army planes will drop on them pictures of General MacArthur and Hirohito in palsey-walsey attitudes, to convince them that hostilities have ceased." Phila. *Bulletin,* Feb. 17, 8/3.

paluka   *n.* = **palooka.**

pam   *n.* **1** A panorama. 1927: "Rapid pamming." "The desire to pam." "If pams are to please." "Do not attempt to panoram." *Filmo Topics,* Nov. *Photographer use. Obs.* See **pan. 2** A pamphlet.   *v.i., v.t.* = **pan.**

pan   *n.* **1** The human face. 1799: *DAE.* 1928: "You Have a Most Attractive Pan," title of poem by Samuel Hoffenstein. 1937: "The disappointment was too great for them to keep their pans shut." Weidman, *Wholesale,* 48. Cf. **dead pan. 2** In baseball, the home plate. 1891: "The pitchers put them over the pan. . . ." N.Y. *Sporting Times,* May 23, 5/2. *Archaic since c1925.* **3** An unfavorable review or notice, usu. by a professional critic of a play, novel, or the like; adverse criticism. 1936: "A pan on a show. . . ." A. Green, *Esquire,* Sept. 1949: "If you give 'Carmen Jones' [a play] . . . an out-and-out pan. . . ." Billy Rose, *synd. newsp. col.,* Nov. 4. **4** A panorama. *Some photographer use.* *v.t.* To criticize adversely; to deride; to find fault with; to roast. 1928: "The non-readers of the Saturday Evening Post . . . pan it as a Menace to American Arts and Letters." F. P. Adams, *New Yorker,* Nov. 24, 48. 1951: "The Daily Worker panned his first novel." Leonard Lyons, *synd. newsp. col.*, May 3. 1956: "Now I'll have to give raves to her next 3 pictures good or bad. Because they'll be saying, watch him pan us." Peter Maas, "Night Beat with Walter Winchell," *Collier's*, Nov. 23, 33. *v.i., v.t.* **1** To move one's camera with the moving subject being photographed, so as to eliminate or reduce blur in still photography, or keep the subject in full view with a movie camera. **2** = **pan out.**

pan, on the Being criticized adversely. 1939: "A . . . professor who wasn't there . . . was on the pan. MacSnuff . . . said 'He's an ignoramus!' " Alison Aylesworth, *Better English*, May, 13/1. *Never common.* See **pan.**

pancake *n.* **1** A girl or young woman, esp. a cynical, tough, or hard-boiled one. 1932: ". . . To marry him off to this little red-headed pancake here." Damon Runyon. *A Runyonism.* **2** A humble Negro; an Uncle Tom. *Some Negro use.* *v.t.* In boxing, to knock out; fig., to knock someone flat as a pancake. *Not common.* Cf. **pancake landing.** —**s** *n.pl.* The feet. *Not common.*

pancake landing 1 A heavy, awkward fall; a flat plop, as of a pancake → **2** Specif., in aviation, the act or instance of landing an airplane on its fusilage rather than on its wheels, done when the landing gear is damaged.

pancake turner One who plays and comments on phonograph records for broadcasting; a disc jockey. 1944: "He had to work as pancake turner on the Green web." Cliff Macon, *Collier's*, Sept. 9, 55/2. *Some radio use c1940–c1945; not common.*

pang-wangle *v.i., v.t.* To live or go along cheerfully in spite of minor misfortunes. 1908: "I just pang-wangled home in the rain. . . ." Anon., *Atlantic Monthly*, Nov., 716/1. *Never common; obs.*

panhandle *v.i., v.t.* To beg money from strangers in the street. 1949: "Others, panhandle." Slocum, "Skid Row," *Reader's Digest*, Dec., 29. *Colloq.* —**r pan handler** *n.* A beggar. 1939–40: "This pan handler came up to me and braced me." O'Hara, *Pal Joey*, 39. *Common since c1900.*

panic *v.t.* **1** To elicit great response, esp. applause from an audience by one's performing; to amuse or entertain well. 1929: "He [a performer] panics 'em." B. Sobel. 1930: "[*Variety's*] readiness to innovate new verbs used to panic me but now I ecstasize over it." H. Mother-

well, *Bookman*, 397/2. 1950: " 'Peep Show' is conceived in ribaldry. An old carnival pitchman, Mr. [Mike] Todd [the producer] knows how to panic the rubes." B. Atkinson, N.Y. *Times*, July 9, XI/1. → **2** To make a fool of oneself while trying to impress, persuade, or lie to another. *Usu. in "You panic me" = I consider you, your troubles, and your way of life laughable. The remark is meant to be cruel.* *v.i.* To become confused, frightened, or irrational. —**ky** *adj.* Excellent, very satisfying or exciting. *Jive use c1940; obs.*

panic button See **push the panic button.**

panic rack The pilot's automatic ejection seat in a jet airplane. 1951: "The jockey is in the panic rack and ready to go." AP, May 10.

pan-jerker *n.* A restaurant worker; esp. a fry cook working at a lunch-counter. *Not common.*

pank(y) See **hanky-pank(y).**

pan-lifter *n.* A pot-holder. *Colloq.*

pano *n.* Bread. *Archaic hobo use.* See Appendix, —**o** ending.

pan out To resolve; to resolve into; to turn out; to yield favorable or unfavorable results. 1875: *DAE.* 1903: "We are indebted . . . to the miner when a project is said to fail to 'pan out.' " H. Spencer. 1914: "Socialism . . . may pan out as a new kind of religion." S. Lewis, *Our Mr. Wrenn*, 42. *Colloq. since c1930.*

pansified *adj.* Effeminate; affected.

pansy *n.* **1** A male homosexual, esp. one who plays the female role. 1934: "She would have flown into a rage of protest if someone had bluntly said that her friends . . . were pansies, lied about being Jewish, slept with their sisters. . . ." P. Wylie, *Finnley Wren*, 85. → **2** An effeminate male. *adj.* Effeminate; affected. 1937: "American stage and screen voices in recent years have become so pansy that it is difficult to distinguish an English from an American actor." H. W. Seaman, *Amer. Mercury*, Sept., 51/1.

panther *n.* Inferior liquor, esp. gin. *From "panther sweat."*

panther piss [taboo] Inferior or strong whisky or gin. *Prob. older than "panther sweat" but never as common.*

panther sweat Whisky, esp. when raw or inferior. *Since c1925; may have orig. been a euphem. for "panther piss" or coined individually.* Cf. **tiger sweat.**

pantry   *n.* The stomach. 1950: "Another real fine left to the pantry." Starnes, *Another Mug*, 116. *Mainly sports use, esp. boxing.* Cf. **breadbasket.**

pants   *n.sing.* A man. 1929: "The first pants that picks her up. . . ." J. Auslander, *Hell in Harness. Not common. "Skirt" = girl or woman is prob. used 100 times as much, but it is interesting to note that "pants" and "skirt" have been chosen as the distinguishing clothing representative of the two sexes. Both imply sexual preoccupation on the part of the speaker which may explain why "skirt" is so much more common to the user of slang., usu. a male.* Cf. **hot pants.** Cf. **ants in [one's] pants, smarty-pants, tin pants.**

n.pl.   Trousers. 1893: "Two clipped words there are which have no friends—*gents* and *pants.*" Brander Matthews, *Harper's,* July, 306/2. 1934: "Colloq." *Web.* 1949: "Standard." *Web. Used since c1850; so common since c1920 that "trousers" now seems somewhat affected.*

pants-leg   *n.* A canvas cone used to show wind direction, as at an airport. *c1930; aviation use; archaic.*

pants rabbit   A louse. *Hobo and W.W.I Army use.*

panty-waist   pantywaist   *n.* A sissy; a frail, cowardly, effeminate boy or man. 1951: "The hurt . . . pantywaist ran off a number of copies of his letter. . . ." Bernard DeVoto, *Harper's,* Nov., 96/1. *Common since c1930.* **—ed** *adj.* Effeminate; cowardly. *Said of boys or men.* 1941: "A panty-waisted young bucko. . . ." *Time,* Mar. 24, 52/1.

pap   *n.* **1** Money. 1942: "Revenue from public office. . . ." *DAE. Now dial.* **2** A weekly list of students having unsatisfactory grades or conduct. *Annapolis use since c1925.*

papa   *n.* A male lover. c1922: "Mamma Goes Where Papa Goes," *pop. song.* c1925: "Poor Poppa," and "Papa Better Watch Your Step," *pop. songs.*

pape   *n.* **1** Paper. *Some student use c1830–1880. Obs.* **2** A playing card. *Perhaps from "paper" on which the designs are printed, as this seems older than "paper" = a deck of marked playing cards.* **3** A Roman Catholic. *Not common. Prob. from "Papist."*

paper   *n.* **1** A dollar. *c1930.* → **2** Money. *Not common.* → **3** Specif., counterfeit money. See **lay paper. 4** A pass or free ticket to a theater or circus. See **peddle [one's] papers, walking papers.** *v.t.* **1** To use or disseminate counterfeit money. **2** To pass worthless checks.

1958: "Helped by phony . . . credentials and a blonde, a former stable boy . . . papered Queens and Long Island with $10,000 to $15,000 worth of bum checks." N. Y. *Daily News,* Apr. 16, 60.

paper-belly   *n.* A person unable to drink liquor straight, or one who grimaces after drinking.

paper-hanger   *n.* **1** One who forges checks or passes worthless checks on a nonexistent bank account. *Orig. underworld use, c1915–c1930 = a check forger.* → **2** One who passes counterfeit money.

paper-hanging   *n.* The act of forging or passing bad checks.

paper house   A theater or circus audience containing many persons admitted on free tickets or passes.

paper-pusher   *n.* One who passes counterfeit money. Cf. **paper.**

papers, go peddle [one's]   See **peddle [one's] papers.**

paper-weight   *n.* A clerk in a railroad office or ticket agency. *Railroad use.*

papoose   *n.* A nonunion worker working with union workers. 1956: ". . . Papoose—A nonunion worker." *Labor's Special Lang. from Many Sources. Because the nonunion worker receives the benefits won by the union workers and thus is carried "on their back," as a papoose is traditionally carried by its mother.*

pappy guy   An elderly man; the oldest member of a group, esp. the worker who possesses seniority in a factory or office; an old or aging man; a fatherly man. 1952: "The sports stars . . . are what we once would have regarded as pappy guys, greased for the skids." Robert C. Ruark, *synd. newsp. col.,* June 27.

paradise   *n.* See **Ethiopian paradise.**

paralyzed   *adj.* Drunk, esp. completely drunk; drunk beyond the point of action or memory. 1928: "A paralyzed lady is another matter." *Amer. Mercury,* Aug., 386/2. *Common since c1925.*

parboiled   *adj.* Drunk, *Some use since c1935. One of the less common "cooking" words to = drunk.*

pard   *n.* A partner; a friend. *Colloq. since c1850. From the common pronunciation "pardner."*

park   *v.t.* To put or place someone or something in a convenient place and leave [him, her, it, or them] there for an indefinitely short or long time; to set; to lay or lay down; to hang up [as a garment]; to allow an object to remain stationary or a person to be ignored until wanted. 1924: "What would become of the fraternity if all of us parked ourselves on our tails?..." Marks, *Plastic Age*, 200. 1924: "A writer in an American family magazine ... declared that girls at dances actually 'parked' their corsets before beginning the evening's exercise." G. H. Bonner, *19th Century* [London], Dec., 835. 1926: "Parking your body in a ... bed." Stallings & Anderson, *What Price Glory*, II. 1932: "Twenty years ago nobody ever 'parked' anything. Now even chewing gum can be temporarily 'parked' by the provident." E. Weekley, *Atlantic Monthly*, May, 559. 1944: "He parked his clothes in Mr. Nelson's filing-cabinet...." Ford, *Phila. Murder*, 168. 1947: "They had to be advised to park their shooting-irons outside." A. Boucher, *San Francisco Murders*, 101. *Common since the advent of the automobile and its parking.* *v.i.* **1** To sit, sit down, or be seated and remain so for a while; to remain more or less stationary in a place. 1949: "The fighters looked like marionettes from where we were parked [in the arena]." Paul Jones, Phila. *Bulletin*, July 14, 18. 1951: "He parked behind a desk." Spillane, *Big Kill*, 58. *Since c1925.* → **2** To neck or pet. 1922: "A boy or girl who objects to 'parking' or 'necking' in a dance." Phila *Eve. Bulletin*, Mar. 8. 1950: "... *Boondocks* ... which in Tennessee college circles has been made into a verb as an equivalent for 'to park' and 'to neck.'" *Archaic. Orig. to park one's car, as in a secluded place, for the purpose of necking.*

parlay *n.* **1** In gambling, a wager on two or more events with the stipulation that the wager on the first event plus the winnings will be wagered on the second event, etc.; if the first or any subsequent bet is lost, the whole sum is lost. 1956: "PARLAY— A form of wagering in which the money bet on one horse and the winnings, if any, are bet on one or more other horses." T. Betts, *Across the Board*, 317. *Horse-racing use.* **2** An instance of parlaying. *v.i., v.t.* To understand. *From Fr. "parler" = to speak.* *v.t.* **1** To bet money and, upon winning, to continue betting the original stake and one's winnings; to bet money stipulating that if one wins the original stake one's winnings will automatically be bet on a subsequent wager. *Since c1890; primarily horse racing use.* → **2** When gambling, to keep doubling the amount of one's successive bets until one wins. *Not common.* → **3** Fig., to start with one item or something small and

increase it into a collection or something large. 1950: "I picked up an 8-ball and parlayed it into a poolroom." *Broadway Is My Beat*, CBS network radio, Jan. 14.

parley-voo *v.i., v.t.* **1** To speak or understand a language. *Since W.W.I. Orig. Army use in France. From the Fr. "parlez-vous."* **2** To speak, converse, or confer; to understand.

parlor *n.* The caboose of a railroad train. *Railroad use.*

parlor house A brothel. 1951: "He was a simple man, happy or sad. Always gay in a parlor house ... making the wild and unsanitary love of the mining towns." S. Longstreet, *The Pedlocks*, 68.

parlor pink A mild radical; one who holds mildly liberal political opinions but takes no action to support them; a member of the bourgeois class who inclines toward radical or communistic ideas. See **pink.**

parlor-snake *n.* A ladies' man; a seducer or would-be seducer. 1920: "Introduce her to all the prize parlor-snakes...." Fitzgerald, *This Side of Paradise*, 52. *Student use c1915–c1925; archaic.* See **snake.** Cf. **lounge lizard.** *v.i.* To act like a parlor-snake. 1920: "That means ... parlor-snaking, getting bored...." Fitzgerald, *This Side of Paradise*, 92. *Never common; obs.*

parole See **back-gate parole.**

particular *adj.* Excessive; special. 1846: *DAE; archaic and dial.*

party *n.* **1** A person. *Since c1925.* **2** A female who will, or likes to, neck passionately. *c1925; student use.* → **3** A session of necking. *Student use since c1930.* Cf. **petting party.** → **4** A session of sexual intercourse, esp. a fairly extended period of sexual abandon. *Common since c1935, the most freq. use.* **5** Four orders of any food. *Some lunch-counter waitress use in relaying orders. Thus "a party of Cokes" = four Cokes.* See **cold-meat party, hen party, necktie party, petting party.** *v.i.* To go to a party or parties; to have a good time; to drink, dance, talk, and indulge in general merrymaking. *Student use since c1945.* *v.t.* To entertain a person at a party or series of parties. 1953: "The delegates and guests [at the P.E.N. Congress] ... were partied to a crisp." Harvey Breit, N.Y. *Times Bk. Rev.*, July 12, 8/1.

party boy A young man, esp. a student, who devotes much time, thought, and effort to social activities, courting girls, and going to parties; a student who is not seriously concerned with his studies, but whose main interest in school is the social life. *Student use.*

party girl   A girl or young woman, esp. a student, who devotes much time, thought, and effort to social activities, attracting suitors, and going to parties; a student who is not seriously concerned with her studies, but whose main interest in school is the social life. *Student use. Not as common as "party boy."*

party pooper   party-pooper   *n.* **1** The first person or couple to leave a party; fig., one who causes the end of a party or good time. *Wide student use since before c1945.* → **2** One who so lacks vitality, interest, or personality that his presence is a detriment to the enjoyment of others; a killjoy; a wet blanket. *Not common.* 1956: "No one can call Mr. Bulganin and Mr. Khrushchev party poopers . . . the Russian leaders demonstrated their suavity and cleverness at the . . . party." Earl Wilson, *synd. newsp. col.*, July 5.

pash   *n.* **1** Passion; love. 1924: "If he danced, they . . . insisted that he get some 'pash' into it." Marks, *Plastic Age*, 57. *Some c1920 use; now considered affected.* **2** A person whom one loves or admires, esp. a celebrity who is one's idol. *Some teenager and newsp. columnist use. adj.* Passionate; amorous. 1920: "That isn't as pash as some of the poems." Fitzgerald, *This Side of Paradise*, 52. *Some c1920 use; now considered affected.*

pass   For phrases beginning with "pass," see under the principal word of the phrase.

pass   *n.* A passenger train. *Hobo use. Obs.* See **make a pass at.**   *v.i., v.t.* To pretend; to counterfeit; specif., to win acceptance as a member of a dominant group, race, religion, etc., without meeting the basic requirements; said esp. of Negroes who make lives and careers as members of the white race. 1950: "Louise, the oldest daughter, so fair she could pass . . . happened to be my mother. . . ." A. Lomax, *Mr. Jelly Roll*, 3.

pass at, make a   To make an amorous advance toward. 1942: "He got high one time and made a pass at her." Chandler, *High Window*, 183. *Colloq.*

passion pit   An out-door movie theater whose patrons view films from their cars; a drive-in movie theater. *Student use since c1940. Because such theaters give young couples an opportunity to neck in darkness and relative privacy.*

passion ration   A boy friend. *Attrib. to teenagers, c1945. Typical of the synthetic teenage rhyming sl. indulged in by newsp. columnists.*

pass out   **1** To faint; to become unconscious, esp. from momentary sickness, shock, excessive drinking of alcoholic beverages, or fatigue. 1924: "A man 'passed out cold.' . . ." Marks, *Plastic Age*. 254. 1942: "I never pass out." W. Bolingbroke Johnson, *Widening Stain*, 122. **2** To die; to pass away. 1924: "He left us a whole of a lot of jack when he passed out. . . ." Marks, *Plastic Age*, 12. **3** To fail or flop, said of a performance or entertainment. *Theater use; archaic.*

pass-out   passout   *n.* **1** A distribution, as of things to people. 1932: "When I [a pitchman] have made the pass-out [of merchandise] I take the money. . . ." J. T. Flynn. **2** The act of losing consciousness. 1950: "[=] the . . . act of falling asleep from taking too much liquor." Jack Alexander, *SEP*, Apr. 1, 76/2. **3** A person who has become unconscious by drinking. 1949: "There is small pleasure to be derived from finding yourself with an 18-year-old passout on your hands." *Esquire's Handbook for Hosts*, 272.

pass up   To pass one's studies in college; to receive credit for one's academic studies. 1909: "If a student fails to 'pass up' the minimum number of hours. . . ." Von Engeln, *At Cornell*, 285. *Never common; obs.*

paste   *v.t.* **1** To strike someone a hard blow with the fist. *Somewhat archaic.* → **2** To defeat a sports opponent decisively. 1953: "[The] Philadelphia A's took a 13–10 pasting from the Washington Senators. . . ." AP, Mar. 9. → **3** In baseball, to hit a pitched ball hard and well. **4** To put blame on another; to make a criminal charge against someone. 1943: "There were two . . . things he could paste on them firemen. . . ." Wolfert, *Underworld*, 244.

pasteboard   paste-board   *n.* **1** A ticket of admission, as to a game, prize fight, or circus. 1949: "He studied the coveted pasteboard [ticket to a prize fight]. . . ." Paul Jones, *Phila. Bulletin*, July 14, 18. *Since c1850.* **2** A business card; a calling or visiting card. 1901: "A man's card is his pasteboard." Greenough & Kittredge, 69. *Not common.* **3** A playing card.

past post   **1** To make a bet on a horse race, with a bookie, after the race is over and one knows the result. *No* *longer probable since the advent of nation-wide telegraphed race results. Horseracing use.* → **2** Fig., to be warned or informed too late to act wisely; to be informed after the fact. *Not common.*

pasture *n.* **1** In baseball, the outfield. *Since c1925.* → **2** A baseball park.

pat *adj.* Incapable of being improved or changed; fixed. *Colloq.*

patch See **tire patch.**

pater *n.* Father. *Some jocular U.S. use.*

patootie *n.* **1** A sweetheart. 1948: "New Yorkers . . . tell their patooties how pretty they are. . . ." Lait-Mortimer, *N.Y. Confidential.* From **hot patootie.** **2** A girl, usu. a pretty one. 1950: "A batch of pretty-panned patooties." George Dixon, *col.,* [Syracuse] *Hebr. Jour.,* Jan. 27, 26.

patsy *n.* **1** A weak or cowardly man. **2** The person who is given the blame for any crime, esp. by others who were actually involved. **3** A dupe; a sucker; a pushover; a fall guy. 1930: "He signals patsy." *Amer. Mercury,* Dec., 457. 1939–40: "I do not pretend I am some kind of a patsy. . . ." O'Hara, *Pal Joey,* 33. 1949: "You are . . . a patsy, a quick push, a big softie." Burnett, *Jungle,* 46f. 1953: "You can hardly call a patsy a hero." William Gloves, AP, May 11.

patzer *n.* An inferior chess player. *Although said to be from the Yiddish, there is no Yiddish, German, or Hebrew word or word combination to suggest it. Prob. from "patsy" with the familiar "—er" ending added.*

paw *v.i., v.t.* To caress or attempt to caress another intimately, but roughly and without invitation; to manhandle. 1955: "And if you'd pulled off that goddamned pajama top, and showed me your lovely white body, it would have been *just exactly* the way I said. Your attitude would have been—'See here. Look, but don't touch. . . .' 'Well, what did you think I wanted you to do?' asked Madeleine, with a frosty stare. 'Paw at me, huh?' She puffed at her cigarette. 'Me, paw at you?' said Jimmy." C. Willingham, *To Eat a Peach,* 186. *n.* A human hand. 1934: "You let me get my paws on the money." Chandler, *Finger Man,* 53. 1953: "You put out your paw. . . . Anything can happen to you from a handshake." Hal Boyle, AP, Feb. 5. See **fox paw, south-paw.**

payday, make a To win or obtain a sum of money at a given time, other than

pay for regular work, lit., to make a payday for oneself exclusive of regular earnings. 1950: "He decided to make a payday at a railroad camp. . . . What Harry meant by 'making a payday' was that he was going to win all the money from the people that had worked for it." A. Lomax, *Mr. Jelly Roll,* 106.

pay dirt **1** An area of a playing field that is the scoring objective of either team; the area covered by a goal or bounded by a goal line; the goal itself. *From the literal mining sense of "pay dirt," which appears in the DAE from 1873 on.* **2** Fig., any desired result, as money, a correct answer, the solution of a problem, or the like. 1946: "I didn't hit pay dirt until near the bottom of the second box of discarded telephone directories [where he found the directory he was searching for]." Evans, *Halo in Blood,* 108. 1951: "Between 1934 and now Shellabarger hit pay dirt with his historical novels. . . ." David Dempsey, *N.Y. Times Bk. Rev.,* Nov. 4, 8/3.

pay off To murder. *Some use in fiction.* **pay-off** **payoff** *n., adj.* **1** Payment; specif., the payment of cash, wages, bets, bribery, or graft. 1943: "A crowd waited . . . to be in on the payoff." Wolfert, *Underworld,* 64. 1950: "I saw that in the Navy there's a lot of pay-off [graft]." J. B. Martin, *SEP,* May 27, 20/1. *Since c1925, orig. underworld use.* → **2** Fig., a final result or outcome, specif., a score in a game, a confession of guilt, the crux of a situation, and esp. the point of a story. 1947: "Yesterday he telephones Max . . . to plead: 'Hey, I wanta tell that swell story around down here. Tell me again—what was the pay-off line?'" Don Fairbairn, "In Our Town," *col.,* Phila. *Bulletin,* Oct. 29, 4. → **3** Something unexpected or absurd. → **4** Lit., that which pays off or brings about a desired result, as a winning play in sports.

payola *n.* Pay; esp. graft, blackmail, or extortion money; a payroll. *One of the more common "—ola" words; see Appendix.*

pay through the nose To pay excessively.

pay-wing *n.* A baseball pitcher's pitching arm which, fig., earns his pay.

pazaza **pazzaza** *n.* **1** A piazza. 1921: "A . . . young woman is sittin' on the pazzaza. . . ." Witwer, *Leather,* 148. **2** Money. Cf. **pizzazz.**

P. C. **p. c.** *n.* Percentage, esp. a percentage of gambling or criminal profits. 1956: "P. C. Percentage; also, in off-course [nonracing] argot, the Police Commissioner's squad." T. Betts, *Across the Board*, 318.

p'd off [taboo] = **pissed off**. *A variant of* **peed off**.

pea   *n.* **1** A baseball. 1908: ". . . Batsmen took bites out of a pea." R. L. Hartt in *Atlantic Monthly*, Aug., 229/1. **2** A golf ball. **3** A bullet. *Underworld use; not common.*

peach   *v.i.* To inform against a person. *Since c1850; now considered somewhat archaic.*   *n.* **1** A pretty, attractive, girl or woman. 1865: *DAE.* 1900: "I struck [met] a little peach coming in on the train. . . ." Dreiser, *Sister Carrie*, 37. 1924: "Golly, but Helen was a little peach." Marks, *Plastic Age*, 15. 1934: "A 'lovely' policewoman in Soho Square. She really was a 'peach.' . . ." Sydney A. Clark, *England on £10*, 270. *One of the most common of the sl. words relating to woman or sex while having a standard food meaning. See Appendix, Food and Sex.* → **2** A promiscuous woman. *Fairly common use c1900; obs.* → **3** An admirable or attractive man. → **4** Any agreeable, admirable person, esp. one who will do favors, forego punishing another, or the like. 1914: "Gee! Miss Croubel is a peach." S. Lewis, *Our Mr. Wrenn*, 173. 1929: "You're a peach. I'm sorry I've given you so much trouble." D. Parker, "Big Blonde," reprinted in *The Amer. Twenties*, 162. *Fairly common, esp. in schoolboy use, c1900–1930.* → **5** Anything pleasing, excellent, or admirable. 1910: "Gee, what a peach of a build!" "What a peach of a room!" Johnson, *Varmint*, 39, 151. 1934: "That [enchilada] I had for lunch, it was a peach." Cain, *Postman*, 3. → **6** Something easy to do, as a task or assignment. *Common student use, c1900.* → **7** Ironically, anything inferior or contemptible. *Common student use, c1900.*

—erino   *n.* **1** A pretty girl. 1917: "'Peach' becomes 'nectarine' and then 'peacherino.' " Utter, *Harper's*, June, 66/2. *Fairly common c1910–c1925.* → **2** Anyone or anything highly approved. *Some use c1910–c1925. See Appendix, —erino ending.*   **—y**   *adj.* Excellent; attractive; wonderful; spectacular. 1951: "The reporter hasn't called the composing room and ordered a replate on a peachy murder." Syracuse, N.Y., *Post-Standard*, Aug. 18, 12/6. 1952: "These periscopes are peachy, grandma." Charles Kuhn, "Grandma," *synd. newsp. comic strip*, May 29. *Since c1900. Since c1930 primarily schoolboy use; adults more and more use the word ironically. See Appendix, —y ending.*

peachy-keen   *adj.* **1** Excellent; fine. *More often than not, used ironically. See* **peachy.** **2** All right; fair; not good enough to warrant enthusiasm but adequate. *Fairly common since c1955. This combination of two words formerly associated with youthful enthusiasm to = "just fair" or "adequate" is typical of cool usage.*

peacoat   *n.* A heavy, hip-length, dark blue jacket, which is the official overcoat of a USN enlisted man's uniform. *Orig. USN use; the style has been adopted by civilian clothiers since W.W.II.*

peahead   pea-head   pea head   *n.* A stupid or unthinking person. *Implying that the size of the person's brain is as small as a pea.*

peak   *n.* The head. *Never common in U.S.*

peanut   *adj.* Unimportant; little esteemed. *Since c1840.*   *n.* **1** A small or small-time person. → **2** A small vacuum tube about the size of a peanut shell. *c1930, electronics use; archaic.*   **—s**   *n.pl.* **1** Anything, esp. a business venture, which is unimportant, insignificant, or small. → **2** A small amount of money, esp. a small profit. 1941: "They got you working for peanuts." Schulberg, *Sammy*, 165. 1951: "Almost $16,000,000 in gold had been taken out of the Dahlonega fields. This is peanuts, of course, [compared] to what California produced. . . ." Paul Becker, *New Yorker*, Mar. 10, 114.

peanut gallery   The top gallery or the highest rows of seats in a theater. *Since c1900. Cf.* **nigger heaven.**

peanut-roaster   *n.* **1** A small locomotive. *Railroad use.* **2** An old or ramshackle automobile. *Not common.*

pearl-diver   *n.* A dish washer. *Since c1900. Fairly common jocular use. Orig. hobo use, then Army use; common Army use during W.W.II and fairly common restaurant and lunch-counter use since c1935.*

pea-shooter   *n.* **1** A rifle. **2** A pursuit or fighter pilot. *Some Air Force use since c1940.* → **3** A pursuit or fighter plane. *Some W.W.II Air Force use.*

pea soup   **1** A thick fog. 1953: "[London's] famous pea soup." AP, London, Jan. 23. **2** A worthless person. *Some underworld use.*   **—er**   *n.* **1** = **pea soup.** **2** A French-Canadian. *Not common. Prob. from his traditional fondness for pea soup.*

peat   *n.* = **pete.**

peavie *n.* A newly enlisted Civilian Conservation Corps man. *C.C.C. use. From the peavey he used in lumbering.*

pebble on the beach A person regarded as only one of a multitude. *Used only in sentences given below, esp. the second one:* "There's more than one pebble on the beach" = "There are plenty of other people I can depend on or have as friends, girl friends, or beaus." "You aren't the only pebble on the beach," *said to diminish another's self-esteem. Both uses common since c1910.*

peck *n.* **1** A white person. *Negro use. From "peckerwood."* **2** A brief interlude for a meal, usu. not more than 15 or 20 minutes. *Railroad, bus driver, and truck driver use.* **—erwood** *n.* **1** A poor Southern white person, esp. a farmer; an ignorant, poor, intolerant Southerner; white trash. *Negro use, orig. dial. Southern Negro use.* → **2** A white Southern male. 1956: "Any white man from the South is a 'Peckerwood.'" S. Longstreet, *The Real Jazz Old and New,* 147. *Negro use since c1935; archaic.*

pecker [taboo] *n.* **1** The penis. *Colloq.; rapidly becoming archaic.* → **2** A mischievous boy; a boy full of "piss and vinegar."

pecking order One's comparative degree of aggressiveness, desire to dominate others, or of leadership. *Orig. used by social psychologists = the exact order or aggressiveness demonstrated by animals, esp. by fowls, in eating; thus the strongest or most aggressive eats or pecks first, the second most aggressive eats next and so on down to the weakest, most timid animal, who eats what is left.*

peckings *n.pl.* Food. *Negro use.*

peddle out To sell one's personal belongings, as clothing or shoes, to a secondhand store.

peddle [one's] papers An order to go about one's business; to mind one's own business; to go away; beat it; scram. 1947: "I told him to go peddle his papers...." Hal Boyle, AP, May 19. 1949: "He had been told to peddle his papers elsewhere." Billy Rose, *synd. newsp. col.,* Nov. 21.

peddler *n.* A local or slow freight train. *Hobo use.*

—peddler See Appendix, Suffixes and Suffix Words.

pee [taboo] *v., n.* = **piss.**

pee'd off [taboo] = **pissed off.** A variant of **peed off.**

peed off **pee'd off** **p'd off** [taboo] Fed up; irritated; angry; depressed; teed off. *Army use since c1940; common W.W.II Armed Forces use. Fairly common, not as pop. as "pissed off." May be from and is definitely reinforced by the now archaic "peeved off." Cf.* **teed off.**

pee-eye *n.* A pimp. *From spelling the first two letters, "p" and "i."*

pee-head = **peahead.**

peek *n.* In horse-racing, third place; the act of finishing in third place. 1939: "Nobody will give you a price on the peek." Runyon. *v.i.* **1** To finish in third place. **2** = **peep.**

peel *v.t.* To arrest. *Obs. From "peeler (2)." v.i.* To undress; esp. to do a striptease on the stage. *Colloq.* **—er** *n.* **1** Any remarkable person or thing. 1823: *DAE; obs. by c1890.* **2** A policeman. 1871: *DAE; obs. by c1890. From the Brit. term.* **3** A strip-tease dancer, a stripper. 1950: "[A show] full of grinders, peelers, and bumpers...." L. Sobol, Apr. 2. See Appendix, —er ending.

peel out To leave or depart, esp. quickly or without ceremony. *Since c1955; orig. hot rod and rock and roll use.*

peep *n.* **1** A vocal sound; a word; esp. a critical or annoying utterance. *E.g.,* "I don't want to hear a peep out of you." **2** = **jeep.** *Early in W.W.II, and in some cases all during the war, some units, esp. Armored Forces units, used "peep" = the quarter ton vehicle commonly called the "jeep," reserving "jeep" to designate a larger vehicle. v.i.* = **peek.** **—er** *n.* **1** An eye. *Never common. May be as old as or older than the common "peepers," as shown from the Eng.:* 1888: "Woman ... lands heavily with her left hand on his dexter peeper. ..." Quoted by Charles Mackay, *Blackwood's Edinburgh Mag.,* 698/2. **2** A private detective. 1943: "And don't bother to call your house peeper.... I'm allergic to house peepers." Chandler, *Lady in Lake,* 205. *Since c1930; most freq. found in detective-story fiction.* **—ers** *n.pl.* The eyes. 1906: "I ain't blinked me peepers f'r two days an' nights." Kildare, *Independent,* July, 139. 1931: "My peepers." Queen, *Dutch Shoe,* 181. 1949: "Frankie could never acknowledge that he squinted a bit. 'If anything was wrong with my peepers the army wouldn't of took me,' he argued." N. Algren, *Man with the Golden Arm,* 12. *Colloq. since c1930.* **—s** *n.pl.* The eyes. *Not common. From "peepers."*

peep show   1 A supposedly private or surreptitious view, usu. through a hole in a wall or tent, of nude women, couples engaged in sexual intercourse, or other lewd scenes. *Once traditionally part of small carnivals and often conducted also by brothels, such shows were likely to be hoaxes, the viewer seeing little or nothing but being too embarrassed to complain.* → 2 Any burlesque show, nightclub act, or other lawful entertainment featuring chorus girls in scant attire, strip-tease dances, or the like. 1947: "... A little peep show." N. Algren, "The Face," a short story. 1950: "Peep Show," the title of a lavishly produced review, featuring many burlesque scenes, produced by Mike Todd and having a long run in a first-class N.Y.C. legitimate theater.

peet   *n.* = **pete.**

peeties   *n.pl.* Loaded dice. *Since c1890; from "repeaters."*

peeve   *n.* 1 A cause of annoyance, irritation, or anger. *Often in "my pet peeve."* 1926: "... Peeve ... from the adj. *peevish* ... seems to fill a real need." Louise Pound, *AS*, I, 246. 1933: "The use of 'infer' for 'imply' has long been one of my pet 'peeves.'..." *Letter, Word Study*, Jan., 7/2. 1945: "My Pet Peeves!" *article title*, Harold L. Ickes, *This Week Mag.*, Dec. 29, 2. 2 A grudge; a mad. 1941: "Here was I ... having a peeve on a poor kid...." Schulberg, *Sammy*, 8.   **—d**   *adj.* Annoyed; irritated; angry. 1914: "I'm peeved...." S. Lewis, *Our Mr. Wrenn*, 58. 1947: "He got peeved...." Billy Rose, *synd. newsp. col.*, Nov. 5.

peeved off   *adj.* Angry. *Fairly wide use c1935-W.W.II. Now sounds archaic and affected, as it is considered a euphem. for "peed off," though it is the older of the two terms.*

peewee   *n.* 1 A person of short stature. 1952: "The Bantams, an organization of men who are what they themselves call 'peewees and proud of it' with 5 [foot] 4 [inch] ... Lenny Herman as spokesman." N.Y. *Daily News*, Aug. 13, C16/3. *Colloq.* → 2 Any small farm animal; often used as the name for a small or short animal. 3 A small, clear glass marble. *Schoolboy use.*   **Peewee** *prop.n.* A common nickname for a person of short stature. *Thus Peewee Reese, former Los Angeles Dodger shortstop, and Peewee Russell, distinguished jazz clarinetist.*

peg   *n.* A man with an artificial leg.

From "peg-leg." See **on the peg.**   *v.t.* 1 To classify a person, place, or thing with others of a certain type; to recognize or identify, esp. in reference to faults. 1939-40: "I tho't I could peg a [Lesbian] joint like that from 2 mi. away...." O'Hara, *Pal Joey*, 57. 1946: "She hadn't really pegged me as a guy who would sell out a client...." Evans, *Halo in Blood*, 47. 1949: "An elderly lady ... who pegged him [Herbert Hoover] looked back, and then winked...." *New Yorker*, Nov. 12, 28/3. 1953: "I can't rest till I get him pegged." *Phone Call from a Stranger*, CBS television network play. 2 To taper or bind a pair of trousers toward or at the cuffs. 1943: "Furthermore, pants must be pegged to fit snugly around the ankle." M. Shulman, *Barefoot Boy with Cheek*, 149. *A style first pop. among c1935 jive enthusiasts.*   **—s**   *n.pl.* 1 The legs. 2 Trousers. *Jive use.* See **peg.**

peg, on the   Under arrest, esp. when charged with a misdemeanor. *Some Army use.*

peg boy   [taboo]   1 A young boy or young man kidnaped, kept, and used as the object of anal intercourse by an older man, esp. a sailor (supposedly because such boys were kept sitting on large pegs). *Obs. maritime use.* 2 A male homosexual who takes the feminine role in anal intercourse. *Not common.* 3 A young lackey, such as an apprentice required to run errands.

Peggy   *n.* A nickname for a one-legged man, esp. a beggar. *Orig. hobo use.*

peg leg   A person who wears a wooden leg.   **peg-leg**   *adj.* Wearing a peg leg. 1947: "Watch me pass up that peg-leg gimp." N. Algren, "The Face."

peg out   To die. 1949: "Harrison ... was then 67 ... and actually pegged out in 1841...." H. L. Mencken, *New Yorker*, Oct. 1, 65. *Prob. from the cribbage term.*

Pelican   pelican   *n.* 1 A Louisianan. 1890: *DAE.* 2 A prostitute. 1888: "Tillie Thurman ... who keeps a joint on Basin Street ... is certainly a Pelican of the first water." *The Sunday Sun*, New Orleans, quoted by H. Asbury in *The French Quarter*, 334/1. *Never common; may have been restricted to New Orleans use. Obs.* → 3 A cynical, tough woman. *Some underworld use.* 4 A glutton: a heavy eater. *Some C.C.C., Army, and USN use since c1935.*

pellet   *n.* A ball, usu. a baseball, but

sometimes a football or golf ball. 1908: "One of whom [baseball player] prepared to slay him with a look, if not with the 'pellet.'" Rollin L. Hartt, *Atlantic Monthly*, Aug., 225/1. 1941: "Like to be out on the [golf] course smacking the old pellet." G. Homes, *40 Whacks*, 71. 1952: "[Yankee baseball catcher Yogi] Berra ... searched the premises for the pellet while [member of the Brooklyn Dodger team, Peewee] Reese and ... [Jackie] Robinson came tearing across the plate." AP, Oct. 4.

pelter *n.* **1** A horse, usu. an inferior or cheap one. 1856: *DAE.* 1934: "Mahogany ... is ... not such a bad old pelter...." Runyon. **2** A fast horse.

pen *n.* A prison of any kind, esp. a large state or federal one. 1884: *DAE.* 1893: "I saw one fellow go into Fort Madison 'pen' [Iowa] one day...." J. Flynt. *Orig. hobo use. Common by 1900. Colloq. "Pen" from "penitentiary" reinforced by "pen" = an enclosure, as for animals, and perh. by the Romany "steri-pen" = prison, which is also a possible orig. for "stir."* See Appendix, Shortened Words.

pencil *n.* **1** A baseball bat. 1910: "Austin then came up with his little pencil and wrote out a hit to right field. ..." N.Y. *Evening Sun, Review of Reviews*, July, 117/2. *Never common.* **2** A revolver. *Some underworld use, c1930.* **3** [taboo] The penis.

pencil-pusher *n.* Lit. and fig., one whose work is writing with a pencil, hence, an office clerk or clerical worker; a reporter, a bookkeeper, a navigator on a bomber, and the like; specif., one who works at a desk in an office in a non-executive capacity. 1890: "An office clerk." *DAE.* 1952: "The number of pencil pushers and typists has increased in the past 25 years out of proportion to the increase in factory workers." Sam Dawson, AP, July 9.

pencil-shover *n.* = **pencil-pusher.**

pen-driver = **pen-pusher.** 1889: *DAE.*

penguin *n.* **1** Any nonflying aviator, as an administrative officer. *Air Force use since c1925.* **2** An actor who appears in full dress as part of a crowd scene, but has no lines to speak or important action to perform. *Movie studio use.*

pen-juice *n.* Ink. *Some student use, c1900.*

penman *n.* **1** A forger. **2** A high school student who writes his own letter of excuse for absence and signs his parent's

name to it, or who signs his own report card. *Rock and roll use, c1955.*

pennant *n.* See **Irish pennant.**

Pennsy *n.* **1** The Pennsylvania Railroad. 1953: "Eisenhower ... ate on the Pennsy between Washington and New York." GNS, May 19. **2** A student, faculty member, or alumnus of the Univ. of Pennsylvania.

Pennsylvania feathers Coal or coke. *Some c1915 hobo use.*

Pennsylvania salve Apple butter. *c1920 hobo use.*

penny *n.* A policeman. *From "cop" considered as an abbr. of "copper," from which most U.S. penny coins are made. As do most sl. words for policemen, this conveys contempt and disrespect, as well as a reduction of status to the minimum. Rock and roll and general adolescent use since c1955.*

penny ante Involving only small sums of money; insignificant; unimportant. *From the poker term = a game in which the players ante only a penny to the pot before each hand.*

penny-dog *v.t.* To pester someone, usu. for money or an opinion; to curry favor; to follow. *Dial.* Cf. **dog, hound.** *n.* A foreman or boss of a crew of manual laborers, esp. a foreman in a coal mine. *Dial.*

penny-pincher *n.* A stingy or frugal person.

pennyweight *n.* Jewelry, esp. diamonds. *Some underworld use c1900–c1925.* **—er** **1** A jewel thief. *Underworld use c1900–c1925.* Cf. **pennyweight.** → **2** A shoplifter. *Some underworld use c1910–c1925.*

pen-pusher *n.* Lit. and fig., one whose work is writing with a pen; an office clerk or clerical worker, a bookkeeper, a writer; anyone whose work is done at a desk in an office. *Not as common as "pencil-pusher."*

pen yen *n.* Opium. *Underworld and narcotics addict use since c1920. From the Chinese, entered U.S. sl. via the West Coast, prob. San Francisco.*

peola *n.* A very light-complexioned Negro, esp. a girl or young woman. 1944: "[peola] = a light person, almost white." *The New Cab Calloway's Hepster's Dictionary. Negro use.*

people *n.sing.* A person, esp. a stranger; used in direct address. *Movie use.*

Peoria *n.* Soup, esp. a thin soup made by boiling a few scraps of vegetables or meat in a lot of water. *Hobo use since c1920. From "purée," by folk ety.*

pep   *n.* Energy, vim; enthusiasm, spirit zest; initiative, gumption; the energy and enthusiasm that come from health and high spirits; alertness. 1920: "Lot of pep." Fitzgerald, *This Side of Paradise*, 44. 1925: "Roosevelt had pep." *Eng. Jour.*, Nov., 700. 1929: "No . . . worker is expected to show more speed and pep [than a writer]. . . ." *Nation*, Sept. 4, 240. 1953: "Pep," the trade name of an "energy packed" breakfast food. *Since c1915; wide sl. use during mid-1920's. Common enough since c1930 to be considered colloq. American emphasis on youth, action, and mobility makes pep a major virtue; thus many products are advertised as supplying pep. See under* **pepper-upper.** *From "pepper."* —adj. Descriptive of anything that supplies or evokes pep. 1949: "It was his [Philip Murray's, labor leader] first talk of a pep tour to take him to . . . steel centers." AP, Oct. 12. See **pep rally, pep talk.** —**less** *adj.* Lacking pep. *Since c1925.* —**py** *adj.* 1 Having pep; full of pep; spry; alert. 1952: "[Truman is] peppy as ever." AP, Jan. 5. → 2 Capable of starting quickly or running efficiently at high speeds; said of motors, automobiles, and airplanes. *Since c1925.*

pepped out   *adj.* Lacking in pep; exhausted; beat; bushed. 1920: "I'm tired and pepped out." Fitzgerald, *This Side of Paradise*, 129. *Some c1920 use; obs.*

pepper   *n.* 1 Vitality; vigor; enthusiasm; courage; stamina. 1927: "The old pepper." F. Graham, N.Y. *Sun*. July 18. 1951: "The old moral support is what gives we players the old pepper. . . ." W. Pegler, *synd. newsp. col.*, Oct. 8. *Orig. baseball use, c1920. Still used, though somewhat archaic.* 2 A fast game of pitch-and-catch; infield practice; both uses by baseball players. *Since c1920.* 3 [derog.] A Mexican. *Some use since c1945; this word may some day replace the more derog. "spic" and "wetback." From the assoc. of Mexicans with peppery foods.* —*v.t.* 1 To hit a person with a series of rapid blows. *From "pepper-and-salt."* 2 To throw a baseball fast and straight. 3 To hit a baseball or golf ball sharply.

pepper-and-salt   *v.t.* To hit a person with a series of rapid blows. *Obs. by 1895.* Cf. **pepper.** *n.* A scolding, a severe reprimand. *Obs.*

pepper-upper   *n.* Any person or thing that supplies pep, peps up, or refreshes;

said freq. of persons, but used most freq. in advertisements for various foods, nostrums, etc. 1940: "Harold L. Ickes seems to have receded as the Administration pepper-upper." G. G. Gross in Wash. *Post*, Oct. 27, III, 4/2. 1941: *The Dr. Pepper* [a soft drink] *Orchestra and the Pepper-Uppers* [a choir]. Ntwk. radio prog., Feb. 20. 1941: "Discover this marvelous pepper-upper [Miracle Whip, trade name for a popular salad dressing]." Ntwk. radio prog., *Kraft Music Hall*, Apr. 24. 1941: "Mr. Snow takes a look at the job of work the pepper-uppers [U.S. Army Morale Branch] are doing." Picture caption, *SEP*, Nov. 8, p. 6. 1944: " 'Say, fellows,' said a uniformed pepper-upper to a bunch of G.I. assault troops. . . ." M. Mayer in *Common Sense*, Apr., 140/2. 1945: ". . . Fragrant bath crystals, oils and bubble powders. . . . These bath pepper-uppers go into the tub after you turn off the cold water. . . ." U. Trow in *Amer. Weekly*, July 15, 31/2. 1947: "Pepper-upper . . . Wise Potato Chips." *Advt.*, Phila. *Bulletin*, Jan. 23, 12. *Since c1940.*

pep rally   1 A meeting, either scheduled or spontaneous, at which speakers, cheer leaders, and students try to arouse and display enthusiasm, usu. for their team in an impending sports contest. 1949: "Pep rally" appears at least 20 times in Cornell (Univ.) *Daily Sun. Student use. since c1925.* → 2 A meeting to arouse enthusiasm and confidence among party workers during a political campaign; a meeting to stimulate enthusiasm among workers for their company or its product; any meeting to evoke support for a given cause, goal, or the like. *Since c1940.*

pep talk   An exhortatory harangue designed to arouse enthusiasm, as at a pep rally. 1935: "Mr. Allen . . . delivered a pep talk on the advantages of dictionary skill. . . ." *Word Study*, Dec., 3/1. 1952: "I always had to give myself a pep talk before I went out to sing." Peggy Lee, pop. singer, quoted by Bob Thomas, AP, Aug. 18. *Since c1925.*

pep up   To excite, stimulate, enliven, or put pep into someone or something. 1945: "Pep up your wardrobe with the wardrobe 'Pepper-Upper'—Renuzit, French dry cleaner." *Advt.*, Syracuse (N.Y.) *Herald-Journal*, Sept. 21, 12. 1948: "Winter Wardrobe Pepper-Upper. Here is a charming . . . style [of dress] to pep up your winter wardrobe." S. Lane in Phila. *Bulletin*, Dec. 3, p. 40, 1/2. *Since c1925.*

perambulator *n.* The caboose of a railroad freight train. *Some railroad use.*

perc *v.* = **perk.**

percenter *n.* See **ten-percenter.**

perch *v.i., v.t.* **1** To neck. 1937: "... Now you may 'smooch' or 'perch,' or, reaching the heights of college argot, you may 'pitch and fling woo.' " E. Eldridge, *SEP*, Feb. 20, 89/2. **2** To linger in the company of one of the opposite sex. *Some student use c1900. Never common.*

percolate *v.i.* **1** To become hot and boil over, said of early automobile engines. *c1915–c1925.* → **2** To run smoothly and easily, said of automobiles and motors. *Some use since c1920.* → **3** To think or act efficiently. *Some use since c1925.* **4** To walk, saunter, or stroll. *Some jive use c1935; obs.*

percolator *n.* = **shake.** 1956: "You could always get together and charge a few coins and have a percolator. ... The money paid the rent." S. Longstreet, *The Real Jazz Old and New*, 126.

Percy boy A sissy. 1952: "He never prated about his Oedipus complex like the Percy boys." S. J. Perelman in *New Yorker*, Sept. 20, 36/3.

Percy-pants *n.* A sissy. 1945: " 'We'll handpick our members!' 'Roger! No Percy-pants!' " M. Blosser, *synd. comic strip*, *Freckles*, Sept. 10. See **Percy boy.**

perform [taboo] To commit cunnilingus or fellatio on someone, usu. in a homosexual relationship.

period [taboo] *n.* A girl's or woman's menstrual period. *Universally known.*

perk **perc** *n.* Percolated coffee, as opposed to that boiled in a pan. *Orig. cowboy use; later hobo use.* *v.i.* To function well, to go smoothly; said esp. of motors, as an automobile. *Since c1925. From "percolate."*

perker-upper *n.* = **pepper-upper.**

pernickety *adj.* = **persnickety.**

persnickety **pernickety** *adj.* Fussy; fastidious; punctilious; snobbish. *Since c1890. "Pernickety" is now obs.; "persnickety," once dial., is now colloq.*

persuader *n.* Any weapon, usu. a revolver, but sometimes a policeman's nightstick or a knife. *Most commonly used in movies about the underworld. Some general use since c1850.*

peso *n.* An American dollar. *Some use since c1925. From the lowest denomination*

of Mexican paper currency, which also uses the "$" sign.

pet *v.i., v.t.* To kiss and caress intimately or passionately; to spoon or neck. 1924: "Say, this kid was the hottest little devil I ever met. Pet? My God!" Marks, *Plastic Age*, 10f. 1955: "After a few minutes ... of *torrid* hugging, smooching, and petting. ..." C. Willingham, *To Eat a Peach*, 229. *Very common c1910–c1930. Orig. student use. Replaced "spoon" and was replaced by "neck."* —**ting** *n.* The act or instance of passionate, intimate caressing and kissing. 1924: "... Some drinking and considerable 'petting'—I believe that's what they call it nowadays. ..." W. L. Graves, quoted in *Collier's*, Feb. 1925: " 'Petting' now exists only in the college novels ... 'necking' having taken its place. ..." Bowers, in *Lit. Digest.* 1957: "... The fiancé holds petting privileges (petting is necking with territorial concessions). ..." Frederic Morton, *The Art of Courtship*, 159. *In common oral use until c1930 by students, thereafter wide written and oral use by older groups.* See **pet.**

Pete *n.* See **sneaky Pete.**

pete **peet** **peat** *n.* A safe. 1932: "This is a very soft pete. ... You can open it with a toothpick." Runyon. *Underworld use since c1915. From "peter."*

pete-box *n.* = **pete.**

pete-man *n.* A safe-blower; a safe-cracker. 1931: "... All my safe-blower pals used ... 'pete-men.' " C. Ashleigh in *Everyman*, May 21, 522/1. *Underworld use since c1920.* See **pete.**

peter *n.* **1** A trunk. 1848: criminal use. J. S. Farmer. → **2** A safe. *Archaic; underworld use, replaced by "pete" c1920.* **3** Pills or injections that render one unconscious; knockout drops. 1933: "drug addict use." D. W. Maurer. **4** An automatic repeating device used in telegraphy. *Telegrapher use, c1930; obs.* **5** [taboo] The penis. *Wide use.*

Peter Funk An auctioneer's accomplice who poses as a buyer in order to stimulate bidding or to "buy" items on which the final bid from a genuine customer has not been high enough. *Auction use.*

peter-man **peterman** *n.* = **pete-man.** 1950: "... The petermen of half a century ago." DeBaun, 69. *Some underworld use, prob. obs. by c1920.*

pet peeve An idiosyncratic dislike; a major dislike or annoyance. See **peeve.**

petrified *adj.* Drunk, esp. stupid or insensible as a result of intoxication. 1949: "They ... drink, then pass out petrified." J. B. Martin in *Harper's*, Nov., 62/1.

petting party A period or session of petting, usu. by one couple. 1920: "... That great current American phenomenon, the 'petting party.' " Fitzgerald, *This Side of Paradise*, 64. 1934: "The prowl car takes a slant down [the old road] now and then looking for petting parties." Chandler, *Finger Man*, 40. See **party; pet.**

pez *n.* A head of hair, mustache, or goatee. *Bop musician use since c1946.*

Pfui! *exclam.* = **Phooey!**

phantom *n.* **1** A person who is on a payroll under an assumed name. 1952: "He had been a phantom on the [Grace] line's payroll before that...." N.Y. *Times*, Dec. → **2** A person, usu. a relative or close friend of a public official, who is paid for performing work that is not done or is unnecessary.

phedinkus *n.* Boloney; phonus bolonus. 1935: "I am never in love ... for the way I look at it love is strictly the old phedinkus...." D. Runyon. *Prob. synthetic.*

pheeze **feeze** *v.t.* To pledge a student for membership in a fraternity or sorority. 1856: "He is said to be pheezed or feezed." Hall, *College Words*, 348.

phenagle *v.* = **finagle.**

phenom *n.* A skilled or gifted person, usu. in sports. 1950: "Sawyer's two other 24-year-old [baseball] phenoms. ..." Frank Eck, AP, Sept. 1. *From "phenomenal."*

Phi Beta house The main library of a university or college. *Some college use c1925. Fig., the home or fraternity house where Phi Beta Kappa students live.*

Phi Bete **1** The Phi Beta Kappa society. 1924: "I won't disgrace the fraternity by making Phi Bete...." Marks, *Plastic Age*, 203. **2** A member of Phi Beta Kappa. *Both common student use.* **phi-bete** *v.i., v.t.* To study. *Some c1930 student use. From the honorary scholarly fraternity, Phi Beta Kappa.*

Phillie **Philly** *prop. n.* Philadelphia, Pennsylvania. 1893: "Phillie." J. Flynt. 1952: "In Phillie tomorrow." AP, Sept. 26.

phiz *n.* The face. 1858: "A phiz which reminds you of pickled mackerel." *Harvard Mag.*, May, 170. 1901: "A recognized colloquialism." Greenough &

Kittredge, 62. 1937: "Just by showing your phiz around to the buyers?" Weidman, *Wholesale*, 141. *From "physiognomy."*

phizog *n.* The face. *Not as common as "phiz."*

phlug **phflug** **flug** *n.* **1** A foolish old married woman. 1935: "... An old phflug by the name of Mrs. Abernathy comes running into the dining hall. ..." D. Runyon. *Another Runyonism that sounds "from the Yiddish," but isn't.* → **2** Anything unpleasant; junk; goonk. 1952: "Did you drop some flug in my [coffee] cup?" Movie, *We're Not Married. Not common.*

Phoebe *n.* In crap-shooting, the point 5.

phoney **phony** **fon(e)y** *adj.* **1** Not genuine; fake or faked; counterfeit; insincere. 1902: "Phoney acting." G. Ade, *More Fables in Sl.*, 138. 1930: "A phoney special sheriff's badge." Lavine, *Third Degree*, 68. 1934: "The phoniest look I ever saw." Cain, *Postman*, 74. 1949: "Sidewalk Vendors 'Phony' Card Decks." Headline, N.Y. *Times*, Aug. 28, 63. 1949: "... You—liar! ... You fake! You phony little fake!" A. Miller, *Death of a Salesman*, 121. 1951: "There is no place [in the U.S.] for the phony economics of the chiseler." Chas. E. Wilson, Director of Office of Defense Mobilization, radio address, Feb. 23. *Very common since c1900. The ety. is not clear. P. Tamony (AS, 1937, 108–110) discredits alleged origins from "telephone," "phoo" (a term of contempt), "funny," and "forney" (a cheap jewelry maker), and suggests "fawney" with supporting evidence. Others have traced origin to the Erse "fáinne," while the DAE labels the word "origin uncertain." The rare spelling "fon(e)y" suggests an older usage. "Phoney" occurs today somewhat more commonly than "phony."* **2** Puzzling; confused. *Not common. Since c1920.* *n.* **1** A phoney thing; a fake; a counterfeit. 1902: "... T' git away wit' a phony like dat. ..." C. L. Cullen, 6 *Ex-Tank Tales.* 1941: "This confession is a phony." G. Homes, *40 Whacks*, 127. **2** A phoney person; an insincere person; one whose words and attitudes are assumed in order to impress others; one whose outward habits do not reveal his true character. 1941: "Some phony calling himself a writer...." Cain, *M. Pierce*, 32. 1957: "I have never felt that I lost any real friends because of my outspoken attitude toward foreign policy, the State Department and other sacrosanct institutions; but I did lose a lot of acquaintances. I have always felt that the phonies were weeded out and that the real, warm friends remained." "Robert Vogeler's Own Story," N.Y. *Daily News*, July 30, 22. → **3** A pompous, punctilious person; a snob; a stuffed shirt; one who pretends to be hep but isn't. 1951: "One of the biggest reasons I left Elkton Hills was because I was surrounded by phonies. That's all. They were coming in the goddam windows. For instance, they had this headmaster, Mr. Haas, that was the phoniest bastard I ever met in my life." J. D. Salinger, *Catcher in the Rye*, 16. *Very common since c1935. Wide student use since c1945.* *v.t.* To fake something. 1952: "I ain't phoneying the woids." J. Durante, quoted in *New Yorker*, July 26, 43. **—man** *n.* A peddler, street vendor, or auctioneer of cheap or imitation jewelry. *Carnival, circus, and hobo use.*

phoney up To exaggerate or lie, usu. in filling out official forms, job applications, etc.

phoniness *n.* The quality or state of being phoney; insincerity. 1949: "I am not defending . . . high-toned phoniness." R. B. Heilman, A.A.U.P. *Bulletin*, Winter, 626. 1951: "People are fed up on the phoniness of Hollywood films." Bob Thomas, AP, May 10.

phono *n.* A phonograph. 1948: "You can play the phono. . . ." F. Brown, *Dead Ringer*, 3.

phonus bolonus, (the) *n.* Something or someone phoney or of a quality below that represented; anything cheap, gaudy, or of inferior quality; insincere speech, exaggeration, a line; wrong or misleading advice, a bum steer. 1932: ". . . Nobody will ever again try to hand him the phonus bolonus when he is buying champagne." Runyon. 1948: ". . . The phonus-bolonus which gums up the average backstage musical." B. Rose, *synd. newsp. col.*, June 30. 1950: ". . . Who engineered the phonus-bolonus deal?" Starnes, *Another Mug*, 99. *Usu. with "the." From "phoney" plus "boloney."* See Appendix, Reduplications.

phoo! *exclam.* = **Phooey!**

Phooey! Fooey! Pfui! Fooy! Fuie! *exclam.* A term of contempt, distaste, or disbelief. 1943: "It came out of your own brains. Fuie!" Wolfert, *Underworld*, 113. 1952: ". . . His girl friend says 'Pfui' to education. . . ."

J. McCarten in *New Yorker*, Jan. 5, 65. *Common since c1930. From the Yiddish "fooy," "fooey," reinforced by the Ger. "pfui."*

photo *n.* A photograph. 1863: *DAE. Very common colloq.*

photog fotog *n.* A photographer. 1952: "The Swedish fotogs were actually saving film." R. Montgomery, N.Y. *Daily News*, Aug. 21, C4. *Common since c1930.*

piano *n.* Spare-ribs. *From the resemblance of the bones to piano keys.* 1942: ". . . Cornbread with a piano on a platter." Z. Hurston. *Some Negro use.* See **horse piano**.

piastre *n.* A dollar. *Not common. From French-Canadian use.*

pic *n.* A movie. 1936: "Raft's next pic is *Proud Rider*. . . ." A. Green in *Esquire*, Sept. *Some theater use, orig. pop. by trade paper "Variety." The plural, which is more common, is "pix."*

Piccadilly commando A London prostitute. *A little W.W.II Army use.*

piccolo *n.* **1** [taboo] The penis considered for fellatio. See **piccolo player**. **2** A phonograph; a juke box. *Not common.*

piccolo player [taboo] **1** A male homosexual who plays the active role in oral intercourse. **2** Any woman, esp. a prostitute, who prefers fellatio.

pick a berry See **gooseberry**.

pick 'em up and lay 'em down **1** To dance. c1920: "Pickin' 'em up an' layin' 'em down, learn to do the razzamatazz. . . ." Popular song. **2** To run, esp. to run quickly.

picker-upper *n.* **1** One who or that which picks up; one who picks up, or looks for, a pick-up. 1936: "*Variety* maintains a news staff—not a bunch of press-release picker-uppers." A. Green, "The *Variety* Mugg," *Esquire*, Sept., 162/2. 1941: "A hitch-hiker caught a ride with a man who turned out to be a bootlegger. . . . After a wild ride, the young thumber . . . made a bee-line to the police. The picker-upper was soon arrested." AP, Sept. 14. 1944: ". . . Because her devoted spouse is an avid picker-upper of any hairpins he can find." A. Daley, "Sports of the Times," N.Y. *Times*, Sept. 3, S2/6. 1947: "The machine has two . . . units. The leaf-picker-upper is like an outsized vacuum cleaner." N.Y. *Times*, Nov. 2, S12/6. **2** Any food or drink that, supposedly, gives one energy or vitality; a pepper-upper. 1947: "Energy picker-upper . . . chocolate cookies. . . ." Advt., Phila. *Bulletin*, July 28, 8. 1950: "For a picker-upper . . . milk, malted." Advt. poster for Carnation milk.

picket fence   A dismissal. 1942: "He gave her the picket fence." S. Billingsley in *Harper's Bazaar*, July. *Not common. Based on "the gate."*

picking   *adj.* See **cotton-picking.**

pickle   *n.* **1** A torpedo. *Some W.W.II USN use. From its shape. Cf.* **fish.** → **2** A bullet. 1950: "He fired six pickles at the knob and the stone-dust and splinters flew. . . ." W. Pegler, *synd. newsp. col.,* April 17. *Not common.   v.t.* To ruin or destroy; to kill; fig., to preserve by embalming. 1953: "This will promptly pickle her college chances. . . ." F. Sparks, NEA, Mar. 7.   **—d**   *adj., usu. pred. adj.* Drunk. 1938: ". . . Soused, pickled, and stewed are rather old-fashioned and distinctly not Junior League." R. Connell, *Parade.* 1952: "Go ahead, get pie-eyed, get pickled." Movie, *Never Let Me Go. Since c1900; common by c1920.* See Appendix, Drunk.

pickle-puss   *n.* A sour-faced, disagreeable, or pessimistic person; a sour-puss.

pick-me-up   *n.* **1** A drink or snack, usu. containing sugar, caffein, or alcohol, taken in the supposition that it will provide energy or stimulation. **2** A drink of whisky, esp. as a cure for fatigue or a hangover, to restore confidence, etc. *Colloq.; common use.*

pick-up   pickup   *n.* **1** The act or instance of inviting or taking another into one's automobile for a free ride. *Since c1925; orig. student use.* → **2** A person, usu. a woman, who has accepted a social invitation from a stranger; a person, usu. a man, whose personal social invitation to a stranger has been accepted; a person who has made a date by accosting or by being accosted by a stranger, usu. in the street, a bar, or other public place. *Often, but by no means always, the ultimate purpose of such invitation or acceptance is sexual intercouse.* 1934: ". . . There's plenty of neat pickups around here. . . ." J. T. Farrell, 131. 1941: ". . . [The] uneasy feeling she had of being just a pick-up." Cain, *M. Pierce,* 92. 1957: *Pick-Up on South Street,* movie title. *Student and Army use since c1930; increasing popularity until W.W.II when it became almost stand.* **3** An arrest by the police. 1958: "Pick-up—An arrest for crime, offense, or delinquency. . . ." G. Y. Wells, *Station House Slang.* **4** An

impromptu meal; a drink, esp. of whisky, tea, coffee, or bottled soft drink. **5** = **pick-me-up.** *Not common. adj.* Having met and worked together only for a specif. purpose; organized temporarily until a specif. job is accomplished. *Usu. said of musicians or athletes who are strangers but play together as a band or team for a specif. engagement or game. Orig. Negro use.*

pick up   **1** To arrest. 1871: "When they are picked up for taking horses. . . ." Thornton. *Orig. underworld use, now universally used.* **2** To offer a person a free ride in an automobile; lit., to stop one's car in order to allow another to enter. *Since c1925.* → **3** To meet someone at a specified time and place before proceeding elsewhere. *Colloq.* → **4** To proffer to or to accept a social invitation from a stranger, usu. of the opposite sex. 1957: ". . . She lets the [soldiers] pick her up. . . ." AP, Sept 26. *The connotation is that of sexual activity.* **5** To be alert to or enthusiastic about; to be on the ball. → **6** To comprehend, to understand.

picnic   *n.* **1** An enjoyable or easy task, occupation, or the like; often in the negative "no picnic" = something disagreeable or difficult. → **2** Specif., a satisfying, enjoyable, easily attained experience of necking or sexual intercourse; a "ball"; specif., a prohibited, unrestricted, uninhibited good time or pleasure. *Jive, student, and W.W.II Armed Forces use.* **3** A thoroughly good time; anything enjoyable, as any entertainment or social gathering.

picture   *n.* The human face. 1847: *DAE; obs.*   **—s**   *n.* **1** Playing cards. 1853: *DAE; archaic.* **2** Specif., those playing cards which have pictures on them: kings, queens, and jacks.

picture, the   *n.* A comprehensive understanding or view; a presentation of all the essential facts and relationships pertaining to the subject in hand. *E.g., the question, "Get the picture?"*

picture gallery   **1** The tattooed man in a circus side show. *Circus use.* **2** A file of photographs of known or wanted criminals kept by police departments and other law enforcement agencies.

pie   *n.* Any easy task; anything easy to win or earn; a weak opponent or any complex of factors that produces an easy victory, business success, or the like. 1903: ". . . A confident base-ball rooter a few years ago would have said of a despised rival team, 'They are pie.' "

H. Spencer. 1927: "That's pie for him." Balt. *Sun.*, Apr. 3. See **apple pie, cherry pie, mince pies, sweetie-pie.**

pie card   A union membership card, specif., as shown to a stranger who is a union member in order to borrow money, obtain food and lodging, or the like. *Hobo use c1925.*

piece   *n.* **1** A share; a financial interest in any business, entertainment, or gambling project, as a stage play, a night club, a boxer, etc. 1930: "A piece of the racket." *Amer. Mercury*, Dec., 457. 1939: "He owns a piece of the room [nightclub] where I sing now. . . ." O'Hara, *Pal Joey*, 21. 1946: ". . . A fellow who had a piece of Mike's game. That is to say, he was betting a nickel a point on Michael to [win]. . . ." D. Runyon, *synd. newsp. col.*, Aug. 5. 1950: ". . . Offered to let me buy a small piece of 'As You Like It.' . . ." Billy Rose, *synd. newsp. col.*, Jan. 13. **2** A gun, usu. a pistol or zip gun. *Teenage street-gang use since c1955.* See **artillery.** See Appendix, Sex and Violence. **3** [taboo] The vagina; hence a woman considered sexually or an experience of sexual intercourse. *Short for "piece of ass." Orig. may have been reinforced by "piece of calico" = girl, c1865–c1920.* See **light piece, mouthpiece, sky-piece.**

piece of ass [taboo]   Sexual intercourse; a lay; a woman considered sexually. *Very common, though replaced somewhat by shorter "piece."*

piece of calico = **calico.** *c1865–c1920; obs. May have reinforced orig. of "piece" and "skirt."* Cf. **dry-goods.**

piece of change   piece of jack   An amount of money, usu. said of a pleasing amount, as "a nice piece of change." 1932: ". . . [A] deal that would net him a handsome piece of change." J. T. Farrell, 125. 1942: "To make a nice piece of jack." W. B. Johnson, *Widening Stain*, 240. 1949: "A nice piece of change." *Jack Armstrong*, radio serial, Nov. 2.

piece of cheese   See **cheese.**

piece [someone] off   1 To pay another person part of one's wages in return for a job. **2** To pay a bribe. **3** To lend a small amount of money to a needy friend. *All uses orig. maritime; later underworld use.*

piece of ice   See **ice.**

piece of shit [taboo]   **1** A lie; an exaggeration; an insincere or untruthful statement. **2** An inferior or cheap item of merchandise. **3** A poor or corny performance, inferior work; an entertain-ment abounding in sentimentality and corn. *All uses from "shit."*

piece of tail [taboo] = **piece of ass.**

piece of trade   A prostitute; a promiscuous woman; a woman considered sexually. 1949: "One afternoon he'd been promenading down Augusta Boulevard with some good-natured piece of trade who liked to say, 'I was a lily of the valley in my time and now I'm just Lily of the Alley.' " N. Algren, *Man with the Golden Arm*, 83. *From "piece," extended to include the trade, i.e., prostitution.*

piece up   To divide loot. *Some underworld use.*

pie-eyed   *adj.* **1** Drunk. 1924: "The jane who got pie-eyed." "The pie-eyed [fraternity] brothers." Marks, *Plastic Age*, 136. 1930: " 'The stag at eve' had become, in the order named, lit, spifflicated, and at long last pie-eyed." C. Bragdon in *Outlook*, Oct., 301. *Common since cW.W.I.* **2** Plain; not pretty; said of a girl. *Some student use c1925.* **3** Open-eyed; with eyes wide open, as in surprise. 1940: "Randall was pie-eyed. His mouth moved, but nothing came out of it." Chandler, *Farewell*, 182. *Not common.*

pie-face   *n.* A person with a round face and a blank, funny, or homely expression; a stupid person. *Some teenage use c1920; obs.*

pie in the sky   A bourgeois heaven, concept of heaven, or earthly Utopia. c1920: "There'll be pie in the sky when you die, bye and bye." From a pop. I.W.W. song. *Orig. an epithet used by members of the I.W.W. (International Workers of the World) to taunt nonsympathizers, idealists, conventionally religious opponents, etc.* → **2** Heaven; Utopia. *Cynical use.*

pie wagon   1 A police truck used to transport arrested persons to jail; a Black Maria. *Orig. underworld use, c1900.* → **2** A ship's prison or brig. *Some W.W.I USN use.*

piffed   *adj.* Drunk. *Some use since c1900; now considered affected or archaic.*

pifficated   *adj.* Drunk. *Some use since c1900; never common.*

piffle   *exclam.* Mild exclamation to signify disbelief or indifference; bunk; boloney.   *n.* Drivel; nonsense; bunk. 1905: "So that's the kind of piffle [trifling criticism] actors have to go up against." McHugh, *Search Me*, 52. 1938: "The writers of popular song words have penned some of the most dreadful

piffle. . . ." F. Collins in *Better Eng.*, Oct., 53/1.   **—d**   *adj.* = **piffed.**
pifflicated   *adj.* = **pifficated.**
pig   *n.* **1** A policeman. 1848: criminal use. J. S. Farmer. *Obs.* → **2** A police informer; a stool pigeon. *Underworld use; obs. c1930.* **3** Any fat, sloppy, disfavored person. *Colloq.* **4** A girl or woman having a sloppy appearance; a girl or woman with "sloppy" morals; a passionate or promiscuous woman; any girl or woman. 1930: "Jack spoke of a pig he had recently picked up." J. T. Farrell, 159. 1951: ". . . A young blade said to me, 'Well, I got to pick up the pig at seven.' " F. Colby, *synd. newsp. col.*, Nov. 19. *Common, esp. among male students.* **5** A race horse, esp. a cheap or inferior one. 1944: "The losers 'cry' the long rationales of 'why the hell that pig didn't win.' . . ." *Fortune*, Sept., 142/2. See **pig it.** **6** A railroad engine, esp. one used in switchyards. *Railroad use.* **7** A leather pocketbook or wallet. *From "pigskin." Orig. underworld use.* See **blind pig.**
—gy   *n.* A toe. 1951: "Of feet I know hardly more than that they have piggies on them and come two to a customer in the conventional deal." W. Pegler, *synd. newsp. col.*, Sept. 13. *From the nursery game and rhyme.*   **—pen**   *n.* A roundhouse. *Railroad use.* See **pig.**
—skin   **pig-skin**   *n.* **1** A football. *Though now made of cowhide, footballs were once covered with pigskin. Since c1900; now colloq.* **2** A football player. *Not common.*   *adj.* Pertaining to football.
pig between two sheets   A ham sandwich. *Some lunch-counter use c1925; prob. synthetic.*
pig boat   pigboat   A submarine. 1944: ". . . He'd [a sailor] put in for pigboat duty." C. Macon in *Collier's*, Sept. 16, 64/3. 1946: "The archaic *pigboat* of the First World War owes its survival to old-fashioned journalists on the home front. Submarine men of the present . . . resent the use of this [word]. . . ." Riordan in *Calif. Folk Quart.*, 1945.
pigeon   *n.* **1** A professional gambler. 1886: New Orleans *Lantern*. *Obs.* **2** = **stool-pigeon.** 1934: "Don't come here again. . . . I don't like pigeons." Chandler, *Finger Man*, 14. **3** = **mark.** A victim of a swindle; one who has been duped; an innocent or naive person, one easy to dupe or take advantage of. 1958: ". . . Pigeon. Target or victim of a confidence game." G. Y. Wells, *Station House Slang.* **4** A girl or young woman.

Often used affectionately and possessively, e.g., "My pigeon." Ex. of sl. word used exclusively by men, as are most sl. words for women. See **chick.**
pigeon-eyed   *adj.* Drunk. 1737: "Pidgeon Ey'd." Pa. *Gazette. Obs.*
pig-headed   *adj.* Stubborn; stubborn and uninformed or stupid. *Colloq. since c1920.*
pig-iron   *n.* Whisky, esp. inferior, home-made, or bootleg whisky. *Dial.*
pig it   **1** To stop running or reduce one's running speed owing to fatigue or lack of wind; fig., to run as poorly as a pig. 1935: "The old [race horse] has bum legs and is half out of wind and is apt to pig it any time." Runyon. **2** To withdraw or retire, as from cowardice; to chicken out. *Not common.*
pig-meat   *n.* **1** A girl or woman, esp. an inexperienced but sexually willing girl or an old promiscuous woman. *Orig. Negro use.* See **meat, pig. 2** An old, sickly, or often defeated person, esp. a prize fighter; fig., one ready to die.
pig salve   Lard. *Dial.*
pig's eye   See **in a pig's eye.**
pig's eye, in a   pig's eye, in the   Not at all; never. *Always used after an affirmative statement, to make it negative. Usu. heard as "in a pig's eye," although often written "in the pig's eye."* 1937: "Yeah, we'll get it back. In the pig's eye." Weidman, *Wholesale*, 134.
pig shave   A crew-cut haircut. *Not common.*
pig-sticker   *n.* **1** A bayonet. *W.W.I Army use.* **2** A sword. *Student Reserve Officers Training Corps use since c1920.* **3** A children's sled, esp. an old-fashioned sled with upturned runners in the front. *Dial.* **4** A railroad locomotive's cowcatcher. *Not common.*
pig sweat   **1** Beer. **2** Inferior whisky or liquor of any kind.
pig's wings, the = **cat's meow, the.** *c1920; never common.*
pike   *v.i.* To go; to depart. 1864: *DAE.* 1924: "Say, I've got to pike along." Marks, *Plastic Age*, 18. *Obs.*   *n.* A cement-paved road, as opposed to an unpaved or asphalt road. *c1920–c1935; obs.*
piker   *n.* **1** A stingy person; a miser; a small-minded person who is unwilling to assume risks. *Since c1900; now colloq.* → **2** A coward; one who accepts only easy tasks. *Since c1915.*
pile   *n.* **1** All of one's money, considered collectively. *c1750–c1915.* → **2**

Any large sum of money, usu. belonging to one person or agency; lit., a pile of money.   *v.i.* To run rapidly, usu. in chase. 1948: ". . . She looked back and I piled after her hell to split." Cain, *Moth*, 87. **—s** *n.pl.* A large amount of money; used either absolutely or with "of" followed by "money" or a synonym.

pile of shit [taboo]   **1** Lies; exaggerations; bullshit. **2** Anything worthless, ugly, or dilapidated. **3** A contemptible, worthless person.

pile up   **1** To run aground, said of a ship. *Maritime use.* → **2** To wreck an automobile or airplane. 1948: "After he piled up his car." Evans, *Halo for Satan*, 135. **pile-up**   *n.* An automobile accident or wreck, esp. one involving several cars in one collision. 1958: "The 6-car, end-to-end pile-up on the New Jersey Turnpike. . . ." AP, Oct. 24.

pilfered   *adj.* Drunk. *Dial.*

pilgrim   *n.* = **greenhorn.** 1936: "It is said that upon the Range . . . 'pilgrim' . . . applied . . . to human newcomers." P. A. Rollins, *The Cowboy*, 29. *Western use; obs.*

pill   *n.* **1** An unlikable, obnoxious, insipid, or disagreeable person, esp. a chronic complainer or nuisance. 1871: *DAE.* 1917: "Kaiser Bill—is a pill." Common W.W.I child chant. 1953: "Oh, don't be a pill, Valerie." S. J. Perelman, *New Yorker*, Jan. 31, 24. *Early 19C Eng. sl. = a platitude, a cliché.* **2** A baseball. 1908: ". . . As the 'pill' leaves the [pitcher's] hand. . . ." R. L. Hartt, *Atlantic Monthly*, Aug., 224/2. 1913: "When Schulte 'slams the pill.' " *Nation*, Aug. 21, 161/2. *Colloq. since c1920.* → **3** A golf ball. *Since c1915; now archaic.* **4** An opium pellet, for smoking. **5** A Nembutal capsule. *Drug addict use.* **6** Any sedative. **7** A cigarette. 1927: "Those pills you smoke are terrible." Hammett, *Blood Money*, 87. *c1915–c1930; never common.* **8** A bullet. *Some synthetic use since c1925.* **9** A bomb. 1957: "A Jesuit priest who was a survivor of the A-bombing of Hiroshima 12 years ago . . . said he was drinking coffee when the big pill came down." N.Y. *Daily News*, Aug. 7, 7. *Some W.W.II use.*

pill-bag   *n.* A doctor. *Child use c1920.*

pillow   *n.* **1** A boxing glove. *Some prize fight use since c1900.* **2** In baseball, a base. 1951: ". . . Having drawn a walk to load the pillows." AP, Oct. 10. See **high pillow.**

pillow-puncher   *n.* A maid; lit., one who makes up beds; a cabin girl.

pill pad   **1** A place where addicts gather to smoke opium. *c1925.* See **pad; pill.** → **2** A place where addicts gather to take any kind of drug. *Since c1950.*

pill-peddler   *n.* **1** A physician. 1931: ". . . Not infrequent gynecological phenomena you pill-peddlers are always talking about." Queen, *Dutch Shoe*, 70. **2** A pharmacist or student of pharmacy.

pill-pusher   *n.* = **pill-peddler.** *A later term fairly common in Armed Forces during W.W.II.*

pill-roller   *n.* = **pill-peddler.**

pilot   *n.* **1** A manager of a sports team or athlete. **2** A jockey.

pimp   *n.* **1** A youth who does menial chores at a logging camp, ranch, or mine; a boy who carries water, washes dishes, or the like. *Since c1915.* **2** [derog.] A male prostitute, usu. to homosexuals. *Since c1935; from the assoc. of pimp and prostitute.*   *adj.* Effeminate.

pimple   *n.* **1** The human head. *Orig. prize fight use.* **2** A saddle. 1934: "Society equestrians' use." Weseen.

pimp stick   A cigarette, esp. a ready-made cigarette. *Logger use c1925. When ready-made cigarettes were first introduced on a large scale after W.W.I, they were considered effeminate by many cigar- and pipe-smoking men.*

pin   *v.t.* **1** To become engaged by giving or accepting a fraternity pin. *Student use until c1935.* → **2** To give or accept a fraternity pin as an indication of intention to become engaged, as an indication of possessive interest, or to signify a "going steady" relationship. *Student use since c1935.* 1958: "I was pinned to a Sigma Chi . . . when I met [the girl who later became] my wife." Radio show, *Rate Your Mate*, Sept. 17.

pin, pull the   **1** To quit a job. **2** To leave a town. **3** To leave one's wife, family, or friends. *Orig. a railroad term, "pull the pin" = to uncouple.*

pin a rose on it   Expression used by lunch-countermen in relaying an order to include onion in a sandwich. *Lunch-counter use c1935. Prob. synthetic.*

pinch   *v.t.* **1** To steal, esp. to steal a small item of little value. 1848: criminals' use. J. S. Farmer. 1944: "Who pinched the script?" Ford, *Phila. Murder*, 75. **2** To arrest. 1894: "The bulls . . . were . . . pinchin' the tramps. . . ." J. Flynt. 1907: "I was 'pinched.' " J. London, *My Life.* 1913: "He was pinched for selling whiskey to Indians." Thornton.

1939: "The stores invite ill will if they pinch [amateur thieves] indiscriminately." *Forum*, Dec., 273/2. *Said to be from Ital. sl. "pizzicane" = to pinch, to arrest, but the Eng. seems to be older.* *n.* An arrest. 1907: "A world of 'pinches' and 'get-aways.' " J. London, *The Road*, 159. 1949: "Now you can make your pinch. ..." Movie, *Johnny Allegro*. 1958: "Pinch—An arrest, usually on warrant or complaint." G. Y. Wells, *Station House Slang*. **—er** *n.* See **penny-pincher**.
pinchers *n.pl.* Shoes. *Not common.*
pinch-gut *n.* A miser.
pinch-hit *v.i.* 1 In baseball, to bat as a substitute for the regularly scheduled batter, esp. at a critical point in the game. → 2 To become a substitute for any regular worker, speaker, performer, or the like; to take another's place. *v.t.* To send in a substitute batter in baseball. *E.g.*, *"The manager pinch-hit Jones for Smith."* **pinch hit** *n.* In baseball, a hit obtained by a batter who is pinch-hitting.
pineapple *n.* 1 A German aerial torpedo. *W.W.I Army use; from its shape.* 2 A hand grenade. *Wide W.W.I and W.W.II Army use. From its shape and also from its exterior, which is often knurled or nodulose like a pineapple to give a better grip.* 3 Any small bomb or home-made explosive device, esp. one that can be thrown by hand. 1934: "Nobody tried to throw a pineapple in my lap. ..." Chandler, *Finger Man*, 52. *Underworld use; very common c1930.* Cf. **Chicago pineapple. 4 = crew cut.**
pin [someone's] ears back To defeat; to inflict physical or verbal punishment on; to administer a comeuppance. 1946: "Pine was a flip-lipped bastard who should have had his ears pinned back long ago." Evans, *Halo in Blood*, 96.
pine overcoat A coffin, esp. a cheap one. 1896: ". . . What they call in the army a pine overcoat." Thornton. Cf. **wooden overcoat.**
pine-top *n.* Whisky. *Dial. and obs.*
ping jockey Any military or civilian worker whose job it is to monitor electronic equipment, especially warning or detecting equipment, that gives off audio or visual responses, as radar or sonar devices. *Orig. W.W.II USN use, applied to monitors of sonar detection devices; now applied to any human monitor or receiver of intelligence from electronic devices. Cf.* **blip jockey.**
ping-wing *n.* An injection of a narcotic, usu. into the arm, or "wing."

Narcotic addict use. See Appendix, Rhyming Slang.
pin-head   pinhead *n.* A stupid person. *Colloq. since c1895.*
pink *n.* 1 A white person. *Negro use.* 2 A mild political radical; esp. one sympathetic to, but not actually working for, the international Communist movement. 3 Lit. and fig., the legal certificate of car ownership; fig., the right to drive one's car. *Thus, for traffic law violations one may lose one's "pink." Orig. and mainly hot-rod use. Because such certificates of ownership are often printed on pink paper. adj. =* **pinko. Pink** *n. =* **Pinkerton.** *Some underworld, hobo, and early union use; archaic.* **—ed** *adj.* Slightly drunk. *Not common.* **Pinkerton** *n.* A member of the Pinkerton Detective Agency; the Pinkerton Detective Agency; hence any detective or plainclothesman. 1956: "Albert Levey, the gambler, filed the first in a long series of suits against the owners of Belmont Park. He said he had been falsely arrested by its Pinkertons and wrongly imprisoned by the county police." T. Betts, *Across the Board*, 42. *The Pinkerton Agency was founded by Allan Pinkerton in 1850 and carried on by his descendants. During the Civil War it became a quasi-official intelligence organization for the Union Army. Later the firm supplied alarm systems and guards to private industry, thus incurring the wrath of hobos who had cause to fear Pinkerton guards on railway property and elsewhere. Later still the firm supplied strike-breakers to industry during the period of intense labor disputes in the first decades of the 20C; labor union and radical elements thus joined the hobo and criminal worlds in their fear and hatred of the Pinkertons.* **Pinkie** *n.* A Pinkerton detective; any detective. 1949: "Ashamed 'cause a fellow like me is studying to be a Pinkerton? . . . How you suppose Pinkies get trainin'. . . ." N. Algren, *Man With the Golden Arm*, 111. See **Pinkerton.** **—o** *adj.* Radical or liberal, usu. with the connotation of harmlessness. 1926: "Pinko-liberal." *Time*, Jan. 7, 30. 1941: "Re-elected were pinko James J. Matles [and] . . . pinko Julius Emspak." *Time*, Sept. 15, 17/1. *The meaning of the word has changed as the complexion of the radical movements in the U.S. has changed. Orig. it meant "anarchistic." Since c1945 it has been applied primarily to communist sympathizers, and in cases of heated debate*

*it can come to mean "communist" or
"traitor." On the other hand, it is a word
often used in smear campaigns against
thoroughly respectable liberal politicians.*
n. One suspected of being a political
radical, specif. a communist.

pink, in the   In good health. *Short for
"in the pink of physical condition" or
"in the pink of health."* 1950: "Enjoy
yourself while you're still in the pink."
Popular song, "It's Later Than You
Think."

pink chord   An irritating mistake in
reading or improvising music. *Some
musician use c1935.*

pink loco   See **loco.**

pink slip   A discharge notice; notification to a worker that he has been
dismissed. 1953: "All 1,300 employees
got pink slips today." AP, May 29.
*Common since c1925. From the traditional
printed notice, usu. put in an employee's
pay envelope.* **pinkslip**   *v.t.* To fire;
to dismiss.

pink tea   1 A formal or elaborate
social affair; usu. used jocularly or
slightingly. 1887: *DAE.* 1934: standard
use. *Web.* 2 A social affair restricted to
the elite of any community.

pink-toes   *n.sing.* A light-complexioned Negro girl. *Negro use.*

pinky   *n.* 1 The little finger. 1949: "He
paused and ran his pinkie along his lower
lip." Chandler, *Little Sister*, 247. 1951:
"Pardon my lifted pinky. . . ." Hy
Gardner, N.Y. *Her. Trib. Most common on East Coast. Apparently a
childhood word taken into adult vocabulary.*
2 An attractive, light-skinned Negro
girl. *Negro use.* *adj.* Pertaining to
the little finger; thus the common
"pinky ring" = a ring worn on the
little finger.

pinky-crooker   *n.* A person whose
social mannerisms are affected; specif.,
a person who lifts the little finger of the
hand in which he holds a cup of tea.
1951: "Linden Mulford [said]: 'All we
have is middle-class people, and if you
give them all longhair stuff, you'll find
only the pinky-crookers at the concerts.' "
Time, Apr. 2, 78. *Not common.*

pinochle season   The off-season in
the garment industry; lit., the season
when workers play pinochle instead of
working. 1956: "Garment workers . . .
wait for *pinochle season*, the slack
season." *Labor's Special Lang. from
Many Sources. Amer. Yiddish orig.*

pin [blame for something] on   To
accuse; to impute a wrongdoing to

someone. 1939: "We're going to pin a
murder rap on [him]." E. S. Gardner,
D. A. Draws, 196. 1950: "Police indicated
they had little to pin on them." AP,
Jan. 18.

pins   *n.pl.* The human legs. 1910:
"Roman was knocked clean off his
pins." Johnson, *Varmint*, 127. *Now
colloq.* See **didie pins, hairpin, pull the
pin.**

pin-shot   *n.* An injection of a drug
made with a safety pin and an eyedropper in lieu of a hypodermic needle.
Drug addict use.

pint   *n.* See **half-pint.**

pinto   *n.* 1 A coffin. *Lorenzo D.
Turner's "Africanisms in the Gullah
Dialect" indicates that this word is of
African origin, taken over from slaves
by American whites. Dial.* 2 A piebald
or mottled horse. 1936: "The piebald
. . . deriving his name from a Spanish
word meaning paint, was generally
termed a 'pinto,' but in parts of Texas
was called in good plain English a
'paint horse.' " P. A. Rollins, *The
Cowboy*, 62. *Colloq.; orig. Western use;
from Sp. "pinto" = painted.*

pin-up   *n.* A photograph or other
depiction of a pretty girl. 1949: "He
said the soldiers went for pin-ups in a
big way." UP, Sept. 14. *Although a
pin-up can be a picture of a sweetheart,
the term was most commonly used during
W.W.II to mean a publicity photograph
of a motion-picture actress, usu. attired
and posed in such a way as to accentuate
her sexual appeal. From the custom of
pinning such photographs to tent and
barracks walls.* See **cheesecake, sweater
girl.**   *adj.* Sexually attractive; pretty.

pin-up girl   A sexually attractive
young woman, usu. a movie star, model,
or the like. See **sweater girl.**

pip   *n.* 1 A remarkable or excellent
person or thing; a pippin. 1928: "It's
a pip." Hecht & MacArthur, *Front
Page*, II. 1950: "A pip of a shiner."
J. McNulty, *New Yorker*, Oct. 14.
Common since c1915. → 2 An attractive
young woman. *Archaic.* *adj.* Remarkable; excellent; attractive.   **—peroo**
n. A pip or pippin. 1941: "Oh, what a gal,
a real pipperoo!" From pop. song, "I've
Got a Gal in Kalamazoo." 1942: "I've
got an idea—a great idea—a pipperoo!"
Striebel & McEvoy, *synd. newsp. comic
strip*, "Dixie Dugan," Nov. 18.   *adj.*
Fine, excellent, outstanding. 1945:
"A pipperoo movie was thrilling the
patrons." Chicago *Daily News*, Dec. 29,

1/6. See Appendix, —eroo ending.
—pin   *n.* **1** Any excellent or highly admired person or thing; sometimes used ironically to mean "queer" or "obnoxious." 1900: "She thinks you are a pippin." Upson in *Independent*, 2573/1. 1924: "She's a pippin." A. Lewis in *Lit. Digest*. 1952: "It's a pippin." Lowell Thomas, radio, Feb. 22. **2** Specif., a pretty girl. 1919: "That girl is sure some pippin!" *Lit. Digest*, June 21, 31/1. 1939: "*Pippin* gives place to *peach, cutie,* and *smoothie.*" Hixson, *Word Ways,* 153. *c1910–c1935; archaic, not now as common as the shortened "pip."*
pip, the   *n.* Annoyance jocularly considered as a mythical disease. 1924: "People gave him the pip, that's what they did." Marks, *Plastic Age,* 6. *From the disease of chickens.*
pipe   *n.* **1** A cigar. 1848: criminals' use. J. S. Farmer. *Obs.* **2** A cinch; any operation or task easily performed. 1905: "It's a pipe." McHugh, *Search Me,* 19. 1935: "A college boy has his own code of 'cuts,' 'pipes' [easy courses], and 'dumb Doras.' " K. S. Bennett, *Classical Jour.,* Oct., 39. *From "lead pipe cinch."* **3** A letter, note, or other written message. *Circus use.* **4** A business or social conversation. 1931: "He shoots a pipe that he is doing well." "We had a few pipes." D. W. Maurer. *Carnival pitchman use. From "stovepipe."* **5** A saxophone. *Not common; synthetic jazz use.* See **gobble-pipe, hit the pipe.**   *v.i.* To watch; to reconnoiter. 1848: criminals' use. J. W. Farmer. *Obs.*   *v.t.* **1** To write a letter; to send a message. 1931: "Bill Johnson pipes from Frisco that times are hard." D. W. Maurer. **2** To talk; to tell; to give information. 1939: "But I am not suppose to know that and do not pipe." O'Hara, *Pal Joey,* 21. **3** To look or look at; to notice or observe; to see; esp. to look at something because it is unusual or remarkable. 1907: "I saw three men coming toward me. . . . I piped the lay on the instant." J. London, *My Life.* 1922: "Did yuh pipe her hands?" O'Neill, *Hairy Ape,* 4. 1927: " 'Pipe the Flight' is to watch the parade of coeds." UP.   **—d**   *adj.* Drunk. *Some use c1910–c1930; obs.*   **—s**   *n.pl.* The vocal cords, the larynx, esp. of a singer; fig., any and all organs involved in speaking, singing, or breathing. 1905: "She has the most elegant line of language that ever left the pipes." McHugh, *Search Me,* 94.
pipe, hit the   **1** To smoke opium. → **2**

To smoke any drug, such as a marijuana cigarette.   *n.* The habit of smoking opium. *Not common.* See **pipe.**
pipe course   An easy course, esp. in college. 1951: "You are all freshmen and you may not be familiar with the term 'pipe course.' " M. Shulman, *Dobie Gillis,* 104f.
pipe down   To stop talking; to shut up; to discontinue any kind of noise; often used as a command. 1850: H. Melville, *White-Jacket.* 1926: "Pipe down." "He tried to pipe me down." Stallings & Anderson, *What Price Glory,* I, III. 1939: "The others got sore at him and told him to pipe down. . . ." O'Hara, *Pal Joey,* 4. 1944: "Pipe down about Pete." Ford, *Phila. Murder,* 75. *Orig. USN use; wide USN sl. during W.W.I. By c1925 Army and student use; colloq. since c1930.*
pipe dream   Any plan, scheme, goal, idea, or ideal that is as unrealistic as the dreams of an opium addict after smoking an opium pipe. *Colloq.*
pipe [someone] off   **1** To blacklist a person; to publicize the fact that a person is unwelcome. *From the nautical use.* **2** To complain about someone to the police.
piss   [taboo]   *v.i.* To urinate. *Universally known.*   *n.* Urine. *Universally known.*   *interj.* An expression of disgust.   **—er**   *n.* **1** A difficult or distasteful task; a back-breaker. **2** A small boy, esp. a mischievous one.
piss and vinegar   Energy; vivaciousness; mischievousness. *Not considered taboo.*
piss call [taboo]   The first call in the morning; the signal to get out of bed. *Orig. USN use.*
pissed off [taboo]   Angry; enraged; disgusted; completely and thoroughly exhausted; fed up; unhappy; forlorn. *One of several such terms very widely used by Armed Forces in W.W.II and carried into civilian life afterward. Though still taboo, this term has passed into sophisticated use among the culturally elite or pseudo-elite.*
piss on [someone or something] [taboo]   To act disrespectfully toward; to do anything to injure or denigrate another; a term often used to indicate an intention to ignore another's advice, feelings, etc.; an expression of anger at, disgust with, or rejection of a person or thing.
piss on ice [taboo]   To live well; to be markedly successful or lucky. *Some use since c1950. Because a cake of ice is*

often placed at the bottom of the urinals in the men's rest-rooms of expensive restaurants, bars, etc. Cf. **eat high on the hog.**

pistols   *n.pl.* Severely pegged trousers, as with a zoot suit. *c1935 jive use; archaic.*

piston   *n.* A slide trombone. *Synthetic use.*

pit boss   **1** The foreman of a mining crew. **2** Any foreman. 1956: "The pit bosses, who are foremen. . . ." J. Cannon, *Who Struck John?* 72.

pitch   *n.* **1** A pitchman's or street vendor's place of business or arrangement of wares. A "high pitch" is one set up on a box, wagon, automobile, or the like. A "low pitch" is set on the ground or pavement. 1932: "40,000 men working the sidewalks . . . with high pitch and low pitch." J. T. Flynn. *Pitchman use.* **2** The sales talk or spiel given by a pitchman. 1939: "He [a pitchman] needs a crowd to hear his pitch." *Life,* July 31, 24. 1951: "He [a pitchman] recited part of his pitch." *New Yorker,* Jan. 27, 21. *Pitchman use.* → **3** Any sales talk or speech intended to persuade, convince, or gain sympathy; an exaggerated story; any utterance as a "line," intended to benefit the speaker. 1950: "He'll give you a pitch about a self-defense killing." Radio play, *Yours Truly, Johnny Dollar,* Feb. 3. **4** = **pitchman.** 1949: "The pitch declares." N.Y. *Times,* Aug. 28, 63. *These meanings all were orig. pitchman, carnival, and circus use; they became common by c1930.* **5** Money. *Not common.* **6** A preliminary, exploratory, or speculative amorous gesture or verbal proposition to one of the opposite sex. 1939: "Anyway I never made a pitch with Herta." O'Hara, *Pal Joey,* 28. **7** A specif. situation or state of affairs, or an explanation of it; a proposition, deal, or plan of procedure; the picture; an angle. 1946: "I think I get the pitch; correct me if I'm wrong." Evans, *Halo in Blood,* 22. 1949: "What's the pitch?" Movie, *White Heat. From "pitch" = a sales talk or story. Common since W.W.II.* *v.t.* **1** To sell gadgets, novelties, or other small articles of merchandise on the street or at a fair or carnival by demonstrating one's wares and exhorting passers-by to buy; said of a pitchman. 1943: "Louie . . . pitches kitchen gadgets." Zolotow in *SEP.* 1951: "He pitches household items like the Magic Towell. . . . At a carny, you pitch phonies." *New Yorker,* Jan. 27, 20/3. *Since c1925.* **2** To

give a party; to throw a party. 1932: "When he is pitching parties. . . ." Runyon. 1952: "One of his assistants actually pitched a party for me. . . ." R. C. Ruark, *synd. newsp. col.,* Apr. 8. *v.i.* **1** To sell or to make one's living by selling as a pitchman. **2** To use a spiel or line; to attempt to display charm. **3** To make amorous advances to one of the opposite sex. 1932: ". . . Not a doll such as a guy will start pitching to. . . ." Runyon. **4** To exaggerate; to speak boastingly; to shoot the bull.   **—fork** See **rain pitchforks.**   **—man**   *n.* **1** One who sells gadgets, novelties, or any small items of merchandise on the street or at a fair or carnival by demonstrating his wares and exhorting people to buy. *Since c1925; now colloq.* See **pitch.** → **2** A television announcer who demonstrates a product while exhorting viewers to buy by mail. *Since c1950. In the early days of television some of these announcers were experienced pitchmen from fairs and carnivals.*

pitch, on the = **on the make.** 1949: "Dames! Always on the pitch—always trying to move in." Burnett, *Jungle,* 60. *Not common.*

pitching, in there   **1** Making an effort. *From baseball use.* **2** Working diligently; defending one's rights; not letting oneself be defeated, insulted, or victimized. 1955: "I'm on the go night and day, and I'm in there pitching." C. Willingham, *To Eat a Peach,* 141.

pitch-out   *n.* **1** In baseball, a pitch thrown wide of the plate, enabling the catcher to receive the ball quickly and surely, usu. in order to catch a runner off base or prevent a runner from stealing a base. **2** In football, a short, quick pass over the opponent's linemen; it differs from a regular pass in that the passer throws or pushes the ball from him without cocking his arm.   **pitch out**   To throw a pitch-out in either baseball or football.

pitch (the) woo   To caress passionately; to spoon, smooch, pet, or neck; to make love. 1937: ". . . 'Pitching woo'—known as petting, necking, or sparking in the old days." *Ladies Home Jour.,* Sept., 20. 1951: "And she pitches some more woo with Dr. Jan." S. J. Perelman in *New Yorker,* Oct. 20, 30/1. *Never as common as the synonyms listed above.*

Pittsburgh feathers   Coal. *Hobo use c1915.*

pix   *n.pl.* **1** Motion pictures; the

motion-picture business; the singular is **pic.** *Pop. by trade paper "Variety"; since c1936.* **2** Photographs, esp. the photographs used to illustrate a specif. article or feature in a newspaper or magazine; illustrations; artwork. *Wide newspaper use.* c1950: WPIX, the call letters of a television station in N.Y.C. operated by the N.Y. *Daily News,* a newspaper noted for its photographs.

pixie *n.* An extreme modern woman's hair style consisting of very short hair, almost as short as a man's standard haircut, worn straight and featuring ragged or zig-zag bangs. **pixilated** *adj.* Bewildered; eccentric; crazy; drunk. *Since c1850; mainly dial. Fig., meaning prob. = affected by pixies.*

pizzazz *n.* Power; force; pep; aggression; audacity. 1951: "Rentschler thinks the J-57 [jet engine] has more pizzazz than any other engine. Says he, 'It is more powerful than any jet engine ever flown.'" *Time,* May 28, 91/2.

P.J.'s *n.pl.* Pajamas; a pair of pajamas. *Common written and spoken abbr.*

place *n.* **1** A gathering point, such as a bar, restaurant, a particular apartment, a particular house, esp. the known gathering point of the members of any specific group. **2** Second place in a race or contest. *v.i.* **1** To finish second in a race or contest. → **2** To finish well enough in a race or contest to receive a prize.

plainer *n.* **1** A street beggar; a bum. *Dial.* **2** A chronic complainer. *Dial.*

plank **plank down** **plank up** **plank out** *v.i.,* (usu.) *v.t.* **1** To pay or put down money, esp. cash. 1824: "Plank." *DAE.* 1835: "Plank up." *DAE.* 1850: "Plank down." *DAE.* 1883: "Plank out." *DAE.* 1948: "20th [Century-Fox] planked out only $44,172,178...." *Variety,* Aug. 25, 4/3. 1949: "[He] planked down a cool $8,000,000." R. H. Fetridge in N.Y. *Times,* Sept. 25, F3/3. 1951: "When you plank the cash on the counter for a slice of sirloin...." Advt., *New Yorker,* Dec. 1, 63/1. *All forms colloq.* **2** To slam down; to place. 1938: "An overstuffed chair some admirer had planked down next to the booth." Liebling, *Back Where,* 182.

plank down = **plank.**

planker *n.* A steak, whether a plank steak or not. 1949: "No one could eat the steaks. Seems [the] cooks, in flouring the plankers, used patching plaster." AP, Nov. 26. *Not common.*

plank out = **plank.**

plank-owner *n.* A sailor who has served on one ship for an exceptionally long time, esp. a sailor who has served on a ship since it was commissioned. *Some USN use.*

plank up = **plank.**

plant *v.t.* **1** To bury, as a corpse; to bury or cache an object, goods, or money. *Since c1860.* **2** To hide something. *Orig. underworld use.* → **3** Specif., to secrete incriminating evidence in such a way that when it is found it will tend to cast blame on another person. 1939: "Someone is planting evidence...." "It had been planted on him." E. S. Gardner, *D. A. Draws,* 200, 203. **4** To land a blow, as with the fist. *n.* **1** = **shill.** *Since c1925.* **2** A hiding place; a hideout. *Underworld and hobo use.* → **3** A cache, usu. of stolen money or goods; anything, usu. stolen, that is hidden or stored. **4** A frame-up. 1930: "He tells his superior that he is on a 'plant.'" Lavine, *Third Degree,* 11. **5** A spy; a police spy. **—ing** *n.* A funeral. 1946: "The solemn atmosphere you find at a run-of-the-mill planting...." "I get in on a lot of these plantings—I drive for Reverend Clark." Evans, *Halo in Blood,* 4, 6. *Not common.*

plant show A colored minstrel show; a plantation show. *Carnival and circus use c1915; obs.*

plaster *n.* **1** Butter. *Hobo use c1925.* **2** A banknote, esp. a one-dollar bill. **3** One who follows another; a tail or shadow. 1948: "I went after him. He probably knew he had a plaster by this time." Evans, *Halo for Satan,* 125. **4** A subpoena; a summons; a warrant for arrest. *v.t.* To mortgage, esp. a house. **—ed** *adj.* Drunk. 1928: "...Anyone who gets plastered on a couple of snifters." C. G. Shaw in *New Yorker,* Nov. 17, 27/1. 1934: "You get plastered on every possible occasion." DeJournette in *Esquire,* Apr., 36. 1951: "In one day I may taste as many as 100 different wines. If I swallowed it, I'd be plastered before lunch." Frank Schoonmaker, professional wine-taster, quoted by AP, Aug. 2. 1951: "I got plastered. Man, I was drunk as a lord." R. S. Prather, *Bodies in Bedlam,* 49. *Usu. a pred. adj. Some use since c1880; very pop. c1920–c1940. One of the most common words = drunk.*

plate *n.* **1** An exceptionally well- or stylishly dressed person. *From "fashion plate."* **2** An attractive woman.

A meliorative, modern form of "dish." Both meanings are fairly common. **3** = **platter.** *Never common.* **—s** *n.pl.* The feet. *From "plates of meat" = feet, in rhyming sl.* See Appendix, Rhyming Slang.

plater platter *n.* Any race horse; specif. an inferior race horse. 1923: "These selling platers with a shot of dope in them." Ernest Hemingway, *My Old Man.* 1928: "There had been a close finish between one of James Butler's horses and another plater." A. Minor in *New Yorker*, Nov. 10, 111f. 1956: "PLATERS—Horses that run in claiming races." T. Betts, *Across the Board*, 318. 1956: "He decided to rename the horse Enrico Caruso.... 'How dare you entertain the thought of changing the name of a cheap selling plater to that of a great singer?'" T. Betts, *Across the Board*, 130, 131. 1957: "... Nashua [famous race horse] ... arrived ... like any ordinary plater." *N.Y. Post*, May 18, 65. *A plater is a race horse of any class or quality, though in modern use a horse not of the best class is implied. Orig. "plater" and pronounced with long "a."* Cf. **selling plater.**

platter *n.* **1** = **plater. 2** A modern disc-shaped phonograph record; esp. a recording of jazz or popular music. Some continued general use; now wide rock and roll use. Cf. **disc.** 1943: "Phonograph records are called 'discs' and 'platters.'" M. Shulman, *Barefoot Boy with Cheek*, 149. 1943: "I bought a couple of Crosby platters." H. A. Smith, *Putty Knife*, 163. 1957: *The Platter Party*, name of radio record-playing program. **3** In baseball, home plate. **4** A discus. *Sports use.*

play *n.* **1** = **action.** → **2** Patronage, esp. at a gambling establishment. → **3** An amount of money, or the total bet during a specif. gambling session. **4** A role of leadership or authority; control of a situation. **5** A girl or young woman. *Not common.* See **make a play for.** *v.t.* **1** To date; to go out with; to court. 1925: "That wet smack Davis plays her pretty steady." Bowers in *Lit. Digest. Student use.* **2** To patronize; to do business with. 1951: "My guest and I played the chili place near the St. Louis *Times* almost exclusively." W. Pegler, *synd. newsp. col.*, Jan. 4. **—boy** *n.* A man of any age who is noted for an ostentatious social life, esp. one who is often seen in public with different women, usu. at expensive places of entertainment. 1931: "Hendrik the playboy." Queen,

Dutch Shoe, 104. 1955: *Playboy*, title of a pop. man's magazine dealing with fashions, entertainment, etc. *The term always implies wealth, education, social standing, and sophistication.*

play around **1** To pursue a business venture or occupation without serious attitude or intent. **2** To date, court, or have sexual relations with several members of the opposite sex over a comparatively short period of time; to have sexual relations extramaritally. 1943: "She plays around and I knew Lavery was one of her playmates." Chandler, *Lady in Lake*, 9.

play ball **1** To begin. *From the umpire's traditional order to start a baseball game.* **2** = **play ball with.**

play ball with **1** To co-operate with; to comply with; to do business with, often by way of a compromise; to be fair or honest with. 1939: "He was playing ball with Artrim." Gardner, *D. A. Draws*, 207. **2** To appease; to give in to. 1952: "I was asked to be reasonable. I haughtily refused to give the favorites special things to do. I might have played ball just a little, but I scorned to." Agnes DeMille in *Atlantic Monthly*, Jan., 70/1. *Specif., to be forced to co-operate or comply with another's request in order to receive a favor or preferred treatment, or because of blackmail or extortion.*

play catch with = **play ball with.**

played out **1** Without funds; broke. *From the gambling use.* **2** Tired; exhausted. **3** No longer usable, esp. too well known to be effective, entertaining, or to elicit enthusiasm, usu. said of a type of entertainment, story, play, or the like.

play for, make a To use one's charm to impress one of the opposite sex; to court a girl; to show a romantic interest in one of the opposite sex.

play for keeps = **play hard.**

play games with To deceive; to play one rival against another.

play hard To be tough, mean, immoral, unethical, or dishonest; to do or be willing to do anything to achieve one's goal; said equally of hoodlums, prostitutes, or aggressive businessmen.

play in the family = **play the dozens.** *Not common. Some Negro use.*

play it cool To be deliberately, or to strive to give the impression of being, unemotional, disattached, and invulnerable; to refuse to show and attempt to feel no emotions, eagerness, enthusiasm, or interest, as a defense mechanism, so one will not be disappointed; to keep one's dignity and pride; not to commit oneself; to refuse to commit oneself. 1956: "We asked for a price and the agent 'played it cool.' " *Publication Weekly,* Oct. 22, 1983. 1957: "Play it cool." Tennessee Williams, *Orpheus Descending,* I. *Orig. and mainly cool, far out, and beat use. Some student, teenage, and general use since c1955. See* **cool.**

play the [someone] Lit. & fig., to imitate someone, either in manner, function, or attitude; to demand the status or respect due to a social position or character other than one's own. *Thus to "play the duchess" = to act as if one were wealthy and had social status, lit. to affect the manners of a duchess; to "play the hero" = to act like and expect to be treated as a hero; to "play the whore" = to be sexually promiscuous or to compromise for personal gain.* 1956: "Weaker men did better than Linkhorn in the world. He saw with eyes enviously slow-burning. 'I ain't a-playin' the whore to no man,' he would declare." N. Algren, *A Walk on the Wild Side,* 7.

play the [something] To affect an attitude or feeling. 1932: "It is surprising to . . . all when Miss Midgie plays the chill for Jack. . . . She is still playing plenty of chill for me." D. Runyon, 5. 1935: "It is unnatural for a guy like Fergus to be playing the warm for a guy like Cecil." Runyon, 272f. *Prob. Runyonese.*

play the dozens To slander one's or another's parents. *Some Negro use.*

play with = **play ball with.** 1934: "They said they'd come back and get her, if I didn't play with them." Chandler, *Finger Man,* 47.

play with [oneself] [taboo] **1** To masturbate. 1954: "I was going with girls . . . and I didn't feel the urge to play with myself." H. K. Fink, *Long Journey,* 14. *Mainly boy use. Used jocularly or as a term of derogation by adult men.* **2** To behave stupidly or unrealistically. *Adult male use. From the old tradition that masturbation leads to feeblemindedness.*

plea *n.* See **cop a plea.**

plead the fifth (a five) To refuse to do something; to refuse to state one's opinion, reason, or objection. 1957: "Pleading a five—When one cat refuses to get up on the bandstand and play with another. Derived from taking the Fifth Amendment or refusing to talk."

E. Horne, *For Cool Cats and Far-Out Chicks. Some hip use since c1955. During c1954 several investigations were televised of the U.S. Senate's Criminal Investigation Committee and its Un-American Activities Committee. Thus for the first time the public saw and heard such investigations; many alleged criminals and communists refused to testify "on the ground that it might tend to incriminate me." Refusal to testify for this reason is granted by the Fifth Amendment to the U.S. Constitution, to protect a person from double jeopardy in the courts. Also during c1954, as a result of such refusal to testify, a public controversy raged concerning the wisdom and the implications of refusal to testify by pleading the fifth.*

pleat *n.* See **reet pleat.**

plebe *n.* **1** A college freshman. *Some use c1850; archaic by c1920.* → **2** A first-year student at Annapolis or West Point. 1950: "Plebe." Movie, *The West Point Story.* 1951: "[West Point Football Coach] Blaik is left with his 1950 plebes and a few B-squad members." AP, Aug. 13. *Since c1860; the only common use since c1920.*

pledge *v.t.* To come to an agreement with a student, binding him to join a specif. fraternity or sorority. 1871: *DAE. Common student use.* *v.i.* To promise to join a fraternity. 1887: *DAE. Somewhat archaic.* *n.* A student who has accepted an invitation to join a fraternity. 1949–1952: "Pledge" occurs at least 55 times in Cornell (Univ.) *Daily Sun. Since c1910.*

plenty *adv.* Very; exceedingly; thoroughly. 1939: "I was plenty cautious." Gardner, *D. A. Draws,* 205. 1941: "The man had just been told off plenty." G. Homes, *40 Whacks,* 65.

pling *v.i., v.t.* To beg or beg from. *Hobo use.*

plonk *n.* = **plunk.** **—ed** *adj.* Drunk. 1943: "A few badly plonked soldiers. . . ." *Life,* Aug. 30. *Not common.* See **plunk.**

plow jockey See Appendix, Suffixes and Suffix Words.

plow the deep To sleep.

pluck *v.t.* **1** To rob; to cheat. 1927: "These bimbos once helped pluck a bank." Hammett, *Blood Money,* 61. **2** [taboo] To have sexual intercourse with. *A thinly veiled rhyming euphem. for the taboo "fuck."*

Plug *prop.n.* A nickname applied to any homely man. 1848: J. S. Farmer. *Obs.* **plug** *n.* **1** A hat, esp. a top hat. 1848: J. S. Farmer. *Archaic.* **2** A homely man. *Obs., but see* **plug-ugly.** **3** An inept, unskilled, or clumsy person. 1863: *DAE. Archaic.* **4** A fellow; a guy. 1894: "I'm always willing to be square to a square plug." J. Flynt. *Obs.* **5** An old worthless horse. *Since c1870.* **6** A particularly diligent student. *Common student use c1875–c1900; replaced by "plugger."* **7** A literal translation; a pony. *Some student use c1900.* **8** A silver dollar. *Some use c1900.* **9** A counterfeit coin; a plugged coin. **10** An average or inferior prize fighter. *Common since c1915.* **11** An item of merchandise that is hard to sell. *c1930.* **12** A favorable statement; a recommendation; an advertisement; a blurb. 1939: "I said I certainly [*sic*] would apprisiate [*sic*] him giving me a plug with the owners." J. O'Hara, *Pal Joey,* 39. *Common since c1935.* **13** A throttle on a locomotive. *Railroad use.* *v.i.* **1** To study hard or diligently; to strive with all one's effort. *Student use c1900.* **2** To yell at the players of a team in encouragement or approval; to root. *c1925.* *v.t.* **1** To shoot someone, esp. to kill by shooting. *Since c1925.* **2** To make a favorable remark or recommendation about someone or something, esp. as a means of public promotion; to advertise. 1949: "You mean you want me to plug it?" Billy Rose, *synd. newsp. col.,* Oct. 6. 1950: "Cosmetic manufacturers plugged products to give women ersatz tan." R. Adler in N.Y. *Times Mag.,* July 9, 20/3. **—ger** *n.* **1** A diligent worker or student. *Since c1900. From "plug."* **2** An enthusiast, a fan, or a spectator who freq. extols the good points of a region, idea, sport, team, etc. **3** A hired killer.

plug, pull the **1** To dive; to submerge. *Submarine use.* → **2** To withdraw one's support. → **3** To expose another. → **4** To cause trouble.

plug hat A top hat. *From c1870 to present.*

plug puller A railroad engineer. *Railroad use; obs.*

plug-ugly *n.* **1** A hoodlum; a tough or ugly-looking ruffian. **2** A prize fighter. **3** A strong, ugly, uncouth man; a rowdy; a tough guy. *In use as early as 1857.*

plum *n.* Anything, usu. a job, rank, or title, given in recognition of good work or service; esp. a political job given in recognition of service rendered during a political campaign. **—my** *adj.* Pleasing, satisfying; rich and mellow. 1951: "The rich, plummy voice of [actor]

Edward Arnold...." K. Harris, *Innocents from Abroad,* 199.

plumb **—er** *v.t.* To ruin; to make a mistake that is impossible to correct. 1939: "I tho't I plumbered it...." John O'Hara, *Pal Joey,* 39. **—ing** *n.* **1** A trumpet. *Swing musician use.* **2** The digestive tract; the bowels. 1953: "This mild little medicine will fix your constipation, your stomach, your plumbing...." *Oral,* County Fair, Morgan County, Illinois. *Both uses usu. humorous.*

plump See **smack,** *adv.*

plunging neckline A low V-shaped neckline on a woman's dress, blouse, or the like, usu. intended to reveal part of the breast. *A style pop. c1949 and after.*

plunk **plonk** *n.* **1** Cheap, inferior wine. **2** A dollar, either silver or paper. *c1880.* 1905: "My five thousand plunks. ..." McHugh, *Search Me,* 45. *Orig. from the dull sound of a silver dollar striking a hard surface; archaic.* *v.t.* To shoot. *Since c1890.* Cf. **plank.**

plunk down = **plank down.** To pay money; to hand over in payment. 1934: "Standard." *Web.* 1953: "He plunked down ... $65,000 to ... [author] Herman Wouk...." Bob Thomas, AP, June 2. *One of the few sl. terms that Web. accepts as standard.*

plunkie *n.* A cookhouse waiter. 1947: "Circus use." *Fortune,* July, 108, 133.

plush *adj.* Stylish; luxurious; connotating wealth. Said of a place; esp. a hotel, nightclub, or the like. 1927: "'Plush' indicates ... stylish." UP. 1951: "A swank, plush, exclusive cabaret club...." Westbrook Pegler, *synd. newsp. col.,* Dec. 27. *From the soft textile plush.* *v.i.* To be wealthy; to live luxuriously; to display wealth. *n.* Places, ornaments, materials, etc., that connote wealth. **—ery** *n.* A luxurious and high-priced hotel, nightclub, etc. 1951: Abel Green, *Show Biz,* 570. **—y** *adj.* Sumptuous; elegant; plush. 1952: "Singer Ella Logan at the plushy Casablanca [nightclub]...." Budd Schulberg, *Holiday,* Jan., 31/2. *An ex. of a sl. adj. adding a suffix that does not change its meaning.*

plute *n.* A rich person. 1924: "The tutoring sections were only for the 'plutes.' ..." Marks, *Plastic Age,* 97. *From "plutocrat." Not common.*

p. o. **P. O.** *n.* **1** The stand. abbr. for "Post Office." **2** The written and spoken abbr. for "pissed off." *Since the orig. term is not spoken, this is a euphem. and is not taboo.*

pocket *n.* **1** The place where one keeps money or valuables, whether it be actually one's pocket, purse, safe, etc. **2** A position between two objects so that one's movements are restricted. 1950: "My horse was in a pocket and couldn't move to the [racetrack's inside] rail." *Oral*, Keenland racetrack. See **frame**. **3** An untenable situation; an unsatisfactory business or personal relationship from which one cannot extract oneself. **4** See **highpockets**. **—book** *n.* A pocket-sized, paperbound edition of a book, orig. sold for 25¢ or 35¢. *Colloq.*

pocket cabbage = **cabbage**.

pocket lettuce = **lettuce**.

pocket pool [taboo] The act or instance of touching or playing with the genitals with one's hands in one's pants' pockets. *A derog. and semihumorous accusation made by one boy to another. Usu. limited to the 10–14 age group. Used by adult males only as a jocular accusation.*

poco *n.* An old-clothes man. *Archaic; used as early as c1855.*

pod *n.* Marijuana. 1952: "Diane smoked jive, pod, and tea...." Orville Prescott, N.Y. *Times*, Apr. 29, 25.

p. o.'d *adj.* A written and spoken abbr. for "pissed off." *Prob. more common than "p. o." A euphem.; not taboo. Since W.W.II.*

pogey   pogie   pogy *n.* **1** Any home provided by charity or government funds for the aged, disabled, etc.; a poorhouse; a government home for disabled veterans; an old-age home; a workhouse. 1891: "Tramps' use." J. Flynt. *More recently, confused with and used for "pokey"* = *a jail.* → **2** A jail. See **pokey**.

pogey bait   pogie bait   pogy bait   poggie bait Candy; any kind of sweets. *W.W.I and W.W.II use, primarily by members of Armed Forces.*

poggie *n.* An Army recruit. *Some Army use.* Cf. **pogey bait**.

point *n.* **1** The jaw. *c1925. Prize fight use.* **2** The essence; the meaning. *Pop. in "to get the point"* = *to understand. Colloq.* **3** In sports, a score.

point-head   pointy-head *n.* **1** A hoodlum. **2** A stupid person; one who is not in the know. 1947: "The amazed point-heads...." Billy Rose, *synd. newsp. col.*, Nov. 4. *Implying that one's head comes to a point, and will easily fit into a pointed dunce's cap.* See **egghead**.

poison *n.* **1** A person, situation, or condition that bodes no good for one. **2** Any person, object, or place that seems to bring bad luck. **3** Liquor, esp. inferior liquor. 1840 [1954]: "He drank freely of this beverage [rum]. . . . The poison had taken effect, and he stumbled. . . ." *Behold Me Once More, The Confessions of James Holley Garrison*, ed. by W. M. Merrill, 88. **4** See **lead poison**.

poison pan An ugly or unpopular girl. *Not common.*

poison pen letter An anonymous letter written to expose, intimidate, threaten, or convey obscene suggestions to the recipient; a malicious letter, often containing false information.

poke *n.* **1** A wallet, pocket, or purse. 1939: "There I was with only about $85 in my poke. . . ." John O'Hara, *Pal Joey*, 50. 1958: "Poke—Pocketbook or wallet." G. Y. Wells, *Station House Slang. Underworld, carnival, pitchman, vagabond use.* → **2** A pocket. *Archaic & dial.* → **3** Money; the total amount in one's possession. *Rock and roll use since c1955.* **4** In baseball, a hit. **5** A cowboy. 1951: "Each poke pays his own transportation to the rodeo. . . ." Ithaca N.Y., *Journal*, Sept. 25, 11/2. *From "cowpoke."* → **6** A hired hand. **7** A slow-moving, slow-talking, or slow-thinking person. See **slowpoke**. **8** See **gunpoke**. *v.t.* **1** To herd, as cattle and sheep. **2** To attempt to influence; to attempt to create enthusiasm or promote action. **3** In baseball, to make a hit. 1908: "Sharky poked a bingle." R. L. Heath, *Atlantic Monthly*, Aug., 229/1. 1951: "Jackie Robinson poked a pitch out of the park. . . ." Herb Altschull, AP, Oct. 1. *Most common present use.* **4** To smoke. 1941: "To poke a butt." *Dictionary of Exeter Language*, 28. *Not common.*

poke a tip To give a free show or free gifts to attract a crowd. *Orig. pitchman use, later circus and carnival use.* See **poke, tip**.

poke fun [at] To tease; to chide.

poke-out *n.* **1** Food, esp. a package of food handed out to a tramp begging at back doors. 1894: "He returned with a 'poke-out.' . . ." J. Flynt. 1936: "'Poke-outs' are possible. . . ." H. F. Kane, *New Republic*, July 15, 289/1. *Vagabond and tramp use.* **2** An outdoor dinner cooked over wood or charcoal; a gathering for the purpose of preparing and eating such a meal; any long hike or camping trip which includes such meals. See **cookout**. *From association with "cowpoke" and his way of life, reinforced by "cookout," "smoke-out"; used by Boy Scouts, suburban residents, etc.*

poker face 1 A face lacking in expression. 2 A person who does not show emotion. *Used in poker, where one tries not to reveal his hand by his facial expression.* Cf. **dead pan.**

pokerino *n.* 1 A game of poker played for small stakes. See Appendix, —ino ending. 2 Any small, insignificant game, business deal, or person.

pokey poky poogie *n.* A jail. 1932: "The county pokey...." Damon Runyon. 1949: "J. M. Curley, Mayor of Boston, was sent away to pokey." CBS radio, Nov. 6. See **hokey-pokey.** 1951: "I think in another second I'd have slugged him, even though I knew damn well that would have pleased Kerrigan almost as much as proving a murder rap on me. Any excuse to toss me in the poky." R. S. Prather, *Bodies in Bedlam*, 47. 1958: "All the residents wanted to go to the pokey, claiming they were as guilty as ...." N.Y. *Daily News*, Feb. 20, 6. *adj.* Slow; small, crowded; like a jail or jail cell.

polack Polack [derog.] *n.* A native of Poland; a person of Polish descent. c1600: "He smote the sledded Polacks on the ice." Shakespeare, *Hamlet*, I, i, 63. 1958: "He gets onto cursing all of them ... the wops and the polacks and the niggers." H. E. F. Donohue, "Gentlemen's Game," *Harper's*, Mar., 64. *adj.* Polish.

pole *v.i., v.t.* 1 To study hard. 1851–1915: "College sl." *DAE.* 2 To hit a baseball very hard. 3 To take a consensus of opinion; to put to a vote. *n.* 1 [taboo] The penis. 2 In baseball, a bat. See **bean-pole, up-the-pole.**

police *v.t.* = **police up.**

police up To clean a place or thing; to make a place or thing neat and presentable. *Army use. One can police up a barracks = scrub the floor, make the beds, etc.; police up a parade ground = pick up cigarette butts and trash, etc.; police up one's shoes = shine one's shoes. Wide W.W.II Armed Forces use and carried over into post-war civilian use to a degree.*

polish *n.* 1 Poise, social grace. 2 Newness, freshness. **—er** See **apple polisher, bone polisher, harp polisher.**

polish apples To curry favor. See **apple polisher.**

polished up Drunk. *Not common.*

polish off 1 To finish eating or drinking something. 1916: "After I had polished off a platter of beans." Boston *Post*, quoted in *Lit. Digest*, Mar. 16. 2 To

finish a chore; to finish or get rid of something. 3 To get rid of a person; to kill; to render unconscious. 1949: "They ... polish him off by crowning him with a Coca-Cola bottle." *Life*, Oct. 24, 23.

politician *n.* 1 Any fast, persuasive, charming talker; one with a good spiel or line. → 2 A flatterer; one who courts superiors to win favored treatment. → 3 One who, for any reason, obtains favored treatment, easy jobs, more than his share of praise or rewards, and the like.

politico *n.* A power-hungry politician; an influential and unethical politician. *From the Ital. and Sp. c1940; was usu. used derog.; now becoming the standard abbr. for politician, losing derog. connotation.*

pollack Pollack *n.* = **polack.**
pollock Pollock *n.* = **polack.**
polluted *adj.* Drunk. *Common.*

polly *n.* 1 A woman who enjoys talking and gossiping; a shrew; any fat, old, unpleasant woman. 2 An echo that necessitates retaking a movie or a recording session. 1940: "Hollywood movie use." K. Malvery, *Woman's Home Companion. From "polyphony."*

pomp *n.* 1 Common abbr. for a pompadour. 2 A short haircut. *W.W.II use.* See **crew cut.**

pom-pom [taboo] *n.* Sexual intercourse. *W.W.II Army use in Philippines, Japan, and Pacific Islands.*

ponce *v.i., v.t.* [derog.] To solicit for a prostitute; to pimp. *n.* 1 A pimp; a man supported by a prostitute. → 2 A man who is supported by a woman; a man whose wife works.

pond *n.* 1 Most commonly, the Atlantic Ocean; the Pacific Ocean; any ocean. 1780: *DAE.* 2 See **big pond, herring pond.**

pong [derog.] *n.* A Chinese. *More common in Austral. than U.S.*

pony *n.* 1 A literal translation of a foreign language text, employed without the teacher's knowledge. *Used at least as early as 1827. Very common.* → 2 Any unethical aid, list of answers, etc., used by a student in a test. See **ride a pony.** → 3 Any physical or mental aid, such as a crutch, reference book, hearing aid, or list of telephone numbers. 4 A small glass for liquor or apertifs, often bell-shaped so that the contents can be more easily held, sniffed, and admired. 1949: "A 1 oz. glass." *Esquire's Handbook for Hosts*, 103. *Since c1850.* 5 A small glass of beer;

the glass itself. *Since c1885; colloq.*
6 A race horse. 1907 [1892]: "I had been out to the race-track watching the ponies run. . . ." Jack London, *My Life.*
7 A chorus girl, burlesque dancer, etc.; esp. a small, attractive chorus girl. 1920: "The ponies . . . slumped into place." F. Scott Fitzgerald, *This Side of Paradise*, 61. 1948: "Pony in a burlecue. . . ." F. Brown, *Dead Ringer*, 48. *Orig. theater use. From the prancing movements of such dancers.* *v.i., v.t.* **1** To use a literal translation of a foreign language text without the teacher's knowledge. 1858: "He [the freshman] does not pony, but learns . . . in the legitimate way." *Harvard Magazine*, May, 172. **2** To urge; to hurry. *c1900; college use.*

pony tail   A version of the horse tail style of hair dressing, but for shorter hair. *Very pop. with adolescent girls since c1952.*

pony up   To pay. 1907: ". . . He had ponied up a silver quarter. . . ." Jack London, *The Road*, 211. *Since c1820.*

poo = **hot poo.**   *interj.* A mild or jocular expression of incredulity, often used to show awareness that one is being teased. *Mainly teenage girl use. n.pl.* Feces. *Mainly child use.* See **poop.**

pooch   *n.* A dog. 1951: "A new greeting card shop . . . has a card for . . . your pooch when she presents you with a litter of pups. . . ." AP, N.Y., Oct. 17.   **—y** *n.* = **pooch.**   *adj.* Doggy; dog; doglike. 1953: "Your four-legged little poochy pal delivered it. . . ." Edgar Martin, *synd. comic strip*, "Boots," Mar. 16.

poodle cut   A style of women's hairdressing in which the hair is cut short all around and curled, thus somewhat resembling the coat of a French poodle. *Common high style c1950–c1952; replaced by the Italian cut.*

poodle-faker   *n.* **1** A self-important newly commissioned officer. *W.W.I use.* → **2** A ladies' man; a man who is subservient to women; a gigolo. *Literally one who emulates a lap dog. In Eng., a "male date."*

poogie = **pokey.**

poohed   poohed out   *adj.* Tired; exhausted. *Has been replaced by "bushed."*

poolroom   *n.* An illegal bookmaker's place of business, wherever it is. 1956: "Originally, the place where you played horses was called a poolroom. The term came from auction-pool betting at Brighton Beach and other American race tracks in the early Eighteen

Eighties." T. Betts, *Across the Board*, 97.

poon tang   poontang [taboo]   *n.* The vagina of a Negress or mulatto; a Negro or mulatto woman considered sexually; sexual intercourse with a Negress or mulatto; a Negro piece. 1929: "A fellow's got to have a little Poon Tang." T. Wolfe, *Look Homeward, Angel*, 343. 1947: "Poley looked out the window and saw a pretty Negro girl on the sidewalk. He rammed his elbow into Marquales' side. 'Eye that poon tang there,' he said." C. Willingham, *End as a Man*, 74. *Traditionally considered a Negro use, but fairly common also among Southern whites. Prob. from the Fr. "putain" = prostitute, by way of New Orleans Creoles.*

poo out   To fail; to make a poor showing; to disappoint.

poop   *n.* **1** Information, esp. from an official or authentic source; data; facts. 1952: "The girl's given us the complete poop." G. Cotler in *New Yorker*, Feb. 9, 92. *Wide W.W.II Armed Forces use.* **2** Excrement. *Child bathroom vocabulary.* **3** A disliked, insignificant, or stupid person. 1951: "Catering to a poop like Belfont revolts me." S. Lewis, *World So Wide*, 154. *Not as common in U.S. as in Eng. interj* = **poo.**

pooped   *adj.* Exhausted, fatigued, etc. 1942: "She's pooped." Chandler, *High Window*, 66. *Since c1930. Not now as common as "beat" or "bushed" among students and young adults.*

pooped out = **pooped; bushed.** 1939: ". . . Dragging along as if they were starting to get pooped out." J. T. Farrell, 186. *Archaic and child use.*

poo-poo   *n.* Feces. *Part of the bathroom baby-talk of very young children. v.i.* To defecate. See Appendix, Reduplications.

poop out   To fail, depart, withdraw, etc., esp. as a result of fatigue or cowardice. *Since c1925; somewhat archaic.* See **pooped.**

poop sheet   **1** Any official written announcement, schedule, compilation of data, or the like. *Orig. Army and student use since c1935.* → **2** Any data sheet; a set of written detailed instructions.

poor-boy   *n.* A very large sandwich, made of a small loaf of bread or long roll cut lengthwise and filled with hot or cold meat, cheese, vegetables, and potatoes in separate sections. *The more elaborate poor-boys actually contain all the courses of a full meal, with an appetizer, such as fish, at one end and a dessert of fruit at the* *other. Orig. and still most common in New Orleans, but universally known since c1920.* Cf. **dagwood, Hero, torpedo.**

poor fish Practically anybody at all; the individual person considered under the aspect of his specif. human characteristics, foibles, problems, and the like. 1920: "I let people impose on me here and don't get anything out of it. . . . I keep my temper when they get selfish and *then* they think they pay me back by voting for me. . . . I'm tired of being nice to every poor fish in school." F. S. Fitzgerald, *This Side of Paradise*, 37f.

poor John **poor john** An average man whose fortunes are notably less than he deserves. See **John.**

poor man's [something or someone], (the or **a)** A less famous, less expensive, smaller, or less satisfactory version of something or someone. *The term does not necessarily imply inferiority, though it often does.* 1924: "Another nickname for the town [St. Petersburg, Fla.] is the Poor Man's Palm Beach." R. Lardner in *The American Twenties*, 40f. 1958: "Burton, 'Poor Man's Olivier,' To Portray Heathcliff on TV [headline]. Like Sir Laurence, Burton has successfully portrayed such characters as Hamlet, Henry V, and Toby Belch. On Friday, May 9, he reaches another Olivier plateau when he plays the fierce but romantic Heathcliff in the Dupont 'Show of the Month' version of 'Wuthering Heights' on CBS-TV." *The Morning Telegraph*, Apr. 30, 4.

pop *n.* **1** Father. From "poppa" or "papa." *Colloq. since c1830.* 1943: *familiar use. Web.* **2** A pistol. **3** A piece of popular music. **4** A concert of popular music, esp. a concert played by a fairly large orchestra featuring a mixture of "Tin Pan Alley" songs and light classics. **5** The common written and spoken abbr. for a popsicle, any ice or ice cream frozen on a stick and sold by street vendors or refreshment stands. *v.t.* **1** To pawn or hock. *Not common in the U.S.* **2** To treat or stand treat for food, drink, or the like. *Not common. adj.* **1** The common abbr. for "popular." → **2** Specif., "popular" as used in music to signify commercially mass-produced sentimental songs as opposed to jazz on one hand and classical music on the other. *Thus there are pop singers, pop records, etc.* **—per** *n.* **1** A revolver. *Negro use.* **2** In baseball, a hit between infield and outfield. *Not common.* **—s** *n.* Popular music. Cf. **pop. Pops**

pops *n.* **1** A nickname or term of direct address, applied to any elderly man. *The familiarity of the term is often intended as a compliment, implying that the named person is up to date enough not to object to the jocose term. Much student and teenage use.* **2** A term of direct address to a male of any age. *May be used either complimentarily to one who is hip or condescendingly to one who is square. Jazz, jive, and some cool use. Now becoming somewhat archaic.*

pop bottle An inferior camera or enlarger lens. *Photographer use. The term implies that the instrument in question has been made with glass of a quality only good enough to be made into a cheap bottle.*

pop [one's] cakes = **toss [one's] cookies.** *Not common.*

pop car A small motor-driven railroad car used by section men. *c1934; Western railroad use.*

pop [one's] cork = **blow [one's] top.** 1950: "I didn't expect her to pop her cork either." Dennis Day, radio, Oct. 28.

Pope's nose, the The derrière of a cooked chicken. *Jocular use.*

Popeye *n.* Spinach. *From "Popeye, the Sailor," a comic-strip character who derives his invincible strength from eating spinach. Not common.*

pop off **1** To die. **2** To kill. 1929: ". . . These gangsters pop each other off." Dunning and Abbott, *Broadway*, III. **3** To criticize, complain, brag, rant, or state one's opinions loudly and emotionally; to talk or write volubly. 1951: "I popped off to Brane last night, but I didn't kill him." R. S. Prather, *Bodies in Bedlam*, 47. 1952: "I'm not popping off about the pennant until we get it." Baseball manager Casey Stengel, quoted by AP, Sept. 26. *Since c1930.* **4** To leave or depart. *A little jocular use. The term is considered affected in the U.S.* **pop-off** *n.* **1** An act or instance of popping off. 1944: ". . . In his poppings-off to [the reporters]. . . ." Fowler, *Good Night*, 153. 1950: "Senator McCarthy made a radio speech at Wheeling, W. Va., and it was a typical senatorial pop-off with more wild swings than punches . . . hundreds of other senatorial pop-offs." Ithaca (N.Y.) *Journal*, July 21, 6/1. **2** One who pops off or complains loudly with or without cause, esp. one who does so habitually.

poppa *n.* **1** One's father. *Colloq.* **2** Any elderly man. **3** = **daddy; sugar daddy; sweet papa.**

poppycock   *n.* Nonsense. *c1850.* 1913: "Slang . . . knows how . . . to work the poppycock racket on any daffy squirt or dotty chucklehead or dippy mushhead, on any crazy kioodle or concatenated chump." F. K. Sechrist.

pop quiz   pop test   An unexpected examination.

popskull   *n.* Powerful and inferior liquor, usu. home-made. *Southern mountain and Western plains use.*

pop to   To come to the military position of attention, esp. with great abruptness. 1947: " 'Pop to!' roared Koble. 'Grind those necks back, you Misters [students at a military school]. Come on, Mr. Simmons, stand up hard.' " C. Willingham, *End as a Man*, 15.

pop-up   *n.* In baseball, a slowly hit ball caught by the catcher or an infielder.

porcelain   See **win the porcelain hairnet.**

porcupine   *n.* A frayed wire rope or cable. *W.W.II USN use.*

pork and   An order of pork and beans. *Common lunch-counter use.*

pork-chopper   *n.* A political appointee, union official, or relative or friend of a politician, union officer, or the like, who receives payment for little or no work; one who is put on a payroll as a favor or in return for past services. 1956: "*Pork-chopper*—A union payroller, originally a union official who is in the labor movement, not because of any ideological belief, but for what he can get out of it for himself." *Labor's Special Lang. from Many Sources.*

porker   [derog.]   *n.* A Jew; esp., an orthodox Jew. *From the Jewish abstention from eating pork products.*

porkey   porky   *adj.* **1** Very bad; very poor. **2** Angry.

Port Arthur tuxedo   Khaki pants and shirt; work clothes.

port-side   portside   *adj.* Left-handed. *From the nautical term.*   **—r** *n.* **1** A left-handed baseball pitcher. **2** A left-handed person. 1945: "We despair that portsiders will ever get their rights. . . ." Editorial, Phila. *Record*, Oct. 28, 8/2.

posh   *adj.* Smart; chic; expressive of good, or at least expensive, taste. 1951: "The apartment has recently been redecorated and is now rather posh. . . ." A. Logan in *New Yorker*, Sept. 1, 44. 1952: Said to derive from the initial letters of 'port *out*, *s*tarboard *h*ome,' referring to the preferred location of a

stateroom on a ship going *out* to India and again on a ship coming *home* to England. *Oral*, G.H.R. *Perh. a mnemonic device for travelers' use.*

possie   possey   pozzie   pozzey *n.* Jelly, jam, marmalade. *W.W.I use. Not common in U.S., though very popular in Eng.*

possum belly   An extra storage compartment under a railroad car. *Hobo lingo.*

posted   *adj.* Well informed. *c1840; now colloq.*

post-Elvis   *n.* A type of men's haircut. 1957: "A barber on Governor's Island says that there is no official short Army cut these days. Barbers at military camps are being urged—as an easy transitional haircut—to push what they call a post-Elvis, which has normal sideburns and is somewhat less sinister than an Elvis." H. Mitgang, *About— Men's Haircuts. The reference is to rock and roll singer Elvis Presley, whose long hair was imitated by many adolescent boys.*

post-hole = **load of post-holes.**

pot   *n.* **1** A derby hat. *c1900–c1930; from its shape; obs.* **2** A man. *Never common. From Cockney rhyming sl. "pot and pan"* = *man. See Appendix, Rhyming Slang.* **3** A disliked, self-righteous, self-important person of either sex, but esp. a woman of middle age or over. 1937: "One of the pots that sat at the table on the platform was writing away with a pencil, her head bent down." Weidman, *Wholesale*, 13. 1951: "Whatever the old pot may be, I'm sure he knows how to make it pay." S. Lewis, *World So Wide*, 152. *Since c1930. Although this usage may derive from first two meanings, "pot" more often refers to a woman than a man, thus according with classical psychoanalytic symbol analysis, esp. of the mother image. When used to* = *a man, may be reinforced by "pot-belly."* → **4** An unappealing, unkempt girl. *Common student use since c1935.* **5** A drunkard, esp. a down-and-out drunkard. *Although word usu. means an unkempt tramp, it has some sophisticated use to mean a successful man who is also a heavy drinker. Cf.* **rumpot.** **6** Cheap, inferior, or home-made whisky; *lit.*, whisky that has been made in a pot instead of in a regular distillery. **7** Marijuana, esp. a marijuana cigarette. 1955: "He must be cutting off her supply of heroin and pot." E. Trujillo, *I Love You, I Hate You*, 111. 1956: "Those dope stories—all about how you go around killing old ladies when you smoke a pot." S. Longstreet, *The Real Jazz Old and New*, 146. *Common addict use.* **8** The total amount of money bet at any stage in a hand of poker, i.e., the stakes that will be won by the winner of the hand; the stakes in any gambling game. 1956: "In poker the goulashes' takeout was 5 percent of the pot." T. Betts, *Across the Board*, 121. *Colloq.* **9** A carburetor. *Orig. and mainly sports-car driver and hot rod use.* **10** A small engine. *Miner, logger, and construction worker use since c1930.* **11** A locomotive. *Railroad use since c1930.* **12** An automobile engine. *Wide hot-rod use since c1950.* **13** = **pot-belly. 14** An acetylene welding torch; a blowtorch. *Not common.* **15** An electrical transformer. *Not common. All meanings but the first have come into pop. use since c1930.* *v.t.* **1** To strike someone with the fist. → **2** To hit a baseball or golf ball.

—pot   See Appendix, Suffixes and Suffix Words.

potato   *n.* **1** The head. 1941: "They just stick their potato in every office and say, 'Anything for me today?' " A. J. Liebling in *New Yorker*, Apr. 26, 25/1. 1950: "The deceased falls and bumps his potato on a desk." Starnes, *Another Mug*, 18. → **2** The face, esp. an unattractive face. **3** An unattractive or ugly woman. *Not common.* **4** A dollar. 1934: "... A few potatoes to take care of the old overhead." Runyon, 345. 1948: "You can get this wonderful coat for 497 potatoes." *Time*, quoted in *Word Study*, May, 3/2. **5** A ball, esp. a baseball.

potato grabblers   The hands. *c1850.*

potato-head   *n.* A stupid person. 1952: "I love you, you potato-head!" Movie, *Monkey Business.*

potato masher   A type of German hand grenade. *From its shape. W.W.I use.*

potato-trap   *n.* The mouth. *Boxing sl.*

pot-belly   *n.* **1** A large, protruding abdomen. **2** A man or, infreq., a woman with a large, protruding abdomen; a fat man.

pot boiler   A book, play, article, or the like written merely to earn money, i.e., to keep the author's pot boiling; any work of mediocre quality done by an artist or craftsman who is capable of a better performance.

potch   *n.* A light blow with the open hand, a slap; a spanking. *Used only in speaking to small children.*   *v.t.* To slap or spank a child lightly.

pothooks   *n.pl.* Spurs. *Cowboy use.*

pot liquor   The residue of solids and fluids left in the bottom of a pot after food, esp. greens and ham, have been cooked in it. 1951: "He always smelled slightly of turnip greens, as Miss Amelia rubbed him ... with pot liquor to give him strength." C. McCullers, *The Ballad of the Sad Café*, 22. *Stand. Southern use.*

pot luck   A meal composed of odds and ends or leftovers. *Fig., a meal composed of whatever one is lucky enough to find "in the pot."*

pot-massager   *n.* One who washes pots and pans. *Not common.*

pot out   To fail; said of an engine in a hot-rod car. *Teenage and hot rod use since c1950.* See **pot.**

potsky   *v.i.* To idle, loaf, or putter; to mess around. 1950: "I can't understand how you could potsky around with such stuperstitions [*sic*]." Billy Rose, *synd. newsp. col.*, June 16. *From the Yiddish sl. "potske."*

pot-slinger   *n.* A cook.

pots on, have [one's]   To be potted = drunk. 1934: "... When the King has his pots on ... she ... drives ... the King's horse." Runyon.

potsy   potssy   potsie   *n.* **1** A badge or shield of office, usu. a policeman's. 1943: "Potsies, they called them." Wolfert, *Underworld*, 262. 1952: "This boniface has been wearing his potsy as house dick for only a brief time." R. Smith in N.Y. *Her. Trib.*, Jan 24, 27/1. 1958: "... Potsy. Policeman's term for his shield." G. Y. Wells, *Station House Slang.* → **2** A policeman. c1955: "Potsy," title of a comic strip about a policeman. *Neither of the above two uses are common. May be from the common Irish name "Pat" pronounced with a long Irish "a."* **3** A variation of the children's game of hop scotch: a hopping game played with bean bags and squares marked upon the ground or pavement.

potted   *adj.* **1** Drunk. 1924: "I'd 'a been potted about half the time. ..." "I don't get potted regularly. ..." Marks, *Plastic Age*, 149, 202. *Fairly common. Orig. flapper use.* See Appendix, Drunk. **2** Under the influence of narcotics, esp. marijuana. See **pot.**

potted up = **potted.** 1955: "She was all potted up on something, drink or otherwise." E. Trujillo, *I Love You, I Hate You*, 138.

pottrie   *n.* A type of playing marble, usu. white and opaque, resembling china in appearance. *Prob. from "pottery."*

potty   *n.* **1** A small potlike urinal used to toilet-train children; a toilet. *Baby talk.* **2** Any toilet. *Part of the bathroom vocabulary of small children.* **3** In poker, the pot. See Appendix, —y endings.   *adj.* Slightly crazy; eccentric.

pot-walloper   *n.* **1** One who washes pots. **2** A lumber-camp cook.

pot-wrestler   *n.* **1** A female kitchen servant or worker. *c1815.* **2** A chef. 1947: "No less a pot-wrassler than the King's Own glorified the chick-wagon croquette...." Arthur Baer, *synd. newsp. col.*, Mar. 18.

pound   *n.* Five dollars, esp. when offered to a policeman for a favor or as a bribe. *c1915. Taxi-driver use.*   *v.t.* To walk on a sidewalk or a pavement, esp. on one's beat, as a policeman making his rounds. 1918: "We [policemen] pound the pavement all day and all night...." *Outlook*, Sept., 127/2. 1941: "... Pounding the sidewalks begging for a job...." Schulberg, *Sammy*, 157.   **—er**   *n.* A policeman; lit., one who pounds a beat.

pound brass   To transmit radio messages on a hand key. *Ham radio and Army Signal Corps use.*

pound [one's] ear   To sleep. 1907 [1894]: "'Kip,' 'doss,' 'flop,' 'pound your ear,' all mean ... to sleep." Jack London, *My Life. Orig. hobo argot.* 1927: "Originated with railroaders sleeping in a caboose on a fast-moving train actually pounding their ears." C. Samolar. 1946: "... While I was pounding my ear...." Evans, *Halo in Blood*, 55. See **brass-pounder, hair-pounder.**

pound salt = **pound salt up [one's] ass.** *This euphem. much more common than the full term.*

pound salt up [one's] ass [taboo]   **1** A strong term of rebuke. "*Go pound salt up your ass*" = "*shut up*" or "*stick it up your ass.*" **2** An expression of anger at, contempt for, or rejection of a person. See **stick it (something) up your ass** [taboo].

pound the books   To study intensely. *Some student use since c1935.*

pound the pavement   To walk the streets in search of a job, in order to beg from passers-by, or as a policeman walking his beat; fig., to seek employment.

pour it on   **1** To concentrate or augment one's effort; esp. to intensify one's effort in order to take advantage of an opponent's mistake. **2** To drive an automobile very fast. 1946: "The driver was pouring it on to close the gap between him and the car he was following." Evans, *Halo in Blood*, 2.

pour on the coal   To drive or fly rapidly; to accelerate the speed of a car or plane; to step on the gas. 1950: "The pilot apparently decided to go around [the field] again and poured on the coal." AP, May 18.

pout-out   Engine failure in a hot rod. *Hot rod and some general teenage use since c1955.*

P.O.W.   A prisoner of war. *Wide W.W.II use. An abbr. that is both written and spoken.*   **pow**   *n.* A prisoner of war. 1953: "This Allied-held Chinese pow." AP, Sept. 16. *W.W.II and Korean War use. Written but seldom spoken. From "P.O.W."*

powder   *n.* **1** A drink of liquor. 1921: "I step around to his oasis and knock over a powder with him...." Witwer, *Leather*, 82. **2** A getaway, as from a robbery. 1949: "Bonnie murdered a constable during the powder." A. Hynd, *Public Enemies*, 67. From **run-out powder.** Cf. **take a powder.** See **foolish powder.**   *v.i.* To leave; to go away. Also, to run away; to flee.   *v.t.* To bat a baseball hard. 1951: "... After he had powdered the second pitch thrown by ... Branca...." AP, Oct. 4.

powder, take a   To depart; to run away; to leave without paying one's bill. *From the earlier "take a run-out powder."* 1939–40: "And take a powder out of here that day...." O'Hara, *Pal Joey*, 24.

powder-bag   *n.* A gunner's mate. *W.W.II USN use.*

powder monkey   One who works with blasting powder. *Miner, logger, and construction worker use.*

powder-puff   *n.* A cautious, shifty boxer, as opposed to a heavy hitter. *v.t.* To hit lightly.

powder [one's] puff   To go to the bathroom; to urinate. *Orig. jocular use. In ref. to traditional female excuse when withdrawing to the ladies' room, i.e., to apply make-up.*

power   *n.* An explosive.

power-house   *n.* **1** A strong, successful sports team, esp. a football team. 1952: "Georgia Tech, another powerhouse, warms up against Florida...." Ed Corrigan, AP, Sept. 26. → **2** A strong athlete, esp. a football player. → **3** Any strong, well-built male. → **4** Any group of people or objects that portend success in a game, sports, business, entertainment, etc. *The term can be applied to a hand of cards, the executives of an organization, a line of merchandise, etc.*

pow-wow   *n.* **1** A person in authority; an important person. *Some use c1910– c1925; obs.* **2** A conference; a discussion or debate. *Supposedly from an Amer. Indian word = conjurer, medicineman. Colloq.*

P.R.   Public relations. *A common written and spoken abbr. Since c1940.* See Appendix, Shortened Words.

prad   *n.* A horse. *Obs.*

prairie   *n.* **1** A poorly kept golf course. *Golfer use.* **2** A vacant lot. *Midwestern urban use. Dial.*

prang   *v.t.* **1** To crash or damage a military airplane. → **2** To bomb a target; to destroy a target by bombing from the air.   *v.i.* To crash; to be shot down by antiaircraft fire; to be involved in an airplane accident.   *n.* **1** A crash landing of a military plane. **2** A very successful bombing mission. *Some W.W.II Air Force use. From the Eng. Royal Air Force use.*

prat   **pratt**   *n.* The human posterior. 1923: "Pratt." Hecht & MacArthur, *Front Page*, III. 1946: "He does not fall on his prat." *Time*, Mar. 11, 63/1. *Very old.*   *v.t.* To move behind someone in order to observe him without being seen or to get into a position to rob him. *Underworld use.*

prat fall   **pratfall**   A fall on the backside or rump; said of a person. *Often used esp. of falls taken by clowns in comedy routines. Wide theater use.* 1939: "A perfect pratfall. . . ." Edmund Wilson, *New Republic*, Apr. 26, 332. → **2** A defeat, a pitfall. 1950: ". . . On the principles and pratfalls of the rhyming racket. . . ." Billy Rose, *synd. newsp. col.*, Jan. 9.

prat kick   A hip pocket in a pair of trousers. *Mainly underworld use.* See **kick.**

prayer   *n.* A chance. *Always used with a negative, as in* **hasn't got a prayer.** 1951: "High school boys, unless extremely bright, 'haven't a prayer' of entering West Point without some special assistance. . . ." E. O'Neill and H. Lee, N.Y. *Daily News*, Aug. 9, C3/5.

prayer bones   The knees. *Not common.*

preem   *n.* A first showing of a movie, play, television performance, or the like. 1948: "The mother-daughter act has

been bought by ABC [television network] and set for an Oct. 4 preem." *Variety*, Aug. 25, 1/2. *Common theater use. Written and spoken abbr. for "première."*   *v.i., v.t.* To appear on the stage or on television for the first time; to make a première performance. 1952: "A new hour-long radio show which preems via ABC [network] Sunday, Aug. 17." K. Gardella in N.Y. *Daily News*, Aug. 5, C23/5.   **—ie   preemy**   *n.* A prematurely born baby. 1949: ". . . Saving 75 per cent of the 'preemies' born. The dread eye diseases said to afflict 'preemies' are unfounded. . . . Dr. Hess and his aides keep in close touch with their 'preemies' until they are 16. . . ." N.Y. *Times*, Sept. 25, 48/1,2. *Orig. hospital argot; now widely known.*

pregnant duck = **ruptured duck.**

prelim   *n.* **1** Any written examination, usu. lasting one class period, given during the progress of a college course, as opposed to the final examination at the end of the course. *Common student use. Usu. stressed on the first syllable.* **2** A minor professional boxing bout preceding the main fight. Usu. stressed on the second syllable. *Both abbr. for "preliminary" are written and spoken.*

pre-med   *n.* **1** A premedical student. **2** A premedical course of study. *Common written and spoken abbr.* See Appendix, Shortened Words.

prep   *n.* **1** A preparatory school student; one who is preparing to enter college. *c1880.* **2** In a prep school, a member of the first, or junior, class of students. **3** In college, an undignified upperclass student. **4** A school sports team practice. *All meanings colloq.*   *v.i., v.t.* **1** To prepare for a specific goal or task; to prepare someone or something for a specif. purpose. 1936: "After [movies] have been 'preppin prod' [preparing production] for some time. . . ." A. Green in *Esquire*, Sept. 1949: "A pitcher who has prepped earnestly for many years in the minors." A. Daley in N.Y. *Times*, Sept. 4, 28. *Not common.* **2** To attend a prep school. *Wide student use.* 1920: "Where'd you prep?" Fitzgerald, *This Side of Paradise*, 43. *Colloq.* → **3** In college, to behave like a preparatory school student; to be boisterous. *adj.* Poor; mean. *In all forms, n., v., adj., "prep" is the common abbr. for "prepare," "preparation."*

prep school   **prep-school**   *n.* A preparatory school; usu. a private school on the secondary level which prepares students for college. 1925: "As if they were choosing a prep school for me. . . ." F. S. Fitzgerald, *The Great Gatsby*, 11. *Common student use.* *adj.* Characteristic of or connected with a preparatory school. 1905: *DAE.* 1912: "Prep school reputations." Johnson, *Stover at Yale*, 45. 1924: "A prep-school man." Marks, *Plastic Age*, 9. *Usu. connotes social status, manners, wealth, etc. Sometimes also connotes snobbery since some prep schools are exceedingly expensive and aim expressly to prepare their students for admission to the oldest Eastern universities.*

pres   **Pres** = **prez.**   1956:". . . We should give the President [Eisenhower, after his election to a second term in office] our full support. . . . Let's give three rousing cheers for the Pres!" Al Smith, "Mutt & Jeff," *synd. comic strip*, Nov. 7.

preserved   *adj.* Drunk.

presquawk   *v.t.* To inspect [a piece of work] before an official inspection. *W.W.II airplane factory use.*

press roll   In drumming, a roll that rapidly intensifies in volume. 1956: "A *press roll* is played on snare drums." S. Longstreet, *The Real Jazz Old and New*, 148.

press the bricks   1 To loaf in town; to stand loafing in the street. *Lumberjack use.* → 2 To walk a police beat. 1929: [gangster to policeman] "Go press the bricks." Burnett, *Little Caesar*, 111. Cf. **pound the pavement.**

press the flesh   To shake hands. *Said as one offers to shake hands.* 1948: Movie, *Look for the Silver Lining. Rhyming jive talk.*

pretty   *adj. & adv.* 1 Slightly; considerably; quiet; "little." *As an example of the clichéd, contradictory, and pop. use of "pretty" and "little," James Thurber's humorous ". . . It [a building] was a little big and pretty ugly" will serve as a classic.* 2 = **sitting pretty.**

pretty-boy   *n.* 1 An effeminate, light-complexioned man; a dandy. *Colloq.* 2 A bouncer; a professional strong man. *c1931; circus use. An example of a sl. word taking on a humorous meaning the opposite of the orig. meaning.*

pretty ear   An ear deformed from being hit repeatedly; a cauliflower ear. 1930: ". . . Busted bones and pretty ear." Burnett, *Iron Man*, 9.

pretzel   *n.* 1 A French horn. 2 A German or one of German descent.

pretzel-bender   *n.* 1 A peculiar person; an eccentric; one who thinks in a round-about manner. 2 A player of the French horn. *Musician use. Not common.* 3 A wrestler. 4 A heavy drinker; one who frequents bars.

prex   **Prex**   *n.* = **prexy.** *Some student use c1900; obs. A pseudo-Latin word.* **—y**   **prexie**   *n.* 1 The president of a college, university, or prep school. 1871: "Prexy." *DAE.* 1905: "Prexie." *DAE.* 1909: "The avenue is still, for Prexy is delivering his annual address in the Armory." Von Engeln, *At Cornell*, 58. 1951: ". . . One of whom is now a Morgan partner, another Ohio University's prexy." D. H. Beetle, *GNS*, Sept. 19. *Student use. "Prexie" now seldom used.* 2 The president of a business organization or any other organization. 1948: "Madison Sq. Garden "prexy" Gen. John Reed Kilpatrick." *Variety*, Aug. 25, 1/4. *Both uses almost never cap.* See Appendix, —ie endings.

prez   **Prez**   *n.* 1 A president. 1936: "Mr. Roosevelt . . . is the Prez to *Variety*. So is Harry Cohn, prez of Columbia Picts." A. Green in *Esquire*, Sept. *Not common. A written and spoken abbr.* 2 A nickname for a person who is outstanding in his profession. *Lester Young, renowned jazz saxophonist, was called "Prez" by his admirers.*

prick   *n.* 1 [taboo] The penis. *Very old. Usu. without sexual connotation.* 2 A smug, foolish person; a knave, blackguard; a heel, a rat.

prig   *v.t.* To steal. *n.* A thief. *Underworld use; obs.*

primed   *adj.* Drunk. *c1920; more common in Eng. than in U.S.*

prince   *n.* An agreeable, generous, or noble person of either sex. 1951: "He's crazy about you. He told me he thinks you're a goddam prince." J. D. Salinger, *Catcher in the Rye*, 23.

print   *v.t.* To fingerprint a person, as by the police. 1939: "They printed me." Gardner, *D. A. Draws*, 205. **—s** *n.pl.* A set of fingerprints. 1939: "My prints ain't on that gun. . . ." Gardner, *D. A. Draws*, 170. *Orig. underworld use.*

private eye   1 A private detective. 1949: "In turning the cabbies into 'private eyes' for the police Mr. Keenan said . . . that passengers would not be spied upon. . . ." N.Y. *Times*, July 24, 1/2. 2 A private surveyor. *Surveyor use only.*

privates   *n.pl.* 1 Private homes; residences, esp. in more expensive neighborhoods. *c1880.* 1936: ". . . Beggars who

...like dogs get along better at the 'privates.' " H. F. Kane, *New Republic*, July 15, 289/1. **2** The genitalia. 1940: "He's so fat he hasn't seen his privates for twenty years." C. McCullers, *The Ballad of the Sad Café*, 297.

pro *n.* **1** Probation. *A common written and spoken abbr.* **2** A person who is on probation, from prison, school, or on a job. **3** A Prohibitionist; one who favors the outlawing of the manufacture and sale of alcoholic beverages. *Not common. This abbr. is written but seldom spoken, prob. because it leads to confusion: a "Pro" is against alcoholic beverages, not "pro" = for.* **4** A professional in any field of endeavor, esp. a professional athlete, entertainer, or writer; one who is paid for his work or skill, as opposed to an amateur who performs merely for his pleasure. 1949: "[An amateur baseball player] is ready to turn pro in earnest. ..." D. Parker, N.Y. *Mirror*, Sept. 11, 12/1. 1952: "The greatest thing that can happen to a song writer is to hear his song played and sung by pros." C. Lowry, AP, Feb. 22. *A written and spoken abbr. Very common.* **5** One who is proficient, experienced, or wise; one who possesses courage, confidence. **6** A prostitute. 1941: "He treats all women like pros and all men like enemies." Schulberg, *Sammy*, 234. *This is not an abbr. for "prostitute," but another abbr. for "professional." The cynical implication is that all women can be seduced, the only difference being that prostitutes are professionals.* *prep.* For; in favor of. *From Latin; a stand. usage.* *adj.* **1** Professional; of the nature of a paid worker or player, as opposed to an unpaid one. 1951: "The pro season [in football]." AP, Dec. 2. **2** Proficient. *Both meanings written and spoken abbr. of "professional."* See Appendix, Shortened Words.

prof *n.* **1** A college or university professor. 1914: "I met a prof. there." S. Lewis, *Our Mr. Wrenn*, 149. **2** A teacher or master of any school. *A written and spoken abbr. for "professor."*

—essor *n.* **1** Anyone who wears eyeglasses. **2** An orchestra leader. *Often used jocularly.* **3** The piano player in a bar, brothel, or silent movie house; any piano player. 1950: "I pulled myself together and started playing with the confidence of being in my own circle. 'That boy is marvelous'—this was the remarks of the inmates. They wanted to give me the job of regular professor."

A. Lomax, *Mr. Jelly Roll*, 21. **4** A professional gambler. **5** Any studious person; a book-lover.

prog *n.* Food. *c1840; underworld use. Still used dial.*

progressive *n., adj.* Jazz music based on chord progressions, rather than on a melody. The basis of cool and far out jazz music.

prohi *n.* A Prohibition enforcement officer. 1931: ". . . Cops, prohis, and the boys downtown." J. Sayre, *Hex*, 416. *Obs. A written and spoken abbr. for "prohibition agent."* See Appendix, Shortened Words.

prom *n.* A formal dance or dancing party, usu. one given annually by a college or univ. class or social organization; a ball traditionally held by each class in a college toward the end of the school year. 1894, 1924: *DAE*. 1924: "There was the excitement of the Prom." "He attended neither the fraternity dance nor the Prom." Marks, *Plastic Age*, 135, 136. *Abbr. of "promenade." Now virtually stand.*

promote *v.t.* **1** To steal; to obtain something by cheating or chicanery. *c1915–25; underworld and vagabond use; now common sl.* → **2** To talk [someone] into making a gift or loan. 1934: "If I hadn't . . . begun promoting him for something to drink. . . ." Cain, *Postman*, 58. → **3** To beg something [as food]; to wangle. 1944: ". . . Food which you can promote from a back door and carry off. . . ." Otis Ferguson.

prom-trotter *n.* **1** A very popular girl; esp. a female student who attends many formal dances. 1920: "Phyllis Styles, an intercollegiate prom-trotter. . . ." Fitzgerald, *This Side of Paradise*, 137. *Student use.* → **2** A male student who is very active in college social life; one who goes to all the dances and parties. → **3** A ladies' man.

pronto *adv.* Quickly. *Colloq. From the Sp.*

prop *n.* **1** A property; any article used by an actor in a play or an act, as a pistol, a book, a glass. 1909: ". . . Scenery and props. . . ." G. Chester, *Bobby Burnit*, 219. *Theater use since 1880.* → **2** The stage crew, property man, and circus tent crew foreman. See **props.** **3** An airplane propeller. *Used since W.W.I.* **4** A fist. *adj.* False; staged. *From "property."* **—er** *adj.* Regular; first-rate. **—s** *n.* **1** A man in charge of stage props. *Theater use since 1900.* **2** The human legs. **3** Falsies;

padding worn under a brassière to give a woman the appearance of having large or shapely breasts.

pro-pack   *n.* A small kit or envelope containing a sheath, strong soap, and an astringent, for use as a protection against venereal disease. *Wide W.W.II Armed Forces use. Abbr. for "prophylactic package."*

prophylactic   *n.* A thin rubber sheath worn over the penis during sexual intercourse, usually as a contraceptive device, but legally available only "for prevention of [venereal] disease." *Not as common as "rubber."*

proposition   *v.t.* To approach a person with an offer of employment or to suggest a mutually profitable plan of action, esp. an illegal or unethical job, plan, or action; specif., to ask for sexual favors from a girl or woman, usu. in return for money or other favors to be given her.

prossie   prossy   *n.* A prostitute.

protection   *n.* Bribe money paid to the police, an individual policeman, or politicians, for allowing illegal activities to continue without interference; any money paid to protect the payer without arrest.

protection money = **protection.**

prowl   *v.t.* To frisk a person; to run one's hands over another's clothing, usu. in search of a gun. 1940: "[He] prowled me over carefully with his left hand." Chandler, *Farewell*, 10.

prune   *n.* **1** A slow-witted person; a simpleton; one easily duped. **2** A prudish, scholarly person. → **3** An eccentric; a dreamer. **4** A man; a guy. 1950: "Lt. Spencer Moon .⸫. a very tough prune. ..." Starnes, *Another Mug*. 118. **5** An error; a mistake. *Not common. All meanings used since c1900.* See **full of beans.** **—d**   *adj.* Drunk.

pruneface   *n.* A homely or sad-looking person. *Used specif. as a nickname.* 1953: "Pruneface wants ya [on the phone]. ..." Dick Brooks, *synd. comic strip*, "Jackson Twins," June 2. *Popularized by a pock-marked wrinkle-faced villain in the comic strip "Dick Tracy."*

prune-picker   *n.* A Californian. *c1915. USN and tramp use.*

pruno   *n.* Fermented prune juice; any fermented fruit juice. See Appendix, **—o endings.**

prushun   prushon   *n.* **1** A boy tramp who begs for a mature tramp. *Obscurely from "Prussian."* 1893: "I once

knew a kid, or prushun, who averaged ... $3 a day. ..." J. Flynt, 5. **2** A young homosexual who lives with tramps.

prut   *n.* Dirt, as the sweepings from a floor, deck, or the like.   *exclam.* An expression of contempt, disbelief, etc. See **crut.**

p's and q's   Fig., one's own business, field of endeavor, or interest. Used either in "Mind your (own) p's and q's" = mind your own business, or in "He knows his p's and q's" = he knows his business well, he is skilled in his job. 1958: ". . . What the hell are you staring at, madam, you mind your p's and q's." H. E. F. Donohue, "Gentlemen's Game," *Harper's*, March, 65.

psych   psyche   *n.* **1** Psychology. → **2** A course in the study of psychology. *Student use since c1900; the form "psyche" is archaic. A written and spoken abbr. v.t.* **1** To psychoanalyze a person; to give a person a psychological examination. *Since c1920; never common.* → **2** To discuss the motives of another's words or actions, usu. critically. See Appendix, Shortened Words.

psycho   *n.* **1** A psychopath. *A written and spoken abbr. Seldom used in the correct psychological sense.* → **2** Any psychotic or neurotic. *The most common use.* → **3** An eccentric; a nut. 1942: "He's a psycho case." Chandler, *High Window*, 139. 1951: "I don't want everybody calling us psycho again." AP, Dec.12. 1953: "[She] had been described as a 'psycho' in a police alarm after she handed her husband a gun." AP, June 3.   *adj.* Psychopathic; unbalanced; used to describe anything from mild eccentricity to violent derangement.   **—kick**   *n.* A deeply satisfying erotic response. 1956: "A *psychokick* is an erotic excitement. ..." S. Longstreet, *The Real Jazz Old and New*, 150. See **kick.**

ptomain domain   *n.* An Army mess hall. *Some reported W.W.II Army use. Prob. synthetic.* See Appendix, Rhyming Slang.

P.U.   p.u.   **1** Phew, said on smelling a bad smell, as something rotting. *Colloq. An exaggerated pronunciation of "phew."* **2** "It stinks."

pub   *n.* **1** A saloon. 1952: ". . . After a round of Long Island pubs. ..." N.Y. *Daily News*, Aug. 13, 5/5. *Colloq. since 1900. Much more common in Eng. than U.S.* **2** The standard abbr. for "publisher." **3** The standard abbr. for "publicity."

pub-crawl *v.i.* = **joint hop.** *Since c1935; orig. a Briticism.*

pud *n.* **1** Pudding. *N.W. U.S. dial. Not common.* **2** A disliked person. *College sl. c1920.*

pudding-head *n.* A stupid but lovable person. 1894: *Pudd'nhead Wilson*, novel by Mark Twain.

puddle-jumper *n.* A small or dilapidated vehicle, esp. a public train, bus, or plane that makes short or local trips, stopping at every town.

puff *n.* **1** Life. *Obs. in U.S., still used in Eng.* **2** A weak or cowardly person. See **cream-puff, powder one's puff.** **—er** *n.* **1** A cigar. **2** One who smokes cigars. *Both meanings obs.* **3** The human heart. See **ticker.**

pug *n.* **1** A prize fighter, esp. a small-time prize fighter. *From "pugilist."* **2** Any young tough or mean man.

puka *n.* **1** Any small, private place, such as a pigeonhole in a desk, a safe, a purse, a small suitcase, or the like. **2** [taboo] The female genitals. *Both meanings W.W.II USN use in Pacific. Prob. orig. Polynesian.*

puke *v.i., v.t.* To vomit. *Stand.* *n.* **1** Vomit. → **2** Fig., any object, person, or situation that is so inferior, obnoxious, ugly, or disliked that it makes one vomit.

pull For phrases beginning with "pull," see under the principal word of the phrase.

pull *n.* Influence; favorable standing with people of authority or influence; drag. 1886: ". . . To have a pull with the cops. . . ." New Orleans *Lantern.* 1949: ". . . The B-36 procurement program was surrounded by irregularities and instances of political pull." AP, Washington, D.C., Oct. 18. *Colloq.* See **leg-pull.** *v.t.* **1** To arrest. 1894 [1891]: "I hate to see a lad get pulled for ridin' a train. . . ." J. Flynt. *From "pull in."* **2** To earn; to receive. 1924: ". . . Nor was he . . . proud of his B in English . . . he could have 'pulled' an A." Marks, *Plastic Age*, 111f. See **pull down.** **3** To smoke a cigarette. 1926: "He seen Cooper pulling a fag. . . ." Stallings and Anderson, *What Price Glory*, I. **—er** *n.* **1** A smuggler. **2** One who smokes marijuana cigarettes.

pull down To earn, usu. a specif. sum of money, as a weekly salary.

pullet *n.* A girl or young woman. *c1900; replaced by "chick."*

pulleys *n.pl.* Suspenders.

pull in To arrest. 1894 [1891]: "They [police] pull him in. . . ." J. Flynt.

Pull in your ears! Pull in your neck! 1 Look out! **2** Shut up! **3** Don't be so aggressive. Reconsider. Review the facts.

Pullman See **side-door Pullman.**

pull [it] off **1** To accomplish or obtain, esp. something remarkable, unique, or outrageous. **2** To commit a crime. 1930: ". . . He allies himself with a . . . [group of criminals], and 'pulls off' something worthwhile." Lavine, *Third Degree*, 35.

pull [something] on [a person] To deceive someone. *Colloq.*

pull out To leave; depart. 1949: "Lewis sat in on today's talks. . . . He pulled out after 45 minutes and disappeared." AP, Oct. 19. *Colloq. since c1880.*

pull [something] out of the fire To save from failure or disaster, to turn a potentially disastrous situation into a successful one, to turn defeat into victory; to rescue.

pulp *n.* **1** A magazine printed on cheap, rough, pulp paper. → **2** Any magazine devoted to sensational and ephemeral literature, for instance, cowboy and detective stories. → **3** A story or article of stereotyped design and sensational contents, usu. written for purely commercial ends. *adj.* Like or pertaining to pulp. *Colloq.* Cf. **slick.**

pump pumper *n.* The heart. 1950: "He had a hole through his pump." Movie, *Asphalt Jungle.*

pump, on On credit. *Dial.*

pump-handle *n.* A salute. *W.W.I Army use.*

pumpkin pumkin punkin *n.* **1** An important person. 1852: *DAE. Obs.* See **some pumpkins.** **2** One's steady girl or fiancée. *Obs.* **3** The human head. **4** A small town or rural community; a rustic place; a town in the sticks. 1951: "I never worked the pumpkins." *New Yorker*, Jan. 27, 21/1. *Carnival, circus, and theater use.* **5** A flat tire on an automobile. *Never common.* **6** A football. 1950: "They're really throwin' that punkin around down there." CBS radio network football broadcast, Nov. 11.

pumpkin-head *n.* A stupid person. *Colloq. since 1850.*

pumpkin-roller punkin roller *n.* A farmer. 1951: "Like as not the feller is a punkin roller. . . ." Letter to the editor, *Time*, Feb. 26, 10. *Colloq. since c1905; now archaic and dial.*

punch *n.* **1** A party, either planned or impromptu; any gathering where free food and drinks are served. c1920 [1954]: "When a club paraded it would make several stops called 'punches' during the day at the houses of the members, where there were sandwiches, cold beer, and, of course, lots of whisky." L. Armstrong, *Satchmo, My Life in New Orleans*, 225f. *Obs.* **2** Force; meaning; pungency. See **one-two punch, punch line, Sunday punch.**   *v.t.* **1** To fail at or to ruin something; esp. to fail a course in school. **2** To herd live stock, esp. cattle. 1936: ". . . 'Punching' being the accepted term for the herding of live stock." P. A. Rollins, *The Cowboy*, 39.   **—er**   *n.* **1** A cowboy. 1936: "The cowboy was not always called 'cowboy.' He everywhere was equally known as . . . 'puncher.' . . . Curiously, though the word 'puncher' was created but a comparatively few decades since, its derivation is now unknown unless it relates to the metal-pointed goad occasionally used for stimulating cattle when they were being urged to board railway cars." P. A. Rollins, *The Cowboy*, 39, 40. **2** A telegraph operator. See **bag-puncher, cow-puncher, donkey-puncher, dough-puncher, pillow-puncher.   Punchy**   *prop.n.* A nickname applied disparagingly to any person, implying that he is confused or mentally subnormal from, or as though from, blows on the head.   **punchy** *adj.* **1** = **punch-drunk.** 1937: " 'Slaphappy' or 'punchy' ex-fighters." *Lit. Digest*, Apr. 10, 39. 1939: "Sailor Bob a punchy stumble-bum." O'Hara, *Pal Joey*, 47. **2** Forceful, emphatic, having punch. 1937: "The English language may some day be as colorful and punchy as it was in Elizabethan times." *Lit. Digest*. Dec. 4, 30/3.

punch-drunk   *adj.* **1** Slow or uncertain in thought or actions; not in complete control of one's thoughts and movements, esp. when due to sustained concussions in prize fighting; groggy, dizzy; fig., drunk from being punched on the head freq. Cf. **slap-happy.** → **2** Groggy, dazed, or dizzy for any reason; mentally or emotionally exhausted, esp. from a series of failures or personal misfortunes.

—puncher   See Appendix, Suffixes and Suffix Words.

punch line   **1** The last line, sentence, or part of a joke that gives it meaning and humor. → **2** The last line, sentence, or part of a story, experience, or incident that gives it meaning or an unexpected ending.

punch-out   *n.* A fist fight.   **punch out**   To leave, to quit, to abandon. *From an office or factory worker's punching a time card as he leaves work for the day.*

pungle   pungle up   *v.t.* To pay money. c1850; obs.

punish   *v.t.* To eat or drink copiously. 1943: "I had a bottle along and he punished it." Chandler, *Lady in Lake*, 57f.

punk   *n.* **1** A petty hoodlum; one who thinks he wants to be a hoodlum but lacks real toughness and experience. 1949: "All the cockiness which association with Frankie had lent him, and Frankie's absence had taken away, returned. Dealer was coming home. 'Guys who think they can rough me up, they wake up wit' the cats lookin' at 'em,' he immediately began warning everyone. And spat to emphasize just how tough a Division Street punk could get." N. Algren, *Man with the Golden Arm*, 11. **2** A young or inexperienced person. Specif. a boy tramp or child hobo; a boy, youth, or beginner; a young prisoner; any C.C.C. boy, except an official leader; a child or adolescent of either sex; a youngster. 1939–40: ". . . Around 21 [years old] but Sparky was always a fresh punk. . . ." O'Hara, *Pal Joey*, 62. → **3** An inferior or unimportant person. Specif. a small-time criminal. 1930: ". . . They reached the stage where they thought only 'punks' committed misdemeanors. . . ." Lavine, *Third Degree*, 102. **4** [derog.] A catamite; the young male companion of a sodomite. *Prison, maritime, and tramp use.* **5** An inferior prize fighter, jockey, poolplayer, etc. **6** A lackey; esp. a waiter or porter. **7** A man or guy; esp. a worthless man; a petty criminal. 1934: "We're just two punks, Frank." Cain, *Postman*, 88. **8** Any young circus animal, specif. a baby lion or elephant. *Circus talk.* **9** Bread. 1907: ". . . She gives you a slice of sow-belly an' a chunk of dry 'punk.' " Jack London, *The Road*, 159. *Since c1880; tramp, logger, soldier, and maritime use. May be from the Hindustani, via Brit. Army use.* **10** A liquid or salve sold as a household remedy; patent medicine. 1943: ". . . The punk workers who sell corn removers." Zolotow, *SEP. Pitchman use.*   *adj.* Of poor quality; bad; inferior; unwell. 1931: "The idea strikes me as punk." W. Pegler, *Lit. Digest*   **—er**   *n.* A greenhorn.

punk day   *n.* A day during which

children are admitted to a carnival or circus free; children's day. *c1930; carnival and circus use.*

punk out To quit; to become cowardly; to turn chicken. *Orig. teenage street-gang use; some general teenage use since c1955.*

punk-pusher *n.* The boss of boy workers in a circus. *Circus use.*

punk sergeant A dining-room orderly. *Orig. Army use.*

pup *n.* **1** A young, inexperienced person. **2** A wiener on a roll; a hot dog. **3** A small four-wheeled truck trailer. *Truck-driver use.* See **gutter-pup, hot pup, pup tent, snuggle-pup(py).**

puppy = **pup.**

puppy-dog feet In playing cards, clubs. 1950: "The trump suit will be puppy-dog feet." Starnes, *Another Mug,* 1.

puppy love Preadolescent love. *A disparaging term used by adults. Since c1830; now colloq.*

pups *n.pl.* The feet; the dogs.

pups, have = have kittens. *Since c1900.*

pup tent A small tent suitable for sheltering one or two persons sleeping on the ground. 1953: "The crew loaded pup tents and cooking equipment into motorcycle sidecars." K. Vidor, *A Tree Is a Tree,* 234. *Since c1900 common Army use.*

pup tents Overshoes. *Circus use.*

purey *n.* A kind of clear glass playing marble. *Prob. from "pure."*

purge *n.* A newly arrived prisoner of war; a group of such prisoners. *Used by W.W.II American prisoners of war in German detention camps.*

purp *n.* A dog or pup. 1949: ". . . After the purp solved a few simple problems. . . ." Billy Rose, *synd. newsp. col.,* Dec. 23. *Since c1865.*

purple *adj.* Erotic; lurid. 1953: "Some of the testimony to be elicited from admitted call girls would be too purple for feminine ears." M. Lewis, N.Y. *Her. Trib.,* Feb. 3, 17/4.

purple loco See **loco.**

—pus See Appendix, Suffixes and Suffix Words.

pus-gut *n.* A fat-bellied man. 1950: "You'd better call old pus-gut. . . ." Starnes, *Another Mug,* 125. *Not common.* Cf. **beer-belly, pot-belly.**

push *n.* **1** A crowd of people. 1907: "It was once my fortune to travel a few weeks with a 'push' that numbered 2,000." Jack London, *My Life,* 4. *c1900 to present; never common.* → **2** A gang, esp. a gang of tramps or thugs.

More common in Austral. than U.S. → **3** A gang of neighborhood boys organized to fight other such gangs. 1944: ". . . Beating . . . the gang, called a push, in the next street. . . ." Walter Davenport, *Collier's,* Sept. 23, 12/4. → **4** A fight between boy gangs. *Is being replaced by "rumble."* → **5** A foreman, esp. a logging camp foreman. 1930: "Jigger's first season as a [lumber] camp push. . . ." S. H. Holbrook, *Amer. Mercury,* Oct., 235/2. **6** An easy mark; a pushover. *Not common.* **7** A discharge from one's job; the sack. **8** A major or sustained effort; a critical, determining, or final effort. *Usu. in "the big push."* *v.t.* **1** To drive a motor vehicle; specif. a truck or taxi. 1952: "Pushing a truck." Movie, *Red Ball Express.* 1952: "Pushing a hack all day, I know a backfire when I hear one. . . ." Fred Dickenson, Syracuse, N.Y., *Post-Standard,* Magazine Section, Jan. 13, 12/1. **2** To kill a person. 1948: "We get . . . touchy . . . when one of our boys gets pushed. . . ." Evans, *Halo for Satan,* 98. **3** To approach close to a specified age. 1949: "It's time you're getting some dignity! You're pushing 50." Earl Wilson, *synd. newsp. col.,* Sept. 30. *Colloq.* **4** To sell; to encourage customers to buy or patronize; esp., to hawk merchandise from door to door. *Colloq.* → **5** Specif., to sell or distribute illicit drugs to narcotics addicts; to deal in the illegal narcotics trade. 1949: "'Funny cigarettes ain't all that one pushes,' Frankie observed and thought bitterly: 'If I didn't need a fix now and then. . . .'" N. Algren, *Man with the Golden Arm,* 30. *Addict use; fairly well known.* **6** To distribute or use counterfeit money, as by a counterfeiter; to use worthless checks, as by a check forger. *Underworld use.* **7** To advertise; to publicize; to make known, esp. a product, entertainer, or the like. **8** To smuggle. *v.i.* **1** To carry an advantage too far; to be overly aggressive or enthusiastic. **2** [taboo] To have sexual intercourse. *Not common.* **3** In playing jazz, to obtain all the feeling from a musical passage; to play adroitly. *adj.* Easy. *From "pushover."* **—er** *n.* **1** A foreman. *Logger and construction worker use.* **2** A passer of counterfeit money. *Underworld use.* **3** One who peddles, sells, or distributes illicit narcotics to addicts, esp. marijuana or heroin. 1951: "The so-called 'queen of the Broadway narcotics pushers,' police said, has been arrested with a packet of heroin hidden in her brassière." AP, Aug. 25. 1958: "Dope addicts were all over, and 'pushers' too. Marijuana was easy to get. . . ." N.Y. *Post*, Jan 24, 18. *Common addict use, universally known.*

—over   *n.* **1** A prize fighter who is easily defeated. 1921: "We'll get a eight-round preliminary with some push-over." Witwer, *Leather*, 48. *Prize fight use since c1915.* **2** Any person, group, or team easily defeated in a contest or easily imposed upon. 1938: "We [the American middle class] have always been pushovers." *Amer. Mercury*, Oct., 140/1. *Very common.* → **3** One who is quickly receptive or responsive to persuasion, flattery, a spiel, or a line. 1946: "Goodwin . . . was not averse to . . . flattery; in point of fact, he was, in the vulgar expression, a pushover for it." G. J. Nathan in *Amer. Mercury*, June, 724/1. **4** A girl or woman who is easily seduced; an easy make. 1937:" This [girl] was going to be a pushover." Weidman, *Wholesale*, 101. **5** One who is always receptive to, cannot resist, or is sentimentally attached to any specif. idea, object, or person. **6** Any easy job or task; a cinch. 1936: "There were two ways to do it. One was a pushover." J. Weidman in *Amer. Mercury*, May, 91/2. *All uses common since c1930.*

—y   *adj.* Aggressive; specif., socially aggressive with an obvious or bold desire to become accepted by and part of a wealthy or socially prominent group. 1943: "Pushy people alarmed him." Wolfert, *Underworld*, 234.

push across   **1** To kill or murder. 1950: "He might have pushed Foster across." Movie, *The Sleeping City*. **2** In sports, to score.

push a pen   To do clerical work in an office. 1953: "I am fond of travel. . . . Why should I want to push a pen in an office?" *New Yorker*, Jan. 31, 20/1–2.

—pusher   See Appendix, Suffixes and Suffix Words.

push off   **1** To go away; to beat it. **2** To kill.

push the panic button   To demand a period of fast, efficient, and sometimes creative work; to demand that a job be done rapidly and well. *Usu. said of an employer, esp. in the advertising business, who is trying to meet a business emergency or soothe an irate client. A term assoc. with Madison Avenue.*

push up the daisies   To lie buried in one's grave. *Since c1860.*

puss   *n.* **1** The face. 1930: "One sock

in the puss. . . ." *Amer. Mercury*, Dec., 455. *From the Irish "pus" = mouth.* **2** The mouth. *Not common.* **3** A grimace; a facial expression of pain, anger, annoyance, incredulity, or the like. **4** A disliked youth; specif., an effeminate youth. See **pussy**. Also **drizzle puss, glamor puss, pickle-puss, sour-puss.**

—y   *n.* **1** [taboo] The vagina; coitus. c1915 [1950]: " 'I got a woman lives right back of the jail,/ She got a sign on her window—Pussy For Sale.' " A. Lomax, *Mr. Jelly Roll*, 17. 1947: "Papa's in jail!/ Mama's on bail!/ Baby's on the corner/ Shouting 'pussy for sale!' " W. Saroyan, *Jim Dandy*, 9. 1947: " 'Eye that poontang there,' he said. 'I could eat it with a knife and a fork. Where I come from we call that kind of stuff table pussy.' " Calder Willingham, *End as a Man*, 74. Cf. **piece.** → **2** [derog.] An effeminate man or boy. *Not common.* *adj.* Aroused, sexually or otherwise; agitated. *Not common.*

pussyfoot   *v.i.* To hesitate in giving one's opinion, or in taking action; to vacillate; to avoid being frank and direct in stating one's opinion or conclusions. *Becoming archaic. Pop., and perhaps coined by, Theodore Roosevelt.* Cf. **beat around the bush.**

pussy's twister, the   = **the cat's meow.** *Obs.*

put   For phrases beginning with "put," see under the principal word of the phrase.

put   *v.i.* To vomit. *c1900; obs.*   *v.t.* To accommodate a person sexually. *Usu. with female subject and male object.* c1930: "There was a young girl from Alaska who would put anyone that would ask her. . . ." Well-known limerick. 1937: "With men buyers, you get them put and you can sell them the Brooklyn Bridge." Weidman, *Wholesale*, 130. *Not common.*

put [something] across   **1** To make something understandable; to explain or clarify; specif., to attempt to convince by explaining; to attempt to convince or persuade. **2** To succeed in cheating or taking advantage of another, to hoodwink; to succeed in accomplishing an unethical task.

put [someone or something] down   To reject; to criticize; to scorn. 1956: "I called my dad and he hung up. My folks put me down strong. . . ." S. Longstreet, *The Real Jazz Old and New*, 147. 1958: "Not that I mean to put down the Old Masters [classical composers], but I don't think they can talk to the musically untrained. . . ." John "Dizzy" Gillespie, "The Gillespie Plan," *Jazz World*, March, 5. *c1955; orig. beat use, now common to far out, cool, and hip people.*

put [someone or something] down for (as) To identify or classify. 1956: "When I see a guy with a pull-over sweater under a double-breasted suit, I put him down for an Englishman." J. Cannon, *Who Struck John?* 253.

put-in *n.* Concern, interest, esp. a person's interest in an affair exterior to his personal responsibility. 1853: *DAE.* 1934: "Ambrose seems to be all heated up about this whole matter, although I cannot see where it is any of his put-in." D. Runyon, *Blue Plate Special. Archaic.*

put in [one's] two cents To contribute one's opinion or advice, esp. when not asked to.

put it on the line = **lay it on the line.**

put it over **1** In baseball, to throw a strike; said of the pitcher. *Baseball use.* **2** = **put over.**

put on **1** To eat; to put on the feedbag. 1935: "I once see Miss Beauregard putting on the fried chicken in the Seven Seas restaurant." Runyon. **2** To act affectedly; to conduct oneself ostentatiously; to put on airs. *adj.* Affected. See **feedbag.**

put on lugs = **lugs.**

put on the spot See **on the spot.**

put out **1** To feel angry, humiliated, offended, rejected, insulted, slighted; to be upset because of the words or actions of another. **2** To inconvenience someone. *Very common.* **3** [taboo] To grant sexual favors freely and indiscriminately; to be promiscuous; said of a girl or woman.

put over **1** = **put across.** **2** To make a success of; to popularize.

put [one's] papers in **1** To apply for admission, usu. to apply for admission

to a college or to enlist in the Armed Forces. *Mainly teenage use.* **2** To resign or retire. 1958: "Put one's papers in— To retire from the force." G. Y. Wells, *Station House Slang.*

putter-offer *n.* A procrastinator. 1942: "Had the President figured what his own tax would be? No, admitted Franklin Roosevelt—as weakly as any putter-offer." *Time*, Apr. 20, 14/3. 1950: "Don't be a putter-offer. Buy United States Saving Bonds now." U.S. Treasury Dept advt., NBC radio, Oct. 18. *One of the few —er--er terms.* See Appendix.

putt-putt *n.* **1** An outboard motor for a boat. → **2** Any internal combustion engine of less than five cylinders; any vehicle or device with such an engine, esp. a small car or motor scooter.

putty-head *n.* A fool; a stupid person. *c1850.*

put up **1** To give someone shelter for a night; to invite or allow another to use one's room or home. *Colloq.* **2** To wager money on the outcome of a sporting event; to present one's stakes in support of a wager.

put-up job A prearranged affair; a frame-up. 1952: "This deal was a put-up job!" E. Martin, *synd. comic strip*, "Boots," Feb. 11. *Colloq. since c1925.*

put up or shut up **1** Lit., back up your opinion with a money wager or be silent about it. → **2** Fig., prove your assertion by some definite action or stop making the assertion. 1894: Thornton. *Colloq. Used orig. as an invitation to wager, but now more in anger as a command to shut up.* See **put up.**

put up with [someone or something] To accept or endure a person, situation, or object even though one does not want to. *Colloq.*

pygies *n.pl.* = **P. J.'s.** 1929: "Now, go and get the pygies. . . ." Sturges, *Strictly Dishonorable*, II.

Q

Q. and A. Questions and answers. 1954: "We stalled until we could get the police into our Q. and A. contest." W. R. & F. K. Simpson, *Hockshop*, 127. See Appendix, Shortened Words.

quad *n.* **1** A quadrangle, as the court of a building or buildings, or a campus or part of one. **2** A prison. Cf. **quod.**

quail *n.* **1** A girl or young woman; esp. a sexually attractive girl or young woman. 1952: "A lovely little quail from Arkansas." A. Godfrey, netwk. radio, Mar. 26. *Since c1860. From the Celtic "caile"* = *a girl.* Cf. **San Quentin quail.** **2** A prostitute or promiscuous woman. *Archaic.* **3** A cornet or trumpet. *c1915.*

[1954]: " 'Just listen to that kid blow that quail!' That is what Slippers called my cornet." L. Armstrong, *Satchmo, My Life in New Orleans*, 115. *Some early jazz use; archaic.*

quail-roost *n.* A women's dormitory. *c1900; college use.*

Quaker gun A dummy gun used as a sham to bluff the enemy into thinking a military position is heavily fortified or defended. *Civil War use. Because Quakers are conscientious objectors to war.*

qualley-worker *n.* An itinerant worker who makes wire coat-hangers, bottle-cleaners, etc. *Perhaps from U.S. dial. "quile," "quarl" = coil, as of wire. Tramp use.*

quarterback *v.t.* To manage a business, lead a group of people, or organize a business, group, or plan. *Since c1945; from the football term.*

quee down To quiet down; to shut up. *Mainly archaic prison use; some dial. and some W.W.II Army use.*

queen *n.* **1** A very generous, pleasant, remarkable, or attractive girl or woman. 1932: "Wouldn't it be luck if some ritzy queen fell for him!" J. T. Farrell, "Jazz-Age Clerk." 1951: "What a lady . . . a queen." J. D. Salinger, *Catcher in the Rye*, 57. **2** A male homosexual who plays the female role, esp. one attractive to or pop. with homosexuals who play the male role. *v.i., v.t.* To go on a date or escort a girl. *Some student use since c1915.* **—er** *n.* A ladies' man. *Some c1930 student use; obs.* See Appendix, —er ending.

queer *adj.* **1** Counterfeit. 1848: J. S. Farmer. *Underworld use.* **2** Homosexual; perverted; degenerate; effeminate; specif., homosexual. *Common since c1925, and now so common that the stand. use is avoided; orig. hobo use.* *n.* **1** Counterfeit money. 1954: "Eagle-eyed concessionaires always on the lookout for shovers of the queer." W. R. & F. K. Simpson, *Hockshop*, 232. *Since c1925. Orig. and mainly underworld use.* **2** A male homosexual. *The most common, polite word in use = a homosexual.* Cf. **fag, pansy, queen.** **3** A homosexual of either sex. 1956: ". . . Some girls said that I was queer and that she shouldn't be friendly with me." Letter in Dr. Franzblau's synd. newsp. col., *Human Relations*, May 21. *Very common.* *v.t.* To put one in bad standing; to spoil or ruin something, as one's prospects or a plan, to quash, to cause hindrance or

discontent. 1920: "Food is what queered the party. We ordered a big supper to be sent up at two o'clock. Alec didn't give the waiter a tip, so I guess the little bastard snitched." F. S. Fitzgerald, *This Side of Paradise*, 256. *Since c1915.* **—ie** *n.* An effeminate man, not a homosexual; an odd or eccentric person. 1930: "Any boy showing interest in [classes] is correctly considered a 'queerie.' " L. Morris in *Amer. Mercury*, Oct., 181/1. 1951: "Why then does he want to get his hands on these millions? To pay the wages of a lot of queeries in the State Department?" W. Pegler, *synd. newsp. col.*, Aug. 14. *Not common, owing to confusion with "queer."* See Appendix, —ie ending.

quetch *v.i.* To complain about insignificant things; to nag. *From the stand. Yiddish "kvetch" = to squeeze → Yiddish sl. = to whine.* **—er** *n.* A chronic complainer; an annoying, bothersome person. See Appendix, —er ending.

quetor *n.* **1** A quarter [25¢]. **2** A tip of 25¢; also, a person who gives a tip of 25¢.

quick buck = fast buck.

quickie *n.* **1** A single, quickly drunk drink of whisky, usu. straight whisky, as taken secretly or to bolster up one's courage. **2** [taboo] A short, fast act of sexual intercourse. *Fairly common.* **3** A movie quickly and cheaply made. 1928: "To play in a 'quickie,' one of those overnight film concoctions. . . ." *Picture Play*, Jan., 32. 1956: ". . . On the set where I [Marilyn Monroe] was working in a quickie called 'Don't Bother to Knock.' " Pete Martin, "The New Marilyn Monroe," *SEP*, May 5, 152. **4** A strike not sanctioned by the workers' union; a wildcat strike. 1956: "*Quickie—* A walkout not approved by union officials." *Labor's Special Language from Many Sources.* **5** Anything done or made quickly, as a quick trip, a book written quickly, or the like. 1948: "[Howard] Dietz due back by air from a quickie to Paris last week. . . ." *Variety*, Aug. 25, 54/1. 1949: "A foreign correspondent who has written his slightly sounder quickies for the book club trade and has kept this [book] for the ladies. . . ." R. Shaplen in N.Y. *Times Bk. Rev.*, Sept. 4, 6/4. See Appendix, —ie ending. *adj.* Quick; fast; short. 1950: "The 'quickie' increases, if approved by Congress, would raise the annual take by $3 billion." AP, July 26. 1950: "These quickie personality sketches [in Allen and Shannon's *The Truman Merry-Go-Round*] are packed with information." S. Lubell in N.Y. *Times Bk. Rev.*, Sept. 24. 6/5.

quick one   A hasty drink of liquor. 1949: "I think I'll catch me a quick one at the bar." Movie, *Everybody Does It.*

quick on the draw   Quick-thinking; quick to comprehend. *The image is that of a Western gunfighter.*

quick on the uptake   Quick to comprehend, esp. relationships between people or nuances of likes and dislikes among people at a gathering.

quick-over   *n.* A hasty glance or inspection. *From "quick" plus "once-over."*

quick push   1 A person easy to victimize; an easy mark. *Underworld use.* 2 A sports team or athlete easy to defeat; a profitable business transaction that is simple to carry out. *Not common.*

quiff   *n.* 1 Money. *Some W.W.I USN use, from Brit. Navy sl.* 2 A cheap prostitute; a girl or woman who will join in sexual intercourse with but little persuasion. *Underworld use and some general use since c1925.*

quill   *v.t.* 1 To try to curry favor with a person. *More common in Eng. than in*

U.S. 2 To report a cadet for a delinquency. 1939: *West Point use.* 3 To whistle.

quim   *n.* 1 = **queen.** 2 [taboo] The vagina.

quint   *n.* 1 A basketball team. *From "quintet."* 2 A quintuplet.

quirk   *n.* A student flyer. *W.W.I use.*

quirley   *n.* A cigarette. *Cowboy use.*

quit it out = **cut it out.** *A cute variant, in vogue c1940.*

quiz   *n.* In college, a short examination. *Colloq. since c1860.* See **drop quiz, shotgun quiz.** —**zee**   *n.* One who is quizzed, esp. one who is a contestant on a television quiz game program. 1947: "Asking questions of eager quizzees. . . ." J. Gould in N.Y. *Times,* Dec. 7, X13/1. 1951: "Many other hapless quizzees." E. J. Kahn, Jr., in *New Yorker.* Nov. 24, 116. *Frequent use owing to the many television quiz shows.* See Appendix, —ee ending.

quod   *n.* 1 A prison. 2 = **quad.**

quote   *n.* 1 A quotation. 1927: *AS.* 1934: "Colloq." *Web.* 1945. "The quote of the week." W. Winchell, *synd. newsp. col.,* Dec. 10. *Colloq.* See Appendix, Shortened Words. 2 A quotation **mark.**

R

rabbit   *n.* 1 Salad; esp. a salad composed of greens. 2 The nose of an airplane. *Not common.* 3 Talk. *From "rabbit-and-pork" = talk, in [Cockney] rhyming sl.* —**foot**   *n.* A prisoner who runs away from prison.   *v.i.* To move quickly, to run; specif., to flee, to escape.

rabbit food   Any kind of greens, esp. lettuce; raw salad vegetable(s).

race   See **boat-race, rat race.** *adj.* Pertaining to "race" music.

race music   A simple form of jazz based on the blues, usu. with a melancholy or sometimes religious theme, a heavily accented beat, etc. *Because such music, during the 1920's and 1930's, was issued by the recording companies on records informally known as "race records," intended primarily for sale to Negroes.*

Rachel   *n.* High gear on a motor vehicle. *Army use.*

rack   rack duty   rack time = **sack   sack duty   sack time.** *USN use.*

Rackensaker   *n.* A common soldier, esp. a member of a state volunteer militia group. c1847 [1956]: "Huge fires of discarded supplies were burning, around them the Rackensackers were

gathered, some sleeping, some playing cards, none working." S. E. Chamberlain, "Victory At Buena Vista," *Life,* July 30, 52. *Mainly Mexican War use; obs.*

racket   *n.* 1 Any shady or dishonest business or occupation; a swindle. 1894: "No tramp . . . is so clever at the begging-letter 'racket'. . . ." Josiah Flynt. → 2 Any kind of concession at a carnival or circus. *Carnival and circus sl.* 3 Any legitimate business or occupation. 4 An easy job; an enjoyable way of life. —**eer**   *n.* A person who works in a shady or unethical business; a swindler or extortionist.   *v.i.* To victimize by means of a racket.

racket-jacket   *n.* A zoot suit. *c1935 jive use.* See Appendix, Rhyming Slang.

radish   *n.* A baseball. *Sportswriter use.*

raft   *n.* A large number or quantity of persons or things; a slew. 1935: ". . . He sees a raft of guys and dolls strolling around. . . ." Runyon. *Colloq. since c1830.*

raft, on a   On toast. *Lunch-counter use in relaying an order; not common.*

rag   *n.* 1 An article of clothing, esp. a dress. 1855: *DAE. Still used, mainly in "rags" or "glad rags."* 2 A circus tent;

esp., the main tent of a circus; a "big rag." *Circus use.* **3** A semaphore flag. *USN use.* **4** Lit. and fig., a baseball championship pennant. 1908: "Our boys [baseball players] 'look good for the rag.' " R. L. Hartt in *Atlantic Monthly*, Aug., 229/1. **5** [taboo] A sanitary napkin. *Usu. in "to have the rag on." The above meanings refer to articles of cloth manufacture; the next three meanings refer to things made of paper.* **6** A paper dollar. 1859: Matsell. *Still some use.* **7** A newspaper or magazine; esp., a newspaper or magazine for which the speaker has contempt; orig. and mainly, a newspaper. 1932 [1951]: "This so called revolutionary organ [*The New Masses*] is a horrible rag." O. E. Chubb's diary, quoted by AP, Aug. 20. 1939: "[To a newspaper reporter:] We couldn't get along without your rag." Gardner, *D. A. Draws*, 62. *Universally known.* **8** A playing card; esp., one which does not improve the player's hand. *Additional meanings:* **9** A girl; specif., a man's sweetheart. 1924: "The New York tough called his girl 'me rag.' " A. Lewis in *Lit. Digest*, Feb. 14, 28. *Obs. From "bunch of rags," reinforced by "rag" = sanitary napkin.* **10** A railroad switchman. *Railroad use. From the red flag he holds up.* **11** A simple form or style of highly syncopated music, primarily for the piano, characterized by a lively, accented tempo, the use of breaks, and intricate figures in both treble and bass; a song written or arranged in this style; ragtime. *Strictly speaking, rag preceded jazz and was distinct from it, being mostly written music, developed by trained white musicians c1890–c1905. The style was an influence on early jazz, however, and many rags were adapted to the jazz repertory. In the public mind the two became identified, and "rag" and "ragtime" were used interchangeably with "jazz" until c1925. Since c1890.* See **ragtime.** *v.t.* **1** To steal. *Some c1900 use; obs.* **2** To tease, to banter with; to ride or needle. 1952: "Sometimes we'd rag one another in the rough manner that is safe only for friends." F. G. Patton in *New Yorker*, Mar. 8, 34/2. *Since before 1900; now somewhat archaic.* **3** To play any music in a style resembling ragtime; popularly, to play in a jazzy manner. 1956: "The street bands [in New Orleans c1900] ragged a tune by taking one note and putting two or three in its place." S. Longstreet, *The Real Jazz Old and New*, 7. *Since c1890.* **4** To surprise or

catch a person in a prohibited, forbidden, unethical, or illegal act. *Not common.* *v.i.* **1** To talk nonsense. *Some c1900 student use.* Cf. **chew the rag.** **2** To dance to a rag or to ragtime music with short, quick, jumping steps. *c1915 use; archaic.* **3** To play a rag. **—ger** *n.* **1** A devotee of rag or ragtime music; one who dances well to ragtime music. See **rag.** See Appendix, **—er** ending. → **2** A popular or socially active student. *c1915 student use; obs.* **3** A newspaper reporter. *Some use since c1920.* **—s** *n.pl.* **1** Clothing, esp. new or fancy clothing. 1939: "She got into her rags and by the time she was dressed. . . ." J. O'Hara, *Pal Joey*, 59. *From "rag."* See **glad rags.** **2** Paper money. See **rag.** **—time** *n.* A highly syncopated style of music, esp. for the piano, characterized by a monotonous bass, a heavily accented tempo, and a melody line composed of many short, fast notes. 1956: "Ragtime always held up through all kinds of new piano. It was raggy, rhythmic, double-timed, always fun. The left hand played it in octaves, single or chords, and mostly did the 4/4 over 2/4. The right hand took the melody in a free way. Running ahead or behind the melody added to the variety. In 1904 they had ragtime contests at the St. Louis Fair." S. Longstreet, *The Real Jazz Old and New*, 128. *It is said that the word first appeared in print in 1896 on the cover of the published song, "Oh, I Don't Know, You're Not So Warm," by Bert Williams, but the word was in use among musicians before this.* See **rag.**

rag-chewing *n.* Talking: conversing; esp., talking idly. 1885: *DAE. Still some use.* See **chew the rag.**

raggle *n.* An attractive girl or woman; specif. a sexually attractive young girl; one's girl friend or mistress. *Underworld use.*

rag-head [derog.] *n.* A Hindu or any other Asiatic. *From the turban worn. West Coast use.*

rag off the bush, take the To excel. *c1840; obs.*

rag on, have the [taboo] To be menstruating.

rag out To dress up in one's best, newest, or most colorful clothes. *c1865; orig. jive use.* See **glad rags, rag.**

rag up = **rag out.**

rah *interj.* Hurrah. *Since c1875.* *adj.* = **rah-rah.** 1941: " 'Old P.E.A.,' a rah song." *Dict. of Exeter Lang.*, 27.

rah-rah *adj.* Of or pertaining to a college; collegiate; characteristic of the spirit or feeling of college students, esp. in respect to sporting and social activities. 1914: "Bunches of rah-rah boys." S. Lewis, *Our Mr. Wrenn*, 37. 1951: "College kids have outgrown all that rah-rah stuff." M. Shulman, *Dobie Gillis*, 33. 1956: "A college romance which led to marriage and a baby boy, turned out to be a sour combination yesterday for the 18-year-old blue-eyed mother and the 21-year-old rah-rah-boy pappy." A. Albelli in N.Y. *Daily News*, Nov. 16, 4. *Always used disparagingly.*

rail *n.* **1** A railroad man. *c1895 to present.* **2** A first lieutenant. *From the appearance of his insigne. cW.W.II Air Force use.* Cf. **tracks.** See **third rail.**

railbird *n.* An ardent horse-racing fan; lit., one who sits on or stands close to the railing surrounding a race track; one who times and keeps his own record of the performances of race horses for comparisons of their merits in later races. 1892: *DAE. Still in use.*

railroad *v.t.* To send a person directly to prison without proof of guilt, due process of law, or a fair trial; to send to jail by false evidence or by cheating, tricking, deceiving, or framing. 1877: *DAE.* 1930: "The prisoner is railroaded to jail." Lavine, *Third Degree*, 200. **2** To force or speed up an action without due process, in disregard of regular or accepted procedures, or without the consent of others concerned; to force one's opinion or schemes upon others. 1934: "If all cases were railroaded through that quick. ...." Cain, *Postman*, 76. **3** To hurry, in the preparation of an order of food. *Some lunch-counter use in relaying an order to the cook.* Cf. **horseback.**

railroad tracks An Army captain's insigne bars. Called also **tracks.** *W.W.II use.*

rain cats and dogs = **rain pitchforks.**

rain check **1** A ticket stub or other receipt that allows one to return to see another baseball game if the one the ticket was originally purchased for is canceled because of bad weather. *Since c1890.* **2** Any request or promise to accept an invitation at a later date.

rain pitchforks (darning needles, chicken coops, cats and dogs, hammer handles) To rain in torrents; to rain very heavily. *Colloq.*

raise Cain To cause a disturbance; to show violent anger; to live or enjoy oneself without regard for the conventions; to raise hell. *Since c1840.*

raise hell **1** To celebrate wildly; to enjoy oneself in a wild, boisterous manner, usually with much noise and whisky; to be drunk and boisterous. *Colloq.* **2** To criticize or castigate thoroughly and in anger.

raise sand = **raise Cain.** 1892: *DAE. Still some dial. use.*

rake-off *n.* **1** Chips or money that a gambling house takes as its percentage from the money bet in a gambling game. *These chips or the money may be removed from the center of the gambling table by a croupier's rake.* → **2** A commission, percentage, share, or rebate received by a party to a transaction, esp. an illegitimate or unethical transaction. 1910: "I'll bet he gets a rakeoff." Johnson, *Varmint*, 61. *Still used commonly.*

rake [someone] over the coals To reprimand; to bawl out. *Colloq.*

ral **ral, the** **rail** **rail, the** *n.* Syphilis; a case of syphilis. *Orig. Southern use. Some Armed Forces use. Orig. "ral"; "rail" is a variant.*

rall *n.* A consumptive. *Crook use.*

ram *n.* **1** A demerit. *College use. Not common.* **2** An accomplice of a crook. *More common in Austral. than in U.S.*

ram bam *interj.* = **wham bam.** 1943: "Ram, bam,/Thank you, ma'am." M. Shulman, *Barefoot Boy with Cheek*, 52.

rambling *adj.* Fast-moving. *Esp. said of a railroad train. Vagabond argot.*

rambunctious *adj.* Boisterous; obstreperous. *From c1835 to present.*

ram it [taboo] = **shove it** [taboo].

ramshack **ramshackle** *adj.* Dilapidated; in disorder.

ramstuginous *adj.* Severe; wild; vicious. *c1850; obs.*

R and R **1** Lit., Rest and Rotation; a transfer or leave from a fighting military unit to a base or town removed from the fighting; a short leave or vacation given a soldier from the front lines to a rest camp or town. *Wide W.W.II and Korean Army use.* → **2** A several-day period spent in drinking, sexual activity, or general carousal. *Army use during and since W.W.II.*

rank *v.t.* **1** To say or do anything that discloses another's guilt in a crime; to deal in innuendo. 1928: "She ranked him by busting out with that new fur so soon after the robbery." E. Booth in *Amer. Mercury*, May, 80. **2** To harass, annoy, or ride someone. *Since c1930; common* *teenage use since c1950.* *adj.* Ruined, spoiled; gone awry.

rank, pull To use one's rank or business or social position, usu. in a specif. situation, to exact obedience, respect, favors, hard work, or the like; to be dictatorial or bossy. *Orig. W.W.II Armed Forces use.*

rantankerous *adj.* Cantankerous. *c1832; colloq.*

rap *n.* **1** A rebuke or reprimand; blame, responsibility. 1777: *DAE.* 1949: "The quarrel was not of [Admiral Denfield's] making. But he had to take the rap." Ithaca (N.Y.) *Journal*, Nov. 3, 6/2. → **2** An instance of being identified, arrested, charged, tried, sentenced, punished, or placed in prison as a lawbreaker; the identification of a criminal; the act of charging someone with having committed a crime, or such a charge; an instance of being arrested, or an arrest; a trial; a jail sentence. 1926: "The newest [crime word] is *rap* meaning identification. When one is singled out from a line of suspects as the [guilty person], one is the victim of a 'rap.' To the eminent 'Lord Beaverbrook' we owe this contribution to polite speech." N.Y. *Times*, May 30, quoted in *AS*, 2, 112. 1930: "Gangs with influence can beat about 90% of their 'raps' or arrests." Lavine, *Third Degree*, 228. 1934: "I'd be under a perjury rap—which I couldn't beat. I'd rather be under a murder rap—which I can beat." Chandler, *Finger Man*, 36. 1951: "[Senator Estes] Kefauver [and his Congressional committee] realize that as dope peddling and boot-legging are made more difficult, the crooks will start looking for ways to beat the rap." P. Edson, AP, Sept. 4. *Universally known.* **3** A derogatory or highly critical remark; a complaint. 1930: "Good, honest cops will often take a 'rap' or complaint rather than testify against a fellow cop." Lavine, *Third Degree*, 17. *v.t.* **1** To identify, arrest, charge, try, or sentence an accused lawbreaker or criminal. **2** To kill someone. *Underworld use.*

—per *n.* **1** One who complains or beefs against, identifies, charges, or acts as a witness against a suspected lawbreaker. 1916: "The rapper had told the truth and the jury believed it." *Lit. Digest*, Aug. 19. 1928: "If we could only pull the rapper off. . . ." E. Booth in *Amer. Mercury*, May, 81. *Underworld use; now archaic.* → **2** A judge or prosecutor. *Underworld use; archaic.*

3 A crime for which someone other than the guilty person is punished. 1940: "There were a couple of [gang murders] solved, but they were just rappers." Chandler, *Farewell*, 163. *All meanings from "rap."* See Appendix, —er ending.

rap, take the See **rap.**

rap to **1** To speak to, recognize, or acknowledge acquaintance with someone; to give [someone] a tumble. 1932: "I wish Moosh a hello, and he never raps to me but only bows, and takes my hat." "I do not rap to these old friends of mine at once, and in fact I put the *Journal* up in front of my face." Runyon, 97, 116. *Not common.* **2** To understand or comprehend something; to realize or become aware of something; to tumble. 1935: "He can see that Philly has something on his mind, and right away The Seldom Seen Kid raps to what it is." Runyon, 174. *Not common.*

raspberries! **razzberries!** *interj.* An expression of incredulity or disgust. *Pop. c1925 euphem.; still in use but not common.*

raspberry **razzberry** *n.* **1** A sharp, harsh, contemptuous, derisive, scornful comment, criticism, or rebuke; specif., a vulgar, derisive noise made by sticking the tongue between the lips and then blowing vigorously; the bird, the Bronx cheer. 1921: "The disappointed crowd is givin' him the raspberry, demandin' the knock-out they paid to see." Witwer, *Leather*, 23. 1933: "To give the raspberry or the Bronx cheer. . . ." W. O. McGeehan in N.Y. *Her. Trib.*, June 24. *Colloq.* Cf. **razz.** **2** Something worthless or inferior. *Not common.*

raspberry, give [someone] the See **raspberry.**

rat *n.* **1** A printer not approved by a trade union. *c1850.* **2** A student; esp. a freshman or new student. *c1850.* 1951: "Of all the cadets, the 'rats' of the entering class have the roughest time." *Time*, May 28, 50. *Virginia Military Institute use.* **3** A disliked or despised person. **4** An informer; a squealer. 1917: "In most cases they were 'rats,' and the best tools the keepers had." P. L. Quinlan, *New Republic*, Jan. 13, 294/1. *The most common use. Mainly assoc. with underworld use = police informer, esp. one who informs on his friends for pay or in return for a lesser jail sentence for himself.* → **5** Any distrusted, unethical, selfish, disliked person. **6** A loose woman. 1924: "I admit that

I chase around with rats. . . ." Marks, *Plastic Age*, 155. **7** A railroad train. *Short for "rattler."* See **dock-rat, grease rat, pack-rat.** *v.i.* **1** To desert one's associates. *More common in Eng. than in U.S.* **2** To inform; to squeal. **—ter** *n.* An informer. **—ty** *adj.* Shabby. 1952: "I went out to a fairly ratty bar and had a few drinks. . . ." Ted Robinson, Jr., *Harper's*, Mar., 88/1.

— rat See Appendix, Suffixes and Suffix Words.

rat cheese Any inexpensive, non-processed, common yellow cheese cut on order by a grocer, esp. a large cheese; bulk cheese; store cheese. 1953: ". . . The country store . . . famous for its checker players, pot-bellied stove, cracker barrel and rat cheese . . . is getting . . . rare. . . ." Hal Boyle, AP, Mar. 16.

rate *v.i., v.t.* **1** To be entitled to something; to receive something because one is highly esteemed or well liked. **2** To be highly esteemed. 1949: "What stunt did he ever pull that makes him rate?" Billy Rose, *synd. newsp. col.*, Nov. 28. **—y** *adj.* Superior in manner; snobbish. *c1925. Not common.* "Much of this . . . badgering . . . is in the spirit of fun, and, if so received, it is easy to bear. But woe betide the plebe who is 'ratey.' " A. A. Ageton.

rate with [someone] To be held in high esteem by someone; to be liked or trusted by someone.

rat-face *n.* A sly, underhanded person.

ratherish *adv.* Somewhat. 1862: *DAE.* 1934: Colloq. *Web.*

rat-hole *v.t.* To store up [food, etc.] furtively.

rat on [someone] To inform on or squeal on. 1934: ". . . No power on earth can keep her from ratting on you." Cain, *Postman*, 79.

rat out To withdraw or depart dishonorably. 1941: "I wouldn't feel you were ratting out if you [signed it]." Schulberg, *Sammy*, 190.

rat pack A teenage street gang. 1951: "It looked like three or four of L.A.'s [Los Angeles'] juvenile gangs, sometimes called rat packs, had taken turns going over the place." R. S. Prather, *Bodies in Bedlam*, 61. *Not common.* See Appendix, Rhyming Slang.

rat race **1** Any job, occupation, office, business, or way of life in which action and activity seem more important than specific results or goals. *From the traditional image of laboratory rodents being placed on a treadmill to test their energy; hence fig., a race on a treadmill.* **2** Any occupation, place, social group, or way of life in which success is based on competition and comparison of one's financial and material success with that of others, ignoring personal achievement and satisfaction. **3** Any crowded locale, scene, business, or social function of great confusion. *Orig. a euphemism implying that sanity or productive work is impossible in such a locale, scene, business, or social function.* 1951: "Usually they have become weary of frivolous dates, the rat-race of ordinary social gatherings." Edna Wilder, AP, N.Y., Dec. 14. **4** Specif., a dance or dancing party. *Student and teen-age use.* **5** A full dress review. *W.W.II Army use.* *v.i.* To dance. *c1935; student use. Not common.*

rats! *expl.* An expression of disgust.

rattle *n.* A "deal"; treatment. 1932: ". . . Who always gives everyone a square rattle. . . ." Runyon. *v.i.* To talk aimlessly; to gossip. Used in "to rattle on." *v.t.* To confuse; to bewilder. *Usu. used reflexively in "to get rattled."* See **rattleweed.** **—brain** *n.* A confused, silly, or stupid person. 1924: "Mother would like to travel around but not with an old rattlebrain like you driving." Ring Lardner, "How to Write Short Stories," reprinted in *The American Twenties*, 41. See **rattleweed.** **—brained** *adj.* Silly; stupid; prone to confusion; unable to concentrate or meditate; foolish. See **rattled.** **—d** *adj.* Confused; confused by excitement; foolish; silly. See **loco; rattleweed.** **—r** *n.* **1** A railroad train. 1951: "We're rolling across the country in a very luxurious rattler. . . ." Walter Davenport, *Collier's*, Nov. 17, 8. → **2** A fast freight train; a railroad freight car. *c1915; vagabond use.* **3** A trolley car. **—s** *n.* Small change; silver money. *c1935; underworld use, not common.* **—weed** *n.* = **loco** weed. *Because the seeds in loco weed make a rattling sound. Since eating loco weed makes cattle and horses insane, "loco" = crazy and "rattle" has come to = to confuse.*

rattling *adv.* Exceedingly; extremely. 1930: "This is a rattling good story." A. G. Hays, introduction to *All in the Racket* by William E. Weeks, 13. *adj.* Good quality; first rate. 1934: Web., *adj.*

raunchy **ronchie** *adj.* **1** Sloppy, careless; inept, unskilled; awkward.

1939: "Depending on how good or how 'raunchy' we [Air Force cadets at Randolph Field, Texas] were, we drilled from one to three hours in the torrid heat." R. G. Hubler in *Forum*, July, 45/1. *W.W.II Air Force use.* → **2** Dilapidated, old, worn out, used up; cheap, inferior; ugly, dirty; gaudy; corny. *Teenage use since c1950.* **3** Drunk; drunken. *Fairly common student use.* See Appendix, Drunk.

rave   *v.i.* **1** To express oneself enthusiastically about a person or thing; to gush. 1887: "People are ravin' over the wonderful cures...." New Orleans *Lantern. Colloq.* **2** To denounce.   *n.* **1** An unfavorable criticism. 1905: "... Suppose our friend ... made a rave because the jokes ... were all ancient....' McHugh, *Search Me*, 54. **2** A very favorable or flattering comment, usu. a review of a stage play or the like. *Note that the noun reversed its meaning c1925; the v. is still used to mean two opposite things.* **3** A sweetheart. 1933: "I thought he was the principal rave ... in your young life." H. T. Webster. *adj.* Very favorable; flattering. Usu. in "rave notice." 1949: "... A role that John Barrymore got rave notices for...." Billy Rose, *synd. newsp. col.*, Oct. 21.

raw   *adj.* **1** Inexperienced, crude. **2** Unfair, unjustified. **3** Naked. 1932: "... He puts her in the 'Vanities' and lets her walk around raw...." Runyon. See also **in the raw.** **4** Risqué; tending toward the obscene.

raw, in the   Naked. 1941: "... To go swimming in the raw." Schulberg, *Sammy*, 178.

raw deal   *n.* A particular instance of very unfair or harsh, malicious, or discriminating, treatment of a person or persons. 1952: "... The Academy officers were heaping raw deal after raw deal upon him...." Sloan Wilson, *New Yorker*, Feb. 23, 78. 1956: " 'They gave that kid [22-year-old Abe Telvi, who blinded Victor Riesel] one raw deal!' Carlino exclaimed during his recital of his efforts to get adequate compensation for Telvi." N. Abrams & N. Patterson, N.Y. *Daily News*, Nov. 16, 5.

rawheel   *n.* A tenderfoot. c1849 [1944]: "... A tenderfoot, or rawheel, or whatever you call 'em...." Andy Gordon's diary, W. E. Woodward in *The Way Our People Lived.*

Ray!   Hurray! 1924: "Ray! Ray! Atta girl!" Marks, *Plastic Age*, 26.

razor   *n.* A pun; a clever joke or homily. *c1845; obs.*   *v.t.* To split up loot into shares. 1925: "When loot is divided among criminals it is 'razored.' " McLellan, *Collier's*, Aug. 8.   **—back razor-back**   *n.* **1** A manual laborer; a porter; a janitor; one who does menial labor; specif., a circus roustabout or a member of a train crew. *Circus, hobo, and railroad use.* **2** A Protestant missionary. *Not common.*   **—neck razor-neck**   *n.* An aristocrat; a wealthy, important person. *Obs.*

razz   *n.* = **raspberry.** 1921: "They begin to give him the razz." Witwer, *Leather*, 52. 1934: "He was giving me the razz." Cain, *Postman*, 78. *From "raspberry."* See Appendix, Shortened Words.   *v.t.* To ridicule or express contempt or scorn for anyone; to ride someone; lit., to give someone the raspberry; to make fun of; to heckle, kid, or rib. *From "raspberry" reinforced by "razzle-dazzle."* 1924: "The fellows razzed [ridiculed] the life out of me.... The sophomores and freshmen ... 'razzed' [heckled] each other ... he had laid himself open to a 'royal razzing' [ribbing]...." Marks, *Plastic Age*, 52, 138, 242.   **—berry** = **raspberry.   —amatazz razz-ma-tazz razzmatazz**   *n.* **1** Anything out of date; anything sentimental; anything insincere or corny. 1951: "The player-piano's playin' a razzamatazz." *Popular song*, "The Piano-Roll Blues." 1956: "*Razzmatazz* is corny jazz." S. Longstreet, *The Real Jazz Old and New*, 147. *Being replaced by "jazz."* **2** = **razzle-dazzle.** Planned confusion; obvious advertising; gaudiness. 1950: "Here ... / Is the big gleam, the eye-blinder,/ The splintered firmament of razzmatazz, Manhattan." H. I. Phillips, *The Once Over*, July 11.   *adj.* **1** Acting, dancing, speaking, doing anything in an old-fashioned, outdated, or corny manner. **2** = **rah-rah. 3** Dazzling. 1948: "... One of the most interesting ... razzmatazz careers of our time." Billy Rose, *synd. newsp. col.*, July 14. *Perhaps from the hypothetical reduplication "razz-tazz" with "-ma-" inserted.* Cf. Appendix, Reduplications; Infixes.

razzle-dazzle   *n.* **1** Confusion, bewilderment; that which is not what it seems, that which confuses, bewilders, or deceives. *Since c1900.* **2** Planned deception or confusion, as for a joke or in joshing or as by one sports team in order to confuse another. **3** A business deception or swindle; an instance of cheating. 1928: "Suspecting some sort of razzle-dazzle, the wiser of the two men said he would buy the seats at their box-office value." *New Yorker*, Dec. 15, 24/1f. **4** Excitement; hilarity; glamor. 1946: "They [supermarkets] put razzle-dazzle into the grocery business." *This Week*, Jan. 4, 7/1f. *The above uses all stem from a basic meaning of something outwardly so dazzling that one does not see an inner deception.* **5** Any exciting carnival ride, esp. a carrousel. *Carnival use, not common.* **6** A prostitute. *Some carnival use.* *adj.* Dazzling; spectacular; showy. 1946: "A great many people are reading Mr. Wakeman's razzle-dazzle novel these days." C. V. Terry in N.Y. *Times Bk. Rev.*, Aug. 4, 5/1.

reach-me-down *adj.* Ready-made; hence, cheap, without individuality or sincerity. 1940: "[The city-hall fixers] all had . . . the nice and the reach-me-down manners." Chandler, *Farewell*, 183. **—s** *n.pl.* Ready-made clothes.

read *v.t.* **1** To inspect clothing for lice. 1918: "The soldiers speak of 'reading their shirt.'" McCartney, *Texas Rev.*, 85. **2** To inspect; to patrol; to check up on an area to be sure everything is as it should be. **3** To ascertain, visually by lip reading, what a person is saying to another; to eavesdrop. 1949: "Can you read him? . . . I can't read him." Movie, *White Heat.* **4** To know a person well enough to predict his thoughts and actions. *From fig. to be able to "read [another] like a book."* **5** To give a pilot a reading or navigational data relating to his plane's exact position. *W.W.II Air Force use.* → **6** To locate a friendly plane on a radar scope. *When the plane is "read" or seen on the radar scope, the pilot knows he will be kept on his proper course and that any necessary assistance is nearby. W.W.II Air Force use.* **7** To understand, comprehend, or see; to d.g. *Orig. cool use; a sophisticated, intellectual syn. of "dig" since c1950. Prob. from the "reading" of sheet music, reinforced by the above Air Force uses.* **—er** *n.* **1** A license to do business, esp. for holding a road show or selling pitchman's merchandise. *Carnival and pitchman use.* → **2** Money paid for a license to put on a show in a city. *Carnival and circus use.* **3** A prescription for narcotics. *Dope addict use.* **4** A printed circular describing a man wanted for a crime. 1946: "They got readers out on him and there was quite a hunt. . . ." Evans, *Halo in Blood*, 121. **—ers** *n.pl.* Marked playing cards. 1939: "They catch him with a deck of readers in a poker game." Runyon, 103. 1954: "The cards and dice were crooked, the cards being readers." W. R. & F. K. Simpson, *Hockshop*, 275. *Lit., cards with secret markings on the back, so that the owner of the deck knows which cards his opponents have.*

read [one's] plate **1** To say grace or give thanks at mealtime. *Southern hill use.* **2** To eat in silence; to be forced to eat in silence as a punishment.

ready   **the ready** *n.* Money, esp. cash. 1933: "Take the ready and send it along. . . ." Kieran, *Sat. Rev. of Lit.* 1958: "Out of work recently and without the ready. . . ." N.Y. *Daily News*, Feb. 20, 5. *From "ready cash."* *adj.* **1** Drunk. *Not common.* **2** Satisfactory; perfect. *Negro and jive use.*

ready for Freddie   Ready, esp. for the unexpected, the unknown, or the unusual. *Orig. and pop. in synd. newsp. comic strip "Li'l Abner."* See Appendix, Rhyming Slang.

real *n.* In the game of marbles, a heavy marble with which a player shoots. 1949: "Now, a shooter, or 'real,' as the afficionados call it. . . ." Billy Rose, *synd. newsp. col.*, Aug. 1. *adv.* **1** Very; really. *Colloq. since c1820.* See **for real.** **2** Emphatically; extremely; definitely; sincerely; intensely; genuinely; really. 1950: "I mean by *real* Creole, he was French and Spanish and spoke languages. Like me." A. Lomax, *Mr. Jelly Roll*, 30. 1957: "Real jazz [means] corny, in bad taste." W. James in *Metronome Year Book*, 66. 1957: "My Sugar Daddy is the Real McCoy." N.Y. *Enquirer*, Feb. 4, 9. 1957: "The statuesque lady is an eye-catching trademark. She turned up first in a memorable mailing piece that prompted an enthusiastic comment of 'real cool' from John O'Connor of Grosset and Dunlap." *Publishers' Weekly*, Apr. 22, 17. *Although in use for some time, as in the familiar "real McCoy", "real" became pop. as an adv. with "bop" c1946, and is freq. used by bop and cool groups, most often in "real cool," "real crazy," and "real gone." It indicates that the speaker knows or feels that the following word is genuine and is almost akin to an oath = "I swear it is . . ." Also, once a word* *assoc. with a specif. group gains pop. outside the group, it begins to lose or change connotation; thus, adding "real" is an attempt to qualify the word to its original group usage by members of the group that orig. used it. Although mainly bop and cool use, also some far out and beat use; often used before "fine," "most," "sheer," "weird," "wild."*

real cheese = **cheese.**

real estate 1 Low-grade coal. *Railroad use. Fig., dirt or earth sold as coal.* 2 Dirt, such as gathers on the hands or face.

real George, the See **George**, *adj.*

real gone Emphatically, irrevocably, thoroughly gone. *Cool use.* See **real.**

real McCoy, the 1 Genuine, uncut whisky or liquor. *Prohibition use.* → 2 Anything or any person that is genuine, superior, dependable, or greatly liked. 1951: [during the bagel bakers' strike] "... Toasted seeded rolls, Bialystok rolls ... and egg bagels, a sweeter variety but not the real McCoy, were being thrown into the bagel void with varying degrees of reception." N.Y. *Times,* Dec. 17, 1/6.

ream   rim   *v.t.* 1 [taboo] Lit. and fig., to poke something up another's rectum. *From the stand. "ream."* See **rim.** → 2 To take advantage of, cheat, or swindle another. 1933: "I've got five [tubes of toothpaste] left out of the half dozen you rimmed me into taking." J. T. Farrell, 64. 1938: "A new technique for reaming the customers." Liebling, *Back Where,* 84. 1951: "What a rimming the poor riders [of streetcars] are getting at the hands of the boys in charge." Letter in *Collier's,* Nov. 17, 4/4.

rear   *n.* 1 A single portion or helping of snuff. *Obs.* 2 The posterior.

rear end   The posterior. *A euphemism for "ass." Colloq.* 1937: "She's a pain in the rear end." Weidman, *Wholesale,* 145. 1952: "I would like to ... give you a swift kick in the rear end...." Letter to the editor, N.Y. *Daily News,* Aug. 20, C11/5.

reat   *adj.* = **reet.**

rebop   *n.* = **bebop.** *Archaic, replaced by "bebop" and "bop."*

Red   *n.* 1 A nickname for a red-haired person. 2 A Communist or one with Communist sympathies. *From the red flag used by the international Communist movement. Colloq. since c1940.* 3 Loosely, any political radical.   *adj.* Communistic; radical.   **red**   *n.* A cent; 1¢. 1856: "I hain't a red." Doesticks,

Elephant Club.   adj. Profitable, said of a place. See **red one.** *Carnival and circus use.*

red, in the   Operating a business at a deficit; losing money; in debt. *From the red ink bookkeepers use on the deficit side of the ledger.*

red apple   A nonunion employee; esp., one who courts a boss or plant owner by refusing to join a union. 1956: "A nonunion worker. Rubber workers use the term 'red apple,' from applepolisher." *Labor's Special Lang. from Many Sources. Not common.*

red ball   1 A fast freight train. → 2 Any express train, truck, or bus that is running on schedule and is given priority over slower vehicles. 1951: movie, *Red Ball Express,* about U.S. Army supply trucks.

red carpet   Lit., the red plush carpet traditionally laid out for a king to walk on; fig., elegance, extremely hospitable or preferred treatment. *Usu. in "to roll out the red carpet for [someone]."   adj.* Elegant. 1957: "Jewelry gives you a red carpet elegance." Advt., *Life,* Sept. 9, 17.

redeploy   *v.i.* To go home, or to be discharged from military service. *Some W.W.II Army use. Note that this sl. use is a v.i. while the stand. use is a v.t.*

redeye   red-eye   1 Thick ham gravy. *From its color. Dial.* 2 Inferior or raw whisky; specif., bootlegged whisky; sometimes brandy, rum, or other hard liquor; cheap liquor. 1922: "This fellow paid a thousand dollars for ten cases of red-eye that proved to be nothing but water." S. Lewis, *Babbitt,* reprinted in *The American Twenties,* 229. 1949: "Barrow put down a slug of redeye...." A. Hynd, *Public Enemies,* 44. *c1820 to present.* See **bottle, hit the.** 3 Ketchup. *W.W.I and W.W.II Armed Forces use.*

red face   *Fig.,* a state of embarrassment. 1948: "... The Chief [of Police] had a red face when ... he was found in possession of stolen property...." A. Hynd, *Pinkerton,* 82.   **—d**   *adj.* Embarrassed.

redhead   *n.* A freshman. *From the red hats worn by freshmen in some colleges.*

red horse   Corned beef. *Not common.*

red hot   red-hot   *adj.* 1 Extremely hot. 1956: "Shiekie Miranti brought him this message: 'The people uptown say get this kid out of town; he's red hot.'" N. Abrams & N. Patterson, N.Y. *Daily News,* Nov. 16, 5. *Fig., something* so hot that it is glowing red. **2** Containing accounts of scandals; sensational. 1887: "... A red-hot newsy journal." New Orleans *Lantern.* **3** Lively; pleasing; peppy. **4** Sexy. *n.* **1** A frankfurter. 1930: "Don leaned against the ... red hot stand. ..." J. T. Farrell, 141. **2** A thief. 1932–34: *Maryland prison use.* **3** A stag; a man unaccompanied by a woman. c1942: "Too many red hots at the [Nassau Tavern]." *Princeton Alumni Weekly.* See **hot, hot for.**

red-hot mamma **1** A pretty, lively, sexy, and affectionate female sweetheart. Also called **mamma, hot mamma, sweet mamma.** Cf. **warm baby.** **2** Specif. a type of large, lively, and earthy female singer in vogue c1920.

red ink Red wine. Cf. **ink.** 1948: "... A pint of red ink still sells for two bits. ..." Lait-Mortimer, *N.Y. Confidential,* 89.

red lead **1** Jelly. *Not common.* **2** Tomato ketchup. *c1900 to W.W.II. Maritime, soldier, vagabond, and lunch-counter use. Orig. from the color of red-lead paint, as used on ships.*

red legs An artilleryman. *Soldier use until W.W.II.*

red-letter day An extremely important day; a day when something very personal, important, and eagerly awaited is to happen or has happened. *Lit., a day that is printed in red on the calendar; hence, a day more important than the rest.*

red-light **redlight** *v.t.* **1** To push a person off or out of a moving railroad train; also, to kill by so doing. 1932: "Who'd you red-light, Ferris? ..." Dashiell Hammett, *Too Many Have Lived. Carnival and circus use.* **2** To stop one's automobile and eject a passenger so that he has to walk home under inconvenient or embarrassing circumstances. 1935: "... Making me walk as those Yale guys do the time they redlight me." Runyon.

redline *v.t.* To delete a soldier's name from the payroll, temporarily, because of some irregularity. *Army use.*

Red Mike A woman-hater. *Annapolis use.*

red-neck *n.* A rustic; esp. a poor white Southern farmer. **—ed** *adj.* Angry. *Rural use.*

red noise Tomato soup; a bowl of tomato soup.

red one A place where, or a day when, business is unusually good; good business.

Carnival and circus use. From "red-letter day."

red paint Ketchup.

red tape **1** A training period. *c1920; prize fight use.* **2** Delay caused by duplication of work and office routine, esp. in government; petty routine. *From the red tape used to bind up official government documents.*

red tea Liquor. 1887: New Orleans *Lantern. Never common, now obs.*

reefer *n.* **1** A refrigerated railroad freight car, truck, or ship. *c1925 to present; railroad, trucker, USN, and hobo use.* 1948: [railroad refrigerator car] "Reefers, as the hobos call them." Cain, *Moth,* 79. → **2** A refrigerator; usu. a large commercial refrigerator. *Hobo, W.W.II, USN use.* **3** A marijuana cigarette. 1934: "I smoked a reefer." *Amer. Journal of Psychiatry,* Sept., 313. 1940 [1951]: "The air of the trailer was heavy with the stinks of food and reefers." C. McCullers, *The Heart Is a Lonely Hunter,* reprinted with *The Ballad of the Sad Café,* 422. 1956: "... Reefers ... the marijuana cigarette. ..." S. Longstreet, *The Real Jazz Old and New,* 144. *Now the most common use, generally known to the public. The most common word for marijuana cigarette. c1930 orig. addict, prisoner, and Negro use.* → **4** One who smokes marijuana. **5** A sea apprentice.

reefer weed Marijuana; a marijuana cigarette. *Addict use.*

reek *n.* Paper money. *Obs.*

reeler *n.* A spree. See Appendix, **—er** ending. 1950: "He begins to take his drinks in gulps, and before he realizes it he is off on a reeler." Jack Alexander, *SEP,* Apr. 1, 75/2.

reet **reat** *adj.* **1** Satisfactory; good; correct; pleasing; right; stylish. 1943: "A reat pleat is a right pleat, i.e., a good pleat; and that comes from 'all reat,' which is the rug-cutter's way of saying 'all right.' " *New Yorker,* June 19, 15/1. 1952: " 'You say you found him loose in the streets?' 'Reet!' " M. Blosser, *synd. newsp. comic strip,* "Freckles," Feb. 22. → **2** All right; great; wonderful; extremely attractive, appealing, exciting, satisfying; hep. 1943: "G. M.! [Glenn Miller, orchestra leader] ... he's reet." M. Shulman, *Barefoot Boy with Cheek,* 90. 1954: "With her good looks, she was still 'reet' with me." L. Armstrong, *Satchmo, My Life in New Orleans,* 152. *Both meanings in wide jive use.*

reet pleat A long, narrow pleat, usu.

in a zoot suit, pressed to a sharp point. *Almost always used in the obs. rhyming jive expression "a zoot suit with a reet pleat."* See **reet**. See Appendix, Rhyming Slang.

refrigerator *n.* A prison. Cf. **cooler**. *c1880.*

regular *adj.* **1** Agreeable, pleasant, friendly; fair; in the same social and economic class and with the same general intellectual level and interests as the speaker; liked by the speaker and not considered superior or inferior to him; generally liked by and acceptable to one's fellow men. *Usu. in "regular guy" or "regular fellow."* 1920: "I know I'm not a regular fellow, yet I loathe anybody else that isn't." F. S. Fitzgerald, *This Side of Paradise*, 50. 1924: "He was just one of so many mute and inglorious Babbitts preparing to qualify as regular fellows." E. Boyd, "Aesthete: Model 1924," reprinted in *The American Twenties*, 354. 1930: "So [the cop] usually decides to become a 'regular guy.'" Lavine, *Third Degree*, 161. *Colloq. since c1920. Common since a major goal of Americans became security and social approval.* **2** Having periodic bowel movements; not constipated; specif., having a bowel movement each day. *A euphem. pop. in laxative advertisements.* **3** With the usual or average amount of cream and sugar; said of a cup of coffee. *Orig. lunch-counter use in relaying an order.*

rehash **re-hash** *v.t.* To rediscuss; to talk about the same thing over and over; to talk about the past. 1920: "...The things...they had hashed and rehashed for many a frugal conversational meal." Fitzgerald, *This Side of Paradise*, 134. *Colloq.* *n.* A rediscussion; repeated conversation; a summary. 1947: "... The re-hash of the case in Monday's papers. ..." *San Fran. Murders*, 239. 1953: "... A rehash of stale political charges. ..." AP, July 6.

Reilly's balls = **Kelsey's nuts**.

Remington **remington** *n.* A machine gun. *From the typewriter. Because "Remington" is a well-known brand of typewriter, and the Remington Company also manufactures weapons.*

remover = **paint remover**.

rent party A party given by a person at his apartment or house in order to collect money to pay his rent. *The host thus provides a place to dance and usu. records and a phonograph; the "guests"— friends, neighbors, and even strangers— all contribute a small sum to the host, which he applies toward his rent. Thus the host can pay his rent and his guests can dance for much less money than if they went to a commercial ballroom. Orig. and most pop. with Harlem Negroes during c1930–c1939. The music was almost always jive or swing.* Cf. **rug-cut**, **rug-cutter**.

rep *n.* **1** A reputation, either good or bad. 1873: *DAE.* 1917: "Go get a rep." Utter in *Harper's*, June, 70/1. 1950: "I don't wanna start gettin' the rep a not havin' a big schnozz." Jimmy Durante quoted by M. Zolotow in *SEP*, July 15, 122/2. **2** A disreputable person. *Some c1900 use; obs.* **3** A representative. *Since c1900.* *adj.* Repertory. *Theater use. Usu. in "rep show" or "rep company."*

rep-dep = **repple-depple**. See Appendix, Reduplications.

repeaters *n.pl.* Loaded dice. *Because they repeat a specif. combination of points.*

report = **sugar report**.

repple-depple **repple depple** *n.* A replacement depot where soldiers await assignment or processing. *From "reple.," an abbr. of "replacement," and "deppo," a pronunciation of "depot." W.W.II Army use.* 1946: "The Naples 'repple depple' which processes the G.I. departing from home. ..." J. P. McKnight, AP, Rome, Jan. 7.

reppo depot = **repple-depple**.

rest [one's] jaw To stop talking. 1929: "Aw, rest your jaw." Burnett, *Little Caesar. Not common.*

rest powder Snuff. *Obs.*

retread *n.* **1** A used automobile tire that has had new treads added to it. *Colloq.* → **2** A discharged or retired soldier or sailor who returns to or is recalled to active military service; specif., a W.W.I soldier who also served in W.W.II or a W.W.II soldier who left military service but was recalled for the Korean War. 1949: "Retreads will reune [hold a reunion]." *Amer. Legion Mag.*, Oct., 26. *Army and some USN use during and since W.W.II.*

Reuben *n.* A rustic; a rube or hick. 1905: "I've a couple of new card tricks ... that will leave the Reubens gasping for air." McHugh, *Search Me*, 60. *Orig. carnival and circus use.*

re-up *v.i.* To re-enlist; to sign up again. *c1935; Army use.*

rhinie *n.* A first-year student in a preparatory school. *Perh. from "rhino" = homesick.*

rhino *n.* **1** Money. 1859: Matsell. *Some use since c1850; more common in Eng. than in U.S. From "rind."* See Appendix, —o ending. **2** A feeling of depression or sadness. *Some use since c1925; orig. USN use.* **3** A rhinoceros. See Appendix, Shortened Words. *adj.* **1** Homesick. *Since c1925; orig. USN use.* → **2** Melancholy; depressed, sad; discouraged. **3** Without funds; broke.

rhubarb *n.* **1** A noisy argument, often accompanied by a fight, orig. and esp., on a baseball field; a controversy, dispute, quarrel, squabble, fracas, or short fight. 1948: "Nice guys finish first without resorting to bean-ball throwing, rhubarbs, and umpire baiting." J. Durant in N.Y. *Times Bk. Rev.*, May 30, 10/2. 1950: "The [baseball] umpires became embroiled in a rhubarb that raged around the interpretation of a very complicated rule." *SEP*, May 6, 168/3. 1957: "Willie Gets Frisco [San Francisco] Home After a Racial Rhubarb [headline]: Negro baseball star Willie Mays got his $37,500 home today after a hectic day in which the race issue raised by neighbors was overcome." N.Y. *Daily News*, Nov. 15, 4. *From the custom in the theater, radio, and movies of saying the word "rhubarb" over and over again to simulate angry and menacing talk in crowd scenes.* **2** Orig., in baseball, an error; hence, any blunder, a mistake; a faux pas. *Not common.* **3** A strafing mission or operation carried out by low-flying airplanes. 1943: "When a fighter pilot flies low over France, strafing whatever he finds—trains, troops, airdromes—he is 'on a rhubarb.' " *Time*, Mar. 22, 51. *W.W.II Air Force use. Orig. Royal Air Force use. In allusion to the low-flying pilot's close view of gardens.* *v.i., v.t.* To strafe from a low altitude; to fly at a low altitude. 1944: "Flying for rhubarbing." C. Macon in *Collier's*, Sept. 23, 69/1. *W.W.II Air Force use.*

rhubarbs, the *n.* Small towns; rural areas; the sticks. 1915: "Until I came to Hillsboro I never imagined what the game [of baseball] meant as it's played out in the rhubarbs." G. Patten, *Covering the Look-in Corner*, 291.

rib *v.t.* **1** To tease a person; to make fun of or poke fun at; to josh. **2** To discredit. *Not common.* *n.* **1** A wife. *c1900; from Genesis, reinforced by the verb meaning.* → **2** A girl or woman. *Once stand. and very common; revived as very hip slang c1958.* **3** A remark, prank, or gag that ribs the victim. 1952:

"Wilt said, 'He is a parasite.' Maybe this was a rib. . . ." Red Smith, N.Y. *Her. Trib.*, Jan. 25, 18. **4** Barbecued spareribs. → **5** A piece of meat, whether actually a sparerib or rib roast or not. Specif., a portion of any kind of beef, esp. a steak or a thick slice of roast beef. **6** A complete dinner; hot food. *c1946; bop, progressive musician, and fan use. From "spareribs," reinforced by the concept that "food sticks to the ribs."* 1948: "Don't eat here, after the set we'll go up the street for some ribs." *Oral;* bop musician Dizzy Gillespie.

rib joint A brothel. 1943: "Fracas in a Minneapolis rib joint." M. Shulman, *Barefoot Boy with Cheek*, 192. *Not common. From "tenderloin," reinforced by "crib joint."*

rib-stickers *n.pl.* Beans. *From the phrase "to stick to one's ribs."*

rib-tickler *n.* A joke.

rice-belly [derog.] *n.* A Chinese.

riceman [derog.] *n.* A Chinese. *Not common.*

rich = **stone-rich**.

Richard   richard *n* **1** A deformed man, esp. a hunchback. 1948: J. S. Farmer. *Underworld use. Obs.* **2** A detective. 1952: "Mickey Spillane, who turns out epics about a private richard named Mike Hammer. . . ." R. C. Ruark, *synd. newsp. col.*, Mar. 3. *From "dick."*

Richard Roe = **John Doe**.

ride *v.t.,v.i.* **1** To cheat in an examination by using a literal translation or list of answers. *c1850.* See **pony, ride a pony.** → **2** To cheat or take advantage of. **3** To tease or nag; persecute, harass, or annoy by continuous adverse criticism; to pick on verbally; to use sarcasm against. 1930: [to persecute] "If a keeper . . . attempts to 'ride' [a prisoner]." Lavine, *Third Degree*, 227. 1936: "The cowboy may have disliked to have another person 'ride him,' but the average puncher would not kill for the mere resultant pique." P. A. Rollins, *The Cowboy*, 48. *The most common use.* 1949: [to use sarcasm against] ". . . Thinking just how the critics would ride me." Margaret Mitchell, N.Y. *Times Bk. Rev.*, Aug. 28, 2/2. **4** In sports, to harass or abuse an opponent verbally in the hope of making him nervous and reducing his efficiency. **5** To go on as usual; to remain as is; to stand pat; to forget or ignore something. **6** [taboo] To have sexual intercourse with. 1951: "Have you heard the story of the old Irish woman who was asked if she were ever bedridden? 'Hundreds of times,' she answered, 'and once in a sled!' " S. Longstreet, *The Pedlocks*, 76. **7** To dance; esp., to dance well. *c1935 jive use.* *n.* **1** An easy course of action; the easy way. **2** Anything enjoyable, esp. if free and easy to do. **3** [taboo] Copulation. **4** In jazz music, an improvised passage. See **sleighride, take [someone] for a ride.** **—r** *n.* **1** Specif., a cowboy. 1936: "The cowboy was not always called 'cowboy.' In Wyoming he preferred to be styled a 'rider.' " P. A. Rollins, *The Cowboy*, 39. **2** Specif., a race-horse jockey.

ride, go along for the To join in passively, usually for the fun of it, without making an active contribution.

ride, take [someone] for a **1** To murder. *Orig. to murder in the Chicago gangster style of the 1920's, by forcing the victim to get into a car, driving him to a secluded place, and shooting him.* 1930: "The gang believes that he is getting yellow or soft, and usually takes him for a ride...." Lavine, *Third Degree*, 26. *Archaic form is "take [someone] for a one-way ride."* **2** To deceive or cheat. 1951: "But the one who really took my friend for a ride was the electrician. He used more ... cable ... than ... it takes to build a battleship." Roger W. Babson, *synd. newsp. col.*, Oct. 13. 1956: "Labor 'Taken for Ride' by State Senate [title of editorial]," *New Jersey Labor Herald*, Dec.

ride a pony To use a written sheet of answers, or other unethical device to obtain answers, during a written examination; to use a pony. *Student use; archaic.*

rideout *v.i., v.t.* To play the last chorus of a jazz performance in a free and abandoned, enthusiastic manner. 1956: "*Rideout* is to swing a last chorus." S. Longstreet, *The Real Jazz Old and New*, 149.

ride shanks' mare (pony) To walk. *Very old.*

ride the beam To pretend innocence, as by looking at the ceiling. *W.W.II Army use.*

ride the gravy train = **gravy train.**

ridge-runner *n.* **1** A hillbilly; a mountaineer. **2** A Southern rustic.

riding the air Working at a great height; said of construction workers. 1956: "A carpenter hopes he won't have to spend the day *riding the air*—working up high." *Labor's Special Lang. from Many Sources.*

rif *v.t.* To notify an employee of the termination of his employment; to can, fire, or sack a person. 1950: "Ask any Federal Government employee what it means when he receives his Reduction In Force letter, and he will say, 'I've been riffed.' " Letter in *N.Y. Times Mag.*, Jan. 1, 2. *From the initials of "Reduction In Force."* See Appendix, Shortened Words. *n.* A dismissal from employment.

riff *n.* **1** A slum dweller. *Some c1890 use; obs.* **2** In jazz, an improvisation of a phrase or passage by a soloist or by several musicians playing in close harmony; a repeated figure. 1938: "Gene Krupa's riffs on the [drums]." C. Smith in *Esquire*, 95/2. 1950: "Riffs—meaning figures. No jazz piano player can really play good jazz unless they try to give an imitation of a band, that is, by providing a basis of riffs." A. Lomax, *Mr. Jelly Roll*, 58. *Common jazz use.* → **3** An improvised or impromptu conversation; a conversation in which one improvises on events or happenings; esp. in order to create a favorable impression on the listener; a line; exaggerated, insincere talk. **4** A refrigerated railroad freight car. *Railroad use. From "refrigerated."* See Appendix, Shortened Words.

riffle *n.* In baseball, a hard swing at the ball with the bat, whether or not the ball is hit. 1951: "With batting, if a kid takes a good natural cut at the ball and gives it a really solid riffle, that's the point." H. Lobert in *N.Y. Times Mag.*, Mar. 18, 40. *v.i.,v.t.* To shuffle cards. *Colloq.*

riffle, make a To beg money; to panhandle. *Hobo use; archaic.*

riffle, make the To succeed; to attain a specific goal. *Hobo use.*

rig *v.t.* **1** To prearrange the outcome of something, esp. a sports contest; to throw; to fix. 1933: "Prize-fights or horse-races have been rigged. ..." *Lit. Digest*, July 1. **2** To control the stock market by manipulating prices. *Wall Street use.* *n.* **1** Wearing apparel; esp. eccentric or unusual clothing. *Colloq.* **2** Any bus. *Bus driver use.*

right *adj.* **1** Friendly; fair; reliable. **2** Trustworthy to a criminal group; not associated with the police; not an informer. *Underworld use.* **3** Drunk. *Not common.* See **bang to rights, dead to rights, reet.**

righteous *adj.* **1** Terrific; perfectly

satisfying; wonderful; extremely beautiful, inordinately pleasing. *The most superlative jive word. Negro and jazz use.* **2** Self-righteous, snobbish, superior. *Colloq.* **3** [derog.] Like a white man. *Harlem use.*

righteous moss Hair characteristic of Caucasians. *Harlem use.*

right-foot [derog.] *adj.* Roman Catholic. *n.* A Roman Catholic.

right guy **1** An honest, reliable, fair man. 1939: "With us you are a right guy." J. O'Hara, *Pal Joey*, 33. 1941: "You was a right guy, and I'm not the one to forget it." J. Lilienthal, *Horse Crazy*, 11. → **2** Specif., one who can be trusted by criminals not to inform to the police. *Underworld use since c1925.*

right-handed [derog.] = **right-foot.**

rightho   righto   right-ho
right-o *adv.* Yes; all right; o.k. 1914: " 'Right-o,' added McGarver." S. Lewis, *Our Mr. Wrenn*, 51. 1924: ". . . And that the coaches said that cigarettes were bad for a runner. 'Right-o,' said Carl." " 'Let's go to the movies.' 'Right-o!' " Marks, *Plastic Age*, 11; 24. *Usu. considered Brit., but some U.S. use after W.W.I.*

right joint **1** A fair, reliable, trustworthy nightclub, gambling place, etc. **2** A prison, reformatory, or other institution where the inmates are treated fairly. 1951: "Great Meadow . . . 'a right joint'. . . ." John Lardner, *New Yorker*, Dec. 1, 113.

right money = **smart money.** 1941: "It's the combination of likely lad [jockey] and a good horse . . . that makes 'right money' dig down in its jeans." J. Lilienthal, *Horse Crazy*, 19.

right off the bat At once; initially; instantly. 1944: " 'Lama,' I said right off the bat. . . ." Shulman, *Leather Merchants*, 2.

right up there Close to or almost winning or succeeding; close to being or almost famous.

righty *n.* A right-handed person; in baseball, a right-handed pitcher. See Appendix, —y ending.

rigid Drunk.

rig-out *n.* A garb; an outfit; a get-up, 1928: ". . . To be seen in a waiter's or a chef's rig-out." Niven Busch, Jr., *New Yorker*, Nov. 3, 32/1f. *Used since c1895.*

Rileyed *adj.* Drunk.

rim-rock   rim-rack *v.t.* **1** To kill by forcing or stampeding over a precipice. *Applied to animals. Western ranch use. To rim-rock an enemy's*

herd *of sheep or cattle was about the worst revenge one could take. Obs.* **2** To ruin another or to cause another to fail, usu. by deception.

rinctum *n.* **1** A wrinkle, contrivance, or design. *Some c1890 New England dial. use.* **2** [taboo] The rectum. *Jocular Negro use,* *v.t.* To hurt, damage, or ruin; said of a person or thing. *From "wreck 'em" and "to shove [it] up [one's] rinctum [rectum]." The "—um" = " 'em" (them), so the word is a v.i. and not truly a v.t. "Rinctum" is the form for all tenses and persons.*

rind *n.* **1** Audacity; nerve. *Some c1900 student use. Because an audacious person is said to have a thick skin or "rind"; fig., being immune to the criticism or dislike of others.* **2** Money.

ring *v.t.* To turn on a light. *Some c1910 use; never common.* *v.i.,v.t.* To substitute one horse for another of similar appearance in a race; to put a ringer in a race. 1948: "He was afraid to attempt ringing. . . ." "In selecting a horse to ring. . . ." ". . . To ring horses without fear of detection." "Barrie had rung Aknahton as Hickey at Bowie." A. Hynd, *Pinkerton*, 67; 70; 79; 94. *n.* A telephone call. 1946: "Tell him to give me a ring at the office." Evans, *Halo in Blood*, 162. *Stand. since c1930.*
—er *n.* **1** A person or animal having an appearance closely resembling another; specif. a race horse, illegally substituted for another in a contest, as a race; esp., a superior race horse that resembles or is made to resemble an inferior horse and is substituted for it in a race. 1944: "The chance that 'ringers'—good horses masquerading as poor ones under assumed names—can be sneaked into races. . . ." *Fortune*, Sept., 140/2. *Horse-racing use.* → **2** One who illegally substitutes one horse for another in a race. 1948: "King of the Race Track Ringers [title:] The master horse ringer of them all. . . ." A. Hynd, *Pinkerton*, 65. **3** A double; a dead ringer. 1950: "With the mustache and glasses, Blackmer is a ringer for Teddy [Roosevelt]." AP, July 21. **4** A doorbell. *Hobo use since c1925.*

ring-master *n.* A yardmaster. *Railroad use.*

ring off To stop talking. *c1895, prob. from telephone use.*

ring-tail *n.* **1** A grouchy person. *Hobo use.* **2** A coward; one who cannot be trusted. *More common in Austral. than in U.S.* **3** [derog.] An Italian longshoreman. *Longshoreman use.* **4** [derog.] A Japanese. *W.W.II USN use.*

ring-tailed snorter   A fine, strong, courageous man; a humdinger. 1950: "You'll have to hand it to this . . . secretary of agriculture. . . . He's a ring-tailed snorter." *Editorial*, Ithaca, N.Y., *Journal*, Aug. 1, 6/2. *Since c1830.*

ring the bell   To succeed; to meet with approval or make a hit with someone. *Also, less freq., "hit the bell." From various carnival devices in which a bell rings when a player is successful. Colloq.*

ring-warm   *n.* A boxing enthusiast.

rinktum ditty = **blushing bunny.**

rinky-dink   rinkydink   *n.* **1** Cheap, gaudy merchandise; junk; drek. *Orig. carnival use.* **2** Old, worn, or used merchandise. 1956: "*Rinky-dink* is broken-down stuff." S. Longstreet, *The Real Jazz Old and New*, 147. *Not common.* **3** A cheap place of amusement. 1951: "I think of Sweet Mama Stringbean [Ethel Waters] as she was called when she played the Rinky-dinks for $25 a week." Edward Weeks, *Atlantic Monthly.* Cf. **honky-tonk. 4** A swindle; a runaround. 1942: [*Nightclub use, N.Y.C.*] "Don't give me the rinkydink." S. Billingsley, *Harper's Bazaar*, July. See Appendix, Reduplications.

riot   *n.* **1** An exceedingly successful entertainment or performance. **2** An extremely funny or amusing person. *Colloq.*

rip   *n.* **1** A disreputable person; a debaucher. 1947: "My way was the proper way to treat a rip." J. Stephens in *Amer. Mercury*, June, 660/1. *Colloq.* **2** A demerit; a penalty; a fine. 1958: "Rip—A fine imposed for infraction of police regulations: e.g., 'I got to pay a five-day rip' (fined five days' pay)." G. Y. Wells, *Station House Slang.*

rip-bop   *n.* = **bebop.** *Obs. form.*

ripe   *adj.* **1** Ready, said of plans or schemes; eager, said of a person; ready and eager, esp. to be victimized. *Colloq.* **2** Drunk. See Appendix, Drunk.

ripe suck   One who is easily fooled; a sucker. *Not common.*

ripped up   Angry. *Pre-W.W.II teenage use, now replaced by "pissed off" and other terms.*

ripping   *adj.* Excellent; dandy; corking; swell. 1910: "It's ripping. . . ." Johnson, *Varmint*, 20. *Now somewhat archaic in both Eng. and the U.S.*

ripple   *n.* A noncommissioned officer in the Waves. *W.W.II use.*

rips   *n.pl.* Trousers; slacks. 1947:

"Slacks are rips, pleated slacks are lipped rips. Shorts, of course, are clipped rips." *The Academian*, a school paper, quoted by Don Rose in Phila. *Bulletin*, Jan. 21, 13. *Some teenage use c1945. Resembles, but is not, jive talk.*

ripsnorter   *n.* A remarkable person or thing. *Since c1840; now archaic.* 1951: "The villain is a real ripsnorter." S. J. Perelman, *New Yorker*, Mar. 3, 28/1.

ripsnorting   *adj.* First-rate. 1910: "A rip-snorting . . . newspaper . . . that would put the *Lawrence* out of biz." Johnson, *Varmint*, 128.

rise   *n.* **1** Anger, indignation, vexation, or the like, purposely aroused in a person by an action or statement contrary to his interests, beliefs, or prejudices. *Usu. in "get a rise out of [someone]." Colloq.* **2** A response, usu. in reply to such action. 1949: "I had to say those unpleasant things to get a RISE out of you." Al Capp, *comic strip*, "Li'l Abner," Oct. 28.

rise out of [someone], get a   See **rise.**

ritz   *n.* Wealthy and aristocratic style; swank. *Usu. in "put on the ritz" or in "the ritz."* 1938: " 'Putting on the Ritz' . . . Cesar Ritz . . . a synonym for luxury. The Ritz Hotel . . . opened in Paris in 1898 . . . the word Ritz became a byname for elegance and luxury." Anon., *Better English*, Nov., 50. 1943: ". . . Put on the dog and give him the ritz like this. . . ." Wolfert, *Underworld*, 12. *The words "ritz" and "ritzy" have flourished most in nonritzy circles.*   **—y**   *adj.* **1** Swanky; elegant; luxurious; fancy; plush. 1930: "The ritziest dance hall was the Haymarket." Lavine, *Third Degree*, 172. 1949: "De window of a ritzy fur saloon." C. Gould, *synd. comic strip*, "Dick Tracy," Oct. 13. **2** Wealthy; living luxuriously and elegantly. **3** Proud, snobbish, vain. 1929: " 'Ritzy,' that is, arrogantly proud and vain." B. Sobel, *Bookman*, Apr., 146.

river   *n.* An examination. *c1925, college student, mainly Annapolis, use. From the concept that a river represents the boundary between life and death.*

rivets   *n.* Money.

roach   *n.* **1** A policeman. *Primarily Negro prison use.* **2** A race horse. *Not common.* See **beetle. 3** A marijuana cigarette, esp. the stub of a partially smoked marijuana cigarette. 1956: "The marijuana cigarette which he smokes down to the roach, the smallest butt in the world." S. Longstreet, *The Real Jazz Old and New*, 144.

road, hit the   **1** To travel; to move on again; lit., to enter a highway in order to hitchhike. 1947: "Laura then hit the road with a lurid lecture entitled 'Wolves in the Fold.' " R. O'Brien, *San Francisco Murders*, 41. See **road. 2** To work as a traveling salesman.

road, the   *n.* Lit., the state of or time spent wandering or traveling, as a tourist, traveling salesman, or esp. as a vagabond or hobo. See **hit the road, skid road, wide place in the road.**

road apples   Horse feces, as found on the highway.

road hog   An automobile driver without regard for the rights of other drivers; one who takes more than his share of the road. *Colloq.* See Appendix, Suffixes and Suffix Words.

road louse   A small automobile, esp. a Ford. *c1925; obs.*

road monkey   A repairer of roads. *c1890, still used by loggers.* See Appendix, Suffixes and Suffix Words.

road-stake   *n.* Money for traveling. *Hobo argot.*

roast   *v.t.* To make fun of; to criticize adversely; to pan. 1905: "If he were to roast our Skinski it might hurt our business." McHugh, *Search Me*, 50. *n.* An instance of criticism or bantering; a panning. 1903: "This national love for a good 'roast,' this spirit of mockery . . ." H. Spencer. *Both forms colloq.* See **peanut-roaster.**

roasting-ear wine   Corn whisky. *Midwest use.*

robber   See **belly-robber, dog-robber, stomach-robber.**

robin = **blind robin.**

Robin Hood's barn, go around   To proceed in a roundabout way. *Since c1880.*

Robinson Crusoe   **1** To accomplish or attempt to accomplish a daring or spectacular feat without the knowledge of others. *From the character and title of the famous children's classic.* **2** A person who prefers to work or live alone.

Robinson Crusoe and Friday   *n.pl.* Two theater seats on the aisle. *In allusion to "two on the isle." c1925; theater use.*

rob the cradle   To date or marry a person much younger than oneself. *Colloq.*

rock   *n.* **1** A piece of money. *Until c1840.* **2** A dollar; the sum of $1. *Most common c1920.* 1950: "I want to see you make twenty rocks. . . ." Starnes, *And When She Was Bad*, 142. **3** Any gem, esp.

a diamond. *Underworld use until c1925; now common.* 1951: ". . . To buy that rock?" Movie, *The Racket.* **4** A mistake; an error. *Perh. from "rockhead."* 1952: "Who deserved the rap for the 'rock' that cast the Yankees Friday's World Series game?" AP, Oct. 4. **5** [derog.] A Negro. **6** Any small hard object; esp. dominoes, ice, or ice cubes. 1949: [ice] ". . . One scotch over rocks." Movie, *East Side, West Side.* Cf. **on the rocks.** See **have rocks in [one's] head. 7** A male teenager who is devoted to rock and roll music, fads, and fashions. *Typically such a youth would have a D.A. or Elvis haircut, would wear Levis and a colorful sport-shirt open to the chest for informal wear or a white sport coat for formal wear, and would wear either shoes with thick rubber soles or boots, together with a black leather motorcycle jacket. In the pop. imagination he should, but probably does not, own a hot rod, motorcycle, guitar, and switch-blade knife. He attempts to overcome natural teenage disillusionment with the world and adults by acting and talking boldly, and his speech, gestures, and actions are consciously unrefined, masculine, and assertive. His dress and swagger will, in adult eyes, often appear tough and sneaky while his moments of shyness will seem effeminate. His dress, likes, and personality are directly opposite to those in the Ivy League or cool groups.* 1957: "An 'Elvis' [type of haircut] is worn by teen-agers called 'rocks.' " Herbert Mitgang, *About—Men's Haircuts. Teenage use since c1955.*   *v.i.* **1** To sway, jump, stomp, or swing to music, orig. and specif. jive and swing music; now also to jazz or rock-and-roll music. 1956: "*To rock* is to jump and swing." S. Longstreet, *The Real Jazz Old and New*, 149. *Orig. jive and swing use.* → **2** Specif., to play or dance adroitly to jive or swing music; to be full of music; to be excited or satisfied, esp. by jive or swing music. *Jive and swing use c1935–c1942.* **3** To play or dance to rock-and-roll music. *Teenage use since c1955.*   *v.t.* Fig., to cause a place to resound or vibrate with the swaying, stomping, jumping, or swinging of jive, swing, jazz, or rock-and-roll devotees. 1957: "Yearly the cats and the jazz buffs rock staid Newport [Rhode Island, where there is an annual jazz festival]." R. Sylvester, N.Y. *Daily News*, June 27, 77.   *adj.* **1** Excellent or satisfying, said of jive or swing music or dancing. *Jive and swing use c1935–c1942. From* *"solid."* **2** [derog.] Negroid. See **eight-rock, hot rock, rim rock.   —s** *n.pl.* Ice cubes; chopped ice. *Usu. in "on the rocks" = whisky served in a glass with ice cubes and no water or soda.*

Rock, The   *n.* **1** Alcatraz prison. **2** A nickname for the heavyweight boxing champion or any good boxer.

rock and roll   rock 'n' roll   1 A style of heavily accented, two-beat jazz evolved from "race" music. *Typically, rock and roll music is characterized by the simplest melodic line (usu. based on the blues), by elementary arrangements scored for small groups (often only rhythm and saxophone), by harsh and reedy tones (both from instrumentalists and vocalists), and by lyrics based on adolescent love problems or hillbilly themes. This has been the pop. music among adolescents since c1954, replacing love ballads and swing. First pop. by Alan Freed, N.Y.C. disc jockey, who discovered, advertised, exploited, and acted as impresario for many rock and roll pieces, performers, and concerts.* See **rock.** **2** The dance or dance steps done to rock and roll music. **3** That group of teenagers, or a teenager, who fervently likes rock and roll music; any fad or fashion associated with this large teenage group.   *adj.* Of or pertaining to rock and roll music, fads, or fashions.

rock candy   A diamond; diamonds. See **rock.**

rock crusher   1 One who is or who has been in prison; the occupation of a prisoner. *Used humorously.* **2** An accordion. *c1935, dance musician use; not common.*

rocker, off [one's]   Crazy. 1950: "He had been off his rocker for two or three days." AP, May 29. 1950: "Part of the population of Ohio and Michigan are off their rockers. . . ." John McNulty, *New Yorker*, Dec. 16, 110/3. 1957: " 'I suppose he was off his rocker,' Loncteaux said, as his assailant was led off." H. Wantuch & J. Davis, N.Y. *Daily News*, Sept. 18, 3. *Since c1930; considered the most modern of the "off one's ——" = "crazy" terms; most popular with students.*

rock-happy   *adj.* Crazy owing to living too long on a coral island. 1945: [USN use in Pacific] ". . . A rock-happy bellhop. . . ." Riordan, *Calif. Folk. Quart.*, Oct. 19, 46. See Appendix, Suffixes and Suffix Words.

rockhead   *n.* A stupid person. 1953: "Hey, rockhead! Ya serve one more

drink . . . and yer canned." CBS, television play, *Phone Call from a Stranger.* Cf. **have rocks in one's head.**   *adj.* Stupid. 1951: ". . . Some rock-head hoodlums. . . ." *I, Mobster*, 161.

rock-hound candy   Tobacco. *c1920, college use.*

rocks in [one's, the] head, have   To be lacking in mentality or sanity. *Usu. said to one who has made a ridiculous or audacious suggestion or proposal; usu. posed as a question.* 1951: "You got rocks in the head?" *I, Mobster*, 15. 1951: "Kid, you got rocks in your head?" Max Shulman, *Dobie Gillis*, 40.

rock-slinger   *n.* A mortar operator. *W.W.II Army use.*

rocksy   roxy   *n.* A geologist. *Student use.*

rocky   *adj.* **1** Drunk. *c1730.* **2** Unsteady; woozy; groggy. *Usu. from being beaten up or drinking too much.* 1946: [beaten up] "You look a little rocky, pal." Evans, *Halo in Blood*, 87. 1952: [drunk] "His weakness was a quiet passion for strong drink. . . . But he always came back to work, looking pale and rocky. . . ." Hal Boyle, AP, Jan. 31.

Rocky Mountain canary   A burro; a donkey. *Western use.*

rod   *n.* **1** A revolver or pistol. c1929: "Here's a rod—blow your brains out. . . ." Ernest Booth, *Stealing Through Life. Underworld use until c1925; now common.* **2** A hot rod. 1953: ". . . A restless youth buys a broken-down rod. . . ." Advt. for Felsen's "Street Rod," N.Y. *Times Bk. Rev.*, Aug. 16, 16. **3** A freight train. 1952: "The rod-riders got off nowhere near the station. (Only passengers with tickets, coaches or Pullmans, can afford the luxury of alighting directly at any station anywhere.)" L. Hughes, *Laughing to Keep from Crying*, 60. See **hit the rods, hot rod, long rod, ride the rods, forty-rod.**

rod-man   *n.* A gunman.

rods, grab a handful of   To steal a ride on a freight train; to ride the rods. 1949: "I grabbed myself a handful of rods." Jack Dempsey, *radio program*, WHAM, Oct. 28. *Hobo use since c1915.* See **ride the rods; hit the rods.**

rods, hit the   To catch a free ride on a freight train; to ride the rods. 1949: ". . . No chance of getting away from town unless he wanted to hit the rods. . . ." Burnett, *Jungle*, 20. *Orig. hobo use. Early hobos rode under the freight cars on* *the connecting rods, rather than inside or on top of boxcars.* See **rod, ride the rods.**

rods, ride the   To sneak aboard and ride a freight train, as is done by hobos. *Although hobos now usually ride in cattle cars, between cars, or on the roofs of freight cars, the least likely to be detected and most dangerous place so to ride is on the actual connecting rods, close to the track and wheels, below the body of the cars. Associated with hobo use.*

rod up   To arm; to provide with guns. 1950: "They do not rod up, or arm themselves. . . ." DeBaun, 75.

Roger   *adv.* Yes; o.k. *Orig. W.W.II Air Force and general Armed Forces use in acknowledging radio messages, esp. in a pilot's acknowledgment of instructions relayed by radio from his base. Considerable civilian use after W.W.II.*

Rok   *n.* A South Korean. 1950: "American soldiers now call the South Koreans 'Roks.' This term does not have the disparaging connotation attached to 'gooks.' " *AS*, 25, 297/1. *Wide Korean War use, orig. by the Army. From the initials of "Republic of Korea."* See Appendix, Shortened Words.

roll   *v.t.* **1** To rob a drunk or sleeping person, usu. a drunk. 1873: "Rolling a drunk." A. S. Evans, *A la California*, 298. 1907: "Robbing a drunken man they call 'rolling a stiff.' " J. London, *The Road*, 170. 1949: "The less perilous profession of rolling lushes in the subway. . . .," W. Gibbs in *New Yorker*, Dec. 24, 23/1. *Lit., to roll a prone victim over in order to rob him.* → **2** To rob any person, as by a hold-up, or esp. to rob a prostitute's customer when he is sleeping or has left his clothing unwatched. 1949: "She heard her new friends kidding about rolling guys." *Life*, Oct. 24, 23. **3** To displace another worker. 1943: "Negro firemen on the good runs should be 'rolled' by whites. . . ." *Survey Graphic*, Dec., 500. *Railroad use.* **4** To operate or begin operating a movie camera. *Always in "roll 'em."* 1953: "When a scene starts on an American stage the assistant calls, 'Quiet—and roll 'em.' " K. Vidor, *A Tree Is a Tree*, 235.   *n.* **1** Specif., a roll of banknotes; money, esp. the money one is carrying with him or a sum of money one has saved for a specif. purpose. **2** [taboo] The act of coitus as enjoyed by a male. *Lit., the instance of rolling in bed with a woman.* **3** A piano-roll. 1956: "James P. Johnson was a great man on the rolls. Till 1920 he punched a lot of rolls. After that he

recorded sides." S. Longstreet, *The Real Jazz Old and New*, 129. *Obs.*   **—back** *n.* A reduction in the number of employees or personnel, or a reduction in wages, prices, or material on hand to a previous level." 1956: "*Rollback*—A reduction of wages to a previous level." *Labor's Special Lang. from Many Sources.* **—er**   *n.* **1** A prison guard. **2** One who robs men who are drunk. See **dough-roller, pill-roller, pumpkin-roller.**

roll a big wheel   To scheme or plot anything, as an election or a spree. 1856: "John was always rolling a big wheel." Hall, *College Words*, 395. *Archaic.*

roll bar   An iron bar or frame on an automobile which arcs over the driver or behind the driver's seat to protect him in case the car turns over. *In stand. model cars, this is incorporated as part of the body frame; in hot rod cars, which may have the frame removed, it must be added separately.* 1957: "In sanctioned meets cars must have roll bars over [the] drivers' seats." *Life*, Apr. 29. *Hot rod use.*

roller skate   Any armored vehicle, usu. an Army tank. *W.W.II, more common in Eng. than U.S.*

roll in   To go to bed; to turn in. *Colloq. since c1890.*

roll out   To get up. *An order to get up and get ready for the day's work. cW.W.I much more common than "roll in." Wide Army use in W.W.II.*

roll out the red carpet   To welcome someone enthusiastically and in a manner as elaborate as possible; to prepare for someone's arrival by making elaborate preparations. *Colloq.* See **red carpet.**

rollover   *n.* The last night before a prisoner's release.

roll up [one's] flaps   To stop talking. *W.W.II Army use.* 1944: [flyers' use] "Carey told him to roll up his flaps." Cliff Macon, *Collier's*, Sept. 9, 55/2.

ronchie   *adj.* = **raunchy.**

—roo   See Appendix, **—eroo**, Suffixes and Suffix Words.

roof   See **blow [one's] top, raise the roof.**

roof, out on the   On a drinking spree; drunk. 1943: "I was out on the roof last night and I've got a hangover. . . ." Chandler, *Lady in Lake*, 33. *Not common. A variation of "high," reinforced by "out on the town."*

roof, raise the   **1** To cause a loud or embarrassing disturbance, specif. in making a complaint or in expressing anger or disappointment. **2** To be loud and boisterous; to ignore conventions. **3** = **blow one's top.** *All uses colloq.*

rook *v.t.* To cheat; to misrepresent or overcharge. 1895: "... They would not leave you till you were rooked and beaten." R. L. Stevenson, *The Amateur Emigrant: The Silverado Squatters,* 107. *Colloq. since c1900.* 1951: "A phoney ... who would rook them for two dollars." A. Green, *Show Biz,* 11. *Lit., to take advantage of someone as if he were a newcomer.* *n.* **1** A novice. → **2** An army recruit; a rookie.

rookery *n.* A place frequented by hobos. See Appendix, Suffixes and Suffix Words.

rookie   rookey   rooky *n.* **1** A beginner; a newcomer; an apprentice; one who is new and inexperienced in certain occupations; specif., a new, inexperienced athlete, Army recruit, or policeman. 1928: [athlete] "The rookies and substitutes...." G. H. Ruth, *Babe Ruth's Own Book of Baseball,* 300. 1930: [policeman] "Some rookie receiving very small pay...." Lavine, *Third Degree,* 13. 1941: [Army recruit] "Army Lingo Every Rookie Should Know," *American Mag.,* Jan., 106. **2** A flunkey, esp. [derog.] a prison guard. *c1915; underworld and Army use. Colloq.* *adj.* New in one's work; beginning; esp. new as a policeman, athlete, or Army recruit. 1930: [policeman] "The shooting of 'rookie' Patrolman James A. Broderick. ..." Lavine, *Third Degree,* 102. 1950: [athlete] "Speedy Giant rookie halfback ... rookie tackle...." AP, Sept. 1. 1954: "They gave me the rooky greeting saying, 'Welcome, Newcomer.'" L. Armstrong, *Satchmo, My Life in New Orleans,* 37.

room *n.* **1** Specif., a room or area in a nightclub, restaurant, or hotel in which there is a small stage or cleared space for a performer to entertain patrons at surrounding tables; a nightclub; any place where a nightclub entertainer can perform. **2** = **pad room.**

roost *n.* One's dwelling place.

root *v.i.* **1** To applaud or cheer, esp. for the players in a game. 1912: "We're all rooting for you." Johnson, *Stover at Yale,* 115. *Since c1900.* → **2** To favor or show favor for the success or well-being of a person, team, or cause. *v.t.* To rob; also in "root against" and "root on." 1928: "Bandits who ... rooted on some bank...." E. Booth, *Amer. Mercury,* May, 81. *n.* A cigarette. *From the semihumorous mispronunciation* "ciga-

root" *or from* "cheroot." *c1900.* See **cigaroot.** See **swamp root.** —**er** *n.* One who encourages a person, sports team, or cause; esp. one who cheers or warmly applauds an athlete or a sports team; a fan. 1909: "'Get on to his curves' sprang directly from the rooters ... on the base-ball field. ..." *Scribner's,* Aug., 250/1. *Since c1895.*

root-hog-or-die With either a complete, overwhelming success as a result of hard work or a total failure; complete acceptance, co-operation, work, and sympathy or total rejection. 1955: "It was root-hog-or-die while supporting a Cleveland or Bryan candidacy." H. R. Hoyt, *Town Hall Tonight,* 19. *Dial.* See **go the whole hog.**

rootin'-tootin' *adj.* Noisy; boisterous; exciting; filled with action; exuberant. 1949: "[The book] is actually a rootin'-tootin' romance of blazing six-shooters and gore." H. Birney in N.Y. *Times Bk. Rev.,* Mar. 27, 32. See Appendix, Reduplications.

rooty-toot (-toot) *n.* Old-fashioned music or an outdated style of playing music; corn. *Orig. musician use.* *adj.* Old-fashioned; corny. *Not common.* *interj.* An expression of derision toward something old-fashioned or corny. See Appendix, Reduplications.

rope *n.* A cigar. Cf. **hemp.** *Occasional use in comic papers and by would-be wits.* *v.i., v.t.* To gain the confidence of a person, or pose as a friend, in order to deceive, trick, cheat, or swindle.

rope in To deceive. *Since c1840.*

ropes, know the **1** To be thoroughly familiar with the details of any occupation or enterprise; to be worldly and sophisticated; to know how to fend for oneself. 1912: "I want to know the ropes." Johnson, *Stover at Yale,* 8. **2** To be wise or hep, usu. in a specific field of endeavor. 1957: "... A man who knows the ropes. ..." Robert Wallace, "Crime in the U.S.," *Life,* Sept. 9, 49. *Prob. from nautical use.*

Rosalie *n.* A bayonet. *W.W.I soldier use.*

Roscoe   rosco *n.* A pistol or revolver; any gun that can be easily concealed on a person. Cf. **Oscar.**

rosy *adj.* **1** Drunk; esp. just a little drunk. *c1895.* *Fig. = to feel a rosy glow.* **2** Promising the best; optimistic. *Colloq.*

rot *n.* Nonsense; boloney. Cf. **tommy-rot.** —**gut** *n.* Whisky or other liquor, esp. bootlegged or of inferior quality. *Used since earliest Colonial* *times. Still used in Eng.* 1943: "It's the real stuff—pure Prohibition rotgut." H. A. Smith, *Putty Knife*, 125.　**—ten** *adj.* Very unpleasant; disgusting; of poorest quality; indisposed or in poor health. *Colloq.*　**—ter** *n.* A scoundrel; a cad or bounder. 1924: "I'll never act like a rotter again." Marks, *Plastic Age*, 319. *More common in Eng. than U.S.*

Rotacy = R.O.T.C., Reserve Officers' Training Corps, or a member of this Corps. *Student use.*

Rot-corps *n.* The Reserve Officers' Training Corps.

rot-see　**rotasie** = Rotacy.

rotten-logging *n.* Going on a date; spooning; necking. *From the concept of sitting out the date on a log. Western use. Not common.*

rough *adj.* **1** Obscene, lewd, lascivious. **2** Good-looking; attractive; hard to resist. *Some c1935 student use.* **3** Dangerous; difficult; unpleasant; tough. *Wide use during and since W.W.II.* *n.* An automobile that has been in at least one collision. *Used-car dealer use.*

roughhouse *n.* **1** Boisterous or rowdy behavior; brawling; a scrimmage; a scuffle; horseplay. 1912: "A magnificent scrimmage, popularly known as a 'roughhouse,' ensued. . . ." Johnson, *Stover at Yale*, 81. *Colloq.* **2** Violence. *adj.* Characterized by violence. 1930: "To do rough-house work for the political boss on primary days. . . ." Lavine, *Third Degree*, 36. *v.t.* To subject a person to physical violence; to strongarm. 1952: "The question of whether . . . gun-toting bodyguards rough-housed Swedish citizens. . . ." AP, Aug. 21. *v.i.* To brawl; to engage in horseplay, as that which puts a room in great disorder.

roughneck *n.* **1** An ill-mannered, uncouth, rough person, esp. if burly; a rowdy; a tough guy or hard guy. 1930: "The so-called roughneck is hit with everything but the foundation of the building. . . ." Lavine, *Third Degree*, 4. **2** A working man in a circus; a circus laborer. *Circus use.*

rough stuff **1** Physical violence, such as murder, beating, shooting, or torture. 1930: "Men of the Capone . . . type . . . have graduated from the 'rough stuff' class. . . ." Lavine, *Third Degree*, 33. **2** Obscene literature or talk; profanity. See **rough.**

rough up **1** To beat up or injure someone, esp. to intimidate that person. **2** To produce minor injuries or a mild case of shock, or shake [someone] up, as

an automobile collision, football game, or the like might do.

round = **merry-go-round.**

rounder *n.* Lit., one who frequents or makes the rounds of saloons and other resorts; fig., a debaucher, a roué. c1888: "Clara is well known by the rounders and is a thorough good fellow." *The Sunday Sun*, New Orleans, quoted by H. Asbury, *The French Quarter*, 334/2. 1900: "At Rector's one could encounter politicians, brokers, actors, some rich young 'rounders' of the town." Dreiser, *Carrie*, 31. *Archaic.*

round-head *n.* A Swede; esp., a Swedish immigrant; one of Swedish origin or ancestry. *Archaic.*

round-heel(s)　**roundheel(s)**　**round heel(s)** *n.sing.* **1** An inferior prize fighter. *Some sports use since c1920. Prob. because such a fighter is knocked down frequently and spends so much time on his back that his heels become rounded, but perh. because a person with round-heeled shoes would be easy to push over.* → **2** A woman of easy virtue; a girl or woman easily persuaded to enter into sexual intercourse. 1943: "But little roundheels over there . . . she's a blonde." Chandler, *Lady in Lake*, 35. 1951: "I've just sort of been resenting your idea I would be an easy conquest. I'm not a round-heel like Livy." S. Lewis, *World So Wide*, 239. *Not common.* **—ed** *adj.* Easily defeated; said of a prize fighter.

roundhouse *adj.* Lit. and fig., done with a powerful, circling, sweeping motion of the arm; usu. said of a punch, blow, swing, or the like. 1921: "He [a prize fighter] swung a roundhouse left." Witwer, *Leather*, 56. 1947: "She testified that she threw a roundhouse punch at a farmer-neighbor. 'I hauled off and hit him, and I really hit him.'" AP, Feb. 14. 1949: "This is a time to take a good old-fashioned, round-house swing at a departmental target—the double feature." T. M. Pryor in N.Y. *Times*, Aug. 7, X3/8. *n.* In baseball, a curving pitch.

round robin A sporting contest in which several teams play each other consecutively.

round-the-bend = **around the bend.**

round-tripper *n.* In baseball, a home run. *From the transportation term "round trip."* 1952: "Ralph Kiner tied the score with a round-tripper in the ninth. . . ." Dan Parker, N.Y. *Daily Mirror*, July 8, 21.

round up   **1** To seek out and collect a group or the members of a group; specif., to arrest and bring to jail all the criminals involved in a given crime. 1954: "Fellows were rounded up in a raid on a gambling house or saloon." L. Armstrong, *Satchmo, My Life in New Orleans*, 126. **2** To seek or collect all of a specif. item. **3** To settle; to finish; to square a complaint. 1935: "He is afraid of arrest for theft even though this matter is now supposed to be rounded up with Philly the Weeper." Runyon.

round-up   *n.* **1** The act or an instance of so seeking, collecting, or arresting. *From the Western ranch use when cattle are so collected and brought to a central point.* **2** A settlement of differences by violence or force.

roust   *v.t.* **1** To arrest a person. **2** To raid a place; said of the police.

routine   *n.* **1** One's way of life, general attitude, personality, or philosophy; one's personal kick; that of which one is a devotee, by which one is obsessed, or which one considers as making life worthwhile. *Often in "What's his routine?" = What is he, or what kind of a person is he?* *Prob. from theater use where "routine" = a comedian's, singer's, etc., repertoire. Mainly cool use.* **2** An insincere speech or conversation, esp. on a topic other than that which the listener desires or has requested; an evasion, an alibi, a line.

row = **skid row.**

row-dow   *n.* **1** = **rowdy-dow.** **2** Specif., exaggerated syncopation in jazz; rag or ragtime. *Some c1925 use.* See Appendix, Reduplications.

rowdy-dow(dy)   rowdydow   row-de-dow(dy)   *n.* **1** Noise; excitement; rowdiness. 1832: "Row-de-dow." *DAE.* 1950: "To restore the old rowdy-dow of burlesque, Mr. Mike Todd [producer] and Mr. [Bobby] Clark [comedian] have gathered. . . ." B. Atkinson in N.Y. *Times*, July 9, X1/1. *Archaic.* **2** A fight; a riot; a rhubarb.   *adj.* Noisy; lively; boisterous; rowdy; exciting; violent. 1854: "Rowdy-dowdy." *DAE.* 1928: "Battle the irate citizens in a rowdy-dowdy get-a-way." E. Booth in *Amer. Mercury*, May, 78. 1946: "This rowdy-dow roundup is the wild-cow milking contest." *Time*, July 22, 40. *Archaic. Prob. from "rowdy."* See Appendix, Reduplications.

royal   *adj. & adv.* Thorough(ly); complete(ly); elegant(ly). *Used as a term of emphasis, esp. before taboo words and expressions, most freq. in "a royal screwing."* 1951: "He gave out a big yawn while he said that. Which is something that gives me a royal pain in the ass. I mean if someone *yawns* right while they're asking you to do them a goddam favor." J. D. Salinger, *Catcher in the Rye*, 27.

rub   *n.* **1** A dancing party. *Because a dancing couple have an opportunity to rub against each other. Some c1925 student use.* Cf. **rub joint. 2** A session of necking or petting. *Some c1930 student use.* **3** The gist, point, or moral of a story or conversation. *Usu. in "do you get the rub?" = do you understand?*   *v.t.* To kill or murder. 1939: "Geiger was rubbed." Chandler, *Big Sleep*, 66. *From "rub out."*

rubber   *v.i.* To gaze at, around, or about, as if awed or incredulous, as a tourist at seeing an awesome or unfamiliar sight; to stare impolitely. 1929: "Don't be rubbering at McCorn." Dunning & Abbott, *Broadway*, II. 1939: "In 1896 the verb, *to rubber*, was as racily modern as *hot-cha.*" Hixson, *Word Ways*, 153. *Universally known c1895–c1920. Not now common. From "rubberneck."* See Appendix, Shortened Words.   *n.* **1** An eraser. **2** A rubber band. *Neither use now common among young people in the U.S. due to the universally known following use.* **3** [taboo] A thin rubber sheath worn over the penis during coitus, mainly as a contraceptive device though legally salable in most states only as a prophylactic. 1947: "He went to St. Louis and brought me back a silk bathrobe. He said it was new, but he'd worn it once or twice, he claimed when some business acquaintances came to see him at night. They must have been the kind of business acquaintances that wear brassières and panties because there were a couple of used rubbers rolled up in a nasty handkerchief in the bathrobe pocket." C. Willingham, *End as a Man*, 95. *The most common term for this device.* **4** A professional killer. *From "rub."* **5** Automobile tires. *Fairly well known.* → **6** An automobile. *Not common.*   **—neck**   *n.* **1** A person who looks attentively or stares at something or someone; orig., when turning his head and craning or stretching his neck this way and that to take in more details of the view; one who obtrusively or discourteously gazes, gapes, or gawks. *c1895.* → **2** An inquisitive person. → **3** An innocent, unworldly person; a rustic; a fool. *Fig. = one who is surprised by what he sees.* **4** The observation car on a passenger train. *Railroad use.* *v.i.* To stare; to crane the neck and look around. *c1900; the n. is much more common than the v., but both are becoming archaic.*

rubber check A check that is returned ("bounces") to the writer because there is not enough money in his checking account to cover its value.

rubber drink Fig., a drink of whisky that the imbiber cannot keep down, because he is drunk and sick to his stomach; the last drink taken before one gets sick.

rubber heel A detective; esp. a company detective. Cf. **gumshoe.**

rubberneck wagon A sightseeing bus.

rubber sock **1** A timid, delicate, or cowardly person. *Hobo use.* **2** A new USN recruit; a boot. *W.W.II USN use.*

rube **Rube** *n.* **1** A farmer; a country man; a rustic; a hayseed. *Derisive use. Colloq. Since before 1900. From "Reuben," a traditional rural name.* → **2** An unworldly, naïve, unsophisticated youth or man; a stupid, inexperienced, awkward person; a newcomer; an outsider; hence one easy to victimize. *Colloq. since c1900.* → **3** A resident of any town or city in which a carnival or circus is showing; hence a member of the public, a townsman. 1937: "Child labor laws have forced children [of circus families] into schools. This contact with 'rubes' and 'townies' has given rise to new interests." *Lit. Digest*, Apr. 3, 21. 1950: " 'Peep Show' is conceived in ribaldry. An old carnival pitchman, Mr. [Mike] Todd knows how to panic the rubes." B. Atkinson in N.Y. *Times*, July 9, X1/1. *Carnival and circus use since c1910, somewhat archaic.* Cf. **Hey, Rube!** *adj.* **1** Rustic, rural, small-town; hick. 1950: "A rube police force." Starnes, *And When She Was Bad*, 15. **2** In the manner and dress of a rustic.

rub elbows with To become acquainted with, live among, or mingle with people of a social, intellectual, financial, or cultural level different from one's own; esp., to mingle with those thought to be one's inferiors.

rub joint A cheap dance hall or nightclub that provides girls with whom lonely men can dance. 1956: "Rub joints where the girls danced with whomever

stood them a snort. A bottle of beer was a ticket and, brother, were the dances short!" S. Longstreet, *The Real Jazz Old and New*, 57. *Because the attraction is that the male can rub against the girl with whom he is dancing; it is a common practice for the girls to wear nothing under their dresses.* See **rub.**

rub out To murder a person. 1848: *DAE.* 1949: ". . . Offer prayers to God that you meet such a kindly person as this woman, whose husband you rubbed out." Judge S. S. Leibowitz, quoted by UP, Sept. 15. *Universally known as an underworld term.* **rub-out** *n.* A murder; a killing. 1927: "The hombre she blamed for Paddy's rub-out. . . ." Hammett, *Blood Money*, 118.

ruckus *n.* An uproar; a fight; a rowdy or boisterous celebration. *Since before c1890; dial.*

ructious *adj.* Annoying, annoyed; difficult. 1833: "Annoyed." *DAE.* 1897: "Difficult." *DAE. Archaic.*

ruff *n.* A quarter; the sum of 25¢. *Not common. Perh. because the edge of a quarter is milled or rough.*

rug *n.* A toupee. 1939: "I even wear a little rug up front." J. O'Hara, *Pal Joey*, 62. 1950: "Rug, as it is called in Hollywood." B. Thomas, AP, Mar. 13. *Orig. theater use.*

rug-cut *v.i.* **1** To gain admission to a public ballroom free of charge; to dance without paying, as at a friend's house. *Harlem Negro use c1930–c1939.* Cf. **rent party. 2** To dance to swing music, esp. in a vigorous and athletic manner. *Never common. Orig. jive and swing use c1935.* **—ter** *n.* **1** Orig., a dancer who frequents rent parties, where jive or swing is played. 1942: "Originally a person frequenting house-rent parties, cutting up the rugs of the host with his feet; a person too cheap or poor to patronize regular dance halls." Z. Hurston, 96. *Orig. Harlem Negro use.* → **2** An accomplished jive or swing dancer; a devotee of jive or swing; a jitterbug. 1943: " 'All reat' is the rug-cutter's way of saying 'all right.' " *New Yorker*, June 19, 15/1. 1956: "*Rug-cutter* . . . old-fashioned now." S. Longstreet, *The Real Jazz Old and New*, 150. *May be based on or reinforced by "rug-shaking." Orig. jive and swing use c1935; archaic.* See Appendix, **—er** ending.

rugged *adj.* Dangerous; difficult; unpleasant; "rough." *Orig. W.W.II Army use.*

rug joint   Any elegant, expensive, lavish, ritzy nightclub, restaurant, casino, hotel, or the like. 1956: "It was not a rug joint (a lavishly decorated casino) but rather a 'sawdust parlor.' " J. Scarne, *The Amazing World of John Scarne*, 378f. *Lit., a place with a carpet on the floor.*

rug-shaking   *n.* Dancing the shimmy; shimmying. *c1920 use.*

ruin = **blue ruin.**

rum   *adj.* Bad; dangerous; eccentric, odd. *More common in Eng. than in U.S.*

rum bag   A drunkard. 1946: "Fishing is also used as an alibi by a lot of cowardly rum bags." Jimmy Cannon, quoted by Red Smith, N.Y. *Her. Trib.,* Mar. 30. *Not common.*

rumble   *n.* 1 Danger. *Underworld use c1915–c1930.* → 2 A complaint to the police; information or knowledge of a crime or criminal supplied to the police. 1927: "The neighbors give us the rumble." Hammett, *Blood Money*, 41. 1949: "The cops had gotten a rumble that gangsters were holed up...." A. Hynd, *Public Enemies*, 21. 1957: "The boys [prominent underworld figures] slip into town. You wouldn't think they would be noticed. But some busybody catches on and puts in a rumble." *Life*, Dec. 9, 57. *Underworld use.* → 3 Police interruption or interference in an illegal activity or before a crime is completed; an arrest. 1949: "If there's a rumble, we do the time." Movie, *Johnny Stool Pigeon*. 1958: "Rumble— A search of premises or of a neighborhood for narcotics or narcotics peddlers." G. Y. Wells, *Station House Slang. Underworld use.* 4 A fight or battle, usu. prearranged, between rival teenage street gangs. 1946: "We're going to have a rumble with the Happy Gents tonight. Gang kids call these [planned] fights rumbles." B. Chambers in *Amer. Mercury*, Apr., 480. 1958: "5 Teenagers Injured In Brooklyn Rumble [headline]: Police round up 44 gang members...." N.Y. *World Telegram & Sun*, Apr. 21, 1. *Orig. teenage street gang use. Now fairly well known, esp. in large cities.* *v.i.* To create a disturbance in order to distract attention from confederates while they are committing a crime or escaping. *v.t.* To see, notice, recognize, report, scare, or frustrate [someone] in an attempted robbery. 1939: "Some mugs rumbled us." *Almanac for New Yorkers. Some underworld use since c1925.*

rum-dum   rumdum   rum dum   *adj.* Drunk; stupid or shiftless, as from constant drunkenness. 1927: "... And Rumdum Smith, who killed Left Read." Hammett, *Blood Money*, 46. *Fig., "dumb" with "rum."* See Appendix, Drunk; Reduplications.   *n.* A drunkard; a person who is stupid, shiftless, or confused, as if or as from habitual drunkenness. 1939: "Rupert is by no means a rum-dum." Runyon, 53. 1949: "The cell was full of a drifting flesh-colored light and the murmuring rum-dums were being let out to wash...." N. Algren, *Man with the Golden Arm*, 20.

rum hole   A cheap, dilapidated saloon. *Since c1830.*

rummy   rummie   *n.* 1 A drunkard. 1860: *DAE.* 1941: "What rummies they were getting to be." Cain, *Pierce*, 55. *Colloq.* See Appendix, —y ending. → 2 A stupid, shiftless, or confused person, as if from habitual drunkenness; a worthless person, as a drunk. 1937: "And besides, that rule was only for rummies." Weidman, *Wholesale*, 68. *Not common.* 3 Anything inferior or worthless. *Not common.*

rumpot   *n.* A heavy drinker; a drunkard.

rum-sucker   *n.* A drunkard. 1858: *DAE. Obs.*

run   *n.* 1 A route followed by a vehicle. *Colloq.* 2 A ride, as in a taxi. 3 A race; esp., an automobile race. *v.t.* To drive (someone) by car.

run a book   To have credit or a charge account with a store, esp. a neighborhood grocery store. 1956: "We went to the stores where our people ran a book which meant they had credit." J. Cannon, *Who Struck John?* 32. *Archaic.*

run-around   *n.* A protracted instance of evasion, coyness, or refusal to make a decision; indecisive, evasive, or coy treatment.

run-around, get the   See **give [someone] the run-around.**

run-around, give [someone] the   To stall a person; to evade, sometimes politely or without seeming to; repeatedly to postpone action on a request, as for payment or employment. 1942: "Don't give me the run-around." S. Billingsley, *Harper's Bazaar*, July. 1949: "All he gets is the polite run-around." Drew Pearson, *synd. newsp. col.*, Phila. *Bulletin*, Sept. 9, 52/7. *Orig. theater use.*

run a sandy on [someone]   To play a trick on; to dupe; to swindle. 1939: "Even Ignaz' own mobsters figure the old guy runs something of a sandy on Ignaz." Damon Runyon, *Take It Easy*, 133.

run-down   rundown   *n.* **1** A summary, esp. a brief one. 1949: "A quick run-down on the [football game] scores to the present time." NBC radio newscast, Sept. 28. 1952: "Here is a brief rundown of what happened." AP, Apr. 28. **2** An itemized account; a very detailed explanation. 1952: "The stark run-down of [Vice President Richard Nixon's] household budget was all too familiar." R. C. Ruark, *synd. newsp. col.*, Sept. 29.

rung up   Emotionally upset.

run-in   *n.* **1** An unfriendly encounter; an argument; a quarrel. 1905: "Sorry we had the run-in but it was all my fault." McHugh, *Search Me*, 82. 1943: "After my first run-in with Army regulations. . . ." A. Tauber in *Scholastic*. → **2** An arrest.   **run in**   To arrest someone. 1922: "I'd run you in. . . ." O'Neill, *Hairy Ape*, 7. 1951: " 'Am I going to have to run you in?' the policeman asked." N. Benchley in *New Yorker*, Dec. 15, 94.

run it out   To be personally and objectionably conspicious, esp. by talking; returning too often to one topic. 1920: "Anything which brought an under classman into too glaring light was labelled with the damning brand of 'running it out.' " F. S. Fitzgerald, *This Side of Paradise*, 48.

running shoes, give someone his   To dismiss someone, as a suitor or an employee; to terminate a personal or business relationship, usu. in anger.

run off at the mouth   To talk too much; to shoot off one's mouth. 1951: "A run-of-the-mob gunsel—till he runs off at the mouth!" Advt. for movie, *The Mob*, Sept. 15.

run of the mill   Average; common.

run-out   *n.* Any act of running away; esp. desertion; an escape; a powder. 1928: "The fair charmer has taken 'a run-out with the bank roll.' " E. Booth, *Amer. Mercury*, May, 80.

run-out powder, take a = **take a powder**.

run over [somebody]   To treat another unethically or discourteously; specif., to usurp another's position in order to further one's own success; to tease or ride somebody. 1936: "The cowboy may have disliked to have another person . . . 'run over' him, but the average puncher would not

kill in defense of mere personal pride." P. A. Rollins, *The Cowboy*, 48. *Obs.*

runt   *n.* **1** A very small, short person. 1956: "You're [jockey] Conn McCreary, a fat runt. You're tiny." J. Cannon, *Who Struck John?* 228. *Colloq.* → **2** An incompetent person; a disliked, annoying person. 1958: "Who'd ever think of connecting that runt with THIS deal." *Synd. comic strip*, "Dondi," Feb. 9.

run-through   ` *n.* A rehearsal. 1949: "After the first run-through, Mr. Berlin casually tossed out three songs." N.Y. *Times*, July 10, 1.   **run through** To rehearse; to practice.

ruptured duck   **1** The lapel pin or pocket insigne of an honorably discharged U.S. service man. *Wide W.W.II use. One wing of the eagle extends beyond the rim of the button. Called also "pregnant duck."* **2** An honorable discharge.

rush   *v.i.* **1** To recite perfectly owing to concentrated or careful preparation. *c1845; college use.* **2** To be aggressive; to try too hard; to be overly persistent.   *v.t.* **1** To concentrate one's attention on or devote great attention to any subject, cause, or person. *Orig. college term. c1860.* → **2** To pay romantic attention to a girl or woman; to court; to give a girl the rush act. 1940 [1932]: "He had 'rushed' her, she said, for several months, and they had decided to announce their engagement." Queen, *Tragedy of X*, 45. *Colloq. c1865 to present.* **3** To show marked attention to a student who is eligible for a fraternity or some membership. 1924: "We've got to rush him [for the fraternity] sure." Marks, *Plastic Age*, 62. *Colloq. since c1890.* *n.* **1** A perfect recitation. *c1845; obs.* **2** Acclaim; a series of frequent attentions paid a woman in courtship. 1952: "The boy meets a new girl and . . . appears to want to give her a big rush. . . ." Doris Blake, N.Y. *Daily News*, Aug. 13, C16/3.   **—ee**   *n.* A college student who is being rushed by and for a fraternity or sorority. 1949–52: 'Rushee' occurs at least 108 times in the Cornell (Univ.) *Daily Sun* from Sept., 1949, to Jan. 16, 1952. *Colloq. student use.* See Appendix, —ee ending.

rush act   rush act, the   1 The act of rushing a person. → **2** The act of courting a girl obviously and intensely, as by being extremely attentive, taking her to many parties, showering her with gifts, and the like; fig., trying to rush her into accepting one's proposal of marriage.

rush-in *n.* A meal or drink served to a beggar in a restaurant and paid for with money he has begged on the street. *c1925 hobo use.*

rush (work) the growler   To take a bucket or pail (growler) to a saloon, have it filled with beer, and carry it home; to buy a bucket of beer. 1893: "In New York the act of sending this can from the private house to the public-house [for beer] and back is called *working the growler*;—why?" Brander Matthews in *Harper's*, July, 307/2. 1914: "I'll match you to see who rushes a growler of beer." S. Lewis, *Our Mr. Wrenn*, 208. 1934: "If we were you, we'd 'rush the growler.' " DeJournette in *Esquire*, Apr., 86. *Very common before the invention of refrigerators and bottled beer. Obs.* See **growler.** → **2** To drink beer or whisky, esp. in large quantities or by the bucketful. 1891: "Liquor drinking [is called] 'rushing the growler.' " J. Flynt. *Hobo use.*

Russian [derog.]   *n.* A Southern Negro in the North. 1942: "One of them Russians, eh? Rushed up North here to get away from . . . work." Z. Hurston.

rust bucket   **1** An old or dilapidated USN destroyer. **2** A common, almost affectionate way of referring to any ship. *Usu. in "my rust bucket." Common W.W.II USN use.* See **bucket.** *Prob. reinforced by Sp. "buque" = boat.*

rusticate   *v.t.* To punish a student by expulsion, either permanent or temporary. 1851: Hall, *College Words*, 261. *Now stand.*

rustle   *n.* **1** A slum boy of unknown parentage; a waif. *Archaic.* **2** A baby or young child given to the care of another during the day when its parents are at work or away. Traditionally such children receive little attention and less food. 1944: ". . . A professional granny accepting anywhere from 25¢ to $1 a week for taking in drops, rustles, fetches or whatever you've a mind to call them." Walter Davenport, *Collier's*, Sept. 23, 13. *Since c1880.* **3** A theft. 1950: ". . . The $300,000 rustle that he got away with in . . . New York." W. Pegler, *synd. newsp. col.*, Mar. 2. *From the Western "rustle."*

rustpot = **rust bucket.**

rusty = **cut a rusty.**

rusty-dusty   *n.* **1** Jocularly and fig., anything not active or recently used; hence a person's rump when the speaker feels the person has been idle. 1958: "Some people say Ike is just like Hoover, sitting around on his rusty-dusty doing nothing while you and me is out of work." W. V. Shannon, N.Y. *Post*, May 29, M4. **2** Specif., an old, rusty gun; a prop or toy gun. *Theater and jocular use.*

rutabaga   *n.* **1** A homely or ugly woman. 1939: ". . . Any pancake [girl] may have the same specifications and still be a rutabaga." Runyon. See **potato.** **2** A dollar. 1951: "We've spent 60,000 rutabagas combing the country for their exact doubles!" S. J. Perelman. See **potato.**

rye-sap   *n.* Rye whisky. *Some Midwestern Prohibition use.* See **sap.**

S

—s   See Appendix, Suffixes and Suffix Words.

sack   *v.t.* To discharge a person from his job; to fire a person; to expel; to dismiss. 1856: Hall, *College Words*, 399. 1907: " 'To fire' is more vivid than 'to sack.' " *Living Age*, July, 117/1. 1949: "When asked if he intended to get a new military aide, President Truman replied: 'I do not.' By refusing to sack his aide, the President in effect tells the American people that he sees nothing whatever wrong with General Vaughan's conduct." Phila. *Bulletin*, Sept. 3, 6/1. 1956: ['Disc jockey Jean Shepherd] was sacked last week by his radio station." *Publishers' Weekly*, Aug. 27, 877.   *n.* **1** A discharge or dismissal from a job; usu. in "to get the sack." 1951: "There's no reason why he should be fired . . . or given the sack." C. Stinnett in *SEP*, Dec. 8, 44/1. *Since c1920.* **2** In baseball, a base. *Since c1925.* **3** A bag of golf clubs. *Golfer use since c1930.* **4** A bed or anything used as a bed; often preceded by "the" where "bed" would not be. 1952: ". . . Let me stay in the sack all day." H. Boyle, AP, Dec. 10. 1953: "Kiser raised out of his sack and asked. . . ." B. Price, AP, Mar. 11. *Wide W.W.II Armed Forces use. Universally known and fairly widely used since W.W.II.* → **5** Sleep. **6** A dress style or dress that fits very loosely over the shoulders, waist, and hips, and is gathered or tapered extremely near the hem line.

Common c1957–c1958 use. **7** An unattractive girl; a bag. *Not common.* **8** = **sad sack.** *Some c1930 student use, and some W.W.II Army use. adj.* Sleeping; favorable for sleeping, as in "sack duty," "sack time," etc. *W.W.II Armed Forces use.*

sack, hit the = **hit the hay.** *Very common during and after W.W.II.* See **sack.**

sack-artist *n.* A person who is overfond of sleeping; a lazy person. *Some W.W.II Armed Forces use.*

sack drill Sleep; time spent sleeping. 1945: ". . . Get in some sack drill." Riordan, *Calif. Folk. Quart.,* Oct., 1946. *Some W.W.II Armed Forces use. Not as common as "sack time."*

sack duty Sleep; time spent sleeping. *Some W.W.II Armed Forces use. More common than "sack drill," not as common as "sack time."*

— **sacker** *n.* In baseball, one who plays the specified base. 1950: "Rip Collins, first sacker . . . four second sackers. . . ." Cornell (Univ.) *Daily Sun,* Feb. 7, 8. *Baseball writer and announcer use.* See **sack.** See Appendix, —*er* ending.

sack in To go to bed; to go to sleep. 1951: "Shut up and sack in." *Fighting Coast Guard,* movie. *W.W.II Armed Forces use. Not as common as "sack out."*

sack out **1** To sleep; to go to bed. 1951: "Well, it's time to sack out." Hal Boyle, AP, July 3. **2** To sleep one's fill; to sleep as much as one wishes. *W.W.II Armed Forces use.*

sack rat One who spends most of his spare time napping. *Some W.W.II Armed Forces use.*

sack time **1** Time spent sleeping; time spent loafing or lying around. 1949: "I didn't have any sack time." *Sands of Iwo Jima,* movie. *W.W.II Armed Forces use. Common enough to have carried over into civilian use.* → **2** Bedtime; the time one usually goes to bed. *Civilian use, c1948.* Cf. **sack duty.**

sack up To go to bed. *W.W.II Armed Forces use.*

sad apple A gloomy person, frequently irritable, introverted, or pessimistic; usually a person unnoticed socially; a drip. See **apple.**

saddle blankets Pancakes, griddle cakes, hotcakes. *c1925; Western and hobo use.*

saddle shoes A style of white leather "oxford" shoe having a wide saddle-like brown (or, infrequently, black) leather insert over the instep. *Widely worn by students of both sexes c1940–c1950, and still fairly common.*

sad sack **1** A disliked, noncompanionable person, specif. a maladjusted, confused, blundering, unlucky, introverted, socially undesirable boy or man. *Student use since c1930.* → **2** An unattractive, listless girl; a sack, a bag. *Student use; not common.* → **3** A maladjusted, confused, unlucky, downtrodden, ill-dressed soldier; a soldier who, however well-meaning, cannot manage to stay out of trouble. *Pop. by comic strip, "The Sad Sack," drawn by George Baker for Armed Service publications during W.W.II. Term may be used either derog. or sympathetically. Wide W.W.II Army use.* See **eight-ball, fuck-up.**

safe-cracker *n.* One who blows open or breaks open and robs safes. *Colloq.*

safety *n.* **1** A thin rubber sheath worn over the penis during coitus as a contraceptive or prophylactic. *Not as common as "rubber"; most common c1935.* **2** A bed. *Some c1935 jive use. Lit., a place where one is safe.*

sagaciate *v.i.* To fare, do, get along. *Some c1890 use; dial.*

sagebrusher *n.* **1** A cowboy; a Westerner. *Obs.* **2** A Western movie, novel, radio play, or television play; a horse opera. 1950: ". . . Horse operas, also known as sagebrushers or oaters." Bob Thomas, AP, July 18.

sagway = **segway.**

said See **You said it.**

sail *v.i.* = **sail through.** Cf. **clear sailing.**

sailboats *n.pl.* The human feet. See **boat.**

sail in To attack boldly. 1856: "Slang." *DAE. Usu. "sail into."*

sail into Lit. and fig., to assail, to attack boldly and directly; to criticize severely. 1916: "I will not . . . sail into my contemporaries." Max Eastman.

sailor *n.* A ladies' man, esp. a youth who is or believes he is attractive to the opposite sex. *Teenage use since c1955. Indicates the teenage youth's attitude toward a man in uniform, who is older and more romantic than he and hence may steal a "rock's" girl.*

sail through To accomplish something or succeed easily, esp. easily and quickly.

St. Louis flats *pl.* Shoes made of one piece of leather individually shaped to the wearer's feet, usu. made without heels and designed like a moccasin so that they can be worn without laces.

c1915 [1950]: "Many of them wouldn't wear ready-made shoes. They wore what they called the St. Louis Flats . . . without heels and with gambler designs on the toes." A. Lomax, *Mr. Jelly Roll*, 16. *Obs. Ready-made versions of this style are now pop. and are called "moccasins"; more dressy versions, with heels, have been pop. since c1955 and are called "Italian style," since they were pop. in post-W.W.II Italy; they are also called "low-cut" shoes, because the sides are cut low under the ankle bone.*

Sal   Sally   Sally Ann   *n.* **1** The Salvation Army. 1949: "Sally Ann. . . ." *Abandoned*, movie. *Hobo use since c1920; orig. "Sal." from verbal abbr. of "Salvation."* → **2** Any refuge where free food, shelter, and clothing can be obtained.

salad = **fruit salad.**

salad days   1 The days, years, or period when one was youthful and daring; esp. when a man was a roué or dude. 1957: ". . . The tale an ancient but unwilted flower of Southern dowagerhood told me of her salad days." F. Morton, *The Art of Courtship*, 161. **2** One's youthful or best period of creativity, work, enthusiasm, or vigor. 1957: "In directing [the movie] 'The Pride and the Passion,' Stanley Kramer created a picture as vast, heavily populated, and downright foolish as anything the Master [Cecil B. DeMille] confected in his salad days." *New Yorker*, July 13, 48.

salary wing   A baseball pitcher's pitching arm. *Some sport columnist use. Not common.*

Sally   Sally Ann = **Sal.**

salmagundi   *n.* Any stewlike concoction, esp. a watery meat and vegetable stew, the vegetables usu. being potatoes.

salon mush   Nonjazz music; restricted jazz or semijazz music; lit., music as played quietly and prettily in a salon. 1956: "*Salon mush* [is] concert stuff." S. Longstreet, *The Real Jazz Old and New*, 150. *Synthetic; musician use.*

saloon   *n.* The caboose of a railroad train. *Some railroad use.*   *interj.* Goodby; "so long." *c1945; sometimes used jocularly; from mispronunciation of "so long."* See Appendix, Mispronunciations.

salt   *n.* **1** A sailor; esp., an old or experienced sailor. *Often preceded by "old." Fig., one who has sailed the seas for so long that he is covered with salt from the ocean spray. Archaic; colloq.* **2** Money. *c1910; never common.* See

pepper-and-salt, pound salt.   —y *adj.* **1** Audacious; daring. **2** Hard to accept or believe; lewd, obscene; violent; exciting; titillating. **3** Angry; emotionally upset. *c1940.* See **jump salty. 4** Terrible, horrible; fig., unpalatable. *c1940.* **5** Smart, neat; vivacious, alert, hep. *c1950; these are late jive usages.*

salted down   1 Drunk. *c1850; never common.* **2** Dead.

salt horse   Corned beef; salted dried beef or chipped beef. *Some use since c1850; some Army and lunch-counter use.*

salt mines, the   A mythical place where one is told to go or said to be sent in punishment or isolation; a place where one is required to work very hard; hard, tedious work. *Usu. in "back to the salt mine(s)" = return to work. From the idea that both Czarist and Communist Russia sentence prisoners, esp. political prisoners, to manual labor in the salt mines of Siberia.*

salvage   *v.t.* To steal or loot. *Some W.W.I Army use, by troops stationed in Europe. Such salvaging ranged from a soldier's stealing a bottle of wine from a French farm house to looting an unguarded museum of costly masterpieces. Owing to the comparatively static trench warfare of much of W.W.I, such salvaging was not too widespread. For the more common W.W.II equivalent, see* **liberate.**

salve   *n.* **1** Butter. *Fairly common W.W.I and c1915 hobo, student, and jocular use. Some recurrence during W.W.II.* **2** Exaggeration; sweet talk; a buttering-up; soft soap. 1939: "I handed him a little salve." Gardner, *D. A. Draws*, 17. *Since c1910.* → **3** A bribe, usu. a small bribe of an unethical rather than an illegal type. → **4** Money, esp. money earned from a distasteful or boring job. 1949: "That [$4,100] is nice salve, even after taxes." AP, Oct. 11. *v.t.* To pay; to reward; to bribe.

sambolio   *n.* A dollar; a simoleon. *Obs.*

Sam Brown   Sam Browne   *n.* **1** An officer's belt, including a diagonal section from the right shoulder to the left hip. → **2** An Army or Air Force officer. *Fairly common W.W.II use.*

Sam Hill   Hell. *Usu. in* "What [or why] in Sam Hill. . . ." *Used seriously by older people, jocularly or dial. by those under about 45 years of age. Within another forty years the term will be completely dial. and archaic.*

sammy   *n.* Syrup. *West Point and a*

little Army use, c1940. **Sammy** *n.* **1** An American soldier. 1918: "Nothing more ludicrous than the attempt to foist the name 'Sammy' upon the American soldier. . . . No propaganda can make 'Sammy' popular." McCartney in *Texas Rev. In fact, it never did become pop. in the U.S., despite its use on government posters and patriotic advertisements during W.W.I. It did, however, become pop. among the Brit. troops and in Eng. Obs. Orig. from "Uncle Sam," of course.* **2** Any male Jewish college student; any young Jewish male. *From the common American Jewish name "Samuel" = "Sammy"; reinforced by the Jewish college fraternity Sigma Alpha Mu, whose initials spell "Sam" and whose members are called "Sammys."*

Sammy Vick One who overeats. *c1928, the orig. Sammy [Samuel] Vick was known for his voracious appetite; he was well known in baseball, and thus received the publicity that associates his name with overeating. Not common.*

sand *n.* **1** Courage; stamina; grit; guts. 1893: "From still further west came the use of *sand* to indicate staying power, backbone. . . ." Brander Matthews, *Harper's*, July, 307/2. 1901: ". . . For a time 'He has plenty of sand' was a common expression among speakers of slang. . . ." Greenough & Kittredge, 69. 1954: "You losing your sand, Buck?" W. Henry, *Death of a Legend*, 4. *c1875–1910; now archaic.* **2** Granulated sugar. 1945: [*USN use*] "Joe with cow and sand." Riordan, *Calif. Folk. Quart.*, Oct. 19, 46. *Orig. prison use; mainly prison, hobo, Army, and USN use. Since c1915.* **3** Salt. *Mainly Army, USN, and student use. Since c1930.*

sand and Salt and pepper. *Not common.*

sandbag *n.* A type of W.W.II USN life jacket that resembled a sandbag in appearance. Cf. **Mae West.** *v.t.* To ambush and beat up a person; specif., to sneak up from behind and hit a person over the head. 1958: ". . . I was walking home alone. . . . Crossing through Fort Greene Park, I was sandbagged from behind. I tried to run. Two men hit me again. I came to in [the] hospital. A stab wound in my chest . . . and a plaster stuck on my head. . . ." *Life*, Apr. 28, 76.

sand-pounder *n.* A USN sailor assigned to shore duty.

sand-smeller *n.* An oil geologist. *c1920. Some student use.*

sandwich board A large board or cardboard containing an advertisement and carried through the streets by a sandwich man.

sandwich man A man who is employed to walk the streets carrying a large board or piece of cardboard on which an advertisement is printed; usu. the person wears one such board in front of him and another on his back. *Since before 1900; because the two boards resemble slices of bread; thus the man looks as though he is in a sandwich; also, most such advertisements are for lunch counters.*

sanitary *adj.* Excellent. *Some teenage use since c1955.*

San Quentin quail A sexually attractive girl, orig. and esp. one under the legal age of consent; jail bait. *Fig., a quail who could put a male in San Quentin prison. One of the most common examples of alliterative sl.*

sap *n.* **1** A stupid person; a fool; one easily taken advantage of. 1923: ". . . He was a sap." C. MacArthur, *Rope*. 1925: "What sense is there in substituting . . . 'sap' for fool?" *AS*. 1949: "Don't be a sap." *Johnny Allegro*, movie. *Very common since c1910; from* **saphead.** **2** A club or blackjack; anything used as a club. 1934: "I had been put down with a sap." Chandler, *Finger Man*, 16. 1940: ". . . The sap . . . a nice little tool about five inches long, covered with woven brown leather." Chandler, *Farewell*, 144. 1951: ". . . A sap about a foot long. . . ." Spillane, *Big Kill*, 39. *Since c1920; still retains its underworld connotation.* **3** Whisky. *Fig., that which makes one alive, as if one's veins were running with sap.* See **sap-happy.** *v.t.* To hit a person on the head, esp. with a blackjack and always resulting in unconsciousness. 1949: ". . . One of the others sapped him from behind with the blackjack. . . ." *Life*, Oct. 24, 24. *Since c1930.* **—py** *n.* = **saphead.** *adj.* Foolish, stupid. 1930: ". . . Lay off them sappy songs." Burnett, *Iron Man*, 167. 1953: "Look at that sappy grin!" Henry Fonda, *Bob Hope network radio show*, June 3.

sap-happy *adj.* Drunk. See Appendix, Suffixes and Suffix Words.

saphead **sap-head** *n.* A stupid person; a blockhead; a fool. 1798: *DAE*. 1913: "What an old sap-head I am!" Stratton-Porter, *Harvester*, 559. 1952: ". . . One young woman who just seems to be a saphead." Wolcott Gibbs, *New Yorker*, Jan. 12, 38/1. *Colloq.* **—ed**

adj. Stupid. 1665: Farmer & Henley. *Colloq.*

sap up on [someone]   To beat a person up, esp. when several attack one. *Maritime use.*

sardine box   A Ford car. *c1930; obs.*

sarge   Sarge   *n.* A sergeant, either an Army or police sergeant. 1867: *DAE.* 1953: "I'd like to report a violation, Sarge!" Hershberger, *synd. comic strip,* "Funny Business," Apr. 6. *Colloq.* See Appendix, Shortened Words.

sashay   *v.i.* **1** To keep company with a sweetheart; to court; to date. *Since c1900; archaic.* **2** To move; to go; to wander, to move slowly. *Archaic.*

sass   *n.* Impertinent talk; back talk. 1853: "Colloq." *DAE.*   *v.t.* To speak impertinently to. *Since c1860; colloq.*

sassafras   *n.* Whiskers. 1939: "... He is afraid of the guy with the sassafras." Runyon. *Not common.*

sat, pull   To receive a satisfactory mark or grade. *Student use; often in naval training courses.*

satch   Satch   *n.* **1** Any man with a large mouth. *Often used as a nickname. Freq. applied to Negroes, whose lip and mouth structure gives the appearance of a large mouth. E.g., the distinguished jazz musician, Louis Armstrong, is called "Satch" or "Satchmo." From "satchel," which in turn is from "satchel mouth." →* **2** Fig., any man who talks a lot; esp., a gossip, a politician, or the like; often used as a nickname. 1945: "... In the days when I was fearlessly denouncing old satch [N.Y.C. Mayor Fiorello La Guardia]." W. Pegler, *synd. newsp. col.,* Dec. 13.   **—el   Satchel**   *n.* **1** The buttocks. 1950: "I sure hate to get off this bus—the first time in 3 months I've had a chance to rest my satchel." Garry Moore, CBS radio, Aug. 8. *Since c1910. Not common.* **2** Any man with a large mouth. *Often used as a nickname. Freq. applied to Negroes, whose lip and mouth structure gives the appearance of a very large mouth; e.g., "Satchel" Page, well-known baseball pitcher. Since c1925. From "satchel mouth." Cf.* **satch.** *→* **3** A musician, esp. a jazz musician who plays a wind instrument. *Since c1935. Because of the large number of Negro jazz musicians, perh. reinforced by the fact that older horn players have developed their lips and cheek muscles noticeably through constant playing. →* **4** One who works for a bar, nightclub, or restaurant catering to Negroes or employing jazz musicians. *Mainly Southern use since*

c1935.   *v.t.* To fix, to rig. 1952: "I thought that [prizefighter Ezzard] Charles had won that fight, and to be downright crude about it, I suspect that it was satcheled against him." Dave Egan in Boston (Mass.) *Daily Record,* Sept. 6, 30/1. *From "in the bag."*

satchel-mouth   *n.* A large-mouthed person. *Orig. Negro use.* See **satch, satchel.**

saturated   *adj.* Drunk. 1928: "... All laden with enough liquor to keep them saturated indefinitely." *Amer. Mercury,* Aug., 399/1. *Common since Prohibition. Now being supplanted by other terms.* See Appendix, Drunk.

Saturday-night-itis   *n.* Stiffness in one's arm, owing to having held it in a horizontal position too long, while resting on the back of a couch, chair, or car seat around a girl's shoulders. *Amazingly enough, this word has been reported to have been in common medical use. A good example of an "—itis" word, for a list of which see Appendix.*

Saturday nights   Baked beans. *Dial. and some lunch-counter use.*

sauce   *n.* **1** Gasoline. *Some use when gasoline cars were first introduced. Most common cW.W.I; obs.* **2** Whisky, liquor. 1939–40: "It made him sad and he almost began hitting the sauce...." O'Hara, *Pal Joey,* 370. 1951: "Cagney [actor James] On and Off the Sauce." *Heading of a movie review,* John McCarten, *New Yorker,* Dec. 1, 155. See **apple sauce; bottle, hit the.**

sauce, on the   Drinking large quantities of whisky frequently; addicted to alcoholic beverages. 1956: "... He was already as a kid (like General Grant as a boy) on the sauce in a charming school-boy way." S. Longstreet, *The Real Jazz Old and New,* 102. *See* **sauce.**

sausage   *n.* **1** [derog.] A German soldier. *Some W.W.I use. Never as common with U.S. soldiers as with the Brit.* **2** [derog.] A German. *Some W.W.I use and a very little W.W.II use by older people.* **3** A military observation balloon. *W.W.I Army use. From the shape of the balloon, reinforced by the Fr. "saucisse."* **4** An inferior athlete, esp. one with rippling muscles, as a prize fighter, wrestler, or weight lifter. **5** A prize fighter, esp. an inept prize fighter whose face is swollen, bruised, or scarred from many severe beatings in the ring. 1939: "A fight manager may have a lightweight champion of the world, but he will get more heated up about some sausage who scarcely knows how to hold his hands up if he is a heavyweight." Runyon. Cf. **boloney.** → **6** Any dull, stupid person; one who is as alert as a real sausage. **7** A clue; a hint or inkling. 1950: " 'Does Doctor Peachy know who did it?' 'I don't think Doctor Peachy has a sausage at the moment. Not an inkle....' " Starnes, *Another Mug*, 133. *Not common.*

savage *n.* **1** A stagecoach driver. *c1840; Western use; obs.* **2** An employee, esp. the most menial, lowest paid employee. **3** A rookie policeman; a policeman who is eager to make arrests.

save it **1** [taboo] To protect or save one's virginity; to save one's sexual favors, as for another; said of a girl or young woman. 1951: "She allowed a few liberties. A wet tongue-kiss, a few minutes in their arms on the river bank, a promiscuous leer, but—she was saving it for her husband, or for a rake, some dark-haired, black-eyed gambler who would rape her charmingly on a white bear-skin rug in a mountain lodge." S. Longstreet, *The Pedlocks*, 310. **2** A command or plea to another to stop talking; usu. used as a request to someone to stop telling a long story or change the topic of conversation.

savvy **savvey** *v.t.* To understand. 1933: "... The 'saps' savvy conversation...." H. T. Webster. *Since c1850.* *n.* Understanding; knowledge; worldliness, correct thinking or doing. 1901: "So *savvy* (Sp. *sabe usted*, 'do you know?') is a slang word for 'comprehension.' ..." Greenough & Kittredge, 58. *Since c1865; orig. Western use; colloq.* *adj.* Clever; intelligent; hip. 1945: "... A person ... who is savvy...." Riordan, *Calif. Folk. Quart.*, Oct. 19, 46.

saw *n.* **1** An old story, joke, or saying; a cliché. **2** A ten-dollar bill; the sum of $10. *From "sawbuck."* Cf. **double-saw.** **3** A landlord, esp. of a rooming house. *Negro use.* → **4** Any disagreeable person. *Not common.*

sawbones *n.* **1** A surgeon. *Orig. hobo, lumberjack, USN, and Army use.* → **2** Any physician or medical doctor. 1952: "You could come down with ... leprosy ... without being able to rouse a sawbones." Robert C. Ruark, *synd. newsp. col.*, Sept. 19.

sawbuck *n.* **1** A ten-dollar bill; the sum of ten dollars. *Orig. and prob. the most common use.* **2** A twenty-dollar bill; the sum of twenty dollars.

sawdust *n.* **1** Money. *c1910. Never*

common. **2** Dynamite; any explosive. *Some underworld use; archaic.* **3** Sugar. *Some student use.*

sawdust-eater *n.* **1** A lumberjack; a sawmill worker. *Some hobo and lumberman use.* **2** A carpenter. *Not common.*

sawdust parlor A cheap nightclub, restaurant, bar, or the like. 1956: "It was not a rug joint ... but rather a sawdust parlor (an unpretentious casino)." J. Scarne, *The Amazing World of John Scarne*, 379. *Fig., a place with sawdust on the floor.* Cf. **rug joint.**

sawed *adj.* Drunk. 1833: "Slang, obs." *DAE.*

sawed-off **sawed off** *adj.* **1** Short of stature. *Said of a person.* 1951: "Marsillo—a clowning, swarthy, sawed-off fight manager from Newark...." Jack Cuddy, UP, July 24. *Since c1880.* **2** Rejected, separated, or ostracized from one's work or by one's friends, fellow employees, or society in general. 1958: " 'You're through, frantic boy. You are sawed off.' He disappears from future guest lists." H. Gold, *The Beat Mystique*, 20.

saw gourds To snore; fig. to snore, hence to sleep. *Obs. by 1920.* Cf. **saw wood.**

saw wood **1** To snore. **2** To sleep. *From the resemblance of the sound of snoring to that of wood being sawed; however, this term probably orig. from comic strips, where a drawing of a saw going through a log traditionally is shown to represent both snoring and sound sleep.*

sawyer *n.* A sawed-off shotgun. *Some underworld use c1920.*

sax *n.* A saxophone. 1952: "Arlene married a sax player in the Billy May swing band." D. Walker in N.Y. *Daily News*, Aug. 13, C14/1. *Universally known; common musician use, esp. jazz musician use.* See Appendix, Shortened Words.

say! *interj.* **1** A common greeting. See **What do you say?** **2** An expression used to gain someone's attention, esp. when one is belligerent.

say a mouthful To speak truthfully and to the point; to express an evident view or opinion. *Usu. in "you said a mouthful"* = *what you have said is true and wholly agreeable.*

say-so **say so** *n.* A person's word; a person's recommendation, opinion, conclusion, or the like; oral advice or permission; oral recommendation. 1934: "... No jury'll convict Manny on your say-so alone." Chandler, *Finger Man*, 36. *Since c1800; colloq.*

Says which? *interrog.* What did you say?

Says who? *interj.* A belligerent expression questioning the knowledge, opinion, or authority of another, usu. the listener.

Says you! **Sez you!** *interj.* A belligerent expression questioning the opinion, knowledge, or authority of another; an expression of incredulity, esp. when the speaker does not want to believe that what he has heard is true; "says who?" *Since before c1925.*

say (cry) uncle To give up or in; to surrender; to admit defeat. *Mainly used by boys, as when fighting.*

scab *n.* A worker who refuses to join a union or go on strike; esp., a worker who will cross a union picket line to take the place of a striking worker. 1956: "The American frontier incubated vivid word-making. From this source came words like . . . a 'scab,' who refused to go on strike." *Labor's Special Lang. from Many Sources. Colloq.*

scads **skads** *n.pl.* **1** Money; dollars; profit. 1894: "Slang." *DAE. Obs. by c1915.* → **2** A large quantity of money. *Since c1890.* → **3** A large quantity or number of anything. 1949: "I have scads of study to do at the library." Cartoon, Phila. *Bulletin*, Sept. 9, 52/1. *Since c1920.* Cf. **bags of.**

'scairdy cat = 'fraidy cat.

scale *n.* **1** A louse. *Some Army and prison use since c1910.* **2** A standard hourly or minimum hourly rate of pay for a job. 1958: "Our scale is $2.50 an hour, time and a half for overtime. That's a quarter above the union scale. . . ." IBM machine office mgr., N.Y.C. See **fish scale.**

scalp doily **1** A toupee. *One of the more pop. jocular words for a toupee. Since c1925.* **2** A wig. *Never common.*

scalper *n.* **1** A ticket seller or agent who buys up many tickets to a pop. entertainment or sporting event and then resells them at exorbitant prices; fig., one who is not satisfied with a fair profit, but takes advantage of the public to obtain as high a price or profit as he can. *Universally known.* **2** One who obtains high odds as a bettor and then himself takes bets at lower odds, so that he will profit, win or lose, either as a bettor or as a bookmaker. 1956: "SCALPERS—Those who bet on a horse at high odds and make book

against the same horse at low odds, so that they are able to profit whether the horse wins or loses; practically confined to professional bettors." T. Betts, *Across the Board*, 318. *Gambling use.*

scamping *n.* Idling while one is supposed to be working; goofing off; producing inferior work; working or talking without regard to one's fellow workers, but only to impress one's boss. 1956: "*Scamping*—Bad work habits. Either deliberate failure to perform the job correctly; or, producing too much in the eyes of fellow workers." *Labor's Special Lang. from Many Sources.*

Scandahoovian *n., adj.* Scandinavian.

Scandahoovian dynamite = Scandinavian dynamite.

scandal sheet **1** A payroll. *W.W.II Army use.* **2** A businessman's expense account. *Very common since c1945.*

scandal soup Tea. *Some lunch-counter use. c1930.*

Scandinavian dynamite Snuff, esp. strong snuff; "snoose." *Lumberjack and jocular use; archaic.*

Scandinoovian *n., adj.* Scandinavian.

scare, the *n.* Extortion; the extortion racket. 1930: "We build the sap for the scare." *Amer. Mercury*, 454. *Some underworld use.*

scare strap **scared strap** **1** A safety belt. *Railroad and telephone lineman use since c1900.* → **2** A safety belt on a passenger airliner.

scare up **1** To locate and/or obtain any specific item. **2** To prepare or manufacture any specific item. *Colloq.*

scarf *n.* Food, a meal. *Negro use. Prob. from "scoff."* *v.i.,v.t. = scoff.*

scat *n.* The fast singing of, or the gibberish or meaningless sounds often interpolated into, jazz songs; singing unintelligible sounds to the melody of a standard song. 1946: "[Danny Kaye's] principal asset is his proficiency at scat. His radio signature is: 'Git gat gittle, giddle-di-ap, giddle-de-tommy, riddle de biddle de roop, da-reep, fa-san, skeedle de woo-da, fiddle de wada, reep!'" *Time*, Mar. 11, 63/2. 1950: "Then I'd carry on some of my scat. *Bee-la-bah-bee-bab-a-lee-ba.* People believe Louis Armstrong originated scat. I must take that credit away from him, because I know better. Tony Jackson and myself were using scat for novelty back in 1906 and 1907 when Louis Armstrong was still in the orphan's home." A. Lomax, *Mr. Jelly Roll*, 120. *Many old jazz and pop. singers have claimed the credit for*

*originating scat. The usu. story is that
the singer forgot the lyrics to a song, or
dropped his sheet music, and finished the
song by singing gibberish; this sounds
reasonable, and it is possible that several
singers discovered the virtues of scat for
themselves in this way.*   *v.i.* **1** To sing
scat. 1956: "To 'scat' is to make nonsense sounds to a song a la Louis
Armstrong." S. Longstreet, *The Real
Jazz Old and New*, 147. **2** To go fast;
to drive fast. Teenage and student use.
*From "scat!" the traditional sound by
which one causes cats to jump up and run
away.   adj.* In or pertaining to scat.
1955: ". . . A light-footed example of
precise *scat* singing. . . ." F. Grunfeld,
Music and Recordings, 207.

scatter   *n.* **1** = **scatter-gun.** **2** A
saloon; a drinking joint; a meeting place.
1916: ". . . The 'Duchess' is said to be
running a respectable 'scatter' in Dayton
. . . for reformed criminals. . . ." *Star of
Hope*, quoted in *Lit. Digest*, Aug. 19. →
3 A speakeasy; a saloon or bar that
sells illegal whisky or whisky after
the legal hours. 1935: ". . . The little
scatter that he has up in Harlem. . . ."
Runyon. → **4** An illicit or secluded
meeting place; a hideout. → **5** A room,
apartment, or sleeping place. 1943:
"And don't bother to call your house
peeper and send him up to the scatter."
Chandler, *Lady in Lake*, 205. **6** A small
amount of money, esp. change; chicken
feed. *Not common.*

**scatter-gun   scattergun   scatter
gun**   *n.* **1** A shotgun. 1936: " 'Scatter-
guns,' otherwise shotguns, were occasionally produced by tenderfoots; but they,
unless with sawed-off barrels, loaded with
nails or buckshot, and in the hands of
express messengers, served for the
Westerner only as objects of derision."
P. A. Rollins, *The Cowboy*, 57. 1943:
"If I had my scattergun we'd eat wild
duck this evenin'. . . ." Glenn Allan, *SEP*,
May 22, 93f. *Cowboy use c1875. Because
a shotgun produces a spreading or
scattered shot pattern; perh. also because it can make a mob scatter.*
2 A musket. *c1850; obs.* **3** A machine gun.
W.W.II Army use. **4** A burp gun.
W.W.II Army use.

scatter-joint   *n.* A nightclub. *c1930.*
Cf. **scatter.**

scene   *n.* **1** Any locale, place, or
room where cool music devotees gather
to hear musicians play. *Some cool use.*
→ **2** Any place where cool people meet;
specif., any event which a cool person

attends. 1957: "Scene—Any place where
musicians play or gather; by extension,
any place where people meet or any
event they attend. Thus, 'Let's make the
country scene this week-end.' " E.
Horne, *For Cool Cats and Far-Out
Chicks. Common cool, far-out, and beat
use.*

sch—   See Appendix, Reduplications,
based on repeating a sl. word. Formed
with the Yiddish sound "sch" prefixed
to or replacing the first syllable of the
repeated word.

schatchen   *n.* A marriage broker.
1949: "Its directory listed . . . a gold
buyer, a schatchen, a diamond setter, a
detective agency." Roeburt, *Tough Cop*,
25. *Mainly used by Jews descended from
Central European parentage.*

schiz   *n.* A schizophrenic; schizophrenia. *Pronounced "skitz."* See Appendix, Shortened Words.   **—o**   *n.*
1 = **schiz.** **2** Any of the four basic
types of schizophrenia. 1952: "Docs
find he's a schizo." Photo caption,
N.Y. *Daily News*, Aug. 13, C3/1.   *adj.*
Schizophrenic; afflicted with schizophrenia. See Appendix, —o ending.

schlack   schlag   *adj.* = **schlock.**

schlemazel   schlemasel   *adj.*
Ill-fated, ridden with bad luck; clumsy,
awkward.   *n.* An awkward, clumsy
person. *From the Yiddish.*

schlemiel   schlemihl   *n.* An oaf, a
fool, esp. a stupid, awkward, clumsy
fellow; a jerk. 1941: "Don't talk like a
schlemiel, you schlemiel." Schulberg,
Sammy, 63. 1950: "Brafferton was a
dead hero and Harford was an alive
schlemiel." Starnes, *And When She Was
Bad*, 134. *From the Yiddish; from
"schlemazel."*

schlep   *v.t.* Drag, carry, tote, haul.
1957: "Queen Elizabeth will *schlep* along
95 pieces of baggage on her trip here."
P. Sann, N.Y. *Post*, Sept. 29, M6. *From
the Yiddish.*   *n.* A stupid or awkward
person.   **—per**   *n.* One who is
always looking for a bargain; one who
always has something he wishes to
sell; one who expects many small
favors, free merchandise, gifts, or the like.
From the Yiddish.

schlock   schlack   schlag   *adj.*
Cheaply made; of inferior material,
design, and workmanship; defective;
cheap and gaudy; usu. said of merchandise to be sold.   *n.* Inferior,
cheap, or defective merchandise. *From
the Yiddish "schlock" = a curse.*

schlock joint (shop, store)   A

store that sells cheap, inferior merchandise, often one in which the customer and owner can bargain over prices. *From "schlock."*

schloomp   schlump   schlub   *n.* A foolish, stupid, or unknowing person; a jerk. 1952: "Why, you schlump! You should talk!" Radio, *Adventures of the Falcon*, Mar. 14.   *v.i.* To idle; to waste time; to relax. *From the Yiddish.*

schlub   *n.* = **schloomp.**   *adj.* Second-rate; inferior. 1952: "Schlub— not so good." M. Blosser, *synd. comic strip,* "Freckles," Sept. 19. *From the Yiddish.*

schlump   *n.* = **schloomp.**

schm—   See Appendix, Reduplications.

schmaltz   *n.* **1** Sentiment or sentimentality exploited for commercial reasons; extreme sentimentality; corn; specif., music or a style of music that is sweet and sentimental. 1951: "What makes us weep is that happy combination of good theater and good pathos known as schmaltz." C. O. Skinner in *New Yorker*, Jan. 20, 26/2. *Prob. the most common of the Yiddish "sch—" words used seriously or to give a jocular twist to one's speech. From the Jewish "schmaltz" = chicken fat, used for cooking, hence greasy, slick.* **2** Hair dressing or pomade; goo, gonk. 1956: "I used olive oil for schmaltz. But chicken fat is still the best schmaltz." T. Betts, *Across the Board*, 283.   *v.t.* To do anything as if it were schmaltz or in a schmaltzy way. *Usu. in "schmaltz it up" = to make something more appealing to those who like sentimentality or corn.*   **—y   schmalzy** *adj.* Extremely sentimental, hackneyed, trivial, or corny. 1951: "It is not always the schmalzy moment that dissolves me." C. O. Skinner in *New Yorker*, Jan. 20, 26/3.

schmear   *v.t.* **1** To bribe; to give someone a gift or be exceedingly kind to another in order to obligate him. *From the Yiddish.* **2** To treat someone roughly and with intended violence; to throw another to the ground. *Most freq. as football use = to tackle an opposing player.*   *n.* **1** A bribe. **2** A slander; a complaint; an attempt to expose or ruin another's reputation. *Usu.* "smear."

schmendrick   *n.* A completely foolish, awkward, inept person. 1951: ". . . A schmendrick with a noodle for a brain." A. Hirschfield, *Show Business Is No Business*, 47. *From the Yiddish.*

schmo(e)   shmo(e)   *n.* **1** A foolish, idle person; one easily deceived, a naïve person; a goof. 1947: "I've been standing here like a schmoe for 20 minutes." Fred Allen, radio, Mar. 9. *As in the case of many Yiddish or Yiddish-sounding words, often used for humorous effect. "Schmo(e)" does not appear in Yiddish.* **2** A stubborn person; a disliked person. 1951: "Them big-time schmoes was stockholders in all the blue-chip corporations. *SEP*, Apr. 21, 10/2. **3** An eccentric, a character. *Often used affectionately.*

schmoos   schmoose   schmoozl(e) *v.i.* To talk; to gossip; to discuss or converse; esp. to talk idly, pleasantly, or jocularly. 1953: "It was a quiet time in the delicatessen, so the three of us started schmoosing for a few minutes." J. McNulty in *New Yorker*, Apr. 11, 25/1. 1956: "Garment workers wait for slack season—when they can *schmoose—* idle around, talking. . . ." *Labor's Special Lang. from Many Sources. From the Yiddish "schmoose" = chat.*

schneider   *v.t.* **1** In the card game of gin rummy, to score the winning amount of points, or win a fixed number of games, before one's opponent has scored or won any games. *Since c1940. Card player use.* → **2** To win any game or series of games before one's opponent, or the opposing team, has scored or won a game; to shut out an opponent. *Since c1945.* → **3** To defeat an opponent by a large margin.   *n.* A tailor; a worker in the garment industry. 1956: "Garment workers, who are all *schneiders. . . ." Labor's Special Lang. from Many Sources. From the German and Yiddish = one who cuts (cloth).*

schnook   *n.* A dope, a sap; esp., one who is too meek to stand up for his rights, bargain, or defend himself from being made the butt of a joke, taking the blame, or being cheated. 1949: "Don't be such an apologetic schnook." Jack Benny, radio, Oct. 9. 1951: "All the other *shnooks* in the pen business thought you just had to write a letter to O.P.A. to get a decent ceiling." Quoted by T. Whiteside in *New Yorker*, Feb. 17, 44. 1956: "Real Estater Leo Taylor bought himself a home and paid a commission, just like any other schnook." H. Caen, San Francisco *Examiner*, Apr. 29, S11/1. *From the Yiddish. Like other derisive words from the Yiddish, this is somewhat affectionate, implying that the person is more to be pitied than scorned and a realization that a person may seem* *foolish because he is meek, gentle, and idealistic.*

schnorrer   *n.* One who begs, chisels, or depends on the generosity of others for his living; a beggar or moocher; a chiseler; one who always attempts to bargain to obtain purchased items at a reduced price; a poor relation who expects his relatives to support him; a parasite. 1938: "['Schnorrer' =] a combination of beggar, sponger, and chiseler." A. A. Roback in *Better Eng.*, Feb., 52/2. 1948: "[In the book *A Treasury of Jewish Folklore*] you'll run across the fabulous, motley crew of schlemihls, schlimazls, and schnorrers made famous by Sholom Aleichem." Advt., N.Y. *Times Bk. Rev.*, July 11, 7. *From the Yiddish.*

schnozz   *n.* Lit. and fig., the nose. 1949: "Right on the schnoz [= on time]." Burnett, *Jungle*, 118. 1950: "When you write up da schnozz [said Jimmy Durante] you better make it 4 inches by 5 inches. I don't wanna start gettin' the rep of not havin' a big schnozz." M. Zolotow in *SEP*, July 15, 122/2. *From "schnozzle."* See Appendix, Shortened Words.   **—le   snozzle**   *n.* A nose; usu. a large nose. *From the Ger. "Schnauze" = a dog's snout or muzzle. Reinforced by the Yiddish "schnubbl" = a beak.*   **—ola**   *n.* A nose, esp. a large one. 1937: "A broken nose epidemic hit Dennison. In early contests 5 players broke their schnozzolas." P. Mickelson, AP, Nov. 29. 1950: "[He] caught another one on the schnozzola." *Time*, Apr. 10, 48. *Since c1930 the well-known nickname for comedian Jimmy Durante, known for his large nose.* 1950: "[Jimmy Durante] cherishes his unbeautiful nose. He has copyrighted Schnozzola." M. Zolotow, *SEP*, July 15, 23/3. See Appendix, —ola ending.

school   *n.* A state penitentiary; a "big school." See **big school, prep school.**

schoolmarm   *n.* A forked log. *Lumberjack use.*

scillion = **skillion.**

scissorbill   scissorsbill   scissorbill   *n.* **1** A person whose income is not from wages, as a farm or camp owner, a coupon clipper, or one who has struck oil; a rich person. 1913: "... Among the hobo's many enemies his pet aversion, the scissorbill ... the 'homeguard' worker ... who has some source of income other than wages." *Industrial Worker*, Spokane, Wash., May 1, 5/3. *Logger, hobo, and I.W.W. use. c1910–*

1930. → **2** A worker who lacks class consciousness; one who will not join a labor union; a non-I.W.W. 1956: "*Scissor-bill*—A nonunion worker." *Labor's Special Lang. from Many Sources. I.W.W. use.* **3** A fool, victim, or sucker. *Orig. logger, hobo, and I.W.W. use, by c1930 some underworld use.* **4** A railroad detective. *Hobo use. Reinforced by "bull" and "cinder bull"; sometimes heard as "scissors bull." Orig. of the term is unknown. In orig. logger use it implies a nosy worker, perhaps fig. one whose long nose is ripe for cutting.*

scissors bull = **scissorbill.**

scoff   *v.i., v.t.* **1** To eat. 1936: "I'll take you over to the ... Restaurant so you kin scoff." Tully, *Bruiser*, 27. *Orig. maritime and hobo use; seems to have more Negro than white use. Said to have orig. in Africa.* **2** To drink. 1951: "... The delicacy which ... Truman scoffed a bowl of. ..." W. Pegler, *synd. newsp. col.*, Jan. 4.   *n.* Food. 1938: "... Beef heart is their favorite scoff. ..." Liebling, *Back Where*, 301. *As a n., more common in Eng. than in U.S.*   **—ings**   *n.pl.* Food; meals. 1892 [1907]: "A hard town for 'scoffings,' was what the hoboes called Reno at that time." Jack London, *My Life. Hobo use.*

scollops, put on   To adopt the dress, manners, and customs of a new country, as the U.S.; said of an immigrant.

sconce   *v.t.* To beat another at a game or contest; to embarrass or ignore another; to criticize another. *Affected student use, from the archaic Eng. schoolboys' "sconce" = to fine, give a demerit, or withhold privileges.*

scooch   scrooch   scrouge   scrooge   *v.i.* To move by sliding or shifting one's body.

scoop   *n.* **1** Important news, an important news item, esp. if published first in a given newspaper. 1886: *DAE.* 1949: "... The scoop of the week." Walter Winchell, network radio, Oct. 30. *Standard by c1925.* → **2** Recent, official information; advance information; dope; poop. 1945: "What's the scoop?" Riordan, *Calif. Folk. Quart.*, Oct., 19. *Armed Forces and student use c1940.* **3** A glass of beer. *c1885.* **4** A spoon. *A little lunch-counter use.* **5** A single, half-sphere portion of ice-cream, as scooped out of a large container by a standard-sized, half-spherical ice-cream spoon. *Common lunch-counter use.*   *v.t.* To precede other newspapers in publishing a given news item.

scooping pitch   A change of pitch or key in the middle of playing a piece of jazz music. 1956: "When they are playing jazz and alter pitch between notes, they call it *scooping-pitch* . . . bending." S. Longstreet, *The Real Jazz Old and New*, 149. *Jazz use; not common. In bop, the key may be changed several times during a piece.*

scooter   *n.* An automobile. 1948: "We'll use your scooter, Mac." Evans, *Halo for Satan*, 62. *Not common.*

scope   **'scope**   *n.* A periscope. *Universally used by U.S. Navy; esp. submariner unofficial use. Since c1935.*

scorch   *v.i.* **1** To ride fast, esp. on a bicycle. 1907: "I am on a bicycle. . . . I proceed to scorch to make up for lost time." Jack London, *The Road*, 210. *Very common c1895, when bicycles were very much in vogue.* Cf. **scorcher**. **2** In baseball, to throw a ball very fast and hard.   **—er**   *n.* **1** A critical, telling remark or speech. *Since c1840.* **2** A fast bicyclist. 1947: [1895] "Cycling in the Park was considered very smart, especially on Sunday when the 'scorchers and crackerjacks' were out in full force. Either a man or woman could scorch, but only men might attain the rank of crackerjack." Lenore G. Offord, *San Francisco Murders*, 107. *Since c1895; archaic.* **3** A person given to causing excitement or a sensation. → **4** Any remarkable thing or person; a corker. **5** In baseball, a line drive. **6** Any exceptionally hot, dry day. *Colloq.*

score   *n.* **1** A victim; a mark. **2** A successful instance of robbing, cheating, swindling, gambling, or the like; loot or money obtained by robbing, cheating, swindling, or gambling. 1957: "The old-time tough guys ran wild in the cabarets as soon as they made a big score." J. Cannon, N.Y. *Post*, Oct. 27, 44. *Orig. underworld use.* → **3** The amount of cash or loot stolen, won at gambling, or obtained by cheating or swindling. 1930: "The score was 3 G." *Amer. Mercury*, Dec., 458. 1949: " '[They stole] $20,000.' 'Nice score.' " Radio, *Gangbusters*, Nov. 8. **4** A stealthy meeting to transact illegal or unethical business; one who is to be met at such a meeting; a "hit." *Mainly underworld use.* **5** A share, esp. a share of loot. *Orig. c1930 underworld use.* → **6** An amount won at gambling, usu. a large amount made on one race, one game, or won from one player. 1932: "Regret makes a very nice score for himself one day against the horses.

. . ." Runyon. → **7** Sexual intercourse, esp. as a man wins from a woman by being pleasing and convincing. **8** Narcotics as obtained from a seller; a package of narcotics for sale or newly purchased. **9** The crux of a matter, the main point, the gist of a situation. *Wide student use, c1945.* See **know the score**.   *v.i.* **1** To be liked or admired by another. → **2** To win sexual intercourse with a girl or woman by being agreeable and convincing. **3** To buy or obtain narcotics. 1952: ". . . So's you'll score from him." David Haburd, *H Is for Heroin.* **4** To be or make a success; to impress by succeeding; esp., to please an audience.

score, know the   To be fully aware of current important facts; to be alert and well informed as to realities. 1938: ". . . Dope . . . a guy who doesn't know the score." D. Nowinson, *Better English*, Oct., 8/1. 1948: "You look like a nice smart lad who knows the score." Evans, *Halo for Satan*, 59. 1957: "The writers of the Bible had the sudden and sophisticated knowledge that promiscuity is basic in character deterioration. They knew the score. . . ." Norman Vincent Peale, col. in *Look*, July 9, 58.

Scotchman   *n.* **1** Any thrifty or miserly person. *From the traditional belief that all Scotsmen are thrifty.* **2** A golfer, regardless of his native country. *Some caddy use, because golf orig. and was first pop. in Scotland, reinforced by the caddies' belief that most golfers tip in small, miserly amounts.*

Scotch polo   Golf. *Not common.*

scouse   *n.* Any very cheap, often tasteless dish, such as a poor-quality stew or weak soup. 1914: " 'What's scouse?' 'Beef stew without the beef.' " S. Lewis, *Our Mr. Wrenn*, 43.

scout   *n.* A college servant or waiter. 1851: "Oxford Univ. use and sometimes American college use." Hall, *College Words*, 155. *Obs.*

scout master   **scoutmaster**   *n.* **1** A major radio executive, sponsor, or advertising agency executive. 1944: ". . . A scoutmaster axed [the radio program] as offside. . . ." Cliff Macon, *Collier's*, Sept. 23, 69/1. *Radio studio use.* **2** An overly optimistic, idealistic, pious, or patriotic person; a moralist.

scow   *n.* **1** A large, ugly, and/or unpleasant woman. **2** A large truck.

scrag   *v.t.* **1** To hang a person. *Obs.* → **2** To kill; to murder. 1932: ". . . When he is scragged in Detroit. . . ." Runyon.

1950: "... If they aim at me they will overshoot or undershoot and scrag some scared civilian...." Robert Ruark, *Reader's Digest*, Nov., 57. → **3** To put another person or firm out of business; fig., to kill. 1950: "The beet sugar people ... try to scrag the cane sugar people." Starnes, *Another Mug*, 34. *n.* **1** A professor. *c1930; not common.* **2** An unattractive girl. *Some teenage and student use c1940. From "hag," reinforced by Al Capp's very ugly Scragg family in his synd. comic strip, "Li'l Abner."* —**ging** *n.* A killing; a murder. 1949: "... The Ash Brothers had committed the scragging." A. Hynd, *Public Enemies*, 79.

scram *v.i.* To depart, usu. hastily; to go away, to beat it. *Often used as a command or entreaty.* 1932: "Now, scram! ... Scram, Pappy!" *I Had a Million*, movie. 1944: "If you'll scram, I'd like to get a bath and pack." Ford, *Phila. Murder*, 60. *Underworld, carnival, and circus use since c1900. Became common c1930 and replaced "skedaddle." Said to be from "scramble," but more prob. from Ger. sl. "schrammen" = "beat it." n.* **1** A hasty departure. *Since c1930.* **2** A male Negro. *Not common.* **3** Food. *Not common; some use by U.S. merchant seamen and students, from the Brit. seaman usage.* **4** Any money, clothing, or items hidden and/or ready to be used for a hasty or forced departure. *Underworld and circus use.*

scram-bag *n.* A suitcase packed in readiness for any necessary, sudden departure. *Underworld and circus use.* See **scram**.

scramble **1** A race between hotrods. *Teenage use since c1950.* **2** A teenage dance, party, or meeting. *Teenage use since c1955.* **3** A race, esp. a horse race. *Never common.* **4** A fight between fighter planes; a dog fight. *Some W.W.II Air Force use.* → **5** An alerting of fighter planes and their ground crews defending a specif. area, for which the pilots scramble to their planes and take off in order to be ready for a possible enemy attack. *Air Force jet plane use since c1950; pop. since Korean War.* *v.i.* **1** To rush to one's fighter plane and prepare for an emergency air defense of a specif. area. *Air Force use since c1950; common during Korean War.* → **2** To disperse, flee, depart hastily; usu. a command. *Teenage use since c1950.*

scrambled ears = **cauliflower ears.**

1939: "... He is ... a ... fighter in his day, and now he has a pair of scrambled ears to prove it." Runyon.

scrambled eggs **1** *sing.* The gold braid, leaves, or embroidery worn as part of a senior military officer's uniform; esp., the gold trimming on the bill of a USN or Air Force officer's dress cap. *Wide W.W.II use, may orig. have implied disrespect but usu. did not carry that implication. Also used by the Eng. Royal Air Force during W.W.II, perh. earlier than by American personnel, though the term sounds American. From the resemblance of such gold trimming to a scrambled egg.* → **2** Senior officers. *Some W.W.II USN use, seldom used in other branches of the armed forces.*

scram money Money or an amount of money or cash kept available for a hasty departure. See **scram**.

scrape *n.* A shave.

scraper See **skyscraper**.

scrape the bottom (of the barrel) (of the pickle barrel) To be forced to rely on or choose what is considered an inferior or unreliable plan, idea, or person in a desperate attempt to succeed, as when it is impossible to use, choose, or rely on a plan, idea, or person considered more adept; to have an unusual idea or plan. *Used by baseball announcer Red Barber in his c1945–c1955 radio broadcasts of the old Brooklyn Dodger baseball team games. South. dial.*

scrap heap = **junk heap.**

scrap iron Whisky of inferior quality; cheap liquor.

scratch *n.* **1** Money; available cash; loose banknotes; paper money. 1939: "She also had plenty of scratch, being the bank president's daughter." O'Hara, *Pal Joey*, 11. 1958: "Win or lose, the sensitive horseplayer's soul is scarred indelibly if he misses any bet to raise fresh scratch for his one and only love." N.Y. *Daily News*, Feb. 20, 5. *Since c1915. Lit., that which has to be scratched for, as a chicken scratches for food. Cf.* **chicken feed.** → **2** A loan of money; the act of borrowing money. 1935: "Many citizens are wondering where they are going to make a scratch for the morrow's operations, such as playing the horses." Runyon, 267. **3** [taboo] The vagina; the female crotch. **4** A wound, even when more than "just a scratch." **5** A horse that has been withdrawn from a race after midnight of the night before the race. **6** An unknown, insignificant, or chronically poor person, one who is to be ignored; fig., one who has been scratched off a list of friends or successful people, one who is as insignificant as an actual scratch, or one who is always scratching around for money. **7** A fountain pen. *Not common.* **8** An appointment book or pad of writing paper; a scratch pad. **9** A mention of one's name in a newspaper, esp. a favorable mention that has publicity value to an entertainer or product. *Since c1940.* → **10** An impression left by someone or something, usu. a favorable impression. *v.t.* **1** To withdraw a horse from a race after midnight of the night before the race. 1956: "SCRATCH—To delete, to scratch a horse's name from the entries because of changed track conditions, colic, lameness. . . ." T. Betts, *Across the Board*, 319. **2** To brush against someone or something. **3** To cause physical harm to someone. *v.i.* In sports, to make a score. *Often used in the negative: "He didn't scratch."* **—er** *n.* A forger. *Since c1850; still mainly underworld use.*

scratch for [something]   scratch [something] up   scratch around for [something]   To look for an object, to try to obtain something, to hunt or seek something, esp. money or a much-wanted object; fig., to scratch in the same way a chicken does in searching for food.

scratch gravel   To go or leave quickly, esp. to run; fig., to go so rapidly that one's feet just brush the gravel of the road. *c1850; obs.*

scratch hit   In baseball, a hit that is almost caught, a fluke hit; a one-base hit.

scratch house   A flop house, cheap lodging house, or seaman's quarters. *c1930. Hobo and merchant sailor use. From the lice or bedbugs that are encountered in these places.*

scratch sheet   A small printed sheet or newspaper published daily giving the expected odds, weights, jockeys, and scratches pertaining to horses entered in races for the day. 1956: "William Armstrong, born Senville, published the first scratch sheet that ever appeared on the newsstands of New York. The year was 1917." T. Betts, *Across the Board*, 170.

scraunched   scronched   *adj.* Drunk.

scream   *n.* Anything or anyone that is uproariously funny, as a movie, joke, comedian, or the like. *Since c1930. v.i.* To move rapidly; esp. said of an airplane or car.   **—er**   *n.* **1** A very large or strong person. *c1830–1920; obs.* → **2** Anything remarkable, unusual, or well done. *c1850–1925; archaic.* **3** An exclamation point. *Printer use. Since c1920.* **4** A murder mystery or horror show. *Orig. c1925 radio use, now also movie and television use.* **5** A large or brightly colored advertising plaque or banner; fig., an advertising banner that screams for attention.

screaming meemie   **1** A specific type of small Army rocket launched from a multiple rocket projector on the back of a jeep or truck. *Common Army use since late W.W.II. From the frightening noise and effect such rockets made, similar to the screaming meemies.* **2** So intense or extreme as to cause one to scream or feel effects similar to the screaming meemies. 1953: ". . . Rather than endure another minute of screaming-meemie loneliness." William DuBois, N.Y. *Times*, May 1, 19.

screaming meemies, the   The delirium tremens; the jitters, the heebiejeebies. 1927: "To have the screaming meemies." *New Repub.*, 50, 72. 1945: "Madison [Wis.] is a town that would give the ordinary thrill-seeker the screaming meemies in one quiet week end." G. S. Perry in *SEP*, Jan. 5, 23/1.

screech   *n.* A woman who habitually complains or criticizes; a shrew.   **—er**   *n.* = **screamer.** *c1890–1920; obs.* See Appendix, —er ending.   **—ing**   *adj.* Drunk. *Some use c1920.*

screeve   *n.* **1** A letter. 1939: ". . . Once she writes me a screeve. . . ." Runyon. *Not common.* **2** A movie script writer. *Some movie use.*

screw   *n. Persons:* **1** A prison guard, orig. a turnkey; a prison warden; a watchman; any law enforcement officer; usu. a prison guard. 1821: Farmer & Henley. 1930: "[The warden] is known as a hard-boiled 'screw.' " Lavine, *Third Degree*, 226. 1931: "He croaked a screw at Dannemora." J. Sayre, *Hex*, 415. 1951: "Lefty, the head screw, came into my cell." Radio, *The Steel River Prison Break*, Sept. 5. *Said to be from "screw" = key, but "screw" = guard appears to be the older use. Perh. from the guard considered as a "thumbscrew," used to torture prisoners in order to make them confess.* **2** A college instructor. *Obs. student use.* **3** A foolish person. 1887: "That screw, Baumgarten." *Lantern*, New Orleans. **4** A cowboy or cowpuncher; a ranch worker. *Some Western ranch use since c1925.*

Perh. because a cowpuncher herds or guards cattle, as a prison guard does convicts. Things: **5** A key. 1848: J. S. Farmer. *Still underworld use.* **6** An imperfect or too detailed examination. 1851: Hall, *College Words*, 265. *Obs.* **7** [taboo] An act or instance of coitus. *From the taboo but too old and well known to be sl. v.i., v.t. "to screw" = to have, take, or cause another to have sexual satisfaction through sexual intercourse; to have coitus in the stand., accepted way.* *v.i.* To leave or depart, esp. hastily; to scram. 1932: "And then screw out of town as quick as you can." Runyon, 137. 1939: "And when I finish my last number I screw and go around the corner to have a cup of coffee." O'Hara, *Pal Joey*, 13. 1951: "I told you to get outa here and I mean it. Now go on. Screw." N. Benchley in *New Yorker*, Dec. 15, 93/2. *v.t.* To take advantage of, to treat unfairly; to cheat, trick, or swindle. *Often used in the passive, past tense. Very common, esp. during and since W.W.II. From the taboo but stand. "screw" = to have coitus. The primary word relating sex and cheating.* See Appendix, Sex and Deceit. —**ed** *adj.* **1** Drunk. *Mainly Brit. use.* See Appendix, Drunk. **2** [taboo] Taken advantage of, treated unfairly, cheated, tricked, swindled; fucked. *Fairly common since W.W.II.* See Appendix, Sex and Deceit. —**ing** [taboo] *adj.* = **fucking.**

screw around [taboo]   To idle or loaf; to refuse to think or act seriously; to fuck off. *W.W.II Army use.*

screwball   *n.* **1** In baseball, a pitched curved ball that twists in and out like a corkscrew; any pitched ball that moves in an unusual or unexpected way. → **2** A very eccentric person, one with unusual ideas or beliefs; a person with antisocial beliefs; an insane person; a nut; a crackpot. 1939: " 'Is the guy a Red?' 'I guess so . . . he acts like a screwball.' " J. T. Farrell. 1950: "New York, a catchall for screwballs and semi-screwballs from all over. . . ." Jack Alexander, *SEP*, Apr. 1, 79/2. 1950: "On the N.B.C. network, it is forbidden to call any character a nut; you have to call him a screwball." *New Yorker*, Dec. 23, 15/3. 1951: "We got to the Edmont Hotel, and I checked in. I'd put on my red hunting cap when I was in the cab, just for the hell of it, but I took it off before I checked in. I didn't want to look like a screwball or some-

thing. Which is really ironic. I didn't know then that the goddam hotel was full of perverts and morons. Screwballs all over the place." J. D. Salinger, *Catcher in the Rye*, 49. *Common since c1935; prob. had an intermediate sports usage = an eccentric baseball player. Considered more tolerant than "nut" or "crackpot"; sometimes used affectionately = a close friend with a distinct personality.* → **3** A worthless, harmless person. 1939: "The correct underworld definition is a harmless individual who doesn't amount to anything, but not a 'nut.' " Howsley. **4** Popularized jazz music; jazz music played without verve or enthusiasm for unappreciative listeners who listen to the music only because it is a fad to do so. *c1935; jazz term.* *adj.* Eccentric, crazy; goofy; nutty. 1948: ". . . Screwball antics. . . ." *Time*, July 26, 72.

screwed, blewed, and tattooed [taboo] *adj.* **1** Having dispensed with all social and moral restrictions and enjoying oneself completely and uninhibitedly. **2** Completely deceived and cheated. See **screw.** See Appendix, Sex and Deceit.

screwed-up [taboo]   *adj.* **1** Spoiled; ruined; botched; confused. **2** Ill-fated, unfortunate; neurotic; confused. 1951: "Hamlet was a sad, screwed-up type guy." J. D. Salinger, *Catcher in the Rye*, 90. *Both uses common during and since W.W.II.*

screwjay   *adv.* Ineffectively; slowly and inaccurately. *Not common.*

screw-loose   *n.* A crazy or eccentric person; a nut. See **have a screw loose.**

screw loose, have a   To be mentally unbalanced; more or less crazy; nuts; extremely eccentric; to be a neurotic; to have an obsession. 1926: "He has a screw loose." Schwesinger, *Journal of Applied Psychology*, 255. 1949: "Or was he a man with a screw loose? . . .'" Burnett, *Jungle*, 104. *Since c1900.* See **screwy.**

screw off   screw-off [taboo]   **1** To masturbate. **2** To evade work or one's duty; to idle or loaf; to refuse to think or act seriously; to fuck off.   *n.* = **fuck-off.** *W.W.II Army use. Another of the "screw —" terms that are syns. for "fuck —" terms.*

screw up [taboo]   To cause to fail; to spoil or ruin; esp. to ruin or fail at something due to blundering or errors of judgment; to fuck up. 1951: "You know what the trouble with me is? I can never get really sexy—I mean *really* sexy— with a girl I don't like a lot. I mean I

have to *like* her a lot. If I don't, I sort
of lose my goddam desire for her and all.
Boy, it really screws up my sex life
something awful. My sex life stinks."
J. D. Salinger, *Catcher in the Rye*, 112.
W.W.II Army use. Still in use. **screwup** *n.* A chronic blunderer; one who
can be expected to make a mistake or a
faux pas; an awkward, inept person.
screwy *adj.* 1 Crazy, absurd, unusual, nuts, eccentric, screwball. 1931:
"Newspaper guys are mostly screwy.
. . ." J. Sayre, *Hex*, 416. *Used to refer to
both people and ideas since c1880.*
2 Dizzy; dazed.
screw you [taboo]   *interj.* = **fuck you.**
scribe   *n.* 1 A letter. *Some archaic,
underworld and Negro use.* 2 A writer, esp.
a movie script writer or newspaper
columnist. *Movie and newspaper use.*
v.t. To write. *Although standard as a v.i.,
the word is sl. as a v.t.*
scrim   *n.* A formal or large, well-
organized dance or dancing party. *Some
student use since c1920.* Cf. **hop, scrum.**
v.i. To attend a formal dance or party;
to dance. *Not common. Both uses prob.
from "scrimmage," but may be related to
the Brit. sl. "scrimshank" = to loaf, to
relax.*
scrimey   scrimy   *adj.* Lit. and
fig., filthy; lowdown; no-good. *From
"scummy" + "grimy."* 1951: "Hello,
scrimey." Spillane, *Big Kill*, 119. *Not
common.*
scrip   *n.* 1 A dollar bill. 2 Money.
3 A check forger. *Underworld use, c1930.*
script   *n.* 1 A prescription, almost
always a forged or stolen prescription
for narcotics. *Mainly drug addict use.*
2 A manuscript. See Appendix, Shortened
Words.
scronch   *v.i.* To dance. *Dial.*   **—ed**
adj. Drunk. *Not common.* See Appendix,
Drunk.
scrooch   *v.i.* = **scooch.**   **—ed** *adj.*
Drunk. *Some c1925 use.* See Appendix,
Drunk.
scrooge   *v.i.* = **scooch.**
scroogie   *n.* In baseball, a kind of
screwball pitch (see quote). 1953: "Mickey
Mantle coined a new word to describe
the pitch he hit for [a] home run—'It
was some sort of a scroogie.' ['Preacher']
Roe confirmed Mantle's description. 'It
was a changeup screwball,' the pitcher
said." AP, Oct. 2.
scroot   *n.* A dog, esp. a grayhound.
1952: "But how do we induce that bushy
scroot to start talkin'?" "Major Hoople,"
synd. cartoon, May 20. *Whether synthetic*

*or not, the word seems to appear only in
the Major Hoople cartoons.*
scrouge   *v.i.* = **scooch.**
scrounge   *v.t.* To borrow trifles without expecting to return them; to steal
small inexpensive items; to borrow, bum,
mooch. 1946: ". . . The instructor
managed to 'scrounge'—a new and useful
word offered us by the G.I.—two
additional blackboards. . . ." Thomas H.
Glenn, *Word Study*, Oct., 4/1. 1954:
". . . Sleeping under old houses and
eating what little he could scrounge."
L. Armstrong, *Satchmo, My Life in New
Orleans*, 43. *Taken from Brit. sl. during
W.W.I, grew in popularity and has
become very common since c1940.*   *n.*
1 A habitual borrower; one who is
always asking for the loan of small items
or small sums of money. → 2 One who
asks for small items that others are
about to throw away or sell.   **—r**
n. = **scrounge.** *Since c1940. The more
common form of the n.* See Appendix,
—er ending.
scrounge around   1 To seek after a
particular item or sum of money to
scrounge; to seek out a person in order to
scrounge from him. → 2 To loaf or idle
in a specif. place or near a group of
people, hoping that excitement or
entertainment will be offered; to walk
the streets aimlessly, or to visit a friend,
in the hopes of meeting an attractive
girl, of meeting someone who will offer
a free drink, meal, or entertainment. →
3 To look through a group of familiar
items, such as books, clothing, or to
investigate the contents of an attic,
basement, or closet, in hopes of finding
a useful or interesting object that one
has forgotten or misplaced. *All uses
common since c1940. The first two uses
were pop. pastimes for W.W.II soldiers.
Usu. no urgency in borrowing or finding
is implied; when one scrounges around
one is just passing time aimlessly, hoping
that something exciting or interesting will
present itself.* Cf. **scrounge.**
scroungy   *adj.* Bad; inferior; terrible;
usu. as a result of being very cheap.
See **scrounge.** See Appendix, —y ending.
scrow   scrowl   *v.i.* = **scram.**
Variant of **screw,** *v.i.*
scrowsy   *adj.* Absurd without being
humorous; worthless, useless; contemptible. *Student use c1930; never common.
From "screwy" + "lousy."*
scrozzle   *v.t.* To take advantage of.
*Some 1940 student use. Never common.
Euphem. for "screw."*

scrud *n.* **1** A mythical disease alleged to be very serious, painful, and socially objectionable. *Usu. in "you look like you got the scrud" = you look very sick. Some Army and C.C.C. use since c1935. From "crud."* → **2** [taboo] Any venereal disease. *Not common.*

scruff *v.i.* To eke out a living; to earn just enough to buy necessary food and shelter; to live from hand to mouth. *Orig. carnival use.*

scruffing along = **scruff.**

scrum *n.* A football scrimmage, a football game. *From the Eng. sl. "scrummage" = scrimmage; orig. a Scot. word. Not common.*

scrumptious *adj.* Excellent; wonderful. *Usu. applied to food = delicious; applied to people = well dressed, well groomed, beautiful, or handsome.* 1958: "For a scrumptious dessert fold a half cup of chopped pitted dates into . . . butterscotch pie filling. . . ." "Cooking Hints," *synd. newsp. col.,* Feb. 19. *Since c1820.*

scud **scut** *n.* Hard, boring, or tedious tasks; minor details that are unrewarding and time-consuming.

scuffle *v.i.* **1** To earn one's living by a routine, dull, legitimate job. 1956: "*Scuffle* is to get by." S. Longstreet, *The Real Jazz Old and New,* 147. **2** To dance. *Some jive use, not common.*

scummy *adj.* Contemptible; mean. *c1915; archaic.*

scumster *n.* A vile person. 1935: O. O. McIntyre, *synd. newsp. col.,* June 3. *Not common. From "scum" + "ster"; reinforced by "crumb."* See Appendix, —ster ending.

scunner *n.* A dislike. 1952: ". . . Department store buyers had taken a scunner against the main competitor of Appleby's company. . . ." Charles W. Morton, *Atlantic Monthly,* Aug., 88/3. *Since c1895; dial.*

scupper *n.* **1** A prostitute, esp. a cheap prostitute who walks the streets to solicit business. *W.W.II USN use.* → **2** A girl or woman who can easily be persuaded to have sexual intercourse. *Not common. Cf.* **V-girl.**

scut *n.* **1** A contemptible or mean person. → **2** An inexperienced person; a newcomer, rookie, apprentice, or fraternity pledge. **3** = **scud.**

scuttle *n.* **1** [derog.] A Negro, esp. a Negro taxi passenger. 1929: "Taxi-drivers' use, Chicago. Less frequent than 'hod.' " G. Milburn, *Folk-Say,* 109. **2** A large container, such as a water pitcher, filled with ice cubes for the convenience of whisky drinkers. *Since c1935, mainly hotel bellhop use. In order to avoid the hotel service charge for ordering whisky, many travelers carry their own and merely order such a container of ice cubes, which a bellhop delivers.*

scuttle-butt **scuttlebutt** *n.* **1** The drinking fountain or water bucket on a ship. *Since c1840, USN use. Also Brit. Navy use.* → **2** A rumor, a piece of gossip; a vague, unsubstantiated story; an exaggerated story; rumors, gossip; idle talk. 1945: "Just scuttlebutt." Riordan in *Calif. Folk Quart.,* Oct., 19. 1953: "And worry about a slump, according to business scuttlebutt, is making some unions concentrate on share-the-job plans." S. Dawson, AP, Mar. 16. *USN use since c1935. Because such talk is indulged in during relaxed moments around the drinking fountain. Became common during W.W.II, and is still common. Cf.* **water-cooler talk.**

sea See **half seas over.**

seabee *n.* A member of a USN construction battalion. *Wide W.W.II use. From "C.B.," initials for "Construction Battalion."* See Appendix, Shortened Words.

sea cow Milk, esp. canned milk. *Some W.W.II USN use.*

sea dust Salt. *Since c1925, some USN use; during W.W.II the term was used by lunch-counter waitresses.*

sea food Whisky. *During Prohibition when the sale of whisky was forbidden, it was common to ask one's bootlegger for "sea food," meaning whisky, just in case a law-enforcement officer was listening. Thus, as criminal argot, the word was used to mislead the police or strangers. The use was so pop. that "sea food" must hold the record for an argot word universally known.*

sea-going *adj.* Ornamented to the point of absurdity; unnecessarily large, ornamental, fancy, pompous, or dictatorial; exaggerated. Applied to manufactured objects, such as automobiles, whose basic purpose is obscured by unnecessary size, ornamentation, or added gadgets; said of people with titles of authority who are unnecessarily pompous, dictatorial, or brisk. *For emphasis the noun modified is often not the actual object or person under discussion, but is a substitute of lesser or greater rank. Thus, a "sea-going Ford" = a Cadillac or other larger, fancier car; a "sea-going alderman" = a Senator or political figure much above an*

455 | Second lining

alderman's rank; "sea-going beer" = any drink fancier and more expensive than beer. A relatively new sl. term; has been increasing in pop. since c1955. In the U.S. tradition of deflating, it implies that the object or person is overly equipped, as if fig. ready to undertake a long sea voyage. Orig. based on the familiar "seagoing bellhop."

seagoing bellhop A U.S. marine. *Orig. USN use. From the ornamentation and striped trousers of the U.S. marine dress uniform. The oldest and most common of the "seagoing" terms.*

sea gull 1 Chicken served at a meal; esp., canned or cold-storage chicken; occasionally turkey served at a meal. *Orig. Annapolis use c1925. Had spread to general USN and Marine use during W.W.II.* 2 A girl or woman who follows the fleet or a specif. sailor. *W.W.II USN use. Usu. applied to wives and families but sometimes applied to casual female followers and prostitutes. Because such women follow the fleet as closely as real sea gulls do. Although sometimes implying that the women follow the sailors too closely, the term is often laudatory in that a wife who follows her sailor husband from port to port is considered, by some at least, as the best type of USN wife.* Cf. **gull.** 3 A USN airplane operating from an aircraft carrier. *Some W.W.II USN use.* 4 A hearty or greedy eater. *W.W.II USN use. Because of the voracious appetite of the actual sea gull.* **seagull** *v.i.* To travel by airplane. *W.W.II USN use.*

seal *n.* 1 [derog.] A Negro woman. *c1930.* → 2 [derog.] Any Negro. *c1940; not common.* 3 The nose of an airplane. *W.W.II. Some Air Force and airplane factory use.*

sea lawyer A sailor who pretends to know more than he does, who is argumentative, free with unwanted advice, or who habitually complains. *Since before c1850, when used by Herman Melville in "White-Jacket." Wide W.W.II USN use.*

sea legs Lit. and fig., legs that are used to the pitch and roll of a ship at sea. *Usu. in "to get [one's] sea legs."*

seam squirrel A body louse; a cootie. *Hobo and W.W.I Army use.*

sea pig An obese Marine. *Some W.W.II Marine Corps use.*

search me, [you can] I don't know. 1905: *You Can Search Me* [book title], Hugh McHugh. 1951: "'Oh, why must people . . . chase after money? . . .'

'Search me.'" M. Shulman, *Dobie Gillis*, 155. *Fig. = you can search me and won't find an answer.*

seat *n.* The buttocks. See **hot seat.**

seat-man *n.* 1 A shill. *c1930, circus use.* 2 A professional card dealer. *Because the dealer who works for a gambling house remains seated throughout the game while other players come and go.*

seat of [one's or someone's] pants, by the 1 By instinct. *Mainly an aviation term = flying without instruments, and thus depending on instinct gained through experience.* 2 Succeeding by a slight margin, having succeeded when failure or disaster seemed imminent.

seaweed *n.* 1 Spinach. *USN use since c1925, fairly common during W.W.II.* 2 A merchant sailor. *Some W.W.II Army use.* 3 An ugly girl; a boring girl. *Some c1940 student use.*

sec *n.* 1 A second of time. 1914: "Come here a sec', Billy." S. Lewis, *Our Mr. Wrenn*, 128. 1953: "Tell him to wait a sec!" M. Blosser, *synd. comic strip*, "Freckles," Apr. 13. *Very common.* 2 A secretary. 1930: "His femme secs open the mail." *Variety*, quoted in *Bookman*, 399/1. See Appendix, Shortened Words.

Secesh **secesh** *n.* 1 Secession, specifically the secession of the Confederate States from the Union prior to the Civil War. *c1860; obs.* → 2 A secessionist, a state or citizen of the Confederacy. *c1860; archaic.* *adj.* Pertaining to secession. 1864: ". . . Passed the most violent secesh resolutions." *Congressional Globe*, 2529, quoted in Thornton. See Appendix, Shortened Words.

second fiddle 1 Of inferior rank or standing; one who follows the ideas or policies of others. *Often in the expression "to play second fiddle."* → 2 Second choice, second best, esp. second best sweetheart or one who is second choice. 1952: "The winner [Dwight D. Eisenhower] was definitely second fiddle before the [National Republican] Convention [in Chicago] started." Paul Martin, GNS, July 12. *From the second violinist of symphony orchestras who is second best or follows the lead of the first violinist.*

second John 1 A second lieutenant. *c1945, Army use.* 2 = **John.**

second lining Following someone, esp. in hopes of recognition or of being invited to participate with or for him. c1915 [1954]: "When I was 'second lining'—that is, following the brass bands in parades. . . ." L. Armstrong, *Satchmo, My Life in New Orleans*, 24.

second off Second; secondly. 1948: "First off, it means that people stop short. . . . And, second off, it means that all hands are cheated, readers and authors both." Harvey Breit, N.Y. *Times Bk. Rev.*, Oct. 31, 33/1. *Though "first off" is fairly common and "second off" is sometimes used, there seems to be no "third off," "tenth off," or "seventeenth off," as yet.* See Appendix, —off ending.

seconds *n.sing.* **1** A second or subsequent portion or serving of food available to anyone who wishes to eat more. *Usu. in such phrases as "there's seconds on beans but not for meat." Colloq.* **2** A pot of coffee brewed from coffee grounds that have already been used at least once. **3** Imperfect merchandise sold at lower cost than first-quality goods; slightly damaged or soiled merchandise sold at a discount. 1958: "Cashmere coats—$89. . . . Seconds from a leading manufacturer at a fraction of their usual cost if first quality." Advt. for Klein's dept. store, N.Y.C., Jan. 20. *Very common since c1945.*

second sacker See **sacker**.

section 8 **1** A discharge from military service because one is psychologically unfit. **2** A psychopath; a neurotic; a nut. *W.W.II Armed Forces use. Orig. Section 8 of the W.W.II Armed Forces rules allowed for the discharge of psychopaths or neurotics; such a discharge paper was also called a "Section-8 discharge."*

see *n.* **1** Recognition; a compliment or promotion due to merit. 1958: "See —Recognition from a superior officer." G. Y. Wells, *Station House Slang. Not common.* **2** A visit, esp. a visit for the purpose of inspecting and specif. an inspection of a patrolman's beat by a sergeant. 1930: ". . . A cop . . . would . . . receive numerous 'sees' or visits from the sergeant. . . ." Lavine, *Third Degree*, 159. See **look-see**. *v.t.* **1** To split or give gratuities or graft. 1930: ". . . Some rival has opened a joint . . . and is doing business without 'seeing the cops.' " Lavine, *Third Degree*, 169. *Fig. = to see that another obtains his share of graft.* **2** In poker, to cover a bet or a raise rather than drop out of the game.

see a man about a dog, have to The traditional and jocular excuse to leave a person, group, or room. *Thus = excuse me, I have to leave. c1920 usu. used to excuse oneself to go out and buy bootleg liquor. c1940 usu. used as an excuse to go to the bathroom.*

seed *n.* **1** A youth. 1849: "Slang, obs." *DAE.* →**2** A young man with little ability or promise of future success. *Fig. = a young man who will never grow into anything. c1900; obs.* **3** A poker chip. *c1900; common then but now archaic.* **4** A dollar. *c1930; archaic.* See **birdseed, hayseed, swamp seed**.

seep *n.* A special type of watertight jeep used as an amphibious vehicle by the USN. *W.W.II USN use.*

see red To become angry or enraged. *Colloq.*

see snakes To be drunk. *c1920; not common. In reference to the snakes seen when suffering from delirium tremens.*

see the chaplain To stop complaining; to shut up. *Often in the imperative. Common W.W.II Army use. Fig. = Stop telling me your troubles, because I am not interested; go and tell them to the chaplain.*

See you *interj.* So long; good-by; I'll be seeing you soon. 1952: "The two cadets exchanged the careless 'See you's' that people say when they know they will see each other again in a few hours. . . ." *Life*, Apr. 14, 147/2. *Very common, esp. among students and younger people. Almost as common as "so long" or "good-by," which increasingly are reserved for long trips and serious occasions. Much more common than the now slightly affected " 'by now."* *n.* A frequent customer who usually asks to be waited on by a certain salesman. 1952: ". . . A 'see-you,' which is a customer who always asks to see a particular salesman." G. Millstein, N.Y. *Times Mag.*, Sept. 21, Part 2, 58/2. *Retail salesman use since c1930.*

segway **sagway** *v.t., v.i.* To go; to walk. 1947: "When I sagway up to the roadside abattoir and order the concentric waffle. . . ." Arthur Baer, *synd. newsp. col.*, Mar. 18. *Not common.* (Note also **sugue**, pronunciation almost identical, meaning to change from record to record, fade out, fade in, in such a way that volume is maintained and music is continuous. *Radio and TV use.*)

sell *v.t.* To convince a person; to create enthusiasm; to convince another of the merits of an idea, object, or person; to talk convincingly. 1934: "It took me a half hour to get sold on the job. . . ." Cain, *Postman*, 3. *Since c1920.* Cf. **hard sell, soft sell.** → *v.i.* **1** To cater to the wishes of a group or audience in order to be popular or successful; to compromise one's style or ideals so as to have popular appeal. *Since c1930.* → **2** To be a popular or commercial success, usu. said of an entertainer, play, song, or the like. *Since c1935.* → **3** To have a piece of work or idea accepted by one's employer, superior, or customer. *Since c1940.* *n.* A hoax; a deliberate swindle. 1900: "I professed to believe the Cardiff Giant was a 'sell.' " Arthur T. Vance, *The Real David Harum,* 87. *Colloq. by c1925; now archaic.* **—ing** *adj.* **1** Popular, having wide appeal, highly desirable. *Usu. said of small items that are part of a fad.* **2** Personally appealing; exciting.

selling plater A cheap or inferior racehorse, such as runs in claiming races. *Racetrack use.*

sell out **1** To leave; to move out. → **2** To become a traitor; to compromise one's ideals or beliefs. *Colloq.* → **3** To become a coward; to leave or compromise because of fear. *Colloq.* **4** To accept a bribe; to renounce one's principles for the sake of monetary gain. *Colloq.* **5** To cause exhilaration, to generate excitement. *Not common.* **sellout** **sellout** *n.* **1** An instance of having all tickets sold, as to a football game or a stage show. 1949: "Penn's [the Univ. of Penn.] football season is not a sellout." E. Selby, Phila. *Bulletin,* Sept. 8, 4. **2** Any article of merchandise that has sold out of supply. 1948: "Repeat of a Sell-Out!" *Advt. for Jonas Dept. Store,* N.Y. *Post,* 37, Feb. 26.

sell out to the Yankees **1** To have an accident; to be hospitalized. *Southern use. Dial.* **2** To move from one of the Southern states in order to take a better job in a Northern industrial town. *Negro use.*

sell [one's] saddle To be out of funds; to be extremely poor. *Southwestern use. From the cowboy use; the cowboy's saddle was often his most prized possession, sold only in cases of extreme necessity.*

sem *n.* A young woman. *From "female seminary."* Cf. **fem-sem.** *c1900; student use; archaic.* *v.i., v.t.* To study; to study together. *From "seminar." Some student use, c1920; obs.*

semolia *n.* A stupid or foolish person. *Some Negro use.*

send *v.t.* Fig., to send a person into ecstasy; to thrill, excite, exhilarate, or satisfy a person; to arouse one's enthusiasm. *Orig. used only in ref. to jazz; now*

anything may be the cause. 1956: "Bessie Smith sent him [Bix Beiderbecke]. Bix used to toss his salary on the floor to keep Bessie singing all night." S. Longstreet, *The Real Jazz Old and New,* 104. *Now archaic.* **—er** *n.* **1** An expert swing or jive musician, whose playing sends one. *Orig. c1935 swing and jive use.* → **2** A swing or jive devotee; esp., an attractive, smartly dressed, hep person popular with the opposite sex. *Jive, swing, and some general Negro use until c1942.* → **3** Anything or anyone that thrills, excites, exhilarates, or arouses enthusiasm. 1954: "It's a funny thing how life can be such a drag one minute and a solid sender the next." L. Armstrong, *Satchmo, My Life in New Orleans,* 126. *Some general jazz use. Almost always modified by "solid."*

send in To provide or pay money. 1932: "... She ... is very happy indeed, especially after The Brain gets so he can send in right along." Runyon. *Not common.* **send-in** *n.* An introduction. 1939–40: "... She said she would give me a send-in." O'Hara, *Pal Joey,* 4. *Not common.*

send [one's] laundry out Fig., to stay in one town or job for a reasonable period of time; to stay long enough to send out and wait for the return of one's laundry. 1956: "Pat Paterno, making his singing debut at La Vouvray, can 'send his laundry out,' as they used to say in vaudeville, meaning that he'll be a fixture there for some time." D. Walker, N.Y. *Daily News,* Sept. 27, 73. *Theater use, archaic.*

send-off *n.* **1** The act or an instance of wishing a person well on his departure or beginning of a new job, career, or the like. Often in "a royal send-off" = elaborate well-wishing or an elaborate party to celebrate a departure or new career. **2** A funeral. 1950: "... To give a man a classy send-off. ..." Billy Rose, *synd. newsp. col.,* Apr. 7.

send [one] to the showers **1** In baseball, to remove a player [usu. a pitcher] in favor of another who is more effective; to eject a baseball player from a game for rudeness to the umpires. *Since c1920; because such a removed or ejected player takes a shower and changes to his street clothes.* → **2** To reject a person.

send up To send or sentence to prison.

sensay *adj.* Sensational. 1945: "The charges, if substantiated, will be sensay!"

W. Winchell, *synd. newsp. col.*, June 18, 12/1. *Not common*. Cf. **sensaysh.**
—sh *adj.* Sensational. 1951. " 'Gee, I had a sensaysh time,' she said. . . .'" M. Shulman, *Dobie Gillis*, 53. *Fairly common, though considered affected.*

sent *adj.* **1** Fig., sent into ecstasy, satisfied, or under the influence of marijuana. *Some c1935 addict use.* See **send. 2** Drunk. *Some c1938 use.* See Appendix, Drunk.

seppo *n.* One who has legally separated from his or her spouse. 1951: "That weirdo is a seppo." Earl Wilson, *synd. newsp. col.*, Mar. 15. *Some columnist and theater use. For a list of sl. abbr. and words ending in —o, see Appendix.*

serendipity *n.* The faculty of finding valuable or agreeable things without actually looking for them. *Coined by Horace Walpole in 1754, after the three princes of Serendip who, in their travels, always gained by chance things they did not seek.*

serious, be To be in love with and court one of the opposite sex. *Lit. = "serious" as opposed to dating for fun or merely because one enjoys another's company. Very common.*

serum *n.* Any intoxicating drink, whether good whisky or merely flavored alcohol. *Usu. used humorously. W.W.II Army use.*

session *n.* **1** Specif. = **jam session.** *Jazz musician use.* **2** A dance or social gathering, a jump. *Hip teenage use since c1955.*

set *n.* A dance band's turn or time on stage during a concert or a dance. 1956: "Clarinetist [Tony] Scott opened his set sporting a goatee. He led off with a soft and persuasive 'Memories of You.'" *Metronome*, Apr., 16.

set [someone] back To cost someone money. *Said of a purchase or service, usu. in "How much will it set me back?"* 1905: "How much will it set me back if I order a plain steak? . . ." McHugh, *Search Me*, 23. Cf. **move [someone] back.** *Since c1890. Very common.*

set-down *n.* A full meal, eaten at a table. 1858: "We Americans think that we cannot live unless we have our three 'set-downs,' each day, which is absurd." *Harvard Magazine*, Sept., 281. 1907 [1892]: "I missed many a meal, in spite of the fact that I could 'throw my feet' with the next one when it came to 'slamming a gate' for a 'poke-out' or a 'set-down,' or hitting for a 'light piece'

on the street." Jack London, *My Life. Orig. hobo sl.; archaic since c1920.*

set of drapes A suit of clothing, esp. a new or stylish one. 1956: "A suit of clothing is *a set of drapes*." S. Longstreet, *The Real Jazz Old and New*, 150. *General jazz use; suggests the reet pleat and drape shape of jive clothing. Somewhat archaic.* See **set of threads.**

set of threads A suit of clothing, esp. a new or stylish one as worn by a bop musician. 1956: "He didn't dress in the smart set of threads as some jazzmen did; when he left town, he had on a borrowed pair of pants, and a friend's coat." S. Longstreet, *The Real Jazz Old and New*, 105. *Orig. c1946 bop use; a variant of the older "set of drapes," which it is replacing in general jazz use.*

set over To kill; to murder. 1949: "They have to set a guy over." Burnett, *Jungle*, 192. *Some c1920 underworld use.*

settle *v.t.* **1** To imprison. 1916: "Foley was 'pinched' and 'settled' in San Quentin." *Lit. Digest*, Aug. 19. *Underworld use.* **2** Specif., to take revenge on, get even with, maliciously harm, or ruin someone.

settle [someone's] hash **1** To dispose of someone, usu. by killing. *No longer common.* → **2** To refute, rebuff, or squelch; to deflate someone's enthusiasm or self-righteousness; to point out obvious flaws of character or intellect, usu. in short, telling comments.

set up **1** To provide or supply someone whisky or food, usu. by placing the items, or setting them up, on a bar, as by a bartender. *Since c1870.* → **2** To treat someone to whisky, beer, or food. *Since c1890.* → **3** To treat or stake someone; to pay another's way, ranging from a movie ticket to an expensive trip or investment. → **4** To set silverware, china, and napkins on a table in preparation for a meal. **5** To weaken another so that he may be more readily overcome. 1957: "Valdez [a prize fighter] set his opponent up with a solid left and then crossed his right." AP, Oct. 19. 1958: "Set up by a severe cold in September, his resistance was too low to throw off pneumonia." GNS, Nov. 28. → **6** Fig., to weaken another so that he may be duped or swindled; to lead another to the point of being duped. *Since c1875.* **7** To be wealthy; to be fortunate; to possess or be in a position to possess all facets of happiness. **set-up** *n.* **1** A list of correct answers used by a student in an examination; a crib, a pony. *c1900* *student use. Obs.* **2** Any person easily cheated, tricked, victimized, defeated, fooled, duped, or compromised; one who is easy to convince; a gullible person. 1930: "You guys talk like I was a set-up." Burnett, *Iron Man*, 14. 1941: "[He] was an awful sucker, himself, for a tip. He'd listen to anybody. A set-up, a tout's dream come true." J. Lilienthal, *Horse Crazy*, 27. → **3** An easy task or job; that which can be done, obtained, or fulfilled easily. → **4** A one-day prison sentence. *c1920 underworld use.* **5** The accouterments to a highball or a drink of whisky; a glass containing enough ice for a highball, or a glass and a container of ice, and carbonated water, ginger ale, or another mixer. 1948: "You brought your own makin's and they supplied the set-ups." Lait-Mortimer, *N.Y. Confidential*, 25. *Common since c1920.* → **6** The eating utensils necessary for a meal; silverware and napkins. *Lunch-counter and restaurant use since c1925.* → **7** The accouterments of a meal; bread and butter, salt and pepper, and condiments. *Lunch-counter use since c1930.* **8** An organization; the method of an organization. 1949: ". . . In all respects except size and its co-op set-up." J. Gould in N.Y. *Times*, Oct. 2, 24/2. **9** A set of factors or circumstances. *Since c1930.* **10** A house, office, or room; the floor plan and furnishings of a room, house, or office. *Usu. in the amenity, e.g., "You have a nice set-up here." adj.* **1** Drunk. *Student use; archaic.* **2** Proud, vain. *c1900; some student use. Obs.* **3** Elated; encouraged. *Since c1930.*

seven hundred   700   *n.* A juvenile delinquent; a member of a teenage street gang; juvenile delinquents in general or as a group. 1958: "Two or three [special] schools will be provided for the '700' and for future members of the '700.'" N.Y. *Daily News*, Mar. 6, 3. *Coined in N.Y.C., Feb., 1958. From the approx. 700 juveniles dismissed from the N.Y.C. public school system after a Board of Education ruling went into effect preventing "known ruffians and indicted hoodlums" from attending and disrupting classes. Separate schools were set aside for these approx. 700 students. Reinforced by "the four hundred." adj.* Of, for, or pertaining to juvenile delinquents. 1958: "1st '700' School For Girls Set For Brooklyn [headline]: School Supt. Jansen said today the city's first '700' school for problem girls would open Friday. This makes three such 'temporary' special

schools established for students suspended since the school system's crackdown on classroom troublemakers in February. P. S. 701 Manhattan and P. S. 701 Brooklyn for boys. The girls' school, P. S. 702." N.Y. *Post*, Mar. 26, 6. *The fact that the schools were numbered or named 701 and 702 is from the n. use of '700' given above; these numbers were consciously chosen and were not the next consecutive numbers that normally would have been given the next new schools opened. N.Y.C. use. Whether these uses will continue and spread remains to be seen.*

seventeen   See **file seventeen.**   **—er** *n.* A corpse. *Some underworld use from the Australian underworld term.*

seventy   70   *n.* **1** A large cannon or artillery piece. *From the famous W.W.I "French 75 [mm.]" cannon; archaic.* **2** A phonograph record made to play on a turntable revolving at a speed of 78 revolutions per minute, the old standard for records. See **LP.** → **3** Any old phonograph record. *Not common.*

seventy-eight   See **seventy, 2.**

seventy-five   See **seventy, 1.**

seventy-'leven   *n.* Any fairly large number, usu. under 100; many; an indeterminate number. 1914: "To keep track of seventy-'leven accounts." S. Lewis, *Our Mr. Wrenn*, 11.

seventy-three   *n.* Any standard closing to a message, as "regards," "best wishes," "happy days," etc. *Telegrapher use.*

sewed up   Completely drunk. *Not common in U.S.; from Brit. sl. "sewn-up."*

sewer hog   A ditch digger for a construction company or road-building firm.

sew up   To conclude, finish; to make certain of success, usu. by completing the key arrangements. *Colloq.*

sex   *n.* See **third sex.**   **—y** *adj.* Capable of or promising high speed and maneuverability. *Said of an experimental or new-model airplane. Mainly Air Force use.*

sex job   **1** A female who can be easily possessed; a promiscuous woman; a nymphomaniac. → **2** A sexually attractive woman; a woman one would like to possess. **3** [taboo] Sexual intercourse; several uninterrupted hours of sexual foreplay, intercourse, and variations on intercourse; sexual activity to the point of exhaustion.

sex pot   A female who is extremely

attractive sexually; a woman whose appearance and personality are sexy. 1957: "How pitiful the American who cannot command the smile of a sexpot." F. Morton, *The Art of Courtship*, 156.

Sh A hissed request or command to another to be quiet or shut up. *Colloq.*

shack *n.* 1 A worthless man; one who cannot be trusted. *c1840–c1900; obs.* 2 The caboose of a freight train. *Railroad use.* 3 A brakeman on a freight train. 1907 :"The 'shack' takes a steel coupling-pin...." J. London, *My Life. There are three possible origins: from the days before automatic couplers, when brakemen "shackled" the cars together; from the brakemen's duty of "shaking" hobos awake; from the rear brakeman's position in the "shack" = caboose. Wide railroad, hobo, carnival, and circus use.* 4 Any shack, public place, town, or region where hobos meet. *Hobo use.* 5 A wireless room or office; a radio operator's working quarters. *Radio operator and ham use.* 6 A woman who, though married, lives with a man as his wife; a paramour or mistress with whom a man lives. *Some W.W.II Army use. See* **frau.** *v.i.* 1 To live as a bachelor; to send away one's wife and live alone. *c1890, Southern Negro use. Obs.* 2 To live with a woman other than one's wife. *Replaced by "shack up."*

shack fever 1 Fatigue; sleepiness. *Hobo use.* 2 Fear of hopping a freight, the desire to remain out of sight, failing health, a disgust with the life of a hobo, or anything else that keeps a hobo from traveling. *Hobo use.*

shack job 1 A promiscuous woman; a mistress, esp. a soldier's mistress; a common-law wife. → 2 A sexual liaison of more than temporary duration. 1951: "... Allowing him to sleep with their daughter (this was an early shack-job, not the girl mentioned above)...." J. Lardner in *New Yorker*, Mar. 10, 119. *Common since cW.W.II. See* **shack up.**

shackles *n.* Stew or soup. *c1930; hobo and soldier use.*

shack man 1 A married man. → 2 A man, esp. a soldier, who has a sexual liaison or keeps a mistress in a dwelling for which he pays the rent; a soldier who sleeps with a mistress in their room or apartment instead of sleeping in Army quarters. *Since W.W.II. See* **shack up.**

shack rat A soldier who shacks up. *W.W.II Army use.*

shack up **shack up with** 1 Specif., to provide living quarters for and live with, at least intermittently, ones' mistress; to live with one's mistress or paramour; to have a fairly permanent sexual relationship with a woman; to have a sexual liaison of some duration with the same woman. 1946: "The medicine man had shacked up with a halfbreed cook." *Time*, Oct. 14. 1949: "... About some doll he shacked up with in Kentucky." Morley, *Man Who*, 62. 1957: "If you drink and shack up with strangers you get old at thirty." T. Williams, *Orpheus Descending*, I. 1958: "Kelly's shacking up with a Japanese girl in a house by the river." Movie, *Sayonara. Orig. c1940, truck-driver and traveling salesman use. Became common with soldiers during W.W.II to mean setting up housekeeping with a local woman near an Army base. Universally known civilian use.* → 2 To spend a night or a longer period in intimacy with a woman. → 3 To occupy living quarters; to live, room, or board at a place. 1950: "One friend of mine, his family being grown, got rid of his home and shacked up in a hotel." W. Pegler, *synd. newsp. col.*, May 31. 1951: "I was going to shack up in a hotel for a couple of days and not go home till vacation started." J. D. Salinger, *Catcher in the Rye*, 49.

shade *n.* 1 An umbrella. 1848: J. S. Farmer. *Still some facetious use.* 2 [derog.] A Negro. 1865: "An eye-witness [in Cairo, Ill.] ran out and ordered the 'shade' to 'get off the walk or he would have him fined.' " *Harper's*, Apr., 676/2. *Still used a little.* 3 Protection; a shield. *Not common.* → 4 A receiver of stolen goods; a fence. 1925: "If [the loot] is merchandise, it is sold to a 'fence' or 'shade.' " McLellan in *Collier's*, Aug. 8. *Because the receiver shields the thief by taking the incriminating stolen goods off his hands.*

shad-mouth *n.* 1 A person having a protuberant upper lip. 2 A Negro. *c1935. Negro use; used both derog. and jocularly.*

shadow *n.* 1 [derog.] A Negro. *Very common; also Negro use.* 2 A parasitic follower. *Colloq.* 3 A detective *v.t.* To follow a person surreptitiously; specif., to follow a criminal or criminal suspect in order to know his whereabouts, ascertain his friends and daily routine, and the like; said of policemen and detectives. *Colloq.*

shady *adj.* Dishonest, unethical, untrustworthy. 1948: "... Shady money began to appear at race-tracks...." A. Hynd, *Pinkerton*, 78. *Colloq.*

shaft   *n.* **1** [taboo] A woman considered only sexually; a woman's body; the vagina. 1949: "She wasn't wearing a slip. 'Wow,' he decided at last, 'a shaft like that. . . .' " N. Algren, *Man with the Golden Arm,* 56. *Not common.* **2** An act or an instance of being taken advantage of, unfairly treated, deceived, tricked, cheated, or victimized; a raw deal. *Usu. in* "*to get the (a) shaft.*" *Fig., the image is the taboo one of the final insult, having someone insert something, as a barbed shaft, up one's rectum.* See **up my ass.**   **—s**   *n.pl.* **1** The human legs. *c1900–c1935; orig. underworld use.* → **2** Attractive or sexually appealing female legs. *Since c1935.*

shag   *adj.* **1** With a date or escort. *Usu. in* "*Are you going to a party stag or shag?*" *Fairly common student use since c1940. Some teenage use since c1955.* **2** Worthless. *Not common.*   *v.i.* To depart, esp. rapidly; to run, to hurry. 1856 [1954]: "You'd best shag now. Sun's dropping powerful fast." W. Henry, *Death of a Legend,* 7.   *v.t.* **1** To chase something. 1913: "I was allowed to 'shag' foul balls." C. H. Claudy, *The Battle of Baseball,* 318. 1945: "Shagging rabbits." E. Kasser. *Almost entirely limited to use by boys between 8 and 15 years old.* → **2** To tease or criticize someone continually; to hound someone. *c1930; teenage and student use.*   *n.* **1** [taboo] A party or group of boys and girls, motivated by sexual curiosity, in which looking at and touching the sexual parts of the opposite sex is as important as any intercourse that may result. *Fairly common use by children from about 10 to 13 years of age. Prob. since c1935.* → **2** [taboo] A lewd party; group sexual activity, usu. involving a number of men with one or two women. **3** One's date or escort. *adj., adv., & exclam.* Remarkable; wonderful(ly), very satisfying, great. *Teenage use since c1958.* Cf. **hounds.** **—ger**   *n.* A police shadow. *Lit., one who shags = chases or follows.* See Appendix, *—er ending.*

shake   *n.* **1** A party to which each guest brings a small amount of money to help pay the host's rent; a rent party. 1956: "Depression came. . . . You could always get together and charge a few coins and have a shake . . . the money paid the rent." S. Longstreet, *The Real Jazz Old and New,* 126. See **rug-cutter.** **2** Lit., a shake of the dice; fig., a chance, an opportunity. *Usu. in* "*fair shake.*" **3** The act of blackmailing; a shake-down.

1939: "I can never approve of the shake. . . ." Runyon. 1949: "Don't get me wrong, Dr. Legardie. This isn't any kind of a shake." Chandler, *Little Sister,* 34. See **on the shake. 4** Shakedown money; bribe money; graft. **5** A moment. *Orig. from* "*two shakes of a lamb's tail.*" Cf. **two shakes, half a shake.**   *v.i.* **1** To wiggle one's hips in a lascivious manner. See **bump, grind, shimmy. 2** To dance. *Facetious.*   *v.t.* To shake down someone. 1934: "Burwand was tied to some racket . . . he tried to shake one of the big boys. The big boy backfired. . . . Exit Burwand." Chandler, *Finger Man,* 110. *Since c1920. Perhaps from the Brit. sl.* "*show a leg.*" **—ster**   *n.* A respectable girl; a lady. 1848: "Criminals' use." J. S. Farmer. See Appendix, *—ster ending. Note here the fairly uncommon feminine use of the suffix.*

shake, on the   • Engaged in crime, esp. shakedowns or extortion. 1938: "You knew they was on the shake." Liebling, *Back Where,* 87.

shake, put [someone] on the   shake on [someone], put the   To extort money, as by torture or threat of death; to shake down. 1930: "Put one on the shake." *Amer. Mercury,* Dec., 457. *Underworld use.*

shake, the   *n.* The act or an instance of ridding oneself of an unwanted friend or relationship; refusal or dismissal of a person. *Fig., the act of shaking oneself loose from an attachment or a follower.*

shake a leg   Hurry; make haste. *Often denotes impatience at someone's slowness.*

shake [one's] ankle = **shake a leg.** 1937: "Come on, now, shake your ankle." Weidman, *Wholesale,* 32; also 123. *Not common.*

shake a wicked (mean) calf (hoof, leg) To dance, esp. to dance well or to like to dance. 1920. "Phoebe and I are going to shake a wicked calf." Fitzgerald, *This Side of Paradise,* 119. 1929: "Shake a mean hoof." *Lit. Digest,* Mar. 16, 23. See **mean, wicked.**

shake-down   shakedown   *n.* **1** A night's lodging; a makeshift bed. *Since c1885; archaic.* See **pad. 2** A search or searching of a person or place. 1950: "We gave the room a first-class shakedown." Starnes, *Another Mug,* 171. **3** A demand for money; blackmail; extortion. 1934: "It isn't a shakedown." Chandler, *Finger Man,* 18. 1942: "I had paid my last shake-down." W. B. Johnson, *Widening Stain,* 239. 1949: "Operating a shakedown." Radio serial, *Mr. District Attorney*, Oct. 26. **shake down** **1** To search, esp. a person for contraband or arms. 1950: "A couple of patrolmen to shake down the neighborhood. . . ." Starnes, *And When She Was Bad*, 109. **2** To extort money by blackmail or a confidence game; to work the protection racket. 1930: "Shaking down poor peddlers, newsboys. . . ." Lavine, *Third Degree*, 166. *Very common. Orig. from image of shaking fruit from a tree, or perhaps of turning a person upside down and shaking money out of his pockets.*

shake down the ashes To crank a car or truck. *Archaic.*

shake it up *imp.* Hurry; hurry up; shake a leg. 1927: "We've got to shake it if we want to find our folks at home." Hammett, *Blood Money*, 172.

shake one *imp.* Lit., prepare a milk shake; the usu. instruction relayed by a counterman or waitress in ordering a milk shake. *Lunch-counter use.*

shakes, the *n.pl.* **1** Fever or chills accompanied by trembling. *Since c1840.* **2** An attack of trembling, usu. from anxiety or as the aftermath of excessive drinking or of narcotic use; the heebie-jeebies; the willies. 1927: "To have the shakes." *New Repub.*, 72.

shake-up *n.* **1** A general reassignment of personnel to new tasks or locales; a general firing of old employees in order to hire new ones; a reorganization of personnel or work methods. 1949: "The remedy is a shake-up in the Bureau of the Budget." Ithaca (N.Y.) *Journal*, Oct. 25, 6/2. *Since c1885. Now colloq.* **2** Whisky made by mixing grain alcohol and coloring. *Not common.* **3** A mixture of two or more whiskies or liquors shaken together and drunk. 1956: "A *shakeup* is a mixture of corn whiskey and wine." S. Longstreet, *The Real Jazz Old and New*, 148.

sham *n.* **1** A policeman. *Though it is sometimes claimed this orig. in "shamrock" in ref. to Irish policemen of N.Y.C., it is claimed to be a shortening of "shamus," perhaps reinforced by stand. "sham," showing the underworld's opinion of the police.* **2** A small pillow, as used behind one's back while sitting on a couch or for decoration. 1956: ". . . Two square pillows of the kind they called 'shams.' " N. Algren, *A Walk on the Wild Side*, 13. *Dial.*

shambro *n.* = **shamrock**, the drink. 1949: ". . . At the Pequot Tavern, drinking shambros or hard cider with

beer chasers. . . ." S. Lewis, *The God-Seeker*, 26f. *From "shambrogue," obs. variant of "shamrock."*

shambrogue **Shambrogue** *n.* = **Shamrock**. *Obs.; from "shamrock" plus* [*Irish*] *"brogue."*

shampoo *n.* Champagne. *Some facetious use. Based on the phonetic spelling of "champagne."* See Appendix, —oo ending.

Shamrock **shamrock** *n.* **1** A person of Irish origin or descent. **2** A mixture of stout and whisky. *Traditionally a favorite of the Irish.* *adj.* Irish.

shamus **shammus** **shamos** **shommus** *n.* **1** A policeman; increasingly, a police, hotel, or private detective; also a watchman or guard. 1934: "I think you are a dick, a shamus." Chandler, *Finger Man*, 14. 1940: "Not a real copper [uniformed policeman] at that. Just a cheap shamus." Chandler, *Farewell*, 96. 1950: "Vallon [in Peter Cheyney's *Lady, Beware*] is an English investigator who is almost a British-accented burlesque of the tough American shamus." H. Mills in N.Y. *Times Bk. Rev.*, Sept. 3, 11/1. 1951: "Scores of hoodlums, gunsels, informers, shyster lawyers, and crooked shamuses. . . ." S. J. Perelman in *New Yorker*, Mar. 3, 26/3. *Very common, esp. in detective fiction, since c1930. The spelling "shamus" is much more freq. than the other forms. Prob. from the Hebr. "shomus" = caretaker or synagogue watchman, reinforced by Irish proper names "Shamus" and "Seamas." The most common pronunciation rhymes with "Thomas," but the Irish of N.Y.C. pronounce it "shay-mus."* → **2** A police informer; a stool pigeon. **3** Anyone with minor influence or semi-official status; a political lackey. *It is interesting to note that a similar American Indian word "shaman" = medicine man had the same sl. meaning among Indians.*

shanghai *v.t.* To abduct a man, usu. a sailor, and force him to work as a sailor on one's own ship. 1954: "You were most likely to get slugged and shanghaied out to sea." W. R. & F. K. Simpson, *Hockshop*, 35. *Colloq.*

Shangri La *n.* A mythical land of eternal youth and beauty; an earthly paradise; any place very well liked. *From the novel "Lost Horizon," by James Hilton.*

shank *n.* See **ride shanks' mare.** *v.t.* To stab a person, whether in the leg or not. *Teenage street gang use since c1955.*

shank it   To walk or hike. *c1920; not common in U.S.; much more common in Eng.*

shanks' mare   shanks' pony   1 The legs considered as a means of transportation. See **ride shanks' mare**. **2** Walking as opposed to riding. **3** = **pot luck**. *A fairly recent usage, apparently due to confusion of the orig. sl. meaning.*

shanty   *n.* **1** A shack. *Colloq.* **2** A black eye; a shiner. 1926: "I hung a shanty on the bimbo's eye." Stallings & Anderson, *What Price Glory*, III. **3** The caboose of a freight train. *Railroad use.* *adj.* Poor, common, unrefined, rude, uneducated. *Not common except in "shanty Irish."* 1951: "There was a girl from an Irish family, oh, not shanty Irish. Rich, well-brought-up family." S. Longstreet, *The Pedlocks*, 153. *Usu. applied to people of Irish descent.*

shanty Irish   Poor Irish people, lit or fig., living in shanties or shanty-towns.

shanty-town   *n.* **1** Lit., a town of shacks; a group of shacks and makeshift dwellings on the outskirts of a city, usu. populated by hobos, men out of work, and, esp. in 19C America, poor immigrant laborers. *An old term revived during Depression of the 1930's.* → **2** The poorer or older residential neighborhoods of a community; a dilapidated section of town.

shape   *n.* **1** = **shape-up**. **2** See **drape shape**. **3** A woman's figure, esp. when attractive. *Usu. in "She's got a shape"* = *she has a good figure. c1940, when a good figure meant a slim waist, fairly prominent breasts, and shapely hips and legs.*

shape in with   To associate with; to pal around with. 1951: "He always shaped in with a guy named Hooker." Spillane, *Big Kill*, 37.

shape-up   *n.* The system of hiring longshoremen for a job by choosing men from a group assembled on a dock or at a union hall; the group so assembled. *The term is often, though not always, associated with the practice of paying money to the hiring boss in return for being chosen.* 1952: "A shape-up is the hirin' boss comes out on the pier and hires the men he wants for certain jobs stevedoring." Radio interview, CBS, Nov. 13.

shark   *n.* **1** A student who is unnecessarily absent from a class or lecture; also the absence itself. 1853: Hall, *College Words*, 421. → **2** An expert or exceedingly intelligent student; fig., a student who does not need to attend

classes in order to learn the subject and pass the examination. 1924: "They're sharks and I'm not." Marks, *Plastic Age*, 203. *Student use from c1900–c1925; archaic.* **3** An expert. 1934: "We got to wait for the autopsy and the gun-shark's report." Chandler, *Finger Man*, 136. 1936: "Chic is a shark on show biz lore." A. Green in *Esquire*, Sept. **4** A cheater, esp. a person who uses his skill in a game to deceive his opponent, as a "pool shark" or "card shark." *The usu. method of the shark is to keep his proficiency secret until a novice has been enticed into the game or until the stakes have mounted high, then to use his superior skill to clean out his opponents.* **5** An employment agent; a hiring boss. *Hobo use.*

—shark   See Appendix, Suffixes and Suffix words.

sharp   *n.* **1** An expert, usu. at card games or other gambling games; a shark. 1900: "Hurstwood's a regular sharp." Dreiser, *Carrie*, 81. → **2** One skilled in forms of cheating, esp. in sleight-of-hand with playing cards; a crooked gambler; one who seeks to take, or habitually takes, advantage of others. **3** A used but well-cared-for automobile having extra accessories. *Used-car-dealer use.* *adj.* **1** Mentally alert; witty; quick thinking; smart; wise; in the know; hep. *Fig., having a keen mind that penetrates into problems easily; having a rapier-like wit. Reinforced by the pop. saying, "Sharp as a tack."* **2** Stylish; trim; neatly and smartly dressed; natty; specif., dressed in the latest, or in the latest hep, fashion; attractive and modern. 1951: "He wore bow ties and sharp suits." T. Capote, *Grass Harp*, 21. 1952: "[Mickey] Jelke and Davioni [assoc. with a call girl racket], the latter sharp in a summer suit. . . ." N.Y. *Daily News*, Aug. 26, C4/1. 1954: "I had on a brand new Stetson, my fine black suit and new patent leather shoes. I was a sharp cat." L. Armstrong, *Satchmo, My Life in New Orleans*, 164. **3** Satisfactory, satisfying; attractive or pleasing, esp. to a modern, hep person; all right, o.k. 1939: "I sound like everything was sharp. . . ." O'Hara, *Pal Joey*, 32. *The above two uses are assoc. with jive use, but were all common by c1935. They are in common jazz and fairly common teenage and student use. They imply an all-inclusive or complete approval of a person or thing. To older people, however, "sharp" still carries a connotation of unrefined, garish, and* *daring.* **4** Specif., shrewd and ambitious; aware of, alert to, and using one's intelligence only to take quick advantage of opportunities for personal gain; worldly, sophisticated, and cynical. *1943:* "The only sharp thing to do is to run an unknown." M. Shulman, *Barefoot Boy with Cheek*, 161. *1951:* "All of them are 'sharp'—an all-inclusive adjective that is applied to smart, ambitious parties who have their eyes on the main chance." S. Frank in *SEP*, June 30, 102/4. *This shift in meaning from the first adj. use given above became most apparent during W.W.II.* *adv.* Stylishly; smartly; gaudily. *1951:* "He was dressed sharp, like the wise guys on Broadway." *I, Mobster*, 142. **—ie** *n.* **1** One who dances expertly to swing music; a devotee of swing. *Jitterbug use.* **2** A flashy dresser; a smartly dressed man. *1952:* "Shorts are going exotic. And not just among the sharpies." *AP*, Jan 2. See **sharp. 3** A shrewd, alert person. *1949:* ". . . Whether he'd been a chump or a sharpie." Burnett, *Jungle*, 83. For above uses see **sharp. 4** A cheat or swindler. *1951:* "They told police they were outwitted out of the remaining $15,000 by three 'sharpies.' " *AP*, Oct. 27. See Appendix, **—ie** ending.

—sharp See Appendix, Suffixes and Suffix words.

shatting (shating) on [one's] uppers Doing without money; broke. *1894:* "I's been a moocher, an' now I's shatin' on me uppers." J. Flynt. *1939:* "She has to blow and she's shatting on her uppers. She figures the peeper can get her some dough." Chandler, *Big Sleep*, 160. *Orig. hobo use; archaic.*

shave *v.t.* To defeat, esp. by a small margin; to take advantage of. *1952:* "[N.Y. Yankee baseball team manager Casey] Stengel had no choice but to hand the ball to [pitcher Allie] Reynolds, his only 20-game winner. Reynolds in his best form is a hard man to shave." *AP*, Oct. 4. **—d** *adj.* Drunk. *1851:* "In use at one time or another." Hall, *College Words*, 302. *Never common; obs.* **—r** *n.* A boy, lad, usu. in "little shaver." *1910:* "A little shaver comes in." Johnson, *Varmint*, 270; 304. *1944:* "When I was a little shaver." Fowler, *Good Night*, 38. *Colloq.*

shave-tail *n.* **1** A mule, esp. a young, unbroken, or untried animal. *1870: DAE. Still some farm and lumberjack use. Dial. and archaic.* → **2** An inexperienced young man; a tenderfoot. *1899: DAE.* *Still some ranch and lumberjack use. Dial. and archaic.* **3** A young or newly commissioned second lieutenant in the Army. *Wide W.W.I Army use, prob. from the Army mule corps. Mary Keeley's 1930 ety.—" 'Shavetail' came from West Point, where the senior had his coat tail shaved off, figuratively, when he donned the uniform of a 2nd lieutenant"—does not seem to take into account the earlier meanings of the word.* → **4** Any second lieutenant. *Wide W.W.II Army use.*

shear **sheer** *adj.* = **cool.** *Some bop and cool use c1948–c1955.*

sheba *n.* **1** An attractive girl, esp. a sweetheart. *Student use c1925; obs.* → **2** A tempting but unattainable woman; a vamp. *1932:* "In the Loop [Chicago] there were plenty of shebas to look at." J. T. Farrell, 121. *Archaic.*

shebang *n.* **1** A soldier's tent or quarters; the place where a soldier sleeps and keeps his possessions. *Civil War use, more common with Confederate than with Union troops. Obs.* → **2** A complete residence, office, or place; a collection of all one's possessions; a collection of anything; an entire series of actions. *Usu. in "the whole shebang." Since c1870; now colloq.*

shed *n.* A closed automobile, as opposed to one with no roof. *c1920; obs.* See **wood-shed.**

shee *n.* See **yen-shee.**

sheeny **sheenie** [derog.] *n.* **1** A Jew. *Always derog., implying one who can't be trusted or one who invariably puts his own interests first. Since before 1885; most common c1910–c1925. Prob. from Ger. "schin" = a petty thief, cheat, miser.* **2** A tailor. *c1910; because Jews were traditionally tailors.* *adj.* Jewish. *1914:* "I ain't one of these Sheeny employment bureaus; I'm an American." S. Lewis, *Our Mr. Wrenn*, 38. *1922:* "Yuh Sheeny bum, yuh!" O'Neill, *Hairy Ape*, 7.

sheep leg An old-style pistol. *From its shape; obs.*

sheep-skin **sheepskin** *n.* A diploma. *1858:* ". . . And receive our sheepskins." *Harvard Magazine*, July, 267. *1949:* "With college sheepskins filed away. . . ." *AP*, Sept. 7. *Since at least 1800. By 1900 used at 79 representative colleges as listed in DN, 2, 59. From the vellum orig. used, and still occasionally used, for diplomas. Colloq.*

sheet *n.* **1** A newspaper. *1946:* "One of the evening rags lighted the fuse; now both morning sheets have written it up." Evans, *Halo in Blood*, 74. From the "sheets" of paper, reinforced by hobo use of newspapers to sleep on and under. Cf. **rag**. **2** Specif. = **scratch sheet**. **3** A magazine. *Not common.* **4** [taboo] = **shit**. *Euphem. and jocular use, mimicking Southern Negro pronunciation.* **5** A criminal's dossier, record, or file. 1958: "Sheet—A criminal record." G. Y. Wells, *Station House Slang.*

sheets, the *n.* Money; lit., the amount necessary to secure lodging or a bed for the night. 1929: "You ain't got any clothes or anything when you ain't got the sheets." J. T. Farrell, 154. *Orig. hobo use; not common.*

sheet-writer *n.* **1** A newspaper reporter, rewrite man, or editor. **2** A solicitor of subscriptions to magazines. *Neither use is common.*

sheik *n.* **1** A handsome male lover, esp. if given somewhat to melancholia; a male sweetheart; a ladies' man. 1921: *The Sheik*, a book by Edith M. Hull. 1924: "We hear almost nothing of the matinée idol any more. The 'sheik' has taken his place." A. Lewis in *Lit. Digest. First popularized by Edith Hull's widely read novel; further popularized by Rudolph Valentino's portrayal of the book's hero in the very popular movie of the same name. Very common c1921–c1927. Presented publicly as a dark, dashing, moody person, Valentino was identified as the typical sheik and was called "The Sheik," which may have restricted the usage from further popularity. Obs. →* **2** A small-time gigolo, gambler, or sharpie. 1933: "Murphy, a line man, was gabbing away with two sheiks who wore bell-bottomed trousers." J. T. Farrell, 10. *Archaic.* 1956: "John Held Jr. drew the flapper and her Sheik best. The lad was apple-headed, his hair buttered tight down. He wore bell-bottomed trousers, drove a Stutz Bearcat, and played or danced to jazz a lot." S. Longstreet, *The Real Jazz Old and New*, 95. *v.t.* To captivate, charm, or cajole a woman.

sheive See **shiv.**

shekel *n.* A coin, but esp. a silver dollar. 1889: "Colloq." *DAE. The word became archaic as silver dollars went out of use. Orig. from the Hebr. word, and still in use by Jewish groups.* **—s** *n.pl.* Money, wealth. *Since c1870; still in use.*

shelf, on the **1** Socially inactive; often said of a woman who has broken her engagement to be married. **2** Post-

poned, deferred; esp. for further study or consideration—said of a plan or project. *Business use.*

shell *n.* **1** A vault or safe. *Underworld use; archaic.* **2** An old cow, horse, or other farm animal that has lived past its usefulness. *Some farm use; archaic.* **3** A standard (8-ounce) beer glass. 1950: "He decanted two thirds of a beer shell of bourbon and to this he added about a teaspoon of water." Starnes, *And When She Was Bad*, 25. *Not common.* See **bomb-shell, clamshells.** *v.i., v.t.* To shell out; to pay. 1948: "You're expected to shell at least a buck." Lait-Mortimer, *N.Y. Confidential*, 224. **—s** *n.pl.* Dollars; money; that which is shelled out. *Not common.*

shellacked *adj.* Drunk. 1922: "One of the boys got beautifully shellacked." Phila. *Eve. Bulletin*, Mar. 8. *Somewhat archaic.*

shellacking *n.* **1** A beating. 1930: " 'Shellacking' . . . and numerous other phrases are employed by the police as euphemisms." Lavine, *Third Degree*, 3. **2** A defeat; a complete failure; usu. used in sports to mean a rout or utter defeat. 1952: "Should Black take a shellacking, the National Leaguers are in bad trouble." G. Talbot, AP, Sept. 30.

shell out To pay or contribute; to spend; to pay extortion or bribe money. *Since c1830.* 1941: "You shelled out [$2.50]." G. Homes, *40 Whacks*, 122. 1949: "If you are one of the taxpayers who are paying by installments, get ready to shell out again." AP, Oct. 12. *Since c1820.*

shell-road *v.t.* To put a person out of one's automobile; to leave a person stranded. 1935: "The only time anybody ever hears of [her] doing much walking is the time she is shell-roaded on the Pelham Parkway by some Yale guys when she gets cross with them." Runyon. *Not common.* See **red-light.**

shemale *n.* A female, esp. a disliked, distrusted woman; a bitch.

shemozzle = **shimozzle.**

shenanigans *n.pl.* Tricks, pranks, nonsense; petty cheating or deception. *Since c1870; may be from Irish "sionnochuigham"* = *I play tricks.*

shenannygag *n.* A trick or prank; petty cheating; a deception. *Based on "shenanigans"; not common.*

she-she *n.* A girl or young woman; a chick; orig. a sexually attractive or promiscuous girl or woman native of a

Pacific Island or occupied country. *W.W.II USN and Army use. Based on pigeon Eng.* See Appendix, Reduplications.

she-stuff *n.* **1** Cows, heifers, ewes; any female cattle. *Ranch use.* → **2** Women, esp. women considered as idle, gossipy, etc. → **3** Feminine clothing, talk, gossip, opinion, or the like; anything mainly of interest to women. *c1930.*

shicker See **shikker.**

shiever *n.* A double-crosser. 1925: "The worst thing you can call a crook is a 'shiever.'" McLellan in *Collier's,* Aug. 8. See **shiv.**

shift *v.i., v.t.* To change one's clothes. 1840 [1954]: "... When I was shifting (changing clothes)." *Behold Me Once More, The Confessions of James Holley Garrison,* ed. by W. M. Merrill. *Obs.* **—er** *n.* **1** A grafter; a grifter. *Some use c1920.* **2** A go-between between a thief and a fence; lit., one who shifts loot from a thief to a receiver of stolen goods. *Some underworld use.* → **3** A fence. *Some underworld use.* See Appendix, **—er** ending. **—ie** *n.* An unreliable girl. See Appendix, **—ie** ending.

shiftie-eyed **shifty-eyed** *adj.* Sneaky; mean; untrustworthy.

shikker **shicker** *adj.* Drunk. 1938: "We'll eat good, then we'll get shikker." Liebling, *Back Where,* 274. *From the Yiddish. Some popularity since c1927.* See **on the shikker.** **—ed** *adj.* Drunk. "*Shikker*" plus stand. ending "*—ed.*" *Very common in Australia.* See Appendix, Drunk.

shikker, on the **1** Drunk. **2** Known to be a habitual drunkard. See **shikker.** See Appendix, Drunk.

shill *n.* **1** A confederate of a gambler, con man, pitchman, or auctioneer, or an employee of a gambling house, carnival, circus, or auction room, who acts as a decoy to encourage real customers to gamble, bid, purchase tickets, or the like. Pretending to be a bona fide customer, the shill places bets, makes bids, buys tickets, or pretends to be convinced by a con man, in order to start or encourage real betting, bidding, buying, or confidence. 1948: "The Story of a Red-headed Shill." Advt. for the movie, *House Across the Street.* 1949: "The shill is innocuous-looking." N.Y. *Times,* Aug. 28, 63. 1956: "SHILL—One who lures customers, pretending to be a

customer himself, but who is in the employ of the establishment that is dealing to the customers." T. Betts, *Across the Board,* 319. *Very common since c1925.* See **shillaber.** → **2** A card-player or gambler who is supplied with chips or money by the house so that there will always be enough players for a game. → **3** A pitchman, auctioneer, carnival barker; an advertising or public relations employee; anyone whose job it is to create business or encourage buying through personal appeals or recommendations. *c1945.* → **4** A recommendation or advertisement. 1939: "I go into the diner and partake of a fish that is on the menu, because the steward of the diner weighs in with a strong shill for this fish." Runyon. *Not common.* **5** A policeman's club or nightstick. *Orig. from "shillelagh."* See Appendix, Shortened Words. *v.i.* To act or work as a shill. 1948: "She was going to shill on Walter's wheel." F. Brown, *Dead Ringer,* 156.

shillaber *n.* **1** = **shill.** *Orig. = a booster or satisfied customer. Circus use. Is at least as old as, and may be the orig. of, "shill."* **2** A policeman; one who carries a club or shill. *Not common.*

shim *n.* = **square,** esp. one not hep to rock and roll music. *Mainly rock and roll use since c1955, but some earlier jazz use.*

shimmy *n.* **1** A chemise. 1952: "To persuade the young matron to doff her wet shimmy...." S. J. Perelman in *New Yorker,* Sept. 20, 35/1. *Since at least 1870. Colloq. by 1900. Became archaic with the disappearance of that garment.* **2** A style of dancing, typified by movements somewhat resembling those of coitus, pop. during the 1920's. *c1927:* "I Wish I Could Shimmy Like My Sister Kate," pop. song title. *Archaic.* → **3** Gelatin desserts, jelly, or any similar substance that shakes easily. *Not common.* **4** The gambling game of chemin de fer. 1956: "Six dice tables, four blackjack tables and a 'shimmy' (chemin de fer) table—eleven gambling tables in all." J. Scarne, *The Amazing World of John Scarne,* 379. *Not common.*

shimmy in the snow See **in the snow.**

shimmy pudding Gelatin prepared for eating. See **shimmy.**

shimozzle **shlemozzle** **shemozzle** *n.* A mess; uproar; a fight; confusion. 1947: "The ensuing schlemozzle required the intervention of the Chair before the orator could continue." P. Jones in Phila. *Bulletin*, Feb. 27, 10/6. *Not common in U.S.; more common in Eng. and Canada.*

shin-crack **shincrack** *v.t.* To dance, esp. to jitterbug. *c1940; some student use; not common.*

shindig *n.* **1** A party, gathering, or festival; any event that attracts guests or spectators. 1873: *DAE.* 1957: "Mr. and Mrs. Louis Lorillard, of Newport, and George Wein, of jazz, who run the shindig [the annual Newport Jazz Festival]...." N.Y. *Daily News*, June 27, 77. → **2** A dancing party; a dance. *Since c1925. May orig. have been a Western term ("shin" plus "dig"), but more prob. evolved from "shindy."*

shindy *n.* Noisy confusion; uproar; a ruckus, a row. 1829: "Slang." *DAE. Obs.*

shine *n.* **1** A good recitation; a good grade. 1851: "To make a shine." Hall, *College Words*, 278. **2** [derog.] A Negro. 1907: "A 'shine' is always a negro, so called, possibly, from the high lights on his countenance." J. London, *The Road*, 126f. 1952: "They were Southern shines. Sure, shines—darkies—niggers. ..." L. Hughes, *Laughing to Keep from Crying*, 60. *Mainly Southern use, and still in use.* **3** Whisky; esp. bootleg whisky or moonshine. 1952: "When Prohibition came non-blinding shine sold in fruit jars for 50 cents a quart." R. C. Ruark, *synd. newsp. col.*, Mar. 10. See **monkey-shines, sunshine.** *adj.* [derog.] Negro. 1940: "Another shine killing." Chandler, *Farewell*, 12. *v.i.* To excel; to accomplish something in a conspicuously proficient manner. *Colloq.* See **shine up to [someone].** —**d** *adj.* Drunk. *Not common.* —**r** *n.* **1** A dollar, esp. a silver dollar; any coin. *c1775–c1860; obs.* **2** A black eye; a mouse. 1950: "...A pip of a shiner." J. McNulty in *New Yorker*, Oct. 14. 1953: "Tommy's shiners were the result of a fall downstairs." AP, photo caption, Feb. 20. *Since c1900; very common.* **3** A handsome or charming man who is esp. attractive to women. *Some use c1920.* **4** A shiny, mirrorlike area on a table top, cigarette case, ring, or the like, in which a dishonest card dealer can see the face of each card as he deals. *Gambler use.* **5** A trainman's lantern. *Railroad use.* See **apple-shiner.** —**rs** *n.pl.* Patent-leather shoes. 1922: "Brew's going stepping. Shiners and claw-hammers and

stiff choker, and bear grease on his hair." A. L. Bass. *Obs.*

shine box [derog.] A bar, dancehall, or other amusement or public place owned or chiefly patronized by Negroes.

shine to, take a To take a liking to. *Colloq. since c1840.*

shine up to [someone] To curry favor.

shingle *n.* **1** Lit. and fig., a framed certificate of a medical, law, or other professional degree; a framed certificate of any college or university degree or membership in an organization. **2** A slice of toast. *Some use since c1935. Most common in W.W.II Army use,* "shit on a shingle" [*taboo*].

shinny *n.* = **shiny.** *Dial.* *v.i., v.t.* Lit. and fig., to climb; also, to play the game of shinny; hence, to be active. 1920: "You let your imagination shinny on the side of your desires for a few hours, and then you decide." F. S. Fitzgerald, *This Side of Paradise*, 156. *Now colloq.*

shiny **shinny** *n.* **1** [derog.] A Negro. 1893: "The shiny lives comfortably." J. Flynt. See **shine.** **2** Liquor. See **shine.**

ship *v.t.* To expel a student, to fire an employee, to release anyone from duty. *Not common.* See **battleship.**

shipwreck a pair *imp.* An order to scramble two eggs. *Lunch-counter use in relaying an order. In allusion to "Adam and Eve on a raft."*

shirt *n.* See **boiled shirt, fried shirt, keep [one's] shirt on, skivvy shirt, stuffed shirt.**

shirt on, keep [one's] To be calm; not to be excited or impatient; to await [one's] turn. *In direct discourse, used chiefly in the imperative,* "Keep your shirt on!" *Colloq. since c1850.*

shirttail *n.* An editorial column in a newspaper. 1944: "The boss blurbed [the story] in his shirttail." C. Macon in *Collier's*, Sept. 16, 64/3. *Newspaper use.*

shirttail kin A distant relative, as a fourth cousin. *Mostly dial. use in Southern and Midwestern rural areas.*

shit [*taboo*] *interj.* An expression of strong disgust or disappointment. *n.* **1** Anything inferior, ugly, cheap, or disgusting; esp., merchandise that is of inferior material, workmanship, and general quality. **2** Cant; any talk or writing intended to deceive; unacceptable explanations; insincere talk, esp. an insincere apology or compliment; "sweet talk"; lies; an exaggeration. Cf.

crap, jazz. 3 An entertainment or performance that is inferior, poor, or insincere; esp., commercial sentimentality; an entertainment or performance abounding in sentimentality, sentiment, or corn. 4 An insignificant, unimportant, disreputable person, esp. an aggressive, ambitious, or annoying one. *Usu. preceded by "little."* 5 Luck; the fortunes of life; fate; one's assignment or role in life or a specif. endeavor. *As in "tough shit," "good shit," etc., but usu. bad luck, ill fortune, or mistreatment. v.i., v.t.* Fig., to experience a violent or extreme response; to be shocked, to laugh uproariously, to feel envy, to become enraged, or the like. *Often in "I thought I'd shit" or in "I shit blue (green, or some other color)." adj.* Complete, total. *adv.* Very; completely. *All uses and all "shit —" expressions are, of course, based on the very old, universally known, and stand. but taboo "shit" = feces (n.), to defecate (v.). Wide Armed Forces use during W.W.II, and the general loosening of moral restrictions and taboos has encouraged "shit" uses among all strata of the population.* —ty [taboo] *adj.* 1 Mean; malicious; petty. 2 Tedious; unrewarding; insignificant; routine.

— shit See Appendix, Suffixes and Suffix Words.

shit creek [taboo] See up shit creek without a paddle.

shit for the birds [taboo] = for the birds.

shit green (blue) [taboo] To be shocked, surprised, or enraged.

shit-head [taboo] *n.* 1 A stupid, stubborn, or confused person; a fuck-off. 2 = shit heel.

shit-heel [taboo] *n.* A heel; an untrustworthy person; a chiseler; a parasite; specif., an obnoxious, egotistical person; a smart aleck.

shit in high cotton [taboo] To live more prosperously, pleasantly, or luxuriously than one has formerly; to be enjoying the results of good fortune, success, or prosperity; to eat high off the hog.

shit list [taboo] Fig., a list of persons disliked, considered untrustworthy, or worthless; specif., those persons toward whom an important, influential person bears malice.

shit on [someone or something] [taboo] An expression of strong anger at, disgust with, or rejection of a person or thing. *One of the more common such expressions.*

shit on a shingle [taboo] Creamed chipped beef (dried beef or canned corned beef) on toast. *Wide W.W.II Army use.* See shingle.

shit on wheels [taboo] = hot shit, on wheels.

shit or get off the pot [taboo] A request, a demand, or a comment that another act, obtain a result, bring something to a successful conclusion, or else stop trying and give someone else a chance to do so. *Fairly common among males.* Cf. fish or cut bait.

shit out of luck [taboo] To be too late to obtain whatever is desired; having no opportunity or chance, as for success or gratification; completely without hope; out of luck. See shit.

shiv   chiv   chive   shive   chev   sheive   *n.* 1 A knife, esp. considered as a weapon. 1674: "Chive." Farmer & Henley. 1848: "Chiv." J. S. Farmer. 1929: "A crook who fights with a knife is a chev man." Givens in *SEP.* 1938: "She gets this annonamous [sic] letter sticking the shiv in my back." O'Hara in *New Yorker.* 1949: "He was also packing a shiv." Radio show, *Sam Spade,* Oct. 30. *Since 1925 the spelling has tended toward "shiv." The variant spellings are given above in decreasing order of prominence. Orig. prob. from "shove" plus "shave." Now very common though still retaining an underworld connotation.* → 2 A razor; any object with a sharp cutting blade. *Mainly hobo use. v.t.* To cut; to stab. 1848: J. S. Farmer. 1934: "He died from being shivved by Johnny Mizzoo." Runyon.

shiv artist   chiv artist   A person who habitually uses a knife as a weapon. 1932: "Chiv artist." Runyon. 1944: "Shiv artist." Knoetgen in *Encore,* 338.

shivering Liz   Gelatin dessert. *Some Army, USN, and lunch-counter use.*

Shiver me timbers!   See timber.

shivoo   shivvoo   *n.* A party. *Some Army use since W.W.I. From Fr. "chez vous."*

shlemozzle   *n.* = shimozzle.

shlub   *n.* = schlub. 1956: "Telvi [a hoodlum] had a contract for $500, not to blind Victor Reisel [labor reporter] but to punch some shlub (Yiddish for jerk) around." N. Abrams & N. Patterson, N.Y. *Daily News,* Nov. 16, 5.

shm—   See Appendix, Reduplications.

shmeikle   *v.t.* To swindle; to con; to fast-talk. 1941: "If you let him shmeikle you into this." Schulberg, *Sammy,* 124. *From the Yiddish.*

shmo *n.* = **schmo.**

Shmoo **shmoo** *n.* A mythical animal orig. and pop. by Al Capp in his *synd. newsp. comic strip, "Li'l Abner." These wonderful creatures multiply very rapidly, lay eggs, give milk, when broiled taste like steak, when fried taste like chicken, and lie down and die if one looks at them hungrily; they symbolize the richness of the earth, abundance, or a simple, good life. Reinforced by, and perh. taken from, the Yiddish "shmoo" = profit, esp. unethical profit.* 1950: "So Mr. Jelly Roll's progress across America produces a rebirth of the music business, the orchestras multiplying back down the trail like Shmoos. . . ." A. Lomax, *Mr. Jelly Roll,* 220.

shnook *n.* = **schnook.**

shocker *n.* A shocking, horrifying, or thrilling movie, book, or story; a sensational story. 1953: "A shocker that makes others [movies] sound like baby-talk!" Radio advt., Mar. 14.

shoe *n.* **1** A person who is well dressed. *c1950; used by bop musicians.* → **2** = **hep, sharp.** *Usu. in the expression, "He's a real shoe." c1955; not common.* See **give [someone] his running shoes, gumshoe.**

shoe-dog *n.* A shoe salesman. *Shoe salesman use.*

shoe-string *n.* **1** A small amount of money, esp. if used as working capital. *Colloq.* **2** Wine, esp. cheap red wine. *adj.* Describing a business venture started with little capital.

shommus *n.* = **shamus.**

shoo-fly **shu-fly** *interj.* A mild expression of surprise or recognition of something remarkable or unusual. 1893: "Temporary [slang] phrases which flourish for a few months and then disappear forever leaving no sign, such as *shoo-fly* in America. . . ." Brander Matthews in *Harper's,* July, 304/2. *A term that has reappeared from time to time, usu. without much specif. meaning. It seems to evoke humorous images; has been used enough as a scat sound to be considered as assoc. with that form of singing. For ex., "Shoo-fly pie and apple pan dowdy" was a line from a very pop. song c1945.* *n.* **1** A plainclothes police officer; esp., one assigned to investigate the honesty of uniformed policemen. 1930: ". . . By having 'shoo-flies,' or [police] officers in civilian clothes, pick the [police] men up for violating the rules." Lavine, *Third Degree,* 19. 1958: "Shoo-fly—A plain-clothes policeman set to watch behavior

of other policemen." G. Y. Wells, *Station House Slang. The major use, but not common.* **2** In a mine, a transverse passage; a temporary stretch of railroad track. *Mining and railroad use.*

shoo in To cause or permit an inferior race horse to win a race with superior horses; to fix a horse race so that a specif. horse will win. 1935: "They are going to shoo in 'Never Despair' [a race horse]." Runyon, 235. *Horse-racing use, not common.* **shoo-in** *n.* **1** A horse that is shooed in. 1939: " 'Sharp Practice' [a race horse] wins by so far it looks as if he is a shoo-in." Runyon, 8. *Horse-racing use.* → **2** Any probable winner of a sporting event or contest of any kind; one favored or expected to win easily; a winner. 1951: "Coaches shudder and think back to what happened to Southern California [in football]. The big, powerful Trojans were the shoo-ins of the Pacific Coast Conference, especially after they bounced undefeated California. The Coast title [was] virtually theirs." E. Corrigan, AP, Nov. 12. 1952: "In the preferential poll [for the Republican presidential nominee] Taft looked like a shoo-in over Stassen." AP, May 13.

shook up *adj.* **1** Emotionally agitated, upset; shocked; lit., shaken with fear, worry, or relief. c1957: "All Shook Up." Title of a pop. rock and roll song. 1958: "I expected years in prison . . . they let me go free, boy was I shook up." T. Poston, N.Y. *Post,* Feb. 16, M2. 1958: "I lay back on my lump mattress [in the reformatory], so shook up I could not sleep." *Life,* Apr. 28, 70. *Wide teenage use since c1955. Some general use.* **2** Excited; enthusiastic; extremely happy, pleased, or satisfied; in love. *Wide teenage rock and roll use since c1955.*

shooper *n.* = **shuper.**

shoot *v.t.* **1** To throw a baseball hard. 1912: *DAE. Colloq.* **2** To photograph; to take a photograph of. 1924: "To the movies we are indebted for 'to shoot.' " G. H. Bonner in *19th Century,* Dec., 837. **3** To pass food at the table. *v.i.* **1** As a command = "Go ahead"; "I'm ready"; "Begin"; "Continue"; "Tell me now." 1941: " 'There are three reasons why.' 'Shoot,' said Jerry." A. R. Hilliard, *Justice Be Damned,* 121. *The most common use.* **2** = **shoot the breeze, shoot the bull.** 1944: "If Kane ever got in and started shooting. . . ." Ford, *Phila. Murder,* 78. **3** To take an intravenous injection of a narcotic drug. *Narcotic* *addict use.* See **shoot [one's] breakfast (lunch, dinner, supper, cookies).**

shoot a line To flatter, exaggerate, or lie. See **line.**

shoot [one's] breakfast (lunch, dinner, supper, cookies) To vomit. 1934: "If I'm any judge of color, you're goin' to shoot your cookies." Chandler, *Finger Man,* 46. *Some student use since c1925. Fairly common.*

shoot (the) bull 1 To talk, gossip, chat; to lie, exaggerate, flatter, or boast. See **bull.** 2 = **shoot the breeze.** 1951: "You could see he really felt pretty lousy about flunking me. So I shot the bull for a while." J. D. Salinger, *Catcher in the Rye,* 15. 1953: "You sit on a stoop and talk, stand on a corner, shoot the bull." L. Hughes, *Simple Takes a Wife.* Cf. **bull-shit.**

shoot (the) crap [taboo] = **shoot (the) bull.** 1951: "He was terrifically intelligent. His teachers were always writing letters to my mother, telling her what a pleasure it was having a boy like Allie in their class. And they weren't just shooting the crap. They really meant it." J. D. Salinger, *Catcher in the Rye,* 33. See **crap.**

shooting gallery 1 Any place where an addict or addicts can receive an injection of a narcotic drug; a pad. 1958: "Shooting gallery—A place where a narcotics user can get an injection." G. Y. Wells, *Station House Slang. Addict use.* 2 A gathering or party of addicts who have assembled for the purpose of taking drugs by injection. 1957: "In a fellow musician's hotel room during a 'shooting gallery' (dope party) involving [four people]...." E. Kirkman and H. Lee, N.Y. *Daily News,* Sept. 14, 4/1. *Addict use.*

shooting iron A pistol. 1787: *DAE.* 1936: " 'Shooting iron,' as the West termed the pistol...." P. A. Rollins, *The Cowboy,* 41. *Still some Western farm and ranch use; familiar to all from cowboy movies.* Cf. **iron.**

shooting match All the persons or things concerned in a given matter; the whole shebang. *Usu. in the phrase "the whole shooting match."*

shooting the agate Walking the street looking for fellow hipsters or to pick up a woman for sexual intercourse. *While walking, if one has his hands at his sides with the index finger extended it is a sign of recognition and greeting to fellow hipsters, a cool way of shaking hands; if the thumb is extended, women in the know will realize one is seeking sex.* 1950: "When you shoot the agate, your hands is at your sides with your index fingers stuck out and you kind of struts with it." A. Lomax, *Mr. Jelly Roll,* 16. *Not common.*

shoot the lemon To chat; to shoot the bull. *Not common.*

shoot off [one's] mouth (face, bazoo) To talk, esp. to talk too much and with too little regard for propriety; to disclose a confidence; to express an opinion strongly, esp. one which is insulting or enraging to others, to say what is better left unsaid; to exaggerate or brag; to talk too much, boastfully, or objectionably. 1880: "Mouth." *DAE.* 1938: "You are shooting off your face about what a don Juan you are." O'Hara in *New Yorker.* 1944: "I don't think you ought to go around shooting off your mouth [disclosing a confidence]." Ford, *Phila. Murder,* 118. 1945: "Every time I see Mussolini shooting off his mouth in a news reel...." Mitchell, *McSorley's,* 247. 1946: "...You come busting in here and shoot off your bazoo at me." Evans, *Halo in Blood,* 74.

shoot one 1 An order for a glass of Coca-Cola. *Lunch-counter use in relaying an order.* 2 An order for a cup of coffee. *Lunch-counter use.*

shoot one from the South An order of a glass of strong Coca-Cola, or a glass of Coca-Cola without much ice. *Some lunch-counter use in relaying an order. Because Southerners are supposedly fond of the beverage.*

shoot-out *n.* 1 In the game of dice, the come-out. 2 A gun duel. 1953: "The justly famous shoot-out between the Earps and the Clantons in the O-K Corral." Hoffman Birney, N.Y. *Times,* July 5, 13/2.

shoot the breeze 1 To talk idly or gossip; to gather for the purpose of talking idly; esp., to speculate lackadaisically or relate exaggerated accounts of past events. 1950: "We were sitting outdoors, enjoying ourselves and shooting the breeze." Billy Rose, *synd. newsp. col.,* May 5. 1951: "We were just shootin' the breeze." Radio play, *Cavalcade of America,* Dec. 4. *Wide W.W.II use, bragging, lawyering, and telling tall tales being a favorite occupation of soldiers aboard ship or confined to a base.* → 2 To speak or write windily and emptily; to speak nonsense, to lie, etc. *c1950.*

shoot the works 1 To go to the limit in anything whatever, as to tell all one knows about something, or to spend or gamble all one's money; to go the whole hog. 1928: "It is not my intention to shoot the whole works, but merely to examine a few specimens [of slang] and guess at their meaning." *AS.* 1941: "In whatever pertains to comfort, shoot the works." Cain, *M. Pierce,* 227. 1949: "Until [President Franklin D.] Roosevelt came along and decided to shoot the works." W. Pegler, *synd. newsp. col.,* Oct. 13. → **2** To vomit. *Not common.* → **3** To die. *Not common.*

shoot [one's] wad **1** Lit. and fig., to chance everything on one gamble; to make a final try with all one's resources, failing which one will be defeated. *From dice player use, where one can shoot one's wad or all one's money on one throw of the dice.* → **2** To have one's say; to speak one's piece. → **3** To be finished or through, to have a surfeit. *All uses since c1925.*

shop *n.* An office. 1952: "The office, once known as the 'shop,' is now the 'foundry,' 'store,' or 'delicatessen.'" *Management Rev.,* Oct., 688. See **guzzle-shop, hock-shop, hookshop.**

short *n.* **1** An automobile. 1932: "A 'hot short' is a stolen car." AP, Nov. 2. *c1930. Prob. orig. used in the term "hot short" = a stolen car, or a car stolen to be used as a getaway car by gunmen, thieves, or the like. Prob. orig. in Chicago underworld.* → **2** Any car, esp. a small foreign sports car. 1957: "Short—An automobile." E. Horne, *For Cool Cats and Far-Out Chicks. Orig. c1925 underworld argot, esp. = a stolen car. Hot rod use since c1950.* → **3** A taxi. 1939: "Horsey calls a short, a yellow short." Runyon. *c1930.* → **4** A streetcar or bus. *c1930. Meanings 1, 3, and 4 above were all most common c1930–c1940. They are now archaic, but still used occasionally in an underworld context.* **5** A prisoner who has served nearly all his time; a prisoner whose term is getting short. *Underworld and prison use. c1925.* *v.i., v.t.* Having only a little money; not having enough money for a specif. purpose; lacking a specif. amount of money in order to be able to pay a debt or the required price of something. *adj.* **1** Lacking; missing. *Colloq.* → **2** Specif., without sufficient funds. **—ie** *n.* **1** Any short person. *Used both indirectly and as a term of direct address. Colloq.* **2** Anything that is short, small, or abbreviated. 1936: ". . . Gave rise to ams [amateurs] as a

shortie for tyro thesps." A. Green in *Esquire,* Sept. 1951: "Documentation for this approach to [Erskine] Caldwell is offered with excerpts from 'Tobacco Road,' 'God's Little Acre,' and shorties [short stories]." W. Glover, Ithaca (N.Y.) *Journal,* June 29, 16/4. → **3** A woman's short nightgown. *The style and usage have been common since c1945.* *adj.* Short. *Colloq.* **—s** *n.pl.* Small sums of money; personal belongings. See **shorts, the.**

short-arm *n.* = **short-arm inspection.** *This form became common during W.W.II.*

short-arm drill = **short-arm inspection.**

short-arm inspection **1** A medical inspection of the relaxed penis, usu. for signs of venereal disease. *Common Army use since c1930, the usu. expression during and since W.W.II. The "short-arm" represents the relaxed penis; the term is based on the frequent inspection of the soldier's rifle or "arm."* → **2** Any inspection of the genitals, medical or otherwise. *Some male civilian use since W.W.II.*

short-change artist The operator of a carnival booth or circus side-show who is skilled in cheating customers by returning to them less than their proper change. *Orig. circus use.*

short-ear *n.* An unreligious student; a noisy, roistering fellow. 1851: Hall, *College Words,* 188. *Not common; obs.*

short end See **short end of the stick.** *This form most common since c1945.*

short end of the stick The least desirable lot, the worst of a transaction; an instance of being cheated, ignored, taken advantage of, or receiving unfair or unfavorable treatment. *Very common since c1940. Although the image is that of the short end as opposed to the larger quantity of the large end of a stick, which can be wielded, the etymology is more vulgar: fig., the short end is the end of a stick poked up another's rectum by the one in command of the situation, who holds the other end.*

short hairs [taboo] Lit. and fig., pubic hair.

short hairs, to have (someone, something) by the To be in a ruling, superior, or victorious position over a person; to have a problem solved, to have an action or task almost completed; specif., to have another person in one's power. Cf. **short hairs.**

short-horn *n.* **1** A tenderfoot; a newcomer. 1907: J. London, *The Road*, 173. *Still some Western use.* **2** A student taking a short course in a college of agriculture. *c1920; some student use. Both uses from the common name for a well-known type of beef cattle.*

short of hat size Lacking in intellect; stupid.

short one A single shot of whisky, as opposed to a double; a jigger of whisky; a quick drink.

short pint Any extremely short person; a dwarf. Cf. **half-pint.**

shorts, the *n.* The "trouble" or "sickness" of being without funds. 1932: "He is troubled with the shorts as regards to dough." Runyon. 1952: "I told him I had the shorts. He tried to slip me two C-notes." L. Stander in *Esquire*, June, 84/3. See **short.**

short-sheet *v.i., v.t.* **1** To play any practical joke. *Orig. from the common sailors' prank of folding one sheet in two to simulate both the top and bottom sheet of a bed; when the victim gets into bed, his legs are stopped short by the fold in the sheet.* **2** To give someone the short end of the stick.

short skate A cheapskate. 1953: "He must be a very short skate. A short skate like you've been speakin' of here. . . ." Radio, *Life Begins at 80*, Jan. 7. *Archaic.* **shortskate** *v.i.* To act like a short skate. 1909: "Don't short-skate; buy a season ticket, good for all the games!" O. D. von Engeln, *At Cornell*, 57. *Archaic.*

short-staker *n.* A transient or migratory worker; lit., one who works only long enough to earn a stake in order to move on. *c1920 to present.*

shortstop *v.t.* To stop a serving plate being passed to another at the table in order to help oneself first. *v.i.* To take a customer out of turn; to sell to another salesman's customer. *Retail salesman use.* *n.* At meals, one who helps himself to food that is being passed to someone else.

short-story writer A forger. *Not common.*

short-tail *n.* A nonunion worker. *c1910; railroad use.*

sho-sho gun A small automatic rifle. *Not common.*

shot *n.* **1** Anything small or insignificant. *Usu. in "little shot" = anything from a calf, child, or small tree to a narrow river or a small mountain. From Anglo-Saxon "scot" or "sceot" = a portion,* a tax; *archaic.* **2** A cadaver; a corpse to be dissected by medical students. *c1900 student use; obs.* **3** Money; esp., money owed. *c1900; obs. From "scot" or "sceot" = tax, a portion.* **4** A drink of straight whisky, usu. drunk in one gulp. 1938: ". . . With one of those nickel shots under their belt." Liebling, *Back Where*, 49. *Very common since Prohibition. From "scot" or "sceot" = a portion, a tax.* → **5** An order of Coca-Cola. *Some lunch-counter use in the South and West.* **6** An injection from a hypodermic needle; a portion of a drug to be injected; often preceded by the name of the medicine or disease involved: "penicillin shot," "polio shot," etc. *Colloq.* **7** Specif., a portion of a narcotic drug or an injection of a narcotic drug taken by an addict; a fix. *Since c1930. Mainly addict use; fairly well known to the general public.* **8** A Negro thief or gangster. *Orig. underworld use = a Negro pickpocket; c1930.* **9** A photograph; a snapshot. *Colloq. since c1930.* See **shoot.** **10** An important or influential person; a big shot. 1941: "Known? Hell, he's a shot." Cain, *M. Pierce*, 125. *Not as common as the orig. "big shot."* **11** The act or an instance of detonating an atomic device, usu. in testing atomic bombs. 1956: "The last shot—as the military calls the touching off of any atomic device. . . ." J. Cannon, *Who Struck John?* 259. → **12** The launching of a guided missile or rocket. 1957: "The second attempted launching of the U.S. satellite was postponed today due to ageing of the fuel in the Vanguard rocket. Another shot will be attempted at Cape Canaveral next week." NBC radio, Jan. 27. → **13** The range, flight, or power of a guided missile or rocket. *The above two uses, becoming common with the development of guided missiles and space flight projects c1955, return the usage to its most early sl. meaning, as it was long ago applied to catapults and bow-and-arrow warfare.* **14** An instance or the act of ejaculation; fig., coitus or any form of sexual satisfaction enjoyed by a male. Thus "a shot downstairs (or in the front door)" = coitus; "a shot in the back door" = anal intercourse; and "a shot upstairs" = fellatio. 1956: "Another ad by Countess Willie Piazza brags about her famous Mahogany Hall [brothel in New Orleans' Storyville]. 'The entire house is steamheated, and is the most handsome house of its kind. It's the only one where you get three shots for your money: The shot upstairs,/

The shot downstairs,/ And the shot in the room [at least one of these shots is of whisky]. . . .' " S. Longstreet, *The Real Jazz Old and New*, 60.   *adj.* 1 Drunk; half-shot. 1864: *DAE*. See Appendix, Drunk. *Very common during and since Prohibition.* → 2 Suffering from the after effects of drunkenness; afflicted with a hangover. → 3 Sick; exhausted, tired. 1933: "Say, am I shot!" J. T. Farrell, 62. *Common since c1935.* → 4 Used up, worn out, aged. *Said of objects. Common since c1930.*

shotgun   *n.* 1 Any rapid-fire gun, esp. a machine gun. *Some W.W.II use.* 2 Spicy, peppery sauce. 3 A matchmaker, a marriage broker; fig., anyone who brings lovers together. *A folk ety. from the Jewish word "schatchen" = marriage broker, reinforced by "shotgun wedding."*

shotgun quiz   A short written examination given without warning. *Some student use since c1920.*

shotgun wedding   1 A wedding demanded by a girl's father because he knows the groom to be sexually intimate with his daughter. *Usu. used jocularly. Orig. because irate farmers were supposed to demand that the spoiler of their daughter's virginity marry the girl, and marched the groom to the preacher at gun point.* 2 A wedding hastened or made necessary by the bride's pregnancy.

shot in the arm   1 A hypodermic injection of a narcotic. *Orig. narcotic addict use.* → 2 A drink of whisky, usu. straight whisky, drunk in one swallow. *Since c1930.* → 3 Fig., anything that gives a person new, or esp. renewed, vitality, enthusiasm, determination, or confidence, ranging from dope and whisky to a compliment or a raise in salary; anything that helps one toward success or that contributes to the successful completion of a task. *Since c1935; from "shot" = an injection of a drug.*

shot in the ass [taboo]   1 = **shot in the arm.** 2 A shock or surprise; bad news; a kick in the ass.

shot in the neck   1 Drunk. 1833: "Slang." *DAE. Obs. by 1900.* 2 A drink of straight whisky; a shot. *c1850; archaic since c1900.*

shot-up   *n.* A person who has been wounded by gunfire. 1927: "There are five shot-ups who might be either thugs or spectators." Hammett, *Blood Money*, 22. *Not common.*

shoulder   *n.* See **cold shoulder.**

shoulder-hitter   *n.* A thug; a prize fighter. c1883 [1936]: "The payrolls of all [city] departments were padded with the names of hoodlums and 'shoulder-hitters' who were henchmen of the politicians." H. Asbury, *The French Quarter*, 295. *Since c1850; never common.*

shout   *v.i.* 1 To say something important or well worth listening to. *Usually in "Now you're shouting." Since c1875.* 2 To chant a religious song with emotion; to sing a blues or spiritual in a highly rhythmic manner with key words spoken loudly and in a high voice.   *n.* 1 A religious hymn sung with much emotion and with a heavily accented rhythm; a revival meeting; an informal dance or rhythmic movement accompanying a religious sermon or spiritual. *Although accompanied by handclapping and actual shouting, the sl. "shout" probably comes from the Gullah rather than from the stand. Eng. "shout."* 2 A slow blues as sung by a jazz singer in the traditional manner. *The above usages are assoc. with slavery and postslavery Negro congregations and singers. The Negro spiritual contributed much to the shout as used in jazz.* 3 An exclamation point. *Printer use.*

—er   *n.* A criminal's mistress or girl friend. *Some underworld use c1920.*

shove   *v.t.* 1 To pass counterfeit money. 1935: "Shove the queer." J. Hargan in *Jour. A. & S. Psychol.*, Oct., 364. *Since c1850; usu. in phrase "shove the queer."* 2 To shovel. 1907: "I offered to 'shove' coal to the end of his run." J. London, *The Road*, 140. *Railroad use.* See Appendix, Shortened Words. 3 To kill. 1949: "Who shoved her?" J. Evans, *Halo*, 75.   *v.i.* To depart; to leave; to go away. 1944: "Well, I guess I'll shove. Good-by." Ford, *Phila. Murder*, 180. 1952: " '. . . . And I'm a judge.' 'And I'm Judge Crater' [the doorman said]. 'Now, shove.' " E. J. Kahn, *New Yorker*, Jan. 5, 53. *Since c1870, and therefore older than "shove off."*   **—r**   *n.* One who passes counterfeit money or forged checks. 1889: *DAE.* 1933: "Shovers of the queer." H. T. Webster.

shove it (something) [taboo] = **shove it (something) up your (one's) ass** [taboo]. 1937 [1954]: "Take the job and shove it!" P. di Donato, *Christ in Concrete*, reprinted in *Manhattan*, 135.

shove it (something) up your (one's) ass (rinctum) [taboo] = **stick it (something) up your (one's) ass.** *Sometimes this is less offensive ("shove" is gentler than "stick") and can show less complete refusal and a lesser degree of* *hatred and anger. When said gently, it can even imply a mere postponement rather than refusal or rejection.*

shovel *n.* **1** In golf, a niblick. *Golfing use c1935.* **2** A spoon. See **put to bed with a shovel.** **—er** *n.* A habitual exaggerater. See **shovel the shit.** See Appendix, —er ending.

shovel, put to bed with a Lit., so drunk that one cannot return home and go to bed by oneself, but must be assisted.

shovel the shit [taboo] **1** To lie, exaggerate, or boast frequently or outrageously; to speak much or obvious bull or shit. *Since c1935. Fairly common. Fig., to speak so much shit that it seems to be coming by the shovelful.* **2** To work at unrewarding, tedious tasks. *Not common.* See **shit.**

shove off *v.i.* To leave, depart; to "shove." 1934: "When we shoved off." Cain, *Postman,* 39. *From the boating term.* *imp.* Leave; depart; beat it, scram. 1926: "Shove off!" Stallings & Anderson, *What Price Glory,* II. 1952: "Shove off, lame-brain!" Movie, *What Price Glory.* *v.t.* To murder. 1939: "People got shoved off for their money by their relations." A. Christie, *Sad Cypress,* 44.

shove out for To set out for; to shove off for. *Since c1850.*

show *n.* **1** A prospective customer, client, or guest; one who is expected to show up. *Not common.* **2** An attempt, a try; a business operation, a task or job. *Not common in the U.S.; considered an affected Briticism.* **3** An exposure by a girl or woman of her thighs, breasts, or genitals to boys or men. *Usu. used by boys from 10 to 15 years old.* See **dog show, free show, good show, kid show, plant show.** *v.i.* **1** To appear in person; to appear on the scene; to be present. 1929: "You suppose he'll show?" Burnett, *Little Caesar,* 44. 1934: "He hadn't shown at any of the clubs." Chandler, *Finger Man,* 20.

show a leg **1** To get up from bed. **2** To hurry, to be alert. *Both uses usu. as an order or command; neither common in U.S.*

showboat *v.i.* To show off. 1951: "[Ford Frick] doesn't have [K. M. Landis'] tendency to showboat." AP, Sept. 21.

showcase *n.* **1** An entertainment, theater, nightclub, rehearsal, or performance whose main purpose is to show the merits of the performers to an audience of prospective employers, such as theatrical producers, booking agents,

directors, or the like. → **2** An audience many of whom were admitted on free tickets. *Theater use.*

showdown *n.* **1** The act of bringing facts out into the open where the persons concerned may know of them. 1895: *DAE.* 1934: "Standard." *Web.* → **2** A meeting between two opposing people or parties to settle their disputes; a meeting between two antagonists. *adj.* Crucial, determining. 1949: "The opening game of the showdown Yankee–Red Sox series." AP, Sept. 24.

shower *n.* A tip, a gratuity, as given to a waiter or cab driver. *Not common.*

shower down **1** To whip a racehorse; lit., to rain blows down on the horse. 1938: "You shower down and [the horse] sulks." Liebling, *Back Where,* 237. *Jockey and some sportswriter use.* **2** To cough up money; to kick in; to pay; to fork out. 1951: "Altho the public law relieves him of compulsion to shower down, it cannot protect him from persecution." W. Pegler, *synd. newsp. col.,* Nov. 16. *Not common.*

shower-stick *n.* An umbrella. *Some jocular and dial. use.*

show-off *n.* A person given to ostentatious behavior; a braggart. 1949: "Anyone from a creep to a show-off...." *Time,* Oct. 3, 37. 1951: "The supervisor's visit, particularly if advance notice has been given, may provide an opportunity for the show-off." G. W. Couchman in Amer. Assn. of Univ. Profs. *Bulletin,* Spring, 49. *Colloq.* **show off** To act like a show-off. *Colloq.*

show out To brag; to show off. *Dial.*

showroom *n.* A large, expensive automobile. *Not common.*

show-shop *n.* A theater. See **shop.**

show up **1** To make a personal appearance; to arrive. 1888: *DAE.* 1939: "I had to show up to make a touch." Gardner, *D. A. Draws,* 204. *Now colloq.* **2** To expose or reveal someone; to make another person seem inefficient, ridiculous, or inferior. *Colloq.* **3** = **show-up line.** 1949: "Tomorrow morning he appears at show-up." Burnett, *Jungle,* 149.

show-up line A police line-up of suspected criminals, usu. presented for possible identification by witnesses. 1949: "A group [of men] about to be shoved into the show-up line." Burnett, *Jungle,* 2.

shrapnel *n.* Grape-Nuts (trade name of a breakfast cereal). *A little Army use since c1930.*

shrewd dude   A well-dressed, alert boy or man. *A rather artificial example of rhyming sl. attrib. to teenagers.*

shrimp   *n.* Any short person.

shuck   *v.i., v.t.* **1** To undress, esp. to take off one's clothes quickly or in the presence of another or others. **2** = **fake.** 1957: "Shucking—Bluffing, faking, vamping, playing chords when a cat doesn't know the melody." E. Horne, *For Cool Cats and Far-Out Chicks. Some cool and far out use.*

shuffler   *n.* **1** A worker who is out of a job. **2** A migratory worker. **3** A grifter.

shuffle them up   To switch railroad cars. *Railroad use.*

shu-fly = **shoo-fly.**

schuper   shooper   shupper   *n.* A large glass, stein, or schooner of beer. 1907: "What we received was spent for 'shupers' of beer—I don't know how they are spelled, but they are pronounced the way I have spelled them, and they cost three cents. . . . Two foaming shupers were before us." J. London, *My Life. Still some use.*

shush   sush   *v.i.* To hush up; also, to say "Shush" to someone in order to hush him up. 1905: "Oh, sush!" "Sush, now!" McHugh, *Search Me*, 12; 16. *Colloq.*   *v.t.* To hush a person up, as by saying "Sh!" or "Hush!" 1941: "Wally tried to shush her down and Mrs. Gessler tried to shush her down." Cain, *M. Pierce*, 153. *Colloq. From "sh—" plus "hush."*

shut down   shut off   *v.t.* To defeat someone, or a team, in a sporting contest. **shut-down   shut-off** *adj.* Defeated. **shutdown** *n.* A stoppage of work; the temporary closing of a factory. 1949: "Assembly line shutdowns." AP, Oct. 18. *Colloq.*

shut-eye   shuteye   *n.* **1** Sleep. 1929: "And grab about ten good hours of shut-eye." K. Brush, *Young Man*, 136. 1949: "I'm going to get some shut-eye." Burnett, *Jungle*, 51. 1956: "A lot of tired jazzmen going home to get some shuteye." S. Longstreet, *The Real Jazz Old and New*, 79. *Colloq. Common since c1920.* Cf. **eye-shut. 2** Unconsciousness; an act or instance of losing consciousness for any reason; a pass-out. 1927: "To pull a shut-eye [to be unconscious from drunkenness]." *New Repub.*, 72.

shut [one's] face   To stop talking; usu. a command = shut up. *Since c1915; becoming archaic.*

shut [one's] head   shut up [one's] head   To stop talking; usu. a command = shut up. *Since c1860; now archaic and dial.*

shut of   *adj.* Rid of; finished with. 1873 [1954]: "It was Cole [Younger's] turn. . . . 'You [Jesse James] mean that? You really mean that if we get the hundred thousand dollars, you're through and done and shut of robbing?' " W. Henry, *Death of a Legend*, 114. *Now mainly dial.*   *v.t.* To rid oneself of.

shut off = **shut down.**

shut out   **1** In sports, to hold an opposing team scoreless. 1952: "The last time [the Princeton football players] were shut out Penn did it on Nov. 3, 1946." AP, Oct. 10. *Since c1880.* **2** To prevent from gambling or playing, usu. by refusing to take a person's bet; usu. a pred. adj. = to be prevented from participating in a gambling play because one's wager has been placed too late.

shutout   shut-out   *n.* A game in which one team does not score. 1952: "It's a Yank shut-out, 2–0." AP, Oct. 8.

shut-pan   *adj.* Secretive; silent.   *n.* One who does not talk much; one who keeps his thoughts to himself. *c1880; obs.*

shutter   *n.* A sleeping pill; lit., that which shuts one's eyes. *Not common.* See **shutters.**   **—bug**   *n.* A photography enthusiast; a photographer. *The most common of the words ending in "bug."*   **—s** *n.* The eyelids; the eyes.

shutting out = **shutout.** 1952: "We beat him once but he gave us a shutting out I'll never forget." Casey Stengel, manager of New York Yankees, quoted by AP, Sept. 26.

shut [one's] trap   To stop talking; to shut up. *Brought to the colonies by Eng. settlers in 17C.*

shut up   A command or plea to another to stop talking or to talk about a different topic. *Colloq.*

shy guy   A modest or bashful boy or man. c1940: "I'm just a shy guy,/ Wish I were a sly guy." From pop. song, "Shy Guy." See Appendix, Rhyming Slang.

shyster   *n.* **1** A crooked, conniving, small-time lawyer. 1943: ". . . You lousy little shyster bastard." Wolfert, *Underworld*, 494. *Always derog. Since c1885. Colloq.* → **2** Any lawyer.

sibling   *n.* Either a brother or a sister. *This is an excellent example of a sl. word accepted as stand. The Eng. lang. contains no inclusive term to characterize the relationship of those of both sexes born of the same parents. Composed of the AS "sibb" = a relative, plus the arbitrary*

"-ling," the word was coined by scientists in genetics as part of their jargon, for their own use, but became pop. with the increasing public attention to psychology.

sick *v.t.* To vomit. *n.* Nausea. *Both uses colloq.* *adj.* **1** Lit. and fig., dangerously psychopathic; psychopathic, neurotic; needing psychiatric attention. **2** Gruesome, morbid; dwelling on the morbid. *Thus a "sick" joke is humorous because it has an unexpectedly gruesome or morbid ending. Both uses fairly common since c1955. Assoc. with earlier cool and beat use; reinforced by the sound of "sick" in "psychiatry."* **—name** *n.* A nickname, esp. a "sick" nickname. 1958: "The cool cats don't even have names. They have nicknames which they call 'sicknames.' The girls are called Space Machine, Spinner, The Spy." S. Boal, *Cool Swinging in N.Y.*, 26. *Some cool and beat use, not common.*

sick and tired of Completely disgusted with; out of patience with; fed up with. *Colloq.*

sick-'em *n.* Anything; "beans." Always preceded by a negative to = nothing. 1951: "[He did a lot of talking], but he didn't know sick-'em about it." *Oral. Archaic.*

side *n.* **1** Affected manners; airs; lit., the false side of a person's character or personality. 1912: "You put on such a beautiful side." Johnson, *Stover at Yale*, 14. *Not common.* Cf. **front. 2** An actor's lines; a page of script for a play. *Theater use since c1925.* **3** A phonograph record; the piece of music on one side of a phonograph recording. *adj.* Other than one's usual job, girl friend, or the like; e.g., a "side job" is a job, often part time, in addition to one's regular job. *Lit., something held or done on the side or besides something else.* Cf. **get up on the wrong side of bed, portside, Stateside, sunny side up, top-side.**

side, go over the To leave a ship or base without a pass. *Fig. to slip over the side of a ship. A USN variant of "go over the hill."*

side, on the Fig., besides; in addition to one's main or regular job, spouse, or order. Thus one may: work part time "on the side" = to earn extra money while not occupied with one's regular job; have a lover "on the side" = in addition to one's usual or known wife, fiancée, or lover; or order a hamburger in a restaurant with beans "on the side" = in addition to the main order of the hamburger.

sidearms *n.pl.* Salt and pepper; cream and sugar; condiments placed on the table during a meal. *Fairly common Army use during W.W.II and some Armed Forces use since c1925. Because such items supplement the meal as actual sidearms supplement heavier weapons; also reinforced by "side dishes."*

side-bar *adj.* Auxiliary; supplementary; part-time. 1952: "The old-style athlete used to loll between seasons. Now he has a side-bar job, hustling beer or sports equipment." R. C. Ruark, *synd. newsp. col.*, June 27.

sideboards *n.pl.* Side whiskers or sideburns. *Not common.*

side-door Pullman A railroad boxcar. 1907: "I rode into Niagara Falls in a 'side-door Pullman.'" J. London, *My Life. Hobo and railroad use.*

side-kick **sidekick** *n.* **1** A partner; a close friend or comrade; a pal; a buddy. 1951: "Going to stay with old sidekicks Mr. & Mrs. Solly Evans." S. Lewis, *World So Wide*, 36. 1952: "[Actor John] Wayne and his side-kick James Arness play a couple of Marine Corps veterans." O. L. Guernsey in *N.Y. Her. Trib.*, Sept. 18, 27/1. *Common since c1910. A term used mostly by males.* **2** A side pocket in a garment; esp. the side pocket of a pair of trousers. 1916: "Pockets range from 'side kicks' to 'double insiders.'" *Lit. Digest*, Aug. 19. *Orig. pickpocket use.* See **kick.**

side of An à la carte order of some food or dish; an extra order of some food or dish. *Wide lunch-counter use in relaying an order.*

sides *n.pl.* Artificial padding worn over a woman's hips or thighs to simulate a full, attractive figure. c1920 [1954]: "When she undressed she pulled off a pair of 'sides,' artificial hips she wore to give herself a good figure." L. Armstrong, *Satchmo, My Life in New Orleans*, 151. *Obs.*

side-slip *n.* Bread and butter. *Not common.*

sidetrack *v.t.* To arrest.

sidewalks, hit the **1** To look for employment; to go from door to door seeking a job. **2** = **hit the bricks.**

sidewalk superintendent A person who passes the time by watching the construction of a new building or other construction work.

side-wheeler *n.* **1** In baseball, a

left-handed pitcher. → **2** Any left-handed person. **3** In baseball, a pitcher who delivers his pitch with a side-arm motion, as opposed to overhand. **4** A pacer; a horse that paces.

sidewinder   *n.* **1** A hard, swinging blow with the fist, esp. when the fist and arm move in an arc from the body, as opposed to a short, straight blow. *Since c1840.* → **2** A tough, rough man, prone to anger and fighting. → **3** A bodyguard; a hired thug; a gangster's side-kick. 1942: "He mumbled about being followed around by a tall guy with a funny eye. That was Eddie Prue, Morny's sidewinder." Chandler, *High Window*, 192. **4** In logging, a falling tree deflected from its intended course. *Logger use. Orig. all usages derive from the Western sidewinder rattlesnake, which moves by coiling from side to side.*

—sie **—sy**   A suffix, sometimes diminutive, usu. indicating familiarity or affection, but sometimes used whimsically. See Appendix, —ie, —y endings.

sieve   *n.* **1** An old, dilapidated, leaky ship. 1953: "That frog-eating sieve. . . ." N. Benchley in *New Yorker*, Feb. 7, 87. *Very old maritime use.* **2** In sports, a player or team that cannot prevent opponents from scoring. **3** Any house, car, or other possession whose upkeep is high, draining money from the possessor.

siff [taboo]   *n.* = **syph.**

signify   *v.i.* To pretend to have knowledge; to pretend to be hip, esp. when such pretentions cause one to trifle with an important matter. *Mainly Negro use.*

sign-off   *n.* The act of ending a day's broadcasting; said of radio stations. 1949: "Because of the earlier sign-off required by the Federal Communications Commission. . . ." *ABC radio. Now also applied to television.* **sign off** To shut up, usu. a command or entreaty to shut up. *Since c1930; orig. from the radio use.*

sign-out   *n.* The act of signing one's name upon leaving a place; also, a name so signed. *Colloq.*

sign-up   *n.* **1** Registration by signing one's name. 1949–51: "Sign-up" occurs in this use at least 206 times in the Cornell (Univ.) *Daily Sun* during these 3 years. → **2** Fig., the act of joining or giving one's support to an organization, political party, or other group.

silk   *n.* **1** Barbed wire. *Some ranch* and farm use. **2** A kerchief or muffler. See **hit the silk.**

silk, hit the   To make a parachute jump; to bail out of an aircraft. 1944: "Carey hit the silk. . . ." *Collier's*, Sept. 9, 55/2. *Common W.W.II paratroop and Air Force use.*

silk broad   A white girl. *Some Negro use.*

silver   *n.* Small change; coins; pennies, nickels, dimes, quarters, and fifty-cent pieces.

silver Jeff   **1** A quarter; the sum of 25¢. **2** A nickel; the sum of 5¢. *Both meanings in rock-and-roll use since c1955. Because the face of Thomas Jefferson appears on the U.S. silver quarter and on modern nickels.*

silver wing   A fifty-cent piece; the sum of 50¢. *Rock-and-roll and general teenage use since c1955. Because an eagle with spreading wings appears on the U.S. silver fifty-cent piece.*

simmer down   **simmer off**   To become calm; to quiet down; to stop being frivolous or boisterous and prepare to think or work seriously. *Usu. as a request or a command.*

simoleon   *n.* A dollar. *Usu. in the plural = dollars, money.* 1950: ". . . And walk away with 200 simoleons in my kimono." Radio program, *Lum & Abner*, Jan. 16. 1950: "To you and me 18 million simoleans means the promised land. . . ." Billy Rose, *synd. newsp. col.*, Aug. 23. *Since c1890; somewhat archaic.* See **Simon.**

Simon   **simon**   *n.* A dollar. 1859: "Slang." *DAE. Obs.* See **Simple Simon.**

Simonizer   *n.* See **apple polisher.**

Simon Legree   **1** Any unsympathetic, unkind, or miserly person. *From the villain's name in the very pop. novel, "Uncle Tom's Cabin."* → **2** Any boss, foreman, manager, or one in authority. *Both meanings are also used jocularly.*

simp   *n.* A simpleton; a dumbbell. 1909: "I'd have been a simp to go among that crowd." G. Chester, *Bobby Burnit*, 325. 1950: ". . . A simp of the proportions of Jane Porter. . . ." S. J. Perelman in *New Yorker*, Dec. 23, 20/1. *Since c1900; most common c1915.*

simpatico   *adj.* Sympathetic; understanding; specif., in rapport with the speaker, his cause, or his beliefs. *Since c1955, when several pop. songs about lovers in Italy and in Spanish-speaking countries incorporated the word.*

simple   *adj.* See **stir-crazy.**

Simple Simon   A diamond. 1932:

"I do not see any Simple Simon on your lean and linger." Runyon. See Appendix, Rhyming Slang.

sincere *adj.* **1** Having or deliberately creating a personality that is expertly charming and subtly ingratiating; deliberately, purposely, and subtly amiable, pleasant, and charming, in order to be accepted, liked, successful, or given preferred treatment. *Since c1940; mainly student use. A common bit of serious, albeit jocular, advice is "Whether you mean it or not, be sincere."* **2** Satisfying; well played; said of bop or cool music; cool. *Some early c1946 bop use and some early cool use; obs.*

sing *v.i.* **1** To inform to the police or other officials concerning a crime or criminals; to squeal. 1949: "He might sing like a canary." Movie, *Johnny Stool Pigeon.* 1952: "Vice Prisoners Ready To Sing." Headline, N.Y. *Daily News*, Aug. 21, 1. *Orig. underworld use.* → **2** To confess; to admit one's own guilt. → **3** To give a sales talk; to make a spiel. *Orig. pitchman use.* **—er** *n.* A squealer; a stool pigeon.

single *n.* **1** A one-dollar bill; one dollar. 1936: "I took out my wallet . . . I pulled out two singles. . . ." J. Weidman in *Amer. Mercury*, May, 86. 1950: "She gimme four singles and the rest in change." Movie, *Mr. 880.* **2** One who works alone, without partners. 1949: "Dillinger now became a single." A. Hynd, *Public Enemies*, 33. *Orig. underworld use.* **3** A nightclub or entertainment act composed of one person; a star.

single-jack *n.* A one-legged, one-armed, or one-eyed beggar. 1937: "The detested single-jacks were relegated to a Bowery within a Bowery." H. Johanson in *Atlantic Monthly*, Dec., 773/1.

single-o *adj.* **1** Unmarried; single. 1932: "She thinks I am single-o." Runyon. **2** Single-handed; unassisted. 1950: "There are 'single-o' heist-men." DeBaun, 71. *n.* A lone grifter. *c1930.* *adv.* Alone; by oneself. 1948: ". . . Instead of working single-o as was his custom." Billy Rose, *synd. newsp. col.*, Apr. 7. *One of the most pop. of the "—o" words.* See Appendix, —o ending.

sing out = **sing.** 1949: ". . . And get him to sing out." Roeburt, *Tough Cop*, 124.

sin-hound *n.* A chaplain. *Some prison and Army use c1920. Here the suffix word "hound" has a different connotation*

from its usual sl. use. See Appendix, Suffixes and Suffix Words.

sink *n.* **1** = **sync.** **2** The sea, the ocean. *Some constant maritime use.*

sinker *n.* **1** A (silver) dollar. 1894: "When I left the parson give me the sinker." J. Flynt. *Once common. Obs.* **2** Any kind of wheatcake, buckwheat cake, hot cake, Johnnycake, or pancake. *By c1900 this was the most common usage; obs.* → **3** A hot roll or biscuit, esp. as served at breakfast. *Some use c1900; obs.* **4** A doughnut. 1952: "A couple of sinkers and a cupa cawfee." R. C. Ruark, *synd. newsp. col.*, Apr. 8. *c1900 "sinker" was usu. used to = pancakes, only occasionally to = biscuits, rolls, or doughnuts. From that time on, doughnuts and other quick breakfasts became pop. By c1915 "sinker" = pancake, biscuits, or rolls was archaic; since c1925 "sinker" = doughnuts has become the only and very common usage. Since c1920 a common lunch-counter breakfast has consisted solely of "sinkers and suds" = doughnuts and coffee. The orig. may relate to "sinker" = silver dollar, since pancakes, rolls, biscuits, and doughnuts are all round and apt to be heavy; in the case of doughnuts it is reinforced by the lead sinker used by fishermen, which is often the same shape as a round doughnut, and by the common habit of dunking or sinking the doughnut in a cup of coffee.* **5** A dumpling. *Some W.W.I use, esp. Army use. During W.W.I certain traditional Ger. dishes were often renamed with more "American" names.* **6** In baseball, a pitch thrown in such a manner that it dips downward in its flight as it nears the batter. **7** In baseball, a hit that drops quickly between infield and outfield. *The first of these baseball terms is by far the more common. Both in use since c1940.*

sinkers *n.pl.* A person's feet, esp. if large. *From "boats."*

sis *n.* **1** A sister. 1835: "Colloq." *DAE.* **2** A cowardly, weak, or effeminate boy. *c1900; colloq.* **3** Any girl or young woman. 1957: "Sis—A girl." E. Horne, *For Cool Cats and Far-Out Chicks. From "sister."* See Appendix, Shortened Words. **—sy** **cissy** *n.* **1** A sister. 1855: "Colloq." *DAE. From "sis."* See Appendix, —y endings. **2** A cowardly, weak, or effeminate boy or man. *Colloq.* **3** Any soft drink containing carbonated water or Coca-Cola and artificial flavoring, esp. vanilla flavoring. *Onomatopoetic, from the sound of the carbonated water* *coming from the tap.*   *adj.* Cowardly, effeminate, weak. *Since c1890.*   **—ter** *n.* Any girl or young woman. *Orig. used in exasperation or as direct address to a stranger, often implying anger, disgust, lack of sympathy, or the like.* See **sob sister, weak sister.**

sissy pants   **1** An overly well-behaved boy; a sissy. **2** A squeamish person.

sit   *v.i.* To care for or watch an invalid or child other than one's own; to baby-sit. *Often in the terms "sit with [a child, invalid, or the like]" or "sit for [the parents or usu. guardian or watcher]." Since c1945 has begun to replace "baby-sit."* See **sitter, 3.**   **—ter** *n.* **1** An occasional prostitute; a novice prostitute. *Implying one who spends more time sitting and talking, and hence earns less than an experienced prostitute who spends most of her time lying down. c1880; archaic.* **2** The buttocks; usu. in the expression, "My sitter is tired [from sitting or riding]." *Colloq.* **3** One who sits with and watches over a baby, child, invalid, or the like, while the parents or usu. guardians are away temporarily; a baby-sitter.

sit-down   *n.* **1** A meal, usu. a free meal, eaten while sitting at a table, as on a back porch or the like. 1932: "A back-door sit-down is a meal handed out for the tramp to eat on the porch, or in the yard." R. T. Oliver. *Hobo use since c1850.* **2** A sit-down strike.

sit in   To join a game (usu. of cards), conference, or the like, usu. as a substitute for a regular player or member, but sometimes as an additional member; specif., to join a jazz band and play a few pieces of music with it as a substitute or guest. 1954: "I would sit in with the hustlers who really knew how to gamble." L. Armstrong, *Satchmo, My Life in New Orleans*, 123. 1956: "The most I've [drummer Buddy Rich] ever had playing in a band was with Count Basie, when I had the very good fortune of sitting in with him. I never *worked* for him, but I *sat in* with the band several times." *Metronome*, Apr., 26.

sit on [one's] hands   **1** To refrain from applauding an entertainer, act, or the like. *Theater use since c1920.* **2** To do nothing, esp. to do nothing when action is necessary.

sitter-downer   *n.* **1** A pillow, cushion, or chair that one habitually enjoys sitting on. **2** A garment specially made for a sedentary person. 1936: "The Sitter-

Downer, a slip with an extra panel at the back." Advt. *Neither use is common.*

sit tight   Lit. and fig., to wait patiently, to remain calm; to await results; to take no further action but to depend on success from actions or factors already accomplished. See **tight.**

sitting duck   Lit. and fig., an easy target, as for scandal or malicious action; fig., an easy mark. *Because in hunting a sitting duck is an easy target, as compared to one flying.*

sitting in the catbird seat = **sitting pretty.** *Pop. by baseball announcer "Red" Barber in his c1945–c1955 radio broadcasts of the old Brooklyn Dodger baseball team games. Orig. Southern dial. use.*

sitting pretty   **1** Fig., in a favorable or commanding position; having an advantage; in command of a situation. **2** Successful; wealthy; living comfortably; safe; in an advantageous position; secure. 1926: "Sitting pretty?" Stallings & Anderson, *What Price Glory*, I. 1950: "He's just the same genial idiot whether he is out of luck or sitting pretty." W. W. Rose, *synd. newsp. col.*, Jan. 24. *Common since W.W.I.*

situash   *n.* Situation. 1934: *Dict. Am. Sl.*

sit-upon   *n.* The buttocks. 1953: "Linda doesn't like [the soldiers'] genial pats upon her sit-upon and their hands on her knee." W. C. Rogers, AP, July 16. *A seldom used euphem.*   **—s** *n.pl.* Trousers. *Never common.*

sitzbein   **sitsbein**   *n.pl.* The buttocks, as used for sitting; the rump. *Lit. = "sitting bone"; from the German.*

siwash   *n.* **1** An American Indian; a hunter or prospector or the like who lives like an Indian. *Northwestern use; archaic. From Chinook jargon.* **2** A boisterous person; a person not adjusted to contemporary living. *Since c1930, some ranch and logger use.* **3** [cap.] A generic nickname for a second-rate American college, esp. when considered in the light of its social or athletic activities.

six bits   The sum of 75¢. *Since c1850; still most common in the West. Lit., three times two bits.*

six-by   *n.* Any large truck. *Mainly and orig. truck-driver use. From the stand. truck size, 6×6.*

sixer   *n.* A six-months' prison sentence. *Some underworld use.*

six-gun   *n.* A pistol; esp., a revolver or six-shooter. *Based on "six-shooter."*

six-shooter   *n.* **1** A revolver holding six cartridges. → **2** Any revolver or pistol. 1936: " 'Six-shooter' as the West termed the pistol." P. A. Rollins, *The Cowboy*, 41. *Since c1850.*

sixty-nine [taboo]   *n.* Simultaneous cunnilingus and fellatio. *From the positions of the participants, end to end like "69"; may have entered U.S. sl. from the older French "six-à-neuf."*

six ways to (for) Sunday   In many ways, in all possible ways; thoroughly; completely. *Some use since c1840; often in "I was deceived (cheated, victimized) six ways to Sunday."*

size-up   *n.* An estimate; the act of estimating or judging.

sizzle   *v.i.* To die in the electric chair; to fry.   *n.* An objectionable person. 1949: "A 'sizzle' is a general term describing anyone from a creep to a show-off." *Time*, Oct. 3, 37. *Reputed teenage use. Not common.*   **—r**   *n.* **1** Lit. and fig., anything that is or anyone who is hot or "hot" in any of their usages; anything that is or anyone who is hot, fast, exciting, sexually stimulating, or stolen.   → **2** Specif., a hard blow with the fist; a knockout punch. *c1920 prize fight use.* → **3** Specif., in baseball, a fast, hard-hit, low line drive. → **4** Specif., an exciting, vivacious, sexually tempting woman. → **5** Specif., a burlesque dancer or stripper. → **6** Specif., a sensational or lurid story or scandal. → **7** Specif., a funny joke, usu. one about sex. → **8** Any extremely pop. song, book, or movie, or extremely pop. entertainer, successful athlete, or the like. → **9** Specif., an expensive item of stolen goods; a stolen car; a kidnaped person. **10** An inferior cook; esp., a logging-camp or ranch cook. Cf. **boiler.**

sizzling   *adj.* "Hot" in any of its usages; stolen; paid as a kidnaping ransom. 1949: "To sell some of the sizzling green at a discount." A. Hynd, *Public Enemies*, 128.

sizz-water   *n.* Carbonated water; fizz water. 1905: "The waiter had crowded the sizz-water into the wood alcohol." McHugh, *Search Me*, 12. *From "sizzling."*

skads   *n.* = **scads.**

skag   **scag**   *n.* **1** A cigarette stub or butt. *c1915. Some use.* → **2** A cigarette, a butt. *c1925; some use, mainly college and Army use.* **3** A homely girl or woman. *c1930. Some Negro use.* *v.i.* To smoke a cigarette. *c1925; not common.*

skate   *v.i.* To avoid paying, to evade a creditor. *The image is of a person who skates away, reinforced by "cheap-*

skate."   *n.* **1** An inferior, decrepit, or useless horse. 1890: *DAE.* 1923: "They'd kill that bunch of skates for their hides." E. Hemingway, "My Old Man." *Ranch, farm, and some racing use.* **2** A contemptible person. *Since c1890. From "cheapskate."* **3** A jag; a load (of liquor); usu. in "to have a skate on." 1927: "Have a skate on." *New Repub.*, v. 50, 72. *Since c1910; some c1920 use; now archaic.* See **bull-skate, short skate.**

skate on thin ice   To take chances; to conduct oneself in a manner verging on the questionable or dangerous. *Colloq.*

skaty-eight   *n.* Any indeterminate large number; forty-'leven.

skedaddle   **skeddle**   *n.* A disorderly retreat. 1861: "A grand Skedaddle of Secesh." N.Y. *Trib.*, Oct. 26. *Orig. Civil War use; colloq; archaic.* *v.i.* To depart, esp. to flee; to run, move rapidly. 1909: "*Skidoo*, the present-day equivalent of the older *skedaddle*." Krapp, *Mod. Eng.*, 209. 1951: "Abner Yokum skedaddled by here." Al Capp, *synd. comic strip*, "*Li'l Abner*," Nov. 17. *Archaic.*

skee   *n.* **1** Whisky. 1930: "We heist the plant for 50 cases of skee." *Amer. Mercury*, Dec., 456. *A respelling of "—sky" in "whisky." Mainly dial.* **2** Opium. *Some underworld use c1930.*

skeeter   *n.* A mosquito. *Colloq. since 1850; mainly dial.*

skeezix   **skeezicks**   *n.* A foolish, untrustworthy, or boisterous but lovable youth or child. *c1930:* "Skeezix," a character in pop. synd. comic strip, "Gasoline Alley." *c1850–c1910; obs.*

sker-ewy   *adj.* = **screwy.** *A prime ex. of sl. emphasis by a louder or longer pronunciation of the first syllable.* See **Kee-rect.**

sketch   *n.* = **hot sketch.**

skewgee   *adj.* **1** Confused: uncertain; said of a person. 1897: "Colloq." *DAE. Obs.* **2** Askew: said of things. *Dial.*

skibby [derog.]   *n.* **1** A Japanese or sometimes Chinese prostitute or mistress, esp. one consorting with Occidental men. *Some c1910 Northwest U.S. use. Fairly common W.W.II use by Army, USN, and Air Force men stationed in the Orient.* → **2** Any Oriental man or woman. *Since c1925, some W.W.II use.*

skiboo   **skibo**   **skyboo**   *n.* A hired gunman; one who serves as a gunman to a gang of racketeers. *Some c1930 use; obs.*

skid   *n.* Butter; from its resemblance

in hot weather to grease. *Some use since c1920.* *v.t.* To pass food at the table. *Some student and Army use.* See **hit the skids.**

skid-box   *n.* A receptacle for waste paper or other trash. *Some W.W.II USN use.*

skid grease   Butter. *Some use since c1925; not common.*

skidoo   skiddoo   *v.i. & interj.* **1** Go away; beat it; to depart; to flee. 1905: "Skidoo, skidoo, and quit me, Mr. Josheimer!" McHugh, *Search Me*, 13. 1909: "Skidoo . . . now current slang . . . equivalent of the older *skedaddle.*" Krapp, *Mod. Eng.*, 209. **2** Also used as a humorous nonsense word to attract attention or to attest to the speaker's being modern and wise, this was a very pop. fad word c1905. 1938: "At the beginning of this century every summer resort and street carnival flew banners carrying the senseless word 'Skiddoo!' " C. T. Ryan in *Better Eng.*, Sept., 38/1. *Both uses c1900–c1910; reappeared in "twenty-three skidoo."*

skidoodle   *v.i.* = **skedaddle.**

skid road   skidroad   *n.* **1** A forest trail, path, or a greased log road along which newly cut logs are dragged, orig. by oxen, to an incline or skidway leading to a river, on which the logs will be floated to a lumber mill. 1880: *DAE.* *Logger use, still in use.* → **2** A street or district of a town containing employment agencies, eating places, gambling rooms, and brothels such as cater to or are frequented by loggers, seasonal and migratory workers, and the like; the cheap business street or section of a town. 1932 [1937]: "I headed towards the Skidroad and its cheap eating joints." H. Johanson in *Atlantic Monthly*, Dec., 776/2. *Orig. logger use; hobo and underworld use since c1915.* → **3** = **skid row.** *It is difficult to determine at which meaning or at what period "skid road" became "skid row." Sometimes capitalized.*

skid row   Skid Row   *n.* Any old, dilapidated street or section of a town containing very cheap bars, eating places, and flop houses where the permanently unemployed, vagrants, beggars, petty criminals, derelicts, degenerates, and, mainly, unemployed alcoholics hang out. 1949: "The missions, saloons, and flophouses . . . known as Skid Row." " 'Smoke,' a universal Skid Row drink. . . ." W. J. Slocum, *Collier's*, Aug. 27, 26 f. 1949: "Chicago's 'skid row' along Madison St. . . . 'down

and outers' live in the area." UP, Aug. 30. 1954: ". . . The Bowery [a street in N.Y.C.], the gaudy, gory, sordid model for all this country's Skid Rows." W. R. & F. K. Simpson, *Hockshop*, 35. *A variant of and from "skid road." "Skid row" apparently developed some 60 years after "skid road."*

skids, the   *n.* Fig., the decline, or being on the decline, from success, fame, honesty, good reputation, or sobriety to failure, mediocrity, a life of disappointment, or a bad reputation: the decline from being, or being known as, a successful, useful, or respected member of society to being a failure, a has-been, or a derelict. *In several idioms having to do with the decline, downfall, or ruination of a person or thing; e.g., "to put the skids under (to) [someone]"; "to hit the skids"; "on the skids"; "greased for the skids"; or the like.* 1929: "You sure put the skids under me." Burnett, *Little Caesar*, 120. 1938: "The men on the Bowery had taken to hanging around saloons. Eventually they had hit the skids." Liebling, *Back Where*, 48. 1952: "There are others [movie actors] whose careers have hit the skids after they were released by their [film] studios." B. Thomas, AP, Sept. 26. 1956: "By 1929 Bix [Beiderbecke] was on the way down—not yet on the skids, but the good time and the big time was behind him." S. Longstreet, *The Real Jazz Old and New*, 107. *Fairly common. May be from "skid row."*

skids, hit the   See **skids.**

skids, on the   See **skids.**

skids under (to) [someone or something], put the   To cause someone or something to fail; to cause someone to lose enthusiasm; to ruin a plan; to cause a plan or venture to fail. See **skids.**

skid-top   *n.* A bald man. *Not common.*

skiffle   *n.* = **rent party.** 1956: "Depression came. . . . You could always get together and charge a few coins and have a skiffle . . . the money paid the rent." S. Longstreet, *The Real Jazz Old and New*, 126.

skig   *n.* **1** A pair of old-style, damaged, or odd-sized shoes, for selling which a salesman is paid a bonus. *Retail shoe-salesman use.* → **2** A commission paid a salesman for selling hard-to-sell merchandise; a salesman who specializes in selling hard-to-sell merchandise.

skillet   *n.* A Negro. 1942: "You skillets is trying to promote a meal on me." Z. Hurston. *Negro use.*

skilley   *n.* Gravy; lit., that which is

washed out of the skillet. *Some prison use since c1925; in the U.S. has never = stew or porridge, as it has in Brit. sl.*

skillion   scillion   *n.* An enormous or inconceivably great number. *Often used facetiously.* 1945: "I have a scillion things to say." D. Fairbairn in Phila. *Bulletin*, Dec. 12, 17. *Colloq.*

skimmer   *n.* **1** A hat, esp. a flat-crowned straw hat with a wide brim. *Attrib. to T. A. Dorgan, cartoonist, died 1929; colloq.* **2** In baseball, a ball hit low over the playing field, so that it skims the grass; a grounder.

skin   *n.* **1** The hand as in the act of shaking hands. *In several expressions = Shake hands: e.g., "Give me some skin"; "Hand me that skin"; "Slip me some skin"; "Lay the skin on me"; and the like.* 1953: "Slip me some skin." Ray Noble, CBS radio, Feb. 22. *Assoc. with jive use.* **2** One's life. *Colloq.* **3** A stingy person: a skinflint. **4** A cheat, embezzler, or confidence man. *Archaic.* **5** A shirt. *Underworld use; obs.* **6** A horse, esp. an old or worthless horse; specif., a racehorse. 1923: "They take the first bunch of skins out to gallop." E. Hemingway, "My Old Man." → **7** Any old or worthless farm animal. *Rural use.* **8** A pocketbook; a wallet. *Orig. underworld use; since c1925; from leather of pigskin or cowhide.* **9** A dollar bill; a dollar. 1930: "Five skins is jake." *Amer. Mercury*, Dec., 456. 1951: "One [customer] laid out 190 skins for half a dozen prints." *New Yorker*, Aug. 4, 16/3. Cf. **eel-skin. 10** [taboo] Any thin rubber or animal membrane contraceptive; a condom; a rubber. *Since c1935.* **11** Any drum used in an orchestra or by a jazz musician. *Orig. and still predominantly jazz use; since c1930.* **12** A demerit; an official written reprimand. *Some W.W.II Army and Air Force use; some student use since c1945.* See **get under one's skin, pigskin, sheepskin, give me some skin.**   *v.i.* To cheat in a recitation or examination; to crib or use a pony. 1835: "Slang." *DAE. Student use; obs.* → *v.t.* **1** To cheat; to take unwarranted advantage of. 1953: "You got skinned in that deal." C. Kuhn, *synd. comic strip*, "Grandma," Feb. 14. *Colloq.* **2** To give a demerit, to give an official reprimand; to report for delinquency. *Some W.W.II Army use.* **3** To defeat an opponent or opposing team decisively.   **—ful**   *n.* Fig., containing a skin full of liquor, or having one's skin full of liquor. 1747: "His Skin is full." *Pa. Gazette.* 1922: "Dey bot' got a skinful." O'Neill, *Hairy Ape*, 5.   **—ned** *adj.* Cheated, taken advantage of; having lost all or a large part of one's money to another in a gambling game or a business transaction, usu. a dishonest one.   **—s**   *n.pl.* **1** A set of drums. *Jazz use.* **2** Automobile tires. *Mainly hot-rod use.*   **—t**   *adj.* Without money; broke. *Not common. Apparently from "skinned."*

skin, get under [one's]   To irritate or annoy a person. 1912: "You two have got under my skin...." Johnson, *Stover at Yale*, 283. *Lit. = to annoy as a tick would under the skin.*

skin, give me some   Shake hands; esp. to shake by extending the flat palm of one's hand and brushing a similarly extended palm. *A jive term that caught the popular imagination. Often used as a rhyming term, "Give me some skin, Flynn." Somewhat synthetic.*

skin, give [someone] some   To shake hands with someone. *Usu. in "Give me some skin" = Shake (hands), friend. c1935 jive use; some swing use; occasionally used by teenagers or, esp., writers who write about teenagers.*

skin-beater   *n.* A drummer. 1953: "Red, the reefer-smitten skin beater. ..." J. Kelly in N.Y. *Times Bk. Rev.*, Sept. 13, 33/3. *Since c1930; not common.*

skinch   *v.t.* To cheat; to take unfair advantage of. *Since c1850; archaic.*

skin-head   *n.* A bald man.

skinned mush   A cane. *Pitchman use. From pitchman "mush" = an umbrella, from "mushroom."* Cf. **mush.**

skinner   *n.* A teamster; a driver of horses or mules. *An old Western term still in use on ranches and construction jobs.* See **hack-skinner, mule-skinner.**

—skinner   See Appendix, Suffixes and Suffix Words.

skinny   *n.* A course or class in physics or chemistry. *Annapolis use. c1925.*

skip   *v.t.* To absent oneself from, to cut school or a class, as to do something more pleasant, when one has no officially acceptable excuse for doing so. 1951: "If I let you skip school this afternoon and go for a little walk, will you cut out the crazy stuff? Will you go back to school tomorrow like a good girl?" J. D. Salinger, *Catcher in the Rye*, 155. *Now almost entirely replaced by* **cut.** *v.i., v.t.* To leave a place without paying one's bill or bills; to leave hastily, as a hotel or town, without paying what one owes.   *n.* **1** An Army captain. *From "skipper." Some W.W.I and W.W.II Army use.* **2** A bus driver; a taxi driver. See **skipper.** **3** A dance. *Some c1920 student use.* Cf. **hop.**   —**per**   *n.* **1** Captain, esp. the captain of a ship. *Colloq.* → **2** An Army captain or company commander. *Colloq.* **3** The chief police officer of a precinct. **4** A railroad train conductor. *Some railroad use.*

skippy   *n.* **1** A sissy. *Some Negro use.* **2** [derog.] A Japanese prostitute or promiscuous woman. *Some W.W.II Army use in Japan. From "skibby."*

skippy strike   A workers' method of protesting working conditions by omitting or skipping part of their work or ignoring some items on which they are to work. 1956: *"Skippy strike*—An organized protest by workers on an assembly line when they don't actually leave the plant but, by prearranged plan, assemble only a portion of the material passing through the line. In autos, say, every fourth car would arrive at the end of the line as an unassembled pile of parts." *Labor's Special Lang. from Many Sources.*

skirt   *n.* A girl or young woman. 1922: "A real skirt." O'Neill, *Hairy Ape,* 4. 1951: "[He] will never give any skirt a tumble. . . ." S. Lewis, *World So Wide,* 21. *Very common. Prob. of underworld orig. Some W.W.I use; very wide W.W.II use. Third in pop. to "dame" and "jane."*

skiv   *n.* = **shiv.**

skivvies   *n.pl.* **1** Underwear, either undershirts or underdrawers. **2** Slippers consisting of one strap across the toes and a wooden or rubber sole, usu. used in the shower or on the beach. *Some use since c1945.*

skivvy   *n.* **1** A man's cotton undershirt, esp. the type with short sleeves and a round, close-fitting neckline. *Has replaced "undershirt" in the USN; fairly common civilian use, esp. since W.W.II.* → **2** A pair of men's cotton underdrawers having three buttons or snaps down the front and with short legs. 1947: "Suffering from chafitis? Skivvy-grabitis?" Advt. for underwear, Feb. 25. Cf. **briefs.**

skivvy shirt   = **skivvy.** 1952: "I got tan wash pants, sneakers, some skivvy shirts. . . ." T. Robinson, Jr., in *Harper's,* Mar., 87/2. *Orig. USN use.*

skivvy-waver   *n.* A Navy signalman who uses semaphore flags. *Some jocular W.W.II USN use.* See **skivvy.**

sklonk   *n.* A boring, uninformed person; one who is not hep. *Some student use since c1945.*

sklook [taboo]   *v.i., v.t.* To engage in sexual intercourse. *Some student use c1935; never common.*   —**ing**   *n.* Sexual desire. *c1935; never common.*

skookum   *adj.* Strong; brave; great. 1844: *DAE. Still some logger use. From Chinook jargon.*

skulduggery   *n.* Rascally conduct; scheming or plotting. 1867: *DAE. Colloq.*

skull   *n.* An outstanding student, worker, or performer; an intellectual, a brain; a grind. See **popskull.**

skull-buster   *n.* **1** In college, a very hard course. *Some use since c1920.* **2** A policeman or detective. *Some Negro use since c1930.*

skull-drag   *v.i.,* **1** To study hard. *Some jive student use since c1935.* → **2** To give one's best effort; to think, work, or play with concentration. *Jive use.*

skull play   In baseball, a player's error caused by faulty judgment.

skull practice   In sports, a lecture session, often illustrated with films or blackboard diagrams, explaining a team maneuver or play, analyzing mistakes made in previous games, or detailing the weaknesses of future opponents. *Chiefly football use.*

skunk   *n.* **1** A boy whose duty it is to wake workers in time for them to go on their shift. *Western and railroad use. Orig. the skunk was an apprentice who also lit the morning fire, carried the day's supply of water, etc.* **2** [derog.] A Negro. *Not common.*   *v.t.* **1** To fail to pay a debt; to welsh. 1851: "To skunk a tailor." Hall, *College Words,* 284. **2** In sports, to defeat an opponent without allowing him to score; to shut out; to defeat decisively. 1952: "Well, at least we didn't get skunked." *Oral,* a Cornell Univ. student after Cornell–Colgate football game, 14–7.

skunk egg   An onion. *Still some Western and Southern rural dial. use.*

skunk [someone] out of [something] **1** = **skunk;** welsh. **2** To cheat someone out of something.

sky   *n.* **1** A hat. 1957: "Sky—A hat." E. Horne, *For Cool Cats and Far-Out Chicks. Some c1935 jive use and a little continuing jazz use.* **2** A uniformed policeman or prison guard. *Some, mainly Negro, underworld use since c1930; prob. from the blue uniform.* **3** Water. *A little student use, c1940; never common.* See **pie in the sky.**

skybo(o)   = **skiboo.**

skygodlin *adv.* Diagonally; slantwise. 1869: *DAE. Never common; now archaic and dial.*

sky-hook *n.* A large plastic balloon used in high-altitude, cosmic-ray experiments by the U.S. Navy. 1951: "These balloons, called skyhooks, were first used in 1947." AP, Feb. 13.

sky-hoot *v.i.* 1 To rise; to increase. 1930: "Jigger's reputation as a 'rugged' man skyhooted from this point." S. H. Holbrook in *Amer. Mercury*, Oct., 235/2. *Not common.* 2 To daydream; to idle away the time. 1949: "Betty took advantage of the opportunity and went off sky-hooting on her own." *Fact Detec. Mysteries*, 118. *Not common.*

sky juice 1 Rain. *Some jocular and student use since c1925.* → 2 Water.

skyman *n.* An aviator. *Since c1920.*

sky-parlor *n.* A garret or a room in a garret.

sky piece   skypiece *n.* 1 A hat or cap. 1907: "I took my pick of the 'sky pieces.'" J. London, *My Life.* 1952: "There isn't a chance that the doughboy will go back to the skypiece his father wore to top off his khaki outfit." GNS, June 26. See **sky.** 2 A wig. *Since c1925.*

sky pilot 1 A clergyman of any rank or denomination; a minister, priest, or rabbi. 1891: Thornton. 1909: "An appreciative visitor [to the U.S.], William Archer, has told of the joy to his soul when he first came upon the phrase, 'sky pilot.'" *Scribner's*, Aug. 250/2. *Orig. hobo and Western use, some W.W.I and wide W.W.II use. With the importance of the Air Force in W.W.II, the "pilot" took on a more modern meaning. During W.W.II and since the term has usu. = an Armed Forces chaplain.* 2 A licensed aviation pilot.

sky rug A toupee. *Never common.*

sky scout A chaplain. *Some W.W.II use.* See **sky pilot.**

skyscraper   sky-scraper *n.* 1 A very tall building; fig., a building so tall that it scrapes the sky. 1883: *DAE. Colloq. by c1920.* 1934: "Standard." *Web. Although six- or eight-story buildings with self-supporting masonry walls were called skyscrapers, technically a skyscraper now is any building supported by steel girders or other interior framework, on which the walls are "hung."* 2 In baseball, a very high fly ball or pop fly. 3 A "tall" sandwich with many layers of meat, cheese, and vegetables; any dessert with many layers of ice cream, syrup, nuts, or the like; anything tall in proportion to its width.

skywest *adj.* Helpless; senseless. 1944: "I happened across something that will knock somebody around here skywest." Ford, *Phila. Murder*, 59. *Since c1900; archaic.* *n.* The land of death; Heaven. "To go skywest" = to die. *Some Western use; now obs.*

sky-winder *n.* An Air Corps man; now an Air Force man. *Some W.W.II Army use.*

sky wire 1 A radio antenna. *Radio and U.S. Army Signal Corps use.* 2 A guy wire. *Television use.*

slab *n.* 1 A town or city. 1921: "Say, this slab's a dude of a burg, hey?" Witwer, *Leather*, 164. 2 A bed. *Early jive use, c1935, replaced by "pad."* 3 A dollar. 1953: "Ten slabs for two days' work!" M. Blosser, *synd. comic strip*, "Freckles," May 2. *Not common.* 4 In baseball, the home plate. 5 Bread; a slice of bread.

—bist *n.* A baseball pitcher. 1913: "The failure of the slabbist to put the pill over the plate...." *Washington Post*, quoted in *Lit. Digest*, Sept. 6, 379/2f. *Not common.* See **slab.**

slack season That season during which a specif. manufacturing, wholesale, or retail business is poor. *Thus late spring and early summer are a slack season for the overcoat business. Orig. and mainly garment worker use.* 1956: "Hocus Pocus' line was other people's coats ... he walked into restaurants in winter without an overcoat and came out wearing a heavy one ... he pawned it the next day. In the slack summer season, he rolled drunks." T. Betts, *Across the Board*, 264.

slam *n.* 1 A salute. 1958: "... Slam. A salute." G. Y. Wells, *Station House Slang. Very little Armed Forces use, mainly police use.* 2 An uncomplimentary or mean remark; a dig. 1950: "Blackmer took a slam at the male stars who dress like 'ranch hands.'" AP, July 21. *Since c1895; colloq.* 3 In baseball, a hit. 4 A drink; a slug. 1932: "... A couple of slams of Joe Goss' liquor." Runyon. *From "slam" = "slug" = hit.* *v.t.* 1 To make uncomplimentary or mean remarks about someone; to abuse someone verbally. *Colloq.* 2 In baseball, to hit the ball. 3 To strike or slap someone hard with the hand.

slam a gate To beg food at a house. 1907: "I missed many a meal, in spite of the fact that I could 'throw my feet' with the next one when it came to 'slamming a gate' for a 'poke-out' or a 'set-down,' or hitting for a 'light piece' on the street." J. London, *My Life*. *Hobo use*.

slam-bang   *v.t.* To attack someone. 1888: "Colloq." *DAE*   *n.* A vicious fight. *Boxing use; c1920.*   *adj., adv.* **1** Violent(ly); in an unnecessarily rough or rude manner. *Since c1890.* **2** Thorough(ly); complete(ly); rigorous(ly). 1951: "Connelly has not seemed too enthusiastic about a slam-bang clean-up [of corruption in government]." D. Pearson, *synd. newsp. col.*, Dec. 27. **3** Direct(ly); straightforward(ly). 1950: "The storm was pointed slam-bang at Tampa." AP, Oct. 21.

slammer   *n.* A door; an entrance way. 1938: "Twister to the slammer." *Variety. Jive use c1935, revived by rock and roll groups c1955. Old underworld use.*

slam off   **1** To leave, to depart. *Underworld use c1930.* → **2** To die. 1930: "He slams off with a cold." *Amer. Mercury*, Dec., 457.

slang   *n.* A watch chain. 1916: "White slang" = silver watch chain; "red slang" = gold watch chain. *Star of Hope* (*Lit. Digest*, Aug. 19). *Underworld use; obs. From rhyming sl., "clock and slang" = watch and chain. See Appendix, Rhyming Slang.*

slangwhang   *n.* Nonsense. 1834: *DAE. Obs.* See Appendix, Reduplications.

slant   *n.* **1** A jag; a load (of liquor). *Archaic and dial.* **2** A look. 1922: "Take a slant at dat!" O'Neill, *Hairy Ape*, 5. 1934: "The prowl car takes a slant down[the road] now and then." Chandler, *Finger Man.* 40. **3** A person's opinion or point of view. 1929: "I'd like to meet the lovers/ And get their slant." M. Bishop, *Paramount Poems*, 87. 1951: "Obviously there was something about [Thoreau's] tone or his 'slant' that irritated his contemporaries." J. W. Krutch in N.Y. *Times Bk. Rev.*, May 20, 1/1. *Since c1920.*

slant-eye [derog.]   *n.* An Oriental.

slap   *adv.* Directly, shortly; smack; plump. 1951: ". . . Streets that ended slap in a courtyard." S. Lewis, *World So Wide*, 129. See **smack**.

slap [one's] gums = **beat [one's] gums**.

slap-happy   *adj.* **1** = **punch-drunk**. 1936: "A slap-happy bum." Tully, *Bruiser*, 69. → **2** Dizzy. 1938: ". . . A sample [of talk] designed to knock philologists slap-happy." *Newsweek*, May 23, 22/1. → **3** Exhilarated; elated; dizzy with success or joy.

slapman   *n.* A plainclothes police officer. *Underworld use c1920.*

slapper   *n.* A large person or thing. *Archaic since c1900.*

slap-up   *adj.* Fine, excellent; stylish; complete or thorough. 1939: "She's given you a slap-up education." A. Christie, *Sad Cypress*, 22. 1952: "[Winston Churchill] and his party crossed the Atlantic in slap-up style on the Queen Mary." M. Panter-Downes in *New Yorker*, Jan. 19., 77/1. *Archaic since c1900.*

slap [someone's] wrist   To chastise a person lightly; to scold a person.

slasher   *n.* An overly diligent student; a grind. *Jocular use. Because he is so serious in his studies that he may slash his throat, committing suicide, if he does not receive high scholastic grades. Some student use since c1950.*

slat   *n.* **1** A rib. Cf. **slats**. **2** A thin, angular woman. *Reinforced by "slut."* **3** A sailor, esp. a friendly, boisterous, fun-loving sailor. *Not common.* **4** An exciting, fun-loving person; one who always has a good time. *Not common.* —**s**   *n.pl.* **1** Ribs, esp. those of a person; often in phrases referring to laughter, as "to split, jiggle, or hold one's slats." 1903: "Wouldn't that split your slats?" E. Conradi. 1913: "Wouldn't that jiggle your slats?" F. K. Sechrist. 1928: ". . . Pokes [him] in the slats." Ben Hecht in *New Yorker*, Nov. 3, 44. 1950: "The Nazis and the Communists held their slats. . . ." W. Pegler, *synd. newsp. col.*, July 12. **2** Corsets; a corset. *Obs.*

slathers   *n.pl.* Lots of. 1876: *DAE.* 1907: "It cost the railroads slathers of money. . . ." J. London, *My Life. Archaic and dial.*

slats, hit the = **hit the hay**. *Some Western use, c1915.*

slave   *v.i.* To work.

slave-driver   *n.* **1** A boss, teacher, or one in authority who is disliked for overworking those under him. **2** One's wife. *Jocular use.*

slave market   **1** An employment office. *Orig. hobo and logger use.* **2** In a town or city, a street or district in which employment offices are located.

slave-puncher   *n.* = **slave-driver**. *Some northwestern U.S. use.*

slay   *v.t.* To make a strongly favorable impression on; to win the affection or approval of, esp. by means of superior charm, humor, etc.; to "kill," esp. to cause a person to lose control of his emotions, usu. through laughter. 1938: "Really, A.P., pardon me, this will slay you." H. Broun in *New Repub.*, Sept. 21, 185/2. 1943: "The boys who slay me are the ones who have set pieces to recite when they answer the phone." H. A. Smith, *Putty Knife*, 147. *Very common since c1930.*

sleazy *adj.* **1** Dirty, grimy; filthy; old, dilapidated; in poor condition. 1958: ". . . Dreary buildings in sleazy sections . . . before demolition began for the housing project. . . ." Picture caption, N.Y. *Daily News*, Feb. 20, 26. *Wide student use.* **2** Cheap, inferior; of cheap or inferior material, workmanship, and over-all quality.

sleep *n.* **1** A one-year prison term. *Underworld use since c1920.* **2** A night. **—er** *n.* **1** A night watchman. *Some underworld use since c1930.* **2** A dull course or lecture. *Some student use.* **3** Any entertainment or performer, or any plan, person, or item, which proves to possess greater popular appeal or wider acceptance than was anticipated; esp., a cheaply made movie that wins public acclaim despite little advertising. 1946: " 'My Name Is Julia Ross' is the first 'sleeper' to come to Philadelphia in months. A sleeper is a small-budget, modest 'B' which has not been highly publicized but which turns out to be better than many grade 'A' pictures." Laura Lee in Phila. *Bulletin*, Jan. 2, 5/4. 1951: "Popkin, I hear, has a real 'sleeper' in [the film] 'The Well.' And it didn't cost a fortune to make." Hedda Hopper, *synd. newsp. col.*, Aug. 29. *Common since c1935.* **4** In sports, esp. football, a player who maneuvers deceptively in order to take the ball without being noticed by the opponents; also, the play in which such a maneuver is used. **5** = **dark horse.** **—ville Sleepville** *adj.* Sleepy, asleep. *Assoc. with cool use.* See Appendix, —ville ending. **—y** *adj.* Drunk. *Obs. since c1870.*

sleep with To have sexual intercourse with. 1955: "His belief was that no girl could love a man, until she had slept with the man over a period of time." " 'Besides,' she said, 'why are you so sure I'm not a virgin? I've never slept with a man.' " C. Willingham, *To Eat a Peach*, 208; 230.

sleeve-buttons *n.pl.* Codfish balls. *Some use since c1880.*

sleeve on [someone], put the **1** To arrest someone; to identify someone to the police for arrest. **2** To stop a friend on the street in order to ask for a loan of money; to ask for a contribution or for money owed.

sleighride *n.* **1** An instance of being under the influence of or taking cocaine; cocaine addiction; exhilaration caused by a narcotic, esp. cocaine. *Addict use c1910; archaic; suggested by the image of snow.* **2** An instance of sharing or a chance to share the wealth, power, or success of a person or pop. idea; a successful period in one's life. **3** An instance of being cheated, believing a lie, or being taken advantage of. *Almost always in the expression "taken for a sleighride."* **4** = **raspberry**, a comeuppance. 1949: "What a sleighride the newspapers gave her." Movie, *Lady Takes A Sailor.*

sleighrider *n.* A cocaine addict. *Addict use c1910; archaic.* See **sleighride.**

sleuth *n.* A detective. *Now usu. humorous or archaic-literary.*

slew *n.* A large number or quantity. 1840: *DAE.* 1941: "A slew of cops." G. Homes, *40 Whacks*, 159. *From the Gaelic "sluagh" = a multitude.*

slewed *adj.* Drunk. *Since c1850; more common in Eng. than in U.S.*

slewfoot *n.* **1** A detective or policeman. Cf. **slough-foot.** **2** In baseball, an awkward player. **3** Any clumsy person; a stumblebum.

slice *n.* A share or interest in any profit-making enterprise; a share of loot; a piece. 1948: "Five grand wouldn't get you a slice of her." F. Brown, *Dead Ringer*, 35. *Common since c1920.*

slick *adj.* **1** Glib; smooth-talking; persuasive. See **slicker.** Cf. **smooth.** **2** Clever, shrewd; adroit in business matters. **3** Smart; clever; witty. *Since c1800.* → **4** Good; swell. 1914: "The soup was 'simply slick.' " S. Lewis, *Our Mr. Wrenn*, 158. *Since c1830.* → **5** Crafty; wily; dishonest. 1939: "He's more than a match for any slick city lawyer." Gardner, *D. A. Draws*, 66. *Since c1915.* → **6** Superficial; insincere; pleasant and attractive but not deeply satisfying; widely popular but vapid or merely sensational; commercially produced to win the widest possible acceptance but without concern for artistic or scientific standards. *The most common use since c1940.* *n.* **1** A magazine printed on glossy or coated paper; hence a magazine or book produced for sale to a wide but uncritical audience. 1953: ". . . Magazines (of all kinds, from top slicks to minor pulps)...." A. Boucher in N.Y. *Times Bk. Rev.*, May 31, 15/2. *Colloq.* **2** A used car in good, resalable condition. **—er** *n.* **1** An unethical businessman; a confidence man; a sophisticated, cynical cheat, crook, etc.; a clever cheat. 1951: "I don't admire slickers who peddle get-rich-quick bubbles—so come along quietly." *Synd.* cartoon, "Major Hoople," Oct. 3. *Since c1900; archaic.* Cf. **city slicker.** **2** A glib, clever, socially adroit person, a smoothie, who achieves success by being well-liked and personable. 1920: "The slicker was good-looking and *clean-looking*; he had brains, social brains, that is, and he used all means to get ahead, be popular, admired and never in trouble. He dressed well, was particularly neat in appearance, and derived his name from the fact that his hair was inevitably cut short, soaked in water or tonic, parted in the middle and slicked back as the current fashion indicated." F. S. Fitzgerald, *This Side of Paradise*, 38f. 1920: "You're [a Princeton student] not a slicker." Fitzgerald, *This Side of Paradise*, 38. (Word appears 15 times in *This Side of Paradise.*) *Common c1920 student use.* **3** A stolen and repainted automobile. *Underworld use c1930.* *v.t.* To outsmart dishonestly; to cheat or dupe. 1951: "We are pictured as outsmarted and slickered by Moscow." C. V. Jackson, CBS radio ntwk., Sept. 15. 1953: "A fox tried to slicker him out of [the cheese]." Bing Crosby in *SEP*, Feb. 21, 71. See Appendix, **—er** ending. **—um** *n.* Hair oil or hair dressing, as pomade.

slick chick An attractive, well-dressed, hep girl. 1943: "Thirty-nine 'slick-chicks' traveled 152 miles for a week end of dancing." *Service Stars*, Sept. 1944: "... Fashion adopted by the 'slick chicks' at Sequoia Union High [school]." *Life*, May 15, 76. 1950: " 'Babe,' used in the United States for a slick-chick, a pretty girl...." M. Berger in N.Y. *Times Bk. Rev.*, July 23, 1f. *Orig. a rhyming jive term, c1935. Became common during W.W.II. The orig. connotation was "hep," but now = merely pretty and well dressed.*

slide *v.i.* **1** To make off with; to steal and flee. 1926: "The dip who slid with the tickstick." N.Y. *Times*, May 30. *Not common.* **2** To lose popularity or prestige. *n.* A trouser pocket. *Some underworld use.* **—s** *n.pl.* Shoes. *Some c1935 jive use; some hobo use.*

slide [one's] jib **1** To become irrational, unrealistic, or insane. **2** To be talkative; to talk too much.

sligh *v.t.* To dismantle, as a tent. Cf. **slough.** *Carnival use.*

slim *n.* A police informer. *Some c1930 underworld use.*

slime *n.* **1** Fig., the world of vice or of unrefined, amoral, unethical people and deeds. **2** A worthless, unethical, unrefined person. **3** Specif., scandalous talk or writing; unsubstantiated accusations of vice, scandal, and unethical deeds. See **mud.**

slimer *n.* A freshman. *Some c1900 student use.*

sling *n.* A sling chair, usu. consisting of a (simulated) wrought iron frame over which one butterfly-shaped piece of canvas is fitted, or slung, to form a seat, back, and headrest. *A pop., inexpensive, modern style of chair often found in U.S. homes in the 1950's.* *v.t.* To throw. 1953: "If I sling a snowball at him...." *Synd. comic strip*, "Bugs Bunny," Feb. 11. *Colloq.*

sling a nasty foot (ankle) To dance expertly. 1834: *DAE.* 1874: "She slings the nastiest ankle on old Kentuck[y]." T. L. Nichols, *40 Years of Amer. Life.*

slinger *n.* **1** A waiter or waitress. 1934: "Anybody but a California Bar-B-Q slinger would know that." Cain, *Postman*, 91. *From "hash slinger."* **2** One who slings or throws bull; a bullslinger.

—slinger See Appendix, Suffixes and Suffix Words.

sling hash To work as a waiter or waitress. 1929: "I used to sling their hash." J. Auslander, *Hell in Harness*, 2. 1949: "She slung hash for a couple of weeks." *Life*, Oct. 24, 20. *c1875.*

sling ink To write. 1867: *DAE. Never common.*

sling it To shoot the bull, throw the bull; to have a good line; to exaggerate or lie; to talk, esp. slangily or fashionably. 1948: "Undoubtedly the chief reason for the conversational effectiveness of many individuals is their inherent ability to sling it." A. H. Marckwardt & F. G. Cassidy, *Scribner Handbook of Eng.*, 154.

sling the bull **1** To talk; to take part in a bull session. **2** To shoot the bull, throw the bull; to talk bull proficiently.

slinky *adj.* Sensuous-looking; sinuous; said of a woman; descriptive of a woman who moves with exaggerated and deliberate hip movements. 1943: "One of those slinky glittering females...."

Chandler, *Lady in Lake*, 116. *Common since c1925.*

slip *n., v.* See **pink slip.**

slip-horn *n.* A trombone. *Some early jazz and radio use.*

slip me five An expression meaning "Shake hands." *Some use since W.W.I. The forerunner of* "*give me some skin.*" Cf. **five.**

slipper *v.i.* To reform and conform; said of a criminal. 1925: "When a crook is reformed he is 'slippered.' " McLellan in *Collier's*, Aug. 8. *Underworld use.*

slippery *adj.* Deceitful, untrustworthy; cunning. *Colloq.*

slippy *adj.* Quick.

slipstick *n.* **1** A slide rule. *Student use since c1930; engineer, surveyor, and Army use since c1940.* **2** A trombone. *Early radio use; a synthetic jazz term.*

slip the clutch To talk or talk critically; to talk too much. *Not common.*

slip [one's] trolley To become irrational, obsessive, or insane.

slip-up *n.* An accident; a mistake; an oversight. 1854: *DAE.* 1950: "There must have been some 'mistake,' a 'slip-up,' by some junior executive." GNS, Sept. 9.

slob *n.* **1** A fat or ungainly person, esp. one of unattractive or untidy appearance. 1910: "You great, fat slob!" Johnson, *Varmint*, 116. 1934: "Two guys came around. ... One was a big slob with a chin that stuck out like a shelf." Chandler, Finger Man, 24. *From "sloppy."* **2** A hopelessly ineffectual person. → **3** An untalented, congenitally average person; any common man whose chance of happiness or success is no better than another's. 1937: "Just another poor slob." Weidman, *Wholesale*, 211. *Very common since c1935.*

slobber *v.i.* = **slobber a bibful.**

slobber a bibful To talk a great deal; to say a mouthful. *Since c1920; now archaic.*

slob-foot *n.* An awkward person. *Some c1915 student use.*

slop *n.* **1** A policeman. *From pronouncing the word as spelled backwards: "ecilop" = slop. Some underworld use since c1915. More common in Eng. than in U.S.* See Appendix, Back Slang. **2** A cheap saloon or restaurant; lit., a saloon or restaurant that serves slop. 1951: ". . . Tending bar in some slop down by the tracks." R. Bissell, *A Stretch on the River*, 67. **—ped** *adj.* Drunk. 1907: "The Erie County pen was the only place where a man could get

'slopped' and not be arrested." J. London, *My Life. Archaic.* **—py** *adj.* **1** Drunk. *Fairly common.* **2** Slovenly. *Colloq. since c1930.* *n.* A sweater. 1947: "In 'teen-agers' talk, a sweater is a sloppy. With buttons it is a spotted sloppy. Buttons down the front make it a stummy spotted sloppy. A V-neck sweater is a slotted sloppy; with the other kind it is a stubby sloppy." *The Academian*, a school paper, quoted by Don Rose in Phila. *Bulletin*, Jan. 21, 13. *Not common.* Cf. **sloppy Joe.** **—s** *n.pl.* Beer. *Hobo use, c1910.*

slop chest A ship's store of tobacco, candy, beer, and miscellaneous supplies. *Maritime use.*

slop-chute *n.* A saloon or tavern.

slope *v.i.* **1** To flee; to run away; to leave. *Since c1840. Not common.* → **2** To escape from jail. *Hobo and some underworld use.*

slopie slopy Slopie Slopy *n.* [derog.] A Chinese. *Some W.W.II use by Armed Forces in the Pacific theater. Prob. from the slanting eyes.*

slopped over Drunk. *Not common.*

slopping-up *n.* A spree; a drinking party. 1894: "The 'bums' intended to have a great 'slopping-up.' ..." J. Flynt. *Orig. hobo use; not common.*

sloppy Joe A long, loose-fitting pullover sweater. *A pop. style with female students c1940, usu. worn several sizes too large.*

sloppy Joe's Any cheap restaurant or lunch counter serving cheap food quickly. *Since c1940.*

slosh *v.t.* To hit. *n.* A blow. *Neither use common in U.S.*

sloshed *adj.* Drunk. 1953: "He saw a youngish man in a bar, a little sloshed and pouring out his troubles to the bartender." *New Yorker*, May 16, 27/3. *More common in Eng. than in U.S.*

slot *n.* **1** A position or place. *Mainly sports and gambling use. In baseball, a player may win a "slot" on the team; in horseracing, a horse may finish in the third "slot."* Cf. **in the slot. 2** A slot machine. 1951: "The slots are going day and night." R. Bissell, *A Stretch on the River*, 81.

slot, in the **1** In baseball, waiting to take a turn at bat; lit., in the chalked box, or slot, reserved for the next batter. Cf. **on deck. 2** Ready to perform next; ready or alert to take one's turn.

slough *v.t.* **1** To lock. *Underworld use since c1880. Also "unslough" = unlock.* → **2** To lock up, hence to imprison or arrest. → **3** To dismantle in preparation for moving, as tents or booths. *Circus use.* → **4** To discontinue; to close or close up, as a carnival concession or the like. 1948: "His job in the side show had been sloughed in many towns." "The law sloughs some of our best concessions." F. Brown, *Dead Ringer*, 2; 18f. **5** To disperse or dismiss, as a crowd. 1943: "When a pitchman is surrounded by [people who do not buy his wares], he finds it necessary to 'slough the joint'— that is, to hint gently that they should disperse." Zolotow in *SEP*. **6** To hit a person hard, esp. with the fist. 1934: "I ain't sloughed anybody." J. T. Farrell, 132.   *v.i.* To depart; to beat it.   *n.* **1** An arrest; the official act of closing a carnival, saloon, or the like, usu. by withdrawing its license or permit. → **2** A policeman.

slough-foot   *v.i.* To walk slew-footed-ly; to walk with the toes not pointing toward one's objective. 1950: "[The airedale] slough-footed away." Starnes, *Another Mug*, 107.

slough up   To arrest. 1894: "I've boozed around this town for seven years, and I've not been sloughed up yet." J. Flynt.

slow, take it   To be careful or cautious.

slow-beat guy   An objectionable fellow; a wet smack.

slow bell, take it on the   To take it easy; to refuse, to decline, as a drink or extra work. *Sailor use. Not common.*

slow burn   The act or an instance of becoming enraged slowly or by gradual stages, as opposed to flipping one's lid all at once. 1951: "His slow burn at a Minnesota prof's constant use of the name when he was a student...." *New Yorker*, Mar. 3, 22/2. *Since c1930. From the comedian Leon Carroll, whose famous "slow burn" = a facial expression which gradually became that of intense anger, was very well known in the late 1930's.*

slow coach   A dull, stupid fellow. *Some c1850 student use.*

slow drag   A formal or boring dance. *Some teenage and student use.* See **drag.**

slow on the draw   Slow to comprehend or recognize; dull-witted.

slowpoke   *n.* A person who acts or moves slowly. 1934: "... An old slow-poke?" P. Wylie, *Finnley Wren*, 142. *Colloq.*

sludge   *n.* Nonsense, drivel, blah. *Not common.*

sluff   *v.i., v.t.* To eat. *Not common.*

slug   *n.* **1** A bullet. 1956: "The bullet struck Boswell in the left side of the neck just above the shoulder. Doctors said they're still unable to remove the slug." N.Y. *Post*, July 11, 2. **2** A dough-nut, a sinker. **3** A dollar. 1950: "... To do the job at 125 slugs a week for the Paramounts." AP, June 22. *Since c1875; from hobo to carnival and circus and then to theater use; now common.* **4** A key. *c1900; not common.* **5** A drink or swallow of something, esp. whisky. 1945: "... Rubbing your buttons against a bar and ordering a slug of old step-mother." W. Pegler, *synd. newsp. col.*, Dec. 13. *From the Gaelic "slog" = a swallow.* **6** A blow. See **put the slug on [someone].** **7** A fellow, esp. a disliked man. 1948: "Well, of all the cheap, chiseling suh-lugs!" Cain, *Moth*, 56. **8** A disciplinary penalty, usu. a walking penalty, imposed upon a West Point cadet. 1952: "In spite of the Point's stiff schedule of 'slugs,' a cadet will occasionally stay out all night." *Life*, Apr. 14, 156.   *v.t.* **1** To hit; to fight; to battle. *Colloq.* **2** In baseball, to hit a pitched ball hard, esp. to do so consistently.   **—ged** *adj.* Drunk. 1951: "Here, you guys, drink some ale. I want you really slugged when we shoot the scene." S. J. Perelman in *New Yorker*, Feb. 10, 28. *Not common.* Cf. **slug.**   **—ger** *n.* **1** In baseball, a player who is consistently a good hitter, esp. of home runs; a long-ball hitter. 1891: "Then he was a slugger from Sluggerville." N.Y. *Sporting Times*, July 11, 3/4. 1953: "The departure of slugger Vern Stephens." AP, Feb. 10. **2** A boxer; a prize fighter. *Colloq.* **3** One who drinks whisky habitually. 1951: "The liquor sluggers drive five miles down the road and load up with a case or two." K. Harris, *Innocents from Abroad*, 88. *Not common.* **4** An ear-to-ear chin beard, as worn by a stage Irishman.

slug-fest   *n.* **1** A vicious or exciting prize fight. *Since c1920.* **2** A baseball game in which many hits and runs are scored. *Since c1935.*

slug-nutty   *adj.* Punch-drunk; punchy. 1937: "'Slug-nutty' fighters are often very talkative." *Lit. Digest*, Apr. 10, 40.

slug on [someone], put the   **1** To hit, slug, or attack someone physically. 1951: "Pepper Martin has been fined for putting the slug on a heckling fan." A. Daley, N.Y. *Times*, Aug. 28, 26. → **2** To attack someone verbally; to criticize or give someone a bad recommendation.

1946: " 'Fishing is the vice of the rummy.' Mr. Cannon needn't think he can get away with putting the slug on rummies." Red Smith, *N.Y. Her. Trib.*, Mar. 30.

sluice the worries   To drink a large quantity of liquor.

slum   *n.* **1** Any meat-and-vegetable stew, esp. one made of boiled salt-beef and potatoes. 1847: "Yale College use." Hall, *College Words*, 432. *Primarily hobo and Army use. See* **slumgullion.** → **2** Rations; inferior, mass-produced food. *Prison and Army use since c1925.* **3** A package of bank bills. *Never common in U.S.; obs.* **4** A worthless or uncouth fellow; *fig.*, one raised in a slum area. 1910: "Is that bunch of slums going to be here?" Johnson, *Varmint*, 294. *Never common; archaic.* **5** Cheap merchandise, as jewelry or gilded plaster book ends, sold at stands or given as prizes in games of chance or skill. *Carnival and circus use. Since c1920; in the U.S. the word has never = a swindle, as it does in Brit. sl. adj.* Cheap; inferior and gaudy. 1946: ". . . A guy buys a slum ring for ten cents." S. S. Jacobs in *Mag. Digest*, Aug., 89/2.   **—gudgeon**   *n.* Hash, stew, slumgullion.   **—gullion**   *n.* **1** A tasteless or poor-tasting drink. 1872: *DAE.* **2** Any meat and vegetable stew. 1953: "Hoboes carry a silver spoon in their pockets—to dig into hobo camp slumgullion." AP, Mar. 30. *Orig. and primarily hobo use. More common than "slum." Prob. from "salmagundi."* **—ming**   *n.* The act or an instance of visiting a skid row or slum area as a spectator, out of curiosity, and to enjoy doing something unusual that will give one a topic of conversation later. 1950: ". . . Millionaires right in those honkeytonks. Called themselves slumming, I guess, but they were there just the same, nudging elbows with all the big bums—the longshoremen and the illiterate." A. Lomax, *Mr. Jelly Roll*, 49. *Usu. said of wealthy people.*

slum-burner   *n.* A cook. *Some Army use; not common.*

slum-diver   *n.* A soldier. *Not common; may be synthetic.*

slup   *v.i., v.t.* = **slurp.** 1949: "[The cat] slupped up the milk in no time." G. Hunter in *Christian Science Monitor*, Aug. 13, 10/2. *Not common.*

slurf   *v.i., v.t.* = **slurp.**

slurp   *v.i., v.t.* To drink or eat noisily. 1951: "Slurping porridge from a wooden spoon." O. Nash in *New Yorker*, Oct. 20, 30. *Common since c1925.   n.* **1** =

apple-polisher. *Some student use c1940.* **2** In jazz, a glissando. 1956: ". . . *Slurp . . . a glissando.*" S. Longstreet, *The Real Jazz Old and New*, 150. *Some jazz use. Because the sound resembles a person slurping food.*   **—y**   *adj.* Semiliquid; said of food or drink of such a consistency as to cause noisy ingestion. 1942: "We had jellied tomato bouillon. Usually this stuff looks like a lot of slick slurpy nothing." *The Family Circle*, Aug. 10, 10.

slush   *n.* **1** Sentiment, esp. an obvious display of sentiment. **2** Drivel; trivial remarks; corn. *Colloq.* **3** Hash. *Some prison use.* **4** = **slush fund,** money in a slush fund.

slushers   *n.pl.* Tire chains, as used on cars and trucks to gain traction on snowy, slushy, or icy roads. *Some garage and filling station use.*

slush fund   A fund or sum of money set aside for political purposes, to use to buy influence or votes, or to use in bribery. *Since c1860; colloq.* 1950: "The use of slush funds to defeat selected victims running for re-election to the senate and house." W. Pegler, *synd. newsp. col.*, July 11.

slush pump   A trombone. 1943: "Awful fine slush pump . . . you ought to dig that." M. Shulman, *Barefoot Boy with Cheek*, 90. *Some jazz use, mostly synthetic. Some musician and radio use since c1935.*

slut lamp = **bitch lamp.** 1956: "Byron called it a 'slut lamp.' But Fitz always said 'light the grease,' and let it go at that." N. Algren, *A Walk on the Wild Side*, 34.

sly   *adj.* Remarkable; excellent. *Archaic since c1925.*

sm—   See Appendix, Reduplications.

smack   *n.* **1** A hit, a slap. *Colloq.* **2** A dollar. *Hobo use. From* **smacker.** **3** A kiss.   *adj.* Satisfactory, as an answer to a question. 1924: "Smack for Carl." Marks, *Plastic Age*, 101. *Not common. adv.* Directly; precisely; on the mark, sharply; suddenly. See **wet smack.** **—er**   *n.* **1** A dollar. 1921: "Hundred smackers." Witwer, *Leather*, 149. 1952: ". . . Having to cough up a thousand smackers." L. Thomas, CBS radio, Apr. 9. *From the sound of a silver dollar as dropped on a counter. In Eng. sl. = a pound sterling.* **2** A kiss. 1951: "Slip me a smacker, sister." Jimmy Durante, CBS radio, Sept. 30.   **—o**   *n.* A hoodlum. 1944: "Few if any of these Harlem smackos have actual war-production jobs." W. Davenport in

Collier's, Sept. 23, 92/2. *Not common. Some Negro use.* See Appendix, —o ending. *interj.* **1** A sound imitative of a hit or slap. **2** A sound imitative of a kiss.

smack down *v.t.* **1** To reprimand severely. **2** To cause another to lose, or to lose, status; to get one's comeuppance.

small *adj.* **1** Cheap, stingy, petty. **2** Impolite, unsociable; quick to take offense and slow to apologize.

small-arm(s) inspection = **short-arm inspection.** 1946: "While you were in the Army you must have taken your clothes off thousands of times for small-arms inspections." M. Shulman, *Zebra Derby*, 111.

small beer An insignificant person, plan, task, or amount; small potatoes.

small bread A small or insufficient amount of money. 1957: "A small sum of money also called small bread." E. Horne, *For Cool Cats and Far-Out Chicks. Some cool and far out use.* See **bread.**

small fry **1** Children; a child of either sex. *Colloq.* **2** An unimportant person or group of persons; persons lacking influence or prestige, such as unknown entertainers, employees working on minor jobs, petty criminals, etc. 1900: "A large [dressing room] with conveniences not enjoyed by the small fry [actors] overhead." Dreiser, *Carrie*, 293. *Colloq. From the stand. "fry" = young fish.* **small-fry** *adj.* Unimportant; minor, petty; lacking influence or prestige. 1941: "Small-fry writers like me." Schulberg, *Sammy*, 133.

small one **1** Specif., a small drink of whisky. *Colloq.* **2** A minor complaint or reprimand. 1958: ". . . Small one. A minor complaint of a superior against a cop." G. Y. Wells, *Station House Slang. Not common.*

small pipe An alto saxophone. 1957: "Small pipe—An alto saxophone." E. Horne, *For Cool Cats and Far-Out Chicks. Synthetic jazz use.*

small pot An unimportant person. 1950: "Deane was succeeded in the hot seat by a very small pot from the State Department." Starnes, *And When She Was Bad*, 59. *From "small potatoes" reinforced by "pot."* Cf. **big pot.**

small potatoes **1** A small amount of money; peanuts. 1836: *DAE.* 1951: "I received $120,000 [to appear in a movie], which is no small potatoes." Danny Thomas, quoted by AP, Aug. 3. → **2** Any unimportant, insignificant, inconse-

quential, minor, or petty person, idea, attitude, object, etc.; a small business; small profit or financial gain, esp. as compared with what one expects from future endeavors. *Since c1850.*

small time A theater or circuit of theaters in which low-salaried vaudeville acts are staged more than twice a day. *Theater use since c1915.* **small-time** *adj.* **1** Minor, petty, unimportant; poorly paid; bush league. 1930: "One of the [prison] keepers, a small-time political power. . . ." Lavine, *Third Degree*, 221. **2** With small ambitions or opportunities; on a small scale; lacking in importance, influence, or prestige; without fame or notoriety. 1956: "The Big Ring contained small-time racketeers, among them a Brooklyn gang of hoodlums." T. Betts, *Across the Board*, 30. Cf. the antyn. **big-time.**

smarm *v.t.* To flatter. *Some dial. use. Not as common as in Brit. sl.*

smart aleck A person who has too much self-confidence; one who thinks he knows everything; an obnoxious extrovert. 1873: *DAE. Now stand.*

smart as paint Very clever; very smart. 1955: ". . . Thinks he's smart as paint. And he *is* smart." C. Willingham, *To Eat a Peach*, 142.

smart cookie See **cookie.**

smart guy A know-it-all, a wise guy, a wiseacre or smart aleck.

smart money Money bet or invested by those in the know, or by influential or wealthy people who are supposedly in a position to know that their bet or investment will be profitable.

smart number See **number.**

smarty *n.* A smart-aleck, one who is overconfident of his knowledge or intellectual prowess; a wise guy. 1874: Thornton. 1914: "I *will* bid seven on hearts, smarty!" S. Lewis, *Our Mr. Wrenn*, 186. 1952: "I'll wear what I want to, smarty!" H. Boyle, AP, Aug. 22. *adj., adv.* In the manner of a smart aleck.

smarty-pants *n., n.pl.* **1** = **smart aleck.** → **2** A snob, esp. an intellectual snob. 1941: ". . . Dance with one of those Vassar smarty-pants." Schulberg, *Sammy*, 70.

smash *n.* **1** A total failure, esp. in reciting. *Some student use c1850. Some cool and beat use c1955.* → **2** A popular success; a very successful play, movie, or the like; a hit. 1948: "[The movie] 'Key Largo' is an unqualified smash." *Variety*, Aug. 25, 1/3. *adj.* Extremely successful. *Usu. in the redundant* **smash**

hit. **—ed** *adj.* Drunk. *Never common in the U.S. Obs.* See Appendix, Drunk. **—er** *n.* Anything very large, extraordinary, or remarkable; esp., anything remarkably attractive or entertaining. 1949: "I thought the book was a smasher." A. J. Liebling in *N.Y. Times Bk. Rev.*, Aug. 28, 17. **—ing** *adj.* Wonderful, entertaining, tremendously successful or gratifying. *Although Brit., had some c1920 popularity in the U.S. and is still known and used.*

smash hit An extremely successful, popular entertainment, esp. a play or a popular song; an extremely popular or well received entertainer or performance.

smear *v.t.* **1** To knock out. *Prize fight use since c1920.* → **2** To defeat decisively. → **3** To murder; to rub out. **4** To destroy or attempt to destroy the good reputation of another, esp. by making false or exaggerated accusations; to degrade or slander. **5** To bribe, esp. to bribe an underling to persuade his superior to do something beneficial to the briber; to buy the influence or support of another. **6** To offer a kickback. Cf. **schmear.** *n.* **1** Hash. *Obs.* **2** An act or instance of attacking another's reputation; an unsupported accusation; an attempt to destroy another's reputation. 1950: "The smear said Gen. MacArthur had sore need of his services." W. Pegler, *synd. newsp. col.*, Sept. 4. *All uses from or reinforced by "schmear."*

smeller *n.* The nose. 1923: ". . . Getting a sock on his smeller." C. MacArthur, *Rope.*

smell the stuff To take cocaine by sniffing. 1949: "You must be smelling the stuff!" Roeburt, *Tough Cop*, 85.

smidgen *n.* A small amount. *Colloq. since c1845.*

smile *n.* A drink of whisky. *Some use c1850–c1900; obs.* *v.i.* To drink, esp. to drink whisky. *Some use c1850; obs.*

—smith See Appendix, Suffixes and Suffix words.

smoke *n.* **1** A cigarette. *Very common.* **2** A marijuana cigarette. 1946 [1951]: "Made crazy one night by a marijuana cigarette, by something called smoke or snow." C. McCullers, *Ballad of the Sad Café*, 788. *Addict use, not common.* See **smoke, the. 3** A cigarette, cigar, or pipeful of tobacco. 1924: "The 'smokes' were free." Marks, *Plastic Age*, 114. *Colloq.* **4** [derog.] A Negro. **5** Any substandard whisky or wine; rubbing alcohol, wood alcohol, or the like, used as a beverage, esp. denatured alcohol

and water shaken together in a bottle. 1949: "Empty tin cans labeled 'Do not take internally, Will cause blindness' (but the hobos drink it anyway—'smoke' they call it. . . .)" "They lay around in the jungles, drink that smoke, then pass out petrified." J. B. Martin in *Harper's*, Nov., 62/1. **6** A railroad fireman. *Railroad use.* **7** Perfume. *Not common.* *v.t.* **1** To look at, look over, or notice. *Since c1930; not common.* **2** To shoot a person. *Underworld use since c1945.* *v.i.* To be angry; fig., to be burning with anger. **—d** *adj.* Drunk. *c1850; obs.* **—r** *n.* A locomotive. *Railroad use. From the days of wood-and-coal-burning locomotives.*

smoke, the *n.* Opium. 1956: "He mixed with studs shying a toy of opium. But there isn't much record that he went for the smoke himself." S. Longstreet, *The Real Jazz Old and New*, 104. *Addict use, archaic.*

smoke-ball *n.* In baseball, a ball pitched very fast.

smoke-eater *n.* **1** A fireman, a fire-fighter. *Common since c1930.* **2** A welder. *Some factory use since c1940.*

smoke factory An opium den. 1905: "A ride through this tunnel on a hot day will put you over on Woosey Avenue quicker than a No. 9 pill in Hop Lee's smoke factory." McHugh, *Search Me*, 33f. *Synthetic.*

smoke-out *n.* = **cook-out.**

smoke [something or someone] out To find a person or obtain information, esp. when the person is hidden or the information withheld.

smoke pad See **pad.** 1956: ". . . Smoke pad, the cot on which the [opium-] smoking is done." S. Longstreet, *The Real Jazz Old and New*, 145.

smoke-stack *v.t.* To assume authority over a person. *Maritime use.*

smoke-up *n.* An official notice that a student is failing his studies. *Some c1925 student use.*

smoke wagon 1 A railroad train. *Some use since c1850.* → **2** An automobile. *c1915; not common.* **3** A gun; a revolver; any pistol; any firearm. *Some hobo and underworld use c1910–c1930.*

smoky [derog.] *adj.* Negro; Negroid. 1949: "The spades are moving in and it's getting smokier every day." N. Algren, *Man with the Golden Arm*, 33. See **smoke.**

smoky seat = **old smoky.**

smooch smooge smouge *v.i., v.t.* **1** To smudge, smear, or make dirty.

c1825–c1875. **2** To cheat on an examination, esp. by copying another student's answers or by using a pony. *Some student use c1900.* → **3** To take; to borrow, esp. to borrow an item too insignificant to return; to mooch; to steal. 1941: "Then she went over to the cash box [and] smooched four $10 bills." Cain, *M. Pierce,* 152. **4** To kiss and caress; to pet or neck. 1937: "Once upon a time you 'spooned,' then you 'petted,' after that you 'necked'—still the most widely used term—but now you may 'smooch' or 'perch' or, reaching the heights of college argot, you may 'pitch and fling woo.' " E. Eldridge in *SEP,* Feb. 20, 89/2. 1951: "College kids are still smooching. ..." M. Shulman, *Dobie Gillis,* 33 f. 1955: "After a few minutes of *torrid* hugging and smooching. ..." C. Willingham, *To Eat A Peach,* 229. *n.* A kiss; kissing and caressing; necking. 1945: " 'I'd rather have hooch/And a bit of a smooch.' When I asked [an Australian girl] what 'smooch' meant, she replied: 'Don't you know your own American slang?' " H. Boyle, AP, Oct. 27. **—er** *n.* **1** A habitual borrower; one who borrows or takes things without returning them; one who mooches. **2** A man or woman, usu. of student age, who will or likes to kiss and caress; one who indulges in smooching or necking. **—ing** *n.* Kissing; necking. 1949: "Good luck with the smooching!" Fibber McGee, radio, Oct. 18.

smooth *adj.* **1** Pleasing, personable, attractive; well and inconspicuously groomed; socially adroit, adaptable; shrewd; persuasive. 1924: "Preparatory school boys, carelessly at ease, well dressed, or, as the college argot has it, 'smooth.' ..." Marks, *Plastic Age,* 7. 1937: "Boy, she was smooth." Weidman, *Wholesale,* 149. 1943: "Petey Loadsafun, the smoothest freshman on campus. You couldn't possibly get a candidate half as smooth as Loadsafun." M. Shulman, *Barefoot Boy with Cheek,* 161. *Wide student use since before 1900; usu. said of a person whom the speaker finds attractive; sometimes used in scorn of one whom the speaker finds glib and crafty.* **2** Pleasing; excellent; esp. of, with, or having pleasing sentiment. c1940 [1952]: " 'Isn't it just too smooth.' That one was employed by Miss [Shirley] Temple as a description of 'Romeo and Juliet.' " J. Crosby in *N.Y. Her. Trib.,* Apr. 9, 29/1. **—ie** **—y** *n.* A smooth person, usu. a youth or girl whom

the opposite sex finds attractive; sometimes one found to be glib or crafty; a slicker. 1938: "He [the intellectual] abhors the 'smoothy,' in whom he sees the signs of cultural decay." N. A. Faris, in *Word Study,* Dec., 3/2. 1951: "You think you're such a smoothie." S. Lewis, *World So Wide,* 6. See Appendix, —ie, —y endings.

smooth apple   See **apple; smooth.**

smooth article   A person who is smooth (in any sl. sense); a slicker. 1913: " 'Smooth article' is equivocal." F. K. Sechrist. 1941: "Jerry, who still retained much of the informal expressiveness of undergraduate phraseology, thought of Dr. Hugo Barker as a 'smooth article.' " A. R. Hilliard, *Justice Be Damned,* 95 f.

smooth operator   =   **slicker.** See **smooth.**

smoudge   *n.* A rough, uncouth, unkempt person; a smoocher. 1907: "Those outside my circle [in Oakland, Cal.] called me 'tough,' 'hoodlum,' 'smoudge,' 'thief.' " J. London, *The Road,* 152f. *May be a further variant of "smouge" = "smooch."* Cf. **smoocher.**

smouge = **smooch.**

smudge [derog.]   *adj.* Negro. *Not common; suggested by "smoke."*

smush   *n.* The human mouth. 1932: "Lily gives me a big kiss right in the smush. ..." Runyon. *From "mush" = mouth, with excrescent "s."*

smutch   *n.* An escape made by sneaking away. *Not common.*

snack   *n.* An easy victim. *Some underworld use since c1935, not as common in U.S. underworld as in Australia.*

snafu   *n.* A mistake, usu. large and obvious; an instance of confusion; a situation confused by a lack of intelligent direction; stupidity; any unnecessarily complex plan, action, or thinking. 1957: "The acquisition of rights of way [for pipe lines] has brought about more snafus than pipe-liners care to remember." A. Lansing in *Collier's,* Jan. 4, 28. 1957: "A trailer truck went under a too-low viaduct [getting stuck in it and] snarling rush hour traffic on four main routes. The snafu occurred at Markwood Road, just west of Queens Blvd." N.Y. *Daily News,* Nov. 5, 5. *Orig. Army use c1940; very wide W.W.II Armed Forces use and some postwar civilian use. From the initials of "situation normal—all fucked up." The orig. Army connotation was that the situation was "fucked up" owing to an excess of Army rules and routine. The orig. is forgotten or ignored*

so that the word is not considered taboo.
See Appendix, Shortened Words.   *adj.*
Confused; snarled; haywire; completely
mistaken; ruined, spoiled.   *v.i., v.t.*
To ruin; to make a mistake; to confuse;
to goof; to foul up or fuck up.

snail   *n.* A cinnamon roll shaped like
a snail shell. *Some maritime and West
Coast lunch-counter use since c1930.*

snake   *n.* **1** A girl or young woman.
" 'Snake!' said Herbie aghast. Cliff
explained, '... That's what they call
girls in the Navy.' " Herman Wouk, *The
City Boy*, 225. *Fairly common W.W.I
USN use; now archaic.* **2** One who
excels in anything, esp. a diligent
student. *Some student use since c1900;
some c1935 jive use.* **3** A treacherous
person. *Colloq.* → **4** A male, usu. a youth
who pursues and deceives many girls.
1951: "Her boy friend, a notorious
fraternity 'snake' ... has done her dirt."
Cornell (Univ.) *Daily Sun*, Oct. 13, 2.
Some student use since c1925. Cf. **parlor
snake.** → **5** A deceitful or fickle girl or
woman. *Obs.* **6** A railroad yard switchman. *Common railroad use.* **7** Whisky,
esp. inferior whisky. *Since c1930; not
common.* Cf. **snake poison, snake
ranch. 8** A policeman. *Some teenage gang
use since c1940.*   *v.i.* To leave un-
obtrusively; to sneak away. 1944: "He
snakes out of here without an overcoat."
Ford, *Phila. Murder*, 169.

snake, the   *n.* The subway; a subway
train. *Not common.*

snake eyes   **1** In dice, the point of
two, each die face having one spot
showing. → **2** Less commonly, the die
face having two spots. *From the image
of the two black spots accentuated against
the white background.* **3** Tapioca. *Army,
prison, and some student use since c1935.*

snake poison   Whisky. 1889: *DAE.
Archaic and dial.*

snake ranch   *n.* **1** Any cheap, dirty
saloon or bar; a joint; a dive. *Orig.
maritime use.* **2** A brothel. *Orig. maritime
use.*

snake's hips, the   Any superior or
remarkable person or thing. 1932: "She
was the dogs, the snake's hips...."
J. T. Farrell, 127. 1933: "[Esoteric
speech] is the caste mark, or if you
insist upon being old-fashioned, the
snake's hips!" H. T. Webster. *In vogue
c1920–c1930; obs.* Cf. **the cat's meow,
the dogs, the end, the most.**

snake's toenails, the = **the snake's
hips.**

snap   *n.* **1** Energy, vitality, pep. *Now
mainly dial.* **2** A snapshot or photograph.
1893: *DAE. Obs. since c1930.* **2** An easy
task, course of study, examination, or the
like; a cinch. 1924: "He had one [class]
in music—partly because it was a 'snap.' "
Marks, *Plastic Age*, 287. 1953: "This
[act] ought to be a snap to get through
[the state legislature]." GNS, Feb. 17.
Common since c1900. **3** A teacher who
gives an easy course. *Common student use
since c1900.* **4** An advantage. *Common
c1900–c1915; obs.*   *adj.* Easy of
accomplishment; easy. Cf. **snap course.**
—ped   *adj.* Drunk. *c1850; obs.*   **—per**
n. **1** A photographer, esp. an amateur
one. *Archaic.* **2** The point of a story or
joke; a quip or witticism. 1951: "The
final snapper was that [Lubben] never
got his income tax paid by his ex-
partners, either." E. Kefauver in Fargo
(N. Dak.) *Forum*, July 24, 4/3. *Archaic.*
3 A match. *Not common.*   **—pers**
n.pl. Teeth. 1951: "People who think
they can tell the age of anything by
its teeth are kind of up against it when
it comes to fish. Not that some fish are
not well stocked with snappers. But
teeth don't help." D. Henderson, AP,
Sept. 22.   **—pily**   *adv.* Neatly;
attractively; nattily. 1932: "Two snap-
pily dressed young fellows." J. T.
Farrell, 126. *Not common.*   **—py**
adj., adv. **1** Quick(ly). *Usu. in "make it
snappy." Colloq.* **2** Neat(ly); smart(ly);
attractive(ly). 1937: "Some dizzy broad
that must have been a snappy number
[once]." Weidman, *Wholesale*, 8. 1953:
"Prime Minister Churchill ... wearing
a snappy light gray suit, walked from
... his home ... to an automobile."
AP, July 24.

snap [one's] cap   To become excited
or flustered; to flip one's lid. *Some use
since c1940; not as common as to "flip
one's lid."*

snap course   An easy course, esp.
in college. 1900: Used in 29 U.S. colleges,
as listed in *Dial. Notes*, 2, 61. 1940:
"At this time of year, students begin to
'grind' even in a 'snap' course." P. M.
Heffron in *Quart. Jour. of Speech*, Apr.,
261. 1952: "His heavily attended snap
course is good for a laugh." C. W.
Morton in *Atlantic Monthly*, Apr., 88/3.
Wide student use since c1895.

snap into it   To hurry up, to do
something with increased energy or
enthusiasm. 1929: "Now, snap into it."
Sturges, *Strictly Dishonorable*, I.

snap it up   To hurry. 1934: "Drop

over to the main drag and snap it up."
Chandler, *Finger Man*, 30.

snap out of it   To come out of an
inattentive or despondent mood; to
become alert or active. *Since c1920.*

snare   *v.t.* To steal. *Not common in
U.S.*

snarky   snorky   *adj.* Elegant;
ritzy. 1941: "It's a snarky one [auto-
mobile]—a super-dooper." Radio, *Fibber
McGee*, Nov. 18. *Dial.*

snatch   *v.t.* **1** To arrest. 1860: *DAE.*
2 To kidnap; to steal. *Since c1925.*
n. **1** An arrest. **2** A theft or kidnaping;
the item stolen or person kidnaped.
1945: ". . . Or pay any share of a
$50,000 ransom to get him back from a
snatch." "Possibly the union should
carry snatch-insurance on a man in such
an exposed position." W. Pegler, *synd.
newsp. col.*, Dec. 20. → **3** A theft, specif.
of merchandise from a retail store. 1939:
"A piece of paper covering the slit [in
a box used by a shoplifter] was rolled
aside in the course of a snatch." R. W.
Woods in *Forum*, Dec., 275/2. **4** A
payroll. *Underworld use since c1940.*
5 The rump or buttocks of horses and
cattle. *Farmer use.* → **6** [taboo] A
woman's crotch. → **7** [taboo] The vagina.
Common since c1935.   **—er**   *n.* **1** A
policeman. *Some underworld, jive, and
teenage use since c1935.* **2** A conductor of a
horse-drawn streetcar. 1885: "The conductor is often called a 'snatcher' (i.e.,
because his characteristic duty is constantly to pull or snatch the bell-strap, to
stop or go on.)" Walt Whitman in *North
Am. Rev.*, Nov., 434. *Obs.* **3** A kidnaper.
1935: "The guy is a dog snatcher."
Runyon. **4** A detective on the police
force. *Not common.* See **cradle-snatcher,
ducat-snatcher.**

snatch, the   *n.* The act or instance
of kidnaping; the act or instance of
stealing. 1958: "His [Communist China's
Premier Chou En-lai] fellow conspirators
showed their true gangster coloration by
putting the snatch on a South Korean
DC-3 airliner." N.Y. *Daily News*, Feb.
20, 37.

**snatch on [someone or something],
put the**   **1** To arrest someone. **2** To
kidnap someone. **3** To take, seize, or
steal something. 1950: "The Treasury
Department is going to put the snatch
on virtually the entire 40 grand."
Billy Rose, *synd. newsp. col.*, Apr. 26.

snazzy   *adj.* **1** Stylish, in the latest
fashion, modern, classy, nifty, ritzy;
colorful, exciting; attractive, agreeable,

pleasing. 1942: "Snazzy colors that
boys like." Sears, Roebuck catalog.
1947: "Pretty snazzy weather we're
having, eh?" Billy Rose, *synd. newsp.
col.*, May 8. 1949: "In Dallas, the
Cokesbury Book Store opened a snazzy
annex." B. Cerf in *Sat. Rev. Lit.*, Oct. 15,
4/1. **2** Gaudy; in bad taste. *This usage
increasing since c1940.*

sneaker   *n.* A motorboat. *Some c1920
underworld use, because motorboats were
used to sneak contraband whisky into the
country during Prohibition.*

sneakers   *n.pl.* **1** Rubber-soled canvas
shoes; tennis shoes. 1909: "[They] called
'em 'sneakers' now." *Baseball Mag.*, Aug.,
23/1. 1911: *NED*, Suppl. 1914: ". . . Firm
in his rubber sneakers. . . ." S. Lewis,
Our Mr. Wrenn, 51. 1945: "She was
wearing a sweater, a shirt, short socks,
and sneakers." E. B. White, *Stuart
Little*, 118. *This style of shoe became
very pop. with school children in the late
1930's and by 1950 was also a stand.
adult's sport shoe. Now stand.* **2** Automobile or truck tires. *Some garage and
truck-driver use.*

sneaks   *n.pl.* = **sneakers.** *Since c1915;
fairly common.*

sneaky pete   sneaky Pete   **1** Any
of various illegal alcoholic beverages,
ranging from home-made whisky, flavored alcohol, and fortified wine to bootlegged moonshine. 1949: ". . . A group
which was discussing the effects of
'sneaky-pete.' " W. J. Slocum in *Collier's*,
Sept. 3, 40. *Since c1940.* **2** Cheap, raw
whisky. 1958: "All the gang piled into
the Ritz bar and polished off a whole
row of 'sneaky pete.' " *Life*, Apr. 28, 75.
*Some use, from confusion with the orig.
meaning.* → **3** Wine, usu. a cheap red
Burgundy, mixed with carbonated water
and ice; any cheap wine. 1952: ". . . A
pint of forty-cent wine known under the
generic title of 'Sneaky Pete.' " *Commonwealth*, Dec. 12, 253. *Since c1945.*
4 Specif., wine, freq. or usu. muscatel,
reinforced or fortified and apparently
habit-forming when so prepared; distributed in pint bottles, which are called
jugs, for quick, low-price sale. *Hobo use.*
1950: ". . . Full of that cheap wine they
call 'sneaky pete.' " A. Lomax, *Mr.
Jelly Roll*, 230. Cf. **jug.**

sneeze   *v.t.* To kidnap; to seize and
hold. 1935: "You are such a guy as is
apt to sneeze a dog." Runyon. 1952: "It
won't do merely to sneeze his luggage
or put a flyer on him after he has taken
it on the swift." Red Smith, N.Y. *Her.*

Trib., Jan. 24, 27/1. *Orig. underworld use, c1920.* *n.* **1** A kidnaping. 1946: "People who have so little regard for the law that they put the sneeze on a respectable businessman...." Evans, *Halo in Blood*, 81. *Since c1935.* **2** The act of seizing and holding, hence esp. an arrest. *Underworld use, c1925.* **—r** *n.* A jail. 1944: "This sailor is still in the sneezer." *Collier's*, July 1, 4/2.

snick *v.t.* To flick. 1946: "I stopped and snicked cigarette ash onto the rug." Evans, *Halo in Blood*, 139. *Not common.*

snide *adj.* Contemptible, sneaky; underhanded, mean, low, cheap; insincere, phoney, assuming a superior attitude. 1887: "Dat snide hash house." New Orleans *Lantern*. 1949: "The Administration is beginning to resemble a kind of snide Harding Administration." L. Bromfield in Phila. *Bulletin*, Sept. 3, 7/6. 1951: "If I had to choose between the repellent McCarthy and the snide 'McStassen' [Harold Stassen], I would instantly choose the former." H. L. Ickes in *New Repub.*, Oct. 29, 10/1. 1953: "A woman gets nothing but snide remarks about her driving skills." C. Lowry, AP, Sept. 24. *Common by c1900. Now colloq.* *n.* A contemptible or underhanded person. *Since c1900.*

sniff *v.t.* To inhale powdered narcotics. *Addict use, becoming archaic.* **—er** *n.* **1** A cocaine addict. 1928: "... The Baron was 'a sniffer' himself." *Amer. Mercury*, Aug., 485. *Not common.* **2** A handkerchief. **—y** *adj.* Snobbish; acting in a superior manner. 1949: "Even the sniffiest of [lexicographers]. ..." H. L. Mencken in *New Yorker*, Oct. 1, 63/1. *From the traditional snobbish posture of holding one's head high, with one's nose pointed upward, as if in disdain or sniffing an unpleasant odor.*

snifter *n.* **1** A drink of whisky. 1848: *DAE.* 1928: "... Plastered on a couple of snifters." C. G. Shaw in *New Yorker*, Nov. 17, 27/1. **2** A large brandy glass shaped like a bowl with a stem on it. *Since c1935; colloq. So shaped to allow one to warm brandy or liqueur with the hands and thus sniff the fumes.* **3** A cocaine addict.

snipe *n.* **1** A cigar or cigarette butt; the discarded remnant of a cigar or cigarette. 1894: "This 'snipe' chewing and smoking is most popular...." J. Flynt. *Orig. hobo use. Until cW.W.I = cigar butt; after the introduction of cigarettes term was used for either cigar or cigarette butts.* **2** A railroad track laborer.

Cf. **gandy dancer, king-snipe.** *Since c1915. Hobo, logger, and railroad use.* **3** A fireman or other member of a ship's engine-room gang. *Since c1920; some W.W.II USN use.* **4** = **gutter-snipe.** **5** A nonexistent animal; any mythical creature. *From the hoax of snipe hunting, in which an uninitiated person is left to watch for a "snipe," usu. at night and in a woods or field, while his supposed hunting companions, the hoaxers, leave him to discover the joke.* *v.t.* To steal. *Hobo and underworld use since c1915.* **—r** *n.* **1** A thief who robs unoccupied houses, a shoplifter, a semi-professional pickpocket. *Since c1925.* Cf. **snipe. 2** A collector of cigar or cigarette butts. *Hobo use.*

sniptious *adj.* Attractive; stylish. *Dial.*

snitch *v.t.* **1** To steal or take small items. *Common since c1920.* *v.i.* To inform against, betray, squeal, esp. to another's superior or teacher. *Common since c1920.* *n.* **1** An informer; a stool pigeon. 1928: "Patsy was a stool-pigeon and a snitch." Asbury, *Gangs of N.Y.*, 208. **2** A theft. *In the U.S. never used in the Australian sense of "a dislike."* **—er** *n.* An informer.

snitch-wise *adv., adj.* Diagonally; crosswise. *Archaic and dial.*

snitzy *adj.* Excellent, first class, modern and attractive. *Perhaps from "snazzy" plus "ritzy." Not common.*

snizzle *n.* A sneeze. 1949: "... To cure a pachyderm's wheezles and snizzles. ..." E. Selby, Phila. *Bulletin*, Sept. 8, 4/1. *Some jocular use.*

snoff *n.* A week-end girl friend, not one's steady. 1949: "A 'snoff' is not a girl with whom he goes regularly, only on weekends. 'Snoff' stands for 'Saturday night only, friend, female.'" Denver *Post*, Apr. 17. *An excellent example of synthetic sl., here based on the initials of a phrase. See Appendix, Shortened Words.*

snollygoster *n.* **1** A politician who relies on oratory rather than knowledge or ability; a politician who speaks much and does little. **2** An inept, talkative, or unethical lawyer; a shyster. *Both uses since c1860. Mainly dial.*

snooker *v.t.* To cheat, swindle, deceive. 1948: "Or, once Baijan disappeared, Wirtz would have realized he'd been snookered and he might let out a yell." Evans, *Halo for Satan*, 174. *Always used in passive.*

snoop *n.* A detective. 1948: "Private

snoop, hunh?" Evans, *Halo for Satan*, 34. *Not common.*   **—er**   *n.* A private detective. *Not common.*

snoose   Snoose   *n.* A potent, moist snuff. *It is usu. chewed or dipped rather than snuffed. Primarily logger use; orig. with Scandinavian lumber camp workers. "Snoose" is a specif. brand name of one such snuff.*

snoot   *n.* The human nose. 1949: ". . . Pokin' him one in the snoot." A. Kober in *New Yorker*, Nov. 5, 87. *Since c1875. Usu. used in ref. to the nose of a disliked person.*   *v.t.* To treat with disdain; to snub a person. 1950: "People who snoot goat milk. . . ." Starnes, *Another Mug*, 82. See **have a snoot full.** **—y**   *adj.* Snobbish; having a high opinion of oneself and a low opinion of others; stuck up. 1936: "Josie Arlington, the snootiest madame in America." H. Asbury, *The French Quarter*, 338. 1948: ". . . Astronomers, a generally vain and snooty class of men." H. L. Mencken in *New Yorker. Fig., with one's nose held high. Colloq.*

snoot full, have [get] a   To be under the influence of alcohol; to be drunk. 1936: "Then I met a lot of other reporters and I got a snoot full." Tully, *Bruiser*, 77. *Since c1920.* See Appendix, Drunk.

snooze   *v.i.* To sleep. *Since c1850; colloq. since c1900.*   *n.* A sleep, esp. a short sleep or a nap. 1907: "The blind was not comfortable enough to suit me for a snooze." J. London, *The Road*, 132. *Colloq. since c1900.*

snorky   See **snarky.**

snort   *n.* **1** A drink of liquor, esp. a drink of neat whisky. 1929: "Who's ready for another short snort?" K. Brush, *Young Man*, 45. 1943: "All hands had another snort." H. A. Smith, *Putty Knife*, 53. *Common since c1915; from "snorter."* → **2** A small piece of anything; a short distance. *Since c1935.* **—er**   *n.* **1** A drink of neat whisky. *Since at least c1800, now archaic in favor of "snort."* → **2** Anything or any person that is strong, big, exceptional, noisy, or the like. *Since c1830; archaic.* Cf. **rip-snorter.**

snort-pipe   *n.* The exhaust pipe of an automobile or motorcycle. *Not common.*

snow   *n.* **1** Cocaine crystals. 1956: "Not all jazz-players smoke marijuana or opium, or sniff snow." S. Longstreet, *The Real Jazz Old and New*, 144. *Orig. West Coast addict use. From the white appearance of the crystals. "Almost obs. among underworld addicts." D. W.*

Maurer. → **2** Cocaine in any form. 1930: "Take a sniff of snow." "A shot of snow." Weeks, *Racket*, 38; 161. *Very common.* → **3** Any habit-forming narcotic. **4** Whipped cream. *A little student use since c1935.* **5** Deceptive, exaggerated, or flattering talk. See **snow job. 6** Rapidly moving white or black dots on a television screen, caused by interference or faulty reception. *Since c1945.*   *v.i.* **1** To talk, usu. to repeat what one has just said. *Almost always in the expression, "Snow again. I didn't get your drift." Some use since c1920.* **2** To exaggerate; to misrepresent or purposely confuse; to talk or write at length on a subject to a person who is uninformed in order to deceive or impress that person. See **snow job, snow under.**   **—ed**   *adj.* **1** Under the influence of a narcotic, esp. cocaine; doped, drugged. 1934: "She looked snowed, weaved around funny. . . ." Chandler, *Finger Man*, 121. **2** Deceived; influenced by exaggerated, deceptive talk; influenced by a snow job. *Common since cW.W.II.*

snow, in the   With whipped cream. *Waiter use in relaying orders. Thus "shimmy in the snow" = gelatin dessert with whipped cream. Not common.*

snowball   *n.* **1** [derog.] A Negro, esp. an elderly, white-haired Negro. *Some use c1850–c1900; obs.* **2** A hydrangea flower cluster. *Because of the rounded shape and usu. white tint. Colloq.* **3** Cocaine crystals. *Since c1930; addict use.* See **snow. 4** = **snowbird.**   *v.i., v.t.* To grow or increase rapidly; fig., to build up as a snowball does when rolled down a slope in wet, clinging snow. 1951: "Soon the racket [of cheating the government out of paychecks] began to snowball." *Time*, Feb. 26, 25/1.

snowball chance   A very slight chance; no chance at all. *From the saying "as much chance as a snowball in hell."*

snowbird   snow bird   *n.* **1** A hobo or migratory worker temporarily working or living in the South to escape winter in the North. *Since c1920; orig. hobo use.* **2** A cocaine addict, esp. one who sniffs cocaine crystals. 1930: "Nelly's eyes had a glassy, far-away look. Snow bird, he thought to himself." Weeks, *Racket*, 91. *Addict use.* See **snow.** → **3** Any narcotics addict.

snowdrop   *n.* A member of the Army's Military Police. 1945: "General Eisenhower said, 'I see some of my own snowdrops on the stage.' " *N.Y. World-Telegram*, May 16, 15. *From the uniform,* *which includes white helmets, white gloves, white belts, and white puttees.*

snowed in   snowed up   1 Doped, drugged. *Addict use since c1925.* See **snow. 2** Deceived by insincere talk. See **snow job.**

snowed under Burdened by an excess of work or responsibilities; fig., being burdened or obscured by an abundance of anything. 1920: "Every one who knew him liked him—but what he stood for (and he came to stand for more all the time) came under the lash of many tongues, until a frailer man than he would have been snowed under." F. S. Fitzgerald, *This Side of Paradise,* 133.

snowed up = **snowed in.**

snow-flier *n.* = **snowbird.** *Some hobo use.*

snow job Persuasive, insincere talk or writing; usu. talk that exaggerates, deceives, or flatters for the purpose of impressing the speaker's importance or knowledge on an attractive member of the opposite sex, a new acquaintance, a business superior, or a client; a line. 1947: "You should have heard his snow job." H. Boyle, AP, May 19. 1950: "Don't let Slattery give you a snow job and get you into trouble." Movie, *Halls of Montezuma. From "snow under." Very common during and since W.W.II.*

snowshoe *n.* **1** A person who cannot be trusted, esp. such a person who has an innocent appearance. *Not common. From the early days of horse-race betting; one who had unmelted snow on his shoes had just entered the betting establishment, hence he might already know the winner of a race on which he was betting. This was one of the easiest forms of past-posting a bookie.* → **2** A detective; a plainclothes policeman. *Reinforced by the image of large feet traditionally assoc. with policemen.* Cf. **flat foot. 3** A cup of hot chocolate, usu. with whipped cream on top. *Some lunch-counter use c1930.* See **snowstorm.**

snowstorm *n.* **1** A party held for the purpose of taking narcotics, esp. cocaine; a drug-induced trance. 1930: "Me broad gets caught in a snowstorm." *Amer. Mercury,* Dec., 455. **2** Whipped cream. *Some student use since c1925.*

snowstorm, in a With plenty of whipped cream. *Lunch-counter use.* See **in the snow.**

snow under   1 To overwhelm with work, advice, or the like. 1880: *DAE.* **2** To talk persuasively but insincerely in order to impress or deceive another.

1943: "If she falls for [the line], she's been snowed under." A. Ostrow. *Replaced by "snow."*

snozzle *n.* = **schnozzle. —d** *adj.* Drunk. *From "snozzle" = nose, "snort," and "have a snootful." Not common in the U.S.* See Appendix, Drunk.

snub *v.t.* To tie, to tie up; to make fast. 1856 [1954]: "Take that rope and snub him [a dog] to yonder sapling. Snub him good and short." W. Henry, *Death of a Legend,* 11. *Now dial.*

snubbed *adj.* Drunk. *Obs.*

snub out To extinguish a cigarette by firmly pressing, tapping, or rubbing the lighted end against a steady surface, as the bottom of an ashtray. 1939: "He snubbed his cigarette out carefully, over and over...." Chandler, *Big Sleep,* 152. 1951: "I snubbed the butt out in my saucer." Spillane, *Big Kill,* 142.

snuff-dipper *n.* A lignite-burning locomotive. *Railroad use; archaic.*

snuffy *adj.* Drunk. *Archaic.*

snug *n.* A small, easily concealed revolver. *Underworld use.*

snuggle-pup *n.* A sweetheart of either sex; one who necks. *Jocular and teenage use, c1920; archaic.* **—py** *n.* = **snuggle-pup.** 1933: "I glimmed him with a snuggle-puppy." H. T. Webster.

snurge *v.i.* To sneak away, esp. in order to avoid work. *Prob. synthetic.*

So?   1 An expression showing lack of interest, rejection, refusal to comprehend, or refusal to agree with another that something is important, worthy of becoming excited about, or remarkable. *This use resembles Yiddish speech patterns and rhythms.* **2** An interrogatory word with an exceedingly wide range of use. Usu. used in reply to a statement, it may be an expression of interest, a request for further information, a term of disbelief, etc. See **how-come-ye-so, say-so, so-and-so, so long, so-so, so's your old man.**

soak *v.t.* **1** To pawn. 1882: "Colloq." *DAE. Archaic.* **2** To strike, to sock. 1905: "... To soak you in the midriff with a rusty patent leather [shoe]...." McHugh, *Search Me,* 11. 1914: "Why don't you soak him?" S. Lewis, *Our Mr. Wrenn,* 13. *Common student use by c1895; obs.* **3** To make a person pay heavily; to overcharge; to penalize heavily, as by a jail sentence or high taxes; fig., to inflict punishment on. 1907: "I knew that if the police 'pinched' me again, I'd get good and 'soaked.'" J. London, *The*

Road, 165. 1951: "It was a good case of how soak-the-rich corporation taxes wind up right in the pocketbooks of all of us." AP, Aug. 9, 6/2. **4** To borrow. *Some student use c1910.* See **go soak yourself.**   *n.* **1** A drunkard; a habitual drinker. *Common since c1900; from "soaked."* → **2** A drunken spree or binge. 1951: "He goes out on a binge . . . a really good soak with the boys." K. Harris, *Innocents from Abroad*, 87. **—ed**   *adj.* Drunk. 1737: *DAE.* 1926: "He ain't soaked." Stallings & Anderson, *What Price Glory*, I. *Common since its first use, the word's popularity rises and falls every decade or so; periods of most recent popularity include c1900 and c1920. With the rise of many competing sl. syns. during Prohibition, the word has lost some of its oral popularity, though still universally known.*

soaker   *n.* A diaper cover, usu. a hand-knitted one; a pilch.

soak yourself, go   A rejoinder signifying disbelief or annoyance.

so-and-so   *n.* **1** A euphem. for any of several strongly derog. epithets for a contemptible person, usu. a male, esp. "son-of-a-bitch." 1938: "I think I'll sue the so-and-so." H. Broun in *New Repub.*, Aug. 17, 45/1. → **2** Any male friend; a guy, a fellow. 1948: "I'd be a silly so-and-so if I should ever let you go." From a pop. song. *As many curse words and epithets, this is used jocularly in greeting close friends.*

soap   *n.* **1** Money, esp. money used for bribery. 1836: *DAE.* 1926: "[In] 1880 'soap' was used by the Republicans as a cipher for 'money' in their compaign dispatches." L. C. Wimberly in *AS*, 2, 135. Cf. **grease. 2 = soft soap.** *Since c1930.* See **no soap.**   *v.t.* To flatter; fig., to give someone "soft soap." 1952: "Brewster was one of those Republicans who soaped Vivien. . . ." W. Pegler, *synd. newsp. col.*, June 20.

soap-box   *n.* Lit. and fig., the traditional box which a public orator stands on while making a, usu. political, speech or harangue. *In such expressions as "Where's your soap-box?" = You're talking like a public orator.*

soap-grease   *n.* Money of any kind. *Some dial. use.* See **grease, soap.**

soap opera   1 A daily dramatic serial program broadcast by radio, usu. lasting fifteen minutes each day, concerning fictitious domestic crises and troubles and often characterized by little action and much sentiment. 1949:

"A couple of girls out of Los Angeles use soap opera as a form of speed-up for the ironing. They turn the radio to CBS and condemn themselves to soap opera until the job's done. . . . A new soap opera which threatens to out-misery all the others put together. . . ." J. Crosby, *synd. newsp. col.*, Aug. 6. *Because such programs are often sponsored by manufacturers of soap.* **2** Any real situation, crisis, or burden of troubles that resembles that usu. heard on a soap opera radio program.   *adj.* Like or pertaining to the situations, crises, or burden of troubles and ill fortune heard on a radio soap opera. 1952: "The average man and woman in this country live a soap-opera existence. [They] travel from crisis to crisis, with bills unpaid, with emergencies, with hopeless troubles." R. C. Ruark, *synd. newsp. col.*, Sept. 29.

soapy-eyed   *adj.* Drunk. *Not common.* See Appendix, Drunk.

s. o. b.   S. O. B.   sob [taboo] *n.* = **son of a bitch.** See Appendix, Shortened Words.

sob-sister   sobsister   sob sister   *n.* **1** A woman news reporter who appeals to readers' sympathies with her accounts of pathetic happenings; a newspaper woman who reports on events of human interest, esp. one whose writing contains much sentimentality. 1938: "The sobsisters [have given us the word] function. . . ." C. T. Ryan in *Better Eng.*, Sept., 40/1. *Since c1925.* **2** Any woman who resorts to tears, the retelling of personal sad experiences, or sentimental stories to gain attention or sympathy; any woman or man who excuses present failure on the basis of personal defeats in the past. → **3** An actress who plays sentimental or sympathetic roles.   *adj.* Sentimental. *Often used to describe sentimental plays, stories, movies, etc.*

sob story   Any very sad story, esp. a recital of personal misfortunes calculated to arouse sympathy in the listener.

sob stuff   Stories of personal sadness, esp. when used to gain sympathy or favor; sentimentality, esp. in writing or before an audience. 1930: "Eppingham had prepared to lay on the sob stuff [in presenting his case to a jury] with a trowel." Weeks, *Racket*, 196.

socdollager = sockdollager.

sock   *v.t.* **1** To hit, as with the fist or a club. 1921: ". . . Bein' socked to dreamland." Witwer, *Leather*, 44. See

sockdollager. → **2** Fig., to deliver a hard blow, as bad news, a surprise, or the like. **3** To save money, fig., by putting it away in a sock. 1951: "The American people socked away $3,200,000 in the year's second quarter." B. Garrett, GNS, Oct. 27. → **4** To earn money, usu. said of a business, play, or the like, rather than of a person.   *n.* **1** A blow, esp. one given with the fist. 1928: "To land another sock on Mr. Renault's nose." B. Hecht in *New Yorker*, Nov. 3, 42. → **2** Fig., a blow, as by a concerted effort, the result of work, events, or the like. 1945: "Strategists are counting upon [rockets] for a large part of the knockout sock against the Nazis and the Japs." F. Carey, AP, Feb. 5. → **3** Fig., that which is very successful with one attempt, as a knockout blow; any person or effort making a quick and spectacular success; esp. a very successful play, movie, song, entertainer, or the like; a hit. 1939: "He said he understood I was a sock the last 2 rooms [nightclubs] I worked." O'Hara, *Pal Joey*, 38f. 1948: "...Changed [the film] from a near-flop to a b. o. sock." *Variety*, Aug. 25, 1/5. **4** A guy, esp. one who is foolish or who can be cheated easily. See **wet sock.** *Since c1920.* **5** In baseball, a hit. *Common since c1925.* **6** A money receptacle, as a bag, box, safe, or the like. *Underworld use since c1930.* → **7** Fig., a place where money is kept, as a savings account at a bank; money saved, a nest egg. 1951: "Every dollar which he [President Truman] will receive for the current four-year term will go into the family sock." W. Pegler, *synd. newsp. col.*, Aug. 14. → **8** A sum of money, esp. a large sum. 1949: "Quigley lost a big sock horse-gambling." Burnett, *Jungle*, 23.   *adj.* Very successful financially. 1947: A sock show can make a million." Billy Rose, *synd. newsp. col.*, May 15.   **—er**   *n.* **1** Anything of exceptional size, force, impact, or value; anything extreme. 1952: "We had six winters above normal from 1927–28 to 1932–33, then came a socker. February of 1934 was the coldest month ever known in New York." R. Sullivan in N.Y. *Sunday News*, Oct. 5, C22/1. *Most common c1890; archaic.* See **sockdollager, sockeroo.** **2** A baseball player who usu. hits the ball hard; a slugger. 1953: "The long-ball hitting Red Sox line-up that earned the name of 'the sockers.'" AP, Feb. 10. See **sock.**   **—eroo**   *n.* Anything of

extraordinary excellence, esp. something having, fig., a sock, punch, or wallop; a smash hit, as a very profitable stage show, movie, or song. 1942: "The act [put on by the Dionne quintuplets for the Victory Loan Drive] was an old-fashioned Hippodrome sockeroo." *Time*, Nov. 9, 77/2. 1948: "One Lone Sockeroo [column heading:] During 1947 there were 10 pix from plays, with Paramount's 'Dear Ruth' ($450,000) the only real sockeroo." H. Golden in *Variety*, Aug. 25, 22/2. See **sock.** *More common than "socker."*   *adj.* Hard-hitting; smashing; very successful. 1947: "The House Civil Service Committee is putting some sockeroo catches in the President's plan to check the loyalty of all Federal employees." D. Pearson, *synd. newsp. col.*, June 23. *c1940; one of the few "—eroo" words in common use.* See Appendix, —eroo ending.   **—ing** *adv.* Excessively. *Some use c1890; now considered affected.*   **—o!**   *interj.* An imitative expression signifying the impact of a blow; used fig. to express the sensation of a sudden and signal success in any endeavor. 1929: "He's inside the room. Socko! This is the quickest way of saying he punches the villain in the jaw." W. Root. *Freq. oral use.* See **sock, sockdollager.**   **—o**   *n.* **1** A punch or hard blow, esp. to the jaw. *Prize fighter use since c1925.* See **sock.** Cf. **socko!** **2** A great success, esp. a great financial success in the field of entertainment; a sock, a hit. *Orig. theater use; not as common as the adj.*   *v.t.* **1** To deliver a hard blow, esp. a punch on the jaw. *Prize fighter use.* **2** To make a great or quick success. *Orig. theater use.*   *adj.* Very successful, esp. successful financially. 1952: "A movie which rated the industry's supreme accolade—socko box-office." J. Bacon, AP, Sept. 24. *Most common use, pop. by "Variety," a theater trade paper.*   *adv.* Very well; most profitably. 1948: "U.S. film people reject these [British] films for the American market and yet find they do socko in their native heath." *Variety*, Aug. 25, 5/1–2. See Appendix, —o ending. *All uses prob. reinforced by "sockdollager."*

sockdollager   socdollager   sock-dolager   *n.* **1** Any remarkable, large, or strong person or thing; the ultimate in anything. 1838: *DAE.* 1893: "'Sockdollager,' once quite current, was an uneducated transposition of 'doxologer,' which was the familiar New England rendering of 'doxology,' the verse used at the conclusion of every hymn. It became a triumphant winding up of the whole act of worship. Now a 'soc-dollager' was the term for anything which left nothing else to follow, a knockdown blow, a decisive, over-whelming finish, to which no reply was possible." Anon. in *Atlantic Monthly*, Mar., 425. *Obs.* Cf. **sock.** 2 A hard blow, esp. with the fist. *c1840–c1900.* Cf. **sock.**

soda jerk   One, usu. a youth, who prepares and dispenses refreshments at a soda fountain. 1949: "She worked for a while as a soda jerk." *Life*, Oct. 24, 20. *Colloq.*

soda jerker = soda jerk. 1945: "In those days . . . 1887 . . . a druggist was a chemist and not a soda jerker." J. B. Martin. 1947: "Harold Korb was the champion soda jerker of the United States . . . he sure knew how to make a soda." E. Pyle, *Home Country*, 153. See Appendix, —er ending.

soda squirt = soda jerk. *Some Western use, c1915.*

sod-buster   *n.*   A farmer. 1952: "You're nothing but a sod-buster." Movie, *Shane*. *Some use since c1890; orig. Western use; used derog. by ranchers, cowboys, and herders.*

sod widow   A widow whose husband has died, as opposed to a grass widow whose husband is merely away or divorced. *Mainly dial.* Cf. **golf widow, grass widow.**

sofa lizard   1 A male student who stays at home to avoid spending money for a social engagement or date. *Some student use, c1925.* → 2 A male who does not take his girl friend to social engage-ments, movies, dances, or the like, preferring to visit her at her home, usu. to save the expense of taking the girl anywhere. → 3 A male who prefers to visit a girl at home, in order to neck or pet with her in private; one who necks or pets ardently. See **lounge lizard.**

soft   *n.* Easy money.

soft, the   *n.* Money. 1939: "A nice package of the soft." Runyon. *Perh. from the softness of used paper money or of "dough," or from "soft money."*

soft-head   *n.* A person who can be easily convinced or dominated; one who cannot or does not make his own deci-sions. *Not common.*

softhorn   *n.* = **greenhorn.** *Some use c1830–c1900; archaic.*

softie   softy   *n.* An excessively trusting, generous, or sentimental person;

one who gives sympathy easily; a dupe, pushover, or soft touch. 1949: "You are a patsy, a quick push, a big softie." Burnett, *Jungle*, 46f.

soft money   1 Paper currency. *Some use since c1860.* 2 The currency of a nation suffering from inflation; inflated currency; currency that is easy to earn or borrow but that is not worth its face value in purchasing power. *Common since c1940.* Cf. **hard money.**

soft-pedal   *v.t.* To de-emphasize; usu. in ref. to an opinion or intelligence that will evoke an unfavorable public res-ponse. 1957: "But there have been times when even my friends advised me to soft-pedal my criticisms. They meant well. They didn't want me, Lucille, and our two sons, Robert Jr. and William, to be hurt." N.Y. *Daily News*, July 30, 22. *From the soft pedal on a piano.*

soft sell   The act or an instance of selling or advertising merchandise in a friendly, soft-spoken, indirect, self-effac-ing, or genteel manner. *Orig. Madison Avenue use. Often applied to television commercials.*

soft-shell   *adj.* Lenient; holding less severe beliefs; pseudo. *Thus a "soft-shell Baptist" is one with modern and moderate attitudes toward dancing, for example, which the orig. church banned; a "soft-shell egghead" is a pseudo-intellectual.*

soft soap   Flattery; flattering or sentimental talk or writing used to gain sympathy or information. *Since c1830.*

soft-soap   *v.t., v.i.* To speak or write flattery to someone; to appeal to another's sentiment; to snow.

soft touch   1 One who, on request, lends or gives money readily and/or generously. 1939: "You get the reputa-tion of being a soft touch." O'Hara, *Pal Joey*, 44. 1949: *Mr. Soft Touch*, title of a movie. → 2 A person who is easily convinced, cheated, or influenced. → 3 An easy task or job; money earned at an easy task or job. *c1940.*

softy   See **softie.**

s. o. l.   S. O. L. [taboo] = **shit out of luck.** *This abbr. is as common as the full expression.* See Appendix, Shortened Words.

Sol   *n.* The sun. *Often in "old Sol," "big Sol," etc. Colloq.*   **sol**   *n.* Soli-tary confinement in prison. 1930: "He draws sol till he's [crazy]." *Amer. Mercury*, Dec., 456.

soldier   *n.* 1 An empty whisky or

beer bottle. See **dead soldier.** 2 A customer or fare who tips heavily. *Some use since c1935.* *v.i.* **1** To shirk one's duty or assigned tasks; to goldbrick. *Army use since c1820; some W.W.I and W.W.II use, but becoming archaic.* 1940 [1951]: "Louis was supposed to be on duty behind the counter. But he soldiered on the job and the place was deserted." Carson McCullers, *The Heart Is a Lonely Hunter*, reprinted with *The Ballad of the Sad Café*, 493–494. **2** To fulfill one's duties, to shoulder one's responsibilities. *Prob. owing to confusion with "shoulder," reinforced by civilian concept of a soldier doing his duty.*

solid *adj.* Great; wonderful, marvelous; exciting, eliciting one's enthusiasm; perfect, excellent. 1943: "G. M. [Glenn Miller]! . . . Man, what solid jive." M. Shulman, *Barefoot Boy with Cheek*, 90. 1946: "Terms that are on their way out of use by jazz musicians and jazz fans are *low-down, solid....*" M. Berger. 1954: "It's a funny thing how life can be such a drag one minute and a solid sender the next." L. Armstrong, *Satchmo, My Life in New Orleans*, 126. *Orig. Harlem jive use. c1935; mainly jive and swing use, widely pop. in jazz and student contexts.* Cf. **solid sender.** *n.* A trusted friend. *c1920 underworld use. adv.* Surely; definitely. *Usu. = "I agree," "You're correct in every way." Often used as a one-word reply to a statement; mainly jive use since c1935. Orig. Harlem jive talk.*

solid, Jackson = **solid.** *The "Jackson" merely serves to reiterate the "solid."* See **Jackson.**

solid ivory **1** Fig., a person's head considered as solid bone or ivory and without brains. *Often accompanied by the gesture of tapping the person in question on his head, sometimes while making a sharp hitting noise, to illustrate the point. In common use since c1900, esp. by young boys.* **2** A bonehead.

solid sender **1** See **sender.** **2** An adroit swing musician; an exciting, satisfying, well-liked piece or arrangement of swing music. *Swing use, c1935–c1942.* → **3** An attractive, sympathetic, alert, hep person, esp., but not necessarily, if a devotee of swing.

solitaire *n.* Suicide.

solo *n.* The act of confessing guilt. *c1920, underworld use.* Cf. **sing.** *v.i.* To live alone; to act independently. *Colloq.*

So long Good-by. *Colloq. since c1850;*

prob. from the Arabic "salaam" and the Hebrew "sholom."

some *adv.* Somewhat; very; rapidly. *Since c1800; colloq.* 1907: "It was a fast freight, and she went some." J. London, *The Road*, 212. 1914: "They'll keep you some busy!" S. Lewis, *Our Mr. Wrenn*, 239. *n.* A great deal. 1850: "Colloq." *DAE.* *adj.* Remarkably good or remarkably bad; may express endearment, surprise, irony, astonishment, etc. 1926: "I can recall about 25 years ago, every school boy was considered a 'hayseed' who could not emphasize his admiration for a person or a thing by the use of 'some.'" C. T. Ryan. 1943: "You've got some line." Wolfert, *Underworld*, 205. *Colloq. since c1850.*

somebody, a *n.* An important, influential, famous, notorious, notable, successful, ambitious, or distinguished individual; a person whose life has meaning or value to society. 1958: "Leroy was a somebody . . . he wasn't a nobody." H. Macleod in N.Y. *Post*, Jan. 24, 5.

some pumpkins *sing.* **1** An important person or thing; an admirable person or thing. 1913: "He is some pumpkins." F. K. Sechrist. *Used only as a pred. nominative. Since c1850, has been extremely pop. Though still in use by older people, young adults prefer stronger terms.* → **2** Audacious, mischievous; clever. *Often used with an affectionate connotation, esp. by older people when talking of children. Archaic and dial.*

something *adv.* Exceedingly. 1914: "He just cusses her out something fierce." S. Lewis, *Our Mr. Wrenn*, 191. *Colloq. n.* An important or remarkable person or thing, a "somebody." *Often used ironically or in the negative when used for persons, as "You think you're something, don't you?" = You're disgusting or insignificant. Always = remarkable when applied to objects or events, usually in "Isn't that something?"*

something damp A drink of whisky. *Not common.*

something else Greater than great; beyond description. 1957: "Something else—A phenomenon so special that it defies description. Thus, when asked if the music is great . . . a cat may reply, 'No, man, not that: it was something else.'" E. Horne, *For Cool Cats and Far-Out Chicks. Some far-out use.*

something on the ball Ability; merit. 1941: ". . . To help a guy with something on the ball." Schulberg, *Sammy*, 124. See **on the ball**.

something on the hip   Whisky, esp. as carried in a bottle or hip flask. *Some c1920 use.*

sona'bitch'u [derog.] = **son of a bitch**. *Said rapidly and slurred to sound like "something bit you." Used by schoolboys as a jocular euphem.*

song   *n.* **1** A confession. See **sing**. **2** A story of personal misfortune, an excuse, an exaggerated story or lie; any, usu. long-winded, personal recital motivated by a desire for sympathy. 1952: "Some bum will brace you with a long song of utter inconsequence." R. C. Ruark, *synd. newsp. col.*, Mar. 5. *From "song and dance."*

song and dance   **1** A rigmarole; nonsense, bunk. 1900: *DAE.* → **2** An exaggerated story or lie told to elicit sympathy; an alibi; a spiel, a snow job. 1951: "There was a long song and dance when he introduced me, about how I was a businessman." *I, Mobster*, 138. *Prob. orig. theater use*

song-bird   *n.* **1** A female vocalist. *Colloq.* **2** One who confesses, informs, or "sings." *Some underworld use.*

son of a b = **son of a bitch**. *A euphem.*

son of a bitch [taboo]   **1** [derog.] A despicable man; sometimes, but rarely, a despicable woman; a bastard. *One of the most pop. insulting epithets in U.S. use.* → **2** A rascal, a scalawag; a guy. *Jocular use, often as part of a greeting between friends.* **3** A troublesome, annoying, or hard task or job; a task impossible to accomplish. *Very common since c1940.* **4** An oath of disgust, disappointment, or anger. *adj.* Annoying, nasty, troublesome. *In no use is the term now understood to cast aspersion upon the subject's mother.*

son of a gun = **son of a bitch**. *A once common euphem., now rarely used by young people.*

son of a so-and-so   **1** = **son of a bitch**. *An infreq. euphem.* **2** = **so-and-so**.

soogan   *n.* = **sugan**.

soogie   sujee   soujge   *n.* A mixture of soap, caustic soda, and water used for washing painted surfaces, esp. on board a ship. 1944: "A bucket of 'soujge.'" *Time*, Jan. 10, 4. *Since c1900; common USN and maritime use; common W.W.I and W.W.II use. Perhaps from the Chinese "soji" but prob. from the Hindustani "suji" or "soojee," a thick mixture of granulated wheat and* water or milk, eaten as gruel, which the washing mixture somewhat resembles. *v.t.* To wash or scrub the walls, or bulkheads, of a ship. 1951: "I was sooging down the walls in [the captain's] cabin." R. Bissell, *Stretch on River*, 48. *Common USN and maritime use.*

soogie moogie   sujee-mujee   *n.* = **soogie**. 1945: "Soon Sailor Slobodkin found himself loading sargo, eating slop and doing soogie moogie (scrubbing paint work) with a crew." *Time*, Dec. 31, 96. See Appendix, Reduplications.

Sooner   *n.* A native of Australia.   **sooner**   *n.* Anything cheap, as clothing, or shabby, as a person; anything mongrel. *Some Negro use.*

soot   *n.* A powdered explosive. *Not common. From Brit. sl. "soot" = gunpowder, from its appearance.*

S. O. P.   s. o. p.   Standard operating procedure; the correct, official way in which something must be done. *Fairly common W.W.II Armed Forces use, and some postwar civilian use.* See Appendix, Shortened Words.

sop   *n.* A habitual drunkard; an alcoholic.   **—py**   *adj.* Sentimental.

soph   *n.* **1** A sophomore student. 1778: *DAE.* 1949–1952: Occurs at least 48 times in Cornell (Univ.) *Daily Sun.* **2** Immature; childish. *Since before 1800.* *adj.* Sophomore. 1949–1952: Occurs at least 76 times in Cornell (Univ.) *Daily Sun. Since c1780.* See Appendix, Shortened Words.   **—omore**   *n.* An athlete in his second year of professional competition.   *adj.* Immature, unsophisticated, childish.

sore   *adj.* **1** Annoyed; irritated. *Colloq.* → **2** Angry. 1887: "[He] feels sore of it yet." New Orleans *Lantern*. 1922: "I was sore." O'Neill, *Hairy Ape*, 4. 1944: "I'm getting pretty sore." Ford, *Phila. Murder*, 59. *Colloq.*

sored up   Angry. 1932: "He is sored up more than somewhat." Runyon, 22. *Not common.*

sore-head   sorehead   *n.* One who angers easily, or complains loudly and frequently; one who frequently feels cheated, neglected or disappointed; a person who has a grudge. *Since c1850.*

sorry   See **I'm sorry**.

sorts   *n.pl.* Marked cards; a deck of marked cards. 1956: "'Sorts'—cards with a mark on the backs of the aces and the kings." T. Betts, *Across the Board*, 234. *Not common.*

S O S   S. O. S.   *n.* **1** Lit. and fig., a distress signal; fig., a request for aid, as in finishing a task successfully or in extracting oneself from an embarrassing situation. *From the Morse Code telegraph and radio distress signal. Usu. thought to be the initials for "save our souls" or "save our ship," the letters actually represent no words, but were chosen because they are easy to transmit and understand without confusion.* **2** [taboo] The usual routine tasks, procedures, or glib talk; the usual unfairness, deception, or bull; the usual shit. *Some W.W.II Army use. From the initials for "same old shit," reinforced jocularly by the Morse Code distress signal.* See Appendix, Shortened Words.

soshed *adj.* Drunk. 1928: "He was never soshed." B. de Casseres in *Amer. Mercury*, May, 103. *Not common.* See Appendix, Drunk.

so-so *adj.* All right, neither exceptionally good nor bad; as good as can be expected; average. Often in reply to the greeting, "How are things with you?"

So's your old man An expression used in scornful or contemptuous reply to any remark that arouses disbelief. *Orig. West Coast use, c1915.*

soujge *n.* = **soogie.**

soul kiss A long passionate, open-mouthed kiss, during which a lover's tongue licks, caresses, or explores the tongue and mouth of the beloved.

sound *v.t.* To taunt or insult someone, usu. a rival; to goad someone into a fight. *Teenage street-gang use since c1955.*

sound off *v.i.* **1** To state one's name; to drill or march while counting off the procedure in unison to the rhythm of the work; to speak when ordered to do so. *W.W.II Army use.* **2** To talk, esp. to complain or expostulate at length; to list one's complaints or opinions verbally. 1949: "Its leaders have sounded off on various issues before they knew what they were talking about." P. Jones in Phila. *Bulletin*, Sept. 1, 14. 1953: "Please forgive me for sounding off where love is concerned!" E. Martin, *synd. comic strip*, "Boots and Her Buddies," Feb. 3. *Wide use during and since W.W.II. Orig. Army use.* **3** To boast; to brag. *Orig. W.W.II Army use.*

soup *n.* **1** Nitroglycerine. → **2** Dynamite. **3** The developing solution used in photography. *Photographer use.* **4** Molten lead, steel, or other construction metals. *Refining and factory use.* **5** Water as taken aboard a moving locomotive. See **jerk soup. 6** Fuel used to power fast airplanes or cars; esp., a

special fuel used only for powerful motors. *v.t.* = **soup up.** 1956: "Souping the Stock [Car] Engine [title:] Explains fully the 5 paths to power. Covers everything from road to track engines. Effective theories on speed tuning." Advt. for *Floyd Clymer Motorbooks.*

soup, in the = **in hot water.** *Orig. jocular use, now common.*

soup-and-fish *n.* A man's formal evening suit of clothes; a tuxedo. 1922: "Getting into the soup-and-fish...." S. Lewis, *Babbitt.* 1948: "You will see more men informal than in soup and fish." Lait-Mortimer, *N.Y. Confidential*, 213.

soupbone *n.* A baseball pitcher's pitching arm. *Since c1920.*

souped up *adj.* **1** Containing added horsepower or a potentially greater speed or rate of acceleration than when originally manufactured; said of a car or engine. 1949: "A Ford with a souped-up motor...." A. Hynd, *Public Enemies*, 29. 1957: "Teen-age infatuation with souped-up cars in which speed-crazy kids raced...." *Life*, Apr. 29. → **2** Accelerated; improved; done, presented, or performed in a faster, more exciting way than usual; made gaudy or flashy.

souper *n.* **1** = **soupbone.** See **pea-souper. 2** = **super**, a watch.

soup house An inferior restaurant. *Orig. hobo use.*

soup job A fast car or airplane. *Student and Air Force use.*

soup jockey A waiter or waitress.

soup-strainer *n.* A mustache. *Some jocular use.*

soup up *v.t.* To increase the horsepower, speed, efficiency, or rate of acceleration of a car engine or airplane. 1949: "He souped up the motors." A. Hynd, *Public Enemies*, 22. *Universally known; wide hot-rod use since c1950.*

soupy *adj.* Sentimental, unduly idealistic, unreal, mushy. *Said of movies, plays, books, attitudes, etc.* *n.* Mess call. *A little Army use during W.W.II.*

sour *n.* **1** A sharp verbal reprimand or criticism. *c1900; never common.* **2** A lemon. *Not common.* *adj.* **1** Disagreeable; unhappy; pessimistic. *Colloq.* **2** Wrong; suspicious; unethical; illegal. *Colloq.*

sour, in In disfavor; in trouble; to make a bad start.

sour apples Unsuccessfully; poorly. In such expressions as, "He can't pitch for sour apples" = he pitches poorly. Used alone or in several phrases indicating incredulity or lack of faith in another's ability. *Dial. and archaic.*

sour-ball   *n.* A chronic grumbler; a pessimist.

sour-belly   *n.* = **sour-ball**. *Not common.*

sourdough   *n.* Counterfeit money. 1946: "The sourdough boys don't usually shoot so high. People have a habit of looking sharp at C notes." Evans, *Halo in Blood*, 100. *From "sour" plus "dough." Not common; prob. synthetic.*

sourdough tourist   An outdoor camper.

sour-pan   *n.* = **sour-puss**. 1942: "He'd change into a sour-pan, grunting in response to greetings." *Amer. Mercury*, Oct., 438/1.

sour-puss   sourpuss   sour puss *n.* A person who is or who looks disagreeable; one who habitually frowns or scowls and seldom smiles. 1947: "Out front will be the regular assortment of first-night sourpusses and professional runners down." Phila. *Bulletin*, Dec. 2, 59. 1951: "He has a serious face and he never smiles. People think he's a sour puss." N.Y. *Daily News*, Aug. 30, C11/3.

sour-top   *n.* = **sour-puss**. *Not common.*

souse   *n.* **1** A drunkard; a known habitual drunkard. 1949: "Yer old man was a souse and a chaser." Movie, *Mr. Soft Touch*. 1958: "A wonderful thyroid substance called triiodothyronine sobered up the souse in 30 minutes." P. Sann, N.Y. *Post*, Apr. 13, M6. *Very common since c1900.* **2** A drunken spree; a jag. 1905: "We think of the many beautiful souses we have [had]. . . ." McHugh, *Search Me*, 12. *Archaic.* → **3** Fig., a state of intoxication, from whatever cause. 1928: "Economic and religious saviors give [man] a new kind of emotional souse." B. de Casseres in *Amer. Mercury*, May 99/1. *Not common.*   **—d**   *adj.* Drunk. See Appendix, Drunk. 1926: "Stews who sought to have the world accept them at their soused face-value." G. J. Nathan in *Amer. Mercury*, Jan., 105/2. 1948: "He'll get soused." Movie, *They Live by Night. Used as a pred. adj. about three times as freq. as attrib. Prob. the most common sl. word for "drunk." Since c1900; very common by c1915.*

soused to the gills = **soused**.

southpaw   south-paw   *n.* **1** The left hand or arm of a left-handed person, esp. a baseball pitcher. 1885: "Morris' quick throw over to first with that

south-paw of his. . . ." *Sporting Life*, Jan. 14, 4/3. → **2** A left-handed baseball player, esp. a pitcher. 1908: "The management has selected a 'south-paw' to man first base." R. L. Hartt in *Atlantic Monthly*, Aug., 225/2. 1951: "Southpaw Warren Spahn pitched his 17th victory. . . ." AP, Aug. 27. *Since c1890.* → **3** Any left-handed person. *adj.* Left-handed. 1951: "[Randy Turpin] has switched to a southpaw stance for his 11th round of boxing against Phillips." H. Fullerton, AP, Sept. 6.

south with [something], go   To steal or abscond with something. 1943: [steal] "She went south with a couple of silk pieces." D. Hammett, *Asst. Murderer*. 1948: [abscond with] "If I should run across any manuscript . . . I won't go south with it." Evans, *Halo for Satan*, 14.

sow   *n.* **1** A nickel. → **2** Any coin. *Never common. Prob. from the French "sou."* **3** Any young, unkempt female, esp. if promiscuous. *Some student use.* Cf. **pig.**

sow-belly   *n.* Bacon or fat salt pork. *Dial. and colloq.*

So what?   An expression showing lack of interest, or inability or refusal to comprehend the pertinence or enthusiasm generated by a speech, act, object, or idea.

sozzled   *adj.* Drunk. *Since c1880.*

space bandit   A press agent. *Because they try to get their clients' names in the limited space of newspaper columns. Theater use since c1940.*

spade   *n.* [derog.] A Negro, esp. a very dark-skinned Negro. 1931: "The plutes compromised with the blacks/ the spades inhabited Harlem and let the/ ofays have Wall Street to themselves." Bob Brown in *Amer. Mercury*, Dec., 407/2. 1956: "A 'spade' is a Negro." S. Longstreet, *The Real Jazz Old and New*, 147. *Common since c1920.   v.t.* To shovel. 1929: "He's spadin' diamonds." G. Jones.

spades, in   Par excellence; in the extreme; doubled. 1934: "He is a bum in spades. . . ." Runyon.

spaghetti   *n.* **1** [derog.] An Italian; a Latin; a Latin American. See **spig. 2** Fire hose, esp. when lines of it lie scattered around a fire. 1945: "A [fireman] will always 'Lay Spaghetti' when running out the hose." Advt. in *New Yorker*, Mar. 31, 41/3. **3** A specif. type of television antenna and antenna lead-in wire. *Since c1950.*

spaginzy [derog.]   *n.* A Negro. 1956:

"... A 'spaginzy' is a Negro." S. Long-street, *The Real Jazz Old and New*, 147. *Not common.* Cf. **spade.**

spam cluster The shoulder patch of the Army Service Forces. *From "Spam," trade name of a canned meat. Some W.W.II Army use.*

Spanish athlete One who "throws the bull." *A pun based on the Spanish love of bull-fighting. Not common.*

Spanish-walk *v.t.* To force a person to walk by holding him, as by the coat collar and the seat of the pants, and pushing him in the desired direction, esp. out a doorway. 1949: "Mike Spanish-walked him swiftly across the little place and out the door." Burnett, *Jungle*, 54. Cf. **walk Spanish.**

spank *v.t.* To defeat, esp. in a game.

spanking new Brand new, completely new.

spare *n.* In bowling, the situation of having knocked down all the pins with two consecutive rolls of the ball.

spare tire *n.* 1 Excess fatty tissue in the region of the human waist. *From the resemblance of such a roll of fat to the extra or spare tire carried in an automobile for emergency use. Jocular and euphem. use since c1925.* 2 An extra person, one whose presence is not needed or wanted, as a fifth person at a bridge game. *Since c1945.* → 3 Any dull, disliked individual; a bore.

spark *v.i., v.t.* 1 To court. 1813: *DAE. From "spark it."* → 2 To kiss and caress; to indulge in sexual play. *Replaced "spark it" c1865; shared popularity with "spoon" c1900–c1920 and with "pet" c1920; replaced by "neck" c1935.* 3 To lead, esp. to provide inspiration, encouragement, and an example to one's co-workers or team-mates. 1956: "Willy Mays sparked an eighth inning Giant [baseball team] drive by stealing second [base]." AP, July 21. Cf. **spark-plug.**

—ing *n.* Courting. 1804: *DAE.* 1937: "Known as petting, necking, or sparking in the old days." *Ladies' Home Jour.*, Sept. 20. *Archaic.*

spark it *v.i., v.t.* = **spark.** *Since c1780; superseded by "spark" by c1865. Still some dial. and archaic use.*

sparkler *n.* 1 A diamond; a diamond ring; any gem or gem-set jewelry. 2 A long, thin firecracker which, when lighted, emits a shower of silver or gold sparks for a fairly long time. *The safest and least noisy firecracker, it is preferred by parents but not by children. Children's use since c1935.*

spark-plug spark plug *n.* A member of a group, esp. of a sports team, who leads other members by providing inspiration, encouragement, or a good example. 1943: "Mr. Fadiman himself is a splendid spark-plug." H. A. Smith, *Putty Knife*, 141. Cf. **spark.**

sparks *n.sing.* A ship's radio operator; often a nickname. 1958: "I was in the radio room sending the Captain's message when he came in and yelled, 'Hey, Sparks, do you know we're landing in France?' " *Oral*, Alfred F. Hoyt, ex-merchant marine radio operator, during *W.W.II. USN and maritime use since c1915.*

sparky *adj.* Wonderful, delightful. *Said of a person. Not common.*

sparrow cop A policeman in disfavor with his superiors and assigned to a park to guard the grass. *Not common.*

sparrowgrass *n.* Asparagus. *By folk ety. Dial.*

speak *n.* 1 = **speakeasy.** 1930: "Better grade speaks in Times Square...." *Variety* quoted in *Bookman*, 398/1. → 2 A cheap saloon. 1941: "All they give you in these speaks is smoke." Cain, *M. Pierce*, 26. 1950: "A sawdust speak on Third Ave." Billy Rose, *synd. newsp. col.*, Jan 18. *v.i.* To express oneself well by any means other than speaking, esp. by playing far-out music adroitly. 1957: "He sure did speak—He played well." E. Horne, *For Cool Cats and Far-Out Chicks. Some far-out use.*

—o *n.* = **speakeasy.** 1931: "One thing that puts a speako over...." J. Sayre, *Hex*, 415. 1941: "... Making the grand tour of all the speakos he knows. ..." Cain, *M. Pierce*, 25.

speakeasy speak-easy *n.* 1 A saloon, bar, restaurant, or nightclub selling alcoholic beverages without a license or after legal hours; esp. an unlicensed saloon selling bootlegged whisky. 1931: *Speakeasy Stories*, a magazine. 1944: "It had been a speak-easy once." Ford, *Phila. Murder*, 105. *Since c1900, very common during Prohibition.* Cf. **free-and-easy.** 2 A silencer on a gun, esp. a Maxim silencer. *Some underworld use c1930.*

speaker *n.* A gun. *Some Negro underworld use.*

speakie *n.* A movie with a sound track, a talkie. *Movie use c1925.* See Appendix, **—ie** endings.

speak [one's] piece 1 To propose marriage. *Since c1920.* 2 To complain, to enumerate one's grievances. *Colloq.*

spear *v.t.* To beg; to accept free

drinks or food. *Some use since c1915; orig. hobo use.* *n.* A fork.

spec *n.* **1** Commercial speculation. 1794: *DAE.* → **2** A speculator, esp. a speculator in land or in theater tickets to successful plays. 1943: "All the important ticket specs are known to the box-office men." M. Zolotow in *SEP*, Nov. 20. **3** The spectacle that opens a circus performance; the grand entry of the circus troupe into the main tent. 1949: "Mrs. Webster rode an elephant in the 'spec.' " H. Basso in *New Yorker*, Nov. 5, 61. *Orig. circus use.* *v.i.* To memorize, esp. to memorize a lesson or the correct answer to a test question. *Some student use since c1935.*

special *n.* A very large, highly spiced, all beef frankfurter; an old-fashioned, home-made style of frankfurter with an honest beef and garlic flavor, as opposed to the mild mass-produced hot dog. *Orig. by people of German and Jewish descent. This all-beef frankfurter is assoc. with kosher delicatessens.*

speck bum A completely helpless, degenerate bum. *Hobo use since c1920.*

specks *n.pl.* **1** = specs. **2** Pepper, as used on food. *Some W.W.II Army use, not common.*

specs *n.pl.* **1** The common abbr. for "spectacles"; eyeglasses. 1878: "We'll have to put on magnifying specs." Newsp., Pottsville, Pa. 1913: "Where's my old specs, Maw?" *SEP*, Jan. 25, 11. *Now somewhat archaic.* **2** The common abbr. for "specifications" in industry and manufacturing. 1958: "The specs for the book called for coated stock." *Oral*, a production manager for a book publishing firm. *Common during and since W.W.II.* See Appendix, Shortened Words.

spectacular *n.* A lavishly produced television show, usu. featuring color transmission, many famous entertainers, lasting an hour and a half or longer, and not part of a regularly scheduled program. *Television use since c1955; now generally known.*

speed *n.* A person with a reputation for being fast, wild, undisciplined, or daring; a hedonist; one who does not observe social conventions or seek a reputation of honor, sobriety, or chastity. 1920: "She was accustomed to be thus followed by her past. She was a 'Speed,' was she? Well—let them find out." "He learned that some of the boys she went with in Baltimore were 'terrible speeds' and came to dances in states of artificial stimulation; most of them were twenty or so, and drove alluring red Stutzes. A good half of them seemed to have already flunked out of various schools and colleges." F. S. Fitzgerald, *This Side of Paradise*, 71. *Wide c1920 student use.*

—y *n.* **1** A delivery boy; a messenger; often used as a nickname. **2** A special-delivery letter or package. *Some post office and office use since c1940.* *adj.* Fast; immoral; dissipated; loose-living.

speedball **speed-ball** *n.* **1** A fast-working, efficient person. *Colloq.* **2** Cheap, potent wine; a glass of such wine. *Hobo use since c1920.* **3** An injection of a mixture of, or the mixture of, cocaine and morphine, to increase the charge or kick. *Narcotic addict use since c1930.*

speed-boy *n.* A fast-running, agile athlete. *Sportswriter use.*

speed merchant A fast, agile athlete. 1951: "[He] had a glass arm and he certainly was no speed merchant." Van Sickle in Ithaca (N.Y.) *Journal*, Aug. 9, 21/1.

speed-up *n.* An act or instance of increasing speed; esp. an order for increased production in a factory or office. 1934: "Colloq." *Web.*

spell out To explain something step by step, as one spells a word. 1943: "Are you a schoolboy I have to spell out everything for you?" Wolfert, *Underworld*, 115. 1951: ". . . Creation of a commission of distinguished citizens to spell out the difference between right and wrong in public offices." G. M. Kelly, AP, Nov. 2.

sphere *n.* **1** A baseball. 1951: "A 27-year-old who smacked the sphere as [Walter] Dropo did last season." H. Grayson, NEA, June 30. *Since c1910.* **2** A golf ball; any ball. *Since c1920.*

spheroid *n.* A baseball. 1951: "Hitting the ball is just as important as slugging the spheroid." AP, Sept. 19. *Not as old or as common as "sphere."*

spic **spick** **spig** **spiggoty** [derog.] *n.* **1** An Italian; an American of Italian ancestry. 1941: "Wop or spig. . . ." Cain, *M. Pierce*, 91. *Shortened from "spaghetti," reinforced by the traditional phrase "No spika da English." Never as common as "wop"; since c1915 this meaning seldom used.* → **2** A Spaniard; an American of Spanish ancestry; hence a Puerto Rican, a Mexican, a person from Latin America. 1934: "Don't go dumb on me, spig [a Mexican]." Chandler, *Finger Man*, 49. 1943: "Female spick [Spaniard], short, fat. . . ." Wolfert,

Underworld, 251. *Since c1915 this meaning has been by far the most common and the most common derog. word = Spanish or of Spanish ancestry. With the increase in the number of Puerto Ricans moving to the U.S., esp. to N.Y.C., since c1940, the word has tended to mean "Puerto Rican" on the eastern coast. With the influx of Mexican migratory workers into the U.S. Southwest since c1945, the word has tended to mean "Mexican" in that section of the country. Since most of the Central and South Americans in the U.S. are tourists or businessmen possessing prestige, wealth, or culture, this derog. term is seldom applied to them. As the meaning shifted from "Italian" to "Spaniard", c1915, the variant "spiggoty" has become obs., and "spig" has become archaic. → 3* A German. 1926: "... Spiggoty [a German]." Stallings & Anderson, *What Price Glory*, II. *Some W.W.I use. Obs.* → **4** A Filipino, Hawaiian, or other Pacific island native. *A little USN and Marine Corps use W.W.I–c1940. Obs.* Cf. **ğook.** → **5** Any foreigner or one of foreign birth or ancestry. *Not common.*

spic and span   **1** A couple, as lovers, of which the male or female is Puerto Rican and the other a Negro. **2** Mixed Puerto Rican and Negro, as a neighborhood. *From "spic" and the abbr. "Span."* = *Spanish, but based on the well-known phrase "spick-and-span" = new or clean, plus the pop. trademarked detergent "Spic and Span."*

spick   *n.* = **spic.**

spider   *n.* **1** A silk worker. *Some use since c1920.* **2** A small, round, plastic insert placed in the center hole of a phonograph record so that it will fit a smaller-diameter record-player spindle. *Used to fit older records, with large center holes, to modern narrow spindles made for LP records. Since c1945.*

spiel   *n.* **1** An eloquent speech, talk, or story used to persuade or convince the listener; esp. such a talk that exaggerates or purposely confuses the facts; an emotional sales talk; a line, a pitch. 1907: "But wait till my turn comes; I'll give his honor a 'spiel.' " J. London, *My Life. Common since c1900. From the Ger. "spiel" = play.* **2** Specif., a circus barker's talk on sideshow attractions; also, a pitchman's sales talk. **3** Specif., advertising copy to be read on the radio. *Since c1940.*   **—er**   *n.* **1** An eloquent, persuasive talker; one who gives a spiel. 1918: "A real accomplished spieler." M. Doolittle in *Outlook*, Nov.,

433. **2** A circus barker; a pitchman. **3** A radio or television announcer, esp. one who reads commercials. See Appendix, —er ending.   **—ing**   *n.* Giving a spiel.

spiff   *adj.* = **spiffy.** *c1910. Not common. n.* A bonus paid to a retail salesman for selling old or hard-to-sell merchandise. *Some retail store use.*

spiffed   *adj.* Drunk. 1950: "He was spiffed." Movie, *Harvey. Orig. northwestern U.S. use, c1915. Not common.*

spiffed out   Dressed up in one's best clothes. *From "spiffy."*

spifflicated   *adj.* Drunk. 1930: "The 'stag at eve' had become, in the order named, lit, spifflicated, and at long last pie-eyed. . . ." C. Bragdon in *Outlook*, Oct., 301. 1952: "A slightly spifflicated gent. . . ." H. Gardner, N.Y. *Her Trib.*, Aug. 22, 15/4. *Since c1920.*

spiffy   *adj.* Splendid, esp. of splendid, fashionable, or colorful appearance; snazzy. 1950: "New Model Buggy for Amish Is Spiffy." Headline, Cleveland *Plain Dealer*, Mar. 25, 6. *More common in Eng. than U.S.*   *adv.* Well. 1941: "They don't translate so spiffy." "Bugs" Baer.

spig   *n.* = **spic.**

spiggoty   *n.* = **spic.**

spike   *v.t.* **1** To fortify a drink by adding an alcoholic beverage. *Since c1900; common since c1920.* → **2** To add poison to a drink. 1950: "The murder syndicate began to spike his drinks." Billy Rose, *synd. newsp. col.*, Jan. 18. *Not common.* **3** = **spike [someone's] ğun. 4** In baseball, to cut or injure another player with the spikes on one's playing shoes.   *n.* A prison. *A little underworld use, c1930. More common in Eng.*   **—r**   *n.* A glass of lemon phosphate. *Some lunch-counter use, c1930.*

spiked beer   **1** Beer that has been artificially aged, as by being subjected to an electric charge. *The most common use.* **2** A glass of beer to which whisky has been added.

spike [someone's] ğun   To stop another from reaching a goal; to spoil someone's chance for success; to deny another pleasure; to punish. *From the sabotaging technique of driving a spike into the vent of a gun barrel, to prevent firing of the piece.*

spill   *v.t.* **1** To cause a person to fall; to throw, trip, tackle, or push another so that he falls. 1893: "[A Mississippi steamboat mate to a traveler:] If you don't tote your plunder off that gang-plank right smart, I'll spill you in the drink." *Atlantic Monthly*, Mar., 425/2. *Colloq.* **2** To disclose information; to confess or inform. 1927: "That's all I'm spilling." Hammett, *Blood Money*, 25. *v.i.* **1** To talk, esp. to enumerate grievances or give one's candid opinion. → **2** To inform; to confess, to squeal or sing. 1951: "[He] spilled to the crime commission." Movie, *The Racket.*   *n.* A railroad station. *Some underworld use c1930.*

spill [one's] guts   1 To tell everything one knows. *Orig. hobo use, c1920.* **2** To inform. 1949: "You spilled your guts." Movie, *Red Light.*

spill-quirley   *n.* A cigarette. *Some archaic Western use.*

spill the beans   To reveal a secret inadvertently; to spoil a plan or the like by saying the wrong thing. *Colloq. Since c1920.*

spin   *v.i.*, To dance. *c1935 jive use.*   *v.t.* **1** To place a phonograph record on a record player turntable and play it. **2** To deceive; to lie to; to break a promise to. 1950: "I don't like to have folks spin me. You know what I mean?" "I wouldn't spin you." Starnes, *Another Mug*, 27. *Not common.*

spinach   *n.* **1** A beard. *Since c1900.* Cf. **lip fern.** **2** Money. *Never as common as "cabbage" or "lettuce."* **3** Nonsense, bunk, boloney, cant, exaggeration, lies. 1933: *Fashion Is Spinach.* Title of a book by Elizabeth Hawes. *From a Carl Rose cartoon in the "New Yorker," Dec. 8, 1928, which showed a mother saying to her child, "It's broccoli," and the child replying, "I say it's spinach and the hell with it." The line "I say it's spinach" became a pop. expression.* 1951: "You could put up with this spinach." R. Bissell, *Stretch on the River*, 123. *Often used as an epithet of scorn or abuse.*

spine   *n.* The flat board at the peak of a railroad freight car's roof, on which hobos and trainworkers walk. 1956: "You could get through Alabama all right provided you didn't stand on the spine like a tourist and wave at the sheriff. And stayed off the A. & W. P." N. Algren, *A Walk on the Wild Side*, 17.

spin in   To go to bed; to take a nap. *Some use since W.W.I. Not as common as "turn in."*

spink   *v.t.* To defeat. 1910: "Two out. One more and we spink 'em." Johnson, *Varmint*, 84. *Never common. Prob. as a variant of "spank."*

spinner   *n.* A truck-driver. *Truck-driver use.*

spitball   *n.* **1** A wad of paper chewed into a small ball or impregnated with saliva, so that it is compact and hard, and can be thrown. *Small boy and young student use. Throwing such spitballs, when the teacher isn't looking, is a pop. pastime of mischievous students. Now somewhat archaic.* → **2** = **spitter.**

spitbox   *n.* A spittoon. 1827: *DAE.*

spitter   *n.* A pitched baseball, which the pitcher has spat upon, in order to make it harder to hit; such a pitch. 1956: "... A controversial pitch known as a 'spitter.'" N.Y. *Post*, Aug. 2, 44.

spiv   *n.* One who profits by obtaining (often illegally) and selling rationed or scarce items during wartime; a merchant on the black market. *Some W.W.II use, orig. and mainly Eng. = thief.*

spivot   *n.* A young woman. 1939: "Well, I had this little mouse, a very nice little spivot that belongs to the college crowd at the Northwestern U." O'Hara, *Pal Joey*, 36. *Not common.*

spizzerinktum   spizzerinctum   *n.* Vigor; pep. 1950: "The fellow who put foresight, science, and spizzerinktum into their business. ..." H. E. Babcock in *Amer. Agric.*, Mar., 4. 1953: "'Spizzerinctum,' which was a word that was popular in some of the older and snappier circles along the Eastern seaboard." St. C. McKelway, *New Yorker*, Feb. 21., 32/2.

spla   *n.* Whipped cream. *Some lunch-counter use, c1930.*

splash   *n.* **1** A bowl of soup. *Some lunch-counter use.* **2** Water; a glass of water. 1950: "Only Scotch and splash." Starnes, *Another Mug*, 112. **3** Water; an ocean or lake; a bath. **4** A remarkable success or newsworthy action or statement leading to fame; noteworthy success or acceptance. *Usu. in "to make a splash."* **5** A military plane shot down in combat. *Some W.W.II Air Force use.*   *v.i.* To bathe.   *v.t.* **1** To publicize someone or something widely. **2** To shoot down an enemy airplane. *Some W.W.II Air Force use.*

splice   *v.t.* To marry. 1939: "Crying to be spliced." J. Auslander, *Hell in Harness*, 6. *Used as early as 1751 by Smollett, pop. by newsp. columnist Walter Winchell.*

splice the main brace   To drink whisky; to have or offer a drink of whisky. 1850: *White-Jacket*, by Herman Melville. 1940: "I can tell him enough

Navy yarns to fill a book—provided the main brace is spliced occasionally." J. H. Jennings in *Life*, Nov. 18, 6.

splinter *n.* A very thin person. 1953: "But lookit this splinter, with no more hips than a starvin' snake!" J. R. Williams, *synd. cartoon*, "Out Our Way," Feb. 14. *Not common.*

split *n.* **1** A small bottle of wine or beer, usu. containing six or eight ounces. *Colloq.* **2** In bowling, any pattern of pins left upright after the ball has been bowled, in which pattern two or more standing pins are separated by enough space so that they cannot be knocked down directly with one ball. *v.i.* To leave a place or gathering; fig., to split oneself off from a group or place. *Used by cool, beat, and rock-and-roll members since c1955.* Cf. **cut out.**

split one An order for a banana split. *Some lunch-counter use in relaying orders since c1935.*

splits, the *n.sing.* The act of lowering one's body to the ground by spreading one's legs apart, while keeping the legs and body rigid and the knees unbent.

split-up *n.* **1** A quarrel ending with each of two persons going his own way. 1837: *DAE.* 1929: "Me and the old man had a split-up." Burnett, *Little Caesar*, 182. → **2** A divorce; the legal separation of a married couple.

split week **1** A week in which a performer works several consecutive days in one theater or town and the rest of the week in another. *Theater use.* → **2** In the card game of poker, a straight with the middle card missing.

sploud *adj.* Excited, high-spirited, happy. *Not common.*

Spokane *n.* Pork-and-beans. *Archaic hobo use.*

spon *n.* Money. *Some use c1900. From "spondulics."* **—dulics spondulix** *n.pl.* Money. 1860: "Spangles and spondulics were in direct ratio to each other." Phila. *Press*, Jan. 5. 1910: "He's just loaded with the spondulix." Johnson, *Varmint*, 60. *Archaic.* *v.t.* To enrich; to pay, loan, or give money to another. *c1870–c1900; obs.*

sponge *n.* **1** A parasitic person; a moocher; one who lives off or takes advantage of another's generosity; a chronic borrower. *Used by Shakespeare, 1598.* 1922: "You avoided college boys, sponges. . . ." F. S. Fitzgerald, "All the Sad Young Men," reprinted in *The American Twenties*, 131. *Colloq.* Cf. **free loader.** **2** A drunkard; one who

frequently takes large quantities of whisky. 1952: "You sponge!" Movie, *The Clown* *v.i.*, *v.t.* To borrow, esp. without the intention of repaying. *Colloq.* **—r** *n.* A parasitic person; a sponge. 1894: "There is one more city tramp that I must catalogue. It is the 'sponger.' " J. Flynt.

spoof *v.i.*, *v.t.* To hoax, to tease, to kid. 1914: "He was just spoofing." S. Lewis, *Our Mr. Wrenn*, 128. *n.* A hoax; an instance of teasing, a joke. 1929: ". . . As the name of a game . . . then as a general name for humbug or hoax, 'spoof' is traced back to the comedian A. Roberts." Otto Jespersen.

spook *n.* **1** [derog.] A Negro. *White man use.* **2** [derog.] A white man. 1947: "[Spoken by a Negro:] What would I want an oil-hair spook for?" N. Algren, "The Face." *Negro use. Although the term has been said to have orig. with Negro jazz musicians, or even Harlem jive groups, it is much older.* **3** A girl, esp. an ugly or shy girl. c1942: "Are you having a spook for the Yale mingle?" *Princeton Alumni Weekly. Not common.* **4** An insurance or safety officer. *Truckdriver use. Not common.* **5** A quiet, introspective, introverted student, esp. one on the fringe of an intellectual group; a creep. *Wide student use c1945.* → **6** One who, though boring and shy, tries to gain entry into a group or social set by currying favor with its members. *Some student use.* **7** A reckless, dangerous auto driver. *Not common.* *v.t.* **1** To scare; to haunt; to follow, esp. in a sly, sneaky way. **2** To impart bad luck. *Student use.* **—ed** *adj.* **1** Burdened with ill fortune or bad luck. *Fig., as if a ghost or spook has hexed one. Some use since c1935; fairly common student use c1945.* **2** Uneasy, fearful, nervous, esp. without a reason or known cause. *Fig., as if one felt an intangible presence.* **—erican** *n.* A person of Puerto Rican and American Negro parentage. *Some N.Y.C. use since c1950. From welding "spook" and "Rican."*

spoon *v.i.* To demonstrate affection, said of engaged or dating couples; to kiss and fondle; to neck; to pet. *c1900 very popular; now archaic and replaced by "neck" and "pet."* See **greasy spoon.** **—er** *n.* One who spoons; a lover. *Archaic.* **—y** *adj.* **1** Romantic, affectionate; displaying affection, as by spooning or petting. 1924: "She stroked my hand and I guess we got kind of spoony." R. Lardner, "How to Write

Short Stories," reprinted in *The American Twenties*, 53. → **2** In love with. See Appendix, —y ending. **3** Neat in appearance. *West Point use.* **4** Silly; weak. **5** Excellent; swell. *W.W.II Army use. Not common.*

spoon up   To put in order; to clean up. *West Point use.*

spoops   spoopsy   *n.* A weak, silly, foolish fellow. *c1850, college use; obs.*

sport   *n.* **1** A handsome, generous, carefree, wisecracking, stylishly dressed roué; an irresponsible lover of wine, women, gambling, and gaiety; one who is eager for a good time, no matter how much it costs or how many responsibilities he must ignore to have it; one obsessed with creating the impression of being carefree, generous, and having fun. 1895 [1947]: "He was . . . 'a sport from the word go. Women, wine, the coursing track, all that went to make up the life of a genuine sport was his.'" Quoted in *San Fran. Murders*, 110. c1915 [1954]: "Those sports gave me so much [money] that I had to borrow hats to hold it all." L. Armstrong, *Satchmo, My Life in New Orleans*, 48. 1950: "Sports like Willie the Pleaser, Chinee Morris (the best-looking guy in the District), Ed Mochez (who left a hundred and ten suits when he died). . . . These guys were all gamblers, and had all the best women." A. Lomax, *Mr. Jelly Roll*, 46f. → **2** A term of somewhat disrespectful and belligerent address to a stranger. *Archaic.* **3** An agreeable, accommodating, fair person; regular fellow. 1950: "I just want to be a good sport and get along with people." H. Boyle, AP, July 20.   **—ing**   *n.* The act or an instance of acting like a sport, of visiting bars, brothels, gambling casinos, and the like. c1920 [1954]: "The night Mayann and I went sporting . . . we went to Spanol's tonk . . . making the rounds." L. Armstrong, *Satchmo, My Life in New Orleans*, 199.   **—y**   *adj.* Garish; flamboyant; unrestrained. *Usu. said of personalities, clothing, and/or automobiles.*

sporting house   A brothel. 1939: "Sporting House Rag." Title of a jazz song by Jelly Roll Morton.

sport the oak   sport one's oak   To close the door of one's room to show that one does not wish to be disturbed; fig., to keep one's confidences to oneself; to refuse to share a good time. *Some c1900 use; from Brit. univ. sl.*

spot   *n.* **1** A small portion of whisky. **2** A short sleep. **3** A restaurant, bar,

nightclub, or other public place of entertainment. **4** A map. *Some c1940 underworld use.* **5** A little of something; a bit. *More common in Eng. than in U.S.* **6** A banknote of low denomination. *But only when used in the following:* **deuce-spot** *or* **two-spot** = *a* $2 *bill;* **five-spot** = *a* $5 *bill;* **ten-spot** = *a* $10 *bill. The term is never used with currency of larger denominations, prob. because larger bills represent more than a "spot" of money. See* **C note.** **7** A short prison sentence; "years" when preceded by a number. *Thus a* **one-spot** = *a one-year sentence; a* **two-spot** = *a two-year term in prison, and so forth.* 1907: "He had done 'one,' 'two,' and 'five spots' in various . . . penitentiaries. . . ." Jack London, *My Life.* **8** Any dangerous or difficult situation. See **put on the spot.** *v.t.* **1** To put on the spot. → **2** To kill. 1939: "That's enough to spot a guy for." Chandler, *Big. Sleep*, 74. *Underworld use.*

spot, hit the   To satisfy; esp. to satisfy the appetite or the taste; said of food or drink.

spot, on the   **1** In danger; in a dangerous position; in peril of death. *Obs. Prob. from the old pirate practice of using the ace of spades playing card, having one printed "spot," as a threat or notice to an informer or coward that he was to be killed.* **2** In danger of meeting with failure, being embarrassed, or losing an opportunity to succeed. **3** Called upon to produce successful results within a short duration of time, or under some other handicap.

spot, put on the   **1** To murder. *Obs. Prob. from the old pirate practice of drawing cards to see who would perform a distasteful or dangerous task, such as the murder of an informer or coward. This use later became that given under the entry* **on the spot. 2** See **on the spot,** all uses.

spotlight   *n.* Fig., that which reveals or brings something to the attention of the public. 1956: "A bright spotlight on some of the greatest talents in the Duke's band." From an advt. for a phonograph recording by Duke Ellington and his band, *Metronome*, Apr., 34.

spots   *n.pl.* **1** Musical notes, as printed on sheet music. *Some musician use.* 1948: "I can learn to play the spots." F. Brown. *Dead Ringer*, 28. **2** Leopards; spotted horses. *Circus use.* **3** The picture cards, jacks, queens, kings, and aces, of a deck of cards. *Archaic.* **4** A deck of playing cards. *Archaic.*

spread   *n.* **1** A newspaper. *c1850, orig.*

underworld use. → **2** Specif., facing pages in an open newspaper, magazine, or book. → **3** An article or a writeup in a newspaper or magazine, esp. when favorable to a person or idea; advertising, publicity. **4** A feast or dinner. *Colloq.*

spread for [someone] [taboo] To enter into or be willing be enter into coitus with a man for either romantic or monetary reasons.

spread it on thick To exaggerate; to flatter. *c1865 to present.*

spring *v.t.* **1** To obtain another's release from jail; to release from jail; to pardon, to parole, or help to escape. c1920 [1954]: "Whenever a crowd of fellows were rounded up in a raid on a gambling house, the proprietor knew how to 'spring' them, that is, get them out of jail." L. Armstrong, *Satchmo, My Life in New Orleans*, 126. 1949: "I don't even ask how come you're in. I just come to spring you." N. Algren, *Man with the Golden Arm*, 29. **2** To treat a person to food or drink. **3** To do something so that it will be a surprise. 1949: "John L. Lewis is preparing to spring a dramatic move...." Lowell Thomas, radio news program, Nov. 1. *v.i.* **1** To obtain a release from jail; to escape from jail. **2** To begin working; to open for business. *Pitchman and some carnival use.* *n.* **1** A loan of money. → **2** A raise in salary. *Not common.* **—er** *n.* **1** A bondsman. **2** A physical education instructor. *W.W.II USN use; not common.*

spring chicken **1** A young inexperienced person. *Always used in "no spring chicken."* 1907 [1894]: "I was no spring chicken in the way of the world...." Jack London, *My Life. c1880.* **2** A young woman. *Always used in "[she's] no spring chicken." The most common use.*

spring fever A feeling of melancholy, inducing romantic daydreaming and reducing one's working efficiency, which young people traditionally have during the first warm days of spring; a feeling of melancholy inspired by the first days of spring, when one wishes to be wandering lazily out of doors rather than working in the material world. *Colloq.*

spring with To introduce something new to one's friends or to the public. 1950: "Eddie suddenly squares his debts and springs with a new car. ..." DeBaun, 71.

sprout *n.* A young son or daughter. 1951: "A girl out your way has married

... and is coming home with a sprout." *Harper's*, July, 36/1.

sprout wings **1** To do a good deed. **2** To die.

spruce *n.* A sucker. *Some c1930 use; obs.*

spruce spruce up *v.i.* To make oneself neat in appearance. 1900. "He spruced around their chambers, preparatory to going downtown. ...." Dreiser, *Carrie*, 123. *Colloq.* *v.t.* To clean up or make a room neat; to redecorate. *Colloq.*

spruce about To go out into society; to step out; to go stepping. 1900: "Since his money-feathers were beginning to grow again he felt like sprucing about." Dreiser, *Carrie*, 228. *Not common.*

sprung Drunk. *c1835.*

spud *n.* **1** A spade. *Dial.* **2** A potato. *Colloq.* *v.i., v.t.* To spade; to dig. 1952: "To people in many sections of the country SPUD is just another name for potato, but the meaning in Texas oil language is to spud an oil well—to dig the first few feet." J. Randolph, *Texas Brags*, 54.

spudge around To move or work fast; to be alert, active. 1920: "If she would only spudge around, get her work done. ..." *Scribner's*, Aug., 247.

Sput sput *n.* = **Sputnik.** 1957: "Sput 2 No Surprise [headline:] News of Russia's second successful satellite launching today came as no surprise to American builders. ..." N.Y. *Daily News*, Nov. 4.

Sputnik Sputnick *n.* A man-made earth satellite. *When Russia launched the first such satellite in Oct., 1957, U.S. newspapers quickly termed it a "Sputnik" or "Sputnik 1," from the jocular or even "cute" sound of the word, implying "sput" from "sputter" plus the diminutive "—nik." The word is actually a corruption of the Russian sl. word for the satellite and = "little fellow traveler" ("fellow traveler" in space and "fellow traveler" in communism).*

squab *n.* A girl or young woman. *Some use since c1925.* See **chick, quail.**

squack [derog.] *n.* A native girl of the Pacific. *W.W.II USN use.*

squad = **goon squad.**

squadrol *n.* A policeman; a group of policemen. *Some underworld use.*

square *n.* **1** A full meal; a satisfying, filling meal. 1894: "I've had my three squares every day." J. Flynt. *Still common.* **2** A person scorned because he is not in the know or, esp., not cognizant of, wise to, or aware of the modern interests, activities, groups, fashions, or fads which the speaker considers vital; one who is or persists in being unworldly, unsophisticated, naïve, old-fashioned, ignorant of current trends and interests, or unenlightened; a patron considered as a sucker; one easy to deceive, trick, or victimize because of his lack of worldly wisdom or knowledge of modern attitudes; one who accepts or believes without question all the pop. cultural, ethical, political, religious, and social rationalizations and mendacity; orig. and specif., one who is not aware of, or has no, or is probably incapable of feeling, sympathy toward or appreciation or understanding of bop and, later, cool and far-out music, or of bop, cool, far-out, and beat attitudes or fashions; one who is not, and is incapable of being, hip; still later, one who has no sympathy for or understanding of teenage interests, esp. of rock-and-roll attitudes; one who accepts or likes commercial sentiment, sentimentality, and corn, esp. in music and entertainment; an uncritical spectator of entertainment and life, whose values, standards, and judgments are those popularly prevailing. 1943: "That G. L. [Guy Lombardo, orchestra leader] . . . strictly a square." M. Shulman, *Barefoot Boy with Cheek*, 90. 1949: "I can't sing. But sometimes I do a little vocal number for the squares." Mary Lou Williams, outstanding jazz pianist, quoted in N.Y. *Times*, Aug. 28, X5/5. 1956: "The 'squares,' the unenlightened, don't get it." S. Longstreet, *The Real Jazz Old and New*, 147. *A very little and late jive use; some Negro and prison use by c1940. Orig. the meanings solidified and the word pop. as a bop use c1946, with later cool use. Now common general jazz use, and teenage and student use. One of the most widely accepted words orig. pop. by bop and cool groups. Earlier evolution from such expressions as "squarehead" and "square John."* adj. **1** Fair; genuine, authentic; legal. 1932: "No matter what name . . . it is not his square name." Runyon, 7. *Usu. in such expressions as "square deal." Since the evolution of the second meaning, seldom applied to people.* **2** Not hip; possessing any or all of the traits of a square; accepted, patronized, defended, liked, or believed in by squares; of, by, or for squares; pertaining to squares. 1958: "One does not 'join' the hipsters. One

is hip or one is square." "You don't try to convert the square world, you don't enter into that sick rationality, you just ignore 'them.' " E. Burdick, *The Reporter*, Apr. 3, 31f. **3** Conventional, conforming; of, by, for, or pertaining to conventional people, tastes, or desires. *v.t.* To right a wrong; to make amends, as for a previously accomplished illegal, unethical, or unwanted action or result; lit and fig., to substitute or follow an unfair or disastrous deed with a fair, desirable, or successful one; to ask forgiveness for a bad or forbidden deed of someone, to calm another's anger; to re-establish one's good reputation with another. See **square the beef.**

square-head   squarehead   *n.* **1** [derog.] A Scandinavian. *c1910; colloq.* **2** [derog.] A German. *cW.W.II. Not common.* **3** A dull-witted, slow-thinking person. *Some student and child use since c1915.*

square John   square john   1 A self-righteous, easily victimized person. *Some underworld use since before c1930.* **2** A self-righteous person, i.e., one who is not a drug addict. *Some addict use since c1930.* **3** An honest man; one who can be trusted; a gentleman. 1951: "Which was good wages for a square john in those days." *I, Mobster*, 90.

square peg   A misfit. 1930: "They were square pegs who weren't succeeding in their respective positions." Lavine, *Third Degree*, 10.

square shooter   An honest, forthright person.

Squaresville   *n.* Conventional, conforming society. 1958: "The Innocent Nihilists Adrift in Squaresville" [title of article], Eugene Burdick, *The Reporter*, April 3, 31. *Orig. bop use, now associated with beat use.* See **square.** See Appendix, —ville ending.

square the beef   To stop or ease a complaint, as from a victim by returning his money or through influence with the police or politicians. *Orig. and mainly underworld use.*

squash   *n.* The face; usu. an ugly face or one with a displeased expression. 1950: "You should have piped the squash on that mark when he left the flattie all tapped out." AP, Los Angeles, Jan. 12.

squasho [derog.]   *n.* A Negro. See Appendix, —o ending.

squat [taboo]   *v.i.* **1** To sit, to sit down, esp. to sit down in order to pass the time with idle talk; to sit and relax. **2** To defecate. *Often used as a n. in "to take a squat"* = *to defecate.* See **doodle-e-squat, hot squat.**

squat hot Fig., to sit in the hot squat; to die in the electric chair. 1942: "If that crook ever squatted hot, that would be doing something for the country." Cain, *Love's Lovely Counterfeit*, 134.

squaw *n.* **1** A wife. *Colloq.* **2** An ugly prostitute. *W.W.II USN use.*

squawk *v.i.* **1** To complain; to find fault; to express dissatisfaction. *Colloq. since c1875.* **2** To inform. **3** To admit one's guilt, often implicating others; to squeal. 1929: "You know . . . Joe squawked. . . ." Burnett, *Little Caesar*, 158. *v.t.* To inspect another's work, the cleanliness of a barracks, or the like. *Some W.W.II use.* *n.* **1** A complaint. **2** One who complains. **3** A military inspection of barracks, uniforms, or arms. Some *W.W.II Army use.* **—er** *n.* One who complains; a habitual complainer. **—ie** *n.* = **talkie.** *Some early movie use.* See Appendix, —ie ending.

squawk box **1** A radio. *Archaic.* **2** A phonograph. *Not common.* **3** A public address system used to make announcements; the loudspeaker of such a system. *W.W.II USN use; general orders for a ship's crew were given through a public address system.*

squawk-stick *n.* = **squeak-stick.**

squeak *n.* **1** A helper; an assistant. **2** A complaint to the police. **—er** *n.* A close result; a close call.

squeak-stick *n.* A clarinet. *Archaic, never common; synthetic.*

squeal *v.i.* To complain; to protest; to inform to the police. *Since c1900; orig. and mainly underworld use.* *n.* **1** Ham; pork. **2** A complaint, as to the police. 1951: "I [detective] got a squeal to finish up." Movie, *Detective Story.* 1958: "Squeal—A Complaint." G. Y. Wells, *Station House Slang.* **—er** *n.* **1** A complainer; a fault-finder. *Since c1890.* **2** An informer. **3** A compass recorder that automatically shows the distance steered off course. *c1940; maritime use.*

squealer's mark Any scar or mark on the face, as if made by criminals or hoodlums in revenge for the bearer's having squealed.

squeegee **squeegie** *n.* **1** An important person. *Used derisively. Some c1910 use; obs.* **2** A jerk or goof. 1949: "In either sex, of course, only a 'squeegie'

would wear a hat." *Time*, Oct. 3, 37. *Some teenage use reported.* **—d** *adj.* Twisted; askew. *Never common.*

squeeze *n.* **1** Extortion. **2** Graft. See **put the squeeze on.** **—r** *n.* A person who does not give gratuities; a miser.

squeeze-box *n.* An accordion.

squeeze-gun *n.* A pressure riveter.

squeeze on [someone], put the To force, harass, or embarrass someone into doing something; to put the heat on [someone]. 1942: "She hired me to put the squeeze on Linda for a divorce." Chandler, *High Window*, 191.

squeeze one An order for a serving of orange juice. *Lunch-counter use in relaying a customer's order, common since c1930.*

squff *v.i.* To eat heavily; to stuff oneself with food.

squib *n.* **1** A short, usu. one paragraph, advertisement or notice as found in newspapers, magazines, and on boxes and labels of manufactured goods. → **2** A short, often witty, paragraph or notice in a newspaper or magazine, often used to fill up space. 1956: "I told it to a friend of mine, he writes these witty 'squibs.' . . ." W. Pegler, *synd. newsp. col.*, Apr. 30. → **3** A small exaggeration or lie. *Not common.* *v.i.* To speak a small exaggeration or lie; to fib.

squib off *v.t.* To murder. 1939: "The night Joe got squibbed off. . . ." Chandler, *Big Sleep*, 151. *Not common.*

squiffed *adj.* Drunk. *Since c1880; more common in Eng. than U.S.*

squiffy *adj.* Drunk. 1928: "Men of letters . . . will tell you about so-and-so's getting 'squiffy' at a dance. . . ." R. Lynd, *New Statesman*, Feb. 4. *c1890; considered somewhat affected.*

squire *v.t.* To escort a girl or woman; to court a girl or woman. 1956: "Guys who squire dames who lug these satchel-sized handbags have to wind up with cauliflower knees." J. Cannon, *Who Struck John?* 135.

squirrel *v.i.* To weave from side to side while driving a car, esp. a hot rod. *Common hot-rod use since c1950.* *v.t.* **1** To cache something. **2** To climb to the top of a railroad car; to set hand brakes from the roof of a railroad car. *Railroad and hobo use.* *n.* **1** Whisky. *Archaic and dial.* **2** A psychologist; a psychiatrist; one who examines "nuts." **3** A crazy person; an eccentric. 1943: "I seen some squirrels in my life, but you got 'em all beat." H. A. Smith, *Putty Knife*, 35. Cf. **food for the squirrels**. See **seam squirrel**. **4** An irrational, easily confused hot-rod driver; a novice or hesitant hot-rod driver. *Hot-rod use since c1950.* **5** A careless or reckless driver. *Some general teenage use since c1955.* **6** A person who would like to be accepted in a group; one who follows a group and tries to be like its members even though he does not belong and is not accepted. *Mainly teenage use, since c1955. Perh. from hot-rod v. use "squirrel" = to weave from side to side while driving, as most freq. done by a novice or incompetent driver.* **—ly** *adj.* Crazy; eccentric.

squirt *n.* **1** A short man; specif., a short, insignificant man; an insignificant, unimportant person. **2** A youth, esp. a callow, foppish, or presumptuous youth. **3** An easy, quick recitation. *Some archaic student use.* **4** A soda dispenser, a soda jerk. **5** A quarter; the sum of 25¢. *Because it is an insignificant sum.* → **6** Twenty-five dollars. **7** A jet airplane. *c1950.*

squish *n.* **1** Marmalade. **2** Nonsense; cant. *Neither use common.* **—y** *adj.* Sentimental; amorous. 1953: "Everyone knows you're squishy about Miss Spring-time!" Merrill Blosser, *comic strip*, "Freckles," Mar. 7.

squitch *n.* A jinx. 1949: "This is the last time it's going to put the squitch on anybody." Billy Rose, *synd. newsp. col.*, Aug. 1. *Not common.*

stab *n.* A chance; a try. *Colloq.* **—bed** *adj.* Delayed.

stable *n.* **1** Several individual enter-tainers, prize fighters, prostitutes, or the like, serving under one manager or agent. **2** A dilapidated, dirty room, house, or public place.

stable push Inside information; in-formation from influential people or people in the know. 1956: "STABLE PUSH—Inside information regarding a horse's readiness to win a race; it may come from anyone connected with the stable." T. Betts, *Across the Board*, 319. *Orig. and mainly horse-racing use.*

stache = **stash.**

stack *n.* An order of, usu. three, hot cakes. *Lunch-counter use in relaying an order.* *v.t.* To put a room in disorder by overturning and piling up furniture, etc. *c1900, college use.* See **blow one's stack**. **—ed** *adj.* Having a sexu-ally attractive body—said of a girl or

woman; well built—said of people. 1952: "The singer ain't a bad-looking broad, she's well-stacked and sort of young." L. Stander in *Esquire*, June, 131/2.

stack up **1** To wreck a car; to have an accident in a car. *Mainly teenage use, since c1950.* **2** To fare; to get along. Usu. in *"How are you stacking up?"* *Archaic.* **3** To emerge; to develop. *Colloq.* **stack-up** *n.* An auto-mobile accident; a piled-up mess.

stag *n.* **1** A youth or man who attends a social affair without a female partner. **2** A bachelor. **3** A detective. *Negro use.* **4** = **stag party.** 1946: "His shoulders were as broad as the jokes at a Legion stag. . . ." Evans, *Halo in Blood*, 37. *adj.* **1** Unaccompanied by a woman or girl. 1924: "Several of the brothers were [going to the dance] 'stag.' " Marks, *Plastic Age*, 210. → **2** Unaccompanied by a male escort. *v.i.* **1** To attend a social function without escorting a girl. *v.t.* To cut off trouser legs midway between the knee and the ankle, so that the trousers serve as shorts or for swimming.

stage = **up-stage.**

stag line A group of stags at a dance, observing the females for possible danc-ing partners. 1920: "The stag line. . . ." Fitzgerald, *This Side of Paradise*, 97.

stag party **1** A party attended by men only, often for the purpose of viewing obscene performances or movies, telling obscene jokes, and the like. **2** Specif., such a party given in honor of a prospective bridegroom by his friends.

stairs = **upstairs.**

stake *n.* **1** A comparatively large sum of money, esp. a gift; a gift of all the necessities one requires. → **2** An amount of money saved, borrowed, or loaned to be used to start a new business venture, or in prospecting, speculating, or gambling. **3** All of one's money, the total assets of a person or business; the total amount of money hazarded, as in gambling or business; the total amount of money possible to win or earn in a specific venture. 1936: "A stake . . . an unqualified gift . . . might, on occasion, be used in a different sense to denote either one's entire assets, or else the entire amount hazarded in any venture." P. A. Rollins, *The Cowboy*, 34. *Colloq.* *v.t.* **1** To gamble a specif. amount on the successful outcome of something. **2** To loan a person a sum of money to start a new business venture, or to prospect, speculate, or gamble; to loan someone money for a specif. purpose. *Colloq.* **3** To give someone money for a specif. purpose; to treat someone to something. *Colloq.* **4** To prepare a place as a police trap for criminals or suspects; to know or watch a place as a known criminal hangout. 1943: "They had the house staked." Chandler, *Lady in Lake,* 174.

stake out   To watch a suspect continuously and systematically, as by the police. 1951: "He's been staked out often enough to spot it when he's being watched himself." Spillane, *Big Kill,* 91.

stake-out   *n.* A police trap for criminals; a point or points from which the activities of a suspect may be observed by the police. 1943: "Somebody stood behind that green curtain . . . as silently as only a cop on a stake-out knows how to stand." Chandler, *Lady in Lake,* 232. 1949: "The stake-outs continued." Radio program, *Dragnet,* Dec. 8. *This very popular radio program used the word often and made it very common.*

stall   *v.i.* **1** To delay action in order to further one's objective; to wait instead of taking action. *Colloq. since c1900.* **2** To engage in obstructive activities; to loiter or hang about without acting. **3** To work as a pickpocket's stall. *Underworld use.*   *v.t.* To put (someone) off; to distract one's attention from the main issue. 1948: "He kept stalling the woman off with one excuse or another. . . ." A. Hynd, *Pinkerton,* 56. *n.* **1** A pickpocket's assistant; one who diverts the victim's attention, maneuvers him into a position in which he can be readily robbed, and/or helps to conceal the work of the pickpocket. *Underworld use.* → **2** An accomplice of criminals; one who delays interference with a holdup, obstructs pursuers, or distracts attention from the crime; a lookout, esp. one who watches for the police during a crime, in order to warn his fellow criminals to flee. 1930: "A well-dressed young girl . . . makes an excellent lookout or 'stall' for her male companions." Lavine, *Third Degree,* 153. *Underworld use.* **3** Any delaying pretext. *Most common use.* → **4** A pretense, a false alibi. 1939: [pretense] " 'Sometimes when he'd be working, I'd take meals up to him. I think that was just a stall.' 'You mean the meals were for someone else?' 'Yes.' " Gardner, *D. A. Draws,* 72. **5** A refusal. **6** A dilapidated, dirty, or cluttered room. **7** = **stand,** *n.*

stall   stall off   To keep away; to

keep at a distance, usu. by evasion or trickery.

stamps   *n.pl.* Money, usu. paper money. *c1865; obs.*

stanch   stanch out   *v.i.* To step out; to begin.

stand   *v.t.* **1** To treat someone to; to buy for someone. 1914: "She stood him tea and muffins. . . ." Sinclair Lewis, *Our Mr. Wrenn,* 223. **2** To cost a specified amount of money, whether a large or small amount. 1938: "The suit I got on stood me ten cents." Liebling, *Back Where,* 144. 1944: "The purchase of the yacht . . . stood Barrymore $110,000. . . ." Fowler, *Good Night,* 239.   *n.* **1** A robbery. **2** A store; a place of business.

—stand   See Appendix, Suffixes and Suffix Words.

standee   *n.* One who is forced to stand because there are not enough seats to accommodate everyone in a crowded theater or public place. 1856: *DAE.* 1945: "The handful of restaurants which remained open catered to packed tables, with long lines of standees waiting their turns outside the doors." Phila. *Inquirer,* Aug. 17, 5/3. *One of the more common "—ee" words.* See Appendix, —ee ending.

stand-in   *n.* **1** Influence; preferred status. *Colloq. since c1885; archaic, replaced by the shortened form "in."* **2** Orig., one who substitutes for a movie actor in order to perform dangerous or tedious parts of his work; one who knows an actor's role in a play and is ready to substitute for him when necessary. *Theater use.* **3** A substitute; one able and willing to substitute for another.   **stand in**   To act as a substitute (for someone). See **sit in.**

stand in with   To enjoy the esteem and favors of a person or group.

stand-out   *n.* **1** One whose merits, performance, or expected performance seem obviously better than others in his group; esp., one who seems sure to win a contest. **2** A very superior person or thing; anyone or anything outstanding. *Colloq.*

stand pat   **1** To keep one's original five cards in the game of draw poker, in the belief that they are good enough to win the game, rather than to attempt to better an already good combination of cards. **2** To keep a firm, fixed position, opinion, or belief; to attempt to succeed or to finish a task with one's original plan, equipment, personnel, or attitude; to stand fast. See **pat.**

stand-up *adj.* Not afraid but proud to state and defend one's opinions, ideas, and beliefs or the rights of others; frank and honest. 1956: "Harry Truman, who is a stand-up guy, had done what he could." M. Kempton in *N.Y. Post*, Aug. 15, 3. *Fig., one who, like a prize fighter, is not afraid to stand up and fight.*

stand [someone] up 1 To fail to keep an appointment, usu. a date, leaving the person standing and waiting at the appointed place; to break a date without giving advance notice. 1937: "You won't stand me up, now, will you?" Weidman, *Wholesale*, 73. → 2 To break an engagement; to discontinue a love affair. 1929: "He thinks she has given him the go-by [stood him up]." Frank Sullivan, *New Yorker*, Feb. 16, 20/2. 3 A full-length photograph. *Photographer use. Not common.* 4 To underrate someone.

stand up for [someone] 1 To defend another against criticism; to testify to another's honesty, sincerity, or other good qualities. 2 To act as best man for a bridegroom.

stanza *n.* Any unit of time or action, esp. in sports: a round of a prize fight, an inning of a baseball game, a quarter of a football game.

star *n.* A detective. *From the shape of the badge sometimes worn or carried.* Cf. **tin star.** *c1850; obs.* *adj.* Of prime importance; first-class. *Colloq. c1875 mail routes in the U.S. Far West were traveled by horse, stagecoach, and wagon. The private carriers were under government contract to carry the mail with "certainty, celerity, and security." Since these three words were used in all contracts, eventually bookkeepers and lawyers grew tired of writing them over and over and substituted three asterisks (***) for them. From this calligraphic short cut the three nouns began to be called "star birds," from the appearance of the asterisks, and the mail routes they covered, "Star Routes." There were 9,225 Star Routes in 1879–80. The famous case of the U.S. v. Stephen W. Dorsey, c1880–83, concerned political interference in granting the post office's Star Route contracts. This Supreme Court case first pop. the use of "star" in its sl. uses and as the now stand. word = major or best-known performer.*

starboard *adj.* Right-handed, as a baseball pitcher. 1913: "Three of ... Henshaw's starboard flingers had gone wrong. ..." Van Loan, *Lucky Seventh*, 164.

star boarder 1 A specially favored

boarder. *Obs.* → 2 A hearty eater. 3 A person who can be depended on to come home on time; a good husband and father. *Not common.*

starch *n.* 1 Any adulterated drug. 2 Courage, bravery, stamina, boldness, determination. *Fig., that which is needed to give a man backbone and make him stand straight and proud.*

star-gazer *n.* An idealist; one with idealistic but impractical ideas.

starker *n.* A roughneck. 1951: "He is called Julie the Starker because starker means a strong rough guy and ... Julie answers this description. ..." Runyon, *Blonde Mink. Not common.*

starred *adj.* = **star.**

stars and stripes A plate of ham and beans. *Obs.*

stash stache *v.t.* To hide something away; to store up; to save; to cache. 1939-40: [to save, store up] "I had not stashed any dough away." O'Hara, *Pal Joey*, 17. 1941: [to hide away] "I'd stache that jug. ..." Farrell, *synd. newsp. col.*, Jan. 1947: "When I signed the register, I told the hotel clerk to stash the cigarette case away in the vault." Billy Rose, *synd. newsp. col.*, Apr. 30. 1956: "*Stash* is to hide." S. Longstreet, *The Real Jazz Old and New*, 158. *Colloq.; very common.* *n.* 1 A hiding place. 2 A cache. 3 A mustache. 1940: "He had a little red stash, and he pulled it all out a few hairs at a time. ..." D. W. Maurer, *The Big Con*, 123.

stash away = **stash.**

stash it = **stick it.**

state-o *n.* A prison convict's uniform or clothing, provided by the state. 1958: "It griped me to have to put on 'state-o' or official clothes [reformatory uniform]." *Life*, Apr. 28, 69. *Common prison use.* See Appendix, —o ending.

Stateside stateside *n.* The United States, considered one's home. *Fairly common W.W.II Armed Forces use; still some use.* *adj.* From, pertaining to, or resembling the United States, its products and people, or the habits, fashions, and fads of United States citizens. *W.W.II Armed Forces use.* 1944: "A genuine Stateside flavor to the celebration." *Yank*, Dec. 1, 4.

station *n.* In baseball, a base. 1931: "The Crab bingled to center for one station. ..." Pegler, *Lit. Digest.*

Stavin Chain Any highly virile, sexually successful man; any man known for his sexual prowess. c1910: "I'm a wining boy, don't deny my name,/ Pick it up

and shake it like Stavin Chain./ . . ."
From "Wining Boy Blues," by Jelly
Roll Morton. 1950: "Stavin Chain, to
whom [Jelly Roll] Morton compared
himself, lived off women. Hero of a long
rambling ballad, known all through the
Southwest, Stavin Chain's prowess was
sexual." A. Lomax, *Mr. Jelly Roll*, 45.
Some early jazz and dial. use; obs.

steady   *n.* One's regular sweetheart;
a girl's regular or habitual escort or the
girl regularly or habitually escorted by a
boy, to the exclusion of all others.
*Since before c1910. Wide student use and
common general use.* See **go steady.**

steady, go   To date only one member
of the opposite sex, because of a strong
preference for that person's company.
1957: "Going steady means taking out
one girl until a better one comes along."
S. B. Holmes, *Woman's Day*, July, 61.
*Orig. "to go steady" meant that the male
was seriously courting and the female
accepting the courtship; since c1945,
however, it has become a teenage phenomenon merely indicating a mutual crush
or a desire for greater security in the social
environment.*

steal   *n.* **1** A theft. 1944: "I didn't . . .
realize you were . . . bringing up the
Douglas steal at the luncheon." Ford,
Phila. Murder, 190. **2** A bargain; a low
price. *Colloq.*

steam   *v.i.* To become angry. 1950:
"I steam easily." Starnes, *Another Mug*,
7. See **let off steam.**

steam, let (blow) off   To relieve one's
pent-up feelings, usu. resentment, by
talking to someone, usu. excitedly and at
length. *From the lit. use concerning steam
engines, boilers, and the like.* 1949: "I've
blown off steam." *Wom. Home Comp.*,
Nov., 14.

steamboat   *n.* **1** A shoe. **2** A human
foot. *Neither use is common.*

steamed up   **1** Drunk. *c1915; not
common.* **2** Angry. 1952: "If she has a
distasteful job to do, the first thing she
does is get all steamed up about it."
Hal Boyle, AP, Aug. 22. **3** Eager.

steam fiddle   A calliope. *Circus use.*

steam shovel   A potato peeler. *Ironic.
W.W.II Army use.*

steam up   **1** To excite; to induce excitement or enthusiasm by making a person
angry or eager, by promising money,
honor, or some reward. **2** To have
enthusiasm; to be eager.

steel   *v.t.* To stab a person.   *adj.*
White; Caucasian. *Mainly Negro use.* See
off the steel.

steel, off the   Not located near a
railroad track; away from a railroad
track. *Said of towns and people; hobo use;
obs.*

steen   *n., adj.* Any fairly large number;
any cardinal number from 13 to 19
inclusive; umpteen. 1900: ". . . Endless
repetitions are designated as occurring
'steen' times." Upson in *Independent*,
2573/2.

steer   *v.i., v.t.* To solicit or direct
patrons to a gambling casino, bar,
brothel, con game, or the like; to act as a
shill. 1949: "I been steerin' for Schwiefka
all day 'n' he told me I could sleep
here—but he ain't paid me." N. Algren,
Man with the Golden Arm, 10f.   *n.* **1**
Advice or information intended as a
guide; a tip. *Colloq.* Cf. **bum steer.**
2 = **steerer.** 1939: "He is nothing but
a steer for a bust-out joint." Runyon.
—er   *n.* One who leads dupes to
swindlers or gambling houses.

stem   *n.* **1** A, or usu. the, major street
in a town or city. 1927: "The . . . stem
is the principal street from the hobo's
point of view." Edge, *The Main Stem*,
18. *Orig. hobo use; now associated with
theatrical use.* Cf. **main stem. 2** An
opium pipe. *Some opium addict use.*
v.t. To beg from strangers on the street,
or stem. 1927: "Stemming is hobohemian
for panhandling." Edge, *The Main Stem*,
18. *Hobo use.*   **—s**   *n.pl.* A person's
legs; specif., the shapely legs of an
attractive girl or woman.

stemless loco   See **loco weeds.**

stem-winder   **1** A truck requiring
hand cranking. **2** Any excellent, attractive, or remarkable person or thing.
*c1890, archaic. Prob. from the stem-
winding pocket watch, called "the stem-
winder" when first introduced, and considered a remarkable scientific achievement.* **3** = **sidewinder.**

step dancer   A tap dancer. *Archaic.*

step-ins   *n., n.pl.* **1** A woman's underpants. *Colloq.* **2** Men's low-cut, stringless
shoes, which can be slipped on or stepped
into easily. *They are similar to moccasins.*
3 Women's low-cut, nonlaced shoes or
slippers. *Colloq.*

step off   **1** = **step off the carpet. 2**
To die. 1927: "The old man and I are
both due to step off if we're caught."
Hammett, *Blood Money*, 169.

step off the carpet   To marry. *Fig. =
to finish walking down the aisle.*

step off the deep end   **1** To rush into
action without ascertaining the facts or
making preparations; to become involved

in something that one does not understand. **2** To die.

step on it   **1** To hurry; to hurry up. **2** To shut up.

step on the gas = **step on it.**

step out   **1** To go to a party or dance. **2** To go on a date.

step out on [someone]   **1** To date someone other than one's steady. **2** To be sexually unfaithful.

stepper   *n.* A student who devotes much time to social life. *Some c1940 use.*

—ster   See Appendix, Suffixes and Suffix Words.

Stetson   *n.* **1** Any man's hat. *From the pop. manufacturer and brand.* **2** An itinerant worker. *Fig. = one who works a short time, then puts on his hat and leaves. Not common.*

Steven   See **even-Steven.**

stew   *n.* **1** A drunkard. **2** A drinking spree. **3** Chaos; confusion; frustration. **—ed**   *adj.* Drunk. 1949: "One morning she and Frankie had drunk from the same can and gotten stewed." N. Algren, *Man with the Golden Arm,* 82. 1951: "He knew where the Colonel lived from the time he'd taken him home stewed." Peter DeVries, *New Yorker,* Sept. 15, 28/2. *Brought to America by the colonists. Universally known.* See Appendix, Drunk. **—er**   *n.* An old woman. *Not common. From "hen," since an old or tough hen is called a stewer.*

stew-builder   *n.* A cook. *Hobo and logger use.*

stewbum   *n.* An unemployed, homeless street beggar, or hobo, who has reached this lowly position through alcoholism. *Orig. any beggar or hobo, as one who lives on stew; but the association has changed to one who is, or has too often been, stewed.*

stewed to the gills   Very drunk; completely drunk. 1949: ". . . He came in stewed to the gills, with Sparrow holding him up by the belt. . . ." N. Algren, *Man with the Golden Arm,* 88.

stick   *n.* Any fairly long, slim object that resembles a stick. *Specif:* **1** A baseball bat. *c1870.* **2** A baton. **3** A cigarette; esp. a marijuana cigarette, which is slimmer than the usu. tobacco cigarette. 1951: "Talent said the crop was due for harvest. . . . He said it would have made 3,500 marijuana 'sticks' which sell for $1 each." UP, Denver, July 30. 1958: "Marijuana was easy to get—25 cents a 'stick.'" N.Y. *Post,* Jan. 24, 18. *Common addict use. From "stick of tea."* Cf. **dope stick,**

dream-stick, joy-stick, pimp stick. *c1900.* **4** A match. *c1915; not common.* **5** A cane. Cf. **gimp stick.** **6** A ship's mast. 1914: "Stacks and sticks, tonnage and knots." S. Lewis, *Our Mr. Wrenn,* 8. **7** A clarinet. Cf. **gob stick, licorice stick, squeak-stick.** **8** A piece of dynamite. **9** A pole on which electric or telephone wires are strung. *Lineman and railroad use.* **10** A pencil; esp. a radio operator's pencil. **11** A fountain pen. Cf. **ink-stick.** *Pitchman use.* **12** The control lever of an airplane. Cf. **joy-stick.** **13** A slide rule. Cf. **guess stick, slip stick.** **14** An ice cream cone. *Not common.* **15** A billiard cue. 1949: "I'm good with the cue. I lived off the stick three months." N. Algren, *Man with the Golden Arm,* 13. **16** A golf club. 1924: "The golf dudes had their bag of sticks." R. Lardner, "How to Write Short Stories," reprinted in *The American Twenties,* 40. *See* **muck stick, shower-stick, temp-stick, up sticks.** *Also,* any person who might carry a stick or anything resembling a stick. *Specif.:* **17** A policeman, night watchman, guard, or the like who carries a billy club or night stick. **18** One paid to pose as a buyer, customer, or gambling player in order to attract a crowd. *c1930. Carnival and underworld use.* **19** Any tall, thin, ugly person. *Colloq.* **20** A dull, boring person with no interests or enthusiasms. *One who sits like a stick.* **21** In a gambling casino, an employee who rakes the money or chips from the middle of the table after each play and pushes the winners their winnings with a long rake-like stick; a croupier. → **22** = **shill.** 1956: "The man who won the $246.00 was a shill, sometimes referred to as a 'stick.'" J. Scarne, *The Amazing World of John Scarne,* 120.   *v.t.* To sell someone an inferior, useless, or over-priced object; to overcharge; to leave one's bill or debts for another to pay; to leave someone the blame or responsibility for an act. 1914: "Yuh, stick him for a thirty-five-cent bed." S. Lewis, *Our Mr. Wrenn,* 39.   **—er**   *n.* **1** A postage stamp. *Some, mainly underworld, use c1915.* **2** A knife, used as a weapon; one who carries or uses a knife as a weapon. *Underworld use.* **—ing**   *adj.* = **stinking.** c1920 [1954]: "'You been up North blowing that horn o' your'n. I know you're sticking.' He meant I had plenty of money." L. Armstrong, *Satchmo, My Life in New Orleans,* 212.   **—s**   *n.pl.* **1**

Drumsticks used by a drummer, esp. by a jazz drummer. 1950: "The snare drummer throwing his sticks up and bouncing them off the ground. . . ." A. Lomax, *Mr. Jelly Roll*, 10. *General jazz use.* **2** A small town or city; a rural district; the country; the suburbs; a hick town. 1930: [suburbs] "A cop was transferred to the 'sticks.' . . ." Lavine, *Third Degree*, 169. 1949: [a small city] "There's a [theatrical] revue being tried out in the sticks. . . ." H. I. Phillips, Sept. 29. *Orig. vaudeville, now common.* **3** A hobo camp. See **jungle. 4** Legs. **stick, on the = on the ball.**

stick around   To stay near a person or place; to stand by; to loiter. 1949: ". . . To do nothing but stick around the . . . factory. . . ." A. Hynd, *Public Enemies*, 12.

stick it (something) [taboo] **= stick it (something) up your (one's) ass.**

stick it (something) up your (one's) ass [taboo]   Lit. and orig., the strongest reply to the question, "What shall I do with this?" Fig., the strongest reply to, "Do you accept, agree, or like it?" and "Are you interested; what do you think?" Specif., an expression of rejection, refusal, or hatred of an object, plan, action, topic, or person, and of anger and contempt for, or rejection of, the person associated with it. *Universally known. Fairly common use by males in moments of extreme anger or stress.*

stick [one's] neck out   To take a chance; to risk making a mistake; to lay oneself open to attack; to invite trouble. 1941: "Don't stick your neck out too far. . . ." Schulberg, *Sammy*, 181.

stick of gage   A regular or a marijuana cigarette. See **stick; gage.**

stick of tea (T)   A marijuana cigarette. See **tea.** Cf. **stick.**

stick-out   *n.* **1 = stand-out;** a remarkable specimen. **2** A cinch; in sports and gambling, what looks to be a sure winner. 1939: "This Marie Cara Mia is a stick-out. . . ." Runyon. **3** Specif., horse-racing use, a horse that seems obviously superior to other horses in the same race.

stick to one's ribs   To be filling; said of hearty food. *Colloq.*

stickum   *n.* **1** Any adhesive, such as glue. *Colloq.* **2** Specif., hair dressing, pomade.

stick up   To rob; orig., to rob a person at gun point, forcing him to stick up his hands. 1914: "Being 'stuck up' by highwaymen." E. L. Pearson, *Nation*, Aug. 13, 189/2. 1956:

"I hate rich guys. Racket guys got more class when it comes to gambling. They're liable to go out and stick up a bank if they owe you. . . ." J. Cannon, *Who Struck John?* 209.   **stickup   stick-up**   *n.* **1** Armed robbery; a holdup. 1929: "A robbery or a 'stick-up.' " John Gunther, *Harper's*, Oct., 529/1. **2** An armed robber; a holdup man. 1934: "Mallory looked at the dark stick-up and said. . . ." Chandler, *Finger Man*, 94.

stick up for [someone] = stand up for [someone], 1.

sticky   *adj.* **1** Firm; stubborn; difficult. 1926: "Chaplain very sticky on that point." Stallings and Anderson, *What Price Glory*, I. **2** Sentimental; tending toward sentimentality.

sticky end of the stick, the = short end of the stick. 1951: "We'll get the sticky end of the stick if we fail to take Pontdue's offer now." S. Longstreet, *The Pedlocks*, 76.

sticky-fingered   *adj.* **1** Given to stealing. 1952: "I brought back a group photograph. . . . 'What are you—sticky-fingered?' he asked." James Thurber, *New Yorker*, Jan. 5, 21/2. **2** Miserly; holding on to money.

stiff   *adj.* **1** Drunk. 1737: Pa. *Gazette.* 1950: ". . . When the regular piano player got stiff and fell off the stool. . . ." W. Pegler, *synd. newsp. col.*, Apr. 17. 1956: "Getting stiff on the courthouse steps while denouncing the Roman Catholic clergy was a feat which regularly attracted scoffers and true believers alike. For drunk as a dog, Fitz could spout religion." N. Algren, *A Walk on the Wild Side*, 9. *Common use.* See Appendix, Drunk. **2** Formal; not relaxed or at ease. **3** Difficult to solve or accomplish successfully; maximally extreme in content. **4** Forged; said of a check. 1953: " 'I put over a couple of stiff ones,' is the way a paperhanger describes an operation. . . ." Robt. M. Yoder, *SEP*, Apr. 4, 18. *Underworld use.*   *n.* **1** A corpse; a cadaver. 1859: "slang," *DAE.* 1910: "Those who are thrown into professional contact with the deceased habitually refer to them as 'stiffs.' " *Review of Reviews*, July, 116/1. 1945: ". . . Medical students . . . tryin' to get your body to work on . . . stiffs is very scarce. . . ." Saxon, *et al., Gumbo Ya-Ya, La. Folk Tales*, 75. *Common.* **2** A drunken person. 1907: "Robbing a drunken man they call 'rolling a stiff.' " Jack London, *The Road*, 170. → **3** A rough, clumsy, stupid, or overbearing man. Usu. in "big stiff."

1896: "stiff," *DAE.* 1902: "big stiff," *DAE. Still common.* 1934: ". . . The big fat stiff . . . ?" Parker Morell, *Diamond Jim, The Life and Times of James Buchanan Brady,* 30. **4** An average or common man, esp. a manual laborer, factory worker or other man employed for strength or skill rather than intelligence; a fellow, a guy. c1900 [1935]: "board stiff = sandwich man." D. W. Maurer. 1952: Ford [Motor Co.] . . . made good cars cheap and paid working stiffs $5 a day." Stewart Holbrook, N.Y. *Her. Trib. Book Rev.,* Aug. 10, 9/5. 1952: "[Presidents] Hoover and . . . Coolidge always seemed unreal to the ordinary stiff." R. C. Ruark, *synd. newsp. col.,* Sept. 29. → **5** Specif., a hobo, tramp, or vagabond. Often in combinations as "blanket stiff," "bindle stiff," "mission stiff," "railroad stiff," "jungle stiff," and the like. 1893: "Blanket stiff = bindle stiff." J. Flynt in *Century,* Nov., 106. 1907 [1894]: "He bore none of the earmarks of the professional 'stiff.' " J. London, *My Life.* 1927: "No stiff ever got information about a job. . . ." W. Edge, *The Main Stem,* 17. 1945: ". . . The stiffs . . . are . . . bums. They are blank-eyed and slow-moving, and they have no strong desire for anything but sleep." J. Mitchell, *McSorley's,* 21. *Mainly hobo use.* → **6** Specif., a migratory worker. 1926: "*Stiff* is used far more frequently than *boomer.*" James Lance, *Amer. Mercury,* April, xxxii. **7** A deadbeat or moocher, specif., a person who does not tip a taxi driver, waiter, bellhop, or the like; also, a poor tipper. **8** A communication or official document considered as contraband: a message circulated secretly among prisoners; a letter received by a prisoner; a forged check; stolen securities. *Various underworld and prison uses since c1900.* **9** A failure; a flop; anything or anyone that seems assured of failing or being a flop. Specif., a racehorse that will not win a race; a prize fighter who is certain to lose a fight; a book, song, play, or movie that has little appeal and seems assured of becoming a flop. 1935: "There is also a rumor that Follow You [a racehorse] is a stiff in the race. . . ." Runyon, 197. 1949: "Juggy listened to the tune [song] and was disheartened. 'It's a stiff,' he said." I. Johnson, *Amer. Weekly,* Oct. 30, 21/2. **10** A useless person who contributes no ideas, conversation, or enthusiasm to a task or social gathering. → **11** A contestant or team that does not try or has no chance of winning. 1956:

"STIFF—A horse that has not been ridden to win; the jockey may not necessarily know that he has received self-defeating instructions from the trainer. The horse may also have a physical ailment." T. Betts, *Across the Board,* 319.   *v.t.* **1** To fail to tip a person; to refrain from tipping. *Waiter, porter, bellhop, and taxi driver use.* → **2** To cheat, as a waiter, restaurant, or the like, by leaving without paying one's check. 1950: "It was a signal for the waiter to hustle over and put the arm on the customer who was trying to stiff him." M. Zolotow in *SEP,* July 15, 124/3. *adv.* Fig., so dull or boring as to cause sleepiness, sleep, or even death, as in "He bores me stiff."   **—ener** *n.* **1** A knockout punch. *Prize fight use.* **2** In sports, the deciding factor; the winning play or score. **3** A small quantity of whisky added to a drink, usu. an alcoholic one, in order to make it stronger.   **—ing** *adj.* = **jiving.**

stiff card   A formal written invitation.

stiff-neck   *n.* A snob; a self-righteous person.

stillion   *n.* An indefinitely large number. Cf. **zillion.**

stilts   *n.pl.* Legs. *Not common.*

sting   *v.t.* To overcharge; to cheat; to steal.   *n.* Money or stolen goods gained from a crime. *Underworld and Negro use.*   **—er**   *n.* **1** A railroad brakeman or watchman. *Hobo and railroad use.* **2** An obstacle; an unresolved problem; any factor of uncertainty.

stinker   *n.* **1** A contemptible person. *Very common since c1930.* → **2** A term of endearment, applied usu. to children, esp. in "little stinker," and freq. to one's spouse; a mischievous but endearing person. *Since c1945. One of many sl. words used both as a term of contempt and as a term of endearment.* **3** Anything inferior, esp. a boring or badly performed entertainment. *Very common.* **4** In baseball, a hit between infield and outfield. *Not common.* **5** A debauch; an extended social affair, as a dance or party, that continues a long time and nearly exhausts the participants. *Student use, c1950.*   **—oo   stinkaroo**   *adj.* **1** Of inferior quality; esp., boring, badly performed; usu. said of entertainment. 1943: "[The Joe Louis–Buddy Baer fight is] going to be a real stinkeroo." S. Feder, AP, Jan. 6. **2** Despicable; wretched. *n.* Anything of the poorest quality, esp. an entertainment; a stinker. 1947: "Keep a stiff upper lip about the movie, too

If it proves to be a 'stinkeroo' leave the theater quietly or suffer in silence." B. Betz in *Coronet*, Feb., 147/1. *One of the most common "—eroo" words.* See Appendix, —eroo ending.

stinkie   stinky *n.* Common nickname or form of direct address for a disliked, contemptible person. *Common child use.* See **stinker.** See Appendix, —ie, —y endings.

stinking *adj.* **1** Despicable; mean. *Fairly common.* **2** Very wealthy; having an abundance of money; loaded. *Fig., having so much money that one can smell it.* **3** Thoroughly drunk. 1944: "We drank 27 toasts . . . and he got pretty stinking. . . ." Shulman, *Feather Merchants*, 3. **4** Exceedingly.

stinko *adj.* **1** Drunk. **2** Smelly; odoriferous. **3** Unpleasant. **4** Of very inferior quality. See Appendix, —o ending.

stink pot Any disliked or scorned person. *Mainly child use.*

stir   stir, the *n.* A jail; a prison. 1851: Farmer & Henley. 1928: "To get a jolt in the stir." E. Booth in *Amer. Mercury*, May, 81. 1950: "John went to stir." DeBaun, 73. *Orig. and mainly underworld use, but fairly common. From the Anglo-Saxon "styr" = punishment, reinforced by the Romany "steripen" = prison, which is also a possible orig. of the syn. "pen."* *adj.* Prison; prisonlike. 1935: "The young guys [from Harvard and Yale] with the stir haircuts. . . ." Runyon, 299.

stir-crazy   stir-bugs   stir-daffy stir-simple *adj.* Dull-witted or insane as a result of long imprisonment; neurotically maladjusted to prison life; said of convicts. 1938: "Any number of others [prisoners at Alcatraz] were what we call 'stir crazy,' going about their routine like punch-drunk boxers." Convict No. 293, quoted in *Amer. Mercury*, Sept. 13/1. *"Stir-crazy" is the only well-known form; "stir-simple" has fairly common convict use.*

stir-wise *adj.* Well informed or sophisticated, esp. about or by reason of imprisonment. 1939: " 'What does he say?' 'Nothing very much. He's closemouthed and wise—stir-wise. He talks about the weather and the war.' " Gardner, *D. A. Draws*, 102. 1949: "Johnson was stir-wise, a tough man to question." *Fact Detec. Mysteries*, 112.

stitched *Adj.* Drunk. *Obs. in U.S.; still used in Eng.*

stocking = **blue-stocking.**

stomach *v.t.* To accept or believe something disgusting. *Almost always in the negative, e.g.,* "I can't stomach that." *n.* Courage; a lack of squeamishness.

stomach-robber *n.* A logging-camp cook. Cf. **belly-robber.**

stomp *n.* A jazz composition or arrangement with a heavily accented rhythm, usu. in a lively tempo and, during the swing era, repeated riffs. 1905 [1950]: "Porter King, a very dear friend of mine and a marvelous pianist from Florida . . . particularly liked a certain number and so I named it after him, only changed the name backwards and called it *King Porter Stomp*. I don't know what the term 'stomp' means, myself. There wasn't really any meaning, only that people would stamp their feet. However, this tune came to be the outstanding favorite of every great hot band throughout the world that had the accomplishment to play it. [Footnote:] Benny Goodman used *King Porter* as a theme for a number of years." A. Lomax, *Mr. Jelly Roll*, 112.

stone *adv.* Very; completely, thoroughly. *Only when used before certain words.* Cf. **stone blind, stone broke, stone cold, stone dead, stone rich.** **—d** *adj.* **1** Drunk. 1958: "They get themselves stoned on beer." D. Parker, *Esquire*, May, 41. *Wide student use since c1945.* See Appendix, *Drunk.* **2** Under the influence of a narcotic. *Some addict use.* **3** Excited, enthusiastic, ecstatic, surprised, flipped; specif., aroused by a good performance of cool or far-out music. 1956: "*Stoned:* drunk, drugged, captivated, ecstatic, sent out of this world." S. Longstreet, *The Real Jazz Old and New*, 151. *Cool and far-out use. A pop. sophisticated word; wide young adult and student use c1945, though much older.* Cf. **ossified.**

stone— See Appendix, Prefixes and Prefix words.

stone blind Thoroughly drunk.

stone broke Completely penniless. 1907: "The money that is made out of stone-broke tramps." Jack London, *The Road*, 197.

stone cold **1** Very cold. *Said of an object, never the weather.* → **2** Dead.

stone-crusher   stone-crushers *n.* **1** The fists. *Obs.* **2** An infantryman. *W.W.II Army use. Not common.*

stone dead Definitely dead.

stone-fence *n.* Cider with whisky added. *c1850; obs.*

stone rich   Very rich. *Prob. in contrast to "stone broke." Not common.*

stonie   *n.* A smooth, heavy playing marble resembling stone or pottery and usu. used as a shooter. *Some boy use since c1920.* See Appendix, —ie ending.

stood   Stayed. Usu. in **should have stood in bed.**

stood in bed, [one] should have   An expression indicating that one is having or has had such an unsuccessful, unhappy, unrewarding experience or day that it was not worthwhile getting up.

stooge   *n.* **1** A comedian's assistant who acts stupidly or naïvely in order to be a foil for or the butt of the comedian and his jokes. → **2** An underling; esp., one who acts as a puppet for another, saying and doing what he does without question, because he is told to. 1939: "His bail-bond stooges." Gardner, *D. A. Draws,* 204. 1950: "One of these toiling sleuths got a telephone call from a stooge of the underworld." F. Oursler, *synd. newsp. col.,* Aug. 5. **3** An Air Force co-pilot. *Some W.W.II Air Force use.* *v.i.* **1** To play the part of a stooge for an entertainer. 1946: "[Entertainer Danny Kaye] stooged for other entertainers." *Time,* Mar. 11, 66. **2** To act as a stooge or puppet for another. 1939: "We're glad to stooge for [him]." Chandler, *Big Sleep,* 103.

stool   *n.* **1** A plain-clothes policeman. **2** An informer for the police; a stool pigeon. 1934: "He's nothing but a cop's stool." Cain, *Postman,* 72. *A sl. back-clipping.* See **stool pigeon.** *v.t.* **1** To lure. 1932: "Lorelei who ... stools sailors up the rocks to get them wrecked. ..." Runyon. **2** To inform, as to the police. 1949: "... To make me stool on a friend." J. Evans, *Halo,* 121. **—ie**   **stooley** = **stool pigeon.** 1951: "There was stoolies and wire tappers working all over town." *I, Mobster,* 124. See Appendix, —ie ending.

stool pigeon   **1** A person serving as a decoy. *From fact that pigeons were often tied to a stool as a decoy for other pigeons. c1830; obs.* → **2** An informer, usu. a police informer. 1949: movie title, *Johnny Stool Pigeon.* 1952: "He did not know that Chin Poy was what the Government calls 'an underworld agent' and what [the] petitioner calls a 'stool pigeon' for the Bureau of Narcotics." Opinion of the U.S. Supreme Court, on Lee v. United States, 343 U.S. 747, 72 Sup. Ct. 967,96L. Ed. 1270.

stoop   *n.* = **stupe.**

stoopnagel   *n.* A silly, blundering person. 1943: "We developed a class of stoopnagels with Oxford accents." P. Wylie, *Generation of Vipers,* 247.

stop   *n.* A receiver of stolen goods. *Underworld use; has replaced "fence" among most underworld elements.* **—per**   *n.* In boxing, a knockout.

store   *n.* **1** A concession. *Carnival and circus use.* **2** A business office.

store cheese   The most common yellow American cheddar cheese. *So called because such cheese used to be displayed as and sold from large blocks or wheels on the counter of every grocery store.*

storm   *n.* A fit of anger; a ruckus. See **barnstorm, brain storm, in a storm. storm storm out** *v.i.,* **1** To leave a place in anger. *E.g.,* "He really stormed out of here without even saying good-by." **2** To move fast; to drive fast. *Hot-rod use since c1955.*

storm, in a   Excited; confused. *A fig. use. W.W.II Army Air Corps use.*

Storyville   *n.* The famous New Orleans legalized brothel district from 1896 to 1917, where many of the early jazz musicians first played and introduced jazz music; fig., the home of jazz; early jazz; New Orleans style jazz. 1950: "In 1896 a New Orleans alderman, Sidney Story, promulgated a city ordinance which restricted prostitution to [two areas, one was] a thirty-eight block red-light district adjoining Canal Street. Much to the mortification of the alderman, some joker nicknamed the area Storyville. And the name stuck. Storyville it remained until, in 1917, the U.S. Navy finally closed the tenderloin for good. In Jelly Roll's time the District's legal boundaries were: North [*sic*] Robertson, St. Louis, [North] Basin and Iberville (Customhouse) Streets." A. Lomax, *Mr. Jelly Roll,* 38. *Some jazz use; not common.*

stove league   Baseball enthusiasts who discuss the last season until the next. *An allusion to the stove at the center of a conversational group in the once typical country store.*

stove-lid [*derog.*]   *n.* A Negro. *Not common.*

stove pipe   **1** Current gossip. *Orig. railroad use.* **2** A trench mortar. *W.W.I and W.W.II use.* **3** A jet fighter airplane.

stow it   **1** An order or request to stop doing or saying something. **2** = **shove it.** *Both meanings USN use.*

stow the gab   To keep quiet; to shut up. *Orig. USN use.*

straight   *n.* 1 In poker, five consecutively numbered cards, regardless of suit. *Colloq.* 2 A week's engagement for a vaudevillian; a week during which a performer performs every day in the same theater and town, as opposed to a split week. *Vaudeville use; obs.*   *adj.* 1 Undiluted, neat; said of liquor. 2 Honest; normal. *Depending on the context, denotes that the person referred to is not dishonest, not a drug addict, not a homosexual, and so forth. Orig. an antyn. to the stand. "crooked," reinforced by "straightforward." The uses = sexually normal and/or not a drug addict, since c1945, and are gaining in pop.*

straight face   A face showing no expression that might reveal a joke, deception, or secret; specif., a face that does not show laughter, as might reveal a joke or hurt someone's feelings.

straight from the horse's mouth   Authentically; directly from one in the know; said of information, news, or the like. 1949: "I got the tip straight from the horse's mouth." Burnett, *Jungle*, 94.

straight from the shoulder   Honestly, frankly, and to the point.

straight goods   Truth. 1922: "Is all dat straight goods?" O'Neill, *Hairy Ape*, 4.

straight job   A one-piece truck, without a trailer. *Truck driver use.*

straight man   A comedian's accomplice who acts as his foil; a stooge.

straight talk   Honest, sincere, succinct talk.

strap   *n.* A person, esp. a student, whose interests lie almost exclusively in athletics, to the neglect of intellectual interests. *College use.* See **black-strap.**   **—ped**   *adj.* Penniless; without money. 1931: "He happens to be strapped financially. . . ." Queen, *Dutch Shoe*, 49. *Colloq. since c1860.*

strawberries   *n.pl.* 1 Beans. *Logger use.* 2 Prunes. *W.W.I and II Armed Forces use, esp. USN use.* Cf. **Army strawberries.**

strawberry patch   The back end of a railroad caboose seen at night. *Railroad use.*

straw boss   1 The foreman of a crew of manual laborers. *Colloq.* → 2 Any person, esp. a foreman, who gives orders or oversees work but has no power, authority, or executive status with which to support his orders. 3 An assistant boss or foreman. "Origin of term: the boss attended to the grain going into the thresher; the second-man watched after the straw coming out and hence had little to do." H. F. Barker. *Colloq. since c1900 ; orig. hobo use.*

straw-cat   *n.* A harvest worker, esp. a migratory harvest worker.

straw-hat   *adj. n.* A summer theater; summer theaters, actors, or plays. *Also used attrib.* 1936: "A new play that's . . . at a straw hat. . . ." A. Green, *Esquire*, Sept.

street, put it on the   To give out information; to disclose a personal confidence or secret to many people; to let something be known.

Street, the   Variously, any of several well-known, exciting, brightly-lit streets in several major cities in the U.S. Esp., Broadway in New York City. *The connotation is always one of bright lights, excitement, and entertainment; "the Street" is always the center of the theatrical, nightclub, or gambling district of a city.*

street monkey   A member of a marching band. *Some W.W.II Army use.*

strength   *n.* Profit, profits; specif. all possible profits, as can be realized by charging maximum prices while giving minimum value.

stretch   *v.i., v.t.* 1 To hang; to be hanged. 1623: Farmer & Henley. *Obs.* 2 To wait on tables; to serve or be employed as a waiter or waitress. *Some c1915 use. Obs.*   *n.* A prison sentence; time served in prison. 1930: "Doing 'a stretch in the Big House.' " Lavine, *Third Degree*, 194. 1949: "A stretch at Sing Sing." Movie, *Johnny Allegro.* 1958: "Stretch—Time served in prison." G. Y. Wells, *Station House Slang. Universally known.*   **—er**   *n.* 1 The neck. 2 A belt.   **—es**   A pair of suspenders.

stretch one   An order for a large glass of Coca-Cola. *Some lunch-counter use in relaying orders.*

strib   *n.* A prison warden. *Underworld use.*

strictly   *adv.* Very well; excellently; adroitly. *Usu. in ref. to the playing of jazz.*

strictly union = corny. Swing use, said of nonswing music. *Implying that the only requirement necessary to play such music is belonging to the musicians' union, no other talent is needed, and that the musicians are fulfilling the bare minimum requirement in displaying enthusiasm or imagination.*

stride   *n.* A style of jazz piano playing in which the bass alternates between single notes on the first and third beats of the measure and chords, usu. emphasized, on the second and fourth beats of the measure. *A development from ragtime usu. assoc. with Eastern or N.Y.C. jazz and first identified with James P. Johnson.* **—rs** *n.sing.* A pair of trousers. *Negro use.* **—s** *n.* = **striders.** *Hobo, underworld, and maritime use.*

strike *n.* **1** In bowling, the act or an instance of knocking down all the pins with one's first ball. **2** Fig., a refusal to work, play, join a gathering, or the like. *Usu. jocular; from the labor use.* *v.t.* **1** To come upon, esp. unexpectedly; to meet. *Colloq.* **2** To make an urgent appeal or request of someone; to ask someone for a job, loan of money, or the like. **—r** *n.* **1** A soldier who works as an officer's servant. *c1925; Army use, esp. Army officer use.* See **dog-robber.** **2** A helper; an assistant. *W.W.II USN use.* → **3** A sailor who is studying to improve his status; also, one who seeks advancement by flattery rather than by work. *W.W.II USN use.*

strike bedrock To die.

strike-breaker *n.* A substitute sweetheart.

string *n.* **1** A false story. **2** Wire; esp. telegraph wire. *Lineman, telegraph, and railroad use.* **3** A necktie. See **shoestring.** *v.t.* To hoax or deceive; to make false promises. 1928–1929: "Who are you trying to string, anyhow?" Elmer Rice, *Street Scene,* III. *Not now common.*

string, on a To have or hold in reserve; specif., to encourage the attention of one of the opposite sex after one has decided to reject that person or while one has another boy friend or girl friend.

string, pull the In baseball, to pitch a slow ball, esp. after having pitched a fast one.

string along To follow.

string [someone] along = **string.** 1924: "I'm afraid that he's just stringing me along, trying to encourage me...." Marks, *Plastic Age,* 206. *Since c1900.*

string along with [someone] To accept another's decision, opinion, or advice; to be a disciple of; to trust, to be faithful to, to agree with; to follow someone as a leader. 1937: [follow someone as a leader] "As long as you string along with me, your cafeteria days are over." Weidman, *Wholesale,* 6. 1951: [to be faithful to] "You may not be an angel,

but till the day that one comes along, I'll string along with you." *Pop. song,* "I'll String Along with You."

string band A band composed entirely of stringed instruments. 1950: "At the age of seven I was considered one of the best guitarists around, and sometimes I played in the string bands that were common at that time. These little three piece combinations, consisting of bass, mandolin, and guitar, used to play serenades at late hours, from twelve to two." A. Lomax, *Mr. Jelly Roll,* 5. 1956: "By 1890 the classic jazz was here. The small string bands—the combinations of fiddle, guitar, mandolin, string-bass, and sometimes piano...." S. Longstreet, *The Real Jazz Old and New,* 48.

stringbean *n.* Any tall, thin person. *Colloq.*

string of coconuts Money; a wad of paper money. *Carnival use; archaic.*

string up To hang a person. *Colloq.*

string-whanger *n.* A guitarist. 1956: "... Real talk ... *string-whanger* for a guitarist." S. Longstreet, *The Real Jazz Old and New,* 150. *Some jazz use.*

strip *n.* = **drag strip.** *v.t.* To break a bill in making change. *Waiter use.* **—per** *n.* A striptease dancer; a burlesque or nightclub entertainer who disrobes (but usu. not completely) slowly and sensually to music; she may also, but not necessarily, dance, do bumps and grinds, or perform other erotic movements. 1957: "You're looking at a stripper/but before I unzip my zipper...." From "Zip," pop. song, quoted in *Life,* Oct. 14, 97.

Strip, the = **Street, the.** *A newer word, sometimes but not always, referring to a district rather than to a single street. Usu. applied to the main street containing many nightclubs, esp. in Los Angeles and Miami, and specif. to the main street containing gambling houses in Las Vegas.*

striped *adj.* Drunk. *Not common.*

stripes *n.pl.* **1** Tigers. *Circus use.* **2** Noncommissioned officers' rank or insignia. *W.W.II use.* Cf. **one-striper, two-striper, three-striper, two-and-a-half-striper.**

stroll *n.* **1** A road, highway, or street. *c1935 jive use; some Negro use.* **2** Anything that is easy to do. *c1940; Negro and jazz use.*

strong *adj.* **1** Flush with money. *Hobo use.* **2** Providing dishonest profit. *Carnival and circus use.* → **3** Costing 25¢ or more to play or bet. *Carnival use.*

4 Well liked; accepted as an equal; "large." *Theatrical use since c1955.*

strong-arm *n.* **1** A person employed to carry out acts of violence; one who uses physical violence to obtain money or information, as a hoodlum. **2** Violence; physical force. *Since c1830;* see **strong-arm man.** *adj.* Done with violence or physical force. 1930: "Strong-arm work around election time. . . ." Lavine, *Third Degree,* 109. *v.i. and v.t.* To beat a person up; to use violence. 1948: "Mugging . . . in old Chicago days called 'strong-arming.' " Lait-Mortimer, *N.Y. Confidential,* 100.

strong-arm man One employed to beat up people; a hoodlum or thug who uses physical violence of any kind.

struggle *n.* A dance or party. *College and Army use. Not now common.* *v.i.* To dance. *c1925; archaic.*

struggle-buggy *n.* An automobile. *Some late 1920's and c1930 use, esp. by students, in ref. to the attempted male use of the automobile as a private place in which one could attempt to neck with a girl.*

strut (do) [one's] stuff **1** To dance; to dance well. *c1915; archaic.* **2** To do well that which one is specially qualified for or noted for doing; to perform; to act. 1950: "You'll . . . be rarin' to strut your stuff again before the cameras." Billy Rose, *synd. newsp. col.* Sept. 1. Cf. **do [one's] stuff.**

stub *n.* A small, stocky person; esp. a high-school or college girl.

stuck **stuck with** *adj.* **1** Having been sold an inferior or worthless item; overcharged; left to pay another's bill or debt; burdened with the undeserved or unwanted blame or responsibility for something. See **stick.** **2** Left with something useless or embarrassing. 1944: "Mr. Toplady . . . imagine being stuck with a moniker like that all your life." Ford, *Phila. Murder,* 116.

stuck on **1** Infatuated with oneself or a person of the opposite sex, usu. said of youths. 1921: "That feller was *stuck* on yuh, Bess." Witwer, *Leather,* 160. **2** Greatly impressed with the merit or personality of a person.

stuck-up *adj.* Haughty; snobbish; snooty. *Colloq. since c1890.*

stud *n.* **1** Any male; esp. a dude, sport, or roué. → **2** Any hip male. *Orig. jive use; fairly common cool use.*

student *n.* **1** An apprentice; a novice. **2** Specif., a beginning drug addict; a drug addict who does not yet need freq. or large doses; a drug addict with a small

habit. *c1936; addict use.* 1949: "Nor did Louie acknowledge that a student had ceased to be a joy-popper because he had reached a one-a-week compromise with his need. On a quarter grain a week a man was still a student. It wasn't till a man needed a quarter of a grain a day that Louie felt the fellow was safely in the vise." N. Algren, *Man with the Golden Arm,* 31. *Common addict use.*

stuff *v.t.* **1** To sell misrepresented merchandise; to sell merchandise that is not genuine or that is stolen. 1840: *DAE. Underworld use until c1890.* → **2** To deceive, kid, ride, or trick a person; to make a person the butt of a joke. 1861: *DAE. Archaic.* *n.* **1** Money. *Not common.* Cf. **green stuff.** **2** Contraband; stolen goods. *Prob. from the 1st v.t. use, reinforced by "hot stuff." Underworld use.* → **3** Specif., bootlegged or illegal whisky. Now in reference to "good stuff." *Since Prohibition.* **4** Specif., any narcotic, as used by an addict. 1957: "Where's the stuff? I can't wait forever." A. Halsey, *SEP,* Mar. 30, 36. 1958: "Finally he admitted he was on dope. He went to jail for two years . . . he came out and seemed to be off the stuff." N.Y. *Post,* Jan. 24, 18. *Orig. addict use.* Cf. **white stuff.** **5** [taboo] A girl or young woman considered only sexually; tail. 1951: "We'll go to Irene's. Classiest stuff this side of Denver . . . gals all colors, all sizes." S. Longstreet, *The Pedlocks,* 102. See **pussy. 6** One's stock-in-trade, as a comedian's jokes or the types of pitches mastered by a baseball pitcher. **—er** *n.* One who sells misrepresented or stolen merchandise; specif., one who sells cheap or inferior watches at exorbitant prices, claiming they are superior watches. *Often called a "watch stuffer." Underworld use c1840–c1920.* See Appendix, **—er** ending.

stuff, know [one's] = **know [one's] onions.**

stuff cuff A padded cuff on a zoot suit. 1945: "Zoot suit, drape shape, reet pleat, stuff cuff. . . ." L. Feather in *Esquire,* quoted in *Negro Digest,* Aug., 64. See Appendix, Rhyming Slang.

stuffed shirt **stuff shirt** **1** A pompous, pretentious bore who insists on formalities. *Always derog. use, usu. said of a man of wealth or social standing.* → **2** Any superior; any wealthy or socially prominent person.

stumble *v.i.* **1** To make a mistake; to suffer a misfortune. → **2** To be arrested. *Underworld use.*

stumblebum *n.* An unemployed,

homeless street beggar, esp. if alcoholic, who is always or usually in a dazed condition, resembling a trance.

stump *v.t.* **1** To cause to fail in reciting. *College use. c1850; obs.* **2** To confuse, to puzzle, to nonplus. *Colloq.* *n.* **1** A gas-lamp post. Cf. **stump glim.** *c1850; obs.* → **2** A pole carrying electric wires; a telephone pole. *Lineman and railroad use.* **—s** *n.pl.* Legs. *Not common.*

stump glim *n.* A lamp-post. *Obs.*

stump-jumper *n.* A farmer. *Archaic and dial.*

stung *adj.* **1** = **stuck. 2** Cheated, esp. by a merchant; overcharged. 1958: "7 Ways To Pay For Home Improvements. (Tells you how to keep from getting 'stung.')" Advertising leaflet for *The Kiplinger Magazine.*

stunned *adj.* Drunk.

stunner *n.* **1** A first-rate story. **2** A striking person or thing; esp. an attractive woman.

stunning *adj.* **1** Excellent; admirable. → **2** Striking; visually attractive. *Usu. said of women or clothes; most often used by women. Colloq.*

stupe   stoop *n.* A stupid person, a blockhead. 1762: "Stupe." Farmer & Henley. 1941: " 'Take a look, stupe. How would I know where the key was, stupe?' 'Don't call me stupe,' Humphrey said." G. Homes, *40 Whacks*, 46. *Common use. From "stupid."* See Appendix, Shortened words.

stymie *v.t.* To impede; to frustrate. *Orig. a golf term.*

sub *n.* **1** A subaltern. 1756: *DAE.* *Archaic.* **2** A substitute of any kind; now specif. a substitute player on an athletic team, a member of the team whose skills or seniority does not give him priority to play but who is a team member and plays when those with more skill or seniority are resting or injured. 1844: [Generic use.] *DAE.* 1876: [Substitute worker.] *DAE.* 1889: [Substitute player on an athletic team.] *DAE. Colloq. Common sports use, which is the most common use of this word.* **3** A submarine. *Orig. W.W.I use; colloq. since c1920.* **4** A subordinate; an assistant. *Since c1925; not common.* **5** A person with subnormal mentality; an extremely stupid person; an imbecile, moron, or idiot. *Some use since c1930.* *v.i.* To act as a substitute for another person, esp. in a job. 1879: *DAE. Colloq.* *v.t.* To substitute one player of a team for another during an athletic contest, as

by the team coach or manager. See Appendix, Shortened Words. **—deb** *n.* A girl younger than a debutante; a young teenage girl. *Colloq.* **—marine** *n.* A doughnut. *By association with "sinker." Orig. waitress use.* **—s** *n.pl.* The feet. **—way!** *interj., n.* A nickel or a dime tip or gratuity, as given to a food or soft drink vendor; an expression of thanks to the tipper, shouted by the vendor mainly as notice to other customers that tips are being received and appreciated, and notice to co-workers or a supervisor that the money is the vendor's and is not to be put in the management's cash register. *Although most subway fares are now more than a nickel or dime, the word is still used.*

suck *v.i., v.t.* **1** [taboo] To perform cunnilingus or, esp., fellatio. → **2** To curry favor with people in authority. *Although not taboo, prob. from "suck off."* **—er** *n.* **1** A person easily deceived or cheated; an easy victim; a dupe. 1900: "You can go to the deuce . . . I'm no sucker." Dreiser, *Carrie*, 159. *Two American sayings are "There's a sucker born every minute," attrib. to circus owner, P. T. Barnum; and "Never give a sucker an even break," which was also the title of a popular 1941 movie starring W. C. Fields. Colloq. since c1835.* → **2** A fan; one who is vulnerable to a certain type of person, business deal, sport, or gambling game. 1953: "I'm a sucker for a beautiful blonde." George Sanders [movie actor], *AP interview.* **3** A teacher's pet. *Student use.* See **egg-sucker. 4** A lollipop. *Child use; colloq.* *v.t.* To trick someone; to make a sucker or dupe of a person. 1951: "Shooting a killer if I can sucker him into drawing first so it'll look like self-defense." Spillane, *Big Kill*, 14.

suck around   To hang around a place or person with a view of gaining preference or favors.

sucker list   **1** A list of the names of good prospective customers, donors, or the like. 1949: "The [telephone] directory is not intended to be a sucker list, but a smart operator can use it for one." Phila. *Bulletin*, Sept. 3, 6/2. **2** A list of people who are easily, and can be frequently, duped, deceived, or victimized; fig., a list of marks.

suck [someone] in   To deceive; esp. to deceive by making false promises.

suck off [taboo]   **1** To commit cunnilingus or fellatio. → **2** To curry favor with a superior or influential person. *Fig. and scornfully, to be willing to do*

anything to curry favor.
n. A toady; a flatterer.

suck up to [someone]   To curry favor with someone by being exceptionally agreeable, or by doing menial jobs for that person. Cf. **suck off.**

suction   *n.* Influence; good standing with one's superiors; pull.

suction, in a   In love; confused, unrealistic because of being in love.

suds   sudds   *n.pl.* **1** Any alcoholic drink. *Obs.* → **2** Specif., beer. *From the sudslike appearance of the foam. Very common c1915 and still in wide use.* **3** Coffee. *Lunch-counter use.* **4** Money. *Not common.*

suede   *n.* A dark Negro. *Negro use; not common.*

Suffering cats!   *A euphem. for "Suffering Christ!"*

Suffering Christ!   An expletive of surprise, mild anger, or disappointment. *Archaic.*

sugan   soogan   *n.* A quilt; a blanket. *Archaic and dial. Some hobo use.*

sugar   *n.* **1** Money; money available to be spent for pleasures; money easy to obtain; an abundance of money. Cf. **heavy sugar; Sugar Hill; sugar daddy.** → **2** Bribe money. **3** Narcotics: heroin, cocaine, or morphine. **4** A sweetheart. *A term of endearment. Popular song,* "When my sugar goes down the street, the little birdies go 'Tweet, tweet, tweet.'" Cf. **heavy sugar; sugar daddy.** *v.t.* To bribe.

sugar-coat   sugarcoat   *v.t.* To make something be or seem more agreeable than it is; esp., to relay bad news in a gentle way, as while emphasizing more fortunate details; to emphasize the happier, more successful facets of a generally unhappy or unsuccessful situation; to include a reward in a distasteful or tedious task.   **—ed**   *adj.* Made, or made to seem, more pleasant; said of a disgusting, unhappy, unsuccessful, or tedious task, duty, venture, or the like.

sugar daddy   A male sweetheart well provided with money, esp., a wealthy, usu. elderly man who spends money freely on girls; specif., a worldly, sophisticated man, usu. not young and usu. wealthy, who pays the rent and other expenses of a young woman in return for her sexual favors and companionship. 1949: "Mrs. Shawsky must have had a sugar daddy on the side." *Fact Detec. Mysteries,* 65. 1951: "The man who finds that Death stares him in the face becomes, provided he has the means, a

'sugar daddy' to chorines." J. D. Forbes in *Amer. Assn. of Univ. Professors Bulletin,* Spring, 56. 1957: "My [a young actress] Sugar Daddy Is The Real McCoy." Headline, *N.Y. Enquirer,* Feb. 4, 1. Cf. **daddy, John, old man.**

sugar-head   *n.* **1** *A term of endearment. Not common.* **2** Moonshine whisky.

Sugar Hill   sugar hill   *n.* **1** A district with Negro brothels; a Negro brothel. *Fig., a place where money grows.* **2** In N.Y.C., the wealthy neighborhood overlooking Harlem. 1957: "The wealthy whites used to live up there on Sugar Hill; one of my sisters worked as a laundress up there. The other sister she made better money working in a sugar hill in Atlanta [Georgia]." *Oral,* Harlem bartender, Aug. 17.

sugar papa   See **sweet papa.**

sugar report   A letter from a sweetheart, esp. from a girl to a serviceman. *Student and W.W.II Armed Forces use; very common.*

sugue   See **segway.** *From the standard [It.] "segue."*

suit   See **birthday suit, monkey suit, zoot suit.**

suit, the   Lit. and fig., any Armed Forces uniform, specif. an Army uniform. *Some W.W.II use. Usu. in such phrases as "I got the suit" = I have been drafted into the Army; or "I'm going to put on the suit" = I'm going to enlist in the Armed Forces.*

suitcase   *n.* A drum. *Swing musician use.*

sujee   *n.* = **soogie.**

sum-up   *n.* A summary. *Colloq.*

Sunday   *adj. and adv. When used in combination with certain words:* **1** Best, most effective, perfect. *As in* **Sunday clothes, Sunday pitch, Sunday punch, Sunday run.** *Fig., saved for a special day.* **2** Amateurish; part time. *As in* **Sunday driver, Sunday soldier, Sunday thinker.**

Sunday—   See Appendix, Prefixes and and Prefix words.

Sunday clothes   One's best clothes; new or dressy clothing. *Fig., clothes saved for Sunday churchgoing and social functions. From* **Sunday-go-to-meeting-clothes.** *Now archaic and dial.*

Sunday driver   A poor automobile driver; one who drives uncertainly and erratically. *Fig., one who drives very seldom, only on Sundays.*

Sunday pitch   A powerful throw; usu. in baseball, but also any pitch.

Sunday punch   A hard, effective blow

with the fist; any powerful attack. 1932: [a blow] "And lay his Sunday punch on your snoot. . . ." Runyon. 1945: [powerful attack] "The Yanks and their Allies are raising hell with rockets—the 'Sunday punch' weapon of the war." Frank Carey, AP, Feb. 5.

Sunday run   A long distance. *Fig., a long trip between towns in which one has to work and, therefore, a trip taken on a Sunday, when one cannot work. Circus and traveling salesman use.*

Sunday soldier   An Army reservist who is not on active duty. *c1945.*

Sunday thinker   A self-proclaimed visionary; an impractical person; an eccentric. 1943: "Ficco's crazy, a Sunday thinker. Nobody could predict him." Wolfert, *Underworld*, 471.

sun-downer   *n.* A strict disciplinarian; a martinet.

sun-fisher   *n.* A twisting, bucking horse. 1929: "The cowboy talks of eating gravel after he has tried to ride a sun-fisher." *World's Work*, Nov., 40/1.

sunny   *adj.* **1** Happy, pleasant. *Colloq.* **2** See **sunny side up.**

sunny side up   Fried on one side only, so that the yolk remains soft; said of an egg. *Because the yolk is round and yellow, like the sun, and lies on top of an egg fried in this manner. Orig. lunch-counter use in relaying an order; now common.* Cf. **over.**

sunshine   *n.* **1** Gold. *Not common.* **2** Carrots; also, carrots and peas. *Not common.*

super   *n.* **1** A watch, specif. a pocket watch. 1941: "Most modern thieves spell it *super*, not realizing that it is really *souper*, a pun on the older *kettle*, meaning watch." D. W. Maurer. *Underworld use. Archaic.* **2** A supernumerary. *Theater use; archaic.* **3** A superintendent, esp. a worker's overseer. 1943: "The super and the floor bosses yelled. . . ." Wolfert, *Underworld*, 161. → **4** Esp., a combined superintendent, watchman, and janitor of an apartment house or small office building. *The super and his family often live in the building, usu. in the basement, or the super may have a small office with sleeping facilities, rent-free, in return for his work. He acts as a hall janitor, sweeps the lobby, shovels snow, makes minor plumbing and electrical repairs, and, in the case of an apartment house, acts as an intermediary between tenants and the landlord. In many cases, he is an actual building superintendent, but often he is a glorified janitor, in which*

case *"super" can be considered a euphem. adj.* Wonderful; marvelous; very pleasing. 1941: "America's Teen-age Girls Speak Language of Their Own That Is Too Divinely Super." *Life*, Jan. 27, 78. *Young teenage girl use since c1935.*

super-duper   sooper-dooper   *adj.* Colossal; exceedingly large and remarkable; remarkable, esp. for its size or scope. 1940: "After seeing this new M-G-M [Metro-Goldwyn-Mayer] movie studio] sooper-dooper musical smash. . . ." Advt., N.Y. *Times*, Sept. 27, 27.

superman   *n.* A German soldier; always used ironically. *Some W.W.II Army use.*

sure   *adv.* Yes; certainly; surely; I shall. 1909: "How more confidingly is cordial agreement acknowledged than by 'Sure'?" *Scribner's*, Aug., 250/2. 1934: [Now slang]. *Web. Freq. used as a one-word reply. Colloq.*

sure-fire   *adj.* Unfailing; certain of winning applause. *Colloq.*

sure thing   **1** A certainty; a standout. *Colloq. since c1850.* **2** Yes; certainly; surely; I shall. *Colloq. since c1890.*

sush   *v.t.* = **shush.**

swab   *n.* A merchant sailor.   **—bie swabby**   *n.* A sailor. *Usu. used in direct address.* See Appendix, —ie, —y endings.   **—bo   swabo**   *n.* **1** A sailor. *Not common.* See Appendix, —o ending. **2** Zero; no results; the grade of 0%. *c1925; Annapolis and USN use. From the concept that a swabbed deck is completely clean or blank.*

swab down   **1** To wash down the decks of a ship; to clean up something. *Maritime use.* **2** To take a bath; to clean oneself. **swab-downs**   *n.pl.* Epaulets. *Maritime use.*

swacked   *adj.* Drunk. 1950: "The baronet and his hireling were swacked to the eyeballs. . . ." J. Alexander, *SEP*, Apr. 1, 75/1. 1958: "You're not fit to be living out here . . . you're swacked all the time." S. Bellow, *Esquire*, Jan., 114. *Army, USN, and underworld use. More common in Eng. than in the U.S.* See Appendix, Drunk.

swag   *n.* **1** Stolen money or goods; loot. **2** Any article or articles forbidden to prisoners; contraband articles.

swagger   *adj.* Stylish. 1930: "A swagger outfit of clothes. . . ." Lavine, *Third Degree*, 128.   *n.* A vagabond carrying a swag. *Not common in U.S.*

swagman   *n.* A vagabond; a hiker. *From the swag, or bundle, he carries.*

Much more common in Australia than in U.S.

swak **SWAK** **S.W.A.K.** *adj.* Sealed with a kiss. *Written on the back of love letters; fairly common teenage and young student use; from the initials.* See Appendix, Shortened Words.

swallow *v.t.* **1** To believe or accept something false, deceiving, or leading to being tricked, cheated, or taken advantage of. *From the expression "to swallow it hook, line, and sinker."* **2** To believe or accept something. *Often used in the negative, as a refusal to believe or accept something, e.g., "I can't swallow that."* Cf. **stomach.**

swallow the anchor To go ashore permanently; to get a shore job; to leave the USN.

swallow [or eat] the Bible To lie; to swear falsely. 1930: "The police will stick together, stretch conscience and at times 'swallow the Bible,' as the quaint phrase has it . . . to protect some grafter. . . ." Lavine, *Third Degree,* 17. *Archaic and dial.*

swamp angel A lowland hillbilly; one who comes from the swamps. *c1850.*

swamper *n.* **1** A truck driver's helper. → **2** A porter.

swamp-root *n.* **1** Whisky. *Archaic and dial.* **2** Any green vegetable. *Not common.*

swamp seed Rice. *Some W.W.II Armed Forces use; mainly dial.*

swamp water Coffee. *Some W.W.II Army use. Not common.*

swan *v.i.* To leave a position for some trivial reason and without authorization.

swank *adj.* Stylish, elegant, ritzy. 1950: "Carroll's swank offices at East St. Louis have been closed." AP, July 22. *n.* **1** Stylishness; smartness. 1925: "The . . . swank of his riding clothes. . . ." F. Scott Fitzgerald, *The Great Gatsby,* 15. *v.i.* To display stylishness in an ostentatious way. **—s** *n.* Best clothes; dressy clothing. **—y** *adj.* **1** Stylish, esp. in an ostentatious way. → **2** Cultured; luxurious.

swat *v.t.* To hit or to hit at; usu., to hit or to hit at a person lightly or to hit or hit at a small object, such as a baseball. **—s** *n.pl.* = **brushes.** 1950: "And I, myself, by accident, discovered the swats on drums. Out in Los Angeles I had a drummer that hit his snares so loud that one night I gave him a couple of fly swatters for a gag. This drummer

fell in with the joke and used them, but they worked so smooth he kept right on using them. So we have 'the swats' today—a nice soft way to keep your rhythm going." A. Lomax, *Mr. Jelly Roll,* 59. *Many musicians have claimed the credit for inventing swats, or brushes.*

swat flies **1** To beg money from people standing at curbstones or store windows. *Hobo use.* → **2** To do one's job or to do anything in a leisurely manner.

swat-stick *n.* A baseball bat.

swazzled *adj.* Drunk.

sweat *v.t.* **1** = **sweat it out.** **2** To give the third degree to someone. *v.i.* **1** = **sweat it out.** 1943: "Waiting for mail is *sweatin'.* In the services you don't worry or wait, you *sweat.*" A. Ostrow. **2** Fig., to work hard at something; to concentrate consciously on performing, comprehending, speaking, or being hip; to strive for a conscious goal. *This is a key word in cool, far out, and beat use. An underlying principle of these groups is that whatever one does, achieves, or believes should come naturally, from natural talent or understanding. Thus one should be relaxed, at ease, cool, loose, natural, or even beat. If one isn't these things, one can't and shouldn't strive for them, because either you are or you aren't. To sweat means that one has no natural talent at, understanding of, or feeling for these things. Thus, consciously striving for them is an indication that the person is playing music, working, studying, or trying to be something he really isn't, just for material or commercial reasons, social prestige, or acceptance. This is why cool and esp. beat people seem uninterested in others and don't try to convert them to their way of living.* *n.* The third degree. *Some underworld use.*

sweater girl **1** A movie actress or model known primarily for her sexually attractive physique, specif. for large, shapely, prominently displayed breasts. *Sweater girls and prominent breasts were much in vogue during the early 1940's.* See **cheesecake, falsies, glamor girl, pin-up,** and **uplift** for an understanding of this phenomenon. → **2** Any girl or young woman with attractive, shapely breasts; any girl or young woman who, esp. habitually, wears tight-fitting sweaters or other clothing that emphasizes her breasts.

sweating-out *n.* A reprimand from a superior or one in authority. *W.W.II Air Force use, not common.*

sweat it To be bothered or annoyed

by something; to sweat it out. *Rock-and-roll use since c1955.*

sweat it out   sweat [something] sweat out   1 To wait (for something) anxiously and helplessly; to hope for and expect something (to happen) when one has no control over the matter; to wait (one's turn) impatiently or in dread. **2** To question a person in a rough or embarrassing way; to obtain information from a person by intimidation or torture; to give the third degree to someone.

sweatshop   *n.* A dilapidated factory employing unskilled labor, often newly arrived immigrants, for long hours at low pay. 1956: *"Sweatshop*—A place of employment characterized by poor work surroundings, long hours, low pay." *Labor's Special Lang. from Many Sources. Colloq.*

Swede   swede   *n.* 1 A blunderer. **2** A piece of clumsy work.

Swedish fiddle   A crosscut saw. *Logger use. Not common.*

Sweeney   See **Tell it to Sweeney.**

sweep   *n.* The act or an instance of one athlete or team winning a tournament without losing an individual game or contest.   *v.t.* To win a tournament without losing a game or contest.   *v.i.* To flee, esp. from danger or potential discovery. *Some underworld use c1930.*

sweepswinger   *n.* One who rows as a crew member of a racing shell. *Student use.*

sweet   *adj.* **1** Easy and lucrative; said of a job or business. **2** Hospitable; pleasant and homelike. **3** Esp., hip or sympathetic to and appreciative of progressive jazz and its players or off-beat art. 1958: "The 5-Spot [a jazz nightclub in N.Y.C.] is a sweet place, that is, the people come to listen to the music or they'll come to listen to me read poetry, not just to get drunk." K. Rexroth, poet, on "Night Beat," a television interview program, Apr. 14.

sweet—   See Appendix, Prefixes and Prefix words.

Sweet Alice   A glass of milk. *Lunch-counter use. Not common.*

sweet-back   *adj.* Having the attributes of a "sweet man." c1915 [1950]: "They were sweet-back men, I suppose you'd call them—always a bunch of women running after them." A. Lomax, *Mr. Jelly Roll,* 15. *Still some Negro use.*

sweeten up   1 To flatter, cajole, or court a person, in order that the person will like or favor one; specif., to talk or act sweetly to one's lover or superior,

usu. to regain one's good standing after anger or an argument or in preparation for asking a favor. **2** = **sugar-coat.**

sweetened (up) = **sugar-coated;** made happier. 1957: "The story has been sweetened up and the heel [made] only a temporary heel . . . really a good guy." *Life,* Oct. 14, 97.

sweetheart   *n.* **1** A pleasing person. **2** Anything excellent; a honey.   *v.t.* To court, to squire or escort to social functions; to act as a sweetheart. c1915 [1954]: ". . . Whose sister I used to sweetheart." L. Armstrong, *Satchmo, My Life in New Orleans,* 57.

sweetie   *n.* A sweetheart; used as a general term of endearment as well as in reference to one's beloved. 1925: "And Tom's the first sweetie she ever had." F. Scott Fitzgerald, *The Great Gatsby,* 43. 1957: "Uebel to Wed School Sweetie. . . ." Headline, N.Y. *Post,* May 18, 65.

sweetie-pie   *n.* **1** A sweetheart; used most often in direct address. 1944: "No, sweetie-pie." Ford, *Phila. Murder,* 155. 1951: "But his sweetie pie came home in the early hours." AP, Sept. 25. *Now considered corny by young people.* **2** An attractive, pleasing, personable, pert girl. *Some student use c1930–c1940.*

sweet mama   A female lover. *The image is of a dark-complexioned or plump girl or woman, not necessarily young, who is extremely sensuous and generous to her lover. Assoc. with Negro use.* See **sweet man, sweet papa.** See Appendix, Food and Sex.

sweet man   A male lover. *The image is of a dude or sport, who is extremely sensuous and generous to his lover. Assoc. with Negro use.* Cf. **sweet mama.** See Appendix, Food and Sex.

sweet on [someone]   In love with, infatuated with; in love with and hoping to be courted or accepted by someone. 1940: "He was never really sweet on Miss Carlisle." A. Christie, *Sad Cypress,* 122. 1957: "She had been very sweet on a handsome young man from a fine old family." F. Morton, *The Art of Courtship,* 161. *Colloq.*

sweet papa   A combination of "sugar daddy" and "sweet man" in one person.

sweet pea   1 A sweetheart of either sex. **2** One easily duped; a sucker.

sweet potato   An ocarina.

sweets   *n.sing.* Sweetheart; a term of endearment for one's sweetheart; always in direct address. *Some use since c1930. n.pl.* Sweet potatoes, usu. roasted or mashed, served at a meal. *Most often in the combination "ham and sweets."*

sweet-talk *v.i., v.t.* To persuade, or gain an advantage or personal goal, by flattery and glib talk; to sweeten up a person, esp. one of the opposite sex. *n.* Talk intended to sweeten up or persuade a person, esp. one of the opposite sex; a line.

swell *n.* A stylishly dressed person, usu. male; a dandy, dude, or sport; a genteel or refined person; a wealthy, socially prominent person, esp. if somewhat of a dandy or sport. 1955: "We're the cream . . . / . . . a stylish team/And as for swells and colored bells/. . . ." H. R. Hoyt, *Town Hall Tonight*, 202. *Colloq.; becoming archaic.* *adj.* Pleasing; excellent; grand; fine; elegant; stylish; wonderful; enjoyable; friendly; hospitable. 1900: "The hotels are swell." "Fitzgerald and Moy's Adams street place was a truly swell saloon." Dreiser, *Sister Carrie*, 3; 31. 1923: "It sure is one swell day." "He was a hell of a swell fellow when he was sober." C. MacArthur, *Rope*. 1930: "The boys give the fellow a swell funeral." "What a swell commission you made." "The swell time he had with the swell broads in the swell musical comedy. . . ." Lavine, *Third Degree*, 29; 128; 128. *Colloq. since c1880; gained present pop. c1920.* *adv.* Excellently; pleasingly; elegantly; wonderfully; enjoyably; stylishly; hospitably. 1949: "The new owners, who have treated me swell. . . ." AP, Oct. 3.

swelled head = **swellhead.**

swellelegant *adj.* Swell; elegant; esp., swell and elegant. *Has been fairly common, almost a fad word, at various times.*

swellhead *n.* **1** An egotistic or conceited person. *Colloq. since c1850.* **2** Conceit. 1930: "I was afraid you'd get the swellhead." Burnett, *Iron Man*, 18.

swift *adj.* Dissolute; fast. *n.* Speed. 1943: "I've got plenty of swift, if that's what you mean." Chandler, *Lady in Lake*, 219.

swig *n.* A swallow, gulp, or mouthful, esp. of whisky. 1957: ". . . Kentucky mountaineer . . . choking down one test swig. . . ." Advt., *New Yorker*, Nov. 16, 174.

swindle *n.* **1** Money charged, as for a purchase. *c1835; not common.* **2** Any business transaction, task, or job; a deal.

swindle sheet An account ledger kept by a traveling salesman or business executive, listing the business expenses incurred and paid out of his own funds, so that he may be reimbursed by the business firm; an expense account. 1942: "Make that two berths. . . . But only one goes on the swindle sheet. . . ." A. Rowley Hilliard, *Outcast Island*, 111. 1956: "Ask any sales manager . . . they'll do it every swindle sheet." Caption for a drawing of a salesman writing down the cost of an expensive meal on his expense account while eating a hamburger; J. Hatlo, cartoon, *SEP*, Oct. 20, 49. *Fairly common since W.W.II. Orig. so called because exaggerating the cost of, or adding extra, items allows the salesman or executive to make a profit. Reinforced by the fact that an executive may list personal items as necessary for business, with his firm's knowledge; in effect this means that he is taking a lower salary in return for the firm's paying part of his personal living expenses, which thus shows his income as lower than it actually is, so that he will avoid paying full U.S. government income tax.*

swindle stick = **cheat stick.**

swing *v.i.* **1** To hang; to be hanged. *Archaic.* *v.i., v.t.* **1** To create or play swing music adroitly or in an exciting or satisfying way; to play a piece of music in the style of swing. → **2** Satisfactorily composed, arranged, or adroitly played in swing; said of a piece of music. *Can be considered as a v.t. as such a piece of music seems to create itself and continue on its own momentum.* → **3** To seem to be created or grow out of its own natural or inherent design, form, or rhythm; to satisfy or be so perfect, for a given time, place, feeling, or mood, that a thing seems to have grown from the time, place, feeling, or mood; to grow naturally or develop from its own momentum; said orig. of swing music, later of any art, entertainment, or the like. → **4** To attract, excite, satisfy, completely envelop; to be hep, in rapport with, swing music, or with anything or anyone; to demonstrate complete understanding of or appreciation for swing; to be hep, in the groove, or with it. 1956: "[George Shearing's group] proves that jazz doesn't have to be raucous to swing." *Metronome*, Apr., 34. 1957: "Chaucer and Jazz are quite similar; they both swing, they both have the same punch, vitality and guts." R. Shelton, in *Jazz World*, Mar., 10. *Can be considered as v.t., as a thing or person that actually swings the speaker, with excitement, or seems to swing or create itself. Orig. swing use, c1935–c1942. One of the most common* *swing words, later some general jazz, and esp. cool, use. Also fairly well known to the general public.* **n. 1** An initiation, as into a fraternal society. *Some c1920–c1935 student use.* **2** Influence, as with one in authority; preference. *Some c1930 student use.* **3** A style or form of music that evolved in jazz during the early 1930's and which became the most pop. music, esp. for dancing, among students, teenagers, and young adults c1935–c1942. *Swing is usu. played by large bands; the rhythm section keep a fast, breathless tempo and even, unbroken beat; the woodwind section and the brass sections alternate in carrying the melody or in providing a formal rhythmical background while the other section plays arranged variations. Most pieces have one solo, usually a saxophone, trombone, clarinet or trumpet solo. Both pop. love ballads and stand. jazz tunes make up the swing repertory. Thus swing can be considered as jazz arranged and played by a large, rhythmically driving band, with the various reed and brass sections, often playing in unison, taking the place of the individual instruments of earlier jazz bands. It resulted from jazz's moving north from the brothels of New Orleans and being adapted, often by commercial white musicians, for large audiences, nightclub and radio performances, and, most important of all, for dancing. Swing died at the advent of W.W.II. Its now older audience lost interest; sophisticated Ivy League youth turned to bop and cool, seeming to prefer the more complex nondance music played by small groups; and teenagers were first commercially subjected to and then completely captured by rock and roll.* → **4** Collectively, the devotees of swing music; the fashions, fads, moods, and attitudes assoc. with devotees of swing c1935–c1942. **5** A second brakeman on a freight train. *Railroad use since c1935.* **6** A rest period or time off from work, as a worker's lunch period or a ten-minute rest period. 1943: "With two hours' swing in the afternoon for lunch." Wolfert, *Underworld*, 327. See **break. 7 = swing shift.** **—ing** *adj.* Hip; in rapport with modern attitudes; satisfying, exciting or pleasing to a modern, hip person; on the ball. 1956: "Songs for Swingin' Lovers." Title of a record album by Frank Sinatra. *Orig. swing use; some resurrected cool and far-out use.*

swing, in full Performing or working smoothly or perfectly; performing without strain; at maximum efficiency or speed. 1919 [1956]: "Every person shall be spared in whose home a jazz-band is in full swing." Letter dated March 13, 1919, sent by a psychotic murderer, known as "The Axeman," to the editor of the New Orleans *Times-Picayune*, reprinted in *The Real Jazz Old and New*, S. Longstreet, 65.

swinging gate An adroitly playing swing musician completely involved and in rapport with the piece being played and the rest of the performers. 1956: "It can't be, they say, that a group of characters in a session become one single unit making something good, but it happens. Everybody is a solid swinging gate and you're no longer a pickup band —you don't see the mike anymore or worry about the turntable. You're making music." S. Longstreet, *The Real Jazz Old and New*, 135. See **gate.**

swing like a (rusty) gate 1 In baseball, to swing or strike wildly at a pitched ball. **2** To play swing music well; to swing. *Swing use.*

swing out To appear wearing new clothing; to take part in a fancy social gathering. 1851: Hall, *College Words*, 296. *Still some use but becoming archaic.*

swing room A room set aside in a factory in which the workers may eat, smoke, or relax. See **swing.**

swing shift A work period or shift between the standard day and night shifts, usu. beginning in the afternoon and ending in the evening, but sometimes beginning in the early morning and ending in the afternoon; a work crew or group of workers who work during these hours.

swipe *v.t.* **1** To steal a small object, usu. one that can be concealed in the hand; to take without asking permission. 1945: "Nix on swiping anything." E. B. White, *Stuart Little*, 93. **2** To appropriate another's idea, sweetheart, or the like. 1956: "First he swiped my idea for a picnic, then he swiped my girl." *Oral.* **n. 1** A hard sweeping blow, as with the hand or a bludgeon. 1944: "Let somebody . . . take a swipe at him. . . ." B. Cerf, *Amer. Mercury*, Aug., 174/2. **2** A racing stable worker who rubs down horses. **—d** *adj.* Drunk. *Obs.*

swish *n.* **1** A male homosexual, esp. one with obviously feminine traits. 1941: "That fat swish." Schulberg, *Sammy*, 88. *Fairly well known. From the effeminate hip motion made while walking. Perh. reinforced by the Brit. sl. "swish" = fancy, which is known in the U.S.* **2** In

basketball, a field goal. *Not common.*
v.t. Acting, walking, or gesturing as a
homosexual; making effeminate gestures.
switch *v.i.* To give information; to
inform, as to the police. *n.* A knife,
whether a switchblade or not. **—blade**
n. A pocket knife with its long blade
concealed in the handle; on pressing a
button the blade springs out. *Assoc.
with teenage hoodlums and street gangs.
Common since c1945.* **—eroo** *n.* A
switch or reversal of position; a substitu-
tion of one thing for another; an old
story, idea, game, or the like with a new
ending. 1933: [substitution] "We'll pull a
switcheroo. We'll use olives instead of
cherries." H. T. Webster. 1942: [new
ending] "And put the switcheroo on an
old joke or two." Ben Bernie [comedian],
radio program, Jan. 12. 1948: [reversal
of position] "Lincoln, playing it smart,
starting from nothing, first opposing
abolitionism in the Douglas debates and
then making the great switcheroo."
Chas. Y. Harrison, *Nobody's Fool*,
quoted in N.Y. *Times Bk. Rev.*, Sept. 19,
5/2. *One of the most common "–eroo"
words.*
switch-hitter *n.* **1** In baseball, an
ambidextrous batter who bats left-
handed against a right-handed pitcher
and right-handed against a left-handed
pitcher. 1953: "[Mickey] Mantle, the
switch-hitting Oklahoma kid. . . ." AP,
July 6.ᵗ *Colloq.* → **2** One who does two
things well; a versatile person. → **3** A
bisexual person.
switch hog A railroad yardmaster.
swivel *n.* A look; a turning of the head
to get a better look.

swivet, in a Hurried; anxious; nervous; fidgety. 1952: "You can't get
yourself in a swivet over some isolated
instances of mild abuse or error. . . ."
Robt. C. Ruark, *synd. newsp. col.*, March
11. *Since c1890. Dial.*
swizzled swoozzled *adj.* Drunk.
Archaic. Cf. **ding-swizzled.**
swobble *v.i., v.t.* To gulp one's food;
to eat hurriedly. *Negro use.*
swoon = take a dive.
swoony *n.* An attractive boy. *adj.*
Attractive. *Teenage use, c1940. More
often in movies ànd stories about teenagers
than used by teenagers.*
swozzled = swizzled.
swutty = sweetie.
—sy = —sie See Appendix, —sie,
Suffix Words.
sync *n.* An act or instance of synchro-
nizing; the synchronization; of a
movie sound track with the action on the
film, of a flash gun with a camera
shutter, or of the audio and visual components of a television set. *v.t.* To
synchronize one thing with another. See
Appendix, Shortened Words.
syph siff [taboo] *n.* **1** Syphilis.
1947: " 'Why don't you tell us about the
time you got siff from your nigger maid?'
'Harold!' said De Paris. 'Not so vulgar,
please, not so vulgar. Use the scientific
terminology. Syphilis, not siff.' " C.
Willingham, *End as a Man*, 16. *Since
c1910. Wide W.W.II use. This shortening
is taboo, though the complete word is not.*
2 A syphilitic. See Appendix, Shortened
Words.
syringe *n.* **1** A trombone. *Synthetic
sl.* **2** A vaginal douche taken as a birth
control measure.

T

T *n.* = **tea.** See Appendix, Shortened
Words.
tab *n.* **1** A bill, an unpaid bill; the
total amount of money owed on a bill.
1956: "Three- or four-hundred-dollar
tabs for unpaid likker." S. Longstreet,
The Real Jazz Old and New, 105. *Colloq.*
→ **2** A handwritten acknowledgment of a
debt, endorsed by the debtor at the time
and place of incurrence; an IOU. 1956:
"Racket guys got class when it comes
to gambling. They're liable to go out
and stick up a bank if they owe you a
tab." J. Cannon, *Who Struck John?* 209.
v.t. **1** To borrow money. **2** To beg money

or food. *Neither use common. Both uses
reinforced by "tap."* **—s** *n.pl.*
The ears. *Not common.*
table = under the table.
table finisher A glutton. *Archaic.*
tab-lifter *n.* A night-club customer.
Cf. **tab.**
T-bone *n.* **1** A trombone. *Some swing
use; musician use; now archaic.* **2** A
Model T Ford automobile; any early
model Ford automobile. *Teenage hot rod
use since c1950.*
tack *n.* **1** An adviser in a boys'
school; a school dean. **2** A nickel.
Negro use. Not common. **3** The saddle

and all other equipment used by a jockey in racing. **—head** *n.* A stupid person. See **brass tacks, coffin tack.** **—y** *adj.* **1** Drunk. *c1900; archaic.* **2** Not quite respectable. *Orig. U.S. and Sp. use in New Orleans.* → **3** Shabby; dilapidated. **4** Untidy, neglected; unrefined, vulgar. 1955: "She talked in a manner that would be considered a bit countrified, if not slightly tacky." C. Willingham, *To Eat a Peach*, 124. *n.* **1** A neglected, ill-kept, or inferior horse. *Since c1835; dial.* **2** An untidy, neglected, or sloppy person. *Dial.*

tack hammer A large sledge hammer used for driving tent stakes. *Ironic comparison to an actual tack hammer.*

tad *n.* **1** A boy; a child. *Archaic and dial.* **2** An Irish person. *From Irish variants of "Thaddeus." Not common.* **—pole** *n.* A small French child. *W.W.I Army use in France.* Cf. **frog.**

taffy *n.* Flattery; exaggeration; applesauce. *Colloq. since c1880; now obs.*

tag *n.* **1** A person's name; a name. **2** = **dog tag;** an identification tag. **3** A letter smuggled out of prison. *Underworld use.* **4** A warrant for arrest. 1934: "Is there a tag out for me?" Chandler, *Finger Man*, 34. **5** An automobile license plate. 1953: "The Seminoles get special tags with the words 'Seminole Indian' on them instead of the usual letters and numbers. Around 170 tags are given out each year." AP, Tallahassee, Fla., June 2. Cf. **dog tag.** *v.t.* To arrest.

tag-along *n.* An auto trailer. *Not common.*

tail *n.* **1** The human posterior; the buttocks. 1924: "If all of us parked ourselves on our tails. . . ." Marks, *Plastic Age*, 200. 1937: "I hadn't tossed him out on his tail. . . ." Weidman, *Wholesale*, 69. *Since before c1895.* → **2** Fig., a person's trail. 1934: "[The insurance detectives are] right on your tail now." Cain, *Postman*, 61. 1934: "You can pull your shadows off my tail any time you like." Chandler, *Finger Man*, 93. → **3** A person, as a detective, who trails or follows and observes another's actions; a shadow. 1941: "He has a tail on me." G. Homes, *40 Whacks*, 100. 1953: "The security officer was even going to put a tail on the children." J. McCarten in *New Yorker*. Feb. 7, 56. **4** [taboo] The vagina; a girl or woman considered only sexually. *After "piece" the most common word for the combined woman-vagina-coitus concept*

in vulgar use by males. Cf. **cunt, piece, poon tang, pussy.** *v.t.* To follow or trail a person, as a detective might follow a suspect or a robber, an intended victim. 1928: "[Robbers] tailing (not trailing) a jewelry salesman, or a mail truck. . . ." E. Booth in *Amer. Mercury*, May, 81. **—s** *n.pl.* **1** Full dress; a man's formal suit with a long-tailed coat. **2** A tuxedo. 1941: "A well-fed man in tails opened the door." G. Homes, *40 Whacks*, 129. *Colloq.*

tail, have [someone or something] by the **1** = **have [someone] by the balls.** **2** To be in command or control of a situation; to be assured of success. 1951: "There is the matter of personal happiness. Oh, I know all young people are sure they can have it by the tail, permit me that indelicate phrase, but can you and Alice really be happy?" S. Longstreet, *The Pedlocks*, 152.

tail bone The rump; the buttocks. *Usu. jocular use. Made somewhat more pop. by its freq. use in Walt Kelly's synd. newsp. comic strip "Pogo."*

tail-gate *n., adj.* A style of playing jazz which is supposed to resemble the style of the early New Orleans musicians. *Generally speaking, tail-gate jazz may be characterized by ensemble improvisations on stand. jazz compositions, usu. blues, an emphatic beat, usu. accented on the second and fourth beats of the measure, a loud and rough tone, simple harmonies in thirds, etc. The term is supposed to have originated in the practice of New Orleans jazz bands that played in horse-drawn wagons during street parades and political rallies: the tail-gate was left down to make room for the slide trombone. Thus the word is assoc. with jazz in general and specif. with a style of playing the trombone, and refers broadly to a spirited, intense, hot manner of performance.* Cf. **gutbucket.** See **jazz.**

tailor-made *adj.* **1** Made in a factory, according to standard specifications. **2** Fitting one's expectations and abilities; just right. *n.* **1** A suit of factory-made clothes. **2** A plainclothes policeman or detective. **3** A factory-made cigarette as opposed to a hand-rolled one. *Obs. except in the West and some rural areas; some W.W.II Armed Forces use ⟋in overseas areas where factory-made cigarettes were hard to obtain.*

take For phrases beginning with "take," see also under the principal word of the phrase.

take *n.* Gross profit, esp. of a short

term business venture, speculation, entertainment, sporting event, gambling casino, or the like; lit., the money taken in. 1958: "Nevada's take has been hit by a recession . . . its Eastern [gambling] trade now passes up Las Vegas for Havana." N.Y. *Post*, Feb. 12, 38. See **double-take.** *v.t.* **1** To rob, cheat, or swindle a person, esp. out of a comparatively large sum of money; to deceive or trick a person; to "stick" a person. 1932: [rob] "After somebody takes a-jewelry store. . . ." Runyon. 1950: "When a sucker came in, don't worry, he would really be taken. The odds were so much against him, he never had a chance, especially if he played Cotch, the three-card Spanish poker where you deal from the bottom of the deck." A. Lomax, *Mr. Jelly Roll*, 50. **2** To fight someone; to treat roughly; to beat up. *c1925.* See **Don't take any wooden nickels, take someone to the cleaners, what it takes.**

take a gander Take a look at; look over.

take five To take a five-minute or a short rest period from work or, esp., from a theatrical rehearsal; to take a five-minute break.

take it (on the chin) **1** To withstand punishment or abuse; to bear up under attack, strain, or hard work. 1936: "To 'take it' . . . is a matter of credit to the person who does the taking. The fuller form, 'take it on the chin' . . . indicates . . . the origin of the phrase in boxing. . . ." *Word Study*, Oct., 2/1. *Most common in prize fight use.* **2** = **buy,** to agree.

take it big To express any marked emotional response, such as surprise, fear, or pain; to exaggerate one's sentiments.

take it in **1** To take time off from walking a beat. *Said of a patrolman.* 1930: "It is . . . pleasant 'to take it in,' rest in some comfortable place, and smoke. . . ." Lavine, *Third Degree*, 160. **2** To see and do everything that a specific locale or job has to offer; to comprehend.

take it on To eat, esp. to eat voraciously or large quantities.

take off **1** To take a short vacation from work. *Colloq.* **2** To leave or depart, specif. in order to go to, or visit, another place. **3** To bawl out (someone). *Some W.W.II Army use; some student use.* **4** To give oneself an injection of a narcotic drug. *Some addict use.*

take on **1** To make a fuss about some-thing. *Colloq.* **2** To put on airs. *Colloq.* **3** To re-enlist in the Army. *World War II Army use.*

take (someone, something) on To accept a challenge; to fight someone; to accept a difficult or unrewarding task.

take-out *n.* **1** Prepared food, sold by a restaurant, that the patron takes out to eat elsewhere, as at home or at an office. 1941: "Pies she hoped to sell to the 'take-out' trade." Cain, *M. Pierce*, 117. **2** A percentage of the gross profits; one's share of money, esp. profits or loot.

take [someone] to the cleaners Lit. and fig., to take all of another's money, specif. by deception or cheating; often passive use, usu. = to have lost all one's money, esp. at gambling.

talk [one's] ear off To talk a great deal; to bore a person by talking too much. 1952: "Donna talked his ear off. . . ." N.Y. *Daily News*, Aug. 12, C8/2.

talker *n.* **1** A motion picture having a sound track. 1936: "*Variety* calls it a talker, never talkie." A. Green, *Esquire*, Sept. *Theater use. c1928–35 when talking movies were a rarity.* **2** = **barker.** *"Talker," and not "barker," is in wide carnival and circus use.*

talkie *n.* **1** A movie with a sound track. *Very common c1928–35.* See **talker, the talkies. 2** A portable two-way radio telephone used by the Armed Forces in W.W.II. See **walkie-talkie.**

talkies, the Motion pictures; the motion picture industry. *Archaic. From the period in the history of motion pictures when an accompanying sound track was a novelty and major attraction.*

talk-talk *n.* Talk, esp. idle gossip. See Appendix, Reduplications.

talk through [one's] hat To talk nonsense; to lie. *Colloq. since c1885.*

talk turkey To talk plainly and frankly; to discuss the facts. *Colloq. since c1920.*

tallow-pot *n.* A locomotive fireman. *Railroad use.*

tall timbers *n.* An area or vaudeville circuit having no large cities; a rural area. *c1920; theater use.*

tamp up on To beat a person up. *Maritime and underworld use, not common.*

tangle *v.i.* To fight. *Colloq.*

tangle-foot *n., adj.* Whisky, esp. cheap whisky. *Western use, c1860; obs.* 1893: "When we find a Western writer describing the effects of *tangle-foot* whisky, the adjective explains itself. . . ." Brander Matthews, *Harper's*, July, 307/2. **—ed** *adj.* Drunk. *c1860; obs.*

tangle-leg *n., adj.* Liquor, esp. cheap whisky; the unstable gait resulting from consumption of too much liquor. See **tangle-foot.** *Western use, c1860; obs.* **—ged** *adj.* Drunk. *c1860; obs.*

tank *n.* **1** A heavy drinker of beer and liquor; a drunkard. *c1900.* **2** A small town. From **tank town. 3** A jail or cell; specif. a cell for prisoners awaiting investigation, trial, or the like. **Drunk tank** = cell where drunks are kept to sober up. **Fish tank** = cell where suspects or new prisoners are kept. 1939: [jail] "When he goes into the tank as a prisoner. . . ." Gardner, *D.A. Draws*, 208. 1947: [cell for drunken prisoners] "The day a police reporter had to pick him out of the collection in the drunk tank. . . ." Allan R. Bosworth, *San Fran. Murders*, 264. Cf. **fish bowl. 4** The stomach. 1945 [1943]: " 'Tank-ache' = stomach-ache." E. Kasser. **5** A locomotive. *v.i.* To fail. *Not common.* *adj.* Fixed. *Said of a prize fight.* See **tank fight. —ed** *adj.* Drunk. *Colloq. since c1920.* **—y** *n.* A butcher. *W.W.II USN use. Not common.*

tank, go in the To allow oneself to lose a prize fight; to throw a fight. *Suggested by "take a dive."* Cf. **tank fight.**

tank act = **tank fight.**

tanked up = **tanked.**

tank fight A prize fight in which one fighter is paid or bribed to lose, as by his opponent or gamblers; a fixed prize fight; one in which a fighter takes a dive. Cf. **go in the tank.**

tank job = **tank fight.**

tank town A small town; a town too small to have a railroad station, but having a railroad water tank, if little else.

tank up To drink one's fill of liquor; to drink a great deal of liquor. 1925: "I think he'd tanked up a good deal at luncheon. . . ." F. Scott Fitzgerald, *The Great Gatsby*, 32.

tap *v.t.* To borrow, or attempt to borrow, money from someone.

tap out *v.i.* To lose all one's money; specif. gambling; to lose one's money; to become broke. 1939: "Nicely-Nicely does not mention his habit of tapping out any time a 4-to-5 shot comes along, which is as bad a habit as anybody can have." "The character from Bangor, Me., unfortunately taps out on the first proposition and has nothing with which to bet on the second." Runyon, 21; 36.

tapped out Broke. 1950: "The mark left the [gambling game] all tapped out." AP, Jan. 12. 1956: "All of a sudden you're tapped out. You're broke." J. Cannon, *Who Struck John?* 35.

tar *n.* **1** A sailor. *Colloq.* **2** The insides; the stuffing. Usu. in "beat [or knock] the tar out of [someone]." 1930: "Some-one . . . beat the tar out of the thug. . . ." Lavine, *Third Degree*, 111. **3** Opium. **4** Black coffee. *Not common.*

tar bucket A military full-dress hat. *Orig. West Point use.*

Target A The Pentagon Building in Washington, D.C. *Jocular use. In ref. to an atomic attack against the U.S. in any future war.*

tarp *n.* **1** A tarpaulin. See Appendix, Shortened Words. → **2** Specif., a special piece of tarpaulin or canvas used to fit over the seat of a roofless sports car, as protection from rain. *Sports car owner use since c1950.*

tarpaulin muster Passing the hat for contributions of money for a particular purpose; a collection of money for a charitable purpose. *Maritime use. c1940.*

tar-pot [derog.] *n.* A Negro child. *Archaic.*

tart *n.* A prostitute; any promiscuous girl or woman. 1951: "Real fancy night-gown, pink drawers, black lace. . . . Nothing cheap for us like the grimy tarts on Mercury Street." S. Longstreet, *The Pedlocks*, 102. *Colloq., becoming archaic.* See Appendix, Food and Sex.

taste *n.* A small portion or sample of anything. *Colloq.*

ta-ta *interj.* Good-by. *Some use since c1895. Usu. jocular, as it is assoc. with Eng. use and is considered an affectation.* *n.* A machine gun. *Some c1925 under-world use; prob. was synthetic.*

tattler *n.* **1** A night watchman. **2** An alarm clock.

taw *n.* Enough money to finance an enterprise; a stake. 1939: "It is . . . necessary for me to get hold of a taw to make a start." Runyon.

tawny *adj.* Most excellent. *Teenage use.*

taxi up To move closer to someone. *W.W.II Army Air Corps use. Not common.*

TD *n.* In football, a touchdown. *Colloq.*

t'd off *adj.* = **tee'd off.**

tea **T** *n.* **1** Marijuana. Cf. **weed tea. 2** A marijuana cigarette. Often in **stick of tea.** 1940: "Three highballs and three sticks of tea. . . ." Chandler,

Farewell, 60. **3** Any of certain stimulants illegally given to a racehorse to make it run faster. 1951: "Usu. cocaine or strychnine. . . ." D. W. Maurer, *Argot of the Racetrack.*

tead up Under the influence of or high on marijuana.

tea-hound *n.* **1** A ladies' man; a man who devotes much of his time to parties. → **2** A sissy. *College use.*

teakettle *n.* An old locomotive. 1952: "I knew Casey Jones when he was stokin' a switchyard teakettle down at Quincy." Merrill Blosser, "Freckles," *synd. comic strip*, Dec. 17. *Railroad use.*

tea pad Any place where marijuana addicts gather to smoke tea. See **pad.**

tea party A party or gathering of addicts for the purpose of smoking marijuana. 1948: ". . . Marijuana 'tea parties' are little things compared to the barely controlled violence of adults who allowed a world war." E. Burdick, *The Reporter*, Apr. 3, 31. *Some addict use.* Cf. **shooting gallery.**

tear *n.* **1** A spree; a bender. 1949: "Fred wanted to go on a little tear in the big town. . . ." *Fact Detec. Mysteries*, 118. *Note pronunciation "tare."* **2** A pearl. *Note pronunciation "teer."*

tearing up the pea patch Going on a rampage. *Pop. by baseball announcer "Red" Barber in his c1945–c1955 broadcasts of the old Brooklyn Dodgers baseball games. Considered a Southern expression.*

tear-jerker *n.* Something that is created or designed to elicit sadness or tears; specif. an entertainment, as a play or song, full of sadness and sentiment, whose main appeal is that it gives one a good cry; an actor or speaker able to elicit sympathy from his audience. 1935: ". . . A lawyer was imported from California, a magniloquent tear-jerker named Delmas." N. Levy in *Amer. Mercury*, Aug., 400/1. 1950: "The 'tear-jerker' is a paragraph about 'Marty,' who had difficulties in school, fell in with evil companions. . . ." H. G. Doyle in *Pub. of the Amer. Lang. Assoc.*, Feb., 19. 1955: "William A. Brady in 1901 decided that New York's sophisticates would like to see the old tear-jerker [the play 'Uncle Tom's Cabin'] with an all-star cast." H. R. Hoyt, *Town Hall Tonight*, 58. See Appendix, —jerk, —jerker endings.

tear off To have, to obtain; to create, to perform; usu. but not always implies haste stemming from desire, eagerness, or lack of time. *Most freq. in* "tear off a piece (of ass)" [taboo] = have coitus, said of a male; fairly freq. in "tear off some sleep" = to sleep while one is able to or has the time; sometimes in "tear off a piece of music" = to play the piece of music; less freq. in various other expressions. 1950: "The musicians began to tear off a La Conga." Starnes, *Another Mug.* 114. 1951: "Look, you come down and tear off a piece anytime. And the wine—*Asti Spumante*—she is ona me. I stand the wine. The girls, that is up to you." S. Longstreet, *The Pedlocks*, 241.

teaser *n.* A girl or woman who seems to invite a male's attention and favors, but who does not return them when given; a cock teaser [taboo]. 1951: "Once when Jacob saw one of Bonzoni's nieces, he had been tempted to accept Bonzoni's offer to stifle his aches with the best the establishment [a brothel] had to offer. Maybe Bella was right in calling his 'uptown lady' a 'teaser.'" S. Longstreet, *The Pedlocks*, 255.

tea-stick *n.* A marijuana cigarette. 1956: "He mixed with vipers on the reefer-trail . . . but there isn't much record that he went for tea-sticks himself." S. Longstreet, *The Real Jazz Old and New*, 104. *Some addict use.* See **stick; tea.**

tech *n.* A school of technology; a technical institute. *Often in the names of schools, e.g., Georgia Tech.* See Appendix, Shortened Words.

teddy **Teddy** *n.* **1** An Irishman. *c1900. Not common.* **2** A woman's one-piece undergarment, serving as both panties and chemise. *c1920; archaic.*

Tee Dee *n.* = **TD.**

tee'd off **teed off** **t'd off** *adj.* Angry; fed up; disgusted. See **pissed off.** *From "tee-off" reinforced by "pee'd off."*

teed up Drunk.

teen *n.* Teenager. 1951: "Such a project as redecorating one's room . . . is really interesting biz for a teen who loves being busy. . . ." Elaine Cannon, Salt Lake City *Deseret News*, July 30, 1/1. **—ager** **teen-ager** *n.* An adolescent; a person between the ages of 13 and 19, but specif. a high-school student between the ages of 15 and 19. *Colloq. since c1930; stand. since c1945. The U.S. is the only country having a word for members of this age group, and is the only country considering this age group as a separate entity whose influence, fads, and fashions are worthy of* *discussion apart from the adult world. Before c1935 U.S. teenagers considered themselves as, and were considered, young adults and not a special group.* **—er** *n.* Teenager. 1952: "He enjoys . . . a robust health that would be remarkable on a teener." R. C. Ruark, *synd. newsp. col.*, Aug. 25.

tee off (on [someone])   **1** In baseball, to make many hits in a game, or off a specif. pitcher of the opposing team; in prize fighting, to hit one's opponent with many hard blows. *From the golf term.* → **2** To reprimand or criticize a person severely.

telegraph   *v.t.* To make known one's intention by an unintentional, involuntary gesture or word; specif., in boxing, to signal unintentionally the blow that one intends to deliver next, as by a glance or twitch in the arm. 1936: "He'll [a boxer] never get to the top—he telegraphs his punches." Tully, *Bruiser*, 13. 1949: "She was leading up to something; the tone of her voice telegraphed it." J. Evans, *Halo*, 94.

telephone number (bit)   A prison sentence of more than 20 years but less than life. *Underworld use. From the high numbers.*

tell   *n.* Something that indicates or shows; an index. 1934: "The feet and ankles are the big tell in the matter of class. . . ." Runyon. *Not common.*

tell a green (blue) man   **1** = **tell it to the Marines. 2** Tell me the truth; inform me; make me hip. 1956: "When a jazz-player asks you to *tell a green man*, he wants you to put him wise." S. Longstreet, *The Real Jazz Old and New*, 147. *Some jazz use.* See **green.**

tell it to Sweeney   *An expression of disbelief. Fig.* = *"Go tell it to Sweeney. He may believe you. I don't." c1920; now archaic.*

tell it to the Marines   *An expression of disbelief. Fig.* = *"Go tell it to the Marines. They may be strong enough to accept your story. I'm not." c1830.*

tell off   **1** To tip a person off; to inform him in advance of some impending occurrence. **2** To reprimand; rebuke; bawl out. 1941: "The man had just been told off, and told off plenty." G. Homes, *40 Whacks*, 65. *Most common and widely popular meaning. Colloq.*

tell the (cockeyed) world, I'll   Emphatically; that's so very true; you're so completely right. *Fairly common cW.W.I; now archaic.*

tell [someone] what to do with (where

to put, shove, stick) [something] [the "shove" and "stick" forms are taboo] = **you (one) know what you (one) can do with it (something); shove (stick) it (something) up your (one's) ass** [taboo]. 1946: "The first thing I did when I got home was to tell my old boss where to stick my old job." "Green, an upholsterer, said that he was through with upholstering and had told his old boss what to do with his old job." M. Shulman, *Zebra Derby*, 124; 125.

tell [someone] where to get off   To reprimand or rebuke strongly; usu. to tell a person that he is not as important as he believes.

ten   *n.* A ten-dollar bill; the sum of $10.

ten, take   To take a ten-minute rest period from work, or, esp., from a theatrical rehearsal; to take a ten-minute break from marching [Army use], from a rehearsal [theater use], or any job.

ten-carat   *adj.* Big; remarkable, as an atypical specimen or example of something, usu. something bad; thorough. 1936: "No more ten-carat heels were going to tell me sorry." J. Weidman in *Amer. Mercury*, May, 91/2.

tenderloin   *n.* Any section or district of a city that is a center of its night life; an area in which lies the greatest opportunity for graft by corrupt police. Specif., in New York City the old 29th police precinct, from 23rd to 42nd Street west of Broadway. A police officer assigned there was reported to have commented that he had always eaten chuck steak, but henceforth would have tenderloin. *c1895. Subsequently the term has acquired a small particularity as related to prostitution, but has retained its use in relation to gambling and all forms of vice.*

ten-minute man   A go-getter; a fast talker. *Orig. hobo use.*

tenner   *n.* **1** A ten-dollar bill. 1901: Greenough & Kittredge. 1949: ". . . Spent the tenner on Jersey applejack." Billy Rose, *synd. newsp. col.*, Nov. 18. **2** A ten-year prison sentence. *Mainly prison use.* See Appendix, **—er** ending.

tenor = **whisky tenor.**

ten-percenter   *n.* **1** An actor's, performer's, writer's, etc., agent, whose commission is 10% of the money earned by his clients. *Mainly theater use.* **2** One who receives 10% of the loot, profit, or transaction. *Orig. underworld use* = *one who informs thieves of good prospects to rob, and is paid 10% of the loot. This use* *is archaic. Now usu. a politically influential person who obtains political favors or public contracts for his clients, and receives a percentage of the cash value of the favor or contract.* See **five-percenter.** See Appendix, —er ending.

ten-spot *n.* **1** A 10-dollar bill; the sum of $10. 1951: "A ten-spot can't get you past two counters in a grocery store without limping." Hal Boyle, AP, May 1. **2** A 10-year prison sentence. 1928: "I was out . . . after having served a ten-spot." D. Purroy.

tent See **dog tent, pup tent.**

tent Johnny In the Army, a second lieutenant. *c1936; Army and C.C.C. use.*

ten-twenty-thirty *n.* A repertory theater or company of actors. *From the prices of tickets, which were once 10¢, 20¢, and 30¢; archaic.*

ten-vee **10-V** *n., adj.* The worst, the lowest; of the lowest rank. *In analogy with "1-A" = the best.*

—teria See Appendix, —eteria, Suffixes and Suffix Words.

terrible *adj.* Wonderful; great; the best; the most. 1957: "Terrible—The best; the greatest." E. Horne, *For Cool Cats and Far-Out Chicks. Some far-out use.*

terrific *adj.* **1** Wonderful, marvelous; beautiful; remarkable; large; when used as a pred. adj. or attrib. adj. 1939: "You're Slightly Terrific." Pop. song. 1942: "He usually tosses off a script in an hour and a half . . . [the] script is apt to be terrific." *Time,* Nov. 2, 90/2. **2** Very much of a, complete; skilled, experienced; used only to emphasize the following noun. *Thus a "terrific bore," "a terrific actor," etc.* 1930: "Times Square hotel biz is on the terrific fritz." *Variety,* quoted in *Bookman,* 397/2. 1951: "*Terrific* may mean spectacular, beautiful, difficult, pretty, interesting, breath-taking, enormous, frightening, detestable, dull, or adorable." J. N. Hook in *Word Study,* May, 4/2.

terror = **holy terror.**

Texan border, the **Texas border, the** The United States border with Mexico, actually the Mexican border. 1952: "The northern land barrier of the U.S. is usually referred to as the Canadian border, but the southern land border is usually the Texas border." J. Randolph, *Texas Brags,* 55.

Texas leaguer In baseball, a hit falling between the infield and the outfield.

thank-you-(ye-)ma'am **1** = **wham bam.** → **2** A bump or hole in the road, such as causes riders to bounce up and down. *Since at least 1895.*

that ain't hay "That's a lot of money." Always used after a specific sum of money, as "He makes $30,000 a year, and that ain't hay." See **hay.**

that kills it Fig., "That destroys the mood, takes away my enthusiasm, or pleasure; that causes me to reject, refuse, or refrain; that ruins or spoils it; that guarantees failure." *Since c1945. Now fairly common.*

that's all she wrote **that's what she wrote** Fig., "That's all there is, that's all; this is the conclusion; it's finished." *During and since W.W.II. Orig. and lit., ref. to a soldier's last letter from his sweetheart, terminating the relationship.*

that's the (my) boy Fig., an expression of encouragement or pride. *As of a father pointing with pride and saying, "That's my boy who did that."*

that's the way the ball bounces Fig., "That's fate, the fortunes of life, the way things happen." 1957: "'Wow!' exclaimed Pat Boone. 'Maybe some year someone will say I was big, and the person he's talking to will have to be told why I was big and who I was. Guess that's the way the ball bounces.'" S. Skolsky, N.Y. *Post,* Mar. 22, 62. *Said in resignation or commiseration. Orig. very wide Korean War Army use.*

that's what she wrote = **that's all she wrote.**

that way In love. *Usu. in "They are that way about each other." c1940.*

the — *article* **1** Often prefixed to a surname to give the effect of a nickname or to imply that the person has an extremely individual personality or talent and is considered a natural force of nature. 1958: ". . . There are also inflexible conventions about the use of the nicknames. If one cat is referring to another the prefix 'the' is always used. But in speaking directly to the [person] you must drop the article. . . ." Sam Boal, *Cool Swinging in N.Y.,* 26. *Some far-out and beat use. Student use since c1920; also freq. theater and jazz use, esp. cool use. Thus "the Monk" = Thelonius Monk, well-known jazz pianist and composer.* See **sickname. 2** Sometimes prefixed to a place or locale name, often to a shortened or abbreviated form of the name, to indicate one's sophistication and that one is hip and familiar and

accepted there. *Thus "the Village"* =
*N.Y.C.'s Greenwich Village section; "the
Quarter"* = *New Orleans' French Quarter
section; "the Chez"* = *the Chez Paree
nightclub in Chicago; etc.* **3** Used before
specif. words, as indicated in the entries
in this dictionary, to form specif. n.
expressions or to confine a noun's meaning
to one specif. unalterable sl. use. *In such
instances "the" is used to indicate the
sl. meaning; if "a" were used the word
would have its stand. meaning. Thus
"the man"* = *a law enforcement officer,
whereas, of course, "a man" is just two
stand. words from a sentence.*

there   *adj.* Competent; skilled; capable
of performing, or performing, remarkably
well. *E.g., "When it comes to painting a
house (playing football, telling a joke, being
generous, etc.) he's right there." Since
c1925.*

There-I-was   *n.* **1** An exaggerated,
boastful account of one's experiences in
battle. *W.W.II Air Force and Army use,
usu. jocular. From the common beginning
"There I was (in some dangerous,
seemingly helpless situation—from which
the speaker continues to tell how his
heroic courage and superb ingenuity not
only extracted himself and/or his unit
from disaster but killed or captured many
of the enemy, or even won a major
battle)."* → **2** Any exaggerated, boastful
story. *Not common.*

there you go   **1** Fig., "Now you're
talking sense, telling the truth, comprehending fully, learning the knack of it";
"You're right, I agree, that's a good
idea." *Orig. c1935 jive use; mainly
general jazz use; some student and teenage
use.* → **2** Fig., "I know you can do it,
keep trying, you'll succeed, I have the
utmost confidence in your ability."
*Some Korean War Army use; now some
civilian use.*

thick   *adj.* **1** Duncelike. *Obs.* **2** Slow-
thinking. *Colloq.* **3** Incredible; seemingly
exaggerated or a lie.

thimble   *n.* A watch. *Underworld use,
c1850.*

thin   *adj.* **1** Broke; out of funds. *Hobo
and carnival use.* **2** Unsubstantiated.
n. A dime. From **thin dime**.   **—ly**
n. A runner or other track athlete. *From
the physical thinness of such athletes,
reinforced by their being thinly clad.*

thin dime   A dime; the sum of ten
cents. *Always used to emphasize the low
price of a product or ticket of admission or
to underline the poverty or need of one who,
lit. or fig., has only a dime. Thus "thin*

*dime" is used by carnival barkers in their
spiel, "For only the cost of a thin dime, buy
a ticket and see the tattooed lady...."
and by poverty-stricken persons, as in
"I have only a thin dime to my name." In
both cases the thinness of the dime is
mentioned to symbolize its purchasing
power.* See Appendix, Rhyming Terms.

thing   See **old thing, sure thing**.
thinga(ma)jig   **thing(um)abob**
thingumadoo(d)(le)   thingamadoger
thingamadudg(eon)   thingumbob
thinga(ma)nanny   *n.* Used to indicate any item of which the speaker does
not know or has momentarily forgotten
the name; esp., used to ref. to any, usu.
a small, new, or unfamiliar device,
mechanical part, gadget, tool, or ornament; a thing. *Such "omnibus" words
are in general use. The oldest is "thingumbob," in use since at least 1750. The third
syllable, "—ma" or "—a" infix, is usu.
added only after a word has been in common
use for some time. In all cases the second
syllable may be either "e," "a," "u," or
"um."* See Appendix, Infix.

things and stuff   Very well dressed;
very witty. *Negro use.*

thin in the upper crust   Deficient or
defective in mentality.

think-box   *n.* The brain.

thinker   *n.* The brain; the mind. 1949:
"What's on the thinker, pal?" Chandler,
Little Sister, 109.

think-piece   *n.* **1** A thoughtful or
provocative piece of journalistic writing,
as opposed to a factual news account.
2 The head or brain. *Not common.*

think-tank   *n.* = **think-box**.

thin man   = **thin one**. *Rock-and-roll
use since c1955.*

thin one   A dime. From **thin dime**.
1945: "He 'drops the lug' on you for
'a thin one.' " Chas. Carson. *Orig. hobo
use; assoc. with jive use. Because a dime
is the thinnest U.S. coin.*

third = **third degree**. 1934: "He's
giving me a third about some gun he
says I had." Chandler, *Finger Man,* 114.

third degree   Prolonged questioning
and/or rough handling of a person, as by
police, in order to obtain information or
to force a confession of guilt. 1930: "The
Third Degree: A Detailed and Appalling
Exposé of Police Brutality." Lavine,
Third Degree, title page.

third lieutenant   **1** One who has completed officer's training, but has not been
commissioned. *Fig.* = *one below a second
lieutenant.* **2** A sergeant. *W.W.II Army
use.*

third party Any new, completely American, completely political party other than the Republican and Democratic parties. *From time to time such parties are formed, usu. by dissatisfied factions of one of the two major parties. Generally speaking, the Socialist Party is not new enough nor the Communist Party sufficiently American to be called third parties; other organizations, such as the Vegetarian Party, are not completely political; but such parties as the Progressive, the Greenback, and the Socialist Party of 1908–12 were true third parties.*

third rail 1 Any of various strong alcoholic drinks. *From comparing the potency of a drink to the shock gotten from the electrically charged third rail of an electric railroad.* 2 An honest person who cannot be bribed. *From "touch" = bribe; one cannot touch an electrically charged third rail.*

third sacker See **sacker.**

third sex, the 1 Newspaper copyreaders or deskmen who should be completely objective. *c1928: archaic.* 2 Teachers. *As a forgotten, underpaid, and ignored group. c1930; archaic.* 3 Homosexuals. *Now the only common meaning.*

third wheel A useless or unwanted person; one who contributes nothing or is even a detriment to the successful completion of a task or to the enjoyment of a good time, party, or social gathering.

thirteen *n. A word used as a warning that one's employer is nearby. From the belief that 13 is unlucky.* See **barracks thirteen, file thirteen.**

thirty 30 *n.* 1 Orig. used as the last word to signify the end of a telegraph message; hence the end of a newspaper correspondent's dispatch; later, used to signify the end of a newspaper article, then a radio newscaster's broadcast. 1949: "The term 'thirty' originated back in the early days of the telegraph. At the time operators, writing longhand, used the symbol 'XXX' to designate the end of a dispatch filed by a newspaper correspondent. The 'XXX' quickly translated itself into the now familiar 'thirty.'" AP, Oct. 4. *Well known.* → 2 The end of a shift or of a day's work. *Orig. telegrapher use. Not common.* → 3 Death. *Never common.* 4 Good-by. c1940 [1952]: "Okay—thirty for now." From a Shirley Temple film, quoted by J. Crosby, N.Y. *Her. Trib.,* Apr. 9, 29/1.

thirty-day wonder A second lieu-

tenant; one who has become an officer by completing a 30-day officers' training course. *Used ironically. W.W.I and W.W.II use.*

Thirty-four! *imp.* "Go away!" "Don't bother me!" *Said to another salesman who is interfering with a sale. c1930 retail shoe salesman use; obs.*

thirty-one *n.* An order of a glass of lemonade or orangeade. *c1930 lunch-counter use in relaying an order; archaic.*

thirty-three *n.* 1 A customer who will not buy from one salesman and is turned over to another. *c1930 retail shoe salesman use; obs.* 2 An order of ground beefsteak. *Some c1930 lunch-counter use in relaying an order; obs.* 3 A phonograph record made to be played on a turntable that revolves at 33⅓ revolutions per minute. See **LP.**

thou *n.* A thousand dollars. 1927: "A hundred and fifty thou is business." Hammett, *Blood Money,* 89. *Mainly theater, gambling, and underworld use.* See Appendix, Shortened Words.

thousand-miler *n.* A dark-blue shirt, esp. a dark-blue work shirt. *Because it shows less wear and dirt, hence lasts a long time and can be laundered less freq. than others.*

thousand on a plate Beans; a plate of beans.

threads *n.pl.* Clothes, esp. a suit of clothes. *Orig. c1935 jive use; fairly common general jazz and hipster use.*

three-alarm fire *Seldom used in the affirmative.* See **no three-alarm fire.**

three-D 3-D 3D *adj.* Three-dimensional; said of a movie. *n.* A movie that is filmed and projected to give a three-dimensional illusion to the viewers. *Both uses almost always "3-D," seldom if ever spelled out as "three-D." From time to time the movie industry has attempted to perfect, and initiate the public to, 3-D movies. In the early 1950's such a 3-D movie-making process was highly publicized, but the public seemed to resent wearing the special glasses necessary to receive the full 3-D effect, and after the novelty value had worn off, 3-D movies did little business. It was during the publicity campaign for this process and for the movies that the word "3-D" became common. It is now seldom used.*

three-dollar bill 1 An odd or eccentric person; specif., a person who claims to be what he is not or tries to assume the identity of another. *Because there is no such thing as a U.S. three-dollar bill. From the expression "as phoney as* *a three-dollar bill."* → **2** Specif., a homosexual; a sexual pervert.

three-letter man   An effeminate man; specif., a homosexual. *The three letters are "f-a-g" = fag. A pun on the collegiate term "three-letter man" = a student athlete who has lit. and fig. won three letters, each the initial of his school, to be sewn on his sweater, each letter representing the fact that he has been on a school athletic team; thus attesting his skill, strength, and masculinity. Reinforced by "three-dollar bill." Some student use since c1935.*

three-quarter kelt   See **kelt.** *Some Negro use.*

three-sheet   *n.* An advertising circular or handbill; esp., a theater or circus advertising poster. 1905: "Did you ever hear of an actor or a manager getting out a three-sheet which held a newspaper up to ridicule?" McHugh, *Search Me,* 53.   *v.i., v.t.* To boast; to seek publicity; to boast about, to publicize or advertise. 1939: "In three weeks she is his star and he is three-sheeting her as if she is Katharine Cornell." Runyon, 165f. *Very old theater and circus use; still in some archaic use. Because advertising circulars are often folded over twice, as into three sheets.*

three sheets in [*or* to] the wind   Drunk. Also **four sheets in the wind.**

three-striper   *n.* **1** A USN commander. *USN use.* **2** A sergeant. *Army use.*

three-time   *v.t.* To combine in a trio to fight someone or to beat him up. Cf. **two-time.**

thriller-diller = **chiller-diller.** See Appendix, Rhyming Slang.

throttle jockey   See Appendix, Suffixes and Suffix Words.

through the line = **across the board.** *Horse-racing use.* 1956: ". . . Across the board. Through the line, I mean, as I am from Maryland and that's how they say it in this state." T. Betts, *Across the Board,* 273. *Dial.*

through the mill   1 Long and hard practical experience in any field. E.g., "He has been through the mill." **2** To have been frustrated, defeated; to meet with obstacles. *Colloq.*

throw   *n.* The cost per unit or cost per portion of an item; any single-unit price; the unit by which something is sold, as a glassful, a bottle, a ticket, an hour's lesson, a pair of shoes, or the like. 1924: "The meetings [of tutoring sections] were a dollar 'a throw.' " Marks, *Plastic Age,* 97. 1948: "[Champagne] at

$35 a throw [a bottle]." Lait-Mortimer, *N.Y. Confidential,* 27. *Fig., each time the customer throws down his money. Reinforced by crap-shooting term = each throw of, and hence each bet on, the dice.*   *v.t.* **1** To hold or give a social affair, as a dance, luncheon, or party. 1951: "When the head of some foreign country comes to Washington, the President has to throw him a luncheon." P. Edson, NEA, Feb. 14. **2** To lose, or play so as to lose, any sports contest in return for a bribe. 1951: ". . . Star basketball players confess that they have accepted bribes to 'throw' games. . . . Bribed [baseball] players blatantly 'threw' ball games and never were penalized for it." A. Daley in N.Y. *Times,* Mar. 4, 20.   **—away**   *n.* **1** A ticket of admission sold at a reduced price. **2** An advertising circular; a handbill. → **3** A cheap magazine. **4** A short, quickly said joke or witticism, as used by a comedian between his major jokes; an incidental joke or witticism. *Orig. vaudeville use.* → **5** A line in a play or movie which the actor purposely understates or slurs, in order to add realism to the speech. *Theater use.*

throw a fit   To have an extreme emotional reaction, esp. of anger.

throw-down   A rejection. *Some use since c1920; never common.* See **put down.**

throw down on   To draw a gun on someone. 1950: "I told him about Sam throwing down on me with a gun." Starnes, *Another Mug.* 35.

throw [one's] feet   To get food or money by begging; to look for temporary work. 1892 [1907]: "I missed many a meal, in spite of the fact that I could 'throw my feet' with the next one when I came to 'slamming a gate' for a 'poke-out' or a 'set-down,' or hitting for a 'light piece' on the street. . . ." Jack London, *My Life. Hobo use.*

throw in the sponge (towel)   1 To concede defeat; to surrender. *From prize fighting use; a manager whose prize fighter is being badly beaten signifies that he wants to stop the fight, and concede defeat, by actually throwing a towel or sponge into the ring—two items readily at hand since they are used to sponge and dry perspiration off the fighter between rounds.* **2** To die. *Not common.*

throw lead   To shoot or shoot at.

throw leather   To box with gloves. 1936: "I was throwin' leather before you could crawl." Tully, *Bruiser,* 27.

throw-money   *n.* Small change, such

as a tip. 1951: "The swank ... hotels and tailors are down scrambling for throw-money." Westbrook Pegler, *synd. newsp. col.*, Dec. 27.

throw-out *n.* A professional beggar who feigns injury to gain sympathy. *Hobo use.*

throw the book at [someone] **1** To sentence a guilty person to the maximum term of imprisonment. *Orig. underworld use. From the image of a judge sentencing a criminal to every penalty found in books of law.* → **2** To penalize, punish, reprimand, or criticize a person severely. *Fairly common since c1950.* See **book.**

throw the bull = **shoot (the) bull.** To talk nonsense or bull.

throw the hooks **1** = **throw [one's] feet.** **2** *Specif.*, to beg on the street by extending one's hand for a hand-out.

throw the hooks into To cheat; to get the better of someone through deceit. 1939: "It takes ... work to throw the hooks into a life insurance company. ..." Gardner, *D. A. Draws,* 202.

thrush *n.* A singer.

thumb *v.t.* **1** In baseball, to hit the ball over the infield with the bat handle. **2** To hitch-hike. See **green thumb.**

thumb, on the Hitch-hiking. Cf. **thumb.**

thumb a ride = **thumb,** hitch-hike.

thumb-nail *n.* A dollar. *Not common.*

thumbprint *n.* An individual's personality as reflected in his work, plans, or deeds. 1951: "When all the actors in a production begin to look, talk and act like the director, the director has achieved what is known in the theatre as his thumbprint." A. Hirschfield, *Show Business Is No Business,* 30.

thumb-pusher *n.* A hitch-hiker.

Thunderbird! *interj.* **1** An expression of excitement or of a feeling of power, exultation, enthusiasm, or ecstasy. *Used absolutely.* → **2** An expression of recognition, or appreciation, as of a sexually attractive girl, of music, or of a fellow dude, sport, or hipster. *Used absolutely.* **3** "Great!"; "I feel full of vigor and enthusiasm." *In the jive-like rhyming answer to the greeting:* "What's the (good) word?" "Thunderbird!" *Harlem Negro, mainly hipster, use. From the trade name of a cheap and supposedly potent wine,* "Thunderbird," *highly advertised in N.Y.C.'s Harlem, orig. in the Spring of 1957. The advertising slogan was* " 'What's the good word?' 'Thunderbird' [wine]." *Reinforced by the Ford*

Motor Co.'s "Thunderbird" *model sports car. By July 5, 1957, the word was pop. enough to the hip people of N.Y.C.'s Harlem to be used as a fad word, eliciting hip laughter, by the master of ceremonies at the Apollo Theater's stage show (mainly jazz performers).*

thusly *adv.* Thus. 1865: "Humorous [use]." *DAE.* 1921: "This one is a wireless, readin' thusly. ..." Witwer, *Leather,* 128. 1948: "Of his own part as director [of a movie] Mr. [Anatole] Litvak was content to sum up his contribution thusly: 'It was the toughest thing I ever attempted.' " T. M. Pryor in N.Y. *Times,* Nov. 7, X5/8. *Now common serious use. Because many adverbs have the* "—ly" *ending.*

tick *n.* **1** Fig., a minute, a second. *E.g.,* "I'll be there in a tick." *Not common.* **2** A recitation made by an ignoramus. *Obs. college use.* **3** Credit. 1950: "Plenty of canned goods and plenty of tick at the store." W. Pegler, *synd. newsp. col.,* July 12. See **hit the tick, on tick.**

tick, full as a Very drunk. See **full.**

tick, hit the = **hit the hay.** *A sl. variation reinforced by being a rhyming term. Some Southern and Western use.*

tick, on On credit. 1901: "A recognized colloquialism . . . from ticket. Greenough & Kittredge, 62. 1946: "Getting his liquor 'on tick.' " Janney, *Miracle of Bells,* 172. *Mainly dial. More common in Eng. than U.S.*

ticker *n.* **1** A student who recites without knowing what he is talking about. *Obs. college use.* **2** A watch. *Pitchman use.* **3** Courage; stamina. 1935: "I never see a guy with more ticker than Shamus. ..." Runyon. **4** The heart. *Colloq.* 1948 [1954]: "Selena's brother tapped the left side of his chest. 'Ticker,' he said. 'Your heart, ya mean?' Ginnie said. 'What's the matter with it?' " J. D. Salinger, "Just Before the War with the Eskimos," reprinted in *Manhattan,* 29.

ticket *n.* **1** In college, a course of study. *Not common.* **2** A playing card. See **meal ticket.** **3** Official papers showing that one has been paroled from prison or has served all of one's prison sentence. → **4** Official papers discharging one from military service; a discharge from military service. *Some W.W.II use.*

ticket, the *n.* The very thing; the exact thing called for or needed. *In the pleased* "That's the ticket" = *That's what I meant or wanted.*

ticke(t)y-boo *adj.* Perfect; fine, all

right, O.K.; correct. 1950: "Bigart's type of reporting is rather different from the assurances, datelined Tokyo, that everything is going to be tickety-boo eventually." A. J. Liebling, *New Yorker*, Aug. 12, 55. *Not common in U.S., but W.W.II Brit. Army sl., perh. from the Hindustani "teega," reinforced by "ticket, the."*

tickled pink   Exceedingly pleased. *Colloq.*

tickler   *n.* **1** A small liquor flask containing just enough liquor to tease a hearty drinker. *c1800; obs.* **2** A small portion of anything. **3** A mustache. 1929: " 'Them pictures don't look like me.' ... 'Not since you got the tickler off.' ..." Burnett, *Little Caesar*, 170.

tickle the ivories   To play the piano.

ticky   *adj.* = **corny.** 1956: "*Ticky* is another word for corny." S. Longstreet, *The Real Jazz Old and New*, 149. *Some jazz use, never common.*

tiddly   *adj.* Drunk. 1942: "She loses count of her drinks and is liable to get a little tiddly, which is to say, shot or blind." P. Wylie, *Generation of Vipers*, 202. *From rhyming sl. "tiddly-wink" = a drink.* See Appendix, Rhyming Slang; Drunk.

tie a (the) can to (on)   **1** To dismiss a person from service; to sever relations; to can. 1952: "First it was the Braves who tied a can to Tommy Hughes." Raymond Johnson, NEA, July 9. **2** To eliminate or get rid of something.

tied   *adj.* Married.

tied up   **1** Busy; having no free time. **2** Finished.

tie-in   *n.* A connection; a relationship. *Colloq.*

tie-in deal   *n.* A business deal whereby one must also buy or hire a less desirable item or person in order to obtain the desired item or person.

tie into   *v.t.* To attack; to approach or do something with fury, speed, or enthusiasm. 1948: "She put her head back and tied into her drink with the easy grace of a practiced drinker." Evans, *Halo for Satan*, 108.

tie it off   To quit work for the day; to let something remain as it is. *Orig. maritime use.*

tie it up   To finish a job.

tie off   To stop talking; shut up. 1951: "Now tie off, kid!" Movie, *Boots Malone*.

tie on   To eat. Cf. **to tie on the feedbag (nosebag).**

tie one on   To get drunk; to go on a drunken spree. *Very common.*

ties, hit the   To travel by walking along a railroad track. 1907: "It was up to me to hit the ties to Wadsworth, and hit them I did." Jack London, *The Road*, 130.

tiger   *n.* **1** Fig., a strong, virile man easily aroused to anger or passion; a good fighter and/or a "sweet" man. *Freq. a nickname, esp. of prize fighters, or given to "sweet" men by their lovers. The most common use.* **2** In poker, the lowest hand a player can hold. *Orig. from faro use, or fig., because the player must bluff if he is going to win, and thus has "a tiger by the tail," that is, he can be hurt financially.* → **3** An obsession; that vice, talent, or idea which a man must dominate in order to succeed. 1950: "And all his life Jelly Roll held a tiger by the tail. In barrelhouse lingo 'tiger' meant the lowest hand a man could draw in a poker game—seven high, deuce low, and without a pair, straight or flush. It takes nerve to hold onto a tiger and all he had was the music of the Storyville bordellos —it was his tiger and he bet his life on it." A. Lomax, *Mr. Jelly Roll*, 62. **4** Faro. *Since c1845.* **5** A prize fighter or wrestler. *Not common.* See **blind tiger.**

tiger eye   **tiger's eye** = **tiger sweat.** *Perh. reinforced by the faro term.*

tiger meat   Beef. *Synthetic sl.*

tiger sweat   **Tigersweat**   **1** Cheap, raw whisky; esp., unaged, bootleg whisky. 1956: "... Bleary-eyed and shaky after a night of tiger sweat called gin." "... Cheap alcohol, also known as Tigersweat." S. Longstreet, *The Real Jazz Old and New*, 4; 148. Cf. **panther sweat. 2** Beer. *W.W.II Armed Forces use.*

tight   *adj.* **1** Stingy, parsimonious. 1828: *DAE.* 1930: "He is tight in his dealings." Lavine, *Third Degree*, 26. *Colloq. From "tight-fisted," reinforced by "tightwad."* **2** Drunk. 1851: "A very common slang term among [American college] students." Hall, *College Words.* 1907: "Stopped at the cider mill coming over by the hill, Come home "tighter" than a drum, by gosh!" Benjamin Hapgood Burt, "Wal, I Swan" [or "Ebenezer Frye," a song]. 1929: "Little tight, honey? Not going to be sick, are you?" D. Parker, "Big Blonde," reprinted in *The American Twenties*, 150. 1944: "I wasn't especially tight." Fowler, *Good Night*, 343. *Colloq. since c1840. Prob. the most common of the sl. words = drunk.* See Appendix, Drunk. *Also often used in expressions such as "tight* *as a tick.*" **3** Friendly, exceedingly compatible; intimate, in rapport with; said of two people, as co-workers, friends, or lovers. *Most common orig. as c1946 bop and now as cool use. Some student and teenage use since c1950.*

tight as a tick (drum, lord, owl, goat, mink, brassière, ten-day drunk, etc.) Very tight, completely drunk. 1928: "He's tight as a drum." W. Gibbs in *New Yorker*, Nov. 17, 28/1. 1946: "Tight as a ten-day drunk." Evans, *Halo in Blood*, 121. 1951: "At lunch you have two cocktails and feel tight as a tick." J. Berke & V. Wilson in *Collier's*, June 23, 21/2.

tight as Kelsey's nuts [taboo] Very stingy or parsimonious; very tight. *Usu. jocular use, even though derisive. One would expect a Scottish name here, rather than an Irish one, as it is the Scots who are traditionally considered stingy.* See **tight.**

tight as O'Reilly's balls [taboo] = **tight as Kelsey's nuts.**

tight-fisted *adj.* Parsimonious; stingy. *Colloq., becoming archaic.*

tight money = **hard money.**

tight spot Lit. and fig., an unfruitful, embarrassing, disastrous, or dangerous situation from which one will have difficulty extracting oneself or succeeding; a situation in which one needs assistance, luck, or all one's ingenuity to extract oneself or succeed; a potentially disastrous situation.

tightwad *n.* **1** A miser; one who has money and does not readily part with any of it. *From the tightly folded wad of money.* 1916: "Pauline . . . despises the 'tightwads' who have saved money." E. Gilbert, *New Republic*, Nov. 4, 16/2. **2** A thin cut of meat rolled up with bacon strips and fried. *Not common. Found in Northwest.* *adj.* Stingy, miserly. 1945: "Hey, don't be so tightwad with that hootch." S. Lewis, *Cass Timberlane*, 107.

Tijuana Bible A cheap pornographic book; any pornographic item. *Because pornography is sold openly and cheaply in the Mexican border town of Tijuana; many U.S. tourists who spend a day there purchase a pornographic book and bring it back into the U.S. with them, as a novelty. Not common. Mainly Southern Calif. teenage use.*

tile *n.* A hat; esp. a stiff hat. 1862: "A well-worn tile in the place of his new beaver." N.Y. *Observer*, Jan. 9. *Obs.*

tillicum *n.* A friend; a man or person;

people. *Logger and some dial. use. From Chinook jargon.*

timber *interj.* Fig., an expression of success or achievement; also used jocularly when a person drops or breaks something. *From "timber!" as shouted by loggers, in warning and jubilation, when a tree is felled.* *n.* **1** One who sells lead pencils on the street; often a street beggar. 1929: ". . . The timber (who sells pencils on the street). . . ." *World's Work*, Nov., 40. *Hobo and street beggar use.* **2** A baseball bat. *Baseball use, not common.* **3** A toothpick. *Not common.* —**s** *n.pl.* Human bones, esp. the ribs. *From the shipbuilders' term. Used chiefly in the stock expression, "Shiver me timbers!" a common saying of fictional buccaneers.*

time, give [someone] the To have sexual intercourse with someone. 1951: "Most guys just talked about having sexual intercourse with girls all the time, but old Stradlater really did it. I was personally acquainted with at least two girls he gave the time to." J. D. Salinger, *Catcher in the Rye*, 40f. *Not common. Euphem. for* **give it to [someone].**

time, have [oneself] a To have a good time; to enjoy oneself. 1949: ". . . Everybody had himself a time." Billy Rose, *synd. newsp. col.*, July 25.

time, off Out of place; ill-timed; offensive; usu. said of a remark. *Jive use, c1935.*

time of day, not give [someone] the To ignore someone; fig., to dislike or distrust someone so much that one would not tell that person the correct time if he asked. *Always used in the negative. Colloq.*

tin *n.* **1** A policeman's badge. 1958: "Tin—Policeman's term for his shield." G. Y. Wells, *Station House Slang.* → **2** A policeman or detective. *Some underworld use.* **3** Silver money. *c1850; obs. by c1920.* → **4** A trifling amount of money; hay. 1939: "$400 per week, and this is by no means tin." Runyon. *Not common.* Cf. **tin-horn.**

tin-badge *n.* A policeman. *Obs.*

tin can *n.* **1** A depth charge. *Fairly common USN use.* **2** A submarine. *Never common.* **3** A car, esp. an early Ford. *c1920.* **4** Any naval warship; usu. a destroyer; esp. an old destroyer; a submarine chaser. *Orig. humorous ref. to armor plating and because the destroyer was smallest fleet ship in use during W.W.II. Very common W.W.II use.*

Cf. **can.** **tin-can** *v.t.* To dismiss a person from his job. *Replaced by "can."*

tin-can it To run fast. *Ref. to a dog with tin cans tied to its tail. Archaic and dial.*

tin cow **tinned cow** Canned milk. *Hobo use as early as c1930. Some W.W.II Armed Forces use, but not as common as the use in war novels and movies.*

tin-ear *n.* **1** A person who doesn't appreciate music, esp. jazz, swing, or pop. music; a person who is tone deaf. 1956: "... *Tin-ear* is a man who doesn't like swing." S. Longstreet, *The Real Jazz Old and New*, 150. *Not common; c1935 jitterbug use.* **2** A cauliflower ear. *c1920; prize fight use.*

tin fish **1** A submarine. *W.W.I use. Not common.* → **2** A torpedo. *Common W.W.II USN use.*

tinge *n.* A salesman who specializes in sales of undesirable merchandise that earn him bonus payments. *Retail salesman use.*

tin hat A steel trench helmet; a shrapnel helmet. *Common W.W.I Army use; some W.W.II use, but not common.*

tin-horn *n.* **1** A pretentious person who spends little. *c1885.* → **2** A small-time gambler; a cheap, flashy person. 1945: "[New York's Mayor LaGuardia made] denunciations of punks, tin-horns, and gyps...." W. Pegler, *synd. newsp. col.*, Dec. 13.

tinkle *n.* A phone call. *v.i.* To urinate. *Common usage by small children; humorously used by adults.*

tinkle-box *n.* A piano. *Synthetic jazz use.*

tin Lizzie **tin lizzie** **1** An early automobile, esp. a Ford. *c1917.* → **2** Any cheap or dilapidated car, truck, or airplane. 1950: "Six 'tin lizzies' of the Syracuse post-office truck fleet ... will be sold...." Syracuse, N.Y., *Post-Standard*, Aug. 22, 7/2.

Tin Pan Alley Fig., the place where popular songs are written, published, and made into commercial successes; popular music; pertaining to or in the style of a popular song, esp. in the style of songs pop. c1925. *Lit., Tin Pan Alley is the offices, buildings, and rooms located roughly between 48th and 52nd Sts. on 7th Avenue in N.Y. City's Times Square area. Here many composers, arrangers, music publishing companies, and recording studio agents have business offices.*

tin pants Paraffin-treated, waterproof canvas trousers. *Logger and fisherman use.*

tinpot *adj.* Inferior; small time. 1950: "Tinpot Napoleons...." Starnes, *Another Mug*, 113.

tin star A private detective. 1949: "You cheap tin star!" J. Evans, *Halo*, 32.

tintype, not on your No; emphatically no. *Common c1900; archaic. Replaced by "not on your life."*

tip *n.* **1** A small audience or crowd of prospective customers gathered around a pitchman or in front of a carnival sideshow, in response to the spiel or ballyhoo. 1939: "A pitchman must *work a tip* before he can *turn* it." *Life*, July 31, 24. 1948: "He had a small tip, mostly kids." F. Brown, *Dead Ringer*, 30. *Pitchman and carnival use.* → **2** The spiel or ballyhoo made by a pitchman or carnival barker. → **3** Advice, esp. short, succinct advice that can be stated in a sentence or two; information, a fact. 1957: "Our tip to Doc Jansen [Superintendent of N.Y.C. schools] would be to...." Editorial, N.Y. *Daily News*, Sept. 17, 27. → **4** Esp., advance information supposedly from those in the know, as on the expected outcome of a horse-race or sporting event. *v.t.* To inform someone; to tip someone off. 1948: "The room clerk tipped him." Movie, *Scene of the Crime*. **—ped** Drunk. *Never common.*

tip [the, one's] elbow = **bend the elbow.**

tip [one's] mitt To disclose or inadvertently reveal a secret, motive, plan, or the like. 1938: "That would be tipping her mitt too much." H. Broun in *New Repub.*, Oct. 26, 331/1.

tip off To warn of something impending; to put someone wise; to inform, to forewarn; also, to point out a victim to a crook. 1939: "Who tipped Larkin off?" Gardner, *D. A. Draws*, 85. 1950: "Marks are either dug up or tipped off ... pointed out by others. One who tips off marks...." DeBaun, 70. **tip-off** *n.* A forewarning; a clue; a hint. 1929: "Thanks for the tip-off." Dunning & Abbott, *Broadway*, I. 1950: "The tip-off on what's ahead in the way of higher cost of living can be found in the commodities futures markets." S. Dawson, AP, July 18.

tip over **1** To rob or loot, as by criminals; to raid, as by the police. 1952: "Ya wanta help us tip over this bank?" Radio drama, *The Big Histe* [*Hoist*], Dec. 1. **2** To die. *Never common.*

tip-over   *n.* **1** An inferior prize fighter. *Prize fight use since c1920, not common.* **2** A raid, esp. a police raid made, without warrant, on a speakeasy. *Prohibition underworld use.*

tipping grand   *adv.* Walking fast; running; leaving quickly. *Some c1930 prison use.*

tipster   *n.* **1** A professional seller of gambling information; a tout. **2** A pitchman or carnival barker. *Not common.* **3** A radio, television, or newspaper news analyst, a professional stock market analyst, all of whom make their living from forecasting future events and broadcasting their tips, or advice. *Not common.*

tip-top   *adj.* Excellent. *Since before 1900.* See Appendix, Reduplications.

tired   *adj.* **1** Drunk. *Some c1850 use; obs.* See Appendix, Drunk. **2** Untidy; disheveled. *Never common.* **3** Dull, boring; unimaginative; specif., out of fashion, reminiscent or repetitive of things previously seen or heard. *Said of entertainments.*

tire patch   A hotcake; a pancake. *W.W.II Army use. Prob. synthetic sl.*

tissue   *n.* A carbon copy, as of a letter, railroad way-bill, or the like; an original or a carbon copy on thin paper.

tit   *n.* Lit., teat or nipple; fig. used in the plural to = noticeable nipples on shapely, protruding female breasts, as of a sweater girl. 1947: " 'Well,' said Munro. 'That girl ought to go to Hollywood.' 'She couldn't make it out there,' blushed Wilson. 'No tits.' " C. Willingham, *End as a Man*, 93. *Universally used. Applied to both animal teats and human teats. "Teat" is now no longer ever used in referring to women; women have tits or nipples, animals have teats.*

titty-boo   *n.* **1** A wild, undisciplined, young girl. **2** A female juvenile delinquent. **3** A young female prisoner, usu. convicted for nonprofessional, nonviolent crime, such as dope addiction, vandalism, sexual misconduct, etc. 1958: "The titty-boos have the best time of it here." Heard in N.Y.C. Women's House of Detention, an older prisoner speaking of a younger one.

tizzy   *n.* A fit or period of nervousness, anxiety, or confusion. *Dial.*

TKO   *n.* **1** In prize fighting, a technical knockout, resulting from one fighter's having been so injured that he is declared unable to continue the fight, even though he has not actually been knocked out. *Colloq.* See Appendix, Shortened Words. → **2** Fig., a defeat or failure. *Not*

common. *v.t.* **1** To score a TKO against an opponent. → **2** Fig., to defeat; to show to be wrong. 1956: Endocrinology TKO's Freud in the second round." T. Betts, *Across the Board*, 296.

TL   **tl**   *n.* **1** A compliment; esp. a compliment given to a person because one has received a compliment from that person; specif. a compliment relayed from the giver to the person complimented by an intermediary, as when the giver is shy or embarrassed by having made the compliment. *From the archaic and dial. "trade last."* **2** = **ass kisser.** *From the Yiddish-American "tokus licker." Based on "AK" and reinforced by the use of "TL" = compliment. Not common.*

tlac   *n.* Money. *From the Spanish and Mexican "tlaco" = a Spanish coin once worth 1/8 of a "real." Dial.*

toad   *n.* **1** A derail iron. *Railroad use.* **2** A toady; a contemptible youth. *c1940; teen use.* **3** = **toad-hide.** Cf. **frog-skin.** See **car-toad, hop-toad.**   **—y**   *v.i.* To attempt to gain familiarity or favor with one's superiors by flattery or extreme subservience. *n.* One who acts as a lackey to his superiors.

toad-hide   *n.* A piece of paper money. *Not common.*

toady up = **toady.**

toenails   See **snake's toenails.**

tog   *n.* A coat. *Criminal use; obs.* **—s**   *n.pl.* Clothes; clothing. *Colloq.*

together, go   To keep company in courtship. *Said of an unmarried couple. Also "go around together." Colloq.*

Tojo [derog.]   *n.* A Japanese; esp. a Japanese soldier. *W.W.II Armed Forces use. From General Tojo, Japanese war leader.*

toke   *v.i., v.t.* To smoke or take a drag on a cigarette, usu. but not necessarily a marijuana cigarette.   *n.* A drag of (or on) a cigarette, usu. but not necessarily a marijuana cigarette. *Some addict use, even less general use. Lit., a token or sample of a cigarette or smoke.* See Appendix, Shortened Words.

tokus   **tokis**   **tuckus**   **1** The posterior. **2** [taboo] The rectum. *From the Yiddish = "ass."*

tokus (tokis, tuckus) licker [taboo] = **ass kisser.** See **tokus.**

tom   *v.i.* To travel to a town as part of a theatrical troupe, esp. to travel to a small town in order to give only one or a few theatrical performances. *Theater* *use; obs. Orig., lit. and fig., to travel to a town to stage or perform the pop. melodrama "Uncle Tom's Cabin" or a similar melodrama. Reinforced by "tomcat."* See **Tom show, tommer.** —**boy** *n.* A girl, usu. between eight and 15 years old, who enjoys or excels at boys' sports and interests and who has as yet developed little if any feminine interest in clothes or grooming. *Very common.* —**cat** **tom cat** *v.i., v.t.* Orig., to dress up in one's best clothes, as a dude or sport, and walk the street, visit public bars, nightclubs, and the like in search of a female; to seek a female, esp. a promiscuous one; esp., to dress in one's best clothes, visit a girl or young woman, and mix boasting and sweet talk in an attempt to persuade her to enter into sexual activity. *Negro and dial. use.* *n.* A woman-chaser. —**girl** = **tomboy.** *From confusion with the older term.* **Tommer** *n.* 1 Lit., the actor who plays the role of Uncle Tom in *Uncle Tom's Cabin;* fig., any member of a traveling theatrical troupe specializing in performing *Uncle Tom's Cabin* or similar melodramas. 1955: "That strange race of actors known as 'Uncle Tommers' like old soldiers have faded away . . . the 'Tommers' as they were known. You had to be a 'Tommer' to play 'Uncle Tom's Cabin.' A 'Tommer' never played anything but a Tom show." H. R. Hoyt, *Town Hall Tonight,* 57. *Theater use; obs.* See **Tom show, tom.** 2 One who tomcats. *Not common.* —**my** **Tommy** *n.* 1 Bread. *Criminal use; obs.* 2 A prostitute. *Obs.* → 3 A girl; a tomboy. 1949: "The red-haired tommy . . . she'd put him over the jumps." Burnett, *Jungle,* 80: 4 A British soldier. *Very common W.W.I use.* See **Tommy Atkins.** 5 = **Tommy gun.** *Underworld and W.W.II use.* → 6 A machine gunner.

tomato *n.* 1 A very attractive girl or young woman. 1951: "The idea that such a luscious tomato might be mixed up in murder went square against the grain." R. S. Prather, *Bodies in Bedlam,* 23. *Since c1920. The word implies "luscious" = desirable or "ripe" = with a mature, sexually attractive body. Universally known. Not respectful, but like "dame" or "doll" implies no disrespect.* See Appendix, Food and Sex. 2 An inferior prize fighter. *Some prize fight use.* 3 The face; the head. *Since c1920; not common.* 4 A baseball. *Some baseball use, not common.*

tomato can A town constable's or

policeman's badge of office. *Hobo use.* Cf. **tin badge.**

Tom, Dick, and Harry Fig., just any youth or man (men) regardless of worth; a nobody, nobodies. *Usu. in the expression "every Tom, Dick, and Harry."* 1920: "And don't waste a lot of time with the college set—little boys nineteen and twenty years old. I don't mind a prom or a football game, but staying away from advantageous parties to eat in little cafés downtown with Tom, Dick, and Harry. . . ." F. S. Fitzgerald, *This Side of Paradise,* 181. 1943: "It's getting hard enough to handle the votes without letting every Tom, Dick, and Harry in on the election." M. Shulman, *Barefoot Boy with Cheek,* 164.

Tommy Atkins A British soldier. 1943: "The British 'Tommy Atkins' got his nickname from the 'Tommy Atkins' on the sample recruiting forms." A. Ostrow. *"Tommy Atkins" is the British equivalent of our "John Doe" or wartime "G.I. Joe." The full term was used early in W.W.I, but was quickly shortened to "Tommy."*

Tommy gun **tommy gun** Orig. and specif., a Thompson submachine gun; fig., any automatic, portable, machine gun. *Orig. underworld use.*

Tommy-man *n.* A machine-gunner for a criminal gang. *c1930 underworld use.*

tommyrot *n.* Nonsense; boloney. *Colloq. Somewhat archaic.*

Tom show Specif., a performance of the melodrama *Uncle Tom's Cabin;* any melodrama; a theatrical troupe specializing in performing *Uncle Tom's Cabin* and/or similar melodramas. *Mainly theater use.* Cf. **tom, tommer.**

tom-troller *n.* A very big playing marble. *Young boy use. Obs.*

tong *n.* A fraternity house. *From the Chinese. Some West Coast college use.*

tongue *n.* A lawyer; a mouthpiece. 1935: "I consult with Judge Goldstein, who is my tongue, and a very good guy. . . ." Damon Runyon.

tonk *n.* 1 = **honky tonk.** c1915 [1954]: ". . . The cops might close the tonk down any minute." L. Armstrong, *Satchmo, My Life in New Orleans,* 60. 2 A railroad car maintenance or repair man. *Railroad use.*

ton of bricks, hit like a To impress in the extreme; to stun; to awe.

tony *adj.* 1 In, of, or representing the best society or latest fashion. → 2 Assuming the manners, speech, or dress of the best society; conceited; arrogant; egotistical. *Most pop. among Negroes.* **3** Stylish; swanky; high-toned; snobbish. *Colloq. since c1880.* Cf. **high tony.**   *n.* Socially prominent people. 1948: "St. Michael's alley, still inhabited by the tony...." H. L. Mencken.

Toodle-oo   *interj.* Good-by. *Considered Eng. or an affected use. Thus seldom seen in print, but has fairly common serious use among middle-aged women. Jocular use by males.*

took   *adj.* = **stuck.**

tool   *n.* **1** [taboo] The penis. **2** A pickpocket; one who in a mob of pickpockets actually does the removing of the victim's wallet from his pocket; the chief of a mob of pickpockets. *Common underworld use since at least c1920.* **3** One easily victimized or deceived; a stupid person. *Fig., one who can be used, as a tool, by others.*   *v.i.* To loiter; to loaf. *Some c1915 prison and Army use.*   *v.t.* To drive an automobile, esp. speedily and with confidence or skill. 1934: "I climbed into the Buick and tooled it down the ramp." Chandler, *Finger Man,* 19.   **—s**   *n.pl.* **1** Table utensils; a knife, fork, and spoon. *Since c1900. Lit., eating tools.* **2** Golf clubs. *Not common.*

tool-box   *n.* A small railroad depot. *Hobo use.*

tool-man   *n.* A gangster whose work is opening safes. *Not common.*

too much   **1** Beyond logical criticism or comprehension, in either a good or bad sense; ridiculously good or bad. *Fairly common c1935 jive use; fairly well known general use since c1940.* → **2** = **far out;** so intellectually, psychologically, or spiritually removed from standards of criticism, by being unrelated or beyond comparison, that one is awed. *Far-out use since c1955.*

toot   *n.* A spree; esp., a drinking spree. 1858: "Mysterious mentions of 'sprees' or 'toots' are made [by the college freshman] to admiring younger brothers." *Harvard Mag.,* May, 175. *Somewhat archaic.* Cf. **bat.**

toot, on a   On a spree, esp. a drunken spree; carousing. 1927: "People going on...toots." *New Republic,* 50. 1952: "It gave me an excuse to go off on a four-day toot." Actor Humphrey Bogart, quoted by Leonard Lyons, *synd. newsp. col.,* Apr. 7. *Since c1860;* see **toot.**

toothpick   *n.* **1** Any large, long object, as a tree-trunk, steel beam, or the like. 1956: "A carpenter hopes he won't have

to spend the day . . . wrestling *toothpicks*—12 × 12 beams." *Labor's Special Lang. from Many Sources. Typical sl. understatement.* **2** A pocket-knife, esp. a knife with a spring blade; a switchblade. 1948: "'Any of her roomers handy with a toothpick?' . . . 'Toothpick, you said?' 'A knife.'" Evans, *Halo for Satan,* 32. *Since c1850. Mainly teenage street-gang use since c1935.*

tootle   *v.i., v.t.* To play a musical instrument, esp. a wind instrument.

too too   *adj.* Excessively polite, stylish, or affected. 1913: "To be too too." F. K. Sechrist, 445. See Appendix, Reduplications.

toots   *n. sing.* A girl or woman; a female sweetheart; a term of familiarity or endearment usu. used in direct address or as a nickname. 1942: "Not any more, toots, not any more, my precious darling angel." Chandler, *High Window,* 169. *Pronounced with either a short or a long "oo." Somewhat archaic.*

tootsies   *n.pl.* The feet.

tootsie-wootsie   **tootsy-wootsy**   *n.* = **toots,** esp. an attractive girl or as a term of endearment to one's sweetheart. 1952: "What about one of those tootsy-wootsies?" B. Marshall in *SEP,* Mar. 1, 21/2. See Appendix, Reduplications.

tootsy   **tootsie**   *n.* **1** = **toots.** 1932: "Hello, tootsie [a man speaking to his wife]." Runyon, 161. See Appendix, **—ie, —y** endings. **2** A person's foot. *Baby talk and jocular use. From "tootsies."*

toot the ringer   To ring a doorbell. *Hobo use.*

top   *v.t.* **1** To hang a person. 1936: "A colleague sent to the gallows has been *topped.* . . ." Mencken, *Amer. Mag.,* Oct., 72. **2** To kill; to bump off. 1932: "Guys getting topped right and left." Runyon. *Underworld use.* **3** To do something better, to perform better, to tell a funnier joke, or to surpass or prove oneself better than another in any way. *Colloq.*   *n.* **1** A top sergeant. *Some W.W.I Army use.* **2** A tent used in a circus or carnival. 1931: "The only tent called [a tent] is the horse tent . . . sometimes the *horsetop* . . . the cook tent is the *cookhouse.* All others are called *tops.*" G. Milburn in *Amer. Mercury,* Nov., 35, 354. 1948: "The G-top [= gambling tent]." "Freak show top." "The sideshow top." "Our sleeping top." "Chow top." F. Brown, *Dead Ringer,* 2; 3; 5; 19; 21. *Common carnival and circus use.*   *adj.* Best; most competent; having the best reputation; known as a leader. 1936: ". . . In 1887. . . . Everywhere upon the Range the price of a 'top' or first-class horse sagged from twenty-five dollars to fifteen dollars and below." P. A. Rollins, *The Cowboy*, 30. *Colloq.* **—per** *n.* 1 A man's top hat. *Colloq.* 2 A joke, wisecrack, or gag that is funnier than a previous one told by another. 1951: "You have a topper?" "Another topper." "That would have been a topper." Radio, *Can You Top This?* Apr. 10. *Orig. comedian use.* See **top.** 3 A memorable remark or statement to which there can be no answer; a statement so audacious, scandalous, true, wise, or fitting that nothing more can be said on the subject. 1939: "It was a famous historical topper when Josephine was informed that the poor people did not have any bread and she said 'Why don't they eat some cake.' " O'Hara, *Pal Joey*, 32. See **top.** 4 A president of a corporation or association; a member of a board of directors; a boss; an official; an executive. 1948: "[The Motion Picture Association] topper had a six-hour session yesterday with [movie theater] managers. [United Artist movie studio] toppers are keeping silent." *Variety*, Aug. 25, 5/3–4. *Mainly business and financial use.* **—ping** *adj.* First rate. *Considered a Briticism. Not common.* *n.* Dessert; any bakery goods, esp. cake, pie, or pastry. **—s** *n.pl.* 1 Loaded dice. 2 The best of anything, either people or things. *adj.* Of highest quality; wonderful; rated highest. 1937: [a person] "I wish you could print Mencken every month—he's tops." *Letter to editor, Amer. Mercury,* Mar., 383/1. 1939: [things] "A night club like the Chez Paris is tops here. . . ." O'Hara, *Pal Joey*, 16. 1949: "Sanitation Service Is Tops." Headline, N.Y. *Times,* Oct. 2, 64/3. *Colloq.*

top — See Appendix, Prefixes and Prefix Words.

top banana   See **banana.**

top dog   1 In the most desirable position; most important; best; most competent; most desired; having the best reputation for success. 1956: "By 1890 the classic jazz was here, and the New Orleans bands were growing. The small string bands were not top dog anymore." S. Longstreet, *The Real Jazz Old and New*, 48. 2 The chief, leader, boss, etc.; the person in authority.

top-drawer   *adj.* 1 Upper-class; also, first-rate. 1916: "A thing dainty or fresh is spoken of [in Nantucket] as

coming out of the bureau (or top) drawer." *Dial. Notes*, 4, 333. *Regarded as a Briticism.* 2 Most important; known only to high-ranking officials; said of military plans or secrets.

top eliminator   An athlete, entry, or contestant with the best chance to win a contest. *Hot-rod and some general teenage use. From hot-rod use. In some drag races only two hot rods are raced against each other at a time; the loser is eliminated and the winner races another car, until the top eliminator or the only car left is the winner.*

top flat   The head. *Some c1935 jive use.*

Top Kick   top kick   top-kick   1 An Army first sergeant. 1944: "The Top Kick was caught shorthanded. . . ." *Amer. Legion Mag.*, Sept., 25/1. *Common use since cW.W.I.* → 2 One in authority; a boss. **—er** *n.* A first sergeant. *More common in W.W.I than in W.W.II. Never as common as "top-kick."*

Top Knocker   top knocker = **Top Kick.** *Not common.*

top notch   The best of anything; of greatest excellence. *Colloq. since c1830.*

top sergeant   A lesbian who plays the dominant or male role in a homosexual relationship. *Not common.*

top-side   *adv.* Upstairs. *From maritime and USN use. Not common.*

top story   The head.

torch   *n.* 1 A match. *Not common.* 2 A pistol. *Some underworld use since c1925.* 3 Fig., a torch carried by a rejected or unrequited lover; the memory or pain of a rejected or unrequited love. *Usu. in the expression "to carry the torch for (someone)."* → 4 = **torch song.** 1948: "All songs of regret and revenge and love's bitter grief are 'torches.' " Lait-Mortimer, *N.Y. Confidential*, 33. *Theater use.* 5 An arsonist; a professional incendiary; a firebug. 1953: "A 'torch' tampered with one of the phones today. If your suspicions are right, the torch will be close by!" L. Turner, *synd. comic strip*, "Wash Tubbs," Feb. 10. 6 A cigar. 1952: "A real two-dollar torch." A. J. Liebling in *New Yorker*, Sept. 27, 56. **—y** *adj.* In love with someone who does not return the love; fig., smoldering with unrequited love. 1953: "Junie [is] still torchy for the Ragtime Kid." S. J. Perelman in *New Yorker*, Jan. 3, 16/2. See **carry the torch.**

torch song   A pop., sad song about lost or unrequited love. 1952: "If love is returned the [popular] song is a simple ballad; if it is unrequited, the song is a torch song." Haskin News Service, Aug. 12.

—torium See Appendix, —atorium, Suffixes and Suffix Words.

torp *n.* A torpedo. *Some W.W.I and II USN use.* **—edo** *n.* **1** Any automobile, esp. a high-powered one. *Archaic.* **2** An assassin, a hired murderer or gunman, esp. if from out of town and imported to commit a murder; any hoodlum or gangster who thrives on violence. 1949: "The torpedoes who worked for Ciro Terranova, red-handed boss of the Unione Siciliana in Harlem and the Bronx. . . ." *Time,* Nov. 28, 16/2. *Orig. underworld use.* **3** An enormous sandwich made from an entire small loaf of hard-crusted bread, the top and bottom halves spread with butter and mayonnaise and filled with a variety of meats, cheeses, vegetables, and relishes. *From its shape.* Cf. **Dagwood, Coney Island, poor boy, Hero.**

torpedo juice Any raw, inferior home-made alcoholic beverage, esp. as made under adverse conditions and from whatever ingredients one can find. *During W.W.II Armed Forces personnel would occasionally find themselves in a position or locale which gave no access to whisky or other alcoholic beverages. Those who felt a desire for some often used much ingenuity to concoct an alcoholic beverage from the ingredients at hand. The orig. of this term is from a typical recipe, based on pure grain alcohol as drained from a Navy torpedo. Other ingenious recipes include modifying and using the alcohol from engine oil, hair tonics, or medicines, usu. mixing them with fruit juice. Chronic alcoholics also turn to such alcoholic beverages when no others are available, "canned heat" being a favorite form of torpedo juice with them.*

toss *v.t.* To give, hold, have, or put on a social party, dance, luncheon, or the like. 1929: "I'm tossing a little party. . . ." Dunning & Abbott, *Broadway,* I. 1952: "Kendall tossed a cocktail party for a group of us visiting writers and Senators. . . ." N.Y. *Daily News,* Aug. 12, C4/4. Cf. **throw.**

toss [one's] cookies To vomit. 1951: "The cab I had was a real old one that smelled like someone had just tossed his cookies in it. I always get those vomity kind of cabs if I go anywhere late at night." J. D. Salinger, *Catcher in the Rye,* 64. *Very much in fashion, esp. with students, since c1945.*

toss in the towel (sponge) = **throw in the towel (sponge).**

toss it in To surrender; to stop trying; to concede failure. From "throw (toss) in the towel (sponge)."

toss it (something) off **1** To accomplish something quickly or with little effort; specif., to drink a shot of whisky quickly, to write a book or play easily, to sing a song without effort, or the like. **2** To fail to consider another's warning, advice, insult, or compliment.

tote *v.t.* **1** To escort or bring a girl, as to a dance. *Some c1925 student use. From "tote" = carry.* **2** To total. 1942: "'How much does it tote?' 'Over two hundred dollars.'" Cain, *Love's Lovely Counterfeit,* 70. See Appendix, Shortened Words. *n.* An electronic totalizator. 1956: "TOTE—A totalizator, an electric apparatus that registers parimutuel bets; originally this automatic machine totalized votes in Australian elections." T. Betts, *Across the Board,* 320. *Horseracing use.*

tote — See Appendix, Prefixes and Prefix Words.

touch *n.* **1** The act or an instance of asking for a loan of money from a friend; a loan or gift of money obtained by request or begging. 1930: "A quick ten or twenty dollar *touch,* which of course was never intended to be returned." Lavine, *Third Degree,* 109. *Since c1920.* **2** Bribe money; a bribe.

tough *adj.* **1** Conscientious; diligent; persistent. 1930: ". . . A conscientious, or 'tough' [police] sergeant." Lavine, *Third Degree,* 17. **2** Fig., impossible to surpass; the best; the greatest; the most. 1957: "Tough—The best; the greatest." E. Horne, *For Cool Cats and Far-Out Chicks. Some far-out use.* *adv.* Roughly; harshly. **—ie** *n.* **1** A tough hoodlum; a tough guy. 1938: ". . . Getting the toughies off the streets. . . ." O. Ferguson in *New Repub.,* Sept. 21, 188/1. **2** A hard or difficult question to answer or problem to solve. 1951: "This is a toughie." M. Shulman, *Dobie Gillis,* 130. **3** A game or contest difficult to win; an opponent difficult to defeat. 1951: "[The Univ. of] Tennessee [football team] has 3 toughies barring its way to a perfect season." R. Roden, AP, Nov. 13. See Appendix, —ie ending.

tough buck Fig., money earned at hard or strenuous work; hard work, a difficult way to earn money.

tough cookie See **cookie.**

tough guy See **guy.**

tough nut   A hard person to deal with; a stubborn, uncompromising person. 1862: *DAE.* 1912: "He's a tough nut." Johnson, *Stover at Yale*, 133. *Archaic. Prob. from the expression "a tough nut to crack."*

tough shit [taboo]   **1** An expression indicating uninterest in another's problem or ill fortune; an expression refusing sympathy, comfort, or aid to another. **2 = that's the way the ball bounces.**

tour   *n.* One's working day or working shift of eight hours. *Fig., one's daily "tour of duty."*   **—ist**   *n.* **1** One easy to cheat or victimize; a victim, a mark. **2** A lazy worker.

tout   *n.* Specif., one who frequents race tracks to sell tips to bettors; one who sells horse-racing information or acts as an advisor to bettors. 1956: TOUT—A tipster. There are many types and they exist in every area of the thoroughbred pastime; some describe themselves as turf consultants." T. Betts, *Across the Board*, 320.   *v.i.* To give or sell tips or advice on horse races.

tow-line   *n.* One who is extremely generous; one who spends money freely. *Some c1925 hobo use. Because it is advantageous to attach oneself to such a person and follow him around.*

town, go to   **1** To succeed; to perform successfully or well. **2** To respond, perform, plan, work, talk, play, or love without restraint, qualification, or inhibition.

town, on the   **1** Having a good time by enjoying a city's night clubs, theaters, and bars; enjoying all the entertainment a town can offer, esp. in one spree and without being concerned about the cost. 1947: "His wife . . . was out on the town with him." UP, Jan. 27. c1954: *On the Town*, title of popular musical show. 1953: "They're mostly on the town instead of in bed." Irwin Edman, *New Yorker*, Feb. 28, 82. **2** Receiving financial help from government, either city or state; living on public relief money. See **on.**

town, out of   In prison. *Some underworld use.*

townie   towney   *n.* **1** Specif., in a town in which a college or university is located, a resident of the town, as opposed to a student. 1853: *DAE. Still in student use.* **2** A resident of a town in which a carnival or circus is performing, as opposed to a member of the carnival or circus; a carnival or circus spectator. 1937: "Child labor laws have forced

children [of circus families] into schools. . . . This contact with 'rubes' and 'townies' has given rise to new interests." *Lit. Digest*, Apr. 3, 21. 1951: ". . . A fight [of carnival workers] with the townies." W. L. Gresham in N.Y. *Times Bk. Rev.*, Apr. 8, 7/5. *Carnival and circus use. Both uses often derisive.* See Appendix, —ie, —y endings.

track   *n.* A dance hall. *Some c1935 jive use. The Savoy Ballroom in N.Y.C.'s Harlem was widely known as "The Track" to hepsters.*   **—s**   *n.pl.* An Army or Air Force captain's insigne bars. *Some W.W.II use.* Cf. **railroad tracks.**

trade-last   trade-lassie   trade-me-lass   *n.* A compliment given for one received. 1920: "It was based upon some 'trade-lasts' gleaned at dancing-school, to the effect that he was 'awfully good-looking. . . .'" Fitzgerald, *This Side of Paradise*, 12. *Since c1890; archaic since c1930. The orig. of "T.L."*

trailer   *n.* A short film shown after a full-length movie, as a preview of a forthcoming movie, a travelog, or the like. *Movie use since c1925.*

train with   To associate with. 1871: *DAE.* 1900: "Ah, the money it required to train with such [well-dressed people]." Dreiser, *Carrie*, 246f. 1944: "She knew as well as I know now—and I don't train with lawyers—that Malone wasn't going to search the house." Ford, *Phila. Murder*, 113.

tramp   *n.* A promiscuous girl or woman, regardless of social class, marital status, or intelligence. *Thus a tramp can be the cheapest prostitute or a refined married society woman who can't resist men. Colloq.*

tranquilize   *v.t.* To subdue a violent person, as a mental patient. 1958: "Tranquilize—To subdue a violent suspect or prisoner." G. Y. Wells, *Station House Slang. Pop. by the tranquilizer pills taken to calm one's nerves.*

transfusion   *n.* Ketchup. *Never common.* See **blood.**

trap   fish (talk, clam, fly, potato, kissing) trap   *n.* **1** A person's mouth, specif. considered as an organ of speech. The expression "to shut [one's] trap" has been cited as early as 1776. 1853: "Fish trap." *DAE.* 1905: "Dodo won't ever open her talk-trap." McHugh, *Search Me*, 94. 1926: "Shut your trap." Stallings & Anderson, *What Price Glory*, I. 1939: "When she opens her trap she has an accent that is British."

O'Hara, *Pal Joey*, 42f. Cf. **blow off [one's] trap. 2** An automobile; a stolen automobile. *Some c1925 underworld use.* **3** A joint, esp. a nightclub. 1932: "Always around the night traps." Runyon, 19. 1952: "Linken owned a pretty good East Side trap, complete with dim lights, a band and food the waiters set on fire." G. Millstein in N.Y. *Times Bk. Rev.*, July 6, 11/1. **—s** *n.pl.* **Clothes.**
— trap See Appendix, Suffixes and Suffix Words.

travel bars Campaign bars worn on the breast of a military blouse. *Some W.W.II Army use.* Cf. **fruit salad.**

tree *n.* The weekly list of men having unsatisfactory grades or conduct. *Some c1925 Annapolis use. Orig. such a list may have been posted on a tree.* Cf. **bush.**

trey *n.* **1** In playing cards, the three of any suit. *Colloq.* **2** Three dollars. *Not common.*

trial balloon A small-scale test made in preparation for a larger endeavor; specif., a testing of public opinion in a limited area to discover how it will respond in a larger area.

trick *n.* **1** A prostitute's customer; a prostitute's "sale" or business transaction. c1915 [1954]: "... Woman walking the streets for tricks to take to her room." L. Armstrong, *Satchmo, My Life in New Orleans*, 8. c1910–c1920: "Keep a-knockin' but you can't come in./ I hear you knockin', but you can't come in./ I got an all-night trick again;/ I'm busy grindin' so you can't come in./ If you love me, you'll come back again,/ Come back tomorrow at half-past ten. ..." From "Bawdyhouse Blues," a very old jazz song. **2** A prison term. *Convict use since c1915.* **3** The act or an instance of committing a crime; a caper, a robbery. *Underworld use since c1925.* **4** An outdoor show or performance. *c1925 carnival and circus use.*

trigger *n.* A gunman; a trigger man. 1949: "He's the trigger." Movie, *Scene of the Crime. Some underworld use since c1935.* See Appendix, Shortened Words. *v.t.* **1** To motivate; to cause something to happen; to initiate or activate. *Colloq.* **2** To commit, manage, engineer, or take a prominent part in an armed robbery. 1952: "Police said Sims has triggered dozens of holdups in the New York area during the last year." AP, Dec. 10.

trigger man An assassin; a gunman for a criminal mob; a bodyguard. *Underworld use since c1925.*

trilby *v.i.* To leave or depart. *c1935 jitterbug use. From "Trilbys."* **Trilbys Trilbies** *n.pl.* The feet. 1917:" We no longer speak of feet as Trilbys." Utter in *Harper's*, June, 72/1. *From the name of the heroine in DuMaurier's novel "Trilby" (1894), noted for her beautiful feet. Obs.*

trill *v.* To stroll, esp. to strut. *Some Negro use. From "Trilbys."* Cf. **trilby.**

trim *v.t.* To defeat an opponent or opposing team, as in a game, esp. to defeat by a narrow margin.

trip *n.* An arrest; specif. a prison sentence. *Some prison use since c1930. Fig., a trip to prison.*

tripe *n.* **1** Untruthful, exaggerated, or insincere talk. **2** An aesthetically insignificant or vulgar thing. **3** A tripod upon which a peddler sets his display case. 1935: "... A low tripod ... the typical tripe of the street hawker." Collier & Westrate, *The Reign of Soapy Smith*, 1. See Appendix, Shortened Words. **4** Entrails; innards; specif., the lining of the stomach. 1952: "Even if they know he is a liar he doesn't put their tripes in an uproar." W. Pegler, *synd. newsp. col.*, July 31. *Now dial.* **5** Inferior or worthless stuff; esp., worthless speech or writing; boloney, lies, exaggeration. 1924: "How I hate Milton! What th' hell do they have to give us that tripe for?" Marks, *Plastic Age*, 102. 1948: "... Anyone who could make money on 'such tripe.'" *Time*, July 26, 72.

tripper *n.* A tourist. 1914: "The tripper class." S. Lewis, *Our Mr. Wrenn*, 126. *Not as common in U.S. as in Eng.*

troll *n.* A disliked boy. *Some c1940 teenage girl use reported; prob. synthetic. Appar. from the mythical troll, a dwarf or a giant.*

trolley, off [one's] Crazy. 1909: "The electric cars were scarcely running when 'off his trolley' was so neatly descriptive of a certain mental state that it was put into immediate commission." *Scribner's*, Aug., 250/1. 1951: "Three minutes to the boat dock? You're off your trolley." M. Shulman, *Dobie Gillis*, 140. *Since c1900; prob. the oldest of the "off [one's] ——" = crazy terms. Archaic.*

trom *n.* A trombone. 1948: "His hands play an imaginary trom." B. Gottlieb in *Sat. Rev. Lit.*, Oct. 30, 51/1. See Appendix, Shortened Words.

troops *n.pl.* A mob or gang. *Some c1930 underworld use.*

trot   *n.* A student's literal translation; a pony. 1891: *DAE.* 1912: "Don't you use a trot?" Johnson, *Stover at Yale,* 148. 1951: "I'm trying to get into Dante, with a trot." S. Lewis, *World So Wide,* 91. *Student use. Not now common.*   *v.i.* To use a trot or pony. *Obs.*   **—s** *n.pl.* Harness races, whether actually trotting or pacing races; harness racing. 1956: TROTS—An inaccurate colloquialism for harness racing, in which, actually, there are more pacers than trotters." T. Betts, *Across the Board,* 320. *Horse-racing use.   n.sing.* Diarrhea.   **—ters** *n.pl.* **1** The feet; the legs. *Not common.* **2 = trots.**

troupe   *n.* Any criminal or violent gang or mob, as of pickpockets or a teenage street gang. 1958: "Troupe—A group of pickpockets, usu. working together." G. Y. Wells, *Station House Slang.*   **—r**   *n.* **1** Anyone who travels with a circus. *Colloq.* **2** An experienced actor. *Colloq.*

trout   *n.* **= cold fish.**

truck   *v.t.* To haul, to carry. 1950: "The boys around that was jealous of me called my horse a goat and picked him up by his knees and hollered, 'We can truck this horse on our back. You shouldn't be riding the horse, he should be riding you.'" A. Lomax, *Mr. Jelly Roll,* 10. *Colloq.*   *v.i.* **1** To go somewhere; to leave; to move. *Jitterbug use c1935.* **2** To jitterbug.

trumped-up   trumped up   *adj.* Made up, imagined; hence, false. 1952: "He had to flee ignominiously with a trumped-up explanation, for how could he confess the simple truth?" C. Aiken, *Ushant,* 187.

trump up   To make up something out of one's imagination, as a lie or alibi; to make something out of makeshift ingredients or parts, by using one's ingenuity; to use one's imagination or ingenuity to make or create something.

try-on   *n., v.t.* **= try-out.**

try-out   *n.* The act or an instance of giving a person or thing a test or trial, under actual or simulated working conditions, to determine fitness, skill, usefulness, or workability. *Since c1910.* *v.t.* **1** To give a person or thing a test or trial, under actual or simulated working conditions, in order to determine fitness, skill, usefulness, or workability. **2** To submit oneself to a test or trial of one's skill, fitness, or ability, often in competition with others, before a prospective

employer in order to secure a job or, specif., in order to earn a part or role in a theatrical production or place on an athletic team. *Colloq.*

t. s.   T. S.   *n.* **= tough shit.** See Appendix, Shortened Words.

tub   *n.* **1 = bucket,** a ship or vehicle. **2** Specif. **= bathtub. 3** Any 16-ounce beer glass; a beer stein. *Dial.* **4 = tub of lard.** Cf. **tubby.**   **—by**   *n.* A fat person; often as a nickname or in direct address. 1953: "A fat man will laugh himself to death at the ex-tubbies trying to live on lettuce leaves." H. Boyle, AP, Apr. 2. *Affectionate or jocular use, never derisive.*   **—s**   *n.* Drums; a set of drums. 1949: "It's all in the wrist 'n' I got the touch—dice, stud, or with a cue. I even beat the tubs a little 'cause that's in the wrist too." N. Algren, *Man with the Golden Arm,* 11.

tub, in the   In bankruptcy.

tub-of-guts   *n.* **= tub of lard.** 1941: "That tub-o'-guts." G. Homes, *40 Whacks,* 77.

tub of lard   A fat person; esp., a person so fat that he is flabby and ugly; specif., a disliked or obnoxious fat person.

tuckus = tokus.

tugboats   *n.pl.* The feet. *Not common.* Cf. **canal boats.**

tumble   *v.i.* **1** To understand, to recognize; to become or be wise to. 1859: *DAE.* 1934: "I tumbled to what she was really up to." Cain, *Postman,* 91f. **2** To be arrested or sentenced to prison. *Underworld use, archaic.*   *n.* An introduction; a sign of recognition or awareness of another's existence. *Usu. in "to give someone a tumble."* 1921: "The newspaper guys had the Bone Crusher pegged as a plant and wouldn't give him a tumble." Witwer, *Leather,* 154. 1927: "Both [men] knew me, but neither gave me a tumble." Hammett, *Blood Money,* 12. 1953: "If the right boy won't give you [a girl] a tumble, you've got a problem." N.Y. *Times Bk. Rev.,* Feb. 8, 17.

tummy   *n.* The stomach; the abdomen. 1951: "But [girdles] keep the figure controlled, eliminating the protruding tummy." A. Donnelly in Syracuse (N.Y.) *Post-Standard,* Sept. 5, 10/1. 1952: "An elephant died of an outsize tummyache at London Airport." AP, Feb. 23. *From "stomach." Said to be a 19C and Victorian euphem. Used as*

Tuned 556

baby talk and jocularly more than in serious speech. *Colloq.*

tuned *adj.* Drunk. *Some c1925 use.* See Appendix, Drunk.

tune up To get into the proper physical or mechanical condition for a contest or task, as by exercise, practice, or making mechanical adjustments; an exercise or practice session, as part of one's conditioning for a contest or task; a warm-up. 1957: "Tuning up [hot rods] for the [drag] race at Santa Ana...." *Life*, Apr. 29, 132.

tunk *n.* An informal banquet or eating or drinking spree; an informal gathering at which light refreshments are served. 1951: "These [social] meetings, usually over coffee and doughnuts, are known locally as tunks, a word of undetermined origin and peculiar to Colgate [University]." Syracuse (N.Y.) *Post-Standard*, pictorial sect., May 27, 4. *Assoc. with Colgate Univ. since c1900; perh. from "tunket."* **—et** *n.* Hell. *Often in "What in tunket?"* 1871: *DAE. Now dial.*

turd [taboo] = **shit,** a person. *From the taboo "turd" = a feces.*

turf *n.* **1** The sidewalk; a street. *c1935 jive use.* **2** The neighborhood, or city blocks, controlled by a teenage street gang; a teenage street gang's territory, which is defended against the encroachment of other gangs. 1958: "I tried to imagine my Deacons [name of a teenage street gang] pacing the turf (gang territory) or talking about me." *Life*, Apr. 28, 70.

turf, on the **1** Engaged in prostitution. c1863 [1936]: "During [Kate Townsend's] early years 'on the turf,' as the saying went, she was ... thrifty and ambitious...." Herbert Asbury, *The French Quarter*, 271f. → **2** Without funds; having little money; being in such dire need of money that one lit. or fig. considers prostitution to obtain funds.

turf-cutter [derog.] *n.* A disliked, unrefined Irishman or one of Irish descent. *From the gathering of peat, used as fuel, in the poorer sections of Ireland.*

Turk **turk** *n.* **1** A strong man; a large, strong, energetic, overbearing man; a man quickly aroused to anger; a stubborn man, one hard to deal with. *Orig. applied mainly to and used by the Irish and people of Irish descent. Now fairly common; often a nickname given to a prize fighter. From the Gaelic "torc" = a wild boar.* **2** A sexual degenerate; specif., an active pederast. *Because this form of perversion was once thought to be prevalent among Turks.* **3** A turkey. See Appendix, Shortened Words.

turkey *n.* **1** See **have a turkey on [one's] back. 2** Money earned or obtained easily; profit, gravy; an easy task; an advantage. 1873: *DAE. Obs. Turkeys are considered comparatively easy to catch.* → **3** A fifty-cent piece. *From the eagle on the coin. Obs.* **4** Pretentious or pompous speech or writing. 1880: *DAE. Obs.* See the antonymous expression **talk turkey. 5** Any suitcase or valise in which one carries personal belongings, esp. a canvas bag or a hobo's bindle. 1909: "A [Colorado] desert miner calls his valise a 'turkey.'" *Outlook*, Jan. 2, 19/1. *Archaic.* **6** Any of various cheap meats, meat dishes, fish or fowl, regarded as inferior to turkey, esp. bacon, hash, or canned tuna fish; specif., chicken. *Some jocular use at the table.* Cf. **Irish turkey. 7** An inferior entertainment, esp. a stage play that is exceptionally dull, badly written and produced, and a financial failure; a flop. 1944: "The management prudently kept the turkey [the play *My Dear Children*] out of town." Fowler, *Good Night*, 388. 1951: "Genuine stars generally can attract an audience no matter what [motion] picture they are in (unless it's a real turkey)." B. Thomas, AP, Feb. 23. *Since before c1930. The most common use.* → **8** Any worthless, useless, unsuitable thing. 1941: "The beach in front was studded with rocks and was therefore unsuitable to swimming. For all ordinary purposes it was simply a turkey." Cain, *M. Pierce*, 176. 1951: "After all, the treasury realizes that this law is a turkey." W. Pegler, synd. newsp. col., Aug. 22. → **9** An ineffective, incompetent, objectionable or disliked person. 1951: "So, if you got a collector [of internal revenue] through the civil service system who was a real turkey, you'd be stuck with that turkey practically until he died." D. Larsen, NEA, Nov. 30. *Some student use since before c1945.* → **10** = **square.** *Some bop, cool, and even teenage use.*

turkey on [one's] back, have a **1** To be drunk. 1851: Hall, *College Words. Never common. Obs.* **2** = **monkey on one's back.**

turkey-shoot *n.* An easy task; a task that is easy to perform successfully; now specif., an airplane attack that is highly destructive of enemy aircraft. 1945: "The great [battle of the] Marianas Turkey-Shoot." Riordan in *Calif. Folk. Quart.*, Oct., 19. *Very old; because* *turkeys are slow to show fear and hence are easy to get close to. Specif., war use, some W.W.II USN and Air Force use.*

turn   *v.t.* To earn or solicit money; to accomplish a task for money. *Thus a waiter is said "to turn a tip" = to have worked for or received a tip for his services.* Cf. **turn the tip.**

turn a trick   See **trick.**

turn blue (green)   1 = **drop dead.** *Pop. c1948 by actress-comedienne Judy Holliday.* 2 = **shit green (blue).**

turned on = **high,** from whisky or a narcotic. 1956: "'I'm really turned on, man,' she cried. 'I'm higher than a giraffe's toupee.'" S. Longstreet, *The Real Jazz Old and New,* 146. *Not common.* See **turn on.**

Turner   *n.* A German; a person of German ancestry. *From the German immigrant fraternal and athletic society called "The Turners."*

turn in   To go to bed; to go to sleep. *Colloq.*

turnip   *n.* A pocket watch. *Underworld and dial. use since c1885.*

turn off   To rob a place successfully. 1948: "When a bank was turned off...." A. Hynd, *Pinkerton,* 12. *Some underworld use.*

turn off [someone's] water   To stop a person from talking, esp. from boasting or exaggerating, as by a direct refutation or a witty or insulting remark; to prevent another from beginning a project or from succeeding, esp. when his project or success is undesirable or unwarranted; esp., to prevent a person from achieving an advantage, reputation or success that is unearned.

turn on   To begin smoking a marijuana cigarette; to smoke a marijuana cigarette; to take a narcotic or to be under the influence of a narcotic. *Narcotic addict use.*

turn on the heat   To strive for or pursue anything vigorously; to use all one's talent, skill, or influence to succeed; to become exciting; to strive to arouse another's passion; to search diligently for a criminal; to make it hard for a criminal to escape; to intimidate a person; to begin shooting a gun. *Many various meanings based on "heat" and "hot."*

turn-out   turnout   *n.* 1 A crowd or audience, esp. a large one; spectators, guests. *Colloq. Fig., those who have turned out to see or be present at an entertainment, spectacle, or gathering.* 2 The acquittal of an arrested person.

1930: "If this [arrest] results in 'turn-outs.' ..." Lavine, *Third Degree,* 210. *Underworld use.* 3 A suit of clothes.

turnover   *n.* 1 The number or percentage of people or items replaced during a specif. time. *Thus the turnover of a factory's employees may be 20% a year, the turnover for a specif. table in a restaurant may be two customers per hour, or a merchant may have a turnover of his entire stock twice a year.* 2 The night before one's release from prison. Cf. **rollover.**

turn the tip   The accomplishment of the talker or spieler, after he has collected a "tip" or crowd by means of his bally, in turning or directing its attention to the product he has for sale.

turn turtle   *v.i., v.t.* 1 Lit., to turn or be turned upside down; fig., to be helpless or defenseless. 1951: "The expression 'to turn turtle' is a monument to their [Mascarene turtles] utter defenselessness: they had only to be tipped over on their backs to be helpless." J. Williams, *Fall of the Sparrow,* 39. 2 To retreat or turn back when necessary; to become cowardly, to turn chicken.

turn [someone] up   To turn a person over to the police; to inform to the police, as to who committed a crime or where the criminals are hiding. 1929: "Maybe you better turn me up." Burnett, *Little Caesar,* 177. 1940: "Somebody turned him up." Chandler, *Farewell,* 32.

turn up [one's] toes (to the daisies)   To die.

turtle   *n.* 1 An armored car, as used to deliver money to or from a bank. *Some underworld use.* 2 An unemployed actor. 1951: "...A couple of turtles (laid-off actors) basking in the sun...." A. Green, *Show Biz,* 10. *Theater use, not common.* See **turn turtle.**

turtle doves   A pair of lovers.

tush   *n.* A light complexioned Negro; a mulatto. *Negro use.*   *adj.* 1 Belligerent, malicious; dangerous. 2 Belonging to high society; wealthy, sophisticated, and influential; ritzy. *Some Negro use.*

—eroon(y)   *n.* Money. *Some Negro and jive use. Reinforced by "tush," but prob. of an earlier orig.* See Appendix, —y ending.

tux   *n.* A tuxedo; a man's formal evening dress suit; sometimes a man's formal afternoon, dining, or evening ensemble consisting of a white or black formal dinner jacket, black trousers with satin seam stripe, and a black bow tie.

1949: "[He] stopped wearing his tux to banquets." Phila. *Bulletin*, Sept. 2, 4/1. *Colloq.* See Appendix, Shortened Words.

tuxedo *n.* A straitjacket, as used to restrain a violent prisoner or mental patient.

tuxedo junction A public place catering to swing devotees; any place, as a dance hall, record store, or lunch-counter, where swing fans gather. *c1940 swing use.*

tweed *n.* A girl or young woman. *Usu. complimentary. Not common.*

tweeter *n.* A small paper-cone loudspeaker that vibrates electromagnetically to reproduce high frequencies without distortion, used in addition to other speakers in a high-fidelity phonograph or sound-reproducing system. *Common hi-fi use since c1950.* Cf. **woofer.**

twelve-hour leggings Puttees, esp. as worn by timekeepers and foremen. *Contemptuous use by laborers and hobos.* Cf. **open-shop pants.**

twenty *n.* A twenty-dollar bill; the sum of $20.

twenty-one *n.* An order of a glass of limeade or orangeade. *c1935 lunch-counter use in relaying orders.*

twenty-three! *exclam.* = **twenty-three skidoo!** *Common c1900–c1910; obs.*

twenty-three skid(d)oo! 23 skid(d)oo! *exclam.* A mild expression of recognition, incredulity, surprise, or pleasure, as at something remarkable or attractive; also used as an expression of rejection or refusal, sometimes as = "Go away!" "Beat it!" or "I don't care." 1926: "[Approx. 25 years ago] appeared in my vocabulary that effective but horrible '23-Skiddoo.' Pennants and arm bands at shore resorts, parks and county fairs, bore either [23] or the word 'Skiddoo.' In time the numerals became synonymous with and connotative of the whole expression." C. T. Ryan, *AS*, 2/92. *Like "shoo-fly," "twenty-three skiddoo" was often used without specif. meaning. It was in male use c1900–c1910, orig. among students and sophisticated young adults. It was perh. the first truly national fad expression and one of the most pop. fad expressions to appear in the U.S. Almost fifty years after it has had any serious use, it is still universally known and remembered. Ironically, it is now assoc. with the 1920's and is freq. used to convey the spirit of the 1920's in novels and plays of the period.*

twerp **twirp** *n.* A person of either sex but esp. a male who is or is thought to be peculiar, insignificant, objectionable, weird, or the like. 1945: ". . . An ill-mannered, foul-mouthed little twirp." W. Pegler, *synd. newsp. col.*, Dec. 13. 1952: "That little twirp?—the hell with him. It may be that some of the novels which the public is ignoring are by little twirps." B. De Voto in *Harper's*, Feb., 68/2. *Wide teenage and student use c1930–c1945. Still some use, now mostly adult use.*

twiddle *v.i.* To chat; to converse idly. 1951: "That's a hell of a crummy place to stop and twiddle!" *New Yorker*, Jan. 6, 23/2.

twig *n.* A tree. *v.t.* To punish. 1910: "You'll get twigged for a midnight spread." Johnson, *Varmint*, 300. *Fig., to punish a child or youth by using the rod.*

twin pots **1** Dual carburetors installed in a car. → **2** A car with dual carburetors. *Hot-rod use since c1950.* See **pot.**

twins, the *n.pl.* A set of, or the, salt and pepper shakers. *Some c1930 lunch-counter use.*

twirl *v.i., v.t.* In baseball, to pitch. *n.* A duplicate or skeleton key. *Mainly underworld use.* **—y** *adj.* Crazy. *Not common.*

twirp *n.* = **twerp.**

twist *n.* A girl or young woman. 1947: "You ought to be all right at snatchin' twists' purses too." N. Algren, "The Face," 29/2. *From rhyming sl. "twist and twirl" = girl.* See Appendix, Rhyming Slang. **—ed** *adj.* A little abnormal, mentally or emotionally; showing some neurotic or psychopathologic symptoms; at best, confused, at the worst, "sick." **—er** *n.* **1** A tornado. *Fairly common dial. use.* **2** A key. *Usu. in "the twister to the slammer." Orig. some underworld use, but mainly c1935 jitterbug use.* **3** A raid by the police. **4** A drunken spree. 1950: "The rest have stretched out their periods of sobriety between twisters." J. Alexander in *SEP*, Apr. 1, 18/3. *Suggested by "bender." Not common. Reinforced by "twister" = tornado.*

two-a-day *n.* = **big time.** *Vaudeville use. Because the more important theaters in large cities had two complete vaudeville performances a day.*

two and a half An order of a small glass of milk. *c1930 lunch-counter use in relaying an order.*

two-and-a(one)-half-striper *n.* A Naval lieutenant commander. *USN use.*

two-bit *adj.* **1** Lit., worth twenty-five cents. *1802: DAE.* 1924: "Two-bit limit." Marks, *Plastic Age*, 232. → **2** Cheap, inferior, insignificant; small-time; tin-horn. 1929: "These two-bit wops." Burnett, *Little Caesar*, 172. 1939: "A two-bit piece." O'Hara, *Pal Joey*, 39. 1949: "The two-bit bureaucrats." Billy Rose, *synd. newsp. col.*, Sept. 12.

two bits A quarter; the sum of 25¢. *1730: DAE.* c1850 [1957]: "I gave him two bits (twenty-five cents) to take the horse back." T. H. Henry, *Buckskin and Blanket Days*, 26. *Colloq.*

two-case note A two-dollar bill. *Not common.* See **case-note.**

two cents' (worth), [one's] One's opinion, advice, or remark.

twofer *n.* **1** A cigar that sells at the price of "two for 5¢"; a cheap cigar. **2** A ticket, usu. theater, that admits two for the price of one. *Both uses from "two for . . ."*

two percenter See **five percenter, ten percenter.**

two shakes (of a lamb's tail) Fig., a minute, a second; a very short time. *E.g., "I'll be there in two shakes."*

two-spot *n.* A two-dollar bill.

two-stemmer *n.* A large town. *Fig., a town having two main stems. Not common.*

two-step(per) *n.* A chicken. *c1925 hobo use. Prob. from its way of walking.*

two-striper *n.* **1** A Naval lieutenant, senior grade. *USN use.* **2** A corporal. *Some W.W.II Army use.*

two-time *v.t.* **1** To join with one other person and fight or beat up a third person. *Not common.* **2** To double-cross someone, esp. in affairs of the heart; specif., to deceive one's sweetheart or spouse by being unfaithful. 1952: "Two-Timing Boy Wrecks Girl's Dream." Headline, N.Y. *Daily News*, Aug. 16, C16/3. *Colloq.*

two-time loser **1** A person who has been convicted and sent to prison twice. 1939: "He's a two-time loser." Gardner, *D. A. Draws*, 162. *In some states a third conviction for a major crime carries a mandatory sentence of life imprisonment.* **2** A twice-divorced person. 1953: "It [marital advice] does sound odd coming from a two-time loser." B. Thomas, AP, Feb. 12. *Usu. jocular use.*

tyee *n., adj.* Chief. *Orig. logger use. From Chinook jargon.*

typewriter *n.* A machine gun; specif., an automatic, portable machine gun. *Some Army use since W.W.I. Underworld use since c1920. Specif. W.W.II Army use = a .30 caliber machine gun.*

tzuris *n.sing.* Ill fortune, esp. chronic ill fortune or bad luck; problems. 1956: "During a long streak of tzuris (misery) with cards and horses. . . ." T. Betts, *Across the Board*, 103. *From the Yiddish "tzuris" (plural) = troubles, specif. problems.*

U

ubble-gubble *n.* Meaningless talk; gibberish. 1942: "Casti's ubble-gubble into phonographs is nonsense." W. B. Johnson, *Widening Stain*, 31. See Appendix, Reduplications.

ugly *adj.* Mean; despicable; said of a person or act.

umbay *n.* A bum. *From Pig Latin.* See Appendix, Little Languages.

ump *n.* An umpire. *Baseball use since c1910.* See Appendix, Shortened Words. *v.i.* To act as an umpire.

umpchay *n.* A chump. a sucker; a dupe. *From Pig Latin.* See Appendix, Little Languages.

umpire *n.* **1** An inspector. *Some factory use.* **2** A legal or labor relations mediator.

umpteen **umteen** *n., adj.* **1** Any unspecified cardinal number from 13 to 19 inclusive. *Not common.* **2** Any large indeterminate number; used to suggest quantity too great to count. 1952: "When you've exhausted all the encomia in your vocabulary on umpteen reviews of [detective stories]. . . ." A. Boucher, N.Y. *Times Bk. Rev.*, May 4, 20/3.

umpteenth **umteenth** *adj.* **1** Any unspecified ordinal number from 13th to 19th inclusive. *Not common.* **2** Any large indeterminate ordinal number. 1945: "Here's the umpteenth development in the battle. . . ." AP, July 24.

umpty *n., adj.* Any unspecified number ending in "—ty" from 20 to 90 inclusive. 1938: ". . . Page umpty-nine." E. Knight, *Flying Yorkshireman.* 1945: "The umpty-fifth regiment." B. Mauldin, *Up Front.*

umpty-umpth *adj.* Any unspecified ordinal number from the 24th to the 99th inclusive. 1937: "Making the same speech for the umpty-umpth time. . . ."

Eleanor Roosevelt in *Ladies' Home Journal*, Dec. 1949: "The umpty-umpth revision. . . ." B. Cerf in *Sat. Rev. Lit.*, Dec. 10.

unc *n.* **1** Uncle. 1951: "Mom! Dad! Unc! Aunt!" Advt., N.Y. *Times Mag.*, Nov. 18, 76/2. See Appendix, Shortened Words. **2** = **uncle**, all meanings.

uncle *n.* **1** A pawnbroker. 1607: used by Eng. dramatist John Dekker. 1954: "These Simpson nephews . . . were responsible for the word 'uncle' becoming a slang synonym of pawnbroker. When offered unfamiliar collateral . . . they would tell the customer, 'I'll have to ask my uncle.'" W. R. & F. K. Simpson, *Hockshop*, 27. → **2** A receiver of stolen goods; a fence. *Underworld use.* **3** Any elderly male Negro. *Since before the Civil War.* **4** A Federal law enforcement agent, esp. a narcotics agent. *Underworld and narcotic addict use. From "Uncle Sam."*

Uncle Dudley I; myself; me. *Dial.*

Uncle Sam **1** The United States of America; the government, power, or authority of the United States. *From the bewhiskered symbol of the United States.* **2** A federal law-enforcement agent or agency. *Underworld use.*

Uncle Sam's party Payday, esp. for federal employees. *Some W.W.II Army use.*

Uncle Tom [derog.] A sycophantic Negro; a meek or ambitious Negro who defers to, and curries the favor of, white people, either for personal gain, from habit, or usu. in an attempt to appease whites who are anti-Negro in feeling; a Negro who casts himself as inferior to white people. 1956: "An 'Uncle Tom' is one who caters to white taste." S. Longstreet, *The Real Jazz Old and New*, 47. *Orig. Negro use. From the chief character in Harriet Beecher Stowe's "Uncle Tom's Cabin."* 1957: "He's [musician Louis Armstrong] . . . the No. 1 Uncle Tom! The worst in the U.S." Thurgood Marshall, famed civil-rights lawyer and NAACP [National Association for the Advancement of Colored People] counsel, quoted by Mike Wallace, *newsp. col.*, N.Y. *Post*, Sept. 30, 38. *v.i., v.t.* To act servilely toward whites; said of a Negro.

Uncle Tommer(s) = **tommer**. *Theater use; obs.*

Uncle Whiskers *n.* = **whiskers**.

uncool *adj.* Not cool; square; hyperemotional, obnoxious, loud, rude, uncouth. *Fairly common cool use.* "Cool" is one of the few *sl. words used with prefixes. Though not common enough to deserve entries in this dictionary, "precool," "procool," and "anticool" are also used by cool groups.*

under For phrases beginning with "under," see under the principal word of the phrase.

under, get out from **1** To recoup one's gambling losses; to recoup one's business losses; to pay off one's debts. **2** To extract oneself from a failing, embarrassing, or unpleasant enterprise, job, or relationship.

under [one's] belt Successfully accomplished; as part of one's experience; to one's credit. *Colloq.*

undergrad *n.* **1** An undergraduate student in college. **2** A university course for undergraduate students. See Appendix, Shortened Words.

under [one's] hat *adj.* Secret; confidential; often in "keep it under your hat." 1908: *DAE.* 1930: "Well, here it is, but it's strictly under the hat, see?" J. Sayre, *Amer. Mercury*, Dec., 415/1. 1941: "This is under your hat." G. Homes, *40 Whacks*, 88.

underpinnings *n.pl.* The human legs. *Since c1850.*

understandings *n.pl.* The human feet or legs. 1833: *DAE. Not common.*

under the daisies See **push up the daisies**.

under the table *adj.* **1** Drunk. *Colloq.* See Appendix, Drunk. **2** Involving illegal or unethical payment or bribery. *From notion of bribe money passed under the table.*

undies *n.pl.* Underwear, specif. women's underpants. 1920: "[A term] now in vogue." W. J. Hawthorn in *Sat. Rev. Lit.*, July 31, 94/1. 1942: "She gave Mrs. Grundies/ A glimpse of her undies." W. B. Johnson, *Widening Stain*, 35. See Appendix, —ie endings.

unfrocked *adj.* Dismissed or barred from a professional society or pursuit; without recognition or status, esp. stripped of recognition as by a professional society, union, or governing body. 1949: "We got an unfrocked psychiatrist to write a paper proving it was harmful to the libido." S. J. Perelman, *Listen to the Mockingbird*, 122. *Usu. jocular use.*

ungepotch(ket, ed) *adj.* Accomplished in spite of many blunders or much confusion; untidy, sloppy, nonprofessional, makeshift. *From the Yiddish.*

unhep *adj.* Not hep; square. 1950:

". . . Faith, devotion, and other such unhep subjects." Billy Rose, *synd. newsp. col.*, Jan. 4. 1951: "Unhep audiences." A. Green, *Show Biz*, 570. *With "cool," "hep" is one of few sl. words that take stand. prefixes.*

unhipped *adj.* = **unhep**. *Jive use since c1935.*

unkjay *n.* = **junkie**. 1949: "He'd seen them coming in the rain, the unkjays, with their peculiar rigid, panicky walk, wearing some policeman's castoff rubbers, no socks at all, a pair of Salvation Army pants a size too small or a size too large and a pajama top for a shirt—but with twenty dollars clutched in the sweating palm for that big twenty-dollar fix." N. Algren, *Man with the Golden Arm*, 78. *From Pig Latin.* See Appendix, Little Languages.

unmentionables *n.pl.* **1** Trousers; a pair of trousers. 1830: *DAE. Obs. by 1900.* **2** Underclothing. 1910: "Each [boy] was required to don upper and lower unmentionables." Johnson, *Varmint*, 221f. *Now jocular use only.* **3** Specif., women's underpants and brassières.

un poco A little; a small quantity or portion. *From the Sp.*

unrooster *v.t.* To tame a horse to work after he has wintered on the range. *Southwestern cowboy use.*

unshoed *adj.* Dressed cheaply or in bad taste. *Some student use since c1950.*

unslough *v.t.* **1** To extract a watch from a vest or pants pocket, as by a pickpocket. *Underworld use.* → **2** Fig., to separate a person and his money or valuables; to steal; to win or take by cheating or chicanery.

unwell *adj.* Menstruating. *An old and familiar euphem. Colloq.*

unwhisperables *n.pl.* = **unmentionables.** *Never common.*

up *n.* A prospective buyer. 1949: "The hottest salesman who ever turned a looker into an up." N.Y. *Times*, May 1. 62. *Some retail salesman use. From the command "Up!" given a salesman when a prospective buyer appears.* *adj.* Fried on one side so that the yoke remains soft; said of an egg. *Orig. lunch-counter use.* See **sunny side up.**

—up See Appendix, Suffixes and Suffix Words.

up [one's] alley To be entirely within one's capabilities or interest; to be one's natural task.

Up anchor! *imp.* Get out! *Orig. Annapolis use, c1925. Still some USN use.*

up-and-down *n.* A look or regard; a visual inspection, usu. of a person. 1950: "The tray-toter gave me the slow up-and-down." Billy Rose, *synd. newsp. col.*, Mar. 27.

up and go, get Ambition and vitality; energy, enthusiasm, gumption. *Usu. complimentary and used in the phrase, "He has a lot of get up and go."*

up and up Honest; trustworthy; fair-minded. 1929: "It's an up and up place." "She's an up and up girl." Burnett, *Little Caesar*, 13, 28. See **on the up and up.**

up and up, on the / on the up-and-up *adj.* Honest; fair; legitimate; sincere; permissible; on the level. 1930: "One of our . . . police inspectors, who was always on the 'up and up,' whenever a 'church bazaar' was advertised, would . . . prevent the boys from doing business on a large scale." Lavine, *Third Degree*, 201. 1935: "I almost wonder if the whole bunch of 'em are on the up and up. . . ." S. Lewis, *Scribner's*, Aug., 68/2. 1942: "This is strictly on the up-and-up." W. B. Johnson, *Widening Stain*, 240. 1950: "It's really quite on the up-and-up . . . [to] pick up the [canasta] stock pile and count it." O. Jacoby, NEA, Apr. 26. *adv.* Honestly; legitimately; sincerely. See **up and up.**

up [one's] ass [taboo] **1** Fig., being treated perversely; being taken advantage of, unfairly treated, cheated, or victimized; the final insult. As in "I was really cheated, right up my ass." **2** = **up your ass.**

up a tree In a dilemma; caught in a predicament. *Since c1825. From the notion of a person chased up a tree by a wild animal.*

up-beat **upbeat** *n.* **1** The first note or beat of a musical composition; lit., the first note played when the conductor raises his baton. → **2** The first note or notes of a musical theme whenever they are repeated within a single composition. → **3** A familiar, well-liked passage in music. *adj.* Entertaining rather than dramatic; familiar, colorful, fast-moving; happy; said of movies, books, plays, etc. 1958: "A triumph of upbeat pictures over the downbeat." AP, Mar. 24. *Common since c1940.* Cf. **downbeat, offbeat.**

up-chuck **upchuck** *v.i., v.t.* To vomit. *Since c1925. Orig. student use. Considered a smart and sophisticated term c1935, esp. when applied to sickness* *that had been induced by overdrinking.*

update *v.t.* To furnish with up-to-date information. 1952: "He updated me on a couple of gimmicks. . . ." John Crosby, N.Y. *Her. Trib.*, Mar. 14, 21/2. *adj.* Up to date.

up in the bucks Wealthy. 1930: "He wished that he was up in the bucks." J. T. Farrell, *Short Stories*, 161. *Somewhat archaic.*

up in the morning and put [him] to bed at night, get [someone] To follow someone; to shadow or tail as by the police. *Not common.*

uplift *n.* A brassière or style of brassière that lifts a woman's breasts so severely that they protrude and become prominent. *An item and style very popular c1940–c1948 and necessary to the sweater girl. During this period prominent and shapely breasts were considered most desirable and sexually attractive. The breast-emphasized female figure was first pop. by Jane Russell in the movie "The Outlaw." For her the producer of the movie, Howard Hughes, designed a very severe uplift.* Cf. **falsies.**

up on the town Obs. form of **on the town.**

—upper See Appendix, Suffixes and Suffix Words.

upper plate An old person; specif. any person whom an adolescent considers old. *In ref. to false teeth. Some student use c1940.*

upper story The brain; head. 1938: "Dope [means] an individual who has definite shortcomings in the upper story." D. Nowinson, *Better Eng.*, Oct., 8/1. *Common since c1910.* Cf. **top story, upstairs.**

uppity *adj.* **1** Snobbish, aloof; having a superior manner; presumptuous. *Colloq.* → **2** [derog.] Truculent toward white people, contumelious, audacious, unlike an Uncle Tom; said of Negroes. 1955: "This nigger received some kind of education at some colored college, and he's pretty damned uppity. In fact, he's just about the most uppity colored fellow I ever ran into in my life." C. Willingham, *To Eat a Peach*, 142. *Mainly Southern use.* *n.* Society folk; the ostentatiously wealthy. 1956: "The *uppity*, the ritzy folk, don't know the half of it about jazz talk." S. Longstreet, *The Real Jazz Old and New*, 148. *Orig. Negro use; never common.*

up shit creek (without a paddle) [taboo] Out of luck; in a hopeless predicament. *Although the shortened form "up the creek" is common, the full orig. term is seldom heard now. Orig. from homosexual usage, meaning that one has encountered difficulties or has been discovered while engaged in anal intercourse.*

up-stage **upstage** *v.t.* **1** To steal the attention of the audience from another actor, as by standing upstage or in front of him. *Old theater use; very common.* → **2** To ignore or snub a person; to treat another coldly. 1921: "Nada Nice has upstaged the Kid . . . at your orders." Witwer, *Leather*, 176. *Since c1910.* → **3** To become or be angry at someone. *Some c1920 use.* *adj.* Aloof, snobbish; vain; fig., affecting the manner of a theatrical star. 1929: " 'Upstage' has taken on the additional meaning of 'ritzy', that is, arrogantly proud and vain." B. Sobel.

upstairs *n., adv.* In the head, brain, or mind. 1950: "He's got nothin' upstairs but solid knuckle." Movie, *Asphalt Jungle.* 1952: "George III . . . became a little balmy upstairs after losing America." H. Boyle, AP, Mar. 11.

up stakes To leave a place, esp. to leave town hurriedly. *Since c1840. Possibly from circus use: "stakes" = tent stakes; or perhaps from old Western use: "stakes" = money, accumulated possessions, bindle.*

up sticks = **up stakes.**

upsweep *n.* A women's hairdressing style in which the hair is brushed upward toward the crown. 1945: "Long hair's out of style anyhow, ain't it?/ Now it's tie it up high with curls./ So gimme an upsweep, Minnie./ I'll show them girls." Gwendolyn Brooks, *A Street in Bronzeville*, 35.

uptake *n.* See **quick on the uptake.**

up the creek Out of luck; in a predicament; in trouble, in difficulty; close to failure or ruin. 1937: "If we get stuck with all those dresses, then you guys'll be up the creek for good. You'll *never* get your dough." Weidman, *Wholesale*, 188. 1943: "His father, already well up the creek. . . ." P. Wylie, *Generation of Vipers*, 269. 1951: "How 'bout writing a composition for me, for English? I'll be up the creek if I don't get the goddam thing in by Monday." J. D. Salinger, *Catcher in the Rye*, 26. *Very common, esp. among students. A euphem. for "up shit creek without a paddle," though many who use it do not know the taboo origin of the term.*

up the pole = **on the wagon.** *Some*

maritime use; never common. This is the opposite of the Brit. use = drunk.

up there   Heaven. 1954: *Somebody Likes Me Up There*, title of prize fighter Rocky Graziano's autobiography.

up the river   In prison. *Orig. underworld use; pop. since c1935. From Sing Sing prison, which is up the Hudson river from New York City.*

up thine with turpentine [taboo]   See **up your (one's) ass** [taboo]. See Appendix, Rhyming Slang.

up to here   up to there   1 *Lit.,* filled with food; full, capable of eating no more. *Often accompanied by a gesture of pointing to the throat or chin, implying that the stomach is full to that level.* → **2** Fig., surfeited with another's talk, actions, etc.; bored, disgusted, fed up.

up to (the) snuff (mustard)   Equal to the usu. or desired quality or standard.

up to the gills   Drunk; full of liquor. See Appendix, Drunk.

uptown lady   1 A woman who is, or assumes the attitudes of being, wealthy, socially prominent, well educated, and worldly. *Not common; some Negro use.* **2** A girl or woman who allows passionate petting, including fondling of her breasts, but who will let her admirer's hands stray no further downward than to her waistline. *Not common.*

up your (one's) ass [taboo]   **1** = **stick it up your ass.** → **2** An expression of disgust, disbelief, rejection, etc. *Like most taboo sl., this can be used jocularly among friends. Sometimes followed by "with sandpaper (gauze, salt, turpentine)" for emphasis.*

up yours   [taboo] = **up your ass.** *Note the shortening from "stick it up your ass" to "up your ass" to "up yours."* Cf. **stick it.**

use [one's] bean = **use [one's] head.** 1924: "You certainly used the old bean." Marks, *Plastic Age*, 10. See **bean.**

used-to-be   *n.* = **has-been.** 1853: *DAE. Colloq.*

use [one's] head   To think; to take thought. 1950: "The Army . . . also teaches a man to use his head and to do the best he can." Soldier quoted by H. Boyle, AP, July 20. *Colloq.*

user   *n.* A narcotics addict. See Appendix, —er ending.

use the needle   To have a narcotic addiction; to be a drug addict. 1956: "Sherlock Holmes . . . a guy with two habits—playing the fiddle and using the needle. . . ." J. Cannon, *Who Struck John?* 199.

ush   *v.i.* To work as an usher. *Since c1890.* See Appendix, Shortened Words.

ut   *adj.* Extreme, esp. in ref. to the manners of the socially elite or to the affectations of a social climber. *From "utter(ly)."* See Appendix, Shortened Words.

utmost, the = **most, the.** *Some cool use.*

V

vacation   *n.* A prison sentence. 1930: ". . . Who won a 20 years' vacation in the Big House." Lavine, *Third Degree,* 223.

vag   *n.* **1** A vagrant, a tramp; a jobless person; often defined legally by municipal courts as a person without a permanent job, without a permanent home address, and with less than a specific amount of money (usu. $15) in his possession. 1894: "America can almost compete with England in the number of her 'city vags.' " J. Flynt. 1895: *DAE.* 1947: "The police . . . at once bagged her as a 'vag.' " John Bruce, *San. Fran. Murders,* 206. *The word is derog., connoting a petty criminal or an incompetent.* **2** Vagrancy; a charge of vagrancy. 1950: "We'll book him on

vag." Movie, *Asphalt Jungle.*   *v.t.* To arrest a person for vagrancy; to sentence a person convicted of vagrancy. See Appendix, Shortened Words.

valentine   *n.* **1** An official written notice to a college student warning him of the danger of dismissal because of poor scholastic work. 1900: *DAE. Never common; obs.* **2** A written warning to an employee who has done poor work; a notification of dismissal from a job. 1930: "The captain . . . may distribute a few complaints or 'valentines' for dereliction of duties." Lavine, *Third Degree,* 16.

valentino   Valentino   *n.* Love, esp. passionate love; coitus. 1958: ". . . I saw Clarice during my leave, and we made terrific valentino when her mother's back was turned." "A Gang Leader's Redemption," *Life*, April 28, 75. *Some teenage use, never common. From the famous 1920's movie lover and idol Rudolph Valentino.*

vamose vamoose *v.t.* To leave a place, town, or region. 1847: "vamoose," *DAE.* *v.i.* To depart, esp. to depart quickly; to flee; to beat it. 1848: "vamose," *DAE.* 1868: "vamoose," *DAE.* 1901: "So *vamos* is a proper Mexican word [Sp. "let us go"], but when it is quoted and used by Americans for 'depart' (*vamoose*) . . . it becomes slang." Greenough & Kittredge, 58. *Both uses colloq.*

vamp *n.* A seductive or sexually aggressive woman; one who entices men; an attractive woman with a strong come-on. 1920: "The flirt had become the 'baby vamp.' " Fitzgerald, *This Side of Paradise*, 65f. *v.t.* To seduce or influence a man through sexual appeal. 1924: "She's vamping you, Harold!" Marks, *Plastic Age*, 28. 1928: "I haven't tried to vamp Sam. . . ." E. Rice, *Street Scene*, II. *Both uses were common c1915–1930. Orig. from the very popular movie, "A Fool There Was" (1914), in which actress Theda Bara played a vampire; the vamp concept included her mannerisms, dress, speech, etc. Now colloq. and prob. archaic.*

van *n.* **1** A railroad caboose. *Railroad use.* **2** A mining or logging camp store. *Because orig. it was in a wagon, truck, or railroad car. Miner and logger use.* **3** Vanilla ice cream; an order of vanilla ice cream. *Some lunch-counter use in relaying an order.* See Appendix, Shortened Words.

vanilla *interj.* An expression of disbelief. *Usu. jocular, used when the suspected lie or exaggeration is of no great consequence.* *n.* **1** Unfounded talk, rumors; lies or exaggeration; bull. **2** An attractive girl. *Some c1935 use. Orig. lunch-counter use, a call used by waiters to direct attention of other employees to an attractive girl.*

varnish *n.* = **varnished car.**

varnished car *n.* **1** A railroad passenger car, whether a coach or sleeping car. → **2** A passenger train; a fast express train, whether passenger or freight. *Both meanings railroad use.*

varnish remover *n.* **1** Strong coffee. **2** Whisky, esp. inferior, cheap, or homemade whisky. Cf. **paint remover.**

varsity *n., adj.* A univ., college, or student team or group, usu. an athletic team. *Colloq. From a Brit. pronunciation of "university." In U.S. the word never = university.*

vaude *n.* Vaudeville. 1951: Green, *Show Biz From Vaude to Video. Since at least 1915.* See Appendix, Shortened Words.

V.D. VD *n.* Venereal disease; a case of venereal disease, esp. syphilis. *Common since W.W.II when the Armed Forces used the abbr. in educational anti-venereal-disease campaigns among servicemen.* 1956: "Increase in Teen VD Sparks Health Study," N.Y. *Daily News*, Nov. 16, headline. See Appendix, Shortened Words.

veal cutlet A man's overcoat. *Not common. Perhaps from the thick breaded coating in which the cutlets are cooked.*

veeno *n.* = **vino.**

veep *n., adj.* A vice-president. 1949: "The 'Veep'—this is the name Mr. Barkley's irreverent descendants have put upon him, because they do not like the jaw-filling title 'Mr. Vice President'— is ready." Wm. S. White, N.Y. *Times Mag.*, Sept. 4, 12/4. 1951: "Three members of the Dodgers' official family feel very happy. They are Veep Fresco Thompson, Coach Jake Pitler, and [Manager Charley] Dressen." AP, Sept. 22. *First pop. applied to U.S. Vice-President Alben Barkley. From the stand. abbr. "V.P."*

vehicle *n.* A rocket; esp. a rocket, or part of a rocket, used to carry instruments, another rocket, or explosives to a great height. *Since c1952.*

vein *n.* A double bass, esp. when used to play modern jazz. 1957: "Vein—The double bass." E. Horne, *For Cool Cats and Far-Out Chicks. Some far-out use.*

velvet *n.* Net profit; money in excess of that expected; winnings; hence any money. 1909: "There are substantial money returns—'velvet,' in student parlance—for those who secure places on at least two of these [publications]." Von Engeln, *At Cornell*, 294. 1930: "In order to be able to work on 'velvet.' . . ." Lavine, *Third Degree*, 173.

verbal diarrhea A mythical disease which causes one to talk too much. 1947: "You've got verbal diarrhea, with these . . . speeches. . . ." C. Willingham, *End as a Man*, 228.

Vermont *n.* Maple syrup. *Some c1925 lunch-counter use; now archaic.*

Vermont charity Sympathy. *Hobo use since c1915; archaic.*

verse *n.* A round in prize fighting;

an inning in baseball. *Not common.* See **stanza.**

vessel-man *n.* A pot washer. *W.W.II USN use. Prob. synthetic.*

vestibule *n.* The rump, the buttocks. 1935: "He unhooks the horse from the motorcycle, and gives it a good kick in the vestibule." D. Runyon, 180. *Jocular use.*

vet *n.* **1** An alumnus. *Some student use since c1910; not common.* **2** An experienced professional athlete or worker; a person who is thoroughly competent in a specific line of endeavor. **3** The stand. abbr. for "veterinarian" or "veterinary." **4** A veteran of the Armed Forces; an ex-soldier. 1949: "I'm a combat vet. Purple Heart. Good Conduct." N. Algren, *Man with the Golden Arm*, 92. *Since W.W.I, but pop. only since W.W.II.* *adj.* Experienced; thoroughly competent as the result of long employment in a specific vocation. 1936: "The vet producer of scouting plays. . . ." A. Green in *Esquire*, Sept.

V-girl *n.* **1** A girl or young woman who dispenses sexual favors in the professed cause of patriotism, esp. one in frequent contact with soldiers, sailors, etc., through being employed on an Armed Forces post or in a nearby establishment; a woman who accords sexual favors to servicemen through being impressed by the glamor of uniforms or service ratings; a nonprofessional prostitute catering to servicemen. *Common W.W.II use. From abbr. of "Victory girl."* Cf. **B-girl.** → **2** A girl or young woman who has or is suspected of having a venereal disease. *W.W.II Armed Forces use. Reinforced by the "V" of "V.D."*

vibes *n.* The vibraphone or vibraharp. *Jazz use.*

vic *n.* **1** A convict; a con. *Orig. and primarily still prison and underworld use.* **2** A victrola; a phonograph. *Obs.*

Victory girl *n.* **1** A girl or woman who worked in a war plant during W.W.II or performed other work necessary to the war effort. *Early W.W.II use. Quickly became archaic owing to rapid change in meaning to* → **2** = **V-girl.**

viggerish **vigorish** *n.* The money or percentage of money paid, lost, won, or earned in illegal dealings; specif. the rate of interest paid on money borrowed from a loan shark, the betting percentage in favor of a gambling house, or a share in the proceeds of a criminal enterprise. 1956: "VIGGERISH—The rate of in-

terest on money borrowed from a loan shark. . . ." T. Betts, *Across the Board*, 320. 1957: "The point difference between the bets is the bookie's percentage, the vigorish." S. Friedlander, "Gambling," N.Y. *Post*, Oct. 15, 56.

—vill, —ville See Appendix, Suffixes and Suffix Words.

vinblink *n.* = **vinegar blink.**

vine *n.* A suit of clothes; any clothing. *Orig. prison use = civilian or nonprison clothes, c1930; by c1935 in wide jive use and soon changed to "vines."* **—s** *n.pl.* Clothing, esp. smart or hip clothes. 1957: "Vines—Clothes. Formerly, threads." E. Horne, *For Cool Cats and Far-Out Chicks. Some far-out use; prison use c1930.* See **vine.**

vinegar blink White wine, esp. cheap or inferior white wine. *Some hobo and vino use. Orig. W.W.I Army use as a corruption of the Fr. "vin blanc."*

vino **veeno** **wino** *n.* **1** Wine, esp. cheap or inferior wine and usu. red wine. *Orig. hobo and some West Coast use since c1925, from the Sp. Not common until reinforced by W.W.II Army use among troops stationed in Italy, but now very common.* **2** See **wino.**

violets *n.pl.* Cabbage. *Some lunch-counter use. In ironic allusion to the smell when cooking. In Eng. "violets" = onions.*

V.I.P. **vip** *n.* A big shot, a person of importance, usu. an Army officer, business executive, politician, or visiting dignitary. *Orig. W.W.II Army use. From the initials for "Very Important Person." The separate initials more common than the word in both speech and writing.* See Appendix, Shortened Words.

viper *n.* **1** A person who lives for or by narcotics, esp. marijuana; a marijuana addict; a marijuana pusher. 1956: "The best of it [marijuana] comes from Mexico. It's a big business and the vipers, its peddlers and users. . . ." S. Longstreet, *The Real Jazz Old and New*, 144. *Narcotic addict use since c1935.*

virgin coke *n.* A glass of Coca-Cola with cherry-flavored syrup added. *Some lunch-counter and student use.* See **cherry.**

Virginia weed **Virginian weed** Tobacco. 1821: "Virginian weed." *DAE.* 1833: "Virginia weed." *DAE. Some use until c1865; obs.*

virtue *n.* = **virgin coke.** *Some lunch-counter use; not common.*

visiting fireman **1** An influential or free-spending out-of-town visitor, often a member of a group holding a convention. 1951: "He meets a good many distinguished visiting firemen." *New Yorker*, Mar. 24, 22/2. *Colloq.* 2 A yokel or rustic visiting a large city. *Not common.*

vocals, give with (the)   To sing [songs]. 1939–40: "I give with vocals

and wolf around in a nite club." O'Hara, *Pal Joey*, 60.

voos [taboo]   *n.pl.* Human female breasts, esp. of a sexually attractive young woman. *Not common.* Cf. **boobs, headlights.**

vulcanized   *adj.* Drunk. *Some use since c1925.* See Appendix, Drunk.

W

wack   whack   *n.* One who is wacky; an extreme eccentric; a screwball, a nut. 1939: "The pecular [*sic*] local people. . . . Two wacks if ever I saw one. . . ." O'Hara, *Pal Joey*, 40.

wacky   whacky   *adj.* Eccentric; nutty; crazy. 1939: "You think I am going wacky. . . ? O'Hara, *Pal Joey*, 22f. 1951: "The National Safety Council . . . annually collects whacky accidents. . . ." NEA Service, Dec. 13. *n.* Jazz or swing music of the wildest kind. *Some c1920 use; obs.*

— -wacky   See Appendix, Suffixes and Suffix Words.

wad   *n.* 1 Lit., a roll or wad of paper money; money, esp. a lot of it or all that one has. 1814: *DAE.* 1900: " 'Made a lot of money, hasn't he?' 'Yes, wads of it.' " Dreiser, *Carrie*, 34f. 1951: "I was pretty loaded. My grandmother'd just sent me this wad about a week before. I have this grandmother that's quite lavish with her dough." J. D. Salinger, *Catcher in the Rye*, 43. 2 The mouth. *Some use c1885–c1920; obs.*

wafers   *n.pl.* Money. *Never common.*

waffle   *n.* 1 A difficult or dangerous task; the object of a dangerous task, or whatever causes it to be dangerous. *Some c1910 use; obs.* 2 A disliked person, esp. an old person with wrinkled skin. 1934: "[Her] papa is a mean old waffle. . . ." D. Runyon, 447. *Never common.* 3 A woman; a broad. *Not common.*

waffle-iron   *n.* A grating in a sidewalk.

wag [taboo]   *n.* The penis, esp. a little boy's penis.

wag [one's] chin   To talk. 1927: "To be seen waggin' your chin with a sleuth. . . ." Hammett, *Blood Money*, 28.

wagon   *n.* 1 A USN ship. *W.W.I USN use; some W.W.II USN use.* See **battlewagon.** 2 = **paddy wagon.** 3 A revolver. *Some c1930 underworld use. From "smoke wagon."*

wagon, off the   Having resumed the use of alcoholic beverages after a period of abstinence. 1952: "Like the bartenders, they fall off the wagon." A. J. Liebling in *New Yorker.* See **on the wagon.**

wagon, on the [water]   Not drinking alcoholic beverages, either for a short or a long period. 1905: "He pulled a few snake tricks . . . and in five minutes he had all the members of the Highball Association climbing on the water wagon." McHugh, *Search Me*, 19f. 1924: "Carver was on the wagon. . . ." Marks, *Plastic Age*, 273. 1946: "Monty didn't drink, and Clifton James went on the wagon for the Empire." *This Week Mag.*, Dec. 21, 11/4. *Also used in various expressions, as "go on the [water] wagon," "climb on the [water] wagon," "hop on the wagon," "put [someone] on the wagon." Also, contrariwise, "fall off the wagon" = to resume one's drinking. These "wagon" idioms have long been universally popular. The "water" is now somewhat archaic.*

wagon wheel   A silver dollar. *Obs.*

wahoo   *n.* A yahoo; a rustic; a simp or yap.

Wahoo   *n.* Hawaii. *Orig. USN use from Oahu Island, the part of Hawaii best known to USN sailors and to tourists.*

wah-wah   *n.* Loosely, any sound resembling the human voice; specif., an exaggerated vibrato produced by brass instrument musicians using a particular kind of mute. 1950: "There were many other imitations of animal sounds we used—such as wah-wahs on trumpets and trombones." Alan Lomax, *Mr. Jelly Roll*, 59. *Old jazz use.*

wail   *v.i.* 1 To play any musical instrument or style of jazz intensely and adroitly. 1955: ". . . We were wailing but nobody had a tape [recording] machine." Nat Hentoff, "Jazz Records." in F. V. Grunfeld, *Music and Recordings*,

197. *Some general jazz use since c1930, esp. applied to the blues, but not pop. until c1950, then by cool and far-out use.* → **2** To be exciting and satisfying; to do anything well. 1956: "I love Bach. Mozart? No comment. Mendelssohn? How square can you get? I want it modern. I want to go to Sweden where it really wails." S. Longstreet, *The Real Jazz Old and New*, 146. *Far out use.* **3** To depart quickly; to flee. *Beat use.*

wailing wall   A chaplain's office. *Some W.W.II Army use.*

wait up   When walking or running, to stop and wait for someone to catch up.

wake-up   *n.* The last day of a prison sentence. *Some prison use.*

walk   *n.* A customer who has walked out of a store without buying anything. *Retail salesman use.*   *v.i.* To play jazz music, or to play it well, esp. in an ensemble; said of a band or a section of a band. 1957: "They really walk—The rhythm section really swings." E. Horne, *For Cool Cats and Far-Out Chicks. Far-out use since c1955. Possibly related to old jazz associations with "cakewalk."*   **—ing**   *adj.* Describing an order of food that is taken by the purchaser to be eaten elsewhere. *Some lunch-counter use since c1945. Used by waiters in relaying orders to indicate that purchase must be wrapped and put in a paper bag.*

walk-around   *n.* A comedy routine performed by a circus clown while walking around the ring of the circus tent. *Circus use since c1915.*

walk-away   walkaway   *n.* **1** Change left behind absent-mindedly by a purchaser, esp. a ticket purchaser. *Orig. circus use.* → **2** Money acquired by a ticket seller by short-changing the public. *Carnival use.* **3** An athletic contest that is certain to be won by one player or team because of inequality in the skill or prowess of the opponents; a cinch. Cf. **walkover.**

walkie-talkie   *n.* A small, portable radio-telephone. *Such instruments were in wide use in U.S. Army during W.W.II and have since been adopted in many commercial undertakings. Very common sl. term; now almost stand.* See Appendix, Rhyming Terms.

walking dandruff   *n.* Lice; cooties. Cf. **seam squirrel.**

walking papers   **1** A dismissal, whether written or not; a discharge. 1825:

DAE. 1949: "Two baseball veterans got their walking papers today...." AP, Oct. 4. *Colloq.* **2** Dismissal or rejection by one's sweetheart or a friend.

walking ticket = walking papers. 1835: *DAE. Still some use but never common.*

walk-on   *n.* In a play or movie, a nonspeaking actor or part. *Theater use, universally known.*

walk out   To court a girl; lit., to take a girl out for a walk, both for amusement and privacy. *Rural use.*   **walk-out walkout**   *n.* A strike by union employees against an employer. *Colloq.*

walkover   walk-over   *n.* An easy victory. 1904: "It looked like a walk-over for Clarence, but ... Lancelot got the decision." McHugh, *Search Me*, 42. *Colloq.*

walk [someone] Spanish   To force someone to leave, usu. from a public place, by lifting him by his coat or shirt collar to a walking position and propelling him toward the door. 1825: *DAE.* 1929: "Smith [a bouncer] . . . was an expert at walking 'em Spanish." Winkler in *New Yorker*, Feb. 9, 42.

walk-up   *n.* **1** A room or apartment higher than the main floor and reached by stairs only. 1942: "Second-floor walk-ups over stores...." Chandler, *High Window*, 149. **2** An elevatorless residential building of at least two floors.

wall, go over the   To escape from prison.

wall-eyed   *adj.* Drunk. *From stand. meaning = strabismic.*

wall-flower   wallflower   *n.* **1** A person, usu. a girl or woman, who is not popular or who is shy; lit., one who attends a dance but does not take part and sits by the wall watching the others. 1934: "The homely and ugly girls who were called wall-flowers." J. T. Farrell, 99. *Colloq. since c1910.* **2** One who idles inside a saloon hoping to be offered a free drink. *Some W.W.II Army use. Obs.*

wallie   wally   *n.* **1** A youth whose hair has a patent-leather luster; a ladies' man; a gigolo. 1922: "Some wallie tried to horn in on our gang." Phila. *Eve. Bulletin*, Mar. 8. *c1920; obs.* **2** A town sport or gambler. *Hobo use. Obs.* **3** A short, fat person. *Some student use c1930.*

wallop   *n.* **1** In baseball, a hit. **2** A thrill of pleasurable excitement; a kick. *Somewhat archaic.*   *v.t.* To hit a baseball hard; sometimes to hit anything with force.

wallpaper *n.* Counterfeit paper money; any discredited paper currency. *Not common.*

walrus *n.* 1 A short, fat person. *Some use since c1925.* → 2 An awkward person; specif., one who cannot swim; also specif., one who does not know how to dance. *Some student use since c1935.*

waltz *n.* A round of boxing; a "stanza." *Sportswriter use.* *v.i.* In boxing, to spar lightly, to clinch, to fight unaggressively; said of both boxers in a match.

wampum *n.* Money. *Orig. a folk etymology for the Indian word for money.*

wang [taboo] *n.* The penis. *Not common.*

wangan **wannigan** *n.* 1 A place for storing camp supplies. 1848: *DAE. Still some logger use.* 2 Money owed to the supply store keeper by lumberjacks. *Both uses orig. a folk etymology of an Indian word.*

wangle *v.t.* To obtain something by bartering; to acquire something by devious means, deceit, or influence. 1919: " 'Wangle' . . . was a humorous euphemism before the war [W.W.I]." E. A. Barker in *Athenaeum*, July 11, 582. 1949: "President Truman has given [Cyrus S.] Ching a free hand in trying to wangle agreements." N. Walker, AP, Oct. 25. *n.* The act or instance of wangling. 1943: "[People of New York City] have made a precise science out of the wangle." H. A. Smith, *Putty Knife*, 120. *Never common.*

wanted *adj.* Sought for arrest by the police; used absolutely. *Colloq.*

wapsed down *adj.* 1 Knocked down or ruined by a storm; said of crops. *Rural use. Dial.* → 2 Drunk. *Rural use. Dial.* See Appendix, Drunk.

war club A baseball bat. *Synthetic.*

—ward See Appendix, Suffixes and Suffix Words.

ward heeler The lowest-ranking officer of a political organization; a political worker who canvasses a city ward or district for his party during an election campaign. *Colloq.*

war horse **warhorse** *n.* 1 Generally, a veteran; one who, though old, is still active or enthusiastic, usu. in ref. to a specif. job, goal, vocation, etc. *Colloq.* 2 A determined female; esp. a fat, stubborn, vociferous woman. *Not common.*

warm baby An affectionate or ama-

tive woman. *Some student use c1900; common in 1920's; now archaic.* See **hot.**

warm [someone's] ear To talk to a person, esp. volubly or excitedly.

warmer-upper *n.* Something that warms a person, as clothing or, more usu., a drink of liquor or hot coffee, tea, or cocoa. 1944: "Wonderful warmer-upper/ 4-button coat sweater. . . ." Advt. in N.Y. *Herald Trib.*, Aug. 29, 5/6. 1947: "Now try it as a warmer-upper—a hot drink [heated tomato juice] your folks will go for. . . ." Advt., *SEP*, Nov. 15, 139. *One of the more common "—er-—er" words, for which see Appendix.*

warm up To get into the proper physical condition for a contest or task; an exercise or practice session, as part of one's conditioning for performing a task or in a contest. *Colloq.*

warm wise To become informed, or to become aware of the facts or conditions; to become hip. 1905: "We young fellows begin to warm wise to ourselves. . . ." McHugh, *Search Me*, 12.

war paint 1 Cosmetics; specif., lipstick, powder, and rouge. 1869: *DAE. Orig. jocular use, now almost stand.* → 2 Jewels; furs; feminine finery. *Not common.*

wart *n.* An olive. *Some lunch-counter and bartender use.*

wash *n.* A chaser, as of water or beer, following a drink of liquor. 1951: "What for a wash?" R. Bissell, *Stretch on the River*, 139. **—er** *n.* A saloon or tavern.

wash-out **washout** *n.* 1 A failure; a fiasco; a misfit; a bankrupt; applied to either persons or enterprises. *Taken into U.S. sl. from Brit. sl. during W.W.I.* → 2 A person who is a failure in a social or sporting context; a wallflower. *Since c1920; most common student use c1925.* → 3 The act or instance of damaging an airplane while landing. *Aviator use c1925.* → 4 A student pilot, esp. in the Air Force, who has been expelled or eliminated from flight training, usu. owing to failure in a course or examination. 1949: "The inability to learn military flying is the major cause for the large number of 'washouts.' . . ." N.Y. *Times*, Sept. 25, 65/5. *Universally known W.W.II Air Force use.* **wash out** 1 To fail; to be rejected; to lose or be beaten in a sports or other contest. → 2 To lose all one's money; to go broke. *c1920.* 1954: "I would sit in with . . . hustlers who really knew how to gamble. I always got washed out." Louis Armstrong,

Satchmo, My Life in New Orleans, 123.
→ **3** Specif., to fail or be eliminated in a course of flight training. 1944: "I was an aviation cadet. . . . Then I was washed out on a slight technicality." Shulman, *Feather Merchants,* 41. *Since c1935; common W.W.II Air Force use.* **4** To kill someone, either deliberately or accidentally.

washtub-weeper   *n.* = **soap opera.** See Appendix, Rhyming Terms.

wash up   **1** To bring a piece of work to a successful or favorable completion. 1929: "I know how I can wash [the story] up," K. Brush, *Young Man,* 67. *From the notion of a worker washing his hands at the end of a day's work.* **2** To finish something, as a job, a career, a friendship, etc. **3** To lose a chance of success; to fail; to nullify or cancel; to become obsolete or unfashionable. *Usu. in the passive, as "to be all washed up."* 1928: "I'm all washed up. . . ." Hecht & MacArthur, *Front Page,* III. 1939: "They said act of God and fire, etc., wash up a contract automatically. . . ." O'Hara, *Pal Joey,* 32. 1941: "Borden is all washed up [i.e., through with his pianist's career because of losing a hand]." G. Homes, *40 Whacks,* 60.

waste   *v.t.* To defeat completely; to beat up thoroughly; lit. and fig., to lay waste, to destroy. *Orig. teenage street-gang use; general teenage use since c1955.*
—d   *adj.* **1** To be a narcotics addict *Narcotics addict and cool use.* **2** Without funds; broke. *Cool and beat use since c1950, rock-and-roll use since c1955.*

watch   *n.* See **graveyard watch.**
—er   *n.* See **clock-watcher.**

water   *n.* See **blanko water, fire water, giggle water, Gordon water, hot water, jerk-water, push water, whoopee water.**

water, in deep   In difficulty or trouble; faced with a problem which one is probably not experienced, intelligent, or aggressive enough to surmount; in difficulty or trouble or faced with a problem for which one is not prepared. *From the image of a swimmer in deep water (above his head) and unable to reach shore.*

water, in hot   In trouble, esp. in trouble from having incurred the wrath of those in authority. *Fig., in a pot just boiling with trouble.*

waterboy   *n.* **1** An inept prize fighter, esp. one who can be induced to take a dive. *Implying that the fighter is fit only to carry water for a real athlete or to take*

a dive in a tank fight. *Not common.* **2** One who courts his superiors, esp. one who is willing to take on menial tasks in the hope of winning favor; a yes-man or ass-kisser.

water-cooler talk   Rumors, gossip; exaggerated stories, esp. as heard in an office or factory. *c1945. Not common. Because such talk is attrib. to employees who gather around the office or factory water cooler or drinking fountain. Cf.* **scuttlebutt,** *which is much more common.*

water lily   A fireman. *Prob. synthetic.*

waterman   *n.* = **waterboy.** 1939: "These matches are with watermen, who plunge in swiftly when Jones waves at them." Runyon.

watermelon   *n.* The oval outline drawn on the ground or pavement and used as the ring in the game of marbles. *Boy use, 8–12 age group. Since at least 1900. With the population shift from rural to urban areas, boys see fewer watermelons and play marbles less; hence the word is seldom heard now.*

water wagon   See **on the wagon.**

wave   *n.* See **brain wave.**

waver   *n.* See **flag-waver.**

wavy navy   **1** The British Navy. *Some W.W.II use. From the wavy stripes worn on British Naval Reserve uniforms.* **2** The Waves. *Some W.W.II use.*

wax   *v.t.* **1** To excel; to overcome. *Colloq. since c1850.* **2** To make a phonograph record; to record for the making of a phonograph record. *A recording technician can wax an orchestra or musician; the orchestra or musician is waxing a piece of music. Common since c1925.* *n.* A phonograph record. 1939: "I am going to play the tune and cut a wax of it." O'Hara, *Pal Joey,* 55. *Orig. radio and musician use, c1925. Cf.* **platter.**

wax, put on   To record phonographically; to wax. 1956: ". . . While jazz grew and the recording companies put the Stone Age stuff of jazz on wax." S. Longstreet, *The Real Jazz Old and New,* 10.

waxie   **waxy**   *n.* A harness maker or repairman. *Obs. except for circus use.*

way   *n.* See **forty ways for Sunday, in a big way, that way.**

way, in a big   Enthusiastically; to a great extent. 1949: [enthusiastically] "He said the soldiers went for pin-ups 'in a big way.'" UP, Sept. 14. 1949: [to a great extent] "But I don't can [fruit, vegetables] in a big way. . . ." Syracuse *Herald Journal,* Sept. 30, 14/1.

way car   The caboose of a freight train. *Railroad use.*

way-out   **1** In progressive jazz, descriptive of the state of a musician who loses consciousness of everything except the development of his improvisation, esp. when his playing is based on extremely complex chord progressions; far gone. *Assoc. with advanced jazz of the late 1940's and 1950's.* **2** Descriptive of the manners, dress, etc., associated with avant-garde jazz musicians and their followers. **3** Excellent, extremely satisfying, esp. in the sense of being individualistic, creative, unusual, unsentimental. *Replacing the earlier hep and cool.* **4** Removed from reality; under the influence of narcotics. *All meanings have evolved since c1955; the last meaning indicates that the term has already begun to degenerate as it has passed from the small clique of musicians with whom it originated to their followers and thence to the general public.*

way-up   *adj.* Very good, excellent, esp. in the sense of high-class or of high social standing. 1900: "It's a way-up, swell place." Dreiser, *Carrie*, 78. *Colloq. since c1870; archaic since c1920.*

weak-jointed   *adj.* Drunk. *Obs.*

weak sister   **1** An undependable or cowardly person. *Usu. in reference to a man; colloq. since c1860.* **2** An effeminate man. *Not common.*

wearies, the   *n.pl.* A feeling of weariness and despair; a melancholy feeling; a subdued form of the heebie-jeebies. 1956: "He saw their nightfires burn. . . . 'I'm getting the evening wearies,' he decided. . . ." N. Algren, *A Walk on the Wild Side*, 18. *Dial.*

Weary Willie   A tramp or hobo. See **Willie.**

weasel   *n.* **1** An informer. *Prison and underworld use since c1920.* → **2** A sneak; one who courts superiors; an inferior man. *Usu. applied to small, thin males, the word retains its physical connotation; since c1925.* **3** A small amphibious truck used by the U.S. Navy in W.W.II. *v.i.* To inform. *Prison and underworld use since c1925.*

weasel out   To withdraw from a group or from the obligations imposed by the group; to renege on a promise, usu. for cowardly or selfish reasons. *Colloq.*

weasel-word   *v.i.* To speak nonsense in such a way that it appears to be true or pertinent. *Not common.*

weather, under the   **1** Suffering the aftereffects of having been drunk or having consumed too much whisky the night before; suffering from a hangover. *Common use.* → **2** Drunk. 1944: "I'm a little under the weather." Fowler, *Good Night*, 72. *Colloq. since c1930.* See Appendix, Drunk. *Fairly common.* **3** Menstruating; suffering from dysmenorrhea.

weaver   *n.* A wife. 1945: "I could never get by with one of those 'night call' excuses. My weaver's too smart." L. F. McHugh. *Not common.*

web   *n.* A radio or television broadcasting network. 1944: "He had to work as pancake turner on the Green web." C. Macon in *Collier's*, Sept. 9, 55/2. *Radio use since c1930.*

wee   *v.i.* = **wee-wee.** See **peewee.**

weed   *n.* **1** Tobacco. *Since at least 1600.* → **2** A cigar; a cheap or inferior cigar. 1858: *DAE.* 1952: "The weed was lit evenly." R. C. Ruark, *synd. newsp. col.*, Apr. 28. 1958: "He [Mike Todd] eyed Press Agent Harry Sobel smoking a cigar, and said, 'Throw that weed away and have a good one!' " E. Wilson, N.Y. *Post*, Mar. 26, 55. See **weed, the.** *Archaic.* **3** A cigarette. *Common since c1920.* **4** A marijuana cigarette. *Addict use since c1930.* *v.t.* **1** To give or hand over something. **2** To remove money, usu. from a stolen wallet or the like. 1916: ". . . To abstract a 'poke' . . . and weed it in security. . . ." *Star of Hope, Lit. Digest*, Aug. 19. *Orig. pickpocket use.* **—head**   *n.* A marijuana addict. See **weed.** Cf. **hophead.** **—ing**   *n.* Petty thievery. **—s**   *n.pl.* **1** A suit of clothes, esp. a new and gaudy suit which the wearer considers dapper. *Orig. jive use. Possibly related to stand. weeds, as in "widow's weeds."* **2** Clothing of any kind. Cf. **vine, vines.**

weed, the   *n.* **1** Tobacco. *c1700; obs.* **2** Marijuana. *Since c1925. Narcotic addict use.*

weed monkey   **1** A prostitute, esp. a cheap one. *Orig. Southern mountain dial. Not common.* **2** A dilapidated automobile. *Orig. Southern mountain use. Not common.*

weed off   To remove money from a roll of banknotes; to "weed" a purse. 1932: "Saro whips out a bundle of scratch and weeds off twenty-five large coarse notes." Runyon. Cf. **weed.**

weeds, the   *n.pl.* A hobo camp; a jungle. *Hobo use.*

weed tea   Marijuana.

weed to   To give money, esp. to one's moneyless friends. Cf. **weed.**

weenchy   *adj.* Tiny; teeny-weeny. 1943: "Just a weenchy . . . little dash of perfume. . . ." Wolfert, *Underworld,* 415. *Dial. use since c1900.*

weenie   weeney   weinie   wienie   wiener   weener   *n.* **1** A wiener-wurst or frankfurter; a hot-dog. 1920: "Wienie." S. Lewis, *Main Street,* 287. 1926: "Weenie." Schwesinger, *Jour. of Applied Psych.,* 261. 1952: "But this weinie and [sauer] kraut combination is not the usual one." M. Meade in N.Y. *Daily News,* Aug. 13, C17/4. *Colloq.* **2** That which threatens success; anything that may cause failure or disappointment; the kicker, the catch. *Since c1925. May have orig. in vaudeville or the movie industry, perh. in ref. to the large bladders used by comics to hit one another over the head in slapstick comedies. Such bladders are the descendants of the mock phallus wielded by ancient Greek comedians.* **3** The act or result of being cheated or taken advantage of; losing or not obtaining what one has expected to gain; the short end of the stick. *Usu. in "I got the wienie." In this context the word definitely has a phallic meaning. Very common since c1940.* **4** [taboo] The relaxed penis. *Jocularly reinforced by "teeny weeny." The last three meanings are related by phallic connotations, which once again relate sex and food.* **5** A disliked person; a jerk. *Another term that seems to relate sex and food, and sex and deceit.* See Appendix, Food and Sex; Sex and Deceit.

weeper   *n.* A movie, play, book, or song that makes the audience cry; a tear-jerker. 1952: "No more tearjerkers for Jane Wyman. She wants happy pictures. . . . After all, it was the weepers that established her as a top Hollywood star." Bob Thomas, AP, Aug. 15. See Appendix, —er ending.

Weepers!   *exclam.* = **Jeepers!** 1953: "I mean . . . [money I] tossed away on sweaters, Weepers!" Haenigsen, comic strip, "Penny," Feb. 3. *Assoc. with teenagers, the term's gentility suggests its synthetic nature. Widely used in literature about teenagers.*

weepie   weepy   *n.* = **weeper.** 1949: "The day-time weepies have been greatly enriched by a new soap opera which threatens to out-misery all the others put together." J. Crosby in Phila. *Eve. Bulletin,* Aug. 6, 16. See Appendix, —ie ending.

weeps   *n.pl.* Tears. 1921: "She's on the brinks [*sic*] of weeps." Witwer, *Leather,* 155.

weeps, put on the   To cry. See **weeps.**

weevil   *n.* Rice. *Some W.W.II USN use.*

wee-wee   *v.i.* To urinate. *Used euphem. by adults in talking to small children; one of the first words many children learn. Used jocularly in adult conversation.*   *n.* Urine. 1941: ". . . Specimen of wee-wee . . . taking it to the hospital for a urinalysis." C. McCullers, *Reflections in a Golden Eye,* reprinted with *The Ballad of the Sad Café,* 555.

weight   *n.* See **paperweight.**   **—er**   *n.* See **penny-weighter.**

weinie   *n.* See **weenie.**

weird   *adj.* Orig. cool use = eliciting a unique emotional response; cool. *Bop and cool use. c1946–c1953. Somewhat archaic.* Cf. **crazy.** See **cool.**   **—ie**

weirdy   *n.* A weird, eccentric, or unusual person, object, work of art, or the like. 1949: "He's a weirdy, all right." Burnett, *Jungle,* 11. *Very common since c1950, now part of every young person's vocabulary. The word applies equally well to introverts, geniuses, homosexuals, abstract painters and their products, bird watchers, etc., and may be applied to any nonconformist.*

welch   *v.i.* = **welsh.**

well   See **dough well done with cow to cover, fare-thee-well, fare-ye-well, fare-you-well.**

well-fixed   well fixed   *adj.* Wealthy, well-to-do. 1822: *DAE. Colloq.*

well-heeled   well heeled   *adj.* **1** Wealthy. 1951: "Mr. Smith personifies the average fairly well-heeled, middle-aged American male." *New Yorker,* Sept. 1, 69/1. **2** Armed; carrying weapons. 1950: "He's always well heeled." CBS radio show, *Gangbusters,* Jan. 14. See **heeled.**

well oiled   well-oiled   *adj.* Drunk. 1924: ". . . If he kept her 'well oiled with hooch.' " Marks, *Plastic Age,* 251. 1930: "If . . . he happened to be well oiled, as was usually the case. . . ." S. H. Holbrook in *Amer. Mercury,* Oct., 233/2. *Fairly common since c1920. The "well" does not necessarily imply any greater degree of drunkenness than "oiled" alone. This more emphatic form is now more common than the plain "oiled."* See Appendix, Drunk. See **oiled.**

welsh   welch   *v.i.* To fail to keep a promise or meet an obligation; esp. to fail to pay a gambling debt. 1905: "Say, are you going to welsh on me?'' McHugh, *Search Me*, 67. *Colloq.*   *n.* An instance of welshing. 1951: "Link can't take a welsh so he looks around for a way to get his dough.'' Spillane, *Big Kill*, 97. **—er**   *n.* One who welshes; one who loses a bet but does not pay it.

wench   *n.*   Any girl; specif. an attractive or vivacious girl. *Although a very old word, "wench" is so archaic that its widespread revival among young people marks it as sl.*

west   See **galley-west, go west, skywest. —ern Western**   *n.* **1** Any historical or pseudohistorical book, play, or movie about the early history and development of the Western U.S. *A number of strict conventions have arisen to govern the form of the Western, thus making it a distinct and clearly recognizable genre in pop. Am. literature. Colloq.* **2** Eggs fried or scrambled with chopped ham, onions, and green peppers, served either as an omelette or as the filling for a sandwich. *Colloq.* **3** A glass of Coca-Cola with chocolate flavoring added. *Lunch-counter use.*

West Coast   **1** The musicians, credos, arrangements, characteristics, fashions, and fads associated with the highly intellectual, cool jazz music developed on the West Coast in the late 1940's. *Jazz use.* See **cool. 2** New, unusual, and satisfying. *Briefly popular c1950 when the West Coast (progressive or cool) school of independent jazz musicians excited jazz circles with their revolutionary forms and style.*

wet   *adj.* **1** Inferior or objectionable in any way; unpleasing; worthless; stupid; unfashionable, as in dress or manner; overdressed; boastful; etc. 1924: "They voted [Shaw's *Candida*] a 'wet' show.'' "A man is wet if he isn't a 'regular' guy. . . .'' Marks, *Plastic Age*, 94. *Very common c1915–1930. Now archaic.* **2** = **all wet.** *Not common.* **3** Specif. describing the state of an infant whose diaper is wet with urine. **4** Drunk. *Not common.* See Appendix, Drunk. **5** Describing itinerant workers who have entered the U.S. illegally, usu. applied to Mexican immigrants. See **wetback.** *v.i., v.t.* To urinate. Said of children and pets. *Colloq. euphem. and baby talk.*   *n.* **1** A drink of whisky. *Obs.* **2** One who favors the legal manufacture and sale of alcoholic beverages. Cf. **dry.**

wet, get   To work under water, as a diver. *Not common.*

wetback   wet back   *n.* An immi-

grant who has entered the country illegally, esp. a Mexican itinerant worker in the southwestern U.S. 1948: "To us, an American's as good as a wetback, who is a Mexican that we don't know how he got here.'' Cain, *Moth*, 111. 1951: "Some 500,000 of these 'wetbacks' were caught by the Border Patrol last year.'' G. Hill in N.Y. *Times*, Mar. 25, 1/3. *Orig. because most such Mexicans swim the Rio Grande river. Most such illegal immigrants enter to work as migratory workers during the harvest season to earn wages higher than those paid in Mexico; they return to Mexico at the end of the season. In the past they have been exploited by their U.S. employers and discriminated against as foreigners and scabs. Recently, however, the U.S. government and various western and southwestern farming co-operatives, canneries, and food packing companies have arranged for a specific number of such Mexican migratory workers to enter the U.S. and work at fair wages during the harvest season.*

wet behind the ears   Innocent, inexperienced, uninitiated, unsophisticated. *Prob. in allusion to new-born animals or human infants not yet altogether dry.* See **wet-nose.**

wet blanket   One who habitually deters or discourages others from having fun; one whose presence prevents others from having fun or enjoying a party or social gathering; one who emphasizes dangers and problems, thus lessening the high spirits or enthusiasm of others; a person, esp. a prude, who subverts the gaiety or levity of a gathering; a pessimist. See **killjoy.**

wet cattle = **wetback.**   *Not common.*

wet deck [taboo]   Fig., a woman who has just completed coitus with one man and is willing to have coitus with another; usu. said of prostitutes. *Orig. maritime use.*

wet [one's] goozle (throat, whistle)   To drink whisky.

wet-head   *n.* An unsophisticated, inexperienced, or uninitiated person; a youth; a rustic. See **wet-nose.**

wet hen   **1** A prostitute. *Obs.* **2** A disagreeable person; a termagant or shrew; a wet blanket. See **mad as a wet hen.**

wet hen, mad as a   Extremely angry.

wet-nose   *adj.* Young and inexperienced; green. *Lit., one who still needs to have his nose wiped by his mother. In use* *before 1860; archaic.* *n.* An inexperienced person; a yokel; a youth.

wet smack **1** A disliked person, esp. a bore, a kill-joy, or a wet blanket. 1933: "The other frail said he was a wet smack. . . ." H. T. Webster. 1942: "A 'slow-beat guy' is a good, old-fashioned wet smack." S. Billingsley in *Harper's Bazaar,* July. 1943: "A drip is nothing but a wet smack." Mackenzie in the N.Y. *Times Mag.* Cf. **drip, wet blanket. 2** One who drinks intoxicating liquor. *Not common. Orig. from a misinterpretation of the first meaning.*

wet sock **1** A jerk; a dull, dreary person. **2** A limp, flaccid handshake.

whack *n.* **1** A try; a chance; an opportunity. 1891: *DAE.* 1944: "He was given a whack at drama reviewing." B. Cerf in *Amer. Mercury,* Aug., 175/2. *Colloq.* **2** A hit, a punch, a thrust. → **3** In baseball, a hit. *v.t.* **1** To hit or punch. **2** To chop with a knife or cleaver. See **out of whack, wack.** **—ed** *adj.* = **bushed.** *Not common. Orig. Brit. sl.* **—y** *adj.* = **wacky.**

whack, on On minimum rations. *Maritime use.*

whack, out of Out of order; not functioning properly. 1899: *DAE; colloq.*

whack out To lose all one's money at gambling. 1956: "WHACK OUT— To go broke." T. Betts, *Across the Board,* 320.

whack up To divide or cut into even shares; to distribute loot or gambling winnings.

whacky-brained *adj.* = **whacky.** *Not common.*

whacky Willies Those members of an audience who applaud by cheering and whistling.

whale *n.* Any large or fat person. *adj.* Large; gross; excellent. *Used esp. in phrase* "a whale of a [*person or thing*]." *Since c1900.* **—r** *n.* A very large person or animal. 1833: *DAE. Colloq.*

wham *v.t.* To hit; to whack. 1930: "And the whamming [of prisoners] continues." Lavine, *Third Degree,* 48.

wham-bam *adj., adv.* Quick(ly) and rough(ly); displaying more energy and enthusiasm than finesse. *v.t.* [taboo] To have sexual intercourse, esp. quickly and without tenderness. See Appendix, Reduplications.

wham bam (thank-you (ye)-ma'am) [taboo] Fig., coitus, esp. quick, unemotional coitus as with a strange woman. *Since before c1895.* See **thank-you (ye)-ma'am.**

whammo! **whamo!** *interj., n.* Indicating force, shock, violence, or surprise; a sudden, violent blow. 1945: "'Ring out the tidings, Grandpa!' and the old gent spit on his hands, and Whammo! went the Liberty Bell." C. Fisher in Phila. *Record,* July 4, 11/1. 1951: "And then when I was off guard—whammo!" *Fibber McGee & Molly,* radio, Apr. 10. See Appendix, —o ending.

whammy *n.* **1** The evil eye. *Pop. by Al Capp, cartoonist, who created "Eagle Eye Feegle," a character who could put people into a trance by looking at them; his stare with one eye is called the "whammy," but in emergencies he uses both eyes, i.e., the "double whammy." From comic strip "Li'l Abner."* **2** Fig., a burden, a threat of failure, a jinx, bad luck. 1952: "His right to run for Vice-President with a whammy of ordinary indebtedness over his head." R. C. Ruark, *synd. newsp. col.,* Sept. 29.

whammy on [someone or something], put the **1** Lit. and fig., to render someone unconscious or motionless; to make something useless; to overpower someone, or overrule a plan. 1949: "So what's put the whammy on the N[ational] S[cience] F[oundation] bill?" H. Alexander, Phila. *Bulletin,* Sept. 9, 21/8. *Pop. by Al Capp's comic strip character "Eagle Eye Feegle," whose whammy stare can render a person motionless and speechless, from the synd. newsp. comic strip "Li'l Abner."* → **2** To wish someone ill fortune; to criticize someone or something, esp. by predicting failure. 1947: "I wrote several pieces putting the whammy on landlords." Billy Rose, *synd. newsp. col.,* Mar. 7.

whang *v.i., v.t.* To shoot, fire, blaze, bang. 1950: "[He] hauled out a revolver and whanged away at the knob on a Grecian urn." W. Pegler, *synd. newsp. col.,* Apr. 17. *n.* [taboo] The penis.

what See **so what, you-know-what.**

whatchamacallit = **thingamajig.** *Prob. the most common of the omnibus terms.* See Appendix, Infix.

What cooks? = **What's cooking?** See **cook.** 1952: "What cooks, Jimmy?" L. Stander in *Esquire,* June, 131/1.

What do you say? A conventional greeting that needs no reply. *Common since c1920. Prob. orig. in western U.S. Usu. slurred rapidly and accented on last word to distinguish it from a true question.*

what-for *n.* A beating, a thrashing; a bawling out; any punishment. 1907: "If he got fresh two or three of us would pitch on him and give him 'what-for.' "

J. London, *My Life*. 1950: "I gave him what-for." Starnes, *Another Mug*, 83. 1952: "A sadistic desire to watch the big shots get what for." J. Crosby in N.Y. *Her. Trib.*, June 20, 17/2.

What gives? **1** A common greeting. **2** "What's happening?" "What did I do to make you say or do that?" See **give; What's up? 3** = **What's new?** *Perhaps a lit. translation of the Ger. "was ist los?"* 1939: "What gives, I asked her. . . ." O'Hara, *Pal Joey*, 43. 1949: " 'What gives?' he croaked in an annoyed tone." Chandler, *Little Sister*, 21.

what it takes **1** Ability, strength, courage, any quality needed for a particular task; e.g., "He has what it takes." *Colloq.* **2** Money. *Fairly common c1920.* **3** Sex appeal. *The most common meaning since c1940.*

What say? = **What do you say?**

What's cooking? **1** A common greeting = "What's new with you?" "What news is there?" as of mutual friends and interests. **2** "What's going on here?" "What's happening or being planned?" *Orig. jive and swing use. Very common c1938–c1945, esp. student and Army use. Still in use.* See **cook.**

what's it(s) = **thingamajig.** *A more modern word.*

What's new? A common greeting requiring no answer.

What's up? "What's happening or being planned?" "What's going on here?"

What's with [something] A query meaning, "What's happened to [something]?" "What are the facts or your opinion about [something]?" "How do you explain [something]?" 1939: "Nick[,] what's with the free food? Explain." O'Hara, *Pal Joey*, 41. *Prob. orig. by Yiddish-speaking Americans.*

What's with you? **What's the matter with you?** **How are things with you?** **How about you?** Common greetings = "How are you?" *The speech pattern indicates that these phrases prob. orig. among Yiddish-speaking people.*

What the hell(?) **1** Emphatically what? **2** An interj. indicating anger, surprise, disappointment, etc. **3** What's the difference? Why? What's the use? I don't care.

What the Sam Hill? **1** Emphatically what? 1954: "What the Sam Hill is eating you?" W. Henry, *Death of a Legend*, 178. **2** An interj. indicating angry surprise. *Colloq. Somewhat archaic. Prob. a euphem. for "what the hell!"*

what-you-may-call-it **whatchama-**

callit *n.* = **thingamajig** *Colloq.*

whatzis *n.* Any object whose name is not known or remembered; a gadget. *A corruption of "What's this?"*

wheat *n.* An unsophisticated person; an innocent youth; a rustic. *Some use c1900.* **—s** *n.pl.* Wheatcakes; pancakes. 1932: "Lighter than a stack of wheats." Runyon.

whee *n.* = **humdinger.** 1952: "Small fry had a whee of a time squirting the [fire-extinguishing] chemicals all over the room." G. Lewis, Syracuse *Post-Standard*, Mar. 11, 16/4. *Not common.* *v.t.* To prod; to goad or stimulate; to prompt. 1949: "And did that whee him up to do his Christmas shopping early?" *SEP*, Dec. 3, 3/3. *Not common.*

wheel *n.* **1** A silver dollar. 1807: *DAE. Some use until c1900.* Cf. **cartwheel, wagon wheel. 2** A business transaction. *c1900.* **3** An important or popular person; a leader. → **4** A person in authority. *v.i., v.t.* To drive a vehicle at high speed. *Since c1940.* **—er** *n.* **1** A long-barreled .45 caliber pistol, once commonly used by police. **2** An expert automobile driver. *Not common.* **3** A motorcyclist, esp. a motorcycle policeman. 1946: "A park wheeler was getting off the seat of his motorcycle without hurry." Evans, *Halo in Blood*, 2. **4** An automobile. *Not common.* **5** = **big wheel.** **wheel.** See **side-wheeler. —s** *n.pl.* **1** The legs. *Not common.* **2** A car. *Hot-rod use since c1950; some general teenage use since c1955.* See **have wheels in [one's] head.**

wheel and deal To act independently, without restrictions or supervision; specif., to act independently, dynamically, and often ruthlessly or unethically, in business or social affairs.

wheeler-dealer *n.* Fig., one who wheels and deals; an adroit, quick-witted, scheming person; a person with many business or social interests.

wheel-man *n.* A skillful driver, esp. one who drives criminals away from a robbery; the driver of a get-away car.

wheels, on **1** Emphatically; definitely; with enthusiasm. *E.g.,* "*Will I come to the party? I'll be there on wheels.*" **2** = **with knobs on.** *A modern hep variant. Some student, teenage, and young adult use since c1940.*

wheels in [one's] head, have To be crazy. *Some use c1925–1935; replaced by "have rocks in one's head."*

wheep *n.* A small glass of beer; a beer chaser.

wheeze *n.* An old, familiar joke; a chestnut. 1929: "Governor Smith even remembered a wheeze I pulled." Groucho Marx in *New Yorker*, Feb. 2, 62. 1950: "This tired little wheeze got a big play." Billy Rose, *synd. newsp. col.*, Feb. 17.

wherewithal, the *n.* Money.

which See **Says which?**

whicker *v.t.* To trick, cheat, or deceive. *Not common.*

whiff *v.i.* In baseball, to strike at a pitched ball and miss. *Since c1920.* *v.i.*, *v.t.* **1** To strike out. 1951: "Vic Raschi [a pitcher] whiffed 12 batters in gaining his 15th win of the year." Acme Telephoto caption, July 30. **2** To kill. 1939: "He wasn't alone when you whiffed him." Chandler, *Big Sleep*, 75. *Not common.* *n.* In baseball and golf, an unsuccessful attempt to hit the ball. 1952: "On the first tee he took a careful stance and then fanned the air four times. After the fourth whiff he growled, 'This is the hardest course I ever played.'" H. T. Webster in N.Y. *Her. Trib.*, May 15, 21/6–7.

whiffer *n.* A flute, esp. as used in progressive jazz. 1957: "Whiffer—A flute." E. Horne, *For Cool Cats and Far-Out Chicks*. *Prob. synthetic.*

whiffle-board *n.* A pinball machine. *Some use since c1935.*

whimsy-whamsy *n.* A whim; capriciousness. 1945: "Underneath his whimsy-whamsy, he's the coldest-hearted rich man's lawyer . . . in Minnesota." S. Lewis, *Cass Timberlane*, 302. See Appendix, Reduplications, —y—y endings.

whim-wham **whimwham** *n.* A whim. 1946: "A man who has been converted . . . to the Marxian whimwham . . . seems to me to be carrying his right to make an ass of himself too far." H. L. Mencken, quoted in *Life*, Aug. 5, 51. *Since c1870; not common.* See Appendix, Reduplications.

whing-ding *n.* = **wing-ding.**

whinnick *v.i.* To refuse to fulfill a promise; to renege. *c1850; obs.*

whipped *adj.* Drunk; unconscious from intoxication. *c1800; archaic.*

whipped-up **whipped up** *adj.* Exhausted, beat. *Some far out use since c1955.*

whippersnapper *n.* A slight, unimportant but pretentious person. 1951: "These young whippersnappers you meet nowadays." S. J. Perelman in *New Yorker*, Mar. 3, 28/3.

whips and jingles A hangover. 1953: "I woke up with a case of the whips and jingles." Bing Crosby, *SEP*, Feb. 14. *Not common.* See **whipped.**

whipsey *adj.* Drunk. *Never common; archaic.*

whip the cat **1** To work as an itinerant shoemaker, etc. *Since c1850; archaic.* **2** To make a fuss or a commotion. *Some use c1925; obs.*

whip the dog To shirk one's duty. *Maritime use.*

whip through [a specif. task] To complete quickly and easily; to dash off.

whip up **1** To form a plan or create or make something quickly. *Most often used in ref. to cooking, as to whip up a cake.* **2** To speak or write in order to incite others to action, esp. violence; to elicit strong emotions, to attempt to create enthusiasm or strong feelings; esp. to create anger in a person or group against a person, idea, or contemplated action.

whirly-bird **whirlybird** **whirly bird** *n., adj.* A helicopter. 1957: "The whirly-bird pilots went off to a nearby constructions site. . . ." J. C. Clark, "We Were Trapped by Radioactive Fallout," *SEP*, July 20, 19. Cf. **egg-beater.**

whisker [taboo] *n.* A woman, considered solely as an object of sexual gratification; a promiscuous woman; a prostitute. Cf. **bush.** **—s** *n.pl.* **1** The jaw, chin, or cheeks. *Primarily prize fighter use. Since c1920.* **2** Any elderly man, whether whiskered or not. *Colloq.* **3** Seniority, esp. union seniority in a trade. *Since c1925.* **4** Artificial eyelashes. **5** = **cat's whiskers.** **6** = **Whiskers.**

Whiskers **Mr. (Uncle) Whiskers** **the old man with the whiskers** *n.* The U.S. government, or any of its law-enforcement officers, such as an internal revenue man, a narcotics agent, an FBI agent, or the like. 1939: "Do we get our percent. of the gross [sale of liberty bonds] but Charley said not with Mr. Whiskers at the gate, nobody cuts in on Mr. Whiskers." O'Hara, *Pal Joey*, 25. 1948: "You can't do business with Uncle Whiskers." Lait-Mortimer, *N.Y. Confidential*, 180. *Common underworld use since c1930. From the whiskers on the cartoon figure of Uncle Sam.*

whisky tenor A husky tenor voice, as if made husky from too much drinking; a falsetto voice, a voice that is being forced to sound like a tenor's.

1924: "Adeline's sweetness was extolled by unsure barytones and 'whisky' tenors." Marks, *Plastic Age*, 138.

whispering campaign   A concerted effort to discredit a person or agency by originating malicious or false rumors. 1949: ". . . To start a whispering campaign against your product. . . ." S. J. Perelman, *Listen to the Mocking Bird*, 120.

whisper joint   A speakeasy. *c1920; not common.*

whisper-low   *n.* A speakeasy. *c1920; not common.*

whistle bait   An attractive woman. 1951: "She has a beautiful face, a figure that is whistle-bait. . . ." B. Thomas, AP, Nov. 26. *Very common c1945. From the custom of whistling to signify approval of a woman's appearance.*

whistle-head   *n.* A boy. 1944: "A tough whistle-head of ten." W. Davenport in *Collier's*, Sept. 23, 12/4. *Not common.*

whistle jerk   1 A boy or man employed to operate a signal whistle for a work crew. *Logger use.* → 2 An Army corporal. *Some W.W.II use. Because drill commands were sometimes given by whistle signals.*

whistle-punk   *n.* = **whistle jerk.**

whistler   *n.* 1 A police car. *Some underworld use since c1930.* 2 A police informer. *Underworld and police use since c1935.*

whistle stop   A very small town. *Lit. and fig., a town so small that a train does not regularly receive passengers there.*

white   *adj.* Ethical, honest, fair; faithful, dependable, decent; friendly, regular. 1910: "It had been white of the Angel to offer. . . ." Johnson, *Varmint*, 120. 1924: "She isn't a lady—but she's white, white as hell." Marks, *Plastic Age*, 54. 1951: "The teaching staff . . . always referred to Doctor Sontag as 'a mighty white Jew.'" S. Longstreet, *The Pedlocks*, 300. *Since c1860.*   *adv.* Fairly. *Since c1900.*   *n.* 1 Silver, esp. as a medium of exchange. *Obs.* 2 Alcohol used for making bootleg whisky. 1931: "So much a case for perscription [*sic*] rye. So much for white to cut it with." J. Sayre, *Hex*, 416. *Since c1900; most common c1920.* Cf. **white line, white mule.** → 3 Gin, esp. bootlegged or cheap gin. *Some use since c1920.* 4 Any white wine. *Colloq.* 5 White bread. 6 Vanilla ice cream. 7 Any of various thick white sauces and syrups, such as cream sauce, marshmallow syrup, and

the like. 8 Cocaine. *Since c1945. From "white stuff."*

white bread = **bread.**

white collar   Of or pert. to office work and workers, mainly clerical. *Colloq.*

white cow   1 A vanilla milk shake. *Since c1930.* 2 A vanilla ice cream soda, made with both vanilla syrup and vanilla ice cream. *Since c1950.*

white-face   *n.* A circus clown. *Circus use.*

white-haired boy   white-headed boy = **fair-haired boy.** 1928: "White-haired boy." Hecht & MacArthur, *Front Page*, II. 1941: "The white-haired boy of the happy family." Schulberg, *Sammy*, 181.

white hope   1 A white prize fighter who may be good enough to win a championship. *Prize fighter use since c1910 in ref. to a white boxer able to beat Negro Jack Johnson.* 2 Anyone, esp. a politician, athlete, or entertainer, whose accomplishments may bring fame or respect to his native town or country, his ethnic group, his school, etc.

white horse = **white mule.** *Dial.*

white hot   Wanted by the police for having committed a major crime. 1949: "Floyd became white hot." Hynd, *Public Enemies*, 87. See **heat.**

whitehouse   white house   *n.* 1 The home of one's employer. *Not common.* 2 Vanilla ice cream with cherries in it or on it. *In ref. to legend of George Washington and the cherry tree.*

white lightning   Cheap, inferior, homemade, or bootleg whisky, usu. uncolored corn whisky. 1940: "He had a pint of bootleg white lightning. . . ." C. McCullers, *The Heart Is a Lonely Hunter*, reprinted in *The Ballad of the Sad Café*, 294. *Mainly Southern use.* Cf. **white mule.**

white line   Flavored or diluted grain alcohol drunk as liquor; bootleg or homemade whisky. *Orig. hobo use.*

white loco   See **loco weeds.**

white meat   1 Any easy task; anything that can be acquired easily or with pleasure. *Because the white meat of a fowl is considered the choice part for eating.* 2 [taboo] A white female considered as an easy sexual conquest; the pudendum of a white woman. Cf. **meat, dark meat.** 3 Any white woman whose time or presence is for hire for legitimate purposes, usu. an actress or singer. *Since c1935. Mainly theater use.*

white money   Silver coins. *Some W.W.II Army use.* See **white.**

white mule   Diluted or flavored grain alcohol used as liquor; cheap or bootleg whisky. *Common since c1920. Orig. Southern use. From the kick of the drink, presumably like a mule's.*

white one   A shirt of any color.

white sidewall   **white sidewall haircut**   A haircut so short on the sides that the scalp shows through. 1957: "The young airman sentenced to four months in prison for refusing to get a 'white sidewall' haircut was released today and said he probably would disobey the order again." N.Y. *Post,* July 25, 3.

white slave   Any young woman who has been kidnaped and forced to enter prostitution by an organized criminal group. 1857: *The White Slave,* a play by Bartley Campbell set in the year 1857; first performed in 1882.   **—er**   A criminal organizer of trade in prostitution.

white stuff   1 Cocaine. *Since c1920; mainly underworld use.* 2 Alcohol used in making bootleg whisky. *c1920.* 3 = **snow.** 4 Morphine. *Narcotic addict use.*

white trash   A poor Southern white farmer or laborer; the class of poor Southern whites generically considered. Cf. **peckerwood. white-trash** *adj.* Descriptive of poverty and ignorance among Southern white rural folk. *Colloq.*

whitewash   *n.* 1 In sports, a defeat in which the losing team is scoreless. *Since c1860.* 2 Fig., an instance of whitewashing, i.e., covering up or glossing over a misdeed; esp. used in politics to refer to an opinion, report, or public statement intended to excuse a misdeed or exonerate an unethical or inefficient person. 1950: "Several Republican senators reported that the report was a 'whitewash' of [Senator] McCarthy's charges." AP, July 20.   *v.t.* 1 To defeat an opponent utterly. 2 To conceal in public the bad record of a prominent figure, esp. a politician; to proclaim the innocence of a person who is really guilty; to influence public opinion favorably in the case of a reprehensible action.

white-wing   *n.* A man, often white-coated, who works as a street-sweeper.

whiz   *n.* 1 A short written examination given in a school class; a quiz. 2 Any person who is remarkably proficient, intelligent, talented, industrious, or successful in a specif. field; an expert, a shark, a go-getter. 1949: "The town's most promising high school football whiz." AP, Oct. 26. 1951: "Mr. Cotterell is a whiz at exterior (as opposed to psychological) characterization." J. Brooks in N.Y. *Times Bk. Rev.,* Feb. 18, 4/5. *Common since at least c1900. From "wizard," reinforced by "whiz" = to go fast.* 3 A remarkable specimen of anything. 1920: " 'Wonderful night.' 'It's a whiz.' " Fitzgerald, *This Side of Paradise,* 45. 4 Any member of a mob of professional pickpockets, usu. excluding the star member who actually removes the wallet or money from the victim's pocket. *Since c1920.* 5 The air used in air brakes. *Railroad use.* 6 Energy, vigor, pep, vim, zing.   *v.i., v.t.* 1 To pick pockets. *Some underworld use.* 2 To drive an automobile rapidly or recklessly.   **—zer**   *n.* 1 A member of a mob of pickpockets; a whiz. *Underworld use; archaic.* See Appendix, —er ending. 2 The propeller of an airplane; the screw of a ship. *Not common.*

whiz-bang   *n.* 1 A high-velocity, antipersonnel shrapnel shell. *W.W.I use. Orig. Brit. Army sl. From whizzing sound of such shells during flight, followed immediately by an explosion.* 2 A mixture of morphine and cocaine, or an injection of this mixture. *Drug addict use since c1930. Because the effect is sudden and explosive.* See **bang.** 3 = **whiz.** 1949: "In time [the baseball players] will all be varsity whizbangs." A. Daley in N.Y. *Times,* Sept. 4, 4S. 4 Anything remarkable. 5 A joke, esp. a hilarious one. c1914: "Captain Billy's Whiz Bang," *orig. a mimeographed sheet of jokes to cheer up wounded veterans of W.W.I in hospitals, later printed and sold on newsstands. Captain Billy was "Billy" Fawcett, of Fawcett Publications.* 1955: *Captain Billy's Whiz Bang,* [title], an anthology of the best humor from the orig. "Whiz Bang."

whiz-dinger   *n.* = **whiz** plus **humdinger.** 1950: "I have just throwed together a whiz-dinger of a shrimp creole." Starnes, *And When She Was Bad,* 176. *Not common.*

whodunit   *n.* A work of prose fiction in which the narrative is based on the solution of a problem posed by the discovery of a crime, usu. a murder; a detective story or murder mystery; any movie, play, book, radio script, or the like based on such a story. 1936: "Sid Silverman decides to call 'em 'whodunits.' " A. Green in *Esquire,* Sept. 1946: "I coined the word 'whodunit' while in the employ of *Variety*. It was along about 1935 or 1936." Wolfe Kaufman in *Word Study*, Apr., 3/1. 1946: Ascribed to P. G. Wodehouse [c1930] by D. B. Chidsey in *AS*, Oct. 1953: "A conventional whodunit." A. Boucher in N.Y. *Times Bk. Rev.*, July 5, 10/1,2. *As for the coining of the word, whodunit remains a mystery. From the illit. "Who done it?"*

whole-hog *adv.* Completely; thoroughly.

whole hog, go the thoroughly, completely; to go the limit; to take a bold step. *Since c1830.*

whomp *v.t.* To defeat decisively. *From "whop" = whip.*

whomp up To create, construct, or imagine; to cook up, whip up. 1950: "Instead of getting sleep, I whomped me up one heck of a nightmare." Billy Rose, *synd. newsp. col.*, Sept. 18. 1952: "When [the British] sit down to whomp up a movie it comes out adult and worthy of watching." R. C. Ruark, *synd. newsp. col.*, Aug. 28.

whoop-de-do   hoopty-doo   hoop-de-doo *interj.* An expression of surprise or joy. *Obs.* *n.* Exuberance; noisy confusion; celebration; a lavish display of emotions or material wealth; advertising, ballyhoo. 1936: "The room still holds its pink bloom and the chandeliers give it all a gay sense of flossy whoop-de-doo." *Esquire*, Sept., 20. 1941: "But, in spite of this whoop-de-do, West Hartfordians' emotions were mixed." *Time*, Oct. 27, 45/1. 1948: "A fine splatter of rhetorical exuberance and chartless hoop-de-doo." M. Wylie in N.Y. *Times Bk. Rev.*, Sept. 12, 23/2. See Appendix, Reduplications.

whoop-de-doodle *n., adj.* Ballyhoo; inflated, insincere praise; whoop-de-do. 1932: "The racketeering, gossiping, whoop-de-doodle thing, it is a piece of stinking fish. . . ." "I am going to change this [phrase] . . . chiefly because 'whoop-de-doodle' does not belong to my own way of speech and is probably Menckenian." Thomas Wolfe in letters to J. R. Meade, Apr. 21 and July 7, pub. in *Atlantic Monthly*, Nov., 1950, 83/1,2.

whoopee *n.* **1** Wild merrymaking, excitement, exultation. Often in "making whoopee." c1930: "Making Whoopee," pop. song. 1930: "The visiting Butter and Egg Men [had] their whoopee in New York." C. Bragdon in *Outlook*, Oct., 301/1. *Much more common c1930–c1935 than later. From the interj., which has*

been common since *c1860.* → **2** Whisky. *c1930.*

whoopee water Liquor or wine, esp. champagne.

whooper-dooper *n.* A spree; a spell of merrymaking. 1941: "In the dream, he finds himself off on a rousing whooper-dooper." J. Alexander in *SEP*, Mar. 1, 11/1. *Since c1930.* *adj.* Excellent. See Appendix, Reduplications.

whoops and jingles = **screaming meemies.** 1927: "To have the whoops and jingles." *New Repub.*, v. 50. *Not common.*

whoosh *v.i.* To fly or drive rapidly. 1953: "The 6-jet atom bomber whooshed from Maine to [England]." AP, July 28. **—ed** *adj.* Drunk. *Not common.*

whop *v.t.* **1** To strike a blow, as with the fist. *Dial. Imitative of the sound of a blow.* **2** To beat or defeat another, lit. or fig. *Reinforced by corrupting "to whip."* *n.* **1** A blow, as with the fist. **2** A fall. *Dial.* **—per** *n.* **1** Anything large or outsized. 1951: "A turtle of such immense size that six men could sit on its shell . . . the Mauritius tortoise must have been a whopper." J. Williams, *Fall of the Sparrow*, 39. *Colloq.* **2** A lie or exaggeration, esp. a story obviously falsified for humorous effect. *Colloq.*

whore *n.* **1** Any man or woman who compromises his beliefs or talents for personal advantage. **2** Any person who changes lovers, jobs, friends, ideals, beliefs, etc., frequently, esp. for personal gain or comfort.

whore-hopper [taboo] *n.* A man who frequently patronizes prostitutes; a man obsessed by the need to enjoy sexual intercourse with as many women, and as often, as possible. 1947: "This kid wasn't any whore-hopper. . . . He'd never had a piece of tail." C. Willingham, *End as a Man*, 108.

whorehouse *adj.* In a sensuous or gaudy manner, as befitting a brothel. 1951: "It was a very old, terrific record that this colored girl singer, Estelle Fletcher, made about twenty years ago. She sings it very Dixieland and whorehouse, and it doesn't sound at all mushy." J. D. Salinger, *Catcher in the Rye*, 89. *The n. "whorehouse" = brothel is stand. though taboo.*

whose its = **thingamajig.** *A more modern word.*

whozis *n.* **1** Any person or object whose name is unknown or forgotten. 1938: "There should be a whozis [i.e., a tilde] over the first *n* [in *Piñon*]. . . ."

A. H. Holt, *American Place Names.* → **2** Any gadget. *From "Who is this?"* Cf. **whatzis.**

whump   *v.t.* **1** To defeat by a large margin. **2** To attack; to strike a telling blow against. *Used both lit. and fig.* 1939: "Taft sturdily whumped at the New Deal's 'insane deficit policy.' " *Life*, Dec. 11, 26.

why, sure   Certainly; surely.

wi   *n.* See **kiwi.**

wick   *n.* A worker who lacks class consciousness; a scissorbill. 1926: 'Wick' reported second to 'scissorbill' in freq. of use. J. Lance in *Amer. Mercury*, Apr., xxx. *An I.W.W. term; obs.*

wicked   *adj.* Excellent in any way; potent, strong, capable; "fierce," keen, "mean." *Often used as an attrib. modifier of the direct object in a simple clause.* 1920: ". . . Shakes a wicked calf [dances well]." Fitzgerald, *This Side of Paradise*, 119. 1922: "He can shake a wicked spatula [is a good pharmacist]." A. L. Bass. *Orig. cool use = intellectually or psychologically so satisfying that one becomes exhausted; cool.* See **cool.**

wicker   *v.t.* To throw into a (wicker) wastebasket; to discard. *Prob. synthetic.*

wick-willie   *n.* A jet plane pilot. *Some Air Force use since c1950.*

widdie   *n.* In card-playing, a widow, or spare hand. 1914: "High bid takes the cat—widdie, you know—and discards." S. Lewis, *Our Mr. Wrenn*, 186.

wide open   **1** Without protection or defense; lit., open to assault, failure, disappointment, etc. *Colloq.* **2** Unrestricted by police or other authority; freely given over to all manner of illegal activity; said of a city, district, region, etc.

wide place in the road   A small town. 1956: "A Wide Place in the Road." Title of an article, *Look* magazine. *Since c1935. Orig. Western and truck driver use.*

widget   *n.* **1** A gadget. *Since c1920.* → **2** Any useless device attached to an automobile, to a garment, or the like, in order to cause a change in style; trimming. *Orig. New York City garment district use.*

widow   *n.* **1** Any extra or spare item that exists by itself. Thus, in publishing, a widow is a short line that appears at the top of a page; in cards, a widow is an extra hand or kitty. **2** A woman whose husband is alive but often away from home. *Often preceded by a word that indicates the husband's reason for being*

away, as "*golf widow.*" See **grass widow, sod widow.**

widow-maker   *n.* **1** Anything, such as a specif. task or machine, that endangers a workman. *Thus in logging a widow-maker is a dangerous hanging limb or dead tree; in mining it is a diamond drill.* **2** A gunman. *Not common.*

wiener   *n.* **1** = **weenie.** *Short for "wienerwurst." Stand. use. This is the most common use of the word.* **2** = **weenie,** in all sl. senses.

wienie   *n.* = **weenie.**

wif = **wiff.**

wife   *n.* **1** A roommate, usu. one who shares a college dormitory room. *College use c1910–c1935.* **2** One's best girl friend; one's steady. *Some student use since c1920.*

wiff   **wif**   *n.* **1** A wife. 1948: "Slang includes intentional mispronunciations such as *wiff* for 'wife.' . . ." A. H. Marckwardt & F. G. Cassidy, *Scribner Hndbk. of Eng.*, 151. See Appendix, Corruptions. **2** A glance, look, or cursory examination.   *v.i.* In baseball, to strike out. Cf. **whiff.**

wig   *n.* **1** A judge. *Obs.* **2** Bobbed hair. *Some c1920 use.* **3** A head of hair. *Colloq.* **4** One's head, brain, or mentality. *Jive use since c1935; often used in jive expressions, e.g., "don't blow your wig," etc.* **5** An intellectual; a studious person. *Student use since c1940.* **6** A progressive jazz musician. *Cool and far out use since c1955.* **7** A white person. *Negro use; in ref. to the long straight hair of the white race.*   *v.i.* To talk, esp. to talk idly or foolishly. *Jive use since c1935.*   *v.t.* **1** To annoy someone; to be a nuisance. *Jive use since c1935.* **2** To play cool or way out jazz music. *Cool use since c1955.* **3** To experience ecstasy from listening to music. **4** To experience ecstasy from any cause; to be well satisfied with someone or something; to be in rapport with someone; to dig something. *Cool uses.*

wiggle   *v.i.* To dance.   *n.* A dance. 1945: "Can I have this wiggle?" E. Kasser. See **get a wiggle on.**

wiggle [move] [hustle] [hump] on, get a   Hurry up. 1926: "Tell him to damn well get a wiggle on." Stallings and Anderson, *What Price Glory*, I. *All in use c1900 to present; "get a wiggle on" and "get a move on" are much more common than other variants.*

wiggle-waggle   *v.i.* **1** To sway. *Western use since c1860.* **2** To gossip; lit., to move one's tongue back and forth rapidly.

wigwag *n.* A railway grade-crossing signal. See Appendix, Reduplications.

wild *adj.* **1** = Very eager or enthusiastic. *Usu. in "wild about" or "wild over."* 1956: "Here's the new lemon flavored cough drop everyone's wild about." *Advt. in N.Y. Post,* Oct. 4, 17. *Since c1920.* **3** Exciting and satisfying; unusual and satisfying. *Orig. cool, jive use; far out use.* See **hog wild.**

wild about [someone] In love with, attracted to, infatuated with someone or something. *Colloq. since c1920.*

wildcat *v.i.* To work secretly or with a secret plan or goal in order to gain an advantage; specif., to prospect for oil or minerals secretly on another's property in order to buy the property at a low price if valuable discoveries are made. 1955: "It was considered smart business to keep the play a secret until the eve of the performance. . . . This system . . . was known as wildcatting. . . ." H. R. Hoyt, *Town Hall Tonight,* 19. *adj.* **1** Spirited; active, energetic; fun-loving and independent beyond the bounds of social approval; usu. said of a girl or young woman. *Colloq.* **2** Secret; unknown to or unsanctioned by the person most concerned; said of an oil well or mine discovered on someone else's property; done by an individual or small group without the support of or in opposition to a larger or parent group; unsanctioned, illegal, unlicensed. Thus a wildcat bus is an unlicensed bus, a wildcat strike is one not openly sanctioned by the workers' union, and a wildcat oil well is one drilled for speculative purposes, often on land which is not owned or leased by the driller. *Since c1930.* *n.* **1** A person who is easily angered or aroused. *Colloq.* **2** An unofficial strike by union workers. 1956: "*Wildcat*—A walkout not approved by union officials." *Labor's Special Language from Many Sources.*

wildcat's ankle A person highly approved of. *Some use c1920.*

wild mare's milk Whisky. *Some jocular Western use.*

William *n.* **1** A Confederate $100 bill. *Some Civil War use. Obs. From "Bill,"* nickname for *William.* **2** Any banknote. 1887: "[He] lost his five dollar William." *New Orleans Lantern. Jocular use; obs.*

William Shears A worker who lacks class consciousness. *An I.W.W. term. From synonymous "scissorbill" ("Shears" for scissor; "William" for bill). Obs.*

willie Willie *n.* **1** A bindle stiff. c1920: "We're Two Weary Willies." Song title. *From "Weary Willie."* **2** Beef, esp. canned or preserved beef. 1926: ". . . Two sacks of bread, one of canned willie. . . ." Stallings & Anderson, *What Price Glory,* II. *Primarily Army use, since W.W.I.* **3** A male homosexual. *Some use since c1930.* See **doowhistle.**

willies, the Willies, the *n.pl.* Nervousness; fear; nervous uneasiness or discomfort, esp. when due to uncertainty, fear, or the aftermath of too much drinking; the creeps, the jim-jams. 1903: "If the shade of Lindley Murray be given 'the Willies,' when it goes up against a new arrival in the limbo of departed rhetoricians. . . ." H. Spencer. 1943: "He couldn't appear like that, all soft and womanish from the willies." Wolfert, *Underworld,* 166. 1947: "He had the hangover willies from too much bottle worship." H. Boyle, *synd. newsp. col.,* May 19. 1951: "For years her friends' shoptalk gave him the willies." G. T. Hellman in *New Yorker,* June 2, 64/2. *Common since c1895. Since c1940 has been partially replaced by "the jitters" and "the heebie jeebies."*

willy-boy Willy-boy *n.* A sissy. 1914: "He's one of these here Willy-boy actors." S. Lewis, *Our Mr. Wrenn,* 162. 1943: "I'm getting to be a regular willy-boy." Wolfert, *Underworld,* 392.

willy-nilly *adj., adv.* Unplanned, unorganized; haphazard(ly); uncertain(ly); occasionally. 1934: "She's happy about herself. Oh, willy-nilly. . . ." P. Wylie, *Finnley Wren,* 175.

wilted *adj.* Drunk. *Not common.*

Wimpy wimpy *n.* A hamburger sandwich. *From the hamburgerophagous "Wimpy," a character in the comic strip "Popeye the Sailor."*

wim-wams *n.pl.* = **jim-jams.** 1946: "Kittenish dames give us the wim-wams." *Time,* Oct. 28, 50/2.

win *n.* A victory, esp. in sports. 1938: "A win in the Kentucky Derby. . . ." Liebling, *Back Where,* 223. *Common colloq. since c1900. pret., past part.* Won. 1921: "Till K. O. Krause win $28." ". . . Would of win me around 20,000." Witwer, *Leather,* 3; 7. 1944: ". . . 'How I got touted off the horse that win it.' (Seasoned [racetrack] fans spurn the past tense.)" *Fortune,* Sept., 142/2. *Sports and gambling use.*

Winchell *n.* A sound-recording worker. *From Walter Winchell, a radio broadcaster who wears earphones during his broadcast, as does such a worker.*

Winchester *n.* A rifle, regardless of

the manufacturer. 1936: "After the early seventies the rifle, regardless of its make, was usually called a 'Winchester,' though this particular term, because of its similarity to the name of a well-known condiment, was occasionally paraphrased into 'worchestershire.' " P. A. Rollins, *The Cowboy*, 57. *Since c1870; from the name of the famous arms manufacturing company.*

wind   *n.* **1** Air brakes. *Some railroad use.* **2** The "air." See **give [someone] the wind.**

wind, give [someone] the   **1** To discard or jilt a suitor with great suddenness. **2** To dismiss or fire someone precipitately. **3** To brake a moving vehicle suddenly and sharply.

windbag   *n.* **1** A talkative or garrulous person; esp. one who talks pompously. 1953: ". . . A windbag who shoots the gab." J. R. Williams, *synd. cartoon*, "Out Our Way," May 8. *Colloq. Often refers to an old person or a politician.* See **hot air. 2** An inner tube for a pneumatic tire. *Auto factory use.*

wind-box   wind box   *n.* An organ or accordion. 1952: "I recall a small vogue for the [song] 'Letter Edged in Black' on the old wind box." R. C. Ruark, *synd. newsp. col.*, Mar. 26.

winder   *n.* See **sidewinder, sky-winder, stemwinder.**

winder-upper   *n.* A song or other musical piece played last on a radio program; the piece that winds up a program. 1942: ". . . And a winder-upper that should give you plenty of action." CBS radio, *The Glenn Miller Program*, Feb. 11. 1945: "That's the winder-upper, listeners." ABC radio, July 28. *Common radio use since c1930.*

winding = **wing-ding.**

winding boy   wining boy   A man sexually pop. with women; an adroit male lover. [1950]: ". . . 'Right there was where I [Jelly Roll Morton, a famous jazz musician and composer] got my new name—Wining Boy.' . . . Johnny St. Cyr was more than a shade embarrassed when asked what the nick-name meant. He said, . . . 'Wining Boy is a bit on the vulgar side. Let's see—how could I put it—means a fellow that makes good jazz with the women.' " A. Lomax, *Mr. Jelly Roll*, 44. *Orig. New Orleans Creole use. Obs.*

wind-jammer   *n.* **1** A talkative person; a boaster. *Some student use c1920.* **2** A musician who plays a wind instru-

ment. 1920: "The spectacled wind-jammers of the orchestra." Fitzgerald, *This Side of Paradise*, 64. *Never common.* → **3** Specif., an Army bugler. *Some Army use.* → **4** Specif., a musician in a circus band. *Circus use since c1930.*

windmill   *n.* **1** A talkative person. *Not common.* See **hot air.** Cf. **windbag. 2** A helicopter. *Not common.* Cf. **egg-beater.** 1952: "The helicopter will be used for aerial spraying of crops. The versatile 'windmill' recently has been adapted to produce sprays." GNS, Sept. 11.

window, out the   **1** Lost; forfeited; destroyed; gone out of one's possession; said of the goods, fame, career, etc., of one who has lost everything, usu. at one sweep. **2** Sold out as soon as put on display; said of merchandise.

window-light   *n.* An eye. 1926: "He'll put out your window-lights." Schwesinger in *Jour. of Applied Psych.*, 259. *Not common.*

windows   *n.pl.* Eyeglasses.

wind pudding   Nothing to eat. *Usu. in phrase "to live on wind pudding"* = *to have nothing to eat and no means of getting anything. Hobo use.*

wind-sucker   *n.* A boaster. *Some c1920 use.*

wind up   To bring something to a conclusion; to complete a task or assignment successfully. *Colloq.*

wind-wagon   *n.* An airplane. *Prob. synthetic.*

windy   *adj.* **1** Nervous. *Not common in U.S., though some W.W.I use from Brit. Army sl.* **2** Talkative; boastful. *Colloq.*   *n.* **1** A talkative person; esp. one who lies or exaggerates. *Since c1930.* **2** An exaggerated story; a lie. *Not common.*

wineeo   *n.* = **wino.** 1949: ". . . The 'winos' (or 'wineeos' as some Chicagoans call them). . . ." W. J. Slocum in *Collier's*, Aug. 27, 60.

wing   whing   *n.* An arm, esp. a baseball pitcher's pitching arm. *Mainly sports and jocular use. Since c1920. Has never* = *a penny, as in Brit. sl.* See **pay-wing, tin wing, white-wing.**   *v.t.* To wound, hit, or nick with a gunshot, not necessarily in the arm. 1944: "Shot missed him, winged the looking-glass." Ford, *Phila. Murder*, 186. 1950: "You were winged by something big—.45 [caliber] maybe— and all it did was peel off some scalp." Starnes, *And When She Was Bad*, 49. *Common during and since* the Civil War. **—s** n.pl. Cocaine. *From its effect. Some West Coast use since c1920.*

wing-ding wingding whing-ding whingding n. **1** A fit, esp. an epileptic fit; a fit induced by drugs; a faked fit used to gain sympathy. *Orig. hobo, prison, and drug addict use. Since c1920.* → **2** A violent fit of anger, frustration, or nervousness; a loud emotional outburst. 1946: "You're going to throw a wing-ding they'll hear in Detroit." Evans, *Halo in Blood*, 148. *Since c1935.* **3** A ruckus; any noisy or exciting incident; a commotion, esp. a noisy celebration or argument. 1949: "We are not sure just what the Festival is to be, but some sort of native whingding no doubt." Editorial, *SEP*, Mar. 5, 10/3. *The most common use. Since c1940.* **4** A gadget; a dingus; a doodad. **5** A hat. 1941: "Slipping on her wing-ding." *Life*, Jan. 27, 78. *Not common.* adj. Boisterous, noisy, exciting; uninhibited. 1948: "They're building up to a wing-ding celebration in Independence, Missouri, tonight." Frank Burkholzer, NBC radio, Nov. 3. v.i., v.t. To hurry. 1945: "A spy feller will come to New York with an atomic bomb. He'll sneak it under the flooring in some rooming house before wing-dinging it back across the ocean." D. Fairbairn in Phila. *Bulletin*, Dec. 31, 8. *Not common.*

wing-dinger n. **1** One who has or fakes a fit. 1933: Drug addict use. D. W. Maurer. **2** An uninhibited, boisterous celebration or celebrator. **3** Anything remarkable. Cf. **humdinger.**

wingdoodle n. A thingamajig. 1947: "... Push in this dingus, step on this wingdoodle...." Billy Rose, *synd. newsp. col.*, Jan. 2. *Not common. Perhaps synthetic.*

wing-heavy adj. Drunk. *Not common.*

wing-waiter n. A postman, esp. a prison mail-carrier. *Never common; some underworld use.*

Wingy prop. n. A nickname often applied to a one-armed man, esp. a beggar.

wink n. See **forty winks.**

winkus n. A wink, sign, or spoken code word, given as approval, warning, or the like. *From "wink" plus Latin ending "—us."*

wino n. **1** A grape picker; a vineyard worker. *Some hobo use.* **2** A habitual wine drunkard, esp. a jobless alcoholic who favors cheap wine because it gives the most kick for a little money. 1931: "The [American hobo] term [wino] is one of

contempt and is used of those broken-down dipsomaniac ex-hoboes or ex-workers who used to drink themselves silly by buying ten-cent tins of sour cheap wine in the 'wine-dumps' of California." C. Ashleigh in *Everyman*, May 21, 520/3. 1941: "... A couple of 'winos' who had been drinking cheap sherry in the bar." G. Homes, *40 Whacks*, 77. 1951: "The Jollity Theater in Minneapolis is patronized largely by vagrants, winos, dehorns, grifters...." M. Shulman, *Dobie Gillis*, 215. *Since c1920.* → **3** Any drunkard.

win out To win; esp. to succeed as a result of perseverance and against odds. 1902: "De Bird of Time will win out in a walk." Coley, *Rubaiyat of the East Side*, 1. 11. *Since c1890; colloq.*

win [one's] spurs To be accepted as an experienced and trustworthy worker and person; to become a professional; to prove by an action or series of actions that one is experienced enough to be considered no longer a novice. *From the cowboy use.*

win the porcelain hairnet win the fur-lined bathtub win the tinfoil doorknob win the cast-iron overshoes win the barbwire garter win the solid gold chamber pot Phrases used ironically on the occasion of a remarkable action by someone else; fig., to win a strikingly useless prize for doing something well, to perform a useless action in a superior manner.

wipe n. **1** A handkerchief. **2** One who washes or wipes cars or dishes; thus "car-wipe," "dish-wipe," etc.

wipe it off 1 An order to stop smiling or joking, to concentrate on the business at hand and be serious; fig., to wipe a smile off one's face. *A common W.W.II Army order, by sergeants getting soldiers ready for inspection or marching. Some civilian use since W.W.II.* → **2** A command to be serious and pay attention; an order to stop all frivolous activity and merriment. *Wide W.W.II Army and USN use.* **3** To forget and forgive; to make retribution. *Fig., to wipe the slate clean.*

wipe off 1 To kill, to murder. 1939: "He'll wipe you off." Chandler, *Big Sleep*, 72. *Not as common as "wipe out."* **2** To destroy; lit. and fig., to wipe someone or something off the map.

wipe [someone] off the slate = **wipe out.** 1951: "Sometimes you had to wipe them off the slate entirely." *I, Mobster*, 82. *Not common.*

wipe out To kill or murder; to eradicate a person or a group. *Underworld use since c1925, pop. in fiction and the movies; some W.W.II use. Colloq.*

wiper *n.* A gunman; a hired killer. *Underworld use since c1930. From "wipe out."* See Appendix, —er ending.

wire *n.* **1** A trick, artifice, stratagem. *Some c1850 student use; obs.* Cf. **pull wires**. **2** A pickpocket; that member of a gang of pickpockets who does the actual stealing. 1928: "The *wire* who abstracts the objective from the victim's *kick*. . . ." E. Booth in *Amer. Mercury*, May, 78. *Common underworld use since c1920.* **3** A lackey, esp. one who helps a prisoner communicate with his friends outside prison. *Prison use c1925.* **4** A warning, as of impending arrest; also, information; advice. 1930: "The real thieves get 'a wire,' and play poker." Lavine, *Third Degree*, 210. **5** A telegram. *Colloq.* See **haywire, live wire**.

wire city A jail; a wire enclosure around a prison stockade, esp. an Army guardhouse or prisoner-of-war stockade. *Some Army use.*

wire-puller *n.* A person who uses influence, stratagems, or the influence of others in order to obtain a desired result; specif., one who obtains a desired result by political influence; an "operator." 1833: *DAE*. 1952: "Grunewald, bigtime wire-puller in the tangled Washington bureaucracy. . . ." *N.Y. Daily News*, Aug. 13, C2/1-2.

wires, pull To use influence or pull to obtain favors.

wiry *adj.* Artful. *Some c1950 student use.* Cf. **wire**.

wisdom box A yardmaster's office. *Railroad use.* See **knowledge box**.

wise *adj.* Informed; alert; on the inside; cognizant of the true course of events even if it is not immediately apparent; hip. 1906: "I'm a wise blokie." Kildare in *Independent*, July, 142/1. 1914: "Get wise, son!" S. Lewis, *Our Mr. Wrenn*, 58. 1939: "He's close-mouthed and wise—stir-wise." Gardner, *D. A. Draws*, 102. *v.t.* To wise [someone] up; to inform someone of pertinent facts or information.

wise, get **1** See **wise**. **2** To be or become impertinent, impudent, or fresh. **3** = **get next to [someone]**. 1951: "I asked her if Mr. Cudahy—that was the booze hound's name—had ever tried to get wise with her. She was pretty young, but she had this terrific figure, and I wouldn't've put it past that Cudahy

bastard." J. D. Salinger, *Catcher in the Rye*, 62. **4** = **get next to [oneself]**.

wise, put [someone] **1** To inform someone of another's personal attitude, feelings, or ideas; to warn, caution, or advise someone. **2** To inform someone of a group attitude, basic concept, or point of view, esp. in order generally to enlighten the person, or make the person more alert, receptive, or hip. *Fairly common student and young adult use. In both uses, the person put wise is considered of inferior intellect, experience, or sensitivity to the speaker.* **3** = **wise up**.

wise apple = **wise guy**. Cf. **apple**.

wisecrack   wise-crack *n.* A bright, smart, witty, or sarcastic remark; an impertinence; a joke, esp. when it emphasizes another's shortcomings. 1929: " 'Wisecrack' is a grand word. It had only to be invented to be indispensable; and it will be no better a decade hence, when the dictionaries have blessed it, than it is at this moment." W. Follett in *Bookman*, 301/2. 1929: " . . . At least two wisecracks in the first paragraph. . . ." *Nation*, Sept. 4, 240. 1949: "Back in 1916, I watched [Will Rogers] twirl a rope and heard him toss out some wisecracks (only I don't think the word had yet come in)." J. T. Winterich in *Sat. Rev. Lit.*, Oct. 15, 19/1. *The late columnist O. O. McIntyre attrib. this coinage to comedian Chic Sale. Since c1920.* *v.i.* To utter a wisecrack. See **crack wise**. 1924: "The crowd filed out, 'wise-cracking' about the picture." Marks, *Plastic Age*, 28.

wisecracker   wise cracker *n.* One who wisecracks; a joker. 1924: "Carl, the flippant, the voluble, the 'wise-cracker.' . . ." Marks, *Plastic Age*, 113. 1945: " 'The Table' [at the Algonquin Hotel in N.Y.C., at which Alexander Woollcott and his friends lunched, became] the arena of the wisecrackers. In fact, there is a legend, probably baseless, that the term originated there." S. A. Adams, quoted in *Word Study*, Dec., 7/2.

wise guy **1** A person, usu. a male, who is aware of contemporary happenings; one who is hep; most freq. used ironically. *Since c1910.* → **2** A person who thinks he knows everything, a smart aleck; one who says everything he thinks, one who gives advice and criticism freely; a troublemaker. 1930: "A man known as a 'wise guy,' or troublemaker." Lavine, *Third Degree*, 88f. 1949: "The wise guys said Frank didn't stand a chance." Phila. *Bulletin*,

Sept. 2, 4/1. *Since c1910, common since c1925.* **3** An egoistic extrovert, often with a cynical and superficial philosophy of life, who delights in offering sarcastic suggestions and making jokes at the expense of the pride of others.

wiseheimer *n., adj.* = **wisenheimer.** 1937: "Some wiseheimer American newspaper man has tagged ['a chicken in every pot'] onto President Hoover." E. E. Ericson. *Some use since c1925.*

wise hombre = **wise guy.** *Some Western use, but esp. in Western fiction.*

wisenheimer *n.* A smart aleck; a wise guy; a know-it-all. 1951: "The way an old-time carny handles a tough wisenheimer with the aid of a hammer. . . ." W. L. Gresham in N.Y. *Times Bk. Rev.,* Apr. 8, 7/5. *Since c1920. Still some use but rapidly becoming archaic.*

wise up To become informed, to see the point of something; to give someone information that is of personal benefit to him; to tip someone off; to warn a person of the real consequences of his actions, utterances, etc. 1924: "My adviser was a good scout and wised me up." Marks, *Plastic Age,* 23.

wish book A mail order catalogue. *Since c1930; jocular and rural use.*

wishy-washy *adj.* Vacillating, faltering, weak. 1951: "The wishy-washy player keeps putting off the evil day." O. Jacoby, *synd. newsp. col.,* "Canasta," Mar. 3. *Colloq.*

witch *n.* **1** [derog.] An unattractive, disagreeable, or unpopular woman. *Colloq.* **2** Any girl or young woman. *Colloq. since c1925; mainly student use.* **3** [derog.] A bitch; an obstinate woman; a woman who takes pleasure in arousing sexual aspirations that she will not satisfy; an unfaithful woman. *A euphem. for "bitch."*

—with *prep.* → *n.* Used to signify the second half of a conventional combination; e.g. "hamburger with" = a hamburger with onions, "coffee with" = coffee with cream, etc. *Common lunch-counter use since c1935.* Cf. **—and.**

with [something], give To give or give out something. 1951: "He wouldn't give with the information. . . ." *I, Mobster,* 74.

with a bang Very successfully; with popular acceptance.

with a fine (sharp) pencil As economically or as cheaply as possible. *Not common.*

with balls on [taboo] = **with bells on.** *A modern, masculine, usu. jocular variation.*

with bells = **with bells on.** 1941: "I'll be here Thursday. With bells." Cain, *M. Pierce,* 97.

with bells on Dressed in one's best and in a gala mood. c1909: "I've got rings on my fingers and bells on my toes, . . ." from pop. song. *The image seems to suggest that of a court jester. Archaic, except in the more general* **with knobs (bells, tits) on.**

with it **1** Officially connected with or employed by a carnival or circus. 1933: "To get with it was to join the outfit." H. T. Webster. 1951: "Dan Mannix saw his chance to be 'with it' [a carnival] and grabbed the opportunity." W. L. Gresham in New York *Times Bk. Rev.,* Apr. 8, 7/4. *Carnival and circus use since c1930.* **2** Appreciative of and sympathetic to jazz; in rapport with, esp. jive or swing; hep. See **get with it.** **3** Alert, spirited, wise, hip. **4** Aware and appreciative of the manner, speech, and fads used by cool or far out musicians and their adherents; hip to the jazz, esp. cool, genre. *Cool use since c1950; beat use.*

with it, get To get on the ball; to get going; to get busy.

with knobs (bells, tits) on Definitely, emphatically; with enthusiasm and in the proper mood, dress, and condition. *Often in "I'll be there with knobs on," in accepting an invitation. Since at least c1935. From "with bells on." Usu. follows an accusation or oath. See* **knobs.**

without a paddle See **up the (shit) creek (without a paddle).**

with tits on = **with knobs on.**

wiz *n.* = **whiz.** *Obs. spelling.*

wizard *n.* A person who excels at a specif. function, usu. intellectual or mechanical; a whiz. *Colloq. adj.* Excellent, marvelous, wonderful. *Some U.S. use but never as common as in Eng.*

wob **Wob** *n.* = **wobbly,** a member of the I.W.W. 1926: "WOBS PULL STRIKE." Heading, *Amer. Mercury,* Jan., 62.

wobble-shop *n.* A saloon. *Never common.*

wobbly **Wobbly** *n.* **1** A member of the I.W.W. (Industrial Workers of the World), an early and radical union. 1922: "Join the Wobblies." O'Neill, *Hairy Ape,* 6. 1926: "*Wobbly,* although [unofficial], is the usual designation of a member by his fellows and himself." S. H. Holbrook in *Amer. Mercury,* Jan., 62. 1956: "*Wobbly*—A member of the Industrial Workers of the World. . . . An old IWW member gives this account of how the expression 'wobbly' came about: 'In Vancouver, in 1911, we had a number of Chinese members, and one restaurant keeper would trust any member for meals. He could not pronounce the letter w, but called it wobble, and would ask: "You I. Wobble Wobble?" And when the card was shown credit was unlimited. Thereafter the laughing term among us was "I Wobbly Wobbly." ' " *Labor's Special Language from Many Sources. Archaic.* → **2** Any exceptionally earnest or emotional labor organizer, agitator, or union member. *Some use since c1930.*

wog   Wog [derog.]   *n.* A native of India, esp. a native laborer. *Some W.W.II Army and Air Corps use, mainly among the "Flying Tigers."*

wolf   *n.* **1** A male homosexual seducer; an aggressive male homosexual. 1917: "The sodomist, the degenerate, the homosexual 'wolf.' . . ." P. L. Quinlan in *New Repub.*, Jan. 13, 293/2. *Prison and hobo use.* → **2** A youth or man who habitually pursues women; a sexually aggressive male; a seducer or would-be seducer; a youth or man who appropriates the girl friends or wives of others; a ladies' man; a man with a psychological need to prove his masculinity or potency by seduction or attempted seduction of a great many women. *This use evolved c1930 and was stand. by c1945. Great student popularity by c1940 and wide W.W.II use. Orig. containing derog. overtones of "seducer," it now is considered complimentary by youths who wish to be known as ladies' men, and is often used jocularly. Thus the meaning of the word, prob. along with pop. conceptions of morality, changed during W.W.II.* → **3** A female who pursues males, a sexually aggressive girl or woman. *Not common.* See **wolfess. 4** A railroad worker who is not a member of the Railroad Brotherhood (union). *From "lone wolf." Railroad use.* · *v.i.,v.t.* **1** To appropriate another's girl friend or boy friend. 1929: "The college boy (in 1929) knows a smoothie who wolfed on a friend and creamed his lady." *World's Work*, Nov., 40. **2** To be, or act as, a heterosexual wolf. 1939: "I give with the vocals and wolf around in a nite club." O'Hara, *Pal Joey*, 60.   **—ess**   *n.* **1** A girl or woman who is sexually aggressive or predatory; a seductress or would-be seductress. 1945: Do Wolfesses Always Win? . . . A nice girl hasn't got a chance with a wolfess around." Phila. *Bulletin*, Nov. 27, 42/1. 1946: "A wolfess who,

asked why she went out with young men, replied, 'You can't hock memories.' " E. Wilson, *synd. newsp. col.*, Apr. 27. *Not common, but some newsp. use.* → **2** A girl with sex appeal. *Some student use.*

wolf whistle   A whistle to show awareness of, approval of, and sometimes an invitation to a sexually attractive woman. *The wolf whistle is commonly a brief rising note followed immediately by a longer descending note. Most common during W.W.II.* See **wolf.**

woman   *n.* See **little woman, old woman.**

woman-chaser   *n.* A ladies' man; a libertine.

womp   *v.t.* To beat or defeat another person or team severely.   *n.* In television, a glare from some white object, as a shirt front, within range of the camera lens; a "bloom." *Television use since c1945.*

wonder   *n.* See **ninety-day wonder, thirty-day wonder.**

woo   *n.* Passionate lovemaking short of coitus; necking. *Archaic.* See **pitch woo.**

wood   wood, the   *n.* The actual bar in a nightclub or saloon. 1952: "In a club-and-bar joint, a customer yelled to the man behind the wood. . . ." N.Y. *Daily News*, Aug. 25, C4/3. See **saw wood.**

wood butcher   1 A carpenter, esp. an incompetent one. 1888: *DAE. Still some use.* → **2** In the U.S. Navy, a carpenter's mate. *W.W.I and II use.* **3** A poor golf player. *Some golf use since c1935.*

wood-chopper   *n.* A xylophonist. *Not common.*

wooden coat   = **wooden overcoat.** 1859: *DAE.*

wooden-head   *n.* A stupid person, a blockhead. *Colloq.*

wooden Indian   1 A person who is silent, stupid, or otherwise similar to the figure of the wooden Indian once displayed in front of cigar stores. *c1900–c1925; obs.* **2** A loafer, an idler. *Not common.*

wooden kimona   wooden kimono = **wooden overcoat.** *Some underworld and fictional use since c1930.*

wooden nickels, Don't take any   An expression meaning, "Good-by; take care of yourself; protect yourself from trouble." *A c1920 fad phrase.*

wooden overcoat   A coffin. *Some use since c1860.* Cf. **pine overcoat, wooden coat.**

wooden shoe A German or Dutch prize fighter. *c1920 boxing use; obs.*

woodfish *n.pl.* Mushrooms. *Dial.*

wood-head *n.* A lumberjack. *Hobo use.*

woodpile woodpile *n.* A xylophone or marimba. 1953: "Marimbas? Oh, that wood-pile out there?" A. Godfrey, radio, Jan. 26. *Some radio use since c1935.* 1956: " . . . Woodpile for xylophone is real [jazz] talk. . . ." S. Longstreet, *The Real Jazz Old and New*, 150. *Jazz usage.* **—r** *n.* A xylophonist. *Not common. Some early radio and jazz use.*

wood-pusher *n.* An inferior chess player. Cf. **patzer.**

wood-pussy *n.* A polecat. *Dial.*

woods woods, the *n.pl.* Small towns; the sticks. *Not common.* See **bull of the woods.**

wood-shed *n.* A rehearsal for a radio program, esp. an arduous rehearsal. 1945: "What a woodshed!" CBS *Listeners' Guide. Radio use since c1935. v.i.,v.t.* To work, practice, or play alone; to seek quiet or solitude. 1956: "Bix [Beiderbecke] did plenty of wood-shedding, playing alone, to some recording on the family Victrola." S. Longstreet, *The Real Jazz Old and New*, 101. *From the archaic and rural image of the woodshed as the place where a boy could retire to smoke or otherwise occupy himself without detection.*

woody *adj.* Insane, esp. from drinking inferior whisky, or from long drug addiction. *Not common. Perh. from wood alcohol (methanol or methyl alcohol).*

woof *v.i.* To talk foolishly or aimlessly. *Usu. used in the negative = to talk sense or to the point.* 1941: "I ain't woofin'. I'm not fooling." *Life*, Jan. 27, 78. 1945: "You ain't just a-woofin'." Riordan in *Calif. Folk. Quart.*, Oct., 19. *Orig. jive use, from the sound of a dog's barking, c1935; mainly student use, though common in Armed Forces during W.W.II. v.t.* To eat rapidly. *Always in "to woof one's food." Colloq.* **—er** *n.* **1** One who woofs habitually. *Some c1935 jive use.* **2** A breathy singer; a singer whose breathing can be heard through a microphone. *Radio use.* **3** A small paper-cone speaker that vibrates electromagnetically to reproduce low frequencies without distortion, used in addition to other speaker in a high-fidelity phonograph or sound-reproducing system. *Common hi-fi enthusiast use since c1950.* Cf. **tweeter.**

woof-hound *n.* A swing-music fan. *Some c1935 jitterbug use.*

woofits *n.pl.* A hangover. *Never common.*

woofled *adj.* Drunk. 1945: "The former boxing champ, once an idol, woofled nightly and looking for trouble. . . ." W. Winchell, *synd. newsp. col.*, Nov. 20.

woofle water Whisky. *Never common.*

woof-woof *n.* A battalion sergeant major. *Some W.W.II Army use. Because a sergeant major barks commands.*

wool *v.t.* To beat or thrash severely. 1845: *DAE. Obs. by c1900. n.* The hair on any human head. **—lies —ies** *n.pl.* **1** = **willies. 2** Wool underwear, esp. men's woolen underwear with long sleeves and legs. *Since this item is considered old-fashioned and rustic by most youths and city dwellers, the word is most often used in a jocular way.* **—ly —y** *n.* **1** [derog.] A Negro. See **woolly-head. 2** A sheep.

woolly-head [derog.] *n.* A Negro. *Since c1825.*

woolly loco See **loco weeds.**

wool over [one's] eyes, pull the To deceive a person. *Colloq. since c1900.*

woo-woo! *interj.* An expression of approval of an attractive girl. *Pop. by the movie comedian Hugh Herbert; archaic. Replaced by the wolf whistle.*

woozily *adv.* In a woozy manner. 1940: "I balanced myself woozily on the flat of my hands." Chandler, *Farewell*, 52. 1952: "When [the elephant] tottered woozily off a plane from Tripoli. . . ." AP, Feb. 23.

woozle *v.i., v.t.* To confuse; to exaggerate; to misrepresent; to talk or write vaguely. *Not common.*

woozle water Whisky. 1949: "Despite the enormous quantities of woozle-water he consumed, he never let his audience down." Billy Rose, *synd. newsp. col.*, Nov. 18. *Not common.*

woozy wuzzy *adj.* **1** Mentally befogged, dazed; confused. 1924: "Come on to bed. You'll just get woozy if you stay up any longer." Marks, *Plastic Age*, 107. 1940: " . . . Still woozy from that crack on the head." Chandler, *Farewell*, 63. 1944: "Some woozy tourist." Fowler, *Good Night*, 169. *Common since c1890.* **2** Drunk. 1908: *DAE.* 1941: "I was feeling pretty woozy from all that liquor." Schulberg, *Sammy*, 58. **3** Uncouth; acting in an impolite, irrational manner. *Some c1915 student use.* **4** Psychologically uncomfortable; affected by eeriness or weirdness. *Since c1930.* **5** Dizzy, faint. *Colloq.*

wop Wop *n.* **1** An uncouth, ill-bred, aggressive person. *Some c1910 use. Obs.* → **2** [derog.] An Italian or person, usu. male, of Italian descent. 1924: "He decided that he looked like a 'blond wop.'" Marks, *Plastic Age,* 193. 1937 [1954]: "And why don't you turn that skinny old Nick loose, and put a young wop in his place!" Pietro di Donato, *Christ in Concrete,* reprinted in *Manhattan,* ed. by S. Krim, 138. 1951: "A master-sergeant from Brooklyn, half-wop and half-Mick." 1957: "I'm a wop from San Marino. . . ." Tennessee Williams, *Orpheus Descending,* I. 1958: "I've met wops and they're not greasy." H. E. F. Donohue, "Gentlemen's Game," *Harper's,* Mar., 65. *Since c1915; became common during the 1920's, during which time it usu. implied an illiterate Italian immigrant working as a day laborer. As do many such derog. terms, this appeared freq. in plays, the dramatist using it for shock effect. Thus it is used in the following successful plays of the 1920's: O'Neill's* Hairy Ape, *1922; Hecht & MacArthur's* Front Page, *1928; Elmer Rice's* Street Scene, *1928; and Sturges'* Strictly Dishonorable, *1929. From the Sp. "guapo" = a tough, brave man, through Sicilian "guappo." According to a letter from Joseph Vesley, 1957, the Italians themselves now use the word "guappo" in a derog. sense to mean Sicilian. The word "wop" is usu. not cap.* Cf. **dago.** → **3** [derog.] Any foreigner, except an Englishman, Frenchman, or German; esp. an unskilled laborer from Southern Europe, specif., a Greek. → **4** [derog.] The Italian language. 1932: "The wop yelling very loud, and maybe cussing us in wop for all I know." D. Runyon. Cf. **dago. 5** Time, less than a month, served by a prisoner. *Some c1925 underworld use. adj.* [derog.] Italian. 1941: "Big wop tenor." Cain, *M. Pierce,* 217.

wop-stick wopstick *n.* A clarinet. 1956: " . . . Words that the jazzmen don't use much, but which most people think are real jazz words . . . *wop-stick* for clarinet. . . ." S. Longstreet, *The Real Jazz Old and New,* 150. *Synthetic jazz use. Because clarinets are supposed to be favored by Italian musicians.* See **wop.** Cf. **licorice stick.**

Worcestershire *n.* A rifle. *Cowboy use c1875.* See **Winchester.**

work *n.* See **dirty work, shoot the works.**

work [one's] bolt To talk idly. *c1935 Army use. From the practice operating of an unloaded rifle.*

workhouse *n.* A ship. *Maritime use.*

Workie *n.* A member of any political party with a strong labor following or an overt connection with labor unions, called a "Workingman's Party." 1830 [1950]: "On the eve of the 1830's, spontaneous Workingman's parties had sprung up. 'Workie' leaders . . . were frank apostles of inevitable class warfare." W. H. Hale, *Horace Greeley,* 36. *Obs.*

workout *n.* **1** A party. *Student use c1925; obs.* **2** A beating. 1930: "The same gangster will either whimper or scream with fear when the 'workout' begins." Lavine, *Third Degree,* 5. *Underworld and prison use.* **3** A task, game, or exercise that tests endurance; a task that leaves one exhausted.

work over To beat someone, usu. in order to gain information or in retaliation; to rough up someone.

works, gum up the To ruin something, as a job or chance of success or making a good impression; to fail to take full advantage of one's opportunity; to commit a *faux pas.*

works, the *n.* **1** Everything available; the complete operation available as part of a service; a complete account. 1939: "Potatoes and salad and red beets, etc. Also butter and bread. The works." O'Hara, *Pal Joey,* 37. 1952: "Verne, the barber, gave them the works—shave, haircut, massage, and tonic." H. Boyle, AP, Aug. 9. *Common since c1930.* See **shoot the works.** *Widely used to mean many different things in many contexts; thus in lunch-counter parlance "the works" are all the possible condiments and trimmings on a hamburger or hot dog; in garage use it means all possible accessories for an automobile; in a restaurant "the works" is a full course meal; in a barbershop "the works" is a haircut, shave, shampoo, manicure, shoe shine, and any other available service.* **2** A killing, beating, roughing up. See **give [someone] the works. 3** Sexual intercourse, esp. if extremely varied or satisfying. *Some use c1935–c1945; obs.*

work the growler = **rush the growler.**

work the stem To beg on the streets. *Hobo use.* Cf. **stem.**

world *n.* See **around the world, dead to the world, out of this world, tell the (cockeyed) world.**

world, out of the = **out of this world.** 1948: "It tasted out of the world." F. Brown, *Dead Ringer*, 38. *Not common.*

world, out of this Perfect; extremely beautiful, moving, etc.; wonderful; too good to be true; extremely happy; heavenly. 1921: "She had a figure which was out of this world." Witwer, *Leather*, 94. 1953: "Even the Songs [in the movie *Peter Pan*] Are Out of This World!" *Nationally circulated newsp. advt.*, Apr.

world-beater *n.* A champion. 1893: *DAE.* 1940: "Sometimes I think you're a world-beater." Chandler, *Farewell*, 158. *Colloq.*

worm *n.* 1 A disliked, untrustworthy fellow; a cad, a deceiver. *Colloq.* 2 Stolen silk. *Underworld use c1925.* *v.t.* To cache. 1925: "When loot is cached it is 'wormed.'" McLellan in *Collier's*, Aug. 8. *Obs. underworld use.* *v.i.* To study. *Some jive use since c1935.* **—s** *n.pl.* Macaroni or spaghetti. *Some student and Armed Forces use since c1925.*

worm out of To retreat or withdraw from a difficult situation; to renege on a promise or obligation; fig., to crawl or sneak away from a problem or distasteful duty.

worry, I [one] should "I don't care." "I have no reason for alarm or concern." "I am not concerned." *Colloq.*

worry wart One who worries excessively and unnecessarily; a brooder; an introvert.

wow *n.* 1 Any remarkable and exciting person or thing; often used as a one-word comment showing awareness of or appreciation of a remarkable thing or person, esp. a sexually attractive girl. 1921: "It would be a wow of a scrap [prize fight]." Witwer, *Leather*, 78f. 1929: " 'She was born bad.' . . . A wow of a line!" K. Brush, *Young Man*, 29. *Since c1925.* → 2 A sensational or striking success, usu. said of popular entertainment or entertainers. *Common since c1935; orig. a theater term.* 3 A slow, wavering tone resulting from imperfect sound reproducing equipment, as a phonograph turntable that revolves unevenly. *Used by high-fidelity enthusiasts since c1950.* *v.t.* To elicit enthusiastic approval, esp. from an audience. 1929: "Success makes the actor jubilant. He 'wows 'em.'" B. Sobel. 1945: "The young university-bound Wisconsinite . . . wondering if he'll make a fraternity and whether or not he'll wow the girls." G. S. Perry in *SEP*, Jan. 5, 23/1-2. *Since c1925.* **—dow** *n.* A dancing party; a party;

any instance or period of excitement, confusion, or pleasure. *Associated with 1920 use; archaic.* *adj.* = **wow.**

wowser *n.* A formal person; a killjoy; a stuffed shirt. 1928: "Men of letters, who would swoon at the sight of a split infinitive, such wowsers they are in regard to pure English, will in conversation address you as 'Old thing' . . ." R. Lynd in *New Statesman*, Feb. 4. *From the Australian sl. use, where orig., c1890, a "wowser" = a prohibitionist or a missionary.*

—wrangler See Appendix, Suffixes and Suffix Words.

wrap it up 1 To conclude any task or operation successfully. 2 To strike the winning blow, fig., in a contest or competition.

wrap-up *n.* 1 A customer who buys readily. 1952: "The ideal customer is known as a 'wrap-up,' which is self-explanatory." G. Millstein in N.Y. *Times Mag.*, Sept. 21, 58/3. *Retail salesman use since c1930.* → 2 An easy sale. → 3 An inferior item wrapped or sealed before it is purchased by a customer, then misrepresented as a better item by the salesman. *Since c1935.* → 4 Any item sold to the customer before he sees it, esp. items purchased by mail, by sending in money to radio and television advertisers, and the like. *Advertising, radio, and television use since c1950.* → 5 Fig., any easy task; anything at which one's success is assured; a certainty, a sure thing, a cinch; said of a task or sports contest. → 6 Fig., a packaging; a presentation of several things as though packaged. 7 A conclusion, an ending; a summary and conclusion. 1951: "This is the 11:30 P.M. wrap-up of the news." NBC radio.

wreath *n.* Cabbage. *Some c1935 lunch-counter use.*

wreck *n.* 1 A dilapidated vehicle, as an automobile. → 2 A person who is fatigued, indisposed, dissipated, or the like. *Colloq. since c1930.* *v.t.* 1 To scramble eggs. *Lunch-counter use, used in relaying a customer's order, e.g., "Wreck two."* 2 To change a banknote into coins of equivalent value. 1937: "Wreck a buck." *Variety*, Sept. 27, 63. → 3 To spend an amount of money quickly, esp. for a good time.

wren *n.* A girl or woman. *Since c1925; not as common as "chick."*

wrestle *n.* A dance. *Dial.* *v.i.* To dance. *Some jocular student use since c1925, but mainly found in stories and* *articles about teenagers. Thus mainly synthetic.*

—wrestler   See Appendix, Suffixes and Suffix Words.

wringer   *n.* See **finger-wringer, put [someone] through the wringer.**

wringer, put [someone] through the 1 To try someone severely; to subject someone to an exhausting period of questioning. **2 = put the heat on [someone].**

wring-jaw   *n.* Hard cider. *c1800–c1850; obs.*

wrinkle   *n.* **1** The mother of one's sweetheart. *Synthetic use c1920.* **2** Style or fashion. *Usu. in phrase, "the latest wrinkle."* **3** An ingenious or unusual idea, method, or approach to a problem. *Usu. in "That's a new wrinkle."*

wrinkle-rod   *n.* A crankshaft. *Factory use since c1940. Now hot-rod use.*

wrist-slapper   *n.* An effeminate or affected youth or man; a goody-goody. 1913: "He was one of those mushy-looking, soft-spoken, biscuit-haired, white-livered, young wrist-slappers; with a complexion as ruddy as a pail of lard." F. K. Sechrist. Cf. **slap [someone's] wrist.**

writ   *n.* A written examination. *West Point use.*

write-in   *adj.* Written on a ballot at the time of voting; said of a candidate's name that does not appear on the prepared ballot.

write-up   *n.* A written account or article, as in a newspaper, esp. a written account or review of a product, celebrity, entertainment, or the like. 1885: *DAE.* 1939: "I figure you have seen the write-ups." O'Hara, *Pal Joey*, 3.

wrong   *adj.* **1** Contrary to the underworld code. *Criminal use since c1925.* **2** Not trustworthy; dishonest; habitually or congenitally criminal. 1949: "... You're guilty the second that spotlight hits you 'cause you're a wrong guy in a wrong neighborhood out at the wrong hour." N. Algren, *Man with the Golden Arm*, 26.   *n.* An informer. *Some underworld use.*

wrong number   **1** A mistaken idea or concept. **2** A psychopath; a dangerous person. **3** A dishonest or untrustworthy person. See **wrong.** *All meanings from the stand. phrase for a wrong connection on a telephone circuit.*

wrong side of [the] bed, get up on the To be in a bad mood or in bad temper; to be peevish or fretful. *Usu. in "You must have got up on the wrong side of bed this morning."*

wuzzy   *adj.* **1** Mean; contrary. *Dial. since c1875.* **2** Confused; faint; woozy.

X

X   *n.* **1** A signature. *Colloq. From the ancient custom of allowing illiterates to sign documents with a cross, thus signifying their obligation under God to carry out the terms of the agreement; the cross eventually degenerated into an "x."* **2** The common written symbol for a kiss, usu. put at the bottom of a letter. *Colloq.* **3** An unknown person, esp. one who wishes to conceal his identity; a criminal boss; Mr. Big. See **x.**   **x**   *n.* **1** Any unknown quantity. *A stand. math. symbol.* → **2** Any unknown or untried factor that may influence the outcome of a business venture, sports contest, or the like.

x-factor   *n.* = **x.**

x marks the spot   A common expression meaning, fig., "That is where it is" or "That is the place where something is located, even though not actually marked with an 'x.' "

x out   **1** Lit., to delete words from a written contract by typing "x's" over them; to erase or delete any material from a written document. **2** To cancel, to nullify.

XX = double-cross. 1939–40: "I know you gave me the XX...." O'Hara, *Pal Joey*, 64.

Y

—y   —ie   See Appendix, —ie, —y, Suffixes and Suffix Words.

yack = yak.

yackety-yak   yakitty-yak   *n.* Use-

less, voluble talk; stupid chatter; gab. 1949: "... If [the State Department] would stop its incessant yakitty-yak...." Rep. Clevenger, quoted by AP, Apr. 6.

v.i. To talk too much; to talk loudly, volubly, or stupidly. See Appendix, Reduplications. *More common than "yak-yak."*

ya(c)k-ya(c)k   ya(c)k-ya(c)k-ya(c)k *n.* Talk; esp. idle talk, gossip. 1946: "... All they can talk about ... yack-yack-yack is their own specialty." AP, Jan. 9.   *v.i., v.t.* To talk; esp. idly or ineffectually; to gossip. 1950: "Neither is [spanking] worse than the practice of sparing the rod and yak-yakking and explaining all the time. . . ." AP, Aug. 3. 1956: "... Everybody is yakking out an opinion on whether he [Dwight Eisenhower] should now reconsider his candidacy [for a second presidential term]. . . ." "Science, Sickness, and Character." *Life,* editorial, June 18, 56. See Appendix, Reduplications. *Not as common as "yackety-yak."*

yaffle *v.t.* To steal. *Dial. and some maritime use.*

yaffner *n.* A dishonest, untrustworthy, sneaky person. *Some c1935 Negro use.*

yak   yack   yock   yuk   yuck *n.* **1** A friend or pal, esp. one who can be depended upon or used. *Some underworld use.* **2** A stupid or innocent person; a dope; a rustic. 1943: "[Yuck] now means a dope of any description." H. A. Smith, *Putty Knife,* 156. *Since c1920; made somewhat pop. by the comedian Fred Allen.* See **yop.** **3** A watch. *Some underworld use.* **4** A laugh, esp. a deep, long laugh; more esp. a laugh produced in an audience by a professional entertainer. 1949: "It makes me furious when I have a corny line and it gets a yock." Comedienne Eve Arden, quoted in *N.Y. Times,* Sept. 4, 7/6. **5** A joke, esp. a very funny joke.   *v.i., v.t.* **1** To talk; to chat, gossip, or banter. 1951: "The students were seated on the floor, still yocking away." M. Shulman, *Dobie Gillis,* 76. *Usu. "yak," often reduplicated.* See **yak-yak, yackety-yak.** **2** To laugh. 1951: "There'd be Don, yockin' it up like crazy ... he's so hysterical with laughter." A. Kober in *New Yorker,* May 12, 32/3.

yam *v.i., v.t.* **1** To eat. *Negro use; archaic. From "yam," a staple in the diet of slaves.* **2** To talk too much. *Not common. From "yammer."*   **—mer** *v.i.* To talk vociferously; to complain, whine, nag, etc.   *n.* Talk, esp. idle or nagging talk.

yan *n.* = **yannigan.**   **—nigan** *n.* A professional baseball player; esp.

a young inexperienced athlete who has just joined a team; a crude or uncouth baseball player. *Baseball use. From "yannigan bag."*

yang *n.* **1** A hurry. *Dial. Obs.* **2** [taboo] The penis.

Yank *n.* **1** A citizen of the U.S. c1847 [1956]: "... With half a dozen armed men, inquiring after the 'Yank' and swearing to have his life. . . ." Samuel E. Chamberlain, "My Confession," *Life,* July 23. *From the now stand.* "Yankee." **2** A United States soldier. *Orig. W.W.I use from Brit. sl.*   **yank** *v.t.* **1** To arrest. 1891 [1894]: "The bulls ... don't care to yank a tramp unless they have to." J. Flynt. **2** To relieve a person of his duties because he has failed to produce satisfactory results.   **—ee** *v.t.* To cheat; to deceive someone. *c1800–c1865; obs.*

yannigan bag A home-made or carpet bag in which loggers, prospectors, and traveling performers used to carry their possessions. *Obs.*

yap *n.* **1** A stupid, inferior, or contemptible person; a boob or sap. 1903: "He's a yap." E. Conradi, 372. 1929: "Just a no-account yap. . . ." Burnett, *Little Caesar,* 177. *c1900; archaic since c1930. From "yok."* **2** A rustic; a farmer. *Some c1900 hobo use.* **3** The victim of a criminal undertaking, esp. a pickpocket's victim. *Some underworld use since c1920.* **4** The mouth, considered only as the organ of speech. 1937: "Every time you open your yap to say something. . . ." Weidman, *Wholesale,* 7. 1952: "And if you open your yap once more, I'll jug you!" Fagaly & Shorten, "There Oughta Be a Law!" *synd. newsp. cartoon,* Feb. 2. *The most common use. Since c1900.* Cf. **blow off [one's] yap.** **5** A request; a complaint.   *v.i.* **1** To talk, esp. to talk idly or without thought; to nag; to gossip. 1937: "You've been yapping away. . . ." Weidman, *Wholesale,* 19. 1958: "He would come home with a little jag on, yapping in a phony cheerful way. . . ." H. E. F. Donohue, "Gentlemen's Game," *Harper's,* Mar., 60. **2** To complain; to protest.

yap, open [one's] See **yap.**

Yarborough *n.* In card games, a worthless or losing hand.

yard *n.* **1** A $100 bill; the sum of $100. 1929: "'How much?' 'Five yards. He wanted a grand at first. I beat him down.'" Dunning & Abbott, *Broadway,* I. *Orig. underworld use; since c1920; obs.* **2** A $1,000 bill; the sum of $1,000.

Underworld use since c1930, replacing first meaning.

—yard   See Appendix, Suffixes and Suffix Words.

yard bird   yardbird   *n.* **1** In the Army, a raw recruit; a rookie. *Army use. Because recruits are confined to camp during their basic training.* **2** A soldier, sailor, or marine who freq. is punished for violations of regulations, such punishment usu. being confinement to camp and assignment to duty of cleaning the parade ground or yard; a soldier assigned to manual labor or menial chores. *Armed Forces use.* **3** An infantryman; any soldier. *Some newsp. use.* **4** A prisoner, a convict. *The great jazz musician Charlie "Yardbird" Parker was nicknamed when he served a prison sentence for narcotics addiction; later the name was shortened to "The Bird" and many references to it occur in cool and bop usage during late 1940's and early 1950's; cf., for instance, the many jazz compositions entitled "Ornithology" or variants thereof and the famous N.Y.C. night club called "Birdland."* 1956: "A yardbird is a low mug...." S. Longstreet, *The Real Jazz Old and New,* 148. *The most common use. Because most prisons are built around yards where prisoners exercise. Cf.* **jailbird.**

yard bull   1 A railroad guard or detective assigned to duty in a freight yard. **2** A prison guard. See **bull.**

yard dog   A mean or uncouth person.

yard goat   A railroad switching engine. *Railroad use.* See **hog.**

yard goose   A railroad switchman. *Railroad use.* Cf. **yard goat, yardpig.**

yard hack = **yard bull.** *Some prison use.*

yard patrol   1 The prisoners in a jail; a prisoner in a jail; a yardbird. **2** The police who patrol a jail; a prison guard.

yardpig   1 A railroad switching engine. 1951: "It was a short, heavy work train, with what they called a yardpig for an engine, hooked on backwards for better traction." S. Longstreet, *The Pedlocks,* 119. **2** = **yardbird.**

yatata yatata   Monotonous talk; idle chatter.   *v.i.* To talk idly and at length. 1947: "Mustn't yatata yatata yatata in the public library." W. Saroyan, *Jim Dandy,* 10.

yatter   *n.* Talk; chatter. 1952: "The yatter against a military man in the White House...." *Time,* Jan. 21, 15/3. *v.i.* To talk loquaciously or inanely.

yawp   yaup   *n.* Foolish talk. 1835:

"yaup," *DAE.* 1884: "yawp," *DAE. Obs. by c1910.   v.i.* To talk loudly. 1872: *DAE. Obs. by c1910.*

yea big   yea high   1 This big, or this high, accompanied with the spreading of the hands to indicate the size; very large or high, overwhelmingly large or tall. **2** Not very big or high. *A sophisticated fad phrase since c1955.*

yea bo   *adv.* Yes. 1927: "*Yebo,* with *e* pronounced as in *they,* is the Zulu word for *yes.* . . . It is . . . easy to recognize the Zulu *yebo* in the *yea bo* of our streets." S. V. Byington, *AS,* 332. *In vogue c1925–c1930. Obs.*

yeah   *adv.* Yes. 1939: "Don't say 'yeah.' It's common." Chandler, *Big Sleep,* 134. *Colloq.* See Appendix, Corruptions.

year   *n.* A banknote; a dollar. Thus "5 years" = a $5 bill or five dollars. *Orig. underworld use.*   **—ling**   *n.* **1** At West Point, one who has begun his second year of studies. 1944: "His femme fell for a [West Point] yearling." C. Macon in *Collier's,* Sept. 23, 69/1. Cf. **plebe.** **2** An Army draftee or recruit. *Some use immediately before W.W.II when the Selective Service law required only one year's duty. Obs.*

yegg   *n.* **1** A safe-blower, orig. an itinerant one. *Orig. hobo, then underworld, use; now in common use but shunned by underworld. Said to be from John Yegg, traditionally the first safecracker to employ nitroglycerine.* **2** Any thief who travels as a hobo, using the freights. *Hobo use.* **3** Any thief.

Yehuda   *n.* A Jew. *From the Arabic* "*yahudi*" = *Jew. The plural is* "*Yehudim." Not derog.; used almost exclusively by Jews.*

yellow   *adj.* **1** Cowardly. *Since c1850. Colloq.* **2** [derog.] Describing a light-complexioned Negro. 1955: "You know that baker we hired. The yellow boy.... This nigger received some kind of education." C. Willingham, *To Eat a Peach,* 141f.   *n.* **1** Cowardice. 1896: *DAE.* **2** [derog.] A Negro, esp. a light-skinned Negress. **3** A gold watch. *Hobo use; archaic.* **4** Butter. *Not common.*   **—ness**   *n.* Cowardice. 1951: "I hate fist fights. I don't mind getting hit so much—although I'm not crazy about it, naturally—but what scares me most in a fist fight is the guy's face. I can't stand looking at the other guy's face, is my trouble. It wouldn't be so bad if you could both be blindfolded or something. It's a funny kind of yellowness, when you come to

think of it, but it's yellowness, all right."
J. D. Salinger, *Catcher in the Rye*, 70.
yellow-back   *n.* A banknote; specif.,
a gold certificate. 1930: "Uncle Sam's
yellowbacks will act as an open sesame.
..." Lavine, *Third Degree*, 222. *Obs.*
See **greenback**.
yellow-bellied   *adj.* Cowardly. 1924:
"Yellow-bellied quitters." Marks, *Plastic
Age*, 75. 1945: "You, you yellow-bellied
jerk." Mitchell, *McSorley's*, 25. c1847
[1956]: "... I will serve the yellow-
bellied Mexicans the same. ..." Samuel
E. Chamberlain, "My Confession," *Life*,
July 23. *Most common among adolescents
and young students.*
yellow-belly   *n.* A coward. See **yellow**.
yellow boy   1 A gold coin. 1809: *DAE.*
Obs. by c1900. 2 = **yellow-back**.
yellow dog   An inferior or worthless
person or thing. *Some use since c1900.*
yellow dog contract   A contract
required by employers of prospective
employees forbidding them to join a
union. 1956: "The American frontier
incubated vivid word-making. ... From
this source came ... phrases like 'yellow
dog contract,' which has been echoed by
the U.S. Supreme Court in precedent-
making decisions. It means a pledge,
now illegal, that employees, before being
hired, had to sign binding themselves
not to join a union." *Labor's Special
Lang. from Many Sources.*
yellow girl   A mulatto girl or woman;
a light-skinned Negress, esp. if sexually
attractive. *Since c1865; both Negro and
white use.*
yellow jacket   A Nembutal (trade
mark) capsule. *Orig. narcotic addict use.*
yellow-leg   *n.* A U.S. Army cavalryman. *From c1890 to W.W.I; obs.*
yen   *n.* A strong craving, yearning, or
desire; a habit. 1930: "He's got a yen
for faro. ..." "A strong yen for your
woman." Burnett, *Iron Man*, 156, 180.
1951: "If I had not ... had a yen to put
on paper what I was saying in class. ..."
R. P. Basler in A.A.U.P. *Bulletin*, Aut.,
587. *Orig. West Coast and hobo use. From
the Chinese word for opium. Cf.* **yen-shee**.
v.i. To desire; to crave. 1950: "I've
yenned to own a Rolls Royce." Billy
Rose, *synd. newsp. col.*, Aug. 7. *Perhaps
reinforced by stand. "yearn."*
yenems   *n.* Another's possession freely
offered; *freq.* used jocularly in reference
to cigarettes: "My brand of cigarettes is
yenems" = whatever brand someone
offers me. *Transliterated Yiddish.*
yen-hok   **yen-hook**   *n.* The

implement used in preparing opium for
smoking and putting it into the pipe.
Opium addict use.
yen-shee   *n.* 1 Opium, as used by
addicts; *orig.* the cake of opium "dottle"
at the bottom of a smoked opium pipe.
1947: "Lin [pleaded] that he be allowed
his daily pipe of 'yen-shee.' ..." A.
Meyers, *San Fran. Murders*, 255. *Opium
addict use; universally known. From the
Chinese word for opium.* → 2 Heroin.
Some addict use.
yentz   *v.t.* To cheat; to fleece. 1930:
"They try to yentz me out of my end."
Amer. Mercury, Dec., 458. 1952: "Yentz-
ing a business friend." M. Lipsius, *SEP*,
Feb. 23, 145/3. *From the Yiddish.*
v.i. To fornicate. *Not common.* **—er**
n. A cheater; one who cannot be trusted.
yen-yen   *n.* A strong craving for
narcotic drugs; *lit.*, a "yen" for "yen-
shee" or another drug. *Some addict use.*
See Appendix, Reduplications.
yep   *adv.* Yes. *Colloq. since c1840.*
—pir   yepper   *adv.* Yes, sir. 1945:
"Yeppir, we have these scarce ... wools."
Advt., Phila. *Bulletin*, Oct. 25, 9. *Not
common.*
yesca   *n.* Marijuana, as taken by
addicts. *Addict use.*
yes-girl   *n.* A sexually compliant
young woman. 1929: "Just a yes-girl!"
K. Brush, *Young Man*, 32.
yes-man   *n.* An employee whose main
function is to endorse his superior's
decisions and opinions; an acquiescent
subordinate; an ass-kisser. 1951: "Joe
Davies, Roosevelt's yes-man at the
Kremlin...." W. Pegler, *synd. newsp.
col.*, Aug. 14. *Orig. c1925 prob. in Hollywood where the term was early used to mean
an assistant director.*
yesterday, today, and forever   Hash.
Lunch-counter use, *usu.* jocular. *Implies
that one pot of hash is maintained, to
which each day's leftovers are added ad
infinitum.*
yet   *adv.* 1 Sometimes used after a
gerund that is preceded by "still";
a redundant use which adds emphasis,
immediacy, or impatience to the sentence. Thus "He's still sleeping yet."
2 = **already**.
Yid   yid   *n.* [derog.] A Jew. 1951:
"At Princeton, when some boy was not
admitted to a secret society ... because
he was a 'Yid' or ... had ... Jewish
blood. ..." S. Longstreet, *The Pedlocks*,
149. *From the Yiddish "yid" = Jew,
universally known since c1910. Cf.* **Hebe.**
ying-yang   [taboo]   *n.* The penis.

Sophisticated jocular use, referring to the Hindu symbol of continuity and fertility.

yippie *n.* A yard or harbor patrol craft. *W.W.II USN use. From the initials "Y.P."* Cf. **yard patrol.**

yock *n.* = **yak.**

yockydock *n.* Narcotics. 1956: "Whisky's bad enough. But this fink's on the old yockydock." J. Cannon, *Who Struck John?* 202. *Not common.*

yodeler *n.* **1** In baseball, a third-base coach. *Some baseball use. Because the third-base coach shouts instructions to baserunners.* **2** An informer; a criminal who gives information to the police. Cf. **sing.**

yok *n.* **1** A laugh, esp. a long, loud laugh. **2** A joke, esp. a very funny joke. *v.i.* To laugh, esp. to laugh loud and long. See **yak.**

yoot *n.* A teenage hoodlum; a member of a teenage street gang; a juvenile delinquent. 1957: "Cop Shot; 3 Yoots* Held. [Headline]. . . . (* Yoot: a young punk; a juvenile no-goodnik.)" N.Y. *World Telegram and Sun,* Aug. 16. *Synthetic. From a corruption of "youth," perhaps with the "oo" of "hood" or "zoot suit."*

yop *n.* A rude, vulgar fellow. 1887: "The yops." New Orleans *Lantern. Obs.* Cf. **yap.**

you bet Sure(ly); certainly; an expression of affirmation. *Colloq. since c1870.*

you bet you = **you bet.**

You can say that again = **You said it.**

you-know-what *n.* Anything so obvious from the context that it need not be named; specif., money or sex.

you (one) know what you (one) can do with it (something) = **shove it (something) up your (one's) ass** [taboo]. *This is the only nontaboo form of the expression.*

young *adj.* Small. 1932: "What does she have in her hand but a young base-

ball bat. . . ." D. Runyon, 161. 1940: "Anyone who wins on that play may make a young fortune." D. W. Maurer, *The Big Con,* 267. *Used often to qualify a hyperbole.* **—ster** *n.* A second-year cadet at the U.S. Naval Academy.

young horse Roast beef. *Some prison, student, and Army use.*

Your Aunt Mitty! An exclam. of derision or disbelief. *Pop. c1890; obs.*

Your mother wears Army boots! An exclam. of derision. *Orig. a strong W.W.II term of derision; now mainly jocular.*

yours (his, hers, etc.**), get** To get punished; to be found out; to fail. *Usu. implying that the punishment or failure will be deserved.* See **get [one's] lumps.**

yours truly I; me; the speaker or writer. 1912: Johnson, *Stover at Yale,* 353.

You said it Emphatically yes; "I agree with you"; "You are right."

yo-yo *n.* A compromising person; one whose political opinions and ideas change as necessary for personal gain; a free-loader. 1947: "One of the yo-yo boys sitting next to me. . . ." H. Boyle, *synd. newsp. col.,* May 19. *From the toy that winds and unwinds in a vacillating manner.*

yuck yuk = **yak.**

yuk-yuk *n.* Empty, idle, or stupid talk. 1947: "In the midst of all the political yuk-yuk that dins around us, there is a young man who is fighting . . . a campaign for common sense." N.Y. *Times Bk. Rev.,* Dec. 7, 35/3. See Appendix, Reduplications.

yum yum-yum *exclam.* An expression signifying delight, usu. in ref. to a specif. sensory perception, as of taste, smell, etc. **yum-yum** *n.* **1** Food. *Baby talk.* **2** Sweets. *Used by young children.* **—my** *adj.* **1** Delicious. *Orig. baby talk, in vogue c1930 and again c1955.* → **2** Good, satisfactory, pleasing, attractive. *Mainly schoolgirl use.*

Z

zagger *n.* A cheap watch. *Jewelry salesman use.*

zaks *n.pl.* Trousers having narrow cuffs and often extremely tapered, as worn by teenagers. *Not common.*

zam *n.* An examination. *Some c1915 student use.* See Appendix, Shortened Words.

zap *v.t.* To kill. *Never common.*

zazoo *n.* A fellow; a guy. 1948: "The bediamonded stranger gazed . . . incredulously. When the Swiss gustily attacked his soup, the 'zazoo' angrily departed. . . ." E. Snow, *SEP,* Feb. 14, 12.

zazzle *n.* Sex appeal, esp. in an

exaggerated degree. 1950: "They've got zazzle! It starts where sex appeal stops." *Movie advt.*, "Free for All." *Orig. Negro use.*

zazzy *adj.* Sexually attractive. *Some c1940 student use. Prob. variant from "jazzy."*

zebra *n.* **1** A convict. *From the traditional striped uniform worn by prisoners. Never common.* **2** A non-commissioned Army officer. *Some W.W.II Army use. From the chevrons designating noncommissioned rank.*

Zelda *n.* A female square. *Some cool and beat use since c1950.*

Zen hipster *n.* A hipster or esp. a member of the beat generation who adheres to Zen Buddhism. 1958: "In recent years some have taken to calling themselves Zen Hipsters, and Zen Buddhism has spread like the Asian flu, so that now you can open your fortune cookie in one of the real cool Chinese restaurants in San Francisco and find a slip of paper with the straight poop: 'Dig that crazy Zen sukiyaki. Only a square eats Chinese food.' " Herbert Gold, *The Beat Mystique*, 86.

Zepp *n.* A Zeppelin. *Orig. W.W.I Army use.* See Appendix, Shortened Words.

zero hour **1** The exact time at which a planned action begins, usu. in ref. to military operations. *W.W.II use.* → **2** An appointed, dangerous, or critical time.

Zex! *interj.* = **Cheese it!**

zib *n.* A stupid person with unknown political or personal opinions; a nondescript nincompoop. *Not common.*

zig(g)abo(o) *n.* = **jigaboo.**

ziggetty! *exclam.* = **hot diggity-dam!** 1944: " 'Ziggetty!' he said." Shulman, *Feather Merchants*, 90.

zig-zag *n.* A Naval executive officer. *Some archaic USN use. From his striped sleeve insignia.* *adj.* Drunk. *Some W.W.I Army use.*

zig-zig *n.* Sexual intercourse. *One of several reduplications = coitus that were fairly common with W.W.II Armed Forces, usu. from folk etymologies of native terms in occupied territories.* See Appendix, Reduplications. *v.i.* To have sexual intercourse.

zilch *n.* Gibberish; double talk; meaningless language. *Never common.*

zillion *n.* An exceedingly large indeterminate number; a larger number than can be imagined. 1952: "A zillion dollars. That's a million trillion." Movie,

Monkey Business. **—aire** *n.* One who has a zillion dollars; a person whose wealth is of mythical proportions.

zing *n.* **1** Vitality, zest, animation; pep. 1945: "With plenty of zing in both the . . . V-8 engine and the powerful Six." Advt. for Ford automobiles, Phila. *Bulletin*, 32. *Since W.W.I.* **2** A veto; a blackball; a vote against, or a dismissal or rejection. 1935: "His newspaper will give him the heave-o as soon as Fergus gets the opportunity to drop the zing on him. . . ." D. Runyon, 267. *Never common.* *adj.* Chic; attractive; appealing. **—y** *adj.* Having zing; full of energy or ambition. *Mainly adolescent use.*

zings, the *n.pl.* **1** The unpleasant aftereffect of excessive drinking; a hangover; the shakes. **2** = **heebie-jeebies.** *Neither meaning common.*

zip *n.* **1** A mark or grade of zero. *Student use c1900; archaic.* **2** Vitality; vim; energy; zing. 1948: "There is a zip and a zing here. . . ." Lait-Mortimer, *N.Y. Confidential*, 11. *Colloq.* **3** Syrup; molasses. *Dial.* **4** Sugar. *Dial.* *v.i., v.t.* To shut up. *From "zip(per) your lip."* **—po** *n.* Zip; zing; vim. 1942: "[Songsters] were grinding out 5¢ tunes with all the old zippo they could muster." *Time*, Feb. 9, 41/1. *adj.* Having zip; peppy; snappy. 1953: "If she's that zippo, who am I not to join them?" M. Blosser, *synd. newsp. comic strip*, "Freckles," Jan. 23. See Appendix, **—o** endings. **—py** *adj.* Peppy.

zip fuel Any high-energy jet airplane fuel.

zip gun A home-made or makeshift gun, usu. consisting of a metal pipe for a barrel, a wooden stock, and some spring or elastic material to actuate a firing pin. *Wide use by teenage street gangs.* 1951: ". . . A zip gun—the kind kids make themselves. . . ." H. Lee in *Pageant*, Apr., 35/2.

zizzy *n.* Sleep; rest; esp. a rest period. *Some W.W.II Army use, from Brit. Army sl.*

zombie *n.* **1** A weird looking person; a person exhibiting eccentric behavior; emphatically a character. *From the traditional "zombie" = a walking corpse. Student use since c1940.* → **2** An unpopular, disliked person. *Student use, most common c1940–c1950.* **3** A putatively strong alcoholic mixed drink.

zoo *n.* The caboose of a freight train. *Some railroad use.*

zool *n.* Anything attractive, well made,

or satisfying. *Rock and roll use since c1945.* **—ie zooly** *adj.* Excellent; satisfying. *Rock and roll use since c1955.* See **zool. —ix** *n.* Syrup. *Dial.* **—o** *n.* = **Zulu**, a Negro.

zoom *v.i., v.t.* To get something without paying for it. *adj.* Free; gratis.

zoom buggy An automobile. *Some c1945 adolescent use; archaic.*

zoot *interj.* **1** An expression of encouragement shouted by devotees to jive musicians as they play. *Some c1935–c1940 jive use.* → **2** An expression of recognition, agreement, or satisfaction. *Some jive use c1935–c1940.* **—y zootie** *adj.* Fashionable; attractive; up to date; dressed in the style of the zoot suit. 1956: "... Zooty—fashionable." S. Longstreet, *The Real Jazz Old and New*, 150. *Orig. c1935 jive use; mostly obs. by c1950.* Cf. **zoot suit.** *n.* A dude.

zoot snoot **1** A large nose; a person who has a large nose. *Based on "zoot suit."* See Appendix, Rhyming Terms. **2** An overly curious person; a gossip or snoop.

zoot suit   **zoot soot**   An extreme style of dress; typically a man's suit with drape shape jacket having heavily padded shoulders, large lapels, many buttons on the sleeves, and high-waisted trousers with sharp pleats, cut full in the legs and tapered sharply to the narrow cuffs. Both the term and the style were assoc. with jive elements during late 1930's and early 1940's. 1942: "Jelly got into his zoot suit with the reet pleats." Z. Hurston, 85. 1953: "The police ... fanned out from headquarters. ... Some were garbed in short sleeve shirts, others in zoot suits." AP,

July 8. *Obs. The zoot suit is either in a bright colored, garish pattern or is black with vertical white stripes. A zoot suit need not be a suit, but may be a jacket and trouser ensemble in the style described above; in such an ensemble, the jacket and trousers are usually in vividly contrasting colors and conflicting patterns. Typically, a zoot suit is worn with a wide satin-finished tie, in bright colors and a bold pattern, a dark-colored or pastel shirt, a wide-brimmed hat, a knee-length key chain, and with an unfolded handkerchief protruding from the breast pocket. Usu. associated with c1935–c1940 hepcats. The suit style was actually created and publicized by manufacturers of men's clothing. During the early part of W.W.II the style, somewhat modified, found some small popularity with students, teenagers, and business men. Perhaps it was a reaction to the drabness of the war and its uniforms. It is doubtful if the style would ever have become widely popular, but in any case it was discontinued owing to wartime restrictions on materials. Zoot suits are still seen on some young atavistic hepcats and have some popularity with young Puerto Rican immigrants.*

zoot suiter Lit., one who wears a zoot suit. Fig., a youth or young man whose brashness, personality, tastes, or friends suggest that he is capable of wearing a zoot suit; a hep and brash young man.

zowie *n.* Zest; energy; *joie de vivre.* 1946: "... Full of zing, full of zest, full of zowie." Movie, *Mad Wednesday.*

zuch *n.* An informer; a stool pigeon. *Underworld use since c1940.*

Zulu *n.* [derog.] A Negro.

INTRODUCTION TO THE APPENDIX

by Stuart Berg Flexner

Note: The reader will find that frequent reference to the appropriate Appendix word lists will illustrate further the various sections of this Introduction.

Major Sub-Groups Contributing to American Slang

Approximately half of the entries in this dictionary can be traced directly to some forty-five general sub-groups of our culture: airplane pilots (both commercial and military), mechanics, and subsidiary aircraft workers; advertising and public-relations workers; auctioneers; baseball players and fans; carnival and circus workers; college students; construction-crew workers; convicts; cowboys and ranchers; criminals (especially the separate groups of car stealers, confidence men, counterfeiters, pickpockets, professional thieves, safe crackers, and suppliers of illegal alcoholic beverages); financial-district employees and dealers in stocks and bonds; fishing and hunting enthusiasts; football players and fans; café society; gamblers and players of cards, dice, etc.; garage and filling-station workers; golfers and caddies; grade-school students; high-school students and general teen-agers (including rock-and-roll and hot-rod fans); hoboes, tramps, and vagabonds; horseracing bookies, jockeys, and bettors; hotel employees; immigrants (especially the separate groups of Dutch, German, Polish, Hungarian, Irish, and Yiddish- and Spanish-speaking immigrants); itinerant farm workers and fruit pickers; jazz musicians and fans (including the separate groups attached to Dixieland, jive, swing, bop, and cool); journalists; law-enforcement officers (both local and federal); loggers and sawmill workers; longshoremen; miners (especially of coal) and prospectors; narcotic addicts; photographers (both professional and amateur); plumbers, carpenters, and radio and television repairmen; politicians (both local and national); post-office employees; pre-school-age children; railroad workers (including separate groups of engineers, firemen, brakemen, conductors, and section hands); retail salesmen (especially those separate groups who sell automobiles, furniture, jewelry, men's clothing, and shoes); sailors (including the separate groups of merchant marine and U.S. Navy); servers of food and drink; show business performers, agents and stage-crew workers (including separate groups of vaudeville, burlesque, legitimate theater, radio, motion picture, and television workers); soldiers (both of the regular army and wartime draftees); teen-age street-gang members; telegraphers; traveling salesmen; truck drivers, and bus and taxi drivers; union organizers and members; and unskilled factory workers (especially the separate groups in automotive, clothing, electronic, and small consumer-goods factories).

The Mechanical Formation of New Words

In modern English, all words, including slang, are created in several well-defined ways. To create new words[1] we can change the meaning, form, pronunciation, or part of speech of old ones; we can borrow from foreign languages; we can coin new combinations of old words and word parts; or we can consciously contrive some type of code device or acrostic based on known words. These methods are briefly discussed below.

Changes in Meaning

The most important and common source of "new" words is the reservoir of standard speech. Most new words are formed by changing the meaning of old ones, either by generalizing their meaning through the linguistic processes of concatenation or radiation, or by specializing their original meanings. In both cases the spelling of the new word remains the same as the old, though a very slight change in pronunciation or stress may occur.

GENERALIZATION. Generalization includes any process by which a single word comes to have more than one meaning. One process of generalization is *radiation*, the linguistic means by which an old word takes on new meanings, each directly related to the origi-

---

[1] The language of the most primitive humans ever studied contains a range and variety of sounds infinitely greater than the sounds made by even the highest animals. For a list of animal vocabulary sounds, see G. Révész, *Ursprung und Vorgeschichte der Sprache* (Francke Verlag, Bern, Switzerland, 1946). Herbert Spencer calculated that there are 108,264 possible monosyllables in English; Otto Jesperson (*Monosyllabism in English*, Oxford University Press, New York, 1929, pp. 8-9) says over 158,000 are possible, though of course only a relatively few are used and others are too close in sound to be useful. The number of possible polysyllabic combinations of all these monosyllables is truly infinite.

nal concept. A classic example of generalization by radiation is the word *hand* and its various standard, cant, and slang meanings. Thus *hand* = a pledge of betrothal, handwriting, assistance ("give me a hand"); a person employed as a laborer ("hired hand," "farm hand," "section hand"); the assortment of playing cards held by one player; to guide, give, or pass ("hand me that plate"); a hand's breadth (approximately four inches, as "that horse is sixteen hands high"); and so forth. Each meaning or word is directly related to the basic concept and word of *hand*. Each meaning radiates from the central concept as the spokes of a wheel radiate from the hub.

The other process of generalization is *concatenation*, the linguistic means by which an old word takes on a series of new meanings, each *not* directly related to the basic concept but rather related to a previous new meaning. A classic example of generalization by concatenation is the word *cardinal* and its various meanings. Originally from the Latin and French and = hinge, the word took on the meaning "of basic or prime importance," as in "cardinal number"; then it came to mean a person of chief importance, specifically a "cardinal" of the Roman Catholic Church; then the word was used to describe the yellowish-scarlet color associated with the robe of a cardinal; from which it came to mean an American bird of this color; and later even came to be the name of the St. Louis Cardinals, a baseball team, whose symbol is this bird. Thus by concatenation *cardinal* = of first importance, a councilor to the pope, a color, a bird, and a baseball team. Each of these meanings has generalized from the previous one but none is directly related to the basic concept and word *cardinalis* = hinge. Each word is catenated, or linked, to the previous one, like the links in a chain.

Examples of generalization in slang include: *applesauce, bird, the blues, doll, hot, pineapple, skins,* and *zombie.*

SPECIALIZATION. Specialization, occurring less frequently than generalization, is the reverse process, whereby a word loses some of its various meanings to become identified with but one concept. *Boat* is more and more restricted to its nautical use of a small, open craft; its once more general use, to mean various boat-shaped vessels, as a "gravy boat," is slowly disappearing. *Corn* once meant grain of any type; now it refers to but one specific type. *Liquor* once meant any liquid, but it is now well on its way to a specialized meaning of "an alcoholic beverage" only.

Specialization often results from taking only one psychological connotation of a word and using it as the prime denotation. The standard *frantic* = mentally deranged or insane is almost extinct and the earlier suggestion of "frenzied" is now its prime mean-

ing. Specialization in slang has given us *the chair, gay,* and *moll.*

Much *apparent* specialization is actually the result of radiation or concatenation, or of only a local specialization for a specific social group or in the mind of an individual. For example, *horn* and *round* have many meanings gained through generalization, but specific individuals may use them in primarily one specialized way. Thus *horn* has one primary meaning to an automobile mechanic, a different primary meaning to a jazz musician, another to a blacksmith, a saddle maker, a hi-fi enthusiast, a cuckold, or a bullfight fan. *Round* also has many generalized meanings, though but one primary meaning to a boxer, a different primary meaning to a butcher, bridge player, bartender, singer, draftsman, mathematician, cowboy, or a pistol shooter. No matter how many generalized meanings, then, a word has, every time it is used the situation and sense of the sentence limits it to but one meaning. This is not true specialization.

METAPHOR. Generalization and specialization are merely linguistic tags which include the formation of new meanings by metaphor and figurative use (the various meanings of the radiated *hand* and the concatenated *cardinal* are due to metaphorical and figurative uses). *Bean pole* is a single radiation from a basic image and is a direct metaphorical use.

Slang often generalizes from old words by using metaphors which illustrate the pathetic fallacy. By giving inanimate objects living characteristics, music can *swing* itself or a car can be *crazy*. The contrary process, however, is more frequent: a person is equated with an inanimate object (which incidentally is somewhat characteristic of the *cool* and *beat* philosophies), so that a man can be a *blue-stocking, stuffed shirt, a tin-horn;* or he can even be *fried* or *hardboiled,* can *bounce* like a rubber ball, or even be a *rock* or *square.*

DEGRADATION AND ELEVATION In the process of changing its meaning, a word can change in pejorative or meliorative ways; it can be degraded or elevated to refer to something of lesser or greater dignity than before. The usual process seems to be degradation. Thus *counterfeiter* once meant *imitator, libel* once referred to a brief written item, and *pirate* once meant merely an adventurer. Elevation has seen *angel* arise from its early meaning of messenger; *knight* gained dignity from its original reference to youth; and *steward* once meant *pig keeper*. In slang, *lady's room* (though actually a euphemism) and *queer* are excellent examples of degradation; *egghead* and *pad* have been elevated.

Changes in Form—Lengthening

New words may be formed by lengthening old words: by compounding and blending old words or word elements, and by affixing suffixes and prefixes.

COMPOUNDING. A common method of forming new words in all Germanic branches of the Indo-European family of languages (including English) is by joining two words together, as *daisy* from "day's eye," *world* from the Old English "wer-eld" = "age of man," and the more modern *railroad*. Compounds of two nouns, as in the above examples, are called "kennings." However, any two parts of speech may be combined in any order: as the noun and adjective *ice-cold* and *blueberry;* adverb and noun *underdog* and *head-on;* noun and verb *sideswipe* and *playboy;* (the examples show that either element may be placed first). Compounds of other parts of speech include: *kickoff, Italian cut,* etc. Such combinations may be made from two standard or two slang words, or a standard and a slang word: *baby-sit, hep-cat,* or *hot shot,* and result in either a standard or a slang word. In such combinations one word eventually loses its stress and may lose its identity; the outstanding examples of this are ——*like,* which in many combinations has long ago been reduced to the adverbial ending -ly, and the multiple compound of "God be with ye", in which each word has lost its identity and the expression has become *good-by.* Compounds are common in English though they often evolve very slowly. Complete acceptance or fairly old use of a compound expression is often shown by its being written as one word; less accepted compounds often retain a hyphen; the least accepted or newer ones are written as very familiar two-word phrases. Slang has certain words which frequently recur in compound formations; in this dictionary these are called *suffix words* and *prefix words,* since they are added and have the influence of suffixes and prefixes.

SUFFIXES, SUFFIX WORDS, PREFIXES, PREFIX WORDS. New words are readily formed by affixing a variety of suffixes and prefixes. This is probably one of the oldest methods of word making: primitives used it to create polysyllabic words, it was common in Greek and Latin, and is still common in all Germanic languages. Although once disallowed by purists, today native and borrowed roots and affixes from various sources are freely joined. A classic example of joining roots and affixes from various sources to make one word is *remacadamized:* *re-* from Latin, *mac* from Celtic, *adam* from Hebrew, *-ize* from Greek via French, and only the *-d* from native English origin. New words formed from affixing suffixes and prefixes are called derivations in linguistics, as they are derived by adding an affix to a full word.

Both standard and slang words are formed by adding suffixes or prefixes to old root words. The past tense is formed from verb roots by adding *-ed;* nouns of agency are formed by adding *-er, -ster,* or *-ess* (feminine); separation from, out of, off, away, reversing, or undoing are noted by prefixing *de-;* and so forth. When such standard and familiar affixes are added to slang words, the meaning of the new word is obvious from knowing the meaning of the root word and the usual influence of the affix. Most such words therefore are not listed in this dictionary.

Non-standard speech, however, does have certain affixes and affix words (common blend-word elements) which constantly recur, such as: —*eteria,* —*crazy,* —*itis,* —*jockey, old*— and *Sunday*— (as in *cleaneteria, boy-crazy, Republicanitis, disc jockey, old thing,* and *Sunday driver*). Some such formations are slang and popular, and they are entered in this dictionary. Separate lists of some such words in the Appendix, and each list is introduced by a brief description of the meaning and popularity of the affixes and affix words. These Appendix lists could be enlarged indefinitely, as the process for forming the words gives unlimited opportunity to coin nonce words, fad words, and unimportant neologisms; all words in the Appendix lists have been found in two sources that have been published at least five years apart.

Many of the suffixes are interchangeable, so that giving all possible variations is impossible as well as useless. Thus, besides the common *luncheonette,* we have *lunchatorium, lunchery, lunchette, luncheteria,* etc. Besides the common affixes and affix words listed in the Appendix, there are many others: thus *aloha* (Hawaiian for "love") has been popularized by steamship and travel companies and by the song "Aloha Oe" ("Love to Thee," written by the last native queen Liliuokalani); it has seen a little use as *aloha* = hello in the United States, and has become a very minor prefix word = welcome, welcoming, hospitality, in *aloha dance, aloha party,* and *aloha week,* given by college social groups during the beginning of the school term. Also the French *bon voyage* has minor use as a prefix word blend-element = farewell, e.g., in *bon voyage dance* and *bon voyage party,* given by friends to those about to embark or merely move away, and by a ship for its passengers on the last night of a cruise or trip.

Affix words are usually monosyllables, or polysyllables with a hard stress on the first syllable. Often suffix words are added to degrade the original word. For example, there are many suffix words for people of limited or confused minds: —*buggy,* —*bugs,* —*crazy,* —*daffy,* —*dippy,* —*dizzy,* —*wacky.* The new word created by adding affixes and affix words to an old word is usually an adjective or a noun.

BLEND WORDS, also called portmanteau

words, are formed by telescoping two word elements into one word. Often the first part of one word is joined to the second part of another word where the two words have a common sound, usually a middle vowel. There are two kinds of blend words: those naturally evolving or coined, which are accepted and serve a purpose as individual words, their individual elements being forgotten; and individual coinages which are seldom accepted and in which the listener need recall the two separate elements before ascertaining the meaning of the blend (this last kind is discussed later under *Individual Coinages*).

Useful and accepted standard words include: *motel* (motorist + hotel), *motorcade* (motorcar + cavalcade), and *smog* (smoke + fog). Blends are not common in slang; even the two most common *mingy* (mean + stingy) and *scrowsy* (screwy + lousy) are seldom heard.

Changes in Form—Shortening

New words are also formed by shortening old words. Since the tendency in all English, and particularly in slang, is toward short, informal usage, shortenings are common. A word may be shortened by back clipping, front clipping, or abbreviation. After becoming a back clipping or front clipping, a word can change further by taking suffixes and by being respelled. Phrases are also clipped and abbreviated; after being abbreviated, a phrase is sometimes further changed by becoming an acronym.

BACK CLIPPING. The most common way of shortening is to clip a syllable or syllables from the back of a word to form a *stump word*. Standard speech has *math*(ematics) and *memo*(random), among many others. Slang has *cig*(arette), *homo*(sexual), *hood*(lum), *sis*(ter) since 1835, *sis*(sy) since 1910, etc.[2] A word is back clipped as soon as enough syllables are given to make the word intelligible: the stump word is often a first syllable representation of a three (or more) syllable noun. Back clippings are often made from words originally having a strongly accented first syllable; a great many back clippings clip off Greek and Latin endings, such as *-gram, -ology*, etc. Many of these back clippings refer to common, every-day items; many occur in student speech, such as *path*(ology), *photo*(graph), *quad*(rangle), *trig*(onometry). Show business seems to feel that two-syllable representations of adjectives make them more forceful: *colos*(sal), *magnif*(icent), *sensay* (sensational), etc.

Back clippings are also frequent in nicknames for products *(Caddy* for Cadillac) and for place names *(Chi* for Chicago, *Pennsy* for Pennsylvania, etc.).[2] Some back clippings take the -o suffix ending *(ammo* for ammunition, *beano* for beanery) either as a true suffix or as a substitute for a back vowel. Some stump words are respelled or corrupted: *fave* (favorite), *letch* (lecher), *looey* (lieutenant), *lube* (lubrication), *mike* (microphone), *nabe* (neighbor), *natch* (naturally), etc.

BACK FORMATIONS.[3] A specific type of back clippings are back formations. They are words formed by clipping the *-er, -or, -ar*, or *-r* from the end of a noun to form a verb, in the mistaken assumption that the dropped ending was a suffix of agency. What remains of the word is assumed to be a verb stem, but is actually a newly created one. Thus we have the newly created verbs of *to auth* (from author), *to burgle* (from burglar)[4], *to orate* (from oration), *to ush* (from usher), etc.

Cropping what is mistakenly assumed to be a suffix is not limited to mistaken suffixes of agency. English has mistakenly assumed the *-y* in *greedy* was an adverbial suffix and clipped it to form *greed;* has mistakenly assumed the *-ing* on *groveling* was a present participial suffix and clipped it to get *grovel;* has mistakenly assumed the *-s* in the word *peas* was a plural suffix and clipped it to get *pea* (this was done in the sixteenth century) just as some people now assume the *-s* in Portuguese is a plural suffix and clip it to form the new word *Portugee*. Similar misconceptions have also given us the stump words *diagnose* (diagnosis), *jell*(y), and *resurrect*(ion).

Thousands of back clippings exist in modern speech, some standard, some slang, some colloquial; any polysyllabic word having an accented first syllable can readily be so shortened, so that many nonce words, fad words, and neologisms exist, and many thousands more are possible: thus this dictionary lists but a few of the more common, representative slang back clippings and back formations. A further list is given in the Appendix.

FRONT CLIPPINGS. New words are also formed by clipping the front syllable or syllables from an old word. Old and standard front clippings include (a)*mend*, (de)*spite*, (peri)*wig*, etc. Slang has (be)*bop*, *croot* (from recruit), (con)*fess*, (tele)*gram*, etc.

Such forms are infrequent compared to back clippings. Front clippings are usually formed by clipping an unaccented front syllable or syllables from a two-, three- or

---

[2] See Jonathan Swift's diatribe against earlier back clippings: in The Tatler, Sept. 28, 1710, No. 230, he objects to *hipps* (hypochondriacs), *mobb* (*mobile vulgus*, from which we get *mob*), *pozz* (positive) and *rep*(utation), among others.

[3] The term was Sir James Murray's. For a discussion and list of back formations, see Otto Jespersen's "A Few Back Formations," *English Studies*, LXX, 1935, pp. 117-122.

[4] Probably coined by W. S. Gilbert in his "When the enterprising burglar's not a-burgling"—line from song in *The Pirates of Penzance.*

four-syllable noun to obtain a noun stump-word. Many front clippings are obtained by dropping what is or what is assumed to be a prefix; once established as words, such front clippings may also further change by taking standard suffixes and by being re-spelled. Adult front clippings[5] often seem more colorful than back clippings because they are rarer, are often made from less common words, and their original word is harder to identify by the uninitiated.

COMBINATION FRONT AND BACK CLIPPINGS. Both front and back clippings sometimes occur in English. The most common such word is *still* (from di*still*ery). Slang has *gate* (alli*gate*or), *tec* (from de*tec*tive), etc. Combined clippings are not common; most were probably first back clippings from which front clippings were then made.

CLIPPED PHRASES. Sometimes phrases are also front or back clipped. An early example is *spark it* of 1780, appearing as *spark* by 1800. Most phrase clippings are, however, comparatively recent, usually omitting the last word or words of a phrase (similar to back clipping a word). Phrase clipping has been especially popular since World War II in both standard and slang speech. Many of these phrase clippings are actually clippings of the second part of a compound which is written as two words: *bull* (shit), *flats* (flat-heeled shoes), *jet* (jet-propelled air-plane), *kings* (king-sized cigarettes), *nylons* (nylon stockings), etc. Many of these first word representations of a phrase take an -*s* suffix, either as a generic term or to show affection or familiarity.

Clipped phrases are common in lunch-counter use, where the shortest form in re-laying an order is not only the quickest way but the most intelligible above working noises: *a cup* (of coffee), *black* (coffee), *Danish* (pastry), *french* (fried potatoes), *with* (cream or onions), etc. Clipped phrases are also popular with cool and beat groups, who dislike long, obvious or direct state-ments, as *it's* (the truth), *it's been* (an en-joyable party), etc.

The above are all back clippings of phrases, but front clippings also exist: (menstrual) *period*, (down) *with it*, etc.

Multiple-word place names are also short-ened, often taking a specifying "the" be-fore the short form: *the* (West) *Point*, *the* (French) *Quarter* in New Orleans, *the* (Greenwich) *Village* in New York City, etc.

Some phrases may be shortened by clip-ping either the first or the last word(s). *Heebie-jeebies* can be clipped to either

---

[5] See Otto Jespersen, *Language, Its Nature, Devel-opment and Origin*, Macmillan, 1949, pp. 169-71. He points out that adults usually form back clip-pings, children prefer front clippings. An adult says enough of a word to identify it (*prof* from professor), whereas a child says the part of a word he remembers or can pronounce easily ('*fes-sor* from professor).

heebies or to *jeebies*, and the complete ex-pression *up shit creek without a paddle* can become either *up the creek* or (less fre-quently) *without a paddle*. Such clippings can also omit a taboo word, as *up yours* = *up your ass*, leaving something of a eu-phemism. Rhyming slang also clips its phrases, but for reasons of secrecy rather than brevity (see Rhyming Slang below).

ABBREVIATIONS AND ACRONYMS. Because slang is primarily spoken rather than writ-ten, comparatively few abbreviations exist for single words. *C* (for cocaine and perhaps for century notes = $100), *H* (for "horse" or heroin), and *M* (for morphine) are un-usual. Common abbreviations for standard words are, of course, not slang, nor are ab-breviations for place names (as N.Y., W.Va., etc).

Slang phrases, however, are frequently abbreviated into the initial letters for each word. Thus there are the written and spoken slang abbreviations of *A.W.O.L.* (absent *without* leave), *BS* (bull shit), *G.A.C.* (grilled American cheese sandwich), *G.I.* (from either general issue or govern-ment issue), *p.o* (pissed off) *s.o.l.* (shit out of luck), etc. Slang phrase abbreviations are short and forceful; many originate in lunch-counter, army, and obscene masculine phrases (where they are also partial eu-phemisms). Slang also forms a few mock abbreviations by phonetically substituting letters for words, as in *I.O.U.* In all such phrase abbreviations the individual letters are usually followed by a period and each letter is pronounced separately in speaking.

The letters forming an abbreviation for the words of a phrase may be run together to form, and be pronounced as, a new word; words so formed are called *acronyms*. Thus the letters forming the abbreviation *a.w.o.l.* are frequently run together to form the word *awol* and the letters forming the ab-breviation *snafu* (situation normal: all fucked up) are always run together as the word *snafu*.

Most frequently, standard acronyms rep-resent the abbreviations for the words in the name of a government, military, or in-ternational agency. When acronyms refer to such proper names they are called tip-names. Both abbreviations and tip-names became exceedingly popular during Frank-lin D. Roosevelt's New Deal with its many "alphabet agencies." The popularity con-tinued during World War II and today many international groups and government agen-cies are abbreviated or have tip-names. Thus C.C.C. (Civilian Conservation Corps), N.R.A. (National Recovery Administration), W.P.A. (Works Progress Administration), WAVES (Women Accepted for Voluntary Emergency Service), CARE (Co-operative for American Remittances to Europe), UNESCO (United Nations Educational, Scientific and Cultural Organization),

I.C.B.M. (*intercontinental ballistics missile*), ARCAS (*all-purpose rocket carrier for atmospheric soundings*), etc. Many such abbreviations and acronyms become standard immediately because they carry the sanction of government, scientific, military, and international agencies.

In any shortening (back and front clippings, abbreviations and acronyms), the short form usually has the same denotation as the original full word or term. In standard use the short form may convey an official, less personal connotation than the full expression. In slang, on the contrary, the short form may connote less formality and respect than the full form. Usually, when abbreviations or acronyms are made from words or phrases the full form remains in the language, the short form serving only as a synonym. However, *C, G.I., snafu,* and some other slang abbreviations and acronyms have replaced full forms almost completely.

Changes in Pronunciation

New words may be formed by changing the pronunciation (and sometimes the spelling) of older words. This is done by making simple changes in stress, corrupting an older word, or adding an infix between the syllables of an older word.

SIMPLE CHANGES IN PRONUNCIATION. A slang word formed from a standard word by generalization or specialization is sometimes pronounced slightly differently from the original usage. This change is usually so minor that it does not affect the spelling. Sometimes the slang usage is said louder or is somewhat stressed in the sentence whereas the standard usage is not. More often, however, the actual pronunciation is not altered, but the standard speech rhythm of the whole sentence is. The slightly different pronunciation tells the listener that the slang, rather than the standard, meaning is intended.

Thus in standard, though ungrammatical use, one says "It's a real cool day" (= "It's a very chilly day,") with emphasis on the main words: *it's, real cool,* and *day* about equal, or with just a slightly greater stress on *real.* If the day is exceedingly chilly we will put a strong emphasis on *real* and *day.* The sentence has a rising pitch, the last three words being pronounced more fully and slowly as "It'sa real cool day." In the slang "It's a real cool day" (in which *real cool* takes on its post-1946 slang use), *real* always receives a very strong emphasis and the standard *day* receives almost none, almost being swallowed. The slang *real cool,* virtually run together as one word, takes the emphasis of the sentence and is also the peak of the sentence's pitch. Thus "It'sa REAL COOL day." In like manner the standard interrogation "WHAT do YOU SAY?" (= "what is your opinion?") when

used as a slang greeting becomes "Whatda-ya SAY!"

These changes come more often when we use a word new to us or when we are speaking to a stranger. Thus, one who infrequently uses the slang word *hip* might distinguish it from the standard "hip" by saying: "He's very HIP," the last word rising in intonation, almost as if a faint question were implied. But one who uses the slang word frequently and naturally, and one whose friends use the slang word frequently and naturally, will say the sentence flatly: "He's very hip."

CORRUPTIONS. A word's pronunciation or meaning may be corrupted to form a new word, though this happens very seldom. A classic example of corruption of the meaning of a word is the standard *exotic,* which means "introduced from or indigenous to a foreign region." The word has been generalized to mean "unusual," and often corrupted to mean "mildly erotic." Thus a strip-tease dancer is often advertised as "exotic," either by popular misconception of the original meaning of the word or by erroneously confusing *exotic* and *erotic.*

Two words sounding alike are occasionally confused in slang, and they may eventually result in a new pronunciation combining a slurred version of each. Thus *boff* may be confused with or melded into the pronunciation of *bop* and slang's *heart* and *hard* corrupted to one slurred pronunciation of "hardt." Other new words formed by corruptions in pronunciation are *leaves* for *Levis* and *kayducer* for *conductor.*

Examples of corrupted pronunciations (which often change the spelling) that do *not* result in new words, include *foist* and *boid* for *first* and *bird* (exaggerated and jocular slurs on a Brooklyn accent), and *nerts* for *nuts* (an expletive perhaps partially euphemistic as well as jocular). Standard *correct* is corrupted into *kee-rect,* popularized by a comic strip character and having some use among students who consider the corruption more emphatic than the original word. *Keed* for *kid* is used in the same emphatic way. Such corruptions as *impredicable* and *worrization* are more often used in jocular imitation of rustic speech than in rustic speech itself. None of these are truly new words since all depend on the existence of the original word for understanding and meaning. Most obvious corruptions are conscious attempts at humor, mockery, or flippancy, as *automobubble, bootician, gyrene, kaydet, martooni,* etc.

Another type of corruption could be called "jocular folk etymology." (See Borrowings and Folk Etymology below.) This type of sophisticated corruption is formed by purposely giving a jocular mispronunciation to a foreign, complicated, or technical term to make it resemble a much less dignified term: *fox paw* for *faux pas, olive oil* for *au revoir* (somewhat popular after World War I), *sickey-ackey* for *psychiatry, very close veins* for *varicose veins*, etc. Such conscious corruptions may be in vogue for a while, or they may represent obvious, hence constantly recurring, nonce words.

Changes in meaning are seldom the result of ignorance or unconscious corruptions: they are usually due to conscious generalization or specialization. Changes in form through sheer ignorance seem limited to true folk etymologies. Only some of the most common corruptions are given in this dictionary.

Infixes are affixes stuck into the middle of a word, between syllables. Infixes, especially those which are not words, are rare in English. The only popular ones are -*ma*-, -*ama*-, and -*a*-. The last two of these are probably only variations of -*ma*-: sometimes -*ama*- is just the common -*ma*- infix with an initial vowel glide to bridge a preceding consonant into the -*ma*- sound; and after this vowel glide is added, the initial -*ma*- may be dropped, leaving the infix -*a*-. The infix -*ma*- is a nondenotative syllable of unknown origin, usually inserted after the second syllable of a three- or four-syllable word. It is often inserted in a learned word for humorous or flippant effect, making a long or pompous word even more so; thus most infixed words are jocular corruptions, as *elomacution* and *stratemagee*. Infixes also occur in many omnibus words, as *thingamajig*, and in some onomatopoeia, as *ting-a-ling*. The -*ma*-, -*ama*-, or -*a*- never changes the meaning of a word. Even as jocular corruptions, infixes have never been popular in the United States, *razzamatazz* having been the most popular. All the words in the Appendix list appeared at least four times in print between 1947 and 1952 when the three major infixes seem to have had a very minor rise in popularity.

Changes in the Part of Speech

Shifting the use of a word from its common or historical grammatical function to another part of speech is called *functional shift*. Functional shifts occur in all levels of the language; the new word thus formed may be standard, colloquial, or slang. A functional shift changes neither the meaning nor the form of a word; it merely changes or extends its grammatical function.[6]

Such standard nouns as *chin, ditch, eye, ink, jaw,* and *stomach* all have slang or colloquial uses as verbs.[6] The standard verbs *break, catch, combine, hit, kick, kill, sell, show,* and *smoke* all have colloquial or slang uses as nouns (even though these standard verbs may have standard noun forms: *com-*

bine *v., combination n.*; or *kill v., killing n.*). Creating new words by functional shift usually makes shorter forms than those in existence; such forms are often originated or popularized by newspaper headline writers.

A recent tendency is to make occupational, technical, and military nouns into rather sonorous verbs: *to process, to requisition, to remainder,* and *to service* being obvious examples. Of these, only the last has taken on a specialized or new meaning (to grease, adjust, or make minor repairs to a piece of machinery or electronic equipment).

When a word is shifted, the part of speech used by the speaker can often be ascertained from his pronunciation of it: he may accent certain syllables, voice final consonants, or stress certain words and phrases. In standard use, the verbs *to abuse* and *to house* have voiced final consonants; the nouns *an abuse* and *a house* do not. In similar manner there is a difference in stress between the verbs *to object, to present,* and *to subject* and the nouns *an object, a present,* and *a subject.* Such functional shifts are not as readily apparent in writing, where the reader has not the speaker's pronunciation as an aid. Though a standard word which undergoes functional shift does not necessarily become slang, many standard words used in a grammatical function different from the expected could be considered slang. Furthermore, slang words are often used *as slang* in several different parts of speech. Since almost any noun, verb, adjective, or adverb can undergo functional shift, all such new forms are not listed in the dictionary.

Borrowings

New words and word elements enter English by being borrowed from foreign languages. Such borrowings, or loan words, may enter with their original form and meaning; but English usage usually changes their connotation, pronunciation, and spelling. Borrowings come from every language and country: —*burger, butt, calaboose, chisel, juke,* —*nik, punk, shmo,* and *yen* respectively being borrowed from the German, Dutch, Spanish, Turkish, African, Russian, English, Yiddish, and Chinese. American slang has taken *hooch* and *pow-wow* from the Indians and *cinch, loco* and the suffixes —*eteria* and —*eroo* from the Spanish of the Southwest.

Folk etymology is the study of the process whereby a foreign (or any unfamiliar) word is changed in popular use so that it can be pronounced as a familiar, meaningful English word or word element. It is an attempt to pronounce an unfamiliar word in a familiar way, changing unfamiliar syllables or word elements to those having approximate sounds in one's native tongue. When this is done, the familiar sound elements used need have no relation to the meaning of the word, though often folk etymology evolves similar

---

[6] In particular, nouns standing for parts of the body and colors, and the most common verbs undergo frequent functional shift. See Krapp, *Modern English,* pp. 197-199 and Jespersen, *Growth and Structure,* p. 16ff. for more extensive lists.

sounding elements that seem to make the word more meaningful. Thus the Old French *mouscheron* has become *mushroom*: the two familiar word elements are used to approximate the foreign sounds, but the item itself has nothing to do with either *mush* or *room*. However, the French *appentis* was folk etymologized into *penthouse*, whose second familiar element helps make the word meaningful and visual.

True folk etymology evolves slowly; people first attempt to give the foreign borrowing its foreign pronounciation, but gradually popular use evolves a new pronunciation and spelling (though the word may enter English already changed, by an honest confusion on the part of the original sub-group users). Jocular corruptions resemble folk etymologies, but are conscious attempts at humor (see Corruptions, above).

Important groups introducing foreign borrowings now include naval and merchant sailors, overseas members of the armed forces, devotees of foreign movies and plays, and tourists and students returning to the United States after work, study, or vacation periods abroad.

Direct foreign borrowings have recently appeared in English. Due to modern communications a foreign word can suddenly be presented to the dominant culture any morning in its newspapers or on its radio and television programs. *Sputnik* was introduced directly without the help of immigrants, soldiers, or travelers: immediately thereafter were evolved a group of words taking the Russian *—nik* ending, as *beatnik*. Such direct borrowings of words and word elements will probably increase in the future.

Euphemisms and Taboo Words

Since euphemisms are acceptable, mild, or pleasant words and phrases substituted for taboo, harsh, or unpleasant ones, they occur more often in standard usage than in slang. Slang has no "genteelisms" for sex words, but *minced forms* of oaths, expletives, and ejaculations do occur. Children, teen-agers, women, elderly people and less successful people still popularize and use minced forms, both old and new: *Creepers!*, *darned*, *for Pete's sake*, *Holy cow*, *Jeez*, etc. Such euphemisms are used for social rather than religious or personal reasons. Curses and oaths using the name of God, Jesus and religious and infernal images seem to be losing popularity in favor of the one-word epithets referring to excrement or sex. The wane of deep religious feeling is evident even in our oaths: a good ripe *God damn* or *hell* doesn't present a realistic picture to the modern or the young mind; such expressions are no longer personal or strong enough. In slang, words once generally taboo no longer are, due to a broader acceptance of once-taboo ideas and images and to a forgetting of the excrement or sexual images on which some

terms are based. Most of us now hear *snafu* and *up the creek* in mixed society. A "taboo" word now seldom refers to a word which a person would never utter — today a taboo word is simply not used in polite conversation. New taboo words are rare — probably the newest category contains the many *—shit* words, as *bull shit*, *chicken shit*, *horse shit*, etc.

Slang has its euphemisms, including the abbreviations of *BS*, *s.o.l.*, etc., and such clippings as *up the creek*, *up yours*, etc. It also has many dignity-bursting words. These short, pithy terms are, in a broad sense, somewhat euphemistic: they add humor or reality to situations which otherwise would be morbid, dangerous, sad, or taken too seriously. In this sense the earthy slang word can be just as pleasing or kind as actual self-conscious euphemisms or sonorous phrases. None of us wants to die, but when we do at least some of us would rather *fall out*, *go west*, or *cash in our chips* than *pass away* or *succumb*. None of us wants to be called "stupid," but if we have to be some of us would prefer to be good-naturedly *kookie* or *square* rather than the Victorian *naturally innocent* or *not bright*.

Individual Coinages

Individuals can and do coin new words. More important than individual coinages, however, are words and expressions popularized by individuals. In the past, writers were the major coiners and popularizers of new words. Since the late nineteenth century, however, new words and expressions have been coined and popularized almost exclusively by scientists (such as Darwin's *atoll*, Huxley's *agnostic*), politicians (such as Theodore Roosevelt's *lunatic fringe*, Woodrow Wilson's *self-determination*, Franklin Roosevelt's *New Deal*, Winston Churchill's *iron curtain*); celebrities; newspaper, radio, and television commentators; and more recently by comic-strip cartoonists and television comedians.

BLEND WORDS AS COINAGES. (Blend words have been discussed previously in this Appendix under Changes in Form—Lengthening). Most coinages are based on familiar word elements and are compoundings or blend words. The more topical, or fad word coinages are often blend words, as *alcoholiday*, *ambisextrous*, *anecdotage*, *cinemactress*, *insinuendo*, *Japanazi* and *shamateur*. These are favorites with newspaper columnists and radio and television commentators, but they have little popular use. Over a period of time such coined blend words turn out more picturesque than apt, more topical than useful. Many blend words are so obvious that they are really only constantly reappearing *nonce* words or clever neologisms: unless they have seen some lasting popularity they are not listed in this dictionary. Some blend words, however, have attained the status of artificial or synthetic slang.

Synthetic and Artificial Slang

SYNTHETIC SLANG. Within the past forty years, because of the effectiveness of mass communication, coinages are popular as synthetic slang. Writers, commentators, and entertainers often create personal neologisms and catch phrases to add color and individuality to their columns or shows or to convey the appearance of authentic popular speech.

Thus columnist and newscaster Walter Winchell has coined and made widely known such synthetic blend words as *infanticipate* (= anticipating a baby, pregnant) and *Renovate* (= renewing one's single status in the divorce center of Reno, Nevada). Damon Runyon coined and made widely known many synthetic words, as the rhyming mock-Latin *phonus-balonus* (a combination of *phoney* and *baloney*). Abel Green, editor of the theatrical trade paper *Variety*, has coined many words used only in that paper, usually for the sake of their brevity and a breezy style.

Although such synthetically popularized words have occasionally risen to the status of true slang, most, rarely in general use, are short lived. They are synthetic in every sense: they are widely known only because of the popularity of the coiner; they are not generally useful in most people's everyday life; and by their commercial and topical association one can use them only self-consciously or for a short period of time. This last criticism especially applies to the synthetic slang of comedians or disc jockeys catering to teen-agers. Comedians often coin and popularize meaningless epithets or catch phrases as joke punch lines or as repetitious jokes. Thus within the last 15 years such synthetic expressions as *Hey Abbott!, Coming Mother!, I dood it!* and *you're a good one* have seen some short-lived generalized use.

These synthetically created and popularized fad words and expressions are not, of course, true slang, though some briefly attain wide popularity. Many could be called counter words or expressions.

ARTIFICIAL SLANG. Besides the conscious creation of synthetic slang by popular columnists, writers, celebrities, and entertainers, little used or archaic words are given artificial popularity through sheer ignorance. Certain colorful, but truly argot, archaic, or recurring nonce words are thought to be slang, and they are thus in wide use by various types of writers, especially movie script writers, who do not know what terms are actually in current oral use. Such words as *gat* = *gun* or *moll* = *a criminal's female companion* have in the past been known to all readers of murder mysteries and viewers of crime movies, even though they have not been used by criminals for at least thirty years and were never widely used by anyone. Certain rarely used Armed Forces words, such as *battery acid* and *tar water* both = *coffee* and *bovine extract* = milk are at best recurring nonce words and never popular enough to be called jargon or cant, much less slang. But they have nevertheless been pounced upon by journalists and script writers and added to their store of words as part of the common vocabulary of all soldiers. In like manner, writers and critics of the jazz music scene have artificially popularized such actually little-used words as *lip-splitter* = *a musician, a trumpet*, or *a high note* and *slipstick* = *slide trombone*.

Such terms are omitted from this dictionary unless they have enjoyed some real popularity.

Trade names, slogans, and punch lines often share some of the synthetic fad use discussed above. Many modern descriptive trade names are coined by manufacturers and advertising men, resulting in such blend words as *Fastred* (dye), *Glo-Coat* (wax), *No-Nox* (gasoline), *Polishine* (a polish that also shines), etc. These and other non-blend coinages, such as *Kodak*, may become generally popular, but they are never slang.

Many commercial advertising slogans have generalized in meaning and become fad expressions. Sometimes such slogans are given a sneering or lewd twist.

Royal Crown Cola's rhyming soft-drink slogan "best by (taste) test" generalized in meaning to have some c1945 fad use—"I like it," said of any food, dress, person, hobby, etc. Chevrolet's rhyming slogan of "eye it, try it, buy it" finds some generalized use = to looking at, trying, or sampling anything, from food to sexual intercourse. Maxwell House's coffee slogan—"good to the last drop"—has seen some generalized use = "thoroughly or completely good or enjoyable."

Political slogans also may take on generalized meaning and become popular. *Tippecanoe and Tyler too* caught the popular imagination and is still heard = "this is even more wonderful than I expected," or more recently, since the slogan has become so old, to = "that's very old fashioned." The more recent "I like Ike" campaign slogan for Dwight ("Ike") Eisenhower is sometimes used to = "I don't know why but I just like it," referring to anything from apple pie to Zen Buddhism.

Besides the repeated catch phrases of comedians, jokes in popular circulation often have punch lines whose meanings generalize so that the lines are used in popular speech. These punch lines remind the listener of the joke, thus adding a specific humorous image to a situation and expressing one's meaning quickly. Many such used punch lines from current or perenially popular jokes, of course, carry taboo connotations, enabling the speaker to express mockery, deflate pomposity, or circumvent propriety by their use. For example, a popular joke concerns an extremely passionate rabbit who in his excitement attempts to make love to an iron statue of a female rabbit. The punch line for this joke *wham bam,* (*thank-you*(ye)-*ma'am*) has been generalized to imply any hurried or rough love making and further to mean any hasty, confused, action-filled activity or situation.

Creating New Words and Expressions by Sound

The creation and popularity of some new words and expressions seem to be based on pleasing sounds, which add to the ease of uttering and remembering the words. Such formations include onomatopoeia, reduplications, and rhyming terms.[7]

ONOMATOPOEIA. Onomatopoetic or echoic words are formed by vocally imitating a sound that occurs in nature, then letting this vocalization name the actual sound or object or action with which it is associated. For example, *Buzz* = the sound of a bee; it is also the sound of a telephone's ringing and thus, figuratively in slang, has come to = a telephone call. *Bow-wow* is the word for the sound of a dog's barking, and also = dog. English has a fair number of both standard and slang onomatopoetic words: *bow-wow* and *ki-yi* for *dog, bash, bop, clinks* (ice cubes), *moo* (*cow,* from the Old English *cu* which may itself have been echoic for a cow's lowing), *putt-putt* (*motorboat,* etc.).

Onomatopoetic expressions may account for a greater part of primitive vocabularies than of civilized languages, and are certainly among the first and more frequently used words found in the vocabularies of young children: *choo-choo=train; tick-tock=clock, watch,* and the like.

Besides basic onomatopoeia, adults also use some echoic words figuratively or with extended meanings. Thus there are many reduplicated echoic words meaning talk, especially idle talk, gossip, or the crowd noises made by a group of chattering people, such as *bibble-babble, buzz-buzz, chitter* (*-chatter*)*, jibber* (*-jabber*)*, ubble-gubble, yak*(ety)-*yak*(ety), etc. Many such echoic words also suggest mockery:

bang(*-bang*), used by adults not only to mean a gunshot or a gun, but figuratively to = drop dead.

boo-hoo, the sound of crying, is usually used mockingly by adults to mean "I'm not sorry at all."

clink, besides denoting a sound, is extended

to = a highball or the clinking of glasses in a toast.

ding-a-ling, besides meaning a bell and its sound, is used figuratively in slang to = a stupid, punch-drunk, or crazy person, one who hears bells when there are none.

flip-flop, besides denoting a wet object, such as a fish, flopping about, is used figuratively in slang to = vacillation of thought or opinion.

meow(*-meow*), besides denoting the sound that a cat makes and a cat itself, is used to indicate that another person is making catty remarks.

moo(*-moo*), besides indicating a cow's lowing and a cow, is used by adults as a comment on seeing a fat woman.

sizzle, besides indicating the sound of frying or broiling, also has some figurative slang adult use to = *appeal,* from the advertising admonition of "don't sell the steak, sell the sizzle."

REDUPLICATIONS. Reduplication is the process by which a new word is formed from a repetition of a radical element in an older word. The repetition is usually of an initial element, sometimes accompanied by a change in the radical vowel. This is one of the oldest methods of word formation. In the early stages of many Indo-European languages, and especially those of the Germanic branches, reduplication often intensifies verbs or puts action in the past or past perfect tense.

For this dictionary, a reduplication is considered any process whereby a word, syllable, or sound is repeated as part of an additional syllable in a word or as an additional word or word element in a compound word or phrase. Many reduplications are onomatopoetic words, as *bow-wow, ding-dong,* etc. The basic element may have no meaning alone, as *flim-flam, hanky-panky.* Or the original element (usually the first word of a hyphenated form) may have meaning alone but be reduplicated for emphasis, as *buddy-buddy, okey-dokey.* Many reduplications are expressions of approval, elation, or exuberance, as *haha, hear-hear!, woo-woo.* A familiar suffix may be added to either or both elements as *yum*(*my*)-*yum*(*my*).

As the above examples show, there are three basic types of reduplications. Reduplications of the first order contain a basic sound, syllable, or word exactly repeated. This is the most common form of reduplication. Besides including many onomatopoetic and children's words, it covers much pidgin or simplified English, and foreign folk borrowings of English words, as *chop-chop, fuck-fuck, she-she.*

In the second order of reduplications, a word, syllable, or basic sound is repeated with the addition of or a simple change in an initial consonant, such as *abba-dabba, itsy-bitsy, boo-hoo.* This is often done (in accompaniment with an affectionate *-ey* or *-y* suffix) to a person's first name to form a

---

[7] Although the formation of onomatopoeia, reduplications, and rhyming terms are completely separate processes, their final forms are often similar. Many onomatopoetic terms and all reduplications actually rhyme within themselves, and some onomatopoetic and rhyming terms contain reduplication.

nickname used in direct address, as *Barney-Warney, Janie-Wanie*, etc. Second order reduplications also occasionally include an infix, as *razzmatazz*. Many fad words, counters, and nonsense words of the 1920's were second order reduplications, and many were associated with carnival use, as *hoop-de-doop, hoop-a-doop, kinxiwinx, row-dow*.

In the second order of reduplications, the most common change in the initial consonant is to *w* (the second most common consonant substituted or added is *d*): *footsie-wootsie, jobsie-wobsie, nasty-wasty*. Such "baby talk" forms are associated with children, pets, or other loved ones. They are usually children's or childish words, often taking the further diminutive or affectionate *-ie, -ey, -y* suffix.

Another and completely separate form of second order reduplication adds or substitutes *sch-, schm-*, or less frequently *sc-, scm*, or *sm-* as an initial consonant sound before the second element: *actor-schmactor, cold-schmold*. This *sch(m)*— sound is associated with Yiddish; such reduplication always indicates dislike, disinterest, mockery, or an attempt to deflate pomposity; it is a vocal way of shrugging one's shoulders, of indicating "so what?" or "who cares?" The *sch(m)*—sound may be added to a person's first or last name, as *Danny-Schmanny, Johnson-Schmonson, Vera-Schmera*, to mean "discount Danny, Johnson, or Vera, their opinions, beliefs, talents; they are not vital, interesting, smart, talented, or worthy of considering or talking about — who cares about them?" Similarly, *actor-schmactor* means "he's not a good enough actor to be called an actor" or "he's a fine and famous actor but who cares, what has that got to do with it, I'm as important as he is, so don't bother me with him or what he thinks."

In the third order of reduplications, a word, syllable, or basic sound is repeated with a change in its initial or radical vowel. This vowel is almost always an *i* which changes to an *a* or less frequently to an *o*. Such third order reduplications include some fad, nonsense, and argot words, as *ephus-uphus-ophus, nickety-nockety, tinkery-tonkery*, etc., as well as the more common words in the Appendix list.

It is possible to make reduplications from almost any word. Only the most common and representative are placed in this dictionary, and other, less common but frequently heard, ones are in the Appendix list. Every entry in the Appendix list has been encountered in at least two sources published five years apart.

RHYMING TERMS. Unintentional rhyming terms occur on all levels of speech. Standard English contains a number of accidental rhyming terms so familiar that we are not conscious that they rhyme, such as *blackjack, grandstand, payday, sure cure*, etc. Unintentional rhyming terms in slang include *BVD's, D.T.'s, hot shot, nit-wit, rough stuff*.

Slang also contains terms which are deliberately contrived to rhyme, even at the expense of forced meaning. There has at times been a slangster cult (among teenagers, students, and armed-forces personnel) to create and use rhyming terms as often as possible, but intentional rhyming terms are usually associated with jive use and many could be called jive rhyming terms.[8] Intentional rhyming terms are usually formed from two monosyllable or two two-syllable words both strongly accented on the first syllable; the first word is usually an adjective and the second a noun; and often one word, at least, is used in an extremely exaggerated or figurative way in the search for a rhyming word: thus, *classis chassis, fat cat, handsome ransom, zoot suit*. Such terms are usually full rhyme, and they resemble reduplications of the second order. In fact, when such intentional rhyming terms contain a meaningless element or nonsense word to make the rhyme, they are actually reduplications of the second order, as *Herkimer-Jerkimer, ooly-drooly*.

Although usually full rhyme, both unintentional and intentional rhyming terms may be based on alliteration, as *cow college, greetings, gates, gyp joint, San Quentin quail*. Slant or partial rhyming terms also occur, as *dead beat, hot rod, weed tea*.

Intentional rhyming terms associated with teen-agers are often derogatory or critical, such as *eager beaver* and *gruesome twosome*. Besides the common two-word phrases, much longer phrases and clauses exist, usually in jive rhyming terms, such as *like your tail, Nightingale* or the thirteen-word line *like the farmer and the 'tator, plant you now and dig you later*.

Code and Cryptic Slang

New words may be formed from various code or cryptic devices: one word may be used to convey the meaning of another word with which it has no obvious relation, or a word may be so respelled or distorted by adding meaningless syllables and letters that it actually becomes something of a new word. Such formations include Cockney and Australian rhyming slang, back slang, and little languages.

RHYMING SLANG. True rhyming slang was originally a secret argot depending on rhyme as a device. Originating with Cockney street vendors, petty thieves, and criminals during the early and mid-nineteenth century,[9] it spread to Australia with the early

---

[8] Such forms would more properly be called "rhyming slang," but this phrase has been pre-empted by a specific type of rhyming argot described later.

[9] John Camden Hotten was the first to write on Cockney Rhyming Slang, in 1858; he concluded it was then about fifteen years old, though most scholars give it a much earlier date. For a discussion of Cockney Rhyming Slang, see Julian Franklyn, *The Cockney*, pp. 291-95.

penal colonists and is usually called Cockney or Australian Rhyming Slang (although some of its terms originated in Ireland and a few in New Zealand). Its major use is in the argot of old-time professional criminals, though a few of its terms are known to most members of the underworld. Outside of its argot use, rhyming slang is not widely known in America, though a few instances occur in the writings of Damon Runyon and in scattered articles and fiction concerning crime.

Rhyming slang is typically formed by substituting a phrase whose last word rhymes with the actual word the speaker wants to convey but does not choose to use. Usually a two-word phrase or a phrase having two nouns connected by a conjunction or preposition, usually by *and*, is used; each phrase, of course, is stylized and can have but one cryptic meaning. To make the rhyming code less obvious as well as shorter, the last and rhyming part of the substitute phrase is often dropped, leaving as rhyming slang a word that does not rhyme with the word replaced. Thus *plates of meat* = *feet* (the last word *meat* of the phrase rhyming with *feet*, the word conveyed), but the rhyming word and preposition can be dropped leaving *plates* = *feet*. In like manner, *twist and twirl* = *girl*, which is back clipped to *twist* = *girl* (this word is the major contribution that rhyming slang has made to general slang). With such shortenings, the initiate will know the longer phrase, which rhymes, but the uninitiate will see no rhyme and have no clue as to the word conveyed. (In the Appendix list the full rhyming slang phrase is given along with any shortened forms.) Also, the original rhyme is often made to a now obsolete or purely argot word, thus *coat and badge* = *to cadge* (to beg), *Johnny Ronce* = *ponce* (pimp).

Rhyming slang is one of the most picturesque and imaginative side-streams of our language. Besides including some archaic British terms, its national origin is obvious in such conveyed words as *quid* and *shilling*. Most rhyming slang terms convey everyday nouns, as *bread*, *chair*, *shirt*, *talk*, *water*, etc. If no rhyming words were readily available, real or fictitious names, or even numbers, were used, as *Aristotle* = *bottle*, *Betty Lee* = *tea*, *Bo Peep* = *sleep*, *forty-four* or *five to four* or *fifty-four* = *whore*, *Richard the Third* = *bird*.

Besides the rhyme, many rhyming slang phrases contain words having images or connotations applicable to the word conveyed, thus *plates of meat* = *feet* not only rhymes but the phrase suggests the image of a platter, which is vaguely foot-shaped, and *meat* has the connotation of flesh.

BACK SLANG is formed by respelling a word backward, from right to left, placing the last letter first, and so on. Thus, *enob* = *bone* (penis) and *yob* = *boy* or *youth*. Be-

cause this is a process of respelling, back slang originates in code writing rather than speech; such respelling and pronunciation is a common children's game and code. Any word can be spelled backward, but only a few have gained even a small degree of popularity with their new form. All back-slang words mean the same as their original, properly spelled base words, though often only one meaning or connotation is implied. Sometimes in spelling a word backward a letter or syllable is dropped, added, or slightly changed for greater ease in pronunciation or to effect a pun, thus *ecilop* or even *e-slop* may = *police*.

(A unique word, and not true back slang, is *bassackwards*. This is actually a Spoonerism formed by transposing the initial consonant of the second syllable to the beginning of the word; it is, as well, something of a euphemism. Such non-back slang respellings and pronunciations are not popular, but some such nonce-word formations and punning respellings do occur.)

LITTLE LANGUAGES. Dozens of little languages exist; in the aggregate they are known to several millions of English-speaking people, though very seldom used. Little languages are vocabularies formed from known words by adding specific meaningless sounds or groups of letters at the beginning or end of a word, or more frequently before or after each syllable or before or after consonants or vowels. This may be accompanied by some respelling or reordering of syllables of the word. Little languages are used to conceal the speaker's meaning from outsiders, but often this is done to amuse rather than for secrecy. Many little languages are known to children who form and use them as code; some are quite old and have been handed down from generation to generation of children; a few little languages are jargon or argot formations.

Pig Latin (also called Hog Latin and Dog Latin) is the best-known little language; it is familiar to almost every child and dates to at least the early 1770's. Pig Latin demonstrates the formation of most little languages: it is formed by transposing the letter order of a word and, more typically, by adding a meaningless syllable. Basically, Pig Latin is formed by taking the first letter of a word and putting it last and adding an *-ay* to it. For example: "ouyay ankay alktay igpay Atinlay" = "you can talk pig Latin."

As are most such primarily children's-code little languages, pig Latin is usually formed from one- or two-syllable simple words. Differences exist in its formation, depending on local uses and the adeptness of the neighborhood group in using it (thus the first letter is usually put last, but in more complicated forms the last vowel or diphthong may be put first, or the first vowel or diphthong and all that follows is put first, so that the word *Latin* may be rendered either by *Atinlay* or much less frequently by *Inlatay*, etc). Pig Latin has contributed more words to general slang than all other little languages combined, including *amscray = scram* and *ixnay = nix*. (*Offsteered* is unique in that it resembles and seems based on pig Latin, but is not.)

Gree, Na and *Skimono jive* are representative and the most popular of the simplest forms of children's little languages. Gree and Na are formed merely by adding a syllable (*-gree* or *-na*) after every word, or in a more advanced form, after every syllable. Thus: "yougree cangree talkgree Greegree" = "you can talk Gree," and "youna canna talkna Nana" = "you can talk Na." Skimono jive has nothing to do with jive or jive talk; to form it, *sk-* is merely added before every word, or in a more advanced form, before every syllable. Thus: "sk-you sk-can sk-talk sk-skimono sk-jive" = "you can talk skimono jive."

Ong is representative of a slightly more difficult group of little languages, which are therefore popular with older children. In these the meaningless syllable or sound is added to every consonant (or sometimes only between consonants and vowels) and is sometimes also placed before initial vowels beginning a word. In this case the added sound is *-ong* and "yong-ou cong-a-nong tong-a-long-kong Onong-gong" = "you can talk Ong."

Pelf Latin and *Carnese* are the most popular and representative of the next, slightly more difficult, group of little languages. In these an extra syllable or sound is inserted after every consonant or vowel or (usually amounting to the same thing) before every consonant or vowel: in some variations the added sound may be placed only before or after key or stressed letters, most often after a consonant beginning a new syllable. Pelf Latin (also called Alfalfa) is a children's-code little language. It is formed by placing an *-lf* after each vowel or diphthong and then repeating that vowel or diphthong. Thus: "*youlfou calfan talfalk Pelfelf*

Lalfatilfin" (or "*Lalfatin*") = "*you can talk Pelf Latin.*"

Carnese (also called Goon Language or Goon Talk) is not carnival jargon and cant but a true little-language argot originated and used by carnival workers. As with most little languages, it is easy to decipher when seen, but confusing when heard spoken very rapidly by initiates. Basically, it is formed by adding an *—eeiz, —eeaz, —ez,* or *-az* sound between each consonant and vowel. Thus: "*yeeizou keeizan teeizalk Keeizarn-eeizese.*" = "*you can talk Carnese.*" The only important Carnese word added to general slang is *mezonny* (m-eeiz-oney) = *money.* Other Carnese words heard occasionally in somewhat general use are *beazeer = beer* and *reazing = ring.*

Tutnee or *tutnese* is representative of advanced forms which are the hardest to decipher of the familiar little languages. Basically, consonants may be followed by an inserted sound (*-u-* in this case) and then may be repeated (thus *t* would become *tut*). Certain consonants, especially liquids, however, may be followed by specific sounds or syllables; and initial vowels may be preceded by, and final vowels followed by, added consonants, in Tutnee by *-t* or *-d*. Also a double letter may be indicated by preceding the single letter with a nonsense word or syllable. Thus in one form of Tutnee: "*yack-o-yud cause-a-nun tut-a-lul-kuk Tut-yud-tut-nun -squir-e*" = "*you can talk Tutnee.*"

Hundreds of such little languages exist, and neighborhood children often devise their own, using whatever added syllables or sounds appeal to them.[10]

---

[10] Double talk is not a little language, and it is not even used to convey meaning. It is a humorous device usually consisting of ordinary English sentences, rhythms, stresses and syllables in which an expected meaningful word is replaced by a meaningless sound that resembles a sound common in meaningful speech. Thus one would say: "Yesterday I was walking down the bedistran to broint a little stillicide—not much you understand —just franzity. Suddenly a large renlif passed me and we trazzled together for a short erloff."

WORD LISTS

Contents

Word Lists

The following lists include both words defined in this dictionary and many other words not considered true slang or popular enough to be entered in the text. Many recurring nonce words, neologisms, colloquial, argot, obsolete, and archaic words are included here, however, to demonstrate various methods of word formation. These lists are only representative. Each word has been encountered in at least two sources published five years apart. An asterisk following an item indicates that that item appears in the text proper. Definitions (following a dash) are given only when an item does not appear in the text and the meaning is not obvious.

Affixes

Suffixes

—ama, —rama. A new noun-forming suffix since c1950, from "panorama." It refers to any motion-picture process in which an exceptionally wide viewing screen is used. Since c1955, this suffix has been used to = any long, expensive, spectacular commercial entertainment, as *circusama, telerama*, etc.

—arino. See **—ino** below.

—aroo. See **—eroo** below.

—ateria. See **—eteria** below.

—atorium, —torium, —orium. From "emp*orium*" reinforced by "audi*torium*." A noun-forming suffix referring to a place where a service is performed, usually for male customers, and often to an inexpensive shop using the ending pompously or jocularly.

barbatorium — barbershop
bathatorium — public bath
bobatorium — beauty parlor
drinkatorium — bar
hatatorium — men's hat shop
healthatorium — gymnasium; vegetarian restaurant
kanditorium — candy store
lubritorium — automobile repair shop

motortorium — garage
pantatorium (pantorium) — men's clothing store
printorium — store that sells art prints
restatorium — lunch counter
restorium — rest room
shavatorium — barbershop
shineatorium — shoe-shine parlor
suitatorium — men's clothing store

—dom. A noun-forming suffix figuratively = the realm, era, or time of. Popular with columnists, it is more often written than spoken.

fandom
flapperdom
froshdom
gagdom
hamdom
hickdom
hitdom
hucksterdom
moviedom*
pitchdom
pledgedom
post-debdom
prepdom
pugdom
sheikdom
stuffed-shirtdom
suckerdom
swelldom
swingdom
trampdom
white-collardom
yeggdom

—ed. An adjective-forming suffix added to nouns = having the characteristics of, figuratively full of, or possessed of. It is frequently added to the second element of a compound form, as *meat-headed, panty-waisted*, etc. It is sometimes added to a noun compounded with *—up*, as *boozed-up*. This suffix also has another, minor slang use = to have been processed or put through a specific process, as *Arthur Murrayed* = to have taken a dancing course at an "Arthur Murray" dance studio, and *Elizabeth Ardened* = to have taken a beauty course at an "Elizabeth Arden" studio.

—ee. A noun-forming suf-

fix added to nouns and verbs usually = the object of an action, as *deceivee, investigatee, kissee*. It was widely used during World War II, as *draftee, evacuee, trainee*. The suffix often refers to one who suffers, as *amputee, accidentee*. In slang *—ee* may mean the doer as well as the object of an action: *cursee* or *flunkee* usually = one who is cursed or flunked, but sometimes it refers to the one who curses or the teacher who flunks a student.

accidentee
adoptee
advisee
amputee
analyzee
assassinee
auditionee
awardee
baby-sittee
barberee
bargainee
beatee
beateree
biographee
bombee
boree
bossee
bouncee
buckeree
bustee
concentrationee
conductee
conferee
conscriptee
contractee
cookee*
crack-upee
cursee
datee
deceivee
deflatee
deludee
departee*
deportee
detainee
disappointee
dischargee
draftee*
eliminee
endowee
enlistee
enrollee
escapee
evacuee
evictee
firee

610

fixee
flickee
flirtee
floggee
flunkee*
foldee
foolee
forgettee
freebee*
freezee
furloughee
garglee
gazee
giftee
goodbyee*
hangee
happenee
hazee
holdupee
honoree
inductee
internee
interviewee
investigatee
invitee
jestee
jigamaree*
jokee
kibitzee
kickee
kissee
knockee
laughee
lovee
maskee*
mesmeree
murderee
observee
pinee
pollee
purgee
questionee
quizzee*
reservee
retiredee
retiree
returnee
rushee*
saloonee
salvagee
screenee
selectee
sendee
sentencee
separatee
shavee
shoutee
sittee
slurree
snubbee
sockee
spankee
squeezee
standee*
staree
startee
starvee
stranglee

sufferee
testee
tippee
tossee
trainee
transferee
tryoutee
tutee
tutoree
waitee
wishee
yank-ee

—er and **—er —er.** A noun-forming suffix usually added to nouns, sometimes to verbs and adverbs. Probably the most popular suffix, it is used literally and figuratively in several ways: as a person or thing associated with *(hasher, junker, page-oner)*; as simply a person or thing *(fifteener, keener)*; as a person or thing doing something *(baby-sitter, buck-passer)*. It is used in shortened forms *(hummer* for *humdinger)*, or it is used to add length to convey a more slangy, colloquial, or flippant effect *(gasser* for *gas)*.

The *—er —er* form could be called a rhyming term or a reduplication. When the *—er* suffix does not indicate agency (as in *killer-diller)*, the word is removed to the list of Reduplications. The *—er —er* formations are usually awkward synonyms for shorter words *(usher-inner* for *usher)*.

aginer
air-breather*
airer — broadcaster
ambulance chaser*
apple knocker*
apple-shiner*
arm-waver*
ass kisser*
baby kisser*
baby-lifter*
baby-sitter*
backer-up
baggage smasher*
bagger*
bag-puncher*
ball-breaker*
ball-buster*
banger*
barker*
barn-burner*
barn-stormer*
bat carrier*
bealer*
bean-baller — pitcher known

for throwing "bean balls"
bean-eater*
beaner*
bean-shooter*
beater*
beefeater*
beefer*
beer-jerker*
beer-slinger*
beezer*
bell-ringer*
belly-buster*
belly-flopper*
belly-robber*
belly-smacker*
belly-whopper*
bench warmer*
bender*
bicker*
biffer*
big-timer*
billiard drinker*
biscuit-roller*
biscuit-shooter*
blackbaiter*
blackbirder*
blaster*
bleeder*
blind-pigger*
blinger*
blister*
blooper*
blotter*
blower*
boater*
bobby-socker*
body-snatcher*
bog-hopper*
bog-trotter*
boiler*
boiler-maker*
bomber*
bone-bender*
bone-breaker*
bone-cracker*
bone-crusher*
bone-eater*
boner*
bone-shaker*
bonzer*
boodler*
boomer*
boondocker*
booster*
booter*
bootlegger*
bootlicker*
booze-fighter*
boozer
bouncer*
boxer*
brain picker*
brass pounder*
breech loader*
breezer*
briar-hopper*
broken-striper*
bronco buster*

bronco peeler*
bronco snapper*
bronco twister*
brown-noser*
bruiser*
bubble-chaser*
bubble dancer*
bucker*
buck-passer
buffer*
bugger*
builder*
build-Germany-upper
bug-hunter*
bugle-warmer*
bulldozer*
bull fiddler — bass-viol player (euphem. bull shitter)
bull-fighter*
bullshitter*
bullshooter*
bullstaller*
bummer*
bumper*
bunco-steerer*
bun-duster*
bunion-breeder*
burner*
busher*
buster*
butcher*
button chopper*
buzzer*
cackler*
cager*
cake-cutter*
cake-eater*
campus butcher*
cannon fodder*
can-opener*
caper*
capper*
car catcher*
carder*
cement-mixer*
chain-smoker*
chair-warmer*
chalk-eater*
chaser*
cheater*
check bouncer*
checker*
cheese eater*
cherry picker*
chiller*
china-clipper*
China cracker*
chirper*
chiseler*
chopper*
Christer*
chronicker*
chucker*
chucker-out
cinder crusher*
circuit slugger*
city slicker*
clacker*

clanker*
cleaner*
cleaner-up
cleffer*
cliffdweller*
cliffhanger*
clincher*
clinker*
clipper*
clocker*
clock watcher*
clodhopper*
clog dancer*
cloud buster*
clouter*
clover-kicker*
club-winder*
clunker*
cobber*
cob-roller*
cock sucker*
cock teaser*
coffee cooler*
coffee grinder*
come-outer
comer*
coming-upper
comma-counter*
conk-buster*
cooker*
cookie-cutter*
cookie pusher*
cooler*
cop-caller
copper*
cop-spotter
corker*
corn cracker*
corn-stealer*
counter-jumper*
cracker*
cradle-robber*
cradle-snatcher*
crammer*
crape-hanger*
crapper*
crasher*
cruller*
creaker*
cream-puff hitter*
creeper*
crip-faker*
croaker*
crooker*
cropper*
cruncher*
crupper*
crusher*
cutter*
daisy-cutter*
damper*
dancer*
dangler*
deader*
dead ringer*
deceiver*
deemer*
deener*

designer*
destroyer*
detainer*
deucer*
diamond-cracker*
diamond-thrower*
dicer*
diller*
dimmer*
diner-out
ding-donger*
dinger*
dipper*
dishwasher*
disker — a disk jockey
diver*
dock-walloper*
dog-chaser*
dog-naper*
do-gooder*
dog-robber*
dolly dancer*
donagher*
donnicker*
dooker*
doper
dosser*
double-crosser*
double-decker*
double-header*
dough-puncher*
dough-roller*
down-and-outer*
downer*
dragger*
dreamer*
drifter*
driver*
drooler*
dropper*
drum-beater*
drummer*
dualer*
ducat-snatcher*
duck-hustler*
dude heaver*
duffer*
duster*
dust-raiser*
dynamiter*
ear-banger*
ear-bender*
ear duster*
egg beater*
egg-sucker*
elbow-bender*
elephant-hunter*
equalizer*
essence peddler*
eye-opener*
faker*
fanner*
fast talker*
feather duster*
feeler*
fellow traveler*
fence-hanger*
fender — one who defends his

rights or others'
fifteener — fifteen-year-old; teenager
file-boner*
filler-in
finagler*
finger popper*
finger-wringer*
firecracker*
fire-eater*
fire-goer-to
first reader*
first sacker
fish eater*
fish-wrapper*
fiver*
five-per-center*
fixer*
flag-waver*
flamethrower*
flanker*
flapper*
flattener*
flesh peddler*
flicker*
flim-flammer*
flinger*
flivver*
floater*
flogger*
flounce-in-and-outer
flunker
fluter*
fly-chaser*
fog-cutter*
follow-upper
fork-hander*
forth-holder
four-bagger*
four-flusher*
four-striper*
free-loader*
free-rider — freshman
fresher — freshman
fritterer-away
fritzer*
frog-eater*
frog-sticker*
fucker — disliked person; a "fuck off"
fudger — cheater, welcher
furper*
fusser*
gabber*
gaffer*
gagger*
gandy dancer*
gaper*
garbage-kisser*
gardener*
gasper*
gasser*
gate-crasher*
gazer*
gear-jammer*
geezer*
getter*
getter-by

getter-up
giddy-apper*
gimper*
glad hander*
glim worker*
glommer*
goer*
go-getter*
gold bricker*
gold-digger*
golfer*
goner*
gonger*
goober-grabber*
gooder*
good-looker*
goofer*
goose-drownder*
grabber*
grafter*
grand slammer*
grandstander*
grass-clipper*
grass-cutter*
grasshopper*
gravel crusher*
grease-burner*
greaser*
gridder — football player
grifter*
grinder*
griper*
grizzler*
groaner*
grounder*
ground-gripper*
grouser*
growler*
grub-choker*
grumbler*
grunt-and-groaner*
grunter*
gum-beater*
gummer*
gutser — strenuous task
gutter*
gypper*
hack-driver*
hacker*
hack-skinner*
hair-pounder*
ham-and-egger*
ham-fatter*
ham-hanger*
hand grenader*
handshaker*
hangarounder
hanger-on
hanger-out
hard-rocker*
harp-polisher*
hash-burner*
hash driver*
hasher*
hash-slinger*
hatchet-thrower*
hay-burner*
hay-eater*

haymaker*
hayseeder*
hay-shaker*
headbeater*
header*
head hunter*
head shrinker*
heater*
heat-packer*
heaver*
heavy-sticker*
hedgehopper*
heeler*
heister*
hell-bender*
heller*
hell-raiser*
herder*
herring-choker*
high-binder*
highgrader*
high-hatter*
high roller*
hijacker*
hiker*
hitter*
hog-caller*
hogger*
hoister
holder-down
homer*
honey-cooler*
hoofer*
hooker*
hooker-off
hooker-on
hopper*
hot-rodder
howler*
hugger-mugger*
hummer — humdinger
hurry-upper
hustler*
ice-breaker — that which puts people in an informal mood
in-and-outer*
in-betweener
in-comer
ink-slinger*
in-or-outer
Irisher*
ivory-hunter*
ivory-thumper*
jabber*
jackroller*
jammer*
jaw-breaker*
jaw-cracker*
Jayhawker*
jaywalker*
jeeter*
jig-chaser*
jobber
jocker*
joe-darter*
joker*
josher*

josser*
joy-popper*
joy-rider*
juicer*
joy-popper
juice jerker
junker*
keener*
keister*
kennebecker*
key-swinger*
kibitzer*
kidder*
kidney-buster*
kike-killer*
killer*
kinker*
kisser*
klupper*
knee-bender*
knocker*
knocker-out
knocker-up
knucker*
knuckle-buster*
knuckle-duster*
knuckler*
kosher*
lagger*
lamster*
laugher-off
layer-out
leader-on
left-winger*
legiter — one who earns an
    honest living; stage show,
    stage actor
lexer*
licker-in
lifer*
lifter-up
lime-juicer*
lip-splitter*
listener*
lollygagger*
loner*
looker*
looker-after
looker-on
looper*
lot hopper*
lug-clipper*
lugger*
lumper
lung-duster*
lunger*
lung-fogger*
lusher*
lush-roller*
lush-worker*
mackerel-snapper*
mainliner*
make-upper
man-catcher*
marker*
marsh-jumper
masher*
meat-burner*

meat-grinder*
megger*
meter-reader*
mitt-flopper*
mitt-glommer*
mittreader*
mixer*
mixer-upping
moll buzzer*
momzer*
monkey-chaser*
moocher*
mooner*
moonshiner*
mopper-up
mop-squeezer*
mouser*
mucker*
muckraker*
mudder*
mud-kicker*
mugger*
mule-skinner*
muscler-in
musher*
mush-faker*
muzzle-loader*
muzzler*
necker
nicker*
nigger*
nipper*
nit-picker*
nobbler*
no-gooder
no-hitter*
nutser
oat-burner*
oater*
oil-burner*
oncer*
one-lunger*
oner*
one-srtiper*
opener*
outcaster
out-of-stater
out-of-towner*
overnighter*
ozoner*
page-oner — a celebrity
palooker*
pancake turner*
panhandler*
pan-lifter*
pan-jerker*
paper-hanger*
party pooper*
patzer*
pea-souper
peanut-roaster*
pearl-diver*
pea-shooter*
pecker*
peddler*
peeler*
peeper*
pelter*

pencil-pusher*
pencil-shover*
pen-driver*
penny-pincher
pennyweighter*
pepper-upper*
percenter*
persuader*
peter*
photogger — photographer
picker-out
picker-up
pig-sticker*
piker*
pill-peddler*
pill-pusher*
pill-roller*
pincher*
pillow-puncher*
pinch-hitter
pinky-crooker*
pisser*
plainer*
planker*
plank-owner*
plater*
plinger
plugger*
plug puller*
poodle-faker*
pop-inner
popper*
pork-chopper*
porker — pig
port-sider*
potato masher*
pot boiler*
pot-massager*
pot-slinger*
pot-walloper*
pot-wrestler*
pounder*
pourer-off
pretzel-bender*
prom-trotter*
prune-picker*
puddle-jumper*
puffer*
puller*
pulse-upperer
pumper*
pumpkin-roller*
punker*
pusher*
putter-in
qualley-worker*
queener*
quetcher*
Rackensaker*
ragger*
rapper*
ratter*
rattler*
reader*
reefer*
reeler*
rib-tickler*
rider*

ringer*
ring-master*
ring-tailed snorter*
rip-snorter*
rock crusher*
roller*
rooter*
roper — cowboy; shill
rotter*
rounder*
round-tripper*
rubber*
rug-cutter*
rum-sucker*
runner-down
runner-up
rusher
— sacker*
safe-cracker*
sagebrusher*
sand-pounder*
sand-smeller*
sawyer*
sawdust-eater*
scalper*
scatter*
schlepper*
schneider*
schnorrer*
schuper*
scooter*
scorcher*
scratcher*
screamer*
screecher*
scrounger*
scunner*
scupper*
secesher — Southerner
second sacker*
selling plater*
sell-outer
sender*
seventeener*
shagger*
shaker-off
shaver*
sheet-writer*
shiever*
shifter*
shillaber*
shiner*
shocker*
shoestringer — insignificant
  businessman or entertainer
shooper*
shooter — bull shooter
short-staker*
short-story writer*
shoulder-hitter*
shouter*
shoveler*
shover*
shower*
shuffler*
shutter*
side kicker — sidekick
side-wheeler*

sidewinder*
Simonizer*
singer*
sinker*
sit-downer
sitter*
sitter-in
sitter-out
sitter-up
sixer*
six-shooter*
sizzler*
skimmer*
skin-beater*
skinner*
skipper*
skivvy-waver*
skull-buster*
skyscraper*
sky-winder*
slammer*
slapper*
slasher*
slave-driver*
slave-puncher*
sleeper*
sleighrider*
slicker*
slider — slow pitch curving
  away from a baseball batter
slimer*
slinger*
slow-downer
slugger*
slum-burner*
slum-diver*
slusher
smacker*
small-timer
smasher*
smeller*
smoke-eater*
smoker*
smoocher*
smoother-over
snapper*
snapper-back
snapper-up
snatcher*
sneaker*
sneeyer — a jail
sneezer*
sniffer*
snifter*
sniper*
snitcher*
snollygoster*
snooker*
snooper*
snorter*
snower — bull shit artist
snow-flier*
snuff-dipper
soaker*
soap-boxer — ardent supporter for a cause; politician
sockdollager*

socker*
soda jerker*
sod-buster*
solid sender*
Sooner*
souper*
spam cluster*
sparkler*
speaker*
speeder-up
spider*
spieler*
spiker*
spinner*
spitter*
splinter*
sponger*
spooner*
springer*
squaker — a companion
square shooter*
squawker*
squeaker*
squeeler*
squeezer*
stander-by
star boarder*
star-gazer*
starker*
stay-a-whiler
stay-upper
steerer*
stem-winder*
step dancer*
stepper*
stew-builder*
stewer*
sticker*
stiffener*
stinger*
stinker*
stomach-robber*
stone-crusher*
stopper*
stretcher*
striders — trousers
strike-breaker*
striker*
string-whanger*
stripper*
stroller-by
stuffer*
stump-jumper*
sucker*
Sunday driver*
Sunday soldier*
Sunday thinker*
sun-downer*
sun-fisher*
super-dooper*
swamper*
sweeper-up
sweepswinger*
switch-hitter*
table finisher*
table-hopper
tab-lifter*
tack hammer*

talker*
taker-over
talker-back
tattler*
tear-jerker*
tear-upper
teaser*
teenager*
teener*
tenner*
ten-percenter*
Texas leaguer*
thinker*
third sacker*
thousand-miler*
three-striper*
thriller-diller*
thumber — hitch-hiker
thumb-pusher*
ticker*
tickler*
timber*
tipster*
tokus licker*
Tommer*
tom-troller*
top kicker*
topper*
Top Knocker*
top-notcher
torcher — torch singer
tosser-away
towner — town dweller
trailer*
tray-toter
trigger*
tripper*
trotters — feet; legs
trouper*
tryer-out
tuner-in
turner-back
turner-out
turf-cutter*
tweeter*
twicer
twinner — a "dead ringer"
twirler — a "twirl"
twister*
two-and-a-half-striper*
twoer — two-year prison sentence
two percenter*
two-stemmer*
two-stepper*
two-striper*
two-time loser*
two-timer
typewriter*
Uncle Tommer*
user*
usher-inner
varnish remover*
vauder — vaudeville performer
viper*
waker-up
wall-flower*

wallpaper*
ward heeler*
warmer-upper*
washer*
washtub-weeper*
watcher*
waver*
waxer — one who records a phonograph record
weak sister*
weaver*
weeper*
weighter*
welsher*
whaler*
wheeler*
wheeler-dealer*
whicker*
wicker*
whiffer*
whippersnapper*
whisker*
whistler*
white slaver*
whiz-dinger*
whizzer*
whooper-dooper*
whopper*
whore-hopper*
widow-maker*
wiener*
winder*
winder-up — that which concludes
wind-jammer*
wind-sucker
wing-dinger*
wing-waiter*
wiper*
wire-puller*
wisecracker*
wisenheimer*
wood butcher*
wood-chopper*
woodpiler*
wood-pusher*
woofer*
word-slinger
world-beater*
wowser*
yammer*
yatter*
yawner-at
yentzer*
yodeler*
zagger*
zoot suiter*

adder-upper
backer-upper
barker-atter
bawler-outer
bender-downer
blower-offer
blower-downer
bracer-upper
breaker-downer
breaker-upper*

brightener-upper
bringer-outer
builder-upper*
butter-inner
buttoner-upper
checker-upper
chiller-diller*
cheerer-upper
cleaner-outer
cleaner-upper
closer-upper
cooker-upper
cracker-downer
cutter-in-arounder
cutter-upper
digger-upper
diner-outer
disher-outer
disher-upper
doper-outer
dreamer-upper
dresser-upper
dryer-outer
dryer-upper
drifter-througher
dropper-inner
ducker-inner
ducker-outer
eater-outer
eker-outer
ender-upper
evener-upper
fighter-backer
filler-inner
filler-outer
filler-upper
finder-outer
finisher-upper
fixer-upper
freshener-upper
fresher-upper
getter-outer
getter-upper
giver-awayer
giver-inner
giver-outer
giver-upper
goer-to-bedder
hanger-onner
hanger-upper
helper-outer
hider-outer
hipper-dipper*
holder-downer
holder-outer
holder-upper
hooper-dooper*
hopper-upper
ice breaker-upper
hooper-dooper*
jacker-upper*
jammer-upper
jotter-downer
jumper-outer
jumper-upper
keeper-in-officer
kicker-downer
kicker-offer

kicker-upper
killer-diller*
knocker-outer
lacer-upper
layer-outer
lifter-upper
liver-arounder
liver-upper
livener-upper
looker-afterer
looker-arounder
looker-atter
looker-upper
maker-upper
meter-reader*
mixer-upper
mopper-upper
mover-abouter
mover-inner
musser-upper
opener-upper*
orderer-abouter
passer-arounder
passer-byer
pepper-upper*
perker-upper*
picker-offer
picker-outer
picker-upper*
pinner-downer
plugger-upper
pointer-outer
puller-inner
puller-upper
pumper-upper
pusher-arounder
pusher-backer
pusher-outer
putter-awayer
putter-downer
putter-offer*
putter-outer
putter-to-bedder
putter-upper
reader-alouder
reader-in-bedder
roper-inner
rooter-outer
rounder-upper
runner-upper
screwer-inner
scrubber-upper
sender-inner
setter-upper
sewer-inner
shaker-downer
shaker-upper
shaper-upper
shiner-upper
shipper-upper
shooter-upper
sitter-downer*
sitter-outer
sizer-upper
slammer-downer
smeller-outer
smuggler-outer
soother-downer

snapper-backer
spader-upper
speaker-outer
speaker-upper
speeder-upper
stander-upper
starter-offer
starter-outer
stayer-upper
sticker-outer
stirrer-upper
straightener-outer
striker-outer
super-duper*
sweeper-upper
taker-awayer
taker-inner
taker-on-the-chinner
taker-outer
tearer-downer
tester-outer
thinker-upper
thriller-diller*
topper-offer
tripper-upper
tuner-inner
tuner-upper
turner-inner
waker-upper
walker-outer
walker-upper
warmer-upper
waver-offer
whooper-upper
winder-upper*
wiser-upper
wrapper-upper

—eria. See —eteria below.
—erino. See —ino below.
—eroo, —aroo, —roo, —oo.
Originally from the Span-
ish —ero (as in the borrowing buckeroo), this suffix
often = the standard —er
suffix of agency. Often the
—oo is added to words al-
ready having the —er end-
ing (dilleroo, jokeroo). Especially in theatrical use,
it indicates hyperbole (bofferoo, flopperoo). It sometimes conveys familiarity,
almost as a diminutive (aceroo, bounceroo). Occasionally it = the standard —ese
ending (Japaroo for Japa-
nese).

aceroo — ace; first; best
antseroo
babyroo
baggeroo
beameroo, on the
bingeroo
biteroo
blabberoo
bofferoo
boozeroo
bopperoo

bossaroo
bounceroo
brusheroo
buckeroo*
buddyroo*
bummaroo
bungaroo
bunkaroo
cabberoo
champeroo
checkeroo
cheferoo
chickeroo
chilleroo
chumperoo
clamperoo
cleareroo
clickaroo
Congaroo*
conneroo
cookeroo
crosseroo
crusheroo
cufferoo*
darberoo
dilleroo
dingeroo
diveroo
dollaroo
dreamaroo
dreameroo
dripperoo
drooperoo
fakeroo
finkeroo
fixeroo
fizzeroo
flatteroo
flipperoo
flopperoo*
gaggeroo
gazaroo
gutseroo
gypperoo
hammeroo
howleroo
humdingeroo
ickeroo
jackeroo*
Japaroo
jazzeroo
jiggeroo
jim-danderoo
jitteroo
jitterbuggaroo
jivaroo
jobberoo
jokeroo
juggaroo
jumperoo
kickeroo
killer-dilleroo
kisseroo
laugheroo
luckeroo
magoo*
mazoo*
mixuperoo

nifteroo
niggeroo
paineroo
payeroo
peacheroo
pepperoo
phraseroo
pipperoo*
pluckeroo
pokeroo
puncheroo
punkeroo
quickeroo
quizzeroo
rancheroo
raveroo
razzeroo
sapperoo
scatteroo
scooteroo
scrammeroo
screamaroo
skiboo*
skidoo*
skipperoo
sleeperoo
smackeroo
smasheroo
smelleroo
snackeroo
snapperoo
snoozeroo
sockeroo*
spotteroo
squatteroo
squeezeroo
staggeroo
stinkeroo*
stooperoo
storkeroo
stripperoo
stufferoo
successeroo
sugaroo
swingaroo
switcheroo*
swooneroo
tipperoo
titty-boo*
toodle-oo*
topperoo
tougheroo
twenty-three skidoo!*
twisteroo
vibaroo
Waacaroo
wackaroo
washeroo
whackeroo
whangeroo
whipperoo
whizzeroo
zipparoo
zoomeroo

—ery. Forming nouns from nouns and occasionally from verbs, this suffix usually signifies a place where something is served or sold *(bootery)*, or a place that is associated with, known for, or provides the facilities for *(dancery)*. The suffix is also used to = the state or condition of, or the qualities or acts characteristic of that denoted by, the root word *(claptrappery, snidery)*.

appetite-killery
beanery*
beer-guzzery
bootery — shoe store
boozery
brainery*
cakery
cannery*
car-washery
claptrappery
crookery
cut-uppery
dancery
debunkery
diskery
doggery — hot-dog stand; kennel
doughnuttery
drinkery
drunkery
duckery
eatery
fishery*
gassery — tavern, where one can get "gassed"
flimflammery
flubdubbery
guzzlery*
ham-and-eggery*
hashery*
hi-jinkery
hoodwinkery
hoofery
hot-doggery
jerkery
lunchery
mendery — tailor's shop
minkery — fur store
nightery*
notchery*
plattery
plushery*
skulduggery*
snidery
sniggery
sockdolagery
spivery
rookery*
stitchery
terpery
tine-bendery
toggery — clothing store
wise-crackery

—ess. This is a suffix used to form a feminine noun, and hence the counterpart of —er and —or. The formation is non-standard when made on non-standard roots or when a feminine noun or doer is so unusual as to be noteworthy *(muggess, wolfess)*.

ambassadress
barberess
bishopess
brokeress
bubbess
burgheress
centauress
conductress
detractress
editress
electress
high-hatress
legionairess
loaferess
Martianess
muggess
mulatress
niggeress
oafess
paintress
photographess
portress
pythoness
receptioness
rectress
suicidess
translatress
trooperess
veepess
wolfess*

—ese. A noun-forming suffix which denotes a style of speaking or writing peculiar to a given region, occupation, publication, mode of communication, or individual. When referring to an individual's mode of speech, his vocabulary is usually meant, rather than his accent or other speech mannerisms.

Brooklynese
cablese
cowpuncherese
filmese — literary style used in subtitles of silent movies
gangsterese
golfese
guide-bookese
journalese
junglese — speech used in hobo "jungles"
Madison Avenuese
Manhattanese
Pentagonese
Runyonese
soda-jerkerese
Winchellese

—eteria, —teria, —eria, —ateria. A noun-forming suffix

indicating a place of business offering goods or services specified by the root word. As it is most commonly applied to inexpensive eating places serving quick lunches, *—eteria* is interchangeable with *—atorium*, *—ette* (the standard diminutive), and *—ery*. Thus *lunchateria, lunchatorium, lunchette,* and *lunchery* are equal in meaning and probably in popularity.

basketeria
bobateria — beauty parlor
bookateria
cafeteria
chocolateria
cleaneteria
drygoodsteria
fruiteria
grocerteria
hatateria
healtheteria — vegetarian restaurant; a gymnasium
icecreamateria
luncheteria
marketeria
mototeria
radioteria
restauranteria
roadeteria — roadside restaurant
serveteria — any of several types of self-service stores, esp. a small grocery or drugstore
shaveteria
smoketeria — a cigarette, cigar, and pipe store
sodateria — a soft-drink counter
valeteria — a cleaning and tailoring shop

—ey. See **—ie** below.

—ian. As in standard use this is an adjective-forming suffix usually = one who is, lives or works in or at, or is an adherent of or believer in whatever the root signifies. It is used to form non-standard words only when the root is non-standard or when the new adjective formed is so unusual as to be noteworthy *(earthian)*.

—ico. An adjective suffix taken from the Spanish and Italian to = one who is. Since c1945 this ending has seen some increased sophisticated use, often in an attempt to intensify the standard *—ic* suffix. This *magnifico, romantico,* and *simpatico* have seen some popular use to describe people who are more "magnificent," "romantic," or "sympathetic" than these common words convey. *Politico* (= a complete politician, usually an aggressive and unscrupulous one) is unique in having derogatory connotations.

—ie, —ey, —y and **—sie, —sey, —sy.** This suffix (especially in its more extreme form, *—sie*) is primarily used as a noun-forming diminutive indicating small size, affection, or familiarity *(beddy, footsie, nightie)*. Such formations frequently refer to parts of the body, familiar items of clothing, love games, and children's games. The suffix is almost always added to both elements of the "baby talk" second-order reduplications (see below). It is also commonly used in direct familiar address *(dearie, sweetie)*; in familiar nicknames *(Fatty)*; in forming nicknames from proper names *(Archie)*; and in nicknames from place, regional, and trade names *(Chevvie, Dixie)*. Besides their diminutive use, *—ie* and *—sie* are adjective-forming suffixes *(baldie, sharpie, weirdie)*.

acey-deucey*
Arky*
assy*
auntie*
Aussie
baddie*
baldy*
beaky
beanie*
beddy
beekie*
benny*
Betsy*
biddy*
biggie*
binny*
birdie*
bitchy*
bleenie*
blinkie*
blokie
bloody*
(go) blooey*
bodgie*
bogie*
boobie*

boogie*
boogie-woogie*
bookie*
bootie*
boozy*
bossy*
brakie*
brainy*
brighty
brookie*
Brownie*
bubie*
buddy*
buggy*
bully*
bummy*
bungey*
bunkie*
bunny*
burly*
burnie*
busy*
buzzey*
cabbie*
Caddy*
cagey*
cally*
canned goods*
carny*
catty*
chappie*
cheapie*
cheeky*
cheesy*
Chevvie
chickie*
Chinkie — a Chinese; Chinese
chinny*
chintzy*
chippie*
chivey*
chokey*
chum-buddy*
ciggie — cigarette
civvies*
classy*
coachie
cokie*
comfy
commie*
conchie*
cookie*
cootie*
corny*
couzie*
cracky*
crappy*
creamie*
credie — credit; a credit card
creepy*
crimpy*
crockie*
crumby*
crusty*
cubby*
curbie*
cushy*
cutie*

cuzzy*
dadsie
dearie*
debbie — debutante
deepie*
depthie*
dewey*
dexie*
didie*
diffy*
dilly*
dippy*
dirty*
divvy*
Dixie*
doggie*
dolly
doosy*
dopey*
dotty*
dovey*
draggy*
drippy*
drooly*
drunky
duckie*
duddy*
dukie*
dummy*
dusty*
Eytie*
falsie*
fanny
fastie — in baseball, a fast pitch; a "fast" talker or "operator"
fatty
fishy*
flashy*
flattie*
floozie*
flossy*
flukey*
flunkey*
folksy
footie
footsie*
frankie — frankfurter
freebie*
freshie*
froggie*
frommie — that which is from someone or something
fruity*
frumpy*
fuzzy*
gabby*
Gangey*
gassy*
gazooney*
giftie
girlie*
glassie
goalie
goaty*
goodie*
gooey*
goodie

goofy*
gooky
goonie*
goulie*
grabby*
greenie*
gunny*
gutty*
hackie*
haggy*
halfy*
handie — something "handed out" or "handed down"; hand
hankie*
hefty*
Heinie
hickey*
high-hatty*
hinkty*
hivey*
holly*
homey*
hooksie
hooky*
hubby*
huffy*
hunkie*
icky*
iffy*
Ikey
immie*
indeedy*
indie*
jakey
jammy*
jazzy*
jeepy*
jimmy*
jinny*
jittery*
jobbie — jobber, commercial middleman
joey*
jumpy*
junkie*
junky
keptie*
(go) kerflooie*
Kewie*
kicksie
kiddie*
kinky*
kippy*
kitty*
kneesies*
knobby*
kooky*
kriegie*
lacy*
lambie*
lambie-pie*
lay chickie*
leery*
leftie*
lifties*
limey*
limmy*

lippy*
lizzie*
longies*
looey*
loony*
loopy*
louie*
lousy*
lovey-dovey*
lumpy*
Maggie*
malarkey*
marksie
matie*
maulie*
mazoomy — money
meany*
messy*
middy*
miffy*
Minnie*
mockie*
mocky*
mollie*
mommy
mooney — daydreaming due to love or "spring fever"; lackadaisical; moody; not alert
mootie — term of endearment, Mother
Motzy*
movie*
moxie*
mushy*
nappy*
nellie*
nervy*
newie — anything new, esp. joke or song
Newfie — person from Newfoundland; Newfoundland
newsie*
newy*
nightie*
nightie-night
nixie*
nobby*
nookie*
nudie*
numbie*
nutty*
Okie*
oldie*
onesie-twosie — children's game, a form of "jacks"
oogly*
pally*
palsie
panicky*
pappy
patootie*
patsy*
peachy*
peppy*
persnickety
Phillie
piggy

pilly
Pinkie*
pinky*
plummy*
plunkie*
plushy*
pogey*
poggie*
pokey*
poky — jail
poochy*
popsie
porkey*
possie*
potsy*
potty*
preemie*
prexie*
prossie*
prowlie
punchy
punky
pupsie
pushy
pussy*
queerie*
quickie*
ratey*
ratty*
raunchy*
righty*
ritzy*
rocksy*
rocky*
rookie*
roomie
rosy*
roughie
rummy*
salty*
sappy*
schizie
schmaltzy*
screaming meemie*
screwy*
scrimey*
scroogie*
scroungy*
scrowsy*
scummy*
sexy*
shady*
shanty*
sharpie*
sheetie
shiftie*
shippy
shitty*
shortie*
singie
sissy*
skibby*
skilley*
skippy*
skivvy*
sleazy*
slinky*
slippy*

slopie*
slug-nutty*
slurpy*
smart cookie*
smarty*
smellie
smoky*
smoothie*
snazzy*
sniffy*
snitzy*
snooty*
snorky*
sobbie — anything which elicits sympathy or sentimentality
softy*
soppy*
soupy*
sparky*
speakie*
spill-quirley*
sporty*
squawkie*
squishy*
staley
steady*
steelie — steel playing marble
sticky*
stiffy
stinkie*
stonie*
stoolie*
strictly*
sunny*
swabbie*
swaddie
swanky*
sweetie*
sweetie-pie*
swiftie
swoony*
tacky*
taffy*
talkie*
tanky*
tappie — one who works with
  a cane; "punchy"
tawny*
teeny-weeny
teensty-weensty — teeny-
  weeny
thickie
ticky*
tippy-toe(s)
toady*
to-and-fromie — that which
  has seen many owners; a
  thing or person previously
  rejected by others
tootsy*
toughie*
torchy*
tough cookie*
townie*
tusheroony*
twirly*

two-bitsey
undies*
wacky*
wallie*
waxie*
weenchy*
weenie*
weepie*
weirdy*
whacky*
whammy*
wharfy — "dock rat"
widdie*
wifie
Willie
willies*
Wingy*
wiry*
wisey
woody*
woozy*
Workie*
Yalie — a student or graduate of Yale; a lock that is
  hard to open
yummy*
zazzy*
zingy*
zippy*
zizzy*
zombie*
zoolie*
zoomie — "zoom" lens in a
  television or movie camera; that which causes enthusiasm
zooty*
zowie*

—iffic, —ific. From "terrific" (colloquial use = *tremendous*) this forced ad-
jective-forming suffix has
gained a little popularity
with advertising copywrit-
ers. Originally a blend element in *superific (super +
terrific)* the *—ific* is now
sometimes added to adjec-
tives to form superlatives
or to brand names or articles of food or clothing to
indicate mass appeal or
satisfaction. Thus we have
*cheeseific, delishific, shirtif-
fic,* and *superduperific.*

—ini. See **—ino** below.

**—ino, —erino, —arino, —or-
ino, —ini, —ina.** Borrowed
primarily from the Italian
and to a lesser degree from
the Spanish, this noun-
forming suffix seldom de-
notes the diminutive of the
root to which it is attached.
It is now primarily used
as an intensive to denote
a remarkable specimen,
and sometimes is merely

an ornamental or comic suffix having semantic force but no significance. The frequency of Italian and Spanish - American family names ending in —*ino* in the United States has familiarized Americans in general with this suffix and helped popularize it.

bambino*
buckarino — a dollar; a "buck"
cakerino
hooferino
casino
cincherino — a cinch (as early as 1905)
corkerino
dingerino
pajamorino — a parade of pajama-clad students the night before a big football game
palomino
peacherino*
pipperino = pipperoo
pokerino*
schnozzolino
sockerino — a great success
whiskerino — an old man; any man wearing whiskers
—ish. This is primarily an adjective - forming suffix which when added to nouns = —*like* or —*esque*, and when added to a previously existing adjective or adverb has the adverbial meaning of *approximately*, *more or less*, *rather*, or *somewhat* (in British use this suffix = "fair, so-so, no more than adequate or satisfactory"). —*ish* is also added to nouns to form a noun denoting an approximate time of day, as *eight-thirtyish*, *five-ish*, *noonish*.
appealish
auntyish
ballet-ish
boobish
Boweryish
bride-and-groomish
bullish*
careerish
dawnish
dime-novelish
doodaddish — useless
eight-thirtyish
fairytale-ish
fiendish
fattish
fortyish
fiveish
four-effish — somewhat physi-

cally inferior or unfit (from Selective Service classification 4F)
goodish
heebyjeebyish
hellish
H. G. Wellsish
ivory-towerish
large-ish — largish
Oscar Levantish
lipstickish
Matisse-ish
Mickey Mouse-ish
movieish
nine-ish
ninety-ish
noonish
oldish
old-retainerish
pickish — particular in small things
pseudo-Maughamish
ratherish*
retainerish
schmo-ish
sevenish
sex-appealish
shortish
sixtyish
smartish — somewhat or almost stylish
spectaclish
standoffish
stiffish
told-you-so-ish
white-ish
womanish
Woppish
—itis. In standard use this noun-forming suffix denotes a disease; in non-standard use it denotes an imaginary or figurative disease, obsession, desire, preference, or compulsion for, or a fear of that which is indicated by the root.
acceleratoritis
accidentitis
adjectivitis
ain't-supposed-to-itis
air-conditionitis
Americanitis
armchairitis
arrangementitis
baggage-itis
balloonitis
barkitis
beerbellyitis
benefititis
betitis
bible-itis
big-shotitis
bite-itis
blinditis
blue-itis
bonditis
bookitis

bowlitis
brass-railitis
budgetitis
Catalina-itis
celebrity-itis
cellaritis
Charlestonitis — a frequent desire to dance the "Charleston," a pop. dance associated with the 1920's
clientitis
comicitis
commentatoritis
committeeitis
complimentitis
compressionitis
conventionitis
conversationitis
corditis
couponitis
crankcase-itis
crossword-puzzle-itis
culturitis
dance-itis
deanitis
depressionitis
divorcitis
double-featuritis
double-entendritis
economitis
electionitis
engagementitis
expansionitis
finalitis
finditis
fiscalitis
fixitis
flapperitis
flivveritis
flunkitis
frivolitis
fumble-itis
functionitis
futuritis
ghostitis
gluttonitis
gobbledygookitis
golfitis
Hitleritis
Hollywooditis
hospitalitis
in-law-itis
interviewitis
ironitis
jungle-itis
jitterbugitis
klanitis
knowledge-itis
let-George-do-it-itis
limerickitis
loanitis
lyricitis
MacArthuritis
mah-jong-itis
mailmanitis
manuscriptitis
microphonitis
monotonitis

motorcaritis
motoritis
museumitis
New Yorkitis
nicotinitis
opening-game-itis
Oxforditis
parolitis
peace-itis
pepitis
Perónitis
Phi-Beta-Kappa-itis
Philippinitis
Picasso-itis
pickle-itis
platformitis
playitis
plugitis
pocketbookitis
poweritis
presidentitis
professoritis
proletarianitis
promotionitis
pronounitis
puppyitis
pyramiditis
radioitis
Republicanitis
rhythmitis
routinitis
Saturday-night-itis*
schedulitis
securititis
senioritis
Shavianitis
shelteritis
shooting-galleryitis
shovelitis
sleeve-itis
spectatoritis
speeditis
squirmitis
stage-itis
Stallinitis
suffixitis
swimmingitis
symbolitis
synonymitis
tee-itis
telephonitis
termitis
theateritis
three-letteritis
tire-itis
title-itis
Townsenditis
traileritis
turnitis
uncle-itis
unionitis
vacationitis
verbitis
Washingtonitis
weatheritis
week-enditis
whatitis
Winchellitis

wire-itis

—loo. The least popular of suffixes, this can be added to nouns and adjectives purely for emphasis. It is heard most frequently among older members of the professional underworld, gamblers, and habitual card players (and may have originated in or be related to the old card game of *loo* or be a variant of the —*eroo* suffix from Spanish). The only —*loo* words heard with any frequency are *fakeloo* = obviously fake, very phoney, and *jakeloo* = very jake, very ok, fine.

—nik. This is actually a noun-forming suffix borrowed from the Yiddish diminutive —*ik, —nik* (the opposite of the Yiddish suffix —*nyak* = large, thorough) and the Russian diminutive —*nik*. The Yiddish diminutive actually = insignificant, bothersome, and is found in the borrowing *nudnik* as well as the formations of *do-goodnik* and *no-goodnik*. The Russian suffix was directly borrowed in *sputnik* and in later words for manmade satellites, including *muttnik* and *lunnik* (a manmade satellite of the moon). The post-1955 *beatnik* uses the suffix in a derogatory way, but the emergence and acceptance of this word followed so closely the acceptance of *sputnik* that it probably owes more to the Russian than to the Yiddish.

—nocracy. See **—ocracy** below.

—o. This suffix seldom denotes anything, but it gives the word a familiar, colloquial, flippant, or slangy connotation. About a third of the —*o* words use the letter as a true suffix (*crumbo, floppo, kiddo, single-o*); many —*o* formations, however, actually result from or accompany back clippings (*ammo, clemo*). Approximately a tenth of the —*o* words are not suffix formations at all but are two syllable back clippings of standard words

taken from the Greek or Latin (*dipso, hippo, phono, steno*). Other —*o* words are borrowings: Spanish via Mexico (*dinero, gringo, loco*), Gypsy (*pano*), Irish (*boyo*).

afto — afternoon
Americano*
ammo*
Balto — Baltimore, Maryland
beano
beauto
blanko water*
blindo — drunk
blotto*
bobbo
boffo*
boko*
botto — bottle
boppo*
boyo*
bozo*
bronco*
browno
bucko*
buddy-o
bunco*
busto
cheerio*
chino*
Chino — a Chinese
chromo*
clemo*
clicko — successful
clucko — a "dumb cluck"
combo*
commo — common
commo*
commando*
como — commotion
compo*
coppo — policeman
creepo — a "creep"
crumb-o*
cuffo*
Daddy-o*
deado
deano*
demo — demonstration
Demo — Democrat
desperado*
dildo*
dimmo*
dinero — money (*from the Sp.*)
dingo*
dino*
dipso* — dipsomaniac
doggo*
doggo — dog
dollo — dollar
double-o*
drinko
dumbo*
eggo — a bald man; an "egghead"
endo

evo — evening
Fatso*
feeblo — feeble-minded person
firo —pyromaniac
eco — economics
floppo — a failure
foldo — failing, unsuccessful
fungo
gabbo — one who "gabs"
geepo*
geezo*
ginzo*
gismo*
glasso
goodo
grappo*
greefo*
gringo
Gypo*
gyppo*
happenso*
heave-o
husho
jacko
jeppo*
jippo*
jolly-o*
jumbo*
keeno
kiddo*
lemo — lemonade
lesbo*
limo — lemonade; Britisher ("limey")
lobo*
loco — locomotive
magnifico
mayo*
medico*
melo — melodrama
mojo — a narcotic, esp. morphine
mucko
niggero
oppo — opposition; opponent
pano*
phono — phonograph; telephone; phoney
pinko*
pino
ploppo
poco — little; a little
politico — a politician
pruno*
psycho — psychopath(ic)
punko — bread; "punk"
queero
ratto — to inform
recco — reconnoiter
reso — reservation
rhino*
righto
romantico
sambolio*
sappo
schizo*
scram(m)o

seamo — seamanship
seppo*
single-o*
skibo*
skybo*
slingo
smacko*
smoke-o — cigarette
socko*
solo*
speako*
spello
squasho*
state-o*
steno — stenographer
stiffo — forged check
stingo — liquor, esp. rum
stinko*
stoolo— stool pigeon
swabo*
trampo
veeno*
ventro — ventriloquist
vino*
weirdo — weird person
wetto — person who is "all wet"
whacko
whammo*
wino*
wrongo — person who cannot be trusted
zingo
zippo*

—ocracy, —nocracy. One of the least used noun-forming suffixes, this is from "dem*ocracy*" (indirectly from the Greek *kratein* = *to rule*). It is added to nouns to = the world, era, or time of, and thus has the same meaning as the shorter and more popular *–dom. Flapperocracy* was somewhat popular c1925 and *jazznocracy* was the title of a popular record of the swing-music era.

—ola, —olo. This popular suffix of Italian origin seldom denotes anything; it is usually a decorative lengthener giving slangy, colloquial, or flippant connotations. It is primarily a noun-forming suffix (*payola*), though it can produce adjectives (*hipola*) and even verbs. The variant *—olo* appears very seldom; *boffolo* is probably the most common.
boffola*
breezola — "the air"
brickola
brushola — the brush-off
bustola — a "flop"

chairola
clinkola
coffola
crapola
cuffola, on the
cupola*
dazzola-dizzola
dreamola
fivola
flopola
G-ola — one-thousand dollars
hepola
hipola
mayola — mayonnaise
mazoola*
mickola — mick, Mickey Finn
muggola — a mug
payola*
peola*
porchola
schnozzola*
scrambola
scramola
slugola
smackola
snortola — a "shot" or short drink of whiskey
stinkerola
stinkola
stoolola — informer or stool pigeon
torchola
whamola — a very successful gag
—oo. See **—eroo** above. (Also see **—loo** above.)
—orino. See **—ino** above.
—orium. See **—atorium** above.
—roo. See **—eroo** above.
—s. This diminutive suffix is sometimes added to a one-syllable word by which a person or thing is familiarly called, to convey affectionate regard for or familiarity toward a specified person or thing. Thus the affectionate nicknames of *Babs, Fats*, etc. This **—s** may be considered a shortened form of the better-known suffix *—sie, —sey, —sy* and is a shade less emotional or sentimental than *—sie, —sey, —sy* or *—ie, —ey, —y*. It also appears as a suffix on certain slang words which have no singular forms, always being noun plurals. This *glims* = *eyes*, though there is no singular "glim" = "eye." In such cases the *—s* is the standard plural suffix which is always an integral part of the word.
babes*
Babs

bags*
benders*
Bermudas*
blues, the*
boobies*
boobs*
booms*
briefs*
bubbies*
bubs*
canal boats*
chaps*
cheaters*
chops*
curtains*
digs*
dogs*
droopers*
ducks*
duds*
dukes*
eagers, the*
falsies*
Fats*
fingers*
flats*
flickers*
flicks*
freckles*
folks, the
gams*
gates*
gents, the*
gimmies, the*
glims*
globes*
goods, the*
gramps*
hots, the*
jim-jams*
knockers*
lily whites*
lungs*
moms*
pops*
privates*
shorts*
sparks*
strides*
swanks*
sweets*
threads*
toots*
tootsies*
undies*
willies, the*

—sie, —sey, —sy. See under —e, —ey, —y above.

—ster. This noun-forming suffix was originally the female suffix of agency (still seen in such standard words as *spinster*), but in modern times is joined to nouns, and less frequently to adjectives and verbs, as a male suffix of agency similar to —*er*. In modern use the —*ster* suffix often carries a derogatory or deprecatory connotation.

bangster — a cheap race horse; one who bangs
bankster
bugster
clubster
crimester
croonster
dopester*
dragster*
fibster
filmster
finster
funster
gagster
gangster*
go-awayster
gonster
gowster*
gridster
gypster*
hepster*
hipster*
hoaxster
homester
hoopster
huckster — advertising executive, a writer of advertising copy
jamster
jiltster
jobster*
jokester
lamster*
mobster*
mugster — a "mug"; hoodlum
netster
oldster
pepster
pollster
pulpster — a writer, editor, or publisher of "pulp"
punster
quipster
rankster
rhymster
ringster
rinkster
roughster
scumster*
shackster
shakester*
sharpster
shyster*
slangster
speedster
siuntster
swingster
thugster
tipster*
trickster
tunester — writer of pop. songs; singer
wordster — writer, usu. newsp. columnist
Zen hipster*

—sy. See —**ie**, —**ey**, —**y** above.

—teria. See **eteria** above.

—torium. See —**atorium** above.

—ville. This noun-forming suffix has seen a little figurative use = village (*Hooverville*). Since c1955, however, it has been in wide bop and cool use, and it is now enjoying some theatrical use = figuratively a place where or a state in which someone or something is (*Dullville* or *Hicksville, Endsville, Nadaville, nowhereville, sleepyville, squareville*). The suffix is also often added to outdated or trite slang words and counters in an attempt to make them sound more modern, sophisticated, and hip (*strictly from Cornville* instead of *corny*). An —*s*— is often inserted between the root word and the —*ville* so that *sleepville* and *sleepsville* both exist. The phrases "strictly from ——ville" are frequent counters of approval or disapproval. The suffix has, of course, been used as the last element in nicknames for towns for many years. Thus both *Derbyville* and *Sluggerville are nick-* names for Louisville, Kentucky, home of the Kentucky Derby and the city where many professional baseball bats are made. See Nicknames, Placenames, and Group Names below.

—ward. As in standard use this suffix denotes literal and figurative direction or tendency; in standard use it is added to adverbs (*downward, upward*) and nouns (*homeward*). In nonstandard use —*ward* is usually added to standard nouns, specific formations being non-standard only because of their rareness (*Chinaward, usward*).
Americanward
bedward
Chinaward
Cornellward
Frenchward
Godward
marketward
slumward
usward

—y. See **—ie, —ey, —y** above.

Suffix Words

—alley. The street, district, or section of a town where a specific type of people live or where a specific item can be bought or found. The oldest of such terms is the circus *clown alley;* in more general use *shoe-store alley* or *used-car alley* = a street or section of a town where shoe-stores or used-car lots predominate (such a street may also be called *—row*). Similarly, *drunk alley* would be a street, section, or neighborhood where drunken derelicts are found; Italian alley a predominantly Italian neighborhood, etc. In these uses the connotation of "crowded" or "narrow" is used. In another use *—alley* = *—jungle* (see below), depending on the connotation of "dark" or "frightening."

—Anonymous. Literally or jocularly, an organization founded to cure its members of a vice or for charitable purposes. Based on the successful *Alcoholics Anonymous,* whose members help prevent one another from returning to alcoholism, we now have *Narcotics Addicts Anonymous, Divorcees Anonymous* (who help one another make emotional adjustments after becoming divorced), and the charitable *Fathers Anonymous* (a legitimate organization whose members serve as foster fathers to underprivileged children). The *Anonymous* is seldom preceded by a hyphen, and is almost always capitalized as part of the organization's name. This suffix word has been used since c1950.

—ape. A noun-forming suffix word literally and figuratively = a driver or laborer. It suggests a large, hulking man; it is a fairly old American suffix, and in the past it often applied to immigrant laborers. The oldest continuing forma-

tion is probably *wood-ape* = logger. More recent formations are *cat-ape* = a tractor driver in a construction crew, *ring-ape* = prize-fighter or wrestler, *truck-ape* = truck driver. This suffix word is less popular than —jockey and —monkey (see below).

—around, —arounder. These suffix words are often added to verbs to suggest wasting time, or attempting to do, or actually doing, something aimlessly or half-heartedly. *—arounder* occurs in the *—er* and the *—er —er* suffix lists (see below).

bat around*
beat around*
belt around*
bum around*
buzz around the barrel*
clown around*
come around*
drive around
fool around*
floss around*
fuck around
futz around*
get the run-around*
give (someone) the run-around*
go around together*
go around with (someone)*
hang around*
hell around*
horse around*
house around*
June around*
kid around
knock around*
louse around*
mess around*
monkey around*
pal around (with)*
play around*
run-around*
screw around*
scrounge around*
spudge around*
stick around*
suck around*
walk-around*

—artist. Literally and figuratively, one more or less skilled at something, one who habitually does, seeks, or provides the thing denoted by the root word. *—artist* = exaggerated, egocentric, or insincere talk is used especially after slang words *(bull-shit artist, hot-air artist).*

booze artist

bullshit artist*
bunco artist*
clip-artist*
dit-da artist*
gyp artist*
heat artist*
hot-air artist
make-out artist*
sack-artist*
shiv artist*
short-change artist*

—atter. One who does something "at" another person or an object, as a *looker-atter.* Fairly common as neologisms and nonce-word noun formations taking the *—er, —er —er* suffix (see above).

—awayer. One who goes, or does something, "away," as *goer-awayer* or a *thrower-awayer.* Fairly common as neologisms and nonce-word noun formations taking the *—er, —er —er* suffix (see above).

—backer. One who returns (comes back) or supports (backs). Common as neologisms and nonce-word noun formations taking the *—er* and *—er —er* suffix (see above).

—bait. This suffix word = that which or the one who tempts, elicits, or is especially worthy of. It was most popular c1940-c1945 with teenagers and students.

alligator bait*
barber bait*
bottle bait — tempting whiskey
bullet bait*
crowbait*
date bait*
draft bait*
dream bait*
fly-bait*
jail bait*
museum bait — old or valuable item; old person
pneumonia bait
pogey bait*
whistle bait*
wolf bait

—bird. In general, this suffix word can be placed after any adjective to = man, fellow, guy *(grease-bird, queer bird).* However, the connotation of a bird in a cage suggests a man in prison, and so with certain groups and in certain combinations *—bird* has the connotation of convict or ex-convict (it may be a front clipping from *yardbird* or *jailbird*). Thus the nickname "Bird" is often from "Yardbird," as with the famous jazz musician and innovator Charley "Yardbird" or "Bird" Parker, for whom the famous *Birdland* jazz night club was named. In recent times, besides Charley Parker, television comedian George Gobel has helped give this suffix word popularity in his "Well, I'll be a dirty bird" (see *Synthetic Fad Expressions* below).

—box. Figuratively a "box" that accomplishes or does what the root word indicates. Often it = the human skull, and sometimes it = a person figuratively considered as a container or source *(chatter-box).*

bandbox*
bitch box*
brain-box*
butter-box*
chatterbox*
coal box*
cold-meat box*
dimbox*
dreambox*
feedbox information*
gitbox*
god box*
goola box*
goon-box*
groan box*
juice-box*
knowledge-box*
pete-box*
sardine box*
shine box*
skid-box*
soap-box*
spitbox*
squawk box*
squeeze-box*
think-box*
tinkle-box*
tool-box*
wind-box*
wisdom box*

—boy. This suffix word has several connotations = male or man. It usually suggests a young, romantic, handsome, intelligent, or aggressive man *(bright boy, fair-haired boy, fly boy).* Sometimes it means an influential and often dishonest middle-aged or elderly man, or a small thin, sharp-featured man, especially a thug or a tough. It sometimes conveys an affectionate or friendly connotation, especially in direct address, as in "How are things with you, Johnny-boy?" Occasionally it suggests the heartiness or bigness that goes with certain things *(big boy =* hamburger sandwich containing two hamburgers and many condiments). Recently it has replaced *—butcher =* vendor *(coffee boy, paperboy).*

B-boy*
big boy*
bingo-boy*
bloomer boy*
blow-boy*
blue-eyed boy*
bright boy — smart, alert, or "hep" youth or man, *often used mockingly*
busboy*
cowboy*
doughboy*
drugstore cowboy*
fair-haired boy
fly-boy*
hatchet-boy*
Jewboy*
Joe-boy*
lover-boy*
Mamma's boy*
mammy boy*
Noah's boy*
number one boy*
party boy*
peg boy*
Percy boy*
playboy*
poor-boy*
pretty-boy*
speed-boy*
tomboy*
waterboy*
white-haired boy*
willy-boy*
winding boy*
yellow boy — a comparatively fair Negro, esp. a mulatto
wolf boy — a "wolf"

—bug, —buggy, —bugs. Basically *—bug =* one who is "crazy" *for* something, an enthusiast, fan, devotee, or follower of the thing or person named in the root. One may be a *money-bug* (1904:DAE), but usually *—bug* refers to an enthusiast of a popular hobby *(shutter-bug),* a form of mass entertainment *(movie bug),* or a popular writer or entertainer *(Arthur Miller bug, Stan Kenton bug). Jitterbug* is probably the most popular of the *—bug* words *(jitter =* dancing to early swing or even jive music). Sometimes the suffix word is used to mean one who habitually does something *(bar-bug, litterbug).* The standard *—y* adjective-forming suffix can be added to any word in the following list. Independently, however, the noun forming suffix word *—buggy =* vehicle *(air-buggy, gas-buggy).* The suffix word, especially when it is spelled *—bugs,* can mean crazy *from,* as in *stir-bugs =* crazy, or partially insane, from having spent too much time in jail.

Arthur Miller bug
camera-bug
bedbug*
big bug*
car-bug
doodle-bug*
firebug*
football-bug
hi-fi bug
jitterbug*
money-bug
litterbug*
radio-bug
Stan Kenton bug
platter-bug
shutterbug*

—burger. From the popular "ham*burger*," this noun-forming suffix word was probably first applied to other items as a blend-word element. It means any hot sandwich served on a bun, often toasted, with many condiments. The root word usually gives the name of the filler for for sandwich *(beefburger, shrimpburger).* Sometimes, however, a lunch counter will specialize in one type of "burger," naming it after the establishment, owner, or cook *(Joeburger).* Occasionally a "burger" is associated with a famous person, event, or historic spot *(Ikeburger).* Special ingredients or condiments will affect the choice of a root word *(Chineseburger,* containing rice; *Mexican-burger*, containing chile), and sometimes the root will merely emphasize its tastiness *(Giantburger, Yummyburger)*.

beef-burger
catfish-burger
cheeseburger
chicken-burger
chile-burger
double-burger — two hamburgers on one bun
fish-burger
hamburger*
Ike-burger — special hamburger somewhat pop. during first presidential campaign of Dwight D. Eisenhower
mutton-burger
sausage-burger
steak-burger
steer-burger
sturgeon-burger
super-burger — very large hamburger
turkey-burger
western-burger — usually a small steak; may be a Western omelet

—butcher. An old-fashioned, almost obsolete suffix word = *vendor*, probably from circus vendors; especially one who hawks or sells food or drink in the street or at sporting events *(beer butcher, candy butcher, coffee butcher, "Coke" butcher, paper* (newspaper) *butcher)*. This suffix word is seldom attached to the root noun which indicates what is sold. It has been largely replaced by —*boy*.

—chaser. This suffix word refers to one who pursues for his own pleasure or is obsessed with the person or item indicated by the root word. Most often, the root word is a slang synonym = woman, sex, or some item associated with a woman or sex. All —*chaser* words, of course, have an —*er* suffix (see above).

ambulance chaser*
broad-chaser
cunt-chaser
dog-chaser*
fly-chaser*
girl-chaser
jig-chaser*
man-chaser

monkey-chaser*
skirt-chaser
tail-chaser
woman-chaser*

—crazy. This suffix word means obsessed with, having a liking for, being devoted to (see —*bug* above) or a habitual pursuer of (see —*chaser* above). Like —*bug*, —*crazy* can suggest one is "crazy" *from* something *(booze crazy)*. This suffix has been most popular with teenagers c1940-c1950; —*crazy* and its synonyms, —*bugs*, —*daffy*, —*dippy*, —*dizzy*, —*happy*, —*mad*, —*nutty*, and —*wacky* have been the most popular teenage suffix words.

booze-crazy
boy-crazy
car-crazy
girl-crazy
house-crazy
jazz-crazy
movie-crazy
speed-crazy
stir-crazy*

—daffy. A less frequently heard synonym for —*crazy* (see above), this suffix word can also be used to = "crazy" about *(doll-daffy)* or crazy from *(stir-daffy)*. Unlike —*crazy*, —*daffy* is often attached to its root word by a hyphen.

—dippy. Another synonym for the suffix word —*crazy* (see above). Thus one can also be *doll-dippy* in favor of a woman or *stir-dippy* from prison.

—dizzy. Another synonym for —*crazy*. This suffix word, however, sometimes carries the connotation that one is only temporarily obsessed with someone or something; thus to be *doll-dizzy* is less serious than to be *doll-crazy*. In like manner, when —*dizzy* is used to mean crazy *from*, it often implies a lesser degree of bewilderment or confusion than does —*crazy* or —*bugs*.

—dog. Although *dog* is a slang word that stands by itself, it is used with the same general denotation as a suffix word. As a compounding element —*dog* = man, guy, fellow, often with the connotation of a

roué or good fortune. It thus conveys admiration or envy *(handsome dog)*. Sometimes —*dog* suggests extreme individuality or eccentricity *(crazy dog)*.

bird dog*
choke-dog*
crazy dog
dirty dog
dumb dog
funny dog
handsome dog
low dog
lucky dog
mean dog
penny-dog*
sad dog
sexy dog
shoe-dog*
smart dog
stupid dog
top dog*
yard dog*
yellow dog*

—down, —downer. This is an old noun-forming suffix word = a contest of stamina, knowledge, or courage in which all but the winner are finally eliminated. The suffix word is most familiar in *spelldown* (a spelling contest in which the winner remains standing to meet the next challenger and the loser returns to his seat and sits "down"). The 1920's saw the *dancedown*, and modern hot rodders call the game of chicken a *ridedown*. The compounding element is also used to mean to put, drop, or plunk down. This meaning is most frequently heard in the bop and cool (and sometimes student) use of *put-down* = to ignore a friend or rebuff someone. —*downer* is found in some neologisms and reoccurring nonce words, and all these can be classified as having the —*er* or the —*er —er* suffix (see above).

bringdown*
brush-down*
buckle down*
burn down*
button down*
call down*
chow down*
clamp down*
closed down*
comedown
countdown*

crack down*
dance-down
dressing down*
fall down*
fuzz-down
go-down*
hairdown*
hand-me-down*
hoedown*
Jew down*
knockdown*
knuckle-down*
lay-down*
low-down*
one down*
pad down*
pipe down*
plank down*
plunk down
pull down*
put-down
quee down*
ride-down
run-down*
salted down*
set-down*
shake-down*
showdown*
shower down*
shuck-down
shut down*
simmer down*
sing-down
sit-down*
smack down*
spell-down
swab down*
throw-down*
throw down on*
wasped down*

—driver. In standard use "driver" = one who drives a vehicle; in non-standard suffix-word use it figuratively = one who causes to move, works with, peddles, or sells, as in *pen-driver* = clerk or *coat-driver* = coat salesman. The use of *—driver* = *peddler* or *salesman* is primarily in New York City. *—driver* also has the connotation of slave-*driver*, figuratively one who directs or bosses others; thus it can = foreman as in *gang-driver*. All *—driver* words, of course, have the *—er* suffix (see above).

—eater. This suffix word is used in many formations to designate a person's nationality or country of origin by combining with a root word naming a food primarily associated with that nation or country

(*bean-eater*, *frog-eater*). Sometimes the root word indicates an occupation (*hay-eater*) and, by extension, a general personality (*cake-eater*).

ball-eater — proficient baseball fielder
bean-eater*
beefeater*
beef-eater — Englishman
cake-eater
cheese-eater*
clay-eater*
fire-eater*
fish-eater*
frog-eater*
hay-eater — farmer
leather-eater — prizefighter
mud-eater — infantryman; construction-crew worker
neater eater
maneater — vamp
smoke-eater*

—eyed. This suffix word means having the character of, or being in the condition of, the state suggested by the root word. This is also a common suffix word used in formations = drunk (*bleary-eyed*, *pie-eyed*). See Synonyms for Drunk below.

bleary-eyed
bug-eyed*
clear-eyed
cock-eyed*
cross-eyed*
evil-eyed
glassy-eyed*
hoary-eyed*
orie-eyed*
owl-eyed*
owly-eyed*
pie-eyed*
pigeon-eyed*
sad-eyed
shifty-eyed
straight-eyed
soapy-eyed*
wall-eyed*

—factory. A suffix word referring to any place that serves or produces quantity rather than quality. The strong connotation is that something is done quickly and impersonally in a situation where such factory attitudes should not be applicable (*brain factory*, *Ph.D. factory*). It is also used to = any office, or store where one earns wages (*ad factory* = advertising agency; *money factory* = any place that

has good salaries).
ad-factory — advertising agency
angel-factory*
bone-factory*
brain-factory — university or college
doughnut factory*
fight-factory — prize-fight arena or gym
food-factory — restaurant
gargle factory*
horse-factory — race track
jag factory*
lunch-factory — luncheonette
match factory*
money-factory — place where one earns a living
nut factory*
Ph.D.-factory — university
sex-factory — brothel; burlesque show; movie studio
slave factory — office or factory
sleep-factory — hotel; esp. flophouse

—fest. Actually a blend-word element from the German *Fest* "festival," this suffix word = any session or period of uninterrupted, unrestrained, often exuberant and immoderate activity.

bat-fest
bull-fest*
cake-fest
chin-fest*
dance-fest
drink-fest
food-fest
fuck-fest
gab-fest*
hitfest*
jazz-fest
love-fest
shoe-fest
slug-fest
talk-fest

—fiend. This suffix word originally = one addicted to, in habitual need of (*cigarette fiend*, *dope fiend*); but since c1940 it has seen wide popularity as a synonym for *—bug* (see above).

book fiend
cigarette fiend
cigar fiend
coffee fiend
coke fiend
dope fiend
hop fiend*
jazz fiend
movie fiend
record fiend

—fighter. One who is addicted to or an habitual consumer of that indicated by the root word, with, however, periods of self-recrimination, sincere resolutions to reform, and sometimes violent attempts to break (or "fight") the addiction or habit. Most —*fighters* have the habit of "hitting the bottle," *booze fighter* being the most common of these formations *(bar fighter, beer fighter, bottle fighter, whiskey fighter)*. There are, however, *dope fighters* and, less serious, *cigar fighters*.

—**guard.** A noun-forming suffix word, always applied as the last syllable to a rootword, means literally and figuratively a guardian. It is usually applied to conservative or pompous people, as *dumbguard* = any person group considered unenlightened or "nonhip."

—**happy.** This suffix word adjective has been added to hundreds of nouns since c1935, especially during World War II. Although the basic connotation "joyous" is usually present, its denotation may = excited, exhilarated; dazzled, dizzy, or drunk; elated from being "crazy" about, obsessed with, or desirous of (see —*bugs*, —*crazy*, etc. above). The suggestion is less of insanity or confusion than of dazzled, dizzy, or goofy. Sometimes —*happy* extends its meaning to = "crazy" from boredom or nervousness. As a slang word word *happy* = joyously or slightly drunk, and this meaning is behind all the connotations of —*happy*.

adjective-happy
auto-happy
bar-happy
bomb-happy
brass-happy
buck-happy
cab-happy
car-happy
cactus-happy
coin-happy
coop-happy*
dit-happy
dollar-happy
dough-happy
flak-happy

footlight-happy
gin-happy
glacier-happy
hate-happy
headline-happy
heat-happy
Hitler-happy — obsessed with the person or ideas of dictator Adolf Hitler
Hooper-happy — Dazzled by having a high "Hooper rating" (a popularity poll rating television entertainers)
hypo-happy — obsessed by one's hobby of photography, in which "hypo" is used in the development of prints
island-happy — jittery from having lived on an island too long
jive-happy
jungle-happy
power-happy
rag-happy — constantly practicing naval signaling with semaphore flags
rock-happy*
saki-happy
sand-happy
sap-happy — drunk
scrap-happy — crazy from fighting; eager to fight
skirt-happy — obsessed by women and sex
slap-happy — "punch-drunk"
strike-happy
stripe-happy
trigger-happy
wire-happy — peculiar or eccentric from long imprisonment as a prisoner of war in Germany during WWII

—**head.** —*head* refers to one's intelligence, usually in a derogatory sense and often by describing figuratively the head's size or shape *(dumb-head, pea-head)*; to one's personality or view of life *(big-head, egg-head, fat-head)*; to one's habits or enthusiasms *(hop-head, lush-head)*; or to one's present state *(sleepy head)*.

apple-head*
bad head
BB head
bake-head*
balloon-head*
banana-head*
bean-head*
big head*
blizzard head*
blockhead*

blubberhead*
bonehead*
bucket-head*
bullhead*
bunhead*
burr-head*
busthead*
cabbage-head*
cheesehead*
chicken-head*
chowderhead*
chucklehead*
cluckhead*
clunkhead*
coke head*
crazy head
deadhead*
dough-head*
dumb-head*
dunce-head
egghead*
empty-head
fat-head*
felt-head
flange-head*
flathead*
ginhead*
good head*
hammerhead*
handkerchief-head*
happy head
hard-head*
hog-head*
hophead*
hothead*
jar-head*
jerk-head
jughead*
kinky-head*
knothead*
knucklehead*
krauthead*
lard-head*
lazy-head
lead-head
leatherhead*
lunk-head*
lush-head
mallet-head*
meathead*
moon-head*
mud-head*
muscle-head*
mush-head*
muttonhead*
nut head
niggerhead*
noodle-head*
numb-head*
old head*
ox-head
peahead*
pin-head*
piss-head
point-head*
potato-head*
pudding-head*
pumpkin-head*

putty-head*
rag-head*
redhead*
rockhead*
round-head*
saphead*
sharp-head
shit-head*
skin-head*
sleepy head
soft-head*
sore-head*
square-head*
stupid-head
sugar-head*
swellhead*
tack head*
tackhead*
weedhead*
wet-head*
whistle-head*
wooden-head*
wood-head*
woof-head*
woolly-head*

—heister. Figuratively and literally = one who lifts, this suffix word is used in two ways. It can = one known for stealing or borrowing a specific item indicated by the root *(car-heister, cigarette heister)* or, more frequently, one who lifts frequent glasses of beer or alcoholic beverages to his lips *(beer-heister, booze-heister)*. Neither use is common.

—hog. This suffix word = one who, like a hog, takes or seeks more than his share. From the basic *road hog* = an automobile driver who uses more than a single road lane, we have *air hog, bed hog, beer hog, chow hog,* and others. When, however, *—hog* follows the name of a specific food or beverage it has a meaning similar to *—fiend* or *—hound.*

—hop, —hopper. These suffix words = *—jerk, —jerker* (see below), as in *bellhop* and *soda-hopper.* As a separate slang word = dancing party, *—hop* often follows adjectives or nouns indicating the time, place, kind, or sponsor *(Friday-night hop, Junior class hop)* in teenage and student use. There has been some artificial use of *—hopper* = teenage dancer or jitterbug.

—horrors. This suffix word

= fear of or an obsession or insanity resulting from the persons, objects, or experiences indicated by the root word. It is in most common use among criminals, convicts, alcoholics, and addicts.
booze horrors
bull horrors
chuck horrors*
hop horrors
road horrors
stir horrors

—hound. This suffix word = one obsessed with or known for pursuing, having, consuming, or using that which the root word indicates. The most common phrase is *chow-hound,* widely used by the armed forces during World War II. The formation conveys a suggestion of voluntary preference, with the thing sought or consumed considered more pleasurable than habit-forming. A *rum-hound* relishes alcohol but is not an alcoholic.
booze hound*
chow hound*
comma-hound
gas hound*
gash-hound
grog-hound*
jake-hound
lush-hound
meal-hound
nicotine-hound
pink-tea hound
rock-hound
rum-hound
sin-hound*
tea-hound*
thrill-hound
woof-hound*

—house. This suffix word generally = any place where one can obtain that indicated by the root word, or any place which houses that indicated by the root word. It is most commonly used in *whorehouse* and other slang synonyms for brothel.
bandhouse*
barrel-house*
bed house*
big house*
bughouse*
call house*
can-house*
cat house*
crazy house*
crumb house*

dice house*
doghouse*
doss house*
doughnut house*
flea house*
flophouse*
fun-house
funny house*
gas house*
greenhouse*
grind house*
hash-house*
henhouse*
iron house*
jail house
joy house*
jug-house — jail, tavern
juke house*
lighthouse*
monkey-house*
notch-house*
nut house*
opera house*
padhouse*
paper house*
parlor house*
power-house*
scratch house*
snort-house
soup house*
sporting house*
station house
whitehouse*
whorehouse*
workhouse*

—how. This suffix word appears in expressions which represent entire expressions or feelings, as in the affirmative rejoinder *and how!* or the toast *here's how.* Since c1945, it has also become common as a shortening for "how to do it" in the word *know-how* = ability, experience, technical capacity.

—in, —inner. Found in many neologisms and nonce words taking the *—er, —er* *—er* suffix (see above).

—jag. Similar to *—fest* (see above), *—jag* = any session or period of uninterrupted and unrestrained activity. The connotation, however, is of a fit rather than of a feast. The suffix word conveys a suggestion of compulsion *(crying jag), candy jag, cigarette jag.*

—jerk, —jerker. This suffix word = one who prepares and serves or who merely serves, especially one who tends a counter or bar serving food and drink *(beer-jerker, counter-jerk-*

er, *ice-cream jerk, suds jerker*). The basic, and still most common formation is *soda-jerk*. The *—jerker* form is archaic and now rarely heard. The origin of the *—jerk* suffix was probably in brothel usage, where a jerk was a callow youngster not old enough to have intercourse; derived from *jerk* or *jerk off*, to masturbate. It has later been applied to other situations, including those mentioned.

—job. Suggesting a new and impersonal manufactured item this suffix = a person or item that is especially typical or attractive of its kind *(frail job* = girl); an item, object, or situation containing that indicated by the root word *(fizz job)*; or, more generally, any activity, in which case *—job* often takes the place of the standard *—ing* to form nouns from verbs *(blow job, snow job)*. The first use is by far the most common, and can be added to any adjective; thus, a new car could be called *big job, cute job, fast job, good-looking job, nice job*, etc.

blow job*
con job*
cowboy job*
fizz job*
frail job*
gow job*
hayeater*
hay-eater job*
mental job*
put-up job*
sex job*
shack job*
snow job*
soup job*
tank job*

—jockey. This suffix word = one who drives or rides that indicated by the root word *(jet jockey* = jet airplane pilot) or, more figuratively, one who herds or works with that indicated by root word *(highball jockey* = "herds" highballs at a bar, *juice jockey* = electrician).
bean jockey — a lunch counter waiter
bench jockey — mechanic; substitute athlete who spends most of his time on the players' bench waiting to play
blip jockey*
desk jockey*
disc jockey*
dit-da jockey*
highball jockey*
highway jockey
hog-jockey*
jalopy jockey
jeep-jockey*
jet jockey — pilot of a jet airplane, esp. of a jet fighter plane
juice jockey*
ping jockey*
plow jockey*
slide-rule jockey — accountant, engineer, or mathematician
slipstick jockey — radio or radar technician
soup jockey*
swab jockey — sailor
tank-jockey
taxi jockey
throttle jockey*

—joint. This suffix word refers to a commercial establishment known for that indicated by the root word. Often deprecatory, sometimes merely familiar or jocular, *—joint* is usually reserved for restaurants, nightclubs, and bars. Since c1955 *—joint* increasingly = a public place patronized mainly by the type of people indicated by the root word *(beat joint, homo joint)*.
beer-joint*
beat joint — restaurant, cafe, bar, etc., where "beat" people congregate
big joint*
booze joint
bop joint — a cafe, nightclub, bar, etc. where bop music is played
bust-out joint*
call joint*
chippie joint*
clip-joint*
coffee-and-cake-joint*
creep-joint*
crumb joint*
doughnut joint*
drop joint*
feed joint
flat-joint*
flop joint
grab-joint*
grease joint*
gyp joint*
ham joint*
homo joint
hopjoint*
jam joint
juice-joint*
lead joint
mitt joint*
mug joint*
nautch-joint*
one-arm joint*
rib joint*
right joint*
rub joint*
rug joint*
scatter-joint*
schlock joint*
stuss joint
whisper joint*

—jumper. Like *—hop*, this suffix word is a little-used modern variant for *—jerk, —jerker* (see above), as *soda-jumper, counter jumper*. It is also used familiarly, affectionately, or jocularly to = a small or dilapidated vehicle *(puddle-jumper)*. Very recently, it has had some use = automobile mechanic, dealer, or salesman, though commonly *car-jumper* refers to a drive-in waiter.

—jungle. This suffix word refers to any place where jungle morality and the survival of the strongest prevail. It can refer to any actual place *(asphalt jungle)* or some facet of modern life *(Washington jungle* = politics). It derives from the old-time hobo use of *jungle*, a camp along the railroad tracks.
asphalt jungle
blackboard jungle
garment jungle
Hollywood jungle
political jungle
Wall Street jungle
Washington jungle

—killer. Interchangeable with *—eater* and *—fighter* (see above), *—killer* refers to one who is very successful with or who consumes much of that indicated by root word. Before c1935 it was commonly used by advertising copy writers to = that which stops or cures *(pain killer, pimple killer)*, and it is still used for cheaper patent medicines.
beer-killer
booze-killer
car killer
headache-killer
lady-killer*

pain-killer
pimple-killer
whiskey-killer
—**king.** This suffix word =
an outstanding success, or
leader, in any endeavor. In
business —*king* usually
means the most successful
and wealthy man, often
controlling an entire industry (*car king, match king,
shoe king*). In entertainment —*king* suggests success and popularity of the
moment, the setter of
styles and leader of fashions. By itself *king* is sometimes used as a nickname
or in direct address.
—**lawyer.** This suffix word =
one who gives advice or
states his opinions fre-
quently and at length,
without being asked to do
so; any pompous talker,
especially one who assumes
technical knowledge, edu-
cation, or information
which he does not have.
This suffix word saw wide
armed forces use during
World War II (*barracks
lawyer, sea lawyer*).
armchair lawyer
barracks lawyer
church lawyer
football lawyer
forecastle lawyer*
guardhouse lawyer*
jackleg lawyer*
office lawyer
sea lawyer*
—**mad.** Another suffix word
= *crazy* (see above), the
choice —*mad* usually seems
to be for alliterative reasons, as in *money-mad* (the
most common use) and
movie mad.
—**man.** This suffix word now
has several general uses.
It = —*butcher* and —*boy*
(see above) in meaning one
who sells or hawks, with
the root word indicating
the item sold ("Coke"
man). This extends an
older, often standard use
of —*man* = one who sells,
supplies, serves, or pre-
pares something (*meat man*
= butcher). These stand-
ard formations are not listed below. In most non-
standard uses, however,
—*man* = one who strongly
prefers, admires, or is successful at or with that in-

dicated by the root word.
The preference is usually
for food, drink, specific
brands of merchandise, a
sport, a masculine habit, or
a part of a female's anatomy; it is often a lifelong
preference or habit rather
than a fad. The suffix word
is also used as if it were a
suffix of agency (*finger
man, steer man*). Some-
times it suggests merely an
association (*butter-and-
eggs man* = successful,
small town businessman).
In bop, cool, beat, and student groups, *man* is often
used as a term of direct
address.
anchor man*
ass man*
bad man*
bagman*
baseball man — baseball fan
big man*
bindle man*
birdman*
blue man*
bottle-man*
bottom man*
box man*
bug man*
bumpman*
caveman*
chain-man*
Chinaman*
coffee man — one who con-
sumes much coffee; coffee
vendor
coke man — one who con-
sumes much Coca-Cola
company man*
con man*
croaksman*
cunt man — man whose in-
terest in women is simply
and directly sexual
finger man*
fireman*
Ford man — one who prefers
Ford cars; Ford dealer or
salesman
G-man*
hammer-man*
hatchet-man — hired killer;
one who fires or dismisses
another
heist man*
he-man
horn man — jazz trumpeter
hot man*
iceman*
iron man*
jigger-man*
knucksman*
ladies' man*
lady's man

landsman*
leg man*
lumberman*
man's man — manly man
meat-and-potatoes man —
one who likes plain foods
or simple things
meat-man — butcher; wres-
tler; thug; undertaker
mug man — mugger
penman*
pete-man*
peter-man*
phoneyman*
pipe man — man who prefers
the pipe or smokes it frequently
pitchman*
rod-man*
sandwich man*
seat-man*
sex man
shack man*
skyman*
slapman*
steer man — shill
straight man*
strong-arm man*
superman*
swagman*
sweet man*
ten-minute man*
thin man*
three-letter man*
Tommy-man*
tool-man*
trigger man*
vessel-man*
visiting fireman*
waterman*
wheel-man*
white-collar man, white-shirt
man — office worker
yes-man*
—**mill.** This suffix word has
the connotation —*joint*
(see above), but is much
older and always = a place
where whiskey is sold. It
was first used in *rum-mill*
(c1850) and also appears
in *grog-mill* and *jag-mill*
(1904: *DAE*). It is widely
used only in *gin-mill*.
—**mind.** From and often =
"master*mind*," this suffix
word is of minor impor-
tance. It = an intellectual
motivator or leader in any
field of endeavor (*movie-
mind*). This suffix word may
also be added to an adjective describing intelligence
to form a noun (*dumb-
mind, smart-mind*).
—**monkey.** This suffix word
= laborer (*powder monkey
= blaster, road monk·*

laborer on a highway con-
struction crew), and often
specifically = *mechanic
(grease monkey)*. It also
may be used to = *—jockey*
(see above).

air monkey
broom-monkey
company monkey
dit-da monkey
grease-monkey
powder monkey*
road monkey*
weed monkey*
wheel-monkey

—nut, —nutty. This suffix
word, like *—bug* = one who
is "crazy" for something,
an enthusiast, fan, devotee,
follower of the thing or
person named in the root
word. *—nut* suggests more
dignity than *—bug;* it is
usually applied to one who
is a fan or enthusiast of an
established hobby *(dog nut,
stamp nut, tennis nut).*
—nut and *—bug* are by far
the most common slang
suffix words for fan or enthusiast, and are more generally accepted than *—crazy,
—daffy, —dippy, —fiend,
—happy, —hound, —mad,
—shark,* etc. *—bug* is never
used to imply drug addic-
tion or alcoholism.

baseball nut
bridge nut
car nut
clothes nut
dog nut
football nut
French nut
golf nut
horse nut
jazz nut
movie nut
pizza nut
plane nut
poker nut
stamp nut
tennis nut
tough nut*

—off, —offer. Adding this
suffix word to verbs, usually transitive, results in
many slang and idiomatic
formations. It conveys a
literal and figurative connotation of moving away
or of removing from by
means of distance, time, or
relation; of suspending or
ending an action or rela-
tion *(lay off, knock off, kiss
off).* The suffix word also
= to give off or broadcast,

usually in anger or as a
rebuff *(pop off, tell off),*
and sometimes it has a reflexive connotation *(fuck
off).* The *—er* form is often
used in nonce words and
neologisms (see *—er,* and
—er —er above).

back off*
ball off*
base, off (one's)*
blast off*
blip off*
blow-off*
brassed-off*
break-off*
breeze off*
brown off*
browned off*
brush off*
bump off*
burn off*
buzz off*
California kiss-off*
calk off*
caulk off*
cheesed off*
chew (someone's) ear off*
chill off*
come off it*
conk off*
cool off*
cork off*
cut it off*
dance off*
dope off*
fall off*
first off*
flub off*
fluff off*
fuck off*
get off*
goof off*
kick-off — beginning; to begin
hedge off*
iron off*
jab-off*
jack off*
jazz up (something)*
jerk off*
kick off*
kiss off*
knock off*
lay off*
New York kiss-off
next off*
pair-off*
pay off*
peed off*
peeved off*
pissed off*
polish off*
pop off*
pull (it) off*
push off*
rake-off*
ring off*

screw off*
second off*
send-off*
shoot off (one's) mouth*
shove off*
show-off*
shut off*
sign-off*
simmer off*
slam off*
sound off*
squib off*
stall off*
step off*
step off the carpet*
step off the deep end*
suck off*
take off*
talk (one's) ear off*
t'd off*
tear off*
tee'd off*
tee off on (someone)*
tell off*
tie it off*
tie off*
tip off*
toss it off*
turn off*
weed off*
wipe off*

—orchard. Never a common
suffix word, *—orchard* = a
place where that indicated
by the root is found or,
figuratively, stored. It is
used most often in argot
formations and hobo cant.
The most commonly heard
—orchard formations are
bone orchard = *cemetery;
egg orchard* = *farmyard,
hencoop; junk orchard* =
junk heap, city dump.

—out, —outer. This suffix
word retains in slang formations much of its standard meaning = away from,
or beyond the limits of.
Hence it may suggest be-
yond the limits of endur-
ance *(crap out, pooped
out),* beyond consciousness
(knock out, pass out), over
a physical boundary *(chucker out),* beyond normal size
(stretch out), out of sight
or beyond embarrassment
or penalty *(lie out, weasel
out, welch out)* and, in recent bop and cool use, beyond the limits of mundane
existence *(far out, way
out).* The formation with
—outer has the *—er* suffix of
agency, and is found in
many nonce words and ne-

ologisms (see —*er* and —*er*
  —*er* above).
bail out*
batch out*
bat out*
bawl out*
beat-out*
bilge out*
black out*
blot out*
blow-out*
boff out*
boil out*
bone out*
buck out
bug out
bum-out
burned-out
bust out
butt out
case out
chew out
chicken out
chucker-out
clean out
conk out
cook-out*
cool out*
cop out*
crap out*
crash out*
crumped out*
crush out*
cut it out*
cut out*
dig out*
dish it out*
dish out*
dog out*
doll out*
dope out*
drag out*
dressing out*
dropout*
dugout*
fade out*
fallout*
far out*
feel out*
flake out*
flat out*
flunk out*
fucked out*
go out*
grub out*
guyed out*
handout*
hangout*
help-out*
hide-out*
hold out*
honk-out*
iron out*
jack out*
join out*
killout*
kiss out*
knocked out*

knockout*
laid out*
let out*
lie out
light out*
loan-out*
lucked out*
lug out*
make out*
melted out*
muscle out*
nose out*
ooze out*
pan out*
pass out*
peddle out*
peel out*
peg out*
pepped out*
pitch-out*
plank out*
played out*
poke-out*
poo out*
pooped out*
poop out*
punch-out*
pot out*
pout-out*
pull out*
punk out*
put out*
rag out*
rat out*
rideout*
rig-out*
roll out*
rub out*
run-out*
sack out*
shell out*
shoot-out*
shove out for*
show out*
shut out*
shutting out*
sign-out*
sing out*
smoke-out
snub out*
spell out*
spiffed out*
stake out*
stanch out*
stand-out*
step out*
step out on (someone)*
stick (one's) neck out*
stick-out*
stretch-out
sweating-out*
sweat it out*
swing off*
take a run-out powder*
take-out*
tap out*
tapped out*
throw-out*

try-out*
turn-out*
walk out*
wash-out*
way-out*
weasel out*
welch out
whack out*
win out*
wipe out*
workout*
x out*

—**over.** This suffix word =
full to capacity or over-
flowing, usually referring
to alcoholic capacity
(*slopped over* = drunk) or
to one's emotions (*boiled
over* = angry). It is also
used to = retained longer
or postponed to (*hold over*),
or to = the effects of
drinking too much (*hung
over*). As are many other
prepositions (around, at,
in, up, etc.), *over* is found
in colloquial expressions
(*come on over*).

—**packer.** This suffix word =
one who or that which carries. Probably *heat packer*
= gun, gunman is the best
known —*packer* word,
though it is found in some
other minor uses (*weight
packer* = a person who
"carries a lot of weight").

—**peddler.** Literally one who
travels about selling his
wares from place to place,
this suffix word figuratively
= one who sells legally
(*car peddler*) or illegally
(*dope peddler*); one who
serves or deals in some-
thing (*sock-peddler*) =
prize fighter); and since
c1950 especially, one who
advertises, sponsors, or advocates (*culture peddler*).
book peddler
car peddler
culture peddler
democracy peddler
dope peddler
dress peddler
gospel peddler
pill peddler*
shoe peddler
sock peddler — a prize fighter
suit peddler
used-car peddler

—**piss.** This somewhat taboo
suffix word literally =
urine, and figuratively =
any beverage considered
inferior, inordinately
strong, or raw to the

throat, usually a bootleg whiskey but sometimes coffee, soup, etc. The root word is often a strong or ferocious animal to indicate the strength or rawness of the drink (*panther piss* = raw whiskey, the most common —*piss* term; *lion piss*). Sometimes domestic animals are used to suggest a weaker but also noxious drink (*horse piss* = inferior or weak wine, coffee, or soup). The suffix word is considered somewhat rustic. Though usually deprecatory, it is sometimes used as a compliment when referring to good, strong whiskey.

—**pot.** A person figuratively considered as filled with, a receptacle of, characterized by, or exuding that indicated by the root word (*sex pot, stink pot*). Young teenagers or children use it as a mild insult; among adults it can be used affectionately or familiarly in direct address. —*pot* is also, less frequently, used to = a place considered as filled with or a receptacle of (*flesh pot*).

coal-pot*
crackpot
fleshpot*
fusspot
gluepot*
grease-pot*
joepot*
quack-pot
rumpot*
rustpot*
sex pot*
small pot*
stink pot*
swill pot
tallow-pot*
tinpot*

—**puncher.** This suffix word has two nonstandard meanings. It can = —*driver* (see above) as in *slave-puncher*, or it can = *fighter* (see above) as in *beer-puncher* and *booze puncher*.

—**pusher.** This suffix word = one who sells or is a —*peddler* (see above); one who drives, uses, or is associated with something (*hack-pusher, leather-pusher*); or one who has a strong, masculine or weak, effeminate personality

(*cookie-pusher*).
bell-pusher — door-to-door salesman, who spends his time ringing doorbells
cookie-pusher*
diamond-pusher*
dope pusher
gospel-pusher*
grease-pusher*
diamond-pusher
hack-pusher — cab driver
leather-pusher — prize fighter
paper-pusher*
pencil-pusher*
pen-pusher*
pill-pusher*
punk-pusher*
thumb-pusher
wood-pusher

—**puss.** As a word *puss* literally means a person's face, but as a suffix word —*puss* figuratively = person. The root word is usually an adjective, often referring to the sense of taste (see Preface), and the entire phrase is usually affectionate except for the most common formation, *sour puss*. The —*puss* serves the same purpose as adding the adjective suffix —*ous* or —*y* to root nouns (*glamour puss* = a glamorous person; *sugar puss* = sugary or sweet person) and has the same effect as adding the article *a* before an adjective (*cutie puss* = a cutie; *sweetie puss* = a sweetie).

—**rat.** This suffix word = man, but always with the deprecatory connotation of unworthy, dishonest, sneaky, etc. The root word often indicates the place or town with which such a person is associated or where he works as in the most common such formation, *wharf rat* (or *dock rat*). —*rat* also = informer, as in *bull rat* = police informer and *company rat* = employer's informer.

—**shark.** One who knows a topic thoroughly and is enthusiastic, even mildly obsessed, about it (*gospel shark*, 1885: *DAE*). In this sense —*shark* = fiend and —*hound* (see above). It has also taken on the meaning of one who uses his knowledge in order to make a

profit from it in either an ethical or unethical way (*card shark, poker shark*). Thus —*shark* now has the primary connotation of one who attempts to take advantage of another, often by fraud (*loan shark*). —*shark* may be reinforced by —*sharp* (see below).
bridge shark
business shark
card shark*
cinder shark*
dice shark
gospel shark
job shark*
loan shark
opera shark
poker shark
pool shark

—**sharp.** This suffix is a synonym for —*shark* and carries both the connotation of "one adept at" and of "a cheat." It is a front clipping from *sharper* = a swindler or a cheating gambler, reinforced by —*shark*.

—**shit.** This taboo suffix word is used in deprecatory formations which indicate lies, exaggerations, or unworthy tasks (*bull shit*). As a counter it sees wide use = any idea, concept, or attitude which is accepted or rejected (*good shit, stupid shit*).
bad shit*
big shit*
bullshit*
chicken shit*
good shit*
horse shit*
hot shit*
mean shit
simple shit
stupid shit
tough shit*

—**shop.** Probably based on the common *hockshop*, this suffix word = any place where that indicated by the root word may be bought, sold, obtained, or imparted.
gospel shop — a church
guzzle shop*
hockshop*
hookshop*
show-shop*
swap shop*

—**skinner.** This suffix word was most common in the colloquial *mule-skinner* = mule-driver. Here —*skinner* is similar to the modern

—*jockey* (see above), but the connotation is of the driver flaying the skin off the mules with his long whip. In modern use *cat-skinner* = driver of a caterpillar tractor is the only important word using —*skinner*, the connotation of "taming" being retained.

—**slinger.** Literally = one who casts forth or who serves, this suffix word is a synonym for —*jerk, jerker* (see above). —*slinger* often, but not always, has the connotation of a server in a cheap or even direputable place where service is not considered important. This suffix word figuratively = one who casts forth or broadcasts that indicated by or associated with the root noun (*gun-slinger* = *gunman, ink-slinger* = *writer*).

beer-slinger*
booze-slinger
bull-slinger
diddy-dum slinger
grub-slinger*
gun-slinger*
hash-slinger*
ink-slinger*
leather-slinger
lightning-slinger*
pot-slinger*
psalm-slinger
rock-slinger*
suds-slinger
word-slinger

—**smith.** This suffix word is the Anglo-Saxon *smith* = one who forges with a hammer, as in the standard *tinsmith*, and the most common *blacksmith*, which has kept this suffix word popular. In non-standard use —*smith* has generalized to = one who creates, forms, or makes. The connotation is usually of one who creates popular entertainment, with the emphasis on craft rather than art (*tune-smith* = song writer, *word-smith* = popular writer, lyricist, or newspaper columnist.

—**spot.** This suffix word refers to a monetary note or a playing card whose number is indicated by the root word (*five spot, ten spot* = a five or ten dollar bill, or a five or ten of a

playing card in any suit). It also = the specific place indicated by the root word, usually an entertainment place, often a night club (*hotspot, nightspot*). The connotation is one of excitement or popularity.

—**stand.** This suffix word = literally a stall where things are sold, and figuratively any place, such as a street corner, where something may be obtained or a person be found, as in the standard *cab-stand* and *newspaper-stand*, the somewhat colloquial *hack-stand* and *hot-dog stand*, or the carnival jargon *bally-stand*.

—**trap.** This suffix word literally = a place where one may be trapped or endangered (*fire trap*), and figuratively it = a place where one may be cheated (*tourist trap*), a person that takes advantage of another (*man trap*), or a place infested (*rat trap*).

clam trap*
fish trap*
fly trap*
flea trap*
fire-trap
girl trap
man trap
mousetrap*
potato-trap*
soldier trap
rat-trap
talk trap*
tourist-trap

—**up,** —**upper.** As a suffix word with a variety of uses, —*up* retains much of its standard meanings. It is most commonly added to verbs or nouns to form phrases serving as verbs or adjectives that figuratively = to fill or be filled or loaded, often to capacity (*beer up, fed up, study up*). Specifically —*up* often = to add or fill with energy, strength, or alertness (*beef up, pep up, straighten up*). The second basic use of —*up* literally and figuratively = to obtain or collect, or to come together for a specific purpose (*bum up, match up, pick up, pile up, think up,* and *write up*). The suffix word is also used to = an agitated or confused state (*fucked up,*

shook up), the least dignified of these formations. It enjoyed wide armed forces use during and since World War II and wide teenage and student use since c1945. The —*er* suffix of agency is often added to make —*upper*; it is found in many neologisms and nonce words. See —*er* and —*er* —*er* ending above.

ante up*
back up*
balled up*
ball up*
bang-up*
barreled up*
beaten-up*
beat up*
beef up*
beer up*
bitch up (something)*
blown up
blow-up*
boil up*
bollixed up*
bone up*
booze up*
break up*
brush up*
buck up*
buddy up*
buddy up to (someone)*
bug up*
build-up*
bum up — obtain, find, beg
burn (someone) up*
bus up*
butter up*
button up*
call up*
canned up*
change-up*
chewed up*
choke up*
clam up*
clean up*
closed up*
close up*
coked up*
cook up*
cough up*
cover-up*
crack up*
cream up*
cross-up*
crumb up*
cut up*
dig up*
dime up*
divvy up*
dog up*
doll up*
done up*
do up*
dream up*

drink up
drive up*
dry up*
dude up*
dummy up*
dustup*
eat up
egg up*
fed up
feel up*
'fess up
fired up*
fire up*
fix-up*
flare up*
fog up*
follow up*
fouled up*
foulup*
frame up*
frog up*
fucked up*
fuck up*
full up*
furp up*
futzed up*
gang up
gas up*
gat up*
geared up*
geed up*
get (one's) dander up*
get-up*
ginned up*
goof up*
go up*
gowed-up*
gum up*
gummixed up*
gussied up*
ham up*
hang up*
hard up*
head-up*
het (heated) up — angry, excited
hitch-up*
hold-up*
hole up*
hoosier up*
hop up*
hopped up*
hung up*
hyped-up*
iron up*
jack up*
jammed up*
jam-up*
jazz up — make more exciting, appealing, or modern; increase the speed of
jet up*
jolly-up*
juiced up*
jumped-up*
kick-up*
knock up*
lash-up*

liquored up*
lock up*
louse up*
luck up*
lushed up*
make up
match up
mess up*
mix-up*
mob up — to form a mob for a specific purpose
mop-up*
muck up*
mug up*
mulled up*
nickel up*
one up*
open up*
pass up*
pep up*
phoney up*
pick-up*
piece up*
pile up*
pin-up*
plank up*
police up*
polished up*
pony up*
pop-up*
potted up*
pungle up*
put up*
read up
re-up*
riled up
ripped up*
rod up*
rough up*
round up*
rung up*
sack up*
sap up on (someone)*
scare up*
screwed-up*
screw up*
send up*
set up*
sewed up*
sew up*
shack up*
shake it up*
shake-up*
shape-up*
shine up to (someone)*
shook up*
shot-up*
show up*
show-up line*
shuffle them up*
shut up*
sign-up*
size-up*
slap-up*
slip-up*
smoke-up*
snafu up
snap it up*

snowed up*
sored up*
souped up*
soup up*
speed-up*
split-up*
spoon up*
spruce up*
stack up*
stand-up*
steamed up*
steam up*
stick up*
stick up for (someone)*
straighten up — to become serious, honest, alert, or responsible
string up*
stuck-up
study up
suck up to (someone)*
suit up — to dress, esp. to don the clothes suitable to a specific sport or occupation
sum up
tanked up*
tank up*
taxi up*
tead up*
teed up*
think up
tied up*
tie it up*
tighten up — to become nervous, suffer from stage fright
toughen up
trump(ed) up*
tumble up — "tumble," recognize
tune up*
turn (someone) up*
up*
wait up*
wake-up*
walk-up*
warm up*
wash up*
way-up*
whack up*
whipped-up*
whip up*
whomp up*
wind up*
wise up*
wrap-up*
write-up*
—wacky. This is another of the —*crazy* and —*mad* synonyms (see above). It may mean "crazy" about, or obsessed with (*car-wacky, wench-wacky*), or "crazy" from (*booze-wacky, stir-wacky*).
—wrangler. This suffix word with a Western connota-

tion (*wrangler* = one who broke and handled horses) is used literally and figuratively to = one who creates, works with, or serves (*coke wrangler* = soda jerk, *song wrangler* = song writer). It is also used with the same meaning as the more common —*fighter* (see above) in such formations as *booze wrangler* and *bottle wrangler*.

—**wrestler.** This suffix word is a synonym for —*fighter* (see above) and is used in such formations as *booze-wrestler* and *pot-wrestler* (one fighting against excessive eating and over-weight). It is less common than —*fighter* and more common than —*wrangler*.

—**yard.** This suffix word = any place where that indicated by the root word may be found in quantity, a residing or storage place. It is a synonym for —*orchard* (see above), and is found mainly in *boneyard* = cemetery.

Prefixes

Prefixes are not common in slang formations.

de.— The prefix *de—* is affixed to standard and nonstandard nouns to form verbs which = to deprive, steal, cheat, or take the item indicated by the root word (this item may be an object, but it is often knowledge, innocence, or some other personal characteristic.) These formations have humorous argot usages, the two most common being to *depocketbook* = to pick a man's pocket of his wallet or, less frequently, to steal a woman's purse, and to *derube* = to teach a person to be wiser in the ways of the world by making him a victim of a confidence game, cheating him in gambling, or otherwise victimizing him. The prefix is also used in several taboo words and oaths, the two most common being to *deball* = to castrate, used as an oath or threat against someone, and to *devirginize*, used as a threat or boast in male

conversation about women. All these formations, besides being humorous, are euphemistic.

ex—. This prefix has its standard meanings when affixed to nonstandard words. It is attached to slang and colloquial nouns to = former or one-time, often with the connotation of being old, or no longer desired, useful, or worthwhile.

ex-boyfriend
ex-carny*
ex-con
ex-flame
ex-girlfriend
ex-hood
ex-husband
ex-hoofer
ex-pal
ex-pug
ex-star
ex-tubby*
ex-vic*

sch—, schm—. This can be considered a slang prefix when it is affixed to standard or slang words. It is also found in many Yiddish borrowings. See Introduction to Appendix above for further discussion, and see Reduplications: Second Order Reduplications below.

schlemiel
schlepper
schlunk
schmaltz
schmear
schmendrick
schmo
schmoo
schnook
shlock shop

Prefix Words

Prefix words in slang are not as common as suffix words. For a further discussion, see Introduction to Appendix above.

armchair—. This prefix word serves as an adjective = one who gives advice or opinion after the fact or without experience, knowledge, or participation. It usually precedes nouns representing leaders, with the connotation that the person wishes to give commands from a safe, comfortable, irrefutable position. It is most often used in the phrase *armchair*

general. *Monday-morning quarterback* is a similar construction.

circus—. This prefix word serves as an adjective = spectacular, exciting, elaborate, garish, specifically created or done in a spectacular manner to impress others. Thus *circus catch* = a spectacular or exciting catch made in baseball, sometimes one which the fielder makes look harder than it actually is in order to impress the spectators with his skill; and *circus meal* = a large, fancy meal, perhaps to impress guests or prospective boarders. This prefix word has been largely replaced by *grandstand* (see below).

for—. This preposition is added before common adjectives as an intensifier without altering their meaning *(for certain, for free)* or to take the place of the standard —*ly* suffix in changing an adjective to an adverb *(for real* = *really)*. *for—* is never followed by a hyphen.

for certain
for free*
for good
for honest
for it*
for kicks*
for real*
for serious*
for sure
for the cuff*
for the birds*

glass—. This prefix word serves as an adjective = weak, liable to break or be damaged easily. Commonly used in *glass jaw*, it is usually applied to parts of the body, especially those where a specific prize-fighter is vulnerable (glass-nose). In baseball, *glass arm* = a pitcher's arm liable to tire, cramp, or become sore.

grandstand—. This is a synonym for *circus* = (see above), which it has now largely replaced. Most frequently found in baseball use, it most commonly appears in *grandstand act*, *grandstand catch*, and *grandstand play*.

half—. Almost always found

in deprecatory formations which apply to people, *half—* = partially. It conveys, however, the strong connotation that the person to whom it applies is on his way toward being fully defined by the root word, as in the standard half-wit.

half-asleep
half-assed*
half-baked*
half-buck*
half-cocked*
half-corned*
half-cracked
half-crazy
half-crocked
half-dead
half-gone
half-nuts
half-pint*
half-portion*
half-screwed*
half shaved*
half-shot*
half-slewed*
half-snaped*
half-sprung*
half-stewed*
half the bay over*
half under*

John—, Johnny—. Originally and still primarily argot, *John—* is a personalized element used before a noun which otherwise would be capitalized and preceded by The. Sometimes it is used simply to indicate a criminal or a victim. Though it is less common, *Johnny—* may be used instead of *John—*.

John Bates — a dupe or victim
John Fate
John Law
John Right — a righteous person, originally a dupe
John (Q.) Public
John Yegg — a yegg, a fellow criminal

mister—. This prefix word is primarily a synonym for *John— (Mister Law =* The Law, a policeman; *Mister Right; Mister Wrong =* a disliked, untrustworthy person). The most frequently heard is Mister Big = the mastermind or head of a criminal organization, or any person in absolute control. In theatrical use the prefix word = a leader or a star *(Mister*

Show Business, Mister Television).

Monday morning—. See arm-chair—.

oh—. Originally the standard interjection indicating surprise, grief, or desire, this is used as a true prefix word before many oaths, especially taboo ones. Strongly vocalized and without any real meaning, *oh—* actually softens the oath *(oh God, oh hell, oh shit)* from a merely explosive interjection to an expression containing some resignation, understanding, and sympathy.

old—. Placed before several standard and nonstandard nouns which loosely = friend this prefix word suggests easy familiarity, long intimacy, or sympathy.

old bean*
old boy*
old buddy
old chap*
old chum
old fellow*
old file*
old fruit*
old gal
old girl
old goat*
old hat*
old head*
old lady*
old man*
old miss*
old smoky*
old sock*
old socks*
old soldier
old thing*
old top*
old woman*

on—. This preposition is used in certain phrase formations when followed by *the* and a noun to = addicted to or in the habit of consuming that indicated by the noun, usually narcotics or whiskey. Sometimes the formation = to be, in the state of, living the life of *(on the blink, on the lam).*

on the arm*
on the ball*
on the beam*
on the Bill Daley*
on the blink*

on the bottle
on the bum*
on the burrole*
on the bush*
on the button*
on the carpet*
on the cob*
on the cops*
on the cuff*
on the dead*
on the dot*
on the double*
on the dry*
on the Erie*
on the finger*
on the fire*
on the fritz*
on the go*
on the grift*
on the heavy*
on the hook*
on the house*
on the lam*
on the lee lurch*
on the legit*
on the level*
on the make*
on the mat*
on the needle*
on the nose*
on the pan*
on the peg*
on the rocks*
on the ropes — down and out
on the shake*
on the shelf*
on the shikker*
on the side*
on the skids*
on the spot*
on the stick*
on the stuff
on the thumb*
on the town*
on the up and up*
on the wagon*

out—. Besides its wide colloquial use in many expressions containing slang words, *out—* is used as a prefix word in many compoundings to = out do, to surpass, to be better than another. Thus *outact, outdrive, outplay, outyell* and many other neologisms and reoccurring nonce uses in which the root is slang, as *outblow* (jazz use), *outnut* (to be more "crazy" than another), etc.

real—. As a prefix word *real—* has wide use before bop, cool, and beat slang adjectives where it = intensely, quintessentially *(i.e.,* a much stronger state than that represented by "very" and "really"). It is most frequently used in phrases of approval, but sometimes it is placed before a noun representing an annoyance or a dislike *(real sick)*. See Introduction to Appendix for discussion of *real*.

real beat
real cool
real crazy
real dragged
real fine
real George, the*
real gone*
real high
real jazzy
real McCoy, the*
real messy
real sharp
real sheer
real sick
real strong
real swinging
real wild
real weird

stone——. In certain specific formations noun *stone* is used as an adjective = completely, totally, utterly. Thus the standard *stone blind* = totally blind, and slang's *stone broke, stone dead,* and *stone rich*. Since *stone—* is always followed by a word which implies totally or completely, it is primarily used for emphasis.

Sunday——. This prefix word has two general uses. In its oldest use it = one's best, literally that saved as if for special Sunday use *(Sunday clothes, Sunday pitch* = a baseball pitcher's best type of pitch). It is also used to = that which is unused or one who is inexperienced, hence inept *(Sunday driver)* and, by extension, one who is enthusiastic under favorable conditions but becomes easily discouraged when facing defeat *(Sunday soldier)*.

Sunday best*
Sunday clothes*
Sunday driver*
Sunday-go-to-meeting-
    clothes*
Sunday pitch*
Sunday punch*
Sunday run*
Sunday shirt
Sunday shoes
Sunday soldier*
Sunday suit
Sunday thinker*

sweet——. This prefix word is based on a figurative use of *sweet* and on a front clipping from "*sweet*heart." It loosely = kind, considerate and in slang often has the further meaning of passionate *(sweet man)* or profitable, easy, cushy *(sweet deal)*.

top——. This prefix word = in command or control, as a boss, leader, or favored person; or outstanding as an athlete or entertainer *(top sergeant, top dog, top man)*.

tote——. From its colloquial verb use = to carry by hand and from its colloquial noun use = the one who carries or the item or load carried, *tote—* is used as a prefix word in compoundings to = that which carries, as a vehicle *(tote-wagon* = wagon). More recently, as a clipping from totaling or totalizator, it has come to = one who or that which is used to make calculations *(tote-machine, tote-board, tote stick)*.

Infixes

For a discussion of infixes see the Introduction to the Appendix.

elomacution
flipmagilder — a "chiseler"
hickeymadoodle — a thinga-
    majig
ouchimagoocha — Spanish or
    Mexican style lovemaking,
    jocular use = passionate
    love-making
photomagenic
psycholomagee
razzamatazz*
razzmatazz*
s n o o z e m a r o o e d — d r u n k
    from snooze = sleep + sl.
    suffix — eroo (dial. use)
stratemagee
thingamadoger*
thingamadudgeon*
thingamajig*
thingamananny*
thingumabob*
thingumadoodle*
whatchamacallit*

Shortened Forms

For a discussion of the various types of shortened forms see the Introduction

to the Appendix.

Back clippings and back formations

ad
aggie — agricultural college
    or student
alum*
am*
ambish*
ammo*
anat — anatomy
ank — to walk (from ankle)
amp*
ape*
Aussie
auth — author; to write
auto*
babe*
bach*
bally*
barb*
bar-keep*
beaut*
benny*
biff — "biffer," girl
bike*
bim*
bio — biology
bish — bishop; to serve as
    a bishop
biz*
bizad — business administra-
    tion
black — black coffee, a cup
    of black coffee
black and white — black and
    white ice cream soda
blitz*
block*
blou — blouse
bogue*
boob*
boog*
boogie*
bootie*
bot*
bra*
bran*
Brit*
bronc*
brud*
buck*
bucker*
bud*
buff*
bull*
bunk*
burg*
burgle*
burly*
Butch*
buttle — to serve as a but-
    ler
cackle*
cad*
Caddy*
caf(f) — cafeteria; *café;*
    caffein

calc — calculus
calic*
cally*
cap*
carny*
cat*
cat's, the*
cauli — cauliflower
celeb*
cert — certainly; certainty; forged certified check
champ*
chank*
Chev(ie) — Chevrolet car
chick*
chiz — chiseler
choc — chocolate
chromo*
cig*
circ — circumstance
cit*
civvies*
clemo*
coco*
co-ed*
coff — coffee
coffee and*
coke*
coloss — colossal
combo*
comfy
commie*
commem — commemorative (issue of a postage stamp)
commish — commission; police commissioner
commo*
comp*
compet — competitor; competition
competish — competition
compo*
con*
conchie*
confab*
con game*
con job*
con man*
coop*
cop*
corp — corporal
cos — cosmopolitan
cosmo*
cou*
cox — coxswain (of a rowing crew)
cred — credential; credit
crew*
crip*
cuke*
cyc — cyclorama
deac*
deb*
deck, dec — declamation
def — definitely
defi*
delish*
delly*

demi-rep*
Demo*
demo*
dent — student of dentistry; dentistry
depresh — depression (financial)
dexie*
diag*
diff*
differ*
dill*
dinah*
dine*
dinge*
dip*
dipper*
dipso*
distrib — distributor
divvy*
doc*
dorm*
dough*
draw one — draw (pour) one cup of coffee
duck*
dupe*
eco, econ, ec — economics
ed — education; editor
emote*
English*
enorm — enormous
ent — entomology
ex*
exam
exec*
exhib — exhibitor (of movies); exhibition
fan*
fave — favorite
fed*
feeb*
fem*
filthy*
fin*
fistful*
flat*
flip*
fliv*
fool
forty-eight*
frank — frankfurter
frat*
French*
fresh, frosh*
frivol*
fuddy
gab
gam
gard — gardenia
gas
gat
gate*
gen — generator; general
gent*
geom — geometry
glad — gladiola
gon*

goody*
googs*
goon*
gorill*
gorm*
goulie*
grad*
grid*
Guin*
gump*
gunny — gunny sack
gym*
gyp*
hack*
ham and*
hankie*
hard top*
heavy*
Hebe*
heebies — heebie-jeebies
heff*
hi fi*
hippo*
hog*
hoke*
home ec — home economics
homo*
hon*
hood*
hook*
hyp*
hypo*
igg*
imposs — impossible
impresh — impression
indie*
info*
inorgan — inorganic chemistry
inter*
intro*
invite*
iso*
jalop*
janit — to work as a janitor
Jap — Japanese
Jeez*
jerk*
jiff*
jig*
jims — jim-jams
jit*
jock*
jun(e) — (college) junior
juve — juvenile
kay*
lab*
legit*
lemo*
les*
letch — lecher, lecherous
libe*
lieut*
lit*
loco*
low fi*
lube*

lunk — lunkhead
mack*
mag*
mage, maje — Major
magnif — magnificent
mansh — mansion
Marge*
ma(r)ma*
marv, marvie — marvelous
Mary, mary, mari — marijuana
max*
may*
mayo*
mazoo*
med*
medic*
melo*
Mex*
mick— micrometer
mickey — Mickey Finn
middy*
mig — migratory worker
mike*
miss*
mitt*
mix*
mo*
moke — mocha
mon*
monk*
mono — monogram
monog — monogamous
moo — moola
morph*
mouse— "mouser"
mush — mushroom; umbrella
nabe — neighborhood
nanny — nanny goat
natch*
neb— nebbish
nick*
nig*
nightie*
Nip *
noncom*
obit*
off*
on — on toast
on the dead — on the (dead) level
one-arm — one-arm joint
oof — offtish
op*
ope*
opposish — opposition
oral — oral examination
org*
organ — organic chemistry
ork*
pack*
pan — panoramic
Pan-Hel — Pan-Hellenic Association
panther — panther sweat (piss)
pape*
pard*

pash*
path — pathology
peck — peckerwood (white person)
peel — peeler
peeps*
peeve — peevish
peg*
pen*
Pennsy*
pep*
perk*
pete — peter
phenom*
Phi Bete — Phi Beta Kappa, a member of Phi Beta Kappa
phil — philosophy
Phillie*
phono*
photo*
photog*
phys ed — physical education
pic*
piece*
Pink*
pip*
pix*
polly*
poly ec, pol econ — political economy
poly sci — political science
pomp*
pop*
pos — positively
possesh — possession
post — postgraduate
pot — pot belly
pound salt*
pre — preliminary; prerequisite
pred — prediction; predecessor
preem — premiere
preemie — premature baby
prelim*
pre-med*
prep*
pres*
presh — precious
prez*
pro*
prob — problem
proc — proclamation
prod — product; prodigy
prof*
prohi*
prom*
prop*
pro-pack*
proposish— proposition
prossie — prostitute
psych*
psycho*
pub*
pull sat*
put on — put on the feedbag

quad*
quint*
quote*
rag — ragtime
razz*
recap — recapitulation
recco, recon — reconnaissance
rec(k) — recreation
reefer*
ref(f) — referee
refer, reffer — reformatory inmate or ex-inmate
reg — regulation
relig — religion
re-org — reorganization
rep*
res — resident
reune — reunion
rheo — rheostat
rhino*
ridic — ridiculous
rook*
rube*
Sal*
san — sanatorium
san, sand — sandwich
sand and*
sap*
sarge*
sat — satisfactory
satch*
saw*
sax*
schiz, schizo* — schizophrenic
schnozz*
sci — science
script*
sculpt
sec*
Secesh*
seconds — second helpings of food
sem*
sensay*
sensaysh*
seppo — one separated, esp. from one's spouse
sham*
shove it — shove it up your ass
side (of) — a side order of
siff*
situash*
skip — skipper
slum — slumgullion
smack — smacker
small pot — small potatoes
snap — snapshot
soc — sociology
sol*
soldier*
som — sombrero
soph*
spark*
speak*
spec*
specks*

spic and span*
spiff*
spig*
spla*
spon*
steno(g)— stenographer;
stenography
stool,-ie — stool pigeon
stupe*
sub*
subdeb*
subsid — subsidiary company
sun—sundae
super*
sync*
syph*
tad*
tarp*
tech*
teen*
tele — television
temp — temperature, temporary
terp — dancer (terpsichore)
terrif — terrific
thesp — actor (thespian)
thou*
tin horn — tin-horn gambler
toke*
torp*
tote*
trig — trigonometry
trigger*
tripe*
trom*
trou— trousers
turk*
tute — tutor
tux*
twit — chatter, talk (twitter)
typer — machine gun (typewriter)
umbrel(l)
ump*
unc*
undergrad*
up the (shit) creek — up the
(shit) creek without a paddle
up yours — up your ass
ush*
ut*
vac — vacuum
vag*
vamp*
van*
vaude*
vet*
vibes*
vil (le) — village
waf — waffle
wheats — wheat cakes
weiner*
with — with potatoes, with
onions, with cream, etc.
wob*
vrit*
yan*

zam*
Zepp*
Front clippings
bird*
bo*
bone*
bop*
box*
brow*
chute— parachute
copter — helicopter
cot — apricot
Creepers!*
croot*
cut A*
cutor*
dike*
doke*
dust*
dusts*
fes(s) — confess
fess(or) — professor
form — racing form
'gator*
goat*
gram — telegram, radiogram
jack — blackjack
jeebies*
jerk*
jock*
juane*
kraut*
legger*
moll*
morphadite*
muck*
mum*
nail*
nig*
otie*
peeties*
peter — repeater
pipe — stovepipe
roll — piano-roll
scope*
scrape*
sheet — scratch sheet
shine* — moonshine
shine — moonshine*
skate*
skee*
skeeter*
slinger*
soap*
soldier*
sorry*
stairs*
star*
stem*
stick*
stocking*
strip*
tini — Martini (cocktail)
thuse— enthuse (a college
rally or pep meeting)
tonk*
tub*
wave*

wet*
wheel*
without a paddle*
Abbreviations and acronyms
AA*
ac-dc*
A.K.*
A.W.O.L.*
b.a.*
b.l.t.*
BS*
BMOC*
BTO*
B.V.D.'s*
C*
C-note*
C.O. — commanding officer;
conscientious objector
C-speck*
c.t.*
D.A.*
D.D. — drop dead; daily
double
D and D*
D.I.*
DJ*
D.O.A.*
D.T.'s*
f.f.*
F.F.V.*
f.o.
flak* — flieger abwehr kan-
one (Ger., "anti-aircraft
artillery")
G*
G.A.C.*
g.d.*
G.I.*
g.j.*
H*
I.O.U.*
j.a.t.o.*
John L's*
K.O.*
LP*
L's the*
M*
M. C. — a master of cere-
monies
MG*
Mig*
M.R. — motivational research
N.G.*
O*
O.B. — obie (argot for "ho-
bo")
O.D.*
o.j.*
O.P.*
P.C.*
P.D.Q. — pretty damn quick
P.F.C. — private first class
p.i. (pee-eye) — pimp
P.J.'s*
p.o.*
P.O.W.*
P.R.*
P.U. — phew

Q. and A.*
Q.T., q.t. — quiet, confidential, secret
R and D — research and development program
R and R*
rif*
Rok*
R.O.T.C. —Reserve Officers' Training Corps
seabee*
snafu*
snoff*
s.o.b.*
s.o.l.*
S.O.P.*
S.O.S.*
swak*
T*
TD*
three-D*
TKO*
t.l.*
t.s.*
V.D.*
V.I.P.*

Reduplications

For a discussion of the various types of reduplications see the Introduction to the Appendix.

First order reduplications

ack-ack*
baa-baa
baddy-baddy — A villain, usu. of a television play or movie
bang-bang*
bee-bee*
beep-beep
beer-beer
blah-blah*
blankety-blank*
boing-boing*
boo-boo*
boom-boom*
bouncy-bouncy*
buckety-buckety — cheap, inferior
buddy-buddy*
buzz-buzz*
by-by — good-by
chi-chi*
chin-chin — talk
chip-chip — expression meant to remind the listener not to be too self-satisfied or pleased
choo-choo
chop-chop*
coo-coo*
dee-dee*
din-din — dinner
dust-dust*
fig-fig — sexual intercourse
fly-fly boy — a military pilot
foo-foo*
footie-footie*

footsy-footsy*
frou-frou*
fuck(y)-fuck — sexual intercourse
fuss-fuss — a fuss
gabble-gabble
gaga*
gee-gee*
gigi*
goody-goody*
goo-goo*
goodie-goodie
Gusy-Gusy*
haba haba*
haha*
ho-ho
housie-housie — house
hubba-hubba*
hush-hush*
jig-jig*
juju*
la-la*
lulu*
mama
meow-meow — expression showing disapproval of the "catty" remarks of others
mo-mo*
moo-moo — cow (childrens' use)
mop mop*
nice(y)-nice*
night(y)-night
papa
pat-pat
pee-pee
pip-pip — a greeting, usu. mocking the English
pom-pom*
pooh-pooh
poo-poo*
putt-putt
quack-quack
rah-rah*
she-she*
so-so*
sucky-suck — fellatio
talk-talk*
ta-ta*
tick-tick
tick-tock
too too*
tum-tum — tummy
tweet-tweet
wah-wah*
wee-wee*
woof-woof*
woo-woo!*
yak-yak*
yatata yatata*
yen-yen*
yo-yo*
yuk-yuk*
yum-yum*
zig-zig*

Second order reduplications

abba-dabba — abracadabra

abracadabra
beddie-weddie*
boogie-woogie*
boogily-woogily*
boo hoo
bow-wow*
boz-woz*
chiller-diller*
dizzy-wizzy*
ducky-wucky — fine, wonderful
even-Steven*
fiddle-faddle*
footsie-wootsie*
fuddy-duddy*
fusty-dusty — fuddy-duddy
handsy-wandsy — hands
hanky-panky*
heebie-jeebies*
Hell's bells*
herkimer-jerkimer — jerk
hipper-dipper*
hocus-pocus*
hoddy-doddy*
hoity-toity*
hokey-pokey*
holly-golly*
honky-tonk(y)*
hoop-de-doop*
hooper-dooper*
hootchie cootchie*
hoovus-goovus — hip; the groove
hotsie-totsie*
huff-duff*
hugger-mugger*
hully-gully*
humpty-dumpty*
hunkie dunkie — fine, O.K.
hurdy-gurdy*
itsy-bitsy
jeepers creepers*
jeezy-peezy*
jobsie-wobsie — job
Joe Blow*
kicksie-wicksie*
killer-diller*
lovey-dovey*
mumbo-jumbo
nasty-wasty
okey-dokey*
okle-dokle*
oofty-goofty
ooly-drooly*
palsy-walsy*
peewee*
petsy-wetsy
phonus-bolonus*
piggy-wiggy
ping-wing*
poolsie-woolsie — game of rotation pool
poopsie-woopsie
popsy-wopsy
racket-jacket*
rangle-dangle — festoon, fringe, dangling ornament; to wrangle or argue

razzle-dazzle*
rep-dep*
repple-depple*
rinky-dink(y)*
roly-poly
root(y)-toot-toot*
row-dow — row
rowdy-dow(dy)-row-dow
rum-dum*
rusty-dusty*
sacky-dacky — "sack" or bed
slangwhang*
soogie moogie*
sooper-dooper*
spooky-wooky
starvie-warvie — to starve
super-duper*
teen(s)y-ween(s)y
teeny weeny
thriller-diller*
tootsie-wootsie*
ubble-gubble*
walkie-talkie*
wham-bam*
whing-ding*
whoop-de-do(op)*
whooper-dooper*
willy-nilly*
wing-ding*
yock(y) dock*

actor-schmactor
barrister-schmarrister
boom-schmoom
careful-schmareful
case-schmase
century-schmentury
Chippendale-shmippendale
coat-schmoat
cold-schmold
cricket-schmicket
dance-schmance
dancer-schmancer
Dixie-Schmixie
even-schmeeven
fancy-schmancy
fielder-schmielder
finish-schminish
fire-schmire
junior-schmunior
lesson-schmesson
lie-schmie
manner-schmanner
megacycle-schmegacycle
messenger-schmessenger
music-schmusic
patter-schmatter
picture-schmicture
point-schmoint
princess-schmincess
rat-schmat
right-shmight
rocket-schmocket
sergeant-schmergeant
spot-schmot
stage-smage
unguent-schmunguent
vital-schmital

wax-schmax
whimsy-schmimsy
wonderful-schmunderful
zodiac-schmodiac
Third order reduplications
akey-okey*
bibble-babble*
bing-bang*
chatter-chitter — chatter;
 idle talk
chitchat*
dilly-dally*
ding-dang*
ding-dong*
dingle-dangle — the penis;
 anything that dangles, as
 a festoon or ornament
drizzle-drazzle — a "drip,"
 drizzle
fiddle-faddle — nonsense,
 "fiddlesticks"
fizz-fuzz*
flim-flam*
flip-flop*
Hot-diggity-doggity!
Hot ziggity sack!
jibber-jabber*
jiggery-pokery — pranks,
 mischievous fun; deception
jim-jam*
jing-jang*
jingle-jangle*
mish-mash*
mish-mosh*
row-dow*
rowdy-dowdy*
tip-top*
tittle-tattle
whimsy-whamsy*
whim-wham*
wiggle-waggle*
wigwag*
wim-wams*
wishy-washy*
yig-yag — sexual intercourse
ying-yang*
zig-zag*

**Rhyming Terms and
Rhyming Slang**
For a discussion of rhyming
 terms and rhyming slang,
 see the Introduction to the
 Appendix.
Unintentional rhyming terms
ac-dc*
A.K.*
back-slack — regress
back-slapper
belly-button
B.V.D.'s
cheap Joe — cheap or miserly
 person
chitchat*
chow hound*
claptrap*
cow college — agricultural
 college; small rural college
crumb-bum*

c.t.*
dead beat*
deadhead*
double-trouble*
D.T.'s
flubdub*
gift of gab*
greasy grind*
gussie mollie*
gyp joint
harlot's hello, a*
hi fi*
hip chick*
honky-tonk
hot rod*
hot-shot*
hot spot*
hot squat — electric chair
howdy-doody
hustle-bustle
jail bait*
jeep-jockey*
King Kong*
king pin*
kissing-kin*
kiwi*
lead-head — stupid person
Leaping Lena*
loco da poco — a little crazy;
 eccentric
nickle-nurser — miser
niff-naw*
nitwit
olive oil — soothing or exaggerated talk
pang-wangle*
party-pooper*
past post*
peddle (one's) papers*
pickle-puss*
plug-ugly*
pocket pool*
pot out — engine failure in
 a hot rod
pug ugly — plug ugly
Rackensacker*
rat pack*
rootin'-tootin'*
rough stuff*
rum-dum*
sad sack*
sneaky Pete*
sure cure
swap-shop
San Quentin quail*
screaming meemie*
scuttle-butt*
seabee*
slap-happy*
thin dime*
weed tea — marijuana
worry wart*
**Intentional and jive
rhyming terms**
Abe's cabe*
acey-deucey*
bag with a sag — girl with an
 unattractive shape

beat feet — to hurry
bee's knees*
belly brass*
boogie-woogie
brag-rags*
bullet bait*
bull's wool*
cakes sakes — order of hot
 cakes and eggs
case-ace*
celler-smeller
chiller-diller*
chopped top*
chopper-copper — greedy eater
classy chassis*
copper dropper — gun
crumb bun
culture vulture*
curl girl — cute girl
date bait*
date mate*
dizzy Lizzie — scatterbrained
 female
dizzy-wizzy*
double-trouble*
drape shape*
duck-butt*
eager beaver*
eighter from Decatur
eighty-six*
even-Steven
face lace — whiskers
fag hag — female chain
 smoker
fancy-nancy — sissy
fat cat*
fem-sem*
finger-wringer*
flip (one's) lid*
flubdub*
flub the dub*
fly-guy
fly pie*
footsie wootsie*
frame-dame*
freak-beak —large nose
fuck a duck*
fuddy-duddy*
git-flip — guitar
give me some skin, Flynn —
 shake hands with me
glad lad*
glad pad — a "pad," esp. an
 attractive room or apartment, or one during a
 party
glad rags*
going to the function at Tuxedo Junction — going to a
 dance or party
goober-grabber*
greetings gate(s) — hello
gruesome twosome*
guzzlery guzzery*
handsome ransom*
Hell's bells*
hen-pen*

Herkimer Jerkimer*
hick dick*
hit the tick — to go to bed
hootchie cootchie*
hot shot*
hot squat*
hunky-chunk*
I'm alive 'cause I dig the jive
 — expression of enthusi-
 asm or self-satisfaction
in like Flynn*
Jeepers creepers*
jug-mug — convict, person in
 jail
ken-ten*
killer-diller*
ki-yi*
khaki-wacky — soldier-
 crazy
la(h)-de-da(h)*
laid, relaid, and parlayed*
lame-brain*
lane from Spokane*
large charge*
legal beagle*
legal eagle*
lens lice*
like the bear, nowhere —
 nowhere
like your tail, nightingale —
 greeting to an attractive
 girl
loose as a goose*
loud shroud — colorful
 ("loud") clothing
lush mush — good food; good
 "line"; attractive face
meter-reader*
Mike and Ike*
mince pies (the eyes)*
mojo*
mole hole — photographic
 darkroom
mop-chop — type of haircut
neater-eater — neat, fastidious, calm person; one who
 is liked or hip
nitwit*
passion ration*
pen yen*
pill pad*
ping-wing*
ptomain domain*
rabbit habit — sexual intercourse
racket-jacket*
ram bam*
ram, bam, thank you, ma'am*
rasher-splasher —rash person, attention-seeker; i.e.,
 one who is rash and causes
 a "splash"
ready for Freddie*
reet pleat*
rootin'-tootin'
rooty-toot
rum-dum — a rummy or wino
rusty-dusty*

saki-happy
San Quentin quail
screwed, blewed, and
 tattooed*
screwy Louie — scatterbrained youth
see you later, alligator*
shoot me the flame, Jane
shoot (pass) me the sherbert,
 Herbert
shrewd dude*
shy guy*
silly billy — silly person
Simple Simon*
skaty eight*
skirty flirty — girl crazy
slick chick*
snap (one's) cap*
sock frock — best suit
solid sender*
spin a hen — to dance
spin a wren — to dance
square from Delaware —a
 square
squawky-talkie — walkie-
 talkie
sticky icky — a square, an
 icky person
stinky pinky — a rhyming
 game
stubble trouble — difficulty in
 shaving
stuff cuff*
sudsy-dudsy — laundromat
superduper(ific)
super-snooper — G-man
thriller-diller*
town clown — rural policeman, sheriff, or constable
trig the wig — think fast, be
 alert
up thine with turpentine*
WAC hack — cough
walkie-talkie*
washtub-weeper*
wavy navy — the WAVES
wham-bam — ram-bam
whacky Willies*
what's your story, morning
 glory?
wheel and deal*
wheeler-dealer*
zoot snoot*
zoot suit*

**Rhyming slang (Cockney
and Australian)**
almond rocks — socks
apples and pairs — stairs
Aristotle — a bottle
babbling brook, babbler —
 crook
ball-of-chalk — walk; scram;
 beat it
balmy breeze — cheese
bees and honey* — money
Betty Lee — tea
birch broom — room
Bo Peep — sleep

bottle and stopper — policeman (copper)
bowl of chalk — talk
bows and arrows — sparrows
bug and flea — tea
bull and cow — row, quarrel
bullock's horn — pawn
bushel and peck — neck
butter and beers — ears
Cain and Abel — table
cheese and kisses — the Mrs. (one's wife)
chevy chase — face
china plate, china — one's mate
clock and slang — watch and chain
coat and badge — beg (cadge)
coke-frame — woman (dame)
cough and sneeze — cheese
daisy roots — boots
Dicky Dirt — shirt
dickory dock — sock
didn't oughter — water
Duke of Kent — rent
Duke of York — talk
Earl of Cork — talk; walk
elephant's trunk, elephant-(')s — drunk
false alarm — arm
Father O'Flynn — the chin
fiddle and flute, fiddle, fiddler — suit of clothes
fisherman's daughter — water
fields of wheat, fields — street
five to two, fifty-two — Jew
five to four — whore
flowery dell, flowery — prison cell
flying kite — night
forty-four*
German bands — hands
give and take — cake
hammer and nail, hammer — to trail, follow, tail
happy half-hours — flowers
heart(s) of oak — broke
Hector's pecking — necking
holy friar — liar
hook — crook
husband and wife — knife
I'm afloat — coat
I'm a wreck — a check
I suppose — nose
Isabeller — umbrella
Joe Blake — steak
the Joe Blakes, the Joes — the shakes
John Hop — policeman (cop)
Johnny Horner — corner
Johnny Ronce — pimp (ponce)
jug and pail — jail
Lady Godiva — five dollars (a fiver)

laughed-and-sang — slang
lean and fat — hat
lean and linger — finger
lean and lurch — church
Lilley and Skinner — dinner
Lincoln's Inn — five dollars (a fin)
linen draper — newspaper
loaf of bread, loaf — head
Lord Mayor — chair
love and kisses — the Mrs. (one's wife)
lump of chalk — talk
lump of lead — head
mariner's grave — shave
Martin-le Grand — hand
Mary Ann —-fist (hand)
Mike Malone — alone
mince pies, pies — eyes
monkey nut — shelter, home (hut)
most unwilling — shilling
Mother Hubbard — cupboard
Mr. McGimp, McGimp — a pimp
mutton pie — eye
Nancy Lee — Flea
needle and pin — gin
never fear — beer
north and south — mouth
Oliver Twist, Oliver — fist
one and one — thief ("gon"); gun
one another — mother
Oscar Asche — money (cash)
Oxford scholar — a dollar
Pat Malone — alone
pen and ink — stink
pies — eyes
pig's ear — beer
plates of meat, plates — feet
plow the deep — sleep
Pope of Rome — home
pot and pan, pot — man; father, husband
raspberry tart, raspberry — heart; fart
ratcatcher's daughter — water
Richard the Third — the "bird"
Robin Hood — good
roll me in the gutter — butter
Rory O'More — floor; door
Rosie Lee, Rosie — tea
round the houses — trousers
salmon and trout — mouth
saucepan lid — quid
shovel and broom — room
Simple Simon — diamond
six to four, sixty-four — whore
skin and blister — sister
sky rocket, sky — pocket
sorrowful tale — jail
stand at ease — cheese

steam tug — bug
stone mason — basin
storm and strife — wife
strike me dead — bread
sugar and honey — money
sweet pea — tea
tea-leaf — petty thief
tit for tat, titfer — hat
Tom Thumb — rum
tiddlywink, tiddly — drink; drunk
Tommy O'Rann — food ("scran," obs. argot)
trouble and strife, trouble — wife
turtle doves — gloves
twist and twirl — girl
twos and threes — knees
Uncle Dick — sick
Uncle Ned — bed
Walter Scott — pot
weasel and stoat — overcoat
weeping willow — pillow
whistle and flute, whistle — suit of clothes
whisper and talk, whisper — walk
Wilkie Bards — cards
you and me — tea

Back Slang and Pig Latin

For a discussion of back slang and Pig Latin see the Introduction to the Appendix.

Back slang

brad*
elttob
enob*
myrrh* — rum
paos — soap; flattery, soft-soap
scob — box
slop*
tuots
yennep
yob

Pig Latin

amscray*
ellybay*
illthray
ixnay*
oday*
ofay*
ogfray*
umbay*
umpchay*
unkjay*
uzzfay — "fuzz," policeman, police

Onomatopoeia

For a discussion of onomatopoeia see the Introduction to the Appendix.

baa — sheep
bam*
bang-bang*
barf*
bebop*

beep*
bibble-babble — gossip, idle talk
bloop*
blubber*
boing*
bong*
boom-boom*
booms*
burp*
burp gun*
buzz*
buzz-buzz*
chewallop*
chitter (-chatter), chatter (-chitter)
choo-choo — train
chug-a-lug*
clink*
clonk*
clunk*
crawk*
crump*
ding-dong*
ding-a-ling*
dit-da artist*
fizz — sound of gas escaping from a liquid; hence, carbonated water
gibble (-gibble), gabble (-gabble) — idle talk
ha-ha, ho-ho — joke, witticism; that isn't funny
jibber (-jabber) — idle talk
jingle (-jangle) — coins, change, money
ki-yi — dog
la-di-da, lah-de-dah — sound of humming; disinterest, laziness
plunk — sound of falling object; *uttered in disappointment*
pow — "you ought to be hit"
putt-putt*
quack-quack — duck; nonsense, idle talk
putt(y)-putt(y) — motor boat, motor scooter, delapidated car
sissy*
sizzle (-sozzle) — sound of frying; appeal, attraction
slup*
slurf*
slurp*
smacko*
smooch*
squawk*
swish*
smack(er)*
tick-tick — watch; the time
tick-tock — clock; the time
ubble-gubble*
whack*
wham*
wham-bam*
whammo*

whang*
whiz-bang*
woof*
woof-woof*
yack-yack*
yackety-yak*
yammer (-yammer)
yuk-yuk

Blend Words, Corruptions, Redundancies, Omnibus Terms, Nonce and Nonsense Words

The following lists contain words which are more interesting to linguists than widely used or useful in general speech. Thousands of similar examples were collected but are not included here, since they are mere curiosities. The following lists, therefore, are simply representative.

Blend words or telescoping. For a discussion of blend words see the Introduction to the Appendix.

ambisextrous — bisexual + ambidextrous
airmada — airplane + armada
beaujeeful*
brunch*
cigaroot*
confab*
Dixiecrat*
domecon*
galumphing — gallop + triumphing
gate*
gyrene*
Homberg Heaven*
hozey*
jamoke*
Japanazi— Japanese + Nazi
mingy — mean + stingy
motel — motorist + hotel
motorcade — motor car + cavalcade
newt*
nymphokick*
quick-over*
repple-depple*
scrowsy*
shambrogue*
shemale*
slithy — lithe + slimy
smog — smoke + fog
snark — snake + shark
snitzy — snazzy + ritzy
spookerican*
tripewriter — tripe + typewriter

Corruptions and mispronunciations.
For a discussion of corruptions see the Introduction to the Appendix.

all reet*

anyhoo*
attaboy!*
automobubble — automobile
bamfoozle — to bamboozle
barn door*
beaujeeful*
bimps — beans
bladder*
bootician — beautician
broad*
brud*
buffaloo — buffalo
burleycue*
burnese*
bylow*
camel flags*
cat lick*
confisticate*
cove*
cowcumber — cucumber; pickle
deduck*
devoon
dimmer*
faloosie — floosie
fever*
foozle*
fox paw*
frosh*
gidget*
googs*
gool*
goulashes*
grooby*
grut*
gummixed up*
gyrine*
heesh*
heist*
inpredicable — not predictable
kaydet*
kayducer*
keed*
kee-rect*
leaves*
lesbine*
martooni*
Mary Warner*
messy bucket*
Monkey Ward*
mott — mort (a woman)
Motzy*
murky bucket — *merci beaucoups*
napoo*
nerts!*
olive oil*
oogle*
ossifer*
pazaza*
peerade — parade
preem*
purp — pup
sagway*
savvy*
Scandahoovian*
Scandahoovian dynamite*

Scandinoovian*
scarf*
segway*
shimmy*
shivoo*
sickey-ackey — psychiatry
slud — slid
stromberry, strawmberry —
  strawberry
whozis*
wiff*
yeah*
yoot*

Redundancies. Though they
are not actual linguistic
formations, redundancies
are found in many non-
standard words and expressions. Thus the reduplication *hustle-bustle* contains
two words generally mean-
ing the same thing. The
blend word *superific* (super
+ terrific) combine two
words of similar meanings;
and the phrase *smash hit*
contains a noun which carries a strong connotation
of what the modifying ad-
jective denotes. Redundancies are common in the
speech of those who use
much slang.

Omnibus terms. These terms,
frequently heard in non-
standard speech, are especially used to = any ob-
ject; an "it." Sometimes an
omnibus term replaces a
word momentarily forgot-
ten, or a word too technical
for informal use.

all*
and such*
any old*
boodle*
caboodle*
dingbat*
dingus*
do-dad*
do-funny*
do-hinky*
doohickey*
doojigger*
doowhistle*
doowillie*
ducrot*
deep
flukum*
gadget*
gaff*
gidget*
gilguy*
gilhickey*
gilhooley*
gillion*
gimmick*
gismo*

gob*
googol*
gubbins*
hickey*
hickeymadoodle
hootenanny*
item
jigamaree*
jillion*
John Doe*
kajody*
kit and boodle*
kit and caboodle*
larry*
number*
one*
poor fish*
scads*
scillion*
skads*
skaty-eight*
skillion*
slathers*
slew*
smidgen*
steen*
stillion*
thingumabob,* thingamabob
thingamajig,* thigamajig
umpteen*
umpteenth*
umpty*
umpty-umpth*
what's it*
what-you-may-call-it*
whatzis*
whichamacallit
whose its*
whozis*
widget*
wing-ding*
wingdoodle*
zillion*

Nonce and nonsense words.
These are not important or
particularly interesting
since they contribute little
to our knowledge of formation and use of words.
Some nonce words, how-
ever, reappear frequently,
and though created by the
user each time they are
used, they become more
than mere nonce words.
Most nonce words, blend
words, corruptions, neologisms, or other coinages
based on topical events
may seem to be nonsense
words to a later reader. A
few examples follow.

ambisexual — bisexual
baffle-gab*
conbobberation — disturb-
  ance
discombobulate — to disturb
  or confuse

faloosie — floosie
posilutely — positively +
  absolutely
gilgadget — gadget
Episcopalopian — an Epis-
  copalian
kidoodle — to neck, "pet";
  cheat or deceive
monowongler — one who
  monopolizes conversation
sagaciate — to fare, do, get
  along
Scowegian — Scandinavian
  seaman or ship (*blend-
  ing Scandinavian and
  Norwegian*)
shoo fly
snifflcate — to sniff
stifflicated — drunk
stupor-man — unattractive,
  dull youth (*pun on "superman"*)
swellelegant*
swingadilla — swing music
thingamananny
tired*
23-skid(d)oo

**Nicknames, Place Names,
  and Group Names**
Nicknames and familiar
names for people, places,
and groups have been gen-
erally omitted from this
dictionary. They are, however, part of nonstandard
American speech, and many
can be considered slang.

Nicknames. Personal nicknames usually fall into one
of three classes: the common shortenings of a per-
son's full name (*Joe* for
Joseph), the physically descriptive nicknames (*Slim*),
and nicknames describing,
or at the least quickly
identifying, a strong personality, a leader, a celebrity (*B. G., Brown Bomb-
er*). A short representative
list from this third class is
given here.

B.G. — Benny Goodman
Bird, the Yardbird, the —
  Charlie Parker, jazz
  musician
Brown Bomber — Joe Louis,
  prize fighter
Frankie — Frank Sinatra
Ike — Dwight D. Eisenhower
J.C. — Jesus Christ (*jocular
  use*)
Little Caesar — James Caesar
  Petrillo
Little Flower, the — Fiorello
  La Guardia
Mister Show Biz — applied
  to various leading com-

posers, comedians, singers,
etc.
Ray, the — Benny Goodman,
because of his piercing eyes
(an early nickname super-
seded by B.G.)
Schnozzola — Jimmy Durante
Stan the Man — Stan Ken-
ton; Stan Musial
Teddy Four-Eyes —
Theodore Roosevelt
Place names. The place names
in most common use are
shortened forms: standard
abbreviations (*L.A.* = Los
Angeles); front clippings
(*Vegas* = Las Vegas) and
back clippings (*Minnie* =
Minneapolis). Some blends
of shortened forms and familiar elements also exist
(*Frisco*). Place names for
cities are often literally
or figuratively descriptive
(*Big Windy* = Chicago),
and many of these nick-
names were originated by,
and are still known only to,
hobos. A few representa-
tive nicknames for places
are given here.
Alabama*
Balto — Baltimore, Md.
Beantown — Boston, Mass.
Berdoo, San Berdoo — San
Bernardino, Calif.
Big Apple, the
Big D*
Big Ditch, the*
big drink*
big pond, the*
Big Windy — Chicago, Ill.
Channel City — Santa Barb-
ara, Calif.
Chappie-quack — Chappaqua,
N.Y.
Chi — Chiago, Ill.
Cincy — Cincinnati, Ohio
coast*
Crabtown — Annapolis, Md.
Derbyville — Louisville, Ky.
home of the Kentucky
Derby
Dixie*
Dixieland*
Down Under*
down yonder*
Frisco*
Galilee*
herring pond*
Jax*
Kasey, Casey, K.C. — Kan-
sas City, Kan.
Lake, the*
Lousy Anne — Louisiana
Minnie*
Orleans — New Orleans, La.
Pennsy — Pennsylvania; the

Pennsylvania Railroad
Phillie*
pond*
Stateside*
Pocaloo, Poca — Pocatello,
Idaho
Sac — Sacramento, Calif.
Spoke — Spokane, Wash.
Stirville — Ossining, N.Y.,
home of Sing Sing pris-
on
Tac — Tacoma, Wash.
T-town — Tijuana, Mexico
Vegas — Las Vegas, Nev.
Yap-town — Cleveland, Ohio
Group names. There are
group nicknames for every
nationality, race, and religion. Most of them are
derogatory. Many origi-
nated to express resent-
ment toward new immi-
grant groups. These derogatory terms are almost
"fighting words" when
used in direct address
(*Hebe, nigger, spick,* etc.).
Others when used among
friends, carry only jocular
connotation (*greaser,
Hunkie, mick,* etc.). There
are, of course, some group
names which are not de-
rogatory in any sense
(*Aussie*).
Abie*
ape*
Arab*
Aussie*
beef-eater*
black*
blue*
blue-gum*
blue-skin*
Boche*
bohunk*
boogie*
border, the*
buck*
bucket-head*
buckra*
buffalo*
buggy*
burr-head*
butter-box*
Canuck*
cat lick*
Chico — Filipino
chili-eater, chili-picker —
Mexican
Chinee*
Chink*
chino*
chocolate*
chocolate drop*
chow*
chub*
clay eater*

clink*
clipped dick*
cloak-and-suiter*
cluck*
coon*
coosie*
covess dinge*
cuffee*
dago*
dange broad*
dap*
dark cloud*
darky*
dee-donk*
digger*
dingbat*
dinge*
dingey*
dino*
domino*
Eytie*
dago*
Dutchman
eagle-beak*
eightball*
eight-rock*
face*
fay*
fisheater*
flange-head*
flip*
frank*
Fritz*
frog*
frog-eater*
froggie*
fuzzy — Negro
Galitzianer
Galway*
Gange*
Geechee*
Geechie*
geese*
ginny*
ginzo*
goober-grabber*
goo-goo*
gook*
goon*
goonie*
goum*
Goy*
gray*
grease-ball*
greaser*
Greek*
gringo*
Guin*
Guinea*
Gypo*
hack*
Hans*
handkerchief-head*
hard-head*
harp*
hatchet-thrower*
hay-eater*
headlight*

Hebe*
Heinie*
herring-choker*
high yellow*
hinkty*
hoofer*
hook-nose*
Hun*
Hunkie*
Ikey*
ink*
Irisher*
itch*
Jap*
jar-head*
jazz-bo*
Jerry*
Jewboy*
jibagoo*
jigaboo*
Jim Crow*
jit*
Kange*
Kazoo*
kelt*
kike*
kinky-head*
kraut*
krauthead*
lemon*
limburger*
lime-juicer*
limey*
litvak*
Mex*
mick*
mickey*
Miss Anne*
Mister Charlie*
mocha*
mochalie*
mockie*
moke*
monk*
mose*
moss*
Motzy*
nap*
nappy*
narrowback*
Newfie*
nigger*
niggra*
Nip*
ofay*
ogfray*
oiler*
Okie*
oofay*
paddy*
pale*
pape*
pea souper*
peck*
peckerwood*
peewee*
Pelican*
peola*

pepper*
pink*
pink-toes*
pinky*
polack*
pong*
porker*
prune-picker*
rag-head*
rice-belly*
riceman*
right-foot*
ring-tail*
rock*
Rok*
zig*
zigaboo*
Russian*
Sammy*
satch*
sausage*
scram*
scuttle*
seal*
shade*
shad-mouth*
shadow*
sheeny*
shine*
shinny*
shiny*
shot*
silk broad*
skibby*
skillet*
skippy
skunk*
slant-eye*
slopie*
smoke*
smoky*
smudge*
snowball*
Sooner*
spade*
spaghetti*
spaginzy*
spic*
spic and span*
spick*
spig*
spiggoty*
spook*
spookerican*
squack*
squarehead — Swede
squasho*
steel*
stove-lid*
suede*
tar-pot*
teddy*
Tojo*
Turk*
turf-cutter*
Turner*
tush*
uncle*

Uncle Tom*
Uncle Tommer*
wetback*
white trash*
wog*
woolly*
woolly-head*
wop*
Yehuda*
yellow*
yellow girl*
Yid*
Zulu*

Children's Bathroom Vocabulary

The dictionary does not include the slang of very young children. Many children's words are onomatopoeia (see onomatopoeia list above and the Introduction to the Appendix), such as *bow-wow*, *choo-choo*, or are reduplications, especially of the first order (see above). Children's bathroom vocabulary is carried over into adult slang more frequently than is to be expected. It is always semijocular and always to some extent euphemistic. The adult's penchant for becoming a child while urinating or defecating is seen in the strictly adult expressions *little boy's room* and *little girl's room*.

boom-boom*
ca-ca — to defecate; faeces
cis-cis — to urinate; urine
gig*
number one*
number two*
pee-pee — to urinate; urine
poop*
poo-poo*
potty*
sis-sis — cis-cis
tinkle*
wag*
wee*
wee-wee*

Synonyms for Drunk

The concept having the most slang synonyms is *drunk*. This vast number of *drunk* words does not necessarily mean that Americans are obsessed with drinking, though we seem obsessed with talking about it. Many of these words are quite old: *half-seas over* and *oiled* were recorded at least as early as 1737 according to the *DAE*, *bent* in 1833, *boozed* in 1887. Later immigrant groups brought their own words for drink and drunkenness, and it seems that some, during their first period of adjustment had a fair number of members who turned to whiskey as a compensation for the rejection they suffered as newcomers in a strange land. Most of the words for drunk, however, originated or became popular during Prohibition. Most drunk words are based on the following figurative uses or images: of being "high," of being happy, content, bright, or conspicuous; of being unconscious or dead; of staggering, especially as a sailor or on rough seas; of being physically bent or beaten; of being bottled or cooked. There are a few strictly nonsense words *(pifflicated, swazzled)*.

alkied*
all geezed up*
aped*
balmy*
bamboozled*
basted*
battered*
bay, over the*
behind the cork*
bent*
biggy*
bleary-eyed
blind*
blinded*
blink, on the*
bloated*
blotto*
blown*
blown up*
blue*
blue around the gills*
blue-eyed*
boiled*
boozed*
boozed up*
boozy*
bottled*
bowzed*
bowzered*
breezy*
bridgey*
bruised*
bungey*
bunned*
buried*
burn with a low blue flame*
buzzed*
buzzey*
caged*

canned*
canned up*
carry a (heavy) load*
cat*
clobbered*
cocked*
cock-eyed*
comfortable*
cooked*
corked*
corned*
crocked*
cronk*
crump*
crumped
crumped out*
cuckooed*
cut*
dagged*
damaged*
D and D*
dead to the world*
decks awash*
ding-swizzled*
discouraged*
disguised*
draw a blank*
drunk*
edged*
elevated*
embalmed*
faint*
feel good*
feel no pain*
fired up*
fish-eyed
fishy*
floating*
flooey*
fogmatic*
folded
four sheets to (in) the wind*
foxed*
fractured*
frazzled*
fresh*
fried*
fried up
full*
full as an egg*
full as a tick*
fuzzled*
fuzzy
gaged*
gassed*
gay
gayed
geared up*
geezed*
ginned*
ginned up*
glassy
glassy eyed*
glowed
glued*
gone*
greased*
grogged*

guyed out*
guzzled*
half-cocked*
half-corned*
half-crocked*
half-screwed*
half seas over*
half shaved*
half-shot*
half-slewed*
half-snaped*
half-sprung*
half-stewed*
half the bay over*
half the bay under
half under*
hammered*
hang one on*
happy*
have a bag on*
have a bun on*
have a can on
have a glow on
have an edge on*
have a package on*
have a snoot full*
have (one's) gage up
have (one's) pots on*
heeled*
high*
high as a kite*
higher than a kite*
high lonesome*
hipped*
hoary-eyed*
hooted*
hot*
how-come-ye-so*
illuminated*
in the gutter*
in (one's) cups*
jagged*
jammed*
jazzed*
jingled*
jolly*
jugged
jug-steamed*
juiced*
juiced up*
killed
kited*
knocked for a loop
knocked out*
laid out*
lathered*
limp*
lined
liquored*
liquored up*
lit*
lit to the gills*
lit to the guards*
lit up
lit up like a Christmas tree
   (Main Street, Times Square,
   Broadway, a store window,
   a church, etc.)

loaded*
loaded for bear*
loaded to the gills (the muzzle, the plimsoll mark, etc.)*
looped*
looped-legged*
loopy*
lubricated*
lush*
lushed*
lushed up*
mellow*
melted*
merry*
mokus*
mulled*
mulled up*
oiled*
on the lee lurch*
on the sauce*
on the shikker*
organized*
orie-eyed*
ossified*
out like a light*
out on the roof*
overboard*
overset*
owly-eyed*
packaged*
paralyzed*
parboiled*
petrified*
pickled*
pie-eyed*
piffed*
pifficated*
piffled*
pifflicated*
pigeon-eyed*
pilfered*
pinked*
piped*
pixilated*
plastered*
plonked*
polished up*
polluted*
potted*
potted up*
potty
perserved*
primed*
pruned*
raunchy*
ready*
rigid*
Rileyed*
ripe*
rocky*
rosy*
rum-dum*
salted down*
sap-happy*
sapped
saturated*
sawed*
scraunched*

screaming*
screeching*
screwed*
scronched*
sent*
set-up*
sewed up*
shaved*
shellacked*
shikker*
shikkered*
shined*
shot*
shot in the neck*
slewed*
slopped*
slopped over*
sloppy*
sloshed*
slugged*
smashed*
smoked*
snapped*
snozzled*
snubbed*
snuffy*
soaked*
soshed*
soused*
soused to the gills*
sozzled*
spiffed*
spifflicated*
sprung*
squiffed*
squiffy*
stewed*
stewed up
stewed to the gills*
sticked
stiff*
stinking*
stinkarooed
stinko*
stitched*
stone blind*
stoned*
striped*
stunned*
swacked*
swazzled*
swiped*
swizzled*
swozzled*
tangle-footed*
tangle-legged*
tanked*
tanked up*
teed up*
three sheets in the wind*
tiddly*
tie one on*
tight*
tight as a tick, etc.*
tipped*
tuned*
turned on*
under the table*

under the weather*
up to the gills*
vulcanized*
wall-eyed*
wapsed down*
weak-jointed*
well oiled*
wet*
whipped*
whipsey*
whooshed*
wilted*
wing-heavy*
woofled*
woozy*
zig-zag*

Sex and Food; Sex, Cheating, and Failure; Sex and Deceit

For a discussion, see the preface and the Introduction to the Appendix.

Sex and food
banana*
banana peeled, have (one's)*
barbecue*
beefcake*
biscuit*
bread*
cabbage*
cake*
capon*
cheesecake*
cheese bun
cherry*
cherry picker*
chick*
chicken*
cold biscuit*
cold fish*
cook*
cookie*
cop a cherry*
cush*
dark meat*
dish*
dog biscuit*
eat*
fine dinner*
fruit*
fruitcake*
fudge*
gobbledygooker*
ground rations*
gum drop*
hair pie*
honey*
honey-fuck*
hot tamale*
jelly*
jelly bean*
jelly-roll*
lambie-pie*
meat*
muffin*
muffins*
mush*
nuts*

peach*
picnic*
pigeon
pig-meat*
quail*
squab*
sugar papa*
sweetie*
sweetie-pie*
sweet mama*
sweet man*
sweet on (someone)*
sweet papa*
sweets*
tart*
tomato*
weenie*
white meat*
virgin coke*
Sex, cheating, and failure
ball-breaker*
ball-buster*
bang*
cheating*
fire blanks*
fuck*

fucked*
fucked up*
fuck off*
fuck you!*
futzed up*
gang shag*
gang shay*
gash*
give it to (someone)*
have*
hustle*
jab
jerk off*
knock up*
laid, relaid, and parlayed
lay*
made*
make*
monkey business*
mug*
piece*
pluk*
push*
prick*
roll*
royal fucking

royal screwing
score*
screw*
screwed*
screwed, blewed, and
  tattooed*
screwed up*
screw you!*
snafu*
suck off*
suck you!
tear off a piece
trick*
turn a trick*
Synthetic Fad Expressions
For a discussion, see the Introduction to the Appendix.
Coming Mother!
Hey Abbott!
Hi Ho Silver!
I dood it!
Say hey!
What's up, Doc?
You're a good one!

SELECTED BIBLIOGRAPHY

Abbreviations

AP   Associated Press
AS   *American Speech*
Cent. Mag.   *Century Magazine*
DAE   *Dictionary of American English*
DN   *Dialect Notes*
DOA   *Dictionary of Americanisms*
INS   International News Service
NAL   New American Library
NANA   North American Newspaper Alliance

N.E.A.   Newspaper Enterprise Association
NED   *A New English Dictionary on Historical Principles*
OED   *Oxford English Dictionary*
SEP   *Saturday Evening Post*
SR, SRL   Saturday Review (of Literature)
UP   United Press
Web   *Webster's New International Dictionary*

(See also Quotations and Citations, page xvii.)

Abbott, George. *See* Dunning.
Abramowitz, Isidore. "Soldier Speech." *Sat. Rev. of Lit.*, Oct. 4, 1941.
Adams, Ramon F. "Southwestern Cowboy Argot," repr. in *AS*, Dec. 1927.
Ageton, Arthur A. "Annapolis, Cradle of the Navy," *National Geographic Mag.*, June, 1936.
Alexander, Henry. "Words and the War." *AS*, Dec., 1944.
Alexander, Jack. "The Drunkard's Best Friend." *SEP*, Apr. 1, 1950.
Algren, Nelson. "The Face on the Barroom Floor." *Amer. Mercury*, Jan. 1947.
———. *The Man with the Golden Arm.* Pocket Books, 1951 (Doubleday, 1949).

———. *A Walk On the Wild Side.* Crest Books, 1957 (Farrar, Straus & Cudahy, 1956).
All About Eve. Movie, 1950.
Amend, Ottilie. "Theatrical Lingo." *AS*, Oct., 1927
Anderson, Maxwell. *See* Stallings.
Angel, Anne. "Golf Gab." *AS*, Sept., 1926.
Anon. "The American Ganguage." *Lit. Digest*, Apr. 9, 1932.
———. "Argot: Peculiar Class Phraseology." *Rev. of Reviews*, July, 1910.
———. "Army Lingo. . . ." *Amer. Mag.*, Jan., 1944.
———. "Army Mess-Hall Slang." *SEP*, Nov. 28, 1942.

———. "Army Slang, 1943 Edition." *Reader's Digest,* Feb., 1943.

———. "As They Say in the AAF." *N. Y. Times Mag.,* July 2, 1944.

———. "Auto Racing." *Fortune,* Sept., 1947.

———. "Ball Talk." *N. Y. Times Mag.,* July 14, 1946.

———. "A Billion Across the Board." *Fortune,* Sept., 1944.

———. "Carrier Chatter." *Collier's,* Nov. 27, 1943.

———. "Charlie Parker, 1920-1955." *The Metronome Year Book,* 1956.

———. "The Circus." *Fortune,* July, 1947.

———. "Circus Time." *Lit. Digest,* Apr. 3, 1937.

———. "College Dialect." *Harvard Mag.,* May, 1858.

———. "Conscience . . . Makes Cowards." *SEP,* Apr. 21, 1951.

———. "Do You Speak Yegg?" *Lit. Digest,* Aug. 19, 1916.

———. "The Drag Racing Rage." *Life,* Apr. 29, 1957.

———. "The Drinkers Dictionary." *Penna. Gazette,* Jan. 6, 1736/7, repr. in *AS,* Apr., 1937.

———. "English and Baseball." *Nation,* Aug. 21, 1913.

———. "Fashions in Slang." *World's Work,* Nov., 1929.

———. "Federal Writers Go Slumming." *Lit. Digest,* Dec. 4, 1937.

———. "Flapper-Filology—the New Language." Phila. *Evening Bulletin,* Mar. 8, 1922. Repr. in *Dialect Notes,* v. 5.

———. "Food Slang." Baltimore *Sun,* Apr. 3, 1927.

———. [Glossary, "Is Zat So?" Program.] *AS,* May, 1926, p. 462.

———. "Glossary of Army Slang." *AS,* Oct., 1941.

———. "Glossary of the Big Show." *SEP,* Mar. 25, 1939.

———. [Glossary of Tramp Language.] *AS,* Jan., 1926.

— ——. "Hobo Hegemony." *Lit. Digest,* Apr. 10, 1937.

———. *I, Mobster.* Fawcett, 1951.

———. "Is Your Sub-Deb Slang Up-to-Date?" *Ladies' Home Jour.,* Dec., 1944.

———. "Jabberwocky." *Time,* July 26, 1943.

———. "Jargon: Talk in Wall Street." *Newsweek,* July 4, 1936.

———. [Jive Talk.] *Time,* Feb. 10, 1947.

———. "Juvenile Delinquency." *Life,* Apr. 8, 1946.

———. "Labor's Special Language from Many Sources." *Business Week,* May 19, 1956.

———. "The Language of Advertising." *Management Rev.,* Oct., 1952.

———. "The Language of the Jitterbug." *Variety,* repr. in *Better Eng.,* Nov., 1938.

———. "Language of the Speakeasy." *N. Y. Sunday News,* Nov. 3, 1929. Repr. in *AS,* Dec., 1930.

———. "Leatherneck Lingo." *Time,* July 19, 1943.

———. "Lexicon of Prohibition." *New Republic,* Mar. 9, 1927.

———. "Lunch-Wagon Slanguage." *World's Work,* Feb., 1932.

———. "Manhattan Hackie." *Fortune,* July, 1939.

———. "Mechanized [Army] Dialect." *Newsweek,* July 7, 1941.

———. "My Mother's Slang." *Scribner's,* Aug., 1920.

———. "New Saws for Old." *Nation,* Sept., 4, 1929.

———. [Nomenclature of the Short-Order Restaurant.] *Wm. Feather Mag.,* July, 1926.

———. [On Curb Hopping.] *Variety,* Sept., 27, 1937.

———. "Only Saps Work." *Amer. Mercury,* Oct., 1938.

———. "Off the Playground." *Rocky Mountain News,* Apr. 21, 1926, repr. in *AS.*

———. "Our Boarding House—with Major Hoople." *N.E.A. Service Cartoons.*

———. "An Overlooked Conversational Asset." *Scribner's,* Aug., 1909.

———. "Peril of the Baseball Lingo." *Lit. Digest,* Sept. 6, 1913.

———. " 'Pitch' Is a Thing You Get Stuck In." *N. Y. Times,* Aug. 28, 1949.

———. "Pitchmen Find Business." *Life,* July 31, 1939.

———. "Prison Argot." *N. Y. Times Mag.,* Jan. 25, 1942.

———. "Quick-Lunch Lingo." *Lit. Digest,* Mar. 18, 1916.

———. "Radio Lingo." *AS,* Apr., 1938.

———. [Railroad Terms.] *AS,* Jan. 1926.

———. "San Quentin." *Life,* Oct. 27, 1947.

———. "Service Slanguage." *Amer. Legion Mag.,* Feb., Apr., 1946.

———. "Slang." *Atlantic Mo.,* Mar., 1893.

———. "Slang." *Living Age,* Apr. 22, 1905.

———. "Slang." *Living Age,* Nov. 10, 1917.

———. "Slang Current on Various Campuses." *Ladies' Home Jour.,* Sept., 1937.

———. "Slang of the Airmen." *Lit. Digest,* June 23, 1917.

———. "Slang Used in [film] *Ball of Fire.*" *Life,* Dec. 15, 1941.

———. "Soldier Slanguage." *Newsweek,* Nov. 18, 1940.

———. [Some Current Terms.] *AS.,* Feb., 1926.

———. "Spring Sunshine in Harvard." *The Harvard Mag.,* May, 1858.

———. "Subdebese." *Life,* Jan. 27, 1941.

———. "Theatricalisms." *N. Y. World,* July 24, 1927.

———. "Truckman Talk." *Rev. of Reviews,* June, 1937.

———. "Underworld Evolves . . . Patter." *N. Y. Times,* Oct. 10, 1926, Sect. 8.

———. "An Up Jells a Deal." *N. Y. Times,* May 1, 1949. [Used-car dealer's slang.]

———. "Waiters' Lingo." *The New York Weekly,* June 23, 1884.

——. "War Slang." *Living Age*, Oct. 14, 1916.

——. "The Weed [Marijuana]." *Time*, July 19, 1943.

——. "[West Point] Cadet Slang." *Better Eng.*, Jan., 1939.

——. "Where You Goin', Bub?" *Time*, Oct. 3, 1949.

——. "Why Worry About Slang?" *AS*, Feb., 1928.

——. "With It." *New Yorker*, Jan. 27, 1951. [Pitchman on TV.]

——. "Word Coinage and Slang." *Living Age*, July, 1907.

——. "You've Had It." *Time*, Mar. 22, 1943. [Flyers' Slang.]

——. "Zoot Lore." *New Yorker*, June 19, 1943.

Anson, Lyman, and Clifford Funkhouser. "The Rails Have a Word for It." *SEP*, June 13, 1942.

Arbolino, Jack G. "Navy Yard Talk." *AS*, Dec., 1942.

Armstrong, John. "Serving the Gentry." *Amer. Mercury*, Aug., 1928.

Armstrong, Louis. *Satchmo*. Prentice-Hall, 1954.

Arnold, Jane W. "The Language of Delinquent Boys." *AS*, Apr., 1947.

Asbury, Herbert. *The Gangs of New York*. Knopf, 1928.

The Asphalt Jungle. Movie, 1950.

Auslander, Joseph. *Hell in Harness*. Doubleday, Doran, 1929.

Axley, Lowry. " 'Drunk' Again." *AS*, Aug., 1929.

B., J. A. "WAC Talk:" *Collier's*, Apr. 8, 1944.

Babbitt, Eugene H. "College Words and Phrases." *Dialect Notes*, v. 2 (1900), 3-70.

Babbitt, Hal. "Shipyard Terms. . . ." *AS*, Oct., 1944.

Baer, Arthur ('Bugs'). "One Word Led to Another." Phila. *Inquirer*, Mar. 18, 1947.

Bailey, Oran B. "A Glossary of Café Terms." *AS*, Dec., 1943.

Bainbridge, John. "Toots's World," *New Yorker*, Nov. 11, 18, 25, 1950.

Banks, Ruth. "Idioms of the Present-Day American Negro." *AS*, Dec., 1938.

Barker, Howard F. "More Hobo Lingo." *AS*, Sept., 1927.

Barkley, Dorothy. "Hospital Talk." *AS*, Apr., 1927.

Bass, Altha Leah (Bierbower). "The University Tongue." *Harper's*, Mar. 1922.

Batie, Russell V. "Railroad Lingo." *AS*, Feb., 1934.

Baugh, Albert C. *A History of the English Language*. Appleton-Century, 1935.

Bayles, William D. "War Slang." *SEP*, May 9, 1942.

Beath, Paul Robert. "Aviation Lingo." *AS*, Apr., 1930.

——. [Review of *American Slang*], *AS*, Aug., 1932.

Beebe, Lucius. *Highball: a Pageant of Trains*. Appleton-Century, 1945.

Beirne, Francis F. "Newspaper English." *AS*, Oct., 1926.

Bellow, Saul. *Seize the Day*. Viking, 1956.

Benardete, Dolores. "Professorial Speech—New Style." *AS*, Mar., 1927.

Bender, James F. "Lingo of the Big Top." *N. Y. Times Mag.*, Apr. 8, 1945.

Benjamin, Philip. "Gang Slang." *N. Y. Times Mag.*, Oct. 20, 1957.

Bentley, Harold W. "Linguistic Concoctions of the Soda Jerker." *AS*, Feb., 1936.

Bentley, Julian T. "The Fifth Estate Vocabulary." *AS*, Apr., 1937.

Berger, Meyer. "The Beggars Are Coming." *New Yorker*, Mar. 11, 1939.

——. "Mokers, Babes, and Spivs." *N. Y. Times Book Rev.*, July 23, 1950.

Berger, Morroe. "Army Language." *AS*, Dec., 1945.

——. "Some Excesses of Slang Compilers." *AS*, Oct., 1946.

Berrey, Lester V. "Fashions in Language." *Esquire*, Oct., 1934.

——. "Air Slang." *Current History and Forum*, Feb. 13, 1941.

——. See DeJournette.

Berry, Edward. "Sawmill Talk. . . ." *AS*, Oct., 1927.

Betts, Toney. *Across the Board*. Citadel, 1956.

Beukema, Herman. "West Point and the Gray-Clad Corps." *Nat. Geographic Mag.*, June, 1936.

Billingsley, Sherman. "The Stork Club Dictionary." *Harper's Bazaar*, July, 1942.

Billman, J. I. "Army Words." *AS*, July, 1926.

Bisgaier, Paul. "Speech in the Post Office [in N.Y.C.]." *AS*, Apr., 1932.

Bishop, Joseph W., Jr. "American Army Speech in the European Theater." *AS*, Dec., 1946.

Bishop, Morris G. *See* Johnson, W. Bolingbroke.

Bissell, Richard. *A Stretch on the River*. Little, Brown, 1950.

Bloomfield, Leonard. *Language*. Holt, 1933.

Blosser, Merrill. "Freckles," comic strip. N.E.A. Service.

Boal, Sam. "Cool Swinging in New York." *Playboy*, Feb., 1958.

Boardman, Fon W., Jr. "Political Name Calling." *AS*, Dec. 1940.

Bolinger, Dwight L. "Neologisms." *AS*, Feb., 1941.

——. "Among the New Words." *AS*, Apr., 1941 to Feb., 1944, many issues.

Booth, Ernest. "The Language of the Underworld." *Amer. Mercury*, May, 1928.

Boroff, David. "A Study of Reformatory Argot." *AS*, Oct., 1951.

Botkin, B. A. "The Lore of the Lizzie Label." *AS*, Dec., 1930.

Bowen, Edwin W. "What Is Slang?" *Popular Science Mon.*, Feb., 1906.

Bowers, Fredson. "College Slang a Language All Its Own." *Lit. Digest*, Mar. 14, 1925.

Boyle, Hal. "Three Co-Eds. . . ." Phila. *Bulletin*, May 19, 1947.

――――. [Many AP articles and columns, July 20, 1950 through 1953].

Brackbill, Hervey. "Midshipman Jargon." *AS*, Aug., 1928.

――――. "Some Telegraphers' Terms." *AS*, Apr., 1929.

Bradley, Gene. "More Jargon of the Amateur Photographer." *AS*, Dec., 1941.

Bradley, Henry. *On the Relations Between Spoken and Written Language*. Oxford, 1919.

Bromberg, Erik I. "Shoe-Store Terms." *AS*, Apr., 1938.

Bromberg, Walter. "Marihuana Intoxication: A Clinical Study. . . ." *Amer. Jour. of Psychiatry*, Sept., 1934.

Brooks, Gwendolyn. *A Street in Bronzeville*. Harper, 1945.

Broun, Heywood. "Shoot the Works." *New Republic*, 7 issues, Aug. 17 to Oct. 26, 1938.

Brown, Barbara. "The Great American Slanguage." *Outlook and Independent*, Nov. 12, 1930.

Brown, Bob. "National Festival. . . ." *Amer. Mercury*, Dec., 1931.

Brown, Carlton. "Confidence Games." *Life*, Aug. 12, 1946.

Brown, Fredric. *The Dead Ringer*. Bantam, 1949 (Dutton, 1948).

Brown, Ivor J. C. *I Give You My Word*. Dutton, 1948.

――――. *Just Another Word*. Dutton, 1945.

――――. *Say the Word*. Dutton, 1948.

――――. *A Word in Your Ear*. Dutton, 1945.

Browne, Howard. *See* Evans.

Bruce, John. "The Flapjack Murder" in *San Francisco Murders*. Bantam, 1947.

Brush, Katharine. *Young Man of Manhattan*. Reprint ed., 1949 (Farrar, 1929).

――――. "Primer for Civilians. . . ." *Reader's Digest*, Sept., 1944.

Buckner, Mary Dale. "Ranch Diction. . . ." *AS*, Feb., 1933.

Burgess, Gelett. "Birth Pangs of Slang." *Lit. Digest*, Aug. 5, 1933.

Burke, James P. "The Argot of the Racketeers." *Amer. Mercury*, Dec., 1930.

Burke, William J. *Literature of Slang*. New York Public Library, 1939.

Burley, Dan. *Dan Burley's Original Handbook of Harlem Jive*. No publisher, 1944.

Burnett, W. R. *The Asphalt Jungle*. Knopf, 1949.

――――. *Iron Man*. Reprint ed., 1949, (Dial, 1930).

――――. *Little Caesar*. Reprint ed. 1945 (Dial, 1929).

Burnham, Josephine M. "Observations on Indefinite Numbering." *AS*, Feb., 1951.

――――. "Three Hard-Worked Suffixes." *AS*, Feb., 1927.

Byington, Steven T. "Baby-Talk English." *AS*, Oct., 1931.

Cahill, Margaret Erskine. "A Caddy's Compedium [of golf terms]." *AS*, Apr., 1937.

Cain, James M. *The Embezzler*. Knopf, 1940.

――――. *Love's Lovely Counterfeit*. Avon, 1952 (Knopf, 1942).

――――. *Mildred Pierce*. NAL, 1948 (Knopf, 1941).

――――. *The Moth*. 1950 (1948).

――――. *The Postman Always Rings Twice*. Pocket Books, 1947 (Knopf, 1934).

Camp, Elwood. W. "C[ivilian] C[onservation] C[orps] Speech." *AS*, Feb., 1937.

Can You Top This? ABC-WCAE, Apr. 10, 1951.

Canby, Henry Seidel. "College Life in the Nineties." *Harper's*, Feb., 1936.

Cannon, Jimmy. *Who Struck John?* Dial, 1956.

Capote, Truman. *The Grass Harp*. Signet, 1953 (Random, 1951).

Carlile, John S. "Some Radio Terms." *Fortune*, May, 1938.

Carpenter, Edwin H., Jr. "Some Notes on Army Language." *AS*, Dec., 1946.

Carr, Dorothy. "Some Annapolis Slang." *AS*, Feb., 1939.

Carson, Charles. "One Underworld." *Author and Journalist*, Nov., 1945.

Carter, Wilmoth A. "Nicknames and Minority Groups. *Phylon* (Atlanta Univ.), 3d quarter, 1944.

Cason, Clarence E. " 'Horsefeathers': a Synthesis." *AS*, Dec., 1928.

Cassidy, F. G. *See* Marckwardt.

Chandler, Raymond. "Smart-Aleck Kill." *Black Mask Mag.*, June, 1934, repr. in *Finger Man*, 1946.

――――. "Finger Man." *Black Mask Mag.*, Oct., 1934, repr. in *Finger Man*, 1946.

――――. *The Big Sleep*. Pocket Books, 1950 (Knopf, 1939).

――――. *Farewell, My Lovely*. Pocket Books, 1943 (Knopf, 1940).

――――. *The High Window*. Pocket Books, 1945 (Knopf, 1942).

――――. *The Lady in the Lake*. Pocket Books, 1946 (Knopf, 1943).

――――. *The Little Sister*. Pocket Books, 1951 (Houghton, 1949).

――――. "The Simple Art of Murder." *Atlantic Mon.*, 1944.

Chase, George D. "Lists from Maine." *Dialect Notes*, v. 4 (1913).

Chase, Stuart. *The Tyranny of Words*. Harcourt, Brace, 1938.

Chidsey, Donald Barr. "Some Lexicographical Notes." *AS*, Oct., 1946.

Chrétien, C. Douglas. "Comments on Naval Slang." *Western Folklore*, Apr. 1947.

Christie, Agatha. *Sad Cypress*. Dodd, 1939.

Clark, A. Bess. "Slang: A Lesson in Ninth-Grade Composition." *English Jour.*, Sept., 1925.

Clark, Bert. *See* Smith, Maurice G.

Clark, J. W. "Lumberjack Lingo." *AS*, Oct., 1931.

Clarke, R. M. *See* Shidler.

Cleator, P. E. Quoted by H. L. Mencken,

"Notes on American." *Word Study*, May, 1946.

Colburn, Dorothy. "Newspaper Nomenclature." *AS*, Feb., 1927.

Colby, Elbridge. [Book review.] *AS*, Jan., 1926.

———. "Soldier Speech." *AS*, Feb., 1936.

Coley, Louis B. "Rubaiyat of the East Side." *Commentator*, Jan., 1902.

Collier, William Ross, and Westrate, Edwin Victor. *The Reign of Soapy Smith*. Doubleday, 1935.

Colodny, I. See Hixson.

Conkle, E. P. "Carnival Slang." *AS*, Feb., 1928.

Connell, Richard. "The Vocabulary of Drinking." *Better Eng.*, July-Aug., 1938.

Conradi, Edward. "Children's Interests in Words, Slang, Stories." *Ped. Sem.*, Sept., 1903.

Cons, C. Lynn. "The Jargon of Jazz." *Amer. Mercury*, May, 1936.

Cook, Pauline. "Informal Library Language." *AS*, Dec., 1941.

Cornyn, William Stewart. "Hotel Slang." *AS*, Oct., 1939.

Cottrell, W. F., and H. C. Montgomery. "A Glossary of Railroad Terms." *AS*, Oct., 1943.

Coulson, Edwin R. "Aeroplane Factory English." *AS*, Apr., 1938.

Courtney, Thomas J. "Hot Shorts." *SEP*, Nov. 30, 1935.

Cowden, R. W. "Slanging English Words." *English Jour.*, Nov., 1925.

Craigie, Sir William A., and Hulbert, James R., eds. *A Dictionary of American English on Historical Principles*. Univ. of Chicago Press, 1938-1944, 4 vols.

Crane, T. F. "Painting the Town Red." *Sci. Mon.*, June, 1924.

Crosby, Bing. "Call Me Lucky." *SEP*, Feb. 14, 1953.

Crosby, John. "Radio and Television" [column]. N. Y. *Her. Trib.*, Apr. 9, 1952.

Crow, C. L. See Northup.

Culbertson, Ely. "Terms in Contract Bridge." *AS*, Feb., 1934.

Cummings, Parke. "What Was That Word?" *Collier's*, Aug. 2, 1952.

Curtiss, Philip Everett. "The Psychology of Tripe." *Harper's*, Aug. 1929.

D., G. H. "College English." *AS*, June, 1929.

D., J. "Dude. . . ." *AS*, Apr., 1935.

Dailey, Daphne. [What Leathernecks Mean], *Amer Mag.*, July, 1942.

Daley, Arthur. "Sports of the *Times*." *N. Y. Times*, Sept. 4, 1949.

———. "Sports Are Honest. . . ." *N. Y. Times Mag.*, Mar. 4, 1951.

———. "World Series Thrills. . . . *N. Y. Times Mag.*, Sept. 28, 1952.

Daly, Sheila John. "Teen-Age Problems." Syracuse, N. Y. *Post-Standard*, Aug. 22, 1950.

Danner, James W. "C.C.C. Slang." *AS*, Apr., 1940.

———. "Glossary of CCC Slang." *Rotarian*, July, 1941.

Danton, George H. "Americana." *AS*, Apr., 1930.

Daughrity, Kenneth L. "Handed-Down Campus Expressions." *AS*, Dec., 1930.

Davenport, Walter. "Harlem, Dense and Dangerous." *Collier's*, Sept. 23, 1944.

Davidson, Levette Jay. "C.C.C. Chatter." *AS*, Apr., 1940.

———. "Folklore in Modern Speech." *AS*, Dec., 1950.

Davis, Elrick B. "Paul Bunyan Talk." *AS*, Dec., 1942.

Day, A. Grove. "American Naval Slang A Hundred Years Ago." *U. S. Naval Institute Proceedings*, 1942.

DeBaun, Everett. "The Heist. . . ." *Harper's*, Feb., 1950.

DeBrul, E. Lloyd. *Evolution of the Speech Apparatus*. Charles C. Thomas, Springfield, Ill., 1958.

de Casseres, Benjamin. "Polemic Against Sobriety." *Amer. Mercury*, May, 1928.

de Crespigny, Claude. "Word Mania." *AS*, June, 1928.

DeJournette, Jean, and Berrey, Lester V. "Poppings of the Corks." *Esquire*, Apr., 1934.

de Kerchove, Rene. *International Maritime Dictionary*. Van Nostrand, 1948.

De Lannoy, William C., and Masterson, Elisabeth. "Teen-Age Hophead Jargon." *AS*, Feb., 1952.

Dickinson, Jean. "Telephone Workers' Jargon." *AS*, Apr., 1941.

Dickinson, M. B. "Words from . . . Diaries [1840-1863]." *AS*, Oct., 1951.

Dictionary of American English. See Craigie.

Dixon, George. "The Washington Scene." Syndicated Column, Jan. 27, 1950.

Donavan, James A., Jr. "Jargon of Marihuana Addicts." *AS*, Oct., 1940.

Douds, J. B. "Hamlet and the G. I." *The CEA Critic*, Nov., 1949.

Dreiser, Theodore. *Sister Carrie*. 1900.

Dunlap, A. R. "GI Lingo." *AS*, Apr., 1945.

Dunning, Philip, and Abbott, George. *Broadway*. Doubleday, 1927.

Eads, Jane. "Economy Campaign . . . Brings New Words." Newspapers, Aug. 25, 1953.

Eastman, Max. "Poetic Education and Slang." *New Republic*, Dec. 16, 1916.

Edge, William. *The Main Stem*. Vanguard, 1927.

Eikel, Fred. "Language of the Underworld." *AS*, May, 1951.

Eldridge, Elizabeth. "Sheepskin Deep." *SEP*, Feb. 20, 1937.

Eliason, Norman E. "Some Negro Terms. *AS*, Apr., 1938.

Elkin, Frederick. "The Soldier's Language." *Amer. Jour. of Sociology*, Mar., 1946.

Ellson, Hal. *Duke*. Popular Library, 1950 (Scribner, 1949).

Emerson, O. F. *History of the English Language*. Macmillan, 1894.

———. *See* Monroe, B. S.; Northrup, C. S.

Ensworth, Bob. "G. I. Laughter." *Amer. Legion Mag.*, Sept., 1944.

Ericson, Eston E. "Beauty-Parlor Slang." *AS*, Dec., 1941.

Evans, John, *pseud. of* Howard Browne. *Halo in Blood*. Reprint ed., 1946.

———. *Halo in Brass*. Pocket Books, 1950 (Bobbs, 1949).

———. *Halo for Satan*. Bantam, 1950 (Bobbs, 1948).

Everybody Does It. Movie, crt. 1949.

Fairbairn, Don. Phila. *Eve. Bulletin*, Dec., 1945, Mar., Apr., May, 1947.

Farmer, John Stephen. *See* Tefft.

Farmer, John Stephen, and Henley, W. E. *A Dictionary of Slang and Colloquial English*. Dutton, 1905. [One vol. abridgment of *Slang and Its Analogues*, 7 vols., 1890-1904.]

Farrell, James T. *Short Stories*. Vanguard, 1946.

Fast, Howard. *The American*. Duell, Sloan and Pearce, 1946.

Faulkner, W. G. "How the 'Movies' Corrupt the English Language." *Lit. Digest*, July 19, 1913.

Feather, Leonard. "Jazz Millionaire." *Esquire*, May, 1957.

Fibber McGee and Molly. Radio show, Apr. 10, 1951, etc.

Fineberg, Martin. [Examples of rhyming slang.] *Newsweek*, Nov. 21, 1949.

Fink, Harold Kenneth. *Long Journey*. Julian Press, N.Y., 1954.

Fitzgerald, F. Scott. *The Great Gatsby*. Bantam, 1951 (Scribner's, 1925).

———. *This Side of Paradise*. Dell, 1954 (Scribner, 1920).

Flynn, John T. "Something for Nothing." *Collier's*, Oct. 8, 1932.

Flynt, Josiah. "The American Tramp." *Contemporary Rev.* (London), Aug., 1891.

———. "The City Tramp." *Century Mag.*, Mar., 1894.

———. "The Tramp at Home." *Century Mag.*, Feb., 1894.

———. "Tramping with Tramps." *Century Mag.*, Nov., 1893.

Ford, Leslie, *pseud. The Philadelphia Murder Story*. Reprint ed., 1945 (Scribner, 1944).

Fowler, Gene. *Good Night, Sweet Prince*. Reprint ed., 1947 (Viking, 1944).

Fowler, H. W. *A Dictionary of Modern English Usage*. Oxford, 1926.

Franck, Russell C. "Words the Gob Uses." *N. Y. Times Mag.*, July 12, 1942.

Frank, Glenn. "Slang and Jargon." *Century Mag.*, Nov., 1920.

Frank, Stanley. "Refugee from Burlesque." *SEP*, Mar. 15, 1952.

Franklyn, Julian. *The Cockney*. Macmillan, 1953.

———. "Reaction to Rhyme." *Contemporary Rev.*, Nov., 1941.

Frazier, George. "Broadwayese." *Life*, Oct. 4, 1943.

———. "Doubletalk." *Life*, July 5, 1943.

Freeman, Oscar L. "Slang It!" *Better Eng.*, July-Aug., 1939.

Fry, Macon. "Ham Lingo." *AS*, Oct., 1929.

Fuller, Norman. *See* Smith, Maurice G.

Funkhouser, Clifford. *See* Anson.

G., F. "Airman's Lingo." *N. Y. Times Mag.*, June 4, 1944.

G., P. "Confessions of a Bus-Booster, I, II." *New Yorker*, Dec. 8, 15, 1928.

Gable, J. Harris. "American Stage-Hand Language." *AS*, Oct., 1928.

Gaines, Ervin J. "Talking Under Water. . . ." *AS*, Feb., 1948.

Gangbusters. Radio play, Jan. 28, 1950, etc.

Gardner, Erle Stanley. *The D. A. Draws a Circle*. Pocket Books, 1946 (Morrow, 1939).

Gardner, Hy. "Early Bird on Broadway." *Synd. Newsp. col.*, N. Y. *Her. Trib.*, Dec. 12, 1951, etc.

Garrett, Robert Max "A Word-List from the Northwest, I, II." *Dialect Notes*, v. 5.

Geikie, A. Constable. "Canadian English." *The Canadian Jour. of Industry, Science, and Art*, Sept., 1857.

Gibbs, Wolcott. "Virtuoso." *New Yorker*, Nov. 17, 1928.

Gillet, Joseph E. "Lexicographical Notes." *AS*, Apr., 1939.

Gillilan, Strickland. "Additions to the Mother Tongue Developed by the Automobile." *Lit. Digest*, May 22, 1920.

Givens, Charles G. "The Chatter of Guns." *SEP*, Apr. 13, 1929.

Gleason, H. A. *An Introduction to Descriptive Linguistics*. Holt, 1955.

Godwin, Murray. "Whence Phony?" *Sat. Rev. of Lit.*, Aug. 26, 1933.

Gold, Herbert. "The Beat Mystique: What It Is—Whence It Came." *Playboy*, Feb., 1958.

Gould, Paul. "A Glossary of Taxicab Words and Phrases." *New Yorker*, Nov. 3, 1928.

Graham, Frank. "Talking about Baseball." N. Y. *Sun*, July 18, 1927.

Gray, Hugh. "Rhyming Slang." *Bookman* (London), Oct., 1934.

Green, Abel. "The Variety Mugg." *Esquire*, Sept., 1936.

———, and Laurie, Joe, Jr. *Show Biz from Vaude to Video*. Holt, 1951.

Greenough, James Bradstreet, and Kittredge, George Lyman, *Words and Their Ways in English Speech*. Macmillan, 1901.

Gregory, Eloise C. "A City Surveying Vocabulary." *AS*, Oct., 1950.

Greig, John Young Thomson. *Breaking Priscian's Head: or English as She Will Be Spoke and Wrote*. London, Kegan Paul, 1928.

Gresham, William Lindsay. [Review of a book on carnivals.] *N. Y. Times Book Rev.*, Apr. 8, 1951.

Griffin, Frank Loxley. "Learn English. . . ." *Atlantic Mon.*, June, 1932.

Grose, Francis. *A Classical Dictionary of the Vulgar Tongue*, 1785. Edited by Eric Partridge. Oxford, 1931.

Haas, Kenneth B. "Trade Jargon." *AS*, Feb., 1939.

Hale, William Harlan. *Horace Greeley.* Harper, 1950.

Hall, Benjamin Homer. *A Collection of College Words and Customs.* J. Bartlett, 1851, 1856.

Halsey Jr., Ashley. "The Lady Cops of the Dope Squad." *SEP*, Mar. 30, 1957.

Hamann, Fred. "Stillers' Argot." *AS*, Oct., 1946.

Hamilton, Delbert W. "Pacific War Language." *AS*, Feb., 1947.

Hammett, Dashiell. "The Assistant Murderer" in *A Man Called Spade and Other Stories.* c. 1944.

———. *Blood Money.* Reprint ed., 1951 (World, 1943).

Handsaker, Gene. AP item, June 22, 1950.

Hardin, Achsah. "Volstead English." *AS*, Dec., 1931.

Hargan, James. "The Psychology of Prison Language." *Jour. of A. & S. Psychol.*, Oct.-Dec., 1935.

Hart, James Morgan. "Notes from Cincinnati [and elsewhere]." *Dialect Notes*, v. 1 (1890).

Hartt, Rollin Lynde. "The National Game." *Atlantic Mon.*, Aug., 1908.

Harvey, Bartle T. "Addenda. . . ." *Dialect Notes*, v. 4 (1914).

———. "Navy Slang." *Dialect Notes*, v. 4 (1914).

———. "A Word-List from the Northwest." *Dialect Notes*, v. 4 (1913).

Hayakawa, S. I. *Language in Thought and Action.* Harcourt, Brace, 1949.

———, (ed). *Language, Meaning and Maturity.* Harper, 1954.

Haynes, Jack Ellis. *Haynes Guide: Handbook of Yellowstone National Park.* Bozeman, Montana, 1949 (51st edn.)

Haynes, Renée. "Class Dialects." *Contemporary Rev.*, Aug., 1941.

Healey, Jack. "Fo'c'sle Lingo." *AS*, Apr., 1928.

Hearn, Edmond. "A Blurb for Slang." *AS*, Dec., 1928.

Hecht, Ben. "The Philoolooloo Bird." *New Yorker*, Nov. 3, 1928.

———, and MacArthur, Charles. *The Front Page.* Covici, 1928.

Heffron, Pearl White. "Slang—Slag or Steel." *Quart. Jour. of Speech*, Apr., 1940.

Hellman, Geoffrey T. "Hi There, Whitney Griswold." *New Yorker*, Jan. 10, 1953.

Hemingway, Ernest. "The Killers." Scribner's, 1927.

———. "My Old Man," in *In Our Time* (Scribner, 1930).

Henry, O., *pseud. Cabbages and Kings.* (Doubleday, 1925).

Henry, Will. *Death of a Legend.* Random, 1954.

Herzberg, Richard A. "Army Slang." *Word Study*, Apr., 1943.

Hilliard, Alec Rowley. *Justice Be Damned.* Farrar & Rinehart, 1941.

———. *Outcast Island.* Farrar, 1942.

Hills, E. C. "Irradiation of Certain Suffixes." *AS*, Oct., 1925.

Hine, William H. "English Behind the Walls." *Better Eng.*, Dec., 1939.

Hirschfeld, Al. Show Business Is no Business. Simon & Schuster, 1951.

Hixson, Jerome C., and Colodny, I. *Word Ways: A Study of Our Living Language.* Amer. Book Co., 1939.

Hobart, G. V. *See* McHugh.

Hobo News, The. Newark, N. J., Dec., 1951.

Hockett, Charles F. *A Course in Modern Linguistics.* Macmillian, 1958.

Hogan, Pendleton. "Pentagonese." *Collier's*, Nov. 24, 1951.

Hoijer, H. (ed.) *Language in Culture.* Univ. of Chicago Press, 1954.

Holbrook, Stewart H. "Hercules in the Woods." *Amer. Mercury*, Oct., 1930.

———. "Wobbly Talk." *Amer. Mercury*, Jan., 1926.

Holiday Inn. Movie, 1942.

Holmes, John Clellon. "The Philosophy of the Beat Generation." *Esquire*, Feb., 1958.

Homes, Geoffrey. *Forty Whacks.* Morrow, 1941, repr. as *"Stiffs Don't Vote.* 1947.

Hook, J. N. "Today's College English, III." *Word Study*, May, 1951.

Hope, Bob, NBC-WBZ, Feb. 18, 1953, and other dates.

Hornberger, Theodore. "The Automobile and American English." *AS*, Apr., 1930.

Horne, Elliot. "For Cool Cats and Far-Out Chicks." *N. Y. Times Mag.*, Aug. 18, 1957.

Hornstein, Lillian Herlands. "Park Patter." *AS*, Dec., 1940.

Horowitz, Mayer. "Slang of the American Paratrooper." *AS*, Oct.-Dec., 1948.

Howsley, L. B. *Argot: a Dictionary of Underworld Slang.* Columbia Pub. Co., 1939.

Hoyt, Harlowe R. *Town Hall Tonight.* Prentice Hall, 1955.

Huddle, Franklin P. "Baseball Jargon." *AS*, Apr., 1943.

Hughes, Dorothy. "Note on Feet and Shoes." *AS*, Feb., 1935.

Hughes, Langston. *Laughing to Keep from Crying.* Holt, 1952.

Hulbert, J. R. *See* Craigie.

Hulburd, David. *"H" Is for Heroin.* Doubleday, 1952.

Hurston, Zora Neale. "Story in Harlem Slang." *Amer. Mercury*, July, 1942.

Hutchens, John K. (ed.). *The American Twenties.* Lippincott, 1952.

Hutson, Arthur E. "Gaelic Loan-Words in American," *AS*, Feb., 1947.

Hynd, Alan. *The Pinkerton Case Book.* NAL, 1948.

———. *We Are the Public Enemies.* 1949.

If I Had a Million. Movie, crt. 1932.

Irwin, Godfrey. *American Tramp and Underworld Slang*. Scholartis Press, 1931.

Israel, Nedra Karen. "Super-Service Slang." *AS*, Dec., 1938.

Jack Armstrong Program. WJZ, Nov. 2, 1949.

Jackson, Joseph Henry. "Other Than A Good One," etc., in *San Francisco Murders*. 1948 (1947).

Jacobs, Stanley S. "A $7000 Income from a Suitcase." *Mag. Digest*, Aug., 1946.

Jacobsen, Carl. "Jargon of the Road." *AS*, Oct., 1936.

James, Thelma. "Detroit Automobile Slang." *AS*, Oct., 1941.

Janney, Russell. *The Miracle of the Bells*. Prentice-Hall, 1946.

Jennings, J. H. "Navy Humor." *Life*, Nov. 18, 1940.

Jensen, Oliver. "The Navy's Humor. . . ." *Life*, Oct. 28, 1940.

Jespersen, Otto. *Growth and Structure of the English Language*. Appleton, 1923.

———. *Language: Its Nature, Development, and Origin*. Holt, 1924.

———. *Monosyllabism in English*. Oxford, 1929.

Johanson, Hugo. "Snipe Hunting." *Atlantic Mon.*, Dec., 1937.

Johnny Allegro. Movie, 1949.

Johnny Stool Pigeon. Movie, ca. 1949.

Johnson, Guy B. "Double Meaning in the Popular Negro Blues," *Jour. A. & S. Psych.*, Apr.-June 1927.

Johnson, Mac R. "New Lexicon for [Korean] War." *N. Y. Her. Trib.*, Dec. 16, 1951.

Johnson, Owen. *Stover at Yale*. Stokes, 1912.

———. *The Varmint*. Baker & Taylor, 1910.

Johnson, W. Bolingbroke, *pseud.* of Morris G. Bishop. *The Widening Stain*. Knopf, 1942.

Johnston, Alva. "The Billboard. . . ." *New Yorker*, Sept. 12, 1936.

Johnston, Robert. "Slanguage of Amateur Photographers." *AS*, Dec., 1940.

Jones, Claude E. "A Note on Sailor Slang." *AS*, Feb., 1935.

Jones, Grover. "Railroad Lingo. . . ." *Bookman*, July, 1929.

Jones, Joe J. "More Slang." *AS*, Apr., 1930.

Jones, Joseph. "More on Marble Names and Games." *AS*, Apr., 1935.

Jones, Paul. "Candid Shots." Column, Phila. *Eve. Bulletin* Jan. 7, 1946, Sept. 2, 1949, many issues.

Kallich, Martin. "World War II Slang of Maladjustment." *AS*, Oct., 1946.

Kane, Elisha K. "The Jargon of the Underworld." *Dialect Notes*, v. 5 (1927).

Kane, H. F. "A Brief Manual of Beggary." *New Republic*, July 15, 1936.

Kansas City Confidential. Movie, crt. 1952.

Kasser, Edmund. "The Growth and Decline of a . . . Slang Vocabulary. . . ." *Jour. of Genetic Psychol.*, 1945.

Keeley, Mary Paxton. "A.E.F. English." *AS*, June, 1930.

Kendall, Park, and Viney, Johnny. *A Dictionary of Army and Navy Slang*. Mill, 1941.

Kennedy, Arthur G. *Current English*. Ginn, 1935.

———. "Hothouse Words Versus Slang." *AS*, July, 1927.

Kent, Hugh. "Variety." *Amer. Mercury*, Dec., 1926.

Kieran, John. "The Sportsman's Lexicon." *Sat. Rev. of Lit.*, July 22, 1933.

Kildare, Owen F. "The Jargon of Low Literature." *Independent*, July 19, 1906.

Kilgallen, James L. "Newspaper English." *Better Eng.*, Feb., 1938.

Kinkead, Eugene. "Sixteen." *New Yorker*, Nov. 10, 1951.

Kittredge, G. L. *See* Greenough.

Klass, Joe. [Vocabulary of prisoners of war.] *AS*, Dec., 1944.

Klein, Edward. "The Beat Generation." N.Y. *Daily News*, Feb. 19, 1958.

Klein, Nicholas. "Hobo Lingo." *AS*, Sept. 1926.

Knoetgen, John Alfred. "Longshoreman's Lingo." *Encore*, Sept.-Oct., 1944.

Kober, Arthur. *New Yorker*, Nov. 5, 1949.

Krapp, George Philip. *Modern English: Its Growth and Present Use*. Scribner, 1909.

———. *The English Language in America*. Appleton-Century, 1925.

Krim, Seymour (ed.). *Manhattan: Stories from the Heart of a Great City*. Bantam, 1954.

Kuethe, J. Louis. "Modern Slang." *AS*, Dec., 1936.

———. "Prisoner Parlance." *AS*, Feb. 1934.

Lady Takes a Sailor. Movie, 1949.

Lait, Jack, and Mortimer, Lee. *Chicago: Confidential*. Crown, 1950.

———. *New York: Confidential*. Reprint ed., 1950. (Ziff-Davis, 1948).

Lambert, Mildred E. "Studies in Stylistics." *AS*, June, 1929.

Lance, James. [I. W. W. terms.] *Amer. Mercury*, Apr., 1926.

Lanning, Emil. "Lousy." *AS*, Apr., 1928.

Lardner, John. "The Lexicographers in Stir." *New Yorker*, Dec. 1, 1951.

Larsen, Swen A. "The Vocabulary of Poker." *AS*, May, 1951.

Laurie, Joe. *See* Green.

Lavine, Emanuel H. *The Third Degree: a Detailed . . . Exposé of Police Brutality*. Vanguard, 1930.

Leacock, Stephen. "Our 'Living Language': a Defense." N.Y. *Times Mag.*, Feb. 26, 1939.

Lee, Gretchen. "In Sporting Parlance." *AS*, Apr., 1926.

———. "Trouper Talk." *AS*, Oct., 1925.

Lehman, Benjamin H. "A Word List from California." *Dialect Notes*, v. 5.

———. "A Word List from Northwestern U.S." *Dialect Notes*, v. 5.

———. "Additional Words. . . ." *Ibid.*

Leichty, V. E. "Some Composing Room Terms." *AS*, Dec., 1938.

Leitzell, Ted. [Broadcasting-studio argot.] *Newsweek*, May 23, 1938.

Leonard, Arthur N. "Lists from Maine." *Dialect Notes*, v. 4 (1913).

Lewis, Ada. "Slang in Evolution." *Lit. Digest*, Feb. 14, 1925.

Lewis, Sinclair. *Babbitt*. Harcourt, Brace, 1922.

————. "Onward, Sons of Ingersoll!" *Scribner's*, Aug., 1935.

————. *Our Mr. Wrenn*. Crowell, 1951 (1914).

————. *World So Wide*. Random, 1951.

Liebling, A. J. *Back Where I Came From*. Sheridan, 1938.

————. "A Day with the [Turf] Analysts." *New Yorker*, Mar. 15, 1952.

————. "Five-Star Schoolmaster." *New Yorker*, Mar. 10, 1951.

————. "Masters of the Midway." *New Yorker*, Aug. 12 and 19, 1939.

————. "Yea, Verily." *New Yorker*, Sept. 27, 1952.

Lilienthal, Jesse. *Horse Crazy*. Somerset, 1941.

Lindsay, Charles. "The Idiom of the Sheep Range." *AS*, June, 1931.

————. "The Nomenclature of the Popular Song." *AS*, June, 1928.

Livingston, J. A. "Wall St. Needs Noah Webster. . . ." Phila. *Eve. Bulletin*, Sept. 13, 1949.

Loehr, Rodney C. "Some Notes on Army Speech." *AS*, Feb., 1948.

Lomax, Alan. *Mister Jelly Roll*. Grove, 1956 (Duell, Sloan & Pearce, 1950).

London, Jack. "My Life in the Underworld." *Cosmopolitan Mag.*, May through Oct., 1907.

————. *The Road*. Macmillan, 1907. [Rprt. of "My Life . . ." with 3 new chapters added.]

Long, Percy Waldron. "Fields for Collectors." *Dialect Notes*, v. 5 (1922).

Longstreet, Stephen. *The Pedlocks*. Pocket Books, 1953 (Simon & Schuster, 1951).

————. *The Real Jazz Old and New*. La. State Univ. Press, 1956.

Lopushansky, Joseph and Michael. "Mining Town Terms." *AS*, June, 1929.

Lorwin, Irving R. "Police Parlance." N.Y. *Times Mag.*, Dec. 15, 1946.

Lovette, Leland P. "Nautical Words and Naval Expressions." in *Naval Customs, Tradition and Usage*. U.S. Naval Institute, 1939.

Lucas, E. V. *Clouds and Silver*. G. H. Doran, 1916.

Lumiansky, R. M. "New Orleans Slang in the 1880's." *AS*, Feb., 1950.

Lynd, Robert. "The King's English and the Prince's American." *Living Age*, Mar. 15, 1928.

M., S. Q. [Sailor talk.] *AS*, Oct., 1926.

Mabey, Richard A. "The English of the Court Room. . . ." *AS*, Feb., 1926.

MacArthur, Charles. "Rope." *Smart Set*, Nov., 1923, repr. in *Amer. Mercury*, Feb., 1937.

————. *See* Hecht.

Macaulay, Rose. *Orphan Island*. Boni & Liveright, 1925.

Mackay, Charles. "English Slang and French Argot. . . ." *Blackwood's Edinburgh Mag.*, May, 1888.

Mackenzie, Catherine. "Teen-Age Slang." N.Y. *Times Mag.*, Dec. 5, 1943.

Macon, Cliff. "Jogging Your Jargon, I-II-III-IV." *Collier's*, Sept. 9, 16, 23, 30, 1944.

Mad Wednesday. Movie, crt. 1946.

Marano, Al. "Glidepath Glossary." N.Y.

Marples, Morris. *University Slang*. London, Williams & Norgate, 1950.

Martin, Douglas S. "Business Jargon. . . ." *Living Age*, Aug. 8, 1914.

Martin, J. B., in *SEP*, May 27, 1950.

Martin, Pete. "Hollywood Says. . . ." *SEP*, Apr. 1, 1950.

————. "They're Taking the Kinks Out of Rinks." *SEP*, May 13, 1944.

Martin Kane, Private Eye. WOR, Sept. 4, 1949, etc.

Masterson, Elisabeth. *See* DeLannoy.

Matsell, George. *Vocabulum*. 1859.

Matthews, Brander. "American English and British English," *Scribner's*, Nov., 1920.

————. "The Function of Slang." *Harper's*, July, 1893.

————. "New Words Born of the War." *Munsey's Mag.*, Apr., 1919.

Times Mag., Oct. 30, 1949.

Marckwardt, Albert H. *Introduction to the English Language*. New York, 1942.

————, and F. G. Cassidy. *Scribner Handbook of English*. Scribner, 1948.

Marks, Percy. *The Plastic Age*. Century, 1924.

Mathews, M. M. *A Dictionary of Americanisms*. Univ. of Chicago Press, 1951.

Matthews, William. "Early New England Words." *AS*, Oct., 1940.

Maurer, David W. "The Argot of Forgery." *AS*, Dec., 1941.

————. "The Argot of the . . . Narcotic Addict." *AS*, 1936.

————. "The Argot of the Underworld." *AS*, Dec., 1931.

————. *The Big Con*. Pocket Books, 1949 (Bobbs, 1940).

————. "Carnival Cant." *AS*, June, 1931.

————. "Junker Lingo. . . ." *AS*, Apr., 1933.

————. "The Lingo of the Good-People." *AS*, Feb., 1935.

————. "Schoonerisms. . . ." *AS*, June, 1930.

————, and Vogel, V. H. *Narcotics and Narcotics Addiction*. Thomas, 1954.

Maxfield, Ezra Kempton. "Maine List." *Dialect Notes*, v. 5 (1926).

Mayer, Lloyd. "She Was Glad She Was Educated." *SEP*, repr. in *Word Study*, Sept., 1930.

Mays, Brock. "Aviation Slang." *Popular Science Mon.*, May, 1928.

McAtee, W. L. ". . . Speech of . . . Old-Timers." *AS*, Oct., 1943.

McCarten, John. "The Current Cinema." *New Yorker*, Dec. 1, 1951.

McCartney, Eugene S. "Additions to a Volume on . . . Slang. . . ," *Papers of Mich. Acad. of Science*, 1928.

———. "Trench Talk." *Texas Rev.*, Oct., 1918.

———. ". . . War Slang." *Papers of Mich. Acad. of Science*, 1923.

McCullers, Carson. *The Ballad of the Sad Café* Houghton Mifflin, 1951.

McDavid, R. I. "A Citadel Glossary." *AS*, Feb., 1939.

———. "Provincial Sayings. . . ." *AS*, Feb., 1943.

McFarland, James R. "Army Vocabulary." *Amer. Legion Mag.*, May, 1946.

McFerran, Doris. "Radio Has a Word for It." *Amer. Mercury*, Nov., 1941.

———. "Railroaders Have a Word for It." *Amer. Mercury*, June, 1942.

———. "Truck Drivers Have a Word for It." *Amer. Mercury*, Apr., 1941.

McHugh, Hugh, *pseud.* of George Vere Hobart. *You Can Search Me.* Dillingham, 1905.

McHugh, LeRoy F. "The Peacock Case—1936" in *Chicago Murders* 1947 (1945).

McKnight, G. H. *Modern English in the Making.* New York, 1928.

———. *English Words and Their Background.* New York, 1923.

McLaughlin, W. A. "Some Current Substitutes for 'Irish' " *Dialect Notes*, v. 4 (1914).

McLellan, Howard. "It's Greek to You—But the Crooks 'Get' It." *Collier's*, Aug. 8, 1925.

McLemore, Henry. "Runyonese." *Look*, repr. in *Word Study*, Oct., 1942.

McNeil, Steve. "High-Pressure Girl." *SEP*, Aug. 10, 1957.

McNulty, John. "A Reporter in Bed." *New Yorker*, Oct. 14, 1950.

McPhee, Marguerite C. "College Slang." *AS*, Dec., 1927.

———. "Anatomical Verbs." *AS*, Oct., 1951.

Mead, Shepherd. *The Big Ball of Wax.* Simon & Schuster, 1954.

Mellen, Ida M. "Words from Sea Animals." *AS*, Apr., 1927.

Melville, A. H. "An Investigation of the Function and Use of Slang." *Ped. Sem.*, Mar., 1912.

Melville, Herman. *White-Jacket: The World in a Man-of-War.* Harper, 1850.

Mencken, H. L. *The American Language.* 3d ed. Knopf, 1923; 4th ed., 1936; *Supplement I*, 1945; *Supplement II*, 1948.

———. "Designations for Colored Folk." *AS*, Oct., 1944.

———. "Postscripts to the American Language: the Vocabulary of the Drinking Chamber." *New Yorker*, Nov. 6, 1948.

———. "Such Language!" *Amer. Mag.*, Oct., 1936.

———. "Video Verbiage." *New Yorker*, Dec. 11, 1948.

———. "War Slang, 1940." *Reader's Digest*, May, 1940.

Meredith, Mamie. "The Human Head in Slang." *AS*, June, 1928.

Merryweather, L. W. "The Argot of an Orphans' Home." *AS*, Aug., 1932.

Milburn, George. "Circus Words." *Amer. Mercury*, Nov., 1931.

———. "Convicts' Jargon." *AS*, Aug., 1931.

———. "The Taxi Talk," in *Folk-Say.* Norman, Okla., 1929.

Miller, Arthur. *Death of a Salesman.* Viking, 1949.

Miller, Charles. "Furniture Lingo." *AS*, Dec., 1930.

Miller, Edwin H. "More Air Force Slang." *AS*, Dec., 1946.

Millstein, Gilbert. "[Clothing-] Salesman's-Eye View of the Customer." *N. Y. Times Mag.*, Sept. 21, 1952.

Misfeldt, Orlo H. "Argot of the Sea." *AS*, Dec., 1940.

———. "Timberland Terminology," *AS*, Oct., 1941.

Mitchell, Joseph. *McSorley's Wonderful Saloon.* 1945 (1938-43).

Mitgang, Herbert. "*About—Men's Haircuts.*" *N.Y. Times Mag.*, June 2, 1957.

Monroe, B. S., and O. F. Emerson. "General List [of terms] B." *Dialect Notes*, v. 1 (1895).

Montgomery, H. C. *See* Cottrell.

Moore, Helen R. "The Lingo of the Mining Camp." *AS*, Nov., 1926.

Morgan, B. Q. "Simile and Metaphor in American Speech." *AS*, Feb., 1926.

Morley, Christopher. *The Man Who Made Friends with Himself.* Doubleday, 1949.

Morris, Bernard. "The Lingo of Bus Drivers." *AS*, Dec., 1938.

Morse, James Herbert. "The New Vocabularly." *The Independent*, Oct. 1, 1908.

Morse, William R. "Stanford [Univ.] Expressions." *AS*, Mar., 1937.

Mortimer, Lee. *See* Lait.

Morton, Frederic. "The Art of Courtship." *Holiday*, Mar., 1957.

Moss, Arnold. "Jewels from a Box Office." *AS*, Oct., 1936.

Mr. Soft Touch. Movie, crt. 1949.

Mullen, Kate. "Westernisms." *AS*, 1925.

Mulvey, Kay. "Hollywood Slang." *Wom. Home Comp.* Aug., 1940.

Mulvey, Ruth. "Pitchmen's Cant." *AS*, Apr., 1942.

Nathan, George Jean. "Clinical Notes." *Amer. Mercury*, 1926.

———. "England and the American Language." *Amer. Mercury*, 1926.

Neill, Frank. "This Film 'Bad Man.' . . ." *Phila. Eve. Bulletin*, Aug. 31, 1949.

Nelson, Victor Folke. "Addenda to 'Junker Lingo' " *AS*, Oct., 1933.

Nevins, Allan (ed.). *America Through British Eyes.* Oxford. 1948.

A New English Dictionary on Historical Principles (known as the *Oxford English Dictionary*). Oxford, 1884-1928, reissued with *Supplement*, 1933.

New Yorker, various issues.

New York *Times*, various issues.
Noble, Kendrick, *et al.* [Army, Navy, and Air Force terms in World War II.] *Word Study*, Apr., 1944.
Northrup, C. S., and Emerson, O. F., Crow, C. L., Zimmerman, H. E., *et al.* "Word-List." *Dialect Notes*, v. 1 (1896).
Norton, Theodore E. "Modern American Usage." *AS*, Dec., 1936.
Nye, Russel B. "A Musician's Word List." *AS*, Feb., 1937.
O., Y. "The American Slanguage." *Living Age*, Nov. 15, 1926.
Offord, Lenore G. "Eleven Days' Wonder," in *San Francisco Murders*. 1949.
———. "The Gifts of Cordelia," In *San Francisco Murders*. 1948. (1947).
Ogden, C. K., and Richards, I. A. *The Meaning of Meaning*. 6th ed. Harcourt, Brace, 1944.
O'Hara, John. "Ex-Pal." *New Yorker*, Nov. 26, 1938.
———. *Pal Joey*. NAL, 1951 (Random, 1939, 1940).
O. Henry, *See* Henry, O.
Oliver, N. T. *See* Stout.
Oliver, Robert T. "Junglese." *AS*, June, 1932.
———. "Electionisms of 1936." *AS*, Feb., 1936.
Once More, My Darling. Movie, 1949.
O'Neill, Eugene. *The Hairy Ape*. Liveright, 1922.
Osgood, Henry Osborne. "Jazz." *AS*, July, 1926.
Ostrow, Albert A. "Service Men's Slang." *Amer. Mercury*, Nov., 1943.
Oxford English Dictionary. See *New English Dictionary on Historical Principles*.
Partridge, Eric. *Dictionary of Slang and Unconventional English*. London, 1937.
———. *Dictionary of the Underworld*. London, 1949.
Pedersen, Holger. *Linguistic Science in the Nineteenth Century*. Harvard Univ. Press, 1931.
Perry, Albert. "Movie Talk." *AS*, June, 1928.
Pegler, Westbrook, various articles in newspapers, 1931 and 1945-53.
Perelman, S. J. *Listen to the Mocking Bird*. Simon & Schuster, 1949.
———. Nine articles in *New Yorker*, Sept. 30, 1950, to Jan. 3, 1953.
Perkins, Anne E. "Vanishing Expressions. . . ." *AS*, Dec., 1927.
Petersen, Sarah Christine. "Yellowstone Park Language." *AS*, Oct., 1931.
Phone Call from a Stranger. CBS, Jan. 5, 1953.
Physteriss, Mr., *pseud.* "Our Mother Tongue." *Princeton Alumni Weekly*, repr. in *Word Study*, Feb., 1942.
Pingry, Carl, and Randolph, Vance. "Kansas University Slang." *AS*, Feb., 1928.
Pollock, F. Walter. "On Commercial Correspondence." *AS*, Nov., 1926.
———. "Courtship Slang." *AS*, Jan. 1927.

———. "The Current Expansion of Slang." *AS*, Dec., 1926.
Porter, Bernard H. "Truck Driver Lingo." *AS*, Apr., 1942.
Pound, Louise. "Word-List from Nebraska" *Dialect Notes*, v. 4 (1916).
———. "American Euphemisms for Dying, Death, and Burial." *AS*, Oct., 1936.
———. " 'Blah' and Its Synonyms." *AS*, Apr., 1929.
———. "The Value of English Linguistics. . . ." *AS*, Nov., 1925.
———. "Vogue Affixes in Present-Day Word-Coinage." *Dialect Notes*, v. 5 (1916-8).
Powell, E. Alexander. "The Elegant Eighties." *Atlantic Mon.*, Aug., 1938.
Prather, Richard S. *Bodies in Bedlam*. Fawcett, 1951.
Prenner, Manuel. "Slang Synonyms for 'Drunk.' " *AS*, Dec., 1928.
———. "Slang Terms for Money." *AS*, June, 1929.
———. "More Slang Words for 'Drunk.' " *AS*, Aug., 1929.
———. " 'Drunk' in Slang—Addenda." *AS*, Feb., 1941.
Prescott, Russell T. "Middlewestern Farm English," *AS*, Apr., 1937.
Purroy, David. "On the Lam." *Amer. Mercury*, Aug., 1928.
Pyle, Ernie. *Home Country*. Sloane, 1947.
Queen, Ellery, *pseud. The Dutch Shoe Mystery*. Pocket Books, 1952 (Stokes 1931).
———. *Hammett Homicides*. 1946.
———. *The Tragedy of X*. Avon, 1952 (Viking, 1932).
Quinlan, Patrick L. "The Trenton Penitentiary." *New Republic*, Jan. 13, 1917.
The Racket. Movie, 1951.
Ramsaye, Terry. "Movie Jargon." *AS*, Apr., 1926.
Randolph, John. *Texas Brags*. John Randolph, 1952.
Randolph, Vance. "Wet Words in Kansas." *AS*, June, 1929.
———. See Pingry.
Read, Allen Walker. "Watch-Stuffer." *AS*, Oct., 1941.
———. "The Word Harvest of '44." *Sat. Rev. of Lt.*, Mar. 10, 1945.
Révész, G. *Ursprung und Vorgeschichte der Sprache*. Bern, Switzerland, 1946.
Red Light. Movie, 1949.
Rice, Elmer. *Street Scene*. French, 1928-29.
Richardson, C. B. W. "Elegy for a Dying Tongue." *Scribner's*, Aug., 1935.
Rickenbacker, Eddie. "Gimpers, Goophers, and Other New Aviation Wrinkles. . . ." *Lit. Digest*, Aug. 24, 1918.
Riding High. Movie, crt. 1950.
Ridings, Joseph Willard. "Use of Slang in Newspaper Sports Writing." *Jour. Quart.*, Dec., 1934.
Riordan, John Lancaster. "American Naval 'Slanguage' in the Pacific in 1945." *Calif. Folk. Quart.*, Oct., 1946.

———. "A. V. G. [Flying Tigers] Lingo." *AS*, Feb., 1948.

———. "Radar Slang Terms." *AS*, Apr., 1947.

———. "Soda Fountain Lingo." *Calif. Folk. Quart.*, Jan., 1945.

———. "Some 'G. I. Alphabet Soup.'" *As*, Apr., 1947.

———. "Some Notes on Army Slang." *AS*, Oct., 1947.

Roback, A. A. "You Speak Yiddish, Too!" *Better Eng.*, Feb., 1938.

Robbins, Rossell Hope. "Social Awareness and Semantic Change." *AS*, Apr., 1949.

Robinson, Ted, Jr. "How to Disappear." *Harper's*, Mar., 1952.

Rockwell, Harold E. "Color Stuff." *AS*, Oct., 1927.

———. "Going to Press." *AS*, Dec., 1928.

Roeburt, John. *Tough Cop*. Simon & Schuster, 1949.

Rogers, Fern Jo. "Occupational Jargon." *AS*, Feb., 1944.

Rollins, P. A. *The Cowboy*, rev. ed. Scribner's, 1936.

Root, Wells. "Socko, Whamo and Sonk!: The Effect of the Movies . . . on the English Language." *Bookman*, Feb., 1929.

Rose, Billy. "Pitching Horseshoes." Syndicated newspaper column, Jan. 2, 1947, to Dec. 4, 1950, various issues.

Rose, Don. "Stuff and Nonsense." Column, Phila. *Eve. Bulletin*, various issues.

Rothenberg, Julius G. "A Devoted Reader Kibitzes the Lexicographers." *Word Study*, Feb., 1942.

———. "'Peanuts! The Pickle Dealers.'" *AS*, Oct., 1941.

———. "Some American Idioms from the Yiddish." *AS*, Feb., 1943.

Roulier, Joseph B. "Service Lore: Army Vocabulary." *N.Y. Folk. Quart.*, Spring, 1948.

Ruark, Robert C., syndicated column, Mar., 1952, to Oct., 1953, various issues.

Runyon, Damon. *Blue Plate Special*. Reprinted. 1944. (Stokes, 1934).

———. Guys and Dolls. Pocket Books, 1944 (Stokes, 1932).

———. *Money from Home*. Reprint ed, 1944 (Stokes, 1935).

———. *Take It Easy*. Stokes, 1939.

———. Syndicated newspaper column, May 24 to Sept. 14, 1946, various issues.

Russell, Elsa. "Slang—Face to Face." *English Jour.*, Nov., 1934.

Russell, I. Willis. "Among the New Words." *AS*, Oct., 1947, Feb. and May, 1951, etc.

———, *et al.* "Words and Meanings, New." *Britannica Book of the Year* c.1946-53, various issues.

Russell, Jason Almus. "Colgate University Slang." *AS*, Feb., 1930.

———. "Erie Canal Colloquial Expressions." *AS*, Dec., 1930.

Ryan, Calvin T. "From 'Quoz' to 'Razzberries.'" *AS*, Nov., 1926.

———. "You Said It!" *Better Eng.*, Sept., 1938.

Salinger, J. D. *The Catcher in the Rye.* NAL, 1953 (Little, Brown, 1945).

Salpeter, Harry. "O! O! McIntyre." *Outlook and Independent*, Sept. 3, 1930.

Salt Lake City Utah *Deseret News*, various issues.

Sam Spade. WCBS radio program.

Samolar, Charlie. "The Argot of the Vagabond." *AS*, June, 1927.

Samuels, V. "Baseball Slang." *AS*, Feb., 1927.

Sands of Iwo Jima. Movie, 1949.

Saroyan, William. *Jim Dandy*. Harcourt, Brace, 1947.

Saul, Vernon W. "The Vocabulary of Bums." *AS*, June, 1929.

Savage, Howard J. "College Slang Words and Phrases from Bryn Mawr College." *Dialect Notes*, v. 5 (1922).

Saxon, Lyle, Dryer, Edward, and Tallant, Robert. *Gumbo Yu-Yu, A Collection of Louisiana Folk Tales*. Houghton Mifflin, 1945.

Sayre, Joel. "Bong Soir." *Amer. Mercury*, Dec., 1930.

———. "A Hex on the House." *Amer. Mercury*, Dec., 1931.

Scarne, John. *The Amazing World of John Scarne*. Crown, 1956.

Scene of the Crime. Movie, crt. 1949.

Scheer, James F. "Housecleaning Your Talk." *Better Eng.*, Sept., 1938.

Schlauch, Margaret. "Hollywood Slang in Spanish Translations." *AS*, Feb., 1939.

Schulberg, Budd. *What Makes Sammy Run?* Bantam, 1949. (Random House, 1941).

———. "Florida's Gold Coast." *Holiday*, Jan., 1952.

Schullian, Dorothy May. "College Slang." *School & Society*, Sept. 4, 1943.

Schultz, John Richie. "Chautauqua Talk." *AS*, Aug., 1932.

———. "Railroad Terms." *AS*, Apr., 1937.

Schultz, William Eben. "College Abbreviations." *AS*, Feb., 1930.

———. "Equivalents for Reproof." *AS*, Dec., 1937.

Schumach, Murray. "On the Pitch with a Sidewalk Florist." *N.Y. Times Mag.*, May 16, 1943.

Schuyler, Jack. "Hipped to the Tip." *Current History and Forum*, Nov. 7, 1940.

Schwesinger, Gladys C. "Slang as an Indication of Character." *Jour. of Applied Psych.*, June, 1926.

Sebastian, Hugh. "Negro Slang in Lincoln University." *AS*, Dec., 1934.

Sechrist, Frank K. "The Psychology of Unconventional Language." *Ped. Sem.*, Dec., 1913.

Seidleman, Morton. "Survivals in Negro Vocabulary." *AS*, Oct., 1937.

Selby, Earl. "In Our Town." Column, Phila. *Eve. Bulletin*, 1949, various issues.

Shafer, Robert. "Air Force Slang." *AS*, Oct., 1945.

——. "The Language of West Coast Culinary Workers." *AS*, 1946.

Shaw, Arnold. "West Coast Jazz." *Esquire*, Sept., 1956.

Shepherd, William G. "I Wonder Who's Driving Her Now?" *Jour. of American Insurance*, Feb., 1929.

Shidler, John Ashton, and Clarke, R. M. "Stanfordiana." *AS*, Feb., 1932.

——. "More Stanford Expressions." *AS*, Aug., 1932.

Shnee, Charles. *They Live by Night*. Screen play, 1948.

Shop Philosopher, *pseud*. [Synonyms of 'blah.'] *AS*, Apr., 1929.

Shulman, David. "Baseball's Bright Lexicon." *AS*, Feb., 1951.

Shulman, Max. *Barefoot Boy with Cheek*. Blakiston, 1943.

——. *The Feather Merchants*. Pocket Books, 1950 (Doubleday, 1944).

——. *The Many Loves of Dobie Gillis*. Doubleday, 1951.

——. *The Zebra Derby*. Pocket Books, 1952 (Doubleday, 1946).

Sidney, F. H. "Hobo Cant." *Dialect Notes*, v. 5 (1919).

—— "Railroad Terms." *Dialect Notes*, v. 4 (1916).

Simons, Hi. "A Prison Dictionary. . . ." *AS*, Oct., 1933.

Simpson, William R., Simpson, Florence K., with Samuels, Charles. *Hockshop*. Random, 1954.

Slocum, William J. "Skid Row." *Collier's*, Aug. 27 and Sept. 3, 1949.

Smart, Alice. "Department Store Technical Expressions." *AS*, Dec., 1938.

Smith, Carleton. "On the Record." *Esquire*, Nov., 1938.

Smith, Grace Partridge. "Speech Currents in 'Egypt.'" *AS*, Oct., 1942.

Smith, H. Allen. *Life in a Putty Knife Factory*. NAL, 1949 (Doubleday, 1945).

Smith, Logan P. *The English Language*. Holt, 1912.

Smith, Maurice G., Fuller, Norman and Clark, Bert. "Crook Argot." *AS*, Feb., 1928.

Smith, Red. "Views of Sport." N.Y. *Herald Tribune Syndicate*.

Smith, Stan. "Woods and Waters." N.Y. *Daily News*, various columns.

Snapp, D. V. "The Lingo of Railroad Linemen." *AS*, Feb., 1938.

Sobel, Bernard. "The Language of the Theatre." *Bookman*, Apr., 1929.

Sobol, Louis. "Passing of Manhattan's Montmartre." *Home* (Sunday supplement), Apr. 2, 1950.

Spectorsky, A. C. "Saloon Street, Chicago." N.Y. *Times Book Rev.*, Sept. 11, 1949.

Spencer, Gilmore. "Current College Slang." *Univ. of Virginia Mag.*, Oct., 1926.

Spencer, Herman. "Language in the Making: a Defense of Slang." *Booklovers Mag.*, Dec., 1903.

Spillane, Mickey. *The Big Kill*. Signet, 1951.

Stallings, Laurence, and Anderson, Maxwell. *What Price Glory?* Harcourt, 1926.

Stander, Lionel. "All I Need Is a Break." *Esquire*, June, 1952.

Starnes, Richard. *Another Mug for the Bier*. Pocket Books, 1952 (Lippincott, 1951).

——*And When She Was Bad She Was Murdered*. Pocket Books, 1951 (Lippincott, 1950).

Stavis, Barrie. [Army food terms.] *Sat. Rev. of Lit.*, Nov. 24, 1945.

Steadman, J. M. "Affected and Effeminate Words." *AS*, Feb., 1938.

——. "A North Carolina Word-List." *Dialect Notes*, v. 5 (1918).

[Steele, St. George.] "Recruits' Primer of Trench Idiom." *Lit. Digest*, Oct. 27, 1917.

Steig, J. A. [Jazz music terms.] *AS*, Oct., 1937, p. 179n.

Stevens, James. "Logger Talk." *AS*, Dec., 1925.

Stinnett, Caskie. "A Verb Can Be . . . Transitive. . . ." *SEP*, Dec. 8, 1951.

Stinson, Robert. "Said the Marine to the Jap." *SEP*, Mar. 20, 1943.

Stork, Willis. "Varying the Football Jargon." *AS*, Oct., 1934.

Stout, Wesley Winans, and N. T. Oliver. "Alagazam. . . ." *SEP*, Oct. 19, 1929.

Strong, K. W. "Radio Slanguage." *Better Eng.*, Mar., 1940.

Stuckey, E. F. "How the Navy Talks." *Author & Journalist*, Oct., 1942.

Sturges, Preston. *Strictly Dishonorable*. Liveright, 1929.

Swanberg, W. A. (ed.). *Fact Detective Mysteries*. 1949.

Talbot, Gayle. "Pitchless Brooklyn. . . ." AP, Sept. 30, 1952.

Tamony, Peter. "The Origin of 'Phoney.'" *AS*, Apr., 1937.

Tauber, Abraham. "G. I. Jive." *Scholastic*, Apr. 5, 1943.

Tefft, B. F. "The Flash Language." *The Ladies' Repository* (Cincinnati), Oct., 1848. [Sometimes attributed to John Stephen Farmer.]

Terrill, Nate. "The Argot of Outdoor Booby Traps." *AS*, Oct., 1950.

Terry, C. V. "A Girl, a Flask and a Coonskin," N. Y. *Times Book Rev.*, Oct. 19, 1952.

Thomas, Macklin. "A Note on 'Baloney.'" AS, Dec., 1935.

Thompson, E. E. *Our Changing Language*. pamph., 1940.

Thornton, Richard H. [Specimen passage of an American glossary.]*Dialect Notes*, v. 5.

——. "An American Glossary, Vol. III." *Dialect Notes*, v. 6 (1931-39).

Time, various issues.

Trapped. Movie, 1949.

Troubridge, Sir St. Vincent. "Some Notes on Rhyming Argot." *AS*, Feb., 1946.

Trout, Bob. "Some Notes on . . . 'War Words.' " *AS*, Dec., 1944.

Trujillo, Emanuel. *I Love You, I Hate You.* Levy, 1955.

Tully, Jim. *The Bruiser.* Reprint ed., 1946 (Greenberg, 1936).

Tunison, J. S. "Newspaper Jargon." *Dialect Notes*, v. 1 (1892).

Turner, Lorenzo Dow. *Africanisms in the Gullah Dialect.* Univ. of Chicago Press, 1949.

Tysell, Helen Trace. "The English of the Comic Cartoons." *AS*, Feb., 1935.

Tyson, Raymond. "Variety." *AS*, Dec., 1937.

Umland, Rudolph. "Nebraska Cowboy Talk." *AS*, Feb., 1942.

———. [Packinghouse] Words from South Omaha." *AS*, Oct., 1941.

UP articles, various dates.

Up Front. Movie, crt. 1951.

Utter, Robert P. "Our Upstart Speech." *Harper's*, June, 1917.

Van Vechten, Carl. *Nigger Heaven.* Knopf, 1926.

Vidor, King. *A Tree Is a Tree.* Harcourt, 1953.

Vizetelly, Frank H. "Flappers' Words and Others." *Lit. Digest*, Nov. 1, 1924.

———. "A Ramble in the Garden of Words." *AS*, Oct., 1925.

von Engeln, Oskar Dietrich. *At Cornell.* Artil, 1909.

Voorhees, T. V. "Slang." *Educational Rev.*, June, 1926.

Vorse, Mary Heaton. "The Pirates' Nest of New York." *Harper's*, Apr., 1952.

Wallace, Robert. "Crime in the U.S." *Life*, Sept. 9, 1957.

Wallop, Douglass, *Night Life.* Norton, 1953.

Warner, James H. "A Word List from Arkansas." *AS*, Feb., 1938.

Warner, Robert. "Turk." *Amer. Mercury*, Oct., 1942.

Warnock, Elsie L. "Terms of Approbation and Eulogy in American . . . Speech." *Dialect Notes*, v. 4 (1913).

———. "Terms of Disparagement in the . . . Speech of High School Pupils. . . ." *Dialect Notes*, v. 5 (1919).

Watt, William W. *An American Rhetoric.* Rinehart, 1952.

Webb, H. Brook. "The Slang of Jazz." *AS*, Oct., 1937.

Weber, Robert H. "Smokers' Slang." *AS*, Oct., 1940.

Webster, Harold Tucker. "They Don't Speak Our Language." *Forum*, Dec., 1933.

———. *The Best of H. T. Webster.* Simon & Schuster, 1953.

Webster's New International Dictionary, 1929 ed.; 2d ed., 1934; supplements 1927, 1939-50; *Webster's Collegiate Dictionary*, 1949 and earlier eds. Merriam.

Weekley, Ernest. "English as She Will Be Spoke." *Atlantic*, May, 1932.

Weeks, William E. *All in the Racket.* C. Boni, 1930.

Weidman, Jerome. "Portrait of a Gentleman." *Amer. Mercury*, May, 1936.

———. *I Can Get It For You Wholesale!* Reprint ed. 1949 (Simon & Schuster 1937).

Weitzel, Anthony. "Woodland Avenue English." *Better Eng.*, Nov., 1938.

Welker, Robert H. "GI Jargon. . . ." *Sat. Rev. of Lit.* Nov. 3, 1945.

Wells, George Y. "Station House Slang." *N. Y. Times Mag.*, Mar. 16, 1958.

Wells, Whitney Hastings. "Words Used in the Drug Traffic." *Dialect Notes*, v. 5 (1922-23).

Wentworth, Harold. *American Dialect Dictionary.* Crowell, 1944.

———. " 'Moola' and 'Moo,' Recent Terms for Money." *AS*, Dec., 1952.

We're Not Married. Movie, 1952.

Werner, William L. "Tad Dorgan Is Dead." *AS*, Aug., 1929.

Weseen, Maurice H. *A Dictionary of American Slang.* Crowell, 1934.

West, V. Royce. " 'Scram'—A Swell Five-Letter Woid." *AS*, Oct., 1937.

The West Point Story. Movie, crt. 1950.

White, Beatrice. "The Talkies and English Speech." *AS*, Apr., 1932.

White, Elwyn Brooks. *Stuart Little.* Harper, 1945.

White, Percy W. "A Circus List." *AS*, Feb., 1926.

———. "More About the Language of the Lot." *AS*, June, 1928.

———. "Stage Terms." *AS*, May, 1926.

White, William. "Whitman College Slang." *AS*, Apr., 1943.

White Heat. Movie, crt. 1949.

Whitman, Walt. "Slang in America." *The North Am. Rev.*, Nov., 1885.

Whorf, B. L. *Language, Thought, and Reality.* J. B. Carroll (ed.) Technology Press, M.I.T., and Wiley, 1956.

Willens, Doris. "It's Oogley, Also Bong." *N.Y. Times Mag.*, Mar. 6, 1949.

Willingham, Calder. *End as a Man.* Avon, 1950 (Vanguard, 1947).

———. *To Eat a Peach.* Dial, 1955.

Wilson, Douglas E. "Remarks on 'Glossary of Army Slang.' " *AS*, Feb., 1942.

Wilson, Earl. "It Happened Last Night." Syndicated newspaper column, various issues.

Wilson, Edmund. "The Playwright in Paradise." *New Republic*, Apr. 26, 1939.

Wilstach, John. "New Words." *Sat. Rev. of Lit.* July 18, 1931.

Wimberly, Lowry Charles. "American Political Cant." *AS*, Dec., 1926.

Winchell, Walter. Syndicated columns.

Winkler, John K. "That Was New York: Some Bounce Easy." *New Yorker*, Feb. 9, 1929.

Withington, Robert. " 'Lady,' 'Woman,' and 'Person.' " *AS*, Apr., 1937.

———. "Neologisms and a Need." *AS*, Feb., 1939.

Witman, Fred. "Jewelry Auction Jargon." *AS*, June, 1928.

Wittmann, Elisabeth. "Clipped Words: A Study of Back-Formations and Curtailments in Present-Day English." *Dialect Notes*, v. 4 (1914).

Witwer, Harry Charles. *The Leather Pushers*. Popular Library, 1950 (Grosset & Dunlap, 1921).

Wolfert, Ira. *The Underworld*. Bantam, 1950 (Hill & Wang, 1943, under title *Tucker's People*).

Wolverton, Charles. "Mysteries of the Carnival Language." *Amer. Mercury*, June, 1935.

Wood, Kenneth P. "The Vocabulary of Failure." *Better Eng.*, Nov., 1938.

Woofter, Carey. ". . . Words and Phrases from . . . West Virginia." *AS*, May, 1927.

Work, James A. "The American Slanguage." *Educational Rev.*, Apr., 1927.

Wouk, Herman. *The City Boy*. Doubleday, 1952.

WPA Federal Writers' Project. [Underworld lingo] in *Almanac for New Yorkers*, repr. in *Better Eng.*, Apr., 1939.

Wyer, Charles A. "If You've Been Reefed. . . ." N.Y. *Sun*, Aug. 7, 1946.

Wylie, Philip. *Finnley Wren*. American, 1949 (Rinehart, 1934).

———. *Generation of Vipers*. Rinehart, 1943.

Yeaman, M. V. P. "Speech Degeneracy." *AS*, Nov., 1925.

Yenne, Herbert. "Prison Lingo." *AS*, Mar., 1927.

Yoder, Robert M. "You'd Never Think They Were Crooks." *SEP*, Apr. 4, 1953.

Yust, Walter. *Ten Eventful Years*. Encyclopaedia Britannica.

Zeisler, Karl F. "Newspaper Authors Never Arrive." *Amer. Mercury*, May, 1935.

Zimmerman, H. E. *See* Northup.

———. "The Forty Thieves." *Reader's Digest*, Jan., 1944.

———. "The Great Schnozzola." *SEP*, July 15, 1950.

Zolotow, Maurice. "Pitchman." *SEP*, Sept. 25, 1943.

Zuger, John A. "Technical Terms in the Game of Marbles." *AS*, Feb., 1934.

PREFACE TO THE SUPPLEMENT

THIS SUPPLEMENT includes all of the material that appeared in the first Supplement of 1967 plus about 1,500 new slang terms and definitions that have become current since then.

Language follows life, and the newer slang reflects recent national concerns, new social subgroups, and changing attitudes. Thus, the Supplement now offers terms from the Nixon/Watergate era (*game plan*, *plumber*, *stonewall*), military and political terms from the Vietnam war (*birdfarm*, *hardhat*), and general slang from aerospace and astronaut use (*glitch*, *go*). New and old social subgroups are represented by terms of the Women's Liberation Movement (*male chauvinist pig*) and young radicals (*right on*, *trashing*); in continued borrowings from the Yiddish (*schlep*, *klutz*); and in the slang of rapidly expanding groups of skiers, surfers, sports-car enthusiasts, etc. (*ho-dad*, *low rider*, *baldy*). Changing attitudes are seen in the increasingly familiar slang of homosexuals who, encouraged by the Gay Liberation Movement, have *come out of the closet*, and in the transition from the mid-1960s slang of Black militancy (*honkey*, *the man*, *walk wide*) to terms of Black solidarity and pride (*Afro*, *blood brother*). Thus, time and the human mind find new objects, events, ideas, and attitudes, causing society to fragment into more occupational, recreational, intellectual, social, and personality groups, each adding its terms to the American vocabulary.

Socially, the major continuing trend is in coinages of the seventeen-to-twenty-four age group, because it is both the largest group and the one most eagerly receptive to, or impressed by, new ideas, attitudes, and styles. In the last fifteen years youth has introduced a vast flow of drug words (*grass*, *acid*, *meth*, *speed*, *high*, *upper*, *downer*) into slang. This Supplement now labels such terms *drug culture* rather than *addict's use* because drugs and drug terms are now a larger part of the subculture than *addict's use* would imply.

The most important overall cultural trend as seen in the Supplement is the recent emphasis on the right to be oneself, the freedom of personality which is the *do-your-own-thing*, *let-it-all-hang-out* attitude. This has led people to become *Vietniks*, *swingles* and *veggies*, militant consumers and *ecofreaks*; to join Women's Lib; to wear *Afros*; to stop being *closet queens*. This freedom to be oneself has lead to new sexual freedom, not only for *swingers* or in *skin flicks* and *porn*, but in the marital bed and in living-room conversation. Thus many words for sex acts, parts of the body, and defecation labeled *taboo* in this book are much less proscribed than formerly. Increasingly, women as well as men use these once-completely-taboo words in home and office, and many of the words now appear regularly in weekly newsmagazines, on television talk shows, and in movies. If the trend continues the dictionary label *taboo* may become archaic, because most people will consider few words taboo in their lives or vocabulary.

The Supplement also reflects an increased blurring of the parts of speech. Words entered as adverbs in the original book are now recorded as adjectives (a very *now* thing to do); nouns have become verbs and interjections have become nouns (*hot dog!* is now *hot dogger*).

Finally, slang itself is becoming more acceptable and its use is criticized less by parents and teachers. The gap between standard and slang usage is narrowing, perhaps possibly disappearing. In twenty or thirty years, if this trend continues, perhaps the public and lexicographers will no longer distinguish between slang and standard words, and most words now considered slang will appear in standard dictionaries—making a specific slang collection as this unnecessary, an artifact of a time when social distinctions were made in language.

Many people have contributed to this Supplement, ranging from scholars to uneducated people totally immersed in the worlds of drugs and crime. I would like to thank all of them equally. I am also deeply grateful to the many readers of previous editions of this book who wrote to suggest additions and corrections.

STUART BERG FLEXNER

Note: An asterisk (*) after a word in the Supplement indicates that the word, or other meanings of it, is defined in the original text.

SUPPLEMENT

*by Stuart Berg Flexner, Sheila Brantley,
and Herbert Gilbert*

A

A*   *n.* **1** Amphetamine. **2** LSD; acid. *Drug culture.*

A-bomb*   *n.* A combination of drugs, typically marijuana or hashish and opium, rolled in a wrapper and smoked like a cigarette. *Drug culture.*

A-bone   *n.* A Model A Ford. *Hot-rod use since c1950.* Cf. **T-bone.***

Acapulco gold   A high-grade marijuana grown near Acapulco, Mexico, and having leaves with a golden hue. *Drug culture.*

accommodation collar   An arrest made to fulfill a quota set by a superior police officer, usu. in response to pressure for strong police action against criminals.

ace*   *n.* **1** A hole-in-one. *Golf use.* **2** A single, unaccompanied customer, esp. in a restaurant; a table for one, in a restaurant. 1961: ". . . eating alone at tables for one in a corner, the tables the waiters call aces." Tennessee Williams, *Night of the Iguana,* Act II. **3** A grilled cheese sandwich. *Lunch-counter use.* **4** The academic grade A. *Some student use.* **5** A very close friend; buddy; pal. *Orig. teenage street-gang use.* **6** A marijuana cigarette. *Drug culture.* **7** A man who favors flamboyant, up-to-the-minute clothes, shoes, etc. *Chiefly Negro use. v.t.* To do something perfectly; to accomplish something without errors or mistakes. 1959: "To make a perfect score on a test is to *ace it.*" L. P. Boone, "Gator Slang," *American Speech,* May, 156.

ace buddy   A good friend. 1969: "Look, Paps, you're my ace buddy and all that but I've already told you about Jack, so cool it. . . ." Richard Farina, *Been Down So Long It Looks Like Up To Me* (Dell), 109. *Negro use.*

ace in   **1** To use strategy in getting oneself into a good or profitable situation. **2** To understand.

acid   *n.* = **LSD.**   1974: "We once believed no government agent would take acid because his situation was too schizophrenic for psychedelic truth serum." Stew Albert, "Agents I Have Known," *Crawdaddy,* July, 65.

acid freak = **acid head.**

acid head   acidhead   A habitual user of LSD. *Drug culture.*

acidless trip   A nickname for sensitivity training. *Critics of the movement think that sensitivity training is not a valid method for helping people to understand their own feelings and to communicate closely with others. Rather, participants are considered to be on a self-indulgent emotional "trip," or looking for "instant intimacy," resulting in little permanent social or psychological value. "Acidless trip" is also applied in a more positive sense to encounter groups that have had some success in treating drug addicts.*

acid pad = **shooting gallery.***

acid rock   A form of very loud rock music having a pronounced beat and featuring electronic sound effects. It is often atonal and without a perceptible melody. To the uninitiated the titles and lyrics may be unintelligible. Named after "acid" (LSD), it may be accompanied by blinking colored lights to simulate a psychedelic experience. *Late 1960s use.*

action*   *n.* Sexual intercourse. 1968: "I therefore denounced the idea of conjugal visits as inherently unfair; single prisoners needed and deserved action just as married prisoners did." Eldridge Cleaver, *Soul on Ice,* 6.

A.D.   *n.* A drug addict. *The letters are reversed in order to avoid confusion with "D.A.," abbr. for District Attorney. Drug culture.*

affirm   *adj.* Affirmative.   *n.* An affirmation: an affirmative reply. *Orig. U.S. Air Force use in the Vietnam war.*

African black   A grade of marijuana grown in Africa. *Drug culture.*

Afro   *n.* **1** A natural, sometimes

bushy, hair style worn by many Negroes of both sexes and by some whites with very curly hair. The hair may be fairly short and follow the natural contours of the head or may be quite long, so as to give an exaggerated bouffant effect like that of a large fur cap. **2** A Negro from Africa. *In use since the 1840s.* **3** Any Negro. *adj.* **1** African. **2** Negro.

Afro-Saxon *n.* A Negro who has the life-style and values of the dominant white society. *Some Negro use.* Cf. **Oreo.**

age out (of a drug addict) To reach an age, usu. in the thirties or forties, when drugs no longer have the desired effect, and the user gradually withdraws from them voluntarily. *Drug culture.* Cf. **burning out.**

agfay *n.* Pig Latin euphem. for **fag*** (def. 2).

aggressive *adj.* Very good; wonderful. *Some cool and student use.*

A-head *n.* **1** A frequent user of amphetamines. **2** = **acid head.**

—aholic See Appendix to the Supplement, Suffixes.

airplane* *n.* = **roach clip.**

all-originals scene A gathering, meeting, party, etc., attended by Negroes only. *Negro use.*

amp* *n.* **1** An amplifier, as of a high-fidelity phonograph. **2** An ampoule of a drug. *Drug culture.*

angel* *n.* **1** A misleading image on a radar screen, usually in vague white shadows, and often caused by bird flights, unusual atmospheric conditions, or faults in the radar's electronic circuitry. *Armed Forces use.* **2** A helicopter, esp. one flying near an aircraft carrier to rescue pilots who may crash into the sea during takeoff or landing. 1965: "Any driver being launched or recovered from the carrier is protected by 'angels'— helicopters that hover near bow or stern to snatch him from a ditched plane." N.Y. *Times,* June 1. *Orig. Navy use in the Vietnam war.*

angel dust **1** A powdered form of PCP, a tranquilizer derived from formaldehyde, used in veterinary medicine. It is taken to obtain a high either by being sniffed or by being rolled tightly into a small cigarette and smoked. **2** Synthetic heroin. *Drug culture.*

Angelino **Angeleno** *n.* A resident of Los Angeles. 1973: "If New York is hip city, then Los Angeles must be superhip city, because Angelinos utilize bankruptcy to a greater degree than any other city in the country." J. I. Meyer, *New York,* Sept. 10, 55.

animal* *n.* An athlete. *Student use.*

antifreeze *n.* Heroin. *Drug culture.*

antsy *adj.* Restless; nervous, jittery. 1974: "Although he sometimes gets up-tight, often starts projects and doesn't finish them and gets 'antsy' when he's not working, she describes him as the ideal husband." Ponchitta, *Ebony,* April, 64. *From the earlier expression "to have ants in one's pants."*

Anzac *n.* An Australian or New Zealand soldier; any Australian or New Zealander. *Since W.W.I; an acronym of "Australian and New Zealand Army Corps." Colloq.*

A-OK **A-Okay** **A-O.K.** *adj.* Favorable; perfect. *adv.* Perfectly suitable, agreeable, congenial, very fine; better than just O.K. 1961: " 'A-okay,' as everybody now knows, means all's well, everything functioning perfectly." Omaha *World-Herald,* May 8, 12m/2. *From "A-1"* plus "O.K." Orig. aerospace use, pop. by use in the televised launching of the flight of Alan B. Shepard, Jr., in 1961 as well as by the other first seven U.S. astronauts, to signify that all electronic circuits were functioning properly in a spaceship and that it was ready for launching.* Cf. **go** (def. 1).

ape* *adj.* **1** Frenzied; uncontrolled; wild. *Common student use.* Cf. **go ape.** **2** = **ape shit.**

ape hangers High, swooping handlebars originally made for motorcycles, but now also adapted for bicycles.

ape shit [taboo] **1** Having a strong liking for an object, person, hobby, etc.; obsessed with an idea or goal. **2** = **ape.** *Fairly common student use; often in the expression "go ape."* See **go ape.**

Apple, the *n.* New York City. 1974: "Both groups are symptomatic of young musicians storming into the Apple, abandoning studio and rock bands to play difficult, improvisatory music." Gary Giddins, letter to the editor, *Village Voice,* May 2, 69. *Mostly jazz and rock musician use.* Cf. **Big apple*** (def. 1).

applejack cap A round, usu. bright-colored cap with a wide peak and a pompom on top, worn mostly by young Negro and Puerto Rican men.

A.R. *n.* Armed robbery. *Police use.*

arm [taboo] *n.* The penis. Cf. **Long-arm inspection,* short-arm inspection.***

artsy-craftsy *adj.* Pretentiously and self-consciously artistic; overdone, cute.

1968: "He wanted to shoot it 50 times in different ways and I told him flat out, no. Don't get artsy-craftsy with me. I can't do a big dramatic scene 50 times with poignancy." *TV Guide*, April 4, 32. *In use since the early 1950s.*

ARVN   Arvn   *n.* The Army of the Republic of Vietnam; one of its soldiers. *An acronym pronounced to rhyme with "Marvin." Armed Forces use in Vietnam.*

ASP   *n.* = **WASP.** 1965: " '. . . the correct term is ASP; all Anglo-Saxons are white, so why be redundant?' " New York Mayor John Lindsay, quoted in *Time*, Nov. 12, 31B.

—ass   See Appendix to the Supplement, Suffix Words.

ass-fuck [taboo]   *v.t.* To perform anal intercourse.   *n.* Anal intercourse.

asshole   ass-hole [taboo]   *n.*   **1** = **asshole buddy.** 1963: ". . . me and all the ass-holes—you know—all us neighborhood guys." T. Rubin, *Sweet Daddy*, 8. **2** fool; stupid person. 1965: "Oh, Christ, what ass-holes be Americans." Norman Mailer, *Partisan Review*, Fall, 64.

asshole buddy [taboo]   A very close friend.

ass in a sling* [have, get (one's)] [taboo] To be in trouble or difficulty, esp. to be in the bad graces of one's superior.

ass peddler [taboo]   A prostitute of either sex.

ass-sucker [taboo]   *n.* = **ass-kisser.***

ass-wipe   ass-wiper [taboo]   *n.* Toilet paper or a substitute for it.

attitude   *n.* A resentful, hostile manner, either toward people in general or toward a specific group. *A person who "catches a quick attitude" is one who is easily angered and ready to fight. Mostly black and prison use.*

Augustus Owsley = **Owsley acid.**

Aunt   Jane   A sycophantic Negro woman; a female "Uncle Tom."*

Aunt Jemima = **Aunt Jane.**

Aunt Tom [derog.]   A woman who does not support or is not in sympathy with the women's liberation movement. 1968: "A group of militant ladies are agitating to forbid U.S. newspapers from running separate Male and Female want ads. Borrowing their rhetoric from the Negro civil rights movement, they call the practice segregation by sex, describing it as 'Jane Crow' treatment, and call any ladies who tolerate it 'Aunt Toms.' " *Life*, Dec. 6, 48. *Not common.*

Aztec two-step = **Montezuma's revenge.**

azul   *n.*   **1** A policeman; cop. **2** The police. *From the Sp. = blue, from the color of the uniform. Popularized by American Spanish-speaking youth.*

B

B   *n.* = **bee.***

baby*   *n.* A term of address equivalent to "pal" or "friend." *Since about the mid-1930s, "baby" has often been used without regard to the sex of the person addressed or to the degree of personal relationship, esp. in show business.*

baby blues   The eyes. 1974: "Something tells me, Ferguson, that you're not making me this offer because of my great big baby blues." Cartoon, *New Yorker*, Aug. 19, 47. *Jocular use for eyes of any color.*

baby-sit*   *v.i., v.t.*   **1** To serve as a guide to someone undergoing a psychedelic drug experience. *Drug culture.* See also **guru** (def. 3). **2** To lend support to someone at a time of trouble; to help someone work out personal problems.

baby-sitter*   *n.* A destroyer, esp. one accompanying an aircraft carrier. 1965: ". . . the 'babysitters' (screening destroyers) are close by." N.Y. *Times*, June 1. *Navy use in Vietnam war.*

bachelor mother   **1** A woman who is both unwed and a mother, by choice. **2** A mother who raises her children alone, being separated, divorced, or widowed. Cf. **bachelor girl.***

back-burner   *adj.* Of less importance; secondary. 1974: "The Republicans are floundering, and very worried. [President] Ford is going to go zipping through. The issue of his competence is now a back-burner crisis." E. Drew, *New Yorker*, Mar. 18, 46. *From the image of the back burners of a cook stove where foods are often left to simmer, the front burners being used for foods that require stirring and watching.*

back-door man   A married woman's lover. *Orig. Negro use, often featured in blues songs.*

back off*   To be ejected from or asked to leave a public place, such as a bar.

back time   The unserved part of a prison sentence which a parole violator must serve if brought back to prison. *Prison use.*

back-track *v.i., v.t.* = **boot.**

bad-mouth *v.t.* To criticize severely or persistently. —**er** *n.* A person who bad-mouths others.

bad news* 1 Any unfortunate or unpleasant situation or event. 2 A depressing or undesirable person.

bad nigger A black person who gains the respect of his own people by refusing to accept oppression from whites. 1965: "The best songs were sung at the funerals for the 'bad niggers.' I learned that a bad nigger was a nigger who 'didn't take no shit from nobody' and even the 'crackers' didn't mess with him." Claude Brown, *Manchild in the Promised Land*, 47. *Negro use only.*

bad scene Something unpleasant, esp. an unpleasant experience.

bad talk Pessimistic comments. *Negro and some Southern use.*

bad trip 1 An unpleasant or depressing experience with drugs, esp. LSD. *Drug culture.* 2 Any unpleasant experience.

bag* *n.* 1 One's disposition or recurring mood, behavior pattern, or way of life; that niche to which one has assigned oneself; that which one currently is or feels. *Thus a person can be known for frequently having "angry bags" or "sad bags," may be in a "jazz bag" or "the cool bag" or a musician may be in or play in the "blues bag." Orig. jazz use to designate the school of jazz to which a musician belonged.* 2 One's special or current interest, obsession, talent, enthusiasm, or liking; one's vocation, hobby, habit, or vice; that which one prefers above all else; one's "kick."* 1965: "Bag: What you're hung up on. I'm in a Bogart bag . . ." "A Cursory Glossary to the Off-beat Side of Now," *Harper's Bazaar*, April, 143. 1965: "A bag is one's current hangup or particular interest, talent, thing." *Mademoiselle* editor Carol Nicklaus, quoted in N.Y. *Times*, Dec. 27. *Jazz, beat, student, and teenage use.* 3 An environment or social milieu; a clique or group. 1962: "That fox comes out of a very intellectual bag." W. M. Kelley, "If You're Woke You Dig It," N.Y. *Times Mag.*, May 20, 45. *Orig. Negro use; now common beat and student use.* 4 A portion or addict's supply of narcotics, often wrapped in a paper or small envelope. *Orig. a grain of heroin or an amount of heroin costing $5 or less. Is replacing "deck."* *The usual quantities or sizes of "bags" are: "trey" = $3*

worth (*esp. cocaine and heroin*); "nickel bag" = $5 worth (*esp. marijuana, cocaine, or heroin*); "dime bag" = $10 worth (*esp. marijuana, cocaine, or heroin*); "half load" = fifteen $3 "bags" (*esp. cocaine and heroin*); and "bundle" = twenty-five $5 "bags" (*esp. cocaine and heroin*). *Prices indicate the cost to the addict. Drug culture.* *v.i.* To pursue one's own pleasure or gratification above all else; to do as one pleases; to indulge in a vice, such as drug addiction; to act amorally. *Mainly Negro use.* *v.t.* 1 To be absent from; quit. 2 To resign oneself to a loss, failure, etc.; to fail, ruin, lose, or be defeated at or by something. *Student use since c1960.* —**ged.** *adj.* Drunk. —**gies** *n. pl.* 1 A pair of loose-fitting boxer-type men's swimming trunks. 1963: "To all, 'baggies' are the loose-legged boxer swim trunks worn by the boys." "Surf's Up," *Time*, Aug. 9, 49. *Surfer use.* 2 Full trousers with very wide cuffs, popular with students and others in the early 1970s and resembling the styles of the 1930s.

bag ass [taboo] To leave hurriedly; to get out; to hurry up. *Orig. Navy use.*

bag job A burglary; specif., an illegal search or seizure of secret or personal documents by government agents presumably to secure evidence of espionage or other threats to the national security, but often to discredit someone. 1973: "They [the logs of telephone taps on newsmen and NSC staff] finally wound up in the comparative security of John Ehrlichman's safe at the White House. Hoover's rage, when in July 1971 he found out that someone had done a *bag job* (i.e. burgled) his precious files, was apparently worth seeing." McCrystal et al., *Watergate*, 50.

bag lady **bag woman** 1 A woman who wanders about the streets collecting discarded objects and carrying them home in shopping bags. 1974: "A bag lady whose tiny room was crammed with garbage." N.Y. *Post*, Sept. 27, 3. 2 A homeless woman, often elderly, who lives in parks, train and bus stations, or any place that offers some shelter, and who carries her worldly possessions in shopping bags. 3 The female equivalent of **bagman.***

bagman* *n.* A person who sells drugs; a pusher. *Drug culture.*

baldy **baldie*** *n.* A worn automobile tire having little or no tread left.

ball* [taboo] *v.i., v.t.* 1 To have

sexual intercourse (with). 1971: "It may be that you are being balled every single day and morning for weeks on end and you are so sexualized, so turned on and so aware of men's bodies. . . ." *Sexual Behavior*, Oct., 31. **2** To introduce cocaine or other stimulants into the body via the genitalia. *Drug culture.*

ball game **1** A situation or condition. 1973: "No, I don't believe the European economy must follow the U.S. into a depression. It is no longer, as you say, the same ball game." *Forbes*, July 1, 36. **2** A competition. 1970: "At the half time it's NBC ahead in the network ratings ball game on every count—NBC says." Richard Doan, *TV Guide*, Jan. 3, A-1. **3** A center of interest or activity. 1969: "One key adviser called the Liberal party nomination 'the ball game,' in many ways.'" *N.Y. Times*, April 12, 1.

balloon* *n.* The common toy balloon used as a receptacle for heroin. *Drug culture.*

ball park Approximation in quantity, degree, quality, etc. *An estimate "within the ball park" is within acceptable limits, or is close to what is desired or expected.*

ball-park *adj.* Approximate, rough; inexact, but close enough to suit a particular purpose. *Usu. descriptive of a guess or estimate.*

balls* [taboo] *n. pl.* Boldness; nerve; courage. 1968: "They have balls but not soul." Richard Goldstein, *Village Voice*, June 20, 30.

ballsy [taboo] *adj.* Courageous; bold; nervy. 1967: ". . . you need balls to slap a [electronic] bug on someone. It's a very ballsy thing to do." William Tell, *True*, Feb., 54. **—iness** *n.* Courage; guts.

ball wracker [taboo] = **ball-buster.***

bam *n.* A mixture of a depressant and a stimulant, esp. of a barbiturate and an amphetamine. *From b(arbiturate) + a(mphetamine). Drug culture.*

bamboo curtain = **iron curtain,*** as applied to the Chinese People's Republic.

bananas *adj.* **1** Crazy; insane. **2** Wildly excited. *Usu. in expression "go bananas."*

band-aid *adj.* Serving to patch up or keep together temporarily. *n.* A temporary or stopgap measure. *From the trade name "Band-Aid," a small adhesive-backed bandage.*

B and D **B/D** Bondage and discipline. 1974: "Real-life S/M [sado-masochism] activity, unlike the clichés

of S/M fiction, rarely is bizarre or extreme; most of it involves biting, hitting, slapping, and the like, rather than heavy B and D (bondage and discipline)." M. Hunt, *Playboy*, Mar., 183.

bandit* *n.* **1** Any enemy. **2** Fig., an unsolved problem or anything that blocks or hinders attainment of a goal. *From orig. use by W.W. II officers responsible for designing and testing new planes, rockets, electronic devices, etc. Not common.* **3** An aggressive homosexual who often resorts to violence. *Prison use.*

banger* *n.* A cylinder in an automobile engine. 1965: "*Four-banger* four cylinder engine." Tom Medley, *Hot Rod Jargon. Always preceded by a number. Hot-rod use.*

bankable *adj.* Worth money, serving as collateral, as the use of a name of a well-known or successful person whose support of, or participation in, a project insures its success. 1968: "A bankable actor is one with whose name a producer can raise enough money to make a film." *Look*, Aug. 6, 68.

barber chair The adjustable seat, equipped with many electronic circuits, breathing apparatus, etc., used by an astronaut in a spacecraft. *Aerospace use.*

Barbie Doll A typical all-American conformist, esp. a "WASP"; a dehumanized person. 1972: "Our Barbie Doll president, with his Barbie doll wife and his box full of Barbie doll children is also America's answer to the monstrous Mr. Hyde." Hunter S. Thompson, reprinted in *Rolling Stone*, Sept. 12, 1974, 39. 1973: "The present Gigi [in Lerner and Lowe's *Gigi*], Karen Wolfe, is a Barbie doll who has been programmed to sing, dance, and fall in love . . ." *Time*, Nov. 26, 79. *From the trade name for a widely advertised, very popular, teenaged, blue-eyed, blond plastic doll for little girls.*

barbs *n. pl.* Barbiturates. *Drug culture.*

barhop bar hop = **joint hop.***

barn *n.* Any summer theater in a rural district, whether an actual barn, an impromptu theater, or a well-equipped legitimate theater.

barrel, in the Fired from a job or in danger of being fired. 1973: "The first guy who blows the assignment is said to be 'in the barrel.'" *Sat. Rev.*, Mar., 1.

barry *n.* A baritone saxophone. *Some musician use; from "baritone."*

baseball Annie A young female fan of a baseball team. 1973: "Some players have come here with their wives, a dangerous practice; the 'baseball Annies' of Phoenix, a breed of minor league groupies, are a fairly comely lot and a number of players have dallied with them from time to time." *Wall Street Journal*, Aug. 30, 8. *Baseball use.* Cf. **groupie.**

basket* *n.* **1** [taboo] The male genitalia, esp. when prominently displayed through tight pants. *Formerly "basket" referred only to the scrotum. Homosexual use.* **2** A bribe given to a hiring boss to assure oneself of being hired. *Orig. Italian-American use.*

Basra belly Diarrhea. *Used by travelers in the Middle East.*

bazoom *n.* The female breasts. *A jocular mispronunciation of "bosom."*

bazoongies *n. pl.* Breasts, esp. large, shapely breasts. *1960s and 1970s student use.*

B.C. Birth control.

beach bunny An attractive girl who may or may not surf, but spends much time with surfers. *Surfer use.* Cf. **bunny.**

beads, the *n.* Fate; destiny. 1963: ". . . fate, or whatever else you called it: 'the beads.' " J. Rechy, *City of Night*, 356.

bean bag A small canvas bag filled with bird-shot, sand, or a similar material, fired from a rifle and used as a missile to drive rioters back without severely wounding or killing them. 1970: "Another refinement has been added to the nation's riot-control arsenal: the bean bag. . . . It emits from the rifle muzzle at 120mph., expands to 4.5 inches in diameter, and socks with the impact of a lead hamburger." John Reedy, *Commonweal*, Sept. 18, 450.

bear* *n.* **1** A capsule containing a narcotic drug. *Drug culture.* **2** A difficult course. *Some student use.*

beard* *n.* **1** A bearded man; also called "beardie." **2** One who places a bet for another, to conceal the identity of the real bettor.

beatle *n.* = **beetle** (defs. 1, 2).

beat off [taboo] To masturbate. *Male teenage use.*

beat the meat [taboo] = **beat the dummy.***

beautiful *interj.* That's good! That's fine! *An expression of approval.*

beautiful people People of the international social set; the "jet set."

beaver* [taboo] *n.* The female genitals. So-called because the triangle of pubic hair resembles the "beaver" beard.

beaver-shooter *n.* A man obsessed with looking at female genitals. 1970: "A beaver shooter is, at bottom, a Peeping Tom. . . . I've seen guys chin themselves on transoms, drill holes in doors, even shove a mirror under a door." Jim Bouton, *Ball Four* (World), 36.

beaver shot [taboo] **1** A photograph showing the pudenda, esp. one revealing the vagina. **2 spread beaver.**

bee* *n.* A quantity of a drug sufficient to fill a penny match box: a unit of measurement used in selling narcotics. *Drug culture.*

Beeb *n.* The B.B.C., or British Broadcasting Corporation. *Chiefly Brit. use.*

beef* *n.* A popular or attractive girl. 1966: "A real popular girl is 'my beef, my woman, a nice chick'. . . ." "Teens," by June Gray, Dayton (Ohio) *News*, Jan. 16, 4. *Teenage use. Not common.*

beefcakery *n.* Photography displaying the male physique, now often completely nude.

beerbust beerburst *n.* A beer party. 1962: "It was supposed to be a party— a beerburst. . . . Unfortunately, the beer was hot. . . ." James Jones, *The Thin Red Line*, 428.

be-in *n.* A large, usu. peaceable gathering of young people, esp. hippies, in which they act freely and spontaneously. 1967: "The 'Be-in' was organized two weeks ago, after a San Francisco 'Be-in' attracted more than 100,000 persons on Jan. 14. . . ." Bernard Weintraub, N.Y. *Times*, March 27, 24. *Late 1960s hippie and student use.*

bells *n.pl.* Bell-bottom trousers.

belly stand belly platform = bally stand.*

benny* *n.* Intoxication as a result of using Benzedrine, a trade name for an amphetamine. *Drug culture.*

bent* *adj.* **1** Under the influence of drugs or alcohol. **2** Homosexual. *So-called because a homosexual is not "straight."**

bent out of shape = bent (def. 1).

bet [one's] ass [taboo] Certainly. *Based on the old expression "bet your boots."*

bevels *n.pl.* A pair of crooked dice with some of the edges beveled to influence the roll.

bi *n., adj.* Bisexual.

Bible-banger *n.* A strait-laced Protestant, esp. a Fundamentalist. 1973: "If they show a so-called adult movie, they cut it to shreds first, to ensure that it doesn't offend some Bible-banger in Mississippi." *Playboy*, Dec., 94.

bicho [taboo]   *n.* The penis. *From the Sp.*

Big*   *adj.* An admiring or affectionate epithet used with proper names in direct address, generally among males. 1964: ". . . at any number of schools, a person may be greeted as *Big Dan*, or *Big Dave*, or *Big Joe*, and so on, depending on his name. . . ." L. Poston, "Some Problems in the Study of Campus Slang," *American Speech*, May, 119. *Widespread student use.*

big-ass   bigass [taboo]   *adj.* **1** Large; pretentiously big. 1965: "Abraham opened the door of his bigass Cadillac. . . ." H. Selby, Jr., *Last Exit to Brooklyn*, 226. **2** Pretentious or extreme.

big bloke = bloke.

Big C   Cancer. 1973: "Her father evidently has cancer, bone cancer. . . . Foumi's brother Yataka had called a Japanese doctor here. He suggested it all sounded like Big C." Josh Greenfeld, *A Child Called Noah* (Warner), 51. *Euphem.*

big D = LSD.   *Drug culture.*

Big Enchilada   big enchilada   The head man; chief of operations; boss. 1974: "The Big Enchilada is tied up with the Chief Honcho at the moment, but the Little Enchilada can see you now." Cartoon caption, *New Yorker*, June 24, 27. *Used in the Watergate tapes by H. R. Haldeman to describe President Nixon's Attorney General John Mitchell.*

big H   Heroin. *Drug culture.*

Big Harry   Heroin. *Drug culture.*

big John*   A policeman or (collectively) the police. *Drug culture.*

big nickel   The sum of $5,000, esp. as a wager. *Orig. gambling use.* Cf. **small nickel.**

big one*   The sum of $1,000, esp. as a wager. *Orig. gambling use.*

bigs   *n.pl.* The major leagues. *Baseball use.*

big wienie = top dog.* *Some hot-rod and student use.*

bill*   *n.* **= scissorbill*** (defs. 1–3). *Mainly I.W.W. use. Obs.*

binders   *n.pl.* The brakes on an automobile. *Some police, hot-rod, and student use.*

bio   *n.* A biography, esp. a very brief one for a yearbook, directory, publicity release, etc. 1970: "By now Jenny had read my bio in the program. I made triple sure that Vic Claman, the manager, saw that she got one." Erich Segal, *Love Story*, 7.

bird*   *n.* **1** Any airplane. **2** A girl friend, steady date, or fiancée. *Orig. Negro use, some student use since c1962.* **3** [taboo] The middle finger when raised straight up, meaning "fuck you." *Usu. in the phrase* "give someone the bird." **4** A helicopter. 1972: " 'I ask my crew maintenance chief if the bird is ready,' he explained. 'If he says it is, I go. . . .' " Drew Middleton, N.Y. *Times*, Dec. 24, 2. *Short for* "whirly-bird." *

bird circuit   A tour of gay bars; the circuit of such bars across the country. *Homosexual use.*

bird dog*   A small-time bettor who frequents the company of professional gamblers to learn which way they are betting on sporting events in order to bet the same way. *Gambling use.*

birdfarm   *n.* An aircraft carrier. 1965: "The days are gone when a carrier was called a flattop. The craft is now a 'birdfarm.' " N.Y. *Times*, June 1. *Navy use in Vietnam war.* Cf. **bird** (def. 1).

bird's eye   A small package containing a narcotic drug. *Drug culture.*

birk   *n.* A stupid or slow-thinking person. *Some teenage use.*

bitch*   *n.* **1** A pleasant or remarkable thing or event. *Often used as an expression of approval:* "That's a bitch!" = "That's fine!" **2** A male homosexual, esp. one who is viciously gossipy, sarcastic, etc. **—ing**   *adj.* Excellent; very good; fine.

bite the bullet   To face a painful or unpleasant situation with fortitude. 1968: "When President Johnson asked Congress today to 'bite the bullet' and pass a tax increase, he was referring to an old practice used . . . to perform painful operations on soldiers in the field. . . . The wounded man would be given a bullet to hold between his teeth and asked to bite it and take his mind off the pain." N.Y. *Times*, May 4, 17.

black camp   A prison in which most of the inmates are Negroes. *Prison use.*

black money = 1 skim. *Gambling use.* **2** Funds that nave been illegally obtained, as by graft by a politician, which must be "laundered" into apparently legitimate capital before being spent. See **launder.** Cf. **white money.**

black operator   A secret agent. 1973: "At the Central Intelligence Agency, he [Howard Hunt] was a 'black operator' who never quite made it." N.Y. *Times Mag.*, June 3, 11.

blackshoe   *n.* Any member of the crew of an aircraft carrier whose duty is concerned with sailing and servicing the carrier; a sailor on an aircraft carrier, rather than a member of the air crew. 1965: ". . . the 'black-shoes' . . . sail and service the carrier." *N.Y. Times,* June 1. *Navy use.* Cf. **snipe.**

blade* *n.* A knife considered as a weapon, esp. a "switchblade."* *Orig. Negro and teenage street-gang use.*

blah* *adj.* Uncomfortable or weary. 1974: ". . . fever, chills, sore throat, swollen glands, abdominal pain, headache, rash, stiff neck, and an allover 'blah' feeling." Morris Fishbein, M.D., *Family Health,* Feb., 14. **—s, the** *n.* A state of boredom, weariness, or malaise. 1969: "The radicals are suffering from a case of the blahs, the liberals are frustrated and there seems to be no movement in any direction except back toward oneself." Joseph McBride, *Life,* Dec. 12, 40.

blank *n.* **1** Nothing; no result. See **draw a blank.* 2** A weakened or diluted narcotic drug, or a non-narcotic powder substance sold as a narcotic drug. *Drug culture.*

blast* *v.t.* To use or take narcotics. 1958: "I spotted this stud in an opium den./ . . . He said I was ripe/To start blasting opium/From a water pipe." H. Braddy, "Anonymous Verses." *Drug culture. v.i.* To accelerate, drive very fast, or pass another car.

blasting party = blast party.*

blaxploitation *n.* The commercial exploitation and utilization of interest in Negroes, esp. in films. 1974: "With few exceptions most of the blaxploitation films following in the wake of 'Shaft' and 'Superfly' have been shoddy ripoffs of the very audience that supports them with unquestioning enthusiasm." George Morris, *Village Voice,* July 18, 69.

bleeding heart A person regarded as being excessively or ostentatiously soft-hearted. *Prob. a fig. extension of a garden plant of the genus* Dicentra, *which has clusters of deep pink or reddish drooping heart-shaped flowers. Disparaging use.*

blind* *adj.* Uncircumcised. *Homosexual use.*

blip* *n.* One of the luminous signals appearing on a radar screen. 1967: "Birds can cause blips on radar screens, *i.e.,* flash alarms affecting our aerial sentry system." Philip Wagner, *Harper's,* April, 82. *v.t.* To censor a word or remark on a television or radio program by automatically erasing it from the tape. 1968: "The program, which is

taped only a few hours before it is televised, always has a censor in attendance. Occasionally Mr. Carson's lines are 'blipped.'" N.Y. *Times,* April 29, 86.

blissed out In a state of extreme spiritual exaltation or bliss. 1973: "At this very moment, in fact, a 'soul rush' of blissed-out young pilgrims is heading for the Western mecca of The Most Important Movement in the History of Mankind." Daniel St. Albin Greene, "A Little Prophet, A Bit of Profit," *National Observer,* Nov. 3, 1.

blitzed *adj.* Drunk.

blivit *n.* Anything unnecessary, confused, or annoying. *Lit. defined as "10 pounds of shit in a 5-pound bag." Orig. W.W.II Army use. The word is seldom heard except when the speaker uses it in order to define it; hence the word is actually a joke.*

blockbust *v.t.* To persuade white property owners to sell their homes quickly and often below true value for fear that Negroes will move into the area. **—er** *n.* **1** A real estate agent or agency who practices blockbusting. **2** A great success. 1973: "'The Godfather' . . . proved for the first time that a gangster movie can be a box-office blockbuster in the class of 'The Sound of Music.'" *Sat. Rev.: Art,* Jan., 46.

bloke* *n.* Cocaine. *Drug culture.*

blood* *n.* A fellow Negro. 1973: ". . . An' these cats they threw me in with . . . well, we was all bloods. . . ." D. Evans, *Black World,* April, 66. *Prob. short for "blood brother." Negro use.*

blood brother **1** A fellow member of one's racial, religious, national, ethnic, or social group. **2** A fellow Negro. *Negro use only; the most common use since c1962.*

blow* *n.* An inhalation of heroin or cocaine. *Drug culture. v.t.* **1** To smoke marijuana. **2** To inhale a narcotic drug. *Drug culture.* **—er** *n.* A supercharger for an automobile engine. *Hot-rod use.* **—n** *adj.* (of a car engine) equipped with or using a supercharger. *Hot-rod use.*

blow a fix To lose part or all of an injected narcotic by missing the vein, the drug being thus diffused in the tissues. *Drug culture.*

blow a stick (hay,* jive,* pot,* tea*) To smoke marijuana. *Drug culture.*

blow [someone] away To impress someone greatly. 1974: "I saw him at a concert in L.A. and asked if he'd come down and put some slide on 'Good Day in Hell,' but with every take he just blew us all away." David Rensin, "Rollin' & Tumblin': The Eagles Have Stopped Takin' It Easy," *Crawdaddy*, July, 29.

blow [one's] cool   1 To lose one's composure; to release pent-up feelings, esp. by shouting, weeping, laughing, etc. **2** To become flustered, esp. in a social situation; to become excited or angry. See **cool*** (def. *adj.* 1, 2).

blow [one's] cover   To have one's hiding place or true identity revealed so as to place one in a situation of peril or embarrassment. 1974: "Somewhere in the Hollywood Hills they abandoned both the van and Matthews. The problem was that with their cover blown they had nowhere to go—and it may never be known how the SLA decided to take refuge in the house on 54th St." *Newsweek*, May 27, 21.

blow it out [taboo]   An expression of anger or disbelief at another's lies, exaggerations, or optimism. *Fig., in ref. to another's statement that is not worthy of words but should have been expressed by "blowing it out your asshole." Armed Forces use since W.W.II. Many variations, including the Navy's "blow it out your barracks bag," and the Air Force's euphem. "blow it out your tailpipe," etc.*

blow [one's] mind   1 To lose one's composure; lose control of oneself; esp. to express strong feelings or emotions or to release pent-up feelings; specif. to scream or shout in joy, anger, fear, etc. **2** To be deeply and emotionally stirred or impressed; to be overwhelmed with feeling; esp. to be overwhelmed by a sincere statement, loving gesture, musical performance, etc. *Jazz, Negro, beat, and student use.* See **blow [one's] top.***

blown out   High on drugs. *Drug culture.*

B.L.T.   A bacon-lettuce-and-tomato sandwich. *Lunch-counter use.*

bluebird   *n.* A policeman. *Some Negro use.*

blue box   An illegal electronic device applied to a telephone to permit a caller to bypass charges when making long-distance calls. 1974: "Rock musician Ike Turner and three other persons have been arrested in connection with the alleged use of an electronic 'blue box' to avoid telephone tolls." *Arizona Wildcat*, March 28, 12.

blue cheer = **LSD**. *Drug culture.*

bluecoat   *n.* A policeman. 1932: "And he told the damn bluecoat that if he would take off the star, he'd punch him

all over the corner." J. T. Farrell, *Young Lonigan*, 95.

blue-devil = **blue heaven**. *Drug culture.*

blue flags = **LSD**. *Drug culture.*

blue flick = **blue movie**.

bluegrass   *n.* Country music, esp. of the southern U.S., played at a very fast tempo and without the use of amplifiers. *A typical Bluegrass band includes a mandolin, a five-string banjo, a guitar, a violin, and a string bass. The instrumental numbers emphasize the mandolin, banjo, and violin, while the guitar and the string bass provide the "bottom," or bass. The songs are mainly of a ballad nature, sometimes based on old traditional themes, sometimes on modern events and situations. The term "Bluegrass" came into wide vogue in the mid-1960s when such country music, long known in the South, became very much of an "in thing" among young, sophisticated people. Named after the Bluegrass State, Kentucky, and helped to nationwide popularity by the Bluegrass Boys, a band founded by Bill Monroe and well-known in the 1940s and 1950s.*

blue heaven   A capsule of Amytal, trade name for a type of barbiturate. *From the color of the capsule. Drug culture.*

blue movie   A pornographic motion picture.

blue velvet   A mixture of paregoric, which contains opium and Pyribenzamine, a trade name for an antihistamine, to be injected. *Drug culture.*

bobtail*   *n.* A truck or a tractor without its semi-trailer. *Some trucker use.*

bod   *n.* **1** A person. *Orig. Brit. use. Now some U.S. student use.* **2** the body; physique.

body-shake = **skin-search**.

Bogners   *n.pl.* A pair of ski pants. *From the trade name "Bogner's," makers of ski clothing. Skier use.*

bogue*   *adj.* In need of narcotics; suffering from a craving for narcotics. 1960: " 'I'm bogue, but I ain't gonna indulge. I'm trying to kick [the habit].' " C. Cooper, *The Scene*, 13. *Drug culture.*

boiler room   *n.* = **bucket shop.*** *Orig. stock market use.*

bolter   *v.i.* To miss the arresting cables while attempting to land an airplane on an aircraft carrier. 1965: "The air officer was talking about the pilot . . . of an incoming F-4 intercepter who had missed the arresting cables on the flight deck (boltered)." *N.Y. Times*, June 1. *Navy use in Vietnam war.*

bomb*   *n.* **1** Anything that causes or

is a sudden success or failure. *Thus a "bomb" may be either a home-run or a strike-out in baseball, and in the entertainment world an instantaneously successful song, play, performance, etc., or one that is a complete failure.* **2** A great amount of money. *v.t.* **1** To do something extremely well, as to write a good examination. **2** To do something very poorly; usu., to fail an examination. *Mainly student use.* **—ed** *adj.* Drunk. *Common student use.*

bombed out   Very high on narcotics. *Drug culture.*

bombita   *n.* Any amphetamine pill or capsule used by addicts. *From the Sp. = "little bomb." Drug culture.*

bongoed   *adj.* Drunk.

bonkers   *adj.* Crazy; mad. 1973: "A powerhouse team like the Reds is liable to go bonkers losing a pennant to the Mets." Larry Merchant, N.Y. *Post,* Oct. 9. *Usu. in phrase "go bonkers." Orig. Brit. use.*

boo*   *n.* Marijuana.

boob*   *n.* A mistake; blunder.

boob tube   A television set. Cf. **tube, the.**

boodle*   *v.i.* = **neck*** (def. 2). *Collegiate use c1915.*

boogie*   *v.i.* To move the body in time to rock-and-roll music. 1974: "During the 'Sunshine Medley,' Amanda boogies and bangs a tambourine while her 39 sisters sit on steps and force shattered smiles." Greg Mitchell, "Inside Miss U.S.A.," *Crawdaddy,* Sept., 62.

boogie*   **booger**   *n.* See **bugger** (def. 1).

boondagger   *n.* A tough woman or an aggressive female homosexual. 1972: ". . . Some of the girls didn't like that, especially the boondaggers, you know, like bulls that come offa the street that they dress in men's clothes and all that, you know, hard. They may break his arm or somethin' like that. . . ." Inmate of the Bedford Hills Correctional Facility, N.Y., quoted in L. Berry, *Prison,* 24. Cf. **bulldyke.***

boonie   **booney**   *n.* Any remote, unpopulated area; "boondocks." *From* **boondocks.*** *Usu. in the expression "the boonies."*

boot*   *v.i., v.t.* To inject a narcotic gradually into a vein, by drawing blood mixed with the drug repeatedly back into the syringe, and discharging the mixture again into the vein, to heighten the drug's initial effect. 1965: ". . . he squeezed in a few drops, let it back up

into the eyedropper again, squeezed in a little more, let it back up, squeezed in more, and continued the in-and-out process until the fluid in the dropper was dark red with blood. Then he shot it all in and withdrew the needle. The technique, known as 'booting,' is believed to prolong the drug's initial effect." James Mills, "We Are All Animals," *Reader's Digest,* June, 230. *Drug culture. n.* A Negro. *Negro use.* **—s**   **1** A shoeshine boy. → **2** A male Negro. *Archaic. Because Negroes were often shoeshine boys.*

boot strapper   One who achieves success by his own efforts. 1974: ". . . southeastern Queens, traditionally a haven for black 'boot strappers'—teachers, city workers, professionals, businessmen who have to struggle to make it." George Vecsey, N.Y. *Times,* Feb. 21, 37. *From the old expression "lift (or raise) oneself by the (or one's own) boot straps."*

bop cap = **applejack cap.**

bop off   To leave; to depart. *Some student use; not common.*

boss*   *n.* Anyone or anything thought to be the most wonderful, exciting, or best in a specific field of endeavor. *adj.* **1** Major; best; best known. *Usu. applied to an entertainer or professional athlete to indicate his superiority in his field.* **2** Excellent; wonderful; fine. 1965: "Daddy-O, who was 'in the groove' back in the class of '40 . . . discovers that 'wig' and 'boss' have come to mean what he used to call 'great' . . ." N.Y. *Times,* Dec. 27. *Orig. Negro and jazz musician use; teenage use since c1960.*

bosshead   *n.* The boss, foreman, or head of a project or work detail.

boss trick = **champagne trick.**

B.O.T.   Balance of time. *The balance remaining of an original sentence which a parole violator must serve. Prison use.*

bottle, the*   *n.* Prostitution, esp. male prostitution. *Probably from the Cockney rhyming sl. "bottle and glass" = "ass."*

bottom-end   *n.* The crankshaft, main bearings, and connecting rod bearings of an automobile engine. *Hot-rod use.*

bottomless   *adj.* **1** Of or pertaining to a female entertainer or waitress who works nude, both without a "top" to cover her breasts or a "bottom" to cover the rest of her. **2** Of or pertaining to a bar or restaurant employing such entertainers or waitresses. *Based on "topless."* See **topless.**

bottom line   **1** The figure representing profit or loss (usu. net). → **2** The result of any computation, esp. one expressed in dollars, as total cost. **3** Any important decision, judgment, conclusion, etc. **4** A fundamental or crucial point of fact; the heart of the matter. **5** A crucial or turning point in the course of events; a critical moment or development. *Orig. accounting use, from its customary position on statements.*

bottom out   To get as bad or as low as possible, after which there can be only a turn for the better. 1973: "Obviously, there is a growing belief that the stock market has finally bottomed out after this year's disastrous decline. . . ." Charles Strand, N.Y. *Post*, July 12, 53. "Still shocked by the Cox firing and the 18-minute gap in a Watergate tape, Republicans have grown wary indeed. 'If it ever bottoms out, we might be all right,' says Kansas' Dole. 'But the coconuts keep dropping.' " *Time*, Dec. 17, 16.

bottoms   *n.pl.* A pair of shoes; shoes. *Now replaced by "ends."*

bottom woman   The woman in a pimp's stable of prostitutes who is the favorite and the most dependable. *Prostitute use.*

bounce off [someone]   To try out a new idea on another person to get his reaction or opinion; also, to bandy about concepts or impressions. 1974: "But Paul [McCartney] is very much a team-work person. He doesn't like working just on his own. He still gets nervous. He likes working with people, bouncing off people and having them bounce off him." Paul Gambaccini, *Rolling Stone*, Jan. 31, 34.

box*   *n.* **1** An unfeeling, stupid person; a "square."* *Some far-out use since c1960; an extension of "square."* **2** A radio.   —**ed**   *adj.* **1** Drunk. *Common student use.* **2** In jail.

box office   Having great popular appeal; predictably successful (said of actors, directors, writers, plays, films, etc.). 1964: "This is the terrible sort of depressing thing people do, just because you're no longer box office. . . ." Roddy McDowall, quoted by Gerald Nachman, New York *Post*, Nov. 29, 31. *Theatrical use.*

boy*   *n.* Heroin. 1960: "But now *he* had the boy; he could lie around up in his crib . . . drugged to the verge of insensibility. . . ." C. Cooper, *The Scene*, 12. *Drug culture.* Cf. **girl** (def. 2).

braburner [derog.]   *n.* A very militant feminist. 1973: "The media decided to henceforth label feminists as 'braburners'—a term that made the movement pretty darn mad." *Esquire*, July, 76. *From the supposed practice of burning brassieres in public as a protest against the use of women as sex objects.*

brain drain   A significant loss of intellectuals or professionals from a country, locality, organization, etc., because of their dissatisfaction or the expectation of betterment elsewhere. *Orig. Brit. use during the period of austerity following W.W.II.*

—**break**   See Appendix to the Supplement, Suffix Words.

break [one's] **balls** [taboo]   **1** To be annoying to or demanding of one; to be hard to do or accomplish; to cause one to suffer or to make one extremely uncomfortable. 1965: ". . . he thought she was making a reference to the weather and said, 'God, yes, this heat is breaking my balls.' " Tennessee Williams, "Mama's Old Stucco House," *Esquire*, Jan., 87. **2** To try very hard. Cf. **ball-breaker**.*

break luck   To succeed in getting the first customer of the day (or night). *Prostitute use.*

break out the jams = **kick out the jams.**

break up*   To laugh or cause to laugh uncontrollably. 1967: "As the struggling elder comics who hang out there tell it, they 'break up' every audience they play to and they don't know what it is . . . to bomb." Eugene Boe, *Playbill*, Nov., 15.

breastworks   *n.pl.* The female breasts considered as sexual objects.

brew   *n.* Beer; a glass, bottle, or can of beer.

brick*   *n.* A kilogram (2.2 pounds) of tightly packed marijuana.

brickyard   *n.* The Indianapolis, Ind., Speedway. *Automobile racing use.*

bright*   *n.* A light-complexioned Negro or a mulatto. *Negro use.*

bringdown   bring down*   *n.* A critical or cutting remark; that which depresses one or deflates one's ego. Cf. **putdown**.

bring [someone] **down**   To depress; sadden. 1965: "Don't Bring me Down: Don't drug me. Don't give me any grief." "A Cursory Glossary to the Offbeat Side of Now," *Harper's Bazaar*, April, 143. *Common jazz musician use since c1958, student use since c1960.*

bring up   To vomit; specif. to vomit food or drink that has disagreed with one.

bring up to speed   To brief; to give necessary facts, information, etc., to someone before a meeting, hearing, etc. *Perhaps from an early radio broadcasting practice of warming up a phonograph's turntable in advance to avoid having it run too slowly at the beginning of a record. Some Watergate use.*

bro'   *n.* A form of address equivalent to "pal" or "friend," etc., but not as common as "man" or "baby." *Short for "brother." Orig. Negro use but now also some student use.*

brodie   Brodie*   A flop, complete fiasco, or failure.

brother*   *n.* A male Negro; a "blood brother." *Negro use only. Cf.* **sister.**

brown* [taboo]   *v.i., v.t.* To have, permit, or prefer heterosexual anal intercourse.

brown-bagger   *n.* A married man, esp. a white-collar worker. *Fig., one who carries his lunch to work in a brown paper bag.*

brown hole [taboo]   *v.i., v.t.* = **brown.**

Brownie point   Credit gained, esp. by obsequious behavior and flattering one's superiors. *From "Brownie," a junior girl scout in ref. to points earned for certain achievements.*

brutal   *adj.* Very good, exceptional, great. *Mainly student use.*

B-side   *n.* = **flip side.***

B.T.   B   and   T   A bacon-and-tomato sandwich. *Lunch-counter use.*

bubblegum   *adj.* Appealing to young adolescents and pre-teenagers; specif., pertaining to a type of rock music with simple lyrics that appeals to this age group.   *n.* Rock music for young adolescents and pre-adolescents.   **—er**   *n.* A young adolescent or pre-adolescent. *From the widespread use of bubblegum by youngsters in this age group.*

buck*   *n.* The sum of $100, esp. a wager. *Orig. gambling use.*

buckwheater   *n.* A beginner, novice, or greenhorn.* *Mainly lumberjack use.*

buddy-buddy*   *adj.* Very friendly. 1965: "He is not buddy-buddy . . . although he . . . insisted that the photographers take their pictures together . . . ." Irwin Shaw, "Tittle Fading Back . . ." *Esquire*, Jan., 34.

buddy store   A military tanker refueling ship or plane, or a fuel supply base. *Air Force and Navy use in Vietnam.*

budge   *n.* Liquor; whiskey. 1874: "Like a sober old judge I'd lave [sic] off the budge. . . ." "I'll Never Get Drunk Any More," (song) in *Musical Americana,*

No. 5059, Microsurance, Inc., Philadelphia. [Quoted in Ruth Keen, "A Word Study of *Musical Americana,*" *American Speech,* May 1965, 128.] *Obs.*

buff*   *adj.* Naked.

bug*   *n.* **1** A joker in a deck of playing cards; any wild card in a poker game. **2** A girl. 1965: ". . . boys prowl for *bugs.*" *Time,* Jan. 1, 75. *Student use.* **3** A small, two-man vehicle designed for exploration of the lunar surface. 1962: "From this vehicle [an Apollo spacecraft], a small two-man lunar excursion vehicle commonly known as the 'bug' would be detached from the mother craft. . . ." N.Y. *Times,* July 15, E7/8. *Aerospace use.*

bugger*   *n.* **1** A piece of solidified mucus picked or blown from the nose. Also **booger, boogie. 2** An expert in electronic eavesdropping. 1974: ". . . 'the best bugger on the West Coast' ought to be as anonymous as possible." Jay Cocks, *Time,* April 16, 90.

buggy whip   **1** A long radio antenna on an automobile. **2** A transmitter antenna on a police car.

bughouse*   *adj.* Insane; crazy.

bull* [taboo]   *n.* A "bulldyke."*

bull-dagger [taboo]   *n.* = **bulldyke.***

bullhead*   *n.* A railroad conductor. *Some railroad use.*

bull horn   An electronic megaphone, loudspeaker, or public-address system, esp. as used aboard a ship to relay orders from officers to enlisted men on or below decks. *Orig. W.W.II Navy use.*

—bum   See Appendix to the Supplement, Suffix Words.

bummed out   Discouraged or irritated.

bummer*   *n.* **1** A bad experience; specif., an unpleasant or depressing experience with a drug, as LSD. **2** Any unpleasant or bad situation.

bumper   *n.* The coupling mechanism on a railroad car. *Railroad and hobo use.*

bum trip = **bad trip.**

bundle*   *n.* Twenty-five $5 packets of a narcotic, esp. twenty-five "nickel bags" of marijuana, heroin, or cocaine. *Drug culture. Cf.* **bag.**

bung hole [taboo]   **1** The anus. **2** To have, permit, or prefer anal intercourse.

bunk*   *v.t.* To be absent from, quit, or leave something.

bunny*   **bunnie**   *n.* **1** Any girl, esp. a pert, attractive one. **2** A girl who may or may not surf, ski, etc., but who associates closely with men who do; esp. a feminine and sexually submissive girl who attaches herself to a particular sport, hobby, field of interest, etc., not only because she finds the men active in it exciting but also in order to express her identity with a group and a way of life which the activity symbolizes. *Used in combinations indicating in the first word the particular activity, as "beach bunny" or "surf bunny" = a girl who spends much time with surfers, "ski bunny" or "snow bunny" = a girl who spends much time with skiers, "jazz bunny" = a girl who spends much time with jazz musicians or enthusiasts, etc.*

bunny fuck [taboo] **1** To engage in a quick act of sexual intercourse. Cf. **wham-bam.*** **2** To stall or lag: waste time.

buns [taboo]   *n.pl.* The buttocks. 1973: "The male dancers in our show have fantastic bodies, and I know most of them are gay, but they still turn me on. Like, I'll grab Ron's or Alan's buns sometimes and they're firm and hard . . . ." *Playboy*, Dec., 268.

burn* *n.* A cigarette, or the act of smoking tobacco. *v.t.* **1** To cook or heat food. **2** To perform well; to act quickly or efficiently. *Negro use.* **3** To borrow; to beg.

burning out   The phenomenon of an older addict's voluntary withdrawal from drugs after many years of use. *Drug culture.* Cf. **age out.**

burn rubber   To leave; esp. to leave rapidly. *From the image of rubber tires burning from a quick acceleration. Since c1955.*

bush* *n.* **1** Marijuana; "grass." *Drug culture.* **2** Afro.

bust* *n.* An arrest. 1973: "At the time of Robert Mitchum's marijuana bust she wrote, 'He could still be cured, providing he wanted to be.'" A. J. Langguth, *Sat. Rev.: Art*, Mar., 33.

v.t. To arrest. 1973: "'I'll have you busted,' Skin said. 'I swear to God, this is grand larceny. This is extortion.'" M. Rogers, *Playboy*, April, 178.

bust a cap   **1** To take a narcotic, esp. heroin. 1960: "'Why don't you bust a cap with me? It's choice.'" C. Copper, *The Scene*, 15. *Drug culture.* **2** To discharge a gun.

bust [one's] ass [taboo] = **bust a gut.***
but [one's] nuts [taboo] = **bust a gut.***
butter-and-egg man* = **angel** (def. 2).*

butterhead   butter head *n.* **1** A Negro who degrades his race, or embarrasses his race or other Negroes. *Negro use only.* **2** Any stupid, rude, or unsophisticated person. *Student use since c1962.*

button* *n.* **1** A small amount. 1961: "There exists some traffic [between Mexico and El Paso, Texas] however, in 'buttons,' or small amounts." H. Braddy, "Running Contraband on the Rio Grande," *Southern Folklore Quarterly*, June, 107. *Orig. a Mafia word; now common underworld use.* **2** A policeman's badge. *Police use.* **3** The rounded top of the peyote plant.

button-down *adj.* Conventional and conservative in dress, manners, and attitudes. 1967: "The button-down, dispassionate, country club racism of the *nouveau riche* . . ." Paul Good, *Nation*, Nov. 28, 571. *From the button-down shirt collars worn by conventional men in the 1960s when many young people adopted blue jeans, T-shirts, etc., as their preferred apparel.*

button man = **soldier.**
B.Y.O.B.   BYOB   Bring your own bottle or booze. *An invitation to come to a party and supply your own liquor.*

C

C* [taboo]   *n.* A woman considered as a sexual object; "cunt."* *Not common.*

caballo *n.* Heroin. *From the Sp. = horse, a slang word for heroin. Drug culture.*

cake* *n.* A person. *Used in phrases such as "he's a sad cake," or "she's a wild piece of cake." Some Negro use.*

California tilt   An automobile having its front end lower than its rear end; an automobile whose hood slopes downward toward the front; the style or

actual downward slope of such an automobile. *Usu. found on cars assembled or modified by their owners. Hot-rod and car-buff use.*

Cambo *adj.* Cambodian. *Armed Forces use.*

campfire boy   An opium addict. *Reoccurring nonce use.*

camp it up   **1** To behave effeminately; to exhibit obvious effeminate gestures, speech, mannerisms, etc.; to display homosexual characteristics blatantly.

2 To take part in a wild party or similar social gathering, esp. of homosexuals. *Homosexual use since c1945.*

cancer stick   A cigarette. *Some facetious use since c1956.*

candy*   *n.* **1** Hashish. *Drug culture.* **2** A sugar cube of LSD; LSD. *Drug culture.* **3** Any drug, esp. a barbiturate drug. *From the earlier use = cocaine.*

candy ass   *n.* **1** One who is timid, irresolute, or markedly unaggressive. **2** A coward.

candy-assed   candyass   *adj.* **1** Timid; irresolute, markedly unaggressive. 1974: "It's a pretty candy-assed biker who worries about what other people think." *Playboy*, March, 45. **2** Cowardly.

candy man   A drug pusher or dealer. *Drug culture.*

canvas back   **1** A hobo. **2** A rural youth newly arrived in the city. *Fig.. anyone who carries his possessions in a gunny sack on his back. Reinforced by the image of a migratory duck.*

cap*   *v.t., v.i.* **1** To open or use a capsule of narcotics. **2** To buy narcotics; "cop." 1958: "I made it slowly back to town;/I capped me some more pot." H. Braddy, "Anonymous Verses." *Drug culture.*   *n.* A capsule of LSD. *From the older addict use = a capsule of heroin. "Caps" vary in size from the large type common in the East to the smaller, more concentrated capsules common on the West Coast, and variously called "West Coast caps," "Tijuana caps," "Mexican caps," "Frisco caps," etc. Drug culture and student use.*

capo   *n.* A captain or head of a local unit of the Mafia. *Underworld use.*

capper   *n.* The final part; end; conclusion; climax.

Castro   *n.* A beard; esp. a full beard. *Some student use since c1960, after the Cuban leader Fidel Castro and his original rebel forces, who grew beards while fighting guerrilla warfare.*

Cat   *n.* A Cadillac car. 1945: "Tia Juana pulled up in his long green Cat and parked in a No Parking zone." C. B. Himes, *if he hollers let him go*, 43. *Mainly Negro use. From "Caddy."*

catch a rail   = **take gas.** *Surfer use.*

chaff   *n.* Insolent, exaggerated, or senseless talk.

chain-drink   *v.i., v.t.* To drink a beverage continuously, draining one glass and then immediately refilling it. 1974: ". . . leave all that out and remember only that Hugh Hefner is a man who chain-drinks Pepsis." Carolyn See, "Nude

Times I," *New Times*, Feb. 22, 30. *Formed by analogy with "chain-smoke."**

chalk talk   **1** An informal intellectual discussion, as between a professor and his students. **2** Any lecture or discussion of an analytic nature; specif. a briefing at which a football coach draws chalk diagrams on a blackboard to illustrate individual plays, or a talk, by a mathematician or physicist, illustrated by written formulae on a blackboard. *From the chalk-writing image.* Cf. **skull session.**

champagne trick   A rich or high-paying customer of a prostitute. 1973: "I take only champagne tricks, $100 an hour. My men are all very well dressed and successful, with styled hair and young wives in Southampton, that group." Gail Sheehy, author of *The Liberated Call Girl*, excerpted in *Penthouse*, Aug., 108. *Prostitute use.*

charge account   **1** Access to bond money needed for posting as bail. **2** Any person or organization that may be called upon to post bail bond. *Some prostitute and Negro use.*

charged up   Under the influence of a drug. *Drug culture.*

charger   *n.* A driver, esp. of a hot rod. *Some hot-rod use.*

Charley Goon   A policeman. *Some archaic underworld use and some Negro use.* See **Charley*** (def. 3), **goon*** (def. 3).

Charlie*   *n.* **1** The Viet Cong or any Viet Cong soldier; "Victor Charlie." The "V.C." → **2** Any enemy. *Armed Forces use in Vietnam. The abbr. "V.C." was lengthened to the communication phrase "Victor Charlie" and then shortened to "Charlie."*   **—s**   *n.pl.* C-rations. *Army use. From the communications symbol "Charlie" = C.*

Charlie Nebs   **1** The police; policemen. *Some archaic underworld use.* **2** A policeman. *Some Negro use.* See **Charley*** (def. 3).

chaser*   *n.* A prison guard. *Prison use.*

cheapie*   *adj.* Cheap; obtained, bought, sold, or produced cheaply. 1973: ". . . X-rated movies and cheapie rip-offs of *The Godfather*." T. Meehan, *Sat. Rev.*, Feb., 50.

cheap shot   A mean or contemptible act or remark.

cheaters*   *n.pl.* **1** = **falsies*** **2** Any padding worn by a woman to improve her figure, as over the thighs, buttocks, etc.

cheat sheet   A set of written answers used by a student to cheat during an examination; a "pony"* or "crib."*

cheese* _n._ **1** An attractive girl or young woman. _From "cheesecake."*_ _Some student use._ **2** Goals; rewards. _Usu. in phrase "get [one's] cheese." Mainly West Coast use._ _adj._ Traitorous; cowardly; "chicken."* _Some teenage use._

cher _adj._ Personable; attractive; knowledgeable about currently popular fashions, tastes, trends, etc. _From the French "cher" = dear. Teenage use._

chew [someone's] ass out [taboo] = chew out.*

chica _n._ A girl or woman; a "chick."* _From the Sp. = little girl. Puerto Rican street use._

Chicago piano A Thompson submachine gun. _Some synthetic use in movies and detective fiction._

chi-chi chichi* [taboo] _n._ **1** The female breasts; "tits"* considered as sexual objects. → **2** Anything sexually stimulating; a sexually attractive woman. _From "chisai chichi," a corruption of the Japanese for "little breasts." Some post-W.W.II and more Korean war Armed Forces use._

chicken* _n._ A boy in his pre-teens or early teens as an object of sexual gratification by an adult homosexual.

chickenhawk _n._ An adult male who seeks out teenage boys for homosexual purposes. 1973: "Henry is, in his own words, a 'chickenhawk,' a man who likes sex with 'chickens'—that is, boys in their middle teens." George Vecsey, N.Y. _Times,_ Mar. 30, 43.

chicken switch chicken button **1** A switch or button that destroys a malfunctioning rocket in flight. → **2** A switch or button that an astronaut can use to cause his capsule to be ejected from a malfunctioning rocket. → **3** A switch that a pilot can use to cause his seat or his cockpit to be ejected from a jet plane in an emergency. _From chicken* = afraid._

chickie _n._ A young woman; girl.

chicklet _n._ A girl; "chick."*

chief* _n._ = LSD. _Drug culture._

chili _adj._ Mexican; Mexican style. _Most commonly in the combinations "chili whore" = Mexican prostitute, "chili food" = Mexican-style food, "chili boots" = Mexican-style, high-heeled, hand-tooled boots._

chili-bowl* A slovenly, dirty person, a stupid or embarrassing person.

chill* _n._ A beer; a glass, bottle, or can of cold beer. 1965: "A chill: a beer," _Newsweek,_ May 3, 25. _Some student use._

china* _n._ A cup of tea. _Lunch-counter use._

chintzy* _adj._ Stingy, cheap.

chippy* _v.i., v.t._ To take narcotics only for an occasional thrill or to show that one is "hip."* _Said of nonaddicts, "students,"* and "joy-poppers."* Drug culture._

chocha [taboo] _n._ = cunt.* _From the Sp. Some Puerto Rican street-gang use._

choi oy An interjection of disgust, dismay, disappointment, etc. _From the Vietnamese. Army use in Vietnam._

chop* _n._ Food. —ped _adj._ Of a car, having the chassis lowered or the fenders removed or both; of a motorcycle, having the front brake and fender removed, the wheel fork extended forward, and the handlebars raised. _Hot-rod and motorcycle use._ —per _n._ A "chopped" car or motorcycle. _Hot-rod and motorcycle use._ —s _n._ **1** Musical ability or technique. _Some jazz musician use; an extension of "chops"* = the mouth; the lips._ → **2** Talent, skill, or technique; esp. a seemingly inborn ability to succeed at some specific type of endeavor. _Orig. theatrical use; became more pop. far-out use c1962._

Christmas tree* The control panel in a submarine. _W.W.II Navy use._

church key A bottle or can opener, esp. as used to open a container of beer.

chuzpa chutzpa hutzpa _n._ Impudence, gall. _From the Yiddish._

ciao _interj._ **1** Goodby. **2** Hello. _From the Italian. Very common use among students and young adults since c1955._

circle jerk [taboo] A sex party of mutual masturbation, either all boys or boys and girls. _Adolescent and young teenage use._ See jerk off* (def. 1).

citizen _n._ A person who belongs to a more prosaic, conservative group than one's own; a "square."* _Thus, to a Negro a white may be a "citizen," to a convict an honest man who has never been in jail is a "citizen," etc._

—city See Appendix to the Supplement, Suffix Words.

clam* _n._ A sour or wrong note. _Jazz musician use._

clank _v.i._ = clank up. —ed _adj._ Tired; exhausted; depressed or despondent. _Some student use since c1960._

clank up clank To cease to function through fear, anxiety, nervousness, etc. 1961: "The expression _to clank_ or _to clank up_ means 'to freeze up,' to make errors because of fright or temporary shock." James L. Jackson, "Notes on

Air Force Academy Language," *American Speech*, May, 148. *Some student use.*

clean* *adj.* 1 Free from addiction to drugs. 2 Well-dressed. 1965: "Danny, he was really clean. He had new clothes; he was really dressed." Claude Brown, *Manchild in the Promised Land*, 246. *Negro use.*

clean on To beat up; to defeat in a fight. 1932: "He was cleaning on Three-Star fair, much to the delight of the gang." J. T. Farrell, *Young Lonigan*, 93. *From the colloq. "clean up on."*

clear up To stop using drugs; get help in withdrawing from drugs. *Drug culture.*

click* *n.* A kilometer (about 5/8 of a mile). *Armed Forces use.*

clit [taboo] *n.* The clitoris.

close* *adj.* Very satisfying; wonderful; "far out."* *Some far-out and student use since c1960, from the jazz musician use of "close"* (def. 3) of the 1950s.*

closet liberal A liberal, esp. in politics, who conceals his liberalism. 1973: "The 'relaxed, easy' fellow who was known around the White House as a 'closet liberal,' . . . was nowhere to be seen in the Caucus Room. . . ." Douglas E. Kneeland, N.Y. *Times*, July 25, 26.

closet queen A person who keeps his homosexuality a secret.

closet queer = closet queen.

clout* *n.* Great influence or power. 1968: "Note: a bill to abolish the board was sponsored in the last Congress by Sen. Strom Thurmond, whose role in Nixon's nomination and election will give him extra clout in the new one." *Newsweek*, Dec. 16, 75. 1973: "Open refrigerator units in supermarkets . . . are major sources of wasted energy. Use your clout as a customer and complain to the store manager. . . ." *Family Health*, Sept., 35.

clutch* *n.* An unpleasant, cheap, or despicable person. 1961: "[Among waiters] a nontipper is universally called a 'stiff,' while . . . in Kansas City . . . [he is also] a 'clutch'. . . ." "The Outstretched Palm," *Time*, June 23, 45. *v.i.* = clutch up. **—ed** *adj.* Nervous; tense. **—y** *adj.* 1 Tending to become tense, nervous, anxious, etc. 2 Nerve-wracking; difficult; dangerous.

clutch up *v.i.* To get nervous; to cease to function through fear, anxiety, nervousness, etc.

clyde *n.* = square* (def. 2).

coast *v.i.* To be under the influence of or feel the effects of a narcotic drug. *Drug culture.*

cobbler *n.* 1 A forger of passports. *Some recent Central Intelligence Agency and underworld use.* Cf. **shoe** (def. 3). → 2 A forger; one who engraves, prints, or distributes counterfeit money, bonds, etc. *Underworld use.*

cockamainie cockamamie *adj.* Absurd, quixotic, crazy, unusual. 1966: "When I make a statement on canvas, I'm not just doing cockamamie drawings." Bob Kane, creator of Batman, quoted by Gerald Nachman, N.Y. *Post*, Jan. 9, 31.

cocksman [taboo] *n.* A man known for constantly seeking sexual intercourse; a man obsessed with having as much sexual intercourse as possible with as many different women as possible; an "ass man."* *From the pun on "coxswain" and "cock"* (def. 1).

cock-sucking [taboo & derog.] *adj.* Despicable; disgusting; base. *Prob. outranked only by "mother-fucking" as a term of violent disapproval, usu. of a person only.*

cocktail *n.* A cigarette containing marijuana and tobacco, the marijuana being inserted into the end of an ordinary cigarette. *Drug culture.*

colaholic *n.* A person who drinks an inordinate amount of cola. 1974: "In their responses to open-ended questions, many colaholics revealed that they would find it difficult to give up the habit. One student wrote, 'I can't possibly imagine not drinking it. . . .' " P. Horn, *Psychology*, Jan., 92.

come* [taboo] *n.* An orgasm.

come down 1 To experience the loss of the effects of a drug, esp. a stimulant drug. 1973: "He was drunk; he seemed agitated and very tired, as if he had just come down off methedrine." J. Bradshaw, *Playboy*, June, 205. 2 To happen. 1969: "At night, the kids huddle together in filthy apartments, inject dope from dirty needles and wander in the streets, armed and 'ready for whatever trouble's gonna come down.' " John Luce, "Haight-Ashbury Today," *Esquire*, July, 118. 3 To become firmly entrenched, as a drug habit. 1965: "When a chick's habit came down on her, she'd usually end up down in the 'marketplace' . . . where all the whores hung out." Claude Brown, *Manchild in the Promised Land*, 184.

comedown* come-down *n.* Cessation of the effects of a drug experience. 1972: "I cooled it with Quaalude. . . . the comedown wasn't too bad, but the cravings of a bliss freak always catch up with you. . . ." John Steinbeck IV, *Sat. Rev.*, Oct., 38.

come out   Begin an active homosexual life. *One who has "come out" has overcome doubts and anxieties about homosexuality or has decided, in spite of them, to begin seeking partners of the same sex. The term is sometimes used in the sense of "make public one's homosexuality," but one who has "come out" may want to keep that side of his or her life secret from "straight"* friends and relatives.* 1973: "By that time their twenty-year marriage had come apart, and their eldest son had 'come out' as a homosexual." Shana Alexander, *Newsweek*, Jan. 22, 28. *Homosexual use.* Cf. **come out of the closet** (def. 1).

come out of the closet   **1** To make an open declaration of one's homosexuality, either by explicit statement or by actions intended to have the same effect. Cf. **closet queen; come out.** → **2** Usu. of a public figure or organization, to admit to, or to make known, something (as an action, a position on an issue, etc.) which has been kept secret or not openly professed.

commfu   *n.* Complete monumental military fuck-up.* *W.W.II Armed Forces use; euphem. acronym formed by analogy with "snafu."**

Company, the   *n.* The Central Intelligence Agency, the Federal Bureau of Investigation, or a metropolitan police force. *May have orig. from the abbreviation CIA = Central Intelligence Agency, which abbreviation stands for "Company" ("Compañia") in Sp. Orig. Central Intelligence Agency use; now some underworld use.*

Comsymp   *n.* Communist sympathizer; fellow traveler. *A coinage of Robert Welch, founder of the John Birch Society. Usu. disparaging.*

conk*   *v.t.* (of Negroes) To apply a mixture containing lye to the hair in order to straighten it.   *n.* Hair treated in this way. 1964: "I couldn't get over marveling at how their hair was straight and shiny like white men's hair; Ella told me this was called a 'conk.' " *Autobiography of Malcolm X* (Grove), 43. *Since the "black is beautiful" concept made the "Afro" or "natural" popular, conking is less common than it was before the 1960s.*

connect   *v.i.* To buy or obtain narcotics, marijuana, or other contraband. *Drug culture.* See **connection.***

coño   *interj.* = damn, hell. *From the Sp.*

constant companion   A lover. 1965: ". . . Existentialist Jean-Paul Sartre . . . and Novelist Simone de Beauvoir . . . have been constant companions. . . ." *Time*, Jan. 15, 36. *Euphem.*

contact high   The feeling of being high in the presence of those using drugs without using any oneself. 1968: "At Big Nig's in San Jose, a lot of the kids . . . did not take LSD that night, although there were enough heads at Big Nig's stoned on various things to create that sympathetic vibration known as the 'contact high.' " Tom Wolfe, *The Electric Kool-Aid Acid Test* (Bantam), 215. *Drug culture.*

contract*   *n.* An assignment, order, or obligation; esp. a major or dangerous job, as the paid killing of another. 1963: "The CHAIRMAN: 'What was your first contract . . . after you became a member of Cosa Nostra?' MR. VALACHI: 'Joe Baker.' The CHAIRMAN: 'You had a contract to kill Joe Baker?' MR. VALACHI: 'That is right.' " U.S. Senate. *Organized Crime and Illicit Traffic in Narcotics*, 188. (The Joseph Valachi testimony.) *Underworld use.*

cook*   *v.t.* To dissolve a narcotic in water over a flame before injecting it. *Drug culture.*   **—er**   *n.*   **1** A small container, as a bottle top, used for heating and dissolving a drug with water prior to injection. 1965: "He empties a little bag of heroin into water in the cooker, heats it with a match to dissolve the drug and injects the mixture." James Mills, "We Are All Animals," *Reader's Digest*, June, 227. *Drug culture.*   **2** A refinery or chemical plant that processes heroin from raw opium, as those in S.E. Asia, Marseilles, etc.

cook up a pill   To prepare opium for smoking. *Drug culture.*

cool*   *n.* A state of mind characterized by detachment, disdain for emotional involvement, and a distant and reserved rather than enthusiastic attitude toward persons and ideas: composure. 1965: "On Not Losing One's Cool About the Young," title of editorial, *Time*, Dec. 24, 16. 1965: "I lost my cool at the Birdland Discotheque," advt. for Birdland nightclub, a major home of bop and cool jazz in New York City during the 1950s and early 1960s, when it became a discotheque. *This noun use was the last use of the word "cool" by the cool groups that flourished in the mid-1950s, the mood and groups dissolving c1965.*   *v.t.* To ignore; to be aloof from, unconcerned with, or disdainful of a person, idea, belief, statement, etc. 1962: "His girl friend . . . had been cooling him of late. She had always cooled him, in fact; she was practically not a girl friend at all." *New Yorker*, July 28, 24. *v.i.* To die. 1964: " 'He cooled about a year ago. Don't you read the obituary columns?' " John O'Hara, "The Whole Cherry Pie," *The Horse Knows the Way*, 417.

cool out* [taboo] To have sexual intercourse. *Some Negro and beat use.*

coonjin coongin *v.t.* **1** To carry, lift, or esp. to load a bale of cotton on a boat or truck. *Archaic Negro use in South.* **2** To work, think, or try hard at anything; to be forced or tricked into working or making a profit for another. *The image of hard work is due to the weight of a cotton bale: 500 pounds. Some Southern Negro use.*

coop *v.i.* **1** (of a policeman) To take a nap or sleep inside one's police car during a duty shift, esp. a night shift. 1973: "Will the city parks ultimately be fenced? And would the cops Clark Whelton found cooping on Washington Square West be more inspired to do their job in the park if there was a fence?" Mary Perot Nichols, *Village Voice*, April 26, 3. **2** = **goof off.***

cooze coozie [taboo] *n.* A female considered as a sexual object; the vagina; sexual intercourse. *Pop. before c1925, replaced by "cunt"* and "tail."**

cop *v.i., v.t.* To obtain or buy narcotics. 1965: "The pusher has appeared, and soon, one by one, they [the junkies] will make their round-about way to him to 'cop.' " James Mills, "We Are All Animals." *Reader's Digest*, June, 232. *Drug culture.*

co-pilot *n.* Amphetamine. *Drug culture.*

cop out* **1** To renege or withdraw from involvement in some action, plan, task, etc.; to cease to be actively engaged in an endeavor; to evade a question or an issue; to break a promise. **2** To compromise or abandon one's ideals, principles, etc.

cop-out *n.* An act or instance of copping out. 1973: "When I question Open Admissions on the basis of Heller's statement that standards will inevitably go down, he says that 'arguing over standards is a "cop-out." ' " Peter Sourain, *Nation*, Feb. 12, 209.

cop shop A police station.

cop [some] z's To take a nap. 1964: " 'Well, my man, I'll get on, got to peck a little, and cop me some z's—' And the hustler went up Seventh Avenue. . . . He was going to eat, then he would get some sleep." *Autobiography of Malcolm X*, (Grove), 310. See **zizz.**

corazon *n.* Courage; manliness. *From the Sp. = heart, often in the phrase "puro corazon" = all heart. Teenage street-gang use, pop. by Puerto Rican youth.* See **heart*** (def. 1).

Corine *n.* Cocaine. *Drug culture.*

corksacking *adj.* Euphem. for the taboo **cock-sucking.** 1972: "I have already had several abusive phone calls, telling me to eff off back to effing Russia, you effing corksacking limey effer." Anthony Burgess, N.Y. *Times Mag.*, Oct. 29, 28.

corn* *n.* Large-grained snow, as formed by alternate freezing and thaw-ing. *Such snow is the best for skiing. Skier use.*

corn-hole [taboo] *v.t.* To perform anal intercourse either as a homosexual or as a heterosexual. *Prison and Armed Forces use.*

corn-pone *adj.* Southern; esp. with a Southern accent or attitudes.

cornrow *n.* **1** An African hairstyle of American Negroes in which the hair is arranged in rows of flat, small braids. **2** A row of such braids. *v.t.* To arrange (the hair) in cornrows. 1973: "From ghetto streets to college cam-puses, with-it black women—and more and more black men—are putting their hair into African-style 'cornrows,' in-tricate patterns of braids all over the skull separated by half-inch parts. . . ." *Newsweek*, Feb. 26, 44.

cotics *n.* Narcotics. *Drug culture.*

cotton *n.* **1** Amphetamine in any form; specif. cotton saturated with Benzedrine and inhaled by an addict. **2** Anything saturated with a drug that can be inhaled. *Drug culture.*

cotton curtain The South; "Dixie."* *Formed by humorous analogy with "iron curtain."* Some Negro and jazz use.*

cotton freak A drug addict who in-hales his drug. *Orig. one who inhaled Benzedrine from a piece of cotton saturated with it. Drug culture.* See **cotton.**

cotton mouth Dryness of the mouth as experienced by someone who is frightened, has a hangover, etc.

cover* *n.* **1** A version of a popular piece of music recorded by performers other than those who originally made it famous and/or composed it. 1974: "Tanya Tucker's third album, like the first two, contain many covers of recent country chart-busters. . . ." Ken Barnes, *Rolling Stone*, April 25, 62. **2** An assumed identity or role used by a spy, criminal, etc., to conceal activities. 1973: "To improve his [Howard Hunt's] cover he 'resigned' from the agency [the CIA] and traveled first to Mexico and then to Miami, posing as a writer who had suddenly come into a windfall inheritance." McCrystal et al., *Watergate*, 56.

cowabunga!   *interj.* An exhortative or victorous cry used by surfers while riding waves. *Surfer use.*

cowboy*   *n.* A reckless driver.

cow peeler   A cowboy. *Some Western use since c1880.*

crabs* [taboo]   *n.* Syphilis; "syph."

crack*   *v.t.* To open, as with a bottle opener or can opener. 1963: "Now and then someone would . . . crack a can of juice." Sterling Hayden, *Wanderer*, 50.

crackers   *adj.* **1** Crazy; mad. 1971: "It was completely crackers, but it was a hit and sounded great on the stage." H. Roberts, *The Rolling Stone Interviews*, 161. *Orig. Brit. use.* **2** Very fond of. *Orig. Brit. use.*

crack on [something or someone]   To prove something or convince someone of; to present facts, arguments, or evidence to support one's idea, belief, or statement. *Some Negro and jazz musician use.*

cram it [taboo]   = **stick it.***

crank out   To produce something, usu. mechanically or laboriously. 1973: "Now, with the kind of junk the studios are cranking out—and the jacked-up prices they're charging—the average family is staying home and watching television." J. Bell, *Good Housekeeping*, Feb., 34.

crank up   To get started; to bring into being or operation.

crash*   *v.i.* **1** To sleep or reside at a place, typically for a single night or just a few days and without invitation. 1973: "I was just riding around the country on my motorcycle, and I heard about this place and hoped maybe I could crash here for a day or two. But after three days I wanted to stay." P. Curtis, *Family Circle*, May, 61. **2** = **flake out.** **3** To pass out drunk. *Student use.* **—ed**   *adj.* Drunk.

crash pad   A place, as a room or apartment, where one may sleep or stay for a night or a few days; temporary quarters. 1973: "His first act on being hired, in 1964, was to rule the long sofa

in the office out of bounds for sleeping, thereby discouraging itinerant filmmakers, homeless poets, and hangers-on of all kinds from using the room as a crash pad." Calvin Tompkins, *New Yorker*, Jan. 6, 40.

crazies   *n.pl.* **1** Extremely radical members of a group; fanatics. **2** A habitually irrational or destructive person.

crazy*   *n.* An inmate of an insane asylum or someone temporarily confined to a psychiatric ward of a hospital.

cream*   *v.t.* To beat up, severely injure, or kill.   *n.* [taboo] Semen.

cream [one's] jeans   **1** = **cream*** (def. 2). **2** [taboo] To be in a state of excitement or ecstasy, esp. to be in a state of sexual excitement so that one fig. has an orgasm. *Fairly common student rhyming use of the 1930s. From "cream" = semen and "jeans" = trousers.*

CREEP   *n.* An acronym contrived from "CRP," official abbr. for the Committee for the Reelection of the President, founded to promote a second term for Richard M. Nixon. 1973: "He [McCord] discussed intelligence data furnished him by the Internal Security Division, which was regularly feeding such information to CREEP . . ." F. J. Donner, *Nation*, Nov. 19, 430.

creeps, the*   *n.* The feeling of discomfort, esp. itching, caused by low pressure, as in a submarine or in a space capsule.

crib*   *n.* A room, apartment, or other living quarters; a "pad."* 1960: " 'Nobody's home at my crib. . . .' " C. Cooper, *The Scene*, 15. *"Crib" is replacing "pad"* in Negro, jazz musician, far-out and student use. The connotation is that of a small, cramped room ("crib,"* def. 4) rather than a baby's bed. Obs. since it was underworld use c1890, this is a prime example of a word becoming pop. with one subgroup long after it has become obs. with another.*

Crow Jim   Strong antiwhite prejudice among Negroes. 1962: "The anti-white attitude of the . . . black Nationalists has spilled over into jazz, in the form of the reverse prejudice known as Crow Jim. . . . Today Muslim-inspired Negroes . . . advise their colleagues not to hire white sidemen." Jean P. Le Blanc, "Jazz: The Happy Sound Is Dying," *Esquire*, April, 144. *A reverse form of Jim Crow* (def. 3). Orig. Negro jazz musician use.*

cruise   *v.i., v.t.* **1** To walk, drive a car,

ride a motorcycle, etc., slowly through a particular area in order to survey the general activity, social prospects, etc., esp. in search of a sex partner; to move about in a place, usually a crowded or public place, party, etc., in search of a sex partner; to look for a "pick-up."* **2** To make a subtle, tentative, usually unspoken sexual approach to someone.

crunch *n.* **1** A crisis. 1970: "The first few months of the magazine remain in my mind as a waking nightmare of impossible deadlines. . . . Then came the political conventions that summer, and more crunches." Clay Felker, *New York*, April 6, 4. **2** A critical financial squeeze. 1973: "A 'crunch' . . . is characterized by a skyrocketing of interest rates and a choking off of the availability of credit." Leonard Silk, N.Y. *Times*, July 31, 37. **3** Stress or conflict between dissenting groups or elements. 1966: "And it is important also to recognize that while the 'crunch' between press and Government is inevitable in American affairs, the hope of easing its consequences is as dependent upon the talent and attitude of the Government as upon the self-restraint of the press." Jack Raymond, N.Y. *Times Mag.*, Feb. 13, 93.

crutch* *n.* = **roach clip** (def. 2).

crying room An imaginary room to which one retires to weep after a big disappointment, defeat, etc. Cf. **crying towel.***

cube* *n.* A sugar cube containing LSD. *Habitual users' and student use.*

culo [taboo] *n.* The anus, rectum, or buttocks; the "ass."* *From the Sp.*

cunt cap [taboo] The standard army enlisted-man's cloth cap when worn with a crease or pleat in the front terminal peak. *Army use.* Cf. **tit cap.**

cup of coffee A very short stay, as a short visit with friends or a stay with a club in the major leagues by a player brought up from a minor-league team. *Meaning about as much time as it takes to drink a cup of coffee.*

curse, the *n.* Menstruation; the days or a period during which a woman menstruates.

curve killer A superior student; one who gets very high grades. *Student use, deriving from the practice of grading "on the curve."*

cut* *v.t.* To share; to live in, pay for, share the responsibility of, etc., with another or others. *n.* **1** A phonograph recording session. 1964: " '[I] made a few cuts,' . . . 'what's that, cuts?' . . . 'Recording dates.' " John O'Hara, "In the Mist," *The Horse Knows the Way*, 185. **2** A band on a long-playing phonograph record containing a separate selection. 1973: "Todd Rundgren's new one contains 11 cuts and 53 minutes of music on one disc." *Playboy*, July, 38. **3** A phonograph record. 1973: "The group reaches its apotheosis on 'I'm a Madman' . . . and does this cut ever rock!" Allen Levy, *Changes*, Dec./Jan., 32.

cutesy cutesie *adj.* Sickeningly or self-consciously cute or coy.

cutesy-poo *adj.* An intensive of **cutesy.** 1973: ". . . I feel like a rotten old cynic saying anything narsty about so cutesy-poo an endeavor as [the movie] *The Optimists.* After all, it gives Peter Sellers, complete with putty nose, a chance to run a Goon Show gamut as a busker. . . ." Judith Crist, *New York*, Oct. 22, 104.

cut-offs *n.pl.* Pants, usu. blue jeans, cut off above the knees and left unhemmed and unraveled to produce fringes.

cut the mustard **1** To succeed in performing or accomplishing something. 1973: ". . . the schools tossed the blame on the Black students, claiming that 'they just couldn't cut the mustard.' " *Jet*, Nov. 8, 36. **2** To be of importance. 1974: ". . . while Clifford Irving may be a celebrity throughout the United States, he cuts little mustard here on Ibiza." G. Bocca, *Playgirl*, March, 67. *This expression is almost always used with a qualifying negative. It dates back at least to 1904, when the phrase "up to mustard" = up to standards or up to the mark, was also used. Since W.W.I men have increasingly used "can't cut the mustard" to mean unable to perform sexually or unable to have an erection.*

D

D *n.* A dollar.

daddy* *n.* The most respected performer in a field; a person whose work or personality is so unique and successful that others seek to imitate him. 1964: ". . . imitation of the 'daddy' spreads through the ranks. . . . Trumpeters try to play like Miles Davis. And hold their horns like Miles. And dress like Miles." *Time*, Feb. 28, 45.

dark*   *adj.* With less than the usual amount of cream added, said of a cup of coffee. *Lunch-counter use. Colloq.*

dash*   *n.* The dashboard of an automobile. *Colloq.*

daylight   *v.i.* To work at a second job during the day to add to one's income or experience when one's principal job is performed at night. 1973: ". . . and Barbara Earp, who is daylighting in an ad agency as a producer of commercials." *Playboy*, Oct., 142. *Formed by analogy with the older and more popular "moon-light."*

deadhead*   *adj.* Empty or unused, as a truck, train, or cargo ship, factory or warehouse, a telephone or telegraph line, a radio frequency or television channel, etc.

deadneck   *n.* A stupid person, a "jerk."* 1932: "They were awake and lively; they weren't deadnecks." J. T. Farrell, *Young Lonigan*, 166. *Fig.*, one who is *"dead" from the neck up.*

deadpan*   *v.t.* To make an ironic or humorous statement while maintaining an expressionless face. 1968: "But mostly Kennedy husbanded his passion and laced his speeches with one-liners kidding himself and the whole political process. With kids packing his audiences, he deadpanned: 'I promise to lower the voting age to 6.' " *Newsweek*, May 28, 32.

deal [someone] a poor deck   **1** To treat a person in a cruel, unfair, or exploitive way. **2** To be ill-fated, to be born poor, untalented, ugly, etc. 1973: "Take a thirty-year-old nurse who's not married, who's been shit upon, used by various doctors, who's bitter and thinks she's been dealt a poor deck." A. T. Fleming, *Playgirl*, Nov., 84.

deck*   *n.* Three grains of heroin; an amount of heroin worth $5 or more. *Drug culture.* Cf. **bag.**

deep six*   **deep-six**   *v.t.* To throw overboard or into deep water; to throw away; discard. 1973: "Last summer, when the Watergate culprits plotted their cover-up their first thoughts were to destroy all incriminating documents. . . . One White House disposal crew even unblushingly planned to deep six a file in the Potomac." Jack Anderson, col., N.Y. *Post*, Aug. 22, 33. *Since the Watergate scandals this term has gained new currency in the sense of getting rid of embarrassing or incriminating material.*

From the earlier phrase "give [something] the deep six," an extension of the nautical term "deep six," burial at sea prob. in six or more fathoms of water.

Delhi belly   Diarrhea. *Used by travelers in India.*

demo*   *n.* A protest demonstration.

detox   *v.i., v.t.* To detoxify from drugs; cure from taking drugs. 1972: " 'We can detox a heroin addict on an outpatient basis in three weeks,' said Eddie Morris of New York City's Addiction Services Administration. . . ." Gary Hoenig, N.Y. *Times*, Dec. 24, Sec. IV, 10.

deuce*   *n.* A powerful or good-looking hot rod, specif. a 1932 Ford. *Hot-rod use since c1940.*

deuce it   **1** To come second in order; esp. in vaudeville, to work as the second act on the bill, usu. assigned to one of the least known or least interesting acts. **2** To do something as a twosome; to become engaged; to date a member of the opposite sex.

devil's tar   Oil. 1958: "In 1818 David Beatty, drilling for salt water in Wayne County, Kentucky, struck oil instead. [When it] caught fire . . . Beatty and his neighbors immediately dubbed the noxious liquid *devil's tar.*" Lalia P. Boone, "From 'Devil's Tar' to 'Liquid Gold,' " *American Speech*, Dec., 304. *Fairly common use c1820–1850. Obs.*

dew*   *n.* Marijuana. *Drug culture.*

dicey   *adj.* Risky; chancy; hazardous. 1969: ". . . a European businessman in Kenya's capital of Nairobi said: 'Let's face it. African investment is dicey. Why risk your shareholders' money?' " *Newsweek*, Jan. 20, 73. *From "dice," regarded as a game of chance. Orig. Brit. slang.*

dicky licker [derog. & taboo]   A person who performs fellatio on a homosexual. *Heterosexual use.*

diddle* [taboo]   *v.i., v.t.* To have or perform any type of sexual act or activity. Thus, the limerick: "There was a young man from Eau Claire/Who diddled his wife on the stair. . . ."

diddly   *adj.* Worthless, silly, mediocre, insignificant. *Some student use.*

diddlybop   *v.i.* **1** To waste time; pass the time in idle chatter. → **2** To do anything pleasant, entertaining, or exciting.   *n.* A diversion; any social gathering, entertainment, etc., whether to pass the time idly or to enjoy oneself doing something exciting. *Some student use.* See **diddle.***

diddly-shit [taboo]   *adj.* Trivial; worthless.   *n.* = **shit*** (defs. 1, 2, 4).

die on [one's] feet   To fail or cease functioning; flop.

dime   *n.* **1** A ten-year prison sentence. *Some underworld use.* Cf. **nickel. 2** The sum of $1,000, esp. a wager. *Orig. gambling use.*

dime bag   Ten dollars' worth of a drug, as a half-ounce of marijuana. *Drug culture and student use.* See **bag.**

dinch   *v.t.* To extinguish a cigarette.

dingbat*   *n.* An inept, stupid, or inane person. 1973: "[the television series] 'All in the Family' . . . was re-exported to the BBC complete with 'Polack pinko meatheads' . . . 'dingbats' and 'spades'. . . ." D. Taylor, *Punch*, May 2, 627.

dingy-dingy   *adj.* Crazy; "nuts."* *Armed Forces use in Korea.*

dink* [derog.]   *n.* A Vietnamese. *Armed Forces use in the Vietnam war.* Cf. **gook, slope, zip.**

dip*   *n.* A slovenly or untidy person. *Some teenage use.*

dipshit [taboo]   *n.* A stupid, ill-mannered, socially unacceptable person; a bumpkin, "jerk,"* or "square."*

dipso   *n.* A dipsomaniac; an alcoholic.

dirty*   *adj.* **1** Addicted to drugs. **2** Having drugs in one's possession.

dirty dozens   Long, jivelike, usually rhyming phrases in response and answer, usually disparaging, obscene, etc. *Negro and teenage street-gang use.* Cf. **play the dozens.***

dirty old man   **1** An obscene or lustful man, esp. an old one, but the term can be applied to a man of any age. **2** A homosexual whose partner is much younger than himself. 1968: "Christopher is 20 years younger than Leo. . . . He asks Leo to be his dirty old man, and Leo complies." N.Y. *Times*, May 31, 27. *Homosexual use.*

dirty pool   Unfair, dishonest, or unethical behavior. 1968: "The incident that almost wrecked him triggered ugly accusations of dirty pool." Stanley Frank, *TV Guide*, Aug. 17, 13.

dirty tricks   Dishonest or underhanded practices; unfair, disruptive tactics; malicious acts intended to discredit or handicap an opponent. 1974: "The President would also make into federal crimes many 'dirty tricks' in presidential and congressional elections. Among them: disseminating false instructions to workers, organizing slander campaigns, and rigging opinion polls." *Time*, Mar. 18, 17.

disappear   *v.i.* To be murdered, esp. in such a way that no trace of the crime or the body is found. 1963: "The CHAIRMAN: 'Does that "disappear" mean that that is about the end of him?' MR. VALACHI: 'It meant that in our language, that he had ordered his death.' " U.S. Senate. *Organized Crime and Illicit Traffic in Narcotics*, 88. (The Joseph Valachi testimony.) *Underworld use.*

disco   *n.* A discotheque, a small, intimate nightclub where patrons dance to live music or to records. *Very popular in the 1960s.*

dish*   *v.i.* To gossip; chat. 1965: "She sat and dished with the girls . . ." H. Selby, Jr., *Last Exit to Brooklyn*, 225.

dishy   *adj.* Pretty; desirable. 1968: "Chabrol's 'Les Bonnes Femmes' defined very exactly what it is to be a dishy girl bored stiff with selling electrical equipment." Penelope Gilliatt, *New Yorker*, Sept. 14, 194. Cf. **dish.***

dispatchers   *n.pl.* A pair of dice that are loaded or in some other way crooked.

ditty bop   **ditty bob**   *n.* A stupid, crude, or unsophisticated Negro; a "butterhead." *Negro use only.*

DMT   Dimethyltryptamine, a hallucinogen similar to LSD but having an effect usually lasting less than an hour. *Drug culture.*

do*   *v.t.* Use; take. 1973: "Almost all the premies I talked with in New York and Boston and Houston reported that they'd done a great deal of dope before encountering the Divine Light movement." Nora Sayre, *New Times*, Dec. 28, 48. *Drug culture.* —*n.* A hairdo; coiffure.

do a number on   Disparage; speak or write of with contempt or disrespect.

dodge   *n.* An illegal or unethical way of earning a living; racket; profession or calling. 1951: " 'Poor Miss Sarah! I wonder why a refined doll like her is mixed up in the [Salvation Army] Mission dodge.' " Jo Swerling, Abe Burrows, and Frank Loesser, *Guys and Dolls*, Act I, Scene 1.

dog*   *n.* **1** The academic grade D. *Some student use.* **2** An opponent or team expected to lose. *From "*underdog.*" Gambling use.* —**gie**   *n.* A sailor or merchant seaman. *Not common.*

Dog, the   *n.* = **Hound, the.**

dog collar*   A collar having the opening at the back, as worn by priests.

doggy bag   **doggie bag**   A bag given a diner in a restaurant to take home leftovers, presumably for a pet.

doghouse*   *n.* A bulge or rounded extension on the surface of a rocket or missile for containing scientific instruments. *Aerospace use.*

dolce vita   Dolce Vita   1 A decadent way of life. → **2** An easy, sophisticated, fun-filled life; a way of life characterized by wealth, leisure, a sophisticated social milieu, exciting amusements and parties, etc.; sophisticated enjoyment and excitement. 1965: "Join the Mustangers. Enjoy a lot of *dolce vita* at a low, low price." Ford Motor Co. advt., *Reader's Digest*, Sept. → **3** Wealthy, sophisticated, and exciting. *From the Italian (lit., "sweet life"); orig. from the title and subject of Federico Fellini's film, "La Dolce Vita."*

doll*   dolly   *n.* An amphetamine or barbiturate drug in pill form. *Drug culture.*

dolly   *n.* = **doll*** (defs. 1, 2).

donar   donah   *n.* A girl, esp. one's steady girl or fiancée, or a girl attached to a teenage street gang. *Prob. from the Italian "donna" = lady. In Brit. Cockney use since c1900 and in U.S. street-gang use since c1955.*

donkey roast   A large, elaborate, festive, or noisy party, celebration, etc. 1964: ". . . the . . . benefit party at $100 a ticket . . . promises to be a real fine donkey roast . . ." Lael Scott and David Murray, "Who's Who and Where," N.Y. *Post*, Dec. 31, 3.

doo   *n.* = **do-dad.***

doojee   *n.* Heroin. *Drug culture.*

doolie   *n.* A first-year cadet at the U.S. Air Force Academy. 1965: ". . . life at the Academy seemed to keep its old cadences—doolies doubletimed to classes. . . ." *Newsweek*, Feb. 8, 84. *Air Force use.*

do [one's] number   **1** Speak or write about a matter in which one has a special interest, usu. with the implication that one has expounded on the subject often enough to have become irksome or a bore to others. **2** Display a pattern of behavior expected of those with a particular reputation or those of a certain social standing, profession, rank, etc.; act a role.

do [one's] (own) thing   To follow one's special interests and inclinations without heeding opinions and conventions. 1973: "Doing your own thing may be all right in prescribed doses for the more cosseted darlings of the middle class home, but it is precious little help to less fortunate offspring." A. J. H. Brown, *Spectator*, Jan. 13, 56.

dopenik   *n.* A person addicted to narcotics. *Drug culture.*

doper   *n.* A dope addict. 1972: "A $500,000 advertising campaign ushered in the new era—radio and TV alerting dopers of every stripe that where the penalties had been stiff, they now would be feudal." Timothy Ferris, "Rockefeller's Law: A New Era of Feudalism?" *Rolling Stone*, Oct. 11, 6. *Drug culture.*

do-rag   *n.* A rag or scarf worn over a processed hairdo, or "conk," to protect it. 1965: "A young mechanic, who took grim joy in looting and throwing rocks, wears a 'do-rag' on his new hair-do as he pours out hatred of whites, especially white cops." *Life*, Aug. 27, 65. *Negro use.* See **conk.**

dork   [taboo]   The penis. *Mainly adolescent and student use.*

dosed   *adj.* Infected with a venereal disease, esp. gonorrhea or syphilis. 1966: "What's going to happen is that you'll get dosed, as if I'm telling you something you don't already know." Richard Fariña, *Been Down So Long It Looks Like Up To Me* (Dell), 109.

double-clutcher   *n.* **1** A driver skilled enough to shift gears by double-clutching. *Trucker use.* **2** [taboo] = **mother fucker.** *Orig. Negro use; pop. by Negro construction workers during the Korean war.* **—ing**   *adj.* [taboo] = **mother fucking.**

doublet   *n.* Any fake or imitation item sold as genuine; specif., glass sold as a precious stone. *Orig. glass with a thin layer of diamond pasted on top so it would pass the scratch test.*

doublet stone = **doublet.**

do up*   To inject, smoke, or sniff narcotics; to take drugs. *Drug culture.*

dove*   *n.* A person who advocates peace or a nonbelligerent national policy. **—ish**   *adj.* Peaceful, nonbelligerent. 1968: "In his Delphic pronouncements on the war, Richard Nixon leaves more and more room for dovish interpretations." Stewart Alsop, *SEP*, April 20, 20. *The most recent use referred to a person advocating negotiating in Vietnam, withdrawal of U.S. troops, or keeping the Vietnam war to the smallest possible scale. The dove of peace is a common metaphor and art symbol. Colloq.* Cf. **hawk.**

down*   *adj.* **1** Sympathetic and "hip;"* "cool"* and understanding; in rapport with oneself. **2** Excellent; appealing to or satisfying one's deeper emotions. **3** Ready, prepared; spontaneous or uninhibited. *Mainly Negro and teenage use.* **4** Negative; depressing;

pessimistic. 1973: " 'Hell,' Irving said, 'that sounds like a dumb-ass approach to your life story. I don't see the point of making such a "down" picture. . . .' " Xaviera Hollander, *Xaviera*, 401. *n.* = **downer.** *v.t.* **1** To criticize. 1971: "But when I started out my friends downed me for listening to country music. . . ." H. E. Roberts, *Rolling Stone Interviews*, 390. **2** To sell.

down-dressed *adj.* Designed, made, adapted, etc., to avoid an appearance of luxury or dressiness. *By analogy with "dressed up."*

downer **down** *n.* **1** A depressant drug, esp. a barbiturate; sedative. *Drug culture.* **2** A depressing or negative experience. Cf. **upper.**

down home **1** The South; "Dixie;"* Southern. → **2** Southern racial prejudice; white Southern traditions and culture.

down-home *adj.* Of or pertaining to the customs, traditions, and culture of the Southern U.S. 1965: "He was getting away from all that old down-home stuff, and he didn't go for hearing it all the time around the house." Claude Brown, *Manchild in the Promised Land*, 269. 1974: "As we parted he [Sen. Howard Baker of Tennessee] reached up, and in a friendly, down-home way, clapped me on the back." Tim Cahill, *Rolling Stone*, Feb. 14, 34. *Orig. Negro use in the North, often sarcastic, but now quite common general use, usu. in a positive sense.*

down on all fours At a very low point. 1973: "Very shortly, Dupont found itself down on all fours with the rest of the industry." M. Ways, *Fortune*, Jan., 70.

downputter *n.* A person who disparages or criticizes another person or a thing. See **put-down.**

down-thumb *v.t.* Disapprove of, veto. 1968: "We down-thumbed the shaky marriage last December. Then came this announcement of the final split. . . ." *McCall's*, Aug., 43. *From the "thumbs down" sign, said to have been used in ancient Rome as a signal that a gladiator's life was not to be spared.*

down trip = **bad trip.**

DPT Dipropylphyptamine, a hallucinogen similar to LSD but having an effect lasting only for an hour or two and considered somewhat safer. *Drug culture.*

drag* *n.* Transvestite clothing. *adj.* Of, pertaining to, or wearing transvestite clothing, esp. female dress, jewelry, and cosmetics as worn by transvestite male homosexuals. *Used either in combination. as in "drag-queen," or as a modifier, as in "drag party."* *v.i.* To dress as a transvestite. *Orig. homosexual use. Now commonly known.*

drag party A party given by and for transvestites, almost always male homosexuals, who may attend in the dress of the opposite sex; any party for homosexuals.

drag-queen *n.* **1** A male homosexual who frequently dresses or is esp. fond of dressing as a woman. 1965: "*drag-queen* A homosexual accustomed to wearing female attire." A. F. Niemoeller, "A Glossary of Homosexual Slang," *Fact*, Jan.-Feb., 26. See "**drag.**" **2** A male homosexual who blatantly affects female gestures, speech patterns, etc.

dragsville *n.* = **dullsville.**

D-rays *n.pl.* Sunshine. c1968: "I went to Central Park to soak up some D-rays. . . ." James Simon Kunen, *The Strawberry Statement* (Avon), 129. *From Vitamin D, which is activated by exposure to sunlight. Not common.*

dream beads Opium pellets; opium. *From the beadlike pellets formed during heating. Drug culture. Obs.*

dress-off *n.* A contest, esp. among young flashily dressed men, to determine who is the best dressed. *Chiefly Negro use.*

Dr. Feelgood A physician who gives his patients renewed energy and a feeling of well-being by administering, usu. on a regular basis, injections of stimulants, esp. amphetamines, often combined with vitamins and hormones. 1972: "Almost all agree that however they perceive the effects of amphetamine, it initially makes them feel good. Thus the term 'Dr. Feelgood' is used to designate almost any doctor who relies heavily on the use of amphetamines or other stimulants in his practice." *Newsweek*, Dec. 8, 73.

driver* *n.* An airplane pilot. *Navy and Air Force use, esp. in the Vietnam war.*

drive [someone] up the wall To harass or torment; drive crazy. 1973: "Sir: Mr. Nixon should not resign. He should be impeached, and if this fails, leave him alone and let him get to work. Quit driving him up the wall." J. J. Roget, Letter, *Time*, Dec. 2, 6.

drop* *n.* **1** A place for the temporary storage of stolen or illegal goods. **2** A place where secret messages, letters, etc., may be left for another person, as a spy, drug peddlers, etc. *v.t.* To ingest any drug, esp. LSD. 1969: "Asked what the Transcendental Students wanted to make of society, one member said, 'We want a society where you can smoke grass (marijuana) and drop acid (LSD) . . . .'" N.Y. *Times*, Sept. 22, 26.

drop beads   1 To use certain homosexual "in" words while talking with another person to discover if he is also homosexual.   2 To reveal oneself as being homosexual unintentionally during a conversation. *Homosexual use.*

drop hairpins = **drop beads**.

drop-in*   n. A person not registered at a college or university who audits classes without paying fees and joins in other school activities. 1965: "Everybody has heard of school dropouts—Hank's a college drop-in. NBC did some research on college drop-ins, unregistered students who audit courses without paying for them. . . ." Dick Kallman, *Seventeen*, Sept., 54. *Student use.*

drop [one's] load [taboo]   1 To ejaculate. 2 = **dump a load.***

drop out   To remove oneself from the competitive commerical world or from traditional society and its mores, as by becoming a hippie, moving to a rural area and living a rustic life, becoming a confirmed drug addict, etc.

drug   v.t. To depress, bother, or bore: "bug,"* "drag;"* to make [someone] unhappy.   n. = **drag*** (def. 11).

druggy   druggie   n. A person who experiments with narcotic drugs; also, anyone who takes drugs. *Drug culture.*

drughead   n. A heavy user of drugs. 1968: "Finally, even hip philosophy of social oneness and all-encompassing love . . . began to sound steadily hollow with every front-page report of violence by some freaked-out drughead." Paul Horn, *Look*, Feb. 6, 76. *Drug culture.*

drum*   n. Eardrum. 1958: "[To] POP A DRUM [is] slang for 'rupture an ear drum' through excessive water pressure." Rex S. Burns, "Water Words," *American Speech*, Oct., 238.

dry fuck [taboo]   1 To go through the motions of sexual intercourse without penetration, usu. without removing the clothes. *Junior-high-school and high-school student use.* 2 Unsatisfying sexual intercourse, as when done hurriedly or without emotional involvement, esp. when it does not result in ejaculation or orgasm.

dry hump [taboo] = **dry fuck**.

duals   n.pl. A pair of wheels and tires mounted as one unit on a truck axle. *Trucker use.*

dubee   duby   n. A marijuana cigarette. *Drug culture.*

dubok   n. An ostensibly respectable person or place of business used to transact illegal business or to hide stolen goods or contraband; a "drop."* *A cold-war word taken from the Russian = oak tree, first used by the Central Intelligence Agency and now spreading to the underworld.*

dude*   n. A man; fellow, guy; any male person. 1973: "I'm sittin' in the bus stop . . . just me an' these three other dudes. . . ." D. Evans, *Black World*, Apr., 65. *Negro use.*

duke*   v.i.   1 To fight with the fists. *Orig. Negro use; then teenage gang use.* 2 To be involved in any kind of action, to argue, to "party,"* etc. *Negro use.*

dullsville   n. Fig., the place from which all dull things emanate; the epitome of dullness. *Thus: "This party is dullsville" or "This party is from dullsville" = "This party is very dull." adj.* Dullest; most "square."*

dumb act   Any performance without words, as a tap-dance act, juggling act, etc. *Vaudeville use, archaic.*

dumb-ass   adj. Stupid; tiresome.   n. A stupid person. 1973: "It is difficult for the average black to understand how a dumb-ass like Newton can have a following. While he bullshits and enjoys himself in his $650-a-month apartment, those he claims he's trying to help still go hungry." David Jackson, Letter, *Playboy*, Aug., 12. *As in "bad-ass" the suffix "-ass" is used as an intensive.*

dum-dum   dumdum   dumb-dumb n. A stupid or foolish person.   adj. Stupid or foolish. *Popularized by the comedian Don Rickles.*

dummy*   n. = **blank** (def. 2).

dump*   v.t. To kill.

duner   n. A driver of or rider in a dune buggy; a dune buggy enthusiast. 1974: "Once having camped . . ., duners go out on runs—trips by a half-dozen dune buggies. . . ." Calvin Trillin, *New Yorker*, Mar. 11, 106.

dykey   adj. (of a woman) Tough and mannish; Lesbian. 1967: "June Buckridge (Beryl Reid) is a short, squat, frizzy-haired Lesbian who guzzles gin out of water glasses, chainsmokes little cigars and keeps a stringy blonde baby doll. . . . But once a day, dykey June turns into Sister George, district nurse, darling of British housewives, the saintly star of a BBC soap serial called *Applehurst." Playboy*, Jan., 30.

dynamite*   *n.* Heroin of good quality. 1965: ". . . a connection who deals in

good-quality stuff—'dynamite,' . . ." James Mills, "We Are All Animals," *Reader's Digest*, June, 227. *Drug culture.*

E

eagle*   *n.* The academic grade E. *Some student use.*

early-bird   *n.* **1** One who habitually arises early in the morning. *From the saying "the early bird catches the worm."* **2** An early arrival; one who habitually arrives early. **3** The first scheduled, or an early train, bus, airplane flight, etc. *adj.* **1** Performed or scheduled for very early in the morning, as a class, meeting, etc. **2** For the benefit of those who arrive very early or too early. *Many parking-lot offices have a sign above a slot in the door reading "Early-bird key drop" as a convenience for those who wish to park their cars and leave their keys before the attendant arrives.*

ease on   ease out   To leave; to depart. *Some student use.*

eatin' stuff [taboo] = **table grade.**

eat shit [taboo]   **1** To be subservient or submissive; to be willing to do or believe anything in order to keep one's job, status, a friend, etc. **2** To believe in; support; be in favor of or enthusiastic about. 1965: ". . . you really eat this shit, don't you!" C. D. B. Bryan, *P. S. Wilkinson*, 9.

ecofreak   *n.* A vigorous supporter of ecological programs.

eff   *A euphem. for the word "fuck" in its various parts of speech and in various phrases, hence, "effer," "effing," "eff off."* 1972: "I am in no danger of suffering from loneliness. I have already had several abusive phone calls, telling me to eff off back to effing Russia, you effing, corksacking limey effer. This is because I suggested some time ago . . . that America would be better off for a bit of socialized medicine." Anthony Burgess, N.Y. *Times Mag.*, Oct. 29, 28.

egads button   egads switch = chicken switch.

eggbeater*   *n.* An outboard motor. 1965: "There are the purists who wouldn't be caught dead with an egg-beater on their [sail] boat." Robert W. Carrick, "Outboard Wells for the Small Auxiliary," *Yachting*, Jan., 77.

ego trip   An act performed primarily to build up or gratify one's ego. 1973: "The pie thrower, who had concealed his

missile beneath a box of flowers, said the guru was on an ego trip and 'I wanted to show he was mortal.' " *Time*, Aug. 20, 43.   **—per**   A person who goes on ego trips.

ego-trip   *v.i.* To do something to gratify one's ego; act selfishly.

eighty-six*   *v.t.* Lit. and fig., to reject or disqualify a person; to ignore, insult, or tease someone; to eject someone from a place or group, esp. from a bar, against his will. 1963: "I'll have you eight-sixed out of this bar." J. Rechy, *City of Night*, 173.

elephant ears*   Large, thick metal discs added to a missile's outer shell to reinforce it, to distribute the heat caused by friction in flight, and to stabilize the flight orbit. *Aerospace use.*

ends   *n.pl.* **1** A pair of shoes; shoes. 1961: "When a hipster buys clothes, he begins with 'ends' or 'shoes.' " E. Horne, "The Words for the Music," 39. *Jazz musician use.* **2** Money.

endsville   *n.* = **the end;***   **the most.***   *adj.* Fine, most exciting, most satisfying. *Orig. cool and beat use. Has replaced the earlier "endville."***

evergreen   *n.* An old favorite, such as a song.

evil*   *adj.* Spiteful, gossipy, sarcastic, "bitchy."*** *Orig. homosexual use.*

exhibeesh   *n.* = **exhibición.**

exhibición   *n.* A lewd performance of sexual acts, presented before an audience, involving either live actors or a film. 1965: ". . . those legendary pre-Castro *exhibiciós* [sic] starring 'Superman,' 'Hercules' and 'Tarzan.' " "After Hours" column, *Playboy*, June, 19. *From the Sp. = exhibition.*

eyeball to eyeball   Face to face; confronting one another, esp. in a tense situation or atmosphere. 1962: "We're eyeball to eyeball, and I think the other fellow just blinked." Dean Rusk, *SEP*, Dec. 8, 16.

eye-opener*   *n.* An addict's first injection of the day. *Drug culture.*

eyes only   A direction on a memorandum or letter that the contents are to be read only by the addressee, because the material is sensitive or confidential. *Short for the older direction*

"For your eyes only," which is often abbrev. as F.Y.O.

F

fab *adj.* Very thrilling or satisfying: excellent, great, wonderful. *From "fabulous." Common student and teenage use since c1963.*

face* *n.* **1** A celebrity; a well-known person. *Orig. show-business use.* **2** A person. 1961: "Bad face . . . i.e., a surly, mean, no-good cat." E. Horne, "The Words for the Music," 39. *Some hipster and student use.*

fack *v.i.* To tell the truth; to speak facts. 1963: "Negroes know . . . that facking means speaking facts, telling the truth." "Beyond the Ears of the Greys," *Time*, Aug. 2, 14. *Negro use.*

fade* *n.* **1** A white person. **2** A Negro who prefers white sexual partners, white friends, or white attitudes. *Negro use only.*

fag bag A woman married to a homosexual. *Homosexual use.* Cf. **fag hag.**

faggotry *n.* Homosexuality. 1973: "To a Midwestern boy faggotry was at the very least a terrible embarrassment." R. A. Arthur, *Esquire*, Nov., 42.

faggot's moll = **fag hag.**

fag hag A heterosexual woman or girl who seeks out the company of homosexual men. 1969: " . . . I'd hazard a guess that you're simply a Faggot's Moll, Fag Hag, or Fruit Fly. . . . A girl who enjoys the company and attention of males-who-go-to-bed-with-males is generally quite hung up about sex and afraid of getting fucked, not to mention a more complicated relationship." Una Sex, *Screw*, Aug. 18, 16. *Formerly, a female who smoked cigarettes, from the earlier common use of "fag"* * *to mean a cigarette.* Cf. **fag bag.**

fail *n.* A failure by a broker to deliver or receive stock certificates, etc., by the customary settlement date, usu. 5 days, after buying or selling. 1973: "The main measuring device for the seriousness of back-office trouble was the amount of what Wall Street calls 'fails.' " *New Yorker*, July 2, 35. *Wall Street use.*

fake off To idle or shirk; "goof off."*

fake [someone] out To bluff or deceive; to mislead intentionally.

fall in (up, by, out) = **fall down*** 1961: "Fall (in, out, by, up). To arrive or enter. Thus, 'The bash is in the base-

ment, Dad. Fall up anytime.' " E. Horne, "The Words for the Music," 39.

fall off the roof To begin a menstrual period. *Common since c1925.*

fall out* To go to sleep.

fan* *v.t.* To jiggle a coin return lever on a public pay phone in hopes of dislodging coins. **—ner** *n.* A person who does this habitually. *Telephone company use.*

fanny-dipper An ordinary swimmer, as opposed to a surfer. *Surfer use.* See **fanny.***

farmer *n.* A stupid or ill-mannered person; a dolt. *Not common.*

farmisht *adj.* Mixed up; in a state of conflicting emotions; emotionally ambiguous. *From the Yiddish.*

fast food Hamburgers, hot dogs, pizza, fried chicken, etc., esp. when dispensed by chain restaurants in which they are the principal menu items.

fast-food *adj.* Pertaining to fare such as hamburgers, hot dogs, fried chicken, etc., or to the chain restaurants that sell such fare. 1974: "The fast-food pollution [in Paris] isn't new, or—hedonist faithful pray—fatal." G. Greene, *New York*, July 8, 76.

fat* *n.* A fat person. 1973: "I met the other 18 women or fellow fats (excepting the six skinnies) at the 'cocktail hour,' before an open fire." A. D. Botorff, *The National Observer*, July 21, 8. *Usu. pl.*

fat city An excellent condition, state, or mood. 1965: "When Johnny came marching home from college this Christmas and announced he was in 'fat city' . . . ." N.Y. *Times*, Dec. 27. *Student and teenage use.*

fat farm A resort that has weight-reducing programs and menus; a resort for overweight people.

father fucker [taboo] = **mother fucker.** *Some homosexual use.*

faunet   faunlet *n.* An adolescent or pre-adolescent boy as a homosexual sex object. *Formed on analogy with "nymphet." Homosexual use.*

fave   fave rave *n.* A favorite, as a song, film, etc. 1973: "The unique French-based vocal group scats Mozart, Vivaldi, Bach, and other fave raves." *Sat. Rev.: Art*, Mar., 50.

Fed* *n.* The Federal government or one of its agencies or departments, esp. the Federal Reserve Board.

Feeb **feeb*** **Feebie** *n.* An agent of the Federal Bureau of Investigation (FBI). 1973: "When it comes down to it, in fact, the narcs speak condescendingly even about the agents of the Federal Bureau of Investigation, whom they call 'Feebs.'" Fred C. Shapiro, N.Y. *Times Mag.,* Feb. 25, 56. *Prob. from a transferred pronunciation of "feeb,"* *slang for a feeble-minded person.*

feel a draft 1 To sense a feeling of racial prejudice against oneself. *Negro use; orig. pop. by jazz musician Lester Young.* 2 To sense a lack of welcome or a feeling of dislike or rejection emanating from another. *Both uses from the image of "cold."* Cf. **cold shoulder.***

fem* **femme** *n.* 1 In a Lesbian couple, the one who plays the female role. 2 A male homosexual who is effeminate in appearance and mannerisms and usu. takes the less dominant role. *Homosexual use.*

fingerfuck [taboo] *v.t., v.i.* To masturbate or sexually stimulate a girl or woman manually. *Mainly teenage use.* See **fuck.***

fink out 1 To withdraw from or refuse to support a project, activity, scheme, etc. 2 To become untrustworthy. 3 To fail utterly. See **fink.***

fink-out *n.* An act of finking out; cop-out.

fire on To strike another person; hit. c1968: " . . . so Huey stepped back and broke the bottle over his head. All the dudes were standing on the corner just looking at this one dude Huey had fired on." Bobby Seale, *Seize the Time,* 16. *Negro use.*

fish* *n.* A heterosexual woman. *Lesbian and male homosexual use.*

fishball *n.* An unpleasant, cheap or despicable person. *Not common.*

fishwife *n.* The legal wife of a male homosexual. *Homosexual use.*

fit* *n.* = **works.** *Prob. short for "outfit." Drug culture.*

five pointer 1 A superior student. 2 A high grade received on a test or for an academic course. *From the five-pointed gold star assoc. with excellence, formerly pasted by teachers on superior papers and report cards, reinforced by stand. and slang "star." Student use.*

flack* *n.* = **flak.*** *v.i.* To act as a publicity agent. **—ery** *n.* Publicity. 1970: "A White House insider's name,

with enough flackery, can be sold like mouthwash." Hugh Sidey, *Life,* Feb. 13, 2.

flack out 1 To fall asleep; to become unconscious, as from drunkenness or from lack of oxygen in an airplane or while scuba or skin diving, etc. 2 To be tired or despondent. 3 To die. *Orig. cool and beat use.*

flag* *v.i., v.t.* To fail an examination or course. *Some college student use.*

flagger *n.* A person who summons, or "flags,"* a taxicab. *Taxicab driver use.*

flag it To flunk an examination or course in school. *Some college student use.*

flag-up *adj.* Of or pertaining to a taxicab ride in which the driver fails to start up the fare meter, thus enabling him to pocket the entire fare illegally. *Taxi industry use.* Cf. **gyp.**

flak* **flack** *n.* Severe criticism. 1972: "Back at the post office Joe took considerable flak from white co-workers angered by the verdict." Catherine Breslin, *New York,* May 29, 61. 1973: "Being married to a Torontonian, I get a lot of 'flack' from Americans who say it is only a matter of time until Toronto is infested with our big-city dilemmas. . . ." Ellen Rose Starr, Letter, *Newsweek,* April 16, 6. *Fig. use of "flak," antiaircraft gunfire.*

flake *adj.* Uninhibited, imaginative; having a colorful, highly individual personality. *Orig. and mainly baseball use.* *n.* 1 A colorful, highly individual personality or style; a "screwball"* or eccentric personality or style. 1964: "In the last three years, the Yankees [New York baseball team] have acquired . . . [an] amount of 'flake' in the person of such young players as Joe Pepitone, Jim Bouton, Phil Linz. . . ." Leonard Koppett, N.Y. *Times,* April 26. 2 Cocaine. *Drug culture. v.t.* To frame someone; arrest on trumped-up charges. *Police use.* **flakey** **flaky** *adj.* 1 Colorful; eccentric. 2 Screwy; crazy. 3 Easygoing; carefree.

flaked-out *adj.* Asleep or unconscious, as from exhaustion or excess of drugs or alcohol.

flake off Go away; "beat it."* 1966: "Want to brush off such friends? Suggest that they . . . flake off. . . ." June Gray, "Teens," Dayton (Ohio) *News,* Jan. 16, 4. *Student and teenage use.*

flake out 1 To leave; to depart. *Jazz musician use.* 2 To fail.

flake-out *n.* A complete failure; flop.

flap* *v.i.* To become anxious or

confused. 1973: " 'It's an effective side of Ehrlichman,' his former coworker mused. . . . 'I've seen him under hostile pressure before. He doesn't flap nor does he become a doormat.' " Douglas E. Kneeland, N.Y. *Times*, July 25, 26. See **unflappable**.

flares   *n.pl.* Flared trousers or slacks.

flash*   *adj.* Excellent, wonderful, great. *Some teenage use. Orig. from the Brit. sl. meaning.*   *v.i.* **1** To vomit. *Some student use.* **2** To undergo an hallucinatory experience, esp. after an injection of narcotics. *Drug culture.* **3** To feel the sudden intensely pleasurable effects of an injected narcotic drug. *Drug culture.* **4** To have a sudden idea or notion. *n.* **1** The sensation experienced by a person soon after heroin has been injected into a mainline blood vessel. *Drug culture.* **2** A thrill, a feeling of excitement or pleasure; "buzz."* *Some far-out and student use.* **3** Great personal style; charisma. 1972: "It was a serious bit of theater, an introduction to Jimmy's 'flash'—what others might call style. . . . Flash is in the clothes, the cars, the eyes, the walk, the talk." Richard Woodley, *Dealer: Portrait of a Cocaine Merchant*, (Warner), 11. **4** A sudden idea or impulse. 1973: " . . . but not before assuring Kroft that if he should get a sudden flash to commit Cat to *In Concert* and wants to call her . . . that's fine." Stuart Werbin, *Rolling Stone*, Oct. 25, 13. **5** A thing one is "turned on" to; one's "bag." His current 'flash,' as he calls it, tends toward gaucho suits . . . " Lindsay Van Gelder and Larry Kleinman, N.Y. *Post*, Feb. 15, 47.

flashback   *n.* A hallucination or sensation originally induced by LSD but recurring some time after the drug experience has ended. *Drug culture.*

flash on   To recall, recollect; bring to mind, esp. suddenly. 1974: "KSAN kept playing it and I kept digging it. . . . Eventually I flashed on the fact that I actually knew the song from somewhere . . . " Ralph J. Gleason, "Perspectives: The Endless Blues Mystery," *Rolling Stone*, Jan. 3, 11.

flash rider   A professional broncobuster; one who breaks and trains wild horses. *Orig. c1870 cowboy use.*

flash roll   A sum of money that is suddenly exposed to view as proof that its holder is ready to do business. 1973: "[Narcotics agents] . . . fill out evidence reports, daily work reports, surveillance reports, and separate fiscal forms for money advanced as a 'flash roll' to be shown, but not passed, to pushers." Fred C. Shapiro, N.Y. *Times Mag.*, Feb. 25, 48.

flatbacker   *n.* A prostitute. 1974: "His prostitutes are well known for being unhooked flatbackers, that is, they are nonaddicts and they make their money exclusively by performing sexual acts. . . ." Francis A. J. Ianni, *Black Mafia*, 32.

flathead*   *n.* An L-head or side-valve engine. *Hot-rod use.*

flat-out   *adj.* Complete, utter, total. 1964: "Marina Oswald . . . was . . . burdened by a . . . husband who was a flat-out failure in every way." *Time*, Nov. 27, 33.   *adv.* Directly; straight. 1973: " . . . and the bear looked up and came at them flat-out." B. Branham, *Sports Afield*, June, 88.

flats*   *n.pl.* A pair of crooked dice having flat, beveled edges; crooked dice. *Some gambler use.*

flavor*   *n.* A sexually attractive woman. *Some Negro use.*

flea powder = blank (def. 2).

flesh flick = skin flick.

flic   *n.* A policeman. 1973: "If the *flic* had the slightest suspicion he was following a much-wanted safe-cracker, would he remain across the street, marching along so sedately?" R. Fish, *Playboy*, April, 128. *From the Fr. Some U.S. use.*

flick*   *n.* A knife, esp. a switchblade knife. *More common in Britain than in the U.S., esp. among Brit. Teddy Boys.*

flight   *n.* = **trip.** *Drug culture and student use.*

flip-flop*   *v.i.* To change direction, attitude, a decision, etc. 1972: " . . . so [Senator Edward] Kennedy flip-flopped again. . . . 'There are no circumstances under which I would accept a nomination for any national office this year.' " *Time*, July 3, 13.

flip out   **1 = freak out** (def. 3). **2** To lose one's temper or cause someone to lose his. **3** To become or cause to become extremely upset; to lose self-control; to react violently; to "flip."*

flip-out   *n.* An instance of becoming extremely upset or out of touch with reality. 1973: "There Harriet has a minor flip-out and flees her 'excessively suicide-proof' room. . . ." *New Yorker*, July 2, 76.

flit*   *n.* A male homosexual; a male exhibiting female mannerisms.   **—ty**

adj. Homosexual; effeminate. *Considered less derog. than "queer"* because the connotation is more often of effeminate mannerisms than of sexual acts.*

flog the dummy (meat sausage) [taboo] = **beat the dummy.***

flong [one's] dong [taboo]   To masturbate. 1974: "If it weren't for flonging my dong, I don't know what I'd do." Cartoon caption, *Playgirl*, March, 142. Cf. **beat the dummy,*** **beat the meat.**

floss   *n.* Spun sugar; cotton candy. *Carnival and circus use.*

flower children   flower people   Hippies, typically young, who stress love and peace, and who sometimes wear or carry flowers to symbolize these attributes. *1960s.*

flower power   1 Love and peace, the central beliefs of the flower children. 2 The conventions or life-style of the flower children. *1960s.*

fluff*   *v.t.* To criticize severely or harshly.

flush*   *v.t.* To ignore, reject, or dismiss someone, usually socially.   *v.i.* To flunk an examination or course in school. *Student use.*

flush it   To flunk an examination or course in school. *Common student use.*

fly*   *adj.* Very stylish and attractive. 1972: " 'Look,' he said, 'okay, here's a young man, looks like he's under thirty, driving a Cadillac that's fly. . . .' " Richard Woodley, *Dealer: Portrait of a Cocaine Merchant* (Warner), 91. Cf. **superfly.**   *v.i.* 1 To take narcotics. *Drug culture.* 2 To experience the exhilarating effects of a narcotic drug. *Drug culture.* 3 To be convincing; go over. 1973: "It [Nixon's speech] didn't fly. 'It's not going over with the American people any more than it went over here.' " C. Manion, *National Review*, Sept. 14, 998.

Foggy Bottom   The U.S. State Department. 1965: "On Capitol Hill . . . the majority of congressmen have little affinity for the 'career boys' of Foggy Bottom . . . " Henry Serrano Villard, *Affairs at State* (Thomas Y. Crowell Co.), 9. *In ref. to the main State Department offices, located near the Potomac river on a section of land called "Foggy Bottom," the imagery being humorously transferred to the State Department.*

foil   *n.* A small packet of narcotics. *Drug culture.*

folkie   *n.* A folk singer.

folknik   *n.* A fan of folk music or of folk-music performers.

foodaholic   *n.* An overweight person who is addicted to food, esp. fattening food.

foot-in-mouth disease   A tendency to be gauche, indiscreet, or careless in what one says; the habit of "putting one's foot in one's mouth." *Humorously based on the veterinary term "foot-and-mouth disease."*

foot in [one's] mouth, put [one's] = **foot in it, put [one's].***

foot it = **hoof it*** (defs. 1, 2).

forked-eight   *n.* A V8 engine or a car having such an engine; a "bent eight." *Hot-rod use.*

for openers   for starters   To begin with; as a beginning.

forwards   *n.pl.* Pills containing amphetamine or its derivatives. *Drug culture.*

four pointer   1 A grade of A on an examination or for a course of study. →2 A superior student. *Because in many colleges and universities a grade of A is worth four points toward graduation. Student use.* Cf. **five pointer.**

fox   *n.* An energetic, attractive, desirable girl, esp. one having a happy and alert personality. *Orig. Negro use. Popularized into white use during 1963 by heavyweight boxer Cassius Clay, later Muhammad Ali.* Cf. **hammer.**   **—y** *adj.* Attractive and desirable. 1974: "She was 22 years old, a real foxy little chick with auburn hair." Joe Eszterhas, "The Prisons of War," *Rolling Stone*, Mar. 28, 33. *Said only of girls and women.*

fragging   *n.* The intentional killing or wounding of a superior officer, as with a fragmentation grenade, by his own troops. *Armed Forces use in Vietnam.*

frat*   *n.* A male student who accepts middle-class norms of conduct and dress; a typical "square"* student. 1965: "A 'frat' in teenage jargon is a youth who dresses neatly and conforms to accepted patterns of behavior." N.Y. *Times*, Dec. 4. *Student and teenage use.*

—freak   See Appendix to the Supplement, Suffix Words.

freak*   *n.* 1 A person who abandons conventional values and attitudes; specif., a hippie. 2 A person of marked individualistic attitudes and life-style. 3 An enthusiast or devotee. 4 A drug addict.

freak out   1 To cause or to undergo intense hallucinations or other reactions after taking an hallucinogenic drug. *Drug culture.* 2 To undergo experiences that resemble hallucinations, as when watching psychedelic visual effects. **3** To be out of touch with reality, esp. as a result of taking drugs; to become irrational. *Drug culture.* **4** To become or make one very stimulated or excited, as if under the influence of drugs. **5** To abandon conventional values and attitudes; to become or act like a hippie.

freak-out   *n.* **1** An act or instance of freaking out. **2** A person who is freaked out, esp. as a result of taking drugs. **3** A bad experience; bad trip. **4** A meeting or group of hippies.

freak trick   A man who engages in unusual or brutal sexual activities with a prostitute. 1972: "A scrawny white hooker who had been the victim of a 'freak trick'—a customer who gets his kicks from brutally beating girls—was nursing her wounds." Xaviera Hollander, *The Happy Hooker,* 4.

freaky   *adj.* Of or pertaining to freaks or freak-outs; unusual, "far-out." * 1973: "They remind us of corporation executives or investment bankers. There is nothing bohemian, or beat, or hippie, or freaky about them. They are straights; uptight." *Sat. Rev.: Art,* Jan., 24.

free people   freeworld people   1 People outside of prison, as distinguished from prison inmates. **2** Collectively, prison guards, officials, and personnel. *Prison use.*

freeworld   *n.* The world outside of prison; civilian life as distinguished from prison life. *Prison use.*

French* [taboo]   *v.i., v.t.* To commit fellatio or cunnilingus. Cf. **French Way.***

fresh and sweet   Just released from jail. *Said of prostitutes. Prostitute use.*

friendly   *n.* A member, ship, airplane, etc., of one's own or an ally's armed forces; villagers or guerrillas friendly to one's own side during a war. 1964: "Friendlies—Generally the ARVN or civil guard troops but sometimes used to designate townspeople who cooperate with the Americans or the Saigon government." N.Y. *Times,* Sept. 4. *Some W.W.II and Korean war Armed Forces use; very common Armed Forces use in the Vietnam war.*

fringes   *n.pl.* Fringe benefits; any benefits or remunerations, other than salary, granted to employees, such as bonuses, paid vacations, paid holidays, pensions, employer-paid insurance and medical plans, etc. *Labor union use since c1960.*

frit   *n.* A homosexual.

'fro = **Afro.**

frog*   *n.* **1** An unpleasant, cheap, or despicable person. **2** An introverted, boring, or old-fashioned person; a "drip"* or "square."* 1965: "Anybody who still wears [saddle shoes] is . . . a 'frog' . . . " N.Y. *Times,* Dec. 27. *Student and teenage use.*

from the git-go   from the get-go From the very beginning. 1972: "'Cause if this motherfucker goes to jail he goes to jail. It was his bust from the git-go." Richard Woodley, *Dealer: Portrait of a Cocaine Merchant* (Warner), 102. *Prob. combination of the old term "from the word go" (from the very beginning) with "get up and go" (energy, initiative).*

front-end   *adj.* On or pertaining to that portion of a midway which is near the main entrance. *Carnival and circus use.*

fruit fly = **fag hag.**

fruit machine = **one-armed bandit.*** *From the tiny pictures of various fruits on the wheels of many slot machines. Chiefly Brit.*

fruit picker   A man who considers himself heterosexual and is considered so by others, but who occasionally seeks out homosexuals for sexual satisfaction. *Homosexual use.*

fruit salad*   A mixture of tranquilizers, painkillers, barbiturates, amphetamines, and other drugs, esp. as collected from the family medicine cabinet and experimented with secretly by adolescents at so-called "fruit salad parties." *Prob. from the variety of bright colors of capsules and pills. Drug culture of early 1960s.*

FTA   Fuck the Army. *Army use since c1960, as a counter expression to disliked orders, rules, etc.* See **fuck.***

fubar   *adj.* Fucked up beyond all recognition.   *n.* = **snafu.*** *W.W.II Armed Forces use; euphem. acronym formed by analogy with "snafu."** See **fucked up.***

fubb   *adj.* Fucked up beyond (all) belief   *n.* = **snafu.*** *W.W.II Armed Forces use; euphem. acronym formed by analogy with "snafu."** See **fucked up.***

fubis   Fuck you, buddy, I'm shipping (out). *Army use since c1960, as a counter expression to a disliked person, order, etc.; euphem. acronym.* See **fuck.***

fuck film [taboo]   A pornographic motion picture, esp. one that consists chiefly of explicit scenes of sexual intercourse. Cf. **nudie** (def. 1); **skin flick.**

fucking-A [taboo]   *interj.* = "That's right"; "I agree completely."

fuck off [taboo]   *interj.* = "Go away"; "leave me alone"; "shut up".

fumtu   *adj.* Fucked up more than usual.   *n.* = **snafu.*** *W.W.II Armed Forces use; euphem. acronym formed by analogy with "snafu."** See **fucked up.***

fun—   See Appendix to the Supplement, Prefix Words.

fun and games   **1** A good time, as a party; a pleasant experience. → **2** Necking, foreplay, or sexual intercourse. **3** A difficult, annoying, or embarrassing task. *Used facetiously.*

Fun City   fun city   Any large city; specif., New York City. 1967: " 'People planning a vacation in Fun City,' [Mayor Lindsay] noted, 'must realize that taxis are no easier to get than orchestra seats to "Cabaret." We urge visitors to write ahead several months in advance for taxi reservations....' " *N.Y. Times*, June 27, 38. *A humorous or sardonic nickname frequently used by John Lindsay, mayor of New York City in the late 1960s and early 1970s, although he denied coining it.*

funk*   *v.i.* **1** To fail, esp. to fail an examination; "flunk."* **2** to be thrown into a panic. *Orig. Brit. use.*   *n.* A style of jazz reflecting elements of Negro culture, such as spirituals, African rhythms, etc. *In vogue with some Negro jazz musicians since c1957, partly in order to maintain something that white musicians had not appropriated.*

—iness   *n.* The melancholy, pensive, or bittersweet mood associated with the blues. 1965: "Cannonball's [Cannonball Adderley's] alto sax has lost its old, zesty funkiness...." *Time*, Feb. 19, 3.

—y   *adj.* **1** Old-fashioned; specif., playing jazz in its older New Orleans style, emphasizing rhythm and uncomplicated breaks. 1961: "The other [criticism of jazz musician Dave Brubeck] is that he isn't 'funky' or old-fashioned and committed to jazz in its pure form, as native American folk art...." R. Rice, "Profiles [of Dave Brubeck]," *New Yorker*, June 3, 42. *Orig. Negro use.* **2** Sad or depressing, as jazz music played slowly, in a low register, or in a minor key; melancholy, pensive, or bittersweet, like the mood produced by the blues. *Jazz musician and Negro use.* **3** Emotional; without restraint, form, or goal. **4** Inferior or obnoxious, said of a person, performance, or manufactured object. *Mainly Negro use.* **5** Groovy; swinging.

funny farm = **funny house*** (def. 1).

funsie   funsey   *n.* Any task that is difficult, requires special effort, or that leaves one exhausted. *Teenage and student ironic use.*

fur [taboo]   *n.* The vagina.

furry   *adj.* Hair-raising; terrifying; scary. *Prob. from association of fur with human hair.*

G

gaff*   *v.t.* To cheat someone; spec., to shortchange a customer and pocket the money, or to withhold for oneself money from the sale of a ticket of admission that should be put in the cashbox. *Orig. and mainly carnival use.*

gaffer*   *n.* **1** One's father. 1932: "Studs felt that Mr. O'Brien was different from his own gaffer." J. T. Farrell, *Young Lonigan*, 95. **2** A foreman. *Some I.W.W. use. Archaic.*

gago   *n.* A non-Gypsy. *Gypsy use.*

game plan   A plan, usu. involved, for achieving a goal. *Orig., a plan or strategy for winning a game in sports. Popularized in its present sense during the Watergate hearings before the Senate Select Committee on Presidential Campaign Activities in 1973.*

gang bang [taboo] = **gang shay.***

gangster*   *n.* A marijuana cigarette.

1960: " 'Just go on and smoke that gangster and be real cool.' " C. Cooper, *The Scene*, 219. *Drug culture.*

ganja   *n.* A type of strong marijuana obtained from a cultivated strain of the Indian hemp plant. *Orig. West Indian use.*

garbage down   To eat; "chow down."* *Orig. W.W.II Navy use; now Navy and some student use.*

garbage furniture = **street furniture.**

gavar   *n.* The art or technique of picking pockets. *Gypsy use.*

gay*   *n.* A homosexual person. *The adjective senses became current in the 1950s and the noun sense in the 1960s.*

gay lib   Gay Lib   Gay Liberation, a movement of male and female homosexuals working as a minority group to obtain freedom from discrimination, demanding equal opportunities in jobs, housing, etc. 1973: "I once did a joke about the Mafia joining forces with the gay lib group in New York, so that now with the kiss of death you get dinner and an evening of dancing." Bob Hope, *Playboy*, Dec., 104.

G.B.   g.b. = **Goof ball*** (def. 1). *Drug culture.*

gear   *adj.* Excellent, wonderful, great. 1964: "For what 17's like, their current vocabulary includes 'fabulous,' as well as 'gear' and 'tuff,' both of which also mean fabulous." N.Y. *Times*, Nov. 1, sect. B, 100. *Popular teenage use since c1960. n.* Something spectacular, exciting, or entertaining. *Teenage use.*

geezy addict   An addict who takes any drug that is available. *Drug culture.*

george*   *v.t.* To lure or invite into sexual activity. 1960: "One of the girls georged him, just for kicks, just to see if he was as good a producer as a braggart." C. Cooper, *The Scene*, 31.

geronimo!   *interj.* Used to express surprise, pleasure, or triumphant achievement. *From the cry used by W.W.II paratroopers upon jumping (after the name of the Indian chief). Since c1945 it has replaced "eureka!" among students and young people.*

get [one's] back up   To become angry; to sulk. 1962: "Just don't get your back up. . . . I haven't got the energy to fight tonight." J. Edgar Grove, "Forgiveness," *Esquire*, Dec., 58.

get behind [something]   To experience a pleasurable drug-induced high. *Usu. in the phrase "get behind it." Drug culture.*

get down on [someone] [taboo] = **1 go down on [someone]**.* **2** To scold; upbraid. c1965: "Mama used to get down on me about hanging out with Reno. She'd say that she knew he'd be going to jail one day soon and that I'd be going with him." Claude Brown, *Manchild in the Promised Land*, 160.

get it on   1 To become aroused sexually; also, to have sexual relations. Cf. **hard on**.* **2** To be very intense about something; greatly enjoy doing something. 1974: "For me, the groove is three, five, 15 guys in a studio just get it on together." Ringo Starr, quoted by Gay Search, *Rolling Stone*, Jan. 17, 10. **3** To begin something; get going. *Often in the imperative.*

get it [all] together. See **together.**

get it up [taboo]   To achieve and hold an erection. 1973: "I think I can get it up twice or three times a day, providing it makes me a few more bucks than

hacking a cab for twelve hours." Xaviera Hollander, *Xaviera*, 53.

get [one's] jollies = **get [one's] kicks** 1962: "The owner of this place [a resort hotel] gets his jollies by walking around most of the day in a Sioux war bonnet. . . ." Douglas Welch, "Squirrel Cage" (synd. column), Nov. 3.

get [one's] kicks   To do that which is personally satisfying, amusing, or thrilling; to indulge in one's preferred vice, form of entertainment, habit, or relaxation.

get off   1 To obtain relief or pleasure by obtaining or injecting a dose of narcotics. *Drug culture.* **2** To drop formally out of a college or university but to remain on campus or in the vicinity taking advantage of some aspects of the academic community. *Student use.* **3** To derive pleasure from; enjoy greatly. 1973: " 'All of our musical landmarks came before CSN&Y,' he says. 'I remember buying their album and getting off. . . .' " David Rensin, "America: What This Band Needs Is a Hat Trick," *Rolling Stone*, Nov. 8, 20.

get [one's] rocks (nuts) off [taboo]   To ejaculate. 1973: "That made it possible for people who'd never be caught dead at a 42nd Street skinflick to get their rocks off and feel intellectual about it at the same time." Ed McCormack, *Changes*, Dec.-Jan., 17.

gevalt   gevald   *interj.* = Oh! *An expression of dismay, protest, astonishment, etc.* 1973: "He breaks open a mezuzah—nothing inside—*gevalt!*—but a piece of paper that says, 'Made in Japan.' " R. Alter, *Commentary*, Jan., 80. *From the Yiddish.*

Gibson Girl   A hand-cranked emergency radio transmitter. 1965: "Tons of hand-cranked 'SOS' transmitters were built for World War II. Because of their curvy chasses they were dubbed 'Gibson Girls.' " "What Radiotelephone?" *Yachting*, Jan., 80. *Orig. and mainly W.W.II Armed Forces use.*

gidget*   *n.* A pert, attractive young woman. *Derived from "gadget"** (*def. 3*) *but pop. by Frederick Kohner's novel* Gidget (*1957*), *and subsequent movies and the TV show based on it.*

gig*   *n.* **1** Any job, as in an office, factory, etc., esp. a dull, menial, or temporary job while awaiting more exciting or satisfying work. *Orig. jazz musician use; far-out and student use since c1960.* **2** = **bag** (def. 2). *v.i.* To play an engagement as a musician. 1974: "The next few years found Hound Dog gigging around the Delta. . . ." James Litke, *Rolling Stone*, Sept. 12, 28.

gin *n.* A street fight or "rumble."* *Some Negro and teenage gang use.*

ginger-peachy *adj.* Fine and admirable in a conventional or sentimental way; "peachy-keen."* *Often used ironically, as a criticism, in order to show the speaker's sophisticated superiority to the person, object, or idea referred to. One of several archaic terms thus used.*

gink* *n.* A dull, ineffectual, or insignificant person; a "jerk."*

girl* *n.* **1** A male homosexual. *Homosexual use.* **2** Cocaine. 1960: " 'Boy is the junkie term for heroin; they call cocaine girl because it gives 'em a sexual job when they take a shot.' " C. Cooper, *The Scene*, 54. *Drug culture.*

G.I.s Diarrhea. 1963: "An all-night bout with the G.I.s left him weak and weary. . . ." *Time*, July 5, 45. *Prob. a shortened euphem. for the taboo "G.I. shits,"* but may be an abbreviation of "gastrointestinal." Unlike "G.I. shits," this term need not mean diarrhea caused by dysentery or tropical diseases but can refer to even a mildly upset stomach. Common since c1955.*

give a flying fuck [taboo] To care about; be concerned with. 1974: "I frankly don't give a flying fuck about the long-range effect of this thing on me, personally." Hunter S. Thompson, *Rolling Stone*, Feb. 28, 42. *Usu. in the negative. Orig. 1940s use, in expressions such as "give a flying fuck at a rolling doughnut," "give a flying fuck at a running rabbit," etc.*

give [someone or something] a miss To avoid; keep away from. 1973: "Unlike those in Paris, the girls here make little pretence of enjoying your company. . . . Give these girls a miss." *Pan American Travel Guide*, 49.

give [someone] five To slap another's hand as a sign of agreement. 1965: "Reno put out his hand for me to give him five, and I slapped it." Claude Brown, *Manchild in the Promised Land*, 412. *Negro use.*

give [someone] head [taboo] To perform fellatio. 1975: "We have it from an unimpeachable historical source that a number of Henry the Eighth's wives gave head." "Playboy's Party Jokes," *Playboy*, Apr., 116.

give [someone] the hairy eyeball To glance or stare fiercely or threateningly;

glare, glower. *Mostly high-school student use in the 1960s.*

glazed *adj.* Drunk. *Orig. jazz musician use; now student use.*

glitch *n.* Any mechanical defect, malfunction, problem, or emergency. 1965: "Despite such 'glitches' (a spaceman's word for irritating disturbances). . . ." *Time*, July 23, 37. *Orig. aerospace use.*

glitter *n.* An elaborate, showy style of dress and makeup indulged in by certain (usu. male) rock stars. It derives its effects from sequins or false diamonds applied to the face and parts of the body, dyed hair, rouge and mascara, and costumes of rich and brightly colored material, often in the form of space suits.

glitter rock The rock music composed by or played by rock groups who wear "glitter."

glom* *v.t.* To take a look at. 1972: "Or walk around the corner to glom old smack heads, woozy winos and degenerates. . . ." Jon Horn, "Glomming the Apple," N.Y. *Times*, Oct. 15, 4. *n.* A look or glance.

glossy *n.* = **slick*** (def. 1). 1973: " . . . and the warring baronesses—the more or less 'legendary' female editors of the powerful 'glossies.' " K. Fraser, *New Yorker*, June 16, 86.

go* *adj.* **1** Favorable; O.K.; ready to begin. 1962: "As the astronauts say . . . all signs are go in the National [Baseball] League." *Sporting News*, April 11, 1. *From use by the orig. seven U.S. astronauts to signify that a spacecraft was functioning properly and ready to be launched. Has replaced "A-OK."* **2** = **swinging.*** 1963: " . . . beatniks, whose heavy black turtle-neck sweaters had never looked particularly go with white tennis socks. . . ." *Time*, Jan. 4, 40.

go ape **1** To lose emotional or mental control; to behave irrationally. 1961: "The exaggerated, unflattering connotation of wild, self-dirtying activity was ascribed to individuals or organizations that had *gone ape* during the Second World War. . . ." L. Jackson, "Amelioration of Some Slang Terms: Have Present Teenagers 'Gone Ape' or 'Chicken'?" *American Speech*, May, 150. **2** To exhibit enthusiasm; to become excited, frenzied or wild. 1965: " . . . people are going quietly ape over the girl [Modesty Blaise, a British comic strip character]." Helen Gurley Brown, "Step into My Parlor," *Cosmopolitan*, Nov., 8. *Common student use. See* **ape**.

go ape shit [taboo] = **go ape.**

go down and do tricks [taboo] **1** = **go down on [someone].** * → **2** To commit any heterosexual perversion.

gofer   go-for   *n.* An employee in an office, construction site, etc., part of whose duties are to run errands for other employees. 1974: "Jennifer says she was hired to be trained for the position of legislative assistant, but after a couple of months she found she was running the robo machine and acting as a receptionist, secretary, and general go-for." Nicholas Von Hoffman, col. N.Y. *Post*, July 30, 31. *From a person's being requested to "go for" coffee, etc.*

goggle-eye   *n.* = **redeye*** (def. 2).

go-go   *adj.* **1** Of or pertaining to a discotheque and its music and dancing. **2** Modish, faddish; esp. of or pertaining to the styles worn typically by patrons of discotheques; flashy, garish. 1966: "The kids don't want me in go-go boots and stretch tights." *Time*, May 13, 69. **3** (of stocks, business, etc.) Promising rapid growth or profits; vigorous, energetic. 1967: "Concern centers mainly on speculation of the mutual funds—the so-called 'go-go' or 'performance' funds." *U.S. News & World Report*, Nov. 20, 63. 1973: "Religion is a really go-go growth industry these days, at least the publishing part of it." L. R. Hills, *Esquire*, Dec., 210.   *n.* Dancing performed in a discotheque. *From the French phrase "à go-go," meaning galore, from the original Parisian discotheque, Whisky à go-go. Since early 1960s.*

go-go girl   go-go dancer   A girl employed to perform provocative dances in a discotheque or small nightclub, usu. on a small stage or raised platform.

gold   *n.* **1** A very high grade of marijuana. See **Acapulco gold.** *Drug culture.* **2** Money. *Some jazz and student use.*   **—en**   *adj.* **1** Easy to accomplish, excel at, or make a high grade in. *Student use.* **2** Lucky; having good luck, talent, easy tasks or assignments; sure of success; certain to obtain fame, wealth, a high rank, or a desired goal. **3** Fine; superb; excellent.

Goldberg [derog.]   *n.* A Jew, specif., one who employs Negroes for domestic, janitorial, or other menial labor. 1965: "I use to have nightmares, man, about bein' old . . . sweeping the floors for Goldberg in that dress house of his." Claude Brown, *Manchild in the Promised Land*, 286. *Negro use.* See **schvartze.**

golden-ager   *n.* **1** An old or retired person, esp. one active in clubs, societies, etc. **2** A member of a community for retired persons. *From the cliché that the aged are in the "golden years" of their lives.*

golden oldie   A popular song of the past, esp. a song that has gained new popularity from reissued records or tapes. 1973: " . . . crank up a . . . golden oldie like 'Honeysuckle Rose' by the immortal Fats Waller." F. P. Tullus, *New Yorker*, Aug. 13, 27. *From the gold record which symbolizes that a record has sold a million copies.*

golden shower [taboo]   The voiding of urine onto the body of a person for whom it is a form of sexual excitement. *Mainly homosexual and prostitute use.*

goldfinger   *n.* A type of synthetic heroin. *From the Ian Fleming novel* Goldfinger, *about master spy James Bond, and the pop. movie based on it in the early 1960s. Drug culture.*

goma   *n.* Crude opium. *Drug culture.*

gomer   gomar   *n.* A first-year or naive Air Force cadet. *Air Force use.*

gonif* *n.* A homosexual.

Go-No Go   Go-No-Go   Pertaining to that moment in a missile launching when the operation must either be canceled or allowed to continue toward completion without the possibility of cancellation. *Aerospace use.* Cf. **go.**

good hair   Straight or almost straight shiny hair like that of white people. *Negro use. This concept became less popular with the rise of the civil rights movement and the subsequent consciousness-raising among Negroes.*

go off [taboo]   To ejaculate; to have an orgasm.

gook* *adj.* Cheap, flashy, inferior. *n.* [derog.] A Vietnamese. *Armed Forces use in Vietnam.* Cf. **dink, slope, zip.** **—y**   *adj.* Sticky, messy, or greasy. 1965: "The feel is fantastic. Greaseless. Nongooky." Revlon lipstick advt., *McCall's*, March, 11.

Gooney Bird   The DC-3 airplane; "the three." 1966: " . . . pilots everywhere refer to it [the DC-3] with great affection as the 'Gooney Bird' after the albatross whose great powers of flight and ubiquity are legendary." N.Y. *Post*, Jan. 21. *Airplane pilots' use.*

goopus   *n.* A stupid, undesirable person; a "square,"* a "goof."* *Some adolescent and teenage use.* See **goop.***

goosey [taboo]   *adj.* Sensitive in the anal region; susceptible to being "goosed."* 1932: "Hennessey was goosey anyway, and he jumped." J. T. Farrell, *Young Lonigan*, 29.

go out of [one's] skull 1 To become very tense or nervous. 1967: " 'We get up at 6 A.M.,' Jay said. 'In the series I am pretending to be an Indian beggar boy, so they spend an hour putting on my face and body makeup and you can go out of your skull while they're doing that.' " Robert Musel, *TV Guide*, Dec. 23, 16. 2 To become very excited, be overcome with emotion. 3 To become bored.

gorilla* *v.t.* 1 To steal, esp. by strong-arm methods; hold up. 1965: " . . . if you let somebody gorilla you out of some money . . . you got your ass beat when you came back home." Claude Brown, *Manchild in the Promised Land*, 255. 2 To beat (someone) up.

go to Denmark To have an operation to change one's sex. *From the fact that Christine Jorgenson, one of the first well-known transsexuals, received her medical treatment in Denmark in the 1950s.*

go up* To become high on narcotics; be under the influence of a drug. *Drug culture and student use.*

goyische *adj.* Gentile. 1967: " . . . every spring . . . they sent him and my mother for a hotsy-totsy free weekend in Atlantic City, to a fancy goyische hotel. . . ." Philip Roth, *Portnoy's Complaint*, 6. *From the Yiddish.* See **goy.***

goyisheh kop [derog.] Gentile brains or ways of thinking, esp. in a Jewish person. 1973: "It has been suggested that Garelik's greatest value is that he, personally, has destroyed the stereotype that all Jews are intelligent. That's all we need—the first Jewish Mayor will be one with a *goyisheh kop*." Dick Schaap, *New York*, Jan. 1, 47. *From the Yiddish. Lit., "a Gentile head."*

grab* *v.t.* To cause a strong emotional response in; to interest, startle; to obsess. *n.* A policeman. *Never common.* **—ber** *n.* Any extremely interesting, provocative, or startling comment, person, piece of news, book, movie, play, or performance; that which interests, stirs, or obsesses someone.

granny dress A floor-length dress, usu. with long sleeves and a high neckline, worn by girls and young women since about 1965 in imitation of earlier rustic styles like "granny" (grandmother) might have worn.

granny glasses Small, round, steel- or gold-rimmed eyeglasses worn since about 1965 in imitation of earlier rustic styles like "granny" (grandmother) might have worn.

grass* *n.* Marijuana. 1965: "Youth scandalizes proud suburbs with grass parties—grass being one of the hippiest synonyms for marijuana." "On Not Losing One's Cool about the Young," editorial, *Time*, Dec. 24, 16. *Drug culture and student use since c1960. Replacing "pot"* as the most common sl. word for "marijuana."*

grasseater *n.* A corrupt policeman who accepts graft money when it is offered, but who does not demand it. 1974: " 'The grasseaters are turning themselves in and cooperating fully,' the source said. 'The meateaters are going to get the full blame.' " N.Y. *Post*, Oct. 3, 1. *Police and underworld use.* Cf. **meateater.**

grasshopper* *n.* A person who smokes marijuana. *Drug culture.*

gray [derog.] *adj.* White; Caucasian. 1968: "What about that gray girl in San Jose who had your nose wide open?" Eldridge Cleaver, *Soul on Ice*, 9.

grayhound *v.i.* To run, esp. in escape or pursuit.

greatsie greatsy *adj.* = **ginger-peachy.**

Greek* [taboo] *v.i., v.t.* To have heterosexual anal intercourse.

green, the *n.* The unbroken forward part of a wave. *Surfer use.*

greenie* *n.* Dextroamphetamine sulfate, a heart-shaped, green pep pill, a stimulant believed to be in wide use among athletes, esp. professionals.

gremlin *n.* 1 A beginner or person past the beginning stage, but not yet of expert caliber. 1961: "If [a beginning surfer's] surfing career goes well, he will be a 'gremlin' in a few years. . . ." *Life*, Sept. 1, 51. 2 A person (usu. a girl) who hangs out with surfers but does not surf; a "beach bunny." 1963: "The true surfer is scornful of the . . . 'gremmies' (gremlins, usually girls), those hangers-on who may never get wet. . . ." "Surf's Up!" *Time*, Aug. 9, 49. 3 Any annoying troublemaker, parasite, or hanger-on. *An extension of the orig. use in the Armed Forces during W.W.II, from the Air Force use = an invisible imp who caused malfunctions, problems, or confusion. Pop. c1950s through surfer use; now common, esp. in student and Armed Forces use.*

gremmie *n.* = **gremlin.** *Mainly student and Armed Forces use.*

grinder*   *n.* A parade ground or drill field. 1963: "The drill field is the *grinder.*" Albert F. Moe, "Anent 'Marine Corps Slang,' " *American Speech,* Feb., 78. *Marine Corps use.*

gripe [one's] ass (balls)   To annoy one greatly. *The expression may conclude with ref. to any real or imaginary part of the body (left nut, middle kidney, butt, spleen, teeth, etc.), as if the annoyance caused physical pain. Taboo parts of the body are most commonly named, then those parts most easily hurt, as the extremities. Expressions containing taboo parts of the body are taboo.*

grit*   *v.i.* To eat.   *n.* Food. *Some Negro use.*

groaty   **grotty**   *adj.* Slovenly; ugly. *Teenage use. From "grotesque."*

grok   *v.i., v.t.* To experience empathy; to establish rapport with, to communicate on a deep and sympathetic level. 1968: " . . . but instead they are all rapping and grokking over the sound it made . . . as if they had synched into a never-before-heard thing, a unique thing. . . ." Tom Wolfe, *The Electric Kool-Aid Acid Test,* (Bantam) 76. 1968: " . . . he met her at an acid-rock ball and she grokked him, this ultracool miss loaded with experience and bereft of emotion. . . ." *Playboy,* June, 80. *Coined by Robert A. Heinlein as a "Martian" term in his popular 1961 science-fiction novel* Stranger in a Strange Land. *Wide hippie and student use, esp. in the late 1960s.*

groot   *n.* = **peanut gallery.***   1964: " . . . he would climb the stairs to the peanut gallery—the groot, it was called in some towns—and look down at the balcony. . . ." John O'Hara, "Arnold Stone," *The Horse Knows the Way,* 32–33.

groove*   *n.* **1** Any habit, preference, or habitually exciting or satisfying activity; one's "kick"* or "bag." **2** Anything that is considered exciting, satisfying, fashionable, or "hip."*   1965: "Your hat is a groove." "A Cursory Glossary to the Off-beat Side of Now," *Harper's Bazaar,* April, 143.   *v.i.* To do, hear, look at, or experience something with great intensity and enjoyment. 1968: "To groove means to yield yourself to the flow of activity around you. To be 'with it,' as a phonograph needle is 'with' the record groove. . . ." N.Y. *Times,* May 12, d 15. 1971: "Sun along Third Avenue eddies up her legs and arms like drops of oil in her joinings.

She walks for blocks grooving on Reality." Gail Sheehy, *Speed Is of the Essence,* 49.   *v.t.* To like; enjoy. 1966: "They see the spade cats going with ofay chicks and they don't groove it." Rose DeWolf, *Village Voice,* Sept. 22, 9. **—er**   *n.* A person who grooves. *Orig. 1960s hippie, student, and musician use.*

gross out   To offend or abuse a person, as by the use of obscene or crude language, gestures, etc.

group-grope   *n.* **1** A group of people, of either both or the same sex, engaged in touching or caressing one another, but stopping short of sexual acts. → **2** Any group of persons or things closely, or too closely, allied. 1970: "Next month . . . Harvard will re-establish an independent department of sociology, ending 24 years of interdisciplinary group-grope (sociologists, psychologists, anthropologists) under the 'social relations' umbrella." John Leonard, N.Y. *Times,* June 3, 43.

groupie   *n.* **1** A girl who seeks out, or follows on tour, star entertainers, esp. members of rock groups or pop singers, in order to gain prestige through sexual favors. 1970: "A national magazine . . . features a story about 'groupies,' an In but not original behavioral phenomenon consisting of youthful females committing sexual aggression against juvenile rock musicians, and involving haphazard lovemaking at any price and in every possible way, reminiscent of dedicated autograph collecting." Leopold Tyrmand, "Reflections," *New Yorker,* Feb. 28, 92. → **2** An ardent fan; a demonstrative admirer; a hero worshiper. 1973: "Fill that room with 1500 assorted lawmen, law groupies (male) and their elegantly coiffured women and you have the Texas Ranger Sesquicentennial Anniversary Celebration." Chet Flippo, "Law and Order Groupies of Texas," *Rolling Stone,* Sept. 27, 8.

grunge   **grunch**   *n.* A dull or boring person.   *adj.* **1** Very ugly or slovenly. **2** Dull or boring. *Mainly teenage use.*

grungy   *adj.* Shabby; dirty; worn. 1973: "I put down in my grungy little notebook that Max Frisch was a wise man." C. Vetter, *Playboy,* April, 172.

grunt*   *v.i.* To defecate. *Used euphem. by adults in speaking to small children; also some adult use.*   *n.* An Army infantryman; soldier. *Orig. Marine Corps use in the Vietnam war.*

guide = **guru** (def. 3).

guilty big   Undergoing or in need of psychiatric treatment.

gump light A miner's lantern or lamp. *Some miner use.*

gun* *n.* A long, heavy surfboard. *Surfer use.*

gung-ho, *adj.* **1** Innocently and uncritically enthusiastic, optimistic, patriotic, zealous, devoted, or eager; childishly believing; having unrestrained enthusiasm; fanatic. 1962: " 'There isn't much gung-ho Communism here (in Russia),' says an American." *Time*, Nov. 19, 43. **2** Lacking sophistication; appealing to noncritical judgment; emotional. *Orig. W.W.II use, from the Chinese "keng ho" = awe-inspiring (lit. "more fiery"). Now almost always used with a connotation of disapprobation which it did not orig. carry in W.W.II.*

guru *n.* **1** A psychiatrist. *From Sanskrit = venerable one, via India, spiritual leader or teacher. Orig. humorous use.* **2** An acknowledged leader, expert, or authority in some field; specif., a charismatic or spiritual leader or guide who attracts a considerable following. 1968: "Frequently they become leaders of the New Left, turning for guidance to gurus such as Paul Goodman and Herbert Marcuse who do profess to have answers to the Big Questions." John Fischer, *Harper's*, Aug., 11. 1973: "That genial guru of the right, Barry Goldwater . . . " Tom Wicker, N.Y. *Times*, Sept. 16, Sect. IV, 15. **3** One who supervises, comforts, or supports someone undergoing an experience with a psychedelic drug. *Drug culture.*

gut— See Appendix to the Supplement, Prefix Words.

gut* *adj.* **1** Fundamental, basic; central. 1969: "The gut issues in the forthcoming election are not dramatic ones." *Newsweek*, May 26, 48. **2** Intuitive, spontaneous, not consciously reasoned; strongly or profoundly felt. 1969: " . . . if there is one thing common to . . . all races, all ages, in America today, it is this deep, gut feeling that they want to be part of things, . . ." W. H. Honan, N.Y. *Times Mag.*, Jan. 19, 73. **3** Easy, not difficult, "snap."* 1969: "Or a prospective engineer will look for a 'gut' humanities course where the professor is said to put on a good show." David Riesman, *American Scholar*, Summer, 378.

gutty* *adj.* **1** Eliciting an emotional response; strongly evocative or emotional. **2** essential; basic; appealing to or arising from a basic emotion, feeling, motivation, etc. **3** Powerful; capable of great force or high speed; having a powerful engine. *Automotive use.*

gyp* *n.* A taxicab whose driver carries a passenger to his destination without starting up the fare meter, thereby enabling the driver to pocket the fare illegally. *Taxi industry use.* Cf. **flag-up.**

gyppy tummy Diarrhea.

gypsy *n.* **1** A taxicab operating without a taxi license. **2** A trucker who owns and drives his own truck and obtains freight wherever possible. → **3** An owner-driven truck, esp. one operating without Interstate Commerce Commission authority. *Trucker use.*

H

hack* *v.t.* To cope or deal with successfully. 1966: "A sophomore at Ivy League Sheldon College, John Fist . . . can't hack it any more. Boring lectures about 'The Greek Ideal.' Finky roommates as dull as footballs." Webster Schott, *Life*, Mar. 18, 17. *Often with "it" as the object.*

hack around To do nothing in particular; to wander about; to idle. 1965: " 'Hacking around' (which can be roughly translated as 'fooling around' or 'doing nothing') is a favorite teen-age pastime." Phyllis Lee Levin, "Family Business in Brief," N.Y. *Times Mag.*, April 4, 99. *Student and teenage use.*

hacked *adj.* Annoyed.

Haight, the *n.* = **Hashbury.**

hairy* *adj.* Difficult to cope with; dangerous, treacherous, tortuous; difficult; exciting; challenging. *Said of an assignment, task, situation, etc.; of a place, such as a battlefield, racetrack, etc.: of people; and of objects.* *n.* A youth or man with very long hair, sometimes with sideburns and a beard. 1971: "Three young hairies with rich homes in their walks, pulling what they call 'street furniture' (other people's throwaways) on wooden dollies." Gail Sheehy, *Speed Is of the Essence*, 23.

half-and-half [taboo] *n.* Fellatio followed by conventional sexual intercourse. *Orig. prostitute use.*

half load Fifteen $3 packets, or

"bags," of a narcotic, esp. cocaine or heroin. *Drug culture.* Cf. **bag.**

hame   *n.* An unpleasant job, esp. a menial task or a job in which one cannot make the best use of one's talent; "gig." 1961: "Hame—Any unpleasant job, from mowing the lawn to playing trumpet in a Mickey Mouse band." E. Horne, "The Words for the Music," 39.

hammer*   *n.* A pretty, sexually desirable girl. *Negro use.* Cf. **fox.**

H and C   A mixture of heroin and cocaine. *Drug culture.*

handkerchief head   1 A black male who wears a scarf or handkerchief to protect his "conk," or processed hairdo. → 2 A person who is a traitor to his own race. *Negro use, esp. before the mid-1960s.*

hang in there   hang in   To refuse to give in or give up; persist, esp. tenaciously. 1973: "The way those tough Bronx mothers wouldn't have quit. The way my mother would have hung in there." B. J. Friedman, *Playboy,* Oct., 172. 1974: "Rose Mary Woods is hanging in, but her friends say it has been difficult." Nora Ephron, *New York,* March 18, 39.

hang loose   To be relaxed or nonchalant; to keep "cool."* *The opposite of being "up tight."*

hang out*   To let the entire truth or all the facts be known without holding back anything. 1973: "As the current saying goes, NCR has it all hanging out." *Forbes,* July 15, 50. *Often used in the phrase "let it all hang out." Orig. Negro use, but later general use, esp. in the Watergate scandals.*

hang-out*   **hang-out road**   *n.* Disclosure of the complete truth. 1974: " . . . the President and his aides decided to change their strategy to what was described as a 'modified limited hang-out'—meaning a response that would satisfy Watergate investigators while disclosing as little as possible." *Newsweek,* July 22, 19. *Formed from "(let it all) hang out" and often used in the phrase "go the hang-out road."*

hang tough   To persevere; refuse to give up. 1972: "You've got a friend at Chase Manhattan, if you've still got a Traveler's Check to cash. Otherwise: hang tough." Jon Horn, "Glomming the Apple: A How-to Story," *N.Y. Times,* Oct. 15, 22.

hang up*   **hang-up**   *n.* 1 A mental block; a psychological disturbance or problem. 2 The cause of a psychological disturbance; that which one is obsessed by or extremely emotional about; a special enthusiasm or interest; that person, thing, idea, etc., on which a person is "hung up." 3 An annoyance, bother, hindrance, encumbrance; anything that or anyone who is burdensome, annoying, bothersome, or irritating. 1965: "You couldn't carry around an amplifier and electric guitar and expect to survive, it was just too much of a hang-up." Bob Dylan, in an interview in *N.Y. Post,* Dec. 1, 8C. *v.i.* To commit suicide by hanging. *Prison use.*

happening   *n.* A staged but usu. partly improvised event that, through shock or novelty, engages the audience's attention and often its participation. *1960s use when this form of entertainment was very popular.* —s   *n.pl.* Narcotics; drugs. 1958: "*Junk, gage, happenings, pod* and *tea* [all mean] narcotics." M. Crane. "Vox Bop." *Some jazz musician and drug culture use. Not common.*

hard-core   *adj.* Of or pertaining to pornography in which sexual acts are described at length and in earthy language or (as in photographs, live shows, and motion pictures) depicted frankly rather than simulated.   *n.* Shortened form of "hard-core pornography." 1974: "Rolls Royce of Hard-Core." Advt. for pornographic film, *The Village Voice,* Aug. 15, 68. Cf. **soft-core.**

hard drug   A drug, such as heroin, and morphine, that is addictive and harmful to health. Cf. **soft drug.**

hard-hat   hardhat   *n.* 1 A full-time Viet Cong soldier, as opposed to a guerrilla or reservist. 1965: " . . . some 50,000 are 'hard-hats' (full-time fighters), another 100,000 are local guerrillas who can be ordered up from farm or village as needed." *Time,* Aug. 6, 28. *Armed Forces use in the Vietnam war.* 2 A construction worker. *From the hard helmet worn as a protection for the head.* → 3 An ultraconservative patriot, esp. one who believes in squelching liberal and radical factions, often by violence. *Since early 1960s when construction workers frequently clashed with student anti-war demonstrators.*

hard legs   A man or youth; cat; dude. *Negro use.*

hardnose*   *n.* A tough, determined person.

hard-road freak   A wandering youth who has utterly rejected the establishment and who typically has had several arrests, as for vagrancy, the sale or possession of drugs, etc.

hard rock A form of rock music with a simple driving beat, usu. performed by a band of instruments with the electric guitar predominating, and usu. greatly amplified.

hard stuff = hard drug. *Drug culture.*

Hare Krishna kids Hare Krishna people Young people who belong to a U.S. cult, the International Society for Krishna Consciousness (ISKON), dedicated to the worship of the Hindu deity Krishna. The men wear saffron-colored dhotis and the women many-hued saris. Often they may be seen dancing on city streets chanting the love mantra, "Hare Krishna."

harp* *n.* A harmonica. *Musician use.*

hash* *n.* 1 Hashish. *Drug culture and student use.* → 2 Marijuana or any other narcotic. *Some drug culture use since c1960.* *adj.* Wonderful; "cool"*; "swinging."* *Beat use since c1963.*

Hashbury *n.* Haight-Ashbury, a section of San Francisco, populated by large numbers of hippies, esp. during the 1960s. *From a blend of "Haight-Ashbury" plus a probable word play on "hash," slang for hashish.*

hash head A frequent user of hashish or marijuana. *Drug culture.*

hassle* *v.i.* To quarrel or argue. *v.t.* 1 Harass; to treat roughly. 1973: "Condon disappeared and I went to an assistant D.A. and told him I wanted to discuss being hassled by the police." A. Aurthur, *Esquire*, Feb., 10. 2 To obtain drugs with great difficulty. *Drug culture.*

hat* *n.* A woman, specif. one's wife or girl friend. *Not common.* See **wear a hat.**

hatchet job 1 A malicious verbal or written attack against a person, organization, etc. 1964: "By the hatchet job is meant here, not just a few surly growls about a particular book, but a calculated attempt to demolish the author, to blow him out of the water, to plant his career with salt." Wilfred Sheed, *Commonweal*, March 6, 691. *Prob. late 1950s on.* Cf. **hatchet-man.*** 2 A firing or dismissal, as of an employee.

hauler *n.* A very fast car, esp. a hot rod. 1965: "Hauler—A car that's really fast." Fort Worth, Texas, *Morning Star-Telegram*, July 16. *Hot-rod use.*

have a thing about To be obsessed with; to have a strong liking or dislike for; to be devoted to or hate.

have [something] going for [one] To

have as an asset. 1973: "As is clearly evident in Darrach's article, Fischer is a horse's ass. I'm happy he can play chess, because it's apparently all he's got going for him." Ann Hotton, *Playboy*, Oct., 16.

have it all together See **together.**

have [one's] nose open 1 To be blindly in love; to be infatuated; to be attracted sexually to someone. 1974: "She's got his nose open so wide you could run a tractor through it." "Sanford and Son," NBC situation comedy rerun, July 12. *From the image of a stallion, bull, etc., with its nostrils distended while in a state of sexual excitement. Negro use.*

hawk* *n.* A person who advocates a war or a belligerent national policy. *Orig. from John C. Calhoun's "War Hawks" political party of 1812, revived in modern use during the Cuban missile crisis of 1961 and common in ref. to those seeking escalation of the Vietnam war. Colloq.* —**ish** *adj.* Advocating a war or a belligerent national policy. 1965: "These people, 18 percent of the total, are as hawkish as Lyndon Johnson. . . ." Stewart Alsop, *SEP*, Oct. 23, 30. —**ishness** *n.* The advocation or promotion of a war; belligerence. 1968: "A few of the Republicans objected to Nixon's hawkishness. . . ." John Bird, *SEP*, Mar. 23, 82. Cf. **dove.**

head* *n.* 1 A ship's toilet or bathroom. *From "bulkhead." Orig. maritime use. Colloq.* → 2 Any toilet or bathroom. *Common since W.W.II.* 3 A narcotics addict or habitual user of a nonaddictive drug. *Also used in combinations with specific drugs, as "acid head."* 4 A feeling of euphoria produced by a drug; a high. 1972: "Anything to get a head. They sniff nail polish in here. Lady in the commissary, I think she gonna stop sellin' nail polish. . . ." Inmate in the Bedford Hills Correctional Facility, N.Y., quoted by Leonard J. Berry, *Prison*, 241.

head comic Any of various underground comic books designed for teenagers and young adults, esp. to be read during the smoking of marijuana. Head comics ridicule sex and feature bizarre situations, black humor, puns.

head job [taboo] = **blow job*** (def. 1).

head kit The collection of articles (syringe, needle, etc.) used by a drug addict. *Drug culture.*

head shop A small shop dealing in various accessories of the drug culture, such as "roach clips" and water pipes, and in other items for hippies and the youth cult, such as psychedelic posters, incense, candles, organic food products, etc.

heavenly blue   Morning-glory seeds. *Drug culture.*

heavy* *adj.* **1** Crooked, illegal. **2** Wonderful, fine, "cool."* **3** Deep; meaningful. 1971: "But the heaviest art form on the planet is certainly films." David Crosby quoted by Ben Fong-Torres, *Rolling Stone Interviews* (Paperback Library), 416. **4** Prominent; important. 1973: "Cain is from Boston, his family very heavy into potato chips." A. Aurthur, *Esquire*, Feb., 18. *adv.* Very much. 1971: "I'm heavy into property, in property management." Chuck Berry quoted by Greil Marcus, *Rolling Stone Interviews* (Paperback Library), 186. *n.* A large wave, esp. one excellent for surfing. 1961: "[Surfers wait] for the sea to act up and produce a 'good set of heavies' (big, rideable waves)." *Life*, Sept. 1, 51. *Surfer use.*

heavy metal   A type of very loud, dense blues music that uses electronic instruments, drums, and many amplifiers.

heel* *v.t.* To serve as an apprentice, esp. said of a student serving as an apprentice in a campus activity, such as on the student newspaper, to work at a campus job in return for free room and board in a dormitory or for part of one's tuition. *The object of the v.t. is always the occupation or place of work: thus a student "heels the newspaper," "heels the campus cafeteria," etc.* *n.* An apprentice worker; often a student or a worker who does menial jobs   **—er.** *n.* A young or apprentice reporter. *Some newspaper use.*

hen* *n.* A young woman; a "chick."*

herb *n.* Marijuana. *Drug culture.*

hick* [derog.]   *n.* A Puerto Rican.

high* *n.* **1** The pleasurable feeling from taking drugs. *Drug culture.* **2** An exhilarated feeling; euphoria.

high-hat* *n.* = **sock.** *Some musician use.*

Hill, the   *n.* **1** Capitol Hill in Washington, D.C.; site of the U.S. Capitol, where Congress meets. → **2** Congress, or its acts, rules, and opinions. *Colloq.*

hip-huggers   *n.pl.* Pants that hug the hips and have a very low waistline, usu. well below the navel.

hippie **hippy** *n.* One of a group of people, usu. young, who withdraws from and rejects the values of modern middle-class society. Hippies typically wear unconventional clothing, let their hair and often their beards grow long, use marijuana and psychedelic drugs, and often live in communes. *Chiefly 1960s use, although aspects of the hippie life style are still very much in evidence among many young people of the 1970s.*

hippiedom **hipdom** *n.* **1** The world and life style of hippies. **2** Hippies considered as a group.

hip-pocket bookie   A bookie who deals only with a few clients who place large bets. *Because he doesn't need an expensive establishment; all of his "business" papers fit in his hip pocket. Gambling use.*

hit* *v.t.* **1** To deal a card to a player, esp. an extra card which the player requests, as in draw poker. **2** To serve a drink to someone, usu. an alcoholic drink; esp. to serve someone a second portion, to refill someone's glass. 1962: "He signaled the bartender. 'Hit us again.'" J. Edgar Grove, "Forgiveness," *Esquire*, Dec., 66. **3** To beg or borrow from. **4** To murder. *Underworld use.* *n.* **1** A premeditated murder; a planned murder. *Underworld use.* **2** A dose of a drug. 1971: " . . . the current price of cocaine was about $10 'a hit.'" Harold M. Schmeck, Jr., N.Y. *Times*, Nov. 15, 82. *Drug culture.* **3** A tobacco cigarette into which heroin has been introduced. 1971: " . . . G.I.'s sit smoking the mixed tobacco-and-heroin cigarettes called 'hits.'" Iver Peterson, N.Y. *Times*, May 17, 12. *Drug culture.* **4** An injection of a narcotic drug. *Drug culture.*

hitch* *v.i., v.t.* = **hitch-hike.*** *n.* A ride, usually as a result of hitch-hiking, but not necessarily.

hit man   A man hired to kill someone; a hired assassin. *Underworld use.*

hit on   To try to sell someone something, often a useless, defective, or over-priced item; to annoy by soliciting, arguing, flirting, etc.; to attempt to force one's attention, ideas, or merchandise on another; to pester.

hitter* *n.* = **hit man.**

hit the bricks   To walk out of a plant, factory, etc., on strike. 1964: " . . . the United Auto Workers hit the bricks against giant General Motors. . . ." *Time*, Oct. 2, 111.

hit the panic button = **push the panic button.**

Hoagy   *n.* = **Hero*** (def. 1).

hocky* **hooky** **hookey** *n.* **1** = **shit.*** 1960: "Great big blooping hunks of dog hocky." William Styron, *Set This House on Fire* (Random House),

53. *A euphem. for the taboo "shit" in all its lit. and fig. uses, both stand. and sl.* **2** [taboo] Semen; "come."* **3** Any unappetizing food; food having an unappetizing appearance.

ho-dad   hodad   ho dad   ho-daddy *n.* **1** A boastful but amateurish person; a wise guy; an objectionable, unpopular person who pretends to be "hip,"* knowledgeable, or expert. 1961: "A new vocabulary has sprung up, with such words as . . . 'ho-daddy' (intruding wise guy)." *Life,* Sept. 1, 48. **2** A person not active in a sport, hobby, field of interest, etc., who spends much time with those who are active, enjoying a false feeling of excitement and belonging. 1963: "The true surfer is scornful of the 'ho-daddies' . . . those hangers-on who may never get wet . . . but like to immerse themselves in [surfer] jargon. . . ." "Surf's Up!" *Time,* Aug. 9, 49. **3** A person who gets no fun from life, esp. a dedicated white-collar worker; a stuffy "square."* *Orig. surfer use; now common sports and student use.*

hog* *n.* **1** A locomotive engineer. *Some railroad use. A shortened form of "hog-head,"* from "hog"* = a locomotive.* **2** A Harley-Davidson motorcycle. *Motorcycle use.* **3** A large car, esp. a Cadillac. 1960: " 'Yeah, I got a Hog,' he said, ' . . . A Cadillac . . . ' " C. Cooper, *The Scene,* 223. **4** = **PCP.**

hog, on the Without money, broke. *Some hobo use.*

ho-hum *adj.* Unexciting or mediocre; so-so. 1973: "Griffin writes, 'late-night TV, first-position ho-hum sex and the dregs of countless six-packs.' " Russell J. Battaglia, Letter, *Playboy,* Nov., 14. *n.* 1974: "Have a bucket of chicken / Have a barrel of fun, / Goodbye ho-hum . . ." Advt. jingle for Kentucky Fried Chicken.

hoke up To create something with a faked or artificial value. 1968: " . . . and on the afternoon he [LeMay] retired from the Air Force, FAA administrator Najeeb Halaby hoked up a special ceremony in which he presented LeMay with a private pilot's license." Robert G. Sherrill, *Nation,* Oct. 28, 422.

hold* *v.i.* To have narcotics in one's possession. *Drug culture.*

Holy fuck! [taboo] = **Holy cow!***
Holy shit! [taboo] = **Holy cow!***

home boy (girl, people) A person, met elsewhere, who comes from one's own hometown. *Chiefly Negro student use at Southern colleges.*

home plate The airfield, landing strip, or aircraft carrier on which an airplane or crew is based and to which the plane returns after successful flights. *Mainly Air Force use, since c1960.*

honcho *n.* The boss; the man in charge of any work or detail; a leader or organizer. *v.t.* To boss, lead, or organize. *Orig. Armed Forces use in Korea; now common Armed Forces use.*

honey bucket Any container used to carry fertilizer or excrement. *Orig. rural use, common Army use in W.W.II.*

Hong Kong dog Diarrhea. *Used by travelers in the Far East. From Hong Kong + "dog," a popular dance of the early 1960s.*

honky   honkie [derog.] *n.* A white person. *Negro use.*

hooch* *n.* **1** A Korean house, room, or esp. a shack inhabited by a prostitute. 1964: "The girls . . . giggle timidly and plead: 'Come on to my hooch.' " *Time,* Oct. 16, 48. *Armed Forces use in Korea.* **2** A typical Vietnamese village hut of woven straw, branches, leaves, corrugated tin, etc. *Armed Forces use in Vietnam.* → **3** An American barracks, esp. a quonset-style barracks in South Vietnam. 1964: "Hooches—The huts woven from banana leaves and roofed with straw or corrugated tin that are the standard housing for Vietnamese outside the cities. Some Americans have appropriated the term for their own quonset-styled barracks." N.Y. *Times,* Sept. 4. *From the Japanese "uchi" = a house. Armed Forces use in Vietnam.*

hoo-ha* *n.* Uproar; tumult. 1973: "Peter Brook, in case you're wondering what all the hoo-ha is about, shook up Broadway a few years ago with his direction of the athletic 'A Midsummer Night's Dream,' and 'Marat/Sade' before that." A. Sainer, *Village Voice,* Sept. 13, 67.

hook* *v.t.* To grab, find, or locate. *v.i.* To engage in prostitution. 1973: "All showgirls are automatically categorized as know-nothing sex-fiend hookers. . . . You say, 'I'm a showgirl,' they say, 'Oh, you hang your tits out and hook.' " *Playboy,* Dec., 257.

hootch *n.* = **hooch.***

hootchee   hotchee [taboo] *n.* The penis. *Armed Forces use in Korea.*

hopsan *n.* A taxi. *Armed Forces use in Korea.*

hopscotch *v.i.* To move or travel from one place to another, usu. rapidly and over long distances. 1972: "The show, already filmed, hopscotches from Toronto and Boston to Lake Tahoe and Las Vegas to sample night-club and theater opening-night performances." Richard K. Doan, *TV Guide*, Dec. 16, A-1.

horn* *n.* A telephone. *Usu. in the expression "on the horn."* **—er** *n.* A person who sniffs large amounts of cocaine and thus has a running, tender nose because the drug destroys nasal mucous membranes.

horse* *n.* A prison guard who is paid by inmates to smuggle out letters and smuggle in tobacco and other contraband articles. *Prison use.* *v.t.* To haze someone; specif., to haze a college freshman or new fraternity member. *College use c1915.* **—s** *n.pl.* A pair of dishonest or loaded dice; specif. mismatched dice that can produce only specific combinations. 1961: "Paul P. Karnov, president of the H. E. Hason Co. . . . testified that his firm sells from 15 to 20 different types of loaded dice. . . . Karnov explained the use of 'horses,' mismatched dice that turn up only certain combinations." Associated Press, Aug. 22.

horse cock [taboo] Bologna or any other cylindrical cold cuts. *Orig. W.W.II Navy use.*

hospital *n.* A jail. *Central Intelligence Agency use; some recent underworld use.* Cf. **ill.**

hot and cold = **H and C.**

hot dog* = **hot dogger** (def. 2).

hot dogger *n.* **1** A skilled surfer, esp. one who performs stunts or tricks while surfing; a "hot dog"* (def. 3). 1961: "Almost every wave carries a 'hot dogger' doing tricks. . . ." *Life*, Sept. 1, 48. *Surfer use.* **2** An expert skier proficient in **hot-dog skiing.** *Skier use.*

hot-dogging *n.* **1** Expert surfing performed by a highly skilled surfer. *Surfer use.* **2** A type of skiing that features acrobatic stunts, such as somersaults, twists, turns, etc., rather than speed. *Perhaps because such expert or acrobatic performers were once considered to be showing off, wanting onlookers to say "hot dog!", an exclamation of approval or surprise since 1905. However, it could come from the 1890s expression "to hot dog it" = to walk fast, move quickly. Skier use.*

hot pants* Very brief shorts for women and girls, often made of soft materials in bright colors. *Late 1960s and early 1970s use.*

hot shit* [taboo] A big shot; an

aggressive, successful, self-important person. 1974: "If I could remember a couple of things that Bob Dylan said to me backstage in 1964, I could write something sensitive and probing like all the rest of these hot shits lately." Letter, *Rolling Stone*, April 11, 7. *Always used disparagingly.*

hot shot* *n.* A narcotic injection that is fatal because of an impurity in it or because poison has been added to it. 1960: " 'You got a hot shot! You're dead, you snitchin' bastard!' " C. Cooper, *The Scene*, 19. *Drug culture.*

hot walker A groom who walks a racehorse to cool it down after a race or workout. *Horse race use.*

Hound, the *n.* A Greyhound bus. *Orig. trucker use; now some motorcycle, Negro, and student use.*

hound dog A man who thinks of little else but sex; a woman-chaser. *Southern hill use, but pop. by rock-and-roll singers, esp. Elvis Presley in his pop. song "Hound Dog," c1958.*

hubba-hubba* **huba-huba** *adv.* Quickly; on the double. *Some Armed Forces use since W.W.II.*

Huey *n.* The helicopter, Utility, Model 1-B. 1964: "Huey—The Helicopter, Utility, Model 1-B . . . a combination of shuttle bus, supply truck, ambulance and weapon of war." N.Y. *Times*, Sept. 16, 4. *Army and Air Force use, esp. in Vietnam.*

huffer *n.* A supercharger for an automobile; "blower." *Some hot-rod use.*

hummy *adj.* Content; happy; esp. content or happy because one is innocent and not aware of danger, expense, or possible disappointment. *adv.* Happily, contentedly; with innocent expectation. *Negro use.*

hump* *n.* **1** A worthless or insignificant person. 1963: "You're gonna make out, kid. . . . You ain't like the rest of us humps." Sterling Hayden, *Wanderer*, 163. **2** [taboo] Coitus; a woman considered sexually; a "lay."* 1965: "I hear she's a good hump." H. Selby, Jr., *Last Exit to Brooklyn*, 18. **—ery** [taboo] *n.* Sexual intercourse. 1973: " . . . locally the D.A. slammed down on homosexual humpery . . . while in sunny Los Angeles the MPAA refused to change the X rating on *Fritz the Cat* on the ground that it depicted 'anthropomorphic humpery.' " Judith Crist, *New York*, Jan. 1, 50.

hung* *adj.* **1** Annoyed; peeved. **2**

Tired; exhausted. *Some jazz use.* **3** = **hung over.*** **4** [taboo] = **hung like a bull.**

hung like a bull [taboo]   Having an exceptionally large penis. *Many nonce expressions are based on this by substituting other animals for "bull" and associating the size of that animal, its virility, or its sexual habits with a man's penis, virility, or sexual life. Thus a man who is "hung like a chicken" has a small penis, a man who is "hung like a rabbit" desires or has frequent but quick sexual intercourse. All such expressions are taboo.*

hung up (on)***   Obsessed (with); frustrated or stymied by; unable to live, act, think or function normally (because of); esp. extremely emotional about, fond of, or devoted to. 1965: "I'm hung up on fried rice...." "A Cursory Glossary to the Off-beat Side of Now," *Harper's Bazaar*, April, 143.

hunky   *adj.* Sexually attracted to women.

hurt   *v.i.* To be in dire straits of one sort or another; to be in trouble. 1959: "[A student who has had] a raw deal from any ... source ... *has been had* or *he's had his*, and he hurts." L. P. Boone, "Gator Slang," *American Speech*, May,

155.   *v.t.* To kill; to wound seriously or beat up badly. *Teenage street-gang use.*

husband   *n.* **1** A pimp in relation to his stable of prostitutes, esp. in relation to his favorite one. *Prostitute use.* **2** The more domineering or "masculine" partner in a homosexual relationship, male or female. *Homosexual use.* Cf. **wife.**

hustle***   *n.* A robbery. 1970: "You know I can't pay out five bills for a wash if I wasn't planning a hustle." Lawrence Sanders, *The Anderson Tapes*, 60.

hutzpa   *n.* = **chuzpa.**

hype***   *n.* Advertising that achieves its end by tricks or gimmicks. 1973: "About 10 days ago, without any advance p.r. hype, a one-hour quasi-documentary opened that has everyone agog ..." H. Smith, *Village Voice*, Sept. 13, 50. **2** A person or thing promoted by hype. **3** A swindle; sham. **4** A lie. **5** An addict who injects drugs. *v.t.* **1** = **hype up** (def. 1). **2** To trick; deceive. **—r**   *n.* A promoter; advertiser. *From the older "hype," a hypodermic needle.*

hype artist = **hyper.**

hype up   **1** To promote by tricks or gimmicks. **2** To arouse; excite.

I

ice***   *v.i.* To become or remain silent. *v.t.* **1** To ignore or pay no attention to. **2** To kill. *Underworld use.*   *adj.* Good; very fine; great. *Prob. from "cool"* (*def. 4*) = *satisfying.*

ice cream habit   The occasional use of drugs. *Drug culture.*

ID   I.D.   *v.t.* To establish the identity of; identify.

idiot board   A cue card; a large card held up out of the range of a television camera to prompt performing actors. 1955: " 'Idiot boards' are held out of camera range to prompt forgetful performers." *SEP*, Sept. 24, 29. *Television use c1945–1960.* Cf. **idiot girl.**

idiot box   A television set.

idiot girl   A girl who works in a television studio and holds cue cards for the performers. 1955: "Girls who hold ... up [cue cards] are called 'idiot girls.' " *SEP*, Sept. 24, 29. *Television use c1945–1960.* Cf. **idiot board.**

ill   *adj.* Arrested on suspicion or for questioning; jailed. *Underworld and*

Central Intelligence Agency use. Cf. **hospital.**

—in   See Appendix to the Supplement, Suffix Words.

I'll drink to that   I agree with you; yes indeed.

in front   In advance; paid or requiring payment in advance. *Orig. underworld and theatrical use.*

innocent [derog.]   *n.* A liberal, white supporter of the Negro civil rights movement. *Negro use.*

in orbit = **way out*****(def. 3). *Mainly teenage use.*

into   *prep.* Involved with; absorbed in. 1974: "A great many ... of Guru Maharaj Ji's converts in the United States formerly were active in the anti-war movement. Many thousands were 'into' the drug culture." D. Snell, *Sat. Rev.: World*, Feb. 9, 21.

invent   *v.t.* To steal. 1974: "The text describes Mailer's interviews with the ghetto artists, who told him about 'inventing' (stealing) the paint from the stores, going into the train yards at night...." *Publishers Weekly*, Feb. 11, 44.

Isro *n.* A hairstyle, similar to the Afro, worn by young Jews.

J

J *n.* A marijuana cigarette. *From the J in "Mary Jane."* * *Drug culture.*

jack around To waste time; to fool around; to engage in horseplay. *From "jack off."* * *Some student use.*

jack up* **1** = **shoot up** (def. 1). *Drug culture.* **2** To hold up someone in order to rob him. **3** To beat someone up. **4** (of the police) To search and interrogate a suspect. *Mainly Negro use.*

jag house A brothel of male prostitutes catering to male homosexuals.

jailhouse lawyer A prisoner who, whether well-informed or not, is given to discussion of his own legal rights and affairs and those of fellow inmates. 1969: "In those four years, DiLorenzo became an avid reader of good literature and a 'jailhouse lawyer.'" Edward Ranzal, N.Y. *Times*, Aug. 1, 67. *Prison use.* Cf. **guardhouse lawyer.***

jake flake An undesirable, insignificant, or tiresome person. *Not common.*

jam* *adj.* Heterosexual. *Homosexual use.*

jammer *n.* A musician who participates in a jam, or jam session. 1974: "Almost from the start of the tour, in Chicago, January 3, there had been rumors that a 'superstar jam' in New York, the likely jammers being the four ex-Beatles, Leon Russell, Mick Jagger, and a few other 'friends.'" Loraine Alterman and Ben Fong-Torres, "Dylan's Star-Studded Homecoming," *Rolling Stone*, Mar. 14, 17.

Jane Crow Discrimination against women. 1968: "Borrowing their rhetoric from the Negro civil rights movement, they call the practice segregation by sex, describing it as 'Jane Crow' treatment...." *Life*, Dec. 6, 48. *Formed on analogy with "Jim Crow,"* * *discrimination against blacks.*

janfu *n.* Joint Army-Navy fuck up. *W.W.II Armed Forces use; euphem. acronym formed by analogy with "snafu."* * See **"fucked up"** (def. 3).

jank *v.i.* To change altitude and direction simultaneously so as to avoid antiaircraft fire. 1965: "I was janking ... when I got hit by ground fire." *Time*, April 23, 23. *Air Force use, orig. in Vietnam.* Cf. **jink.**

jap* *v.t.* = **jap (Jap), pull a.*** *Current teenage use. A shortened form of the older phrase, which is now obs.* *n.* An ambush; surprise attack.

jawbone* *v.i.* To persuade; urge. *n.* A specific instance of jawboning. **—ing** *n.* Strong pressure or persuasion to do something; specif., urging on the part of a U.S. president or other prominent official to business and labor unions to hold down spending, prices, and wages as a way of fighting inflation. *From moving the jawbone in talking with overtones of David slaying Goliath with the jawbone of an ass. 1970s use; "jawboning" is the most commonly used form.*

jay* *n.* = **J.**

jay smoke = **J.**

jazz* *n.* **1** Lit. and fig., ornamentation; trimmings; anything added to improve the appearance of something. **2** The usual, expected argument, story idea, plan, etc.; routine insincerity; middle-class mendacity. *Esp. in the expression "and all that jazz," which is used to = "et cetera."*

J.B. = **Stetson.*** *Some railroad and hobo use.*

jellybean* *n.* An overdressed man; one who dresses flashily according to the latest fad, esp. a man who wears bright and varied colors. *c1910–c1925.*

Jersey green A type of marijuana. *Drug culture and student use.*

Jesus Freak Jesus People A member or members of the Jesus Movement or Revolution, a Protestant movement among young people, esp. ex-hippies and drug addicts, which stresses traditional fundamentalist beliefs and practices, the literal interpretation of the Bible, a deep personal commitment to Jesus Christ, and evangelical preaching and witnessing. 1974: "In this light the herds of Jesus Freaks, and all the other herds, are as much a product of the New Left action as is anything else we set out deliberately to inspire." Michael Rossman, *Rolling Stone*, May 9, 9.

Jesus Movement Jesus Revolution See **Jesus Freak.**

jet set The international group of wealthy, chic people who move about from one expensive resort to another.

1966: "Last week, at the age of 82, Valletta turned the wheel over to Gianni Agnelli, 45, grandson of Fiat's founder and a charter member of the international jet set." *Time*, May 6, 102. *Since the inauguration of transoceanic jet passenger flights in the 1950s.*

jink *v.i.* To dodge enemy planes, antiaircraft fire, etc., by following a zigzag course. *Air Force use, orig. in the Vietnam war.* Cf. **jank.**

jive* *v.t.* **1** To tease; joke with. **2** To deceive. *Orig. Negro use.*

jive stick A marijuana cigarette. *Drug culture.*

jizz [taboo] = **jism*** (def.1).

jock* *n.* **1** An athletic supporter; a jockstrap. **2** An athlete, esp. a college athlete. *Common student use. From "jockstrap" and the slang "jockstrap."*

jockstrap *v.i.* To travel widely and make a meager living in the lower brackets of the sporting world; esp. to make one's living in small towns as a prizefighter or wrestler. *n.* An athlete, esp. a student athlete. *Not common; replaced by the shortened "jock." Some student use.*

Jodie **jodie** *n.* A civilian male; one who has been rejected by or deferred from the draft. *W.W.II Army use.*

Joe Storch = **Joe Zilsch.*** See **storch.**

John* **john** *n.* A customer of a female prostitute.

Johnny Reb = **Rebel.**

Johnny Trots = **The trots*** (diarrhea).

jollies *n.pl.* Thrills or excitement; "kicks."* 1965: " . . . we concluded . . . that people who drive Buicks are getting some kind of jollies that Pontiac and Mercury owners can never really know or feel." Allan Sherman, "Sex and the Single Sherman," *Playboy*, July, 151.

Jones **jones** *n.* **1** A drug habit. 1970: "A lanky, good-looking youth who now works at two jobs to keep up with the 'Jones'. . . ." Joseph Lelyveld, N.Y. *Times*, Jan. 12, 1. **2** Any intense interest in something. *Drug culture.*

josan *n.* A girl friend. *Armed Forces use in Korea.*

jostle *v.i., v.t.* To pick pockets. 1973: " . . . the researcher asked for further details on a junkie vocation known as 'jostling,' a sophisticated form of pickpocketing." James M. Markham, N.Y. *Times Mag.*. Mar. 18, 39. —**r** *n.* A pickpocket.

joy pop To take narcotic injections

irregularly, usu. by injecting under the skin. *Drug culture.* See **skin pop.**

joystick* [taboo] *n.* The penis.

J smoke = **J.**

jug* *n.* A carburetor. *Some hot-rod use.* —**s** *n.pl.* The female breasts considered as sexual objects.

juggler *n.* = **pusher*** (def. 3). *Drug culture.*

juice* *n.* **1** = **pop.** **2** Influence; pull; clout. 1973: "Don't claim to have juice. Telling a cop that you're a nephew of Harold Stassen . . . isn't going to help." George Frazier, "Beating a Bust," *Rolling Stone*, Aug. 16, 23. *v.t.* To excite, encourage, inspire; to enliven; to increase one's confidence in. 1964: " 'A thing like that can really juice you up,' said [athlete Dallas] Long. . . ." *Time*, Oct. 23, 61.

juice dealer An underworld usurer; a racketeer who loans money at exorbitant interest to gamblers who have lost; an underworld boss who loans money at illegally high rates of interest to gamblers, gambling casinos, bookies, etc., so that they can pay winners or expand their businesses. Cf. **juice man.** See **juice*** (def. 2).

juicehead *n.* A heavy drinker. See **juice*** (def. 1).

juice loan A loan made by a "juice man."

juice man An underworld money and loan collector; specif. a hoodlum employed to collect a gambling debt or loan by intimidation or to beat up or kill one who does not pay. 1961: "The body of a man believed to be William ('Action') Jackson . . . a 'juice man' (loan collector) for syndicate hoodlum bosses was found last night. . . ." Chicago *Daily Tribune*, Aug. 12, 1. See **juice*** (def. 2).

jumping *adj.* Of a place, gathering, etc., pulsating with excitement and activity. *Orig. jive use.*

jungle bunny [derog.] A Negro.

junked up = **hopped up.***

junker *n.* A drug pusher, esp. a heroin pusher. *Drug culture.*

junk food Food such as potato chips, popcorn, sugar-coated cereals, and similar snacks, that have little or no nutritional value and provide mostly "empty calories."

junk mail Mail, usu. third class, consisting of advertising circulars or pleas for financial contributions, sometimes addressed to "occupant."

K

karma   *n.* = **vibrations.** *From the term in Buddhism and Hinduism meaning the doctrine of responsibility for all one's acts in all reincarnations.*

katusa   *n.* **1** A Korean soldier attached to the U.S. Army. *An acronym for "Korean attached to U.S. Army."* **2** Any South Korean soldier. *Armed Forces use in Korea.*

kee   See **key** (def. 2).

keep the faith (baby)   *interj.* Be optimistic and courageous despite what happens; be steadfast. *An expression uttered at parting. Popularized in the mid-1960s by Harlem's Adam Clayton Powell at the time of his self-imposed exile in the Bahamas and his expulsion from Congress. Orig. Negro use.*

key   *n.* **1** A typical Ivy League student; one who assumes the dress, manners, attitudes, etc., associated with the typical Ivy League student. *Has replaced "white shoe" since c1955. Prob. from the image of a fraternity key or pin.* **2** A kilo (2.2 pounds) of marijuana. *Drug culture.* Also **kee, ki.**

ki   See **key** (def. 2).

kick down   To shift to a lower gear. *Mainly truck drivers' use; some automobile racing and sports car use.*

kick out the jams   To act in a completely unrestrained way; let loose with everything one has. 1974: "With 'On the Border,' they kick out the jams once again, the stuff that made their first album rock and roll." Bruce Malamut, *Crawdaddy*, July, 74.

kick party   A party or gathering where LSD is used. *Drug culture.*

kicks*   *n.pl.* Shoes. *Jazz musician use.*

kick stick   A marijuana cigarette. *Drug culture.*

kicky   *adj.* **1** Very chic and up to the minute. 1967: "[the store has] been redecorated to display more effectively a lot of kicky clothes, many of them imports." N.Y. *Times*, April 3, 36. **2** Very exciting; far out; full of "kicks." 1967: "It's very kicky to be able to drive right over sand dunes, so it's easy to understand why so many people have flipped out over dune buggies." *Playboy*, Dec., 155.

kilo connection   A wholesale drug pusher, the first of what may be a chain of distributors who cut the potency of a drug, esp. heroin. The kilo connection usually doubles the volume by mixing a kilo of nearly pure heroin with an equal amount of adulterant. *Drug culture.*

kimble   *v.i.* To try hard to be liked, popular, etc. *Some student use, mainly synthetic.*

kink   *n.* **1** A person with deviant or bizarre sexual tastes. **2** A deviant sexual practice or preference. 1974: " . . . a Nazi with a kink for prepubescent girls." Andrew Bailey, *Rolling Stone*, April 11, 12.   **—y***   *adj.* **1** Pertaining to or appealing to sexually deviant tastes. **2** Sexually deviant. **3** Bizarre; peculiar. 1974: " . . . because there was no offense so kinky that the Maximum Enchilada and his consigliores wouldn't commit it. . . ." Geoffrey Wolff, Review of *All the President's Men* by Carl Bernstein and Bob Woodward, *New Times*, June 28, 63.

kiss ass   [taboo]   **1** One who obsequiously curries favor, as from his superiors. *A variant form of the older and more common "ass kisser."* **2** Flattery, esp. to curry favor.

kiss-ass   [taboo]   *adj.* Obsequiously flattering. " . . . I feared the worst: another kiss-ass review of an extremely bad album. . . ." Letter, *Rolling Stone*, Sept. 27, 4.

kitsch   *n.* Slick, pretentious literature or art having little esthetic value but appealing strongly to modern tastes; bad taste. 1973: "A 300-acre complex of rococo gingerbread spires, towers, minarets and balconies resembling a landlocked Mississippi showboat tossed hopelessly off course on a bed of rocks and boulders, it stands unchallenged as a masterpiece of kitsch." *Playboy*, Nov., 20.   **—y**   *adj.* Shallow and pretentious; slick; in bad taste. 1973: "There is Visconti's kitschy film, *Death in Venice*, in which Gustav von Aschenbach accompanied by lush string and harp music of the 'Adagietto' from Mahler's Fifth Symphony, succumbs to decadence. . . ." H. Gross, *American Scholar*, June, 484. *From the Ger. word = gaudy trash.*

Kitty*   *n.* A Cadillac car. 1945: " . . . we talked about cars for a time. . . . The boy . . . said, 'Of course if I had my way I'd take a Kitty.' " C. B. Himes, *if he hollers let him go* (Doubleday), 42.

Mainly Negro use. From "Caddy"* via "Cat."

klepto *n.* A kleptomaniac.

klick klik *n.* = **click.** *Armed Forces use in the Vietnam war.*

klutz *n.* A stupid, worthless person. **—y** *adj.* Stupid and awkward. 1973: "You see all these girls in their twenties who have IQ's of 150 and handle their work so well, but in personal life they're like eight-year-olds. Then you meet a girl who's klutzy in her job, but *she* can hold a man." J. Wilkie, *Playgirl*, Oct., 55. *From the Yiddish (Ger. Klotz = lump, block).*

knee-jerk *adj.* Reacting in an expected and automatic way. 1967: "The ABM decision can be seen . . . as one more gesture to the knee-jerk hawks in the Congress. . . ." William Jackson, *New Republic*, Oct. 28, 16. *n.* A person who reacts in an expected or automatic way. 1969: "The most notorious Congressman from Iowa is cranky old H. R. Gross, a seventy-year-old knee-jerk best remembered for castigating the Reverend Bill Moyers for dancing the frug in the White House. . . ." Larry L. King,

Harper's, Mar., 52. *From the reflex kick produced in the lower leg by tapping the tendon below the kneecap.*

knock* *v.t.* To have under control; to be assured of having solved a problem or having gained a desired result; esp., in student use, to be certain of passing an examination or a course. *Since c1955.* **—er** *n.* An important, prominent, or influential person, or one who talks and acts as if his words and views are important and influential. 1966: " . . . knocker [means] a big shot, either real or imagined, and you pronounce that first 'k.' " Charles McHarry, N.Y. *Daily News*, Jan. 12.

knocked out* Under the influence of a drug. *Drug culture.*

knock [one's] socks off To overwhelm. 1973: "Dressing sexy is great, but it's undressing sexy that really knocks your socks off." *Playboy*, Dec., 77.

kook* *n.* A beginning or inexperienced surfer. *Some surfer use.*

kvetch *v.i.* To complain, whine, be overly concerned with the negative. *n.* A person who complains or whines habitually. *From the Yiddish.*

L

laid-back *adj.* Relaxed; low-keyed. 1974: "I had seen Bonnie Raitt as a woman with the blues, a sort of laid-back, not-insane Janis Joplin." Vince Aletti, "Bonnie Raitt: Back to the Kitchen?" *Village Voice*, Aug. 22, 59.

lame *n.* A "square,"* one not cognizant of modern attitudes and fads. 1974: "If I had only known sooner that Maharaj Ji was turned on to Steve Miller Band's 'Your Saving Grace,' I might not have been as quick to judge him as a lame." Letter, *Rolling Stone*, April 25, 7. *adj.* Not in the know; naive; unaware of current fashions, attitudes, interests, etc., but not completely out of touch with them and hence capable of learning; somewhat "square."*

large for *adj.* Enthusiastic about; having a liking or strong desire for.

larky *adj.* Playful; frolicsome. *Orig. Brit.*

later *interj.* Goodby. *Shortened form of "See you later, (Alligator)."*

launching pad = shooting gallery.*

launder *v.t.* To transfer, funnel, or convert funds, as from one account to

another or one currency to another, to conceal the source of origin of the money; specif., to transfer illegally obtained funds from one bank account to one or more other bank accounts to conceal where the funds came from. 1973: "The account held money that had been 'laundered' by being siphoned from this country into Mexico and returned under an alias for use by the Nixon re-election committee. . . ." W. Barthelmes, *Commonweal*, July 27, 403.

laundry* *n.* Any banking institution, company, or other organization through which funds, esp. illegally obtained funds, are conveyed for the purpose of concealing the source or origin of the funds. See **launder.**

laundry list A list, usu. long, of items, subjects, etc., to be discussed or acted on.

lay a batch In driving or racing a car, to leave black rubber marks during acceleration. *Hot-rod use.*

lay [something] on [someone] 1 To present an idea, point of view, etc., to someone. 1968: "And the sisters laid the revolutionary ideology right on them."

Bobby Seale, *Seize the Time*, 396. **2** To tell something to someone, inform someone of something. *Orig. Negro use.*

lay rubber   In driving or racing a car, to spin the wheels on the pavement, as in making a fast start, skidding, etc. *Automobile racing and hot-rod use.*

leaf *   *n.* Cocaine. *Drug culture.*

least, the   *n.* The worst.   *adj.* Worthless or dull; "square."* Cf. **the most.** *

leather *   *adj.* Of or pertaining to sadists and masochists, whether heterosexual or homosexual; affecting leather jackets, boots, chain bracelets, etc., signifying that one is a sadist or masochist; sadistic or masochistic.

left-handed *   *adj.* Homosexual.

leg *   *n.* An Army infantryman. *Facetious and derog. paratrooper use, esp. in Vietnam.*

lemon *   **lemonade**   *n.* = **blank** (def. 2).

letch *   **lech**   *v.i.* To desire strongly; lust after. 1970: "When Henry goes letching after Anne, old Wolsey is likely to wink. . . ." Vincent Canby, N.Y. *Times*, Jan. 21, 37.

let it all hang out   **1** To be utterly free of inhibition; keep nothing repressed or suppressed. 1973: "We were all seated in my living room, having something to drink, but you could feel the tension in the air. I decided to let it all hang out. 'James,' I said, 'tell me—are you gay?'" Xaviera Hollander, *Xaviera!*, 52. **2** To reveal the whole truth; confess everything. Cf. **hang out.**

lez = **les.** *

libber   *n.* A member of Women's Liberation. 1973: "'You mean those nuts that burn their bras and walk around all disheveled and hate men? They're crazy. Crazy.' Thus—in Ms magazine, of all places—did Golda Meir vent her view of women's libbers." *Newsweek*, Mar. 26, 46.

lid *   *n.* One ounce of marijuana. 1973: "When the police have gone ahead and lifted out the back seat and found a lid of marijuana, the smart smoker lets his lawyer explain how it got there." Michael Stepanian, "Beating a Bust," *Rolling Stone*, Aug. 16, 25. *Drug culture.*

Life, the   **life, the**   *n.* Prostitution; specif., prostitution as a business. 1974: "The pimp's job, as is generally understood by those in the Life, is not only to make money. He is primarily responsible for spending and displaying the wealth that his women bring in. . . ." Francis A. J. Ianni, *Black Mafia*, 35.

light *   *adj.* With extra cream added;

said of a cup of coffee. *Lunch-counter use. Colloq.*

lightfooted   *adj.* Homosexual. *Fairly common since c1955.* Cf. **limp wrist.** *

like fun = **like hell.** *   1959: "When the prostitute says 'Like fun you are,' Holden comments: 'It was a funny thing to say. . . . You'd think a prostitute . . . would say 'Like hell you are.'" Donald P. Costello, "The Language of *The Catcher in the Rye*," *American Speech*, Oct., 179. *Colloq.*

limo   *n.* A limousine. 1973: "Senator William Proxmire, chairman of a Senate appropriations subcommittee, disapproves of this vast fleet (789 limos) of luxury transportation." *Sat. Rev./World*, Nov. 20, 8.

lip-sync   *v.i., v.t.* To move the lips silently in synchronization with words, esp. of a song, produced by a tape, phonograph record, or an unseen performer. 1967: "When I got home from the movies, I'd pantomime what I had seen. My parents bought recordings of the musicals, and I would lip-sync to them." Melodie Johnson, *TV Guide*, Jan. 7, 16. 1968: "Having taped his lines before the show, he lip-synched his pronouncements and with broad gestures mimed Christ from the beatitudes to the last cry from the cross." *Newsweek*, Sept. 30, 68.

little cheese   An unimportant person. *Based on "big cheese."* * Not common.*

little Michael   **little Mike** = **Mickey Finn.** *

loid   *v.t.* **1** To unlock a door with a celluloid strip, as a burglar. *From "celluloid." Underworld use; the method and the word are replacing "jimmy."* **2** To rob a building or an apartment.

longhair *   *n.* A young man with long hair, esp. a hippy. 1973: "He went along to the bank with another longhair, a member of our commune." J. Jerome, *American Scholar*, June, 434.

long hitter   A heavy drinker.

loo   *n.* A toilet. *Chiefly Brit.*

love drug   A drug regarded as being an aphrodisiac, esp. Methaqualone, a trade name for a nonbarbiturate muscle relaxer. *Drug culture.*

love-in   *n.* A gathering, usu. of young people, to promote mutual love and understanding. 1967: "The hippies are happening. Ed Sanders of the Fugs is on a cover of *Life*. Tulsa, Okla., which went for Barry Goldwater by 30,000 votes, recently had its first love-in." Jack

Low

Newfield, *Nation*, June 26, 809. *Hippie and student use in 1960s.*

low*   *n.* A bad reaction to a drug. *Drug culture.*

low-belly strippers   Marked playing cards. *Gambler use.*

low rider   **1** A person who drives a car with a lowered suspension. **2** A car with a lowered suspension. **3** A motorcyclist who drives with the handlebars adjusted high so as to give the impression that he is riding low on the motorcycle. **4** A youth from a ghetto, usu. a tough ghetto youth. *Negro use.* **5** A prison hoodlum who tries to force other prisoners into paying for protection. 1972: "There are what the blacks call low riders, these people who run around pushing their weight around, threatening the weak. . . ." Leonard J. Berry, quoting Warden Louis S. Nelson, *Prison*, 44. *Prison use.*

lox   *n.* Liquid oxygen, esp. as used as a rocket fuel. 1959: "*Lox* [is] . . . short for liquid oxygen." Thomas J. Fleming, "Space Slanguage," *American Weekly*, Aug. 30, 2. *From combining the first letters of the words, reinforced by the stand.* "*lox*" = *smoked salmon. Early rocket and aerospace use.*

LSD   **LSD-25**   Lysergic acid diethylamide (D-lysergic acid diethylamide tartrate). *A potent but non-addictive hallucinogenic drug. It is tasteless, odorless, colorless, and water-soluble. The initials are taken from the original Ger.* name "*Lyserg-Säure-Diaethylamid.*" *The drug was created in 1938 by Dr. Albert Hofmann of the Sandoz Research Laboratories in Basel, Switzerland, on the 2nd day of the 5th month (May 2), hence the medical code name "LSD-25." Commonly known since c1962 when addicts, students, and others seeking new experiences began to use it by swallowing it in capsules or in small sugar cubes, 100 micrograms being the average beginner's dose, 300 micrograms the average dose of a habitual user. It causes hallucinations, illusions, and euphoria, initially accompanied by slight nausea, dilation of the pupils, etc., that last from four to eight hours. For several hours after this psychedelic period the user alternates between the hallucinogenic state and reality, followed by a period of fatigue and tension that may last up to 24 hours. About 5% of those who try LSD, prob. latent schizophrenics, suffer prolonged, severe, and dangerous psychotic reactions. Possession or use of the drug is illegal in some states. Cf.* **acid head, cap, cube, tab, trip** (def. 1).

lude   *n.* Quaalude, the trade name of a depressant drug, or "downer." *Drug culture.*

lunch   **lunchie**   **lunchy**   *adj.* Stupid; inadequate. 1963: " . . . a lunch guy might as well be out to lunch for all the good he's doing . . . " Robert I. Scott, " 'Qualm' as Verb, 'Lunch' as Adjective," *American Speech*, May, 159. *Some student use.* See **out to lunch.***

lunker   *adj.* Big; heavy. *Archaic.*

M

ma-and-pa   See **mom-and-pop.**

Ma Bell   A wry nickname for the American Telephone & Telegraph Company; the Bell System. 1973: "As it has turned out, the quality of some phone lines is often below what Ma Bell promised." T. Alexander, *Fortune*, Feb., 130. *It has replaced the older "Maw Bell."*

macaroni*   *n.* **1** A dandy. *Obs., but still known from the song "Yankee Doodle."* **2** Any long, thin, flexible item that fig. resembles macaroni, specif. long, thin copper rods, various types of flexible tubing, radio antennas, etc.

machismo   *n.* Male pride; strong and aggressive masculinity; virility. 1965: "Unfortunately, that form of birth control [rhythm method] has proved far too sophisticated for Latin America's widely uneducated masses. Another factor is machismo, a he-man complex that makes sexual prowess and large families—in and out of wedlock—a matter of male pride." *Time*, Aug. 20, 34. *In Spain and Latin America "machismo" is the traditional belief in male superiority and dominance.*

macho   *n.* A virile and aggressive man. *adj.* Full of masculine pride; virile; manly. 1973: "[Author Norman Mailer's] theory that men impart their substance and qualities into women along with their semen is a typical macho Mailerism. . . ." Pauline Kael, book review of *Marilyn*, by Norman Mailer, N.Y. *Times* Book Review, July 22, 2. *From Mex. Sp.* = *male.*

machodrama   *n.* A motion picture or

play glorifying male supremacy through extreme violence and debasement of women.

macht nichts = mox nix.

mackman   *n.* A pimp; a "mack."* 1960: "Once she had spent almost a week at the apartment of a new pimp. . . . Suppose she just . . . went back to . . . that young mackman?" C. Cooper, *The Scene*, 208.

maggot   *n.* A cigarette butt. 1963: " . . . Red took a mighty drag on her cigarette, covered both eyes with one arm, then snapped the maggot over the rail. . . ." Sterling Hayden, *Wanderer*, 41.

main   *v.i., v.t.* = mainline.*

make*   [taboo]   *n.* A woman considered only as a sexual object; a "lay."* *Generally in the phrase "an easy make."*

make it*   To be satisfied; to be true to one's personal inner needs and values. 1965: " 'I was playing rock 'n' roll when I was 13 and 14 and 15, but I had to quit when I was 16 or 17 because I just couldn't make it that way.' . . . Q. 'By "making it," do you mean making commercial success?' A. 'No, no, that's not it, making money. It's being able to be nice and not hurt anybody.' " Bob Dylan, in an interview, N.Y. *Post*, Dec. 1, 8C.

make like   To imitate; to pretend to be; to act in a manner resembling someone or something. *For example, "make like Einstein" = "act intelligently" or "be smart."*

make noises   To express one's ideas, feelings, etc., vocally, esp. indirectly.

make out*   To neck heavily or passionately.

make the scene*   **1** To arrive, appear, or be at a particular place or gathering. **2** To succeed; achieve something. **3** To do something; experience something.

male chauvinist pig   [derog.] = A male chauvinist; a man who believes that men are superior to women.

mama   *n.* **1** Any woman or girl. **2** A sexually attractive or sexually available woman or girl. *Orig. Negro use.* Cf. **red-hot mamma.*** **3** A girl or woman who belongs to a motorcycle gang. 1965: "There is one girl to every four or five Angels [member of the Hell's Angels motorcycle gang], and the turnover is terrific. If a girl wants to be a mama and 'pull a train,' which means make herself available to everyone, then she'll be welcome at any Angel party." *SEP*, Nov. 20, 36.

mama-and-papa   *adj.* = ma-and-pa.

Mama-san   *n.* See under —san.

Man, the*   *n.* **1** Anyone in authority; anyone to whom respect is due; one's employer. → **2** Anyone to whom obedience is owed or granted through fear; specif. the police, a drug addict's peddler, an underworld vice boss, etc. → **3** Any person who sells narcotics: a "pusher"* or "connection."* *Drug culture.* **4** A white man, esp. one in a position of authority, as a policeman, employer, etc.; white people, the white race; the white establishment, society, or culture, etc. *An extension of "the Man"* = the law. Negro use only.*

manhole cover   Any large, round, flat object, esp. a pancake, but also a plate, phonograph record, etc.

marbles   [taboo]   *n.pl.* The testicles. *Not common.*

marge*   *n.* A female homosexual who takes the passive, female role. *Lesbian use.*

maricon   *n.* A male homosexual. *From the Sp.; often used as an interj. having a force equivalent to that of "bastard."**

marshmallow   [derog.]   *n.* A white person. 1969: "New businessmen joining Breadbasket are questioned by an 'attunement' committee to make sure they are black through and through—no Oreos, or, worse, an Oreo fronting for a 'marshmallow' need apply—and treat their Negro employees accordingly." Richard Levine, *Harper's*, Mar., 63. *Negro use.* See **Oreo.**   **—s**   *n.pl.* = **marshmallow shoes.**

marshmallow shoes   Shoes with very thick white platform soles, worn chiefly by youths and girls.

mask*   *n.* Large wraparound sunglasses as worn by hot rodders, traffic policemen, etc. *Some teenage and police use.*

massage parlor   An establishment that ostensibly offers massage treatments but in fact engages young women to perform a variety of sexual services for male customers. Cf. **rap club.**

Mau Mau   A Negro who belongs to or supports one of the more militant Negro nationalist organizations, esp. the Black Muslims. *From the name of the African terrorist organization that fought against the white government of Kenya during the 1950s before that country obtained its independence. Negro use.*

mavin   **maven**   *n.* An expert or connoisseur in any field. 1970: "There I was, happily shlepping pizzas to a steady and growing clientele of pizza mavins, when all of a sudden the Underground Gourmet and *New York* Magazine named my little pizza store as the best in New York." Larry Goldberg, *New York*, June 15, 7. *From the Yiddish.* See **mayvin.***

maxi   *n.*   **1** An ankle-length skirt or coat. **2** The fashion of skirts and coats with an ankle-length hemline. 1968: "What is happening to hemlines ? . . . Is the new length a midi or a maxi ?" *Life*, Feb. 16, 69.   *adj.*   Ankle-length. 1968: "They go with long black pants under a maxi black coat. . . ." Gloria Emerson, N.Y. *Times*, Jan. 30, 32. *Chiefly 1960s use, when the style was popular.* See **midi; mini.**

M.C.   *v.t.* = **emcee.*** 1973: " . . . the 25th anniversary party in 1961 that was M.C.'d by . . . Bob Hope. . . ." *New York*, Jan. 15, 49.

MCP   **m.c.p.** [derog.] = **male chauvinist pig.**

M.D.   *n.* Dr. Pepper, a soft drink. *Lunch-counter use.*

MDA   *n.* Methyl diamphetamine, a stimulant having some effects similar to those of LSD. *Drug culture.*

meat*   *n.* **1** [taboo] The penis. *Mainly teenage use.* **2** A strong but stupid person; one whose physical deeds overshadow his mental powers; esp. a professional or college athlete. *Student use.* **3** A male considered as a sexual object; homosexual gratification. *Homosexual use.* **4** The amount of tread on an automobile tire. *Orig. automobile racing and teenage use.*

meateater   **meat eater**   A corrupt policeman who actively and aggressively seeks graft money. 1972: "Meat eaters, probably only a small percentage of the force, spend a good deal of their working hours aggressively seeking out situations they can exploit for financial gain. . . ." N.Y. *Times*, Dec. 31, Sec. IV, 2. Cf. **grasseater.**

meat rack   A gathering place, usu. public, where male homosexuals seek out partners. *Homosexual use.*

megillah   *n.* **1** Something considered as a whole, esp. a tedious, lengthy, excessively detailed speech, account, explanation, etc. **2** The complete details. 1966: "Megillah also means the entire thing, but it is used differently. . . . When you say 'Let's not have the megillah,' you're saying 'Spare me the details.' " Charles McHarry, N.Y. *Daily News*, Jan. 12. *Usu. in the expression*

"the whole megillah." *From the Hebrew "megillah"* = *scroll, "The Megillah"* = *The Book of Esther.*

mellow*   *n.* A close friend.   *adj.* **1** Relaxed. **2** Very friendly; intimate. *Mainly Negro use.*

mellow out   **1** To mellow; relax; take a rest. **2** To become subdued. 1974: "Critics . . . were saying he'd mellowed out . . . 'drained the venom from his voice.' " Ben Fong-Torres "Knockin' on Dylan's Door," *Rolling Stone*, Feb. 14, 38. *Mainly musician use.*

member   *n.* A fellow Negro. *Negro use only.*

mensch   *n.* One who is honorable, decent, upright, responsible, etc.; a person to be looked up to and respected. 1968: "[Dress designer Pauline] Trigere, almost alone, is mensch enough to candidly dismiss the misogynous midi, saying, 'No midis—I tried some but it didn't come off.' " Stephanie Harrington, *Village Voice*, Feb. 22, 21. *From the Yiddish.*

men's lib   **Men's Lib**   Men's Liberation, the male counterpart of Women's Liberation. 1973: "Only men's lib and women's lib together can alert society to the unnecessary damage and frustration caused by the continued lack of social support for a wider field of activity for women." R. Park, *American Scholar*, Jan., 142.

mesc   *n.* Mescaline. *Drug culture.*

mess over [someone]   To infringe upon the freedom or actions of someone. 1965: "Cats used to say it [dealing drugs in Harlem] made them feel better than being down there, being messed over by Goldberg all the time. . . ." Claude Brown, *Manchild in the Promised Land*, 286. *Negro use.*

metal   *n.* = **heavy metal.**   *v.i.* To play heavy metal. 1974: "And nobody can metal like Blue Oyster Cult." Bruce Malamut, *Crawdaddy*, July, 84. **—lurgist**   *n.* A person who plays heavy metal.

meth   *n.* Methedrine (a trade name). *Drug culture.*

meth head   **meth freak**   A habitual user of Methedrine (a trade name). *Drug culture.*

Mexican red   A type of marijuana. *Drug culture and student use.*

m.f.   [taboo]   *n.* = **mother fucker.** 1968: "Of all the people, why'd they kill Malcolm ? Why'n't they kill some of them Uncle Tomming m.f.'s ?" Eldridge Cleaver, *Soul on Ice*, 51.

mice   *n.pl.* Children; in terms of being watchers of programs tailored to their interests and of becoming consumers of the products advertised on such programs. *From the pop. children's program* "The Mouseketeers" *of the 1950s, revived and rerun in 1975. Television use.*

Mickey Mouse   mickey mouse* 1 Cheap, shoddy, or inferior; unfair, confused, or senseless; mean or "lousy."* **2** Simple; easy; childlike. 1958: "At Michigan State . . . a 'Mickey Mouse course' means a '*snap* course.' "* M. Crane, "Vox Bop." **3** Foolish; inconsequential. *Mainly student use.* **4** An easy task; specif. an easy course in college, one that is of slight educational value and almost impossible to fail; "crib,"* "gut,"* "pipe."* *Student use.* **5** Action, behavior, etc., that is unnecessary, cowardly, confused, etc.; a mistake. 1965: "Logistically so far, the only big Mickey Mouse . . . was a brief shortage of . . . jungle boots. . . ." *Time,* Dec. 10, 33/34. *Mainly Armed Forces use.* **6** [derog.] A white person. *Negro use.* **7** To waste time; fool around. 1973: "And the commissioner warns, 'We can't Mickey Mouse around while faced with technological challenges from other countries.' " R. G. Hummerstone, *Fortune,* May, 264.

milk [taboo]   *v.t.* To masturbate.

midi   *n.* **1** A skirt or coat reaching to about the middle of the calf. 1971: ". . . Sawyer passed a bus stop at which half a dozen young women were queued. 'Thank God,' he said. . . . 'No maxis, no midis.' " John Bainbridge, *New Yorker,* Aug. 14, 47. **2** The fashion of skirts and coats with a mid-calf hemline. 1968: ". . . some hemlines are coming down—to a midcalf length dubbed midi. . . ." *Life,* Feb. 16, 69. *adj.* Reaching to the mid-calf. *Chiefly 1960s use.* See **mini; maxi.**

mike* *n.* A microgram (millionth of a gram). 1973: "You won't believe this, but I feel like I've been up on 300 mikes of acid for three weeks." *Sat. Rev./Society,* May, 56.

mince   *n.* A person who is considered unfashionable or not in touch with currently popular modes of dress, behavior, etc.; a bore; a "drip."* 1965: "Anybody who still wears them [saddle shoes] is . . . a 'mince,' . . . That's bad." *N.Y. Times,* Dec. 27. *Teenage use.*

mind-bender   *n.* = **mind-blower.**
mind-bending   *adj.* = **mind-blowing.**
mind-blower   *n.* **1** A hallucinogenic

drug. **2** Something exciting, beautiful, shocking, etc.; something that overwhelms or changes one, as an experience, a book, an idea, etc. *Drug culture and student use.*

mind-blowing   *adj.* **1** Hallucinogenic. **2** Overwhelming; exciting, shocking. *Drug culture and student use.*

mind-fuck [taboo]   *v.t.* To manipulate others to believe and act as one does, without any consideration for them. *n.* = **mind fucker** (def. 1). **—er** *n.* **1** A person who manipulates others. **2** An upsetting or disturbing situation.

mini   *n.* **1** A very short dress, skirt, or coat ending several inches above the knee. **2** The fashion of wearing such short skirts. *adj.* Very short; several inches above the knee. *Chiefly 1960s use.* See **midi; maxi.**

mink* *n.* **1** An attractive, pert girl. **2** A girl friend, esp. a very attractive one. *Negro use.* Cf. **fox. 3** The pudenda or the area of female pubic hair; a very attractive or high-class "beaver."

mintie   *adj.* Homosexual; exhibiting or affecting mannerisms of the opposite sex; "gay"* or "queer."* *n.* A homosexual, esp. an aggressive or masculine Lesbian. *Orig. homosexual use.*

mishegoss   meshegoss   *n.* Absurdity; craziness. 1967: " '. . . I assure you, Alex, you are never going to hear such a mishegoss of mixed-up crap and disgusting nonsense as the Christian religion in your entire life.' " Philip Roth, *Portnoy's Complaint,* 40. *From the Yiddish, the noun form of* "mishugah."

mishugah   mishoogeh   *adj.* Mad, "nuts,"* crazy; witless. 1966: ". . . mishoogeh or mishugah . . . spelled either way means crazy." Charles McHarry, *N.Y. Daily News,* Jan. 12. *From the Yiddish.*

Mister Tom   A Negro who seeks or has achieved middle-class white values or assimilation into white society or culture. *Negro use.* Cf. **Uncle Tom.***

M.J.   *n.* Marijuana. *From the initials for* "Mary Jane," *an older name.*

mod   *adj.* Very fashionable and chic in dress, music, tastes, etc. 1966: "Daliah Levy . . . shows off her attributes in a mod wardrobe. . . ." Bosley Crowther, *N.Y. Times,* Dec. 20, 58. *From the Brit.* "mod," *an avant-garde style of fashion originating on Carnaby St., London, in the early 1960s.*

mojo* *n.* A charm; esp. a sack of herbs, feathers, entrails, etc., worn to bring good luck or to break a hex. *Archaic Negro use.*

mola *n.* A homosexual.

mom-and-pop *adj.* Of or pertaining to a small business establishment, often a retail store, owned and managed by a family. *Less common forms are "ma-and-pa" and "mama-and-papa."*

monkey dish A small serving dish or bowl, as a salad bowl, a bowl for peanuts, etc.

mono *n.* Mononucleosis. *Widespread student use.*

monster *n.* 1 A drug that acts on the central nervous system. *Drug culture.* 2 A big seller, esp. a recording.

Montezuma's revenge Diarrhea. 1974: "We got good water here that won't give you no Montezuma's revenge." "Sanford and Son," TV comedy, Aug. 15. *Used by tourists in Mexico. In use since the 1930s.* See **touristas.**

moon* *v.i., v.t.* To exhibit one's naked buttocks, or "moons," as a defiant or humorous gesture, usu. at a window. *Mostly student use.*

moonlight *v.i.* To work at a second, often part-time, job in order to supplement the salary from one's regular job. 1961: "Moonlighting—Is the Two-Job Husband a Threat to . . . Home and Happiness?" From the cover of *True Story* mag., March. *Because the second job is often done in the evening after the usual day's work. Pop. during and since W.W.II.* Cf. **daylight.**

moonman *n.* An astronaut who journeys to, explores, or lives on, the moon. 1965: "On its approach to the spot where an American Moonman would be most likely to land, Ranger 8 flashed more than 7,000 close-up pictures back. . . ." N.Y. *Journal-American,* Feb. 21, 1.

moose* *n.* A prostitute. *Armed Forces use in Korea. From the Japanese "musume" = girl.*

mope* *n.* A fool; a stupid person. 1932: "They had a lot of pep, and weren't a bunch of mopes." J. T. Farrell, *Young Lonigan,* 166.

MOR **M.O.R.** *adj.* Middle-of-the-road. *Applied to popular music that is not too loud and does not have offensive lyrics so that it appeals to people with conservative tastes. Musician use.*

mossback *n.* An unsophisticated person; "hick"* or "hayseed."*

mother* *n.* 1 The social leader, spokesman, or most attractive member of a group of homosexuals. → 2 Any

homosexual or effeminate man. *Almost always used derisively, even by homosexuals themselves.* 3 The leader, the most necessary member, or the one who gives others a sense of security in any illegal or immoral relationship; specif. one who peddles narcotics, a pimp, a madam of a brothel, one who carries a gun in a gang fight, etc. *These slang degenerations of the stand. "mother" used to show a psychologically dependent relationship have become fairly common in subgroup use since c1965.* 4 [taboo] = **mother fucker.** 1965: "And the cops and every mother other one of 'em cries Foul. . . ." Hoke Norris, "Look Away," *Playboy,* July, 133. *The most common variant.* 5 A fine, interesting, or remarkable event, object, or person.

—ing *adj.* = **mother fucking.** 1963: "The [recaptured] prisoner shrugged . . . 'I was doin' awright till you put them motherin' dogs [bloodhounds] on me.' " R. Lorning, "A Quiet Night in Jail," *Esquire,* May, 127.

mother fucker [taboo] 1 A low, despicable, base person. *This is now the most derog. of all common U.S. epithets. Similar epithets are common in Sp. ("chinga tu madre"), It., Port., and Grk. In Latin-Catholic countries "mother" has long been a common element in taboo oaths, but often refers to the Holy Virgin ("Mother of God") and the connotation of "fuck"* = to cheat. The U.S. use seems to have no religious base, "mother" being one's own mother and the meaning of "fuck" being sexual; thus the U.S. use is obscene rather than blasphemous. However, the incest image is purely fig., never lit. Applied to any disliked man, and sometimes to women. The dislike may apply to any characteristic: selfishness, rudeness, laziness, unethical behavior, etc. Often applied to those of superior wealth, rank, etc., but also to equals and inferiors. Orig. strong Negro use and association, spreading to gen. male population in the Armed Forces during W.W.II and esp. during the Korean war, from Negro construction battalion workers. Since c1950, has gradually begun to replace the older, hence weakened, derog. "bastard"* and "son of a bitch."* Has many variant forms, some humorous, all formed on two-word expressions, each word having two syllables, such as: mother eater, mother dangler, mother flunker, mother grabber, mother helper, mother joker, mother kisser, mother lover, mother nudger, mother pisser, mother rucker, and many more. Many variants* *do not even contain the word "mother," as* "triple-clutcher." *Very common.* **2** A familiar, jocular, even affectionate term of address between males. *The use of derog. terms as jocular address is common in U.S. slang, as "bastard."* Cf. **muh-fuh.**

mother fucking [taboo]   **1** Despicable; base; undesirable; inferior, ugly, or disgusting. **2** Dangerous; annoying or harsh; distasteful; unpleasant; difficult to accomplish; causing anger or hard work. *Like "mother fucker," this was orig. Negro use, pop. to gen. male use during W.W.II, and increased in pop. rapidly during and since the Korean war. As an adj., is applied to people, events, objects, etc., to express one's disgust. Also has many variants.* See **mother fucker.**

mothergrabber [taboo]   *n.* A euphem. for **motherfucker.**

mothergrabbing [taboo]   *adj.* = **mother fucking.** 1962: "He's a jerkoff. A goddam mothergrabbing jerkoff." James Jones, *The Thin Red Line*, 60. 1963: "He [actor Steve McQueen] was TV's Hessian headhunter in *Wanted—Dead or Alive*, serving as what he describes as 'three hard mothergrabbin' years, but I learned my trade. . . .' " *Time*, June 28, 24.

mother's day   Mother's Day   The day, usu. once a month, when one receives one's regular welfare or relief check. 1972: "So it was on the first day of June, 1969, that Egan and I drove to the 81st Precinct, arriving at 8 a.m. We had picked this day because it was 'Mothers' [sic] Day,' the day when the welfare checks arrived. . . ." Robin Moore, "Why They Got Popeye," *New York*, Jan. 31, 28.

mouth off   To talk; make remarks; converse.

mox nix   It doesn't matter; it doesn't make any difference; it's not important. *Corruption of Ger. "es macht nichts." Post-W.W.II Army use in Ger., some civilian use since c1950.*

Mr. Clean   An honest, conscientious person; specif., a politician whose methods of running his campaign and collecting funds are above reproach. *From the trade mark of a popular household liquid cleaner of the same name.*

MTA   A Medical-Technical Assistant. *Specif. a medical student, intern, or orderly in charge of clinic or hospital supplies when a registered doctor is not on duty, as at night; hence any nonofficial who is responsible for or has access to drugs. Drug culture and prison use.*

muh-fuh [taboo]   *n.* = **mother fucker.** 1974: "I had a .22 in my bag because I was headed for the New Lots and them muh-fuhs are superbad." Dalton James, "Confessions of a Hustler," *Village Voice*, July 11, 23. *Humorously based on a stereotyped Negro pronunciation of* "mother fucker."

mui   *n.* A talisman or charm, as a devil's head, a tiny snake, etc. *Gypsy use.*

mule*   *n.* A narcotics smuggler. 1974: "Couriers—'mules' in the trade—carry coke in picture frames and sealed in the sides of suitcases. . . ." Ann Crittenden and Michael Ruby, "Cocaine: the Champagne of Drugs," N.Y. *Times*, Sept. 1, 17. *In earlier underworld use a mule was any smuggler or carrier of contraband or illegal goods.*

munchies   *n.pl.* Snacks eaten after using marijuana. *Usu. in the phrase "to have the munchies," meaning to be hungry, esp. for sweets and starches, as one often is after smoking marijuana. Drug culture. The word is also a punning reference to the Munchkins in* The Wizard of Oz, *who start Dorothy off on her dreamlike trip down the yellow brick road to see the wizard.*

murphy*   *n.* Any confidence game in which the victim is left with a sealed envelope which he expects to contain a list of prostitutes, places to obtain narcotics, sure-thing stock-market or racing tips, or his share of money from an unethical or get-rich-quick scheme, etc., but which contains newspaper, scrap paper, or blank paper instead. *v.t.* To fleece a victim by such a confidence game. 1964: ". . . Mayor Smitherman, a segregationist leader in Selma, and . . . a Selma lawyer . . . were 'murphyed' by the Negro confidence man at 2:30 A.M. today." N.Y. *Times*, April 6, 1.

my ass [taboo]   An expression of strong disbelief or opposition.

N

nabe   *n.* A neighborhood motion-picture theater; a local theater as opposed to a big city, downtown or first-run movie house. 1970: ". . . almost all the current films—from *I Am Curious (Yellow)* to *Easy Rider*—eventually make their way to the nabes." A. D. Coleman, *New York*, June 8, 35.

nail* *n.* A hypodermic needle. *Drug culture.*

'Nam   Nam   *n.* Vietnam. 1970: "These Cambodians seem like real nice people. Not like the gooks back in 'Nam who always got their goddam hands out." Murray Sayle, London *Times*, June 14, 8. *Orig. Armed Forces use in the Vietnam war.*

name of the game   **1** The important thing; the thing that matters most. 1973: "*Hit!* is a smashingly photographed, smartly acted tale of vengeance in the international drug trade. Going after the big guys is the name of the game. . . . " *Playboy*, Dec., 30. **2** The true situation; the way it is or the way it has to be.

narco   narc   *n.* An agent of the police narcotics squad; a narcotics detective. 1960: "The Beat Generation has marijuana and the ritual of dodging the 'narcos'—the narcotics squad." John Ciardi, "Epitaph for the Dead Beats," *Sat. Rev.,* Feb. 6, 11. *Drug culture. From "narcotics squad," reinforced by "nark."**

natural   *n.* = **Afro.**

neat* *adj.* Adroit; "keen,"* "swell."* *Although assoc. with the 1920s and said strongly as if it were sl., this is one of the stand. meanings of the word.*

nebbie   *n.* = **nimby.**

nemmie   nemish   *n.* = **nimby.**

nerd   nurd   *n.* A contemptible, undesirable, or unpleasant person, esp. one who is not in the know; a "square."* 1965: "*Nurd* a person who is not in the know, a square, not hip." Tom Medley, *Hot Rod Jargon. Teenage use.*

nick* *v.t.* To steal. *Orig. Brit.*

nickel* *n.* **1** A five-year prison sentence. *Some underworld use.* Cf. **dime.** **2** = **nickel note.*** See also **big nickel; small nickel.**

nickel bag   Five dollars' worth of a drug, as a quarter-ounce of marijuana. *Drug culture.* See **bag.**

nigger-pot   *n.* = **moonshine*** (def. 1). *Some Southern use.*

nimby   nimbie   *n.* Nembutal (a trade name) or any barbiturate. Also nebbie, nemmie, and nemish. *Drug culture.*

nine-to-five   *n.* A regular, usu. salaried, job customarily starting at nine o'clock in the morning and ending at five o'clock in the afternoon.   *v.i.* To be

regularly employed. 1972: " 'I think Jimmy always aspired to be a hustler,' a friend said. 'Even when he was nine-to-fiving.' " Richard Woodley, *Dealer: Portrait of a Cocaine Merchant* (Warner), 119.   **—r**   *n.* **1** A person who is steadily employed. → **2** A reliable, responsible person. **3** A regular job.

nitro   *n.* **1** Nitroglycerin, esp. as used in blowing open a safe. *Commonly used in crime movies and books.* **2** Nitromethane, esp. as used as a fuel additive for automobiles. *Hot-rod and racing use.*

nitty-gritty   *n.* The basics or essentials of any situation, predicament, action, etc., esp. the hard, unvarnished facts, "brass tacks,"* or harsh realities. 1963: "Negroes . . . know perfectly well that the nitty-gritty of a situation is the essentials of it." "Beyond the Ears of the Greys," *Time*, Aug. 2, 14. *Orig. Negro use.*

nod* *n.* A comatose state experienced by an addict after an injection of narcotics. 1965: "When the heroin addict . . . gets a sufficiently powerful shot he goes on a 'nod'—his head drooping, eyelids heavy." James Mills, "We Are All Animals," *Reader's Digest*, June, 232. *Drug culture.*

no-go   no go   *adj.* **1** Not functioning well; not ready to proceed. *Orig. aerospace use.* Cf. **go.** **2** Useless or unavailing.

no-no   *n.* Something one should not do, say, etc.; something forbidden, esp. by reason of custom. 1970: "But the company says mustaches are a no-no—and even though they've gone all the way to the president of the place, nobody seems to be chief in charge of mustaches." *Charlotte Observer*, May 20. *From "no, no," the parental admonition to young children.*

nose cone   The ultimate; anything sensational or remarkable. *Because the nose cone of a space rocket is as "far out"* as one can get. Some teenage use c1961.*

nose job   nose bob   Plastic surgery to correct an overly large or misshapen nose.

nosh   *v.i., v.t.* To eat snacks; nibble. *n.* A snack; a little something eaten between meals.   **—er**   *n.* A person who snacks frequently. *From the Yiddish.*

no-show* *adj.* Designating a worker, esp. on a public payroll, who collects a salary without reporting for work; also, designating a nonexistent worker entered on a payroll whose salary is collected by a corrupt official.

no sweat   No problem; with no difficulty; easily. *Usu. as a reply to a question or to a statement expressing doubt.*

now   *adj.* **1** In the very latest style, fashion, etc.; modern. 1969: ". . . it was a beautiful decade, a really weird time for tripping out on now words, on today's zonked-out speech patterns." "The Freaks Had a Word for It," *Newsweek*, Dec. 29, 18. **2** Aware and concerned with what is new or current. 1973: "Thanks to the Beverly Hills Health Club, I'm a member of the Right On, Now Generation, except I still talk about going back to teach at Bowdoin, just as soon as I have my fill of all this." Gail Sheehy, "The Liberated Call Girl," *Penthouse*, Aug., 112. *"Now" as an adj. sounded very hip in the 1960s, yet all slang uses are so close to the standard adv. meanings it's surprising the use became slang rather than standard.*

no way   *interj.* In no way; impossible. *Often a reply to a question asking for something.*

nowhere   *adj.* Dull, "square,"* not "hip."* 1959: "If you're not with it, you're nowhere." L. Lipton, *The Holy Barbarians*, 317. *Orig. cool and far-out use.*

nudie   *n.* **1** A play or motion picture in which the performers appear in the nude. Cf. **skin flick. 2** A publication, esp. a magazine, featuring photographs of nudes. Cf. **skin magazine.**

nuke   *n.* A nuclear weapon.

number*   *n.* **1** An activity that one engages in as a profession, avocation, etc. **2** A marijuana cigarette. *Drug culture.* **3** A psychological trick or tactic; game. 1973: "You know the first thing a good shrink teaches you is to stop fooling yourself. . . . When he's pulling one of his numbers, he knows what he's doing." Quoted by Hendrik Hertzberg, *New York*, Dec. 10, 74. **4** A casual homosexual lover. *Homosexual use.* See also **do a number on; do [one's] number.**

Number One*   **number one**   **1** The part of a stage in front of the big drop curtain where stars perform or a master of ceremonies introduces the next act; the preferred part of a stage, closest to the audience, where a performer may best be seen. *Vaudeville use. Archaic.* **2** Very good; best. *Orig. Armed Forces use in Korea.* Cf. **number ten.**

number ten   Very bad; the worst. *Orig. Armed Forces use in Korea.* Cf. **number one.**

number two*   Second in rank, importance, influence, power, etc.

nurd = **nerd.**

nut*   *n.* **1** A share in the graft collected by policemen. **2** Any illegal payoff, as a bribe, to a policeman. 1971: "At plainclothes school, he recalled, many of his fellow students complained about being off the street for the 30 days of schooling because they missed what they called 'the nut'—payoffs to the police." Martin Arnold, "Crusading Policeman," N.Y. *Times*, May 11, 27.

nutbox   *n.* = **nut house.***

nuts and bolts   The fundamental issues; the basics. 1973: "Ball interviewed twenty-five diplomats and military experts. . . . Much useful information came, he says, 'from men who are dealing with the nuts and bolts of negotiations.' " Editorial, *Fortune*, Feb., 51.

nuts-and-bolts   *adj.* Basic or fundamental; also, practical.

O

O.B.U.   One Big Union. *I.W.W. use. Obs.*

O.D.*   **OD**   *n.* An overdose of a narcotic. *Drug culture.* *v.i.* To become ill or die from an overdose of a narcotic drug. *Drug culture.*

off   *v.t.* **1** To kill or destroy. 1973: "The Organization had ordered him to mess up a couple of guys, but instead he offed them." John Godey, *The Taking of Pelham One Two Three*, 109. *First heard by most Americans in the mid-60s in the chants of radicals, esp. during clashes with police that arose out of racial disturbances and protests against the war in* S.E. Asia: *"off the pigs," "kill the police."* **2** To have sexual intercourse with. 1968: "You may not believe this . . . when I off a nigger bitch, I close my eyes and concentrate real hard, and pretty soon I get to believing that I'm riding one of them bucking blondes." Eldridge Cleaver, *Soul on Ice*, 160-61.

off artist   A thief.

off-putting   *adj.* **1** Repelling, disgusting; unattractive; unappealing. 1968: "Nor do I find pubic hair particularly interesting or arousing. . . . Nor do I find it ugly or off-putting." Alan Brien, *New Statesman*, April 5, 447. **2** Causing doubt, discomfort, or anxiety. 1968: ". . . though he was one of the most charming, witty, and sociable gentlemen alive, he also had a surprising defensiveness, an off-putting chip on the shoulder that made me wary of him." *Esquire,* July, 111. *Considered effete in the 1940s, this adjective based on the expression "to put one off," gained some currency in the 1960s.*

off the wall 1 Unusual; way out. 1974: ". . . his off-the-wall sense of humor and his enormous scatological vocabulary." Jon Landau, "Films: The Last Detail," *Rolling Stone,* Mar. 14, 70. **2** Insane; out of one's mind. 1972: "Deputy Inspector Martin Duffy said Mrs. Morea was 'very, very distraught—really incoherent, off the wall.' " N.Y. *Times,* July 5, 79.

oil spot In the war in Vietnam, a village or area, esp. one that has just been captured or pacified, used as a center from which to spread civilian and military influence farther into the hostile area. 1964: "Oil Spot—The first village in a hostile area to be won over by the Government. Its troops and civilian cadre then attempt to extend their influence in a widening circle, using the pacified village as their base." N.Y. *Times,* Sept. 16, 4. *Armed Forces use in Vietnam.*

oink *n.* A law-enforcement officer; policeman. *Not common.* Cf. **pig.***

old Joe *n.* Any venereal disease, esp. syphilis or gonorrhea. 1963: ". . . twice I got old Joe, you know, a dose. . . ." T. Rubin, *Sweet Daddy,* 110.

old lady* A mistress or girl friend.

old man* **1** A woman's steady boyfriend. **2** A "sugar daddy."* **3** A prostitute's pimp. *Prostitute use.*

Old Sparky The electric chair. *Prison and criminal use. Not common.*

old-timey *adj.* Old-fashioned, esp. in a pleasant and nostalgic way. 1973: "There will be an enormous tree, dripping with old-timey decorations, and an elaborate spun-sugar house presides over the lobby for the holidays." Nancy Winters, *New York,* Oct. 29, 90.

one-eye *n.* **1** = **hillbilly.*** *Because family inbreeding, as in isolated areas, is popularly believed to make the eyes of children of each succeeding generation grow closer together. Archaic and rural use.* → **2** A stupid person; a mentally defective person, as a moron. **3** An automobile driving with only one headlight. *Some police use.*

one-liner *n.* A brief joke in a single

sentence; a joke which is virtually its own punch line.

one thou **one thousand** The worst; even worse than "number 10." *Orig Armed Forces use in Vietnam.*

one-up* *adj.* Being in a better state or position than another or others. *v.t.* To gain ascendancy over. 1967: "But pedantry wasn't my point. . . . Furthermore, I wasn't trying to one-up Arthur Schwarts." Martin Williams, *Down Beat,* Sept. 7, 14. See **one-upmanship.**

one-upmanship *n.* The urge to get or stay ahead of another or others in knowledge, skill, achievement, possessions, etc. 1964: "The write-in vote for Bob Kennedy . . . injected an ominous note of party conflict into a scramble that until then had been a wide-open but good-humored game of political one-upmanship." Tom Wicker, *SEP,* April 25, 76. *From the title of a book (1952) by Stephen Potter, British humorist.*

on the cheap At minimum cost; very inexpensively; cheaply.

on the make* **1** To be available for sexual intercourse; promiscuous. 1961: "We will shimmy/ And we will shake,/ But please don't think/ We're on the make." Song "Hello Everybody," sung by burlesque chorus girls in N.Y. City production *This Was Burlesque.* → **2** To be willing to say or do anything in order to attain success, fame, money, etc.; ambitious and immoral. → **3** Habitually dishonest, said of an opportunist. 1962: ". . . Editor Ed Pooley . . . who has spent 30 years fighting everything from pigeons to cops on the make." *Time,* Oct. 19, 51. See **make.***

on the pad (of a policeman) Taking graft, accepting graft. See **pad.**

on the rims With the absolute minimum amount of money necessary; on the borderline of poverty; cheaply, as cheaply as possible. *Thus one may live, travel, or operate a business "on the rims." The image is that of an automobile without the luxury of tires.*

on the take Receiving illegal money, bribes, graft, kickbacks, or the like.

Op-Ed page **op-ed page** A page of a newspaper featuring columns and other special articles, usu. opposite the editorial page. *Shortened form of "opposite editorial."*

open [one's] head To make one understand things more clearly and to experience things more deeply. 1973: "Now, I listen to everyone—including my own children. I didn't have them for a reason, didn't really plan them at all. But watching them—seeing the growing up of children—is wonderful and amazing, and it's opened my head." J. Bell, *Good Housekeeping*, April, 184.

Orange Sunshine   A famous brand of illegally manufactured LSD in the form of orange tablets. 1974: "Within months after the lab at Windsor went into operation, 'Orange Sunshine' began to appear in acid-starved New York City and in New England communes." Mary Jo Warth, "The story of the acid profiteers," *Village Voice*, Aug. 22, 8. *Drug culture.*

orbs   *n.pl.*   Eyes or eyeballs. 1973: "If Tony Glover thinks those early Stones pix look quaint now, wait'll he fixes his orbs on the glitter crew in 18 months." Gene Sculatti, Letter, *Rolling Stone*, Sept. 27, 4.

Oreo   [derog.]   *n.*   A Negro whose values, life style, etc., are indistinguishable from those of the white establishment. 1969: ". . . successful black businessmen who were regarded as 'Oreos' after the cookie that is black on the outside and white within." Allan T. Demaree, *Fortune*, April, 184. *From the trade name of a chocolate cookie with a vanilla cream filling. Negro use.*

ouch   *n.* A wound or injury. 1962: "A very serious injury is a *big* ouch." D. Dempsey, "The Language of Traffic Policemen," *American Speech*, Dec., 271.

ounce man   **1** A drug dealer who cuts,

or adulterates, heroin. **2** (in the heroin distribution system) A connection; a drug retailer who buys from a "kilo connection." *Drug culture.*

out*   *adj.* **1** Not modern, popular, or in accord with modern tastes, fads, or trends. *Colloq.* **2** Uninformed; not "hip;"* "square."* **3** Openly homosexual. Cf. **come out of the closet.**

out-front   *adj.* Honest; sincere. 1968: ". . . a community of intelligent, very open, out-front people who cared deeply for one another. . . ." Tom Wolfe, *The Electric Kool-Aid Acid Test* (Bantam), 47.

out of it   **1** With little or no chance to win or succeed; not considered capable of succeeding; not worthy of regard or respect. **2** Elated, happy. **3** Not concerned with mundane things, as when under the influence of a drug, obsession, all-consuming idea, etc.; in a state of euphoria. **4** Not "with it";* stupid; "square."*

out of sight = way out*   1965: "Out of sight: As far out as you can get." "A Cursory Glossary to the Off-beat Side of Now," *Harper's Bazaar*, April, 173. *An extension of "far out."**

out to lunch*   **1** Bizarre; insane. **2** (of people) Unaware of what's going on around one; out of it.

Owsley acid   **Owsley's acid**   **owsley**   High-quality LSD. *Named after Augustus Owsley, who illegally manufactured a high-potency LSD. Drug culture.*

P

P   **pee***   **pea***   Any of various basic units of foreign currency beginning with the letter "p," esp. the Mexican peso or the Vietnamese piaster. 1966: ". . . 'pees' (South Vietnamese piasters worth roughly a penny). . . ." *Time*, March 4, 41.

packtripper   *n.* A backpacker.

pad*   *n.* **1** Graft, usu. money, shared by policemen or other law-enforcement officers. **2** A list of persons from whom graft is collected. *Usu. with "the." From a pad or tablet of paper containing the names of policemen to whom graft is distributed.* See **on the pad.**

paddy*   **patty**   *n.* **1** A worthless or lazy person. *Orig. hobo use.* **2** A white person, esp. one despised. *Negro use only.*

paddy boy   **patty boy**   [derog.]   A white man; "paddy." *Negro use.*

pad out   To go to sleep. *Some beat and student use since the 1950s when "pad"* (def. 4) gained currency.*

paleface*   *n.* A white homosexual. *Negro homosexual use.*

Panamanian red = Mexican red.

panman   *n.* A drummer in a steel band. *Musician use.*

Papa-san   *n.* See under **—san.**

paper*   *v.t.* **1** To distribute many free tickets or passes to a theater, auditorium, etc., in order to ensure a large audience. *Theatrical use.* **2** To write up parking tickets. *Police use.*   *n.* A small packet containing a narcotic drug. *Drug culture.*

paper over   To gloss over or conceal. 1974: "If the tiff were nothing but a clash of personalities . . . it might be quickly papered over." *Newsweek*, Feb. 25, 75.

paper tiger A person or thing appearing to be strong, threatening, etc., but which is really ineffectual and lacking in power. 1965: "I disagreed with nearly all of Mr. Hoffer's conclusions but one. That is where he stated that the Negro is doing battle with a paper tiger when he aims his wrath at the white liberal." N.Y. *Times Mag.*, April 25, 110. *Orig. used by Communist China in referring to the United States, from an old Oriental saying.*

parakeet [derog.] *n.* A Puerto Rican.

pasty pastie *n.* One of a pair of small circular pieces of adhesive material, often decorated with sequins, etc., applied to the nipples by a burlesque performer, exotic dancer, etc., in order to satisfy laws banning the display of bare breasts, or as a gesture of propriety. *Burlesque and theatrical use.*

pato *n.* A male homosexual. *From the Sp. Not common. Cf. maricon.*

pay dues 1 Fig., to put in a period of apprenticeship, as holding a series of menial jobs while working one's way toward a specific goal. 2 To have to work hard, lose money, suffer, or in some other way find oneself paying the penalty for past mistakes, work hastily done, or for entering into ill-considered relationships or bad habits. *Thus, a convict is "paying dues," as is a drug addict who is trying to break his addiction, as is a student who is suffering over a lost girl or retaking a course he failed to pass.*

payola * *n.* Bribery money paid by recording companies, singers, etc., to disc jockeys for promoting and playing their records so they will become popular. 1961: "On November 6, 1959, a letter . . . from Burton Lane, president of the American Guild of Authors and Composers, was released to the press . . . [It] described wholesale commercial bribery in the radio, television, and music industries. . . . [It] gave mass circulation to *payola*, a word that had been a part of the highly specialized argot of the music business." William Randle, "Payola," *American Speech*, May, 104. *Common in the music industry since the 1930s.*

PCP Phencyclidine. *A potent tranquilizer used in veterinary medicine, esp. for hogs, but smoked illegally by young people to get a high. See **angel dust** (def. 1).*

p.d.q. 1 Pretty damn quick. 1964: " '. . . he changed her mind for her p.d.q.,' said Maisie. 'What is p.d.q.?' said Betty Lewis. 'Oh, you're such a child, Betty. That's old-time slang for pretty damn quick.' " John O'Hara, "The Jet Set," *The Horse Knows the Way*, 227. 2 Pretty damn cute. *Some student use. c1940.*

P.D.R. *Physicians' Desk Reference*, a handbook listing drugs by their chemical and brand names and by manufacturer. It is useful to addicts in obtaining drug information. *Drug culture.*

peacenik *n.* A person who shows his opposition to a war by joining peace demonstrations and marches specif., a vigorous opponent of American involvement in the Vietnam war. *Usu. disparaging.*

peck * *v.i.* To eat. *Negro use.*

pecks *n.pl.* Food. *Teenage gang and addict use. Prob. derives from "peckings"* * = *food; orig. Negro use.*

peek freak A voyeur; a peeping Tom.

peepers * *n.pl.* Sunglasses. 1974: "In the morning I'd come in through the employee door with one of my peepers on and my hair smoothed down. Then I'd flake to the john and comb my hair out and slip on my regular glasses." Dalton James, "Confessions of a Hustler," *Village Voice*, July 11, 23.

penetrate *v.t.* To break and enter; to break into or enter a room, apartment, building, etc., secretly and without permission. *Some Central Intelligence Agency and underworld use.*

penny * *n.* A dollar bill. *Never common. Some jazz use.*

people, the *n.* = **kilo connection.**

pep pill Any amphetamine pill. 1966: ". . . amphetamines (pep pills) . . ." N.Y. *Post*, Jan. 28, 13.

perk * *n.* An incidental benefit of a job or position, as a service, privilege, fringe benefit, money, etc., beyond what is earned as salary or wages. 1974: " 'That's not cheap,' I warned Selwyn. 'Nixon likes a lot of perks, such as servants, chauffeurs, secretaries. . . .' " Art Buchwald, synd. newsp. col., Oct. 17. *From "perquisite."*

petnapper *n.* A person guilty of petnapping. *Based on kidnapper and the more common "dognapper."* *

P.G. *n.* Paregoric. *Drug culture.*

Philadelphia bank roll A roll of $1 bills with a $10 or $20 bill wrapped around the outside. See **Michigan roll.** *

pick *n.* A phonograph.

pick 'em An expression that means teams or opponents are rated about even; gambling odds of even money. *Gambling use.*

piddle   *v.i.* To piss.* *Colloq.*

piece*   *n.* **1** An ounce of heroin or other narcotic. 1965: "He buys heroin in 'pieces' (ounces), cuts it, and bags it. . . ." James Mills, "We Are All Animals," *Reader's Digest*, June, 228. *Drug culture.* **2** A graffito painted on the outside surface of a subway car. 1974: "A train rumbles into the station and we all pause to view its pieces." Michael Blaine, "The Kids Behind Graffiti," *Wisdom's Child*, Aug. 19, 7.

piece of cake   Any task or duty that is easy to perform. *Orig. Brit. use.*

piece of goods = **calico.***   *Variant of* "*piece of calico*."* Cf. **dry-goods.***

piece of the action   A portion or share in something, esp. a financial venture. 1968: "It was not long before he formed his own production company and persuaded CBS—by threatening to quit the program—to let his company have a piece of the *Gunsmoke* [television series] action." Leslie Raddatz, *TV Guide*, Aug. 17, 17.

pig*   *n.* A bigot, racist, or fascist; anyone who contributes to the oppression of a people. *Pop. by the Black Panthers about 1967.*

pigeon*   *n.* A counterfeit, void, or useless bill, ticket, or pass that is used, sold, or cashed as if it were good; esp. a losing ticket on a race, lottery, etc., that is sold or cashed as a winning ticket.

pillhead   *n.* A person who habitually takes tranquilizers, amphetamines, barbiturates, or similar drugs in pill form. *Drug culture.*

pillow talk   Intimate, confidential, heart-to-heart talk, as that practiced by married people and lovers while in bed.

pimple lights   *n.pl.* Parking lights on a truck tractor. *Some trucker use.*

pimpmobile   *n.* A pimp's automobile, typically a large, expensive, custom-built auto having ostentatious or gaudy interior and exterior colors and ornamentations.

pin*   *v.t.* **1** To pursue a member of the opposite sex in hopes of romance and/or sex. **2** To understand another person, and that person's motive, thoroughly; to be able to predict what another person will say, do, or think, esp. for the purpose of taking countermeasures. **3** To know, recognize; to look at, survey. 1963: ". . . two . . . marines walk into the bar—they weren't queer . . . just pinning the queer scene. . . ." J. Rechy, *City of Night*, 196.   *n.* A thin or very short marijuana cigarette. *Drug culture.*

—ned   *adj.* Constricted (said of the pupils of the eyes). 1965: "When the heroin addict is high, his pupils are 'pinned,' constricted. . . ." James Mills, "We Are All Animals," *Reader's Digest*, June, 232. *Drug culture.*

pincers   *n.pl.* The eyes. *Some student use since c1964, esp. among young teenagers. Pop. by Brit. singing group the Beatles.*

pinga   [taboo]   *n.* The penis. *From the Sp. Considered more vulgar than "bicho."*

pipe*   *n.* **1** A telephone. **2** The part of a wave that is fastest, where the water rolls over and downward. *Surfer use.*   *v.t.* To strike (someone) on the head, as with a metal pipe. 1972: ". . . I was wondering if one night someone was gonna pipe me, stab me. . . ." Inmate, California State Prison at San Quentin, quoted by Leonard J. Berry, *Prison*, 235.

piss [something] **away**   To waste; spend foolishly or recklessly. 1970: ". . . and then they went and pissed the money away on other things." Lawrence Sanders, *The Anderson Tapes*, 51.

piss poor   Very poor, wrong, or weak; disgustingly poor, bad, inefficient, etc. *Like "piss and vinegar,"* this is a *"piss" expression usu. considered not taboo.* See **piss.***

pix*   *n.* A homosexual.

pizzazz*   *n.* **1** Any item or trimming designed mainly to attract attention or give a gaudy appearance; specif. chromium strips, oversized grills and headlights, etc., that give automobiles a sporty or new look. **2** Loud, colorful, aggressive advertising or salesmanship.   *adj.* Sporty; flashy; esp. used to refer to automobiles having unnecessary gadgets reminiscent of true sport or racing cars, such as bucket seats, manual four-speed gearshifts, etc.

plasma   *n.* Rocket fuel. 1959: "Birds . . . use a lot of *plasma*—but it's not available for transfusions. It refers to a highly charged gas. . . ." Thomas J. Fleming, "Space Slanguage," *American Weekly*, Aug. 30, 2. *Aerospace use.*

plastic   *adj.* Artificial; fake; hoked-up. 1973: ". . . Charlie Russell saw in California a chilling vision of the future. From his casual remarks and humorous yarns an unflattering picture emerges of a plastic society. . . ." B. W. Dippie, *American Heritage*, April, 14.

plastic hippie   A part-time, or "weekend," hippie who likes to adopt on occasion hippie attire and mannerisms, but who is not committed to the hippie life-style or beliefs.

platforms   *n.pl.* = **pyramids.**

play checkers   To keep changing seats in a motion picture theater in search of a potential sexual partner. If, after making overtures to a likely prospect, the "player" is rejected, he moves to another seat, etc. *Homosexual use.*

player   *n.* **1** A bettor. *Gambling use.* **2** One who is promiscuous, esp. a married person who engages in wife- or husband-swapping, group sex, etc. **3** A pimp. 1974: "Normally, he would drive down to the YMCA in the early afternoon to work out, perhaps shoot baskets with some of his fellow 'players' (as pimps refer to themselves) and relax for a while in the steam room." Francis A. J. Ianni, *Black Mafia*, 28.

play on down   To go from one place to another. 1958: "The *cat* . . . jumps into his short . . . and plays on down to [his chick's] *pad.*" M. Crane, "Vox Bop." *Jazz and beat use.*

play smacky lips   **play smacky mouth** To kiss or neck. *Student and teenage use. Not common.*

plonk*   *n.* A boring or socially awkward person.

pluck*   *n.* = **plunk.***

plug*   *n.* An advertisement or favorable statement, specif. one that is received free of charge. *Orig. advertising and show business use; now common.* **—ged** *adj.* Angry. *Most common c1935.* **—ola**   *n.* **1** Compensation given television performers, producers, writers, etc., for mentioning a manufacturer's product in the course of a program. *Payment may be in cash but is usu. in kind, the person receiving the car, or refrigerator, etc., mentioned. Orig. television use, now also applied to movie directors, newspaper writers, etc.; coined by analogy with the more pop. "payola."* **2** The free advertisement or favorable comment or review itself; a "plug."

plugged-in   *adj.* = **turned-on** (defs. 1, 2).

plumber*   *n.* A member of the White House group supervised by President Nixon's domestic advisor John Ehrlichman, and originally called Special Investigators Unit, organized in 1971 to stop "leaks" of top-secret information to the newspapers after the unauthorized release of the Pentagon Papers (sensitive documents about the war in Vietnam), and to investigate other matters relating to national security. Members of the group were involved in the break-in of the Democratic Party's headquarters at the Watergate complex in Washington in 1972. *From the fact that plumbers are employed to stop leaks.*

pocket litter   The usual contents of a man's pockets or of his pockets and wallet, including change, keys, credit cards. 1973: "HUNT: . . . I probably need just a driver's license and some pocket litter. . . ." Quoted from a secret taped interview between Howard Hunt and Gen. Robert Cushman, C.I.A. McCrystal, et al., *Watergate*, 50.

pogey*   **pogie**   **pogy**   *n.* **1** Free food, as given out by a charity; food or food packages as sent by parents or friends to a student, soldier, or prisoner away from home, esp. sweets. **2** A homosexual. *Because gifts of food or sweets may be used to tempt another into a homosexual relationship.* Cf. **pogey bait.***

point*   *n.* **1** A hypodermic needle; "spike." *Drug culture.* **2** One who serves as a lookout, esp. one who warns an accomplice in the act of committing a crime that someone is coming. *From military use, the "point man" being a point or lookout in advance of a body of troops.*

point man = **point** (def. 2).

pointy head*   **pointy-head**   *n.* An intellectual. 1968: "It [Middle America] may agree that the 'pointy heads' are impractical as politicians, but it reserves its right to admire them for their achievements in other disciplines." *Newsweek*, Nov. 18, 52.   **—ed**   *adj.* Of, for, or characteristic of intellectuals. *Usu. disparaging.*

pol   *n.* A politician. 1973: ". . . the scold [Vice President Spiro Agnew] of the effete snobs and the tomentose radic-libs had in fact turned out to be only another pol on the take." *Newsweek*, Oct. 22, 35. *Usu. disparaging.*

poler   *n.* = **grind.*** 1962: "To the bulk of the undergraduates, however, he [Princeton student Edmund Wilson] was a withdrawn . . . 'poler' or grind, a smug, conceited little fellow. . . ." Andrew Turnbull, *Scott Fitzgerald*, 59. *Student use, most common c1915.*

poop scooper   **pooper scooper**   A shovel designed for collecting the excrement of dogs, in order to keep the streets clean. *Some humorous use.*

poor mouth   An exaggerated plea of poverty. 1965: "And it is hard to talk poor mouth just after the papers have written of your daughter's coming-out party for 2,000 guests." N.Y. *Times*, July 29, 16.

poor-mouth   *v.i., v.t.*   1 To plead poverty, usu. in an exaggerated way. → 2 To belittle one's position, opportunities, etc. 1968: "Richard Nixon often poor-mouthed his chances during the primaries. In New Hampshire he said he would be happy with 35% when he knew public and private polls showed him getting nearly double that." John Rekkanen, *Life*, July 19, 62b. 3 = **bad-mouth.** 1970: "I'm not going around poor-mouthing the war or showing how I feel all the time." Soldier quoted by Alvin Shuster, N.Y. *Times*, Oct. 23, 17. **—er**   *n.* A person who poor-mouths.

pop*   *n.* Nitromethane or any other fuel additive for automobiles and hot rods. 1965: ". . . Nitromethane and other fuel additives . . . called pop." Fort Worth, Texas, *Morning Star-Telegram*, July 16. *Automobile racing and hot-rod use.*   *v.i.* 1 To take narcotics or a shot of narcotics by injection. *Drug culture.* 2 Sexual intercourse.   *v.t.* 1 To swallow (pills), esp. habitually. 2 To have sexual intercourse with.

popout   *n.* A mass-produced surfboard. *Surfer use.*

pop party   A gathering or party for the purpose of injecting drugs. *Drug culture.*

pop polloi   The common people; the masses. *A blend of "populace" and "hoi polloi." Not common.*

pop wine   Any usu. sweet, fruit-flavored, low-alcohol wine, esp. that favored by young people.

porno   **porn**   *n.* Pornography. *adj.* Pornographic.

porny   *adj.* Pornographic.

potato digger   An undesirable person; a "square."*

pothead   *n.* A marijuana user. *From "pot"** = *marijuana. Drug culture.*

pothunter   *n.* A person who scavenges, usually illegally, in abandoned buildings, deserted farms, ghost towns, etc. 1973: "Another group of pothunters, as ghost-town thieves are called, yanked out a cabin porch in Boulder Flat . . . in order to steal a wood-burning stove." *Wall Street Journal*, July 16, 1.

pot party = **blast party.***

pound* [taboo]   *v.i., v.t.* To have sexual intercourse.

poundcake   *n.* A beautiful or desirable girl. *From "pound"* + *"cake."*

pound sand = **pound salt.***

pow*   *n.* = **clout.** 1969: "A thicker pay envelope is too easily thinned by

taxes and inflation—two sly thieves who can only be apprehended by government action, that is, by political 'pow.' " Gus Tyler, *New Leader*, July 21, 13.

preggers   *adj.* Pregnant. *Chiefly Brit.*

preppy   **preppie**   *n.* A student or graduate of a preparatory school.   *adj.* Typical of the manners and attitudes of a preparatory school boy: ". . . the lanky one says, 'I'm St. John Hunt.' The handshake is firm and preppy. The grin is not." Julia Cameron, "Life Without Father," *Rolling Stone*, Jan. 31, 27.

pressure cooker   A situation or place in which a person is subjected to great stress, crowding, noise, etc. 1973: "These men had a good deal in common even before they were put into the pressure cooker [West Point] on the Hudson." Gore Vidal, *New York Review of Books*, Oct 18, 21.

prick teaser   **prickteaser** [taboo]   *n.* = **cock teaser.***

pro*   *n.* A prophylactic for the prevention of venereal disease. *Orig. W.W.II Armed Forces use.*

process   *n.* = **conk.**

prosty   **prostie**   *n.* A prostitute; "prossie."* 1965: "Eduardo De Filippo . . . is the principal adaptor of his own play about a retired prosty who has been a rich man's mistress for 20 years." *Playboy*, March, 34.

prune*   *v.t.* To out-accelerate another driver in a drag race. *Hot-rod use.*

pseud   *n.* A fake or phony person or thing. *From the prefix "pseudo."*

psych*   *v.t.* 1 To make someone anxious, confused, or nervous. 1973: " 'I'm going to psych her [tennis player Billie Jean King] right out of her socks.' " Bobby Riggs, quoted before a much-publicized match between the two, *Newsweek*, Sept. 10, 44. 2 To outsmart another person.   *v.i.* To be excited, elated, or full of nervous energy. 1974: "Another plus is Isis' ability to inspire each other. . . . They smile at one another, jump around, whistle, boogie, and are generally so psyched that elation becomes their bottom line. . . ." Susan Shapiro, "Records: Isis," *Crawdaddy*, July, 72.

psych out   1 To lose control through fear; to lose one's nerve. 1963: ". . . *psyched out* [is a] slang term applied to losing one's nerve. . . ." Horst Jarka, "The Language of Skiers," 205. 2 To understand someone; to discover someone's deeper psychological motivations.

psych [oneself] up   To prepare oneself

mentally. 1974: "When a long-lengthed, bristled fellow comes in for the shearing, the hair dressers said they know he's been psyching himself up for the appointment. . . ." A. Fisher, *Arizona Wildcat*, Mar. 28, 9.

psywar *n.* Psychological warfare. 1973: "The KGB is carrying on an impressively orchestrated psywar operation against the dissidents." *New Republic*, Dec. 21, 1397.

p.t. **P.T.** [taboo] = **prick teaser.** *Based on "c.t."**

pucker *n.* Fear. *From the taboo "pucker assed."*

pucker assed [taboo] Afraid; frightened.

pud* *n.* **1** [taboo] The penis. *From "pudding." Some archaic and rural Southern use.* **2** An easy course; a "snap."* *Some student use.* *adj.* Easy to pass or make a good grade in, as a course or test. *Some student use; never common.*

pudding *n.* **1** [taboo] The penis, esp. as used for masturbation. *Of Brit. orig., some archaic Southern and rural use; prob. the orig. of "pudding head,"* from the old superstition that masturbation leads to feeblemindedness.* **2** Money. *Some student use since c1964, esp. among young teenagers. Pop. by the Brit. singing group the Beatles.*

puff* *n.* Lit. and fig. a free advertisement; a favorable mention of a product or brand name in a news report; a favorable mention of a business firm or individual; a "squib."* *v.t.* To extol or praise highly, esp. an article for sale. 1965: "There is little need for us to puff this book. . . ." Advt. for *Hart's Guide to New York City*, *Sat. Rev.*, March 13, 116. **—ery** *n.* **1** Free advertising. **2** Extravagant praise or commendation, esp. in advertising or promotional material.

pull a train Of a girl, to have sexual intercourse with several males consecutively. *Orig. West Coast motorcycle club (Hell's Angels) use; now some student use.*

purple heart Any barbiturate or mixture of a barbiturate and morphine used as a narcotic by addicts, esp. a Nembutal (trademark) capsule; a "goof ball"* or "yellow jacket."* *Orig. W.W.II Army addict use, when the addicts would take or mix any drugs they could obtain from military medical supplies.*

push the panic button* To become momentarily immobilized through fear,

anxiety, nervousness, etc.; to become panicky, unnerved, or irrational.

pussy butterfly [taboo] A specific intrauterine device (I.U.D.).

pussycat *n.* An agreeable or sweet person of either sex; "doll."* *Sometimes used as a term of endearment in direct address. Orig. theatrical use.*

pussy whipped Henpecked; dominated by one's wife or girl friend.

puta [taboo] *n.* A prostitute; a girl willing to have sexual intercourse with any youth who asks her. *From the taboo Sp. "puta" = prostitute. N.Y., Phila., and Pittsburgh teenage street-gang use, introduced by Puerto Rican youths; also some Los Angeles teenage street-gang use, introduced by Mexican youths. Since c1950. For the relation of Sp. "puta" to Fr. "putain," see the much earlier "poon tang."**

put-down *n.* An act, remark, etc., intended to disparage or humiliate someone or something. 1973: "This is a typical [Debbie] Reynolds self-put-down —'The nobody-ever-wanted-me, I-wasn't-particularly-talented . . . Blues.' " Liz Smith, *Good Housekeeping*, Aug., 165.

put-on* *n.* **1** A person who fakes good taste; class, or being "hip."* 1965: "*He's the biggest put-on since Murph the Surf.*" "A Cursory Glossary to the Off-beat Side of Now," *Harper's Bazaar*, April, 173. **2** An act, remark, etc., intended to deceive, mislead, or tease someone, usually with humorous intent. 1964: "He [Thelonius Monk] has a great reputation in the jazz world as a master of the 'put-on,' a mildly cruel art invented by hipsters as a means of toying with squares." *Time*, Feb. 28, 56. *adj.* Feigned; pretended.

put [someone] on To tease, make fun of, or play for a fool; to misrepresent something to; to convince someone that something fake is real. 1965: "A parent . . . might ask . . . 'Are you putting me on?' or 'pulling my leg.' " *N.Y. Times*, Dec. 27. *One of the most common slang expressions to gain currency since c1956. Orig. student and swinger use.*

put-on artist = **put-on** (def. 1).

putz *n.* = **schmuck.** *From the Yiddish.*

PX **1** Post Exchange, a government-owned store, similar to a department store, located on a military base and selling articles to military personnel at prices generally lower than retail prices elsewhere. **2** Standardized; common. *Some Army use.* **—ies** *n.pl.* =

falsies.* *Armed Forces use, orig. in Korea, because such American items can only be obtained in a "PX."*

pyramids *n.pl.* Shoes with very thick platform soles and heels sometimes 6 inches high, worn by flashily dressed young men and women. *Early 1970s use.*

Q

Q, the *n.* The Chicago, Burlington and Quincy Railroad. *Hobo use. Obs.*

quad* *n.* Any automobile having four headlights. **—s** *n.pl.* A set of four headlights on an automobile.

qualm *v.t.* To bother or disturb. *Some student use.*

queer for To have an inordinate or uncontrollable liking for something, ranging from a type of work to music, clothes, hobbies, food, etc. *Not taboo, orig. used without any homosexual implication though now occasionally used with* humorous or ironic homosexual connotation. See **queer*** (*adj.*, def. 2).

quick *adj., adv.* Tight; snugly. 1964: " 'The sweater fits you quick,' she said. . . . 'A little quick, but I can still get it on.' " John O'Hara, "Aunt Fran," *The Horse Knows the Way*, 65.

quick-and-dirty = **greasy spoon.***

quill* *n.* A folded matchbox cover used to hold heroin or cocaine when it is sniffed into the nose. *Drug culture.*

quit it To die. *Some Negro use.*

R

rack* *n.* = **pad*** (defs. 1–4); **crib.** *Some beat and student use.* **—ed** *adj.* Under control; mastered; sure of success or of the desired result; confident of passing an examination or course. *From the billiard image of racking up winning points.*

racket* *n.* A party or social gathering, esp. a rough or drunken one. 1965: ". . . a couplea gangbangs at beer rackets. . . ." H. Selby, Jr., *Last Exit to Brooklyn*, 260.

rack out To lie down and go to sleep; to go to bed, retire.

rad *n.* A radical, esp. a campus radical of the late 1960s.

Radical Chic **radical chic** The fashion for socialites to entertain and cultivate members of radical or controversial groups, such as the Black Panthers.

radiclib **radic-lib** **radic lib** **rad-lib** *n.* A radical liberal in politics. 1970: "In his panic at finding himself the first *Republican* to be impartially Agnewthematized as a 'radiclib,' he has lost whatever ear he may have had for subtleties." Brock Brower, *Life*, Oct. 16, 28.

rag top **rag-top** *n.* An automobile with a convertible top; a "chopped top."*

rag trade The clothing industry; garment trade. **—er** *n.* A clothing retailer.

rain *v.i.* To complain. *Orig. Negro use.*

rainmaker *n.* A powerful and successful lobbyist. 1969: "In the parlance of Capitol lobbyists, all such well-connected persons are 'rainmakers' capable of making their employer's cause prosper in the desert of Washington regulation." *Newsweek*, Feb. 3, 69.

raisin *n.* **1** A Negro. *From the dark color.* **2** An old person, esp. a woman. *From the wrinkles.*

raked *adj.* Of a modified car or hot rod, having the front end lower than the rear end. *Hot-rod use.*

ralph **ralph up** To vomit; throw up. 1974: "He ralphs up the downers and the quarts of beer." Joe Gallick, "Station House Groupies," *Village Voice*, July 11, 19.

R and R* = **rock and roll.***

rap* *v.i.* **1** To converse, esp. in an open and frank manner. **2** To sympathize; be in accord. *n.* Informal conversation; talk. **—per** *n.* A person who raps; member of a rap group.

rap club **rap parlor** **rap studio** An establishment that ostensibly offers conversation and companionship but in fact engages young women to perform a variety of sexual services for their male customers. 1973: "In the face of a crackdown on street prostitution many of the girls . . . are taking shelter in 'rap clubs'—which have replaced massage parlors in the sex-for-sale world. . . ." N.Y. *Post*, June 22, 7. Cf. **massage parlor.**

rap group   A discussion group.

rap session   1 = **bull session.*** 2 A group discussion, esp. by a rap group.

rap sheet   A police record. 1968: ". . . they had some sheets of paper that I had to fill out; one for my property and for receiving mail, and one for listing all my arrests. The last one is called a rap sheet." Bobby Seale, *Seize the Time*, 316.

rat*   *v.i.* To wander; to idle or loaf. 1964: " 'Where else have you been since I saw you . . . ?' 'Oh, I don't know. Ratting around.' " John O'Hara, "In the Mist," *The Horse Knows the Way*, 185.

rat fink   A treacherous, despicable, or unpleasant person. *Pop. by theatrical use.* See **rat;* fink.***

rat fuck [taboo]   1 Unacceptable to established social, moral, or cultural traditions or beliefs and therefore considered rebellious, individual, and good; shocking to middle-class values and thus humorous or expressive of oneself. → 2 = **far out*** (defs. 4, 5, 6). 3 To have a good time; to enjoy oneself in a personal and satisfying way. → 4 To idle or loaf, to "rat." *Orig. West Coast student use, esp. at Stanford Univ. and the Berkeley campus of the Univ. of Calif. Increasingly pop. student use, esp. in the abbr. form "R.F."*

rave-up   *n.* A boisterous, freewheeling get-together; a wild party. *Chiefly Brit.*

reader*   *n.* = **script*** (def. 1). *Drug culture.*

ream [someone] out   ream [some-one's] ass out [taboo] = **chew out.**

Reb   *n.* = **Rebel.**

Rebel   *n.* A white Southerner. *Commonly used among non-Southerners as a jocular epithet. Orig. derog.; from the Civil War's "Johnny Rebel" = Confederate soldier. Colloq.*

redassed   red-assed   *adj.* Angry; furious. 1974: " 'And my wife is real redassed at me,' Joe says. 'Johnette says I'm never home. . . .' " Joe Eszterhaus, "Claw Men From Outer Space," *Rolling Stone*, Jan. 17, 46.

red devil   Seconal, trade name of a barbiturate. *Drug culture.*

reenter   *v.i.* To cease feeling the effects of a drug; return from a drug "trip" (def. 1); be off a drug "high."* *Drug culture.*

reentry   *n.* The return from a drug "trip" (def. 1). *From the astronaut use. Drug culture.*

regs   *n.pl.* Regulations.

rehab   *adj., n.* Rehabilitation. 1972: "What they need is more work release and rehab centers. In other words, put you out to work in the community." Inmate at Bucks County Prison, quoted by Leonard J. Berry, *Prison*, 155.

rejasing   *n.* The practice of putting cast-off, rubbish, etc., to new uses. *Acronym formed from "reusing junk as something else."*

retard   *n.* A person who is mentally retarded.

rev up   *v.t.* 1 To increase in activity; step up the pace of. 2 To stir up; stimulate. *From "rev," a revolution, as of a motor or engine and "rev up," to increase the speed of a motor or engine.*

R.F.   1 = **rat fink.** *Not common.* 2 A "royal fucking." *Some euphem. use.* See **royal,* fuck.*** 3 = **rat fuck.** *An increasingly common euphem. Student use.*

ricky-tick   ricky-ticky   *adj.* 1 Pertaining to the jumpy popular music of the 1920s; ragtime. 2 Old-fashioned; corny.

ride*   *n.* 1 A horse race. 2 An automobile race. 3 = **trip** (def. 1). *LSD users and student use.*

rif*   *n.* A demotion.   *v.t.* To demote. 1965: ". . . former captains who . . . had been 'rif'd' back to sergeants." C. D. B. Bryan, *P. S. Wilkinson*, 12.

right on   right-on   *interj.* A fervent exclamation of affirmation and approval, originating with the Black Panther Party. *Mainly 1960s use.* → *adj.* Performing, operating, etc., very well; perfect. 1970: "Michael Caine, giving his best performance since *Alfie*, is right on as the medic who goes the antiestablishment route with intelligence." Judith Crist, *New York*, May 25, 61.

rigor   *n.* Lack of enthusiasm; coldness in attitude; an unwillingness to perform. *From "rigor mortis" and punning on "vigor." In theatrical use before c1960 but more common thereafter, with the pronunciation "riguh" in imitation of President John F. Kennedy's pronunciation and frequent use of the word "vigor," in his Boston accent.*

rip*   *n.* Stolen goods; loot. 1974: "The other time I was riding the Seventh Avenue with my week's rip in a large expensive suitcase." Dalton James, "Confessions of a hustler," *Village Voice*, July 11, 23.   *v.t.* = **rip off.**

rip off   *v.t.* 1 To steal. 2 To appropriate as one's own, esp. as a form of political or social protest against a supposed injustice or exploitation. 1973: "In defying the law, some young people claim not only innocence of wrong-doing but a special kind of moral superiority. 'Ripping off the Establishment,' they insist, is a political act." Joyce Brothers, *Good Housekeeping*, Feb., 66. **3** To kill.

rip-off   ripoff   *n.* **1** An act or instance of stealing; a theft. **2** Exploitation of a person or group of persons, esp. for financial gain. **3** Something fraudulent. **4** A business or corporation that overcharges for products or services. **5** Something copied; an imitation; also, a parody.

rip-off artist   A robber, thief, or confidence man.

roach*   *n.* An unattractive or unpopular girl. *Student use.*

roach clip   roach holder   Any tweezerlike clip for holding a butt of a marijuana cigarette that is too small to be held in the fingers. See **roach*** (def. 3).

roadie   roadster   *n.* A member of an entourage that travels with a rock band to handle bookings and related matters. 1974: " 'We had to cancel a gig in Roanoke, Virginia, because the stage couldn't support the drums,' a roadie proclaimed proudly." Judith Sims, "ELP . . . What? ELP! . . . What? ELP . . . ," *Rolling Stone*, April 25, 12.

road people   People, typically young, who have left their homes and roots and travel about from place to place either by riding in live-in vans or by hitchhiking carrying a backpack. 1973: "The biographies of some road people tend to display a continual inability to adjust throughout their lives to socially accepted modes of behavior. . . . Road people are in a sense confirmed outsiders. . . ." Abraham Miller, *Society*, July-August, 17. Cf. **street people.**

roadster   *n.* = **roadie.**

rock*   *v.t.* To surprise; shock; stun.

rocker   *n.* **1** A performer of rock-and-roll* music. **2** A song with rock-and-roll

characteristics. 1973: "The record set includes classic country rockers, sometimes with an old-timey flavor, as in 'Dixie Lullaby'. . . ." *Playboy*, Oct., 42.

rocks* [taboo]   *n.pl.* The testicles. See **get [one's] rocks off.**

rod* [taboo]   *n.* The penis.

roll in the hay   Sexual intercourse. *Usu. humorous use because of its rustic connotation.*

romp   *v.t.* **1** To smash or break something. → **2** To fight or quarrel with someone.   *n.* A fight. *From the Sp. reflexive verb "romper(se)" = to break. Orig. N.Y.C. teenage street-gang use, introduced by Puerto Rican youths.*

root*   *n.* A marijuana cigarette.

rooty   *adj.* Sexually aroused or passionate; "horny";* rutty.

rosebud [taboo]   *n.* The anus. *Mostly homosexual use.*

rosewood   *n.* A policeman's nightstick; a "billy."* *Orig. underworld argot, now mainly Negro use.*

rough trade   *n.* A tough or sadistic homosexual, as one who affects meanness, wears boots, etc.; a male homosexual who prefers anal intercourse for sadistic reasons; a male prostitute who caters to such homosexuals. 1965: " 'The gay boys call us "rough trade"! We're the ones they date. . . . We're the ones they buy presents for. . . .' " Shel Silverstein, "Silverstein on Fire Island," *Playboy*, Aug. *Orig. homosexual use.* See **trade** (def. 2).

round-eye   *n.* An Occidental woman, as opposed to an Oriental. *Armed Forces use in Japan and Korea.*

rug merchant   A spy. *Humorous ref. to the fact that spies often pose as foreign traders. Cold war use since c1960.*

run on the rims = **on the rims.**

rush*   *n.* **1** The sudden intensely pleasurable feeling produced after the injection of a narcotic drug. *Drug culture.* Cf. **flash. 2** Any intensely pleasurable feeling.

S

S.A.   **1** Sex appeal. *Applied most often to women, but can be applied to men. Often used to describe movie stars, celebrities, etc., but also used in ordinary conversation about people one knows.* **2** Santa Anita racetrack. **3** San Antonio, Texas.

sadie-maisie   *n.* = **S and M.**

salt*   *n.* Heroin in powder form. *Drug culture.*

salt and pepper   Marijuana that is impure or of poor quality. *Drug culture.*

Sam   sam   *adj.* Having sex appeal and magnetism, usu. said of a male. *n.* **1** Masculine sex appeal and magnetism; a male with sex appeal and magnetism. 1965: " . . . coeds search for their *Sam*—sex appeal plus magnetism. . . ." *Time*, Jan. 1, 57. *Student use.* **2** A federal narcotics agent. *From "Uncle Sam." Drug culture.*

—san One in charge. *Orig. Armed Forces use in Korea. This suffix is used to follow an English or pidgin word to = the top one or boss. Thus "Mama-san" = boss mother, the madam of a brothel; "Papa-san" = the man in charge, etc.*

sandbag* *v.i., v.t.* To win a race; drive very fast. *Hot-rod use.*

S and M **1** Lit., sadism and masochism; a sadist and a masochist; any sexual pervert; sexual perversions of any sort. *Orig. homosexual use; some general use since c1962.* **2** A slave master, the dominant person in a sado-masochistic relationship.

sao *n.* A repulsive, disagreeable, dishonest, or stupid person. *From the Vietnamese. Armed Forces use in Vietnam.*

sapfu *adj.* Surpassing all previous fuck ups. *n.* = **snafu.*** *W.W.II Armed Forces use; euphem. acronym formed by analogy with "snafu."* See **fuck up*** (def. 3).

sapphire *n.* An unpopular, unattractive Negro girl. *Negro use.*

Saturday night special A cheap, small-caliber handgun that is easily bought in a gun store or ordered by mail. 1974: "Since a great many of these purchases were made to satisfy the passions of Saturday Night, Detroit lawmen began to refer to the weapons as 'Saturday night specials.'" Robert Blair Kaiser, *Rolling Stone*, Feb. 28, 62.

savage* *adj.* The very best, excellent, superlative. 1965: "Degrees of superiority at Colorado College . . . work up toward . . . savage." *Time*, Jan. 1, 56. *Student use.*

scag *n.* Heroin. *Drug culture.*

scag jones A heroin habit. 1973: "Even unguarded brooms don't last long around this building because the junkies steal them and sell them to janitors for a quarter to support their 'scag jones.' . . ." Claude Brown, "The Group," N.Y. *Times Mag.*, Dec. 16, 79. *Drug culture.*

scam *n.* A swindle, esp. a dishonest carnival concession or game of chance. *Carnival use.* *v.t.* To swindle; to rob or cheat, usu. of a small sum of money. 1963: "He . . . worked . . . as a carny huckster. . . . 'It was a full scam. My boss was scammin' from the public and

I was scammin' from him.'" *Time*, June 28, 34. **—mer** See **skammer.**

scared shitless [taboo] Extremely scared; anxious; frightened. 1963: "And the [television] producer is scared shitless of the sponsor." Sterling Hayden, *Wanderer*, 243.

scene* *n.* **1** The setting or milieu associated with a specific activity or group of people. 1968: "The Beatles were also responsible for the bohemianization of the rock 'scene'. . . ." Ellen Willis, *New Yorker*, July 6, 56. **2** Experience.

schatzi **schanzi** *n.* A German girl friend; a German prostitute. *From Ger. "schatz" = treasure, diminutive = sweetheart. Post-W.W.II Army use from soldiers stationed in Germany.*

schizo* **schizy** **schizzy** *adj.* Crazy; psychotic. *From "schizophrenia."* See **schiz.***

schlang **schlong** *n.* = **prick*** (defs. 1, 2). *From the Yiddish.*

schlep* **shlep** *v.i.* To move or proceed slowly or with difficulty. 1973: "Ralph Nader was furious. He had just shuttled into New York, schlepped through ridiculous crosstown traffic and arrived an hour late for a private West Side gathering. . . ." P. Nobile, *Esquire*, Dec., 178. *n.* **1** A difficult or wearisome trip, walk, etc. 1974: "We've loved our old town house on East 32nd Street, even with the four-flight schlep to the editorial offices. . . ." *New York*, April 8, 4. **2** = **schlepper.*** **—py** *adj.* Stupid or awkward.

schmatte **schmattah** **shmatte** **shmotte** *n.* A shoddy or worn-out garment, hat, etc.; lit., a rag. 1973: "She had on a tired old schmattah and I was wearing an expensive knitted pants suit." Xaviera Hollander, *Xaviera!*, 87. *From the Yiddish.*

schmegeggy *n.* **1** A sap;* drip;* whiner. 1967: "My own mother . . . greets me over the phone with the following salutation: 'Well, how's my lover?' . . . And it never occurs to her, if I'm her lover, who is he, the schmegeggy she lives with?" Philip Roth, *Portnoy's Complaint*, 97. **2** Nonsense; claptrap. *Yiddish slang.*

schmuck = **prick*** (defs. 1, 2). *From the Yiddish.*

schtoonk *n.* A contemptible person; "stinker."* *From the Yiddish.*

schussboom *v.i.* To ski downhill at great speed. **—er** *n.* A person who schussbooms.

schvartze   shvartzeh   schwartze
n. **1** A Negro. **2** A Negro woman. 1967:
"She [my mother] sews, she knits, she
darns—she irons better even than the
schvartze. . . ." Philip Roth, *Portnoy's
Complaint*, 12. *From the Yiddish word
for "black."*

schvartzer   schwartzer   *n.* A Negro
man, esp. an employee of Jews. *From the
Yiddish word for "black."*

sci-fi   *n., adj.* Science fiction.

scobe   *n.* A Negro. *Negro use.*

scope on   scope out   To look at;
watch. 1971: "Two black youths, who
moved easily through the Belmont
Avenue market 'scoping on the foxy
sisters,' or looking at the pretty girls. . . ."
Thomas A. Johnson, "Brownsville Back
to Normal Despair," N.Y. *Times*, May 8,
59.

score*   *n.* **1** A planned murder.
Underworld use. **2** A prostitute's paying
customer. *Male and female prostitute
use.*   *v.t.* To murder. *Underworld use.*
v.i. To find a paying customer. *Male and
female prostitute use.*

scratch*   *n.* In horse racing, a ticket
on a horse withdrawn from a race. 1974:
"The girl said she found one 'scratch'—a
ticket worth a $2 refund since it was bet
on a horse that had not started." Gerald
Eskenazi, "Minors Are Found Betting
With OTB," N.Y. *Times*, Jan. 25, 26.

screech*   *n.* Cheap, inferior whiskey,
esp. homemade or bootlegged; "rotgut."*

screwup*   *n.* A blunder; something
that is the result of a blunder or series of
blunders.

script*   *n.* A doctor's prescription.

scrub   *v.t.* **1** Fig., to wash away a
score or mark; to tie, eliminate, or
eradicate an opponent's score. *Colloq.*
2 To cancel or stop, usually referring to
a sports contest or a missile-launching
operation; to ignore or forget a person,
deed, or idea; to fire an employee; to
cancel a planned action; to postpone an
activity; to eliminate a plan from consideration. *Fig., to wash something out of
existence, similar to the image of "wiping
a slate clean."*

scrub club   Any group, factory, office,
scientific, or business project, etc., that
has proved inefficient or had many
failures. See **scrub.**

scruffy   *adj.* Dirty and unkempt;
slovenly. 1973: " . . . there is sure to be
at least one bearded, sad-eyed, scruffy-
looking lad who comes up after class and
says: 'I was really interested in what you

had to say today—it sorta made me
wanta cry.' " A. Goldman, *New York*,
Aug. 27, 26.

scuffle*   *n.* = **scruff.*** *In the transition
from carnival to general theatrical use
"scruff" has become "scuffle."*

scum [taboo]   *n.* Semen; "jism";*
"come."*

scumbag [taboo]   *n.* A condom; "rubber."* See **scum.**

scuzzy   *adj.* Dirty; filthy. 1973:
" . . . your white middle-class American
audience doesn't really care two pins
about the righting of wrongs among a
bunch of scuzzy Moroccan A-rabs. . . ."
M. Feingold, *Village Voice*, Sept. 13, 64.

seafood*   *n.* A sailor considered as a
sex object. *Homosexual use.*

security blanket   An object, person,
place, etc., that has the effect of reducing
or preventing anxiety. 1974: "Zeigler
instead is, by one in-house assessment,
Mr. Nixon's 'security blanket'. . . ."
Newsweek, Jan. 21, 24. *From the blanket
carried by young children as a comforting
object or a defense against anxiety.*

seed   *n.* = **roach*** (def. 3).

seg   *n.* A person who advocates racial
segregation; a segregationist.

send up*   To make a parody of;
satirize; make fun of.

send-up   *n.* A parody; an instance of
mocking, teasing, or pulling someone's
leg; an instance of "putting on" someone.

session*   *n.* The time during which
one is high on a drug. *Usu. refers to
LSD. Drug culture.*

set*   *n.* **1** A small party or social
gathering; a personal conversation; a
good time shared with good friends. *Some
jazz, beat, and Negro use.* **2** A drug dose
consisting of 2 Seconals (a trade name)
and one amphetamine. *Drug culture.*
3 A jam session lasting for about 30
minutes. *Jazz musician use.* **4** A discussion. 1968: "He never said get those
Panthers out of here with those guns,
never said that all through the whole
set." Bobby Seale, *Seize the Time*, 176.
Mainly Negro use. **5** The group of songs
or selections musicians play during one,
approx. 45-minute, period. *Musician
use.*

sexpert   *n.* A therapist who treats
people with sexual problems. 1973: "The
behavioristic sexpert would call this
situational homosexuality." *Playboy*,
May, 68.

sexploitation   *n.* The commercial exploitation of interest in sex, esp. through the use of pornography.

shades *n.pl.* A pair of sunglasses; sunglasses. *Orig. bop musician use c1948–c1955; now mainly beat and student use.*

shaft* *v.t.* To take advantage of; to victimize; to deceive.

shag ass [taboo]   To leave, esp. to leave abruptly; "cut out,"* "haul ass."*

shake* *v.t.* To make a thorough search of a person, room, etc., as for contraband. *From the older expression "shake down"** (def. 1).*

shank* *n.* 1 A knife. 2 A prostitute.

shaved* *adj.* Of a car, having the ornamentation and unnecessary hardware removed. *Hot-rod use.*

sheep-dip *n.* Cheap, inferior liquor.

sheik* *v.t.* To tease; to deceive in a joking way. 1965: "A parent . . . might ask, 'Are you sheiking me, Ralph?' . . . for 'Are you putting me on?' or 'pulling my leg.'" N.Y. *Times*, Dec. 27.

shikse   shiksa   shikseh *n.* A non-Jewish girl or young woman. 1967: "That Alice was so blatantly a shikse caused no end of grief in Heshie's household, and even in my own. . . ." Philip Roth, *Portnoy's Complaint*, 54. *From the Yiddish.*

shirt*   shirty *adj.* Excellent, great, wonderful. 1965: "That's a shirt skirt." "A Cursory Glossary of the Off-beat Side of Now," *Harper's Bazaar*, April, 173. *Some student use.*

shit* [taboo]   *n.* Narcotics, drugs, specif. heroin. 1958: "I bet they're [junkies are] capping right now from their man/And shooting up as much shit as they can." H. Braddy, "Anonymous Verses." 1962: " . . . The New York Board of Regents has denied [a license] . . . to *The Connection* because [the producers of the movie] . . . insisted on retaining the word 'shit' as junkie slang for heroin." Dwight MacDonald, "Films" column, *Esquire*, Nov., 56. *Drug culture.* *v.t.* To exaggerate or lie to.

shit-ass [taboo]   *n.* 1 A contemptible person. 2 = shit-heel.*

shit-faced [taboo]   *adj.* Drunk. *Common student use.*

shit for the birds [taboo]   1 Nonsense, lies, exaggeration. 2 = for the birds.* See shit.*

shit hits the fan [taboo]   A crisis or uproar; trouble; a very tense situation. 1970: " 'Oh, you are looking for trouble, my son, and you are going to find it, too! The shit is going to hit the fan, buddy, and you ain't going to like it one

bit.' " Philip Roth, "Salad Days," *Modern Occasion*, Fall, 33. *From an old joke about a person who, not finding a bathroom in an upstairs room, defecates into a hole in the floor; upon rejoining a group downstairs he is asked, "Where were you when the shit hit the fan?"*

shit hook [taboo] = shit-heel.*

shitkicker [taboo]   *n.* 1 A farmer or other rural inhabitant. *Because of the manure found on farms.* 2 A western movie. **—s** *n.pl.* Heavy farm boots.

shit-stick [taboo]   *n.* A despicable, stupid, or worthless person.

shitter [taboo]   *n.* A toilet.

shlep   See schlep.

shlubbo   *n.* = zhlub.

shmatte   See schmatte.

shmeck   shmack   smack   *n.* Heroin. *Drug culture.*

shmee   *n.* Heroin. *Drug culture.*

shmotte   See schmatte.

shoe* *n.* 1 A plainclothes policeman or a detective. *From "gumshoe."** Mainly underworld use.* 2 = white shoe. 3 A forged passport. *Some recent Central Intelligence Agency and underworld use.* Cf. cobbler. 4 An automobile tire. *Orig. racing driver and mechanic use.*

shook   *adj.* = shook up.*

shoot [someone] down   1 To ruin someone's chance to win or succeed. 2 To deflate someone's ego; to put someone to shame, as by pointing out a lie, exaggeration, or character flaw. 3 To defeat, outdo, or best. *Mainly student use.*

shoot-'em-up   *n.* A grade-B western movie. 1972: "In the leisure time after supper, until Lights Out at 10, while the rest of the prison gambled for cigarettes, slurped Tang or watched shoot-'em-ups on TV . . . I would sit alone on the back steps of the dormitory. . . ." Ralph Ginzburg, N.Y. *Times Mag.*, Dec. 3, 39.

shoot off   1 [taboo] To ejaculate. 2 = shoot off [one's] mouth.*

shoot-out   *n.* = shoot-up (def. 2).

shoot up   To inject a narcotic drug. *Drug culture.*

shoot-up   *n.* 1 An act or instance of injecting a drug. *Drug culture.* 2 A gun battle.

short* *v.t.* To inhale heroin or cocaine in crystal form. *Drug culture.*

short fuse   A quick temper; lack of patience. *Usu. in phrase "have a short fuse," to get angry or excited easily; to blow up.*

short heist   Any small-time thievery, fraud, or illegal activity, as stealing food from supermarket shelves, stealing an unwatched purse or coat, etc.; petty larceny.

short list = **shit list.** *

shot *   *n.* One's habit, hobby, or vice; one's penchant, "kick," * or "bag." *Since c1960.*

showbiz   *n.* Show business; the theater, motion pictures, television, etc., as an industry or profession.

showboat *   *v.t.* To take advantage of one's superior rank; to bully or exact patronage from an inferior.

shpilkehs   *n.pl.* The jitters; restlessness; nervousness. *Usu. in the phrase "have shpilkehs." From the Yiddish.*

shrink   *n.* = **head shrinker.** *   *Orig. Calif. use c1960.*

shtick   *n.* **1** A special talent, attainment, or ability; a typical trait or characteristic. 1966: "The rest of it is the atmosphere of the factory, an enormous, dark, cluttered loft, a lot of it papered in shiny tinfoil, which is a [painter Andy] Warhol shtick." Leonard Shecter, *N.Y. Post,* Feb. 23, 38. **2** A part, detail, item, etc., that is attractive and appealing and has its own individuality and essence; a "bit." * 1965: "To my surprise, it [a small part in a film] turned out to be a nice little *shtick.*" Actor John McGiver, quoted by Gerald Nachman, *N.Y. Post,* Feb. 7, 29. **3** That which attracts, appeals, elicits a response, etc.; "gimmick." * 1966: "The *shtick* is that the taped remarks [on a comedy recording] of a number of political figures are tacked onto questions dreamed up by writers. . . ." *Playboy,* Feb., 37. *From the Yiddish.*

shtup [taboo]   *v.t.* Have sexual intercourse with. 1967: " . . . With those legs—why, of course he was shtupping her. . . . Wasn't he?" Philip Roth, *Portnoy's Complaint,* 83.   *n.* **1** The sexual act. **2** A woman who fornicates. *From the Yiddish.*

shuck *   *n.* **1** = **bullshit** * (def. 2). **2** = **rip-off** (*n.* defs.). **3** A person who is insincere or hypocritical. **4** An ex-convict.   *v.i.* To joke with; kid around with.   *v.t.* **1** To deceive. **2** To swindle. **3** To tease. *Orig. Negro use.*

shuffle   *v.i.* To fight; to have a "rumble." * *Teenage street-gang use.*

shun-pike   *v.i.* To travel by back roads rather than on turnpikes. *Lit.,* to shun the turnpikes. **—er**   *n.* A person who travels by back roads. 1973: "I turned shunpiker for the return

home. . . . At 35, 40, and 50 m.p.h., children see flocks of sheep, hex signs on barns and tree-lined main avenues of towns. . . ." David W. Hacker, *Wall Street Journal,* July 14, 12.

sick *   *adj.* To be in need of an injection of narcotics. *Drug culture.*   *n.* The extreme physical discomfort and craving felt by a drug addict in need of a drug. *Drug culture.*

side *   *n.* A single band on a long-playing record.

sideswipe   *n.* A critical or derogatory remark or observation, esp. an oblique one. 1965: " . . . J. Edgar Hoover took a sideswipe at 'restrictive court decisions affecting police prevention and enforcement activity.' " Yale Kamiser, *N.Y. Times Mag.,* Nov. 7, 110.

silk *   *n.* A white person. *From the smooth texture of the hair. Some Negro use.* Cf. **silk broad.** *

sister   *n.* **1** A female Negro. *Negro use only.* Cf. **brother.** **2** A member of the Women's Liberation Movement; a feminist. 1973: "The sisters in the movement do not much like [Washington columnist] Sally Quinn, nor do they wish her well on television." Aaron Latham, *New York,* July 16, 23. **3** A Negro homosexual. *Homosexual use.*

sister act   **1** Sexual relations between two homosexuals who have the same tastes and proclivities. **2** Sexual relations between a male homosexual and a woman. *Homosexual use.*

sitcom   *n.* A television situation comedy show. 1973: "But for a few wrenching moments, 'Maude' stands tall in the new family of sitcoms." Harry F. Waters, *Newsweek,* Sept. 24, 66.

sit fat   To be in a powerful, successful, or commanding position.

sit in *   To participate in a "sit-in."

sit-in   *n.* **1** A demonstration of protest in which Negroes, often accompanied by white liberals, enter and sit down in restaurants and other establishments from which Negroes, esp. in the South, were systematically excluded. *Early 1960s.* → **2** Any similar organized protest in which the participants sit in seats or on the floor and refuse to move until their demands are met.   **—er** *n.* A person who sits in.

sitter *   *n.* = **guru** (def. 3).

sitzfleisch   *n.* Perseverance. *Based on Ger. and lit.* = *sitting flesh or buttocks, used only fig. to* = *the patience to sit in one place until a problem is solved.*

sitzpower   *n.* = **sitzfleisch.**

siwash* *v.t.* **1** To blacklist. **2** To prohibit someone from buying liquor. *Orig. Chinook jargon, from "Siwash" = "American Indian." Northwestern use.*

skag* *n.* Someone or something foolish, undesirable, repulsive, dull, or insignificant. 1964: " . . . 'skag' . . . means what 'jerk' used to mean to their [teenagers'] parents." N.Y. *Times*, Nov. 1, Sect. B, 100. *Teenage use.*

skammer scammer *n.* A person who earns his living dishonestly, esp. by his wits, as a confidence man, swindler, smuggler, etc. 1974: "Trader Red was a dope smuggler, or skammer, as he preferred to be called." Gary Cartwright, "Dirty Dealing in the Lone Star State," *Rolling Stone*, Sept. 26, 91. See **scam.**

ski bunny An attractive girl who may or may not ski, but spends much time with skiers. *Some skier use.* Cf. **bunny.**

skim *n.* Income, usually gross winnings, that is not reported by a gambling casino to state or federal revenue collectors. *From the image of skimming the cream off whole milk. Gambling use.*
—ming *n.* **1** The illegal act or process of concealing a portion of the gross or take, as from a legal gambling establishment, to avoid payment of taxes on the removed portion. **2** The process by which illegally gained money, as from heroin trafficking, is invested in a legal business, the profits from which being declared as taxable income.

skim board A round or oval disc used in riding shallow water or a spent wave on the slope of a beach. *Surfer use.*

skin* *n.* **1** An automobile or truck tire, esp. one with a worn-out or smooth tread. 1961: "*Skin*—a worn-out tire still being used." R. Hanley, "Truck Drivers' Language," *American Speech*, Dec., 273. *Orig. truck-driver and hot-rod use.* **2** A person; "head"* (def. 4). *v.t.* To disarm a person or a military device. *Armed Forces, underworld, and police use.* *v.i., v.t.* = **skin pop.** **—ned** *adj.* Unarmed, said of a person who habitually carries a weapon, or esp. of a military vehicle whose guns, rocket launchers, etc., have been removed to increase its speed for reconnaissance missions. *Armed Forces, underworld, and police use.* **—ny** *n.* Information; inside or authentic information; the facts; the "poop."* *Mainly student use.*

skin flick A motion picture featuring nude performers; a pornographic movie. Cf. **flesh flick, fuck film, nudie** (def. 1).

skin-head* *n.* **1** A man with a shaved head or a closely cropped head of hair. → **2** A Marine recruit.

skin house A burlesque theater or a movie theater showing burlesque movies.

skin magazine A magazine containing photographs of nudes of either sex, esp. one that is intended to arouse or titillate; a pornographic magazine. Cf. **nudie** (def. 2).

skinny-dip *v.i.* To swim in the nude. *n.* A swim in the nude. **—per** *n.* One who swims in the nude. *From the 18th century use of "dipping" for "swimming."*

skin pop To take an intramuscular injection of narcotics, as opposed to an injection taken directly into a vein. 1958: "Since my veins are all hardened,/I'll have to skin pop. . . ." H. Braddy, "Anonymous Verses." *Drug culture.* **—per** *n.* A person who takes drugs in this way. *Drug culture.*

skin-search *v.t.* To perform a thorough examination of a naked person for evidence of hypodermic needle marks or for contraband (as drugs) hidden in the cavities of the body. *n.* An act or instance of skin-searching.

skull session 1 = **skull practice.*** → **2** A group discussion or briefing session. 1969: "To make certain that his position was clearly understood, Mr. Johnson [President Lyndon B. Johnson] held two separate 'skull sessions' with six members of the U.S. negotiating team. . . ." *Newsweek*, May 20, 29. Cf. **chalk talk.**

skunk* *n.* Any unidentified and possibly hostile object seen on a radar screen. *Navy use.*

skycap *n.* A porter who carries baggage for travelers at an airport. *Formed on analogy with the older term "red cap," a railway station porter.*

skyjack *v.i., v.t.* To seize control of an aircraft, usu. during flight, and force the pilot to fly it to a destination other than its scheduled one or to hold the plane, crew, and/or passengers for ransom. *n.* An instance of seizing control of an aircraft. **—er** *n.* A person who skyjacks an aircraft. *Formed on analogy by the earlier "hijack." Since the late 1960s.*

slag *v.t.* To criticize severely. 1974: "I think it was good copy at the time to slag everything. Everybody was getting slagged, the Beatles were getting slagged." Paul Gambaccini quoting Paul McCartney, "The Rolling Stone Interview," *Rolling Stone*, Jan. 31, 34.

slam* **slammer** *n.* Jail; a jail. *Some Negro and beat use.*

slat* *n.* A ski. *Skier use.*

slave* *n.* A job, esp. a menial, poorly paid job. 1965: "I had gotten out of the garment center and that was the place where everybody worked. Cats used to call it a 'slave.'" Claude Brown, *Manchild in the Promised Land,* 177.

sleeper* *n.* A sleeping pill, esp. a barbiturate; loosely, any sedative. *Drug culture.*

sleighride* *v.i.* To take cocaine. *Drug culture.*

slice* *v.t.* To cheat, as by overcharging.

slick* *n.* An automobile tire with but little tread left; a wide, smooth-tread tire, esp. as used in hot-rod races. *Hot-rod use.*

slide* *v.i.* To depart; go away. *Mostly Negro use.*

slim* *n.* A tobacco cigarette; a "straight"* or "square."* *Some jazz musician use.*

slope* [derog.] *n.* An Oriental. 1971: "But hearing it [the term 'nigger'] bandied about in the comfortable setting of his fraternity house recalled scenes near Chu Lai. . . . 'It was there that I first heard of dinks, slopes, and gooks.'" Daniel Long, *New Yorker,* Sept. 4, 43. *From the appearance of the eyes, a later version of the term "slant-eye."* *Armed Forces use in the Vietnam war.* Cf. **dink, gook, zip.**

sloppy Joe* Hamburger meat cooked in small particles instead of a patty and served with a spicy barbecue sauce, usu. on an open-faced bun.

slurb *n.* A suburban area that has many cheaply built or poorly kept houses, and often has ill-planned and unattractive business areas containing gas stations, used-car lots, etc. *From a blending of "slum" and "suburb."*

SM S/M = S and M.

smack* = shmeck.

small change = small potatoes.*

smallest room, the The bathroom; restroom. *A facetious euphem.*

small nickel The sum of $500, esp. as a wager. *Orig. gambling use.* Cf. **big nickel.**

smarmy *adj.* Smug and ingratiating; unctuous. 1973: "Its official name is 'the Workshop,' and it is run by a rather smarmy doctor and a highly officious nurse." T. Kalem, *Time,* Dec. 17, 96. *Orig. Brit. slang.*

smart ass A smart aleck;* a know-it-all.

smart bomb A bomb, first used in 1972 in Vietnam by the U.S. Air Force, equipped with a laser-guidance system, television camera, or other sensor or guidance system which accurately focuses on a predetermined target, as a bridge or factory.

smarts *n.pl.* **1** Intelligence; sense. 1973: "If they had any smarts, they would have put a silencer on a gun and pumped a bullet in his head." D. Fisher, *Playboy,* Apr., 210. **2** An instance of brashness, of being a "smart aleck,"* or of being aware of something one is not supposed to be. *Often in the expression "to have a case of the smarts."*

smash* *n.* Wine. *Mostly Negro use.*

smashing* *n.* Kissing or "necking."* 1965: "'Smashing' is not the British superlative, but means kissing." N.Y. *Times,* Dec. 27. *Teenage use.*

smoke* *n.* Lies, big talk, exaggeration, or flattery.

Smoky *n.* A state highway policeman. 1974: "Truckers . . . keep Don advised for the location of 'Smokies' . . . so he'll know when to gear the tour bus down from its maximum speed of 82 mph." Chet Flippo, *Rolling Stone,* Sept. 26, 86. *Prob. from U.S. Forestry Service symbol, Smoky the bear, who wears a wide-brimmed ranger's hat similar to those of many state policemen. Mainly trucker use.*

snake* *n.* An unpleasant, cheap, or despicable person. *v.t.* To get into trouble. *Usu. in the expression "to get snaked." Some Negro use.*

snap* *v.i.* To laugh; to mock or tease. *Some Negro and beat use.*

snapper *n.* **1** A punch line. 1969: "The word factory's resident pro for zingers and snappers (as punchlines are known in the trade) is, of course, Safire [William Safire, speech writer for President Nixon and later political columnist]." William H. Honan, N.Y. *Times Mag.,* Jan. 19, 73. **2** [taboo] The foreskin. *Homosexual use.* **3** [taboo] The vagina.

sneak *v.t.* To show a new motion picture at a sneak preview to gauge its effect on an audience. 1974: "We sneaked it in several cities. Audiences loved it. Only a loud minority protested it. . . ." B. M. Williams, *Psychology,* Feb., 102. *n.* A sneak preview of a motion picture.

snipe* *n.* Any member of an aircraft carrier who services and maintains the airplanes. 1965: " . . . 'snipes' . . . service and maintain their flying crews' birds. . . ." N.Y. *Times*, June 1. *Navy use*. Cf. **blackshoe.**

snop *n.* Marijuana. *Drug culture.*

snort* *v.i., v.t.* To take a narcotic by inhaling or smoking. 1958: "Since ma was a viper/and daddy would snort,/ There wasn't much more/I had to be taught." H. Braddy, "Anonymous Verses." *Drug culture.*

snow bunny = **ski bunny**. *Some skier use*. Cf. **bunny.**

snuff *v.t.* To kill someone; fig., to snuff out another's life.

soap* **soaper** *n.* = **soap opera.***

sobe *adj.* Sober. *Some student use since c1960.*

sock* *n.* A drummer's set of double cymbals operated by a foot pedal, as used in dance and jazz bands. *Musician use.*

socked in *adj.* Of an airport, unable to allow landings because of fog, rain, snow, etc.

sock it to [someone] **1** To attack vigorously. 1974: "One reader wrote in saying, 'Thanks for socking it to Barbie, that all-American plastic tart.' " Caryl Rivers, *Rolling Stone*, July 4, 9. **2** To impress or excite greatly. 1971: " . . . Aretha is the last word. . . . Aretha will sock it to you." **3** = **sock*** (*v.t.* def. 2). 1973: "Some congressional liberals would like to sock it to business by taking away the tax reductions . . . received under Nixon." R. Loving, Jr., *Fortune*, April, 142. *Popularized by the television show "Laugh-in" of the late 1960s and early 1970s, in which a young woman shouts, "Sock it to me!" and is usu. doused with a pail of water.*

soft-core *adj.* Pertaining to pornography that is not highly explicit, or in which sexual acts are simulated. Cf. **hard-core.**

soft drug A drug, such as marijuana, milder types of hashish, and mescaline, that is usu. thought of as being neither physically addictive nor a serious hazard to health. Cf. **hard drug.**

soft legs A girl or woman. *Negro use.*

soldier* *n.* One of the lowest ranking members of the Mafia; a hired thug. *Underworld use.*

sop* *v.i.* To drink, esp. to drink beer or liquor. *From such older phrases as "sopping it up" = to drink large quantities of beer or liquor.*

sopor *n.* Methaqualone, a trade name

of a muscle relaxer and non-barbiturate. *From "soporific." Drug culture.*

soul— See Appendix to the Supplement, Prefix Words.

soul *adj.* **1** Negro; pertaining to or having the essence of things, feelings, moods, etc., that are considered to be basically Negro; esp. having or expressing authentic sensitivity, emotional sincerity, a feeling of "the blues,"* etc., which status-seeking, commercialized, puritanical white Americans do not have. 1962: "In the strictest sense, 'soul' is a synonym for 'Negro.' The basic assumption being that the things it is used to describe are either totally or fundamentally Negro and that to whatever extent they are not, they still emulate the Negro or a Negro-ness." Ralph J. Gleason, "Lively Arts," San Francisco *Chronicle*: *Datebook*, April 22, 19. *Orig. Negro use; wide musician use; now common.* **2** Not segregated; welcoming, catering to, or friendly to Negroes. *Negro use only.* See Appendix to the Supplement, Prefix Words: **soul—**. *n.* Profound and authentic sensitivity, feeling, or sincerity.

soul brother A male Negro; a "blood brother." *Negro use only.* See Appendix to the Supplement, Prefix Words, **soul—**.

Soul City Harlem. *Negro use.* See Appendix to the Supplement, Prefix Words, **soul—**.

soul food **1** Food that is generally associated with the South, as black-eyed peas, hominy grits, ham hocks, etc. **2** Anything sincerely, profoundly, and personally satisfying, ranging from sex and love to music. *Still mainly Negro use.* See Appendix to the Supplement, Prefix Words, **soul—**.

soul music Modern jazz that is based upon or emphasizes blues or Negro gospel music. 1962: "[Soul music is] small combo jazz, modern in style but with emphasis on gospel music and the blues and played with the same feeling as gospel music." Ralph J. Gleason, "Lively Arts," San Francisco *Chronicle*: *Datebook*, April 8, 19. See Appendix to the Supplement, Prefix Words, **soul—**.

soul sister A female Negro. *Negro use only.* Cf. **soul brother.** See Appendix to the Supplement, Prefix Words, **soul—**.

Soulville = **Soul City**. *Negro and jazz use.* See Appendix to the Supplement, Prefix Words, **soul—**; Suffixes, **—ville.**

soundproof bra A padded brassiere.

soup* *n.* Foam formed by a breaker;

the froth or foamy part of a wave. 1965: "Surfers . . . drive to Galveston to . . . find a big wave with lots of soup, or white water." Houston, Texas, *Chronicle*, Sept. 5. *Surfer use.*

spaced-out *adj.* **1** Under heavy influence of a narcotic drug. *Drug culture.* **2** Not in touch with reality.

spacey *adj.* = **spaced-out.**

spaghetti bangbang A motion picture about underworld wars, esp. among the Mafia. 1974: "What with *The Valachi Papers* and *Crazy Joe* under his belt, Dino De Laurentiis is deep into the spaghetti bangbang with *Three Tough Guys.*" Judith Crist, *New York*, March 18, 67.

spaghetti Western A film with the traditional American western themes and settings produced and directed by Italian film-makers, usu. on location in Europe.

speed* *n.* An amphetamine, esp. Methedrine (a trade name). *Drug culture.* Cf. **speedball*** (def. 3).

speedfreak *n.* A habitual user of amphetamines and related stimulant drugs. *Drug culture.*

spider* *n.* A skillet, esp. an iron skillet as used by hunters, hikers, etc.

spike* *n.* A hypodermic needle or syringe, esp. a homemade one used by a narcotics addict. *Drug culture.*

spill* [derog.] *n.* A Negro or a Puerto Rican; esp. a person of half Negro and half Puerto Rican descent. *Since c1945.*

splay *n.* Marijuana. *Some drug culture.*

splib *n.* A Negro. *Negro use.*

spliff *n.* A marijuana cigarette. *Drug culture.*

split* *v.t.* To hit someone, esp. to knock a person out with one's fists or a weapon. **—ter** *n.* A person, esp. a young person, who runs away from home to live in the street or in hippie communes or to take drugs. *Since 1960s.*

split beaver [taboo] = **spread beaver.**

spook* *n.* **1** A psychiatrist. *Not common.* **2** A spy. *Not common.* **—ed** *adj.* Annoyed; bothered. *Some jazz and beat use.*

spoon* *n.* **1** The nose-to-tail bow or curve in a surfboard. *Surfer use.* **2** Two grams or 1/16 ounce of heroin. *Drug culture.*

spread beaver [taboo] **1** A woman's genitals seen with her legs wide open, as in a pornographic photograph. **2** A look at a woman's genitals or her underpants because she is sitting with her knees apart.

springbutt *n.* An overly diligent or enthusiastic person; an "eager beaver." *

square* *n.* **1** A regular tobacco cigarette, esp. as opposed to a marijuana cigarette; a "straight" or "slim." *An extension of "square"* = not "hip."* Orig. addict use. Some Negro, hip, and student use since c1960.* → **2** A person who does not use or approve of others using drugs, esp. marijuana. *Addict and student use.*

square broad A young woman who is not a prostitute. 1971: "The pimp's total control over his women starts from the moment he takes a 'square broad' (a non-prostitute) and 'turns her out' (initiates her)." "The Pimping Game," *Time*, Jan. 11, 54.

square one The starting place; original situation or condition. *Usu. in the phrase "back to (at) square one," in ref. to board games in which a player is so penalized.*

squat* *n.* = **zot.**

squeeze the eagle To be stingy with money; be parsimonious. *Gambling and Negro use.* See **eagle day.***

s.s. *n.* A suspended sentence. *Drug culture and underworld use.*

stack* *n.* An exhaust pipe on an automobile. *Usu. in the expression "twin stacks" = a dual exhaust, as orig. on some European and sports cars.*

stagflation *n.* A combination of economic stagnation and inflation. *A blend of "stagnation" and "inflation."*

stallion *n.* **1** = **stud.* 2** A beautiful, sexually appealing girl, esp. one who is large. *Negro use.*

stand tall To be ready for an inspection; to be prepared; to have things under control. *Army use.*

starkers *adj.* Naked; in the nude. *Usu. in phrase "in the starkers." Orig. Brit. use.*

stash* *n.* **1** A person's supply of drugs for his own use. **2** A hiding place in which a drug dealer keeps his merchandise, processes it, and packages it for sale. *Drug culture.*

stay [taboo] *v.i.* To maintain an erection.

steam* *n.* Bootleg whiskey; a drink of bootleg whiskey. 1962: " . . . he made a point of calling it booze in the aggregate and an individual drink he called a steam." John O'Hara, "The Bucket of Blood," *The Cape Cod Lighter*, 15. *Most common c1920s.*

stick* *n.* **1** A ski; a ski pole. *Skier use.* **2** A surfboard. *Some surfer use.* **3** A manual gearshift on an automobile, attached to the floorboards. **—s** *n.pl.* A pair or set of various sporting equipment, as golf clubs, fishing rods, etc.

stinkpot *n.* A motor-propelled yacht or boat. *Sailboater use.*

stink with To have an abundance of.

stompers *n.pl.* A pair of shoes; shoes. *Some jazz musician use, replaced by "ends."*

stone* *adj.* Absolute; complete. 1973: "He is so good at it that I'm afraid he might get hit with one of them and be sidetracked into a straight career. . . . And that would be a stone drag." Ralph J. Gleason, *Rolling Stone*, Sept. 27, 9. *From the older adverbial use of "stone"* * *as in "stone deaf," "stone broke,"* * *etc.*

stonewall *v.t.* To employ delaying or obstructive tactics. 1974: "No other word exists to describe its meaning: 'filibuster' . . . means to delay, or talk, to death, but to stonewall has come to mean something else—to rigidly resist inquiry, to make obfuscation a policy." William Safire, "The Word Watchers," N.Y. *Times*, Aug. 15, 33. *n.* An instance of stonewalling. *Orig. Brit. cricket term, later used in a political sense. Also from "Stonewall" Jackson, the nickname of the Confederate General Thomas J. Jackson, referring to his standing firm under enemy fire. Watergate use.*

stooper *n.* A hanger-on at a race track or off-track betting parlor who searches for discarded tickets that may be turned in for money. 1974: "The girl said she had become a stooper after she saw 'some of the other kids from around the corner' hanging around the parlors." Gerald Eskenazi, "Minors Are Found Betting With OTB," N.Y. *Times*, Jan. 25, 26. *From the posture assumed when searching for tickets on the floor.*

storch *n.* 1 An ordinary man; a guy. **2** = **mark.***

STP *n.* A synthetic drug (2-5-methoxy-4-methylamphetamine) which, in large doses, produces hallucinogenic effects of long duration. *The initials properly stand for Serenity, Tranquillity, and Peace.* 1973: "The name was taken from that of the proprietary oil additive, said to increase pep and power in automobile engines." *Scientific American*, Oct., 130. *Drug culture.*

straight* *adj.* Having taken an injection of a narcotic and thus able to go about one's business, esp. said of a drug

addict after his first injection in the morning. 1965: "Once the addict has had his shot and is 'straight' he may become admirably, though briefly, industrious. . . ." James Mills, "We Are All Animals," *Reader's Digest*, June, 232. *Drug culture.* *n.* A regular tobacco cigarette, esp. as opposed to one containing marijuana; a "square." *Orig. drug culture use.*

straight arrow A person who is honest, sincere, and upright. 1970: "Naturally he thinks it is his son with the long hair and the funny clothes who turned his daughter on to drugs; just as naturally it turns out the boy is a straight arrow. . . ." Richard Schickel, *Life*, Sept. 4, 11. *From the old term "straight as an arrow" with the slang use of "straight"* * *(def. 2).*

straight-arrow *adj.* Honest, sincere, and upright.

straighten [someone] *v.t.* **1** To obtain a narcotic for or administer a narcotic to. *Drug culture.* → **2** To help; aid. *Some beat and student use.*

straight up (of alcoholic drinks, esp. cocktails) Served without ice cubes; not on the rocks.

streak *v.i.* To run in the nude through a public area. *v.t.* To disrupt a gathering or public event by running in the nude past or through a crowd. *n.* An incident of streaking, esp. by a number of participants. **—er** *n.* A person who streaks. *This short-lived fad started on university campuses and received a great deal of publicity in the first three or four months of 1974.*

Street,* **the** *n.* **1** = **Number One.*** *Vaudeville use. Archaic.* Cf. **2** The world outside of prison; normal free life or society. *Some underworld use.* **3** Society or the world as a place of violence, immorality, cruelty, etc., *Mainly Negro use.* **4** Wall Street. as the world of U.S. finance. 1974: "The Street Waits for [President Gerald] Ford's Message." Headline, N.Y. *Post*, Oct. 8, 56.

street furniture Discarded furniture found in the street and appropriated for one's own use or to sell.

street people **1** Slum dwellers who, esp. during the summer, spend much of their time sitting on building steps, standing on the sidewalk talking, or visiting neighbors and local stores; the local people of a crowded neighborhood. *The common meaning in the mid-1960s.* **2** People, usu. young people and esp. hippies, without a permanent residence, who survive by cadging food and shelter from others. *The only common use since the late 1960s.* Cf. **road people.**

street time 1 The period during which a convict is either on parole or on probation. 2 A period between two prison terms; the time a habitual criminal spends outside of prison. *Prison use.*

stretch out To play a musical instrument without restraint; to become completely uninhibited; to express one's emotions intensely and without restraint. 1961: "When a cat stretches out, he can make the moon on his own thrust or horn." E. Horne, "The Words for the Music," 39. *Jazz musician use. Lit., to play "riffs"* or improvise after the orig. harmonic statement in jazz, to leave the written bars of harmony and stretch one's own imagination and technique in improvising on it.*

strip-search *n., v.* = **skin-search.**

stroke *v.t.* To flatter, usu. in order to persuade or manipulate. 1973: "But the outstanding problem was how to persuade [FBI Director] Mr. Hoover of the illogic of his objections. First: 'Mr. Hoover should be called in privately for a stroking session at which the President [Nixon] explains the decision he had made, thanks Mr. Hoover for his candid advice and past cooperation, and indicates he is counting on Edgar's cooperation in implementing the new report. . . .' " McCrystal, et al., *Watergate*, 43. *Orig. Negro use.*

strung out 1 Disturbed, worried, concerned; involved with psychological problems. *Some Negro use.* 2 = **have [one's] nose [open].** *Negro use.* 3 Sick and disturbed or thin, weak, and nervous from a lack of or long use of narcotics. *Drug culture and student use.* 4 To be addicted to narcotics; to be "high"* on a drug. 1965: "Indeed, if one spends time talking to marijuana users, one can only conclude that the entire college population is 'strung out' thrice weekly." Nora Ephron, "Campus '65 . . . All That Talk about Marijuana," N.Y. *Post*, Dec. 3, 45. 1966: "Then . . . I began using drugs regularly. Every day, every day. I . . . got fairly well strung out, fairly well addicted." David Lyle, "The Logistics of Junk," *Esquire*, March, 60. *Drug culture and student use.*

sub* subby submarine *n.* = **Hero.** *Because the long sandwich with tapering ends resembles a submarine's shape.*

submarine watching = **necking.*** *Some student use. Popularized by rock-and-roll announcer Murray the K.*

suck* *n.* Special influence or favor which has been purposefully curried. *Usu. found in the phrases, "to get suck" or "to have suck."* *v.i.* To be a failure; be of poor quality; be unpleasant. 1973: "The point is, *Angel Clare* is a failure as an album. It sucks. Maybe Artie [Garfunkel] should go back to making movies. . . ." Linda A. Solomon, Letter, *Rolling Stone*, Nov. 8, 7. *Said of things or situations rather than of people.*

sugar* *n.* = **LSD.**

sunshades *n.pl.* A pair of sunglasses; sunglasses; "shades." *Neither as old nor as common as "shades."*

sunshine* *n.* = **Orange Sunshine.**

super— See Appendix to the Supplement, Prefix Words.

superfly *adj.* Very wonderful, desirable, or attractive. 1972: "See, you cut coke with lactose or dextrose, or both. I add a little of another thing which makes my coke superfly." Richard Woodley, *Dealer: Portrait of a Cocaine Merchant*, 46. *Became popular after the 1972 motion picture* Super Fly, *about a cocaine dealer in Harlem. Mainly Negro use.* Cf. **fly.**

superjock *n.* An outstanding male athlete, esp. a football star. Cf. **jock, jockstrap.**

surf bunny = **beach bunny.** *Surfer use.* Cf. **bunny.**

swave *adj.* Fine, wonderful, splendid. *Teenage and student use.*

sweat* *v.t.* To make a problem of; be anxious about. 1974: " 'Jesus, man. You don't even have a meter. You're really taking a chance.' Pause. 'Well, don't sweat it. Look, is a buck and a quarter okay?' " *New York*, April 8, 70.

sweetheart contract sweetheart agreement A contract, drawn up between an employer and a labor union, that benefits both the employer and the union but usu. does not help the worker.

sweet tooth Addiction to narcotics. *Some drug culture use, based on the standard meaning = a craving or extreme liking for sweets.*

swing* *n.* A short or hurried journey that includes several stops or visits in one region of a country or continent. *Now usu. applied to travelers who use jet airplanes to hasten their trips. Colloq.* *v.i.* 1 To belong; to run with a gang. *Teenage street-gang use.* 2 To follow, cultivate, be in rapport with, or embody currently fashionable attitudes and tastes; to be a member of a vanguard that is considered socially and culturally stylish, sophisticated, etc. **3** To be active and exciting. **4** To be sexually promiscuous, esp. to engage in group sex and the swapping of sexual partners. **—er** *n.* **1** A person who inhabits a socially fashionable world and whose taste in dress, music, entertainment and places of entertainment, resorts, etc., reflects what is considered modern, stylish, youthful, and sophisticated. *A new and very pop. use, and an American type since c1961.* **2** Any person who cultivates or who is representative of, or a leader in, what is considered fashionable, sophisticated, etc., within a given social framework. 1965: "To the bored, vacant-eyed teen-agers . . . Charles Howard Schmid, Jr., 23, was known as a swinger. . . . Schmid went to bizarre lengths to build his image. . . . He dyed his hair raven black, wore pancake makeup, pale cream lipstick and mascara." *Time*, Nov. 26, 27. **3** A promiscuous person, esp. one who engages in group sex and the swapping

of sexual partners. **—ing** *adj.* Fashionably lively; tasteful, sophisticated, modern; avant-garde; following, representing, or embodying whatever is currently considered most sophisticated, exciting, etc.

swing both ways   To be bisexual.

swingles   *n.pl.* Single persons, usu. young, who pursue a fashionable, often frenetic life style with much partying, drinking, and sexual adventures. *Usu. in the pl. and in such phrases as "swingles bar" or "swingles scene." A blend of "swinging" and "single."*

swingman   *n.* A dealer in illicit drugs; a "connection."* *Drug culture.*

swipe*   *n.* Any homemade alcoholic beverage, esp. raw, inferior whiskey or wine. 1962: " . . . a private's pay could afford only the homemade bootleg mess made by the natives out of fruit and called 'swipe.' " James Jones, *The Thin Red Line*, 422.

switched-on   *adj.* = **turned-on** (defs. 1, 2).

switch on   **1** = **turn on**. **2** To be part of the modern scene; to be "hip";* to enjoy modern fads, music, etc.

T

tab*   *n.* A capsule containing LSD. *From "tablet." Drug culture.*

table grade [taboo]   Sexually attractive, said of a woman or specif. of her vagina, legs, or breasts. *Lit. and fig., so sexually attractive or submissively feminine that one drools at the mouth and would like to perform cunnilingus.*

table-hop   *v.i.* To go from one restaurant table to another, or others, to visit with friends.

tach   *n.* Tachometer.

tailgate*   **tail-gate**   *v.i.* To drive a motor vehicle too closely behind the vehicle in front.

take a leak   To "piss."* *Very common.*

take gas   To lose control of one's surfboard while riding a wave and fall into the water.

take [someone's] mind   To disturb someone, to upset someone psychologically; to obsess someone. *Mainly Negro and beat use.*

take off*   To rob. 1960: " ' . . . we took off a bar. We came in through the roof.' " C. Cooper, *The Scene*, 220. *Underworld and police use.*

takeoff   **take-off**   *n.* = **rip-off** (def. 1).

takeoff artist = **rip-off artist**.

tap*   *n.* The act of, or a device for, secretly listening to or, esp., recording the telephone conversations of others. 1966: " ' . . . the FBI publicly acknowledges the number of taps it has across the country at any one time. Once I was ordered to pull out a tap because one was being installed in another city. . . . But I was at the same time ordered to install a bug to replace the tap.' " Former FBI Agent William Turner, quoted in "Crisis in Law Enforcement," *Playboy*, March, 56.   *v.t.* To listen to or record telephone conversation secretly or to do so to a specific telephone, address, or person. *From the earlier "wiretap."*

tar beach   A roof, esp. of an apartment building, used for sunbathing.

tarfu   *adj.* (Things are really) fucked up.   *n.* = **snafu.*** *W.W.II Armed Forces use; euphem. acronym formed by analogy with "snafu." See **fucked up*** (def. 3).

taste*   *n.* **1** A share or percentage of profits. *Theatrical use.* **2** Any alcoholic drink. *Usu. as offered by a host as "would you like a taste?" or in ordering from a*

bartender, *"Give me a taste of bourbon."*
3 [taboo] Sexual intercourse; coitus.
TCB   T.C.B.   Take care of business.
1973: "Where he is always to be found
TCB'ing (takin' care of business, an old
ghetto phrase which originally meant to
copulate. . .)." Alfonso X. Donalson,
New Times, Nov. 2, 41. *Negro use.*
teenybop   teenybopper   *n.* A stereo-
typed teenage rock-and-roll enthusiast;
a teenager considered as an annoying,
insignificant, undesirable, boring burden.
1965: "A 'teeny-bop' translates as a
teen-age R & R nut who wears $3.98
boots, a transistor at the ear and who
wigs out over the Stones, the Turtles,
the Beatles, and anything else with a
concussive 4/4 beat." N.Y. *Times*, Dec.
27. *Orig. Negro use.*
teeny-rocker   *n.* = teenybop.
teeny-tiny   *n.* A girl in the early teens;
specif., a teenybop or teenybopper.
adj. Tiny; very small.
tell it like it is   To tell the whole
truth; tell everything, without regard
for the consequences. 1968: "Everyone
who's anyone will want *Black Rage*, by
Negro psychiatrists William H. Grier
and Price M. Cobbs, who tell it like it
is." *McCall's*, Dec., 86.
ten cents = dime bag. *Drug culture.*
that's the way the cookie crumbles =
that's the way the ball bounces.* *The*
most pop. of many variations, all
beginning with "that's the way—" followed
by a mundane or humorous action such
as: "—the bread rises," "—the doughnut
rolls," "—the elephant farts" [taboo],
"—the fish fry," "—the frogs fuck"
[taboo], *"—the ink spills," "—the mothers*
muck" (mainly Brit. use; taboo as U.S.
use; see "mother"), "—the owls hoot,"
"—the pill breaks," "—the stars shine,"
"—the wine spills." The last words are
often created on the spur of the moment as
nonce expressions and may contain images
that are taken from popular sayings,
jokes, etc.
THC   *n.*   Tetrahydrocannabinol in
liquid form, the chemical intoxicant in
marijuana that produces the "high."*
thing*   *n.* Something for which one
has a strong interest or appeal. 1968:
"Thousands of kids were moving into
San Francisco for a life based on LSD
and the psychedelic thing. Thing was
the major abstract word in Haight-
Ashbury. It could mean anything, ism,
life styles, habits, leanings, causes,
sexual organs. . . ." Tom Wolfe, *The*

Electric Kool-Aid Acid Test (Bantam),
10. See **do [one's] (own) thing.**
think tank*   An organization, corpora-
tion, or center engaged in research, esp.
intensive theoretical or problem-solving
research involving disciplines, usu. for a
typed teenage rock-and-roll enthusiast;
governmental body or a business. *An*
extension of the obsolete slang sense of
"think tank" meaning the brain. Informal.
Three, the   The DC-3 airplane; the
"Gooney Bird." 1966: "The airlines call
it simply, 'the Three.' " N.Y. *Post*, Jan.
21. *Mainly airplane pilot use.*
throw a bop into [someone] [taboo]   To
have sexual relations with. 1973: " . . .
it's inevitable that someone is going to
want to throw a bop into someone else's
wife. . . ." R. Hills, rev. of John
Updike's *Couples*, *Esquire*, April, 38.
thud   *n.* 1 An airplane crash; esp. the
act or an instance of being shot down by
an enemy aircraft or by antiaircraft fire.
Orig. Air Force use in the Vietnam war.
2 An F-105 Thunderchief jet fighter
plane. *Air Force use in Vietnam. So-*
called because of their record of being shot
down in the Vietnam war.
thumb   *n.* A marijuana cigarette. *So-*
called because one sucks it. Drug culture.
ticked off = tee'd off.*
tick [someone] off   To annoy; to make
angry. *Usu. in the passive.*
tight-ass   *n.* A person who is tense and
uneasy. 1970: " 'Jenny Cavilleri,'
answered Ray. 'Wonky music type.' 'I
know that one,' said another, 'a real
tight-ass.' " Erich Segal, *Love Story*, 15.
—ed   *adj.* Tense; "up tight."
tip*   *v.i., v.t.* 1 To be sexually unfaith-
ful to one's spouse or current lover; to
"cheat."* → **2** [taboo] To have sexual
intercourse (with).   *n.* 1 [taboo] An
act or instance of sexual intercourse.
2 An attractive, pert girl; a "chick";*
"fox." *Orig. Negro and jazz musician*
use; now becoming beat and student use.
tish   *v.t.* Lit. and fig., to pad something
with tissue paper; specif. to wrap bills of
large denomination around a tissue-
paper core so that one appears to have
more money than one actually has; gen.
used to imply any physical exaggeration,
as to make an automobile look longer
than it is by adding large bumpers, for a
woman to wear a padded brassiere, etc.
Orig. and mainly carnival use.
tit cap [taboo]   The standard Army
enlisted-man's cloth cap, when worn
with front and back terminal peaks

standing up rather than creased or pleated. *Army use.* Cf. **cunt cap.**

tits   *adj.* Great; terrific; very enjoyable.

tits-and-ass [taboo]   *adj.* Of, being, or pertaining to commercial photographs of nude young women.

t. o.'d = tee'd off. *   *Based on "p. o.'d."* *

toe-jabber   *n.* A knife considered as a weapon. 1962: "I seen you pull the toe-jabber on him. . . ." John O'Hara, "The Bucket of Blood," *The Cape Cod Lighter*, 23. *Not common.*

together   *adj.* **1** Free of distractions and confusion; without anxiety; composed. *Often in phrases "get it all together" and "have it all together."* **2** Harmonious; in tune. 1969: " 'It was a very together class by the end of the year,' said one student. . . ." N.Y. *Times*, Sept. 22, 26. **3** Stylish. *Negro use.* **4** Socially adept. *Orig. Negro use.*

Tom *   *n.* = **Uncle Tom.** * *Negro use.*

Tom   tom   *v.i.* = **Uncle Tom.** * 1973: "He glared at them, and they looked back at him startled. 'You stupid niggers, you too *young* to be Tomming. Get your eyes straight and look the man in the fucking eye.' " John Godey, *The Taking of Pelham One Two Three*, 86.

tommy *   *n.* A tomato or a slice of tomato. *Lunch-counter use.*

ton   *n.* Specif., a speed of 100 miles per hour; any high speed. *Orig. motorcycle racing use = an average speed of 100 m.p.h. during a race or over a measured course. Some teenage and automobile racing use since c1960.*

tool *   *n.* A diligent, overstudious student; a "grind." * *Student use.*

topless   *adj.* **1** Of or pertaining to female entertainers and waitresses who work with the breasts bare. **2** Of or pertaining to a bar or restaurant employing such entertainers and waitresses. 1974: " . . . He would never meet you at his home, only at bars and only if they were topless." David Harris, "Hogtown Justice," *Rolling Stone*, Feb. 14, 47. See **bottomless.**

topsider   *n.* **1** A naval officer or deckhand, one whose duty is topside or on the bridge rather than below deck. **2** A person having a high position, esp. in government.

toss *   *v.t.* = **shake.**

total   *v.t.* **1** To demolish completely, as an automobile in a wreck. **2** To put someone out of action, as in a contact sport; physically injure someone. 1970:

" 'Jenny, please, I'm trying to concentrate!' 'On what?' 'On how I'm gonna total that bastard Al Redding.' " Erich Segal, *Love Story*, 9.   *n.* A wreck, esp. a demolished automobile. *From the expression "a total wreck."*

touch dancing   Ballroom dancing, such as the fox trot, waltz, tango, etc., in which the partners hold one another, as opposed to various dances since the 1950s in which the partners face, but do not touch.

touchdown   *n.* The landing of an airplane, lit. and fig. the moment the wheels touch the runway. Cf. **wheels-up.**

touchie-feelie   *adj.* Of or pertaining to any movement or group which employs sensitivity training as a means for deepening understanding of oneself and others. 1973: "They're all part of the touchie-feelie movement, but some require strict self-discipline." Wesley Pruden, Jr., *National Observer*, July 28, 21. *So-called from the practice of touching and feeling one another to break down inhibitions between members of the group.*

tough cat   A man who has great success with women. *Negro use.*

tour guide = **guru** (def. 3).

touristas, the   turistas, the   *n.* Diarrhea. *This post-W.W.II term is replacing "G.I.s" as more Americans travel abroad as tourists. Based on Sp. word formation; prob. first used by tourists returning from Mexico. Changes in water, food, altitude, and time zones often upset travelers' stomachs, and the term need not imply a serious illness or contact with tainted food or drink.*

tracks *   *n.pl.* Scars or marks on the arm or leg caused by repeated puncturing with hypodermic injections. 1965: "In summer, they [addicts] alone wear long sleeves (to cover their 'tracks'—needle marks)." James Mills, "We Are All Animals," *Reader's Digest*, June, 232. *Drug culture.*

trad   *adj.* Traditional.

trade   *n.* A man or woman considered sexually, esp. in a commercial sense; a "piece." * *Orig. prostitute and homosexual use.*

tragic magic   Heroin. 1972: " 'My partner's thing is dope,' Jimmy said when we were alone. 'You know, duji, scag, tragic magic. I don't dig the heroin thing personally.' " Richard Woodley, *Dealer: Portrait of a Cocaine Merchant* (Warner), 18. *Drug culture.*

trank   tranx   *n.* A tranquilizer, a pill or capsule containing a tranquilizer.

trash   *n.* An act or instance of vandalism.   *v.t.* **1** To treat or abandon as worthless. **2** To subject to wanton destruction; vandalize. **3** To beat someone up.   *v.i.* To pick up furniture placed in the street for disposal by the department of sanitation either for one's own use or to sell.   **—er**   *n.* **1** A vandal. **2** A person who collects discarded furniture in the street.   **—ing** *n.* Vandalism.

tref   **treff**   **trif**   **triff**   *n.* A clandestine meeting to transact illegal business, such as to plan a robbery, distribute illegal drugs or weapons, etc. *From the Ger. "das treffen" = meeting. Not used in the underworld until after W.W.II. Prob. orig. came to U.S. Central Intelligence Agency from German spies and thence spread to the underworld.*

trembler   *n.* A prison inmate who is very fearful of other prisoners, usu. a man who has committed only one crime, esp. one of passion, and does not identify with criminals. *Prison use.*

trendy   *adj.* Forming or following a fashionable trend or trends.   *n.* A person who forms or follows a fashionable trend or trends.

trey*   A $3 packet of a narcotic, esp. a $3 "bag" of cocaine. *Drug culture.* Cf. **bag**.

trick* (of prostitutes)   *v.t.* To receive as a customer for sexual purposes. 1973: "Once she had tricked a john from Macon [Georgia]." *Playboy,* Dec., 314. *Prostitute use.*

trif   **triff**   *n.* = **tref**.

trip*   *n.* **1** An instance of being under the influence of a drug, esp. LSD. 1966: "LSD users like beat poet Allen Ginsberg (30 trips), psychologist Ralph Metzner ("many trips"). . . ." "LSD: Who Takes It and Why?" Barbara Yuncker, N.Y. *Post,* April 17, 29. *Drug culture and student use.* **2** Any activity, outing, period of time, or way of life. *Some beat and student use since c1965.*

triple-clutcher   *n.* **1** A driver skilled enough to employ triple-clutching. *Trucker use.* **2** [taboo] = **mother fucker**. *A typical two-word, four-syllable euphem. variant on the taboo "mother fucker." Prob. orig. in W.W.II; pop. during the Korean war by Negro construction battalion truck drivers.*   **—ing** *adj.* [taboo] = **mother fucking**.

tripped-out   *adj.* Under the influence or as if under the influence of a psychedelic drug. 1974: "But 'Celine and Julie' is not about what happens as much as it is about who it happens to, and Berto & Labourier, whether on a tripped-out laughing jag, performing in a musical magic act . . . make the film work smoothly." Fred Barron, "Film: The Cannes Was On," *Crawdaddy,* Sept., 86.

truck drivers   Amphetamines. *From their use by truck drivers to keep awake during long hauls. Drug culture.*

tsuris   *n.pl.* Worries; troubles; problems. 1974: "If [Howard] Samuels, with all his *tsuris,* wins the Democratic nomination, it will have to be as much by default as by clever design." M. Kramer, *New York,* April 8. *From the Yiddish.*

tube   *n.* **1** A telephone. *Not common.* **2** A subway tunnel, system, or train. *From the Brit. use. Not common.* **3** The inside curve of a wave. *Surfer use.*

tube, the   *n.* **1** Television considered as a medium. 1965: "She started modeling for TV spiels back in 1948 and now . . . is making a name for herself as a singer on the tube. . . ." N.Y. *Sunday News,* Oct. 4, 2. **2** A television set. *Orig. teenager use c1955; increasing use since c1960. From the cathode-ray oscilloscope "tube" that is the basis, and forms the screen, of television receivers.*

tube it   To flunk an examination or course in school. *Student use.*

tuff   *adj.* **1** = **tough*** (def. 2). 1964: "For what 17's like, their current glossary includes 'fabulous' as well as 'gear' and 'tuff,' both of which also mean fabulous." N.Y. *Times,* Nov. 1, Sect. B, 100. 1965: "Tuff—good or great." Houston, Texas, *Chronicle,* Sept. 5. *Very pop. student and teenage use since c1962.* → **2** Good-looking, energetic, and popular. *Student and teenage use.*

tuifu   *n.* The ultimate in fuck-ups. *W.W.II Armed Forces use; euphem. acronym formed by analogy with "snafu."***

tullies, the   *n.pl.* Remote or rural areas. *From "tule" or "tule land" = Southwestern regions covered with tule bulrushes.*

tuned in   **1** Skillful; expert; aware of problems and solutions in one's work. **2** Aware; knowing; in rapport with modern attitudes, fads, etc. *Teenage and synthetic use; one of many words "squares"* consider "hip."**

tune in   To become aware, interested, and involved. See **tuned in**.

tune out   To cease being involved; to turn one's mind, feelings, etc., away from.

tunnel   *v.i.* To go into hiding, as to escape capture by the police; to hide out.

turkey*   *n.* = **blank** (def. 2).

turn [someone] around   To change a person's attitudes, habits, outlook, etc., either positively or negatively.

turned-off   *adj.* **1** No longer under the influence of drugs. *Drug culture.* **2** Uninterested. **3** Sick of; tired of.

turned-on   *adj.* **1** Possessed with a knowledge of and appreciation for what is new; alert and responsive to modern fashions, ideas, life-styles, etc. **2** Stimulated, excited, or elated. **3** Under the influence of drugs. *Drug culture.*

turn [someone] off   To bore; depress. See **turn [someone] on.**

turn [someone] on   **1** To introduce; to arouse someone's curiosity or interest in something. 1959: "He turned me on to Zen." L. Lipton, *The Holy Barbarians* (Julian Messner), 318. **2** To supply someone with something, as a drink, cigarette, advice, etc. **3** To become or get "high"* on narcotics. → **4** To arouse or excite sexually; to be sexually appealing to someone. **5** To excite, stimulate, or thrill someone; to cause to become interested, enthusiastic, alert, happy, etc. 1965: "Bach really turns me on." "A Cursory Glossary to the Off-beat Side of Now," *Harper's Bazaar*, April, 173. *One of the most common sl. expressions to gain pop. since c1960. Orig. addict, jazz musician, and student use; now common.* See **turn on.***

turn-on   *n.* **1** A person or thing that is interesting, exciting, or stimulating. 1973: "But perhaps the most interesting thing about the book is the fact that the few women I gave it to read for a while and then exclaimed, 'Wow, this is a real turn-on.' " Howard Smith and Tracy Young, *Village Voice*, June 7, 41. **2** Excitement; exhilaration; euphoria.

turn out*   = **pull a train**, esp. for the first time.

tushie   **tushy**   **tush** [taboo]   *n.* = The buttocks, "fanny."* 1974: " . . . he shakes his tushie with elegant languor." Jon Hodenfield, synd. col., N.Y. *Post*, July 23, 14. *From the Yiddish "tochis" or "tuchis," buttocks.*

T.V.   **TV**   A transvestite. 1965: "TVs are not as feminine as they themselves think they are." *The Realist*, March, 24. *Not common.*

twat   *n.* **1** [taboo] The vagina, a vagina; a girl or woman considered as a sexual object; "cunt."* *Usu. used in a gentler, more relaxed, more humorous way than "cunt,"* "ass,"* or "piece."** **2** The buttocks of either a man or a woman. *Not common.*

twenty-five   **25** = **LSD.** *The number that is part of the abbr. chemical name.*

twink   *n.* **1** An effeminate male; a homosexual; a "queer."* **2** Any odd, socially unacceptable person. *Not common.*

twisted*   *adj.* **1** High on narcotics. 1960: " ' . . . twisted . . . that's when he's so high he doesn't know where the hell he is.' " C. Cooper, *The Scene*, 55. *Drug culture.* **2** Drunk.

U

underground   *adj.* Opposed to, or unsanctioned by, conventional social standards; relating to the codes and life styles of those (usu. young people) who are in rebellion against, or disdainful of, conservative social mores, esp. hippies, street people, crazies, sexual swingers, those involved in the drug culture or in radical political or artistic movements, etc.; relating to publications, motion pictures, works of art, etc., produced by or for such groups. *n.* The world of such groups, considered as a counterculture—anti-establishment, radical, or avant-garde.

unflappable   *adj.* Calm and clear-thinking; lit., so competent and calm that one cannot become confused or make a mistake in an emergency. *Orig. Air Force use. The opposite term "flappable" has never existed.*

unglued   *adj.* **1** Frantic, out of control, disorganized, wild. **2** Insane, crazy.

unisex   *adj.* (of clothes, hair styles, etc.) Designed or suitable for both males and females; not distinguishable as to sex. 1968: "In Europe and in the U.S., with-it young couples . . . are finding that looking alike is good fashion as well as good fun. The unisex trend was launched by the era's pacesetters, the teen-agers, back when the Beatles came to fame." Helen Carlton, *Life*, June 21, 87.   *n.* The belief that sexuality is an unimportant or repressive characteristic and that men and women should have identical life styles, attitudes, clothing, etc., sometimes also coupled with the belief that sexual partners should be chosen without regard to gender.

unreal   *adj.* Unbelievably wonderful; great; excellent. 1965: "Like great. *She's real unreal.*" "A Cursory Glossary to the Off-beat Side of Now," *Harper's Bazaar*, April, 173. *Cool, beat, and student use.*

unscrewed   *adj.* = **unglued.**

untogether   **un-together**   *adj.* **1** Functioning poorly intellectually or emotionally. 1970: "Joanna the Army captain's daughter whose head is put permanently un-together by electro-shock and insulin treatments. . . ." N.Y. *Times*, Oct. 23, 39. **2** Lacking social know-how or appeal. **3** Being out of date or shabby. *Orig. Negro use.*

unzip   *v.t.* **1** To overcome someone's defenses; to break down resistance. **2** To solve a problem, find a solution for; to organize or accomplish successfully. **—ped**   *adj.* = **unglued.**

up*   *adj.* Under the influence of a narcotic; "high."* 1965: " . . . waiting for time to pass, as it does when you're up on bennie. . . ." H. Selby, Jr., *Last Exit to Brooklyn*, 52. *Drug culture and student use.*

up front   **up-front**   *adv.* In advance. 1972: "But I never asked for cash 'up front,' because that strikes me as too whorish." Xaviera Hollander, *The Happy Hooker*, 131.   *adj.* Honest, truthful; out in the open. 1973: " . . . she's intelligent, politically aware, and very up-front about who she is and what she thinks." James Nolan, "The Third Sex," *Ramparts*, Dec., 26.

upper   **up***   *n.* **1** Any stimulant drug, esp. an amphetamine. *Drug culture.* **2** A pleasant or exciting experience. Cf. **downer.**

up-South   *adj.*   Northern.   1973: "Among white social scientists there is an overemphasis on the effects of the down-South slavery of yesteryear on the Black psyche, and a corresponding underemphasis on what can be called 'up-South' slavery of today." P. Taylor, *Black World*, May, 6. *Orig. Negro use, with the implication that racism in the North is as bad as it is in the South.*

up the ass   [taboo]   Completely; thoroughly. 1971: "I could play almost every song, man, I know country music up the ass on the guitar. I could play about every country style guitar there is." Jann Wenner, "Mike Bloomfield," *The Rolling Stone Interviews*, 52.

uptick   *n.* **1** A rise, as in stock prices. → **2** An improvement. 1974: "His [President Nixon's] apparent uptick in spirit was contagious among his people; they insisted that he is fully in command of his job." *Newsweek*, May 10, 3.

up tight   **1** Thoroughly known, re-membered, or familiar, as a piece of music to be played by a jazz musician or the information necessary to pass an exam or course in school. *Orig. jazz musician use; now student use.* → **2** = **hip;*** **with it.*** *Beat and student use.* **3** O.K.; fine; everything is great. *Some cool and student use.* **4** In or pertaining to the Madison Avenue or Ivy League style of dress, esp. button-down shirts, vests, etc. *Some jazz and Negro use.* **5** Tense; "hung up."*

urb   *n.* A large city, esp. a sophisti-cated, modern city where "hip"* people and "swingers" may find culture, excite-ment, jazz nightclubs, discotheques, bohemian neighborhoods, etc., as San Francisco, New York, London, etc. *Some use by "swingers," musicians, and beat people. From "urban."*

use   *v.i.* To be a drug addict; take narcotics or a dose of narcotics. 1960: " 'Why don't you bust a cap with me? It's choice. I used this morning and I'm still nice.' " C. Cooper, *The Scene*, 15. *Drug culture.* See **user.***

V

varoom   *n., v.i.* = **vroom.**
Vatican roulette   The rhythm method of birth control.
V.C.   **1** The Viet Cong or one of its soldiers, guerrillas, or supporters in South Vietnam. *Orig. Armed Forces use in Vietnam.* **2** A stupid, inept, or irresponsible soldier. 1964: "V.C.—They are of course the Vietcong, the enemy.

But when a private displeases his sergeant, he may hear 'you knucklehead V.C.!' " Jack Langguth column, dated South Vietnam, N.Y. *Times*, Sept. 16, 4. *Armed Forces use in Vietnam.*
veggy   *adj.* Vegetarian.   *n.* A vege-tarian.   **—ies**   *n.pl.* Vegetables.
vette   *n.* A Corvette automobile. *Main-ly hot-rod use.*

vibes* *n.pl.* = **vibrations.** 1973: "The vibes were good that morning for our reunion, and when he left, I recall making positive—if hasty—predictions about what a great year it was going to be." Evelyn Shelby, Editorial, *Sat. Rev./ Ed.,* Feb., 39.

vibrations *n.pl.* **1** One's awareness that a situation, thing, or another person or persons may or may not be in harmony with oneself; intuition, feeling. **2** Ambience, mood, atmosphere.

Victor Charlie = **V.C.** (def. 1). *Armed Forces use in Vietnam. From the communications symbols "Victor" = V and "Charlie" = C.*

Vietnik *n.* A person who actively opposed U.S. participation in the Vietnam war. 1966: "The latest Vietnik demonstration on the campus of the University of California at Berkeley. . . ." *Time,* Feb. 18, 49. *Usu. derog.; most common in pro-Vietnam war tabloid newspapers. Based on "beatnik,"* and reinforced by being made to rhyme with it.*

vig *n.* = **viggerish.*** *Underworld use.*

vig ounce = **piece** (def. 1).

vote with one's feet To express one's rejection or disapproval of a situation, condition, etc., by abruptly leaving or escaping from it. 1973: "From 1946 to 1961 East Germany lost nearly one-tenth of its population to West Berlin and West Germany as nearly three million people voted with their feet." *N.Y. Times,* July 6, 23.

vroom *n.* The roar of the engine of an automobile or motorcycle at high speeds. *v.i.* To move or accelerate with such a roar.

W

waffle *v.i.* To talk, write, or act in an indecisive or equivocating way. 1964: "It is probable that Goldwater will back away from or waffle around even this position as he approaches responsibility for his party's policies." Richard Rovere, *New Yorker,* June 13, 115. *n.* Indecisive, equivocating, or ambiguous talk or writing. *Orig. Brit.*

waffle-stompers *n.pl.* Hiking boots, esp. heavy and clumsy ones. *So-called because the footprint left by the skid-preventing gridlike sole has the pattern of a waffle.*

walk* *v.i.* **1** To get out of jail. **2** To be acquitted of a criminal charge. *Underworld and prison use.*

walk heavy **1** To be important; to be in a position to command or intimidate others. **2** To have or assume an appearance of importance or superiority. *Orig. Negro use. Cf.* **weight, walk soft.**

walk soft To act in a modest and humble manner. *Cf.* **walk heavy.**

walk wide To be careful; to be on one's guard. 1888: "You'd better walk wide." Troy, Alabama, *Enquirer,* July 28. [Quoted in William Warren Rogers. "Deep South Slang in the 1880s," *American Speech,* Feb. 1962, 76.] *Now mainly Negro and some beat use.*

wall-to-wall *adj.* All-embracing; complete; sweeping. 1972: "For *A Clockwork Orange,* Anthony Burgess created a wall-to-wall nightmare in which society dissolves into violence and repression." Stefan Kanfer, "Sispeak: A Msguided Attempt to Change Herstory," *Time,* Oct. 23, 79. *A fig. sense of term describing carpeting covering every inch of a floor.*

Walter Mitty A person, usu. of unexceptional abilities and unassuming appearance, who lives in a fantasy world in which he is brilliant, famous, courageous, etc. 1973: "Walter Cronkite is a Walter Mitty in reverse: He is a famous man who has fantasies of being ordinary." Critic Ron Powers, *Playboy,* June, 68. *From the character in James Thurber's short story "The Secret Life of Walter Mitty."*

waltz* *n.* Something accomplished with little effort or difficulty; a cinch.

wank off To masturbate. *Mostly Brit.*

wash* *v.i.* To stand put to the test; to hold up under scrutiny. 1965: "I see that the government's going after the tobacco industry again. Well, it just won't wash." Gerald Walker, *Atlantic,* Feb., 122. 1973: "And in case The Voice hasn't heard yet, the stereotype of gay males as child molesters just doesn't wash anymore." Craig Rodwell, Letter, *Village Voice,* Feb. 22, 77. *The expression "it won't wash" goes back to the 1840s. Usu. in the negative.*

WASP wasp *n.* A white Anglo-Saxon Protestant; specif. a member of the dominant American middle class who is descended from the earlier northern European settlers of the country, as opposed to one belonging to a racial or religious minority or someone of more recent immigrant stock. *Often used derog., usu. to refer to an average, noncreative, noncritical American who enjoys traditional American values, beliefs, fashions, entertainment, etc., unquestioningly.*   *adj.* Of, pertaining to, or suitable for WASPs. 1965: " . . . Westchester and Darien and places like that, WASP country. . . ." N.Y. *Herald Tribune, Book Week,* Feb. 7, 1.

waste*   *v.t.* To kill.   **—d** *adj.* Emotionally and physically exhausted; beat; down-and-out. 1965: "He felt that life was over for him. 'Look, Sonny, I'm already through. Like, I'm wasted. You got somethin' to live for, but me, I can't lose no more.' " Claude Brown, *Manchild in the Promised Land,* 170.

water hole   watering hole   A bar or tavern.

wax*   *v.t.* **1** To beat up, injure severely, or kill. **2** To defeat decisively, as in a sports contest, military operation, etc.; "zap."*   **—ing** *n.* A beating. *Underworld, police, and some Armed Forces use.*

wear a hat   To have a girl friend; to be married; fig., to be or become respectable. *Archaic except in theatrical use.* Cf. **hat.**

wear two hats   To play a dual role; perform two jobs or activities at the same time. 1965: "Except for Chairman Wheeler, each of these men wears two hats: one as topbraid officer of his service, the other as a member of the Joint Chiefs." *Time,* Feb. 5, 23. 1974: "Rockefeller to Wear Two Hats?" David S. Broder, Headline, N.Y. *Post,* Sept. 27, 2.

weathercock   *v.i.* Of an airplane or missile, to tend to turn in the direction of the wind. *Aerospace and Air Force use.*

weedhead*   *n.* A marijuana user. *From "weed" = "marijuana." Drug culture.*

weejuns   *n.pl.* Moccasin-style loafers (shoes). 1965: " . . . weejuns (loafers)." Houston, Texas, *Chronicle.* Sept. 5. *From the trademark. Teenage use.*

weekend hippie = **plastic hippie.**

weight*   *n.* **1** Influence. 1963: "We have an expression, you have money, you have weight." U.S. Senate. *Organized Crime and Illicit Traffic in Narcotics,* 301. (The Joseph Valachi testimony.) *Some underworld use.* **2** An ounce of marijuana or heroin. *Drug culture.*

weirdo   *n.* = **weirdie.***

well-hung   *adj.* Having a very large penis. 1974: "What you react to, first,

are the artsy drawings, in color, of a man (well-hung) and a woman (slender but with bosoms) going through a 30-page sexual exhibition. . . ." Anne Schneider, Rev. of *The Joy of Sex, New Times,* Feb. 22, 67.

whack*   *v.t.* To dilute a drug, esp. heroin and cocaine; cut a drug. *Drug culture.*

whack off   To masturbate.

whale*   **Whale** *n.* The A-3 Skywarrior, a twin-jet military airplane used to refuel other airplanes in flight.

what else is new?   An expression showing a lack of interest in the oft-repeated complaints or anecdotes of another.

what [or that] makes [one] tick   That which guides or influences one's behavior; that which causes one to act in a specific way. 1974: " 'My business is gambling,' he says. 'It's that gambling instinct that makes me tick.' " G. Clark, *Esquire,* Feb., 72.

what's going down?   What's happening? What's going on? *The phrase is also employed as a greeting calling for no particular response.*

what's the scam?   What's up? What's happening?

wheels-up   *n.* The departure of an airplane from a runway, the takeoff of an airplane. *Orig. and still in pilot use = the retraction of the wheels into the body of the airplane after it is airborne.*

when the eagle flies   Payday. *Negro use.* Cf. **eagle day;* day the eagle shits.***

where it's at   **1** Where the exciting, trend-setting, successful, or satisfying events, people, ideas, etc., are. **2** Where the ultimate truth lies; where the unvarnished facts are; where the heart of the matter is. 1968: "And suddenly it dawns on me. This is really where it's at. This is the real Elvis story. This is the language—the only language that he speaks. . . ." Dwight Whitney, *TV Guide,* Nov. 30, 48.

where [one] lives   One's deep, personal, innermost feelings. 1974: "Fonda's conversation eludes both the esoteric and banal, and has that Will Rogers' sense of immediacy, an ability to capture the moment and zap you where you live." S. Shevey, *Playgirl,* Mar., 57.

where the action is   **1** The center or area of greatest activity, importance, etc. **2** = **where it's at** (def. 1).

whip out   To perform a prescribed greeting or stance, usu. from respect. *Orig. = to shake hands; at military* *schools = to stand at attention, present arms, etc.*

whipsaw   *v.t.* **1** To defeat an opponent easily. **2** To beat up another person badly. **3** To accomplish any task easily or rapidly.

whistle blower   A person who informs against another to the authorities; stool pigeon; tattletale.

white*   *adj.* Not good, lacking in feeling. 1965: " . . . someone who is not good is 'white.' " Sybil Burton, quoted by Nora Ephron, N.Y. *Post*, June 20, 23. *Orig. Negro jazz use.*

white buck   white bucks = white shoe.

white flight   The increasing tendency of white, middle-class people to flee to the suburbs or surrounding countryside in order to escape from the hazards of city life.

white lightning* = LSD.

white money*   Funds that have been illegally obtained, as by a politician, and have been "laundered" to conceal their origin and thus appear legitimate. See **launder.** Cf. **black money.**

white nigger   [derog.]   A white person who champions civil rights for Negroes.

white shoe   **white shoes**   **1** An archetypal student of the Ivy League. **2** Having or affecting the dress, manners, attitudes, etc., of the Ivy League. *Pop. at Princeton at varying intervals since c1915; general student use c1945–1955 only. From the white buckskin shoes that were part of the typical student's dress.* Cf. **key** (def. 1).

Whitey   **whitey**   *n.* A white person; white men, the white race; the white establishment, culture, society, etc. *Now the most common urban Negro sl. word for white man.*

whittle   *v.i., v.t.* To perform an operation on someone; perform surgery.

whiz kid   A bright, extremely able young person who achieves success at an early age. *Formed by analogy with "quiz kid," one of the precocious children who participated in a radio question-and-answer show, "Quiz Kids," of the late 1930s.*

whole schmear, the   **whole schmeer, the**   The entire thing; the whole deal; the whole story. 1970: "Tommy, I want a complete list of everyone who lives in the place or who works there. . . . Names, ages, business they're in, daily schedules—the whole schmear." Lawrence Sanders, *The Anderson Tapes*, 23. *From the Yiddish "to smear, to spread."*

wife*   *n.* **1** A prostitute in a pimp's stable, often the favorite one. 1971: " . . . She is his favorite 'wife' at the moment; he stops in to see her at least once a day." Lesley Oelsner, "World of the City Prostitute Is a Tough and Lonely Place," N.Y. *Times*, Aug. 9, 33. *Prostitute use.* **2** The less aggressive or "feminine" member of a homosexual relationship, male or female. *Homosexual use.* Cf. **husband.**

wig*   *n.* **1** A thrilling or satisfying experience, a "ball."* 1962: "A wig is something that excites. . . ." Ralph J. Gleason, "Lively Arts," San Francisco *Chronicle: Datebook*, Apr. 15, 19. *Some jazz use.* **2** A crazy or far-out person. *v.i., v.t.* To be, become, or make thrilled, excited, frenzied, etc.   *adj.* Excellent, wonderful, great. 1965: "Daddy-O, who was 'in the groove' back in the class of '40 . . . discovers that 'wig' . . . [has] come to mean what he used to call 'great'. . . ." N.Y. *Times*, Dec. 27. *Teenage use.*

wigged out   **1** Removed from reality. **2** Very high from the influence of narcotics. *Drug culture.* **3** Excited about something or someone.

wig out   To react with unrestrained enthusiasm and appreciation; to be excited, aroused, or thrilled; to "flip"* or "dig"* completely. 1965: "A teenybop . . . wigs out over the Stones, the Turtles, the Beatles, and anything else with a concussive 4/4 beat." N.Y. *Times*, Dec. 27. *Orig. jazz, Negro, and cool use; now some teenage use.*

Willie Fudd   The WF-2 propeller-driven airplane, designed and used as a flying radar center. *Navy use in Vietnam.*

wimp   *n.* An introverted, boring, overly solicitous person; a meek, passive person; one who is out of touch with current ideas, trends, fads, etc.; a "drip"* or "mince." *Some teenage and student use.*

wing it   **1** To leave; depart. **2** To start; get going. *Teenage and student use.* **3** To play music, esp. swing or jazz, without notes; to improvise. **4** To do or produce something extemporaneously, e.g., cook without a recipe, improvise words or stage business while acting.

wipe*   *v.t.* To defeat or trounce an opponent.

wipe out*   To lose control of one's surfboard while riding a wave and fall into the water. *Used in the active voice, as in "I wiped out." Surfer use.*   **—ed**

out   1 Conforming, dull; "square."* *Some beat use.* 2 Drunk. *Student use.* 3 Very high from the effects of a drug. *Drug culture.* 4 Tired; exhausted.

wired   wired up   *adj.* 1 High on a drug or alcohol. 2 Very excited; happy. 3 Nervous. *Prob. orig. Negro use.*

wiretap   *n., v.t.* = **tap.**

wise ass = **smart ass.**

woke   *adj.* = **hip.*** *Negro use.*

wonk   *n.* An unattractive, boring person. 1970: "Who could Jenny be talking to . . . ? Some musical wonk?" Erich Segal, *Love Story,* 26.   **—y** *adj.* Unattractive; boring.

work* [taboo]   *n.* Sexual intercourse. *Some jazz and far-out use.*   **—s** *n.pl.* The paraphernalia used to prepare and inject a drug: an eyedropper, hypodermic needle, and "cooker." 1965: "When he awakes in the morning he reaches instantly for his 'works'— eyedropper, needle . . . and bottle top."

James Mills, "We Are All Animals," *Reader's Digest,* June, 227. *Drug culture.*

workaholic   *n.* A person who has a compulsive need to work and who becomes anxious when idle. 1973: "This type of person is a work freak, a 'workaholic'. . . . Work is his whole life and he can't seem to enjoy anything else. He can no more give up work than an alcoholic can give up booze." Francis L. Clark, *National Observer,* June 30, 8.

working   girl   A prostitute. *Orig. prostitute use.*

workshoe   *adj.* Rugged, solid, long-lasting, dependable. 1964: " . . . the money these workshoe Macks earn year after year. . . ." Advt. for Mack Trucks, Inc., *Time,* Nov. 20.

wrecked   *adj.* Under the extreme influence of alcohol or narcotics.

wuzzy*   *n.* A girl. *Some teenage use, via Brit. rock-and-roll use, from the Fr.* "*oiseau*" = *bird.*

Y

Y   *n.* The symbol, often painted or written on walls of buildings, of the Youth International Party, the members of which are known as "yippies." See **yippie.**

yakky   *adj.* Talkative; noisy.

yantsy   *adj.* = **antsy.**

yard*   *v.i.* To have sexual relations with someone other than one's spouse or current lover; to be unfaithful; to "cheat."* 1960: "He tried to go to bed with her several times, but she didn't like him. She told him she didn't like to yard on her man. . . ." C. Cooper, *The Scene,* 34.

yellow sunshine = **LSD.** See **Orange Sunshine.**

yenta   *n.* A talkative or gossipy woman. 1966: " . . . yenta . . . a female blabbermouth." Charles McHarry, N.Y. *Daily News,* Jan. 12. *From the Yiddish.*

yippie   *n.* A hippie who is a member of the Youth International Party, a loosely organized radical political group active in the late 1960s, esp. at the Democratic Convention in Chicago in 1968.

yoke   *v.i., v.t.* To mug a person by attacking him from behind and placing a knife at his throat. 1973: "That night on the Boardwalk, they decided to 'yoke' the old man with the hearing aid." Barry Cunningham, "Muggers and Victims," N.Y. *Post,* April 24, 33. *Underworld use.*

yold   *n.* A gullible person, a dupe. 1966: " . . . yold, which rhymes with cold . . . means a chump." Charles McHarry, N.Y. *Daily News,* Jan. 12. *From the Yiddish.*

you [you'd] better believe it   Yes; of course; indeed. *Used as a rejoinder when one person makes an observation and the other wishes to agree emphatically.*

yo-yo*   **yoyo**   *n.* 1 A stupid, incompetent, or undesirable person; a "jerk."* *Orig. teenage and student use.* 2 A gullible person; a dupe.   *v.i.* To fluctuate in opinion, action, etc.; vacillate.   *adj.* Fluctuating; vacillating. *From the trade name for a toplike toy that can be made to roll up and down on a string.*

Z

Z   *n.* An ounce of a narcotic drug. *Drug culture.*

zaftig   *adj.* See **zoftig.**

zap*   *v.t.* 1 To shoot someone. *Under-*

world, teenage street-gang, and Armed Forces use. → **2** To defeat decisively, as in a sports contest, a military operation, etc. **3** To confront, esp. verbally. **4** To impress deeply. *v.i.* To go or move quickly. *n.* **1** Vigor; vitality; zip. **2** A confrontation. 1972: "Despite six zaps, New York's Mayor Lindsay has consistently refused to meet with any homosexual delegation." Faubion Bowers, *Sat. Rev.*, Feb. 12, 26. *interj.* Used, often repetitively, to express a sudden occurrence, action, change, etc.

zero cool Very "cool"*; as "cool" as possible. 1965: "The ancient *real cool* is still admired . . . but the University of Florida has gone on to *zero cool.* . . ." *Time*, Jan. 1, 56. *Some student use.*

zhlub zhlob *n.* A boorish, insensitive person. **—by** *adj.* Boorish; coarse. 1972: "Even the Kismet Inn, a classic tie-up and tie-on booze station for the zhlubby middle-aged boat owners from the other side . . . has now become a swinging singles bar." Albert Goldman, "I Have Seen the Future—and It's Fire Island," *New York*, July 24, 26. *From the Yiddish, orig. from the Slavic.*

zilch* *n.* **1** A completely dull, ineffectual, unattractive, or insignificant person. **2** Nothing; zero. 1969: "The city . . . has turned its smaller islands into zilch. Generally speaking, New York has the poorest yachting waterfront, mile for mile, of any first-class seaport in the country." Morten Lund, *New York*, Aug. 11, 41.

zing* *v.i.* To go or proceed quickly; zip. 1973: "As pure escapist entertainment, however, the movie zings right along. . . ." *Playboy*, May, 44. **—er** *n.* **1** A punch line or witty saying. 1970: "[Television talk show host Dick] Cavett's wit is his moat. . . . In casual chatter the zingers are just as fast and frequent as they are on the show." Brad Darrach, *Life*, Oct. 30, 40. **2** Any sharp retort.

zip* *n.* **1** A score of zero; no score. **2** [derog.] A Vietnamese. *From the acronym for z(ero) i(ntelligence) p(otential). Armed Forces use in the Vietnam war. Cf.* **dink, gook, slope.**

zit *n.* A pimple, esp. on the face or neck.

zit doctor A dermatologist.

zizz *v.i.* To doze; snooze. *n.* A short nap. *From the sound of a sleeping person's snoring or even breathing, esp. as represented in comic strips by "z-z-z-z-." Orig. Brit. Cf.* **saw wood.***

Z-Latin *n.* = **carny*** (def. 3).

zoftig zaftig *adj.* Plump in a sexually attractive or pleasing way, said of a woman. 1966: " . . . zoftig . . . pleasantly plump and pretty. . . ." Charles McHarry, N.Y. *Daily News*, Jan. 12. *From the Yiddish.*

zonked *adj.* Drunk; dead drunk. 1961: "Zonked—one step past being stoned. . . ." E. Horne, "The Words for the Music," 39. *Student use.*

zonked out Very high on drugs. *Drug culture and student use.*

zonkers *adj.* Extremely excited; wild; crazy. *Usu. in phrase "to go zonkers."*

zoo* *n.* Any jungle or jungle area. *Army and Marine use in Vietnam.*

zot *n.* A grade or a score of zero; "zip." *Student use.*

APPENDIX TO THE SUPPLEMENT
Word Lists

The criteria used for including words in the following lists are the same as those used for the original volume (see p. 610). An asterisk (*) placed after a boldface heading indicates the word list is a continuation of a list in the original appendix, where an explanation of the list and other similar list words will be found. A dagger (†) placed after an individual list word indicates that the word is defined fully in this supplement.

Affixes

Suffixes

—aholic. The use of this suffix to describe forms of overindulgence or abnormal craving other than alcoholism has become somewhat popular in recent years.
colaholic†
foodaholic†
pillaholic
sleepaholic
workaholic†

—ama, —rama.* This suffix has become increasingly popular in advertising and merchandising, its meaning having become more general to include any playground, amusement park, store, or esp. a national or international show where a product, activity, or sightseeing attraction is on display.
Adventurama — amusement park
Aquarama — aquarium
Autorama — international automobile exhibition
Liquorama — liquor store
Motorama — automobile show
Newsorama — newsreel theater

—er.*
ball wracker†
Bible-banger†
Bircher — member of John Birch Society
brainstormer
brown-bagger†
buckwheater†
bulldogger — steer wrestler
butt-twitcher
capper†
charger†
cobbler†
cribber — one who cheats on exams
doper†
double-clutcher†
downer†
downputter†
duner†
fanny-dipper†
father fucker†
five pointer†
flagger†
flatbacker†
four pointer†
golden-ager†
grabber†
grasshopper†
hauler†
hot dogger†
hot walker†
huffer†
jammer†
juggler†
junker†
libber†
long hitter†
low rider†
lunker†
mind blower†
mother fucker†
nosher†
poler†
potato digger†
prick teaser†
rocker†
rock 'n' roller
side-armer — baseball pitch or pitcher
sleeper†
splitter†
stooper†
swinger†
toe-jabber†
topsider†

trembler†
triple-clutcher†
upper†
whistle blower†
wildcatter
—eroo.*
bitcheroo
—ese.*
gobbledygookese
officialese
—ie, —ey, —y and —sie, —sey, —sy.*
antsy†
artsy-craftsy†
baddy
baggies†
boonie†
cheapie†
doolie†
druggy†
dykey†
flitty†
folkie†
funsie†
ginger-peachy†
glossy†
goosey†
greatsie†
greenie†
gremmie†
groaty†
groupie†
hippie†
hocky†
hummy†
jollies†
larky†
mintie†
nudie†
old-timey†
pasty†
preppy†
prosty†
schizy, schizzy†
subby†
tommy†
trendy†
tullies†
veggy†
Whitey†
yippie†
—nik.* The development of *—nik* words has been documented by J. B. Rudnyckyj, " 'Sputnik' and —nik Derivatives in the

Present Language of North America" (see the bibliography). The popularity of *beatnik* has made —*nik* a fairly common suffix and —*nik* words are now more commonly formed by analogy with *beatnik* rather than with *sputnik*. The —*nik* suffix is now often used to denote a person who does not accept middle-class political, moral, social, and religious beliefs and values. It most often is used to form nouns denoting a college student who is unkempt, dresses in old, sloppy clothes, believes in love more than accepted sexual morality, is a pacifist and a political liberal, and has substituted marijuana for the whiskey that older Americans may use to achieve euphoria. It most common such word of the mid-1960s is *Vietnik*. —*nik* is also seeing some use to indicate a fan, enthusiast, or frequenter of, as in *discothequenik*.

discothequenik
dopenik†
folknik†
neatnik — a worrisomely neat person
peacenik†
protestnik — student who marches in civil rights or pacifist demonstrations
quitnik — one who advocated withdrawal of U.S. troops from Vietnam
sicknik — a psychologically sick person
Vietnik†
—**o.***
Afro†
amazo
capo†
cheapo
demo†
disco†
freako
Isro†
klepto†
limo†
pervo
porno†
schizo†
sleazo
weirdo†
—**ola.*** The popular use of *payola* in the late 1950s has caused many words to be formed by analogy with it. Thus —*ola* has now gained an additional meaning = a

bribe, a business or political favor, political patronage, etc.
bribeola
favorola
fixola
flushola
freeola
ghostola — a ghost-written speech, book, etc.
grabola
nayola — do-nothingism
plugola†
sockola
—**s.***
bevels†
binders†
bottoms†
breastworks†
Charlies†
crackers†
duals†
ends†
flares†
flats†
fringes†
happenings†
hip-huggers†
kicks†
marbles†
marshmallows†
orbs†
pecks†
peepers†
pyramids†
shades†
smarts†
sticks†
stompers†
sunshades†
touristas, the†
waffle stompers†
—**ville.*** During the first half of the 1960s—*ville* saw fairly wide use as a synthetic beat, cool, and teenage suffix, esp. by newspaper columnists. The —*s*— insert has become more common and most —*ville* words are now printed with an initial lower-case letter rather than a capital letter.
beatsville
dragsville†
Dreamsville
dullsville†
endsville†
gloomsville
hickville
illsville
jakeville
lootville
movieville
mudville — small towns
slickville
Soulville†
squaresville

teensville
yokelville
youthville

Suffix Words

—**ass.** This suffix has gained currency since the 1960s in a non-taboo sense to intensify the word to which it is joined, either solidly, with a hyphen, or as a separate word. Adjectives sometimes are followed by "—assed."
badass
big-ass†
dumb-ass†
funky-ass
hard ass
smart ass†
wise ass†
—**boy.***
campfire boy†
—**bum.** This suffix word is similar to —*bug* and —*nut* in noting a fan or enthusiast. However, —*bum* implies that the enthusiast has degraded himself in the pursuit of his special interest and = lit. or fig. someone who has become a bum by forsaking or slighting job, family life, and other interests to devote as much time as possible to his special interest, usually a sport but sometimes a hobby. The true —*bum* has no regular employment but ekes out an existence by taking odd jobs or by sponging from other enthusiasts.
beach bum
jazz bum
ski bum
surf bum
—**city.** A suffix that sometimes refers to a specific place known for an industry, etc., and at other times may simply describe a state of mind or a lifestyle.
fat city†
Fun City†
movie city — Hollywood
Soul City†
—**freak.** Like —*bug* or —*nut*, this suffix word = one who is an enthusiast, fan, devotee, etc., of the thing named in the root word.
coffee freak
cola freak
ecofreak†

food freak
Jesus Freak†
peek freak†
rock freak
speedfreak†
—head.*
acid head†
A-head†
bosshead†
bullhead†
butterhead†
drughead†
handkerchief head†
hash head†
juicehead†
meth head†
pillhead†
pothead†
—in.* Formations with —*in* as a suffix word have become popular since c1960, when civil rights protests began to gain national attention. *Sit-in* was the first such word to gain currency and many others have since been formed by analogy with it. Orig. these —*in* words referred to a protest for Negro integration and equality in which demonstrators, either Negroes or Negroes and whites, entered a segregated place, as a luncheonette (the orig. *sit-in*), or performed some action which was prohibited by segregation customs or laws, in order to protest publicly the customs or to force arrest so that the legality of the laws could be tested in court. The range and context of such —*in* formations are shown in the following two quotes:

"At a meeting commemorating the Greensboro sit-in, a Winston-Salem minister ticked off a long list of 'ins' that are still to come. Among them: pray-ins, apply-ins . . . buy-ins . . . study-ins and bury-ins." (*Time*, Feb. 10, 1961, p. 18.)

"[A Civil Rights leader] called for walk-ins in art galleries and museums, drive-ins at segregated motels and roadside ice cream stands, sit-ins in court rooms, study-ins at segregated schools, and bury-ins to integrate cemeteries." (Tuscaloosa *News*, May 18, 1961, p. 2.)

The use of —*in* has now expanded to include any protest in which demonstrators enter or remain in a place to protest any custom, law, or official policy or to gain support and publicity for a civil right, pacifism, etc.
apply-in — applying for a job in or admission to a segregated place of business or school
be-in†
buy-in — Negroes buying homes in segregated neighborhoods
chain-in — demonstrators chain or tie themselves together
drive-in
drop-in†
fish-in — by American Indians and supporters against fishing and conservation laws that ignore Indian treaty rights
join-in — joining segregated organizations
kneel-in — Negroes entering segregated churches to attend services
lie-in — demonstrators lie down to block traffic on a road or the access to a building
love-in†
marry-in — interracial marriage or applying for wedding license to protest or test miscegenation laws
pedal-in — demonstrators ride bicycles
play-in — Negro children using segregated parks and recreation areas
pray-in — demonstrators pray or Negroes enter segregated churches to attend services
puff-in — smoking marijuana in a demonstration in front of a police station, court, etc., to protest drug laws
read-in — using segregated library facilities
ride-in — riding segregated buses
sit-in†
stall-in — stalling automobiles to block traffic
stand-in — standing in line to enter segregated facilities
study-in
swim-in — swimming at segregated pools
wade-in — using segregated beaches or swimming pools

walk-in
—jockey.*
backwoods jockey — rustic, farmer
bus jockey
chopper jockey — helicopter pilot
elevator jockey
mop-jockey — sailor, considered as swabbing decks
motorboat jockey
pole jockey — telephone lineman
rocket jockey — astronaut
switchboard jockey
—killer.*
curve killer†
—man.*
cocksman†
juice man†
mackman†
moonman†
—off.*
beat off †
bop off †
dress-off †
fake off †
flake off †
get off †
go off †
mouth off †
rip off †
shoot off †
take off †
ticked off †
tick [someone] off †
turned-off †
turn [someone] off †
wank off
—out.*
blissed out†
blow it out†
bummed out†
cop out†
crank out†
drop out†
ease out†
fake [someone] out†
fink out†
flack out†
flake out†
flat-out†
flip out†
freak out†
gross out†
hang out†
mellow out†
pad out†
psych out†
rack out†
ream [someone] out†
spaced-out†
stretch out†
strung out†
tripped-out†
tune out†
turn out†
whip out†
wigged out†

wig out†
zonked out†
—stand.*
belly stand†
—up.*
bring up†
camp it up†
clank up†
clear up†
clutch up†
crank up†
get [one's] back up†
hoke up†
hype up†
junked up†
screwup†
send up†
shoot up†
zing up†

Prefix Words

fun—. This adjective prefix word has become popular since c1960. It generally means that the following noun is in some way pleasant, relaxing, or excitingly enjoyable. It is widely used by advertisers who know they can sell a product that is "fun" easier than one that is useful, with the further connotation of modernity. In general conversation, however, *fun—* is often used in a humorous, facetious, or derogatory way = conventional, boring, tedious, or even self-consciously sophisticated or faked spontaneity.

fun car — an inexpensive car or sports car
Fun City†
fun crowd
fun group
fun guy
fun hat
fun night — night of special attractions at an amusement park, theater, etc.
fun party
fun piece — informal, humorous, or light article, story, or other piece of writing
fun thing
fun time
fun type — a jolly extrovert

gut—. This adjective prefix has become popular since the late 1960s. It means that the noun following is (1) easy or simple (2) highly relevant (3) appealing to or arising from a basic emotion.

gut course — a very easy school course of study
gut feeling — a strong inner feeling
gut issue — an important, relevant issue
gut reaction — a reaction from the depths of one's feelings

soul—. This adjective prefix word indicates that the following noun pertains to Negroes or to things, moods, feelings, etc., which are considered basically Negro. Although this use is not new (*Soul City* and *soul food* have been used by Negroes for years) it has gained currency since the modern Negro civil rights movement began in the early 1960s, esp. with the use of *soul force* = moral or ethical integrity by the Rev. Dr. Martin Luther King, Jr. This use of *soul—* = Negro has also expanded to refer to things, places, organizations, etc., which are associated with Negro integration or equality. Since c1962 *soul—* has also expanded to indicate authentic sensibility, emotional sincerity, honesty, etc. as relating to Negroes, jazz and popular musicians and singers, cool and beat people, and others considered still able to express and appreciate individual feelings and integrity.

soul brother†
Soul City†
soul food†
soul force
soul friend
soul hotel — a hotel where Negroes are welcome
soul music†
soul sister†
Soulville†

super—. This adjective prefix has become very popular since the 1960s. It has the meaning of "unusually fine for its kind," or, in the case of adjectives, "very much so."

supercop
superfly†
superhero
superjock†
superstud

Shortened Forms

Back clippings and back formations*

affirm†
anthro — anthropology
barry†
bi†
bio†
bod†
boonie†
bro'†
Cambo†
Cat†
cheese†
civ — civilization
clit†
dash†
detox†
dipso†
disco†
doo†
exhibeesh†
fab†
groaty, grotty†
gyp†
hash†
hitch†
jock†
Johnny Reb†
klepto†
letch, lech†
lib — liberation
mesc†
meth†
mod†
mono†
mother†
nabe†
narco, narc†
nimby†
nitro†
nuke†
one thou†
pet — petroleum
pol†
prosty†
psywar†
pucker†
pud†
rad†
Reb†
rehab†
rigor†
seg†
shook†
showbiz†
shrink†
sobe†
tach†
tish†
trad†
trank†
urb†
vibes†

Front clippings*

bill†
Charlie†

drum†
head†
later†
loid†
lude†
Nam†
shoe†
tap†
Tom†
vette†

Abbreviations and acronyms*

Action — American Council to Improve Our Neighborhoods
Anzac†
A.R.†
A.R.A. — Aerial Rocket Artillery
ARVN†
ASP†
B and D†
B.C.†
BEM — bug-eyed monster, in science fiction
Big C†
big D†
big H†
B.L.T.†
B.O.T.†
B.T.†
B.Y.O.B.†
B.Y.O.L. — bring your own liquor
commfu†
CORE — Congress of Racial Equality
c.p.b. — certified pure bull
CREEP†
D†
DMT†
D.O. — double-overhead, automobile camshaft
DPT†
EEI — essential elements of information, as photographs and other data supplied to military intelligence
fac — forward air control; forward air controller (Armed Forces use, esp. in Vietnam)
FTA†
fubar†
fubb†
fubis†
fumtu†
G.B.†
H and C†
ID†
J†
janfu†
katusa†
lox†
LSD†
M.C.†
MCP†

M.D.†
MDA†
m.f.†
M.J.†
MOR†
MTA†
O-and-O — one-and-only
O.B.U.†
O.D.†
P†
p.d.q.†
P.D.R.†
P.G.†
p.t.†
PX†
R and R†
rejasing†
S.A.†
Sam†
S and M†
sapfu†
SNCC — Student Nonviolent Coordinating Committee
s.s.†
S.S.T. — supersonic transport
STP†
tacair — tactical air power
tarfu
TCB†
THC†
T.L.C. — tender loving care
T.O. — traffic officer
t.o.'d†
tuifu†
T.V.†
V.C.†
veenaf — South Vietnamese Air Force
WASP†
Y†
Z†

Reduplications
First order reduplications*

dingy-dingy†
dum-dum†
go-go†
Mau Mau†
no-no†

Second order reduplications*

Delhi belly†
megaton-schmegaton
Santa-schmanta

Rhyming Terms and Rhyming Slang

Unintentional rhyming terms*

circle jerk†
jet set†

Intentional and jive rhyming terms*

beat the meat†

boob tube†
brain drain†
chalk talk†
cheat sheet†
cop shop†
cream [one's] jeans†
fag bag†
fag hag†
flong [one's] dong†
gang bang†
jake flake†
kick stick†
nitty-gritty†
no-go†
no-show†
panman†
peek freak†
ricky-ticky†
sci-fi†
scrub club†
tragic magic†
white flight†

Rhyming slang (Cockney and Australian)*

Cockney rhyming slang has been exceptionally well covered in J. Franklyn, *A Dictionary of Rhyming Slang* (see the bibliography).
bottle and glass — arse, ass
cobbler awls — balls (testes)
Joe Hunt — cunt

Nicknames, Place Names, and Group Names

Nicknames* Nicknames for specific things, esp. manufactured products, and specifically for such items as airplanes and weapons, are becoming increasingly popular. A short, representative list is given here.
Gibson Girl†
Gooney Bird†
Hound, the†
Huey†
Q, the†
Three, the†
whale†
Willie Fudd†
Place names*
Apple, the†
bamboo curtain†
brickyard†
Fun City†
Hashbury†
Hill, the†
Old Al — the Mississippi River
Old big strong — the Mississippi River
Old Man River — the Mississippi River

San Berdoo — San Bernardino, Calif.

Street, the†

Group names*

ASP†
Charlie†
hard-hat†
Hare Krishna kids†
hick†
parakeet†
round-eye†
spill†
splib†
WASP†
Whitey†

Children's Bathroom Vocabulary*

grunt†
piddle†

Synonyms for Drunk*

Slang synonyms for *drunk* continue to appear with amazing frequency. Recent additions are often from the vocabulary of college students. Slang synonyms for *drunk* are increasingly taking on the additional meaning = under the influence of drugs, so that many of the words in this list, and in the list of *drunk* words in the original volume, now also mean high on narcotics or hallucinogens. The main *drunk* words that also = to be under the influence of a drug or hallucinogenic agent are: *aped, bent, blind, blue, buried, buzzed, gassed, glued, have a bag on, high* (the most common by far), *laid out, limp, lit, loaded, shot, smashed, stiff, stoned* (the second most common). The use of these *drunk* words to apply to the *high* or euphoria obtained from drugs, esp. among college students, is a strong indication that the present college generation may take drugs for some of the same reasons that older generations drank whiskey, and to obtain some of the same reactions. The drunkard's son does not necessarily become an addict, but it is quite possible that the couples who remember wild drinking parties of the 1920s, '30s, and '40s have grandchildren or children who will remember parties at which they smoked *grass* or took LSD *trips.*

bagged†
blitzed†
bombed†
bongoed†
boxed†
crashed†
featured
flaked out†
frozen
glazed†
have a brass eye
have a kick in the guts
have a rubber drink
have a skate on
have a skinful
have a slant on
have [one's] flag out
horseback
in the bag
leaping
nimtopsical
over the bay
owled
plowed
pull a Daniel Boone
pull a shut-eye
shit-faced†
tore down
tore up
twisted†
wiped out†
zonked†
zozzled

Sex and Food, Etc.*

beef†
cream†
flavor†
poundcake†
pudding†
table grade†
taste†

Selected Bibliography

(Bibliographic entries for the original volume begin on page 655.
See also *Quotations and citations*, page xvii.)

Ackerman, Louise M. "Carnival Talk." *AS*, Dec. 1960.

Algeo, John. "A Fun Thing." *AS*, May 1962.

Anon. *Acronyms and Initialisms Dictionary*, 2nd ed. Gale Research Co., 1965.

——. "The Anonymous Society." *Time*, July 28, 1961.

——. *Automotive Styling Terminology.* Chrysler Corporation: Engineering Division, Technical Information Services, Oct. 3, 1960.

——. "Beyond the Ears of the Greys." *Time*, Aug. 2, 1963.

——. "A Cursory Glossary to the Off-beat Side of Now." *Harper's Bazaar*, April 1965.

——. *First Facts about Drugs.* U.S. Dept. of Health, Education, and Welfare: Food and Drug Administration; FDA Publication No. 21, Nov. 1963, rev. Aug. 1964.

——. "The Mad Happy Surfers." *Life*, Sept. 1, 1961.

——. "Senators Survey Low-belly Strippers." *Life*, Sept. 1, 1961.

——. "Surf's Up!" *Time*, Aug. 9, 1963.

——. *Truck Drivers' Dictionary.* Pamphlet of the American Trucking Association, n.d.

Babcock, C. Merton. "Americanisms in the Novels of Sinclair Lewis." *AS*, May 1960.

——. "The Echo of a Whistle." *Western Folklore*, Jan. 1960.

Barnhart, Clarence L., Steinmetz, Sol, and Barnhart, Robert K. *The Barnhart Dictionary of New English Since 1963.* Clarence L. Barnhart/Harper Row, 1973.

Bernstein, Theodore M. "Now It's 'Watch Your Slanguage.' " N.Y. *Times Mag.*, Feb. 28, 1960.

Berry, Leonard J. *Prison.* Subsistence Press, 1972.

Boone, Lalia P. "Gator (Univ. of Florida) Slang." *AS*, May 1959.

Braddy, Haldeen. "The Anonymous Verses of a Narcotics Addict." *Southern Folklore Quarterly*, Sept. 1958.

Brenni, Vito Joseph. *American English, a Bibliography.* Univ. of Pennsylvania Press, 1964.

Brown, Claude. *Manchild in the Promised Land.* Macmillan, 1965.

Bryan, C. D. B. *P. S. Wilkinson.* Harper & Row, 1965.

Claerbaut, David. *Black Jargon in White America.* William B. Eerdman's Publishing Co., 1972.

Clausen, Connie. *I Love You Honey, But the Season's Over.* Avon, 1962 (Holt, Rinehart and Winston, 1961).

Cleaver, Eldridge. *Soul on Ice.* Dell, 1969 (McGraw-Hill, 1968).

Cooper, Clarence L., Jr. *The Scene.* Crest, 1962 (Crown, 1960).

Crane, Maurice A. "Vox Bop." *AS*, Oct. 1958.

Cray, Ed. "Ethnic and Place Names as Derisive Adjectives." *Western Folklore*, Jan. 1962.

Dempsey, Don. "The Language of Traffic Policemen." *AS*, Dec. 1962.

Dempsey, Jack, Considine, Bob, and Slocum, Bill. *Dempsey.* Avon, 1960 (Simon and Schuster, 1960).

Dickson, Paul. *The Great American Ice Cream Book.* Atheneum, 1973.

Dietterle, Otto C. "Road Talk." *N.Y. Folklore Quarterly*, Fall 1959.

Di Petto, Adam. "Strictly Youthsville." *N.Y. Sunday News*, Nov. 28, 1965.

Dundes, Alan and Porter, C. Fayne. "American Indian Student Slang." *AS*, Dec. 1963.

——— and Schonhorn, Manuel R. "Kansas University Slang: A New Generation." *AS*, Oct. 1963.

Einstein, Stanley. *The Use and Misuse of Drugs.* Wadsworth Publishing Company, Inc., 1970.

Ephron, Nora. "Campus '65—All That Talk About Marijuana." N.Y. *Post*, Dec. 3, 1965.

Farrell, James T. *Young Lonigan* (in *Studs Lonigan*). Modern Library, 1938 (*Young Lonigan*, Vanguard, 1932).

Franklyn, Julian. *A Dictionary of Rhyming Slang.* Routledge & Kegan Paul, 1960.

Geller, Allen and Boas, Maxwell. *The Drug Beat.* McGraw-Hill, 1969 (paperback ed.).

Godey, John. *The Taking of Pelham One Two Three.* Dell, 1973 (Putnam, 1973).

Gohdes, Clarence. "American Liquor Lingo of Days Gone By." *Georgia Review*, Spring 1959.

Griffin, Junius. "The Last Word from Soul City." N.Y. *Times Mag.*, Aug. 23, 1964.

Hanley, Roberta, "Truck Drivers' Language in the Northwest." *AS*, Dec. 1961.

Hayden, Sterling. *Wanderer.* Bantam, 1964 (Knopf, 1963).

Himes, Chester B. *if he hollers let him go.* Berkeley, 1955 (Doubleday, 1945).

Hollander, Xaviera. *The Happy Hooker.* Dell, 1972 (paperback orig.).

———. *Xaviera!* Warner, 1973 (Artistae-Stiftung, 1973).

Horman, Richard E. and Fox, Allen M. *Drug Awareness*, Avon, 1970.

Horne, Elliot. "The Words for the Music." N.Y. *Times Mag.*, June 25, 1961.

Ianni, Francis A. J. *Black Mafia.* Simon and Schuster, 1974.

Jarka, Horst. "The Language of Skiers." *AS*, Oct. 1963.

Jones, James. *The Thin Red Line.* Signet, 1964 (Scribners, 1962).

Kelley, William Melvin. "If You're Woke You Dig It." N.Y. *Times Mag.*, May 20, 1962.

Kunen, James Simon. *The Strawberry Statement.* Avon, 1970 (Random House, 1968).

Landy, Eugene E. *The Underground Dictionary.* Simon and Schuster, 1971 (paperback ed.).

Lees, Gene. "Show Business Lexicon." *Show Business Illustrated*, Jan. 23, 1962.

Lewis, Sinclair. *Arrowsmith.* Harcourt, Brace, 1925.

———. *Main Street.* Harcourt, Brace, 1920.

Lipton, Lawrence. *The Holy Barbarians.* Julian Messner, 1959.

Lyle, David. "The Logistics of Junk." *Esquire*, March 1966.

McCrystal, Cal, et al. *Watergate.* Ballantine, 1973 (The Sunday Times [London], 1973).

Medley, Tom, ed. *Hot Rod Jargon.* Capitol Records pamphlet, 1965.

Mencken, H. L. *The American Language.* 4th ed. and 2 supplements, abridged, with annotations and new material by Raven I. McDavid and David W. Maurer. Knopf, 1963.

Mills, James. "We Are All Animals." *Reader's Digest*, June 1965.

Millstein, Gilbert. "Why They Race with Fate—Talk of the Track." N.Y. *Times Mag.*, May 24, 1959.

Monteiro, George. "Truckers' Language in Rhode Island." *AS*, Feb. 1963.

Niemoeller, A. F. "A Glossary of Homosexual Slang." *Fact*, Jan.-Feb. 1965.

O'Hara, John. *The Cape Cod Lighter.* Bantam Books, 1962 (Random House, 1962).

———. *The Horse Knows the Way.* Random House, 1964.

Poston, Lawrence, III. "Some Problems in the Study of Campus Slang." *AS*, May 1964.

Preuss, Fritz. "Das Wortfeld *sit-in*." *Die Neueren Sprachen*, July 1962.

Rechy, John. *City of Night.* Grove Press, 1963 (paperback ed.).

Roberts, Hermese E. *The Third Ear: A Black Glossary.* Better-Speech Institute of America, Inc., 1971.

————. *The Rolling Stone Interviews*. Paperback Library, 1971.

Roth, Philip. *Portnoy's Complaint*. Random House, 1967.

Rubin, Theodore Isaac. *Sweet Daddy*. Ballantine Books, 1963.

Rudnyckyj, J. B. " 'Sputnik' and -nik Derivatives in the Present Language of North America." *Études slaves et esteuropéenes*, Autumn-Winter 1959-60.

Salisbury, Harrison E. *The Shook-up Generation*. Harper & Bros., 1958.

Sanders, Lawrence. *The Anderson Tapes*. G. P. Putnam's Sons, 1970.

Sanderson, James L. "Lingua Cosa Nostra." *AS*, Dec. 1964.

Scully, Frank. "Scully's Scrapbook." *Variety*, Aug. 21, 1963.

Seale, Bobby. *Seize the Time*. Vintage Books, 1970 (Random House, 1968).

Segal, Erich. *Love Story*. Signet, 1970 (Harper & Row, 1970).

Selby, Hubert, Jr. *Last Exit to Brooklyn*. Grove Press, 1965 (paperback ed.).

Sheehy, Gail. *Speed Is of the Essence*. Pocket Books, 1971 (paperback orig.).

Sontag, Susan. "Notes on Camp." *Partisan Review*, Fall 1964.

Spillane, Mickey. *The Snake*. Signet, 1964 (Dutton, 1964).

U.S. Senate, Committee on Government Operations. Hearings before the Permanent Subcommittee on Investigations. *Organized Crime and Illicit Traffic in Narcotics:* Part I. 1963.

Williams, Tennessee. *Night of the Iguana*. Two River Enterprises, Inc., 1961.

Wolfe, Tom. *The Electric Kool-Aid Acid Test*. Bantam, 1969 (Farrar, Straus and Giroux, 1968).

Woodbridge, Hensley C. "Slang in Farrell's 'Young Lonigan.' " *AS*, Oct. 1961.

Woodley, Richard. *Dealer: Portrait of a Cocaine Merchant*. Warner Paperback, 1972 (Holt, Rinehart & Winston, 1971).

ANNE
CARROLL
MOORE

BOOKS BY

Frances Clarke Sayers

ANNE CARROLL MOORE   1972
ANTHOLOGY OF CHILDREN'S LITERATURE
(*with Evelyn Sickels*)   1970
SUMMONED BY BOOKS   1965

ANNE CARROLL MOORE

A Biography by

FRANCES CLARKE SAYERS

Atheneum

NEW YORK

1972

For Storer

These pages betray her secret; which is that she was naturally exuberant. And her power came, as all power comes, from the control and direction of exuberance.

G. K. CHESTERTON *Preface to* Love & Friendship *and* Other Early Works *by Jane Austen*

Is it not possible that the ultimate end is gaiety, music and a dance of joy—

JAMES STEPHENS

FOREWORD

Every reader for reading's own sake car-
ries his own smoke screen, assumes his own
protective coloring. If it were not so, then
the children's rooms of public libraries
would become mere laboratories or experi-
ment stations instead of theaters in which
books live and move and play their various
parts in daily human experience.

ACM

 the turn of the century, to use a phrase cherished by Anne Carroll Moore, a new concept of reading
in relation to children came into being. It followed fast
on the growth of the Free Public Library in the United
States. Destined to move beyond the walls of the public
library and to become essential to formal education in
its own country, its influence as a natural, spontaneous,
and informal enhancement of the lives of children gave
it such appeal to the traditional European mind as to make
it widely copied and imitated in England, France, Belgium, Sweden, Russia; in India, Japan, and other countries
of the East, as well as in Latin America.

That concept, taken for granted now some seventy
years after the fact, was the radical idea that children

be given free access to books in public libraries, without hindrance of age or capacity to read, and with minimal concern for cleanliness of hands.

One hundred years after the declaration of American Independence, the American Library Association was founded in Philadelphia, at the Philadelphia Centennial Exhibition. The librarians meeting there were, for the most part, administrators of college and university collections or librarians of private libraries supported by subscription. But all over the country, men and women were beginning to organize in churches, in trade unions, in sewing circles, and athletic clubs, in village and town meetings, for the purpose of making books available to everyone with the support of local tax monies. Andrew Carnegie gave impetus to the public-library movement with his gift of free public-library buildings. His largess, continuing from 1881 until 1917, resulted in a stereotype of library architecture, the greystone fronts rising like a national monument in towns and cities across the land.

Free books for everyone! That was the exhilarating idea, an ideal born of a young country whose founding fathers had recognized from the beginning that in a democracy education of the populace was a necessity for survival.

But the children were denied entry. They were considered to be unequal to the ideal. Straightway, they made their own persistent and unorganized demands, knocking upon doors that were not open to them. They literally climbed upon window sills to peer in at their elders, who sat at soap-yellow tables in high-ceilinged, mustard-colored rooms, or emerged from the building with armloads of books after a mysterious ceremonial ritual at the desk in the rotunda, involving rubber stamps and little boxes of pads purpled with ink.

With the rise of public libraries in the country, an awareness of an undefined responsibility began to trouble the minds of librarians, the responsibility of choice. Which books should be purchased for any given community? The responsibility vexes the professional thinking to this day. The question could be more easily defined and more readily answered in relation to children whose tastes were unformed and who were helpless in the face of authority. But whoever serves children in any capacity, no matter how tangentially, is haunted by an awareness of a commitment to the future. Dealing with adults, one works with the here and now. Each child, however, wraps about him the promise or the threat of all that is yet to happen. When, therefore, in 1882 Caroline Hewins, librarian of the Young Men's Institute of Hartford, Connecticut, presented to the American Library Association a report on the melodramatic, sensational quality of the reading of boys and girls, she found a receptive conscience in the profession at large and an awakened concern for the minds of the young.

By 1894, when the American Library Association met at Lake Placid, New York, eager but bewildered administrators took heed when Miss Lutie Stearns, of the Milwaukee Public Library, read a "Report on the Reading of the Young," which declared for a policy of abolishing age limitations, presented the necessity of providing special rooms for the young, staffed by attendants "*who liked children*" and were prepared to serve them with the same standards of excellence as obtained in libraries for adults.

The young women who found themselves assigned to those first rooms for children in their respective libraries soon discovered that nothing in their previous training or experience with books and people had prepared them for this new commitment to children and books. It was to involve them in heretofore undiscovered skills, attitudes, and subject matter. Their accustomed patterns of thought regarding librarianship were shaken with such violence as to force them to become innovators, improvisors, and pioneers in a whole new area of being. They worked before the days of child psychology and child study, with all the catch phrases ready to the tongue. They functioned without the benefit of professional library schools with their varied courses in library work with children, and floundered in a confusion of purpose and direction.

Out of this confusion was to emerge a new profession. It introduced a philosophy of education that functioned independently of pedagogy, created an undiscovered rapprochement between the world of the adult and the child, and brought into being a tradition, uniquely American, that was to excite the admiration of countries around the world. It reached outside the library walls to publishers' inner sanctums, bombarding them with certain knowledge of the demands of children and direct experience of their capabilities. The breed of librarians born of this profession acclaimed standards of taste and judgment with such consistency as to influence the production of books for children and to involve, on their behalf, writers and artists of significant magnitude.

One person more than any other gave shape and content to the new profession, to the greatest degree and in fullest measure: Anne Carroll Moore, of Brooklyn's Pratt Institute and the New York Public Library. To be sure, confluence of period and place set the stage for her achievement, but the color and character of her accomplishment derived from the quality of her imagination; her courage and stubborn determination; her shrewd,

New England practicality; her logical, analytical mind, which, like a pyrotechnical display, could turn and light up the sky with its rocketing commitment to joy.

From time to time, certain few artists transcend the magnitude of their unique inspiration to emerge not as artists in a given field but as profound prophets who reveal in a blaze of light some splendid affirmation at the heart of life: Isaac Stern at the violin, Artur Rubenstein at the piano, Picasso in all his manifold manifestations. Anne Carroll Moore was one of these. She lived and moved beyond the prescribed condition of her art: children, books, and the utmost reach of the public library.

ACKNOWLEDGMENTS

*M*y indebtedness for help in writing this book is great and includes many people. A large portion of gratitude is due the nieces of Anne Carroll Moore, Constance Moore Willey and Ruth Moore Owen, of Saco, Maine; and Rachel Moore Warren and Margaret Moore Bedell, of Northampton, Massachusetts. They provided family records and letters, offered New England hospitality as setting for interviews and reminiscences, and took me to haunts known and loved by Anne Moore.

I am grateful to two cousins, Dudley and Storer Lunt, whom Anne claimed as nephews by virtue of their devotion to her. Each read the manuscript with critical but sympathetic care. The book owes its origin to Storer Lunt, who suggested that it be written and then stood faithfully by through long years of waiting for its completion.

Anne Carroll Moore was prolific in her letter writing, and many recipients husbanded her letters through the years. To this circumstance I am indebted for floods of letters generously lent to me by the following: Bertha Mahony Miller, Siri Andrews, Katherine Carnes, Lillian Smith, Virginia Bowman King and her daughters, Ruth Sawyer Durand, Ruth Hill Viguers, Marcia Dalphin, Alexandra Sanford, and Margaret Warren Brown, Anne Carroll Moore's great-niece.

Certain of Miss Moore's friends wrote their impressions of her, and these gave me valuable syntheses of her effect upon a variety of people. Among these were Anne T. Eaton, Louise Seaman Bechtel, Martha Peterson, Florence Little, Julia Carter, Eulalie Steinmetz Ross, and Nancy Bedell Massey, Anne Carroll Moore's great-niece.

Special gratitude is due Flora Cutler Cohn, whose records of the early years were complete and substantiated by newspaper clippings of the time, and Alexandra Sanford, who went on many an errand in New York City to fasten upon some fact. I wish to thank Marjeanne Blinn, of Los Angeles, who checked and rechecked facts of place and time, and Louise Bruckner and Betty Izant, whose typing dignified the appearance of my scrawled pages. To the cat Flan I am grateful for the comfort of his frequent presence. Whatever courage, determination, and discipline I was able to muster in writing this book I owe to the support of my sister Marie V. Clarke, who sustained me also with food and drink and a daily bouquet of fresh flowers.

To E. B. White and the New York *Times* I am indebted for permission to reprint a part of an article appearing in the Book Review section of that paper. The Literary Trustees of Walter de la Mare and the British Society of Authors as their representative gave permission to reprint the poem of Walter de la Mare, "Not I," which appears as a chapter heading. A great measure of gratitude is due to *The Horn Book*, its editor, Paul Heins, and to Mary E. Manthorne, President of the Horn Book Company, for permission to quote without limit from its pages and publications.

CONTENTS

ILLUSTRATIONS

(between pages 144 and 145)

Anne Carroll Moore as an infant
Anne Carroll Moore at the age of seven
Luther Sanborn Moore
Sarah Hidden Barker Moore
Almira Boardman Barker
Alderwood
Anne Carroll Moore as a young lady
Anne Carroll Moore as a student, 1892
Anne Carroll Moore with Flora Cutler, Marit Blehr, and Alice Tyler
Anne Carroll Moore as the Supervisor of Children's Rooms, New York Public Library, 1906
Anne Carroll Moore as the Superintendent of Work with Children, in the thirties
Children applying for library books
The academic procession at Pratt Institute, 1955
Anne Carroll Moore with Anne Carroll Peterson, in the fifties

ANNE CARROLL MOORE

1

ANCESTRY

*Once upon a time, Creation, Eternity, a
hundred years ago, a century ago, my birthday—these are familiar phrases to children
who have lived at the crossroads of life and
literature.*

ACM

ANNE CARROLL MOORE was born on July 12, 1871,
in Limerick, Maine, York County, southwesterly as the
state stands on the map, the youngest in a family of ten
children. Seven brothers had preceded her and two sisters who had died in the first years of their infancy.
When her mother felt that the birth of her tenth child
was near, she called to one of her sons and asked him to
fetch the doctor. "I'll not go," he replied, "unless you
promise it will be a girl."

She was christened *Annie* Carroll Moore, a name
adapted from that of one of the maiden aunts who lived
with the family in the wide, generous house, Aunt Ann
Eliza. The name was changed to Anne Carroll Moore
some fifty years later to avoid confusion with a teacher
at Columbia's Teachers College, Annie E. Moore, who

not only had a similar name but was in a related field of work. Both women were publishing books on the reading of children in the same period. At the suggestion of her editor, Eugene Saxton of George H. Doran Company, "Annie" became "Anne" when her second book appeared, *New Roads to Childhood* (George H. Doran Company, 1923). In certain untidy bibliographies, even today, a confusion exists between the two writers.

Carroll seems not to have been a family name but was chosen, apparently, because her mother liked the sound of it. It was an appropriate choice, with its connotation of Christmas and music, its foreshadowing of a lilting quality, characterizing her walk, the gestures of her hands, her voice and manner of speaking.

The landscape of Maine, the blue reaches of its sky, the hills that lift themselves to mountain heights, the thousand ponds and deeply wooded stretches, the boisterous coast and islanded shore, the rivers and valleys rich in Indian names, these constitute a national heritage threading through the literature of America to such an extent that even those who have never been there claim the state of Maine as a birthright of the American experience.

For Anne Moore it was inescapable. Maine was both root and refuge, especially its woods, fields, mountains, and country roads. These things she wrote of often with moving intensity.

> I had always loved the Cornish road for its woods and rushing brooks and, most of all, because it led straight on to the White Mountains. From its open stretches on a clear day, I could see Mount Washington white with snow.[1]

The roads to Cornish and Limington, linking small New England villages together, were the roads she knew as a

child, and she was to travel them many times in her lifetime. They were destined to take her well-nigh around
the world and bring her home again, where

> Spring still lingered with a gift of pink lady's-slipper in
> the Maine woods, and white lilacs and lilies-of-the-valley
> were blooming under the Christmas trees in the Old
> World garden of my childhood. Mount Washington rose
> white with snow in the distance and warm and clear and
> blue the June day held past, present, and future in its keep-
> ing.

Her lifelong reliance upon flowers was the result of
childhood freedom to roam woods and fields as she
pleased as well as of having had the good luck to be born
into a family of garden-loving people. It was a strong
and characteristic trait, not altogether typically American. She loved and employed flowers as do the Mexican
people, who depend upon them for fiesta, propitiation,
or merely for the humble comfort of holding them in
the hand; or in the manner of Northern people, the
Russians and the Scandinavians, for whom bouquets of
garden flowers, innocent of arrangements, are the natural
accompaniment of celebration and ceremony.

It was no affectation but a response to a need born of
instinct, like hunger or thirst, and it became a basic
premise in her philosophy of work with children. Time
and again she speaks of children and books "in natural
surroundings." She meant just that, asking of each Children's Room under her jurisdiction that, periodically in
the year's calendar of events, some gesture from the
earth, some small token of root and flower, be made the
focal point in the arranged environment where children
and books were brought together.

The wisdom of her insistence on flowers can scarcely
be realized unless one has watched with one's own eyes

the response of city-bred children to the actuality of blossom and flowering branch. To see children standing in line, waiting their turn to "smell the roses" (every flower is a rose to many of the children in New York); or to have a child ask, "Miss, the next time you go to the country, will you bring me a little dirt? I've got a seed"; or to realize that for one boy the experience of seeing a single spray of bleeding hearts in a small vase was literally beyond his belief; "Miss," he asked the librarian, "did you *make* that?"—incidents such as these reveal the enormity of the gap between millions of children and an elemental knowledge of nature.

In the early days at Pratt Institute, Anne Moore proved her point:

> Very early in the work of satisfying children with books, I had discovered how many of the stories and poems known and loved by me as a child were meaningless to children who had never seen the country in springtime, and whose parents seemed to have forgotten their childhood. The "nature study" of the schools was as yet unfortified by botanical specimens, or by the expanding resources of the Children's Museum of Brooklyn.

The recognition of nature even crept into her criticism:

> I believe the secret of Mr. Altsheler's appeal lies in a deep love of nature, the ability to select from historical sources subjects of strong human interest, a natural gift for story-telling, and great modesty.

Anyone even remotely associated with Anne Moore could scarcely escape the contagion of her involvement with the flowering earth. A cataloguer in the library of the University of Southern California recently recalled a spring day in New York when she had been a member of the staff of the New York Public Library, undergoing one of those interminable "In-Service Training" sessions. Miss Moore had been scheduled to speak on the goals of library work with children. She had come into the room carrying a basket of spring flowers. The flowers and the weather had quite undone her, she announced, and though she was supposed to talk about the Children's Division, she had decided, instead, to make them a present of the spring by reading aloud the poetry of the season. "I've never forgotten it," said the California librarian, some forty years after the event.

This bright fixation had its beginning in the garden of her childhood, a large rectangular plot as wide as the depth of the house, bordered to the north by a stand of pine to break the wind. Anne spoke of the pines as Christmas trees. Good New England stone walls marked the separation from the open fields, orchards, and hills, and the road streamed beyond to the front entrance of the house, circled and branched off into a second road that led into the gaping mouth of the huge barn. A summer house—the fashionable gazebo of the period—added its open-work decor to the abundance of roses that grew there with all the other country flowers. "An Old World garden," Anne calls it, over and over again.

It was her mother who supervised the planting of the garden. "Born with a green thumb, she could bring the most reluctant plant to bud and blossom," Anne wrote of her. "She had the only greenhouse for miles around, and a gift of flowers from her hand was precious to many a visitor." But the allotted space for the garden had been part of the large design that originated in the mind of her father, Luther Sanborn Moore.

As a young man, Luther Moore walked three miles each way between the villages of Newfield and Limerick in order to attend Limerick Academy. He passed a stretch of woodland on that walk, bordered by an alderswamp, "not outside the village but skirting the heart of it." This was the place he determined to make his own. It was precisely right for a young man with courage and vision, attached to the land as was his farming father before him, who saw in the swampland the possibility of a farm, bountiful in fields and orchards. He was promised to the law, and in the course of time he came to practice his profession with distinction, establishing headquarters in Limerick. But the farm remained central to his being, and countless others were to know and remember it, engulfed in the warmth of life that it sustained.

In due time the swamp was drained—by immigrants, one hundred strong, from famine-stricken Ireland, brought by Luther from a sailing ship in Boston Harbor —and turned into a hayfield, with the great hay barn in its center. The large, three-storied, multiroomed house was built upon a stone foundation that stands to this day, though the house has long since gone. Other generous barns were built, orchards planted, and the sown fields stretched away to the ascending hills. He called the place Alderwood, and to it he brought his bride, Sarah Hidden Barker, daughter of Deacon Simeon Barker, of Limerick's Congregational Church, and Almira Boardman Barker, of Newburyport, Massachusetts. The wedding date was June 11, 1846. The bride was twenty years old and the groom twenty-five.

Luther Moore had been born in Newfield in 1821, the son of a prosperous farmer who sent his son to Limerick Academy after he had exhausted the resources of the local school. According to the testimony of one of his contemporaries at the Academy, he "recited his Virgil with distinction and gave every indication of being a

first rate scholar." After the Academy, his father sent
him to Harvard to study law. But a break in his health
made it necessary for him to abandon Harvard, to study
on his own, at his own pace, with a prescribed amount
of time to be spent out of doors. He returned to his
father's farm and read law in Newfield with Nathan
Clifford, who was later to become an Associate Justice of
the Supreme Court of the United States.

After Luther was admitted to the bar in 1844, he
opened an office in Stetson, Maine, but in less than two
years he returned to Limerick, established an office there,
built Alderwood, brought home his bride, and there he
remained for the rest of his days except for his terms in
office in the State Assembly. By the time he was thirty
he had become president of the Maine Senate and made
his influence felt in the matters most important to the
state—education and intensive and experimental farming.
Later he served as trustee of the State Agricultural College, which was destined to become the University of
Maine.

In reading scraps of letters left to his heirs, one feels
the presence of a man who was reserved and reticent
except in the presence of his family. He must have been
an unusual father, with a breadth of view that transcends
the limits of a country upbringing. At no point does he
seem to have assumed the role of authoritarian patriarch
one would expect of the time and circumstance. As for
his relationship with Anne, it was little short of idolatry
on the part of each. She inherited his keenness of mind,
his analytical and logical bent, his stubborn determination
and reticence, too, in certain matters. The companionship between them Anne herself has described in scattered pieces of writing that make one wish she might
have found it possible to write her autobiography.

I am quite sure that my father had no conscious thought of imparting lessons to me as we drove or walked about the country. It was my companionship he sought, not my improvement or instruction, and his invitations always meant a good time. . . .

When his business was finished he would often say: "Now we will go home another way, a little longer and not as good a road—one of the old roads with a beautiful view. I haven't been over it for a long time." Sometimes he shared with me the pictures memory gave back from the road, more often we drove for miles in "social silence." . . .

On such a day, if it fell upon a Sunday, my father would stroll out of the garden and across the barnyard to the wide-open door of the stable to be greeted by joyous whinnying and stamping. "Quiet, Pocahontas, quiet," he would say as he led the horse from her stall, and if I appeared in the doorway I was greeted with an invitation after my own heart. "There's a man I must ride over to the eastern end of the town to see on a little matter of business. Will you come with me—just for the ride? I should love your company." . . .

I did not care to be read to, except by my father, who read just as he talked and seemed to like the same books and pictures I did. The *Nursery* was his favorite magazine, I firmly believed, not because he said it was, but because he seemed so interested in it. I associate with his reading the most beautiful parts of the Bible, Aesop's *Fables*, interspersed with proverbs, nonsense verses, old songs and hymns, a great deal of poetry, stories out of the lives of great men, and many stories of child life. He had a keen sense of dramatic values, a power of mimicry of animals and human beings, a strong sense of humor, and an intimate knowledge of men in their various forms of social and political organization. Moreover, he possessed the rare faculty of complete identification with the emotional life of childhood in all its stages of growth and change, and the imagination to know when to create a diversion. Since my intuitions have been at all times keener than my powers of external observation, I identified myself in turn with the childhood of my father. I seemed to have known him well as a little boy. That I was like him in certain qualities of mind, I was to learn in maturity; that I shared his emotional life, I knew as well at four or five years old as at his death, when I was twenty.

What infinite pleasure Luther Moore must have had in this child of his late years! He had been fifty when she was born. Moreover, she was his only daughter whom he was to enjoy all through her childhood and to know as a young woman of character. He saw himself mirrored in the small person seated beside him in the Concord buggy, and the sympathy between them ran deep. But the little girl, her gray eyes set far apart, her peaked eyebrows like small triangles set above them as though she were forever pleased and astonished by what she saw— this small person, with her delicate bones and slender body, gave back to him also the reflection of his wife, Sarah Hidden. It was from her mother, Sarah Hidden Barker, that Anne inherited her predilection for diversion, her social grace, and her splendid generosity of self and earthly goods.

Sarah Hidden Barker Moore, Anne's mother, was the second daughter of Almira Boardman of Newburyport, Massachusetts, and Simeon Barker of Limerick, Maine. There is a story behind that name, Sarah Hidden, which bears telling. When Almira Boardman was a young girl, her dearest friend was one Sarah Hidden, daughter of Parson Samuel Hidden of Tamworth, New Hampshire. It was she who had been engaged to marry young Deacon Barker of the Congregational Church at Limerick, and the date of the wedding had been set. When the doctors told her that she would not survive until the day, she sent for Almira Boardman and suggested that Almira assume responsibility for the happiness of Deacon Barker.

It was a plan which, in the face of the inevitable, Almira and Simeon came to adopt. In memory of the Sarah Hidden they both had loved, they gave their daughter her name.

The Barkers traced their beginnings in America to one James Barker, who came from England with Ezekial Rogers on the ship *Desire*, which landed in Salem, Massachusetts, in 1638.

The origins of the Boardman family date back to the boyhood of one William Boardman, born in Cambridge, England, in 1614, who came as a child to New England with his mother and stepfather. The name William Boardman persisted into the eighteenth century, and the record of a William Boardman's wedding to Rachel Wiggin still stands in the books of Newburyport. It took place on Saturday, April 9, 1785, at ten o'clock in the morning. Rachel Wiggin Boardman was Almira Boardman's mother. She lived to be ninety-nine years of age and was the subject of tales and legends in the family, having gone to live with her Great-Aunt Rachel at the age of fourteen, following the death of her mother. Rachel Wiggin Boardman's husband was a sea captain, sailing out of Newburyport in the great sailing days. It was she and her aunt before her who established "Rachel" as a name in the Moore-Boardman-Barker family, and the name persists to the present time.

Doubtless the English origins of her mother's people were responsible for Anne Moore's love of English life and English ways. She was an Anglophile almost to the last drop of her blood. But the Irish strain was there through her father.

The story of the first coming of the Irish into Maine and New Hampshire was ever a romantic story to me, for it must have been they who brought the old songs I loved and the fiddles for dancing—my own ancestor, once fondly though fabulously pictured as Tom Moore, the poet, with his harp, being among them. There is a round-topped hill in Limerick which I often climbed to take a look at the world when spring was coming up the valley. And from this hill I came to see more and more clearly, with no premature vanishing of fairies from mountain or glen—a little procession of hard-fisted, warm-hearted Irishmen moving up the valley with shovels, pickaxes and hoes, turning bogs and rocky pasture lands into green fields and flower gardens and then marching down toward the sea again for fresh conquests.

Whatever I know or feel about poetry and history had its beginnings in romantic associations such as these, and while my sharing of Irish poetry with children has been at all times spontaneous and by no means confined to St. Patrick's day and May Eve it is between these two dates that I . . . feel the Old World spell coming over me and the desire to share treasures that have their roots deep down in the childhood of the world.

"Be glad you're Irish," she once said to Bertha Mahony Miller, that elfin, powerful woman who founded *The Horn Book* and accomplished gigantic tasks of distinguished publishing in the world of children's books. Anne gathered together all of her Irish heritage in a fervor of celebration on each St. Patrick's Day. She followed the parade the length of Fifth Avenue, stopping at St. Patrick's Cathedral at some point in the morning. She plastered paper shamrocks on all the letters that left her hand in the week of March 17, and there were special parties of her own—as well as the feasts of the telling of Irish stories and the reading of Irish poetry in the Children's Rooms of the city's libraries. For her, spring always came wearing a leprechaun's hat.

A good account of a St. Patrick's Day celebration is given in a letter to Virginia King in 1943. Anne was retired, but the pace and variety were typical of The Day as she usually celebrated it:

> Mrs. Durand and I had a marvelous St. Patrick's Celebration beginning with a story hour attended by 300 children and adults at Bruce Branch Tuesday Evn'g—Fire on the hearth—Yellow primroses—the Room looked as lovely as I've ever seen it—Next morning Pontifical Mass at St. Patrick's with the 69th Regiment pouring in after the Color Guard from a misty Fifth Avenue. Glorious music —taps—the roll of drums—a service one will always remember.[2]
>
> Jacqueline Overton for luncheon afterward in the Louis XIV Restaurant—Rockefeller Plaza. Miss Florence Overton kept home by bad weather. We sent her yellow tulips, forgetmenots & a pot of shamrock. We caught glimpses of the procession under umbrellas and then Mrs. D. and I saw *Dark Eyes*. You would love it. . . . We ended the day with broiled lobster at 34th & 3d Ave.[3]

2

ALDERWOOD

*There are no satisfactions comparable to
a free and spacious childhood with a clear
title to one's own good name at maturity.*

ACM

To HAVE BEEN the only daughter and the youngest child growing up in a family of seven brothers might well have tempted a small girl to adopt the habits of a tomboy by way of compensation for not having been born a boy in the first place. The concomitant danger of an excess of admiration from brothers and an adoring father might have resulted in an accentuation of femininity, creating a small daughter full of wiles and graces, interested chiefly in dolls and the domestic concerns of a diminutive play-pretending mistress of a home and garden.

The child Anne seems characteristically to have gone her own way, assimilating the best of both masculine and feminine worlds. She was not physically robust (her brothers called her "Shrimp"). The stark realities of farm life and the strenuous activities in which her brothers engaged seem to have left little impression on her. Sheep, lambs, cows, and horses were her favorite animals. All her life she regretted the fact that she had never learned to ride horseback when she was young, but horsemanship was not an accepted pastime, even on prosperous American farms, since the animals were considered mainly in relation to the work of farming or were bred to be good carriage horses. Dogs she loved, though nowhere in her writing does she call by name a single memorable canine character. She abhorred cats and feared them all her life long. Her brothers, when they teased her, threatened to throw a cat on her and held this awful power over her all through her childhood.

But the winter sports she shared with them—all the exhilaration of snow and winter winds. She writes of it in *Nicholas: A Manhattan Christmas Story*. The chapter "New Year's Eve in Maine" gives the full flavor of childhood's remembered winters, besides a glimpse of the house in Portland she loved second only to her own Alderwood.

In the story, Nicholas and Ann Caraway are riding a Pullman coach from New York to Portland, and Ann, who is to sleep in the upper berth, says to him:

> When I go up and lie down in the top berth, Nicholas, I'll forget all about New York. I'll see only the White Mountains covered with snow and a lovely old garden with Christmas trees growing all around it and then, far away in the sky, the wonderful Northern Lights will stream down.
>
> And after that I'll begin to see all the boys and girls I ever knew, skating and coasting, first in the daylight, then by moonlight, and I'll see great bonfires blazing on the ice, and then I'll sail away on an ice boat, and the next thing I know, Nicholas, I'll be waking up—not in my old home in the country, but in a city that seemed like a fairy city when I was a little girl because Ben's grandfather and

grandmother gave my brothers and me such wonderful times there.

The next morning the two travelers are met with a sleigh. The tale continues:

> Ben Star tucked the big buffalo robes about them and away dashed the old sleigh with its jingling bells. Up the steep side of Cassidy's Hill raced the horses.
>
> Morning was just breaking over the city and Ben Star told Nicholas to look back and see the white smoke rising from the freight-yard at the foot of the Western Promenade.
>
> "You can't see the harbor from here," he said, "but there's Cape Elizabeth beyond [Fore River]."
>
> "And there's the old grey house on the hill with the little windows like eyes near the roof, and the cupola on top. . . ."

The toboggan rides were high drama as well as a lesson on the conduct of life. In *My Roads to Childhood*, she gives account of the following experience:

> This hill by the Baptist Church marks the entrance to the old burial ground with its beautiful view across the Ossipee Valley to the mountains. It was also the starting point for the most thrilling bobsled adventures of my youth. The slide led straight down the precipitous hill to Main Street with its peril of single and double sleighs, and slow-moving ox sleds. Turning a sharp corner, the challenge was to make three more hills, two of them very steep ones, to "the Factory" a mile distant without going off the road. The way was fraught with danger at every turn. The proudest winter of my life was the one I was chosen to sit next to the steering genius who managed the bobsled. His words of caution, "Don't scream if we do go off the road. Sit tight and expect a happy landing next time," have been worth cherishing for many another adventure.

She was well aware of the life her brothers were leading even though she may not have been an invited com-

panion on some of the outdoor adventures. Her way of
wooing their interest was to hoard cakes of maple sugar
in the dresser drawers of her doll's bureau, to be produced at strategic moments as bribes as well as gifts of
the heart. She followed them about the house, "from
library to attic," where in addition to bound volumes of
St. Nicholas, Our Young Folks, and Harper's Magazine
they had a cache of The Police Gazette and other unfamiliar sources of information, and these she read in
sweet companionship with them, especially on rainy days
when the drain pipe's tinny music broke the silence and
heightened the secrecy and daring.

Whatever the extent of her companionship with her
brothers, it was to give her rare understanding of boys
and men and to tilt the balance of her sympathy toward
the male in any matters of judgment. Her profession by
its nature dealt largely with women, but her friendships
with men were numerous, encompassing young men as
well as her contemporaries. She was, in many ways, a
man's woman, having a rare gift for comradeship; feminine, perceptive, gay, and sympathetic, but without exacting a toll of homage and idolatry, which women, in
almost every relationship with any male, barely escape
expecting to some degree. Every aspect of her personality
was delicate and feminine, but her processes of thought
were direct, logical, and decisive. She reasoned with masculine strength and spoke out without regard for consequences. Her colleague and friend Anne T. Eaton, that
inspired librarian of Lincoln School, at Teachers College,
Columbia University, has well described the quality of
the mind of Anne Carroll Moore. "I knew I could go to
her for advice and get it. I loved the way her mind
worked, there was no hesitation, no 'let me think this
over.' She knew on the spot what she thought and it was

always right. . . ." "The vigorous, critical mind that can purge, stimulate and invite," wrote Ruth Sawyer of her in *The Way of the Storyteller*.

Such surge of life swept through that bountiful house as to absorb a child's interest in all manner of incidents and people. "Beyond the White Mountains lay the world," she writes of the time in retrospect, "but I felt in no haste to explore it, I was too fearful of missing something vitally interesting at home." Her older brothers had already left home when Anne was born. As she grew up, they returned for visits with wives and children. Cousins on both sides of the family from Newfield and Portland came for visits and parties. Anne's nieces, Rachel Moore (Warren) and Margaret Moore (Bedell), the children of Anne's brother Harry, remember from their childhood the look of the place. They tell their children and grandchildren the inconsequential tales that echo the tone of life there and are the stuff of legend: how Anne's mother deplored the habit the boys had of waiting until food was on the table before they bethought them to go to the barn to feed the horses. Her most vivid memory of her sons, she said, had been their departing backs as she stood at the doorway to call them to dinner. "Harry, Walter, Luther—whatever your names are— come back—food's on the table"; the story of Aunt Carrie shouting out, "Come quick, Harry's swallowed the sugar bowl" (it was in reality a small decorative knob on the lid); the remembrance of Aunt Ann Eliza, who had a genius for cooking and insisted on carrying on even when her sight began to fail, until the day when the dish rag was served up at the table as part of the main course. It was she who sang as she worked, and filled the house with the measured sound of old hymns; the account of Cousin Alice arriving from Portland for a visit, behind a span of white horses. The steeds were mud-splattered and in need of grooming. Emissaries were sent throughout the town in search of lemons with which to whiten and cleanse them, to the astonishment of the natives.

The house in Portland, Maine, was the home of the most cherished cousin, Alice (Storer) Lunt, ten years older than Anne, who was, on Anne's own confession, "dearer to me than any sister." Anne looked up to her in the years when the difference between ten and twenty was great and claimed her as beloved friend and confidante in terms of equality in the years after sixteen, at which time the decade between them shrank into oblivion. Alice's sons, Dudley and Storer Lunt, and Dudley's children in their turn, were destined to give Anne long devotion that bridged the generations and the vagaries of fate and fortune—a regard that transcended family loyalties and the responsibility the young may feel for the elderly. Day by day and year by year, to the very last, when the years of Anne's life numbered close to ninety, it was the Lunt family who renewed her commitment to the present and kept fresh and vital the interests that bound her to the contemporary scene. Even though Anne was by character and endowment an ageless person, it was their companionship that kept the banners of her spirit flying to the end. The home of the Dudley Lunts in Wilmington, Delaware, was in the later years the natural base for the celebration of traditional holidays. In the comradeship of Storer Lunt, for many years the bachelor of the family and head of the noted publishing firm of W. W. Norton & Company, Anne found an ongoing fervor for books and reading that matched her own and a mind honed to the sharp edge of argument and debate in matters of critical opinion. It was Anne who had persuaded him in the first place to enter the field of book publishing.

In their youth, Anne was to Storer and Dudley an exhilarating comrade whose judgment, advice, and common sense proved trustworthy over the years, whose gaiety and perception colored their own reactions to the business of living. In Storer's case, the relationship came full circle in the years of his maturity, with Anne the recipient of counsel, succor, and endless felicities.

It had all begun at Alderwood with frequent visits between the families of the Barker sisters, Mary Thomas Barker Storer of Portland, and Sarah Hidden Barker Moore of Limerick. Alderwood was the focal point in the lives of "The Barker Girls." There were six of them altogether, three of whom lived at Alderwood and one, Almira, who was married from that house in an apple-green corded silk dress which she left to Anne in her will. It served Anne as costume and ceremonial well nigh all her life. She wore it on state occasions of her own and for appropriate public appearances. When the New York Public Library celebrated its fortieth anniversary in 1935, there appeared in various newspapers throughout the country a picture of Anne in Almira's apple-green dress, with her classmate from Pratt Institute, Mollie Leavitt, also on the staff of the New York Public Library, dressed in the grandeur of forty years past.

The house was also blessed with the presence of a grandmother, Sarah's mother, Almira Boardman Barker. Anne writes of her in *My Roads to Childhood:*

> Always my grandmother remained a city-bred lady of great personal charm. I was twelve when she died at the age of eighty-four. Quite unconsciously she set a standard, for I have never met anyone who grew old so graciously in the homes of her children. Everything she did, whether it was fine needlework or the dipping of her laces in a

china bowl filled with gum-arabic water, was done in such a fascinating way. That she had been a beauty in her Newburyport days was still evident. As for her stories of Lord Timothy Dexter with his strange doings, his mock funeral and his speculations in warming pans for the West Indies, they were a source of unending delight to my brothers and me.

It was our grandmother who read *Uncle Tom's Cabin* aloud to us while we listened, spellbound. My father adored her (his own mother had died when he was sixteen) and she returned his affection and confidence with a single exception. She did not approve of divorce. How often I heard her say, as he was leaving to attend court, "Promise me that you will not divorce anyone this time."

The real strength of Alderwood and the life engendered there lay in the relationship between Anne's father and mother. A handful of letters written by Luther to his wife when he was at Augusta, the state capital, or when Sarah was off on visits to relatives in Boston, one or two of the children tagging along, reveal an equality of judgment shared between them, as well as the love honestly and tenderly declared. Luther showed no hesitation in discussing with his wife details of trials and courtroom procedures, nor of any other matters which concerned him. Among the earliest letters extant are several written from Augusta in the spring of 1854, when Luther Moore was, at thirty-three, president of the State Senate, struggling to gain support for academies of the state, especially the one at Limerick. Their eldest son, Charley, was six years old; a daughter born in 1852 had died within a week of her birth, and Sarah was to have another son in July of that year.

Augusta Sunday Aprl 9th/54

My dear Sarah.

Yours of the 6th was rec'd yesterday morn & I was rejoiced to hear that your father was so comfortable. hope it will continue so, but I fear the warm weather will tend to weaken and reduce him. Remember me to him & tell him I hope to see him better when I get home. It is a dark, rainy, gloomy day here & as I have a slight cold I've concluded not to go to church today, thinking it would be quite as well to keep in. I am lonely enough here. Such a Sabbath as this & can only sit and think of that *home* which is *so dear and precious* to me. What an unhappy man should I be without such a home. When I think of it, I *see & feel how much* I am indebted to you *my dear wife* for my happiness & I hope I may be truly grateful to the great Author of all good for the blessings I enjoy. I've no doubt you are sitting and thinking of me today—how I wish I was with you & Charley. I never wanted to see you both more than now. The time is rapidly passing away & I shall soon be home to *remain* as you say you wish me to. We are turning off the business quite rapidly. Members are getting anxious to go home & I've no doubt we shall adjourn as early as Wednesday of next week. My duties are growing more laborious, tho' I think I feel better the more I have to do. Next week we shall have two sessions a day. We meet at 9 A.M. now instead of 10. Most of the Committees have got through the business referred to them & reported finally. The Committees on the Judiciary & Education are about all who have not reported. The Com. on Education will report finally on Tuesday morning. Mr. Abbott told me last night that they would report in favor of Limerick Academy a half township of land. It will be a desperate struggle to get them tho'. but I think it can be carried. I shall spare no pains or *means* that will insure success & I think I can manage to save 2000$ clear out of it for the Academy but of this I am not certain—the whole thing may fail. If the Dr. inquires about it you may tell him what I've stated about it. . . . I am sorry to hear that you don't feel any better—fear you don't take proper care of yourself. Hope you are well by this time. Charley seems to have got into the notion of writing again—am glad of it for it does me good to see the marks his dear little fingers have traced. I'm afraid Lorenzo will have some trouble about hay to last till I get home. I did not say anything about it in *his* letter. Mr. Bangs has not returned. If it was important for him to be here at all it is now I should think. Quite a number of ministers have gone for good. It don't rain this P.M. & I'm going to church.

I suppose you'll expect this tomorrow night, so I'll mail this P.M.

Give my love to all the family and believe me as

> Ever *your own*
> *Luther*

Trouble, anxiety, and the vagaries of human behavior must have existed in so large a family, but there is small echo of them in the letters that are extant. A disastrous libel suit involving Luther Moore is known to have been a matter of concern. He was completely exonerated by the courts, but the cost must have been great. Sarah considered the desirability of leaving Limerick after the suffering and notoriety, but Luther held for staying, knowing the allegations to be false no matter what the decision of the courts might have been.

It was probably this case that marked the beginning of a continuing and nagging worry over money. The maiden sisters in the household moved to Boston, found a house on Blagden Street right behind the Boston Public Library, and maintained themselves as managers of an excellent rooming house. Anne and her mother were frequent visitors there. Letters from Luther to Sarah during those years bespeak the generosity of the man. No matter what the state of the family finances, he could not deny Sarah her extravagances of dress.

> Limerick April 25, 1878
> [Anne was nine years old]

My dear Wife—

Your letter is rec'd & we are glad to hear from you & Annie. We are all well and you need not worry about any of us. . . . Now as to your dress I think you had better

get it & have it made up while you are there. You must not
worry about the cost. It is my wish that you get it. . . . I
want you to write me Saturday what day we should meet
you next week. Whether Monday, Tuesday or Wednesday. Loran wants you to come home—wants to see you &
Annie & so we all do. The other boys are doing well. . . .

Give Annie good kisses for me—

Yours
L.

I have just sent Arthur 16$ that he asked for.

In October of that same year, Sarah was once more in
Boston, this time without Annie. Luther never complained of her absences beyond declaring his loneliness,
which is rebuke by compliment rather than by acrimony.
In a letter from Limerick, dated October 17, he reports
on the crops: the apples picked, 700 to 800 bushels, the
corn husked, the boys well pleased with their crops, and
the corn house full. He continues:

> Everything goes on nicely, only it seems so odd and lone-
> some without you. Margaret says she can stay as well as
> not next week, and so we have talked it all over and we all
> think you ought to stay until you have made all your visits
> and seen all you wish to. It has been 27 years since you and
> I were in Boston and as you will be too old to go 27 years
> hence you had better make the most of the present oppor-
> tunity now you are there—Annie is just like a little kitten
> as good as can be only she wants to see her mother Write
> often.
>
> As ever   Luther

On June 11, 1881, when Anne was ten, she and her
mother and brother Luther, Anne's senior by two years,
were away from home, whether in Boston or some other
place is not clear in the letter, but obviously it was after
some tragic circumstance in the family had occurred.
Luther Senior wrote on that day. It was the thirty-fifth

wedding anniversary of Sarah and Luther, and he comments on that fact:

Limerick, June 11, 1881

My dear Wife.

I rec'd your letter & was very glad to get it. . . . I hope you are all well & will keep so. I want you to use what money you need & I will make up what you have to borrow when I come in. I realize how lonely it is there now —it seems to be something you can feel in every part of the house. There is a great void—the light of that household has gone out. Am glad Annie and Lu are happy & contented. Kiss them for me & tell them how much I miss them. We are all getting along nicely so far have all been in & abed before 10 o'clock. Arthur seems to take a great deal of fancy to Mary & is very attentive. She is happy & contented I don't want Aunt Sarah to trouble about her. And so far I am glad to say there has been peace in the household We shall work on the road Monday & Tuesday —I have watered everything in the Green House & will look carefully after it. I have been thinking a good deal to-day & this evening about this day 35 years ago & what changes have taken place— It does not seem so long it has run so smoothly that we have hardly taken note of time, & but for the fact that our children have grown into men we could not realize it— Shall we see 15 yrs more together? I hope so, for I have a great desire to see all the boys settled in life. I shall write Galvin this evening so if anything new occurs I can write it, but give yourself no uneasiness about us as we are all doing well—

Yours as Ever
Luther

Among the varieties of people, with all the tangential relationships they brought into the household, Anne was given time and space in which to grow. She was not sent to school until she was past seven, and at ten she was precipitated into the Academy to make what she could of it. In a letter to her niece, Rachel Moore Warren, written in 1924, covering these matters, she said:

It took the courage of conviction to keep the child I was out of school until past seven, and when elementary teachers were of poor caliber to send her ahead of all her companions to what was virtually High School at ten. I didn't want to go but the case was not open for argument. I was told to try it. Looking back, I think that it was remarkable that any Mother with limited school education and in the midst of all her cares could see so clearly the essentials to be grasped, that she recognized so immediately the people qualified to supply them, in some measure, at least, and cared not a rap not a button for what masqueraded as school systems in her day.

At the Academy she found herself once more in the minority, there being a predominance of boys among the students. The practice of reciting aloud was in force at that time, and Anne listened eagerly, acquainting her ears with the sounds of Latin and Greek as well as the poetry and prose of English masters. Northrop Frye, in his book *The Well Tempered Critic*, describes the results of such educational procedure as the Academy sustained in terms so applicable to Anne as to seem to have been written about her:

> Literary education of this kind, its rhythm and leisure slowly soaking into the body and its wit and concreteness into the mind, can do something to develop a speaking and writing prose style that comes out of the depths of personality and is a genuine expression of it.

No doubt it was the Academy that gave Anne early control of a lucid style in speaking and writing that was to make her a distinctive critic and essayist in her day. She herself gives account of her discovered pleasure in the study of Latin and of the young teacher who made it possible:

> My own most vivid remembrance of entering the teens is of beginning the study of Latin. Up to the age of thir-

teen I had held out against Latin, chiefly because a brother two years older than I denounced its uselessness with such eloquence.

"There's no use in Latin. Just a waste of time," he would say, inviting hours of argument with a brother two years older than he, who maintained that no one could be educated without the study of Latin, and no one would want to be who had once mastered the technique and was able to read Virgil, Cicero, and Horace just as he read other books.

And while the battle over languages—dead and living— was still raging, came a new principal to the old academy. He it was who persuaded me to begin the study of Latin. "Why not give it a fair trial?" he said, and proceeded to make the first year of Latin so delightful that it remains the most potent influence upon my outlook during those impressionable years.

Less skillful as a teacher of all things to all types of minds than his predecessor in this old New England academy, the new principal was an ardent lover of literature and language, with a charm of personality which gave him place at once in the life of the village.

To him the year of teaching was an interlude between college and a professional school. He shared both generously and acceptably his love of Latin for its own sake. I do not remember that this young man in his early twenties ever made a direct suggestion to me to read a book. The invitation lay rather in his own personal habit. Along with the newspapers, magazines, and books of the day, he seemed always to be reading some classic as well, and since he was a member of our own household for the year and left his books lying about, I made my first perplexed acquaintance with Dante that winter and began to read Shakespeare with new eyes after listening to some admirable reading of his lines by members of a Shakespeare club to which I was too young to belong. I had previously read through a one volume Shakespeare in very much the same mood and temper as I had read the Bible through—to see what it was like and to say that I had done it in a company of my peers.

All the days of Alderwood! They were, for Anne, the ultima Thule. Because she had lived at the start of life with intense joy, in a world where grace, trust, and love were the accepted norm, the search for home need never again be undertaken. Most women on their own in life strive to possess themselves of a permanent dwelling place. Not Anne. She was free to move about the world. Like the opera singer in Gilda Varesi's play *Enter Madam*, who created a home in any place with the deployment of certain scarves, shawls, and draperies, Anne needed only a clutch of symbolic possessions to feel safely rooted anywhere.

In New York she lived in countless places: rented rooms, clubs, hotels in neighborhoods she found congenial, studio apartments. In one such she asked the landlord for a mousetrap, troubled as she was by a small beastie. He said he had no mousetrap, but he offered to lend her his cat for as long as might be necessary. Greenwich Village and Gramercy Park were favored haunts, and she found an apartment greatly to her liking in one of the old houses of Chelsea, set back from the street, with wrought-iron balconies and balustrades, dispirited ivy on display, and scraggly flowers dauntless among old bricks. The degree of comfort, elegance, or lack of it mattered little to her. At the peak of her career she holed up for a time in a dark back room, looking out on a brick wall, at the old Woodstock Hotel on Broadway, the better to aid financially a young grand-niece in her year at library school. Because she possessed Alderwood and was in turn possessed by it, "all places were alike to her." Except "The Balcony." That was yet to come.

In a birthday letter written to her goddaughter, Alice Campbell King, from Berkeley, California, in 1942, she speaks of the subject of birthright:

I love San Francisco and I feel very happy to be here for a time but I can never love any city as I love New York, nor any real countryside as I love New England and Old England, just as I fancy you will never love any part of our dear country as you love the South where you first saw the light. But it is something to take with you through all the birthdays to come that you never lose your birthright even when you are living somewhere else and that I think makes life wonderful at all times and in all places and assures a welcome wherever we go.

"None of us ever escape the first few years of our lives." It is not Anne who speaks but Lizette Woodworth Reese in her book *A Victorian Village,* which Anne revered and quoted in her review of it in the New York *Herald Tribune.* The quotation continues: "They make a mold into which we are cast, and though it may be broken, and we be turned loose, some remnant of it, some intangible evil or lovely thing, or both, will remain with us, like the odor to a flower or the smoothness of a piece of ivory."

The mold in which Anne was cast predisposed her to expectancies of joy and triumph. ("Admit to no discouragement" was her initial advice to her immediate successor at the New York Public Library.) That she considered disappointment, tragedy, sorrow, and woe almost as matters of personal disgrace to be borne privately and in silence was due in large measure to the tone and flavor of those first years. It was not that she denied the existence of tragedy or attempted to soften or explain it. She knew it well, having ample share of it in her lifetime. Her awareness of it increased through her sympathy with all those whom she cherished. Countless people confided in her their utmost sorrow. She never betrayed them for the sake of tales to be told, but held their woes in secret as she held her own. No one made better comrade in sorrow. She voiced no wisdom or advice, gave no homilies of consolation. She was there if needed, her presence testimony to the larger harmony she could never deny, having experienced in her early years a world beautiful in its proportions, peopled by men and women intent on giving life itself the delineation of intuitive art. In one of the most memorable biographical passages that occur often in her discussion of books, she writes of the first decade:

> I was not a bookish child, I discovered, although I had always cared to read. I have no recollection of any process or method by which I learned to read, but I hold a very vivid recollection of the first book from which I read. It was a large print edition of the Gospel of St. John. The time was early evening, and I went to bed thrilled with the discovery and the beauty of the words. I told no one until I could read well. I may have been five or even six years old, I have never been sure, but I recall very definitely that I brought to the reading of poetry, the psalms and the prophets strong impressions of the beauty of the country about me. Beyond Mt. Washington lay the world, just out of sight, and beyond the low horizon line to the southeast lay the sea. I had seen the sea, but I had not seen the world, and I was always wondering about it.
>
> This sense of wonder and mystery, the beauty of nature, the passing from night to day, the speaking voices of the people about me, the sound of music, are present in my earliest recollections. I had a keen interest in pictures and I was always seeing things in pictures. I had no gift for drawing, and the mechanics of writing was extremely difficult for me. I shall never be able to unearth a manuscript written before the age of ten. My early literary compositions were all scribbled and dispatched by post. I never had a doubt that what I whispered as I scribbled was read by the cousin or brother to whom it was sent. Writing, like going to school, was a social experience full of news of people and of what they said and did. Never did

I write out of deeper emotions. I hated goodness in books, and the tendency to get everybody to behave alike, in life or in books.

"Are you a citizen of New York?" a Cockney lad asked Anne at the David Copperfield Library in London, the year 1922. The first two chapters of her book *New Roads to Childhood* tell the story of that library. The lad could as well have asked, "Are you a citizen of the world?" and the answer could have been the same, "I am." Work with the children of New York and their parents made Anne a world citizen. She responded to the diverse cultures and convictions with characteristic eagerness. Her regard and respect was never vitiated by pity. She understood the million variations fate composes upon the theme of existence, and welcomed entrance through every door her work opened to her. Here again it was Alderwood that had prepared her for all that was to come. In one of the most eloquent passages she ever wrote, and perhaps the most quoted, she tells the truth of it:

> Nearly everything that happens in novels had happened in the village where I grew up. Here were romance and mystery, beauty and terror, here lived cowards, liars, thieves, and adulterers, as well as men and women of character and definite achievement. I had seen with my own eyes, heard with my own ears and felt with strong feelings of my own the human drama in which I was playing a part long before I was fifteen.
>
> A frank determination to know all that can happen to human beings in books or in life is quite different from a prurient curiosity. Feeling under obligation myself, I have never been shocked to find other boys and girls, similarly impelled to find out all that they can.

Those Sunday-morning rides with her father had taken Anne among foreigners, the poor, the workers in the woolen mills, so that her experience of life, even in Limerick, lay beyond the boundaries of her schooling and the social life of a small New England village. Lawyers, like doctors, know the crooked and the straight of life. Anne must have listened and observed with that rare degree of intensity she brought to bear upon every action of her life.

The breadth of view, the courage and compassion did not derive from the heritage of her father alone. In the plot of the Limerick cemetery where the Moores are buried—"planted," Anne would have said, a New England term that pleased her, bold statement of fact that it is yet holding promise of transfiguration—in that place stands a small headstone marking the grave of a young woman, a minister's wife who had run off with her lover. After a time she returned, with her child, to suffer such scorn as to bring to mind the anguish of Hester in *The Scarlet Letter*. When she died soon after, no one would give her Christian burial or space in any hallowed ground. It was Sarah Hidden Moore who insisted that the Moore plot receive her to lie for the ages under winter snows, among summer's lilies of the valley, black-eyed Susans, daisies, and wild honeysuckle that tangle there with indiscriminate beatitude over the graves of the Moores and the young, passionate outcast.

BRADFORD

I was brought under the spell of historical perspective in the midst of natural phenomena. . . .

The plain truths of today are discounted by the amazing discoveries and inventions of tomorrow. We may as well take on trust that there is a truth of emotion as well as of fact. ACM

𝓑RADFORD, MASSACHUSETTS, is one of the villages clustered in the northernmost and narrowest corner of the state, lying among benign hills, the Merrimac curving through the region to the sea and the transcendental elms of New England reaching skyward. Rowley, Bradford, Haverhill, and Boxford—stout English names that rumble on the tongue like the old refrain "Rowley, powley, gammon and spinach."

The Haverhill *Observer* of April 27, 1803, announced the founding of a new academy erected in Bradford "half a mile from Haverhill bridge":

under the care of the best instructors; and will be opened on Wednesday the first day of June, which contains two apartments, one for the Males, the other for Females. In the Male apartment will be taught the English, Latin and

Greek languages; Reading, Writing, Geography, Arithmetic, and all other necessary branches of School Education. In the Female will be Embroidery, and all other forms of needlework together with Drawing and Painting. The tuition will be placed on so low terms as barely to defray the necessary expences with the help of the Interest of a Considerable Fund appropriated for that purpose. Boarding will also be very low, and every attention will be paid to form the minds of youth to virtuous and religious habits, and secure them from every kind of immorality. Such as are disposed to commit their children to their care, may depend upon their punctuality, and every favor will be acknowledged.[1]

Academies were indigenous to New England. The difficulties of establishing state-supported schools were manifold even when laws were passed for the maintenance of them and fines imposed for failure to conform to the law. The academy made certain that some form of classical education was established in community after community. Funds were raised among the citizens by various means, sometimes by lotteries or by land grants from the state. "Academies were never 'free' in the sense of admitting students without the payment of tuition, but they were free to all who could qualify for admission and were never operated for private gain."

Hard work on the part of a few families of Bradford had preceded the appearance of the announcement in the *Observer*, including the adoption of rules and regulations, drawn up by committee. The by-laws were comprehensive, covering points of procedure as well as rules of conduct for the students. Consider the qualifications set forth for the choice of suitable persons to conduct the school:

Art. 1. The immediate care of the Instruction of this Institution shall be committed to a Preceptor and Preceptress appointed by the Proprietors of the Institution.

Art. 2. The instruction in the female Apartment may be suspended whenever the Proprietors Judge necessary.

Art. 3. No person shall be appointed Preceptor of this Academy who has not received a publick education who does not Sustain a good moral charictor and reputed a Gentleman of good abilitys.

Art. 4. No young lady shall sustain the Office of Preceptress who is not a Reputable person well versed in the Science of Belles lettres, Embroidery, and all kind of fine needle work.

Article 2 allows rather comfortably for the suspension of female education. The ironic fact remains that from the beginning the female students outnumbered the males, and in 1836 all attempt to educate the young male was abandoned. The school became the Bradford Academy for Women and exists to this day as a junior college for women.

By the time Anne Moore entered Bradford in 1889, the school had attained a position of leadership. Anne E. Johnson, a woman of considerable intellect and character, was nearing the end of her nineteen-year period as principal. In her time she had established stringent scholastic standards for those who hoped to acquire a diploma at graduation. Latin, science, mathematics, logic were required, and, in the senior year, metaphysics and theology were added. Many of the students attended the academy as "specials"—"The giddy, giddy specials," as they were known—taking such electives as appealed to them with no thought of a credential of any kind. The rigidity gave way somewhat under the influence of Ida C. Allen, who became assistant principal in 1888 (later she was to succeed Miss Johnson), for she supported greater freedom of choice in the matter of courses available to those who hoped to graduate, and by her own enthusiasm for art as a fact of everyday life as well as a subject of study she was to enhance and enliven the actuality of school life.

Anne, with the credentials from Limerick Academy behind her, was able to encompass in two years the courses necessary for obtaining the diploma, graduating from Bradford in 1891. The experience of Bradford was pivotal to the life of Anne Carroll Moore. Its progress through the decades of her lifetime, its hold upon succeeding generations of young women were matters that commanded her ardor and devotion. She loved the place. She noted every change in the landscape, rejoiced in the new buildings—the President's House, the distinctive chapel, designed by Charles Stone, which seemed to have grown from the pines that surrounded it. Successive presidents and alumnae secretaries came to know her friendship, and she returned to the campus for special celebrations in the life of the school and particularly upon the graduation of two young women who had chosen Bradford because of their association with ACM. Anne Lunt, daughter of Dudley Lunt, was one; the other, Alice Campbell King, the daughter of Virginia Bowman King, once a children's librarian in the New York Public Library for whom Anne bore great affection. The college recorded through the pages of its alumnae bulletins the succeeding honors that were heaped upon ACM in her lifetime and crowned these garlands of laurels by bestowing upon her the Jean Pond Trophy (June 2, 1956), whose only other recipient had been Jean Pond herself, the beloved teacher, assistant principal, and vice-principal of Bradford.

Anne's memories of Bradford and tributes to her years there were recurring subjects in her speaking as well as her writing. Among the scraps of notes salvaged from the tangled conglomeration of her papers there emerged an early talk written in 1900 (she was twenty-nine years old), when ACM was midway in her career at the Pratt Institute Library and nine years distant from the Bradford graduation. It is not known for what occasion the talk was created, but the topic to which Anne addressed herself was: Is There a Place for Bradford Academy among the Educational Institutions of Today? Such parts of it as reflect the life at Bradford in her day are included here:

Before attempting to give answer to this question, it has seemed to me necessary to go back to the years of my own school experience and in the light of subsequent events, to mention some of the characteristic features of the school as I knew it in the years 1890 & 1891.

First of all, I should mention its *social opportunity.* Among the students, numbering 150 or more, of those years there were girls from Western cities and from New England farms and villages, from southern plantations and from northern manufacturing towns, from foreign missionary fields and from Back Bay in Boston, from the plains of Texas and from Fifth Avenue in New York. These various elements mixed and mingled in one great homogeneous life—some of them becoming friends for a life time while others merely enjoyed pleasant acquaintance for the time or perhaps did not care for one another at all but learned, notwithstanding lack of personal affection, to respect character and a certain wholesome disregard for the false and the pretentious. The assimilation of such a social experience distinguishes in later life the woman who is able to get on with all kinds of people from the one who is confined to the narrow range of her native town or the town of her adoption or to a certain section in a large city. (There is quite as much of provincialism existing in our large cities as in out-of-the-way country districts.) . . .

The course of study as I knew it was as strong in the essential features of metaphysics, English and American literature and general history as the work in most women's colleges of the time. . . .

In the subjects I have mentioned I feel that I owe to my

teachers a lasting debt of gratitude. The course in literature was then given by Miss Allen, the present principal,
whose love for the subject was communicated to her pupils in a marked degree. The history was given by Miss
Pond, a true disciple of Miss Annie E. Johnson's mental
and moral philosophy: Paley's *Natural Theology*, Fisher's
Evidence of Christianity and, shall I add, a philosophy of
life which has been a blessing and an inspiration to every
girl who is privileged to receive her instructions.

These were Anne's beliefs in 1900. Half a century beyond—in 1952—she wrote of Bradford once again: "I
owe a lasting debt to Bradford of the nineties for whatever I have been able to contribute to my profession of
librarianship."

ACM was no seeker of office, but she served as president of the New York Bradford Club for two terms
(1916–1920) and was class recorder in her own right and
as aid to her erstwhile roommate and lifetime friend, Alice
Gale Hobson, whose house and hospitality at Little
Boar's Head, New Hampshire, was a continuing pleasure.

Her devotion increased in the latter years, especially
subsequent to the coming of Dorothy Bell as principal in
1940. Miss Moore's letters to her, to Jean Pond and Jane
Runyan, alumnae association secretary, reveal an almost
childlike reliance upon their pride in her accomplishments and in the honors heaped upon her. Bradford
became a substitute for the lost parents who could not
know how far-reaching was the heritage they had given
her.

> 476 Fifth Avenue
> New York
> May 22, 1932.

Dear Jean Pond:
  It now seems certain that I will not be able to celebrate
the fortieth anniversary of the class at Bradford. Since I
began celebrating it nearly a year ago in California with

Winnifred [Winnifred M. Lyman] and continued to do so throughout 1931 it is not far from my thoughts. Until very recent events changed my vacation plans I had hoped to be with you. One of the events, which may not be told until June 8th, is that the trustees of Pratt Institute have asked if they may confer a "Diploma of Honor" upon me and have requested that I be there to receive it in person. I'm really very pleased to have that form of recognition of my work after twenty six years across the river. There's a reality about it often missing from an honorary degree. . . .

I was at Simmons for a lecture last Monday and spent the night with Grace [Grace E. Goodwin], and after seeing how impossible it would be for her to be away from home I am the more reconciled to holding over our reunion. The last one was too perfect to take chances. . . . We all missed you at the New York luncheon.

With love and millions of good wishes for the coming days.

Anne Moore.

3 Mitchell Place
June 10, 1932.

Dear Jean Pond:

You may like to see the Citation even tho' I may not let out of my keeping the Diploma of Honor itself. It's a beautiful one and for the first time I feel like having it framed since it means so much.

It was given for the first time last year to a man who has done remarkable things with Radio. Apparently I'm the first woman to receive it and it was a complete surprise to Miss Rathbone, the head of the Pratt Library School. In short, a direct act of the Trustees which is a triumph for the children and their books to be thus recognized. The Academy of Music was packed and Dean Gauss of Princeton gave a very fine address. Mr. Harold Pratt proved a delightful shepherd to guide my steps to the front row on the platform. Mr. Frederick Pratt, now the President, and probably responsible for my appearance was highly pleased that strict confidence had been kept and that Pratt Library Staff were speculating as to why I had come until they looked at the program. . . .

The one regret I felt was that Miss Plummer could not be there to see the work with children chosen out of the whole library field for this recognition. She was the first to accord it departmental status on equal terms and on its own base rather than as an appendage of a circulation dept. "You can do with it whatever you have it in you to do," was all she said in starting me off.

I hope the girls didn't freeze at Commencement and that it was as always a great success. I wish I might have been there but you can see I'm sure that it was the year for Pratt Institute and now I'm working at top speed on *Nicholas and the Golden Goose* which is to be published this fall.

Officially, I'm away on vacation—actually at the Panhellenic until I can turn over the ms. It's a great life after you get your second or third wind.

With greetings to your sister and my love always

Anne Moore

Twenty-three years later, in 1955, Pratt Institute honored ACM once again, and once again Anne reported the matter with pride, this time in a letter to Miss Bell:

35 Fifth Avenue
New York
May 21, 1955

Dear Miss Bell:

May has been such a heavenly month that I've been on the wing from its first weekend with dogwood and azaleas in Wilmington to Float Night with the whole campus in bloom at Smith the past week. I was contemplating Bradford commencement when the President of Pratt Institute telephoned me to say that the trustees had voted to confer a Litt.D. on me as one of the first group of Alumni to be given honorary degrees. Needless to say I was surprised and unbelieving until a confirming letter came next day. So I'll be going to Brooklyn to receive it on June 3rd instead of to Bradford. You may be sure that I'll be taking Bradford memories along with me and thinking with deep pleasure and satisfaction of your welcome to the new President's House. What a relief it must be to you at all times. With my love and good wishes

Anne Carroll Moore.

Every visit to Bradford campus invigorated her spirit and gave her fresh impetus and vision. In 1950, when she was in the last stages of recuperating from a vicious bout of pneumonia, she insisted on going to the commencement at Bradford. With the consent of her doctor, Anne took off. It was understood that she could be scheduled for no gatherings, free to go or stay as she pleased. She reported to Maria Cimino, in the New York Public Library's Central Children's Room, that some of the students came to call on her early one morning, unofficially and unannounced. They were eager to meet a graduate of 1891, they said, and to see what she was like. Anne opened the door to them, her hair in curl papers, saying, "Well, you see she is still vain enough to care how she looks." If she were following her customary procedure, those "curl papers" were scraps of pink tissue paper peculiar to packages originating at Lord & Taylor of New York.

Seven years later, in 1957, when ACM was seventy-nine, she went once more to a Bradford commencement, Storer Lunt simplifying the intricacies of travel by driving her there. A letter to Jane Runyan tells the story. The words and music are familiar, a variation on ACM's repeated theme of triumph and exaltation.

The Grosvenor
35 Fifth Avenue
New York

May 7, 1957

Dear Jane Runyan:

Before the Commencement Announcement came I was about to write and break the news of my new lease of life

—fairly bursting with health the past two weeks and eager to see the President's House and to tell the rest of the Alumnae how much I'm enjoying the Jean Pond trophy. Having seen Round the World in 80 days and The Waltz of the Toreadors (with Sir Ralph valiantly playing his part in spite of his larynx) I feel up to anything that doesn't involve standing or much stair-climbing. If a bed should be possible at the Infirmary it would be wonderful. If not, perhaps you will find one that doesn't involve too much "to and fro" so I enclose the card. I would even like to arrive on Thursday to avoid the crowd and have a bit more time but I'm not yet sure how I'll come whether by train or motor.

After a winter of hibernation it is marvelous to feel and I'm told, to look as I do. My love to Miss Bell. I thought of you both especially at Easter—it was a very beautiful one here and after 8 o'clock service at the Church of the Ascension I had the two King girls for luncheon here with primroses from their Mother's garden in Biltmore [North Carolina].

With love and anticipation

Anne Carroll Moore

No continuing relationship could have been happier for Anne than that which Bradford afforded, symbolizing by its very nature the polarization of her life: her intense attachment to the strengths and traditions of the past, her eager commitment to the future with its ongoing promises. But Anne herself revealed the deepest core and cause of the matter in a letter to Miss Bell, written on May Day, 1953. There she disclosed that her graduation day, June 11, 1891, which her mother and father had celebrated with her at Bradford in great pride, had also been the forty-fifth anniversary of their wedding. Anne was to hold to that day forever because it was destined to be the last such family reunion she was to know.

As for Anne's days at Bradford as a student, there are extant none of her letters to her parents, but the few existing letters that they wrote her show Anne to have been a somewhat strong-willed and stubborn young lady, suffering the complaint of most young people—namely, a certain dereliction in acknowledging receipt of funds and a never-ending need for money.

Alderwood was a lonely place for Sarah Hidden and Luther Moore, with Anne, their youngest child, gone from home. Anne's father arranged frequent visits to Bradford and sent apples from the orchards of Alderwood for midnight eating. He and Anne made plans to go to Boston together, but the plan came to naught, as is revealed in the following letters.

Limerick Oct. 16, 1889

My dear Annie:

I shall leave here tomorrow & take the P.M. train for Berwick & stop at Harry's all night and Friday AM go to Bradford by the train you spoke of last week as due at 12 & then take your 2 o'clock train for Boston, hoping to have your company. I see no reason why we can't go this time. I shall put up a box of apples express and take with me to the depot and send along by express. You had better not open until your return from Boston. The box will get to you before I do I suppose. I suppose there is some man about who can take it to your room.

As ever Lovingly.
L. S. Moore

Limerick Oct. 20, 1889

My dear Annie:

Your good letter was received. I am sorry that I am not feeling well enough to go to Boston tomorrow. My cold has been very bad & I cough a good deal, but am getting over it. I want to feel well when I go or I do not enjoy it. So I have concluded to defer my visit for a week when I hope the weather and other conditions will be more favorable. Should I not be able to go then I will send you some money so you may go to Boston yourself and get your books. I enclose one dollar for pin money. Until then—

Affectionately yours
L. S. Moore

Boston was a temptation for Anne. She went for Thanksgiving in 1889, apparently ignoring her father's disappointment in not having her at home.

Limerick   Nov. 11, 1889

My dear Annie:

Your good letter is received & is none the less welcome because of the request for money. I know you cannot live without it. And I am sure you will not waste it. . . . I send you enclosed five dollars of which please acknowledge receipt. As soon as it comes to hand. We are all well & would much enjoy your being with us Thanksgiving Day, at any rate you have a cordial invitation. I know you will not come, but it does really seem that you ought to be here. We will have to have our turkey for a week.

Write me how much money you will need for your trip to Boston for you are bound to go I very well know not withstanding your invitation here. . . .

The girls at Bradford had somewhere heard a lecture by Sir Henry Morton Stanley, the rescuer of David Livingstone in Africa, as Luther's letter of January 21 reveals.

Limerick   Jan. 21, 1891

My dear Annie:

Of course I was delighted with your letter. It was so good, so entertaining and withal written so plainly that it more than satisfied. Your description of Stanley's return was at times almost an impersonation, I would have been glad to have heard & seen him, but when in Portland, the weather was so bad that I did not think best to risk the exposure. I am glad you had the opportunity. I see the girls at Wellesley had a great time with Mrs. Stanley. Too bad you could not have seen her. Should like to drop in and surprise you some day. I suppose the thought that money may be needed ought to occur to me without suggestion so I enclose five dollars but don't be surprised and think that any radical change has taken place in me, for this is only a freak, but I hope you won't take it as an indication of mental unsoundness. Let us know you get it.

Yours as ever,
L. S. Moore

On February 15, 1891, Anne's mother wrote a letter that began in contemplation, for she was mindful of the fact that her eldest son, her first child, Charles William Moore, dead at twenty-five, had been lost to her for eight long years.

Feb 15: '91

My dear Annie:

I must say a few words to you tonight. It has been one of my hard days [the] anniversary of my dear Charley's leaving me. It did not seem then that I could live without him. . . . How I have missed him, no-one can tell. . . . He never seems very far away from me. He was so fond of you . . . [and] never so happy as when you were about him. You were doubly dear to me then & ever since. . . .

Your father had a great time over your letter. Thinks you write the best letters of anyone—so natural & easy. [He] says you are the brightest of any of them. Now he has done it, has he not! Do not let it lift you up too much . . . I hope you will succeed with your essay & that you will attend to it right away before you get any more popcorn feeds. Do not think that will strengthen you much. . . .

I should have enjoyed seeing the camellias. I do think them so beautiful. Have tried hard to raise them. Mean to try again some time.

Miss Allen is very good to give you so much time. Talk with her as you have opportunity about your future studies for I do not expect you will be willing to stop where you are.

We go on the same old way. [I] am looking forward to your coming home. Now what should we do were it not for anticipation. . . . I suppose you didn't have any Valentines. Do not worry about the dress it will come right somehow. I must stop now so this can be mailed. Be sure not to get sick.

Your loving Mother.

At Bradford it was customary to award each year to two members of the graduating class a prize in the amount of twenty-five dollars, one for "the greatest progress in culture and scholarship" and the second for the best essay. In the class of 1891, Miss Almira D. Locke was deemed to have made the greatest progress, and Miss Irene Tyler won the prize for the best essay. But Miss Annie C. Moore had submitted a paper on "Birds of History and Literature" which so stirred the judges as to necessitate their breaking with precedent to the extent of awarding her a special prize of twenty dollars.

"All along the fields of literature," it began, "fresh avenues of thought are opening not only fragrant with perfume of flowers, but musical with the song of birds." Two portions of that paper dimly foreshadow certain interests in Anne's future. One, a reference to Hans Christian Andersen: "Thanks to Hans Christian Andersen, other birds will always hover about our childhood; no purer moral was ever taught than by the story of The Ugly Duckling, yet the childish mind receives its impress all unconsciously, years after the story comes again, its beauty in no wise impaired by the teaching now so plain."

The second is a small tribute to owls, "the most picturesque and human of all birds," a trio of which were to head up her pages of criticism of children's books in the New York *Herald Tribune* "Books" and *The Horn*

Book and to give title to the three subsequent volumes of essays, *The Three Owls.*

Anne left Bradford, knowing well that her formal education was at an end. She longed to go to Smith, as she confessed years later in a letter to her niece, Rachel Moore Warren, but she knew it was a financial impossibility.

Two professions were generally open to the unmarried woman of that era. She could become a teacher or a missionary. Bradford, with its traditional sympathy for the mission field, had no doubt exposed Anne to the possibilities of such a life. As for teaching, Miss Allen had assured Anne of her ability to teach should she wish. But Anne was drawn to neither pursuit.

After the festivities of graduation, Anne went to Boston to visit the aunts and to have as gay a time as possible. When she returned to Limerick she announced that she was going into her father's law office to read law. In light of the fact that opportunities for women lawyers were all but nonexistent, it was a decision that was hardly practicable. But Anne was adamant in her choice.

Part of ACM's fascination lay in her audacity. She was no rebel, no nonconformist. Custom, propriety, and, above all, a certain style and elegance were greatly important to her, yet she was capable of spurts of outlandish behavior. Sometimes it was no more than an act of spontaneous mischief, such as she perpetrated in Los Angeles when her friend "Cousin Oscar," [2] Althea Warren, director of the Los Angeles Public Library, Gladys English, head of work with children in that library, and several others met her at the railway station early in the morning. They were all invited to breakfast at the station restaurant, a pleasant place then in the heyday of

Fred Harvey's reign as restaurateur. As the group was being ushered to the table, a waitress passed them in the aisle carrying a large tray with glasses of fresh orange juice. Anne, as she walked, scooped up a glass in each hand without a moment's break in her tread and joined the others. At times high-handed arrogance took command, as when in St. Paul, Minnesota, she ordered the hotel management to clear her room of its abnormally overstuffed plush furniture and replace it with something simple and less conducive to nightmare.

Inventiveness was part of that audacity, as when she lit upon the scheme of extracting money for the Bradford Endowment Fund, not from her classmates and other alumnae but by addressing her pleas to their grown sons, who were thus invited to honor their mothers. She would "undertake gigantic tasks for honor's sake," eschewing common sense to work with no resource at her command other than her own strength and imagination. Such was her achievement of organizing and managing a lecture series in New York for Marie Shedlock of England at the time of the First World War. The determination to read law with her father was an early indication of characteristically absolute and independent action. Her audacity was destined to bring her grave encounters as well as gay and inconsequential ones, and in one instance her action bordered on the heroic.

Six months were allotted to the Moores, father and daughter in "partnership," from July 1891 to January 1892. Four months before Anne's graduation from Bradford, her father had written to her as follows:

Limerick, Feb. 3rd. 1891

My dear Annie:
Your good letter just received and I hasten to comply with your request as I can as well spare the money now as

later and I don't want you to have to count the few coins you have like a devout Catholic his beads. I enclose five dollars which acknowledge as soon as received. What shall we do with you when school days are over? I think we will keep you a while ourselves. Though I wish we were able to give you as good privileges as the country affords. Its growing dark and I must go home. All well.

Aft. yours. L.S.M.

"Its growing dark and I must go home."

The winter of 1891–1892 was severe beyond memory. An epidemic of influenza raged through the countryside. Luther Sanborn Moore died of it on January 14, 1892. Two days later Anne's mother, Sarah Hidden, succumbed to the scourge. The years of being the cherished only daughter had come to an end and Alderwood was all but gone.

4

PRATT INSTITUTE: THE STUDENT YEAR

Librarianship offers release for creative, intelligent social relationships which know no geographical boundaries—freedom to enjoy and share the books one loves.

ACM

NOT UNTIL four years after the death of her father and mother did Anne discover the direction her life was to take. She stumbled through the first dark year with the help of Alice Lunt, who came immediately from Portland at the time she was most needed. When word of the double tragedy reached her, she got out of her own sickbed and drove by sleigh the fifty miles to Limerick to help the distraught household. Anne's elder brother, Harry Moore, meanwhile, had become principal of Limerick Academy. He and his wife, whom Anne held in great affection, and their two little girls, Rachel and Margaret, came to live in Alderwood and filled the echoing rooms with new life. Anne weighed the possibility of teaching at the Academy with her brother. Before she could undertake it, the cherished sister-in-law died in childbirth, and Anne found herself mistress of Alderwood, with the responsibility of caring for two children, aged five and seven. For two and one half years she was immersed in the tasks and cares of a household and a family, neither of which was hers in actuality.

If there was in Anne's life an all-encompassing romance, she kept it well hidden. Nowhere in her correspondence—and letter writing was for Anne a plenary and endemic necessity—nowhere does she give any hint of having known the troubled joy of being young and in love. Nothing less than the grand passion would have sufficed. In everything she accomplished, in every encounter with people or circumstances, extremes of intensity governed her reaction. It was all or nothing, acceptance or rejection, with small room for compromise and little patience with the shading of "yes and no."

"I don't suppose you got any Valentines," her mother had written when Anne was at Bradford, as though it were too much to expect of her. The matter of marriage seemed never to have occurred to her father. "I do not worry about you," he said to her when she came out of Bradford, "because I feel sure you will always be rich in the love of friends." There was a legend in the family, known to Constance and Ruth Moore, the daughters of Anne's brother Luther. Their version of the tale was that Aunt Annie had once been engaged to a young man. She appeared at the breakfast table one morning and announced to the assembled family that his name was never again to be mentioned by anyone. Furthermore, Dudley Lunt remembers that once in his young manhood Anne hinted at a love affair that she brought to an end without the consolation of having shared with anyone the strain and anguish it entailed. These are stories told and dimly remembered, but the nature of legend and myth is to disclose truths of feeling and response that transcend the actuality of fact.

Certain pictures show Anne lovely in her youth with ethereal beauty. Tall, graceful, and slender: "jimp" is the word for her, borrowed from balladry, encompassing delicacy in its meaning, as well as grace and elegance. She had ample opportunity for meeting young men, with seven brothers in the house at one time or another offering her the friendship of their companions. In a letter written to a friend in 1943 she refers to a possibility of marriage.

> I hope you had a happy Thanksgiving Day and that we may soon meet again or "together" as Nancy Bedell's mother [Margaret Moore] and her sister expressed it when they felt I might marry and leave them. That was long ago and far away. . . .

At a time of crisis when she felt called upon to explain certain matters in a letter to Franklin Hopper, the director of the New York Public Library, she again intimated that a proposal of marriage had come in that period when she was absorbed in the care of her nieces and implied that she had chosen the children as a matter of duty. Whether she was motivated in her choice by her New England conscience, her devotion to the children or whether the children afforded a welcome escape from the possibility of marriage must remain a matter of conjecture.

In the fourth year of the interim period at Limerick, Harry Moore married a second time, choosing for his bride a classmate of Anne's from Bradford, for whom Anne never felt the degree of affection she had given to her first sister-in-law, though she befriended her in generous fashion.

Somewhere Anne caught the rumor of librarianship as a profession for women. Public libraries were in their first period of ascendancy. She learned that the New York Regents' examinations for entrance to library school were scheduled to be given in Boston, and she decided to try them. Off she went, telling no one of her intent, facing, as was customary with her, ordeal or dubious adventure in secret and silent encounter.

In a long, revelatory letter to Miss Bell, Anne gave her own account.

> Six weeks or more later I received a pass card and with it a letter stating that admission Board at the State Library School at Albany had made a ruling to admit only college graduates. A circular of the Pratt Institute Library School was enclosed. A church centennial was being observed in Limerick and a young minister who became later the minister of the Park Street Church in Boston, made the chief address. I decided to consult him knowing that he had had a church in Brooklyn. He said very frankly that he knew nothing about library teaching—very few people did in the nineties—but that a year in Brooklyn and New York City would be worth far more to me than a year in Albany. My father had been of great help to him when he had his start in Limerick and he was determined that I at once begin a life of my own for my father's sake as well as my own. He lost no time in writing to Pratt Institute that very night [stating] that I should be admitted on the Regents Examination record and told me I would embarrass him very much if I didn't do likewise. It gave me just the push that was needed.

Pratt Institute first opened its doors to students in 1887. Founded by a family of successful industrialists, eager to make a contribution to the city and the neighborhood in which they had prospered, Pratt was envisioned as a technical school, designed to offer courses to young people for whom college was not a possibility.

Architecture, art, engineering, home economics, and library science were the subjects that comprised the early course of study.

Anne entered Pratt in September of 1895 and moved for the first time beyond the environs of New England. She was twenty-four years old. The century was turning upon the axis of its last five years. An air of hope and the promise of expansion characterized the period. Brooklyn streets were in a state of eruption, a subway under construction beneath the cobblestones, and Pratt Institute on Ryerson Street was itself undergoing a change and signs of growth, a new library being well under way by the time Anne arrived.

Many of Anne's recollections of Pratt are preserved on a series of "P" slips she assembled as notes from which to speak at the fiftieth anniversary of her class in 1946.

Why is it that in all library literature there is no research into the origin or etymology of that ubiquitous piece of paper, measuring five inches by three, called a "P" slip, without which no library can function? The computer can hardly hope to equal its usefulness. The librarian's dependence on it often becomes a lifetime habit. So it was with Anne. If none were at hand, she created a similitude by cutting stationery down to size.

The talk ACM gave at the fiftieth anniversary of her class appears in the Pratt Graduates' Association *News Letter*, February 1947, but the "P" slip as source material is used in the following instance.

Having accounted for all twenty members of the class of '96, ten of whom were living, Anne began by saying that she intended to show "the reasons why our relationship to Pratt Institute has endured for fifty years."

There follow then quotations from the letters of absent classmates, the introduction of some of those present, chiefly Mollie Leavitt, who in 1946 had only recently retired from the New York Public Library after forty-two years in charge of Gifts and Welfare. Then vignettes of faculty and students peel off the packet of "P" slips, the order of their coming unpredictable since the slips are unnumbered. Here they are in part.

Mary Wright Plummer. Of all American librarians of her time she was the one who made the strongest impression abroad. Her professional papers were read by librarians in all parts of the world—of the 1890's & early 1900's. Linguist and poet and a natural student of the literature of other countries Miss Plummer was chosen as the United States delegate to the International Congress of Librarians held in Paris in 1900. For 2 months she was in charge of a graphic Exhibit at the Paris Exposition printing two papers in French. One on cooperation between public librarians & public schools in the U.S. The other on Bibliography. Miss Plummer's clear perception of international relationships and her warm friendships with European librarians and writers contributed definitely to the cosmopolitan atmosphere of the library and of the whole Institute. Educators from all over the world were visiting Pratt Institute for new ideas in demonstrable terms & the free library, thanks to Miss Plummer's interpretation, proved one of the most interesting of those ideas.

Mildred (Collar) Gardner, a director of The Redwood Library of Newport, R.I., whose interest in civic affairs has been continuous from her resignation as a librarian to be married in 1911.

Mrs. Gardner as a student had the temerity to challenge the instructor in cataloguing at every turn. She had no respect for a model catalogue as such. She brought an incisive scholarly mind to bear on every problem and was at once the admiration and the terror of an instructor who had accepted rules without allowing for exception.

Caroline Weeks, Registrar of Pratt Institute 1895. A genius in human relationships and the most selfless person I have ever known. We met in a boarding house on Ryerson Street in the latter half of my student year and achieved a rare friendship.

Mary L. Avery, Lecturer, Editor of *Pratt Institute Monthly*. Severe in manner, outstanding—when speaking of books, she said, "You must at least hold these books in your hands with a realization of what they are."

Pratt Institute was only eight years old when we took our course in the old class room across the street. The School of Domestic Science was on the floor above and beaten biscuits were literally pounded out over our heads. . . .

The ironic truth of the matter is that, while at Pratt, work with children interested Anne Moore very little. At first she was drawn to the fascination of research and reference work. But the ultimate appeal lay in the new concept of County Library Service, under the directorship of the State Library. Soon after she graduated from Pratt in June 1896 she set out for Augusta, Maine, to see what the prospect might be. But Maine was then far from a beginning in state organization. The best the State Library could offer was an invitation to return "some day" to address the State Legislature on the advantages of a statewide basis for library service.

Meanwhile, Anna Barnard White, Anne's classmate at Pratt, with whom she had shared the office of class president, accepted Miss Plummer's offer to head up the new Children's Library of Pratt Institute. The work was hardly begun, a matter of two or three months, when Miss White resigned. Mary Wright Plummer wrote to Anne, inviting her to return to Pratt, this time as a member of the library staff, to direct the work of the Children's Library. Anne was there within four days.

That was in the fall of 1896. On February 23, 1897, Anne sat down to address herself to the task of writing her stint of a round-robin letter to the classmates at Bradford. "Dear Birdlings," it began, and after explaining reasons for her desultory past she regaled them with the following account:

Oh girls. I've got so much to say I don't know where to begin. If I stopped to think I might be chilled by the fear that you would not be interested in everything. . . .

One of my classmates who had been taken on the Library Staff after graduation basely deserted the profession but opened the door of my future and here I am in Brooklyn. . . . [On] the nineteenth of June I became possessed of another roll of parchment. Two weeks before commencement I received a letter from the Superintendent of Schools in the State of Maine asking me if I would deliver a series of talks upon "Library Methods of Study" before the Summer School to be held in Saco. Having long before determined to undertake the first piece of work which presented itself I saw no way of escape though I had no more idea how it was to be accomplished than a babe in arms.

People were so comforting. "It will be such good experience," they said. . . .

I had undertaken library work because it seemed to present a quiet congenial life with the seamy side underneath and [now] at the outset I must appear as a *female lecturer* in miniature.

There was little time to "reason why" and I fell to collecting material to take home with me.

In the midst of it my brother was married in Philadelphia and I appeared as bridesmaid for the last time.

I left Pratt with some reluctance for I had grown to care for the place and the people though I've no affection for Brooklyn.

On my way home I visited libraries in Hartford, Worcester and Boston, picking up lists and "Brillianti" for my lecturing. I reached Limerick a day ahead of the bridal pair, opened the house and tried to blazon welcome on the family shield. The next three weeks were busy enough. I initiated my new sister into the mysteries of house keeping, made jelly, preserves, did everything but sew by day and worked up my papers at night.

Fancy, girls, any one of you seated on a *platform* while a man introduced the next speaker as "Miss Moore from Pratt's Polytechnical Institution, Brooklyn, New York." I was scared but I made up my mind to one thing. I would interest those people in something even though I sent my notes to the winds and after the first morning I used them hardly at all. I found a very pretty little library in the school building, where the Summer School was held. Here I displayed lists, books, all the illustrative material I could gather, and here people came to talk after the more formal talk down stairs. I really enjoyed it very much especially the "side talks." . . .

I spent ten days in Portland after this. Visited the State Library in Augusta on invitation of the Librarian. The poor man was quite taken aback when he saw me. We had had some correspondence and he evidently thought me on the shady side of "somewhat."

"There—there's a circus in town today," he stammered. "Wouldn't you like to see the parade?" Of course I would and did. When luncheon hour came I was delivered into the hands of a young assistant who had previously been summoned to entertain me by showing me pictures.

We went not to a hotel nor yet to a restaurant but to the young man's house where I was warmly welcomed with "We're always glad to see Ernie's friends even though they are library cranks."

Time forbids a description of the visit and how I was entertained. Ernie drove me out to the Insane Asylum in the afternoon and facetiously introduced me to the librarian of the City library as "a young lady we hope to have speak before the legislature this winter." He suggested my spending the last of August at Popham Beach where he was to spend his vacation. The family objected to the same as open to misconstruction and I decided to take a journey to Cleveland instead. This is not a letter of travel but it might easily become crowded with incident should I describe that trip to the edge of the west [Cleveland], my first journey beyond New York. I left Boston with a party, names of whom were well known to me at the start, but I cannot call up the figures of some of them, notably the elephantine soul who occupied the lower half of my section, without a rush of something like tears.

We had one common end in view, to attend the annual meeting of the American Library Association held in Cleveland from Sept. 1–4, 1896. Arrived in Cleveland, we found the Hollander, our headquarters, swarming with a Bryan Convention. Alas, for the solitude of my own apartment, engaged two weeks before. I was forced to share with a gaunt female from the State of "Ioway." My first impression—she in red flannel petticoat attired, one or two other nondescript articles of dress not to be mentioned in these pages—was not conducive to *Sisterly* affection. I love the human race but when it comes to sleeping with them promiscuously, I am reluctant.

She was State Librarian by the way, got in through a political pull for she is no more fitted to care for the interests of a state institution than—words fail me. There was a reception at the Hollander that night and I met many delightful people. When at last I sought my chamber I found "Ioway" in nightly attire, hair in leads, *chewing* gum.

"Now you never suspicioned did you, that I was a married woman." I certainly never did, I rejoined with a glance of relief at the cot in the extreme corner. I was not to sleep with her.

"Yes, I've got two grown girls." "You, you must have been married very young," I faltered. "A good deal younger than I mean the girls to be," with unction. "Are your daughters engaged in library work?" "No, they isn't as yet, one's been taken' lessons in physical culture 'n the other in Elocution but just as soon as they get rested up I shall set them to work on travelling libraries. The bill passed our legislature last spring." . . .

On the way home, I stopped at Buffalo and had a lovely day at Niagara. I was winding up with a very good time in Boston, seeing everybody and [buying] a few things when I received the letter which put an end to my wanderings and brought me back to Pratt.

I had a very short time for goodbys. It is better so—

only three days in Limerick.

And now for my work which is all engrossing.

Our new library was opened last June and here in a big room, flooded with sunlight on bright days and crowded with children on grey days, I am living some of the most satisfying days of my life. . . .

I have all nationalities common to large cities. The majority of the children are of the poor middle class but there are many extreme cases. There are some children from the best families also and from them all it seems to me in time one may gain a fairly composite idea of child life. . . .

I dissipate by going to New York. I have all day Tuesday to go where I please. I learned to ride a wheel in the fall and enjoy it immensely though I'm not as secure as I might be and hope to be.

Just now I'm attending some art lectures on Wednesday afternoons. There are a thousand things one sighs to do at Pratt but my hours are long and I have to be careful. I have spun out a long thread. . . .

Congratulations to them as fits to 'em. . . . Whenever a body comes to New York do let her sound her trumpet.

With the best of good wishes

Yours at last.

Annie Carroll Moore

Certain distinctive traits of mind and temperament are revealed in this letter: the quick eye to mark details; the ear, tuned to dialogue and rhythms of speech; the decisive judgment of people; the prejudice against the Middle West which never quite left her although it was later mitigated by her association with the university at Ames, Iowa; the energy which led her to encompass multiple tasks in a day and enabled her to pursue proffered opportunities for adventure to the limits of her physical strength.

5

PRATT INSTITUTE: THE PROFESSIONAL YEARS

Out of this vivid sense of the reality of the Andersen stories that I loved best and their association with the affairs of my own everyday life I stepped into the children's room of a public library and found there an ideal spot to continue my celebration of Hans Andersen's birthday, for a children's room is more like a garden than any spot I know. ACM

$\mathcal{I}$T was high good fortune that brought Anne Carroll Moore and Mary Wright Plummer into partnership at a time when education for librarianship was at its beginning and work with children seething to discover its definitive form and philosophy.

Miss Plummer had been given full responsibility for planning the library building at Pratt and for determining the scope of its work. Two far-reaching innovations were the product of her imaginative approach: one, a room designated as a library for children, not as an afterthought but initiated on the drawing board of the architect; secondly, an art reference library for general use, including in its collection slides and prints as well as books.

In the person of ACM these new directions were to find a single focus. Children, books, and pictures—these were for her a major triad. She made good use of the art department at Pratt, enkindling in the children a response to the whole spectrum of art, through the exhibitions they saw on the walls of their library and through the illustrations in their picture books.

When Anne went to Pratt to head up the children's library, her knowledge of children was limited to the all but total recall of her own childhood, to chance accounts of childhood she had encountered in her reading, to the direct experience accrued to her through her care of and devotion to her nieces, Rachel and Margaret Moore, and to the association with her brother Luther's children, Constance and Ruth. As for her knowledge of children's reading, of the books they chose on their own or of those available for them, she had only the remembrance of her own reading ready at hand as aid and understanding. At this precise point of ignorance Anne Moore showed a proclivity that was to give her wisdom all her life long. Whenever she hungered for knowledge of any subject she straightway sought out the deepest origins of the matter. More than thorough study and research were involved. What she pursued was living proof, the very headwaters of accomplishment and personality. The vitality of that distinctive list, "A Choice of a Hobby," which she made for Compton's Pictured Encyclopedia in 1934 and revised from time to time, was due to the fact that she consulted first off not the literature of the subject but the men and women, the boys and girls, whose hobbies were vivid in their lives. The circus chapter in *Nicholas: A Manhattan Christmas Story* derives its validity not from her years of attending circuses, circus buff though she was, but from hours spent behind scenes, an actuality she brought off with the help of Mr. Edwin Norwood, for long years the publicity director for Barnum & Bailey. She talked with clowns and knew the giraffes by their given names! As for riding on the back of the great tortoise at the Bronx Zoo, a feat her hero Nicholas accomplished easily, being eight inches high, she herself essayed the adventure, the better to catch the feel of it.

Her judgment of current books was never an isolated factor performed within the limits of the time in which she chanced to read them. Whenever she was elated by book or illustrations, stirred by the intensity of the writing or captivated by signs of freshness and originality, she set about to discover the roots of the inspiration by seeking to know, on her own terms, the authors and artists as well as editors and publishers, whom she held accountable for format and design. Consequently, her criticism was illuminated by a sense of kinship with those secret inner wells of being that give artists and authors their power and their distinctive coloration. As for the writers dead and gone, she delved and dug for every scrap of information about them, biographical and critical, read their books in toto with the zeal of an avid scholar, and in her travels trudged the country paths and city streets they had walked in their lifetimes. She retrieved them from the dead past, presenting them as living personalities, breathing, palpable, and relevant, in her lectures to students at Pratt and later to the staff of the children's librarians in New York. George MacDonald, Laura E. Richards, Washington Irving, Sarah Orne Jewett, Julia Horatia Ewing, Henry Longfellow—what gifts she made of them!

At the Pratt Institute Free Library, in 1896, the first subject marked for investigation in the mind of ACM was childhood itself. The children's room had been functioning for only a few months when Anne took charge of it. Neighborhood children came in large numbers, the novelty of the adventure of taking one's own books off the shelves still bright and exciting, and there were crowds of children of diversified backgrounds demanding the services of the new librarian. But ACM was not content to observe only the children within the environs of the library. She was determined to know all she possibly could about childhood. She went where the children were: to the schools, the settlement houses, and the streets—New York as well as Brooklyn, the area of her investigation.

Chief among the innovations in education at that time was the kindergarten, first recognized as a part of public education in the United States in 1873. The movement, predating nursery-school programs, was based on the philosophy of its founder, the German educator Friedrich Wilhelm Froebel, who held that the education of young children between the ages of four and six should derive from the natural instincts and activities of the children themselves. Play was the keynote of the schema. The profession attracted numbers of teachers who by an excess of enthusiasm created a stereotype of the kindergarten teacher as a person dedicated to the service of children but often sentimental in her approach to them.

The settlement-house movement in America, an outgrowth of a philosophy of social service originating in England in 1884 with the founding of London's Toynbee Hall, was initiated in New York in 1886, when the Neighborhood Guild Settlement House was established, later becoming the University Settlement. Jane Addams' famed Hull House in Chicago came into existence in 1889. The turmoil of the industrial cities that swallowed up the great migrations of people from Middle and Eastern Europe in the years spanning the nineteenth and twentieth centuries was alleviated and given a modicum of order through the work of the settlement houses with their programs of athletics, drama, informal education, their social clubs, and their concern for the Americanization of the hordes of seeking people.

From her first exploration of these haunts of children, Anne acquired a knowledge of child psychology and behavior and studied at the same time the varieties of approaches to children on the part of the adults who worked with them. Her mind was so honed to the differentiation between these concerns with children as to give her own liminal profession—Library Work with Children—distinctive form and clear direction.

The reports of Miss Moore's decade at Pratt, together with certain articles she wrote for professional journals, reveal the sunrise of her vision "a ribbon at a time." A portion of the first annual report, ending June 30, 1897, runs:

> The order of the room has constantly improved, and certain of the older children have been of much assistance in making the social atmosphere of the room what it should be.
>
> Nevertheless, there is nothing of the school about the Children's Library. As one boy expressed it, "It's better'n any school 'cause you don't have to learn anything if you don't want to." Our part is of course to lead them to "want to," and to make the caring as easy and as agreeable as possible by providing quiet and ready assistance and the best books.
>
> For, after all, the library should not forget that its true

function in the work of education is to provide the means found in books and instruction in their use. Let us use kindergarten methods as far as they help us to this end, and by all means let us have the kindergarten spirit; but let us not turn the Children's Library into a kindergarten, a creche, or a club. Clubs may easily grow out of the Children's Library, and it is most desirable that they should; but the Library itself should be sought as a mental resource, it seems to us, and if we can educate one generation of children to regard it in this way, the problem of self-education is not far from being solved. . . .

Our whole doctrine, in fact, may be summed up by this: Make routine subservient to the gaining of the main object, and take time to judge when it is proper to make exceptions to the rules. Of course we are liable to the feeling of over-much responsibility that all sociological work brings to the worker; but we try to preserve patience and serenity and to realize that the books themselves are accomplishing much. . . .

The report of 1898 reveals the first appearance of the pledge which later became established practice in the New York Public Library. To this day, every child, on receiving a library card in the New York Public Library, writes his name beneath a pledge in an impressive, large black book. The Pratt version read as follows:

By writing my name in this register, I pledge myself to take good care of all the books I draw from this library, to pay all fines and damages rightly charged against me, and to obey all the rules of the Children's Library and Reading Room.

The ceremony of the pledge proved to be one of the strongest psychological bonds between children and their libraries. By the time ACM inaugurated it in New York, she had perfected the wording. The matter is told with simple dignity, omitting any hint of punitive action:

When I write my name in this book I promise to take good care of the books I use at home and in the library, and to obey the rules of the library.

The staffs of the children's rooms in the New York Public Library were admonished to remember that for most children library membership is their first independent act of citizenship. As such, it involves a reciprocal responsibility: the granting of a privilege and the obligation to abide by the rules that make the privilege possible. It was good to come upon confirmation of her theory as recently as 1969 in Philip Roth's tribute to the Central Library of Newark, when the existence of that library was threatened. He wrote in the *Wilson Library Bulletin* of April of that year:

Why I had to care for the books I borrowed, return them unscarred and on time, was because they weren't our property alone, they were *everybody's*.

This idea had as much to do with civilizing me as any idea I was ever to come upon in the books themselves.

The assistants in charge of registering children at entrance desks were instructed never to treat the signing of the pledge as mere routine. Time and attention were to be given to each event, with full awareness of what that moment meant to the child, no matter how long the line of children waiting to come to grips with the pledge, the pen, and the hard precision of setting one's name on a given line.

"There's something about writing your name in a big, black book that is remembered," ACM said. She lived to know the truth of it. During two world wars more than one soldier on leave or returning home from the war sought out the branch children's room of his boyhood and asked to see his name written in the book when he had first joined. What they sought—their lost child-

hood, some symbol of the past, some token of identity—
wise librarians did not seek to know but gladly dug in
basement files to find the book recording the long-gone
year.

The Children's Library at Pratt was open in the evening for the use of older children. Because of the prox-
imity of the Adult Department, circulation of books to
children with the resulting hullabaloo was not permitted
in the evening hours. Anne observed the pleasure these
children found in a place sacred to desultory reading as
well as to the serious business of "looking up things."
She resolved to reserve some corner of the library for
such pursuits during the daytime as well.

When in time the idea was translated to the New York
Public Library, increased benefits accrued from it. The
"Reading Room" of each children's library proffered
reference books, to be sure, but offered for display small
collections of costly books, rich in illustration, books
bright in their original bindings, escaping the conformity of library buckram and the ignominy of pasted book
pockets and date slips. All this was before the great plas-
tic-cover revolution! Children were free to explore fine
editions on their own and to read the pivotal books of
the years as represented in these non-circulating collections. The books were immediately available also for exhibitions, for classroom visits and book talks, or as sources
for the storyteller.

When book budgets were cut to the bone, as they
were during the 1929 depression, a token copy of the
new titles was available in reading-room collections. It
was no uncommon sight in the thin days of the thirties
to see varicolored pieces of paper o'ertopping the edges
of books on the shelves, each with the name of a child
on it, marking the places of itinerant readers. Over the

years each children's room acquired a nucleus of distinguished books. When the Second World War swept thousands of titles into the limbo of "out of print," a record of the years existed in these reading-room collections, a living, continuous history of children's books in the twentieth century.

For a person who never confessed to boredom, Anne Carroll Moore held a curious concern lest children suffer from it in their reading as well as in their often cramped and meager lives. She knew that a sustained habit of monotony can destroy the curiosity of a child, dull his powers of perception, and cripple his ability to respond to wonder and delight. The threat of dullness and disinterest she circumvented not by heaping one excitement on another but by creating a variety of events in the life of the Children's Library. Exhibitions were a continuing source of renewal, and Anne became expert in the choice of their subject matter and the manner of presentation.

> We have found it a good plan to show natural objects in the room and interest the children first in these, then in books about them. In this way the books and pictures "come real" as a little fellow expressed it.

So reads an early report.

The calendar of the year—seasons and holidays—was a natural incentive for the building of exhibitions and offered an opportunity to create appropriate and inciting reading lists. No matter how elaborate or ambitious the exhibition and the special occasions staged around it, the objective of reading was never forgotten. All activity was subservient to that ideal and served only to enlarge and heighten the private pleasure of the book.

The scope of the exhibitions grew with the years and came to include the interests of the librarian as well as those of the children who thus found themselves involved in such matters as *Queen Victoria and Her Reign* and *Japanese Prints and the Art of Japan.* The exhibition of Japanese prints in the Pratt Children's Library turned the minds of all observers to Japan. Mr. A. M. Kashiwa, whom Anne had consulted as authority, visited the room often, enchanting the children with the formality of his friendship and the grace and ritual of his bows.

The Spanish-American War was foremost in the minds of Americans in 1899. The hard fact of war Anne translated into an exhibition on heroism. For the climactic event, which she often introduced midway of an exhibition, she invited Dr. C. Hanford Henderson, director of the Pratt Institute High School, to speak to the children on heroism. The boys and girls discussed the subject among themselves, and some expressed themselves in writing. Certain statements, deemed by Anne to be significant, were preserved in the chronicles of the library.

One lad of fourteen, an ardent reader at Pratt since his eleventh year, commented on the subject in this fashion:

> In ancient times a brave man only was a hero but now, in modern times, a hero has to be both brave and good morally and virtually.

His interest in the Children's Library outlived his childhood. When he had gone off to college at Cornell and later to Germany to study, he asked that the plant he had once given his mother as a birthday gift be taken to the Children's Library. There it stood in a southern window, overlooking the playground—a living reminder of that shy and serious boy who named the toy boats he sailed in Prospect Park after characters from the *Leather Stocking Tales.*

These "innovations" are not outmoded. Certain immutable truths emerge from a long perusal of the reports of ACM's decade at Pratt. They are pertinent to the world today, even necessary as counterattack on the dilemma of the overstimulated, "outer-directed," fast-paced, increasingly mechanized life of the contemporary child. The need for a place of one's own in a public institution still exists for children. The chance to see and hear interesting adults in the reality of flesh and blood, to meet them on terms of equality outside the instructional environment of home and school, without the interruptions of commercials—this remains for children an experience that dignifies them as persons and touches their imaginations with quickening immediacy.

As for the art of making an exhibit, ACM was to write on that topic with verve and solid good sense in one of her lead editorials for her page of criticism—"The Three Owls" of the New York *Herald Tribune*—in the issue of January 27, 1929. Since it is not included in the three volumes she herself culled from the pages of "The Three Owls," it deserves the permanency of print here.

We hear a good deal about creative reading and writing, creative art and creative education, but we are still too often bored by static and ill-chosen exhibitions of books and prints.

Interested, as I am, in the whole subject of children's books and in the manner of their evolution and production, I am not inspirited by the sight of precious and perishable little Newbery and Isaiah Thomas volumes stretched painfully wide open one against another, lying flat like pressed flowers in black, coffin-like exhibition cases with no point of contrast or living historical association. Neither the collector's instinct nor the cataloguer's meticulous arrangement achieves the kind of exhibition one likes to look at for sheer pleasure of looking—the kind of exhibition that draws one back for another look before it is too late—the kind from which one brings away ideas. Since New Year's I have been five times to see the exhibition of children's books at the Grolier Club arranged by Ruth Granniss, librarian of the club, with the assistance of Mrs. Haight.

As an exhibition of the subject for the special student it is by no means complete; as an introduction of it to the casual visitor, as a reminder to the historian or scholar that children's books have a place in the scheme of things, as a tonic for jaded authors, artists, publishers, librarians or booksellers it is delightfully free from the besetting sins of book exhibitions in general. It is so well placed that it is possible to take in the plan of it at a glance, yet it achieves variety, continuity, color, freshness and contrast, as well as definite chronology stretching from the Gutenberg Bible, and illustrated German and Italian editions of Aesop dated 1480 and 1485, to the Ernest Shepard originals for Winnie the Pooh.

The majority of the books stand up in groups composed of their kind rather than lie down in rows so similar as all to look alike. The standing arrangement is made possible by the deep three-tier cases of glass shelving about the walls of the room. The effectiveness and variety in the presentation of the subject are the fruit of years of experience in the selection of rare books and prints applied to the subject too seldom related to such liberal sources. [Mrs.] Granniss admitted that she had had her doubts about being able to make this exhibit definitely interesting and admitted that it had taken a good deal of time and a vast amount of daily weeding while assembling the material. Any true exhibition has to grow under the eye and the hand until it takes on form and meaning. It is a fascinating form of art, that of exhibition making, whether achieved with a single book or manuscript like this or groups of books in library or bookshop.

Once the Children's Library was established as a focal point in the community, ACM turned her attention to the neighborhood schools, seeking ways of serving teachers and pupils alike within the limitations of the library resources.

In the *Library Journal* of April 1902—Helen Haines was editor of the publication at that time—there appeared an article written by Miss Moore entitled "Visits to Public Schools." It chronicles experience so universal in the lives of children's librarians at one point or another as to be timeless in interest and in the wisdom of its conclusions.

> The subject of co-operation between librarian and schools from the standpoint of the supply of books and methods of circulating them has been admirably presented from time to time by librarians who have been doing organized work with schools for many years. The object of this paper is to present the social side of the most admirable experience in unorganized work with the elementary schools of a large city. . . .

There follow accounts of the number of public schools in Brooklyn, the relationship between Pratt Library and the newly established Brooklyn Public Library and the status of cooperation with the schools, which was practically nonexistent. The report continues:

> We were not prepared to supply school duplicates nor to send books to the schools.
>
> We were prepared to receive the teachers and the children at the library and to give them every possible means of assistance in connection with their school work as well as in their general reading. Our problem then was to make children and teachers really want to come.
>
> We wrote letters of invitation to school principals and teachers, telling them that the library would be glad to lend assistance in various branches of the school work, particularly in the study of English, in nature study, history, geography, etc. The letters sent to school principals received little more notice than a general circular. They

were usually read at the opening exercises of the school and were sometimes passed about among the teachers. The letters sent to individual teachers brought more satisfactory results. Many of them visited the library and procured application blanks for their classes and teachers' cards for themselves.

In order to get a better idea of actual conditions in the schools and a better knowledge of the reading ability of the average child in a given grade, it was decided that the children's librarian should visit five representative schools noted upon our list. Out of the 130 schools 50 at least have been represented in our records.

The school visits began in the principal's office, where half a precious morning was sometimes spent before an opportunity of speaking to the chief functionary could be granted. The visitor was invariably treated with great politeness, the library was spoken of as an important part of an admirable institution doing noble educational work, but there was no apparent desire on the school side for a union of forces. The request to visit certain classes was readily granted, and the principal frequently offered to conduct the visitor through the building. One such visit, at the very beginning of the work, filled her with great awe of the "system." The tour of the building was made in breathless haste, and there was no time for visits to the class room. We simply rushed through the rooms. How might one hope to penetrate walls of apparent impenetrability and really come to know the inmates? That even such a visit might have results was a great surprise but was evidenced by the return of one of our old boys with several new ones, who were introduced after this fashion:

"These fellers here want to join. I told 'em about the lib'ry. I left my card here and forgot all about it. When I saw our principal *chase* you through our school yesterday I thought I'd like to belong again. I told the teacher you was from Pratt's, and she said she guessed she would come to the lib'ry some day. She's never seen it." . . .

From this introductory round of visits we gathered a good deal of practical information concerning the conditions under which public school work is done and the various ways of doing it, as expressed by the personalities of the teachers as well as by the attitude of the children. We enlarged our circle of acquaintance very appreciably and found here and there a teacher with the book sense and the child sense so united that her work was an inspiration. . . .

A year later . . . the visitor presented herself at one of these same schools, feeling sure that this time she would be asked to say something to the children.

Vain hope! The principal received her with the most polite expressions of interest and said he himself would take great pleasure in speaking of the exhibition [in the library] at the opening exercises of the school, to which no invitation was extended.

On her way down stairs the visitor, feeling very dubious about ever making what she considered successful school visits, was attracted by the strains of a violin. Looking through the stairway window she saw an old man, with the sunniest smile, standing in the midst of a room full of happy-faced children and drawing his bow across his fiddle as if he loved it and could not help it. Presently they all began to sing, quite naturally and spontaneously. One felt at once, even through dingy glass, that the relations were absolutely harmonious between the children, the teacher, and the old violin player.

A teacher who passed on the stairs was asked if the old man came often to the school.

"Oh, yes," she said, "he teaches the children music and they look forward to his coming with the greatest delight." The incident, trivial though it may seem, was full of suggestion for the matter at hand. It was quite evident, if he had any other business the old violin player had left it all behind when he came into the school room. He came to make music, and he played till the children wanted to sing. While we cannot hope to strike the same chord with library books and library privileges that is reached by a violin note, for the charm of music is more subtle than the charm of books, may we not hope to so master the technique of our subject as to be able to present its essence as the violin player presented his melody, rather than the exercises which have made more perfect melody possible?

Books must seem to us like real life, and human experiences must seem like chapters from unwritten books.

There is a certain technique of library visits to schools which seems to me to consist in taking things exactly as one finds them and adapting one's self so completely and cheerfully to the situation, whether it means sitting in an office, standing in a passage way, rushing through class rooms, receiving polite but immediate dismissal, or having pleasant talks with children and teachers, as to make it seem the most natural experience in the world while it lasts, and to make it the basis for future experiences. Theories, methods, the habit of looking too early for results, and above all, an aggressive or a too retiring personality, must be got rid of at any cost if we are to beget a love for books and win confidence and respect for our ways of giving them into the hands of those who want them, or who may be induced to want them. . . .

Always diligent in her pursuit of the dramatic as a means of increasing the pleasure of children in books, ACM found storytelling a bright promise of rich associative experience for the children at Pratt. From the beginning of her work she had taken advantage of every opportunity to talk to children about reading and to speak to them out of her own enthusiasm and discoveries in the evening when the room was closed to the circulation of books. She often read aloud. A splendid reader she, to the end of her days, the voice alive, alert to every nuance of meaning, paced to perfection, and never a tinge of artificiality in it. She related to them events in her own life and in the life of her father and told them about the boyhood of Frederick Pratt, the founder of the Pratt Institute, and of his childhood spent in the region where they themselves now enjoyed a library. The children's response was immediate. They described such periods of conversation as times of "telling things."

It must be remembered that storytelling as it is known today did not exist in the early 1900s. The mode of the day was something known as elocution, painful in its gaucheries of overdramatization and rampant sentimentality. These were anathema to Anne. She was sensitive too to the difference between telling things and teaching things, recognizing that children resent, particularly in the freedom of the library, any hint of being purposefully and systematically instructed.

With her usual thoroughness, she began to experiment with storytelling and to expand the range of special occasions staged for the children at Pratt. One program was devoted to the subject of dogs, and only boys and girls who owned dogs were given a ticket of admission. At another time Dan Beard, that genius of *The Boys' Handbook* and a founder of the Boy Scouts of America, was the star performer, the audience limited to boys who had known and used his books. She searched among students at Pratt in the kindergarten training class and other departments for people whom she felt might have a gift for storytelling or for talking directly to children of their own experiences with such conviction as to involve the listeners in the intensity of their initial emotion.

Why ACM did not herself attempt storytelling remains a secret unrevealed. She held an uncanny rapport with children, her response to the dramatic was eager and intuitive, and certainly she was endowed with the gifts of a natural storyteller. Perhaps some New England reticence constrained her. That she was dedicated to storytelling and to those who could tell stories to good effect was demonstrated throughout the years of her professional life.

In the *Library Journal* of April 1905 there is her account of the experiments at Pratt, touching on such practical matters as the arrangement of seating, size of groups, the control of the audience by school grade, age, or interest, including consideration of the inspirational heights to which storytellers aspire as well as reporting on the measured and proven results of tale-telling. At one point in the article ACM gives an account of a Christmas story hour to which she had invited a kindergarten teacher as storyteller. The guest performer arrived bringing with her three students in training. All four of them told stories. The brief paragraph describing this incident reveals one source of ACM's fascination, the antithetical turn of her mind. She could speak extensively of fairy godmothers, the lighting of wishing candles or of other small rituals in her private mythology and in the same breath pronounce so solid and so sensible a judgment as to thrust the bemused reader or listener into the cold shock of common sense.

> After the storyteller had gone, the children lingered to say Merry Christmas and I lighted them out at the door telling them they might wish on the candle as they passed under it and that when they had all gone, I would blow out their wishes which they must not tell until they came true. I would not advise inviting more than one person to tell stories on the same evening. It gives to the story hour too much of the nature of an entertainment.

Typical of many of ACM's reports, her conclusions transcend the time in which they appeared.

> Generalization from particular experience is a dangerous thing unless that experience is grounded upon principles strong enough to withstand the shock of change of circumstance or condition. I am fully aware that such a story hour as I have described would not fit every library. If it had been made with that intention it would not fit in the place where it belongs. I firmly believe, however, that

some kind of a story hour is both physically possible and highly desirable in every library where work with children is being done, whether it be a small and poor library or a rich and institutionalized one. The first essential is that someone shall believe in it heart and soul, and since the weight of that belief lies far back in childhood, there is no alternative but to get back into one's own childhood; the next step is to muster all one's resources and prepare to make them tell toward the desired object; and finally, to take all the things one is unable to do personally, find people who can do them and so order the work that it will seem an easy and a pleasant thing to come into it as a story-teller. It need not take eight years to make the start —eight months or even eight weeks might be sufficient in a town where one had lived always and in such relation with people as to know their real gifts and to be able to claim a share in them. I have given emphasis to the presence of flowers, pictures, lighted candles and other things which might be considered non-essentials to story-teller and to children. If to another they seem trivial I can only say "I see it so," for I believe the final test of every story hour will be, not whether the story was perfectly told, but whether it was told in a way to create associations in the minds of the children that will abide with them forever.

The definitive event which was to fix for all time in Anne's mind the image of perfection in storytelling was being staged in 1900 in the fashionable ballroom of Sherry's[1] in Manhattan, put to use in the afternoons as the setting for a series of polite lectures on varied topics and gentle recitals by *artistes*. The impresario of these occasions was a Mrs. Charlotte Osgood Mason, who as early as 1900 had been importuned by Dr. Earl Barnes[2] to present in recital a certain Marie Shedlock of England. He had spoken of her as "an elocutionist," and consequently Mrs. Mason had avoided meeting her as long as she possibly could. The day came when meet her she must. She found herself confronted by a petite and beautiful woman of charming presence whose manner of speech was music to the ear, the accent English with certain intonations that were unmistakably French.

A remarkable woman, Marie Shedlock, who at the age of forty-five abandoned teaching in one of London's most successful public day schools for girls to launch herself in the professional world as a lecturer and to emerge eventually as a performer of rare subtlety and grace. Since she was born in Boulogne of English parentage, educated in France and Germany, hers was an international childhood. Her father's profession made it mandatory for the family to move about the countries of Europe. He was an engineer and at one time was involved in the construction of the first railroad in France, built under the direction of the English engineering genius, Isambard Brunel.

When Marie Shedlock came to America, she had in her repertoire one lecture, "The Fun and Philosophy of Hans Christian Andersen." She told certain of Andersen's stories in the course of her talk, and in this storytelling Mrs. Mason recognized a unique talent. In her small person Marie Shedlock combined the French mastery of precise and polished gesture, a heritage from the Continental theater of mime, with the English habit of literature and storytelling as distinct from dramatic reading. These were the gifts she brought to bear upon the humor, pathos, and poetic irony of H. C. Andersen. Seldom has his genius been as richly served.

"I was completely captivated," wrote Mrs. Mason in her memoirs of the affair, "and felt there could be nothing more beautiful to do for the precise and hide-bound little children of the social set in New York than to have some afternoon at Sherry's with little Marie telling her stories in her inimitable way."

The critics acclaimed Marie Shedlock as well as did

the children. "Every tale of the seven was admirably chosen and admirably told," wrote the critic of the New York *Morning Post,* "simply and with little gesture, but every now and then some delicious little bit of hokus-pokus, worthy of Madam Yvette Guilbert." [3]

From 1900 until 1907, Marie Shedlock toured the United States, going as far inland as Iowa, loving the Midwest and finding herself beloved there.

It was not ACM who encountered Miss Shedlock at Sherry's but Mary Wright Plummer. She lost no time in presenting her as speaker to the trustees and faculty members at Pratt in the year 1902. She came again the following year to tell stories to the children in the Children's Library. In 1906, when Anne was at the beginning of her work in the New York Public Library, Marie Shedlock appeared once more at Pratt, this time telling Hans Christian Andersen's "The Nightingale." Among her listeners was a student in the library school, Anna Cogswell Tyler, who was enchanted with what she heard and decided then and there on the direction her life was to take: she would become a storyteller. She it was who two years later was chosen by ACM to head up storytelling in the New York Public Library. For this reason, Anne was to write in "The Three Owls" in 1927:

> Storytelling in the New York Public Library has its roots in Miss Shedlock's rendering of "The Nightingale" twenty-five years ago.

For this reason, too, the birthday of Miss Shedlock is celebrated in the New York Public Library. On the fifth of May, or thereabouts, the storytellers gather at Staten Island, where there are still patches of green surrounding certain of the branch libraries and even a garden here and there, to hear stories told, one by a gifted experienced storyteller on the staff and others by newcomers to the scene. It is an occasion observed with a tradition and ceremony of its own, marking the end of the winter storytelling in branch libraries and the beginning of the hot city summer when the storytellers take to city parks and playgrounds, heroic troopers that they are, to tell their stories to children.

It is not clear at what point the friendship between Anne and Marie Shedlock developed, but it probably occurred sometime within the period of Miss Shedlock's first American tour. Letters passed between them in a faithful stream as long as Miss Shedlock lived, and hers was a long life. As was the custom with ACM, she bestowed names of her own contriving on certain of her cherished intimates, holding with W. H. Auden that "It is our right and duty, as it was Adam's, to give names to all things, and to any thing or creature which arouses our affection, we desire to give a proper name." [4] Because Miss Shedlock often appeared in recitals wearing a costume reminiscent of the French *Ma Mère l'Oye*, the peaked hat of the traditional fairy godmother on her silver hair, Anne spoke of her as the Fairy Godmother of Storytelling in America. Needless to say, the not infrequent use of the title annoyed those who could not stomach such play of fancy in the midst of articles of serious criticism and analysis. But Marie Shedlock was not without gifts of her own in this jest of accolade by name. "Pony" was the term of endearment by which she addressed Anne. How she happened on this choice is not known, but something of the stamina and steadfastness usually associated with the small and slender-boned beast, the pony, is somehow appropriate, and ponies too are of the breed of Pegasus.

Marie Shedlock returned to America in 1915, escaping the heartbreak of war in England, to undertake a second lecture tour, having added to her accomplishment her book *The Art of the Story Teller*, a classic in its field. That tour was conceived in the mind of ACM. She organized it with the help of a committee she herself chose, and gathered together funds for financing it so that the maximum amount of profit might accrue to Marie Shedlock. The multitudinous details of schedules in Boston, Philadelphia, and Pittsburgh, transportation, fees, the hiring of suitable halls, publicity, the supervision of program printing, the selling of tickets—all this she blithely accomplished with such help as she could muster from her office and staff in the New York Public Library.

For five years Anne sheltered, in one way or another, upheld, and promoted Marie Shedlock in the United States. Not until 1920 did Miss Shedlock return to England, too ill at the last to fulfill her scheduled final recital. Nothing daunted, ACM sold tickets for an imaginary recital and sent after her a "Fairy Ship" of messages from hundreds of people all over the world and with it a "small gift of gold."

Once more she was to inaugurate a great scheme in behalf of Marie Shedlock. It was ACM, working through Anne Morgan's Committee for Devastated France, who arranged in 1922 to have Miss Shedlock return to France to visit the libraries established by the committee. There the delighted villagers, children and adults alike, gathered in the barrack schools and libraries in huts set amid the wrecked and dismal aftermath of war, to hear "Fée Marraine" tell her stories in their own tongue.

From a scrap of paper on which ACM had written some largely illegible notes on Miss Shedlock, a few sentences emerge with clarity:

No one who has ever heard her will forget her, whether dressed in the traditional robes of a fairy godmother or in the lovely silver brocade chosen for her by Ellen Terry herself or in the everyday cloak and hat in which she walked the streets of American cities and towns and entered the *baraque* schools of war-stricken villages in France.

A List of Books Recommended for a Children's Library is hardly a title to stir the blood, but to hold in one's hand the tattered twenty-one-page pamphlet by that name, prepared for the Iowa Library Commission in 1902, is to be deeply moved, as is often true when one stumbles upon some token of a beginning destined for significant fulfillment. "With a Few Practical Suggestions as to the Selection and Purchase of Children's Books," the subtitle continues. "Compiled by Annie Carroll Moore, Children's Librarian, Pratt Free Institute Library, Brooklyn, New York, and instructor of the Iowa Summer School."

It was Alice Tyler, the noted head of Iowa's State Library Commission, who enticed Anne to the Midwest on a teaching assignment for three consecutive summers —1902 to 1905. The book list was the capstone of that venture.

How few the books worthy of mention in 1902 as being appropriate for the expenditure of funds in a public library. Twelve titles in the picture-book section by seven artists, but two of the seven were French: Boutet de Monvel and Vimar. This consideration of foreign picture books was revolutionary in 1902 and gives early promise of ACM's regard for the pictorial no matter what language the text might employ. The foreword to the list is full of suggestions for book selections in the library, with great emphasis put on the necessity for du-

plication of good titles rather than using titles which
have only a modicum of worth. Interesting, too, is her
observation that

> Children's literature as a whole has not yet been cast
> into sufficiently permanent form to make it seem possible
> to compile a brief general list which shall have more than
> timely interest or value; and therefore many of the books
> entered in this list should be replaced by better books
> on the same subjects as soon as better books are pub-
> lished. . . .
>
> When the necessity for duplication is clearly recognized
> in starting children's libraries, and the best books to meet
> the conditions are selected for duplication and a sufficient
> number of duplicates is provided to give every child the
> right book at the right time the problem of children's
> reading will be solved. This solution cannot be reached,
> however, until we have something approximating perma-
> nent literature for children, and that we shall *never* have if
> we base the selection of children's books on the ephemeral
> interests of children rather than on the fundamental inter-
> ests of child nature.

The Iowa list contained no notes, with one exception,
the *Heart of Oak Books* in six volumes. But in that one
note the art of annotation of which ACM was master is
clearly discerned. Brilliant in its brevity, describing scope
and content of the books, it conveys at the same time the
larger purpose of reading itself:

> A collection of traditional rhymes and stories for children,
> and of master-pieces of poetry and prose for use at home
> and in school, chosen with special reference to the cultiva-
> tion of the imagination and the development of a taste for
> good reading.

" 'Choosing is creating'—an ancient Persian proverb,"
according to a scrap of paper on which ACM wrote the
words, turning it loose in a melee of scribbled disorder,

her sure-fire system for preserving aphorism and quotations she judged memorable. For Anne the choosing of titles for a list was an act of creation commanding the full powers of mind and spirit and revealing the tone, conviction, knowledge, and judgment of the compiler. Her own lists were vivid and rich in their variety. She knew everything about the books she chose and a great deal about the men and women who wrote them. The annotations, sure and incisive, reveal the separate and distinctive gifts each book proffers the seeking reader. As with well nigh every piece of work Anne accomplished, the prevailing mood governing it can be defined in one word—exhilaration. Take, for example, her "Seven Stories High," created originally as an accompaniment to an article on reading for Compton's Pictured Encyclopedia in 1932. Books for a child's own library was its theme. It appeared as a distinctive reprint year after year, the revisions being made by ACM throughout the years of its publication. In all probability it influenced more homes, schools, libraries, and bookshops than any other book list of its era, and more than one school of librarianship used it as a text of perfection. The annual appearance of her "Children's Books Suggested As Holiday Gifts" issued by the New York Public Library represented her wise and discerning choice of the year's output, and publishers, authors, and artists alike hoped beyond hope that the books for which they were responsible would find a place on the Christmas lists of her choosing (1918–1941).

In the matter of lists, as in many other professional concerns, Anne's mentor was Caroline M. Hewins, that redoubtable New Englander, librarian of the Hartford Public Library, who had fallen in love with libraries through diligent use of the institutions in the course of her work for a Mr. William Seavey, principal of a school, for whom she did research at the Boston Atheneum. She became the conscience of the American Library Association as far as work with children was concerned.

"What are you doing to encourage a love of reading in boys and girls?" she asked of twenty-five leading libraries in 1882 and, in the light of their own poor showing, stirred up action and reaction in many places. That same year, 1882, saw the publication of Miss Hewins' *List of Books for Boys and Girls*, published by the American Library Association, of which ACM wrote in *Roads to Childhood:*

> It was out of print before my time but I look upon the discovery of a stray copy of it as a milestone on the long path leading up to the appraisal of children's books.

ACM attended Miss Hewins' lectures as a student at Pratt when the reading of children was not uppermost in her mind. However, when she herself entered the world of children's books, she found in Caroline Hewins a sympathetic counselor and a continuing source of wisdom.

As in the case of many other people whom Anne encountered casually or in the pursuit of a common interest, enduring ties of friendship were the result. This was a recurring refrain in Anne's relationship with numerous people. The gift of her friendship was seldom superficially bestowed or sustained. Fortune and time served only to increase the measure of her devotion. So it was with Caroline Hewins. She spoke of ACM as "Little Anne"—"Dear Little Anne," the salutation of her letters —but ACM found no need for any other appellation than the name of Caroline Hewins. Miss Hewins formed the habit of appearing in New York for Children's Book

Week celebrations and for the Halloween storytelling. Often ACM called on her to perform what she defined as her only parlor accomplishment—namely, the recitation of Peter Piper picking his peck of peppers, from A to Z. Long years after the death of Miss Hewins, ACM, presenting the famous alphabet on some occasion recalling her memory, read it aloud. Marcia Brown, noted picture-book artist of the present day, was in the audience and was inspired to make her brilliantly absurd, robust drawings for the rhymes, resulting in a distinguished picture book which she dedicated to ACM.

The decade at Pratt gave Anne Carroll Moore time in which to search *Roads to Childhood,* many of which she herself had cleared in the wilderness, pioneer that she was. These roads have been traveled ever since by librarians and by others who aspire to serve, capture, and enthrall the minds and imaginations of children through reading.

In Howard Pyle's story "The Swan Maiden," when the three impossible tasks had been accomplished and the Swan Maiden rescued from wicked enchantment, the prince found himself in possession of three magical eggs harrowed from the nest of the crow. "Take the first egg," the Swan Maiden said to him, "and break it in your hand," and he broke the first egg in his hand and there was a minute castle. "Set it on the ground," she said, and he put it on the ground. Before their eyes it grew into a splendid palace—life-size in all proportion.

So it was with ACM. A decade of experience, thought, and imaginative experimentation encapsulated in her mind a golden embryo that needed only space in which to grow to its full meaning and magnificence. Time and space were soon forthcoming.

6

AT HOME AND ABROAD

The great pleasure of travel lies in discovering whatever one has the capacity to recognize and enjoy in its own setting.

ACM

IN THE year 1897 it was considered daring and somewhat hazardous for two young women to set up housekeeping on their own. Anne Moore and Mildred Collar accomplished it and had, as Anne described it years later, "the time of our lives."

Both young women were on the staff of the Pratt Institute Library, Anne in the Children's Library, Mildred Collar a teacher in the Library School. The apartment was on the top floor of a brownstone house, 335 Lafayette Street, within walking distance of the library. Their good friend and former classmate Carolyn Weeks lived down the block in a house twin to theirs. The two places lay in easy access of each other, a brief walk across the rooftops affording a comfortable route with entrance through the skylights, eliminating the stairs.

Anne must have been responsible for the cooking, an

art she pursued with passionate devotion whenever time and opportunity were favorable. Records of the venture are infrequent, but the impression remains of much gaiety and wide and warm hospitality. Echoes of parties float through the letters she wrote to her nieces during this time. She describes, in a letter to Rachel written on April 22, 1900, an Easter Monday party:

> I spent Monday morning making cake—nut cake baked in little heart and shamrock-shaped tins; these frosted with maple sugar to melt in your mouth. I went to the library at one—worked until five and then came home to make sandwiches—chopped walnuts with mayonnaise dressing and lettuce—"love drops" and fruit punch and to help deck the house. The dining room looked very pretty with asparagus fern strewn along the walls, a grate full of wood, pine cones and green boughs; Miss Weeks' brass candlesticks on the table under the china [The china consisted of a tea set of beautiful luster ware which had belonged to Anne's grandmother and which was kept on a shelf]; green candles there and on the mantel. The punch bowl was set on a patch of ferns with cousin Alice's violets scattered over them. Dishes of green "pillows" at the corner of the table and a few of the glasses in their green and white crimped cases, all ready to serve with. The punch was the best I ever made and I think the color was lovely—from plum preserve juice (my own recipe). I'll lend it you after we get the house cleaned.

In a letter to Virginia Bowman King, written in the 1930s, the memories of those days are vivid on the page. She speaks of Carolyn Weeks, saying, "She and I always had a May party in our apartment for library school students when we drowned their cares in a superlative fruit punch and in English poetry."

As recently as 1962 those parties came to light in the seventy-fifth anniversary issue of the *Pratt Alumnus*. In that number old graduates had been invited to contribute

brief accounts of their recollections of days at Pratt. Mrs.
Berth Trube Dean, graduate of the Library School, class
of 1900, wrote:

> The most vivid impression was of two dynamic, radiant
> young women—apparently close friends—whose memory
> and friendship I have carried through life: Anne Carroll
> Moore and Mildred Collar. Miss Moore was head of the
> Children's Library which she had organized in a charac-
> teristically attractive room a few years previously. The
> class for children's librarians was a revelation, for it pio-
> neered many new fields—including the physical features of
> children's rooms. But the appraisal and selection of the
> books themselves was the main thing; and this involved the
> appraisal of the author, editor, illustrator, translator and
> other points until then hidden. I can still feel the inspira-
> tion of Miss Moore's guidance. She had an imaginative
> quality, hard to catch in a practical way but so out-reach-
> ing . . . as to take one on wings. At the same time, for the
> more realistic-minded she could be baffling to frustration.
> She planned activities outside class to imbue us (I think)
> with the joy of youth. We had, for instance, a May Day
> party with a May Queen. Always something that had a
> touch of beauty. In the spring, also, she and Miss Collar
> took us out to the swamps of Long Island to gather wild
> azalea and hear the marsh birds sing.

It was Mildred Collar who conceived an idea and gave
it voice—the year, 1901. "We need a change of scene,"
she declared and suggested a trip to England, Scotland,
and Ireland. They counted their money. It amounted to
three hundred dollars apiece. With this fortune in their
pockets they set sail from New York on July 13, returning by the same ship nine weeks later. On the day
before they sailed, July 12, Anne's birthday, they closed
the apartment and went to Manhattan to stay the night
at Everett House. A Mr. Upjohn (whose identity remains unknown) took them to dinner and afterward to
the Victories Paradise Gardens on Forty-second Street,

where they enjoyed a variety show that included, as Anne reported in the first entry of her traveler's journal, "A clever ventriloquist, musical dogs, a shocking Italian dancer and a very tame wire-walking."

On the day of sailing, "M. [Mildred] woke with a sick headache"—an entry that was to recur often in the journal. "M. was still feeling badly at ten o'clock so I called a hansom and we drove to the boat, stopping at Lord & Taylors to pick up a parcel."

Friends were dockside and streamed over the ship, including Aunt Carrie and the Blairs, the Scottish family whose son, as a small boy, was one of the children in the library whom Anne was to hold in her memory all her life. The voyage was not a markedly pleasant one. "M." recovered from her headache, but by three o'clock of the day they sailed the sea had turned rough and Anne endured her first attack of seasickness, a plague that was spasmodically to make her wretched throughout the voyage.

There were few congenial people aboard. Anne concerned herself with the children among them. She filled the pages of her journal with accounts of weather, the moods of the sea, the stars at night, and the shifting, silent clouds by day. But intermittently there appeared sharp vignettes of passengers observed, especially those who sat at the table with them.

> Mr. Malkey and son are from Texas on a tour to the Continent and the Holy Land. Mr. M, a very warm-hearted and interesting man, with tales of the Ku Klux to tell. He isn't quite fifty but looks a good fifteen years older, has had nine children and amassed a considerable fortune and he says after this trip he shall feel that he can turn up his toes to the daisies and die with a clear conscience.
>
> He hasn't shaved since he came on board and both he and the boy are so thinly clad, they look half frozen most

of the time. They eat from the dish nearest at hand whether it is raisins or turnips, figs or baked beans. The boy is a lanky thing all arms and legs and often begins his meal with ice cream.

Eleven days at sea! The ship landed in Glasgow on July 24, and the real adventure began. No thought of making reservations had apparently entered the minds of the two travelers. They put their trust in a system of Temperance Hotels known to abound throughout the British Isles. As soon as they cleared customs they went by cab to Glasgow's Waverly Temperance Hotel. It was filled up, the city being *en fête* and crowded because of the Glasgow International Exhibition. One of the stewards on shipboard had taken the precaution of furnishing them with an address in case of emergency, so they went straightway to 24 St. Vincent Crescent and came upon a lovely, clean house with a big brass bell and brass plate on the door, the name Mrs. Croel inscribed thereon. Mrs. Croel appeared, "A fine old lady with high white cap, followed by a frolicsome kitten which leaped upon my neck three or four times before I could get away," Anne reports. But there were no rooms there. They were passed on to a Miss Granger nearby, where they found a room, with breakfast, for half a crown each. But such a room! Anne describes it:

> A large room, furnished as a dining room—a huge sideboard (really a fine piece of furniture) taking up nearly one side of a great, square room—two big windows with green blinds inside, a mantel shelf on the other side and further along a very untidy-looking bed, a long dining table covered with red felt in the center of the room, a big sofa across one corner—some heavy chairs and pictures hung thick all over the walls: oil paintings, chromos, photographs of the royal family and Miss Granger's family intermingled with heads in various poses. . . .

. . . We sat down in the general untidyness—the room had not been swept nor dusted and sheets and pillow slips were very dirty—feeling thankful to be settled anywhere for we were rocking from the motion of the steamer and confused with the strange sights as we had been driven through the city.

By tram, charabanc, coach, cab, and steamer they toured Scotland: Edinburgh, Callander, the Trossachs, Oban, Ayr (to see the cottage of Robert Burns. ACM did not like it—"too fixed up," she reported), enduring their fortunes in hostelry, fair and foul, with great good nature. Anne was the cannier of the two regarding matters of business and arrangement. It was she who inquired at hotels concerning rates, rejecting out of hand the more costly, and it was she who made initial inspection of rooms before Mildred disembarked from whatever conveyance accommodated them at the time. Always believing in the luck of the lone adventurer, Anne often wandered off on haphazard jaunts by herself, leaving Mildred to her own devices, which were likely to be founded on Baedeker. They were both splendid walkers. "Eight miles there and back" was as nothing to them, equipped as they were with short walking skirts and fortified with buns and Abernathy biscuits. The sharpness of their hunger is reflected in Anne's journal, which is peppered with accounts of culinary triumphs and disasters.

We took a tram to Princes Street and went to the Edinburgh Cafe where we had a most satisfying luncheon: one order of mutton cutlets, one of mushroom cutlet (there are two to each), one of salmon mayonnaise we might have dispensed with. I had a glass of delicious milk and a spice cake while M. had tea. . . .

Dinner was served at seven. Tomato soup, roast mutton, boiled potatoes, pear and raspberry jelly with whipped cream in the middle. Delicious. Crackers and cheese. . . .

Miss B. gave us tea downstairs. Bad marmalade, poor bread—made better by toasting at our suggestion—and the only two biscuits she had in the house. . . .

A gray morning on the water. Breakfast at 7:30. Ham and eggs wilted by the cooking. Paid twelve shillings for this decayed hospitality.

After Scotland came the Lake Country, London itself, and Ireland the last bit before the journey home. Anne kept a journal of the Irish visit in a small notebook especially bound in green moire silk, but aside from a spirited account of the horse show in Dublin, her joy on catching sight of the Limerick hills from the train, and a magnificent breakfast at Cork ("Porridge, boiled salmon, bacon and sausage, toast and marmalade—coffee pretty weak"), the record of Ireland is one of sights the usual tourist sees.

We hurried back to our car (from Blarney Castle) and were driven back to Cork by another road past St. Ann's of the Shadows but the bells didn't sound.

In spite of the Irish blood of the Moores coursing her veins, seldom in Ireland did the bells sound for Anne. It was England that proved to be her spirit's place. So it remained for her as long as she lived.

On August 2 they had started out from Keswick, England, by coach and four, the scarlet-coated driver causing Anne some uneasiness because his face was as red as his coat and his breath was heavy with the scent of whiskey.

The four horses pulled each a different way and the hill leading out of Keswick was tremendous. He raced the horses all the way up and we clung to the seats. He proved to be a fine driver and the ride was most beautiful. We stopped at the little old church at Wythburn, and went in-

side. We came down over a long hill into the vale of Grasmere and drove up before the Rothary Hotel about six
thirty (in the evening).

The hotel, Anne discovered, was much too costly. She
left M. sitting in front of its door while she set out to
find lodgings. Someone had given her an address, but on
inquiry Anne discovered that the house had been sold to
an artist who had no interest in letting lodgings. The man
in the shop where Anne had made inquiry assured her
that any house in Grasmere would be safe for two young
ladies to stay since every home was respectable. So she
went, in the summer evening, from door to door, finding
refuge at last in the Baisbrown's Book and Shoe Shop.
Mrs. Baisbrown had two sleeping rooms, front and back,
the back one having two beds: two shillings each overnight and fifteen shillings by the week, including attendance and light cooking. Anne took the back room
and went to fetch Mildred.

By seven-thirty they were dining at the Moss Hotel,
just around the corner from their lodgings, and found the
meal good and well served. M. went early to bed, but
the indefatigable Anne took a letter to the post office,
walking through the churchyard of St. Oswald's en route.
The choir boys were rehearsing. On the way back Anne
went into the little stone church to have a look at it,
choir practice being over. She talked to the organist, who
lingered there alone. It was he who spoke of the rush-
bearing service to be celebrated next evening. He urged
her to come and to see the procession "so quaint and such
an old custom," he said but did not explain.

Mildred was abed next morning, and Anne, making
sure Mildred was to have toast and tea sent up to her,
breakfasted well at the hotel and then started out on a
walk. "I spoke to everyone I met by the way," she wrote

in her journal, "and everything about the little village seemed wonderfully familiar."

Having purchased a penny volume of Wordsworth's poetry, she made straight for the churchyard, deserted at this hour of the day, and wandered there until she came upon the poet's grave. She mused there awhile, then meandered through the village, coming at last upon Dove Cottage.

> A nice old lady, Mrs. Dixon, took me in and showed me all the rooms. Very pretty, especially Wordsworth's study which opens out into the garden. Mrs. Dixon waited very patiently while I wandered about the garden and told me to pick a bit of white heather for good luck. She said she was having a hard time to get them gingerbread baked for the Rushbearing she had had so many visitors. When I asked what the Rushbearing really was she told me to sit down on the garden seat and she would tell me about it.

Anne records the tale as Mrs. Dixon told it:

> In ancient times there was no carpet to the church not even a stone floor and every year after the hay was gathered the farmers brought loads of rushes and strewed the church with them to take the place of a carpet. After the church floor was laid 'twas changed to a kind of procession. Every child in the parish has a flower piece, a cross or a wreath or what not and fetches it to the church wall about four o'clock in the afternoon—the band plays and the children march round the village with their "bearings" then they all go into the church and have service and afterwards they go to the school and each of 'em gets 2 penny worth o' gingerbread and a new sixpence. I've made the gingerbread for Rushbearing for 40 years.

All unknowing, the young ladies from Brooklyn had stumbled onto the observance of an ancient ceremony, scheduled to begin that very afternoon. Anne, having rested as she listened to Mrs. Dixon, started afresh up the hill to "The Wishing Gate" ("the second gate at the right after passing a farmhouse"). There, looking down on Grasmere Lake, she read Wordsworth's poem and made wishes of her own.

> Yea! even the Stranger from afar,
> Reclining on this moss-grown bar,
>   Unknowing, and unknown,
> The infection of the ground partakes,
> Longing for his Beloved—who makes
>   All happiness her own.

The realist Anne, having feasted Anne the romanticist on the haunts of the poet and his poetry, noted in her journal that that Wishing Gate was not mossy at all and was badly defaced with the carving of many initials. Moreover, the gingerbread she bought on her way home —Mrs. Dixon's gingerbread—"was the soft kind. Pretty heavy!"

By four o'clock the children had begun to gather near the old church wall, each with his bearing

> wrought with reeds, mosses, feathery grasses, bright-hued garden flowers and wild flowers. The old church wall bloomed from end to end.

Two hundred children marched in the procession, carrying such a variety of flower-bedecked banners, garlands, and symbolic floral pieces as to bedazzle the eye, but Anne in her journal noted and described dozens of them to the last flower and petal. After winding its way around the village, the procession marched through the doors of the church and the arches beyond, the children fanning out to place their bearings along the dim stone walls of the church interior. A brief service followed. There was the singing of the rush-bearing hymn and a short prayer. Then the children dashed to the school

yard for the distribution of pennies and gingerbread—
two squares to every child and each square bearing the
name of St. Oswald. The celebration continued through
Sunday and Monday with services in the church on the
Sabbath, and Maypole dancing, games, and contests on
Monday with the awarding of trophies and prizes.

Anne was captivated and enthralled by every part of
it. Homage to tradition was for her a law of life, and
heights of exhilaration the natural concomitant of celebration, ceremony, pageantry, and procession. In addition
there had been the children. By the end of the celebration, Anne knew scores of them by name and could
match child to parent, having conversed with many people at various stages of the proceedings. Small wonder
that Grasmere and the north of England were for her
beloved regions to which she returned on every trip to
England.

> There is I find a very definite connection between my
> childhood and girlhood in New England and my feeling
> so completely at home in the North of England as soon as
> I entered it in 1901—not as a tourist, but as one to whom
> it *belonged*—lock, stock and barrel

she wrote Bertha Miller in 1945, when they explored together the possibility of Anne's writing an autobiographi-
cal book for the Horn Book publications. She continued:

> I have always felt that way about England, and since it
> stems from literature and history rather than family, my
> childhood and youth may hold something of value to those
> who are searching for signs and values in this critical time!

Unhappily this plan came to naught. But England
loomed large in all that ACM thought, felt, and accomplished. As for the children at Pratt Free Library, shortly
after Anne's homecoming they were enjoying an exhibi-

tion of the rush-bearing ceremony and hearing from Mildred as well as Anne vivid accounts of the idyll of Grasmere.

In 1902 Anne's beloved brother Harry Vane Moore died at the age of forty-eight, leaving a young widow and two daughters. The affairs of the family were, for a time, in some disarray. Luther Moore, Anne's youngest brother, a brilliant young attorney at Saco, Maine, offered assistance at every possible point. As for Anne, she invited her sister-in-law and the two girls to make their home with her in the apartment on Lafayette Street in Brooklyn. It was a characteristically generous and highly impractical solution. However, more than once in her life, Anne flouted common sense with stunning audacity in behalf of a cause or a person important to her, and as often as not, like the seemingly foolish youngest son in all the folk and fairy tales, she brought off the affair successfully.

To the professional activity which increased for Anne as her reputation grew now was added the challenge of two young minds to be introduced to all the theater, art, books, and music that could be crowded upon them. Rachel was fourteen years old and Margaret two years younger. Anne longed to open doors to her brother's children and so she did, sacrificing reserves of strength and emotion in the process and impoverishing her pocketbook. As for the nieces, looking back on their years with Anne, their memories of the time were not altogether happy. Often they felt themselves dragged a long and tiresome way from Brooklyn to Manhattan, to operas and exhibitions that only partially held their interest. Even comforted as they were by chicken patties at Purcells and treated to other extravagant delicacies, tension and anxiety often accompanied the festivity. With

Auntie, there was the possibility of failure to respond with the degree of intensity she demanded and the subsequent endurance of her displeasure, implied though seldom spoken. They knew something of the frustration which the student at Pratt had acknowledged in her tribute to ACM. Hers was a brilliant sun, and the satellites orbiting around it rejoiced in its brilliance and governed themselves accordingly, but certain planets moving beyond that sun's circadian rhythms felt themselves deprived of an illumination which yet lay within their reach.

In the house in Brooklyn it was Anne who called the turn of events. The parties were Anne's parties. It was she who decided when the girls should appear in Kate Greenaway costumes. It was she who made up the guest list.

This was a fiercely loyal family. Anne's affection for her nieces, her great-nieces and nephews was both torment and delight to her, as it must have been for them. With the cruelty of youth, they often resented her insistence on a view of life uniquely her own, but their loyalty and love endured. As for Anne, her generosity toward them was unremitting, her faith in them unending, her love indisputable.

In her wisdom and with the years, Anne came to understand the truth of the matter. Writing to Bertha Miller, in the summer of 1939, she said:

> Perhaps the hardest thing we have to learn is that we may not judge others in terms of ourselves but rather in terms of their capacity and understanding.

7

THE NEW YORK PUBLIC LIBRARY

> *Without fee or questioning, the Public
> Library offers every living soul the cer-
> tainty of knowledge, playgrounds for the
> mind and habitation for the spirit. As soon
> as a child can enjoy pictures in a book, the
> doors open.*
>
> ANON.

THE CONCEPT of a scholarly free reference library, its
resources open to the public of New York City, first
took form in the mind of a New England lawyer and
schoolmaster. His name was Joseph Green Cogswell,
professor of geology at Harvard and assistant librarian
there from 1820 to 1823. He had been one of the group
of brilliant students at Harvard that included George
Bancroft, Edward Everett, and George Ticknor.[1] In the
company of these men he traveled to Europe and studied at German universities, noting with special interest
the resources of the great libraries he encountered there.
At Weimar the young Americans repeatedly visited

Goethe, who was at that time a lonely, aging man. Much drawn to young Cogswell, Goethe made a commemorative gift of his collected works to the Harvard Library as tribute to his friend. In later years Cogswell with Bancroft founded a famous private school, Round Hill, at Northampton, Massachusetts. When ill health forced him into partial retirement, he accepted the invitation of a New York banker, Samuel Ward, three of whose sons had been students at Round Hill, to make his home with the Ward family, thus becoming part-time tutor and full-time friend-in-residence at the fashionable address of the Wards at Broadway and Bond Street.

Through his hosts Mr. Cogswell came to know John Jacob Astor, who by this time (1838) was seventy-five years old, somewhat unhappy in his retirement, and perplexed by the problem of deciding upon a suitable memorial to himself, one that would perpetuate his memory and at the same time afford some benefit to his adopted country, he having come to America from Germany and made a great fortune in the early days of the fur trade. He had toyed with the idea of building an actual monument to himself in Washington, D.C. Then he met Mr. Cogswell, who, in a letter to a friend, reported on these matters in January 1833:

> I have seen a great deal of Mr. Astor, having dined with him twice at his own house, and three times at his son's. He is not the mere accumulator of dollars, as I supposed him; he talks well on many subjects and shows a great interest in the arts and literature. I meet Halleck[2] there often, and some other pleasant visitors.

Six months later he wrote to George Ticknor:

> Early in January Mr. Astor consulted me about an appropriation of some three or four hundred thousand dollars, which he intended to leave for public purposes, and I

urged him to give it for a library, which I finally brought him to agree to do, and I have been at work ever since, settling all the points which have arisen in the progress of the affair. It is now so nearly arranged that he has promised me to sign the last paper to-day, and if so I shall see you in Boston early next week. Had I not foreseen that this object would never have been affected unless someone had been at the old gentleman's elbow, to push him on, I should have left New York long since. It is not made public at present, but I think it will be in a week or two. In the meanwhile say nothing about it.

Public announcement was made in Boston the following week and by circuitous routes finally reached the New York papers. That was in 1838. Had Mr. Cogswell foreseen the years of delay, the dilly-dallying on the part of Mr. Astor, who with increasing age found it difficult to hold to one plan above another for any length of time, he would have lost heart completely. Meanwhile, Mr. Cogswell purchased books, made buying trips to Europe, and somehow endured the frustrations of an impatient man. In 1842, four years after the initial announcement of the plan for a library, Washington Irving, having been appointed Minister to Spain, asked Mr. Cogswell to accompany him as Secretary of the Legation. When Cogswell's departure was almost an actuality, Mr. Astor, in fear of losing his companionship and his services, promised to complete plans for the library, guaranteed Cogswell the office of Librarianship and proffered financial support for his labors meanwhile and so held him in New York. Six years later, in 1848, the library was still a nebulous possibility. In March of that year Mr. Astor died, but the library was assured existence by the terms of his will. On January 10, 1854, sixteen years after the idea was first implanted in the mind of Mr. Astor, the Astor Library in Lafayette Place opened its doors to the public of New York City, the librarian himself standing inside the railing to give directions to the visitors. The details of the event were described in a letter to George Ticknor:

> The library has been open now about ten days, and harassing days they have been to me, one unbroken string of questions from morning till night, requiring constant and wearing repetition of the same answers. At nine a.m. I take my stand inside the railing and there I remain as a fixture until half-past four. They all look wistfully at the books, and ask, "can't we go into the alcoves and up to the second story," and, when I answer, "No," they break out into a railing accusation. But it's no use, I tell them, "You can't do it." I know not what I should have done if I had not hit upon this plan of a close corporation. It would have crazed me to have seen a crowd ranging lawlessly among the books, and throwing everything into confusion.

As for the reading of the young—boys fourteen years and older were allowed entry—Mr. Cogswell bewailed their choice of books in a further letter, his complaint falling strangely, indeed, on the ears of the librarian of today:

> . . . The readers average from one to two hundred daily, and they read excellent books, except the young fry, who employ all the hours they are out of school in reading the trashy, as Scott, Cooper, Dickens, *Punch* and the *Illustrated News*. Even this is better than spinning street yarns, and as long as they continue perfectly orderly and quiet, as they now are, I shall not object to their amusing themselves with poor books.

In the course of time the nucleus of the Astor Library drew within the radius of its influence two great additional resources of books and funds. First, the Lenox Library, established like the Astor as a memorial to the wealth and general distinction of a successful financier, one John Lenox, son of a Scottish merchant and importer. He found his chief pleasure in book collecting, among his enthusiasms the poet Milton, the Bible, and the acquisition of multiple editions of a favorite book of his, Bunyan's *Pilgrim's Progress*. "Original and peculiar" as a collector, so he was described by his purchasing agent, but fervent, knowledgeable, and widely read.

Samuel Jones Tilden, lifelong bachelor, once Governor of New York, whose disputed candidacy for the office of President in 1876 forms a curious chapter in American history, left nearly five million dollars to the city of New York, to be incorporated in a fund known as the Tilden Trust, "with capacity to establish and maintain a free library and reading room in the City of New York." The legacy was reduced to two and a half million after the legal squabbling of his relatives had subsided. By great good fortune and the perspicacity of distinguished boards of trustees, the three library foundations were bound together in a signed Agreement of Consolidation on May 23, 1895.

In December of that year, Dr. John Shaw Billings, noted Army surgeon of the Civil War, subsequently organizer of the Surgeons' General Library in Washington, which he brought to great distinction, was named director of the New York Public Library. On March 25 of the following year, 1896, the board of trustees of the New York Public Library, Astor, Lenox, and Tilden Foundation, addressed to the Mayor, Aldermen, and Commonalty of the City of New York, a document describing "the meager and unsatisfactory provision existing in the City of New York either for scholars and students in a reference library, or for home reading through a library of circulation," comparing the small expenditures supplied by New York to this cause of public education with the more ample means afforded like causes by lesser cities of the Eastern seaboard:

> . . . What is necessary for real public interest and lasting public benefit is a great central library of reference and exhibit, and in addition, the public must be provided with the means of procuring books for home reading within some reasonable distance of their residence.

It is to be noted that the site for such a library is mentioned for the first time officially in this document:

> No site within the control of the City could accomplish the ends in view as well as that of the Reservoir upon Fifth Avenue between Fortieth and Forty-Second Street.

A certain fire and eloquence informs this plea for public support, with its tables and statistics and other documentary evidence giving the history of the past as well as a plan for the future, culminating in this last paragraph:

> When we consider the extent to which an institution of the character proposed may fairly be expected to strengthen the police, diminish crime, raise public standards of morality, attract to our City men from every industry and every walk of life, add to the operative power of our people, and extend the influence of our Commonwealth, it can hardly be regarded otherwise than a privilege for the City to share in the work.

John Bigelow was president of the Board of Library Trustees at that time, having come into the picture as a trustee of the Tilden Trust. Accomplished professional writer and distinguished diplomat during the Civil War, he had served in France and was credited with preventing that country's recognition of the Confederacy. No doubt it was his rhetoric that spawned such extravagant declarations of faith in the accomplishment of libraries and librarianship. John Bigelow lived to be ninety-four years old, and it was into his hands that the Mayor of New York, on May 23, 1911, delivered the keys of the great Central Building at the celebration of its opening to the city. He died in December of that year.

For five years after the directorship of Dr. Billings, the scope of the library was limited to reference service. It was not forgotten, however, that the second Article of the Agreement of Consolidation of the three foundations read as follows:

> The said new corporation shall establish and maintain a free public library and reading room in the City of New York, with such branches as may be deemed advisable.

From this brief, formal statement was to come the drama and sheer humanity of the greatest public library system in the world, its diversified pattern of administration and its imaginative concept of public service destined to enliven and inform the life of three boroughs of the city—Richmond, the Bronx, and Manhattan—and to set an example to the world.

By the year 1900 the city brought pressure to bear upon Dr. Billings toward the fulfillment of the promise made at the time of consolidation, demanding a calendar of action and proposing to assume part of the financial burden. Consequently Dr. Billings, with a plan for unification of a library of circulation in mind, sent to fourteen of the existing subscription libraries in the city, privately financed or, in a few instances, receiving aid from the city, asking them to give full accounting of their financial status and holdings and putting to them, as it were, the familiar question from the Lobster Quadrille: "Will you, won't you, will you, won't you, won't you join the dance?" The cause of centralization was expedited by the gifts of Andrew Carnegie, who in a brief letter to Dr. Billings, dated March 1, 1901, offered to give the city sixty-five branch libraries. "Sixty-five libraries at one stroke probably breaks the record," he wrote, sounding like the valiant Little Tailor of Grimm's *Fairy Tales*, who killed seven at a blow, "but this is the day of big operations and New York is soon to be the biggest of the Cities."

Now and then, when Anne Carroll Moore was Director of Work with Children in the New York Public Library, at the monthly meeting of Children's Librarians, she began proceedings with roll call, not by names of staff members but by names of the branch libraries: Aguilar, Cathedral, Chatham Square, Epiphany, Harlem, Hudson Park, etc., through the complete litany. Her sympathy for the mystique of the names of things, the tone of her voice, and the rhythm of the syllables as she spoke them conveyed a sense of history though the subject was never formally presented in lecture or program. One came to know the founding personalities, the character of the neighborhoods, the multicolored life of New York branch libraries as ACM knew and cherished them: the Harlem branch, its origins going back to the time of Harlem as a township in its own right when monies accrued to the library from the sale of the land of Harlem Commons as early as 1820; Washington Heights, begun in 1868, supported by shares and subscriptions, where a boys' and girls' library made an early appearance, its subscription rate being five cents per week for those under sixteen; Aguilar Free Library Society, organized in 1886, to serve "those who were actually interested in Jewish communal affairs." So runs the tale away.

By national groups, by church affiliations, by parish

house and synagogue, by labor-union affiliation, by settlement house, by public schools, by Czech Sokol clubs meeting in gymnasiums, by German clubs and debating societies, by philanthropists and scholars—by such diverse shouts and murmurs were demands made for books and reading in New York during the mid-1800s.

One splendid system, the New York Free Circulating Library, originated at Grace Church in 1878, the setting a sewing class for young girls whose taste in reading was deemed to be deplorable. In an effort to improve matters, certain women of the church undertook to read aloud as the group learned to sew.

Two decades later, in 1899, the New York Free Circulating Library claimed eleven branches throughout the city, and by that time the use of the libraries by children was so marked that in several branches a separate room was set aside for them.

This well-organized system stood ready as the sound basis of operation for the New York Public Library when the year of consolidation among the City's circulating libraries came to pass. On the very day, March 3, 1901, that Andrew Carnegie wrote his letter to Dr. Billings, promising a clutch of branch libraries, Arthur E. Bostwick, formerly a chief librarian of the New York Free Circulating Library and of the Brooklyn Public Library, was appointed head of the newly organized Circulation Department of the New York Public Library.

The title of doctor, which his associates invariably used in speaking to or of Arthur Bostwick, was his due, since he held a Ph.D. from Yale (1883) in the physical sciences. Degrees of such magnitude were not common in the library profession of that time, and, no doubt, the staff of the New York Public Library spoke of their tandem directors in one proud breath as Dr. Billings and

Dr. Bostwick. Certainly Dr. Bostwick was not the pedant wearing his honors conspicuously. It was not he who insisted on the title.

New England by birth, he was very much a man of the world, welcomed and consulted in far places. His knowledge of science did not preclude an interest in literature. Before he became a librarian he had distinguished himself as editor and literary adviser on *The Forum*, Appleton's *Cyclopedia of American Biography*, and the *Literary Digest*. He was a genial man, gracious and comfortable in encounter, and Anne Carroll Moore was to find in him a decisive administrator, generous in sympathy and in understanding. The friendship between them was sustained throughout their lives. She dedicated the second of her "Roads to Childhood Books," *New Roads to Childhood*, "To Arthur Bostwick, whose zest for exploring new roads lights up every turn in the long road of an old friendship."

In 1905, after four years of creating a Department of Circulation in the New York Public Library, Dr. Bostwick held work with children as top priority for the library. On December 20 of that year, Dr. Bostwick wrote to Miss Annie Carroll Moore of the Pratt Free Institute Library asking her to call at his office the following week, as he wished to discuss with her the possibility of her coming to the New York Public Library to direct the work with children. The opportunity came at the time when life for Anne had come to a peak, presenting a natural point of division. A decade of accomplishment at Pratt lay behind her, but the growth and development of the Brooklyn Public Library, founded in 1903, was bound to overwhelm and absorb the service of Pratt Free Institute Library as a public library. Anne Carroll Moore might well have found herself at that period of time in a *cul-de-sac*.

As for her personal life, there was no longer need for her to maintain a home base for her nieces. Rachel, the older of the girls, had gone off to college at Bryn Mawr. Physically Anne was spent, her spirit much depleted. She was too ill to go to Manhattan. Consequently Dr. Bostwick wrote asking if he might call upon her at her home on Lafayette Street. When the day came, she was flat on her back, suffering what her cherished Dr. Butler diagnosed as emotional exhaustion. She received Dr. Bostwick in this unbecoming state of collapse, but the news Dr. Bostwick brought was exhilarating to the point of intoxication. He was tired, he said, of having to send hundreds of people inquiring about library work with children across the Brooklyn Bridge for their answers. Would she come to Manhattan and take over the untidy and more or less haphazardly organized work with children, giving it the direction she deemed best suited to the great metropolitan center?

Rivalries existed in this fair enterprise of library work with children. The public libraries of Pittsburgh and Cleveland were generally acknowledged to be leaders in this field, and their activities dominated the reports in professional journals. Anne was aware of this. In a letter to her niece reporting the great news, Anne revealed the scope of her ambition. "It's the one place I have ever felt that I might be induced to consider if I could have right of way, for taken in a big way it would knock the spots out of any other like position in the country."

Dr. Butler recommended a long period of rest before signing on. Mr. Bostwick suggested September 1, 1906, as a probable date for beginning. Anne closed up her share of the apartment, stuffed her unpaid bills, alarming in their plenitude as a result of her generosity to the family, into a shoe box, shoved it under the bed, and took off for England, on the *Minnehaha*, March 3, 1906. The mooing of cows accompanied her across the Atlantic, for she was sailing on a cattle boat, under Captain Robinson, in whom Anne discovered, of all things, a fellow devotee of Mrs. Gaskell's *Cranford*.

She had hoped for the full panoply of an English spring and summer when she set sail from Brooklyn, but London in March was cold, and after two weeks she abandoned it and went to Ventnor on the Isle of Wight. In the footsteps of Tennyson, she journeyed to Freshwater, seeking the house where he had lived and visiting the church he must have frequented. She sat in the pew she thought was Tennyson's and was confirmed in her choice by the sexton, "Though of course Miss," he confided to her, "him never come to church nor Lady Tennyson neither."

Her lively journal of these months from March until the middle of July recounts trips to Knutsford, where *Cranford* had its roots, and long walks with a Miss Hollins, who had known Mrs. Gaskell. She was there for May Day and found the celebration somewhat tarnished in its performance, with artificial flowers and gaudily colored feathers used in the procession, though the Morris dances were still beautiful in their authentic costume and tradition. The heath was populated by traveling caravans of carnival folk. Through her chance acquaintance with a churchly woman who visited the sick and the poor, Anne found herself concerned about a performer in one of the wagons, a young woman who shared a wagon with the show's "fat lady" and a snake charmer. The poor soul was dying, according to all reports, and lived on nothing but champagne. Then one day a man in one of the other wagons came to visit her.

He turned to Anne's friend and asked, "Is she going to die?" And the woman nodded her head in assent, whereupon the man turned to the patient in the bunk and shouted, "Don't be such a God damn fool as to die on the road" and stomped out. Anne records all this in her journal, initialing the profanity by way of polite abbreviation, and reports that immediately thereafter the woman showed signs of recovering.

Anne returned to Grasmere to revive old memories and went for the first time to Ambleside, which she loathed. Even though she had paid a week's lodging in advance, which the landlady refused to refund to her, she decided to abandon the place for Troutbeck, four miles distant, a village she had discovered on her own. There she found a countryside, a house, and a room full of comfort and inner consolation. She was to hold that place very dear forever after.

From March until the middle of July she wandered from lodging house to country inn, took residence in a women's club in London or visited friends held over in her affection from the first English journey with Mildred Collar in 1901. Long, solitary walks were her delight, as well as the other traveler's joy that was abundantly hers, the ability to become a part of the life of room, house, garden, country lane, or city street, wherever she found herself.

The precise and carefully kept journal of those months must often have given ACM pleasure in rereading. The honest love of good food was chronicled there and people, clear and sharply drawn, with glimpses of landscape and the English spring to "flash upon the inward eye."

> Gathered my first sprig of hawthorne and a shaft of yellow broome. . . . Saw daisies just peeping out in the fields. Primroses beside a little stream and blackthorn just

coming out in the hedgerows. The birds sang divinely and I began to feel happy. . . . The young lambs were a delight to see. Lots of primroses to left and right but not many trees nor were they far along in age. . . . We took the road past Buddle's and further on toward the lighthouse—nearly down to it having met some children who told us that primroses grew very thick down there. I got out and scouted through a hedge and over a rough pasture until I began to find such heaps and heaps I took off my hat and filled it and then I went on and scrambled over a very high stone wall and found myself beside a primrose-bordered stream with a bank of violets stretched blue above the yellow flowers. I never saw anything so beautiful and I sat down and filled myself full of it.

Not all the scenes are those of wood and stream. Anne spent Easter in London. On the Saturday before the day, she had risen betimes at her club and made her way to Covent Garden Market before anyone else was astir.

What fun it was to see the market wagons unloading and the donkey carts loading up. I dodged barrels, baskets, hampers of fruit and vegetables right and left being the only woman on the scene. Everybody was jolly and nice 'though very busy. I made my way through to the fruit and flower markets where I spent most of the time and before I left people were pouring in to buy Easter flowers. I had my hands full long before I could find a basket which I finally did at a shop outside the market. I lined it with maiden hair and filled it with forget-me-nots, most lovely white tulips with delicate green edges, lilies of the valley, yellow roses, a dozen bunches of violets and some feathery lavender flower. Then I took it on my arm and walked home trying in vain to get tea or coffee at an Egyptian restaurant that I passed.

On Easter Sunday she put on her gray silk and walked down through Trafalgar Square to Westminster Abbey, lingering outside to hear the chimes. After service, she walked through St. James's Park, "which was perfectly

beautiful with all the flowers and the trees just bursting
into every shade of green and yellow. I came out through
the Cloisters of Westminster and walked past the Houses
of Parliament before entering St. James's Park. Stopped
long enough for a view at the upper edge."

On Easter Monday Anne was to catch the first view
of a spot in London that she was to enjoy time and again:
Hampstead Heath.

> Monday a perfect day. . . . I planned to go on Hamp-
> stead Heath joined by Miss Ogle. We start off a little past
> eleven by the new Tube and bus top. Everybody wears a
> holiday face. We have luncheon at a confectioners quite
> by ourselves and then walked to the Heath a mile or more.
> Punch and Judy shows were the first sights to be seen
> and I was delighted to see one again. Soon we came to
> the Coster boys and girls dancing in the road 4 in a line
> opposite 4, to the music of barrel organs. Such clothes,
> purple velvet, shirts trimmed with jet or fur, robin's egg
> blue cashmere waists black velvet capes and hats with
> blue, pink, yellow or green ostrich feathers nearly a yard
> long. . . .

The last page of the journal was full up before the
journey was done. She wrote it in the lodging at Troutbeck.

> I believe it is the most beautiful day since I came to the
> Lakes—so clear yet with lovely clouds. I stopped to chat
> in the kitchen with Mr & Mrs Browne—saw my scone
> toasted and buttered and then had my tea at the long table
> in the hall and then I came up to sit in my little oak room
> in the gloaming. There is a young moon tonight, and Miss
> Clara brought my supper here between 8 and 9 and then I
> lighted three candles and by their light I am writing the
> last pages in the red book my dear girl gave me when I
> sailed away. What another girl I feel with this new
> strength and spirit and what a happy record is here con-
> tained!

Five months in England! For Anne, in the face of a strenuous new assignment, no better preparation could have been devised by doctor, sage, or philosopher. On September 1, 1906, she crossed the Brooklyn Bridge to Manhattan, refreshed, renewed in spirit, joyously determined, and destined to be numbered among the most distinguished of Knickerbockers.

8

THE FIRST DECADE

I have never wished to formulate a scheme of library service to children. My chief interest has been in discovering and putting to work personalities who have something special to contribute—the more varied the contribution the better for the work—for it should never become static.

ACM

$\mathcal{T}$HE NEW YORK PUBLIC LIBRARY was a wilderness in the library world of 1906." So ACM described it in a letter of recollection. She knew a sinking of the heart when she found herself stationed in her office, a bleak room on the third floor of the Muhlenberg Branch Library at 209 West 23rd Street after the warmth and color of Pratt. "Old friends came and wept to find me without any visible environment, in an office space absent of children or any signs that children ever existed," she continued, "but I was having the time of my life."

Her assignment paralleled somewhat the work of Dr. Bostwick, as head of the Circulation Department. For her, too, the first imperative was to unite under a single supervisory head all those who in any way had been

assigned to work with children. The category included
the branch librarians as well as the assistants scheduled to
staff the children's rooms. The latter more readily welcomed a clear directive and a consistent philosophy of
procedure than did the branch librarians, who found it
one thing to have surrendered authority to Dr. Bostwick,
a man of parts, as it were, and quite another to yield
autonomy and authority to a young woman, midway in
her thirties, whose area of supervision infringed on their
own. That was bitter medicine on the tongue.

"I had been resented, rejected by most of the Branch
Librarians who did not want to be supervised, who were
untrained for their work and had to be met on such terms
as I could devise," she wrote in retrospect.

One day Dr. Bostwick asked her, "How is it you and
Miss B. have come to an understanding?" (Miss B. was
famed for her recalcitrance.) "I would never have
thought it possible."

"It's very simple," ACM records herself as saying. "She
has no interest in and no knowledge of library organization. I talk with her about books and plays and Woodrow
Wilson and she lets me do anything I want to with work
with children in her branch."

Anne Moore was a gifted diplomat as well as a psychologist whose knowledge of people was innate and
intuitive. She knew when to be conciliatory and when to
remain adamant. There was no wavering. Once she had
arrived at an opinion or fixed her goals of accomplishment, nothing could shake the strength of her belief in
her own infallibility. She had what the French call *la
grande confiance*. As well as admitting to no discouragement, she admitted to no mistakes; seldom did she apologize for any action. The closest she allowed herself to
come to an admission of regret was to say, "I did not

fully understand." A tenet of belief she proffered many a person was "Never deprecate yourself," and a show of humility was not a trait she counted among the beatitudes. She had upon her, however, that certain bloom which J. M. Barrie has defined in *What Every Woman Knows* as "charm." Few turned a deaf ear to her, and none could ignore her high originality.

During the first month of September, Anne went "on trek" to the thirty-six branch libraries of the city. By elevated railroad, subway, streetcar, and horse car (these did not entirely disappear from the streets of New York until 1907), trailing her long black skirts bound in horsehair braid as first defense against the dust and filth of city streets, slim in white tailored shirtwaist with narrow stiff collar, Anne went her daily journeys. City travel held no weariness for her. In all the more than thirty years of her life in the New York Public Library, she undertook such excursions with seemingly tireless energy, the burden lightened in the later years by an extravagance of taxis. In that first September she met the library personnel and listened to them, her eyes meanwhile alert to the character of every nook and cranny. She noted the space allotted to work with children, the appearance of the room (if there were a room), the initial impact of the place on the mind of a visitor, making notes in a small brown notebook remarkable for the range of topics marking its pages. Her immediate staff, the assistants who worked with children, were a heterogeneous lot seemingly blown together by a careless wind, whom she inherited from the past. She found them working to enforce discipline under the stigma of the sign SILENCE. Disparate though their methods were, they were united by one enormous concern—the theft of books from library shelves.

On these visits Anne sniffed out the quality of the book collections, noting the lack of judgment or any clear policy of selection, the remnants of Sunday-school libraries and cheap sensationalism showing through the skeletal beginnings of professional concern for the books children read.

One month after her arrival in Manhattan, she called her first meeting of assistants in charge of children's rooms—the place, the Tompkins Square branch; the date, October 1906. Her introductory speech is outlined in part in the brown notebook:

It is not my purpose to present an historical sketch of library work with children, nor to make general statements as to its value. I have chosen instead to set out before you such aspects of the work as seem to me of the first importance in shaping work with children in the New York Public Library. First the selection of books. It does matter what books we put on the shelves of the Children's Room. Second, personal responsibility. Successful work in a public library is based upon demonstrated knowledge of children and of children's books. All problems connected with the work fall under these two heads.

The first step to the knowledge of children is to have been a real child and to hold so vivid a recollection of the experience as to enable one to understand children and to meet them on their own ground. The next step is to have accomplished the difficult task of growing up so successfully that the experience becomes part of one's stock in trade. To the general intelligence, judgment, tact, enthusiasm and devotion required by other departments of library work, the work with children calls for the stronger sense of proportion, for clearer demands upon one's sympathies and disciplinary powers, at a time in the day when the initial power of most persons is depleted by the earlier work of the day.

In the late afternoon there is a peculiar and a very exhausting nervous strain about the general government of a children's library arising chiefly from the effort to do too many things at one time or from the attempt to turn off work too rapidly or from a failure to plan work with care or from the distinct physical limitation of the place in which the work is done. To escape this strain the sense of proportion of the children's librarian must be abnormally developed. . . . So far as I know limitation in space has never been recognized in public library service of children. What are some of the results of lack of system in children's work?

We have resorted to *devices* to secure what it is impossible to secure by any other means than by a definite recognition of the nature of the work and of its demands upon those who are to carry it on. A silence sign will never secure a quiet children's room. In my opinion it is a hindrance to that end. The best evaluative list of books or picture bulletin made will not take the place of a firsthand recommendation from a children's librarian who is capable of evaluating the *person* who is to make use of it.

No badge or button of club or league pledged to the care of books will take the place of a rock foundation of belief in the possibility of teaching children to take care of the books and that theft can be stopped, backed by as big a rock of determination to secure the desired end in every individual membership in the library.[1]

Nor do I believe that a glass partition which may prevent some loss of books from the children will take the place of the eternal vigilance which is the first requisite of every successful children's librarian. The question of loss of books from the shelves of the children's rooms of libraries is the burning question in the administration of them for the current year and the best energies of the administrative head of your children's rooms will be directed toward a full statement if not a solution to this problem. All special features in children's work, valuable though they may be, will be recommended most conservatively until the question of a library membership to which is attached greater personal responsibility on the part of the children themselves and of the assistants in charge of the work has been settled and until we have arrived at a more substantial agreement as to whether the selection of books is to be based upon discriminating knowledge or merely supplying the popular demand without reference to the development of taste and feeling for books.

Anne had the answers to the problems her assistants faced. She had solved them on a stage of smaller dimension at Pratt. But she issued no decrees from the heights of her authority, no directional policies announcing step-by-step procedures. Master of finesse, she chose instead to give them the illusion of independent thinking on their part, thus fully involving them in the procedures. She furnished clues which led them to foregone conclusions. "Library membership to which is attached greater responsibility on the part of the children themselves." This led straight to the self-registering scheme she had conceived at Pratt. In the matter of book selection, she issued no master list with directions for wholesale discarding of titles. Instead, she turned out their minds to romp in the wide fields of an enduring professional quandary: "whether the selection of books is to be based upon discriminating knowledge or merely supplying the popular demand without reference to the development of taste and feeling for books."

She insisted that books be read at a furious pace and with discerning judgment. The "P" slips of the period yield scattered records of questions to be answered and judgments proposed.

> How far are children going to be influenced by the books they find in a public library?
> The education of children begins at the open shelves.
> Choose children's books for their vitality, and stand by until they find their market.
> Try reading aloud.
> Books about girls should be as interesting as girls are.
> Look for fidelity to life and essential atmosphere.

Tenderness without sentimentality, humor without vulgarity.

Avoid the facetious, condescending, artificial.

Is the book conceived for children or grown-ups?

Age is no criterion of mental condition and capacity.

Book Selection—History.

Look for the dramatic. The story must be vividly told.

Facts in children's histories should agree with those established by more recent scholarship so far as possible. This need not exclude historical events which have been discovered to be legends which are true to human nature if not historical fact.

The incidental value of history is the conveying of facts.

Chief value to stimulate the imagination in the noble and heroic and to broaden the horizon by pictures of life under experiences foreign to their condition.

Historical interest for children lies in the event rather than in the conclusions drawn from it.

Avoid those histories which gain dramatic interest by appeal to prejudice. Especially true of American histories.

These were notes for subjects under discussion in the years 1907, 1908, and upward. Certain principles of administration are scribbled on note paper, as viable now as they were in 1910.

Fundamentals in successful administration.

See the end purpose clearly.

Have complete mastery of essential detail in order to feel free.

Have as full and varied a book stock as possible.

Keep your room attractive and alive: This is accomplished by your relations with children, their parents and other adults, and with the staff.

Keep alive to books on all sides. Know bookshops, reviews and reviewers. Cultivate an attitude of learning and a capacity for no end of surprise.

Ask yourself, "Am I doing this to please myself, the adult public or the children?"

Do not get Branch bound!

In support of this last item of advice, ACM scheduled the monthly staff meetings at different branch libraries throughout the city. The expedient and economical plan, after 1911, would have been to hold all monthly meetings at the Central Library. It was often suggested that this be done. But ACM pursued the greater wisdom of creating an informed staff, each member of which might know the work as a whole, the city as a unit in its diversity, and have the opportunity of observing every branch library in its own situation. Assistants were soon convinced that it was well worth the effort of arising early in the morning on the appointed days and traveling miles to and from the Bronx or Staten Island to see fresh neighborhoods and gather new strength from comrades in arms.

ACM feared once again the old threat of boredom, this time among the assistants. How often her sheer humanity broke through in unexpected places! In the first week of her retirement, when she held long conversations with her successor, she said of these monthly meetings, "Don't hold them in meeting to the last minute. They want to go to lunch with each other. Give them time."

By 1908—two years after her arrival in New York from her recuperative journey to England—ACM had gained professional status for the children's librarians within the organization, established a "Children's Librarian Grade" with fixed salary rate, defined the qualifications for acceptance in the grade, and had begun in earnest the building of a professional staff. Anna Cogswell Tyler, a graduate of Pratt Institute Library School, came in that year to give form and content to storytelling procedures and to develop a brilliant program of reading clubs that was unequaled in library history. Marcia Dalphin, also a Pratt graduate, who ultimately brought to such a degree of perfection the art of relating books and reading to a community—Rye, New York— as to become a legend in her own time, came in 1907. Julia Carter was another graduate brought across the bridge from Brooklyn in that same year. She remembers well those days and gives her own report of the training period:

> I think of Anne Moore's teaching as having four parts and I call them "The Four Respects."
>
> The first respect was for the children. We were to think of and respect them as individuals and neither talk down to them nor call them pet names. We were to answer their requests for books, but were also to suggest other titles to them to give them a new and wider knowledge. Also, if the children wished for more adult titles, we were to consider requests and try to satisfy them.
>
> The second respect was for the books which were on our shelves. They were to be well-written, and none of them were to be rewritten in words of one syllable. If the books were factual, the authenticity of the author and his background was to be checked. If a story was imaginative, it was to be purely so and not have reality mixed up with fantasy. All books were to be sincerely and clearly written.
>
> The third respect was for our fellow workers. We were told again and again to remember that we were but a part of the whole. The branch work concerned all of us and all were to receive due credit and respect for their share in it. We were to know something of the other library departments, ask for and give cooperation. I well remember Miss Moore's advice along this line. I had been given a difficult assignment and could not obtain from the branch staff the measure of support I needed in completing the routine work of the children's room. I appealed to Miss Moore for help, asking her to use the authority of her position to bring pressure to bear on the branch staff. She replied, "I know the situation and I could give my order but that would not help. You must go back to the

branch and influence those people on your own so that they will want to do as you wish themselves and not by my order." After restless nights and many gray hairs I managed it and the cooperation lasted.

The fourth respect was for the professional standing of the Children's Librarian. They were not to be dictated to by others against their better judgment. Miss Moore felt that children's librarians were the best trained and most informed staff members on the subject of children's books and reading. The children were to be allowed free use of books, and not just to use those that some authority thought belonged to their age group or to their school grade.

With this nucleus of professional help, Anne undertook to bring the other staff members to a point of eligibility for the professional classification. Only one among the twenty-seven was a college graduate; fourteen had taught in high schools; two were formerly kindergarten teachers; four had previously had some experience working in libraries. ACM set them to reading, she herself inciting them to fervor with lectures, her own and those of invited speakers.

A certain amount of anxiety was entailed in working under ACM. There was exhilaration, to be sure, for her enthusiasm was contagious. The larger vision, the ultimate goal of the work was never sacrificed to petty tasks and routine performances. She expected everyone to function at the peak of his abilities; nor could she tolerate complacency or listlessness in an assistant, and she manifested her lack of sympathy with attacks of the doldrums in several ways. One of her most effective methods was a clearing of the throat, a kind of humming under the breath that signaled irrevocable dismissal of one's person as well as one's opinions and lack of interest in whatever was being said.

She was unwittingly prone to expose such traits as those which beset the mouse in Grimm's fairy tale "The Cat and the Mouse Who Set Up Housekeeping. " You may remember that after the two partners had gathered enough fat to last through the winter, the question arose as to a safe place in which to store it. "The mouse knew she could never think of a place," runs the tale. In every instance the mouse found herself predestined for inadequacy. So it was with many who felt themselves intimidated in the presence of ACM. Tension and constraint were the result, and these led certain members of the staff to frame their opinions in terms they deemed pleasing to ACM. A very human trait, this! Sometimes ACM was taken in by it, though none was quicker than she to welcome the honest, outspoken ideas of a sincere person.

Certain other workers under her direction felt themselves ignored. Year after year they pursued their work, but nothing they did or described in their monthly "informal reports," those small essays that recorded the daily life of the children's rooms, often with moving effect, won them praise or recognition. One accomplished librarian, Priscilla Edie, confronted ACM with the fact. "Is there anything wrong with my work?" she asked. "You never remark upon it." To which ACM replied, "If there were anything amiss, I would have told you."

Sometimes a shaft of wit was both probe and suture. One young assistant was sent by the branch librarian to ACM for reprimand because, impetuous girl, she had been surprised in the embrace of the janitor (it was before the days of custodians), he compounding the crime by his married status. The young woman's defense was that she could not be responsible for the effect of her *considerable* good looks upon the male psyche. "Apparently you have had very little experience in handling men," said ACM, deflating the young woman's vanity and ending the interview.

Miss Moore was adept at recognizing the weakest attributes in character and temperament. She could thrust thorn to the quick on occasion. Nor did she spare those whom she most greatly cherished and on whom she depended in the largest measure. Scarcely anyone escaped, at one point or another, an encounter of great bitterness in a relationship with her. "But no one ever held it against her," said Anne Eaton when the matter was once under discussion. Some suffered at her hands and some were destroyed; but the gift of her friendship, the lasting lifelong strength of her support, the eagerness with which she brought people to a realization of latent abilities of which they themselves were unaware—these were incomparable, outweighing all else. Pages could be filled with the names of those whom she discovered in their chrysalis state, to whom she gave encouragement and in whose subsequent triumphs she rejoiced. She held no one in fealty to herself or to the New York Public Library. In the first years of her work she surrendered her chief assistant, Mary Douglas, to the St. Louis Public Library when Dr. Bostwick became a director of that institution. Visting librarians came for periods of work, and these too were carriers of ACM's spirit and philosophy. Her influence spread across the country: Siri Andrews in the Pacific Northwest; Lillian Smith of the Boys' and Girls' Library at Toronto; Jacqueline Overton in the distinctive Bacon Memorial Library at Westbury, Long Island; Marcia Dalphin in Rye, New York; Katherine Carnes in Atlanta, Georgia; Rosemary Livsey in California. During the First World War a flock of children's librarians was released to Anne

Morgan's American Committee for Devastated France, where libraries were a prime concern in the restoration of French village life: Jessie Carson, Alice Keats O'Connor, Marianne Greene chief among them.

The publishing field was to know the influence of Anne through members of her staff who became editors of children's books: Marian Fiery and Margaret McElderry. Writers developed among the group: Eleanor Estes, Helen Forbes, Eugenia Garson, Pura Belpré, Florence Adams, Mary Gould Davis, Anna Cogswell Tyler, Harriet Wright, Maria Cimino, Ruth Hill Viguers, Alexandra Sanford, Ruth Giles Lontoft, Shirley Barker, and Claire Huchet Bishop.

The year 1907 brought Anne her first encounter with someone peculiarly worthy of her friendship, Valfrid Palmgren Munch-Petersen, that vibrant scholar-librarian from Sweden, who came to the United States in August of that year, sent by her government to study the public-library movement. She was in the country for only six months, but it was time enough. She visited libraries on the Eastern seaboard, attended library conventions, counseled with leaders in the movement, interviewed Andrew Carnegie and the President of the United States, Theodore Roosevelt, who gave her ardent testimony as to his belief in public libraries.

Early in these months she came upon an aspect of library work of which she had not dreamed: library work with children. It was Anne Carroll Moore, in the second year of her appointment at the New York Public Library, who indoctrinated her. With Anne, Valfrid saw the children reading in an exuberance of pleasure, without hindrance or restriction, without commitment to age, school grade, or prescribed theories of education. With Anne, she watched the lines of black-stockinged children waiting for the doors of libraries to open, the story hours, the clustered heads bending over small tables piled with books, and all the solitary readers and searchers of shelves, grazing like sheep in some paradisiacal pasture. When she returned to Sweden, Valfrid Palmgren was determined that the children of Stockholm should have an equal chance with the children of the New World. Public libraries got under way in Sweden in 1909. But not until 1911 did the first children's library in Scandinavia, indeed in Europe, open its doors on December 4, at 65 Drottninggatan, Stockholm. Anne herself was a visitor to that library in 1912 when she went as a delegate to the Library Association of the United Kingdom in Liverpool and made a detour to Stockholm. There she saw the image of the American library carried across the sea by the devotion of her great friend, Valfrid Palmgren.

Theirs was a friendship that endured for five decades. They saw each other three times in that period, but though space, wars, and turns of fate separated them, they never lost touch. Valfrid Palmgren married a distinguished Dane, lived in Copenhagen, and became a professor at the university there, reared a family, lost a son in the Loyalist cause in Spain, and knew at first hand life under the Nazi invasion. The friendship was inherited by the second generation. Finn Munch-Petersen, Valfrid's son, represented his country at the United Nations in New York. Many were the feasts of food and good talk ACM shared with him and his attractive wife. It happened to Anne more than once in her lifetime, this claiming of her friendship by succeeding generations: the grandsons of her classmates at Bradford; the children and grandchildren of L. Leslie Brooke in England; the Petersons of Utah, who adopted her as a member of the tribe to the third and fourth generations.

Ruth Sawyer Durand, writer and storyteller and among the staunchest of Anne's friends, first appeared on the scene in 1910, coming to Anne with a letter of introduction from Alice Tyler of the Iowa Library Commission. In a 1951 letter of recollection Anne wrote:

> I casually took her along with me to the Hudson Park Branch Library for a Christmas story hour. She told "The Voyage of the Wee Red Cap" for the first time before it had appeared in print. As you know, we have been the warmest and most understanding of friends ever since. We look for the same things in a storyteller, a diction free from the dictionary, a voice from the lower reaches rather than the higher brackets, and a *real re-creation* of the story for an audience of one or one hundred. Mrs. Durand knows infinitely more than I do about placement and development of the voice. I only know that the majority of storytellers I hear do not give me pleasure as a listener and I also know as a children's librarian that a well-modulated voice is the most effective means of control of any problem that can arise in a public library.

Anne gave to friendship a dimension of sensibility that few could equal. She wore it as a talisman like Hans in the old tale who carried the Golden Goose under his arm as he went to the palace to make the princess laugh. Whoever so much as touched a feather of it found himself held fast to the bird. And, in turn, the person touching him could not pull away. The result was a motley parade of men, women, and children, held together by the power of the great bird. Anne never doubted that her friends were held in such a manner to each other as well as to herself. She wove and interwove the fates and fortunes of her friends, issuing orders and commands in behalf of them all. "Write a letter, send a message, perhaps a visit would be helpful." And dates and addresses were included. "Command performances," Helen Masten called these directives, she as head of the Central Children's Room happily bearing the burden for fulfilling many of them. One young assistant embarking from New York for a week's sail down the coast to Texas was astonished to find herself the center of much attention at the time of the ship's departure. People she barely knew appeared in considerable numbers, showering her with gifts. Not until years later did she realize that the vacationing Miss Moore had suggested the bon voyage be celebrated in gala fashion. No system of notation, no birthday-book entries jogged Anne's memory in relation to the celebrations her friends enjoyed, the tragedies they might endure. Only in the multiple pages of her affection and concern were the data recorded.

Five years of innovative accomplishment in the New York Public Library lay behind ACM when the great bronze doors of the library at Forty-second Street and Fifth Avenue swung open to the world for the first time on May 23, 1911. The first day was celebrated with dedicatory ceremonies, followed by an open house for several thousand invited guests. The largest marble building ever built in the country, it had been metamorphosed from the waters of the old Croton Reservoir that had stood on that ground since 1842. A noble structure, it was "simple in design, Renaissance in style, based upon classic principles and modern in character," to quote one of the architects responsible for the accomplishment, Mr. Hastings of Carrère and Hastings.

That May day was warm for spring, and the cool marble spaciousness of the rotunda was doubly welcome to the six hundred guests seated there in that great arena.

None other than the President of the United States, William Howard Taft, was among the galaxy of speakers. Crowds on Fifth Avenue waited to catch a glimpse of him. The people lining Fortieth Street cheered the police-escorted cars that crowded into the entry there, but no one was aware of the President's actual arrival at the doors of the Forty-second Street entrance. He was escorted to an elevator, the building boasting two, their handsome bronze doors bearing an intricate design of the caduceus as a subtle tribute to Dr. Billings.

The procession formed in the trustees' room on the third floor, making an impressive entrance as they walked two by two down one of the grandiose stairways to the rotunda, Dr. Billings and his assistant, Edwin Anderson, leading the procession, which included an appropriate allotment of governors, mayors, park commissioners, architects, etc., the glory culminating at last in the presence of William Howard Taft and John Bigelow, president of the Board of Library Trustees, described in the press as "the oldest man in public service," he being ninety-four years old.

The only speaker who could be heard from the rear seats was President Taft. His perceptive understanding of the effort involved in the founding of this library was exceedingly human and refreshing.

It is to the librarians and trustees of these various foundations that I would convey my profound felicitations. Everyone who has had to deal with human nature knows the difficulty of securing from those who are independent in control of any organization, however large or small, a willingness to subordinate their own importance and their own freedom by a union of that which is in their custody with similar trust in the custody of others, even in order to render all the trust more effective in the accomplishment of their original purposes.

It was that aged, aged man, Mr. John Bigelow, whose speech must have struck home for ACM. He recounted his dealings with Mr. Tilden, who hesitated to make his contribution when he learned from the annual report of the Boston Public Library that 90 percent of the books taken from it during the year of its opening had been works of fiction. "He asked me," said Mr. Bigelow, "whether it was really worth his while to devote so much or indeed any money whatever to fostering an abnormal appetite for imaginative literature."

Mr. Bigelow answered the argument by quoting Mother Goose!

> I said to him in substance that probably the first printed writing that ever made a lodgment in his mind was the reading, or hearing recited or sung, the melody of Mother Goose; that it never occurred to him that there was any incongruity in
> > Hi Diddle Diddle
> > The cat and the fiddle
> > The cow jumped over the moon
> or
> > The dish ran away with the spoon . . .

The real luxury of a printed book consists in the degree its contents are capable of interesting us. To create a genuine taste for that luxury, therefore, everyone must begin by reading what interests him, and imaginative literature is far more captivating to all people in whom a genuine taste for printed literature has not yet been formed.

The following day, May 24, the corridors of the great temple were aflood with people, and books were circulated at the prescribed places. The Central Children's Room staff were horrified to discover that some few rows of books had been shelved without pockets and date slips in place, but otherwise all went well. ACM's report for the year of the great opening reads:

The opening of the new Central Children's Room on May 24th is the most significant feature of the year's work and marks an advanced step in the general development of work with children. . . . The fact that for the first time in the development of special work for children in The New York Public Library we now have in one builidng the offices of administration of this work, a children's room with such an equipment of books and furniture and people as makes it possible to give a very practical idea of the work the library is doing in the interests of the boys and girls of the city, and to direct visitors who wish to study special phases of the work to the points most favorable for observation and consultation with experienced workers in widely varied districts covered by the forty branch libraries. To the cumulative experience of the branch children's rooms the Central Children's Room owes much of its vitality.

It was a surprise to the greater number of adults to be admitted to the Children's Room in the central building on equal terms with the children in the use of the books and in the personal attention of the assistants, and they have availed themselves of their privileges in increasing numbers, but with unusual regard for the comfort and convenience of the children. . . . Visitors from European countries attracted by what appealed to them as "a new idea in education" and requesting detailed information concerning children's libraries and children's books have been a large segment of the public. Correspondents for foreign papers and magazines have written of the work in several languages and European visitors during the past three months speak of having read of these accounts and of noting children's libraries as among the most interesting things to be seen in America.

CHILDREN'S ROW: THE CENTRAL CHILDREN'S ROOM

As I came out of Wiseman's Street,
The air was thick with driving sleet;
Crossing over Proudman's Square,
Cold louring clouds obscured the air;
But as I turned towards Goodman's Lane,
The burning sun came out again;
And on the roof of Children's Row
In solemn glory shone the snow.
There did I lodge; there hope to die:
Envying no man—no, not I.

WALTER DE LA MARE

FROM THE BEGINNING when plans were under way for a central library building designed as a fitting structure for a reference collection of heroic magnitude, children's books were considered a necessity by trustees and director alike. The Central Children's Room was allotted spacious quarters, and its book collections and activities were fully financed by Reference Department funds from 1911 until the middle 1940s. Then, in the cause of economy, it was summarily relinquished to that segment of the library supported by city funds and its ultimate demise as part of the central building thereby assured.

An early plan designated the room on the main floor now assigned to periodicals as the appointed place. But the northeast corner of the building paralleling Forty-second Street on the ground level, with one secluded window looking out on Fifth Avenue beyond a stretch of shrubbery, offered easier access to children and gave them space set apart from the rest of the library. In actuality, the space measured about 3,390 square feet. It consisted of two rectangular rooms, their symmetry refreshingly broken by an arched alcove stretching between. Here tables and chairs built for the picture-book set were in perfect proportion and the inset of a wide three-sided window seat, with polished wood paneling at back and sides, offered a tempting area for sliding as well as an invitation to be seated. Here cherished old books of the past were housed in a glass-doored bookcase that stood against one wall. Above it hung fine old English prints, the "Cries of London," and the portrait of an eighteenth-century duchess. Framed small pictures from Randolph Caldecott's books hung on the wood paneling of the window seat. In the minds of certain of the staff they were associated with Lord Dunsany, the Irish playwright, because upon walking into the Children's Room one morning in the company of ACM and catching sight of those pictures, he shook his cane at them with all six feet of his vigor and shouted aloud, "My Lord! Caldecott! Why, I had them as a child." In the shelter of this many-cornered place, the smallest clientele found within hand's reach a choice of picture books for home borrowing.

The wider of the two rooms was given over to books

for use in the library, a perpetual and changing exhibition of the soaring significance of children's books. The shelves on the north wall held the picture books of the world freshly arranged each morning not in classified order, being only haphazardly shelved by national origin, but in such a way as to show covers and contents to good advantage, and laid flat every evening that their spines might know a period of respite. Each of the windows in this room harbored a small window seat. "What I loved about that room," a noted professor of English at the University of California at Los Angeles remarked in 1960 in a tribute of remembrance, "was the window seats. You could sit there all day and read and nobody on your back." The Fifth Avenue window was set in an alcove that stood one step above the floor level. In the course of time, this became a proscenium, framing a succession of celebrations and celebrities: musicians, puppeteers, and poets; artists, editors, publishers; actors, playwrights, and magicians; storytellers and ballad singers; novelists and essayists. From that alcove Kate Douglas Wiggin as speaker inaugurated the first Book Week meeting in the Children's Room in November 1919. The bright procession of the years is encapsulated in the names of those who celebrated Book Week, St. Nicholas Eve, story hours, or other occasions in that room, addressing audiences of adults for whom books and children were a vital and a joyous concern: Ethel Parton, Laura Benét, Stephen Vincent Benét, Marie Shedlock, Margery Bianco, Wanda Gág, Edgar and Ingri Parin d'Aulaire, Thomas Handforth, Anne Thaxter Eaton, William Pène DuBois, Nora Archibald Smith, Lizette Woodworth Reese, Boris Artzybasheff, Padraic Colum, Ludwig Bemelmans, Ruth Sawyer Durand, Dorothy P. Lathrop, Lynd Ward, Constance Lindsay Skinner, Anne Parrish, René D'Harnoncourt, Reginald Birch, Evelyn Scott, Theodore Seuss Geisel, Edward Ardizzone, Louise Seaman Bechtel, Frederic Melcher, Carl Sandburg, Elizabeth Janet Grey, James Daugherty, Paul Honoré, Isabel de Palencia, Monica Shannon, Pamela Travers.

As for the children, coming as they often did two by two, representatives from the branch libraries that stretched from the Bronx to the farthest reaches of Staten Island, what sights and sounds awaited them in that place: Susan Bloch, daughter of the composer, playing on ancient instruments, the lute and the viola da gamba, time and again as a gesture of gratitude for childhood days spent in the Children's Room; Kurt Wiese, drawing "The Five Chinese Brothers" before their very eyes; Walter de la Mare, reading from his play *Crossings* and his own choice of poems from *Peacock Pie;*

(Overheard in the Children's Room of the Harlem Library: "Was you down to the big library yesterday?"

"No, what was there?"

"*Walter* was there and he read some of his poems.")

Hendrik Willem van Loon, historian, in celebration of his book *The Songs We Sing*, playing his fiddle to the accompaniment of a small, garishly decorated piano borrowed from a neighboring night club for the occasion; Walter Wilkinson, the noted English puppeteer; Eleanor Farjeon, in New York for the opening of her play *The Two Bouquets*, written in collaboration with her brother, reciting Sussex rhymes to the children; Katharine Adams, in the heyday of her popularity as a writer for girls, speaking to an audience of them on the eve of her wedding day and her departure for Ireland, and the bridegroom himself, sitting in their midst.

The boys had their turn, three hundred strong of them, members of the boys' clubs in branch libraries, when they came to hear Corinne Roosevelt Robinson speak of her recollections of her brother, Colonel Theodore Roosevelt, in the days when he was a "rough rider"; John Mulholland, the magician, staging a costumed performance; James Stephens, the Irish poet, in full control of a different magic.

Louise Seaman Bechtel in her *Books in Search of Children* writes of this occasion:

> How well I remember a day in the twenties, in this room, when Miss Moore lit the candles and introduced that great Irishman, James Stephens. He was famous for his adult poetry and novels like *The Crock of Gold*. We [Macmillan] had just published his robustly retold *Irish Fairy Tales* and I hoped he would tell those stories. There were mostly children present who seemed awed at Stephens' gnome-like figure and that long, dour face of his. Then, in his beautiful Dublin-English voice, he began reciting his adult poetry. He said poems like:
>
> > Come with me, under my coat,
> > And we will drink our fill
> > Of the milk of the white goat,
> > Or wine if it be thy will. . . .
>
> Next to me sat a rough-looking boy of about twelve. At the end of each poem, he gave me a dig with his sharp elbow. Once he muttered, "I *never* heard *nothing* like this!" At the end, he seized my arm. "Gee!" he cried, "Gee, what a man! He sure does know his onions!"
>
> To see that boy touched by genius, surprised by greatness—I shall never forget it.

The "new" poetry of the twenties burst upon the heads of children when Louis Untermeyer gave them pieces from his anthology, *This Singing World*, the children listening long past the closing hour of the library to be finally turned out on the arrival of the wheeled steel cart of steaming suds and Tony with his mop come to wash the floor.

More beautiful than gold that floor of tile imported from the red quarry of Wales. No free-standing book stacks broke the full sweep of it. Light was reflected from it in warm effulgence. The walls of the room above the book shelves were painted in neutral colors, a fitting background for changing exhibitions. There was a time when N. C. Wyeth longed to paint a mural across the alcove of the Fifth Avenue window, having chosen the story of "Rip Van Winkle" as his subject. Miss Moore must have been tempted to accept so generous an offer, but she decided against it, knowing that a mural was more or less fixed for all time and must forever dominate or vitiate exhibitions of a different mood and character. The full series of N. C. Wyeth's illustrations for *Robin Hood* hung in the room for many a long year, having been given as a gift to the Children's Room. But styles changed in children's-book illustrations, and those changes were reflected through the decades marking the life of the room, for neither ACM nor the staff she assembled there were people who showed any tendency, as far as art was concerned, "to get stuck in a period," as one critic put it.

One of the advantages accruing to ACM by the fact that the Central Children's Room was supported by private rather than public funds was the freedom it gave her in choice of staff. She was not bound by the rules of the city which forbade the employment of anyone who was not a citizen, nor by the complexities of professional requirements as the New York Public Library System became more standardized in its employment policies. She was free to select assistants in accordance with her strongest propensities—namely, by intuition and by a response to traits of personality. As a result, a succession of young women of unusual gifts, aptitudes, manifold backgrounds, and varied educational experience headed up the Central Children's Room from its inception, or were members of its staff. Flora G. Cutler, the first head, was one of Alice Tyler's most brilliant students from the Library School in Iowa. She was given eight months' intensive experience and training under ACM before she was appointed to that position. Marit Blehr of Norway, daughter of a diplomat who was Prime Minister of Norway; Jessie Sibley, an early professional librarian; Leonore St. John Power, native New Yorker, with gifts of originality, invention, and a ready response to merriment and diversity; Helen Masten, who brought to librarianship innate good judgment, an easy understanding of children, and a rare concern for the public, child and adult alike; Maria Cimino, Italian in heritage, singer by avocation, storyteller *par excellence*, and an artist in her creation of exhibitions. For many years Nadia Rodzianko was an assistant in that room. Russian by birth and heritage, she was a legend in the minds of the public and staff alike, her beauty and compassion memorable attributes. Claire Huchet Bishop, French by birth though American by marriage, served intermittently on the staff of the Children's Room. She became a noted writer of children's books, her two stories "Pancakes Paris" and "Twenty and Ten" lasting contributions to contemporary accounts of children of the Second World War. Summer schedules were upheld by professional librarians from various parts of the country who welcomed a turn of duty in that room and looked upon it as something of a vacation. Katherine Carnes, librarian of the Wesleyan College at Macon, Georgia, having once been a member of the staff, came summer after summer. In a letter of reminiscence she writes:

> The time in the Central Children's Room set its mark on me for life. The emphasis on exhibits, flowers, colors

"As wise as a child three years old"

Anne at seven holding a basket. She was always to be fascinated by baskets, with their assurance of color and promise of surprise.

Luther Sanborn Moore

Sarah Hidden Barker Moore

Almira Boardman Barker, Anne's maternal grandmother, a great lady who had been a beauty in her day

Alderwood. The front entrance to the great house.

The student at Bradford, 1892

Anne is second from the right, Flora Cutler beside her; at the far left is Marit Blehr, and next to her, Alice Tyler, of Iowa—all properly hatted and veiled for a picnic at Coney Island.

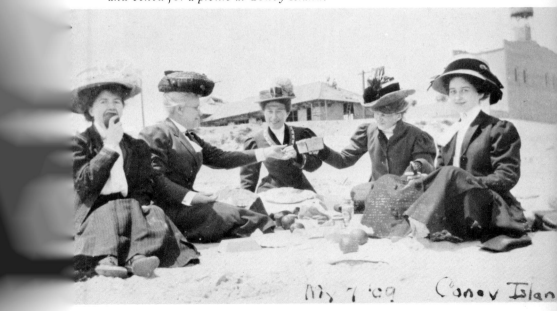

Portrait of Anne in the apple-green, corded silk wedding dress of her young aunt, Almira Barker.

The Supervisor of Children's Rooms in her first office of the
New York Public Library, 1906

*The Superintendent of
Work with Children of the
New York Public Library in
the golden era of the thirties*

"*When I write my name in this book, I promise . . .*"

The academic procession at Pratt Institute, 1955, when Anne Carroll Moore was mad[e] a Doctor of Letters

Anne Carroll Moore with Anne Carroll Peterson, her namesake, Washington, D.C., in the early 1950s

and light were all secondary to the emphasis on reading. How Miss Moore kept us on our toes about books! And not only books but the theatre and the multi-colored life of the city. Relentlessly she steered us toward the stars. Not one of us who followed her could ever be a mere drudge again.

Many a nonprofessional assistant found her talents developed and put to good use in the Central Children's Room. A name recurring in the reports is that of Katherine Seymour of Chazy, New York. Splendid woodsman she, a certain flavor of the out-of-doors permeating her storytelling, the vitality of her puppetry putting to shame the precious and finicky approach of some professionals in the field. Librarians from abroad asked to serve in the Children's Room for a space of time, welcoming the experience and the opportunity of association with Anne Carroll Moore: Mlle. Blanche Weber of the Institute of International Education in Geneva; Lydia Duproir of France; and Lillian Smith, the renowned head of the Boys' and Girls' Library of Toronto notable among them.

Every children's room in the city held "CH"—the designated abbreviation for the Central Children's Room in the Library Directory of Branches and Departments —in high regard, as a symbol of perfection and a source of refreshment. The majority of assistants spent some period of indoctrination there—days, weeks, or months— at the beginning of their assignments to the library system. All librarians in the system looked to CH with an air of expectancy as an arena where great and special events were celebrated, Book Week staff meetings, the Christmas staff meetings, St. Nicholas Eve celebrations, evening meetings of note and import.

In 1918 the American Book Sellers' Association, the

Booksellers' League of New York, the Women's National Book Association, and the New York Public Library contrived among them a significant series of meetings in CH. The chairman and originator of the project was Ben W. Huebsch, a prince among publishers who first launched into print Sherwood Anderson and other eagles in American literature and who founded with Albert J. Nock the distinguished liberal journal *The Freeman* (1920–1924), which has yet to be equaled in this land. His name is not often mentioned in relation to books for children, yet it was he who foresaw in 1918 the brilliance of the future for children's books and recognized the need for book publishers and booksellers to forswear ignorance of the subject and to inform themselves. It was he who asked ACM to prepare and deliver a series of lectures to a group of as distinguished book people as could be found in the city of New York— heads of publishing firms, editors, booksellers and librarians, writers, journalists, and artists. Tickets were available on request and each occasion drew a full house. Eight lectures in all were given, the first, "Children's Books; How a special literature for children originated, its growth and its expansion by subject." Then followed lectures on "Fairy Tales: their defenders and objectors"; "Histories: the readable and the reliable"; "Books about the War"; "Boys' books"; "Girls' stories"; "Illustrated Books, including picture books for little children"; and the final lecture of the series, the "Holiday Books of 1918." A watershed in the history of children's books in America was that year 1918, with Children's Book Week to be inaugurated the next year and Macmillan, the publisher, announcing its special and separate department, the first of its kind, for the publishing of children's books, under Louise Seaman Bechtel. The Central Children's

Room, meanwhile, after almost a decade of existence, stood ready to offer its resources and the proven validity of its founding philosophy.

With the passing of the years, the stacks and offices alike in the Central Building bulged with expanding collections, and some departments looked with covetous eyes upon the wide area of the Children's Room. Business librarians, from time to time, importuned the director of the library to surrender the space of the Children's Room to the greater need of business research. The claws of that argument were clipped somewhat by records showing the use of the room by publishers, writers, artists, interior decorators, stage designers, costume designers, textile and wallpaper designers, choreographers, and many others for whom the arts were a matter of business. Because children themselves did not use the room in comparable numbers to those served by the branch libraries situated in crowded residential neighborhoods, casual observers asked, "But where are the children?" Some library officials found it difficult to weigh the measurable count of bodies present and books circulated against such immeasurable assets as a philosophy of education given bone and sinew, proven by demonstration, the reach of its influence international in scope.

The children who were habitués of the room either came great distances, on book pilgrimage, or from the streets bounding Fifth Avenue, east and west, which were business districts not heavily populated by families. The children, being few in number, were well known to the staff, who watched their reading with interest born of intimacy. ACM knew many of the children also because she made it almost a daily habit to stop by CH as she entered or left the building, and the children who frequented the library became her friends, among them the fair-haired, beautiful Farren children, Constance, Mary, George, and Julian, their parents both in the theater. Miss Moore's book *Nicholas: A Manhattan Christmas Story* grew out of encounters with children there. One lonely child from Belgium, Aimée, spent nearly the whole of every day in the Central Children's Room, both parents struggling to make a living in the war years of 1918 and beyond and finding in the Children's Room a haven for their child.

On the southern wall of the Reference Room a bank of shelves was reserved for the display of books related to exhibitions. What diversity of interest was represented there through all the years and what a record of generosity on the part of "Cooperating Agencies," to use a term favored by sociologists. The seasonal subjects and those that became traditional thread the accounts of the annual reports: Spring, Heroes, Old Valentines; Feasts and Holidays, diversified by the celebration of such matters as Kites and Kite Flying; Toy Theaters, Pirates and Buccaneers; but unexpected excitement is discovered amid all the poetic, imaginative topics related to the humanities in such events as "an exhibition on aviation, lent by the Aero Club of America; a transportation exhibition, with small models of gasoline engines, ocean liners, electric and steam engines, lent by the New York Central Railroad and the New York Society of Model Engineers; a whaling exhibition for ship models lent by the Whaling Museum of New Bedford, Massachusetts; an exhibit of push-about boats in a miniature harbor, small motor boats, and sailing ship models made and lent by Mr. Paul Revere Stevens of Portland, Maine."

Long before the neighboring glass house of the United Nations ennobled the East River of New York, the Central Children's Room dramatized its allegiance to internationalism not only in its book collection, its staff, and its exhibitions, but also in its daily responses to the children and adults of the multi-nationed city.

On one occasion an exhibition stretched from April through October. That was the year 1933, when the Children's Room was *en fête* in the cause of internationalism. Children's books published in England, Ireland, France, Germany, Czechoslovakia, and the United States were successively represented, and each exhibit was accompanied by informative talks and discussion. The brilliance of the whole venture permeates the perfectly matter-of-fact account as Miss Moore states it in the annual report, which reads in part as follows:

To the exhibition of French books selected and arranged by Mrs. Claire Huchet Bishop, additional distinction was given by the inclusion of paintings of circus subjects, drawings, and lithographs, by Edy Legrand, lent by the Sterner Galleries. The Vildrac Galleries in Paris also lent original drawings by this artist for *Les Lunettes de Lion.* Three talks about French children's books and their illustrators were given by Mrs. Bishop. Many teachers of French in public and private schools availed themselves of the opportunity to discuss their reading lists and add fresh titles to school collections.

The twenty-second birthday of the children's room was celebrated during the French exhibition with a Guignol show given by the courtesy of the French Line. The theatre and the puppets were brought to the room from the *Île de France.* Two hundred children under ten years old, from the branch libraries and the Extension Division, were introduced to Guignol and spent a memorable afternoon. It mattered not at all that the play was in the French language, the pantomime being perfectly understood by children who knew not a word of French.

Contemporary German books were selected and arranged by Ernest Eisele, who lent from his own collection a number of *Images d'Épinal.* These, with some drawings by Wilhelm Busch from the Prints Collection, made interesting points of contrast with modern books. Mr. Eisele opened the exhibition with a discussion of "International Trends and German Children's Books of the Twentieth Century." Dr. Hellmut Lehmann-Haupt gave a lecture on "Modern Illustration and the Color Printing of Children's Books in Germany," illustrating his talk with a selection from the books shown in the exhibition. "German Books for American Children" were discussed by Anne Thaxter Eaton and May Massee.

The exhibition of Czech children's books, selected by Mrs. Jan Matulka from the Czechoslovak collection of the Webster Branch, was opened with a special program on July 12th. Dr. Jaroslav Novák, Consul General of Czechoslovakia, who was the guest of honor, spoke of the unconquerable love of books which had persisted in his country for centuries and of his own first impressions of the children's rooms in American libraries, with their free access to books and their natural ways of fostering new interests in reading.

The principal influence in Czech children's books and their illustration spring from folk lore and folk life. The vivid decorative sense applied to the making of even the books which are cheapest in price was well brought out in the selection. Paintings in oil and in water colors by Jan Matulka, representing the countryside associated with national folk legends, provided a colorful background. The importance attached to childhood as shown in the work of the artists Ales and Manes and the provision for a special literature for children made by the Czechoslovak Government of today gave entirely new impressions of the country of Comenius to many visitors from summer schools. . . .

The event that triggered this celebration was an exhibition held in the main exhibition room of the library, arranged by the Metropolitan Museum of Art and the New York Public Library, its subject: "Children's Books of Yesterday, an Exhibition from Many Countries." The catalogue was written by ACM and shows her at her bibliographic best.

> The books have been chosen, not primarily for textual merit, but for their originality, their rarity and historical significance, for qualities of colorful illustration and ingenious design, for their power of invoking lively memories of childhood and youth. . . .
>
> Pause for a moment before a quaint little book of spiritual instruction printed by Hugh Newman at The Grasshopper in the Poultry, London, 1696, and read these lines under the portrait frontispiece of the most redoubtable of parents:
>
> > Learn little children,
> > Born to live today;
> > Art cannot make our glass of time to stay.
> > Live much in little space of time, for why,
> > You're not born to live, but born to dye.
>
> Born to live is the most inspiriting testimony of the adjoining case to which Dr. Hoffman, wise parent and physician of the 1840's, contributes his *Struwwelpeter*. It was Dr. Hoffman who first uncurbed the comic spirit and mixed enough genuine fun with behavior problems to anticipate the comic strip by half a century. The famous picture book made by Dr. Hoffman for his three-year-old son is here shown, side by side, with that inimitable French book of manners, *La Civilité*, illustrated by Boutet de Monvel.
>
> By such sharp contrasts, as well as by familiar trails of association, one is made aware of changing attitudes toward childhood in different centuries and of the changing form and perishable substance of children's books in many lands.

No demonstration in the world could have been more fortuitously staged than was Work with Children in the New York Public Library, with the office of its founding chief—Room 105, as it was known—on one floor and on the floor below the actuality of her inspiration made visual in every facet of its character down to the minutest subtlety of its concept. The Central Children's Room became a show place of the city. The pages of its guest books attest to the diversity of notables who lingered there awhile.

Two years after the opening of the Children's Room, the International Exhibition of Modern Art in the 69th Regiment Armory sent shock waves through the whole of American culture and brought many visitors to the city, eager to know at first hand the power of its insurgency. Among such visitors was a petite young woman from Boston. She was secretary to the president of the Women's Educational and Industrial Union, an organization that, in addition to selling jams and jellies in its exchange, concerned itself with the wages of women in industry and the betterment of their working conditions. Her name was Bertha Mahony. A friend suggested to her that after having known the heady experience of Duchamp's "Nude Descending a Staircase" and other revolutionary pictures, she might find it reassuring to visit the new library at Forty-second Street, especially the Children's Room. She made the pilgrimage alone, and as she sat in the Children's Room, watching children and adults enjoying the place on terms of equality, it came into her mind that a bookshop similarly dedicated to a celebration of books, in a like atmosphere of freedom of choice, would be a grand undertaking in the cause of education for the Women's Industrial Union. By 1916 the bookshop was a reality in Boston, with Bertha Mahony in charge of it.

Anne Carroll Moore did not leave entirely to chance the discovery of the Central Children's Room by men and women whom she knew would recognize its quality. When she read in the newspapers or heard from the gossip of literary circles that some noted person was in the city, or expected, she wrote or telephoned them, inviting them to meet her in the Central Children's Room. By this means such notables as Ethel Sidgewick and May Sinclair had come at her invitation and remained to be caught in the net of her friendship. In 1920 E. V. Lucas, the noted English essayist, visited New York. Author of *Old Fashioned Tales* and *Forgotten Tales of Long Ago*, he had also written two books for children, *The Slow Coach* and *Anne's Terrible Good Nature*. ACM wrote a letter of invitation to him and had in reply the following:

May 26, 1920

Dear Miss Moore:

I wish I had seen you to congratulate you on the Room: but I am a diffident person and had no introductory document. So instead I walked about and admired, and then settled down in a chair and read for half an hour in a book which I had not seen for years and which I don't mind saying for all my diffidence I found amusing: *Anne's Terrible Good Nature*.

I shall tell some English librarians about your triumph. Believe me

Yours sincerely
E.V. Lucas

They never met face to face, but he like many another responded to her importunity and found the encounter memorable.

She captured Arthur Rackham on the very eve of his departure for England, he having been in New York to be lionized at certain exhibitions of his pictures. Anne, in company with a young artist, Joseph Paget-Fredericks, whose pictures were on display in the Children's Room, pursued him to the gallery—it was Scott and Fowles' of Fifth Avenue—on the chance of finding him there only to discover that he, meanwhile, in answer to her invitation, had gone to the library, a last-minute response to her invitation. ACM's account of the matter read:

> We fairly flew down Fifth Avenue and arrived breathless in the Children's Room to find Arthur Rackham, no other, tall, spare, matter-of-fact, looking at the drawings of the young artist with critical yet discerning eyes.[1]

No, he had never seen New York alight from the Brooklyn side, and he had nothing to do "but kick up his heels" between the moment of his encounter with Anne until the midnight sailing of his ship the *Olympic*. They dined at the grill in the Breevoort Hotel. Then Anne hailed a taxi and in this, her accustomed coach, she crossed and recrossed, with Arthur Rackham and the artist, the Brooklyn and Manhattan bridges until time to take him to the ship.

The most audacious of Anne's pursuits for the glory of the Children's Room had as its objective a king, a queen, and a young prince. In 1919 the officials of the city designated the New York Public Library as the most appropriate place in which to welcome in public reception the notables of the world who came to visit the United States at war's end. The Fifth Avenue entrance was uncluttered, the noble staircases on either side marble parentheses enclosing the rotunda that marked the entrance into the main exhibition room. There the king, Albert of Belgium, and Queen Elizabeth and the prince, Duke of Bravant, were to be honored.

It was unthinkable that a flesh-and-blood king, queen, and prince should enter the library and be deprived of so much as a glimpse of the Children's Room and in turn that children, steeped in the lore of kings, queens, and princes, should miss by a flight of stairs the sight of three such beings at one and the same time. Inquiry revealed that such, indeed, was to be the fact. Anne Carroll Moore approached all the chairmen of the Planning and Arrangement Committees, including the dignitaries of the Office of the Mayor, but the answer was the same. The schedule was too crowded; it would be late in the day when they reached the library. "There is no way, Miss Moore, by means of which the party can visit the Children's Room."

No way! When the hour arrived for the reception, ACM said to one of the assistants in the room, "Let's go upstairs and see." Crowds of people stood in orderly lines in the great room, a path cleared between for the royal procession. Anne and her companion pushed forward to the front of the crowd. It was apparent that the queen, walking to the king's left, would pass very close to them. When the moment came, Anne stepped forward and said to the queen, "Ask to see the Children's library. It isn't on the schedule."

Six o'clock was the hour of closing for the Children's Room. On this day, at 5:45 P.M., three policemen shouldered themselves through the door of the room and behind them came the king, the queen, and the young prince, followed by a flurry of equerries and ladies-in-waiting, one among them squealing with delight as she seated herself on a succession of the small chairs in the Picture Book Room. The queen, in her turn, cried out in happy recognition of the great French histories by Job that stood on the picture-book shelves. "I brought my children up on those books," she said. The heroic king in military uniform shook hands with the children and listened to what they had to say. The Duke of Bravant was the practical member of the family. "Who pays for all this?" he asked. ACM told them of Aimée, who had only just returned to Belgium. Queen Elizabeth asked for the child's address and said she would write her upon her return. There is no way of knowing whether she did or not, but among Anne's papers there is a far from perfunctory note written by a lady-in-waiting at the request of the queen, thanking her for having had the wit to have gotten the queen to the Children's Room on unscheduled time.

"When the curtain goes up, the scene must be there." Anne had overheard Arthur Rackham speak these words of advice to the artist in the Children's Room on that day of pursuit and the bridges. In the first quarter of this century, when curtains were rising on library work with children all over America and in Europe as well, the scene was there: the Central Children's Room, ordered, inspired, and incomparable. Time is a cruel scene shifter, working secretly and in silence, all the more easily when none survives to keep the stage light burning. Anne knew this. "As long as you are here," she said to her immediate successor, "the room will be safe."

Now it no longer exists in the central building; but beyond the curtain descending, the action and attitudes engendered there persist on countless stages of the mind. No child, be he Hindu, Dane, or Ghanaian, in school or public libraries, wherever books are made available to him—no child, lifting his eyes for a moment from the pages of his book, but pays homage to CH though he knows nothing of its existence. Such is the measure of the drama once played against the scene of the Central Children's Room.

THE SHADOW OF
THE TOWER

> *Whatever disagreement there may be as
> to the scope of the phrase "due process of
> law," there can be no doubt that it embraces
> the fundamental conception of a fair trial,
> with opportunity to be heard. Mob law does
> not become due process of law by securing
> the assent of a terrorized jury. We are not
> speaking of mere disorder, but of a case
> where the processes of justice are actually
> subverted.*
>
> JUSTICE OLIVER WENDELL HOLMES

A LARGE PACKET of crumbling newspaper clippings
lay among the hoarded memorabilia of Anne Carroll
Moore. It gave account of the Leo Frank case, a *cause
célèbre* in its time that resulted in a wave of anti-Semitism
and demonstrated the heights of nobility and the depths
of depravity that human beings are capable of attaining
under stress. Like the Sacco-Vanzetti case of the twenties,
the controversy surrounding the trial and conviction of
the accused swept through the body politic, dividing the

country, arousing the consciences of men and women throughout the world, and leaving a bitter heritage of guilt that has increased with the years as continuing investigation and study substantiate the belief held by many that, in these cases, the cause of justice was subverted by prejudice, bigotry, and hysteria.

Even at a distance of fifty-five years, to read these yellowed columns of print is to be shadowed by the anguished terror of those whom the Furies pursue without pity. The shriek of Oedipus, the cry of Lear—"Horror! horror! horror"—ring in the memory, echoing as they do from the streets of Atlanta, Georgia, U.S.A. The image of Prometheus that Leo Frank invoked on his own behalf in an open letter to his enemy, Joseph Brown, ex-Governor of Georgia, proved tragically appropriate. "I remembered that when Prometheus was bound to the rock, it was the vulture, and not the eagle, that struck its beak into his vitals."

Confederate Memorial Day, like its counterpart, Decoration Day in the North, is dedicated to the memory of the soldier dead. The day is numinous in the South, commemorating as it does the loss of the Confederacy as well as the death of heroes.

On one Confederate Memorial Day, April 26, 1913, the curtain rose with epic irony upon the tragedy of Leo Frank. On that day a thirteen-year-old girl, Mary Phagan, was murdered, her mutilated body discovered in the basement of the pencil factory where she was employed. The superintendent and part owner of that factory was Leo Frank, a young man who had come to Atlanta from New York after some months of technical study in Europe, to establish and manage a pencil factory founded by his family. He had married an Atlanta girl and was held in highest esteem by the Jewish community of the city, serving on the board of managers of the Hebrew Orphans' Home and as president of B'nai B'rith. When he was accused of the murder he went to trial confident that in a matter of weeks his innocence would be a proven fact. The evidence against him was circumstantial and patently contrived. In the natural order of things it would have been proved beyond a doubt that he could not have committed this crime, but the times were not ordinary. A confluence of inimical events and circumstances, largely out of the past, compounded his doom. Old habits of thought obtained in the South as yet not bound to the North by ties of two great shared national wars. The War Between the States remained the ultimate tragedy in the minds of the Southerners. Atlanta was adjusting to a new industrialism, resented because it destroyed old patterns of life. The rural poor, black and white alike, flocked into the city in search of work. A rising crime rate overwhelmed the constabulary, which, in that fateful spring, was held accountable for a shameful record of unsolved and unpunished crimes. In this most recent case of murder, the least clue was seized upon with a fervor of hope for quick conviction and with careless regard for thorough investigation. At best, anybody from the North was considered an outsider. Leo Frank was regarded not only as an outsider but as a representative of the unwelcome industrial infiltration, and in addition he bore the ancient stigma of the Jew. Neither he nor his lawyers were prepared for the raging antagonism and bigotry of the populace that surfaced in the Atlanta of 1913. After a trial of four months he was found guilty and condemned to be hanged.

Not until the preparations for his first appeal were under way did the case of Leo Frank command the attention of the press in the North. Not until then did his lawyers ask him for the names of people who had known him in his youth. Among the first names he recalled was that of a librarian at Pratt Institute Library in Brooklyn. He wondered if she were still there. The lawyers found her in New York. By this means ACM came to the realization that the Leo Frank who sought her aid was the boy she had known and cherished since the day of her first encounter with him. He it was who had marked his departure with the gift of a plant to the Children's Library. He it was who had named his toy boats after the characters of the *Leather Stocking Tales*. His was the definition of heroism preserved in the reports of the Pratt Free Library:

> In ancient times a brave man only was a hero but now in modern times a hero has to be both brave and good morally and virtually.

Immediately Anne began a correspondence that lasted until the end. She undertook a campaign in his behalf. It never occurred to her that, as this world goes, she was a person without means in a position of limited influence. She inaugurated petitions. She wrote articles and letters describing the boyhood of Leo Frank as she had known it. One such letter was published in the New York *Times* in March 1914 and reprinted at least twice during the years that followed. The faculty of the Pratt High School where Leo Frank had gone as a boy were enlisted in the cause at Anne's request. Old letters of commendation written to Leo's father and mother by teachers and the superintendent of the school were resurrected from the file and sent with a petition signed by fourteen former teachers. These were to be presented to the Governor of the state and the Prison Commission at an appropriate time.

For all the tragedy of the situation, ACM could not forget that she was a librarian eager for testimonies to the influence of books on the character of man and boy. Late in 1914 she had apparently asked Frank to tell her what he had enjoyed as a boy. By this time the handwritten letters from Leo had given way to typewritten notes because his correspondence had become voluminous. On December 17 he wrote:

> . . . You must excuse me if I cannot comply with your wish and enumerate the books which appealed most to me when I was a young boy. When once more I am in New York I will be glad to do so and talk with you on this.

The trials went on. The first appeal for a new trial was denied by Judge Leonard Roan, who declared even as he handed down a decision against Frank that he was not certain of the man's guilt. For the second time, Leo Frank was given the death sentence. This time the date was set for April 17, 1914, his birthday. The State Supreme Court, in its turn, upheld Judge Roan's ruling, denying a new trial. When at last the case was debated before the Supreme Court of the nation, it too rejected the plan for a new trial, the decision based not on the question of Frank's guilt or innocence but on a technicality concerning the legality of the procedure in the original trial. For the fourth time Leo Frank was condemned to death, the date set for the hanging June 22, 1915.

The last refuge for Frank was a pardon or commutation of sentence by the Governor, John M. Slaton. Frank wanted to ask for a pardon, but in the face of mob violence which threatened to overwhelm the city, his lawyers thought the wiser plan a petition for commutation of sentence to life imprisonment. Meanwhile, Frank was held in the Tower, the Atlanta prison situated within sight of the capitol building. There he held strange court, for men and women of note came to see him by the dozens and wrote to him out of their deep sympathy and interest and concern: artists, stars of opera and stage, professors, senators, judges, journalists and reporters. More than one hundred thousand pleas for clemency flooded the Governor's office and the office of the Prison Commission.

At this point Anne went to the director of the New York Public Library, Edwin Anderson, and asked for a leave of absence. She intended to go to Atlanta to present in person petitions to the Governor and to visit Frank in prison. If the library were not willing to grant her the time, she declared herself ready to submit her resignation. Mr. Anderson was sympathetic to her cause, granted her a leave with the stipulation that the New York Public Library, as an institution, not be involved. Anne arrived in Atlanta on June 13. She spent eight days there, going to the home of the Franks immediately after settling in at a hotel. She had known Leo's mother in the Brooklyn days, but now she met his wife and father for the first time. Many relatives of the Franks had gathered in Atlanta to await the outcome of the hearing, which Governor Slaton held just four days before the end of his term. Anne talked with Frank's lawyers, who urged her to persist in seeking an audience with the Governor. She consulted with Rabbi David Marx and with many other Georgians of influence, Jew and Gentile alike, who were working in the cause of Leo Frank, and every evening was spent in the Tower in conversation with Leo and the men and women who gathered there.

On Thursday of that week she finally resigned herself to the fact that she could not reach the Governor. She took a trolley out to Lake Gatlin by way of comforting herself and there gathered boughs of Georgia pine to take with her to the Tower that evening. Her own words tell the story of that time:

For nearly two years I wanted a favorable opportunity to visit him in prison, fearing lest in the desire to give evidence of my friendship I might prove only one more source of trial and persecution. On April 29th, 1915 he had written: "Never fear that I will falter in this fight. I am fighting for name, honor and life, for loved relatives and friends. To me life without honor is unsufferable. I know I have builded right. My faith is undaunted; and while I do not at this moment know how, and while the future stretches dark before my mental vision, I feel intuitively that I will yet win the name, freedom, honor and life which are mine rightfully."

When the final hearing before the Governor began on June 12th, within ten days set for the execution, I went to Atlanta unannounced. I had never been inside a prison and as I wished to come into Mr. Frank's presence without announcement I went first to the home of his wife who accompanied me to the Tower of the prison in which he was confined. It was evening and I steeled my nerves for a trying ordeal. But as one door after another was opened for our admission and I observed the courtesy and respect of the attendants toward Mrs. Frank, I began to feel, what I afterward found to be true, that the sheriff was a man among his men whether jailors or prisoners.

Mr. Frank received me as I might have received him had he come unexpectedly into the library where we had first met and where all our previous encounters had taken place. We began where we left off for to each the other seemed unchanged.

Had I needed any visible sign of his innocence I should have found it at the first handclasp and look into his eyes. The years had developed the man from the boy but the heart and the smile of the boy remained with a deepened sense of the meaning of my visit. . . . The bars which had seemed so terrible as I pictured the restriction of the liberty of an innocent man became the sign of his safety and security as I remembered "the mass-meeting against Frank" I had seen in front of the Capitol, only a block away, that very Sunday afternoon. His presence radiated cheer and affection as he introduced a friend of his boy-hood to friends he had made in Atlanta.

I went back to my hotel with an easier mind than I had known for two years. I remained in Atlanta eight days. I visited Mr. Frank every day and found him always cheer-ful, serene and hopeful, as ready to listen to others as to talk himself but with a fund of conversation as rich and in-exhaustible as it was varied and interesting. . . .

Monday morning's paper, June 21, brought news of Governor Slaton's decree of commutation. In the face of public feeling, his was an act of enormous courage that cost him, as he knew it would, his political future. Slaton had been the fair-haired boy of Georgia politics, elected to office "on a tidal wave of popularity, enthusiasm un-precedented in Georgia's annals." By this one act he be-came the enemy of the mob who clamored for his death. For the first time in the history of the country, the militia was called out to protect the Governor of a state.

Frank's lawyers called Anne at her hotel Monday morning and advised her not to visit the capitol. Frank, meanwhile, at the Governor's instruction, had been smuggled out of the Tower and transferred to the prison farm at Milledgeville. Anne had spent the day with mem-bers of the Frank family, who, in the evening, drove her along the river. "Moonlight on the river," she wrote in her notepaper diary, "and the mob on Peachtree Road."

She saw Leo for the last time in the Tower Sunday evening, only hours before his transfer from the place. What he said to her then was to compensate beyond telling for all the talk about books he had been unable to give her previously. She rushed back to the hotel to scribble down on the inevitable piece of notepaper the gist of the matter, dated it, and slipped it carelessly among her records of the visit.

> A librarian's work is very intangible. I have been thinking of this since you have been here and I want you to know before you go away how it seems in the life of one man, brought almost to the breaking point by the bitterest experience of life. What you did for me thro' the Library has gone to make up the *reserve force* I have relied upon to carry me thro' this. It is inexhaustible in itself but the renewal of it by your presence at this time has given me such a realization of your own faith in the ideal as inspires me anew.

The return to New York was almost joyous. Now there would be time for Leo Frank to prove his innocence. He wrote two letters to her from Milledgeville, the first on July 2:

Office of Warden
State Prison Farm
    Milledgeville,   July 2, 1915
      Georgia   Friday

My dear Miss Moore:
Your letter of 6/28 brought to me its message of cheer and inspiration. I was so glad to hear from one whose helpful friendship meant so much to me during those last trying hours in the "Tower." It was the voice and presence of the long ago, infusing spirit and exhorting manhood for the last final test—a test that tries the staunchest of mere human flesh. However, thank God, I passed successfully and with whole skin through the ordeal and I am now with ever increasing strength facing the new conditions.
I am gradually adjusting myself to "stripes" and the new environment. There is much to study of human nature here and I will make the most of it. I have gained in weight and my color is getting better daily. I have good appetite and

I sleep well. I have been given certain tasks in the Prison Building which do not over tax my strength. This too gives me enough exercise to keep me in trim.

The Warden and his staff are kindly and solicitous. I know I shall get on famously with them. This is the breathing spell in the present phase of my life to gain the strength and reserve for the spurt to freedom, vindication and that honor which is justly and rightfully mine.

Suffering, mental especially, is the "fining-pot" of experience, the leavening influence in Life. I should be better—more efficient because of this ordeal.

Won't you please send me the addresses of ——. I wish to write to them.

With every good wish, I am

Cordially,
Leo M. Frank

The second letter, dated July 17, 1915, follows:

Office of Warden
STATE PRISON FARM
   J. E. SMITH, Warden
   JOHN SAYE, Asst. Warden
Milledgeville, Georgia   July 17th, 1915

My dear Miss Moore:

I have your letters of July 5 & 13 & was certainly glad to hear from you. Was indeed grieved to hear that your sister-in-law passed away. I thank you for the book of views of N.Y. City as well as the other printed matter. I was waiting for the addresses you so kindly sent to me.

I am glad to report that I continue well, and am daily improving in health and strength. In my spare moments, I attend to my correspondence, read the papers & occasionally a magazine. Occasionally, too, I operate the Victrola whereby I can, thro' the ingenuity of modern science, bring Caruso, Alda, Farrar, et al. within the confines of the State Prison.

On last Wednesday, my dear Lucille visited me and remained in the vicinity. She will stay possibly until the beginning of next week. You know how comforting and pleasurable it is to me to have my wife near, & where the opportunity is given me each day of seeing her for an hour or two.

I still continue to get letters from friends all over the U.S.A. enclosing clippings in praise of Gov. Slaton's action. He will surely be a big national political figure some day in the future.

I hear frequently from my good friends in Atlanta & several have already visited me here. The officials here are kindness itself, for which, all things considered I am truly thankful.

I assure you I shall be glad to hear from you at any time the spirit moves you. We must keep in touch, one with the other.

With cordial regards & good wishes in which dear Lucille joins me, I am

Sincerely

LEO M. FRANK

Give my greetings to all inquiring friends.

In the night of that very day, July 17, one of the prisoners who worked in the kitchen in Milledgeville and thus had access to knives attacked Frank as he lay sleeping and all but slashed his throat from ear to ear. Two fellow prisoners, who were doctors, clamped the jugular vein and stopped the hemorrhage. "I am going to live," he said. "I must live. I must vindicate myself."

One month after this attempt on Frank's life, on August 16, twenty-five men broke into the prison, overpowered the guards and the warden, took Leo Frank to Marietta, the home of Mary Phagan, and there lynched him.

Anne was on vacation in New England when the terrible news reached her. She made straightway for Portland, Maine, and Cousin Alice. There she found succor, a welcoming room, a stretch of silence, and the summer sky and weather to heal her spirit.

Timeless and contemporary are the words she wrote:

Not until we become fully alive to the social, political and racial issues behind the tragedy can we realize that the father, husband, son or brother of any one of us might find himself in such a situation as Leo Frank faced in Georgia.

NICHOLAS

Every critic should try to create some-
thing once in a lifetime, regardless of conse-
quence. It's more difficult than praising or
finding fault with the work of other people;
it's more fun; it heightens appreciation of all
that is admirable in any sincere attempt to
tell something new and different in story or
pictures; and it enlarges one's sympathies
for things which do not "come off."

ACM

I T WAS TOLD of Louis Couperous, the Dutch novelist
whose series of novels, *Small Souls,* created a stir in the
twenties, that his walking stick had become to him so
much of a person as to oblige him, when spending a solitary evening at the theater, to purchase two seats, one for
himself and one for his cane. The habit of endowing inanimate objects with life is as ancient as man himself.
Anthropology bears witness to the fact that for primitive
man every stone and tree, the very pots in which he
cooked food, his weapons and his drums, all shared with
him the common factor—life. Children never hesitate to
bring alive in their imaginations toys, sticks, or teapots,

according to their whim, nor to invent imaginary companions, according to their need. That such objects should speak with voices of their own follows the manner of their genesis.

The release of emotion through a surrogate person or object is an oft-told tale in literature and in life. Cyrano de Bergerac could speak the depth of his love for Roxanne only through the voice of another; in *Lili*, the musical play of our own time, based on the novel of Paul Gallico, *The Man Who Hated People*, the puppet declared his love while the puppeteer himself was locked speechless in his own person. The measure of the ventriloquist's appeal lies in the degree of wit, raillery, and impudence his dummy is permitted beyond the character and personality of the performer. The mystique of the inanimate embraces also the power of the symbolic. Hans Christian Andersen, that master magician of endowing the inanimate with life, understood the beneficence of symbols that accrue to themselves the past and the future, holding in their singularity essences and epiphanies. The amulet, the mascot, the lucky sixpence, and the rabbit's foot—these are symbols at the lowest level of meaning. At the highest level are the holy insignia of all religions, signifying in their design and patterns the long history of man's spiritual desiring.

There was an object in the life of Anne Moore. It began as a means whereby to catch the immediate attention of children. As Superintendent of Work with Children, she was expected to appear at the special events scheduled in the children's rooms, from Throgs Neck in the Bronx to the far reaches of Staten Island: Christmas story hours everywhere, Halloween at Harlem Branch, St. Patrick's Day at George Bruce, the Feast of Lights at Seward Park, H. C. Andersen's birthday at Hamilton

Fish, the Polish celebrations at Tompkins Square, the Czech story hour at Webster, puppet plays at Jackson Square, peep shows at Aguilar, the Cranford Reading Club at Fordham—bookish affairs and fetes created by an imaginative staff to bring drama into the quiet business of reading and to heighten the common day for thousands of children who trudged up and down the steep stairways of branch libraries to second floors, day after day, in search of pleasure and diversion.

The long journeys by subways, elevateds, buses or ferries, and taxi reduced by not one iota Anne's expectancy of pleasure in these events. She never ceased to be refreshed by the response of the children. Invariably she sat where she could watch their faces, straight on.

On each of these occasions, before the main event, as it were, the Superintendent of Work with Children was introduced to the audience and expected to speak to them. Now, it is no easy matter to address to good effect a group of children who, like John Gilpin, are "on pleasure bent." How many adults can accomplish it without condescension or without assuming that ghastly tone of exaggerated enthusiasm which is too often deemed appropriate to such an affair? For a storyteller, the initial approach is easy—"Once upon a time." But Anne was no storyteller in the accepted or professional sense. She knew instinctively what to say to children, but to be able to produce and hold aloft some object which aroused curiosity and held immediate attention was to capture the group quickly and entire. "I have brought someone with me," she would announce, opening up one of her copious handbags, or fumbling in some colorful subsidiary basket, bag, or carry-all hanging on her arm, to produce at last the figure of Nicholas.

For Anne, the wooden figure of Nicholas came to embody all children she had known or encountered in New York City, in Louisiana and Texas, in Boston and in Brooklyn, in Utah, Minnesota, California and the Pacific Northwest, in Canada, England, Scandinavia, and France. He symbolized the essence of childhood itself.

As the years passed, an accrual of memories and associations gathered about him. He acquired a symbolic patina, like the walnuts the Chinese fondle in their hands for a lifetime, and became a token of the richness of life which time and her own genius and incomparable capacity for friendship had bestowed upon her.

Nicholas came into being on the day before Christmas, 1920, when the staff of the Central Children's Room gathered up attractive trifles to send up to Room 105, ACM's office, by way of saying Merry Christmas to Miss Moore. Leonore Power was in charge of the room at that time, and in the course of her meanderings through the Gourmet Shop at Bloomingdale's she had come upon the sturdy wooden figure of a Dutch boy, designed as a toy, about eight inches high, his arms and legs articulated at shoulders and hips. His costume was of splendid stuff, first-rate homespun wool, blue trousers, a gray jacket, stitched about the edge with red yarn. He wore a minuscular gray woolen scarf about his neck, tied at a giddy angle, and a helmetlike wooden hat, permanently attached to his head by the woodcutter's skill. (Anne spoke of it as resembling the caps worn by the French *poilu*.) Miss Power bought him on the spur of the moment and set him atop the basket of delectables sent upstairs to the office.

Anne loved him at first sight. He could stand free of support since his feet were formed of wooden blocks, and his seemingly mittened hands were scooped out into small hollows, only the thumbs protruding. Anne discovered at once that the hands were capable of holding objects, small trinkets, birthday-cake candles, and many of the inconsequential trifles that are the delight of children. ". . . his hands were the kind of hands you want to shake or to fill full of things to give away" was Anne's own description of him.

He was immediately established as a tradition. Obviously Dutch, she called him Nicholas Knickerbocker after the patron saint of the Dutch, who had founded New York, and Washington Irving's well-loved Knickerbockers. The association with Christmas was natural since he had made his initial appearance on Christmas Eve. Moreover, he could easily be carried in her handbag, and it was there he took up more or less permanent residence.

Three points of extravagance marked Anne's wardrobe, no matter how tired or worn her workaday clothes might be: shoes, gloves, and handbags. The shoes were costly, setting off her narrow feet, her ankles, delicate-boned and slim, her legs tight-fleshed and shapely even in old age. The gloves were invariably of handsome soft leather. They were often lost, since she carried rather than wore them. The handbags were copious, conservatively elegant, of the finest leather, or they were of beautiful fabrics: wool, silk, and quilted stuffs.

As for the contents of her purses, no gathering of cosmetics was there. Who ever saw her powder her nose or reconstruct her hair, which was straight, fine in texture, and apt to be troublesome about the face, unless the need were absolute? She was one who dressed as appropriately as possible for the day's work, but, once assembled, never gave the matter a second thought. Her purse contained no career woman's notebook and pencil, no calendar or date book. There were eyeglasses—usually knocking about on their own without benefit of protective case—

a clutch of gloves, a dust of invisible hairpins, a changing collection of snapshots of children—nieces, nephews, and friends—and letters. When she opened her purse in one's presence, one knew something interesting was about to be shared.

The slender fingers—uncluttered by any ring, sensitive and thin at the tips, the nails astonishingly narrow from base to rim, with scant half moons visible—fluttered the current file, made their choice, and the listener would share for a moment a fragment of the wide and far-reaching world of ACM: a letter from her friend, the distinguished scholar and librarian Valfrid Munch-Petersen of Copenhagen; scraps of comments from Beatrix Potter or L. Leslie Brooke or Walter de la Mare, in England; news of Maria Cimino, on leave in the jungles of South America with her anthropologist husband, Will Lipkind; a letter from Marit Blehr in Norway; news of Leonore Power Mendelson, by then living in Yokohama, or of Mary Gould Davis, summering in Brittany, or Ruth Sawyer, on a folk-tale-gathering trip in Spain.

To have a letter of one's own produced from that file was a mark of distinction. If ACM read aloud from a letter one had written to her, friends made note of it and quickly reported it to the writer, recognizing it as accolade, indeed.

"I have brought someone with me," Anne would say, holding up Nicholas, who was seemingly alive in her hand. She recounted his adventures with such zest and conviction as to involve the audience in all she said. Nicholas was no imparter of knowledge. He was never used as nucleus for giving information. He gave rise to no such question as "How many of you know where Holland is?" The events he reported were apt to have happened to Anne herself: some encounter that had occurred on the way to a branch library, a ride over Brooklyn Bridge by moonlight, a book lately read, or an account of a personality recently come to town—all told with an eye for childlike drama and particularization such as might well have been encompassed by an alert boy from a far country on his first visit to New York. For Anne, like her description of Miss Harriet Friend in a book she was yet to write, "made little stories when she talked." Later, when Nicholas had become an established personality with two books of personal history behind him, he was to display manifold treasure, such marvels of the miniature as to bring forth from the children exclamations of wonder. At the end of her talk Anne might anchor in each of the wooden hands a small birthday-cake candle, light them, and invite the children to blow out their wishes upon them. The flickering uncertainty of candle-light never ceases to cast a spell upon children and adults alike, its wavering flame a reminder of man's first triumph over the dark, its brief light, burning close to the certainty of extinction, a confirmation of his courage. At any rate, children everywhere would blow across Anne's little lights, utterly convinced of the Dutch magic she and Nicholas had at their command.

Soon the children asked questions, as they often do after some experience has touched them to the quick and set them on the philosopher's quest for reality.

"Is he real?" they asked.

"Does he come alive at night?"

"He isn't real, is he?"

One day, in the Central Children's Room, when Anne was sitting in the Fifth Avenue window seat with Annie Astor of Ninth Avenue and her friend, Carlotta Lorenze of Third Avenue, the reality of Nicholas was the topic of conjecture and debate. It was the Italian child who had no whit of skepticism. "Why don't you write a book about Nicholas?" she said, sensing perhaps the indisputable proof of print. The suggestion tumbled about in Anne's mind and took root. She brought it to fruition in two books, *Nicholas: A Manhattan Christmas Story* (G. P. Putnam's & Sons, 1924) and *Nicholas and the Golden Goose* (G. P. Putnam's & Sons, 1932).

A bold and original design was called for to embrace the world of Nicholas as Anne felt it. She sought to distill the essence of New York in the twenties, to translate her own life, profession, and friendships into the state of awareness and wonder that children often attain in the best of their reading years, the middle years between eight and twelve. Searching for a schema, her mind turned, as it often did, to that small milestone among books for children, *Miss Muffet's Christmas Party*, a fantasy of well-known characters in children's books which was at the same time a penetrating piece of criticism of the literature of childhood. Its author was Dr. Samuel McCord Crothers, a noted clergyman, whose essays on literature combined clear-headed observation with charm, scholarship, and genuine love of reading.

The *dramatis personae* of Dr. Crothers' story was limited to characters in books and stories. Anne's cast of characters included the living and the dead, characters of fiction and fantasy as well as the supernatural beings of folklore: members of the staff of the New York Public Library, thinly disguised, doormen and mop-men, heroes of history, writers, artists, the very statuary lining the halls of the Central Building, children she knew, sometimes given fictitious names, sometimes appearing as themselves, pictures come to life from the walls of the Children's Room and the Prints Division. Scarcely a corner of the great Central Building but was transmogrified

by the alchemy of her passionate response to the place
and the reaches of its influence.

"It takes courage and determination to give a big party
and mix EVERYBODY up with EVERYBODY and give EVERY-
BODY a good time," Mary Mapes Dodge is quoted as saying in the chapter "Brownie's Big Party," one of the
most breathless episodes of *Nicholas*. What a document
for the celebration of some golden anniversary of the library the reprinting of that chapter would be with a
small *roman à clef* for people, books, and things, by way
of clarification.

Anne Carroll Moore, the fantasist, like others before
her and since, wrote out of the passionate enjoyment of
an experience of life. It was the same force that begot *The
Wind in the Willows*, by Kenneth Grahame, and W. W.
Tarn's *Treasure of the Isle of Mist* and Robert Lawson's
Rabbit Hill. Each of these books fixes for all time the
gratitude of its author for certain gifts of life. For Kenneth Grahame, it was the pleasure he had in the English
landscape, comradeship, and the felicities of English
country life; for W. W. Tarn, the love of Scottish earth,
which he knew as a geologist as well as a poet; for Robert
Lawson, his delight in his own place and the character of
the Connecticut countryside.

For Anne, there were countless beatitudes: the child
she had been, children, books, friends, the New York
Public Library, which she treasured, stone by stone,
branch by branch, and the city and the life it encompassed—all these she prized. Bridges, taxis, flowers, food
and wine, wind and weather, Maine, pageants and parades, circuses and balloons, ceremonies and celebrations,
costumes, parties, surprises, small delights of sight and
sound and taste: all these she cherished, and, being a
woman "of courage and determination," she did not

hesitate to bring together disparate parts. There is no plot, no prescribed conflict and resolution, no quest and consummation in her books, but character, personalities galore, atmosphere and sense of place, all crowned by a high mood of festival.

The hero is Nicholas, a very real boy in many respects: "I will stay on one condition," he says. "That I am free to come and go when I feel like it and not fussed over—" The heroine, his companion and confidante, is one Ann Caraway, "a lady of no particular age" who is reported to "make things happen, any time, not just at Christmas."

"To make things happen"—there is as brief and as accurate a self-portrait as one is likely to come upon in a lifetime. Ann Caraway is recognizably Anne herself, and many who loved her called her by that name after the appearance of the books. It came, fittingly enough, straight out of Walter de la Mare's *Peacock Pie*. Anne had brought home from England an early copy of the book. As was the custom with books she loved and revered, she had spread among the staff so happy a contagion of her own delight in it as to have created an awareness of it in many a mind. One night at dinner, at the Woman's City Club when it was housed in the beautiful mansion on Madison Avenue, one of Stanford White's architectural triumphs, ACM was discussing with a group of colleagues the problem of a name for herself in the book she was writing and someone said, out of the blue, "Old King Caraway supped on cake—" And there it was!

The writing of Nicholas was undertaken in a period of increased activity in her life. She began it in 1918, at the peak of her assignments of criticism for *The Bookman*, when the library was recovering from shortages of staff and all the dislocation caused by the war years. It absorbed her utterly, as any piece of writing out of one's deepest self is bound to do, and she fought for space and time in which to bring it off. For a while she took a room on one of the topmost floors of the Commodore Hotel, which gave her the necessary sense of remoteness, yet was within walking distance of her office. The view of the East River, to say nothing of the towers of the city at night, refreshed her eyes as well as her spirit. There she would write and then summon some friend at a late hour in the evening to read aloud what she had written and to order up from room service dishes of chocolate ice cream and raspberry ice served cheek by jowl.

A summer at the McDowell Colony gave her a breathing spell. Originally the two books had been planned as one, but Anne soon discovered that there was too much material for one volume, and since the story broke naturally into two halves, one centered in New York, the other in France and England, it was decided to publish *Nicholas: A Manhattan Christmas Story* as the first volume with a sequel to follow.

The choice of Jay Van Everen, a young Czech artist, as illustrator was the happiest ever, for in his strong black-and-white line pictures, reminiscent of woodcuts, he established a precise balance between the realism of the text and all that was implied in its fantasy. He too was a lover of the city, who caught the spirit of place in decorative excursions of his own. The book appeared in September 1924, its bright red cover, its fascinating end papers of Van Everen's Map of New York, its jolly square size—all distinctive and fitting. What joy she had in it, sending it *broadcast* to members of the family and to half a hundred friends the world over! Each such copy was no idle gift. She seldom inscribed any book she gave as a gift in a perfunctory way. No "All best wishes" or

"Merry Christmas" but always she wrote words that re-affirmed the relationship between donor and donee, and no recipient of books from her could ever again be satis-fied with the clichés of friendship.

Brentano's Book Store, which in 1924 was at Twenty-seventh Street and Fifth Avenue, arranged in one of its windows a pyramid of copies of the book. Anne hailed a cab on a Sunday evening and drove down to see it. She asked the driver to wait until she had her fill of pleasure in the sight. There can hardly be a moment in the life of any author to equal that of seeing, for the first time, mul-tiple copies of his book, displayed in the window of one of the country's greatest bookstores, on one of the world's richest and most fabled avenues. When she stepped back into the cab, she said to the driver, "I wrote that book." "Yeah?" he replied, casting half an eye on the display. Then he said, "My God, lady, did you write them all?"

Geoffrey Parsons, chief editorial writer of the New York *Herald Tribune*, reviewed *Nicholas: A Manhattan Christmas Story* for "The Three Owls," in a perceptive piece that conveys his understanding of Anne's intent and its fulfillment. It is given here in its entirety, for the sake of the book and for its revelation of the man, one of the noted journalists of his day, who did not disdain to write a piece about a book for children. The review appeared in the New York *Herald Tribune* of September 28, 1924. The plight of the great cities, it is interesting to note, concerned Geoffrey Parsons as long ago as the 1920s:

> There is a man, a hard-working writer of politics and such truck, who every once in a while drives his car down a certain street, collects an assorted carload of strange chil-dren and takes them off for a party. He is a little man with a serious, wistful face and he is never more serious than

when he is driving off with his picnickers. That is probably why they like him—he is quite himself with them, making no more effort than if they were grown-up.

"Why do you go off with those kids?" he was once asked.

"To hear somebody tell me the truth," he answered. "When I get confused and tangled they make it all clear again."

There is the same touch in Miss Moore's "Nicholas." Every grown-up knows what a cruel, jangling maze of steel and speed is Manhattan Island. Once, years ago, one loved it for its leisurely homeliness and its friendly corners. Now one works in it, is thrilled and appalled by it. The city has been lost in the machine. It is the peculiar and unexpected gift of Miss Moore's book that it recaptures the old magic of the town and makes New York warm in one's heart, whether the heart happens to be young or old.

Her method is the method of the carload of children. She tells the truth about the city with the clear-seeing eye of a child, relighting old beacons, discovering new magic in every elevated train, behind each shop window. Would you believe that New York could be made into a party, a gorgeous, gigantic children's party, with candles and icing and music and fairies? That is just what Miss Moore does. As Mary Mapes Dodge says at the biggest party of all at the library: "It takes courage and determination to give a big party and mix everybody up with everybody and give everybody a good time." Miss Moore and her Brownie have both the courage and skill to live up to this incredibly difficult formula. Everybody inside the pages and in front of the pages does have a good time.

Miss Moore has a flair for parties above all else. She loves them and she eats them as the mouth-watering repasts provided Nicholas testify. In a fairyland cabinet her portfolio would unquestionably be that of Parties and Good Things. Yet there is a mingling of old tales with these present excitements, of time both ruined and riveting, that shows an unusual sensitiveness to the past. Here is a gallant effort and Miss Moore has put all her heart into it. If it does not come through as vividly as does the Manhattan of today, obliteration is the fact that intervenes. Fraunces' Tavern and St. Paul's help among the towers, but the difficulty is great. At any rate, Miss Moore never commits the fatal error of turning didactic. The parties of Washington and the Knickerbockers are either parties or they are nothing.

A rich handful of a book Miss Moore has written that will be equally precious to children who have cut their teeth on New York's skyline and to children afar to whom it is a longed-for fairyland, some day to rise above the horizon. Mr. Jay Van Everen has provided drawings in the manner of woodcuts as understandable as they are understanding of the event and for good measure one of the most engaging maps in and out of fairyland.

The ancient cities—London, Paris, Rome—these belong to the ages and the entire world, loved for their tradition and heritage. Walking the streets of these beloved places, one feels the past coexisting with the present. This is true to a shamelessly small degree in New York. The historic past is largely a lost consideration of American life in the twentieth century. It is thrown out the window, like the proverbial baby with the bath. Anne's desire was to instill in children an awareness of the traditions of New York, that they might be cherished as a universal experience, belonging to the world. She accomplished this to a degree. Much of the book remains timeless even in the face of mammoth changes wrought by the passing years.

By the nature of its theme and structure, the book could never have attained the immediate popularity of a *Pinocchio* or *Mary Poppins* or *Winnie the Pooh*, but for many children *Nicholas* remains a memorable reading experience. The high originality is there, palpable and enduring, and the pervading mood of delight replenishes the spirit and exists beyond the limits of time and place.

Nicholas and the Golden Goose, the second book, did
not appear until 1932. It chronicled, as a matter of fact,
the year 1921 in Anne's life. In that year she went to
France to visit the libraries for children established there
after the First World War by the American Committee
for Devastated France. The committee had been largely
the inspiration of Miss Anne Morgan, the daughter of
Pierpont Morgan, the financier, a philanthropist in her
own right and a great Francophile. She, with the help of
Mrs. A. M. Dike and eight other American women, constituted the original committee. Having gotten the consent and blessing of the French government, they pledged
themselves and their growing staff to render succor to
the people who lived in the thirty smoldering villages
behind the lines held by the Third French Army Corps,
in the years when the war raged uncertainly back and
forth across the country of the Aisne. Theirs was the
first motor corps run by women. The tasks and their accomplishment of them were gigantic, including evacua-
tion of the wounded, the setting up of dispensaries, the
transportation of food and supplies, the organization of
classes for children, and care of the old and sick. By
1919, when most of the immediate physical needs of the
devastated region had been met, the committee enlarged
the scope of its work to include solutions for pressing
social problems and the restoration of the French way of
life. Five categories for service were adopted: Public
Health, Social Service, Agricultural Syndicates, Construction, and Libraries.

It was at this point, Libraries, that Anne Moore became involved. Miss Morgan leaned heavily on her for
advice in this effort, because books for the children were
among the first concern of the French themselves. Anne
Carroll Moore could not go herself, but several of the

most able and gifted children's librarians from the New York Public Library were enlisted in the cause. They were dispatched to France: Alice Keats O'Connor to Soissons, Jessie Carson as an organizing supervisor, Marianne Greene to Anizy-le-Château. The bowls of flowers on the tables, the large black book in which the French children wrote their names when joining the library, the brave displays of picture books opened up on shelves and window sills, the story hours, the reading aloud—all these bespoke the New York Public Library and Anne Carroll Moore. No official reports of the Committee for Devastated France equal the story as Anne tells it in this book.

The visit to France was followed by a sojourn in London, where the doors of artists, writers, and publishers were opened to Anne as an official representative of *The Bookman*, the chief American literary journal of its day. She was welcomed in her own right and bolstered by the knowledge that her solid accomplishment as a critic in its pages had been recognized beyond the borders of the United States.

These were the matters of fact in *Nicholas and the Golden Goose*. The matter of fantasy transpired in a series of letters Nicholas wrote home to the friends of the first book, together with certain adventures reported at first hand. The edged awareness of each of her encounters with people, places, sights, and sounds sustains a mood bordering on exaltation. That was, when one thinks of it, the dominant mood of her life.

With the publication of the books, the influence of Nicholas widened in the world. Children who had read about him made pilgrimages to the Central Library to see the window through which he had made his initial appearance in the first book. Artists, writers, and friends presented him with gifts, many of them exquisite miniatures. Louis Slobodkin, the sculptor-illustrator, gave him a tool chest, the awl and screwdriver, the hammer and saw made to exact scale and in good working order. The beautiful Nadia Rodzianko, whom Anne had discovered and enticed into becoming a member of the staff of the Central Children's Room, gave him a small golden Easter egg from the traditional collection she had brought with her from Russia in the dark days of her escape from the revolution of the Bolsheviks. A telescope, a small heart of purest crystal, a compass, a rabbit good-luck piece were among his treasures. People found pleasure in finding the exquisite and uncommon for Nicholas, as they did for Anne herself. Sometimes the gifts were judged as being quite unacceptable and found no space in the treasure chest. They simply disappeared, for Nicholas, like Anne, judged objects not from the point of view of their value or worth but sharply by the subtle light of taste and the quality of the imagination that had begotten them.

As far as Anne was concerned, Nicholas moved closer to the center of her private mythology, becoming, in her behalf, spokesman and spendthrift *extraordinaire*. Countless gifts were bestowed in his name, parties initiated at his request, extravagances of a hundred delights brought off by the lad. He acquired his own stationery, with the end piece for *Nicholas: A Manhattan Christmas Story* at its masthead, showing Nicholas writing a letter. Letters of gay and special import went out over his signature.

There can be no hedging the fact that for many of her friends and associates, Nicholas was somewhat *hors de combat*. Not everyone was willing to play the game for which Anne invariably called the tune, nor to enjoy the ceremonies of candlelight and other rituals of play she carried off to perfection. The congeries of her masculine friends, especially, were apt to balk at this bit of drama and were embarrassed by it. One or two of the brave among them told her their opinion and advised her to desist, and one good friend of long standing in California, "Cousin Oscar," said to her, "Anne, take that damn doll, lock it in your trunk and forget it." She roared with laughter and told the story on herself. But she remained importunate, using Nicholas in many ways for her own purposes. She judged people by their initial response to Nicholas and their acceptance or rejection of him, as one tests the temper of a friend by the quality of his humor or the depth of his feeling. He served to command a situation, to create a diversion, and to bolster and sustain her own opinions and convictions. "He served to keep her relationships where she wanted them," commented one astute librarian.

When he was lost in one of the hundreds of taxis in New York, certain people with whom she was associated sighed with relief. But the relief was short-lived. The children of the Psychiatric Institute at Presbyterian Hospital asked for him. Eleanor Nave, one of the children's librarians, who had a rare gift of reaching disturbed children through storytelling and puppet plays, had often asked ACM to visit these children to tell them the story of Nicholas. Mrs. Nave could not bear to have them deprived of his presence, and she contrived with the help of a very gifted wood carver to have the original Nicholas copied. The copy was presented to ACM as a gift from the children, appearing inside a box made as a replica of his own book. For a while Anne was troubled by him, and then little by little he merged into the personality of the first, and Nicholas the first and Nicholas the second became one.

The game went on into the mid-forties. When for a

second time Nicholas disappeared, Anne was utterly stricken. "It has been one of the worst summers of my life," she wrote to a friend in Ann Arbor, in a rare disclosure of suffering and unhappiness. Nothing was ever quite the same again. That touchstone was irrevocable.

It was Walter de la Mare who, in the last analysis, defined the role of Nicholas. In the 1940s, at the request of ACM, he invited a friend of hers to tea. He too lived among exquisite miniatures, which his *Memoirs of a Midget* had brought to him from friends and admirers. One could understand the sympathy that existed between these two people, ACM and Walter de la Mare. Each acknowledged childhood as a state of being like no other, each knew the flashing insights of heightened imagination, each lived in a state of acute awareness of the mystery surrounding all that exists, including the inanimate. As the friend was about to depart, Walter de la Mare said, "Give Anne Moore my deep and warmest regards." Then, scanning the face of the visitor with those deep eyes of his that were both kind and searching and recognizing that she was within the circle of belief, he said, "And to her alter ego—Nicholas."

12

BEHIND THE LIBRARY
LIONS

*Why is it that they always think that all
the whole thing amounts to is that for a few
hours in the afternoon after school there is
a mad rush of children, who come and read
story books, and that for the rest of the time
we all sit around and crochet?*

*The two biggest things about it are the
spontaneity of their coming and going, and
the training in discrimination and judgment
which they get by choosing their own
books. Even their unwise choices help. The
sociological aspect of it always interests me
—the way the children come together and
love to be together, the way one comes because others come.*

*The community of interest is what, un-
consciously, appeals to most of the children.
It is the exceptional child who loves to get
off into a corner and read alone, or come in
when the other children are not here. And
out of this develops a distinct educational
value, a something which would be entirely
lost if the comings and goings of the children were regulated or formalized in any
way. A library, for children, should be quite
separate from the formal part of his day,
school and studying and set hours. The library is the only testing ground of the reality of the interest aroused at school.*

*It is nearly twenty years ago since chil-
dren's rooms were started in libraries, and at
first they were simply for circulation, until
the need was felt of a place where children
could read, a place that invited reading, and
where the first early knowledge of literature
and art, the first light of history, through
folk-lore and saga, could be brought to
them, for these are the things which make
for personality and individuality, for the
whole upbuilding of morals and spiritual
life.*

ACM

*T*HE GRANDEUR of the Central Building melted into a
comfortable acceptance by those who daily trod its
marble steps as public or entered by circuitous routes as
habitués of the staff. They created in their time a folklore of the building. The sculptured six figures across the
front attic, created by Paul Bartlett to represent History,
Drama, Poetry, Religion, Romance, and Philosophy, became known as the Tilden girls, and the lions by Edward
Potter, on either side of the first flight of stairs leading
from the avenue to the esplanade, were the butt of many
a joke and jibe. James Daugherty fixed their identity for
all time in his incomparable picture book *Andy and the
Lion* (Viking Press, 1938) by dedicating it to "Lord
Lenox and Lady Astor," his inspiration outweighing the
obvious fact that both of the beasts were male.

For Anne those lions were mastheads of courage and
accomplishment. "Behind the Library Lions" was the
salutation on many a communiqué of good report recounting high deeds and accomplishments. The drudger-
ies, the disappointments, the battles for funds were en-

dured in private, except in official reports. She knew the discouragement of the perfectionist and bore it for the most part in secret, as was her habit.

A long view across the thirty years of her residence behind the lions reveals the magnitude of disasters that swept over ACM—wars and plagues (infantile paralysis in epidemic force), a great depression, budgets cut to the bone, with shelves in the children's rooms as empty of books as were Mother Hubbard's of food, shortages of staff as well as of coal. An *aperçuant* among the reports finds here sad documents of woe:

- The shortage of the supply of books and the worn-out conditions of the collections for circulation in busy branches have led to a thorough inspection of the available resources. The importance of large and continuous additions cannot be too strongly urged as the greatest need of 1914. A general building up of book collections is needed at branches where the circulation use has been declining for a considerable period of time and an increase of twenty-five percent of book stock is needed at each of the ten branches reporting the heaviest circulation use. [1913]
- Thousands of children have been led to expect certain definite things on receipt of their library card. Chief among these expectations is that of choosing a book to take home from well-filled circulation shelves. From the children's standpoint no other library privilege is comparable to this. The story hour, the library reading-room, the club, the book talk to a visiting class from school—each has its place, but the children are disappointed when these cannot be reenforced by books to take home. Everything except books is provided and made accessible in the children's rooms, even to the catalogue of books no longer supplied. [1922]
- Unless prompt and effective measures are taken to increase the existing supply of books by at least one-half, it seems inevitable that the circulation of books to children from several branch libraries must cease and the children's

rooms be used merely as reading rooms. . . . Why do the children keep on coming to a children's room with empty shelves? Unquestionably it is because they like to come and because they still have faith in the Library. This has been kept alive for years largely by the collection of books in the reading rooms, and by story hours.

There is a great and unnatural strain about the continuous administration of a large children's room with so few books.

Such conditions preclude any sound work, but they are sapping the vitality and initiative of the members of the Staff whose knowledge of books and varied experience of work should be free for the training of these younger assistants and students, as well as for proper library service to the children, their parents and teachers. [1923]

• Under existing conditions not only is it impossible to provide duplicates of recent books of fine quality, it is equally impossible to provide the children's classics in sufficient numbers to insure the reading of any one of them to a boy or girl within that span of life when the book is most desired and its influence most potent. [1924]

• A hundred thousand new volumes, at least, are needed to sustain a profitable book service to the homes during the next year. The situation is extremely critical because of the rapidly increasing impoverishment of book stock. It is so far-reaching in its implications as to create a vital need for a revised plan based upon the assignment of available funds according to condition of book stock rather than circulation statistics.

The use of books within the library, both for recreational reading and for reference, has greatly increased at all points. Children in family groups, where numbers have been doubled or trebled to save rent, and rooms are often without heat and adequate light, come day after day to read and to study the next day's lesson with the aid of library books.

"What we should do without the library I don't know," said the wife of a musician who had been for two years without employment. "We love music and books, as a family we love the home life, and these three things keep us

sane while making the rounds in search of employment."
The number of applications signed "not working at present" is a constant reminder of the silent part the library
plays in sustaining the mental life and spirit of those who
continue to turn to it for refreshment and courage to go
on. [1933]

These are among the matters ACM made public in her
reports. Behind the scenes battles were fought in the
cause of adequate salaries for the staff. Interdepartmental
skirmishes were frequent when fields of authority were
disputed between adult and children's departments in
branch libraries. Even within library walls the imperative
of excellence in books for children was sometimes under
attack because purchasing agents saw no reason why
cheap editions of standard titles could not be substituted
for costly books, if the text remained unchanged.

Anne was a fearless and a witty fighter. "Admitting to
no discouragement," she supported on every hand the
great humanistic design she had envisioned for children
in libraries. Consequently the staff, caught up in her exuberance, created and contrived ways of enticing children into an exuberance of reading.

Meanwhile the Lions Roared in Triumph!

• Twenty-two story clubs and reading circles are reported for older girls. Twelve of the number are organized
clubs conducted in the same manner as the boys' clubs. For
two years the girls of the Shakespeare Club read alternately
a Shakespearean play and a modern one. In this manner
they read *The Merchant of Venice* followed by *The Bluebird*; *As You Like It* followed by Percy Mackaye's *The
Scarecrow*; *The Taming of the Shrew* followed by *The
Piper*. They are now reading old English comedies beginning with *She Stoops to Conquer*. Pictures of the countries
in which the scenes of the play are laid and portraits of
the great actors and actresses who have played the leading

roles are used wherever obtainable. The growing appreciation and genuine enjoyment of dramatic literature are fine antidotes for vapid stories. [1912]

• The visit of Miss Marie Shedlock, the English storyteller, has been the event of greatest interest to the storytellers and children. Miss Shedlock first inspired the library story hour in America. On Hans Christian Andersen's birthday Miss Shedlock told his story, "The Steadfast Tin Soldier," and told something of his life to a group of children and their parents in the Central Children's Room. On Shakespeare's birthday she told "The Nightingale" to 270 delegates from the reading clubs assembled at the Central Building. This meeting took the form of a personal greeting from each club by a representative who carried back to the regular meeting of his or her club a full account of the joint meeting. [1915]

• Fortunately, the continuity of the story hour as an integral part of the work of the children's room is assured by the appointment of Mary Gould Davis to succeed Anna Cogswell Tyler. Miss Davis was one of the first of the children's librarians to make this effective connection between the story hour and the children's reading rooms. Her familiarity with all the conditions of work has given her a rare appreciation of the natural place of story-telling in enriching the reading tastes of boys and girls of different races, and a true understanding of what is involved in carrying on a story hour in almost bookless children's rooms. [1923]

• The outstanding event of the year, in which the children of the Extension Division, as well as the children of the Branch Libraries, participated, was the celebration of St. Nicholas Eve (December 5th) in the Central Children's Room. Few of the children had ever visited "the Fifth Avenue Library" before and merely walking up the steps was a great event. Once inside, it seemed the most natural place in the world to meet an English poet, whose birthday they had celebrated in their own libraries in April. No audience quite like it—quite so spontaneous and so varied in racial imagination—has ever assembled in the Library. As he read from "Crossings," his fairy play, and "Peacock

Pie," Walter de la Mare so identified himself with the children that he seemed at one with them, and each of them carried back to the children of the Branch Library from which he came the personal satisfaction of really knowing a living poet. [1924]

• The Fo'c's'le Club at the St. George Branch was inspired by a visit from Gordon Grant, and a loan exhibition of his pictures of ships. This club is keeping a log and imparting its enthusiasm for ships and sailors to a children's room which overlooks the harbor and the road out to sea. The introduction of marionettes at special story hours held at this branch is another enlivening influence of peculiar value in defining and sustaining the relationship of the Italian children living in the neighborhood, and has distinct possibilities in the further development of storytelling in other Staten Island communities.

The broadcasting of stories from Station WEAF was continued at stated intervals by different storytellers. There was an effective celebration of Hans Christian Andersen's birthday, and folk and hero tales of different countries were told. During August, the Supervisor of Work with Children gave a weekly talk on children's books, accompanied by reading from books mentioned. The response indicates that putting books "on the air" if the speaking voice meets the test has increasingly varied and interesting possibilities for libraries. There is, however, an art in the selection of material for transmission as well as the presentation of it. [1925]

• Holidays and anniversaries were generally observed with more than usual festivity.

On an evening in June the boys and girls of Hamilton Fish Park Branch held a colorful "Street Fair" on the roof of the library.

At the 115th Street Branch, Irving's *The Rose of the Alhambra* was presented as a puppet play and at Harlem Library story hours and plays in the Russian language were given.

At the Seward Park Branch, George MacDonald's story, "The Princess and the Goblin," was told with marked effect on the children's own reading.

Midsummer poetry hours at which the children read poems of their own selection were continued in the garden of the Woodstock Branch. On the anniversary of the opening of this branch a spirited dramatization of *Floating Island* was given in the children's room before a large audience of children.

The Poe Literary Club of the Melrose Branch had Percy Mackaye as a guest one evening in January and invited the members of the other library reading clubs to share a reading from his *Tall Tales of the Kentucky Mountains*. Mr. Mackaye proved his competence in handling boys as well as dialect. Asking to have most of the lights turned off, he put on his hat and sat down in a log cabin (figuratively), while the boys grouped close about him seemed to get the full flavor of the unaccustomed American speech along with the humor and drama of the stories.

The Eric Kelly Club of Polish boys was visited by Mr. Kelly, who gave a stirring talk about Poland accompanied by an exhibition of embroideries and objects of art. Parents and friends were invited to attend this opening meeting. [1931]

• At the opening of the annual holiday exhibition of children's books in November, Evelyn Scott, Reginald Birch, Louise Seaman and Bertha Mahony were guests of honor. Miss Scott's fine paper on *Writing for Children* was followed by brief speeches by Mr. Birch, whose black-and-white illustrations for the Gilbert and Sullivan operas were a feature of the exhibition, by Miss Mahony, and Louise Seaman, who paid tribute to the work of Helen Sewell, whose drawings for *A First Bible, Cinderella, Away Goes Sally,* and *Blue Bonnets for Lucinda* were represented in the exhibition.

The original manuscript for Lauren Ford's *A Little Book About God,* drawings by Ludwig Bemelmans for *Hansi,* by F. Luis Mora for *Tono Antonio,* and by Dorothy P. Lathrop for *The Lost Merry Go Round* were also included.

There has always been one basic belief back of the organization of school work in the Circulation Department, i.e., that the function of the public library in its relation to schools is not primarily to supplement the school curriculum, but to offer the schools an expert knowledge of the spontaneous reading interests of young people. During the past decade there has been a steadily increasing appreciation of this service.

The New York City schools have lately become reading-conscious because of extensive reading tests and surveys. Teachers were shocked to discover the low reading score and mediocre reading taste of many of their students. As a result, they are scrutinizing teaching methods and surveying community activities which influence reading such as the radio and the motion picture. Written book reports and credits for supplementary reading are shaking on their foundations. There is a definite drive for more books for young people in the school and public libraries. [1936]

• Early in the year the librarians in charge of children's rooms were authorized to spend one-half of the yearly appropriation for children's books immediately. Collapse of circulation was imminent at several points and staff, as well as the children, were disheartened by fruitless efforts to satisfy readers from bookless shelves.

Word spread like wildfire when the new books came, and children flocked to the branch libraries to reclaim their cards and renew their faith in the Library. Everywhere the book shelves were brightened and for a short time it became possible for boys and girls to find books they had long wanted to read. It was possible also for the librarians to reassert standards of cleanliness and care of books as city property. [1937]

• The year has been a challenging one both for older members of the staff who are able to contrast it with earlier years of unrestricted immigration and for the young college graduates fresh from psychology, sociology or history majors. The latter are seeing for the first time what a public library can mean to a stranger in a strange land and they are thrilled by its possibilities. Refugee children are frequently met at the boat by relatives or friends who have counted their library association as a major interest over a period of years.

No more heartening proof of the value of personalities

in libraries can be offered than the confidence of these self-appointed friends of the Library that a welcome is waiting in the children's rooms where they have been made to feel at home. "You can find a book in any language in the library." "Librarians can speak different languages." "You can learn English quick in a library." "You can listen to stories and look at pictures and sometimes see flowers growing there." "You can forget your troubles in a library." "You will find friends there."

These are a few of the many testimonies offered by those who have come to look upon the public library as belonging to them.

No wonder that for the first time since 1932 the circulation of books to children shows an upward curve, that there is storytelling in the play streets of the city and that significant festivals are celebrated on roof-tops on the lower East Side and in library gardens in The Bronx.

Poverty of book stock has been the cry from year to year. We must build up, restore, provide more generously in order to function. Yet suddenly we have tangible proof that we have functioned in terms of human need at a critical time. We still ask for more books, but no longer in the abstract. We need a great many books for our guests from Europe as well as for the children of New York. [1938]

There was a time when ACM considered resigning from the New York Public Library. She could not work in harmony with Benjamin Adams, the chief of the Circulation Division who followed Dr. Bostwick in that post in 1909. Two years after the opening of the Central Building, she wrote to Dr. Bostwick of her intent and had from him a letter so wise as to be universal in its application to professional affairs. It read in part as follows:

St. Louis. Apr. 4. 1913

Dear Miss Moore:

Your determination to resign, as expressed in your letter of March 30, takes me somewhat by surprise. I know you are not altogether satisfied with things, but I did not know that you had quite reached this point. You have told me nothing specific that seems to me to warrant it. If there has been nothing specific, I think you ought to see that there is some particular issue on which you can tender your resignation. I certainly shouldn't say, "If you don't let me do so-and-so I will resign"; but I should say specifically what I wanted to do and if refused I should resign, with the definite statement that this was the reason for resigning. All this could be done without rancor and leaving the best of feelings, I am sure.

Nobody will believe that you have resigned because you want time for lecturing and like the more independent life. Everyone will cast about for some specific reason and most will conclude that you resigned under some kind of pressure. You had better carry the war into Africa. . . .

That settled the matter. She carried the war "into Africa," with such good effect that several years later when Mr. Adams himself resigned, he wrote her a letter of gratitude, thanking her for her support and acknowledging that many of the reforms which he had brought about she had originated and brought to his attention. She put before him, in 1914, a plan for the reorganization of work with schools, recommending a position of supervisor of work with schools, to be maintained under the Division of Work with Children on the same level as the supervisor of storytelling and the supervisor of work with children in the Extension Division, then known as Traveling Libraries.

One of the most vital and successful libraries that had functioned as an independent institution, later joining the New York Public Library in its period of unification, was the Webster Library, serving an interesting locale made up mainly of Bohemian nationals. Under its librarian, Mr. Edward Gaillard, a vigorous program of service to schools and teachers had been developed, consisting of lending books to teachers and of setting up in the library collections of special interest to them. When in 1903 the library was absorbed in the New York Public Library system, Mr. Gaillard became a member of the Circulation Department, in charge of certain classroom stations in schools and responsible for the selection of books therein. This plan divided the authority of work with children. ACM fought for a more logical organization.

> I would give the School Department what seems to be its logical place in the organization of the live work of the library, dividing it between the Children's Department and the Adult Department with the close cooperation between the Children's Department and Adult Department relationship well-defined. It should be a definite division of the Children's Department and considered a regular feature of its work constituting as it does a large part of the reference work of the Children's Room.

Here in this memorandum of 1914 she declares her philosophy of work with schools.

> There is a great danger of turning a children's library into a school grade extra by the pushing of school work until library attendance ceases to be voluntary. On the day that everybody gets "sent" we lose the most valuable clause in our charter of liberty.

For Anne the words engraved on the heart's core, as far as the children's libraries were concerned, were "individual, spontaneous and voluntary reading." Mabel Williams, that sane and humorous woman whom ACM met at a library convention in Massachusetts and plucked out of a meeting for her own purposes, was responsible for the clear evolution of the distinctive work with schools which characterized the New York Public Li-

brary. It had begun as early as 1910 with the customary
class visits to the libraries, instruction in the use of in-
dexes, and the mysteries of the card catalogue. Under
Mabel Williams a declaration of independence from instruction as such within library walls became an actuality,
and from it emerged a proclamation of benefits that derived from exposure to books and spirited talk about them
by people who had read them and could excite interest
in others. Book talks as a distinct and separate genre, dif-
fering in purpose and invention from the accepted book
review in school, became the subjects of study, critical
appraisal, and analysis, recognized as arts in their own
right. In time the school authorities came to acknowledge that the class visit was an educational experience
larger in influence than reference work on a given assignment or adherence to the lesson plan for the day.

From Mabel Williams' vision, her eyes following
where ACM's had scanned the peaks, the distinctive work
with young people was to emerge with comparable space
and service in branch libraries for children in their
teens as was sustained on behalf of children in the elementary grades. And here also guns were fired in continuous salvos of salute honoring individual reading, spontaneously pursued: for knowledge—and pleasure; for
excitement—and pleasure; for information—and pleasure;
out of curiosity—and pleasure; for experience of life beyond one's own—and pleasure; for the triumph of art
over mediocrity—and pleasure.

All these running tides—work with schools, storytelling and reading clubs, the selection of books, the making
of exhibitions, celebrations, and routines—all these tides
washing the shores of children's lives in Manhattan, the
Bronx, and Staten Island flowed into one small sea at Fifth
Avenue and Forty-second Street, the office of Work with

Children, Room 105. If on judgment day an angel of the
Lord thought it necessary, for some celestial reason, to
bring together all souls, living and dead, who had known
the influence of ACM, no blast of trumpets would be
necessary. Let him but whisper "Room 105" and thousands would rise and assemble.

It was situated on a corridor of the south wing—a small
room, with two great bronze-framed windows on the
north wall, looking out on the court where the book
trucks were loaded. A fountain had once graced that
court, but traffic and cinders rendered it an anachronism,
and its watery refreshment was abandoned. The windows
opened inward, the degree of air admitted controlled by
a great perforated bar and a bolt that supposedly fitted
into the holes. The place knew only extremes of hot and
cold in winter, and in summer the choice of methods lay
between suffocation by heat or by soot and cinders. No
plants would grow there. Countless pots of ivy and philo-
dendron died as if by prearrangement, and ACM learned
to discourage tributes of anything that was rooted and
hopeful.

A table stood between the two windows, on it, leaning
against the wall, a large, somber, dark-framed picture of
children whose beautiful Slavic faces looked out in pensive, dreamlike trance. It was the original of an illustration that had appeared in *The Century Magazine*, designed to accompany a poem by Nora Archibald Smith,
describing her emotions on watching streams of children
coming from the story hour. The artist was W. T. Benda,
noted in the world of theater and art as the creator of
masks of extraordinary beauty. The telephone was on
that table for the moment and such books as happened
to be at the time foremost in the mind of Anne Carroll
Moore. The office did not rate a second telephone until

the year of her retirement in 1941. Every time the telephone summoned her it entailed a scramble from behind the entanglements of her desk, stationed at right angles to the westmost window and given a shadow of privacy by a heavy screen of leather with bright brass studding, a stumble around the chair where the interviewees sat, into the clear space before the table where ACM conducted her affairs in full view of people passing down the corridor and in full sound of an office staff adept at working at their separate tasks as if theirs was an ordinary office instead of the focal point of a disciplined, fascinating, and often joyous world in which one had to be prepared for "no end of surprises."

Bookshelves lined the east and west walls of the room. Rare editions of folk tales and certain basic reference books were comfortably available on the east, while on the western wall particular objects cherished by Anne were housed on shelves partially enclosed in glass: old children's books; the ceremonial doll of the Emperor of Japan and a crystal ball on its plinth, the gifts of Leonore Power, who lived in Japan; a sturdy wooden figure of a troll, from Marit Blehr's Norway, who at the flip of a finger could turn from troll to bear by means of an articulated head. Atop this bookcase stood a very beautiful wooden toy, a gull on wheels. When the wheels were rolled the wings of the gull moved in a verisimilitude of flight. This had been a gift from the children in Utah and was the creation of the art teacher at Logan. Anne cherished it for its unique beauty, as a gift from children, and as a reminder of the legend told among Mormons. In the first years of their settlement in Utah there came a time when their crops were all but destroyed by a plague of grasshoppers, blackening the sun. Suddenly a great flight of gulls winged in from the sea and devoured the pests. For this reason the gull is revered in Utah.

The new books pouring into Room 105 were shelved on the west wall, where they awaited the notice of ACM and assignment by her to members of the staff for review and appraisal. In the space to the left of those shelves stood a card catalogue filled with the rich accumulation of judgments, acceptances, and refusals of thirty-five years' study of books for children. Each review as it came in was read by ACM and either allowed to stand or given the imprint of a dissident opinion. On the other side of the door was a small cabinet for the coat and hat of one person and beyond that the great files that had accumulated in a golden richness through the years. A cluster of small desks like so many ducklings in a crowded nest stood in front of the east wall, and here was "the office" of the Supervisor of Storytelling, "the office" of the first assistant, a junior assistant, and "the office" of the Supervisor of Work with Schools until 1924, when Miss Williams moved to the luxury of an office of her own at the Fifty-eighth Street Branch of the library.

Into that room came trooping on a monthly schedule the children's librarians, each from her respective library. For them it was a time of private conference and discussion with ACM. Then off to the stacks of the library where the new books with typed reviews clipped to their covers awaited perusal and the verdict of acceptance or rejection by these librarians, each responsible to her own book budget and to the environment in which she functioned. ACM was proud of this staff that knew and respected the heritage of neighborhoods they served, addressing their book collections and their activities to the deep and holy origins of race and creed, and enlivening, at the same time, their participation in the contemporary scene.

The influence of Room 105 was to reach out literally across the world in the time of ACM. But the wider field of action never precluded her knowing at any given time the pace of life, the state of the book collection, the titles that were being discarded, the titles purchased, in the furthermost branch library or substation of the Extension Division. She knew at first hand, indefatigable as she was in her visits. She gathered news from her assistants in the office who went "on the road" in pursuit of their duties. She learned from the informal reports, from a hundred subtle clues she never quite defined, as well as from the splendid organization in the office covering these matters. She sensed where the dead spots were and was not above dramatizing their existence. One hapless librarian, returning from her lunch hour, found ACM, hatted and impressively suited, alone in the branch children's room pulling off the shelves books she deemed outmoded and slamming them down on the floor.

Any efficiency engineer studying the flow of traffic in Room 105 would have suffered a nervous breakdown. Small wonder that ACM found it necessary to remain there long after five o'clock to have the place to herself. She read then, to her heart's content, often far into the night, for dinner was a movable feast for her, to be picked up at the Oyster Bar at Grand Central on the way home or at some other restaurant where crowds of theatergoers were refreshing themselves after the performances. There were no regulations, in those days, governing permission to stay late at work, and Mr. O'Brien, the guard at the Fortieth Street entrance, was accustomed to seeing ACM, like a tired ghost, emerge from the doors of the library at odd hours of the night, as was the night watchman on his rounds with his police dogs.

The Central Children's Room did not shut its doors

on the daily public until six o'clock in the evening. If,
between five and six, Anne came across some book she
ached to share, she would call the Children's Room and
summon certain members of the staff to "come up for a
minute." In the excitement of discovery, Anne never
considered whether the librarian had a dinner appointment or whether some hapless suitor, waiting inconspicuously in a window seat for the closing hour, was doomed
to be abandoned without notice. It took more courage
than most could muster to mention these facts to Anne
in the face of her exhilaration. Each such encounter in
the silence of Room 105 was considered to be worth any
sacrifice and not one in a hundred would have escaped
it. When Anne so much as turned the pages of a book,
laying a finger on a chosen spot, it seemed a gesture of
immense import. "Nothing like it has happened before,"
she might say. "Listen." Then she would read "Do you
want a ticket to go away and come back or do you want
a ticket to go away and never come back?" In this wise
the moment, the voice, and Sandburg's *Rootabaga Stories*
became forever fixed in one's recollection of events pleasurable and significant. She had the gift of illumination.
The commonplace as well as the profound took on grace
and sparkle in her companionship, and the quips and
comments that she made clung to the memory. "What
do you do with oddments of butter, Marie?" she asked
the hostess whom she was helping to clear the table. Forever after the term rings in the mind whenever the problem confronts one. "Oddments of butter!" A certain
group of intimates waited, one evening, on dinner for the
arrival of the beautiful May Massee, that genius of an
editor who, to compensate for her enormous endow-
ments, had to sustain a tendency to be late to appointments. Anne sat there twirling between her fingers a

small carnation she had gotten hold of or brought with her. When May at last came in the door, Anne reached up and handed her the flower. "A pink for punctuality," she said. A children's editor of a most affluent publishing house sent out invitations for a gala publisher's party. When the affair came off, it was dismal. On every hand there were signs of an impoverished economy. It was apparent that the children's department was a deprived area as far as the publisher was concerned. The slight of unnecessary austerity chilled the bones of all guests, and the program only compounded their misery. On the way home someone said, "It was exactly like a Sunday-school social." "That's to be expected," said Anne, "whenever anything is announced as 'a gala.' "

Instigator of many a fete and celebration, Anne scorned organized and contrived mirth. The programs she furthered in the library seemed to rise in the head-waters of spontaneity though they occurred on schedule. The annual celebration of certain birthdays—those of Kate Greenaway, Randolph Caldecott, H. C. Andersen, Walter de la Mare, L. Leslie Brooke, Marie Shedlock—gave each librarian an opportunity to frame in space and time the books and pictures of those designated fete-worthy, endowed certain writers and artists with new life in the contemporary world, and created for the children an authentic sense of happening, a cause for joy. Children rise to expectancy like fish to worm, and the simplest gesture of preparation is bait enough to lure and hold them. They are as wise as that citizen of Santa Fe, New Mexico, who when plagued by the recurring question of a tourist, "When does the fiesta begin?" at last answered her, "What does it matter, Madam? The fiesta is in the heart."

Even before the existence of the lions, ACM conceived

the plan of celebrating Christmas in such manner as to
involve children of all creeds. "Everybody's Christmas,"
she termed it. Room 105 sent to each branch children's
room a packet of books, made up of ten or twelve chosen
titles, mostly from the output of the year. Each book was
wrapped as a Christmas package, to be opened on Christmas Eve in the presence of the children. Often the children took a hand in the unwrapping, turn by turn. Nothing equals the pleasure of opening a package, even if one
is involved in the task only vicariously, even though the
contents of the package is certain to be a book! But what
book? Time for guessing what the book might say, for
exchange of opinions, for confessions of enjoyment of
books similar in nature, for questions and comments—
time for talk—was allotted for these important matters.
The books were there in the reading rooms to be used
during all the twelve days of Christmas. Like all drama
begotten of feeling and artfully staged, there was no
evidence of studied preparation. The Christmas packages
were, to the children, a comforting event in a place
where there were books and something was always happening.

One day in the fall of 1918 a newly appointed co-
editor of *Publishers' Weekly* came through the door of
Room 105, bringing with him a handsome, white-haired
man, Franklin K. Mathiews of the Boy Scouts of America. The editor was Frederic Melcher, New Englander,
who as a bookseller in Indianapolis had endeared himself
to a great segment of the Midwest. He knew books. The
Hoosiers loved him for that and for his lack of Bostonian
superiority. He was also the secretary of the American
Booksellers' Association, and it was in that capacity that
Mr. Mathiews had sought his aid. As an officer of the
Boy Scouts of America, Mr. Mathiews had been horrified

at the kinds of books the boys were reading. What could be done about it? He could hardly have found a more sympathetic conspirator than this New Englander. When Frederic Melcher was born into this world, he must have entered reading. He was a genuine lover of books, with such vivid memories of his own boyhood reading as to make him especially susceptible to the plight of those children who were never to know the pleasure of books of genuine spirit. Mr. Melcher thought something could be accomplished by a sustained campaign, nationwide in scope, with a Children's Book Week to be celebrated in schools, libraries, and bookshops across the country. He envisioned, too, a plan to encourage authors of children's books and to entice others into the field. After preliminary talks they had come to Room 105, a location that had gained some repute as a hatching ground. The Three M's—Moore, Mathiews, Melcher! Three musketeers who were troubadours as well and made things hum. Theirs is an oft-told tale, one to be cherished by book people as a living tradition. Children's Book Week gave way to Book Week, fixing on the calendars of the years an opportunity for declaring a celebration in praise of books and reading. The Caldecott and Newbery medals which Frederic Melcher gave to the American Library Association to be awarded annually were the prototypes for the plethora of awards that followed.

The first celebration of Children's Book Week in the New York Public Library was held in the Central Children's Room in 1919, with Kate Douglas Wiggin the speaker of the day. ACM, for this reason, found pleasure in describing Kate Douglas Wiggin as the godmother of Book Week and Frederic Melcher as godfather.

When the war came, the First World War, Anne welcomed America's entry into the arena, thinking of

England and all that country held for her. She could not
but rejoice in the panoply and panache in which the city
was bedecked. New York never looked more beautiful
from Washington Square to Central Park. The splendid
buildings gleamed in marble and Indiana limestone, the
chocolate architecture of the nineties all but gone, with
remnants of great private mansions standing solidly
among the stone façades of skyscrapers that towered toward the stars. The clocklike symmetry of glass and
steel had not yet been announced. Flagpoles lined both
sides of Fifth Avenue with flags of the nations dancing
and shimmering in a clean wind. The city seemed eter-
nally *en fête*, and midway up the avenue the old Tyro-
lean building of Max Schling, the florist, spilled flowers
from window boxes in great profusion.

Children in libraries asked for books on aviation of
which there were none. A list of adult books on the war
was gotten together recommending titles to be purchased
for the children's rooms. Maps and geographies were in
great demand as children sought to know where their
brothers and fathers were "dug in." Anne met the time
as she had met the lesser tragedy of the Spanish-American
War, by stressing the ideals of sacrifice and courage.
Mabel Williams, with the help of the office staff, created
a reading list on the topic of heroism that stands for all
time a distinguished accomplishment among library publications. A club of Jewish boys at Hamilton Fish Park
Library named their club "The Hero Club" and took as
their pledge the final quotation from the heroism list. "I
am a citizen of America and heir to all her greatness and
renown."

As for the library lions, they were never again to see
such sights—parades day after day, with Woodrow Wilson, the President of the United States, in tails and a top

hat, marching at the head of one of them. Bands played on the esplanade; opera singers performed at the tops of their lungs; stars of the theater hawked war bonds hour after hour; ambulances, wooden ships, airplanes were on display; soldiers, sailors, and marines in splendid drill formation; and the immortal Mary Pickford, Charlie Chaplin, and Douglas Fairbanks appeared as a trio. Heroes of all nations, wearing their medals, shouted for victory, the only amplifier being a megaphone. It was as though there were a three-ring circus in the space between the lions, the gaiety gone awry, like an episode experienced in a nightmare.

The rotunda of the library served as a fitting background for special ceremonies. Cardinal Mercier trailed his crimson robes down the steps of the foyer. The French Society of New York borrowed the library to tender a reception for Marshal Joffre and M. Viviani. That day was memorialized in the library unofficially by another event: a child was born on that day in the library, the daughter of Mr. Fedler, the building's maintenance engineer, who lived with his family in the apartment allotted him, a perquisite of his position. They named her Viviani Joffre.

When the war ended, how quickly hope and exhilaration trod upon its heels! All the fiddles began to play! There would certainly never be another war! A renaissance of the arts surged through the country—in the theater, in the writing of novels, in pert and gallant little magazines sprung like crocuses heralding the spring.

Children were involved. Within the next few years, the publishing of their books became the concern of major publishing houses. Louise Seaman at Macmillan, May Massee at Doubleday, Alice Dalgliesh at Scribner's —these three young women were pioneers as heads of departments, the sole concern of which was responsible publishing of books for children.

George H. Doran, publisher, feeling the time propitious, announced in early 1918 the publication of a new literary monthly, *The Bookman*, with Eugene Saxton[1] as one of its editors, to be followed by young, red-headed John Farrar, whose literary bent came via the New York Public Library, his mother having been a staunch and gracious librarian in the Extension Division for a considerable period of time. It was Eugene Saxton who sought out ACM, asking her to assume responsibility for the space in the forthcoming magazine allotted to books for children.

The years of ACM's contribution to *The Bookman* are generally designated as the era that inaugurated in America the reviewing of books for children on a sustained and continuous basis. There has been some hairsplitting among the Ph.D.s as to the validity of the assumption that no reviews of books for children preceded hers. As if it mattered. The truth of the matter is that these essays collected in *My Roads to Childhood* far outreach the term "review." Every critic worth his salt is read not alone for his appraisal of titles, or his critical analysis of a writer's work, but for his account of the tilt of the world as he feels it, the temper of his experience in relation to the common fate of man, revealed in art and literature. *My Roads to Childhood* remains no mere collection of reviews of books, many of which are out of print. Its pages are informed with passion, spirit, and intellectual force, based on a breadth of experience of life and a perceptive reading on many subjects, transcending boundaries of narrow specialization. The portrait of a great personality is here revealed as well as a philosophy of criticism.

The Bookman was sustained from 1918 until 1924, its bright blue cover, its double column of clear print reflecting much of the excitement of the period. "It was courageous of Eugene Saxton to pick me," Anne wrote to Bertha Mahony Miller in retrospect, "for I was no longer young but already middle-aged."

A letter from him in 1922, when he had left *The Bookman* for Harper and Brothers, reflects his pride in that choice:

> I am glad you remember that we started the children's reviews and essays. As I tell J.[ohn] F.[arrar] I grow jealous every now and then when someone points to the great editor apropos of some feature that antedated his coming. I'm not jealous. I couldn't possibly have done what he has accomplished with the magazine and no one knows that better than myself.

When the revised edition of *My Roads* appeared in 1939, ACM sent Mr. Saxton a copy at Christmas time and had from him gracious acknowledgment:

> Dear Miss Moore
> It was very nice of you to remember me in your distribution of Christmas copies of the new edition of *My Roads*. The memories of the very beginnings of those papers go back to the old days when you made your first appearance in *The Bookman* and that seems a long time ago. One of the nicest things about the length of the period is the fact that the book is vital and attractive today. That is sufficiently a rarity in publishing experience to make it noteworthy. I am sure many thousands of young readers have found a new and delightful road into your enchanting country through the pages of this book.

At the time of Anne's retirement, he wrote in part:

> I am glad to know you are to have more time for writing. The personal record will cover a period of New York

literary history when more has been done for the reading of the younger generation—and largely by you—than at any other time. . . .

On July 2, 1943, Anne wrote to Bertha Mahony Miller:

Dear Bertha:

Eugene Saxton's death was such a shock to me I could not pull the Three Owls piece together until yesterday. While we did not often meet in his Harper years I always felt I could rely on his friendship and his sound editorial judgment. There was always a lovely card from him at Christmas time. It did me good to hear Mr. Huebsch say, as we came out from the service at The Little Church Around the Corner, "I feel that half my life has gone." We were all back in 1918 that morning. Stanley and Ted Rinehart asked to take me wherever I wanted to go which was behind the library lions. Later I bought a copy of *Western Star* [by Stephen Vincent Benét] [2] at Scribners and gave the rest of the day to it—a living book—and as I wrote John Farrar, his only consolation for the loss of so dear a friend was the privilege of publishing it.

More than once in her lifetime she was to forge from grief and the ache of remembrance a ritual of reading and to seek solace behind the library lions.

13

A FLIGHT OF OWLS

For next to the pure joy of creating a thing one's self is the discovery of something created by another. The instant recognition and detachment of a piece of original work from a mass of ready-made writing and the presentation of one's findings and conviction constitute the reviewer's main chance. His function is to declare the book's quality and give it a place in association with other books. To the degree that the review stimulates the desire of the reader to read the book to confirm or to differ with the critic will it be contributory to thought, discussion, criticism, fresh creative work. And this, as I see it, is the true objective for the reviewer of children's books no less than for the reviewer in the general field.

For many more years than any of us like to recall children's books, if read at all when written about, were read for ulterior ends. They were considered en masse rather than individually, both in the educational field and in the publishing field. They were tagged for moralistic trends, for a physical age limit, for collateral reading, for anything and everything save appraisal of them as books in relation to books in general.

ACM

ITH THE APPEARANCE of *The Bookman* essays, in the magazine and as separate volumes, such an oncoming tide of people rafted into Room 105 as to create an outward flow of shaping waters that edged on beaches far beyond the margins of the library. Editors, artists, and publishers and their kind might well be expected to find their way into Room 105, but many others came to check all points of the compass with ACM: trustees of libraries in search of librarians attune to children and their books; architects asking for aid in planning children's rooms at the drafting-board level; representatives of foreign governments seeking advice in the selection of books in the English language to serve as interpreters of American life.

One Dutch "navigator"-historian, Hendrik Willem van Loon, came first in gratitude because he found his *Short History of Discovery* acclaimed in *The Bookman* when other reviews and the bookshops themselves gave it little room because it looked strange. His *Story of Mankind* he brought to Room 105 and to the Central Children's Room literally chapter by chapter, as he wrote it, the manuscript, rolled like wallpaper, bulging the pockets of his ample overcoat. In the dedication of *The Songs We Sing*, music arranged by Grace Castagnetta, he crowned his regard for ACM:

This book is dedicated
to
Annie Carroll Moore

in cheerful recognition
of all the many miracles
she has performed
within the delightful realm of
the world of books
where the readers sit in little
chairs
and rest their elbows on diminutive tables
when following the adventures of Ferdinand.
For if that room is now filled
with much more sunshine, gaiety,
beauty and common sense
than ever before,
it is mainly through the efforts of
Annie Carroll Moore
who opened wide the windows
and said
"A little less stuffiness right here
would surely do none of us
any harm."

James Daugherty, muralist turned illustrator and author, in a confrontation with ACM confessed to a love for Washington Irving and a desire to give the Knickerbockers pictorial reality. The result was a splendid collaboration between two Irving buffs, *The Bold Dragoon and Other Ghostly Tales* and *Knickerbocker's History of New York*, appearing in editions edited by ACM and illustrated in full spirit by James Daugherty.

Ann Morgan, the instigator of the Women's Committee for Devastated France after the First World War, leaned on Miss Moore for aid and thirstily absorbed her philosophy of librarianship, and the young clergyman, John Brett Langstaff, who during a period in England conceived the idea of transforming a shabby building where Charles Dickens had once lived into the David Copperfield Library for the tattered children of the Bor-

ough of St. Pancras, asked Miss Moore to serve on his
board of counselors. When the day of presentation came,
on November 1, 1922, Anne was present, in the mansion
house of the Lord Mayor, among the gathering of notables: the Burgomaster of Leyden, bringing with him a
gift of Dutch children's books as a tribute to Dickens; the
French Ambassador with a gift from his country; John
Galsworthy as speaker of the day; and that girl from
Limerick, Maine, Anne Carroll Moore. As was the habit
with Anne, she saw and heard the proceedings with eye
for pomp and decor. In a letter to her great-niece Margaret Warren, Rachel's child, she gave account of it:

> I've written Mother about speaking at the Mansion
> House which is the official residence of the Lord Mayor.
> I had to say, just as Mr. Galsworthy did, "My Lord
> Mayor, My Lady Mayoress, etc." Wasn't it fortunate
> there was a gold collar on my black satin dress since the
> Lord Mayor wore his great jewel and the Burgomaster of
> Leyden his silver chain and the Mayor of St. Pancras a big
> gold chain? I was the only lady who spoke and I expected
> to feel scared to death standing up in the Egyptian Room
> of the Mansion House but it was really quite nice, for
> everyone was interested in David Copperfield's Library—
> and that was what it was all about.

When Mrs. Robert Bacon of Westbury, Long Island,
fixed on the idea of a children's library as the perfect
memorial to her husband, Robert Bacon, formerly this
country's Ambassador to France, her footsteps and those
of the architect led to 105. ACM promised Mrs. Bacon
that she would hold that library under concern as though
it were in truth a branch of the New York Public Library. The initial collection of books was a duplicate of
one chosen by the children's department of the New
York Public Library for English-speaking children of

Rio de Janeiro at the request of Edwin Morgan, Ambassador to Brazil. To this nucleus Mrs. Bacon added many rare illustrated books in the French language as well as in English. "It is, as far as I know, the best and most varied selection of books yet made for a children's library," ACM was to write of it. "Not merely a gift to children of Westbury but a unique contribution to the educational institutions of the whole country." Once again ACM relinquished one of the staunchest and most gifted of librarians, Jacqueline Overton, to head up the library at Westbury.

For two consecutive years—1921 and 1922—the outgoing tides of influence swept Anne to the shores of England and France. There she acquired such wealth of friendships and experience as to refresh her for a lifetime. Of the visit to devastated France, in 1921, Nicholas has made excellent account in the book *Nicholas and the Golden Goose*. In 1922 Anne returned to France to hear her cherished friend, Marie Shedlock, tell stories to the French children in the libraries established by the American committee. Such an event had been conceived in a private dream of ACM and was brought to fulfillment by her persuasive powers. She was a gifted dreamer, brilliant in the practical execution and funding of her dreams.

Only by indirection and in certain letters to her family is there the smallest hint of the depths of feeling Anne must have known when she saw the children in war-torn villages of France enjoying libraries staffed by young women she had trained whose vision derived from her own. The skills with which they adapted the tenets of library work with children to the French psyche and the French need were her skills and hers was the great design formed out of the clay of Pratt and the multiracial city of New York. It is well that she had invented Nicholas to stand as emissary between her and the world, to serve as a voice by means of which she could control the expression of her private ecstasy and her inner pride.

When she went to England from France in 1921 she took with her splendid photographs of the libraries and the children in them. It was of these matters she spoke immediately to the editors and publishers who welcomed her as the major critic of children's books in America without peer in England. Nicholas and his French companions were given space in the London *Times* right beside the court calendar as "most newsworthy story of the day." "How on earth did he get into the *Times?*" asked the astounded Walter de la Mare, in a letter of October 1921.

Three enduring friendships grew and flowered out of that first visit Anne made to England in the role of writer and critic rather than as librarian. The cast of characters was L. Leslie Brooke, Beatrix Potter, and Walter de la Mare. Marie Shedlock introduced her to L. Leslie Brooke, whose pictures of famous trios are definitive, "The Three Bears" and "The Three Little Pigs," and whose "Johnny Crow" with his garden and his garden parties is probably destined to endure as long as laughter itself. In a long letter to Rachel, her niece, written from Grasmere, on June 23, 1921, Anne recalls the first two encounters and announces the possibility of a third:

> I had an enchanting afternoon with a family tea round the dining room table at Leslie Brooke's, Miss Shedlock and Miss Glover, who is an old friend of the Brookes, meeting me there. Mr. B. is quite deaf but adorable and his wife, a daughter of Stafford Brooke, one of the most gracious hostesses I have ever met. You would have loved both the home and the studio, everything was so *real*. Mr.

Brooke and I literally fell into one another's arms and he wants to give me for myself one of his originals. They were immensely pleased with Nicholas, who sat on the easel in the studio. Their eldest son was missing and finally reported lost in the War and one sees the tragedy in their eyes but in no other way.

Last Sunday afternoon I had tea and late supper at Walter de la Mare's. His daughter, "Jinny," a girl of seventeen, met me at Crystal Palace Station and after looking me over and proposing a taxi, finally consented to take me on the top of a tram. We found rather an interesting actor singing verses from *Peacock Pie* which has been set to music by another guest of the afternoon—a very good voice— Mrs. de la Mare had been called to Oxford by the illness of the eldest son, and a daughter just past twenty received me with her father who is very good-looking and likeable. There is a boy of fifteen—a very lovely family altogether. . . .

As for Beatrix Potter, she was reportedly a hard nut to crack, and Mr. Warne, when he delivered to Anne his letter of introduction, hastened to say, "I can only wish you luck." Now it happened that at this time *The Tale of Peter Rabbit* and *The Tale of Benjamin Bunny* were rolling from the presses in French translation, *Pierre Lapin* and *Jeannot Lapin*. Anne bought fifty copies of each and sent them to the children of the library at Soissons. Having mentioned this fact when she posted from Grasmere her letter of introduction to Beatrix Potter, and having promised to show her pictures of the French children and their grandmothers, Anne was immediately invited to luncheon at Castle Cottage in Sawrey, near Ambleside, and given full instructions as to the best route of traveling. ACM tells the story of that visit twice over, one in *Nicholas: A Manhattan Christmas Story* and secondly in a remarkable book to which she was to contribute an appreciation some thirty years later. It shall not be spoiled by telling it here. The fact remains that the two indomitable characters recognized in each other like traits of determination, discernment, and forthright expression of opinion, and their friendship and devotion to each other held until the end of Beatrix Potter's life in 1945. Anne not only had luncheon but stayed for tea and dinner and all night, visiting Hill Top Farm, the first of Beatrix Potter's holdings in the region and the scene of many of her books. Such a state of affairs was characteristic of Anne. She was often an instantaneous visitor, repeatedly coming to a sudden decision to stay when she had previously declared a visit impossible. The aura of a house determined the shift in the winds of her decision. If a pine tree grew in certain proportion to the window through which one saw it, or if the room invited a session at the writing desk, she grew content and happy and announced, "I think I'll stay for a while." She was a visitor easily pleased once she had come to stay. The only inconvenience she could not tolerate was a Murphy bed, that hidden peril that springs from the walls at the touch of a button.

Of the three rare spirits, L. Leslie Brooke was the most merry and most puckish, yet his critical judgments were bold and original. The first letter from Leslie Brooke was written from The Four Winds, Elmhurst, Surrey, on August 4, 1921. After reference to the fact that Anne had chosen for herself one of his original drawings at Warne's, the publisher, the letter continues:

Did Nicholas become a Wordsworthian at Grasmere? He would have kicked, at first, at the absence of childish fun. While such things as
"And three times to the boy, I said
'Why? William, tell me why?'"
would have offended all the cries of child study. But per-

haps if he approached him in the spirit of Lamb's Daddy
Wordsworth they may have come to terms.

I do not know at all when you return to America, we
hope you will not forget us altogether. Johnny Crow must
give you a caw of reminder now and then. (Quite so—as
you say—caws and effect) With our very kind remem-
brances, yours sincerely, L. Leslie Brooke.

In 1927 Leslie Brooke writes to her from Oxford:

And I join with you in your admiration of de la Mare as
poet and editor. Though if the Atlantic were not between
us I should be prepared—greatly daring—to maintain the
position that the introductory story of this book[1] is in the
wrong key. I have no doubt that it is sound allegory for
those who can read allegory—and I am quite sure that it
is most characteristic of one of the chief and most charming qualities in its author—a sense of mental remoteness
and atmosphere charged with strangeness. But it seems to
me that it is just this conscious and abnormal atmosphere
that is the wrong approach to so catholic a collection of
English verse—the boy is a self-conscious little boy and the
original collector was a self-conscious and consequently
lonely man and neither of them embodied the essential
spirit of the main English character. It's like putting a
Rossetti frame on Millais' "Boyhood of Raleigh."

Anne wrote him apparently asking for an expression of
opinion as to the elements that make for greatness in a
picture book. In a letter of September 2, 1928, he quotes
W. H. Hunt as saying, "Draw firm and be jolly," and he
reports himself as looking forward to receiving *Millions
of Cats* because "I do not find that cats come easily myself." The letter continues:

You know as well as I do what elements are essential to
picture books which are to have a perennial interest. . . .
I am not going to be beguiled into platitudes. But to see
how instinctive the inspiration of the very best type of
picture book is, it is worth looking at the first draft by

Caldecott of his *House That Jack Built*. Warne published it some years ago, but it is little known. It is just a series of scribbles but implicit in each scrawl can clearly be found the very dog, cat, rat, etc., that has become classic. Of course Caldecott is an extreme instance of instinctive drawing and though I have seen a sheet covered with "tries" after a special effect of expression in a face—I do not think he had the patient building up that so many have to do before they achieve the appearance of facility. I imagine his plan was rather to tear it up and begin again.

In 1929 Anne had sent him a copy of *Knickerbocker's History of New York* inscribed by both herself and James Daugherty. His hearty response to James Daugherty's illustrations reflects his own spirits and exuberance:

He has got into the contemporary skin of his author in a wonderful way or adapts himself to the same taste in humor and draws all with a line and with a sense of style that are distinctly not essentially of today. I don't know how long it is since I have found such fullblooded gusto. . . . I am especially struck how the work gathers weight as it goes on. I don't see how more force and tension could be put into drawings. [He then cites the pages.] His line looks as though it had come boiling onto the paper—and that is enough for any man's good name.

Rachel Field's *Hitty*, illustrated by Dorothy Lathrop, he dubbed "The Hittiad," and in a letter from Hurstcote, Cumnar, Oxford, January 15, 1930, he gives a fascinating glimpse of how one artist reads the concept of another:

As to the illustrations, there is first of all the craftiness in the choice of them. They are all most carefully confined to Hitty's immediate world, and in that way give a decorative unity to the book which would have been lost had the artist allowed herself to be led aside even once into the human element of the stories and introduced a new standard of proportion and measurement and life. I should never have had her courage and should have come a most prodigious cropper.

Beatrix Potter's letters from 1921 until 1945 are rich documents of her life as Mrs. Heelis, sheepherder, deep in content with her house and the countryside she loved as a child, her farmer-lawyer husband, and her privacy. But there was the agony of the Second World War soon to come. In a letter of 1938 she wrote:

> To think that in one's old age one must hear the sound again. . . . It's different to the last war—seems less to do individually, partly, of course, because we have grown old. This is a war of young people in uniform—and more and more a war of mechanics and chemistry. Last war we were drying foxglove leaves for the druggist; now no demand; so much is synthetic in production. . . . It was a lovely green April, plenty of grass for the sheep, and a good lambing time in spite of the privations of frost and snow. A spring of flowers. The hawthorne hedges on the big thorn bushes of the fell side have been like drifts and patches of snow and the bluebells a sheet of blue. It is un-believable that such a lovely peaceful land should be in shadow. . . .

Her responses to Anne's own books are no polite ac-knowledgments but documented evidence of her pleasure in them. The gift of *Nicholas: A Manhattan Christmas Story* was acknowledged in this wise:

January, 1925

Castle Cottage
Sawrey
Ambleside

Dear Ann Caraway and Nicholas,
    What a delightful book you have made! It was a great surprise when I opened the parcel. I am sure American children will love it and ask for *more*. Do let us hear about Nicholas in France. Ann Caraway need not fear the task;

she can write a book that has wisdom, pathos and fun. Tears and laughter.

My favorite parts are about the Knickerbockers, and General Washington; and I think it is wonderful how cleverly Ann Caraway has worked in two real live—very gentlemanly—young fellows as companions to Nicholas. "Ben" being a small boy is easier.

I had no idea that New York is so "Christmasy"—a real old-fashioned Christmas.

We have had a wet one here, wild, windy and much floods; and influenza in the village; but so far my husband and I have escaped it.

I have no book to send in return; there should have been a painting book for children to colour, but the engravers made a muddle of it.

With congratulations and very kind regards,

> yrs. sincerely,
> Beatrix Heelis

In December of that same year she sent her Christmas greeting via the Bookshop for Boys and Girls in Boston. The letter with its almost Biblical concern for the sheep is so full of her snap and ginger, one cannot resist quoting it:

December 12, '25

> Sawrey
> nr. Ambleside

Dear Miss Carroll Moore,

I do not know the home address of Nicholas: Peter and Flopsy want to wish him a very Merry Christmas and they hope that the Bookshop will be so kind as to pass the message on. We will read his book again on Christmas Eve and think of his merry doings across the Atlantic.

Here—there has already been some old-fashioned weather, 4 weeks hard frost, with skating & hard snow. But it thawed suddenly last Monday, and although the frost had been enjoyable & lovely to look at—I was not sorry to see green grass again. I wonder how the sheep live in countries like U.S.A. and Canada? Ours scrape and dig with feet & heads to get at the rough grass on the hillsides; but frozen snow soon means anxiety to the shepherd and hunger for the sheep. They are next now to eat hay; and there are too many to feed, many hundred in a flock.

There have been two letters recently from Miss Bertha Mahony of the Boston Bookshop, forwarded through Messrs. Warne, and also copies of the "Horn Book." The letter which asks for particulars about "Beatrix Potter" is very perplexing. I have a most intense dislike to advertisement (and I have got on quite well enough without it). And I object to being supposed to be the wife of Sidney Webb, a member of the last socialist government. He married a Miss Beatrice Potter, no relation. There were photographs of him in the newspaper, and it said his wife had written children's books. There has often been confusion between us. I thought it would be best to write this for Mr. Warne, to forward through the New York branch of F. W. Co., to whom Miss Mahony had applied. "Beatrix Potter is Mrs. William Heelis, she lives in the north of England, her home is amongst the mountains & lakes that she has drawn in her picture books. Her husband is a lawyer. They have no family. Mrs. Heelis is in her 60th year. She leads a very busy contented life, living always in the country and managing a large sheep farm on her own land."

I don't think anybody requires to know more about me. In the second letter Miss Mahony asks how I came to write the books. I used to write picture letters to a little invalid boy years and years ago, the eldest child of a friend. Peter was written to him in a letter. He is now a hardworked clergyman in a London parish and I believe he has the letter yet. About 1900 there began to be a fashion for little picture books, and I thought Peter might be worthwhile publishing. But I could not find anyone else who thought so. It was refused by many publishers, and I got a small number printed for myself, with pen & ink illustrations like the scribbles on the original letter. That is the history of Peter Rabbit. I have never been able to understand what is the attraction of the book, but it continues to sell.

The Horn Book is pleasantly written. I wish all such books of gossip—British as well as American—were in equally good taste.

But I *don't* want to be exploited! And I am very grateful to Nicholas for his reticence. . . . Has Nicholas been abroad again?

With kind regards from us both,

yrs. sincerely,
Beatrix Heelis

Throughout the years of their friendship, Anne sent visitors to Sawrey and always they were received with utmost cordiality. "We had a call from Mary Haugh and her husband a week ago," she wrote in 1937 of Mary Haugh Zipprich, one of the best storytellers on the staff of the New York Public Library, with an Irish edge to her tongue and a look of beauty on her face. Beatrix talked to her about storytelling. "I was trying to ask her," Mrs. Heelis wrote, "whether the art of live speech, that speaking storytelling is not the real thing? I expect P[eter] R[abbit] comes nearer to word storytelling than the later books which she probably has to cut and put in her own words." All this was preamble to a lively account in the same letter:

Mrs. Fausler of the New York Metropolitan Museum has been to Messrs. Warne's office, wanting to borrow the Peter Rabbit originals—they are willing to lend them and I have no objection. I don't think the P. R. drawings "represent a very high watermark in the history of book illustration," to quote Mrs. Fausler!! In fact I think them bad, the rabbit on the cover I have always thought a horrid monstrosity—all out of drawing—but undoubtedly it was that first book—P. R. "which hit a mark" of some sort. The much better-executed illustrations of following books of the series did not make the same hit. . . .

The letter returns to the topic of Mary Haugh:

I was very interested to hear her praise *Sister Ann* [a
sly remark on B. P.'s part, this, ACM having told her only
a month previously that she thought *Sister Ann* not
worthy of publication as a book].

I did so much enjoy your visit. You are over my head
intellectually, but you appreciate old-fashioned simple
memories and pleasures. I am glad you and Nicholas had
a pleasant passage back to New York. My love to you
both,

                                              Beatrix Heelis

No small part of the inheritance Anne bequeathed the
generations was her record of friendships. She had a
genius for the gift. The devotion of these three innovators in poetry and art to ACM and her work attuned
children on both sides of the Atlantic to an appreciation
of those who served them with the highest art in drama
and rhyme, poetry and picture. Anne alerted the American public to the distinctive genius of each of these three,
beginning at Pratt in 1903, when Beatrix Potter's *Tailor
of Gloucester* appeared in a packet of books from England. She recognized that the little red books of one
B. Potter were more than toy books and stocking stuf-
fers. Beatrix Potter always resented the tendency of the
English to consider her books little more than the toys
among which they were displayed. Johnny Crow's pre-
emptive position as a folk hero among the picture-book
set was due in great measure to Anne's promotion of the
sturdiness of his characterization, the humor of his pre-
dicaments, and the agility of the line that placed him on
the pages of his books. In the music of Walter de la Mare,
Anne heard reverberations of the threat and the wonder
that is natural to the mysticism of childhood. Her scheme
of celebrating in all the branches of the New York Public
Library the birthdays of Leslie Brooke and Walter de la
Mare was sometimes questioned by newcomers to the

staff who did not at first recognize the cleverness of the idea. Not only did these gentle fetes heighten the common day, but they set a-rattling in the memories of children the names of *Johnny Crow* and *Peacock Pie*, Leslie Brooke and Walter de la Mare, and made them as familiar as the rhymes of Mother Goose.

The letters of Walter de la Mare reveal a mind that mused on visions peculiarly its own and saw, through a half-open doorway, as Henry Beston put it, the haunted possibilities of the undiscovered and the unknown. He was reticent, contained, remote, and surprised that anyone was listening. The measure of his accomplishment seemed never to affect his modesty, and that so great a man should know timidity added to his charm.

"I have only once met Arthur Rackham," he wrote ACM in answer to her letter describing her encounter with the artist, "but I am sure Childs was the right eating house—a good old word which is now almost as obsolete as 'tavern.' It is one of the few restaurants in New York that I have the courage to enter alone (what a confession)."

In a later letter, written on May 6, 1940, in which he addresses her as Anne and signs himself "Yours ever, W. J."—nearly twenty years after the beginning of their friendship—he writes: "I know we share certain theories and convictions about children and childhood and if at any time mine seem to differ with yours, then that will be at my peril."

On each of the April birthdays a cable went to Walter de la Mare, with birthday wishes from the children of New York, the first when he was fifty-one in 1924. Each brought from him a letter rejoicing in the fact that he was thus remembered. Among letters of the latter years one is given here in its entirety:

April 25, 1952   4, South End House,
                                      Montpelier Row,
                                          Twickenham.

Dear Ann,[2]

You were a Dear to remember I'm all but Eighty: so you see how quickly now I'm catching up, but never, never, NEVER shall I manage to squeeze into what's called Time so much as you are doing. As a matter of fact I'm still so attached to my inkpot that I begrudge leaving off for meals. And you know how meals are spent in England just now—BANQUETS. However I manage to keep going, though it is rather reminiscent of my memories of a railway now defunct that used to be called The London Smashum & Turnover Railway.

You will know what a real joy it was to see Pamela Bianco the other day. She looked younger than when she was twelve, I think; though perhaps my fading inward eye may account for the memory of her being twelve. Anyhow she has the same marvellous grey eyes—or grey-blue, or blue-grey, or blue: we had a little argument about it. And she brought me a lovely picture, which fits into my little parlour with perfection. How I wish you could come and see it. Also, how I wish I could come and see *you*. But, alas, it doesn't seem likely now.

How well I recall that Santa Claus feast with you behind the Lions—in the candle-light; some of the pansy faces even.

                                          With my love,
                                          yours ever
                                          W. J.

It was Anne's custom to use narrow strips of paper, seemingly torn from the backs of old envelopes, as markers in books she read. These gave her ready access for quick referral. Then slightly marked in pencil, a wavery line indicated the choice she had made from the page. She seldom removed the papers. They stood yellowing on her bookshelves, tattered pennons marking the pleasure spots of her reading through the years. In her copy of *Come Hither*, that wide and luminous anthology of Walter de la Mare's, the flag stands at page 738, in the section called "About and Roundabout," where erudition and delight are chock-a-block, under the guise of notes. The thin pencil line marks the passage. It is Walter de la Mare's own comment: "Words are but a *means* of conveying poetry from one imagination to another. So may a smile make lovely a plain face; or sunbeams weave a rainbow in the air. Even words themselves may be needless; for two human spirits may hold converse together (of which only the rarest poetry in words or music, paint or stone could *tell*) without one syllable of speech between them." One may surmise that such was the understanding between these two friends, for whom childhood was chief among the bonds they shared.

Three years before *The Bookman* came to an end, day broke for another literary magazine, this one published by the New York *Herald Tribune* as a weekly supplement to the paper, its title *Books*, under the editorship of Stuart Sherman, previously a professor of English at the University of Illinois, who had become critic-at-large. His assistant editor was Irita Van Doren, a vital, vigorous, and charming woman of letters in her own right, who as the wife of Carl Van Doren increased the fame and prestige of that first family of American letters.

The year was 1924. How favorably stood the stars then on Anne's behalf! Her own book for children, *Nicholas: A Manhattan Christmas Story*, was promised for September publication. Six years of contribution to *The Bookman* lay behind her. In that time she had honed to a cutting edge the skills of the reviewer and had so intermingled them with knowledge and intuitive perception as to raise to an apogee of art the criticism of books for children. Interest in the publication of children's books surfaced like a great wave, and authors and artists of enormous gifts rode high on the swing of it, the result a spate of glory in the blackness of the terror-ridden twentieth century. The editors of *Books* knew the time had come to recognize the Lilliputian renaissance in full panoply. They cast their eyes across Fortieth Street and Sixth Avenue to the New York Public Library.

In a letter to the nieces written from Cousin Alice's in Portland and dated September 1924, Anne wrote:

> Did I tell you that I was asked some weeks ago if I would edit a page of criticism of children's books for a new review called *Books* Stuart Sherman is going to edit for the *Herald Tribune*? While I was considering the matter I went down to Westbury, Long Island, to take charge of the Children's Library Mrs. Robert Bacon has given to the town in memory of her husband. . . . When I found Miss Overton needed a vacation, I took part of mine down there. . . . I got the best rest I've had outside of England and I needed it just then.

In that placid and beautiful place Anne drew up her articles of confederation with the *Herald Tribune* and sent them to the editors. The title came first. Five iron owls roosted on the weathervane of the Westbury Library, swinging with the wind. Anne chose three—one to represent the writer, one the artist, and the third, with ruffled feathers, the critic. The page would be called "The Three Owls." No advertising was to appear on the page. Anne was to be responsible for a lead article every week, for the selection of books to be reviewed as well as for the matching of reviewer's talents and interest to the titles under consideration. The date of a book's publication was not to preclude discussion of books of former years. Anne was to have control of the illustrations chosen for the page and to be free from the burden of responsibility for makeup. When there was no immediate reply to this document, Anne decided that the editors could not comply with her demands, so she returned to New York and planned to take off for Portland for the rest of her vacation, but at the last minute she was summoned for a luncheon conference with Irita Van Doren and informed that after a series of conferences all stipulations had been met. "It promises some very good fun," Anne commented in the letter, "if I can continue to regard it as an adventure."

The fun and adventure of "feeding the owls," as she called it, was sustained by Anne from 1924 until 1930. It was no diminution of zest and spirit that grounded the owls, but the Great Depression and the realization on the part of *Books* that a department of books for children could not be further sustained on so splendid and lavish a scale. Anne was invited to continue as a contributing member of the staff, but she decided to cut clear, taking the three owls with her until such time as they found a new roost among the rafters of *The Horn Book*, from which shelter they circled the scene in briefer flight in the form of "The Three Owls' Notebook" from 1936 until the day of her life's end.

The accomplishment of "The Three Owls" under the aegis of the *Herald Tribune*'s *Books* has never been equaled, nor is it likely to be. Vitality infused the pages, born of the diversity in interests, knowledge, and abilities of those who wrote in answer to Anne's request: lawyers, doctors, musicians, poets, engineers, professional magicians, novelists, critics of other great newspapers—Harry Hansen, of the Chicago *Daily News*, Llewellyn Jones of Chicago's *Evening Post*—editors, heads of bookshops, Geoffrey Parsons, May Lamberton Becker, and Will

Cuppy of the *Herald Tribune* staff, John Farrar, editor
and publisher, authors and artists of children's books by
the score. Chart geographically the background of the
contributors. What distances the owls encompassed in
flight to return with freighted wings—England, Scotland, France, in the person of Esther Averill, of the
Domino Press in Paris, with writers, librarians, and acquaintances at focal points in Boston, Fort Worth, Cleveland, Baltimore, Seattle, Los Angeles, Washington, D.C.,
Salem, North Carolina, Logan, Utah, and Santa Fe, New
Mexico. All the divergence of interest, the points of view,
were made adhesive by a "continuity in the manner of
presentation." The group review was abolished as a
matter of principle, those catchpenny listings of titles on
related subjects with their sentence-long notations, their
hurried and harassed summaries. The sense of time and
space was not the least of the charisma of these pages. All
directions in which a book might lead were imaginatively
explored and all accompanying associations disclosed and
laid before the reader, inviting contemplation. Here, for
example, is a piece by ACM on a book by Marian Hurd
McNeely, illustrated by William Siegel, its title *The
Jumping-Off Place*. Now this was not a great book but
a good piece of writing. With what care Anne considers
the title and the author! How far its reach, how genuinely critical, how it sticks in the memory!

> In an earlier story, *Rusty Ruston*, Mrs. McNeely planted
> a garden in Kansas and made it the background for the
> story of a seventeen-year-old girl earning her way to col-
> lege. A living and likable girl was Rusty and her flower
> garden was very real. The story suffered, however, from
> too much sprightliness and exaggeration of character. One
> felt too conscious of the author doing it as one read. In
> short it seemed a made-up vocational story on an essen-
> tially sound base of good ideas.

In *The Jumping-Off Place* Mrs. McNeely has done a more significant and a more permanent piece of work. She has transplanted a family of children, headed by a girl of seventeen and a boy of fifteen, to a homestead in South Dakota to which their uncle had staked a claim. The uncle's death does not deprive them of his counsel, for he has left a notebook of instruction and comment relating to the new life and a sense of his lovable, reliable presence in their midst.

There is more genuine atmosphere and character in this story than we have found in any recent book for girls. The neighboring homesteaders are well characterized and one feels throughout the poignancy of life, death, and unending struggle to conquer the land.

If Mrs. McNeely can write like this she should abandon the practice of introducing irrelevant "light touches" which get in the way of her story. There are a few even in *The Jumping-Off Place* which recall the reader sharply from moments of genuine emotion to the commonplace. But the story itself rings true to prairie and to children. They live there in actuality rather than by hearsay and even one born and bred in the mountains or by the sea comes to feel the call of the prairie and is grateful to Mrs. McNeely for writing a story which will give to New England girls, for example, something truer and more intimately related to their own home life than they are accustomed to find in Western stories. Nor do we stop with New England. This is a book for children of other countries—a true picture of American life.

One feels that girls who have read and liked it will go on of their own accord to *My Antonia* and *The Song of the Lark* of Willa Cather.

Mr. Siegel's pictorial designs for the book are in striking contrast to Beatrice Stevens's for *Betty Leicester* in that they do give an impression of the prairie, while Miss Stevens conveys not a hint of what Maine is like but rather the dress and ways of the '90s, and this we think is unfortunate, since it is by the quality of Maine in the book and the simplicity and naturalness of Betty Leicester herself that the book survives rather than by the story of what happens. After forty years one would have chosen a more effective format for a new edition, but *Betty Leicester* is doubtless good for many years to come and we may yet welcome her in a pictorial setting more like the Maine of Sarah Orne Jewett's stories, on which we fed with delight as they came from the presses, to which we still turn with a deeper realization that she has given back "the very life" of the Maine we carry about with us.

All the drama, changing excitements, the whirligigs and divertisement that emanated from those pages of critical studies were in truth held within the bounds of two major disciplines: the discipline of literature and of form. Anne never confused literature with sociology, pedagogy, psychiatry, and child study, worthy subjects in their own right that are too often emboldened to tromp through books for children, indecent in their weak disguises, to an extent that would not be tolerated in books for the adult. When it came to criticism, Anne held with T. S. Eliot. "We can therefore ask, about any writing which is offered to us as literary criticism, is it aimed toward understanding and enjoyment? If it is not, it may still be a legitimate and useful activity; but it is to be judged as a contribution to psychology, or sociology, or logic, or pedagogy, or some other pursuit—and is to be judged by specialists, not by men of letters."

Early in Anne's career when she was preparing lectures for Iowa and in the first days of Pratt, the word "ought" in relation to the selection of books for children occurs twice but it never appears again. She was not one to prescribe books by rote: grade, age, reading readiness, or "pots of message." When Agnes Hansen, the director of the library school at Pratt, asked ACM what could be done to prepare children for the threat of communism, fascism and all, Anne replied, "You can only give them what you've found to be the highspots of life, and festivity rates very high. That's what you remember when it comes to a vote." "After every war," Anne wrote, "people want to wipe the decks clean and tell children what they ought to think. Little will come of it."

Deeply read in the heritage of English letters, Anne considered books for children within the sweep of her own experience of literature, for literature was her passion. She knew that children felt the pull and tug of it and might be caught for a lifetime in its enduring joy. "The more we know about literature," writes Northrop Frye, "the better the chance that intensity of response and the greatness of the stimulus to it will coincide." In the cause of that transfiguring coincidence Anne Carroll Moore used her strengths and powers to the utmost.

As for form, it was a word writ large in the lexicon of her judgment. For her it included style, direction, freshness of encounter, as well as balance and proportion. A lack of form in personality, in the appearance of a place or of print on a page, the manner in which one brought off one's work, the lack of form was for her ultimate damnation. When the first issue of "The Three Owls" appeared, the headpiece proved to be less than appropriate, and other accidents marred the first issue. Then Anne asked Boris Artzybasheff, the artist-designer, lost to children's books when *Time* magazine gave him the long assignment of making portraits for their covers, to draw three owls for her. He stayed up all night to bring to completion in time for the second issue the magnificent drawing of three owls, wings curved, heads curved, boughs beneath them curved, great tropical trees curved above them, the drawing that later became the end papers for *The Three Owls*, Books Two and Three. Under the signature of this strong embracing, curved design, the forms of picture-making and the writing of books for children were explored in a golden time.

Meanwhile *The Horn Book* of Boston had emerged as the major journal of criticism of books for children. It had begun as a small publicity sheet issued in behalf of the Bookshop for Boys and Girls, which in 1916 became a project of the Women's Educational and Industrial Union. Bertha Mahony was in charge of it, she being the young secretary in the organization who had envisioned a bookshop with a mission: to sell the best children's books available in a setting that invited exploration by the children as well as by adults. By 1924 the four-page leaflet had become a magazine, published four times a year, Bertha Mahony the editor and her assistant editor Elinor Whitney. As the magazine evolved, outdistancing its New England boundaries, it offered critical appraisal of a high order and, as a lagniappe, varied and fascinating articles concerning artists, editors, writers—all the tangential interests of those concerned with the making of books for children.

At the beginning ACM had been skeptical of the Bookshop, but when she saw Miss Mahony in action she knew her to be a woman of uncommon gifts and sensibility. Anne's great-nieces and -nephews, a lively tribe of Bostonians, hold the memories of their visits to the Bookshop with "Auntie" as among the most vivid and blithe of their childhood recollections. On October 1, 1936, *The Horn Book* editors, in friendly agreement with their parent organization, took over the ownership and publishing of the magazine on their own, an act of great daring and courage in the annals of publishing. The Bookshop was surrendered to the Old Corner Bookstore of Boston. It was then that ACM offered "The Three Owls Notebook" to Miss Mahony and Miss Whitney as a gift and as affirmation of her faith in their venture. The pages headed by three diminutive owls soon proved to be a powerful attraction, and it was not long before they flew home to *The Horn Book* with pieces of eight in their beaks.

With the appearance of "The Three Owls," ACM's influence on *The Horn Book* increased beyond the range of her own articles. Bertha Mahony Miller came to depend on her for editorial suggestions as well as criticisms. Anne laid to with customary incisiveness. She was largely responsible for the appearance of special issues dedicated to such people as Marie Shedlock and L. Leslie Brooke, Helen Sewell, Elizabeth MacKinstry, etc. If certain titles were never reviewed, it was because ACM had dropped a word of suggestion. The issue of January–February 1937 elicited thorough and typical analysis from her:

> The Woodstock
> January 20th 1937

Dear B E M.

The Horn Book has just come and its pictorial aspect is fine—excellent make-up. I liked the Editor's own part immensely—"Definition of a Poet" leaves me cold and I wonder how it may leave other readers. Does it tell anybody anything they really want to know? What one wants from a poet is a good *poem* or so at least it seems to me.

"Mountain Woman" is excellent. I hope I can send you a copy of the poetry of New Mexico I had for Christmas from a former assistant now teaching in a Mission School there. There are lovely things in it which would bear reprinting if she is willing and you like them. *The Junior Bible*, with due respect to Edgar Goodspeed & Macmillan, left us longing for a King James version. And so C. C.'s article seems to me a total loss—merely a piece of writing which the Nuns and Brothers, Heaven bless them, would also consider superfluous. The New Children's Bookshop is an interesting commentary from New Russia. The *real leading article* of the number is Esther Averill's. She tells things one wants to know and *knows* far more than she tells. [ACM then discusses an auto-biographical article by Mabel Leigh Hunt.] *It is so incredibly naïf and personal and commonplace.* For goodness sake, B.E.M. and Elinor Whitney, call out your ancestors if necessary to *edit* such an article as that, for you invite more of the same when you fail to do so. Setting a premium on mediocrity is the last thing you want to do. That article makes me fairly *cringe.* Do be careful when editors recommend as I've no doubt Helen Fish did— Which brings me to the Mukerji article which I consider *very important.*

May [Massee] should not attempt it and I've already heard rumors of her passing it on—Entre Nous—very wisely and tactfully. I think it should be done preferably by a man rather than by a woman, who really knows the East—even if you have to *wait.* And I believe in waiting for such a piece. I probably understand the Oriental mind least of any writer of contemporary criticism and kept Mukerji's respect because I *said so little.* I was profoundly moved by the manner of his leaving the world and I am sure many others share my feeling. Don't be in any hurry to estimate his contribution to an enduring literature for children. It is *assured.* Curiously enough I met Mukerji for the first time in the Bookshop for Boys & Girls in Boston. "I wish you wouldn't *preach* so much," said I. "How can I help it since I was educated for the priesthood?" was Mukerji's reply—I think we understood one another there and then but I of all his friends feel least competent to tell what was in his heart when he left this world so suddenly last summer. I wish I might come to Ashburnham before I sail on March 19th. If I can possibly arrange it I will let you know. I cannot as yet set any date. The Annual Report is consuming all my time and thought. With my love to you and William.

As always
Anne Carroll Moore

The two women, Bertha Mahony Miller and Anne Carroll Moore, for all their common heritage of Irish blood and New England tradition, approached argument and debate by opposite directions: Anne, direct, hard-hitting, and straightforward; Bertha, less revealing of her opinions in discussions and full of surprises because one seldom knew from preliminary discussions what final line of action she might pursue. Sessions between the two must have often been stormy, but nothing could shake the measure of affection they shared, based as it was on the respect each bore for the other's intellectual capacity, and many were the days of camaraderie in Boston and New York they celebrated. The role of critic was the most enduring of all Anne's assignments and accomplishments. "The Three Owls" winged out from *The Horn Book* for the last time in the December issue of 1960, and from that flight they did not return.

The critic of books for children is seldom held worthy of recognition by his peers. Men and women of letters admit to their circle, in terms of equality, critics of the dance, theater, films—the whole spectrum of "The Seven Lively Arts"—but books for children run the risk of being strained through the sieve of "stock responses" belonging to pedagogy, science, ethics, and sociology before their legitimacy as literature is considered.

When, for example, *The Three Owls, Second Book* appeared in 1928, the person on the *Saturday Review of Literature* responsible for assigning books to appropriate authorities or critics sent the book to a member of the Child Study Association. The result: a diatribe, in part, against the book because it did not give "proper recognition to the notable progress made by psychologists in determining the influence exerted by the interest, emotions and mental grasp of early childhood in shaping pre-school literature." It was as though a fishmonger had been asked for his appraisal of Eleanor Clark's *The Oysters of Locmariaquer*.

Even that perceptive, sympathetic, and widely cherished writer E. B. White—even he fell victim to the disease of expecting the children's critic to be concerned with dogma rather than with the living stuff of literature, albeit he did so in retrospect. Twenty years after the fact he attributed to ACM attitudes she could never have assumed and ascribed to her words she did not speak.

Well nigh the whole world of letters rejoiced when, in 1945, it was rumored that E. B. White had written a book for children, its title *Stuart Little*. When it appeared it was heralded with trumpets of acclaim and is now considered a classic. Two voices of dissent were heard at the time of publication, one made public, the other stated privately. Malcolm Cowley's criticism appeared as a review in the New York *Times*, October 28, 1945. He praised the book but with certain reservations concerning the fragmented structure of the tale. The second dissident was ACM. At this time she had only the *Horn Book* owls as mouthpiece. So deep was her regard for E. B. White that she could not bring herself to comment on the book in that space. "I was never so disappointed in a book in my life," she wrote Bertha Mahony Miller, "and I choose not to mention it." But out of her deep concern she wrote a letter to Mr. White.

In 1966, as special celebration of its twenty years of abundant life, NBC presented *Stuart Little* on television, with Johnny Carson as off-stage narrator and all the characters played by human actors except Stuart, who, being more mouse than man, was obliged to be represented by an articulated toy.

The New York *Times* of Sunday, March 6, 1966, observed the event with the publication of the history of the book, written by Mr. White himself, a photograph of Johnny Carson and a headline, "The Librarian Said It Was Bad for Children." The article read in part:

A few weeks later, back home in Maine, a letter arrived for me from Anne Carroll Moore, children's librarian emeritus of the New York Public Library. Her letter was long, friendly, urgent, and thoroughly surprising. She said she had read proofs of my forthcoming book called *Stuart Little* and she strongly advised me to withdraw it. She said, as I recall the letter, that the book was non-affirmative, inconclusive, unfit for children, and would harm its author if published. These were strong words, and I was grateful to Miss Moore for having taken the trouble to write them. I thought the matter over, however, and decided that as long as the book satisfied me, I wasn't going to let an expert talk me out of it. It is unnerving to be told you're bad for children; but I detected in Miss Moore's letter an assumption that there are rules governing the writing of juvenile literature—rules as inflexible as the rules for lawn tennis.

Now ACM never mastered the typewriter. She had no recourse to carbon copies, therefore, unless she had employed a typist. When she desired to have a record of certain letters she deemed important, she copied them in her own hand and then carelessly shuffled them among her papers. The letter to E. B. White was one such. There are certain discrepancies between the document and Mr. White's recollection of it.

35 Fifth Avenue
June 20, 1945

Dear Mr. White
Ten days have gone by since I delivered the galleys of *Stuart Little* to Miss Nordstrom. I've written you countless letters in my mind and have destroyed several attempts to put on paper my personal reaction.
I was delighted to be given the opportunity to read E.B.W.'s story in advance of publication and I took up the galleys with anticipation—I laid them down in perplexity and genuine concern. Had the manuscript been sent to me by a publisher for a professional opinion I would have had

to say that it seemed to me a double risk—for publisher and author. Illustrations may help but they cannot supply what seems to be lacking—a completely realized fantasy. After the first chapter I feel the story getting more and more out of hand, the invention becoming labored and Stuart himself staggering out of scale.

By the time I came to the school chapter the two worlds were all mixed up. He might readily pass from one to the other but to keep him alive in both at once proved too much for me to take.

Realizing that E.B.W. had once said in a letter that he could not write on his children's story unless his temperature was up, I thought perhaps the trouble is with me—temperature too low or too high applied to the reading. I put the galleys aside for several days and read them for a second time with certain children at various age levels in mind. Children are more unpredictable than adults and I hold no such belief in the infallibility of their acceptance as do many. It has taken a long time for certain books to win a sure place and it has required the permanent market of libraries and schools to reinforce the publisher's faith in their authors. I fear *Stuart Little* will be very difficult to place in libraries and schools over the country.

The prestige of Mr. White's name will undoubtedly assure an initial sale. It is precisely that element which gives me genuine concern and leads me to write as I have before publication of a book which I feel may become an embarrassment rather than the source of continuing pleasure and rewarding return any book from his pen should command.

Published anonymously it might not matter greatly. Children's books as you well know often pass with the sales of a season. Published under the name of E. B. White at this time it matters a great deal to children's books that the book should have inherent qualities which seem to be left out of this one.

I wish it were possible to talk with you both instead of writing one of the most difficult letters I have ever attempted. Since the book is in press you may wonder why I make the attempt and I can only say because I can't seem to help saying something.

How far beyond the effect upon a child for good or ill are the opinions expressed here. ACM's chief concern was that so true a writer as E. B. White should not appear before children in less than the full regalia of his greatest capabilities. Mr. White was not responsible for the tawdry headline of the article in the New York *Times* announcing the Johnny Carson show, but the sight of it angered those who knew with what passionate devotion ACM had served the highest gifts of writers and artists as well as the potential reach of children as readers.

14

FROM A BALCONY

*Somehow the poetry at the heart of life
only strikes clear when one finds it in the
everyday living of a member of one's own
family—a New England family at that.*

ACM

$\mathcal{T}$HE ROADS of Anne Carroll Moore took her to England and to France, but it was a flight of owls that winged her westward across the Wasatch Mountains to Utah. There she was destined to enliven a region, to set upon it an enduring pattern of taste and sensibility, and to endear herself literally to the generations.

In Salt Lake City, for example, a group of women, one of whom had encountered ACM in 1927, read children's books together for twenty-three years or more, becoming themselves authoritative critics of books their children and their grandchildren read. Mrs. De Fonda Collier, the catalyst of the group, reported in 1961 that it was she who had suggested to the women that they study literature for children. "What's in it?" someone asked. "Well, more than you think," she replied. It had begun in the summer session at Logan, Utah, 1927. "I had a full schedule of required courses in education which did not include literature for children," she recalls, "but I had a free period at ten o'clock. On that first morning I wandered down the hall past the open door of a large, well-filled classroom. There was Anne Carroll Moore. The second day and every day during her stay I was on the front row."

The college at Logan was at that time a state agricultural college, the president of which was Dr. Elmer George Peterson, who in the 1920s was troubled by the fact that the students had little opportunity to encounter the humanities. The head of the English Department, Dr. N. A. Pedersen, held a like concern. It was he whose attention had been caught by a section in the *Herald Tribune Books* called "The Three Owls." "There was such liveliness there," he said as he remembered the time, "such pace, to say nothing of the acumen. I wished there were someone at Logan like that who could incite students to read. When I discovered that Dr. and Mrs. Peterson were scheduled to go to New York, I suggested that they go to the New York Public Library and see who that Miss Moore might turn out to be."

The Petersons[1] appeared in the Central Children's Room on December 5, 1926. Propitious day! St. Nicholas Eve, as Anne numbered it on her private calendar. They had expected to find Miss Moore somewhere in that room. She was summoned from her office. In the interim, before her arrival, Dr. Peterson walked about the room and finally burst out with the words, "Oh, Utah could use a place like this."

She went to Utah for the first time in June 1927. She was told that a room in the college library would be assigned to her as a base of operations. From that center she would be expected to speak to students, faculty, and the general public. Outside of that, hers was a free hand. It was an assignment that well fitted her heart's delight. She commandeered copies of essential titles from the publishers, sending out before her great boxes of books which became in time the basis for the Anne Carroll Moore Library, with a plaque outside the door so naming it, its subsequent support coming from the college library.

By the time Anne arrived in Logan, she had already fallen captive to the landscape as she observed it from the train windows.

There is an Old World spell upon the Wasatch Mountains. I felt it strongly on my first visit to Utah. Crossing the mountains from Ogden to Logan I was reminded now of the land of the Frost Giants in the Waldres of Norway and now of the English Lake Country, so beautiful and so friendly seemed the treeless fells with their soft covering of pungent sagebrush, the green fields and the quiet valleys. The long rows of Lombardy poplars separating the farm lands are a gracious reminder of the Holy Land of which these pioneers were always dreaming as they planted the desert.

The room allotted to her was spacious enough to accommodate five great windows that looked out upon the Wasatch Mountains, and it held welcoming bookshelves along its walls. Anne set about immediately to make it a living and an enticing place. An initial reception was scheduled to be held there. Some of the ladies of the community came to help with the preparations and brought as offering the standard jardinieres of ferns to be set about the room on wrought-iron stands. At the sight of the dreary house-bound pots Anne grew indignant. "Don't be so Bostonian!" she exclaimed. "Bring in things that grow in your gardens and in the countryside." She had seen the farm gardens filled with roses and peonies, and these she hankered for as decorations. A letter to Rachel Moore Warren written after the fact, in July of that year, tells the story:

> I spoke twenty-eight times in ten days including a ward meeting or Mormon Sunday School. I took by request the Mappe of Fairyland and about fifty choice books from my clinic. A specialist in children's health had already changed the physical diet of Utah, and they were no less ready to absorb new kinds of books. It made the usual run of women's clubs of Eastern parent-teacher associations a pallid kind of thing by comparison. When I told how I prized my twenty-five-year-old autographed copy of *Miss Muffet's Christmas Party*, seventy copies were ordered by telegraph in the hope that Dr. Crothers might write in them also. They stole a march on me by sending for *Nicholas* in bulk and I spent the last morning autographing. There was something deeply touching in the response to poetry and romance and pictures.

In August of that year Anne sailed for Europe to attend the international library meeting in Edinburgh, but it was Utah that left the lasting imprint on her spirit and made the year memorable.

In 1931 she returned to Utah to find Martha Peterson, the youngest member of the family, a child of eight. Between them they staged a reading party in the library which Martha remembers as a chief glory of her childhood. She as hostess was charged with the task of putting before each of her eight guests a book she deemed appropriate for her and enjoyable. What possibility for discussion, agreement and debate and flights of enthusiasm this small scheme engendered! It was all capped with actual refreshments that had been carefully chosen to be consumed easily while reading without soiling the pages of the books.

There are no more welcoming people on God's green

earth than the Mormons, and Anne was from the first taken into the community as a beloved person. She was invited to return in June 1938 for the celebration of the school's fiftieth anniversary. A birthday letter to her great-niece, Margaret Warren Brown, written with the sprawl of haste, engenders breathlessness even as it is read thirty-four years after the fact.

Dear Margaret,
   Happy birthday from the snow-capped Wasatch Mountains, with golden wishes gathered from the 50th anniversary celebration of this land-grant college. It's a marvellous place.
   It has been a wonderful week, all told. The weather glorious, cool part of the day as Maine in early October. I arrived in time for the singing of Haydn's Creation on June 3rd. Was met at Ogden by a delegation of children from the Pingree School with bouquets of roses—Nicholas had to appear in the station—the Forty-Niner was ten minutes ahead of schedule so Mr. Peterson and Martha found me surrounded by children. Then came the 50 mile drive over the mountains—Martha is now 15 but essentially the same as at 4, 8 and 12 my previous visits. She is as tall as I am but utterly without self-consciousness and so companionable.
   No time to tell you of the events at which I marched in the procession with nearly a hundred delegates from universities and learned societies. President Sproul of the University of California gave the commencement address. The governor of Utah was there and also spoke. Monday night, Drinkwater's *Lincoln* was played extremely well. . . . There have been banquets, luncheons, and all manner of doings. My clinics came off with a bang and I have given three parties in the library for children.

There follows news of the family and the customary greeting of love and affection, signed Auntie.
   As for the Peterson family, Anne became an auxiliary

member of it. The girls, growing up, paraded their prospective husbands before Anne for her approval, and Chase, one of the sons, graduating from Harvard with many honors, insisted that Anne be there to share with the family all the pomp attending bestowal of hoods and capes. Chase later became Dean of Students at Harvard.

When Martha was married and the mother of a baby girl, she named the child Anne Carroll, telling ACM she had saved the name for this event all her life. Anne felt that this child, more than any other, gave her a hold upon the generations yet to come.

Anne never knew of another namesake—a small Chinese child, Anne Carroll Reicher, whose mother as a student at Pratt fell under the spell of ACM. When she and her husband adopted a Chinese orphan, to add to the family of their own children, Mrs. Reicher knew what name she wished to honor.

The decade of the thirties is remembered by most Americans as the time of the Great Depression, and ACM met manifold administrative problems in the course of affairs at the library, but her own life attained in those years—especially from 1932 to 1938—succeeding periods of rewards for labor of the past. The twenty-fifth anniversary of her coming to the New York Public Library ushered in that special period, and the observance of the day was so attuned to Anne's taste and desire as to seem a dream made actual. The genius of Mary Gould Davis, the Supervisor of Story Telling, was largely responsible for the affair, and she involved all the diligence and talent of the staff to bring about the big party. The scene was the Central Children's Room. On an evening in September 1931 Anne was asked to appear there. She came with Storer Lunt to find the place brilliant with candlelight and flowers, and men and women of the literary world, old friends and out-of-town guests waiting to greet her. She was escorted to the center of the room, and there she was seated in a high, curved rocking chair that had belonged to Washington Irving. Frederic Melcher was master of ceremonies. He announced The Procession of Branches. Winding through the length of the Children's Room they came, the children's librarians, each dressed in the costume representative of the national character of the neighborhoods they served—Italian, Chinese, Czech, German, Serbian—the beautiful Mrs. Rodzianko appearing as she had on the day she was presented to the court of the Czar. Their faces were radiant in the light of the sparklers they carried.

Dr. John Finley, the editor of the New York *Times*, was among the guests. He was so moved by the sight that he rushed out to summon photographers from his paper. Speaking in the mode of the day and from the habit of his masculinity, he said to Miss Davis, "Why aren't these young women married?" To which she replied, "Most of them are."

Everything about the evening conspired to create a heightened festivity. It appeared to be unrehearsed and spontaneous, though Ruth Sawyer Durand told a story, and *The Tinder Box* was given as a puppet play, as was another written for the occasion, *Rootabaga Processional*.

A great portfolio of original drawings made for Anne by artists of the time was put into her hands, and at one point Mr. Melcher poured from a large cornucopia a shower of letters, telegrams, messages from everywhere, into her lap.

"The surprise party was quite the loveliest silver anniversary anyone ever had," Anne wrote in a letter to Jean Pond. "It was so spontaneous and so festive. No speeches but done with a lovely feeling for everything and everybody. Of course I couldn't sleep a wink that night, so I read all the hundreds of telegrams and messages stretching from Maine to California, from Japan to England and France and Italy. As for the portfolio with all the artists' originals, you must come and see for yourself."

Anne was never to forget that evening, and it shone with heightened meaning in the face of what was for her the fiasco of the fiftieth anniversary of the establishment of work with children in the New York Public Library. In 1956 the library published, in Miss Moore's honor, a *Festschrift*, its title *Reading Without Boundaries*. Old friends of Anne's and experienced members of the staff had been asked to write on assigned aspects of work with children. ACM accepted the publication with guarded politeness for a time, but in short order she came to resent it, feeling that the library administration which authorized publication without her knowledge, advice, or consent had exploited her accomplishment for its own pragmatic purposes, with little feeling for or support of the actuality of the past. The campaign she waged against the publication was one of the most bitter and vitriolic of her lifetime. It was cruel treatment of those who in good faith had brought the publication into being, but for Anne Carroll Moore the integrity of an opinion or a principle she held to be true was more important than any other consideration. She was accustomed to sacrificing everything and everybody if in her opinion the cause justified it. If it were cruel, so be it.

A king and a queen were crowned midway of the thirties—George the Sixth of England and his Scottish Queen Elizabeth. What ceremony and panoply a coronation promised! It was ACM for England once again! The year was 1937. The grand-niece had accomplished library school. Anne left the dark room of the Woodstock Hotel and sailed for England on the *Europa,* the date March 14. Three months in England—with a small trip to France besides—stretched before her. She landed on the twenty-fourth at Southampton, sent her baggage on to London, and went to Stonehenge to see it at day's end under a lowering sky.

Old friends awaited her in London: the Brookes family, giving parties and teas in quick succession; the de la Mares; Eleanor Farjeon a hostess for tea and an afternoon; Kathleen Lines escorting Anne to church in the Inner Temple; dinner with Helen Waddell at a Serbian restaurant in Soho.

Old haunts in the Lake Country were revisited, and Beatrix Potter made her a welcome guest once more. Villages within range of London were observed in all their manifestation of decor deemed suitable for the coronation.

The event itself was something of a shambles as far as Anne was concerned, for though good money had been paid out in advance for a seat, there was none forthcoming. Anne wandered from place to place during the procession and pieced out what she had not seen by viewing the whole thing in a cinema. But the city itself was a great sight for all to see, with the old buildings brilliantly lighted every night.

Anne went to the Coronation Ball on her own. The bagpipes played, all the old dances were in swing—merrie old England to the life—and Anne ached to dance in the reels. She met a company of actors there who asked her to have supper with them. They proved to be a charming lot, and Anne blessed her stars for giving her the courage to go places by herself.

When Anne Moore returned to New York in June, the American Library Association met there in annual convention. She was a center of attention, for in addition to all she had to tell she wore, at appropriate times, her coronation cape—a rich black velvet all-enveloping wrap that reached to her ankles. Royal it was too, with its crimson satin lining and an antique silver clasp at the throat. It was made to her order at Liberty's in London and, like the apple-green corded silk of Aunt Allie, it served as ceremonial for the spirit.

The Balcony awaited Anne. Before she sailed for England she had taken a lease on an apartment at the Beverly Hotel, 125 East 50th Street, on the sixteenth floor. A previous stay at the old Panhellenic Building on Mitchell Place had endeared the neighborhood to her, for from a certain height one could see the East River, and that was a source of refreshment. The Beverly had the view. It was an ideal dwelling for a career woman at the top of her success. A large room formed the living area, with a foldaway kitchen attached. French windows opened onto a balcony that could hold six or eight people comfortably crowded. The river shone beyond. Moreover, the facilities of a big hotel lay below floors and could be commandeered in case of large parties.

Second only to Alderwood in Anne's affection, the Balcony came to fulfill a long need. It enabled Anne to spread her hospitality lavishly. Her letters of this ample time are filled with accounts of suppers, teas, dinners, the menus lovingly itemized. The Balcony meant that she could receive in her own place the guests that came to the Children's Room for Book Week. It gave her too the homely satisfaction of being domestic. On St. Nicholas Day, 1938, she wrote to one of the nieces:

> I go to Wilmington on Monday the 26th. So Christmas day, Sunday, the Balcony will hold open house for the family. I'm asking Madeline and her husband—the Bedells

and such Warren-Browns and Willys as may be able to respond. The more the merrier, says Nicholas. Storer unfortunately will be in Wilmington on that day and on Monday.

We had a lovely St. Nicholas Eve in the Children's Room. Mrs. Durand came unexpectedly to tell a story heralded by a box of the loveliest red roses. Miss Massee sent red roses also and the room fairly glowed with their color and fragrance. I had invited the staff for supper at The Balcony and Mrs. Durand came too. Sunday I achieved a really excellent dish of creamed chicken and rice, cranberry sauce and superlative fudge for dessert. Incidentally, I cleaned my silver, sitting in the sunshine of the front window. I had a lovely day remembering lovely things in the lives of my father and mother— Looking back from the world of today there is calm and a sense of permanence. "It is a great thing to live at all and more to live well," wrote my father in the 1890's and it still holds in the 1930's.

As for the Balcony proper, it boasted a set of window boxes. These gave an illusion of country gardens, for Dudley and Storer Lunt kept them filled with privet or boughs fetched from the country, and at Christmas time Storer shopped the tree market for pines the appropriate size, pointed firs against the sky.

One winter's morning Anne rose to close the windows against a blow of wind and saw her Christmas trees topped with snow. She told the young artist, Bob McCloskey, about it and in due time he made a lithograph of the scene, cold, blue and mysterious, that she might keep it always in her mind.

During the years of the Balcony, honors began to accrue unto Anne. The University of Maine conferred upon her a Doctor of Letters in 1940. Anne went in person to receive it, grateful for the fact that in the citation mention was made of her father's service as a trustee of the college when it was the State Agricultural School. Anne had previously held honorary degrees in some disdain. Apparently she had written Dorothy Canfield Fisher of her feeling. Her letter elicited from Mrs. Fisher a memorable rebuttal:

> Let me tell you something in connection with your degree from the University of Maine, which was said to me years ago when I was about to receive an honorary degree. I had said something evidently like what you are feeling about honorary degrees to a friend, a scientist, who answered very seriously that he thought that attitude of half-scorn was entirely wrong, and that every American who had any opportunity to share in an honor granted to other ability than the ability for material success, should leap to take advantage of the opportunity.
>
> It made quite an impression on my mind, and I pass it on to you to think about as you walk across the platform to have the hood dropped round your neck.

The following year, in 1941, the Women's National Book Association bestowed upon Anne the first Constance Lindsay Skinner Medal, an award she cherished because of her friendship for Constance Skinner and because it honored those who celebrated books and reading.

In spite of wars, depressions, and recessions, those years of the thirties—from 1932 to 1938—were distinguished by a renaissance of arts as far as illustration and book design were concerned. Anne Carroll Moore took cognizance of these matters by setting apart in the annual Christmas lists the first few pages wherein she named and described such books in some detail. Among those artists so honored was Dorothy Lathrop. In a letter to Anne, written in 1944, some years after the demise of the Balcony, Dorothy Lathrop makes clear the reason for the special aura that still surrounds the Balcony days.

The time seems very long ago when Rachel [Field] and Elizabeth MacKinstry and Jo and I came to your parties on the Balcony, every one of us so filled with enthusiasm for our work—each one of us looking forward. But not one of us could match your joy of living or keep pace with your adventuring.

I never think of you without seeing bright balloons tugging at their strings, or countless lights shining over a mysteriously humming city, or without a lift of anticipation for adventures just around the corner—around every corner.

15

RUE AND
REMEMBRANCE

Growing old is quite a responsibility . . .
and so many people make such a mess of it.
ACM

ANNE'S RETIREMENT DATE from the New York Public Library was set at October 1, 1941. A flick of the
calendar on September 30, and there was an end to thirty-
five years of being the center of a universe, the boundaries
of which she herself had extended beyond the expectations of any librarian in a comparable position. Hers was
the authoritative voice in the world of children's books.
With the growth of her influence through *The Bookman*,
the *Herald Tribune Books*, and *The Horn Book*, to say
nothing of the book-selection policies of the New York
Public Library, her voice remained in command. When
she retired at seventy, she faced no diminution of her
power, her zest for books and the children who read
them; she knew no waning of her zeal for the discovery
and acclamation of those genuine, original men and

women among the artists and authors who unfurled to the world their separate banners of singularity.

The University of California at Berkeley acknowledged her retirement by inviting her to teach, in the spring semester of 1942, at the Graduate School of Librarianship, with freedom to treat the subject of libraries for children in any way she chose. Sidney B. Mitchell, the director, asked for no commitment of outline or syllabus, which pleased Anne immensely.

Beyond that appointment there were no definite plans for her future, but publishers were quick in their attempts to sign her up. Her autobiography was sought by more than one editor, and she was actually committed to two titles, *Reading Boys Like* and *Reading Girls Like*, as well as a long-postponed biography of Mary Wright Plummer for the American Library Association's series of biographies of noted librarians.

Anne was convinced of her ability to retire. The letters in which she spoke of her plans for the future exuded from their pages the accustomed exhilaration with which she gave account of events in her life. Whatever had happened or was to happen was recorded with an edge of triumphant expectation and a conviction of her own speciality as a person on whom circumstances bestowed distinctive tokens of recognition. "I believe I have had a good time," she wrote to Rachel Moore Warren early on in 1941, "and have felt as free to act on my own initiative as anyone in the U.S.A. I feel no sense of possession and no reluctance to give over. Unlike Miss Hewins I did not marry a library neither that of Pratt Institute nor the N.Y.P.L."

Words well spoken! But how seldom do the turbulent floods of emotion follow the watercourses that reason designs! The actuality of retirement was a shock, and the pain of it was compounded by the fact that she had to surrender the Balcony as a setting and live haphazardly until such time as she should start for California in December. Moreover, she was not clear of Room 105. The files had been systematically cleaned out, but thirty-five years of personal mementoes were everywhere on hand. She could not bring herself to erase them. Consequently, many days in October and November Anne spent in the stacks, where space had been allotted her, sorting books and papers left as unfinished business. She worked in a faded blue voile dress reserved for grime and desolation as she confronted herself and the future in the dusty residue of the past. There she was on the very day of the Children's Room Book Week celebration, having refused all invitations, determined not to appear.

There had been no special retirement party for Anne. The library had staged a collective reception for all staff retiring at that time. Anne had declared she wanted no further fete, ever, after the perfection of the twenty-fifth-anniversary celebration, but the staff gathered informally in the Central Children's Room one evening and presented her with a handsome clutch of baggage in view of her forthcoming trip to California. To the delight of ACM, the collection included a leather jewel case—it resembled a miniature suitcase—and stamped in gold upon it the initials N.K.

The trip to California was charted to touch as many points of the compass of her interest and affection as possible. The strongest and youngest of her friends, hearing account of it, questioned their own abilities to endure the rigor of so widespread an undertaking. But Anne, always an inspired traveler, found her strength renewed by each change of scene, each diverse encounter. First to St. Louis to visit Mary Douglas Carpenter;

to Cincinnati to see Julia Carter; to New Orleans, the ties with library people there strong and lasting; to Abbeville, Louisiana, where she spent Christmas with her cherished great-nephew, Dr. Edgar Warren and his family; to Houston, Texas, and Julia Ideson, librarian of a splendid institution that ACM admired, the Houston Public Library; to San Antonio; to Galveston, Texas, to visit Emma Lee, the noted children's librarian of the Rosenberg Library there; and the family of Anne's blood cousin, Charles Moore, known to his intimates as "Yellow Pine Charlie" because yellow pine had been the chief source of his considerable fortune; and from there she entrained for Los Angeles, for a visit with "Cousin-by-mutual-consent-Oscar" and his daughter, Marie Clarke.

Children had been encountered at each of these points, in library groups and schools as well as in the homes of friends, children spellbound as usual by accounts of Anne Caraway and Nicholas, who exhibited his new treasure chest of miniatures to their delighted eyes.

ACM found the Berkeley campus spacious and welcoming in that year of 1942. She was put up at the Women's Faculty Club, which meant that she walked to classes by a wooded path, the creek running beside for company. With her gift for vivid response to spirit of place she enjoyed the campus, climbed to the top of the Campanile, and became the friend of the young musician who played upon the keyboard to make the bells ring.

As for her lectures, she publicly forswore outline or syllabus, but among her papers there remains an impressive document, including a series of penetrating examination questions, that give the lie to the myth of her completely spontaneous approach to the subject. In all of her life she never spoke for as much as five minutes without knowing exactly what she intended to say and how she intended to say it. The monthly meetings of her library staff were carefully planned and outlined on paper. The Berkeley course was centered on the writers and artists of the twentieth century whom she had known. Some students resented this approach because they had come to the library school to learn how to head up a library for children in the state of California. But others among them were exhilarated, realizing that a quarter of a century of living, vivid experience among major artists and authors was being put into their hands by one who had shaped much of it with her own spirit. They were never to forget it.

Leonore Power Mendelson was living in San Francisco then, and this made possible weekly celebrations of old times in New York, seasoned with the beauty of the Bay cities and the comfort of good food and festivity on every hand. Anne was the great personality on the campus, and there were fitting celebrations in her honor. But a curious note of sorrow runs through her letters of the period, faint but persistent, until at last it emerges, foreign to her but there. She was homesick for New York! She confessed to her niece, Margaret Bedell, that she could not begin her day at Berkeley without first tuning in the radio to hear from Kate Smith what the weather was in New York. "Kate Smith, of all people!" her niece said, astonished at the revelation.

The course at Berkeley ran from the middle of January until May. Anne had no further commitments until late in August, when she had agreed to speak before the Library Association of the Pacific Northwest meeting in Seattle. The time between she determined to spend in writing, and she chose Logan, Utah, with its quiet mountain grandeur, its memories of good encounters and welcoming friends, as a place propitious for fresh beginnings. She went to stay in the home of one of the Peterson family, Mrs. Huhne, who made her so comfortable that Anne reported, in a letter to Ruth Sawyer, that she was tempted to stay indefinitely. The garden, the hammock on the porch, the fresh mountain trout, all the hospitality showered upon her—these she reveled in—but the writing would not come. Mrs. Huhne, remembering that time, spoke of the muted mood in which Anne seemed suspended and of her dismay at finding Anne slumped over her desk, head sunk upon her arms in an unaccustomed show of despair.

But the talk at Seattle was restorative, and ACM set off for home by as roundabout a route as she had followed on her westward journey: to Minneapolis and St. Paul, reaffirming friendships with Della MacGregor and Alice Brown, and to Buffalo on a like quest. When she came home, the beloved city bore a new guise, dim and somber in the half-light of the wartime blackout. Anne found it beautiful and her spirits rose, though she arrived without the slightest idea of where she would go or what her abode would be. Storer Lunt met her at the train. He meanwhile had taken quarters at the Grosvenor Hotel, Fifth Avenue and Tenth Street, in which a few apartments were to be had in the upper reaches of the building. He invited Anne to be his guest at the hotel until such time as she could find a place that appealed to her.

It was a neighborhood she knew and loved of old— a part of Greenwich Village and therefore heir to its color and life but not in the middle of the cluttered, crowded streets, the noise and dirt, all of which one endured for the sake of charm and architectural eccentricity. As a region, it invited walking and poking about. Eighth Street was near, with its small moving-picture theaters, its galleries and shops, chief among them the Washington Square Book Store, boasting an extensive lending library. There were small grocery stores, sausages and cheeses hanging from the ceiling, and stalls of fresh fruit at the entrances; and bakery shops, one of which, on Sixth Avenue, the legendary Ugobono's, Anne had pictured in the pages of *Nicholas*.

> In one of the two windows of Ugobono's pastry shop there was a wonderful thin cake watch, with a chocolate stem winder, pink and white dots for the minutes, and vanilla hands. . . . In the other window were the most fascinating tin boxes and glass bottles swinging from basket hangers. They quickly filled a box with almond cakes and macaroons, panitoni and marrons, and Nicholas bought a big tin box with twenty-four little packages of nougat inside, each with a different picture of Italy on the wrapper.

East of Fifth Avenue there stood the high-ceilinged, old-fashioned charm of Wanamaker's department store, and dark shops full of secondhand books, a wig shop with displays of antique jewelry in the window, and at the corner of Tenth Street and University Place a flower shop that by some act of grace transcended the limits of its show windows, which were free of fixed and set pieces, and seemed actually to bloom and blossom into the street. It was run by Louis Chingo, who knew the taste and judgments of each of his customers. A friend of Anne's, stopping there one day, thought Louis psychic. He recognized for whom the flowers were purchased though she said not a word. She had chosen boughs of hawthorn. "Don't break off the branches," she admonished him. "My God, no," he said. "I wouldn't break anything for Miss Moore."

Restaurants were plentiful thereabouts: Schrafft's, Longchamps, Charles on Sixth Avenue, and Asti's at Twelfth Street, where live song and music enhanced the appetite.

The churches of the region, open-doored and consoling, were indigenous to the neighborhood, leading ministers of the time appearing there and liturgical music abounding in practiced perfection: the Church of the Ascension, directly across the street from the Grosvenor; the Presbyterian Church at Twelfth Street; St. George's and St. Mark's close by.

Friends lived near: Maria Cimino and Will Lipkind around the corner; May Massee, Anne Eaton, and numerous others within walking distance. Recounting all these blessings of familiarity and convenience, Anne decided to take a room on the twelfth floor and settle in on her own. Later she moved to the sixteenth floor, where she could more easily avail herself of the hospitality of Storer Lunt's place when he was absent from the city. There she cooked in his small kitchen and entertained her friends for luncheon, with table set against the window that looked out across the rooftops of the Village to the thread of the Hudson River far beyond and the cranes and smokestacks of great ships in the harbor.

There was work to be done. The "Three Owls" articles for *The Horn Book* kept her *en rapport* with current children's books. Bertha Mahony Miller came increasingly to depend on the advice and criticism of Anne as contributing editor as the time approached for her own signing off from Horn Book responsibilities. ACM's involvement was extensive in the publication of the Horn Book's monumental book on illustrators of the period as well as in other independent ventures of its publishing. Editors consulted ACM on any number of problems. Pratt Institute Library School demanded, by tradition, at least one lecture a year, and Anne became vigorously involved in the administrative affairs of the institution by virtue of the honors its officers had bestowed on her and by her own conviction on certain matters for which she waged active and telling campaigns. The affairs of Bradford and its Alumnae Club concerned her. There were lectures before the New England Library Association, especially at the time tribute was paid to Caroline Hewins; to the New York State Library Association meeting at West Point and various other meetings. Compton's Pictured Encyclopedia relied on her for periodic revisions of her famous lists, which continued to be the major feature of their service to libraries. The English-Speaking Union commanded her interest, as did the wartime programs of Books Across the Sea and the Treasure Chest campaign whereby children's books were shipped by the crate to allies everywhere. Well she might say of herself, "Retiring into activity."

But as for the creation of the two books concerning the reading of boys and girls and the biography of Mary Wright Plummer—nothing seemed to rise up within her and overflow the margins of her inspiration. She left evidences of many a brave try, but come it did not.

Anne was one, apparently, who worked best in the heat of the battle. Gone was the urgency of struggle in the midst of daily complications and complexities involving many people. A kind of loneliness possessed her and an anger that time should have robbed her of her greatest arena—the New York Public Library. She could not forswear responsibility for it.

Came the day, after her return to New York, when

she visited Room 105 for the first time. The staff recognized the light dancing shuffle of her feet on the marble floor long before she appeared in the doorway. They had lifted their eyes in a unison of expectancy at the first sound of the clearing of her throat. There she stood, looking on top of the world, wearing a hat so gay, so much in character, that one wanted to laugh aloud at the charm of it. As she greeted everyone she looked about the office. It was much the same as it had been, but a brass candlestick that had stood on a catalogue case had been moved to the top of a bookcase on the east wall. "The candlestick's in the wrong place," she said. "It should be put back where it was. The catalogue case is lower." It was pointed out that as a matter of actual measurement the catalogue case was the taller of the two locations. "But it *looks* lower on the catalogue case," she said. Then she slouched down in a chair as though she were lounging comfortably at home, slung one slim leg across the other, pushed the French hat to the back of her head, its saucy little streamers gone suddenly absurd, and made her pronouncement, "Push Babette Deutsch's *Walt Whitman*. It's the book of the year."

Anne would not recognize the fact that each of her successors claimed the right to make her own decisions in her own time. She professed to them time and again her eagerness to be of help. The difficulty was that by virtue of her genius and experience she could not resist assuming full control. If she were asked for aid she made no distinction between assistance and command. In a letter to Bertha Mahony Miller, Anne complained of one successor, "She never asks for help. I can understand her wanting to stand on her own feet, but I wish she were not so Spartan about it."

At times Anne knew an anguish of longing for the sight of children in the library, and on such days she would set out on branch visits of her own. She was always an expected and hoped-for guest at the celebrations the children's rooms staged with such diligence the length and breadth of the city, and a fete in her honor held every St. Nicholas Eve in the Central Children's Room created afresh the bond between past and present. But her unannounced presence in a library was sometimes an embarrassment, especially to newly appointed members of the staff who were not always able to cope with her praise or criticism.

The staff met this circumstance with generous spirit and professional aplomb, weighing no set of loyalties against another. But the habit of concern Anne never surrendered. In the last years of her life she wrote to Bertha Mahony Miller, describing a certain exhibition in the Central Children's Room. "It is something I brought off by remote control," she said. The ghost of a chuckle is written there in invisible ink.

Little of this was known outside the library. Her letters of the period read like accounts in the life of a busy debutante. Such arrivals and departures of visitors around the world; such quantities of friends coming to see Anne, bringing, like Squirrel Nutkin's kin, small gifts of homage to Old Owl. No stay-at-home was she! Countless were the theaters enjoyed, the art exhibitions explored and evaluated, the pilgrimages to favorite neighborhoods, to museums and cherished spots, the little zoo in Central Park, the Sheep Meadow, the Shakespeare garden, the feasts consumed at proven restaurants, the walks taken in solitary pleasure, the countless rides on the Staten Island ferry, the bridges encompassed on moonlit nights by taxi and in Storer Lunt's "little red car."

Journeys were embarked on: to Ashburnham and Boston for visits with the Millers; to the Edward King family at Biltmore, North Carolina; to Bradford and to Maine, especially to Saco, where family roots ran deep.

The habit of festivals continued with hardly a month of the year that did not hold one day sacred to some private celebration, not to mention the customary holidays of Christmas and Easter, St. Patrick's Day and Halloween.

Patterns of her birthday celebrations ranged all the way from a small gathering in her own place with champagne at hand through theaters and dinners in New York and Boston to the all but legendary revels that Ruth Sawyer Durand arranged one summer in Maine with her daughter and son-in-law, Peggy and Bob McCloskey. The Durands had built a home called Gull Rock on the coast of Maine at Hancock. Anne gives account of that most gracious time in a letter to Edward and Virginia King:

> Mrs. Durand had hidden my mail since my arrival on the 7th. It now appeared on the breakfast table in a setting of wild roses and strawberries. She rose betimes to make a birthday cake and soon after breakfast we loaded up the car and took off for the island where the McCloskeys lived—a lovely drive of thirty-odd miles through blue hills and over a high toll bridge across Eggemoggin Reach to Little Deer Isle and along a narrow stony road to the cove where Bob awaited us with the dinghy to transport us to the motorboat in which we crossed to the larger of the two islands where their house is. We were met at the dock by a visitor with a wheelbarrow and made our way through Christmas tree woods, past the boathouse, where Bob has his studio, on by a winding fern-bordered path to the house on the other side of the island. It faces Penobscot Bay with Camden Hills in the distance. . . . The fire was already lighted in the big fireplace on the wide terrace of native stone and a birthday table bearing treasures

from all over the island—a tiny Christmas tree, a curious branch of driftwood with seaweed and shells—masses of bayberry, wild strawberries—gave Mrs. Durand a setting for more of the letters and the cards she had held in reserve.

While lobsters writhed in the big copper kettle over the fire we drank numerous healths in the double rounds of old-fashioneds. Luncheon on the terrace with Sally (two in May) waking up in time for the birthday cake and a most wonderful sense of Christmas as well as birthday cheer. The island is perfect. Seven acres of Christmas trees —grassy point—sandspits, on which one can walk at low tide—five beaches—all fascinating to explore.

The Durands went back to Hancock in the late afternoon and next morning the two visitors and David [Durand] left, leaving Nicholas and me alone with Peggy, Bob and Sally for a week. We visited the mainland only once for supplies. That meant a 6 mile crossing to Cape Rosier and a drive of several miles to the store at South Brooksville. We feasted on lobster-clams-mussels with a ham for solid background. Bob rowed us to the smaller island one afternoon to look for wild strawberries. In the evening I read to them from *The Country of the Pointed Firs* which they had not known before but felt its likeness to their own setting. Their house, the only one on the island, was built twenty years ago by an actress and later was sold to some English people. The husband died and his wife sold everything as it stood at a sacrifice. It is spacious and convenient—well heated and they plan to spend the winter there. Bob hopes to pick up his Prix de Rome a year from September and go to Italy taking Peggy and Sally along. . . .

Peggy drove me back to Hancock leaving Sally with Bob overnight. We made a detour from Blue Hill and called on the E. B. Whites at North Brooklin. They have a beautiful place with such delphiniums and other flowers as I haven't seen all summer.

ACM was never one to boast of the number of years she had attained, but when the eighties caught up with her she could not help but acknowledge the fact, and she did so by renewing old pledges to the enjoyment of each day with all the vigor she could summon. She knew a lessening of physical powers—the ears lazy to hear, the eyes to see—and there were recurring bouts of respiratory illnesses, but the spirit sufficed. Moreover, the neighborhood boasted a doctor in whom she had complete confidence, as did hundreds of other Villagers: Dr. Eugenia Ingerman. Anne, with her predilection for the wisdom of the male in such matters, had been skeptical of women in medicine, but when one day she was introduced to Dr. Ingerman in the lobby of the Grosvenor and had seen the strength and compassion in that grave face she knew she had found a rare physician.

Anne professed time and again to an enjoyment of this late decade. "She spoke exultantly of the eighties," Bertha Mahony Miller reported. The degree of her protest had lessened with the years, though she continued to write to authors, editors, artists—anyone whom she considered to have betrayed their own best gifts or the highest goals of excellence in books produced for children.

That she lived among books literally was plain to see, her living quarters chock-a-block with books—books that had been sent to her for review, brought to her for reading by her publisher nephew, or borrowed from the Washington Square Book Store. "The best thing about retirement," Anne wrote to Katherine Carnes in 1954, "is the freedom to read what one really wants to. Only last month I read *Bleak House* for the first time and last summer *War and Peace*, which Maria Cimino says she read in the jungles of Brazil." Accounts of her reading thread the letters she wrote during these years, and the scope of the books mentioned bears witness to the fact that she lived in the thick of things. "I am reading Virginia Woolf's diary with great interest," the letter to

Katherine Carnes continues. "If you haven't, do turn to page 88 and read what she writes of Thomas Hardy. I read it aloud yesterday to someone and we laughed to the point of tears. I've now got to read her books all over again in the light of what she says while writing them."

"My latest reading was Sir Anthony Eden's memoirs," she reported in a letter to Bertha Miller in 1960. "Terribly sad yet containing much of great interest. . . . I was glad I read it before the reviews, thanks to Storer's thoughtfulness." She felt a responsibility for Bertha's selections of books that might appropriately be read aloud to her husband William Miller, and there are wise suggestions all along the line. "I have just begun to read Sholem Asch's *East River* which Siri said seemed to her the best book she read last summer. I found it absorbing and so true to the old East Side I felt I was living with the people of the book. If you haven't read it, let us save it until I come for I am not sure of its appeal to William."

In the last handful of her years—1952 to 1960—four great events crowned Anne's life with such joy that she could do little else but revel in them. The first of these came from England. One day in September 1952 Mr. Arthur Treble, the American representative of the English publishing firm of Frederick Warne, telephoned her and asked if he might come to call, mentioning that he had at hand the manuscript of a proposed book on Beatrix Potter. "It's rather bulky," he said. When he came he set before her a treasure chest—six portfolios containing unpublished drawings by Beatrix Potter, the finished layout for a book tentatively entitled *The Art of Beatrix Potter*, which was in such a state of meticulous perfection as to make one gasp and wonder what extraordinary mind and hand had produced such a piece of work. On the proposed title page, faintly penciled in, were the words, "With an introduction by Anne Carroll Moore."

At this moment Anne must have felt like the Tailor of Gloucester, who, when he beheld the Lord Mayor's wedding coat completed on his work table, could only exclaim, "Oh joy!" A formal letter of invitation to write an appreciation was presented to ACM at the same time from Mr. W. A. Herring of Warne, the very man who had seen all of Beatrix Potter's books through the presses over the long years. ACM knew Mr. Herring of old in London. She had, in fact, put him in a book, for it was he who appears as the make-up man in *Nicholas and the Golden Goose*.

> Here's the make-up man, the make-up man
> Who makes up books as fast as he can.

But who was L. Linder? His was the name of the builder of this celestial dummy of a book. He must have loved Beatrix Potter books all of his life to have produced such a work. ACM made discreet inquiry and in time established with him ties of enduring friendship, held firm by long letters over their years of correspondence.

Mr. Leslie Linder is well known in this day as the man who, among others feats, broke the code in which Beatrix Potter kept her journal and "translated" the minute writing of that document into the fascinating book we know today. He lives in Essex, England, and is by profession an engineer whose specialty is the study of stresses. It was not through a conscious memory of childhood that he came to be obsessed first by the art of Beatrix Potter and then by the character of the artist herself but by an accidental encounter with a battered copy of *Squirrel Nutkin* in a Sunday-school library in which he was involved when he was in his forties. The sight of that one tattered little volume suddenly brought to mind the pleasures he had had in such small red books when he was a child. Not one remained in his possession, the family having cleared away all childish things while he was only seven, and he set out to find all titles, known and unknown. He became positively captivated by the worlds of Beatrix Potter, the worlds in which she lived and the worlds she had engineered. Tales of joyous obsession are always sources of great pleasure. The tale of Leslie Linder is an important one and most endearing. In the appreciation which ACM brought off after a struggle of two years, she told the story of her relationship with Beatrix Potter. But the piece is no mere adventure in nostalgia; it is an incisive criticism of Beatrix Potter's work, a clear statement of the scope of L. Linder's book as it stands and of its future service to the art world. As always happened whenever ACM put pen to paper, something lives and glows there.

In February 1954 she wrote to Katherine Carnes in Atlanta, "You will be glad to know that the Beatrix Potter appreciation got finished at last and I have had two enthusiastic letters from Mr. Linder who says it's even better than he dared hope. The pictures are in proof and I suppose the publication date will be announced in due time by Warne."

It was published in 1955 and immediately went into a second edition. Anne was eighty-four in that year, clear of the book and fully equal to all the year held for her. The second cause for pride originated at Pratt Institute. The trustees voted to confer on her the degree of Doctor of Letters. On June 3, 1955, she walked triumphant in the academic procession, her partner in the march Robert Moses, the famous Parks Commissioner of New York City.

When she was invited to go to Toronto in November to celebrate Young Canada's Book Week, she went off in a new red dress with a black velvet stole and a red hat to match, to such a festival of books, old friends, speeches, theaters and puppet shows, luncheons and banquets, as to intimidate the staunchest soul. After it was over she wrote to Mr. Linder, saying, "I feel as though I could live forever."

Canada had always held a special significance for ACM. It was in Montreal, the year 1900, at a meeting of the American Library Association, that a children's librarians' club was formed with Anne Carroll Moore its president and Mary E. Dousman its secretary. Within months the club had become, at the invitation of the American Library Association, the Children's Librarians' Section and its officers were the first officers of the section. Thirty-four years later, when Siri Andrews was president of the section, the ALA met again in Montreal and at that time Anne delivered a memorable paper, "The Creation and Criticism of Children's Books: a Retrospect and a Forecast." It remains to this day a brilliant summation of the past, but its significance lies in the timeless and ageless truths that were expressed there:

> Having advertised children's books and children themselves to the extent that we have since the war, shall we look upon the mass production and wide distribution of mechanical triumphs of American color reproduction, upon mediocrity, vulgarity, and commonplace unimaginative treatment of theme as acceptable; or shall we continue to search for the intelligence, the wit, the sound basis of creative ideas we associate with the living children's book of any age?

As for Lillian Smith, the genius of the Boys' and Girls' Library in Toronto, she had served apprentice time in the New York Public Library, and she and ACM were bound together by years of friendship and shared admiration for each other. By 1955 Lillian Smith had retired, which meant she could give full strength to the enjoy-

ment of the festivities and, with her successor, Jean
Thompson, oversee the celebration.

This was a working fiesta. ACM was the guest of
S. J. Reginald Saunders, publishers. The executives of
Saunders were careful that there should be periods of rest
for her each day, but there was no diminution of scheduled appearances on account of the years accruing to
the guest of honor. Press, radio, and television each had
a scheduled interview and appearance, with the addition
of a personal appearance at Eaton's big department store.
Anne also spoke before a group of librarians for an hour,
after a buffet luncheon at the Boys' and Girls' House in
the lovely room where the famous Osborne collection
of old children's books is housed, reading letters from
Mr. Linder, talking of Leslie Brooke and Beatrix Potter.
Her letters reveal how great was the release of all her
powers in that setting and tradition with old friends close
at hand. She felt no change of direction in library work
with children as far as Canada was concerned but only
growth and reaffirmation of founding truths. She was
no longer certain of a like turn of affairs in her own
country.

The television interview centered on *The Art of Beatrix Potter*. The interviewer took the book home with
her the night before the screening in order to make a
selection of pictures that would be well served by the
camera. She had confessed to ACM that *The Tailor of
Gloucester* was a favorite of her childhood. All this
meant that ACM felt *en rapport* with the interviewer,
and the affair went off with a blaze of glory, as was
proved by the following day's repercussion from stations coast to coast. She had made her debut on television at the age of eighty-five.

On the way home to New York, as she ate breakfast
in the train diner Sunday morning, a young man paused

as he passed her table. "Did I not see you on television Thursday night?" he said. "I could not resist telling you how delightful it was."

On St. Nicholas Eve of 1959, as if the good saint himself had had a hand in it, Anne Moore received a letter from the Catholic Library Association telling her that she was to be the recipient of the Regina Medal in 1960. This signal honor was created by the Catholic Library Association: "To single out for recognition and emulation those writers, editors, and illustrators who have given unstintingly of their creative genius to children's literature, finding in the field a challenge worthy of their talents and demanding always their very best." It is not limited to any one country or any creed and is to be bestowed not for a single work or series of works but for the entire lifetime work of the individual. The first medal had gone to Eleanor Farjeon. The second was for Anne Carroll Moore, to be presented on April 18, 1960, at a luncheon at the Statler Hilton in New York as part of a Catholic Library Association conference. "It was the most complete surprise I have ever had," she wrote to Bertha Mahony Miller in March of that year. There had been a hiatus in the "Three Owls" pages in *The Horn Book*, due to a period of physical depletion for Anne. As usual, she was invigorated by joy. She describes the thoughtfulness of the committee, Miriam Wessel of the Detroit Public Library and Sister M. Camillus of Mount Mercy College, Pittsburgh, who had first written and then called on her. "Both bore out the spirit of their letter which really touched me deeply and has given me a fresh incentive—the Three Owls will fly again!"

What celebrants of ACM that fair occasion called forth, countrywide—librarians, friends, artists, authors— the whole kit and caboodle of the literary world. The honoree looked frail but beautiful in a blue and green printed silk dress, Margaret Lunt, Dudley's wife, having come up from Wilmington to help in the choice of costume.

Anne did not attempt a speech, since Ruth Sawyer had agreed to accept the honor in her behalf. This she did in splendid fashion, showing in her tribute how boundless was Anne Carroll Moore's world of children's books. ACM contented herself with an airy wave of her hand and a brief "This is the happiest moment of my life."

The exaltation and the vigor continued through the fall, and friends returning from Europe who had not seen her for years found her happy, boasting that her hearing had improved, and able to journey about the city for appropriate festivity. Moreover, during the fall she fulfilled her prophecy that the Owls would fly again and produced a piece for the December *Horn Book*.

But the winter was severe, and Anne fell victim to old bouts of depleting chest colds. The Christmas season found her longing to be astir but unable to battle the blowing corner winds of Tenth Street.

For Anne Carroll Moore, Christmas had always held all the enchantment that a young child finds in it. In addition there was the adult exhilaration of new books pouring from the presses. Every year, as early as in August, Anne drew an anticipatory breath, often choosing to be on hand in that vacation month because the new children's books blossomed then in their bright jackets. She read like a whirlwind and followed the fate of certain titles not only in the reviews but throughout the bookshops of the city, gathering the reactions of buyers and sales people, testing the winds of opinion from every direction.

The twelve days of Christmas she devoted to private

rituals of observance, going from church to church, not as a devout religious person but as a lover of tradition. She found affirmation of her own glee in secular shrines as well as in holy places—the carol service at St. George's Church, where the boys' choir sang the old songs in voices of unearthly beauty; the midnight mass at St. Patrick's; the music at the Church of the Ascension; the golden bells hung at Lord & Taylor; the lighting of the Christmas tree at Rockefeller Plaza and along Park Avenue—even the clang and fury of Woolworth's five-and-dime. Small wonder that she faced Christmas Eve of 1960 with some unhappiness, having been house-bound since the day of the big blizzard, December 12.

She sat surrounded by Christmas roses and boughs of pine from South Carolina, and visitors galore had come to call on the day before Christmas. But nothing could compensate for the deprivation of not seeing with her own eyes the lights that gathered momentum and broke in splendor against the Christmas sky of her beloved city.

When Alexandra Sanford appeared that Christmas Eve, Anne's hopes rose, for here was an old companion skilled in the art of happy prowling, one who, like H. C. Andersen's small hero, was numbered among the staunchest and most steadfast of children's librarians, having first come to the New York Public Library in 1918. She sent account of that Christmas Eve to the "Hunt Breakfast" of *The Horn Book* and it is her story that is told herewith:

> We had a festive dinner in the Grosvenor Bar, then while up in her "Little Book Room" the phone rang to announce callers. They turned out to be Mary Farren Jones and her husband. . . .
> Their visit was brief, as they had to get back to their

children and to trimming their tree. When talk of hat and coat began, I hedged a bit, claimed I could see snowflakes coming down again and the wind coming up. . . . When I suggested the lights would remain all through the holidays and we could go some other evening not so cold, she replied in a tone which put an end to the discussion, "Why, Sandy, it wouldn't be the same." So, well bundled up, off we went in a *big* taxi, after letting several small ones go. It was well heated, so we rolled up Fifth Avenue as far as Fifty-ninth Street to see the fountain illuminated for the first time, in front of the Plaza. Then down the other side of Fifth Avenue to Thirty-fourth Street and over to Eighth Avenue so we could swing around and be on the side near the fascinating scenes like something out of the Arabian Nights, along the second floor windows of Macy's on the Broadway side. Marcia Brown had told her of them, and she wanted to see them. The Venetian one was enchanting. When I said where next? she replied, "Around Gramercy Park." When we passed there last year on Christmas Eve she spoke about where she had lived there with a view of the Park from her high-up window. But she didn't talk much as we rode. . . . Then after bouncing along some dark, bumpy streets we spied that gem of a City Hall she loved, looking superb all illuminated. Then we swung across Brooklyn Bridge, and she leaned forward eagerly not to miss a bit of it. . . .

Then back to Manhattan by way of the Manhattan Bridge, and so to the Grosvenor, but not to bed. Nothing of the sort. If *I* wasn't too tired would I read aloud to her the ballad composed for Helen Masten's party she hadn't been able to attend, but had heard it had been read with gusto? So it was about one-thirty Christmas morning when I reached my diggings!

16

A JOYOUS SUFFICIENCY

> *But that there is a top to a thing and a*
> *bottom to the thing doesn't make it that*
> *there are two things; and that there is a top*
> *called birth and a bottom called death*
> *doesn't make any difference to that which is*
> *free, and sufficient, and joyous, and eternal.*
>
> JAMES STEPHENS

*S*HADOWS FOLLOWED the Christmas lights. In the dusk of the days Anne reached out from her couch for a slim volume of a book and slipped a handful of letters from past decades between its pages. With these epiphanies she confronted the dark.

The book was Walter de la Mare's *O Lovely England*, which Grace Hogarth brought to her from Walter de la Mare in England, and his was one of the letters harbored there. Another had come from Dr. Billings, the first director of the library. Through the years she had cherished the memory of Dr. Butler, the physician of her Pratt days, and his letter she hoarded as talisman. Another came from Dr. George Putnam, who had been Librarian of Congress. A child had written one letter,

Anne Carroll Peterson, her namesake. A card from Storer Lunt and a note from Eugenia Ingerman completed the portfolio.

There was a fall of snow on January 20, 1961. "Those are the white bees swarming," said the old grandmother in *The Snow Queen*. The entire Eastern seaboard was filled with snow. It fell upon the inaugural ceremonies of John F. Kennedy, and a wind blew the page out of the hand of the bare-headed poet Robert Frost even as he read from it. "The land was ours before we were the land's." Early on that day, Anne Carroll Moore "changed worlds."

No funeral marked her death. The Church of the Ascension opened its doors for a memorial service on the first day of February 1961 at four o'clock in the afternoon. The young clergyman explained that usually the Episcopal Church forswore the speaking of tribute to the dead but that an exception had been made in the case of this good neighbor who had enjoyed the informal fellowship of the church for many a day.

He knew Anne Carroll Moore in her last years and saw her as a frail elderly lady with a sharp blue eye. He spoke of her as he saw her, a somewhat whimsical character who loved children, never sensing that whimsy was the least of it. Some among the group longed for tribute to her strength, her endurance and resolve, her clear-sighted wisdom, generosity of spirit, and emotion. Others hoped for a recapitulation of her accomplishment and its far-reaching power. Each remembered in sorrow, in separate recollection, her significance as a friend.

But the family, in their wisdom, and especially Storer Lunt, realized that all held in common gratitude to Anne her love of life at its joyful peaks and at the simple level of small felicities. Therefore, after the solemn words were spoken the group was invited to cross the street to the Grosvenor Hotel for a festive gathering in the Mark Twain Room, where they ate and drank and spoke together. There was sadness, but there was also laughter and glasses raised high in the toast Ann Caraway herself had spoken "to the living in both worlds."

The ashes were taken to Limerick, Maine, over the Memorial Day weekend, to the cemetery where the Moores are gathered. There, on a typical spring day, with wild flowers all about, intermittent showers, patches of blue sky, and billowing wild clouds, Anne was buried. Sprigs of lilac and apple blossoms were laid on the earth and a cluster of lilies of the valley from the Tenth Street flower shop in New York.

A fitting and appropriate epitaph might be spun from the multiple threads revealed in tributes that swept down upon the family of ACM after she was gone. But it was Bertha Mahony Miller, walking across the lawn's green grass at Ashburnham in the half-light of a summer's evening, who said the significant word: "What life she gave us."

NOTES

CHAPTER ONE

1. Many of Anne Carroll Moore's *Bookman* articles were subsequently published in book form by George H. Doran, their titles being *Roads to Childhood* (1920), *New Roads to Childhood* (1923), and *Cross Roads to Childhood* (1926). The three books were combined and brought up to date in 1939 under the title *My Roads to Childhood*, Doubleday, Doran, publisher. The Horn Book, Inc., acquired publishing rights to the title in 1961, and it is currently available in hard cover and paperback. It is from this edition that much quoted material is given here.

A second major source of quotations has been the three volumes comprising a selection of articles from the New York *Herald Tribune Books*, the "Three Owls" section, edited and written by Anne Carroll Moore. The titles are: *The Three Owls: A Book About Children's Books* (The Macmillan Company, 1925); *The Three Owls, Second Book* (Coward-McCann, 1928); *The Three Owls, Third Book* (Coward-McCann, 1931). These titles are no longer in print, invaluable though they are.

2. The friendship between ACM and Ruth Sawyer Durand, distinguished writer and noted storyteller, was a sustaining force in the lives of both women. Anne was friend and adviser, and Ruth for her part offered practical help as well as intellectual counterpoint. Anne had no thimble sense. Ruth Sawyer, on flying visits to New York, between festivals and feasts, would send her skilled needle flying through Anne's wardrobe, setting aright all small disorders.

3. Two daughters of the colorful Overton family, native New Yorkers, contributed to the distinction of the New York Public Library: Florence Overton as head of the Circulation Department and Jacqueline as Children's Librarian.

CHAPTER THREE

1. The accounts of Bradford's founding are taken from Jean Sarah Pond's book *Bradford, A New England School*, Sesquicentennial Edition, revised and supplemented by Dale Mitchell, Bradford, Massachusetts, 1954.

2. "Cousin Oscar" was O. L. Clarke of Galveston, Texas. He first met Miss Moore in 1919 when he visited his daughter Frances, who was an assistant in the Central Children's Room in New York. Before she introduced her father to ACM she exacted a promise of circumspect behavior. He was a great tease, often an embarrassment to his daughters. Upon catching first sight of Anne standing at the telephone in her office Mr. Clarke waved his arm exuberantly and shouted, "Hello, old girl." This was the basis of their lasting friendship.

Subsequently, after ACM had lectured in Houston, Texas, a woman from the audience approached her and said, "Do you know my cousin Oscar? His daughter is in the New York Public Library." From that time forward she called him "Cousin Oscar."

CHAPTER FIVE

1. Louis Sherry was primarily a caterer when he opened his first candy shop and restaurant on New York's Sixth Avenue in 1881. The world of fashion moved northward, up Fifth Avenue, and Sherry's moved with it. In 1898 he built his own lavish establishment on the corner of Fifth Avenue and Forty-fourth Street: twelve stories of elegance, including several restaurants of various types, a splendid ballroom and smaller rooms for public entertaining, a catering and confectionery department, and, in the upper stories, a few lavish apartments for the convenience of a chosen clientele among the great. It was here that Marie Shedlock made her American debut in 1902.

2. Dr. Earl Barnes (1861–1935) was a professor of education at Stanford University who abandoned teaching to devote himself to lecturing and writing. In 1900 he became staff lecturer, London Society for Extension of University Teaching. It was during that period that he came to know Marie Shedlock.

3. Yvette Guilbert, a famous French *chanteuse* who appeared in the United States in the early 1900s.

4. The quotation from W. H. Auden is from his book *Secondary Worlds*, "Words and the Word," Random House, 1968.

CHAPTER SEVEN

The *History of The New York Public Library* by Harry Miller Lydenberg, published by the library in 1923, is the source for the historical background given in this chapter. Dr. Lydenberg was Chief Reference Librarian at the time of the book's publication. He later became director of the library.

1. Each of these young men became famous. George Bancroft (1800–1891) was statesman, diplomat, and historian, his *History of the United States,* in ten volumes, fixing his place among major historians of the world. George Ticknor (1791–1871), "this grand and chilly old scholar," as Van Wyck Brooks describes him in his *New England: Indian Summer,* wrote a distinguished *History of Spanish Literature.* Edward Everett (1794–1865), statesman and orator, was acclaimed at the time for his speech at the dedication of Gettysburg. It remained for the ages to recognize the grandeur of the words Abraham Lincoln spoke on that same day and occasion.

2. Fitz-Greene Halleck (1790–1867) was an American poet who with Joseph Rodman Drake wrote satirical verse. One of his best-known poems, an elegy on the death of his friend Drake, continues to find a place in certain anthologies of poetry.

CHAPTER EIGHT

1. The phrase "No badge or button . . ." was aimed at the practice of the Cleveland Public Library. Children signed a pledge involving clean hands and the care of books and were awarded a badge or button enabling them to make a display of their virtue.

CHAPTER NINE

1. The quotation is from "The Three Owls," appearing in *The Horn Book,* November–December 1939, pp. 369–72.

The event is told in more detail in a long letter Nicholas wrote on his own stationery to Walter de la Mare, dated December 14, 1927, signed Nicholas and A(nn) C(araway).

. . . We saw Arthur Rackham on board the *Olympic* last Friday night after taking him around Brooklyn and Manhattan bridges. His first visit to America. . . .

I had a good deal of fun with Mr. Rackham and a young artist named Paget-Fredericks who says he has met you. . . . Do you remember the young man himself? He needs simplifying in certain ways. He was horrified when A.[nn] C.[araway] suggested Childs as a typically American restaurant when Mr. Rackham asked for one where he might invite us to dine with him. "Better perhaps for breakfast between midnight and five o'clock," said A. C. reflectively and we went eventually to the Brevoort Grill.

CHAPTER TEN

The text of Justice Holmes's dissent is given in Harry Golden's book, *A Little Girl Is Dead* (World, 1965), p. 315. Leonard Dinnerstein's *The Leo Frank Case* (Columbia University, 1968), richly documented, provides an excellent résumé of the case.

In Boston, on September 1, 1915, a great demonstration denouncing the lynching of Frank was held in Faneuil Hall, Asa P. French, a former U.S. District Attorney, acting as chairman. The New York *Herald* described the meeting thus:

> A more impressive cry of indignation was never heard in Boston, and never did Faneuil Hall more fitly perform its function as "the cradle of liberty."

ACM sent to Mr. French a copy of her letter that had appeared in the New York *Times*. He wrote her, on September 3, an account of the Boston meeting:

> I read the letter very early in the proceedings in Faneuil Hall, on Tuesday night, and its effect was marked. It gave an atmosphere to the meeting which it would have otherwise hardly had, I think. I am glad it occurred to you to let me see it.
> We had a crowded hall and a large overflow outside, and the whole thing was successful beyond our expectations. . . .

Anne Carroll Moore continued to fight for the vindication of Leo Frank, offering articles to several magazines of the time, but editors were unwilling to pursue the subject in the immediate future.

ACM sustained her friendship with Leo's father and mother as long as they lived. Judging from the outlines and observations she preserved, it seems probable that she considered writing a biography of Leo Frank.

CHAPTER TWELVE

1. Eugene Saxton, an editor at George H. Doran, was the initial editor of *The Bookman*. He went subsequently to Harper and Brothers (1925), eventually becoming vice-president and secretary of the firm. He was by all counts a talented and sympathetic editor, who abandoned his profession of the law in favor of journalism and publishing.

2. Stephen Vincent Benét's *Western Star* was published by Farrar and Rinehart in 1943, a few months before Eugene Saxton's death. Anne thought of that event in relation to the friendship between the three men—Stephen Benét, John Farrar, and Eugene Saxton.

CHAPTER THIRTEEN

1. The book under discussion was *Come Hither* by Walter de la Mare, "a collection of rhymes and poems for the young of all ages." The introduction is in truth an allegory, purporting to be "The Story of This Book," full of anagramatic names—the scene "Thrae" which is easily "earth" and the region of "The Laps" which becomes "planets." It is a piece of writing that reveals the poet at his eeriest and mystical best, yet it contains sound advice on the reading of poetry. In Anne's copy the thin marginal line that marks the paragraph she wanted to find at a glance stands at the following:

> Having discovered, then, that every poem must have been written as it was written, on purpose, I took a little more pains with those

I cared for least. In some even then I could not piece out the meaning; in others I could not easily catch the beat and rhythm and tune. But I learned to read them very slowly, so as fully and quietly to fill up the time allowed for each line and to listen to its music, and to see and hear all that the words were saying.

2. When "Ann" was used as the name by which Walter de la Mare addressed ACM, it indicated that he was answering a letter from Nicholas, and the Ann was Ann Caraway. When he addressed her in her own person, it was "Anne."

CHAPTER FOURTEEN

1. The summation of ACM's Utah experience and her relation to the Peterson family is movingly told on the fly leaf of her presentation copy of *The Art of Beatrix Potter*, sent to Mrs. Peterson in 1956:

For Phoebe Nebeker Peterson, with whom I explored new roads to childhood in Utah, leading from her beautiful home on College Hill with President Peterson and their children back to her father's and mother's home on the shores of Bear Lake. Truth and Beauty were the guiding stars of a joyous pilgrimage which began in 1927 under the spell of the Wasatch Mountains. The same stars have continued to shine with increasing radiance wherever we meet—Utah—Concord—Boston—Harvard Yard—Alexandria on Easter Day. With love and gratitude for a beautiful friendship and my share in a living child of the Peterson family.

N.Y.   ACM
Sept. 1956

CHRONOLOGY

1871   Anne Carroll Moore born on July 12, at Limerick, Maine.

1881   Entered Limerick Academy.

1889   Graduated from Limerick Academy. Entered Bradford Academy at Bradford, Massachusetts.

1891   Graduated from Bradford Academy, June 1891. Read law with her father from June 1891 until January 1892.

1892   Death of Anne's father and mother.

1895   Entered the Library School of Pratt Free Institute, Brooklyn, New York.

1896   Graduated from Pratt in June. Lectured to teachers in the Summer School at Saco, Maine, at the invitation of the State Superintendent of Schools; the topic: "Library Methods of Study." Appointed head of the library for children, the Pratt Free Library of Brooklyn.

1900   Chosen as President of the first Round Table organization of librarians actually in charge of children's work at the American Library Association's annual meeting in Montreal, Canada.

1901   At the invitation of the American Library Association, the Round Table organization became a section of the Association, with Anne Carroll Moore its first chairman.

First trip to England, Scotland, and Ireland.

1902   Taught at the Iowa State Library Commission Summer School. Her *A List of Books Recommended for a Children's Library* published, for the Iowa State Library Commission.

1906   Appointed to organize work with children in the New York Public Library.

1911   The Central Library opened its doors to the public. The Central Children's Room was established as a major department of a reference library.

1918   Joined the staff of *The Bookman* with responsibility for criticism of books for children in its pages.

1920   *Roads to Childhood* first published.

1921   Journey to England, Belgium, and France to report for the American Library Association on children's work in other countries, she being chairman of a subcommittee on library cooperation with other countries. Report published in the ALA Bulletin of July 1921.

1922   To France for the Marie Shedlock festival of storytelling in the devastated regions, and to England for ceremonies at the opening of the David Copperfield Library.

1924   First appearance of "The Three Owls" in the New York *Herald Tribune Books*. Publication of *Nicholas: A Manhattan Christmas Story*.

1927   Delegate to the International Conference of Librarians at Edinburgh, Scotland.
       First visit as lecturer to the Utah State Agricultural College at Logan, Utah.

1931   The Anne Carroll Moore Children's Library opened in the new library of the Agricultural College at Logan, Utah.

1932   Pratt Institute bestowed upon Anne Carroll Moore a Diploma of Honor in recognition of her eminence as "a commanding influence and authority in the choice of children's literature within and without the library profession."

1940   The first Constance Lindsay Skinner Gold Medal for outstanding work as a pioneer in the field of better books for children was awarded Anne Carroll Moore by the Women's National Book Association and the Booksellers' League of New York.

The University of Maine honored Anne Carroll Moore by bestowing upon her the honorary degree of Doctor of Letters.

1941   Retirement from the New York Public Library. Accepted teaching appointment at the Graduate School of Librarianship at the University of California, Berkeley.

1954   Publication of *The Art of Beatrix Potter*.

1955   The honorary degree of Doctor of Letters awarded Anne Carroll Moore by Pratt Institute.

1960   The Regina Medal of the Catholic Library Association was given to Anne Carroll Moore.

1961   Died on January 20 in New York City.

INDEX

Frances Clarke Sayers

Frances Clarke Sayers is a Texan who, as she says, "happens to have been born in Topeka, Kansas." Her father, an official of the Santa Fe Railroad, was transferred to Galveston. She was brought up there in an atmosphere that combined the aura of the old South with the varieties of internationalism a seaport affords. Her father was a conservative, her mother "a fighting liberal." For Mrs. Sayers and her sister, the household was a lively one.

An article in the *St. Nicholas* magazine, read by Mrs. Sayers when she was ten or twelve, aroused her interest in a new profession for women: children's librarianship. In time she came to be a student at the Carnegie Library School in Pittsburgh. Anne Carroll Moore, the subject of this biography, came to the school as a visiting lecturer and asked Mrs. Sayers to come and work in New York City. For five years, Mrs. Sayers worked in the Central Children's Room of the New York Public Library. Later, after a span of years in California, Mrs. Sayers returned to the New York Public Library as Superintendent of Work with Children from 1941 to 1952. From 1954 to 1964, she was Senior Lecturer in the School of Library Science and the English Department at the University of California in Los Angeles.

Miss Moore, New York, the children of that city, and Alfred Henry Paul Sayers, librarian and bookman whom Mrs. Sayers met there and later married, have, she says, constituted the major themes of her life.

Mrs. Sayers now lives in Ojai, California. She is the author of six books for children: *Bluebonnets for Lucinda, Mr. Tidy Paws, Tag Along Tooloo, Ginny and Custard, Sally Tait,* and *Oscar Lincoln Busby Stokes.* Her adult books are *Summoned by Books* and *Anthology of Children's Literature* (with Evelyn Sickels).